BEGINNING FROM JERUSALEM

CHRISTIANITY IN THE MAKING

Volume 2

BEGINNING FROM JERUSALEM

James D. G. Dunn

WILLIAM B. EERDMANS PUBLISHING COMPANY

GRAND RAPIDS, MICHIGAN / CAMBRIDGE, U.K.

© 2009 James D. G. Dunn

All rights reserved

Published 2009 by

Wm. B. Eerdmans Publishing Co.

2140 Oak Industrial Drive N.E., Grand Rapids, Michigan 49505 /

P.O. Box 163, Cambridge CB3 9PU U.K.

Printed in the United States of America

14 13 12 11 10 09   7 6 5 4 3 2 1

Library of Congress Cataloging-in-Publication Data

Dunn, James D. G., 1939-

Beginning from Jerusalem: Christianity in the making, vol. 2 /

James D. G. Dunn.

p.   cm.

Includes bibliographical references and index.

ISBN 978-0-8028-3932-9 (cloth : alk. paper)

1. Church history — Primitive and early church, ca. 30-600.

2. Bible. N.T. — Criticism, interpretation, etc.   I. Title.

BR162.3.D86 2008

270.1 — dc22

2008028392

www.eerdmans.com

For Catrina,
David
and Fiona

the best of me,
of us

In memoriam
Professor C. F. D. (Charlie) Moule
1909-2008
my doctor-father

Contents

PART SEVEN: THE FIRST PHASE

Contents

PART NINE: THE END OF THE BEGINNING

Maps

Preface

This is the second volume in a projected trilogy *Christianity in the Making,* in which I attempt to trace and examine the history of Christianity's beginnings well into the second century. The first volume, *Jesus Remembered,* focused exclusively on the person to whom the origins of Christianity can undoubtedly be traced. It included an exposition of the critical historical method on which the whole enterprise is undertaken, including recognition of the fact of faith as part of the historical data and of the function of faith as integral to the critical historical dialogue. These methodological considerations continue to guide the historical studies of the present volume. Some of the first volume's critique of the sources available to us for the period is also relevant here.

Volume 2, *Beginning from Jerusalem,* covers from 30 to 70 CE, a much longer period than the (probably) three years of Jesus' mission. These two periods and subjects — Jesus' mission and the first generation of the movement which began from Jesus — are probably the most thoroughly investigated periods and subjects of all history. The amount of secondary literature, particularly over the last thirty years, has grown exponentially and is impossible to cover thoroughly, even in monographs devoted to particular aspects of the much more extensive subject matter. In what follows, of course, I have given primary attention to the source documents and historical data from the period available to us. In addition, I have attempted to draw on or to consider as much as I could of what I deemed to be the most relevant of the secondary literature to illuminate the source material. For the most part I have focused on the more recent secondary literature, principally to ensure that I engage as fully as possible with the current discussion on the numerous individual issues discussed, but also bearing in mind that many of the recent monographs and essays on particular subjects carefully review earlier debates and take up or engage with the most salient points from these earlier debates.

However, so far as possible, as in *Jesus Remembered,* I have endeavoured to limit the interaction with the secondary literature to footnotes. My hope is that the main text will have been kept sufficiently uncluttered to allow those who do not wish to engage with the often interminable disagreements of scholars on individual points to maintain a steady forward momentum in their reading. At the same time, the footnotes should provide at least a start for those who wish to pause or simply to consider these more detailed issues. Even so, I need hardly add, the secondary literature referred to has had to be selective; it has been no part of my intention to provide an exhaustive bibliography — the volume is large enough as it is! No doubt in consequence I have treated several classic expositions too lightly and have missed a fair number of contemporary monographs and articles which may well have influenced my views on one point or another. To any such contributors I give my apology, and I invite them to draw my attention to the more grievous omissions. I should add that, in common with my common practice, in order to limit what would otherwise be an inordinately lengthy bibliography, I have not included dictionary articles in the bibliography.

As part of the enterprise I have thought it necessary to consider in some detail the key texts within the New Testament which relate most closely to this period — particularly the Acts of the Apostles and the letters of Paul. In the case of Paul's letters I regard the treatment offered in the following pages as complementary to my earlier study *The Theology of Paul the Apostle* (Grand Rapids: Eerdmans/Edinburgh: Clark, 1998). In an important sense *The Theology of Paul* was an enterprise which I had to clear out of the way before I could turn to the task of *Christianity in the Making.* In the lecture courses which prepared the way for the trilogy, I had regularly found the progression of the exposition of Christianity's beginnings being sidetracked and stalling because I had to give adequate consideration to Paul's theology. But now, with *The Theology of Paul* out of the way, I can maintain the progress of the story of *Christianity in the Making.* At the same time, I can in effect respond to those critics of *The Theology of Paul* who think that the only way to explore Paul's theology is in terms of each individual letter. It is partly for this reason that I decided that a brief summary statement of the contents of each of Paul's letters would be insufficient for the purposes of this volume — insufficient, that is, to assist the readers of the volume to enter into (so far as possible) Paul's intention and thinking in writing these letters. The fact that we thereby see also Paul's theology, or better his theologizing, as it was being formulated in relation to particular churches and their particular situations is a bonus and should be a reminder of the existential character of Paul's theology/theologizing.

Focusing on particular texts as I have done raised the further bibliographical problem that the production of commentaries on these texts seems to be unending. Fortunately, in most cases there have been two or three substantial and high-quality commentaries recently published on each text. These commentaries almost always include coverage or review of earlier issues and contributions. Rather than attempt a dialogue with the principal commentary tradition stretching back across the generations, therefore, it seemed wiser to me to concentrate my commentary references and dialogue to these two or three commentaries in each case. Of course, it would have been folly to attempt to engage with every exegetical issue of moment in each text, but I hope I have done enough to make readers aware both of the key issues in each case and of the interpretations of the data which differ from my own. In the bibliography I have listed separately the commentaries consulted for each of the key NT texts, which I hope is helpful.

This volume is the principal product of my research since I retired in 2003. Retirement has diminished somewhat the opportunities for personal interaction with colleagues at home and elsewhere. So I am more grateful than I can express to those who were able to respond positively to my tentative requests for other specialists to cast critical eyes over the early drafts of the material. Others, sadly, were already overburdened and had to decline. I am particularly grateful to Loveday Alexander, Anthony Bash, Lutz Doering, John Kloppenborg, Bruce Longenecker, Barry Matlock, Scot McKnight, Bob Morgan, Greg Sterling, Steve Walton and Michael Wolter, some of whom must have spent many hours trailing through my material. They have saved me from many infelicities, spared me more than a few embarrassments, and given me cause to pause and think again at numerous points, and on a goodly number of occasions to re-write. The remaining infelicities are my own. Nor was I persuaded at all points raised, but in most instances I hope that I have been able to strengthen the case made. In all this I include my publisher, William B. Eerdmans, whose willingness to send out various draft chapters to scattered destinations has been exemplary and whose encouragement has been unbounded. I am particularly grateful to my editor, Craig Noll, who has taken immense pains over a massive manuscript to ensure correctness of detail and consistency of style, and who has saved me from many a slip. And above all, I thank my beloved wife, Meta, who both tolerates and encourages my commitment to continuing my teaching and writing ministry.

As the first volume was dedicated to Meta, so this volume is dedicated to our three children, who are indeed the best of us. It goes out with our hope and prayer that it may prove beneficial to those who want to understand the beginnings of Christianity better and to teachers who wish to instruct such seekers after historical truth.

October 2007

PART SIX

WRITING A HISTORY OF CHRISTIANITY'S BEGINNINGS

CHAPTER 20

The Quest for the Historical Church

'The quest of the historical Jesus' is one of the few phrases and concerns to have escaped the 'closed shop' of New Testament and theological specialist scholarship. This is wholly understandable, given the fascination which such an epochal figure is bound to arouse and the diverse outcomes of the quest as it has actually been pursued. This quest has been the principal subject of volume 1, *Jesus Remembered.* But the quest for the historical *church* has been equally fascinating, and equally fraught with possibly challenging or even threatening outcomes. And it has absorbed scholarly research in equal measure, although it has made much less impact outside 'the groves of Academe'.

A curiosity of twentieth-century scholarship has been that the more unknown or unknowable Jesus was claimed to be, the more confident scholars have often been that they knew sufficient about the historical church. The present forms of the Jesus tradition could be assumed to tell us more about the *church(es)* which used the tradition than about *Jesus,* to whom the tradition bore witness. The obvious protest against this argument, that the primitive church(es) were (on such a reckoning) *as much an unknown as Jesus,*[1] was not heard with as much effect as it deserved.

So, what can be said about the initial emergence of Christianity, following the departure of Jesus from the scene? How did this religion which was to shape the history and culture of Europe (and beyond) for the next two millennia come to be? After Jesus, how did it all begin? As these questions indicate, the focus for this volume is on *beginnings,* on the first phase of Christianity's existence. The obvious *terminus ad quem* of this volume is 70 CE, when Jerusalem was captured by the Roman legions of Titus and the Temple destroyed. That date marks the

---

1. This point was made effectively by F. G. Downing, *The Church and Jesus: A Study in History, Philosophy and History* (London: SCM, 1968).

3

formal end of Second Temple Judaism. It coincides roughly with the end of the first generation of Christianity, including the death of the three leading figures in earliest Christianity (Peter, James and Paul), all, probably, in the 60s. And with the Gospel of Mark dated usually to about that time, the date 70 forms a sort of dividing line between the earliest NT writings (the letters of Paul) and the new phase of second-generation Christian writing (most if not all of the rest of the NT!). In the development of Christianity as well as of Judaism, it makes sense to speak of 'pre-70' and 'post-70'. This volume will examine the pre-70 period, Christianity's emergence during the forty years following the epochal events Christians remember as Good Friday and Easter Sunday — 30-70 CE.

By way of introduction, however, it will be both necessary and of cautionary value to provide some definitions and scene-setting. As with 'Judaism' (*Jesus Remembered* §9), we need first to clarify the 'what' of our key term, the subject matter of our investigation (§20.1). And as with the quest of the historical Jesus, a review of the quest for the historical church should be equally salutary in pointing up key issues and findings of continuing relevance and importance (§§20.2-3).

20.1. Defining Terms

It began in Jerusalem. That affirmation certainly summarizes the account of Christianity's beginnings according to the Acts of the Apostles. Whether and the extent to which that Acts account needs to be qualified is a subject addressed in the following chapters (§21.2, §§22-23). But first we must be clear on what is being referred to by 'it'. What was the 'it' which 'began in Jerusalem'?

This question, once asked as a crucial issue for appropriate historical description,[2] is now often passed over as though the definition of the subject matter was self-evident. But even where such a question has been asked, the answer has usually been offered in objectively historicist terms, as though it was primarily a

---

2. See particularly A. Harnack, 'The Names of Christian Believers', *The Mission and Expansion of Christianity in the First Three Centuries* (ET London: Williams and Norgate, 1908; New York: Harper Torchbook, 1962) 399-418; H. J. Cadbury, 'Names for Christians and Christianity in Acts', *Beginnings* 5.375-92; Paul Trebilco referred me also to C. Spicq, 'Les dénominations du Chrétien', *Vie chrétienne et pérégrination selon le Nouveau Testament* (LD 71; Paris: Cerf, 1972) 13-57; J. A. Fitzmyer, 'The Designations of Christians in Acts and Their Significance', in Commission Biblique Pontificale, *Unité et diversité dans l'Église* (Rome: Libreria Editrice Vaticana, 1989) 223-36; and H. Karpp, 'Christennamen', *RAC* 2.1114-38; see also W. Reinbold, *Propaganda und Mission im ältesten Christentum* (FRLANT 188; Göttingen: Vandenhoeck und Ruprecht, 2000) 16-24; and the brief list in R. Bauckham, 'Jesus and the Jerusalem Community', in O. Skarsaune and R. Hvalvik, eds., *Jewish Believers in Jesus: The Early Centuries* (Peabody: Hendrickson, 2007) 55-95 (here 56-59).

matter of listing the names used of the group(s) in view, that is, of describing what names they were known by.[3] To describe the birth of a religious movement *from outside,* with all the hindsight awareness of what that movement became, is of course a thoroughly respectable goal for a historian. The more challenging task, however, is to describe that historical sequence *from within,* to ask how the participants understood themselves and what was happening, when horizons were limited and outcomes unknown.[4] That is not to imply that such in-the-event-provisional views were or should be definitive or of lasting significance. But historical honesty forbids us even more to assume the opposite: that those involved clearly foresaw and worked to achieve what in the event happened. Historical processes, religious movements not excepted, are much more complex and messy than that. The attempt to penetrate into and to clarify something of that complexity and messiness signals both the fascination and the frustration of historical study.

As a matter of procedure, then, we are looking for an appropriate term or terms which will serve as a social description but which will also give us something of an insider's view of developments.

The obvious answer to the opening question (What was the 'it' which 'began in Jerusalem'?), as already implied, is (1) *Christianity.* But here at once we have to take seriously the methodological considerations just voiced; we must pause and grasp the fact that such an answer is strictly speaking anachronistic. That is to say, to use the term 'Christianity' at this stage is historically inaccurate. Properly speaking, 'Christianity' did not yet exist. The term 'Christians' was first coined, as a neologism, some way into Luke's account in the Acts.[5] And the term

---

3. So Harnack and Cadbury (above, n. 2); Fitzmyer is alert to the problem ('Designations' 223-24).

4. I made such an attempt in my *Christology in the Making: A New Testament Inquiry into the Origins of the Doctrine of the Incarnation* (London: SCM, 1980, ²1989; Grand Rapids: Eerdmans, 1996) and was disappointed that such crucial methodological principles (limited horizons and 'conceptuality in transition') were so little appreciated (see 'Foreword to Second Edition' xiv-xvi). I return to the subject at the end of §21.

5. Acts 11.26; 26.28; see also 1 Peter 4.16; Ignatius, *Eph.* 11.2; *Magn.* 4; *Trall.* 6.1; *Rom.* 3.2; *Pol.* 7.3; *Mart. Pol.* 3.2; 10.1; 12.1-2; *Did.* 12.4; *Diogn.* 1.1; 2.6, 10; 4.6; 5.1; 6.1-9; Pliny, *Ep.* 10.96; see also Harnack, *Mission* 411-12 n. 4. The fact that Tacitus (*Ann.* 15.44.2) and Suetonius (*Life of Nero* 16.2) use the term to describe events of the 60s may reflect only early second-century usage; it need not imply that the term was in such wide use in the period described (though see Harnack, *Mission* 413). Cadbury, *Beginnings* 5.383-86, makes an important observation: Luke's statement in Acts that they were called Christians at Antioch 'for the first time *(prōtōs)*' (11.26) must imply his knowledge of subsequent usage (386). However, his further observation that 'the absence of the word from the earliest Christian literature . . . from all the Apostolic Fathers, except Ignatius, suggests that as a matter of fact it was not a name early accepted by the Christians themselves' (386; following Harnack 411 n. 1; 412) appears to

'Christianity' itself first appears in our sources in the 110s,[6] that is, some eighty years after the events narrated by Luke in Acts 1–5, or their historical equivalents. Of course, we can make the working assumption of a direct continuity from the beginnings of 'it' to the 'Christianity' of Ignatius and the subsequent centuries. We can no doubt speak of *'embryonic* Christianity', or *'emergent* Christianity', without falsification.[7] But what we must not do is to allow any use of the term itself ('Christianity') to presume the corollary that the distinctives of full-grown Christianity were already present in these beginnings.[8] To use the term 'Christianity' in description too quickly would pre-empt what is one of the key issues: what *are* the distinctives of Christianity, and *when* did they first emerge? Better not to use the term, heavily freighted with centuries of significance as it is, than to run the risk of pre-judging the historical reality of our subject matter.

If not 'Christianity', then what? We could certainly speak of (2) *the church* ('the quest for the historical church'),[9] principally because from the second century at least it became a prominent if not the preferred self-designation.[10] And such a use would be more immediately validated by the use of the term *(ekklēsia)* within the earliest Christian literature.[11] There is also the possibility that it provides a bridge to Jesus' own intentions[12] and that it reflects the self-designation of the first disciples of Jesus as 'the church *(qahal)* of God'.[13] But here too it is wise

---

be an overstatement in the light of the data listed at the beginning of the note. See further Karpp, 'Christennamen' 1131-37; and below, §24.8d.

6. Ignatius, *Magn.* 10.1-3; *Rom.* 3.3; *Phld.* 6.1; *Mart. Pol.* 10.1. See also below at nn. 120-22.

7. G. Lüdemann, *Primitive Christianity: A Survey of Recent Studies and Some New Proposals* (2002; ET London: Clark, 2003), still prefers the older 'primitive Christianity' (2).

8. Contrast F. C. Baur (below, §20.3a); and note the complexities of the discussion reviewed below (§§20.2-3).

9. In the first half of the twentieth century it was common to speak of 'the primitive church', 'the early Church', etc. E.g., E. von Dobschütz, *Christian Life in the Primitive Church* (London: Williams and Norgate, 1904); B. H. Streeter, *The Primitive Church* (London: Macmillan, 1930).

10. Harnack, *Mission* 408-10.

11. In the NT, 114 times, including 23 in Acts, 62 in the Pauline corpus, and 20 in Revelation; e.g., Matt. 18.17; Acts 5.11; 8.1, 3; etc.; Rom. 16.1, 4-5, 16, 23; 1 Cor. 1.2; 4.17; etc.; Jas. 5.14; Revelation 2–3; *1 Clem.* inscr.; Ignatius, *Eph.* inscr.; *Did.* 4.14; Hermas, *Vis.* 2.4.3.

12. See *Jesus Remembered* §13.3f. Cf. K. Berger, 'Volksversammlung und Gemeinde Gottes. Zu den Anfängen der christlichen Verwendung von "Ekklesia"', *ZTK* 73 (1976) 167-207 (here 187-201).

13. Gal. 1.3; cf. 1 Cor. 15.9; Phil. 3.6; Acts 5.11; 8.1, 3; 12.1; Jas. 5.14. Harnack attributed the introduction of the term to the 'Palestinian communities, which must have described themselves as *qahal*' (*Mission* 407); see also H. Merklein, 'Die Ekklesia Gottes. Der Kirchenbegriff bei Paulus und in Jerusalem', *Studien zu Jesus und Paulus* (WUNT 43;

to pause. For the use of the singular ('the church') is equally fraught with the possibility of misleading significance. For one thing, to speak of 'the church' (singular) implies a unified entity, which has certainly been a theological ideal from early days,[14] and which remains an ecumenical aspiration to this day. But for that very reason its use too early may easily serve as rose-tinted spectacles through which we perceive these beginnings. As noted earlier,[15] it was precisely such an idealized perception of embryonic Christianity which Walter Bauer called into question. And as we have already seen in some detail, perspectives influenced by the Nag Hammadi texts have called even more sharply into question whether there was ever a single (positive) response to Jesus' mission or ever a single 'pure form' either of the Jesus tradition or of 'the early church'.[16] Here again such issues must not be pre-empted by casual use of 'loaded' terms. Perhaps more to the point is the fact that the earliest references use the term ('church') most typically in the plural ('churches'),[17] or to describe an assembly in a particular place.[18] Here again, then, the dangers of anachronism and of unwittingly promoting misleading implications need to be taken seriously. A 'safer' and historically more accurate title for this chapter would be 'the quest for the historical churches'!

Tübingen: Mohr Siebeck, 1987) 296-318 (here 303-13); Fitzmyer, 'Designations' 231-32; also, *The Acts of the Apostles* (AB 31; New York: Doubleday, 1998) 325; P. Stuhlmacher, *Biblische Theologie des Neuen Testaments* (2 vols.; Göttingen: Vandenhoeck und Ruprecht, 1992, 1999) 1.199-200. See also §30.1 below.

14. Eph. 1.22; 3.10, 21; 5.23-25, 27, 29, 32; but apart from Col. 1.18, 24, this use of *ekklēsia* to mean the universal church is exceptional within the Pauline corpus and was probably not in view in 1 Cor. 10.32; 12.28; Gal. 1.13, as is commonly assumed; the ideal in the singular use may reflect the sense of continuity with Israel (the *qahal Yahweh*) rather than a single universal entity (see further my *The Theology of Paul the Apostle* [Grand Rapids: Eerdmans, 1998] 537-43). The concept of 'the catholic = universal church *(hē katholikē ekklēsia)'* appears first in Ignatius, *Smyrn.* 8.2, on which see W. R. Schoedel, *Ignatius of Antioch* (Hermeneia; Philadelphia: Fortress, 1985) 243-44; also *Mart. Pol.* inscr.; 8.1 ('the whole catholic church throughout the world'); 19.2.

15. *Jesus Remembered* §1; see §22 n. 4 below.

16. *Jesus Remembered* §4.7; F. Vouga, *Geschichte des frühen Christentums* (UTB; Tübingen: Francke 1994).

17. Rom. 16.4, 16; 1 Cor. 4.17; 7.17; 11.16; 14.33-34; 16.1, 19; 2 Cor. 8.1, 18-19, 23-24; 11.8, 28; 12.13; Gal. 1.2, 22; Phil. 4.15; 1 Thess. 2.14; 2 Thess. 1.4; also Acts 15.41; 16.5; Revelation 2–3. Acts 9.31 ('the church throughout all Judea and Galilee and Samaria') is exceptional in its use of the singular in reference to a large region (contrast, e.g., 'the churches of Galatia') but may reflect the sense as much (or more) of a unified (single) region (= the land of Israel) as of a single unified church! The usage, however, should not be taken to validate the idea of a national church.

18. Rom. 16.1, 23; 1 Cor. 1.2; 11.18, 22; 14.23; 2 Cor. 1.1; Col. 4.16; 1 Thess. 1.1; 2 Thess. 1.1; a church in someone's house — Rom. 16.5; 1 Cor. 16.1, 19; Col. 4.15; Phlm. 2; typically in Acts (e.g., 8.1; 11.26; 14.23; 20.17).

Other terms appear to be still less satisfactory. (3) *Synagogue (synagōgē)* might not seem to be much of a contender, since the antithesis between 'church' and 'synagogue' is deeply rooted in the history of Christian anti-Jewish polemic.[19] But the term itself was still in transition from 'assembly' to 'place of assembly',[20] and in our period it had not yet become the technical designation for a distinctively *Jewish* 'place of assembly'.[21] So it is no surprise that it appears occasionally in early Christian literature as a description of a 'Christian' gathering.[22] Such a usage, however, simply reminds us that *synagōgē* was not yet a technical term ('synagogue') and still in broader use ('assembly'), and its infrequent appearance in first-century literature for the gatherings of those who identified themselves by reference to Jesus hardly makes it appropriate to serve as the regular reference term for which we are looking. At the same time, these observations provide a further reminder that any attempt to draw out clear lines of definitional distinction, particularly from 'Judaism', for the beginnings of Christianity would be historically irresponsible.

A more hopeful candidate is (4) *disciples (mathētai),* which would certainly provide a link back into the mission of Jesus and his immediate circle.[23] More to the point, in Acts it attains an almost technical status ('the disciples') for those committed to the new body.[24] On the other hand, it does not appear elsewhere in the NT outside the Gospels and Acts. This could suggest that the *first* 'disciples' continued to see/define themselves in terms of their earlier teacher-disciple relationship with Jesus,[25] or that Luke chose to extend that us-

19. Classically in church architecture, contrasting two female figures, the church triumphant and the synagogue defeated, as in Strasbourg cathedral. But the antithesis is already active in Justin, *Dial.* 134.3, and the beginnings of the polemic are elsewhere evident in the second century (details in W. Schrage, *synagōgē, TDNT* 7.838-40); note also the term *aposynagōgos* ('expelled from the synagogue'), which is unknown in nonbiblical literature or the LXX but which appears in John 9.22; 12.42; 16.2 (see below, vol. 3).

20. See *Jesus Remembered* §9.7a.

21. See also §30 nn. 7 and 84 below.

22. Notably Jas. 2.2; possibly in the Synoptic tradition for gatherings of Jesus' followers (see *Jesus Remembered* §9 n. 233); and in the second century see Ignatius, *Pol.* 4.2; Hermas, *Mand.* 11.9-14; *T. Ben.* 11.2 (probably Christian); Justin, *Dial.* 63.5; Irenaeus speaks of the *duae synagogae* as the church and the true Judaism of the old covenant (Schrage, *TDNT* 7.840-41, referring to *Adv. haer.* 4.31.1; see also BDAG, *synagōgē*); Harnack drew particular attention to Epiphanius, *Pan.* 30.18 (*Mission* 408 n. 1).

23. *Jesus Remembered* §§13-14.

24. 'The disciples' — Acts 6.1-2, 7; 9.19, 26, 38; 11.26, 29; 13.52; 14.20, 28; 15.10; 18.23, 27; 19.9, 30; 20.1, 30; 21.4, 16; a 'disciple' — 9.10, 26, 36; 16.1; 21.16; 'to make disciples' — 14.21.

25. K. H. Rengstorf, *mathētēs, TDNT* 4.458. Did Mnason represent such a continuity, as Harnack suggested (*Mission* 400 n. 1) — hence his description as 'an early disciple *(archaios mathētēs)'* (Acts 21.16)? Cadbury, however, notes the surprising absence of the term from Acts

age and image in his own record.[26] But the silence of the rest of the first-century writings hardly suggests that it was a widespread self-description in the first century. And if the suggestion just offered for the initial usage is sound, the same silence may well suggest in turn that a self-understanding in terms of disciple-to-teacher, familiar in the ancient world,[27] was soon perceived as inadequate among the first 'Christians'.[28] That in itself would be a highly significant conclusion to be able to draw, and we shall have to return to the issue as we proceed.

In NT literature (5) *believers* is actually the first collective term to be used of the emergent community,[29] and it well catches what was evidently a key distinguishing feature of the earliest groups. As such it will be the most obvious term for us to use, not least because its usage seems to have been so distinctive

---

1–5 and rightly observes that in Acts the term is detached from Jesus; whereas in Luke's Gospel a genitive referring to Jesus is expressed or implied, only once in Acts has the noun a possessive reference, 'the disciples of the Lord' (9.1), and 'the disciple(s)' is used without explicit addition (*Beginnings* 5.377); see also Fitzmyer, 'Designations' 227-29. Since talk of someone's 'disciples' was familiar in the ancient world (BDAG, *mathētēs* 2), to speak simply of 'the disciples' indicates an insider's perspective.

26. Cadbury observes the 'contrast' between 'the twelve' and 'the crowd *(plēthos)* of the disciples' in Acts 6.2 (*Beginnings* 5.376-77).

27. BDAG, *mathētēs* 2; Fitzmyer, *Acts* 346.

28. Harnack's observation that 'disciple' subsequently became a title of honour, particularly for the original disciples, but also for martyrs ('truly a disciple' — Ignatius, *Rom.* 4.2), is still valid. 'The term "disciples" fell into disuse, because it no longer expressed the relationship in which Christians now found themselves placed. It meant at once too little and too much' (*Mission* 400-401).

29. *Hoi pisteuontes* ('those who believe') — Acts 2.44; Rom. 3.22; 1 Cor. 14.22; 1 Thess. 1.7; 2.10, 13; Hermas, *Sim.* 8.3.3; Origen, *c. Cels.* 1.13.34
   hoi pisteusantes ('those who believed/became believers') — Acts 2.44 v.l.; 4.32; 2 Thess. 1.10; Hermas, *Sim.* 9.19.1; 9.22.1
   hoi pepisteukotes ('those who had become [and remained] believers') — Acts 15.5; 18.27; 19.18; 21.20, 25
   pistos/pistē ('believing, faithful') — Acts 16.1, 15; 1 Cor. 7.25; 2 Cor. 6.15; 1 Tim. 4.10; 5.16; 6.2; Tit. 1.6
   hoi pistoi ('the believers/faithful') — Acts 10.45; 12.3 D; 1 Tim. 4.3, 12; Ignatius, *Eph.* 21.2; *Magn.* 5.2; *Mart. Pol.* 12.3; 13.2; Celsus, *c. Cels.* 1.9.
See further *PGL, pistos;* Harnack, *Mission* 403-404 n. 4; see also Spicq, 'Dénominations' 17-19.

But *hē pistis* ('the faith') appears only in the later NT writings — 1 Tim. 1.19; 3.9; 4.1, 6; 5.8; 6.10, 12, 21; 2 Tim. 2.18; 3.8; 4.7; Tit. 1.13; Jude 3. The otherwise unique language of Galatians (1.23; 3.23, 25, 26; 6.10) probably indicates Paul's claim that the new phase in divinely ordered history (3.23) was distinctively characterized by faith (the faith which his gospel called for), rather than referring to a body of belief as in the later usage; see my *The Epistle to the Galatians* (BNTC; London: Black, 1993) 84, 197, 202.

for its time.[30] More to the point, central to any inquiry into Christianity in the making must be the *what* and the *when* of such faith: what were the content and direction of that faith at any one time, how distinctive, how diverse was it? and can we trace the way(s) in which this believing developed through these earliest years? Bearing in mind the conclusion already reached, that Jesus himself was remembered as calling for 'faith', but not for faith in himself as such,[31] the issues call for sensitive handling. Do we see here that crucial transition already accomplished, from believing *in response to* Jesus to believing *in* Jesus?[32] If so, we must inquire how that came about. Here not least we will have to take care lest we beg too many questions in the terms we use.

Alternatively we could use the longer, more cumbersome phrase (6) *those who call upon the name of the Lord*. The phrase certainly has the ring of a self-description in a number of passages[33] and reflects the influence of Joel 2.32 (LXX 3.5).[34] The first believers presumably saw themselves in the light of the Joel passage, in somewhat the way that the Qumran community saw itself in the light of Habakkuk (1QpHab). This suggests that Luke had good reason to date its influence very early when he attached it to his account of the events of the day of Pentecost (Acts 2.17-21). 'To call on (the name of) God' in prayer is, of course, language regularly used in Greek as well as Hebrew religion.[35] What

---

30. 'This active sense of the adjective instead of its usual passive sense as faithful, trustworthy, is notable and hardly to be found outside of Christianity' (Cadbury, *Beginnings* 5.382). Similarly R. Bultmann, *The Theology of the New Testament* (2 vols.; ET London: SCM, 1952, 1955): 'In Christianity, for the first time, "faith" became the prevailing term for man's relationship to the divine; in Christianity, but not before it, "faith" came to be understood as the attitude which through and through governs the life of the religious man' (89), though Bultmann also maintains that 'faith as a personal relation to the person of Christ is an idea that was at first foreign to the earliest Christian message' (92). To similar effect Robin Lane Fox, *Pagans and Christians* (1986; London: Penguin, 1988): '"to anyone brought up on classical Greek philosophy, faith was the lowest grade of religion . . . the state of mind of the uneducated" [quoting E. R. Dodds] . . . . no group of pagans ever called themselves "the faithful": the term remains one of the few ways of distinguishing Jewish and Christian epitaphs from those which are pagan' (31).

31. *Jesus Remembered* §13.2b.

32. I choose this formulation in preference to the contrast between believing *with* Jesus and believing *in* Jesus, favoured by Liberalism old and new (cf. 'the Jesus of history' vs. 'the Christ of faith', below, §20.2b).

33. Acts 9.14, 21; 1 Cor. 1.2; 2 Tim. 2.22. It thus 'becomes a technical expression for "Christians"' (H. Conzelmann, *1 Corinthians* [Hermeneia; Philadelphia: Fortress, 1976] 23).

34. Acts 2.21; Rom. 10.12-14.

35. Gen. 13.4; 21.33; 26.25; Pss. 80.18; 99.6; 105.1; 116.4; Isa. 64.7; Zeph. 3.9; *T. Jud.* 24.6; *Pss. Sol.* 15.1. The phrase becomes a self-identifying title ('those who call on the Lord') in Pss. 79.6; 86.5; 145.18; Jer. 10.25; Zech. 13.9; *T. Dan* 5.11; 6.3; *Pss. Sol.* 2.36; 6.1; 9.6; cf. *Jos. Asen.* 11.9, 17-18 with Acts 22.16 and Rom. 10.13. See also K. L. Schmidt, *kaleō, TDNT* 3.498, 499-501; BDAG, *epikaleō;* Spicq, 'Dénominations' 45-49.

made the early Christian usage so distinctive is that 'the Lord' whose name is called upon is more often than not Jesus,[36] a fact which will call for further attention below.[37]

What other terms can we use with historical responsibility? (7) *Brothers* is certainly a term much used, all the way across the spectrum covered by the NT writings.[38] Moreover, if Mark 3.31-35 recalls an episode from Jesus' mission,[39] the term also spans the gap between pre-Easter mission and post-Easter expansion, and more effectively than 'disciples'. Its value also is that it characterizes the movement within which it was used as a (fictive) family association, and that certainly tells us something about the character of the movement as perceived (felt) from within.[40] The trouble is that the usage was not distinctive of the new movement, since such usage is attested within other religious communities, including Qumran.[41] And while the term works well in personal address and to denote internal relationships within the movement,[42] there is little encouragement in NT usage (apart from 1 Peter) to speak of the new movement as 'the brotherhood'.[43]

(8) *Saints* is another descriptive term used particularly in the Pauline letters and in Revelation.[44] But this too is a term which makes sense only from within

---

36. Explicitly Acts 7.59; 9.14, 21; 22.16; Rom. 10.9-13; 1 Cor. 1.2.

37. See further below, §§23.2a, 4d.

38. Or 'brothers and sisters' (NRSV) if we want to avoid the gender-specific restrictiveness which the term now conveys to so many; but 'sister' was used in its own right from the first (Rom. 16.1; 1 Cor. 7.15; 9.5; Phlm. 2; Jas. 2.15; Ignatius, *Pol.* 5.1; *2 Clem.* 12.5; Hermas, *Vis.* 2.2.3; 2.3.1), including the full address 'brothers and sisters' (*2 Clem.* 19.1; 20.2).

39. See *Jesus Remembered* §14.7.

40. E.g., Rom. 8.29; 16.23; 1 Cor. 5.11; 1 Thess. 3.2; 1 Pet. 5.12; *1 Clem.* 4.7; Ignatius, *Eph.* 10.3; *Smyrn.* 12.1; *Barn.* 2.10; Hermas, *Vis.* 2.4.1; in Acts note 1.15-16; 6.3; 9.30; 10.23; 11.1, 12, 29; 12.17; 14.2; 15.1, 3, 7, 13, 22-23, 32-33, 36, 40; 17.6, 10, 14; 18.18, 27; 21.7, 17, 20; 28.14-15. See also W. Schenk, 'Die ältesten Selbstverständnis christlicher Gruppen im ersten Jahrhundert', *ANRW* 2.26.2 (1995) 1355-1467 (here 1375-82).

41. Josephus, *War* 2.122; 1QS 6.10, 22; CD 6.20; 7.1-2; 1QSa 1.18; 1QM 13.1; 15.4, 7; in Acts note 2.29, 37; 3.17, 22; 7.2, 23, 25-26, 37; 13.15, 26, 38; 22.1, 5; 23.1, 5-6; 28.17, 21; see further BDAG, *adelphos* 2a; K. H. Schelkle, *RAC* 2.631-40; *NDIEC* 2.49-50; and below, §30 n. 49.

42. Characteristically in Paul — Rom. 1.13; 7.1, 4; 8.12; etc.

43. *adelphotēs* ('brotherhood, fellowship') — 1 Pet. 2.17; 5.9; *1 Clem.* 2.4. Otherwise Matthew comes closest — Matt. 5.22-24; 7.3-5; 18.15, 21, 35. Note also Christians/the church as 'the *oikos* (household, family) of God' (1 Tim. 3.15; Heb. 3.2-6; 1 Pet. 4.17). Harnack points out the later tendency to restrict the title 'brothers' to the clergy and confessors (cf. n. 28 above) — 'the surest index of the growing organization and privileges of the churches' (*Mission* 406-407 and n. 1).

44. Paul regularly addresses his readers as 'saints' (Rom. 1.7; 1 Cor. 1.2; 2 Cor. 1.1; Phil. 1.1; also Eph. 1.1). The spasmodic occurrence in Acts (Acts 9.13, 32, 41; 26.10; cf. 20.32;

the movement, as a way of claiming participation in the heritage of Israel.[45] Since it embodies a claim to theological status,[46] it does not serve well as a social description of the movement which made the claim. The gradual disappearance of the term after the middle of the second century, noted by Harnack, signals both a shift to a more polemical attitude towards Israel and the growing tendency, once again (as with 'disciple' and 'brother'), to restrict the term to special sub-groups within Christianity ('holy orders').[47]

Not listed by Cadbury, but as obvious a contender as 'saints' is (9) *the elect,* 'the chosen' (people/ones), a central term in Jewish self-understanding,[48] including not least the Dead Sea sect.[49] In earliest Christian use it serves to advance Paul's concern to demonstrate continuity between his converts and the Israel of old;[50] and the use of the term elsewhere in earliest Christianity indicates that Paul was not alone in that concern.[51] Whether, like 'saints', the usage was a claim to *participate* in Israel's heritage, or rather *to take it over,* is an issue which will have to be confronted later.[52] At any rate, like 'saints' it describes a theologi-

---

26.18) may provide an insight into its early usage (see n. 45). See also Schenk, 'Selbst-verständnis' 1384-92.

45. 'Saints' (= those set apart/'sanctified' to God) is a self-designation for the people of Israel peculiar to the tradition of Israel (e.g., Pss. 16.3; 34.9; Dan. 7.18; 8.24; Tob. 8.15; Wis. 18.9; 1QSb 3.2; 1QM 3.5; see further *ABD* 3.238-39). Harnack lists other names which reflect the same claim to Israel's heritage — 'God's people', 'Israel in spirit', 'the seed of Abraham', 'the chosen people', 'the twelve tribes', 'the elect', 'the servants of God' — but notes that they never became technical terms (*Mission* 402-403). See further Spicq, 'Dénominations' 19-29, 41-45.

46. Other factions within Second Temple Judaism used the term in self-designation as a way of making the same claim, in effect, to be or to represent Israel (*Pss. Sol.* 17.26; 1QS 5.13; 8.17, 20, 23; 9.8; *1 En.* 38.4-5; 43.4 v.l.; 48.1; 50.1; etc.).

47. Harnack, *Mission* 405.

48. 1 Chron. 16.13; Ps. 105.6; Isa. 43.20; 45.4; 65.9, 15, 22; Tob. 8.15; Sir. 46.1; 47.22; Wis. 3.9; 4.15; *Jub.* 1.29; *1 En.* 1.3, 8; 5.7-8; 25.5; 93.2.

49. 1QpHab 10.13; 1QS 8.6; 1QM 12.1, 4; 1QH 10[= 2].13; CD 4.3-4.

50. Paul speaks of believers as the 'elect' *(hoi eklektoi)* only occasionally (Rom. 8.33; Col. 3.12; but also 2 Tim. 2.10; Tit. 1.1); but note his use of the closely related *eklogē* ('selection, the selected') in Rom. 9.11 and 11.5, 7, 28 (also 1 Thess. 1.4). From a different root but similar in effect is Paul's talk of 'the called' *(hoi klētoi)* — Rom. 1.6-7; 8.28; 1 Cor. 1.2, 24; also Jude 1 and Rev. 17.14 (K. L. Schmidt, *kaleō, TDNT* 3.494), which is a term of self-definition also at Qumran (1QM 3.2; 4.10-11; cf. 1QSa 2.2, 11; 1QM 2.7; CD 2.11; 4.3-4); note how central to the first part of the discussion of Israel (Romans 9–11) is the divine call *(kaleō)* (9.7, 12, 24-25); see further BDAG, *kaleō* 4.

51. Mark 13.20, 22, 27/Matt. 24.22, 24, 31; 1 Pet. 1.1; 2.9; 2 John 1, 13; Rev. 17.14; and popular in *1 Clement* and Hermas, *Vision* (BDAG, *eklektos* 1). See further Spicq, 'Dénominations' 29-35, who also includes those 'beloved of God' (Rom. 1.7; cf. 9.25; Col. 3.12; 1 Thess. 1.4; 2 Thess. 2.13) (35-41).

52. The challenge is even sharper with the tendentious descriptions: 'the people of God'

cal claim, meaningful only in an intra-Jewish dialogue and hardly serviceable as a social description.

It is possible that the earliest community of believers in Jerusalem thought of themselves as (10) *the poor,* as those referred to, for example, by the Psalmist (Pss. 69.32; 72.2). Such a self-reference may be implied or echoed in Paul's explanation of the need for a collection to be made for 'the poor among the saints in Jerusalem' (Rom. 15.26).[53] In so doing they would have been claiming to be among the poor and oppressed who are God's special care, in much the same way as those behind the *Psalms of Solomon* and the sectarians at Qumran did.[54] It would also be a further mark of asserted continuity with Jesus' mission to 'the poor'.[55]

Other terms of self-designation listed by Cadbury do not call for much consideration, as being too episodic or context specific to provide a general term of description, particularly (11) *friends,*[56] (12) *the just/righteous,*[57] and (13) *those being saved*[58] — all highly expressive of an insider's self-definition.

But four other terms come closer to what we are looking for — that is, a term which was used by others ('outsiders') in the earliest days as a means of referring to the movement, but one which also characterizes its members and what they stood for. Three occur only in Acts, and the fourth virtually so (in its capacity as a referent to the earliest believers); but in this case that may indicate a temporary and/or local use which actually preserves an early, hesitant usage that may soon have been left behind.

The first is (14) *the way (hodos)* — the first believers as those 'belonging to the way, both men and women'.[59] The image clearly reflects the Hebrew idiom of conduct as walking *(halak)* along a path, an imagery, untypical of Greek

---

(Acts 15.14, citing Amos 9.11-12; Rom. 9.25 and 1 Pet. 2.10, both using Hos. 2.25; Heb. 4.9, a midrashic inference drawn from Deut. 31.7 and Josh. 22.4; Rev. 18.4, echoing Jer. 50.8 and 51.45); 'the twelve tribes in the diaspora' (Jas. 1.1; cf. 1 Pet. 1.1); and 'the seed of Abraham' (Gal. 3.16, 19, 29; Rom. 4.13-18).

53. See further my *Romans* (WBC 38; Dallas: Word, 1988) 875-76; and below, §33.4.

54. See *Jesus Remembered* §13 n. 144. The link forward to the Ebionites ('poor men') is also important (see, e.g., Karpp, 'Christennamen' 1117).

55. *Jesus Remembered* §13.4.

56. Particularly 3 John 15; possibly also Acts 27.3; and cf. Luke 12.4; John 11.11; 15.14-15 (see Harnack, *Mission* 419-21).

57. Acts 14.2 D; 1 Pet. 3.12; 4.18; cf. Matt. 10.41; 13.43; Luke 1.17.

58. Luke 13.23; Acts 2.47; 1 Cor. 1.18; 2 Cor. 2.15; Fitzmyer, 'Designations' 226; Fitzmyer includes 'witnesses of the risen Christ' (224), 'the flock' (Acts 20.28-29; 1 Pet. 5.2-3), 'the company *(plēthos)*' (Acts 4.32; 6.2, 5; 15.2, 30; Ignatius, *Smyrn.* 8.2) and 'fellowship' (Acts 2.42) (226-27). Other possible names are reviewed by Karpp, 'Christennamen' 1122-30.

59. Acts 9.2; see also 19.9, 23; 22.4; 24.14, 22; cf. 18.25-26; 2 Pet. 2.2; possibly reflected in 1 Cor. 12.31.

thought, which Paul continued to use[60] — hence the new movement as a 'way' of life, of living. The association of ideas between conduct as 'walking' and the resulting way of life as a 'path' followed is clear in Qumran thought; Qumran usage, in fact, provides the closest parallel to the term as it appears in Acts.[61] More striking is the fact that the Qumranites evidently drew their inspiration for the usage from Isa. 40.3: 'In the desert prepare the way *(derek)* . . .' (1QS 8.14). Since it is precisely this text which the early Jesus tradition related to the Baptist (Mark 1.3 pars.), the intriguing possibility emerges of a linkage in thought from Qumran, through the Baptist, to the earliest Christian community.[62] Alternatively put, there is the possibility of a similar sense of the vision of Isaiah 40 having achieved eschatological fulfilment in each of the three parties: 'the way of the Lord' had been realized. The imagery can hardly have been unrelated to the motif of *two* ways, traditional throughout the ancient world, where choice has to be made between one and another;[63] but no doubt it was the Jewish version which most bore upon the earliest disciples, as implied by the tradition of Matt. 7.13-14 in particular.[64] In which case the implication of the title ('the Way') is that those who claimed the title thereby asserted also that they had made the right choice and that theirs was the (only) way to salvation.

Not least in significance is Luke's description of Jesus' followers as a (15) *sect (hairesis)* (Acts 24.14; 28.22), 'the sect of *the Nazarenes*' (Acts 24.5). This presumably indicates that Luke regarded Jesus' early disciples as a 'sect' (or party, faction, school of thought),[65] like the 'sect' of the Sadducees (5.17) and the 'sect of the Pharisees' (15.5; 26.5). This in turn suggests that among fellow Jews, Jesus' disciples, as soon as they were perceived as a significant body, were regarded as yet another of the factions which were a feature of late Second Temple Judaism, as distinctive, and as 'sectarian', as better-known factions like the Pharisees.

(16) *Nazarenes* (Acts 24.5) puts us still more closely in touch with a distinctively Jewish way of describing the first believers. It was a natural tendency

---

60. See *Jesus Remembered* §9 n. 68; Dunn, *Theology of Paul* 643 nn. 82-84.

61. See particularly the absolute use ('the way') in 1QS 9.17-18, 21; 10.21; CD 1.13; 2.6; the Qumranites liked to think of themselves as 'the perfect of way *(derek)*', who 'walk in perfection of way *(derek)*' (1QS 4.22; 8.10, 18, 21; 9.5).

62. See also Fitzmyer, 'Designations' 229-30; also Fitzmyer, *Acts* 423-24, with further bibliography.

63. See H. D. Betz, *The Sermon on the Mount* (Hermeneia; Minneapolis: Fortress, 1995) 521-23.

64. Especially Deut. 30.15-16; see also, e.g., Josh. 24.15; Ps. 1.6; Prov. 15.19. Note also the implication of John 14.6 and the prominence of the motif in the Apostolic Fathers (particularly *Did.* 1–6 and *Barn.* 18–20) (W. Michaelis, *hodos, TDNT* 5.70-75, 78-96).

65. See *Jesus Remembered* §9 n. 44.

to designate Jesus' disciples as followers of the man from Nazareth, the Nazarene.[66] So far as we can tell, the name gained no currency outside Jewish Christian tradition. But within that tradition it retained its vitality. As H. H. Schaeder observes, 'Nazarenes' persisted as the name for Syrian Christians, and was adopted also by the Persians, the Armenians and later the Arabs.[67]

Here, finally, should be mentioned also (17) *Galileans,* which occurs only twice in Acts (1.11; 2.7), but which appears later as a term of scorn by outsiders.[68] Like 'Nazarenes', the term similarly links the movement back to its origins in Jesus' Galilean mission.[69] And, a point worth noting, it probably provides confirmation that the earliest leadership of the movement was provided by Galileans. But this inference itself raises again an issue (was there a Galilean 'church', or distinctive Galilean community — 'the Q community'?) to which we must return (§22.1).

Even such a cursory survey of terms actually used within the earliest traditions for infant Christianity is sufficient to highlight a number of important considerations, worthy of note before we go any further.

First, there is *no single term* which served to designate or describe those who participated in the sequel to the death of Jesus and its immediate aftermath. That fact itself should give us pause. To use one of these terms on our own part, predominantly or as the consistent referent and definition of what is in view, would be misleading. For similar reasons it might be equally objectionable to use a single term of our own choosing (like 'group', 'community', or 'movement'), since such terms import their own word-pictures and associations which may equally prejudge the evaluation of the material. Of course, it would be easy to become over-sensitive on the subject; on any subject or issue we cannot avoid using language whose word-pictures and associations may not quite 'fit' and may even skew the description which employs that language. The more realistic inference to be drawn is that we will be wise to use a variety of descriptive terms, just as Acts does, so that no single image becomes fixed and unduly normative.

---

66. F. F. Bruce, *New Testament History* (London: Marshall, Morgan and Scott, 1972) 214 (with bibliography, n. 41); Fitzmyer, 'Designations' 234-35; see also *Jesus Remembered* §9 n. 272.

67. Jerome, *Ep.* 112.13; H. H. Schaeder, *Nazarēnos, Nazōraios, TDNT* 4.874-75; see further 875-78; note the developed form of the famous twelfth benediction (*Shemoneh 'Esreh,* Palestinian recension): '. . . may the Nazarenes and the heretics perish quickly . . .' (Schürer, *History* 2.461). On the pre-Christian Jewish sect of the Nasarenes referred to by Epiphanius, *Pan.* 18; 29.6, see Harnack, *Mission* 402-403, and Schaeder 879.

68. Epictetus, 4.7.6 (quoted below, §21.1b); Julian, *Contra Galilaeos* (Julian continually links Galileans with Jews, while aware that they are different); and further Harnack, *Mission* 402; *GLAJJ* 1.541 n. 1, 528, 539, 541, 543, 550, 557-58, 572; see also §26 n. 97 below.

69. Cf. particularly the account of Peter's denial (Mark 14.70 pars.; *Jesus Remembered* §17 n. 54); Luke 23.6; and *Jesus Remembered* §§9.6-9.

Second, as an immediate corollary of greater significance, we should also note that the variety of terms used is an indication of the *inchoate character* of the group of first disciples. The range of terms just reviewed evidently indicated various facets of their corporate identity, but we should not assume that from the first these various facets cohered into a single 'Christian' identity. 'Identity' is a term naturally reached for at this point, and one which is in great vogue today in such discussions. Here it is especially appropriate, since the sociologists rightly remind us that identity is multiform — the single individual who is a daughter, a sister, a wife, a mother, a pupil, a teacher, a colleague, a friend, and so on.[70]

The implication is clear: the 'Christianity' which was beginning to emerge in the early 30s was not a single 'thing' but a whole sequence of relationships, of emerging perspectives of attitude and belief, of developing patterns of interaction and worship, of conduct and mission. A key question for us, then, is not so much whether we can speak of a single thing (movement, church, body of believers) but whether the various and diverse facets caught by the terms reviewed above (and more recent alternatives) form a coherent whole, or rather cloak a diversity which from the first could hardly be described as a unity.

Third, one such factor for coherence — indeed, arguably the chief factor for coherence (in *prima facie* terms) — is present in a number of the terms reviewed, namely, the *continuity with the mission of Jesus*. The feature is most obvious in 'disciples', 'brothers' and 'the poor', but also in 'Christians', 'Nazarenes' and 'Galileans', and is probably implicit in talk of the 'church' and 'the way'. During Jesus' mission Jesus himself, and their personal relation with him as his followers or disciples, was sufficient of itself to identify them. But with Jesus no longer 'on stage', that identifying factor (cf. Acts 4.13) would quickly lose its effect. The more striking feature, then, is given by the phrase 'those who call upon the name of the Lord (Jesus)', where the relationship is transformed from that of disciple to that of devotee or even worshipper. Self-identification by reference not only to Jesus, but to Jesus as Lord, constituted a massive step in the basic self-understanding of the early disciple groups, to which careful consideration will have to be given in due course. This will include the role of formulae like 'in his name', the way Jesus was spoken about in preaching and apologetic, the issue of whether and how quickly Jesus was worshipped, and (more controversially) the use made of the Jesus tradition.[71]

Fourth, another factor for coherence, which certainly holds together a number of the aspects reviewed above, is their *distinctively Jewish character* — particularly 'church', 'synagogue', 'saints', 'elect', 'poor', 'way' and 'sect of the Nazarenes'. The perspective from 'inside' Second Temple Judaism which such

---

70. See further below, §29.2.
71. See below, §§23.2; 23.4; 29.7d.

terms express indicates clearly enough that in the beginning, embryonic Christianity was self-consciously Jewish in its self-designation and claims and was so perceived during that beginning period. We recall, of course, that Second Temple Judaism itself was diverse in character.[72] The point is that in the beginning, the new movement which was embryonic Christianity was part of that diversity, wholly 'inside' the diversity of first-century Second Temple Judaism. That is a large conclusion to draw from what is merely a survey of names, and it will have to be tested and qualified as we proceed. Whether, and the extent to which, that preliminary conclusion (drawn only from terms of description and designation) is confirmed by our further investigations is a major concern of this volume. And if confirmed, the question of the conclusion's significance for an ongoing understanding of Christianity becomes one of the most important questions for the whole three-volume exercise.

20.2. From Jesus to Paul

The last two observations (the link to Jesus, and the Jewish character of the emerging sect) nicely introduce the two main puzzles which have intrigued students of Christianity's beginnings for more than two centuries. One is how to *bridge the gap (or gulf) between Jesus and Paul:* to explain how it was that Jesus' message of the kingdom became Paul's gospel of the crucified Jesus as Lord; how Jesus, the preacher of the good news, became its content; how the gospel *of* Jesus became the gospel *about* Jesus. The other puzzle or challenge is to *explain how a Jewish sect became a Gentile religion:* how a mission so much within the diversity of Second Temple Judaism became a movement which broke through the boundaries marking out that Judaism to emerge as a predominantly Gentile religion; how a kingdom preaching so much directed to the restoration of Israel became a claim by Gentiles to participate in, even to take over, Israel's name and heritage.

In his work on Jesus, E. P. Sanders made much of what he called 'Klausner's test' of a good hypothesis regarding Jesus' intention: the hypothesis 'should situate Jesus believably in Judaism and yet explain why the movement initiated by him eventually broke with Judaism'.[73] That is indeed a good test of a Jesus hypothesis. But it applies equally to any attempt to reconstruct Christianity in the making, and to 'the quest of the historical church' as much as to 'the quest of the

---

72. *Jesus Remembered* §9.

73. E. P. Sanders, *Jesus and Judaism* (London: SCM, 1985) 3, 18-19, referring to J. Klausner, *Jesus of Nazareth: His Life, Times and Teaching* (ET London: George Allen and Unwin, 1925) 369.

historical Jesus'. A good hypothesis regarding Christianity's beginnings should equally be required to explain how Christianity emerged from Jesus and how the movement which thus emerged within the matrix of Second Temple Judaism so quickly broke out of that matrix. And always the underlying issue is that same tantalizing question about identity: did the developments remain true to the initiating impulse provided by/embodied in Jesus? and did emerging Christianity retain the same identity throughout or evolve into a different species?

The heart of the first conundrum is christology. It is the other side of what I characterized as 'the flight from dogma' in volume 1.[74] There we looked at the reaction against the Christ of dogma, the Christ of faith, a reaction which initially fuelled the quest of the historical Jesus. Here it is the fact that high claims were being made for Christ from a very early period,[75] which provokes questioning and fuels suspicions. 'From Jesus to Paul' signals puzzlement that such a transformation could have been effected so speedily and encourages scepticism that it could have so happened without either some deceit or serious damage to the fundamentals of Jesus' own mission and message.

a. Hermann Reimarus

As with the quest of the historical Jesus, it was the English Deist Thomas Chubb[76] and the German rationalist Hermann Reimarus who first drew attention to the discontinuity between the message of Jesus and the early teachings of Christianity. And as in the former case, it was Reimarus who provided the most penetrating and devastating of the critiques. As regards christology, he urged that Jesus 'was born a Jew and intended to remain one';[77]

> it was not his intention to present a triune God or to make himself God's equal . . . nor did he intend to introduce a new doctrine that would deviate from Judaism.

74. *Jesus Remembered* §4.

75. M. Hengel, *The Son of God* (ET London: SCM, 1976), famously commented on the fact that the 'apotheosis of the crucified Jesus' must already have taken place in the forties [referring to the 'hymn' quoted by Paul in Phil. 2.6-11]: 'one is tempted to say *that more happened in this period of less than two decades than in the whole of the next seven centuries, up to the time when the doctrine of the early church was completed*' (2).

76. Chubb distinguished the gospel preached by Christ sharply from accounts of his suffering, death, resurrection and ascension and any doctrines founded thereon (such as Christ's meritorious suffering and heavenly intercession); extract in W. G. Kümmel, *The New Testament: The History of the Investigation of Its Problems* (ET Nashville: Abingdon, 1972) 55-56.

77. C. H. Talbert, *Reimarus Fragments* (Philadelphia: Fortress, 1970/London: SCM, 1971) 71-72. For fuller details see *Jesus Remembered* §4.2 and n. 15.

When Jesus calls himself God's Son he means to imply only that he is the Christ or Messiah particularly loved by God;

it is the apostles who first sought something greater in this term.[78]

In regard to the law, Reimarus's conclusion is

that the apostles taught and acted exactly the reverse of what their master had intended, taught, and commanded, since they released not only the heathen from the law but also those who had converted from Judaism. . . . the apostles strayed completely from their master in their teaching and in their lives, abandoning his religion and his intention and introducing a completely new system.[79]

Referring to Jesus' proclamation of the kingdom, Reimarus concludes:

only after Jesus' death did the disciples grasp the doctrine of a spiritual suffering savior of all mankind. Consequently, after Jesus' death the apostles changed their previous doctrine of his teaching and deeds and only then for the first time ceased hoping in him as a temporal and powerful redeemer of the people of Israel. . . . Now, however, that their hope is disappointed, in a few days they alter their entire doctrine and make of Jesus a suffering savior for all mankind; then they change their facts accordingly.[80]

Not content to insert the knife so expertly between the intention of Jesus and the subsequent teaching of his followers, Reimarus gave it a final savage twist. The explanation for the transition and transformation is crude. The motives which had led the disciples first to follow Jesus were those of worldly ambition, hopes of future wealth and power, lands and worldly goods (Matt. 19.29). When with Jesus, they had been well cared for by his friends and supporters; they grew out of the habit of working. But when Jesus died, only poverty and disgrace awaited them — until they realized that it need not end. It was this desire for wealth and worldly advantage which motivated them to fabricate the resurrection (they themselves removed Jesus' body) and the doctrines so strange to and at odds with the intention and message of Jesus.[81]

Reimarus's own final attempt to bridge the gulf from Jesus to Paul was a sad travesty, probably more indicative of his own long-concealed disillusion with the traditional claims of Christianity than of a fair-minded reading of the data.

78. Talbert, *Reimarus* 96, 88, 84.
79. Talbert, *Reimarus* 101-102.
80. Talbert, *Reimarus* 129, 134.
81. Talbert, *Reimarus* 240-54 (Matt. 19.29 is cited on 145).

But he again put his finger on features of the data, puzzles and tensions, which cannot be ignored in any attempt to explain how the move from Jesus to Paul came about so quickly. The issues he raised have not achieved a final resolution, so that his bringing them to focus remains one of Reimarus's major contributions to the Jesus/Paul debate.

- The more fully Jesus is set within the Judaism of his time, including the expectations of Jewish apocalypticism, the more pressing becomes the question: How and why did the beliefs about and claims regarding the divine status of Jesus come about? And are they at odds with any convictions Jesus is remembered as having uttered about himself?
- The more fully Jesus is set within the Judaism of his time, as a Torah-observant Jew who did not teach against the law, the more pressing becomes the question: How and why did it prove acceptable to leading disciples like Peter and John when Paul insisted that Torah-observance should not be required of Gentile converts?
- The more fully Jesus' teaching on the kingdom of God is set within the Judaism of his time, as proclaiming the fulfilment of Israel's hope of redemption, the more pressing becomes the question: How and why did a gospel for all, particularly the belief in Jesus' death as a sacrifice for all, first emerge?

The questions are posed avoiding some of Reimarus's more outdated language. But they are his questions, and they continue to demand attention.

b. The Jesus of History vs. the Christ of Faith

As a result of the rationalist challenge to traditional Christian dogma, the contrast, if not outright antithesis, between Jesus' own intention and what earliest Christianity made of him became a central preoccupation through most of the following two centuries. But to set 'the Jesus of history' over against 'the Christ of faith' required the historian of Christianity's beginnings not only to penetrate (and leave behind) the latter in order to rediscover the former ('the quest of the historical Jesus'). It required the historian also to explain how it was that a Jesus so different from the Christ of faith nevertheless became the Christ of faith and so speedily.

   David Friedrich Strauss first posed the issue sharply in these terms. His extensive and biting critique of Schleiermacher's *Life of Christ* was in fact entitled *The Christ of Faith and the Jesus of History*.[82] In his Foreword he characterizes

---

82. D. F. Strauss, *Der Christus des Glaubens und der Jesus der Geschichte* (Berlin:

Schleiermacher's christology as 'a last attempt to make the churchly Christ acceptable to the modern world' and responds cuttingly: 'Schleiermacher's Christ is as little a real man as is the Christ of the church'.

> The illusion . . . that Jesus could have been a man in the full sense and still as a single person stand above the whole of humanity, is the chain which still blocks the harbor of Christian theology against the open sea of rational science.[83]

Strauss was not concerned with the historical issue of how Jesus became 'the Christ of the church'. His critique was directed against Schleiermacher's dependence on John's Gospel 'as apostolic and trustworthy'.[84] But the implication is clear that the rift between the Jesus of history and the Christ of faith is already mirrored in the contrast between the Synoptics and John's Gospel. In the Fourth Gospel the Jesus of history is already lost behind the Christ of faith.[85]

When subsequently the great historian of Christian dogma, and greater historian, *Adolf Harnack* addressed the equivalent question, he attributed the transition to Paul. In a famous sentence he insisted that 'the Gospel, as Jesus proclaimed it, has to do with the Father only and not with the Son'. And he later quotes Wellhausen approvingly: 'Paul's especial work was to transform the Gospel of the kingdom into the Gospel of Jesus Christ, so that the Gospel is no longer the prophecy of the coming of the kingdom but its actual fulfilment by Jesus Christ'.[86] Here the challenge is as stark in its own way as that made by Reimarus: Jesus claimed no significance for himself; it was Paul, well before the Fourth Evangelist, who created the Christ of faith.

Another who made the contrast between the Jesus of history and the Christ of faith central to his analysis was *Martin Kähler* in his critique of 'the so-called historical Jesus' in favour of 'the historic biblical Christ'.[87]

Duncker, 1865), ET *The Christ of Faith and the Jesus of History* (Philadelphia: Fortress, 1977) translated and edited, with Introduction by L. E. Keck.

83. Strauss, *Christ of Faith* 4-5 (further ch. 2).

84. Strauss, *Christ of Faith* ch. 3.

85. Robert Morgan reminds me that already in 1835 in Strauss's *The Life of Jesus Critically Examined* (ET 1846; Philadelphia: Fortress, 1972), the Jesus of history is lost behind the Christ of faith in the Synoptics; see *Jesus Remembered* 29-34.

86. A. Harnack, *What Is Christianity?* (ET London: Williams and Norgate, 1900; ET 1901, ³1904) 147, 180-81.

87. *Der sogennante historische Jesus und der geschichtliche biblische Christus* (1892), ET *The So-Called Historical Jesus and the Historic Biblical Christ,* ed. C. E. Braaten (Philadelphia: Fortress, 1964). Kähler, of course, regarded the antithesis between the Jesus of history and the Christ of faith very differently from Strauss; for Kähler, the positive side of the antithesis was the latter. See *Jesus Remembered* §§4.5b, 5.2.

The risen Lord is not the historical Jesus *behind* the Gospels, but the Christ of the apostolic preaching, of the *whole* New Testament.

The real Christ, that is, the Christ who has exercised an influence in history . . . *is the Christ who is preached.* The Christ who is preached . . . is precisely the Christ of faith.

The recollection of the days of his flesh and the confession of his eternal significance and of what he offers to us are not separated in the New Testament.

The passionately held dogma about the Savior vouches for the reliability of the picture transmitted to us by the biblical proclamation of Jesus as the Christ.[88]

Whereas Strauss saw the transition to 'the Christ of faith' most clearly in John's Gospel, and Harnack saw it already happening in Paul, Kähler saw it in 'the apostolic preaching'. He dismissed the possibility of retrieving a 'historical Jesus' who was different from 'the biblical Christ' because the only Jesus proclaimed by the NT writers, including all the Gospel writers, is 'the Christ of faith'. Kähler thus inaugurated a theme which ran through two further generations of German scholarship: the NT writings as the preaching of the early church, with the implication that the transition to 'the Christ of faith' had already happened in the first preaching of Christ.

Rudolf Bultmann built directly upon Kähler when he justified his No to 'the quest of the historical Jesus' by insisting that Christ 'meets us in the word of preaching and nowhere else. The faith of Easter is just this — faith in the word of preaching. . . . The word of preaching confronts us as the word of God. It is not for us to question its credentials'.[89]

So once again it is the effectiveness of preaching, the existential challenge which was its self-authentication for Bultmann, which provided sufficient indication that it must have been so from the first. Now the Jesus of history/Christ of faith antithesis is recast as the antithesis between the historical Jesus and the kerygmatic Christ, with the implication that already with the earliest kerygma (the faith of Easter so defined) the decisive transition from one to the other had taken place; from the first, the myth (of cross and resurrection) had begun to obscure and to prevent access to the historical person.

Here again issues are being posed which cannot be ignored:

- the contrast between the Synoptic Jesus and the Johannine Jesus;

---

88. Kähler, *The So-Called Historical Jesus* 65, 66, 83-84, 95 (his emphasis).

89. R. Bultmann, 'New Testament and Mythology', in H. W. Bartsch, ed., *Kerygma and Myth* (London: SPCK, 1957) 1-44 (here 41). See further *Jesus Remembered* §5.3.

- the difficulty of squaring Jesus' focus on the kingdom of God with Paul's focus on Jesus;
- the challenge that the biblical Christ cannot or should not be correlated with the Jesus of Galilee and that the proclamation of Christ provides its own authentication.

I have already countered much of the thrust of this antithesis between the Jesus of history and the Christ of faith by arguing that faith did not first begin with Easter, and that the continuity of *impact* made by Jesus, before as well as beyond Easter, points to a greater continuity between the two than has usually been recognized.[90] But the contrasts and the disjunctions just noted are not resolved by that counter-thrust, so that a challenge for any attempt to analyze Christianity's beginnings is to describe, to explain as much as possible, and to understand if possible, the developments in christology which to a large extent determined the development of Christianity.

c. The Christology of Jesus?

The issues and challenges which focused in christology are already clear. But it is instructive to follow the debate further and to reflect briefly on its implications for the present study.

C. F. D. Moule provided a helpful diagrammatic illustration of how the contrast between 'the Jesus of history' and 'the Lord of faith' was treated in the late nineteenth-century quest and by Bultmann.[91] If we regard them as two concepts, they can be represented as circles on opposite sides of a dividing line:

In the understanding of Harnack and his fellow Liberals, faith should be focused in the left-hand circle and cut off more emphatically from the right-hand circle:

---

90. *Jesus Remembered* 129-34, 239-42.

91. C. F. D. Moule, *The Phenomenon of the New Testament* (London: SCM, 1967) 44-45.

For Bultmann, by contrast, the emphasis should fall on the right-hand circle, and the dividing line be drawn even thicker:

Moule's illustration can be extended into the subsequent phase of the discussion. For in the post-Bultmannian generation the attempt was made to elide the dividing barrier, to find already in Jesus' message an implicit christology.[92] There is no gap between Jesus' preaching of the kingdom and Paul's gospel, since, in a classic formulation by Ernst Käsemann, 'the issue in justification is none other than the kingdom of God that Jesus preached. . . . God's Basileia is the content of the Pauline doctrine of justification'.[93] The thrust of such argument can be illustrated by showing the circles as touching at least tangentially, or even overlapping:

To formulate the matter thus, however, is in danger of simply confusing an issue which was formulated more clearly by Harnack and Bultmann, however misleadingly. For Jesus was proclaimed in the post-Easter communities in a way that, so far as we can tell, he never proclaimed himself; faith was called for in Christ in a way that Jesus never called for faith in himself; claims were soon made for Jesus that he never made for himself. Even when the evidence of the Jesus tradition is pressed as hard as it seems able to bear, there is still a substan-

92. See *Jesus Remembered* §5.4, where I note *inter alia* that in debate with his pupils, Bultmann had accepted that Jesus' own preaching contained an implicit christology.

93. E. Käsemann, *Perspectives on Paul* (1969; ET London: SCM, 1971) 75, as cited approvingly by P. Stuhlmacher, *Revisiting Paul's Doctrine of Justification* (Downers Grove: InterVarsity, 2001) 52; see also E. Jüngel, *Paulus und Jesus* (Tübingen: Mohr Siebeck, ³1967) — Paul's teaching on justification makes explicit the christology which was implicit in the proclamation of Jesus (283).

tial gap between Jesus' own remembered self-estimation and the proclamation of Paul.[94] And to press it harder runs the risk of hearing only the elaborated form of the tradition and not the originating voice of Jesus himself. So the question remains: why and how did it come about that Jesus was so proclaimed? Alternatively, why or how did it come about that such richer overtones came to be heard in the Jesus tradition? The fact that the 'new quest' of the historical Jesus seems to have come unstuck or become bogged down on problems of methodology[95] is not unrelated to the fact that it has reached an impasse on the issue of continuity and discontinuity in the christology of the Jesus tradition.

d. The Question of Eschatology

In discussing the transition from Jesus to Paul it is rarely possible to side-step the issue of eschatology for very long. For the more Jesus' talk of the coming of the kingdom is seen in terms of *imminent expectation* (*à la* Schweitzer), the more pressing the question: in what sense if any did what in the event happened meet the expectation of Jesus? Alfred Loisy's famous quip still has bite: 'Jesus proclaimed the kingdom, and it was the Church that came'.[96] The suggestion that Paul's teaching on 'justification' somehow continues Jesus' teaching on the kingdom[97] seems to be another (less ironic) attempt to resolve the failure of imminent expectation. And so far as the issue elides into the issue of Jesus' own parousia (coming again, from heaven), I have already suggested that the idea may have emerged, in part at least, from a merging of Jesus' own remembered hope of vindication with his equally remembered parables of owners who depart only to return unexpectedly.[98] But in any case, that could only be part of the answer, and the question will require further exploration.

Equally pressing on Paul's side has been the problem of 'the delay of the parousia', already signalled by Reimarus[99] and frequently reappearing in 'the century of eschatology'.[100] Was the delay of the parousia a major determining factor in the shaping of early Christian theology?[101] Can it be used to explain the

94. *Jesus Remembered* §§15-17.

95. *Jesus Remembered* §5.4.

96. A. Loisy, *The Gospel and the Church* (London: Isbister, 1903) 166.

97. See above, n. 93.

98. *Jesus Remembered* §16.4f.

99. 'If Christ neither has nor does come again to reward the faithful in his kingdom, then our belief is as useless as it is false' (Talbert, *Reimarus Fragments* 228).

100. I mean, of course, the twentieth century. See, e.g., J. Plevnik, *Paul and the Parousia: An Exegetical and Theological Investigation* (Peabody: Hendrickson, 1996).

101. Particularly M. Werner, *The Formation of Christian Dogma* (1941; ET London: Black, 1957).

development of Paul's theology?[102] Does it provide a framework by means of which NT documents can be temporally located: the more intense the expectation, the earlier the writing; the less intense the expectation, the later the writing?[103] The question of failed expectation, already aired in *Jesus Remembered*,[104] raises its head again and cannot be ignored or lightly dismissed.

If we approach the question from the other side, the aspect of *realized expectation,* the problems of continuity/discontinuity appear equally fraught. No one of the past generation has posed the issue quite so sharply as Ernst Käsemann as he developed his own distinctive reconstruction of the theological impulses shaping Christianity's beginnings. His basic argument is that Jesus himself did not share the Baptist's apocalyptic imminent expectation; rather he 'proclaimed the immediacy of the God who was near at hand'. It was Easter and the reception of the Spirit which caused primitive Christianity to (in a sense) replace Jesus' preaching about the God at hand with 'a new apocalyptic'. Hence one of Käsemann's famous *dicta:* 'Apocalyptic was the mother of all Christian theology'.[105] The challenge thus posed by Käsemann is clear: if, in simple terms, Jesus was non-apocalyptic, even though set between an apocalyptic Baptist and an apocalyptic primitive community, from what source does this apocalypticism, so determinative of subsequent Christian theology, derive? To affirm both that 'apocalyptic was the mother of all Christian theology' and that Jesus was non-apocalyptic seems to cut Jesus off from what followed him and to attribute the decisive impulse for Christianity to experiences whose connection back to Jesus may have been no more than accidental.

e. Recent Debates

The two strands of the most recent phase of 'the quest of the historical Jesus'[106] have not advanced the issue very much. On the contrary, they have posed the

---

102. Famously in C. H. Dodd, 'The Mind of Paul', *New Testament Studies* (Manchester: Manchester University, 1953) 67-128.

103. Such a 'rule' has been a major factor in determining when 'early Catholicism' emerged (see below, §20.3a), and equally so in the famous characterization of the theology of Luke by H. Conzelmann, *The Theology of St. Luke* (1953, ²1957; ET London: Faber and Faber, 1961). J. A. T. Robinson made an analogous attempt to use awareness of the fall of Jerusalem as the clue to whether NT writings should be dated pre- or post-70, in *Redating the New Testament* (London: SCM, 1976).

104. *Jesus Remembered* §12.6d-e.

105. E. Käsemann, 'The Beginnings of Christian Theology' (1960), *New Testament Questions of Today* (ET London: SCM, 1969) 82-107 (here 101-102); see also the following essay, 'On the Subject of Primitive Christian Apocalyptic' (1962), 108-37.

106. *Jesus Remembered* §§4.7, 5.5.

same questions afresh. For on this issue both strands simply restate the dilemma as posed by the Liberal Protestants a century ago. On the one hand, what I have characterized as 'the neo-Liberal quest'[107] finds Jesus to be (simply) a subversive sage and thus substantially distant from the crucified and risen Christ of Paul — with no real link from the one to the other beyond the assertion that there were radically different responses to Jesus. The further corollary, implicit or explicit, is that the Christ of Paul's and of Mark's Gospel is a corruption of the 'original' Galilean good news. On the other hand, the so-called third quest of the historical Jesus — that is, in the terms I have been using, the quest for Jesus the Jew[108] — may seem similarly to restore the emphasis to the pre-Easter Jesus. The conse-quent dilemma is that *the more Jewish we see Jesus to have been, the harder it is to understand how and why the Christ of dogma emerged;* where the latter ob-scured and blocked the way back to the former, now the former may seem to ob-scure and to form a block on the way forward to the latter.

Looked at from the side of primitive Christianity, the issues are evidently complementary. On the one hand, a current argument runs strongly that there was a continuing Galilean community of Jesus' disciples who maintained his subver-sive wisdom teaching and mission and who showed no interest in a gospel of cross and resurrection.[109] And on the other, a forceful theological argument runs along the line of Barth and Käsemann to insist that Paul's 'revelation of Jesus Christ' (Gal. 1.12) breaks through all historical continuity and transposes the whole process of salvation to a new plane ('new creation').[110] Here the question of continuity between Jesus and Paul merges into the question of the diversity and disparity of the several groups and communities which constituted them-selves by some reference to Jesus of Nazareth.

The issue of continuity has been posed most sharply in contemporary con-troversy on how speedily a very high christology emerged. As we shall observe below, there is a substantial consensus in recent scholarship that christology de-veloped within a Jewish matrix (§20.3e). But was it the case that Paul (and his predecessors?) already thought of Jesus as pre-existent, partner in creation,[111] indeed as Yahweh,[112] or as included within the identity of the one God?[113] Or is

107. *Jesus Remembered* §4.7.

108. *Jesus Remembered* §5.5.

109. See *Jesus Remembered,* particularly §7.4b; and below, §21 n. 135.

110. See particularly J. L. Martyn, *Galatians* (AB 33A; New York: Doubleday, 1997); and further below, §31.7.

111. A. T. Hanson, *The Image of the Invisible God* (London: SCM, 1982); J. Haber-mann, *Präexistenzaussagen im Neuen Testament* (Frankfurt: Lang, 1990).

112. D. B. Capes, *Old Testament Yahweh Texts in Paul's Christology* (WUNT 2.47; Tübingen: Mohr Siebeck, 1992).

113. R. J. Bauckham, *God Crucified: Monotheism and Christology in the New Testa-*

the use of wisdom language for Christ, the reference of 'Yahweh texts' to Christ, and the devotion offered through Christ[114] to be understood not quite so straightforwardly?[115] If the former, then indeed the forward gap to later dogma is much diminished, but the backward gap to Jesus' own self-claims increases dramatically and the significance of his pre-passion mission recedes into the distance.

In short, however much we may question the various formulations of the confrontation between the Jesus of history and the Christ of faith (and I have already made the point that 'faith' did not first begin at Easter), the fact that the confrontation continues to be formulated and reformulated points to a continuing and unresolved issue. Several facets have been highlighted in the preceding review:

- How can we explain the transition from the Synoptic Jesus to the Johannine Jesus?
- What is the significance of the relative disappearance or demotion within earliest Christianity of the theme so central to Jesus' message, that is, his proclamation of the kingdom of God?
- To what extent (if at all!) did Jesus' own message influence the Pauline gospel and continue to be part of early Christian teaching?
- How and why did the transition from Jesus the proclaimer to Jesus the proclaimed come about?
- Did Easter primarily confirm and supplement what was remembered as a growing conviction of Jesus himself regarding his own role, or did it break upon a barely formed faith with the force of revelation, shifting perceptions of Jesus to an entirely different plane?
- Did the developments in christology proceed so apace as to cast the significance of Jesus of Nazareth into deeply increasing shadow from the beginning?

In sum, the debate on continuity and discontinuity between the pre-Easter Jesus and the post-Easter Christ, between the message of the former and the gospel about the latter, shifts back and forward without much progress. Can we move it forward?

---

ment (Carlisle: Paternoster, 1998); a much larger-scale monograph is promised in the near future.

114. L. W. Hurtado, *Lord Jesus Christ: Devotion to Jesus in Earliest Christianity* (Grand Rapids: Eerdmans, 2003).

115. See discussion in my *Theology of Paul* §§10-11; and further below, §§23.4d and 29.7d.

20.3. From Jewish Sect to Gentile Religion

The debate on whether christology properly so called began with Jesus or only after his death is only one issue within a wider discussion — the make-or-break issue as it proved to be, but not the only crux. That wider discussion concerns *the relation of Christianity to Judaism.* The aspect which bears most immediately on our concerns is the question *how and why Christianity emerged from Judaism* — the second half of 'Klausner's test'.[116]

The question is posed immediately by our opening analysis of terms which might be used to describe the beginnings of Christianity. I have already noted the distinctively Jewish character of many of these terms, particularly 'church', 'synagogue', 'saints', 'elect', 'poor', 'way' and 'sect of the Nazarenes' (§20.1), and those mentioned in n. 52 above — 'the people of God', 'the twelve tribes' and 'the seed of Abraham'. And I have not even mentioned the most controversial title of all — 'Israel'.[117] The use of such terminology among the first believers requires that the initial question be sharpened: How was a group or groups who used such language of themselves perceived and understood by others in relation to the heritage which gave them such language? Even sharper: How did those who used such language of themselves understand themselves in relation to that heritage and to other claimants on that heritage? On the face of it, this is 'intra-Jewish' or 'intra-Israel' language. But were those who used it perceived by others as *within* Judaism? Did those who used it perceive themselves as within Judaism? Or was the sect of the Nazarenes attempting to make exclusive claims on Israel's heritage, analogous to those of the Qumran community: these epithets belong to us and nobody else?[118] Did this new sect simply extend the factionalism already apparent within Second Temple Judaism?[119]

The sharpness of the issue is nicely posed by the context of thought in which the term 'Christianity' itself first appears. For it seems to be the case that Ignatius introduced that term precisely as a way of marking off this relatively

116. See n. 73 above.

117. I omitted it partly because the data are finally unclear in their implications, but also because their inclusion would be unnecessarily provocative at too early a stage in the discussion. The key NT data are the possible implications of Rom. 9.6 (an 'Israel' within 'Israel' or beyond 'Israel'?); 1 Cor. 10.18 (does reference to 'Israel according to the flesh' imply the assumption that there was another Israel?); Gal. 6.16 (who is 'the Israel of God' here?). But the claim that Christians/the church *is* Israel is certainly explicit later — e.g., Justin, *Dial.* 123.7 and 135.3; see further *PGL, Israēl* 4.

118. Though note the qualifications called for by M. Bockmuehl, '1QS and Salvation at Qumran', in D. A. Carson et al., eds., *Justification and Variegated Nomism.* Vol. 1 (see below, n. 223) 381-414.

119. See *Jesus Remembered* §9.4.

new entity from the more established 'Judaism'. *Christianismos* ('Christianity') was to be understood as something distinctive and different from *Ioudaïsmos* ('Judaism').[120] There is an interesting and somewhat ironic progression here: as the name *Ioudaïsmos* ('Judaism') was initially introduced to define what it referred to over against and in opposition to *Hellēnismos* ('Hellenism'),[121] so the name 'Christianity' was initially introduced to define its referent over against and in opposition to 'Judaism'. As the Maccabean rebellion in effect defined 'Judaism' as 'not-Hellenism', so Ignatius in effect defined 'Christianity' as 'not-Judaism'.[122]

That definitional usage already represented what became the principal claim of Christianity in relation to Judaism: that Christianity had superseded Judaism, had taken over Israel's status as 'the people of God', and had drained all the substance, leaving 'Judaism' only the husk.[123] I have already observed the extent to which that attitude has perverted Jewish/Christian relations throughout most of Christianity's history, and how in particular it influenced 'the quest of the historical Jesus'.[124] And we shall have to look more closely at the question of how and when this Christian 'supersessionism' first appeared.[125] The question here is whether that attitude was innate within, integral to the movement, which became designated 'Christianity', from its inception. How did that movement in its earliest days relate to the larger religious entity, Second Temple Judaism, within which it emerged? To ask, How did Christianity emerge from Judaism? is also to ask, What in the earliest days of its emergence was the character and identity of that movement?

As with the subject of christology (§20.2), so with the larger issue of how and why Christianity emerged from (or 'broke with') Judaism, it is instructive to recall the extent to which this issue has shaped the study of Christianity's origins over the past two centuries. To be more precise: there are two sides to the question, because there were two sides to the process. Not only the increasing *detachment* of Christianity *from Judaism,* but (note again the irony) the increasing *attachment* of Christianity *to Hellenism.* That is a shorthand formulation. But it highlights the twin concerns which have motivated researchers into Christian-

---

120. 'It is out of place to talk of Jesus Christ and to judaize. For Christianity did not believe in Judaism, but Judaism in Christianity . . .' (Ignatius, *Magn.* 10.3). 'But if anyone interprets Judaism to you, do not listen to him; for it is better to hear Christianity from a man who is circumcised, than Judaism from one uncircumcised' (*Phld.* 6.1).

121. See *Jesus Remembered* §9.2a.

122. See further K.-W. Niebuhr, '"Judentum" und "Christentum" bei Paulus und Ignatius von Antiochien', *ZNW* 85 (1994) 218-33, especially 224-33.

123. This will be a major issue in vol. 3.

124. *Jesus Remembered* §5.5.

125. This is also an issue which cannot be adequately tackled until vol. 3.

ity's beginnings for most of the last two hundred years. As Christianity became more and more distinct from Judaism, it became more and more Gentile, more and more Greek, more and more attuned to the religious-philosophical debates of the Greco-Roman world. How to explain this twin-motored process: how much repulsion or expulsion on the one side; how much attraction and assimilation on the other? A brief survey of the to-ing and fro-ing debate on such questions will give us further insight into the dynamics of the more narrowly focused Jesus-to-Paul and christological debates.

a. F. C. Baur

As Hermann Reimarus inaugurated the quest of the historical Jesus, so Ferdinand Christian Baur is the key figure in the quest of the historical church.[126] Already in the opening pages of his study of Paul he announced his programmatic question:

> The idea [of Christianity] found in the bounds of the national Judaism the chief obstacle to its universal historical realization. How these bounds were broken through, how Christianity, instead of remaining a mere form of Judaism, although a progressive one, asserted itself as a separate, independent principle, broke loose from it, and took its stand as a new enfranchised form of religious thought and life, essentially different from all the national peculiarities of Judaism is the ultimate, most important point of the primitive history of Christianity.[127]

As Baur himself subsequently related,[128] it was his study of Paul's letters to Corinth which provided the insight that the key to the whole question lay in the relation of the apostle Paul to the older apostles. Whereas the traditional as-

---

126. In what follows I use some of the material of my *The Partings of the Way between Christianity and Judaism and Their Significance for the Character of Christianity* (London: SCM/Philadelphia: TPI, 1991, ²2006) §1. Like my earlier *Unity and Diversity in the New Testament: An Inquiry into the Character of Earliest Christianity* (London: SCM, 1977, ²1990, ³2006), *Partings* was an attempt to clarify the nature of earliest Christianity. Unfortunately the significance of the full title of *Partings . . . and Their Significance for the Character of Christianity,* as an inquiry intended primarily to remind (and instruct) Christians of/on the Jewish origins and character of Christianity, has not been adequately appreciated (see the Preface to the second edition of *Partings,* particularly xxviii-xxix).

127. F. C. Baur, *Paulus. Der Apostel Jesu Christi* (Stuttgart, 1845), ET *Paul: The Apostle of Jesus Christ,* vol. 1 (London: Williams and Norgate, 1873) 3.

128. F. C. Baur, 'Die Einleitung in das Neue Testament als theologische Wissenschaft', *Theologische Jahrbücher* 10 (1851) 294-95, quoted by Kümmel, *New Testament* 127-28.

sumption had been of complete harmony between all the apostles, the Corinthians epistles, starting with the slogans of 1 Cor. 1.12, provided evidence of sharp opposition between a Petrine party and a Pauline party, of a Jewish Christianity which was fundamentally hostile to Paul and his Gentile mission.[129] From this insight grew the full thesis of the history of earliest Christianity as a long-running conflict between Pauline and Jewish Christianity, with NT documents dated in accordance with where they fitted into the history of this conflict. In particular, the historical value of Acts could not be defended, since it depicts Paul and Peter as closely similar in message and conviction, that is, a Paul who is manifestly different from the Paul of the Epistles. The Acts of the Apostles must derive, therefore, from a later period when attempts were being made to reconcile the conflicting views of the two factions.[130] And the epistles of Ignatius and Polycarp could not be authentic simply because a date for them in the second decade of the second century did not fit within this paradigm of a sustained conflict between these factions which was reconciled only later in the second century.

As the quotation from his *Paul* book shows, Baur was operating with a prejudicial distinction between 'particularism' and 'universalism', that is, between *Jewish* particularism and *Christian* universalism. And this came to full expression in his *Church History* in the following decade.[131] Here the self-confidence, not to say arrogance, of Christian Europe appear full grown in un-

---

129. F. C. Baur, 'Die Christuspartei in der Korinthischen Gemeinde, der Gegensatz des petrinischen und paulinischen Christentums in der ältesten Kirche, der Apostel Petrus in Rom', *Tübinger Zeitschrift für Theologie* 4 (1831) 61-206. His crucial finding was that 'two opposing parties with a very distinct difference of views had come into being as early as those early times in which Christianity had yet hardly begun to break through the narrow bounds of Judaism and to open up for itself a successful field of work in the pagan world' (cited by Kümmel, *New Testament* 129-30). Baur argued that the Christ party and the Cephas party in 1 Cor. 1.12 were one and the same, so that the slogans attested only two parties. It was J. Weiss, *1 Korinther* (KEK; Göttingen: Vandenhoeck und Ruprecht, 1910), who effectively destroyed that argument: if there was a party making exclusive claims on Christ, then Paul's rejoinders in 1.13 and 3.23 would simply have played into their hands (15-17).

130. The Acts of the Apostles 'is the attempt of a Paulinist to facilitate and bring about the *rapprochement* and union of the two opposing parties by representing Paul as Petrine as possible and, on the other hand, Peter as Pauline as possible' (F. C. Baur, 'Über den Ursprung des Episcopats in der Christlichen Kirche', *Tübinger Zeitschrift für Theologie* 3 [1838] 141, cited by Kümmel, *New Testament* 133-34). See Baur's more developed and more critical view in his *Paul* 5-14, in which he dismissed the historical value of Acts in favour of primary reliance on Paul's own letters (see further Kümmel, *New Testament* 133-36). On the issue of the historical value of Acts, see below, §21.2c.

131. F. C. Baur, *Das Christenthum und die christliche Kirche der drei ersten Jahrhunderts* (Tübingen, 1853), ET 2 vols. *The Church History of the First Three Centuries* (London: Williams and Norgate, 1878, 1879).

lovely synthesis: Christianity was 'universal' and 'absolute'; Judaism, as other forms of religion, was defective and limited, one-sided and finite.[132]

> Here then we meet again the characteristic feature of the Christian principle. It looks beyond the outward, the accidental, the particular, and rises to the universal, the unconditioned, the essential . . . the all-commanding universalism of its spirit and aims. . . . [Paul was] the first to lay down expressly and distinctly the principle of Christian universalism as a thing essentially opposed to Jewish particularism.[133]

Such a formulation well expressed the hubris of nineteenth- and early twentieth-century European scholarship, though regrettably the particularist/universalist contrast has extended well into the present day as a Christian criticism of Judaism.[134] But as an analysis of the historical process by which Christianity emerged into full flower, Baur's tendentious reconstruction could not stand.

In English-speaking scholarship no one more radically undermined Baur's schema than *J. B. Lightfoot*.[135] Despite popular misunderstanding on the issue, Lightfoot did not oppose Baur root and branch. In his penetrating essay 'St. Paul and the Three' he did not hesitate to speak of 'the systematic hatred of St. Paul [as] an important fact, which we are too apt to overlook, but without which the whole history of the Apostolic ages will be misread and misunderstood'.[136] 'Pharisaic Ebionism' (as he calls it) 'was a disease in the Church of the Circumcision from the first'.[137]

---

132. *Church History* 5-6; 'The universalism of Christianity is essentially nothing but that universal form of consciousness at which the development of mankind had arrived at the time when Christianity appeared' (5).

133. *Church History* 33, 43, 47.

134. For its inappropriateness see particularly N. A. Dahl, 'The One God of Jews and Gentiles (Romans 3.29-30)', *Studies in Paul* (Minneapolis: Augsburg, 1977) 178-91; A. F. Segal, 'Universalism in Judaism and Christianity', in T. Engberg-Pedersen, ed., *Paul in His Hellenistic Context* (Minneapolis: Fortress, 1995) 1-29; J. D. Levenson, 'The Universal Horizon of Biblical Particularism', in M. G. Brett, ed., *Ethnicity and the Bible* (Leiden: Brill, 1996) 143-69; J. D. G. Dunn, 'Was Judaism Particularist or Universalist?', in J. Neusner and A. J. Avery-Peck, eds., *Judaism in Late Antiquity*. Part 3, vol. 2: *Where We Stand: Issues and Debates in Ancient Judaism* (Leiden: Brill, 1999) 57-73. From the Jewish side D. Boyarin, *A Radical Jew: Paul and the Politics of Identity* (Berkeley: University of California, 1994), takes up the issues in a way which challenges both sides (particularly chs. 2-3).

135. An attractively told account was given in the Firth Lectures delivered in the University of Nottingham in 1962 by Stephen Neill, published as *The Interpretation of the New Testament* (Oxford: Oxford University, 1964), here ch. 2.

136. J. B. Lightfoot, 'St. Paul and the Three', *Saint Paul's Epistle to the Galatians* (London: Macmillan, 1865) 292-374 (here 311).

137. *Galatians* 322-23.

The crucial difference between Baur and Lightfoot, rather, lay in their hermeneutical approach to the NT documents. Baur began from the undisputed Pauline letters and, *reading them through the lenses of an idealist philosophy,* extrapolated what he found there into a grid for the first two centuries of Christianity's history, into which the rest of the NT documents had to be fitted. Lightfoot's response was that of the classic *historical exegete,* who subjected the NT texts to rigorously critical analysis, drawing on his unrivalled knowledge of ancient languages and writings.[138] Nothing demonstrated the effectiveness of the latter technique more than Lightfoot's massive three-volume study of Ignatius and Polycarp, in which he completely undermined the Baurian attempt to date these documents late in the second century in order to fit Baur's schema.[139] What emerged, however, was not a complete destruction of Baur, rather what C. K. Barrett characterizes as Lightfoot's 'modified Baurian position'; but its effect was certainly the destruction of the *chronology* of the Tübingen school.[140]

In German scholarship the revision of Baur proceeded more rapidly.[141] The course of the revision was already signalled by Baur's one-time admirer *Albrecht Ritschl.* In the second edition of his attempt to trace the origin of the ancient Catholic Church,[142] Ritschl demonstrated that early Christian history should not be conceived in terms of two monolithic blocks (Petrine and Pauline Christianity) grinding against each other. Peter (and the original apostles) should be distinguished from the opponents of Paul (the 'Judaizers').[143] And there was also a Gentile Christianity distinct from Paul and little influenced by him.

138. See also B. N. Kaye, 'Lightfoot and Baur on Early Christianity', *NovT* 26 (1984) 193-224; and further J. D. G. Dunn, 'Lightfoot in Retrospect', *The Lightfoot Centenary Lectures: To Commemorate the Life and Work of Bishop J. B. Lightfoot (1828-89), Durham University Journal* 94 (1992) 71-94.

139. J. B. Lightfoot, *The Apostolic Fathers.* Part 1: *S. Clement of Rome* (2 vols.; London: Macmillan, 1869, ²1890); part 2: *S. Ignatius, S. Polycarp* (3 vols.; London: Macmillan, 1885, ²1889).

140. C. K. Barrett, 'Quomodo historia conscribenda sit', *NTS* 28 (1982) 303-20 (here 310, 313-14); see also his 'Joseph Barber Lightfoot as Biblical Commentator', *Lightfoot Centenary Lectures* 53-70, reprinted in his *Jesus and the Word, and Other Essays* (Edinburgh: Clark, 1995) 15-34. Barrett's own 'modified Baurian position' is evident in his 'Paul: Councils and Controversies', in M. Hengel and C. K. Barrett, *Conflicts and Challenges in Early Christianity* (Harrisburg: Trinity Press International, 1999) 42-74, especially 51-53.

141. See the reviews by A. C. McGiffert, 'The Historical Criticism of Acts in Germany', *Beginnings* 2.363-95; E. Haenchen, ET *The Acts of the Apostles* (Oxford: Blackwell, 1971) 15-24.

142. A. Ritschl, *Die Entstehung der altkatholischen Kirche* (Bonn, 1850, ²1857).

143. In reference to the Jerusalem agreement (Gal. 2.1-10), however, Baur had recognized that there were two sections in Jewish Christianity, the one more strict, the other more liberal (*Paul* 131-33).

Whereas Baur saw the Catholic/Protestant schism as a reflection of the Petrine/Pauline schism, Ritschl saw Gentile Christianity as the root of early Catholicism.[144]

The double thrust here signalled provided an agenda which lasted through most of the twentieth century. On the one hand, the spectrum of earliest Christianity was seen to be more and more complex, running from Judaizers at one end, through Peter and the twelve, through Hellenistic Jews and Hellenistic Gentiles, to Paul and the more radical gnosticizing Christians beyond. More attention has been paid to the intervening positions on the spectrum — to the Hellenists (Acts 6.1),[145] to the distinctive features of the gospel of the church at Antioch,[146] to the phenomenon of the 'God-fearers' as the bridge into Gentile circles,[147] and now also to James.[148] And it is not without significance that some of the most thoroughgoing acceptance of this diversity is to be seen in attempts to trace the development of christology, precisely as a movement along such a spectrum.[149] On the other hand, the debate on how the ancient Catholic Church emerged, transposed itself steadily into a debate on 'early Catholicism', what it was, and how soon and how extensively the latter could be discerned within the NT itself.[150]

All this is tantamount to acknowledging the lasting importance of Baur's initial insight: that substantial tensions and conflicts were a feature of earliest Christianity's development, as fierce as, if not more so than, the tensions and conflicts elsewhere within Second Temple Judaism. Baur sustained the myth of earliest Christian history as a clearly identifiable 'Christianity' (or 'Christian principle') breaking loose from 'Judaism'. But he banished for all time the 'myth of Christian beginnings' as an ideal period of church unity and unified expansion.[151] The reconciling tendencies of Acts need not be postponed till the second quarter of the second century. But as Lightfoot acknowledged, even less can the hostility generated within the mother church against the work of Paul be post-

---

144. *Entstehung* 22-23; see further Kümmel, *New Testament* 162-67, with an extensive abstract.

145. See below, §24.

146. See below, §24.9.

147. See below, §29.5c.

148. See below, particularly §36.

149. F. Hahn, *Christologische Hoheitstitel* (Göttingen: Vandenhoeck und Ruprecht, 1963, [5]1995), ET *The Titles of Jesus in Christology* (London: Lutterworth, 1969); R. H. Fuller, *The Foundations of New Testament Christology* (London: Lutterworth, 1965).

150. See V. Fusco, 'La discussione sul protocattolicesimo nel Nuovo Testamento. Un capitolo di storia dell'esegesi', *ANRW* 2.26.2 (1995) 1645-91; also my *Unity and Diversity* ch. 14, including pp. xxix-xxx of the second edition (= xlvii-xlix of the third edition).

151. I echo the title of R. L. Wilken, *The Myth of Christian Beginnings* (London: SCM, 1979).

poned to the Ebionites of the second and subsequent centuries.[152] As Barrett observes, the challenge of Baur regarding the Pauline period readily dovetails with the challenge of Bauer regarding the post-Pauline period.[153] And more recently the repeated claims of Michael Goulder, that early Christianity is the tale of two competing missions,[154] shows that the central thrust of Baur's thesis still commands respect for its potential explanatory power.

In short, the making of Christianity was evidently much more confused and contested (from within!) than has traditionally been recognized. The clarification of just how 'confused and contested' must be a major concern of volumes 2 and 3.

b. The History-of-Religions School

Around the turn of the twentieth century, attention swung away from the question of Christianity's emergence from Judaism to Christianity's embrace of Hellenism.

Harnack had characterized the development of Christianity in terms of 'Hellenization', regarding the conception and development of dogma as the work of 'the Greek (or Hellenic) spirit', a spirit which was hardly dominant in the NT itself.[155] But the history-of-religions school emerged with the insistence that from the start Christianity could only be adequately understood within the context of the other religions of the time, and (here was the key point) *as influenced*

---

152. 'The great battle with this form of error [Ebionism] seems to have been fought out at an early date, in the lifetime of the Apostles themselves and in the age immediately following' (Lightfoot, *Galatians* 336).

153. C. K. Barrett, 'Pauline Controversies in the Post-Pauline Period', *NTS* 20 (1974) 229-45, reprinted in *Jesus and the Word* 195-212 (particularly 208). Barrett could be fittingly described as Durham's twentieth-century Lightfoot. My own *Unity and Diversity* was stimulated by Bauer's work (see also *Jesus Remembered* §1 n. 21).

154. M. D. Goulder, *A Tale of Two Missions* (London: SCM, 1994); also *Paul and the Competing Mission in Corinth* (Peabody: Hendrickson, 2001). Also to be mentioned here is G. Lüdemann, *Opposition to Paul in Jewish Christianity* (Minneapolis: Fortress, 1989).

155. See Kümmel, *New Testament* 178-79. Harnack worked with a very clear distinction between the gospel and dogma: 'Dogma in its conception and development is a work of the Greek spirit on the soil of the Gospel' (*History of Dogma.* Vol. 1 [1886, ET 1894; New York: Dover, 1961] 17). He regarded 'the influx of Hellenism, of the Greek spirit, and the union of the Gospel with it' as 'the greatest fact in the history of the Church in the second century', the first stage of which influx he was able to date to about 130 (*What Is Christianity?* 203-204). As Kümmel observes, such a thesis completely isolates early Christianity within its environment and does not allow it 'to have any decisive effect on the subsequent development of the Church' (178, 206).

by them. In particular, the Christianity which began to spread beyond Palestine was already showing the influence of pagan ideas.[156] This influence was most evident in two areas of emergent Christianity — cultic ritual and Christ mysticism.

It was *Wilhelm Heitmüller* who posed the challenge most sharply in terms of the Pauline understanding of baptism and Lord's Supper.[157] The very use of the formula 'in the name of' in the baptismal ritual reflects the widespread belief in the religions of the time (Judaism as well) that the 'name' was a bearer of power and magic.[158] And the Eucharist reflects the primitive concept of devouring the godhead, most clearly attested in the Dionysiac mystery cult.[159] At the heart of this new thrust was the growing conviction that Christianity itself was a syncretistic religion[160] — that it was in appearance and effect one more mystery cult emerging from the East into the Greco-Roman world, sharing with other mystery cults the foundational belief in a dying and rising god, like Attis, and in the cultic (sacramental) means by which the destiny of that god could be participated in.[161]

That early assessment proved too bold and had to be considerably qualified by more careful analysis.[162] (1) We know so little about the mysteries themselves

156. P. Wendland, *Die hellenistisch-römische Kultur in ihren Beziehungen zu Judentum und Christentum* (HNT 1, 2; Tübingen: Mohr Siebeck, 1907): 'already in early Christian literature . . . borrowings of pagan ideas and motifs, reminiscences of, and relationships to, the Hellenistic conceptual world [increase] with the progressive stages of its development' (cited by Kümmel, *New Testament* 247).

157. Prior to Heitmüller, mention should be made Otto Pfleiderer, one of the last of Baur's pupils, who was subsequently hailed as 'the father of history-of-religion theology in Germany' (Kümmel, *New Testament* 207); see Pfleiderer's *Primitive Christianity* (London: Williams and Norgate, 1906) and the brief discussion in J. Z. Smith, *Drudgery Divine: On the Comparison of Early Christianities and the Religions of Late Antiquity* (Chicago: University of Chicago, 1990) 93-99.

158. W. Heitmüller, *'Im Namen Jesu'. Eine sprach- und religionsgeschichtliche Untersuchung zum Neuen Testament, speziell zur altchristlichen Taufe* (Göttingen, 1903).

159. W. Heitmüller, *Taufe und Abendmahl bei Paulus. Darstellung und religions-geschichtliche Beleuchtung* (Göttingen, 1903); see Kümmel, *New Testament* 255-57.

160. Explicitly stated by H. Gunkel, *Zum religionsgeschichtlichen Verständnis des Neuen Testaments* (Göttingen, 1903) 1, 95; see the lengthy abstract in Kümmel, *New Testament* 258-59.

161. For recent treatments of the mystery cults see W. Burkert, *Ancient Mystery Cults* (Cambridge: Harvard University, 1987); E. Ferguson, *Backgrounds of Early Christianity* (Grand Rapids: Eerdmans, 1987, [2]1993) 235-82; H.-J. Klauck, *The Religious Context of Early Christianity: A Guide to Graeco-Roman Religions* (1995, 1996; ET Edinburgh: Clark, 2000) 81-249. For a good collection of ancient texts on the theme see M. W. Meyer, ed., *The Ancient Mysteries: A Sourcebook; Sacred Texts of the Mystery Religions of the Ancient Mediterranean World* (San Francisco: Harper, 1987).

162. H. A. A. Kennedy, *St. Paul and the Mystery Religions* (London: Hodder and

(they were good at keeping their mysteries secret!); poorly discerned analogies hardly provide proof of genetic dependence.[163] From what we can discern, (2) water rituals, as in initiation to the Isis cult, seem to have served as preliminary purifications and did not constitute part of the initiation itself. (3) The motivation seems to have been more in terms of deliverance from the terrors of the afterlife than of redemption from sin. (4) No clear concept of a mystical identification with the cult deity is evident, more that of re-enacting the fate of the god. (5) While the idea of a meal presided over by the god provides some kind of parallel (1 Cor. 10.20-21), the Dionysiac ritual of 'eating raw meat' hardly provides a precedent for the Lord's Supper. (6) Not least, there are more obvious source-influences for the characteristic (Pauline) features in the Jewish background of Jesus' own mission: 'baptism' as metaphor for Jesus' death;[164] the table-fellowship, and particularly the last supper of Jesus and his disciples.[165]

Nevertheless, scholars have justifiably shown themselves unwilling to return to a concept of early Christianity as wholly isolated and distinct from the religious culture and ethos of the day. Paul himself evidently saw a dangerous parallel between the chaotic enthusiasm of the Corinthian worship (1 Cor. 14.23) and the abandoned ecstasy of the Dionysiac cult (12.2). The suggestion that the bread and wine, consumed in a wrong spirit, could have destructive effect (11.29-30) has an unnerving ring. And as we shall see, social-anthropological appreciation of the function of rites of passage, of experiences of conversion and liminality, of eating rituals as community defining, and of the pervasiveness of magical beliefs and practices in the ancient world has reinforced the fundamental history-of-religions' conviction that unless the resonances between earliest

---

Stoughton, 1914); A. D. Nock, 'Early Gentile Christianity and Its Hellenistic Background' (1928) and 'Hellenistic Mysteries and Christian Sacraments' (1952), in J. Z. Stewart, ed., *Essays on Religion and the Ancient World* (Oxford: Clarendon, 1972) 1.49-133 and 2.791-820; B. Metzger, 'Considerations of Methodology in the Study of the Mystery Religions and Early Christianity', *HTR* 48 (1955) 1-20; G. Wagner, *Pauline Baptism and the Pagan Mysteries* (ET Edinburgh: Oliver and Boyd, 1967); A. J. M. Wedderburn, *Baptism and Resurrection: Studies in Pauline Theology against Its Graeco-Roman Background* (WUNT 44; Tübingen: Mohr Siebeck, 1987); Ferguson, *Backgrounds* 279-82. See also M. Hengel, 'Early Christianity as a Jewish-Messianic, Universalistic Movement', in M. Hengel and C. K. Barrett, *Conflicts and Challenges in Early Christianity* (Harrisburg: Trinity Press International, 1999) 1-41. But the repeated warnings of Smith against undeclared agendas to 'insulate' early Christianity from its environment and to maintain its 'uniqueness' (*Drudgery Divine* chs. 2-5) need to be constantly borne in mind.

163. It was A. Deissmann, *Light from the Ancient East* (1908, ⁴1923; ET London: Hodder and Stoughton, 1927), who first posed the issue sharply: 'Is it analogy or is it genealogy?' (265-66).

164. *Jesus Remembered* §§17.4d, 17.5c.

165. *Jesus Remembered* §17.4e. See further my *Theology of Paul* 445-52, 601-608.

Christianity and its religious environment are properly recognized, the history of earliest Christianity cannot be adequately appreciated.[166] Nor can we wholly ignore the fact that polemical reconstructions of Christianity's beginnings still attempt to rework the earlier crude thesis of direct influence from the mysteries to explain the origin for the Christian sacraments of baptism and eucharist.[167] Here then is another major item for our ongoing agenda.

The other most striking feature of the history-of-religions approach to the NT was the switch of focus from doctrine and morality to religion and experience. A crucial factor was the reassessment of christological development in terms of 'Christ mysticism'.[168] Here the main player was *Wilhelm Bousset*. In his great work on the development of Christian belief about Jesus, *Kyrios Christos,*[169] Bousset made several breakthroughs. In particular, he brought home the recognition that between Jesus and Paul must be interposed both the primitive Palestinian community and the Hellenistic communities of Antioch, Damascus and Tarsus.[170] From that time forward no study of Christianity's beginnings could ignore the greater complexity of the transition from Jesus to Paul. He was also the most impressive executive of William Wrede's programmatic call for the study of earliest Christianity not as the history of doctrine but as the history of religion, a study which broke through the boundaries of the NT canon,[171] in Bousset's case extending to Irenaeus.

But Bousset's principal contribution was to emphasize the intensity of religious feeling which comes to expression in the mysticism of Paul's frequent 'in Christ' formula. 'Behind Paul's mysticism of the *en Christō einai* there stands the living experience of the Kyrios Christos present in worship and in the practical life of the community'; 'for Paul Christ becomes the supra-terrestrial power which supports and fills with its presence his whole life'.[172] With this, Jesus' ethical religion of the forgiveness of sins has been left behind.[173] Nor is it merely a matter of cult mysticism, of sacraments influenced by mystery cults, for Paul de-

166. See further below, n. 197.

167. H. Maccoby, *Paul and Hellenism* (London: SCM, 1991) chs. 3-4 (particularly 65, 73, 123-26); G. A. Wells, *The Jesus Myth* (Chicago: Open Court, 1999).

168. 'Paul as a mystic — this great theme of the *religionsgeschichtliche Schule*' (U. Luz, 'Paul as Mystic', in G. N. Stanton et al., eds., *The Holy Spirit and Christian Origins,* J. D. G. Dunn FS [Grand Rapids: Eerdmans, 2004] 131-43 [here 132]).

169. W. Bousset, *Kyrios Christos* (1913, ²1921; ET Nashville: Abingdon, 1970).

170. Bousset, *Kyrios Christos* 119, where Bousset expresses his agreement with W. Heitmüller, 'Zum Problem Paulus und Jesus', *ZNW* 13 (1913) 320-37.

171. W. Wrede, *The Task and Methods of 'New Testament Theology'* (Göttingen: Vandenhoeck und Ruprecht, 1897), ET in R. Morgan, *The Nature of New Testament Theology* (London: SCM, 1973) 68-116.

172. Bousset, *Kyrios Christos* 156, 154.

173. Bousset, *Kyrios Christos* 182.

veloped a personal mysticism out of cultic mysticism.[174] In such experiences in worship, where a supernatural divine power (the Spirit) seizes a person and works charismatic gifts through him, Spirit-mysticism and Christ-mysticism are one and the same.[175]

The characterization of these developments in terms of 'mysticism' probably diminished the appeal of Bousset's formulation, since mysticism has typically come to be regarded with suspicion in academic circles,[176] and too much emphasis on ecstatic religious experience evokes memories of the Reformation Schwärmer for most of those within a mainline Christian tradition.[177] But Bousset had opened a more inviting door.

c. The Quest for Pre-Christian Gnosticism

Behind the individual myths of the dying and rising god Bousset saw the more fundamental Gnostic myth of the Primal Man who sinks down into matter and is again liberated from it, a myth most clearly expressed in the Hermetic tractate 'Poimandres' and in the Naassene hymn (Hippolytus, *Ref.* 5.10.2).[178] This is the context of oriental mysticism, within whose context Pauline mysticism had to be understood. Alternatively expressed, the Primal Man is a cosmic power which has sunk down into matter to produce that mixture between higher and lower, good and evil elements which human beings experience in inward struggle. Salvation consists in bringing knowledge *(gnōsis)* to the fragmented 'light-souls' as to their true nature, thus liberating them to ascend once more to be reunited in the world of light.[179]

This claim became an important starting point for the very influential *Theology of the New Testament* of *Rudolf Bultmann,* with its assumption that the full-blown Gnostic myth was in widespread existence before Paul.[180] Here was the

174. Bousset, *Kyrios Christos* 157; 'it is just his achievement to have re-formed into individual mysticism, ethicized, and transposed out of the cult into the total personal life that cultic and community mysticism, in the ardor of experience' (157).

175. Bousset, *Kyrios Christos* 160-63.

176. See, e.g., R. Bultmann, 'Mysticism in the New Testament', in J. Pelikan, ed., *Twentieth-Century Theology in the Making.* Vol. 2: *The Theological Dialogue: Issues and Resources* (London: Collins Fontana, 1970) 368-73 (ET of *RGG* article); and further my *Theology of Paul* 390-96.

177. J. Ashton, *The Religion of Paul the Apostle* (New Haven: Yale University, 2000), revives the early history-of-religions interest in Paul's religion rather than his theology.

178. Texts in C. K. Barrett, *The New Testament Background: Selected Documents* (London: SPCK, 1961) 82-90, and R. M. Grant, ed., *Gnosticism: An Anthology* (London: Collins, 1961) 115.

179. Bousset, *Kyrios Christos* 190-98.

180. Bultmann, *Theology* 1.164-83.

explanation for the already pre-Pauline concept of salvation: Christ identified as the light person who brings the vital Gnosis to those held captive, modelled not simply on the pattern of the dying and rising god, but also on the full-blown pattern of a descending and re-ascending redeemer (most clear in Phil. 2.6-11). Christ was the Man (Adam), the spiritual man, who overcomes the damage done by the psychic man (the first Adam) (1 Cor. 15.44-49). Here too was why Christians were classed as 'spirituals *(pneumatikoi)*', as opposed to 'soulish *(psychikoi)*' (1 Cor. 2.13-15).[181] The same source provided Paul with his concept of the body of Christ.[182]

The problem with all this has been that the full-blown Gnostic redeemer myth here inferred is nowhere clearly attested before the second century CE. There are terms used *(gnōsis, pneumatikos)*. There are partial parallels, like talk of the descent and ascent of divine Wisdom in *1 Enoch* 42. But the thesis has to assume that the pre-Christian sources provide evidence of a broken myth, fragments of a disintegrated myth. That is to say, the full myth has to be presupposed before such features can be designated fragments.[183] On the face of it, a more likely hypothesis is that the full myth is itself a later amalgamation of such earlier elements. The Jewish Adam myth seems itself to have influenced Poimandres.[184] In 1 Cor. 15.44-49 Christ, the spiritual man, is the *last* Adam, not the first; this is Jewish eschatology, not Platonic or Gnostic cosmology.[185] And the first redeemer figures as such do not appear till the second century — probably Christianity's contribution to syncretistic Gnosticism![186]

Despite such crippling facts, the quest for pre-Christian Gnosticism continued into the second half of the twentieth century. The debate shifted from the question whether Gnosticism influenced Paul; or was it only his churches which were influenced? The embarrassment of attributing Paul's gospel to Gnostic influences could be circumvented by attributing it to his opponents! Where Baur could characterize all Paul's opponents as 'Judaizers',[187] now they were to be

---

181. The explanation had already been provided by R. Reitzenstein, *Hellenistic Mystery Religions: Their Basic Ideas and Significance* (1910; ET Pittsburgh: Pickwick, 1978).

182. Developed by Bultmann's pupil E. Käsemann, *Leib und Leib Christi. Eine Untersuchung zur paulinischen Begrifflichkeit* (Tübingen: Mohr, 1933).

183. C. Colpe, *Die religionsgeschichtliche Schule. Darstellung und Kritik ihres Bildes vom gnostischen Erlösermythus* (Göttingen: Vandenhoeck und Ruprecht, 1961).

184. C. H. Dodd, *The Bible and the Greeks* (London: Hodder and Stoughton, 1935) part 2.

185. See further my *Christology* 123-25 and xviii.

186. 'The most obvious explanation of the origin of the Gnostic redeemer is that he was modelled after the Christian conception of Jesus. It seems significant that we know no redeemer before Jesus, while we encounter other redeemers (Simon Magus, Menander) immediately after his time' (Grant, *Gnosticism* 18).

187. At the time of Paul 'judaize' was a term used for Gentiles who sympathized with

characterized as 'Gnostics'. Not surprisingly, 1 Corinthians offered itself as an inviting location, with its talk of 'spirituals', its hint of realized eschatology (4.8) and dualistic asceticism (7.1), the confident talk of 'knowledge' (8.1-2), and denial of resurrection or resurrection body (15.12, 35).[188] And later Pauline epistles like Ephesians could be characterized as using modified Gnostic terminology to defeat Gnostic opponents.[189] But the truth is that the quest for pre-Christian Gnostic influence on the development of first-century Christian thought has run into the sand.[190] To be fair, the much later Nag Hammadi documents have prevented the debate from being dismissed altogether.[191] In consequence, we will have to keep it on the agenda. But it will not be a lead item.

d. A Sociological Perspective

A natural expression of a history-of-religions perspective was to examine Christianity's beginnings as a social phenomenon, involving groups and interaction with and between different social structures and processes. To some extent the path was pioneered by Edwin Hatch before the flowering of the history-of-religions school by his relating the organization of the early churches to the social groupings of the classical world.[192] But the impulse was presumably not helped by Troeltsch's early observation that 'the rise of Christianity is a religious and not a social phenomenon', and his concern not to give ground to a Marxist

---

Judaism and adopted some Jewish customs (see below, §27.4a[iii]); the usage introduced in the nineteenth century and dominant since (Judaizers as Christian Jews who insisted that Gentile converts had to be circumcised and keep the law) was unknown in the first century.

188. Particularly W. Schmithals, *Die Gnosis in Korinth* (FRLANT 48; Göttingen: Vandenhoeck und Ruprecht, 1965), ET *Gnosticism in Corinth* (Nashville: Abingdon, 1971); also *Theologiegeschichte des Urchristentums. Eine problemgeschichtliche Darstellung* (Stuttgart: Kohlhammer, 1994) e.g., ch. 7.

189. See H. Merkel, 'Der Epheserbrief in der neueren Diskussion', *ANRW* 2.25.4 (1987) 3176-3212.

190. See, e.g., P. Perkins, *Gnosticism and the New Testament* (Minneapolis: Fortress, 1993) particularly 74-92; M. Hengel, 'Paulus und die Frage einer vorchristlichen Gnosis', *Paulus und Jakobus* (Tübingen: Mohr Siebeck, 2002) 473-510; and the discussion by K. L. King, *What Is Gnosticism?* (Cambridge: Harvard University, 2003). A. J. M. Wedderburn, *A History of the First Christians* (London: Clark, 2004), concludes his note on the subject: 'there is increasingly little room for gnosis as an independent entity existing prior to early Christianity' (64-66).

191. Particularly the *Gospel of Philip* 58.17-22; 71.9-17, and the *Sophia of Jesus Christ* 100-101; but the thesis still depends on the non-sequitur reasoning that 'independent means prior'.

192. E. Hatch, *The Organization of the Early Christian Churches* (London: Longmans, 1888).

social analysis, in terms of class struggle.[193] In fact it took another fifty years for a sociological interest to re-emerge.[194] However, since the pioneering studies of the Corinthian church by *Gerd Theissen,*[195] the sociological path has become a major highway for scholarly monographs. The Acts portrayal of the earliest Jerusalem church might not provide enough information (or give enough confidence) to make possible a sociological analysis. Reconstruction of the *Sitz im Leben* of the Gospels can rarely rise above the speculative. But the letters of Paul, with their immediacy and directness of address to particular churches and situations, have been more fruitful.

The sociological approach has enabled better understanding of the social dynamics of small groups meeting in private houses, often small tenement apartments, in the cities where Paul principally operated. What was the proportion of well-to-do and low born, of slaves and slave-owners, of Jews and non-Jews? What did it mean for Paul to work with his own hands to support himself? How did the patron/client and honour/shame conventions of the Mediterranean world impact on the conduct and relationships within the Pauline churches? What about the status of women within the house churches and their role in ministry within these churches? How did the first Christian groups survive or thrive within often hostile environments? What boundaries did they draw round themselves, and what movement did they permit through these boundaries?[196] Such

193. E. Troeltsch, *The Social Teaching of the Christian Churches* (1912; ET London: George Allen and Unwin, 1931) 43. G. Theissen, 'Sociological Research into the New Testament', *Social Reality and the Early Christians* (Minneapolis: Augsburg Fortress, 1992) 1-29, discusses 'the declining interest in social history during the era of dialectical theology, 1920-1970' (8-15). On the suspicion of Marxist influence as the principal reason why social-scientific approaches to NT studies fell out of favour during that period, see J. G. Crossley, *Why Christianity Happened: A Sociohistorical Account of Christian Origins (26-50 CE)* (Louisville: Westminster John Knox, 2006) 5-21.

194. E. A. Judge, *The Social Patterns of Christian Groups in the First Century* (London: Tyndale, 1960), about which Theissen commented, 'This little book deserves a place of honor in the history of modern sociological exegesis' (*Social Reality* 19 n. 23).

195. G. Theissen, *The Social Setting of Pauline Christianity* (Philadelphia: Fortress, 1982).

196. See particularly J. K. Chow, *Patronage and Power: A Study of Social Networks in Corinth* (JSNTS 75; Sheffield: JSOT, 1992); R. F. Hock, *The Social Context of Paul's Ministry: Tentmaking and Apostleship* (Philadelphia: Fortress, 1980); D. G. Horrell, *The Social Ethos of the Corinthian Correspondence: Interests and Ideology from 1 Corinthians to 1 Clement* (Edinburgh: Clark, 1996); B. J. Malina, *The New Testament World: Insights from Cultural Anthropology* (London: SCM, 1983); W. A. Meeks, *The First Urban Christians: The Social World of the Apostle Paul* (New Haven: Yale University, 1983). On the dangers of misusing sociological models — what E. A. Judge, 'The Social Identity of the First Christians: A Question of Method in Religious History', *JRH* 11 (1980) 201-17, described as the 'sociological fallacy' (210) — see Horrell, *Social Ethos* 11-18; B. Holmberg, 'The Methods of Historical Reconstruction in

questions are obviously of considerable importance in any attempt to give a full description of the making of Christianity.

In an equivalent psychological and social-anthropological approach to Christian beginnings, an obvious candidate for closer inspection was the prominence of Spirit and Spirit phenomena. By reading Paul's account of the effects of the Spirit within his churches, Hermann Gunkel had shifted the perception of 'spirit' from the idealist world spirit of Hegel to something much more primitive — the experience of empowering.[197] This understanding of the Spirit in terms of experience became fundamental to analysis of Spirit language in the NT,[198] and Max Weber's portrayal of the charismatic leader[199] provided an obvious link-point. But the link was not much exploited, and the emergence of Pentecostalism in the first half of the twentieth century may have contributed to scholarship's neglect of the aspect; this Spirit was *too* primitive a concept! Käsemann's recognition of the importance of enthusiasm as a (dangerous) feature in earliest Christianity[200] was the main outcome in scholarly study of Christianity's beginnings, though the growth of the so-called charismatic movement in the second half of the twentieth century

---

the Scholarly "Recovery" of Corinthian Christianity', in E. Adams and D. G. Horrell, eds., *Christianity at Corinth: The Quest for the Pauline Church* (Louisville: Westminster John Knox, 2004) 255-71 (here 267-69): 'Models should not be seen as ideas that a scholar starts from and lets his research be guided by, but rather as the results of empirical research, which serve to simplify, abstract, or generalize the findings obtained, so that they can be further tested elsewhere' (269); 'models or theories cannot substitute for evidence, by filling in gaps in the data, as it were' (270). J. T. Sanders, *Schismatics, Sectarians, Dissidents, Deviants: The First One Hundred Years of Jewish-Christian Relations* (London: SCM, 1993), makes a swinging attack on the use made of Mary Douglas's group/grid model, particularly by Malina (106-13). He is similarly critical of the use made of Troeltsch's church/sect model (114-25) but finds deviance theory more to the point (129-51); he is more gently critiqued in turn by J. M. G. Barclay, 'Deviance and Apostasy', in P. F. Esler, ed., *Modelling Early Christianity: Social-Scientific Studies of the New Testament in Its Context* (London: Routledge, 1995) 114-27.

197. H. Gunkel, *Die Wirkungen des Heiligen Geistes nach der populären Anschauung der apostolischen Zeit und der Lehre des Apostels* (Göttingen: Vandenhoeck und Ruprecht, 1888), ET *The Influence of the Holy Spirit: The Popular View of the Apostolic Age and the Teaching of the Apostle Paul* (Philadelphia: Fortress, 1979).

198. See, e.g., H. Bertrams, *Das Wesen des Geistes nach der Anschauung des Apostels Paulus* (Münster, 1913) ch. 2; H. W. Robinson, *The Christian Experience of the Holy Spirit* (London: Nisbet, 1928); 'Long before the Spirit was a theme of doctrine, he was a fact in the experience of the community' (E. Schweizer, *TDNT* 6.396); L. T. Johnson, *Religious Experience in Earliest Christianity* (Minneapolis: Fortress, 1998) 6-16, though note his subtitle — *A Missing Dimension in New Testament Studies*.

199. See particularly M. Weber, *The Theory of Social and Economic Organizations* (ET New York: Free Press, 1947) 358-92. Theissen observes that Weber's term 'charisma' 'has proved so useful in connection with so many phenomena that we cannot now get along without it' ('Sociological Research' 20).

200. See above, n. 105.

aroused an equivalent interest in the charismatic and experiential dimension of Paul's writings in Pauline scholarship.[201] However, the more we recognize that earliest Christianity was in some important sense a movement of the Spirit, the more important it will be to keep this dimension in mind as we proceed.

Not unrelated was a famous debate between *Rudolph Sohm* and Adolf Harnack which spanned the turn of the twentieth century — in effect, complementary to the debate on 'early Catholicism'. Sohm sharpened an already recognized contrast between 'function' and 'office' in early church organization into a sharp antithesis between 'charisma' and 'canon law' *(Kirchenrecht)*. His argument, based principally on Paul, was that 'the organization of Christendom is not a legal one, but a charismatic organization'; 'Christendom is organized through the distribution of spiritual gifts'.[202] For Sohm the displacement of charismatic structure by human Kirchenrecht, first visible in *1 Clement* (late first century CE), marked a 'fall' from the apostolic to the sub-apostolic age. In contrast, Harnack recognized the tension between Spirit and office but saw it not as sequential rather as simultaneous, charismatic functions and administrative offices operating in tension more or less from the first.[203] This too is a debate which revived in the second half of the twentieth century,[204] with the 'early catholicism' issue restated in terms provided from Weber's sociology, as to whether the 'routinization' or 'institutionalization' of charisma is best conceived as a second-generation development or as already a feature within Paul's own churches.[205] Here too we will be unable to ignore various aspects of the charisma/office tension and debate in what follows.

Another older and related interest which was reinforced by history-of-religions motivation was in the influence of ancient rhetoric on Paul. This was another way of approach to Paul's letters, other than viewing them as primarily statements of theology, which came to the fore in the great commentary on 1 Corinthians by Johannes Weiss.[206] But here once again it was an interest which

---

201. See particularly J. D. G. Dunn, *Jesus and the Spirit: A Study of the Religious and Charismatic Experience of Jesus and the First Christians* (London: SCM, 1975; Grand Rapids: Eerdmans, 1997); G. D. Fee, *God's Empowering Presence: The Holy Spirit in the Letters of Paul* (Peabody: Hendrickson, 1994).

202. R. Sohm, *Kirchenrecht* (1892; Munich: Duncker und Humblot, 1923) 1.1, 26.

203. A. Harnack, *The Constitution and Law of the Church in the First Two Centuries* (London: Williams and Norgate, 1910).

204. E.g., Bultmann, *Theology* 2.95-118; H. von Campenhausen, *Ecclesiastical Authority and Spiritual Power in the Church of the First Three Centuries* (1953; ET London: Black, 1969); E. Schweizer, *Church Order in the New Testament* (ET London: SCM, 1961).

205. See particularly M. Y. MacDonald, *The Pauline Churches: A Socio-Historical Study of Institutionalization in the Pauline and Deutero-Pauline Writings* (SNTSMS 60; Cambridge: Cambridge University, 1988).

206. Weiss, *1 Korinther* (1910).

sputtered only fitfully during the middle decades of the twentieth century when the programmes of Barthian (and Bultmannian) kerygmatic theology largely dominated university faculties of theology. However, it too has revived in the closing decades of that century, kick-(re)started by Hans Dieter Betz,[207] and much stimulated by interaction with the lively postmodern debates within the field of literary criticism. It is increasingly evident that familiarity with ancient epistolary and rhetorical conventions helps illuminate the terms, idioms and strategies employed by Paul and the likely effects he sought to evoke in his readers.[208]

When we add the steadily accumulating archaeological finds (structures, artefacts, inscriptions),[209] the ever closer attention paid over recent years to major cities which feature in the early expansion of Christianity (Jerusalem, Antioch, Rome, Ephesus, Corinth),[210] and a growing appreciation of the character of diaspora Judaism,[211] the prospects of achieving a fairly full coverage of Christianity's beginnings become steadily brighter.

e. The Wheel Comes Full Circle

The quest for a pre-Christian Gnostic Redeemer myth has been something of a parenthesis within the last two centuries of inquiry into Christian origins. The sociological approach has absorbed and maintains most of the energy of the earlier history-of-religions concern. But in the last generation the interest in trying better to understand why and how Christianity emerged in its distinctive form from within Judaism has re-appeared as a central issue. Klausner's test still requires to be passed.

In christology a major wave of research has been devoted to examining the

207. H. D. Betz, *Galatians* (Hermeneia; Philadelphia: Fortress, 1979).

208. See, e.g., R. N. Longenecker, *Galatians* (WBC 41; Dallas: Word, 1990); M. M. Mitchell, *Paul and the Rhetoric of Reconciliation: An Exegetical Investigation of the Language and Composition of 1 Corinthians* (Louisville: Westminster John Knox, 1993).

209. See, e.g., E. M. Meyers, ed., *The Oxford Encyclopedia of Archaeology in the Near East* (New York: Oxford, 1997); and the volumes of *NDIEC*.

210. See, e.g., B. Mazar, *The Mountain of the Lord: Excavating in Jerusalem* (New York: Doubleday, 1975); W. A. Meeks and R. L. Wilken, *Jews and Christians in Antioch in the First Four Centuries of the Common Era* (Missoula: Scholars, 1978); P. Lampe, *From Paul to Valentinus: Christians at Rome in the First Two Centuries* (Minneapolis: Fortress, 2003); H. Koester, ed., *Ephesos: Metropolis of Asia* (HTS 41; Cambridge: Harvard Divinity School, 1995, 2004); D. N. Schowalter and S. J. Friesen, eds., *Urban Religion in Roman Corinth* (HTS 53; Cambridge: Harvard University, 2005).

211. Particularly J. M. G. Barclay, *Jews in the Mediterranean Diaspora from Alexander to Trajan (323 BCE–117 CE)* (Edinburgh: Clark, 1996).

antecedents and possibly prototypes for what Christians were soon saying about Christ — exalted heroes (like Enoch or Elijah) or glorious angels or divine intermediary agencies (notably Wisdom).[212] With such precedents, and plenty of allusions to one or other of them in the NT material, there seems little or no need to look further. But how to explain the consequent break with Judaism? Maurice Casey argues that it was an inevitable consequence of trying to transplant Jewish categories into Gentile soil.[213] Larry Hurtado roots the explanation in the Christ-devotion of the earliest communities, which likewise broke through the monotheistic constraints of Second Temple Judaism.[214] My own explanation figures the reason not so much in a Christianity which broke away from Judaism as in a rabbinic Judaism which drew the boundaries of Judaism more tightly to leave nascent Christianity (but also other forms of Second Temple Judaism) outside these boundaries.[215]

In terms of mysticism, the growing awareness that Jewish (merkabah) mysticism was already being practised at the time of Paul has brought the category back into play with renewed explanatory power. There is no reason whatsoever to regard 'mysticism' as evidence *per se* of non-Jewish (oriental) influences. The evidence of 2 Cor. 12.1-4 is clear enough for Paul. And if, as seems likely, 2 Cor. 4.4-6 reflects Paul's own conversion experience, it can provide the basis of an argument that Paul's whole perception of Christ emerged directly from that visionary experience.[216]

On the issue of the decisive influences on Paul's theology, the tide began to turn with the work of W. D. Davies, who protested against the undue history-of-religions concentration on Paul's Hellenistic background and insisted that the key to understanding Paul was his Jewish origins.[217] However, there was a major

212. Dunn, *Christology;* C. Rowland, *The Open Heaven: A Study of Apocalyptic in Judaism and Early Christianity* (London: SPCK, 1982); L. W. Hurtado, *One God, One Lord: Early Christian Devotion and Ancient Jewish Monotheism* (Philadelphia: Fortress, 1988); A. Chester, *Messiah and Exaltation: Jewish Messianic and Visionary Traditions and New Testament Christology* (WUNT 207; Tübingen: Mohr Siebeck, 2007).

213. P. M. Casey, *From Jewish Prophet to Gentile God: The Origin and Development of New Testament Christology* (Cambridge: Clarke, 1991).

214. Hurtado, *One God, One Lord.* Like Bousset, Hurtado recognizes the importance of the experience of Christ-veneration within the earliest Christian assemblies, and in *Lord Jesus Christ* he addresses the same challenge as Bousset in tracing its outworking in Christianity's developing christology.

215. Dunn, *Partings.*

216. Particularly S. Kim, *The Origin of Paul's Gospel* (WUNT 2.4; Tübingen: Mohr Siebeck, 1981, ²1984); also *Paul and the New Perspective: Second Thoughts on the Origin of Paul's Gospel* (WUNT 140; Tübingen: Mohr Siebeck, 2002); A. F. Segal, *Paul the Convert: The Apostolate and Apostasy of Saul the Pharisee* (New Haven: Yale University, 1990).

217. W. D. Davies, *Paul and Rabbinic Judaism* (London: SPCK, 1948, ⁴1981). The dis-

stumbling block in any attempt to shed light on Paul from that source — namely, the deeply rooted, albeit unconscious, prejudice in so much Christian scholarship against Judaism. Judaism was what Paul had turned away from, was it not? His conversion had surely liberated Paul from the slavery of the law and from a legalistic Pharisaism. Was not his central doctrine, justification by faith, formulated precisely in opposition to a Judaism which taught that justification depended on one's own efforts ('works')? Thus it could be said that the history-of-religions school had in effect continued to be motivated by Baur's conception of Christianity as a universal religion which could become itself only by freeing itself from the narrow particularistic bonds of Judaism. So far as the history-of-religions school and its heirs were concerned, it was the influence of the universal spirit of Hellenism which had saved infant Christianity from a Jewish childhood of stunted growth and enabled it to achieve maturity.

Every so often, voices were raised against such a parody both of Second Temple Judaism and of Paul's debt to his Jewish heritage.[218] But not until *E. P. Sanders* attacked the parody in a bare-knuckled way did the wrong-headedness of much of the earlier disregard of Paul's Jewish background become widely recognized, although the bluntness of his polemic provoked considerable resentment, particularly within German scholarship.[219] Sanders observed that the starting point for Judaism's self-understanding as the people of God (both Second Temple Judaism and rabbinic Judaism) was the covenant made by God with Israel; the covenant was nowhere regarded in Jewish writings as an achievement of human merit. And although Jews had the responsibility to maintain their covenant standing by obedience to the law, the repeated emphasis on repentance, as well as the centrality of a sacrificial system which provided atonement for the repentant within Israel's 'pattern of religion', meant that the characterization of that religion as legalistic and merit-based was misconceived, unjustified and prejudicial. Sanders coined the phrase 'covenantal nomism' to embrace both aspects — the divine initiative of God's choice of a 'not people' (covenant) and the response of obedience required from that people (law/nomism).

This was 'the new perspective on Paul'. In reality it was a new perspective on Paul's 'Judaism'. But it called for a new perspective on Paul himself. If Paul was not reacting to a legalistic Judaism which understood salvation to be depen-

---

covery of the DSS was, of course, a decisive factor more generally, though of less immediate influence on the evaluation of Paul's theology and religion, until the publication of 4QMMT in 1994; see, e.g., my 'Paul and the Dead Sea Scrolls', in J. H. Charlesworth, ed., *Caves of Enlightenment: Proceedings of the American School of Oriental Research Dead Sea Scrolls Jubilee Symposium (1947-97)* (North Richmond Hills: Bibal, 1998) 105-27; on 4QMMT see below, §27.4b.

218. Particularly G. F. Moore, 'Christian Writers on Judaism', *HTR* 14 (1922) 197-254.

219. E. P. Sanders, *Paul and Palestinian Judaism* (London: SCM, 1977).

dent ultimately on human achievement, then to what was he reacting? Sanders himself saw Paul's reaction to be essentially confused or inconsistent.[220] But I have argued that the new perspective sheds light on Paul's theology by allowing us to see the target against which its polemical thrust was directed: not against the idea of achieving God's acceptance by the merit of personal achievement (good works) but against the Jewish intention to safeguard the privilege of covenant status from being dissipated or contaminated by contact with non-Jews. Paul was reacting primarily against the exclusivism which he himself had previously fought to maintain. In particular, he was reacting against the conviction (shared by most other Christian Jews) that 'works of the law', such as (or particularly) circumcision and laws of clean and unclean, continued to prescribe the terms of covenant relationship for Gentiles as well as Jews. In and from this conflict, Paul's doctrine of justification by faith alone achieved its initial classic expression (Gal. 2.1-21). It was precisely as 'apostle to the Gentiles' that Paul formulated the doctrine of justification.[221]

In the last decade the responses have come thick and fast. In a thorough study, Friedrich Avemarie has observed that the rabbinic evidence is more mixed than Sanders allowed and argues consequently that Sanders has pushed the covenant side of his 'covenantal nomism' too hard.[222] It has been pointed out that the language of 'justification' should be used in reference not only to the initial acceptance through faith but also to the final judgment, and that there is a greater conditionality in the Jewish understanding of justification than Sanders allowed — a belief expressed often enough that salvation does depend on obedience.[223] The key passage, Rom. 4.4-5, serves as a strong redoubt from which the reinterpreted theology of Paul can be assailed.[224]

---

220. E. P. Sanders, *Paul, the Law and the Jewish People* (Philadelphia: Fortress, 1983); more pointedly, H. Räisänen, *Paul and the Law* (WUNT 29; Tübingen: Mohr Siebeck, 1983).

221. J. D. G. Dunn, 'The New Perspective on Paul' (1983), *Jesus, Paul and the Law: Studies in Mark and Galatians* (London: SPCK, 1990) 183-214; more recently *Theology of Paul* ch. 14 (intervening bibliography on pp. 334-35); insufficiently appreciated has been the earlier K. Stendahl, *Paul among Jews and Gentiles* (Philadelphia: Fortress, 1977). See further below, §§27.2-5.

222. F. Avemarie, *Tora und Leben. Untersuchungen zur Heilsbedeutung der Tora in der frühen rabbinischen Literatur* (TSAJ 55; Tübingen: Mohr Siebeck, 1996).

223. Stuhlmacher, *Revisiting Paul's Doctrine of Justification;* D. A. Carson et al., eds., *Justification and Variegated Nomism.* Vol. 1: *The Complexities of Second Temple Judaism* (WUNT 2.140; Tübingen: Mohr Siebeck, 2001); vol. 2: *The Paradoxes of Paul* (WUNT 2.181; Tübingen: Mohr Siebeck, 2004); S. J. Gathercole, *Where Is Boasting? Early Jewish Soteriology and Paul's Response in Romans 1–5* (Grand Rapids: Eerdmans, 2002); Kim, *Paul and the New Perspective;* see also A. A. Das, *Paul and the Jews* (Peabody: Hendrickson, 2003).

224. See particularly S. Westerholm, *Israel's Law and the Church's Faith: Paul and His Recent Interpreters* (Grand Rapids: Eerdmans, 1988), revised as *Perspectives Old and New on*

Underlying all this ongoing debate is the crucial historical question — a question, indeed, on which the whole course of earliest Christianity dramatically turned. What was it that caused the first Christian evangelists to take the gospel to non-Jews? What was it that brought about the breakthrough to the Gentiles — a development so momentous for Christianity itself and indeed for European history? And why, in taking this step, did they make the revolutionary decision not to treat the Gentile converts as proselytes, not to require of them circumcision and full obedience to the law? The issue behind the theological debate around the 'new perspective' is the historical question of what happened in this crucial turn of events, and why. If we can clarify that question, we will assuredly have discovered the single most important key to unlock the mystery of how a Jewish messianic sect became a predominantly Gentile religion.

Inevitably, then, much of this volume will have to focus attention on Paul. For Paul stands at, indeed in himself constitutes, that critical juncture — Paul, the Jew become believer in Jesus Messiah, the Pharisaic zealot become apostle to the Gentiles. Paul the paradox: *apostle for* Israel, or *apostate from* Israel? Of course we will begin by attempting to sketch out the developments from the first Christian Easter prior to Paul's decisive contribution, which, after all, includes the crucial breakthrough to the Gentiles. But the historical circumstances of that breakthrough are very obscure, and it is on the evidence provided by Paul that the resolution of the historical as well as the theological issues hangs. Without that resolution the most important developments in the beginnings of Christianity will remain an enigma.

Of course Paul was not the only Christian Jew involved in the initial outreach of the new movement beyond Palestine and the land of Israel. We must resist the temptation to treat Acts as though it provides the whole story of emergent Christianity's earliest development. What were obviously important developments in Antioch and Syria are only hinted at in Acts. We hear nothing of the beginnings of Christianity in Alexandria and Egypt. Paul's letter to Rome implies the establishment of churches, of whose origin and foundation we can only guess. Lest the picture become too drastically skewed, we will have to inquire into such developments as best we can, both in this volume and in volume 3. But the key considerations remain: it is Paul who is credited with the most significant expansion of the infant movement; it is letters of Paul which (almost) alone have survived from the first generation of Christianity; and the collection and preser-

---

Paul: The "Lutheran" Paul and His Critics (Grand Rapids: Eerdmans, 2004). I respond to these criticisms in *The New Perspective on Paul* (WUNT 185; Tübingen: Mohr Siebeck, 2005; revised edition, Grand Rapids: Eerdmans, 2008) ch. 1; see also M. Bachmann, ed., *Lutherische und Neue Paulusperspektive* (WUNT 182; Tübingen: Mohr Siebeck, 2005); and B. W. Longenecker, 'On Critiquing the "New Perspective" on Paul: A Case Study', *ZNW* 96 (2005) 263-71.

vation of his letters assuredly indicates that the impact he made was highly valued more or less from the first by those who proved themselves to be the movers and shapers of Christianity.

So the key question remains: how and why did Christianity emerge from Second Temple Judaism? With its corollary: in emerging more fully into the Hellenistic world, to what extent did the new movement change in character and become something different?

CHAPTER 21

The Sources

As with the first phase of our inquiry (into the mission of Jesus),[1] so with the next phase, we cannot proceed without asking what should count as sources for our information regarding the first generation of 'Christianity' (30-70 CE). The most obviously inviting answer is the NT writing which on the face of it seems to be devoted to providing that information — the Acts of the Apostles. But the reference to Baur in the preceding chapter (§20.3a) has already alerted us to the likelihood that Acts is far from a straightforward purveyor of historical information.

Right at the outset we should be alert to two problems regarding the value of Acts: the tensions between (1) the story of Acts and what Paul himself tells us in his letters of his own mission and (2) the concentration of Acts latterly on Paul. In the first case, there is the question whether Paul's account of events is to be preferred over Acts. The answer has almost always been firmly that Paul's first-hand account must take precedence over Luke's at best second-hand account.[2] The only caution to be observed is that Paul should hardly be regarded as providing a dispassionate view; on the contrary, his strength of feeling is evident on page after page of his letters. So it may not be a straight choice between Paul and Acts when their accounts diverge.[3]

In the second case we are indeed in a quandary. We can assume neither that Luke tells the whole story of early mission nor that Paul was the only mission beyond Palestine nor that the sweep of his mission round the northeast quadrant of the Mediterranean was the only region into which the message of Jesus penetrated. But we have almost no information about the earliest spread of the mes-

---

1. *Jesus Remembered* §7.
2. See further below, §28.1a.
3. Cf. the discussion by D. Wenham, 'Acts and the Pauline Corpus II: The Evidence of Parallels', *BAFCS* 1.215-58.

sage in Syria beyond Antioch or to the east, nor about developments in Alexandria, Egypt, and the North African coast. Investigation of the beginnings of Christianity in these regions is best left till we can draw on the firmer evidence from the second century.[4]

But there is a third source on which we can draw, and for which the study of the Jesus tradition as oral tradition in volume 1 has prepared us: that is, the information we can glean from the Jesus tradition itself about the way it was used and developed in the earliest years following Jesus. Here the question, already partially discussed in *Jesus Remembered,* will emerge again: whether the various forms and emphases of these traditions attest different and divergent movements, all of which stemmed from the initial impact Jesus made, and whether all of them can be justly termed 'early Christian' or 'proto-Christian' — with secondary effects for the definition and coherence of 'Christianity'. In particular, we recall from volume 1 that the Q material is generally regarded by Q specialists as attesting the vitality of a post-Easter Galilean community or communities, but one somewhat divergent from the mainline tradition evidenced in Mark and Paul.

As in §7, however, it is appropriate to begin by assembling the few references to the embryonic Christianity of this period which are to be found outside specifically Christian sources.

21.1. External Sources

The following sources are usually cited in this connection.[5]

a. Josephus (37-ca. 100)

Josephus nowhere mentions 'Christians' in his writings.[6] This is noteworthy, first, since he writes extensively about his people, the Jews, and their history. And secondly, because he was living in Rome, as part of the emperor's household (*Life* 423, 428-29), when he wrote his Jewish history *(Jewish Antiquities)* in the 90s. This suggests (at most) that Josephus was unaware of 'Christians' or did

---

4. See below, vol. 3.

5. See also S. Benko, 'Pagan Criticism of Christianity during the First Two Centuries', *ANRW* 2.23.2 (1980) 1055-1118; E. Ferguson, 556-70; R. M. Grant, *Second-Century Christianity: A Collection of Fragments* (Louisville: Westminster John Knox, ²2003) 3-12; and further R. Wilken, *The Christians as the Romans Saw Them* (New Haven: Yale University, ²2003).

6. The most useful introduction to Josephus in relation to Christianity's beginnings is S. Mason, *Josephus and the New Testament* (1992; Peabody: Hendrickson, ²2003).

not think them worthy of note as a significant or troublesome sect within or related to Judaism, even in Rome. The observation may be significant, given the other references about to be reviewed and given that the Christian letter of Clement (*1 Clement*) was written at about the same time as the *Antiquities* and attests a substantial Christian presence in the city.[7] While little can be made of Josephus's silence on this point, it suggests nonetheless the relative invisibility of Christian groups within the great cities of the Mediterranean. Two generations beyond the events of 30 in Jerusalem, the growth and expansion of the Nazarenes/Galileans/Christians, which must have been continuing apace during this period, had yet to impinge on the consciousness of writers and social commentators of the time. That would soon change!

The only information Josephus provides is his brief account of the summary execution of James the brother of Jesus in Jerusalem, in 62.[8] Ananus, the recently appointed high priest, had seized the opportunity given by the interval between the death of one Roman procurator, Festus, and the arrival of his successor, Albinus, to act against James: 'Ananus convened a sanhedrin of judges and brought before it the brother of Jesus, the so-called Christ *(ton adelphon Iēsou tou legomenou Christou)*, James by name, and certain others. He accused them of having transgressed the law and handed them over to be stoned' (*Ant.* 20.200). We will have to examine the political motivation behind Ananus's action later,[9] and particularly what the episode tells us about the standing of James within Jerusalem and any political involvement of James himself within Judean politics in a period of increasing tension. The point here is that for the first time a prominent Christian features within a non-Christian history and is identified by his association with 'Jesus, the so-called Christ'.[10] Two generations from their beginnings, Christians were beginning to break surface in non-Christian history.

There are no references to Christians or Christianity in non-Christian Greco-Roman sources prior to the second century (Epictetus, Tacitus, Suetonius, Pliny). However, the first two use the term when writing of events in Rome in the 60s, and so they call for attention here.

---

7. *First Clement* provides next to no indication of the status of the sending church (Rome), but the self-conscious authority claimed in writing to the troubled church in Corinth (particularly 57.1-2) implies that Clement himself had a firm and strong base in Rome; cf. H. E. Lona, *Der erste Clemensbrief* (KEK; Göttingen: Vandenhoeck und Ruprecht, 1998) 84.

8. Already referred to in *Jesus Remembered* §7.1.

9. See §36.2 below.

10. *Ho legomenos Christos* can either denote 'he who is called Christ/Messiah' (as in *Jesus Remembered* §7.1) or strike a more reserved note: 'the so-called Christ' (as here); see BDAG 590.

b. Epictetus (ca. 55-135)

As a slave of Epaphroditus, Nero's freedman and secretary, Epictetus had been permitted to attend the lectures of the Stoic teacher Musonius Rufus. After being granted his freedom, he began himself to teach philosophy in Rome and subsequently, when banished by Domitian, at Nicopolis. His teaching in Nicopolis, probably in the first decade of the second century, was recorded by his pupil Flavius Arrianus, a Roman administrator.[11] Epictetus refers to Christians only once, as 'Galileans' (4.7.6), but a second passage has been interpreted as referring to Christians (2.9.19-21), probably wrongly.

> Therefore, if madness can produce this attitude [of detachment] toward these things [death, loss of family, property], and also habit, as with the Galileans, can no one learn from reason and demonstration that God has made all things in the universe, and the whole universe itself, to be unhindered and complete in itself, and the parts of it to serve the needs of the whole. (4.7.6)

Two features are worthy of comment. First, the unusual name 'Galileans' indicates an awareness among the more cultured classes that the new movement had originated either in the otherwise rather obscure region of Galilee or that its initial membership or leadership consisted principally of Galileans — an interesting observation in itself.[12] Second, this group was sufficiently large to have impressed itself upon the consciousness of a teacher like Epictetus, and to have impressed him with their readiness to lose property, family and even life itself in the cause to which they were committed as Galileans. A reference to Christian calmness and resolution under persecution is presumably implicit.

> Why, then, do you call yourself a Stoic, why do you deceive the multitude, why do you act the part of a Jew, when you are a Greek? Do you not see in what sense men are severally called Jew, Syrian or Egyptian? For example, whenever we see a man halting between two faiths, we are in the habit of saying, 'He is not a Jew, he is only acting the part'. But when he adopts the attitude of mind of the man who has been baptized and has made his choice, then he both is a Jew in fact and is also called one. So we also are counterfeit 'Baptists' *(parabaptistai)*. Ostensibly Jews, but in reality something else, not in sympathy with our own reason, far from applying the principles which we profess, yet priding ourselves upon them as being men who know them. (2.9.19-21)

11. *OCD*³ 532.
12. See also above, §20.1(17).

Assuming that baptism had already become established as part of proselyte conversion by this time, a reference to proselytes is most likely.[13] It is well known that many non-Jews in Rome (and elsewhere) were attracted to the synagogue by the Jewish understanding of God, the Jewish moral code and practices like the Sabbath day of rest.[14] But a cautionary note may be in order, since 'baptism' had probably been longer established as a distinctive feature of conversion to the new 'sect' within Judaism. The passage, then, may just refer to Christians and attest to the confusion in the minds of onlookers on whether the new movement was (still) bound up with the religion of the Jews. Given the overlap between the terms 'Galilean' and 'Jew' observed in volume 1,[15] it is not altogether unlikely that Epictetus thought of 'Galileans' also as 'Jews'.

c. Tacitus (ca. 56-ca. 120)

Chronologically the first reference, already noted[16] but now given in full, is to those chosen by Emperor Nero as scapegoats for the fire of Rome in 64, though Tacitus himself was probably writing during the second decade of the second century.[17]

> To scotch the rumour [that the fire had taken place to order], Nero substituted as culprits, and punished with the utmost refinements of cruelty a class of men, loathed for their vices *(per flagitia invisos),* whom the crowd styled Christians *(Chrestianos).* (3) Christus, the founder of the name, had undergone the death penalty in the reign of Tiberius, by sentence of the procurator Pontius Pilate, and the pernicious superstition *(exitiabilis superstitio)* was checked for a moment, only to break out once more, not merely in Judea, the home of the disease, but in the capital itself, where all things horrible or shameful in the world collect and find a vogue. (4) First, then, those who confessed *(fatebantur)* were arrested; next, on their disclosures vast numbers *(multitudo ingens)* were convicted, not so much on the count of arson as for hatred of the human race *(odio humani generis).* And derision accompanied their end: they were covered with wild beasts' skins and torn to death by dogs; or they were fastened on crosses, and, when daylight failed, were burned to serve as lamps by night. (5) Nero had offered his gardens for the spectacle, and gave an exhibition in his Circus, mixing with the crowd in the

13. See *GLAJJ* 1.543-44.
14. See below, §29.5c.
15. See *Jesus Remembered* §9.6.
16. *Jesus Remembered* §7.1.
17. *OCD*³ 1469-71.

habit of a charioteer, or mounted on his car. Hence, in spite of a guilt, which had earned the most exemplary punishment, there arose a sentiment of pity, due to the impression that they were being sacrificed not for the welfare of the state but to the ferocity of a single man. (*Annals* 15.44.2-5)[18]

Several observations are called for. First, Tacitus asserts that the name 'Christians' was already current; the name was used by the crowd.[19] The explanation of its derivation from 'Christus' is presumably added by Tacitus,[20] so the knowledge he evidences of the movement's spread beyond Judea is probably his, and not necessarily current at the time being described. But the confession extracted *(fatebantur)* was probably to being Christian (cf. Pliny, *Ep.* 10.96.2-3) rather than to arson (Tacitus did not think them guilty of the latter),[21] or, probably to be more precise, to being a member of the group who were being blamed for the disaster.

Second, Tacitus's account indicates that there was a sizeable body of these 'Christians' in Rome by the early 60s. Whatever we make of his vivid language (*multitudo ingens,* 'a vast multitude'), if his account has any factual basis whatever, the procession of victims for the games and for the sick parody of executions must have amounted to a substantial number. Evidently those first arrested were tortured to divulge the names of others. Even so, it is likely that those thus martyred were a minority of the full number of Christians in Rome prior to the fire. So should we be thinking of several hundred 'Christians' already in Rome by the mid-60s?[22]

Third, Tacitus's disgust with sects originating in the orient is clearly evident (15.44.3), but the charge of 'hatred of the human race' is a standard charge against the Jews.[23] So it is quite likely that Tacitus at least saw the Christians as a

18. I have adapted the translation in *GLAJJ* 2.89. It should be appreciated that 'the word "superstition" is relative, for it may be taken to mean indulgence in beliefs or practices which have been abandoned by general, or at least by educated, opinion of the time'; Virgil implies that it denotes 'unenlightened and meaningless worship' (*Aen.* 8.187), perhaps with special reference to oriental cults of his day. Juvenal, *Sat.* 14.96, uses it of the observance of some Jewish rites, especially the Sabbath, by those who were neither Jews nor proselytes (*OCD*[2] 1023-24; see also *OCD*[3] 1456).

19. Ambivalence between *Chrestus* and *Christus, Chrestianoi* and *Christianoi* was a feature of this period; see *GLAJJ* 2.92; R. E. Van Voorst, *Jesus outside the New Testament* (Grand Rapids: Eerdmans, 2000) 43-44.

20. See further *Jesus Remembered* §7.1.

21. So most — e.g., J. Stevenson, ed., *A New Eusebius* (London: SPCK, 1960) 3; *GLAJJ* 2.93.

22. See further below, §37 at nn. 237 and 238.

23. See details in *GLAJJ* 2.93. 'It cannot be mere coincidence, that the *odium humani generis* with which Tacitus charges the Christians in the *Annals* 15.44 is nearly the same expression that he uses concerning the Jews in *Histories* 5.5.1' (Benko, 'Pagan Criticism' 1064).

form of Judaism, even though they could be distinguished more precisely as 'Christians', as the next excerpt may confirm.[24]

Tacitus is possibly the source for the later account by the Christian writer Sulpicius Severus of the climax to the siege of Jerusalem:[25]

> Others, and Titus himself, expressed their opinion that the Temple should be destroyed without delay, in order that the religion of the Jews and Christians should be more completely exterminated. For those religions, though opposed to one another, derive from the same founders; the Christians stemmed from the Jews *(Christianos ex Judaeis)* and the extirpation of the root would easily cause the offspring to perish.

If the comment does go back to Tacitus, it is noteworthy that he attributes the opinion to Titus, in the year 70, that Jews and Christians formed a single religion *(religio,* singular), and that the destruction of the Jerusalem Temple would hasten their extermination. Here Christians are still understood as part of the Jewish religion. The second sentence, in contrast, was probably Tacitus's own explanatory comment. For it now speaks of two *religiones,* seeing them as 'opposed to one another', even though Christians stemmed from Jews. The ambivalence suggests that Christian identity emerging in that period was both confused and confusing: were 'Christians' the same as Jews, or a separate religion? Had Gentile converts become members of a Jewish sect? The same question will arise in various forms repeatedly throughout volume 2 and will still press upon us in volume 3.

d. Suetonius (ca. 70-ca. 140)

A brief reference by Suetonius[26] to the expulsion of the Jews from Rome, probably in 49,[27] since they 'constantly made disturbances because of the instigator

---

24. E. A. Judge, 'Judaism and the Rise of Christianity: A Roman Perspective', *TynB* 45 (1994) 355-68, however, observes that 'the vague phrase *genus hominum* ("a class of people") plainly displays his [Tacitus's] lack of any correlation with people he had already treated' (360 n. 4). There is no substantive indication that Jews (other than Christian Jews) were also accused of arson, or that it was Jews who began the rumour of Christian culpability, for which *1 Clem.* *6.1-2* provides no support (*GLAJJ* 2.91; and see §35 n. 36 below). That Nero was responsible for the fire was maintained by Pliny the Elder (*Nat. Hist.* 17.5) and Suetonius (*Nero* 38.1). See further §35.2 below.

25. So argued in *GLAJJ* 2.64-67. The manuscript of Tacitus's *Annals* breaks off in book 16, when his account had reached the year 66, before the outbreak of the Jewish revolt.

26. *OCD*³ 1451-52.

27. On the issue of the date of the expulsion of Jews from Rome, see below, §28.1b at nn. 29-41.

Chrestus *(impulsore Chresto)*' *(Divus Claudius* 25.4), has already been cited.[28] Assuming, as most do, that the passage conveys a confused account of distur-bances in Rome *regarding* Christ (not caused *by* Christ),[29] that again tells us something about the beginnings of Christianity in Rome. It would appear that the teaching of Jesus, or more likely claims that Jesus was the Christ (Messiah), caused such disturbances within the Jewish community of Rome that the authori-ties resolved the situation simply by expelling (a number of) Jews, or perhaps simply the ringleaders — both those who confessed Jesus as Messiah and those who rejected the claim.[30] Alternatively, the trouble was caused by Jewish mis-sionary activity among non-Jewish Romans; that is, Jews in Rome were pro-claiming Jesus as the Christ to their non-Jewish neighbours and associates.[31]

One of the most intriguing connections between sources is provided by Acts 18.2, since it links the couple who became Paul's closest associates, Priscilla and Aquila, to the expulsion of Jews from Rome. The suggestion lies close to hand that Priscilla and Aquila were among the Christian Jews who were expelled from Rome because of the furore caused by their preaching or witness-ing within one or more of the Roman synagogues or in wider outreach.[32] If the date of the expulsion is indeed 49, it means that we can trace the beginnings of Christianity in Rome as early as (probably) the mid-40s — only fifteen or so years after Jesus' death. We also gain a clear impression of the vigour and persis-tence of early evangelistic efforts, whether solely within the Jewish community or beyond, of the reaction which they caused ('disturbances'), and of the prompt-ness with which the Roman authorities dealt with such threats to public order and/or traditional ways.

Suetonius's reference to the persecution by Nero is much briefer than the

---

28. *Jesus Remembered* §7.1.

29. See particularly the discussion in Van Voorst, *Jesus* 30-39, in dispute particularly with S. Benko, 'The Edict of Claudius of A.D. 49', *TZ* 25 (1969) 406-18 (also 'Pagan Criticism' 1056-62) (who argues that Chrestus was a Jewish radical active in Rome at the time), and with other bibliography. I follow Van Voorst here in translating 'instigator', rather than the normal 'instigation' (as in §7.1). On the confusion of 'Chrestus' with 'Christus' see J. A. Fitzmyer, *Romans* (AB 33; New York: Doubleday, 1993) 31, and above, n. 19.

30. See my *Romans* (WBC 38; Dallas: Word, 1988) xlviii-xlix (with bibliography).

31. L. H. Feldman, *Jew and Gentile in the Ancient World* (Princeton: Princeton Univer-sity, 1993) 300-304, followed by Van Voorst, *Jesus* 37: 'it is clear that Roman authorities typi-cally saw the spread of Judaism among the native populace as an offense that merited expul-sion' (37). There had been a previous expulsion of Jews by Tiberius in 19 CE because 'they were converting *(methistantōn)* many of the natives to their ways' (Cassius Dio 57.18.5a; cf. Tacitus, *Ann.* 2.85.4 — 'the proscription of Egyptian and Jewish rites'; Suetonius, *Tiberius* 36 — 'he abolished foreign cults, especially the Egyptian and Jewish rites . . . [and] banished [Jews] from the city'). See further below, §24 n. 247.

32. See further below, §28 n. 40.

account of Tacitus: 'Punishment was inflicted on the Christians *(Christiani)*, a class *(genus)* of men given to a new and evil-doing/nefarious/criminal *(maleficus)* superstition' *(Nero* 16.2). This comes in a list of various regulations imposed by Nero for the public good and is not linked with the episode of the fire of Rome. It thus reflects the same impression given by Tacitus that the Christians were widely regarded, by educated Romans at least, as a public menace. Again this tells us more about the repugnance which well-born Romans like Tacitus and Suetonius felt towards foreign sects contaminating Roman traditional ways and beliefs than about the *Christiani* themselves. The tendency to vilify Judaism and Christianity in particular as threateningly strange and foreign religious traditions runs through Greco-Roman literature of the period.[33] At least, then, through such references we gain a sense of the antipathy and hostility with which the first Christians were confronted as their distinctive identity emerged more clearly.

e. Pliny (ca. 61-113)

Gaius Plinius Caecilius Secundus was appointed governor of Bithynia Pontus by Emperor Trajan in 111, with a commission to restore law and order in the province (he died in 113).[34] His custom was to refer all cases to Trajan where he was uncertain how to proceed. One of these was the Christians. The letter asking for advice on this subject contains such a range of information that it is worth quoting at length, both for present purposes and for later reference.

> I have never attended trials of Christians; therefore, I do not know what is to be investigated and what kind of punishment to apply. I am very doubtful whether any discrimination should be made because of age, or young people should not be distinguished from grownups, whether pardon should be given to the penitent, or if he was a Christian once he would not gain anything by renouncing it; should the name itself *(nomen ipsum)* without crimes, or the crimes associated with the name be punished? In the meantime, I followed this method with those who were accused before me as Christians. I asked them whether they were Christians. Those who confessed I asked again and a third time, warning them of capital punishment; those who persevered I commanded to be led off to execution, for I had no doubt that whatever it were they believed in, stubbornness and inflexible obstinacy should be punished. There were others of similar folly, whom I ordered to be sent to the City, because they were Roman citizens.

33. See most recently P. Schäfer, *Judeophobia: Attitudes toward the Jews in the Ancient World* (Cambridge: Harvard University, 1997); texts in *GLAJJ;* and further below, §29 n. 165.
    34. *OCD*³ 1198.

As it usually happens, the fact of the investigation caused the charges to be more widespread and varied. An anonymous list was published containing the names of many. Those who denied that they are or were Christians I have dismissed, when they invoked the gods . . . and made offering of frankincense and wine to your image . . . and furthermore cursed Christ. It is said that those who are really Christians cannot be forced to do any of these things.

Others who were named by the informer said that they were Christians and then denied it; they were once but then ceased to be, some three years ago, some many years ago, some even twenty years ago. All these too venerated your statue and the images of the gods and cursed Christ. They also asserted that all of their guilt or error was that they used to come together on a certain day before daylight to sing a song with responses to Christ as a god, to bind themselves mutually by a solemn oath *(sacramentum),* not to commit any crime, but to avoid theft, robbery, adultery, not to break a trust or deny a deposit when they are called for it. After these practices it was their custom to separate and then come together again to take food but an ordinary and harmless kind, and they even gave up this practice after my edict, when, in response to your order, I forbade associations. This convinced me that it was all the more necessary to find out what the truth was by the torture of two female slaves who were called deaconesses. I found nothing else but a depraved and excessive superstition.

[deferring further action till he had consulted with Trajan, because of the numbers involved] Many from all age groups and all classes and from both sexes are, and will be, brought to trial. Not only cities but villages and farming districts are affected by the contagion of that disease, but it seems possible to stop and correct it. It is agreed that the temples which were almost deserted began now to be filled and the sacred festivals after a long intermission are again performed, the meat of sacrificial victims is again on sale and until now there were very few buyers.[35]

The letter confirms that the name 'Christian' was by then (112) well established, the appropriate and recognized way to identify those referred to. Notable is Pliny's hesitation on whether it was a criminal offence to own to the name itself. Equally notable is Pliny's action, despite his hesitancy, but approved by Trajan, to punish by execution those who did confess to the name.[36] The crime 'associated with the name', presumably, was the unwillingness to invoke the tra-

35. Pliny, *Ep.* 10.96 (following Benko's translation). Trajan's reply commends Pliny's practice, though ruling that the Christians are not to be sought out and warning that anonymous lists or accusations should not have any place in criminal procedures (*Ep.* 10.97).
36. See further Benko, 'Pagan Criticism' 1071-76.

ditional gods and to venerate Trajan's image, which was tantamount to rejection of the sovereign rights of the emperor. Roman citizens were sent to Rome to be dealt with. To be noted also is the degree to which Roman justice depended, in this case at least, on 'informers'.[37]

A second important piece of information is how widespread and influential the Christians had become: 'many from all age groups and all classes and from both sexes' were involved; 'not only cities but villages and farming districts are affected'; temples had been almost deserted, the sacred festivals had not been observed for a long time, and the temples had not been producing the meat of sacrificial victims for the meat markets since there were so few buyers. This information, it should be noted, comes not from a piece of exaggerated propaganda by a rabid opponent of Christianity but from a formal report to the emperor, seeking the latter's advice, and therefore motivated to give a careful description of the situation pertaining in order to receive the advice appropriate to that situation. If we take Pliny's report with the seriousness it deserves, it is hard to escape the impression that Christianity had spread widely in the region and that it took some vigorous persecution on Pliny's part to counter its influence. To be noted also is that Trajan's reply shows him to be quite familiar with the issues, implying, presumably, that the spread and influence of Christianity was no news to Trajan. Moreover, Pliny could have attended earlier trials, presumably in Rome, where he had served as one of Trajan's advisers. This implies both that such trials were becoming quite frequent but also that they were not so common that someone of Pliny's rank was bound to have had some knowledge and experience of procedures and of how the issues were being dealt with.

A third point of note is that the confrontation between loyalty to Jesus as Lord and Emperor Trajan was an already established factor for Christians. Pliny had heard that 'those who are really Christians cannot be forced to do any of these things' (invoke the gods, venerate the emperor). Equally striking is the fact that many of those accused of being 'Christian' were quick to deny it. The implication of the second and third points is that while many had been drawn to Christianity by its success, a considerable proportion of them did not qualify as 'really Christian'. This is a point to remember as we trace the makings of Christianity: not only was there consistent and substantial growth, but there were many who moved out again from the new sect. The margins will have been very porous, with movement in both directions.

37. 'The expression which he uses in this connection *(Christiani deferebantur)* is a legal *terminus technicus,* the verb *defero* means to "inform against somebody" or, to begin a prosecution. Who were the informers? We are not told and we can only suppose . . . that they may have been Jews, or sectarian Christians, or perhaps even businessmen who suffered financial loss because the spread of Christianity resulted in a decline in the demand for sacrificial items' (Benko, 'Pagan Criticism' 1070).

Finally, we should not fail to notice the descriptions of these early Christian meetings in Bithynia in the second decade of the second century.

- They met twice 'on a certain day' (presumably Sunday): once for worship and renewing their commitment, the second time for a shared meal.
- The worship included 'a song with responses to Christ as a god'; but from what Pliny had been told, the meal consisted simply in 'ordinary' food.
- The teaching or exhortation given at the first meeting was not on doctrinal matters but on concerns of social and ethical responsibility — 'not to commit any crime, but to avoid theft, robbery, adultery, not to break a trust or deny a deposit when they are called for it'.
- The only officials or ministries mentioned were the 'two female slaves who were called deaconesses'.

The information is meagre and itself fragmentary, but as a 'snapshot' it is fascinating, and invaluable when added to the other information still available to us.

f. Cassius Dio (ca. 160-230)

In a much-debated passage (67.14.1-3) Cassius Dio[38] describes how Emperor Domitian executed his cousin Flavius Clemens in 96. The charge against both Flavius Clemens and his wife, Flavia Domitilla, was 'atheism, a charge on which many others who had drifted into [*or* made shipwreck on] Jewish ways were condemned', some of whom were put to death, and the rest deprived of their property. Domitilla, also a relative of the emperor, was merely banished. There is nothing to indicate that Flavius Clemens and his wife became Christians, since, as we shall see, Jewish customs proved perennially attractive to certain inquiring non-Jews over the years.[39] However, the possibility that it was what we might call Christian Judaism which was in view cannot be wholly ruled out. So long as the Christian message was not clearly distinct from historic Judaism, it would share the attraction of Judaism's ancient lineage, a matter of importance for truth-seekers. And if Christianity was already growing more rapidly among non-Jews than among Jews, as seems already to have been the case forty years earlier, then the likelihood of high-born Romans coming into contact with Christian non-Jews is presumably higher than their having close contact with non-Roman Jews.

The issue is so obscure that nothing can be made of it beyond the further possible indication that Christianity would not have appeared very different from Judaism at this time, and the confirmation that the attraction of Jewish customs

---

38. *OCD*³ 299-300. For the passage, see *GLAJJ* 2.379-84.
39. See again below, §29.5c.

to many non-Jews must surely have been a factor in the spread of the Jewish Nazarene sect among non-Jews.

In short, the historian who had no access to Christian sources would have to be content with minimal information about the beginnings of Christianity. At the same time, such sources as there are certainly attest a movement identifiable by reference to one Christus or Chrestus which originated in Judea, was a branch of the religion of the Jews, and already in the 60s had a substantial and distinctive presence in the capital city, Rome. Beyond that we have to resort to Christian sources.

21.2. The Acts of the Apostles

'The Acts of the Apostles' *(praxeis apostolōn, acta apostolorum)* is a very old title for the work. It was used by Irenaeus *(Adv. haer.* 3.13.3), the Muratorian Canon (line 34), and the so-called Anti-Marcionite Prologue to Luke,[40] and presumably provided the precedent for the apocryphal acts of individual apostles which began to appear towards the end of the second century.[41] So the title probably became established about the middle of the second century.[42] As such it attests the high esteem in which the 'apostles' were already held at that time.[43] Even though 'The Acts of the Apostles' deals in effect only with the acts of Peter (only so far) and of Paul, and its account of the expansion of the new movement is limited to following Paul's footsteps through the Aegean and finally to Rome, it evidently soon (within two or three generations) came to be regarded as the definitive account of the beginnings of Christianity, 'the apostolic age'.

a. Author and Date of Writing

Acts is the second of a two-volume work — Luke-Acts. This is clearly signalled in the opening sentence of the latter volume (1.1-2), as also by the stylistic char-

---

40. Irenaeus ca. 130-ca. 200; Muratorian fragment, see below, n. 47; on the Anti-Marcionite Prologues see E. Haenchen, ET *The Acts of the Apostles* (Oxford: Blackwell, 1971) 10-12.

41. Schneemelcher, *NTA* vol. 2. Hegesippus, who is described by Eusebius as 'coming from the first successors *(diadochē)* of the apostles' *(HE* 2.23.3) and who was in Rome until the 170s or 180s (4.11.7), gave his five books the title *Pente hypomnēmata ekklēsiastikōn praxeōn* (Five Treatises on the Acts of the Church) (K. Lake, *Eusebius, Ecclesiastical History,* LCL [1926] xlvi), possibly also under the influence of Acts.

42. *Beginnings* 4.1-2; D. E. Aune, *The New Testament in Its Literary Environment* (Philadelphia: Westminster, 1987) 78.

43. W. Bienert, in Schneemelcher, *NTA* 2.5-27. The title of the *Didache* ('The Teaching of the Apostles') is not attested till later (K. Niederwimmer, *Die Didache* [Göttingen: Vandenhoeck und Ruprecht, ²1993] 81-82).

acteristics which permeate both volumes,[44] and is confirmed by the several obviously deliberate points of parallel between the two volumes which effectively lock them together.[45] We can therefore take the prologue to the Gospel (Luke 1.1-4) and conclude that the claim of careful research after sources and eyewitness information indicated there applies also to the Acts.[46]

Neither volume tells us who their author was. According to the same late second-century witnesses (Irenaeus, the Muratorian fragment and the anti-Marcionite prologue to Luke),[47] however, the tradition has been that the author was Luke, the one described as 'the beloved physician' in Col. 4.14 (cf. 2 Tim. 4.11; Phlm. 24).[48] The evidence available to us from Acts does not make possible a firm

44. H. J. Cadbury, *The Making of Luke-Acts* (New York: Macmillan, 1927). That Luke and Acts were written by the same author is still the major consensus; see J. Verheyden, 'The Unity of Luke-Acts', in J. Verheyden, ed., *The Unity of Luke-Acts* (BETL 142; Leuven: Leuven University, 1999) 3-56. The most substantial challenge is by R. Pervo and M. C. Parsons, *Rethinking the Unity of Luke and Acts* (Minneapolis: Fortress, 1993).

45. *Luke*   *Acts*
   3.21-22   2.1-4
   4.14-21   2.14-39/13.16-41
   4.40   28.9
   5.17-26   3.1-10/14.8-11
   8.40-56   9.36-41/20.9-12
   22.66-71   6.8-15
   22.69   7.56
   23.34, 46   7.59-60

See M. D. Goulder, *Type and History in Acts* (London: SPCK, 1964) ch. 4; C. H. Talbert, *Literary Patterns, Theological Themes and the Genre of Luke-Acts* (SBLDS 20; Missoula: Scholars, 1974) 16-18; D. Marguerat, *The First Christian Historian: Writing the 'Acts of the Apostles'* (SNTSMS 121; Cambridge: Cambridge University, 2002) ch. 3; note also J. B. Green, 'Internal Repetition in Luke-Acts: Contemporary Narratology and Lucan Historiography', in B. Witherington, ed., *History, Literature and Society in the Book of Acts* (Cambridge: Cambridge University, 1996) 283-99.

46. See particularly H. J. Cadbury, 'Commentary on the Preface of Luke', *Beginnings* 2.489-510 (here 492); I. H. Marshall, 'Acts and the "Former Treatise"', *BAFCS* 1.163-82.

47. The date of the Muratorian fragment is disputed, but the consensus is late second century; see, e.g., F. F. Bruce, *The Acts of the Apostles* (Grand Rapids: Eerdmans, ³1990) 1-2; *ODCC*³ 846-47, 1126.

48. Irenaeus, *Adv. haer.* 3.1.1 — 'Luke, the travelling companion of Paul, wrote down the gospel as proclaimed by him [Paul]'; Muratorian Canon lines 3-6 — 'Luke the physician, after the ascension of Christ, after Paul had taken him along as a learned person, wrote in his own name according to his [Paul's] perspective' (both as quoted by U. Schnelle, *The History and Theology of the New Testament Writings* [London: SCM, 1998] 240); the anti-Marcionite prologue to Luke — 'Luke . . . a Syrian from Antioch, by profession a physician, the disciple of the apostles, and later a follower of Paul until his martyrdom'. For the original texts see K. Aland, *Synopsis Quattuor Evangeliorum* (Stuttgart: Württembergische Bibelanstalt, 1964) 533, 538. The title *euangelion kata Loukan* is found at the end of the Gospel in the oldest extant

judgment on the point.[49] But the presence of passages written in the first person plural ('we/us' sections) in the second (the Pauline) half of the narrative gives the strong impression that the narrator was personally present at and involved in the events described (16.10-17; 20.5-15; 21.8-18; 27.1–28.16). To be sure, it is customary in critical scholarship to ascribe this feature to artistic invention or literary convention,[50] but the abruptness of the transitions from third person to first person and back again is more obviously explained in terms of personal presence and absence, and overall it is hard to avoid the conclusion that the narrator intended his readers to infer his personal involvement in the episodes described.[51]

---

ms of it, p[75], a papyrus codex dating from 175-225; see J. A. Fitzmyer, *The Gospel according to Luke* (AB 28, 2 vols.; New York: Doubleday, 1981, 1985) 35-36. J. Jervell, *Die Apostelgeschichte* (KEK; Göttingen: Vandenhoeck und Ruprecht, 1998), observes: 'It was normal to publish a book with both the title and the name of the author' (57-58). For a full review of testimony from the patristic period see H. J. Cadbury, 'The Tradition', *Beginnings* 2.209-64; Aland, *Synopsis* 531-48; C. K. Barrett, *The Acts of the Apostles* (ICC, 2 vols.; Edinburgh: Clark, 1994, 1998) 1.30-48; A. Gregory, *The Reception of Luke and Acts in the Period before Irenaeus* (WUNT 2.169; Tübingen: Mohr Siebeck, 2003). For the tradition that Luke came from Antioch, of equal age (late second century), see, e.g., Fitzmyer, *Luke* 1.45-47.

49. Jervell represents a recent tendency to dispute the more traditional view that Luke was a Gentile Christian and insists, on the basis of the internal evidence, that he was a Jewish Christian, or at least a God-fearer with roots in Hellenistic-Jewish Christianity (*Apg* 84).

50. For example, W. G. Kümmel, *Introduction to the New Testament* (Nashville: Abingdon, 1975) 184-85; V. K. Robbins, 'The We-Passages and Ancient Sea Voyages', in C. H. Talbert, ed., *Perspectives on Luke-Acts* (Edinburgh: Clark, 1978) 215-42; Schnelle, *History* 267-70; bibliography in Fitzmyer, *Acts* 99. But why would Luke simply incorporate units of travel narrative unassociated with the characters of his own narrative and written in the first person, without either eliminating the 'we/us' to make the incorporated material conform to the rest of his narrative, or expanding the motif to imply eye-witness testimony for more important parts of his account? Luke is a better story-teller than that. See further J. A. Fitzmyer, 'The Authorship of Luke-Acts Reconsidered', *Luke the Theologian: Aspects of His Teaching* (London: Chapman, 1989) 1-26 (here 16-22); also *Acts* 100-103.

51. J. Dupont, *The Sources of Acts: The Present Position* (London: Darton, Longman and Todd, 1964) 167; W. C. van Unnik, 'Luke's Second Book and the Rules of Hellenistic Historiography', in J. Kremer, ed., *Les Actes des Apôtres. Tradition, redaction, théologie* (BETL 48; Gembloux: Duculot, 1979) 37-60: 'In introducing this simple "we" Luke indicates that he had been in the company of Paul; . . . An ancient reader could not draw any other conclusion from these data' (41-42); similarly M. Hengel, *Acts and the History of Earliest Christianity* (London: SCM, 1979) 66; Bruce, *Acts* 3-5; Aune, *New Testament* 123-24; and particularly the thorough discussion by C.-J. Thornton, *Der Zeuge des Zeugen. Lukas als Historiker der Paulusreisen* (WUNT 56; Tübingen: Mohr Siebeck, 1991): 'The We-narratives of Acts contain nothing which readers in antiquity would not have held to be completely realistic. In them they would be able to recognize only an account of actual experiences of the author. If the author had not taken part in the journeys described in the We-form his stories about them would — according to the ancient understanding also — be lies' (141). Thornton (176) and Aune (124) refer to the instructive parallel of Polybius 36.12; see earlier discussion in J. Moffatt, *An Intro-*

Some have thought to date Luke's composition before the death of Paul,[52] others into the second century,[53] but a date in the middle or towards the end of the second generation of Christianity (the 80s or early 90s)[54] fits best with the evidence: (1) a volume written some time after the Gospel of Luke, itself usually thought to be dependent on Mark's Gospel (usually dated to the late 60s or early 70s), (2) by someone who had probably been a companion of Paul, and (3) whose portrayal of earliest Christianity seems to reflect the concerns of the post-Pauline generation after that stormy petrel had disappeared from the scene (vividly indicated in 20.25-31).

All NT writings come down to us in different textual forms, from manuscripts and translations dating chiefly from the fourth century onwards. Usually the differences between them, though multitudinous, are insignificant. But in the case of Acts, a text form of Acts (usually called the 'Western' text) can be discerned which consistently seeks to clarify and smooth the underlying text by numerous elaborations.[55] These almost certainly do not belong to the original text

---

duction to the Literature of the New Testament (Edinburgh: Clark, [3]1918) 294-96. Fitzmyer lists the 'modern interpreters who recognize the Luke of church tradition as the author of Acts' (*Acts* 51). Particular mention should be made of A. Harnack, *Luke the Physician: The Author of the Third Gospel and the Acts of the Apostles* (London: Williams and Norgate, 1907) 26-120; also *The Date of the Acts and of the Synoptic Gospels* (London: Williams and Norgate, 1911) 1-29. It should be noted that in Dibelius's view, the 'we' indicates that the author of Acts participated in the events recorded (M. Dibelius, *Paul,* edited and completed by W. G. Kümmel [London: Longmans, 1953] 9-10). See further below, n. 94 and §§21.2c-d.

52. See, e.g., E. J. Schnabel, *Early Christian Mission* (Downers Grove: InterVarsity, 2004) 30-32 and n. 86. But the fact that Acts ends without recounting Paul's martyrdom is amenable to other explanations — e.g., the narrative having climaxed in his account of how the gospel came to Rome, Luke preferred to 'fade out' his narrative with his picture of Paul still actively preaching the kingdom (28.30-31). Bruce observes that 'the story of the early expansion of Christianity has no single natural conclusion: Luke chooses to conclude his narrative with Paul's uninhibited preaching of the gospel in Rome' (*Acts* 13). Van Unnik points out that according to the standards of the time, the end of Acts was a good one ('Luke's Second Book and the Rules of Hellenistic Historiography' 52). See further Bruce's eminently sensible discussion (*Acts* 12-18); for summary review of the options see Fitzmyer, *Acts* 51-55.

53. Most recently C. Mount, *Pauline Christianity: Luke-Acts and the Legacy of Paul* (NovTSupp 104; Leiden: Brill, 2002); J. Tyson, *Marcion and Luke-Acts: A Defining Struggle* (Columbia: University of South Carolina, 2006). Earlier bibliography for both views appears in Kümmel, *Introduction* 186, and Fitzmyer, *Acts* 52-54.

54. The current consensus — e.g., Schnelle, *History* 260; Fitzmyer, *Acts* 54.

55. Brief details in Schnelle, *History* 263-64. For fuller details and discussion see Haenchen, *Acts* 50-60; B. M. Metzger, *A Textual Commentary on the Greek New Testament* (London: United Bible Societies, 1971, 1975) 259-72; P. Head, 'Acts and the Problem of Its Texts', *BAFCS* 1.2-29; J. Read-Heimerdinger, *The Bezan Text of Acts* (JSNTS 236; London: Sheffield Academic, 2002). Barrett concludes: 'Can it be simply that the Western text is not a redaction but a tendency to paraphrase and to enhance, and that in Acts copyists felt a greater

but are often interesting and tell us how Acts was received and used within early Western Christianity.

b. The Question of Genre

Since the rise of modern historiography,[56] there has been considerable discussion regarding the genre of Acts and the implications of the decision made for the historical value of Luke's account. There is almost universal agreement, despite numerous qualifications, that it has to be accorded the title 'history' in at least some sense.[57] But the qualifications do confuse and diminish the finding. So some clarifications are necessary.

---

freedom especially in the narrative portions (where the variants are more frequent and divergent) than they did in regard to the life and teaching of Jesus and the letters of the apostles?' (28). For a valuable recent review and discussion see T. Nicklas and M. Tilly, eds., *The Book of Acts as Church History: Text, Textual Traditions and Ancient Interpretations* (BZNW 120; Berlin: de Gruyter, 2003).

56. See *Jesus Remembered* §6 (particularly §6.3).

57. 'That the author of Acts is the first Christian historian is a widely accepted view [*Auffassung*] in New Testament and ancient historical research' (J. Schröter, 'Lukas als Historiograph. Das lukanische Doppelwerk und die Entdeckung der christlichen Heilsgeschichte', in E.-M. Becker, ed., *Die antike Historiographie und die Anfänge der christlichen Geschichtsschreibung* [BZNW 129; Berlin: de Gruyter, 2005] 237-62 [here 246-47]). See particularly Hengel, *Acts;* G. E. Sterling, *Historiography and Self-Definition: Josephus, Luke-Acts and Apologetic Historiography* (NovTSupp 64; Leiden: Brill, 1992); C. K. Rothschild, *Luke-Acts and the Rhetoric of History* (WUNT 2.175; Tübingen: Mohr Siebeck, 2004); other bibliography in L. C. Alexander, 'The Preface to Acts and the Historians', in Witherington, ed., *History* 73-103 (here 95 n. 54), reprinted in L. C. Alexander, *Acts in Its Ancient Literary Context: A Classicist Looks at the Acts of the Apostles* (LNTS 298; London: Clark International, 2005) 21-42 (here 37 n. 54). C. Breytenbach, *Paulus und Barnabas in der Provinz Galatien* (AGAJU 38; Leiden: Brill, 1996), comments on the divergence between German and British Acts scholarship and on the degree to which the latter interact with ancient historians, and observes that form classification is too quickly taken to be a judgment on historicity (5-12). But Jervell notes that recent German scholarship has shown a renewed interest in Luke as historian (*Apg* 50), though Schnabel gives examples of continuing scepticism on the subject (*Mission* 22-23). Still valuable is the earlier review of 'The Greek and Jewish Traditions of Writing History' by H. J. Cadbury and the editors, in *Beginnings* 2.7-29. See also D. W. Palmer, 'Acts and the Ancient Historical Monograph', *BAFCS* 1-29; B. Witherington, *The Acts of the Apostles: A Socio-Rhetorical Commentary* (Grand Rapids: Eerdmans, 1998) 2-39. Kümmel, *Introduction* 161-62, asserts that Acts 'is not "a real historical work" (E. Meyer) nor its author "the first Christian historian" (M. Dibelius)', but his reasons, somewhat astonishingly, are that (1) Acts is the second volume of a two-volume work, and (2) 'so many of the marks of real historical writing are missing — completeness of material, exactitude of historical detail, consistent chronology, biographical interest', a yardstick which would disqualify not a few ancient historians.

First, there is no single ideal type of ancient 'historian'. Almost all recent attempts to characterize by categorizing the Gospels and the Epistles fail because the documents of the NT fit no single template.[58] So it is with Luke's Acts. We may be sure that his concern was not to conform to a particular type but simply(!) to tell the story of Christianity's beginnings.[59] Evidently he was sufficiently aware of how such a story should or might be told[60] in his use of standard or typical techniques, for example, by including speeches at appropriate points and by interspersing summary statements every so often (to keep the plot moving

58. See further *Jesus Remembered* 184-86 and below, §29.8b.

59. Cf. Cadbury: 'Those who told or wrote about Jesus and the apostles were not imitating literary models, but were following the natural trend of motives and purposes which influenced the material' (*Making of Luke-Acts* 49). Recent discussion illustrates the tendency and problem of over-categorizing. Sterling defines his sub-set '*apologetic* history' as 'the story of a people in an extended prose narrative written by a member of the group who follows the group's own traditions but Hellenizes them in an effort to establish the identity of the group within the setting of the larger world' (*Historiography* 17). Acts itself could fit that definition ('an effort to provide . . . a definition of who they were' [19]), though the precedents Sterling cites have a characteristically nationalistic emphasis (16) — not least the Hellenistic Jewish historians cited (223; Josephus on pp. 308-309), hence his description of Acts as 'the story of Christianity, i.e., of a people' (349) (cf. Rothschild, *Luke-Acts* 51-53). Alexander ('Preface'; see also 'The Acts of the Apostles as an Apologetic Text', in *Acts in Its Ancient Literary Context* 183-206) also prefers 'apologetic historiography' to E. Plümacher's 'historical monograph' (which Plümacher draws from Cicero and Sallust) — E. Plümacher, 'Die Apostelgeschichte als historische Monographie', in Kremer, ed., *Les Actes des Apôtres* 457-66. Hubert Cancik, 'The History of Culture, Religion, and Institutions in Ancient Historiography: Philological Observations concerning Luke's History', *JBL* 116 (1997) 673-95, suggests the sub-category 'institutional history': Luke-Acts as 'a history that narrates the origin and spread of an institution' (673), but the term 'institution' still rings of the older argument that Acts represents an early-catholicizing phase *(Frühkatholizismus)* of Christian history (see §20 n. 150 above) and does not give sufficient weight to Luke's emphasis on the boundary-breaking character of the Spirit's direction; this is an issue for vol. 3. Marguerat prefers a 'narrative of beginnings' (*First Christian Historian* 29-31). Jervell argues for 'salvation history' ('The Future of the Past: Luke's Vision of Salvation History and Its Bearing on His Writing of History', in Witherington, ed., *History* 104-26 [here 110]), but in his commentary he opts for 'tragic history', referring to Plümacher's *Lukas* 255-58, and Thornton, *Zeuge* 153ff. (*Apg.* 78). Aune prefers the less specific 'general history' (*New Testament* 77). A. J. M. Wedderburn, 'Zur Frage der Gattung der Apostelgeschichte', in H. Lichtenberger, ed., *Geschichte — Tradition — Reflexion.* Vol. 3: *Frühes Christentum,* M. Hengel FS (Tübingen: Mohr Siebeck, 1996) 302-22, concludes that Acts is *sui generis* (319). The fluidity of the genres with which Luke and Acts have been identified is rightly emphasized by J. B. Green, *The Gospel of Luke* (Grand Rapids: Eerdmans, 1997) 4-6; and for a fuller listing of options canvassed see S. Shauf, *Theology as History, History as Theology: Paul in Ephesus in Acts 19* (BZNW 133; Berlin: de Gruyter, 2005) 60-62.

60. Central to Rothschild's thesis is the rhetorical character of ancient historiography (see n. 69 below); she cites appropriately 2 Macc. 15.39 (*Luke-Acts* 3 n. 10).

along).[61] But use of such techniques makes him neither a better nor a poorer historian so far as the broad outline of his story is concerned.

Second, the discussion of sources, which was very prominent in the early decades of the twentieth century, soon reached an impasse.[62] Luke's style in Acts is so consistent and so characteristically Lukan that there is no real possibility of disentangling any sources.[63] At the same time, we may recall Luke's respect for the sources used in compiling his Gospel — a fact borne home to us by the evident parallels with Mark and Matthew. The fact that similar sources are not detectable in Acts is not simply a consequence of Acts having no parallel document but strongly suggests that Luke's sources were seldom literary and probably much more a matter of reports made personally to Luke.[64] Here we need to re-enforce a point argued at length in *Jesus Remembered:*[65] that to think of sources (only) as written, or of a writer's dependence on oral reports as though they were copied (the literary paradigm), is a failure of historical realism. So to assume is to misunderstand the character of a society where tradition was preserved and information communicated orally, with the sort of 'performance variations' which the diversity of the Synoptic tradition attests. More to the point, so to assume does too little credit to the quality of Luke himself as a superb raconteur, of which the three (different) accounts of Paul's conversion (Acts 9, 22, 26)[66] and the mounting climax of the 'Pauline passion narrative' (chs. 21–28) are superb examples.

Third, the debate which superseded the discussion of sources was dominated by the issue whether Acts was history or kerygma or theology. As in the case of the quest of the historical Jesus,[67] the working assumption evidently was

---

61. Acts 2.42-47; 4.32-35; 5.11-16; 6.7; 9.31; 12.24; 16.5; 19.20; 28.30-31.

62. Dupont's thorough examination of *The Sources of Acts* concluded: 'Despite the most careful and detailed research, it has not been possible to define any of the sources used by the author of Acts in a way which will meet with widespread agreement among critics' (166). Haenchen's discussion becomes fully realistic only when it moves beyond the question of written sources (*Acts* 81-88). See reviews in Kümmel, *Introduction* 174-78; Fitzmyer, *Acts* 81-85.

63. See n. 44 above.

64. 'The author had very rich oral sources at his disposal. . . . The widespread idea that conditions were unfavourable for the forming of tradition over the earliest period, so that only sparse material was available to Luke, is not correct' (Jervell, *Apg* 64; see further 64-66).

65. *Jesus Remembered,* especially §8; also 'Altering the Default Setting: Re-envisaging the Early Transmission of the Jesus Tradition', *NTS* 49 (2003) 139-75, reprinted in *A New Perspective on Jesus: What the Quest for the Historical Jesus Missed* (Grand Rapids: Baker, 2005) 79-125.

66. *Jesus Remembered* 210-12; see also A. M. Schwemer, 'Erinnerung und Legende. Die Berufung des Paulus und ihre Darstellung in der Apostelgeschichte', in L. T. Stuckenbruck et al., eds., *Memory in the Bible and Antiquity* (WUNT 212; Tübingen: Mohr Siebeck, 2007) 277-98.

67. *Jesus Remembered* §4; *New Perspective on Jesus* ch. 1.

that Acts could not be both history and theology without the history being diminished or corrupted.[68] But good history has never been simply a matter of pedantic communication of information. Clare Rothschild properly emphasizes both that historians have always used rhetorical techniques to persuade readers of the credibility of what they write[69] and that 'theology is thoroughly integrated in the composition of ancient historical works'.[70] And Todd Penner similarly draws attention to the rhetorical character of ancient historiography: 'They placed their emphasis less on the *fundamenta* and more on the plausibility of their representation' — history *as* rhetoric, not simply using rhetorical devices.[71] Modern historians, of course, are hardly less biased, tendentious and rhetorical (endeavoring

68. Hengel speaks similarly of a 'flight from history' (*Acts* viii; cf. *Jesus Remembered* §5). As Wrede posed the antithesis in regard to the Synoptic Gospels (theology, and therefore not history; *Jesus Remembered* 50), so Franz Overbeck had already posed the same antithesis for Acts: *either* history *or* theology; theology, and therefore *not* history (Rothschild, *Luke-Acts* 25-26, 29-32, drawing particularly on J. A. Overbeck, *History against Theology: An Analysis of the Life and Thought of Franz Overbeck* [Chicago PhD, 1975]). The weight of Harnack's conservative scholarship stemmed the sceptical tide during the first half of the twentieth century — see his *Luke the Physician,* also *Die Apostelgeschichte* (Leipzig: Hinrich, 1908); also *Date of Acts.* Most influential in the second half of the twentieth century have been M. Dibelius, *Studies in the Acts of the Apostles* (London: SCM, 1956), and H. Conzelmann, *Die Mitte der Zeit* (Tübingen: Mohr Siebeck, 1953, [2]1957), significantly translated as *The Theology of St. Luke* (New York: Harper and Brothers, 1960); see also T. Penner, *In Praise of Christian Origins: Stephen and the Hellenists in Lukan Apologetic Historiography* (Emory Studies in Early Christianity; New York: Clark International, 2004) 44-50.

69. See her thesis statement in *Luke-Acts* 61 and conclusion on 291; she cites with effect S. Hornblower, 'Narratology and Narrative Techniques in Thucydides', in S. Hornblower, ed., *Greek Historiography* (Oxford: Clarendon, 1994) 131-66: 'By examining the techniques of historical presentation we do not necessarily imply that the subject-matter of that presentation is true or false. True facts can be presented rhetorically or non-rhetorically. Or rather, true facts may be presented with a rhetoric which is more or less obtrusive' (133); and L. H. Feldman, *Josephus' Interpretation of the Bible* (Berkeley: University of California, 1998): 'by the time of Josephus, virtually all historiography was . . . actually rhetorical' (9) (Rothschild, *Luke-Acts* 75-76). Rothschild was following a lead given by van Unnik, 'Luke's Second Book and the Rules of Hellenistic Historiography' 46-59. See also P. E. Satterthwaite, 'Acts against the Background of Classical Rhetoric', *BAFCS* 1.337-79; Witherington, *Acts* 39-49.

70. Rothschild, *Luke-Acts* 6, 24, with reference particularly to F. M. Cornford, *Thucydides Mythistoricus* (1907; New York: Greenwood, 1969); and C. W. Fornara, *The Nature of History in Ancient Greece and Rome* (Berkeley: University of California, 1983) 77-90. Similarly Hengel: 'By far the majority of ancient historians agree that history is not the work of men alone' (*Acts* 51-52).

71. *In Praise of Christian Origins* ch. 3, particularly 123-26, 129 (quotation from 217). The rhetorical character of ancient (and Luke's) historiography has become a prominent emphasis in recent study; in addition see D. P. Moessner, ed., *Jesus and the Heritage of Israel* (Harrisburg: Trinity Press International, 1999), particularly D. D. Schmidt, 'Rhetorical Influences and Genre: Luke's Preface and the Rhetoric of Hellenistic Historiography' (27-60).

to persuade) in their reconstructions and portrayals of characters and events than ancient historians; we may think, for example, of the current diverse historical recountings and evaluations of such figures as Richard III or, more recently, Winston Churchill or Margaret Thatcher in British history. So there should be no difficulty in recognizing that Luke had a theological agenda, a *Tendenz,* but that need not indicate that he was a poor historian, only that he read the information he had from a particular perspective;[72] hence the common alternative title for the volume, 'The Acts of the Holy Spirit'.[73]

Finally, we should beware of judging Luke's Acts by the canons of modern historiography. It is not that ancient historians were any less interested in what had happened in significant periods and events of the past than are modern historians. But modern historians have far more extensive source material and more refined methods (not least a concept of copyright), whereas an ancient historian like Luke did not have reference works or, unlike some of his contemporaries, access to official archives.[74] He had to rely on first-hand accounts and reports from earlier decades; he does not even show awareness of Paul's letters.[75] It should occasion no surprise, therefore, when the information he uses is at times confused or false, as in the apparent blunder about the Quirinius census (Luke 2.2),[76] or the much-cited allusion to Theudas in Acts 5.36,[77] or that his numbers are usually to be taken with a grain of salt.[78] Similar examples can be pointed out for

72. If the task of the historian is to be defined as giving meaning to events, forming historical materials into a history, with the unavoidable element of interpretation involved, then Luke fulfils the role of a historian (cf. Schröter, 'Lukas als Historiograph' 247-50, 254; Marguerat, *First Christian Historian* 5-7, and further 8-13, 21; Shauf, *Theology as History* 66-80).

73. As in F. F. Bruce, *The Book of the Acts* (London: Marshall, Morgan and Scott, 1954) 33; see also Marguerat, *First Christian Historian* ch. 6; and below, §22 n. 52.

74. In a private communication Greg Sterling adds: 'It did not occur to ancient historians to visit archives and conduct research. They rewrote the accounts of others. This is a fundamental difference between ancient and modern historiography'.

75. For the chief considerations see, e.g., G. Lüdemann, *Early Christianity according to the Traditions in Acts: A Commentary* (London: SCM, 1989) 7-9.

76. See *Jesus Remembered* 344 and n. 29. The location of the Italica Cohort in Caesarea in the 30s (Acts 10.1) is another possible blunder, but the issue is disputed (see below, §26 n. 47).

77. C. Hemer, *The Book of Acts in the Setting of Hellenistic History* (WUNT 49; Tübingen: Mohr Siebeck, 1989), attempts to ease the problem (162-63); and further P. Barnett, *The Birth of Christianity: The First Twenty Years* (Grand Rapids: Eerdmans, 2005) 199-200. Mason wonders whether Luke knew Josephus or a narrative like that of Josephus (*Josephus* 277-82).

78. E.g., Haenchen, *Acts* 188-89. It is easy to forget how difficult it is to achieve a realistic estimate of the size of a crowd. Many a protest organizer today will estimate crowds two or three times larger than the estimate of the supervising police. In the Iran-Iraq war of the 1980s each side regularly reported huge casualties sustained by the other side.

other ancient historians without diminishing the overall regard in which their historical work is held. Acts should be accorded the same courtesy.

c. Historical Value

The issue is not whether Acts is 'good' history by modern standards but primarily whether it may be reckoned as responsible history writing in the ancient world. What would Luke's readers have expected from him? How would they have read Acts? We can derive the answer in large part from the NT itself. On the one hand there are good grounds for respecting the broad sweep of his account of Christianity's beginnings.

(1) The language of Luke's prologue (Luke 1.1-4) is conventional.[79] That signifies both Luke's awareness of these conventions and his intention to follow them. Thus his aim was to write a 'narrative or account *(diēgēsis)* concerning the events *(pragmatōn)* which have come to fruition among us' (Luke 1.1). The term *diēgēsis (narratio)* signifies a record of events set in narrative sequence and could be related specifically to writing history.[80] In Luke's case it is not a claim to some kind of objective impartiality, of course. As his use of the cognate verb *(diēgeomai)* reminds us (Acts 9.27; 12.17),[81] his concern was to tell his story as the narrative of God's working out his purpose.[82] The equivalent term used in Acts 1.1, 'the former word *(logos)*', takes up its striking use in Luke 1.2 (the

79. See particularly L. Alexander, *The Preface to Luke's Gospel: Literary Convention and Social Convention in Luke 1.1-4 and Acts 1.1* (SNTSMS 78; Cambridge: Cambridge University, 1993); but note Sterling's brief critique (*Historiography* 340-41); also Rothschild, *Luke-Acts* 68 n. 31. On the bearing of the Gospel preface to the subject (that it would not of itself suggest that the following work belonged to the genre of 'Hellenistic historiography') see Alexander, 'Preface', and her response to critiques of *Preface* in *Acts in Its Ancient Literary Context* 12-19. For parallels between Luke's preface and Josephus's preface see Mason, *Josephus* 252-59.

80. Josephus, *Life* 336; Plutarch, *Mor.* 1093B; Lucian, *Historia* 55; details in Fitzmyer, *Luke* 1.292; Alexander, *Preface* 111; BDAG 245. '*Diēgēsin peri tōn . . . pragmatōn, . . .* these are more or less technical terms in historiography' (van Unnik, 'Luke's Second Book and the Rules of Hellenistic Historiography' 40); 'by substituting the term "narrative" for Mark's "gospel", Luke indicated his intention to write history' (Aune, *New Testament* 116).

81. Green, *Luke* 38. H. Schürmann, *Das Lukasevangelium 1,1–9,50* (HTKNT; Freiburg: Herder, 1969), suggests that Luke may have intended an allusion to Hab. 1.5 (7-8).

82. See particularly J. T. Squires, *The Plan of God in Luke-Acts* (SNTSMS 76; Cambridge: Cambridge University, 1993). *Pace* Rothschild (*Luke-Acts* chs. 5-6, particularly 148-49, 185-89, 212), the rhetorical effectiveness of the motifs of fulfilled prediction and *dei* ('it is necessary') enhance rather than diminish Squires's case. See also Marguerat, *First Christian Historian* ch. 5; Shauf, *Theology as History* 286-99.

diēgēsis handed down by 'those who from the beginning were eyewitnesses and servants of the word')[83] and carries the same implication even more clearly, since Luke liked to summarize the events he describes as 'the word of God growing/ spreading' (Acts 6.7; 12.24; 19.20).

The claim to 'eyewitness' *(autoptēs)* testimony in support of historical writing is precisely the point at which Luke's prologue seems to be vulnerable to the criticism of being merely conventional.[84] But Samuel Byrskog has argued that autopsy *(autopsia)* in fact was regarded (both valued and used) as an essential means by which the major Greek and Roman historians reached back to the past.[85] And Luke's language indicates one who both recognized his own lack of involvement in so much of what he was about to relate and the value he placed on the testimony of those who had been personally involved.[86] His own concerns at this point are confirmed by his accounts of the choice of a twelfth apostle to replace Judas and of Peter's and Paul's subsequent testimony: the new apostle had to be someone who had been part of the group of disciples from the beginning (Acts 1.21); Peter and John could not help but speak of what they had seen and heard (4.20); Paul was to be a witness of what he had seen (26.16). Similarly to be noted is Luke's emphasis on the fact that the preaching of the word was on the basis of personal experience (1.8, 22; 10.39), not least of the resurrected Jesus (1.22; 2.32; 3.15; 5.32; 10.41; 13.31; 26.16).

So too Luke's objective to 'follow through *(parakoloutheō)*[87] everything carefully *(akribōs)*[88] from the first' and 'to write an orderly account' (Luke

83. Too little noticed is the fact that Luke's use of *logos* here is already halfway to the much more familiar *logos* of John's prologue (John 1.1-18) (see further my *Christology* 232).

84. Alexander, *Preface:* 'the convention of *autopsia*' (34-41); Green, *Luke* 41.

85. S. Byrskog, *Story as History — History as Story* (WUNT 123; Tübingen: Mohr Siebeck, 2000) 48-65 (citing Herodotus, Thucydides, Polybius, Josephus and Tacitus). See also Cadbury, *Beginnings* 2.498-500; Rothschild, *Luke-Acts* 64, 222-25, who also notes the diverse ways in which Luke-Acts emphasizes reliance on eyewitnesses (226-31, 240-45); R. Bauckham, *Jesus and the Eyewitnesses: The Gospels as Eyewitness Testimony* (Grand Rapids: Eerdmans, 2006) — on the Lukan preface (116-24); M. Hengel, 'Der Lukasprolog und seine Augenzeugen. Die Apostel, Petrus und die Frauen', in Stuckenbruck et al., eds., *Memory in the Bible and Antiquity* 195-242.

86. The Greek implies that the two terms refer to the same group of people — those who had been 'the original eyewitnesses and ministers of the word' (Fitzmyer, *Luke* 294).

87. BDAG's note should be observed: 'Luke does not specify the means whereby he was able to assert his thorough familiarity [a rendering such as "research" or "investigate" depends on an interpretation of the context and not on the semantic content of *p.*]. It can be assumed that some of it was derived from the kinds of sources cited in vs. 2' (767). See further D. P. Moessner, 'The Appeal and Power of Poetics (Luke 1:1-4)', in D. P. Moessner, ed., *Jesus and the Heritage of Israel* 84-123 (here 85-97): 'Luke highlights the credentials of one steeped in the events, traditions, and reports that he orders into a narrative' (96).

88. D. L. Balch, *'akribōs . . . grapsai* (Luke 1:3)', in Moessner, ed., *Jesus and the Heri-*

1.3)[89] can presumably be referred to Acts as well.[90] The very selectivity or sparseness of his basic account (Acts 2–5 is built round only four episodes; the sequence chs. 8–12 is very episodic) can be taken as evidence for a degree of care and discrimination too seldom accorded to Luke. There is no good reason, then, to doubt that Luke endeavoured to act out the programme he laid out in Luke 1.1-4 for his second volume as well.[91] At the same time, it is again worth noting that he was not looking for unbiased witnesses but for the testimony of those whose lives had been transformed by 'the word' and who had committed themselves to its service.

(2) These deductions are strengthened by the 'we' passages in Acts. They certainly provide *prima facie* evidence that the author was personally present during the sequences described (the beginning and end of Paul's Aegean mission and his final arrival in and departure from Palestine).[92] But one of the implications

---

tage of Israel 229-50, argues implausibly that *akribōs* should be translated 'fully' (229-39); but see BDAG 39.

89. See again Cadbury, *Beginnings* 2.501-505; Fitzmyer, *Luke* 1.296-99; Rothschild, *Luke-Acts* 67-68 n. 31, 84 n. 96, 98. Sterling summarizes Josephus, *Ant.* 14.2-3: 'more than anything else . . . the main objective must be *akribeias*' (*Historiography* 243-44).

90. See further D. Moessner, 'The Meaning of *kathexēs* in the Lukan Prologue as a Key to the Distinctive Contribution of Luke's Narrative among the "Many"', in F. Van Segbroeck et al., eds., *The Four Gospels 1992*, F. Neirynck FS (3 vols.; Leuven: Leuven University, 1992) 2.1513-28; also 'Appeal and Power' 97-114.

91. In arguing that 'it is very difficult, if not impossible, to move beyond the framework, order, characterization, and style of the narrative to a concrete bedrock of assured reliable and verifiable data', Penner (*Praise* 111) is in danger of replacing the earlier antithesis (history vs. theology) with a history vs. rhetoric antithesis (though he would see it in terms of history *as* rhetoric, truthfulness as utility — 216-17). But it is more possible to distinguish veracity from verisimilitude than Penner allows: as we shall see over the next few pages, it is possible to identify both accurate data in Acts and Luke's own tendentious interests. And if Luke did rely on first-hand reports, as again and again seems to be the case, in line with his stated aim of drawing on eyewitness tradition (see above, n. 85), that redounds more to his credit as a historian even when the reports raise more questions than they answer. It will be one of the repeated challenges in the use of Acts in *Beginning from Jerusalem* to inquire as to where Luke most likely derived his information from.

92. 'The evidence within the text itself compels the belief that the author of Acts made use of travel notes that he himself had written and that the "we" was simply retained from the notes themselves' (R. Jewett, *Dating Paul's Life* [London: SCM, 1979] 17). 'It must be acknowledged that the force of these texts is to claim that the author was present. . . . The "we" passages appear so unobtrusively that the most natural way to read them is still the quiet presence of the author or a source' (Sterling, *Historiography* 324-26). Contrast Rothschild, *Luke-Acts* 264-67: 'The author of Luke-Acts inserts "we" to indulge the audience in a fantasy meant to transport them beyond argument to belief' (267); but did the move to Macedonia (Acts 16.10-12) and the later itinerary down the coast of Asia Minor (20.5-15) really require such authentication? and the absence of 'we/us' throughout Paul's imprisonment and trials is surely more surprising in such a 'fantasy' than its presence at the beginning and end of the period. In a

which can obviously be drawn from them also is that the author had opportunity to consult participants in the early phases of his story. According to the first 'we' passage (16.10-17) he spent some time in the company of Silas, one of the 'leading men among the brothers' (15.22), that is, in this case the Jerusalem disciples. According to the third 'we' passage (21.8-18), he stayed in Caesarea for several days with Philip (21.8, 10), one of the leaders of the Hellenist group which emerged in ch. 6 and the evangelist of Samaria (ch. 8); there he encountered the prophet Agabus (21.10), who would have provided another link with the earlier history of both Jerusalem and Antioch (11.27-28); and on the way to Jerusalem itself he stayed at the house of Mnason of Cyprus, 'an early disciple' (21.16). The lack of first-hand ('we') reports during Paul's imprisonment in Jerusalem and Caesarea (22–26) is surprising but could have a number of explanations, and the 'we' of 27.1 may be sufficient for the conclusion that the author must have spent some time in Caesarea,[93] during which he would have had plenty of opportunity to consult 'those who from the beginning were eyewitnesses and servants of the word'. A reasonable deduction, therefore, is that Luke both had personal involvement with Paul's mission and that he was able to draw on first-hand (eyewitness) reports for at least much of the substance of the earlier episodes which he narrates in Acts.[94]

---

review of the extra-biblical literary evidence, S. E. Porter, 'The "We" Passages', *BAFCS* 2.545-74, revised in *The Paul of Acts* (WUNT 115; Tübingen: Mohr Siebeck, 1999) ch. 2, concludes that there is no literary precedent which explains the usage but that the author of Luke-Acts was utilizing a previously written 'we' source, probably not written by himself (573-74; *Paul* 27); but the thesis of a 'we' source incorporated and departed from so abruptly is hardly as persuasive as that of an author who, in the narrative he retells, signals his personal involvement by using the first person and his lack of personal involvement by dropping it. Cf. J. Wehnert, *Die Wir-Passagen der Apostelgeschichte* (Göttingen: Vandenhoeck und Ruprecht, 1989). See also above, n. 51, and on Paul's voyage to Rome see further below, §34.3.

93. The absence of 'we' between 21.18 and 27.1 need not imply that Luke had been absent for the duration of Paul's time in custody; in accordance with his normal technique, Luke in these final chapters focuses almost exclusively on Paul himself. However, there is no problem in assuming that Luke had other business affairs to attend to and was absent for much or most of the time; and he probably would have been debarred from attending Paul during the several hearings to which Paul had to submit.

94. A. J. M. Wedderburn, 'The "We"-Passages in Acts: On the Horns of a Dilemma', *ZNW* 93 (2002) 78-98, effectively discredits other literary solutions (81-85, 88-93). However, (1) he is puzzled why the author does not identify himself (as do, e.g., Thucydides, Julius Caesar and Josephus) (80-81), and (2) he follows Vielhauer in finding the Acts portrayal of Paul in regard to the law too much at odds with the evidence of Paul's letters to be credible (85-87): 'attempts to argue that the author of Acts had indeed accompanied Paul, despite the widely different portrayal of Paul, stretch our credulity too far' (87). But (1) Acts is a sequel to an equally anonymous Gospel, which may simply be following the model provided by (anonymous) Mark. And (2) Paul's attitude to the law was much more complex, even convoluted, than reference to polemical passages like Gal. 2.12 and 6.15 suggests; Paul also wrote passages like Rom. 3.31, 7.14, 8.4, 13.8-10 and

At this point we may recall Luke's technique in writing his former volume, the Gospel of Luke. Without detracting from the point already made above — that talk of his 'sources' should not be limited, as so often, to consideration of written sources — the fact remains that Luke's use of written sources is such as to allow us to recognize (Mark) or reconstruct (Q) these sources with a fair degree of confidence. That tells us much both about Luke's desire to carry out his task in accordance with the standards he set himself (Luke 1.1-4) and about his success in doing so. And if the main thesis of *Jesus Remembered* is on the right lines, then it also follows that Luke was a faithful transmitter (as well as providing an innovative performance) of the traditions he learned about Jesus, in oral as well as written form. The failure to detect written sources for Acts, then, or sources whose format was already so fixed as still to show clearly through Luke's use of them, in no way counts against the reliability of Luke's transmission of what he himself may have heard and witnessed.[95]

(3) Often overlooked in assessments of Acts is the degree of concurrence between Acts and the data to be gleaned from Paul's letters as to his basic movements. The point can be documented effectively in a chart on the following pages.[96]

The details will be reviewed as we proceed. But the overall impression strongly suggests that the author of Acts was well informed about Paul's life and mission.

(4) It is a striking fact that whereas with the Gospel of Luke there are only a few details which can be correlated with information from non-biblical sources, in the case of the Acts of Luke the number of such details is substantial.[97] For exam-

---

1 Cor. 7.19. To present Paul in a non-polemical light may be a surprising perspective, but it has more plausibility than Luke is usually given credit for and hardly rules out the possibility that the author of Luke-Acts was a personal companion for some of Paul's mission. Wedderburn's own solution is to hypothesize that the author of Luke-Acts was a disciple of an obscure travelling companion of Paul and that the 'we' indicates those points of the narrative where he knew that his source had been present (94-98). But would a disciple have left his revered teacher's identity so obscure? The simplest solution remains the 'we' of the author's personal reminiscence.

95. The fact that Luke 1.1-4 relates to both volumes of Luke-Acts, and that Luke relied on written as well as oral sources in writing his Gospel, does not diminish the effectiveness of the claim to eyewitness testimony in writing Acts; it suggests, rather, that Luke reckoned the Jesus tradition as he knew it, in written as well as oral forms, to have the character of eyewitness testimony.

96. The chart was suggested to me in a private communication by Greg Sterling, and I have gladly adopted it, though slightly adapted to accord with my own reckoning of the sequence of events.

97. For an overview see W. W. Gasque, *A History of the Criticism of the Acts of the Apostles* (Tübingen: Mohr Siebeck/Grand Rapids: Eerdmans, 1975) chs. 6 and 7; more recently, the brief treatments of Bruce, *Acts* 31-33; Hemer, *Book of Acts* 3-14; Fitzmyer, *Acts* 126-27.

Activity/Locale	Pauline Corpus	Acts
Pre-Christian		
Lineage	2 Cor. 11.22; Phil. 3.4-5; Rom. 11.1	
Tarsus		22.2 (cf. also 9.30; 11.25)
Educated in Jerusalem		22.3
Pharisee	Phil. 3.5 (cf. Gal. 1.14)	23.6; 26.5
Persecutor	Gal. 1.13; Phil. 3.6	7.58; 8.1
Early Christian		
Call/Conversion	Gal. 1.15-16; 1 Cor. 15.9-10; Phil. 3.4-11	9.1-22; 22.1-21; 26.1-18
Arabia	Gal. 1.17	
Damascus	Gal. 1.17; 2 Cor. 11.32-33	9.23-25
Jerusalem	Gal. 1.18-19	9.26-29
Caesarea		9.30
Tarsus		9.30
Antioch		11.26
Jerusalem		11.30; 12.25
Initial Journey		
Antioch		13.1-3
Seleucia		13.4
Salamis		13.5
New Paphos		13.6-12
Perga of Pamphylia		13.13
Antioch of Pisidia	Gal. 1.21; 4.13; *cf. 2 Tim. 3.11*	13.14-52
Iconium	*Cf. 2 Tim. 3.11*	14.1-7
Lystra	*Cf. 2 Tim. 3.11*	14.8-20
Derbe		14.20
Lystra, Iconium, Antioch		14.21-23
Perga, Attalia		14.25
Antioch		14.26-28
Jerusalem Conference		
Jerusalem	Gal. 2.1-10	15.1-29
Antioch	Gal. 2.11-14	15.36-39

European Missionary Journey

Syria and Cilicia		15.41
Derbe and Lystra		16.1-5
Phrygia and Galatia		16.6
Mysia		16.7-8
Troas		16.8-10
Samothrace		16.11
Neapolis		16.11
Philippi	1 Thess. 2.2; Phil. 4.15	16.12-40
Amphipolis and Apollonia		17.1
Thessalonica	1 Thess. 2.1-12; Phil. 4.15	17.1-9
Beroea		17.10-14
Athens	1 Thess. 3.1-6	17.15-34
Corinth	1 Cor. 3.6; 4.15	18.1-17
Cenchrea		18.18
Ephesus		18.19-21
Caesarea		18.22

Collection Journey

Galatia and Phrygia		18.23
Ephesus	1 Cor. 16.8	19.1-40
Corinth	2 Cor. 13.1-2 (cf. 2 Cor. 1.15-16; 2.1-2, 5-8; 7.11-12; 12.14, 19-21)	
Ephesus	2 Cor. 2.3-4, 9; 7.8-13	
Troas	2 Cor. 2.12-13	
Macedonia	2 Cor. 7.5-7	20.1
Illyricum	Rom. 15.19	
Corinth/Greece	Rom. 15.26; 16.1	20.2
Macedonia/Philippi		20.3-6a
Troas		20.6b-12
Assos, Mitylene, Chios, Samos		20.13-15
Miletus		20.16-38
Cos, Rhodes, Patara		21.1-2
Tyre		21.3-6
Ptolemais		21.7
Caesarea		21.8-14
Jerusalem	Rom. 15.25	21.15

ple, the striking account of the death of Herod Agrippa I (Acts 12.20-23) is paralleled in its main details by Josephus (*Ant.* 19.343-46) and must have been the subject of many a story-teller's performance. Luke's knowledge of it, as no doubt Josephus's, probably came from such 'common knowledge', not from any literary source, with Luke's own 'take' on the story most evident in the final verse (12.23).

A feature worth noting is that examples of these correlations become frequent from the beginning of the 'we' passages onwards. Indeed, since William Ramsay was converted to a high view of the reliability of Acts,[98] students of Acts have regularly been impressed by Luke's historical accuracy on various small details on which a writer with no personal experience of the events he narrates might well have stumbled. Luke knows that Herod Antipas was only titled 'tetrarch' of Galilee (Acts 13.1), whereas Agrippa I and II were both properly titled 'king' (12.1; 25.13), since both were granted the royal title by Gaius and Claudius. He uses the correct title 'proconsul' for the Roman governors of Cyprus, Sergius Paulus (13.7), and of Corinth, Gallio (18.12), the only NT writer to use the proper Greek equivalent *(anthypatos)* of the Latin *proconsul,* governor of a senatorial province,[99] whereas Felix and Festus were only procurators of Judea, governor *(hēgemōn)* of a minor province (23.24; 26.30). Philippi is correctly described as a 'colony' *(kolōnia,* 16.12) and its chief magistrates praetors *(stratēgoi,* 16.20). The city magistrates of Thessalonica, however, are properly designated 'politarchs' *(politarchai,* 17.6), a title which Luke could not have derived from literary sources, since it is not attested in Greek literature known to us, though we know the title from Macedonian inscriptions.[100] His report of an expulsion of the Jews from Rome by Claudius (18.2) is confirmed by the famous report of Suetonius cited above (§21.1[d]). His knowledge of the several Ephesian officials named in Acts 19 is exact — proconsul (19.38), secretary of

98. Ramsay records his change of mind several times — W. M. Ramsay, *St. Paul the Traveller and the Roman Citizen* (London: Hodder and Stoughton, 1896) 8; more fully *The Bearing of Recent Discovery on the Trustworthiness of the New Testament* (London: Hodder and Stoughton, 1915) 37-63. The pivot on which his view turned was the realization that the topographical information provided by Acts 14.6 was, after all, accurate for the time of Paul (39-44). His further study convinced him that 'Luke's history is unsurpassed in respect of its trustworthiness' and that 'the book [of Acts] could bear the most minute scrutiny as an authority for the facts of the Aegean world' (*Bearing* 81, 85). Ramsay in effect dedicated his scholarship to disproving the 'North Galatian' theory (see further below, §31 nn. 31-33).

99. Already noted by J. B. Lightfoot, 'Discoveries Illustrating the Acts of the Apostles' (1878), reprinted in his *Essays on the Work Entitled Supernatural Religion* (London: Macmillan, 1889) 291-302 (here 291-94): 'At any given time it would be impossible to say without contemporary, or at least very exact historical knowledge whether a particular province was governed by a proconsul or a propraetor' (292).

100. See *NDIEC* 2.34-35; G. H. R. Horsley, 'Politarchs', *ABD* 5.384-89; also 'The Politarchs', *BAFCS* 2.419-31.

state/town clerk (*grammateus,* 19.35), and Asiarchs (*asiarchoi,* 19.31), men of status within the civic administration;[101] and he uses the correct term, *agoraios,* for a provincial assize in Ephesus (19.38).[102] And his knowledge of the rights of Roman citizenship and of judicial procedures reflects the conditions of the middle decades of the first century, not those of the later decades, during which he probably wrote Acts.[103]

Also worth noting is the extent to which Josephus in particular confirms many of Luke's details which otherwise we might attribute to his story-telling imagination: the rebels, Judas of Galilee and Theudas (5.36-37 — even if Luke is confused as to their dates), and the 'Egyptian' (21.38);[104] not only the dating of the procuratorships of Felix and Festus in Judea (23.24; 24.27)[105] and the identity of the high priest Ananias (23.2; 24.1),[106] as well as the names of Felix's wife (Drusilla, 24.24) and of Agrippa II's wife (Bernice, 25.13),[107] but also his characterization of Felix, Festus and Agrippa II.

In an age when there were no almanacs providing ready information regarding titles and dates of officials and no easy access to official records by someone of Luke's likely rank and status, the slips already indicated are readily explicable. At the same time, the accuracy of such details and representations as have just been listed can hardly be better explained than by Luke's own involvement with those caught up in the events (or with the events themselves), or by his having access to eyewitness accounts of the events.[108]

---

101. On the institution of the Asiarchs see particularly the still valuable note by L. R. Taylor, 'The Asiarchs', *Beginnings* 5.256-62; now also R. A. Kearsley, *NDIEC* 4.46-55; and 'The Asiarchs', *BAFCS* 2.363-76; summarized in §32 n. 131 below. As A. N. Sherwin-White, *Roman Society and Roman Law in the New Testament* (Oxford: Clarendon, 1963), notes: 'If the author of Acts had not known the peculiarities of the organization of Asia, he might well have made an error' (90).

102. Lightfoot, 'Discoveries' 297-301. He concludes: 'We are justified in saying that ancient literature has preserved no picture of the Ephesus of imperial times . . . comparable for its life-like truthfulness to the narrative of St. Paul's sojourn there in Acts' (301). Similarly Sherwin-White: 'The author of Acts is very well informed about the finer points of municipal institutions at Ephesus in the first and second centuries AD. He even uses the correct technical term *ennomos ekklēsia* to distinguish the regularly appointed meetings of the people from the present concourse' (*Roman Society* 87). For more recent comments to the same effect see §32 n. 134 below.

103. Sherwin-White, *Roman Society* 172-89.

104. Josephus, *Ant.* 18.4-10; 20.97-98, 169-72.

105. Josephus, *War* 2.247, 271-72; *Ant.* 20.137-44, 189-94, 197, 200; also Suetonius, *Claudius* 28; Tacitus, *Ann.* 12.54; *Hist.* 2.2.

106. Josephus, *Ant.* 20.103, 131, 205-13.

107. Josephus, *War* 2.217, 220; *Ant.* 19.354-55; 20.138-45; Suetonius, *Claudius* 28; *Titus* 7.1; Tacitus, *Hist.* 2.2.

108. The judgment of Ramsay was affirmed by Harnack: 'Not only in its major features

d. Tendentious History

At the same time, several of Luke's *Tendenzen* are clear.

(1) I have already noted Luke's concern to tell his story as the narrative of God's working out his purpose.[109] The point can be elaborated in terms of Acts as salvation history, as a continuation and fulfilment of the biblical history of Israel, as Jacob Jervell and others have argued,[110] as illustrated by Luke's sustained interest in the theme of the kingdom of God[111] and by the emphases of several key passages.[112] This concern includes justification for the development of the mission (by a Jewish 'sect') as a mission to Gentiles[113] and the apologetic reassurance that the movement's expansion did not threaten Roman authority in any degree.[114]

---

is it [Acts] a genuinely historical work, but also in the majority of the details it contains it is reliable' (*Apg* 222), and more recently by the ancient historian Sherwin-White: 'Any attempt to reject its [Acts'] basic historicity in matters of detail must now appear absurd' (*Roman Society* 189). See further Hemer, *Book of Acts* ch. 4; also R. Riesner, *Paul's Early Period* (1994; Grand Rapids: Eerdmans, 1998) 327-33. C. K. Barrett, 'The Historicity of Acts', *JTS* 50 (1999) 515-34, finds himself obliged to conclude: 'We cannot prove that it happened in the way Luke describes, but if it did not it must have happened in a similar way or the result could not have been what it was' (534). Schröter concludes that the historical value of Acts is not overall *(pauschal)* but only in individual cases ('Lukas als Historiograph' 260).

109. See n. 82 above.

110. See above, n. 59, and further particularly Jervell's earlier *Luke and the People of God: A New Look at Luke-Acts* (Minneapolis: Augsburg, 1972); also *The Theology of the Acts of the Apostles* (Cambridge: Cambridge University, 1996) ch. 3; see also G. Lohfink, *Die Sammlung Israels. Eine Untersuchung zur lukanischen Ekklesiologie* (Munich: Kösel, 1971); R. Maddox, *The Purpose of Luke-Acts* (Edinburgh: Clark, 1982) ch. 2; J. Schröter, 'Heil für die Heiden und Israel. Zum Zusammenhang von Christologie und Volk Gottes bei Lukas', in C. Breytenbach and J. Schröter eds., *Die Apostelgeschichte und die hellenistische Geschichtsschreibung,* E. Plümacher FS (AGAJU 57; Leiden: Brill, 2004) 285-308; also 'Lukas als Historiograph'. Cf. Marguerat's refinement: Luke's 'achievement consists in placing Christianity at the intersection of the continuity and the rupture with Israel' (*First Christian Historian* 131, and ch. 7).

111. Acts 1.3, 6; 8.12; 14.22; 19.8; 20.25; 28.23, 31; note its functioning as an inclusio (1.3; 28.31), and the significance of the question in 1.6, diverted but not disowned.

112. Acts 3.19-26; 15.14-17; 28.23-31; see further my 'The Book of Acts as Salvation History', in J. Frey et al., eds., *Heil und Geschichte. Die Geschichtsbezogenheit des Heils und das Problem der Heilsgeschichte in der biblischen Tradition und in der theologischen Deutung* (WUNT; Tübingen: Mohr Siebeck, forthcoming).

113. Particularly noteworthy is the exceptional prominence Acts gives both to the conversion/commissioning of Paul (Acts 9, 22, 26) and to the conversion of the Roman centurion Cornelius (10.1–11.18; 15.7-11).

114. Acts 16.35-39; 18.12-17; 19.21-41; 25.19, 25; 26.30-32; 28.31 ('unhindered'). See also P. W. Walasky, *'And So We Came to Rome': The Political Perspective of St. Luke*

(2) Luke's artistic contrivance is attested by a number of features. As already noted, Acts is structured to bring out the parallel with the Gospel.[115] Various elements in the Gospel clearly look forward to Luke's second volume (Luke 2.32; 3.6; 4.24-27; 12.11-12; 21.12-15; 22.32; 24.47-49).[116] Less frequently noted are the number of features in the Gospel which Luke chose to omit or to refer to only briefly because, evidently, he wanted to reserve their impact till Acts. Thus, although his Gospel uses much of Mark's Gospel as one of its sources, Luke nevertheless omitted the accusation at Jesus' trial that Jesus had threatened to destroy the Temple (Mark 14.58), presumably because he wanted to reserve the confrontation and split over the Temple till the Stephen episode (chs. 6–7).[117] Likewise, Luke omitted Mark 7, the episode which in Mark spells the end of the ritual distinction between clean and unclean (Mark 7.19), presumably because he wanted to reserve the full impact of Peter's 'conversion' on this point until the Cornelius episode (Acts 10).[118] So too Luke may have omitted the account of John the Baptist's death in Mark 6.17-29 because he did not want to anticipate and thus diminish the impact of Acts 24.24-26. Finally we may note that he restricted the allusion to Isa. 6.9-10 in Luke 8.10 (contrast Mark 4.12 and Matt. 13.14-15), presumably because he wished to reserve the impact of the full quotation of Isa. 6.9-10 till Acts 28.25-27. As a feature of Luke's technique we may compare his holding back of the information in 22.17-20 from his first telling of Paul's conversion-commission for this more dramatic second telling.

(3) Luke's structuring within Acts itself is still more evident. He obviously makes a point of setting the two chief actors in his drama in parallel.[119] That he

---

(SNTSMS 49; Cambridge: Cambridge University, 1983), though see also R. J. Cassidy, *Society and Politics in the Acts of the Apostles* (Maryknoll: Orbis, 1988); C. Burfeind, 'Paulus *muss* nach Rom. Zur politischen Dimension der Apostelgeschichte', *NTS* 46 (2000) 75-91.

115. Acts 1/Luke 1–2; Acts 2.1-4/Luke 3.21-22; Acts 2.14-36/Luke 4.14-27; and so on, till Acts 21–28/Luke's passion narrative. See also n. 45 above.

116. See further C. K. Barrett, 'The Third Gospel as a Preface to Acts? Some Reflections', in Van Segbroeck et al., eds., *The Four Gospels* 2.1451-66.

117. See further below, §24.4c. Luke 19.46 also omits 'for all nations' (Mark 11.17); Acts will show that the Temple is not to have that function.

118. See below, §26.3.

119. *Peter*   *Paul*

Peter	*Paul*
2.22-39	13.26-41
3.1-10	14.8-11
4.8	13.9
5.1-11	13.6-12
5.15	19.12
8.17	19.6
8.18-24	19.13-20
9.32-34	28.8

takes time to tell the story of the conversion of Cornelius twice (10.1–11.18) shows how important he thought it to be in providing the crucial precedent for mission to the Gentiles (15.7-11; contrast Paul's account of the same or equivalent decision in Gal. 2.7-9). Indeed, it is difficult to escape the impression that the episodes of Paul's conversion (Acts 9) and of Cornelius' conversion (10.1–11.18) have been deliberately inserted by Luke into the account of the Hellenist-led expansion (8.4-40; 11.19-26), thereby diminishing the credit due to the Hellenists for the breakthrough to the Gentiles (passed over very briefly in 11.20). At the very least, such retellings within the same volume tell us much of what Luke regarded as good historical as well as good story-telling technique.[120]

(4) In Acts, Luke's freedom in constructing the various reports on which he relied into a coherent and compelling story is also shown by various features:

- a degree of idealization or romanticization of the first Jerusalem community (Acts 2.41-47; 4.32-35);[121]
- his practice of telescoping events;[122]
- his playing down the probable seriousness of the crisis for the Jerusalem church occasioned by the activities of the Hellenists and Stephen in particular (chs. 6–8);[123]
- his smoothing out initial relations between Paul and the Jerusalem church (9.23-30);
- his ignoring the confrontations between Paul and other Christian Jews at Antioch (Gal. 2.11-16) and Galatia (Galatians);

9.36-41	20.9-12
10.25	14.11-13; 28.6
12.6-11	16.25-34

The observation of such parallels goes back to M. Schneckenburger, *Über den Zweck der Apostelgeschichte* (Bern, 1841) and became an important building block in the Tübingen school's explanation of the role of Acts in their reconstruction of the early history of Christianity (see above, §20.3a; Baur, *Paul* 98-100, 164-74, 198, 201-203). See, e.g., the brief review by Kümmel, *Introduction* 160-61, and the fuller review by Gasque, *History* ch. 2.

120. Hengel points out that 'chronology was not the basis for every historical account' and 'could be largely dispensed with' in the biographies of the time (*Acts* 16–17).

121. See below, §23.

122. Resurrection appearances ceased after forty days (Acts 1.1-11; contrast 1 Cor. 15.5-8; see below, §22.2); the length of time before going to Jerusalem (Acts 9.23-30; contrast Gal. 1.18-20; see below, §25.5a); the puzzle of Paul's second visit to Jerusalem (Acts 11.29-30; contrast Gal. 1.21–2.1; see below, §25.5g); the 'apostolic decree' (Acts 15.28-29; contrast Gal. 2.6; see below, §27.3); appointment of elders from the first (Acts 14.23; elders do not appear in Pauline churches till the Pastorals); (only) three weeks in Thessalonica (Acts 17.1-15; contrast 1 Thess. 2.9 and Phil. 4.16).

123. See below, §24.

- his failure to mention Paul's letter-writing activity[124] and the tensions they indicate, particularly in Paul's relations with the church in Corinth (see, e.g., 2 Cor. 2.12-13; 7.5-7);
- his side-lining of the principal reason why Paul made his final journey to Jerusalem (to deliver the collection).[125]

Luke evidently had a different agenda from that of Paul, Luke presumably wanting to highlight the unity of the Nazarene sect in its expansion,[126] whereas Paul's letters were occasioned more by the conflicts and tensions which his church planting occasioned. So too we should not be surprised at the different details and divergent tendencies as between Luke's portrayal of his great hero and the self-portrayal of Paul himself in his letters;[127] that even the closest collaborators

124. A. Lindemann, *Paulus im ältesten Christentum* (Tübingen: Mohr Siebeck, 1979), answers the question whether Luke knew the Pauline letters with a cautious Yes (163-73).

125. Only briefly hinted at in Acts 24.17; contrast the importance of the collection for Paul, as indicated in the several references to it in his principal letters (Rom. 15.25-28; 1 Cor. 16.1-4; 2 Corinthians 8–9). See further below, §33.4.

126. The object is achieved (1) by emphasizing the centrality and oversight of the Jerusalem church (as in 8.14 and 11.22; the solution to the long-running problem of table-fellowship between Jews and Gentiles provided by the 'apostolic decree' in 15.20, 29) and of 'the apostles' (1.26; 2.42; 8.1; 9.27; 11.1; 15.2, 6, 22-23; 16.4), (2) by drawing a discrete veil over the tensions provoked by 'the Hellenists' (6.1) and Stephen (8.2), not to mention those involving Paul (already mentioned), and (3) by portraying Paul as law-observant (16.1-3; 18.18; 20.6, 16; 21.24-26) in contrast to the reports regarding him (21.20-21). For discussion of the reasons why Luke wrote Acts, see vol. 3; briefly in my *The Acts of the Apostles* (Peterborough: Epworth, 1996) xi-xiv.

127. In a neglected article, Olof Linton, 'The Third Aspect: A Neglected Point of View', *ST* 3 (1949) 79-95, noted that there are some points in common between the account of Paul *contested* by the apostle himself and Luke's representation of him, notably in Paul's relations with Jerusalem (n. 122 above). Note in particular how the qualifications for an 'apostle' in Acts 1.21-22 would exclude Paul (14.4, 14 notwithstanding), something Paul vigorously disputes (Gal. 1.1); Luke seems to be suggesting in Acts 9.23-27 what Paul so vehemently denied in Gal. 1.18-20; and a report such as Luke records in Acts 16.3 may have provoked Paul's protest in Gal. 5.11. Linton concluded that Luke deliberately painted a more conciliatory picture of Paul: he 'wanted to correct Paul slightly in order to make him better' (95); similarly Haenchen, *Acts* 88-89. This seems to me a better reading of the tensions in the overlapping and divergent material between Acts and Paul than the more famous article by P. Vielhauer, 'On the "Paulinism" of Acts', in L. E. Keck and J. L. Martyn eds., *Studies in Luke-Acts,* P. Schubert FS (Nashville: Abingdon, 1966) 33-50 (on which see Fitzmyer, Luke 50-51; Porter, *Paul of Acts* 199-205). Similarly Haenchen, *Acts* 112-16, makes no allowance for Paul's rhetoric; and Kümmel, *Introduction* 179-84, refuses to recognize that Luke could have had his own theological perspective and an evaluation of Paul different from Paul's own. Still valuable is P.-G. Müller's review of the history of research in 'Der "Paulinismus" in der Apg', in K. Kertelge ed., *Paulus in den neutestamentlichen Spätschriften* (QD 89; Freiburg: Herder, 1981) 157-201; and in the same volume see also K. Löning, 'Paulinismus in der Apg' 202-34.

in a great enterprise have different impressions and divergent evaluations of their common endeavours is a recurrent feature of history both ancient and modern.[128] The solution, indeed, may lie in the fact that Luke drew consistently on traditions which reflected the perspective of the Jerusalem church, both its centrality as *the* mother church of the whole movement stemming from Jesus, and its consequent claim to have the authority to direct expansion and developments beyond Jerusalem.[129] That is, such emphases probably reflect not so much an 'early catholicism' of Luke himself[130] as Luke's concern to interweave the perspective of the Jerusalem church with the mission outreach of his main hero, Paul, in an integrated and (relatively) harmonious portrayal of Christianity's beginnings.

(5) I might add my own sense of a degree of naïvete in Luke's account of spiritual or ecstatic phenomena. He narrates episodes of belief in the healing efficacy of Peter's shadow (5.15) and of handkerchiefs and aprons touched by Paul (19.12) without comment — though that may say more of the enthusiastic atmosphere engendered in the earliest days of the Christian mission.[131] He talks of 'signs and wonders' in an uncritical way (2.43; 4.30; 5.12; 6.8; 8.13; 14.3; 15.12), even though other NT writers show themselves hesitant to take 'signs and wonders' as straightforward proof of divine power and approval.[132] And he shows none of Paul's hesitations regarding glossolalia (2.4, 8; 10.46; 19.6) or of the need for prophecy to be evaluated (contrast 20.22 with 21.4).[133]

None of this need diminish the value of Luke's Acts as a source for historical information,[134] though in what follows I will have occasion frequently to la-

---

128. Cf. Riesner: 'The historiographic problem seems not to be that Luke simply invented whatever he needed, but rather that he often passed over in silence things he thought were either unpleasant or secondary' (*Paul's Early Period* 413).

129. See further below, §36.1.

130. This was a popular way of categorizing Luke's perspective in the middle of the twentieth century; so particularly E. Käsemann, 'The Disciples of John the Baptist in Ephesus' (1952), *Essays on New Testament Themes* (London: SCM, 1964) 136-48; also 'New Testament Questions of Today' (1957), *New Testament Questions of Today* (London: SCM, 1969) 1-22.

131. See further below, §23.2g.

132. Mark 13.22/Matt. 24.24 (Luke omits the reference!); John 4.48; 2 Cor. 12.12; 2 Thess. 2.9. See my *Unity and Diversity* 181-82. Luke's uncritical acceptance of reports of 'wonders' marks him off most clearly from the more rigorous standards of Thucydides and Polybius, though 'popular' historians had no such hesitations (see Penner, *Praise* 130-35).

133. Contrast Paul with regard to glossolalia (1 Corinthians 14) and on the need for prophecy to be tested and evaluated (1 Cor. 12.10; 14.29; 1 Thess. 5.20-22). See further my *Jesus and the Spirit* 233-36, 246-48.

134. Cf. J. Weiss, *Das Urchristentum* (1914), ET *Earliest Christianity* (1937; New York: Harper Torchbook, 1959) 148. 'That something is formulated in Lukan style in no way means that Luke had not begun further back with tradition' (Breytenbach, *Paulus und Barnabas* 14, 29-30, echoing Bultmann).

ment the inadequacies of Luke's account. No doubt it is necessary to discount, or at least to take account of, the 'spin' which Luke puts on his narrative, but the twenty-first-century reader (or viewer) of historical studies and portrayals is well accustomed to doing so. It is of first importance in all this that we neither attribute to Luke an unrealistically idealistic quality as an ancient historian nor assume that his mistakes and *Tendenzen* show him to be unworthy of the title 'historian'.[135]

21.3. The Speeches in Acts

The most sensitive area of unease over Luke's portrayal of Christian origins is the speeches or sermons, which constitute a major feature of his narrative (they take up about 30 percent of the space) and which carry the most heavy weight of the book's theology.[136] At this point, conventions of ancient historiography differ most markedly from those of the modern period. In ancient historiography speeches served not only to indicate what the person was known to have said but also what the writer thought he was likely to have said (or should have said). They also played a role within the drama of the unfolding narrative, being included for rhetorical effect, to entertain as well as to inform the reader; the ancient historians show varying degrees of responsibility and irresponsibility in this practice.[137] For example, Josephus, a contemporary of Luke, places two

---

135. The volume of seminar papers by R. Cameron and M. P. Miller, *Redescribing Christian Origins* (Atlanta: SBL, 2004), which dispenses with Acts and attempts to build its redescription on the flawed hypothesis of a Q community simply runs out of steam, floundering in a swamp of further implausible hypotheses (frank self-assessments on 418, 415, 435, 448, 490) — thus, presumably, puncturing the confidence of the seminar's *éminence grise,* Burton Mack, expressed in his *The Christian Myth* (New York: Continuum, 2001): 'The seminar is poised to make a significant contribution both to early Christian studies and to studies in the theory of myth and social formation' (215); see further my review in *JBL* 124 (2005) 760-64. Crossley, engaged in a somewhat analogous enterprise — to free the historical investigation of Christianity's origins from the over-involvement of Christians and 'to provide a thoroughly (socio-)historical explanation for the rise of Christianity without having to resort to theological reasons' — is also dismissive: 'many of Mack's arguments . . . are incredibly implausible' (*Why Christianity Happened* 32-33). Lüdemann similarly questions whether Vouga's *Geschichte des frühen Christentums* 'is not replacing tradition (Acts) with wandering imagination (e.g., that of non-apocalyptic Galilean followers of Jesus)', 'a mishmash of almost incomprehensible new conjectures' (*Primitive Christianity* 18, 23). Sanders, *Schismatics,* seems to have an almost pathological disdain for the historical value of Acts.

136. Dibelius, 'The Speeches in Acts and Ancient Historiography' (1949), *Studies* 138-85, counted twenty-four speeches (150). M. L. Soards, *The Speeches in Acts* (Louisville: Westminster John Knox, 1994), briefly analyzes thirty-six speeches.

137. R. E. Brown, *An Introduction to the New Testament* (New York: Doubleday, 1997) cites the much-quoted Lucian of Samosata, *How to Write History* 58: 'If some one has to be

quite different speeches in the mouth of Herod in his parallel accounts of the same episode (*War* 1.373-79; *Ant.* 15.127-46).[138] At this point the line between the ancient historian and the dramatist becomes quite fine, and the ancient history becomes somewhat closer to the historical novel than to the modern history, where much stricter controls apply over what can and cannot, should and should not, be attributed.[139] Much quoted in discussions on this question are the words of the Greek historian Thucydides, often regarded as the greatest of ancient historians.[140] In his *History of the Peloponnesian War* 1.22.1 he writes:

> As to the speeches which were made either before or during the war, it was hard for me, and for others who reported them to me, to recollect the exact words. I have therefore put into the mouth of each speaker the sentiments proper to the occasion, expressed as I thought he would be likely to express them, while at the same time I endeavoured, as nearly as I could, to give the general import of what was actually said.[141]

---

brought in to give a speech, above all let his language suit his person and his subject. . . . It is then, however, that you can exercise your rhetoric and show your eloquence'. Brown comments: 'Most moderns would regard this process as not truly historical, but evidently Lucian thought it was reconcilable with what he wrote earlier (*How* 39): "The sole task of the historian is to tell it just as it happened"' (318 n. 94). See also van Unnik, 'Luke's Second Book and the Rules of Hellenistic Historiography' 58-59; C. Gempf, 'Public Speaking and Published Accounts', and B. W. Winter, 'Official Proceedings and the Forensic Speeches in Acts 24–26', *BAFCS* 1.259-303 and 305-36 respectively; on Lucian, and on Polybius and Dionysius of Halicarnassus on the function of speeches in history, see also Penner, *Praise* 170-74, 212-14. On the speeches in Josephus see Mason, *Josephus* 260-61.

138. Dibelius, *Studies* 139. Cadbury notes that 'when Livy follows Polybius for the facts of his narrative he almost regularly makes a change in the occasion and form of his speeches' (*Beginnings* 2.13), with further examples (13-14).

139. Although 'the line between historical novel and novelistic history is much more porous than we might like to admit' (Penner, *Praise* 138), it would be unfair both to Luke's intention and to what he actually wrote to liken Acts to a historical novel; contrast R. I. Pervo, *Profit with Delight: The Literary Genre of the Acts of the Apostles* (Philadelphia: Fortress, 1987). See Porter's critique of Pervo and Robbins (n. 50 above) in *Paul of Acts* 14-24. As Wedderburn observes: 'The writer of this double work seems to evince a seriousness of purpose alien to historical novels in the ancient world' (*History* 12).

140. W. C. McCoy, 'In the Shadow of Thucydides', in Witherington, ed., *History* 3-23: 'Thucydides has become a barometer by which to gauge the writing of history both past and present' (3).

141. Bruce, *Acts* 34, following the translation of B. Jowett. 'Thucydides was claiming that he presented his speech-makers as saying what it seemed likely that they *did* say (not what they might have said), adhering as closely as he could to what he knew of what they actually spoke' (Witherington, *History* 25). He notes the finding of Fornara, *Nature of History* 154-55, that it was *not* a convention of ancient historians to invent speeches out of their own heads, as is so often presupposed (27).

In Acts we can see fairly clearly how Luke worked within these ancient conventions.[142] First, to make the point once again, in all cases the style of the speeches is *Lukan* through and through; they are, properly speaking, Lukan compositions.[143] Second, in almost all cases we cannot but be impressed by the combination of brevity (speeches which take only three or four minutes to deliver) and roundedness; they are neither outlines nor abbreviations but cameos, finely crafted miniatures.[144] Third: at the same time, however, in most cases there is an individuality and distinctiveness of material used which points to the conclusion that *Luke has been able to draw on and incorporate tradition* — not necessarily any record or specific recollection as such but tradition related to and, in Luke's considered judgment, representative of the individual's views and well suited to the occasion. In consequence, it would be unwise to focus on the first two features and conclude that the speeches simply reflect Luke's own interests or that he imposes his own perspective entirely on the material.[145] The speeches of Acts do show clear indications of non-Lukan material, which is presumably the result of his inquiries and which therefore probably provide source material for earliest Christian proclamation and teaching, but only if used with care. They represent Luke's impression of the episodes and characters he describes, though it is history and theology seen through Luke's eyes and reflecting also his own concerns.

So important is the material potentially offered by the Acts speeches for our better appreciation of the earliest Christian proclamation and theology that it

142. 'Luke follows the tradition of historical writing so closely that we must assume that he has read the historians' (Dibelius, *Studies* 183). E. Plümacher draws a particular parallel with Dionysius of Halicarnassus, in 'The Mission Speeches in Acts and Dionysius of Halicarnassus', in Moessner, ed., *Jesus and the Heritage of Israel* 251-66: 'The Lukan conception of the mission speeches as factors determining the course of history is identical with that of Dionysius' (258).

143. See above, n. 44; Haenchen, *Acts* 80.

144. Dibelius observed the same feature in a large number of the speeches in Xenophon's *Hellenica* (*Studies* 143-44).

145. 'This type of Christian sermon certainly seems to have been customary in the author's day (about A.D. 90). This is how the gospel is preached and ought to be preached!' (Dibelius, *Studies* 165, referring to the 'missionary speeches' of Acts 2, 3, 10 and 13). Typical of Dibelius was his conclusion: 'In the last analysis . . . [Luke] is not an historian but a preacher' (183). Dibelius's conclusion was taken further by U. Wilckens, *Die Missionsreden der Apostelgeschichte* (WMANT 5; Neukirchen-Vluyn: Neukirchener, ²1963), who concludes: 'The apostolic speeches of Acts are in a very obvious sense summaries of (Luke's) theological conception; they are not to be valued as witnesses of older, far less the oldest early Christian theology, but as Lukan theology of the closing years of the first century' (186). Similarly E. Schweizer, 'Concerning the Speeches in Acts', in L. E. Keck and J. L. Martyn, eds., *Studies in Luke-Acts* (Nashville: Abingdon, 1966) 208-16. Dibelius and Wilckens are followed by Jervell, *Apg* 152.

is worth taking time to examine some of the key examples. Here we look at the three principal speeches or sermons attributed to Peter.[146]

a. Acts 2.14-36/39 — Peter's Pentecost Speech

There are several indications that Luke was able to draw on earlier tradition.

(1) The speech is a good example of a Jewish sermon — a midrash on Joel 2.28-32, with supporting texts from the Psalms, and with Acts 2.39 (alluding again to Joel) rounding it off.[147]

(2) The full quotation from Joel is only alluded to elsewhere in the NT,[148] which suggests that the fuller thought given by the whole passage early on became an established part of Christian tradition. Ps. 16.8-11, quoted in 2.25-28, could be part of Luke's own theological armoury: it is used only here and in Acts 13.35. But Ps. 110.1 (quoted in 2.34-35) certainly belongs to early Christian reflection on what had happened to Jesus.[149]

(3) The eschatology is surprisingly primitive as compared with the rest of Acts. It is generally reckoned that Luke pulls back from the belief that the coming (again) of Christ was imminent: he seems to qualify such expectation elsewhere,[150] and in the perspective of Acts the church seems to be set for a long haul,[151] an eschatology of 'the last things' rather than of expectation that 'the end is nigh'.[152] So it is noteworthy that Peter's speech retains that primitive note of imminent expectation: the quotation from Joel replaces the Hebrew 'afterwards' by the much more pregnant 'in the last days' (*en tais eschatais hēmerais,* 2.17);[153]

---

146. I will look more closely at other Acts speeches in the sequence provided by Acts (§§27, 31, 33).

147. Cf. J. Bowker, 'Speeches in Acts: A Study in Proem and Yelammadenu Form', *NTS* 14 (1967-68) 96-111.

148. Particularly Rom. 10.13 and Tit. 3.6.

149. See below, §23.4d. Note particularly Mark 12.36; 1 Cor. 15.25; Heb. 1.13.

150. Notably Luke 19.11; 21.24; Acts 1.6-7.

151. This is a principal thesis of Conzelmann, *Theology;* a brief treatment appears in my *Unity and Diversity* §71.2.

152. Note, e.g., that the threat of final judgment seems less urgent in Acts 10.42 and 17.31.

153. Cf. Isa. 2.2; Mic. 4.1; see below, §22 n. 139. Luke also adds 'and they shall prophesy' at the end of 2.18. This could well be Luke's own addition, since he elsewhere emphasizes the importance of prophecy ('prophet' occurs fifty-nine times in Luke-Acts), including the Spirit's role as inspirer of prophecy (Luke 1.67; Acts 19.6). But the Spirit of prophecy is a traditional understanding of the Spirit (cf. particularly Num. 11.29) which was widely shared in earliest Christianity (1 Cor. 12.10; 14.1-5; 1 Thess. 5.19-20; 1 Pet. 1.10-11; Rev. 19.10).

and 2.19-20 retain the apocalyptic imagery of cosmic convulsion, which heightens the expectation. The impression given by the passage, that 'the great and terrible day of the Lord' (the day of judgment) was imminent, again indicates very early tradition.

(4) The christology itself seems primitive at a number of points. The personal name 'Jesus the Nazarene' (2.22), 'Jesus' (2.32), 'this Jesus' (2.36) is quickly lost elsewhere in the NT behind the more formal 'Christ' or 'Lord'. Jesus is described in remarkably un-divine language as 'a man attested by God', his success spoken of in terms of 'signs that God did through him' (2.22). The oath referred to in 2.30 probably alludes to Ps. 89.4 and thus recalls the promise to David in 2 Sam. 7.12-16, a promise which seems to have reverberated in Jesus' hearing before the Jewish council;[154] in which case it would almost certainly have been in play from the beginning in early Christian thought. 'The Messiah' is still a title (2.31), whereas elsewhere in the NT it has become more or less a proper name, 'Jesus Christ'. Quite remarkable is the depiction of Jesus as the bestower of the Spirit, consequent upon his exaltation (2.33) — an expectation which probably reflects the influence of Jesus' predecessor, John the Baptist,[155] but which hardly appears elsewhere in the NT. In some ways most striking of all, the resurrection/ascension is cited as evidence that 'God has made him both Lord and Messiah' (*kai kyrion auton kai Christon epoiēsen ho theos,* 2.36). Such an affirmation is quite likely in the first flush of enthusiasm, but any suggestion that Jesus was *made* Messiah only at his resurrection was soon excluded by more carefully worded formulations.[156] Given that at the period of Luke's writing christology was much more developed, it must be judged unlikely that Luke was attempting to promote these emphases. It is much more likely that he drew them from traditions or memories which his inquiry (or common knowledge) had brought to light.

The conclusion seems clear, then. However much Peter's first sermon owes to Luke's compositional technique, it is very likely that he was able to draw on very early sources for his composition. It remains unlikely that any initial preaching would have been so brief. But it is not an outline or a summary: it contains a complete and rounded argument. Consequently we may imagine Luke carefully inquiring of those who remembered the earliest preaching of the Jerusalem church and crafting the sermon from these memories and from emphases which had lasted from the earliest period of Christianity's beginnings in Jerusalem to his own day.

---

154. *Jesus Remembered* 619-20, 632-34, 710-11.
155. Mark 1.8 pars.; cf. Acts 1.5. See further below, §23.4e.
156. But cf. Acts 13.33; Heb. 1.5; 5.5.

b. Acts 3.11-26 — Peter's Preaching in the Temple

Here again Luke seems to have been able to draw on some very old tradition in framing this sermon. Above all, the christology hardly occurs anywhere else in the NT and has a distinctively primitive ring, particularly the titles used of Jesus.

(1) He is called *pais,* 'servant' (3.13, 26). The language is almost certainly drawn from the LXX of Isa. 52.13: 'my servant *(pais)* . . . will be glorified'; the idea of God glorifying Jesus is quite exceptional in the NT outside John's Gospel, and in the NT the title *pais* for Jesus is limited to Acts 3–4 (also 4.25, 27, 30).[157] This allusion to the famous Servant song of Isa. 52.13–53.12 is probably very early, since it expresses only a theology of suffering and vindication (3.13-15), whereas other allusions to it in connection with Jesus' suffering, while still early, use it to express a theology of atonement.[158]

(2) He is also called 'the holy and just one' (3.14), epithets seldom used of Jesus elsewhere.[159]

(3) Equally uncommon, he is called the *archēgos,* 'leader' or 'originator' (3.15; 5.31), a title which appears elsewhere only in Heb. 2.10 and 12.2.

(4) Noteworthy is the Semitic train of thought in 3.19-20. In 3.19 the Greek idea of repentance is supplemented by the Hebrew understanding of turning round, or turning back *(šub)* — a radical change of direction, a turning round of direction of life.[160] And in 3.20-21 there continues to be strong indication of a train of thought first formulated by someone to whom Semitic idiom came naturally — 'from the face of the Lord [= God]', 'send the Messiah appointed for you', 'all that God spoke by the mouth of his holy prophets'.

(5) Even more striking is the fact that 3.19-21 contain several ancient motifs: the call for a repentance which will secure times of refreshing, the return of Jesus and universal restoration;[161] and 'the Lord', clearly God is meant, who will send the Christ, now in heaven awaiting his recall onto the earth's stage. Whatever the precise reference in the phrases, we can say that the portrayal is of Jesus received by heaven and just awaiting the signal to return as the Christ to bring

157. Bibliography in BDAG 750-51, to which should be added Cadbury's discussion in *Beginnings* 5.364-70. Barrett is in error when he denies that *pais* occurs in the LXX of Isaiah 53 (*Acts* 194).

158. Cf. Mark 10.45; Rom. 4.24-25; 1 Pet. 2.22-25. See further below, §23.4g and §23.5.

159. 'Holy' — Luke 4.34; John 6.69; 'just' — Matt. 27.19; Acts 7.52; 22.14; 1 John 2.1.

160. See *Jesus Remembered* 498-500.

161. The two 'time' phrases, 'times of refreshing' and 'times for restoration', are without parallel in the rest of the NT. Since we lack the information to fill out their meaning and to distinguish them from each other, it remains uncertain how the two should be related to each other.

about and be part of the times of refreshing and of restoration of all things. As with 2.17, this is an eschatology, and an imminent eschatology, which Luke does not seem to promote elsewhere. All told, the language catches rather effectively a sense of trembling, expectant excitement at the prospect of the Christ recently departed but ready to return soon to bring history to a climax. It should occasion little surprise that J. A. T. Robinson characterized this as 'the most primitive christology of all'.[162]

(6) Also striking is the presentation of Jesus as the fulfilment of Moses' promise that the Lord God would raise up a prophet like himself (3.22-23, referring to Deut. 18.15-16),[163] a promise explicitly cited elsewhere only at 7.37. The promise of a prophet like Moses was surprisingly not much reflected on in the Jewish writings of the period.[164] But the Deuteronomy 18 texts seem to have attracted early Christian attention. And that early reflection, though it never became a central feature of christology ('prophet' being deemed an inadequate term to describe Christ's significance), nevertheless left traces at various points in the tradition.[165]

(7) And quite unique in the NT is the closing argument that Jesus as God's servant fulfils the covenant promise to Abraham, of blessing for all the nations (Gen. 22.18), but to Israel first (3.24-26).[166]

It is difficult to avoid the conclusion that Luke had some very old tradition at his disposal in framing this speech of Peter. The fact that he has evidently made an effort to uncover and use such material is a clear indication that he felt under some constraint in formulating such speeches. The very marked primitiveness of the christology indicates that Luke was probably conscious of some dangers of anachronism and that he did not intend the sermon to be a model for preaching in his own day.[167] We can say no more than that, and need say no more than that. So far as Luke and his readers were concerned, it would not matter whether Peter said just these words on just that occasion. It was enough that the words gave a fair representation of what Peter would or might have said at that stage.

---

162. J. A. T. Robinson, 'The Most Primitive Christology of All?', *Twelve New Testament Studies* (London: SCM, 1962) 139-53.

163. The quotation in 3.22-23 is a combination of Deut. 18.15-16, 19 and Lev. 23.29. Lev. 23.29 originally had nothing to do with the hope of a prophet like Moses, which makes the combination of such a severe warning with the prophet-like-Moses prophecy all the more powerful: it is response to the new Moses which determines membership of the people.

164. But see *Jesus Remembered* 656; Barrett, *Acts* 208; Fitzmyer, *Acts* 289-90.

165. Cf. Mark 9.7; John 1.25; 6.14; 7.52.

166. The text evokes the repeated promise to Abraham, Isaac and Jacob (Gen. 12.3; 18.18; 22.18; 26.4; 28.14), though the particular citation is drawn immediately from Gen. 22.18 and 26.4. Cf. §36.1b below.

167. *Pace* the persistent view of Dibelius, Wilckens and Schweizer (above, n. 145).

c. Acts 10.34-43 — Peter's Address to Cornelius

The third sermon of Peter falls in the second half of the story of the conversion of the Gentile centurion Cornelius. As usual, it is a fine Lukan cameo; it would take little more than a minute to deliver. As 10.44 suggests and as 11.15 states explicitly, the speech had hardly started when the Spirit intervened. But as usual with the Lukan speech cameos, this one is a nicely rounded whole, where nothing more need be said.

The structure is clear enough. The main body of the speech (10.36-43) is built round five scriptural allusions —

- 10.34 — Deut. 10.17 (God is not partial) — a fundamental principle of Jewish justice, often echoed in early Jewish literature.[168]
- 10.36 — Ps. 107.20 ('he sent out his word and healed them').
- 10.36 — less clearly, Isa. 52.7 ('. . . those who preach peace'). Both the 10.36 texts may well have belonged to an early arsenal of Christian texts: Ps. 107.20 is echoed again in 13.26, and Isa. 52.7 is cited in Rom. 10.15 as part of a catena of texts.
- 10.38 — Isa. 61.1 ('anointed with the Holy Spirit').
- 10.39 — Deut. 21.22 ('hanged on a tree'). That this was part of early polemic against belief in a crucified Messiah may be implied by Gal. 3.13 — 'Cursed is everyone who hangs on a tree' (cf. 1 Cor. 1.23). This polemic was possibly part of Paul's motivation as a persecutor. Such a play on Deuteronomy is not developed elsewhere.

These are followed by the now familiar rehearsal of Jesus' death and resurrection and by an implicit call for belief and promise of forgiveness. It contains the same Lukan, but also possibly older features: Jewish responsibility for Jesus' execution (10.39);[169] the theme of witness thrice repeated (10.39, 41, 43); the resurrection as something 'manifest' (10.40, 41); the mention of Jesus' name (10.43); but now also a more distant, less urgent eschatology (10.42), suggestive of a longer time perspective.

But once again there are primitive features.

1. The Israel-centredness of the message (10.36, 42).[170]
2. 'You know', perhaps implying a Judean audience (10.36).

168. 2 Chron. 19.7; Sir. 35.12-13; *Jub.* 5.16; 21.4; 30.16; 33.18; *1 En.* 63.8; *Pss. Sol.* 2.18; Pseudo-Philo 20.4; *2 Bar.* 13.8; 44.4; as also Paul (Rom. 2.11).

169. J. A. Weatherly, *Jewish Responsibility for the Death of Jesus in Luke-Acts* (JSNTS 106; Sheffield: Sheffield Academic, 1994), concludes that Luke was using tradition with this emphasis (242).

170. Cf. Acts 3.25 (see above, §21.3b).

3. The setting of John the Baptist and his baptism at, and as, the beginning of Jesus' mission (10.37; cf. 1.22; 13.24).[171]

4. Jesus is identified as 'the one from Nazareth' (10.38), still needing to be identified, a more weighty title not yet assumed (cf. 2.22).

5. God anointed him with the Spirit and power (10.38). In other words, he is presented as an inspired prophet — a primitive christology. The echo of Isa. 61.1 may reflect Jesus' own self-understanding as implied in Luke 6.20 and 7.22 but is not characteristic of the heightened christology of the second generation.[172]

6. Jesus' mission of healing is described in restrained terms (good deeds and exorcisms), and his success is again attributed to the fact that 'God was with him' (10.38; cf. 2.22). The description is one which might have come from the mouth of any sympathetic observer of Jesus' ministry. The juxtaposition of this very moderate portrayal of Jesus with the final confessional claim of 10.36 is striking.

7. The suffering-reversal theme — they put him to death, but God raised him (10.39-40) — not yet a doctrine of atonement. 'On the third day' (10.40) is unparalleled in Acts, but it is already enshrined in the early confessional formula received by Paul after his conversion (1 Cor. 15.4).

8. That Jesus had been appointed 'judge of the living and the dead' is a distinctive feature. It could be early: that God had chosen to give others a share in his role as final judge is reflected in Jewish speculation of the period in regard to such great heroes as Enoch and Abel,[173] as well as in very early Christian tradition (Luke 22.30; 1 Cor. 6.2); and the identification of Jesus with the man-like figure ('one like a son of man') in the vision of Dan. 7.13-14 would have reinforced the link in the case of Jesus. On the other hand, the formulation is remarkably lacking in any sense of urgency (so also 17.31; contrast 3.19-20) and reads more like a doctrine of the last things framed in the light of Jesus' return having been much delayed.[174]

9. The scriptural allusions noted above, round which the speech has been moulded, all appear early in Christian reflection about Jesus and his death and are not characteristic of the heightened christology of subsequent years.[175]

171. See also *A New Perspective on Jesus* 124 and n. 93.

172. See *Jesus Remembered* 516-17; though Luke himself made the claim more explicit in his version of Jesus' sermon in the synagogue of Nazareth (Luke 4.17-21, 24), and in his Gospel he emphasizes how much the possibility that Jesus was a prophet was canvassed during his mission (Luke 7.16, 39; 9.8, 19; 13.33; 24.19).

173. *Jub.* 4.17-24; *1 Enoch* 12–16; *T. Abr.* [A] 13.3-10; *T. Abr.* [B] 10; 11.2; *2 En.* 22.8; 11QMelch. 13-14; see further my 'Jesus the Judge', *The New Perspective on Paul* ch. 18.

174. But cf. 1 Pet. 4.5 and 2 Tim. 4.1.

175. See further §23.5. Cf. G. N. Stanton, *Jesus of Nazareth in New Testament*

In addition, 10.34-35 look like an introduction added to already existing material to fit it to the context: the jump from 10.35 to 36 is rather abrupt ('As for the word which he sent . . .').[176] It is possible, indeed, that verses 34-35 and 43 have been added to an already fairly coherent torso.[177]

One plausible hypothesis which takes all the above details into account is that Luke has moulded his cameo on some tradition of early preaching to Gentile God-fearers.[178] This would explain the slight tension between the more traditional formulations and the more universal dimension evident in 10.34-35, 36c, 39 ('the country of the Jews') and 43 ('all who believe'). At all events, it does appear as though Luke has again followed Thucydides' practice of putting 'into the mouth of each speaker the sentiments proper to the occasion', expressed as he thought the speaker would be likely to express them, while at the same time he endeavoured, as nearly as he could, 'to give the general import of what was actually said'.[179]

For the value of these speeches (and others in Acts) as testimony to what the first disciples believed, preached and taught in the earliest days of Christianity, it is

Preaching (SNTSMS 27; Cambridge: Cambridge University, 1974) ch. 3: 'Peter's speech to Cornelius shows that early communities grouped together passages of Scripture to expound and defend their interpretation not only of the death, resurrection and exaltation of Jesus, but also of his earthly ministry' (84). In particular, 'Ps. 107:20 seems to have been a *testimonium* used in the early church to point to the significance of the ministry of Jesus' (75); Stanton also suggests that Peter's speech originally included a longer citation from Psalm 107 (73).

176. On the awkwardness of the Greek see Barrett, *Acts* 1.521-22. Fitzmyer comments: 'If this part of the speech were merely a resume of the Lukan Gospel and nothing more, one would have to explain why Luke has written such miserable Greek at this point (vv. 36-38)' (*Acts* 459-60).

177. The emphasis on prophets bearing witness (10.43) is a constant theme of the Acts speeches and reflects also Luke 24.25-27, 44-48. Passages in mind could be Isa. 33.24, 55.7 and/or Jer. 31.34. The call for repentance is lacking, since it refers usually to responsibility for the death of the Christ. But it is replaced by a call for belief, with the Pauline emphasis on '*all* who believe' again underlining the tension with 'the people' of v. 42 (as again in 3.25-26). The phrase is a further variation on Luke's belief formulae: here 'believe in (or into) him', giving more the force of commitment to the person named (such as would normally be expressed in baptism). To this invitation is attached the promise of forgiveness of (presumably a much wider range of unspecified) sins. 'Through his name' is the characteristic emphasis of 2.38 and 4.12.

178. C. H. Dodd argued that 10.34-43 'represents the form of *kerygma* used by the primitive Church in its earliest approaches to a wider public' (*The Apostolic Preaching and Its Developments* [London: Hodder and Stoughton, 1936, 1944] 27-28; also 'The Framework of the Gospel Narrative', *New Testament Studies* [Manchester: Manchester University, 1953] 1-11 [here 9]; see also Bruce, *Acts* 261).

179. In view of the evidence marshalled above, such a conclusion is preferable to that of Dibelius (*Studies* 110-11) and Wilckens (*Missionsreden* 46-50) that the speech is a wholly Lukan composition; similarly Lüdemann speaks of the 'redactional origin of the speech throughout' (*Early Christianity* 128).

not necessary to argue or to assume that Peter actually said the words attributed to him. I have indicated my reasons for concluding that they are not: in terms of the historiographical principles then operative, Luke would not have thought it necessary, nor would his audiences have assumed it to be necessary, for the speeches to be verbatim as delivered. The cameo effect, two- to three-minute miniatures, is hardly likely to reflect actual speeches or sermons; the evidence is clear that both Luke's style and his own distinctive theological concerns shape and structure the passages in question. To make the historical value of these speeches depend on their being *de facto* transcripts of what was said on the occasions described is to obscure and distort their real value.

At the same time, the evidence that Luke has been able to draw on early material in his composition of these speeches is equally or even more difficult to deny or refute.[180] How did he gain access to such material? Not because there were written versions of these speeches available to him, which would imply a literary society and environment such as we have seen to be wholly unlikely for the beginnings of Christianity.[181] Nor, I suggest, because they were preserved as fixed or stable forms still current in the communities of Luke's time; C. F. Evans famously observed that, in contrast to the Jesus tradition, no *Sitz im Leben* can be posited for the repetition and preservation of the apostles' speeches in the early phase of Christianity's growth.[182] Once again, however, the discussion can be too easily diverted or miss the way because Luke's access to genuinely primitive material is conceived in literary or quasi-literary terms, as though it was only a choice between the implausibility of a tradition fixed (in effect written down) and the unlikelihood of some individual disciple being able to remember the terms and themes of sermons delivered about fifty years earlier. But in the oral society, which we must envisage for the earliest Christian groups and communi-

---

180. H. J. Cadbury, 'The Speeches in Acts', *Beginnings* 5.402-27, concludes: 'Like Thucydides and the other best composers of speeches he [Luke] attempted to present what the speakers were likely to have said. . . . They indicate at least what seemed to a well-informed Christian of the next generation the main outline of the Christian message as first presented by Jesus' followers in Palestine and in the cities of the Mediterranean world' (426-27).

181. See n. 62 above.

182. C. F. Evans, 'The Kerygma', *JTS* 7 (1956) 25-41. Jervell summarizes Evans — 'It is not conceivable that the apostles' speeches were repeated year after year, and a Sitz im Leben may not be discerned for their preservation' (*Apg* 68) — but goes on to qualify the point (70-72). In contrast, R. Bauckham, 'Kerygmatic Summaries in the Speeches of Acts', in Witherington, ed., *History* 154-84, goes beyond Dodd's famous attempt in his *Apostolic Preaching* to reconstruct traditional kerygmatic summaries used by Luke and argues that 'in his summaries of the history of Jesus in these speeches Luke follows a form — I shall call it the kerygmatic summary — which was very traditional but also very flexible and variable' (190), building his case on parallels with other 'kerygmatic summaries' particularly in the *Ascension of Isaiah* and Ignatius of Antioch.

ties, it is readily and appropriately possible to envisage the speeches, sermons and teaching of leading figures (the apostles) providing material, themes and emphases, claims and arguments, which were taken up by those who emerged as teachers and elders of the individual groups and communities in their own preaching and teaching.[183] Many of these emphases and arguments would have been superseded by further reflection and instruction within these communities and as the movement they represented spread and developed. But Luke would have had little difficulty in finding older teachers and elders who could still recall these emphases and arguments of earlier days, even though the living tradition of the churches had now left them behind. My claim, then, is that a thesis along these lines makes best sense of all the evidence available to us in the early speeches of Acts.

21.4. The Letters of Paul

Throughout the modern attempts to trace the beginnings of Christianity, much the most valued source has been the letters of Paul. The reason is straightforward: Paul's letters provide a first-hand witness to events of the first generation; whereas Acts is at best second-hand for the majority of its account, and in the view of many is entirely derivative. Even if those who believe that the 'we/us' passages in Acts attest personal involvement in the events/travels described are correct, for his account of the pre-Pauline growth of the new movement Luke would have had to rely on second- or third-hand testimony. The *strength* of setting Paul and Luke in contrast is that Paul was himself actively involved in several of the key decisions which proved formative of Christianity, both its expansion and its theology. His testimony inevitably stands to the fore.[184] The *weakness* of such a contrast between Paul and Luke is its forgetfulness that Paul was a controversial figure in that expansion and a passionate exponent of an understanding of the gospel, and of its implications, which other believers in Messiah Jesus found it hard fully to accept. Paul, in other words, cannot be regarded as a dispassionate witness in what he records.[185] Luke of course had his own perspective on the events he records. But so had Paul! Neither is straightforwardly 'historical'; their theological perspective shapes each of their accounts.[186] All that being said, the crucial fact remains that Paul's letters have a prime claim to our attention.

183. Similar observations were already made by Moffatt, *Introduction* 306.

184. The prioritizing of Paul's letters over Acts goes back to Baur, *Paul* 5-14.

185. 'It has not been sufficiently taken into account that Galatians is anything but an objective and unprejudiced autobiographical document, but is rather a highly subjective controversial tract' (Weiss, *Earliest Christianity* 158; see also 258-59).

186. See again further below, §28.1a.

a. Which Letters Were Written by Paul Himself?

The question must be clarified, since, as several of the letters indicate, Paul probably always used a secretary or scribe; that is, he dictated his letters, usually adding a greeting at the end in his own hand.[187] That fact in turn raises the question of how much the secretary/scribe contributed to the writing of any of the letters of Paul. Usually a scribe would simply record or transcribe the dictation. But a secretary might be given greater responsibility. For example, in preparing a final draft from a rough dictation copy, the author could leave it to the secretary to make minor changes in form or content. There could even be occasions when a secretary, long accustomed to the letter writer's thought and concerns, might be trusted to write in the name of the letter writer. Moreover, seven of Paul's letters indicate joint authorship, raising the possibility that the co-author(s) may have contributed their own language or sentiments.[188] The question at the head of the paragraph, therefore, should be reformulated: Which letters are written in Paul's own words?[189]

The large consensus for most of the last century is that the letters attributed to Paul in the New Testament can safely be divided into two or three categories:

1. seven undisputed letters — Romans, 1 and 2 Corinthians, Galatians, Philippians, 1 Thessalonians and Philemon;
2. two letters of uncertain authorship — Colossians and 2 Thessalonians;
3. four letters usually attributed to the generation following Paul — Ephesians and the Pastoral Epistles (1 and 2 Timothy and Titus).

(1) In the first group, the indications of co-authorship have not distracted from the general conclusion that the letters are genuinely Paul's. Even if the sentiments recorded can be attributed to more than Paul, they can certainly be attributed to Paul himself. And the fact that Paul links no other name with his in the writing of Romans (Tertius names himself as scribe — Rom. 16.22) presumably indicates that he wanted Romans to be regarded as especially and distinctively the expression of his own views. Where disagreement arises among commentators is over the integrity of some of the letters: was the letter composed as we now have it, or is the letter which we have the result of a later editor combining two or three separate letters? There are vigorous disputes on the subject, particularly in the cases of 2 Corinthians and Philippians.[190] Even so, however, the vari-

---

187. Rom. 16.22; 1 Cor. 16.21; Gal. 6.11; Col. 4.18; 2 Thess. 3.17; Phlm. 19.

188. 1 Corinthians (Sosthenes), 2 Corinthians (Timothy), Philippians (Timothy), Colossians (Timothy), 1 and 2 Thessalonians (Silvanus and Timothy), Philemon (Timothy).

189. I go into all this in more detail in §29.8c below.

190. See below, §§32.7a and 34.4a.

ous elements are usually recognized to be authentic (parts of) letters written or dictated by Paul. I will take up the issue in each case later.

(2) Of the two letters in the second category, my own inclination is to take as a working hypothesis that they are both from Paul himself but that their present form may owe more to the secretary than in the case of the first group. In the case of Colossians in particular, the rather distinctive vocabulary may well indicate that Paul (in prison) left the framing of the letter to someone else (Timothy?) but was able to show his approval (and authorization) by appending his own words at the end (Col. 4.18).[191]

(3) In the remaining four I find myself of the same mind as the majority of scholars, who regard them as pseudonymous.[192] By using a word which some regard as controversial, I indicate my belief that the letters were written after Paul's death, but written by close disciples in what they (and the recipients) regarded as acceptable, even as authoritative, statements of Paul's views in the changing circumstances of their time. That is to say, I distinguish these letters from the second group, Colossians in particular, in that while both groups were probably penned by others, Paul himself was no longer alive (as in the case of Colossians) to give his approval of what had been written in his own name. In other words, the practice of pseudonymity just envisaged was in no sense an attempt to deceive the recipients but accorded with the standards and practices of the time.[193] I offer this explanation of my rationale at this point, since I need to explain why I refer to Ephesians only at the end of this volume (§37.1) and do not draw on the Pastorals as such, but not to foreclose the fuller discussion of the issue of pseudonymity, which will be necessary in volume 3.

The value of the letters of Paul is inestimable for the information they provide, much of it by way of allusion and inference. On a number of occasions he indicates that he had received and passed on tradition, using the technical terms for receiving *(paralambanō)* and passing on *(paradidōmi)* tradition, clearly implying that this was an important facet both of beginning a new life as a Christian (catechesis) and of founding a new church.[194]

---

191. See below, §34.6b.

192. See below, §37 n. 208.

193. See below, §37 n. 209.

194. *paralambanō* — 1 Cor. 11.23; 15.1, 3; Gal. 1.9; Phil. 4.9; Col. 2.6; 1 Thess. 2.13; 4.1; 2 Thess. 3.6; *paradidōmi* — Rom. 6.17; 1 Cor. 11.2, 23; 15.3; *paradosis* (tradition) — 1 Cor. 11.2; 2 Thess. 2.15; 3.6.

b. Autobiographical Elements

The information is brief but covers a wide swathe of Paul's life prior to the writing of his letters:[195]

- an Israelite/Hebrew — Rom. 11.1; 2 Cor. 11.22; Phil. 3.5
- pre-Christian past — Gal. 1.13-14; Phil. 3.4-6
- persecution — 1 Cor. 15.9; Gal. 1.13; Phil. 3.6
- conversion/commission/apostleship — 1 Cor. 9.1; 15.8, 10; 2 Cor. 4.4, 6; Gal. 1.1, 12, 15-16
- time in Arabia — Gal. 1.17
- early relations with Jerusalem — Gal. 1.17-20
- early mission — Gal. 1.21-23
- second visit to Jerusalem/Jerusalem council — Gal. 2.1-10
- an important incident at Antioch — Gal. 2.11-14/17
- preaching to Gentiles — Rom. 10.14-17; 11.13; 1 Cor. 15.1-11; 2 Cor. 5.18-21; Gal. 1.6-9; 1 Thess. 1.9-10
- principles of his mission — Rom. 11.13-15; 15.20; 2 Cor. 10.12-16; Gal. 2.9
- perils of mission — 2 Cor. 11.23-28
- the goal of Spain — Rom. 15.23-24, 28
- the commitment of the collection — Rom. 15.26-31; 1 Cor. 16.1-4; 2 Corinthians 8-9; Gal. 2.10
- Paul's theology/theologizing — his letters themselves!

This material obviously provides an agenda to be worked through when the time comes to focus on Paul's part in the making of Christianity.

c. References to the Judaism of the Time

Given that Christianity did emerge from within the diversity of Second Temple Judaism, it is also worth itemizing the information which Paul's letters provide regarding that Judaism, not least for the light it sheds on the character of Christianity itself (as an offspring of Second Temple Judaism). Paul, after all, is the

---

195. E.-M. Becker, 'Autobiographisches bei Paulus', in E.-M. Becker and P. Pilhofer, eds., *Biographie und Persönlichkeit des Paulus* (WUNT 187; Tübingen: Mohr Siebeck, 2005) 67-87, provides a fuller listing of autobiographical statements and texts (82-83). I have already noted the points of congruence between Acts and Paul's letters regarding Paul's movements (§21.2c[3]).

only Pharisee we know of whose personal writings from the period prior to the destruction of the Temple we still have.[196] To be sure, present-day Jews usually do not regard Paul as a Jewish witness; in their eyes he was an apostate and cannot be regarded as a representative Jew in any acceptable sense. But such views are largely determined by the post–Second Temple understanding of Judaism shaped by the Mishnah, Talmudim and Midrashim — classic (rabbinic) Judaism. Paul, on the other hand, bears testimony to Second Temple Judaism in at least some of its diversity, the Judaism, we might say, from which both Christianity and rabbinic Judaism emerged.[197] Indeed, his letters provide some of the best witness available to us 'from inside' the last forty or so years of Second Temple Judaism — as do, of course, the Synoptic Gospels. Together with the Dead Sea Scrolls and various pseudepigrapha, these NT writings can properly be classified as *Jewish* documents, attesting the rich variety in the last hundred years of Second Temple Judaism.[198] Paul, in other words, regarded his as an authentically Jewish voice within the religious cacophony of the first-century Hellenistic world, and as such his witness as a late Second Temple Jew deserves a fresh hearing.[199]

His testimony on this subject naturally overlaps with the early autobiographical elements, since he first appears on the scene as a Pharisee. Prominent in the following list are the items which functioned as the most distinctive identity markers of Second Temple Judaism and which Paul's treatment implies were of first importance for his fellow Jews, including most of his fellow Jewish believers in Jesus Messiah, and in some cases of continuing importance for Paul himself:

- credal belief (Deut. 6.4) that God is one — Rom. 3.30; 1 Cor. 8.6; Gal. 3.20
- God as creator — Rom. 1.25; 4.17; 11.36; 1 Cor. 8.6; 10.26; Col. 1.15
- total antipathy to idolatry — Rom. 1.18, 20, 23; 1 Cor. 5.10-11; 6.9; 8.7, 10; 10.7, 14; Gal. 5.20; 1 Thess. 1.9
- Israel's election — Rom. 3.1-4; 9.4-13; 11.5-7, 28-29
- identity as 'Hebrews' — 2 Cor. 11.22; Phil. 3.5
- the law as a defining feature — Rom. 2.12-23; 3.19; 7.1, 12, 14, 16; 8.4; 9.31; 10.5; 13.8-10; 1 Cor. 9.20; Gal. 3.19-24; 4.4-5; 5.3, 14; Phil. 3.5-6
- 'zeal' for the law — Rom. 10.2; Gal. 1.13-14; Phil. 3.6

196. Josephus claims to have begun to govern his life by the rules of the Pharisees in his nineteenth year (*Life* 12), but all his writing falls in the period 70-100 (see above, §21.1a).

197. Hence the evocative title of A. F. Segal, *Rebecca's Children: Judaism and Christianity in the Roman World* (Cambridge: Harvard University, 1986).

198. Segal, *Paul the Convert* xi-xvi; Hengel, 'Early Christianity' 21-28.

199. See also S. Meissner, *Die Heimholung des Ketzers. Studien zur jüdischen Auseinandersetzung mit Paulus* (WUNT 2.87; Tübingen: Mohr Siebeck, 1996).

- high evaluation of ancestral traditions — Gal. 1.14; Col. 2.8
- importance of 'works of (doing) the law' — Rom. 2.13; Gal. 2.14-16; 3.10
- especially of circumcision — Rom. 2.25–3.2; Gal. 5.2-3; 6.12-13; Phil. 3.3, 5
- 'the circumcision' = Jews/Israel generally — Rom. 3.30; 15.8; Gal. 2.7-9; Phil. 3.3
- importance of food laws — Rom. 14.2-3, 20; Gal. 2.11-14
- the Sabbath — Rom. 14.5-6; 1 Cor. 16.2; Gal. 4.10; Col. 2.16
- hostility to sexual license *(porneia)* — 1 Cor. 5.1; 6.15-20; 10.8; 2 Cor. 12.21; Gal. 5.19; Col. 3.5
- the (Jerusalem) cult and Temple — Rom. 5.2; 12.1-2; 15.16; 1 Cor. 10.18; 2 Cor. 6.16; 2 Thess. 2.4
- the authority of Scripture — *(kathōs) gegraptai* ('as it is written') over 30 times.

This list could be extended, and, of course, most of the references require some exegesis for their full relevance to become clear.[200] In particular, many of the allusions would have been contentious, because Paul was in process of redefining or reconfiguring these identity markers in the light of his new faith in Christ. But even with these defects, the list provides an interesting peep-hole into the self-understanding and priorities of the Judaism of Paul's time.

d. Knowledge of Jesus Assumed

The fact that Paul shows so little interest in the pre-passion life of Jesus is notorious in 'life of Jesus' research. But too little account is taken of the indications that he was able to *assume* knowledge of Jesus and the character of his mission. Here we must take seriously the fact that Paul in every case was writing to churches and individuals who had been baptized *in the name of Jesus* and put through at least some basic catechesis or teaching regarding (we cannot but suppose) Jesus himself, the *Christ* whose followers they were becoming known as (Christians). This basic teaching included, no doubt, the character of Jesus' mission and some at least of his central teaching, as well as the significance of his death and resurrection. Such *a priori* likelihood is confirmed by allusions to Jesus which could be appreciated by the recipients of Paul's letters only if they could fill out the allusions from their earlier instruction.[201]

---

200. See further *Theology of Paul,* and below, particularly §§27.2-5, 31.7, 32.5, 33.3.
201. What J. M. Foley has called 'metonymic references' (J. M. Foley, *Immanent Art:*

At several points Paul appeals to the model or pattern which the Jesus tradition provided. In Rom. 6.17 Paul refers the auditors of his letter to 'the pattern of teaching *(typos didachēs)*' to which they had been handed over. All agree that the reference is to the catechetical teaching given to new converts. But *typos* in Paul's letters almost always has a personal reference — a particular individual (or individuals) providing a pattern of conduct.[202] And talk of converts being handed over *to* the *typos* makes better sense both if the reference was to a person (cf. Phil. 3.17; 2 Thess. 3.9) and if the person was Christ (the handing over to the new Lord named in baptism).[203] The clear implication is that the information provided regarding Jesus' conduct and the character of his mission gave new converts a pattern for their own conduct. The same point emerges from Col. 2.6-7, where the text is best translated, 'As you received [the tradition of] the Christ Jesus the Lord, continue to walk in him . . . just as you were taught' (similarly Eph. 4.20).[204] Again the clear implication is that catechetical teaching about Jesus gave new converts a clear pattern for the new way of living which they had embraced.

This likelihood is strengthened by Rom. 15.1-3, where Christ is referred to as providing the pattern of love of neighbour, which presumably would evoke a wider range of stories about Jesus and his teaching than only his passion. Notable here is the parallel with Gal. 6.2, where similar compassion towards the failing is called for, with the implication that 'the law of Christ' is summed up in the command to love the neighbour (Gal. 5.14).[205] Again the implication is that Jesus' teaching on the importance of love of neighbour (Mark 12.31 pars.) and the embodiment of such love in his concern for sinners (Matt. 11.19/Luke 7.34) provided the Christian equivalent of the law, namely, 'the law of Christ' (Gal. 6.2).[206] Consequently we need not be surprised to read Paul exhorting the Corinthians to 'be imitators of me, as I am of Christ' (1 Cor. 11.1; cf. 1 Thess. 1.6).

From Structure to Meaning in Traditional Oral Epic [Bloomington: Indiana University, 1991] 6-13, 42-45), referred to in my 'Altering the Default Setting' 152 = *New Perspective on Jesus* 95.

202. Rom. 5.14; Phil. 3.17; 1 Thess. 1.7; 2 Thess. 3.9; also 1 Tim. 4.12; Tit. 2.7; 1 Pet. 5.3; Ignatius, *Magn.* 6.2; otherwise only 1 Cor. 10.6.

203. See further my *Romans* 343-44.

204. See my *The Epistles to the Colossians and to Philemon* (NIGTC; Grand Rapids: Eerdmans, 1996) 138-41.

205. *Theology of Paul* 653-55.

206. Some find it necessary to stress that *nomos* here is not to be taken in the sense of 'law', as though Christ or the Jesus tradition or the love command in particular was a legal requirement like the ten commandments. But the facts remain that Paul was playing on the word *nomos* and that Gal. 5.14 echoes Jesus' remembered assertion that love of neighbour is one of the two greatest commandments, that is, of the law/Torah (Mark 12.31). See further below, §31 n. 395.

'Imitation of Christ' was not simply a keynote of mediaeval piety; Christ's priorities in life as well as death evidently provided a pattern for Paul's own life and mission. This is the clear implication also of Phil. 2.6-11: 'Let the same mind be in you that was in Christ Jesus' (similarly 2 Cor. 8.9).[207]

Within this general evocation of the character of Jesus' whole mission we find allusion to particular features and aspects of his life and character:

- a Jew, descendant of Abraham and David — Rom. 1.3; 9.5; Gal. 3.16
- law-observant — Rom. 15.8; Gal. 4.4
- had brothers, including James — 1 Cor. 9.5; Gal. 1.19
- knew poverty — 2 Cor. 8.9
- known for his meekness and gentleness — 2 Cor. 10.1
- he instituted a memorial meal on the night of his betrayal — 1 Cor. 11.23-25
- echoes of Jesus' teaching.[208]

e. Allusions to Pre-Pauline Christian Beliefs and Worship

One of the more fascinating lines of research through the twentieth century has been the attempt to discern by means of Paul's letters what the state of the movement or sect was to which Paul was converted before he made his distinctive impact on it. The major and most fruitful outcome has been the clarification of various *kerygmatic and confessional formulae* which Paul seems to draw into his own writing,[209] notably Rom. 1.3-4, 10.9 and 1 Cor. 15.3-5/7.

Rom. 1.3-4 — . . . the gospel of God . . . concerning his Son
Who was descended from the seed of David in terms of the flesh,
and who was appointed Son of God in power in terms of the Spirit

207. The translation of Phil. 2.5 is disputed; see, e.g., M. Bockmuehl, *The Epistle to the Philippians* (BNTC; London: Black, 1997) 121-24.

208. Details in *Jesus Remembered* 182 n. 48; bibliography in *Theology of Paul* 182; add D. C. Allison, *The Jesus Tradition in Q* (Harrisburg: Trinity Press International, 1997) ch. 4. For a more negative view of Paul's knowledge and use of Jesus tradition, see J. Becker, *Paul: Apostle to the Gentiles* (Louisville: John Knox, 1993) 112-24.

209. A. Seeberg, *Der Katechismus der Urchristenheit* (1903; republished Munich: Kaiser, 1966); A. M. Hunter, *Paul and His Predecessors* (London: SCM, 1940, ²1961) chs. 2-3; V. H. Neufeld, *The Earliest Christian Confessions* (NTTS 5; Grand Rapids: Eerdmans, 1963); W. Kramer, *Christ, Lord, Son of God* (London: SCM, 1966); K. Wengst, *Christologische Formeln und Lieder des Urchristentums* (Gütersloh: Gütersloher, 1972) 55-143; R. N. Longenecker, *New Wine into Fresh Wineskins: Contextualizing the Early Christian Confessions* (Peabody: Hendrickson, 1999). E. E. Ellis, *The Making of the New Testament Documents* (Leiden: Brill, 1999), attempts to identify preformed traditions in all the Pauline letters (69-117).

of holiness
as from the resurrection of the dead.[210]

Rom. 10.9 — If you confess with your mouth, 'Jesus is Lord',
and believe in your heart that 'God raised him from the dead',
you will be saved.[211]

1 Cor. 15.3-5/7 — I handed on *(paredōka)* to you as of first importance
what I in turn had received *(parelabon):*
that Christ died for our sins in accordance with the Scriptures,
and that he was buried,
and that he was raised on the third day in accordance with the
Scriptures,
and that he appeared to Cephas, then to the twelve.
Then he appeared to more than five hundred brothers at the same
time. . . .
Then he appeared to James, then to all the apostles.[212]

Several variations of formulae which probably served as semi-credal assertions or liturgical responses can be detected simply by the regularity of their form
and the frequency with which they are repeated:

* resurrection formulae — 'God raised him from the dead'[213]
* 'died for' formulae — 'Christ died for us'[214]

210. Similar balanced formulae (son of David, son of God) are evident in 2 Tim. 2.8 and
Ignatius, *Smyrn.* 1.1, and may provide the core for the tradition lying behind the birth narratives
(see *Jesus Remembered* §11.1 at nn. 34-35).

211. Rom. 10.9 clearly expresses a long-established summary of the agreed response to
inquirers (Romans was sent to a church Paul had never visited), as confirmed by the even more
impressive array of parallels (1 Cor. 8.6; 12.3; 2 Cor. 4.5; Phil. 2.11; Col. 2.6; see also Eph. 4.5;
Acts 2.36; 10.36; John 20.28). 'Jesus is Lord' may be the earliest Christian confession that we
have (O. Cullmann, *The Earliest Christian Confessions* [London: Lutterworth, 1949]; Neufeld,
Confessions 51).

212. For the debate on how full the version received by Paul was, see, e.g., G. Strecker,
Theology of the New Testament (1996; Berlin: de Gruyter, 2000) 74-78; W. Schrage,
1 Korinther (EKK 7/4; Düsseldorf: Benziger, 2001) 53-54. See further below, §23.4.

213. Rom. 4.24-25; 7.4; 8.11; 10.9; 1 Cor. 6.14; 15.4, 12, 20; 2 Cor. 4.14; Gal. 1.1; Col.
2.12; 1 Thess. 1.10; see also Eph. 1.20; 2 Tim. 2.8; 1 Pet. 1.21; Acts 3.15; 4.10; 5.30; 10.40;
13.30, 37. P. Pokorny, *The Genesis of Christology: Foundations for a Theology of the New Testament* (Edinburgh: Clark, 1987): 'The statements about awakening or resurrection of Jesus are
the oldest component parts of the more detailed extant formulae' (73).

214. Rom. 5.6, 8; 14.15; 1 Cor. 8.11; 15.3; 2 Cor. 5.14-15; 1 Thess. 5.10; see also
Ignatius, *Trall.* 2.1.

- 'handed over *(paradidōmi)*' formulae — 'he was handed (*or* handed himself) over (for our sins)'[215]
- combined formulae — 'Christ died and was raised'.[216]

Equally fruitful have been the attempts to discern *liturgical material* which Paul echoes or refers to,[217] although there has been some tendency to 'pan-liturgism' in some of the attempts.[218]

- baptism in the name of Christ — 1 Cor. 1.13
- received tradition *(parelabon)* of the Lord's Supper — 1 Cor. 11.23-26
- established prayer language (Aramaic) — *abba* (Rom. 8.15; Gal. 4.6); *amēn* (1 Cor. 14.16); *Marana tha* (1 Cor. 16.22)
- hymns/hymnic material — Phil. 2.6-11; Col. 1.15-20[219]
- exposition of Scripture — notably Ps. 110.1 (1 Cor. 15.25) and Isaiah 53 (Rom. 4.25).[220]

In the second half of the twentieth century attempts were made to flesh out the traditions which Paul inherited as typically 'Hellenist' (Acts 6.1) or specifically 'Antiochene', on the basis of the Acts reports that Paul was associated for a number of years with the church of Antioch (Acts 11.25-26; 13.1).[221] This and other controversial issues lying behind many of these references will provide matter for fuller discussion below.[222] For the moment it is sufficient to note

215. Rom. 4.25; 8.32; 1 Cor. 11.23; Gal. 1.4; 2.20; see also Eph. 5.2, 25; 1 Tim. 2.6; Tit. 2.14; *1 Clem.* 16.7.

216. Rom. 4.25; 8.34; (14.9); 1 Cor. 15.3-4; 2 Cor. 5.15; 13.4; 1 Thess. 4.14.

217. G. Delling, *Worship in the New Testament* (1952; London: Darton, Longman and Todd, 1962); Wengst, *Christologische Formeln* 144-208; R. Deichgräber, *Gotteshymnus und Christushymnus in der frühen Christenheit* (Göttingen: Vandenhoeck und Ruprecht, 1967); J. T. Sanders, *The New Testament Christological Hymns: Their Historical Religious Background* (SNTSMS 15; Cambridge: Cambridge University, 1971).

218. I use the phrase 'pan-liturgism' in *Unity and Diversity* §36, drawn from W. C. van Unnik, 'Dominus Vobiscum: The Background of a Liturgical Formula', in A. J. B. Higgins, ed., *New Testament Essays: Studies in Memory of T. W. Manson* (Manchester: Manchester University, 1959) 270-305 (here 272).

219. Wengst identifies other Christ hymns — John 1.1-18; Eph. 2.14-16; Col. 2.13-15; 1 Tim. 3.16; Heb. 1.3; 1 Pet. 1.20; 3.18, 22; Ignatius, *Eph.* 19.2-3 (*Christologische Formeln* 144-208); similarly Sanders, *Hymns*. Deichgräber adds several hymns to God — Rom. 11.33-36; 2 Cor. 1.3-4; Eph. 1.3-14; 1 Pet. 1.3-5; Col. 1.12-14 (*Gotteshymnus* 60-105).

220. See below, §§23.4d and 23.5. Paul himself was an expert expositor of Scripture (classic examples in Rom. 4.3-25; 10.6-9; 2 Cor. 3.7-18), but he was able to assume familiarity with both the text (LXX) and the acceptance of the importance of such exposition among the recipients of his letters.

221. See further below, §24 n. 278.

222. See below, §§24.9 and 25.5e.

that the list provides some indication of the emphases and practices which Paul inherited.

f. Paraenesis and Life-Style

That baptism in the name of Jesus carried with it a commitment to Jesus as Lord and to a pattern of living which accorded with that lordship — to what Paul describes as a slave-like obedience to righteousness (Rom. 6.15-22) — should be obvious. What is interesting here is how much of the resulting paraenesis draws on tradition, implying that Paul here too took over much that had already been accepted as expected of Christian living. Indeed, the language of passing on/receiving tradition occurs most often in Paul's letters in reference to paraenesis, advice and exhortation regarding the character of life which Paul expected of his converts,[223] the way of living appropriate for those who have responded to the calling *(klēsis)* of Christ.[224]

Some paraenesis draws heavily on Jewish tradition. It is well known, for example, that Paul's treatment in 1 Corinthians 5–6 and 8–10 reflects Jewish antipathy both to sexual licence and to idolatry.[225] But less well appreciated is the degree to which Rom. 12.9-21 draws on the wisdom that diaspora Jews had learned over the centuries on how to live in a hostile environment.[226] Again, it is well recognized that Paul's various vice- and virtue-lists echo patterns of ethical exhortation long traditional in Greco-Roman as well as Jewish moral teaching.[227] And the fact that Paul can sum up the highest moral aspiration simply in terms of 'doing good' (Rom. 2.10) is a reminder that 'the good' was an ideal shared by many.[228] Not least we should recall that much of the Jesus tradition referred to above in §21.4d would contain ethical instruction explicitly or implicitly. In particular, it is worth remembering that in dealing with the question of

223. Of the references in n. 194 above, six have in view ethical conduct (1 Cor. 11.2; Phil. 4.9; Col. 2.6; 1 Thess. 4.1; 2 Thess. 2.15; 3.6).

224. *Kaleō* — Rom. 8.30; 9.12, 24; 1 Cor. 1.9; 7.15, 17-18, 20-22, 24; Gal. 1.6; 5.8, 13; Col. 3.15; 1 Thess. 2.12; 4.7; 5.24; 2 Thess. 2.14; also Eph. 4.1, 4; 1 Tim. 6.12; 2 Tim. 1.9; *klēsis* — Rom. 11.29; 1 Cor. 1.26; 7.20; 2 Thess. 1.11; also Eph. 1.18; 4.1, 4; 2 Tim. 1.9. Response to such a call carried with it obligation to an appropriate code of conduct, which is especially clear in 1 Cor. 7.15, 17, 19, 21; Gal. 5.8, 13; Eph. 4.1; 1 Thess. 2.12; 4.7; 2 Thess. 1.11; 1 Tim. 6.12.

225. See above, §21.4c; and further B. S. Rosner, *Paul, Scripture and Ethics: A Study of 1 Corinthians 5–7* (Grand Rapids: Baker, 1999).

226. See my *Romans* 738, and §33 n. 250 below.

227. Rom. 1.29-31; 13.13; 1 Cor. 5.10-11; 6.9-10; 2 Cor. 6.6; 12.20; Gal. 5.19-21, 22-23; Phil. 4.8; Col. 3.5, 8, 12. See further my *Theology of Paul* 662-67.

228. See further my *Romans* 86, 88.

marriage and divorce Paul's first recourse is to the distinctive teaching of Jesus (1 Cor. 7.10). And he sums up the case for his looking to his churches for financial support by recalling another instruction from the Jesus tradition (9.14).

In none of the above are we given to understand that Paul was saying something new or distinctive of his own moral stance, which naturally suggests that this, or most of it, was teaching shared with the earlier groups of disciples and may have been part of the tradition which he himself first received when he converted to the Christ-sect. At the very least we can envisage basic ethical instruction given to new converts as they formed themselves into a new church, some intensive teaching on the character of living which should match their new calling and profession, a teaching drawn from both Jewish wisdom and from Jesus tradition, often compatible with the best ethical teaching of the moral philosophers of the time, and already characteristic of the new movement before Paul made his principal contribution.[229]

g. Leadership in the Pre-Pauline Churches

From what must count as among the earliest traditions received by Paul, that is, when he was converted (1 Cor. 15.3-5/7), we gain the impression (1) that Cephas (Peter) was the most prominent of the continuing disciples (15.5), (2) that there was a leading circle, 'the twelve' (15.5), and (3) that James (brother of Jesus) was also a prominent figure (15.7). (4) 'All the apostles' (15.7, 9) seems to be a larger group than 'the twelve', since elsewhere it is clear that Paul regards as numbered among these 'apostles' figures like Andronicus and Junia (Rom. 16.7), Apollos (1 Cor. 4.9), Barnabas (Gal. 2.8-9) and Silvanus (1 Thess. 2.6-7), not to mention Paul himself (1 Cor. 9.1; 15.8-9)!

Paul's autobiographical narrative in Galatians 1–2 provides some clarification of the picture of the early leadership of the Jerusalem church, the mother church. Cephas/Peter again seems to be the leading figure on Paul's first visit to Jerusalem after his conversion, that is, four to six years after Jesus' crucifixion (1.18), with James, the Lord's brother, and 'the apostles' again given prominent mention (1.19). More striking is the fact that by the time of Paul's second visit to Jerusalem, the order of precedence seems to have changed, with the triumvirate or triarchy now named as James, Cephas and John (2.9). And in the subsequent

---

229. See further below, §29.7i. In the 1940s there were several attempts to find evidence of a firm pattern of early catechetical instruction from the NT epistles (Colossians, Ephesians, 1 Peter, James, etc.); see particularly P. Carrington, *The Primitive Christian Catechism* (Cambridge: Cambridge University, 1940); E. G. Selwyn, *The First Epistle of St. Peter* (London: Macmillan, 1947) 363-466. See further below on James and 1 Peter (§§37.2-3).

incident at Antioch Cephas is depicted as giving way before some message from James (2.11-12). 'The twelve' make no appearance in the Pauline letters apart from 1 Cor. 15.5. And, rather intriguing, we find no mention of 'elders' in the undisputed Paulines.[230]

Most intriguing, however, is the identity of those Paul describes as 'false brothers' (Gal. 2.4), the opponents of Paul's mission in Galatia, whom he describes as 'agitators' (Gal. 1.7; 5.10, 12), the 'false apostles' who were causing trouble in the Corinthian church (2 Cor. 11.13-15), and 'the dogs', 'the evilworkers' warned against in Phil. 3.2. These do not necessarily constitute a single group, and their identity is subject for further discussion below. But since one prominent theory is that one or more of them refer directly or indirectly to the leadership of the Jerusalem church, I mention them here for completeness.[231] At the very least we gain some vivid glimpses of the tensions and disputes which marked Paul's mission, or, more exactly and more to the point, which his mission provoked with others who thought of themselves as preachers of the gospel (Gal. 1.8-9) and 'apostles of Christ' (2 Cor. 11.13). Any suggestion that Christianity began with an idyllic apostolic age, with all apostles working in close harmony all the time, begins at once to look very doubtful.[232] More to the present point, from the controversies in which Paul was engaged with those in the movement before him, we gain a clear impression of a pre-Pauline movement more comfortably Jewish or traditionally Jewish in character than Paul himself found acceptable, into which Paul's missionary work among non-Jews introduced severe strains and disruption.

h. Indications of the Character of the Churches Addressed

Not least of the value of Paul's letters is the fact that they tell us a good deal about the churches and groups to which Paul wrote. 1 Corinthians in particular 'lifts the lid off' an early Christian church (in this case a first-generation church) as no other document from the early centuries does. One of the most intriguing features of Paul's letters is that they constitute one side and one part of what must have been some sort of dialogue between Paul and these churches. In most cases they are the product of a dialogue which had already run for several years — and which probably ran on beyond the letters themselves. And here again the Corinthian correspondence may be particularly valuable, since the canonical letters comprise at least two and perhaps as many as four or five separate letters written

---

230. Despite Acts 11.30; 14.23; Jas. 5.14; 1 Pet. 5.1, 5. See also §27.1f below.
231. See further below, §32.7b.
232. My *Unity and Diversity* was intended to undermine such an assumption.

in the course of a few years; in addition, we have *1 Clement* written to the church of Corinth some forty years later. In consequence we may be able to glean insights stretching across the first two generations of its existence.[233]

I include this section here for completeness, to underline how much we are dependent on Paul's letters for our knowledge of the beginnings of Christianity, but also how much we may learn from them across a fairly wide spectrum of our inquiry. At the same time, inclusion of this section gives me opportunity to reinforce an earlier point: that Paul is not a dispassionate and wholly objective witness to the character and self-understanding of these churches. He was an advocate, an evangelist, seeking to persuade the recipients of his letters to see things from his perspective. Since we have only one side of each of the dialogues, we can 'see' these churches only through Paul's eyes.[234] To reconstruct the other side of the dialogue is a painstaking and hazardous business. 'Mirror-reading' allows a great deal of divergence in reading what are often ambiguous and ambivalent signs.[235]

All this is simply to observe that the information regarding Paul's churches is extensive, but it is wrapped up within his letters and often is not easy to disentangle from his rhetoric — which is also a way of pointing out how demanding is the agenda which lies before us.

21.5. Jesus Tradition

Finally, among the sources of our knowledge of the earliest phases of what became known as 'Christianity' we must not forget the Jesus tradition. This was, of course, the principal source for volume 1. But the forty-or-so-year gap between Jesus and the written Gospels was not empty of Jesus tradition. The stream of tradition did not disappear underground for several decades only to re-emerge when Mark put pen to papyrus.[236] It is only realistic to assume that the Jesus tradition was the subject of reflection and use (to say no more) during the period of our present concern (30-70). So if we can gain some sense of how the Jesus tradition was handled during that period, it should tell us something more about the first Christian churches.

233. See particularly Horrell, *The Social Ethos of the Corinthian Correspondence*.

234. Readers of vol. 1 will recognize a parallel with the Gospels: we can only 'see' Jesus of Nazareth through the eyes of those who recorded the Jesus tradition (*Jesus Remembered* §6).

235. Often cited in this connection is J. M. G. Barclay, 'Mirror-Reading a Polemical Letter: Galatians as a Test Case', *JSNT* 31 (1987) 73-93.

236. As Vincent Taylor, *The Formation of the Gospel Tradition* (London: Macmillan, ²1935), famously observed, 'If the Form-Critics are right, the disciples must have been translated to heaven immediately after the Resurrection' (41).

In fact, the emergence of form criticism in the 1920s started with the observation that it was the early churches who first put the Jesus tradition into its enduring forms, and that their doing so tells us what were the concerns and needs and priorities of those who thus formed the Jesus tradition. Rudolf Bultmann famously ordered the Jesus tradition into the various categories which he deduced to have been the categories used by the early Christians when the tradition was still in oral form. He divided the Jesus tradition into the two self-evident categories of sayings and narrative. The sayings he subdivided into two subcategories: apophthegms (conflict, didactic and biographical), though many prefer the alternative title 'pronouncement stories' — that is, episodes in the mission of Jesus which climax with a saying of Jesus;[237] and dominical sayings (wisdom sayings, prophetic and apocalyptic sayings, legal sayings and church rules, 'I' sayings, similitudes and similar forms). The narrative tradition he subdivided into miracle stories (healings and nature miracles) and historical stories and legends (particularly the infancy, passion and Easter narratives).[238]

This procedure gave a major impulse to the working assumption of most of those using the form-critical tool that the earliest forms of the Jesus tradition were individual and often fragmentary sayings[239] — an assumption which I have already criticized severely.[240] The assumption may also have been a significant factor in the transition from form criticism to redaction criticism, which became a feature of the second half of the twentieth century. After all, so little can be said about a string of individual sayings isolated from the only context we know them to have had (their still-present contexts in the Gospels). It is much more productive to concentrate rather on how Matthew and Luke redacted the earlier tradition as it had already been processed (written down) by Mark and Q.

Instead of focusing on each unit of tradition and trying to deduce from its form the life-setting which gave it or determined that form, C. F. D. Moule came at the form-critical task from a different angle. He discerned from the NT itself

---

237. Taylor is usually credited with offering this alternative title (*Formation* ch. 4).

238. To give a flavour of Bultmann's procedure I list the apophthegms examined under the heading 'conflict and didactic sayings':
- occasioned by Jesus' healings — Mark 2.1-12; 3.1-6, 22-30; Luke 13.10-17; 14.1-6
- occasioned by Jesus' or the disciples' conduct — Mark 2.15-17, 18-22, 23-28; 7.1-23; 11.27-33; Luke 7.36-50
- the Master is questioned — Matt. 11.2-19/Luke 7.18-35; Mark 9.38-40; 10.17-31, 35-45; 11.20-25; 12.28-34; Luke 9.51-56; 12.13-14; 13.1-5; 17.20-21
- questions asked by opponents — Mark 10.2-12; 12.13-17, 18-27

239. The assumption was simply taken over by the Jesus Seminar: '. . . those fragments of tradition that bear the imprint of orality: short, provocative, memorable, oft-repeated phrases, sentences, and stories' (R. W. Funk and R. W. Hoover, *The Five Gospels: The Search for the Authentic Words of Jesus* [New York: Macmillan/Polebridge, 1993] 4).

240. See *Jesus Remembered* 127-28, 193-95, 241-42, 245-48.

large contexts in which it may be assumed that the Jesus (and other) traditions functioned: the church at worship, the church explaining itself, and the church under attack.[241] His attempt was to understand better 'the birth of the New Testament': 'It is to the circumstances and needs of the worshipping, working, suffering community that one must look if one is to explain the genesis of Christian literature'.[242] But by reminding us of such *a priori* obvious contexts, he indicated historically realistic settings for the early stages of the Jesus tradition, for the use and performance of the Jesus tradition, which do not depend on the unrealistic assumption that the earliest stage is conceivable only in terms of individual units of tradition.

For my own part, I have already argued that a natural tendency among teachers, and any others responsible for maintaining a community's distinctive oral tradition, would be to group material of the same sort. In what would inevitably have been a fairly expansive repertoire of foundational traditions, it would be natural for teachers to hold in mind a sequence of sub-repertoires — pronouncement stories, kingdom parables, stories of healings, and so on. This obvious *a priori* is borne out by what we find in the Synoptic Gospels.

a. Individual Stories and Sayings

In arguing as I have in the preceding paragraph, I do not intend to imply that stories about Jesus and teachings of Jesus were remembered and used *only* in blocks and collections of like material. On the contrary, there were no doubt many individual elements which had made a strong impression on a particular person or group and which in themselves maintained a special vitality for that person or group. We may instance the 'floating' logion 'He who has ears to hear, let him hear',[243] or the saying about salt (Mark 9.49-50 pars.), or again, sayings of Jesus which were not retained within the Gospels (Acts 20.35; *GTh* 82).[244] I have already suggested that the example of Jesus' prayer form, 'Abba, Father', must have become so firmly established within the first, Aramaic-speaking congregations that the usage passed on in that Aramaic form into the Greek-speaking churches (Rom. 8.15; Gal. 4.6). And I have little doubt that the Lord's prayer (Matt. 6.9-13/Luke 11.2-4) was maintained as a much-repeated unit of tradition, alone or with other liturgical material, and was a feature of Christian worship from the first.[245]

---

241. C. F. D. Moule, *The Birth of the New Testament* (London: Black, 1962, [3]1981).
242. Moule, *Birth* 270.
243. *Jesus Remembered* 462 n. 379.
244. *Jesus Remembered* 172.
245. *Jesus Remembered* 226-28.

As for narratives, there is a strong indication that the story of the woman who anointed Jesus as he sat at table (Mark 14.3-9 par.) was told repeatedly. The story ends with Jesus saying, 'Wherever the gospel is proclaimed in the whole world, what she has done will be told in remembrance of her' (14.9). Similarly the story of the healing of Bartimaeus (Mark 10.46-52 pars.) would naturally have had a special significance for Bartimaeus himself — which may be why Mark's account still retains his name (10.46).[246] Likewise stories with named characters, such as the calling of Levi/Matthew (Mark 2.14 pars.), Peter's denial of Jesus (Mark 14.53-54, 66-72 pars.), and Jesus' burial in the tomb of Joseph of Arimathea (Mark 15.42-47 pars.),[247] may well hold the position that they do within the Jesus tradition because they were particularly dear to or poignant for those named. In like manner the mention that Simon of Cyrene, remembered as the one compelled to carry Jesus' cross, was the father of Alexander and Rufus both strongly implies that Alexander and Rufus were well known in Christian circles and suggests the importance of the episode for them in their own remembering of Jesus.[248]

At this point it may be appropriate to raise the question of why the tradition as a whole has not been attributed to particular teachers, or specifically to the immediate disciples of Jesus. To be sure, two of the four canonical Gospels have traditionally been attributed to two of the twelve (Matthew and John), and the claim deserves respect.[249] But there has evidently been no attempt made within these Gospels themselves (apart, it would appear, from the references to the somewhat mysterious 'beloved disciple' in John's Gospel) to identify the teacher or teachers responsible for the transmission of the tradition making up these Gospels.[250] This suggests that it was the tradition itself which carried the stamp of authority in its face and which did not require to be labelled and attributed. Here we may observe something of a parallel between the early rabbinic traditions and the Jesus tradition. A feature of the former is that while some of the oral tradition is specifically attributed to a named teacher, the majority is anonymous.[251] Here

246. '. . . within the disciple circles it may well have been Bartimaeus's own testimony which provided the initial and enduring form of the tradition' (*Jesus Remembered* 643).

247. *Jesus Remembered* 774 n. 54, 782; also the women at Jesus' tomb (832-34).

248. Bauckham stresses the continuing role of such individuals personally involved in telling and retelling their stories (*Jesus and the Eyewitnesses* ch. 3).

249. See further below, vol. 3. In the meantime I need refer only to M. Hengel, *The Four Gospels and the One Gospel of Jesus Christ* (London: SCM, 2000). On the attribution of the *Gospel of Thomas* to Thomas see Schneemelcher, *NTA* 110-11.

250. Bauckham contests this conclusion (*Jesus and the Eyewitnesses,* particularly chs. 6-7).

251. J. Neusner, *The Rabbinic Traditions about the Pharisees before 70* A.D. (3 vols.; Leiden: Brill, 1971).

The Sources

too, in other words, there may be evidence of the way the Jesus tradition was communicated and passed on from the first. No doubt the first disciples and apostles were authoritative sources for the Jesus tradition. But evidently it was not thought necessary to label this tradition as derived from Peter and that tradition as derived from James, and so on. The anonymity of the early tradition, in other words, does not amount to a refutation of apostolic responsibility for the earliest teaching and narrating of the Jesus tradition but is a reminder that the Jesus tradition was important for the first Christians as *Jesus'* tradition, and not the Jesus tradition of any one apostle or teacher.[252]

This point needs to be borne in mind by those who think that in *Jesus Remembered* I have given too much credit to anonymous groups of disciples and churches for their part in maintaining the vitality of the Jesus tradition in the period prior to its being written down and not enough credit to the apostles.[253] I thought I made it plain in *Jesus Remembered,* however, that the primary sources of the Jesus tradition had to be the first disciples, particularly the twelve ('the teaching of the apostles' — Acts 2.42).[254] And I have no doubt that their fingerprints were all over the earliest forms of the tradition. But I have equally no doubt that as the movement spread, the role of local teachers became equally im-

252. Paul is equally silent on the actual traditions he received from Peter (Gal. 1.18) and fails to attribute the tradition of 1 Cor. 15.3-5/7 to any individual. This is also of a piece, of course, with his failure to attribute Jesus tradition explicitly to Jesus, but in that case he could assume that its status as *Jesus* tradition would have been widely familiar (see further *Jesus Remembered* 183-84).

253. B. Gerhardsson, 'The Secret of the Transmission of the Unwritten Jesus Tradition', *NTS* 51 (2005) 1-18, principally in critique of *Jesus Remembered,* whose 'orality approach' he largely dismisses (18); cf. Gerhardsson's pupil Byrskog, *Story as History,* who in turn has influenced R. Bauckham, 'The Eyewitnesses and the Gospel Tradition', *JSHJ* 1 (2003) 28-60; also *Jesus and the Eyewitnesses.* I respond to both Gerhardsson and Bauckham in 'Eyewitnesses and the Oral Jesus Tradition', *JSHJ* 6 (2008) 85-105. In response to Barnett's somewhat dismissive critique of *Jesus Remembered* (*Birth* 117 n. 27), it should be noted that *diēgēsis* in Luke 1.1 simply refers to 'an orderly description of facts, events or words' and can refer to other than a *written* narrative, including oral recitals (BDAG 245; see further Fitzmyer, *Luke I-IX* 292); the syntax of 1.1-3 does not make clear (despite Barnett 118 n. 28) whether the earlier *diēgēseis* had been written or otherwise. It is precisely against Barnett's assumption — that unless the earliest Jesus tradition was in *writing,* it is lost to us — that the 'oral' thesis of *Jesus Remembered* was developed. (In total antithesis to my thesis, Barnett regards a study 'based on the culture of orality' as effectively closing off 'any pathway to the actual teaching of Jesus' [136].) In discussion of that thesis, it should be recalled that the *given* is the 'same yet different' character of the Synoptic tradition; the issue is not whether teaching and performance, written and oral, are mutually exclusive explanations for this character but what is the best overall explanation.

254. *Jesus Remembered,* particularly 128-33, 239-43; and see further the index entry 'Jesus: impact of'.

portant for the maintaining and shaping of the tradition, at least at the local level. To repeat, presumably the awareness that the tradition was *Jesus'* tradition evidently made it less a matter of consequence who was performing the tradition at any one time.[255]

b. Groupings of Jesus' Teachings

In addition to individual items of tradition we may note again various collections of sayings material:[256]

- beatitudes — Matt. 5.3, 4, 6, 11, 12; Luke 6.20b, 21b, 22, 23
- following Jesus — Matt. 8.19-22; Luke 9.57-62
- the new and the old — Matt. 9.14-17; Mark 2.18-22; Luke 5.33-39
- parables of light and judgment — Mark 4.21-25; Luke 8.16-18[257]
- Jesus and the Baptist — Matt. 11.2-19; Luke 7.18-35[258]
- Jesus and exorcisms — Matt. 12.24-26; Mark 3.22-29; Luke 11.15-26[259]
- the cost of discipleship — Matt. 16.24-27; Mark 8.34-38; Luke 9.23-26[260]
- parables of crisis — Matt. 24.42–25.13; Mark 13.33-37; Luke 12.35-46.[261]

As noted in the passages of *Jesus Remembered* referred to above, the fact that these groupings are far from identical between the written Gospels strongly suggests that the Evangelists have not derived each from single written sources. Rather, the more appropriate inference is that several such collections on particular topics or themes were in circulation (in the repertoires of various apostles and

255. On other criticism of *Jesus Remembered,* particularly that I did not pay attention to contemporary theories of memory, see my 'Social Memory and the Oral Jesus Tradition', in Stuckenbruck et al., eds., *Memory in the Bible and Antiquity* 179-94; also 'On History, Memory and Eyewitnesses: In Response to Bengt Holmberg and Samuel Byrskog', *JSNT* 26 (2004) 473-87.

256. *Jesus Remembered* 246-47. See also U. Wilckens, *Theologie des Neuen Testaments.* Vol. 1: *Geschichte der urchristlichen Theologie* (4 vols.; Neukirchen-Vluyn: Neukirchener, 2003) 1/2.210-29.

257. In *Jesus Remembered* 246 n. 295 I note that the sayings have also been preserved separately in Q material (Matt. 5.15/Luke 11.33; Matt. 10.26/Luke 12.2; Matt. 7.2/Luke 6.38b; Matt. 25.29/Luke 19.26).

258. *Jesus Remembered* 445-46.

259. *Jesus Remembered* 456-57.

260. In *Jesus Remembered* 246 n. 294 I note that the sayings have also been preserved separately in Q material (Matt. 10.38/Luke 14.27; Matt. 10.39/Luke 17.33; Matt. 10.33/Luke 12.9).

261. *Jesus Remembered* 428-29.

church teachers) and that the Evangelists knew different collections or more than one. Here I want to note that such groupings of similar or homogeneous material were made and were preserved in the written Gospels. There is no reason whatsoever to assume that such groupings were made only at the time the Jesus tradition was transcribed, and no reason not to infer that such groupings, as a natural pedagogical technique, were a feature of the oral traditioning process more or less from the first.

c. The Evidence of Early Clusters in Q Material

I assume that we can speak of a recognizable Q collection of Jesus tradition, however clear or unclear are its boundaries, and that it was formulated as the Q collection mainly in the 40s and 50s of the first century.[262] The very character of the Q material, basically a collection of Jesus' teaching, suggests a procedure for retaining the Jesus tradition among the early Christian groups and churches and a process for its transmission. It is not possible to deduce from the recognizable Q material with much confidence the phases of that procedure and process. But it is at least plausible that the procedure and the process were more or less consistent from the first.

As we saw in volume 1, the most influential study of Q in recent years has been that of John Kloppenborg, *The Formation of Q*.[263] Kloppenborg's analysis of the 'sapiential speeches in Q'[264] leads him to the conclusion that 'a collection of sapiential speeches and admonitions was the formative element in Q', a collection 'subsequently augmented by the addition and interpolation of apophthegms and prophetic words which pronounced doom over impenitent Israel'.[265] This 'formative stratum', which can be conveniently designated Q^1, consists of six 'wisdom speeches', 'united not by the themes typical of the main redaction [Q^2], but by paraenetic, hortatory, and instructional concerns'.[266] The six 'wisdom speeches' he lists as:[267]

---

262. See above, *Jesus Remembered* §7.4 (147-60); cf. Allison, *Jesus Tradition in Q* ch. 1.

263. J. S. Kloppenborg, *The Formation of Q: Trajectories in Ancient Wisdom Collections* (Philadelphia: Fortress, 1987); see also his masterful *Excavating Q: The History and Setting of the Sayings Gospel* (Minneapolis: Fortress, 2000).

264. Kloppenborg, *Formation* ch. 5.

265. Kloppenborg, *Formation* 244.

266. Kloppenborg, *Formation* 317; *Excavating Q* 146. I follow the convention of listing the shared Matthew/Luke passages by reference only to the Luke versions.

267. Kloppenborg, *Formation* ch. 5, summarized and amended in *Excavating Q* 146. That six collections of aphoristic sayings lie behind Q was already suggested by D. Zeller, *Die weisheitlichen Mahnsprüche bei den Synoptikern* (Würzburg: Echter, 1977) 191-92 (Q 6.20-23,

1. Q 6.20b-23b, 27-35, 36-45, 46-49;
2. Q 9.57-60, (61-62); 10.2-11, 16, (23-24?);[268]
3. Q 11.2-4, 9-13;
4. Q 12:2-7, 11-12;
5. Q 12.22b-31, 33-34 (13.18-19, 20-21?);[269] and probably
6. Q 13.24; 14.26-27; 17.33; 14.34-35.

I do not want to make much depend on this particular theory, but it hardly stretches historical imagination to deduce that the Q material consists of an aggregation of material already in use and circulation. And Kloppenborg's thesis at least illustrates the sort of thing which must have happened. Kloppenborg himself is clear that 'tradition-history is not convertible with literary history', and that his concern is only with the latter; the judgment that material is redactional, secondary, is a *literary* judgment and need not imply anything about the *historical* origin or emergence of the tradition in view.[270] So he certainly does not wish his analysis necessarily to imply that redactional material from the secondary compositional phase cannot be dominical. And by the same token, it need not follow that material from Q^1 is necessarily the oldest material in the Q tradition. On the other hand, some of the Q material must have been current from the earliest days of the new movement (unless we make the improbable assumption that nothing of Jesus' teaching was remembered by his first disciples). And Kloppenborg's Q^1 passages are as good a sample as any of what that material might have been or included.

In a close study of the Q^1 passages[271] I have argued (1) that the Q^1 material consists of groups of teaching material, clusters of wisdom sayings and exhortations, used by teachers in the early Christian communities in their oral teaching role

31, 36, 43-46; 10.2-8a, 9-11a, 12, 16(?); 11.2-4; 12.2-3, 8-9, 10; Matt. 6.25-33, 19-21; Q 12.35-37(?), 39-40). R. A. Piper, *Wisdom in the Q-tradition: The Aphoristic Teaching of Jesus* (SNTSMS 61; Cambridge: Cambridge University, 1989), identified five aphoristic collections: Q 11.9-13; 12.22-31; 6.37-42; 6.43-45; 12.2-9; to which he added Luke 6.27-36 and 16.9-13.

268. Kloppenborg regards 10.23-24 as part of the secondary redaction of Q, along with 10.21-22 (*Formation* 201-203), but with some qualification (*Excavating Q* 147 n. 63).

269. In 'Jesus and the Parables of Jesus in Q', in R. A. Piper, ed., *The Gospel behind the Gospels: Current Studies on Q* (NovTSupp 75; Leiden: Brill, 1995) 275-319, Kloppenborg suggests that Q 13.18-21 (which was not treated in his analysis of Q^1 in *Formation* 223 n. 214) was perhaps added to Q 12.2-12, 13-14, 16-21, 22-31, 33-34, in the formative layer of Q (311).

270. Kloppenborg, *Formation* 244-45. He has continued to make this point in subsequent writing — most recently 'Discursive Practices in the Sayings Gospel Q and the Quest of the Historical Jesus', in A. Lindemann, ed., *The Sayings Source Q and the Historical Jesus* (Leuven: Leuven University, 2001) 149-90.

271. Dunn, 'Q^1 as Oral Tradition', in M. Bockmuehl and D. A. Hagner, eds., *The Written Gospel*, G. N. Stanton FS (Cambridge: Cambridge University, 2005) 45-69.

within these communities; (2) that the use made of this material by Matthew and Luke attests the flexible or variable character of the oral tradition used in such teaching — hence the difficulty which the compilers of the Q document have typically experienced in reconstructing the Q text for this material;[272] and (3) it is very unlikely that the Q[1] material formed a coherent unit or single collection used as such in the several communities which we can assume to have been familiar with it.

For example, the material in the first group identified by Kloppenborg forms the core of what is generally known as *the sermon on the plain* (the Q equivalent or portion of Matthew's sermon on the mount):

- Matt. 5.3-6, 11-12/Luke 6.20b-23b/*GTh* 54, 68, 69
- Matt. 5.39-47; 7.12/Luke 6.27-35/*Did.* 1.3-5
- Matt. 7.16; 12.35/Luke 6.43-45/*GTh* 45
- Matt. 5.48; 7.1-5; 10.24/Luke 6.36-42/*GTh* 26, 34
- Matt. 7.21, 24-27/Luke 6.46-49.

One can easily envisage this material as typical of the clusters of Jesus' teaching held within a teacher's portfolio — a group of beatitudes, two groups of sayings about attitudes to others (response to hostility, and criticizing others), aphorisms about character and conduct, and the parable of the wise and foolish house builders. At the same time, the fact that the material is ordered differently in Matthew and Luke, that some of the material is retained by Matthew outside the sermon on the mount (Matt. 10.24; 12.35), and that other material has not been retained in the *Gospel of Thomas,* is a reminder of how flexible was the use of such teaching material in oral performance.[273]

The concern for *discipleship and mission,* a concern which was probably characteristic of the Nazarene sect from the first, makes a natural second cluster:

- Matt. 8.19-22/Luke 9.57-62
- Matt. 9.37-38; 10.7-16/Luke 10.2-11/*GTh* 14, 39, 73
- Matt. 10.40/Luke 10.16/John 13.20.

The fact that Mark 6.7-13 constitutes a variant and overlapping mission commission again reminds us that such material was by no means set in stone but was probably taken up and rehearsed in various permutations in different missionary situations.[274]

---

272. J. M. Robinson, P. Hoffmann, and J. S. Kloppenborg, eds., *The Critical Edition of Q* (The International Q Project; Leuven: Peeters, 2000).

273. See also Allison, *Jesus Tradition in Q* 79-95.

274. It is commonly deduced that the two commissions in Luke 9.1-5 and 10.1-12 re-

Equally natural would it have been for early teachers to cherish Jesus' instruction on *prayer:*

- Matt. 6.9-13/Luke 11.2-4
- Matt. 7.7-11/Luke 11.9-13;

Jesus' *encouragement to fearless confession:*

- Matt. 10.26-31/Luke 12.2-7
- Matt. 10.19-20/Luke 12.11-12/Mark 13.11/John 14.26;

and Jesus' teaching on the *right priorities:*

- Matt. 6.25-33/Luke 12.22-31/*GTh* 36
- Matt. 6.19-21/Luke 12.33-34.

But Kloppenborg's final cluster can hardly be cited as evidence of a cluster prior to Q (Q 13.24; 14.26-27; 17.33; 14.34-35).

Again I should perhaps stress that such material cannot be definitely identified as very early Christian clusters of Jesus tradition, but it is the sort of material which could have been expected to feature in the repertoire of Christian apostles and teachers from the first. And to the extent that such clusters can be identified as clusters already in use and circulation prior to the more elaborate collection we know as Q, to that extent at least we have evidence of the sort of teaching material which presumably constituted significant portions of the teaching of the earliest Christian groups and churches. Not only so, but here again it may be important to note that the tradition is not attributed to any named teacher but was evidently drawn from what in effect must have been the common (but in varied formats) store of many churches from the first.

d. The Evidence of Pre-Markan Material

By common agreement the other earliest and written formation of the Jesus tradition is the Gospel of Mark.[275] Here too, and still more plausibly, we can talk of pre-Markan material on which Mark evidently drew in composing his Gospel. In so saying I by no means intend to imply that Mark was merely a collector of pre-

---

flect two different settings, the latter perhaps the broader perspective of Jesus' mission commission reformulated for a more extensive mission to Gentiles. See also *Jesus Remembered* 247.

275. See again *Jesus Remembered* 143-46.

formed material. Not at all. The composition and theology of the Gospel of Mark will be a subject for later analysis.[276] But it is no denigration of Mark's authorship to recognize that he was able to and did edit earlier material. Here too I have no illusions that this material can be extracted with full confidence as to its content and extent. As already noted, redaction criticism of Mark — that is, disentangling Mark's editorial contributions from his inherited material — is extraordinarily difficult.[277] Whereas with Matthew and Luke we have Mark as a source, and therefore the clear possibility of comparing source with edited source, in the case of Mark we have to distinguish Markan source from Markan redaction in the same document. And there are few reliable criteria for recognizing Markan redaction which can be applied across the sweep of Mark's Gospel. Nevertheless it is inherently likely that Mark did draw on pre-formed material, and it is worth looking at some examples which have been suggested.

In fact, I have already indicated an outline of the pre-formed material on which Mark possibly drew.[278] So, as with the proposed Q^1 material, we may well be able to gain some more insight into how the Jesus tradition was handled in the earliest days of the Jesus movement.

- 1.21-38   Twenty-four hours in the ministry of Jesus
- 2.1–3.6   Jesus in controversy in Galilee
- 4.2-33   Parables of Jesus
- 4.35–5.43; 6.32-52   Miracles of Jesus round the lake
- 10.2-31   Marriage, children and discipleship
- 12.13-37   Jesus in controversy in Jerusalem
- 13.1-32   The little apocalypse
- 14.1–15.47   The passion narrative.

Mark 2.1–3.6 provides a good example of how one of the twelve or an early disciple may have grouped a number of *controversy stories* together to form a dramatic sequence culminating in a plot to destroy Jesus (3.6).[279] Such a cluster of five stories could serve as a teaching performance to instruct new Christians on how Jesus responded to attacks and thus to provide them with an example of how they should respond in similar circumstances. The sequence probably documents an early heightening of christological interest, with em-

276. See below, vol. 3.

277. *Jesus Remembered* 155.

278. *Jesus Remembered* 247, where I refer particularly (n. 300) to H. W. Kuhn, *Ältere Sammlungen im Markusevangelium* (Göttingen: Vandenhoeck und Ruprecht, 1971).

279. See also my 'Mark 2.1–3.6: A Bridge between Jesus and Paul on the Question of the Law', *NTS* 30 (1984) 395-415, reprinted in my *Jesus, Paul and the Law* (London: SPCK, 1990) 10-31, with additional notes (32-36).

phasis on the authority of the Son of Man (2.10, 28), now seen as a title (but 'Son of Man' did not become established as a title in ongoing christological reflection).[280] It highlights Jesus' relation to 'sinners' (2.15-17), language which had resonance only in Jewish circles.[281] It indicates some no doubt early confusion on the question whether Christians should continue to fast (2.18-20).[282] And it reflects a situation where the Sabbath was still seen as important and where the issue was not *whether* but *how* to observe the Sabbath (2.23–3.5); in other words, the story evidently took its present shape within a Palestinian situation and before observance of holy days became an issue (Gal. 4.10; Rom. 14.5; Col. 2.16).[283] There is no reason, then, why the cluster may not have been put into its present sequence within the first ten years of the life of the Jesus movement.

As already suggested above (§21.5b), *parables of Jesus* were obvious teaching material in the first Christian communities. Mark 4.2-33 appears to be a collection of such parables which Mark has fitted into his narrative, first by setting the scene, as he liked to do, beside the sea (4.1), and finally by rounding the collection off with an allusion to his secrecy motif (4.34).[284] We may even be able to detect how the collection of parables was developed in successive performances over the years before Mark became aware of it. In what follows I offer one possible scenario:

• The early phase of the collection consisted of simply two or three parables about seeds and growth: the sower (vv. 3-8), the seed growing secretly (vv. 26-29) and the mustard seed (vv. 30-32); they would have been attracted to each other by their obvious thematic and verbal links. Q attests a different collection (Matt. 13.31-33/Luke 13.18-21), on which Matthew and Luke were able to draw.[285]

• At some point an interpretation became an established attachment to the parable of the sower (vv. 13-20). That the interpretation emerged within the traditioning process is generally accepted, since the vocabulary is char-

---

280. 'Mark 2.1–3.6' 26; *Jesus Remembered* 737-39, and review of the never-ending debate (734-36).

281. *Jesus Remembered* 528-32.

282. Whatever the earliest Christian practice (Mark 2.18-19 pars.), *Did.* 8.1 shows that fasting was resumed as a typically Christian discipline (as Mark 2.20 pars. and Matt. 6.16-18 also imply).

283. 'Mark 2.1–3.6' 21-23.

284. It is noticeable that Matthew omits v. 34, as he does vv. 26-29, often a sign of Matthew's awareness of Markan redaction; see further my 'Matthew's Awareness of Markan Redaction', in Van Segbroeck et al., eds., *The Four Gospels* 3.1349-59.

285. See *Jesus Remembered* 462-64.

acteristically Christian.[286] And that it became part of the parable collection
earlier than vv. 10-12 is likely, since v. 13 refers directly back to the parable of the sower ('this parable'), whereas v. 10 broadens out the discussion
to parables in general ('the parables').

- The short parabolic sayings (vv. 21-22, 24-25) were probably used independently, since, as we have noted (above, n. 257), the matching Q material is scattered through Matthew and Luke. But at some point they were
  drawn in to make a larger collection of parables.
- Possibly the collection was rounded off at a pre-Markan stage by adding an
  introduction (v. 2) and conclusion (v. 33).
- V. 9 ('He who has ears to hear, let him hear') is an example of a characteristic saying of Jesus which seems to have been dropped somewhat randomly, or perhaps better, spontaneously, into performances of Jesus tradition, but without always gaining an established place within particular
  repertoires; in this case it is repeated at v. 23, though not by Matthew and
  Luke.[287]
- Apart from the further introduction and conclusion (vv. 1, 34), the indications of Mark's own hand are probably clearest in the addition of vv. 10-12,
  to provide a (Markan) theory of parables.[288]

To make the point again: I do not offer this as a firm proposal of the composition-
history of Mark 4.1-34. My thesis is of several teaching occasions in the different
groups and churches of early disciples where the collections and clusters of like
material (in this case parables) were varied in content and use from performance
to performance. What I do propose is (1) that collections of like material were
probably a feature of the earliest Christian teaching from the first, (2) that the
collections would have been varied and overlapping from church to church,
(3) that the aggregating of such teaching material into larger repertoires was
probably inevitable, and some of these repertoires probably became fairly firmly
established over the sort of period in view in this volume (30-40 years), and
(4) that Mark was able to draw on one of these in composing his Gospel. There is
no good reason to conclude that the pre-Markan collection was already in written
form at any stage in its composition history.

Similarly, it is to be expected that apostles and teachers would gather to-

286. Particularly 'the word', which is hardly characteristic of Jesus' own language in the
Jesus tradition, but which is used eight times in 4.13-20. See further *Jesus Remembered* 492-93
n. 16.

287. See again *Jesus Remembered* 462 n. 379.

288. That is not to imply that vv. 11-12 could not have been words of Jesus remembered
by his disciples (*Jesus Remembered* 493-96); as Kloppenborg has noted more than once, literary history is not the same as tradition history (above, n. 270).

gether, into what today would be a single folder, a collection of *stories of Jesus' miracle-working power*. It would seem that here too Mark could draw on such a collection:

- the stilling of the storm (4.35-41)
- the healing of the Gerasene demoniac (5.1-20)
- the healing/raising of Jairus's daughter (5.21-43)
- the feeding of the five thousand (6.32-44)
- Jesus walks on the water (6.45-52).

They are all thematically linked (Jesus' power over a range of life-threatening forces); they are chronologically linked as a sequence of to and fro crossings of the lake by boat;[289] and the collection is framed at beginning and end by miracles which actually take place on the lake itself. Again it is not necessary to argue that this must have been a pre-Markan collection, in whole or in part, but such a hypothesis makes good sense of the evidence available to us, and it is the sort of thing which, *a priori,* we would have expected. In Mark the summary of 6.53-56 rounds off the sequence, though it is less evident that the paragraph was part of the earlier collection.

Such data (a collection of miracle stories) have been taken as evidence of a miracle source available to Mark which was concerned to present Jesus primarily, or possibly even exclusively, as a miracle worker. From this it can then be argued that among the early respondents to Jesus there were groups/communities which regarded Jesus primarily, or possibly exclusively, as a miracle worker, a *theios anēr* ('divine man'), in the language of the thesis being argued. Mark can then be presented as seeking to correct the divine-man christology by presenting Jesus as the suffering Son of Man.[290] The thesis itself is matter for volume 3. Here I simply need to recall the critique of the 'Q community', and of the 'one document per community' fallacy already offered in volume 1.[291] In my view it is simply fanciful to deduce the character of a group or church solely from a *single* hypothetical document or collection of material, and almost equally unacceptable to assume that such a group/church possessed only *one* document or collection of traditions concerning Jesus. In complete contrast, it is highly plausible to see here evidence of a straightforward collection of miracle stories, grouped together for pedagogical convenience and providing only one part of a

289. Note the repetition of *eis to peran,* 'to the other side', in 4.35; 5.1, 21; 6.45.

290. E.g., H. Koester, 'One Jesus and Four Primitive Gospels', in J. M. Robinson and H. Koester, *Trajectories through Early Christianity* (Philadelphia: Fortress, 1971) 158-204 (here 187-93).

291. *Jesus Remembered* 149-52.

much richer repertoire of Jesus tradition drawn on by apostles and teachers in their preaching and teaching.

To cite one other example briefly from the pre-Markan material, the so-called little apocalypse (ch. 13) probably provides evidence of how Jesus' forebodings in regard to the Temple were the subject of considerable reflection among the first disciple groups and communities[292] and how the material was reworked not a few times in face of the various threats and challenges which confronted the Jews of Palestine in the decades prior to the Jewish revolt of 66-70/73. One threat which must certainly have resonated with the talk of 'the desolating sacrilege set up where it ought not to be' (13.14) was the crisis provoked by the decision of Emperor Gaius Caligula to have a statue of himself erected in the Jerusalem Temple, less than ten years after Jesus' death.[293] Mark's record includes the sort of interjection into the retelling of the Jesus tradition at this point ('let the reader understand') which was very likely to have been a feature of Christian teaching in the face of such a horrific prospect.

In short, such material in Mark is not best explained on the hypothesis that Mark took over (or collected) material which was previously unco-ordinated and known only in small units. Even if Papias's account of Mark putting into order Peter's preaching/teaching is only one possible explanation,[294] it is still highly likely that at the very least Mark was able to draw on the repertoires of more than one teacher, and that such repertoires contained various collections of Jesus tradition, which could be disaggregated to choose an appropriate aphorism or story, or combined with other material as was appropriate to the occasion. That some of this was already in writing is quite possible, but the data themselves, as used by the three Synoptic Evangelists in diverse patterns and differing locations, suggest more the flexibility of oral tradition and varied performance.

e. Indications of Narrative Interest

Finally, should we assume that the apostles and first teachers of the Jesus tradition performed the tradition only in thematic collections (or individual items)? The earliest form critics took over the findings of K. L. Schmidt that chronologi-

292. See *Jesus Remembered* 417-19.

293. Referred to briefly in *Jesus Remembered* 296. For the belief that Mark 13.14 was inspired by the Caligula affair, see the bibliography in G. R. Beasley-Murray, *Jesus and the Last Days: The Interpretation of the Olivet Discourse* (Peabody: Hendrickson, 1993) 415 n. 111 (and further 407-16); Barnett, *Birth* 35-36; and particularly G. Theissen, *The Gospels in Context: Social and Political History in the Synoptic Tradition* (ET Minneapolis: Fortress, 1991) 151-65. See also below, §26.5a.

294. See *Jesus Remembered* 44 n. 90, 146 and 223 n. 216.

cal and topographical references in Mark were the contribution of Mark himself. From this they deduced that the earliest Christians had no biographical interest in Jesus.[295] However justified this particular finding was in its own terms, it was too quickly understood to imply that the first Christian tradents had no narrative interest in Jesus' mission and that Mark was the first to give the tradition a narrative flow.

Once again, however, a thesis based on some evidence was in danger of being driven across the evidence as a whole and pushed into historical implausibility. For it is simply implausible to assume (or deduce from such evidence) that the first Christians had no interest in the character and mission of the one after whom they became named (Christ-people). The evidence already considered of the circulation and use of the Jesus tradition prior to its transcription is evidence sufficient to the contrary. But again we have to ask whether there was any narrative interest in Jesus' life and mission. Was there concern to tell the Jesus tradition as a story or stories about Jesus, with the character of a story, a beginning, middle and end, plot and characterization? Common sense (awareness that human curiosity is universal) strongly suggests a positive answer. Because the Jesus tradition comes down to us in the narrative form provided by Mark and his successors, it is harder to document earlier narrative interest than we might have expected. But there are some indications. I have touched on the passages which I have in mind at various points in *Jesus Remembered,* so again it may be sufficient simply to list them:

- John the Baptist as the beginning of Jesus' mission (Mark 1.1)[296]
- twenty-four hours in the life of Jesus (Mark 1.21-38)
- growing opposition to Jesus (Mark 2.1–3.6)
- a succession of miracles round the sea (Mark 4.35–5.43; 6.32-52)
- mission to the regions beyond Lower Galilee (Mark 7.24-37; 8.27-30)
- journey from Galilee to Jerusalem (Mark 10.1, 32, 46)
- the final week/passion narrative (Mark 11–15).

Some of these indicators can, of course, be attributed to Mark. But others are either well embedded in the body of the tradition or shared with other versions of the tradition. And in any case, does the evidence oblige us to deduce that in providing such narrative indicators Mark was introducing a completely unprecedented innovation? I think not. Rather, Mark is better portrayed as a performer of Jesus tradition, in the sequence of teachers and tradents from whom he derived

---

295. See further *Jesus Remembered* 74-75.

296. *Jesus Remembered* 352-55; 'Altering the Default Setting' 174 = *New Perspective on Jesus* 124.

and with whom he shared so much of that tradition. Mark's is, of course, a very sophisticated performance in comparison with his predecessors, and as a *written* performance it has endured. But there is sufficient reason to conclude alternatively that much of the earlier forms and performances of the Jesus tradition expressed a similar, if less well-developed, narrative interest. All the world loves a good story. And the story of Jesus, his mission, teaching and miracles, must have been a major part of the tradition with which apostles endowed new church foundations and probably provided a degree of narrative framework within which teachers in these churches could retain and recount the Jesus tradition as circumstances occasioned.

In sum, the Jesus tradition, even in the developed written form in which it has come down to us, provides a further contribution to our knowledge of the earliest Christian groups and churches. It is true, of course, that the overview just conducted carries us well across the full sweep of thirty to forty years before the Jesus tradition was substantially put into writing. My whole argument, however, is that the process indicated in this section did not begin only late in the day but was a feature of the use made of the Jesus tradition throughout the first generation of Christianity. To be more specific: we can tell from the Synoptic tradition (1) *that* the first Christians must have mediated the tradition which stems from Jesus' mission and ended in the Synoptic Gospels (so it must have been important to them), (2) something of *how* they remembered Jesus and made use of the Jesus tradition (the forms and clusters), and (3) *what* they derived from the memory of Jesus that was important for their living, witness and worship. As suggested by Moule's analysis, this last evidently included material for prayer, teaching on discipleship and priorities, edifying stories and challenging parables, content for preaching and evangelism, and instruction and example for dealing with the questions, controversies and challenges with which they must have been confronted.[297]

21.6. Conclusion — and a Note on Procedure

The prospect of gaining well-grounded historical insights into the beginnings of Christianity prior to the impact made by Paul is often regarded as minimal. And it is true both that external sources tell us hardly anything and that a superficial view of Acts can lead to much too inflated expectations. But we have also seen that the Acts of the Apostles is likely to provide more reliable historical data than the previously dominant theology-and-therefore-not-history school of NT schol-

---

297. On the issue of (an)other stream(s) of Jesus tradition than those which flowed into the Gospel tradition, see below, §22.1b.

arship has been willing to recognize. Even the speeches which Luke has put in the mouths of his characters have given strong evidence of pre-Lukan and probably primitive detail. And we are not dependent on Luke's Acts alone. For it is not hard to push beneath the surface of Paul's letters to uncover references and allusions to a wide range of material which he inherited and which attests facets of Christianity's earliest history partly confirmed and partly contested by Luke. Nor should we forget the stream of Jesus tradition which evidently ran alongside the Lukan and pre-Pauline sources but which presumably was largely taken for granted by both, since Acts and the Pauline letters were not in the business of passing it on as such.

All told, then, the sources for the second phase of *Christianity in the Making,* including its first decade or two, are more robust than we might have imagined at the beginning of this chapter, and we can embark on Part Seven with good prospects.

First, however, a note on procedure. The opening chapters of *Beginning from Jerusalem* have followed the pattern of Parts One and Two of the first volume — including a review of 'the quest for the historical church' and an analysis of the sources and character of the tradition available to us for the period 30-70. At this point, however, I change tack to some degree. For in *Jesus Remembered* I took some pains to fill out the historical context of Jesus' mission (§9) before proceeding to a study of the mission of Jesus itself. It is tempting to do the same at this, the equivalent point of volume 2. In that case I would have attempted to provide an overview of the political, social and religious contexts within which earliest Christianity began to make its way, including some description of the western Jewish diaspora, the main cities where Christianity became established (Jerusalem, Antioch, Ephesus, Corinth, Rome), the social conditions of the first Christians, and the main philosophical and religious competition which they faced.[298]

That is not the course I intend to pursue, however. Ever since I first conceived the project, now underway as *Christianity in the Making,* I found myself returning again and again to an observation which I recall being made years ago by Edwin Judge, in regard to the genre of 'New Testament history'.[299] Such histories, Judge observed, give the modern reader a 'bird's-eye view' of the period under review. They enable the reader to know what was happening in Rome at the same time as something else was happening in Jerusalem. They can cross-

---

298. Following the lead, e.g., of H. Koester, *Introduction to the New Testament.* Vol. 1: *History, Culture and Religion of the Hellenistic Age;* vol. 2: *History and Literature of Early Christianity* (Berlin: de Gruyter, 1980; ET Philadelphia: Fortress, 1982).

299. Judge was referring, I think, primarily to Bruce's *New Testament History.*

reference events later as well as earlier than the events described. They can draw on writings, scrolls and inscriptions which might have been totally unknown to the actors in the narrative they were relating. They can view events from different historical perspectives. The problem is that by so doing they prevent the reader from entering *inside* the historical processes being described. The reader becomes like the audience of a melodrama, who can see the danger threatening the hero and heroine when they themselves are oblivious to it. Or like the person watching the video recording of a crucial football match full of tension and excitement who, because he knows the outcome of the match, can never really enter into the finger-gnawing anxieties of those who saw the match 'live'. So with a history of early Christianity, where it is already well known that Christianity was going to triumph and become the state religion of the Roman Empire, how can the reader enter adequately into the uncertainties and fears of the first Christians?

To achieve a history of Christianity's beginnings truly 'from inside' is, of course, impossible. Twenty-first-century readers cannot abstract themselves from their own history in order to look at an earlier portion of history with complete objectivity. What can be done, however, is to attempt to operate so far as possible *within the horizons* of the first Christians themselves, to hold ourselves as unaware of what was happening outside Palestine as the first disciples, to enter with Paul into Ephesus or Rome as for the first time, to overhear the first believers reflecting on the significance of Jesus the Christ without knowing where it was going to end, and so on. I admit that the attempt is hazardous, perhaps foolhardy. As noted above, I made a first venture down this road in my earlier *Christology in the Making* and was rather disappointed that my attempt to carry through my analysis with a view to the 'historical context of meaning' of key terms, and the fact that their horizon of meaning was in process of being pushed back ('conceptuality in transition'), was not more appreciated.[300] But I still believe the attempt is worthwhile and cherish the hope of enabling readers to experience something of Christianity in the making 'from inside' the historical process, with something of the existential excitement of a living experience, and not simply the clinical interest of a historical or theological pathologist. It is the chief reason why I have taken the risk of using a similar title for these volumes — *Christology in the Making* and *Christianity in the Making* — since my primary interest is to appreciate more fully the process of 'coming to be' in both cases.

In consequence, my procedure will be to 'set the scene' for each stage of the new movement as we come to it. For example, rather than describe diaspora Judaism straight away, it is more appropriate to let the reality of diaspora Judaism impinge little by little on us, in a faint reflection of how that reality must have increasingly impinged on the earliest disciples (§§24, 27, 29). Likewise,

300. See above, §20 n. 4.

Paul's extension of his mission to Corinth is the appropriate place to provide a description of what he would have seen and experienced there (§31). In effect, what might have been a large chapter on 'The Historical Context' will be broken up and its items treated severally so far as is necessary to understand better the developments which were taking place at each stage of development. By so doing my hope is that the shock and surprise of many of these developments will become more apparent, and we will be the better able to appreciate the boldness of those who ventured into what was for them an uncertain future. In §20.1 I have already indicated something of the problem: when did 'Christianity' begin? can we use a title or descriptor which is historically more accurate? Our task now, so far as possible, is to live through the making and coming to be of Christianity, to see how 'Christianity' gained the content of that title and what its character in thus coming to be was — and is.

PART SEVEN

THE FIRST PHASE

CHAPTER 22

Beginning in Jerusalem

22.1. One Community or Several?

How did Christianity, or infant Christianity, first emerge? At first sight the answer seems straightforward: Luke's account in the first few chapters of Acts tells the story of the beginnings of the church in Jerusalem, and that church is the beginning of a new religion, the mother church of Christianity. On the information provided by Luke we can even date the birth of the church to a specific day and even time — the feast of Pentecost, fifty days after the Passover at which Jesus was crucified, just before nine o'clock in the morning (Acts 2.1, 15)!

However, the matter is not so straightforward as Luke's beguiling portrayal suggests. There are two main considerations.

a. Cautionary Tales from the History of Religions

We cannot begin with the assumption that Christianity is unique in its emergence as a religious force in the world. The fact is that first beginnings are typically much more confused and complicated than later devotees of the religion or movement usually like to acknowledge. Since Christianity emerged from within the matrix of the long-established Second Temple Judaism, the nearest parallels in this case are probably the development of new denominations within Christianity itself. The emergence of the Reformation in the sixteenth century, of Methodism in the eighteenth, and of Pentecostalism in the twentieth all share features with the first appearance of infant Christianity as being a renewal movement within a larger parent body (or tradition) which grew to become independent of its parent.[1]

---

1. The 'parent bodies' in the first two cases are obvious — the Western mediaeval (Ro-

But in each case the emergence was far from straightforward, and what emerged is hard to describe as a single entity.

So far as the emergence of Protestantism is concerned, it is not only the somewhat divergent tracks of Lutheranism and the Reformed churches that we have to trace. Also to be included are Anglicanism (the Reformation in England), Congregationalists, Anabaptists and other more radical reformers, and such precursors as the Hussites in Bohemia and the Waldensians in Italy, not to mention the Brethren of the Common Life in the Netherlands. As regards the emergence of Methodism, consideration has to be given to George Whitefield as well as the Wesley brothers, to the Countess of Huntingdon's Connexion, the Methodist New Connexion and the early development of the Primitive Methodist tradition. And then there are evangelical sympathizers who remained within the Church of England, and the development of episcopal Methodism in the United States. So far as Pentecostalism is concerned, its emergence cannot be traced simply to the Pentecost-like revival at Azusa Street in Los Angeles in 1906. The Assemblies of God can look back to that beginning, but the Church of God (Cleveland) has a different story of beginnings, and the Pentecostal Holiness tradition different again. In Britain, as well as the Assemblies of God, we have the Elim Pentecostal churches and the Apostolic Church, each with their own account of their origins.[2]

One might wonder, therefore, without being overly suspicious, whether Luke's presentation of a single day and place of origin for the whole of what was to follow (Christianity) is the consequence of his looking back at these origins through rose-tinted spectacles. Or, more culpably, perhaps he has adopted a partisan stance, giving exclusive attention to what was a much messier and more fragmented beginning. Possibly even his narrative has a polemical edge, not simply to affirm the beginning in Jerusalem, but also, by deliberate silence on the subject, to deny that there was any other source or origin for the movement whose origins and initial expansion he has set out to describe.

Such speculation is intended simply to remind readers that they may be approaching the evidence regarding Christianity's beginnings with assumptions which need to be examined, to indicate possibilities which cannot be excluded *a priori,* and to help open ears and eyes to all the implications and overtones which the evidence may contain. In the opening section of the whole work[3] I recalled Walter Bauer's challenge to the traditional view, that the earliest forms of Christianity in various major Mediterranean centres had been uniformly 'orthodox',

---

man) Catholic Church and the Church of England. In the third case we should speak rather of the more diffuse Holiness movement of the nineteenth century in North America.

2. Since the last of the three examples may be less well known, I need cite only W. J. Hollenweger, *The Pentecostals* (London: SCM, 1972), and V. Synan, *The Holiness-Pentecostal Movement in the United States* (Grand Rapids: Eerdmans, 1971, [2]1997).

3. *Jesus Remembered* §1.

and that 'heresy' had always appeared later as a corruption of the pure original. Bauer argued to the contrary that the earliest forms of Christianity had been much more of a 'mixed bag' than had previously been thought. 'Orthodoxy', he maintained, was the faction which won, and which had succeeded in superimposing its account of Christian origins by blotting out all memory and record of alternative accounts.[4] Without assuming that Bauer's argument is correct — it has been subjected to considerable criticism[5] — the fact that there is such an argument to be had regarding Christianity in the second century should be a warning to us that we cannot rule out the propriety of a similar discussion in regard to the emergence of Christianity in the first century.

b. Hints within the New Testament

In present-day scholarship on the beginnings of Christianity a major and well-regarded hypothesis postulates the existence of a community of Jesus' followers who continued to exist in Galilee through the 40s and 50s, and who maintained a memory of Jesus and of his teaching which was quite independent of the traditions that go to make up Mark's Gospel, climaxing as it does with Jesus' passion. This is the so-called Q community which we met in §7 of *Jesus Remembered* — the argument being that the Q material, focusing as it does on Jesus' teaching but lacking a passion narrative, attests a community which saw Jesus only as a teacher of wisdom and saw nothing of the significance in Jesus' death which Mark attributes to it. I have already indicated that I find this hypothesis almost entirely unconvincing.[6] The assumption that a community knew or possessed only *one* document or type of Jesus tradition is already far-fetched (did they choose to ignore traditions of Jesus' doings and to cherish only traditions of Jesus' teaching?). Even more far-fetched is the assumption that this document

---

4. W. Bauer, *Rechtgläubigkeit und Ketzerei im ältesten Christentum* (1934, [2]1964), ET *Orthodoxy and Heresy in Earliest Christianity* (Philadelphia: Fortress, 1971). See also Wilken, *Myth*. For a stimulating reposing of the 'orthodoxy/heresy' issue from the Jewish side, see D. Boyarin, *Border Lines: The Partition of Judaeo-Christianity* (Philadelphia: University of Pennsylvania, 2004).

5. See, e.g., T. A. Robinson, *The Bauer Thesis Examined: The Geography of Heresy in the Early Christian Church* (Lewiston: Mellen, 1988).

6. See also the critique of A. J. Hultgren, *The Rise of Normative Christianity* (Minneapolis: Fortress, 1994) 31-41. My criticism extends to J. Schröter, 'Jerusalem und Galiläa. Überlegungen zur Verhältnisbestimmung von Pluralität und Kohärenz für die Konstruktion einer Geschichte des frühen Christentums', *NovT* 42 (2000) 127-59, though his concluding description of 'plurality within a coherence' (159) is a welcome advance on Koester's finding that 'the mission and expansion of Christianity in the first years and decades after the death of Jesus was a phenomenon that utterly lacked unity' (*Introduction* 2.94).

defines the community and that the community's character and distinguishing emphases can be read from this one document. The hypothesis becomes increasingly fanciful when we recall that the extent and content of Q are open to considerable debate, not to mention the lack of clarity as to when the Q material was put into writing. I remain of the view that the best explanation of Jesus tradition which bears a strongly Galilean stamp and which displays little or no sign of a passion-oriented perspective is that it took its present form already during Jesus' Galilee mission.[7]

All that being said, however, the advocates of a Q community are not the only ones in twentieth-century scholarship who hypothesized the existence of an ongoing Galilean community independent of Jerusalem.[8] Not least to be considered is the strange silence regarding a continuing presence of disciples of Jesus in Galilee; the only reference to the 'church . . . of Galilee' appears in Acts 9.31. One would have thought that the impact made by Jesus among the villages of Galilee would have had a more lasting effect than that one mention seems to indicate.[9] Could it be, then, that there is something more to the 'Q community in Galilee' hypothesis than I have allowed? Could it be that Acts and the other NT writers draw a veil of silence over the 'Christianity' of Galilee because the lasting effect of Jesus' mission in Galilee itself took a form which Luke and others in the mainstream chose not to record? Broadening the issue, should Bauer's argument about the in-

7. See *Jesus Remembered* §7.4; also *New Perspective on Jesus* 26-28. See also M. Frenschkowski, 'Galiläa oder Jerusalem? Die topographischen und politischen Hintergründe der Logienquelle', in Lindemann, ed., *The Sayings Source Q and the Historical Jesus* 535-59; B. A. Pearson, 'A Q Community in Galilee?', *NTS* 50 (2004) 476-94.

8. E. Lohmeyer, *Galiläa und Jerusalem* (Göttingen: Vandenhoeck und Ruprecht, 1936); L. E. Elliott-Binns, *Galilean Christianity* (London: SCM, 1956) 43-53; W. Schmithals, *Paul and James* (1963; London: SCM, 1965): 'Not Jerusalem, but Galilee is the home of Christianity' (33); L. Schenke, *Die Urgemeinde. Geschichtliche und theologische Entwicklung* (Stuttgart: Kohlhammer, 1990), envisages little groups of Jesus' disciples scattered over the whole of Palestine which after Easter formed the first 'Christian' communities (23; and further chs. 9-10). The earlier response to such theses is already clear in Weiss: 'Contrary to the popular view, "the Galilean tradition" must be looked upon as a product of fantasy' (*Earliest Christianity* 1.18); L. Goppelt, *Apostolic and Post-Apostolic Times* (London: Black, 1970), summed up the debate bluntly: 'There was no "Galilean Church" which developed its own tradition different from that of Jerusalem' (22); M. Hengel and A. M. Schwemer, *Paul between Damascus and Antioch* (London: SCM, 1997): 'It is a misuse of the form-critical approach on the basis of the Gospels to invent as the founders of the mission to the Gentiles post-Easter Galilean communities which were particularly active in mission after Easter' (30-31).

9. Rabbinic traditions refer to *minim* ('heretics') in Galilean settings, which probably at least include Christians (Christian Jews); see the documentation and discussion in R. T. Herford, *Christianity in Talmud and Midrash* (London: Williams and Norgate, 1903). But though they were still (a contested) part of the Jewish communities, there is no way of knowing whether they originated in Jesus' original mission or only later. I will return to the issue in vol. 3.

choate diversity of the origin of second-century Christianity be pushed more firmly back into the first century, as James Robinson and Helmut Koester attempted to do by tracing different 'trajectories' back into the NT writings themselves?[10] The agenda pursued by Burton Mack is an extreme example of the same logic.[11]

The plot thickens a little more when we recall hints elsewhere within the NT that other groups were known about, groups which identified themselves by reference to Jesus but did not recognize their own origins in Jerusalem. I think particularly of the curious little episode recalled in Mark 9.38-40/Luke 9.49-50 — someone who performed exorcisms 'in the name of Jesus' but who 'did not follow with us'. The episode is set within Jesus' ministry, which I see no reason to question. But was it also retained and recycled as guidance for the first Christians when they in turn were confronted by followers of Jesus who 'did not follow with us'? Then there are the equally curious episodes recorded in Acts 18.24–19.7. First, Apollos, who 'had been instructed in the way of the Lord' but knew only the baptism of John, and who needed to be instructed 'more accurately' (18.25-26). How could that have been so for someone belonging to a mainstream which flowed only through the Jerusalem Pentecost? And then the twelve 'disciples', who also knew only the baptism of John, but who had 'not even heard that there is a Holy Spirit' (19.2-3), let alone about Pentecost. Where did such disciples come from? In what sense were they 'disciples' if they knew so little?[12] Others speculate whether the troubles which confronted Paul in Corinth and elsewhere are to be traced not to non-Christian sources but rather to variant Christian sources.[13] But sufficient cause to doubt whether Luke is telling us the whole story in the Acts has already been indicated. And it gains some strength from the earlier observations regarding Luke's willingness to draw a veil over some of the less savoury episodes in the history which he has chosen to relate.[14]

Above all, perhaps, are the indications within Luke's own account of the earliest days in Jerusalem that he is giving a somewhat selective and slanted account. But this deserves closer examination.

---

10. Robinson and Koester, *Trajectories,* especially the essays by Koester — '*Gnōmai Diaphoroi:* The Origin and Nature of Diversification in the History of Early Christianity' (reprinted from *HTR* 58 [1965] 279-318) and 'One Jesus and Four Primitive Gospels' (reprinted from *HTR* 161 [1968] 203-47). I will return to the apocryphal Gospels in vol. 3; in the meantime I refer to *Jesus Remembered* §§7.6, 8.

11. Mack, *The Christian Myth;* I have already referred to the complete failure of the agenda to produce any worthwhile results (§21 n. 135 above).

12. In *Jesus and the Spirit* I note that Luke does not explain the origin of the community in Damascus (9.2, 10, 19), which those cited in n. 8 above attribute to influence from Galilee (137 and n. 8). But the implication of 8.1-3 and 9.1-2 is that the disciples in Damascus had fled there from Jerusalem.

13. See, e.g., Robinson and Koester, *Trajectories* 40-46.

14. See above, §21.2d(4).

22.2. Between Easter and Pentecost

Luke fills the fifty days prior to his account of Christianity's 'launch-pad' on the day of Pentecost (Acts 2) by narrating appearances Jesus made to his disciples (1.1-8), Jesus being taken up to heaven (the 'ascension') after forty days (1.9-11), the disciples' sojourn in 'the upper room' in Jerusalem (1.12-15), and the election of a successor to Judas (1.15-26). In this case it is particularly difficult to gain a clear historical perspective. Indeed, to the parallels already noted between Luke's Gospel and Luke's Acts,[15] we might well add the parallel between Luke 1–2 and Acts 1. The difficulties in discerning the oldest tradition in the opening chapters of Luke's first volume meant that a historical account of Jesus had to begin effectively with his mission.[16] So in attempting a historical account of Christianity's beginnings we encounter a similar problem of finding firm historical ground in the equivalent opening to Luke's second volume.

Acts 1 provides a sequence of important test cases for any historical reconstruction of Christianity's beginnings, so it requires some attention. A number of questions immediately arise.

a. Were Appearances of Jesus Limited to Jerusalem? (Acts 1.1-8)

One feature attracts our attention immediately, in view of the preceding reflections (§22.1). It is the fact that Luke confines the appearances of Jesus exclusively to Jerusalem. The point is not so explicit in the Acts account. But it was already made clear in the closing paragraphs of the preceding Gospel, where the disciples on the evening of the first day of resurrection appearances (in Jerusalem) are explicitly told to 'sit tight *(kathisate)*/stay in Jerusalem until you have been clothed with power from on high [at Pentecost]' (Luke 24.49). The Acts account echoes the explicit instruction: 'While he was in their company he [Jesus] ordered them not to leave Jerusalem, but to wait for the promise of the Father [Pentecost]' (Acts 1.4). For anyone aware of the recollections of appearances in Galilee, appearances attested by the other three Evangelists,[17] Luke's repeated emphasis on this point must have come across oddly.

Not only so, but Luke seems to have gone out of his way to exclude any tradition of appearances in Galilee. Noteworthy is what happens to Mark's account of the young man at the tomb commanding the women, 'Go, tell his disciples and Peter that *he is going ahead of you to Galilee; there you will see him, just as he*

15. See above, §21 n. 45.
16. See above, *Jesus Remembered* §11.1.
17. Details in *Jesus Remembered* §18.3.

told you' (Mark 16.7, referring back to 14.28). In this he is followed by Matthew (Matt. 28.7). But Luke has instead: 'Remember *how he told you, while he was still in Galilee,* that the Son of Man must be handed over . . .' (Luke 24.6-8). Since Luke has simply omitted the earlier Markan promise ('After I am raised up, I will go before you to Galilee' — Mark 14.28), it is hard to avoid the conclusion that Luke has deliberately edited Mark at this point.[18] In which case the implication clearly is that Luke wanted to focus the events of these forty days around Jerusalem[19] and took steps deliberately to exclude accounts of appearances elsewhere.

The motivation will hardly have been simply a concern for tidiness. There is evidently a theological intention at work here. It is evident also in the way the narrative of the first five chapters of Acts focuses exclusively on Jerusalem, and in the way the Jerusalem leadership of the young church monitors and approves the first three great breakthroughs in Christian mission.[20] We can guess already that Luke wanted to maintain the theological and ecclesiastical point that Jerusalem was the centre and fountainhead of Christian mission, thus probably reflecting the Jerusalem church's own perspective, but also maintaining the continuity of the new movement with the Israel of old.[21] But should we also deduce that Luke was seeking thereby to silence the voices of witnesses to other beginnings, or other claimants to be the beginning of what became Christianity?

b. Why Forty Days? (Acts 1.1-8)

In Acts (contrast Luke 24.50-51), Luke is quite explicit as to the length of the period of resurrection appearances — 'during forty days' (Acts 1.3; cf. 13.31 — 'for many days'). Here too there is some tension with the other Gospels, in which appearances in Jerusalem take place on the day of resurrection itself, apart from John 20.26-29, which takes place one week later. At the same time, inclusion of the Galilean appearance tradition inevitably extends the time line by a significant amount; the John 21 tradition seems to imply that some time has elapsed prior to the appearance (21.3). But the real problem arises when we take into account the early tradition recorded by Paul in 1 Cor. 15.5-8, since it seems to envisage a lon-

18. E.g., I. H. Marshall, *The Gospel of Luke* (NIGTC; Exeter: Paternoster, 1978) 886; Fitzmyer, *Luke* 1545. Weiss, however, maintained that '"the Galilean tradition" [that is, of a "flight to Galilee"] must be looked upon as a product of fantasy' (*Earliest Christianity* 16-20).

19. Since Emmaus was only about seven miles from Jerusalem, that is about three hours on foot from Jerusalem, the account of Luke 24.13-32 does not weaken the focus on Jerusalem, especially since the sequel was an immediate return of the two concerned to Jerusalem (24.33).

20. Acts 8.14-25; 11.1-18, 25-26.

21. See further Fitzmyer, *Luke* 164-68, and below, n. 48.

ger period of appearances well beyond forty days, assuming, as seems most probable,[22] that the list is set out in part at least in chronological sequence.[23]

- The appearance to 'more than five hundred brothers at once' (1 Cor. 15.6) presupposes a larger number of disciples than ever is envisaged in the forty-day period; presumably it took place after the initial expansion of the new movement was under way — on Luke's timetable, post-Pentecost.
- The appearance to James is indeterminable (cf. Acts 1.14),[24] but the appearance to 'all the apostles' (1 Cor. 15.7) seems to presuppose the emergence of a larger group who believed themselves to be called to mission ('apostles'), whose commissioning probably marked and helps explain the first major outreach beyond Jerusalem.[25]
- The appearance to Paul himself (15.8) is generally reckoned as taking place roughly between eighteen months and three years following the resurrection.[26] A little thought indicates the unlikelihood of Paul's claim to such an appearance being accepted (by deeply suspicious disciples) after such a lengthy interval,[27] had the only other recognized appearances ceased long before, after forty days.[28]

In the light of these considerations, it is more likely that Luke was trying to restrict the number of recognized appearances than to expand it. The way he does this is by limiting the appearances to the forty days of Acts 1.1-11. In so doing, of course, he effectively excludes Paul himself from the list of apostle-making appearances and witnesses to Christ's resurrection (1.21-22) — and deliberately

22. The sequence of *eita . . . epeita . . . epeita . . . eita* ('then . . . then . . . then . . . then'), followed by *eschaton de pantōn* ('last of all'), is most naturally read as a chronological sequence (BDAG 361).

23. E.g., H. Grass, *Ostergeschehen und Osterberichte* (Göttingen: Vandenhoeck und Ruprecht, 1956) 96-98; R. H. Fuller, *The Formation of the Resurrection Narratives* (London: SPCK, 1972) 28-29; C. Wolff, *Der erste Brief des Paulus an die Korinther.* Vol. 2 (THNT; Berlin: Evangelische, 1982) 166.

24. See *Jesus Remembered* 862-64. Wilckens thinks that the appearance to James probably happened in Nazareth (*Theologie* 1/2.129).

25. As already noted, the circle of 'apostles' was more extensive than the twelve, including Andronicus and Junia (Rom. 16.7), that is, including women (Stuhlmacher, *Biblische Theologie* 1.212), Apollos (1 Cor. 4.9), Barnabas (Gal. 2.8-9) and Silvanus (1 Thess. 2.6-7). For bibliography on 'apostle' see §29 nn. 47, 49 below; on Barnabas see particularly M. Öhler, *Barnabas. Die historische Person und ihre Rezeption in der Apostelgeschichte* (WUNT 156; Tübingen: Mohr Siebeck, 2003) 10-15.

26. See below, §28.1.

27. As indicated by Luke (Acts 9.26) and hinted at by Paul himself (Gal. 1.18-20).

28. See further my *Jesus and the Spirit* 143-46.

so, it would seem: despite 14.4, 14, Luke apparently did not count Paul as ranked fully on a par with the twelve![29] At the same time, we should recognize that Paul too bears witness to a perceived need to restrict recognized and apostle-making appearances. The appearance to himself was 'last of all *(eschaton de pantōn)*, and he made it into the fast-closing circle of apostle-making appearances only by being unnaturally forced in his new birth *(ektrōma,* 'abortion' — 1 Cor. 15.8).[30] So already a danger may have been perceived of the tradition of resurrection appearances being exploited to provide authorization or legitimation for other claimants on the memory and traditions of Jesus.[31]

Why forty days? Why not thirty, or fifty? The answers here can only be guesswork. Of course it is possible that Luke simply takes up the various 'forty' traditions — Israel's forty years in the wilderness (Exod. 16.35), Moses' sojourn on Mount Sinai for forty days and forty nights (Exod. 24.18), David's reign for forty years (1 Kings 2.11), Elijah's forty-day journey to Mount Horeb (1 Kings 19.8), Jesus' temptations in the wilderness (Mark 1.13) — and settles on forty days for his own narrative.[32] My own guess is that the tradition of the first Pentecost was already sufficiently established — that is, of the first great experience of the Spirit in collective Christian memory, as having happened on the next pilgrim feast (Pentecost).[33] Forty days would be the most obvious round number before fifty.[34]

Whatever Luke's reason for choosing a forty-day period for the resurrection appearances, we should note another theological consideration at work. The

---

29. See, e.g., the discussion in Barrett, *Acts* 1.671-72. Should we see here evidence (§21 n. 127) that Luke was influenced by a tradition hostile to Paul's claims to apostolic status? This tradition eventuates in the polemic of *Epistula Petri* 2.3; ps-Clem., *Hom.* 17.18-19 (see my *Unity and Diversity* §54.2b).

30. Dunn, *Jesus and the Spirit* 101-102. Discussion in A. C. Thiselton, *1 Corinthians* (NIGTC; Grand Rapids: Eerdmans, 2000) 1208-10. See also below, §25 n. 142.

31. We also know of later traditions in Gnostic circles which stretched the period of appearances still further: eighteen months, according to Irenaeus *(Adv. haer.* 1.3.2; 1.30.14); 550 days, according to *The Apocryphon of James* (Schneemelcher, *NTA* 291); 545 days, according to *Asc. Isa.* 9.16 — which, as Harnack noted, could allow the inclusion of Paul's conversion; for details see K. Lake, 'The Ascension', *Beginnings* 5.20; A. Grillmeier, *Christ in Christian Tradition.* Vol. 1: *From the Apostolic Age to Chalcedon (AD 451)* (London: Mowbrays, ²1975) 75-76.

32. This is the most common explanation for the forty days in treatments of the ascension in Luke (e.g., Jervell, *Apg.* 111).

33. Dunn, *Jesus and the Spirit* 139-42; and further below (§22.3).

34. G. Lohfink, *Die Himmelfahrt Jesu. Untersuchungen zu den Himmelfahrts- und Erhöhungstexten bei Lukas* (Munich: Kösel, 1971) 184-86; S. G. Wilson, *The Gentiles and the Gentile Mission in Luke-Acts* (SNTSMS 23; Cambridge: Cambridge University, 1973): 'It is not the forty days which forces Luke to date the coming of the Spirit at Pentecost, but the date of Pentecost which forces him to use the forty days' (100); contrast Haenchen, *Acts* 141 n. 1, 172, 174.

gap of ten days served to mark off clearly the time of Jesus from the time of the Spirit, the appearances of the risen Jesus from the outpouring of the Spirit.[35] In a way analogous to the need to limit the period for recognizable resurrection appearances, there may already have been a recognition of the need to make a clear distinction between resurrection appearances and experiences of the Spirit's inspiration or commissioning (cf. Acts 2.1-4; 4.8, 31; 10.19-20; 13.3).[36] The reason would again be obvious: from earliest days the claim to a resurrection appearance carried with it a claim to authorization and legitimation which far exceeded the significance that could be claimed for any Spirit experience.[37]

This discussion does not add much clarification to the issue of whether Luke has applied too much force to the traditions of Christianity's beginnings by restricting his account of the appearances of Jesus to Jerusalem and to such a limited period. But it does highlight the intense theological concerns which seem to have shaped his narrative of these beginnings.

c. Distinctive Lukan Emphases in Acts 1.1-8

Also worth noting are other features that bear clear signs of Lukan concerns which he evidently wished to press home upon his readers.

(1) Luke takes some pains to stress the continuity between Jesus' doings and teachings recounted in his first volume and what was said by Jesus during the forty-day period.[38] The period of Jesus' mission stretched from the beginning

---

35. Contrast J. F. Maile, 'The Ascension in Luke-Acts', *TynB* 37 (1986) 29-59 (here 48-54) — 'a vehicle for conveying Luke's theology of continuity'; W. Kasper, *Jesus the Christ* (London: Burns and Oates, 1977) — the ascension as providing an overlap between the Easter story and the beginning of the church (148). This is not to deny that, at the same time, the disciples as 'witnesses' do provide an important element of continuity (Lohfink, *Himmelfahrt* 267-72).

36. Cf. Conzelmann, *Theology of St. Luke* 203-204; Fitzmyer, *Acts* 208-11. This in contrast to the often-repeated thesis of E. von Dobschütz, *Ostern und Pfingsten* (Leipzig, 1903) 31-43, that the account of Pentecost began as a variant on the appearance to more than five hundred (1 Cor. 15.6); but see J. Kremer, *Pfingstbericht und Pfingstgeschehen. Eine exegetische Untersuchung zu Apg. 2,1-13* (SBS 63/64; Stuttgart: KBW, 1973) 232-37, and my *Jesus and the Spirit* 144-46 (other bibliography 397 n. 40; Barrett, *Acts* 109, and Wedderburn, *History* 26, show some sympathy with the hypothesis). G. Kretschmar documents a tradition in the Syrian and Palestinian churches (as early as the third and fourth century) in which ascension and Pentecost fall on the same day — 'Himmelfahrt und Pfingsten', *ZKG* 66 (1954-55) 209-53 — which, if earlier, could conceivably provide some motivation for Luke's clear separation of the two.

37. Compare, for example, the much stronger claims made by Paul in Gal. 1.11-12, 15-16 and 1 Cor. 9.1-2, than what he argues for in 1 Cor. 7.40.

38. On the implication of *ērxato* (the gospel as what Jesus *began* to do and teach), see Barrett, *Acts* 66-67; contrast Haenchen, *Acts* 137 n. 4.

in the Gospel (Acts 1.1), not just until his passion, but 'until the day when he was taken up' (1.2, 22). Moreover, the subject of Jesus' discourse with the disciples during the forty days is described as 'the kingdom of God' (1.3), the central motif of Jesus' teaching.[39] By being so specific, Luke not only indicates continuity between Jesus' pre-Easter message and his post-Easter teaching, but he also excludes the possibility of a post-Easter teaching which was in addition to or at odds with the teaching already presented in the Gospel.[40] In addition, Luke goes out of his way to indicate that 'the kingdom of God' continued to be a feature of earliest Christian preaching and teaching.[41] Particularly noticeable is the fact that 1.3 forms an *inclusio* with 28.31: the final note of Paul's preaching ('proclaiming the kingdom of God') matches the chief and last topic of Jesus' instruction. This is presumably Luke's way of indicating that although the post-Easter proclamation focused on Jesus' death and resurrection, the content and central concerns of Jesus' pre-Easter preaching and teaching continued to be a fundamental feature of the post-Easter preaching and teaching (2.42).

(2) The tangibility of the resurrection appearances: Jesus 'presented himself alive to them [the disciples] with many convincing proofs' (1.3). What Luke had in mind, presumably, is illustrated by his account of the resurrection appearance to the disciples gathered on the evening of the first Easter Sunday (Luke 24.38-43).[42] The tensions thus set up with other perceptions of Jesus' resurrection I have already commented on.[43]

(3) In his first volume Luke had given additional prominence to the twelve disciples by referring to them as '(the) apostles' more frequently than Mark and Matthew.[44] In the second volume they are immediately reintroduced on centre stage: the instructions of the risen Jesus were given 'through the Holy Spirit to the apostles whom he had chosen' (1.2).[45] This double affirmation of their status (chosen by Jesus himself; instructions inspired by the Spirit)[46] signals the apos-

---

39. *Jesus Remembered* §12.

40. Jervell, *Apg.* 111 n. 24. We need not infer that divergent teaching attributed to the risen Christ was already in circulation (see n. 31; though see R. Pesch, *Die Apostelgeschichte* [EKK; Zürich: Benziger, 1986] 1.63). But at least Luke was aware of such a possibility (Acts 20.30).

41. So also 8.12; 14.22; 19.8; 20.25; 28.23, 31.

42. Elsewhere I have noted Luke's predilection for the eye-catching miracle and the tangibility of the spiritual; see my *Unity and Diversity* 180-84; and above, §21.2d(5).

43. *Jesus Remembered* §18.5b.

44. Matt. 10.2; Mark 3.14 and 6.30; but Luke 6.13; 9.10; 11.49; 17.5; 22.14; 24.10.

45. The order of the words in Greek makes for a degree of ambiguity; but see Barrett, *Acts* 69.

46. The oddity of attributing the risen Jesus' instructions to inspiration by the Spirit is rarely noted; there is no immediate parallel in the Gospel (cf. Luke 4.14, 18; 10.21). The words of a prophet or apostle might need the confirmative phrase ('through the Holy Spirit'), but the risen Jesus? Is this Luke's way of acknowledging both that the mode by which instructions

tles' central role as the focus of authority and continuity in the narrative about to be unfolded. These observations, of course, add to the considerations already adduced under §22.2a and b.

(4) Luke also takes the opportunity to raise a question regarding the kingdom which remained unanswered in the Gospel:[47] 'Is this the time when the kingdom will be restored to Israel?' (1.6). Interestingly, the question itself is not given a clear answer: Jesus dismisses speculation about timing, though not the thought itself (1.7), and instead redirects the disciples' attention to the task and responsibility before them (1.8). But the 'Israel-dimension' of the disciples' ongoing task is frequently referred to in the subsequent narrative,[48] and it is no surprise for the attentive reader that in the final scenes of Acts Paul expresses his motivation and ambition in terms of 'the hope of Israel' (28.20).

(5) The fact that talk of the kingdom (1.3, 6-7) alternates with the promise of the Spirit (1.5, 8), and that the question about the kingdom is framed by that promise, is probably intended to suggest that the two hang together and that the promised Spirit is in fact the presence and activity of God's royal power.[49] As in the mission of Jesus, the present activity of God's kingly power foreshadows the kingdom still to come.[50]

(6) The promise of the Spirit is given special attention. In Luke's formulation the imminent experience of Pentecost is presented as the disciples being baptized in the Holy Spirit (1.5), as the Baptist had predicted at the beginning of Luke's first volume (Luke 3.16).[51] Thus here too Luke clamps the two volumes of his writing firmly together. But thereby Luke also indicates how fundamental is the experience of the Spirit in his understanding of what effects participation in the new movement to be launched with the Pentecost experience.[52]

---

were received during the period of resurrection appearances was not quite as in the days of Jesus' (pre-Easter) mission, and also that the risen Christ was still dependent on the Spirit and not yet ascended/exalted to become bestower of the Spirit (2.33)?

47. *Jesus Remembered* 886; and note Luke 22.29-30 and 24.21. The tense used by Luke in Acts 1.6 implies a repeated asking of the question.

48. Note particularly 2.39; 3.25-26; 5.31; 9.15; 10.36; 13.23; 15.15-18; 23.6; 26.6-7.

49. 'The earliest Christians regarded the outpouring of the Spirit as a sign that the end of the world [*sic*] was at hand. With this in mind it is easy to understand why they should ask, "Is the kingdom coming now, at the same time as the Spirit?"' (Haenchen, *Acts* 143). See also my 'Spirit and Kingdom', *ExpT* 82 (1970-71) 36-40.

50. 'It is the Spirit of God's kingdom which is meant, that is, the power which brings about the kingdom' (Jervell, *Apg.* 112; and further 114).

51. It is unclear why Luke recalls the promise as one made by Jesus, despite the facts that in Luke 3.16 the prophecy is made by the Baptist and that in the Gospel Luke nowhere recalls Jesus as repeating the promise on his own account. On the imagery of the original Baptist prediction see *Jesus Remembered* 366-69.

52. Hence 2.38-39; 8.15-17; 9.17; 10.44-48; 11.15-18; 15.8-9; 19.2-6. See further my

(7) As is generally recognized, Acts 1.8 provides a programme note for what is to follow: a story beginning in Jerusalem (Acts 2–7), continuing through Judea and Samaria (8–12), and thence to 'the end of the earth' (13–28).[53] Acts 1.8 also is Luke's account of the risen Jesus' commissioning for mission of those to whom he appeared, a characteristic feature of resurrection appearance stories.[54] As such, it gives Luke the opportunity to strike the first note of his witness motif, a prominent feature of his apologia for the reliability of the testimony forthrightly given in the pages that follow. The coming Spirit would empower, that is, make the more effective, their witness both to what Jesus had done (10.39) and particularly to his resurrection.[55] Apparently only 'the apostles' are in view, though 1.22 indicates that the circle of witnesses in the event was larger, and Luke was careful to include Paul as a witness of what he 'had seen and heard' (22.15; 26.16).

Where Luke's agenda is so clear, questions regarding the extent to which he was able to draw on reminiscences of the period, and the extent to which he did so, are bound to remain the more obscure.

d. What Did Luke Understand by the Ascension? (Acts 1.9-11)

The climax of Luke's account of the forty days of Jesus appearing is, of course, 'the day when Jesus was taken up (into heaven)' (1.2, 11, 22),[56] that is, the 'as-

---

Baptism in the Holy Spirit (London: SCM, 1970) ch. 4. Surprisingly, Fitzmyer thinks the confrontation and testimony of the twelve with and to the twelve tribes of Israel (cf. 2.14 and 36) 'are far more important than the reception of Spirit baptism' (*Acts* 232). Contrast Barrett: 'The Holy Spirit is one of the most major themes of Acts; some would say the central and most important theme' (*Acts* 74).

53. The plural ('ends of the earth') is more common, but there may be an allusion to Isa. 49.6 — the Servant to be 'a light to the nations, that my salvation may reach to the end of the earth'. The same text is quoted in Acts 13.47 as a slogan for the mission to which Paul especially is called (26.17-18, echoing Isa. 42.6-7). Conceivably Luke had Rome in mind (the unusual singular is used in reference to Rome in *Pss. Sol.* 8.15), which would help explain why Acts ends with Paul fulfilling his mission in Rome. E. E. Ellis, '"The End of the Earth" (Acts 1:8)', *BBR* 1 (1991) 123-32, argues that 'Luke signals his knowledge of a (prospective) Pauline mission to Spain and his intention to make it part of his narrative' (132), but he remains puzzled as to why Luke does not then include such a mission (he dates Acts to the mid-60s). Schnabel argues for a broad reference — 'literally to the farthest reaches of the inhabited world (known at that time)' (*Mission* 372). See the brief discussion in Barrett, *Acts* 80, and Fitzmyer, *Acts* 206-207; other bibliography is in Jervell, *Apg.* 116 n. 54.

54. See *Jesus Remembered* 859, 864-65.

55. Luke 24.46-48; Acts 1.8, 22; 2.32; 3.15; 4.20, 33; 5.32; 10.39, 41; 13.31; 18.5; 20.21, 24; 22.15, 18, 20; 23.11; 26.16; 28.23.

56. On the text of 1.2 see particularly Metzger, *Textual Commentary* 273-77; M. C. Parsons, 'The Text of Acts 1:2 Reconsidered', *CBQ* 50 (1988) 58-71; A. W. Zwiep, 'The Text of

cension'.[57] Here again questions at once arise, since the Acts account of the ascension is unique within the NT.[58]

(1) In the Gospels there is little or no chronological separation of resurrection and ascension. Matthew does not narrate an ascension as such and gives no weight to chronological considerations in his retelling of the final episodes of his Gospel (Matt. 28.16-20). In his Gospel Luke was evidently content to leave the impression that Christ 'was carried up into heaven' on the day of the resurrection itself (Luke 24.50-51). And John similarly talks of an ascension happening on the day of resurrection (John 20.17), though he also includes an appearance a week later (20.26-29); and the appendix includes a presumably subsequent appearance of Jesus in Galilee (21.1-23), though both episodes tail off without indicating what happened next to Jesus himself.

(2) Elsewhere in the NT the somewhat different imagery used implies a single movement of resurrection-exaltation.[59] For example, Peter's speech in Acts 2: 'this Jesus God raised up, and of that all of us are witnesses. Being therefore exalted at the right hand of God . . .' (Acts 2.32-33). According to the Philippian hymn, 'He became obedient to death, even death on a cross. Therefore God also highly exalted him' (Phil. 2.8-9). The whole imagery of Hebrews is of an entry into the heavenly sanctuary as a priest bearing the sacrificial blood (his own): 'When he had made purification for sins, he sat down at the right hand of the Majesty on high' (Heb. 1.3; etc). And the theology of John's Gospel is of a single act of glorification, of ascension and of being lifted up, which begins with the cross and climaxes in heaven.[60]

So why is it only in Acts that we have such a clear distinction and separation (forty days) between resurrection and ascension? The simplest answer is that Luke wanted to mark a definite and undisputable end to the sequence of resurrection appearances.[61] This is presumably the reason why he went out of his way to

---

the Ascension Narratives (Luke 24.50-53; Acts 1.1-2, 9-11)', *NTS* 42 (1996) 219-44 (here 234-38).

57. For form-critical discussion as to which genre Luke's account best fits into — heavenly journey, assumption, exaltation, rapture — see Lohfink, *Die Himmelfahrt Jesu,* and A. W. Zwiep, *The Ascension of the Messiah in Lukan Christology* (NovTSupp 87; Leiden: Brill, 1997). Both agree that in form-critical terms Luke's ascension story belongs to the rapture *(Entrückung)* type of ascension. See also below, n. 67.

58. J. G. Davies, *He Ascended into Heaven* (Bampton Lectures 1958; London: Lutterworth, 1958), notes that Harnack's judgment on this point (that the ascension had no separate place in the primitive tradition) was highly influential on English scholarship and largely explains the relative neglect of the subject in Britain during the first half of the twentieth century (9-10).

59. See, e.g., Zwiep, *Ascension* ch. 4.

60. See, e.g., R. E. Brown, *The Gospel according to John* (i-xii) (AB 29; New York: Doubleday, 1966) 145-46.

61. For an alternative, possibly complementary explanation in terms of Luke's rhetorical

stress the visibility of Jesus' final departure before witnesses.[62] No less than five times in the three verses Luke emphasizes that the disciples *saw* what was happening.[63] This also accords with what some have called Luke's 'absentee christology', the ascension marking Jesus' departure and subsequent absence from earth,[64] or the transition from physical presence to presence in and through his name (Acts 3–4).[65]

For a historical inquiry all this raises further awkward questions. How did Luke conceive of Jesus' resurrected corporeality? Where did he think the risen Jesus was when he was not visible to the disciples? Acts 1.4, 'while he was staying/eating with them' *(synalizomenos),*[66] could be taken to indicate lengthy periods of Jesus' visible sojourn, though the implication of the parallel episodes in Luke's Gospel is that appearances were of relatively short duration (Luke 24.31, 51). But if the risen body of Christ was no less physical than the crucified body of Christ (Luke 24.39), then what does that say about its alternate visibility and (presumably) invisibility during the forty-day period? Or was Jesus' state during the forty days conceived as some kind of transitional state, and did his ascension result in a yet further different state of being? During the forty days was he located on earth, having not yet ascended to heaven, de-materialized or somehow 'in hiding'? Or again, if the ascension is intended to mark Christ's first going up to heaven — the appearances lasted 'until the day when he was taken up' (1.2, 22), that is, 'into heaven' (1.11)[67] — presumably he was thought of as not yet in

---

technique, see B. W. Longenecker, *Rhetoric at the Boundaries: The Art and Theology of New Testament Chain-Link Transitions* (Waco: Baylor University, 2005) 221 and n. 16.

62. Lohfink, *Himmelfahrt* 81-98.

63. A. Weiser, *Die Apostelgeschichte* (ÖTKNT 5/1; Gütersloh: Gütersloher, 1981) 57 — '. . . as they were watching . . . out of their sight . . . they were gazing into heaven . . . looking up into heaven . . . as you saw him go into heaven'.

64. C. F. D. Moule, 'The Christology of Acts', in Keck and Martyn, eds., *Studies in Luke-Acts* 159-85 (here 179-80).

65. Cf. M. C. Parsons, *The Departure of Jesus in Luke-Acts: The Ascension Narratives in Context* (JSNTS 21; Sheffield: JSOT, 1987) 161-62. A. W. Zwiep, 'Assumptus est in caelum: Rapture and Heavenly Exaltation in Early Judaism and Luke-Acts', in F. Avemarie and H. Lichtenberger, eds., *Auferstehung — Resurrection* (WUNT 135; Tübingen: Mohr Siebeck, 2001) 323-49, argues that the Jewish genre of rapture stories implies that the ascension for Luke was not an act of enthronement or apotheosis; 'Jewish rapture candidates are kept in preservation to fulfil some task in the end time' (348); we may think at once of Acts 3.20-21.

66. Whatever the precise meaning of *synalizomenos* (see, e.g., Barrett, *Acts* 71-72; Fitzmyer, *Acts* 203; BDAG 964), Acts 10.41 presumably tells the same story: they 'ate and drank with him after he rose from the dead'. As noted in *Jesus Remembered,* a shared meal is a feature common to a number of resurrection appearance stories (859-60).

67. *Analambanō* had already become almost a technical term for rapture to heaven (2 Kgs. 2.10-11; Sir. 48.9; 49.14; 1 Macc. 2.58; Philo, *Mos.* 2.291; *T. Job* 39.11-12; *T. Abr.* [A] 7.7; [B] 4.4; 7.16; so also Mark 16.19; *1 Clem.* 5.7).

heaven (not yet ascended), or as not disappearing to heaven between resurrection appearances.[68] Such questions may seem to be crude and even crass, echoing the critical scepticism of a D. F. Strauss,[69] but it is Luke's own account, with his insistence on 'convincing proofs' (Acts 1.3), which prompts them![70]

In all this we should recall that Luke could operate only within the conceptuality possible for him, in which heaven was conceived as literally 'up there', and departure into heaven could only be conceived in terms of 'being taken up', a literal ascension. It is not simply a matter of literary genre which Luke could choose to operate or dispense with. Rather, the typical mind-set and worldview of the time *conditioned what was actually seen* and how the recording of such seeings was conceptualized.[71] Since there is little doubt that Jesus was seen by not a few after his death, however these seeings are interpreted,[72] and since the sequence of seeings ceased at some point, as Paul agrees (1 Cor. 15.8 — 'last of all'), we can easily envisage the last appearance ending with what was seen as a departure into heaven.[73] Was, then, the ascension simply Jesus' 'farewell' appearance?[74]

68. Bruce acknowledges such questions, arguing that Jesus' enthronement at God's right hand was not postponed to the fortieth day, that the intervals between appearances are not to be thought of as 'spent in some earth-bound state', and that his resurrection appearances 'were visitations from that eternal order to which his "body of glory" now belonged' (*Acts* 103). But does such harmonizing of different NT authors do sufficient justice to Luke's own purpose in Acts 1? Similarly Zwiep, *Ascension* ch. 5; but the language of 1.2, 22 hardly suggests this interpretation ('until the day he was taken up to heaven'), and 2.33 implies that Jesus 'received the Holy Spirit' only after his exaltation, which in Acts 1–2 can only refer to the ascension of 1.9-11. Fitzmyer sees the decisive clue in Luke 24.46: 'The risen Christ now appears from "glory", i.e. . . . from the glorious presence of the Father' (*Acts* 200). Contrast B. Donne, *Christ Ascended: A Study in the Significance of the Ascension of Jesus Christ in the New Testament* (Exeter: Paternoster, 1983), who is motivated by similar concerns as Bruce but argues that 'there does not seem to be sufficient Scriptural evidence to suggest that each appearance was a descent from heaven of a Lord who had ascended to heaven the moment he was raised from death' (8); Barrett, *Acts* 64.

69. Strauss, *Life of Jesus* 749-52.

70. We need to bear in mind here again Luke's consistently materialistic conceptualization of spiritual phenomena (*Jesus and the Spirit* 121-22).

71. Pesch does not allow for this when he writes: 'The visible "wonder" is neither an empty grave nor a man travelling like a rocket to heaven, but the gathering established by Jesus itself (1.14), in which all who believe and do not doubt "see" their exalted Lord, who is really present invisibly in their midst and who binds all with one another through his Spirit' (*Apg.* 75). See further my 'The Ascension of Jesus: A Test Case for Hermeneutics', in Avemarie and Lichtenberger, eds., *Auferstehung — Resurrection* 301-22 (here 311-22). This could apply also to the cloud as 'an apocalyptic stage prop' (Fitzmyer, *Acts* 210); 'the cloud is obviously the typical rapture cloud [of] Hellenistic and Jewish assumption stories' (Zwiep, *Ascension* 104).

72. See *Jesus Remembered* §18.5c.

73. All the more so if at least some of the appearances were perceived as 'from heaven' (see *Jesus Remembered* 858 and n. 144).

74. A. M. Ramsey, 'What Was the Ascension?', *SNTSBull.* 2 (1951) 43-50 (here 44);

We can make no further progress on such questions, and to focus solely on them is to miss the point, which all talk of Jesus' ascension obviously counted as much the more important — hence the unconcern evinced over such questions in our sources.[75] For the main point was the theological significance of what the ascension was asserting. It was evidently seen early on as of crucial importance that Jesus had not simply been raised from the dead, the beginning of or first to experience 'the resurrection of the dead', but also that he had been exalted to heaven. It is because the first Christians found it necessary to claim these *two* things for the once-crucified Jesus (exalted to heaven, as well as raised from the dead) that Luke evidently thought it appropriate to retell the tradition of Jesus' resurrection appearances so as to state in a fresh and clear way the fact that *both* claims were important and that one should not be subsumed within the other.[76] We will have to return to this point below (§23.4d).

e. Who Was Present? (Acts 1.12-15)

Luke, having left a ten-day gap between ascension and Pentecost, fills it first with a note of who constituted the disciple band at that stage. He repeats the list already provided in Luke 6.14-16, with two alterations. The initial four have been re-ordered; the two sets of brothers have been separated. John (brother of James) is listed second to Peter; this no doubt foreshadows the close association of Peter and John in the following chapters (3.1-11; 4.13, 19; 8.14). James (brother of John) comes third, as before, also foreshadowing his future prominence (12.2). Andrew heads the list of the remaining eight, all of whom make no future appearance in Luke's account.[77] The other alteration is, of course, the omission of Judas Iscariot, an omission which Luke goes on immediately to explain (1.15-19).

The focus is on the remaining eleven disciples, who are the subject of the main verb in 1.14 ('they were all with one mind devoting themselves to prayer'),

---

Bruce, *Acts* 103; Fitzmyer, *Luke* 1588; Zwiep, 'Assumptus est in caelum' 348. Cf. Lüdemann: 'Underlying this [1.9-11] is a tradition the form of which can no longer be recognized' (*Early Christianity* 29; also 30-31).

75. Haenchen describes the account as 'unsentimental, almost uncannily austere' (*Acts* 151).

76. Zwiep confuses the issue by distinguishing the ascension ('rapture') sharply from the resurrection ('exaltation') — 'the Lukan ascension story is not a narrative description of the *exaltatio ad dexteram Dei*' ('Assumptus est in caelum' 348, and n. 65 above). But as already noted, it is difficult to credit that Luke did not intend his readers to understand Jesus' exaltation to the right hand of God and reception of the Holy Spirit (Acts 2.33) as a reference to the ascension described in 1.9-11.

77. On Jesus' choice of twelve see *Jesus Remembered* §13.3b; and further below, §22.2f.

as presumably they were in 1.12-13. Luke, however, adds that (an unspecified number of) women were with them (presumably those mentioned in Luke 23.55 and partially named in 24.10), and Jesus' mother Mary and his brothers. Two things are of note here. First, that James, brother of Jesus, is not explicitly named, though no doubt included; and thereafter he is never explicitly stated to be the brother of Jesus (contrast Gal. 1.19). That is somewhat curious, given that the listing of the eleven reflects the subsequent prominence of Peter and John in particular, and that James, brother of Jesus, soon emerged into similar prominence (12.17; 15.13-21; 21.18). Luke's silence at this point has to be added to the implication that the appearances of the forty days were limited to 'the apostles' (1.2). Together, these suggest that if Luke knew of the well-established tradition of an appearance to this James (1 Cor. 15.7), perhaps he also knew that it came later in the sequence of 1 Cor. 15.5-7.[78] Also to be noted is the implication that James, Jesus' brother, was (like Paul) not one of 'the apostles'; the implication of Luke 8.19-21 is that he would have failed the criterion to qualify as one of the apostles (1.21-22). In this brief paragraph, therefore, the primacy of Peter among the apostles and the first disciples is subtly safeguarded.

The other curiosity is that no resurrection appearance is recalled as having been made to Mary, Jesus' mother. She too is excluded from the appearances indicated in 1.1-11. But in addition there is no mention of such an appearance in the (authorized) list of witnesses in 1 Cor. 15.5-7, or (more surprisingly) in any of the Gospels; that privilege is given to unnamed women in Matt. 28.8-10 and specifically to Mary of Magdala (John 20.11-18).[79] I do not know whether anything should be made of this.

Equally surprising is the mention of a 'crowd about 120 in number'. The clause interrupts the beginning of Peter's speech, in parenthetical fashion, as we today might provide additional information in a footnote, which may suggest that Luke here cites information which his inquiries had gleaned.[80] But where did they come from? Were they all local disciples (and sympathizers), like Cleopas and the

---

78. See above, §22.2b. The implication need not be that James was converted by the appearance of Jesus; quite possibly James and other members of Jesus' family had joined Jesus' disciples in the latter stages of his mission; so particularly R. B. Ward, 'James of Jerusalem in the First Two Centuries', *ANRW* 2.26.1 (1992) 779-812 (here 786-91); R. Bauckham, *Jude and the Relatives of Jesus in the Early Church* (Edinburgh: Clark, 1990) 46-57; and J. Painter, *Just James: The Brother of Jesus in History and Tradition* (Columbia: University of South Carolina, 1997) 11-41.

79. 'It is clear that Luke either has no information, or is not concerned to provide information, about Mary in the post-resurrection period' (Barrett, *Acts* 89).

80. 'It is difficult to think that any writer would willingly interrupt himself in this way, and it is therefore natural to suppose that at this point Luke was incorporating a statement from one source into another which he was in the main following' (Barrett, *Acts* 1.95).

other in Luke 24.13-35? — only the eleven apostles, and presumably the few others capable of being appointed apostles, are identified as Galileans (1.11, 21-22). And how did they live during that period? 'The room upstairs/upper room' (*to hyperōon* — 1.13) was presumably provided by a local supporter,[81] though at least the women would have been lodged elsewhere. And the meeting of 120 (presumably not in the open, as in the outer court of the Temple) would have required a substantial room as well. Luke, of course, does not bother himself with such issues, but the verisimilitude of his narrative actually hangs to a substantial extent on them. We will have to return to them as Luke's narrative continues to unfold.

f. The End and Replacement of Judas (Acts 1.15-26)

The other event which fills out the ten-day wait for Pentecost is the mending of the rupture in the circle of the twelve apostles. The rupture, of course, had been caused by the defection of Judas, 'who became a guide to those who arrested Jesus' (1.16), despite the fact that he had been numbered with them (as one of the twelve) and had been allotted his share in 'this ministry' (1.17), and by Judas's subsequent death (1.18). The account of Judas's end, which Luke inserts (1.18-19) somewhat awkwardly into Peter's speech (1.16-22), is strikingly at odds with the only other early account of Judas's death, in Matt. 27.3-10. As already noted, the divergence probably indicates that the details of Judas's death were of little concern to the early Christians.[82] Matthew clearly uses the version known to him as another example of his 'fulfilment of prophecy' motif and adapts the details of the story to bring out the degree of fulfilment most fully.[83] Luke, on the other hand, takes the opportunity to depict the gruesome character of Judas's death, in the tradition of 'thus perish those who act in defiance of God'.[84] The main point

81. Did Luke think of it as the same room *(anagaion)* where the last supper was celebrated (Luke 22.12)? Fitzmyer notes that the traditional view assumes it was the same room and locates it in the house of Mary, the mother of John Mark (Acts 12.12) (*Acts* 213), though see also Barrett, *Acts* 86-87. See further §23 n. 40 below.

82. *Jesus Remembered* 224 n. 218. All that the variant traditions have held constant is (1) that Judas had died an ignominious death, (2) that a field had been bought with the reward given to Judas for his betrayal of Jesus, and (3) that the field was known as the 'field/place of blood' (*Akeldamach* — on which see Fitzmyer, *Acts* 224-25). Both accounts mention that the name of the field was well known locally (Matt. 27.8; Acts 1.19); that is, they were drawing on a tradition not specifically Christian. See further A. W. Zwiep, *Judas and the Choice of Matthias* (WUNT 2.187; Tübingen: Mohr Siebeck, 2004) ch. 5.

83. See my *Unity and Diversity* 92-93.

84. The most famous cases include Jezebel (2 Kgs. 9.30-37), Antiochus IV (2 Macc. 9.5-29), Herod the Great (Josephus, *War* 1.656, 665; *Ant.* 17.168-69) and Herod Agrippa (Acts 12.23). See also K. Lake, 'The Death of Judas', *Beginnings* 5.22-30; Zwiep, *Judas* ch. 3. See also below, §26 n. 140.

for Luke, however, was evidently to explain why there was a place to be filled (one of the twelve) and to recount the rationale for its being filled.

The motivation is clearly to complete again the broken circle of the twelve. The implication, obvious to anyone knowledgeable about Israel's history and constitution, is no doubt the same as with Jesus' original choice of twelve — namely, that the twelve immediate disciples of Jesus somehow represented the twelve tribes of Israel and thus were a focus for a reconstitution of Israel, the eschatological restoration of Israel to be the people that God had appointed them to be (cf. particularly Luke 22.29-30).[85] This inference dovetails neatly with the implications already drawn above, from 1.6 in particular.[86] Luke evidently saw it as important that the twelve should be complete, and that it should have been done prior to the empowering of the Spirit, possibly even as a necessary prerequisite for Pentecost.

The only indication Luke gives of the role to be fulfilled by the twelve is his description of it as 'this ministry (and apostleship)' (1.17, 25). He uses the same term in 6.4 for the twelve's special responsibility ('the ministry of the word'), including, presumably, 'the teaching of the apostles' (2.42). Once again, the implication is of the twelve apostles constituting the constitutive and authoritative core of the community which was to emerge and which was already in embryo in the 120.

Luke also succeeds in giving a flavour of the kind of reasoning which must have been a feature of the earliest community/ies. He depicts Peter as drawing his guidance on what should be done directly from Scripture (1.16), citing Pss. 69.25 and 109.8.[87] The quotations may strike us as odd and as pulled out of context, but they come from imprecatory psalms, which call down judgments from

---

85. *Jesus Remembered* §§13.3, 14.9b; on Luke 22.29-30 see 416 n. 178, 420 n. 205, 510-11, 820. Cf. particularly K. H. Rengstorf, 'The Election of Matthias: Acts 1.15ff.', in W. Klassen and G. F. Snyder, eds., *Current Issues in New Testament Interpretation,* O. A. Piper FS (New York: Harper and Row, 1962) 178-92: 'by completing their number, which is the number of the twelve tribes of Israel, they have made perfectly obvious the continuing unbroken claims of Jesus on Israel as his people' (188). 'When Peter "stood up with the Eleven" (2.14) and confronted the Jews, the "twelve apostles" confronted the "twelve tribes of Israel" (Luke 22.29; cf. Acts 2.36, "the whole house of Israel") and functioned as their judges, thus echoing what the Lucan Jesus predicted at the Last Supper' (Fitzmyer, *Acts* 234). See also, e.g., Pesch, *Apg.* 91; Jervell, *Apg.* 125; and further, M. E. Fuller, *The Restoration of Israel: Israel's Regathering and the Fate of the Nations in Early Jewish Literature and Luke-Acts* (BZNW 138; Berlin: de Gruyter, 2006).

86. See above at n. 21 and §22.2c(4).

87. Cf. particularly Luke 4.17-21; 24.44; and the frequent citing of Scripture in the speeches of Acts (2.17-21, 25-28, 34-35; 3.22-25; 4.24-26; 7.3, 5-6, 18, 27-28, 33-35, 37, 40, 42-43, 49-50; etc.). But the pre-occupation was evidently widespread in the first communities (see below, §23.2b[1]).

God on the psalmist's enemies and the wicked.[88] The earlier part of Psalm 69 in particular was evidently soon seen to foreshadow the suffering and rejection of Jesus,[89] and it strains historical imagination not at all to envisage the first disciples turning precisely to such psalms to help express their distress and to help them make sense of what had happened. Indeed, I have already suggested that the first retellings of the story of Jesus' crucifixion were already framed round the meaning which the psalms gave to it.[90] So I do not regard it as at all implausible that Peter should find in Psalm 69 and the similar Psalm 109 guidance on what should be done in respect of the one who had proved so decisively to be their enemy.

Luke's account, however, leaves three further questions hanging. One is fairly minor. The tradition received by Paul on his conversion numbered an appearance to 'the twelve' second only to the appearance to Cephas (1 Cor. 15.5). That reinforces the importance for the earliest community of there having been a complete 'twelve' to constitute it (as representing eschatological Israel). But in view of the undisputed tradition about Judas's defection, it can only be explained on the hypothesis that 'the twelve' quickly became established as *a designation for the core group of disciples,* even though initially only eleven strong.[91] Luke had in fact spoken accurately of 'the eleven' remaining disciples in Luke 24.9, 33, but his limitation of the appearances to (only) eleven in Acts 1.1-11 also, strictly speaking, excludes the appearance to 'the twelve'. The anomaly is more apparent than real, since the two 'candidates' to fill the now vacant twelfth place had themselves to be witnesses of Jesus' resurrection (1.22).[92] So the implication is that those favoured with an appearance must have included at least a number of the 120 (1.15), despite Luke's focusing the appearance traditions only on the eleven.

More striking is the question why only Joseph Barsabbas and Matthias (1.23) are named as candidates for the vacant twelfth apostleship. Or rather, the question is, given his subsequent prominence, why not James, the brother of

88. The fact that the LXX text of the psalms is presupposed is not a decisive indication that such texts were not considered in the earliest (Aramaic-speaking) community (*pace* Haenchen, *Acts* 161), since, naturally, Luke would have transposed any such usage into the text familiar to him (LXX).

89. Cf. Ps. 69.21 with Mark 15.23, 36 pars.

90. *Jesus Remembered* 777-78.

91. Lüdemann, *Early Christianity* 37, cites Meyer's illuminating parallel from antiquity: 'Antony and Octavian remain *triumviri* even after Lepidus has been deposed' (E. Meyer, *Ursprung und Anfänge des Christentums* [3 vols.; Stuttgart: J. G. Cotta, 1921, 1923] 1.297 n. 2). Similarly, Xenophon, *Hellenica* 2.4.23, still speaks of 'the thirty' even though two have already been put to death (BDAG 266).

92. 'The chief point here is not the resurrection as an actual event, but the meaning of the resurrection as the "hope of Israel"' (Jervell, *Apg.* 127).

Jesus? In the first generation of Christianity there were only two others who rank in significance with members of the original twelve — James, brother of Jesus, and Saul, who becomes Paul. Paul was hardly a contender for the twelfth position at this stage, but James was present (according to 1.14), and 1 Cor. 15.7 credits him with a personal resurrection appearance. Even with the restrictive criteria of 1.22, Luke could surely have regarded him as a fit person for the role. But no, it is two otherwise unknown figures who are candidates, one of whom is appointed.[93] Once again, then, early involvement of James within the new movement (when and how) is left with a question mark against it.

Most striking of all is the obvious question: Why was the vacant twelfth place filled up during the ten-day gap between Jesus' presence with them and the coming of the Spirit at Pentecost? One would have thought that if the completion of the twelve was so important, then the risen Jesus himself might have made his own appointment; Luke after all had given some emphasis to the importance of the fact that Jesus himself had chosen the apostles (1.2). It was equally important that Paul was appointed directly by the risen Jesus (9.15; 26.16-18).[94] Alternatively, the obvious appointer other than Jesus would be the Holy Spirit (as in 13.2-4). It is altogether curious that Luke, having made such a point of the interregnum between ascension and Pentecost, nevertheless chooses to narrate the appointment of Judas's replacement during that interregnum, and using methods (the lot) which appointment by Jesus or the Spirit would have rendered unnecessary and outmoded. The oddity of the event from Luke's own perspective is, of course, a positive indicator that he was drawing on tradition here,[95] and that there was a community memory of an action taken in the uncertain period before they became confident of the Spirit's guidance (contrast the later failure, or — perhaps better — positive decision, not to replace James, the brother of John — 12.2).[96] But the account itself leaves one wondering whether Luke was trying to signal something deficient in the appointment of Judas's replacement,[97] even

93. However, nothing should be made of the subsequent silence in Acts and other early Christian literature regarding Matthias, since the same silence envelops eight of the other eleven apostles. On later speculation about the two men's subsequent roles see, e.g., Fitzmyer, *Acts* 226-27; Zwiep, *Judas* 159-63.

94. The answer that the lots are a way of allowing *God* to determine the twelfth apostle (as in Haenchen, *Acts* 164) is inadequate, since all the other apostles (including Paul!) are chosen by Christ himself.

95. See particularly the review by Weiser, *Apg.* 64-66.

96. Though Wedderburn points out that 'James, as a martyr, could still fulfil his role as eschatological judge' (*History* 23). 'Matthias was not chosen because Judas had died, but because he had become an apostate' (Zwiep, *Judas* 179).

97. Decision-making by casting lots is not attested elsewhere in the NT. For the various uses for which lots were thrown see W. Foerster, *TDNT* 3.758-59, 761. They were still in use at this time, as Josephus confirms (*War* 4.153). Zwiep concludes that the procedure was 'quite ap-

while, at the same time, signalling the importance of the twelve apostles as constitutive of the new movement in its role of forwarding and fulfilling Israel's destiny. Once again, in telling his tale of Christianity's beginnings as he does, Luke leaves a number of loose ends dangling and questions prompted but unanswered.

g. Conclusion

So, in summary, what did Luke hope to achieve in this opening chapter of his second volume? He certainly makes a number of strong affirmations, explicitly or implicitly, the most important being:

- the centrality of Jerusalem for the beginning of Christianity
- the constitutive function and authority of the apostles, that is, the twelve apostles
- the status of the new movement as continuing Israel's role and mission
- Acts as continuing Jesus' mission and message (the kingdom of God)
- the necessity for Spirit-empowered witness if the programme of mission is to be accomplished
- the resurrection appearances as very tangible
- the resurrection appearances as ended after a short time
- the importance of distinguishing Jesus' resurrection from his being taken up into heaven
- the clear distinction and gap between ascension and Pentecost.

This was Luke's way of setting the scene for the 'big bang' which was to be Pentecost. His freedom in telling this story is not out of line with the kind of freedom we have had to envisage in the retellings of Jesus' mission which lie behind and which are represented in the Synoptic Gospels, as we saw in *Jesus Remembered.*

Equally evident are the historical data on which and from which Luke has shaped his retelling. These are attested elsewhere in earliest Christian tradition and would have been either immediately familiar to Luke from his own experience of Christian fellowship and worship or standard features of the reminiscences of those involved from the beginning:

- Jesus being seen (resurrection appearances) by a number of his disciples (more than the eleven) in and around Jerusalem after his crucifixion
- a characteristic conviction that Jesus had also commissioned those to whom he appeared

---

propriate in the given circumstances from Luke's perspective . . . the perfect "biblical" scenario' (*Judas* 171).

- the cessation of these sightings after some time
- continued reflection on Jesus' message of God's kingly rule in relation to Israel
- from early on a recognition of the importance of 'the twelve'
- the early appreciation that Jesus had been more than raised from the dead; he had been taken up into heaven as well
- the shameful death of Judas Iscariot
- a searching of the Scriptures to help make sense of what had happened and what now needed to be done
- the possibility that in the period before the first disciples gained self-confidence (Spirit-confidence!) they took steps to fill the place vacated by Judas Iscariot.

Finally, it is necessary to remind ourselves of where Luke's retelling of these shared traditions raises a number of questions and leaves them unanswered:

- How can Luke's account be correlated with the traditions of other sightings of Jesus (resurrection appearances) in Galilee (not to mention Paul's claim — 1 Cor. 15.8) (§22.2a)?
- If the limitation of the appearances to forty days cannot be sustained, what are the consequences for Luke's clear gap and distinction between them and Pentecost (§22.2b)?
- In the light of Luke's contrivances (and of the first-century worldview), how are we to think of 'the ascension' (§22.2d)?
- When and how did Jesus' own family come to associate themselves with the continuing group of disciples (§22.2e)?

A final issue sets us up nicely for the next phase of investigation: was Luke's positioning of the election of a twelfth apostle, at a time when neither Jesus was still perceived as present among them nor the Spirit understood to be yet given to them, intended (1) negatively, to indicate the inadequacies of decisions made in that in-between time, or (2) positively, to underscore (by contrast) the necessity for the infant church to rely rather (a) on the tradition of Jesus' teaching and (b) on the guidance of the Spirit?

22.3. Pentecost

Luke's account of the first Christian Pentecost (Acts 2.1-13) is one of his most famous and influential narratives. With a few deft strokes he paints a riveting scene. When the feast of Pentecost dawned, the disciples were all together (presumably all 120 — 1.15?).[98] Suddenly a sound like a violent wind *(pnoē biaia)* comes from heaven and fills the whole house where they were sitting (2.2).[99] And 'divided tongues, just like fire', appear to them, one sitting on each of them.[100] They are all 'filled with the Holy Spirit and begin to speak with 'other tongues *(heterais glōssais)*' as the Spirit gives them to speak (2.1-4). A crowd of devout Jews, living *(katoikountes)* in Jerusalem, but from the diaspora, are attracted by the sound *(phōnē)* and gather in bewilderment, since each one hears the mighty deeds of God being spoken in his own language (2.5-6, 11). Some dismiss what is being said as the babble of drunkards (2.13), and their snide comment gives Peter his cue for the first Christian sermon (2.14-36) — the implication presumably being that in the meantime the disciples had spilled out from the house into some open space.[101] The sermon so convicts the hearers that no less than 3,000 are converted and baptized (2.37-41).

Given the captivating power of the scene thus painted, anyone with Christian convictions, or even simply sympathies, can hardly fail to wish that it all happened just as Luke records it. But questions similar to those posed by the preceding chapter of Acts (§22.2) immediately arise.

a. Luke's Theological Agenda

Three features catch the attention.

(1) Luke's concern to cement a link with his previous volume (the Gospel) is very evident. As the mission of Jesus depended on the prior anointing of the Spirit (Luke 3.22; 4.18; Acts 10.38), so the mission of the apostles depended similarly on their being empowered by the same Spirit (Luke 24.49; Acts 1.8). As the Gospel of Jesus only really began with Luke 3–4, so the Acts of the Apostles only really begins with Acts 2.[102]

---

98. J. Dupont, 'The First Christian Pentecost', *The Salvation of the Gentiles: Studies in the Acts of the Apostles* (1967; New York: Paulist, 1979) 35-59, suggests that '1.13-14 constituted the original and normal introduction to the Pentecost narrative, but it became separated from that narrative' by the insertion of 1.15-26 (38).

99. Luke does not bother to say where the house *(oikos)* was — presumably the same place as in 1.13.

100. 'Luke probably means that one tongue-like flame rested upon each person' (Barrett, *Acts* 114). Haenchen draws attention to *1 En.* 14.8-15 and 71.5 (*Acts* 168 n. 2).

101. A court of the Temple is suggested quite often — see, e.g., Kremer, *Pfingstbericht* 98 n. 34 — but unless the *oikos* is envisaged as contiguous with the outer court, such a substantial shift of scene may be ruled out by Luke's albeit sparse narrative. Luke always refers to the Temple as *to hieron* (2.46; 3.1-3, 8, 10; 4.1; 5.20-21, 24-25, 42; etc.; Haenchen, *Acts* 168 n. 1; Kremer 104).

102. See also Longenecker, *Rhetoric at the Boundaries* 215-26, and §21 n. 45 above.

Moreover, the Pentecostal coming of the Spirit is explicitly identified as the fulfilment of the promise made by the Baptist in Luke 3.16 and repeated by Jesus (Acts 1.5). Although the tradition in Luke 3.16 envisaged being baptized in the Spirit and fire as a fiercely purgative experience,[103] Luke evidently had no qualms in portraying that ministry as completed in the very different experience of being filled with the Spirit, an experience of exultation rather than of purgation.[104] The implication that Jesus now at last fulfils the Baptist's prediction is made explicit in Peter's speech (Acts 2.33), with important corollaries as regards the status thereby attributed to the risen, and now ascended, Jesus.[105] Not that Luke ignores the dual elements of the Baptist's prediction — *ruach/pneuma* (wind/Spirit) and fire (Luke 3.16). It is surely not a mere coincidence that the event/experience of Pentecost involves a hearing of wind *(pnoē)* and a seeing of fire — albeit a sound *as it were (hōsper)* of wind, and tongues *like (hōsei)* fire (Acts 2.2-3). Perhaps, then, Luke intended to indicate thereby that the fulfilment of the Baptist's prediction, though different from the Baptist's expectation, was nevertheless to be understood as the genuine fulfilment of what the Baptist had looked for.[106]

(2) A second indication of Luke's theological agenda is his depiction of the crowd who were attracted by the noise as drawn from 'every nation under heaven' (2.5). Setting aside the obvious hyperbole (from *every* nation under heaven?), Luke clearly presents the scene as the beginning of the fulfilment of Simeon's original prophecy (Luke 1.30-32), the disciples at Pentecost already representing the 'all flesh' of Joel's prediction (Acts 2.17, 21), and as foreshadowing the universal mission which was to follow (1.8; 2.21, 39; 3.25; 4.12; etc.).[107] The scope of the outreach foreshadowed is given more precision by 'the catalogue of nations' which Luke inserts somewhat awkwardly into the exclamation of the crowd (2.9-11), the crowd functioning in effect as the chorus in the unfolding drama. The issue of where Luke derived the list of names from,[108] the

---

103. *Jesus Remembered* 366-69.

104. In *Jesus Remembered* 803-804 I suggested that Jesus himself may have begun the process of re-interpreting the Baptist's prediction, as implied by Luke 12.49-50.

105. See further below, §23.4e.

106. Central to the early Christian message, after all, was the claim that despite the difference between Jesus' mission and the Baptist's expectation of 'the coming one', Jesus was indeed the one prophesied by John (see *Jesus Remembered* 439-55).

107. But Luke does preserve the breakthrough character of Peter's mission to Cornelius — 'even on Gentiles' (10.45), 'even to Gentiles' (11.18) — by making it clear that at Pentecost itself only 'devout Jews' (2.5) are in view. Jervell pushes the point too hard: 'The list of nations shows clearly that it's all about world Judaism, not about the world' (*Apg.* 134-36, though also 137).

108. It is important to note that the list does not presage Luke's subsequent account — no mention of Syria, Macedonia or Achaia, for example, or inclusion of areas to the east. But

degree of artificiality in envisaging the crowd so speaking,[109] and the various elements of inconsistency involved — Jews residing in Jerusalem(!), 'residents' in Mesopotamia (2.9) 'residing' in Jerusalem (2.5), and the inclusion of 'Judea' in the list (2.9)[110] — should not be allowed to detract from Luke's main point: that from the very first day the good news of Jesus' resurrection[111] was being heard by a wide range of diaspora Jews.

(3) Most striking for most readers of Luke's account is the report that those thus filled with the Spirit spoke in foreign languages. That they did so speak is the most obvious way to understand what Luke wrote. For obvious reasons some have attempted to diminish the miraculous character of the event thus understood, usually by envisaging a miracle of hearing, rather than of speaking.[112] The inference of 2.13, that some heard only a drunken babble, gives the argument some weight. But so far as Luke himself was concerned, his choice of wording in 2.6 and 11 is hard to construe other than as intended to convey a miraculous speaking in foreign languages, presumably hitherto (and still) unknown to the speakers themselves. The key word, *glōssa* (2.4, 11), means 'tongue', with the secondary meaning, as in English, of 'language'. The fuller phrase, *heterai glōssai* (2.4), can hardly be understood other than as 'other languages', just as the fuller phrase, *hēmeterai glōssai* (2.11), can hardly be understood other than

---

why such a list (derived from where?) unless it matched up with inquiries Luke made as to the range of nationalities in the earliest Jerusalem community? See further Haenchen, *Acts* 169-70 n. 5; B. M. Metzger, 'Ancient Astrological Geography and Acts 2:9-11', in W. W. Gasque and R. P. Martin, eds., *Apostolic History and the Gospel*, F. F. Bruce FS (Exeter: Paternoster, 1970) 123-33; Fitzmyer, *Acts* 240-43. R. Bauckham, 'James and the Jerusalem Church', *BAFCS* 4.415-80, plausibly finds in the list of nations a Jerusalem-centred perspective (419-22). G. Gilbert, 'The List of Nations in Acts 2: Roman Propaganda and the Lukan Response', *JBL* 121 (2002) 497-529, sees the list as Luke's critique of the geographical catalogues which celebrated Rome's imperial power and his alternative vision of universal authority (518-19).

109. K. Lake, 'The Day of Pentecost', *Beginnings* 5.111-21: 'It is unlikely that any body of men witnessing the phenomena described ever made a speech in which they gave a complete catalogue of the nations from which they had been taken' (120).

110. See particularly A. J. M. Wedderburn, 'Traditions and Redaction in Acts 2.1-13', *JSNT* 55 (1994) 27-54 (here 39-48).

111. The reference here is not so much to 'the mighty deeds of God' (2.11) as to the sermon which follows (in the vernacular?) to the same audience (2.14-36), although, of course, Luke may well have intended to imply that the resurrection of Jesus was one, if not the chiefmost, of God's 'mighty deeds'; but the phrase itself reflects characteristic Jewish usage (as in Deut. 11.2; Ps. 71.19; 105.1; 106.21; Sir. 17.8-9; 18.4; 36.10; 42.21).

112. Cf. Bruce: 'The disciples, suddenly delivered from the peculiarities of their Galilean speech, praised God and rehearsed his mighty works in such a way that each hearer recognized with surprise his own language or dialect' (*Acts* 115). Others in Kremer, *Pfingstbericht* 136 n. 148; now also P. Barnett, *Jesus and the Rise of Early Christianity: A History of New Testament Times* (Downers Grove: InterVarsity, 1999) 197.

as 'our languages'. The second reference, it is true, is recorded as what the crowd hear (2.11), and similarly in 2.6 — 'each one heard them speaking in his own native language *(dialektos)*'. But the first reference is Luke's own description of what happened: 'they began to speak in other languages' (2.4).[113]

The rationale of Luke's understanding of this effect (or manifestation) of the Spirit's coming upon the disciples is presumably to reinforce the preceding point. The Spirit enabled or inspired a speaking which could be understood by a wide range of the crowd (2.8-11), though not all (2.13), a crowd which could be regarded as to some extent representative of all the nations under heaven. In other words, the outpouring of the Spirit on the day of Pentecost was to reinforce and enable a worship (and proclamation?) which was meaningful to a wide range of nationalities.[114]

Can we fairly read more in (or into) Luke's narrative?

b. The Theological Significance of Pentecost

'Pentecost', which means literally 'fiftieth', is short for *hē pentēkostē hēmera*, 'the fiftieth day', referring to the festival celebrated on the fiftieth day after Passover; it was the second great pilgrim feast in the Jewish calendar.[115] The significance of Pentecost seems to have been developing during the period before and after Jesus. It had already become the feast of covenant renewal in *Jub.* 6.17-21 and probably also in the Qumran community (cf. 1QS 1.16–2.18), an association already implied in 2 Chron. 15.10-12.[116] This almost certainly meant a link be-

---

113. The superficially attractive suggestion that Luke saw Pentecost as the reverse of the curse of Babel (Gen. 11.6-9) is unlikely; Pentecost was not the restoration of a single, universal language. Luke, of course, does not concern himself with the thought that diaspora Jews resident in Jerusalem would have had a common language — Greek!

114. Surprisingly, Jervell deduces from the repetition of *apophthengomai* in 2.14, as well as 2.4, that 'the speech of Peter, 2.14ff., is obviously to be understood as tongues-speech' (*Apg.* 134). But Haenchen had already pointed out that *apophthengomai* means 'to speak in a solemn or inspired way, but not ecstatic speech' (*Acts* 168 n. 3).

115. Pentecost began as a harvest festival, when the firstfruits of the wheat harvest were presented to Yahweh, and was celebrated seven weeks after the beginning of the barley harvest (hence 'Feast of Weeks'). For more details see Exod. 23.16; 34.22; Lev. 23.15-21; Num. 28.26-31; Deut. 16.9-12; Tob. 2.1; 2 Macc. 12.32; 4Q196 frag. 2.10; Philo, *Decal.* 160; *Spec. Leg.* 2.176-88; Josephus, *War* 1.253; 2.42; 6.299; *Ant.* 3.252-57; 13.252; 14.337; 17.254; E. Lohse, *TDNT* 6.45-48.

116. See, e.g., Kremer, *Pfingstbericht* 14-18; Schürer, *History* 2.582, 595; M. A. Knibb, *The Qumran Community* (Cambridge: Cambridge University, 1987) 88-89; H. Stegemann, *The Library of Qumran* (1993; Grand Rapids: Eerdmans, 1998) 108, 164-65; Fitzmyer, *Acts* 233-34. Barrett comments that *Jub.* 6.17-18 seems to refer only to the covenant with Noah, not to

tween Pentecost and the covenant of Sinai in particular: both Exod. 19.1 (the Sinai covenant) and 2 Chron. 15.10 (the renewal of the covenant) specify 'the third month' (the month during which Pentecost was celebrated).

In Philo, the Sinai traditions are themselves developed. The heavenly voice at Sinai (Exod. 19.16-19) 'sounded forth like the breath *(pneuma)* through a trumpet'; 'the flame became articulate speech in the language familiar to the audience' (*Decal.* 33, 46). However, Philo did not associate the Sinai revelation with Pentecost. Subsequently, in rabbinic Judaism, these two developments do come together. The association of Pentecost with the giving of the Law becomes explicit (*b. Pesaḥ.* 68b), and the words of Rabbi Yohanan are frequently quoted (in various forms): the (one) voice (at Sinai) divided into (seven voices and these into) seventy languages (so that all the nations heard in their own language).[117] However, the link between Pentecost and Sinai is not documented before the second century and Rabbi Yohanan (who died in 279).

Such parallels have been familiar to students of Acts for more than one hundred years and naturally raise the question whether, and if so by how much, Luke's account of the first Christian Pentecost has been influenced by such traditions. Was Luke familiar not simply with the idea of Pentecost as the festival of covenant renewal but also with a speculation regarding Sinai which thought of the fiery revelation of Sinai as given in language which was understandable to those gathered at the foot of the mountain? And if so, did he incorporate elements of that speculation into his narrative in order to present the first Christian Pentecost, the outpouring of the Spirit predicted by Joel and other prophets, as in effect the Christian equivalent of Israel's Sinai experience? Or, to put the issue more sharply, did Luke make use of such traditions in order to present Pentecost as (1) the equivalent foundational event for the new movement, (2) thereby implying not only that Pentecost was the fulfilment of prophetic hope for a new covenant,[118] but also (3) that the Spirit had in effect replaced the Torah as the determining factor for the new sect's life and faith?[119] The point, of course, would

---

that with Moses (*Acts* 111), but Wedderburn observes that for *Jubilees* 'God's covenant with Noah, Abraham and Moses seems to be one covenant, renewed at Pentecost' ('Traditions and Redaction' 34; also Kremer 15-16). See further Lohse, *TDNT* 6.48-49.

117. Lake, *Beginnings* 5.115-16; Haenchen, *Acts* 173-74; Kremer, *Pfingstbericht* 241-53.

118. Notably Jer. 31.31-34 and Ezek. 36.26-27. Note the thesis of M. Turner, *Power from on High: The Spirit in Israel's Restoration and Witness in Luke-Acts* (Sheffield: Sheffield Academic, 1996), that the coming of the Spirit at Pentecost is part of the traditional expectation for the restoration of Israel. J. M. Scott, 'Acts 2:9-11 as an Anticipation of the Mission to the Nations', in J. Ådna and H. Kvalbein, eds., *The Mission of the Early Church to Jews and Gentiles* (WUNT 127; Tübingen: Mohr Siebeck, 2000) 87-123, concludes: 'It can hardly be a coincidence that the first names listed in Acts 2:9-11 are peoples and places to which Israel and Judah had been exiled centuries earlier' (123).

119. Jervell, however, thinks that for Luke law and Spirit belong closely together (*Apg.*

be that if Luke's narrative is the product of such influence, then it becomes all the more difficult to attribute such detail (particularly the fire and the many languages) to any kind of historical reminiscence available to Luke.

What we can say with some confidence is that Pentecost had already become the feast of covenant renewal within Jewish tradition and praxis. Given that the covenant for Israel was so much identified with the Torah,[120] the feast of Pentecost would presumably have included celebration of the law-giving at Sinai. Such an association was inevitable from the time that festivals became also celebrations of Israel's history.[121] The dating of the Sinai revelation to the third month (six to ten weeks after the Passover) must clearly have suggested the association. And the custom of reading Exodus 19 at the Feast of Pentecost may possibly have become established in the century before Jesus.[122] Consequently, whether Luke himself was aware of these associations, many of his readers would have been, so that it would be difficult for a Jew (as were all the first disciples of Jesus) to hear this account without thinking of the outpouring of the Spirit at Pentecost as God's renewing of his covenant (with Israel) or indeed as establishing his new covenant.[123]

Beyond that, the historical foundations become exceedingly shaky. The Acts 2 tradition is significantly different from the rabbinic reflection on Sinai.[124] The earlier the reflection, the greater the differences from Acts 2. Philo's treat-

---

132 and 133 n. 149, 139); he finds support in the tradition behind Eph. 4.7-8 (citing Ps. 68.17-18, with its reference to Sinai) (138-39); see also §23 n. 100 below.

120. The tie-in between election, covenant and law was a fundamental and persistent theme of Jewish self-understanding, as illustrated by ben Sira (Sir. 17.11-17; 24.23; 28.7; 39.8; 42.2; 44.19-20; 45.5, 7, 15, 17, 24-25), *Jubilees* (1.4-5, 9-10, 12, 14, 29; 2.21; 6.4-16; 14.17-20; 15.4-16, 19-21, 25-29, 34; 16.14; 19.29; 20.3; etc.), the Damascus Document (CD 1.4-5, 15-18, 20; 3.2-4, 10-16; 4.7-10; 6.2-5; etc.) and Pseudo-Philo (*LAB* 4.5, 11; 7.4; 8.3; 9.3-4, 7-8, 13, 15; 10.2; 11.1-5; etc.). *Mek. Exod.* 20.6 — 'By covenant is meant nothing other than the Torah' — well represents subsequent rabbinic thought (see further Str-B 3.126-33).

121. Passover — cf. Exod. 12.12-13, 17, 23-27, 39; Tabernacles — Lev. 23.43.

122. Lohse, *TDNT* 6.47 n. 19.

123. The evidence of Luke's only two 'covenant' references in Acts is ambiguous: 3.25 gives some scope for a putative Lukan theology of new covenant, but 7.8 identifies the covenant with Abraham as 'the covenant of circumcision'; contrast Galatians 3 and Romans 4. But neither does Paul have much of a 'covenant theology'; see my 'Did Paul Have a Covenant Theology? Reflections on Romans 9.4 and 11.27', *The New Perspective on Paul* ch. 20. Note however the thesis of S. McKnight, 'Covenant and Spirit: The Origins of the New Covenant Hermeneutic', in Stanton et al., eds., *The Holy Spirit and Christian Origins* 41-54: 'The new covenant hermeneutic owes its origins to the pneumatic experiences of early Jerusalem-based followers of Jesus' (51).

124. Sinai — one heavenly voice from the mountain, proclaiming the law, in seventy languages; Pentecost — many human voices, inspired by the Spirit to praise God, in many languages.

ment of Exodus 19 appears to be simply his own (typical) exposition of a biblical narrative (contrast Heb. 12.19), and the possible points of contact with Acts 2 are minimal. At the same time, the fact that the recognition of a link between Pentecost and Sinai cannot be traced back in rabbinic tradition before the second century CE is not decisive against the view that such a link had already been made earlier. The rabbis' silence may simply reflect their lower regard for Pentecost, which in turn may be due to a reaction on their part against the high esteem accorded to Pentecost in the 'heterodox Judaisms' of the time. I have already noted Pentecost's significance at Qumran;[125] we know that the Therapeutae regarded Pentecost as the chief feast of the year (Philo, *Vit. Cont.* 65-66),[126] a view which Philo may well have shared (*Spec. Leg.* 2.176-87); and the importance attached by Christians is evident in the Acts 2 story itself.[127]

How much does all this bear on the significance of Luke's Pentecost narrative? The most interesting aspect of the whole debate is the more or less complete absence from that narrative of any clear indication that Luke wanted his readers to hear such overtones, far less that he had shaped his narrative to make them explicit.[128] Of course, present-day hermeneutics encourages us to recognize that a text once written may well set bells ringing and activate associations for readers of which the author was completely unaware. But our inquiry is into the sources on which Luke drew, the historical foundations for his narratives. And in that respect it can only be said that there is no evidence of any great weight that Luke's narrative was the product of his drawing on current reflection and speculation regarding the giving of the Torah. The covenant associations

125. See n. 115 above.

126. Schürer, *History* 2.592-93, 595.

127. Wedderburn, 'Traditions and Redaction', thinks that echoes of Jewish traditions concerning the giving of the law and covenant at Sinai are too clear in Acts 2.1-13 to be coincidental but notes that Luke betrays no awareness of the parallels. His solution is to envisage a three-stage development of the tradition, with the associations of the day of Pentecost influencing Luke's *predecessors,* those who formulated the tradition which Luke drew upon.

128. Fitzmyer, *Acts* 234, draws attention to J. Dupont, 'La nouvelle Pentecôte (Ac 2,1-11). Fête de la Pentecôte', *Nouvelles études sur les Actes des Apôtres* (LD 118; Paris: Cerf, 1984) 193-98, who notes several verbal allusions in Acts 2 to Exodus 19–20: 'together' (2.1; Exod. 19.8), 'sound' (2.2, 6; Exod. 19.16), 'fire' (2.3; Exod. 19.18), 'from heaven' (Exod. 20.22) (already in Dupont, 'First Christian Pentecost' 38-42). But the first two are at best incidental details, whereas to be effective, an allusion would have had to evoke the shuddering awesomeness of the Exodus account — thunder and lightning and thick cloud, a loud and sustained trumpet blast (which Philo took up), and smoke like the smoke of a kiln. Wind and fire were more widely understood to signify the presence of the divine (Exod. 3.2-6; 13.21; 19.16-18; 24.17; 1 Kgs. 19.11-12; Ps. 104.4; Isa. 66.15; Ezek. 1.4; Kremer, *Pfingstbericht* 102, 106, 113-14, 238-40); 'these belong to the general vocabulary of Old Testament and Jewish theophanies' (Kremer 239); see also *Jesus Remembered* 366-67.

which already attached to Pentecost may be another matter, but the point here is that they were attached to the feast itself, rather than in any obvious way to Luke's account. Indeed they may be part of the historical associations of the first Christian Pentecost, even if Luke chose not to make anything of them!

c. The Historical Foundations of Luke's Account of Pentecost

What then can we say about the historical data on which Luke has built his narrative in Acts 2?[129]

(1) The movement which became Christianity began as an enthusiastic sect within Second Temple Judaism. This is clearly the testimony of Luke's Acts,[130] even if Luke himself makes more of the tangibility of these experiences than others would have preferred.[131] And Luke's testimony is confirmed by Paul, who talks freely, if more circumspectly, about speaking in tongues (1 Corinthians 14), who warns against quenching the Spirit (1 Thess. 5.19), who can boast, should that be considered desirable, about his many visions and revelations (2 Cor. 12.1, 7), and who does not hesitate to claim signs and wonders wrought by the power of the Spirit (Rom. 15.19; Gal. 3.5). Occasional further references confirm the broad picture — such as Eph. 5.18, which, by setting drunkenness in contrast with being filled with the Spirit, suggests experiences similar to that of Pentecost (cf. Acts 2.13); Heb. 2.4, which attests experiences of 'signs and wonders and various miracles, and apportionments *(merismois)* of the Holy Spirit'; and John, who uses experientially rich imagery in describing 'worship in Spirit and truth' (John 4.23-24, in the light of 4.14 and 7.38-39).[132]

It is not without significance for the historian of religious movements that such characteristics — ecstatic experience, visions, prophecy and amazing healings (miracles) — can be matched with similar experiences in the beginnings of the three illustrative parallels cited above in §22.1a (particularly the radical Ref-

129. In some of the points below, particularly (3) and (4), I draw on my earlier *Jesus and the Spirit* 138-40.

130. Ecstasy — 2.1-4; 8.17-18; 10.44-46; 11.15; 19.6; inspired speech — 4.8, 31; 5.32; 6.3, 5, 10; 11.28; 13.9; 20.23; 21.4, 11; glossolalia — 2.4; 10.46; 19.6; visions — 7.55; 9.10; 10.3-6, 10-16; 16.9-10; 18.9; 22.17-18; 26.19 ('ecstatic', 10.10; 11.5; 22.17); inspired guidance — 8.29, 39; 10.19; 11.12; 13.2, 4; 15.28; 16.6-7; 19.21; 20.22; healings — 3.1-10; 8.7; 9.18, 33-34, 36-41 (through Peter's shadow, 5.15-16, and through cloths and aprons touched by Paul, 19.11-12); miracles of judgment — 5.1-11; 13.8-11; 19.13-16.

131. See above, §21 n. 132, and further my *Unity and Diversity* 176-84. For the visionary element in the Pentecost experience (sight and sound), see my *Jesus and the Spirit* 147-48.

132. See also Kremer, *Pfingstbericht* 28-59. Cf. Pokorny: 'This spontaneous joy with its ecstatic expression was thus evidently a more elemental reaction to the Easter event than the formulated acclamation and confessional phrases' (*Genesis* 117).

ormation and Pentecostalism). It may be disconcerting for some, but in describing earliest Christianity as an 'enthusiastic sect', it is difficult to avoid the connotations which *Schwärmerei* ('enthusiasm') gained as a result of the radical Reformation.[133] And if 'enthusiasm' proves to be an unsatisfactory description because of its seventeenth- and eighteenth-century overtones of excess and hints of fanaticism, then we simply have to substitute some term like 'overtly spiritual' or the more twentieth-century 'charismatic' (or even 'Pentecostal'!). At any rate, it was the kind of fervent renewal movement which makes those who cherish and who live by older, established traditions distinctly uneasy or even hostile.[134]

Without labouring the issue of appropriate descriptive language, the point is that such characteristics which so typified the movement must have begun to appear for the first time at some stage, and to do so in a way which set a pattern for those who then and subsequently joined that movement (much as the 1906 Azusa Street experience set a pattern for so many Pentecostals). This suggests that those who designate Pentecost as 'the first outbreak of inspired mass ecstasy' within Christianity are probably on the correct track.[135] That there was such an experience, recognized as experience of God's Spirit and shared by those who became the initial leaders of the movement, is highly probable.[136] Luke's account of Pentecost is presumably his account of that experience.

(2) We can be confident that such experiences, and not just those of ecstasy and inspiration (Acts 9.31; 13.52), were understood from the first as experiences of the Spirit of God *in fulfilment of prophetic hope*. Luke's initial emphasis on Pentecost as the fulfilment of 'the promise of the Father' (Luke 24.49; Acts 1.4), the promise of the Spirit (2.33, 39), is by no means his alone or a distinctively Lukan emphasis.

- We find the same emphasis in Gal. 3.14 and Eph. 1.13;
- 2 Cor. 3.3 echoes Ezek. 11.19, 1 Thess. 4.8 echoes Ezek. 36.26-27, and Rev. 11.11 echoes Ezek. 37.5, 10;
- 1 Pet. 4.14 draws on the language of Isa. 11.2;

133. See my 'Enthusiasm', *The Encyclopedia of Religion* (New York: Macmillan, 1987) 5.118-24, reprinted in *The Christ and the Spirit*. Vol. 2: *Pneumatology* (Grand Rapids: Eerdmans, 1998) 32-42.

134. Cf. the brief review in Pesch, *Apg.* 1.109-13.

135. Lohse, *TDNT* 6.51; Goppelt, *Apostolic* 22. Kremer does not like the characterization 'mass ecstasy' and prefers to speak of the 'waiting apostles deeply stirred *(ergriffen)* by an overwhelming power which they explained as the promised Holy Spirit sent by the exalted Lord' (*Pfingstbericht* 263, 267).

136. H. Conzelmann, *History of Primitive Christianity* (Nashville: Abingdon, 1973): 'It remains as a probable historical kernel that the power of the Spirit was experienced in the primitive community' (49).

- Joel's image of the Spirit 'outpoured' (Acts 2.17-18) is reflected also in Rom. 5.5 and Tit. 3.6;
- Paul takes for granted that every Christian has been 'baptized in the Spirit' (1 Cor. 12.13);
- John 20.22, the so-called Johannine Pentecost, uses language unique in the biblical tradition *(emphysaō)* to Gen. 2.7 and Ezek. 37.9.[137]

In other words, the sense that they were now enjoying what had been expected for the age to come (in shorthand, the eschatological Spirit) was widespread among the first Christian communities.

One of the most striking features of Luke's account in Acts 2 is the modification to the prophecy of Joel which he incorporates into Peter's speech. For, as already noted,[138] Joel's prophecy had begun with the more ambiguous 'after this' (Joel 2.28 = 3.1 Heb.; Greek 'after these things'). But Acts 2.17 cites Joel as saying 'in the last days'.[139] The feature is striking, since, apart from the second sermon of Peter (3.19-21), there is little indication of eschatological enthusiasm (a sense of belonging to the time of the end) in Luke's narrative.[140] The likelihood, then, is that the emphasis came to Luke in the traditions which he drew together to write his narrative. This sense of realized hope (realized eschatology) may well, of course, reflect Jesus' own claims regarding the already-present activity of God's kingly rule.[141] But almost certainly it would have been stimulated by the twin events which the disciples had now experienced — the evidence of end-time resurrection having already begun (with Jesus' resurrection), and the evidence of the prophesied Spirit now outpoured. These are aspects of earliest Christianity to which we will have to return below (§§23.4a, e).

---

137. Dunn, *Baptism in the Holy Spirit* 180; see further M. M. Thompson, 'The Breath of Life: John 20:22-23 Once More', in Stanton et al., eds., *The Holy Spirit and Christian Origins* 69-78.

138. See above, §21 at n. 153.

139. The alteration is usually attributed to Luke (e.g., Metzger, *Textual Commentary* 295), presumably his recognition of the eschatological excitement which marked the earliest community. Haenchen argues that 'after these things' is the original: 'In Lucan theology the last days do not begin as soon as the Spirit has been poured out!' (*Acts* 179); but see F. Mussner, '"In den letzten Tagen" (Apg. 2,17a)', *BZ* 5 (1961) 263-65; others in Jervell, *Apg.* 143 n. 207.

140. See below, §23.4f. Fitzmyer insists that Conzelmann's three-phase division of Lukan salvation-history (the period of Israel, the period of Jesus, the period of the church) has to be maintained, even if slightly modified (*Acts* 201, referring back to his *Luke* 181-87 and to Conzelmann, *Theology of St. Luke* 12-17); that is, Luke saw salvation history as stretching for a further period (the period of the church) before its end in the parousia (coming again) of Jesus (Luke 21.27; Acts 1.11; 3.20-21). For some reflections on the meaning we can or should give to the term 'eschatological', see *Jesus Remembered* 398-401.

141. See again *Jesus Remembered* §12.5.

(3) But where did 'the first mass ecstasy' take place? That there was such an experience/event in Jerusalem is very likely. The key fact here is that Jerusalem was clearly regarded widely within the new movement as its centre. No alternative centre or geographical point of origin is even hinted at in any document or source available to us.[142] Critical here, once again, is the testimony of Paul. As already hinted, and as we shall see more fully in due course, Paul did not regard himself as particularly dependent on Jerusalem and may even have been at times quite (or very) hostile to its emissaries.[143] Yet he acknowledges Jerusalem's primacy, authority and fountainhead status on several occasions (notably Gal. 2.1-10 and Rom. 15.25-27). Had there been another centre or originating locus for Christianity, Paul would surely have given us some hint to that effect. The fact that no such hint can be found in his letters (he mentions Antioch only in Gal. 2.11) can only mean that Jerusalem was where it all began to happen.[144]

A notable fact is that the leaders in Jerusalem were, and from the first, Galileans — Peter, James and John, and soon James the brother of Jesus (§23.3 below). That Jesus' Galilean disciples should have abandoned so completely the region where Jesus had conducted his most successful mission (Galilee) is quite remarkable.[145] The reason, we can guess, was that Jerusalem was the most obvious location of the next great phase of the eschatological drama and climax which had begun to unfold on Easter day.[146] But whatever the reason, the consequence seems to have been that Galilee was denuded of the most important of Jesus' original disciples and consequently did not feature as a major part of the new movement or even as an alternative form of it. Here too we are driven to conclude that it all began in Jerusalem.[147]

(4) And when? Two considerations push us towards the Pentecost follow-

---

142. The play on 'Jerusalem' — the 'heavenly Jerusalem' etc. (Gal. 4.25-26; Heb. 12.22; Rev. 3.12; 21.2, 10; see further *PGL* 671) — could only be sustained if the earthly Jerusalem had in fact been the *fons et origo* of Christianity.

143. See further below, §§27.2-6, 31.7, 32.7 and 34.4.

144. The attempt of contributors to Cameron and Miller, *Redescribing Christian Origins* part 2, to locate Christian origins *away* from Jerusalem provides a fascinating example of tendentious argument which finds only what it wants to find in the data: particularly the attempts to play down what appear to be obvious inferences from Pauline texts (Gal. 1.18; 2.1-14; Rom. 15.19, 25-26), and to find evidence which supports an alternative hypothesis of the decisive developments somewhere else (anywhere, it would appear, other than Jerusalem).

145. J. Becker, *Jesus of Nazareth* (Berlin: de Gruyter, 1998), observes that 'if Jesus had predicted the destruction of the temple or had pronounced God's judgment on Jerusalem, the earliest post-Easter church would probably have established itself in Galilee rather than in Jerusalem' (334).

146. See below, §23.4f.

147. For those who reach a similar conclusion see my *Jesus and the Spirit* 396 n. 33; and see nn. 7-8 above.

ing Jesus' crucifixion. One is that the timescale for the early years can be sketched out with a fair degree of confidence. Paul must have been converted within two or three years of Jesus' death.[148] But in the months prior to Paul's conversion we have to envisage the period covered by Acts 2–8, including Paul's persecution of the new sect, the reasons which incited him to that persecution, and the events which preceded. But had belief in Jesus' resurrection taken some months (even years) to become established, as is sometimes suggested, it would be difficult, not to say impossible, for the events prior to Paul's conversion to have taken place. The pressure of historical reconstruction pushes us inexorably back to a date for the 'first mass ecstasy' sometime around the Pentecost of Luke's account.

Add to that the fact that, as many have pointed out, early Christianity took over only two Jewish feasts, namely Passover and Pentecost (cf. Acts 20.16; 1 Cor. 16.8), which implies that something special for the first Christians happened at Pentecost as well as at Easter.[149]

Moreover, the feast of Pentecost provides another point of resolution or convergence for one of the major anomalies behind Luke's account — I refer to the tradition of resurrection appearances in Galilee, not just in Jerusalem, as Luke would have it. For Pentecost was the next great pilgrim feast for Jews, indeed it was the climax of the festal period which began with Passover.[150] So, for those who had been revitalized by appearances in Galilee, and who thought of Jerusalem as the obvious location for the following or final act in the divine drama begun with Jesus' resurrection,[151] the feast of Pentecost following Jesus' resurrection was the obvious time for that expectation to be realized. For those thinking to return to Jerusalem from Galilee in the light of Jesus being seen alive from the dead, there could be no more propitious time than Pentecost.[152] Such an outcome would be sufficient to resolve the anomaly of appearances in Galilee as well as Jerusalem and could explain why Luke was able to ignore the former as he did — in the event they did not make any difference to the main thrust of Luke's narrative.

Earlier I asked, Why forty days? Why did Luke confine the resurrection appearances to forty days? I already suggested one reason might be that the fifty days of Pentecost was an already fixed date within Luke's tradition; Luke then simply settled on forty days as the next significant figure lower than fifty (§22.2b above). The above considerations give that suggestion more weight. The conclu-

148. See below, §28.1d.
149. Jervell, *Apg.* 138, with further bibliography n. 186.
150. Lohse, *TDNT* 6.45-48.
151. See again below, §§23.4a, f.
152. Cf. C. F. D. Moule, 'The Post-resurrection Appearances in the Light of Festival Pilgrimages', *NTS* 4 (1957-58) 58-61; Wedderburn, *History* 26-27.

sion that the event which Luke has retold in his Acts 2 account actually happened on the Pentecost following the Passover of Jesus' execution has a surprisingly substantial historical feel to it. If the ascension 'began' as the last resurrection appearance of Jesus (§22.2d), then Pentecost 'began' as the first (Christian) experience of the Spirit.[153]

(5) Infant Christianity drew to itself a large number of adherents or converts very quickly; Paul's persecution, within a year or two of Jesus' death, is sufficient confirmation that the new sect was soon seen as becoming too popular and threateningly influential. Even if Luke's figures in 2.41 and 4.4 may have to be discounted, as with almost all such ancient estimates, the rapid growth of the new movement is a substantive historical fact which should not be discounted. That being so, the most obvious historical explanation for this is not in terms of some hidden transition to an evangelistic outreach, without further stimulus. Much more obvious is some 'big bang' which galvanized disciples and attracted interested inquirers to their ranks. Acts 2 is Luke's version of the 'big bang'.

Luke's account of the crowd at Pentecost as 'from every nation under heaven' (Acts 2.5) is certainly exaggerated (hyperbole). But he also describes them as 'devout Jews . . . living in Jerusalem' (2.5), that is, not (only as) pilgrims attending the feast from abroad. Luke evidently had in view the fact that a goodly number of Jews from the diaspora had settled in Jerusalem. And although he develops the point — the promise to the inquirers responding to Peter's speech (2.39) is described as 'for you, for your children, and for all who are far away *(eis makran)*'[154] — the implication that the first adherents or converts to the new movement included a significant number of diaspora Jews is probably soundly based. The confirmation comes in incidental details in Luke's subsequent narrative which are almost certainly derived from information which Luke acquired and which do not reflect any specifically Lukan agenda. We soon meet Joseph Barnabas, who is a native of Cyprus but who had evidently settled in Jerusalem and who may have owned land in or around Jerusalem (4.36-37); and I have already mentioned Mnason, 'an early disciple', also from Cyprus and also an owner of property near Jerusalem (21.16). Most notably, in Acts 6 Luke abruptly introduces his readers to the fact that the first community in Jerusalem included 'Hellenists' as well as 'Hebrews' (6.1). As we shall see shortly (§24), the term 'Hellenists' almost certainly refers (at least predominantly) to diaspora Jews who had settled in Jerusalem. These indications that the new renewal movement

---

153. 'Luke was not the first to connect the descent of the Holy Spirit on the apostles with the feast of Pentecost' (Kremer, *Pfingstbericht* 260); contrast G. Schille, *Die Apostelgeschichte des Lukas* (THNT 5; Berlin: Evangelische, 1983), who argues that Luke derived his account from an early Christian cult aetiology for Pentecost as a Christian festival (96-98).

154. See below, §23 n. 279.

within Second Temple Judaism was not a narrowly Palestinian or Aramaic-speaking sect, but from the first included substantial numbers of Greek-speaking Jews from outside the land of Israel, are important pointers to the distinctive character of embryonic Christianity.

(6) History-of-religion parallels may also suggest a historical foundation to Luke's account of those filled with the Spirit speaking in unknown foreign languages. Early Pentecostalism, for example, produced many an account of individuals hearing those 'filled with the Spirit' speaking in languages unknown to the speakers but known to some hearers.[155] What is interesting about such reports is that they are modern examples of oral tradition. Such reports are notoriously difficult to track down; they usually come to the inquirer at second or third (or more) hand. The point is that such reports were fairly commonplace in the twentieth-century movement which most closely parallels (and, of course, was largely inspired by) Luke's account in Acts 2. It is not necessary, then, to conclude that Luke's account (of speaking foreign languages) is nothing more than Luke's invention, in service of his theology. It is entirely feasible that Luke heard such reports regarding Pentecost, and even that during his inquiries he met individuals who themselves claimed that what they heard on the day of Pentecost was indeed foreign languages.[156]

Those who have followed with me through *Jesus Remembered* may recall that the argument here is similar to that regarding the miracles of Jesus in §15.7c. There I warned against the assumption that any report of a 'miracle' was bound to be a later interpretation of an event or a report. There is no reason to doubt that at least some healings were *experienced as a miracle*. So here, we certainly cannot rule out the likelihood that Luke received reports about or even from those who, present at the Pentecost event, claimed to have heard the first disciples speaking 'in our own languages' (2.11). We may question whether Luke was wise to take such reports at face value;[157] what we cannot simply conclude is that Luke has invented the whole account.

d. Conclusion

What we find, then, in or through or underlying Luke's account of the first Christian Pentecost, is the shared memory of the initial burst of spiritual renewal and

---

155. See my *Jesus and the Spirit* 399 n. 83.

156. See further my *Jesus and the Spirit* 148-52; similarly Barrett, *Acts* 116; cf. C. Colpe, 'The Oldest Jewish-Christian Community', in J. Becker, ed., *Christian Beginnings* (1987; Louisville: Westminster John Knox, 1993) 75-102 (here 82).

157. See again §21 n. 132 above.

enthusiasm which launched the movement which became Christianity. That it took place in Jerusalem itself is very likely, and at the time of the feast of Pentecost following Jesus' death is quite probable. That it took the form of the core disciples enjoying an experience of spiritual ecstasy is most probable, including the phenomenon of glossolalia, quite possibly heard by some as the languages of their homeland. And that it resulted in many local Jews, including those who had returned from the diaspora, attaching themselves to the movement is hardly to be disputed.

Most important of all for embryonic Christianity, this experience was no doubt a major factor in ensuring that first-generation Christianity understood itself as *quintessentially a movement of the Spirit of God,* as the fulfilment of the ancient prophetic hope of a people (God's people Israel) renewed by the Spirit, and on whom the Spirit had been outpoured, to inspire praise and prophecy and witness and conduct. The focus on Jesus, which soon showed itself to be a dominant feature of the new movement's self-understanding, should not cause us to ignore or sideline this twin aspect of infant Christianity. If resurrection and ascension remind us that entirely constitutive of Christianity was the Christian understanding of what had happened to Jesus, Pentecost should never allow us to forget that Christianity understood itself in the first instance as a religion of the Spirit.[158]

---

158. J. Gnilka, *Die frühen Christen. Ursprünge und Anfang der Kirche* (Freiburg: Herder, 1999), in effect makes the same point when he devotes the first two sections of his treatment of 'Die frühe Kirche' to 'Bekenntnisbildung' ('confession formation') and 'Das Wirken des Gottesgeistes' ('the effect of God's Spirit') (219-48). See also Wilckens, *Theologie* 1/2.168-75; and further my *New Testament Theology* (LBT; Nashville: Abingdon, 2009) §2.4.

CHAPTER 23

The Earliest Community

Whatever the precise details of the emergence of the first Christian community in Jerusalem, we certainly have to speak of such a community in existence within not many months from Jesus' death. The conviction that God had raised Jesus from the dead, together with the spiritual enthusiasm attributed to the Spirit promised for the new age, engendered an embryonic new sect which soon attracted (1) new adherents and (2) a growing opposition from the Temple authorities. Even if all or most of the details provided by Acts 2.41–5.42 are discounted or put through a sceptically critical sieve, the undeniable evidence of Saul's persecution (Gal. 1.13-14, 23) is sufficient indication of both facts.

23.1. The Social Character of the First Christian Community

What can we say about this first Christian community? Some initial scene-setting is in order. At this stage I need only concern myself with the first half of the period — roughly 30 to the death of Agrippa I in 44 (Acts 12.20-23).

a. The Social Context of Jerusalem

We know a fair amount regarding the setting of the first Christian community in Jerusalem — both from ancient sources (Philo and Josephus in particular) and from archaeology.

In terms of political power, we know that Rome was at that time maintaining direct rule over Judea, as it did from 6 to 41 and again from 44 till the beginning of the Jewish revolt in 66, with the brief intermission of Agrippa I as king of Judea (41-44). We know that during this period imperial policy was generally sympathetic to the Jews, partly as a consequence of Jewish support for Julius

Caesar,[1] and partly because Herod Agrippa I was a friend of the imperial family.[2] We know that Pontius Pilate continued in office as prefect until 37, when he was recalled, and that Judea was a subordinate region within the province of Syria.[3] We know that the military rule of Rome did not bear particularly heavily on Judea: the prefect resided at Caesarea, coming to Jerusalem itself only on particular occasions, especially during the main Jewish festivals, when he resided in Herod's palace. The troops under his command were auxiliaries, mostly recruited locally, but exclusively from the non-Jewish inhabitants of the country, since Jews had been exempt from military service since the time of Caesar. Only one cohort was stationed in Jerusalem itself (cf. Acts 21.31).[4] Pilate himself had provoked two damaging confrontations centred on Jerusalem, apparently early in his period of office (between 26 and 30 — during Jesus' mission!),[5] but otherwise he seems to have hardly interfered in internal affairs.[6] Little of all this impinged directly on the new sect: Pilate does not appear again in the story of infant Christianity; however, Herod Agrippa makes a brief but potentially devastating intervention during his brief reign over Judea (12.1-19).

On the religious front, we know that principal authority lay with the high priest and with the families from which the high priest was usually drawn.[7] Currently the house of Annas (= Ananus) held ascendancy, with Joseph Caiaphas, Annas's son-in-law, in post from 18 to 37.[8] The high priest, his predecessors

1. Schürer, *History* 1.271-76.

2. See below, §26.5b. The exceptions were the period of Sejanus's power, under Tiberias — Sejanus was dismissed by Tiberias in 31 and Sejanus's anti-Jewish policy reversed (Philo, *Legat.* 159-61) — and Caligula's attempt to have a statue of himself erected in the Jerusalem Temple in 39-40 (see Schürer, *History* 1.343 n. 17, 394-96).

3. Schürer, *History* 1.358-60.

4. More details in Schürer, *History* 1.361-66.

5. Pilate tried to bring military standards with images of the emperor into Jerusalem, and he used money from the treasury to construct an aqueduct to bring water into Jerusalem (Josephus, *Ant.* 18.55-59, 60-62); Josephus dates the episodes to about the time of Jesus' mission (18.63-64). For discussion see H. K. Bond, *Pontius Pilate in History and Interpretation* (SNTSMS 100; Cambridge: Cambridge University, 1998).

6. See *Jesus Remembered* 308-309.

7. Josephus speaks of 'those families from which in turn the high priests had always been drawn' (*War* 4.148). The families of Phiabi, Boethus, Annas and Kamith provided no less than twenty-two of the twenty-five high priests who held office during the period between the end of the Hasmoneans and the beginning of the Jewish revolt; see J. Jeremias, *Jerusalem in the Time of Jesus* (London: SCM, 1969) 194-98, 377-78; Schürer, *History* 2.229-32; E. P. Sanders, *Judaism: Practice and Belief, 63 BCE–66 CE* (London: SCM, 1992) 328. Under Rome 'the high priest governed the temple and Jerusalem, and it is probable that he effectively governed Judaea' (Sanders, *Judaism* 323).

8. See particularly H. K. Bond, *Caiaphas: Friend of Rome and Judge of Jesus?* (Louisville: Westminster John Knox, 2004) here especially 74-77.

and members of the noble families from which the high priests were selected will almost certainly be in view in the several references in Acts 4–5 to 'the high priest's family' (4.6), 'the high priests' (4.23; 5.17, 24) and 'the high priest and those with him' (5.21).[9] Associated with them we sometimes read of the 'elders' (4.5, 8, 23), presumably (lay) heads of the leading (land-owning) families, though power clearly lay primarily with the high priests.[10] The high priest had the authority to convene a council to consider matters of state and legal issues, to advise or decide policy. Whether this council *(synedrion)* should be called 'the Sanhedrin' at this stage is a matter of some dispute,[11] but it is certainly such a council which is in view in the opening chapters of Acts (as in the hearing which had resulted in Jesus being handed over to Pilate).[12] The presence of the distinguished Pharisee Gamaliel, grandson of the still more famous Hillel, in the council of 5.34 is certainly entirely plausible.[13] That he should have given advice which ran somewhat contrary to the hostility attributed to the high priests (5.33-39) is consistent with the tensions we know to have existed between the high priestly (Sadducean) faction and the Pharisees in such a council (cf. 23.6-9).[14]

The basis for the authority and power of the high priest and high priestly

9. The John (or Jonathan) of 4.6 is presumably the son of Annas/Ananus, who succeeded Caiaphas as high priest in 36 or 37; Alexander (4.6), otherwise unknown, was probably another relative of Annas/Ananus (Bond, *Caiaphas* 75). See also Mason, *Josephus* 188-90.

10. Jeremias, *Jerusalem* 222-28; Sanders, *Judaism* 329; see also p. 330: 'Aristocratic priests are sometimes named . . . ; important laymen are seldom named'. *Archontes* ('rulers, magistrates') probably included both priests and laymen (3.17; 4.5, 8, 26).

11. It has been traditional to speak of 'the Sanhedrin' (E. Lohse, *TDNT* 7.862-66; Schürer, *History* 2.199-226), consisting of the high priests as the leading personalities, but also 'elders', scribes (professional lawyers) and at least a number of Pharisees; but Sanders prefers to speak of 'a council' rather than 'the Sanhedrin' (*Judaism* 472-88; see *Jesus Remembered* 271 n. 75), in agreement with J. S. McLaren, *Power and Politics in Palestine: The Jews and the Governing of Their Land, 100 BC–AD 70* (JSNTS 63; Sheffield: Sheffield Academic, 1991) — an ad hoc body commissioned for a specific task (217).

12. Luke 22.66; Acts 4.15; 5.21, 27, 34, 41; 6.12, 15.

13. Schürer, *History* 2.367-68.

14. The error which placed Judas the Galilean 'after' Theudas (5.36-37) is, of course, Luke's own (see above, §21 at n. 77), but that the new movement aroused some sympathy among Pharisees is confirmed by 15.5 (cf. Gal. 2.4) and 23.6-9; so Luke's portrayal of Gamaliel should not be dismissed out of hand. 'Luke has a historian's concern for verisimilitude. Gamaliel appears as a shrewd popular politician, weighing popular piety against administrative needs' (S. Mason, 'Chief Priests, Sadducees, Pharisees and Sanhedrin in Acts', *BAFCS* 4.115-77 [here 150-51]; see further 174-77, on the points of agreement between Luke and Josephus in his depiction of these groups). See also P. J. Tomson, 'Gamaliel's Counsel and the Apologetic Strategy of Luke-Acts', in J. Verheyden, ed., *The Unity of Luke-Acts* (BETL 142; Leuven: Leuven University, 1999) 585-604.

families was, of course, the Temple. As already noted,[15] Judea was in effect a temple state; the territory was what was deemed necessary to support the temple cult.[16] Jerusalem stood on no trade route or river or vital shoreline; its importance lay entirely in its Temple.[17] The Temple itself on the huge platform engineered by Herod the Great dominated the city, and those who controlled the Temple controlled the lifeblood of the city.[18] The income generated through the sacrificial cult, the Temple tax which flowed in from all over the diaspora, and the pilgrim traffic must have been immense.[19] The Temple also functioned as a bank, where vast private funds were deposited.[20] The Temple itself was still in process of being built, involving a huge number of trades and workmen.[21] Apart from the royal palaces and garrison, more or less all trade and commerce would be directly or indirectly dependent on the Temple. It should occasion no surprise, then, that the Temple provides the setting and occasion for action throughout Acts 3–7 and that the chief interaction is with the Temple authorities.

Beyond this the historian has to begin to scrape around for hard data. The gleanings from archaeological investigations are disappointingly meagre, the devastations of 70 and 135 having so completely destroyed the city. Apart from the Temple mount/platform itself, particularly the still-recent excavations at its southwest corner,[22] and a good idea of where the city walls must have been (the first wall at least),[23] it has proved remarkably difficult to gain a clear picture of

15. *Jesus Remembered* 287-88.

16. 'All cattle found in the vicinity of Jerusalem . . . were without exception regarded as destined for sacrifice (M. Shek. 7.4)' (Jeremias, *Jerusalem* 57).

17. Jerusalem 'lay in a part of the country quite extraordinarily unfavourable for trade'; 'Judaea played no part in world trade' (Jeremias, *Jerusalem* 27, 54).

18. The Temple's strategic importance is underlined by the role it played both in the Maccabean uprising against the Syrians and in the Jewish revolt of 66-70, which Josephus's *War* so vividly recounts.

19. Jeremias, *Jerusalem* 27-29; M. Goodman, 'The Pilgrimage Economy of Jerusalem in the Second Temple Period', *Judaism in the Roman World: Collected Essays* (Leiden: Brill, 2007) 59-67.

20. 2 Macc. 3.6, 10-12, 15; 4 Macc. 4.3, 6-7; Josephus, *War* 6.282.

21. Josephus notes that over 18,000 workmen were put out of work when the Temple was finally completed in the period 62-64 (*Ant.* 20.219).

22. J. Murphy-O'Connor, *The Holy Land* (Oxford: Oxford University, [4]1998) 96-103; see also D. Bahat, 'The Herodian Temple', *CHJ* 3.38-58.

23. The first wall embraced the city of David and Mount Zion; the route of the second wall, built by Herod the Great, is less clear but enclosed the district to the north of the Temple. Agrippa began to build a third wall enclosing a much larger area of northern suburbs during his brief reign. See Josephus's description of the course of the three walls (*War* 5.142-47, with further description of the strength of the third wall, 148-75); maps and diagrams in M. Ben-Dov, *Historical Atlas of Jerusalem* (2000; New York: Continuum, 2002) 102-25; see also Mazar, *The Mountain of the Lord* 204-209; Sanders, *Judaism* 125, 306.

the structure of the city. We know the site of the Antonia fortress and of the pools Siloam and Bethzatha/Bethesda (John 5.1-9), and we can guess the location of some of the markets/bazaars.[24] We know where the palaces of Herod and the kings of Adiabene must have been, as also the site of the Hasmonean palace. Moreover, the restoration of the Jewish quarter in the old city since 1967 has uncovered evidence of wealthy residences in the Upper City and overlooking the Tyropoean Valley, at that time still making a fairly deep incision between the Temple mount and the Upper City.[25] Josephus's mention of 'the gate of the Essenes' (*War* 5.145), by implication at the southwest corner of the city, has given rise to speculation regarding an Essene quarter in that section of the city, close to where 'the upper room' of the last supper has been traditionally located.[26] Beyond that, however, more or less all is guesswork.[27]

All this means that it is very difficult to reconstruct a picture of the immediate social context and conditions in which the first Christian community in Jerusalem began to flourish. We know nothing of where they might have lived and met (apart from the Temple court), or what their social standing and occupations were.[28] The narrative thread of Acts could be sustained without Luke having to

24. Jeremias, *Jerusalem* 18-21. Jeremias reckons that the city had 25,000-30,000 inhabitants at the time of Jesus (27, 84). Pseudo-Hecataeus estimated 120,000 (Josephus, *Ap.* 1.197), but Mazar notes that this figure would have included the suburbs and outlying villages (*Mountain of the Lord* 210), and Sanders feels unable to comment further (*Judaism* 125), though he goes on to estimate crowds of between 300,000 and 500,000 attending the festivals in Jerusalem (128). The most recent discussions estimate a settled population of at least 60,000 — D. A. Fiensy, 'The Composition of the Jerusalem Church', *BAFCS* 4.213-36 (214 and n. 3); W. Reinhardt, 'The Population Size of Jerusalem and the Numerical Growth of the Jerusalem Church', *BAFCS* 4.237-65 (240-59).

25. See Murphy-O'Connor, *The Holy Land* 73-76; L. Ritmeyer and K. Ritmeyer, *Jerusalem in the Year 30* A.D. (Jerusalem: Carta, 2004).

26. See R. Riesner, 'Das Jerusalemer Essenerviertel und die Urgemeinde. Josephus, Bellum Judaicum V 145; 11Q Miqdasch 46, 13-16; Apostelgeschichte 1-6 und die Archäologie', *ANRW* 2.26.2 (1995) 1775-1922; also 'Synagogues in Jerusalem', *BAFCS* 4.179-211 (here 206-207); J. Murphy-O'Connor, 'The Cenacle — Topographical Setting for Acts 2:44-45', *BAFCS* 4.303-21. See also below, n. 45.

27. In 1979 I asked Professor Nahman Avigad, who had been responsible for excavations in the Upper City, how much of the model of the old city in the grounds of the Holy Land Hotel was based on archaeological findings; apart from the Temple platform, he reckoned only 5 percent was archaeologically reliable. Ben-Dov's *Historical Atlas* 102-25 contains some excellent suggested reconstructions of some of the main features of the pre-70 city; and the Ritmeyers' *Jerusalem* contains excellent photographs and diagrams. See also Schnabel, *Mission* 417-20.

28. Jeremias, *Jerusalem,* provides much information about the industries and commerce of Jerusalem — domestic goods, food, trades and guilds, pilgrim traffic — and about the economic circumstances of the people of Jerusalem, though his treatment is heavily dependent on rabbinic sources. He notes that typically 'a large section of the population lived chiefly or en-

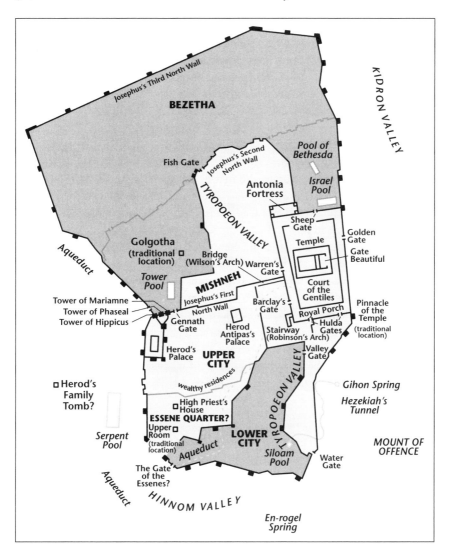

Jerusalem in the First Century

trouble about such questions, even if the result is that he produced a somewhat dream-like sequence, which intensifies the impression of an idealized recon-struction. But the information he provides nevertheless does enable us to make some relevant observations and to flesh out his account with plausibly historical imagination.

b. Who Were the First Christians?

However accurate, or inaccurate, the figures provided by Acts 2.41 (3,000 con-verts) and 4.4 (5,000 believers), the new Jerusalem sect must have grown quickly. But who were these first Christians, from what strata of Jerusalem soci-ety did they come, and how did they support themselves? Our information does not provide even the beginnings of a comprehensive picture, but it does sketch a number of outlines.

Worth repeating is the striking fact already noted: that the core group of disciples were Galileans (1.11; 2.7). Did they live with relatives or friends or some local residents who were already disciples? And how did they support themselves?[29] Even if they all lived 'by faith', their economic survival must have depended on income from some sources.[30]

We also soon hear of 'a large number of priests'[31] who 'became obedient to the faith' (6.7) and later of 'some of the sect of Pharisees who had believed'

---

tirely on charity or relief' and that in the time of Jesus Jerusalem 'was already a centre for mendicancy' (111-12, 116-18; see also 126-34). See also Mazar, *Mountain of the Lord* 210-16, and Fiensy's section on the social groups in Jerusalem ('Composition' 215-26). Fiensy summa-rizes: 'Thus Jerusalem in our period of consideration (30-66 AD) was inhabited by a population varied in its socio-economic composition. The wealthier class tended to live in the Upper City and the lower class in the Lower City or the burgeoning New Town. Many in the submerged class were probably homeless and wandered the streets and alleys begging or otherwise lived on the outskirts of the city' (226).

29. 'In Jerusalem they scarcely had any choice but to earn their own and their families' keep as day-labourers or servants' (Haenchen, *Acts* 234-35). Or were James and John able to draw on income from their father's fishing business, which had a number of employees (Mark 1.19-20)?

30. An interesting feature of the list of nations in Acts 2.9-11 is that it does not include Galileans (though it does include Judeans!). So although Galileans came to the pilgrim festivals (*Jesus Remembered* 296), Luke's account gives no scope for Galilean believers returning to Galilee after the festival.

31. Jeremias reckons there must have about 18,000 priests and Levites operative in the Judaism of Jesus' day, of whom at least 7,200 would be priests, and he envisages a substantial 'social gulf' between the priestly aristocracy and the 'ordinary' priests (*Jerusalem* 180-81, 198-207). See also Schürer, *History* 2.238-50.

(15.5), the latter finding confirmation in Paul's reference to 'false brothers' in Gal. 2.4. So we can well imagine priests being able to depend on income from tithes and share in firstfruits and Temple offerings,[32] and Pharisees would typically have been able to follow some trade.[33]

Women are frequently mentioned among the disciples:

- 'certain women, including Mary, the mother of Jesus' (Acts 1.14)
- the daughters and female servants/slaves of Joel's prophecy (2.17-18)
- Sapphira, wife of Ananias (5.1-10)
- 'great numbers [of disciples] both men and women' (5.14)
- the Hellenist widows (6.1)
- the victims of Saul's persecution, 'both men and women' (8.3; 9.2; 22.4)
- Tabitha/Dorcas (9.36-41)
- Mary, mother of John Mark
- the servant Rhoda (12.12-15).

We also know of some property owners among the first Christians:

- the owner of the colt (Luke 19.29-31)
- supporters in Bethany (Mark 14.3; cf. Luke 19.29; 24.50)
- the owner of the upper room (Luke 22.12 = Acts 1.13?)
- Simon of Cyrene, who owned a farm outside Jerusalem (Mark 15.21)
- the disciples in Emmaus (Luke 24.13, 29)
- Peter, who was able to provide guest hospitality for Paul in Jerusalem (Gal. 1.18)
- Barnabas, who sold a field (4.37)[34]
- Ananias and Sapphira, who likewise had property or land to sell (5.1)
- Mary, mother of John Mark, who owned a substantial property with a gate and servants (12.12-13)[35]
- Mnason of Cyprus, who had a house outside Jerusalem where Paul stayed during his final journey to Jerusalem (21.16).[36]

---

32. Schürer, *History* 2.257-74; Sanders, *Judaism* 146-57, 170-82.

33. Sanders, *Judaism* 404-406.

34. Haenchen notes, however, that the property sold might have been in Cyprus (*Acts* 232).

35. 'It is striking that no man is mentioned as husband of Mary and father of Mark; somewhere behind Luke's narrative lies a tradition of a Christian family in Jerusalem where the father either was already dead or had not become a Christian' (Barrett, *Acts* 1.583).

36. Ms D places the location in 'a certain village', presumably somewhere between Caesarea and Jerusalem; the journey would take at least two days. Bruce assumes Mnason lived in Jerusalem (*Acts* 443), but the more natural sense of Acts 21.17 is that Paul's party only arrived in Jerusalem following their overnight stay with Mnason.

In addition, three other comments in Acts point to ownership of property:

- The first disciples met day by day in one another's houses *(kat' oikon)* (2.46; 5.42).
- The whole community was able to meet, presumably in some privacy (15.6, 12).
- James 'and all the elders' were able to receive Paul's party when they arrived in Jerusalem (21.18).

Such information is extremely sketchy[37] and gives us next to no idea of how the individuals named made their living. But no doubt they included landlords and businessmen, landowners and tradesmen, scribes and stall holders. And judging by the later reference to 'the poor of the saints in Jerusalem' (Rom. 15.26), the new sect presumably attracted not a few of Jerusalem's mendicants. All this is guesswork, but David Fiensy may well be correct in deducing that 'nearly all levels of society were represented' in the Jerusalem church.[38]

c. Where Did They Meet?

Even if the numbers indicated in Acts 2.41 and 4.4 have to be taken with a grain of salt, the rapid expansion of the new sect is hardly to be disputed — as already noted. But where could such a rapidly growing sect meet? (1) *Epi to auto* (1.15; 2.1, 44; 4.26), 'at the same place, together',[39] certainly implies large communal gatherings. But only the Temple courts would have provided sufficient room for very large gatherings (Solomon's portico/colonnade, Acts 5.12), and teaching (2.42) given there would have been very public and was bound to have an evangelistic or apologetic slant. Would the Temple authorities have tolerated such very large gatherings? In the light of this consideration, we should probably ask whether the whole body of disciples met or attempted to meet as a single group. (2) 'The upper room' (1.13) could presumably accommodate quite a large gathering, but nothing like the numbers suggested from 2.41, 47 onwards. Did it function effectively as a synagogue, a gathering place?[40] And if so, should we

---

37. Bauckham lists forty-five names who were certainly or probably members of the Jerusalem church ('Jesus and the Jerusalem Community' 81-92).

38. Fiensy, 'Composition' 213, 226-30.

39. See below, n. 125.

40. Riesner notes that *hyperōon* is used of upper rooms in a synagogue (the third-century synagogue inscription from Stobi, in Dalmatia) and that upper rooms appear also in rabbinic literature as a preferred meeting place of teachers. He goes on to suggest that the upper room in Jerusalem (Acts 1.15) 'was in the eyes of Luke some kind of Christian synagogue'

conceive of a number of such Christian synagogues/assemblies from the first? In which case, different members of the twelve presumably functioned as synagogue leaders/teachers. (3) The other locations specified are various disciples' homes (2.46; 5.42), which presumably implies a network of house groups or house churches, with many of the original disciples sharing the leadership and teaching responsibility.

In any case, as the history of renewal movements suggests, we should not assume that clear structures and patterns of common life became established and formalized very quickly. On the contrary, with new recruits being won to the new movement on a daily or weekly basis, there must have been considerable '*ad-hoc*ery'. The one organizational model which did emerge (the community of goods) seems to have quickly buckled under the strain (6.1), and the sequence well illustrates the sort of problems that any quickly growing sect is liable to face.

d. The Community of Goods

In economic terms the most striking feature of the new sect, according to Acts, was the fact that 'they held everything in common' (2.44); 'no one ever claimed any possession as his own, but all things were common for them' (4.32). Here again Luke shows an understandable tendency to look back on this beginning through rose-tinted spectacles — property and belongings were sold and the proceeds distributed to any who had need (2.45); 'there was never any needy person among them' (4.34)[41] — though, to be fair, he goes on to record that the administration of the common fund soon broke down (6.1).

This description of 'primitive communism' has provoked a good deal of scepticism, for not always sound reasons.[42] But it is entirely plausible in its basic

---

('Synagogues in Jerusalem' 200, 206). 'The tradition of veneration [of a Christian building on Mount Zion] must go back to the 1st century when highly idealistic Christians shared a common life in the home of a wealthy believer in the most affluent quarter of Jerusalem' (Murphy-O'Connor, 'The Cenacle' 303). See also R. W. Gehring, *House Church and Mission* (Peabody: Hendrickson, 2004) 65-69.

41. The language seems to echo that of Deut. 15.4, presumably deliberately.

42. 'A narrative to which historical credibility must be denied as a whole' (Baur, *Paul* 32). Cf. Haenchen's review of the discussion of the two summary passages (2.42-47 and 4.32-37) (*Acts* 193-96, 232-35): 'The summaries appear to flow entirely from the pen of Luke' (195); 'Luke is here suggesting that the primitive Church also realized the *Greek* communal ideal!' (233, referring to Plato and Aristotle — references in Pesch, *Apg.* 1.184-85, and Barrett, *Acts* 1.168-69); similarly Jervell, *Apg.* 156, but with qualification (191). M. Öhler, 'Die Jerusalemer Urgemeinde im Spiegel des antiken Vereinswesens', *NTS* 51 (2005) 393-415, draws parallels with the voluntary associations of the time (see further §30.3 below) and sug-

details. The Qumran community, which would certainly be known to at least many of the Jerusalem believers, also practised a common ownership of property, and novitiates were required to turn over all their possessions to the community (1QS 6.19-22).[43] Philo also speaks in two places of groups of Essenes living in villages or cities of Palestine who did not retain private property but held everything in common and passed wages to a common treasurer.[44] Elsewhere Philo also devotes a tract to a description of an ascetic community near Alexandria, the Therapeutae, who *inter alia* 'gave away their possessions instead of wasting them' (*Vit. Cont.* 16). It would be exceedingly blinkered to suppose that these parallels functioned only at a literary level, inspiring Luke (or his source) to incorporate a similar report in his account of Christianity's beginnings.[45] Rather we should see here further evidence of the sort of spiritual enthusiasm which expresses itself in a strong and even extravagant commitment to one another. After all, Jesus was remembered as one who had given high priority to ministry to the poor,[46] and the cautionary tale of the rich young man who could not rise to the challenge of selling all that he had and distributing it to the poor is treasured in all three Synoptic Gospels (Luke 18.18-23 pars.). Inspiration was already there in Israel's system of 'poor relief' (cf. Jas. 1.27).[47] In later centuries similar impulses resulted in the creation of Christian monasticism. Hermits and vows of communal poverty are not simply curious historical or literary phenomena but are further demonstrations of how experiences and movements of spiritual re-

gests that 'Luke presents the ideal community as an invitation to his readers to emulate', particularly the equality between rich and poor and the daily shared meal (415).

43. The Qumran community's discipline of members not owning any private possessions was well known in the ancient world; see Pliny, *Nat. Hist.* 5.73; Philo, *Prob.* 86; Josephus, *War* 2.122.

44. Philo, *Hypothetica* 11.4-12; 'they all have a single treasury and common disbursements; their clothes are held in common and also their food through their institution of common meals. In no other community can we find the custom of sharing roof, life and board more firmly established in actual practice. . . . For all the wages which they earn in the day's work they do not keep as their private property, but throw them into the common stock and allow the benefit thus accruing to be shared by those who wish to use it' (*Prob.* 86).

45. See further B. Capper, 'The Palestinian Cultural Context of Earliest Christian Community of Goods', *BAFCS* 4.323-56; also 'Community of Goods in the Early Jerusalem Church', *ANRW* 2.26.2 (1995) 1730-74. The proximity of 'the upper room' (the Cenacle) to the Essene gate (and Essene quarter?) suggests to Capper the conduit for Essene influence on the nascent Christian church (341-42).

46. Particularly by Luke — Luke (3.11); 4.18; 6.20; 7.22; 12.33; 14.13, 21; 16.19-31; 18.22; 19.8. See also M. Hengel, *Property and Riches in the Early Church* (London: SCM, 1974) 31-35.

47. Jeremias, *Jerusalem* 126-33: 'There can be no doubt therefore that these arrangements served as a model for the primitive Church' (131). Jervell emphasizes that the actions fulfilled the law (*Apg.* 156, 191).

newal can radically re-motivate those caught up in the new fervour to self-sacrificial commitment and an intensely altruistic life-style. It should occasion no surprise whatsoever that Luke reports the community of goods as the almost immediate sequel of the experience of Pentecost.[48]

An interesting feature of Luke's account is its distinctive character — another indication, probably, that he draws his account from memories of the initial enthusiasm of the Jerusalem community, rather than from the different models provided to him in Qumran or the Essenes generally (or Plato). For Luke does *not* say that all believers sold off all property and possessions and contributed the proceeds to the common fund (unlike Qumran, where the handing over of property at the novitiate stage was obligatory).[49] Rather his description envisages members of the new sect selling off possessions and goods as need arose for more funds (2.45; 4.35).[50] And although 4.34 could be understood to say that all those who had property sold it all and brought the proceeds to the apostles, the sequel indicates otherwise. Joseph Barnabas is singled out for special mention because he had sold a field and brought (all) the money thereby raised to the apostles (4.37). His contribution is probably mentioned because it was unusually generous, or was the first large gift;[51] but even so, it is nowhere implied that he sold off all the land belonging to him. Likewise in the immediate sequel (5.1-10) the sin of Ananias and Sapphira is not that they held back some of the proceeds of their sale of property but that they pretended to give all the proceeds to the apostles, whereas in fact they had retained some of them (5.3-4, 8-9).[52] And I have already referred to those, like John Mark's mother, Mary, who still owned a substantial house (12.12), without any hint that they had breached the spirit of the sect's community spirit.

48. See also S. S. Bartchy, 'Community of Goods in Acts: Idealization or Social Reality?', in B. A. Pearson, ed., *The Future of Early Christianity,* H. Koester FS (Minneapolis: Fortress, 1991) 309-18. 'Luke describes not an early Christian "community of goods" but the renunciation of monetary assets for the sake of the poor' (Schnabel, *Mission* 413).

49. See again 1QS 6.19-22. Capper sees in Acts 5.4 a parallel to the phased novitiate at Qumran ('Community of Goods' 338-40); but it is inaccurate to describe the possessions and earnings handed over to Qumran treasury (1QS 6.19-20) as still 'in the power' of the novitiate, even though they would be returned to him if he decided to withdraw before the end of his second year.

50. He uses imperfect tenses in 2.45: 'they used to sell *(epipraskon)* and distribute *(diemerizon)* . . .'; 'the practice was to sell and distribute . . .'; Lake and Cadbury, *Beginnings* 4.29; K. Lake, 'The Communism of Acts 2 and 4–6 and the Appointment of the Seven', *Beginnings* 5.140-51 (here 140-41); Haenchen, *Acts* 192; Barrett, *Acts* 1.169. Similarly in 4.35.

51. Jeremias, *Jerusalem* 130 n. 19. Öhler argues that Barnabas had lived in Jerusalem for a long time, perhaps had been born there, and that he had been a disciple already before Easter (*Barnabas* 139-67, 479).

52. See further below, §23.2g.

So the community of goods was much more voluntary than, say, Qumran,[53] and property was sold, apparently, only in order to maintain the common fund, from which the poorer members of the community could be supported.[54] Nevertheless, the practice seems somewhat over-casual, in that according to Luke the common fund was sustained not from income but by the sale of capital goods (2.45; 4.34-37). If so, such a policy was hardly a model for the long term: simply to continue to dispense with property holdings and possessions was a recipe for communal poverty in the not-too-distant future, given not least the regularity of famines in the region.[55] On the other hand, such a policy could be sustained, at least in the short term, by the continual acquisition of new recruits,[56] whose additional commitment would help sustain the fund, even if support for the poor was a continual drain.[57]

Probably we should understand the community of goods in the earliest community both as a spontaneous expression of the mutual affection which their shared experience engendered and as an indication that their future horizon was quite limited. In other words, they did not plan their communal life-style for the long term, because they expected the risen and exalted Jesus to return soon and 'the restoration of all things' (3.21).[58] This in turn may have coincided in their thinking with the hoped-for restoration of the kingdom to Israel (1.6). We need hardly assume that their expectation was at all clear, let alone detailed, on the subject; a euphoric optimism would be sufficient to explain the seemingly casual, not to say careless, forward planning involved in the community of goods as described by Luke. At all events, we certainly cannot exclude the likelihood that repeated sales of property, together with growing demands on the common fund, constituted a major factor in the subsequent relative poverty of the Jerusalem church (cf. 11.29; Rom. 15.26-27).[59]

---

53. See also K.-J. Kim, *Stewardship and Almsgiving in Luke's Theology* (JSNTS 155; Sheffield: Sheffield Academic, 1998) 234-52.

54. The admonition made to Paul in Gal. 2.10 and his subsequent concern to collect funds for the poor in the Jerusalem church (Rom. 15.26; cf. Jas. 2.2-6) suggest that welfare relief was a major concern of the Jerusalem church.

55. Jeremias, *Jerusalem* 140-44; see further below, §25 n. 242.

56. According to Philo, the Essenes eschewed marriage: 'no Essene takes a wife' (*Hypothetica* 11.14). Cf. the Shakers, who did not practise marriage and who depended on new recruits and being given charge of orphan children for the continuation of their communities.

57. Widows would form a major group of recipients, as Acts 6.1 suggests (cf. 9.39-41; and subsequently particularly 1 Tim. 5.3-16); 'many Jews came to Jerusalem to die and be buried in the Holy City, and their widows had no families to look after them' (Haenchen, *Acts* 235).

58. See further below, §23.4f. 'There was no need to take thought for the morrow since there would not be one' (Barrett, *Acts* 1.168).

59. Weiss, *Earliest Christianity* 72-73; Haenchen, *Acts* 235, who also refers to Troeltsch's portrayal of the 'primitive Christian love-communism', whose collapse led to its later financial crisis (233); Hengel, *Property* 31-34.

23.2. The Religious Character of the First Christian Community

We may take it for granted that whatever the social composition of the first Christian gatherings in Jerusalem, their motivation was primarily religious — that is, the principal motivation grew out of the twin experiences of 'resurrection appearances' and religious enthusiasm, together with the interpretations which these experiences engendered (Jesus exalted to heaven, and the Spirit now out-poured as promised for the age to come). The immediate sequel to the account of Pentecost (Acts 2.41-47) contains a number of indicators of the character of the community which began to emerge. The passage is a Lukan summary, but most of the characteristics he highlights are confirmed elsewhere, and they are certainly consistent with what we have already deduced about the new sect.[60]

a. Baptism in the Name of Jesus

According to Luke, Peter ended his first sermon by calling on his hearers to 're-pent, and be baptized in the name of Jesus Christ for the forgiveness of your sins, and you will receive the gift of the Holy Spirit' (2.38). Those who responded were promptly baptized — about 3,000 individuals (2.41)! This, we could say, marks the formal inauguration of the new sect. The account, however, raises a number of questions, which can be focused in two in particular.

First, why baptism at all? If we read Luke-Acts in straight sequence, there has been no forewarning that baptism would be a feature in the sequel which is Acts. The Baptist had contrasted his baptizing in water with the coming one's ex-pected baptizing in Spirit and fire (Luke 3.16). And Luke gives no hint that Jesus himself had continued John's practice of baptism.[61] Nor does the risen Christ in Luke commission a Christian form of baptism, as he does in Matthew (Matt. 28.19). On the contrary, by reiterating the Baptist's prediction of the disciples soon to be baptized in Holy Spirit, once again in contrast to John's baptizing in water (Acts 1.5), Luke seems to imply that the experience of Pentecost would be the complete fulfilment of the Baptist's prediction, leaving no room or necessity for a continuation of John's baptism in water. And yet he promptly records that Peter called his audience to be baptized. What are we to make of this?

A popular view early in the twentieth century was that experience of the

---

60. In reference to 2.42 Barrett comments: 'The idealizing is in the participle *proskarterountes* ['persisted steadily'] . . . There is no ground for doubting the outline of Luke's account; if he had not given it we should doubtless have conjectured something of the kind' (*Acts* 166).

61. See also *Jesus Remembered* 606-607.

Spirit (being baptized in the Spirit) was originally understood to be the fulfilment of John's baptism, and that water baptism was reintroduced only with the Hellenists some years down the line.[62] But that solution is rendered implausible by the fact that (water) baptism is everywhere taken for granted in earliest Christian sources. In particular, Paul, our earliest first-hand witness, simply assumes that all believers have been baptized;[63] evidently it did not occur to him that there might be such a person as an unbaptized Christian.[64] The fact that the 'we all' of Rom. 6.3-4 and 1 Cor. 12.13 must have included Paul himself indicates that when Paul was converted, at most two or three years from the beginnings referred to in Acts 2, baptism was an already established practice for the new sect. The practice is hardly likely to have been a new innovation which distinguished new believers from others.

We are driven back to the conclusion, therefore, that Luke is correct in depicting baptism as a feature of the new sect from the beginning. Why they reintroduced a practice which Jesus himself seems to have moved on from[65] remains something of a puzzle. The most likely solution is that the first Christian community believed that the risen Christ had so instructed them. That is to say, the root of Matt. 28.19 is probably a memory of a revelation experienced as from on high, or specifically of the risen Christ's commission including a command to baptize those who responded to the proclamation of the good news about him.[66] That Luke chose not to narrate such a commission is slightly odd. But as we have seen, Luke does have a habit of leaving certain developments to be related at a later time,[67] and he may have thought that his readership would recognize the im-

62. Weiss, *Earliest Christianity* 50-51, 172-73, 196 n. 12; Foakes-Jackson and Lake, eds., *Beginnings* 1.332-44. Pokorny finds in the NT 'traces of a brief period in which faith in Jesus in important parts of the Church was not bound up with water baptism' (*Genesis* 208). Cf. F. Avemarie, *Die Tauferzählungen der Apostelgeschichte* (WUNT 139; Tübingen: Mohr Siebeck, 2002) 265-66; Jervell, *Apg.* 113; Wedderburn, *History* 35.

63. 1 Cor. 1.13-15; Rom. 6.4. The use of the imagery of being baptized in the Spirit (1 Cor. 12.13) or into Christ's death (Rom. 6.3) and the understanding of the Israelites' passage through the Red Sea as a kind of baptism (1 Cor. 10.2) likewise presuppose that baptism was the regular rite of initiation for converts. Outside Paul note particularly 1 Pet. 3.21 and Heb. 6.2.

64. The question put by Paul in Acts 19.2, which assumes that all 'disciples' will have been baptized, is therefore entirely consistent with the Paul of the Epistles.

65. *Jesus Remembered* 606-607.

66. G. R. Beasley-Murray, *Baptism in the New Testament* (London: Macmillan, 1963) 83-84 — the full discussion (77-92) remains valuable; F. Hahn, *Mission in the New Testament* (London: SCM, 1965) 63-68; Goppelt, *Apostolic* 41; P. Stuhlmacher, 'Matt 28:16-20 and the Course of Mission in the Apostolic and Postapostolic Age', in Ådna and Kvalbein, eds., *The Mission of the Early Church* 17-43. The addition of Mark 13.10 to the tradition of the 'little apocalypse' probably reflects the same later reflection (Hahn, *Mission* 70-74; *Jesus Remembered* 435-36).

67. See above, §21.2d(2).

plication of Luke 24.47 ('repentance and forgiveness of sins to be proclaimed in his name to all nations') and so find Acts 2.38, 41 unsurprising.[68]

Second, how was this baptism understood? The formulation of Acts 2.38 is strikingly evocative of what is recalled of the Baptist's ministry: repentance, baptism, forgiveness of sins, and the promise of the Spirit (Luke 3.3, 16).[69] The implication may well be, therefore, that Christian baptism was initially understood as a resumption or re-working of John's baptism, but with the promised Spirit (being baptized in Spirit) understood (and experienced!) as its immediate fulfilment.[70] This would certainly help explain the various sequels to 2.38, 41 in Acts itself, which have occasioned endless discussion.[71] For each of them serves in different ways to bring out the belief that the gift of the Spirit was to be expected in close conjunction with baptism: the Samaritans, who had 'only been baptized in the name of the Lord Jesus' but lacked the Spirit, necessitating apostolic intervention (8.16-17); Cornelius and his friends, whose being baptized in the Spirit nevertheless did not render baptism in the name of Jesus Christ unnecessary (10.47-48); and the Ephesian 'disciples', whose ignorance of the Spirit showed that their baptism of repentance had not been fulfilled (as had the apostles by Pentecost?) and that it was necessary for them to go through the whole procedure. Luke, of course, is making his own point in all this — Acts 2.38 as a kind of model conversion-and-initiation.[72] But Paul's continued use of the metaphor of

68. See also Avemarie, *Tauferzählungen* 212-13. The fact that Jesus himself was recalled as having been baptized by John and his own reception of the Spirit as having been closely related to that baptism (Mark 1.9-11 pars.) may have been a factor (e.g., Gnilka, *Die frühen Christen* 286-87). Wilckens thinks the association between John's baptism and the Pentecost experience (predicted by the Baptist) provides the answer (*Theologie* 1/2.185-87).

69. Luke 3.3 — John came 'preaching a baptism of repentance for the forgiveness of sins'; 3.16 — 'I baptize you with water; . . . he will baptize you in holy spirit and fire'. See further *Jesus Remembered* 357-62.

70. 'The meaning of baptism can hardly have been different from that of John's baptism, which Jesus and his first "disciples" had themselves received' (Bultmann, *Theology* 1.39). It is perhaps significant that the first mention of baptism appears on the lips of Peter, who presumably had himself become a disciple of Jesus through John's baptism (as implied by John 1.35-42 with 3.22); H. Kraft, *Die Entstehung des Christentums* (Darmstadt: Wissenschaftliche Buchgesellschaft, 1981) 216.

71. These sequels were the subject of my original doctoral dissertation, *Baptism in the Holy Spirit,* from whose main thrust I see no reason to depart. So I remain dubious as to whether the textual evidence actually allows us to conclude that the Spirit was bestowed through baptism (as, e.g., by Conzelmann, *History* 49-50; Colpe, 'Oldest Jewish-Christian Community' 83-84); Wilckens typically shows more concern to bind the gift of the Spirit to the ritual act than any of the NT writers he draws on (*Theologie* 1/2.179-82). See the recent discussions by Turner, *Power from on High* ch. 12; Avemarie, *Tauferzählungen* 129-74.

72. 'The normative unity of baptism and reception of the Spirit' (Avemarie, *Tauferzählungen* 138-44).

baptism for union with Christ and for the endowment with the Spirit (Rom. 6.3-4; 1 Cor. 12.13) confirms that acceptance of baptism must have been the occasion of profound religious experiences for many typical converts. And it would occasion no surprise whatsoever if it was induction into the highly charged religious atmosphere of the first Christian community which established that pattern.

In some ways the most striking feature of this new rite of baptism was that it was performed 'in the name of Jesus'.[73] It is this phrase which marks off the Christian rite most sharply from that of the Baptist. How did it come into use? An attractive inference is that with Jesus now absent, baptism 'in his name' was seen to be the way to signal entry into discipleship of this Jesus. That could provide a further explanation for the reintroduction of baptism: whereas during Jesus' own mission discipleship involved some degree of physical attachment to him, in Jesus' absence the act of being baptized gave an equivalent tangibility to the commitment to discipleship. In any event, the phrase must have indicated the baptisand's putting himself/herself under the authority, and power, which 'the name of Jesus' expressed.[74] This is the clear implication of 1 Cor. 1.12-15, where 'baptism in the name of' is understood to imply membership in the faction of the one named. It goes a long way to explaining how the name 'Christians' emerged (Acts 11.26) — Christians as those who belonged to the faction of Christ, who rallied under the name of Jesus Christ.[75] And it is consistent with the description of Christians as 'those who called on the name of the Lord Jesus' (1 Cor. 1.2; Rom. 10.12-14), language which appears also in Acts (2.21; 9.14, 21; 15.17). That baptism would be the occasion for or expression of the first 'calling on his name', as explicitly in Paul's own baptism (22.16), is the logical conclusion.[76]

The social implications should also not be ignored, for they would have been obvious from the first.[77] Baptism in the name of Jesus was not the first of a regular practice of ritual ablution, as would have been the case with an initiate to

---

73. 'In *(epi)* the name of Jesus Christ' (2.38); 'in *(en)* the name of Jesus Christ' (10.48); 'in *(eis)* the name of the Lord Jesus' (8.16; 19.5; by implication, 1 Cor. 1.13, 15). The 1 Corinthian references again confirm that this formula had already become a standard rubric for Christian baptism.

74. So, e.g., Haenchen, *Acts* 184; Stuhlmacher, *Biblische Theologie* 1.218, 220; Barrett, *Acts* 1.154; Jervell, *Apg.* 150. L. Hartman, *'Into the Name of the Lord Jesus': Baptism in the Early Church* (Edinburgh: Clark, 1997) 37-50, argues for a rather innocuous meaning for the phrase, as signifying little more than 'in reference to Jesus' ('with regard to', 'having in mind'), but he ignores Acts 3–4, with its focus on the authority and power of the name (see below, §23.4d).

75. See above, §20 n. 5, and below, §24.8d.

76. Similarly Avemarie, *Tauferzählungen* 41-43.

77. Baptism of a substantial number would have required access to a major supply of water, like the pools of Siloam or Bethzatha — that is, a very public ritual.

the Qumran community. Like the Baptist's rite, it was a once-only rite. And more clearly than with the Baptist, it was an initiation rite, a rite marking the baptisand's transfer into a new grouping, a new sect, a sect marked by a committed discipleship of Jesus and, presumably, by acknowledgment of his messiahship ('in the name of Jesus Christ') and submission to his lordship ('in the name of the Lord Jesus').[78] However that commitment was played out, and we are in process of exploring the subject, it was the commitment expressed initially in baptism 'in the name of Jesus' which must have marked them out most clearly within the setting of Jerusalem. Notwithstanding the importance of seeing the first Christians as Jews and as full members of the society of late Second Temple Judaism, it is also important to recognize from the first the role of baptism 'in the name of Jesus' in the group formation and boundary marking which was in due course to result in Christianity's distinct and separate identity among the religions of antiquity.

b. The Teaching of the Apostles (Acts 2.42)

An obvious bonding element in a newly emerging sect would be the convictions and teaching which distinguished them as a group. Principal among these, of course, would be beliefs regarding the Jesus in whose name they had been baptized, into whose discipleship they had entered. We will go into the beliefs regarding Jesus in more detail in §§23.4-5. Here it is important to recognize the sources of the teaching and how 'the apostles' handled them. On *a priori* grounds we can assume that there would have been two foci in particular — (1) the *Scriptures* (what Christians call the OT) and (2) the *traditions about Jesus,* for which the disciples who had been closest to Jesus would be the prime sources and exponents.[79]

(1) Luke portrays the newly risen Christ as 'interpreting' to his Emmaus disciples 'the things about himself in all the Scriptures' (Luke 24.25-27; also 44-46) and reports them recalling how their hearts burned within them while Jesus opened the Scriptures to them (24.32). Peter's second speech likewise starts with the claim that in Jesus God had fulfilled what he had foretold through all the prophets (Acts 3.18). And subsequently Luke describes the Jews of Berea as 'examining the Scriptures every day to see whether these things [the Christian asser-

---

78. See further below, §23.4d.

79. Pesch, *Apg.* 1.133; Gnilka, *Die frühen Christen* 268-72. Barnett is one of the few who treat both elements with the seriousness they deserve: he cites Moule (*Birth* 69), who comments that collections of biblical passages were 'drawn together round Jesus, as a magnet collects iron filings', and notes the importance given to collecting the oracles and acts of Jesus (*Jesus* 200-207).

tions regarding Jesus] were so' (17.11). Whatever we make of Luke's details, the stories must reflect something at least of the curiosity (to put it no more strongly) which almost inevitably drove the first disciples to try to correlate what they had experienced with what Scripture taught or had previously led them to expect.[80] The Scriptures were too important to their already formed religious identity, which Jesus' own handling of Scripture would, if anything, have reinforced at some depth,[81] for them to even begin to think that what they had experienced somehow rendered the Scriptures of their people passé or no longer relevant.[82]

We have already seen that in the speeches/sermons attributed to Peter, Luke has been able to draw on interpretations of the sort of Scriptures that the first Christians must have turned to for solace and instruction. Ps. 16.8-11 appears only in 2.25-28 and 13.35, but as a psalm of David it would have provided an obvious quarry for investigation, and the sparsity of usage may indicate a text tried but then discarded, rather than a later somewhat idiosyncratic usage of Luke.[83] Psalm 89, probably alluded to in 2.30, became early established in Christian theologizing, as reflected in the widespread allusions to it elsewhere in the NT.[84] Deut. 18.15-16 is cited only in 3.22-23 and 7.37, but it would have provided an obvious reference point in any survey of Scripture in such a hunt for meaning, and it is echoed in the Synoptics' account of Jesus' transfiguration,[85] whose telling may itself echo the convictions which derived from resurrection

80. The classic study of B. Lindars, *New Testament Apologetic: The Doctrinal Significance of the Old Testament Quotations* (London: SCM, 1961), looked for the earliest use of the Scriptures by the first followers of Jesus in their apologetic on behalf of Jesus (252). D. Juel, *Messianic Exegesis: Christological Interpretation of the Old Testament in Early Christianity* (Philadelphia: Fortress, 1988), however, argues that the earliest use of Scripture was not to defend the gospel (already formulated) but in effect to understand and formulate the gospel itself; his principal thesis is that 'the beginning of Christian reflection can be traced to interpretations of Israel's Scriptures, and the major focus of that scriptural interpretation was Jesus, the crucified and risen Messiah' (1). Schenke cites a range of passages on which the first Christians may have reflected (*Urgemeinde* 100-107; and further chs. 12-13).

81. *Jesus Remembered* §§9.9c and 14.4.

82. 'There is no doubt that in the earliest Church the proving of Old Testament predictions was practised, sometimes for edification, sometimes for missionary purposes, but especially for apologetic reasons. . . . In 1 Cor. 10:11 the principle that proof from prophecy is to be sought in "us", the Church, is clearly formulated (cf. "for our sake" . . . 1 Cor. 9:10 and Rom. 15:4)' (Bultmann, *Theology* 1.41-42).

83. 'The study of the intricate biblical background of the speech in Acts 2 has shown the survival of a very primitive argument for the messiahship of Jesus from the fact of the Resurrection' (Lindars, *Apologetic* 44).

84. Juel, *Messianic Exegesis* 107-10, referring principally to Luke 1.51 (89.11), Luke 1.69 (89.24), John 12.34 (89.36), Acts 2.30 (89.4), Col. 1.5 (89.27), Heb. 11.26 and 1 Pet. 4.14 (89.50-51), and Rev. 1.5 (89.27, 37).

85. *Jesus Remembered* 491 n. 7; 656, 665.

appearances.[86] And the five scriptural allusions round which Peter's sermon to Cornelius is constructed provide an instructive illustration of the sort of interweaving of texts which can well be envisaged in the Jewish context of Christianity's beginnings.[87]

Very significantly, if what I have already suggested is on the right lines, the first attempts to tell the story of Jesus' passion probably drew upon such newly illuminating Scriptures to shed light on the events themselves — particularly Psalms 22 and 69.[88] Given both that the issue of Jesus' messianic status must have arisen during his mission[89] and that the title 'Christ' became established so quickly for members of the new sect (their first formal title is 'Christ-ians', Acts 11.26), we can only infer that the messiahship of Jesus was a prominent part of earliest Christian theologizing, in which key passages like Ps. 2.7 and 2 Sam. 7.12-14 would almost certainly have played a role, as reflected in Acts 13.23, 33 and the early confessional formula used by Paul in Rom. 1.3-4.[90] And if indeed the visions of Dan. 7.9-14 had influenced Jesus' own expectation, then it would no doubt have helped dictate the suffering-vindication theme which is a feature of the Acts sermons (see further §23.4g). Again, as we shall see further below (§23.4d), Ps. 110.1 must have played a substantial part in shaping christological thinking from very early on,[91] possibly also from early on in conjunction with Ps. 8.4-6.[92] And whatever the role of Isaiah 53 in shaping Jesus' own thought,[93] it seems to have come in quite prominently and soon, as reflected in Acts 8.32-33, and in the confessional formulation echoed in Rom. 4.25.[94] Similarly the rejected-stone passage (Ps. 118.22) would probably have early on been drawn

86. *Jesus Remembered* 665-66.

87. Deut. 10.17; Ps. 107.20; Isa. 52.7(?); Isa. 61.1; Deut. 21.22; see above, §21.3c and n. 175.

88. *Jesus Remembered* 777-79. 'The so-called passion psalms — Psalms 22, 69, and possibly 31 — were from an early date employed to tell the story of Jesus' death' (Juel, *Messianic Exegesis* 116).

89. *Jesus Remembered* §15.3.

90. See further Juel, *Messianic Exegesis* ch. 3.

91. Lindars, *Apologetic* 45-51: Ps. 110.1 'was perhaps the most important of the scriptures used with the argument from literal fulfilment'; 'the argument in Acts 2 preserves the original and fundamental use of Ps. 110.1' (45, 47); Juel, *Messianic Exegesis* ch. 6. See further below, n. 240.

92. Lindars, *Apologetic* 50-51; Dunn, *Theology of Paul* 248-49.

93. *Jesus Remembered* 809-18, 820.

94. M. Hengel, *The Atonement: A Study of the Origins of the Doctrine in the New Testament* (London: SCM, 1981) 35-36; O. Hofius, 'The Fourth Servant Song in the New Testament Letters', in B. Janowski and P. Stuhlmacher, eds., *The Suffering Servant: Isaiah 53 in Jewish and Christian Sources* (Grand Rapids: Eerdmans, 2004) 163-88 (here 180-82); see also *Jesus Remembered* 811 n. 221, and further below, §23.5.

upon to express the early Christian sense of Jesus' rejection and vindication, as Acts 4.11 suggests, possibly in early conjunction with other stone passages,[95] as Rom. 9.33 and 1 Pet. 2.4-8 imply.[96] In this last case we can probably see an example of a scriptural passage (Ps. 118.22-23) being drawn in to elaborate the Jesus tradition itself (Mark 12.10-11 pars.).[97] The likelihood that the first Christians began to assemble catenas of scriptural passages or collections of 'testimonia' (for the use of teachers instructing new converts) has been made more likely by the discovery of such testimonia collections among the Dead Sea Scrolls (4Q174-177).[98]

The other principal feature of earliest Christianity — their experience understood as experience of the promised eschatological Spirit — must have gained illumination from the Joel prophecy, as Acts 2.17-21 suggests.[99] The echoes of 'outpouring' imagery in connection with the Spirit (Rom. 5.5; Tit. 3.6) probably reflect the way the Joel language entered into early Christian vocabulary. And the phrase 'calling upon the name of the Lord' as a description of believers is also taken from the Joel passage (Joel 3.5), indicating again its formative influence on early Christian reflection. That Paul was able to make allusions to passages like Ezek. 11.19 and 37.14 (2 Cor. 3.3; 1 Thess. 4.8) likewise suggests that such passages and their language became formative in earliest Christian understanding of the significance of what they were experiencing and of the new movement of which they were part.[100]

I do not for a moment suggest that all such passages used in very early Christian self-understanding reflection, catechetical instruction and apologetic emerged in and through 'the teaching of the apostles' as reported in Acts 2.42. But reflection on and interpretation of such passages must have been part of the teaching which began from the first to shape the self-understanding and message of the first Christian communities.

---

95. Isa. 8.14, 28.16; and possibly Dan. 2.34.

96. See also Lindars, *Apologetic* 169-86.

97. *Jesus Remembered* 721-22 n. 67.

98. On the whole subject see M. C. Albi, *'And Scripture Cannot Be Broken': The Form and Function of the Early Christian* Testimonia *Collections* (NovTSupp 96; Leiden: Brill, 1999).

99. Joel 2.28-32 'is one of many eschatological passages used by the early Christians . . . to support their claim to be living in the Last Days and to possess the Spirit' (Lindars, *Apologetic* 37).

100. Several argue that behind Acts 2.33 lies the interpretation of Ps. 68.19 on which Eph. 4.8-10 draws in its version of the Pentecost tradition, e.g., Lindars, *Apologetic* 51-59; J. Dupont, 'Ascension du Christ et don de l'Esprit d'après Actes 2:33', in B. Lindars and S. S. Smalley, eds., *Christ and Spirit in the New Testament,* C. F. D. Moule FS (Cambridge: Cambridge University, 1973) 219-28; Barrett, *Acts* 149-50 (others in Fitzmyer, *Acts* 259); see also §22 n. 119 above; Fitzmyer, however, thinks the verbal echoes 'are so minimal as to be nonexistent' (259).

(2) Equally we can safely assume that much attention would have been devoted to the traditions of what Jesus did and taught. We can hardly assume that the revolution in the first disciples' thinking about Jesus, which the realization that Jesus had been raised from the dead and the experience of Pentecost must have occasioned, caused them to forget or marginalize or discount the memories of Jesus' mission, in response to which they had first come to discipleship.[101] On the contrary, those newly attracted to discipleship would presumably want to learn more about this Jesus or to refresh or correct such knowledge as they already possessed. After all, they had been baptized 'in his name'. Who their leader was and what he expected of his disciples would inevitably be among their first questions. The bare statement of Jesus' death and resurrection (as in 1 Cor. 15.3-5) would hardly be sufficient to satisfy such natural curiosity.[102] The picture which I sketched of disciple groups, already during Jesus' mission sharing impressions of Jesus and beginning to formulate Jesus tradition,[103] readily elides into gatherings of new converts/recruits faithfully absorbing the teaching of the apostles and other of the 120(?) disciples (including women) who had followed Jesus throughout his mission.[104]

I have already indicated the sort of material retained within the Synoptic

101. Similarly Wilckens, *Theologie* 1/2.163-64, 196-203, who draws attention to Matt. 23.10 and points out that the resurrection and exaltation of Jesus would have confirmed and reinforced the authority of Jesus' pre-Easter mission and teaching (199); contrast the scanty treatment by F. Hahn, *Theologie des Neuen Testaments* (2 vols.; Tübingen: Mohr Siebeck, 2002) 1.144-46.

102. 'In the ancient world it was impossible to proclaim as Son of God and redeemer of the world a man who had died on the cross, i.e. had suffered the shameful death of a common criminal, without giving a clear account of his activity, his suffering and his death. . . . It was only possible to describe the exalted Jesus by telling of the earthly Jesus' (Hengel, *Acts* 43-44). See also Hengel, 'Eye-Witness Memory and the Writing of the Gospels', in M. Bockmuehl and D. A. Hagner, eds., *The Written Gospel*, G. N. Stanton FS (Cambridge: Cambridge University, 2005) 70-96: 'Without the narration of Jesus tradition the stereotyped "kerygma" would have been incomprehensible to the church from the beginning' (75-76).

103. *Jesus Remembered* 239-43, also 180-81. L. M. White, *From Jesus to Christianity* (San Francisco: HarperSanFrancisco, 2004), gives more recognition than most to the oral character of the early tradition: 'The majority [of the sources of information] were oral traditions repeated and preserved within the congregations themselves. . . . Our earliest sources regarding the foundations of the movement occur in situations where they were also reminiscing about Jesus himself' (118).

104. W. R. Farmer, 'James the Lord's Brother, according to Paul', in B. Chilton and C. A. Evans, eds., *James the Just and Christian Origins* (Leiden: Brill, 1999) 133-53, suggests that 'James could have represented the family of Jesus in the apostolic monitoring of the translation of Jesus' teaching into the languages in which Jesus himself had not taught . . . where the proper nuancing of his idiomatic expressions required a first-hand acquaintance with the linguistic culture in which his speech was formed' (141-42).

tradition which must have provided a large part of the 'syllabus' for such new disciples (§21.5).[105] The story of Jesus being anointed by a woman as he sat at table (Mark 14.3-9) would have had a particular poignancy while the memory of Jesus' execution and burial was still fresh.[106] Personal testimonies of a Matthew or a Bartimaeus or a Simon of Cyrene would probably have been a regular feature of such gatherings. The challenge to costly discipleship was no doubt the impetus for such clusters as Luke 9.57-62 and Mark 8.34-37, the latter given added shock-value by the memory of what had happened to Jesus himself. Similarly we may appropriately envisage parables like the new and the old (Mark 2.21-22 pars.) and the treasure in the field and the pearl of great price (Matt. 13.44-46) resonating richly with the initial sense of participating in a whole new beginning (the age of resurrection and Spirit).[107] Jesus' instruction about carefree trust in God's provision (Matt. 6.25-33/Luke 12.22-31) may have been a factor in the early community of goods. And no doubt the memory of Jesus' practice of table-fellowship[108] prompted the similar practices attested of the earliest community (§23.2d). Here too we should recall Luke's insistence that the disciples continued to be preoccupied with the principal topic of Jesus' teaching, the kingdom of God, and not just in the period prior to Pentecost (§22.2c). That the topic had ceased to be a front-line issue by the time of Paul's letters, functioning more as a formula for future expectation,[109] should not be taken to indicate a lack of continuity between Jesus' teaching and that of the apostles, but rather that the continuity soon came to be maintained in formulaic terms.

As soon as the new movement's message began to provoke opposition, we can well imagine Jesus' encouragement to fearless confession[110] becoming a prominent element in the teaching 'syllabus'. And the stories of how Jesus handled himself in controversy would have been valued for the instruction they provided (Mark 2.1–3.5). In the case of the Sabbath controversies (Mark 2.23–3.5 pars.), it is evident that the stories have taken their final shape in a Jewish context, since they assume that the Sabbath is still to be observed; the possibility, as in the Gentile churches, that 'all days are alike' (Rom. 14.5) is not yet envisaged. Matt. 15.11, 17-18 (in comparison with Mark 7.15, 18-20) indicates how Jesus' teaching on the real sources of impurity could be (and was) interpreted in a way

---

105. Cf. Schenke, *Urgemeinde* 164-74.

106. Mark took it for granted that the story was already widely known.

107. See *Jesus Remembered* 442-43.

108. *Jesus Remembered* §14.8; if Paul's attitude in Antioch (Gal. 2.11-17) reflects a knowledge of Jesus' practice of eating with 'sinners' (*Theology of Paul* 192), then Paul must have learned of this practice when he was instructed as a catechumen.

109. 1 Cor. 6.9-10; 15.50; Gal. 5.21; Eph. 5.5; 1 Thess. 2.12; 2 Thess. 1.5.

110. Matt. 10.26-31/Luke 12.2-7; Matt. 10.19-20/Luke 12.11-12/Mark 13.11/John 14.26.

that did not challenge the purity law as such.[111] And passages like Matt. 5.23-24, 15.11 and 23.25 attest a living memory of Jesus' teaching among those who still attended the Temple and for whom purity was still an issue. Again, since exorcisms and healings continued to be performed in the earliest Christian communities,[112] it may well be that we should see an echo of the Spirit enthusiasm among the earliest communities in the retelling of Jesus' healings and in the recollection of Jesus' teaching about his exorcisms (Mark 3.22-29 pars.).[113]

Most interesting of all are the indications of how the Jesus tradition itself was shaped or interpreted in the light of Easter faith. We have already noted the likelihood that the rejected-stone testimony (Ps. 118.22) was an early addition to the parable of the wicked tenants (Mark 12.1-9 pars.).[114] And it is commonly and reasonably deduced that Mark 2.20 was an interpretative addition to Jesus' teaching on the inappropriateness of fasting (Mark 2.19): that the death and departure of Jesus was soon seen as a reason for the resumption of the spiritual discipline of fasting.[115] Such an identification of Jesus as the bridegroom of Jesus' parable is of a piece with extensive christological renderings of other elements of the Jesus tradition. As I shall note further below, the most obvious instance is the transition from a self-referential 'the son of man' to the christological title 'the Son of Man'.[116] And I have already suggested that the expectation of Jesus' return (parousia) may have transformed Jesus' expectation of a vindicatory coming *to* heaven into the Christian hope of a coming (again) *from* heaven, and caused the master/householder/bridegroom of the 'parables of crisis'[117] to be read/heard as an allegory for Jesus.[118] Perhaps it would be more accurate to deduce that it was such elements in the Jesus tradition which confirmed or even sparked off the initial conviction that Jesus would return from heaven. Who was the returning master/householder/bridegroom? Who else but Jesus himself!

In other cases the signs of how the Jesus tradition was used and interpreted are clearly later. For example, any implication of a wider mission or of contrast or comparability with Cynic philosophers in the enduring forms of the commissioning instructions (Mark 6.7-13 pars.)[119] probably reflects subsequent use and

---

111. See *Jesus Remembered* 574-75.

112. E.g., Acts 3.1-10; 8.6-7; 9.33-41; 16.18; Rom. 15.19; Gal. 3.5; Heb. 2.4.

113. Cf. J. Boring, *The Continuing Voice of Jesus: Christian Prophecy and the Gospel Tradition* (Louisville: Westminster John Knox, 1991) 213.

114. Above at n. 97.

115. *Jesus Remembered* 442 n. 288.

116. See below, §23.4f.

117. *Jesus Remembered* §12.4g.

118. *Jesus Remembered* 754, 757-58, 761.

119. The disciples are forbidden to take a *pēra*, the 'begging bag' (Mark 6.8 pars.) which

reworking of the commissioning at a time when mission beyond the boundaries of Israel began to be seriously considered and implemented. And the suggestion is very plausible that the crisis over Caligula's proposal to erect a statue of himself in the Temple (39) was the occasion for a fresh formulation of the tradition making up the eschatological discourse commonly known as the 'little apocalypse' (Mark 13).[120] But for the rest of the above examples there is good reason to believe that the use and re-use of Jesus tradition began within the earliest Christian community in Jerusalem, as part of 'the teaching of the apostles'.

c. The Fellowship (Acts 2.42)

That Luke should describe the first believers as devoting themselves to 'the fellowship *(koinōnia)*' is fascinating. It is the only time Luke uses the word, but it was a favourite term with Paul.[121] For Paul the term denoted 'participation in', the act or experience of sharing — hence, the shared experience of the Spirit (2 Cor. 13.13; Phil. 2.1), the act of sharing in the Lord's Supper (1 Cor. 10.16), and so on.[122] Luke's usage seems to lapse into the derivative (and now popular) sense of the 'fellowship, community' which is the expression and outcome of that sharing.[123] But in the context, the immediate sequel to Pentecost, his single usage still retains the central thought of a community brought into existence by the shared experience of the Spirit.[124]

Similar overtones are evident in two other phrases used by Luke repeatedly in these opening chapters — *epi to auto* ('together, in the same place, at the same time, with one accord')[125] and *homothymadon* ('with one mind/purpose/impulse').[126] No doubt there is a touch of idealization in Luke's presentation, but it is more likely to reflect the rose-tinted memories of some of the participants than to be due solely to Luke himself.

---

characterized Cynic itinerant preachers (BDAG 811); see further *Jesus Remembered* 159 nn. 96 and 247.

120. *Jesus Remembered* 417-18, and above, §21 n. 293.

121. *Koinōnia* — Rom. 15.26; 1 Cor. 1.9; 10.16; 2 Cor. 6.14; 8.4; 9.13; 13.13; Gal. 2.9; Phil. 1.5; 2.1; 3.10; Phlm. 6; *koinōneō* — Rom. 12.13; 15.27; Gal. 6.6; Phil. 4.15.

122. See my *Theology of Paul* 561 and n. 153; BDAG 552-53.

123. Cf. Barrett, *Acts* 163-64; Fitzmyer, *Acts* 269 ('communal form of life').

124. Cf. Pesch, *Apg.* 1.133.

125. Acts 1.15; 2.1, 44. See Bruce, *Acts* 108, 132; BDAG 153. On 2.47 see Bruce 133; Barrett, *Acts* 172-73.

126. Acts 1.14; 2.46; 4.24; 5.12. Luke uses the term ten times, elsewhere in the NT only Rom. 15.6. See BDAG 706; Barrett, *Acts* 88-89; S. Walton, '*Homothymadon* in Acts: Colocation, Common Action or "Of One heart and Mind?"', in P. J. Williams et al., eds., *The New Testament in Its First-Century Setting,* B. W. Winter FS (Grand Rapids: Eerdmans, 2004) 89-105.

We see a sample of such communal feeling and shared experience in the *Abba* prayer, presumably inspired by Jesus' own example.[127] Rom. 8.15 and Gal. 4.6 are sufficient proof that the prayer had become firmly established in Aramaic form and that it was a widespread feature of early Christian devotion; the letters were written to widely disparate congregations, and yet the 'we' of Rom. 8.15 and the 'you' of Gal. 4.6 assume a common and familiar experience. The pattern can only have become established in the Aramaic-speaking mother communities of Judea. What is striking is that both Pauline passages take it as given that the *Abba* prayer expresses the same experience of the Spirit, and they draw the same deduction that those who so pray are bonded in a shared relationship of son and heir. It is hardly pressing the evidence to deduce that it was such a character of experience which must have drawn the new converts together, a fellowship born of and expressive of their shared experience of the Spirit, and a bonding factor of immense psychological and social power.[128]

Another hint of the same bonding power of the experienced Spirit is given in Luke's description of the table-fellowship of the first Christians in their several homes *(kat' oikon)* 'full of exultation and simplicity of heart *(en agalliasei kai apheloteti kardias)*' (2.46). The term *agalliasis* appears only in religious writings, frequently in the Psalms, and indicates the exultant joy and fervour which often characterized, and still today in Middle Eastern countries characterizes, religious festivals.[129] It is noticeable that Luke uses the equivalent verb *(agalliaō)* to describe Jesus' exultation 'in the Holy Spirit' at the reported success of the returning missionaries (Luke 10.21), in a passage whose description of Jesus comes closer than any other to the effect of the experience of the Spirit of Pentecost (10.18-21). Such intensity of emotion and/or expression is implied also in the verb used by Paul on both occasions to describe the *Abba* prayer which marked out the first Christians (Rom. 8.15; Gal. 4.6) — *krazein,* whose first meaning is 'to make a vehement cry'.[130]

---

127. *Jesus Remembered* 711-18.

128. 'So the first Christians had experiences sufficiently strong to build their group identity on them and so to differentiate themselves from the world around them'; 'the first phase consisted in the shock of enthusiastic joy and the experience of the Spirit' (Pokorny, *Genesis* 156, 169).

129. E.g., Job 8.21; Pss. 30.5; 42.4; 45.7, 15; 47.1; 65.12; 100.2; 105.43; 107.22; 118.15; 126.2, 5, 6; 132.9, 16; see BDAG 4. For Bultmann the word 'characterises the consciousness of the community that it is the community of the last time constituted by the saving act of God' (*TDNT* 1.20); it 'probably means the mood of eschatological joy' (*Theology* 1.40). The mood is well expressed in the canticles of Luke 1–2.

130. BDAG 563. Weiss still catches the mood better than most (*Earliest Christianity* 40-44): 'A tempestuous enthusiasm, an overwhelming intensity of feeling, an immediate awareness of the presence of God, an incomparable sense of power and an irresistible control over the will and inner spirit and even the physical condition of other men — these are ineradicable features of historic early Christianity' (42-43).

It is probably not a matter of coincidence that Paul also uses the term *koinōnia* in connection with the collection.[131] The vivid sense that the Gentile believers had been granted to participate in the same spiritual reality (Rom. 15.27) clearly motivated the unusual sense of concern in churches round the Aegean for fellow believers, even though hundreds of miles distant. There should be no surprise, then, that Luke uses *koinōnia* in close conjunction with his description of the community of goods (Acts 2.42-45). The strong and emotionally rooted conviction that they were now all rejoicing in the same experience of the outpoured Spirit was no doubt a major motivational factor in the setting up of the community fund.[132] Here indeed was a spiritual community, whose committed spirituality was plain to see.

d. The Breaking of Bread (Acts 2.42, 46)

It has been customary among commentators to assume that the reference here is to 'the cultic meals of the early Christians'[133] — that is, to be more explicit, meals which included remembrance and re-enactment of Jesus' 'last supper'.[134] And it is certainly the case that Paul both uses the 'breaking bread' formulation for the bread part of the Lord's Supper (1 Cor. 10.16) and takes it for granted that the elements of the Lord's Supper are received in the course of a meal (11.20-26) — that is, the meal beginning with the breaking of bread, in the usual way, and the cup reserved till 'after dinner' (11.25). Moreover, Paul's other most significant use of *koinōnia* comes precisely in this same context, to describe the act of sharing in the body and blood of the Christ (10.16). Besides which, Paul's reception of the tradition of Jesus' last meal with his disciples implies a practice of commemoration of that meal already well established by the time Paul received his instruction.[135] So the most obvious inference to draw from all this is that the memory of Jesus' last meal with his disciples remained fresh among his first disciples and that they made a practice of commemorating this last meal from early on. If the command 'Do this in memory of me' (Luke 22.19; 1 Cor. 11.24, 25) was not part of the original memory of Jesus' own words,[136] then we have a further case of a tradition elaborated in the use made of it, and probably in the still very early days of the first community.

131. Rom. 15.26; 2 Cor. 8.4; 9.13. See further below, §33.4d.
132. See also U. Wendel, *Gemeinde in Kraft. Das Gemeindeverständnis in den Summarien der Apostelgeschichte* (Neukirchen-Vluyn: Neukirchener, 1998) 134-61.
133. BDAG 546.
134. On which see *Jesus Remembered* 771-73, 804-805.
135. See my *Theology of Paul* §22, particularly 606-608; *Jesus Remembered* 230 n. 241.
136. See, e.g., my *Theology of Paul* 607-608.

In Luke's formulation, however, he probably had in view the practice of eating daily meals together. 'Breaking of bread' simply describes everyday meals by metonymic reference to the initial action by which the head of the household gave the signal to begin the meal.[137] This is probably what is in view in the three other references in Acts. In the first two, Paul and his friends break bread on Sunday (20.7), after which Paul goes on speaking till midnight; Eutychus is ministered to after his fall, they break bread again (20.11), and Paul continues to converse with them till dawn — two meals within half a day seem to be what Luke had in mind. And the third appears after their boat had been driven day after day before a fierce wind, when no food had been eaten for many days; at which point Paul breaks bread and begins to eat, with the result that, much encouraged, the whole company partakes of food (27.35-36); Luke presumably intends us to think of at least a rudimentary meal giving the boat crew and passengers essential nourishment.[138]

Rather than designating the meals referred to in Acts 2.42, 46 as cultic meals, it would be better to see in them the resumption of a characteristic feature of Jesus' mission and discipleship.[139] His table-fellowship had been notorious, and when he had had occasion to act as host, it was he who began the meal by saying the blessing over the bread, breaking it (as in Mark 6.41 pars.; cf. Luke 24.30), and distributing it to the rest of those present. It is the spontaneity ('from home to home')[140] and the delight in the company of others who had shared the same life-transforming experience (2.46) which is in view here, not formal cultic rituals.[141] So we should probably also infer that the meals were not for believers only, 'closed' to 'outsiders', but were open, as had been Jesus' table-fellowship,

137. If not taken over from Jewish usage in this sense ('breaking of bread' = the whole meal), then presumably Luke's usage here was a Christian development (cf. Barrett, *Acts* 165-66). In 2.46 'sharing their food/taking their meals' is presumably resumptive of 'breaking bread in their [various] homes' (but see also Fitzmyer, *Acts* 270-71).

138. See further below, §34 n. 179. Stuhlmacher ignores 27.35-36 (*Biblische Theologie* 1.210).

139. J. Jeremias, *The Eucharistic Words of Jesus* (London: SCM, 1966): 'The meals of the Early Church were not originally repetitions of the last meal which Jesus celebrated with his disciples, but of the daily table fellowship of the disciples with him' (66). Cf. Stuhlmacher, *Biblische Theologie* 1.206-10; Jervell, *Apg.* 155. However, Jeremias goes on to advocate the translation of *koinōnia* in 2.42 as '(table) fellowship', referring to the Agape: 'then "the breaking of bread" must mean the subsequent Eucharist' (119-20). But see Haenchen, *Acts* 191 and n. 2; and above, §23.2c.

140. Surprisingly Schnabel seems to think that meals were shared not only in private houses but also 'on the occasion of their daily visits to the temple' (*Mission* 414).

141. We may well envisage it was during such gatherings that the stories of Jesus' meals, particularly the feeding of the five thousand (Mark 6.32-44 pars.), were given their lasting shape.

with acquaintances and inquirers readily welcome to participate and thus to hear more about Jesus. Such meals may well have been as effective evangelistically as the more formal preaching.

This does not mean that two quite distinct traditions are to be detected in the earliest years — a more festive, enthusiastic, eschatological celebration round the meal table as implied by the Acts narrative (perhaps with no wine and no words of institution), and a 'Pauline' cultic type more focused on the death of Jesus (perhaps more influenced by the mystery cults).[142] But the thesis presupposes both that Paul's formulation (1 Cor. 11.23-26) was an innovation, which is a misreading of the language of tradition 'received' (11.23); and that the Last Supper tradition was thought of as distinct from the memory (and continuation) of Jesus' table-fellowship practice, which has to be read into the data.[143] Perhaps, as I have suggested elsewhere,[144] the commemoration of the Last/Lord's Supper was initially an annual celebration, the Christian version of the Passover — reflected in the degree to which the Last Supper is presented as a Passover meal in the Synoptics (cf. 1 Cor. 5.7); according to Origen and Epiphanius,[145] the Ebionites celebrated it as an annual festival, possibly as a throwback to early Jerusalem practice. But in any case we should not assume a uniformity of practice across the expanding range of early churches,[146] and it would certainly be a mistake to read the earliest traditions in the light of the high theology of the Eucharist which developed in subsequent centuries, since such a reading presupposes a clear distinction between everyday meals and a eucharistic celebration, which is almost certainly anachronistic.[147]

142. The most famous version of this thesis was by H. Lietzmann, *Mass and Lord's Supper: A Study in the History of the Liturgy* (1926; ET Leiden: Brill, 1953-55, 1979) chs. 15-16; earlier Weiss, *Earliest Christianity* 56-66. Lohmeyer modified this by distinguishing between a Galilean tradition of bread-breaking, reflecting Jesus' own practice of table-fellowship, and a Jerusalem tradition stemming from the Last Supper tradition ('Das Abendmahl in der Urgemeinde', *JBL* 56 [1937] 217-52). See also §20 at n. 162.

143. See also *Jesus Remembered* 229-31, 771-73, and above, §20 n. 167.

144. *Unity and Diversity* §40.2.

145. Origen, *In Matt. comm. ser.* 79; Epiphanius, *Pan.* 30.16.1.

146. It should be recalled that our sources reveal variant forms of 'the words of institution' (*Jesus Remembered* 229-30).

147. Lietzmann's thesis has not won much support; see, e.g., E. Schweizer, *The Lord's Supper according to the New Testament* (Philadelphia: Fortress, 1967) 23-28; I. H. Marshall, *Last Supper and Lord's Supper* (Exeter: Paternoster, 1980) 130-33; P. F. Bradshaw, *The Search for the Origins of Christian Worship* (Oxford: Oxford University, 1992) 51-55; Hahn, *Theologie* 1.157.

e. The Prayers (Acts 2.42)

Prayer is a prominent theme in Luke,[148] but there is no reason to doubt that Jesus was remembered as a man of prayer, who taught his disciples to pray as a fundamental aspect of their discipleship.[149] So we need not question Luke's report that prayer was a high priority for the first disciples.[150] It would have been a 'natural' expression of the same shared experience and exultation already noted. No doubt during these early months the Lord's prayer would already begin to undergo the liturgical development noted earlier,[151] and the *Abba* prayer would become established in its Aramaic form. We may envisage the house groups indicated in 2.46 including fairly spontaneous times of worship and prayer (2.47), as well as providing occasions for teaching and commemoration of the last supper. The informality still evident in the Corinthian church (1 Cor. 14.26) may give us some idea of what fellowship meetings were like from the beginning. No hint is given, however, that Sunday soon emerged as a particularly special day within their daily gatherings (2.46).[152]

The most striking reference to prayer, however, is Acts 3.1 — the information that Peter and John used to go up *(anebainon)* into the Temple at the hour of prayer, the ninth hour (= three o'clock in the afternoon). This presumably indicates that the principal leaders of the new sect participated in the worship offered in the Temple, in its formal 'services'; no other reason is given for their going up into the Temple at that time. It should be recalled that worship then could be summed up simply as a communal praying: hence the description of a synagogue as a 'prayer(-house)';[153] hence too, probably, the indication of a certain formality — 'the prayers'.[154] All this is consistent with the earlier note that 'every day' *(kath' hēmeran)* the members of this new sect 'spent much time *(proskarterountes)* together in the temple' (2.46). Indeed, the leaders at least of the new sect seem never to have been out of the Temple for long (3.11; 4.1; 5.12, 20-21, 42). Of course, the Temple was the largest social space in Jerusalem, ideal as a meeting point for a

---

148. Luke 3.21; 5.15; 6.12; 9.18, 28-29; 11.1-2; 18.1, 10-11; 22.40-41, (44), 46.

149. *Jesus Remembered* 554-55, 711-18.

150. Particularly Acts 1.14, 24; 2.42; 6.4, 6; 8.15; 9.11, 40; 10.9; 11.5; 12.5, 12; 13.3; etc.

151. *Jesus Remembered* 226-28.

152. *Pace* Colpe, 'Oldest Jewish-Christian Community' 85.

153. Data in *Jesus Remembered* 304 n. 226.

154. 'The prayers are above all those offered together with the Jewish congregation' (Haenchen, *Acts* 191); 'the prayers were familiar Jewish prayers' (Barrett, *Acts* 166); similarly Jervell, *Apg.* 155. See particularly D. K. Falk, 'Jewish Prayer Literature and the Jerusalem Church in Acts', *BAFCS* 4.267-301 (here 269-76, 285-92); and further P. F. Bradshaw, *Daily Prayer in the Early Church* (London: SPCK, 1981) ch. 2.

large group (3.11; 5.12), and according to Luke their leaders went there principally to bear witness to their new faith (4.1-2, 18; 5.20-21, 25, 28, 42). But no hint is given of any criticism of the Temple or of the Temple cult; would 'the [new] faith' have proved so attractive to 'a great many priests' (6.7) had the first disciples in effect already disowned the Temple?[155] Luke was evidently quite content to leave the impression that as the new pattern of worship and community was beginning to take shape in believers' homes, at the same time they continued to value and participate in the Temple ritual and times of prayer (3.1).[156] Since we hear of synagogues also in Jerusalem (cf. 6.9),[157] we may infer that these home meetings would have been regarded, by authorities and participants, as informal equivalents.

f. 'The Church of God'

The fact that Paul explicitly recalls his persecution as persecution of 'the church of God' (1 Cor. 15.9; Gal. 1.13) could mean one of two things. Either this was how the Jerusalem and Judean churches (Gal. 1.22-24) thought of themselves, or the realization that he was actually persecuting 'the church of God' was a shocking aspect of Paul's conversion. If the former, it would imply that the first believers already saw themselves as the eschatological expression of the people of God, the *qahal Yahweh/Israel*.[158] This opens up the possibility that Jesus was remembered as so speaking of his group of disciples;[159] it ties in with the idea of (some of) the Jerusalem leadership as 'pillars' of the eschatological temple[160] and helps explain why Paul used the term *ekklēsia* consistently for all his churches.[161]

g. A Holy Conventicle

A notable feature of Luke's description of the earliest Jerusalem community is his repeated talk of 'fear' or 'awe' which the new sect and its doings evoked

155. See also §24 n. 88 below.

156. Note also Luke's reference to 'a Sabbath day's journey' in 1.12; 'Luke is concerned to depict the apostles as Christians still observant of their Jewish obligations' (Fitzmyer, *Acts* 213).

157. See below, §24 at n. 30.

158. W. Kraus, *Zwischen Jerusalem und Antiochia. Die "Hellenisten", Paulus und die Aufnahme der Heiden in das endzeitliche Gottesvolk* (SBS 179; Stuttgart: Katholisches Bibelwerk, 1999) 33-38.

159. See *Jesus Remembered* 513-14.

160. See below at n. 202 and at n. 322.

161. See below and further §30.1.

among the people of Jerusalem: 'awe *(phobos)* came upon everyone, because many signs and wonders were happening through the apostles' (2.43); 'great fear *(phobos megas)* came upon the whole church and everyone who heard the shocking story of Ananias and Sapphira' (5.5, 11).[162]

'Signs and wonders' is a favourite term of Luke, drawn from the same Joel prophecy (2.19 = Joel 2.30). Undoubtedly it indicates Luke's own (rather uncritical) evaluation of miraculous healings.[163] But it is equally without doubt that 'extraordinary deeds' happened within the earliest Christian communities;[164] we need only recall such personal recollections of Paul as Gal. 3.5 and Rom. 15.19. Luke goes on to narrate only one such healing — of the man lame from birth at the Beautiful Gate of the Temple (3.1-10).[165] The story presumably came to him in Jerusalem tradition or personal recollections of some already active in or recruited to the new movement at that time. Luke signals its importance by attaching to it a second sermon of Peter (3.11-26), almost certainly drawing on at least some memories of the emphases of the time.[166] And he goes on to present the healing miracle as the occasion for the first confrontation between Peter and John and the Temple authorities (4.1-22). But even if Luke has made a typical episode out of such memories, we can be confident that such (a) healing(s) did occur, and that opposition to the new movement from the high priestly leadership did begin quite soon — probably because the doings of the new community were coming to public attention and its success in winning support was being seen as something of a threat to the authority of the high priests.

The point I want to draw attention to here, however, is the impression which Luke gives of what we might call the *numinous* character of the new sect. Such extraordinary deeds evidently evoked a sense of fear or awe (2.43).[167] Those who witnessed the healing of the lame man were 'utterly astonished *(ekthamboi)*' (3.11). Prominent in chs. 3–4 is reference to 'the name' of Jesus Christ (3.6, 16; 4.7, 10, 12, 17, 18, 30). As representing the presence of one recently crucified but now raised from the dead and exalted to heaven, or so the first Christians proclaimed, 'the name' must have evoked the same sense of the

162. Colpe draws attention to the 'ecstatic motivations' and 'ecstatic complexity' of the oldest congregation ('Oldest Jewish-Christian Community' 76).

163. See again §21.2d(5) above.

164. See *Jesus Remembered* §15.7.

165. Which gate is referred to is a matter of dispute: most think the Nicanor Gate, which gave access on the east from the Court of the Gentiles to the Court of the Women; see discussion in K. Lake, *Beginnings* 5.479-86; Barrett, *Acts* 179-80; Fitzmyer, *Acts* 277-78.

166. See above, §21.3b.

167. 'Here there is some genuine fear of further supernatural events. . . . *egineto* (imperfect) describes a state; not *fear came upon* (as at 5.5, 11, *egeneto*) but *fear lay upon*, as a continuous condition' (Barrett, *Acts* 166-67).

numinous, of the presence and power of the 'holy' — especially as 'the name of Jesus Christ' was proving so effective in winning recruits to the new sect (2.21, 38, 41), as well as in effecting (a) miraculous cure(s) (3.6, 16; 4.10, 30).[168] We can readily, and without strain, envisage a milieu in which the spiritual realm was perceived as having an almost tangible presence of raw, uncontainable energy, and where the new sect seemed to have a kind of aura of the holy — what Rudolf Otto referred to as the *mysterium tremendum et fascinans*.[169]

Something like this, I believe, lies behind the disturbing story of Ananias and Sapphira, where the couple, having determined to hold back (as they were perfectly entitled to do) some of the proceeds of a sale of land and lied about it, were struck dead in the presence of Peter (5.1-11). It is idle to assume that a rational analysis can penetrate to the heart of this story. For it seems basically to be an account of the devastating results which ensue from an infringement of the holy. In the ancient world such holiness was perceived as adhering particularly to the holy place or the holy object, set apart to God and therefore touched with something of the fearful power of his very presence. Classic examples are the restrictions on the people to prevent them approaching or touching Mount Sinai (Exod. 19.10-25), the cautionary tales of Nadab and Abihu (Lev. 10.1-3) and of Achan (Josh. 7), and the equally unnerving story of Uzzah's fate when he tried to steady the ark of the covenant (2 Sam. 6.6-7).[170] The Temple itself was the focus of holiness within the religion of Israel (Acts 6.13),[171] and its consecration was recalled as another experience of the holy (2 Chron. 7.1-3). Such folk memories could only serve to heighten a sense of the presence of such holy power surrounding the leaders of a new sect vibrant with fresh spirituality and seemingly able to tap into previously untapped resources of spiritual energy (and physical power). Subsequently Paul seems to show both a similar willing-

---

168. 'There is power in names, because they both participate in the reality named and give definition and identity to that reality. That is, name and named exist in a mutual relationship in which the power of the former is shared with the being of the latter' (F. M. Denny, 'Names and Naming', *Encyclopedia of Religion* [16 vols.; New York: Macmillan, 1987] 10.300-301). The equivalence of name and person is illustrated by comparing 3.6 ('in the name of Jesus Christ of Nazareth, stand up and walk') and 9.34 ('Jesus Christ heals you; get up and make your bed'); but note the warning contained in the story of 19.13-16. See further S. New, *Beginnings* 5.121-23; H. Bietenhard, *TDNT* 5.243, 250-51, 253-58, 269-70, 277; D. E. Aune, 'Magic in Early Christianity', *ANRW* 2.23.2 (1980) 1507-57 (here 1545-49); Barrett, *Acts* 182-83.

169. R. Otto, *The Idea of the Holy* (London: Oxford University, 1923).

170. Several commentators include 1 Kgs. 14.1-18 but ignore 2 Sam. 6.6-7 — e.g., Barrett, *Acts* 263, and Fitzmyer, *Acts* 319. Marguerat argues that the typological model is not so much Achan as Adam and Eve: 'Luke wants to inform his readers that *the original sin in the Church is a sin of money*' (*First Christian Historian* 172-78, here 176).

171. *Jesus Remembered* 788-89.

ness to play the same role as Peter in regard to another one guilty of grave sin (1 Cor. 5.3-5),[172] and concern for the potentially lethal effect of unworthy partaking of the Lord's Supper (11.29-30).[173] So we should not regard these as merely folk tales plucked by Luke from random sources to create an impression on his readers. Rather they are better regarded as folk memories retained and retold in the gatherings of early Christians, particularly by those who remembered the highly charged spiritual atmosphere of the earliest days of the Jerusalem church.[174]

This way of looking at Acts 3–5 may even explain Luke's further summary account of the earliest community subsequent to the awful fate of Ananias and Sapphira (5.12-16): more 'signs and wonders' (5.12); a kind of protective aura surrounding the new sect (5.13), attracting new recruits (5.14);[175] and a spiritual, healing power emanating from Peter (5.15-16), as it had from Jesus (Luke 8.44-46).[176] It was an atmosphere in which a story like the miraculous release of (all) the apostles from prison and their subsequent return to the Temple (Acts 5.17-26) could emerge and thrive. That is, once again, we should not be content simply to label this latter story as belonging to the genre of miraculous prison escape stories[177] and as-

172. See my *Jesus and the Spirit* 166; Conzelmann, *1 Corinthians* 97-98; discussion in Schrage, *1 Korinther* 1.374-78; Thiselton, *1 Corinthians* 395-400.

173. *Theology of Paul* 612-13; careful statements in Schrage, *1 Korinther* 3.52-53; Thiselton, *1 Corinthians* 894-97.

174. Fitzmyer's helpful review of discussion of Acts 5.1-11 (*Acts* 316-20) shows how little this dimension of the story has been considered in that discussion. That the story could have been told without apparently raising the obvious moral issues posed (e.g., by Haenchen, *Acts* 239-41) simply reminds us that similar issues are posed by 2 Sam. 6.6-7 and 1 Cor. 11.29-30. As Lüdemann observes in the same connection, '1 Cor. 5 makes one think!' (*Early Christianity* 66). Infringement of the holy cuts across moral categories; as Otto observed, '*qadosh* or *sanctus* is not originally a *moral* category at all' (*Idea* 54). At this point talk of 'excommunication' and parallels with the discipline exercised at Qumran (cf., e.g., Jervell, *Apg.* 199 nn. 537, 538) break down.

175. 'After the great *phobos* aroused by the punishing of the couple, one would expect the Jews to sense the *mysterium tremendum* and apprehensively keep their distance. . . . Thus a contradiction inevitably arose: on the one hand an awestruck reserve, on the other great missionary successes' (Haenchen, *Acts* 244). Why a 'contradiction'? Haenchen has forgotten Otto's fuller formula — *mysterium tremendum et fascinans*.

176. On 5.15-16 Haenchen writes, 'This idea of the Apostle is so heightened as to be fantastic' (*Acts* 246); did he ever discuss such a story with Christians from West or East Africa? See, e.g., the range of considerations opened up by P. W. van der Horst, 'Peter's Shadow: The Religio-Historical Background of Acts 5.15', *NTS* 23 (1976-77) 204-12.

177. Acts 12.6-11; 16.25-26. See particularly O. Weinrich, 'Gebet und Wunder. Zwei Abhandlungen zur Religions- und Literaturgeschichte', *Religionsgeschichtliche Studien* (Darmstadt: Wissenschaftliche Buchgesellschaft, 1968) 147-79; J. B. Weaver, *Plots of Epiphany: Prison-Escape in Acts of the Apostles* (BZNW 131; Berlin: de Gruyter, 2004), who notes that di-

sume consequently that Luke has somewhat arbitrarily inserted this example of the genre at this point. Rather, I believe, we should see here further evidence of the euphoric (some might prefer 'febrile') attitudes and experiences of the earliest Christian community in Jerusalem, with their levels of spiritual awareness raised and their meetings carried out in a highly charged atmosphere of excitement, enthusiasm and expectation.[178]

23.3. Leadership

What can we say about the leadership of the first Christian community in its earliest beginnings? Although almost all detail is lost in the mists of time, some broad features are still visible.

a. The Twelve

The twelve tribes, as denoting the fullness of Israel, evidently remained significant in early Christianity, as Jas. 1.1 and Rev. 21.12 attest. As already noted, the only obvious way to interpret the significance of Jesus' choice of twelve disciples was that he saw them as representing (the twelve tribes of) Israel, at least in God's eschatological intent.[179] The same rationale must lie behind the prominence of 'the twelve' in the earliest records of Christianity. The most notable testimony is 1 Cor. 15.5, the resurrection appearance to 'the twelve', which already counted as established tradition at the time of Paul's conversion. And the status accorded to 'the twelve apostles' in Rev. 21.14 confirms that by the end of the first century the role of 'the twelve' was seen as truly foundational for Christianity.[180]

The obvious inference to be drawn from this is that the twelve disciples chosen by Jesus, or the eleven, either as such or as restored to twelve by a replacement for Judas,[181] were in the beginning seen as the core of the new sect.

---

rect influence from Euripides' *Bacchae* has often been detected in Gamaliel's warning against becoming 'God-fighters *(theomachoi)*' (5.39) (132-48). See also §31 n. 76 below.

178. Similar considerations can even apply to Luke's description of 'the place in which they were gathered together (being) shaken *(esaleuthē)*' (Acts 4.31); see my *Jesus and the Spirit* 188 n. 150 (407), 192.

179. *Jesus Remembered* 510-11, and above, §22.2f.

180. In the full title of the *Didache,* 'The Teaching of the Twelve Apostles', or more fully, 'The Teaching of the Lord through the Twelve Apostles to the Gentiles', the word 'twelve' may be a later addition (see above, §21 n. 43).

181. See above, §22.2f.

Those recruited to the new movement would have cohered round them to participate in the Israel of the new age which had now dawned with Jesus' resurrection.[182] All this strongly indicates that Luke's representation of 'the twelve' as
the unifying and coordinating leadership of the new community (Acts 6.2) must
be a fair representation of what was the case in at least some measure in the earliest days. In other words, the enduring value of the symbol of 'the twelve' probably indicates that the role of the twelve was an effective reality in the beginning and established the power of the symbol in the folk memory of the early
Christians.[183]

More than that we cannot say. The fact that memory of who the twelve actually were soon became confused[184] probably means that as the timescale
lengthened before the return of Christ, and the Gentile mission slackened the focus on Israel as such, so the significance of the twelve faded.[185] Certainly it is
striking how little interest the NT writers display in the identity of the twelve.
And even Luke, by giving emphasis to 'the apostles' rather than 'the twelve'
(even though he had in view the twelve apostles), seems to want to play down the
role of 'the twelve' as such in the earliest days. We should probably infer, therefore, that the role of 'the twelve' was soon rendered nugatory by the rapid expansion of the new movement and the changes which ensued.[186]

182. W. Horbury, 'The Twelve and the Phylarchs', *NTS* 32 (1986) 503-27, suggests
that the twelve princes of the tribes, 'phylarchs' (Num. 1.4-16; 7.2; Philo, *Fug.* 73; Josephus,
Ant. 3.220), provided the model for the twelve, with particular reference to Matt. 19.28.
Bauckham adds: 'We can take it as certain that the Twelve, the phylarchs of the eschatological Israel (Mt. 19:28; Lk. 22:29-30), would have taken up residence in Jerusalem precisely
because of their and its eschatological significance' ('James and the Jerusalem Church' 439;
also 422-27).

183. 'Even the Twelve are not so much a governing body as the symbolic representation
of the nature of the church as God's people of the end-time' (Conzelmann, *History* 56). See also
S. S. Bartchy, 'Divine Power, Community Formation, and Leadership in the Acts of the Apostles', in R. N. Longenecker, ed., *Community Formation in the Early Church and in the Church
Today* (Peabody: Hendrickson, 2002) 89-104.

184. *Jesus Remembered* §13.3b (507-11); Bauckham, however, *Eyewitnesses* ch. 5, argues differently — 'The lists show, not carelessness about the precise membership of the
Twelve, but quite the opposite: great care to preserve precisely the way they were known in
their own milieu during the ministry of Jesus and in the early Jerusalem church' (108).

185. 'That the role of the Twelve paled into almost complete oblivion is easier to explain
if it was an earlier institution which was superseded by a new and wider circle constituted by
the risen Christ' (Wedderburn, *History* 23).

186. Schnabel wants to put as much weight as possible on the apocryphal Acts to support his view that the apostles generally were engaged in extensive missionary work (*Mission*
372-76, 469-98, 526-33, ch. 22 *passim*), but such traditions — that the twelve (other than Peter)
were involved in extensive mission — most likely belong to the realm of legend as churches in
different regions sought to claim an apostolic foundation (see, e.g., Reinbold, *Propaganda* 253-

b. Peter

Luke gives almost exclusive prominence to the leadership of Peter in the opening chapters of Acts.[187] This accords well not only with his prominence during the mission of Jesus[188] but also with the tradition of his being the first to whom Jesus appeared (1 Cor. 15.5).[189] The name 'Cephas' for Peter, which is obviously old,[190] most obviously relates to the idea of Peter as the 'foundation-stone' of the church founded by Jesus (Matt. 16.18);[191] that Peter and only Peter is thus remembered can only adequately be explained if Peter had indeed a foundational role in the formation of Christianity.[192]

The pre-eminence of Peter is further confirmed by Paul's testimony that he went up to Jerusalem, three years after his conversion, precisely in order 'to get to know Cephas', that is, to become acquainted with Peter and to learn from him (Gal. 1.18).[193] There can be little doubt, then, that Peter's subsequent status in Christianity's history reflects his status at the first or from the first as the recognized leader or spokesman of 'the twelve' and 'the apostles'. It is noticeable, for example, that the laying of offerings 'at the apostles' feet' in Acts 5.2-3 meant coming face to face with Peter. His role no doubt included a principal responsibility and authority in 'the teaching of the apostles' (Acts 2.42),[194] as again confirmed by Paul's wording in Gal. 1.18, and in providing a lead in the preaching and healings of the earliest days and in the confrontation with the Temple authorities (the principal themes of Acts 3–5). Beyond that, once again the data provide no basis for further speculation. But we will certainly have to return to Peter as the story of Christianity's beginnings continues to unfold (§26).

---

64). However, extensive missionary work by others of the first disciples than Luke records is supported not only by 1 Cor. 9.5 but also by the fact that the mission instructions in Mark 6.6-12 pars. appear to have been much used and reworked.

187. Acts 1.15; 2.14, 37-38; 3.1-6, 12; 4.8, 19; 5.3-9, 15, 29.

188. *Jesus Remembered* 540, 645.

189. *Jesus Remembered* §18.3(3) (843-46).

190. Apart from Gal. 2.7-8, Paul refers to Peter always as Cephas (1 Cor. 1.12; 3.22; 9.5; 15.5; Gal. 1.18; 2.9, 11, 14). The use of Peter's nickname 'Cephas' (Aramaic *Cepha* = Greek *Petros* — Mark 3.16 pars.) in 1 Cor. 15.5 and Gal. 1.18 evidently reflects the same early time period as 'the twelve'.

191. M. Hengel, *Der unterschätzte Petrus* (Tübingen: Mohr Siebeck, 2006) 30-39.

192. Hengel, *Petrus* 45-58 and further 84-92, 128.

193. The basic meaning of *historeō* is 'to inquire into, or about, or from'; see my *Galatians* 73. 'When the object is personal it is hard to exclude the idea of a getting to know which includes getting to know *about,* a knowledge which enables an informed opinion or judgment about the person and his significance' (73).

194. See above, §23.2b.

c. James and John

Of the twelve apostles mentioned, the two sons of Zebedee are the most enigmatic. I have already observed that with Peter they seem to have formed an inner circle of Jesus' disciples.[195] That status probably continued into the embryonic sect, though in the list of Acts 1.13 the reversal of order (John and James, instead of James and John) prefigures the relative attention devoted to them by Luke.

John appears regularly in Acts 3–4 (mentioned six times by name), but always as Peter's companion, sometimes almost as an afterthought (3.4) or as a kind of reflex (4.13, 19; 8.14). This may simply be a consequence of Luke's style; later on Paul in a similar way overshadows Silas (16.25–17.13). But it may also reflect some remembered difference of temperament. At all events, after 8.14 John does not feature again as a participant in Luke's drama. His early status is also indicated by Paul, as one of the 'pillar apostles' in Jerusalem (Gal. 2.9). But beyond that we can say no more without becoming embroiled in the discussion about the Johannine writings in the NT, to which we shall return in volume 3.

James, brother of John, is mentioned only once, after the initial list of Acts 1.13. During his brief reign as king over the reunited kingdom of Herod the Great (41-44), Herod Agrippa had this James 'killed with a sword' (12.2). This reads like an official execution[196] and presumably implies an intensification of the opposition to the new movement.[197] To be noted here, however, is the implication that James was a prominent figure in the new movement. In which case it is particularly noteworthy that Luke records only the fact of his death, in contrast to the story about Peter which follows (12.3-17), and in still more striking contrast to the attention devoted earlier to the martyrdom of Stephen (ch. 7). Why Luke did not take the opportunity to give a fuller account of the death of one of Jesus' intimates is not clear. It may count in his favour as a reliable historian that he did *not* spin a more elaborate tale round the only data that he may have been able to glean. But his silence beyond the bare fact does raise unanswerable questions as to why the memories of or stemming from the earliest community were not fuller at this point or on the role and stature of James.[198]

---

195. *Jesus Remembered* 540.

196. Discussion in Barrett, *Acts* 1.574-75.

197. See below, §§24.4, 25.2, and further §26.5c.

198. As noted above, §22 n. 96, James brother of John is not replaced to maintain the full complement of 'the twelve' — unless Luke implies that the twelfth seat was filled by James, brother of Jesus (reference to the two Jameses forms a kind of inclusio in 12.1-17).

d. James the Brother of Jesus

James the brother of Jesus is mentioned by Paul in Gal. 1.19 as someone Paul saw when he visited Jerusalem in the mid 30s. But the reference may only reflect his subsequent importance, not least in the events recorded in Galatians 2, and need not imply a prominence already achieved. On the other hand, he is the only one other than Peter to be granted a personal appearance of the risen Jesus (1 Cor. 15.7). And as the eldest brother of Jesus, he would naturally be accorded a prominence within the new movement from when he first began to associate with it.[199] When that was remains obscure (see above, §22.2e), but his non-appearance in Luke's narrative before Acts 12.17 may well suggest that his emergence to prominence took some time. Since 12.17 seems to indicate Peter's departure from Jerusalem,[200] Luke may even be suggesting that this was the moment of transition from Peter's pre-eminence in Jerusalem to that of James.[201] Most striking of all is the fact that this James is acknowledged by Paul to constitute with Peter and John three 'pillar' apostles (Gal. 2.9), a term which suggests that these three leading apostles were regarded as 'pillars in the [eschatological] temple' (as in Rev. 3.12).[202] The point here is that James, the brother of Jesus, was being accorded that role (and numbered with the two surviving intimates of Jesus) some time before Paul made his second journey to Jerusalem, that is, within about fifteen years of the first Christian Easter. The evidence of Galatians 2 and Acts 15, however, takes us beyond the period of our initial review (about 30-44), so I will say no more at this point. But James, like Peter, is a massive figure in the beginnings of Christianity and will feature prominently in the unfolding narrative of Christianity in the making.[203]

---

199. The subsequent tradition of the caliphate, where succession is through brother rather than son (as today in Saudi Arabia), is sometimes appealed to (e.g., Colpe, 'Earliest Jewish-Christian Community' 98).

200. Luke says, enigmatically, that Peter 'left and went to another place' (12.17); see below, §26 n. 130.

201. W. Pratscher, *Der Herrenbruder Jakobus und die Jakobustradition* (FRLANT 139; Göttingen: Vandenhoeck und Ruprecht, 1987) 74-77.

202. See further *Jesus Remembered* 514; Bauckham, 'James and the Jerusalem Church' 441-48, though he presumes on the basis of Prov. 9.1 that the pillars were a group of seven (447-48). Pratscher suggests that the group of pillars emerged as a compromise between the old twelve- or Cephas-tradition (1 Cor. 15.5) and the more recent James-tradition (1 Cor. 15.7), though with Cephas still accorded the leading role (*Herrenbruder* 68-70).

203. See below, particularly §36.

e. Who Else?

'Elders' are first mentioned as leaders in the Jerusalem church in Acts 11.30, but they become prominent, twinned with 'the apostles' ('the apostles and the elders'), only in the account of the council in Jerusalem and in its aftermath (15.2-6, 22-23; 16.4; 21.18). This relatively late reversion to the more typical structure of Jewish communities and synagogues[204] is perhaps a further indication that the first flush of eschatological enthusiasm, where organization could be *ad hoc* (4.32-37; 6.1-6), soon gave way to the recognition of the need for a more regularly constituted leadership group.[205] Since the appearance of elders coincides quite closely with the emergence of James the brother of Jesus to first place in the Jerusalem church, perhaps we should also see the influence of James asserting a more traditional pattern of leadership (cf. Jas. 5.14). But all this is thinly based speculation.

The other leadership group to appear in the early chapters of Acts is the seven appointed in 6.3-6, but they belong to the story of the Hellenists, as does Stephen, to whom we will devote §24.

The status and influence of Mary the mother of Jesus during this period are not attested, but her continuing presence is implied (1.14), and presumably she had some influence, not least in forming and shaping some of the early Jesus tradition.

The only other person deserving of mention in the early years of the Jerusalem leadership is Barnabas, since he first appears as a prominent contributor to the common fund in 4.36, and again as emissary from the Jerusalem church to the

---

204. Bultmann, *Theology* 2.101; G. Bornkamm, *TDNT* 6.662-63; BDAG 862; Hengel and Schwemer, *Paul* 254; and the more extensive thesis of J. T. Burtchaell, *From Synagogue to Church: Public Services and Offices in the Earliest Christian Communities* (Cambridge: Cambridge University, 1992); note the reference to elders in the Theodotus inscription (§24 n. 30). 'Elder' could be more a title of respect (for the wisdom of age and experience) than a title of formal office, but some leadership status is certainly implied; see R. A. Campbell, *The Elders: Seniority within Earliest Christianity* (Edinburgh: Clark, 1994), who suggests that those in view may have been leaders of the Jerusalem house churches (159-63); similarly Gehring, *House Church* 101-105.

205. It is often deduced that the persecution of Herod Agrippa in Acts 12 marked the end of the leadership of the twelve and the transition to James and the elders; see particularly Bauckham, 'James and the Jerusalem Church' 432-41. Bauckham also suggests that the elders may have taken over the financial responsibilities which had been earlier passed to the seven of Acts 6.1-6 (429-30). Note also Bauckham's earlier conjecture, in *Jude and the Relatives of Jesus in the Early Church* (Edinburgh: Clark, 1990), that the body of elders, twelve in number, took over from the initial leadership of the twelve (apostles), absorbing those of the latter who continued to reside in Jerusalem; he even attempts to identify some of them, drawing on the names in Eusebius's list of the bishops of Jerusalem (*HE* 4.5.3) — John, Matthias, Philip, Zacchaeus and Justus (Barsabbas) (74-76).

breakthrough in Antioch (11.22) — a role equivalent to that of Peter and John in 8.14. But he too deserves fuller attention at a later stage (§27.2), not least as a major force for mutual acceptance and recognition in the tensions which began to disfigure the new movement when the fresh new dawn gave way to the heat of the day.

23.4. Beliefs about Jesus

The one clearly distinguishing feature of the new movement was their convictions regarding Jesus, that is, the belief that in Jesus something of epochal importance had taken place and that he himself was now to be seen as the key player in the climax of God's purpose for Israel and the world.[206] But what were these beliefs? As already observed, most of 'the quest for the historical Jesus' has been driven by the sense that the later creedal statement and dogmas about Jesus obscured the reality of what actually was.[207] The same applies by extension to 'the quest for the historical church'. The assumption in both cases has been that the creedal and dogmatic beliefs emerged only over time and that they therefore distance the historical researcher from the, by inference, much simpler and less sophisticated views of the very first Christians. It is important, therefore, to be as clear as possible on what the earliest beliefs about Jesus actually were, lest questers for the historical church(es) make a mistake similar to that which regarded any recognition of the role of faith as a barrier to historical knowledge of Jesus and of the impact he made during his mission.

a. The Resurrection of the Dead

It is beyond dispute that the core claim of the first Christians is that God had raised Jesus from the dead. Whatever we make of the resurrection narratives in the Gospels, no one can realistically dispute that, at least from very early days after Jesus' crucifixion, individuals believed that Jesus had appeared to them, alive from the dead. It is equally evident that such experiences convinced them that in Jesus resurrection had happened.[208] The claim that Jesus had been raised from

206. The thesis of Barnett, *Birth,* is that 'the birth of Christianity and the birth of christology are inseparable, both as to time and essence. Christianity *is* christology'; his 'reasonable assumption is that christology changed little from the first Easter to the end of Paul's letters' (8). Paul's 'christology in all essential points was not of his own making but was formulated by those who were believers before him. . . . It was christology that gave birth to Christianity, not the reverse' (26).

207. *Jesus Remembered* ch. 4.

208. *Jesus Remembered* ch. 18.

the dead is the central and principal message of the preaching in Acts.[209] That Luke is drawing on firm memories of earliest preaching and apologetics is confirmed by the various kerygmatic and confessional formulae reviewed in §21.4e, which have a principal focus in the assertion that God raised Jesus from the dead. We can be quite confident, then, that Jesus' resurrection was from the first a prominent and distinctive feature of earliest Christian belief and functioned as a defining identity marker of the new sect which gathered round his name.

The point which needs to be underlined here is that Jesus' resurrection does not seem to have been perceived, initially at any rate, as an isolated or exceptional event, but rather as the beginning of the resurrection expected at the end of the age prior to the final judgment.[210] I have already cited the key data:[211]

- Rom. 1.4 — the early creedal statement that Jesus' appointment as Son of God in power was 'from the resurrection *of* the dead' (*not* 'from his resurrection *from* the dead')
- 1 Cor. 15.20, 23 — that Paul continues to think of Jesus' resurrection as the firstfruits = beginning of the harvest of (the general) resurrection presumably reflects a very early (the earliest) understanding of Jesus' resurrection as literally the beginning of the final resurrection.[212]
- Matt. 27.52-53 — the report of the dead saints being raised at the time of Jesus' resurrection ('after his resurrection they came out of the tombs . . . and appeared to many') has the feel of a legend which grew out of the same understanding of Jesus' resurrection as the catalyst for the general resurrection of the saints.

The point, then, is that the resurrection of Jesus was at the first probably seen as ushering in the new age, the end time which had been long seen as the climax of God's purpose in creation and for Israel in particular.[213] The resurrection had begun! The end-time harvest had begun to be reaped. The final denouement itself

209. Acts 1.22; 2.24-32; 3.15, (22, 26); 4.2, 10, 33; 5.30; (7.37); 10.40-41; 13.30-37; 17.3, 18, 31-32; 23.6; 24.15, 21; 26.8, 23. See also Pokorny, *Genesis* 66-68.

210. On the 'end-point' (or 'end-stage') character of the resurrection of the dead see N. T. Wright, *The Resurrection of the Son of God* (London: SPCK, 2003), particularly 200-206.

211. *Jesus Remembered* 868-70.

212. The Spirit was also understood as the firstfruits of the resurrection (Rom. 8.23). As Weiss observed: 'When the "first fruits" have been harvested, there can be no doubt that the full crop is about to be gathered in' (*Earliest Christianity* 40).

213. For Jewish 'eschatological' expectation see *Jesus Remembered* 390-404. Lüdemann, *Primitive Christianity* 7-10, refers particularly to the eschatological interpretation of early Christianity in Schenke, *Die Urgemeinde*; 'Schenke always understands the resurrection of Jesus in the context of the dawn of the end-time, during which the general resurrection was expected' (9).

could not long be delayed. This understanding would go a long way to explain the feverish and numinous atmosphere which we have already seen as reflected in Luke's account (Acts 2–5). This is what is meant when the term 'eschatological' is used to describe the first community and its message. At the beginning it carried all the overtones of final expectation in process of being realized, with the full consummation imminent.

b. Redefinition of Messiahship

We can be quite specific here. For one thing, we know that the title 'Christ' (the Greek form of the Hebrew *Mashiah*) soon became so attached to Jesus as to be already established as a proper name for Jesus in the earliest writings of the NT (the letters of Paul)[214] — Jesus *Christ,* a step beyond *Messiah* Jesus. This must mean that the claim that Jesus was Messiah had long since become so obvious in Christian circles as to need no further affirmation or defence. This, in turn, must mean that the claim became a defining feature of the new movement from earliest days, and probably from the first.[215] The fact that members of the new sect were given the title 'Christians' in Antioch (Acts 11.26), probably within the first ten years of Christianity's existence, designating the followers of 'the way' (9.2) as 'Christ's people',[216] confirms that 'Christ' was seen as the chief identity marker of the new sect. And the deduction is the same: the claim that Jesus was 'the Christ' had very quickly become one of the central defining characteristics of the new movement. We should note in passing here that the speed with which the political designation 'Messiah' transposed into the Greek proper name 'Christ' probably defused the

214. See my *Theology of Paul* 197-99, though I note that some of Paul's references show that the titular usage was not altogether lost.

215. The most implausible of the several theses tried out in Cameron and Miller, eds., *Redescribing Christian Origins,* are those which attempt to argue that Paul's use of *christos* cannot be explained from any messianic conception of Jesus (289); '"the messianic concept" seems to have "played no role at the beginning of the Christian experiment"' (290, quoting B. Mack). Similarly, the suggestion that Paul used *christos* only as a proper name and without titular significance is simply incredible, when texts like Rom. 1.2-3 and 9.5 are considered; Miller at least seems to recognize the difficulty of imagining how *christos* could have become a name without assuming knowledge of its titular significance and readily assumes that its connotations were royal (310, 316, 326, also 452-53)! Contrast, e.g., the conclusion of M. Hengel, 'Erwägungen zum Sprachgebrauch von *Christos* bei Paulus und in der "vorpaulinischen" Überlieferung', in M. D. Hooker and S. G. Wilson, eds., *Paul and Paulinism,* C. K. Barrett FS (London: SPCK, 1982) 135-59: 'It cannot be doubted that both Paul and his readers understood the messianic significance of the term, although clearly it was not a matter of controversy for them' (159).

216. See above, §20.1(1), and below, §24.8d.

politically potential threat of calling Jesus (the) Christ; had 'Christ' been understood as a messianic/royal title, presumably the Antiochene authorities would have been more hostile to the sect they designated 'Christians'.

The other controlling factor is the twin but contrasting fact that the issue of Jesus as Messiah must have been raised during Jesus' mission and that he was denounced to Pilate as a messianic pretender. Jesus was crucified as a would-be Messiah, with all the overtones of a royal claim being made to the throne of Israel in defiance of Rome.[217] It is this firm historical fact which makes it unlikely that the primitive elements in Peter's first two speeches should be interpreted as asserting that Jesus was first appointed Messiah at his resurrection/exaltation. Acts 2.36, 'God has made him both Lord and Messiah', can certainly be taken that way,[218] but in the light of the evidence just noted regarding Jesus' mission and death, the expression should probably be taken more as an enthusiastic expression of the realization that Jesus was far more important than they had previously recognized. The verb 'made' *(poiein)* is an all-purpose verb, like English 'put' or German 'machen', and is probably being used as casually as the English and German equivalents. Perhaps we should even paraphrase 2.36 as 'God has made him Lord as well as Messiah'.[219]

Given these two parameters within which interpretation must work, the more obvious conclusion to draw is that Jesus' death and resurrection defined 'Messiah' in a new way. As already pointed out, Jesus did not fit the typical Jewish expectation of Messiah; he was not the Messiah his contemporaries were hoping for.[220] Yet the issue of whether he was Messiah was already clearly posed during his mission and could not be escaped, despite his death. Had that not been the case, it is doubtful whether Jesus would ever have been regarded as Messiah. As Nils Dahl argued in his definitive study, the resurrection itself was not sufficient reason to attach for the first time the epithet 'Messiah' to a crucified man.[221] We

217. See the full discussion in *Jesus Remembered* §§15.3-4.

218. See Weiss, *Earliest Christianity* 31, 118-19; Bousset, *Kyrios Christos* 33; Bultmann, *Theology* 1.43; E. Schweizer, *Erniedrigung und Erhöhung bei Jesus und seinen Nachfolgern* (Zürich: Zwingli, ²1962) 59-60; M. de Jonge, *Christology in Context: The Earliest Christian Response to Jesus* (Philadelphia: Westminster, 1988) 110; Barrett, *Acts* 151-52 (This is 'clear proof that Luke is at this point using a source; he would not have chosen to express himself in this way').

219. On Acts 3.20 see below, §23.4f.

220. *Jesus Remembered* 647-54.

221. N. Dahl, 'The Crucified Messiah', *Jesus the Christ: The Historical Origins of Christological Doctrine,* ed. D. H. Juel (Minneapolis: Fortress, 1991) 27-47, referred to in *Jesus Remembered* 626-27; similarly Stuhlmacher, *Biblische Theologie* 1.185. Jewish thought could embrace the conviction that other heroes of the past had been exalted to heaven without implying that they were of messianic status — e.g., the righteous (Wis. 5.5, 15-16), Adam and Abel (*T. Abr.* 11, 13), Ezra (*4 Ezra* 14.9), Baruch (*2 Bar.* 13.3; etc.).

should not think, then, that the crucified Jesus became the Messiah of Jewish expectation by virtue of his resurrection. Rather we should say, the fact that Messiah
Jesus had been crucified and raised from the dead necessitated the re-evaluation of
messiahship and redefinition of what Jesus' role as Messiah had to be.[222] It now
appeared, in the light of Jesus' death, that the Messiah should after all suffer (Luke
24.26-27, 46; Acts 3.18; 17.3). This process of redefinition, as we have already
observed, was most likely to have been an integral part of 'the teaching of the
apostles' (§23.2b). Here again we should note that this theological redefinition of
'Christ' probably absorbed Christian interest in the name and deflected any suspicion on the part of the Roman authorities that a political claim was being made
thereby.[223]

c. Appointment as Son of God in Power

The designation of Jesus as 'God's Son' appears surprisingly infrequently in the
Acts traditions and the earliest NT writings.[224] But the more explicit articulation
is well rooted in memories of Jesus' own prayer to God as 'Abba, Father',[225] and
the formal deduction from that as to Jesus' status as God's Son was no doubt
quickly drawn in earliest Christian reflection, as Gal. 4.6 indicates. Particularly
noticeable is the close match between Acts 9.20, Gal. 1.16 and 1 Thess. 1.10:
Paul's understanding of his conversion as a commission to preach God's Son
among the Gentiles (Gal. 1.16) ties neatly into Luke's summary of Paul's initial
Christian preaching, 'that Jesus is the Son of God' (Acts 9.20), and into the earliest summary we have from Paul himself of his preaching of God's Son soon to
come from heaven (1 Thess. 1.10). So the indications are good that Jesus was understood in more formal terms as the Son of God more or less from the first.

Here however we find a feature similar to that noted in the case of Jesus as
Messiah (referring to Acts 2.36), for several of the early references to Jesus as
God's Son seem to indicate that Jesus became God's Son (only) as a result of his
resurrection. The citation of Ps. 2.7, 'You are my Son, today I have begotten

222. The point is all the more significant when we remember Weiss's observation of the
'unheard-of' character of the proclamation of Jesus as Messiah: 'None of the Messianic movements of the time had survived the fall of their leaders (as Gamaliel's words imply, in Acts
5:35ff)' (*Earliest Christianity* 14).

223. This may also help explain why 'Son of David' features so little in earliest
christological reflection, apart from Rom. 1.3, where the *kata sarka* ('in terms of the flesh')
may have a slightly negative overtone (see my *Romans* 12-13).

224. Acts 9.20; 13.33; Rom. 1.3-4, 9; 5.10; 8.3, 29, 32; 1 Cor. 1.9; 15.28; Gal. 1.16;
2.20; 4.4, 6; Col. 1.13; 1 Thess. 1.10; also Eph. 2.2; and not at all in James or 1 Peter.

225. *Jesus Remembered* 711-18.

you', with explicit reference to the resurrection in Acts 13.33, is given added strength by its similar use in Heb. 1.5 and 5.5. And Paul at the beginning of Romans probably cites an earlier formula which speaks of Jesus being 'appointed Son of God in power as from the resurrection of the dead' (Rom. 1.4).[226] Once again, however, as with 'Messiah', it is unlikely that the first Christians thereby set themselves in opposition to the belief that Jesus carried through his mission as God's Son; the memory of his *Abba* prayer was too fresh and firmly rooted. Presumably, therefore, the language expressed the surprise and delight occasioned by Jesus' resurrection and the sense that Jesus thereby had been exalted to a new status, publicly honoured as his Son by God. Paul, who talks of Jesus 'having been appointed *(horisthentos)*',[227] hardly thinks of the event as giving Jesus a status as Son for the first time: both parts of the formula, including his life on earth, describe Jesus' sonship (1.3-4).[228] For him at least, the resurrection marked an enhancement, not an initial bestowal, of Jesus' sonship — 'Son of God *in power*'. Rom. 1.4, therefore, is more an exaltation than a resurrection formula.

d. Jesus' Exaltation as Lord

With 'Messiah/Christ' soon losing its titular significance, the most important title for Jesus which emerged was 'Lord'. It certainly has that significance for Paul,[229] but it must have become established well before Paul. Most noticeable is the continued use of the Aramaic form *mar* in 1 Cor. 16.22,[230] which presumably indicates that the title became quickly fixed in the Aramaic-speaking communities of Palestine.[231] In fact there are strong indications that it was Jesus' resurrection and exaltation which were seen as establishing Jesus as Lord. What is probably an established baptismal confession echoed in Rom. 10.9 links the affirmation that

226. See my *Christology in the Making* 33-36.

227. See my *Romans* 13-14.

228. 'The supposed two-stage adoptionistic Christology presumed to lie behind Rom 1:3-4 has no more life setting in early Christianity than the adoptionism suspected behind Mark 1:9-11 par.' (Stuhlmacher, *Biblische Theologie* 1.188).

229. See my *Theology of Paul* 244-52.

230. *Maranatha* can be rendered as either *marana tha* or *maran atha,* both meaning 'Our Lord, come!' See Conzelmann, *1 Corinthians* 300-301; Stuhlmacher, *Biblische Theologie* 1.183.

231. 1 Cor. 16.22 was the fatal flaw in Bousset's attempt to maintain that '*ho kyrios* in the religious sense for Jesus is conceivable only on the soil of the Hellenistic communities' (*Kyrios Christos* 128); Bultmann tried to defend Bousset by arguing that the 'Lord' of 1 Cor. 16.22 referred originally to God (*Theology* 1.51-52). See further C. F. D. Moule, *The Origin of Christology* (Cambridge: Cambridge University, 1977) 36-43.

'Jesus is Lord' with and presumably as the expression of the belief that 'God has raised him from the dead'.[232] The hymn or hymnic passage used by Paul in Phil. 2.6-11 attributes Jesus' lordship to his exaltation following his death.[233] And Acts 2.36 ('God has made him both Lord and Christ') similarly thinks in terms of an installation to the status of Lord as a consequence of his exaltation (2.33).[234] An interesting confirmation of the perceived link between Jesus' resurrection and his installation as Lord is the way Luke deliberately reserves the title 'Lord' on the lips of Jesus' contemporaries till after his resurrection.[235]

In this case the determinative influence seems to have been Ps. 110.1, 'The Lord said to my Lord, "Sit at my right hand until I make your enemies your footstool"'. Whether or not Jesus himself made play with this text (Mark 12.35-37 pars.),[236] there can be no doubt that it played a key role in earliest Christian reflection on Jesus' status.[237] The prominence of the text across the board, in explicit quotation and implicit allusion,[238] is best explained on the hypothesis that it provided some of the clearest answers to the initial questions as to what Jesus' resurrection said about his status. I have already suggested that we can see some of that reflection in the way in which Ps. 110.1 has been drawn into the tradition of Mark 14.62 pars.[239] Whether or not it had featured in Jewish reflection regarding the hoped-for Messiah prior to this, it was evidently just this text which provided the key to the major puzzles which Jesus' death and resurrection posed to his first followers.[240]

If I may speculate further, it probably was this text which brought home the importance of understanding what had happened to Jesus not simply as resurrection (the beginning of the harvest of dead people) but also as exaltation. As risen

232. See §21 n. 211.

233. See §21 n. 217 and further below.

234. See also above, §23.4b.

235. Moule, 'The Christology of Acts', in response to Conzelmann's assertion of Luke's 'promiscuous use of titles' (*Theology of Luke* 171 n. 1).

236. *Jesus Remembered* 634-35, 651.

237. See again my *Theology of Paul the Apostle* 246-49, with further bibliography in n. 58.

238. Mark 12.36 pars.; 14.62 pars.; Acts 2.34-35; Rom. 8.34; 1 Cor. 15.25; Eph. 1.20; Col. 3.1; Heb. 1.3, 13; 8.1; 10.12; 12.2; 1 Pet. 3.22; fuller listing in Albi, *'Scripture Cannot Be Broken'* 217-19.

239. *Jesus Remembered* 749-51, 758, 761; cf. Albi, *'Scripture Cannot Be Broken'* 229-30.

240. See particularly D. M. Hay, *Glory at the Right Hand: Psalm 110 in Early Christianity* (SBLMS 18; Nashville: Abingdon, 1973); Juel, *Messianic Exegesis* 135-50; M. Hengel, '"Sit at My Right Hand!" The Enthronement of Christ at the Right Hand of God and Psalm 110.1', *Studies in Early Christology* (Edinburgh: Clark, 1995) 119-225; Albi, *'Scripture Cannot Be Broken'* 216-36.

from the dead, he had also been taken up to heaven, and not merely to be vindicated before God (like the earlier martyrs and righteous), but to assume his seat 'at God's right hand'. How could the first believers have come to such a conclusion without Ps. 110.1?! The *sessio ad dexteram Patris* is so long established in Christian creedal confession that it is difficult for those well versed in Christian tradition to appreciate how stunning a conclusion and affirmation this was when it was first made, and of one who had been crucified.[241] As I have already suggested, this is the lasting importance of Luke's clear distinction between resurrection and ascension, that the two are not the same. And even if earlier formulations blurred the distinction,[242] in many cases it was the exalted status of the resurrected-ascended Jesus which was the main emphasis of the blurred formulation, most notably in the Philippian hymn (Phil. 2.8-11).

In such a context, of course, the title 'Lord' carried with it overtones of authority, mastery and supremacy. How this was perceived as working out in the earliest community is probably indicated by the importance of 'the name' of Jesus, since it was the name which authorized baptism and effected healing.[243] Those who baptized and healed acted on the authority of Jesus, that is, of Jesus raised from the dead (Acts 3.15-16; 4.10-11). And those baptized, calling upon the name of the Lord Jesus (22.16; 1 Cor. 1.2), thereby submitted to his lordship and became his bond servants. How well thought-through were the implications of this usage is unclear: is Acts 4.12[244] an enthusiastic encomium expressive of

241. There are some near parallels with the legendary figures (see above, §21 n. 173 and §23 n. 221), but nothing quite like this. G. Jossa, *Jews or Christians? The Followers of Jesus in Search of Their Own Identity* (WUNT 202; Tübingen: Mohr Siebeck, 2006): 'The assertion of the heavenly exaltation of Jesus (and of Jesus crucified) in fact puts the group of his disciples in a completely different situation from that of the other Jewish groups of the time' (68); 'To the Christ is attributed a lordship that goes far beyond the powers customarily recognized to the Messiah of Israel' (93). Chester also warns that earliest christology cannot be explained by a simple correlation between Jesus and any of the intermediary figures of late Second Temple Jewish theologizing, even though they attest that the barrier between the divine and human spheres was becoming increasingly permeable; he concludes that 'the phenomenon of earliest christology can only be understood as developing within a Jewish context, and that Jewish intermediary figures constitute a central and integral part of that context . . . [and] that it is the early visionary experiences of the resurrected Jesus, as transformed and set alongside God in the heavenly world, that are crucially important for the development of christology' (*Messiah and Exaltation* 119-20). Contrast J. Carleton Paget, 'Jewish Christianity', *CHJ* 3.731-75: 'At that early stage there was no sense on their part that a commitment to Jesus implied anything negative about their continuing commitment to their inherited faith' (742).

242. See above, §22.2d.

243. See above, §§23.2a, g.

244. 'There is salvation in no one else; for there is no other name under heaven and given among men by which we are to be saved'. On the obscurities of the Greek see Barrett, *Acts* 1.232-33.

the excitement of what the first Christians were experiencing and beginning to appreciate, or is its 'exclusivity'[245] reflective rather of the more developed theology of Luke's own time (cf. 10.36c)? Equally unclear is whether and how quickly this affirmation of Jesus' lordship was seen to constitute a real political threat. But it is significant that the earliest opposition recorded by Luke is of the rulers and high priestly families formally forbidding Peter and John to speak any more 'in this name' (Acts 4.17-18; 5.28, 40). The implications of a lordship which called for different priorities from those of the current rulers evidently became quickly apparent.

The most striking aspect of the attribution to Jesus of rule 'at God's right hand' is the way scriptural texts which spoke of God as 'Lord' began to be used of Jesus. This is usually commented on in relation to Paul's theology, with particular reference to the key passages 1 Cor. 8.4-6 and Phil. 2.9-11,[246] principally because it seems to indicate that Paul thought of Jesus in terms of God.[247] But Phil. 2.9-11 is probably a quotation of an earlier hymn or poem. And 1 Cor. 1.2 may well be using a well-established definition of Christians as 'those who call upon the name of the Lord', in probable echo of Joel 2.32, where 'the Lord' is Yahweh. Most striking of all, the same feature appears in Peter's first speech in Acts 2. The speech is bracketed with references to Joel's prophecy (2.17-21, 39),[248] and the climactic scriptural quotation is of Ps. 110.1 (2.34-35); so a logical deduction is that the Lord who calls them and on whom they call is to be understood as the exalted Lord Jesus.

How much christological significance should we read into all this, and for the very early days of the new community? The key once again is probably Ps. 110.1, for that text envisages two Lords — the Lord God, and another exalted to God's right hand and described as 'my Lord'. It would be entirely understandable if the first Christians allowed this text to determine the language they used for Jesus, and if their initial use of 'Lord' in reference to Jesus made somewhat indiscriminate use of other appropriate 'Lord' texts.[249] Ps. 110.1, after all, indi-

---

245. Schnabel, *Mission* 421-23.

246. See my *Theology of Paul* 245-46, 251-52, 253.

247. See particularly Capes, *Old Testament Yahweh Texts;* also 'YHWH Texts and Monotheism in Paul's Christology', in L. T. Stuckenbruck and W. E. S. North, eds., *Early Jewish and Christian Monotheism* (JSNTS 263; London: Clark International, 2004) 120-37; Bauckham, *God* Crucified; cf. Fitzmyer, *Acts* 260-61; and see further below, §23.4h.

248. Barrett, *Acts* 1.156.

249. In Acts 2.20-36 'the Lord' is Yahweh in 2.20, 25 and 34a, while Christ is clearly in view in 2.34b and 36. In 2.21 and 39 'the Lord' is presumably the Yahweh of Joel 2.32 ('the Lord our God'), though Rom. 10.13 shows that the Joel text was also (subsequently?) applied to Christ. The prayer in 1.24 probably addresses God as *kardiognōstēs,* 'one who knows the heart', as in the word's only other occurrence (15.8; cf. Luke 16.15) (see Fitzmyer, *Acts* 227 and those cited there; otherwise Barrett, *Acts* 1.103), though Luke does recall the episode

cated that Jesus had been exalted to God's right hand, no less. Such exaltation called for full submission to one whose enemies God would soon make his footstool. It is unlikely, then, that the use of 'Lord' for Jesus reflects deep thinking about the divine status or deity of the exalted Jesus, at least at this initial stage, more a somewhat unreflective use of Ps. 110.1 in reference to Jesus as the second Lord installed by the Lord God at his right hand.[250] But, of course, the possibilities opened up by this early interpretation of Ps. 110.1 became a major seam for subsequent christology.

e. Bestower of the Spirit

One of the most striking, and most neglected, of the assertions made regarding the exalted Jesus is the claim attributed to Peter that on being exalted at God's right hand, Jesus had received from the Father the promise of the Holy Spirit and had poured out this Spirit at Pentecost (Acts 2.33). That is, it was the exalted Christ, not God himself, who had poured out the end-time Spirit. Of course, Luke understands this as the fulfilment of the Baptist's prediction (1.5), itself unprecedented.[251] But the exaltation of Jesus transposed this expectation onto a different plane. For now was being attributed to the exalted Jesus the role hitherto assumed to be possible only for God, that of bestowing his own Spirit on human beings.[252] Jewish thought was familiar with the idea that other divine roles might

---

where Jesus knows the inner thoughts of hearts (Luke 5.22; 9.47). On the whole subject see my '*KYRIOS* in Acts', in C. Landmesser et al., eds., *Jesus Christus als die Mitte der Schrift*, O. Hofius FS (Berlin: de Gruyter, 1997) 363-78. G. Schneider, 'Gott und Christus als *KYRIOS* nach der Apostelgeschichte', in J. Zmijewski and E. Nellessen, eds., *Begegnung mit dem Wort*, H. Zimmermann FS (Bonn, 1980) 161-73, concludes that there is no mixing in the use of *kyrios* in Luke-Acts, since reference is either to God or to Jesus each time (171). Cadbury's final comments are judicious (*Beginnings* 5.374).

250. 'We are dealing here [2.36] with an unreflecting Christology . . . not yet submitted to such theological criticism as Paul was able to provide. He who shares the throne of God shares his deity; and he who is God is what he is from and to eternity — otherwise he is not God. This truth, evident as it is, was not immediately perceived; the staggering fact of the resurrection . . . both marked a contrast with the earthly life of Jesus and set his disciples in search of some terminology that might not seem wholly inadequate' (Barrett, *Acts* 1.152).

251. See my 'Spirit-and-Fire Baptism', *NovT* 14 (1972) 81-92, reprinted in my *The Christ and the Spirit*. Vol. 2: *Pneumatology* (Grand Rapids: Eerdmans, 1998) 93-102; also *Jesus Remembered* 366-71. Influence from the Baptist's expectation seems more likely than that Ps. 68.19 was so quickly applied to Pentecost (though the two suggestions are not incompatible) (see above, n. 100); when Eph. 4.8 takes up the Psalm it is only in terms of the exalted Christ giving gifts, ministry gifts to humans, not the Spirit as such.

252. Classically Isa. 44.3; Ezek. 36.26-27; 39.29; as well as Joel 2.28-29. Similarly, Acts 5.31 attributes the giving of repentance to the exalted Jesus, while 11.18 attributes it to God.

be attributed to human beings. In particular, the suggestion that fabled heroes of the past, like Adam and Abel, Enoch and Melchizedek, were already glorious heavenly beings sitting on thrones and ready to take part in the final judgment is one which we meet in several writings of the period.[253] Jesus himself was remembered as anticipating that his immediate circle of disciples would 'sit on thrones and judge the twelve tribes of Israel' (Matt. 19.28/Luke 22.30). And Paul expected the saints to judge the world (1 Cor. 6.2). But this was qualitatively different. For where *God* was so uniformly understood to be the one who gives the Spirit, the reattribution of the gift of the Spirit to *Christ,* albeit having received the promised Spirit from the Father (2.33), was an astonishing development. It is, after all, *the Spirit of God* that we are talking about. Nothing in Jewish religion and theology prepares us for such a development.[254]

Perhaps it is significant that Paul does not follow suit. In Paul's writings it is always God who is described as the one who gives the Spirit.[255] And even if Luke was drawing on very early kerygmatic material in his crafting of the sermon of Acts 2.14-39, he too does not make much of the claim, beyond the repetition of the assertion that Pentecost was the fulfilment of the Baptist's expectation of one to come who would baptize in Holy Spirit (Acts 1.5; 11.16).[256] Possibly, then, the attribution of the Spirit to the exalted Christ was not regarded as something very distinctive, simply the Lord God sharing another of his functions with the exalted Lord Christ. The Baptist's expectation of the coming one as baptizer in the Spirit might not have seemed to require a radical redefinition or reattribution of *divine* functions. Nevertheless, if Acts 2.33 stands as a somewhat isolated fragment of some very early reflection on the christological significance of Pentecost — and its very isolation within early Christian theologizing marks it out as such a remnant — then it speaks all the more forceably of the kind of volcanic eruption which Pentecost precipitated, spewing out insights and claims, some of which were neither taken up nor developed further, at least until the Fourth Evangelist.[257]

---

253. See §21 n. 173 above.

254. See particularly M. Turner, 'The Spirit of Christ and "Divine" Christology', in J. B. Green and M. Turner, eds., *Jesus of Nazareth: Lord and Christ,* I. H. Marshall FS (Grand Rapids: Eerdmans, 1994) 413-36; Schnabel, *Mission* 401; cf. Wilckens, *Theologie* 1/2.173-75.

255. 1 Cor. 2.12; 2 Cor. 1.21-22; 5.5; Gal. 3.5; 4.6; 1 Thess. 4.8; Eph. 1.17; cf. the 'divine passives' of Rom. 5.5 and 1 Cor. 12.13.

256. In the light of the Baptist's expectation it is doubtful whether the gift of the Spirit was ever unconnected with the heavenly working of Jesus (*pace* Hahn, *Titles* 98).

257. See further my 'Towards the Spirit of Christ: The Emergence of the Distinctive Features of Christian Pneumatology', in M. Welker, ed., *The Work of the Spirit: Pneumatology and Pentecostalism* (Grand Rapids: Eerdmans, 2006) 3-26.

f. Soon Coming (Son of Man)

If Acts 2.33-36 contains the most striking indications of earliest christology in Peter's first speech, then 3.19-21 is the most striking passage in his second speech, perhaps even to be regarded as 'the most primitive christology of all'.[258] The central feature is the assertion that Messiah Jesus was now in heaven and would remain there 'until the time of the universal restoration that God announced long ago through his holy prophets' (3.21).[259] Although the imminence of the expected return is not a necessary corollary,[260] it is difficult to avoid the implication that Israel's repentance would be a vital signal for Jesus to return (3.19-20). This is all the more striking, since in the later speeches Jesus' role as judge seems to have become more an affirmation of faith than a near expectation (10.42; 17.31). So it does not seem to be a particularly Lukan theme, a fact which strengthens the likelihood that he has drawn on early tradition at this point (3.19-21) rather than moulding material to express his own views.[261]

At all events, the sense of imminent expectation is strong throughout the early Christian tradition. The Aramaic prayer preserved in 1 Cor. 16.22 expresses longing for the Lord (Jesus) to come. The earliest echo of Paul's preaching likewise talks of waiting for God's Son (to return) from heaven (1 Thess. 1.10), and it is very likely that the problem addressed by Paul in this his earliest letter (4.13-18) was occasioned by the Thessalonians' assumption that Jesus would have come (again) before any of their number had died.[262] I have already noted the assumption implicit in the conceptualization of what had happened to Jesus as 'resurrection', namely that his resurrection was the beginning of the end-time resurrection, again implying a very short-term perspective (§23.4a). Not only so, but

---

258. See above, §21 n. 162. Throughout the twentieth century it was regularly inferred that the earliest concept of Jesus as Messiah was as coming Messiah (usually merged with the coming Son of Man); Bousset, *Kyrios Christos* 45-52 ('the Messiah–Son of Man faith'); Bultmann, *Theology* 1.33-37, 49 ('Jesus' importance as Messiah–Son of Man lies not at all in what he did in the past, but entirely in what is expected of him for the future'); Hahn, *Titles* 161-62 ('the messianic status of Jesus was therefore not at first confessed in view of his resurrection and exaltation, but relatively to his authoritative action at the coming parousia'); similarly Fuller, *Foundations* 158-60. But see §21.3b above.

259. For the significance of *apokatastaseōs pantōn,* 'restoration of all things', see Fitzmyer, *Acts* 288-89; 'probably it refers generically to an awaited universal cosmic restoration, often mentioned vaguely in Jewish prophetic and apocalyptic writings'; he cites Mal. 3.24; Isa. 62.1-5; 65.17; 66.22; *1 En.* 45.4-5; 96.3; *4 Ezra* 7.75, 91-95; *T. Mos.* 10.10 (289).

260. 'As Weiser points out, it is not so much that repentance will hasten the parousia; it is necessary if the time of salvation is to come at all' (Barrett, *Acts* 203).

261. Cf. 2.17 (see above, §21 at n. 153).

262. See further below, §31.5, and on Paul's sense of eschatological apostleship (§29.3e).

the end-time Spirit had already been, or had begun to be, poured out (§22.3c); as with Jesus(?),[263] the consummation could not long be delayed. Also relevant is the likelihood that such anticipation provides a good explanation for what seems to be the equally short-term thinking behind the community of goods (§23.1c). And I refer to my earlier suggestion that one of the earliest interpretations likely to have been read and heard from the Jesus tradition was that the returning master/householder/bridegroom of the 'parables of crisis' was none other than Jesus himself (above at n. 118).[264]

Most striking are the indications from the Jesus tradition itself of how Jesus' self-referential 'son of man' became, in the process of tradition, Jesus 'the Son of Man'.[265] Since the title 'Son of Man' has left no trace in other earliest tradition, beyond Acts 7.56,[266] we have to deduce that the Jesus tradition usage did not spark off a Son of Man christology independent of the Jesus tradition,[267] and that this development within the Jesus tradition itself was very early. At this point the key feature is the further likelihood that the earliest performances of the Jesus tradition changed what I called the 'direction of travel';[268] that is, the likelihood that Jesus' expectation of a vindicatory coming *to* heaven was transformed into the Christian hope of his coming (again) *from* heaven; or, more fully, that Jesus' hope expressed in the language of Daniel's vision of the one like a son of man's coming to the 'Ancient of Days' in heaven (Dan. 7.13-14) was quickly reinterpreted, in the light of Jesus' vindication already secured, to become the Christian hope of Jesus as the Son of Man coming back from heaven.

If we ask why the expectation of Jesus' parousia from heaven emerged in the first place, the answer is not immediately clear. Other dead saints and heroes of the past were understood to have been exalted to heaven without the corollary being drawn that they would return from heaven.[269] Part of the answer may lie in

---

263. *Jesus Remembered* 479.

264. See again *Jesus Remembered* §12.4g and 754, 757-58, 761; see now also M. Casey, *The Solution to the 'Son of Man' Problem* (LNTS 343; London: Clark International, 2007) ch. 11.

265. *Jesus Remembered* 759-61; those who believe that Jesus thought of the coming Son of Man as someone other than himself would rather say that the post-Easter disciples took the step of identifying Jesus with the Son of Man (cf., e.g., Hahn, *Titles* 33-34; Schenke, *Urgemeinde* 127-29, 137).

266. The phrase 'son of man' in Heb. 2.6 (Ps. 8.4) and Rev. 1.13 and 14.14 (Dan. 7.13) is not titular but simply quotes or echoes the two scriptural passages where it appears.

267. See further my *Christology in the Making* 90-92.

268. *Jesus Remembered* 757-58.

269. Noteworthy is the fact that those who were expected to return from heaven — Elijah (Mal. 3.1-3; 4.5; Sir. 48.10-11; Mark 6.15 par.; 8.28 pars) and in some circles Enoch (*1 En.* 90.31; *Apoc. Elij.* 5.32; Rev. 11.3-4) — had not died and therefore could be 'held in reserve' (as it were) for further service on earth.

the natural desire (or fear) that a particularly significant figure on the stage of history will reappear on stage; we need instance only the Nero redivivus 'scare' which featured in the latter decades of the first century.[270] A more likely answer would be that the belief was received as a matter of revelation during the period of the resurrection appearances, although only the Fourth Gospel (John 21.22) and Luke's account of Jesus' ascension (Acts 1.11) refer to it, and only the latter as a point of instruction. Perhaps more significant is the fact that Paul refers his instruction regarding the manner of Jesus' parousia to a 'word of the Lord' (1 Thess. 4.15), that is, probably, a prophetic utterance given in a gathering concerned about the sort of problem posed by the unexpected death of Christians prior to the parousia which the Thessalonian believers put to Paul (4.13).[271]

My own guess is that Jesus was not initially remembered as speaking of his return, either during his mission or during his post-resurrection instructions. But on first reflection, following Jesus' departure, his 'parables of crisis' immediately invited the interpretation that Jesus had in fact spoken there, in veiled terms, of his own return; and so the parables came almost at once to be understood as expressing Jesus' own understanding and intention in the matter. Either simultaneously, or as a consequence, the reflection on Jesus as the Son of Man drew the inference that his expected 'coming on clouds' (Mark 13.26 pars.; 14.62 par.) should be understood as a coming (again) to earth. If there is anything in this, we should also note that the hope of parousia was not dependent on a Son of Man christology but quickly became affirmed of Jesus as Messiah (Acts 3.20), as God's Son (1 Thess. 1.10), and as Lord (1 Cor. 16.22).

A further factor might well be that in the early Christian search for Scriptures which shed light on their post-Easter situation, Mal. 3.1 came alive in a new way. For it predicted that 'the Lord whom you seek will suddenly come to his temple'. This passage soon became woven into the reflection on John the Baptist (Matt. 11.3, 10/Luke 7.19, 27; Mark 1.2),[272] so any attempt to make best sense of the relation of the Baptist to Jesus, and of Jesus' own final focus on the temple (Mark 11.17 pars.),[273] might well have lighted on Mal. 3.1. An important aspect of this hypothesis is that it would help explain why the Galilean disciples seem to have returned to Jerusalem (for Pentecost?), to have settled there and to have continued attending the Temple; indeed, no person of religious sentiment would settle in Jerusalem unless to be near the Temple.[274] The reasoning suggests itself,

---

270. See D. Aune, *Revelation* (WBC 52; Nashville: Nelson, 1997, 1998) 737-40.

271. See my *Theology of Paul* 303-304, where I note that the (prophetic) 'word of the Lord' might have been stimulated by the Jesus tradition preserved in Mark 13 — another example of how the Jesus tradition was reflected on and not simply passed on (see above, §21.5).

272. See *Jesus Remembered* 353, 370, 451.

273. *Jesus Remembered* 636-40, 650.

274. 'If Jerusalem with its Temple were not still a focus of the disciples' hope, it must be

then, that the first Christian hope was for Jesus to return to the Temple, or possibly to the nearby Mount of Olives (Zech. 14.4). Luke himself anticipated a longer period before the final events — the agenda of Acts 1.8 had to be carried out first.[275] But his use of the early material of 3.19-21 indicates that he did not wish to obliterate the earliest imminent expectation entirely, and Conzelmann's famous suggestion that for Luke the Spirit was the solution to the problem (delay) of the parousia, the 'substitute' *(Ersatz)* for the imminent parousia,[276] misses the mark insofar as it downplays overmuch the eschatological excitement which Luke shows Pentecost to have provoked — the outpouring of the Spirit as itself the mark of 'the last days' (2.17).[277]

Not least of importance is the fact that such an expectation would go a long way to explaining what appears in the initial phase of the new movement (Acts 1–5) to be a remarkable unreadiness to evangelize beyond the boundaries of Jerusalem.[278] Of course, the feature could be explained in terms of Luke's own phasing of the first-generation expansion of Christianity; he delays talk of expansion till the persecution following Stephen's martyrdom (8.1-4).[279] Even so, however, the exclusive focus on Jerusalem in chs. 1–7 and the portrayal of the initial expansion as a providential by-product of the persecution (8.4) do seem odd in the light of the programme laid out in 1.8. Was there, then, a lack of evangelistic impulse and outreach within the earliest Christian congregations in Jerusalem simply because the return of the Messiah was expected imminently? Perhaps the simplest way of reading the somewhat confusing data is that the hope for restoration of the kingdom to Israel (1.6) continued to be a dominant factor in the earliest Jerusalem community (the restoration would obviously be focused on Jerusalem), and 1.8 represents an awareness of the need for outreach which grew only slowly within the new sect and which became a contentious issue within it.

At all events, whatever the origins and content of the belief in Jesus' immi-

---

asked why they based themselves in this city, despite the danger to themselves' (Wedderburn, *History* 31).

275. Conzelmann, *Theology of Luke* 95-136; cf. Haenchen: '[Luke] has decisively renounced all expectation of an imminent end' (*Acts* 143).

276. Conzelmann, *Theology of Luke* 95, 135-36; similarly Haenchen, *Acts* 179.

277. Pesch, *Apg.* 1.70; and see above, §21.3a(3) and §22.3c; 'An eschatological-apocalyptic enthusiasm which as far as we know is unprecedented in Jewish history between the return from exile and the Talmudic period' (Hengel and Schwemer, *Paul* 28).

278. 'The mission to the heathen was not regarded as an obligation by the Jerusalem Church' (Bultmann, *Theology* 1.55). Even if Matt. 10.5-6 is dominical (*Jesus Remembered* 435, 511, 515, 537), it was presumably preserved (only in Matthew's circle) as expressing and justifying(?) a continuing conservative attitude towards Gentile mission.

279. In which case the promise 'to you who are far off' (2.39) could be predictive for Luke (like 1.8), though as an original formulation it may have had primarily the Jews of the diaspora in view (cf. 2.5; Joel 2.32), as in Isa. 57.19, which it also may echo.

nent parousia, it was clearly a major and prominent aspect of earliest Christian belief about Jesus,[280] though not the most important.[281] As such, it is a further important indicator of the enthusiastic and feverish mind-set and motivations of the first Christian community in Jerusalem.

g. Other Early Evaluations of Jesus

Of the other primitive titular references to Jesus retained in the early speeches of Acts, 'holy and just one' (3.14) and 'leader' (3.15, 31)[282] do not add much to our appreciation of earliest christology (§21.3b), though 'Saviour' (5.31) implies at least one who leads his people out of peril, like the saviours of old.[283] More interesting are the echoes of prophet christology: the quotations of Deut. 18.15-16 in Acts 3.22-23 and 7.37 and the description of Jesus as a Spirit-inspired prophet in 10.38 (similarly 2.22). As already noted (§21.3b[6]), 'prophet' was subsequently perceived to be a title inadequate to express Jesus' full status. So it probably did feature in earliest Christian attempts to understand Jesus,[284] presumably in continuity with Jesus' own remembered willingness to refer to his own mission in prophet terms.[285] However, it provides further evidence of the first community's casting around for appropriate categories and language to speak of Jesus.

Most interesting of all, however, is the designation of Jesus as God's *pais,* 'servant' (3.13, 26; 4.25, 27, 30). As already noted (§21.3b), the language is almost certainly drawn from the LXX of Isa. 52.13: 'my servant *(pais)* . . . will be glorified'. It is notable, however, that this allusion to the famous Servant song of

---

280. The larger point is not in dispute, although Hahn, *Titles,* and Fuller, *Foundations* ch. 6, over-schematize the development of thought, inferring that Jesus' exaltation did not become a fact of christological significance till the Hellenistic community, since the Palestinian community was focused on his parousia.

281. 'Without doubt the witness to Jesus' resurrection and not the announcement of the imminent parousia had been the focal point' (Goppelt, *Apostolic* 37).

282. More detail and bibliography are in Barrett, *Acts* 197-98, 290; Fitzmyer, *Acts* 286. When Jesus is called 'leader of life', that is, 'leader *to* life' (Barrett 198), the picture evoked is that of Heb. 2.10.

283. Judg. 3.9, 15; Neh. 9.27; the difference in the latter case is that God gave Israel saviours when they cried out to him, whereas Jesus saves by giving repentance as well as forgiveness of sins, as presumably was evident in the earliest community in the numbers who repented (2.38-41; 3.19–4.4). The breadth of usage of the epithet, also of deserving persons (BDAG 985), makes it unlikely that it was first used of Jesus in deliberate challenge to the imperial cult (early discussion in Cadbury, *Beginnings* 5.371 and n. 2).

284. Hahn, *Titles* 372-88: 'The conception of Jesus as the eschatological Moses played an important role in Palestinian tradition' (383); similarly Fuller, *Foundations* 169.

285. See *Jesus Remembered* §15.6 (660-66).

Isa. 52.13–53.12 expresses only a theology of suffering and vindication (3.13-15), whereas other allusions to it in connection with Jesus' suffering, while still early, use it to express a theology of atonement.[286] Similarly the references to Jesus being hung on a tree (5.30; 10.39; cf. 13.29), with their allusion to Deut. 21.22-23,[287] presumably have in mind the shame to which the criminal's corpse was subjected, although Luke certainly makes no effort to match the theological implications which Paul draws from the Deuteronomy passage in Gal. 3.13.[288] The consistent and persistent theme of the early chapters of Acts is summed up in the repeated charge: 'You had Jesus executed, but God raised him from the dead'.[289]

h. Christ Devotion

Larry Hurtado has maintained that what he calls 'Christ devotion' can be dated back to the earliest days of Christianity.[290] And that there was 'devotion' to the exalted Jesus from the first can hardly be doubted. Jesus had been exalted to God's right hand, and in accordance with Ps. 110.1, his enemies would soon be forced to submit to him. He had been vindicated as Israel's Messiah and installed as God's Son in power. He was and had become their Lord. The outpouring of *God's* Spirit was attributed to his agency. He was coming soon to manifest his heavenly authority. His disciples identified themselves by acting on the authority of his name.[291] So wholly understandably, they called upon him as their Lord

286. Cf. Mark 10.45; Rom. 4.24-25; 1 Pet. 2.22-25; on 1 Cor. 15.3b see §23.5a below.

287. See particularly Fitzmyer, *Acts* 337.

288. But see D. P. Moessner, 'The "Script" of the Scriptures in Acts: Suffering as God's "Plan" *(boulē)* for the World for the "Release of Sins"', in Witherington, ed., *History* 218-50.

289. Acts 2.23-24; 3.14-15; 5.30-31; 13.28-30. 'Allusions to Isaiah seem more likely to have provided Jesus' followers with a way of speaking of Jesus' death and vindication. . . . Perhaps, therefore, we should speak not of the Suffering Servant but of the "rejected and vindicated servant", acknowledging that Isaiah 52–53 was important primarily as a way of speaking about Jesus' humiliation and exaltation' (Juel, *Messianic Exegesis* 132-33). 'It is God's act of vindication after suffering that gives significance to the Servant' (Barrett, *Acts* 194).

290. Hurtado, *Lord Jesus Christ,* particularly ch. 3; see also his *How on Earth Did Jesus Become a God? Historical Questions about Earliest Devotion to Jesus* (Grand Rapids: Eerdmans, 2005). Weiss was also convinced that the earliest disciples 'already . . . ventured to pray to [their exalted Lord]. This is the most significant step of all in the history of the origins of Christianity, the advance to the "Jesus-religion"' (*Earliest Christianity* 37); he traced it back to 'the continuing influence of the personality of Jesus' (39).

291. Hurtado presses his case strongly here: 'I propose that the early Christian use of Jesus' name represents a novel adaptation of this Jewish "monotheistic" concern and religious practice. Early Christians saw Jesus as the *uniquely* significant agent of the one God, and in their piety they extended the exclusivity of the one God to take in God's uniquely important representative' (*Lord Jesus Christ* 204).

(1 Cor. 1.2) and pleaded with him as their Lord to return soon (1 Cor. 16.22). On almost any definition, this all qualifies as 'Christ devotion'.

Whether the reverence thereby clearly indicated should be further described as 'worship' is probably another question. If 'worship' is defined as that which can appropriately be offered only to (a) god, then it is not clear that worship was offered to Jesus in the earliest phase of the Christian movement.[292] The crucial role of Ps. 110.1 in the earliest christological development allowed full recognition of the exalted Jesus as God's 'right-hand man', his 'viceroy' or 'grand vizier', and as such worthy of all reverence, honour and obedience. But it also implied God's lordship as something distinct and still more ineffable. Luke reflects something of this when he preserves the early formulation of Acts 3.20 speaking of 'the Lord' (= God) sending the Messiah, that is, Jesus, just as does Paul in his repeated talk of 'the *God* and Father of our *Lord* Jesus Christ'.[293] Indeed, on the only occasion that Paul makes any attempt to spell out the relation between the two Lords implied by Ps. 110.1 (1 Cor. 15.24-28), he makes clear the transcendent finality of God's godness (15.28). It must be subject to the severest doubt that anything like such serious thought had been given to the subject before Paul, himself the first great Christian theologian.[294]

We should probably recognize, then, the unreflective nature of the earliest christology. Some of the amazing statements made about Jesus and scriptural passages applied to him are probably best seen as expressions of exultant enthusiasm and deep reverence before the one who had so recently walked the hills and lakeside of Galilee. And their instinctive response launched the Christian estimate of Jesus' significance at once onto a high and rising trajectory. But the evidence should make us hesitate to say more.

292. J. L. North, 'Jesus and Worship, God and Sacrifice', in Stuckenbruck and North, eds., *Early Jewish and Christian Monotheism* 186-202, points out that 'worship *(proskynēsis)*' is too imprecise to point necessarily to the conclusion that Jesus is divine and argues that it was *sacrifice to* rather than *proskynēsis* of the deity that was the differentia of divinity. In the same volume, L. T. Stuckenbruck, '"Angels" and "God": Exploring the Limits of Early Jewish Monotheism' 45-70, observes that some Jewish sources could tolerate venerative language directed to angelic beings, while retaining a wholly monotheistic focus. And W. Horbury, 'Jewish and Christian Monotheism in the Herodian Age' 16-44, concludes that 'the conditions of the Herodian age . . . were suited to interpretation of Jewish monotheism in ways that rigorous monotheists might have avoided, and did later seek to avoid' (44).

293. See further my *Theology of Paul* 244-60; and below, §29.7d.

294. Hurtado does not reflect sufficiently on how the relationship of the two Lords of Ps. 110.1 to each other would have been perceived (*Lord Jesus Christ* 179-85), and greater clarification of the relation of 'cultic devotion' (his key term) and 'worship' is necessary; see further my review in *ExpT* 116 (2004-5) 193-96 and below, §29.7d. Jossa is even more unrestrained in his assertion that the earliest Palestinian community already 'worshipped' Jesus as Lord (*Jews or Christians?* 71-74).

23.5. The Significance of Jesus' Death

An important issue remains. How did the first Christians regard Jesus' death? In particular, how soon did they attribute a saving significance to Jesus' death? Or, to be more precise, how soon did they regard Jesus' death as a (or the) sacrifice in effective atonement for (their) sins? I have already shown how difficult it is to draw the conclusion from our available texts that Jesus himself foresaw his death in those terms, despite the strong advocacy of some that Isaiah 53 can be shown or inferred to have influenced his thinking on the subject.[295] But in 1 Cor. 15.3b Paul recalls that the message which he received at the time of or soon after his conversion[296] contained as its first article 'that Christ died for our sins in accordance with the Scriptures'. The fuller formula is well structured and evidently the product of some careful, agreed and mature consensus,[297] and takes us back to within a year or two of Christianity's own emergence.

a. 1 Cor. 15.3

In a religious tradition for which it was axiomatic that sins required atonement by sacrifice, a formulation like this can only mean that Jesus' death was already being understood in sacrificial terms. The same implication can be drawn from the final phrase, 'in accordance with the Scriptures'. It is true that the Scriptures provided various precedents or models on which an understanding of Jesus' death as having a positive outcome could be based — covenant sacrifice or Passover sacrifice (neither properly described as 'for sins'), righteous sufferer or martyr.[298] But the 'for our sins' pushes the allusion firmly towards the scriptural regulations for sin offering and Day of Atonement, or to other models insofar as they absorbed or merged with sacrificial imagery.[299] An allusion specifically to Isaiah 53 is not necessary for the sacrificial allusion to be loud and clear.[300]

---

295. *Jesus Remembered* §17.5d; the volume edited by Janowski and Stuhlmacher referred to there (811 n. 221) is now available in English translation (see above, n. 94).

296. Presumably Damascus or Antioch (Gal. 1.17; Acts 11.25-26).

297. See above, §21.4e n. 212.

298. These, I suggested, were categories which can be shown with greater clarity or probability to have shaped Jesus' own references to his impending death; see again *Jesus Remembered* §17.5.

299. Most strikingly 4 Macc. 17.22. Contrast Hahn, *Theologie* 1.152-53 (the thought was of a 'non-cultic atonement').

300. The case for seeing an intended echo of Isa. 53.4-6, 8, 11-12 (particularly 53.5) behind 1 Cor. 15.3b ('Christ died for our sins in accordance with the scriptures') has been strongly pressed in recent years; see Hofius, 'The Fourth Servant Song' 177-80; W. R. Farmer,

The understanding of Jesus' death as atoning sacrifice was evidently an article of faith which Paul took over wholeheartedly.[301] It is obvious from the way he refers to the theme that the understanding was widely shared and not disputed in early Christian circles.[302] For one thing he frequently draws on other earlier formulae, whose wide acceptance and resonance he could take for granted.[303] And for another, Paul never found it necessary to expound in any detail his own belief in Jesus' death as atoning sacrifice.[304] Paul, it would appear then, did not regard the teaching on Jesus' death 'for our sins' as distinctively his own, nor did he see any need much to elaborate it. In short, more than in any other matter of earliest Christian doctrine, we can read a consensus of early Christian theology on Jesus' death from Paul's writings.

There has been a long-running debate regarding the 1 Cor. 15.3b formula on whether an Aramaic version can be discerned under the Greek formulation — the key issues being the lack of a Semitic equivalent to 'according to the Scriptures', and whether anarthrous *Christos* could be a translation from Aramaic.[305] Although we should not forget that an Aramaic form could be rendered faithfully in Greek without being a *literal* translation of the Aramaic, we might expect a creedal formula to be more rigid. Even so, Acts attests the presence of Hellenist converts in Jerusalem from very early days (Acts 6.1), that is, presumably, diaspora Jews who had settled in Jerusalem but who spoke only Greek — hence 'Hellenists' = Greek-speakers.[306] In other words, it is entirely plausible to envis-

---

'Reflections on Isaiah 53 and Christian Origins', in W. H. Bellinger and W. R. Farmer, eds., *Jesus and the Suffering Servant: Isaiah 53 and Christian Origins* (Harrisburg: Trinity Press International, 1998) 260-80 (here 263). Hengel is equally convinced that 'Isa. 53 had an influence on the origin and shaping of the earliest kerygma' (*Atonement* 59-60, also 36-39). Others are less convinced that a specific allusion need be inferred; see the discussion with bibliography in Thiselton, *1 Corinthians* 1190-92; and Schrage, *1 Korinther* 4.32-34. S. G. F. Brandon, *The Fall of Jerusalem and the Christian Church* (London: SPCK, 1951), thought that 'soteriological possibilities of the Suffering Servant concept were not developed by Jewish Christians, since emphasis on the Crucifixion was calculated to constitute an obstacle to Pharisaic sympathy and support' (xiv, 77).

301. See my *Theology of Paul the Apostle* 207-23.

302. Hengel, *Atonement* 53-54.

303. Rom. 4.25; 5.6, 8; 8.32; 14.15; 1 Cor. 8.11; 11.24; 2 Cor. 5.14-15; Gal. 1.4; 2.20; 1 Thess. 5.10. See further above, §21.4e. Rom. 4.25 might be enough to tip the conclusion in favour of a conscious allusion in 1 Cor. 15.3 to Isaiah 53 (Hengel, *Atonement* 35-38). M. D. Hooker, 'Did the Use of Isaiah 53 to Interpret His Mission Begin with Jesus?', in Bellinger and Farmer, eds., *Jesus and the Suffering Servant* 88-103, now accepts that Rom. 4.25 contains a clear echo of Isaiah 53 (101-103), an echo she had not recognized in her *Jesus and the Servant* (London: SPCK, 1959).

304. Contrast Hebrews, particularly 9.1–10.18.

305. See Pokorny, *Genesis* 64 n. 4; and Schrage's brief review (*1 Korinther* 4.23-24).

306. See further below, §24.2.

age the confessional formula being composed by and for the Greek-speaking converts, but already in Jerusalem and still very early.

In sum, then, the answer provided to our question by an initial probe into the pre-Pauline formula enables us to trace belief in Jesus' death as atoning sacrifice to the earliest days of the Jerusalem church, though the earliest traceable formula suggests that the formula may have been coined by Greek-speaking believers. Should we therefore deduce as a further corollary that the belief itself was first formulated by the Christian Hellenists?

b. The Testimony of Acts

There is something of a puzzle here. It is clear enough that Jesus was understood to have died 'for our sins' from very early on. Yet, at the same time, there is an awkward gap between the events surrounding Jesus' death and the earliest formulae evidenced in the Pauline letters, a gap which such evidence as we have in the Acts of the earliest Jerusalem church seems to leave empty. The gap seems to mark a discontinuity in the evidence and poses the question 'When?' more sharply.

The sharpness of the issue is inescapable. For if the first Christians believed Jesus' death to be an atoning sacrifice and remembered Jesus as instructing them so to believe, then that must have deeply affected their attitude to the practice of sin offerings and annual Day of Atonement rituals of the Jerusalem temple. If Jesus' death was an effective sin offering, indeed *the* effective sin offering, then the unavoidable conclusion was that the Temple atonement ritual had thereby been rendered unnecessary and passé, that Jesus' death had wholly replaced the Temple cult as a way of dealing with sin. The conclusions to be drawn by Hebrews in due course (Heb. 10.1-10) would already have been drawn at the very dawn of the Christian movement. In which case, to continue to attend the Temple and to depend on its ritual would have been to deny the validity of the gospel and the effectiveness of Jesus' death 'for sins'; it would have been tantamount to apostasy, as again Hebrews was soon to point out (6.4-8; 10.26-31).

But it is precisely this conclusion which, according to Acts, the first Christians did *not* draw. According to Luke, the first Jerusalem Christians *did* continue to attend the Temple. Peter and John were going[307] to the temple 'at the hour of prayer, the ninth hour' (Acts 3.1), that is, the hour at which the afternoon Tamid sacrifice was offered.[308] This sacrifice of a male lamb, twice a day, was probably

---

307. Acts 3.1 could be translated 'Peter and John used to go into the Temple at the hour of prayer, the ninth hour' (cf. 2.46).

308. Josephus, *Ant.* 14.65; Dan. 9.21. Prayer at the time of sacrifice was the common practice (Falk, 'Jewish Prayer Literature' 296-97).

not thought of as atoning.[309] But it was evidently regarded as essential for the continuing welfare of Israel, including the diaspora.[310] The first Christians' continued association with this integral part of the Temple cult cannot but raise the question whether the understanding of Jesus' death as the final sacrifice had yet taken hold in the thought and consequent practice of his first followers. Moreover, we surely have to infer that the first believers in Messiah Jesus continued to pay the Temple tax, as they remembered Jesus doing (Matt. 17.24-27), and that tax paid for the Temple sacrifices, including the sin offerings (Neh. 10.32-33). Some argue that for Luke the Temple was a place of preaching and prayer only, no longer a place of sacrifice.[311] But there is no hint of a concern to preach in 2.46; and to preach in effect against the cult at the time of the evening sacrifice would assuredly have aroused greater hostility (and differently directed) than is envisaged in chs. 3–4. And if the purpose was to pray privately, the ninth hour was precisely the time that anyone going to the Temple for that purpose would avoid; 'the hour of prayer' was the time for public prayer, and anyone going to the Temple at that time was thereby publicly associating himself with that prayer.[312] Anyone who still prized the Temple as 'the house of God' but who thought of its sacrificial ritual as obsolete would have gone to the Temple at any other time to preach or for his devotions, *not* at the ninth hour.[313] This line of reflection tells decisively against the possibility that Jesus intended to establish a new cult in place of the Temple. For in that case his closest disciples, as represented here by Peter and John, must have wholly misunderstood his intention in the matter.[314]

---

309. Sanders, *Judaism* 104-105.

310. It was paid for by the Temple tax, which flowed in from all male Jews, including those living in the diaspora. These twice-daily sacrifices were or included offerings on behalf of the nation and of Caesar; the decision to abandon 'the customary offering for their rulers' laid the foundation for the first Jewish revolt (Josephus, *War* 2.197, 409-10).

311. Hengel, *Atonement* 57; G. Schneider, *Die Apostelgeschichte* (HTKNT, 2 vols.; Freiburg: Herder, 1980, 1982) 1.288-89, 299; cited approvingly by Pesch, *Apg.* 1.37.

312. Barrett, *Acts* 1.178; Fitzmyer makes the obvious deduction from 2.46 that they frequented the Temple together and shared in its prayers, sacrifices and services; 'even though they had been baptized as followers of the risen Christ, they continued to be exemplary Jews, seeing no contradiction in this' (*Acts* 272).

313. It may be argued that much of the sacrificial cult was not concerned with atonement, so that an atoning significance could have been attributed to Jesus' death without affecting participation in the rest of the cult (cf. R. Bauckham, 'The Parting of the Ways: What Happened and Why', *ST* 47 [1993] 135-51 [here 150-51 n. 37]; Wedderburn, *History* 206 n. 54). But would such a sharp disjunction within the sacrificial cult have occurred to Jesus' followers? Not according to Luke (see on 21.23-24, 26 below).

314. M. Bockmuehl, *This Jesus: Martyr, Lord, Messiah* (Edinburgh: Clark, 1994) 75 and 201-202 n. 50; J. Klawans, 'Interpreting the Last Supper: Sacrifice, Spiritualization and Anti-

That the implications of Acts 3.1 are not at odds with Luke's own understanding of the situation in Jerusalem is confirmed by his later account of the Jerusalem church. For he records Paul himself as affirming that he prayed in the Jerusalem Temple after his conversion (22.17). And according to Luke's account, James subsequently, when he had long been established as undisputed leader of the Jerusalem church, affirmed to Paul that myriads of Jews had come to faith, 'and all are zealots for the law' (21.20). No one living in Jerusalem could be so described who did not avail himself of the Temple cult. It is impossible that there were 'zealots for the law' in Jerusalem who did not observe the rituals of atonement, and almost as impossible that they could have tolerated any fellow believing Jews who discounted or dismissed the Temple cult so central to the law.

This is also the implication of the sequel in which Paul himself participated in the Temple rituals (21.23-24, 26). According to Luke, at James's suggestion Paul joined with four men who were under a vow; he purified himself with them and paid their expenses, in order that they might shave their heads. The circumstances envisaged are presumably those covered by the legislation in Num. 6.9-12, where a Nazirite's 'separation' has been defiled by contact with a corpse; the defilement required a seven-day purification and the shaving of the previously uncut hair; and on the eighth day the offering of two turtledoves or young pigeons, the one as a sin offering, the other as a burnt offering in atonement for his sin.[315] It is unclear whether Paul counted himself as similarly 'under a vow' (cf. Acts 18.18) or as unclean and required to offer sacrifice for himself. Some sort of compromise was evidently involved — but to what extent would it have constituted a departure from what he himself believed (cf. 1 Cor. 9.20-21)?[316] In any case, Paul 'went along with' those who observed the cult, including the offering of sacrifice for sin.[317] And even if Paul had herein acted out of character, the action is portrayed as very much in character with the faith and practice of the Jerusalem community itself. Is it possible that a community which so acted also be-

---

Sacrifice', *NTS* 48 (2002) 1-12 (here 9-10). Contrast Hengel, who thinks it 'probable that from the beginning the Jewish Christians adopted a fundamentally detached attitude to the cult' (*Atonement* 56), but who ignores the evidence of 2.46 and 3.1 completely at this point. S. McKnight, *Jesus and His Death: Historiography, the Historical Jesus, and Atonement Theory* (Waco: Baylor University, 2005), reviews the development of atonement theology after Jesus (339-74), without grappling with the particular issue posed here.

315. The Nazirite vow apparently became a very popular way to express thanksgiving for divine favours in the latter years of the Second Temple; tradition records Bernice, the sister of Herod Agrippa II, and Helena, the queen of Adiabene, a proselyte, as making the vow (see further G. Mayer, *nzr, TDOT* 9.309-10).

316. See the discussion in Barrett, *Acts* 1011-13; Fitzmyer, *Acts* 694; Porter, *The Paul of Acts* 180-82; and further below, §34.1a.

317. Wilckens ignores this detail (*Theologie* 1/2.189 n. 59).

lieved that Jesus' death was an atoning sacrifice which ended all such sacrifices? Do we have to envisage that the bulk of the Jerusalem believers had already relapsed into traditional Judaism? Or is it simpler to deduce that the understanding of Jesus' death as an atoning sacrifice had never been clearly expounded in the church of Jerusalem?[318]

c. Lukan Theology or Reflection of Early Emphases?

The deductions just outlined could be countered by detecting in all this a feature of Luke's own theology rather than a historical account. For one thing, Luke seems to avoid or to play down any idea of Jesus' death as an atonement for sins in his account of the earliest preaching.[319] And since Baur, a recurring claim is that Luke attempted to reconcile diverging strands of Christianity by, *inter alia,* re-judaizing Paul.[320] In such a case, Luke's account of the earliest period of Christianity cannot be expected to provide any historical data that would bridge the gap between Jesus' death and the early confessions of Jesus' death as 'for our sins'.

On the other hand, there are indications elsewhere that Luke's account of the Jerusalem community's continued participation in the Temple cult is indeed firmly rooted in historical memory.

(1) The very fact that Jerusalem was and remained the mother church of Christianity from the first is significant. As already noted, since Jerusalem itself existed primarily for the Temple and to service the Temple cult, the only reason why Galileans would relocate themselves in Jerusalem would be the desirability of close proximity to the Temple.[321] And even if that was only because they expected the climactic events of the age to take place there, Temple and Zion were inextricable concepts in such expectation.

---

318. 'It is reasonable to suppose that the particular *emphasis* upon Jesus' death as atoning for sins that we find developed in Paul may not have been made in the early Jewish Christian setting' (Hurtado, *Lord Jesus Christ* 186).

319. See Acts 2.23-24; 3.14-15; 4.10; 5.30; 8.32-33; 10.39-40; 13.28-30; on Luke 22.27 see *Jesus Remembered* 812-14. See further H. J. Sellner, *Das Heil Gottes. Studien zur Soteriologie des lukanischen Doppelwerks* (BZNW 152; Berlin: de Gruyter, 2007) ch. 10, which discusses the significance of Jesus' death for salvation, though not in terms of atonement.

320. See, e.g., Gasque, *History of Criticism of Acts* chs. 4-5, who quotes Jülicher's neat refinement of the theme: 'Paul was not Judaized, nor Peter Paulinized, rather Paul and Peter were Lucanized, i.e. Catholicized' (101).

321. See above, §22.3c. 'For the Jerusalem believers, the temple was thoroughly a component-feature of their faith and piety *as followers of Jesus*' (Hurtado, *Lord Jesus Christ* 197).

(2) If the designation of James, Peter and John as 'pillar' apostles in Gal. 2.9 does indeed imply that they were regarded as 'pillars in the [eschatological] temple',[322] the implication presumably was of a community in continuity with the Jerusalem Temple.[323] Jesus' symbolic purification of the Temple is remembered as pointing in the same direction — for it to serve as 'a house of prayer for all nations' (Mark 11.15-17 pars.).[324]

(3) Those who opposed Paul's Gentile mission so vigorously on behalf of the law[325] were unlikely to abstract the Temple cult so central to the Torah from their zeal for the law. On the other hand, the fact that the Temple cult does not feature in the disputes of Paul tells against such a hypothesis, though since the disputes took place in the diaspora, loyalty to the Temple cult may not have been a practical issue anyway.

(4) Hebrews does however attest that the tangibility of the Temple cult must have proved a strong attraction to many Gentile Christians.[326] If *all* Christians had renounced the Temple cult, including those living in Jerusalem and Judea, then it is hardly likely that Gentile believers (if it is such who are addressed in Hebrews) would have been so attracted to it as part of their faith in Christ. Such Gentiles would surely have bypassed the Christian sect entirely and embraced Judaism itself.

(5) It is important here to recall that the Jesus tradition contains a saying which envisages continued recourse to the provisions of the Temple cult: 'If you are offering your gift at the altar, and there remember that your brother has something against you, leave your gift there before the altar and go; first be reconciled to your brother, and then come and offer your gift' (Matt. 5.23-24). The term 'gift' *(dōron)*, of course, need not signify a sacrifice as such, but the phrase used here, 'bring an offering, offer a gift', is more or less a technical term for participation in the Temple sacrificial cult, as its regular use in Leviticus makes clear.[327] The point is that this instruction was remembered as part of Jesus' teaching. Had Jesus turned his face against the Temple sacrificial system, it is hardly likely that such a saying would have been preserved. Those who took it seriously as practical advice for their daily living presumably continued to observe the cult to which it referred. Were they then misguided? Had they relapsed into traditional Jewish observance despite Jesus' teaching, or despite a deduction drawn from the

---

322. See above, §23.3d, and further below, §36.1.

323. Qumran's thought of itself as functioning in lieu of the corrupt Temple did not mean that the Temple played no further part in their expectations — as 11QTemple attests.

324. *Jesus Remembered* 636-40, 650.

325. Particularly in Galatia and Philippi (§§31.7 and 34.4 below).

326. See vol. 3.

327. BDAG 267; W. D. Davies and D. C. Allison, *Matthew* (ICC, 3 vols.; Edinburgh: Clark, 1988, 1991, 1997) 1.516-17.

death of Jesus from earliest days? Or is Matt. 5.23-24 simply further attestation to the fact that the understanding of Jesus' death as atoning sacrifice had not yet emerged among those who treasured the saying?

(6) In addition it should be noted that Luke was hardly antagonistic to the thought of Jesus' death as necessary for salvation, as the admittedly confusing reference in Acts 20.28 ('the church of God which he obtained [*periepoiēsato*] through the blood of his own') indicates.[328] So Luke's failure to reproduce 1 Cor. 15.3b in any of the evangelistic preaching he records probably owes more to the tradition which he received than to his own predilections.

(7) Finally, it should be recalled that Luke's allusions to the Servant of Isaiah seem all to be in service of its predominant suffering-vindication theme (§23.4g), as even more clearly the only explicit quotation of Isa. 53.7 in Acts 8.32;[329] the thought of Jesus' death as atoning for sin is not yet clearly present.[330]

The most obvious conclusion to draw from all this is that the theme of Jesus' vindication and exaltation dominated the earliest horizons of the first Christian reflection on what had happened to Jesus. He had suffered the most barbaric and humiliating of deaths.[331] But God had raised him from the dead. By raising him from the dead, God had shown Jesus to have suffered unjustly, like the Servant of Isaiah, and had vindicated him, as Isaiah 53 had foretold. It would appear, then, that the understanding of Jesus' death as sacrifice for sins may have emerged initially not with the first Aramaic-speaking disciples but more likely with the Greek-speaking Hellenists, from whom Paul learned his 1 Corinthians 15 catechism and to whom §24 will be devoted.

---

328. 'V. 28 shows that he [Luke] presupposes the conception of [Jesus'] vicarious death as more or less self-evident, even if it does not play a central role in his own theological thought' (Pesch, *Apg.* 1.204-205, citing J. Roloff); 'the mention of "blood" must refer to the vicarious shedding of the blood of Jesus' (Fitzmyer, *Acts* 680); further discussion in Barrett, *Acts* 976-77; see further below, §33 n. 397.

329. J. B. Green, *The Death of Jesus* (WUNT 2.33; Tübingen: Mohr Siebeck, 1988): 'Apparently, for earliest Christianity, the highest priority was on proving that Jesus' death was no surprise to God and constituted no contradiction of the christological claims that had been and were being advanced. The idea that Jesus died "for us" evidently constituted one very early and important means of making this point clear' (320-23).

330. See above, §23.4g. Cf. Hahn, *Theologie* 1.152-53, 158, 169-70. P. Stuhlmacher, 'Isaiah 53 in the Gospels and Acts', in Janowski and Stuhlmacher, *The Suffering Servant* 147-62, argues that without the larger concept of Jesus as God's Servant, 'it would be impossible to understand the language of the forgiveness of sins that came through Jesus' mission as the *pais Theou*', referring to Acts 3.13, 19, with 2.38; 5.31; 10.43; etc. (156). But the point is not so clear, since 2.38 seems to pick up from the language of the Baptist (see above, §23.2a), who seems to have promised forgiveness independently of sin offering or other atoning ritual (*Jesus Remembered* 358-60).

331. M. Hengel, *Crucifixion* (London: SCM, 1977).

23.6. In Sum — a Messianic Sect

Most studies of Christianity's beginnings give only a few pages to the earliest Jerusalem community.[332] There is so little material available, and Luke's account in Acts 1–5 can so easily be discounted as an idealization. In some contrast, however, it is my belief that a fairly substantial outline can be extracted and constructed, not only (1) by setting the scene within the larger history of the period, but also (2) by drawing on the information, including the many inferences and allusions, provided by our earliest Christian witness, Paul; (3) by fairly obvious deductions about the way the Jesus tradition must have been used from earliest days; and (4) by taking seriously the impression given by Acts 1–5 either as reflective of the information Luke had gleaned about the period or as his own well-informed attempt at verisimilitude in the sketch he provided.

Of course, much of the data are uncontrollable so far as any accuracy or precision of dating is concerned. But in some cases we have been able to highlight elements which were clearly established more or less from the beginning (Jesus as raised from the dead and taken up to heaven, Jesus as Messiah, baptism in his name, Jesus' parousia), or which do not seem to have been taken up subsequently (Son of Man christology, prophet christology), or which were developed in different ways in subsequent years (attitude to the Temple, the significance of Jesus' death). And in others it is an obvious deduction that patterns and trends must have become established more or less from the beginning (interpretation of Scripture in the light of what had happened, formation and use of the Jesus tradition, patterns of worship and witness), even if we cannot be sure what particular elements were present from the beginning. The resulting picture is not insubstantial.

To sum up, we could ask what is the most appropriate shorthand description of the new movement generated by Jesus' mission, death and resurrection? A 'messianic sect' is the most obvious candidate.

It was a *'sect'* in the sense used by Luke and Josephus *(hairesis)*.[333] Like Pharisees and Sadducees it functioned within the parent body of Second Temple Judaism, within which Jesus had also functioned. It was a 'sect' in the sense that it began as a faction within first-century Judaism, in disagreement with other factions, but not in denial of their status as also part of Judaism — rather as opposing political parties in Britain today recognize other parties as legitimate, but as

332. 'The history of the primitive church remains almost wholly unknown' (Conzelmann, *History* 33).

333. See above, §20.1(15). J. H. Elliott, 'The Jewish Messianic Movement', in Esler, ed., *Modelling Early Christianity* 75-95, traces 'the shift from faction to sect' (79-84). White provides a helpful discussion of the distinction between 'sect' and 'cult' (*From Jesus to Christianity* 129-31).

variant expressions of commitment to the same democratic ideal of British society. Unlike Qumran it did not deny opponents any status as part of the Israel of God; it was not a 'sect' in that sense, a subdivision of the 'church' of Judaism which disowned the parent body. It occasions no historical strain when Luke depicts the charge against Peter and John in terms of disagreement regarding the resurrection (4.2), as later when Luke has Paul calling upon the support of his erstwhile Pharisaic colleagues on the same dispute (23.6-9). It was not the existence of the new movement which was initially questioned by the Temple authorities, but their beliefs.

It was a *messianic* sect in that their most distinguishing feature was their beliefs regarding Jesus — that as Messiah, God had raised him from the dead, and that they identified themselves by his name, by calling upon his name and acting in the authority of his name. Here again the issue was not the existence of the new movement, nor even their affiliation to this Jesus, but their freedom and boldness to proclaim him as risen from the dead and as calling others to submit to his lordship.

Other terms are almost as equally appropriate — particularly 'eschatological', 'enthusiastic' and/or 'spiritual'. We simply will fail to appreciate the character of earliest Christianity if we do not give real content to the term 'eschatological' (or an alternative, should one prove more suitable).[334] The continuing emphasis on the kingdom of God and its restoration, the continuing significance of 'the twelve', the convictions that with Jesus God's Messiah had already come and that in what had happened to Jesus 'the resurrection of the dead' had begun, the sense of the Spirit outpoured on them as the fulfilment of promises for 'the last days', the hope of Jesus' parousia — all of them integral to the self-understanding of infant Christianity, and all expressing and evoking an attitude of excited realization and expectation.[335] That overwhelming intuition of a new age having dawned, of God's final purposes for his people and his creation in process of being fulfilled, is difficult for us two thousand years later to comprehend, but without some empathetic apprehension of it we will not begin to understand the beliefs and motivations of the first Christian communities.

Similarly the 'enthusiasm'. Here too we have to recognize that characteristic of the earliest Christian community/ies was the experience (or conceptualized experience) of being empowered 'from on high', of inspiration giving words to say, of enabling to work extraordinary deeds. However inadequately, the term

---

334. White, e.g., prefers 'an apocalyptic Jewish sect' (*From Jesus to Christianity* 128).

335. 'When regarded from the history-of-religions point of view, the earliest Church presents itself as an eschatological sect within Judaism, distinguished from other sects and trends . . . especially by the fact that it is conscious of being already the called and chosen Congregation of the end of days' (Bultmann, *Theology* 1.42).

'enthusiasm' does encapsulate the fervency of the first disciples and the excitement they seem to have engendered from the first. The modern rationalist who discounts or dismisses all such claims as *Schwärmerei* will naturally attribute these phenomena to untraceable socio-psychological factors as sufficient explanation. But the reality of the experiences as conceptualized should not be denied, and their significance for our understanding of Christianity's beginnings should not be understated. The impact and expansion of twentieth-century Pentecostalism (in various forms) in Latin America, Africa and Southeast Asia has made heirs of older Christian theological traditions realize that there are aspects and dimensions of pneumatology which need to be reassessed. The equivalent impact and expansion in the first century is what is in view here, and it too calls for the same sort of reassessment of the traditional understandings of Christianity's beginnings.

One other way of describing these beginnings should not be neglected — a renewal or revivalist movement within late Second Temple Judaism. These events and beliefs in themselves did not mark any kind of rupture within the diverse fabric of Second Temple Judaism. Most of the features, indeed, can be paralleled with the Qumran sect: the 'Teacher of Righteousness' as having a quasi-messianic status; the eschatology, with its claim that old prophecies had the sect's future firmly in view; even the enthusiasm as expressed in their belief that they were experiencing the promised end-time Spirit[336] and in the Songs of the Sabbath Sacrifice. The difference was not so much that Qumran was more focused on the law, for we have seen that, so far as we can tell, the earliest community seem to have remained equally focused, in their own terms ('zealots for the law', Acts 21.20). Rather that Qumran was more sectarian, more exclusive, more dismissive of all other Jews.[337] This is also to say that the embryonic Christian movement had the greater potential to bring renewal to the rest of Second Temple Judaism. How long that potential remained alive and relevant is another story.

336. 1QS 4.20-23; 1QH 15[=7].6-7; 17[=9].32; 20[=12].12; CD 5.11; 7.3-4.
337. Goppelt observes that 'Jesus' disciples did not consider themselves, as did the Essenes and Pharisees, to be the *True* Israel. . . . Rather they considered themselves to be the *New* Israel upon whom God's salvation had already dawned' (*Apostolic* 28).

CHAPTER 24

The Hellenists and the First Outreach

As we begin to move beyond the earliest beginnings of Christianity, we are confronted with an interesting feature. Luke, in planning this next phase of Acts, seems to have been able to draw on three sets of traditions: (1) traditions regarding the 'Hellenists' and the spread of the new movement beyond Jerusalem; (2) traditions surrounding the emergence of Paul on the scene; and (3) traditions about Peter and his missionary work. The slightly odd thing is the degree of independence between them: we do not know how to relate them chronologically — which came first? Luke does provide some links — particularly through Peter and Barnabas — though, as we shall see, these are among the more problematic passages for the historian of earliest Christianity. But their relative independence is largely unaffected, which is probably a testimony to Luke's concern to let his sources speak for themselves as much as possible within his overall scheme.

More to the point here, Luke evidently endeavoured to maintain a strong measure of chronological progression by turning from one sequence of traditions to another, intercalating, rather than interweaving. He inserts the accounts of Paul's conversion and of Peter's mission into the narrative of the Hellenists; the account of the breakthrough in Antioch has to be told before the stories of Paul and of Peter can be further unfolded. We therefore have a choice at this point: either to follow Luke's example — in effect the account of Acts; or to trace out each of the three groupings of tradition to gain a better sense of their coherence and of their contribution as coherent groupings to our better understanding of the making of Christianity. It is the latter alternative I choose to follow. It has the disadvantage that in each case the story probably takes us beyond the first decade, or indeed well into the 40s, before we have to turn the clock some way back to pick up the next strand. But in keeping the strands thus apart we are better able to appreciate their historical value and to evaluate the links Luke has provided.

We start with the Hellenists, as Luke invites us to do.

24.1. A New Phase

'In these days, when the disciples were increasing in number, there arose a complaint from the Hellenists against the Hebrews, to the effect that their widows
were being neglected in the daily (provision of) aid' (Acts 6.1). With these
words Luke introduces one of the most intriguing phases of earliest Christianity.
The idyll of a rapidly growing body of believers, their divinely approved status
attested and their integrity protected by a perceptible aura of holiness, their
preaching in Temple and household undaunted, and opposition from the Temple
authorities in disarray, is interrupted by the jarring note of domestic strife. The
hitherto united body of believers is shown to be made up of at least two disparate groups — Hellenists and Hebrews (6.1). The hitherto undisputed leadership
of 'the apostles' appointed by Jesus (or by lot) has to be supplemented by seven
men elected by the whole community (6.2-6). A new figure of charismatic stature (Stephen), one of the seven (not one of the twelve), emerges centre stage
(6.8-15), with Peter (and John) no longer to be seen. The speech attributed to
Stephen is the longest in the book (7.2-53), and his death precipitates both a
persecution and an outreach of the message hardly in view within the first phase
(8.1-4). And the next figure to emerge on centre stage seems to come from the
same group of seven (Philip), to whom is attributed a dramatic breakthrough
with Judeans' old enemies, the Samaritans (8.4-25), and the first fully Gentile
conversion — a eunuch, no less (8.26-40). Still more striking is the report that
the same circumstances and impulses (the dispersion caused by the persecution)
resulted in the still wider preaching of the word and particularly the establishment of a church in the major metropolis of the eastern Empire, Syrian Antioch
(11.19-26).[1]

There is a general consensus in scholarship on the view that Luke has
been able to draw on source material for this section of his narrative.[2] It is
likely, in fact, that Luke was provided with a fairly coherent narrative — in oral
memory, not necessarily in writing — which ran from the appointment of the
seven to the founding of the Antioch church. Such a narrative would probably
be part of the Antioch church's own story (foundation narrative), and any contact which Luke had with that church or members of that church would have enabled him to learn the basic outline of the story and to frame it, as ever, in his

1. In concluding that 'the importance attributed to the Hellenists in modern scholarship
is a product of its own theological and historical commitments, and may have very little to do
with the actual realities of life in the early church', Penner gives too little weight to this sequence of events, which follows from the introduction of the Hellenists and the activities of
Stephen (*Praise* 331).

2. 'That Luke begins at 6.1 to follow a fresh tradition (some would say, a fresh written
source . . .) is agreed by almost all students of Acts' (Barrett, *Acts* 1.305).

own terms. In Acts itself, the continuity of the story seems to have been broken by Luke inserting his accounts of the conversion of Paul and the mission of Peter (9.1–11.18), but the repetition of the language of 8.4 in 11.19 is probably sufficient indication that at the latter point Luke consciously returned to his earlier (oral) narrative sources.[3]

The indications that Luke has drawn on, and in his own retelling has been constrained by, such source material are numerous.

- The terms 'Hellenists' and 'Hebrews' are introduced without explanation as self-evident.[4]
- The suggestion of some dissension (6.1) runs counter to the note regularly struck in chs. 1–5 — *homothymadon,* 'with one mind/purpose/impulse' (1.14; 2.1 v. l.; 2.46; 4.24; 5.12). Why would Luke introduce such a note of discord on his own initiative?
- The resort to election rather than (divine) appointment (6.3-6) implies some decline from Luke's carefully crafted portrayal of the theocracy of the first phase.
- The names of the seven elected most likely came to Luke from his informants regarding the whole episode, since he himself shows no further interest in five of the seven; they are even more ephemeral than the ten of the apostles who receive no mention after ch. 1.[5]
- The occasion for the election of the seven immediately passes out of view, and the Stephen who emerges centre stage is hardly a 'waiter' at tables. Why would Luke attribute the emergence of Stephen (and Philip) to these circumstances were it not that he had good tradition to that effect?[6]

---

3. 8.4 — 'Now those who were scattered went from place to place, proclaiming the word *(hoi men oun diasparentes dielthon euangelizomenoi ton logon)*';

11.19 — 'Now those who were scattered . . . went from place to place . . . speaking the word *(hoi men oun diasparentes . . . dielthon . . . lalountes ton logon)'*.
Cf., e.g., Barrett, *Acts* 1.547; Fitzmyer, *Acts* 474.

4. 'The list in v. 5 and the *abrupt* introduction of Hebrews and Hellenists best suggest a written tradition' (Lüdemann, *Early Christianity* 78); 'much of the wording of this verse [6.1] is non-Lucan, which suggests that he has derived it from a source' (Fitzmyer, *Acts* 348).

5. 'The bedrock tradition of this section is the list of the Seven in v. 5' (Lüdemann, *Early Christianity* 77); 'we should perhaps conclude that if Luke did not see the names on paper they must have belonged to a very well known and influential group' (Barrett, *Acts* 1.314). See further below, §24.3.

6. 'If Luke invented it he told his story badly by first inventing a setting and then immediately leaving it — the poor widows are soon abandoned. It is quite understandable that men who were in fact connected with the distribution of alms should grow into preachers and controversialists but it would be bad writing first of all to make up a job for them and then represent them as neglecting it for another' (Barrett, *Acts* 1.306).

- The reference to a synagogue in Jerusalem (6.9) is somewhat unexpected, given that Jerusalem existed for and to maintain its Temple.[7]
- The opponents of Stephen are shown as his fellow Hellenists (6.9-14), not the high priestly authorities of chs. 3–5.[8]
- The accusation against Stephen (6.14) is further testimony to a tradition of something Jesus was remembered as having said which was disturbing for the first Christians — treated as false testimony in Mark 14.57-58 and Acts 6.13-14, but in effect acknowledged in John 2.19.[9]
- The speech attributed to Stephen (ch. 7) is unique in Acts and provides hints that Luke was able to draw on material appropriate to the outcome; and the attitude to the Temple expressed in the speech is markedly at odds with the picture drawn throughout chs. 1–5.[10]
- There is a perceptible Temple motif running through these chapters: the accusation against Stephen (6.14), the critique of the Temple in Stephen's speech (7.48), and Philip's ministry (ch. 8) to the devotees of a different Temple (Samarians) as also to a eunuch (debarred from the congregation of Israel).[11]
- The divine protection afforded to Peter and John (5.19-21) is not extended to Stephen (7.57-60).
- That Saul/Paul was the arch-persecutor of the earliest believers is confirmed by Paul himself (1 Cor. 15.9; Gal. 1.13, 23; Phil. 3.6 — 'the persecutor').
- Various linguistic peculiarities suggest a vocabulary provided by others: in particular, the term 'disciple' appears for the first time in 6.1;[12] the apostles are called 'the twelve' for the only time in Acts (6.2);[13] the phrase 'full *(plērēs)* of the Spirit' occurs only in this material (6.3, 5, [8]; 11.24); the term 'grace *(charis)*' is characteristic of the material (6.8; 7.10, 46; 11.23) and prefigures Paul's usage more than Luke's earlier use; and the narrative climaxes in the first appearance of the title 'Christians' (11.26).

7. But see below, n. 30.

8. 'There is nothing to oblige Luke to introduce these men, unless there was a tradition he could not ignore' (Haenchen, *Acts* 273).

9. See *Jesus Remembered* 631-33; 'a strong case can be made for the belief that Jesus did foretell the destruction of the Temple' (Barrett, *Acts* 1.329)

10. See below, §24.5. It can hardly be an accident that Luke chooses to record at precisely this point — 6.7 (between the election of the seven and the description of Stephen's controversial ministry) — that 'a great crowd of priests became obedient to the faith', thus preparing for and reinforcing the Temple motif of these chapters.

11. See further below, §24.7.

12. 6.1, 2, 7; 9.1, 10, 19, 25-26; 11.26.

13. Barrett, *Acts* 1.310-11.

In short, the rounded story of Acts 6.1–8.40 with 11.19-26, starting with the 'Hellenists' and ending with the 'Christians', is evidently structured (probably from an Antioch perspective) to narrate one of the most crucial transitionary phases in the emergence of Christianity.[14]

We can be fairly confident, then, that Luke drew the thread (and at least some of the language) of his narrative for this second phase of his own story from accounts which were framed as a direct outcome of the episodes narrated. That he was thereby able to push forward his own agenda[15] is neither surprising nor does it detract from this conclusion; his 'agenda' may at least partly have been shaped by the findings of his own research.[16] More problematic is the likelihood that Luke has chosen in his telling to pass over in rather cursory fashion features of his story (elements which were part of the accounts he received) which detracted too much from his own attempt to portray a mission which went forward without serious internal divisions. We know Luke was quite capable of doing so from the fact that his narrative says nothing of the sharp confrontation involving Paul in Antioch (Gal. 2.11-17), or of the subsequent challenges to Paul's mission from other preachers of the gospel in Galatia and elsewhere.[17] And the abruptness and brevity of his account, both of Stephen's emergence and of his demise (Acts 6.8; 7.57-60), and of the critical breakthrough in Antioch (11.20), raises some suspicion that Luke has refrained from being clearer and more explicit at these points for his own good reasons. Consequently, the attempt to trace the history behind the account provided has to take something of the character of a detective story, where everything depends on what we make of the few clues Luke has left us. The investigation has all the fascination of a good detective novel![18]

The first task is to gain a clearer sense of who were involved in the opening sequence.

---

14. See also T. Seland, 'Once More — the Hellenists, Hebrews, and Stephen: Conflict and Conflict-Management in Acts 6–7', in P. Borgen et al., eds., *Recruitment, Conquest, and Conflict: Strategies in Judaism, Early Christianity, and the Greco-Roman World* (Atlanta: Scholars, 1998) 169-207 (here 195-99).

15. E.g., Philip's mission in Acts 8 obviously takes forward the commission of 1.8 (Samaria).

16. 'It was knowledge of these developments which no doubt caused Luke to frame his table of contents as he did in 1.8 ("in all Judaea and Samaria")' (Dunn, *Acts* 79).

17. 2 Cor. 11.4-5; Gal. 1.6-7; Phil. 1.15-17. In Luke's account the challenges all come from without, not least from 'the Jews'.

18. Penner's main thesis, that Luke's primary concern was to demonstrate the praiseworthiness of the community in dealing with a crisis (Acts 6.1), is again set up in too antithetical terms, as though Luke could not also be playing down some reported early tensions or disagreements in the earliest Jerusalem community, and as though recognition of such aims unavoidably 'obscures, if not prevents, any reasonable assessment of its [the narrative's] historicity' (*Praise* 262-87, particularly 275-76 and 286).

24.2. Who Were the Hellenists?

The abrupt juxtaposition of the referents 'Hellenists' and 'Hebrews' is very telling. The word 'Hellenist' *(Hellēnistēs)* means 'one who uses the Greek language'.[19] Equivalently, the word 'Hebrew' *(Hebraios)* presumably means 'one who speaks Hebrew or Aramaic'.[20] But there is more to it.

a. Greek-Speakers

First, we know that Greek was quite commonly spoken (or understood) in and around Jerusalem, that is, by Jews as well as any other incomers.[21] So the distinction between Greek-speakers and Aramaic-speakers cannot mean that the latter ('Hebrews') could speak only Aramaic and understood no Greek. But it could mean that the former ('Hellenists') in effect spoke only Greek and did not understand much if any Aramaic.[22] This could well be the case if, as is most likely, the Hellenists were Jews from the diaspora who had settled in Jerusalem and who functioned only in Greek, the international *lingua franca* of the Mediterranean world.[23] Hengel envis-

19. BDAG 319; see further Barrett, *Acts* 1.308; Fitzmyer, *Acts* 347; H. A. Brehm, 'The Meaning of *Hellēnistēs* in Acts in Light of a Diachronic Analysis of *hellēnizein*', in S. E. Porter and D. A. Carson, eds., *Discourse Analysis and Other Topics in Biblical Greek* (JSNTS 113; Sheffield: Sheffield Academic, 1995) 180-99. The point is not in dispute; Cadbury's attempt to argue that Luke uses *Hellēnistai* as synonymous with *ethnē* or *Hellēnes,* Gentiles or Greeks *(Beginnings* 5.59-74), has not proved convincing.

20. Cf. BDAG 269-70; Lüdemann, *Early Christianity* 78; Barrett, *Acts* 1.308. Barrett does not give enough weight to the fact that the two terms 'Hebrews' and 'Hellenists' are set in some contrast.

21. More than a third of the ossuary inscriptions from this period found in Jerusalem are written in Greek; see especially M. Hengel, *The 'Hellenization' of Judaea in the First Century after Christ* (London: SCM, 1989) 9-11, and on the 'Hellenization' of the ruling class in Jerusalem (ch. 4).

22. C. F. D. Moule, 'Once More, Who Were the Hellenists?', *ExpT* 70 (1958-59) 100-102; M. Hengel, *Between Jesus and Paul* (London: SCM, 1983) 8-11; P. F. Esler, *Community and Gospel in Luke-Acts: The Social and Political Motivations of Lucan Theology* (SNTSMS 57; Cambridge: Cambridge University, 1987) 138-39; H. Räisänen, 'Die "Hellenisten" der Urgemeinde', *ANRW* 2.26.2 (1995) 1468-1514 (here 1477-78). Räisänen envisages Andrew and Philip as possible go-betweens (cf. John 12.20-22), also Barnabas (1478).

23. Haenchen, *Acts* 260-61, 266-67; Schneider, *Apg.* 1.423; N. Walter, 'Apostelgeschichte 6.1 und die Anfänge der Urgemeinde in Jerusalem', *NTS* 29 (1983) 370-93; H.-W. Neudorfer, *Der Stephanuskreis in der Forschungsgeschichte seit F. C. Baur* (Giessen: Brunnen, 1983) 220-23, 293, 309-10, 329-31 (tabulation 81-85). Fitzmyer questions the logic of this inference, given the evidence of Greek inscriptions on ossuaries found in Jerusalem *(Acts* 347), but Jews resident in Jerusalem who could function only in Greek (the most likely hypothesis, as

ages diaspora Jews who had retired to Jerusalem[24] — an aspiration (to return to the mother country) which emigrant communities the world over also know only too well.[25]

The probability that such was indeed the case is immediately strengthened by the reference in 6.9 to 'the synagogue of the Libertini[26] and Cyrenians[27] and Alexandrians and others from Cilicia[28] and Asia', including, no doubt the diaspora Jews resident in Jerusalem to which Luke referred in 2.5-11. The Libertini (or 'freedmen'), a Latin term, would probably be the descendants of Jews who had been taken captive from Judea into slavery, following the conquest of Jerusalem by Pompey in 62 BCE, and who subsequently had been freed (Philo, *Leg.* 155).[29] That there was a synagogue which was known in these terms presumably

---

Fitzmyer agrees) are hardly likely to have been native to the region (as Fitzmyer seems also to agree — 350).

24. Hengel, *Between Jesus and Paul* 12, 16, 18. Hengel's evaluation of the passage has been highly influential; see Penner, *Praise* 29-39. Hengel reckons that, given a population of between 80,000 and 100,000, the inscriptional evidence suggests a number of between 8,000 and 16,000 Greek-speaking Jews in greater Jerusalem (*'Hellenization'* 10). In *Paul* 160, he and Schwemer cite epitaphs of two Jewish Tarsians found in Jaffa. In his Nachtrag to the original 'Zwischen Jesus und Paul' essay, Hengel reasserts his claim that the Hellenists provide sufficient bridge between Paul and the earliest community and make redundant hypotheses of a pre-Pauline Gentile Christian community (*Paulus und Jakobus* [Tübingen: Mohr Siebeck, 2002] 58-62).

25. N. T. Wright has reminded us of how important to the Jews of the Second Temple period was the hope of 'return from exile', the hope of restoration to the land of Israel for the scattered tribes of Israel; see *Jesus Remembered* 473. Schnabel ignores this factor when he argues that diaspora Jews 'hardly would have settled in the Jewish capital if they were unable or unwilling to communicate in Aramaic' (*Mission* 654); today many English-speakers retire to Spain without knowing or having any intention of learning Spanish.

26. There must have been a substantial body of such freedmen, whose identity was given precisely by their slave origins, rather than the country from which they had come. Hengel reckons that the prestige which Herod the Great's achievements brought to Jerusalem would presumably have facilitated the return of prominent diaspora Jews to Jerusalem (*'Hellenization'* 13, 32-35).

27. Fitzmyer notes that the burial site of a Jewish family from Cyrene has been discovered in Jerusalem (*Acts* 358), citing N. Avigad, 'A Depository of Inscribed Ossuaries in the Kidron Valley', *IEJ* 12 (1962) 1-12. The Simon of Mark 15.21 came from Cyrene, as presumably also his two sons, Alexander and Rufus.

28. Saul/Paul, of course, was from Cilicia, and his sister is later said to be resident in Jerusalem (23.16). Bruce wonders whether Saul himself had attended this synagogue, or whether (as a 'Hebrew of the Hebrews') he would have preferred one where the worship was conducted in Hebrew (*Acts* 187). It is natural to wonder whether Saul/Paul himself had been one of those who disputed with Stephen.

29. Schürer, *History* 2.428 n. 8. Slaves were regularly manumitted (freed) after a period of service. Tacitus tells of '4,000 descendants of enfranchised slaves *(libertini)*, [who were] tainted with that superstition *(ea superstitione infecta)*' (*Ann.*2.85.4); that is, they had become

indicates not only that the diaspora returnees frequented a particular synagogue but also that it was known as 'theirs'.[30] It is, of course, entirely understandable that a monolingual community should clump together for communal activities in a city where the language of everyday life was unfamiliar to them; the experience is as common today as it has been in the past.

The name 'Hebrew' is surprising in the context of Jerusalem. Who would designate representatives of the majority Aramaic-speaking population as 'Aramaic-speakers'? The most logical answer is that this was a term used by the *non*-Aramaic speakers. So today in a British city the local native residents might well use a term like 'the Urdu-speakers' for a minority language group but would hardly refer to themselves as 'the English-speakers', whereas an immigrant group conscious of its failings in the native language might conceivably desig- nate a faction of the native population as 'the English-speakers'.[31] Similarly, Paul's designation of Jews and Gentiles as 'the circumcision' and 'the uncir- cumcision' certainly betrays a Jewish perspective;[32] no Greek would classify himself as 'the uncircumcision', only one who claimed that circumcision was something to be prized (and therefore the lack of circumcision to be a negative identity marker). The inference, then, is that *the contrast of 'Hellenist' and 'He- brew' is expressive of a Hellenist perspective*[33] — an observation which adds fur-

---

proselytes (or possibly simply God-fearers) (see text and commentary in *GLAJJ* 2.68-73). Lake and Cadbury wonder whether Paul might have been a *libertinus* (*Beginnings* 4.68).

30. Only one synagogue seems to be intended, though the Greek could imply more (cf. 24.12), or at least two different groups *(tōn ek . . . tōn apo . . .)*; discussion in Bruce, *Acts* 187; Barrett, *Acts* 1.324; earlier discussion in Neudorfer, *Stephanuskreis* 158-63, 266-69; bibliogra- phy in Jervell, *Apg.* 225 n. 663. There is archaeological evidence of a synagogue in Jerusalem founded by one Theodotus for the benefit of Jews who came from abroad, though the age of the inscription is disputed; but see Riesner, 'Synagogues in Jerusalem' 192-200, and J. S. Kloppenborg, 'Dating Theodotus (*CIJ* II 1404)', *JJS* 51 (2000) 243-80, referred to in *Jesus Re- membered* 303 n. 220, and revised as 'The Theodotus Synagogue Inscription and the Problem of First-Century Synagogue Buildings', in J. H. Charlesworth, ed., *Jesus and Archaeology* (Grand Rapids: Eerdmans, 2006) 236-82; Hemer also thinks it 'certainly pre-70' (*Book of Acts* 176). The text of the inscription can be found in various publications and has been frequently discussed; in addition to Riesner and Kloppenborg, see, e.g., Lake and Cadbury, *Beginnings* 4.67-68; Hengel, *Between Jesus and Paul* 17-18; *NDIEC* 7.89.

31. This takes further Hengel's observation that the *Hellēnistai* were 'a phenomenon limited to Jerusalem', since 'for the Greek-speaking Diaspora the use of *Hellēnistēs* would be meaningless, as here the use of Greek as a mother tongue was taken for granted' (*Between Jesus and Paul* 8).

32. As expressly stated in Eph. 2.11.

33. Cf. R. Pesch et al., '"Hellenisten" und "Hebräer"', *BZ* 23 (1979) 87-92. As K. Lön- ing, 'The Circle of Stephen and Its Mission', in Becker, ed., *Christian Beginnings* 103-31, ob- serves, 'the actual meaning [of "Hellenists"] only results when one contrasts "Hellenists" with "Hebrews"' (105).

ther strength to the probability that Luke was able for these chapters to draw on memories and accounts framed by self-styled 'Hellenists'. This in turn suggests that what follows is indeed *an account provided from a Hellenist perspective,* indeed by 'Hellenists', and that the title of this chapter ('The Hellenists . . .') is an entirely fair assessment of their role in what follows.

b. Returned Diaspora Jews

Second, several further deductions are quite in order. Language, it can safely be asserted, is an expression of culture. So, if Greek was the only language of 'the Hellenists', it must mean that their culture and attitudes were 'Hellenist' in character.[34] This is entirely consistent with the hypothesis that the Hellenists in Acts 6.1 were Jews who had returned from the diaspora. As diaspora Jews who functioned only in Greek, their life-style and ethos would reflect Hellenistic perspectives and values in at least some degree. The observation must at once be qualified by the fact that they had returned (retired?) to Jerusalem; they were not so enamoured of diaspora life and culture![35] Even so, however, their ability to function only in Greek must signify that their social and communication networks in the diaspora had included only other Greek-speakers.[36]

'Hebrew', on the other hand, while hardly appropriate as a self-reference in a Jerusalem context, as we have just seen in the preceding section (a), is entirely understandable in a diaspora context. This latter is the context for the only other two occurrences of the word in the NT (2 Cor. 11.22; Phil. 3.5). In each case Paul speaks from the perspective of a Jew brought up in the diaspora who insisted on maintaining his Jewish identity, in learning and speaking Hebrew/ Aramaic, even though living in a Greek environment. Whereas 'Hebrew' as a self-description in Jerusalem makes not much sense, it is entirely understandable in a diaspora context.

The point can be put more strongly. The designation 'Hebrew' is something of an archaism; as G. Harvey notes, 'The name "Hebrew" was conventionally associated with traditionalism or conservatism'.[37] In other words, use of the term in self-reference by a diaspora Jew surely indicates a determination to

---

34. Weiser, *Apg.* 165; G. Harvey, *The True Israel: Uses of the Names Jew, Hebrew, and Israel in Ancient Jewish Literature and Early Christian Literature* (AGAJU 35; Leiden: Brill, 1996) 135-36.

35. The attempt to root any Hellenist opposition to the Temple in their diaspora origin requires much more careful statement; cf. Walter, 'Apostelgeschichte 6.1' 376-77, 384.

36. On the degree of integration accepted or achieved by many diaspora Jews in local society and culture, see below, §29.5b.

37. Harvey, *The True Israel* 146.

maintain traditional Jewish identity in the face of the enticing but corruptible influences (as seen from a 'Hebrew' perspective) of Hellenism. This was no doubt
the attitude of Paul himself, as indicated particularly by his self-reference in Phil.
3.5 — 'a Hebrew of the Hebrews' — denoting Paul's earlier determination to
identify himself as completely as possible with the ancient origins and character
of his people.[38] It follows that use of the term 'Hebrews' by diaspora Jews to designate a group of fellow Jesus-believers in Jerusalem most likely indicates *a diaspora Jewish attribution of traditional and conservative attitudes to those so
designated.*

Here we should recall the antipathy to things Hellenistic which gave birth
to the term 'Judaism' and which characterized those who gave the term its living
expression.[39] For the self-designation 'Hebrew' presumably indicates an even
deeper hostility to 'Hellenism'.[40] And the designation of others as 'Hebrews' by
self-styled 'Hellenists' presumably indicates a Hellenist perception of such antipathy. Or to put the point in reverse. If 'Judaism' had been formed as the national and religious expression of determination *not* to be swept into an undifferentiated 'Hellenism', it is likely that suspicion of things Hellenistic continued to
be a constitutional element in Jewish character and a gut feeling for many Palestinian Jews.[41]

The conclusion to which all this ineluctably leads us is that *the terms 'Hel-*

38. So most commentators on Philippians; see, e.g., J. Gnilka, *Der Philipperbrief*
(HTKNT 10.3; Freiburg: Herder, [2]1976) 189-90.

39. *Ioudaïsmos* was coined precisely in antithesis to *Hellēnismos;* see *Jesus Remembered* 261, and further below, §§25.1d and 29.2a.

40. To be noted is the fact that Paul describes his former life both as 'a Hebrew of the
Hebrews' (Phil. 3.5) and as 'in Judaism' (Gal. 1.13-14), both expressed in his violent persecution of 'the church of God', in particular, probably, the Hellenists; see below, §25.2.

41. It was M. Simon, *St. Stephen and the Hellenists in the Primitive Church* (London:
Longmans, Green, 1958), who drew my attention to this connection (12-13). The point is not
disturbed by recognition of the degree to which Hellenism had penetrated into Palestine and
into Palestinian Judaism; it has been one of the great contributions of M. Hengel to indicate that
a simplistic antithesis between Palestinian Judaism and Hellenistic Judaism is not possible (*Judaism and Hellenism* [London: SCM, 1974]); also *'Hellenization';* also 'Judaism and Hellenism Revisited', in J. J. Collins and G. E. Sterling, eds., *Hellenism in the Land of Israel* (Notre
Dame: University of Notre Dame, 2001) 6-37; though note also J. J. Collins, 'Cult and Culture:
The Limits of Hellenization in Judaea', in the same volume, 38-61. On the contrary, the very
fact of such a degree of penetration would feed the suspicions of many more traditional Jews
that Jewish society and religion had become too 'Hellenized'. At the same time, Esler's warning against assuming that diaspora Judaism as such could be assumed to be less loyal to the
Temple and the law (*Community and Gospel* 145-48) should be heeded. See also the essays by
W. A. Meeks, D. B. Martin and P. S. Alexander on the problematic character and ideological
abuse of the Judaism/Hellenism 'divide', in T. Engberg-Pedersen, ed., *Paul beyond the Juda-
ism/Hellenism Divide* (Louisville: Westminster John Knox, 2001) chs. 1-3.

lenists' and 'Hebrews' indicate a degree of suspicion and possibly even hostility between the two groups thus denoted. The Hellenists more than likely looked down on the Hebrews as parochial and traditionalist. Equally, the Hebrews probably regarded the Hellenists as those who were diluting and compromising key traditions of their shared faith and praxis as Jews. The attitudes are classically caught by Paul in his counsel to a situation in Rome which can be not unfairly characterized as a clash of Hebrew/Hellenist attitudes and praxis on food laws and holy days (Rom. 14.3-5).[42] The possibility that Luke is not giving us a full picture thus becomes more than a possibility (one sentence!), and any suspicion that there was more to the Hellenists/Hebrews distinction than Luke has told us becomes a good deal firmer.

c. Their Complaint

What can be deduced from the report of the Hellenists' complaint? The very term and phrase used is interesting. *Gongysmos* denotes an 'utterance made in a low tone of voice, behind-the-scenes talk', and so 'complaint', displeasure expressed in murmuring.[43] The implication is of a group who felt themselves to be hard done by and who voiced their complaints among themselves for some time before bringing them to the surface. And the 'murmuring' was directed not against the leadership but against 'the Hebrews'. Again the implication is of two fairly distinct groups, with the feelings of resentment of the one group ('us') directed against the 'them' of the other group.

The complaints were because the Hellenist widows were being overlooked, neglected *(paretheōrounto)*[44] in the daily distributions from the common fund referred to earlier in Luke's narrative (2.44-45; 4.32, 34-35).[45] The social context indi-

---

42. See further my *Romans* 799-802; and below, §33.3f.

43. BDAG 204, classically for the murmurings of Israel in the wilderness (Exod. 16.7, 8, 9, 12; Num. 17.5, 10).

44. Note the imperfect tense; it had been going on for some time. D adds *tōn Hebraiōn* — 'in the daily distribution "of the Hebrews"'.

45. In subsequent rabbinic tradition distribution of alms included 'a weekly dole to the poor of the city, and consisted of food and clothing'; Jeremias assumes this was already the practice and served as a model 'for the primitive Church' (*Jerusalem* 131-32). The issue is important, since, if there was already a well-developed practice of charitable distribution in Jerusalem, the Hellenist widows could have depended on that practice (cf. Lüdemann, *Early Christianity* 75-76); Walter, indeed, assumes that the breakdown in welfare relief referred to in 6.1 was a breakdown in the city-wide system ('Apostelgeschichte 6.1'); however, the situation reflected in the tradition of the new sect's common fund and in the specifics here — not to mention the subsequent traditions of 11.27-30 and Paul's collection for 'the poor among the saints in Jerusalem' (Rom. 15.26) — suggests that the practice was not so developed as Jeremias suggests. Capper, e.g., observes that

cated is fairly easy to elucidate. Since marriage of girls in young teenage to older men was common practice, many of these wives were widowed when they were still relatively young.[46] In the case of men who had returned with their wives from the diaspora, there would no doubt have been many such instances. And their plight — in a still not very familiar city, caught in a monolingual community, and, evidently in the cases in view, left with few personal resources and no relatives to call upon — is fairly easy to imagine.[47] While we may imagine that many diaspora Jews returning to Jerusalem would have been wealthy, Luke's account indicates that the Hellenist widows attracted to the new sect included many who were not so.[48]

The fact that it was the Hellenist widows who were being neglected (and not widows generally) strengthens the likelihood that the two groups (Hebrews and Hellenists) lived separate lives, socially and perhaps geographically (by district) in Jerusalem. In other words, the breakdown of such a system of distribution from the common fund as had developed was not occasioned simply by the growth of numbers associating themselves with the new sect (all baptized?). A crucial factor was that the two groups were in significant degree separate or disjoint from each other.[49]

---

the rabbinic system envisaged a weekly dole, whereas here the talk is of a daily distribution ('Community of Goods' 351). 'There was, presumably, a more established system of poor relief with Jerusalem for all poor, but perhaps it was already a point of principle that those who had aligned themselves with the new movement should look to it for support' (Dunn, *Acts* 81). 'One should not represent the poor relief as a comprehensive (city-wide) system, but as the institution of smaller synagogue communities' (Pesch, *Apg.* 1.233). How much may we deduce from *T. Job* 10 ('I established in my house thirty tables spread at all hours, for strangers only. I also used to maintain twelve other tables set for the widows')? See further D. Seccombe, 'Was There Organized Charity in Jerusalem before the Christians?', *JTS* 29 (1978) 140-43; Walter, 'Apostelgeschichte 6.1' 379-80; M. Goodman, *The Ruling Class of Judaea: The Origins of the Jewish Revolt against Rome AD 66-70* (Cambridge: Cambridge University, 1987) 65-66.

46. 'The lot of the widow, often reduced to poverty by the death of her husband, was a topic to which the law and the prophets often spoke (Deut 14:29; 24:17; 26:12; Isa. 1:23; 10:2; Jer 7:6; 22:3; Mal 3:5)' (Fitzmyer, *Acts* 345).

47. 'Perhaps the number of Hellenistic widows was relatively large, for many pious Jews in the evening of their days settled in Jerusalem so as to be buried near the Holy City; the widows of such men had no relatives at hand to look after them and tended to become dependent on public charity' (Haenchen, *Acts* 261).

48. The higher-status residents in Jerusalem were probably more strongly influenced by the international and more sophisticated culture of Hellenism (as evidenced in the palaces and wealthy mansions known to have been in Jerusalem at this time). But it would be too facile to set the Hellenist/Hebrew distinctions into a class framework (Hellenists from the wealthy upper-class, worldly sophisticates; Hebrews from the poorer, lower classes). At the very least, the Hellenist widows may have exemplified the well-known trait of 'genteel poverty'. See also F. S. Spencer, 'Neglected Widows in Acts 6:1-7', *CBQ* 56 (1994) 715-33.

49. Theological differences were not necessarily already a factor, as has often been suggested (see Neudorfer, *Stephanuskreis* 310, tabulation 99-101).

How else could it be that the Hellenist widows (and only they?) were being thus neglected?[50] Here again the impression is given of two distinct groups or factions, with resentment growing among the first against the second ('murmuring'), while the second viewed the first with some suspicion.

All in all, it is hard to escape the conclusion that the terminology and details, which Luke learned and which he has communicated in the briefest of accounts, nevertheless 'give the game away'. Already within not many months of the new sect's beginning, there emerged a significant degree of factionalism. To speak of 'schism', as Haenchen did,[51] is far too precipitate. But equally, Craig Hill's attempt to deny that there was anything much amiss[52] simply ignores or suppresses the clear implications of the terminology used and the situation envisaged.[53] The idyll, such as it had been in historical reality, was indeed at an end. The reality of 'church' as it has been known for centuries, and as the *qahal Israel* had been long accustomed to,[54] (re)asserted itself — that is, the reality of groups who have come to their shared faith from different backgrounds, who find it most congenial to practise their

50. 'The "Hellenist" widows were left out simply because the distribution took place within the gatherings of the Aramaic-speaking Christians, and the "Hellenist" widows did not take part in these because they could not follow what was said' (Wedderburn, *History* 45). Contrast Wilckens, who resists the implication that Hebrews and Hellenists worshipped separately and who even suggests that the common worship language was Greek (*Theologie* 1/2.231-32), which hardly explains the primary data, the fact that the earliest Christian community in Jerusalem could be described as two groups distinguished by their language usage.

51. E. Haenchen, 'The Book of Acts as Source Material for the History of Early Christianity', in L. E. Keck and J. L. Martyn, eds., *Studies in Luke-Acts* (Nashville: Abingdon, 1966) 258-78: 'the first confessional schism in church history' (264) — a provocative phrase which I used to head my earlier discussion of the Hellenist episode in *Unity and Diversity* §60.

52. C. C. Hill, *Hellenists and Hebrews: Reappraising Division within the Earliest Church* (Minneapolis: Fortress, 1992), sets out to question the four points of wide consensus: 'that the Hellenists and Hebrews were distinctive ideological groups, that Stephen, the Hellenist leader, spoke against the temple . . . , that he was put to death for his liberal (or radical) views, and that the Hellenists and not the Hebrews were persecuted by the Jews' (11-12). Bauckham follows Hill to a large extent — e.g., 'Jesus and the Jerusalem Community' 63-64.

53. For example, the recognition that *Hellēnistēs* means 'Greek-speaking Jew from the Diaspora' (*Hellenists and Hebrews* 24), without following through the likelihood that the Hellenists could function in effect *only* in Greek (nn. 19, 22 above) and without reflecting on the juxtaposition of 'Hebrew' over against 'Hellenist', is simply not good enough. It is true that Stephen's death and the subsequent persecution need not shed any light on Hebrew/Hellenist tension (31, 34), but if the Temple was an issue between Stephen and his fellow Hellenists (which Hill also questions), it is hard avoid the corollary that the Hebrews would have been critical of Stephen's views. See also Lüdemann's critique (*Primitive Christianity* 58-59).

54. See *Jesus Remembered* §9.4.

shared faith differently, and between whom readily grow up suspicions and resentments, which in due course can become hostile factionalism and eventually schism. The poisonous brew had only begun to be mixed and heated, but vital elements were already present and the process was, even thus early, already under way.

24.3. The Seven

Whatever the historical circumstances behind his narrative, Luke hastens to indicate how the young Jerusalem church responded to this first internal challenge. 'The twelve' take charge, call together 'the crowd of the disciples' (6.2), 'the whole community' (6.5) — all 5,000 plus (4.4; 5.14)?! They set out the priorities: the twelve's responsibility to attend to 'the word of God' (presumably both preaching and teaching) must take precedence over 'waiting on tables' (6.2, 4). The crowd should therefore scrutinize their own ranks to find *(episkepsasthe)*[55] men of good reputation *(martyroumenous)*, 'full of *(plēreis)* the Spirit and of wisdom', whom the twelve will then put in charge of (dealing with) this need (6.3), that is, to ensure that the Hellenist widows are included in the daily distribution from the community of goods. The crowd then choose seven men, present them to the apostles, and praying, lay their hands on them (6.6).[56]

Who were these seven, whose names must have come to Luke from the source(s) which provided the basic information on which he drew for this section? All their names are Greek,[57] which suggests that they were all from among 'the Greek-speakers'.[58] The deduction is by no means certain: some of Jesus'

---

55. B reads *episkepsōmetha*, 'let us choose', presumably an attempt to have the situation resolved solely by 'the twelve'; the reading is preferred by Lake and Cadbury (*Beginnings* 4.65) but runs counter to the further description in vv. 5-6 (cf. Metzger, *Textual Commentary* 337).

56. The syntax is most obviously read as indicating that it was the same subject (the whole community) who prayed and laid on hands. This could well have been Luke's intention — the setting apart for ministry thus enacted being seen as the responsibility of the community as a whole (cf. 13.3; perhaps in echo of Num. 8.10). Most assume that Luke's formulation has been rather casual, since he must have intended to say that it was the apostles who laid on hands; but given Luke's concern to stress the authority of the apostles, it is all the more significant that he has left his account as ambiguous as he has (see further Barrett, *Acts* 1.315-16). From a subsequent ecclesiological perspective it is natural to see here the first 'ordination' (see, e.g., those cited by Jervell, *Apg.* 219 n. 636), but the danger of an anachronistic reading-back is substantial. Luke 'reports the origin of Church offices neither here nor elsewhere' (Goppelt, *Apostolic* 55). See also n. 65 below.

57. Details in Barrett, *Acts* 1.314-15, with repeated reference to the documentation from *IG* provided by E. Preuschen, *Die Apostelgeschichte* (HNT; Tübingen: Mohr Siebeck, 1912) 36.

58. This is the general consensus — e.g., Bruce, *Acts* 183; Pesch, *Apg.* 1.229; Jervell, *Apg.* 219.

own disciples also had Greek names — Andrew *(Andreas)* and Philip *(Philippos)*.[59] But the sequel (chs. 6–8), in which Stephen and Philip play the lead roles, is part of the narrative running through to 11.19-26, which strongly suggests that the first two mentioned in the list of 6.5, Stephen and Philip, were themselves from the group who provided Luke with the story which is told from their perspective.[60] The last of the seven, Nicolaus, is described as a proselyte, that is, a Gentile (a native Greek-speaker) who had fully converted to Judaism; he was moreover an 'Antiochene', indicating a further link with Antioch. And the substantial evidence of names used in Israel (from inscriptions and other texts) shows that only two of the names were familiar within Israel (Philip and Nicanor). So it is a fair deduction that the seven all belonged to the group designated 'the Hellenists' in 6.1.

This highlights a somewhat curious feature: that the whole community (Hebrews as well as Hellenists) may have elected only Hellenists. Which in turn suggests that administration of the common fund across the whole community was not what was in view, but in effect ministry only among the Hellenist segment of the community. Luke indeed says that the seven were appointed to meet 'this need', that is, the neglect of the Hellenist widows.[61]

In which case, we can probably make a further deduction. Those who spoke only Greek would presumably have met separately from the Aramaic-speakers, in Greek-speaking homes (cf. 2.46; 5.42). Consequently, the seven may have been the leaders of the Hellenist house churches.[62] It could be, indeed, that

59. Andrew — Mark 1.16 par.; 1.29; 3.18 pars.; 13.3; John 1.40, 44; 6.8; 12.22; Acts 1.13; Philip — Mark 3.18 pars.; John 1.43-46, 48; 6.5, 7; 12.21-22; 14.8-9; Acts 1.13.

60. There is a strong consensus that Stephen himself was a Hellenist (Neudorfer, *Stephanuskreis* 252-54, 293, 311), questioned by M. H. Scharlemann, *Stephen: A Singular Saint* (AnBib 34; Rome: Pontifical Biblical Institute, 1968) 54.

61. 'The solution to the dispute was *not* the integration of the "hellenist" widows *into* the "daily distribution" of the "Hebrew" congregation, but rather the establishment of officers to organize care within the hellenist community, which clearly had no arrangements of any kind for the care of its poor' (Capper, 'Community of Goods' 353-54). Esler suggests an underlying history where the seven set up a separate fund which they used to support their own poor, and so a deepening separation between the two groups (*Community and Gospel* 141-45). G. Theissen, 'Hellenisten und Hebräer (Apg. 6,1-6). Gab eine Spaltung der Urgemeinde?', in H. Lichtenberger, ed., *Geschichte — Tradition — Reflexion,* M. Hengel FS. Vol. 3: *Frühes Christentum* (Tübingen: Mohr Siebeck, 1996) 323-43, argues that behind Luke's narrative lies the development of local organization (in Jerusalem) alongside the wandering-missionary role of the apostles. However, the argument depends too much on the implausible earlier thesis that the disciples of Jesus were wandering charismatics, without established bases (see *Jesus Remembered* 54-56, 244, 558-59).

62. Hengel, *Between Jesus and Paul* 12-17; suggested earlier by Simon — 'the leading body' of a (more liberal) synagogue (*St. Stephen* 9).

the choice of just seven indicates that there were seven Greek-speaking house groups/congregations.[63] This would also mean that the seven were seen as representative leaders of the Hellenist believers, analogous to the leadership provided by the twelve of the church as a whole (but more effectively for the Hebrews!); hence they can be called 'the seven' (21.8) in parallel or some equivalence to 'the twelve' (6.2).[64] It would also help explain how it was that those appointed as table-waiters became such vigorous leaders in evangelism (Stephen and Philip).[65]

In all this, the indications continue to mount that Luke was telling his story from a Hellenist or Antiochene perspective:

- The use of the term 'the disciples', which first appears in 6.1, suggests that it was initially a self-description within Hellenist circles (6.1, 2, 7; 9.1, 10, 19, 25-26; 11.26).
- The juxtaposition of 'the seven' with 'the twelve' mirrors the opening juxtaposition of 'the Hellenists' and 'the Hebrews', again suggesting that both the latter terms — 'the Hebrews' and 'the twelve', which occurs in Acts only at 6.2 — were Hellenist ways of referring to the 'others'.
- The men chosen were to be 'full of the Spirit and of wisdom'. Both terms occur only in the 'Hellenist section' of Luke's narrative ('full of the Spirit' — 6.3, 5; 7.55; 11.24; 'wisdom' — 6.3, 10; 7.10, 22), which again suggests that Luke's use here is drawn from a Hellenist or Antiochene source.
- The contrast with Luke's usual verbal phrase ('filled with the Spirit' for a particular occasion) may also suggest that the Hellenist source had a concept of a more settled level of inspiration (contrast 4.8 with 7.55 and 11.24). The full phrase certainly envisages one whose inspiration, insight and discernment was exceptionally well matured.[66]

---

63. Barrett wonders whether there is sufficient evidence of a Jewish custom of appointing seven to carry out some task (*Acts* 1.312); Fitzmyer thinks not (*Acts* 349).

64. Neudorfer notes that this parallel was first suggested by Wellhausen, and that the role of the seven as leaders of the Hellenist (house) groups goes back to Loisy (*Stephanuskreis* 112-13, tabulation 124-25).

65. It is unlikely that Luke intended to describe here the first appointment of 'deacons'; he uses only the noun *diakonia* (service) (6.1; but also 6.4) and the verb *diakoneō* (to serve) (6.2) and does not describe the seven as 'deacons' *(diakonoi)*. As Barrett observes, 'It is impossible that anyone should set out to give an account of the origin of the diaconate without calling its first holders deacons' (*Acts* 1.304). Luke describes only an appointment to ministry: in this instance, to table-waiting. Haenchen notes that 'the collection from Antioch was received in Jerusalem not by deacons but by the presbyters (11.30)' (*Acts* 266). See also n. 56 above.

66. There are echoes in all this of Num. 11.16-30 and 27.16-23 and possibly also Exod. 31.3 and 35.31.

At all events, if only Hellenists were chosen, just as only the Hellenist widows had been neglected, then the suggestion of a church already marked by two distinct groups is strong. Diversity — in language and culture, and presumably in social composition too — was part of the first church more or less from the first. There was never a time when Christianity did not know the tensions which come from diversity of culture and viewpoint and defects in organization!

24.4. Stephen

a. When Did Stephen Emerge on the Scene?

Luke makes no attempt to date these early events (contrast Luke 2.1-2; 3.1-2). Prior to Acts 12 his chronological sequencing is reasonably clear, but the number of months and years covered between ch. 2 and ch. 12 is left confusingly vague. Here in particular Luke provides no indication as to how soon the domestic crisis of 6.1 arose and how soon it was that Stephen came to prominence. His insertion of one of his summaries between 6.6 (the appointment of the seven) and 6.8 (the emergence of Stephen) suggests something of a time lag between the two events. The only firm givens, relatively speaking, are the dates we can attach to Paul's career.[67] And since Pauline chronology suggests a date for Paul's conversion no more than about two to three years after Jesus' crucifixion, the important corollary is that all the events covered in Acts prior to Paul's conversion have to be reckoned as falling within that time frame. These events include an active period of persecution by Saul/Paul, which must have stretched over a number of weeks at least — sufficiently intensive and extensive for him to have gained a reputation as 'the persecutor' (Gal. 1.23). Add in the events which must have aroused Saul/Paul's persecuting ire, and (possibly many) more weeks and months come into view. We should probably reckon, then, with the domestic crisis emerging within the first year of the new sect's beginning, and Stephen coming to prominence within no more than eighteen months from Jesus' death.[68]

---

67. See below, §28.1.

68. A date of 31/32 is favoured by A. Strobel, *Die Stunde der Wahrheit. Untersuchungen zum Strafverfahren gegen Jesus* (WUNT 1.21; Tübingen: Mohr Siebeck, 1980) 88; Riesner, *Paul's Early Period* 59-63, 71; H.-W. Neudorfer, 'The Speech of Stephen', in I. H. Marshall and D. Peterson, eds., *Witness to the Gospel: The Theology of Acts* (Grand Rapids: Eerdmans, 1998) 275-94 (here 277). Bruce notes C. H. Turner's observation that by means of his succession of progress reports (6.7; 9.31; 12.24; 16.5; 19.20; 28.31), Luke divides Acts into six 'panels' which cover on an average five years each (*Acts* 185, referring to *HDB* 1.421-23). But if Paul's conversion (Acts 9) took place within two or three years of the first Good Friday and Easter (see again below, §28.1), then 6.7 does not fit neatly within that scheme. Similarly, the

b. Stephen's Ministry

The most striking feature of Stephen's ministry, so far as this study is concerned, is not the fact that he seems (soon?) to have been spending more time working miracles and arguing with others (6.8-10).[69] The interest in 'signs and wonders' which Luke evinces through his narrative[70] may have been shared with or encouraged by a similar interest on the part of his Hellenist source (6.8; 8.6, 13). And no doubt, as already observed,[71] in the charismatic fervour of the early days there were many reports of amazing events ('extraordinary deeds') and wonderful healings. Stephen, who is repeatedly reported as being 'full of faith and the Holy Spirit' (6.5), 'full of grace and power' (6.8), 'full of the Holy Spirit' (7.55), and as speaking with irrefutable 'wisdom and Spirit' (6.10), is thus presented as the most sustainedly and effective charismatic figure in the whole of the NT! So it need hardly be doubted that Luke's portrayal of Stephen is drawn from the memory of a powerfully persuasive charismatic performer.

What is particularly of interest here, however, is that Stephen's mission of evangelism, or at any rate of dialogue and debate, seems to have been entirely within the circle of diaspora Jews — as indicated by the specific mention of the synagogue which served the bulk of the diaspora Jews resident in Jerusalem.[72] A point of possible confusion needs to be clarified at this point. For the term 'Hellenists' in 6.1 obviously refers to diaspora Jews who had come to faith in Jesus as

---

attempt to date the execution of Stephen to the interregnum following the recall to Rome of the prefect Pilate (36-37) would make the conversion of Paul 'impossibly late' (Barrett, *Acts* 1.381-82; similarly Pesch, *Apg.* 1.267; Fitzmyer, *Acts* 391, treats the suggestion more positively). But in any case, the prefect would not have been in Jerusalem at this time (the lynching did not take place during a pilgrim festival), so the Jerusalem garrison would have been relatively small (§23 at n. 4) and would not necessarily have thought it necessary to become involved in what would appear from their perspective to be a minor internal disturbance; at any rate, the Roman authorities seem to have taken little notice of Saul/Paul's subsequent persecution, once again, no doubt, regarding it as an internal matter without political ramifications. N. H. Taylor, 'Stephen, the Temple, and Early Christian Eschatology', *RB* 110 (2003) 62-85, favours a date at the time of the crisis caused by Caligula's attempt to have his statue erected in the Temple, but the 'bad fit' with what we know of the persecution following Stephen's death is even worse.

69. Löning suggests the historical likelihood that 'the circle of the Seven, headed by Stephen, played an active missionary role in Jerusalem from the very beginning' ('Circle of Stephen' 107).

70. See above, §21 at n. 132.

71. See above, §23.2g.

72. The main concentrations of Jews within the western diaspora were in precisely the territories indicated in 6.9 — Alexandria and Cyrenaica on the southern shores of the Mediterranean, Syria-Cilicia and Asia Minor on the northeast shores, and freedmen, most of whose slave ancestry would have achieved their liberty in Rome itself. See further below, §27 n. 181. On the famous Theodotus inscription see above, n. 30.

Messiah, that is, an inner-Christian referent. But 'Hellenists' = 'Greek-speakers' can refer to Greek-speakers more widely — Greek-speaking Jews presumably in 9.29, and Greek-speakers = Greeks, it would appear in Luke's (and the NT's) only other use of the term, in 11.20.[73] This reminds us that the Hellenists of 6.1 were only some (few or many?) of the diaspora Jews who had taken up residence in Jerusalem. The believing (Christian) Hellenists were only part of the larger group of Greek-speaking Jews who had returned from the diaspora. So what is indicated in 6.9 could properly be referred to as *an inner-Hellenist disputation*, a disputation presumably carried out in Greek, by and among those who could function effectively only in Greek.

From this we may further deduce that the disputation was not only caused by the fact that some of the diaspora Jews had become believers in Jesus Messiah but may have been occasioned also by tensions and disagreements within the Greek-speaking community in Jerusalem. Two possibilities call for mention. One is that there may have been something of a generation gap involved. I have already indicated that (the bulk of) the Greek-speakers had presumably returned from the diaspora, many/most of them to retire there in Jerusalem. In which case, the possibility arises that at least several families' younger members resented having been brought from some multicultural metropolis, on the Mediterranean or on some international trade route, to what was a very much out-of-the-way Jerusalem, easily despised by those more accustomed to the 'bright lights' of an Alexandria, Antioch, Ephesus, or Rome as a cultural back-water. All that we need further assume on this possibility is that Stephen was of a younger generation than most of the other Greek-speakers, and was something of a 'young Turk'. Of course, this is entirely speculation. But in the absence of more information some speculation is unavoidable if we are to gain a clearer picture.

The other possibility, which gains more credibility from the sequence, is that a major cause of tension between Stephen and his disputants was the Temple. For, of course, the primary reason why diaspora Jews would have returned to Jerusalem was to be near the Temple, if only to be buried in close proximity to the Temple.[74] Had there been generational tensions within the larger Hellenist community, therefore, they could easily focus on the Jerusalem Temple — resentment at the cause of the return from the diaspora. At all events, whatever the reasons and factors involved, what is in view is clearly a sharp and even bitter dispute within the ranks of the diaspora Jews settled in Jerusalem.

---

73. See further below, §24.8b.

74. 'Jerusalem was without doubt one of the most impressive and famous cities in the Roman empire, and even for pagans was surrounded with an almost "mystical" aura' (Hengel, *'Hellenization'* 13).

c. The Accusations against Stephen

Here we come to a further point of interest. For the resentment caused by Stephen's arguments, so Luke indicates, was not occasioned by a message which focused on Jesus' death and resurrection (as in the sermons of chs. 2–5). Rather the accusation was that Stephen 'was speaking blasphemous words against Moses and God' (6.11); 'this man never stops talking against (this) holy place and the law' (6.13).[75] The role Stephen is reported as attributing to Jesus of Nazareth was as the one who 'will destroy this place and change the customs which Moses handed down to us' (6.14).[76]

The echoes of the accusations brought against Jesus himself are manifest: that Jesus was heard saying he would destroy the Temple, that the accusation is attributed to 'false witnesses' (6.13),[77] and that he was accused of blasphemy (Mark 14.57-59, 64 par.). What is noticeable is that Luke omitted the first and last of these elements from his own account of Jesus' trial before the council (Luke 22.66-71). As elsewhere, Luke evidently chose to hold back these elements of the record of Jesus' trial in order to include them at this point.[78] The implications are clear: that Luke knew well the standard account of Jesus' trial circulating (not least in Mark's Gospel) among many Christian congregations, but also, more important here, that he nevertheless wanted to portray Stephen as accused of mounting the first full-blown attack on the Temple ('this holy place') and Moses.

Whether the blasphemy charge had in view anything equivalent to Mark 14.62 (which Luke 22.67-71 does not describe as 'blasphemy') is unclear. Certainly the dramatic close to the trial and execution of Stephen suggests that it did (7.55-56).[79] But the focus of the accusations in 6.13-14 is on the attack on 'this

75. 'These are new charges, which have not been levelled against the Twelve or other Christians up to this point in the Lucan story' (Fitzmyer, *Acts* 363-64).

76. On the possibility that in this paragraph Luke was drawing on two versions of what had happened, see Barrett, *Acts* 1.321, 380.

77. Attribution of the charge to false witnesses is an obvious way to devalue or undercut the opposition to Stephen; cf. Deut. 19.16-19; Pss. 27.12; 35.11; Prov. 24.28; classic are the cautionary tales of Naboth (1 Kings 21) and Susanna. See also G. N. Stanton, 'Stephen in Lucan Perspective', in E. A. Livingstone, ed., *Studia Biblica 1978.* Vol. 3 (JSNTS 3; Sheffield, JSOT, 1980) 345-60 (here 347-48), and K. Haacker, 'Die Stellung des Stephanus in der Geschichte des Urchristentums', *ANRW* 2.26.2 (1995) 1515-53 (here 1523-29). Haacker notes the possibility that an important element in the conflict round Stephen was the hostility of the Jerusalem priestly hierarchy towards what would appear to them as essentially a pious lay movement stemming from Galilee (1520-21).

78. See above, §21.2d(2).

79. B. Wander, *Trennungsprozesse zwischen Frühen Christentum und Judentum im 1. Jh. n. Chr* (Tübingen: Francke, 1994) 137-40.

holy place' (the Temple, as in Ps. 24.3). For residents in Jerusalem, especially those who had abandoned life in the diaspora precisely in order to be near the Temple, this would indeed be a kind of blasphemy, not to say a calling in question their own very reason for existence in the holy city. And since so much of the Mosaic legislation had to do with the functioning of the Temple and its cult, what was perceived as an attack on the Temple would certainly be perceived also as an attack on Moses and 'the customs that Moses handed down to us'.[80]

This raises a contentious issue: whether Stephen (and the Hellenists) had already engaged in a radical critique of the law. A positive answer is given by several commentators[81] on the basis that Saul/Paul persecuted Stephen's associates out of 'zeal for the law' (not quite what Paul says in Gal. 1.13-14 and Phil. 3.6); but as we shall see, Paul's language is rather more nuanced. And as we shall see more immediately, the speech attributed to Stephen also focuses his attack on the Temple and not on Moses.[82] So it is worth staying with the probability that the primary or most sensitive accusation against Stephen was that he criticized the Temple.[83]

80. Josephus also speaks of blasphemy against Moses (*War* 2.145); see also *Jesus Remembered* 751. 'It is self-evident that talk against Moses is also talk against God, so blasphemy' (Jervell, *Apg.* 226).

81. A strong strand of German scholarship takes this position, no doubt encouraged by such evidence of a precedent in what they take to be Paul's even more radical critique of the law; see, e.g., Bultmann, *Theology* 1.54-56, 109; Schmithals, *Paul and James* 25-27; Conzelmann, *History* 59; Hengel, already in his *Judaism and Hellenism* 1.313-14 = *Judentum und Hellenismus* (WUNT 10; Tübingen: Mohr Siebeck, ³1988) 569-70, and frequently assumed thereafter (as *passim* in Acts ch. 6), but more carefully in Hengel and Schwemer, *Paul* 88-89; Pesch, *Apg.* 1.239-40; Lüdemann, *Early Christianity* 78, 82, 85; Schenke, *Urgemeinde* 176-83; Wedderburn, *History* 49-54; 'it was the charismatic experience of the exalted Christ at the right hand of the Father, thus faith in the role of the Son of Man and Lord that challenged the Mosaic Law as the instrument of reconciliation, and thus determined the break with official Judaism' (Jossa, *Jews or Christians?* 82-84). Räisänen ('Hellenisten' 1473, 1485) and Jervell (*Apg.* 226-28) protest strongly against this view; see also Kraus, *Zwischen Jerusalem und Antiochia* 41-42; and Penner's critique of Hengel (*Praise* 23-29).

82. J. Carleton Paget, 'Jewish Christianity', *CHJ* 3.731-75, also points out that the *kai* in 6.14 could be epexegetic; 'that is, the phrase "and change the customs of Moses" could relate exclusively to what Jesus will do to the temple' (743).

83. K. Berger, *Theologiegeschichte des Urchristentums. Theologie des Neuen Testaments* (Tübingen: Francke, 1994) 140-42; Kraus, *Zwischen Jerusalem und Antiochia* 44-55. But against the view that the Hellenists (diaspora Jews) generally were more 'liberal' in regard to the law, Jervell rightly points out that such diaspora Jews 'were drawn to Jerusalem because of their faithfulness to the law' (*Apg.* 222, questioning those referred to in 216 n. 609). See also H. Räisänen, '"The Hellenists": A Bridge between Jesus and Paul?', *Jesus, Paul and Torah: Collected Essays* (JSNTS 43; Sheffield: JSOT, 1992) 149-202 (here 177); also 'Hellenisten' 1486-88; Barrett, *Acts* 1.337-38.

In fact, as we saw in *Jesus Remembered,* Acts 6.14 greatly strengthens the probability that Jesus was remembered as predicting the destruction of the Temple and, in some forms of the tradition, as speaking of his own role in that destruction.[84] The memory of Jesus having said something about the Temple's (imminent) destruction was still alive, and not simply among his followers. It is somewhat surprising, therefore, that the earliest Jerusalem congregations of Jesus messianists seem to have remained close to the Temple and to have continued regularly to attend and gather there.[85] In contrast, Stephen is remembered as having taken up what seems, therefore, to have been a neglected aspect of Jesus' teaching and brought it to the fore, and forceably.[86] Johannes Weiss may well have been on the right track when he claimed that 'Stephen thereby tore open a wound which the original disciples would gladly have seen healed over'.[87]

If so, such a critique of the Temple (as it would have been perceived to be) would be seen as directed against Stephen's own Greek-speaking community — but presumably also in some degree against his fellow Jesus-believers. This no doubt would be part of the reason for the epithet 'Hebrews' being used (by the Stephen faction within the Hellenists) against the more traditionally minded and practising believers of chs. 2–5. The epithet would be appropriate precisely in reference to those who saw themselves, and were seen by others, as remaining defiantly loyal to their traditions — among which, of course, continuing commitment to the Temple and its cult would be part.[88] In short, the history which may

84. See again *Jesus Remembered* 631-33.

85. See above, §23.2e and §23.5b.

86. Given Luke's own otherwise positive view of the Temple, and given that he goes out of his way to dismiss the accusations against Stephen as false, it is hardly likely that Luke has invented the accusation in the first place — much more likely that such accusations were remembered as part of the traditions about Stephen and that Luke attempts here (and in ch. 7) to set the record straight. Luke's defence of Stephen from these accusations as 'false' need not imply that Luke did not regard 7.44-48 as an attack on the Temple, as Stanton argues ('Stephen' 348, 351-52), only that Stephen's critique of the Temple (see at n. 124 below) was no more (but no less) weighty than that of Jesus himself.

87. Weiss, *Earliest Christianity* 168.

88. Could this be part of the reason why the accusations brought against both Jesus and Stephen are remembered as 'false witness' — that the tradition of Jesus speaking against the Temple was something of an embarrassment within the earliest Jerusalem community? We may again ask: would 'a great crowd of priests' have been attracted to a faith (6.7) which regarded the Temple as passé (see further Dunn, *Acts* 85)? As Esler points out: 'There is no hint in the text that the priests gave up their priesthood in becoming Christians' (*Community and Gospel* 140). 'The adhesion of so many priests would strengthen the ties which bound a large proportion of the believers to the temple order; this would heighten the tension between them and those Hellenists who shared Stephen's negative estimate of the temple' (Bruce, *Acts* 185). See also B. F. Meyer, *The Early Christians: Their World Mission and Self-Discovery* (Wilmington: Glazier, 1986) chs. 4-5.

be emerging seems to show a Stephen who may have been engaged in active disagreement on two fronts: both explicitly with his fellow Hellenists and implicitly, as a Hellenist, with 'the Hebrews' — and both on the same issue, of whether continuing loyalty to and participation in the Temple cult was being true to what Jesus himself had said (and done) in regard to the Temple.

The plot grows ever thicker.

d. Stephen's Death

The climax of the story of Stephen is his summary execution — the first Christian martyr (7.54-60). Here too the echo of Jesus' passion is clear and obviously deliberate on the part of Luke. Most striking is Stephen's final vision of Jesus, explicitly identified as 'the Son of Man', standing at the right hand of God (7.55-56). In other words, what Stephen sees is the fulfilment of the expectation attributed to Jesus at his trial ('from now on the Son of Man will be seated at the right hand of the power of God' — Luke 22.69 pars.).[89] Stephen's trial is not just an echo of Jesus' trial, but in effect it rounds off the business of Jesus' trial and demonstrates that Jesus' seemingly hopeless hope (in the circumstances of his arrest and trial) had indeed been wonderfully realized.[90]

Almost equally striking, however, are the strong resemblances between the final words of Stephen and those of Jesus, at least according to Luke, but not recalled by others:[91]

- Jesus: 'Father, into your hands I place my spirit' (Luke 23.46);
  Stephen: 'Lord Jesus, receive my spirit' (Acts 7.59)
- Jesus: 'Father, forgive them, for they don't know what they're doing' (Luke 23.34);[92]
  Stephen: 'Lord, do not hold this sin against them' (Acts 7.60).

Once again, this can hardly be coincidental: the manner of Stephen's death is a re-run of Jesus' death, the repetition serving to highlight what Luke regarded as

89. See *Jesus Remembered* §17.6.

90. The reason why Jesus is seen as '*standing* at the right hand of God' (7.55) is unclear — perhaps to speak on behalf of or even to welcome his dying disciple; Barrett (*Acts* 1.384-85) and Fitzmyer (*Acts* 392-93) review a range of suggestions; earlier discussion in Neudorfer, *Stephanuskries* 199-207, 283-87, 313-14. N. Chibici-Revneanu, 'Ein himmlischer Stehplatz. Die Haltung Jesu in der Stephanusvision (Apg 7.55-56) und ihre Bedeutung', *NTS* 53 (2007) 459-88, suggests that the portrayal is the result of the motif of the martyrs and suffering righteous in heaven being combined with the imagery of Ps. 110.1. See also below, n. 191.

91. See *Jesus Remembered* 779-80.

92. See again *Jesus Remembered* 780 n. 86.

the key features of both — namely, calmness and confidence in the face of hope-less odds, and a sure sense of God's overruling purpose. That Stephen appeals to the Lord Jesus, where Jesus had appealed to his Father, confirms that for Luke's Stephen Jesus had indeed been exalted to God's right hand and as the Son of Man could act as God's executive and plenipotentiary.

It is not possible to determine how much of this final scene is due to Luke's artistry. Certainly the points just noted would be evident only to those who knew the Gospels' passion narrative — not just any version of it, but only the one which Luke himself knew or crafted. So we can hardly attribute these points with any confidence to Luke's Hellenist rapporteur. But the martyrdom of Stephen is unlikely to have been a figment of Luke's imagination: martyrdom is too poi-gnant and sensitive a subject to be treated so lightly; the early martyrdoms are seen through a haze of hagiography (cf. 6.15),[93] but it would be a hard-hearted critic who denied that such martyrdoms took place. In fact, the parallel with Jesus' trial and death breaks down, in that while Luke depicts the hearing af-forded to Stephen as a formal session before the council (6.12), his execution is attributed to the fury of an uncontrolled mob (7.57-58).[94] Moreover, the recur-rence of one of the Hellenist fingerprints in 7.55 ('full [plērēs] of the Holy Spirit')[95] suggests strongly that Luke has here elaborated an account he received from his sources. And it would also be somewhat odd if Luke contrived a Son of Man reference at just this point and nowhere else.[96]

The issue is beyond firm proof. But when we put together the indications in the accusations brought against Stephen (§24.4c) with those in Stephen's death scene, the probability grows that something along the following lines lies at the historical heart of the Stephen episode: that Stephen was indeed remembered as taking up a neglected strand of Jesus' teaching (Jesus heralding the destruction of the Temple), one indeed which may well have caused some embarrassment for many in the earliest phase of the new movement; and that it was Stephen's persis-tence in emphasizing that element of Jesus' teaching which brought down upon

---

93. Cf., e.g., 2 Macc. 7; 4 Macc.; *Mart. Pol.;* the martyrs of Lyons and Vienne (Eusebius, *HE* 5.1.3-63).

94. Stoning is the penalty for blasphemy according to Lev. 24.11-16, 23; see further Fitzmyer, *Acts* 391, 393, who justifiably rebukes Haenchen (*Acts* 296) for 'naively' assuming that the Mishnaic regulations relating to execution by stoning (*m. Sanh.* 6.3-4) were already in operation.

95. Translations should observe such distinctiveness in vocabulary; contrast NRSV and Fitzmyer (*Acts* 392), who both translate 'filled with the Holy Spirit', as though the formulation was precisely the same as in 4.8 and 13.9.

96. Conceivably the elaboration of 'son of man' references in the Jesus tradition into the Son of Man references which we have in the Gospels was the work of Hellenist translators of the Aramaic tradition into Greek. See further below, §24.9a, b.

his head the murderous wrath of a community whose faith and livelihood focused entirely on the Temple.[97]

One remaining issue is also tantalizingly beyond firm conclusion. Luke records that 'a young man named Saul' was party to Stephen's execution (7.58) and that the same Saul thereafter took the lead in 'ravaging of the church' (8.3). That Saul/Paul was indeed in Jerusalem at the time is quite probable, and his own admissions as persecutor-in-chief of the Jesus-believers makes the initial episode plausible.[98] But Paul himself gives no hint of such early involvement, and the link to the sequel (Acts 9) which the episode provides is a little too convenient in the narrative sequence for us to be sure that there is more to it than that.[99] So we can only note its detail and move on to firmer ground.

But there is still one important element in the Stephen sequence which demands attention.

24.5. The Speech Attributed to Stephen

Luke has taken the opportunity to include a (relatively speaking) very long speech within the formal setting of Stephen's hearing before the council (6.12, 15). As with all the speeches in Acts, the question Where did Luke get this speech from? should not be ignored.[100]

a. A Hellenist Tract?

The comment has often been made by commentators on Acts and on its speeches that the speech attributed to Stephen fits its context poorly.[101] Apart from anything else, it goes on at such length before addressing the charges brought against Stephen, and then answers them only obliquely. But by now we should have ceased to think of an Acts speech as though it was (and was intended by Luke as) some kind of verbatim report of the events narrated — which is actually the mea-

---

97. The parallel with the summary execution of James the brother of Jesus in 62 is often noted; see below, §36.2.

98. Barrett wonders whether the (or an) account of Stephen's death attests the 'deep impression' made by Stephen's death on Saul (*Acts* 1.381). See further below, §25.2.

99. The assumption is common that Paul combines two separate traditions — the death of Stephen and the persecution by Paul (e.g., Jervell, *Apg.* 256).

100. See above, §21.3.

101. E.g., Haenchen, *Acts* 286-88; Barrett, *Acts* 1.335. The observations of Dibelius on what he saw as the irrelevance and pointlessness of the speech ('Speeches in Acts' 167-68) have been very influential; e.g., Haenchen, *Acts* 287-88. But see Penner, *Praise* 303-27.

sure by which so many judgments are made in regard to the speech's potential contribution to our knowledge of an episode like Stephen's. So what should we make of the speech in Acts 7?

On the one side it is important to recognize that the speech's rendering in Greek is crucial to the argument:

- 7.42b-43 = LXX of Amos 5.25-27, with 'beyond Damascus' replaced by 'beyond Babylon'.[102]
- In 7.45 the speech refers to *Iēsous,* the Greek rendering of 'Joshua', but in the speech the allusion to or foreshadowing of 'Jesus' is obvious.
- This strengthens the probability that the earlier reference to 'the *ekklēsia* in the wilderness' (7.38; cf. Deut. 9.10; 18.16; 23.1) is a similar allusion to and foreshadowing of the 'church'.
- And the still earlier note that God gave 'salvation *(sōtēria)* through his (Moses') hand' (7.25) gains a similarly pregnant overtone.

That Stephen could have sustained such a discourse only in Greek (being a Hellenist = Greek-speaker) is, of course, hardly surprising. But it is hardly plausible that any such formal hearing before a *synedrion* in Jerusalem was conducted in Greek or that a judicial body allowed themselves to be addressed at such length in Greek.[103] Moreover, as several have shown,[104] Luke has certainly put the speech into his own words.[105] So it is hardly likely that the whole speech as such was derived from some memory or record of the proceedings.

On the other side, there are various indications that the speech is hardly Luke's own.

- Its content is unique in Acts, it is much longer than his usual speeches, it is hardly overtly Christian till the end, and even then it lacks the usual call for repentance and faith.

102. Details in Haenchen, *Acts* 284 and n. 1; Barrett, *Acts* 1.368-71.

103. 'Nobody will maintain that Stephen sought to persuade the High Council with a LXX text which diverges widely from the Hebrew' (Haenchen, *Acts* 289). Note also a further marked difference with the trial of Jesus, which is recorded with extreme brevity.

104. E. Richard, *Acts 6:1–8:4: The Author's Method of Composition* (SBLDS 41; Missoula: Scholars, 1978). Worth considering, however, is the possibility that Luke derived one of his own favourite phrases ('signs and wonders') from this source. For 'signs and wonders' were a marked feature of Moses' rescue of his people (particularly Exod. 7.3; cf. Ps. 105.27) and a regular feature of retellings of Moses' story (e.g., *Jub.* 48.4, 12).

105. As Hengel notes: 'The ancient historian took pride in so reshaping his sources that his model could no longer be recognized, and the mark of his own individual style emerged all the more clearly' (*Between Jesus and Paul* 4).

- It contains features which read like a somewhat unorthodox account of Israel's history — particularly the burial of Abraham, Isaac and Jacob in Shechem (Samaria) rather than in Hebron, as Israel's official history recorded (7.16).[106]
- The lack of any hint of anxiety over circumcision ('the covenant of circumcision' — 7.8) reflects a period prior to Paul.[107]
- The allusion in 7.46-47 to 2 Sam. 7.1-14 indicates a link with the accusations against both Jesus and Stephen.[108]
- And not least, the denunciation of the Temple in 7.48 runs quite counter to Luke's otherwise consistently positive appraisal of the Temple.[109]

The best explanation of both sets of data is probably that Luke was able to use a Hellenist source, perhaps a Hellenist tract, which expressed a Hellenist view of Israel's history and of the Temple in particular.[110] This would be wholly

106. According to Gen. 49.30-31 and 50.13 the place of burial of the patriarchs was at Machpelah, that is, modern Hebron. Possibly there has been some confusion between Gen. 23.3-20 and Gen. 33.19, correlated with the record of Joseph's burial at Shechem in Josh. 24.32 (discussion in Barrett, *Acts* 1.351). Alternatively, the speech here may be following a variant tradition of the Samaritans, which claimed that the sacred burial site was Shechem (in Samaria!). In which case we would have a further indication that the speech or tract was shaped by Samaritan tradition subsequent to Philip's successful mission — another chapter in the account which Hellenists gave of their own doings and to which Luke was given access. In 7.32 the plural 'your fathers' is also in accord with the Samaritan Pentateuch rather than the Hebrew and LXX ('your father'). The expectation of a 'prophet like Moses' was prominent in Samaritan theology (see below, §24.7b and n. 170). Scharlemann conveniently summarizes 'the Samarian overtones in Stephen's discourse' (*Stephen* 50). But the suggestion of a distinctively Samaritan source is now generally dismissed (see particularly K. Haacker, 'Samaritan, Samaria', *NIDNTT* 3.464-66, and G. Schneider, 'Stephanus, die Hellenisten und Samaria', in Kremer, ed., *Les Actes des Apôtres* 215-40; also *Apg.* 1.412-13; also, e.g., Bruce, *Acts* 191, 196; Barrett, *Acts* 1.361; Fitzmyer, *Acts* 368).

107. Contrast Paul's insistence that God's *earlier* dealings were decisive in Romans 4: Gen. 15.6 is not referred to here; and Paul would have hesitated to describe the promise given to Abraham as 'the covenant of circumcision'. Contrast *Jub.* 15.25-34.

108. See below, n. 122.

109. Luke 1.8-23; 2.22-38, 41-50; 24.53; Acts 2.46; 3.1; 5.42 (*pace* Taylor, 'Stephen' 73-74). See further below, §24.5b.

110. Fitzmyer is typical of a moderate consensus: 'In its present form it is certainly a Lucan composition, but it builds on inherited tradition, possibly Antiochene' (*Acts* 365); similarly Wilckens, *Theologie* 1/2.236; Hengel, somewhat surprisingly, thinks that a connection directly with Stephen and the Hellenists is 'extremely dubious', though perhaps he gives too much weight to the 'directly' (*Between Jesus and Paul* 19); Jervell briefly reviews attempts to distinguish Lukan redaction (*Apg.* 249-50); Lüdemann confidently discerns Lukan redaction and sees no need to discuss the traditions or history behind the speech (*Early Christianity* 86-89); similarly, Hill regards the speech as a Lukan composition (following Richard), which al-

in line with the historiographical practice of the time.[111] And since Stephen was remembered as a leading Hellenist and as having suffered martyrdom for his attitude to 'the holy place', that would no doubt have been ground enough for the speech to be regarded as representative of the views which had brought about Stephen's death.[112]

What, then, should we make of the speech and its awkwardness in the sequence of Acts 6–7?

b. The Purpose of the Speech

The speech belongs to a familiar genre: the rehearsal of the (sacred) history which has formed a people's identity and self-understanding. The story, particularly the story of its beginnings, says what the people is, how it is constituted, what it stands for. Virgil's *Aeneid* did this for the Rome of Augustus. The story of Muhammed plays the same role for Islam. The account of the Pilgrim Fathers and the Declaration of Independence have the same significance for the United States of America. Similarly for Israel. The telling and retelling of the story of the patriarchs, the exodus and the wilderness wanderings constitute Israel's identity. That is why so much of the Torah (the Law) is in the form of story, why the principal feast of Passover is actually a reliving the story of the foundation event of the exodus. Recognition of this fact is vital to a proper understanding of Stephen's speech in Acts 7. Some have thought it a rather dull rehearsal of Israel's early history. They fail to appreciate the power of the story of origins.

The key to understanding the speech attributed to Stephen, then, is to note the way Israel's story is told by the speech — where it concentrates, and what it adds or omits. Since the story has such power to express and define Israel's identity (so already Deut. 6.20-24 and 26.5-9), a careful retelling can reinforce that identity or reshape that identity. Thus, for example, the retelling of Neh. 9.6-31 encourages a proper sense of penitence before the covenant God, and the retellings of Psalms 105 and 106 re-create a spirit of devotion to the covenant God. The retelling by the book of *Jubilees* (written about 150 BCE) reinforces a strict interpretation of the Law and abhorrence of Gentile practices. And the retelling in visionary guise in the dream visions of *1 Enoch* 83-90 (some time before

---

lows no possibility of deriving a coherent pre-Lukan theology from it (*Hellenists and Hebrews* 50-101). The debate is reviewed in Penner, *Praise* 86-90.

111. See again §21.3.

112. 'The most probable explanation . . . is that Luke gives us, in outline, a "Hellenist" sermon, the sort of sermon that might be preached in a "Hellenist", Diaspora synagogue, and could easily be taken over and used when Hellenist Jews became Hellenist Jewish Christians' (Barrett, *Acts* 1.338).

Jubilees) encourages a sense of trust in the overarching and climactic purpose of God. So with the retelling of Acts 7. Perhaps the closest parallel in terms of selectivity and *Tendenz* is the Essene reading of Israel's history in CD 2.14–6.2.

Analysis of Stephen's speech indicates a double theme.

(1) The rejection of God's servants — Joseph (7.9), Moses (7.23-29, 35, 39) and the prophets (7.52) — finds its climax in the rejection of (Jesus)[113] 'the Righteous One' (7.52).[114] This is fully in line with the repeated emphasis of the earlier speeches.[115] In particular, the 'but God' of 7.9 echoes the 'but God' of 2.24. And the emphasis on the hope of a prophet like Moses (7.37) echoes the same hope in 3.22-23. On this point Stephen has said nothing worse or more challenging than Peter and John before him.[116] More provocative, however, is the second theme woven into the first and given more prominence.

(2) The rejection of the Temple as necessary to guarantee God's presence. There are several striking features of the speech here.

(i) The bulk of the speech focuses on the period prior to the entry into the promised land and the building of the Temple (7.2-46). In the course of the retelling, the emphasis is made repeatedly that God was with them, outside the promised land. He appeared to Abraham in Mesopotamia (7.2). Abraham himself had no inheritance in the land (7.5).[117] God was with Joseph in Egypt (7.9). God appeared to Moses at Mount Sinai, on holy land far from the promised land (7.30-33), and gave the congregation (*ekklēsia*, 'church') in the wilderness 'living oracles' (7.38). The implication of this telling of Israel's story is clear: promised land or sacred site is not necessary to ensure the presence of God with his people.[118]

(ii) Conversely, a direct line is drawn from the sin of the golden calf at Sinai (7.41) to the worship of the host of heaven (7.42),[119] for which Amos blamed the Babylonian exile (7.42-43). These two episodes were regarded within Israel

---

113. 'Luke aligns Stephen carefully *with* Moses: Stephen, like Moses, the prophets, Jesus (and Paul) is rejected by part of Israel' (Stanton, 'Stephen' 349).

114. This is an early way of speaking of Jesus, though not exclusive to Hellenist believers (3.14; 22.14).

115. Acts 2.23; 3.13-15; 4.10; 5.30.

116. See further Stanton, 'Stephen' 354-57; H. A. Brehm, 'Vindicating the Rejected One: Stephen's Speech as a Critique of the Jewish Leaders', in C. A. Evans and J. A. Sanders, eds., *Early Christian Interpretation of the Scriptures of Israel* (JSNTS 148; Sheffield: Sheffield Academic, 1997) 266-99.

117. 'So Abraham becomes a wanderer, and the reader learns that the worship of God is not tied to any individual place' (Fitzmyer, *Acts* 366).

118. Cf. Löning, 'Circle of Stephen' 111. See also G. E. Sterling, '"Opening the Scriptures": The Legitimation of the Jewish Diaspora and the Early Christian Mission', in Moessner, ed., *Jesus and the Heritage of Israel* 199-225.

119. God 'handed them over (*paredōken*)' to idolatry — the very language Paul uses in Rom. 1.24-25.

as the two lowest points of Israel's story, the nadir of Israel's failures.[120] Stephen's speech in effect ignores all the history of the settlement in Canaan and the monarchy and sums up the span of Israel's intervening history by these two nadir points. Israel's worship has always been flawed.[121]

(iii) These two points, the one more implicit, the other almost explicit, are summed up in the penultimate paragraph (7.44-50). The period of the wilderness, and of God's presence with them in the wilderness, was encapsulated in 'the tent of testimony' (e.g., Exod. 27.21), which had been made in accordance with the heavenly blueprint (7.44; Exod. 25.40). That focus for divine presence had continued right through the reign of Israel's greatest king, David (7.45-46).[122] The subsequent building of the Temple by Solomon (7.47) was fundamentally misconceived, or embodied a false perception of God (7.48-50).[123] What transforms the proper deference of Solomon in 1 Kgs. 8.27, and of Isa. 66.1-2 cited in 7.49-50, into a more radical critique is the fact that the Temple is described in more or less the same terms as those used for the golden calf in 7.41.[124] In such a context 'made with hands' is an astonishing term to find in a Jewish description of the Jerusalem Temple, for *to cheiropoiēton* was Hellenistic Judaism's dismissive description of 'the idol'.[125] The implied criticism is hard to avoid: the attitude of Stephen's accusers to the Temple was nothing short of idolatrous![126]

120. Jer. 7.18; 19.13; Amos 5.25; Wis. 14.12-27; Rom. 1.24-25; 1 Cor. 10.7-9.

121. Cf. Simon, *St. Stephen* 48-56: 'the idolatry of the royal period is rooted in, and is in continuity with, the idolatry already initiated in the wilderness' (56).

122. The allusion in 7.46-47 to 2 Sam. 7.1-14 links with the idea of an eschatologically rebuilt Temple (4Q174 [4Q Flor] 1.10-12) and thus evokes the same circle of thought that is implied in the accusations against both Jesus (Mark 14.58) and Stephen (Acts 6.14); see further *Jesus Remembered* 448, 620 and n. 20.

123. Cf. W. Manson, *The Epistle to the Hebrews* (London: Hodder and Stoughton, 1951), who over-interprets the contrast: 'The mobile sanctuary of the early days corresponds with the idea of the ever-onward call of God to His people, the static temple does not'; 'Israel has been tempted to identify its salvation with historical and earthly securities and fixtures, and Stephen cannot but see the same danger in the attitude of the "Hebrew" brethren in the Church' (35).

124. 7.41 — 'the idol, the works of their hands *(to eidōlon, ta erga tōn cheirōn autōn)*'; 7.48 — 'the Most High does not dwell in what is made with hands *(en cheiropoiētois)*'. Note the echo of the language used in Deut. 4.28, Ps. 115.4, Jer. 1.16 and Wis. 13.10; also the contrast between what *God* has made ('my hand', *hē cheir mou* — 7.50) and what is *man*-made *(cheiropoiēton); and to 7.41 add 19.26.

125. Lev. 26.1, 30; Isa. 2.18; 10.11; etc.; Dan. 5.4, 23; Jdt. 8.18; Wis. 14.8; Philo, *Mos.* 1.303; 2.165, 168 (though Philo does not hesitate to speak of the Temple in the same context as *cheiropoiēton* — *Mos.* 2.88); *Sib. Or.* 3.605-606, 722; 4.28a; see also, e.g., Ps. 115.4 and Isa. 2.8. In the LXX *cheiropoiētos* almost always stands for the Hebrew *'elil,* on which see H. D. Preuss, *'elil, TDOT* 1.285-87.

126. 'Stephen's words would have had a blasphemous ring for Jews' (Haenchen, *Acts*

In the final climactic sentence the two themes come together (7.51-53): their failure to acknowledge Jesus is of a piece with their idolatrous attitude to the Temple.[127] Far from being faithful to their law, their misconception of both Temple and Jesus was a failure both to keep the law and to hear the Holy Spirit.

This is the retelling of Israel's story which Stephen's speech expresses. The Holy Spirit and Jesus, appearing at the climactic point (7.51-52), reinforce Luke's repeated emphasis that these two are the central features of the new Christian sect.[128] The sovereign purpose of God directing affairs is a still more constant theme.[129] But now in addition, or in contrast, the continuity which the Temple had provided is radically questioned, and the line of continuity begins to be redefined — particularly in terms of a God who is known to his people in lands afar and without dependence on the holy place of the Temple as such. Not only so, but there seems to be something of a recoil from the continued devotion which the first believers had continued to pay through and by attending the Temple. The Temple is presented, not least by contrast to the mobile tent, as a serious hindrance and embodiment of a false perception of God's presence. The way is thus prepared for the next phase in the Christian mission (Acts 8), itself occasioned by the expulsion of the followers of Stephen from Jerusalem. That this retelling of Israel's story is from a Hellenist perspective, part of the Antioch church's explanation and justification for its existence (outside the land), is an obvious corollary.

---

285). 'To associate such language with the Temple must have been highly offensive in Jewish ears' (Barrett, *Acts* 1.373, and further 374). 'This misguided act has made Yahweh like a heathen idol' (Fitzmyer, *Acts* 367, 384). 'The unmistakable association of the language in 7:41 (making idols "with their hands") with 7:48 (the temple made "with human hands") undermines the numerous attempts by scholars to avoid the serious (and seemingly un-Lukan) association of the temple with idolatry' (Penner, *Praise* 98). In resisting this corollary, E. Larsson, 'Temple-Criticism and the Jewish Heritage: Some Reflexions on Acts 6–7', *NTS* 39 (1993) 379-95, observes that such a condemnatory note would fall on the tent as well as the Temple (391); but against the Temple as *cheiropoiētos* (7.48) Luke sets the tent as made 'according to the pattern he [Moses] had seen [on Sinai]' (7.44). Hill equally ignores the tie between 7.41 and 7.48 (*Hellenists and Hebrews* 69-81).

127. Haenchen is hardly justified in describing the speech as an 'anti-Jewish diatribe' (*Acts* 290), since it is mostly uncontroversial, and its climax echoes some of the Scriptures' own summary of Israel's earlier failures (Exod. 33.3, 5; Num. 27.14; 1 Kgs. 19.10, 14; 2 Chron. 36.16; Neh. 9.26; Isa. 63.10); the accusation of 'uncircumcised hearts and ears' (7.51) is drawn from, e.g., Lev. 26.41 and Jer. 6.10; the rejection of the prophets (7.52) is a common theme in Jewish thought (details in Fitzmyer, *Acts* 385; *Jesus Remembered* 417 n. 184; see also "The Lives of the Prophets," in *OTP* 2.385-99); and invective of one faction against others is hardly strange within Second Temple Judaism (e.g., 1QS 2.4-10; CD 8.4-10; *Pss. Sol.* 1.8; 2.3; 8.12). But 7.48, following on so closely to 7.41, does give a distinctive edge to the critique here.

128. As I noted above, particularly §22.3d.

129. Acts 7.2, 6-7, 9, 17, 25, 32, 35, 37, 42, 45-46. See above, §21 n. 82.

So far as the theology of the speech is concerned, a final point is worth noting. For all that the speech seems to criticize the Temple, it does not criticize the law.[130] Moses is presented as the hero of Israel's story: nearly half the speech is devoted to him.[131] The promise to Abraham was fulfilled in the time of Moses (7.17). Moses is presented as one specially favoured by God (7.20); he 'was instructed in all the wisdom of the Egyptians and was powerful in words and deeds' (7.22);[132] he brought salvation *(sōtēria)* to God's people (7.25); God sent him as both 'ruler and liberator' to Israel (7.35); he provides the prophet pattern for the Christ (7.37). It was an angel that spoke with him on Mount Sinai; the law he received there is described as 'living oracles' (7.38).[133] The law was not at issue between Stephen and his accusers; their failure was not devotion to the law but failure to keep it (7.52-53). In short, so far as Luke was concerned, there was no breach over the law at this stage. That would come later (Acts 15).

c. The Speech as Testimony to the Crisis Occasioned by Stephen

The most striking consequence of the analysis just conducted is that the speech can now be seen to complement the rest of Luke's story of Stephen. Also we can see that the two chapters (Acts 6 and 7) provide confirmation of the deductions being drawn independently of each.

(1) Stephen was remembered as a charismatic figure within the Greek-speaking (diaspora) community in Jerusalem, one who incensed the more tra-

---

130. Schneider, *Apg.* 1.416; S. G. Wilson, *Luke and the Law* (SNTSMS 50; Cambridge: Cambridge University, 1983) 62-63; Pesch, *Apg.* 1.247; Berger, *Theologiegeschichte* 146-47; Haacker, 'Stephanus' 1533-34. See also n. 81 above.

131. The speech 'can be described as "Moseocentric" much more than Christocentric' (Simon, *St. Stephen* 45).

132. 7.22 has no parallel in Exodus but represents well the sort of glorification of Moses which was a feature of Jewish, particularly Hellenistic (or diaspora) Jewish, apologetic in that period, as exemplified by Artapanus and Eupolemus; see J. J. Collins, *Between Athens and Jerusalem: Jewish Identity in the Hellenistic Diaspora* (New York: Crossroad, 1983) ch. 1; and further J. G. Gager, *Moses in Greco-Roman Paganism* (SBLMS 16; Nashville: Abingdon, 1972) ch. 1; also D. C. Allison, *The New Moses: A Matthean Typology* (Edinburgh: Clark, 1993), particularly ch. 2. Barrett refers to Philo, *Mos.*, Ezekiel's *Exagoge* and the paintings in the synagogue of Dura-Europos (*Acts* 1.338). That Moses was 'a powerful speaker' runs counter to Exod. 4.10-16 — and contrasts with Paul (2 Cor. 10.10)!

133. That is, also, 'oracles for life/living' (Deut. 30.15-20; 32.47). As elsewhere in both Jewish and Christian tradition, the participation of angels in the giving of the law is a wholly positive motif (7.53; Deut. 33.2 LXX; *Jub.* 1.29–2.1; Josephus, *Ant.* 15.136; Heb. 2.2; cf. Gal. 3.19).

ditionally minded of that community by vigorously reviving Jesus' critique of the Temple, or at least Jesus' prediction of the Temple's imminent destruction.[134]

(2) The furore aroused by Stephen was primarily an inner-Greek-speaking-diaspora-Jewish one within Jerusalem. On such a contentious subject, however, where the Temple was so vital to both Jerusalemites' identity and livelihood, it would hardly be surprising that the passions of the Jerusalem mob were quickly inflamed and that Stephen was executed as an outcome of popular outrage at what he seemed to stand for.

(3) The break and contrast between Acts 2–5 and Acts 6–7 also suggest that Stephen and his views posed serious questions to the main body of Jesus-believers in Jerusalem ('the Hebrews').[135] The contrast is evident both in the attitudes to the Temple, but also in the different outcomes of defiance of the authorities in council *(synedrion)*. If Stephen had been as outspoken as 6.9-10 and 7.51-53 indicate, did the recognized leaders of the new sect wholly approve (cf. 4.19-20; 5.29)? Did they try to intervene on Stephen's behalf — or did the crisis unfold too rapidly for them to become involved?[136] To entitle the episode 'the first schism' within the Christian movement[137] is certainly over-bold, but can the possibility, even likelihood, be excluded that Stephen's views put him out of favour not only with the non-believing Hellenists but with the believing Hebrews as well?[138] This is a possibility which could shed light on the next sequence of events in the history of infant Christianity.

---

134. '. . . a towering theological genius endowed with prophetic insights that turned out to be too revolutionary for general acceptance' (Scharlemann, *Stephen* 187-88).

135. If Stanton is correct in his insistence that the focus of the speech attributed to Stephen is on the fact that the Most High does not dwell in the Temple (7.48) ('Stephen' 352; followed by Haacker, 'Stephanus' 1538), then it still amounts to a critique of fellow believers who continued to be bound to the Temple.

136. It is curious that Luke does not specify who buried Stephen, beyond describing them as 'devout men' (8.2). That certainly refers to devout Jews who would regard the burial of an executed or unclaimed corpse as an act of piety (cf. Luke 23.50-53). But does he mean any of the 'Hebrews' or 'Hellenists' of 6.1? Inserting the notice *(after* 8.1) suggests that he did not intend his readers to identify them as believers in Jesus. ('Since, according to Luke all the Christians have fled, it can only be "devout" non-Christian Jews who now bury Stephen' [Haenchen, *Acts* 294].) But, again given 8.1, why not the apostles?! Barrett notes that 'the church' of v. 3 stands in close connection with the devout men of v. 2, but 'there is no attempt to relate them to each other' (*Acts* 1.393).

137. See n. 51 above.

138. Jervell does not reckon sufficiently with this likelihood (*Apg.* 245).

24.6. The First Persecution — against Whom Was It Directed?

Luke reports that Stephen's execution was the beginning of 'a great persecution against the church in Jerusalem', the result being that 'everyone was scattered throughout the countryside of Judea and Samaria, except the apostles' (8.1). This verse forms a kind of headline, to be followed by more precise detail: the burial of and lamentation for Stephen (8.2); the description of Saul's persecution — punitive house raids, men and women being hauled off to prison (8.3);[139] and the much fuller description of the initial consequences of the dispersion to Samaria (8.4-25).

An oddity in the headline verse immediately catches the eye: Luke's assertion that 'the apostles' were untouched by the persecution, despite the ferocity indicated in 8.3. What attempt to repress a movement, and to do so with such ferocity, would leave the leadership of the movement unscathed? Such a policy of repression, persecution and pogrom was hardly new in the ancient world, and its tactics were well rehearsed and practised. The first rule was (and is!) almost invariably to 'take out' the leaders, to lop off the heads of the tallest poppies and leave the rest leaderless,[140] that is, much less effective and/or more vulnerable to the policy of repression (cf. 12.1-4). It is hard to imagine a policy such as that indicated in 8.3 which did not make 'the apostles' a priority target.[141]

Conceivably the apostles could have sheltered with friends and sympathizers. But Luke's account envisages a clean sweep ('everyone'), which simply highlights more sharply the oddity of his account: that the persecution succeeded in targeting everyone else (at least in that it drove them from Jerusalem) *except* the apostles; they were the *only* ones exempted! Alternatively, we no doubt should in some degree discount Luke's 'everyone' as a characteristic Lukan hyperbole.[142] That is to say, the persecution may have caused a significant, even mass exodus of Jesus-believers from Jerusalem, but by no means all members of or sympathizers with the new sect left Jerusalem.[143] Even so, the fact that 'the

139. 'The fierceness of the language here ('was ravaging the church'; cf. 2 Chron. 16.10 and Ps. 80.13) matches the fierceness of Paul's own recollection (Gal. 1.13; cf. Acts 9.21; 22.4; 26.10-11)' (Dunn, *Acts* 106); see also Lake and Cadbury, *Beginnings* 4.88; Barrett, *Acts* 1.393.

140. The allusion is to Livy, *Hist.* 1.54, recalling Herodotus's account of Thrasybulus in his *Hist.* 5.92.

141. '. . . impossible to understand' (Simon, *St. Stephen* 27); Luke's assertion is 'false and impossible' (Jervell, *Apg.* 257). Fitzmyer, however, apparently sees no problem (*Acts* 397).

142. E.g., Luke 4.15, 22, 28, 36-37; 5.17; 6.17, 19; Acts 2.5, 47; there is an interesting and significant parallel in Acts 18.2 — few think that 'all Jews' were ordered to leave Rome (see below, §28.1b at n. 40). Barrett quotes Calvin: 'It is certain that they were not all scattered' (*Acts* 1.391).

143. Cf. Bauckham, 'James and the Jerusalem Church' 428-29; followed by Schnabel, *Mission* 671. Barnett insists that Acts 8.1 'should be taken to mean that both "Hebrews" and

apostles' escaped scot-free remains a puzzle, especially as Luke makes no attempt to attribute their being so unscathed to divine intervention (cf. 5.19;
16.26).[144]

The implausibility of the scenario sketched by Luke encourages a quest for
an alternative.

We can start from a sure base: that there was a persecution directed against
the new sect. Paul's own ready confession that he himself had persecuted and attempted to destroy the church of God (Gal. 1.13; 1 Cor. 15.9) puts the matter beyond dispute. Paul himself does not specify the locale of his persecution, and
there is some dispute on the matter. His claim to be 'unknown by sight to the
churches of Judea' (Gal. 1.22) could be taken to mean that he was not involved in
any persecution in Judea itself, [145] or that the targets of his persecution were Hellenists, who generally fled beyond Judea. On the other hand, Paul immediately
goes on to report what the Judean churches said when they heard of his conversion: 'He who was once *our* persecutor now preaches the faith he once tried to
destroy' (1.23 my emphasis).[146] A persecution within Judea, directed by Saul/
Paul but involving minimal face-to-face contact with those affected, is probably
the best explanation.

That such a persecution was directed from Jerusalem is also likely. Saul, as

----

"Hellenists" were driven out' (*Birth* 73), but had earlier noted that 'the church in Jerusalem appears to be an increasingly "Hebrew" church, whereas the "Hellenists" in Israel more or less
disappear from sight' (67).

144. Haenchen also notes the impression of some confusion in Luke's narrative indicated by his insertion of 9.31 (a church at peace and growing) between the two references to
'those scattered' by the persecution in 8.4 and 11.19 (*Acts* 266).

145. Gal. 1.22 ('I was still unknown by sight to the churches of Judea') is hardly sufficient grounds either to deny that Saul had spent time in Jerusalem and had been well known
there, or to affirm that his persecuting activity must have been outside Judea (*pace*
R. Bultmann, 'Paul' [1930], *Existence and Faith* [London: Collins Fontana, 1964] 130-72 [here
131]; J. Knox, *Chapters in a Life of Paul* [London: SCM, 1950, ²1989] 22; G. Bornkamm, *Paul*
[London: Hodder and Stoughton, 1969] 15; Haenchen, *Acts* 297-98, 625; Becker, *Paul* 38-39).
It is hardly difficult to envisage circumstances where followers of Jesus did not know him
(Hengel, *Pre-Christian Paul* 23-24; K.-W. Niebuhr, *Heidenapostel aus Israel* [WUNT 62;
Tübingen: Mohr Siebeck, 1992] 58-59), or where a persecution of Hellenists (causing them to
flee beyond Judea) left the more traditional churches of Judea largely unscathed. So also
Murphy-O'Connor, *Paul: A Critical Life* (Oxford: Clarendon, 1996) 54; Hengel and
Schwemer, *Paul* 37-38; Kraus, *Zwischen Jerusalem und Antioch* 32-33. See further my
Galatians 81.

146. If Hellenists were the target and not Judeans, then Gal. 1.22 attests a striking sense
of unity between the Judean churches and the persecuted Hellenists; in the perspective of the
Judean churches, he who persecuted (Hellenist) believers was 'our persecutor'. Wilckens
points out that when Paul recalled persecuting 'the church of God' (Gal. 1.13), he would have
meant (or included) the early community in Jerusalem (*Theologie* 1/2.242-43).

a Pharisee, would see Jerusalem as his natural base.[147] Such early disquiet among Temple authorities at the new sect's claims, as is indicated in Acts 4–5, would certainly have been deepened by a Stephen taking up Jesus' predictions regarding the Temple. And if the views expressed in the speech of Acts 7 do represent Hellenist believers' attitude to the Temple, then the same logic as had impelled the action against Jesus himself would presumably have been applied with redoubled force: the removal of Jesus himself from the scene had not dampened down what would be too easily represented as dangerous anti-Temple rhetoric. Moreover, whereas the counsel of a leading Pharisee like Gamaliel may have tempered and restrained more ruthless action against the new sect, at least as led by Peter and John (Acts 5.33-39), the emergence of a much more radical voice from within the sect of the Pharisees — even one of Gamaliel's own pupils (22.3)! — could have greatly strengthened the hands of the 'hawks' in the high-priestly-dominated council. In short, a policy of vigorous repression, initially at least directed by Saul from within Jerusalem, and directed against the resurgence of Jesus' perceived attack on the Temple, can be readily envisaged on good historical grounds and with very plausible historical speculation.[148]

This line of thought may go some way to explain the anomalous 'all were scattered . . . except the apostles' (8.1), from which this section started. For I have already noted the likelihood that the information on which Luke drew for this section of his narrative originated from Hellenist sources and expressed a Hellenist perspective. So it could be that the 'all/everyone' expresses the same perspective and had primary reference to those who actually bore the brunt of the persecution — the Hellenists whom Stephen represented and for whom Stephen spoke (or was thought to speak).[149] The original leaders of the new sect ('the apostles'), on the other hand, were seen to live in continuing attachment to the Temple and so were not targeted in the wave of persecution. The sequel, at least as told by Luke, seems to bear out these speculations: the person who takes the next decisive step forward is not one of 'the apostles' but one of those scattered by the persecution — indeed, Philip, one of the seven (Hellenist leaders) appointed in 6.5 and presumably, therefore, perceived as a collaborator with Stephen; whereas 'the apostles' remain in Jerusalem, apparently untroubled by any of the persecution and able to meet, take counsel and act on that counsel (8.14).[150]

147. See below, §25.1f.
148. On Saul's persecution and its rationale, see below, §25.2. It is most curious that Hill's discussion of the 'severe persecution' referred to in Acts 8.1b takes no account whatsoever of Gal. 1.13-14 (*Hellenists and Hebrews* 32-39); see also Räisänen's critique of Hill ('Hellenisten' 1476).
149. Haenchen, however, thinks that only the Hellenist leaders left the city (*Acts* 297).
150. Bauckham sees Luke's main point to be that 'the persecution did not bring their

In the light of these considerations, and the clues and hints followed up through the last two sections (§§24.4-5), a plausible scenario emerges with some strength. (1) The Hellenist believers in Jerusalem were distinctive within the wider body of the new sect. They presumably operated only in Greek. Their worship and life together would have been in some measure apart from the bulk of other believers. The seven chosen to deal with the crisis over distribution from the common fund may already have been their *de facto* leaders. (2) Within the ranks of the Jesus-Messiah Hellenists, there was a marked reaction against the Temple, as the (continuing) focus of God's presence. This negative attitude was typified and probably articulated most forceably by Stephen. (3) These views were not shared by those whom the Hellenist believers classified as 'Hebrews'. The very title suggests that Hellenists like Stephen would have regarded the Hebrew believers as traditionalist and backward looking, and not least in their attitude to and continued participation in the Temple cult. In other words, we should probably recognize a marked divide, even gulf, in understanding and sympathy opening up between 'the Hebrews' and the Hellenists represented by Stephen. (4) Consequently, when Stephen's views resulted in his being summarily executed, it may be that the Hebrews were not altogether surprised and even that they had no desire to defend the views he had argued for.

All this builds up to the probable answer to the question at the head of this section: when the persecution followed, it was primarily directed against the Greek-speaking followers of Stephen and not against the new sect as a whole.[151] Those who fled from Jerusalem may well have included more than just 'the Hellenists'. But it should occasion no surprise if a diaspora Saul directed his main zeal against other diaspora Jews, whom he would presumably have seen as at the polar opposite end of the spectrum from his own excessive zeal for the traditions of the ancestors (Gal. 1.14).[152] Moreover, the testimony of Paul, as well as Luke, is that subsequently Jerusalem became the bastion of conservative opinion and practice within the new sect (Gal. 2.12; Acts 21.20), which must mean that however indiscriminate the initial persecution within Jerusalem itself, 'the Hebrews' were able to return to Jerusalem and to continue operating there, in continuing attachment to the Temple and (most of) 'the customs that Moses handed down', and that it was only 'the Hebrews' and not 'the Hellenists' who returned in any strength to Jerusalem.

In short, the most likely conclusion is that the initial persecution was in effect

---

[the apostles'] leadership of the Jerusalem church to an end' ('James and the Jerusalem Church' 428-29).

151. So most, e.g., Simon, *St. Stephen* 27-28; Hengel, *Between Jesus and Paul* 13; Wilson, *Gentiles* ch. 5; Esler, *Community and Gospel* 139-40; Barrett, *Acts* 390; Jervell, *Apg.* 221-22.

152. See again below, §25.2c.

a radical sharpening of the tensions within the Greek-speaking diaspora community in Jerusalem already caused by Hellenist views regarding the Temple (6.9-11). That is, it was non-believing Hellenists who, in the light of the blasphemy being proclaimed by Stephen and his followers, took the radical step of trying to suppress that blasphemy under the leadership of a zealous young Pharisee named Saul.

24.7. The Mission of Philip

Luke's account proceeds immediately to the mission of Philip, as the first positive outcome of the wave of persecution (8.4-5). Given the Hellenist character of the whole narrative, the Philip in view must be the member of the seven (Hellenist leaders?) named in 6.5, described subsequently as 'Philip the evangelist' (21.8), rather than the apostle Philip, mentioned in 1.13. The significance of Philip's mission was the success which he achieved in Samaria, already signalled in the headline of 8.1. That, of course, matches Luke's own programme outlined in 1.8 ('in all Judea and Samaria'), but there is no good reason to doubt that Samaria, given its proximity to Jerusalem, was one of the areas to which those scattered in the persecution fled. Missionary success in Samaria is also reflected elsewhere in Christian sources (notably John 4.39-42).[153] And there is no obvious reason why Luke should, of his own initiative, have chosen to credit the otherwise relatively obscure Philip with the breakthrough in Samaria (8.4-13) and the first Gentile conversion (8.26-39).[154] So once again we should probably hear Luke, himself a great story-teller, moulding his tale on the stories he learned from churches who traced their beginnings to those 'scattered abroad' by the persecution.[155]

a. Samaria

To appreciate the importance of Philip's mission it is necessary to recall the troubled history of Judea's relationship with Samaria. Formerly the northern kingdom (Israel), after the united kingdom of David and Solomon had been split in two following Solomon's death, Samaria had been devastated and depopulated by the Assyrians in 722 BCE. The more mixed people settled by the Assyrians

153. It was O. Cullmann, 'Samaria and the Origins of the Christian Mission', *The Early Church* (London: SCM, 1956) 183-92, who suggested that the prior ministry of the 'others' referred to in John 4.38 probably was an allusion to the missionary work of the Hellenists; taken up by Simon, *St. Stephen* 36-37.

154. 'The mission in Samaria carried on by the Hellenist Philip is in all probability a historical fact' (Lüdemann, *Early Christianity* 100).

155. The 'we' source had some association with Caesarea (21.8-16; 27.1), where Luke's own tale leaves Philip (8.40; 21.8-9).

adopted the religion of their new country and regarded themselves as full heirs of the religion whose central lawgiver and prophet was Moses.[156] They maintained their own version of the Pentateuch (arguably an earlier version than that of the Hebrew Bible)[157] and established their own temple on Mount Gerizim (Josephus, *Ant.* 11.302-25), claiming the precedence of Joshua 24.[158] Consequently they are remembered (in the canonical Jewish tradition) as less than sympathetic to the exiles who returned from Babylon to resettle in Judea (Ezra 4) and who under the leadership of Ezra in effect laid exclusive claim to their version of the Pentateuch and Mosaic inheritance. The Maccabean revolt against the Syrian overlordship of the region did not initially affect the Samaritans. But when the Hasmonean John Hyrcanus began to expand the territory of little Judea and to reclaim the northern territories which had formerly been part of the united Davidic kingdom, he made a point of destroying the temple on Mount Gerizim (in 128 BCE). In so doing he thus condemned and rendered invalid the Samaritan form of Israel's earlier religion. As already noted, it was probably about this time that the term *Ioudaios* began to broaden from a geographical referent ('Judean') to include a more religious content ('Jew').[159] The failure of the Hasmonean policy at this point was marked by their failure to draw Samaria into this new category ('Jew') and into the religio-nationalist 'Judaism' which emerged from the Maccabean/Hasmonean period. The contrasting success of the same policy in regard to Galilee[160] made the stubborn persistence of the Samaritans in maintaining their own tradition of pre-Judaism all the more marked.

In political terms Samaria was regarded as part of the same territory as Judea, both part of Herod the Great's kingdom,[161] and after the deposition of

---

156. See Schürer, *History* 2.16-20; T. H. Gaster, 'Samaritans', *IDB* 4.190-95; Haacker, 'Samaritan' 3.449-53; F. Dexinger, 'Limits of Tolerance in Judaism: The Samaritan Example', in E. P. Sanders et al., eds., *Jewish and Christian Self-Definition.* Vol. 2: *Aspects of Judaism in the Graeco-Roman Period* (London: SCM, 1981) 88-114; J. D. Purvis, 'The Samaritans and Judaism', in R. A. Kraft and G. W. E. Nickelsburg, eds., *Early Judaism and Its Modern Interpreters* (Atlanta: Scholars, 1986) 81-98; also 'The Samaritans', *CHJ* 2.591-613; R. T. Anderson, 'Samaritans', *ABD* 5.941-43. We know of Samaritan colonies elsewhere in Palestine, in Alexandria (Josephus, *Ant.* 12.7-10; 13.74-79), also in Thessalonica and Rome, and from inscriptional evidence we know that there was a Samaritan community on the island of Delos (in the Aegean), who called themselves 'Israelites' (Schürer, *History* 3.66-67, 70-71, 81; *NDIEC* 8.148-51).

157. See B. K. Waltke, 'Samaritan Pentateuch', *ABD* 5.932-40.

158. 'It was this contention [that Shechem/Gerizim was the divinely ordained center of Israel's cultic life], not simply the existence of a Samaritan temple, which drove the permanent wedge between the Samaritans and the Jews' (Purvis, 'The Samaritans' 89).

159. See *Jesus Remembered* §9.2.

160. See *Jesus Remembered* §9.6.

161. It was Herod who had rebuilt the city of Samaria and renamed it Sebaste (Josephus, *War* 1.403; *Ant.* 15.296-98).

Archelaus, falling under the rule of the prefect in Caesarea.[162] Indeed, it was Pilate's mishandling of a disturbance in Samaria, during the period covered in this chapter, which resulted in his recall to Rome (Josephus, *Ant.* 18.85-89).[163] But the tensions between Judea and Samaria persisted and are reflected in the various references to Samaria and Samaritans in the Jesus tradition.[164] The step of taking the proclamation of Jesus Messiah to them as well constituted a significant step across a major boundary — not simply, as with Jesus, a breaking down of internal boundaries (in relation to 'sinners'), or responding sympathetically to non-Jews who appealed to him,[165] but a deliberate stepping across (Philip goes to a/ the city of Samaria),[166] one of the boundaries by which Judaism had defined itself as Jew and not Samaritan![167]

b. The Evangelist/Apostle of Samaria

Luke's account starts in a straightforward way. Philip 'proclaimed the Messiah' (8.5), that is, Jesus as Messiah,[168] and 'the good news concerning the kingdom of

162. Schürer, *History* 2.163.

163. See further Schürer, *History* 1.361 n. 36, 386-87.

164. *Matt. 10.5* — Samaritans are explicitly excluded from 'the lost sheep of the house of Israel' ('traces of an early Jerusalem polemic against the mission of Philip'? — Räisänen, 'Hellenisten' 1497);

Luke 9.52-54 — a Samaritan village refuses Jesus hospitality 'because his face was set toward Jerusalem', and the brothers James and John respond by proposing to command fire from heaven to consume them;

John 4.4-26 — Jesus' encounter with the Samaritan woman presupposes deeply rooted hostility between Jews and Samaritans ('Jews do not share things in common with Samaritans'; Samaritans worship what they do not know);

John 8.48 — to call someone a 'Samaritan' is an accusation and insult equivalent to denouncing him as possessed by a demon.

165. *Jesus Remembered* §§13.5, 7.

166. The 'city' in view was perhaps Sebaste (previously Samaria), though it had become predominantly pagan (Schürer, *History* 2.162-63); others have thus preferred Neapolis (Nablus, the ancient Shechem), Shechem being the main centre for the Samaritan religion (Bruce, *Acts* 216; Haenchen, *Acts* 301-302, cites Wellhausen, Zahn and Meyer), or Sychar (John 4.5); see further Hengel, *Between Jesus and Paul* 123-26; Schnabel, *Mission* 676-77. On the unclarity of the text (did the text include the definite article?), see Metzger, *Textual Commentary* 355-56; Barrett, *Acts* 1.402-403.

167. In Matt. 10.5-6 we should note the irony (historical, political and theological) of a command to go only to 'the lost sheep of the house of Israel' and to 'enter no town of the Samaritans', since *Samaria* was the capital of what had been the old northern kingdom of *Israel*!

168. F. S. Spencer, *The Portrait of Philip in Acts* (JSNTS 67; Sheffield: JSOT, 1992):

God and the name of Jesus Christ' (8.12).[169] And he exercised a very successful ministry of exorcism and healing (8.7, 13). Both elements are likely to have come from the traditions Luke received.

- Luke usually refers to Jesus as 'Jesus Christ', and to leave 'the Christ/Messiah' unidentified as he does in 8.5 is quite exceptional.
- The Samaritans probably had their own version of messianic hope, referred to in their Scriptures as 'the Taheb';[170] indeed, Luke's report may be sufficient indication that this hope was already lively among the Samaritans and that Philip made his evangelistic appeal by claiming that this hope had now been realized in Jesus.
- This same circle of expectation may have been reflected back into the material on which Luke drew to craft Stephen's speech, since the speech makes great play of the expectation of a prophet like Moses (7.37), an expectation which also features strongly in Samaritan theology.[171]
- Although Luke gives particular prominence to 'signs and wonders' wrought by the characters in his tale,[172] here he speaks simply of 'signs' (8.6), or 'signs and great miracles' (8.13). More to the point, his description of Philip's ministry as one of exorcising unclean spirits is not so typical of Acts and unusually vivid (8.7 — 'crying with loud shrieks'; cf. 5.16; 16.18).

Here once again, then, we should probably infer that Luke has shaped his narrative round reports he received from his (Hellenist) informants.[173]

The impression of a straightforward narrative, however, soon fades. Simon,

---

'Used here with the definite article, Christ should no doubt be understood in the titular sense of "the Christ" or "the messiah"' (38).

169. See further Spencer, *Philip* 39-44.

170. See Gaster, 'Samaritans' 194; J. Macdonald, *The Theology of the Samaritans* (London: SCM, 1964) 362-71; J. Bowman, *Samaritan Documents Relating to Their History, Religion and Life* (Pittsburgh: Pickwick, 1976) 257-58, 267-71; S. Isser, 'The Samaritans and Their Sects', *CHJ* 3.569-95 (here 591-93).

171. Macdonald, *Theology of the Samaritans* 160, 197-98, 363 n. 1, 443.

172. See above, §21 at n. 132.

173. It has been characteristic of research on the Samaritan episode to infer that Luke has combined two separate traditions; see, e.g., the discussion and conclusion of A. von Dobbeler, *Der Evangelist Philippus in der Geschichte des Urchristentums* (Tübingen: Francke, 2000) ch. 1; he concludes that 'in the background of both traditions stand actual historical events, which here have found their narrative outcome' (103). See further C. R. Matthews, *Philip: Apostle and Evangelist* (NovTSupp 105; Leiden: Brill, 2002) chs. 2-3, who concludes: 'Philip was remembered as one who proclaimed the gospel to non-Jews, or more particularly to those who could be identified as marginalized' (94).

a magician, is introduced as one of Philip's most important converts (8.9-13), but only to prepare the reader for the weighty confrontation between Simon and Peter which follows (8.18-24). A serious defect is identified in Philip's ministry — his converts did not receive the Spirit — though not as part of the story of Philip, which is told as a success story from start to finish (8.6-13), but only as a kind of flashback in the sequel (8.16). And in the sequel the focus is fixed exclusively on Peter (and John), with Philip wholly absent from the picture — almost as though two (or more!) quite separate stories have been inexpertly joined into one.[174] Both features demand some attention; I will take them in the order of the second half of the narrative (8.14-24).

c. The Delay of the Spirit

For those interested in Luke's understanding of Christian initiation and the beginnings of Christian baptism, this episode is something of a puzzle. We may infer that Acts 2.38 indicates what Luke would have taken to be the normal process of becoming and being recognized as a member of the new sect: repentance/belief and baptism in the name of Jesus Christ, followed by the gift of the Spirit. And such a pattern, implying at least a close conjunction of baptism and the gift of the Spirit, holds for all the rest of Luke's reports of conversions.[175] But here the reader is confronted with a considerable gap between the two, separated at least by the time taken for news to be reported back to the apostles in Jerusalem (during a bout of persecution?) and for Peter and John to be dispatched to Samaria. Indeed, Luke's account draws explicit attention to the anomaly in his flashback verse: the Samaritans 'had only been baptized (*monon de bebap-*

---

174. Lake and Cadbury, *Beginnings* 4.88. Jervell briefly lists the various hypotheses that have been offered (*Apg.* 267 n. 825); and see Matthews, *Philip* 54-64. Barrett thinks it 'more likely that there should have been available to Luke a number of scraps of information about Simon than that there should have been two distinct and sharply contrasting stories' (*Acts* 1.399). As Matthews observes, 'Had there been an original tradition that attributed the conversion of Samaria to Peter and John, a later tradition, which credited the same accomplishment to a "lesser figure", would hardly have arisen' (*Philip* 41).

175. Acts 2.38; 9.17-18; 10.47; 19.2, 5-6. The passage here in ch. 8 has been important for both the developing theology and the practice of confirmation (see, e.g., Pesch, *Apg.* 1.280-81; Barrett, *Acts* 1.400), though at best we may see this passage as the first case of laying on of hands being used as a kind of supplement to baptism — and for the classic Pentecostal separation between conversion/baptism and the subsequent gift of the Spirit. On the latter see my *Baptism in the Holy Spirit* ch. 5, also 'Baptism in the Spirit: A Response to Pentecostal Scholarship on Luke-Acts', *JPT* 3 (1993) 3-27, reprinted in my *The Christ and the Spirit.* Vol. 2: *Pneumatology* (Grand Rapids: Eerdmans, 1998) 222-42; and M. Turner, 'The Spirit and Salvation in Luke-Acts', in Stanton et al., eds., *The Holy Spirit and Christian Origins* 103-16.

tismenoi) in the name of the Lord Jesus', and the Spirit had 'not yet *(oudepō)* fallen upon any of them' (8.16). Only when Peter (and John) pray and lay hands on the Samaritan converts do they receive the Spirit (8.15, 17), though, apparently, without any further instruction.

The episode can, of course, be attributed to Luke's contrivance: he presumably wanted to show that the breakthrough in Samaria was soon brought under Jerusalem's authority — even if that meant in some degree disparaging what his source reported as a highly successful missionary effort on the part of Philip. On the other hand, would he have felt free arbitrarily to pull so far apart what he may have believed to be a divinely ordered linkage (baptism and the Spirit), to subordinate divine order to ecclesiastical order? The strong balance of his narrative elsewhere should certainly count against that.[176] My own suggestion — that Luke intended his readers to recognize that the Samaritans' faith had been defective,[177] that is, that they should not have been baptized so precipitously — has not won much support.[178] Certainly the fact that Luke does not report Peter and John as providing further instruction (contrast even 19.4) weakens the suggestion. And the total absence of Philip from the scene remains unresolved, unless explained by Luke's preferring to focus only on the lead actors in any scene.[179]

The more important factor, it seems to me, is that Luke evidently saw the gift of the Spirit as the crucial factor in entry into the new sect. In each case where Luke takes the trouble to speak about the (initial) reception of the Spirit, it forms the crucial moment and climax of any longer process involved in conversion and initiation.[180] Moreover, it should always be recalled that in the earliest days of the new movement, reception of the Spirit was seen as a significant, transformative and sometimes eye-catching experience on the part of the recipient;[181] the Spirit was first experienced before being believed in, and the experi-

---

176. In any debate between Luke 'the enthusiast' and Luke 'the early Catholic', the former wins by a substantial margin.

177. *Baptism in the Holy Spirit* 63-68. Normally Luke says 'they believed (on/in) the Lord/God' (5.14; 9.42; 10.43; 11.17; 16.31, 34; 18.8), but here Luke says 'they believed Philip' (8.12). 'That faith was directed to Philip is exceptional and may be Luke's way of signalling that all was not right with the Samaritans' response' (Dunn, *Acts* 110).

178. See, e.g., Schnabel, *Mission* 679-80. But Barrett notes that Stählin thought that Simon's '"faith" was no true faith, his conversion no genuine conversion' (*Acts* 1.409). And Fitzmyer observes that Eusebius thought that Simon 'feigned faith in Christ even to the point of baptism' (*HE* 2.1.11; Fitzmyer, *Acts* 405) — the point being that Luke makes no distinction between the Samaritans' belief and baptism and Simon's (8.13).

179. See above, §23.3c.

180. 2.38; 10.44-48 (baptism as secondary consideration, its appropriateness rendered indisputable by the outpouring of the Spirit); 19.1-6.

181. 'Luke knows of no silent comings of the Spirit!' (Dunn, *Acts* 111); see further my *Baptism* 66-67; *Jesus and the Spirit* ch. 7; also *Theology of Paul* §16.

ence helped shape the belief.[182] It may be, then, that the mission to Samaria misfired or malfunctioned, for whatever reason (now only to be guessed at), in that what had been the normal pattern hitherto and what continued to be the normal pattern in Paul's mission (cf. Gal. 3.2-5) did not eventuate in Samaria. The manifestations which were thought to signal the entry of the Spirit into converts' lives did not happen. In such circumstances the sequence of events outlined in 8.14 could have transpired, with the results indicated in 8.15-17 — not necessarily in close chronological sequence with Philip's mission, but as one of the steps taken by initiative from Jerusalem to draw into their own circle what might well otherwise have become splinter movements diverging from the Jerusalem-directed mainstream.

The issue is too shrouded in uncertainty for any firm conclusion to be possible. But the possibility that Luke's own theological agenda (to emphasize Jerusalem's central role) actually coincides in this instance with an initial attempt by the Jerusalem apostleship to assert leadership or supervision over the movement now beginning to expand from Jerusalem should not be lightly dismissed.[183] And in any case, the effectiveness of charismatic ministries and the importance of the experience of the Spirit in the initial expansion of Christianity are evident, whatever the precise historical details.

d. Peter's Confrontation with Simon the Magician

The other, still more riveting aspect of the story, or twin stories, is the introduction it provides to Simon Magus, Simon the magician. Simon is one of the most interesting figures of the ancient world. In the second century the Christian apologist Justin Martyr, himself from Samaria, names Simon's home town as Gitta and reports that his people venerated Simon as the supreme God (*Apology* 1.26.3).[184] That may be an exaggeration, but other second- and third-century sources[185] identify Simon as the founder of the Simonian Gnostics, and that claim may be ultimately sound. How much of this may be reflected in Luke's

---

182. See my *Theology of Paul* §16, and further *Jesus and the Spirit*.

183. If we are to assume that persecution was happening all this while, any report that the new sect was welcoming Samaritan deviants would almost certainly increase the suspicions of the high priestly hierarchy that the new sect was beginning to threaten traditional boundary lines. But quite how Luke saw the events of Acts 8 fitting into the Saul-directed persecution is by no means clear. It would be unwise to assume that narrative (or modern chapter) progression reflects historical chronological progression.

184. Justin himself came from Nablus/Neapolis/Shechem.

185. See, e.g., G. Lüdemann, *Untersuchungen zur simonianischen Gnosis* (Göttingen: Vandenhoeck und Ruprecht, 1975) 98-102; Barrett 405, also 416.

narrative is now impossible to say.[186] Of course the outcome is told from a Christian perspective. And Luke uses the episode to demonstrate Christianity's difference from, superiority to and triumph over magic (*mageia* — 8.11).[187] But that there was an encounter between the historical Simon and early Christian missionaries is entirely possible.

The title attributed to Simon ('The Great Power' — 8.10) has an authentic ring. In a monotheistic system 'the power' could stand for God (as in Mark 14.62).[188] At this period, however, there was considerable speculation about how God, or the Most High God, interacted with the world and with humanity. Philo, the Jewish philosopher from Alexandria, shows how a sophisticated monotheism could use language of the 'powers' to describe the diverse ways in which the divine impacts on the earthly and human (rather like the idea of divine Wisdom, or even the Spirit within wider Judaism).[189] But to envisage a system of powers, of which one could be called 'Great', may reflect an early example of what became characteristic of Gnostic systems in the following centuries, where intermediate figures of decreasing divinity help explain the manifest gulf between the divine and the human.[190] Luke takes some care to distinguish Simon's own claim for

186. See particularly K. Beyschlag, *Simon Magus und die christliche Gnosis* (WUNT 16; Tübingen: Mohr Siebeck, 1974); R. M. Wilson, 'Simon and Gnostic Origins', in Kremer, ed., *Les Actes des Apôtres* 485-91.

187. See also Acts 13.6-11; 16.16-18; 19.18-19. BDAG defines *mageia* as 'a rite or rites ordinarily using incantations designed to influence/control transcendental powers' (608). The implication of Luke's account is that 'magic' tries to manipulate the divine by use of special formulae and techniques (8.19) which could be written down in books, learned and used by would-be practitioners (19.13, 18-19). The Christian practice of laying on hands or exorcism may look very much the same, and indeed may have a very similar effect (cf. 8.9-11 with 8.6, 8 and 13), but one of Luke's primary concerns in relating the episodes of 8.17-24 and 19.13-16 is to make clear the difference (see further Aune, 'Magic'; S. R. Garrett, *The Demise of the Devil: Magic and the Demonic in Luke's Writings* [Minneapolis: Fortress, 1989] 19-36 and ch. 3; H.-J. Klauck, *Magic and Paganism in Early Christianity: The World of the Acts of the Apostles* [London: Clark, 2000] 14-19; see also N. Janowitz, *Magic in the Roman World* [London: Routledge, 2001]).

188. See *Jesus Remembered* 749 n. 180.

189. See my *Christology in the Making* 225, with bibliography in nn. 45 and 47; Schürer, *History* 3.881-85. See further Barrett, *Acts* 1.406-408. H. G. Kippenberg, *Garizim und Synagoge. Traditionsgeschichtliche Untersuchungen zur samaritanischen Religion der aramäische Periode* (Berlin: de Gruyter, 1971) 329-48, and J. E. Fossum, *The Name of God and the Angel of the Lord: Samaritan and Jewish Concepts of Intermediation and the Origin of Gnosticism* (WUNT 36; Tübingen: Mohr Siebeck, 1985) 171-72, both regard 'the Great Power' as a Samaritan title for God.

190. See also the data summarized in Bruce, *Acts* 219; Jervell, *Apg.* 261 n. 799. The suggestion of G. Lüdemann, 'The Acts of the Apostles and the Beginnings of Simonian Gnosis', *NTS* 33 (1987) 420-26, that the term *epinoia* ('thought') in 8.22 contains an allusion to Simon's

himself ('saying that he was someone great' — 8.9) from the popular opinion of him, that he was some sort of manifestation or embodiment of 'the Great Power' (8.10).[191] But how significant that is remains unclear.[192]

There is a striking contrast between the two halves of the twin episodes. In the first, Philip proves himself much the more impressive instrument or channel of divine powers (*dynameis* — 8.13); Simon, a famous performer himself who had amazed others (8.11), is depicted as amazed at Philip's (by implication) even more astounding miracles; he pays court to Philip and is even baptized by him (8.13). The sequel, however, shows him up as a charlatan. What had kept him close to Philip was the desire to learn the secrets of Philip's success; baptism was presumably a means to ingratiate himself with Philip.[193] His primary concern was to improve his magical act — specifically to learn the trick of causing the effects and spiritual manifestations which he saw resulting from Peter's and John's ministry (8.18-19).[194] Peter's response is outright dismissal and denunciation: Simon has no part in what had been happening (8.21);[195] he was still 'in the gall of bitterness and the chains of wickedness' (8.23).[196]

Luke having thus shown Simon to be entirely trounced and wholly insincere leaves the door ajar for a possibly favourable resolution (8.24) but breaks his

---

feminine companion in Simonian Gnosis, however, strains the evidence much too far, as his own review of other data indicates (424). Lüdemann is remarkably confident that the bedrock of the tradition about Simon in Acts 8 is 'the worship of Simon as a god and the existence of *epinoia* as his syzygos' (*Early Christianity* 101-102). See also Spencer, *Philip* 90-91.

191. An intriguing link is suggested by Isser's note that Simon 'also called himself "The Standing One" *(ho hestos),* signifying eternal endurance, apparently a translation of the term *qa'em*'. Isser suggests 'this usage is a reinterpretation of the term *qa'em* which literally means "standing one" and was used in [Samaritan literature] to describe Moses' standing before God (Deut. 5:28 [31?]; cf. Exod. 33:21)' ('The Samaritans and Their Sects' 594). The twofold link with Jesus as the Moses-prophet (Acts 7.37) and Stephen's vision of the Son of Man 'standing' beside God (7.55-56) might suggest a stronger Samaritan background to the Hellenist traditions in Acts 7–8 than has so far been recognized (see above, n. 106).

192. Haenchen goes well beyond the evidence in concluding, 'Simon declared that [the supreme] deity had come to earth in his person for the redemption of men' (*Acts* 303).

193. Cf. Avemarie, *Tauferzählungen* 51-54.

194. Simon saw that the Spirit was given 'through the laying on of the apostles' hands (8.18), but Luke immediately contrasts this with Simon's magical perception of what happened (8.19). Note the similar contrast in 19.11-16.

195. Luke says, 'no part or lot in this matter *(en tō logō)*', on which Haenchen comments: 'The *logos* in which Simon is refused a share is Christianity' (*Acts* 305); similarly Jervell, *Apg.* 265. Presumably the reader is to understand that Simon, although one of the baptized, had not himself had hands laid on him by Peter and John, and so had not himself received (the experience of) the Spirit.

196. The language of 8.21 and 23 is drawn from a sequence of scriptural passages — Deut. 12.12 and 14.27, 29; Ps. 78.37; Deut. 29.18.

story off at that point (contrast 5.5, 10 and 13.11). Was that deliberate, we may wonder? Could it be that Luke knew other stories which were already circulating about Simon, and thus invited the reader to seek a resolution in his own time rather than in story-time? At all events, it would be a fairer assessment of Luke's story-telling abilities to deduce something of the sort, rather than to conclude that Luke could not bring his tale to a satisfactory conclusion.[197]

Instead, Luke rounds off his Samaritan episode not by reverting to Philip but by attributing the further evangelism of Samaritan villages to Peter and John (8.25). From Luke's perspective, and presumably also Jerusalem's, whose spokesman Luke is in this, it was important to be able to recount that the expansion into Samaria was brought under the supervision of the Jerusalem apostles more or less from the first.

e. The First Gentile Convert

Somewhat surprisingly, following what might therefore be seen as a parenthesis (8.14-25), Luke returns to Philip and his conversion of the Ethiopian eunuch (8.26-39). The story is framed by supernatural intervention: it begins with Philip being directed south by 'an angel of the Lord' to the road from Jerusalem to Gaza, which joins the great way of the sea (Via Maris),[198] and it ends with the Spirit of the Lord snatching away *(hērpasen)* Philip, and Philip finding himself *(heurethē)* further north at Azotus.[199] The former is one of the ways in which Luke depicts the divine initiative and guidance which determined the history he narrates.[200] But the latter is exceptional in Acts,[201] though, presumably, one should recognize a deliberate echo of the Elijah cycle of stories (1 Kgs. 18.12; 2 Kgs. 2.16).[202] The

197. Cf. Klauck, *Magic and Paganism* 20-23.

198. The description of the road from Jerusalem to Gaza as 'wilderness' is puzzling, since the desert only begins south of Gaza. Has Luke, or his source, become a little confused on such a detail?

199. Azotus (ancient Ashdod) is twenty miles north of Gaza (Fitzmyer says fifteen kilometers); the detail is presumably derived from the Philip tradition. Caesarea was a further fifty-five miles to the north. See further Schürer, *History* 2.108-109 (Azotus), 115-18 (Caesarea); Hengel, *Between Jesus and Paul* 112-15.

200. Acts 5.19; 10.3; 11.13; 12.7; 27.23.

201. The verb is *harpazō*, 'snatch away, catch up', language used for transportation to heaven in 2 Cor. 12.2 and 1 Thess. 4.17 (also Rev. 12.5); 'was found' adds to the note of unexpectedness. Haenchen (*Acts* 313-14) justifiably critiques what he calls the 'psychological' chorus, who interpret the data in terms of Philip's presumed ecstatic state, e.g., Lake and Cadbury — 'The Christian preacher moves about in a state of ecstasy and hardly knows how he goes from place to place' (*Beginnings* 4.99).

202. See further Spencer, *Philip* 135-41.

effect of the double bracket, however, is to give the story something of the character of a folkloric legend (in which miraculous transportation is more characteristic of the genre). Why Luke should have framed this particular story in just this way is not clear; none of the other major 'moments' in his history have quite this character.[203] But perhaps the significance of this episode provides a clue.

The significance of the episode must lie in the two-word description of the other main character as 'an Ethiopian eunuch'.[204] It should be recalled, first, that a eunuch, who was incapable of receiving circumcision, was debarred from entering 'the assembly *(ekklēsia)* of the Lord' (Deut. 23.1).[205] The story starts, then, with a note of supreme irony. Here is a foreigner who showed himself sympathetic to the religion of Israel, and who may indeed have desired, had it been possible, to become a proselyte.[206] At all events, 'he had come to Jerusalem to worship' (8.27), that is, of course, in the Temple; but, being a Gentile and a eunuch, presumably he had been unable to enter beyond the outer court of the Temple (the court of the Gentiles).[207] The vision of Isa. 56.3-5, which implies the eunuch's disadvantaged status, had not yet been realized.[208] Instead, it is as he was returning *from* Jerusalem that he gains an acceptance which (presumably) had not been possible for him. In other words, the Temple had failed to be 'a house of prayer for all nations' (Isa. 56.7),[209] and it is the representative of the new messianic sect who meets the eunuch's spiritual aspiration and need.[210] The fact that in

203. Contrast, e.g., 10.23-24; 16.10-11.

204. It is true that 'eunuch' (Hebrew *saris*) could refer to a high office, but Luke has taken care to indicate the Ethiopian's office by the second descriptive word, *dynastēs* (court official); see further Spencer, *Philip* 166-67. Luke almost certainly intended his audience to hear/read *eunouchos* in its obvious Greek sense of 'castrated male' (BDAG 409; Barrett, *Acts* 1.424-25). German commentators have tended to tie themselves in knots at this point (e.g., Pesch, *Apg.* 1.289; Jervell, *Apg.* 270-71) on the grounds that Luke could not have intended to narrate the conversion of a non-Jew or non-proselyte prior to Acts 10 (similarly Fitzmyer, *Acts* 410, 412), but such an objection assumes that Luke tailored his source material (or his understanding of it) fairly ruthlessly to fit his scheme; Haenchen gives a more balanced assessment (*Acts* 314).

205. See Cadbury, *Beginnings* 5.66-67 n. 2; but also D. L. Christensen, *Deuteronomy* (WBC 6B; Nashville: Nelson, 2002) 537-38. On the status of the eunuch in ancient society see B. Kedar-Kopfstein, *TDOT* 10.346-47; J. Schneider, *TDNT* 2.765-66; Spencer, *Philip* 167-69.

206. See again n. 204 above. The degree of the eunuch's commitment is shown by his willingness to undertake such a lengthy journey and by his purchase of a scroll that was no doubt expensive, evidently written in Greek.

207. As with the 'Greeks' mentioned in John 12.20.

208. Similarly with Wis. 3.14-15, which would hardly represent the views of the Temple authorities.

209. Again the implication (of Isa. 56.7) is of Gentile access to full participation in the cult, which was in principle denied to Gentiles. See further below, §24.9a.

210. The language of 8.36 may be significant here: 'what is to prevent *(kōluei)* me from

this second Philip episode we again hear an overtone of Temple critique, just as the Samaritan episode contains a hint that rivalry between the two sites claimed for a central sanctuary has been superseded, can hardly be accidental. Luke makes no attempt to bring out these Temple allusions, but for anyone who knew the history of the Judea/Samaria split and of a eunuch's disbarment from the worship of Israel, the overtone could hardly be missed. Here, once again, then, we have an indication of a Temple-coloured thread linking the material in chs. 6–8 closely together. And since Luke makes so little of the link on his own part, we may fairly conclude that conjoining of this material was already accomplished before it came to Luke. It is such data that give substance to the hypothesis of a coherent Hellenist perspective in the source material on which Luke was evidently able to draw for this section of his narrative.

The other factor of significance is that the man was an Ethiopian. At that time Ethiopia (or Nubia), whose territory bordered Egypt to the south (Ezek. 29.10), represented the limit of common geographical knowledge. Isa. 11.11-12 seems to regard it as one of 'the corners of the earth' (cf. Zeph. 3.10); Ethiopians were regarded by Homer as the 'furthermost of men' (*Odyssey* 1.23), and the geographer Strabo placed Ethiopia at the 'extreme limits' of the Roman Empire (*Geog.* 17.2.1).[211] So Philip's winning of the Ethiopian to faith may be intended as the precursor of the gospel reaching to the 'end (last) of the earth' (Acts 1.8). In terms of Luke's programmatic intentions in Acts, this is actually the most astonishing feature. For Luke immediately follows this chapter with an account of Paul's conversion, the one primarily appointed to take the gospel to Gentiles (9.15), which is followed in turn by his account of Peter's conversion of the Gentile Cornelius (ch. 10). For Luke both episodes were absolutely crucial: he relates or draws upon each of them no less than three times.[212] It was Peter's conversion of Cornelius which was the determinative precedent for the church (15.7-11); it was Paul who was commissioned to bear the light to the Gentiles (26.17-18). Why, then, should Luke attribute the first Gentile conversion to Philip? Why should he even allow the suggestion that the goal of the church's expansion ('to the end of the earth') was already being reached out to, and not by Peter, and not by Paul, but by the much less significant Philip?[213] The only obvious answer is that this is how the story was told as it came to Luke. And even if it is Luke who has framed the story with its supernatural beginning and ending, perhaps to suggest that it did not happen in 'real time'(?), the implication remains firm and al-

---

being baptized?' — the implication being that his earlier desires had been frustrated, but now no barrier remained. See further Spencer, *Philip* 171-72, 183-85.

211. Further details in Spencer, *Philip* 149-51; Barrett, *Acts* 1.424.

212. Paul — Acts 9.1-19; 22.3-16; 26.9-18; Cornelius — 10.1-48; 11.1-18; 15.7-9.

213. See again n. 204 above.

most inescapable that Luke's Hellenist source(s) recalled Philip as prominent among their own role of pioneer heroes.[214] Luke, faithful to his sources, gives the credit where credit is due, even if it somewhat cuts across his own intended programme.

Here again Luke leaves the story without an ending. What happened to the eunuch? As a prominent member of the Ethiopian court,[215] he could have exercised some considerable influence. But as with his story of Simon the magician, Luke leaves threads dangling over the edge of his story; he paints pictures with characters disappearing off the edge of his canvas. He invites his readers to imagine what became of them and perhaps to fill in further episodes from their own knowledge and subsequent history. He had no intention of telling a tale which came to an end; the story was to continue in the lives of his hearers.[216]

f. The Significance of Philip's Mission

In telling the story of Philip's mission as he has, Luke has taken good care to absorb Philip into the larger tale he wants to narrate:

- Philip's initial success in winning great support in Samaria is at once qualified by the comment that even though Philip baptized 'in the name of the Lord Jesus', his converts did not receive the Spirit through his ministry.
- His seeming triumph in winning Simon the magician to the faith is shown to be hollow by Simon's request and Peter's denunciation of Simon.
- It is Peter and John who carry through the mission to Samaria (8.25), with Philip entirely removed from the scene.

Is it the case, then, that Luke was willing to downplay, even denigrate, Philip's mission in order to depict it as quickly brought under the Jerusalem apostles' sphere of influence? Perhaps — though, if so, Luke took care to keep Philip off-

---

214. Haenchen, *Acts* 315-16; Lüdemann, *Early Christianity* 105; von Dobbeler, *Philippus* 177-78; Wilckens, *Theologie* 1/2.241.

215. He was *dynastēs Kandakēs* — 'a court official of the Candace', in this case 'in charge of the queen's entire treasury' (v. 27). 'Candace' was probably not the name of the queen but a title of the reigning matriarch — perhaps another slight misunderstanding by Luke or his tradition (detail in BDAG 507; Barrett, *Acts* 1.425). Eunuchs were often employed in high positions of responsibility, not least in service of royal women (cf. Esth. 2.14). Further documentation is in Fitzmyer, *Acts* 412.

216. 'There is no evidence of a first-century church in Ethiopia, though according to Irenaeus, *Adv. Haer.* 4.23.2, and Eusebius, *HE* 2.1.13, the eunuch was the first missionary there' (Barrett, *Acts* 1.422) — presumably as a deduction from this passage!

stage in the Peter and John part of the story. There is no hint of any criticism, explicit or implicit, let alone of confrontation between Philip and the two apostles.

On the other hand, nothing else in Luke's story (8.14-25 apart) seems to be anything other than highly commendatory of Philip:

- It is Philip who makes the initial breakthrough first in Samaria and then in reaching still further beyond to someone wholly outside the mainstream and side-streams of Israeli-Judean tradition.
- His mission is attended by clear signs of divine approval — signs and exorcisms, the manifest intervention of the Spirit (8.29, 39),[217] and what we might properly describe (from Luke's perspective) as the 'gospel of Christian joy' (8.8, 39).[218]
- His message is wholly in accord with what Luke elsewhere indicates to be standard preaching: good news concerning the kingdom of God[219] and the name[220] of Jesus Christ (8.12); the first explicit reference identifying Jesus with the servant of Isaiah 53 (8.32-35) may be significant,[221] but the reference itself (to Isa. 53.7-8) is of a piece with the suffering-vindication treatment of Jesus' death in the earlier speeches.[222]
- Philip's practice in baptizing as soon as belief is declared (8.12) and without further preliminary instruction is wholly characteristic of Luke's account;[223] and if any criticism of Philip's practice or baptism in Samaria is implied by the addition of 8.14-26, then Luke's readiness to record Philip following precisely the same procedure with the eunuch becomes still more of a puzzle.

217. Spencer, *Philip* 44-53.

218. *Chairō* — Acts 5.41; 8.39; 11.23; 13.48; 15.23, 31; *chara* — 8.8; 12.14; 13.52; 15.3.

219. See above, §22 n. 41.

220. See above, §23.4d.

221. See those cited by Barrett, *Acts* 1.429-30; cf. Bruce, *Acts* 227-29; see further §24.9c below.

222. See above, §23.4g. Here it is noteworthy that the quotation stops just before the last line of Isa. 53.8.

223. J. Munck, *Paul and the Salvation of Mankind* (London: SCM, 1959), observes: 'In Acts, as in the rest of the New Testament, there seems to have been no hesitation about baptizing. In a way that is remarkably casual compared with the modern formal ceremony, one baptizes and goes on one's way' (18 n. 1). The scribes responsible for the Western text evidently regarded the account as too brief and added v. 37 — 'And Philip said, "If you believe with all your heart, you may". And he replied, "I believe that Jesus Christ is the Son of God"'. 'Its insertion into the text seems to have been due to the feeling that Philip could not have baptized the Ethiopian without securing a confession of faith' (Metzger, *Textual Commentary* 359-60; see also Barrett, *Acts* 1.433).

In short, Luke probably gleaned these reports from his sources of information regarding the initial outreach of the Hellenists. Beyond integrating them into his Jerusalem-centred mission, Luke seems to have been entirely content to narrate the story of Philip's mission as he heard it without further comment. And it is an impressive story, of a one-man initiative which rolled back the boundaries of the emerging Christian movement both in significant part and in significant principle. Philip joins Stephen and Barnabas as one of the minor heroes of Luke's account of Christianity's beginnings, without whom the story might have taken a very different turn.[224]

Not least of the oddities of Luke's account of Philip's mission is the way he rounds it off — with a picture of Philip preaching along the coast of Judea all the way to Caesarea, where he apparently settled and prospered (21.8).[225] So Philip could be credited also with evangelizing the Judean coast;[226] in contrast to 8.14-25, Peter's mission in 9.32-43 envisages already established groups of disciples in this territory.[227] The oddity is that in Acts 10, when the Gentile centurion seeks to learn more of the gospel, he is told to send to Peter, residing some distance away (10.5-9, 23-24), rather than to Philip, the successful evangelist and already(?) resident in Caesarea itself. Of course we should not assume that Luke's narrative sequence is the same as historical sequence. But Luke's concern to include such details (as 8.40) leaves the reader unclear as to how the overlapping edges of his source material are to be related to one another. That Luke evidently did not worry about such questions does not make him a poor historian; it was (and is) more important that he included such material than that he rubbed away all the rough edges and left subsequent historians of Christianity's origins only with a smooth and uncomplicated account.

24.8. The Breakthrough at Antioch

Following his account of Philip's mission, Luke inserts two key sequences — the conversion of Saul/Paul and its aftermath (Acts 9.1-31), and the conversion of Cornelius with introduction (9.32–11.18). The reasons for the insertion are obvi-

---

224. Philip is 'one of the truly great figures in early Christianity' (Spencer, *Philip* 127). His importance is reflected in the relative prominence he receives in the second century (see Matthews, *Philip*), a subject to which we will have to return in vol. 3.

225. His house was large enough for Philip and four unmarried daughters, with guest accommodation for Paul and his party ('we') (21.8-9).

226. 'All the towns' would include Jewish settlements (cf. 9.32, 36), so it may be significant that Luke mentions only two Hellenistic cities (see further Hengel, *Acts* 79).

227. Spencer suggests a parallel with the mission to Samaria, 'where Philip establishes a beachhead for the gospel, and Peter comes along later to nurture and expand the young congregations' (*Philip* 153; further 'Philip the Forerunner and Peter the Culminator', 220-41).

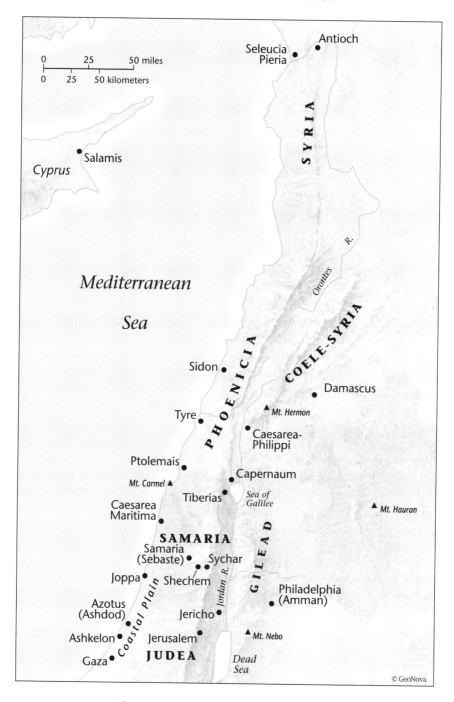

The Mission of Philip and the Hellenists

ous and have already been alluded to: these were the events which transformed the new sect functioning primarily, even exclusively, in Jerusalem and its immediate environs into a powerful missionary movement reaching out beyond Palestine and Judaism; they provide the second surge, including a second Pentecost (11.15-17), without which Christianity as Luke knew it could never have come about. Having given these two episodes full attention, however, Luke evidently reverted to the sources on which he had depended for chs. 6–8: as 8.4 introduced the chapter on Philip's mission, so 11.19 picks up the same thread to introduce the breakthrough in Antioch (11.19-21).[228]

a. Antioch

The dispersion of the believers scattered from Jerusalem took in Judea and Samaria (but not Galilee? — cf. 9.31)[229] and presumably Damascus (9.1-2). But the larger movement seems to have been up the coast, including Phoenicia and the not far distant Cyprus, with Antioch on the Orontes as the most obvious goal and destination (11.19).

Antioch was the major city of the region, the old capital of the Seleucid Empire, now the capital of the Roman province of Syria, the headquarters from which the whole eastern flank of Rome's empire was directed (especially against the constant threat of the Parthians), and the third largest city in the Roman Empire (after Rome and Alexandria). Its population is variously reckoned as between 150,000 and 400,000.[230] Syria had been annexed by Rome, following Pompey's conquest of the East, only a century earlier, and the new province included oversight of Palestine and direct rule of Judea and Samaria; Pontius Pilate, as prefect of Judea, was directly responsible to the governor (legate) in Antioch. The governorship of Syria was one of the most important posts in the empire and was held by a senator of consular rank appointed directly by the emperor. Antioch, in other words, was the political and cultural capital of the whole region and an obvious base for any movement with an eye to expansion.[231]

228. So, e.g., Wedderburn, *History* 71-73, and see above, n. 3. Note also that the description of Barnabas (11.24) matches that of Stephen (6.5; 7.55); and the repeated use of 'church' (8.1, 3; 11.22, 26; 13.1) and 'disciples' (6.1, 2, 7; 11.26, 29). Again, it is not necessary to think of Luke's sources as written.

229. 'Out-of-the-way Galilee, "backwoods" Galilee quickly lost its significance for the further history of earliest Christianity and could not regain it even after the destruction of Jerusalem' (Hengel, *Acts* 76).

230. Hengel and Schwemer reckon 300,000 to be 'a more realistic estimate' (*Paul* 186), and Schnelle thinks between 300,000 and 600,000 (*Paul* 113, citing F. W. Norris, 'Antiochien I', *TRE* 3.99).

231. For more detail here and in the following two paragraphs see Schürer, *History* 3.13-

Antioch was also famous for its proximity to Daphne, the seat of a cult of Artemis and Apollo, and was sometimes called *hē epi Daphnē* (Epidaphna) (Tacitus, *Ann.* 2.83.3). Traditional Romans saw Antioch and other Eastern cities as a source of decadence and immorality, *Daphnici mores* becoming a byword for loose living.[232] Among the many temples and cults, typical of an Eastern city, the emperor cult was already well established in Antioch.[233]

Unsurprisingly, given the history of rule from Antioch (Seleucid and Roman), the links between Judea and Antioch were strong. Herod the Great is credited with the provision of a long colonnaded street paved with polished marble (Josephus, *War* 1.425; *Ant.* 16.148). And many Jews had settled in Antioch, particularly since the Syrian rulers had welcomed them and treated them favourably, in particular, allowing them to follow their own customs and possibly granting them rights equivalent to those of citizenship.[234] Indeed, Josephus observes that of all the diaspora, Syria, and especially Antioch itself, had the largest percentage of Jewish inhabitants (*War* 7.43). They must have prospered there, since Josephus also notes that 'their richly designed and costly offerings formed a splendid ornament to the temple' (*War* 7.45), presumably the Temple in Jerusalem. The Jewish population of Antioch was probably in the region of 30,000 — that is, a major proportion of the total population.[235]

Most interesting of all is Josephus's report that the Jews 'were constantly attracting to their religious ceremonies multitudes of Greeks, and these they [the Jews] had in some measure made to share in their own lot *(moiran hautōn pepoiēnto)*' (*War* 7.45). Earlier Josephus had reported that each of the Syrian cit-

---

14, 141-42; Meeks and Wilken, *Jews and Christians in Antioch* 2-13; I. Levinskaya, *BAFCS* 5.127-35; M. Zetterholm, *The Formation of Christianity in Antioch: A Social-Scientific Approach to the Separation between Judaism and Christianity* (London: Routledge, 2003) ch. 2; Schnabel, *Mission* 782-86; key bibliography in Hengel and Schwemer, *Paul* 430-31 n. 949.

232. Bruce, *Acts* 271.

233. Zetterholm, *Formation* 26-27. On the religious situation in Antioch see further F. W. Norris, 'Antioch on the Orontes as a Religious Center I: Paganism before Constantine', *ANRW* 2.18.4 (1990) 2322-79; Hengel and Schwemer, *Paul* 268-79.

234. Josephus, *War* 7.43-44; *Ant.* 12.119; *Ap.* 2.39; see discussion in E. M. Smallwood, *The Jews under Roman Rule from Pompey to Diocletian* (Leiden: Brill, 1981) 358-60; E. J. Bickerman, *The Jews in the Greek Age* (Cambridge: Harvard University, 1988) 91-92; Hengel and Schwemer, *Paul* 186-88; Zetterholm, *Formation* 32-37.

235. C. H. Kraeling, 'The Jewish Community of Antioch', *JBL* 51 (1932) 130-60, estimated a Jewish population in Antioch between 45,000 and 60,000; Hengel and Schwemer suggest extending the range to 30,000-50,000, probably 'scattered over different parts of the city' (*Paul* 189, 196); Riesner estimates between 20,000 and 60,000, that is, over 10 percent of the population (*Paul's Early Period* 111); Meeks and Wilken, however, estimate a first-century Jewish population of 22,000, on the assumption that the total population was at the lower end of the range mentioned above (*Jews and Christians* 8); Schnelle calculates 20,000-30,000 (*Paul* 113-14).

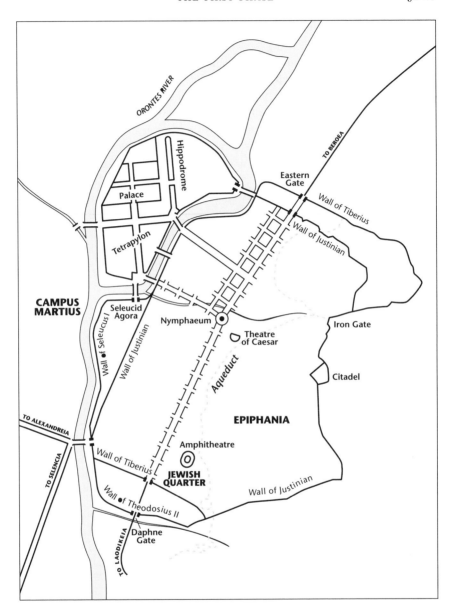

Antioch (in Syria)

ies had its 'Judaizers', that is, Gentiles who adopted a Jewish way of life, and that during the Jewish revolt the Syrians greatly feared those who had become 'mixed up with *(memigmenon)*' the Jewish population (*War* 2.463). Although Josephus's report relates to the events of the 60s, the relationships between Jews and sympathetic non-Jews which his account envisages must have pertained for some time and can probably be taken as a fair indication of the circumstances in which those scattered from Jerusalem found themselves when they came to Antioch.[236] In other words, it is in Antioch that we first meet in significant measure the phenomenon which seems to have been crucial for the expansion of the Jesus messianic movement beyond the boundaries of Judaism. I refer to the presence of Gentile 'Judaizers', or 'God-fearers', or 'God-worshippers' in and around, and to some extent part of, the Jewish community, not least in their participation in religious activities centred on the synagogues.[237] At all events, the overlap of Jews and non-Jews in the diaspora community of Antioch must have been a major factor in the events which Luke proceeds to describe with utmost brevity.

b. Preaching to the Greeks/Greek-Speakers

According to Luke, the scattered Hellenists, as I assume them to have been, initially 'spoke the word to no one except Jews' (Acts 11.19).[238] But some among them, from Cyprus and Cyrene, on arriving in Antioch, 'spoke also to the Greeks/ Greek-speakers, preaching the good news of the Lord Jesus' (11.20). Two points require some clarification here. First, the mention specifically of 'Cypriots and Cyrenians' should not be taken to imply that they were the only diaspora Jews who had fled from Jerusalem — the others being 'Hebrews'. Rather, the more obvious inference is that those who had fled from Jerusalem were all diaspora Jews, and that of these dispersed Hellenists it was the Cypriots and Cyrenians who were remembered as taking the fresh initiative so briefly described.[239]

236. The sixth-century *Chronicle* of Malalas records an outburst of anti-Jewish violence in Antioch in 40 CE, probably in connection with Caligula's attempt to have his statue erected in the Jerusalem Temple (see *Jesus Remembered* 296, and below, §26.5a), which would be early in the establishment of Christianity in Antioch (details in Meeks and Wilken, *Jews and Christians* 4; Levinskaya, *BAFCS* 5.130-32; Hengel and Schwemer, *Paul* 184-85). Malalas is notoriously unreliable, and Josephus naturally paints as positive a picture of Gentile sympathy towards Judaism as he can, but there is no difficulty in envisaging both substantial Gentile attraction to Judaism and a more popular antipathy to things Jewish which occasionally burst out in violence against Jews and their property. See also §26 n. 96 below.

237. See further below, §29.5c.

238. Note that whatever was the Hellenist attitude to the Temple, they had not turned from Judaism or their fellow Jews; see also Jervell, *Apg.* 321-22.

239. Acts 13.1 probably gives us the name of one of those referred to here — 'Lucius of

The other point requiring clarification is the much more difficult question of whom the Cypriot and Cyrenian believers spoke to. In the most ancient copies of Acts the more strongly supported reading is 'Hellenists/Greek-speakers *(Hellēnistas)*'.[240] It seems rather odd that Hellenists (as we assume) spoke to 'Hellenists'. But that was what Stephen had evidently done much earlier in Jerusalem itself (6.9), and (again according to Luke) Paul had done, after his conversion, when he first preached in Jerusalem (9.29). So, on that reading, the action of the Cypriots and Cyrenians does not seem to have been much of an innovation. This presumably explains the alternative reading — not 'Greek-speakers', but 'Greeks *(Hellēnas)*', that is, 'Gentiles', in the contrast made familiar by Paul's letters between 'Jews and Greeks'.[241]

Whatever it was that Luke originally wrote, the key to what he intended must lie in the contrast between the first phase of the dispersed Hellenists' preaching, 'to no one except Jews', and the second phase of preaching 'also to the *Hellēnistas/Hellēnas*'. Whatever the word originally dictated or scribed by Luke, he evidently intended it to stand in contrast to 'only Jews'.[242] Here it is appropriate to recall that *Hellēnistai* referred not to believing Greek-speakers only but also to diaspora Jews who did not believe in Jesus as Messiah. As already noted, the controversy occasioned by Stephen was properly speaking an inner-Hellenist controversy (6.9).[243] And in describing those with whom the converted Paul argued as 'Hellenists' (9.29), Luke obviously intended to refer not to diaspora Jews who belonged to the new sect but to diaspora Jews who disputed the claims of their fellow diaspora Jews, the Hellenists who, like Stephen and the converted Paul, believed and preached the good news of Jesus. The crucial factor here may be, then, that Luke uses *Hellēnistai* primarily as an indicator of language-usage — 'Greek speakers' — and that it is therefore the context which indicates *which* Greek-speakers are in view. In 6.1 it was the Greek-speakers who had become disciples; in 9.29 the diaspora Jews who rejected the claim that Jesus was Messiah, raised from the dead; and in 11.20 it is the Greek-speakers to be distinguished from 'the Jews' (to whom alone the dispersed believers initially spoke), that is, Greeks/non-Jews/Gentiles.[244] Here it is relevant to note that Paul

Cyrene'. With Barnabas also said to be from Cyprus (4.36) and, like Lucius of Cyrene, a leader of the Antiochene church (13.1), we can be confident that the tradition used by Luke here was based on good first-hand information.

240. Metzger, *Textual History* 386-89; Bruce (*Acts* 272) and Fitzmyer (*Acts* 476) prefer *Hellēnas*.

241. Rom. 1.16; 2.9-10; 3.9; 10.12; 1 Cor. 1.22, 24; 10.32; 12.13; Gal. 3.28; Col. 3.11.

242. Kraus, *Zwischen Jerusalem und Antiochia* 62.

243. See above, §24.2.

244. Cf. Metzger, *Textual Commentary* 388-89; Brehm (above, n. 19); Jervell, *Apg.* 322. Barrett allows the different referents of the same term *(Hellēnistai)* too much weight in

characterizes non-Jews as 'Greeks' more often than he does 'Gentiles'; it was their 'Greek-ness' which most distinguished Gentiles from Jews.[245]

Who were these Greek-speaking non-Jews? In the light of Josephus's two reports (referred to in §24.8a), we can confidently conclude that they were among the numerous Judaizing/God-fearing Gentiles who had attached themselves in some measure to (some of) the synagogue(s) of Antioch.[246] The transition from 11.19 to 11.20 did not necessarily involve a change of venue. Perhaps Luke makes so little of the innovation of preaching to such God-fearers because it was, from a story-teller's perspective, such a slight innovation. The dispersed Hellenists preached the good news of Jesus in the Antioch synagogue(s) and found, perhaps somewhat to their own surprise, that the God-fearing Gentile adherents found their message most compelling. Not such an obvious breakthrough, then, as Peter's conversion of Cornelius, attended as it was by visions and explicit guidance from the Spirit.

But even if we can make some sense of Luke's brevity in 11.19-21, we can hardly overstate the significance of the event from the perspective of a later historian of Christianity's beginnings. For one thing, Judaism was not a missionary religion.[247] Pharisees and Essenes were more naturally concerned to win fellow

---

arguing that the 11.20 reference comes from Luke's own hand rather than his source (*Acts* 1.547, 550-51).

245. 'Jew and Greek' — Rom. 1.16; 2.9, 10; 3.9; 10.12; 1 Cor. 1.22, 24; 10.32; 12.13; Gal. 3.28; Col. 3.11; 'Jews and Gentiles' — Rom. 3.29; 9.24; Gal. 2.14-15.

246. Zetterholm reckons there may have been as many as eighteen synagogues (*Formation* 37-38).

247. Against the older view (that Israel *was* a missionary religion), well exemplified by Harnack, *Mission* 9-18; 'this was the "missionary age" of the Jewish Religion' (Goppelt, *Apostolic* 82); 'Pharisaism by the time of Paul had probably become . . . highly missionary' (W. D. Davies, 'Paul: From the Jewish Point of View', *CHJ* 3.678-730 [here 682-83]); restated particularly by Feldman, *Jew and Gentile* ch. 9; other bibliography in J. Carleton Paget, 'Jewish Proselytism at the Time of Christian Origins: Chimera or Reality?', *JSNT* 62 (1996) 65-103 (here 66-67 nn. 4-17). See particularly S. McKnight, *A Light among the Gentiles: Jewish Missionary Activity in the Second Temple Period* (Minneapolis: Fortress, 1991); P. Fredriksen, 'Judaism, the Circumcision of Gentiles, and Apocalyptic Hope: Another Look at Galatians 1 and 2', *JTS* 42 (1991) 532-64 (here 533-48); M. Goodman, *Mission and Conversion: Proselytizing in the Religious History of the Roman Empire* (Oxford: Clarendon, 1994), also 'Jewish Proselytizing in the First Century', *Judaism in the Roman World* 91-116; R. Riesner, 'A Pre-Christian Jewish Mission?', in Ådna and Kvalbein, eds., *The Mission of the Early Church* 211-50; L. J. L. Peerbolte, *Paul the Missionary* (Leuven: Peeters, 2003) ch. 1; Schnabel, *Mission* ch. 6; J. P. Ware, *The Mission of the Church in Paul's Letter to the Philippians in the Context of Ancient Judaism* (NovTSupp 120; Leiden: Brill, 2005) ch. 1 and further chs. 2-3. See also the discussion between L. V. Rutgers, 'Attitudes to Judaism in the Greco-Roman Period: Reflections on Feldman's *Jew and Gentile in the Ancient World*', *JQR* 85 (1995) 361-95, and Feldman, 'Reflections on Rutgers's "Attitude to Judaism in the Greco-Roman Period"', *JQR* 86 (1995) 153-70. Peerbolte

Jews to a stricter devotion to their covenant obligations;[248] they were not in the business of trying to win *non*-Jews to adopt their praxis.[249] Judaism was, after all, the national religion of the Jews; it was not a matter of going out to convert non-Jews to a non-ethnic religion. Israel was very welcoming of God-fearers and proselytes and looked for an influx of the nations to Zion as part of the eschatological home-coming of the diaspora,[250] but an outgoing to persuade Gentiles to come in was not part of the script. So what the Hellenists began to do was exceptional and mind-blowing; *one of the earliest distinctives of Christianity is that it emerged within Second Temple Judaism as a missionary sect.*

For evidently we have to envisage a situation where a large number of Gentiles in Antioch became believers in Jesus Messiah, were (presumably) baptized, and thus attached themselves visibly to the new messianic sect. With 10.44-48 behind (or before) us, we can hardly doubt that Luke understood these Gentiles to have been fully accepted into the new movement, as those who had

---

takes the conclusions of McKnight and Goodman as the starting point for his examination of Paul's contribution to the development of Christianity as a proselytizing religion (for the influence of the earlier view of Harnack, that Christian mission was little more than a development of Jewish mission, and earlier bibliography, see *Paul* 2-6 and nn. 6-10). 'The theory that diaspora Judaism was characterized by missionary activity . . . is an integral part of a larger and decidedly Christian conception of ancient Judaism, in which Judaism is viewed not only as a preparation for the church but also as Christianity *manqué*. Such a conception may have a place in Christian theology but not in Jewish history' (S. J. D. Cohen, 'Adolph Harnack's "The Mission and Expansion of Judaism": Christianity Succeeds Where Judaism Fails', in B. A. Pearson, ed., *The Future of Early Christianity*, H. Koester FS [Minneapolis: Fortress, 1991] 163-69 [here 169]).

248. This is probably where Matt. 23.15 comes in. The readiness of 'scribes and Pharisees' to 'cross sea and land to make a single proselyte' probably refers to the zeal of an Eleazar to ensure that would-be converts to Judaism, like Izates, were converted all the way (Josephus, *Ant.* 20.38-46; see §27 n. 166 below). 'Matthew 23:15 probably has in mind not the conversion of pagan Gentiles to Judaism but the conversion of a God-fearing Gentile to become a proselyte' (Riesner, 'A Pre-Christian Jewish Mission?' 234, further 232-34). The passage may reflect the experience of churches like those in Galatia and Philippi, where traditionalist Jewish believers attempted to persuade the Gentile converts to be circumcised (i.e., become, in the traditionalists' view, full/genuine proselytes).

249. 4QMMT can now be seen as a classic example, written with the explicit hope of persuading fellow Jews to accept and follow the rulings listed in the letter (C26-32).

250. That the attractiveness of Judaism to many Gentiles and Judaism's welcome of such God-fearers and proselytes implies at least some missionary activity is argued by Carleton Paget and J. P. Dickson, *Mission-Commitment in Ancient Judaism and in the Pauline Communities* (WUNT 2.159; Tübingen: Mohr Siebeck, 2003) ch. 1 (on Matt. 23.15 see Paget, 94-98, and Dickson, 39-46); see also Kraus, *Zwischen Jerusalem und Antiochia* 71-81. The challenge to McKnight from P. Borgen, 'Militant and Peaceful Proselytism and Christian Mission', *Early Christianity and Hellenistic Judaism* (Edinburgh: Clark, 1996) 45-69, rests mainly on the few occasions when Jews had sufficient political and military power to enforce proselytism.

been fully accepted by God, despite their lack of circumcision;[251] such an inference is presumably encapsulated in 'the grace of God' which was so evident to Barnabas (11.23). That is to say, the Gentile God-fearers who accepted the Hellenist preaching themselves gained an acceptance and a degree of integration into the new sect which they had never been granted by the Jewish synagogue.[252] The 'judaizing' God-fearer, almost by definition, was so called because he had not (yet) taken the step (circumcision) which would integrate him fully into the Jewish community; he was still (only) a Judaizer, not (yet) a proselyte.

The point is, as with Cornelius, that for such a one to become a full member of a Jewish sect, while yet uncircumcised, was *an innovation which was bound to set the sect on a collision course with mainstream Judaism itself.* And while a single conversion, like that of Cornelius (and his household), could be seen as anomalous, a rapid growth in number of such converts (incomplete converts, from a traditional Jewish perspective) was bound to put a strain on the relations between the new sect and the traditional Judaism from which the new sect was emerging.[253] Apparently the strains did not become evident immediately, for reasons we will explore later,[254] but it would be a failure of historiographical responsibility not to note that a Rubicon was crossed by the innovative evangelism of the Hellenists in Antioch — the acceptance of growing numbers of Gentiles as full members of the new sect without requiring them to be circumcised. We should not infer that some great heart-searching took place before this policy was implemented. More likely the success of the preaching to Gentiles was simply taken as a sign of God's grace upon and through the preaching, and the acceptance of such Gentiles in the gatherings of the Christ people (Christians) raised no questions among the Hellenist believers themselves. Whatever the precise details, we should not let Luke's brevity obscure the significance of what happened in Antioch. Luke gives Peter the principal credit for the breakthrough to the Gentiles, which is why he goes into the Cornelius episode so fully and repeatedly (10.1–11.18).[255] But the Hellenists

251. That circumcision was not required of them is the *communis opinio* (Haenchen, *Acts* 365 and n. 6).

252. Peerbolte, however, wonders whether commensality of Jews and Greeks was already practised before the synagogue of Antioch became involved in the Jesus movement (*Paul* 131, 137); but although 'there is no indication that this commensality of Jews and Greeks started within the Jesus movement', it is an obvious deduction from the importance of shared meals in the Jesus tradition and the practice of the Jerusalem congregation (see above, §23.2d).

253. We may recall again the story of Izates' conversion to Judaism (referred to in n. 248 above). The date of his conversion is unclear, and it may not have happened by this time; even so, the story highlights the tensions between differing attitudes among Jews at this time towards Gentile adherents (see further below, §§27.2-3).

254. See again §§27.2-3 below.

255. Luke devotes sixty-six verses to the Cornelius episode (plus 15.7-11) but only eight to the Antioch breakthrough.

themselves probably told the story differently, and, to his credit, Luke retains their account alongside and within his own, even if weighting it differently. The Gentile mission began with the Hellenists in Antioch.

c. The Role of Barnabas

Re-enter one of the most important of the lesser figures in Luke's narrative. Barnabas had been the first named outside the apostolic circle in the opening months of the new sect's growth (4.36-37). According to Luke, it was Barnabas who broke down the suspicions of the Jerusalem disciples when the recently converted Saul/Paul first came to Jerusalem (9.26-27).[256] And subsequently he is depicted as settled in Antioch, and a leading member of the church there (13.1-2). He must therefore have been a man of substance, with property presumably in both Jerusalem and Antioch.[257] As a Cypriot himself (4.36), Barnabas was perhaps one of those (Hellenists) who had to flee from Jerusalem under the persecution.[258] Alternatively, as a figure of social standing, and therefore with some clout, he may have been exempted from the most serious of the measures taken against the disciples.

Whatever the historical facts, Luke has 'the church in Jerusalem' sending Barnabas to Antioch to check on the developments there (11.22). The implication is that the growth of the sect, and the growing numbers of Gentile disciples, raised similar issues for the Jerusalem leadership as had Philip's success in Samaria. This fits well, of course, with Luke's concern to portray the initial expansion of the new movement as directed or at least approved from Jerusalem. At the same time, however, we need not assume that Barnabas's mission should be attributed to Luke's creativity; Gal. 2.12 confirms the possibility of a delegation from Jerusalem to Antioch. And the fact is that Luke neither hesitates to attribute the breakthrough at Antioch to the unnamed Hellenists from Cyprus and Cyrene nor attempts to produce anything equivalent to 8.14-17. On the contrary, he reports straightforwardly and without ambiguity that Barnabas was wholly satisfied with what he found to be the case at Antioch — as satisfied as Peter had been in the case of Cornelius.[259]

256. On the problems surrounding Luke's report at this point see below, §25.5a.

257. See above, §23 n. 34 and at n. 51.

258. But Hengel and Schwemer have no doubt that he was a 'Hebrew' (*Paul* 213-15), a 'link man' with the Hellenists (216-17). And Öhler notes that, although as a Levite he may have sided with the Hebrews in relation to Stephen, Barnabas's openness to the events in Antioch and his mediating role speak highly of his character (cf. 4.36) (*Barnabas* 219-25, 479-80).

259. The grace of God (11.23) = Spirit falling upon (10.44-48). Note the parallel: Peter's success with Cornelius told in terms of the Spirit coming upon them (11.15-18), whereas Paul's

What we have here is further evidence of the perspective of Luke's sources of information, that is, presumably, his Hellenist or Antiochene sources. Luke incorporates here part of Antioch's own story of its establishment. In that story Barnabas evidently played an important role, for he settled in Antioch and (soon) became a leading member of the church there (11.25-26; 13.1-2). He was remembered as a 'good man, full of the Holy Spirit and of faith' (11.24),[260] who presumably helped consolidate the expansion and establish the new church on a secure basis. Not only so, but as a man of substance and status, held in high regard by the Jerusalem disciples, he was able to establish and himself constitute a bond of friendship and mutual confidence between Jerusalem and the new church in Antioch.[261] This is already hinted at in Luke's report of the famine visit made by Barnabas and Saul/Paul to Jerusalem on behalf of the church in Antioch (11.27-30), and in the later interactions between Jerusalem and Antioch (Gal. 2.1-14), to both of which we must return.[262] Here the point is that Luke's account of the establishment of the church of Antioch must be based on first-hand recollections (of the Antiochenes themselves), which Luke has faithfully reported, and from their own perspective, albeit in briefest outline.

d. The First 'Christians'

The other notable feature of this brief paragraph is the final note, almost a footnote, that 'it was in Antioch that the disciples were first called "Christians"' (11.26). This too Luke passes on and passes over without comment, but it too marked a notable stage of development for the new sect. The only other names used for the new movement by others — 'the way' and 'the sect of the Nazarenes'[263] — indicate that it was viewed from a Jewish perspective as a movement within the Judaism of the day, but without much specification of its character. But the term used here was a new coinage — *Christianoi*, 'Christians'. More important, *Christianoi* is a Greek form of the Latin *Christiani;* that is, the name was almost certainly coined by a Latin-speaker or one accustomed to the Latin formation.[264] This implies that it was coined by the Roman authorities in

---

account of success in Gentile evangelism is put in the same terms as here, the grace of God (Gal. 2.7-9). Which prompts the question: Did Paul learn his distinctive understanding of 'grace' from the Hellenists or from the church in Antioch?

260. Note again the Hellenist fingerprint: like Stephen, *plērēs pneumatos hagiou kai pisteōs* (6.5; 11.24; see above, §24.1); contrast Barrett: 'another Lucanism' (*Acts* 1.553).

261. The principal historical feature which emerges is Barnabas's role as a mediating figure — 'a *Vermittlungsfigur*' (Öhler, *Barnabas* 481-82).

262. See below, §§25.5g, 27.2-4.

263. See above, §20.1.

264. *Pace* E. J. Bickerman, 'The Name of Christians', *HTR* 42 (1949) 109-24, who ar-

Antioch on the analogy of Herodians *(Hērōdianoi)* or Caesarians, the party of Caesar, or possibly members of Caesar's household *(Kaisarianoi)*.[265] The 'Christians' were so called, then, because they were perceived to be partisans of 'Christ', followers of 'Christ', members of the Christ-party.[266] It is worth noting that initially the term appears predominantly in texts which either refer, like Acts 11.26 or 26.8, to Syria (and Palestine) or come from there.[267]

The significance of this development is twofold. For one thing it confirms that the growth of the new movement in Antioch must have had a sufficiently public character (numbers involved, some prominent people, public baptisms?) to catch the attention of the Roman authorities, who were ever vigilant against new groups and societies, which might prove subversive. For another, it confirms that belief in and talk of Jesus as the Messiah *(Christos* in Greek) must have been characteristic of the burgeoning assembly in Antioch. This was the reference that any spies or informants must have heard being made regularly in gatherings of

---

gued for a middle meaning of the verb *chrēmatisai,* 'to style oneself', with the corollary that the disciples of Jesus were the first to so style themselves (123); similarly Spicq, 'Dénominations' 13 n. 1. But see Karpp, 'Christennamen' 1132; H. B. Mattingly, 'The Origin of the Name Christiani', *JTS* 9 (1958) 26-37 (here 28 n. 3); BDAG 1089.

265. B. Reicke observes that the verb used *(chrēmatisai)* has the sense of 'called officially' and translates 11.26, 'for the first time in Antioch the disciples were publicly known as Christians' *(TDNT* 9.481-82). Hengel and Schwemer also suggest that the name could have emerged during the tense period when the unrest caused by Caligula's policy may have made the authorities more vigilant *(Paul* 229-30).

266. 'The Greek-speaking synagogues in Rome used the Greek suffix *-esioi* in their names. The suffix *-ianus* constitutes a political comment. . . . It is not used of the followers of a god. It classifies people as partisans of a political or military leader, and is mildly contemptuous' (Judge, 'Judaism and the Rise of Christianity' 363). See also §21.1d; and further Barrett, *Acts* 1.556-57; Hengel and Schwemer, *Paul* 228-29 and nn. 1171-72, 1185; Fitzmyer, *Acts* 478; D. G. Horrell, 'The Label *Christianos:* 1 Peter 4:16 and the Formation of Christian Identity', *JBL* 126 (2007) 383-91 (see also §37 n. 228 below). 'The element of reservation in some Christians' acceptance of the word militates against its being an original self-designation' (Riesner, *Paul's Early Period* 112); see also §20 n. 5 above. A. M. Schwemer, 'Paulus in Antiochien', *BZ* 42 (1998) 161-80, notes that a recently discovered inscription from the year 20, dealing with the trial against C. Calpurnius Piso, charged with the murder of Germanicus, includes the information that the Roman troops in Syria were divided into *Pisoniani* and *Caesariani,* and that this *senatus consultum* was to be prominently displayed on bronze tablets in the most crowded thoroughfare (171-72). These data undermine Jossa's insistence that the term means 'belonging to' and not merely 'being a follower of', as one might be a follower of Caesar or Herod *(Jews or Christians?* 75-76). White suggests that the name may not have been coined for forty or fifty years or more after the death of Jesus, on the grounds that Paul never uses the name *(From Jesus to Christianity* 121-22), but if it was a label coined by the Antioch authorities, that could provide sufficient explanation for Paul's unwillingness to use it (contrast 1 Peter 4.16).

267. Hengel and Schwemer, *Paul* 226-27 and n. 1158.

the new group(s), and they or the authorities presumably concluded that *Christos* was the name of their leader.[268]

This last observation has, in turn, a double corollary. One is that the term *Christos* was thus early understood as a name rather than as a title. That would be understandable if the Roman authorities in Antioch were relying on reports from Greeks who probably did not understand the titular significance of 'Messiah'. It may also indicate, however, that the titular significance was already being over-laid in the gatherings of the new church as frequent reference to 'Messiah Jesus' or 'Jesus Messiah' *(Christos Iēsous, Iēsous Christos)* transformed the title into a proper name. This would help explain why the titular significance of *Christos* in Paul's letters has fallen largely into the background.[269] It also implies, of course, that the messianic title for Jesus was probably not recognized by the authorities or the name *Christos* seen by them as bearing any political significance. Perhaps the first Christians in Antioch themselves did not press the political connotations of the name, and may even have deliberately sought to avoid or prevent the asso-ciation Messiah = king, which the Jerusalem authorities seem to have exploited when they handed Jesus over to Pilate.[270] Otherwise the Roman authorities in Antioch would probably have been a good deal more worried about the 'Chris-tians' than either Luke's or Paul's accounts of the Antioch church indicates to have been the case. Such considerations must be weighed carefully when the possible political overtones of the earliest Christian gospel are considered.

The other corollary is that the designation of the Antiochene disciples as 'Christians' should not be taken as necessarily indicating recognition by the au-thorities that the 'Christians' were a new religion or had become quite separate and distinct from the Antioch synagogues.[271] Josephus refers to 'the synagogue'

---

268. Cf. Suetonius, *Claudius* 25.4, where the assumption seems to be that 'Chrestus' was the name of the instigator of the disturbances in Rome (see above, §21.1d). A variant spell-ing, *Chrēstianos,* is attested for *Christianos* in fourth-century correspondence and inscriptions from N. Phrygia (*NDIEC* 2.102; 3.98).

269. See below, §29.7b, and above, §23 n. 215.

270. See *Jesus Remembered* §15.3a.

271. Kraus, *Zwischen Jerusalem und Antiochia* 62-64; Jervell, *Apg.* 324-25; Jossa, *Jews or Christians?* 126 ('no distinction was yet made between Jews and Christians'). To refer again to Suetonius: the unrest over Chrestus resulted in the expulsion of (the) *Jews* from Rome (§21.1d). Contrast Becker: 'It is a name that points to the independence of the group . . . an al-ready independent group' (*Paul* 87); and Barrett, who is not untypical, but in fact quite anachro-nistic, when he suggests that the coining of the title 'Christians' already implied that Christians were 'a third race', 'clearly distinguishable from Jews' (*Acts* 1.548, 556); see P. Richardson, *Is-rael in the Apostolic Church* (SNTSMS 10; Cambridge: Cambridge University, 1969). K. Haacker, 'Paul's Life', in J. D. G. Dunn, ed., *The Cambridge Companion to St. Paul* (Cam-bridge: Cambridge University, 2003) 19-33, points out that 'the very form of the term *Christianoi* does not sound like the name of a new cult worshipping Christ: the appropriate

of the Antiochene Jews (*War* 7.44), but with the numbers involved we have to assume that there were many Jewish assemblies *(synagōgai)*, at least some of which probably met in larger private houses. And it is hardly likely that the 'Christians' soon became distinguishable from the 'mixed' groups (Jews, proselytes and God-fearers) who took part in such gatherings.[272] More likely, the name was coined by the authorities to designate what was perceived as a faction within the larger mix of diaspora Jews and their Gentile Judaizers.[273] Its very newness and distinctiveness (signalled precisely by frequent reference to *Christos*) would be sufficient reason for the authorities to take note of these 'Christians'.[274]

It is, of course, ironic that the name 'Christian' derived from the need for suspicious Roman authorities to have a shorthand term by which to refer to those who named Jesus as (the) Christ. The slowness of the name to be taken up by those it designated[275] suggests that the 'Christians' themselves may not have been overly enthusiastic about being thus named. But the name stuck, and as so often happens, it is the nickname by which a movement is first identified by others but in due course becomes the accepted and preferred self-designation.

e. When Did All This Happen?

As with so many of these central chapters of Acts, the question arises as to their relative timing, and the issue of the chronological relationship of these episodes

---

term for such a cultic fellowship would have been *Christastai'* (26). Zetterholm observes that 'since the synagogue was considered as a *collegium* and enjoyed protection, it is highly unlikely that the Jesus movement would organize in any other way than the one that had the approval of the authorities of the city' (*Formation* 99).

272. Hengel and Schwemer assume a clearer 'separation from the synagogue communities', with the 'Christians' perhaps already meeting on 'the first day of the week' (*Paul* 200-204, 225), but they also observe that 'it was always possible to found relatively independent "special synagogues"' (285). An early rupture with the bulk of Antioch synagogues would have made difficult the recruitment of Gentile God-fearers who attended the synagogues, which presumably continued for a long time. In addition, we should note that the overlap between synagogue and church persisted for another three centuries in many parts of the Roman Empire, including Antioch (see further vol. 3; also my *Partings* [²2006] xviii-xxiv).

273. Similarly Wedderburn, *History* 69.

274. J. J. Taylor, 'Why Were the Disciples First Called "Christians" at Antioch?', *RB* 101 (1994) 75-94, notes that the names 'Christ' and 'Christian' first appear in non-Christian sources associated with public disorder (referring to Suetonius, *Claudius* 25.4, and Tacitus, *Ann.* 15.44.2), which suggests that the crisis caused among Jews by Caligula's order to have his effigy erected in the Jerusalem temple (see above, n. 265) may well have caused Roman authorities in the East to look more closely at Jewish groups. See also Schnabel, *Mission* 794-96.

275. See above, §20.1(1), and §24 n. 264.

to one another is posed. It is all the more important in this case, since without the insertion of 9.1–11.18 the obvious implication would be that the missionary outreach of those scattered by Saul's persecution carried the gospel in speedy and unbroken sequence all the way to Antioch. That is, the breakthrough at Antioch would then appear to be quite independent of these two other episodes. And presumably that is how Luke's Hellenist sources told their story; the story of the founding of the church at Antioch did not include a recollection of Paul's conversion or of Peter's mission further south.

Given that the church of Antioch was commissioning missionary work no later than the mid-40s (Acts 13.1-3) and was clearly well established before the Antioch incident (Gal. 2.11-17), we can safely deduce that the breakthrough at Antioch probably happened within the 30s, that is, within the first ten years of Christianity's existence.[276] Indeed, if Saul/Paul was persecuting the new sect already within two or three years of Jesus' crucifixion, then the breakthrough at Antioch could already have been taking place in the mid-30s.[277] Luke's ordering of his narrative makes it impossible to achieve greater clarity.

At issue here, of course, is the question whether Luke has given sufficient credit in his narrative to what happened at Antioch. Has he, in his desire to credit Peter with the decisive or at least archetypal breakthrough to Gentile converts (10.1–11.18), failed to acknowledge that it was at Antioch that the real breakthrough took place? Has he, in his desire to show Peter as the pioneer, failed to do sufficient justice to the unnamed Hellenists and to Barnabas? We will have to return to such questions in §§25 and 26. For the moment it will have to suffice to note, in sum, that the breakthrough at Antioch was of major proportions:

- the first time that the gospel penetrated into a major city of the Roman Empire;
- the establishment of what would prove to be the springboard for extensive mission among Gentiles;
- the first conversions of Gentiles (without requiring them to be circumcised) in substantial numbers;

---

276. 'The traditions behind vv. 19-26 are without doubt historical, namely that the Hellenists began the mission to the Gentiles in Cyprus, Phoenicia and Antioch. . . . Their beginnings might lie in the middle of the 30s' (Lüdemann, *Early Christianity* 137). Hengel and Schwemer suggest a date around 36; 'a year earlier or later is neither here nor there' (*Paul* 172-73). 'Once removed from the straitjacket of Lucan chronology this piece of tradition [11.20] raises the question whether this action may not even antedate the outbreak of persecution against Stephen and his group in Jerusalem' (Wedderburn, *History* 68).

277. Riesner notes that various dates for the founding of the church in Antioch are to be found in tradition — 31/32, 37/38, 41 — which point to a date between 35 and 39 (*Paul's Early Period* 59-60, 110).

• and so also the first fully mixed congregations of Jewish and non-Jewish believers.

At Antioch the new messianic movement focused on Jesus began to modulate into something different — a mutation achieved through the Hellenists, as the sequence (chs. 6–8, 11.19-26) beginning with 'the Hellenists' and ending with 'Christians' suggests. As the believers were first called 'Christians' in Antioch, so we can say with some justification that it was at Antioch that we can begin to speak of the new movement as 'Christianity'.

24.9. A Hellenist/Antiochene Theology?

Is it possible at this distance in time to identify something that can properly be called the theology and praxis of the church in Antioch, or, alternatively, of the Hellenists to whose evangelism the church at Antioch owed its existence? Attempts to move in this direction are in danger of trying to weave too large a cloth from too few threads,[278] but there are at least some indications which are worth pulling together. Whether they amount to a coherent and distinctive expression of earliest Christianity remains a moot point.

a. The Jesus Tradition into Greek

The most obvious starting point is with the identifying character of the *Hellēnistai,* the Greek-speakers — that is, that they functioned in Greek. This

---

278. The most notable attempts have been by J. Becker, *Paul: Apostle to the Gentiles* (Louisville: Westminster John Knox, 1993) 104-12; E. Rau, *Von Jesus zu Paulus. Entwicklung und Rezeption der antiochenischen Theologie im Urchristentum* (Stuttgart: Kohlhammer, 1994); and the still more ambitious discussion in Berger, *Theologiegeschichte* parts 5-11. Cf. the brief outline offered by Neudorfer, *Stephanuskreis* 338-39. W. Schmithals, 'Paulus als Heidenmissionar und das Problem seiner theologischen Entwicklung', in D.-A. Koch, ed., *Jesu Rede von Gott und ihre Nachgeschichte im frühen Christentum,* W. Marxsen FS (Gütersloh: Mohn, 1989) 235-51, thinks that a universalist Christianity had already been attained in Damascus; but as Schnabel points out, the thesis has no basis in the texts of the NT (*Mission* 700, and further 796-97). Schmithals claims to be able to distinguish a 'Damascene (pre-existence) christology' from an 'Antiochene (adoption) christology' (*Theologiegeschichte* ch. 5), though he follows the same fallacious logic of identifying different emphases with different communities. Stanton ('Stephen' 346) and Räisänen ('Hellenisten' 1470) summarize the various suggestions to trace the influence of the Hellenists in other NT literature. But note the cautions of Hengel and Schwemer, *Paul* 286-91, 309 (warning against 'pan-Antiochenism', 286); and Schnelle, *Paul* 116-18; and the more restrained summary treatment of Hahn, *Theologie* 1.166-75.

must mean that the message they heard and were won to came to them in Greek. Which must mean, in turn, that those who successfully evangelized the Hellenists must have been bilingual and thus able to translate the message about and teaching of Jesus into Greek. I do not by any means exclude the possibility that this process of translation of the Aramaic Jesus tradition into Greek was already underway during Jesus' own mission. Nor do I necessarily imply that the translation was undertaken as a formal exercise, directed or managed by a core group of disciples (the apostles), or that it was a literary exercise in the beginning. On the contrary, I suspect that preaching and teaching in Greek was dependent on those, perhaps initially only few, who could function easily in both languages and that there was a good deal of random transmission as individuals talked and communicated in a whole variety of situations. My point is simply that this process seems to have been under way from the very beginning, and that from very early days (weeks and months, rather than years) there was a substantial and growing number of baptized members of the new sect who knew and were familiar with the Jesus tradition in Greek.[279]

Given the character of translation, of course, the inevitable corollary is the extension of the diversity of the Jesus tradition and the way it was heard and understood. Since few if any words in one language overlap exactly with the spectrum of meaning and overtone of the nearest equivalents in another, since grammar and syntax are peculiar each to its own language, and since idiom is very dialect- and culture-sensitive, the very acts of translating the Jesus tradition from Aramaic to Greek would inevitably introduce greater variation and flexibility into the forms and groupings of the Jesus tradition. To recognize this, of course, need not carry the further corollary that the substance of the Jesus tradition was significantly altered. Nor need it imply that the way in which the Jesus tradition was performed and rehearsed in the Greek-speaking gatherings was different in character and content from the performances in Aramaic. Nor does it follow that any control exercised by those who had been the first witnesses or the earliest gatherings of disciples was thereby dissipated. For the Greek-speakers to become members of the Nazarene sect, they must have been sufficiently informed of the beliefs and tradition of the new sect and to have joined their faith and testimony

279. Hengel quite rightly gives considerable emphasis to the role of the Hellenists in interpreting the message of Jesus into the new medium of the Greek language: 'We owe the real bridge between Jesus and Paul to those almost unknown Jewish-Christian "Hellenists"' (*Between Jesus and Paul* 24, 29). The point is taken up by E. Larsson, 'Die Hellenisten und die Urgemeinde', *NTS* 33 (1987) 205-25 (here 207-208, 214-15). Räisänen thinks the time too short for what Hengel envisages ('Hellenisten' 1507-8), but the greater the distance between Jerusalem and the putting of the Jesus tradition into Greek, the greater the difficulty of explaining how it came about. It is much more probable that the process began as soon as the gospel began to be preached to Greek-speakers.

to that of the Aramaic-speakers. What should be acknowledged, however, is that performance and transmission of the Jesus tradition would inevitably have been that much more variable. Indeed, the variability of the Jesus tradition still evident in the Synoptic Gospels in their written form may well go back in greater or lesser degree to those early attempts to translate it from Aramaic into Greek. Given the rather modest amount of variation at the end of the process (the Synoptic Gospels), especially when the obvious editorial redactions of the Evangelists themselves are taken into consideration, it is not at all fanciful to suppose that the major transitions (note the plural) from Aramaic to Greek left a very substantial mark on the tradition in its Greek forms.

How much of the development of the Jesus tradition which was outlined in §21.5 above should be traced to the Hellenists is not at all clear. But some features can be identified with some probability:[280]

- We may suspect that the transition from 'the son of man' to 'the Son of Man' in the tradition was in part at least a result of translating an Aramaic idiom unfamiliar to Greek ears.[281] The fact that the only titular 'Son of Man' reference outside the Gospels appears on the lips of Stephen (Acts 7.56) is perhaps a clue that the title functioned for some time in Hellenist references to the exalted Jesus.
- The sequence Mark 2.1–3.6 may reflect this transition, since it focuses on the authority of Jesus as the Son of Man (2.10, 28) but still assumes the importance of the Sabbath (2.23–3.5).[282]
- In the same sequence, the addition of 2.20 to Mark 2.18-20, implying the resumption of fasting (cf. Acts 13.2-3),[283] should perhaps be attributed to Hellenist reworking of the tradition; presumably with their dispersion from Jerusalem, the Hellenists' expectation of Jesus' imminent return (to the Temple?) slackened.
- The sharper critique of the necessity for ritual purity implied in Mark 7.15, 19 may provide a further example of a Hellenistic tendency, since the whole logic of ritual purity was predicated on the necessity of purity in order to enter the Temple.[284]
- At the beginning of the passion narrative, perhaps it was the Hellenists who made explicit that Jesus' 'cleansing of the Temple' was with a view to its

280. Cf. and contrast Berger, *Theologiegeschichte* 149.
281. See *Jesus Remembered* 739-46.
282. See above at §21 n. 278.
283. *Jesus Remembered* 442 n. 288; Barrett observes that all three references to fasting in Acts (13.2, 3; 14.23) stand in connection with Antioch (*Acts* 1.605).
284. See also *Jesus Remembered* 289-90, 573-77.

    eschatological role as a house of prayer 'for all the nations' (Mark 11.17).[285]

- In the tradition of the hearing before the high priest, the use of *cheiropoiētos* in Mark 14.58 probably reflects the transposition of the tradition into Hellenistic Jewish categories.[286]

- The description of the Son of Man 'standing at the right hand of God' (Acts 7.56) indicates a merging of Dan. 7.13 and Ps. 110.1 and may suggest another point in the Jesus tradition where Hellenist elaboration of the tradition can be detected (Mark 14.62).[287]

- If most of these examples relate to the Markan tradition, it is also worth considering whether it is to the Hellenists that we owe the initial groupings of teaching (in Greek) which were subsequently taken up into the Q source.[288]

b. Developing Christology and Theology

The transition from Aramaic to Greek will also inevitably have involved some degree of mutation in theological and liturgical language.

- We have already noted that the transition from the Aramaic *Messias* to the Greek *Christos* seems to have contributed to the steady loss of the name's titular significance.

- In contrast, the address of Jesus as *mar,* 'Lord', when translated into the Greek *kyrios,* probably gained a richer resonance, given its regular and extensive usage in Greek cults.[289] Stephen is recalled as praying or appealing to Jesus as 'Lord' (7.59-60), and Jesus as having the authority to ascribe/record sins or to refrain from doing so (7.60);[290] though we should also note that in 7.55-56 Jesus 'at the right hand of God' (= the 'my Lord' of Ps. 110.1)[291] is distinguished from 'the glory of God' (different from John 12.41), and that as 'standing' (and not 'sitting'), Jesus is not seen as sharing God's throne. And the final section of the Hellenist narrative (Acts 11.19-26) reports them as 'preaching the good news of the Lord Jesus' (11.20), the only time early evangelism is so described in Acts.

---

285. *Jesus Remembered* 636-40.
286. *Jesus Remembered* 631 n. 89.
287. See *Jesus Remembered* 749-51, 761.
288. See above, §21.5c.
289. For the data see LSJ, *kyrios* B; *NDIEC* 3.33, 35-36. In Acts 25.26 the emperor is referred to simply as 'the Lord'. See also below, §29.4d.
290. Perhaps like Enoch, 'the scribe of righteousness'; see above, §23 at n. 253.
291. See above, §23.4d.

- In contrast also, the reference to Moses-prophet and Son of Man language in the Stephen episode (7.37, 56) — the latter echoed in Hegesippus's account of the execution of James the brother of Jesus[292] — suggest that the Hellenists initially adopted early christological formulations of the first Jerusalem believers.
- Some at least of the confessional and hymnic formulae which Paul echoes in his letters, usually in reference to Jesus,[293] must go back to his Hellenist instructors in the faith and may well have been formulated in Antioch (see further below, §24.9c).[294]
- Worthy of note also is the description of God as *ho hypsistos,* 'the Most High' (7.48), a title for the highest god which appears regularly in Greek writings and inscriptions, and which was an obvious term for Jews to use for God when writing in Greek.[295]
- The fact that the Hellenists had to use the LXX rather than the Hebrew Bible would have had further consequences, given not least the larger scope of the LXX.[296]
- A further possibility is that the formula *baptizesthai eis to onoma,* 'baptized in the name of', first used in (the Hellenist source of) 8.16, reflects a deliberate interpretation of baptism on the analogy of a commercial transaction (as a cheque today transfers something to the possession of the one named).[297]

c. Attitude to the Temple

A second characteristic of the Hellenist traditions of Acts 6–8 is their critical attitude to the Jerusalem Temple. Stephen is remembered as reviving Jesus' talk of the Temple's destruction; the speech attributed to Stephen describes it as idola-

292. See below, §36.2b.

293. See above, §21.4e.

294. E.g., D. Georgi, 'Der vorpaulinische Hymnus Phil. 2,6-11', in E. Dinkler, ed., *Zeit und Geschichte,* R. Bultmann FS (Tübingen: Mohr Siebeck, 1964) 263-93, attributes the hymn to the group round Stephen; H. Merklein, 'Zur Entstehung der urchristlichen Aussage vom präexistenten Sohn Gottes', *Studien zu Jesus und Paulus* (WUNT 43; Tübingen: Mohr Siebeck, 1987) 247-76, argues that the Hellenists were the first to contemplate Jesus' pre-existence.

295. BDAG 1045; Fitzmyer, *Acts* 384. Luke uses the term for God on several occasions in his Gospel, but the only time the term is used for God elsewhere in the Gospels is on the lips of the Gerasene demoniac (Mark 5.7); it appears elsewhere in Acts only in 16.17, again on the lips of a spirit-possessed Gentile!

296. But there is no hint in our sources that the Hellenists introduced the practice of 'allegorical' interpretation of Scripture, as suggested by Berger, *Theologiegeschichte* 141.

297. First suggested by W. Heitmüller, *'Im Name Jesu',* but influential thereafter (see Hartman, *Name* 40 n. 16).

trous; Philip goes to the Samaritans, who still prized the memory of their destroyed temple on Mount Gerizim, and wins them to the new faith, disregarding their renegade status;[298] and then he goes on to accept by baptism one who was wholly unacceptable in the Jerusalem Temple, a Gentile and a eunuch to boot.

The likelihood is that such Hellenist critique of the Temple included critique of the Hebrew traditionalist practice of continuing to resort to and meet in the Temple. And whoever the subsequent persecution targeted, the outcome was that the more traditionalist wing remained in (or returned to) Jerusalem, whereas the Hellenists took the gospel of Jesus with them as they spread out from Jerusalem. As diaspora Jews they would have been accustomed anyway to functioning religiously without constant reference to the Temple and in effect independently of the Temple and the Temple hierarchy. We should probably see, then, the roots of a different attitude to Temple and priesthood, such as we find in Paul,[299] as sunk deeply into Hellenist soil.

Did this critique include the development of a theology of Jesus' death as a sacrifice for sin, and as a sacrifice which rendered the sacrificial cult of the Temple redundant?[300] We have already noted that if Jesus saw any sacrificial connotations of his own anticipated death, it would most likely have been in terms of a covenant sacrifice.[301] Also, the continued attendance of the earliest disciples at the Temple, even after Pentecost, presumably indicates that they did not think of Jesus' death as rendering the Temple cult obsolete.[302] But if the Hellenists turned their back on the Temple, either that could be because they were already developing an understanding of Jesus' death as a sacrifice — indeed, as *the* final atoning sacrifice — or the formulation of such a theology could have been the result of their rejection of the Temple as *the* place for God to encounter his people.

Another factor may be that the theology of martyrdom may have emerged in the first place or have become strongest within diaspora Judaism.[303] In which

298. 'The hiccup over the reception of the Samaritans, which may itself reflect the depth of the hostility between Jew and Samaritan, makes their reception of the Spirit all the more emphatic. The Spirit proves integrative where the Temple had been divisive' (Dunn, *Acts* 102-103).

299. See below, §30 nn. 277 and 243.

300. Pesch, *Apg.* 1.239; Becker, *Paul* 112; Stuhlmacher, *Biblische Theologie* 1.192-95; Räisänen, 'Hellenisten' 1490-91, 1506; Löning, 'Circle of Stephen' 111-12; Hengel and Schwemer, *Paul* 182, 199; Schnabel, *Mission* 661-65; Barnett, *Birth* 75; Wilckens, *Theologie* 1/2.237-38.

301. *Jesus Remembered* 816-18.

302. See above, §23.5.

303. E. Lohse, *Martyrer und Gottesknecht* (Göttingen: Vandenhoeck und Ruprecht, ²1963), suggests that diaspora Judaism developed a martyr theology as a substitute for the sacrificial cult in faraway Jerusalem (71). The martyr parallel may have been present to Jesus in his hope of vindication like that of the martyrs of 2 Maccabees 7; see *Jesus Remembered* 821-

case it would have been a natural step for the Hellenists to think of Jesus' death in these terms and to go down the same road as 4 Maccabees in describing Jesus' death in terms of the Day of Atonement ritual (4 Macc. 17.21-22).[304] Here again there may be a hint in the Hellenist sources on which Luke draws in his composition of chs. 6–8. For we recall that it is only Philip who is credited with the explicit identification of the suffering servant of Isaiah 53 with Jesus (Acts 8.32-35). As noted above, Luke's reference conforms to his own pattern of presenting Jesus' death within a suffering-vindication contrast ('you crucified . . . but God raised').[305] But perhaps Acts 8.32-35 reflects a fuller Hellenist reflection on the death of Jesus as a vicarious sacrifice.

All this is unavoidably speculative, but it may feed instructively into the issue raised earlier, as to whether the gospel as Paul learned it when he was converted, 'that Christ died for our sins' (1 Cor. 15.3), was actually a Hellenist formulation.[306] That is not to say that the theology of Jesus' death as vicarious sacrifice was not accepted by the Jerusalem leadership. There is nothing in our sources to suggest that, and the absence of any indication that such a theology of the cross was controversial within earliest Christianity suggests otherwise. Nonetheless, the fact that Jesus' death as sacrifice was a central feature of Paul's theology may indicate that he saw it as requiring more emphasis than it had originally received.

d. Developing Outreach

Both of the first two items imply a willingness on the part of the Hellenists to develop their understanding both of the Jesus tradition and of the gospel they preached and lived by. That would include the use of the (Jewish) Scriptures in Greek, with translations of the Scriptures they cited following the Greek where it diverged from the Hebrew. It would include also the wider scope of the LXX, with use of a writing like the Wisdom of Solomon, so clearly reflected in Romans 1–2.[307] And it would probably include the beginning of engagement with the wider Greek philosophies and religions. None of that is particularly evi-

---

22, and further M. de Jonge, *Christology in Context: The Earliest Christian Response to Jesus* (Philadelphia: Westminster, 1988) 181-84.

304. Becker, *Paul* 112.

305. See again §23.5c above.

306. Schenke, *Urgemeinde* 334-39; Jossa, *Jews or Christians?* 82-83. It would naturally follow that the pre-Pauline formula which Paul quotes in Rom. 3.25-26 could be a Hellenist formulation (see, e.g., Kraus, *Zwischen Jerusalem und Antiochia* 53-54 [with bibliography], 176-78).

307. See below, §33 nn. 99, 105.

dent in the Hellenist materials Luke has left to us, but the establishment of a church in Antioch and engagement with other Greeks/Greek-speakers there cannot but have led the Hellenists/Antiochenes at least a little way down that path.

Nor should we underplay the contrast which Luke was evidently quite happy to leave with us — between a Jerusalem church which remained rooted in Jerusalem, without any thought or effort to evangelize beyond its walls, and a Hellenist dispersion which preached widely, and with marked success wherever they went. To what extent the third point (§24.9c) dovetails with this one is unclear: it is certainly possible that the turning away from the Temple was also a turning away from hope of an imminent parousia of Messiah Jesus at/to the Temple,[308] that is, a growing belief that the good news of Jesus had to be preached more widely before the Christ would come again (cf. Acts 1.6-8). Here again we can only speculate on the possibility. What is clear, however, is that the beginning of Christian mission, properly speaking, has to be credited to the Hellenists, even if it is the case, as Luke suggests, that the wider initiative in evangelism was a by-product of the persecution. It would be consistent with this line of thought that the next great initiative in the same direction is attributed to the church in Antioch, with Jerusalem being shown, even by Luke, as more of a brake on such initiatives than as urging them forward and initiating further outreach on their own account. In other words, *we should probably credit the Hellenists with turning the new sect within Second Temple Judaism into an evangelistic sect,* the first sustained evangelistic outreach in the history of Israel — a major development indeed.

All this may also help explain what otherwise is a puzzling detail in the tradition Paul received when he was converted. For 1 Cor. 15.5-7 recalls appearances of the risen Christ both to 'the twelve' and to 'all the apostles'. On Luke's terms the distinction remains a puzzle, since he regards 'the twelve' and 'the apostles' as synonymous terms. The solution may lie in the fact that initially 'apostle' had the (to us) less specific meaning of 'missionary'.[309] That is to say, the appearance to 'all the apostles' may be part of Hellenist tradition, recalling that the impulse to evangelize so extensively was in response to (an) appearance(s) of the risen Christ to those who proceeded to distinguish themselves by their successful evangelism and church-founding as they moved away from Jerusalem. Once again we are in the realm of speculation, since our sources are silent on the matter. But we should recall once again also that the understanding of apostleship just outlined (appointed by the risen Christ to evangelize and found churches) was Paul's understanding. So perhaps, here again, we should see evidence of how Paul's understanding of his vocation was shaped by the fact that the

---

308. See above, §23.4f.
309. 'Apostle' is a transliteration, not a translation, of *apostolos.*

first Christians with whom he had anything to do at or following his conversion were themselves Hellenists.

e. The Impact of the Spirit

A prominent feature in the sources on which Luke drew for his account of the Hellenists and of the breakthrough in Antioch is the emphasis placed on the Spirit.[310] In itself, of course, that hardly distinguishes the material of Acts 6–8 and 11.19-26 from the rest of Acts. But the description of individuals as 'full of the Spirit', evidently as a prominent and enduring characteristic (as distinct from Luke's own description of individuals being 'filled with the Spirit' on particular occasions),[311] suggests more than a mere linguistic difference. Possibly also implied is a somewhat different understanding of how the Spirit operates in and on individuals. Certainly Luke's own language focuses primarily on the coming of the Spirit, on the Spirit as acting upon a person.[312] Perhaps, then, the Hellenists thought more of the Spirit as indwelling believers and saw a 'fullness' of the Spirit — evidenced (in the cases in point) in leadership potential (6.3), in effective witness (6.5, 10), in vision (7.55) and in readiness to recognize God's grace even in unexpected circumstances (11.23-24)[313] — as the primary mark of God's presence and ongoing activity in and through a person. Since a similar difference in emphasis distinguishes Luke from Paul in their respective linguistic portrayals of the Spirit's action on, in and through individuals,[314] perhaps here too we can see the soil out of which grew Paul's own understanding of how the Spirit operates.

The possibility gains some little further strength by recalling also the prominence of the talk of 'grace' within the same material.[315] The parallel between Acts 11.23-24 and Gal. 2.8-9 is especially noticeable: the grace of God was so clearly manifested in the successful evangelism of both the unnamed Hellenists in Antioch (Acts 11.21) and of Paul in Syria and Cilicia (Gal. 1.21)[316] that the less warmly disposed pillar apostles in Jerusalem could no more deny it than the sympathetic Barnabas in Antioch.[317] It is more likely, then, that Paul initially

---

310. Acts 6.3, 5, 10; 7.51, 55; 8.7, (15, 17-19), 29, 39; 11.24; note also 13.2, 4.

311. See above, §24.3.

312. Documentation in my *Baptism* 70-72.

313. See also below, §27.1b.

314. Of the terms listed in *Baptism* 70, Paul does not use *eperchesthai* or *epipiptein* ('come upon', 'fall upon') of the Spirit.

315. See above, §24.1.

316. Note also Acts 13.43; 14.3, 26.

317. Haenchen completely underestimates the significance attached to the manifest evi-

drew the term which almost more than any other sums up his theology — 'grace' — from the Hellenists with whom he associated after his conversion, than that Luke's use of the term in these passages is a retrojection of Pauline usage into that earlier period in his narrative. Given the importance of the term within Christian theology generally, that would be a major point of credit which Christianity owes to the Hellenists or Antiochenes.

Contained within these observations is the crucial importance of the decisions made at that time to recognize the hand of God in the conversion of uncircumcised Gentiles, and to accept these converts as full participants in the new body of Christians almost solely on the evidence that they had received the Spirit. It was evidently the clear manifestation of God's grace, of the Spirit's presence, of God's acceptance of uncircumcised Gentiles which was *the* crucial factor in the earliest Christians' recognition that this was the way forward for outreach and to prepare for the coming of the Lord. The point needs to be underlined: given the centuries-old tradition of how non-Jews should be welcomed into the *qahal Israel,* it would have needed some irrefutable sign from God that these traditions should be set aside or bypassed. *The Spirit and grace of God so manifest in Gentile converts was that proof positive, sufficient to convince even traditionalist Jewish believers.* It was the proof of the Spirit which was decisive.[318] At this point it can be seen that those involved in outreach (Peter, the Hellenists, Barnabas and Paul) maintained the Pentecostal character of the new movement and underscored by their evangelism and its effectiveness the distinctively Christian emphasis on the work and experience of the Spirit as central to Christian identity.

f. Attitude to the Law

More ambiguous is the Hellenists' attitude to the law. As we have seen, the thrust of their critique of Jewish tradition seems to have been directed primarily, or even exclusively, against the Temple as the continuing focus of God's presence (and of Christ's imminent parousia?).[319] But such an attitude to the Temple would inevitably carry with it implications for other key elements of the Torah: particularly ritual purity (necessary to enter the Temple) and tithes for priests (to keep them free for Temple duty).[320] Given that piety would usually see the com-

---

dence of the Spirit's activity when he writes of 11.23: 'We cannot explain this renunciation [of the demand for circumcision] simply from the impression made upon him [Barnabas] by the readiness and responsiveness of the Gentiles' (*Acts* 371).

318. See further below, §27.2b and 4d.
319. See above, §24.4c.
320. See above, §23 n. 32.

mandments of the Torah as interlocking, such a substantial treating lightly important elements of the law presumably indicates at least the beginning of a certain detachment from the law, that is, a recognition that the law, including above all the law of circumcision, need not be regarded as still determinative and binding on all (Gentile) converts. The positive references to Moses in the speech attributed to Stephen suggested that a wider critique had not yet been developed, so the more radical critique which Paul was to develop need only be seen as a further radicalisation of the Hellenist critique of the law and traditions bearing on the Temple. But once again we can see factors which probably influenced Paul in at least some degree.

Would not the acceptance that circumcision was unnecessary for a Gentile convert amount to or imply a serious disregard for the law?[321] Yes, of course, to some extent. But two points need to be noted. (1) It was the overwhelming attestation that the Spirit had been received, that effective grace was clearly in operation, which was sufficient to overwhelm any doubts on the issue, even for Torah-loyal Jews like 'those of the circumcision' in Acts 11.2 and James in Gal. 2.7-9.[322] (2) The readiness of the Antioch believing Jews to side with Peter and 'those who came from James' in the Antioch incident (Gal. 2.11-14)[323] clearly implies an unwillingness (on the part of the Hellenist Jews) to press any practice which might clearly merit the description of a 'radical critique of the law'.[324] We have to assume, rather, that there was an in-between phase, between (as we might say) James and Paul, during which Hellenist believers could live with the anomaly of a circumcision-free gospel but still think of themselves in effect as a sect of Second Temple Judaism (exemplified by Peter in Gal. 2.11-14). Their opening the door to Gentiles was necessitated (in their perspective) by the Spirit (1), but they did not press through with the logic that Paul was to bring to the issue.

The anomalous position was probably well represented by the more relaxed attitude to law observance evidently typical in the church in Antioch before the intervention of 'the men from James'. As modern Judaism reminds us, more liberal attitudes to food laws and to table-fellowship with non-Jews can be as Jewish as the more scrupulous practices of the orthodox. And Gal. 2.12 indicates that the church in Antioch had developed a practice where Christian Jews and Christian Gentiles ate freely together and, apparently, without restriction. That practice must be attributed to the Hellenist Jews who made the breakthrough at

321. As in the case of Izates referred to in n. 248 above.
322. See again §27.4d below.
323. See further below, §27.6.
324. Contrast Becker: 'When the Antiochene Christians leave the synagogue with the aim of building an independent Gentile-Christian church life, they give up entirely this part of the observance of the law that separates Jews from Gentiles. Paul takes this decision for granted for the rest of his life' (*Paul* 105).

Antioch, and the willingness of Barnabas to commend what he saw at Antioch presumably included (at least by implication) recognition that God approved of such sharing of meal tables by circumcised and uncircumcised. Luke chose to give no hint of this. But the subsequent confrontation between Peter and Paul in Antioch on this very topic, recalled in Gal. 2.11-17, was probably a long time in coming. I return to the question in §§27.2-4 below.

g. Ecclesiology

The translation of the Jesus tradition into and formulation of the gospel in Greek brought forth the key word *ekklēsia,* which was to become so central to Christian identity as 'church'.[325] But can we also detect the emergence of a distinctive Hellenist concept of church and of church order?

     The answer depends in some degree on what we make of the election and appointment of the seven in Acts 6.3-6. If they were all Hellenists, and in effect leaders of the Hellenists,[326] then to some extent they form a parallel and different structure from Luke's 'apostles', 'the twelve'. After all, in Luke's account, the seven were both elected by the disciples/Hellenists (6.3a) and appointed by the apostles (6.3b).[327] So the concept and practice of ministry are depicted as already developing. And if their role as administrators of the common welfare fund is only partial indication of a much wider leadership role in bearing witness, taking initiative and evangelism, then again the understanding of ministry, of what should be recognized and count as valid/effective ministry, can be seen to be developing, and developing in a non-hierarchical, charismatic direction.

     Probably more can be deduced from the account of the church in Antioch in Acts 13.1-3. At a time when James (brother of Jesus) is shown to have become more or less the undisputed and sole leader in Jerusalem, and the synagogue pattern of rule by elders seems to have emerged,[328] the church in Antioch is depicted as led by a group of five 'prophets and teachers' (13.1).[329] Their worship *(leitourgein)*[330] includes the practice of fasting (13.2-3)[331] and attentiveness to

---

     325. Its first prominent usage in Acts is in the Hellenist material — 7.38; 8.1, 3; 11.22, 26. See also above, §20.1(2).

     326. See above, §24.3.

     327. I leave aside the issue whether the hands laid on them were those of the community or of the apostles (6.6); see n. 56 above.

     328. See above, §23.3e.

     329. Some of them were perhaps affluent householders (Gehring, *House Church* 111).

     330. 'In "ministered to the Lord" Luke has borrowed an expression of special solemnity from LXX as an allusion, above all, to prayer' (Haenchen, *Acts* 395).

     331. See above at n. 283. Bruce, among others, notes the possible implication that fasting makes one more alert for the reception of spiritual communications (*Acts* 294).

the voice of the Spirit,[332] no doubt through one of the prophets (13.2, 4), and a readiness to commission their own missionaries (13.3).[333] This is rather different from the Jerusalem model and, once again, would seem to prepare the way for the more charismatic ordering of the churches which Paul founded. In other words, Paul may have followed the Antioch pattern in talking of his converts coming together regularly in/as 'church' (1 Cor. 11.18).[334]

That only 'prophets' and 'teachers' are mentioned may be significant (this is the only place in Acts where 'teachers' as such appear). The two together imply a balance necessary to the life of any church — an openness to new insight and development inspired by the Spirit (the role of the prophet), balanced by a loyalty to the tradition taught and interpreted (the role of the teacher).[335] No other or higher figure of authority (apostle, elder) is mentioned. Since Luke elsewhere assumes the appointment of elders in the Pauline churches (14.23; 20.17), the portrayal here is hardly of his contriving and assuredly is derived from tradition.

The diversity of the leadership group is also noteworthy: Barnabas first mentioned (embodying the continuity with Jerusalem begun in 11.23-26); Simeon, possibly a black man (Niger = 'black'); Lucius from Cyrene, where there were strong Jewish colonies (cf. 2.10; 11.20); Manaen, a man who may have been brought up with Herod (Antipas) the tetrarch and/or had been his intimate friend *(syntrophos);*[336] and Saul.[337] The Greek may imply that the first three

332. Hengel and Schwemer suggest that 1 Thess. 5.19-20 'indirectly already characterizes the worship in Antioch', and that liturgical celebration on the first day of the week 'is probably already to be presupposed with Paul'. 'The prophetic-ecstatic element [as in 1 Corinthians 14] may have proved at least as attractive as later in Corinth' (*Paul* 202, 197); on the importance of prophecy in earliest Christianity, see further *Paul* 231-40, though I question Hengel and Schwemer's judgment that Luke 'as a "man of order"' . . . was relatively critical of them [prophets]' (231; see above, §21.2d[5]).

333. The 'laying on of hands', it should be noted, was for the mission to which they were sent (13.3), not to a life-long or permanent ministry.

334. See also Rom. 12.6-9; 1 Cor. 12.28; 14.26; 1 Thess. 5.19-22.

335. See my *Jesus and the Spirit* 227-33, 236-38. 'Prophets' were evidently settled members of the church — as subsequently in the Pauline churches (1 Cor. 12.28; 14.29-33), though we also hear of wandering prophets (Acts 11.27; *Did.* 15.1-2); see Lüdemann, *Early Christianity* 148. Hengel and Schwemer rightly caution against any assumption that the boundaries between 'apostle', 'prophet' and 'teacher' were already well defined (*Paul* 234-35); 'basically, men like Paul and Barnabas are apostles, prophets and teachers in one' (237). They also justifiably warn against 'the social romanticism' in the role which Theissen attributes to 'itinerant charismatics'; 'whereas itinerant prophets were active in the small scattered rural communities of Galilee and Judaea, the large cities of Syria called for longer stays and greater stability' (*Paul* 235 and n. 1222).

336. See further BDAG 976; *NDIEC* 3.37-38; also Haenchen, *Acts* 394 n. 5; Bruce, *Acts* 293.

337. There is general agreement that Luke has been able to draw on good tradition for

were designated as the prophets and the last two as the teachers[338] — if so, an interesting status for Saul/Paul in the light of his subsequent work (cf. Stephen and Philip in chs. 6–8). That none of the names match those in 6.5 need not count as evidence against the view that the Antioch church was founded by Hellenists; in a rapidly developing mission new leadership would continually emerge.

Beyond such features we quickly leave even the shaky ground on which these reflections have been based. But even if much of the above is (unavoidably) speculative, the necessary hesitations should not be allowed to diminish the firm conclusion that the establishment of a church at Antioch marked the most significant advance to date in the emergence of earliest Christianity. Whatever the precise details of the Stephen episode and the subsequent dispersal of members of the new sect from Jerusalem, the result was the beginning of a transformation of the sect into a missionary movement. From the Hellenist ranks (Acts 6.1), almost certainly, emerged evangelists (or believers who evangelized), who took the good news of Messiah Jesus first beyond the bounds of Judea, and then to Antioch, the principal metropolis of the region. The church they established there, more or less from the first, in some measure straddled the boundaries between Jew and Greek. From its own leadership emerged *the* apostle to the Gentiles, Saul/Paul, who in turn was to give a decisive stamp to Christian ecclesiology and theology. Much of the groundwork for that foundational work must have been laid in Antioch. Without the unsung entrepreneurs and innovators of 11.20, the sect of the Nazarene might never have become 'Christianity'.

---

the information of 13.1; see, e.g., Lüdemann, *Early Christianity* 147; Barrett, *Acts* 1.599-600; Jervell, *Apg.* 342. 'It is amazing that this expansive enthusiastic-messianic movement did not rapidly fall apart into many sectarian groups' (Hengel and Schwemer, *Paul* 220).

338. So Harnack suggested (see Fitzmyer, *Acts* 496).

CHAPTER 25

The Emergence of Paul

Next to Jesus the most significant figure in the beginnings of Christianity is Saul the Pharisee, who became Paul the apostle. So much so that he has been described as the real founder of Christianity.[1] The reason is simple: the more Jesus is set within Second Temple Judaism, and the more the earliest phase of Christianity is seen as (merely) a (messianic) sect within Second Temple Judaism, the greater the transition to the predominantly Gentile Christianity of the second century onwards. And if any single person was more responsible for that transition than any other, it was Paul, the self-styled 'apostle of the Gentiles' (Rom. 11.13). So his emergence on stage is a moment of extraordinary significance for Christianity in the making and demands much more attention than I give to Barnabas or James or even Peter, despite Peter's greater significance in the longer term in Catholic Christianity.

As already observed, the precise inter-relationship of Paul's emergence with other developments of the first ten years of the new movement's existence is not entirely clear. We have already looked at the Hellenists and the initial expansion associated with them (§24) and will return to look at the early missionary work of Peter (§26). Luke chose to include his account of Saul's conversion as an insertion into his account of the Hellenist expansion (after the evangelisation of Samaria but before the breakthrough in Antioch) and before his account of Peter's mission. And though I have chosen to follow through each strand of tradition (Hellenists, Paul, Peter) to gain a sense of their continuity and coherence which Luke's breaking up of the sequences can easily obscure, there seems to be no good reason to depart from Luke's broad ordering of the main body of events in each sequence (Hellenists, Paul, Peter). So although I have pushed ahead from Acts 8 to the end of the

---

1. W. Wrede, *Paul* (London: Philip Green, 1907): the 'second founder of Christianity', who has, 'compared with the first, exercised beyond all doubt the stronger . . . influence' (180); see further §29 n. 8 below.

Hellenist account of the establishment of the Jesus sect in Antioch (Acts 11.19-26), we return now to pick up the story of Paul, which Luke turned to in Acts 9.

As to dating, it is quite possible to work out a chronology for the life and mission of Saul/Paul, a chronology which for the most part is remarkably secure, with a margin of error of only a few years;[2] but its firmest fixed point is some way ahead in our narrative and analysis. So rather than disrupt the endeavour to stay within the story as it unfolds and within the horizons of the main players, I delay complete consideration of Pauline chronology until the beginning of Part Eight, which is devoted to the role of Paul in the beginnings of Christianity.

25.1. The Early Life and Education of Saul

In this section I will focus initially on the rather sparse information available to us before attempting an overall assessment of the significance of the data for our project.

a. Date of Birth

We have only two clues as to Paul's age. In Acts 7.58 Saul is described as 'a young man *(neanias)*'. And in Phlm. 9 he describes himself as 'an old man *(presbytēs)*'.[3]

Neanias could designate anyone from 24 to 40 years of age.[4] We do not know how much weight to give to Luke's report regarding Saul's involvement in Stephen's death;[5] but even if *neanias* is only Luke's estimate of Paul's status at the time of Stephen's death, his personal acquaintance with Paul later on[6] does at least suggest that, in regard to his age, the description of Saul as *neanias* in about 31 CE was well informed.

As to Paul's own statement in Philemon, in a common (though not univer-

2. The main disagreement is on the issue of whether Paul spent some time in prison in Ephesus and wrote two or more of his 'prison' letters from there; the margin of error for the dating of these letters could be as much as ten years. See further §28.1 below.

3. Despite the unanimity of the Greek witnesses, some prefer the conjectural emendation of *presbeutēs* ('ambassador'), or argue that *presbytēs* itself can mean 'ambassador'. But there is no reason to discard the obvious and regular meaning (BDAG 863; R. F. Hock, 'A Support for His Old Age: Paul's Plea on Behalf of Onesimus', in L. M. White and O. L. Yarbrough, eds., *The Social World of the First Christians,* W. A. Meeks FS [Minneapolis: Fortress, 1995] 67-81; J. D. G. Dunn, *The Epistles to the Colossians and to Philemon* [NIGTC; Grand Rapids: Eerdmans, 1996] 322 n. 3; J. A. Fitzmyer, *The Letter to Philemon* [AB 34C; New York: Doubleday, 2000] 105-106).

4. Fitzmyer cites Diogenes Laertius 8.10 and Philo, *Cher.* 114.

5. See above, §24.4d.

6. See above, §21.2a.

sal) reckoning of the 'seven ages' of a man, *presbytēs* was the second oldest, from 50 to 56.[7] However, given the uncertainty as to the date of Philemon, whether written from Ephesus or from Rome, and as to whether Paul was speaking for accuracy or effect, it is unclear whether calculation for the 50-56 years runs back from ca. 54 (Ephesus) or ca. 61 (Rome).[8] On a strict reckoning, that would give a date for Saul/Paul's birth either ca. 2 BCE–4 CE, or 5-11 CE.[9] Since the latter would make Saul a very young man indeed when he became a persecutor of 'the church of God' (his late 20s), the former is probably more likely.[10] But the uncertainty does not allow much confidence. More to the point, it does not make too much difference to the way the story of Saul/Paul unfolds. So, again we note what can and might be deduced and move on.

b. Tarsus

We learn from Luke that Saul was born in the city of Tarsus (Acts 22.3), and though Paul himself never refers to the city, the other references in Acts are best explained by Luke's having reliable information to the effect that Paul had such a close association with the city (9.30; 11.25; 21.39).[11]

The city of Tarsus, in southeast Asia Minor, had been established as the capital of the Roman province of Cilicia following Pompey's conquest in 67 BCE. Cicero had resided there as proconsul of Cilicia in 51-50 BCE, and it had flourished under Augustus. Its prosperity owed much to the linen industry, and it was a notable centre of commerce.[12] It was also a city of culture. According to Strabo (14.5.131) the people of Tarsus in the first century CE were keen students of philosophy,[13] and Dio Chrysostom, from the generation following Paul, refers to its orators and famous teachers (*Or.* 33.5).[14]

7. BDAG 863; Dunn, *Philemon* 327; Murphy-O'Connor, *Paul* 1-4; Fitzmyer, *Philemon* 105.

8. See further below, §28.1c.

9. See below, §28 n. 56. On Saul/Paul's name see below, §27 n. 35.

10. 'So Paul may have been a few years younger than Jesus' (J. Gnilka, *Paulus von Tarsus. Zeuge und Apostel* [Freiburg: Apostel, 1996] 23).

11. H.-M. Schenke, 'Four Problems in the Life of Paul Reconsidered', in B. A. Pearson, ed., *The Future of Early Christianity,* H. Koester FS (Minneapolis: Fortress, 1991) 319-28, suggests that Paul had been an inhabitant of Damascus, where he was known as Tarseus, 'the man from Tarsus' (319-21).

12. *OCD*[3] 1476; Murphy-O'Connor, *Paul* 33-35.

13. 'The people at Tarsus have devoted themselves so eagerly, not only to philosophy, but also the whole round of education in general, that they have surpassed Athens, Alexandria, or any other place that can be named where there have been schools and lectures of philosophers' (as cited by Murphy-O'Connor, *Paul* 35).

14. More details in F. F. Bruce, *Paul: Apostle of the Free Spirit* (Exeter: Paternoster, 1977)

Jewish colonists had probably been settled in Tarsus in large numbers under the Seleucids. Philo mentions Jewish colonies in Pamphylia, Cilicia, most of Asia up to Bithynia and the corners of Pontus (*Leg.* 281).[15] That there was a strong link between such Jews and Jerusalem is suggested by the fact that Cilicians were one of the groups served by the synagogue(s) referred to in Acts 6.9.[16]

It is possible that the Seleucids had given the Jewish colonists citizenship as a group, enrolling them as a civic 'tribe' *(phylē)*,[17] though the point is greatly disputed. Were it so, this would explain Paul's claim to citizenship of Tarsus (Acts 21.39). Other suggestions to explain this text are that Paul was a citizen because of some service rendered to the city by his father,[18] or that citizenship had been purchased by his father,[19] or that the term *politēs* denotes not full legal citizenship but membership of the Jewish community in Tarsus.[20] Here again it is not necessary to achieve resolution of such a dispute, since it makes little difference to the picture we can build up of the early Paul.

c. A Roman Citizen?

More weighty in its consequences is the issue whether Saul/Paul was a Roman citizen, as claimed in Acts 22.25. A positive answer is regularly denied, by some on the grounds that a Jew was unlikely to have attained Roman citizenship, and that Paul never mentions it, and by others on the grounds that a Roman citizen would never have had to undergo the punishment he tells us he endured ('three times beaten with rods' — 2 Cor. 11.25).[21]

33-36; M. Hengel, *The Pre-Christian Paul* (London: SCM, 1991) 90-91 n. 11; W. W. Gasque, 'Tarsus', *ABD* 6.333-34; 'a metropolitan center of Hellenistic culture' (Schnelle, *Paul* 59).

15. On the extent of the Jewish diaspora see V. Tcherikover, *Hellenistic Civilization and the Jews* (Philadelphia: Jewish Publication Society of America, 1959) 284-95; Schürer, *History* 3.1-86; and further below, §27 n. 181.

16. See also Barrett, *Acts* 2.1026.

17. This was argued particularly by W. M. Ramsay, *The Cities of Paul* (London: Hodder and Stoughton, 1907) 169-86; see further Hemer, *Book of Acts* 122 n. 59; and §24 at n. 234 above.

18. Ramsay, *St. Paul* 31-32.

19. Hengel, *Pre-Christian Paul* 5-6; a substantial property qualification would normally have had to be met. But if Paul was also a Roman citizen (Acts 16.37; §25.1c), the lesser dignity could well have been his by birth also.

20. H. W. Tajra, *The Trial of St. Paul* (WUNT 2.35; Tübingen: Mohr Siebeck, 1989) 78-80. Meeks suggests that 'it may have been possible . . . for individual Jews to find a way to hold Greek citizenship without directly engaging in acts most Jews would regard as idolatrous' (*Urban Christians* 37). See further B. Rapske, *Paul in Roman Custody, BAFCS* 3.72-83.

21. See particularly W. Stegemann, 'War der Apostel Paulus ein römischer Bürger?',

On the former reason for a negative answer, however, there is no reason why a Jew should not have become a citizen, since on manumission the slave of a Roman citizen was granted citizenship. Conceivably, then, Saul/Paul was descended from a native Judean who had been enslaved by Pompey when the latter captured Jerusalem in 63 BCE and subsequently freed and granted citizenship (cf. Philo, *Leg.* 155-57).[22] That Saul's grandfather or father, as a freedman *(libertinus),* had settled in Tarsus for reasons of business or trade is entirely conceivable, given the strong diaspora community already there.[23] Alternatively, it is equally possible that Saul's father gave some signal service to the state or its officials and was awarded with citizenship,[24] or that he had been wealthy enough to purchase citizenship (cf. Acts 22.28).[25] Since Roman citizenship began to be more widely distributed during the late Republic, it could be and was granted to non-Latins far beyond the shores of Italy.[26] A wider dispersal of Roman citizenship was one of the means by which Rome managed to keep its vast empire as united as it did.

On the latter reason, the conflict between Acts 22.25 and 2 Cor. 11.25 should

---

ZNW 78 (1987) 200-229; C. Roetzel, *Paul: The Man and the Myth* (Edinburgh: Clark, 1999) 2, 19-21.

22. Jerome, however, has a tradition to the effect that Paul came to Tarsus with his parents as prisoners of war from Gischala in Galilee *(De vir. ill.* 5; *Comm. in Phlm.* 23); Weiss thought it probable that the tradition had historical roots *(Earliest Christianity* 181 n. 1).

23. See further Lüdemann, *Early Christianity* 240-41; Hemer, *Book of Acts* 127 n. 75; Hengel, *Pre-Christian Paul* 11-15; Murphy-O'Connor, *Paul* 40-41; Riesner, *Paul's Early Period* 147-56 (here 152-53); K. Haacker, *Paulus. Der Werdegang eines Apostels* (SBS 171; Stuttgart: KBW, 1997) 27-44; Rapske, *Paul in Roman Custody* 83-90; also 'Citizenship, Roman', *DNTB* 215-18; S. Legasse, 'Paul's Pre-Christian Career according to Acts', *BAFCS* 4.365-90 (here 368-72); R. Wallace and W. Williams, *The Three Worlds of Paul of Tarsus* (London: Routledge, 1998) 140-42; H. Omerzu, *Der Prozess des Paulus* (BZNW 115; Berlin: de Gruyter, 2002) 17-52; Schnelle, *Paulus* 44-47. E. Ebel, 'Das Leben des Paulus', in O. Wischmeyer, ed., *Paulus* (Tübingen: Francke, 2006) 83-96, presents a concise discussion of pros and cons (89-91).

24. Bruce, *Paul* 37-38. G. Gardner, 'Jewish Leadership and Hellenistic Civic Benefaction in the Second Century B.C.E.', *JBL* 126 (2007) 327-43, observes a notable tradition of Jewish benefaction.

25. Hengel's discussion wisely concludes: 'Here there are many possibilities, but no probabilities' *(Pre-Christian Paul* 15). J. J. Meggitt, *Paul, Poverty and Survival* (Edinburgh: Clark, 1998), insists that Paul belonged to the urban poor and challenges 'the myth of Paul's affluent background' (75-97), but Meggitt overstates his case, here as elsewhere. For a recent brief review of the various evaluations of Paul's social status, see Schnelle, *Paul* 63 n. 34.

26. *OCD*³ 334: 'Roman citizenship came to possess two features which distinguished it from *polis* citizenship and which later surprised Greek observers: the automatic incorporation of freed slaves of Romans into the Roman citizen body; and the ease with which whole communities of outsiders could be admitted as citizens'. G. H. R. Horsley notes that about 50 percent of the identifiable members of a fishing association in Ephesus in the mid-50s were Roman citizens *(NDIEC* 5.108-109).

not be pressed too hard. If the story of Paul and Silas in Philippi has any historical grounding,[27] it shows that incidents could have occurred where Paul's citizenship was either not declared (because he wished to share Jesus' unjust suffering at Roman hands, or because Silas was not a Roman citizen?) or disbelieved/disregarded (Acts 16.22, 37).[28] Rigour of historical judgment must always be tempered by recognition of the anomalies and muddles which must have occurred as frequently in the past as they do today. More to the point here, 'without the appeal to Caesar on the basis of Roman citizenship, it is difficult to explain the transfer of Paul's case to Rome'.[29]

The significance of Paul's Roman citizenship is that it would have given him greater boldness in his mission and would certainly have played a part in his finally being sent to Rome (Acts 25.11-12).[30]

d. Paul the Jew

We come on to much firmer ground with Paul's own claims about his origins in Phil. 3.4-5: 'If anyone else thinks to have confidence in the flesh, I have more: circumcised on the eighth day; (a member) of the people of Israel; (a member) of the tribe of Benjamin . . .'. Here clearly is an expression of 'confidence' *(pepoithēsis)* before God,[31] and confidence 'in the flesh'; such boast in status — status as a member of the covenant people Israel, the physical descendants ('in the flesh') of Abraham, and as heirs of the covenant promises made to and through Abraham (as confirmed by circumcision 'in the flesh') — is hardly likely to have been contrived or even exaggerated.[32]

- 'Circumcised on the eighth day' (in accord with Gen. 17.12). The fact that Paul begins his c.v. thus is a reminder not just that circumcision seems to have been the primary point at issue with the interlopers into the Philippian church. It also affirms Paul's recognition that circumcision was a (if not the)

27. See below, §31.2b.

28. Hengel, *Pre-Christian Paul* 6-7, with examples of such cases and further bibliography in the notes (101-104); similarly Murphy-O'Connor, *Paul* 39-40; further J. C. Lentz, *Luke's Portrait of Paul* (SNTSMS 77; Cambridge: Cambridge University, 1993) ch. 5; Rapske, *Paul in Roman Custody* 129-34.

29. Schnelle, *Paul* 60-61, further 60-62; similarly Gnilka, *Paulus* 25-26; Wedderburn, *History* 83. Rapske cites Epictetus's observation (3.24.41) that 'those who falsely claim Roman citizenship are severely punished' (*Paul in Roman Custody* 87). See also Tajra, *Trial* 81-89.

30. See below, §34 nn. 131 and 138.

31. As in Phil. 1.14; 2.24; also 2 Cor. 1.9; 2 Thess. 3.4; Eph. 3.12.

32. *Pace* H. Maccoby, *The Mythmaker: Paul and the Invention of Christianity* (London: Weidenfeld and Nicolson, 1986) 95-96, who as a hostile propagandist against Paul consistently produces and discusses partial and selective evidence, presented in a highly tendentious way.

defining characteristic of the member of the covenant people,[33] and thus also a 'sign of distinctiveness over against a non-Jewish environment'.[34] Here speaks the Jew conscious of the distinctiveness of his Jewishness.

- '(A member) of the people of Israel' — of direct descent from Abraham, Isaac and Jacob, not a proselyte (similarly Rom. 11.1). Here, clearly, the ground of Paul's confidence before God was his *ethnic identity;* he was an Israelite, belonging to that people which God had chosen for himself out of all the nations (Deut. 32.8-9).
- '(A member) of the tribe of Benjamin' (similarly Rom. 11.1). It is of interest that Paul knew his tribal lineage and that it was a matter of pride for him, a further ground for his confidence before God. Of Jacob's twelve sons only Benjamin had been born in the promised land (Gen. 35.16-18), and only the tribe of Benjamin had remained faithful to Judah and the house of David when the kingdom split after the death of Solomon.[35]
- 'A Hebrew of the Hebrews'. I have already quoted Harvey's observation that 'the name "Hebrew" was conventionally associated with traditionalism or conservatism'.[36] The intensification of the claim — 'a Hebrew of the Hebrews', rather than just 'I am a Hebrew' (as in 2 Cor. 11.2) — must reflect Paul's early determination to maintain his ethnic identity and to identify himself more completely with the ancient origins and character of his people.[37]

All these references to his earliest years surely indicate that Saul was brought up from the first to be a devoutly practising Jew, despite his early years in the diaspora.[38] The fact of his circumcision, that he was proud of his ethnic identity, that his family had preserved some sort of genealogical record, and that he spoke Aramaic/Hebrew (presumably) as well as any native indicates most as-

33. See further §27.2a below.

34. Niebuhr, *Heidenapostel* 105.

35. J. B. Lightfoot, *Philippians* (London: Macmillan, [4]1878) 146-47; P. T. O'Brien, *Philippians* (NIGTC; Grand Rapids: Eerdmans, 1991) 370-71; Bockmuehl, *Philippians* 196. Hengel notes that several prominent Jews could claim descent from Benjamin, including Gamaliel I (Paul's teacher, according to Acts) and adds that 'nowhere do we have comparable information from the Greek-speaking Diaspora' (*Pre-Christian Paul* 26-27). The possibility is certainly strong that Saul (Sha'ul) had been named after the first king of Israel (Saul).

36. See above, §24 n. 37.

37. So most; see, e.g., Gnilka, *Philipperbrief* 189-90; 'a kind of climax of the different elements of his Jewish identity' (Niebuhr, *Heidenapostel* 106-108).

38. Murphy-O'Connor shrewdly observes that 'such concern to affirm his Jewish credentials betrays the expatriate, i.e. a Jew living in the Diaspora' (*Paul* 32). Lentz muses on the difficulty of conceiving 'that Paul could have been born into a Pharisaic family and also have been a citizen of Tarsus and a Roman citizen' (*Paul* ch. 3), but the characterization 'Pharisaic family' weakens his case (see below, §25.1f).

suredly a pious home and an upbringing equivalent in modern times to that of an Orthodox Jew living outside the land of Israel.

e. Paul the Hellenist

But what of Saul/Paul the Hellenist?[39] The fact that Tarsus was such a strong intellectual centre of Hellenist culture, and the likelihood that various cults seem to have thrived there during this period,[40] have led to various speculations regarding Paul's subjection to Hellenizing influences. The facts that Paul could write good Greek and that his letters display a fair degree of rhetorical expertise have encouraged the view that the young Saul's early schooling in Tarsus was foundational for him and that the transition which he wrought in earliest Christianity had its roots in his own straddling the two cultures of Greece and Judea.[41] Such speculation was grist to the early history-of-religions specialists as providing the source for Paul's teaching on Jesus' death and resurrection (the myth of the dying and rising god) and on baptism and the Lord's Supper (modelled on the equivalents in the mystery cults).[42]

However, it is almost impossible to believe that the man who provided the self-testimony of Phil. 3.4-5 could have been a 'Hellenist', in the sense of one who saw the importance not simply of translating the religion of Israel into Greek language but also of integrating Israel's religion into the wider Hellenist culture (the 'Hellenization' against which 'Judaism' had revolted).[43] This 'Hebrew' would have been entirely antagonistic to any ascription to him of the epithet 'Hellenist', beyond that of simply 'Greek-speaker'.

Moreover, there are few signs either that Paul had enjoyed a classical education or, if he had, that it had any lasting effect on him.[44] For example, he hardly

---

39. To this extent I follow the common characterization of Paul as a man of three worlds — Jewish, Greek, Roman — as in M. Grant, *Saint Paul: The Man* (Glasgow: Collins Fount, 1978) 14; B. Witherington, *The Paul Quest: The Renewed Search for the Jew of Tarsus* (Downers Grove: InterVarsity, 1998) ch. 2 ('The Trinity of Paul's Identity'); Wallace and Williams, *The Three Worlds of Paul of Tarsus*.

40. We are still to a large degree dependent on Ramsay, *The Cities of St. Paul* 137-56. B. Chilton, *Rabbi Paul: An Intellectual Biography* (New York: Doubleday, 2004) 9-12, draws on Ramsay in his description of the cult of Tarku.

41. Roetzel argues that 'as a Greek speaker Paul could not avoid being deeply influenced by Hellenistic philosophy and religion' (*Paul* 3).

42. See above, §20.3b; still today Maccoby, *Paul and Hellenism* chs. 3-4 — Paul was acquainted with the mystery-religions in Tarsus, 'a centre of mystery-religion' (115). But see Hengel and Schwemer, *Paul* 167-69: 'So we can doubt whether — apart from the traditional, long-established Dionysus and perhaps Isis — real mystery gods were worshipped at all in Tarsus in the time of Paul' (168).

43. *Jesus Remembered* §9.2a.

44. For a more positive view, see Schnelle, *Paul* 75-83; T. Vegge, *Paulus und das antike*

shares the high Greek evaluation of 'virtue', and he shows no knowledge of classical Greek literature.[45] He knows a few philosophical maxims, but these had become commonplace in everyday life. And the rhetorical skill which he undoubtedly displays could have been picked up by listening to a few public orators in his early travels.[46] To attribute his fluency in Greek and his ability as a persuasive speaker to an education in Tarsus[47] is unnecessary, given not least the presence of Hellenists in Jerusalem, who, as argued above (§24.2), could function effectively only in Greek, and given also that training in rhetoric was a staple of all education throughout the Greek-speaking world.[48]

f. Education in Jerusalem

There is a long-running debate as to whether Saul received his basic education in Tarsus or in Jerusalem.[49] The key texts are Acts 22.3 and 26.4:

- 22.3 — 'I am a Jew, born *(gegennēmenos)* in Tarsus in Cilicia, but *(de)* brought up *(anatethrammenos)* in this city, at the feet of Gamaliel, educated *(pepaideumenos)* strictly *(kata akribeian)* in the ancestral law';

Schulwesen. Schule und Bildung des Paulus (BZNW 134; Berlin: de Gruyter, 2006) part B (conclusions 455-56, 486).

45. Unless we count Acts 17.28 and the popular wisdom of 1 Cor. 15.33.

46. Hengel and Schwemer, *Paul* 169-71: 'In reality, Paul's language and "elements of education" do not go beyond what he could have learned within the Greek-speaking synagogues and in conversation with learned non-Jews, who he did not avoid' (170-71). 'He was only imbued with Greek and pagan ways of thinking to a limited and superficial extent' (Grant, *Saint Paul* 6). 'Not through Greek education, but through study and interpretation of Scripture are Paul's thought and speech determined' (E. Lohse, *Paulus. Eine Biographie* [Munich: Beck, 1996] 22). Similarly Legasse, 'Paul's Pre-Christian Career' 374.

47. Murphy-O'Connor argues that Paul did not leave Tarsus till he was twenty (*Paul* 46-51). Roetzel also questions whether Paul knew or spoke Aramaic and thinks it unlikely that he lived in Jerusalem 'from early childhood well into his adult years' (*Paul* 11-12). Similarly A. du Toit, 'A Tale of Two Cities: "Tarsus or Jerusalem" Revisited', *NTS* 46 (2000) 375-402, reprinted in du Toit, *Focusing on Paul: Persuasion and Theological Design in Romans and Galatians* (BZNW 151; Berlin: de Gruyter, 2007) 3-33.

48. See further Hengel, *Pre-Christian Paul* 2-4, 93-96; he writes in effect to qualify Bornkamm, *Paul* 9-10, who quotes the verdict of the great Greek scholar Wilamowitz-Moellendorf on the quality of Paul's diction: his Greek 'makes his writing a classic of Hellenism'; and Becker, *Paul* 51-56: 'There are several indications that together reinforce the impression that Paul enjoyed the higher education that was available in Hellenism' (55).

49. See particularly W. C. van Unnik, *Tarsus or Jerusalem: The City of Paul's Youth* (London: Epworth, 1962), reprinted in *Sparsa Collecta: Part One* (NovTSupp 29; Leiden: Brill, 1973) 259-320.

- 26.4 — 'All (the) Jews know my way of life *(biōsin)* from my youth, which from the beginning was spent among my own people and in Jerusalem'.

In his classic study, W. C. van Unnik observed that the three participles in 22.3 correspond to the three regular stages in the c.v. of a notable person — birth, childhood and education. The point is that the second stage *(anatrephō,* 'bring up, rear, train') is said to have taken place 'in this city', which in the context of Acts 22 can only mean Jerusalem.[50] That implies, as van Unnik argued, that Saul/Paul's basic education was carried through in Jerusalem. Which would further imply that Saul was sent or brought to Jerusalem at an early age (he had a sister living there, according to Acts 23.16).[51] However, how early is not clear.[52] Acts 26.4 mentions Saul's 'way of life', as a manner of living practised 'from the beginning' throughout his youth *(neotēs)* and well known in Jerusalem. That speaks not so much of childhood as of adolescence, and *biōsis* implies a life-style consciously and responsibly chosen.[53] Both references may tell us no more than Luke's own estimate of Paul's early life in Jerusalem, but it would be foolish to downgrade the value of these data in favour of questionable inferences drawn from elsewhere.[54]

The last clause of 22.3, 'educated *(pepaideumenos)* strictly in the ancestral law at the feet of Gamaliel',[55] refers most obviously to what we would now call Saul's 'higher or tertiary education'.[56] Luke's only other use of the verb de-

50. So most; see particularly Barrett, *Acts* 1034-36. The *de* is therefore probably adversative.

51. 'His parents made sure of an orthodox upbringing for him by arranging for him to spend his formative years in Jerusalem' (Bruce, *Paul* 43); similarly Stuhlmacher, *Biblische Theologie* 1.229-30.

52. Van Unnik thinks very early — 'apparently before he could peep round the corner of the door and certainly before he went roaming on the streets' *(Sparsa Collecta* 301); followed by Haenchen, *Acts* 624-25 and n. 5; Gnilka, *Paulus* 28 (but also 31-32).

53. As implied also in the few other occurrences of the term (LSJ 316; Bruce, *Acts* 497); so here equivalent to *anastrophē* (Gal. 1.13), which BDAG defines as 'conduct expressed according to certain principles' (73). But Schnelle's estimate of Paul coming to Jerusalem aged about fifteen may be too late *(Paul* 69). Chilton is even more removed, suggesting that Paul did not leave Tarsus till he was twenty-one *(Rabbi Paul* 27, 267).

54. See above, §24 n. 145.

55. 'At the feet of Gamaliel' could be taken with the middle clause (as by NRSV, Barrett, *Acts* 1029), but the language ('educated strictly in the ancestral law') refers most obviously to Saul's training as a Pharisee (so the great majority — e.g., REB, NIV, NJB, and Haenchen, *Acts* 624 n. 5; Fitzmyer, *Acts* 705).

56. G. Bertram cites Zahn: 'The third statement does not refer to what we usually call education, but to the student days of a young man destined to be a future rabbi' *(paideuō, TDNT* 5.619 n. 144). According to Hengel, commenting on this passage, Luke 'gives the most accurate and positive accounts of Jewish situations [*Verhältnisse*] of any non-Jew in the ancient world' *(Pre-Christian Paul* 40); 'circumstances' would be better for *Verhältnisse*.

scribes Moses' instruction 'in all the wisdom of the Egyptians' (7.22). And *akribeia* ('exactness, precision') is almost a mark of Pharisaic intent to interpret the law accurately and to conform to it scrupulously.[57]

At this point Luke's account meshes into Paul's own self-characterization of his earlier life, in Phil. 3.5e-6 and Gal. 1.13-14:

- Phil. 3.5 — 'as to the law, a Pharisee', with all the overtones of strictness and separateness which the name evoked.[58] To become a Pharisee was a matter of choice, not of birth. Training to be a Pharisee could only have been carried through in Jerusalem;[59] talk of Pharisees living strictly in the diaspora is a contradiction in terms.[60] If already in Jerusalem, Saul must have put himself under a Pharisaic teacher; the picture of Acts 22.3 is completely plausible.[61]

- Phil. 3.6 — 'as to righteousness which is in the law, blameless *(amemptos)*'. This is a striking expression of the confidence of a strict Pharisee, who saw himself as living before God in accordance with the requirements of God's law. That is, not a 'sinless' life;[62] 'in accordance with the law' will have included availing oneself of the ritual and cultic provisions of the law when impurity and sin blighted the covenant life.[63] This

---

57. See *Jesus Remembered* 269-70 and n. 67.

58. See again *Jesus Remembered* 269-70.

59. See particularly Hengel, *Pre-Christian Paul* 27-34 (notes 118-24); similarly Niebuhr, *Heidenapostel* 55-57; Lohse, *Paulus* 21-22. 'There is no reliable evidence for Pharisees permanently based outside Jerusalem' (Murphy-O'Connor, *Paul* 58).

60. In Acts 23.6 Paul describes himself as 'a Pharisee, son of Pharisees'. This is often taken to imply that there were Pharisees living 'strictly' in the diaspora; see, e.g., the too casual assumption of Dibelius: 'In Tarsus he [Paul] had, in fact, grown up in Pharisaic Judaism' (*Paul* 37). But a more likely understanding of the phrase 'son of a Pharisee' is that it constituted a claim to having been trained as the pupil of a Pharisee — as doctoral postgraduates today still speak of their supervisor as their 'doctor father' (Jeremias, *Jerusalem* 252 n. 26; Rapske, *Paul in Roman Custody* 95-97; Barrett, *Acts* 2.1063).

61. 'If Paul arrived in Jerusalem around AD 15, his sojourn in the city would have coincided with that of Gamaliel I, and it is extremely improbable that Paul or any other Pharisee would have escaped his influence' (Murphy-O'Connor, *Paul* 59). Schnelle notes that Josephus took up his study of the Jewish 'sects' at the age of sixteen (Schnelle, *Paul* 55, referring to Josephus, *Life* 10). Lake and Cadbury were already warning against opposing the historicity of such a claim on the grounds of a 'gross caricature of anything which he could have learnt from Gamaliel' (*Beginnings* 4.278-79). J. Klausner, *From Jesus to Paul* (London: Allen and Unwin, 1943) notes the rabbinic tradition concerning an impudent 'pupil' of Gamaliel who scoffed at Gamaliel's teaching and was convinced that 'that pupil' was none other than Paul (309-11).

62. '*Amemptos* should not be pressed to mean that Paul completely [ful]filled the law or entirely avoided transgressions' (O'Brien, *Philippians* 380); Lightfoot paraphrases the claim, 'I omitted no observance however trivial' (*Philippians* 148).

63. The terms of covenant law included demand for repentance and provision of sacri-

pattern of law-directed living is well caught in Sanders's phrase 'covenantal nomism'.[64]

- Gal. 1.14 — 'I progressed in Judaism[65] beyond many of my contemporaries among my people, being exceedingly zealous for my ancestral traditions'.[66] Here we see an element of competitiveness, of a pre-Christian Paul seeking to outdo his contemporaries in his zealous devotion to and application of the more scrupulous halakhoth of the Pharisees, outdoing even many of his fellow Pharisees.[67] What is evoked is the hot-house of a very intense group of Pharisaic students in Jerusalem or of Saul as a particularly intense devotee to Pharisaic rationale and praxis among others who joined him 'at the feet of Gamaliel' in Jerusalem.[68]

The close match between Paul's own autobiographical reminiscences in Phil. 3.5-6 and Gal. 1.13-14 and Luke's account in Acts 22.3 and 26.4 makes it virtually impossible to doubt that Saul did indeed spend his most formative years of education and training *(paideia)* in Jerusalem.[69]

---

fice and atonement for sin, as Sanders in particularly has reminded us (*Paul and Palestinian Judaism;* see also his *Judaism,* especially 107-10, 271-72).

64. The point is recognized, e.g., by F. Thielman, *Paul and the Law: A Contextual Approach* (Downers Grove: InterVarsity, 1994) 155; M. A. Seifrid, *Justification by Faith: The Origin and Development of a Central Pauline Theme* (NovTSupp 68; Leiden: Brill, 1992) 174; Bockmuehl, *Philippians* 202; D. A. Hagner, 'Paul as a Jewish Believer — according to His Letters', in Skarsaune and Hvalvik, eds., *Jewish Believers in Jesus* 96-120 (here 103). See further my *The New Perspective* §§1.4.1b and 22.4.

65. Michael Wolter reminds me that 'progression in' something (learning, philosophy, virtue) is a biographical pattern which is relatively widespread in Stoic ethics (cf. G. Stählin, *TDNT* 6.705-706).

66. 'The Pharisees passed on to the people certain regulations from the succession of fathers, which had not been written in the laws of Moses' (Josephus, *Ant.* 13.297). A funerary inscription from Italy praising a woman 'who lived a good life in Judaism' (*CIL* 537), which I mistakenly referred to as 'from our period' in *Jesus Remembered* 261, is more likely from the third or fourth century (*JIWE* 2.584).

67. 'The combative tone and competitive spirit are equally characteristic of elite groups' (Murphy-O'Connor, *Paul* 60).

68. If the debate is realistic on whether Saul aligned himself more with the (relatively) more liberal faction of Hillel or with the stricter faction of Shammai (Hengel, *Pre-Christian Paul* 28; bibliography in 118-19 n. 157), this verse presumably tips the debate in favour of the latter, despite the possibility that Gamaliel was the grandson of Hillel (see Schürer, *History* 2.367-69). See also Hengel 40-53; Haacker, *Paulus* 71-77; also 'Paul's Life', in J. D. G. Dunn, ed., *The Cambridge Companion to St. Paul* (Cambridge: Cambridge University, 2003) 19-33 (here 21-23); Hengel and Schwemer, *Paul* 392-93 n. 622; Davies, 'Paul' 687-91. Chilton provides an imaginative account of Gamaliel's influence on Saul, including a postulated break with Gamaliel in 32 over Stephen (*Rabbi Paul* 35-43); note again Klausner's speculation (n. 61 above).

69. Roetzel, *Paul* 24, and J. A. Overman, 'Kata Nomon Pharisaios: A Short History of

At some stage Saul learned the trade of a *skēnopoios,* 'tent-maker' or 'leather-worker' (according to Acts 18.3).[70] That he did have such a trade which required hard manual labour is certainly consistent with Paul's ability to support himself by his own hands[71] and is consistent too with what we know to have been rabbinic practice subsequently (that rabbis should earn their own living). But when he learned such a trade is less clear, and given the silent gap of several years in the late 30s and early 40s in our knowledge of Saul/Paul's biography, we cannot simply assume that he learned the trade as part of his Jerusalem education.[72]

On the issue of whether Paul married, we simply have insufficient information even to attempt an answer.[73] As in the case of Jesus, speculation lacks substantive roots and takes us nowhere.

g. In Sum

The evidence calls on us to envisage Saul as a rather remarkable young man, with roots both in the diaspora and in Jerusalem. With regard to the former:

- he was born in a diaspora city noted for its political and cultural importance;
- he continued to hold citizenship there;
- his family may have been of high social status in Tarsus;
- Luke recalls him returning to Tarsus subsequent to his conversion (Acts 9.30; 11.25), presumably indicating continuing family ties there;
- his mastery of Greek is hardly that of a second language, and his Bible of choice seems to have been the LXX.[74]

Paul's Pharisaism', in J. C. Anderson et al., eds., *Pauline Conversations in Context,* C. J. Roetzel FS (JSNTS 221; London: Sheffield Academic, 2002) 180-93, question whether Paul ever was a Pharisee as such, rather than simply sympathetic to what they stood for. But the self-description of Gal. 1.14 indicates a commitment which well matches the description of both Phil. 3.5 and Acts 22.3.

70. Hock, *Social Context* 20-21; cf. W. Michaelis, *TDNT* 7.393-94; BDAG 928-29; see further P. Lampe, 'Paulus — Zeltmacher', *BZ* 31 (1987) 256-61; Barrett, *Acts* 2.863; Murphy-O'Connor, *Paul* 86-89; and below, n. 216.

71. 1 Thess. 2.9; 1 Cor. 9.18; 2 Cor. 12.13.

72. Hock suggests that Paul learned his trade from his father, starting a two- or three-year apprenticeship at the age of thirteen (*Social Context* 22-25), but Hengel dryly remarks that Hock 'is claiming to know rather too much' (*Pre-Christian Paul* 16; see further 15-17). Schnelle provides further bibliography (*Paul* 47-48). See also below, §29.5d.

73. Murphy-O'Connor says what can be said, and a bit more (*Paul* 62-65).

74. Hengel, *Pre-Christian Paul* 35-37.

In short, Saul's familiarity with Hellenistic culture was not limited to his early years in Tarsus. He could evidently function effectively there whether as a strictly observant Jew or as a neophyte Christian. This suggests an ability, even willingness, to function within a Hellenist context and culture, which probably grew out of a childhood spent in Tarsus. The 'Hebrew of the Hebrews' need not have been so cut off from wider cultural influences as the rhetoric of Phil. 3.4-5 might suggest.

At the same time, even allowing for Paul's rhetoric in Gal. 1.13-14 and Phil. 3.5-6 (emphasizing his youthful zeal in order to highlight, by way of contrast, the full extent of his conversion), it is clear enough that Saul's birth and earliest life in Tarsus gave him the strong roots of an intensely dedicated (orthodox) Jew. It would be natural for a youth with obvious (academic) potential and (religious) commitment to be sent (by willing parents) to Jerusalem for his 'secondary' and higher education, especially if he could lodge with relatives in Jerusalem. In other words, it is likely that Saul came to and settled in Jerusalem as a young adolescent and received his principal education there.[75] That would not exclude continued education in Greek — he may have been one of 'those from Cilicia' mentioned in Acts 6.9, though as a 'Hebrew of the Hebrews' he was not one of those who could function only in Greek.[76] But his higher education was that of a budding Pharisee, and he evidently made it his goal to outshine his fellow students in his zeal for the law and the 'ancestral traditions' and to live in strictest conformity to both the Torah and the Pharisaic halakhoth. As he looked back on that period of his life, even though his Christian evaluation of it was quite different (Phil. 3.7-8), he could still recall the pride he experienced during these years that his life was such an epitome of what a devout Jew's life should be.

25.2. 'The Persecutor' (Gal. 1.23)

As already noted, there is no doubt that Saul was heavily involved in persecution of the embryonic Christian movement. That conclusion is not dependent on Luke's account in Acts 8.3 and 9.1-2, and so it is not disturbed by questions usually raised about the historical reliability of Acts 7.58 and 8.1.[77] Nor indeed is it dependent only on Paul's confession as to his role as persecutor:

75. This is also Hengel's conclusion (*Pre-Christian Paul* 37-39); on the possibility of Jewish Greek education in Jerusalem, see further Hengel 54-62.
76. 'It is likely that Saul of Tarsus, as a Greek-speaking Jew of the Diaspora, belonged to, or was a rabbi in, a "Hellenist" synagogue' (Barnett, *Birth* 20).
77. See above, §24.6.

- 1 Cor. 15.9 — 'I persecuted the church of God';
- Gal. 1.13 — 'I persecuted the church of God in excessive measure and tried to destroy it';
- Phil. 3.6 — 'as to zeal, a persecutor of the church'.

In addition, Paul cites or summarizes reports he evidently heard from or in reference to the churches of Judea about their attitude to himself: 'our former persecutor now preaches the faith which once he tried to destroy' (Gal. 1.23). Ernst Bammel's categorization of the sentence as 'one of the oldest theological statements of Christianity' may be too strong,[78] but there is no reason to doubt that this was indeed the way Saul/Paul was regarded by the earliest churches — Saul, the persecutor *(ho diōkōn)*.

We have already discussed who were the targets of Saul's persecuting zeal,[79] but other questions require discussion also.

a. On Whose Authority?

There is no place for any naïve assumption that Saul, as a young Pharisee (aged about thirty), could command authority on his own account, including powers of arrest (Acts 8.3). As already noted, Pharisees had no authority as Pharisees in the first-century synagogue; and Sanders's vigorous protest against the view that the Pharisees 'ran' Judaism at the time should also be recalled.[80] Such civil authority as the Romans allowed beyond their own ranks was vested in the high priest and his immediate circle (as depicted in Acts 4–5).[81] On the other hand, the information that some senior Pharisees were called to participate in councils convened in Jerusalem by the high priest is sufficiently secure,[82] and we have some evidence of Pharisees being co-opted into official delegations; Josephus's report of the machinations regarding his own commission in Galilee in the early days of the Jewish revolt is a prime case in point (*Life* 197). So it is quite justifiable to envisage a situation where priestly authority had been challenged in terms similar to that which occasioned Jesus' condemnation (Acts 6.14; 7.48), a situation in which a zealous young Pharisee of impeccable credentials was given a free hand, with temple police support, to attempt to extirpate such views by the arrest and expulsion of those who were assumed to hold them.

78. E. Bammel, 'Galater i.23', *ZNW* 59 (1968) 108-12.

79. See again §24.6 above.

80. See *Jesus Remembered* 307-308 and nn. 240 and 244.

81. On 'the competence of the Sanhedrin' see Schürer, *History* 2.218-23; though see above, §23 n. 11.

82. Schürer, *History* 2.210-17.

Luke's report that Saul was given authority to deal with members of the Way in Damascus by bringing them under arrest to Jerusalem (Acts 9.1-2) is usually regarded as highly dubious.[83] In particular, what authority could the high priest in Jerusalem have in a city under quite another jurisdiction? And it certainly reads like one of Luke's 'over the top' exaggerations.[84] Nevertheless, there may be more to it than initially meets the eye. For one thing, Luke attributes the initiative to Saul himself: it was he who went to the high priest and asked for letters of commission (cf. 22.5). Moreover, the letters are said to be addressed 'to the synagogues' (of Damascus). Now, it is quite true that the high priest had no formal jurisdiction over synagogues, least of all in other countries.[85] But he had at least two considerable constraints which he could bring to bear on *archisynagōgoi* and synagogue elders. One was that he was responsible for much of the content and timing of lived-out Judaism; he and his councillors were the ultimate authority in matters of dispute, and it is not at all unlikely that Jerusalem authorities occasionally wrote to diaspora synagogues to encourage them to maintain the traditions and possibly to take sides in some dispute on timing of festivals and the like.[86] The high priest might even have been willing to claim jurisdiction over a 'greater Judea' which included Damascus.[87] In any case, the high priest was not a person whose envoy could be lightly disregarded or dismissed with his mission unfulfilled. The other is that the Temple in Jerusalem held an amazing range of financial deposits for Jews at home and abroad; it was Judaism's 'central bank'.[88] It is quite conceivable, therefore, that any requests were backed, explicitly or implicitly, with threat of financial sanctions. All this is speculative, of course, but the possibility does give more credibility to Luke's account than it usually receives.[89] And we do need to explain how it was that Saul

83. E.g., Knox, *Chapters* 24; Lüdemann, *Early Christianity* 106-107. More sympathetic is Barrett: 'Given the good will of the synagogues in Damascus it would be quite possible for Jews known to be Christians to "disappear" (our own age is familiar with the phenomenon, and the word) and subsequently to find themselves in unwelcome circumstances in Jerusalem' (*Acts* 1.446-47).

84. Hengel, *Acts* 77; Legasse, 'Paul's Pre-Christian Career' 388-89.

85. The right of extradition extended to the high priest by the Roman consul as recorded in 1 Macc. 15.16-21 provides something of a precedent (Bruce, *Paul* 72); but see Barrett, *Acts* 1.446.

86. We will see later that the letter attributed to James in Acts 15.23-29 may well presuppose such a practice on the part of the Jerusalem authorities; see below, §37 n. 115.

87. See below, §36 n. 25.

88. The same was true of other famous temples — e.g., the temple of Artemis in Ephesus (Dio Chrysostom 31.54-55).

89. Hengel and Schwemer also think that Luke exaggerates: 'Rather, Saul will have been sent by one or more Greek-speaking synagogues in Jerusalem to Damascus to help its Jews to stem the pressure from the Jewish-Christian "Hellenists" who had fled there'. But

ended up in Damascus at this phase of his career (Gal. 1.17). Luke provides the answer, however much we have to suspend judgment on the detail of his account (Acts 9.1-2).

How severe was Saul's persecution? Luke reports that Saul 'was ravaging *(elymaineto)* the church' (Acts 8.3) and 'breathing out threats and murder' (9.1); and he has Paul confess that 'I not only locked up many of the saints in prison, but I also cast my vote against them when they were being condemned to death' (26.10). That seems to go beyond the judicial discipline which the synagogue was permitted to exercise — even the 'forty lashes minus one', which Paul attests in 2 Cor. 11.24. Here again, however, Luke's rather florid language is more soundly based than at first appears.[90] For Paul himself describes his persecuting zeal with similar fierceness (Gal. 1.13): he did not simply 'pursue/persecute' the church of God, but he did so *kath' hyperbolēn,* 'to an extraordinary degree, beyond measure, extravagantly, in excess';[91] he had even 'tried to destroy *(eporthoun)*' the church. As P. H. Menoud observes, the verb *porthein* when elsewhere applied to things or people always conveys the idea of material assault (destroying and ravaging cities and territories), or even more violent physical or mental destruction.[92] No doubt Paul too was in danger of exaggerating the language he used as he looked back in some horror at his former life, but even so, 'the use of brute force'[93] can hardly be

---

they add: 'However, it makes good sense that he should have asked for a letter of commendation from the high priest to back him up. The high priest and other heads of the Jewish leading class must have been interested in the restoration of peace in this important Jewish community' (*Paul* 51).

90. For *elymaineto* cf. 2 Chron. 16.10 and Ps. 80.13; also Acts 9.21; 22.4; 26.10-11; and see further BDAG 604; Lake and Cadbury, *Beginnings* 4.88; Barrett, *Acts* 1.393. On 26.10 Barrett cautions against dismissing Luke's language as 'rhetorical' and thinks he 'probably represents at least folk memory of that period' (*Acts* 2.1155-56).

91. A well-known idiom and characteristically Pauline (Rom. 7.13; 1 Cor. 12.31; 2 Cor. 1.8; 4.17). Fredriksen, however, thinks that *kath' hyperbolēn* refers only to Saul/Paul administering the maximum number of stripes permitted by the law (thirty-nine lashes) ('Judaism' 549-50).

92. P. H. Menoud, 'The Meaning of the Verb *porthein* (Gal. 1.13, 23; Acts 9.12)', *Jesus Christ and the Faith* (Pittsburgh: Pickwick, 1978) 47-60; Hengel, *Pre-Christian Paul* 71-72 and n. 308. Luke echoes Paul's use in his Acts 9.21 description. S. A. Cummins, *Paul and the Crucified Christ in Antioch: Maccabean Martyrdom and Galatians 1 and 2* (SNTSMS 114; Cambridge: Cambridge University, 2001), draws attention to the 'notable analogy' of Antiochus IV's 'plundering' Jerusalem and 'destruction' of the martyrs (4 Macc. 4.23; 11.4; the only occurrences of *porthein* in the LXX) (122).

93. Hengel, *Pre-Christian Paul* 72. W. D. Davies seeks to play down the language and ignores the *kath' hyperbolēn* in 'Paul: From the Jewish Point of View', *CHJ* 3.678-730 (here 681-84). Murphy-O'Connor cautions against taking Paul's language too literally ('It articulates the quality of the Apostle's commitment, not the means he employed'), although he still concludes, 'Paul did real damage over a period of time impossible to estimate' (*Paul* 67). And

excluded. In Jerusalem itself, it is not hard to envisage limited police action, led by the fiery young Pharisee, with high priestly backing or at least connivance. The Roman garrison would note and observe, without necessarily recognizing any need to intervene. Elsewhere, and especially outside the territory within which the high priest could exercise his formal authority with some effect, we probably have to envisage Saul leading a delegation urging synagogue leaders to discipline recalcitrant followers of the Way and to do so with all the force at their command.[94] Any less than that and we evacuate Paul's language of its obvious significance and reduce it to empty posturing.

b. Why Did Saul Persecute?

In the past, when the question about the reason for Saul's persecution of Christians has been asked, one or more of three answers have usually been regarded as sufficient.

- He objected violently to the claim that a crucified man was being proclaimed as Messiah.[95] A plausible inference from Gal. 3.13 is that Saul regarded the crucified Jesus as cursed by God; to hail him as Messiah could well have seemed to Saul a kind of blasphemy.[96] The suggestion that the devotion (or worship) already being offered to Jesus by his followers was also a factor is not borne out by Paul's own references to his conversion.[97]

Davies suggests that Paul's attacks 'were more likely to have been in the form of theological argument' ('Paul' 683)! But Legasse has no doubt: 'The vocabulary of Acts, which corresponds to that of the letters, expresses, without any possibility of doubt, violent actions', though he also notes that in his letters Paul never indicates that he was responsible for the death of those he persecuted ('Paul's Pre-Christian Career' 381, 384). See further below, §25.2c.

94. In Acts 26.10-11 Luke has Paul confess that 'by punishing them often in all the synagogues I tried to force them to blaspheme; and since I was so furiously enraged at them, I pursued them even to foreign cities'.

95. 'Christology must have been a point of dispute between Paul and the Christians persecuted by him' (Räisänen, 'Hellenisten' 1501).

96. E.g., Lohse, *Paulus* 59; Barnett, *Jesus* 223-25. The question whether Saul/Paul had heard Jesus during his time in Jerusalem cannot be given a final answer. On the one hand, the possibility can hardly be excluded that Saul had heard Jesus or even witnessed his execution (so, e.g., Weiss, *Earliest Christianity* 187-89; Klausner, *From Jesus to Paul* 313-16). On the other hand, Saul's presumed time of study in Jerusalem may have preceded Jesus' one (or more) visit(s). The famous 2 Cor. 5.16 does not necessarily imply that Paul had 'known' Jesus, as argued by J. Weiss, *Paul and Jesus* (ET London: Harper, 1909) 41-56; even so, however, the knowing 'in a fleshly way' is presumably a reference to Paul's pre-Christian opinion — but formed on what grounds? Cf. Hengel, *Pre-Christian Paul* 63-64.

97. Particularly L. W. Hurtado, 'Pre-70 C.E. Jewish Opposition to Christ-Devotion', *JTS*

- He objected violently to the Hellenists' revival of Jesus' critique of the Temple (Acts 6.14). For a scrupulous Pharisee, the sanctity of the Temple would have forbidden a description of it such as we find in Acts 7.48.[98]
- He saw the first Christians as abusing and abandoning the law, the very centre of his religion as a scrupulous Pharisee, and therefore as threatening Judaism itself.[99] This would fit with his own description of his previous self as 'exceedingly zealous for my ancestral traditions' (Gal. 1.14).

All of these reasons make good sense, and it is hard to doubt that they all played some part in Saul's compulsion to 'destroy' the new movement before what he regarded as the cancer became too established within the body of Israel. But do they provide sufficient explanation? After all, we have already noted that 'the Hebrews' (Acts 6.1) seem to have been able to remain in (or return to) Jerusalem despite their continuing assertion of the messiahship of the crucified Jesus. As for the Hellenists' dismissal of the Temple, that would certainly have provoked strong reaction in Jerusalem itself; but would it have provoked such a pursuit to 'foreign cities' as Luke asserts and Paul himself implies? After all, there must have been many diaspora Jews for whom distance from Jerusalem meant that the Temple could have only marginal importance for their own ongoing praxis of Judaism. And as for the law, the conclusion from our study of the Hellenists (§24) was that apart from the Temple, the law does not seem to have been questioned in principle or to have been spoken of so negatively as Paul was later to do. Noteworthy, for example, is the description of the disciple Ananias of Damascus (one of Saul's putative targets), as 'a devout man in accordance with the law' (Acts 22.12).[100] We are left wondering, therefore, whether these factors, important as they no doubt were, provide sufficient explanation of Saul's persecuting zeal.

---

50 (1999) 35-58, who finds evidence in Gal. 1.15-17, 2 Cor. 3–4 and Phil. 3.4-16 (50-53; also *How on Earth?* 169-72). But 2 Corinthians 3–4 gives no hint of Paul's reasons for his own former hostility; Gal. 1.13-14 is clear that it was zeal for the law which led Paul to persecute the church of God, that is, to persecute those who were departing from and threatening the traditions of the fathers; and what Paul in Philippians 3 recalls turning away from was his confidence in his Jewish identity and in his being a very devoted Pharisee, as indicated also by his persecuting zeal.

98. Wander suggests that the spread of pneumatic experience among the Hellenists would have been seen by Saul as endangering the observation of the Torah's ritual purity regulations (*Trennungsprozesse* 159-63).

99. 'He saw them as apostates of the law' (S. Kim, *The Origin of Paul's Gospel* [WUNT 2.4; Tübingen: Mohr Siebeck, 1981/Grand Rapids: Eerdmans, 1982] 44-46, 51).

100. That Ananias is not a Lukan invention has been well argued by Wilson, *Gentiles* 162-65; N. Taylor, *Paul, Antioch and Jerusalem* (JSNTS 66; Sheffield: Sheffield Academic, 1992) 65-66.

For my own part, I have long concluded that the above explanations miss an important dimension of what Paul had in mind when he attributed his persecution of the church explicitly to his 'zeal'.[101]

c. Saul the Zealot

If there is one word which characterizes the mind-set of the pre-Christian Saul as persecutor, it is the word 'zeal'. This indeed is one of the points where Luke's account and Paul's own reminiscences are in full accord:

- Acts 22.3-4 — '... educated strictly in the ancestral law, being a zealot for God *(zēlōtēs tou theou),* just as all of you are today. And I persecuted this Way to the death . . .'.
- Gal. 1.13-14 — 'I persecuted the church of God in excessive measure and tried to destroy it, and I progressed in Judaism beyond many of my contemporaries among my people, being exceedingly zealous for my ancestral traditions *(zēlōtēs tōn patrikōn mou paradoseōn)*'.
- Phil. 3.6 — '. . . as to zeal *(zēlos)* a persecutor of the church . . .'.

We know that Paul could use the term *zēlos* ('zeal') both positively and negatively.[102] And in two of these three passages the reference is primarily to his devotion to God and to Torah, understood and practised in terms of the Pharisaic halakhoth. Nor should it be inferred that by calling himself a 'zealot *(zēlōtēs)*' Paul was admitting to membership of the radical party which later led the revolt against Rome ('the Zealots').[103] The term 'zealot' only took on such political and

---

101. I set out my argument in several contributions, including 'Paul's Conversion — a Light to Twentieth-Century Disputes', in J. Ådna et al., eds., *Evangelium — Schriftauslegung — Kirche,* P. Stuhlmacher FS (Göttingen: Vandenhoeck und Ruprecht, 1997) 77-93, reprinted in *The New Perspective on Paul* ch. 15; briefly in *Galatians* 60-62. It is surprising that so many have failed to recognize the light shed on this question by the 'zeal' motif. E.g., Gnilka, *Paulus* 37-38; Peerbolte, *Paul* 143-46; Schnelle, *Paul* 85-86; and even Hengel, *Pre-Christian Paul* 84, despite 70-71, *Acts* 83, and his earlier work *The Zealots* (1961, ²1976; ET Edinburgh: Clark, 1989). But see also Haacker, *Paulus* 84-90.

102. Positively ('zeal, ardour') — 2 Cor. 7.7, 11; 9.2; 11.2; negatively ('jealousy, envy') — Rom. 13.13; 1 Cor. 3.3; 2 Cor. 12.20; Gal. 5.20.

103. As J. B. Lightfoot assumed (*Galatians* 81-82); J. Taylor, 'Why Did Paul Persecute the Church?', in G. N. Stanton and G. Stroumsa, eds., *Tolerance and Intolerance in Early Judaism and Christianity* (Cambridge: Cambridge University, 1998) 99-120; cf. M. R. Fairchild, 'Paul's Pre-Christian Zealot Associations: A Re-examination of Gal. 1.14 and Acts 22.3', *NTS* 45 (1999) 514-32. For a brief review of the diverse opinions on the political/nationalist overtones of the term 'zealot', see T. Seland, 'Saul of Tarsus and Early Zealotism: Reading Gal

titular significance ('Zealot') twenty-five or thirty years after Paul's conversion.[104] What is striking in the usage of Phil. 3.6, however, is the fact that Paul clearly remembered his 'zeal' as characterized and most clearly expressed in his persecution of the church — 'as regards zeal, a persecutor'. Moreover, for Saul the Pharisee, 'zeal' had been one of the highest grounds for his confidence 'in the flesh'; this item comes as second only to his 'blamelessness' in what is obviously a climactic list (3.4-6). Not only so, but we should observe the radical change in evaluation which he goes on to indicate (3.7-8). For Paul the Christian, this former 'zeal' was something he could now only regret. What, then, was this 'zeal' which he valued so highly as a very strict Pharisee and which found its highest expression in persecution? In what sense was Paul a 'zealot'?

The clue lies in the earliest use of the motif of 'zeal/jealousy' (Hebrew, *qn'*) in the Torah — Yahweh's own 'zeal/jealousy' in insisting that Israel must not worship any other gods but remain dedicated to him alone.[105] E. Reuter notes that the relationship between Yahweh and his worshippers 'is characterized by an intolerant demand for exclusivity: it is Yahweh's will "to be the only God for Israel, and . . . he is not disposed to share his claim for worship and love with any other divine power"'.[106]

This 'zeal' of Yahweh was seen as requiring and providing the pattern for Israel's own 'zeal' — a 'zeal' for holiness, as Yahweh is holy (Lev. 19.2), that is, a burning concern to maintain Israel's identity as a people set apart to God, a passionate concern to protect Israel's holiness over against other nations. In a sequence of episodes, cherished by many Jews in their folk memory, this zeal was expressed in violent action to prevent or to stem a breach in Israel's set-apartness, its holiness to God — that is, by preventing or countering any adulteration or compromise of Israel's distinctive holiness. God's 'zeal' that Israel should keep herself for God alone was directly mirrored in the 'zeal' which defended and reinforced the boundaries separating Israel from the (other) nations.

The most famous of Israel's 'heroes of zeal' was Phinehas, who, when an Israelite brought a Midianite woman into his tent (into the congregation of

---

1,13-14 in Light of Philo's Writings', *Biblica* 83 (2002) 449-71 (here 450-56). Davies is brusque: 'no such "party" existed in his day' ('Paul' 681).

104. See *Jesus Remembered* 272-73, where I note that Josephus does not use the term 'Zealot' until the revolt itself, and that he uses it earlier in the sense of 'someone who is ardent for a cause', including himself (*Life* 11). In the LXX it is God who is described as a 'zealot' (Exod. 20.5; 34.14; Deut. 4.24; 5.9; 6.15).

105. Exod. 20.5; 34.14; Deut. 4.23-24; 5.9; 6.14-15; 32.21; 11QTemple 2.12-13. Hengel observes that the adjectives are applied only to God (*Zealots* 146).

106. E. Reuter, *qn'*, *TDOT* 13.54, citing von Rad, *Old Testament Theology* 1.208. Paul's plea to the Corinthians, 'I am jealous for you with the jealousy of God' (2 Cor. 11.2), is a direct echo of this divine zeal/jealousy.

Yahweh), forthwith slew them both, 'because he was zealous for God' (Num. 25.6-13); it is no surprise that in Num. 25.11 Phinehas's zeal is understood as a direct reflection of Yahweh's.[107] For this single deed he was often recalled and his zeal praised,[108] and he became the model and inspiration for the later Zealots.[109] Many other heroes were famed for their 'zeal'.

- Simeon and Levi 'burned with zeal for you [God] and abhorred the pollution of their blood' (Jdt. 9.2-4), which referred to their slaughter of the Shechemites after the seduction of their sister Dinah by the son of Hamor (Genesis 34). In *Jubilees* 30 the avenging of Dinah's defilement (vv. 4-5) and protection of Israel's holiness from Gentile defilement (vv. 8, 13-14) was counted to them for righteousness (v. 17).
- Elijah's 'zeal for the Lord' was most fully expressed in his victory over (and execution of!) the prophets of Baal.[110]
- Mattathias sparked the revolt against the Syrians when, 'burning with zeal', 'with zeal for the law, just like Phinehas', he executed the Syrian officer and the fellow Jew who was made to apostatize by offering forbidden sacrifice (1 Macc. 2.23-26). Mattathias rallied the rebellion by crying out, 'Let everyone who is zealous for the law and supports the covenant come with me' (2.27; Josephus, *Ant.* 12.271), and his death-bed testimony is a paean in praise of zeal and the heroes of Israel (1 Macc. 2.51-60).[111]
- Qumran expresses the same understanding of 'zeal' as directed *against* others: 'The closer I approach [God], the more am I filled with zeal *(qn'thi)* against all workers of iniquity and the men of deceit' (Vermes) (1QH 6[= 14].14; similarly 10[= 2].15).

---

107. 'Like Joshua's zeal on behalf of Moses (Nu. 11:29), Phinehas's zeal on behalf of Yahweh realizes Yahweh's own jealousy . . . which otherwise would have consumed all Israel' (Reuter, *qn'*, *TDOT* 13.56). A. Stumpff had already observed (*TDNT* 2.879) that the term ('zeal') is linked with 'anger' (Deut. 29.20) and 'wrath' (Num. 25.11; Ezek. 16.38, 42; 36.6; 38.19; see also 1QH 17[= 9].3; 4Q400 1.1.18; 4Q504 frag. 1-2 col. 3.10-11; 5.5); similarly Hengel, *Zealots* 146-47. The importance of Phinehas as the 'classical' precedent for Paul has been more widely recognized (Haacker, *Paulus* 89 n. 130).

108. Ps. 106.28-31 (the deed was 'reckoned to him as righteousness'); Sir. 45.23-24 ('third in glory for being zealous in the fear of the Lord'); 1 Macc. 2.26, 54 ('Phinehas our ancestor, because he was deeply zealous, received the covenant of everlasting priesthood'); 4 Macc. 18.12.

109. Hengel, *Zealots* ch. 4.

110. 1 Kgs. 18.40; 19.1, 10, 14; Sir. 48.2-3; 1 Macc. 2.58. The prophets of Baal would at least include fellow Israelites who had taken service in the worship of Baal. See also Exod. 32.26-29 and 2 Kgs. 10.16-28.

111. Cummins concludes: 'The collocation of the themes and terms deployed at Galatians 1.13-14 suggests that in his former life as a zealous Pharisee Paul stood firmly in the tradition of the Maccabees' (*Paul and the Crucified Christ* 122).

- Philo bears witness to the same attitude when, writing possibly only a decade or so before Paul's role as a persecutor, he warns that 'there are thousands . . . who are zealots for the laws *(zēlōtai nomōn)*, strictest guardians of the ancestral customs, merciless to those who do anything to subvert them' *(Spec. Leg.* 2.253).[112]
- In the same spirit are the rulings preserved in the Mishnah: 'If a man . . . made an Aramean woman his paramour, the zealots may fall upon him. If a priest served (at the altar) in a state of uncleanness his brethren the priests did not bring him to the court, but the young men among the priests took him outside the Temple court and split open his brain with clubs' *(m. Sanh.* 9.6).[113]

In the light of this evidence, the tradition of 'zeal for the Lord/Torah' was marked by three features in particular:

1. It was sparked by the sight of fellow Jews disregarding the law, particularly when it meant that Israel's set-apartness to God and from the defilement of other nations and their gods was being threatened or compromised.[114]
2. It could be directed against fellow (compromising) Jews as much as against the foreign 'others' whose involvement marked the breach of Israel's boundaries.[115]
3. It regularly involved violence and bloodshed, as necessitated (in the view of the zealots) by the severity of the danger to Israel's exclusive set-apartness to and holiness before God.[116]

---

112. Similarly *Spec. Leg.* 1.54-57: 'But if any members of the nation betray the honour due to the One, they should suffer the utmost penalties. . . . And it is well that all who have a zeal *(zēlos)* for virtue should be permitted to exact penalties offhand and with no delay, without bringing the offender before jury or council or any kind of magistrate at all, and give full scope to the feelings which possess them, that hatred of evil and love of God which urges them to inflict punishment without mercy on the impious' (1.54-55) — instancing Phinehas (1.56). See further Seland, 'Saul of Tarsus' 456-68.

113. Other cases where zeal is expressed in violent action include 2 Sam. 21.2 — '(king) Saul had tried to wipe them [the Gibeonites] out in his zeal for the people of Israel and Judah'; and 2 Kgs. 10.16 — Jehu's 'zeal for the Lord' is expressed in his slaughter of Ahab's supporters. Haacker cites also Exod. 32.26-29 and John 16.2 *(Paulus* 88-89).

114. This aspect of 'zeal' as not simply zeal for the law, but zeal to maintain the set-apartness of Israel is usually missed — e.g., Schnelle, *Paul* 85-86.

115. 'Sinners and lawless men' in 1 Macc. 1.34 and 2.44, 48 certainly included those whom the Maccabees regarded as apostate Jews, Israelites who had abandoned the law; see further my 'Pharisees, Sinners and Jesus', *Jesus, Paul and the Law* (London: SPCK/Louisville: Westminster John Knox, 1990) 61-86 (here 74).

116. As Seland notes, the Philo references confirm the violent character of the 'zeal' in view ('Saul of Tarsus' 466-68).

What is immediately striking about this finding is that the three features provide a remarkably accurate description of Saul's persecution, particularly as directed against fellow Jews (Hellenists) and as to the fierceness with which he himself recalled it. The most interesting corollary, then, is the fact that the first of the three features offers us the answer for our question, 'Why did Saul persecute?' The answer it offers is that Saul persecuted because he regarded the Hellenists (§24) as a threat to Israel's set-apartness to God.[117] That could be described also as zeal for the law, but in this case it was the law in its role as a bulwark against the corruptions and the defilements of other nations.[118]

To draw such an inference it is not necessary to argue that the Hellenists were already launched into their mission to non-Jews (in Samaria or Antioch). Since the Hellenist mission was occasioned by persecution (of Saul, at least according to Acts), on the most probable dating, Saul's persecuting activity must have already been triggered off before the breakthrough in Antioch. Possibly the slighting of the Temple, indicated by the accusation against Stephen and the statement of Hellenist views (Acts 6.14; 7.48), would have been sufficient grounds in itself to rouse Saul's ire.[119] Nor should we disregard or discount the possible echo in the label 'Hellenist' of the Hellenizing policies and practices which roused Mattathias's ire and began the Maccabean rebellion (1 Maccabees 2). Most striking of all, of course, is the record that Saul sought to continue his policy of repression in the synagogues of Damascus (Acts 9.1-2), which indicates that in the course of his persecution (perhaps as a result of it) there had already been an exodus of Jesus followers to Damascus, where, Saul might well suspect, their 'Hellenizing' policies had been taken further.[120]

All that need be assumed, however, is that Saul in his zeal regarded certain attitudes and actions of some (representative) Hellenists as a threat to Israel's

117. In seeking an answer to the question 'Why did mainstream Judaism treat Christianity as deviant?', J. T. Sanders concludes, 'The Jewish leadership punished early Christianity . . . because events were leading the enforcers of Judaic identity to maintain the boundaries of Judaism while the Christians were breaking through those boundaries in one way or another' (*Schismatics* 136-41, 150).

118. Classically expressed in the *Letter of Aristeas* 139-42: 'In his wisdom the legislator [i.e., Moses] . . . surrounded us with unbroken palisades and iron walls to prevent our mixing with any of the other peoples in any matter, being thus kept pure in body and soul. . . . To prevent our being perverted by contact with others or by mixing with bad influences, he hedged us in on all sides with strict observances connected with meat and drink and touch and hearing and sight, after the manner of the Law' (Charlesworth).

119. Weiss regarded it practically certain that Saul had listened in person to debates with Stephen (Acts 6.9-10), and may even have entered into the discussion himself (*Earliest Christianity* 187).

120. Cf. Fredriksen, 'Judaism' 548-58.

separateness,[121] as breaching the protective boundaries formed by the law and maintained by doing the law.[122] If a single episode was sufficient to trigger the violent zeal of Phinehas and Mattathias, we need hardly look for anything more substantial or sustained in the case of Saul.[123] In the sort of fundamentalist mindset which the pre-Christian Saul manifested, even suspicion that Hellenists were acting as 'fifth-columnists' would be sufficient to provoke and justify a repressive and violent reaction.[124] An explanation along these lines seems to me to make best sense of the fact that Paul ascribes his own violent persecution of 'the church of God' to this same 'zeal' (Phil. 3.6). Paul's persecuting zeal was not simply zeal to be the best that he could be (zeal for the law) but a grim determination to maintain Israel's holiness by attacking — 'seeking to destroy'! (Gal. 1.13, 23) — those Jews who (in his view) were beginning to breach Israel's boundaries of set-apartness.

25.3. 'Approaching Damascus, about Noon'

The tradition that Saul was converted 'on the road to Damascus', probably within two or three years of Jesus' crucifixion,[125] has become well established in common parlance as well as for historians of early Christianity. Indeed, a 'Damascus road conversion' is widely used in all sorts of contexts for a sudden turn-about of policy or complete reversal of direction of life. And though Paul himself never says where his conversion took place, the implications of Gal. 1.17 (after his conversion he went immediately to Arabia and afterwards 'returned' to Damascus) are sufficiently coherent with the Acts accounts of the decisive event (Acts 9.3-8; 22.6-11; 26.12-20) to put the matter beyond reasonable doubt.

a. Why Damascus?

That is, why did so many Hellenists, fleeing Jerusalem (8.4), head for Damascus? And why did Saul pursue these Hellenists rather than others? The answers

---

121. It will be recalled that 'Pharisees' was probably something of a nickname — the 'separated ones' (*Jesus Remembered* 268 n. 57).

122. 'He went to Damascus to stop the shameless messianic sectarians who were corrupting the numerous sympathizers there who could easily be led astray' (Hengel and Schwemer, *Paul* 54).

123. 'Can anyone in Paul's time speak at all of so similar a zeal without evoking the spirit of Phinehas?' (Becker, *Paul* 68).

124. Could we compare the violent response provoked by even suspicions of terrorist activity since '9/11' and '7/7' in the United States and Britain?!

125. See below, §28.1.

almost certainly overlap. A major factor is bound to have been the presence of many Jews in Damascus: Josephus reports that 10,500 Jews were killed there at the outbreak of the Jewish revolt and, perhaps more to the point, that the Jews of Damascus had won many converts among the wives of the Damascenes (*War* 2.560-61; cf. 7.368). Another factor may have been that in Damascus the ethnarch of the Arabian king Aretas IV was able to exercise some political and quasi-military force at this time (2 Cor. 11.32):[126] a mission of internal (Jewish) discipline[127] would probably have been more easily executed in situations where Roman rule was less direct; Caesarea and the coastal region (Acts 8.40) would have been under much closer supervision by the Roman authorities. And Damascus historically had close links with Israel, being only about 135 miles from Jerusalem.[128] But why not Samaria (Acts 8)? Perhaps the mission of Philip had been fairly isolated, with most fleeing Hellenists choosing to bypass Samaria. Then why not Galilee? Probably because Galilee was hardly an obvious destination for fleeing Hellenists; and perhaps because the transposition of many or most of Jesus' disciples to Jerusalem left few functioning communities of his earliest disciples.[129] Whether there is any possible linkage in the early history of Qumran is almost totally obscure.[130]

The key point, of course, is that the influence of 'those who belonged to the way' (9.2) had spread to and within the substantial Jewish community of Damascus. These synagogues could already have been influenced directly from Galilee; the distances were such that reports of Jesus' mission in northern Galilee would no doubt have reached Damascus, and not a few Damascene Jews may well have gone to Galilee to hear and see for themselves. But there is no reason to question the basic picture implied by Luke's account: that some/(many?) Hellenists who had departed from Jerusalem during the first wave of persecution ended up in Damascus.[131] That Saul's commission was to the Damascus synagogues sug-

126. See below, §28.1b.

127. See above, §25.2a.

128. On the history of the city and its Jewish community, see further Hengel and Schwemer, *Paul* 55-61.

129. See §24 n. 229. But the question 'Why not Galilee?' must be answered by those who regard Galilee as a centre for early Christianity and as more open to Hellenization than I found to be the case in *Jesus Remembered* §9.6.

130. CD 6.5, 19 speak of 'the converts of Israel, who left the land of Judah and lived in the land of Damascus . . . those who entered the new covenant in the land of Damascus' (also 8.21; 19.33-34; 20.12). For various interpretations of 'Damascus' in CD, see G. Vermes, *An Introduction to the Complete Dead Sea Scrolls* (Minneapolis: Fortress, 1999) 233 n. 8. It is certainly curious that CD 7.12-21 uses the very passage (Amos 5.26-27) which appears in Stephen's speech (Acts 7.42-43, though 7.43 reads 'Babylon' rather than Amos's and CD's 'Damascus') and links it with Balaam's prophecy of a star to come out of Jacob (Num. 24.17).

131. Indications that Luke was able to draw on good tradition here include the reference

gests that Hellenist incomers witnessing to their faith in Messiah Jesus had been sufficient to cause unrest within the Jewish community. And Paul's talk of his motivating 'zeal' further suggests that their testimony had succeeded in attracting and even winning a goodly number of the non-Jewish sympathizers and proselytes who associated with the synagogues. We should probably refrain from talking about a Damascus 'church', as Luke does. Reports of gatherings of 'disciples' (9.10, 19, 25) in different houses, without any schismatic intentions, at which the (in Saul's eyes) subversive views of the Hellenists were being propagated, would have been enough to rouse Saul's zealous ire.[132]

Whatever the reasons, both of those who had fled to Damascus and of Saul the persecutor, the tradition is sufficiently reliable that it was on the way to Damascus (as he was approaching Damascus — 9.3) that the event known as Saul's 'conversion' took place. I have already set out the heart of the three Acts accounts in synoptic fashion (9.1-22; 22.1-21; 26.9-23) and noted both the variations between them and the word-for-word agreement of the core encounter (9.4-6; 22.7-10; 26.14-16) — typical examples, on my view, of the way the tale of Saul's conversion was retold not only by Luke but within the early churches.[133] But, more important for us here, we have Paul's own references back to his conversion — 1 Cor. 9.1, 15.8, 2 Cor. 4.6 (probably), Gal. 1.15-16 and Phil. 3.7-8.

- 1 Cor. 9.1 — 'Am I not apostle? Have I not seen Jesus our Lord?'
- 1 Cor. 15.8 — 'Last of all he appeared as to me, as to one untimely born'.
- 2 Cor. 4.6 — 'It is the God who said, "Let light shine out of darkness", who has shone in our hearts to give the light of the knowledge of the glory of God in the face of Jesus Christ'.[134]

---

to the disciples in Damascus as those of 'the way' (9.2; note also 22.4) and 'the saints' (9.13; cf. 26.10), both of which appear in Acts for the first time here. Ananias (see above, n. 100) need not have been a Hellenist as such, but a local Jew won over by incoming Hellenists (22.12 describes him as 'a devout man according to the law and well spoken of' by all his fellow Jews in Damascus); but according to 22.14, Paul himself associated 'the way' with devotion to the law and the prophets.

132. See also Hengel and Schwemer, *Paul* 80-90; on the unlikelihood that Saul was active as a persecutor in Damascus rather than in Judea, see 341 n. 163.

133. *Jesus Remembered* 210-12. See also A. M. Schwemer, 'Erinnerung und Legende. Die Berufung des Paulus und ihre Darstellung in der Apostelgeschichte', in L. T. Stuckenbruck et al., eds., *Memory in the Bible and Antiquity* (WUNT 212; Tübingen: Mohr Siebeck, 2007) 277-98. Marguerat notes that the three accounts span Luke's account of Paul's mission: 'The history of the Gentile mission unfolds entirely within the space defined by this enlightening event; . . . the narrator makes the conversion of Saul function as a hermeneutical key . . . the emblematic illustration of the fact that through this very break the Christian faith retains a basic faithfulness to the God of the fathers' (*First Christian Historian* 203-204).

134. That 2 Cor. 4.6 does allude to Paul's own conversion is probably a majority view

- Gal. 1.15-16 — 'But when it pleased the one who set me apart from my mother's womb, and called me through his grace, to reveal his Son in me, in order that I might preach him among the Gentiles . . .'.
- Phil. 3.7-8 — 'Whatever gains I had, these I came to regard as loss because of Christ. More than that, I regard everything as loss on account of the surpassing value of knowing Christ Jesus my Lord'.

As we shall see, the degree of correlation of the Acts accounts with Paul's own reminiscences is sufficient for us to draw out the main features of Saul's conversion, for Paul himself, but also as Luke heard and retold it. Besides these, the performance variations between the Acts accounts pale to insignificance.[135]

b. 'Have I Not Seen Jesus Our Lord?' (1 Cor. 9.1)

Paul's conviction that he had seen Jesus can hardly be doubted — that is, Jesus alive from the dead and appearing to him from heaven. He had evidently no doubt that Jesus, risen from the dead, had appeared to him, just as he had appeared to Peter and the twelve before him (1 Cor. 15.8). The retellings in Acts major on the visual aspect too:

- 'a light from heaven' (9.3), Saul blinded and healed (9.8, 18), 'the Lord Jesus appeared to you' (9.17);
- 'a great light from heaven' (22.6), 'I could not see because of the brightness of that light' (22.11), sight regained (22.13), chosen 'to see the Righteous One' (22.14);
- 'a light from heaven, brighter than the sun' (26.13), 'for this purpose I have appeared to you, to appoint you as a servant and witness of what you have seen' (26.16); 'I was not disobedient to the heavenly vision' (26.19).

Not to be ignored is the echo of such descriptions which we find in 2 Cor. 4.6: the light shone, Paul saw the face of Jesus Christ. Nor indeed the fainter echo of Gal. 1.15-16 in Acts 22.14. And the talk of 'knowing Christ Jesus' in Phil. 3.8 is already intensely personal.[136]

---

among commentators; see discussion in M. Thrall, *2 Corinthians* (ICC, 2 vols.; Edinburgh: Clark, 1994, 2000) 316-20, bibliography in 316 n. 878; also Schnelle, *Paulus* 80-81. See further below, §25.4a.

135. To speak of the differences between the Acts accounts as 'discrepancies' or 'disagreements' is to reflect a common misunderstanding of the way oral tradition was (and is) used/performed; see again *Jesus Remembered* §8.

136. Schnelle, *Paulus* 81.

Is the tradition to the effect that Saul recognized Jesus and in that instant was converted to faith in this Jesus? We note that the address in the Acts accounts, *kyrie* ('Lord, sir'), that is, to the figure bathed in light,[137] would have been an appropriate address to such a figure, rather than an immediate confession that this *kyrios* is Jesus; after all, the initial address is a question, 'Who are you, *kyrie?*' (9.5; 22.8; 26.15). But the understanding of his experience as a seeing of Jesus is one which was probably given to him either in the event itself ('I am Jesus whom you are persecuting', part of the story core — 9.5; 22.8; 26.15), or possibly by the Christians with whom he quickly associated. The implication of Paul's own reminiscence (and not just of Luke's account) is that Saul did not go to the synagogue authorities in Damascus, as we might otherwise have expected, but either sought out or was sought out by one or more of those whom he had intended to persecute.[138] So what he saw/experienced must have been sufficiently compelling in itself to cause him to stop short and to change direction. This implies, in turn, that Luke was able to draw on good tradition for much of his account in Acts 9.8-19.

What kind of 'seeing' is a question I have already asked.[139] Here we need simply note again: (1) that unlike other appearances, this one was presumably directly from heaven; (2) that Luke does not hesitate to speak of it as a 'heavenly vision' (Acts 26.19); and (3) that Paul himself speaks of God revealing his Son 'in me' (Gal. 1.16).[140] So a strong visionary and subjective element is not to be denied. The key factor, however, is that Paul experienced the encounter as a *seeing* of Jesus. Even if we were to deduce that his mode of conceptualization was given to him subsequent to the event, that his commitment to the cause he had been persecuting resulted in some 'biographical reconstruction',[141] the fact re-

137. Light, of course, is a common feature of appearances of heavenly figures; see, e.g., the data in Barrett, *Acts* 1.449.

138. Luke does not explain why Saul went or was taken to 'the house of Judas', on 'the street called Straight', and whether Judas was himself a believer (Hengel and Schwemer, *Paul* 81 think not); on Ananias, see again n. 100 above.

139. *Jesus Remembered* 872-74.

140. 'In me' is a preferable rendering of *en emoi* than 'to me', despite BDF §220(1), RSV/NRSV. When Paul wanted to use a dative with the verb 'reveal', he did so (1 Cor. 2.10; 14.30; Phil. 3.15). The 'in me' of Gal. 1.16 matches rather the 'in me' of Gal. 2.20; cf. 2 Cor. 4.6 — 'in our hearts'. B. R. Gaventa, *From Darkness to Light: Aspects of Conversion in the New Testament* (Philadelphia: Fortress, 1986), argues that the parallel of *en tois ethnesin* suggests that the *en* in both cases carries the sense of 'to' (27); the more natural sense of the latter phrase, however, is 'among the Gentiles'.

141. Bibliography in Segal, *Paul the Convert* 28. L. Bormann, 'Autobiographische Fiktionalität bei Paulus', in Becker and Pilhofer, eds., *Biographie und Persönlichkeit des Paulus* 106-24, quotes H. Winter, 'The truth of the autobiography is always only a truth for its author' (113).

mains that this was how Paul thereafter, that is, more or less from the first, understood what had happened to him. His question to the Corinthians (1 Cor. 9.1) obviously demands an affirmative answer: Yes, I saw Jesus our Lord!

c. 'Am I Not an Apostle?' (1 Cor. 9.1)

The other consistent feature of the various references and accounts is that Saul experienced his encounter with the risen Jesus as a commissioning. Almost more important than anything else for Paul's future career was that he understood the event as constituting not simply his commission as an apostle (1 Cor. 9.1; Gal. 1.1) but, more specifically, his commission as an apostle *to the Gentiles* (Rom. 1.5; 15.15-16). This is clearly the implication of 1 Cor. 15.8: the appearance of Christ appointed him as one of the select band of apostles ('last of all') who were commissioned to preach the gospel (15.9-11),[142] where 'apostle' still has its basic sense of 'messenger, envoy', that is, one commissioned and sent to speak on behalf of or to represent (an)other(s).[143] In 2 Cor. 4.6 we have the climax of Paul's comparison and contrast between his own ministry and that of Moses (2.14–4.6). And in Gal. 1.15-16 Paul explicitly states that God's purpose in revealing his Son in him was in order that he might preach the good news *(euangelizesthai)* of Christ among the Gentiles.

Here too the Acts accounts correlate rather closely with Paul's reminiscences: as with the visual element, so the commissioning is a firm part of the repertoire of the retellings of Paul's conversion. Note however the interesting qualification, that whereas the brief dialogue between the heavenly Jesus and Saul belongs to the firm core of the various retellings, the commissioning is the most variable element of all.

- In 9.15 the commissioning is signalled only in the vision to Ananias (Saul is an instrument chosen by God to bring his name before Gentiles), though the implication of the immediate sequel is that Saul had experienced some sort of commission himself (9.20, 27-29).

142. For convenience I repeat the beginning of my note in *Theology of Paul* 331 n. 87: The term *ektrōma* denotes 'premature birth'. Since it could imply the deformity often involved in such a birth, it may have originated as a jibe against Paul by opponents ('freak', 'monstrosity'). Paul probably took it up to indicate that his birth (as a believer) was premature, forced ahead of time, in order that he might be included within the circle of apostles before it closed ('last of all'). See further my *Jesus and the Spirit* 101-102; Fee, *1 Corinthians* 732-34; and below, §29 n. 50. See also M. W. Mitchell, 'Reexamining the "Aborted Apostle": An Exploration of Paul's Self-Description in 1 Corinthians 15.8', *JSNT* 25 (2003) 469-85.

143. See further below, §29.3.

- In the second account the commission is only referred to briefly in the conversion sequence itself ('you will be his witness to all people' — 22.15), and is confirmed later by an explicit vision in the Temple of Jerusalem ('I will send you far away to the Gentiles' — 22.21).
- In the third account, however, the commission is given explicitly and at some length by the risen Jesus himself at the point of encounter on the Damascus road (26.16-18): '. . . the Gentiles, to whom I am sending you, to open their eyes, so that they may turn from darkness to light . . .' (26.17-18).

The constancy of this motif, despite the variation in the way it is presented, assuredly indicates that it was a firm element in the various tellings of Saul/Paul's conversion; Luke had presumably heard the story retold several times, as well as retelling it himself.

What are we to make of all this? It can readily be accepted that Saul's Damascus road experience involved both visual and auditory elements.[144] Whatever precisely he heard, it was evidently sufficient to convince him that he had to join the band of brothers whom he had set out to persecute. No doubt in this, as in the matter of what he had seen, his understanding became clearer over time: it is unlikely, for example, that the language of 'apostleship' would have sprung unbidden to his mind in the first instance. What we can say is that Paul was able to insist with unyielding emphasis, in his letter to the Galatians, that he had received his commissioning directly 'through Jesus Christ' and his gospel directly 'through a revelation of Jesus Christ' (Gal. 1.1, 12), where the correlation with 1.16 (God revealed his Son in me) almost certainly indicates that in the two earlier verses he was also referring to his Damascus road experience. Moreover, Paul naturally thought of himself as 'apostle of the Gentiles' (Rom. 11.13); the 'grace and apostleship' he had received was to bring Gentiles to the obedience of faith (Rom. 1.5; 15.15-16). There is no suggestion that he first saw himself as an apostle and only subsequently (after failed missionary work among fellow Jews?)[145] concluded that his apostleship must, after all, be to the Gentiles.[146] As he looked back, his conviction was clear: the risen Lord had

144. Both elements are a feature of many 'call' testimonies of the prophets — e.g., Isa. 6.1-13; Jer. 1.4-13; Ezek. 2.1-3.13; Amos 7.14–8.3.

145. So argued by F. Watson, *Paul, Judaism and the Gentiles* (SNTSMS 56; Cambridge: Cambridge University, 1986) 28-32; revised (Grand Rapids: Eerdmans, 2007) 69-82; distinctively by Segal, in reference to Romans 7 (*Paul the Convert* ch. 7).

146. Gal. 1.21 with 2.7-9 clearly implies that Paul's earliest missionary work was among Gentiles. On Gal. 1.17 see below (§25.5b). T. L. Donaldson, *Paul and the Gentiles: Remapping the Apostle's Convictional World* (Minneapolis: Fortress, 1997), argues that Gal. 5.11 refers to a time when Paul did preach circumcision (278-84), playing the role of Eleazar in the conversion of Izates (Josephus, *Ant.* 20.43-46), but his thesis does not take sufficient account of

commissioned Saul to be his missionary/apostle to the Gentiles when he encountered Saul on the Damascus road.[147]

d. To the Gentiles

The recognition that Saul understood his encounter on the Damascus road as first
and foremost a call to preach the good news about God's Son to the Gentiles
(Gal. 1.16) has several important corollaries.

(1) The argument as to whether we should speak more properly of Saul's
conversion or of his *commissioning* becomes rather pointless.[148] Of course we
should not think of Saul as converting from one religion to another (Judaism to
Christianity);[149] enough has been said already both about the embryonic state
particularly of the latter, and about the diverse and rather amorphous state of both
at this time, for such oversimplification to be firmly ruled out as totally anachronistic and unacceptable as a historical description.[150] Nevertheless we can hardly
avoid speaking of Paul's experience as a conversion; the *volte-face* of which he
himself speaks (Phil. 3.7) was as clear a 'conversion' as one could imagine.[151]
The only clarification required is that it was a conversion not from one religion to
another but from one form of Second Temple Judaism to another, that is, from
Pharisaism to Jesus messianism — conversion, we might even say, from a closed
Judaism to an open Judaism.[152] We have no reason, then, to set the two catego-

---

the character and targets of Paul's 'zeal' — more likely to oppose the inclusion of Gentile proselytes than to encourage it; cf. his treatment of the theme (286, 290, 292). See my *Galatians*
(BNTC; London: Black, 1993) 278-80; Martyn, *Galatians* 167-68 and 476-77.

147. Here I agree with S. Kim, *The Origin of Paul's Gospel* (WUNT 2.4; Tübingen:
Mohr Siebeck, 1981/Grand Rapids: Eerdmans, ²1984) 60, 65-66, 95. 'It is perfectly clear that
when composing the letter to the Galatians the apostle was convinced that the self-revelation of
the resurrected Jesus near Damascus already contained his commission to the Gentiles'
(Riesner, *Paul's Early Period* 235).

148. Stendahl, *Paul among Jews and Gentiles* 7-23: 'Call Rather Than Conversion'.

149. See, e.g., W. D. Davies, 'Paul and the People of Israel', *NTS* 24 (1977-78) 4-39: 'In
accepting the Jew, Jesus, as the Messiah, Paul did not think in terms of moving into a new religion but of having found the final expression and intent of the Jewish tradition within which he
himself had been born'; 'Paul was not thinking in terms of what we normally call conversion
from one religion to another but of the recognition by Jews of the final or true form of their own
religion' (20, 27).

150. See above, §20.1(1); Roetzel, *Paul* 44-46.

151. 'If such radical changes do not amount to conversion it is hard to know what would
do so' (Barrett, *Acts* 1.442).

152. Segal, *Paul the Convert* 6, 21, 79-84, 113, 117, 147. See also S. J. Chester, *Conversion at Corinth: Perspectives on Conversion in Paul's Theology and the Corinthian Church*

ries in contrast or antithesis. 'Conversion' is more the language of the historian of religion; 'commissioning' is the language of Paul's self-understanding. But the two can easily cohabit the same space.[153]

(2) This emphasis on 'called to the Gentiles' helps explain what otherwise appears to be a straight contradiction between Gal. 1.11-12 and 1 Cor. 15.3:

- Gal. 1.11-12 — 'I did not receive *(parelabon)* the gospel from humans, neither was I taught it, but through a revelation of Jesus Christ';
- 1 Cor. 15.3 — 'I received *(parelabon)* as the gospel (the tradition passed down) that Christ died for our sins . . .'.

The resolution is fairly straightforward. Paul assuredly did not think of his gospel as a different gospel from that agreed upon by Peter, James and John (Gal. 2.2-9); the gospel of 1 Cor. 15.3-4/5 was the gospel which they all preached (15.11). What was different about Paul's gospel was *his conviction that it was open also to Gentiles,* that the gospel he received in the tradition handed down to him at the time of his conversion (1 Cor. 15.3) was the message regarding God's Son which he had been commissioned to deliver to the Gentiles (Gal. 1.16). That was why Paul was such an uncomfortable bedfellow with his fellow apostles: he saw himself as first and foremost 'apostle to the Gentiles'; and so far as Paul himself was concerned, that had been the case from his commissioning itself.

(3) Paul seems deliberately to suggest that this commissioning was wholly in line with the earlier commissioning of Israel's prophets and indeed was a commissioning to fulfil Israel's own mission in regard to the nations. Gal. 1.15-16 is (evidently) framed in order to make clear an echo of Isa. 49.1-6 and Jer. 1.5:

- Gal. 1.15-16 — '. . . the one who set me apart *(aphorisas)* from my mother's womb and called me *(ek koilias mētros mou kai kalesas)* through

---

(London: Clark, 2003) 153-64, though he misses the nuances in Paul's talk of 'Judaism': 'Paul does not conceive himself as simply having exchanged an inferior brand of Judaism for a superior one'; 'it was Judaism *per se* that Paul left behind' (162-63). Rather we need to recognize that 'Judaism', as the term was beginning to emerge, denoted a specific understanding of what we today describe as the much broader phenomenon of 'Second Temple Judaism', an understanding forged by the Maccabean resistance to political and religious Hellenization (see *Jesus Remembered* §§9.1 and 2a); in Paul's case 'Judaism' denoted what we would more accurately describe as 'Pharisaic Judaism' (see further §29.2a below).

153. Hagner criticizes my description of Paul's conversion to 'the necessity of taking the gospel of Christ to the Gentiles': 'it does not do justice to the personal significance of what happened to Paul himself' ('Paul as a Jewish Believer' 102 n. 32). My formulation, however, simply reflects Paul's own recollection of his conversion (Gal. 1.13-16) and in no way detracts from the personal transformation involved for Paul, any more than Gal. 1.13-16 does.

his grace . . . in order that I might preach him among the Gentiles *(en tois ethnesin)* . . .'.

- Jer. 1.5 LXX — Jeremiah expresses his sense of call: 'Before I formed you in the womb *(en koilia)* I knew you, and before you were born I consecrated you; I appointed you a prophet to the nations *(prophētēn eis ethnē)*'.
- Isa. 49.1-6 LXX — The Servant of Yahweh = Israel (49.3) speaks: 'From my mother's womb he called *(ek koilias mētros mou ekalesen)* my name. . . . Behold, I have set you for a covenant of the people, to be for a light of the nations/Gentiles *(eis phōs ethnōn),* for salvation to the end of the earth *(eis sōtērian heōs eschatou tēs gēs)*'.[154]
- There is probably an echo of Isa. 49.6 also in the climax of the third account of Saul's conversion (Acts 26.23), and Luke has Paul and Barnabas explicitly quoting the same passage in Acts 13.47.
- Other allusions in Paul's letters seem to confirm the suggestion that Paul did not hesitate to see his work in terms of the role attributed to the Servant of Second Isaiah.[155]

There can be little doubt, therefore, that Paul saw his conversion as a prophetic commissioning, like that of Jeremiah in Jer. 1.5,[156] and more specifically in terms used for the Servant of Second Isaiah. This continuity between his own vocation and that of Israel (the Servant of Yahweh) was evidently an important part of Paul's self-understanding. What happened on the Damascus road *was* a conversion, a conversion from Saul's previous understanding of how God's will and purpose for Israel was to be carried forward. But Paul saw it as a conversion *to* a better, indeed to the correct, understanding of that will and purpose for Israel. Apostle to the Gentiles, yes, but not thereby an *apostate from* Israel; rather an *apostle of* Israel, commissioned to carry forward Israel's destiny as 'a light to the nations'.[157]

---

154. It will be recalled that the *heōs eschatou tēs gēs* is picked up in Acts 1.8.

155. Rom. 10.16 (= Isa. 53.1); Rom. 15.20-21 (= Isa. 52.15); 2 Cor. 6.1-2 (= Isa. 49.8); Phil. 2.16 (cf. Isa. 49.4). See also T. Holtz, 'Zum Selbstverständnis des Apostels Paulus', *TLZ* 91 (1966) 331-40.

156. See further K. O. Sandnes, *Paul — One of the Prophets?* (WUNT 2.43; Tübingen: Mohr Siebeck, 1991) ch. 5 (but he fails to bring out the 'to the nations' dimension integral to the call); Dunn, *Galatians* 63-64. The *aphorisas* ('set me apart') of Gal. 1.15 may also be a deliberate play on the word which gave the Pharisees their nickname (= 'separated ones') (see again *Jesus Remembered* 268 n. 57): Paul's 'separatism' as a Pharisee in service of the law was replaced by his 'separation' to be an apostle in service of the gospel.

157. See further my 'Paul: Apostate or Apostle of Israel?', *ZNW* 89 (1998) 256-71. The question of how soon this realization came home to Paul is always worth considering (as by Wedderburn, *History* 85), even though it can never finally be resolved. See also A. du Toit, 'Encountering Grace: Towards Understanding the Essence of Paul's Conversion Experience', *Focusing on Paul* 57-75.

(4) Not least of importance is the degree to which this insight into Paul's understanding of his conversion correlates with and helps confirm the hypothesis put forward in §25.2: that Saul's persecuting zeal was the determination to prevent Israel's set-apartness to God being compromised by Hellenist critique of the Temple and/or willingness to lower the barriers of Israel's holiness in regard to Gentiles. It was the shocking realization that he was wholly mistaken in what had been his central motivation (in regard to the followers of Jesus' way) which poleaxed Saul on the Damascus road. The light of heaven exposed a major flaw in his self-understanding, namely, that he was heading in the completely wrong direction (so far as God's will for Israel was concerned). So the description of what happened to Saul as a 'conversion' is entirely appropriate, for Saul did indeed 'convert' (that is, 'turn round') 180 degrees, becoming an advocate of what he had been persecuting (Gal. 1.23): from persecuting those who threatened Israel's boundaries, to a mission which required him to cross them himself; from an attitude essentially dismissive of Gentiles (as subsequently expressed in Eph. 2.12)[158] to a commitment to bring them the good news of Jesus Messiah.

In all this, of course, I am attempting to penetrate some way into Saul's experience of what can indubitably be spoken of as a 'conversion'. How the various factors played and interacted in the event itself — the light, the experience of personal encounter, the sense of commission — and how much is to be attributed to subsequent instruction, later reflection and autobiographical reconstruction is now impossible to determine. As might be expected in regard to such a classic 'conversion', there has been endless speculation on the psychological dynamics involved, though most of it so lacking in firm roots as to be a frustrating and largely fruitless exercise.[159] The point surely to be held on to here is that Paul's conversion transformed him from a zealous and apparently ruthless persecutor of the first Christians into an advocate for the cause he had persecuted, soon to be the most effective missionary in the expansion of the new movement beyond the bounds of Second Temple Judaism. Whatever we may deduce as to Paul's psychological profile, his subsequent career suggests an essentially positive assessment of the conversion experience and its outcome.[160]

---

158. Gentiles as outsiders, 'strangers to the covenants of promise, having no hope and without God in the world' (Eph. 2.12).

159. See, e.g., W. James, *The Varieties of Religious Experience* (1902; London: Collins, Fontana, 1960) 35, 251; Klausner, *From Jesus to Paul* 326-30; C. G. Jung, *Contributions to Analytical Psychology* (ET 1945) 257, cited by C. S. C. Williams, *Acts* (BNTC; London: Black, 1957) 123; W. Sargant, *Battle for the Mind* (London: Pan, 1959) 106; J. G. Gager, 'Some Notes on Paul's Conversion', *NTS* 27 (1981) 697-704; Taylor, *Paul* 69-74. More generally, see Gaventa, *From Darkness to Light*.

160. I am puzzled at the outright hostility to the attribution of any significance to 'reli-

But there is still more to be said about the significance of Saul's conversion experience for his gospel and his subsequent theology.

25.4. The Origin of Paul's Gospel

Seyoon Kim is to be credited with bringing Paul's conversion back into focus as a, if not the, major creative influence on Paul's gospel.[161] It is not difficult to mount a persuasive argument on the subject, on two aspects in particular.[162]

(1) One aspect concerns *Paul's christology,* his understanding of who Jesus was. It is obvious that what Saul/Paul appreciated to be an encounter with Jesus — an understanding given either in the encounter on the road itself or immediately thereafter (as explained by Ananias?) — was bound to transform his understanding of Jesus. Moreover, we may confidently assume that his knowledge of what the first disciples believed about Jesus shaped his conceptualization of who it was who had so encountered him, and from the first. This was the shocking realization which formed the heart of his 'conversion': that what those whom he had been pursuing claimed about Jesus was actually true! They must be right after all!

- That Jesus had been raised from the dead/taken up to heaven would be self-evident in 'a revelation of Jesus Christ' from heaven (Gal. 1.12), understood very quickly as another (final) appearance of the risen Christ (1 Cor. 15.8).
- That he must (therefore) be God's Messiah: according to Acts 9.22 Saul sought to demonstrate his new conviction, that Jesus is the Christ, with the fervour of a new convert;[163] the emphasis on 'Christ crucified', which was to be a feature of Paul's preaching (1 Cor. 1.23; 2.2; Gal. 3.1), probably contains an echo of the opposition he must previously have had to that very message (cf. 1 Cor. 1.23; Gal. 3.13);[164] and his previous 'knowledge of

---

gious experience' for our appreciation of Christianity's beginnings (Cameron, *Redescribing* 16), when the importance of Paul's conversion experience is so obvious.

161. Kim, *Origin of Paul's Gospel,* also *Paul and the New Perspective* chs. 1 and 5, in which Kim responds to my critique of the former volume — '"A Light to the Gentiles": The Significance of the Damascus Road Christophany for Paul', in L. D. Hurst and N. T. Wright, eds., *The Glory of Christ in the New Testament: Studies in Christology,* G. B. Caird FS (Oxford: Clarendon, 1987) 251-66 (here 256-63); I reply in *The New Perspective on Paul,* particularly (2005) 33-37, 81 n. 349, (2008) 36-41, 90 n. 377. See further below, §§27.2-5.

162. Schnelle largely agrees with Kim on the first, but not the second (*Paul* ch. 4). See also R. N. Longenecker, ed., *The Road from Damascus* (Grand Rapids: Eerdmans, 1997).

163. Hengel and Schwemer wonder whether Saul received the first of his five synagogue beatings (2 Cor. 11.24) in Damascus (*Paul* 93).

164. See further my 'Paul's Conversion' 80-82/344-47.

Christ in fleshly terms' (2 Cor. 5.16) probably included a very negative evaluation of 'the Christ' claim made of Jesus.[165]

• That he was (after all) God's Son: the report in Acts that the converted Saul began immediately proclaiming Jesus as 'the Son of God' (Acts 9.20)[166] correlates quite neatly with Paul's own recollection of his conversion as 'God revealing his Son in me' (Gal. 1.16).

• That he had been installed as Lord: Paul's most characteristic mode of referring to Jesus as 'Lord' presumably was rooted in the same experience; he may already have been aware of the significance of Ps. 110.1 for the first Christians and would hardly need persuading of its significance in the light of his own encounter.[167]

• In a logic not clear to us, this christology carried with it the implication that it was good news for Gentiles as well as Jews: Christ had been cursed on the cross 'in order that the blessing of Abraham might come to the Gentiles' (Gal. 3.13-14); Jesus was revealed as God's Son 'in order that (Paul) might preach him among the nations' (Gal. 1.16); Jesus as Lord meant 'Lord of all, generous to all who call upon him' (Rom. 10.12).

How much more can be said on this aspect depends largely on how we evaluate 2 Cor. 4.6: does it allude to Paul's conversion experience, and if so, does it imply that Paul saw Jesus as a figure of divine glory? The resolution of such questions depends in turn on whether 2 Cor. 4.6 reflects an experience similar to that sought or enjoyed by Jewish mystics. There is sufficient indication that a form of merkabah (chariot) mysticism was already practised at this time; that is, Jewish mystics already endeavoured to re-experience the vision which is reported in the first chapter of Ezekiel, to be given to see the divine chariot. Other prophetic visions, particularly Isaiah's vision of 'the Lord sitting on a throne' (Isa. 6.1-6), provided focus for and stimulus to the meditation through which it was hoped that such an experience might be given again.[168] So for anyone who valued mystical experience or dabbled in it himself,[169] to see a figure bathed in heavenly radiance might well have provoked the conclusion that the exalted Je-

---

165. Murphy-O'Connor comments appropriately on 2 Cor. 5.16: 'At one time, manifestly prior to his conversion, he thought about Jesus in a way of which he was later ashamed' (*Paul* 73). See also n. 96 above.

166. Paul's own earliest reference to his preaching likewise speaks of God's Son (1 Thess. 1.9-10).

167. His reference to 'the Lord's brother' in Gal. 1.19 may reflect the language Paul used at the time, two or three years after his conversion, suggesting that Paul quickly slipped into the habit of referring to 'the Lord'.

168. See further, e.g., my *Partings* §11.6b.

169. See below at n. 238.

sus stood *with* God rather than *before* God.[170] To pursue all that is involved here is part of the agenda for a later chapter.[171] Here the question is, How soon did such trains of thought begin to run? or How quickly did they reach such conclusions? Kim presses for an answer, very early, and more or less from the first ('the first half of the 30s').[172] The one problem with that is that 2 Cor. 4.6 is fairly isolated within the Pauline corpus, and confirmation (such as that mentioned above in respect of 'Messiah', 'Son of God' and 'Lord') is lacking. Presumably Paul's reflection on his Damascus road experience was not completed in a few days or weeks, and its significance became deeper over time, particularly as further illumined by subsequent visions (2 Cor. 12.1, 7)[173] and experience of being 'in Christ'. In short, there is insufficient evidence to allow us to decide whether 2 Cor. 4.6 reflects Paul's early or his more mature recollection/evaluation of his Damascus road encounter.

(2) As to other aspects of Paul's gospel, we are little better off. That *Christ died for our sins* was presumably passed on to him more or less at once (1 Cor. 15.3). Whether or not this formula expressed a Hellenist elaboration of an earlier suffering-vindication understanding of Jesus' death,[174] Paul certainly inherited an understanding of Jesus' death as a sacrifice for sins, and on the analogy of the Day of Atonement sacrifices.[175] And the degree to which he treated lightly the Jerusalem Temple strongly suggests that he quickly inferred that it had been rendered less than relevant for his gospel. But again we have to ask, How quickly? Luke records Saul as praying in the Temple after his return to Jerusalem (Acts 22.17), displaying an attitude more like that of Peter and John in Acts 3.1 than that reported of Stephen in Acts 7.48. The issue here becomes entangled with that of Luke's own attitude to the Temple and with the veracity of his report of Saul's return to Jerusalem. So the issue becomes quickly clouded and difficult to resolve.

We can be more confident with regard to Paul's understanding of *the gift of the Spirit* as central to becoming a Christian and indeed constitutive of being a Christian. And this, despite the facts that Luke makes very little of Paul's own reception of the Spirit at his conversion (Acts 9.17) and that Paul himself does not refer to it explicitly in his own allusions back to his conversion. But the constitu-

---

170. Cf. Hengel and Schwemer, *Paul* 39-40 (though note also 105); and particularly Segal, *Paul the Convert* 8-11, 22, ch. 2 ('Paul's Ecstasy'). Cf. also Chilton, *Rabbi Paul* 48-56.

171. See below, §29.7.

172. *Origin of Paul's Gospel* 5-11, 128-36, 223-33: 'At the Damascus revelation Paul realized that Christ . . . is the true Wisdom' (128); 'Paul saw the exalted Christ in glory as the *eikōn tou theou* on the road to Damascus' (193); and further *Paul and the New Perspective* ch. 5.

173. On 2 Cor. 12.1, 7 see below, §25.5f.

174. See above, §24.9c.

175. Rom. 3.25; 4.24-25; 8.3; 2 Cor. 5.21. For the theology of atoning sacrifice in these verses see my *Theology of Paul* §§9.2-3.

tive role of the Spirit in the conversion of those won to the faith by Paul (as in Gal. 3.2, 5) and in their ongoing life as believers is so obvious in Paul[176] that we can hardly doubt that it was so also in Paul's own experience.[177] The argument is the same as in the case of baptism and being 'in Christ'.[178]

What of the theologoumenon regarded by so many as giving the essence of Paul's gospel — *justification by/through faith?* Kim again presses for an 'as early as possible' answer.[179] Here too we can be confident that in terms of the response called for, Saul/Paul's preaching of the gospel to non-Jews, from whenever that was, always placed the primary — indeed, the sole — emphasis on the need to respond with faith. There is no suggestion anywhere that he started with a different emphasis and only subsequently came to appreciate that the gospel could be received simply by believing in the Lord Jesus Christ proclaimed therein. The question is rather whether Paul *developed* that basic insight through his own missionary experience and/or in the light of confrontation with other missionaries. This in fact is what I believe to be the case, though I will have to wait till §27 to demonstrate it.

Bound up with the same issue is the question whether Paul saw his encounter with the risen Christ as requiring a complete break with *the Torah/the Jewish law*. The present-day Tübingen school has tended to assume that the Hellenists' critique amounted to a repudiation of the law in general,[180] with the corollary that Paul's conversion to what he had opposed was a conversion also to their repudiation of the law. Peter Stuhlmacher in particular has argued that Rom. 10.4 ('Christ is the end of the law') was a conclusion which Paul derived directly from his Damascus road encounter.[181] Here again, in my view, the matter is more com-

176. E.g., Gal. 3.2; 1 Cor. 12.13; Rom. 8.9; Phil. 3.3; see further my *Theology of Paul* ch. 16, and below, §29.7g.

177. See particularly G. D. Fee, 'Paul's Conversion as Key to His Understanding of the Spirit', in Longenecker, ed., *The Road from Damascus* 166-83; F. Philip, *The Origins of Pauline Pneumatology* (WUNT 2.194; Tübingen: Mohr Siebeck, 2005) ch. 6.

178. See again my *Theology of Paul* chs. 15 and 17; Schnelle, *Paul* 97-100.

179. Kim, *Origin of Paul's Gospel* 269-74: 'Paul perceived the revelation of the Son of God on the Damascus road as the revelation of God's righteousness apart from the law (Rom. 3.21) immediately' (271); 'One thing is beyond doubt: namely that at the Damascus revelation Paul came to understand that "no man is justified by (works of) the law" and so to see the fundamental problem of the law itself' (283). Hengel and Schwemer are rightly more cautious (*Paul* 101).

180. See above, §24.4c.

181. P. Stuhlmacher, '"The End of the Law": On the Origin and Beginnings of Pauline Theology', *Reconciliation, Law, and Righteousness: Essays in Biblical Theology* (1981; ET Philadelphia: Fortress, 1986) 134-54; *Biblische Theologie* 1.248 and ch. 20: 'before Paul ever taught the justification of the ungodly (cf. Rom 4:5; 5:6), he had experienced it outside Damascus in his own person!' (1.247); see also Kim, *Origin of Paul's Gospel* 3-4 and *passim;*

plex and there was more of a process involved. I have already indicated my conclusion that the Hellenists' critique was more directed against the Temple than against the law.[182] And we shall see later that Paul's developed critique of the law was not quite so black-and-white as many have assumed.[183]

My own suggestion is that the 'zeal' which drove Saul the persecutor gives the most helpful clue: that what he sought to punish were breaches of the law which opened the door of acceptance in a Jewish messianic sect to Gentiles in an undiscriminating way, that what he as a 'separated' Pharisee sought to defend was Israel's 'separateness' (from other nations and to God). In other words, it was the law in its Israel-defining role, its boundary-marking role, which he had attempted to enforce but which he found he could no longer defend when he encountered Christ. Does that mean that Hellenist evangelists had already been admitting Gentiles without requiring them to become proselytes (to be circumcised)? Or did Saul simply perceive that this was the way the Hellenists were inevitably headed? There is nothing in our sources to provide an answer to these questions. All we can say with confidence is that whenever Saul/Paul began to preach the gospel to Gentiles, he did so without requiring them to be circumcised. As previously a Pharisee who would certainly have insisted on the necessity of circumcision from would-be converts, something must have made him conclude otherwise — that is, to adopt a practice either already operating among the Hellenist evangelists or implicit in the gospel revealed to him (Gal. 1.11-12, 16). On this issue too we can hope for greater illumination from the next phase of Saul/Paul's career (§27).[184]

Not a lot of lasting significance hangs on decisions made here. It is clear enough that Saul's experience on the Damascus road triggered a massive and radical transformation in Saul's self-understanding, his understanding of what God required of him, his understanding of his ancestral faith and his understanding of the goals he now had to pursue. The language of Phil. 3.7-9 is no doubt exaggerated, but it certainly attests such a transformation. Whether Saul drew all the conclusions which are expressed in his subsequent writings immediately or soon, or subsequently, over a period of time, matters little for our appreciation of his mature theology. And most of the period before these writings is lost in the mists of time, so that speculation has to stand in for sound exegesis. In which case we have to be content with noting the various pros and cons in each case, and move on.

C. Dietzfelbinger, *Die Berufung des Paulus als Ursprung seiner Theologie* (WMANT 58; Neukirchen-Vluyn: Neukirchener, 1985) 105-106, 118, 125, 145; D. Marguerat, 'Paul et la loi. Le retournement (Philippiens 3,2–4,1)', in A. Dettweiler et al., eds., *Paul, une théologie en construction* (Geneva: Labor et Fides, 2004) 251-75 (here 267-68).

182. See above, §§24.4d and 24.5b.

183. See below, §§31.7 and 33.3.

184. See also Kraus, *Zwischen Jerusalem und Antiochia* 82-105.

25.5. The Immediate Aftermath and Tunnel Period

The immediate aftermath of Saul's conversion is shrouded in confusion, and the period between then and his emergence as a missionary of the church in Antioch (Acts 13.1-3) is like a long Alpine railway tunnel where the train can be glimpsed only occasionally at one or other of the few gaps in the tunnel.

a. Luke versus Paul

To inquire into the sequel to Saul's conversion is to find ourselves caught in one of the major conflicts between the narrative of Acts and Paul's own account. In Acts Luke seems to suggest that the converted Saul left Damascus after a short time there and went directly to Jerusalem, where he was received by 'the apostles' (Acts 9.23-27). The juncture is even tighter in Acts 22, where Paul in his self-testimony, having recounted Ananias's call to him to be baptized, continues, 'After I had returned to Jerusalem . . .' (22.16-17). In contrast, Paul's testimony is sharply different — Gal. 1.16-20:

> [16]. . . in order that I might preach him among the Gentiles, I did not consult immediately with flesh and blood, [17]nor did I go up to Jerusalem to those who were apostles before me, but I went away into Arabia and returned again to Damascus. [18]Then, after three years, I did go up to Jerusalem to get to know Cephas, and I stayed with him fifteen days. [19]Others of the apostles I did not see, but only James the Lord's brother. [20]What I write to you, please note, before God, I am not lying.

The overlap in the two accounts is almost as striking as the contrast. Paul is clearly protesting against a different version of the sequel to his conversion. Why does he deny that he consulted with flesh and blood? The obvious inference is that he was responding to a claim that he *had* done so; the parallel with 1.1 similarly implies that Paul found it necessary to contest (in his opening words!) a claim that his commission came from fellow humans and through human hands (rather than directly from God and through Jesus Christ). And why does he deny that he went up to Jerusalem to those who were apostles before him? The implication is the same: Paul was denying what others said about him, that he had derived his commission and his gospel from the Jerusalem apostles.[185] The point is

---

185. The focus of Paul's defence suggests that 'the apostles' here in view were not the apostles (= missionaries) referred to in 1 Cor. 15.7, but those regarded by others as 'the apostles' (the Jerusalem leadership). This is the one time that Paul's usage comes close to that of Luke, which suggests both that Luke's usage was closer to that of Paul's critics and that Paul speaks concessively here.

that this is precisely what Luke seems to say: that soon after his conversion Paul went up to Jerusalem and consulted with the apostles. So Paul seems to be going out of his way to deny Luke's account!

Paul evidently found it necessary to continue laying out his version. It was only after three years[186] that he went up to Jerusalem, for the first time following his conversion. Even then he stayed only with Cephas (Peter) and otherwise saw only James. The assertion was so important to Paul, and so important to refute the alternative being circulated by others, that he takes a solemn oath on the point there and then: 'what [plural] I write to you, look, before God I am not lying' (1.20).[187]

What are we to make of this? There seems to be no way to avoid the conflict between the two accounts. Luke evidently saw the episode as a means of knitting the converted Saul into the Jerusalem leadership (Acts 9.27), and therefore of sustaining his theme of the centrality of Jerusalem for the beginnings of Christianity. And his account (9.19-25) does leave room for some period of time to have passed before Saul's inelegant exit from Damascus (by basket!).[188] But Luke hardly allows the impression that three years were to elapse (spent in Arabia) before Paul's departure for Jerusalem, and the Acts 22 account gives no hint of such a gap. Perhaps we have to recognize that Acts is not simply or solely a defence of Paul, or, at least, not a defence of Paul in Paul's own terms. Luke evidently did not see himself simply as a spokesman for Paul but was familiar with other views of Paul, including the views of those who opposed Paul's mission and who had misgivings about his gospel.[189] If Luke was fully aware of Paul's

186. 'After three years *(meta etē tria)*' is expressed in the normal Greek idiom (BDAG 637-38). It could denote an interval of fully three years; but since the year from which the counting began would be reckoned as the first year, the period could be anything from not much over two years. See further §28.1b below.

187. 'I am not lying' has the force of a formula of affirmation (Job 6.28; 27.11; Ps. 89.35; 4 Macc. 5.34; Plutarch, *Mor.* 1059A; BDAG 1097; H. Conzelmann, *TDNT* 9.601). Paul uses the formula elsewhere (Rom. 9.1; 2 Cor. 11.31; also 1 Tim. 2.7). For the seriousness of lying within the Jewish tradition see *TDNT* 9.598-600. The addition of 'before God' gives the affirmation the force of a sacred oath, indicating that Paul was willing to stake his whole standing before God on the veracity of what he had just written; see further J. P. Sampley, '"Before God, I Do Not Lie" (Gal. 1.20): Paul's Self-Defence in the Light of Roman Legal Praxis', *NTS* 23 (1977) 477-82.

188. 9.19 — 'after some *(tinas)* days' is vague and imprecise; 9.22 — Saul engaged with 'the Jews who lived in Damascus' for some time; 9.23 — 'after many *(hikanai)* days'. Hengel and Schwemer read these differentiated time notes as positive indicators of Luke's responsible historiography: they 'mark Luke out as a historian and distinguish him from the producers of apostolic romances' (*Paul* 402 n. 701).

189. See further above, §21 n. 127; cf. Betz, *Galatians* 79. Otherwise, Barrett indicates what can be said positively about the traditions drawn on by Luke (*Acts* 1.460-62).

version, he may even have thought there was too much special pleading and *parti pris* in Paul's account of his relationship with Jerusalem. What we may well have, then, is Luke trying to construct an account which was aware of both views, but without excluding either.[190]

b. 'I Went Away into Arabia' (Gal. 1.17)

Both where Saul went and the reason why are unclear and the subject of some dispute.[191] 'Arabia' could refer to anywhere west of Mesopotamia, east and south of Syria and Palestine, including the Isthmus of Suez (cf. 4.25 — the Sinai Peninsula). But the proximity to Damascus (implied by the following clause — 'and returned again to Damascus') points most naturally to the kingdom of Nabatea, immediately to the south of Damascus. And this fits best with our other evidence, including the reference in 2 Cor. 11.32 to King Aretas, who would be the Nabatean king Aretas IV.[192]

More difficult to resolve is the question why Saul went there. It should not be assumed that 'Arabia' meant for Paul desert or semi-desert country. To be sure, some parallel with the tradition of Jesus' forty days in the wilderness is inviting. It would accord with the much more widely attested practice in the history of religions of a period of withdrawal into an uninhabited region following a revelatory or visionary experience, in preparation for some prophet-like or shamanistic role. And the psychological need for such a 'retreat' and reconstruction of his thought world can readily be imagined.[193] It would also fit Paul's emphasis throughout this passage: 'I did not consult with flesh and blood but went away to Arabia'.[194] The only problem is that Arabia/Nabatea at that time was a prosperous region which included a number of towns and was in close proximity to other Decapolis cities (Gerasa, Philadelphia). So it is certainly possible to deduce that Saul went to Arabia 'in order to preach Christ

190. This suggestion could count as a modified version of Baur's famous attempt to portray Luke's narrative as a synthesis of the opposing Petrine and Pauline parties in early Christianity (see above, §20.3a) — that is, an acknowledgment that Baur had recognized an important feature of Luke's presentation.

191. In this section I draw heavily on my *Galatians* 69-71.

192. BDAG 127-28; Murphy-O'Connor, *Paul* 81 (on Aretas, 83-84); Hengel and Schwemer, *Paul* 386-87 n. 571. The precise limits of Nabatean rule during this period are unclear (see below, §28 at n. 19).

193. 'We cannot sufficiently realize how hard and desperate was this destruction of his ideals, this breakdown of his whole scheme of existence' (Weiss, *Earliest Christianity* 194). See especially E. de W. Burton, *Galatians* (ICC; Edinburgh: Clark, 1921) 55-57; Taylor, *Paul* 67-74; Wedderburn, *History* 86-87.

194. Lightfoot, *Galatians* 90.

among the Gentiles'.[195] This too would have served Paul's purpose in the statement of self-defence *(narratio)* which is Gal. 1.12–2.14 (Betz): the implication
being that the gospel preached by him was thus firmly established from the first
(cf. Acts 9.20).[196]

Paul, however, has left the point unclear, and further clarity is not possible.[197] It is idle, for example, to speculate whether his silence on the success (or
otherwise) of what would have been his earliest mission indicates a relative failure on his part, occasioning some re-evaluation of his mission and gospel.[198] The
only point Paul chose to make is that his time in Arabia further underlined his independence from the Jerusalem leadership; in Arabia there was no one whom he
could have consulted.[199] And with that we must be content.

Following an unspecified period in Arabia, Saul 'returned again to Damascus'. Paul has given no indication of the intervals of time at this point, since that
information was irrelevant to his main concern (his relationship with the Jerusalem apostles). The talk of 'return' to Damascus clearly implies that the initial period following his conversion was spent in that city, though if the 'immediately'
of v. 16 does carry forward into v. 17, Saul cannot have remained in Damascus
for any length of time before going off to Arabia. But presumably he was there
long enough to be baptized and received into the gathering of disciples (Acts
22.16) in Damascus; a later baptism would hardly accord with the clear implication of Rom. 6.3-4 that Paul thought of himself ('we') as inaugurated into life in
Christ through baptism.[200] More important, for Paul certainly, was his reception

195. So Bornkamm, *Paul* 27; Betz, *Galatians* 73-74; Bruce, *Paul* 81-82; also *Galatians*
(NIGTC; Grand Rapids: Eerdmans, 1982) 96; Meeks, *Urban Christians* 10; Murphy-
O'Connor, *Paul* 81-82; Lohse, *Paulus* 73; Hengel and Schwemer, *Paul* 107-13; E. A. Knauf,
'Die Arabienreise des Apostels Paulus', in the German edition of Hengel and Schwemer 469-
71; and further Hengel, 'Paulus in Arabien', *Paulus und Jakobus* (Tübingen: Mohr Siebeck,
2002) 193-212 = 'Paul in Arabia', *BBR* 12 (2002) 47-66; Schnabel, *Mission* 1035-45. Since
Paul never alludes to churches in Arabia, the probable corollary is that Paul's earliest missionary work was completely unsuccessful (despite Gal. 2.7-9).

196. For Hengel and Schwemer, the further reference to 'Arabia' in Gal. 4.25 suggests
that Paul gained the fundamental insights regarding the promise to Abraham and its outworking, which he expounds in Galatians 3 and Romans 4, already in Arabia, the territory of Abraham's other son, Ishmael (*Paul* 113-20).

197. Riesner cites Harnack: 'What drove him to Arabia, and what he did there, simply is
beyond the scope of our knowledge' (*Paul's Early Period* 260).

198. See above, nn. 145 and 146.

199. 'The meaning is: he was in Arabia and consequently not in Jerusalem' (Linton,
'Third Aspect' 84). Cf. D. J. Verseput, 'Paul's Gentile Mission and the Jewish Christian Community: A Study of the Narrative in Galatians 1 and 2', *NTS* 39 (1993) 36-58 (here 38-43).

200. Otherwise Taylor, who presses the 'immediately' too hard in arguing that it was
only on his return to Damascus that Saul first made contact with the church of Damascus and

of the Holy Spirit (Acts 9.17); for Paul it was this (a conscious experience of being filled with power from on high) above all which constituted him 'of Christ' (Rom. 8.9). All this correlates sufficiently closely with Acts 9.8-19 for us to be able to discern the basic sequence of events.

Nor do we know how long Saul spent in Arabia before his return to Damascus. It could have been quite a short period; the aorist tense ('I returned') probably excludes any implication of repeated visits to Arabia, using Damascus as a base. To put the same point from the other angle, we do not know how much of the two to three years between his conversion-commissioning and his first visit to Jerusalem (1.18) was spent in Damascus itself. At all events, this opening two-three year period came to an end with Saul's ignominious escape from Damascus. The hasty exit, Paul recalls, was necessitated, since King Aretas was trying to 'seize *(piasai)*' him (2 Cor. 11.32-33), possibly for unrest which he had provoked during his sojourn in Arabia.[201] Luke attributes the flight to opposition from Damascus's Jewish community (Acts 9.23-25); it would not have fitted with Luke's portrayal to suggest that Paul was a political troublemaker.[202] The two accounts could be complementary (the king responding to unrest within or complaints from the important Jewish community).[203] But Luke may be cloaking more serious opposition to Saul (the reasons we do not know), or he may have chosen to focus only on the opposition from within the Jewish community of Damascus. However, Paul says nothing of this in Galatians, since, once again, it was not relevant to the primary purpose of defending his gospel.

c. 'After Three Years I Did Go Up to Jerusalem, to Get to Know Cephas' (Gal. 1.18)

In this section of his brief personal statement Paul is obviously focusing on his relationship with Jerusalem and the Jerusalem apostles; all other details fall out of view. Whatever the precise length of time signified by the 'after three

---

was baptized (*Paul* 66-67, 71). 'Historically, Paul's baptism can hardly have taken place anywhere but in Damascus' (Hengel and Schwemer, *Paul* 43).

201. Full discussion in Hengel and Schwemer, *Paul* 128-32; Thrall, *2 Corinthians* 763-66.

202. 'The ethnarch's intervention would make sense if he had had a hint from his royal lord that he should seize the agitator who had caused offence in his missionary activity in the Nabatean kingdom' (Hengel and Schwemer, *Paul* 128-29).

203. Murphy-O'Connor's judgment that 'Luke's second-hand version . . . is a tissue of implausibilities' (*Paul* 6) is unduly harsh. Nor is it so clear that a surreptitious escape from Damascus indicated only danger from within the city and not from without; Murphy-O'Connor regards the latter suggestion as 'sheer nonsense' (6).

years',[204] the point is clear: his trip to Jerusalem in ca. 35 CE was his first visit to Jerusalem and his first encounter with any of the Jerusalem leadership following his 'revelation of Jesus Christ'; the elapse of time between the two events was long enough to make it obvious to everyone that Paul's understanding of his revelation was already firm prior to his Jerusalem visit and that the Jerusalem apostles made no contribution whatsoever to that understanding. Once again, Paul writes with the clear objective of refuting views which had evidently been put about, to the effect that Paul's gospel was dependent on and derived from the Jerusalem leadership, with the implication that the policy line advocated by the Jerusalem leadership on any points of dispute was to be followed, rather than Paul's.

Interestingly, Paul does not deny contact with the Jerusalem leadership outright. The view which he was opposing was based on knowledge of at least some contact between Paul and the Jerusalem leadership. This is the view, as already suggested, on which Luke probably drew in drafting his own version of events (Acts 9.26-27). For his part, Paul freely acknowledges his first visit to Jerusalem and his having spent two weeks with the leading apostle, Cephas/Peter. Beyond that he acknowledges 'seeing' only James, 'the Lord's brother',[205] nobody else. The lines of the defence are clear: an acknowledgment of the importance of 'those who were apostles before him', of Peter's pre-eminence and of an extensive communication with him, of a brief(?) encounter with James, but otherwise of no contact with anyone else who might be reckoned as of apostolic authority or to have contributed authoritatively to his gospel.[206] What other infer-

---

204. See again §28.1b below.

205. How to translate Gal. 1.19? The *ei mē* introduces an exception — 'except, but only'. But does the exception refer to the whole clause: 'I did not see any of the other apostles (other than Cephas); the only one I did see was James' — that is, James is *not* to be counted as one of the apostles? Or does the exception relate only to 'other of the apostles': 'I did not see other of the apostles, except James'; that is, James was the only other apostle Paul did see? Despite Lightfoot (*Galatians* 84-85; followed by Bruce, *Galatians* 101), the issue is not settled on syntactical grounds, since the 'other' can be fully explained by reference back to Cephas, and the same construction in 1.7 indicates that the relation of the clauses thus linked need not be precise. James falls outside the circle of the apostolic twelve in Luke's own account (Acts 1.26), and Paul may have hesitated to acknowledge that one who remained so rooted in Jerusalem was in fact an apostle = missionary. The point, however, is that Paul did not make James's status clear and may have chosen to be deliberately ambiguous — a notable feature, given Paul's own insistence that he himself was an apostle (Gal. 1.1). See further my *Galatians* 77.

206. It seems impossible to square Acts 9.26-29 with Gal. 1.18-20; the limited exposure which Paul seems to have allowed himself in Jerusalem on that visit (Gal. 1.18-20) is hard to square with Luke's depiction of him as 'going in and out', 'speaking boldly in the name of the Lord Jesus', and arguing with the Hellenists (the Greek-speakers who refused to believe Jesus was Messiah) (Acts 9.28-29). But we should recall that accounts of the same complex sequence

ences we may draw regarding Saul's time in Jerusalem are more intriguing than clear: did he meet only the group of believers who worshipped with Peter (his house church)? Were there larger communal gatherings which Saul or other apostles avoided?[207] Much as we would like Gal. 1.18-19 to shed light on the functioning of the earliest Jerusalem congregation(s), the laser-like narrowness of Paul's focus at this point prevents us from gaining a larger picture.

The most important issue here is what Paul means when he speaks of the purpose of his visit as 'to get to know *(historēsai)*' Cephas/Peter. The verb, *historeō*, appears only here in the NT, and its precise weight is yet one more matter of dispute.[208] The basic meaning is 'to inquire into, or about, or from'.[209] And though the sense can be eroded towards that of a traveller's mere 'sightseeing',[210] the element of 'inquiry' in the 'visit' is usually hard to exclude (e.g., Josephus, *Ant.* 1.203). And when the object is personal, it is equally hard to exclude the idea of a getting to know which includes getting to know *about,* a knowledge which enables an informed opinion or judgment about the person and his significance (Josephus, *War* 6.81; *Ant.* 8.46).[211] Added to this is the information that Saul 'stayed *(epemeina)* with him for fifteen days', a period far exceeding the normal two to three days of traditional hospitality offered to a visitor.[212]

From Paul's careful choice of language we can draw several deductions. (1) Despite Saul's conviction that he had been directly commissioned to preach the gospel which he had formerly tried to extirpate, he nevertheless saw the importance of making contact with Cephas, the most prominent disciple of Jesus' own mission.

---

of events can differ drastically according to the different perspectives of the different witnesses; Hengel and Schwemer draw as much as can be drawn from Luke's account (*Paul* 134-42). And Rom. 15.19 may indicate that Paul did preach in Jerusalem at the beginning of his mission, though Paul could have had in mind his defence of his gospel at the later Jerusalem conference (*Romans* 863). See further my *Galatians* 75.

207. For possible reasons for non-contact with the other apostles, see my *Galatians* 75.

208. Cf., e.g., the different translations: 'visit' (RSV, NRSV, JB), 'meet' (NJB), 'get to know' (NEB/REB), 'get acquainted with' (NIV), 'obtain information from' (GNB).

209. LSJ, *historeō;* so, e.g., Herodotus, *Hist.* 2.19; 3.77; Polybius 3.48.12; Plutarch, *Mor.* 516C; cf. 1 Esdr. 1.33, 42 — 'report'.

210. MM, *historeō.*

211. BDAG 483: 'visit (for the purpose of coming to know someone or something)'. See further my 'The Relationship between Paul and Jerusalem according to Galatians 1 and 2', *NTS* 28 (1982) 461-78, reprinted in *Jesus, Paul and the Law* 108-26 (here 110-13); and the further clarification in 'Once More — Gal. 1.18: *historēsai Kēphan*', *ZNW* 76 (1985) 138-39 = *Jesus, Paul and the Law* 127-28, in response to O. Hofius, 'Gal. 1.18: *historēsai Kēphan*', *ZNW* 75 (1984) 73-85.

212. Paul makes it sound as though he had spent most of the two weeks closeted away with Cephas/Peter. It is likely 'that Paul means us to understand that this was the total length of his stay in Jerusalem' (Wedderburn, *History* 223 n. 39); note again the solemn oath in 1.20 regarding what has just been said (1.18-19).

That must mean that he saw his commissioning as entirely of a piece with Jesus' commissioning of Cephas, and his gospel as the gospel also preached by those appointed apostles before him. (2) 'Getting to know' Cephas, during a two-week stay with Cephas, would assuredly include learning about his time with Jesus, about Peter's part in Jesus' pre-passion mission. Cephas's time with Jesus had been so personally transformative for Peter that, without playing down the importance of the resurrection appearance to Cephas and Peter's role in the initial months of the new sect in Jerusalem, it is no strain whatsoever to conclude that Saul could hardly have spoken of 'getting to know' Cephas without including Peter's own reflections on his time with Jesus. (3) Inevitably included, therefore, would also have been some in-depth induction to the Jesus tradition, whether as formal instruction or simply as Peter reminisced at length on what Jesus did and said.[213] It is no abuse of historical imagination to envisage many hours of conversation between Cephas and Saul during that two-week stay, sufficient to stock Saul's own well-trained mind with many of the traditions he was to pass on in turn to the churches he founded. Here again, no conflict with Paul's assertion in Gal. 1.1, 11-12 need be postulated: the distinctiveness and independence of Paul's gospel as 'to the Gentiles' was hardly compromised by his learning more about Jesus' own mission.[214]

d. Saul's Association with the Church in Antioch

At some point Saul became active in the church in Antioch and, indeed, soon became one of its leaders (Acts 13.1). Luke has it that Paul returned to Tarsus (Acts 9.30), that is, about 36 CE, for an indeterminate period, prior to his being brought from Tarsus to Antioch by Barnabas (11.25-26) and the subsequent mission from Antioch (13–14). Paul, however, covers the whole period (of about thirteen years) in the laconic report, 'Then I went off into the territories of Syria and Cilicia' (Gal. 1.21).[215] That at least allows the correlation of Tarsus in Cilicia and of Antioch in Syria.[216] But it leaves two major issues wholly unclear.

---

213. Murphy-O'Connor agrees (*Paul* 90-93). Hengel and Schwemer argue that the conversation would not all have been one way and that Paul would have impressed Peter with his own understanding of the gospel (*Paul* 147-50). The only problem with this idea is that Paul gives no hint that he had found a willing ally for his views at that early stage and was still concerned subsequently (Gal. 2.2) on the need to gain the backing of Peter and the others.

214. See further my *Galatians* 74. Alternatively, did the exchange include Saul/Paul's reflection on what his own commission was (Wilckens, *Theologie* 1/2.247-48)? In which case the subsequent sharing (Gal. 2.2) would hardly have been a surprise to Peter.

215. Following his usual pattern, Schnabel gives details of the cities in which Paul might have worked, but without any support from tradition to that effect (*Mission* 1049-68); similarly M. Wilson, 'Cilicia: The First Christian Churches in Anatolia', *TynB* 54 (2003) 15-30.

216. Perhaps it was at this time that Paul learned a trade, since, as Murphy-O'Connor ar-

One is the date when Saul linked up with the church in Antioch. Hanging on the answer is the further question whether his missionary work in Syria and Cilicia was carried on by Saul in an independent capacity (as in Arabia?) or in association with Antioch. There are hardly any data to provide a clear answer, but such as there are point to an earlier rather than a later association with Antioch.

- Paul's description of his relationship with the Jerusalem leadership in Galatians 1–2 suggests that he did not strike out as an independent missionary prior to the Jerusalem council and the Antioch incident.[217]
- Saul's work as an evangelist in Syria and Cilicia (Gal. 1.21), even if prior to his linking firmly with the church in Antioch, would probably have been carried out under the aegis or with the approval of the Antioch church (much as we can assume that early evangelism in Judea would have been in concert with the Jerusalem leadership), since Antioch was the capital of the province.[218]
- This fits quite well with the account of Acts, both that Antioch could be regarded as a kind of daughter church of Jerusalem (Acts 11.19-21), or at least as approved by the Jerusalem church (11.22-24), and that Saul functioned as a teacher (and/or prophet) in the Antioch church (Acts 13.1).[219]
- It also fits with the Acts claim that Saul only set out on mission when he was so commissioned in Antioch (13.2-3).

The likelihood, then, is that Saul made contact with the Antioch church at a time soon after his departure from Jerusalem, or after a brief intermission in Tarsus. Either straight away or after a time as a missionary away from Antioch (and brought by Barnabas to Antioch), he became more established in the church in Antioch and emerged as one of its leaders. That, of course, would not exclude the kind of evangelism in the wider region referred to in Gal. 1.21 and 23. A date for Saul's becoming thus established in Antioch about 40 CE, give or

---

gues, Saul's conversion would have deprived him of the resources on which he could depend as a Pharisee (*Paul* 85-86).

217. See below, §27.1.

218. The Roman territories Cilicia and Syria adjoined each other (folded round the northeast corner of the Mediterranean), and eastern Cilicia had been united with Syria as a single province administered from Antioch some sixty years earlier (W. M. Ramsay, *A Historical Commentary on St. Paul's Epistle to the Galatians* [London: Hodder and Stoughton, 1900] 275-78; Bruce, *Galatians* 103; BDAG 977). Given the barrier formed by the Taurus Mountains to the north, it was natural that Cilicia should be linked more with Antioch than with the hinterland of Asia Minor; see further below, §27.1.

219. See above, §24 at n. 335.

take two years on either side, would thus make best sense of the meagre data available.[220]

Since Gal. 1.21 seems to cover the period between Paul's first two visits to Jerusalem, it probably has to make room for what is normally described as 'the first missionary journey' (Acts 13–14).[221] To say the least, the overlap is somewhat tenuous, since the route of that journey takes Barnabas and Saul entirely outside Syria and Cilicia.[222] All we can say is that the rather vague report, 'I went into the regions of Syria and of Cilicia', does not *exclude* a particular venture like that recounted in Acts 13–14 towards the end of the lengthy period in view.[223] Even so, Paul's silence in Gal. 1.21 is slightly odd, if indeed that was the mission which brought the gospel to the Galatians. On the other hand, there may be an allusion to the Galatian mission when Paul a few sentences later notes that he resisted the attempt to have Titus circumcised in Jerusalem 'in order that the truth of the gospel might *remain* for you' (Gal. 2.5), implying that the gospel had already been preached in Galatia prior to the Jerusalem council.[224] Perhaps, then, they did not need reminding at that point in his defence statement, or an explicit reference to Paul's success as a missionary of Antioch would not have sat well with his insistence on the independence of his gospel.[225] Here again the terseness of Paul's reminiscence makes it difficult to lever Acts 13–14 into any interstices.

220. Compare and contrast Hengel and Schwemer, *Paul* 178-79, 261, who think Paul functioned as an independent missionary for between six and seven years (including the time in Arabia) before he became associated with the church in Antioch (Acts 11.25-26 'may indicate that it was not all that easy for Barnabas to find Paul'). But would the Paul we know from his letters have readily functioned under Barnabas's leadership (as Acts 13.1-6 clearly implies; see §27.1a-b below) if he had already enjoyed success as an independent missionary? For Barnabas's influence on Paul see Hengel and Schwemer 205, 218-20, 224. There is no indication that the ecstatic experience referred to in 2 Cor. 12.2-4 (see below, §25.5f) played any part in the move from Tarsus to Antioch (Schnabel, *Mission* 1069).

221. Here I assume that the second Jerusalem visit (Gal. 2.1-10) cannot be equated with the visit referred to in Acts 11.30, that is, prior to 'the first missionary journey'; see below, §27.3a-b.

222. See n. 218 above, and further §27.1.

223. It has to be recalled that Gal. 1.21 was not intended to give a full itinerary of Paul's work prior to his second Jerusalem visit but simply to affirm that during that time he was never in Jerusalem (Weiss, *Earliest Christianity* 203-205; Breytenbach, *Paulus und Barnabas* 88-89). 'With geographical generosity Paul can evidently still include these areas [Pamphylia, Pisidia and Lycaonia, which bordered on Cilicia] under the term *klimata* in the information that he gives in Gal. 1.21' (Hengel and Schwemer, *Paul* 261). Note also that Acts 15.23 addresses the churches of Antioch, Syria and Cilicia, which in context would include the churches of 'the first missionary journey' (Acts 13–14); see further below, §27.3e.

224. Murphy-O'Connor, *Paul* 24.

225. A similar reason may explain why Paul never refers in his subsequent letters to the churches of his early missionary work; see further below, §27.6(3).

At this point historical inquiry simply has to admit that the data are too fragmentary to allow a fuller picture of the tunnel period to emerge.

Two things can be said, however, and with some confidence. (1) Luke seems to be well informed regarding Paul's association with the church in Antioch (Acts 13.1); Paul's stature in the church there, reflected in the Antioch incident of Gal. 2.11-14, is probably sufficient confirmation from our only other source. (2) During this period Paul was engaged for some considerable time in missionary work in the larger region. Paul's own account indicates that he was 'evangelizing' in these territories (Gal. 1.23), and it must have been in and through that preaching that he saw God working through him in effective mission among Gentiles (Gal. 2.2, 7-9). That at least covers the two features of Luke's account — a lengthy period as a leader in the church of Antioch (Acts 13.1) and effective mission among Gentiles (13–14), causing the issue of the terms of acceptance of Gentiles into the new sect to become a cause of sharp dispute (Acts 15.1-2; Gal. 2.1-5). But we are getting ahead of ourselves and will have to pick up the story in §27.

e. Antiochene Influence on Paul's Theology?

I have already discussed the likelihood that the most formative influence on Paul's theology was his encounter with the risen Christ on the road to Damascus (§25.4). Throughout the twentieth century the main alternative explanation has been that a greater influence on Paul's theology was exerted through the pagan syncretism which he confronted in Syria and Cilicia.[226]

There can be little room for doubt that Paul was indeed influenced by the Hellenist/Antiochene theology he found in Antioch (§24.9). So his developing understanding of Jesus and of the gospel he believed himself commissioned to preach would be a blend of several influences:

- his own deep knowledge of his ancestral faith and Scriptures
- the encounter with the exalted Christ on the Damascus road
- the information he gained during his two weeks with Cephas/Peter in Jerusalem
- what he learned from and during his association with the church of Antioch
- his own reflection on his ongoing experience of the Spirit of Christ and on his burgeoning mission.

226. The attempt to reconstruct an 'Antiochene' theology (§24 n. 278) is a much watered down version of the earlier history-of-religions school thesis (see above, §20.3b).

On that basis there is no difficulty in making sense of everything Paul wrote. It is not necessary to hypothesize further influence from traditional Greco-Roman religion, religious philosophy, mystery religion or emperor cult. That Paul was familiar with these other strands of Greco-Roman religiosity is fairly clear at various points in his letters.[227] And it is also true that some of what he writes could have been heard and understood in terms other than those he intended.[228] But the original suggestions of the history-of-religions school of the early twentieth century that his sacramental theology and his gospel of salvation could only be adequately explained by influences from the mystery cults and a presupposed pre-Christian Gnostic Redeemer myth have proved almost wholly groundless, unnecessary hypotheses which read in most of what is then read out.[229]

f. 'I Know a Person in Christ' (2 Cor. 12.2)

Two other details concerning the early period of Saul's association with the church in Antioch call for comment at this point. The first is the enigmatic allusion in 2 Cor. 12.2-4:

> [2]I know a person in Christ who fourteen years ago was caught up to the third heaven — whether in the body I do not know, or out of the body I do not know (God knows). [3]And I know that such a person — whether in the body or apart from the body I do not know (God knows) — [4]was caught up into paradise and heard inexpressible words that no human being is permitted to utter.

By common consent the passage is best seen as autobiographical: Paul recalls one of his own 'visions and revelations' (12.1), one marked by its 'extraordinary character' (12.7). Paul must be describing his own experience, since he was in process of describing the grounds on which he might have grounds for boasting, the 'signs' of apostleship which evidently counted for the 'super-apostles' of 12.11-12. The third-person description is presumably Paul's way of distancing

---

227. E.g., some knowledge of Stoic philosophy is indicated in Rom. 1.20-28 (see, e.g., my *Romans* 57-68), and some engagement with the emperor cult is probably implicit at various points (see below, §29.4d).

228. E.g., talk of 'wisdom', 'knowledge', 'spirituals', 'mature' in 1 Corinthians traded on widely used and variously understood religious terminology; nor should it occasion surprise that Christianity's rituals (baptism, Lord's Supper) would appear to some as the equivalent of similar rituals elsewhere.

229. See above, §20.3b-c.

himself not so much from the experience itself as from the significance which others invested in such experiences.[230]

The value of this information for a historian is that we can date the experience referred to with some precision.[231] Fourteen years before the writing of 2 Corinthians (ca. 55/56) would take us back to about 42.[232] Some have attempted to identify this mystical experience with Saul's conversion experience, and there is an unfortunate tendency to merge Paul's (probable) allusion to the latter in 2 Cor. 4.6 with the experiences alluded to in 12.1, 7, if not the experience of 12.2-4 in particular.[233] But the thesis cannot stand:

- The dating makes it impossible, since the date of Saul's conversion is about ten years earlier (32 or 33).[234]
- Paul himself was quite clear that the Damascus road experience was in a distinct and separate category, the select sequence of experiences usually described as 'resurrection appearances'; in Paul's thinking, it was the Damascus road 'revelation' which made him an apostle (1 Cor. 9.1; 15.8). Paul's description of his Damascus road 'vision' as 'last of all' clearly implies that that sequence of experiences came to an end after his conversion/calling. In contrast, 2 Cor. 12.1, 7 envisages a number of similar 'visions and revelations'.[235]
- Paul's conversion involved a vision from heaven, a shining 'in his heart' (2 Cor. 4.6), a revelation 'in me' (Gal. 1.16), whereas 2 Cor 12.2-4 describes a journey to heaven.
- During his experience Paul heard 'unutterable words', 'unutterable' either because they could not be expressed in human language or because they must not be repeated;[236] either way, the emphasis runs counter to Paul's readiness to speak of his conversion-commissioning (Gal. 1.12, 15-16).[237]

230. See further Thrall, *2 Corinthians* 778-82; M. J. Harris, *2 Corinthians* (NIGTC; Grand Rapids: Eerdmans, 2005) 834-35.

231. 'There is . . . fairly wide agreement that the basic reason for the precise dating is Paul's concern to underline the factuality of the occurrence' (Thrall, *2 Corinthians* 783).

232. To be noted once again is the normal convention of the time (inclusive reckoning), which included both the start and the finish date within the number of years given.

233. C. Buck and G. Taylor, *Saint Paul: A Study in the Development of His Thought* (New York: Scribner's, 1969) 220-26; Segal, *Paul the Convert* ch. 2.

234. It would be only a little less difficult to equate the experience of 2 Cor. 12.2-4 with the vision of Acts 22.17-21, which in Acts chronology took place during Paul's first post-conversion visit to Jerusalem, though Ramsay, e.g., linked the two visions with the Acts 11.30 visit (*St. Paul* 60-64).

235. Note also 2 Cor. 5.13, on which see Thrall, *2 Corinthians* 406.

236. BDAG 134; Thrall, *2 Corinthians* 794; Harris, *2 Corinthians* 843-44.

237. The same applies to attempts to identify 2 Cor. 12.2-4 with either the vision of Acts

The account of 2 Cor. 12.2-4 (or 1-7) is valuable for us, however, since it indicates a striking dimension of Saul's spirituality. He was accustomed to experience 'visions and revelations'. Perhaps, indeed, we should infer that he was an adept in the practice of merkabah mysticism.[238] If so, should we further infer that he had so been trained in the practice in his pre-Christian days as a Pharisee, and that he continued the practice thereafter, 'in Christ'? Certainly we have to date the experience of 2 Cor. 12.2-4 to Paul's post-conversion days. At the same time, the fact that he had to go back fourteen years to recall such an 'extraordinary' vision presumably implies that the 'heavenly journey' of 12.2-4 was exceptional. Nevertheless, the implication of 12.1-7, 11-12 is that Paul continued to enjoy visionary experiences during his evangelistic and pastoral work as an apostle,[239] even if he regarded them as of little significance.[240] There were many 'visions and revelations', 'visions of extraordinary character', in which he could have boasted, had he thought it proper to do so. Both features — that such experiences continued for Paul and that he deemed them of little significance — are important for any attempt to appreciate Paul's spirituality.

g. The Problem of the 'Famine Relief Visit' to Jerusalem (Acts 11.30)

Luke records one other episode which it may be possible to date to Saul's emergence among the leadership in the Antioch church. This is Luke's much-disputed account of a visit from Antioch to Jerusalem undertaken by Barnabas and Saul to bring aid to the Jerusalem disciples in view of an expected severe famine (Acts 11.27-30).[241] This episode suffers from the same problems as afflicted 9.26-30.

22.17-21 or with Acts 13.2-3 (Taylor, *Paul* 91-92). Chilton argues that one of the 'unutterable expressions' heard by Paul was the idea that Gentiles actually became Israelites by baptism, and that Paul initially withheld this information from the Jerusalem leadership (*Rabbi Paul* 142-45).

238. That Paul was familiar with the practice of merkabah mysticism is suggested by J. Bowker, '"Merkabah" Visions and the Visions of Paul', *JSS* 16 (1971) 157-73; see also J. D. Tabor, *Things Unutterable: Paul's Ascent to Paradise in Its Greco-Roman, Judaic, and Early Christian Contexts* (Lanham: University Press of America, 1986); and for more details and bibliography see Harris, *2 Corinthians* 838-46. But see also the cautionary remarks of P. Schäfer, 'New Testament and Hekhalot Literature: The Journey into Heaven in Paul and Merkavah Mysticism', *JJS* 35 (1985) 19-35. Ashton sets Paul's religious experience in the context of shamanism (*Religion* chs. 2-3).

239. Acts recounts several visions which Paul experienced during his missionary work (16.9-10; 18.9-10; 23.11; 27.23). Note also Gal. 2.2 and 2 Cor. 5.13.

240. Compare Paul's attitude to the experience of 'speaking in tongues' (1 Cor. 14.18-19).

241. Barrett points out that Luke could have gained first-hand knowledge (Agabus appears later in 21.10-11, a 'we' passage) but thinks that the prophecy may only have forecast a

It is not that historical records fail to record famines during the reign of Claudius (41-54): there are several such references.[242] Nor the implication that the Jerusalem church had many impoverished members; that is confirmed by Rom. 15.26. It is rather that Paul's own solemn affidavit (Gal. 1.18–2.1) does not allow room for any intermediate visit by Paul to Jerusalem. It is possible that Gal. 2.1-10 refers to that visit (Gal. 2.1-10 = Acts 11.27-30),[243] but as we shall see, the match between Gal. 2.1-10 and Acts 15 is too close to allow them to be pulled apart.[244] More plausible, I think, is the likelihood that such a visit was undertaken by Barnabas, alone[245] or with some other(s), before he and Saul had become a team; and that, possibly confused by the fact that the two subsequently became such a

---

famine in Jerusalem or Judea; 'over the whole inhabited earth' is probably the result of Luke's heightening of the description (*Acts* 1.561). However, B. W. Winter, 'Acts and Food Shortages', *BAFCS* 2.59-78, notes an inscription from 163 CE which speaks of a famine which 'extended over all the world', and wonders whether such a phrase would simply be regarded as 'natural poetic hyperbole' or as a literary convention (65-69).

242. Reviewed by Hemer, *Book of Acts* 164-65; Bruce, *Acts* 276; Barrett, *Acts* 1.563-64; Hengel and Schwemer, *Paul* 240-41; Riesner, *Paul's Early Period* 127-34; Fitzmyer, *Acts* 482. Josephus reports a 'great famine' in Judea in the mid-40s (45 or 46-47), during which Queen (Mother) Helena of Adiabene purchased supplies for Jerusalem and King Izates sent money (*Ant.* 20.51-53, 101; see Feldman's notes in the LCL volume); see further Barrett, who thinks a reference to the famine of 47 is most likely (563, 565). Winter refers to an acute crop failure in Egypt from the autumn of 45 or 46 CE to the following spring (46 or 47) ('Acts and Food Shortages' 63). Hengel and Schwemer think a date in 44/45 is more likely (*Paul* 243); 'between A.D. 44 and 46' (Riesner 134). A Jerusalem visit in the middle of the 40s (unless it was immediately before the famine itself — the famine is only prophesied in 11.28) would come very close to the visit for the Jerusalem consultation (see §28.1 below). In which case, we should also note, the episode would have been subsequent to the events narrated in Acts 12, Herod Agrippa's death being dated to 44.

243. See below, §27.3a.

244. See below, §27.3b. Of other solutions offered (see, e.g., the discussion in Longenecker, *Rhetoric at the Boundaries* 242-52), the most plausible envisage Luke confusing or merging two separate (oral) traditions which he received: possibly one a report of Agabus's prophecy, and the other of Paul's visit with relief for Jerusalem's poor — Luke makes nothing of the later collection apart from Acts 24.17 (Haenchen, *Acts* 378-79); alternatively, one dealing with the questions of circumcision and table-fellowship and the other with the organization and discharge of charitable relief (see Barrett, *Acts* 560); or Luke simply confused traditions about Paul's second visit (Gal. 2.1-10), which included reference to the obligation to almsgiving (2.10) as well as to the subject matter covered in Luke's narrative in Acts 15 (Lüdemann, *Early Christianity* 138). Hengel and Schwemer consider the possibilities that Paul travelled with the delegation but kept out of Jerusalem, because there his life was still in danger or his presence would not have been welcome (*Paul* 242-43), or that he had been involved in the preparation of this collection in Antioch (465 n. 1273).

245. As suggested by Hengel, *Acts* 111. Öhler makes much of the fact that a trip to Jerusalem explains how the Jerusalemite John Mark became part of Barnabas's and Saul's team (Acts 12.25) (*Barnabas* 238-52).

close team, some of those ill-disposed towards Paul later assumed that Saul had accompanied Barnabas on the visit. Some attempt to represent Paul as visiting Jerusalem more frequently, and therefore as more dependent on/subservient to the Jerusalem leadership, is presumably what caused Paul to itemize his Jerusalem visits so scrupulously. Paul's insistence that he remained unknown by sight to the churches of Judea, and that it was only after a further fourteen years that he went again to Jerusalem (Gal. 1.22; 2.1), is another way of saying emphatically, 'I did *not* go to Jerusalem during the intervening years'. Acts 11.27-30 looks to be another passage, then, in which Luke has heard an account of Paul's relationship with Jerusalem which was at odds with Paul's own recollection, but which he has chosen to use (he may not have been familiar with Paul's account of the matter) in order to highlight the strength of continuity between the Jerusalem leadership and Paul's mission to the Gentiles. Once again, however, we are trying to make the bricks of historical fact with a minimal amount of the straw of historical data.

CHAPTER 26

The Mission of Peter

Having followed through the Hellenist and Paul strands of the traditions available to Luke for the first fifteen or so years of his narrative, we pick up, finally, the Peter strand. Peter had been the dominant figure in the first phase of Luke's account of Christianity's beginnings (Acts 1–5) but largely disappears from the scene in the following chapters. His absence during the whole Stephen episode is surprising and slightly perturbing; why did the leading figure of the new sect, who had already demonstrated his fearlessness during the opening exchanges with the Temple authorities (Acts 4–5), not intervene at any point in the deteriorating situation outlined in Acts 6.8-15, or in the crisis of Stephen's 'trial' and lynching? He (and John) are drawn in effectively (by Luke) to make good what was lacking in Philip's mission in Samaria, and to secure the oversight of Jerusalem for the first stage of mission beyond Jerusalem and its environs (Acts 8.14-25). But Peter is not explicitly mentioned at any point in connection with Paul's conversion and its immediate aftermath (9.26-30; contrast Gal. 1.18), or again in Luke's account of the 'famine-relief visit' of 11.27-30. And the turn to pick up the Peter traditions, in each case (9.32; 12.1-3), is rather abrupt. That's fine for us, since a very smooth interconnection would suggest that Luke had been editorially active. And the abruptness in each case is a reminder that Luke's style was simply to turn from one strand of tradition to another, without going out of his way to make a more elegant transition. Even so, Luke's decision not to intrude Peter into the other strands, and the fact of Peter's relative absence from them, does raise questions as to how dominant Peter actually was in these initial days, at least for those who framed the traditions on which Luke drew.

That said, there evidently was a strong strand of tradition regarding Peter available to Luke, and it is that to which he turned (back) in Acts 9.32.

26.1. Mission to 'the Circumcision'

We know from Gal. 2.7-9 that Peter had been active and successful in mission to his fellow Jews in the period prior to the Jerusalem consultation — that is, certainly in the early 40s, and probably in the later 30s also. Indeed, Paul speaks of Peter's 'apostleship *(apostolē)* to the circumcision' (Gal. 2.8) in a way analogous to his later description of himself as 'apostle to the Gentiles' (Rom. 11.13). The slightly strange formality of the language[1] has a threefold implication:

- that Peter believed himself called to a particular assignment *(apostolē)* — to preach the gospel of Jesus Christ among his own people;
- that this apostleship was fully recognized and affirmed by the rest of the Jerusalem leadership: they believed he had been 'entrusted' with this commission (Gal. 2.7);
- and that he had been markedly successful in this mission: God had worked effectively through him (2.8).

This suggests in turn that Peter had been active in this mission for some considerable time.

a. Peter's Commission

Can we say any more about Peter's call to evangelistic outreach? Given the concern so evident in Luke (as well as in Paul) to document Paul's call to mission (§25.3c-d), it is rather striking that Luke evidently did not think it necessary to provide an equivalent account of Peter's call to mission among his own people. Of course, such a call is subsumed within the commission outlined in Acts 1.8 and implicit in the definition of being an apostle (1.22).[2] But the first phase of the new movement (Acts 2–5) gives no hint that Peter saw that commission in terms of outreach beyond Jerusalem.[3] Here too, we do well to remember, much of the

---

1. The un-Pauline phrasing 'the gospel of uncircumcision', '(the gospel) of circumcision' (2.7) and the 'apostleship of the circumcision' (2.8), as well as the sudden intrusion of the name 'Peter' (2.7-8) in a context where Paul consistently uses the name 'Cephas' (1.18; 2.9, 11, 14), has suggested to several commentators that Paul is here (2.7-8) citing a formal agreement reached on the occasion; details and discussion appear in Betz, *Galatians* 96-98.

2. Here again the question arises whether the appearances to Peter and to the twelve (1 Cor. 15.5) were of a different character from the appearance to 'all the apostles' (15.7): were they all experienced or regarded as commissioning appearances (apostle-appointing), or were Peter and the twelve included among 'all the apostles'? See again §25.3c-d above and §29.3 below.

3. The commissions of Matt. 16.18-19 and John 21.15-17 are also more ecclesiastically and pastorally directed than evangelistic in thrust.

impression being thus given could simply be the consequence of Luke's editorial practice of keeping phases distinct;[4] in this case, the commissioning vision to Peter is delayed till Acts 10. It would, however, be valuable to know why and how Peter became so identified with mission to the circumcision.

Perhaps it took the scattering Hellenists to trigger a recognition of the need for mission beyond Jerusalem. As already noted, we should perhaps see a link between the appearance to 'all the apostles' (1 Cor. 15.7) and the Hellenist outreach (Acts 8.4); these 'apostles' believed themselves commissioned to go forth from Jerusalem and to evangelize where they went.[5] Should we also see here any influence from Matt. 10.5-6, the instruction of Jesus preserved, presumably, by Israel-focused 'Hebrews' (cf. Acts 1.6)? That is, did the memory of Jesus' instruction to his original disciples cause something of a reaction to news of the Hellenist evangelism, as it reached into the towns of Samaria explicitly forbidden to the earlier disciples?[6] If so, of course, part of the function of Acts 8.14-25 would be to show Peter as approving and himself active in mission to Samaritans. Another possibility may be suggested by the fact that, apart from Gal. 2.7-8, Paul always speaks of Peter as 'Cephas',[7] evoking Peter's original nickname in its Aramaic form, and perhaps implying a foundational role in the universal spread of the message of 'the church of God' — as spelled out more fully in Matt. 16.18-19.[8] However close to historical reality, or otherwise, such speculation is, something must have set Peter on the evangelistic trail.

b. Peter's Mission in the Judean Coastal Plain (Acts 9.32-43)

The description of Peter's first 'solo' ministry is consistent with Paul's characterization of Peter's mission as to 'the circumcision'.[9] The two locations where he is recalled as ministering, Lydda[10] and Joppa, had traditionally been on the edge of Judea's territory and were predominantly Jewish in population — so that 'all the residents of Lydda' (9.35) could mean all Jews. Joppa (= modern Jaffa), indeed, having been forceably judaized during the Maccabean period (1 Macc.

---

4. See above, §21.2d and the beginning of §24.
5. See above, §22.2b.
6. Cf. Hahn, *Mission* 54-59.
7. 1 Cor. 1.12; 3.22; 9.5; Gal. 1.18; 2.9, 11, 14.
8. See further below, §35.1d.
9. Barnett, *Jesus* 234; cf. further 237-40.
10. Lydda (OT Lod — 1 Chron. 8.12; Ezra 2.33; Neh. 7:37; 11.35) lay on the road from Jerusalem to Joppa, a day's journey from Jerusalem. Josephus describes it as a village 'in size not inferior to a city' (*Ant.* 20.130); it gave its name to the surrounding district (*War* 3.54-55).

13.11), was to become a revolutionary centre at the start of the war of 66 CE.[11] Perhaps, then, following his excursion into Samaritan territory, Peter reverted to Jesus' practice of touring the outer reaches of Judaism's homeland.[12]

For this developing mission of Peter, Luke was evidently able to draw on early recollections. The names (Aeneas, Tabitha/Dorcas)[13] and locations (Lydda, Sharon, Joppa) assuredly came to Luke through local traditions,[14] as also the vivid account of Tabitha's reputation (for her charitable work) and the details of the arrangements made following her death (9.36-37, 39). And the accounts of healing (Aeneas) and resuscitation (Tabitha/Dorcas) would almost certainly have come to him from the same sources.[15] As one who himself had no doubt that such healings took place, Luke simply recounts the tradition, probably more or less as he received it — more or less, we may say, as it was remembered by the early 'saints' in these places (9.32, 41).[16]

The details of the raising of Tabitha by Peter (Acts 9.40) may, however, be a little more contrived. They echo the account of the raising of Jairus's daughter in the Gospel at two points: the expulsion of the crowd (Luke 8.51) and the formula used (personal address and the command to arise — Luke 8.54); still more

11. Josephus, *War* 2.507-508; 3.414-31; further Schürer, *History* 2.3, 112-14; Schnabel, *Mission* 688.

12. *Jesus Remembered* 322-23; S. Freyne, *Jesus, a Jewish Galilean* (London: Clark, 2004) ch. 3. Lydda and Joppa 'are the most important almost purely Jewish places on the coastal plain' (Hengel, *Between Jesus and Paul* 116; see further 116-18).

13. The name 'Aeneas' is not Jewish, but we know that Greek names were regularly used in Jewish circles (see §24 at n. 59), and 'Aineas' does occur in Palestinian inscriptions (BDAG 27). As Barrett notes, Luke 'could hardly have failed to mention the matter if he had thought that Peter was already having dealings with a Gentile' (*Acts* 1.480). Tabitha (Aramaic)/Dorcas (Greek) is a reminder that many in the towns and cities of Palestine were bilingual.

14. M. Hengel, 'The Geography of Palestine in Acts', *BAFCS* 4.27-78, notes that in contrast to Luke's 'inexact knowledge of the geography of Galilee, Samaria and most of Judaea', his 'exact information about the cities of the coastal plain, the road from Jerusalem to Caesarea, and the relations between the Temple and the Antonia fortress in Jerusalem is striking, and is consistent with the view that he had visited Palestine as a companion of Paul' (27).

15. Those whose understanding of how tradition came to Luke remains imprisoned within the constrictions of form-critical methodology are surprised by the incompleteness here of what they assume to have had the form of a miracle story; Luke must have compressed it (e.g., Lüdemann, *Early Christianity* 122).

16. The healing is not particularly spectacular — Aeneas had been afflicted for eight years (contrast the man crippled from birth in 3.2); the healing formula, 'Jesus Christ heals you' (9.34), is unusual in Acts; and the story does not include a note of the conversion of Aeneas himself. It is difficult to see how one could decide whether Aeneas was already a Christian (Haenchen, *Acts* 338) or not (Fitzmyer, *Acts* 444).

closely the Markan account (Mark 5.40-41);[17] and more distantly the accounts of similar recallings to life attributed to Elijah and Elisha.[18] On the other hand the verbs used in the raising formula are different,[19] and Luke's failure to mention 'calling upon Jesus' or 'calling on the name of Jesus', more typical of his own healing accounts, may equally suggest he was drawing on tradition also at this point. Whatever the actual condition of Tabitha, which we have no way now of checking, it was no doubt the widespread understanding of those closest to the event that she had been raised from the dead.[20]

To be noted, however, is the strong impression which Luke gives that any evangelistic success was only a corollary to the success of Peter's pastoral work.[21] Initially his concern is presented as more pastoral in character, expressed among the saints in Lydda and the disciples and saints at Joppa (Acts 9.32, 38, 41).[22] It was the news of his success as a healer (not as a preacher) which caused many to 'turn to the Lord' and to 'believe in the Lord' (9.35, 42).[23] Such an effect is consistent both with what might have been expected and with Luke's consistent emphasis on the faith-generating effect of miracles.

The implication of all this is that Peter had not yet taken the plunge or caught up with Philip in readiness to engage in pioneer missionary work (were 'the saints' converts of Philip? — 8.40).[24] That it took a considerable jolt to his theology and self-understanding before he was prepared to do so is the chief burden of the next episode (10.1–11.18). This probably reflects fairly accurately the serious qualms and hesitation which many of the first Jerusalem-based believers experienced as they contemplated the possibility that their movement was beginning to break through the boundaries which in Jewish perspective God had established to mark out the difference and distinctiveness of their religion (their set-apartness to

17. Translated back into Aramaic, there would be only one letter of difference: *talitha koum* (Mark 5.41); *tabitha koum* (Acts 9.40).

18. 1 Kgs. 17.17-24; 2 Kgs. 4.32-37. Weiser sets out the parallels in tabular form (*Apg.* 238).

19. Luke here, as in 9.34, uses the verb (*anistēmi*) which elsewhere describes Jesus' resurrection.

20. Cf. Pesch, *Apg.* 1.320, 325-26.

21. In Acts 8.25 Luke says nothing about the success (or otherwise) of Peter's (and John's) preaching 'to many villages of the Samaritans'.

22. That Luke refers to Jewish believers in using the terms 'saints' and 'disciples' is almost certain; see above, §20.1(4) and (8). See also Barrett, *Acts* 1.479-80, 482.

23. These are two of the phrases Luke uses to describe conversion: 'turned to the Lord' — 11.21; cf. 14.15; 15.19; 26.18, 20; 'believed on the Lord' — 11.17; 16.31; 22.19. As Haenchen observes, the language indicates that Jews are in view; Gentiles would have 'turned to God' (14.15; 15.19; 26.20) (*Acts* 338).

24. Schnabel shows some concern to maintain that Peter was 'the pioneer missionary in this area' (*Mission* 693).

God).[25] It also probably signals that Peter himself was beginning a broadening process which was to take him away from Jerusalem (on mission among fellow Jews, Gal. 2.7-9), leaving James and the more traditionalist element in control there.[26]

The final narrative note, Peter's staying in Joppa (9.43), prepares for the spectacular next step, to be recounted immediately (ch. 10). But the description of Peter's host in Joppa, Simon,[27] as 'a tanner' may be significant. The smell associated with tanning made the job not only unpleasant but its practitioners unacceptable among those who regarded cultic purity as something to be maintained as far as possible (a tanner's very work involved constant touching of the skins of dead bodies).[28] Does the mention of this fact indicate that Peter was already moving away from his previously Temple-centred focus of worship and ministry (5.42)?[29] This is probably more likely than that Luke expected his readers to pick up such significance from the bare mention here.

26.2. Caesarea as a Pivotal Point

Luke continues to make a second major insertion into the history of Hellenist Christian expansion, which had begun with ch. 8. The account in 9.1-31 had interrupted it to ensure that the conversion of Saul was given due and early prominence. But now an even lengthier insertion opens up (10.1–11.18), an account of Peter's encounter with and successful preaching to the centurion Cornelius and his relatives and friends. The object is plain: to demonstrate that the first breakthrough of the gospel to the Gentiles, or at least the first breakthrough recognized by the Jerusalem church (so the conversion of the Ethiopian eunuch in 8.26-40 does not count), was led by Peter himself.[30]

The decisive proof recited is twofold. First, there are the interlocking visions of Cornelius and of Peter (10.1-23) — an angel instructing Cornelius to send for Peter (10.1-8) and Peter's thrice-repeated vision of a large sheet filled

---

25. In this Luke and Paul agree; see, e.g., Acts 11.2-3; 15.1; 21.20-21; Gal. 2.4, 12-13.

26. See further below, §26.5.d.

27. 'The name must be traditional; pure invention would never have invited confusion by making Simon Peter stay with another Simon' (Barrett, *Acts* 1.486); contrast Lüdemann, *Early Christianity* 123.

28. Str-B 2.695; Jeremias, *Jerusalem* 304-305, 310; Barrett, *Acts* 1.486, with reference particularly to *m. Ket.* 7.10; *b. Pesah.* 65a.

29. The direct influence of Jesus' own openness to other despised individuals ('tax collectors and sinners') should, of course, not be discounted or ignored.

30. Reinbold argues that the Cornelius episode probably did not take place till after the Jerusalem conference (*Propaganda* 55-62); this conclusion is justifiably criticized by Schnabel, *Mission* 707-708.

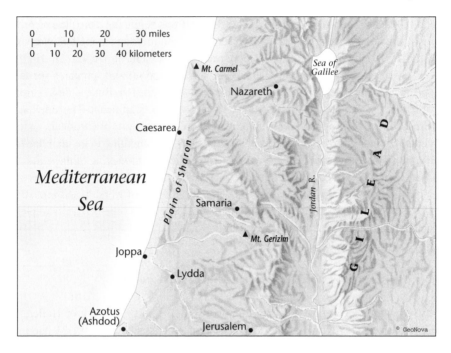

Peter's Mission

with all kinds of animals and birds, accompanied by the command to arise, kill and eat (10.9-16) — both recalled again in the following verses (10.30-32; 11.5-10). As in the case of Ananias (9.10-12), it is the double testimony of divine approval given by the complementary visions which puts the issue beyond doubt: God approves and wills the next step. In Peter's case the significance of the vision (10.14-15) is, exceptionally, confirmed by the prompting of the Spirit (to go to Cornelius) — again twice told (10.19-20; 11.11-12). Second, the account of the Spirit unexpectedly falling upon Cornelius and his companions, while Peter was still preaching to them, is again rehearsed twice for double effect (10.44-47; 11.15-17). The former proof secures Peter's complete acceptance of Cornelius (10.47-48); the latter, that of the Jerusalem apostles and brothers (11.18).

a. Luke and His Tradition

As usual we must ask how much of all this was contrived by Luke and how much is well rooted in history. And as usual the answer is a bit of both.

First, the evidence of Luke's shaping of the record is clear. We need mention only the two most striking points. (1) It is quite possible that the first real breakthrough to Gentiles, in chronological sequence, happened at Antioch (11.19-24), not forgetting the conversion of the Ethiopian eunuch (8.26-39).[31] The problem was that Jerusalem's relation to these (earlier?) developments was a good deal less clear. Whatever the chronology, however, the point is that Luke clearly regarded the decisive breakthrough as the episode in which Peter was personally involved, the breakthrough which Peter himself made. It was crucial for Luke that, not only had the unheard-of step of accepting (eating with, 11.3) and baptizing an uncircumcised Gentile been taken by the leading apostle (10.45-48), but also that Peter had been able to convince his Jerusalem colleagues by recounting the clear evidence of divine approval which had first convinced him (11.1-18). Only so could Luke demonstrate to his readers that this decisive breakthrough into a whole new dimension for the Jesus movement was in full continuity with all that had gone before.

(2) Luke has delayed any confrontation over the question of clean and unclean till this point. In Mark's Gospel the issue is already confronted by Jesus and the challenge to Jewish tradition sharply posed by Jesus in Mark 7.1-23. But Luke has completely omitted that passage from his own Gospel — part of, and quite probably the principal reason for, the 'great omission' (Mark 6.45 to 8.13/26) by Luke in his use of Mark as a primary written source.[32] We have seen him use this technique before, in his delay of the charge of destroying the Temple from the trial of Jesus until the accusation against Stephen (see on 6.14).[33] So here, Luke had evidently decided that the proper place in his two-volume account for the issue to be confronted was in the Peter/Cornelius episode. He did this, presumably, partly out of a concern for an orderly account, but also partly in order to show that the questioning of Judaism's traditional identity markers did not seriously begin until the new movement was already well launched, and even then only at the undeniable insistence of God's direction. In this way he avoids the problem posed when Mark 7.1-23 is juxtaposed with Acts 10.14, but it does sharpen the historical question: if Jesus had indeed spoken as he did in Mark 7.15, 18-19 (with the implication Mark himself draws in 7.19 that no food should be regarded as unclean) and had acted in accord with that teaching, how could Peter say he himself had never contemplated the eating of unclean food (Acts 10.14)?

On the basis of such considerations some have assumed that the story is

---

31. The dating of both episodes is obscure: Antioch, probably in the second half of the 30s (see §24.8e above); Cornelius, some time before Herod Agrippa's entry on the scene (12.1), that is, some time before 41; Fitzmyer agrees with Bruce in dating the episode to 'before 41' (*Acts* 449).

32. On the 'greater omission' see, e.g., Kümmel, *Introduction* 61-62.

33. See above, §§21.2d and 24.4c.

more or less wholly contrived: a rather obscure episode briefly recalled from Peter's early missionary work has been taken over by Luke and elaborated into a
major event whose significance was recognized from the first.[34]

Second, however, there is more to be said for the historical value of Luke's
tradition. (1) Peter's hesitation on the subject of Jew/Gentile relations is attested
also by Paul (Gal. 2.11-12). If Peter was so reluctant to maintain table-fellowship
with Gentile believers, even after the Gentile mission had been given formal approval (Gal. 2.7-9), it is very likely that his reluctance at an earlier date was even
more marked. At the same time, the tendentiousness of Mark's account in Mark
7.15-19 should also be recognized (contrast the Matthean parallel — Matt.
15.11-17) and probably reflects the sharper focus which the Gentile mission
brought to Mark's retelling of the tradition.[35] So Luke may well be representing
in Acts 10.14 the genuine reluctance which Peter had displayed on this question,
a reluctance which had not been challenged until the question of Gentile acceptability was first raised for him personally. And if we accept that the first Christians experienced visions, and that such visions helped form policy and theology,[36] there is no reason in principle why the tradition told to Luke should not
have included a vision which shook Peter out of the attitude of Acts 10.14.[37]

(2) It is unlikely that Luke would have invented on his own novellistic initiative the sequence narrated in 10.44-48. Such a departure (Spirit preceding baptism) from the normal pattern (baptism and Spirit, 2.38) would have made
Cornelius into a precedent uncomfortable for the ecclesiology of Luke's day.[38] It

---

34. So, famously, by M. Dibelius, 'The Conversion of Cornelius', *Studies* 109-22: 'a
straightforward legend of a conversion, comparable in its simple beauty with the legend of
the Ethiopian eunuch' (120); see further the careful analysis of tradition and redaction in
Weiser, *Apg.* 1.253-62; the review by Haenchen, *Acts* 355-57; Jervell, *Apg.* 318-20. In resisting any suggestion that active proselytizing preceded Paul, Peerbolte has to infer that 'the
proclamation of the gospel reached Cornelius through his socio-religious network' (*Paul*
126). Pesch, however, argues strongly for the view that 'the artistic composition is not primarily the work of Luke, but on the whole goes back already to the prelukan tradition' (*Apg.*
1.333-35). And Barrett thinks it 'more probable that what (if anything) Luke universalizes
was a particular local arrangement that could have served, and did serve (15.7-9) as the basis
of a general agreement' (*Acts* 1.535). Wilckens thinks that such an event was an essential
presupposition for the subsequent basic agreement between the Jerusalemites and the
Antiochenes (*Theologie* 1/2.260).

35. See my 'Jesus and Ritual Purity: A Study of the Tradition History of Mark 7.15',
Jesus, Paul and the Law 89-107.

36. Something which can hardly be dismissed in the case of Paul (§§25.3-4).

37. *Pace* Dibelius, *Studies* 111-12; see also below, n. 40.

38. In deducing a primary tradition of the conversion of a Gentile by Peter in Caesarea,
which ends with them being baptized and receiving the Holy Spirit (*Early Christianity* 131),
Lüdemann ignores such considerations.

is more likely, given the enthusiastic character of the new sect, that some early preaching of Peter was attended by charismatic manifestations of the Spirit's presence from Gentile members of the audience; as a 'God-fearer' (10.2),[39] Cornelius would probably have participated in many Jewish gatherings. Such divine attestation is implied in the brief allusion to Peter's ministry to the circumcised in Gal. 2.8.[40] But if that was indeed what happened, then the event had a significance which Peter could not have failed to recognize: the Spirit had fallen on Gentiles, 'even on Gentiles' (10.45), just as it had upon the first disciples at Pentecost (11.15); God had given to Gentiles the same gift as they had received when they had believed in the Lord Jesus Christ (11.17). The conclusion, for a sect which valued such manifestations, was unavoidable. God had accepted them; how could Peter and the other believers obstruct God's clearly signalled will (11.17)?

In other words, whenever it took place (and it must have been early), the event of Cornelius's acceptance by Peter marked a step forward of momentous significance, which can hardly have been ignored at the time.[41] All that Luke seems to have done, therefore, is to bring it into even sharper prominence and, by interposing it before the account of the Hellenists' mission in Antioch, to have ensured that the strongest precedent (acceptance of Gentile Cornelius by the apostle Peter and the Jerusalem church) is given the full glare of attention on centre stage.[42] The basic story itself may have come to Luke together with the traditions lying behind 9.32-43, perhaps part of the founding tradition preserved by the church in Caesarea.[43]

b. Caesarea

Part of the significance of the Cornelius episode is the importance of Caesarea. As usual with Luke, no attempt is made to bring this out (as with Antioch); he

39. See below, n. 54.

40. In Gal. 2.7-9 Paul draws a repeated parallel between Peter's mission and his own — 'just as Peter' (*kathōs Petros*, 2.7); 'through me also' (*kai emoi*, 2.8); 'us to the Gentiles, them to the circumcision' (2.9). The gift and gifts of the Spirit to which Paul refers in Gal. 3.2-5 were evidently equally characteristic of Peter's converts (cf. Acts 10.44-47; 11.15-17).

41. As Haenchen observes, in reference to Dibelius's assumption that 'in the days of the primitive community a Gentile could have been accepted into the fold without such a singular event exciting remark': 'This presupposition . . . is extremely unlikely. It was precisely in the earliest days that the admission of Gentiles must have been most unthinkable to the community' (*Acts* 360-61). See also Avemarie, *Tauferzählungen* 381-94.

42. To speak of 'self-contradiction' between the two tellings of the story, 10.1-48 and 11.1-18 (as Haenchen, *Acts* 355), evinces a failure to appreciate the 'same yet different' character of the oral performance of such stories (and of their transmission).

43. Barrett concludes that Luke has been able to draw on the account given by the church in Caesarea of its own founding by Peter (*Acts* 1.496-97).

simply assumed that his readership will have been aware of it, and the various allusions he makes to it subsequently[44] are evidence enough that he was aware of
its political and economic importance. He himself almost certainly spent some
time in Caesarea (21.8; 27.1), so he will have been familiar with its main features. Its importance dated from its rebuilding by Herod the Great (completed in
13 BCE), who used pioneering science to provide it with a breakwater and an excellent harbour, renaming it in honour of the emperor. It had quickly become
prosperous and one of the major cities of Palestine, and since 6 CE it had been the
headquarters of the Roman prefect and the main garrison for the forces under his
command. More to the point for us, its population and ethos were chiefly Gentile, and although it had a sizeable Jewish population, there was a long-lasting
tension between Jews and Gentiles on questions of citizenship.[45]

For Christianity, then, to establish itself in Caesarea opened up a whole
new horizon for the new movement. There was the possibility of influencing the
Roman garrison, the movers and instruments of Rome's policy in the region. As
the first of the Hellenistic cities in Palestine (that we know of) to be penetrated
by the gospel, the possibility was given of the message reaching beyond the Jewish community (as happened in Antioch). And as a major seaport (thanks to
Herod's harbour) the possibility became immediately real of the message of the
gospel being carried across the Mediterranean to other major ports and cities (including the future great centres of Christianity — Ephesus, Corinth, Rome, Alexandria). Who now can tell how many seeds and how quickly they were carried
abroad from the young plant which was given root by the work of Philip and
other Hellenist evangelists, even prior to Peter's mission?

For Peter himself, mission in Caesarea was itself a significant step beyond
the earlier mission in Lydda and Joppa. Caesarea Maritima was a fitting place for
the episode which Luke describes. His narrative runs unbroken through the
whole chapter. But two stages are clearly distinct: first, Peter's recognition that
God does not make distinctions between human beings in general as to their acceptability or unacceptability on grounds of their basic identity (ethnic, social or

---

44. 12.19; 18.22; 21.8, 16; 23.23, 33; 25.1, 4, 6, 13.

45. Details in Schürer, *History* 2.116-17. 'Caesarea Maritima was Herod's showpiece
city; it was a major outlet to the Mediterranean. It rearranged trade patterns in the area. Produce, trade, and people flowed in both directions; it was a city where Hellenistic and Roman
ideals jostled with Jewish convictions, where Roman, Greek, Jew, Nabatean, and Egyptian
would rub shoulders daily. The city covered 164 acres and included a large number of state-
sponsored or royal structures: the harbor itself with its installations and warehouses; water and
sewage facilities; walls; gates; streets; agora; hippodrome; theatre; amphitheatre; Promontory
Palace; and the Temple of Roma and Augustus hovering over the whole at the focal point of the
harbor' (P. Richardson, *Herod: King of the Jews and Friend of the Romans* [Columbia: University of South Carolina, 1996] 178-79). See also Schnabel, *Mission* 688-90.

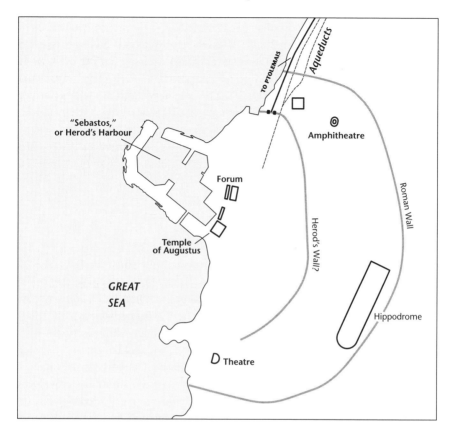

Caesarea

religious); and second, Peter's preaching to Cornelius on the basis of that recognition, with the further consequence of God's visible acceptance of Cornelius and his companions as such. The climax of the first stage comes in Peter's initial address to Cornelius (10.28-29).

26.3. The Conversion of Peter

It is important, then, to grasp that Luke's account falls into two parts and that the first part in the process is the conversion of Peter himself, which also comes in two stages. There is the initial reluctance of a devout Jew to associate with a Gentile. The revelation which Peter receives and the new conviction which comes to him were neither so dramatic nor so traumatic as in the case of Saul (ch. 9). But it was every bit as much a conversion as in Saul's case — a conversion from traditional and deeply rooted convictions which, according to Luke's telling, had completely governed his life till that moment (10.14-15, 28).[46] He was then ready, as not before, to preach the good news of Jesus to this Gentile. The fact that it took the further event of the Spirit's coming upon Cornelius in such an unexpected, unprecedented way to complete Peter's conversion indicates Luke's appreciation of just how major a transformation had taken place in Peter and how epochal a step was being taken by the new movement. The care with which Luke narrates the story is telling. The detail is painstaking. No doubt must be left that this initial step was at God's direct bidding. By way of contrast, we may compare the relatively brief record of other events of potentially comparable significance (8.5-8, 12-13; 11.19-21).

a. Cornelius

The name 'Cornelius' was no doubt part of the tradition which came to Luke. He is clearly understood to have been a Gentile (10.35, 45; 11.1). Since the Roman army recruited widely from nations within the Roman Empire, we do not know what nationality he was, though 'the Italian Cohort' (10.1) was presumably made up originally of Italians. He is located in the Roman administrative capital (Caesarea) and was possibly still a serving officer, with soldiers at his command (10.7). It is true that we lack any record of the Italian Cohort being stationed in Caesarea (but our records are hardly complete).[47] And it would be unlikely for Roman troops to be stationed in Caesarea during the reign of Herod Agrippa (cf. 12.20-23). However, the possibility cannot be excluded that the God-fearing Cornelius had retired from the army and settled with his family[48] in Caesarea (in its own interests the Roman army's terms of settlement for its veterans could be generous). The soldier of 10.7, notably described also as 'devout', may have been a favoured subordinate who had chosen to retire with him.[49]

46. So also Klauck, *Magic and Paganism* 36. I do not imply, of course, that Peter became a follower of or believer in Jesus only at this time.

47. The existence of a cohort by that name is attested only from 69 CE and in Syria (T. R. S. Broughton, 'The Roman Army', in *Beginnings* 5.427-45 [here 441-42]; Schürer, *History* 1.365 n. 54). Lüdemann concludes bluntly that 'the information [of Acts 10.1] is historically incorrect' (*Early Christianity* 126). But Hengel rightly points out that we know too little about military conditions in Palestine to be able to draw any firm conclusion (*Between Jesus and Paul* 203-204 n. 111). See further I. Levinskaya, 'The Italian Cohort in Acts 10:1', in P. J. Williams et al., eds., *The New Testament in Its First-Century Setting*, B. W. Winter FS (Grand Rapids: Eerdmans, 2004) 106-25.

48. The presence of 'relatives' (wife and children?) is indicated in 10.24 (see also 11.14).

49. Broughton, 'Roman Army' 443; Barrett, *Acts* 1.499, 503-504. In which case, of course, the presence of Cornelius in Caesarea would not require or necessarily imply the presence of a *cohors Italica* in Caesarea at that time.

The description of Cornelius (10.2) emphasizes his piety. The terms used indicate that he was one of many Gentiles attracted to Judaism (was that why he had settled in Caesarea?). He feared God and prayed constantly to him. Coming from Luke's pen, this must mean the God of Israel. Cornelius already believed Israel's God to be the one true God. And he gave many alms to the people — a characteristic mark of Jewish piety.[50] This impression is confirmed by the additional information of 10.22, which further describes Cornelius as a 'just/upright' man (cf. Luke 1.6; 2.25; 23.50), 'well spoken of by the whole Jewish nation'. Cornelius is one of Luke's good centurions.[51] By thus demonstrating Cornelius's openness to and then membership in the new movement, Luke can advance (if only slightly) the further objective of showing the growing sect to have been on good terms with the Roman authorities.

Has Luke exaggerated the degree of Cornelius's closeness already to the religion of Israel in order to diminish the gulf which Peter was about to cross and to make the crossing that much less threatening to Jewish traditionalists? Not necessarily. We have many records of other Gentiles who were attracted to Judaism and who 'judaized' in some measure (that is, followed a distinctively Jewish way of life), without going all the way to become proselytes (that is, without being circumcised).[52] Judaism did not seek out such (it was not a missionary religion),[53] but it was very willing to welcome such sympathizers at gatherings for prayer and Torah reading and at festivals. Such Gentile sympathizers are usually called 'God-fearers', which is quite appropriate so long as we do not assume that it was a formal title but simply denotes a dominant attitude of piety.[54] Cornelius's household, included within the description of 'God-fearing', presumably includes his household retainers (10.2). In short, Luke sets the stage for Peter's *volte-face* with great skill, but there is no good reason to doubt that the encounter which was integral to Peter's own conversion actually involved such a one as Cornelius, or indeed 'the historical Cornelius' himself.

---

50. One of the most impressive features of Judaism past and present is the major emphasis it places on provision for the poor and disadvantaged — classically the widow, orphan and stranger (e.g., Deut. 24.10-22; Isa. 10.2; 58.6-7; Jer. 7.6; Mal. 3.5). Almsgiving was therefore a principal act of religious responsibility (e.g., Sir. 3.30; 29.12; Tob. 12.9; 14.11; Matt. 6.2-4); see further below, §27 nn. 188-89.

51. Luke 7.5; 23.47; Acts 27.43. But does that warrant Lüdemann's dismissive judgment, 'For the first Gentile to be converted by Peter to be a centurion fits Luke's apologetic too well to be traditional' (*Early Christianity* 126)?

52. See, e.g., Josephus, *War* 2.462-63; 7.45; *Ap.* 2.282. See further below, §27.4 at n. 251.

53. See above, §24 at n. 247.

54. As in 10.2, 22, 35; also 13.16, 26, 50; 16.14; 17.4, 17; 18.7. See further §29.5c below.

b. The Vision to Peter

The heart of the story is a vision to Peter, received by Peter on the rooftop in Joppa. It is set between the earlier vision to Cornelius (10.3-6)[55] and the subsequent command of the Spirit (10.19-20). The timing of the visions also enhances the spiritual atmosphere: the ninth hour (10.3) was the time of the evening sacrifice in the Temple and the appropriate time for evening prayer (3.1); and Peter is likewise depicted as praying — at midday, an additional (third) hour of prayer,[56] or perhaps simply an opportunity for prayer.

In the vision Peter sees a large sheet *(skeuos)*[57] lowered to the ground by its four corners, and in it 'all kinds of four-footed creatures and reptiles and birds of the air' (10.11-12). It is not stated explicitly, but in the vision (10.11-13) the beasts in the sheet obviously include those regarded as unclean in Jewish law, particularly the reptiles (Lev. 11.1-47). The command to 'kill and eat', without any further discrimination, would therefore have been regarded as reprehensible for a devout Jew. As in a dream, Peter knows, as part of the vision itself, what animals the command refers to (possibly a historical reminiscence). In Luke's account Peter's reaction is strong: 'Certainly not *(mēdamōs),* Lord!' (10.14).[58] He refuses and implicitly rebukes the heavenly visitation.[59] Equally strong is the self-testimony which follows: 'I have never *(oudepote)* eaten anything profane or unclean *(koinon kai akatharton)'*.[60] The emphatic denial is repeated in 11.8 and reflected in 10.28.

Peter here is portrayed as through and through loyal to the ancestral traditions of Second Temple Judaism. Observation of the laws of clean and unclean foods had become a distinctive identifying mark of the Judaism which defined itself by its opposition to Hellenistic/Gentile influences (1 Macc. 1.62-63).[61] The

---

55. The story of Cornelius's vision is retold in 10.30-33 for emphasis, but also to build up the dramatic 'feel' of the story towards its climax. The detail of the angel's clothing has been added (10.30) to provide some variety, which is typical of successive performances of the same tradition.

56. Cf. Ps. 55.17; Dan. 6.10.

57. See BDAG 927.

58. The phrase echoes Ezek. 4.14.

59. Once again 'Lord' is not necessarily Jesus or God as such (cf. 9.5 and 10.4).

60. Both words are commonly used to denote 'unclean' foods (cf. 10.15; 11.19; Rom. 14.14, 20). *Koinos* in ordinary Greek means simply 'common, ordinary'. The sense of 'profane, unclean' derives from the use of *koinos* as equivalent to the biblical *tame'* (e.g., Lev. 11.4-8; Deut. 14.7-10; Judg. 13.4; Hos. 9.3) or *chol* (Lev. 10.10; Ezek. 22.26; 44.23), a step taken subsequent to the LXX rendering of the OT but reflecting the increasing purity concerns of the Maccabean and post-Maccabean period (1 Macc. 1.47, 62). In Mark 7.2, 5, Mark has to explain the unusual use of *koinos* = 'defiled' to his Greek audience.

61. Note the elaboration of this stand taken by the Maccabean martyrs in 4 Maccabees 8–9 (8.12, 29).

heroes and heroines of Israel's popular tales of the period demonstrated their loyalty to their people and religion by refusing to eat the food of Gentiles.[62] Both the Pharisees and still more the Essenes were noted for the strictness with which they protected the purity of the meal table by their various halakhoth (rulings on less clearly defined laws).[63] And the subsequent tensions within the Christian communities of Antioch, Corinth and Rome show just how important dietary rules continued to be for the self-identity of many Jewish Christians.[64]

It is important, then, for the twenty-first-century reader to appreciate that the issue was not a minor matter of insignificant dietary fads. It lay at the heart of Jewish identity. What was at stake was the character of the new movement as a Jewish movement and the process of identity transformation. Was it to remain still loyal to the now traditionally distinctive features of the covenant people? Was it to be loyal to the principles and practices for which martyrs had died and heroes and heroines had been willing to sacrifice everything? Hitherto Peter and his brother apostles and believers in Jerusalem would have assumed the answer to be Yes.[65] But now Peter was faced with one of the most radical rethinks of religious principle imaginable. That is why Luke gives the episode such prominence and tells the story with such care.

The challenge to traditional practice is as sharp as could be: 'What *God* has made *clean*,[66] *you* must not call *profane (ha ho theos ekatharisen, sy mē koinou)*'; the double antithesis drives home the point *(theos/sy, ekatharisen/koinou)* (10.15-16). This is the moment when new religions or sects are born — when what has hitherto been taken for granted as a fundamental and defining principle is called in question and the question is heard as the voice of God. Lest there be any doubt in Peter's or the reader's mind, Luke notes that the revelation was repeated three times.

No wonder Peter was perplexed (10.17-23): how should one evaluate a dream or vision which cut so radically across long-established principles and traditions? The answer is given by the double confirmation. (1) The Spirit tells him (gives him the clear conviction — cf. 13.2 and 16.6) that he should go with the messengers just arrived; the coincidence of his vision and their arrival can hardly be accidental. (2) And the request of the three men reports Cornelius's comple-

---

62. E.g., Dan. 1.8-16; Tob. 1.10-13; Jdt. 10.5; 12.1-20; Add. Esth. 14.17; *Jos. Asen.* 7.1; 8.5.

63. See further *Jesus Remembered* 267-68, 272. For the heightened concerns about the purity laws in the century before Jesus, see, e.g., Jdt. 12.7; *Jub.* 3.8-14; *Pss. Sol.* 8.12, 22; 1QS 3.5; CD 12.19-20.

64. Gal. 2.11-14; 1 Corinthians 8; Romans 14. See also below, §27.3e (the 'apostolic decree').

65. Acts 10.14; 11.3; cf. Gal. 2.12-13.

66. Cf. Lev. 13.6, 13, 17, 23; Mark 7.19.

mentary vision. The conclusion is obvious: Peter's vision of ancient uncleanness nullified by God himself must refer to this God-fearing Gentile, who was calling for him at angelic command.[67]

c. Peter's Conversion

The encounter with Cornelius (10.27-29) is the climax to the first half of the story. Peter's first words to those assembled in Cornelius's house make the crucial point: 'You yourselves know that it is forbidden *(athemitos)*[68] for a Jew to associate with or to visit a foreigner/alien *(allophylos);* but God has shown me that I should not call anyone profane or unclean *(koinon ē akatharton)*' (10.28). The importance of the lesson just learned by Peter is drawn out clearly and should not be missed: not simply could he now eat 'unclean' *meat* with a good conscience, but he must not call any other *person* 'unclean'!

The key to this part of the story is to recognize that Peter was in process of breaching a fundamental guiding principle of Jewish human relationships and communal living: that Jews should keep themselves separate from Gentiles.[69] Of course the practice was not quite so cut and dried, otherwise there could have been no business or social relationships whatsoever between Jews and Gentiles, whether in Israel itself (where many Gentiles had settled — the 'resident aliens' of the OT) or in the diaspora (where Jews were in the minority).[70] As already

67. To be noted is the fact that angel and Spirit can be equally and variously described as the voice of God (cf. 10.5-6 with 10.20).

68. For *athemitos* cf. its use in 2 Macc. 6.5 and 7.1; see further Wilson, *Luke and the Law* 69. Bruce observes that in this context *athemiton* 'might well be rendered "tabu" (cf. 1 Pet. 4.3)' (*Acts* 259).

69. See the material gathered in my 'The Incident at Antioch (Gal. 2.11-18)', *JSNT* 18 (1983) 3-57, reprinted in *Jesus, Paul and the Law* 129-82 (here 137-42, particularly 142); Esler, *Community and Gospel* 73-86. R. J. Bauckham, 'James, Peter, and the Gentiles', in B. Chilton and C. Evans, eds., *The Missions of James, Peter, and Paul* (NovTSupp 115; Leiden: Brill, 2005) 91-142, notes that for most late Second Temple Jews, Gentiles were not *ritually* impure but *morally* impure and profane; 'only a Jew could be holy (not profane)' (91-102).

70. Schürer comments on Acts 10.28: 'The statement . . . does not mean that such an association was forbidden, but that each such association was a cause of defilement' (*History* 2.83-84); see further S. J. D. Cohen, 'Crossing the Boundary and Becoming a Jew' (1989), *The Beginnings of Jewishness* (Berkeley: University of California, 1999) 140-74; E. P. Sanders, 'Jewish Association with Gentiles and Galatians 2.11-14', in R. T. Fortna and B. R. Gaventa, eds., *Studies in Paul and John,* J. L. Martyn FS (Nashville: Abingdon, 1990) 170-88; Segal, *Paul* 231-33 ('there is no law in rabbinic literature that prevents a Jew from eating with a gentile'); P. Borgen, '"Yes", "No", "How Far?": The Participation of Jews and Christians in Pagan Cults', in Engberg-Pedersen, ed., *Paul in His Hellenistic Context* 30-59; Barclay, *Jews in the Mediterranean Diaspora* 434-37; Zetterholm, *Formation* 149-55 ('social intercourse

noted, for example, Josephus observes that in Syria many judaizing Gentiles had become 'mixed up' (literally) with the Jews (*War* 2.463).[71] The fact that many Gentiles 'judaized' must have made possible substantial association between such Gentiles and the local Jews.[72] And the Jews of Caesarea who commended Cornelius so highly (10.22) must have had some association with him. But the principle was nevertheless a basic item of Jewish identity — the fundamental conviction that Israel as a nation had been chosen by God and therefore was required to keep itself separate from other nations to maintain its holiness before the Lord.[73] And the testing point again and again was the meal table, the main expression of hospitality or friendship and the principal occasion for the transmission of impurity.[74]

The point is, then, that Peter had recognized the close correlation of the clean/unclean food laws and the separateness of Jew and Gentile (as clearly spelled out in Lev. 20.24-26).[75] But, more to the point, he had recognized the significance of his vision. As the law of clean and unclean served to embody and defend Israel's separateness, so its abolition meant that the time of Israel's holding itself separate from the nations was over.[76] If no animal was by nature unclean,

---

existed in almost every area of life with one general exception — marriage'). See also below, §27.4.

71. See above, §24.8a.

72. See again n. 70 above, and below, §27.4 at n. 251.

73. E.g., Lev. 20.24-26; Ezra 10.11; *Ep. Aris.* 139-42; Philo, *Mos.* 1.278. This was also the impression given to onlookers; both Diodorus Siculus (34.1.2) and Tacitus (*Hist.* 5.5.1-2) saw Jewish refusal to break bread with others as a mark of their hatred for the rest of the world (texts in *GLAJJ* 1.182-83; 2.19, 26).

74. Hence the assumption and accusation of 11.3; cf. Luke 7.34; 15.1-2; 19.7; Gal. 2.11-14.

75. Lev. 20.22-26:

> [22]You shall keep all my statutes and all my ordinances, and observe them, so that the land to which I bring you to settle in may not vomit you out. [23]You shall not follow the practices of the nations that I am driving out before you. Because they did all these things, I abhorred them. [24]But I have said to you: You shall inherit their land, and I will give it to you to possess, a land flowing with milk and honey. I am the Lord your God; *I have separated you from the peoples.* [25]You shall *therefore* make a distinction between the clean animal and the unclean, and between the unclean bird and the clean; you shall not bring abomination on yourselves by animal or by bird or by anything with which the ground teems, which I have set apart for you to hold unclean. [26]*You shall be holy to me; for I the Lord am holy, and I have separated you from the other peoples to be mine.*

C. Wahlen, 'Peter's Vision and Conflicting Definitions of Purity', *NTS* 51 (2005) 505-18, does not consider Lev. 20.22-26 or its significance for the episode.

76. See also Bauckham, 'Peter, James, and the Gentiles' 104-106, with reference also to *1 Enoch* 85–90 (more fully 102-16). In wondering 'whether Luke has given the vision a mean-

then neither could any human being as such be so designated. Peter was now free to deal with Cornelius as he would have dealt with any fellow Jew.

In short, the gulf which Peter had had to cross was not the vertical one between God and humanity (hence Luke's emphasis on Cornelius's piety) but the horizontal one between Jew and Gentile. The breakdown of the ethnic/religious boundary round Israel was indispensable and integral to the breakthrough of the gospel to the nations at large. The success of God's plan for 'all the families of the earth' (3.25) involved a redefinition of Israel's own identity insofar as it was defined by separation from Gentiles. It was this process of redefinition in which Peter found himself.

Here again we can enjoy the high quality and dramatic character of Luke's story-telling without finding it necessary to deduce from the quality and character that the story has been contrived from start to finish or in its central message. Luke brings his art and skill to the story, but we can almost certainly take from it that Peter traced his openness to mission among Gentiles, as also attested in Gal. 2.6-9, 12a, to some such revelation. Paul attests a more radical turn-about and attributes it equally to a 'revelation' (Gal. 1.12, 16). If Peter's protest in Acts 10.14 is at all soundly based, then it would have equally required a revelation to turn him around.[77] Luke tells the story with all his story-telling artifice, but it was a good story to start with, and one whose significance deserved to be brought out in such a fitting way.

26.4. The Acceptance of Cornelius

The story is only half told. So far, we have seen the removal of the barrier which had prevented Peter from even conceiving of the possibility that the gospel might be for a Gentile. Now Peter was authorized to offer the gospel to Gentile Cornelius as freely as he had to Jerusalem residents. The fuller, climactic mani-

---

ing different from that which it originally bore', Barrett (*Acts* 1.494, 497, 509, 516; cf. Wilson, *Luke and the Law* 68-70) is typical of those who have missed the vital link between unclean animals and unclean persons which Lev. 20.22-26 indicates, and who have thus failed to appreciate the mind-set whose breakthrough is fundamental to the story which Luke received; the critique applies also particularly to Dibelius, *Studies* 112, 118; and Conzelmann, *Apg.* 61-62 (cf. Haenchen, *Acts* 361-62; Lüdemann, *Early Christianity* 126-27, 131-32). That the tie between food as unclean and people as unclean was thus broken did not necessarily signify for Luke that the basic food laws could be lightly ignored (Acts 15.20, 29; 21.25) (cf. Jervell, *Apg.* 306, 316-17; in response to Haenchen, *Acts* 361-62).

77. Lüdemann recognizes the point ironically when he observes that Peter's departure from eating with Gentiles in Gal. 2.12 'would have required the revelation' (*Early Christianity* 132).

festation of God's purpose in Christ could now be opened to Gentiles for their participation in it if they sought it.

This second half of the story also falls into two parts — the speech of Peter and the pouring out of the Spirit on Cornelius and his companions.

a. Peter's Speech and the Theological Tensions (Acts 10.34-43)

I have already analyzed the speech in some detail (§21.3c). Here it is appropriate to focus on the theological tensions which it reveals.

The opening words — 'I truly understand that God shows no partiality, but in every nation anyone who fears him and does what is right is acceptable to him' (10.34-35) — summarize the principal lesson that Peter learned from his recent revelatory experience. Even if the verses are to be attributed to Luke's composition, they highlight the theological tensions which the new understanding of the good news of Jesus was setting up. For the implication of the revelation Peter had received was that the statement of God's impartiality, as in Deut. 10.17, extends to his regard for Gentile as well as Jew. To the impartial God, what makes a person acceptable is not a matter of ethnic heritage or nationality but reverence of God and doing what is right.[78] The insight, of course, stands in some tension with the axiom of Israel's election, and with the emphasis on Israel's set-apartness from the (other) nations. But Peter was not the first, nor was he the last, to experience it within Judaism.[79] So this is the language of the liberated Jew, willing now to recognize that the God-fearer, the one who fears God (10.2), is as acceptable to God as the Jew,[80] without meeting any further stipulation of the law (circumcision in particular). The national boundary round Israel which had hitherto functioned also as a religious boundary had become irrelevant 'in the presence of God'. In other words, the God-fearing Gentile is as ready to receive the blessing which comes through the name of Jesus and the Spirit of God as the God-fearing Jew.

But was Cornelius 'acceptable' to God or already 'accepted' by him? The Greek of 10.35 could have either meaning. The key is the recognition that 'fearing God' and 'doing what is right' (literally 'working righteousness') are classic expressions of what is expected of God's people, of what membership of God's covenant involves.[81] The issue then which Peter confronted is this: if a Gentile

---

78. This is one of the points where Peter comes very close to Paul (Rom. 2.6-11); see further below, §33 at n. 106.

79. Already in Amos 9.7; Jonah; Matt. 3.8-9.

80. Cf. Deut. 10.12; Ps. 2.11; Prov. 1.7; Mal. 4.2.

81. Cf., e.g., Ps. 15.2; Ezek. 18.5-9; Heb. 11.33; James 1.20. See also discussion in Barrett, *Acts* 1.519-21.

displays the spirituality to be expected of the devout member of God's people, how can it be doubted that he or she is acceptable to God? For Luke (and Peter) the test of whether 'acceptable' means 'accepted' would be the gift of the Spirit to Cornelius. The key point, however, is that Cornelius was acceptable to God *even as a Gentile,* and his full acceptance into the messianic Jewish community depended only on his believing and receiving the Spirit, *as a Gentile,* that is, without becoming a proselyte.

The tension continues through the speech. The first two texts drawn on[82] seem to have Israel primarily in view as beneficiaries: to Ps. 107.20 ('he sent out his word and healed them') is added the phrase 'sent to the sons of Israel' (Acts 10.36); and in Isa. 52.7 ('. . . those who preach peace') the proclamation is to Zion as such. This brings out still more the tension implicit in 10.34-35.[83] A blessing focused *on* Israel is becoming a blessing channeled *through* Israel. The identity of the people of promise is being broadened beyond the boundaries of Israel. This is the reconfiguration in Peter's self-understanding which Luke intended the whole episode to express.

The tension is heightened still more by the phrase 'He is Lord of all' (10.36).[84] It was a tension bound up in Israel's own monotheism: if God is one, then he is God of *all* peoples, of Gentile as well as Jew.[85] But the 'Lord' at this point, once again, is clearly Jesus.[86] The message here is twofold. First, the Lord God who had commanded Cornelius (10.33) had shared his lordship with Jesus Christ.[87] Second, this lordship of Christ had brought home to Peter that the lordship of God extended over all, Gentile as well as Jew. In this phrase, then, is encapsulated the redefinition of God as well as of his purpose which, within a few decades, was to begin to pull Christianity apart from the Judaism which shared its common heritage.

All that contributes to the tensions is not explicit or obvious in the speech. It may even be that Luke was not alive to them all. They arise out of the situation in which the speech is set, and out of the interplay of the situation with some of the details of the speech. In other words, Luke's presentation may well reflect, not simply the archetypal situation which posed such questions to the young sect as it bumped up against Judaism's traditional borders, but also the texts and theological reflections which the situation drew from the first disciples — indeed, possibly from Peter himself.

The rest of the speech in the main follows the more characteristic lines and

82. See §21.3c above.
83. As already in 2.39, 3.25 and 4.10, 12.
84. For contemporary parallels see Fitzmyer, *Acts* 463-64.
85. Paul exploited this tension to good effect in Rom. 3.29-30.
86. Cf. 2.21, 36; Rom. 10.12-13.
87. This point was already made in 2.21, 34-36.

emphases of the earlier Acts speeches (10.37-43)[88] — Luke's way, presumably, of bringing out the degree of continuity between the Jerusalem beginnings and the breakthrough from traditional perspectives which he was now unfolding.

b. The Gentile Pentecost (Acts 10.44-48)

The climax of the episode, and what resolves the tensions just outlined, is that the Holy Spirit 'fell upon all who heard the word' (10.44). Here the primacy of the Spirit as the mark of God's acceptance is plain beyond dispute. The implication is clearly that Cornelius had believed (10.43; so explicitly in 11.17 and 15.7, 9). The coming of the Spirit awaited no human regulation or ordering. At the same time, baptism in the name of Jesus Christ is not dispensed with (though not mentioned in the sequel, 11.15-18). In fact, it will not be accidental that the repeated emphases on Cornelius's reception of the Spirit (10.44-47) are bracketed by the double reference to the name of Jesus (10.43, 48). The two primary identity markers of the new movement are interdependent. And thus Cornelius moves from being acceptable to being accepted, and the decisive breakthrough of God's blessing to the nations has taken place. The acceptability of the God-fearer to the God of Israel has become the acceptance of anyone who believes in God through Jesus.

Those with Peter are described as 'the faithful' _(pistoi)_ rather than as 'believers' _(pisteusantes/pisteuontes)_[89] — literally, 'the faithful from circumcision' (10.45). Thereby Luke signals that they represent that portion of the church which continued to regard circumcision as the most distinctive feature of the covenant people (cf. 7.8) and who would thus be most convinced that the fundamental separation between Jew and Gentile marked by circumcision had to be maintained.[90] 'Those of (the) circumcision' were faithful, loyal to Israel's basic calling to be holy and separate, eager to maintain its identity markers and boundaries. The fact that even they were convinced of the Spirit's coming upon the Caesarean Gentiles meant that the fact of the outpoured Spirit was beyond question. The point is reinforced in the sequel: even 'those of the circumcision' who were critical of Peter's eating with uncircumcised Gentiles (11.2-3) were silenced by Peter's retelling of what had happened and praised God, saying, 'Then God has given even to the Gentiles the repentance that leads to life' (11.18).

A particular feature of these three verses (10.44-46) is the emphasis on the

---

88. See again §21.3c above.

89. See above, §20.1(5).

90. Cf. 11.2; 15.1, 5; Gal. 2.12. Paul could distinguish Jews and Gentiles simply as 'the circumcision' and 'the uncircumcision' (Rom. 2.25-26; Gal. 2.7). See also below, §27.2a.

visible impact of the Spirit. The Spirit 'fell upon' them (as in 8.16); something 'hit' them; there was a visible impact of invisible power. The effect was so obvious that those with Peter could not deny or doubt it. The particular evidence mentioned is their speaking in tongues and extolling God. The double echo of the experience and event of Pentecost[91] is obviously deliberate. What happened to Cornelius and his companions was manifestly no different from what had happened to the first disciples on the day of Pentecost. How could 'the faithful from circumcision' affirm the one and deny the other? They couldn't.

It is Peter himself who draws the inevitable conclusion — 'Can anyone withhold the water for baptizing these men who have received the Holy Spirit just as we have?' (10:47). God has so clearly accepted them; the parallel with Pentecost is reiterated ('just as we did' . . .). So how can we refuse them? This could not be dismissed as arbitrary or mindless ecstasy. God's hand in it all was beyond dispute. The question (10.47) is the same as that posed by the eunuch in 8.37: who can forbid what God has so clearly ratified? And the answer is the same: no one. The order here is exceptional: the gift of the Spirit preceded baptism. Luke clearly wants his readers to understand that God had to give so clear an indication of his will, otherwise even Peter might have hesitated to take such a step in the case of Gentiles without first requiring them to be circumcised. At the same time, the prior bestowal of the Spirit did not lead Peter to the conclusion that baptism could or should be dispensed with (10.47). Baptism 'in the name of Jesus Christ' (10.48) closes the circle already drawn with the proclamation of belief in him and of forgiveness of sins in his name and with the outpouring of the Spirit. Where the gift of the Spirit had ratified God's acceptance of Cornelius, now the church of Jews and circumcised must ratify their acceptance of these Gentiles by baptism. As usual the baptism proceeds at once, without further instruction or delay.

Of course Luke has made much of this event, by telling it in very dramatic terms, and by telling it twice. The coming of the Spirit in a very tangible way, with physical manifestations, is very much in accord with his own conception of the Spirit and of the Spirit's working. But something like this must have happened if the presuppositions and traditions of centuries were to be so quickly overturned in the initial expansion of the new messianic sect. The scene is just what we would have had to deduce anyway by reading Gal. 2.7-9 with 3.2-5. It was the Spirit coming so manifestly on Paul's own Galatian converts which put the matter of their acceptance by God beyond dispute too (3.2-5). It was such clear evidence of God's accepting grace to Gentiles which equally convinced the

---

91. 'Poured out' — 2.17-18, 33 and 10.45; speaking in tongues and saying great things of God — 2.4, 11 and 10.46; 'the Holy Spirit fell upon them just as it had upon us at the beginning' (11.15); 'God gave them the same gift that he gave to us' (11.17).

more conservative Jerusalem leadership that Paul's message was the gospel and that he had not been running in vain (2.2, 6-9).[92] So even if the full significance of this episode was not seen at first, even if Luke gave it an archetypal significance it may not have been seen to possess before (cf. Acts 15.7-11), it is still likely that Luke's account is based on good basic tradition.[93] Otherwise, it is as likely that the breakthrough at Antioch would have been met with more immediate hostility and Paul's own mission would have resulted in a far more serious split within the new movement than was the case. Peter's conversion of Cornelius was a — perhaps the most — significant watershed in the early days of the new movement, but it could only happen because Peter himself had been converted!

c. The Acknowledgment of God's Initiative (Acts 11.1-18)

It is important to appreciate that 11.1-18 is not simply a story-teller's self-indulgence in repeating a dramatic tale. The retelling serves a different purpose. It is as much about the acceptance of *Peter* and what he had done as it is about the acceptance of *Cornelius* and what he represented. The second account of the events which climaxed in Cornelius being baptized in the Spirit (11.4-17) is presented as Peter's defence of his own conduct (11.3). And the charge levelled against him is not that he had baptized uncircumcised Gentiles but that he had eaten with them (11.3). *It was Peter's initial action of acceptance, as a Jew of a Gentile, which was the primary issue.* Thus the second account of the epochal event reflects the two stages of the first account. As the first account hung on the conversion of Peter, on the fundamental questioning of Jewish 'separateness' from other nations, on the abandonment of the presumption that non-Jews *per se* are unacceptable to God, so the second account hangs on the Jerusalem apostles' acceptance of Peter in his new conviction and consequent action. Once again Luke underlines just how important were not only the events at Caesarea themselves but also the acceptance of them by the Jerusalem apostles. Thus the unity of the new movement and its continuity with its previous heritage, even through the process of transformation of previously cherished and fundamental beliefs, is maintained.

If the basic outline of the events narrated in ch. 10 was derived from early memories of the church at Caesarea, then the event must have occasioned the sort of misgivings as are expressed in 11.3. It follows also that Peter's unexpected initiative in this case would have had to gain wider acceptance within the Jerusalem church. Whether that approval was of an exception to the rule, or of a principle of

---

92. See also below, §27.3d.

93. 'The table fellowship between him [Cornelius] and the Jews is not the decisive factor, for the uncleanness is overcome through the pneumatic and visionary context' (Wander, *Trennungsprozesse* 282).

more universal significance, would probably have been unclear in the event. So it is not surprising that the issue arises again in 15.1, 5. Luke himself concludes the retelling with a clear indication that a crucial precedent had been recognized (11.18). But no doubt there were others among the apostles and brothers who saw it only as an exception.

26.5. Anxious Times under Herod Agrippa I (Acts 12)

Our knowledge of Peter through the 30s and 40s is also limited by the tunnel period. In fact, Luke's account of Christianity's beginnings through the 30s and early 40s only entwines with non-Christian history of the period at two points: (1) the references to Gamaliel in Acts 5.34 and 22.3[94] and (2) the fuller reference to King Herod Agrippa I in ch. 12. But this means that Luke has chosen to pass over a number of episodes in Syro-Palestine which he could readily have brought in to reinforce one or more of his themes.

a. The Missing Episodes

Of episodes which Luke might have alluded to, either because they offered a fitting lesson for his audience(s) or to help provide verisimilitude to his narrative (cf. Luke 3.1), the following are the most important:[95]

- the brief war between Herod Antipas and the Nabatean Aretas in 36 and the abortive Roman campaign against Aretas in 37 (Josephus, *Ant.* 18.113-15,120-26);
- Pilate's massacre of Samaritans and his consequent downfall in 36-37 (*Ant.* 18.85-89);
- Caiaphas's deposition as high priest by the Syrian legate, Vitellius, on his visit to Jerusalem in 37 (*Ant.* 18.90-95); and
- Caligula's long-running attempt (39-41) to have his effigy set up in the Temple in Jerusalem, provoking intense and substantial protests from Jews within Israel, general alarm in Jewish circles everywhere, and collateral attacks on diaspora Jewish communities, particularly Alexandria and Antioch.[96]

94. See above, §23 nn. 13, 14. But Luke does not name Aretas in his recounting Saul's departure from Damascus (2 Cor. 11.32).

95. Fuller details in Schürer, *History* 1.350, 386-88, 394-97; see also Hengel and Schwemer, *Paul* 181.

96. Josephus, *War* 2.184-203; *Ant.* 18.257-88; see also Philo, *Legat.* 197-338; on the Antioch unrest see above, §24 n. 236.

None of these, of course, was integral to the story Luke was telling. But presumably they did not leave the earliest Christian communities unaffected or unscathed.[97]

Particularly relevant is the crisis which Caligula's provocation must have caused within Jewish communities generally.[98] As already noted, a plausible suggestion is that the tradition in Mark 13, subsequently used by Mark in writing his Gospel, took much of its enduring shape in response to that crisis. The talk of '"the abomination of desolation" set up where it ought not to be' (Mark 13.14) could well be an allusion to Caligula's sacrilegious project, in echo of the reference in Dan. 12.11 to the heathen altar set up in the Jerusalem Temple by the Seleucids in 167 BCE.[99] If so, we may readily deduce that the crisis occasioned by Caligula's command ratcheted up the eschatological fervour among the members of the Jesus sect within these Jewish communities, an intensity of apocalyptic anticipation which is still evident in Mark 13.5-27.[100] Such fervour might explain why Luke has not referred to the episode; in his re-use of the Mark 13 tradition he has transformed Mark 13.14 into a reference to the siege of Jerusalem (Luke 21.20) and indicated that a longer timescale is to be envisaged before the return of the Son of Man (21.24-28). But unless we assume that the earliest Christians in the land of Israel were totally disassociated from the political stresses and other crises of the time, we must judge it likely that their expectations regarding the immediate future, including the coming (again) of their Lord Jesus, reflected these crises in at least some measure. The detail and intensity of Mark 13.5-27 well express the anxieties and hopes that must have been experienced at that time.[101] Luke's silence on the subject leaves a tantalizing hole in our knowledge of Christianity in the making.

---

97. According to the unreliable Malalas, the victims included 'many Jews and Galileans' (text in Levinskaya, *BAFCS* 5.131-32), where 'Galileans' may well reflect an early name for Christians which crops up every so often (see above, §20 n. 68).

98. Already referred to in *Jesus Remembered* 296; Tacitus notes that Caligula's order would have resulted in a full-scale uprising had he not been killed (*Hist.* 5.9.2; see *GLAJJ* 2.21, 29, 51); see further N. H. Taylor, 'Popular Opposition to Caligula in Jewish Palestine', *JSJ* 32 (2001) 54-70. 'It is all the more striking that these events under Caligula, which intensified the apocalyptic fever especially in Eretz Israel and in Syria, were not worth mentioning in the letters of Paul, in Luke or in the Gospels. For not only were Alexandria and a little later the mother country affected by them, but the whole Diaspora, especially in the eastern part of the empire, was shaken' (Hengel and Schwemer, *Paul* 182).

99. 1 Macc. 1.41-64; 2 Macc. 6.1-11; Josephus, *Ant.* 12.253.

100. See above, §21 n. 293.

101. See also *Jesus Remembered* 417-19.

b. Herod Agrippa I (10 BCE–44 CE)

Herod Agrippa I is one of the most fascinating figures to cross the stage of Jewish history at this period. Son of Aristobulus and grandson of Herod the Great, he was named after Marcus Agrippa, Augustus's close friend and deputy in the East. As a boy he had been sent to Rome to be educated. There he had been befriended by the imperial family and moved for a long time in their circles. Towards the end of Tiberias's reign he had made known his support for Caligula and was imprisoned by Tiberius in consequence. On ascending the imperial throne, Caligula had him released at once and continued to show him special favours; in the crisis caused by Caligula's command to have a statue of himself erected in the Temple, Agrippa was able to trade on his close friendship with Caligula and to persuade him to desist from the foolhardy enterprise.[102] And subsequently (41) Agrippa played a significant role in securing the succession of Claudius.[103] For Jews to have had such a representative, however 'secular' he may have been during his time in Rome,[104] must have helped sustain the generally favourable attitude of the Roman authorities to their Jewish subjects.

On his ascent to the imperial throne, Caligula had conferred on Agrippa the former tetrarchies of Philip and of Lysanias, together with the title of king.[105] Subsequently the tetrarchy of Herod Antipas was joined to Agrippa's realm (Josephus, *War* 2.182-83), and when Claudius became emperor, he added Judea and Samaria, so that for the first time since Herod the Great's death (4 BCE) the kingdom of Israel was united under one ruler.[106] Soon thereafter Agrippa was able to intercede effectively with Claudius on behalf of the Jews of Alexandria (*Ant.* 19.279, 288).

On his return to Jerusalem in 41, Agrippa immediately set out to demonstrate his piety, and by so doing won the support of the Pharisees in particular. 'On entering Jerusalem, he offered sacrifices of thanksgiving, omitting none of the ritual enjoined by our law. Accordingly he also arranged for a very considerable number of Nazirites to be shorn' (*Ant.* 19.293-94); that is, he probably covered the costs of fulfilling their vow (cf. Acts 21.24).[107] 'He enjoyed residing in

---

102. Philo, *Legat.* 261-333; Josephus, *Ant.* 18.289-304.

103. Josephus, *War* 2.206-13; *Ant.* 19.236-47.

104. His extravagance had brought him into severe debt (Josephus, *Ant.* 18.143-67). More detail in Schürer, *History* 1.442-45; Smallwood, *The Jews under Roman Rule* 187-93, also 196-97. For a full biographical treatment see D. R. Schwartz, *Agrippa I: The Last King of Judaea* (Tübingen: Mohr Siebeck, 1990).

105. Josephus, *War* 2.181; *Ant.* 18.237-39.

106. Josephus, *War* 2.214-17; *Ant.* 19.274-75. But presumably none of the earliest believers saw in this the answer to the earlier question: 'Lord, is this the time when you will restore the kingdom to Israel?' (Acts 1.6).

107. See also §34 at n. 19 below.

Jerusalem and did so constantly; and he scrupulously observed the traditions of his people. He neglected no rite of purification, and no day passed for him without the prescribed sacrifice' (*Ant.* 19.331).[108]

Agrippa's reign impinges on the Acts account of the Jesus movement at three points.

c. The Execution of James (Acts 12.1-2)

One of the most surprising elements in Luke's narrative is his reference to Agrippa's execution of James, son of Zebedee:

> [1]About that time Herod the king laid his hands on some of those who belonged to the church so as to harm them. [2]He killed James, the brother of John, with the sword.

The surprise, of course, is that the reference should be so brief. Apart from 1.13, this is the only reference to James, brother of John, in Acts.[109] Yet such other indications as there are, all suggest that James was one of the leaders of the earliest Jerusalem church. With Peter and his brother John he is remembered as forming a kind of inner circle within the twelve.[110] And presumably Agrippa targetted James precisely because he was one of the new sect's leaders. Why, then, does Luke pass over his execution so cursorily? The contrast with the amount of attention he devoted to Stephen's lynching (Acts 6–7) is hard to ignore. And the contrast with the space Luke devotes to the various trials and tribulations of Peter in Jerusalem, including those inflicted by Agrippa, is no less striking (Acts 4–5; 12.3-19). Even less notice is given to (the rest of) the 'some' who had violent hands laid on them (roughed up by Agrippa's henchmen?).[111]

One obvious answer, of course, could be that Luke had no fuller report or recollection available to him of that episode.[112] But such a solution simply raises

---

108. 'They were the golden days again for Pharisaism . . . which is why Josephus and the Talmud are unanimous in his praise' (Schürer, *History* 1.446); for fuller detail see the whole section (1.445-54). Smallwood is dismissive: 'superficial piety', 'only a façade', 'as much a pagan at heart as the rest of his family' (*Jews* 194).

109. On the unwarranted suggestion that the original text read '. . . killed James and John his brother', see Bruce, *Acts* 280-81.

110. Mark 3.16-17; 5.37; 9.2; 14.33; Acts 1.13.

111. An epitome of Philip of Side (ca. 430 CE) includes the report that 'Papias in his second book says that John the Divine and James his brother were killed by Jews'; but there is too little supporting evidence that John was martyred at this early date; see further Lake and Cadbury, *Beginnings* 4.133-34; Bruce, *Acts* 280-81; Lüdemann, *Early Christianity* 142-43; Hengel and Schwemer, *Paul* 247.

112. Jervell, *Apg.* 337-38.

the further question, Why so? Why did the Jerusalem church retain no such reminiscence or tradition, particularly of James's death? Was James not such a prominent figure after all, or possibly a more controversial figure? But even so, as the first of the reconstituted twelve to be martyred, one would have thought his death called for greater notice and more comment than Luke has provided. Luke's silence at this point remains an unanswered puzzle. The one more positive corollary is that Luke did not feel free or choose to elaborate a far too skimpy death notice.[113] The brevity of his reference may therefore point more to Luke's conscientiousness as a historian, in recording only the bare information that he had been able to pick up.[114] But the character and role of James, and the regard in which he was held by his fellow believers, remain an enigma. Caught up in the obscurity is the issue of why the vacancy caused by James was not filled, as had been done in the case of Judas (1.15-26). One possibility is that the symbolism of 'the twelve' was already slackening and that the likelihood of deaths happening before the Christ's return had already become accepted.[115]

Agrippa's motive in so arbitrarily executing James may be deduced from Josephus's account of Agrippa's devotion during his residence in Jerusalem.[116] The new sect (especially Stephen and the Hellenists) had already given evidence of disregard for the Temple. And despite any tolerance displayed by Gamaliel (Acts 5.33-39), Saul the persecutor no doubt represented a faction within the Pharisees who were strongly opposed to the new sect. Distinctions between 'Hebrews' and 'Hellenists' (6.1) may well have been lost on someone anxious to display his devotion to the law and the traditions of his people. It is not necessary to infer any particular adverse turn in the relations of the new sect with the Temple authorities and the Pharisees as the occasion for Agrippa's action. It would have been sufficient that Agrippa was looking for opportunities to signal his devotion to both his religion and his nation.[117] Such a hypothesis fits well with the indica-

---

113. Subsequent tradition made good the defect: according to Eusebius, *HE* 2.9.2, Clement of Alexandria knew a tradition that the officer in charge of James was so impressed by James's testimony that he became a Christian himself and then was beheaded with James. Haenchen suggests that Luke played down the martyrdom of James in order to focus attention more fully on Peter and his miraculous liberation (*Acts* 389).

114. No one doubts the historicity of Luke's report.

115. Though, note again Zwiep's observation: 'Matthias was not chosen because Judas had died, but because he had become an apostate' (*Judas* 179).

116. The year of Agrippa's move against James and Peter would therefore be 41 or 42 (Riesner, *Paul's Early Period* 118-21). Schnabel suggests that for his strike against James, Agrippa could look to the precedent of Claudius's action against Jews who proclaimed Jesus as Messiah in Rome (*Mission* 719), but there is no indication that the action of Claudius in 41 (Cassius Dio 60.6.6) was directed against Jews who believed in Jesus as Messiah (see also Schnabel 806-807); contrast Suetonius's report (§21.1d) in reference to 49, and see §28 at n. 33 below.

117. 'His actions in regard to James and Peter may be regarded as part of his role as the

tions that Agrippa saw himself as a leader who could free Israel from Roman rule.[118] In other words, the questions hanging over the new Jesus sect may have provided Agrippa with sufficient reason to single them out for exemplary treatment, demonstrating both his readiness to stamp on any deviation from Israel's traditional practices and his own qualities as a leader capable of prompt and decisive action.

The cursoriness of Luke's account at least seems to mirror the abruptness of Agrippa's summary execution of James. No trial or even hearing is indicated or suggested. Rather what seems to be in view is the ruthless removal ('taking out') of a possible dissident by a remorseless ruler. As we shall see, the acquisition of the territory and power which had not been known since Herod the Great seems to have given Agrippa visions of restoring Israel's greatness. And he would have been well aware that his grandfather had secured his kingdom and authority by acts of similarly pre-emptive ruthlessness. His uncle Herod Antipas had been able to order the execution of John the Baptist with similar arbitrariness (Mark 6.17-29 pars.). That James was executed by beheading ('with a sword') may also indicate that Agrippa saw, or chose to portray, the new sect as something of a threat to his political ambitions.[119] At the same time, the fact that Josephus makes no mention of the episode suggests that such an arbitrary act need occasion no surprise or comment; the Jesus sect was not yet prominent enough for Josephus to notice it.

d. The Imprisonment of Peter (Acts 12.3-19)

Luke pays more heed to the lesser matter of Agrippa's action against Peter. Seeing that the pre-emptive strike against James had gone down well, Agrippa apparently decided that further action against the new sect would increase his favour with the people, or a major faction therein. Luke refers simply to 'the Jews', with a gener-

---

"good Jew" who would naturally be concerned to put down a heretical sect' (Barrett, *Acts* 1.574) — though 'heretical' is an anachronism. Agrippa would no doubt have been aware that his less than honourable earlier escapades (see n. 102 above) were well enough known in Jerusalem. See further Hengel and Schwemer, *Paul* 246-50, who emphasize that Agrippa's motivation was 'above all to secure and keep the good will of the Sadducean priestly party of the nobility who were the political leaders' (249). That James's and Peter's openness to a Gentile mission was a factor (Riesner, *Paul's Early Period* 122-23) is more questionable, but it could help to explain why James the brother of Jesus was not targeted — perhaps because of his already known devotion to the traditional ways; see further A. M. Schwemer, 'Verfolger und Verfolgte bei Paulus. Die Auswirkungen der Verfolgung durch Agrippa I. auf die paulinische Mission', in Becker and Pilhofer, eds., *Biographie und Persönlichkeit des Paulus* 169-91 (here 177-81; cf. 182-91).

118. See further below, §26.5e.
119. Cf. Barrett, *Acts* 1.574-75.

alisation which has since given the impression of anti-Judaism.[120] But this reference to 'the Jews' is the first in his narrative to have a slightly odd ring — slightly odd, since those subject to Agrippa's arbitrary action were also Jews.[121] Perhaps we should see in this an indication of a change of mood among the inhabitants of Jerusalem, of a groundswell of popular opinion, provoked by Caligula's attempted sacrilege and now much quickened both by the reunification of Herod's kingdom (the kingdom of David) under a single ruler and by the evident signs of Agrippa's piety. Inevitably these events must have rekindled dormant hopes of many Jews for a restoration of Israel's sovereignty. That Luke saw Agrippa's decision to act against the leadership of the young sect in this light is strongly implied by Luke's inclusion of the account of Agrippa's frightful death (Acts 12.20-23), an account which otherwise hardly had relevance to the life of the young church. The implication is that the whole of Acts 12 reflects a mounting political crisis occasioned by Agrippa's actions and only resolved by his death.[122]

In which case two important corollaries may be drawn. First, that the phase of persecution to which the Jesus movement was subjected in the early 40s was more political than religious/theological in motivation; the 'way' followed by the Jesus-believers who remained in Jerusalem may not have been particularly different or controversial in the eyes of most traditionalists, but in a situation of mounting national fervour any dissidence could be seen, at popular level not least, as some kind of threat to the bandwagon which was beginning to roll. The other corollary is that in this episode we begin to see what was to become a growing political and nationalist sentiment within Judea which was bound to affect the attitudes of traditionalist Jews towards the new sect; the latter's claims for Jesus as Lord would seem to cut across any nationalist aspirations, and any deviation from loyalty to the traditions and customs which bound the nation together would inevitably be regarded with suspicion.

The episode involving Peter is a classic example of what almost amounts to a distinctive genre of 'miraculous prison escapes'.[123] Peter is arrested, even though during the festival of unleavened bread (Acts 12.3), that is, during the seven days following Passover (Exod. 12.15-20).[124] He is imprisoned under

120. So particularly J. T. Sanders, *The Jews in Luke-Acts* (Philadelphia: Fortress, 1987).

121. The earlier references to 'the Jews' had in view 'the Jews' living in Damascus (9.22, 23) or were appropriate generalisations (Jews = Judeans) in a speech to a Gentile living outside the ancient territory of Judea (10.22, 39).

122. See again further §26.5e below.

123. Weiser, *Apg.* 1.284-85; Barrett, *Acts* 1.580, 581-82; Weaver, *Plots of Epiphany* 149-72; and see above, §23 n. 177. The episode provides one of the parallels between Peter and Paul (cf. 16.25-40).

124. See further Fitzmyer, *Acts* 487. Luke could refer to the whole period as 'the Passover', as in Luke 22.1 and here (Acts 12.4).

close guard (four squads of four soldiers each!) (Acts 12.4), chained between two soldiers (12.6), while the church prays fervently for him (12.5). The night before he is to be produced to the people (for trial or execution), an angel of the Lord appears and a light shines in the cell; Peter is awakened, and his chains fall off (12.7).[125] He rises, dresses, and, led by the angel, passes the several guards, before finding the outer gate opening of its own accord (12.8-10) — not a vision, but really happening (12.9). The angel having left him, Peter goes to the house of Mary, where many believers were gathered and were praying (12.12). An amusing sequence of confusion and misunderstanding follows: the maid recognizing Peter's voice but failing to open the gate, those inside refusing to believe her, and Peter left standing still knocking (12.13-16). Resolution follows, with the regular note of amazement, Peter's narration of 'how the Lord had brought him out of the prison', and Peter's departure 'to another place' (12.17).[126] Equally characteristic of the genre is the confusion caused to those who had acted against Peter, the final savagery of Agrippa sentencing the inefficient guards to death (12.18-19).

This presumably is the story much as Luke heard it. It is not necessary to envisage it being told to him with just these details. The story itself may have been told and retold (performed) in various versions — much as Luke retold the story of Saul's conversion in three different versions. What we can say is that Luke's own retelling shows the hand of a master story-teller (Luke's or another's):

- The drama of the main scene is compelling narratively and visually — the timing (the night before Peter's trial/execution), the closeness of his imprisonment (chains and several guards), both heightening the miraculous character of the release, the chiaroscuro of the angel appearing and the light shining in the dark cell, the chains falling off and the outer gate opening of its own accord.
- Luke (probably) adds a note typical of his own understanding of the tangibility of such heavenly intervention in human affairs — what was happening was real *(alēthes),* not a vision.[127]

---

125. Haenchen notes that 'the taciturn angel has to prod him [Peter] in the ribs . . . to wake him. "Get up, quick!" he says. Now this shows that the account did not originate with Luke, who always has heavenly beings use dignified and, as far as possible, biblical language (cf. the angel's word to Cornelius in 10.4)' (*Acts* 390).

126. Unusually among translations NRSV reads the 'he' of 12.19 as referring to Peter — 'he went down from Judea to Caesarea and stayed there' (12.19). But the Greek is more naturally read as referring to Agrippa, as almost all agree.

127. Lane Fox notes how often visions of the gods are described as 'not in a dream but in waking reality' (*Pagans and Christians* 138, 144, 150-51).

- The sequel with the maid Rhoda is a wonderful story-telling device, allowing the tension of the mysterious escape to be dissipated in the amusement
of Rhoda's confusion, Peter's frustration and the company's amazement.

The story must have been told in these or similar terms over and over again in the
gatherings of the little groups of Jesus-believers in Jerusalem and Judea. Luke
probably heard it several times before he made it his own.

What are we to make of it? It is hard to penetrate through the story-teller's
art (and artifice) to the event which first set the story going. We need not assume
that the artifice must be *later* embellishment of some much more straightforward
tale. On the contrary, I suspect that the story was being told/performed in some
such terms from earliest days.[128] There is no reason to doubt that Peter was imprisoned; it fits too closely in a historical sequence beginning with the execution
of James and ending with the death of Agrippa to leave much room for doubt;
and the final savagery against the guards (12.19) is also consistent with what we
know of the arbitrary powers exercised by rulers in these days. Again, the names
of Mary, John Mark and Rhoda and the location of the prayer meeting in the
(substantial) house of Mary were probably part of the earliest tellings of the
story, and one or other of those named may have provided some of the story's
content.[129] Finally, we may note that the final mysterious note of Peter's departure 'to another place' (12.17) was hardly Luke's contrivance (he locates Peter in
Jerusalem only three chapters later, 15.7-11); instead, it must be part of the score/
script which Luke inherited and may reflect the early formulation of the story
when it was still important to maintain secrecy about Peter's whereabouts.[130] Be-

128. 'The exegetes are all agreed that Luke took this story over without making any major alterations — its style is wholly alien to him, and he was right not to touch it' (Haenchen,
Acts 391); see also n. 123 above.

129. According to 1 Peter 5.13 John Mark was known to Peter, and according to Luke
John Mark was a companion of Paul, though not during any of the 'we' passages (Acts 12.25;
13.13; cf. Col. 4.10); in Phlm. 24 Mark and Luke are named together as Paul's fellow workers
(cf. 2 Tim. 4.11). Barrett refers to Acts 9.32-43 and observes that the 'the cycle of stories about
Peter evidently contained a number of names' (*Acts* 1.570).

130. For suggestions that he headed for Rome (cf. already Eusebius, *HE* 2.14.6) or Mesopotamia or Edessa, see Fitzmyer, *Acts* 489-90, with bibliography; Barrett, *Acts* 587. Haenchen
notes that since Wellhausen (1907), the 'other place' has usually been identified as Antioch
(*Acts* 386 n. 1); cf. Gal. 2.11; Wilckens thinks the towns on the Phoenician coast (Acts 9.32ff.)
are the most plausible reference (*Theologie* 1/2.257 n. 57). That Peter went to Rome at such an
early date (42, 43) is unlikely (see Bruce, *Acts* 287; Hengel and Schwemer, *Paul* 252 and
n. 1319; see also 256-57), though argued for by C. P. Thiede, *Simon Peter* (Exeter: Paternoster,
1986) 153-57 and considered sympathetically by Pesch, *Apg.* 1.368-69, and Schnabel, *Mission*
721-27, 801, 807. O. Cullmann, *Peter: Disciple, Apostle, Martyr* (London: SCM, ²1962),
whom one might have expected to sympathize with the view, summarizes his brief discussion

yond that it is hard to go, and we may have to be content simply with speaking of the mysterious circumstances of Peter's release from prison.[131] Luke perhaps made a point of recording the so-brief notice of James's execution, prior to the elaborate tale of Peter's deliverance, as a reminder that God's sovereign purpose embraces the unexplained tragedy as well as the unexpected turn for the better, and the word of God continues to advance through and beyond both (12.24).[132]

The episode functions in effect as the climax to the sequence of Peter's mission. Its significance for our appreciation of Christianity's beginnings is threefold:

1. Peter drops out from the Jerusalem scene. His final message on departure — 'Report these events to James and the brothers' (12.17) — could be taken as indicating the emergence to sole pre-eminence in the Jerusalem church of James the brother of Jesus, the first precursor of mono-episcopacy.[133]
2. The implication of 12.17, following as it does the account of the conversions of Peter and Cornelius, and in the light of Gal. 2.7-8, may well be that hereafter Peter established himself as a missionary, working for the most part away from Jerusalem, and probably more open to the developments happening in Antioch (11.20-21) and subsequently in Paul's mission (chs. 13–14) than many/most(?) of his fellow believing Jews who remained in Jerusalem (including James).[134]

---

simply: 'the wording does not permit the identification of the "other place" with Rome' (39). And the Protestant-Catholic collaborative volume *Peter in the New Testament,* edited by R. E. Brown, K. P. Donfried and J. Reumann (London: Chapman, 1974), is even more curt: 'There is no scientific support for this tradition, and it does not deserve serious discussion' (48 n. 114).

131. Lüdemann revives Baur's old proposal that 'Agrippa himself released Peter once the unpopularity of his action against James had become clear' (*Early Christianity* 145). Hengel and Schwemer speculate on the possibility that some Pharisaic sympathizers were able to engineer Peter's escape (*Paul* 470 n. 1315).

132. Barrett's questions — 'Were the lives of the soldiers of no consequence? Why should Peter be rescued but not James? Did the church not pray for James? Did those who were praying for Peter not believe that their prayer could be effective? (*Acts* 1.573) — are of course still relevant whether the story is historical or not.

133. In the later episode (five or six years later) involving both Peter and James (brother of Jesus) in Jerusalem, James is obviously understood to be chairman of the gathering (Acts 15.13-29). Paul agrees, in effect, by naming James as first of the three 'pillar apostles' — James, Cephas and John (Gal. 2.9). Similarly Bauckham, 'James and the Jerusalem Church' 434-36: 'The deliberately vague phrase "to another place" signals the fact that Peter's story, though unfinished, is of no further concern to the readers of Acts' (434); 'it is historically very credible that the persecution of Agrippa I (AD 43 or 44) was the point at which the Twelve ceased to be the leadership of the Jerusalem church' (439-41).

134. Cullmann, *Peter* 42. See further below, §35.

3. Not to be overlooked are the hints both of a growing nationalist fervour within Judea, incited by Agrippa, the king of Israel, establishing his residence in Jerusalem, and of a growing hostility to the Nazarean sect, some at least of whose members would presumably have been out of tune with the political manoeuverings which climaxed in Agrippa's downfall.

e. The Death of Agrippa (Acts 12.20-23)

If the story of Peter's escape from prison is a classic example of the 'miraculous prison escape' genre, even more classic is the story of Agrippa's death (in 44) as an example of divine retribution on human hubris. The story was well known, and Josephus's retelling of it is quite close to Luke's, though the two retellings reflect the story-tellers' different perspectives.

Agrippa soon began to flex his political muscles. He set about strengthening Jerusalem's fortifications 'on such a scale as, had it been completed, would have rendered ineffectual all the efforts of the Romans in the subsequent siege' (Josephus, *War* 2.218) but desisted when the Syrian governor reported his actions to Claudius and Claudius rebuked him (*Ant.* 19.326-27). He also began to develop links with other client kings of the region, thus further arousing the suspicions of Marsus, Roman governor of Syria (*Ant.* 19.338-42).[135] Only Luke tells of a delegation from Tyre and Sidon, or of Agrippa's anger (at the unwillingness of these free cities to support his alliance-building?) which occasioned it (Acts 12.20),[136] but the account is consistent with Josephus's report of Agrippa's increasing political activity.

As to the meeting itself (in Caesarea), Luke ignores the more elaborate version known to Josephus, which told how it was Agrippa's glorious apparel, the silver in it glittering in the sunlight, which provoked 'his flatterers' to address him as god (*Ant.* 19.344). Luke's much briefer account refers only to Agrippa's 'royal robes' and suggests, rather less plausibly, that it was the oration given by Agrippa which provoked the crowd to cry out, 'The voice of a god, and not of a mortal' (Acts 12.22). The word Luke uses to refer to the crowd, 'the people (*dēmos*)', is not the word Luke uses elsewhere to denote 'the people of Israel' (as in 12.11). It refers simply to the crowd gathered for the occasion.[137] Thus Luke

135. For further detail on the five kings named by Josephus, see Schürer, *History* 1.448-51 n. 34; also Smallwood, *Jews* 197-98.

136. Agrippa was evidently prepared to use economic sanctions to further his policy: the delegation sought reconciliation because their cities depended on food supplies from Agrippa's territory (12.20).

137. But in Luke's other three uses of the word (17.5; 19.30, 33 — the only occurrences in the NT) it refers to the popular assembly of a Hellenistic city, 'a convocation of citizens called together for the purpose of transacting official business' (BDAG 223).

manages to give the impression that the occasion was Gentile in character, the crowd's mistake being the typically pagan one of failing to distinguish a man from God.

Characteristic of their different perspectives are the different accounts given of Agrippa's actual death by Josephus and Luke. Josephus refers it to 'fate' and describes how Agrippa saw an owl, 'harbinger *(angelos)* of woes', immediately prior to his fatal attack *(Ant.* 19.346-47). Luke attributes Agrippa's death immediately to 'an angel *(angelos)* of the Lord' and provides the reason in succinct terms: 'because he did not give God the glory' (Acts 12.23). God did not brook a man, least of all king of the Jews, claiming share of the glory which is God's alone.[138] The literary and dramatic effect should not be missed, giving the chapter as a whole its unity: God struck down Agrippa in as summary a fashion as Agrippa had struck down James (12.2).

The common features of the accounts of Josephus and Luke could suggest that Agrippa's death (in 44) was caused by peritonitis or poison.[139] But whatever the historical facts, the two accounts provide another good example of the way in which such stories were told and of the 'same yet different' character of oral tradition telling the same story. This is consistent with our findings in regard to the Jesus tradition, but the example here is all the more valuable since the two versions come from two very different authors in pursuit of very different goals. Luke's concern was primarily to describe Agrippa's death as an act of God: 'the angel of the Lord (= God)' was responsible (as in 12.7-10). The precedents were clear, and Agrippa was at fault in failing to heed the warning which they contained.[140] Thus perish all who set themselves against God. From this account many an early Christian will have drawn comfort and strength in the face of political pressure and persecution, and we need not doubt that many of the first Christians who were in a position to contrast the church's 'troubles' under Agrippa with Agrippa's horrific end would have found reassurance and fresh confidence in this recollection of Agrippa's demise. Which is no doubt why Luke included a tale which on the face of it had no immediate relevance to his record of Christianity's growth.

---

138. Klauck wonders whether Luke intended a concealed criticism of the imperial cult of his own time *(Magic and Paganism* 43-44).

139. Worms in the alimentary canal could have hastened Agrippa's death.

140. They include the deliverance of Jerusalem from the Assyrians (2 Kgs. 19.35; Sir. 48.21; 1 Macc. 7.41); the horrific deaths of Antiochus, whose 'body swarmed with worms' (2 Macc. 9.9), and of Herod the Great (Josephus, *Ant.* 17.168-70); not to mention the more 'domestic' cases of Judas (Acts 1.18) and of Ananias and Sapphira (5.5, 10). The prince of Tyre in particular should have served as a warning to any king, lest he say, 'I am god', when he was but a man and no god (Ezek. 28.2, 9). Further details are in Bruce, *Acts* 289; Barrett, *Acts* 1.591-92; Fitzmyer, *Acts* 491; and above, §22 n. 84.

In the event, the fact that the Caesareans and the Sebastenes (Samaria) received the news of Agrippa's death with riotous pleasure (Josephus, *Ant.* 19.356-59) strongly suggests that the stirrings of Judean/Jewish nationalism under Agrippa were regarded with no little trepidation by the Hellenistic cities round Judea's perimeter. And we may well further infer that the wave of nationalist sentiment, presumably stirred up by Agrippa's policies and potentially so threatening to the young church, subsided at least for a time and gave the new movement in its Judean homeland a little more breathing space. At any rate, Claudius did not persevere with the experiment of maintaining a united Israelite kingdom under the rule of descendants of Herod the Great but determined that the whole territory, as earlier only Judea and Samaria, should be administered by a procurator under the supervision of the governor of Syria. Thus nationalist hopes for greater independence from Rome were squashed, though by no means extirpated.

26.6. A Distinctive Petrine Theology?

It is virtually impossible to disentangle a distinctive Petrine theology from the early speeches in Acts. In terms of the historiography of the time (§21.3), all that can safely be deduced from the speeches is that Luke was probably able to draw on such information and echoes of the earliest formulations of the first believers in Jerusalem as were still available to him when he began researching for his second volume. Given Peter's lead role, we can infer that Peter himself was a spokesman for these beliefs and claims, and possibly that Peter himself was responsible for some of the distinctive features. To that degree we could describe the fragments and emphases drawn out in §§23.2b and 23.4 above as expressions of Peter's teaching and theology.[141] Perhaps, as Martin Hengel suggests,[142] we should attribute specifically to Peter's influence such features as

- the resumption of John the Baptist's baptism 'for the forgiveness of sins',
- the use of Ps. 110.1 to hail Jesus as 'Lord' as one of the earliest attempts to understand what had happened to Jesus (Acts 2.33-36; cf. 1 Pet. 3.22), and
- the drawing in of Isaiah 53 to earliest Christian reflection on Jesus' death, as suggested by the *pais* ('servant/child') allusion attributed to Peter in Acts 3.13 and 26 (cf. 1 Pet. 2.22-25).[143]

---

141. See also Hengel, *Petrus* 54-56, and further below, §35.1d. For links in thought between the Peter sermons in Acts and 1 Peter, see Selwyn, *First Peter* 33-36.

142. Hengel, *Petrus* 140-45; similarly Barnett, *Birth* 77, 87-88.

143. So also Cullmann, *Peter* 67-69, who also attributes 'universalism' to Peter from early on (66-67).

The contrast here with Paul is frustrating. Since we have undoubted letters from Paul's hand/dictation and can discern within them use made of and allusions to earlier tradition, we can not only compare Luke's portrayal of Paul with what he himself tells us through his letters but also infer earlier tradition which he received. But again, it is difficult if not impossible to infer from Paul's letters any distinctively *Petrine* traditions that Peter may have passed on to him during their two weeks together in Jerusalem (Gal. 1.18); even the reference to the appearance of the risen Jesus to Peter is limited to two words — *ōphthē Kēpha,* 'he appeared to Peter' (1 Cor. 15.5).[144]

The story is not much developed yet, however, and a fuller assessment of Peter's role and theological contribution to earliest Christianity will become possible later (§35.4). The nearest we may well have to a distinctively Petrine teaching and theology is the letter attributed to him — 1 Peter. If the possibility of discerning any distinctive shape of Peter's gospel and theology is to be realized, it should become clearer when we turn to that letter (§37.3).

144. See also *Jesus Remembered* 843-46.

CHAPTER 27

Crisis and Confrontation

From Acts 13, that is, from about the middle of the 40s, Luke focuses his atten-tion almost exclusively on Saul/Paul and on the mission with which the latter was primarily identified. We know that Peter continued in missionary work,[1] but of that Luke tells us nothing; his intervention at the crucial council described in Acts 15 refers only to Peter's precedent-setting conversion of Cornelius (10–11). And James, brother of Jesus, appears to remain located in Jerusalem, as the leader of the young church there (15.13-21; 21.18-26), although displaying a concern for his 'Gentile brothers' (15.23). The wider concern suggested by 1 Cor. 9.5 (the brothers of the Lord who exercised the right to go about accompa-nied by their wives) and James 1.1 (addressed to 'the twelve tribes in the dias-pora')[2] is nowhere elaborated by Luke. And nothing more is said about evange-lism by unknown Hellenists (or others), like that which led to the establishment of the church in Antioch (Acts 11.20) — even though Luke occasionally twitches back the curtain to give us a glimpse of other missionary work beyond Palestine apart from Paul's.[3] As for any seeding of the new faith in Jesus Messiah in other parts — elsewhere in Syria or Edessa, Alexandria or Cyrene,[4] for example — Luke is silent. From ch. 13 of his narrative, Luke concentrates on the single trail blazed by Paul, ending up in Rome, his account leapfrogging from Jerusalem to Antioch, from Antioch to the Aegean, and from the Aegean to Rome, showing

1. Gal. 2.8-9; 1 Cor. 9.5. Does the existence of a 'Cephas party' in Corinth (1 Cor. 1.12) imply missionary work by Peter in Corinth? Does the opening of 1 Peter (1.1) imply mission-ary work in the regions listed (Pontus, Galatia, Cappadocia, Asia and Bithynia)? On these ques-tions see §32 n. 170 and §37.3a, and further §§35.1b-c below.

2. See further below, §37.2a.

3. Acts 18.25; 19.1; 28.14-15.

4. Particularly intriguing is the string of allusions to Cyrene or Cyrenians among the foundation events of Christianity — Mark 15.21 pars.; Acts 2.10; 6.9; 11.20; 13.1.

hardly any concern even for developments around or extending from these centres.[5] A complete portrayal of Christianity's beginnings, Acts is not. But neither
was it intended to be.

It is simplest if we follow out the trail that Luke has laid down. That procedure has the advantage of being able to draw also on the complementary and often confirmatory testimony of Paul's own letters. After all, between them, Acts
and the undisputed letters of Paul cover nearly one-third of the NT. And Paul is
the only firsthand witness still available to us from the first generation Christians. So it is natural for the historian of Christianity in the making to give them
first attention. Even if we think that Luke often veils as much as he uncovers, it is
still true that the veil lying over the beginnings of Christianity elsewhere is much
thicker and more impenetrable. I shall therefore leave assessment of first generation beginnings beyond the tunnel vision of Luke until the veil begins to be
drawn back in the second century, that is, until volume 3.

27.1. Mission from Antioch (Acts 13–14)

a. A Radical Innovation

Somewhat surprisingly, Acts 13–14 is one of the most contested sequences in
Acts's history. This is partly because of the difficulty of integrating it with Paul's
own testimony, that between his two Jerusalem visits he operated in the regions
of Syria and Cilicia (Gal. 1.21); and partly because various chronologies of
Paul's mission find it hard to fit it in.[6]

Acts 13–14 describe a momentous sequence — the first recorded outreach
of the good news of Jesus Messiah beyond the eastern Mediterranean seaboard.
The missions of Philip and the unknown Hellenists had prepared the way by
reaching beyond Judea and the land of Israel (8.4-25; 11.19). And although the
conversions of the Ethiopian eunuch and of Cornelius and his household may
have been somewhat reactive and exceptional (8.26-39; 10.1–11.18), the breakthrough to the Gentiles in Antioch itself had been extensive and sustained
(11.20-21). But now we have to envisage an evangelistic mission whose intention, presumably, was to continue the outreach thus begun in Antioch — that is,
to preach the gospel to Gentiles as well as to Jews. Such a commission, of course,

---

5. Luke was evidently content to allude to such wider outreach in his summary passages
— 9.31, 35; 11.21, 24; 12.24; 13.49; 16.5; 19.20.

6. See below, §28.1. On the debate in German scholarship whether behind Acts 13–14
lies a source, see Breytenbach, *Paulus und Barnabas* 16-20. Breytenbach himself assumes that
Luke was able to draw on traditions in oral form, impossible to reconstruct (30).

was an integral part of Saul's/Paul's calling; both he himself (Gal. 1.15-16) and Luke were agreed on that.[7] But it is not at all clear when he began to fulfil that calling, or (alternatively expressed) when the full implications of his conversion/calling became clear to him. In particular, it remains tantalizingly unclear how we are to correlate Paul's own testimony regarding his earliest evangelistic preaching (Gal. 1.21-23) with Luke's account in Acts 13–14.[8]

Such obscurity should not blind us to the innovation which Paul's earliest missionary work, aimed (at least in part) at the conversion of non-Jews, was within Second Temple Judaism. As already noted (§24.8b), Judaism was always welcoming and receptive to Gentile God-fearers and proselytes, but it remained an ethnic religion — *Ioudaïsmos* (Judaism), the religion (of course) of *Ioudaioi* (Judeans/Jews). For a Jewish sect to go out of its way to convert non-Jews, to take on some of the aspects of a mystery cult, ready to recruit members from all races and nations,[9] was a step occasionally contemplated,[10] but hitherto never pursued as a sustained or primary strategy. It is this step that Barnabas and Paul are portrayed as undertaking in their mission from Antioch — a crucial turning point in the long-drawn-out process of Christianity's emergence from, increasingly distinctive character within, and eventual separation from its parent religion. For in thus opening the door to Gentiles, and on the same terms as Jews (faith in Jesus Messiah), the process began of Gentilizing that faith. Christianity beginning as a form of evangelistic messianic Judaism thereby began to become something different.

Luke was aware of at least some of the implications of the evangelistic mission he narrates in chs. 13–14. That is presumably why he emphasizes that the mission was commanded by the Holy Spirit. As the acceptance of Cornelius was authorized by the combined authority of heavenly vision and Spirit direction (10.11-16, 19-20), so now the outreach to others like Cornelius was authorized

7. Acts 9.15-16; 22.21; 26.17-18. See above, §25.3c-d.

8. See again above, §25.5d. Acts 13.1, of course, implies a more local work, in the church of Antioch itself — strengthening the likelihood that Gal. 1.21 includes that ministry, as well as the mission from Antioch (Acts 13–14). See further n. 319 below. According to Hengel and Schwemer, 'Acts 13.1ff. indicates a belief that the mission territory of Phoenicia, Syria and Cilicia had been "worked" sufficiently' (*Paul* 265).

9. The traditional religions were all ethnic in character, with religious philosophers ready to recognize that the different names of local deities often referred to the same divine reality. It was part of the strength of the Roman Empire that it was so willing to recognize and honour such ethnic religions. The mystery cults, though local or national in origin, were distinct precisely in that they welcomed participation or membership from a wide range of nations. See further §30.3a below.

10. Positive outreach, as distinct from ready reception, is envisaged only occasionally, Jonah and Isa. 66.19 being the obvious exceptions; see above, §24 n. 247, and further below, §29.3-5.

by the same twofold testimony of heavenly vision (22.21; 26.17-18) and Spirit prompting (13.2, 4). We need not doubt that Luke was drawing on good tradition at this point — the recollection of a specific prophetic utterance during worship (13.2). Prophecy, after all, including 'revelation', was a regular feature of the earliest Christian communities.[11] More to the point, nothing short of what was perceived as clear authorization from on high would have been sufficient to break out beyond what, after all, was a natural and universal assumption: that the Jewish religion was the religion of the Jews, and to join in its worship one had at least to 'judaize' (adopt the distinctive practices of the Jews) or to become a proselyte (that is, be naturalized as a Jew).

At the same time, Luke is clear that the commissioning of Barnabas and Saul was by the hands of the church in Antioch: 'after fasting and praying they laid their hands on them and sent them off' (13.3). Here again the parallel is worth noting: as Peter's response to heavenly vision and Spirit prompting was confirmed by the church in Jerusalem (11.1-18), so the Spirit's commissioning of Barnabas and Saul was channelled through the church in Antioch (13.3).[12] Of these two, the most important, as always for Luke, was the clearly manifest will of the Spirit. But the latter was important too. Also to be noted is that the tradition recalled Barnabas as the leading figure of the two (13.2, 7), and that they went out as missionaries of the church in Antioch.[13] The resulting mission is usually called Paul's 'first missionary journey', although 'missionary journey' is a misleading characterization of the subsequent mission which Saul/Paul undertook.[14] And he did so with the full backing of the Antioch church, and as their emissary.

b. Cyprus (Acts 13.4-12)

Luke traces the course followed by Barnabas and Saul in some detail. First stop was Cyprus, only 60 miles from Seleucia, the port of Antioch. This was a natural first step, since Barnabas himself was a native of the island (Acts 4.36), the earlier Hellenists had already reached Cyprus (11.19), some Cypriots had been

---

11. Prophecy — Acts 2.17-18; 11.27-28; 21.9-11; Rom. 12.6; 1 Cor. 11.4-5; 12.10, 28-29; 14; 1 Thess. 5.20; 'revelation' — 1 Cor. 14.6, 26; 2 Cor. 12.1, 7; Gal. 2.2. Chilton assumes that the Spirit's instruction was heard during 'the communal, prophetic practice of the Merkabah in Antioch' (*Rabbi Paul* 115-16).

12. As Lightfoot maintained (*Galatians* 96), this is presumably when Barnabas and Paul became 'apostles' (as referred to in Acts 14.4, 14), that is, apostles commissioned by the church of Antioch (see further below, n. 108).

13. Barrett, *Acts* 1.601; Öhler, *Barnabas* 267-70.

14. See below, §31.1.

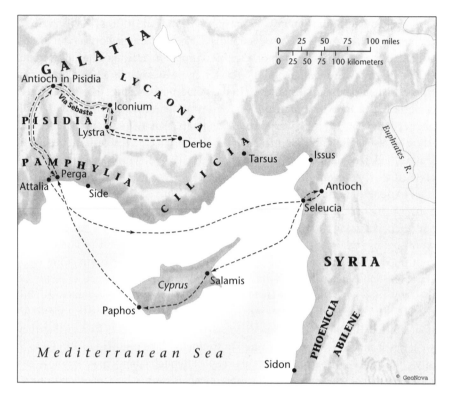

Paul's Antioch Mission

among those who first established the church in Antioch (11.20), and possibly also many Jews had settled in Cyprus (cf. 1 Macc. 15.23).[15]

At Salamis, at the east end of the island, they set what was to become the pattern of their mission, following, indeed, what had presumably been the pattern of the Hellenists' mission leading to the foundation of the church in Antioch: that is, initial preaching in the local synagogues.[16] Some have questioned whether Paul, the apostle to the Gentiles, would indeed have followed this practice.[17] The objection is pe-

15. See further P. W. van der Horst, 'The Jews of Ancient Cyprus', *Jews and Christians in the Graeco-Roman Context* (WUNT 196; Tübingen: Mohr Siebeck, 2006) 28-36. See also T. B. Mitford, 'Roman Cyprus', *ANRW* 2.7.2 (1980) 1285-1384; map with Roman roads at 1288.

16. Acts 13.14; 14.1; 16.13; 17.1, 10, 17; 18.4, 19; 19.8; 28.17, 23. This is 'Luke's version of Paul's "to the Jew first but also to the Greek" (Rom. 1.16)' (Barrett, *Acts* 1.611).

17. E.g., Schmithals, *Paul and Jesus* 60 ('almost impossible to imagine'); Sanders, *Paul, the Law and the Jewish People* 179-90; Meeks, *Urban Christians* 26; Martyn, *Galatians* 213-16; Horrell, *Social Ethos* 75; White, *Jesus to Christianity* 171-72. The possibility apparently does not occur to them that Paul could have seen his mission to Gentiles as most effectively car-

dantic: the Gentiles most likely to be open to the gospel were those Gentiles who had already been attracted to Judaism and attended the local synagogue as sympathizers or 'God-fearers'.[18] Paul's own recollection of how often he suffered under Jewish discipline (five times he had received thirty-nine lashes — 2 Cor. 11.24) confirms that his allegiance to the synagogue continued for a long time.[19] In contrast, the fact that Luke records no opposition from the Cypriot Jews (in any of the synagogues), though such opposition becomes a feature from the next stage onwards (13.45), indicates that Jewish opposition to the gospel was not a Lukan fixation.

Luke's account, and probably the reports that he heard, concentrate on only one episode:[20] the encounter with the magician Elymas in Paphos, at the western end of the island (a week's journey from Salamis); and the conversion of the Roman proconsul, Sergius Paulus. Both are historically plausible. Roman sources tell us of more than one high-born Roman who was attracted by the 'superstitions' stemming from the East.[21] And several Roman rulers had magicians and soothsayers among their personal staff.[22]

---

ried out, initially at least, in the synagogue — that is, directed to winning those Gentiles who were already attracted to Judaism but inhibited by the full demands of the law and circumcision from becoming proselytes. The significance of God-fearing Gentiles for Paul's mission passes them by, and they usually leave a blank when it comes to the question of how Paul actually went about reaching out to Gentiles. J. Gager, *Reinventing Paul* (New York: Oxford University, 2000), thinks that Paul did preach in synagogues, but (only) to Gentiles (51, 68)! See further below, §29.5b, and now also R. Hvalvik, 'Paul as a Jewish Believer — according to the Book of Acts', in Skarsaune and Hvalvik, eds., *Jewish Believers in Jesus* 121-53 (here 124-28).

18. See below, n. 135, and further §29.5c.

19. A. J. Hultgren, *Paul's Gospel and Mission: The Outlook from His Letter to the Romans* (Philadelphia: Fortress, 1985): 'It is difficult to imagine that Paul would have been punished and persecuted if he avoided synagogue communities and lived solely as a gentile among gentile populations' (142).

20. Luke 'seems to possess no concrete tradition of this journey but the Bar-Jesus episode, which he hastens to recount' (Haenchen, *Acts* 402).

21. Seneca mentions autobiographically that in his youth he began to abstain from animal food but that he abandoned the practice because 'some foreign rites were at that time being inaugurated, and abstinence from certain kinds of animal food was set down as proof of interest in the strange cult (*Ep.* 108.22). He refers most probably to the persecution of Jewish and Egyptian rites under Tiberius in 19 CE (Tacitus, *Ann.* 2.85). Texts in *GLAJJ* 1.§189 and 2.§284. For more detail see Smallwood, *Jews* 201-10.

22. Emperor Tiberius, for example, had retained an astrologer, Thrasyllus, among his close advisers, as would have been well known; details in A. D. Nock, 'Paul and the Magus', *Beginnings* 5.164-88 (here 183-84). 'Men of his kind would find it convenient to have a powerful protector' (Barrett, *Acts* 613). Josephus tells us that Felix, when governor of Judea, called on the services of one Atomus, a Jew from Cyprus who professed to be a magician, to persuade Drusilla, with whom he had fallen in love, to leave her husband to marry him (*Ant.* 20.142). Tacitus records that 'the backstairs intrigues of Poppaea [wife of Nero] had employed a number of astrologers whose nefarious activities secured her marriage to the emperor' (*Hist.* 1.22).

Bar-Jesus[23] is the classic example of the *wrong* kind of Jewish integration into the wider religious world (a Jew who was both a 'magician' and a 'false prophet'):

- He is the only one actually described as a *magos,* 'magician', in Acts (13.6), even though the confrontation with magic is one of the main secondary themes in Acts.[24]
- Similarly, he is the only one described as 'a Jewish false prophet' (13.6): the confrontation is not only between miraculous powers (as in the case of Simon in ch. 8), but also between two prophets and the powers of inspiration presupposed (13.1-4).[25] At this point the tradition plugs particularly into the substantial history of false prophecy within Israel and the clearly perceived dangers it posed:[26] Bar-Jesus' opposition to the gospel (13.8), contrasted with Saul's Spirit-filled and devastating denunciation (13.9-11).[27]

The denunciation of the false prophet Bar-Jesus is framed in biblical language and on biblical precedents.[28] That such a denunciation could have its effect in a

23. Bar-Jesus = 'son of Jesus'; in this episode the disciple of and believer in Jesus confronts and defeats the 'son of Jesus'! 'If Luke had invented the story himself, he would never have hit upon *this* name: we have thus here a proof that Luke is following a tradition' (Haenchen, *Acts* 402). Paul addresses him as 'son of the devil' (13.10)!

24. Particularly 8.9-24 and 19.11-20. J. Taylor, 'St. Paul and the Roman Empire: Acts of the Apostles 13–14', *ANRW* 2.26.2 (1995) 1189-1231: 'the island of Cyprus was in fact reputed for *magia*' (1195). Magic was widely practised in the first-century world; see above, §24 n. 187; and further Garrett, *Demise of the Devil* ch. 4.

25. That there were such wandering prophets is well attested elsewhere (cf. 11.27; 21.10; *Did.* 12–13; Josephus, *Ant.* 20.169-71; Lucian, *Alexander the False Prophet*).

26. Classically illustrated in the episodes of 1 Kings 22 and Jeremiah 28; contrast Numbers 23–24. Klauck quotes Jer. 29.9-32, 'which gathers in one single passage all the standard elements of polemic [against false prophets]' (*Magic and Paganism* 48). As so frequently in OT and NT, the recognition of the reality of prophecy is qualified by the recognition of the dangers of false prophecy and the need underlined to test and prove any claim to prophetic powers (see my 'Discernment of Spirits — a Neglected Gift', *The Christ and the Spirit.* Vol. 2: *Pneumatology* [Grand Rapids: Eerdmans, 1998] 311-28; R. W. L. Moberly, *Prophecy and Discernment* [Cambridge: Cambridge University, 2006]).

27. Endless bewilderment has been caused by Luke's note in 13.8 that the other name by which he was known, Elymas, was a translation of Bar-Jesus, since the two have nothing to do with each other. Perhaps 'Elymas' was a kind of nickname, but if so, its point is too obscure for us, though Klauck suggests a derivation from a Semitic root roughly corresponding to 'magician' — *alim,* 'wise man' in Arabic, or *haloma,* 'interpreter of dreams' in Aramaic (*Magic and Paganism* 50). See further Barrett, *Acts* 1.615-16; bibliography in Jervell, *Apg.* 346 n. 416.

28. 13.10 — cf. Prov. 10.9 and Hos. 14.10; Jer. 5.27; Sir. 1.30; 19.26. 13.11 — the ancient accounts of Moses' and Aaron's victory over Pharaoh and his magicians (Exod. 7.4, 5, 17; 9.3), along with the judgment, 'you shall be blind' (cf. Deut. 28.28-29). Weiss regrets the 'intrusion' of the miracle-tale as spoiling 'such a reliable account' (*Earliest Christianity* 215).

context of magic and spiritual power need not be doubted,[29] though Luke, the good story-teller, does not miss the opportunity of heightening the drama.

In contrast stands Sergius Paulus,[30] one of Luke's good Romans.[31] The contrast with Bar-Jesus is deliberate and threefold: the embodiment of Roman authority, 'an intelligent man' (13.7), open to and eager to hear the word of God; against the duplicity of the Jewish magician and false prophet, resisting the missionaries of the word, and trying to turn the proconsul away from the faith they proclaimed.

The result is the conversion of Sergius Paulus. But again, somewhat surprisingly, in view of later episodes, Luke does not stay to narrate any reaction from the Cypriot Jews or any other successes; oddly enough, the twin victories do not seem to have brought other conversions in their wake.[32] Is this simply a case of Luke's reserve, that he wished to hurry on to the next episode?[33] Or does it in fact indicate a striking lack of success in Cyprus?[34] Or was he more restricted by the brevity of his sources than some allow? At any rate, it should be noted that Luke did not compose his narrative on simply repeated formulae or some standard pattern; his tradition may have been sketchy, but he almost certainly had some.

The mention of Paul's second name, or transition from the Jewish 'Saul' to the Greco-Roman 'Paul', comes in curiously at this point (13.9). It is unlikely that it reflects the course of the episode — Paul taking the name of his illustrious convert, as though accepting the status of Sergius Paulus's son or slave (the change is recorded before the proconsul's conversion!).[35] But it could reflect a transition to a mission directed more overtly and immediately to Greeks and Romans, where the Greco-Roman identity might facilitate relationships. Equally,

29. See above, §23.2g.

30. Correctly described as 'proconsul'; see above, §21 n. 99; and further Lake, *Beginnings* 5.455-59; Barrett, *Acts* 1.613-14; A. Nobbs, 'Cyprus', *BAFCS* 2.279-89 (here 282-87); Taylor, 'St. Paul and the Roman Empire' 1192-94.

31. Cf. Acts 10.1-2; 18.14-16; 27.43.

32. Contrast particularly the later victory over magic (19.17-20).

33. Luke omits mention of Sergius Paulus being baptized, but was such a public profession too much for the proconsul?

34. But note already 11.19 and Barnabas's return to Cyprus in 15.39, paralleling Paul's return to the churches founded during the mission from Antioch (16.1-5).

35. Haenchen, *Acts* 399-400 and n. 1; Nobbs, 'Cyprus' 287-89; Taylor, 'St. Paul and the Roman Empire' 1196-98; Riesner, *Paul's Early Period* 143-46; see also Fitzmyer, *Acts* 502-503. On the name 'Paul' see C. Hemer, 'The Name of Paul', *TynB* 36 (1985) 179-83: 'The name "Paulus" itself was a common *cognomen*. . . . In Paul's case, as in that of enfranchised provincials generally, the *cognomen* will have been his ordinary personal name in the Gentile world, his formal designation by *praenomen, nomen,* father's *praenomen,* Roman tribe and *cognomen* being reserved for official documents and remaining unknown to us' (183).

if 'Saul' was the name by which he was known in the Antioch church, the name-change could also reflect a transition in his relationship with Antioch.[36] And it does seem to reflect the emergence of Saul/Paul into the position of leadership in relation to Barnabas, reversing the earlier relationship.

c. Antioch in Pisidia (Acts 13.13-52)

Luke records that the missionary team sailed from Paphos to the south coast of Anatolia and thence to Perga in Pamphylia, and with little more ado headed into the interior.[37] The direction is somewhat surprising since a direct eastern route would have taken them across the coastal plain to Side, which was probably a Jewish centre;[38] or a more westerly fork[39] would have taken them to the large Jewish settlements in the Lycus Valley[40] on the way to Ephesus, the major city of the Roman province of Asia.[41] But perhaps the latter would have taken them too far from their base in Syrian Antioch, whereas the Via Sebaste to Pisidian Antioch (built by Augustus) would allow the option of direct return to Syrian Antioch should they so decide.[42] The brevity of his account leaves two important questions hanging.

(1) Why did John Mark, who had come along as assistant *(hypēretēs)* to Barnabas and Saul (13.5),[43] Barnabas's cousin (Col. 4.10), leave them in Perga and return to Jerusalem (13.13)? Plausible answers include: that he resented Paul's taking over the leadership of the mission from Barnabas; and/or that he was unhappy with the direction they were taking, far more ambitious than a mission to Cyprus.

36. Cf. Barrett, *Acts* 1.609, and further 616; Fitzmyer warns against making too much out of 'this minor detail' (*Acts* 500).

37. For treatment of this region S. Mitchell, *Anatolia: Land, Men, and Gods in Asia Minor* (2 vols.; Oxford: Clarendon, 1993), is indispensable.

38. 1 Macc. 15.23; see also Philo, *Legat.* 281; Acts 2.10; further Schürer, *History* 3.33. But travel beyond Side would have been impractical, if not impossible, either along the coast or into the interior; see R. J. A. Talbert, ed., *Barrington Atlas of the Greek and Roman World* (Princeton: Princeton University, 2000) maps 65-66.

39. Map in Mitchell, *Anatolia* 1.120; Talbert, *Barrington* maps 62, 65.

40. Schürer, *History* 3.27-30.

41. See D. H. French, 'The Roman Road-System of Asia Minor', *ANRW* 2.7.2 (1980) 698-729 (here 706-708).

42. See Mitchell, *Anatolia* 1.70, and the summary overview by D. H. French, 'Acts and the Roman Roads of Asia Minor', *BAFCS* 2.52-53, 55; also J. D. Crossan and J. L. Reed, *In Search of Paul: How Jesus' Apostle Opposed Rome's Empire with God's Kingdom* (San Francisco: HarperSanFrancisco, 2004) 200-201; Schnabel, *Mission* 1074-76.

43. John Mark was the son of Mary, a prominent and wealthy member of the Jerusalem church (Acts 12.12).

(2) Why head into the Anatolian highlands? Again all we can do is suggest plausible answers. One popular suggestion builds on Paul's own recollection that he came to the Galatians[44] in a poor physical condition (Gal. 4.13-14), which allows the inference that Paul found it necessary to leave the coastal region and to head for the higher interior for his health's sake.[45] Another is the somewhat unexpected evidence that Sergius Paulus (governor of Cyprus) was a native of Pisidian Antioch and probably maintained strong family links there, which equally allows the inference that Paul headed for Antioch because he had the possibility of important contacts there — though Luke gives no hint of this.[46] As in so many other instances where Luke skips over large periods and regions in a few words, the inquiring historian is left with more questions than can be answered.

At any rate, Pisidian Antioch did match Paul's idea of an appropriate centre for his preaching. It was 'the principal Roman colony in the Greek East, deliberately modelled, in some respects, on the imperial capital itself'.[47] Probably more to the point for Paul, there was evidently a strong Jewish settlement there and a thriving synagogue community (13.14).[48] As in many other cases, we should not assume that the synagogue was a small back-street affair; the image of the Jewish ghetto from the middle ages should certainly not be projected back to the first three centuries. In some cities we know of through that whole period, the synagogue was (or became) a large and prominent building, indeed a major architectural contribution to the city. Such Jewish communities and synagogues often attracted a fair number of Gentile sympathizers (God-fearers), including prominent citizens and counsellors.[49] Luke's account in 13.50 indicates that the

44. Assuming that the churches spoken of in Acts 13–14 are those addressed in Galatians; see below, §31 n. 32.

45. 'A species of chronic malaria' = the 'thorn in the flesh' of 2 Cor. 12.7 (Ramsay, *St. Paul* 92-97). But an arduous uphill journey in excess of one hundred miles would be very demanding for someone suffering from a malarial fever. A popular suggestion was epilepsy (see, e.g., Dibelius, *Paul* 42-43). Chilton suggests 'herpes zoster' (*Rabbi Paul* 126). See also below, §32 n. 507.

46. Details in Mitchell, *Anatolia* 2.6-7: 'We can hardly avoid the conclusion that the proconsul himself had suggested to Paul that he make it his next port of call, no doubt providing him with letters of introduction to aid his passages and his stay' (7); see also *NDIEC* 4.138-39. The data are surprisingly neglected in Acts commentaries; but see Breytenbach, *Paulus und Barnabas* 38-45; Taylor, 'St. Paul and the Roman Empire' 1205-7; Riesner, *Paul's Early Period* 138-41, 275-76 (the Sergii family tree, 416); Öhler, *Barnabas* 308-309; Crossan and Reed, *Paul* 181-82; Schnabel, *Mission* 1088.

47. Mitchell, *Anatolia* 2.7; 'a Rome in miniature' (Crossan and Reed, *Paul* 204; further 204-209); Schnabel, *Mission* 1098-1103. On the importance of the imperial cult, see below, §29 at n. 124; Ramsay, *Cities of Paul* 285-96, shows little awareness of its importance.

48. See also Schürer, *History* 3.32; Breytenbach, *Paulus und Barnabas* 48-50.

49. See below, §29 n. 188; also §27 n. 136. Here see also Taylor, 'St. Paul and the Roman Empire' 1207-10.

Jewish community in Antioch was able to gain the support of 'devout women of high standing and leading citizens *(tous prōtous)*', which is consistent with what we know.[50] This factor was almost certainly the key to Paul's missionary strategy: to reach out in and through the synagogues to Gentile God-fearers as well as the local Jews.[51]

Luke evidently regarded this first working through of the strategy as archetypal: Paul, invited to speak to the synagogue congregation (13.15), addresses himself to both the resident Jews and the Gentile adherents: 'Fellow Jews, and you who fear God' (13.16, 26). Luke recalls the sermon as being received favourably by 'many Jews[52] and devout proselytes' on the first Sabbath (13.42-43), and as creating wide interest in the city. The result is that on the following Sabbath 'almost the entire city' gathered to hear what Paul had to say (13.44), provoking in turn a more negative reaction from 'the Jews' of Antioch (13.45). We may infer that it was not so much Paul's message which caused the offence to the bulk of Antioch's Jews as its surprising appeal to Antioch's wider citizenry. The fear, presumably, would be of an untried and untested new sect upsetting and undermining the good standing and good relations which the Jewish community had established for itself within the city: minorities were always likely to be anxious about their legal and social standing since local and international politics were so unpredictable.[53]

Equally archetypal is Paul's response: he turns to the Gentiles, many of whom receive the word with gladness and believe (13.46-48). The quotation from Isa. 49.6 (Acts 13.47) expresses a strong Pauline self-understanding: that his commission was of a piece with and towards the fulfilment of Israel's own vocation to be 'a light for the Gentiles'.[54] Although, as Luke tells it, this 'turn to the Gentiles' has a final and irrevocable ring, that would be a too simplistic reading of the narrative.[55] For Luke is equally clear that Paul continued the same

50. P. W. van der Horst, *Ancient Jewish Epitaphs* (Kampen: Kok Pharos, 1991), notes that, according to the available epigraphical data, at least 50 percent of proselytes and about 80 percent of God-fearers were women (109-11, 136-37).

51. See again below, §29.5b.

52. Given that the more typical Jewish response to Paul's preaching elsewhere in Acts is hostile (9.22-23, 29; 13.45, 50; 14.19; 17.5, 13; 18.6, etc.), the response here is strikingly positive.

53. See particularly M. Goodman, 'The Persecution of Paul by Diaspora Jews', *Judaism in the Roman World* 145-52. Probably a more accurate rendering of Luke's phrase 'the Jews' would therefore be 'the Jewish community'.

54. See above, §25.3c-d; note particularly the echo of Isa. 49.1-6 in Paul's recollection of his own commissioning (Gal. 1.15-16). Isa. 49.6 equally ties in with Luke's own view of Paul's mission: 'to the end of the earth' (Isa. 49.6) is the same phrase Luke uses in Acts 1.8.

55. Haenchen's comment that 'this is the moment of divorce between the gospel and Judaism' (*Acts* 417, further 417-18) is much too exaggerated. See also Jervell, *Apg.* 363-64.

practice thereafter (initially preaching in the synagogue in a new town or city).[56]
The point is rather that the scenario repeats (18.6; 28.25-28).[57] This is the character of the message and the lot of the preacher: the message is first and foremost for the people of Israel, and it must always be offered first to the Jews, even if only some of them accept it and the rest reject it. On this point Luke has captured a genuinely Pauline concern: 'to the Jew first and also to the Greek'.[58]

d. Paul's Sermon in Antioch (Acts 13.16-43)

13.13-16 and 42-43 provide the frame for one of the more substantial speeches in Acts, one which matches Peter's first speech (2.14-36, 38-39) both in length and character. The parallel is no doubt deliberate.[59] Paul preaches the same message as Peter:

- the opening paragraph unique to each and appropriate to their respective contexts (13.16-25; 2.14-21);
- the core kerygma focusing on Jesus' death, instigated by his own people, and met by God's vindicatory resurrection ('but God raised him'), with his immediate disciples as witnesses (13.26-31; 2.22-24, 32);
- the fulfilment of prophecy, Ps. 2.7 here serving in the place of Ps. 110.1, but Ps. 16.10 cited by both and invoking the same argument (13.32-37; 2.25-31, 33-36);
- finally the concluding appeal for belief and offer of forgiveness (13.38-41; 2.38-39).

Even more than in ch. 2, the emphasis is on continuity with Israel's past revelation: from the exodus, through the first prophet (Samuel) and first king (Saul), and particularly through David, to David's greater successor (13.17-23);[60] Jesus

---

56. See n. 16 above.

57. 'A programmatic conclusion', 'a recurring pattern' (Barrett, *Acts* 1.625; also 657). Lake and Cadbury wisely comment: 'Far too much attention is paid to Gal. ii.7-9 as though it means that Paul and Barnabas were never to preach to the Jews' (*Beginnings* 4.159).

58. Rom. 1.16; 9.24; 10.12. See also A. Deutschmann, *Synagoge und Gemeindebildung. Christliche Gemeinde und Israel am Beispiel von Apg 13,42-52* (BU 30; Regensburg: Pustet, 2001).

59. Lüdemann also notes the parallel with Jesus' inaugural sermon in Nazareth: 'in both cases they stand almost programmatically at the beginning of the activities of Jesus and Paul' (*Early Christianity* 153).

60. The initial description (13.17-19) is studded with scriptural language, particularly from Deuteronomy, recalling Israel's election as a people and deliverance from Egypt (Deut.

as the fulfilment of promise through John the Baptist and earlier through David (13.23-27, 32-37); the message and the fulfilment are for all Israel (13.23-24).[61] More striking, however, is the way the speech is directed not only to Israel, the direct heirs of Abraham, but also to those who feared God (13.16, 26), sympathetic God-fearing Gentiles.[62] What is striking is that they are included equally in this continuity — 'our fathers' (13.17), 'what God promised to the fathers he has fulfilled to us their children' (13.33), 'brothers' (13.26, 38), 'to us', 'us their children' (13.26, 33). The speech itself expresses an openness which is only hinted at in Peter's earlier speeches (2.39; 3.25; but also 10.34-35).

Here, as usual, Luke's intention was not to present the sermon Paul actually delivered on the occasion, but to provide in cameo form (the perfectly rounded miniature would take a little over three minutes to deliver) an indication of what Paul would/could/should have said on the occasion.[63] The double emphases just noted (continuity with Israel and openness to Gentiles) are certainly Pauline in character. On the other hand, the concluding peroration is much less like Paul: in his letters Paul hardly speaks of 'forgiveness',[64] and 13.39 reads oddly as a report of Paul's view of the law.[65] Yet the tradition, as in Peter's first

---

1.31; 4.34, 37; 5.15; 9.26, 29; 10.15). Distinctive, however, is the thought of Israel made great during their time in Egypt, whereas Deuteronomy recalled them more to their experience of slavery. This, together with the reference to the seven Canaanite nations destroyed before Israel (Deut. 7.1), makes for a double note of exaltation which may well reflect the need felt within diaspora Jewish communities to remind the larger majorities among whom they had settled that their nation had a high pedigree and an impressive history. See also §24 n. 132 above.

61. 'The speech probably reflects the extensive exegetical debate that must have gone on as soon as Jewish Christians began to make their voices heard in the synagogue' (Barrett, *Acts* 1.623). Barrett also draws attention (624) to the degree of correspondence between Paul's sermon and a form of synagogue homily noted by Bowker, 'Speeches in Acts' 96-111; see also Bruce, *Acts* 303.

62. Barrett wants to limit the reference of 'you who fear God' (13.16, 26) to proselytes (*Acts* 1.629-31, 639); cf. 13.43.

63. Schnabel is confident that he can draw on Acts 13.16-41 to illustrate Paul's missionary preaching to a Jewish audience (*Mission* 1380-85).

64. 'Forgiveness' as a concept appears only in the later Paulines, Col. 1.14 and Eph. 1.7 (though we should note also the quotation Paul uses in Rom. 4.7), but it is typical of the Acts sermons (2.38; 5.31; 10.43).

65. The closest would be Rom. 6.7 (using the verb in the same unusual way; cf. Sir. 26.29) and 8.2-3 (saying something the same in different language). Paul would more typically have spoken of deliverance from the power of sin, or indeed of freedom from the law itself (see further Bruce, *Acts* 311-12). It is difficult to avoid the impression that a Pauline sentiment has been only half grasped and used here, and in consequence it is less than clear what the 'everything' is from which the law does not provide freedom. 'On a central question of faith Luke shows his devotion to Paul but less than a full understanding of his theology' (Barrett, *Acts* 1.651).

sermon, is old,[66] and includes what sounds like an early christological use of Ps. 2.7, where God's begetting of Jesus as his son is linked to the resurrection (13.32-33).[67] So Luke exercises some freedom on the matter, as we might expect, either in using pre-formed material, Pauline in character and echo but not Paul's as such, or in the degree of casualness for the terms in which he represents Paul speaking. All this would be quite acceptable for the times, but the sermon provides more of a sidelong glance at Paul than material on which we could reconstruct Paul's earliest preaching with any confidence.

e. Iconium, Lystra and Derbe (Acts 13.50–14.20)

Expelled from Antioch (13.50), it was natural for Paul and Barnabas to head south and eastwards along the Via Sebaste to the two further Augustan foundations, the Roman colonies of Iconium and Lystra — involving sustained travel of at least five days and a further day respectively.[68]

In *Iconium* the pattern is repeated: preaching in the synagogue; 'a great number of Jews and Greeks became believers' (14.1); and the 'disobedient(!)', perhaps better 'unpersuaded Jews' stirring the Gentiles to opposition (14.2). Paul and Barnabas remain 'for a long time', 'speaking boldly for the Lord', presumably still in the synagogue, their witness attested by Luke's favourite 'signs and wonders' (14.3). The city is divided between the resident Jews and 'the apostles' (14.4), and when a plot is laid to attack Paul and Barnabas (14.5), they flee to Lystra (14.6)[69] to continue their mission (14.7). All of which is perfectly plausi-

---

66. See above, §21.3a. Here note the allusion to 2 Sam. 7.12-14 (13.23; cf. 2.29-32); the Baptist as the beginning of the good news (13.24-25; cf. 10.37); the echo of Ps. 107.20 (13.26; cf. 10.36); the cross as 'the tree' (13.29; cf. 5.30; 10.39); the familiar 'they' (the Jerusalemites and their leaders) were responsible for Jesus' death, 'but God raised him from the dead' (13.30; cf. 2.24; 3.15; 10.39-40); the appearances to the first disciples to serve as witnesses to the people (13.31; cf. 3.15; 10.41) — without reference, interestingly, to Paul's own 'resurrection appearance', in some contrast to his own practice in his letters (1 Cor. 9.1; 15.8; Gal. 1.12, 16), but reflecting the fact that in Acts Paul does not qualify as one of the primary witnesses (1.21-22). The final quotation from Hab. 1.5 (13.41) is unusual, but both the Qumran community and the first Christians saw Habakkuk as foreshadowing the crises and opportunities of their own times (1QpHab; use of Hab. 2.4 in Rom. 1.17, Gal. 3.11 and Heb. 10.38).

67. Cf. Heb. 1.5 and 5.5, and the similar ('adoptionistic'-like) emphasis in Rom. 1.4, a passage usually assumed to be a quotation of an early confessional formula; see above, §23.4c.

68. See Mitchell, *Anatolia* 1.76-77 (map between 78 and 79), and the earlier studies by Ramsay, *The Cities of Paul* 317-419. On Lystra as 'a frontier town between Phrygia and Lycaonia' see, e.g., Bruce, *Acts* 319-20. Schnabel gives fuller details on the locations (*Mission* 1108-13).

69. Quite what Luke envisaged by adding 'and to the surrounding countryside' (14.6) is

ble, given the positive attitudes with which at least some leading citizens and/or their wives probably regarded the local synagogue community, and given also the same concern on the part of the Jewish community as a whole that the new teaching would be disruptive of their status and that their standing in these Roman colonies would be somehow jeopardized. In cities where the cult of the emperor was a major feature of the civic life, the proclamation of Jesus as 'Lord' (14.3) was likely to send a shiver up and down many a spine, since it could so easily be represented as in direct antithesis to the loyalty owed to the emperor.[70] Luke would have been well aware of this (17.7-8), but it may not have been an explicit factor in the events in Pisidia and Lycaonia.

In *Lystra* there is no record of a synagogue or of Jewish presence (hence 14.19), so any proclamation (14.7, 9), presumably, would have been in the open market. A miraculous healing (like that in 3.1-10)[71] provides the occasion for a defining encounter between the missionaries to the Gentiles and the representatives of the old gods of classical Greece. The portrayal of the Lystrans is rather condescending, but Luke's skill as a story-teller is clearly in evidence, in the vividness of the visual detail in the scene he presents to the reader. The irony is striking: Jewish missionaries, rejected by their own community in Iconium, are now hailed as the gods of old Greece.[72] The implication is of an upcountry townspeople (they speak in local dialect — 14.11)[73] whose beliefs in the tradi-

---

a puzzle, since he always depicts Paul's mission as centred in cities and the area was not well settled, 'without cities or municipal organisation' (Lake and Cadbury, *Beginnings* 4.163). The note was possibly part of the tradition he received, denoting the outskirts or vicinity of the cities mentioned.

70. 'The imperial high priesthood was the most prominent public position at Iconium' (Mitchell, *Anatolia* 1.116, 104; see the whole chapter — 1.100-117; on Antioch, 1.101, 104-106); 'One cannot avoid the impression that the obstacle which stood in the way of the progress of Christianity, and the force which would have drawn new adherents back to conformity with the prevailing paganism, was the public worship of the emperors' (2.10). See further below, §29 nn. 118, 119.

71. Breytenbach sets out the parallels (*Paulus und Barnabas* 27).

72. There is probably an allusion to the famous tale of Zeus and Hermes entertained unwittingly by the old couple Philemon and Baucis, which may have been linked with this region (Ovid, *Metamorphoses* 8.620-724); see further Haenchen, *Acts* 427 n. 1, 432; Barrett, *Acts* 1.676-77; Breytenbach, *Paulus und Barnabas* 31-38. The episode confirms that Paul was the chief speaker (Hermes was popularly thought of as the messenger of the gods), but there may also be an implication that Barnabas had a more distinguished or venerable appearance (Zeus as the high god). The Greek suggests that the temple was called the temple of 'Zeus outside the city', like the abbey of 'St. Paul outside the Walls' in Rome. Taylor suggests that the two gods Paul and Barnabas were identified with were 'the mysterious Kabeiroi, the *Megaloi Theoi*' ('St. Paul and the Roman Empire' 1219).

73. Since Lystra was a Roman colony, there is no problem in inferring that most or many of any audience would understand Greek well enough, even if the local populace conversed

tional gods of Olympus were simple and heartfelt (the response is of ready welcome and reverence).[74] The key sentence, which provides the principal reason
for telling the story, is 'The gods become like human beings have come down to
us'. It is this which gives Luke the opportunity to stress that the message of Paul
and Barnabas is a message about the one God, Creator of all. He makes no attempt to portray Paul as going on to preach about Jesus: in this first encounter
with Gentile paganism the first priority is the Jewish Christian proclamation of
God.

The story-teller was conscious of the constraints imposed by the scene he
has described (14.15-17). So the speech is brief, and the point is made at once.
The good news is not of human beings with godlike abilities (cf. 10.26), but of
the living God, Creator of everything. The thoroughly Jewish character of the
message is clear:[75] they should turn from such worthless vanity *(mataia),* typically expressed in Gentile idolatry;[76] the only god worthy of worship is 'the living God, who made heaven and earth and the sea and everything that is in
them'.[77] That the God of Israel was also God of all the nations (14.16) is a reminder that Jewish monotheism gives its fundamental creed a universal character.[78] The description of God's providential care (14.17) also echoes typically
(though not exclusively) Jewish reflection on God's goodness in the fruitfulness
of creation.[79]

Most striking is the fact that this axiom of Jewish faith is now presented as
part of the good news (14.15). There had been no shortage of Jewish apologists

---

more naturally in Lycaonian (see further Hemer, *Book of Acts* 110 and n. 23). 'The Lycaonians
understood Greek like their contemporaries all over the Near East, whereas the two missionaries were unacquainted with Lycaonian' (Haenchen, *Acts* 431).

74. See further D. W. J. Gill, 'Acts and Roman Religion', *BAFCS* 2.80-92 (here 81-85):
'Paul and Barnabas are quite likely to have come across a local Lycaonian cult, which itself recast the nature of the deities in the language of the classical world' (84). 'The story named appropriate gods. A statuette of Hermes and an eagle, bird of Zeus, have been found near Lystra;
the two gods are coupled in an inscription from this general region; on a sculptured relief, we
can see how people locally pictured these divinities, round-faced and solemn, with long hair
and flowing beards, a searching gaze and the right hand held prominently across the chest.
Such a Zeus looks uncommonly like our image of a wandering Christian holy man: in these re-
liefs, we, too, can sense the elusive features of a Paul or Barnabas'. 'To all but a few of the
highly educated, the gods were indeed a potential presence whom a miracle might reveal' (Lane
Fox, *Pagans and Christians* 99-100, 140; and further ch. 4, 'Seeing the Gods'). See also Öhler,
Barnabas 345-60.

75. Breytenbach, *Paulus und Barnabas* 53-75.

76. Cf. Jer. 2.5; 8.19; Wis. 13.1; 3 Macc. 6.11; Rom. 1.21.

77. Citing a classic expression of Jewish monotheism (Exod. 20.11; Neh. 9.6; Ps.
146.6). See also Breytenbach, *Paulus und Barnabas* 60-65.

78. Deut. 32.8; Ps. 145.9; Wis. 11.22-24; *1 En.* 84.2.

79. Lev. 26.4; Ps. 147.9; Jer. 5.24. See further on Acts 17.22-31 below (§31.3b).

for their unique monotheism, and diatribes against Gentile idolatry were standard fare within Jewish diaspora communities.[80] But as already noted, Judaism was not an evangelistic religion, and the call to repudiate such (false) conceptions of God was not typically part of Israel's apologia. It was precisely the evangelistic compulsion within earliest Christianity which made it necessary to turn its presupposition of Jewish monotheism into an active part of its proclamation. The gospel of Jesus Messiah is first about God, and about God and creation; the message about Jesus follows from that.

Luke tells the story as ever in his own terms,[81] including the parallel with Peter provided by the healing of the lame man in Lystra (3.1-10; 14.8-10). As to his sources of information, all we can say is that, despite a sophisticated modern western scepticism to the contrary, there is nothing basically implausible in the rather farcical sequence of events and swings of mood recorded.[82] Paul himself recalled one episode in his mission where things went so badly wrong that he was stoned (2 Cor. 11.25),[83] Timothy is known in Christian tradition as a native of Lystra (Acts 16.1) and 2 Tim. 3.11 retains a tradition of persecution at Lystra following a similar hostile response at Antioch and Iconium.[84] So too the argument of 14.15-17 is a variation on Paul's indictment in Rom. 1.20-23, and the need for Gentiles to make the same initial turn from a false understanding of God to the living God is reflected in 1 Thess. 1.9.[85] So once again, Luke has provided a fair representation of the sort of preaching that Paul would most likely have

80. Wisdom of Solomon 11ff.; Epistle of Jeremiah; *Sib. Or.* 3.

81. 'Traces of Luke's style and of his interests are spread fairly evenly through the whole section and as it stands it must be regarded as Luke's own composition' (Barrett, *Acts* 1.664); but Barrett adds that 'Luke had information of various kinds'. Lüdemann finds much evidence of Lukan redaction (*Early Christianity* 159-63) but concludes that 'the missionary journey with the stations of Derbe, Lystra, Iconium and Antioch is a historical fact', referring especially to 14.19-20a (165).

82. See Hengel and Schwemer, *Paul* 443 n. 1095. Haenchen observes that some days must have elapsed before the news reached Antioch and Jews from Antioch came to Lystra and stirred up the crowds, 'but this secondary consideration does not interest the narrator' (*Acts* 429 n. 5). Mitchell thinks the local data confirm 'the historical precision' of the episode (*Anatolia* 2.24). Sanders shows little appreciation of crowd psychology when he judges the sequence 'hardly credible' (*Schismatics* 10).

83. Lüdemann justifiably questions the common assumption that the stoning was in accord with the formal Jewish legal process (*Early Christianity* 165); a mob reaction to slighted religious enthusiasm is more likely, whether with or without Jewish encouragement.

84. Note also the tradition in the *Acts of Paul,* focusing on Antioch and Iconium (*NTA* 2.353-57).

85. 'The Christian message will have been almost incomprehensible to a genuine worshipper of Sarapis or Dionysus or a follower of the "Syrian goddess". By way of preparation, it was still necessary to argue for some form of ethical monotheism before preaching to real pagans' (Hengel, *Acts* 89).

presented in these circumstances. We can hardly say more, but hardly need to say more.

The 'first missionary journey' ended at *Derbe*,[86] to which Paul and Barnabas retreated after Paul's stoning (14.20).[87] Some 60 miles from Lystra, and thus a three- or four-day journey by foot for fit travellers, it would presumably have been more than a little demanding for Paul himself, who, according to 14.19, had been left for dead![88] The road beyond Lystra may not have been paved,[89] and the travel more strenuous as the road climbed up towards the Cilician Gates, the pass through the Taurus mountains into Cilicia. It is not at all clear why the two missionaries did not take that most direct route back to their base in Syrian Antioch. Perhaps the road was too demanding, there may have been no inviting caravan in which to shelter,[90] and having been driven further east than they had intended, Paul and Barnabas may have decided it was wiser to retrace their steps, in the hope that the troubles caused by their preceding visits would have abated.[91] At all events, their stay in Derbe is recalled without detail, beyond noting its uncontested success (14.21).[92]

---

86. On Derbe see Mitchell, *Anatolia* 1.96 and n. 170; as reconstituted by Claudius (about this time), it was also known as Claudioderbe (1.95 and n. 162). On the site of Derbe see particularly B. Van Elderen, 'Some Archaeological Observations on Paul's First Missionary Journey', in W. W. Gasque and R. P. Martin, eds., *Apostolic History and the Gospel,* F. F. Bruce FS (Exeter: Paternoster, 1970) 151-61 (here 156-61).

87. That some Jews (not 'the Jews') should be so antagonistic to a message which seemed to call in question the uniqueness of Israel's election as to travel the distances involved to oppose Paul would be surprising but not incredible (we may recall the vehemence of Paul's own previous hostility to the new movement).

88. Luke's report that Paul was able immediately to return to the city (where had 'the disciples' come from?) and on the very next day to undertake the demanding journey to Derbe inevitably causes some eyebrow raising. Luke was evidently cutting several corners and for some reason chose not to make much at all of the severity of Paul's sufferings. Becker surmises that 'Paul was uncommonly robust' (*Paul* 175). Chilton deduces that Paul's wounds must have taken some eighteen months to heal, which he spent in Derbe, and then returned directly to Tarsus (*Rabbi Paul* 130).

89. French, *BAFCS* 2.53.

90. The incidents that Paul had in mind when he spoke of having been 'often near death' (2 Cor. 11.23f) and in 'danger from bandits' (11.26c) are unknown, but travels through Lycaonia probably provided one or two of them. See below, §28.2b.

91. Ramsay observes that the expulsion of Paul and Barnabas by municipal authorities would be valid only for the officials' twelve months of office (*Cities of St. Paul* 372-74).

92. The verb used, 'make disciples' *(mathēteuō),* is unique in Acts but was probably used in the tradition as it came to Luke.

f. The Retracing of the Steps (Acts 14.21-28)

Luke's main objectives in narrating the mission from Antioch were now more or less complete, concentrated as they were on the confrontation with syncretistic magic, Jewish unbelief and the old religions, expressed particularly in the two speeches attributed to Paul, and setting the pattern of mixed response and rejection from both Jews and Gentiles. The return journey is narrated in the briefest of terms, Luke pausing only to fill in a few details and to confirm the character and success of the mission. The fact that Luke passes over thus so briefly long days of arduous travel simply reminds us that Luke as a good story-teller knew how to retain his audience's attention. And that Paul and Barnabas were able to re-enter cities from which they had recently been ejected need mean only that the opposition had been a crowd phenomenon which subsided as quickly as it had boiled over.

The positive reason for their return is clearly implied in the language used. Paul's letters confirm that he was a church founder who was equally anxious to ensure the upbuilding and maturity of his churches; so a follow-up visit would likely have been one of his priorities (cf. 15.36). The description of the missionaries' consolidation of their converts is given (14.22) in terms regularly used by Luke and Paul: strengthening[93] and encouraging/exhorting.[94] Less characteristic of Luke and more typical of Paul is the concern that his converts should 'remain in the faith', or better, 'remain in their faith',[95] and that suffering was an unavoidable gateway into the inheritance of God's kingdom.[96] Quite probably, then, Luke here recollects the typical concerns and language of Paul the pastor.

The reference to elders being appointed (14.23) creates a historical anomaly. There is no indication from 13.1-3 that elders were a feature of the sending church (Antioch).[97] And in none of the undisputed Pauline letters are elders mentioned, despite the fact that in several cases there were situations or crises in which elders, had there been any, would have been appealed to or called to account. In contrast, elders first appear in the Pauline corpus in the Pastoral Epistles (1 Tim. 5 and Tit. 1.5), generally regarded as written after Paul's death by someone from Paul's circle, and with the same thought of their being appointed

93. Acts 15.32, 41; 16.5; 18.23; Rom. 1.11; 1 Thess. 3.2, 13.

94. Acts 15.32; 16.40; 20.1-2; Rom. 12.1; 15.30; etc.

95. Cf. Acts 11.23; 13.43; 1 Cor. 15.1-2; Gal. 1.6.

96. Cf. Rom. 8.17; 2 Thess. 1.5. For the whole verse cf. particularly 1 Thess. 3.2-4. See further below, §32 at n. 153.

97. 'It is hardly likely that the representatives of the church of Antioch would institute in the daughter churches a kind of ministry that the mother itself did not have' (Barrett, *Acts* 1.666).

by Paul or at his behest. It looks, then, as though Luke, both here and in 20.17, has either assumed the presence from the first of a practice and church structure which had become more common in his own day (the procedures of 13.3 were more 'charismatic'); or he has made more formal the sort of commendation of mature believers such as we find in 1 Thess. 5.12-13 and 1 Cor. 16.15-18; or indeed he has understood the teachers (Gal. 6.6), whom Paul presumably had encouraged to take on their role, as equivalent to 'elders'. Either way it tells us something of the character and objectives of Luke as a historian — a readiness to read the traditions he had from the founding period in a way which brought out the harmony of the early churches and the settled pattern of their organization from the first (cf. 11.30; James 5.14).[98]

The return journey mentions preaching in Perga (14.25),[99] of which nothing had been said in 13.13-14,[100] and omits the Cyprus stage of the missionary journey. The reminder that Syrian Antioch was the place where 'they had been commended to the grace of God for the work which they had now fulfilled' (14.26, alluding back to 13.3) nicely rounds off the mission from Antioch. It also reminds readers that Paul and Barnabas had carried it out as missionaries of the church there (14.4, 14) and that the story of their exploits had been told from an Antiochene perspective.

The report to the church in Antioch (14.27)[101] emphasizes that it was all God's doing, and that it was God who had opened a door of faith to the Gentiles: the image is a favourite of Paul;[102] and the emphasis is one we would expect from Paul (faith as the Gentiles' means of entry into Israel's heritage). The mention of Jewish converts (and of Jewish opposition) was less to the point: the principal significance was the fact that Gentiles had responded in significant numbers and that churches composed substantially, in some cases wholly of Gentiles had been established. A new phase in the development of the new movement and in the transformation of its identity had clearly opened up, with consequences which Luke proceeds to describe.

---

98. But were 'elders' (Jas 5.14) also 'teachers' (3.1) within the Jerusalem-based churches? See also §23.3 above.

99. For details, see Schnabel, *Mission* 1122-24.

100. D. A. Campbell, 'Paul in Pamphylia (Acts 13.13-14a; 14.24b-26): A Critical Note', *NTS* 46 (2000) 595-602, notes that a ship travelling to Perga (13.13-14) would have sailed up the river Cestrus to dock opposite the city, whereas the busier harbour at Attalia (14.24-26) would give a better opportunity to find a passage to Syrian Antioch.

101. The Antioch church was still of a size able to be gathered in a single place (large house).

102. 1 Cor. 16.9; 2 Cor. 2.12; Col. 4.3.

g. Summary Assessment

As on every page of Acts, in chs. 13–14 we see clear evidence of Luke's composition, but also of the tradition that he had been able to draw on for his composition.

Typical examples of Luke's perspective, concerns and technique:

- mission undertaken at the behest of and in the inspiration of the Spirit (13.2, 4, 9 and 52; cf. 1.8; 5.32; 8.29; 10.19-20, 47; 16.6-7);
- a further confrontation with and victory over magic (13.6-11; cf. 8.18-24; 19.18-19);
- supportive Roman authorities (13.7, 12; cf. 18.12-17; 25.25-27; 26.30-32);
- the synagogue as the obvious venue for initial mission (13.5, 14-15; 14.1);[103]
- a sermon (13.16-41) which emphasizes continuity of Jewish heritage and hope through Jesus (cf. e.g., 3.22-25; 15.15-18);
- another which has the artificial ring of many such speeches in ancient historical writings (14.15-17) — hard to imagine as uttered in the circumstances envisaged;[104]
- opposition from 'the Jews' (13.45, 50-51; 14.2, 19; cf. 17.5; 18.12; 19.9; 20.3; 23.12);
- the first instance of the 'turn to the Gentiles' motif (13.46-47; cf. 18.6; 28.25-28);
- further examples of Luke's concern to emphasize that everything takes place in accord with the purpose of God (13.36; cf. 2.23; 5.38-39; 20.27); the believing Gentiles 'had been destined for eternal life' (13.48; cf. 2.47; 3.18-21; 22.14; 26.16);
- the spread of the word (13.49; cf. 6.7; 12.24; 19.20), and disciples full of joy and the Holy Spirit (13.52; cf. 8.39; 9.31; 11.23; 15.3);
- the anachronistic account of Paul and Barnabas 'appointing elders in each church' (14.23).

Notable, not least, are the parallels of Paul with Peter which Luke has contrived in chs. 13–14:

- miracles of judgment (5.1-10; 13.11);
- remarkably similar initial sermons (2.14-36; 13.16-41);
- the healing of a man 'lame from birth (*chōlos ek koilias mētros autou)*' (3.2; 14.8), evoking wonder from the crowd (3.9-11; 14.11-13, 18) and providing opportunity to preach (3.12-26; 14.14-17).

---

103. See nn. 16-18 above.
104. As difficult to envisage as the chorus-like response of the crowd in Acts 2.7-11.

Equally typical, however, is the evidence that Luke was able to draw on reports and reminiscences, perhaps from Paul himself, or indeed from Timothy, who is reported as well known to (and who therefore knew well) the disciples in Lystra and Iconium (16.2). Signs of the tradition which Luke probably received include:[105]

- a prophecy resulting in a completely new strategy (13.2-4);
- the first, easy and obvious step, to Cyprus, Barnabas's homeland (13.4);
- the surprising name Bar-Jesus, and the obscurity of the name Elymas (13.8), the inference being that both were given to Luke in the tradition he received;
- Luke's correct designation of Sergius Paulus as 'proconsul' (13.7), Cyprus being a senatorial province;
- the embarrassment of John Mark's abandoning of the mission (13.13);
- the link between Sergius Paulus and Pisidian Antioch;[106]
- the brief description of the synagogue 'service' in 13.14-15, consistent with what we know of diaspora synagogues at that time from Philo and Josephus;[107]
- the implication that the Jewish communities in Antioch and Iconium had influential sympathizers among the local citizens (13.50; 14.2, 5);
- the recollection in the Pauline churches of Paul's mission through Antioch, Iconium and Lystra (2 Tim. 3.11);
- the reference to Paul and Barnabas as 'the apostles' (14.4, 14), which hardly makes sense within Acts as a whole, given the qualifications for apostleship laid down in 1.22, and Luke's use of the term elsewhere invariably to refer to the twelve in Jerusalem (within whose number Barnabas had not previously been included); the only obvious solution is that Luke's account reflects the story as told from an Antiochene perspective, Paul and Barnabas having been commissioned and sent forth as missionaries of that church (13.3);[108]

---

105. Cf. Breytenbach, *Paulus und Barnabas* 78-83, 94-95; Jervell, *Apg.* 349, 367-68, 380.

106. See above, n. 46.

107. See *Jesus Remembered* 304 nn. 223-26.

108. Similarly Barrett, *Acts* 1.666-67, 671-72; Fitzmyer defends the view that the term comes from Luke's source (*Acts* 526). For 'apostle' as emissary of a particular church see 2 Cor. 8.23 and Phil. 2.25, and note the wider usage indicated in 1 Cor. 15.7 and Rom. 16.7. Wilson observes that 'the casual references in 14:4, 14 show that the word has no polemic significance for him [Luke]' (*Gentiles* 120). A. C. Clark, 'The Role of the Apostles', in Marshall and Peterson, eds., *Witness to the Gospel* 169-90, finds a clear hint that Luke himself saw Paul and Barnabas as playing a role similar to that of the twelve apostles (182-84).

- one of the few close matches between Paul's list of his personal sufferings (2 Cor. 11.23-27) and Luke's account of Paul's mission in Acts (Acts 14.19 = 2 Cor. 11.25b);
- the success of the mission recorded by Luke as probably reflected in the reports and allusions of Gal. 2.7-9 and 3.1-5;
- the presentation of Paul as caring for the churches he founded (Acts 14.22).

We should also note that in putting together his version of the events narrated, Luke has been able to present Paul in ways that accord with Paul's own self-testimony (though least successfully in 13.16-41):

- Paul's understanding of the gospel as 'to the Jew first and also to the Greek' (13.46; cf. Rom. 1.16);
- Paul as fulfilling the mission of the Servant in Isa. 49.6 (Acts 13.47; cf. Gal. 1.15-16);
- the 'sermon' of Acts 14.15-17 as a variation on Paul's indictment in Rom. 1.20-23, and the echo of Paul's evangelistic call to 'turn from idols to the living God' (14.15; 1 Thess. 1.9);
- the echoes of Pauline language of exhortation and of suffering as a necessary preliminary to glory (14.22).[109]

All in all, chs. 13–14 go some way to enhance Luke's status as an ancient historian: his story-line is captivating; it advances his major aims; it draws on good tradition; and its representation of Paul is one that would have drawn few complaints from Paul himself.

27.2. The Crisis

The crisis broke some time after Paul and Barnabas had returned to Antioch, that is, some time in the second half of the 40s. Acts implies that Paul and Barnabas resumed their role as active members of the Antioch church (14.28). Paul himself simply recollects that Barnabas and he went up to Jerusalem fourteen years after his first visit (Gal. 2.1), a period which covered his preaching in 'the regions of Syria and Cilicia' (1.21-23).[110] Whether the meetings in Jerusalem which follow in both accounts are different versions of the same meeting, or different visits, we will discuss below (§27.3). But both accounts agree that the issue which oc-

109. See n. 96 above.
110. See above, §25.5d; and further below, §31.7b.

casioned the meeting (Acts 15.1) or was at its heart (Gal. 2.3-5) was *circumcision:* whether it was necessary for Gentile believers to be circumcised. In the words of Acts 15.5, 'Some of the believers who were from the sect of the Pharisees stood up and said, "It is necessary for them to be circumcised and ordered to keep the law of Moses"'. To appreciate what was at stake here we have to understand why circumcision was so important, why it had been ignored in the early mission to Gentiles, and why the issue took so long to come to the fore.

a. Circumcision

The irreducibly fundamental importance of circumcision for the Jew in the Second Temple period can easily be documented. Nothing could be clearer than Gen. 17.9-14:

> [10]This is my covenant which you shall keep, between me and you and your descendants after you: Every male among you shall be circumcised. [11]... and it shall be a sign of the covenant between me and you. ... [13]So shall my covenant be in your flesh an everlasting covenant. [14]Any uncircumcised male who is not circumcised in the flesh of his foreskin shall be cut off from his people; he has broken my covenant.

The covenant which constituted Israel as a people, the seed of Abraham who had inherited the promises to Abraham and the other patriarchs,[111] the assembly of God *(qahal Yahweh),* was 'the covenant of circumcision' (Acts 7.8); no circumcision, no covenant, no promise, no nation (Gen. 17.10, 12-14).[112]

The importance of circumcision as defining national and religious identity and as an unremovable boundary post was massively reinforced by the Maccabean crisis. Hellenistic antipathy to what Greeks saw as bodily mutilation caused many Jews to abandon this key covenant marker. In the words of 1 Maccabees, 'They built a gymnasium in Jerusalem, according to Gentile custom, and removed the marks of circumcision, and abandoned the holy covenant' (1 Macc. 1.14-15).[113] In the consequent revolt and suppression, circumcision

---

111. See, e.g., Exod. 2.24; 6.8; 32.13; Deut. 1.8; 6.3, 23; 9.5; 26.18-19.

112. On the central importance of the covenant for Israel's self-understanding and religious/national identity, see particularly A. Jaubert, *La notion d'alliance dans le Judaisme* (Paris: Éditions du Seuil, 1963); Sanders, *Paul and Palestinian Judaism* part 1; E. J. Christiansen, *The Covenant in Judaism and Paul: A Study of Ritual Boundaries as Identity Markers* (Leiden: Brill, 1995); briefly in my *Partings* §§2.2-3.

113. 'They concealed the circumcision of their private parts in order to be Greeks even when unclothed' (Josephus, *Ant.* 12.241).

was clearly for many the 'make or break' issue. Thus on the one side, in accordance with the Syrian decree, women who had their children circumcised were put to death with their (circumcised) infants hung from their necks (1 Macc. 1.60-61; 2 Macc. 6.10); enforced abandonment of circumcision was evidently recognized to be the best way to break down the barrier which protected and maintained Israel's distinctiveness. Equally, on the other, the Maccabean rebels made a particular point of forcibly circumcising 'all the uncircumcised boys that they found within the borders of Israel' (1 Macc. 2.46); for them circumcision obviously had the same function as the *sine qua non* of Israel's self-definition.

For the same reason, when, subsequently, the Hasmonean kingdom was able to extend its borders during the period when Syrian power was in decay, they made a particular point of forcibly circumcising the inhabitants of the conquered territories of Galilee and Idumea;[114] evidently it was impossible to conceive of the inhabitants of these territories belonging to Israel unless they had been circumcised. The *Book of Jubilees,* probably written in this period, follows Gen. 17 fairly closely and then continues:

> This law is for all generations for ever . . . it is an eternal ordinance, ordained and written on the heavenly tablets. And everyone who is born, the flesh of whose foreskin is not circumcised on the eighth day, belongs not to the children of the covenant which the Lord made with Abraham, but to the children of destruction. . . . (*Jub.* 15.25-34)

In the light of such traditions and passages the language of Acts 15.1 (the logic of those who pressed for the circumcision of Gentile believers) can readily be understood: 'Unless you are circumcised according to the custom of Moses, you cannot be saved'. In a word, circumcision was essential for salvation.

That circumcision was so crucial for Jews was well recognized in the wider Greco-Roman world and quite often commented on.[115] This is all the more remarkable since it was also well enough known that other peoples practised circumcision, including Samaritans, Arabs and Egyptians.[116] Clearly in the case of

---

114. 'After subduing all the Idumeans [John Hyrcanus] permitted them to remain in their country so long as they had themselves circumcised and were willing to observe the laws of the Judeans/Jews' (Josephus, *Ant.* 13.257-58); likewise Aristobulus with the Itureans (northern Galilee) (13.318); Josephus is able to substantiate his report from the first-century BCE historian Timagenes (13.319; further detail in *GLAJJ* 1.§81). Josephus also describes the later necessity for Azizus, king of Emesa, to be circumcised before he could marry Drusilla, daughter of Herod Agrippa, and how the same Herod's elder daughter, Berenice, induced Polemo, king of Cilicia, to be circumcised in order to marry her (*Ant.* 20.139, 145). See also below, §27.4a.

115. See particularly Petronius, *Satyricon* 102.14; *Fragmenta* 37; Tacitus, *Hist.* 5.5.2; Juvenal, *Sat.* 14.99 — texts in *GLAJJ* 1.§§194, 195; 2.§§281, 301.

116. Herodotus, *Hist.* 2.104.2-3; Strabo, *Geog.* 16.4.9; 17.1.51; Celsus in Origen,

the Jews the rite had been given a particular prominence and significance, at the insistence of Jews themselves, as *essential to the definition and maintenance of their national and religious (covenant) distinctiveness* and the final salvation which members of the covenant could expect. As Tacitus was to put it in his own abrupt manner: 'They adopted circumcision to distinguish themselves from other peoples by this difference' (*Hist.* 5.5.2). Similarly Josephus: God commanded Abraham to practise circumcision 'to the intent that his posterity should be kept from mixing with others' (*Ant.* 1.192). This is no doubt why Paul was able to re-define the Jew/Gentile or Jew/Greek distinction as 'circumcision/uncircum-cision' — Jews as 'the circumcision' (not 'the circumcised'), 'circumcision' standing metonymically for 'Jews', circumcision as *the* defining characteristic of 'the Jew'.[117] Just as, no doubt, it was, in part at least, the distinctively national importance of circumcision which caused Hadrian to ban the rite as part of his response to the Bar Kokhba revolt of 132-135.[118] Subsequently, the ban having been lifted by Hadrian's successor, Antoninus Pius, Justin Martyr could remind his Jewish interlocutor, Trypho, that 'You [Jews] are recognized among other peoples by nothing other than your circumcision in the flesh' (*Dial.* 16.3).

It is entirely understandable, therefore, that circumcision should be re-garded as essential for converts to Judaism, the submission to circumcision as the crucial step of crossing the boundary between Gentile and Jew, the decisive rite by which he who was no son of Abraham became a child of the promise to Abra-ham and a member of the people defined by that promise. It is true that the neces-sity of circumcision, that is, of the ritual act itself, was sometimes questioned.[119] But in each case the answer given is that the rite of circumcision was too funda-mental to be dispensed with.[120] Even the sophisticated, spiritualizing Philo could not think to argue otherwise.[121]

---

c. Cels. 5.41 — texts in *GLAJJ* 1.§§1, 118, 123; 2.§375; in Jewish sources cf. Jer. 9.25-26; Philo, *Spec. Leg.* 1.2; see further Schürer, *History* 1.537-38.

117. Rom. 2.26; 3.30; Gal. 2.7; Col. 3.11.

118. Though again see further Schürer, *History* 1.538-40.

119. Philo, *Migr.* 92; Josephus, *Ant.* 20.38-42.

120. *Migr.* 93-94; *Ant.* 20.43-48. Watson argues too quickly from these data that the practice of not circumcising proselytes was sufficiently widespread to provide a precedent for early Christian mission (*Paul, Judaism and the Gentiles* [²2007] 74-79; he even speaks of 'a tra-ditional Jewish argument for the non-circumcision of Gentiles' — 83 n. 69); but he ignores the bibliography in n. 121 below and the considerations marshalled in §27.2b below (circumcision unnecessary because the Spirit has been given, not because of some Jewish 'traditional' prece-dent).

121. See further L. H. Schiffman, 'At the Crossroads: Tannaitic Perspectives on the Jewish-Christian Schism', *JCSD* 2.115-56 (here 125-27); also *Who Was a Jew?* (Hoboken: Ktav, 1985) 23-25; J. Nolland, 'Uncircumcised Proselytes?', *JSJ* 12 (1981) 173-94; J. J. Col-lins, 'A Symbol of Otherness: Circumcision and Salvation in the First Century', in J. Neusner

In Acts the argument that Gentile believers in Messiah Jesus should be circumcised is attributed to some of the Judea-based believers 'from the sect of the Pharisees' (Act 15.1, 5).[122] In Paul's own account the pressure comes from a group whom he refers to dismissively as 'false brothers smuggled in' (Gal. 2.4), a designation to which we will return. Clearly implied in both cases is that the pressure-group were representative of the more traditional among those who had come to believe in Jesus as Messiah. In view of the data just reviewed, however, it is surprising that only they felt it necessary to raise the issue. When circumcision was so integral to the being of a Jewish male, why did the other Jews involved in the new sect as it began to reach out to Gentiles not simply assume that circumcision was, of course, the rite of entry into the people of God?

b. Why Did the Jewish Evangelists Not Circumcise Gentile Converts?

Here we must revert to one of the most astonishing features of Luke's account of the breakthrough made by Hellenists in Antioch (Acts 11.20-21): that he passes over so briefly the amazing departure from what had been the uniform and (almost) universal treatment of Gentile converts to Israel. As indicated earlier, circumcision cannot have been required of these converts.[123] The subsequent history of the mission to Gentiles, and particularly the crisis which broke in the late 40s, is inexplicable on any other terms. Indeed, it is hardly conceivable that the earliest Gentile admissions to the new sect were on traditional terms, thus setting a pattern of conformity to tradition, and that only subsequently Gentiles began to be admitted without requiring circumcision. If the pattern of conformity had been thus set, departure from that pattern was bound to have raised queries much sooner. Rather, what we have to confront is the implied, but very assured fact, that Gentile believers in Messiah Jesus were accepted without the requirement of circumcision from the first. The historical fact with which we have to reckon is the shocking fact (shocking to almost any Jewish sensibility) that *Jewish missionaries accepted Gentiles as full members of the new messianic sect without demanding that they be circumcised,* that is, without regard to the terms laid down in Gen. 17.9-14 and still regarded as binding on the people of the covenant.

---

and E. S. Frerichs, eds., *'To See Ourselves as Others See Us': Christians, Jews, 'Others' in Late Antiquity* (Chico: Scholars, 1985) 163-86; Schürer, *History* 3.169; McKnight, *Light* 79-82; Cohen, *Beginnings,* index 'circumcision', particularly 39-46. In this section I draw on my *Romans* 119-20.

122. Phil. 3.2-5 still reflects the centrality of circumcision in a Pharisaic perspective; see my *New Perspective on Paul* ch. 22 (here 464-67).

123. See above, §24 n. 251. It might have been expected that the memory of Jesus' openness to Gentiles would have been a factor, but it is not mentioned.

We have already noted the answer to our question: the coming of the Spirit on the Gentile converts (and baptism) made circumcision superfluous.[124] But the point needs to be underlined if we are to appreciate how it was that the Jewish sect became so attractive to Gentiles. The stark, rather disconcertingly 'primitive' fact is that Gentile God-fearers, who heard the gospel preached by these first Jewish missionaries, and who responded to it (believed), thereupon 'received the Spirit'. They experienced a power entering or coming upon them, an experience of love/being loved, and/or joy/exhilaration, and/or peace/forgiveness, and/or praise/prayer, and/or spiritual renewal/new life, a transforming, even visibly transforming experience which others could witness.[125] Such is the testimony of the only two writers who speak of these earliest converts and of what happened when they were converted. We recall that Luke made a point of describing the conversion of Cornelius in such terms: the gift of the Spirit poured out on the uncircumcised Gentiles, as attested by their speaking in tongues and extolling God (Acts 10.45-46), an experience such as had characterized the apostles themselves on the day of Pentecost (10.47; 11.15-17), and a compelling proof for the circumcised believers who had accompanied Peter (10.45-46).[126] And Paul clearly recalls the same sort of thing happening when the Gentiles in Pisidian Antioch, Iconium, Lystra and Derbe believed: they received the Spirit, quite apart from any requirements of the law, an experience to which Paul could appeal as one they could well remember, and one attested or accompanied by miracles (Gal. 3.2, 5).[127] And Luke and Paul are both agreed also, that it was this proof of God accepting Gentiles, while still uncircumcised, which was decisive in the debate which the crisis provoked (Acts 15.7-18; Gal. 2.5-9).

What we have to envisage, therefore, is that the earliest missionaries among Gentiles, whether as God-fearers in a synagogue context, or more directly addressed, found that many of these Gentiles accepted their message regarding Jesus and displayed the effects, physical and moral, which the first believers recognized to be clear evidence that the Spirit of God had entered into or come upon them.[128]

124. See above, §26.4b. That baptism in the name of Christ was early on seen as replacing circumcision may be implied in the understanding of its precursor (the baptism of John, Matt. 3.9/Luke 3.8) and in Col. 2.11-14 (Kraus, *Zwischen Jerusalem und Antiochia* 118-30).

125. For such a range of 'manifestations of the Spirit' for NT writers see my *Jesus and the Spirit* ch. 8 and *Theology of Paul* ch. 16, particularly 430-32.

126. Schnabel surprisingly plays down the significance of 'the unambiguous manifestations of God's Spirit in this particular instance', as over against the 'new revelation from God' (*Mission* 992), but that hardly accords with the emphasis given by Luke to the former in Acts 10.44-48 and 11.15-18.

127. I again assume that the letter to the Galatians was written to these churches; see again §31 n. 32 below.

128. E. W. Stegemann and W. Stegemann, *The Jesus Movement: A Social History of Its*

This they understood to be a sure sign that God had accepted these Gentiles as they were.[129] In Paul's subsequent language, they were displaying evidence that they had been circumcised within, in their hearts (Rom. 2.28-29; Phil. 3.3). This was unheard of in Jewish tradition: Gentiles drawn to Mount Zion as proselytes in the final acts of this age could be assumed to receive the promised eschatological Spirit along with the native Jews; but nothing had been said (because it had not even been conceived?) about them not being first circumcised.[130] Yet in the case of the first missionaries winning Gentiles to faith, we must suppose that they concluded that indeed circumcision was, after all, *un*necessary; the Gentile believers had experienced what the rite of circumcision symbolized;[131] God had eliminated the boundary marked by the rite; there was no more boundary to be crossed, no need for the Gentile believer to become a proselyte. Whether that logic was worked through at the beginning we can no longer tell. But it must have been implicit, otherwise the failure of these missionaries to practise circumcision on the new converts is hard to explain.

The point is worthy of a little more reflection. For Luke makes a point of *not* drawing the same inference with regard to baptism: although Cornelius had already been baptized in the Spirit (Acts 11.15-16), that fact did not make his baptism in water dispensable (10.47-48). The implication, again not clearly drawn in our texts, is that baptism and circumcision were perceived to be of different orders. The first missionaries were not in the business of dispensing with ritual, or pursuing a theology of spiritual reality rendering ritual symbol redundant. The key is probably to be found in the function of circumcision in distinguishing Jew from Gentile, as defining the Gentile as 'other', 'uncircumcised' as denoting 'the outsider', 'uncircumcision' as indicating by definition that lack of

---

First Century (Minneapolis: Fortress, 1999), speak of 'this vaulting of the charismatic fire over the socially well-defined boundaries between Jews and non-Jews', and they quote W. Schluchter: 'instead of the "Spirit" being controlled by the "law", the "Spirit" now controls the "law"' (271-72). In contrast, in his attempt to explain the influx of non-Jews in non-theological terms, that is, in terms of resolving the messy problem of people attracted to the new movement with varying commitment levels, Crossley *(Why Christianity Happened)* ignores what our only informants (Paul and Luke) regarded as critical and decisive. Contrast also Mack's antipathy to religious experience as an explanatory factor, religion for him being a purely social construct *(The Christian Myth* 65-66; see also §25 n. 160 above).

129. The full significance of what was seen as the divine initiative through the Spirit has been too little noted in discussion of the beginnings of the Gentile mission; but see now Philip, *Origins of Pauline Pneumatology* ch. 7.

130. See further Philip, *Origins of Pauline Pneumatology* part 1.

131. The implication of passages like Rom. 2.28-29 and Phil. 3.3 is that Paul and the first Christians generally believed that they had experienced the 'circumcision of the heart' so highly regarded in Jewish writings (Deut. 10.16; Jer. 4.4; 9.25-26; Ezek. 44.9; 1QpHab 11.13; 1QS 5.5; 1QH 10[= 2].18; 21.5[18.20]; Philo, *Spec. Leg.* 1.305).

circumcision was an alien and hopeless condition.[132] It was this boundary which the first missionaries, Peter and Paul, found themselves breaking through, whether they intended it or not. And having thus broken through it, or rather, found that the Spirit had dispensed with it, they evidently thought it unnecessary or indeed a denial of God's manifest grace to re-erect it.

If we are on the right track here, there is still one other question to be answered.

c. Why Was the Question of Circumcision Not Raised by Others Earlier?

If we can take it that the first missionaries to win Gentiles to faith found that the manifest coming of the Spirit on these Gentiles was sufficient reason for them to dispense with circumcision, what about the more traditionalist Jewish believers in Messiah Jesus? We have already had to conclude that there was a spectrum within the early Christian sect — the Hebrews, as over against the Hellenists to whom the expansion of the new sect has to be attributed. How would the Hebrews have viewed the acceptance of Gentiles without requiring circumcision of them? And presumably there were 'those of the sect of the Pharisees' who had been drawn to the new sect prior to their appearance in Luke's narrative (Acts 15.5), as had the many priests mentioned in 6.7. Would they not have raised the issue as soon as uncircumcised Gentiles began to be counted as members of the sect?[133] Gentiles may have been so accepted from the middle or late 30s. Why did the issue only arise, the crisis only break in the second half of the 40s?

The reasons can only be guessed at. My guess[134] is that the believing Gentiles were initially regarded by the Jewish traditionalists as in the same ambiguous situation as Gentile God-fearers, that is, Gentiles who were adherents of the local synagogue and who had adopted some Jewish beliefs and customs, but who had not accepted circumcision.[135] These Gentile sympathizers were evi-

---

132. I echo the language and perspective of Eph. 2.11-12.

133. 'The strange thing is that it [the issue of circumcision] had not already emerged ten or fifteen years earlier [ET mistakenly translates "later"], in the thirties, when Gentile "godfearers" were also already being baptized' (Hengel and Schwemer, *Paul* 266).

134. For earlier statements see my *Partings* (²2006) 164-69, also *New Perspective on Paul* §2.4. Hengel and Schwemer explain the puzzle 'by the sharpening of the former more "liberal" position in Jerusalem and the growth of Zealotism there' (*Paul* 266).

135. Cf. Fredriksen, 'Judaism' 548-58; and see below on 'judaize' (§27.4a). Sufficient detail can be found in my *Romans* xlvii-xlviii and in *Partings* 125. See further F. W. Horn, 'Der Verzicht auf die Beschneidung im frühen Christentum', *NTS* 42 (1996) 479-505; and on Godfearers, see below, §29.5c.

dently quite welcome in the synagogues of the diaspora, the hope being, presumably, that they were on their way to becoming proselytes, much as Juvenal characterizes what must have been a not untypical sequence of events — otherwise Juvenal would not been able to satirize it![136] So initially the Judean-based traditionalist messianic Jews need not have been much disturbed by the accession of the few like Cornelius, devout, God-fearing Gentiles: at worst they could be regarded as anomalous exceptions; at best they marked the beginning of the pilgrimage of Gentiles into Judaism which so many expected at the end of the age.[137] It was only when the number of Gentile converts began to outnumber the believing Jews that alarm bells began to ring. The *exception* (uncircumcised God-fearers) was becoming the *rule* (believing Gentiles).[138] Even if the alarm bells had not been ringing for the Jewish Christian traditionalists earlier, the fact that the Antioch church had sent out Paul and Barnabas on a mission which targetted more directly such God-fearers, and the fact that their mission had been so successful (14.27 — many Gentile converts) would inevitably raise the hitherto unasked question in a sharp form: should not these Gentile converts be circumcised?

This indeed is when (and how) both Luke and Paul explain that the issue was brought up. And there is no reason to dispute their testimony. But I should underline once again how significant is the fact that circumcision had thus been dispensed with. It was indeed one of the defining moments for emerging Christianity. For what had happened is that a new and unheard-of event (Gentiles receiving the Spirit promised to Israel in the age to come) was setting aside a rule which had defined the people of God, a rite which had identified the people of God for centuries, and a practice which had the weight of divine revelation behind it and was unequivocally prescribed in Scripture. It is in such moments, by such uncovenanted experiences of divine grace, through such insights coming as new revelation, that new religions are formed.

27.3. The Council in Jerusalem

Both Paul and Luke agree that the crisis was addressed and resolved in Jerusalem in a meeting involving Paul and Barnabas, James and Peter in particular — Gal. 2.1-10, Acts 15.6-29. Most commentators agree that these two are different ac-

136. Juvenal, *Sat.* 14.96-106: the son of the God-fearing father takes the logical next step of accepting circumcision.

137. Cf. Wilson, *Luke and the Law* 72-73; Martyn, *Galatians* 221. On the expectation see *Jesus Remembered* 394-95.

138. 'Too many Gentiles, too few Jews, and no End in sight' (Fredriksen, 'Judaism' 562).

counts of the *same* meeting. But a significant minority view argues that the Gal. 2.1-10 account describes the earlier trip to Jerusalem referred to in Acts 11.30, and that the letter to the Galatians was written before the council described in Acts 15.[139] The difference is not important theologically, since both agree that the central issue of circumcision was dealt with in the late 40s. And so far as sequencing of the events is concerned, the only real significance is that the Galatians 2 = Acts 11 hypothesis would make Galatians the first of Paul's letters to be preserved and the earliest of the NT writings — matters of no great moment. What is really at stake here is the reliability of Luke's history, and particularly of his reference to 'the apostolic decree' of Acts 15.29.

a. Galatians 2 = Acts 11

The strength of this reconstruction of the central events is threefold:

- It means that both Luke and Paul agree in treating the vital visit to Jerusalem as only Paul's second visit — as Paul insists (Gal. 2.1).
- It avoids awkward problems of correlating Acts 15.6-29 with Gal. 2.1-10, especially Paul's failure to refer to 'the apostolic decree' in Galatians.
- It envisages the Acts 15 council as resolving the further crisis which provoked Paul in Antioch (Gal. 2.11-16).

At the same time, however, the reconstruction causes its own serious problems:

1. The Antioch incident (Gal. 2.11-14) fits into the Acts sequence only with difficulty: if it preceded the mission of Acts 13–14, it is hard to see Paul re-

---

139. Notably Ramsay, *St. Paul* 54-60, 154-55; Bruce, e.g., *Acts* 278, also *Paul* chs. 15 and 17, followed by Mitchell, *Anatolia* 2.4-5; Longenecker, *Galatians,* with full discussion in lxxiii-lxxxviii; Bauckham, 'James and the Jerusalem Church' 469-70, also 'Peter, James, and the Gentiles' 135-39; Barnett, *Jesus* 294-95. Bruce's argument (*Galatians* 115-17) that 2.3-5 refer to later events which took place in Antioch (so that the circumcision issue was not raised at the Jerusalem meeting) has been found unconvincing by most commentators (see, e.g., Longenecker 49-50). P. J. Achtemeier, *The Quest for Unity in the New Testament Church* (Philadelphia: Fortress, 1987), argues for the more complex hypothesis that the agreement reached in Gal. 2.1-10 should be identified with Acts 11.1-18, and that Acts 15 represents a further conference, at which Antioch was represented by a delegation headed by Symeon Niger (Acts 15.14; cf. 13.1), and from which Paul and Barnabas were absent; it was at this conference that 'the apostolic decree' was formulated, as Luke reports (ch. 6). Schnabel's support for Gal. 2 = Acts 11 (*Mission* 987-92) is also confused by his earlier identification of the first 'Jerusalem conference' with Acts 11.1-18 (715-16), without clarifying the relation of 11.18 to 11.30.

aligning himself under Barnabas's leadership after Barnabas's failure (from Paul's perspective) in Antioch; if it followed the Acts 13–14 mission, it provided a different occasion for the Acts 15 meeting from the circumcision crisis indicated in Acts 15.1-5.[140]

2. It is understandable if Luke should have ignored an earlier agreement regarding circumcision reached by Paul and the Jerusalem leadership on the Acts 11.30 trip — on the Galatians 2 = Acts 11 hypothesis, referring to the private *(kat' idian)* meeting described in Gal. 2.2. This would accord with Luke's tendency to postpone reference to a major issue until it became particularly significant or was decisively dealt with.[141] That is, he may have regarded the issue as decisively dealt with only at the (on this hypothesis) later conference which he describes in Acts 15. The only problem is that Paul clearly regarded the Gal. 2.1-10 meeting as achieving a formal agreement with the key Jerusalem leadership (2.7-9), despite fierce opposition (2.4-5), an agreement which would have made further debate on the issue both unnecessary and retrograde.[142] We may have a case here of sacrificing the integrity of the Jerusalem leadership in order to safeguard Luke's reliability.[143]

3. On the Galatians 2 = Acts 11 hypothesis, the attitude ascribed to Peter in Acts 15.10 is remarkably at odds with his conduct in Gal. 2.12, so that one has to envisage a Peter who learns that Jews may eat with Gentiles in Acts 10, is persuaded otherwise in Gal. 2.12, and then claims that the law is a yoke which 'neither we nor our ancestors have been able to bear' (Acts 15.10).[144] It is also hard to imagine the Paul who wrote so dismissively of the Jerusalem apostles in Gal. 2.6, and was so outraged by the conduct of Peter and Barnabas in 2.11-16, acting so meekly as Acts 15.12, 22 and 25 implies.[145]

---

140. See further Barrett, *Acts* 2.xxxvii-xxxviii; Jervell, *Apg.* 342-44. Barrett is also sceptical of attempts (Weiser, *Apg.* 2.368-76, and Pesch, *Apg.* 2.71-75) to distinguish two traditional sources drawn on by Luke (2.710-11).

141. See above, §21.3d(2).

142. In defending the Gal. 2 = Acts 11 option, Schnabel argues that 'there was no in-depth discussion of circumcision during the consultation' (*Mission* 991), ignoring the obvious implications of Gal. 2.3-6.

143. 'In order to preserve Luke's reliability it seems necessary to impugn the good faith of the Jerusalem leadership' (Dunn, *Galatians* 88).

144. Peter 'is described here as something of a Paulinist, though the Paulinism is not accurately portrayed' (Barrett, *Acts* 2.719). Ramsay and others assume that Paul succeeded in persuading Peter in the confrontation of Gal. 2.11-14/17 (*St. Paul* 161-63); but see below, §27.6.

145. Would Paul have accepted that the items listed in 15.20, 29 were 'essentials, compulsory *(epanankes)*' (15.28; BDAG 358)?

b. Galatians 2 = Acts 15

The strengths of the former (a) are, of course, the weaknesses of the latter (b), and vice-versa. If, however, what is at stake is Luke's reliability as a historian of Christianity's beginnings, the question can be fairly asked whether the Galatians 2 = Acts 15 reconstruction does any more damage to Luke's reputation as an ancient historian than the damage we have already registered. And when we take into account Luke's objectives in writing his history (the axes he was trying to grind) does he come out any worse than most historians past and present?

I have already offered a suggestion as to why Luke may have misunderstood the 'famine relief' trip to Jerusalem (Acts 11.30) as involving Saul/Paul as well as Barnabas.[146]

We know that Luke was a good deal more cavalier in his descriptions of Saul/Paul's dealings with Jerusalem (Acts 9.26-30), whereas Paul himself was much more 'uptight' about them and therefore much the more scrupulous in his references to them (Gal. 1.17-2.1). Expressed more positively, Luke was concerned to bring out and emphasize the good and strong relations Paul had with the Jerusalem leadership, whereas Paul was like a cat walking on hot bricks on the same subject (as we shall see shortly). Luke's mix-up over Acts 11.30 (if that's what it was) is no more serious than his account of Paul's first visit to Jerusalem (Acts 9.26-30).

The differences between Acts 15 and Galatians 2 are quite marked, that is true. But the question is whether they nevertheless can stand as accounts of the *same* encounters and agreements from the different perspectives of Luke and Paul.[147] Neither Luke nor Paul was a dispassionate chronicler of these events. *Luke* relates the Jerusalem meeting from the perspective of the Jerusalemites:[148] the lead actors are Peter and James (Acts 15.7-11, 13-21); Barnabas and Paul are passed over in a single sentence (15.12). He narrates it from his own perspective, where Peter's decisive contribution (15.7-11) reflects the central importance Luke gave the Cornelius episode in his own narrative (10.1–11.18), and the im-

146. See above, §25.5g.

147. Lake, after initially being impressed by Ramsay's view, subsequently rejected it (*Beginnings* 5.199-204, here 201). See also Barrett, *Acts* 2.xxxviii-xlii. Despite the differences between the two accounts, Lüdemann, *Early Christianity* 170-72, strongly disputes Dibelius's conclusion that Luke composed Acts 15 on the basis of bare knowledge of a conflict about circumcision of Gentile converts which arose in Antioch and was arbitrated in Jerusalem (*Studies* 98); Lüdemann concludes that 'there is a high degree of historical reliability in the elements of tradition underlying Acts 15.1-35' (172). W. Kirchenschläger, 'Die Entwicklung von Kirche und Kirchenstruktur zur neutestamentlichen Zeit', *ANRW* 2.26.2 (1995) 1277-1356, sets out Gal. 2.1-10 and Acts 15.1-29 in synoptic parallel (1323-24).

148. Cf. Haenchen, *Acts* 461-63; Jervell, *Apg.* 404.

portance he placed on Peter's acceptance of Cornelius as the determinative precedent for the whole Christian mission. *Paul*, on the other hand, recalled his own
contribution to the decision not to require circumcision of Gentile believers as
decisive: the predominantly 'first person' account of Gal. 2.1-10 ('I'/'me' — 2.1,
2, 3, 6, 7, 8, 9, 10) almost entirely eclipses the role of Barnabas (2.1, [5], 9, [10]);
it was Paul through whom God had worked so effectively, the grace given to Paul
that was recognized by the Jerusalem leadership, and Paul who had been entrusted with the gospel for the uncircumcision (2.7-9). Paul evinces here an un-
graciousness which is only partly excusable in the light of Barnabas's subsequent
lapse (2.13): perhaps Barnabas had not been so unyielding as Paul in the critical
confrontation of 2.3-5; or possibly Paul wanted to suppress the fact that he and
Barnabas went to Jerusalem as representatives of the Antioch church.[149]

At all events, once we allow that Luke was likely to recall the Jerusalem
agreement with a different hindsight than Paul, and that Luke was probably
drawing his own account from or choosing to reflect a Jerusalem perspective, it
can be seen to be entirely plausible that Acts 15 and Galatians 2 are accounts of
the same event, with only 'the apostolic decree' as a continuing problem.[150]

c. The Relationship between Paul and Jerusalem

There is a further factor which deserves some attention and which may make it
more likely to see behind the perspectives of Luke and Paul to a shared memory
of a common reality. For in order to appreciate more fully the events behind Gal.
2.1-10 it is necessary to take account of the sensitivities which Paul displays in
describing his relationship with Jerusalem.[151]

We have already noted the contrast between Luke's and Paul's accounts of
his dealings with Jerusalem.[152] Here we might further
note Gal. 1.16 — 'I did not consult immediately with flesh and blood, nor did I go
up to Jerusalem to those who were apostles before me'. In rebutting the charge

---

149. Martyn, *Galatians* 209. 'Barnabas was probably the chief respondent to the
Jerusalemites' (Öhler, *Barnabas* 70-72).

150. See further below, §27.3e.

151. In what follows I draw on my 'The Relationship between Paul and Jerusalem according to Galatians 1 and 2', *NTS* 28 (1982) 461-78, reprinted in *Jesus, Paul and the Law* 108-
26 (Additional Note 126-28). I owe my awakening to 'the dialectic between being independent
of and being acknowledged by Jerusalem (as) the keynote of this important text' [Galatians 1–
2] to B. Holmberg, *Paul and Power: The Structure of Authority in the Primitive Church as reflected in the Pauline Epistles* (Lund: Gleerup, 1977) 14-34 (here 15). See also R. Schäfer,
Paulus bis zum Apostelkonzil (WUNT 2.179; Tübingen: Mohr Siebeck, 2004) 123-49, 175-80,
201-21

152. See above, §25.5a.

that he had received his gospel from the Jerusalem apostles, evidently regarded as the fount of authority by those making the charge, Paul nevertheless acknowledges that authority. The verb 'consult' *(prosanatithēmi)* had a technical meaning, of consulting with someone who was recognized as a qualified interpreter about the significance of some sign — a dream, or omen, or portent, or whatever.[153] So it had the force of 'consult in order to be given a skilled or authoritative interpretation'. The implication is that 'those who were apostles before' Paul were the obvious authorities to consult, had he found it necessary to consult anyone about the meaning of his encounter with Messiah Jesus on the Damascus road.

The implications of Paul's own description of his first post-conversion visit to Jerusalem, so different from Luke's (Acts 9.26-30), are the same: however independently he had received his gospel, 'through a revelation of Jesus Christ' (1.12), Paul had still found it necessary 'to get to know Cephas' (1.18). That, as we have already seen, must have included getting to know him as Jesus' leading disciple and the Jesus tradition of which he was a chief steward.[154] Here the point is, once again, that almost despite himself Paul, writing subsequently, has to acknowledge the seniority of the Jerusalem leadership (Peter at least) and his dependence on Peter for so much of his knowledge of the impact of Jesus which had made Peter to become Cephas.

As to the second Jerusalem visit, the differences between Luke and Paul are similar, but again we can discern behind Paul's account a reality and relationship which he was not altogether comfortable in recalling in Galatians. Luke reports that Paul and Barnabas were appointed by the church of Antioch to lead a delegation to Jerusalem to discuss the issue (whether circumcision should be required of the Gentile converts) with the apostles and elders (Acts 15.1-3).[155] In other words, Paul (and Barnabas) still functioned as emissaries and representatives of the church in Antioch. Paul, on the other hand, makes a point of claiming that he went up to Jerusalem 'in accordance with a revelation' (Gal. 2.2).[156] Thereby Paul in effect declares (again) his independence both of Jerusalem and

153. E.g., Diodorus Siculus relates an odd incident from the life of Alexander and how he 'consulted with seers regarding the sign' (17.116.4); further details are in my 'Relationship' 109-10 and *Galatians* 67-69.

154. See above, §25 nn. 209-11.

155. The 'they' who appointed *(etaxan)* Paul and Barnabas (15.2) are 'the brothers' of 15.1, who are addressed in 15.1b ('Unless you are circumcised in accordance with Mosaic practice you cannot be saved'). That could suggest that only the Gentile members of the Antioch church were in view, or even that the Antioch church had become so predominantly Gentile that the ultimatum of those who had come down from Judea was in effect addressed to the whole Antioch church. Either way, 15.3 confirms that the delegation was 'sent on their way by the church' as such.

156. On the Acts 11 = Galatians 2 hypothesis, the 'revelation' could well be an allusion to the prophecy of Agabus (Acts 11.28).

of Antioch; the former is part of his apologia running through Galatians 1, the latter is consistent with what was probably the outcome of the subsequent confrontation at Antioch (§27.6). The reason for such nuances is suggested by the stated purpose of Paul's visit: 'I laid before them the gospel which I proclaim among the Gentiles . . . lest somehow I was running or had run in vain' (2.2). The implication is that Paul saw the Jerusalem leadership's approval of his gospel as vital to the success or failure of his missionary effort.[157] It was not that he doubted the truth of his gospel; he had emphasized that point sufficiently in ch. 1. It was rather that 'the truth of the gospel' included its continuity with and fulfilment of Israel's hope (Gal. 3.8), so that he could not but be apprehensive lest any disclaimer from Jerusalem of his efforts might cut at the heart of that gospel.[158] Here again, then, we see Paul steering a careful middle course between according the Jerusalem apostles too much authority and denying them the authority which would undercut his own claims.

Most striking of all is the strong assertion of Gal. 2.6. Whereas Luke either ignores entirely the stand Paul took at Jerusalem (Acts 11.30), or passes over it in virtual silence (15.12), Paul indicates that he had had to put up a strong resistance to those who argued for circumcision: he did not yield submission to 'the false brothers', 'not even for an hour' (Gal. 2.5), and his stand was honoured and accepted by James, Peter and John (2.6). But once again the language he uses gives away perhaps more than he intended:

> From those reputed to be something — what they once were makes no difference to me; God shows no partiality — for to me those of repute added nothing.

The formula he uses (*hoi dokountes*, 'those reputed to be something') has a distancing and slightly depreciating note (those held in repute by others, whom others regard as important).[159] The parenthesis confirms the impression. Paul ac-

---

157. 'In laying his gospel before the Jerusalem apostles what he sought was not so much their approval (without which his gospel would have no validity) as their recognition of his gospel's validity, without which his gospel would lose its effectiveness' ('Relationship' 116); see further my *Galatians* 93-94; also Betz, *Galatians* 86 n. 268; R. E. Brown and J. P. Meier, *Antioch and Rome: New Testament Cradles of Catholic Christianity* (London: Chapman, 1983) — 'Paul, for all his defense of his independence, cannot mask the fact that the question is being brought to Jerusalem for a decision' (37); Taylor, *Paul* ch. 4; C. K. Barrett, 'Paul and Jerusalem', *On Paul: Essays on His Life, Work and Influence in the Early Church* (London: Clark, 2003) 1-26 (here 5-6); Wedderburn, *History* 106-107.

158. Cf. Longenecker, *Galatians* 48-49.

159. See Betz, *Galatians* 86-87: 'the expression enables Paul to recognize the *de facto* role which "the men of reputation" play, without compromising his theological stance that God and Christ are the only authority behind his gospel (cf. 1:1, 12, 15-16)' (87).

knowledges their pre-eminence among the Jerusalem leadership, 'what they once were' presumably referring to their role among the disciples of Jesus and in establishing the Jerusalem church itself. But he also affirms that this earlier pre-eminence now (present tense) makes no difference to him, and he implies, rather dismissively, that to accord them too much respect would be contrary to the will and purpose of God.[160] In other words, Paul indicates that he himself has moved on from an earlier esteem for the pillar apostles' authority (as pillars) to a more jaundiced or querulous evaluation of that authority.

The balancing act is spectacular: Paul had admitted in so many words (2.2) that the decision of the Jerusalem leadership had been critical for him; he wished to place the full weight of that authority behind the decision actually made in Jerusalem; he was more than ready to appeal to that authority because of the weight it carried for others.[161] But at the same time he wanted it to be clear that he no longer recognized that authority over himself or his mission. Evidently something had happened between the Jerusalem consultation and the writing of the letter. It takes no great insight to guess that the 'something' was probably the incident at Antioch (2.11-14) and the subsequent attempt to subvert Paul's work in Galatia (1.6-9). It is particularly striking, then, that in the very verse (2.6) where he indicates most clearly the crucial decision taken at Jerusalem (and implying his dependence on it!), Paul made a deliberate point of affirming that the authority of those who made that decision no longer counted for anything with him.[162]

These nuances in Galatians 1–2 are a further reason why it is difficult to conceive of a sequence, Galatians 2.1-10 = Acts 11.30, followed by the Antioch incident (Gal. 2.11-14), followed by Paul writing letter to the Galatians, followed by the Jerusalem council (Acts 15). For in his letter to the Galatians Paul seems to have drawn a firm line between himself and the Jerusalem leadership, even to have 'burnt his boats' so far as his ongoing links with Jerusalem were concerned. Which rings oddly, to put it no more strongly, with Luke's portrayal of Paul submissively accepting the ruling of James in Acts 15.22-30 (contrast Gal. 2.12-14). The greater likelihood, I think, is that Galatians was written after a definitive

---

160. The metaphor ('God shows no partiality') is primarily that of God as judge and could imply some attempt to bribe or to gain his favour by improper means (for references see §33 n. 106). Paul's 'coolness is unmistakable' (Wedderburn, *History* 106).

161. 'The awkwardness of Paul's position was that in order to stress the fact that the pillar apostles accepted his understanding of the gospel and of his vocation he had also to acknowledge their authority to grant that acceptance' (Dunn, *Partings* [²2006] 170).

162. 'In connection with the "men of eminence" this statement more than anything else declares their authority to be an *adiaphoron*. . . . he uses it [the doctrine of *adiaphora*] as a principle here for the purpose of relativizing the authority of the Jerusalem apostles' (Betz, *Galatians* 94).

agreement in Jerusalem, which Paul regarded as licensing him to go about his apostolic mission without further reference to Jerusalem.[163]

d. The Agreement Reached at Jerusalem (according to Paul)

The meeting described by Paul in Gal. 2.1-10 was evidently very fraught and could have turned out differently from what Paul had hoped. 'False brothers' had infiltrated Paul's meeting with the Jerusalem apostles. They must have been regarded as 'brothers' by the Jerusalem leadership, all the more so if the meeting was as 'private' as 2.2 indicates.[164] Paul describes them as 'false', presumably for the same reason that he described the message of the missionaries who were causing trouble in Galatia as 'another gospel' (Gal. 1.6), and later describes the other missionaries who were intervening in Corinth as 'false apostles' (2 Cor. 11.13). That is, they were Christians, Jewish believers in Messiah Jesus, who no doubt had been baptized in the name of Jesus; talk of 'brothers', as of 'gospel' and 'apostles', in these contexts would make no sense otherwise. But the ones referred to had a very different understanding of what acceptance of the gospel demanded of Gentile converts. Paul's language is polemical and hardly conceals his animosity towards them; but even in denouncing them ('false') he concedes their right to make representations on the matter at issue ('brothers').[165]

Whatever the precise circumstances, the issue was circumcision. Paul and Barnabas had brought Titus, a Greek convert, with them, and the 'false brothers' evidently saw Titus as a test case.[166] Paul's language in 2.3 clearly implies a res-

163. See further the next section (§27.3d).

164. The term used by Paul (*pareisaktous* — 'smuggled in, secretly brought in', from *pareisagō*) is a rare term (see Betz, *Galatians* 90 n. 305) and probably indicates an action initiated by others, with James perhaps acting as sponsor for the more traditionalist Jewish believers. It could refer to their entry into the Jesus sect itself, with 2.4 (they 'sneaked in to spy on our freedom') referring to their entry to the meeting itself.

165. The 'false brothers' of Gal. 2.4 are most naturally to be identified with 'some believers who belonged to the sect of the Pharisees' (Acts 15.5). Paul would have known the attitude well 'from inside' (Gal. 1.13-14; Phil. 3.6). Lüdemann reminds us that the 'false brethren' remained members of the Jerusalem church, despite the concordat reached at the Jerusalem conference (*Opposition* 36).

166. The parallel with the case of Izates of Adiabene is close. Having been told that he did not need to be circumcised in order to be a Jew, Izates was then confronted by the more scrupulous Eleazar, with arguments which probably were very similar to those used by the 'false brothers': 'In your ignorance, O king, you are guilty of the greatest offence against the law and thereby against God. For you ought not merely to read the law but also, and even more, to do what is commanded in it. How long will you continue to be uncircumcised? If you have not yet read the law concerning this matter, read it now, so that you may know what an impiety

olute attempt made by the 'false brothers' to 'compel' the circumcision of Titus. In so saying, Paul assuredly does not mean that he gave way gracefully (he did not need to be *'compelled'*);[167] such a response would have wholly undermined Paul's argument and runs entirely counter to 2.5.[168] In each of its uses in Galatians, *anankazō* ('compel') refers to pressure being exercised from the more traditionalist side in regard to Gentile converts (2.14; 6.12). So, the more likely inference is that the *Jerusalem apostles* did not exert the compulsion. Again the nuance should not be missed: the Jerusalem apostles had tried to persuade Paul to accede to the false brothers' demand, but did not insist ('compel'); they were sympathetic to the demand, but recognized the force of Paul's counter-arguments.[169] The implication, of course, is that they could have insisted, and such was their authority within the Jesus sect that it would have been difficult if not disastrous for Paul to refuse.

But Paul did resist, and the first person plural indicates that Barnabas was equally resolute when the 'crunch' came. The line of the counter-argument is clear from 2.7-9 and has already been indicated (§27.2b): the grace of God had proved so manifestly effective for the Gentile converts of Paul and Barnabas, that a circumcision designed to achieve that end was thereby rendered superfluous. With a view to the Galatians, Paul puts the argument in terms of freedom/liberty (2.4), where his thought obviously is of liberty from requirements of the law (5.1). Whether he put his argument in these terms at the Jerusalem council itself must be doubted; if James 1.25 and 2.12 ('the law of liberty') are anything to go by, James would certainly have bridled at the inference. And the language betrays the perspective of Paul the Christian rather the perspective of Saul the Pharisee.[170] In any case, Gal. 2.7-9 imply that the decisive consideration was the undeniable grace and working of God in and among Gentiles through Paul.[171] More

---

it is that you commit' (Josephus, *Ant.* 20.44-45). Watson follows a lonely track in arguing that concern over circumcision arose only at the Antioch incident (Gal. 2.11-14) (*Paul, Judaism and the Gentiles* [²2007] 103-107).

167. So, notably, Weiss, *Earliest Christianity* 270-72; K. Lake, 'The Apostolic Council of Jerusalem', *Beginnings* 5.197. A. D. Nock, *St. Paul* (Oxford: Oxford University, 1938, 1946), suggested that 'Titus, under pressure, but on his own initiative and without consulting Paul, had himself circumcised in the hope of easing a difficult situation' (109).

168. See, e.g., Longenecker, *Galatians* 50; Barrett, 'Paul and Jerusalem' 6-7.

169. 'The counsels of the Apostles of the Circumcision are the hidden rock on which the grammar of the sentence is wrecked' (Lightfoot, *Galatians* 105-106). Paul's fractured train of thought has prompted other explanations; see my *Galatians* 97.

170. For liberty/freedom as motif in Paul, see my *Theology of Paul* 328, 388-89, 434-35, 658-61.

171. Martyn thinks that 2.7-8 contains a kernel of an earlier agreement between Paul and Peter, achieved on Paul's first visit to Jerusalem (1.18) (*Galatians* 212). But had Paul been engaged in mission prior to that meeting (see above, §25.5b)? and, more to the point, if

to the point, the key fact remains that in the event 'to me those of repute added nothing' (2.6).[172] The authority which the Jerusalem apostles certainly had was exercised in Paul's favour. The precise reference of the verb 'added' is unclear, but what is clear is that Titus was *not* circumcised and the pillar apostles agreed formally[173] that the gospel could go to the Gentiles without any requirement of circumcision being laid on those who accepted it and made a faith commitment to Messiah Jesus.[174]

We should not underestimate how astonishing a decision was here made:[175] that Jews, leaders of a Jewish messianic sect, agreed in considered and formal terms that circumcision need no longer be required of Gentiles wishing to be counted full members of that sect — despite Gen. 17.9-14! Anomalies like God-fearing adherents to diaspora synagogues, or even exceptional cases like Cornelius (Acts 10–11) or Izates (*Ant.* 20.38-42), could be winked at so long as their lack of circumcision did not become a public issue or point of principle. But Paul had had the temerity to make Titus a test case, whether by design or under pressure from the 'false brothers'. And the Jerusalem leadership had given him their backing, however hesitantly.[176] Clear scriptural teaching and historic tradition had been set aside and discounted in the light of events clearly perceived as the work of God.

In Paul's presentation of the historic agreement he himself naturally takes

---

he had been so engaged, had he achieved the kind of manifest approval from God which so clearly attended his subsequent evangelistic preaching, without which the recognition of 2.7-9 was unlikely to have been accorded? (And why has no memory of such success been retained?)

172. As in Gal. 1.1, 12, 16-17, 18-20, Paul's firm assertion in 2.6 seems to be directed against a different view of the agreement achieved in Jerusalem: 'they added *(prosanatithēmi)* nothing' has the ring of a refutation of the tradition used by Luke in Acts 15.28 (the decision 'not to lay [*epitithēmi*] any burden beyond the following essentials').

173. For 2.7-9 as a formal agreement, see Bruce, *Paul* 153-54; Betz, *Galatians* 96-98; other bibliography in Schnelle, *Paul* 127 n. 19. 'The right hand of fellowship' (Gal. 2.9) indicates a formal agreement, clearly set out, and not simply a private arrangement or expression of good will; see particularly J. P. Sampley, *Pauline Partnership in Christ* (Philadelphia: Fortress, 1980) ch. 3; and further my *Galatians* 110-11.

174. See also Kraus, *Zwischen Jerusalem und Antiochia* 139-41.

175. Cf. Wilckens, *Theologie* 1/2.266-71.

176. Some hesitancy may be indicated by the fact that whereas Peter's mission is designated as 'the apostleship *(apostolēn)* of the circumcision', Paul's is described only as 'for the Gentiles' (*apostolēn* is not repeated) (2.8). 'The agreement must have recognized Peter's apostleship, but left Paul without a specific title' (Betz, *Galatians* 82, 98). 'The nature of the recognition which Paul received at this conference in Jerusalem could easily have been misunderstood or misrepresented' (Bruce, *Paul* 155). 'Gal. 2:9 contains no acknowledgement of Paul's apostleship but speaks merely of Paul's Gentile mission' (Lüdemann, *Opposition* 37); '. . . unmistakably failing to grant formal apostolicity to Paul's labors' (Martyn, *Galatians* 203).

centre stage, with his rather dismissive comments regarding the apostles 'reputed to be pillars' (Gal. 2.9) casting them in the shadow (2.6). But we should not fail to give credit also to James, Peter and John. For without their assent to Paul's advocacy, without their recognition of the mission to the Gentiles, the missionary outreach of the nascent Christian movement would either have been strangled at birth, or it would have ceased to be attractive to God-fearers who did not want to go all the way to circumcision, or, perhaps more likely, it would have become a renegade sect in *de facto* independence from both its parent Judaism and the Judean Christians.[177] The leadership which they displayed on that occasion, however unwillingly, was absolutely crucial.[178] And James in particular, who is often regarded as a somewhat sinister figure in Paul's account of things (2.12!), should be included in the Gentile Christian applause. For all that he was evidently closer to the traditionalist end of the Christian spectrum, he was ready to acknowledge the grace of God even when it manifested itself unexpectedly and to accept a logic of grace which he probably found uncomfortable in many of its implications.[179]

From Gal. 2.1-10 we glean only two other elements of the agreement made in Jerusalem. The formal agreement as such is briefly stated: the pillar apostles 'gave me and Barnabas the right hand of fellowship, that [literally] we to/for the Gentiles, and they to/for the circumcision *(hēmeis eis ta ethnē, autoi de eis tēn peritomēn)*'. This is generally taken to indicate a division of missionary responsibility, with the main debate being whether the division in view was geographical or ethnic ('we to the Gentiles, they to the Jews').[180] However, neither interpretation makes much sense, since there were far more Jews in the diaspora than in the land of Israel,[181] and since Paul's regular missionary tactic was probably to reach

177. Cf. B. J. Malina and J. H. Neyrey, *Portraits of Paul: An Archaeology of Ancient Personality* (Louisville: Westminster John Knox, 1996): 'In an honor/shame society such as the one in which Paul lived, claims to honor and precedence always required public acknowledgment, lest they be vain claims, ridiculed and leading to shame' (47).

178. 'This recognition of the Antiochian Gentile mission was something astounding, and does all honour to the men of Jerusalem' (Haenchen, *Acts* 467).

179. Murphy-O'Connor suggests that the main reasons for James's acquiescence in the Gal. 2.6-9 agreement were political and practical; 'it was not the moment to insist on principle' (*Paul* 138-41). See further below, §36.1b.

180. See, e.g., discussion in Betz, *Galatians* 100; Bruce, *Galatians* 124-25; Longenecker, *Galatians* 58-59; Murphy-O'Connor, *Paul* 142-44; Schnabel, *Mission* 992-1000. Painter argues that *ethnē* is not used here exclusively for Gentiles and that Paul would have understood the agreement as a universal mission to 'the nations', including the Jews (*Just James* 61-67), but clearly *ethnē* in the sense of 'Gentiles' is in view throughout Galatians 1–2 (Gal. 1.16; 2.2, 8; and most obviously 2:12, 14-15). So that dimension of Paul's commission, or Paul's commission as 'to the Gentiles' = 'uncircumcision' (2.7-8), is obviously in view in 2.9 as well.

181. The relative Jewish populations in the diaspora and in Israel/Palestine during

out to Gentiles through the diaspora synagogues which Gentile God-fearers attended. The absence of a verb in the brief terms of the agreement, and the breadth of meaning possibly in the preposition used *(eis),*[182] suggest a more general division of responsibility: that Paul and Barnabas should act 'for, with respect to' the Gentile mission/believers, while Peter, James and John should act 'for, with respect to' the Jewish mission/believers.[183] And since Paul and Barnabas were at that point in effect representing the interests of the largely/predominantly Gentile church of Antioch,[184] it may well be that we should see in the Jerusalem agreement a formal recognition by each of the other's role: Antioch as representing the interests of and exercising oversight over the mission to Gentiles (which they had been foremost in sponsoring) and the growing number of Gentile converts; Jerusalem as representing the interests of and exercising oversight over the mission to Jews and the equally increasing number of Jews who were becoming members of the new sect (cf. Acts 21.20). Such an understanding of the agreement of Gal. 2.9 would help explain Paul's attitude subsequently to what he evidently regarded as encroachments on his responsibility as agreed at Jerusalem.[185]

Paul recalls the Jerusalem leadership making only one other stipulation — not as part of the formal agreement, but as a kind of addendum: 'with the one proviso *(monon),* that we should remember the poor' (2.10). 'The poor' refer no doubt to those who lacked resources to maintain life even at subsistence level, probably with particular reference to those in Jerusalem itself.[186] Active con-

---

this period are disputed. S. W. Baron, *A Social and Religious History of the Jews.* Vol. 1: *Ancient Times,* part 1 (New York: Columbia University, 1937, ²1952), reckoned about 2,000,000 in Palestine, and over 4,000,000 within the Roman Empire outside Palestine (167-71, 370-72). Tcherikover notes varying estimates (*Hellenistic Civilization and the Jews* 504-505). 'It comes as a startling fact to many that in Paul's time there were more Jews living in the Greek world than there were in Palestine. Scholars all agree on this conclusion. . . . Some reckon that the ratio was five to one; others reckon that it was ten to one' (S. Sandmel, *The Genius of Paul: A Study in History* [1958; Philadelphia: Fortress, 1979] 10). See also §29.5b below.

182. See BDAG 288-91; (5) 'marker of a specific point of reference, *for, to, with respect to, with reference to*' (291).

183. Cf. Hahn: 'The decision . . . does not denote a division into two missionary spheres, nor does it mean that the one side has to devote itself only to Gentiles and the other to Jews; it rather indicates the main emphasis and purpose of the missionary activity' (*Mission* 81).

184. See above, §27.3b-c.

185. Gal. 2.11-14 — see below, §27.4; 2 Cor. 10.13-16 — see below, §29.4b.

186. This is consistent with other data or what we can deduce from them: the strains on the system of 'poor relief' in the Jerusalem church (Acts 6.1); the report of a famine which hit Jerusalem hard (11.29); the subsequent collection made by Paul for 'the poor among the saints in Jerusalem' (Rom. 15.26); see also §23.2d above. 'The poor' was hardly intended as a title for the Jerusalem Christians as a whole; see, e.g., the data in Longenecker, *Galatians* 59. The verb 'remember' may well include a broader concern on behalf of

Crisis and Confrontation

cern for the poor was, of course, a particular and distinctive feature of Jewish law and tradition.[187] More to the point, however, almsgiving was widely understood within Judaism as a central and crucial expression of covenant righteousness;[188] indeed, 'almsgiving' and 'righteousness' could be regarded as synonymous.[189] Accordingly it was regarded as particularly important in the case of God-fearers, those Gentile adherents who had (so far) declined to be circumcised — Cornelius being a classic example (Acts 10.2, 4).[190] Not only so, but the expectation of an incoming of eschatological proselytes to Mount Zion included the expectation that they would come bearing gifts.[191] This suggests that the 'only' qualification added to the agreement in Jerusalem was of particular significance for the traditionalists who acceded to the agreement.[192] For if circumcision was not required of the Gentile believers, what else would bind them into the people of God? The righteousness of almsgiving was just such an obligation, a primary expression of Jewish covenant piety. If Paul and Barnabas could ensure that they inculcated that sense of obligation among those they represented (the Gentile believers), that would ensure that the Gentile converts were indeed accepting traditional Jewish covenant concerns; and it would help the Jewish traditionalist believers to recognize that the abandonment of the requirement of circumcision did not disqualify the Gentile believers from membership of the covenant people.[193]

'the poor'(Taylor, *Paul* 116-22), but the primary thrust of the request no doubt was for financial help.

187. Deut. 24.10-22; Pss. 10.2, 9; 12.5; 14.6; etc.; Isa. 3.14-15; 10.1-2; 58.6-7; Amos 8.4-6; see further *IDB* 3.843-44.

188. Dan. 4.27; Sir. 3.30; 29.12; 40.24; Tob. 4.10; 12.9; 14.11.

189. In the LXX, *eleēmosynē*, 'kind deed, alms, charitable giving', is frequently used to translate Hebrew *sedeq/sᵉdaqah*, 'righteousness' (G. Schrenk, *dikaiosynē, TDNT* 2.196). For subsequent rabbinic tradition see Str-B 4.536-58; R. Garrison, *Redemptive Almsgiving in Early Christianity* (JSNTS 77; Sheffield: JSOT, 1993) 52-59; e.g., the Midrash on Deut. 15.9 elaborates: 'Be careful not to refuse charity, for everyone who refuses charity is put in the same category with idolaters, and he breaks off from him the yoke of heaven, as it is said, "wicked", that is, "without yoke"'.

190. See K. Berger, 'Almosen für Israel. Zum historischen Kontext der paulinischen Kollekte', *NTS* 23 (1976-77) 180-204, particularly 183-92; cf. W. Schmithals, 'Probleme des "Apostelkonzils" (Gal 2,1-10)', *Paulus, die Evangelien und das Urchristentum* (Leiden: Brill, 2004) 5-38 (here 28-31).

191. See below, §33 n. 364. 'Gentile mission and the collection for Jerusalem are component parts of the eschatological event for Israel' (B. Beckheuer, *Paulus und Jerusalem. Kollekte und Mission im theologischen Denken des Heidenapostels* [Frankfurt: Lang, 1997] 85, and further 57-97).

192. Their use of 'remember' may be significant also, since cultic overtones were not far away (O. Michel, *TDNT* 4.682).

193. In setting 2.10 against the background of the Greek tradition of reciprocal benefit-

In short, we should probably see the Jerusalem agreement as containing an element of compromise (as so often in agreements negotiated between disputing parties). The Jerusalem leadership, having acknowledged Paul's mission (however hesitantly), and conceded on the issue of circumcision for Gentiles (perhaps unwillingly), sought to safeguard the principle that the covenant made with God nevertheless laid obligations on the people of the covenant which could not be dispensed with, and that incoming Gentiles should fulfill prophetic expectations. Paul (and Barnabas), for their part, having achieved their primary goal, were willing to concede an obligation which they anyway were eager to maintain.[194]

The problem was, as soon became apparent, that the Jerusalem leadership probably thought that the addendum safeguarded a point of principle: that all believers in Messiah Jesus were obligated to practise righteousness as directed by the Torah, an attitude which has become summed up in the phrase 'covenantal nomism';[195] and that the righteousness of the law still defined the Jesus sect as part of the covenant people. Whereas Paul saw the agreement itself (Gentile believers need not be circumcised) as breaking away from the idea that any practice should be required which marked off Jew from Gentile; the obligation to 'remember the poor' was not one such, but an inheritance from Scripture and tradition which he continued gladly to embrace and affirm.[196]

Curiously, Paul recalls nothing being said about another crucial identity-marker of Jewish covenant obligation — the propriety and rules governing Jew and Gentile eating together.[197] That oversight, if that is what it was, became cru-

---

exchange, S. Joubert, *Paul as Benefactor* (WUNT 2.124; Tübingen: Mohr Siebeck, 2000) 91-103, takes too little account of this theological aspect of the agreement.

194. Bruce finds here support for the Acts 11 = Galatians 2 hypothesis: 2.10 alludes to the reason why Paul and Barnabas had come to Jerusalem (to deliver the famine relief). He translates, '"Only", said they, "please continue to remember the poor"; and in fact I had made a special point of attending to this very matter' (*Paul* 156; further his *Galatians* 126-27). But since the appeal was addressed to both Barnabas and Paul, and the famine relief visit reportedly involved both, Paul's reversion here to the singular ('the very thing which I have eagerly done') is better seen as a reference to his continuing practice of traditional Jewish (and Jesus') concern for the poor (now independently of Barnabas), a concern well exemplified subsequently by the time he gave to making the collection (see below, §33.4).

195. The phrase introduced by E. P. Sanders, *Paul and Palestinian Judaism* (London: SCM, 1977), to characterize the soteriology of Palestinian Judaism (75, 236).

196. Wander suggests that the 'alms-model', rather than one determined by the requirement of ritual purity, was Paul's way of relating his churches to the Petrine mission (*Trennungsprozesse* 196-204).

197. '*Only* (Gal. 2.10): unless the word is discounted one is bound to infer that at this meeting nothing was said — at least, nothing was decided — about meals shared by Jewish and

cial in the sequel episode, the confrontation at Antioch (Gal. 2.11-14), when it became apparent that the agreement achieved at Jerusalem was indeed vulnerable to different interpretations.

To sum up. The Jerusalem agreement had three elements:

- the formal agreement of division of responsibility between two valid missions — to/for the circumcised and to/for the uncircumcised (Gal. 2.9);
- the implied recognition of the validity of a mission to Gentiles which did not require them to be circumcised (2.5-8);
- the addendum that the covenantal obligation of care for the poor should still be in force (2.10).

e. The Agreement Reached in Jerusalem (according to Luke)

Luke's version of the Jerusalem council is notably different. The determinative precedent is provided by Peter's encounter with Cornelius (15.7-9),[198] rather than by the success of Paul's mission (Gal. 2.7-9). The role of Paul and Barnabas is simply confirmatory (Acts 15.12). And the crucial role in securing the acceptance of the precedent is attributed to James (15.13-21), rather than to Paul's resistance of the 'false brothers'.

The ruling given by James focuses on a further precedent, that provided by Scripture (15.16-17) — specifically the text of Amos 9.11-12:

> [16]Afterwards I will return and I will rebuild the tent of David that has fallen down, and I will rebuild its ruins and I will raise it up, [17]in order that the rest of humanity may seek the Lord, even all the Gentiles upon whom my name has been named.

Most striking of all, the qualifications added as a codicil to the agreement (15.20), usually described as 'the apostolic decree',[199] are more extensive than the exhortation to 'remember the poor' that Paul recalled (Gal. 2.10):

Gentile Christians, and that no decrees of abstention were imposed on Gentiles' (Barrett, 'Paul and Jerusalem' 11).

198. Referring back to 10.1–11.18; see above, §26.3-4.

199. The actual terms of 'the apostolic decree' are a matter of some confusion in the textual tradition (see the discussion in Metzger, *Textual Commentary* 429-34; Barrett, *Acts* 2.735-36), though that very confusion is a reminder that the terms of association continued to be debated and revised during the period when, as we may infer, 'the apostolic decree' played a vital role as the basis of mixed churches. See also P. Borgen, 'Catalogues of Vices, the Apostolic Decree, and the Jerusalem Meeting', *Early Christianity* 233-51.

Gentiles who turn to God should abstain from things polluted by (contact with) idols,[200] from fornication *(porneia)*,[201] from that which is strangled *(pnikton)*,[202] and from blood.[203]

200. The noun ('things polluted', *alisgēmata*) occurs only here in the Bible but presumably is equivalent to 'what has been sacrificed to idols *(eidōlothyta)*' in the corresponding letter (15.29; 21.25; and in Paul, 1 Cor. 8.1-10; 10.19, 28 [v.l.]; also Rev. 2.14, 20). The reference, then, is to the fact that in most cities the meat available for purchase in the meat market was supplied primarily from the local temples and from the sacrifices offered there (as in the Jerusalem temple, only part of the animal's carcass would be used in the ceremonies). In most pagan households also, before wine was drunk, a libation to some god or goddess would be poured out. In both cases the problem for devout Jews was that the meat/wine had been consecrated to an idol, and to partake of it would be to tarnish (render unclean) their own dedication to the one God (Exod. 34.15-16). The fear of having anything to do with idolatry was a major determiner of social behaviour for most Jews because of the supreme importance of the first two commandments (Exod. 20.3-6); a whole tractate of the Mishnah was subsequently devoted to the issue *(Aboda Zara)*. Strictly applied, the rule would prohibit most social intercourse with Gentiles and prevent Jews from holding many posts and from participating in civic ceremonies. The care with which Paul deals with the issue in 1 Corinthians 8–10 indicates its sensitivity in the early churches (see below, §32.5e)

201. *Porneia* (also 15.29 and 21.25) is best taken to indicate not just adultery or fornication but every kind of sexual licence, though in this context with special reference to sexual union within the prohibited degrees (Lev. 18.6-18) (see particularly Fitzmyer, *Acts* 557-58). As Paul's own indictment of humanity (seen from a Jewish perspective) indicates (Rom. 1.22-27), a link between idolatry and sexual licence was taken for granted (e.g., Jer. 3.6-8; Ezek. 16.15-46; Wis. 14.12; *T. Reu.* 4.6-8; Rev. 2.14, 20). Israel's own failure over the golden calf at Sinai was remembered as a dreadful warning (Exod. 32.6; 1 Cor. 10.7-8). Paul warns his own converts against *porneia* regularly (e.g., 1 Cor. 6.11, 13, 18; 7.2; 2 Cor. 12.21; Gal. 5.19; Col. 3.5). As these references indicate, the rationale behind the prohibition was not some narrow-minded prudery but the realistic recognition that such lack of self-control usually came to expression also in other self-indulgences and vices.

202. The presence of *pniktos* in the decree has occasioned much discussion; see, e.g., Wilson, *Luke and the Law* 88-101; A. J. M. Wedderburn, 'The "Apostolic Decree": Tradition and Redaction', *NovT* 35 (1993) 362-89. The term probably means 'strangled, choked to death', though it occurs only here (and 15.29 and 21.25) in biblical Greek, and only in these passages in this sense in secular Greek. Here it no doubt refers to the prohibitions in Jewish law against eating the flesh of animals from which the blood had not been properly drained (Gen. 9.4; Lev. 7.26-27; 17.10-14), strangulation killed without allowing the blood to drain from the beast. The importance of adequate provision for kosher meat was one of Israel's traditional identity markers (as still today), part of a complex of food laws which also covered clean and unclean and the dangers of idol meat (cf. 4 Macc. 5.2). It was not a dietary fad but part of the Jewish way of life which identified it as Jewish. The Cornelius episode had called in question the need to retain the laws of clean and unclean (10.11-15), but Jewish sensitivities could be respected by observing the kosher laws.

203. The fourth element, 'blood', could denote murder (cf. Gen. 9.6; Deut. 21.7-8), the shedding of blood rather than the consuming of blood, but probably goes with the previous item and highlights the reasoning behind the kosher laws. It was precisely because 'the life (of the

The differences are such that most commentators conclude that Luke's account cannot be regarded as straightforwardly historical.[204] One hint of this is the fact that the quotation of Amos 9.11-12 (15.16-18) follows the LXX version of Amos in which the crucial line (verse 17a) is quite different in the Hebrew (presumably James did not address the gathering in Greek).[205] But most weighty is the difficulty of squaring the more substantial qualification of Acts 15.20 with Paul's own account in Gal. 2.10; could Paul have made the bold assertion that nothing was added to him (2.6) if the meeting had agreed to require so much in regard to Gentile converts? And would Paul have willingly accepted such a basis for table-fellowship in his predominantly Gentile churches? How could the Antioch incident have unfolded as it did (2.11-14) if 'the apostolic decree' had been already agreed as a basis for Jew/Gentile community?[206] As we shall see, Paul was in strong agreement on two of the four items — avoiding meat sacrificed to idols and *porneia*.[207] But the other two, probably referring to kosher meat, implied a basis in Jewish law rather than in Christ for fellowship among Jewish and Gentile believers, a restrictiveness in table-fellowship between Jew and Greek against which he firmly set his face (Gal. 2.14-16).[208] The fact that

---

animal) is (in) the blood' (Gen. 9.4; Lev. 17.11, 14) that the blood had to be drained away; human dominance over the animal realm permitted human consumption of some animal flesh but not the absorption of their life.

204. The conclusion provides the central thrust of Achtemeier's *Quest for Unity*, particularly chs. 2-5.

205. Amos 9.12 — 'in order that they [Israel] may possess the remnant of Edom'; Acts 15.17 — 'so that the rest of humanity *(hoi kataloipoi tōn anthrōpōn)* may seek the Lord'. Further details appear in Barrett, *Acts* 2.725-28: 'It must be concluded, not with certainty, but with high probability, that the quotation, and probably therefore the whole speech, cannot be attributed to James. . . . It was probably used by Christian Jews who habitually used the OT in Greek' (728). This is a decisive consideration for most commentators (see Jervell, *Apg.* 405 n. 756), though see also Bauckham, 'James and the Jerusalem Church' 455-56; J. Ådna, 'James' Position at the Summit Meeting of the Apostles and the Elders in Jerusalem (Acts 15)', in Ådna and Kvalbein, eds., *The Mission of the Early Church* 125-61, who argues that the Acts quotation reflects a text closer to that of the LXX (128-42); M. Stowasser, 'Am 5,25-27; 9,11f. in der Qumranüberlieferung und in der Apostelgeschichte. Text- und traditionsgeschichtliche Überlegungen zu 4Q171 (Florilegium) III 12/CD VII 16/Apg 7,42b-43; 15,16-18', *ZNW* 92 (2001) 47-63, concludes that a pre-Lukan testimonia collection underlies both Acts passages.

206. The problem is resolved for some by dating the two Gal. 2.1-14 episodes prior to the Jerusalem council (Acts 15) (see particularly §27.3a above). But that solution simply replaces the problem with another: why is the issue which provoked the Acts 15 council still the question of circumcision rather than the explicit issue (table-fellowship) raised at Antioch?

207. Idolatry — 1 Cor. 5.11; 6.9; 10.7, 14; Gal. 5.20 (see further below, §32.5e); *porneia* — 1 Cor. 5.1; 6.13, 18; 7.2; 2 Cor. 12.21; Gal. 5.19; 1 Thess. 4.3.

208. See below, §27.4-5; it is clear from Rom. 14.14 that Paul no longer regarded the

Paul never refers or alludes to such a weighty agreement, either to support his arguments or to dispute elements in it, is also more than a little puzzling.[209] And it is even more difficult to see Paul willingly acting as emissary of the Jerusalem council ('the apostles and elders', that is, of Jerusalem; Antioch is one of the addressees), to take its decree to Antioch, and to the churches he had established (16.4). On the contrary, his correspondence shows clearly that relations with Jerusalem remained tense and unresolved,[210] as even Luke implies (Acts 21.18-26). So, straightforward history Acts 15 is not.

On the other hand, the fact that the two versions of the Jerusalem council are in full accord on three crucial points is probably proof sufficient that they are two versions of the same meeting:

- the determinative precedent of Gentiles receiving the Spirit/grace of God without being circumcised is the same;
- the principal outcome, that it was not necessary for Gentile believers to be circumcised before they could be regarded as full members of the new movement, is also the same (15.19);[211]
- a qualification is added (15.20) which is presented as consistent with the principal outcome.

Moreover, the argument produced by James can hardly be described as un-Pauline. (1) 'God has looked favourably on the Gentiles, to take from among them a people for his name' (15.14).[212] The initiative is attributed to Simeon (Peter), but by using the emotive idea of 'God's people' the speech implies that the calling of Gentiles is of a piece with Israel's own calling and an extension of it — an argu-

---

laws of clean and unclean as binding; nor was he fazed by the thought of unwittingly eating idol-food (1 Cor. 10.25-27).

209. See again further below, §32.5e and §33.3f, Romans 14–15, where Christ himself is the norm.

210. Apart from Galatians itself, we have to consider the likelihood that the traditionalists in Jerusalem were in some way behind Paul's opponents in Corinth and Philippi (2 Corinthians 10–13; Phil. 3.2-16; see below, §32.7b), as they certainly were in view in the apprehension expressed by Paul in Rom. 15.31.

211. 'The Gentile converts must not be pestered; the context makes clear that this means that demands of full legal observance must not be made' (Barrett, *Acts* 2.730). Since the conference had been called explicitly to debate whether it was necessary for the believing Gentiles to be circumcised and to keep the law of Moses (15.5-6), James's words (15.19) should certainly be read as a firm denial that circumcision was necessary.

212. The language is deliberately scriptural in tone: God visited to fulfil his promise and saving purpose (Gen. 21.1; 50.24-25; Exod. 3.16; 4.31; Jdt. 8.33; Luke 1.68; 7.16), to take from the nations a people for his name, that is, for himself (cf. Deut. 14.2; 26.18-19; 32.9; Ps. 135.4).

ment Paul was himself to use with good effect.[213] (2) The scriptural proof or confirmation cited by James (15.15-18) is essentially Amos 9.11-12.[214] It envisages a restoration of Israel with a view to the rest of humankind seeking out the Lord, that is, the Gentiles over whom God's name had been called.[215] What is clearly intended is an understanding of the (or a) people of God in which Jew and Gentile are one, a restored Israel in which 'all other peoples' have part, and into which 'all the Gentiles' called by God in their own right, and not as petitioning proselytes, are integrated (not assimilated) — once again, a very Pauline argument.[216]

So, what can be deduced from all this? Certainly we can see that Luke has produced an account in line with his consistent intention to portray the beginnings of Christianity as essentially harmonious.[217] By thus having *James* both affirm the precedent through *Peter,* and in very *Pauline* terms,[218] Luke was able to provide an account of the agreement reached by these three key figures in Christianity's beginnings and to promote the harmony which he was portraying. James agrees with Paul (15.19) that even for a non-Christian Jew, a genuine turning to God by a Gentile should be sufficient ground for the former to drop most of the ritual barriers to association with the latter and to stop bothering/harassing Gentile converts on the point.

But perhaps more to the point are the indications that Luke has, once again, told his story more from the perspective of Jerusalem than that of Paul. That the precedent was provided by Peter and the determinative ruling given by James accords well with what we learn (also from Acts) of the shifting leadership in the Jerusalem church, as Peter became more committed to mission, leaving the leadership in Jerusalem primarily in James's hands. Also noticeable is that James is presented as finding confirmation of what Simeon/Peter had reported in Scripture,[219] and in such

---

213. Cf. Paul's use of Hos. 2.23 and 1.10 in Rom. 9.24-26.

214. The opening phrase is possibly drawn from Jer. 12.15, and the closing phrase from Isa. 45.21 (e.g., Fitzmyer, *Acts* 555).

215. REB — 'all the Gentiles whom I have claimed for my own' (Acts 15.17).

216. God's 'call' as directed not only to Isaac and Jacob (Rom. 9.7, 11-12) but also to Gentiles (9.24); see my *Theology of Paul* 509-10 and below, §33 n. 209. Paul could have included Amos 9.11 very effectively in his catena of texts in Rom. 15.9-12. It is noteworthy that Qumran also cited Amos 9.11 (CD 7.16; 4Q174/Flor. 1.12-13) in reference to themselves, but only in terms of the restoration of Israel (rebuilding the booth of David, 9.11a); see further Fitzmyer, *Acts* 556, whereas 'James quotes Amos 9:11-12 in order to establish from Scripture that the nations belong to Yahweh as *Gentiles* in the messianic era' (Schnabel, *Mission* 1014).

217. See above, §21.2d.

218. 15.10 also depicts Peter as speaking in Pauline terms (see above, n. 144).

219. 'The issue is a matter of halakhah, which can only be decided from Scripture (cf. *b. B. Mes.* 59b)' (Bauckham, 'James and the Jerusalem Church' 452).

terms as integrated the incoming of the Gentiles with the primary goal of the restoration of Israel.[220]

The terms of 'the apostolic decree' are also indicative of the 'solution' to the problems caused to most believing Jews by the growing number of Gentile believers. For they seem to be based not so much on the 'Noahide laws' (including the prohibition of idolatry, adultery and incest, bloodshed, and eating the flesh of a limb cut from a living animal) which may already have served to provide 'rules of association' between Jews and Gentiles.[221] However, it is now generally recognized that the principal source of 'the apostolic decree' is the legislation regarding 'the resident alien', that is, the non-Jews who were permanently resident in the land of Israel, 'in the midst of' the people.[222] The apostolic decree, in other words, could be regarded as the Jerusalem church's solution to the problem of how to regard God-fearers who became believers in Messiah Jesus and who (evidently) received the Spirit as Gentiles. That is, to treat them in effect as 'resident aliens', Gentiles in the midst of the people, while retaining their identity as Gentiles. In other words, the qualification of the apostolic decree in Luke's version of events was similar in effect to the qualification of the impor-

220. Bauckham justifiably argues that the 'rebuilt tent of David' would have been seen as a reference to the Jerusalem community as the eschatological Temple, the Amos prophecy being read in the 'context of prophecies which associate the eschatological conversion of the Gentile nations with the restoration of the Temple in the messianic age' ('James and the Jerusalem Church' 453-55).

221. On the Noahide laws see particularly D. Novak, *The Image of the Non-Jew in Judaism: An Historical and Constructive Study of the Noahide Laws* (Lewiston: Mellen, 1983); M. Bockmuehl, *Jewish Law in Gentile Churches* (Edinburgh: Clark, 2000) ch. 7. Gen. 9.4-6 had already warned against (1) eating flesh in which the blood still adheres and (2) murder.

222. Lev. 17.8-9, 10-14; 18.26; see also Fitzmyer, *Acts* 557; Kraus, *Zwischen Jerusalem und Antiochia* 148-55; J. Wehnert, *Die Reinheit des "christlichen Gottesvolkes" aus Juden und Heiden* (FRLANT 173; Göttingen: Vandenhoeck und Ruprecht, 1997) 209-38; and further Barrett, *Acts* 2.733-34. Bauckham has effectively demonstrated that the rules drawn from Leviticus 17–18 all referred explicitly to 'the aliens who sojourn in your/their midst' (Lev. 17.8, 10, 12, 13; 18.26); it is the recurrence of this catchword ('in the midst') which explains why just these four laws were seen as indicating how (and the terms on which) Gentile believers could be reckoned as belonging to/with the eschatological people of God ('James and the Jerusalem Church' 458-62, including response to the issues raised by Wilson, *Luke and the Law* 84-87). Bauckham's argument in regard to the speech of James is presented more fully in 'James and the Gentiles (Acts 15.13-21)', in Witherington, ed., *History* 154-84. J. Taylor, 'The Jerusalem Decrees (Acts 15.20, 29 and 21.25) and the Incident at Antioch (Gal 2.11-14)', *NTS* 47 (2001) 372-80, suggests that the Jerusalem decrees can be interpreted both as 'Noahide commandments', implicitly keeping the separation between Jews and Gentiles, and as analogous to the decrees for resident aliens, implicitly allowing Gentiles to associate with Jews under certain conditions; he argues that the two interpretations correspond to the attitudes towards Gentile believers at Antioch manifested by James and Cephas respectively.

tance of almsgiving in Paul's version. In both cases we can see the more tradi-tionalist Jews, led by James, attempting to ensure that the albeit uncircumcised Gentile believers should maintain a pattern of living which fitted with the contin-uing priorities of the Jewish believers.[223]

Similarly the implication of Acts 15.21 (Jews of the diaspora heard Moses being read out Sabbath by Sabbath) is that knowledge and observance of the law was well sustained in diaspora synagogues and was not at all threatened by the compromise proposed. The hope implicit in 'the apostolic decree', then, would be for a mutual respect within the extended communities between Jews who in-sisted on stricter practice and those who consorted with Gentiles on the basis of the rules just proposed. It should be noted, however, that the whole proposal is put from a Jewish perspective and is geared to maintaining relationships in mixed churches on Jewish terms. The thought is not of Christian communities as such, the basis of whose fellowship was their common faith in Christ (note the absence of any overt reference to Jesus). The thought is rather of communities whose basis for fellowship would be continued respect for the law.

One further deduction can be made in regard to the historicity of Luke's account and the origin of 'the apostolic decree'. If Luke's account cannot be squared in detail with Paul's, and if it reflects so strongly a Jerusalem perspec-tive on the problems of mixed congregations, then the most likely inference to be drawn is that this was in fact Jerusalem's version of events, that indeed the theology (15.14-18) and the practice (15.19-20) were those insisted on by Jeru-salem (and by James). But also that they were the theology and practice as they became clear and established in the years following the Jerusalem council.[224] The origin of 'the apostolic decree' in fact is probably indicated by those to whom the letter conveying the decree was addressed (15.29) — the Gentile be-lievers in Antioch, Syria and Cilicia (15.23). These were the churches which be-came established during the period when Paul still fully acknowledged the Jeru-salem leadership's authority (Gal. 1.20; 2.1-2).[225] As I shall argue below, the policy emanating from James (Gal. 2.12-13) probably won the support of the whole church in Antioch, despite Paul's protest.[226] As a result, it would appear that Paul's relationship with the Antioch church was fractured, which presum-ably applied also to the churches which, as closest to Antioch, operated under

223. See again Bauckham, 'James and the Jerusalem Church' 462-67. Cf. Borgen's in-genious thesis ('Catalogues of Vices'): he sets the apostolic decree within the context of cata-logues of vices and virtues as used in teaching Gentiles when they became proselytes and sug-gests that the Jerusalem meeting in effect agreed to remove the requirement of circumcision from such a catalogue (this would be the understanding of James and the others).

224. Cf. Goppelt, *Apostolic* 76-79; Kraus, *Zwischen Jerusalem und Antiochia* 162-63.

225. See above, §§27.1 and 27.3c.

226. See below, §27.6.

Antioch's oversight. Here it may well be significant that Paul never refers again to the churches of Syria and Cilicia:[227] he no longer regarded them as 'his' churches; whereas, as we shall see, he certainly fought to retain his influence in the churches of Galatia.[228]

The decree, then, probably represents the practice which evolved in the mixed (Jew/Gentile) churches which continued under Jerusalem's and Antioch's direct supervision, probably at the direction (as a 'decree') of the Jerusalem leadership. How soon that practice became established is not at all clear, but it need not have been long after Paul's departure on his Aegean mission, and perhaps as a compromise to resolve the problems posed by the Antioch incident.[229] In any case, it would appear that Luke has done here what he did in describing the appointment of elders in the churches founded by the mission from Antioch (14.23). That is, viewing the events from the perspective of his own time, forty or fifty years later, Luke presents the agreed practice which had become established during the intervening years in the mission directed from Antioch (Syria and Cilicia)[230] as the terms of association agreed at the Jerusalem council.[231]

227. The interlude in Antioch 'so darkened Paul's memory of his time in Syria that later he is silent about it in his letters, with the exception of Gal. 1 and 2' (Hengel and Schwemer, *Paul* 267).

228. See below, §31.7.

229. Wedderburn, 'Apostolic Decree' 388-89; Hengel and Schwemer, *Paul* 442 n. 1084; C. K. Barrett, 'Christocentricity at Antioch', *On Paul* 37-54 (here 51). M. Slee, *The Church in Antioch in the First Century C.E.* (JSNTS 244; London: Clark International, 2003), suggests that the decree actually originated in the Antioch church (40-42, 48-49).

230. Paul probably conceded this region to Antioch's sphere of influence, following his break with the church of Antioch (see below, §27.6); Paul's churches developing their own *modus vivendi* for mixed congregations (1 Corinthians 8–10) may have been unaware of them.

231. This hypothesis accords with the majority view; see, e.g., Haenchen: 'a living tradition which was probably even then [at the time of Luke's writing] traced back to the Apostles. . . . These prohibitions must have come into force in a strongly mixed community of the diaspora, where Jewish claims were more moderate and could be satisfied by the four commandments which Moses himself gave to the Gentiles' (*Acts* 470-72); 'both the decree and the accompanying letter . . . were given at a later Council at which Paul was not present' (Wilson, *Gentiles* 191). Fitzmyer follows the interpretation that Acts 15 is a conflation of reports of two separate episodes: a discussion regarding circumcision (= Gal. 2.1-10) and a later consultation, a short time after the 'Council' itself (and after the Antioch incident), which resulted in rulings 'about diet and marital unions for the local churches of Antioch, Syria, and Cilicia' (*Acts* 553, 561-63; patristic references to the decree, 563). An interesting variation is that of D. R. Catchpole, 'Paul, James and the Apostolic Decree', *NTS* 23 (1976-77) 428-44, who suggests that the Antioch incident was occasioned by the arrival of the emissaries from James bringing the demands of the apostolic decree (442); similarly Achte-

This more negative judgment on Luke's account of the Jerusalem meeting carries with it a similar hesitation to take his account of the sequel as straight-forward history — the delivery of the letter containing the 'decree', from 'the apostles and elders' (that is, the Jerusalem leadership)[232] to the church in Antioch, and presumably subsequently to the churches of 'Syria and Cilicia' (15.30, 41) and Galatia (16.4). In other words, it is once again precisely in his description of Paul's dealings with 'the apostles' in Jerusalem, as in his account of Paul's first post-conversion visit to Jerusalem (Acts 9.26-30), that Luke's account becomes most difficult to square with Paul's attitude and clearly expressed sentiments. Here too Luke was probably following a tradition which emanated from Jerusalem and which told a story more conducive to Luke's own point of view. The one element of the tradition which fits with what we know from Paul of his further mission work is the appearance of Silas (15.32), as representing Jerusalem (15.25), but as becoming Paul's associate worker in place of Barnabas (15.40). Luke's tradition is somewhat confused at this point: 15.33 implies that the emissaries from Jerusalem, Judas[233] and Silas, both returned to Jerusalem after completing their commission, whereas Paul and Barnabas remained in Antioch (15.35); with the consequence that Paul's subsequent choice of Silas (15.40) cuts across the account Luke has given.[234] Perhaps, then, the slight confusion is indicative of traditions which did not readily meld into a wholly consistent narrative.[235]

---

meier, *Quest for Unity* ch. 6; Wehnert, *Reinheit* 129-30. But the Acts 10–11 episode implies that eating even with such a God-fearing, judaizing Gentile as Cornelius would not have been acceptable to traditionalist Jewish believers (Acts 11.2); and, in reference to Achtemeier, if indeed Gal. 2.1-10 = Acts 11.1-18, Acts 11.2 also indicates how difficult it would have been to avoid some discussion among the participants and agreement on table-fellowship with Gentiles. Chilton offers the boldly imaginative speculation *e silentio* that Silas broke with Paul in Corinth, that it was Silas's news of what had happened in Macedonia and Achaia which prompted James to issue the 'apostolic decree', and that Silas was James's envoy in bringing the encyclical to Antioch which provoked the Antioch incident (*Rabbi Paul* 167-69).

232. Paul and Barnabas were to act not simply as postmen but also as emissaries by making verbal report of what had been agreed (15.27).

233. Wilson notes that Judas is not mentioned elsewhere in Acts; 'one might have expected Luke to have made more of the role of Paul and Barnabas' (*Gentiles* 187).

234. 15.34 ('But it seemed good to Silas to remain there') is probably a later addition to the text to account for the presence of Silas in Antioch (Metzger, *Textual Commentary* 439; Barrett, *Acts* 2.750).

235. Lost in the confusion is the question of Silas's own attitude to the confrontation in Antioch, unmentioned by Luke. If Luke's account does dovetail with the high standing accorded to Silas by Paul (see below, §29.6), it must mean that Silas sympathized with Paul's attitude, though 1 Pet. 5.12 may also suggest that Silas functioned as some sort of bridge between Paul and Peter (see also §31 n. 36 below).

27.4. Confrontation — the Incident at Antioch

Following the crisis came the confrontation. Some time after the Jerusalem agreement[236] a sequence of events transpired in the church of Antioch which tested the goodwill generated by the Jerusalem agreement to the limit. Oddly enough it was the same issue that, according to Luke, Peter had faced with Cornelius (Acts 10.1–11.18) — the propriety of Jew eating with (uncircumcised) Gentile (11.3). On the assumption that the agreement of Gal. 2.6-10 was reached during the 'famine relief' visit of Acts 11.30, it can be readily seen that Luke's account of the Jerusalem conference in Acts 15 deals with that issue (15.20, 29) — which is the great strength of the Acts 11 = Galatians 2 hypothesis (§27.3a). But on the sequence as Paul himself tells it, the Antioch incident (Gal. 2.11-14) follows on from the Jerusalem agreement (2.6-10), so that the issue posed at Antioch comes as something of a surprise.[237]

The 'clash of the Titans' came about in this way. Peter had evidently come down from Jerusalem to (visit) the church in Antioch. While he was there all the believers, Jew and Gentile, 'were accustomed to eating together',[238] Peter included.[239] Here the correlation of Luke's account and Paul's is straightforward: the Peter whose attitude (to unclean food and persons) was truly expressed in the words of Acts 10.14 ('I have never eaten anything profane or unclean') would never have eaten with Gentiles as a matter of regular practice. But when 'certain from James' came (that is, no doubt, from Jerusalem), Peter 'began to draw back and separate'[240] himself from the common table-fellowship, fol-

---

236. Some have suggested that the Antioch incident (2.11-14) must have preceded the Jerusalem meeting of 2.1-10 (notably Lüdemann, *Paul* 44-80) — the logic being similar to that which infers that Acts 15 must have followed the Antioch incident (see §27.3a above). But Paul has been at such pains to maintain a strict chronology in the preceding episodes that it is unlikely that he would have narrated the Antioch episode out of sequence. See further §28 n. 26 below.

237. My fascination with this episode goes back to the late 1970s; my essay 'The Incident at Antioch' was first delivered as a lecture in 1980, and I have returned to it frequently since (particularly *Partings* §7.5; *Galatians* 115-31; and *The New Perspective on Paul* [2005] 24-25, 28-31, 33-37; [2008] 27-28, 31-34, 36-41).

238. The tense of 'ate together' is imperfect *(synēsthien)*, denoting a customary practice. It is important to notice that Paul does not make the issue dependent on the meals including the Lord's Supper (though presumably some at least did so); the issue was 'simply' the propriety of Jew eating with Gentile at the same table.

239. Esler criticizes my earlier 'Incident at Antioch' essay by arguing that there could not be any table-fellowship between Jews and Gentiles in this period (*Community and Gospel* 76-86). But he greatly oversimplifies the evidence (see above, §26 n. 70; also my response in *Jesus, Paul and the Law* 179-81).

240. Here again the tenses are imperfect *(hypestellen kai aphōrizen)*, indicating not a sudden break but a steady withdrawal.

lowed by the rest of the believing Jews, including even Barnabas, Paul's fellow evangelist in the mission from Antioch (2.12-13). Here the correlation with Acts seems to go awry: why did the one who had outfaced the traditionalist believers in regard to eating with Cornelius (Acts 11.4-18) now back down on the same issue in Gal. 2.12?[241] And why did Barnabas, who had (evidently) backed Paul so firmly in the crisis over Titus in Jerusalem (Gal. 2.5, 'we'), play turncoat over table-fellowship in Antioch?[242] Whatever their reasons, Paul openly confronted Peter (presumably when Peter's gradual withdrawal had become apparent as deliberately intended) and denounced him to his face (Gal. 2.11, 14).[243] His recollection of the confrontation itself seems to pass seamlessly from what he said at Antioch to Peter in person, into what he still wanted to say at the time of writing (2.15-17).[244]

What was the confrontation all about? What was at stake here?[245]

a. Five Key Terms

The intensity of Paul's concerns over what had happened and his feelings of dismay at Peter's conduct can be judged by the outspokenness of his rhetoric: Peter 'stood condemned' (2.11); 'he feared those of the circumcision' (2.12); he 'played the hypocrite' (2.13); he 'was not walking straight towards the truth of the gospel' (2.14).[246] Such emotive language tends to cloud the issue and the fac-

241. Wehnert tries to resolve the tension by setting the Cornelius tradition historically between Gal. 2.1-10 and 2.11-14 (*Reinheit* 265-67, 273). Here again it is possible that where an exception proved acceptable for an occasional ardent God-fearer, the large number of non-Jewish believers involved in Antioch meant that the exception was becoming the rule (§27.2c). The different readings of Jesus' teaching on the cleanness that matters, as between Mark 7 and Matthew 15 (see *Jesus Remembered* 574-75), may well reflect the different weightings being given to the issue of clean/unclean people at this time (cf. Wedderburn, *History* 74-75).

242. Schmithals has no doubt that Paul's disagreement with Barnabas 'formed the real substance of that unfortunate incident in Antioch' (*Paul and James* 71).

243. Given the division of responsibility/authority agreed upon in 2.9 (see above, §27.3d), Paul would have been aggrieved and angered that James was in effect trying to exercise authority in the predominantly Gentile church of Antioch.

244. See, e.g., Betz, *Galatians* 113-14; my *Galatians* 132; Martyn, *Galatians* 246-47. The echo of the confrontation itself runs at least to 2.17 (see below, §a[iv], 'sinner', and n. 260); so also Bauckham, 'Peter, James, and the Gentiles' 125-26.

245. For a variation on what follows see my 'Echoes of Intra-Jewish Polemic in Paul's Letter to the Galatians', *JBL* 112 (1993) 459-77, reprinted in *The New Perspective on Paul* ch. 9, here (2005) 222-32, (2008) 228-38.

246. The harshness of Paul's language indicates that 'the wound remained open' (Hengel, *Petrus* 103).

tors involved.[247] But five terms used by Paul in the fuller account provide important insights.

(i) Peter 'began to *separate* himself'/'was *separating* himself *(aphōrizen heauton)*' from the Gentile believers. Behind the verb *aphorizō* lies the late Hebrew *parash* ('separate'), from which most agree the term 'Pharisees' comes *(perushim,* 'separated ones'), with the clear implication that they were so called because they tried to separate themselves within or even from the rest of Israel in order to maintain the level of purity they deemed necessary.[248] It would appear that *parash/aphorizō* had become almost a technical term for the separation deemed necessary in order to maintain the purity of the cultic community.[249] The same word is used in a document in which a leader or leaders of the Qumran sect seem to be explaining why they had to 'separate *(prshnu)*' from the rest of the people of Israel for such purity reasons (4QMMT C7 = 92). The implication is that Peter was acting from the same sort of motivation that characterized the Pharisees in their practice of 'separatedness', a motivation which Paul could well appreciate (Gal. 1.14), or indeed from a motivation too like that of the Qumranites for comfort. If there is any allusion to the Cornelius tradition (Acts 10–11), then Peter was going back on the revelation given to him regarding the acceptability of Gentiles to God (Acts 10.28), which could help explain the charge of hypocrisy (Gal. 2.13).

(ii) Paul describes Peter's previous conduct — that is, when he 'used to eat with the Gentiles' (2.12) — as *'living like a Gentile* and not like a Jew' (2.14).

---

247. For more detail on each of these phrases, see my *Galatians ad loc.,* particularly 117, 124-25.

248. See *Jesus Remembered* 267-68. That devout Jews in the diaspora were also purity conscious is indicated by Philo, *Spec. Leg.* 3.205-6; *Sib. Or.* 3.591-93; Josephus refers to a long-established privilege of Jewish citizens of Antioch to be given a sum of money instead of the obligatory distribution of oil by the gymnasiarch, since they did not want to use foreign (= impure) oil *(Ant.* 12.120; cf. *War* 2.591; *Life* 74); Rom. 14.14 indicates that the issue of clean/unclean was alive in Rome.

249. Cf. U. Kellermann, *EDNT* 1.184, with reference to Isa. 56.3; *Jub.* 22.16; *Par. Jer.* 6.13-14 (= *4 Bar.* 6.17?). Bauckham also notes Ezra 10.11; Neh. 9.2; 10.28; 13.3; *Ep. Aris.* 151-52; *2 Bar.* 42.5 ('Peter, James, and the Gentiles' 125); the issue was not food but separation (123-25). The attitude and practice impressed itself upon Tacitus *(separate epulis* — *Hist.* 5.5.2). *Jub.* 22.16 is particularly expressive of the attitude:

> Separate yourself from the Gentiles, and do not eat with them,
> And do not perform deeds like theirs. And do not become an associate of theirs.
> Because their deeds are defiled,
> and all their ways are contaminated, and despicable, and abominable.

Paul himself expresses surprisingly similar sentiments in 2 Cor. 6.17 (a modified form of Isa. 52.11 LXX)!

The phrase should not be taken to indicate that Peter and the Jewish believers generally had totally abandoned the law governing relations between Jews and Gentiles.[250] The pattern in Antioch, as Josephus indicates, was for Gentiles to associate with Jews by accepting at least some of the Jewish customs.[251] More directly to the point, we know that such accusations were used in the intra-Jewish polemic of the period.[252] To describe the conduct of the other (the non-sectarian, or other sectarian) Jew as 'acting as the Gentiles act' was an effective way of vilifying conduct of which the sect disapproved.[253] So the phrase used here ('living like a Gentile') is almost certainly drawn from the language used by those who disapproved of Peter's conduct.[254]

(iii) Paul further accuses Peter/Cephas of 'trying to compel the Gentiles to *judaize (ioudaïzein)*' (2.14). 'To judaize' was a quite familiar expression, meaning 'to adopt a (characteristically) Jewish way of life'. As already noted, many non-Jews in the ancient world 'judaized' by attending Jewish synagogues and adopting Jewish customs.[255] In other words, 'judaize' was typically used to describe the

250. Betz speaks of 'Cephas' total emancipation from Judaism' (*Galatians* 112); similarly T. Holtz, 'Der antiochenische Zwischenfall (Gal. 2.11-14)', *NTS* 32 (1986) 344-61 (here 351-52).

251. See again §26 at nn. 69-70 above.

252. In *Jub.* 6.32-35 observance of a festival or ordinance whose date has been wrongly computed is *non*-observance, failure to observe the covenant, 'walking in the feasts of the Gentiles'. Similarly in *1 En.* 82.4-7 'the righteous', 'who walk in the ways of righteousness', mark themselves off clearly from those who 'sin like the sinners' in that they wrongly reckoned the months and feasts and years. *Pss. Sol.* 8.13 condemns the way the Hasmonean Sadducees conducted the Temple rituals: 'There was no sin they left undone in which they did not surpass the Gentiles'.

253. 'From the perspective of the men from James, the modest level of law-observance in the table-fellowship at Antioch was tantamount to abandoning the law altogether' (Dunn, *Partings* [²2006] 174). See further my *Galatians* 128-29. Catchpole ignores the rhetorical exaggeration when he claims that 'it would be quite impossible to describe existence under the Decree as living *ethnikōs*' ('Paul, James and the Apostolic Decree' 441).

254. The polemical overtone of the phrase was overlooked by those who criticized my earlier suggestion that the Gentile believers in Antioch may well have already gone some way towards meeting the traditional scruples of the Jewish believers, as was true generally of 'judaizing' God-fearers; so particularly J. G. Crossley, *The Date of Mark's Gospel: Insights from the Law in Earliest Christianity* (JSNTS 266; London: Clark International, 2004) 141-54.

255. Esther 8.17 LXX — 'many of the Gentiles were circumcised and judaized for fear of the Jews'; Theodotus in Eusebius, *Praep. evang.* 9.22.5 — Jacob would not give Dinah to the son of Hamor 'until all the inhabitants of Shechem were circumcised and judaized'; Josephus, *War* 2.454 — Metilius (commander of the Roman garrison in Jerusalem) 'saved his life by entreaties and promises to judaize and even to be circumcised'; 2.463 — 'each city [of Syria] had its judaizers', suspected during the Jewish revolt because they were too much 'mixed up' with the Jews; Plutarch reports of a freedman named Caecilius who was suspected of 'judaizing' (*Cicero* 7.6; *GLAJJ* 1.566).

way of life which necessarily accompanied circumcision but which might stop short of circumcision, that is, the practice of God-fearers who had not (yet) become proselytes.[256] This latter is presumably what is in view in Gal. 2.14: Peter and the rest of the Jewish believers were putting pressure[257] on the Gentile believers to 'judaize', that is, to adopt a Jewish way of life, or a more complete Jewish way of life than they had hitherto accepted.[258] Whatever the terms on which table-fellowship had hitherto been practiced in the Antioch church, they were no longer deemed acceptable to the Jewish believers; they were not 'Jewish' enough.

(iv) In Paul's sustained protest he makes his plea from a particularly Jewish perspective: 'we are Jews by nature and not Gentile *sinners*' (2.15). 'Sinner', as noted in volume 1, is a term used to denote the law-breaker *(rasa'/hamartōlos);* though in the factionalism of Second Temple Judaism it also denoted other Jews who did not agree with or observe the faction's interpretation of the law (halakhah).[259] Here we need to note that it could also be used to denote the Gentile, who by definition was outside the covenant people, literally 'law-less', an 'out-law'.[260] This is clearly the attitude which Paul strikes in 2.15; the dismissive

---

256. See further Cohen, *Beginnings* 179-85: at the time of Paul *ioudaïzein* was not (yet) used in the sense 'become a Jew', but only as meaning 'to be like', 'to live Jewishly'. See also Cassius Dio 37.17.1, cited below in §29 n. 27.

257. We again meet the idea of 'compel'. Bauckham wonders whether there was any implied threat of Jewish violence ('Peter, James, and the Gentiles' 128-30).

258. P. F. Esler, *Galatians* (London: Routledge, 1998), ignores the evidence of n. 255 and argues that 'judaize' must include the requirement to be circumcised (137-39), as earlier in his *Community and Gospel* 88; followed by Slee, *Church in Antioch* 46-47; similarly Bauckham, 'Peter, James, and the Gentiles' 126. Martyn's observation is sounder: 'We can be sure that the message [of the messengers from James] did not directly and explicitly rescind the formula of the Jerusalem conference with its acknowledgment of the Antioch church's circumcision-free mission. Had it done so, Paul would certainly have pointed that out. . . . The issue of circumcision was not reopened' (*Galatians* 233). 'The issue is not circumcision but purity' (Betz, *Galatians* 104). 'No NT source ever claims that James demanded that Gentile converts be circumcised. . . . Both Acts and Paul connect James with imposing kosher laws on Gentiles' (Brown and Meier, *Antioch and Rome* 37-38). As in his earlier 'Making and Breaking an Agreement Mediterranean Style: A New Reading of Galatians 2:1-14', *BibInt* 3 (1995) 285-314, Esler seems to assume that a social-science appreciation of possible honour-shame considerations gives him license to interpret the episode in a way wholly discreditable to Peter and Barnabas. He thereby lays himself open to the critique of Horrell on the (mis)use of sociological models (*Social Ethos* 11-18); see above, §20 n. 196. See also below on *hoi ek peritomēs* ('those of the circumcision') in Gal. 2.12 (n. 273).

259. See *Jesus Remembered* 528-32. 'The heyday of Jewish sectarianism was from the middle of the second century BCE to the destruction of the temple in 70 CE' (Cohen, *Maccabees to Mishnah* 143).

260. Ps. 9.17; Tob. 13.6; *Jub.* 23.23-24; *Pss. Sol.* 1.1; 2.1-2; Luke 6.33 *(hoi hamartōloi)* = Matt. 5.47 *(hoi ethnikoi);* Mark 14.41 pars.; cf. K. H. Rengstorf, *TDNT* 1.325-26, 328.

note ('Gentile sinners') is hard to miss.[261] Evidently Paul was adopting the sort of language and attitude which lay behind and indeed was expressed in Peter's action. In the spirit of the quasi-legal rhetoric he was using,[262] Paul was looking for common ground with his fellow Jews 'by nature'. The common ground was the Jewishness which they shared, with its too characteristic disparagement of Gentiles as outside the law ('sinners') and beyond the reach of covenanted mercy. Paul's implied charge against Peter was that his withdrawal from table-fellowship with the Gentile believers was tantamount to continuing to regard them in this way, whereas he already knew that Gentile believers were recipients of God's grace and Spirit. Hence Paul's further argument in 2.17: to regard non-observance of the Jewish way of life as 'sin' is to regard Christ, who has accepted such non-observers, as a 'servant of sin'.[263]

(v) The fifth key term is *'works of the law'*, which Paul poses in some antithesis to 'faith in Jesus Christ' (2.16). The phrase 'works of the law' simply denotes doing what the law requires[264] — not simply 'deeds' or 'precepts' but the conduct prescribed by the Torah.[265] As such, the phrase nicely sums up the traditional Jewish understanding of the Jews' covenant relationship with God. God had chosen Israel to be his people and had rescued them from slavery in Egypt. Israel's part in the covenant, Israel's appropriate response to God's electing grace, was to do what he demanded of them — to obey the law (hence the sequence of Exod. 20.1-2). Again the phrase 'covenantal nomism' captures the double emphasis in Jewish self-understanding, with Deuteronomy its classic expression. In Galatians 2 the phrase 'works of the law' is used obviously with a

---

261. H. Merklein, '"Nicht aus Werken des Gesetzes . . .". Eine Auslegung von Gal 2,15-21', *Studien zu Jesus und Paulus,* vol. 2 (WUNT 105; Tübingen: Mohr Siebeck, 1998) 303-15: 'They [Jewish Christians] are "by nature Jews" and therefore — as a matter of course — *not* sinners like the Gentiles' (304).

262. See further my *Galatians* 132-33: Betz regards 2.15-21 as the equivalent of the *propositio,* whose objective in rhetorical practice, according to Quintilian, was to sum up the position so far, including the points of agreement, and to provide a transition to the main stage of the argument following (*Galatians* 114, 121-22).

263. 'Sinners' in 2.17 most obviously echoes the same term in 2.15: if seeking to be justified in Christ and not by works of the law means that we are 'sinners' (because we fail to do what the law demands), then the Christ who has accepted us is a servant of sin. Surely not (2.17). See further my *The New Perspective on Paul* (2005) 13, (2008) 14 and n. 53 (with bibliography); also Cummins, *Paul and the Crucified Christ* 191-92, 207-10.

264. The point is not in dispute; see the bibliography in my *The New Perspective on Paul* (2005) 22, (2008) 24 n. 94; C. A. Evans, 'Paul and "Works of Law" Language in Late Antiquity', in S. E. Porter, ed., *Paul and His Opponents* (Leiden: Brill, 2005) 201-26.

265. See further *The New Perspective on Paul* (2005) 22, (2008) 24 n. 93; also 'The Dialogue Progresses', in M. Bachmann, ed., *Lutherische und Neue Paulusperspektive* (WUNT 182; Tübingen: Mohr Siebeck, 2005) 389-430.

view to the conduct of Peter and the others to which Paul was objecting, and as such is of a piece with the other key terms.[266] In the context of 2.11-17, 'to do the law' meant 'separating' from 'Gentile sinners' and 'living the (distinctively) Jewish way of life'. This is why the phrase here has such a negative tone, although 'doing the law' was/is in itself a good thing.

b. An Illuminating Parallel — 4QMMT

Paul's language in this passage received fresh illumination from the long-delayed publication (in 1994) of 4QMMT, a letter which expressed the sectarian rationale of the Qumran community more clearly than any other.[267] Not only did it use the language and rationale of 'separation', as noted already (MMT C7 = 92). But it also used the phrase 'the works of the law', which hitherto had appeared to be a formulation more or less unique to Paul. Two further features of the letter are particularly relevant here.[268]

One is that the full phrase 'some of the works of the law' clearly refers to the purpose of the letter itself: 'We have also written to you some of the works of the Torah (*miqsat ma'ase ha-torah*) which we think are good for you and for your people' (MMT C26-27 = 112-13). The allusion back to the rather fragmentary beginning of the second section of the letter is beyond dispute: 'These are some of our teachings (*dbrenu*) . . . which are . . . the works which we . . .' (B1-2 = 3). What then follows is a series of halakhic rulings, chiefly relating to the Temple, the priesthood, sacrifices and purity, and regularly introduced with the formula 'We are of the opinion that . . .'.

The parallel with Galatians is quite striking. As in MMT, Paul seems to use the phrase as a summary reference to the rulings (regarding table-fellowship) which seem to have been governing the conduct of Peter and the other Jewish believers (Gal. 2.12). It is true that the 'works' in MMT are all highly technical matters, principally related to the cult, whereas in Gal. 2.16 'the works of the

266. Cummins sets the whole episode against the backcloth of the 'Maccabean martyrs' steadfast adherence to food laws, circumcision, Sabbath observance, and such like' (*Paul and the Crucified Christ* ch. 6 (quotation from 197). The correlation of all five terms is regularly missed, as, e.g., by Wilckens, *Theologie* 1/3.131-42.

267. E. Qimron and J. Strugnell, *Discoveries in the Judean Desert*. Vol. 10: *Qumran Cave 4.V: Miqsat Ma'ase ha-Torah* (Oxford: Clarendon, 1994).

268. I draw here on my '4QMMT and Galatians', *NTS* 43 (1997) 147-53, reprinted in *The New Perspective on Paul* ch. 14; in expanded form, with J. H. Charlesworth, 'Qumran's *Some Works of the Torah* (4Q394-99 [4QMMT]) and Paul's Galatians', in J. H. Charlesworth, ed., *The Bible and the Dead Sea Scrolls*. Vol. 3: *The Scrolls and Christian Origins* (Waco: Baylor University, 2006) 187-201.

law' would seem to be (from a Christian perspective) more weighty matters. But 'the works of the law' which Peter and the other Jewish believers had in effect been 'trying to compel' the Gentile believers to adopt (to 'judaize') (2.14) — food laws governing table-fellowship — were not so very different from the halakhic concerns of Qumran. More to the point, however, is the fact that in both cases the rulings and practices ('works') had been the focal point of disagreement within the community and had been deemed of sufficient importance for one group to 'separate' from the rest of the community.

Even more striking is the third parallel. MMT ends with the hope that 'at the end of time you may rejoice in finding that some of our teachings *(dbrenu)* are true. And it shall be reckoned to you for righteousness in doing what is upright and good before him' (C30-31 = 116-17). Clearly in view are the words/teachings/practices *(dbrenu)* documented in the letter and described a few lines earlier as 'some of the works of the law'. What jumps out from the page, however, is the way in which the phrase 'reckoned for righteousness' is drawn into the letter's exhortation. The phrase is clearly drawn from Gen. 15.6, where 'he [the Lord] reckoned it [Abraham's faith] as righteousness', and it clearly echoes the way Gen. 15.6 was currently understood within Second Temple Judaism — Abraham's *faithfulness* reckoned as righteousness (1 Macc. 2.52).[269] So argues MMT: faithfulness measured by acceptance of the Qumran halakhic rulings will be reckoned as righteousness.

Given the two other parallels between Galatians 2 and 4QMMT, it should perhaps occasion no surprise that Paul also draws on Gen. 15.6 to make his point (Gal. 3.6). But whereas MMT assumes that halakhic *faithfulness* is counted as righteousness, Paul argues in direct opposition: not works of the law, but *faith* (3.2, 5), believing as Abraham believed (3.6-9). And the argument of 3.6-29 is clearly intended to elaborate the thesis which in 2.16 summed up Paul's response to Peter and his rebuke of Peter for making 'works of the law' an essential addendum to faith.

In short, 4QMMT sheds a good deal of light on the attitude which Peter and the other Jewish believers were expressing: that there were 'works of the law' which were crucial to one's standing before and acceptance/affirmation by God. In using just these terms ('separate', 'sinner', 'works of the law') and in drawing in Gen. 15.6, Paul was deliberately echoing and confronting an understanding within Second Temple Judaism that there were key elements of the law which had to be maintained for the sake of individual and corporate righteous-

---

269. The phrase is used similarly of some of Israel's heroes of faithfulness (see above, §25.2c): Phinehas's action in preventing Israel's defilement was 'reckoned to him as righteousness' (Ps. 106.31); righteousness was reckoned to Simeon and Levi for likewise safeguarding Israel from defilement (*Jub.* 30.17).

ness. In Paul's view, Peter and the other Jewish Christians had succumbed to a traditional Jewish perspective on Gentiles which Paul thought they had now left behind and which should have been left behind. Paul presumably was drawing such a conclusion from the agreement recently(?) achieved in Jerusalem (2.6-10). Which brings us to a further conundrum: why did the issue of table-fellowship arise as it did? was a *modus vivendi* for Jewish and Gentile believers not included in the Jerusalem agreement? why did Peter act as he did in Antioch? was it Paul who was going beyond the agreement?

c. The Missing Element in the Jerusalem Agreement

In order to make sense of the sequence Gal. 2.1-10 and 2.11-14, we have to assume that the issue of Jewish and Gentile believers eating together had *not* been raised in the Jerusalem meeting. This is sometimes questioned with the counter-assumption that in Jerusalem Titus must have shared meals with Jewish Christians, and therefore the issue of table-fellowship shared by Jewish and Gentile believers must have been recognized and already resolved in the Jerusalem consultation.[270] But there is no 'must' about it.

For example, we do not know where Paul, Barnabas and Titus lodged during their time in Jerusalem, and whether there were mixed (Hebrew/Hellenist) house groups in Jerusalem; Paul's first post-conversion visit had been very restricted (1.18-19). Alternatively, if there were few Hellenist believers remaining in Jerusalem, perhaps the three had conformed with traditional Jewish practices in regard to table-fellowship during their visit, 'becoming like a Jew among Jews' (1 Cor. 9.20).[271] Another possibility is that mixed groups ate together but not the same food, as with Judith (Jdt. 10.5; 12.17-19) and perhaps in the tenement church(es) of Rome (Rom. 14.2).[272] Or again, what if Titus was regarded as

270. So Esler, *Galatians* 130-34; S. J. Gathercole, 'The Petrine and Pauline *Sola Fide* in Galatians 2', in Bachmann, ed., *Lutherische und Neue Paulusperspektive* 309-27: 'in the events of Gal. 2:1-10 we see a concrete example of Jewish and gentile Christians mixing, to the extent that Titus and the others shared common life' (319).

271. Cf. Acts 16.3; 21.23-26. The *Letter of Aristeas* depicts a meal table where the king of Egypt dined with his Jewish guests and ate the food which had been prepared in accordance with Jewish regulations (*Aristeas* 181). The implication of the subsequent episode (in Antioch) is that if the Gentile Christians had been willing to 'judaize', that is, to accept such strictures as the Jewish believers wanted to observe, then table-fellowship could have been resumed.

272. The Mishnah contains two rulings which presuppose situations at the meal table where non-Jews were present (*m. Ber.* 7.1 and *'Abod. Zar.* 5.5). M. Bockmuehl, 'Antioch and James the Just', in Chilton and Evans, ed., *James the Just and Christian Origins* 155-98, points out that observant Jews had four options: (1) refuse all table-fellowship with Gentiles and refuse to enter a Gentile house; (2) invite Gentiles to their own house and prepare a Jewish meal;

an exception, much as local Roman Catholic authorities today may give permission exceptionally to extend eucharistic fellowship to non-Catholics, or turn a blind eye to its occasional practice, without yielding the principle of no shared eucharist until the church is again united? As a single God-fearing, or judaizing, Gentile, Titus would have provided no precedent for a whole community (Antioch), probably already consisting of a majority of Gentiles, to ignore what devout Jews would regard as essential.

Above all, had the issue been presented in Jerusalem as it was in Antioch, would James and the others have approved of Titus eating with Jews? If, alternatively, the James group objected in Antioch, would they not have objected all the more in Jerusalem? Responsibility cannot simply be shifted to 'those of the circumcision' (Gal. 2.12) playing the role in the Antioch episode equivalent to that of the 'false brothers' in Jerusalem (2.4-5). For if the 'false brothers' had been resisted in Jerusalem, why would they not have been resisted all the more strongly in Antioch, and by Barnabas in particular? Nor can James be easily exonerated from responsibility for the 'schism' in Antioch. It is surely clear enough from Paul's account that the arrival of 'certain from James' was the catalyst for Peter's separating himself from the Gentile believers (2.12).[273] That can only have been because the former disapproved of Peter's table-fellowship with Gentiles and because the disapproval was of sufficient weight for Peter to abandon what had been his habitual practice in Antioch.[274] That weight is surely indicated by the 'from James', which can hardly indicate other than that the authority of James was behind the newcomers, either explicitly or implicitly, either formally or in effect claimed by them.[275]

---

(3) take their own food to a Gentile's house; (4) dine with Gentiles on the explicit or implicit understanding that food they would eat was neither prohibited in the Torah nor tainted with idolatry (165). See again §26 nn. 69, 70 above.

273. Hengel and Schwemer suggest that they would have been identical with the 'elders' who had become prominent in Jerusalem (see §23.3e above) (*Paul* 245). M. D. Nanos, 'What Was at Stake in Peter's "Eating with Gentiles" at Antioch?', in M. D. Nanos, ed., *The Galatians Debate* (Peabody: Hendrickson, 2002) ch. 15, argues implausibly that 'the "certain ones from James" most likely represent(ed) non-Christ-believing interest groups, but with James' permission' (xxxi); there is no reason why *hoi ek peritomēs* ('those of the circumcision') in Gal. 2.12 should not refer to Christ-believing Jews, as the phrase clearly does in Col. 4.11. The phrase, it should be noted, simply characterizes those referred to as native Jews or as devout Jews, not necessarily as advocates of the circumcision of Gentile believers (cf. Acts 10.45; 11.2; Rom. 4.12; Col. 4.11).

274. Hill plausibly suggests that the 'representatives of James' probably said something to the effect: 'You must know that this is not what we agreed to in Jerusalem. Just because Gentiles do not need to live like Jews does not mean that Jews are therefore free to live like Gentiles!' (*Hellenists and Hebrews* 141; followed by Cummins, *Paul and the Crucified Christ* 164-65).

275. Ward argues that Paul's account 'does not necessarily contradict the picture of ami-

479

The only plausible resolution is that the Jerusalem agreement had not covered the issue of mixed (Jew/Gentile) churches — as is perhaps suggested by the implication that 'we for the Gentiles and they for the circumcision' (2.9) was intended (naïvely?) to mark out two discrete responsibilities.[276] The surprise that the issue was not raised is tempered by a number of considerations. One is that the presence of Titus had evidently not raised the issue; in a church (house groups) more or less exclusively Jewish in character, he may simply have conformed, as a guest, to the customs of his hosts. Another is that the crisis confronted in Jerusalem (whether Titus should be circumcised) had been so traumatic that all parties hesitated to raise any other issues lest the (fragile?) agreement be compromised. Another runs along the lines already suggested,[277] that the addendum to the agreement (2.10) was regarded by James as safeguarding the principle of covenantal nomism in regard to association with Gentile believers; they need not be circumcised, but they should be prepared to honour Jewish scruples by themselves 'judaizing'. As I have expressed it elsewhere, it is quite likely that James left the Jerusalem council under the impression that an exception had been permitted rather than a principle conceded.[278]

We should also bear in mind the deteriorating political situation in Judea during this period. The fiasco over Caligula's statue had traumatized Judeans less than a decade earlier and had evidently caused serious unrest in Antioch too.[279] Herod Agrippa's brief reign over the united kingdom (41-44) cannot but have stirred up nationalist sentiment. The succeeding Roman procurators were weak and heavy handed. Cuspius Fadus (44-46?) had demanded that the vestments of the high priest be returned to the Romans for safe-keeping and had confronted the threatened rebellion of Theudas (Josephus, *Ant.* 20.6, 97-99). His successor, the Jewish apostate Tiberius Iulius Alexander (46?-48), crucified James and Simon, sons of Judas the Galilean, presumably because, like their father, they were thought to be fomenting unrest against Roman rule (*Ant.* 20.102). Under his successor, Ventidius Cumanus (48-ca. 52), that is, during the period in view here, the

---

cable relations between Paul and James' ('James of Jerusalem' 784), but he takes too little account of the distancing character of Paul's reference in Gal. 2.6 and of the depth of indignation Paul expresses in regard to Peter's actions and the motivation behind them.

276. 'The Law is not mentioned because its continuing validity is taken for granted' (Martyn, *Galatians* 267-68). See also C. K. Barrett, 'Christocentricity at Antioch', *On Paul* 37-54 (here 49-53); also *Acts* 2.711-12. Bruce comments appositely: 'In our more sophisticated days we are familiar with the device of calculated ambiguity in ecclesiastical as in other agreements; but such ambiguity as inhered in this agreement was not deliberate but inadvertent' (*Galatians* 125). Similarly Martyn, *Galatians* 220-22.

277. See above at §27 n. 197 and further §27.3e.

278. *Partings* (²2006) 172; see further my *Galatians* 122-24.

279. See above, §24 n. 236.

situation continued to deteriorate, with a near riot in Jerusalem resulting in thousands dead (according to Josephus) and increasing banditry in Samaria and elsewhere (*War* 2.223-38; *Ant.* 20.105-24).[280]

Under such circumstances, and given the degree to which nationalist identity and religious identity were so intertwined in Jewish self-understanding, it would be almost inevitable that pressure would have built up on Jewish members of the Jesus sect to demonstrate their loyalty to and continuing high regard for the laws and customs which so constituted these identities.[281] This may already have been a factor in the crisis in Jerusalem itself ('the false brothers'?), and there may be a good deal more than sarcasm in Paul's accusation that Peter acted as he did in Antioch because he 'feared those of the circumcision' (2.12).

d. The Case for Peter

Such considerations allow us to gain a more sympathetic perception of why Peter acted as he did. The historian is in a difficult position here, for Galatians 2 gives only Paul's side of the story, and Acts omits the episode altogether. But unless Peter is to be regarded as completely unprincipled, we must infer that he had good reason for 'separating' from the Gentile believers. After all, it was not he alone who provoked the *de facto* schism, but all the other Jewish believers, and even Barnabas, Paul's co-worker in the mission which had won so many more Gentiles to the faith. So how might Peter have responded to Paul's sharp rebuke in 2.14-16?[282]

1. He would certainly have seen the logic of covenantal nomism: that a Jew was bound by Israel's covenant with God to live in accordance with the law.[283]

---

280. Fuller treatment in Smallwood, *Jews* 257-69.

281. As argued by R. Jewett, 'The Agitators and the Galatian Congregation', *NTS* 17 (1970-71) 198-212 (here 204-206); cf. Hengel and Schwemer, *Paul* 256; 'this agreement was a brittle one, which was liable to be undermined by rising Jewish nationalism' (Wedderburn, *History* 109-10). In just over a decade hence James himself would fall victim to the internecine suspicions of the high priestly faction in the run up to the revolt itself (see below, §36.2). That a delegation from James should have attempted to assert Jerusalem's authority as covering also Antioch may also have been a factor (Taylor, *Paul* 130-31); see also §36 nn. 24, 25 below.

282. In what follows I draw on my earlier treatments of the passage ('The Incident at Antioch' 156-57; *Partings* [²2006] 175-76; *Galatians* 119-24). Cf. Murphy-O'Connor, *Paul* 152; Martyn, *Galatians* 241-43; Lohse, *Paulus* 92-93; Schäfer, *Paulus bis zum Apostelkonzil* 236-38; Hengel, *Petrus* 97-98, 105-16.

283. 'One's attitude and obedience to the Law was the acid test of one's membership in the people of God' (Davies, 'Paul' 703). Cummins suggests that loyalty to all that the Maccabean martyrs exemplified and for which they died may have been a factor for Peter (*Paul and the Crucified Christ* 174-78, 188).

2. He would no doubt have felt the pressure of mounting nationalism. Even if Paul's charge that he 'feared those of the circumcision' (2.12) was unkind and unfair, Peter may well have allowed his judgment to be swayed by the delegation(?) from James.

3. Very likely he would have been concerned for the continuing viability of his own mission to the circumcised (2.9). To be identified as a 'sinner', and not least by those of his own 'sect', would have made him unacceptable to many of his fellow Jews.

4. He may have hoped that the Gentile believers would act as so many God-fearers did in associating with the synagogue, that is, adopted or adapted to Jewish customs. Here again Paul's harsh talk of 'compelling Gentiles to judaize' (2.14) may simply be an unsympathetic reading of Peter's tactic of gradually withdrawing from table-fellowship, in the hope that the Gentiles would come to eat with him, rather than expecting him to sit loose to his ancestral customs. Subsequently, Paul's own counsel to mixed congregations in Corinth and Rome was not so dissimilar (1 Corinthians 8–10; Rom. 14.1–15.6).

All in all, then, we might justifiably think that Peter's policy was rather sensible: he was concerned for the genuine and deeply felt beliefs of his fellow Jews, and he was not really putting much of an additional demand on the Gentiles. The gospel was not at stake: the Gentile believers had received the Spirit and been baptized, without circumcision; now all that was required was to accommodate the scruples of the Jewish believers. Paul disagreed — strongly!

27.5. The Truth of the Gospel

[14]If you, a Jew, 'live like a Gentile and not like a Jew', how is it that you compel the Gentiles to judaize? [15]We are Jews by nature and not 'Gentile sinners', [16]knowing that no person is justified by works of the law but only *(ean mē)* through faith in Jesus Christ; we too have believed in Jesus Christ in order that we might be justified by faith in Christ and not *(ouk)* by works of the law, because by works of the law shall no flesh be justified. (Gal. 2.14-16)

Paul's response to Peter, merging as it does into his continuing reflection on the confrontation (2.14-21), shows Paul striving to bring out what he saw to have been, and to be, at stake in that confrontation.[284]

---

284. Schnelle, *Paul* 136-37, is unjustifiably adamant that Paul could not have said 2.16 at Antioch itself.

a. The Common Ground

I have put a clause of 2.14 and a phrase of 2.15 in quotation marks because it is probable that Paul actually quotes here the language used by the group from James to dissuade Peter from his practice of eating with the Gentile believers in Antioch. The repeated antithesis between Gentile and Jew is particularly striking: Jewish sense of set-apartness from the nations/Gentiles was obviously being appealed to. Peter had been 'living like a Gentile and not like a Jew', which almost certainly echoes the censorious language of the James group in regard to Peter's conduct in eating with the Gentile believers. Similarly, it must be judged doubtful whether Paul would have used the phrase 'Gentile sinners' (Gentiles = sinners) on his own account, whereas, as already seen, the phrase expresses the attitude of those who look out from 'within the law' to those who by definition are out-laws. The two phrases obviously hang together: 'live like a Gentile, that is, a Gentile sinner'. The group from James evidently condemned the Jewish believers as effectively putting themselves in the status of Gentiles. In his response to Peter, Paul picks up the language without comment. It is the starting point for his rebuke.

Equally striking is the way Paul appeals to Peter on the common ground of the gospel: 'we know, we who are Jews and not Gentiles, that no one is justified by works of the law but only through faith in Jesus Christ'. The appeal is twofold. First to their common Jewish heritage ('we are Jews by nature'). As we shall see more fully later,[285] the appeal was presumably to the fact that the teaching on 'justification' was rooted in their common heritage, that their whole standing as Jews was based entirely on God's initiative in choosing Israel to be his people and showing them how to live as his people.[286] The scriptural quotation (or allusion) with which Paul rounds off 2.16 makes the same point: 'no living person will be justified before you' (Ps. 143.2).[287] The theology is thoroughly Jewish: that no one could claim to be sinless before God, worthy of (final) acquittal by reason of the quality of his or her life.[288] Thus Paul indicates that 'justification' is at root a teaching shared by Jews and derived from their common heritage.

285. See below, §33.3a.
286. This is the principal theme of Deuteronomy, the charter of Israel's 'covenantal nomism'.
287. The allusion is repeated in a similar context and is clearer in Rom. 3.20; see further my *Romans* 153-54 and below, §33 n. 117.
288. E.g., Job 9.2; Ps. 14.1-3; Isa. 59.2-15; *1 En.* 81.5; 1QH 17[= 9].14-15. On the tension of covenantal nomism (that final justification did depend in at least some measure on observing the law), see below, *The New Perspective on Paul* (2005) 55-63 and further 63-80, (2008) 60-71 and further 71-89.

Second, however, Paul appeals also to the Christian faith shared between them: 'we know that a person is justified . . . only through faith in Jesus Christ'.[289] The fact of their shared faith, and the fact that it was the ground of their relationship both with God through Christ and with one another and other believers, was the common ground on which they stood.[290] This sentence alone (2.16a) should be sufficient evidence that the 'doctrine of justification through faith' was not a Pauline creation, and not first formulated by Paul for his mission alone or only after his mission had been under way for some time.[291]

b. The Underlying Principle

The issue for Paul was that the two elements from which his rebuke starts had become irreconcilable. Peter's conduct at Antioch had made it clear to Paul that the old Jewish attitude to Gentiles was incompatible with the gospel which they shared. In Paul's eyes Peter's conduct was an attempt to 'compel' Gentile believers to 'judaize', to take on customs characteristic and distinctive of the Jewish way of life (2.14); that is, Peter was requiring 'works of the law' *in addition to* faith in Christ as a *sine qua non* of the gospel, and for the community of believers (2.16).[292]

---

289. I remain firmly convinced that the current fashion to interpret the phrase *pistis Christou* as referring to Christ's faith(fulness) is a misunderstanding, not of the theology behind that interpretation (that Paul understood Jesus' death as an act of 'obedience' is clear from Rom. 5.19), but of the texts being thus interpreted. So far as Galatians is concerned, it should be obvious from 3.6-9 both that the 'faith' *(pistis)* spoken of in 3.7-9 is to be understood in terms of Abraham's believing *(episteusen)* in the headline text (3.6) and that 3.6-9 is an exposition of the *pistis* referred to in the thematic statement of 2.16; see below, §31 n. 352 (also §33 n. 121), and further my *New Perspective on Paul* 39-40 n. 164 (with recent bibliography); also Chester, *Conversion at Corinth* 175-81; D. M. Hay, 'Paul's Understanding of Faith as Participation', in S. E. Porter, ed., *Paul and His Theology* (Leiden: Brill, 2006) 45-76; R. B. Matlock, 'Detheologizing the *pistis Christou* Debate: Cautionary Remarks from a Lexical Semantic Perspective', *NovT* 42 (2000) 1-23; also his '"Even the Demons Believe": Paul and *pistis Christou'*, *CBQ* 64 (2002) 300-318, and 'ΠΙΣΤΙΣ in Galatians 3.26: Neglected Evidence for "Faith in Christ"?', *NTS* 49 (2003) 433-39; R. A. Harrisville, 'Before *pistis Christou*: The Objective Genitive as Good Greek', *NovT* 48 (2006) 353-58.

290. 'A consensus statement of Antiochene theology' (Becker, *Paul* 96, 287-88); 'a standard Jewish view' (Westerholm, *Perspectives* 370); see further M. Theobald, 'Der Kanon von der Rechtfertigung (Gal 2,16; Röm 3,28)', *Studien zum Römerbrief* (WUNT 136; Tübingen: Mohr Siebeck, 2001) 164-225 (here 182-92); Schäfer, *Paulus bis zum Apostelkonzil* 253-65. J. Murphy-O'Connor, 'Gal 2:15-16a: Whose Common Ground?', *RB* 108 (2001) 376-85, observes that Paul attributes to the Christian Jews a theological position which they should have defended, not the one they actually maintained.

291. See again *New Perspective on Paul* 33-37.

292. The confusion between the Jerusalem agreement and the Antioch disagreement is

Paul's tactic is familiar to debaters of all ages. He took his starting point from the episode which had occasioned the confrontation, even echoing the language (probably) used by the James group, and sought to show how their shared understanding of how *God* deals with humankind ran counter to that language and to the attitudes which it expressed. In effect he was appealing to Peter to consider the terms of the gospel which they shared and seeking to draw from Peter an acceptance of the more fundamental principle which he saw enshrined in it.

The tactic may be indicated by Paul's use of the phrase *ean mē* in 2.16a, rather than the subsequent direct denial, *ouk*. The former can mean 'except' (as well as 'but' or 'but only'), so that Paul's appeal could be understood as an acknowledgment of Peter's position: 'we know that no one is justified from works of the law except through faith'; that is, faith in Christ is the fundamental qualification of a belief that works of the law were still essential for justification, or final acquittal, a very natural position for a believing Jew.[293] In other words, the ambiguity of the phrase *ean mē* may reflect the ambiguity of Peter's position: that he was in effect holding both that justification was by faith in Christ and that it was still necessary for believing Jews to observe works of the law (food laws, in the case in point). This understanding of *ean mē* has been criticized, but whatever the precise force of *ean mē* ('except', or 'but'),[294] the key point remains firm: at Antioch Peter acted in a way which implied that it was still necessary for (Jewish) believers to observe (certain key) works of the law, even though he already agreed that justification was by faith in Christ. The point was, therefore,

---

perhaps mirrored in modern discussion as to whether the former was an agreement to recognize *different versions* of the gospel as of equal status (Schnelle, *Paul* 129). Paul would not have accepted such a formulation: from his perspective there was a single, common gospel ('the truth of the gospel'; cf. 1 Cor. 15.11); the disagreement was whether anything further should be required of Gentile believers.

293. *New Perspective on Paul* 189-91 and n. 25, 195-98. F. Mussner, *Der Galaterbrief* (HTKNT 9; Freiburg: Herder, ³1977): 'The Jew would not let the pauline antithesis "faith"/ "works of the law" pass; for him it makes no sense' (170). 'Probably many Jewish Christians did not see their turning to the Messiah Jesus as a soteriological alternative to the principle of the works of the law' (Merklein, '"Nicht aus Werken"' 306). See further Martyn, *Galatians* 264-68.

294. I respond to earlier criticism in the 'Additional Notes' to 'The New Perspective' (207-209, 212). A. A. Das, 'Another Look at *ean mē* in Galatians 2:16', *JBL* 119 (2000) 529-39, comes to my support (the formula is deliberately ambiguous; also his *Paul and the Jews* [Peabody: Hendrickson, 2003] 31-32), though he needs to bear in mind that the belief described in 2.16a seems to be the belief put into practice at Antioch by Peter and the other Christian Jews. In his paper 'Galatians 2:15-16' at the British New Testament Conference in Edinburgh (September 2004), M. C. de Boer gave a preview of his forthcoming New Testament Library commentary on Galatians (Westminster John Knox), in which he similarly argues that 2.15-16a is a *captatio benevolentiae* intended by Paul to win the sympathy of those who disagreed with him by use of the ambiguous *ean mē*.

that the formulation 'no person is justified by works of the law *ean mē* through faith in Jesus Christ' was proving inadequate. The critical gospel principle of justification through believing in Messiah Jesus was not being sufficiently safeguarded and had to be restated with a fresh antithetical sharpness — not faith plus, not both faith and works, but *only* through faith, 'faith in Christ and not *(ouk)* works of the law' (2.16b).[295]

In a similar way, Paul qualifies his final allusion to Ps. 143.2 by adding the key phrase of his polemic: '*by works of the law* shall no flesh be justified' (2.16c). The elaboration of the Psalm text was not unjustified. For if 'no living person/flesh will be justified before God', then the more general principle includes the particular case of one seeking to be justified 'from works of the law'. In other words, here again Paul drives through the confusing ambiguity of Peter's attitude and conduct, as indeed the confusing ambiguity of covenantal nomism, to the core principle, the fundamental axiom on which all else rested: that acceptance by God and God's final verdict on a life does not depend on particular requirements of the law being observed.

For Paul nothing less than 'the truth of the gospel' was at stake in this confrontation, as it had been in the crisis in Jerusalem (2.5, 14).[296] In both instances this truth of the gospel was bound up with 'freedom' — here, freedom from being 'compelled' (2.3-4, 14) to observe requirements (works) of the law deemed to be of continuing importance by Jewish believers. Hence the prominence of the theme of freedom subsequently in the letter and Paul's alarm that their freedom, the truth of the gospel, was being endangered and critically compromised by the other missionaries who had entered Galatia after Paul's departure.[297]

c. The Truth of the Gospel

Given that Gal. 2.16 is the first extant statement of what many would regard as the heart of the Pauline (and Christian) gospel, a few further remarks by way of clarification may be called for.

---

295. See also Schäfer, *Paulus bis zum Apostelkonzil* 253-65, 483-84. Paul 'thinks of the Gentiles as proselytes to an "Israel" whose boundary marker is Christ rather than Torah' (Donaldson, *Paul and the Gentiles* 160); Donaldson's central thesis is that for Paul 'the community of salvation is to be determined by the boundary marker of faith in Christ, and that as a result no other boundary marker — including that set of Torah-prescribed observances marking the boundary between Jew and Gentile — is to be imposed' (161-64 [here 162]).

296. P. Dschulnigg, *Petrus im Neuen Testament* (Stuttgart: Katholisches Bibelwerk, 1996): 'Even the first apostle Cephas, the first witness of the Risen One and leader of the Jewish mission, must let himself be measured against the truth of the gospel' (169).

297. Gal. 2.4; 4.22, 23, 26, 30, 31; 5.1, 13. See further below, §31.7.

It should be clear from his account that Paul did not first attain his belief in justification by faith at Antioch or in response to Peter, or indeed only when confronted by his Galatian opponents.[298] I have already indicated that from his earliest evangelism (whenever that was) Paul almost certainly preached that God's offer of acceptance was to those who received the gospel, believed its good news and committed themselves (in baptism) to Jesus as their Lord. But the sequence of events outlined in Galatians 2 strongly suggests that the issue of faith *versus works* as such did not emerge for some time after the Gentile mission had begun. It was evidently the success of that mission which brought to the surface the question whether justification by faith in Christ Jesus was in any way or degree dependent on observance of the law, on doing the works of the law, on adopting a characteristically Jewish way of life. The development which I see attested in the text is that it was the insistence by traditionalist Jewish believers that at least some key laws were still binding which made it clear that there was an issue here and that it had to be confronted. The circumcision question was resolved with a fair degree of amicableness.[299] But it was the insistence on the laws governing table-fellowship between Jews and non-Jews at Antioch which raised the issue whether faith needed to be complemented by works of the law, *any* works of the law. In other words, Paul's formulation in Gal. 2.16 was, as the context suggests, formulated in response to the crisis at Antioch.[300] The belief that justification was from faith in Christ Jesus was the common ground. The events at Antioch showed Paul that the teaching had to be sharpened — faith in Christ *and not works of the law*.[301]

298. *Pace* Strecker: 'Paul's message of justification was occasioned for the first time by the Galatian crisis and developed in his letter to the Galatians' (*Theology* 139); Schnelle, *Paulus* 132-35, 302-304: 'With Gal. 2.16 Paul takes a decisive step beyond the agreement of the apostolic council and the point at issue in the Antioch incident' (302); also, to some extent, Martyn, who sees Paul's formulation in Gal. 2.16 as Paul's interpretation of the common gospel of justification in polemical response to the nomistic interpretation of that gospel brought by the other missionaries ('the Teachers' in Martyn's terminology) to the Galatians (*Galatians* 268-75). S. Kim seems to think I belong to this camp (see n. 303 below); but see my *New Perspective on Paul* 33-37.

299. Although not for 'the false brothers' of Gal. 2.4 and the trouble-making missionaries attacked in Galatians; Paul saw 'the truth of the gospel' (2.5, 14) as expressed in 'the gospel for the circumcised' — that is, as not requiring or dependent upon Gentiles 'living like Jews' (2.14), that is, here in effect, becoming proselytes.

300. 'It is scarcely imaginable that Paul's companion in Gentile mission, Barnabas, would have wavered at Antioch if earlier he had been exposed to the full force of the polemic [I might add 'and of the theology'] Paul employs in the letter to Galatia' (Seifrid, *Justification by Faith* 180).

301. Similarly K.-W. Niebuhr, 'Die paulinische Rechtfertigungslehre in der gegenwärtigen exegetischen Diskussion', in T. Söding, ed., *Worum geht es in der Rechtfertigungs-*

In earlier treatments of Gal. 2.16 I also pressed the case for seeing 'the works of the law' as referring particularly to the practices which marked out Jews as a people apart from other nations.[302] I do indeed think that the primary or initial reference of the phrase in Gal. 2.16 is to the laws which had been disputed at the Jerusalem council (circumcision) and which had been at issue in Antioch (laws governing the meal table). It was because Peter was in effect demanding that Gentile believers submit to such food laws that Paul accused him of subverting the principle of justification by faith.[303] But the theological principle which Paul states in Gal. 2.16, of course, transcends that particular issue. In defining acceptability to God, and therefore of believers to one another, *nothing* should be added to the gospel's call for faith; faith in Christ alone is the sole basis for Christian unity.[304]

At the same time we should not lose sight of the issue which sparked off this key theological insight: that it was the reality of Jew and Gentile living and working together which was first endangered by failing to appreciate this gospel axiom.[305] In considering the particular issue which occasioned the statement of Gal. 2.16, it should never be forgotten that this was the issue which called forth Paul's classic statement of the gospel. Nor should it be forgotten that *central* to the gospel for Paul was the conviction that it was a gospel for Gentiles and not only for Jews.[306] What was it that roused Paul's anger at Antioch? What was it that he saw as such a threat to the fundamental truth of justification by faith? — precisely the refusal of one group of believers/Christians fully to accept another

---

lehre (Freiburg: Herder, 1999) 105-30 (here 113-14, 128); cf. Martyn's complete argument (*Galatians* 263-75) and Theobald's thesis in 'Kanon'.

302. Particularly 'The New Perspective on Paul', *Jesus, Paul and the Law* 183-214 (191-95), reprinted in *The New Perspective on Paul* ch. 2 — (2005) 98-101, (2008) 108-11; 'Works of the Law and the Curse of the Law (Gal. 3.10-14)', *Jesus, Paul and the Law* 215-41 (219-25), reprinted in *The New Perspective* ch. 3 — (2005) 115-22, (2008) 125-32. For clarification see *Galatians* 135-37 and *The New Perspective* (2005) 22-26, (2008) 23-28.

303. 'For Paul, the behaviour of Peter and Barnabas constitutes their rejection of the doctrine of justification by faith' (N. Dahl, 'The Doctrine of Justification: Its Social Function and Implications' [1964], *Studies in Paul* [Minneapolis: Augsburg, 1977] 95-120 [here 109]); 'with v. 16 Paul makes clear what momentous consequences must result from the renouncing of table-fellowship' (Lohse, *Paulus* 94).

304. In *The New Perspective on Paul* (2005) 31-32, (2008) 34-36 I draw out the ecumenical implications.

305. I draw here on *The New Perspective on Paul* (2005) 26-33, (2008) 29-36. Barnett misses the point in suggesting that the 'new perspective' maintains 'that Paul's gospel is only addressed to the "inclusion of Gentiles", as if Israel had no such need' (*Birth* 63).

306. Kim thinks that by focusing on the Jew/Gentile aspect of Paul's gospel I (or should that be Paul?) reduce it to the status of a pragmatic solution to a problem of relationships among Christians' (*Paul and the New Perspective* 45-53).

group of believers/Christians! The statement of justification which Paul formulated in the wake of the Antioch episode (2.16) at the very least includes the message that justification means that believers must fully accept (eat with) other believers, despite important disagreements on what conduct is appropriate/inappropriate to such faith. Evidently the two dimensions are inextricably interlocked — the vertical and the horizontal, acceptance by God with acceptance of others. To de-prioritize the horizontal emphasis, as 'sociological' and distinct from 'theological',[307] is to miss and to mistake the high priority which Paul placed upon it, as his later writings confirm.[308]

27.6. The Outcome

What happened at Antioch when Paul rebuked Peter so roundly? Did Peter accept Paul's rebuke and he and the rest of the believing Jews resume table-fellowship with the Gentile believers? The traditional reading of the episode is that Peter did indeed respond graciously to Paul, thereby restoring harmony to the church in Antioch.[309] That is a wholly comprehensible interpretation, since Paul here is the voice of the canon, which carries with it the implication that his views prevailed. But it stumbles on one important feature: that *Paul does not tell us that he prevailed!* If he had indeed won the day, we would have expected him so to indicate, 'to blow his own trumpet', however modestly. This is what he did

---

307. See those referred to in *The New Perspective on Paul* (2005) 26-27 n. 109, (2008) 29 n. 110.

308. It is hardly a coincidence that Paul's greatest letter, to the Romans, rounds off with a discussion of this very theme (Rom. 14.1–15.6), summed up in the exhortation to 'welcome one another, just as Christ has welcomed you' (Rom. 15.7). Nor that the letter climaxes in the vision attested by law, prophet and psalmist of Gentiles worshipping and glorifying God together with God's ancient people (15.9-12), a vision being fulfilled through Paul's own mission. Nor should we forget that Paul counted this as the great 'mystery' which had been hidden from the ages and the generations but which had now been revealed in the gospel: that God's purpose from of old had been to include the Gentiles with his people. In Ephesians particularly this is the climactic mystery of the ages, to reveal and implement which Paul had been commissioned: that 'the Gentiles have become fellow heirs, members of the same body' (Eph. 3.6). Christ died to break down the wall, the law with its commandments and ordinances, the wall that divided Jew from Gentile (2.14-16). In him the two have become one, and the church is presented precisely as existing to be *the place where the separated peoples come together as one* (2.17-22). The surmounting of these ancient hostilities was not merely a by-product of the gospel, far less a distraction from the true meaning of the gospel, but *the climactic achievement of the gospel*, the completion of God's purposes from the beginning of time. See also §§31.7b(iii) and 37.1b(ii) below.

309. Most recently Schäfer, *Paulus bis zum Apostelkonzil* 481.

when he prevailed at the earlier meeting in Jerusalem (2.6-10); his resistance there had been crucial to 'the freedom which we have in Christ' (2.4), that is, the freedom of his Galatian addressees. But a triumph in Antioch (if that's what it was) was equally crucial for the Galatian Gentile believers, not least because Paul deemed the truth of the gospel to have been at stake there too (2.14). Paul had pinned his rebuke of Peter on what he regarded as the essential character of faith in Christ as alone the ground for acceptance (of Gentile as well as Jew) by God. If he had been equally successful in that confrontation, there can be little or no doubt that he would have so indicated to the Galatians, as a way of immeasurably strengthening his response to what was a renewal of the old crisis in Galatia.[310]

Instead, as already observed, in Gal. 2.14-21 Paul's response to Peter merges into what he wanted to say to his Galatian audiences in regard to that earlier confrontation. In so doing he leaves the story of that confrontation unfinished, almost as though he restates what he did say more clearly, or even restates the essence of his earlier argument more effectively. The inference is hard to avoid that he did so because he was all too well aware that his earlier argument, his rebuke to Peter, had *not* been successful; his attempt to restore relationships in the Antioch church to what they were before the appearance of the James group failed. Precisely because Paul is the voice of the canon here, some find it hard to draw this inference. But when we bring into the confrontation what Peter's response was likely to have been, the probabilities begin to change. For as we saw, Peter's reasons for his conduct most likely were substantial; that a Jewish minority should be able to look for consideration from a Gentile majority in the circumstances of growing Jewish nationalism was not, after all, unreasonable (§27.4d).

The strong likelihood emerges, therefore, that in the confrontation it was *Peter* who prevailed.[311] That is, it is quite likely that in the event Peter succeeded in persuading ('compel' is Paul's word) the Gentile believers to conform their practice

---

310. 'How triumphantly Paul would have shown the power of his gospel, had he been able to write: "Peter, Barnabas and the other Jewish Christians confessed that I was right, and ate once again with their Gentile brethren"! Here the *argumentum e silentio* is justified for once, as everything urged Paul to speak if he could. And his silence shows that success was denied to him' (Haenchen, *Acts* 476). Similarly Lohse, *Paulus* 96; Wedderburn, *History* 118.

311. Weiss, *Earliest Christianity* 275-76; 'had Peter conceded the justice of Paul's position, Paul must have said so; it would be a trump card in his hand' (Nock, *St. Paul* 110); Conzelmann, *History* 90; Brown and Meier, *Antioch and Rome* 39; '. . . a stunning defeat and damaging loss' (Catchpole, 'Paul, James and the Apostolic Decree' 442); Achtemeier, *Quest for Unity* 58-59 — 'the Jerusalem conference and its decree succeeded only in splitting the gentile mission without in any way mollifying the radical Jewish Christians' (55); 'James, Peter and Barnabas won not only in Antioch but in the early church as a whole' (Holtz, 'Antiochenische Zwischenfall' 355); Becker, *Paul* 97, 169; Öhler, *Barnabas* 85-86.

of table-fellowship to accommodate the scruples of the Jewish believers. After all, if we follow Josephus, there was a strong tradition of Syrian Gentiles 'judaizing' (*War* 2.463); how different was the demand being made by Peter and Barnabas, one of their own leaders? This is the irony of Paul's account of the episode: that table-fellowship may well have been resumed, but on terms approved by James and heartily disapproved of by Paul. Paul was outfaced by Peter; Barnabas did not stand with him as he had in Jerusalem, and the church of Antioch as a whole discounted what Paul thought of as a, if not the, fundamental gospel truth.[312] 'The absent James was a more powerful influence than the present Paul'.[313]

If this entirely plausible scenario is at all close to what happened in Antioch as a result of 'the clash of the Titans', then several corollaries would seem to follow.[314]

(1) Paul had in effect been disowned by the church which had first commissioned him as a missionary.[315] Since Paul continued to believe passionately in the truth of the gospel which in effect had been rejected in Antioch, the relationship could not continue as before. It is not surprising, then, that in his continuing mission, as we shall see, Paul seems to have worked much more as an independent missionary.[316] As elsewhere in his narrative, Luke draws a veil over such tensions and disunity.[317] But we probably have to envisage a breach between Paul and the Antioch church as one of the outcomes of the Antioch confronta-

312. That Peter 'won' the confrontation is probably the dominant view today (see, e.g., those cited in my 'The Incident at Antioch' 173 n. 126; and *Galatians* 130 n. 1; and in Painter, *Just James* 71 [Painter himself is unpersuaded, 71-73]; White, *Jesus to Christianity* 170-71; Joubert, *Paul as Benefactor* 121).

313. C. K. Barrett, *Freedom and Obligation: A Study of the Epistle to the Galatians* (London: SPCK, 1985) 13.

314. As already observed in my 'The Incident at Antioch' 160-61 (bibliography 173 n. 128); *Partings* [²2006] 177-78). Similarly Murphy-O'Connor, *Paul* 158. Again, Schnabel treats the subject with remarkable casualness (*Mission* 1005-6).

315. Sanders's conclusion that the Jewish Christians and Gentile Christians formed separate communions in Antioch (*Schismatics* 154) is unlikely, since apparently the Gentile Christians followed Peter's lead.

316. 'When he writes Galatians . . . he is no longer answerable to or supported by any congregation, unless those of his own founding' (Haenchen, *Acts* 466); see also Wedderburn, *History* 118-20. In private correspondence, Michael Wolter notes the significance of Paul's description of the founding of the church in Philippi, the first church established by Paul following the Antioch incident, as 'the beginning of the gospel' (Phil. 4.15). The characterization by Malina and Neyrey of Paul as 'a typically group-oriented person' — 'Paul is essentially obedient to group norms and group-sanctioned persons' (*Portraits of Paul* 51, 62, 206, 217) — is quite hard to correlate with Paul's stand at Antioch and its outcome; Malina and Neyrey are too ready to generalize from a stereotypical characterization of ancient 'collectivist culture' (214-15).

317. A later visit to Antioch (Acts 18.22-23) need not undermine the scenario being painted; Paul seems to have buried more than one hatchet! See §32.1d below.

tion. By siding with Peter, as I infer, the Antioch church had affirmed its readiness to acknowledge Jerusalem's (James's) authority and had therefore ceased (in Paul's eyes) to champion the cause of Gentile believers. In the division of responsibility agreed in Jerusalem (Gal. 2.9), Antioch had voted itself out of Paul's camp. Paul would probably have concluded that he could no longer serve as one of Antioch's missionaries/'apostles'.

(2) In the circumstances reported in Gal. 2.11-14, and even more if Paul had failed to persuade Peter of the error of his ways, Paul must have felt abandoned by his erstwhile closest colleague, Barnabas. We probably, therefore, have to envisage also a breach between Paul and Barnabas.[318] Luke indeed confirms that such a breach occurred: Paul and Barnabas parted company and engaged in quite separate missions — Barnabas back to Cyprus, and Paul to the churches of Syria and Cilicia (Acts 15.39-41).[319] But the reason Luke gives is entirely different. In Acts the breach occurs because of 'a sharp disagreement *(paroxysmos)*' between Paul and Barnabas over Barnabas's proposal to take John Mark with them on their return (pastoral) visit to the churches they had established (Acts 15.36-39). It may not be necessary to choose between the two reasons for the breach — the one indicated in Luke's account and the other suggested by Paul's account. But here again it is unlikely that Luke has told the whole story.

(3) Another consequence would probably have been a breach between Paul and the churches of Syria and Cilicia with which Paul had worked, and (some of) which Paul may have founded during the initial phase of his missionary work (Gal. 1.21-23). The fact that the letter of Acts 15.23-29 is explicitly addressed to the 'Gentile brothers in Antioch, Syria and Cilicia' (15.23) supports the inference that the churches of Syria and Cilicia (daughter churches of Antioch) followed the lead of the church of Antioch and ceased to support Paul. At all events, it is noteworthy that Paul never refers to these churches thereafter,[320] and they did not participate in the later collection from the Gentile churches for Jerusalem.

318. Taylor, *Paul* 139, and those cited by him (n. 1); Kraus, *Zwischen Jerusalem und Antiochia* 166-67; Öhler, *Barnabas* 55-56, 84-86, 444-54. Hengel and Schwemer infer that in the event Barnabas did accept an 'added' obligation (cf. Gal. 2.6), possibly the terms of the apostolic decree (*Paul* 207).

319. The reference to churches already established in Syria and Cilicia recalls Paul's own description of his early mission in the territories of Syria and Cilicia (Gal. 1.21). Since a possible implication of Acts 15.41 is that Paul and Silas took on the other part of the return visit envisaged by Barnabas (15.36), Barnabas taking the Cyprus part, 15.41 could provide some support for the view that Gal. 1.21 covered the ground (Galatia at least) of the mission from Antioch (Acts 13.14–14.23). Acts 16.1 suggests that Derbe and Lystra lay beyond 'Syria and Cilicia', but Barrett notes the new beginning made in 16.1 — 'probably the beginning of a new source of information' (*Acts* 2.758). See also above, §25 n. 223.

320. Quite likely, however, some of Paul's experience of synagogue discipline (2 Cor. 11.24) refers to these 'years of silence'; see, e.g., Barnett, *Jesus* 248-49.

(4) It would further follow that Paul saw the outcome as constituting an effective breach with the mother church in Jerusalem.[321] As we have seen, in his account of the Jerusalem agreement Paul seems to have been willing to acknowledge the authority of the Jerusalem leaders.[322] The reason is obvious: they had backed him in Jerusalem; their authority could be cited in support of his argument in his letter to the Galatian churches. But we also noted that at the time of writing the letter, Paul's acknowledgment of their status had become more than somewhat jaundiced (Gal. 2.6). Why the change? What had intervened? Almost certainly the answer is the confrontation at Antioch. That, after all, had been occasioned by the arrival of the group/delegation 'from James' (2.12), and no doubt by their manifest disapproval of Jews 'living like Gentiles' (2.14). Paul, in other words, seems to have formulated 'the truth of the gospel' in sharper terms precisely in opposition to the lead being given from Jerusalem. The Jerusalem agreement had not enshrined the truth of the gospel in sufficiently explicit terms. And Paul's attempt to formulate it more explicitly seems to have been rejected or discounted or ignored. It was time for Paul to build what he could on the parts of the Jerusalem agreement which had not been repudiated, and to fulfill his commission to preach the truth of the gospel as he had been given it, without regard to the Jerusalem leadership.[323]

(5) Not least, then, in the double episode narrated in Gal. 2.1-14 (and Acts 15), the crisis at Jerusalem and the confrontation at Antioch, we see a significant shift in the relationships of the three most significant figures in the first generation of Christianity — Peter, James and Paul — and in their authority and influence.

- *James* has emerged as the leader of the Jerusalem church. He chaired the important consultation in Jerusalem; his judgment determined the outcome (Acts 15);[324] his influence in support of a traditionalist understanding of the Jesus Messiah sect reached out to the church at Antioch; and his au-

---

321. Cf. Chilton, with reference to the scenario indicated at the end of §27.3 above: 'The decree of James carried the day, and Paul was now effectively an excommunicant from his own movement' (*Rabbi Paul* 170).

322. See above, §27.3c. In siding with Holtz's opinion that there was no 'radical breach between Paul and the leaders of the original community', Lohse (*Paulus* 96) does not give enough consideration to these hints in Galatians 1–2 that his relationship with Jerusalem had altered over that time period.

323. The breach with Jerusalem, however, should not be exaggerated (Taylor, *Paul* ch. 6).

324. Acts 15.19 — 'Wherefore I give my judgment *(krinō)* that . . .'; 'I decree' (Lake and Cadbury, *Beginnings* 4.177); 'Therefore I have reached the decision that . . .' (NRSV); though *krinō* here may only have the force of 'give my opinion' (BDAG 568; Fitzmyer, *Acts* 556). But the force of *episteilai* (followed by infinitive) in 15.20 is probably that of 'send written instructions'; 'not simply a message or exhortation is conveyed by *orders*' (Barrett, *Acts* 2.730).

thority was acknowledged there, by Peter and the other Jewish believers in Antioch (including Barnabas), and in face of Paul's vigorous protest (Gal. 2.12-14).[325]

- *Peter* no longer appears as the leading apostle and disciple of Jesus: presumably as a consequence of his missionary activity reaching beyond Judea, his role and influence in Jerusalem itself seems to have diminished; more striking still, he seems to have submitted, for whatever reason, to the representations of 'the men from James', even to the extent of refusing (once again) to eat with Gentiles. He probably outfaced Paul at Antioch, and his policy was probably backed there, even by the Gentile believers; but subservient to James and rebuked by Paul, he appears as a somewhat diminished figure.[326]

- *Paul* has come to the end of a period in which he served as a leader and missionary of the Antioch church, a period in which he was willing to acknowledge (with whatever reservations) the authority of the Jerusalem apostles. But the incident at Antioch led him to conclude that 'the truth of the gospel' was being threatened by the policy being advocated from Jerusalem and by the practice being followed at Antioch. His response (in Galatians) was a fresh assertion of his gospel and of his authority to proclaim it, with such backing from the Jerusalem apostles as they felt able to give, but otherwise independently of Jerusalem.

In short, the confrontation at Antioch and its outcome probably marked a very important watershed in the history of earliest Christianity. The possibility of a united or at least mutually complementary missionary effort was seriously undermined. The phase of Jerusalem exercising a recognized and acceptable supervision over the expanding mission was probably curtailed. The church of Antioch ceased to be the chief engine in the outreach to Gentiles. Above all, Paul probably emerged from the shadow of Jerusalem and Antioch to become the 'apostle to the Gentiles'.

---

325. See further §§36.1b-c below.
326. See further §35 below.

PART EIGHT

APOSTLE TO THE GENTILES

CHAPTER 28

Dates, Destinations and Distances

Before we launch into a closer study of the major features of Paul's mission as 'apostle to the Gentiles', it is most helpful at this point to clarify the chronological structure of his mission, as indeed of his life as a whole, and to reflect on the harsh realities of what his mission involved in terms of travel in particular.

28.1. The Chronology of Paul's Life and Mission

a. Introduction

The broad outline of Paul's life and mission is uncontroversial, and if historians of Paul's life and mission were willing to work with a fair degree of latitude of up to about ten years, usually less, there would be little problem. For specific events of ancient history such latitude in regard to what were relatively minor events in the history of the Roman Empire would normally be quite acceptable. And given that Paul's major contribution to the history of Christianity has been the letters that he wrote and the theology he hammered out in his mission and in these letters, it is hardly of great importance to be able to decide finally whether he thought out the theology and wrote a particular letter ten years earlier or later.[1]

---

1. An astonishing weight has been placed on being able to track the development of Paul's thought by means of sequencing his letters in the correct chronological order. Several attempts originated in Göttingen over the past generation. And the ten-year project of the Theology of Paul seminar at the annual SBL meeting in November (1986-95) proved more frustrating than fruitful at this point; see the final essays in E. E. Johnson and D. M. Hay, eds., *Pauline Theology.* Vol. 4: *Looking Back, Pressing On* (Atlanta: Scholars, 1997). G. Tatum, *New Chapters in the Life of Paul: The Relative Chronology of His Career* (CBQMS 41; Washington, D.C.: Catholic Biblical Association of America, 2006), makes everything depend on

A rough outline, then, could be framed somewhat as follows:

- birth some time close to the turn of the epochs to what we now call the Common Era (CE or AD);
- education from adolescence probably in Jerusalem, through the latter 10s and early 20s;
- conversion some time after Jesus' crucifixion, that is, probably the early (but possibly the middle) 30s;
- a substantial interval (Gal. 1.18; 2.1) before he went up to Jerusalem for the second time (after his conversion), late 40s;
- a further period of five to eight years during which he evangelized mainly in the Aegean area and wrote most of his letters, to the mid-50s;
- a final five or so years from arrest in Jerusalem to detention in Rome (Acts 24.27; 28.30) before he disappears from view in the early 60s.

Were it possible to remain contented with such an outline, we could leave it at that and pass on. And, truth to tell, as I have already said — but it is worth repeating — not too much of lasting significance, historically or theologically, hangs upon achieving a more precise date-line. The problems arise, however, because virtually no one is satisfied with even the relative confidence we can have in the broad picture and everyone wants to achieve greater precision. And greater precision is in fact attainable, but at once we become caught up in controversial interpretations of disputed data. The table below, for example, indicates the range covered by some of the more important attempts of the past twenty to thirty years to achieve greater precision.[2]

---

establishing the relative chronology of Paul's letters and suggests the following order: 1 Thessalonians, 1 Corinthians, 2 Corinthians 10–13, Galatians, Philippians, 2 Corinthians 1–9 and Romans (6).

2. Jewett, *Dating* table 162-65; G. Lüdemann, *Paul, Apostle to the Gentiles: Studies in Chronology* (1980; ET Philadelphia: Fortress, 1984) chart 262-63; N. Hyldahl, *Die paulinische Chronologie* (Leiden: Brill, 1986) table 121-22; K. P. Donfried, 'Chronology (New Testament)', *ABD* 1.1011-22 (table 1016); Riesner, *Paul's Early Period* survey 3-28, 318-26 (table 322); Murphy-O'Connor, *Paul* 1-31 (tables 8, 28, 31); Hengel and Schwemer, *Paul* (table xi-xiv); Schnelle, *Paul* 47-56 (table 56); Wedderburn, *History* 99-103 (table 103). Earlier treatments include, e.g., G. Ogg, *The Chronology of the Life of Paul* (London: Epworth, 1968), and A. Suhl, *Paulus und seine Briefe* (Gütersloh: Gütersloher, 1975) 299-345; Knox, *Chapters in a Life of Paul*, offers a date-line very similar to that of Jewett (68); Buck and Taylor's reconstruction is similar to Lüdemann's (*Saint Paul* 214-15); Becker, *Paul* 31, is close to my own suggestions below (apart from the dates of several letters), as also is A. Scriba, 'Von Korinth nach Rom: Die Chronologie der letzten Jahre des Paulus', in F. W. Horn, ed., *Das Ende des Paulus* (BZNW 106; Berlin: de Gruyter, 2001) 157-73 (table 166-67), and Ebel in Wischmeyer, ed., *Paulus* 87; Lohse, *Paulus* 57, is close to Schnelle, though he dates Paul's death to the beginning

	Jewett	Lüdemann	Hyldahl	Donfried	Riesner	Murphy-O'Connor	Hengel/Schwemer	Schnelle	Wedderburn
Birth						6 BCE		ca. 5	
Jesus' death	33 (30)	27 (30)		30	30		30	30	30
Conversion	34 (31)	30 (33)	39/40	33	31/32	33	33	33	31/32
First visit to Jerusalem	37	33 (36)	41/42	36	33/34	37	36	35	33/34
Syria/Cilicia (Galatia + ??)	37-51	34-47 (37-50)	42-53	47-48	34-48	37-?	36-47	ca. 36-47	
Jerusalem council	51	47 (50)	53	49	48	51	48/49	48	45/46
Aegean mission	52-57	48-51/52 (51-54/55)	53-55	50-57	49-57	52-56	49-57	48-56	48-51, 52-57
Arrest and imprisonment	57	52 (55)	55	57	57	56	57	56	57
Journey to Rome	59/60			60	59	61/62	59	59	59-60
Execution	62				62	67	62/64?	64	

The main methodological dispute among chronologists is on the value to be attributed to the information provided by Acts. More or less all agree that Paul's own letters are the primary (firsthand) source, and some attempt to work as exclusively as possible from Paul, with little or no reference to Acts.[3] The majority, however, draw on Acts whenever possible, though with a natural tendency to follow Paul when the information from Acts seems to diverge significantly.[4] The methodological issue is posed, however, when ambiguous data from Paul and/or from nonbiblical sources are made the basis for a view which requires as a corollary that Luke has seriously misunderstood the sequence of events or has deliberately distorted them.[5] Given the earlier discussion and conclusions drawn about Luke the historian (§21.2), such a corollary is highly questionable. It is surely a mistaken procedure to draw conclusions from the ambiguous non-Lukan data without reference to the Lukan data, and then to disparage the Lukan account on the basis of these conclusions. That is an irresponsible way to treat what should be regarded as a valuable source, even allowing for Luke's own *Tendenzen*.[6] The Acts information must be included in the data

---

of 60. Riesner 3-28 provides a helpful analysis of treatments prior to his own (1994); and A. Suhl, 'Paulinische Chronologie im Streit der Meinungen', *ANRW* 2.26.2 (1995) 939-1188, offers a full-scale review of Knox, Suhl, Lüdemann, Jewett and Hyldahl.

3. Lüdemann, *Paul* 21-23. Hyldahl is the most obvious example. 'The general outline of Paul's life must be worked out on the basis of the evidence from the letters and these alone' (Jewett, *Dating* 23).

4. See, e.g., Schnelle's formulation (*Paul* 48).

5. Lüdemann, *Paul* 7, though he does regularly recognize the use of reliable tradition in Acts (*Paul* 23-29), and has developed the point systematically in *Early Christianity*. The 'general rule' drawn by Jewett — 'that material from Acts is usable in the chronological experiment only when it does not conflict with evidence in the letters' (*Dating* 24) — makes good sense, but in practice the operation of the rule often assumes the 'evidence in the letters' is more clear-cut than is the case (Paul was not a dispassionate narrator). Knox, Lüdemann and Murphy-O'Connor provide several examples below — e.g., the unwillingness to recognize how forced an interpretation it is to assume that Gal. 1.21 can include an extensive tour through Macedonia and Achaia (at n. 46 below); or the denial that Barnabas had any part in the mission in Galatia, on the grounds that Paul refers only to his own activities there (Gal. 4.13) (Knox, *Chapters* 60) — despite the parallel of Gal. 2.1-9; or the suggestion that 1 Cor. 15.32 and 2 Cor. 1.8 can be pressed to indicate a breach between Paul and the church in Ephesus, to provide an explanation for Paul's failure to mention Asia's participation in the collection (Lüdemann 86).

6. Similarly Riesner: 'No *a priori* judgments should be made regarding the reliability of the chronological material in Acts' (*Paul's Early Period* 31); he later observes that the 'we' passages and the second part of Acts contain 67 of the approximately 103 pieces of chronological information in Luke-Acts, that is, approximately two-thirds, and that the 'we' passages contain the highest absolute number of pieces of chronological information (323-24). On Luke's tendentiousness see above, §21.2d.

to be examined and correlated before even preliminary conclusions are reached. And I have already indicated several points at which I do not believe such correlation can be achieved with any success.[7] But if the three sources can be shown to blend, however roughly at the edges, then that should be a pointer to the likelihood of the sequence of events having taken place as Luke indicates. That such seems to be the case we have already seen in most cases in earlier chapters, but it is worth pausing long enough to make the point here before proceeding further.

b. Firm and Disputed Points in the Chronology of Paul

When so much cannot be dated with any precision, there is a natural tendency, first, to build the framework round the firmest points in the time line and then, second, to begin to fill in the gaps with the more probable of the other dates and time sequences.

More or less all agree that the firmest points are as follows:

- the crucifixion of Jesus — probably 30, but possibly 33;[8]
- the time periods noted by Paul himself: three years between his conversion and first visit to Jerusalem (Gal. 1.18); a further fourteen years until his second visit (2.1).[9] The fact that time was reckoned inclusively (including both starting date and finishing date) means that 'after *(meta)* three years' (1.18) could mean only about two years,[10] and 'after *(dia)* fourteen years' (2.1) could mean only about 13 years.[11] Nevertheless, a firm total of 15-16 years is probably a good working hypothesis for this crucial period of Paul's life.

---

7. E.g., the forty days of resurrection appearances, the disciples not stirring from Jerusalem (§22.2a-b) and the apostolic decree (§27.3e).

8. *Jesus Remembered* 312; Jewett *(Dating* 26-29) and Barnett *(Birth* 25) are in a minority in favouring 33. The most thorough review of the arguments is provided by Riesner, *Paul's Early Period* 35-58.

9. It has sometimes been suggested that the fourteen years included the three years (most recently, Longenecker, *Galatians* 45), but the sequence of 'then . . . then . . . then' (Gal. 1.18, 21; 2.1) most obviously indicates the successive stages of a chronological sequence, as Jewett in particular has effectively demonstrated *(Dating* 52-54). As Murphy-O'Connor observes, the fourteen years could not include the three years, since the clear implication is of fourteen years without contact with Jerusalem; moreover, the 'again' of 2.1 ('I went up again') most naturally indicates the (14-year) gap between the first and second visit *(Paul* 7-8).

10. See BDAG 637-38.

11. BDAG 224. Murphy-O'Connor's dating depends on reckoning a full fourteen years *(Paul* 8).

- The firmest of all the data is the date of Gallio's proconsulship in Corinth, most likely 51-52.[12] This enables us to date Paul's time in Corinth with remarkable precision (Acts 18.12-17) as 49-51 or 50-52. A date in 51 for the hearing before Gallio (Acts 18.12-17) towards the end of Paul's time in Corinth (that is, following the time note of 18.11) and near the beginning of Gallio's period of office[13] makes best sense of all the data and is about as firm a date as we could realistically hope for.
- Invaluable also are the time spans indicated by Acts for several periods of Paul's life and mission:[14]
  - the eighteen months of his sojourn in Corinth (Acts 18.11), though with important events of unknown duration on either side of that period; an estimate of up to two years in Corinth is appropriate;
  - the three months centred in the synagogue in Ephesus and the further two years in the lecture hall of Tyrannus (Acts 19.8, 10), again with an indeterminate time implied thereafter; an estimate of two-and-a-half to three years seems appropriate;
  - the two years of imprisonment in Caesarea (Acts 24.27),[15] again with a preceding sequence difficult to quantify; the dates here can be correlated

---

12. Referred to in a letter of Claudius preserved in a fragmentary inscription at Delphi; text and discussion in Lake, *Beginnings* 460-64; J. Murphy-O'Connor, *St. Paul's Corinth: Texts and Archaeology* (Wilmington: Glazier, 1983) 141-52, 173-76; also *Paul* 15-22; Taylor, 'Roman Empire' 2484-85; Fitzmyer, *Acts* 621-23; see also Riesner, *Paul's Early Period* 202-207. 'The high level of certainty . . . makes it the pivotal date in the construction of Pauline chronology' (Jewett, *Dating* 38-40); 'the only item in recent discussions of Pauline chronology on which there is general consensus' (Schnelle, *Paul* 49 n. 9). Fitzmyer argues for the dates of Gallio's year of proconsulship as 52-53 (620-23), against the majority view of 51-52 (see the brief survey of views in Thiselton, *1 Corinthians* 29-30).

13. It can be deduced from comments of Seneca, Gallio's brother, and Pliny that Gallio did not complete his term of office (Murphy-O'Connor, *Paul* 19-20).

14. Knox uses an odd *non sequitur* argument that 'because his narrative is liberally interspersed with such phrases as "after many days" or "after some days" [Luke's] occasionally more definite statements are robbed of value as far as the chronological reconstruction of Paul's career is concerned' (*Chapters* 32). D. Slingerland, 'Acts 18:1-18, the Gallio Inscription, and Absolute Pauline Chronology', *SBL* 110 (1991) 439-49, shares Knox's scepticism over Luke's vague statements of time.

15. 'When two years had passed' (24.27) could refer either to Paul's imprisonment or to Felix completing his time in office, the latter then indicating a transition from Felix to Festus which can be dated to 55 (Suhl, *Paulus* 333-38; Lüdemann, *Early Christianity* 250-51; cf. Barrett, *Acts* 2.1118); but the phrase is a genitive absolute, which implies some independence from the two following main clauses, and therefore a reference independent of the transition from Felix to Festus. The phrase is 'usually related to Paul's imprisonment and actually so intended by Luke, who is interested only in Paul's imprisonment' (Haenchen, *Acts* 661; further bibliography in Jervell, *Apg.* 576 n. 263).

with what we know of the appointments of the Roman governors of Judea, Felix (52/53-59/60) and Festus (59/60-62);[16]

○ the two years in detention in Rome (Acts 28.30).

Other dates and time spans can be estimated with a reasonable probability:

• the conversion of Saul/Paul in relation to the resurrection of Jesus and the persecution of the Hellenists. In the former case, the likelihood is that the appearance to Saul was the last (as Paul claimed) of a sequence of 'sightings' which extended over a period of about eighteen months and probably no more than two or at most three years.[17] In the latter case, the persecution of the Hellenists probably began within a short time of the first beginnings of the new sect, quite probably less than two years.[18]

• Paul's escape from Damascus (2 Cor. 11.32-33) can be safely identified with the similar report in Acts 9.25. Since Paul specifies that this happened despite the fact that 'the ethnarch of/under King Aretas was guarding the city of Damascus in order to seize me', the event has to be set within the reign of Aretas IV, the Nabatean king. Unfortunately, for dating purposes, Aretas ruled from 9 BCE (Josephus, *Ant.* 16.294) until 39/40 CE.[19] There is an unresolved debate as to what Paul's description entails and what power Aretas actually had as a client king. Jewett argues strongly that 'the transfer of Damascus to Nabatean control . . . probably occurred during the early years of Caligula's administration', which can hardly have come into effect before the summer of 37.[20] He concludes that Paul's escape must be dated to the period 37-39 and regards this date as 'the cornerstone of my hypothesis'.[21] But Riesner justifiably objects that the archaeological and

---

16. Schürer, *History* 1.460 and n. 17; 467 and n. 43; Jewett, *Dating* 40-44; Hemer, *Book of Acts* 171, 173; Bruce, *Acts* 484; Riesner, *Paul's Early Period* 219-24; Barrett, *Acts* 2.1080-81, 1117-18; Murphy-O'Connor, *Paul* 22-23. Less persuasive are the suggestions that Felix's recall was immediately consequent upon his brother Pallas's fall from favour in Rome, so 55 or 56 (Lake, *Beginnings* 5.464-67; cf. Schwartz, *Studies* 227-31), or that Paul's return with the collection was in response to a famine caused by the sabbatical year 54/55 (Suhl, *Paulus* 327-33; followed by Hyldahl, *Chronologie* 113-15), thus allowing him to be imprisoned before the transition from Felix to Festus (n. 15 above).

17. See above, §22.2b. Note the Gnostic traditions which assume that the resurrection appearances extended over an eighteen-month period (§22 n. 31 above); see also Jewett, *Dating* 29-30; and further Riesner, *Paul's Early Period* 67-74.

18. See above, §24.4a.

19. The date usually given is 40 (Schürer, *History* 1.581), but Jewett (*Dating* 30) and Murphy-O'Connor, (*Paul* 5) prefer 39.

20. Jewett, *Dating* 30-33; followed by Murphy-O'Connor, *Paul* 6-7.

21. Cited by Riesner, *Paul's Early Period* 79. Schenke resolves the problem by arguing

textual data do not allow such confidence regarding Nabatean control over Damascus and cautions against trying to draw too many firm conclusions from 2 Cor. 11.32.[22] All we can say with full confidence is that Paul's escape from Damascus must have taken place in the 30s, presumably either before or after Aretas's brief war with Herod Antipas in 36.[23]

- Douglas Campbell argues that the Chytri inscription from Cyprus should be read as implying a date during or before 37 CE for Paul's encounter with Sergius Paulus (Acts 13), which would call in question the implied Acts dating for the mission to Cyprus.[24] The poor state of the inscription, however, leaves the identity of the persons referred to and their relationship to each other unclear.

- The gap between the Jerusalem council (Gal. 2.1-10) and the incident at Antioch (2.11-14) is likely to have been shorter (a few months) than longer,[25] since one of the things which made Paul so angry was presumably the shortness of the time between the agreement in Jerusalem and the consequent breach of faith by Peter (as Paul saw it).[26]

---

that 'the regions of Syria' (Gal. 1.18) included Damascus, so that the escape from Damascus could have taken place between 37 and 40 ('Four Problems' 324-25).

22. Riesner, *Paul's Early Period* 75-89; Riesner (84-86) draws particularly on the demonstration by E. A. Knauf, 'Zum Ethnarchen des Aretas', *ZNW* 74 (1983) 145-47, that the ethnarch was no more than the leader of the Nabatean population in Damascus, 'a kind of consul' (147). Note too the caution of Schürer, *History* 1.581-82; Wedderburn, *History* 101. And it would be well also to note Knauf's reminder that Aretas was a Bedouin sheik, and the Nabatean territory not a 'nation' or 'state' in the modern sense ('Arabienreise' 467-69).

23. D. A. Campbell, 'An Anchor for Pauline Chronology: Paul's Flight from "the Ethnarch of King Aretas" (2 Corinthians 11:32-33)', *JBL* 121 (2002) 279-302, argues that Aretas's defeat of Antipas was what enabled Aretas to secure his control over Damascus, and that in consequence Paul's ignominious departure from Damascus must be dated to the few months between late 36 and spring 37, when he assumes that Gaius must have ended Aretas's control over Damascus. But see also A. Bunine, 'La date de la première visite de Paul à Jérusalem', *RB* 113 (2006) 436-56, 601-22.

24. D. A. Campbell, 'Possible Inscriptional Attestation to Sergius Paul[l]us (Acts 13:6-12), and the Implications for Pauline Chronology', *JTS* 56 (2005) 1-29.

25. *Pace* Suhl, who argues for the surprisingly early date of 43/44 (before the death of Herod Agrippa) for the Jerusalem council (compressing the three + fourteen of Gal. 1.18 and 2.1 into fourteen), and for a gap of four years before the incident in Antioch (47/48), with the mission in Pisidia and Lycaonia intervening, and a journey to Corinth completed within the year following (*Paulus* 322-23). Hengel and Schwemer favour the view that the first phase of the Aegean mission intervened between the Jerusalem council and the Antioch incident, since 'after the explosion of Gal. 2.11ff., Silas probably could not accompany Paul again as a missionary "companion"' (*Paul* 215-16). Similarly Öhler, *Barnabas* 61-64 (an interval of five or six years between the Jerusalem council and the Antioch incident [77-78]); Wedderburn, *History* 98-99. See also §27 n. 234.

26. Lüdemann's attempt to date the Antioch episode prior to the Jerusalem council (*Paul*

- The travel times of the various journeys Paul took, particularly from Antioch to Corinth, and again to Ephesus, the journeys round the Aegean and the journeys by sea, can all be estimated with some degree of plausibility. Certainly, earlier attempts at dating Paul's mission which ignored the reality of land and sea travel are much less credible for that reason. Of course weather conditions, known restrictions of sea journeys during the seasonal unfavourable weather, and winter conditions preventing travel for several months, affecting particularly the Taurus mountain range and highlands of Asia Minor, have also to be taken into consideration. The lengthy trek from Tarsus, through the Cilician Gates, across Galatia and Phrygia and into Asia Minor must have been especially taxing and must have absorbed many weeks and months.[27]

- The most contentious of the disputed data has been the expulsion of the Jews from Rome by Claudius — referred to in the famous Suetonius quotation (*Claudius* 25.4).[28] This expulsion is usually dated to 49,[29] which meshes nicely with Paul's arrival in Corinth and the subsequent ruling of Gallio (51/52).[30] However, the event is not mentioned by either Josephus or Tacitus in their accounts of the period. So some find it more satisfactory to identify the Suetonius passage with Cassius Dio's report of an early ruling made by Claudius against Jews in Rome (60.6.6), that is, in 41.[31] For Lüdemann, indeed, the dating of the expulsion of Jews from Rome to 41 is the lynchpin of his whole chronology.[32] The argument, however, has serious flaws:

44-80) has won little or no support. For example, it is not at all 'inconceivable that the conference could have bypassed such a fundamental problem of the mixed congregations' (73; see above, §27.2); and as Murphy-O'Connor points out, the depiction of Paul and Barnabas as close colleagues at Jerusalem hardly squares with the painful breach between Paul and Barnabas in Antioch (*Paul* 132). Hengel and Schwemer are similarly dismissive: 'The incident at Antioch is only understandable if it presupposes the agreement in Gal. 2.6-10. Moreover after the break Paul could never in any way have negotiated in Jerusalem in this way together with Barnabas' (*Paul* 441-42 n. 1080).

27. See further below, §28.2.

28. See above, §21.1d.

29. It is also the date given by the fifth-century Christian historian Orosius, who attributes the information to Josephus (*Historiae adversus paganos* 7.6.15-16, cited by Riesner, *Paul's Early Life* 181), but no such reference in Josephus is known, and it is possible that Orosius dated the Suetonius expulsion by reference to Acts 18.2 (Murphy-O'Connor, *Paul* 9-10); Riesner is more positive, but still cautious, in his evaluation of Orosius as a source (180-87).

30. Jewett, *Dating* 36-38.

31. Text in *GLAJJ* 2.367 (§422).

32. Lüdemann, *Paul* 163-71; he continues to maintain the argument vigorously in *Primitive Christianity* 122-24, supported by Levinskaya, *BAFCS* 5.171-77. But Fitzmyer justifiably

- Cassius Dio is quite explicit that Claudius 'did not drive them (the Jews) out, but ordered them, while continuing their traditional mode of life, not to hold meetings' (60.6.6).[33]
- The lesser action against the Jews in Rome is likely at the beginning of Claudius's reign, when he was indebted to and still a close friend of Herod Agrippa;[34] whereas, in the second half of the 40s, following what he must have regarded as Agrippa's treachery,[35] Claudius was likely to be much more hostile to the Jews generally.
- The meshing of the later date with Paul's mission in Corinth (Acts 18.2) is an example of the point made more generally above: that is, it should be reckoned as part of the evidence to be weighed rather than discounted in the light of the questionable identification between Suetonius's account of an expulsion and Cassius Dio's account of restrictions.[36]
- In any case, the extent and effectiveness of the decree of expulsion has to be something of an open question,[37] despite Luke's typically hyperbolic statement that 'all Jews' were ordered to leave Rome (Acts 18.2).[38] Were

---

dismisses Lüdemann's claim that 'most scholars all over the world are agreed' on the date 41 CE as 'exaggerated nonsense' (*Acts* 620).

33. As Lampe, *From Paul to Valentinus* 15, observes, Dio is not correcting a source (Suetonius), as Lüdemann argues (*Paul* 165-66), but comparing Claudius's action with that of Tiberius just over twenty years earlier: '"he did not expel" needs to be completed with "as Tiberius had done"' — referring to the expulsion of Jews by Tiberius in 19 CE (referred to by Suetonius, *Tiberius* 36 and Cassius Dio 57.18.5a — *GLAJJ* 2.§§306 and 419). Lampe goes on to ask, 'Why does Lüdemann give Cassius Dio, who edited his chronological information towards the end of the second century at the earliest, more credence than the Acts 18 chronology which is at least 100 years earlier?' (15). Murphy-O'Connor attempts to support the 'admittedly tenuous' view that Suetonius and Cassius Dio were speaking of the same event by referring to Philo, who completed his *Legatio ad Gaium* while in Rome in 41 CE; Philo's repeated observation that Augustus had never removed the Jews from Rome or forbad their assembling (*Legat.* 156-57) could be a reference to rumours of possible actions by Claudius which Philo heard (*Paul* 10-13; followed by J. Taylor, 'The Roman Empire in the Acts of the Apostles', *ANRW* 2.26.3 [1996] 2436-2500 [here 2478-79]). But Philo's talk of expulsion from Rome could again be a reference back to Tiberius's action in 19 CE, though the talk of forbidding assembly does indeed match the action which Claudius actually did take, according to Cassius Dio.

34. Riesner points to evidence that Claudius was generally friendly towards the Jews during the first year of his reign (*Paul's Early Period* 101).

35. See above, §26.5.

36. For Jewett the corroboration with the Gallio inscription makes this datum (the meeting of Paul and Aquila/Prisca in 49/50) 'of crucial significance' in constructing a Pauline chronology (*Dating* 36-38). Contrast Lüdemann, who concludes that 'the traditions in Acts 18 reflect various visits' (*Paul* 162).

37. See §33 n. 64 below.

38. Luke tends to work with blanket categories when talking about Jews — 'the Jews'

all synagogue congregations affected? Some had prominent pedigrees and backers.[39] Perhaps only some synagogues were affected by the disturbances occasioned by the followers of Christ (Chrestus) and only the leaders of the new (trouble-making) faction (like Aquila and Prisca) were expelled.[40] The more focused and 'local' the decree, the more likely that Josephus and Tacitus could pass over it in silence.

A much-favoured solution to the problem of disharmonious data is to postulate two actions of Claudius, one in 41 and the other 49: the first an early palliative ruling, short-lived and limited in effect; the second more deliberate and drastic after his patience had worn thin and when he was more sure of himself.[41]

c. Disputed Solutions

The most significant disagreements arising from the interpretation of the above data relate to when Paul first extended his mission to Macedonia, the date of the Jerusalem council and Antioch incident in relation to Paul's several comings and goings to and from Jerusalem/Antioch, and the dating and place of writing the 'prison epistles' (Philippians, Colossians and Philemon).

(without discrimination) as the subjects (or objects) of various actions (Acts 13.45, 50; 14.4; 17.5; etc.); cf. his earlier talk of 'all/the whole of Judea' (Luke 5.17; 6.17; 7.17).

39. See below, §33 n. 47.

40. E.g., Lampe, *Paul to Valentinus* 11-15; H. Botermann, *Das Judenedikt des Kaisers Claudius. Römischer Staat und Christiani im 1. Jahrhundert* (Stuttgart: Steiner, 1996) 77. Brown suggests only 'those Jews who were the most vocal on either side of the Christ issue' (Brown and Meier, *Antioch and Rome* 102, 109); Murphy-O'Connor thinks that the edict of Claudius 'concerned only a single synagogue in Rome' (*Paul* 12, 14); 'one or several Roman synagogues' (Riesner, *Paul's Early Life* 195). It is certainly unlikely that Claudius expelled the whole Jewish community (reckoned at more than 40,000), despite Acts 18.2 ('all Jews') (e.g., Pesch, *Apg.* 2.152). See also §33 n. 62 below.

41. A. Momigliano, *Claudius: The Emperor and His Achievement* (Oxford: Clarendon, 1934) 31-37; Bruce, *History* 295-99; Jewett, *Dating* 36-38; Smallwood, *Jews* 210-16; D. Slingerland, 'Acts 18:1-17 and Luedemann's Pauline Chronology', *JBL* 109 (1990) 686-90; Barclay, *Jews in the Mediterranean Diaspora* 303-306; Botermann, *Judenedikt,* particularly 114; E. S. Gruen, *Diaspora: Jews amidst Greeks and Romans* (Cambridge: Harvard University, 2002) 36-39; Omerzu, *Prozess* 229-37; S. Spence, *The Parting of the Ways: The Roman Church as a Case Study* (Leuven: Peeters, 2004) 65-112; S. Cappelletti, *The Jewish Community of Rome from the Second Century BCE to the Third Century CE* (Leiden: Brill, 2006) 69-89. Riesner's thorough study is particularly impressive (*Paul's Early Period* 157-201; on Cassius Dio, 167-79, with other bibliography on this point in nn. 113 and 135); he concludes that the 49 date is the more firmly established (201).

- The suggestion that Paul engaged in an initial mission to Macedonia and Achaia already in the 40s (or even the 30s)[42] depends either on dating the expulsion of Jews from Rome to 41 (Cassius Dio),[43] or on dating such an initial mission prior to the Jerusalem council and Antioch incident.[44] But while the Gal. 1.21 reference (missionary work in Syria and Cilicia) can possibly accommodate a Galatian mission (cf. Gal. 2.5),[45] the suggestion of extensive missionary work much further west (Macedonia and Achaia) can hardly be fitted into Paul's allusion, without either forcing the sense or implying that Paul was, after all, and despite his protest, trying to hide something.[46]

- A consequence of the same interpretations of the data is that the apostolic council and Antioch incident have to be dated to what Luke narrates as Paul's return trip to Jerusalem and Antioch after the mission based in Corinth (Acts 18.22).[47] Here is another example of the methodological criticism made earlier: the Acts account should be part of the data to be considered rather than held in suspense until a judgment is made on the basis of

---

42. 'Paul's founding visit to Macedonia occurred at the end of the 30s' (Lüdemann, *Paul* 201).

43. Lüdemann, *Paul* 59-61; Lüdemann also reads the reference to Paul's mission in Philippi 'in the beginning of the gospel' (Phil. 4.15) as necessarily referring to the initial period of Paul's evangelistic activity (105-106, 199), but even that would be relative to his earlier work in Syria and Cilicia.

44. Murphy-O'Connor accepts both the Cassius Dio date (41) and that Paul first encountered Aquila and Prisca only in 49, assuming that the latter couple wandered around for several years following their expulsion before they met Paul (*Paul* 14-15; similarly *GLAJJ* 2.115-16). But all we know of them suggests rather that they ran their business from major centres (Rome, Corinth, Ephesus), so that expulsion from Rome and arrival in Corinth in the same year (49) makes better sense; see further §31.4b below.

45. See above, §25 n. 223.

46. Longenecker, *Galatians* 40; also lxxv-lxxvii; Hengel and Schwemer treat Lüdemann's thesis with scorn (*Paul* 475-76 n. 1361). See also Riesner, *Paul's Early Period* 269-71. Jewett and Murphy-O'Connor rely too heavily on being able to fix the date of Saul's escape from Damascus to 37. Both hypotheses treat Luke's sequence of events in cavalier fashion (Murphy-O'Connor seems to merge the 'first missionary journey' with the second) and have to infer that Barnabas, who did not accompany Paul on the Macedonian and Achaean mission (though see §29 n. 208 below), nevertheless somewhere reunited with Paul in time for the Jerusalem council so that together they could represent the Gentile mission (Gal. 2.9) (Murphy-O'Connor, *Paul* 131-32); however, Jewett does surmise 'that the material in Acts 13–14 was formed from the Antioch recollections of the reports rendered by Barnabas and Paul at the conclusion of the journey' (*Dating* 12).

47. Schnelle dismisses the trip to Jerusalem (Antioch only), since 'it is opposed to Paul's own statements in the letters' (*Paul* 54); but that is only true if Galatians is dated to the Ephesus period of Paul's Aegean mission (in contrast, see below, §31.7a).

other data and then to all intents and purposes dismissed in corollary fashion as wholly unreliable.[48] But Gal. 2.10 need not imply that the collection began forthwith and was completed within four years.[49] And, as we have already seen, neither the 37 date for Saul's escape from Damascus nor the 41 date for the expulsion of the Jews from Rome is sufficiently firm for Luke's sequencing to be so completely overridden.

• The other significant difference of opinion relates to the dating of Paul's letters:

  ○ If 1 Thessalonians was written before the apostolic council, then it has to be dated to the 40s (41 — Lüdemann) or 50 (Jewett, Murphy-O'Connor).

  ○ If Galatians was written before the apostolic council, it has to be dated to the late 40s;[50] or if its similarity to Romans points to a similar date, then it should be dated to the mid-50s.[51]

  ○ If the 'prison epistles' were written during a postulated Ephesian imprisonment, then they have to be dated to the early to mid 50s; but if written from Rome, they should be dated to the 60s.[52]

  ○ My own view, to be elaborated as we proceed, is that 1 Thessalonians is the earliest extant letter of Paul, written during his eighteen months to two years in Corinth (ca. 50);[53] Galatians was written soon after, also from Corinth (ca. 51); and the 'prison epistles' were written from Rome. The argument in the last case could go either way, but the absence of any reference to the collection, which, as we shall see, was a dominant concern of Paul during the Ephesus-based mission, is probably decisive (just) against dating them to the Ephesus period.

48. Knox (*Chapters* 35-36, 48-52), Jewett (*Dating* 84) and Lüdemann (*Paul* 149-52; *Early Christianity* 206-207) all agree that the journeys to Jerusalem in Acts 11 and 15 are 'triplets of the journey reported in Acts 18:22' (Jewett).

49. This interpretation of Gal. 2.10 is the lynchpin of Knox's reconstruction (*Chapters* 39-40); he dates the Jerusalem conference to 51 and the last (third) trip to Jerusalem as 54 or 55 (68).

50. See, e.g., Bruce, *Galatians* 43-56; Longenecker, *Galatians* lxxii-lxxxviii; Ellis, *Making* 258-59 n. 111.

51. The dominant view in German scholarship; but see §31.7a and n. 300 below.

52. That Philippians and Philemon (and Colossians, if authentic) should be dated to an Ephesian imprisonment is a view strongly supported and perhaps still dominant; see, e.g., Becker, *Paul* 159, 162; others cited in Schnelle, *History* 131 n. 357, 144 n. 405; R. P. Martin in his revision of G. F. Hawthorne, *Philippians* (WBC 43; Nashville: Nelson, 2004), reviews the alternatives and finally settles in favour of an Ephesian provenance for the letter (xxxix-l). The minority view, that Ephesians, Colossians and Philemon should be dated to Paul's imprisonment in Caesarea, is maintained by Robinson, *Redating the New Testament* 61-67, 73-82, and Ellis, *Making* 266-75; see also §34 n. 237.

53. See below, §31 n. 228.

• For the sake of completeness, I should also note the minority view that Paul was released after an initial imprisonment in Rome and either returned to mission in Asia Minor and the Aegean (as could be implied by the Pastoral Epistles) or attempted to fulfil his ambition to reach Spain with the gospel (as could be indicated by *1 Clem.* 5.6-7). That he would have returned eastwards, despite his driving ambition to reach Spain, is less likely: he had completed that phase of his mission (Rom. 15.19, 23); and the Pastorals are generally regarded as post-Pauline.[54] The lack of confirmatory evidence that he did reach Spain does not help, though there is a two-year gap between the end of the Acts narrative and Eusebius's report of Paul's martyrdom during the Nero persecutions (*HE* 2.25.5-8).[55]

d. A Working Outline

There can be no certainty about Paul's early years. But the range sometimes suggested is too wide.[56] It is less likely that someone born several years before the turn from BCE to CE would be described as a *neanias* ('young man') in the early 30s, and he would then be approaching 70 at the time of his death.[57] If he wrote Philemon late in life, he would be well over the age range usually classified as *presbytēs* (Phlm. 9).[58] Alternatively, a birth date well into the first decade CE would make it almost impossible for Saul to be regarded as old enough to be ceded a leading role in the persecution of the Hellenists — still only in his twenties. None of the dates is firm, but in probability terms it makes most sense to think of Paul having been born around the turn from BCE to CE.

Saul's education has already been discussed (§25.1f), and the most likely reading of Acts 22.3 and 26.4 puts him in Jerusalem as an adolescent and completing his education and training as a Pharisee in about the mid-20s. No firmer estimate is possible.

Given the likelihood of Jesus' crucifixion in 30, as most agree,[59] and the

---

54. See, e.g., the review by L. T. Johnson, *The First and Second Letters to Timothy* (AB 35A; New York: Doubleday, 2001) 47-54; and further vol. 3.

55. See further below, §34.7.

56. Ogg was content to say somewhere in the period 5-14 *(Chronology);* Murphy-O'Connor argues for a birth date of ca. 6 BCE *(Paul* 8); and White for a date between 5 BCE and 5 CE *(Jesus to Christianity* 147). Chilton, however, opts for 7 CE *(Rabbi Paul* 267).

57. Murphy-O'Connor thinks he was executed when he was seventy-three.

58. Murphy-O'Connor *(Paul* 4) dates Philemon to Paul's mission in Ephesus (53), but even so, that would put Paul beyond the usual range for a *presbytēs* (between fifty and fifty-six); see further §25.1a.

59. See above, n. 8.

considerations marshalled above regarding the rise of the Hellenists, Saul's persecution and subsequent conversion,[60] we can probably date his conversion to
about 32.

The three years in Arabia (Gal. 1.17-18) and subsequent flight from Damascus would then take us to about 34 or 35.[61] And the 'after fourteen years'
(Gal. 2.1) would indicate a date for the Jerusalem council of about 47/48, with
the Antioch incident following a few months later. The missionary work narrated
in Acts 13–14 can be accommodated within this timescale, but not an otherwise
unrecorded mission in Macedonia and Achaia.[62]

The land journey to Corinth, with stops of indeterminate length at several
places, Philippi and Thessalonica in particular, would point to an arrival in Corinth in late 49 or early 50. It should not be regarded as coincidental or contrived
that this date meshes so neatly with the likely date (49) for the expulsion of
Aquila and Prisca from Rome (Acts 18.2), and that the about two years of mission in Corinth mesh so well with the Gallio date.

If we follow the Acts account, that would indicate a third visit to Jerusalem
and Antioch (Acts 18.22) for visits of indeterminate length in late 51/early 52 and
a return to Ephesus to arrive in late 52 or early 53 (having wintered *en route*).[63]
The further two-and-a-half to three years in Ephesus, the troubled journey through
Macedonia (of indeterminate length) and the three months (wintering?) in Corinth
(Acts 20.3) would bring us well through 56 and probably into 57.

The final trip to Jerusalem then falls in spring or summer 57, to be followed by more than two years in detention in Jerusalem and Caesarea. An attempt to sail to Rome late in the season of 59 would then have resulted in an arrival in Rome in 60, followed by the two years of house arrest, up to 62. Beyond
that date our primary sources fall silent.

We could go into more detail on times and seasons, and all the dates suggested have a touch (sometimes more than a touch) of speculation. But they are
very plausible, even with a margin of error of one or two years either way in sev-

60. See above at n. 17 and §24.4a.

61. The attractiveness of dating the flight from Damascus to 37 (Jewett) is matched if
not outweighed by the easier integration of a 34/35 date with the 'three years' and 'fourteen
years' of Gal. 1.18 and 2.1 and the subsequent Gallio date.

62. Despite Jewett's support (*Dating* 84), Lüdemann hardly provides 'conclusive proof
of Paul's independent mission prior to the Apostolic Conference' (referring to *Paul* 6). On the
contrary, the play which Paul makes in Galatians 1–2 between acknowledging the authority of
the Jerusalem leadership and asserting his independent authority clearly implies that he had
previously acknowledged their authority but now sat much more loose to it. Gal. 2.2 clearly
implies that he went up to Jerusalem (after the fourteen years of mission) with the former attitude; the incident at Antioch would most likely explain his change of attitude (see above,
§27.3c).

63. See further below, §32.1d.

eral cases, and sufficiently secure to give us a framework within which to set the main thrust of Paul's mission. And that will suffice.

In sum:

ca. 1 BCE–2 CE	Birth in Tarsus
ca. 12-26	Education in Jerusalem
31-32	Persecution of Hellenists
32	Conversion
34/35	Flight from Damascus and first visit to Jerusalem
34/35–47/48	Missionary of the church of Antioch
47-48	Jerusalem council and incident at Antioch
49/50–51/52	Mission in Corinth
	(1 and 2 Thessalonians, Galatians)
51/52	Third visit to Jerusalem and Antioch
52/53–55	Mission in Ephesus
	(1 and 2 Corinthians)
56/57	Corinth
	(Romans)
57	Final trip to Jerusalem and arrest
57-59	Detention in Jerusalem and Caesarea
59	Attempt to sail to Rome
60	Arrival in Rome
60-62	House arrest in Rome
	(Philippians, Philemon, Colossians?)
62??	Execution

28.2. Travels and Travails

Paul's journeyings by land and sea were by no means exceptional for his age. Alexander the Great's Macedonians had travelled far to the east, into modern Afghanistan and India. Merchants regularly plied all round the Mediterranean and round the Black Sea, and the great Silk Road of later centuries was already being followed.[64] There were quite strong links between Mediterranean, Celtic and Far Eastern cultures. Roman armies marched hundreds of miles.[65] Nevertheless,

64. For more detail see, e.g., Schnabel, *Mission* 496-97.

65. 'The people of the Roman Empire traveled more extensively and more easily than had anyone before them — or would again until the nineteenth century' (Meeks, *First Urban Christians* 17). See further L. Casson, *Travel in the Ancient World* (London: Allen and Unwin, 1974) ch. 6: 'The first two centuries of the Christian Era were halcyon days for a traveler. He could make his way from the shores of the Euphrates to the border between England and Scotland without crossing a foreign frontier, always within the bounds of one government's juris-

Paul's travelling was substantial, comparable to John Wesley's in eighteenth-century England. And given that he must have made almost all of his land journeys on foot, his feat(!) should not be treated lightly, even as lightly as Luke's narrative does!

a. Travels

We do not know how extensive Paul's travels were during the first phase of his mission in Syria and Cilicia. But if we take the itineraries provided by Luke in Acts 13–21 as a guide, then we have to envisage at least two journeys from Jerusalem and Syrian Antioch to the west coast of Asia Minor, and at least three land journeys in part or whole round the northern part of the Aegean. In addition there were at least two sea journeys from Greece or Asia Minor to Syria-Palestine, several other comings and goings between Jerusalem and Antioch, and the final journey by sea and land to Rome.

The most careful assessment of journey lengths and times has been provided in recent years by Jewett:[66]

Distances	Miles/Kilometers		Time
Jerusalem to Syrian Antioch	373	600	15 days–4 weeks
Syrian Antioch to Derbe	293	471	12 days–3 weeks
Derbe to Iconium	89	144	3-4 days
Iconium to Pisidian Antioch	88	142	3-4 days
Pisidian Antioch to North Galatia	194	312	8 days–2 weeks
North Galatia to Troas	479	771	20 days–6 weeks
Troas to Philippi (by sea)	155	250	3 days
Philippi to Thessalonica	87	140	4 days
Thessalonica to Beroea	43	70	2 days
Beroea to Athens — by land	35	56	
by sea	280	450	10 days–2 weeks

---

diction. A purseful of Roman coins was the only kind of cash he had to carry; they were accepted or could be changed anywhere' (122). 'Travel simply for pleasure, what we would call tourism, was surprisingly well established' (Wallace and Williams, *Three Worlds* 17; and further ch. 3).

66. *Dating* 59-61; for bibliographical basis of his estimates see 138 n. 53 (I have added the figure for miles). Schnabel gives more detailed and differing figures for the distances involved (*Mission* 1125-26; further 1197-99).

Athens to Corinth — by land	10	16	
by sea	47	75	3 days
	2,173	3,497	12-20 weeks

The calculation is bound to be rough and ready for several reasons.

- One is that routes are not always known. In particular, Jewett assumes a North Galatian mission during the Acts 16–18 mission, a hypothesis I regard as improbable.[67] That clearly adds a substantial mileage to the above estimate.

- A second is that we do not know how rapidly Paul was able to travel. We have to assume, I think, that Paul almost always completed land journeys on foot.[68] On the 'Naismith' estimate currently used by ramblers and walkers in the UK, one could expect to cover 2.5 miles (4 km.) in an hour, allowing an extra half-hour for ascent or descent of 500 feet. That would suggest that 20 miles (32 km.) would be the upper limit that one could hope to achieve in a day, and that far only when the terrain was undemanding. For extended journeys the average distance covered per day would be less, about 15 to 20 miles (24 to 32 km.).[69] The evidence suggests that in marches of several weeks even well-trained infantry would have had an upper limit of about 20 miles (30 km.) for a day's march. On forced marches a military contingent could cover substantially more, but after three days of forced marching, soldiers had a day of rest.[70] In consequence we can hardly assume that on a week's journey on foot Paul would have been able to cover more than about 100-120 miles (160-190 km.), even in good conditions.[71] On that estimate Jewett's minimal figures for the distances indicated look to be rather sanguine.

- Calculations must always allow for the exigencies of weather conditions (as

67. See below, §31 n. 32.

68. There are no hints or indications that Paul was normally able to travel by horse or carriage. One exception might be the journey from Philippi to Thessalonica, since Amphipolis and Apollonia seem to be envisaged as interim stations on a three-day journey, which could be completed in three days only if one used a carriage (Riesner, *Paul's Early Period* 313) or on horseback (Taylor, 'Roman Empire' 2458). That the journey from Caesarea to Jerusalem in Acts 21.16 was on horseback is unlikely; see B. M. Rapske, 'Acts, Travel and Shipwreck', *BAFCS* 2.1-47 (here 10-11).

69. Casson, *Travel* 189.

70. Riesner, *Paul's Early Period* 311.

71. Most agree that in the case of longer journeys over fairly normal terrain, a day's journey by foot would cover 15-20 miles, or 20-30 kilometers (Riesner, *Paul's Early Period* 311). Schnabel's summary is, as usual, well informed (*Mission* 632-37).

Jewett does). We can assume, for example, that Paul was unlikely to have attempted the strenuous climb through the Cilician Gate in winter, and the conditions of the Anatolian highlands would likewise inhibit or prohibit much travel in winter. So the journey from Syrian Antioch or Tarsus into Galatia was unlikely to be attempted before the spring or early summer. Similarly for sea journeys. The eastern Mediterranean became increasingly stormy from the end of September, so shipping generally closed down from mid-November to mid-March.[72] Calculations of the length of time taken on Paul's longer journeys, across Anatolia and by sea in particular, have to allow for these factors.[73] Prevailing winds usually favoured west-to-east travel, which, no doubt, is why Paul always returned home by ship.[74]

- The question of Paul's health can never be ignored, even if it cannot be satisfactorily answered. But passages like Gal. 4.13-15 and 2 Cor. 12.7 suggest that he may have suffered from serious ailments at various times. It cannot be simply assumed that Paul would have been able to maintain a steady, let alone a taxing, pace over several days.

- Nor do we know how long Paul stayed at his different locations. Jewett assumes a stay of from one to four weeks in places like Lystra, Iconium and Pisidian Antioch, six to twelve months in North Galatia, three to twelve months in Philippi, three to four months in Thessalonica and two months in Beroea. But if we exclude the North Galatian hypothesis and question the lengths of time hypothesized for Macedonia, the variation from Jewett's timetable becomes quite considerable — a year instead of nearly two years on the minimum timescale, two years rather than four years for the maximum timescale.

If then we abbreviate the time given for the postulated North Galatian mission, we are still left with a total journey in the region of 2,000 miles, or 3,200 kilometers. On the above estimates, including Jewett's estimates for the sea journeys, that would require a minimum of 100 to 140 days, probably longer, simply devoted to travel. Add in the time Paul must have spent in the various centres, rests on the longer legs of the journey, delays while shipping transport was arranged, and we reach a minimum of one year between Syrian Antioch (Jewett estimates from Jerusalem) and Corinth, and probably something nearer eighteen months to two years.[75]

---

72. Jewett, *Dating* 56-57; Rapske, 'Travel' 3; Riesner, *Paul's Early Period* 308.

73. Haenchen lists twelve journeys that Paul made by sea (*Acts* 702-703).

74. Acts 18.18-22; 20.6–21.3; Murphy-O'Connor, *Paul* 165.

75. Jewett thinks Ogg's estimate of eighteen months for the journey 'far too short to be credible' (68-69).

The exercise need not be repeated for Paul's other journeys. The example is sufficient to indicate the difficulties in making such estimates. But when similar estimates are made for the initial Galatian mission (Acts 13–14), the return from Corinth to Jerusalem/Antioch (Acts 18.22-23), the further journey from Antioch to Ephesus,[76] and what became the return journey through Macedonia to Corinth, it can be easily seen that Paul 'clocked up' a very considerable mileage. Whatever else he was, Paul was a seasoned traveller, who must have covered some 3,000-4,000 miles (roughly 5,000-6,000 km.) during his mission.

b. Travails

The most vivid impression of what travel in the ancient world must have involved for Paul is given by his 'boastful' self-testimony in 2 Cor. 11.25-27:

> [25] . . . Three times I was shipwrecked; for a night and a day I was adrift at sea; [26]on frequent journeys, in danger from rivers, danger from bandits, danger from my own people, danger from Gentiles, danger in the city, danger in the desert, danger at sea, danger from false brothers; [27]in toil and hardship, through many a sleepless night, hungry and thirsty, often without food, cold and naked.

The picture is immediately evocative of the sort of conditions which Paul must have known well. 'Danger from rivers', for example, implies that he was not always able to depend on being able to travel by well-made Roman roads. Similarly 'danger from bandits' was a common hazard, even between major centres and even when travelling in company — I have already instanced the possibility that Paul might have had his trips through Lycaonia in mind when he wrote these words.[77] 'Danger in the desert' could imply memories of when weather was bad and water supplies were running low. Similarly 'many a sleepless night, hungry and thirsty, often without food, cold and naked' probably refers to various occasions when the travelling group could not reach or find hospitality for the night and had to make a rough-and-ready camp in the open.

We can, of course, assume that Paul and his companions would usually have been able to depend on hospitality in some town or village. The tradition of hospitality to strangers was deeply rooted in the cultures of the time. Temples and altars were places of sanctuary, and Zeus was frequently called Zeus Xenios, protector of the rights of hospitality (as in 2 Macc. 6.2). The legend of Philemon

---

76. Riesner estimates between sixty and ninety days and assumes that Paul spent the winter somewhere en route (perhaps in Antioch) (*Paul's Early Period* 313).

77. See above, §27 n. 90.

and Baucis (Ovid, *Met.* 8.613-70) characterizes the ideal and may indeed have been evoked in the episode in Lystra (Acts 14.11-13).[78] In Jewish tradition, Abraham was extolled as the model of hospitality because of his entertaining the three heavenly visitors in Genesis 18,[79] and Job also.[80] Synagogues would often serve also as hospices.[81] The episode described in Luke 24.13-33, where the unknown traveller is urged by his companions, 'Stay with us, because it is almost evening and the day is now nearly over' (24.29), can be taken as both typical and characteristic. So it is not surprising, then, that hospitality is attested as a feature of the early Christian mission.[82] And when Paul exhorted the Roman believers to 'aspire to hospitality' (Rom. 12.13), he was probably mindful of the many occasions when he himself had benefited from such hospitality.

Where there were no compatriots or friendly invitations, there were usually inns. In well-settled Roman territory inns *(mansiones)* were spaced about a day's journey apart, that is, about 20-23 miles (30-36 km.) apart.[83] But to reach the next inn would require some eight or nine hours of steady walking, and that may not always have been possible.[84] And anyway inns were often held in bad repute, to be avoided if at all possible.[85] Murphy-O'Connor provides a helpful sketch:[86]

> The rooms were grouped around three or four sides of a courtyard with public rooms on the ground floor and sleeping accommodation above. Those with money to spend could buy privacy, but those with slender purses had to share a room with strangers; how many depended on the number of beds the

78. See above, §27 n. 72.

79. Philo, *Abr.* 107-14; Josephus, *Ant.* 1.196; *1 Clem.* 10.7; probably Heb. 13.2.

80. Job. 31.32; *T. Job* 10.1-3; 25.5; 53.3.

81. The Theodotus inscription from Jerusalem (see *Jesus Remembered* 303 n. 220, and §24 n. 30 above) can be taken as illustrative here: Theodotus 'constructed the synagogue for the reading of the law and the teaching of the commandments and the guest-room and the [upper?] chambers and the installations of water for a hostelry for those needing [them] from abroad'.

82. E.g., Mark 6.8-11 pars.; Acts 16.1-2, 13, 15, 23; 18.3; Rom. 16.2, 23; Phlm 22.

83. Riesner, *Paul's Early Period* 311; Murphy-O'Connor, *Paul* 99; Casson says, on average, between twenty-five and thirty-five miles apart (*Travel* 184-85). The Latin *mansio* could serve also as a measure of the day's journey (LS 1109).

84. Between the *mansiones* were usually very simple hostels, *mutationes* ('changing places') (Casson, *Travel* 184).

85. Plato, *Laws* 918D-919A. 'Inns in general had a reputation for bedbugs, discomfort, rough-houses, and prostitution . . .'; 'innkeeping was classed among disgraceful trades' (*OCD*[3] 759).

86. Murphy-O'Connor, *Paul,* 99, acknowledging indebtedness to Casson's *Travel* ch. 12 (with much fascinating detail). See further *Paul* 96-100, with reference particularly to F. Millar, 'The World of the *Golden Ass*', *JRS* 71 (1981) 63-75, and illuminating quotations from Apuleius, *Metamorphoses* 2.18 and 8.15, 17.

landlord could cram in, or on his or her attitude to guests sleeping on the floor. Unless they wanted to cart baggage with them, guests had to leave it unguarded while they visited the baths and a restaurant.

On board ship, especially on stormy seas, conditions would have been even more stressful; the living accommodation would have been at best cramped, and travelers would have depended on such food rations as they had been able to bring with them. In writing 2 Corinthians 11, Paul could already recall having been shipwrecked and having spent a night and a day adrift. And the description of the travails on the sea journey towards Rome in Acts 27, whatever its historical value as a description of Paul's own experience, can certainly be regarded as a fair account of what seafarers had to be prepared to confront and live through.

Although Luke gives a vivid account of the shipwreck on the journey to Rome, as already noted, he passes over often harsh details of Paul's land journeys in his laconic description of Paul's movement from place to place. And apart from 2 Cor. 11.25-27, Paul himself makes only allusive references to the hardships which were an unavoidable part of such.[87] All of which is much to be regretted, since a more realistic description of the travails as well as the travels of Paul would have given us a better impression of the man himself and of the personal cost of his apostleship.

---

87. See further Becker, *Paul* 170-78.

CHAPTER 29

Paul the Apostle

29.1. The Second Founder of Christianity

I began §27 by noting that Luke's account of Christianity's beginnings focuses more or less exclusively on Paul from Acts 13 onwards. Following the consultation or council at Jerusalem (Acts 15/Gal. 2.1-10), Luke's focus on Paul becomes even tighter and more exclusive. That is certainly regrettable, since it leaves other parts of the earliest Christian outreach and expansion in the dark. For example, we do not know how and when the new movement became rooted in Rome; Paul's letter to Rome presupposes several already well-established groups of Jesus-believers already functioning in the capital city.[1] And it would have been desirable to have fuller information about the 'myriads' of Jews who became believers, 'all zealous for the law', of whom James speaks according to Acts 21.20.[2] On the other hand, the narrowness of Luke's focus on Paul does mean that we have much detail which overall correlates well with what can be deduced regarding Paul's mission from his letters (from Acts 16 onwards)[3] and which therefore provides an invaluable setting within which to read his letters. And for that we are very much in Luke's debt.

The fact is that Paul is the single most important figure to emerge in the first generation of the new messianic sect. If Luke had to choose to focus on only one figure from that generation, it is well that he chose to focus on Paul. What we

1. See below, §33.2b, and above, §26 n. 130.

2. J. Jervell, 'The Mighty Minority', ST 34 (1980) 13-38, reprinted in The Unknown Paul (Minneapolis: Augsburg, 1984) 26-51, justifiably drew attention to 'the mighty minority' (of believing Jews) referred to in Acts 21.20, in building his thesis that Jewish Christianity remained a dominant influence on early Christianity beyond the disaster of 70 CE.

3. A factor which tells more strongly for the view that the author of Acts was a companion of Paul for a fair amount of this period; see §21.2c(3) above.

might have gained by a more cursory treatment of Paul, leaving more room for details of other missions, might well have been outweighed by what we would have lost from our knowledge of Paul's mission. The point is that *Paul's mission following the Jerusalem council was the single most important development in the first decades of Christianity's history.* Paul's mission and the teaching transmitted through his letters did more than anything else to transform embryonic Christianity from a messianic sect quite at home within Second Temple Judaism into a religion hospitable to Greeks, increasingly Gentile in composition, and less and less comfortable with the kind of Judaism which was to survive the ruinous failure of the two Jewish revolts (66-73, 132-35).

The point is obscured by the traditional characterization of Paul's further mission as two more (the second and third) missionary journeys,[4] as though he continued to regard Jerusalem or Antioch as his base of operations. The reality, however, as already indicated, is that his failure to persuade the believers in Antioch not to require more than faith in Christ as the condition of table-fellowship probably resulted in Paul's undertaking his commission (almost wholly) independently of Jerusalem and Antioch, though assuming the agreement of Gal. 2.6-9.[5] As a result of the Antioch incident Paul in effect lost (or disowned or was disowned by) what had been his base. Henceforth he based his operations elsewhere, in two other of the most important and strategic cities in the Roman Empire — Corinth and Ephesus.[6] What has been designated as two missionary journeys, as though Paul was constantly on the move, a wandering charismatic indeed, is much better described as *Paul's Aegean mission.*

This mission, which unfolds through Acts 16–20, was of crucial importance for two reasons in particular. One is the decisive shift westwards. This development alone was sufficient to shift the centre of gravity in earliest Christianity from Jerusalem and the eastern seaboard of the Mediterranean towards the metropolitan centres of Asia Minor, Greece and then Rome. Combined with the increasingly Gentile membership of the churches founded by Paul, this development alone might have been sufficient to ensure the transformation of a Jewish sect into a predominantly Gentile religion. But in the longer term the second reason was even more decisive. For *it was during his Aegean mission that Paul wrote most of his letters* — almost certainly his most important letters, but possibly *all* the letters which can be attributed to Paul himself.[7] And it is these letters,

---

4. As presented more or less universally in maps depicting Paul's mission.

5. See above, §27.6.

6. As we shall see (§32.1), the trip back to Jerusalem and Antioch referred to in Acts 18.22-23 is best seen more as a temporary break in order to maintain good relations (if possible) with these two mother churches than as Paul's 'reporting back' to authorities regarded as supervising or directing his mission.

7. As we shall see, certainly Romans, 1 and 2 Corinthians, 1 (and 2) Thessalonians,

the only Christian writings which can assuredly be dated to the first generation (thirty-five years) of Christianity, which ensured that Paul's legacy would continue to influence and indeed to give Christianity so much of its definitive character.

In other words, the eight or so years of the Aegean mission stand alongside the three years of Jesus' own mission, the first two or three years of the Jerusalem church's existence and the initial expansion led by the Hellenists as the most crucial for Christianity's existence and enduring character. It is the period of the Aegean mission and its lasting outcome, in terms of both churches established and letters composed and circulated, which makes appropriate the title sometimes accorded to Paul — 'the second founder of Christianity'.[8]

It is appropriate, therefore, to devote a whole section of this historical study to Paul's Aegean mission and its outcome. Appropriate too that we should pause further at this point, the beginning of Paul's apostolic mission as an independent missionary, to reflect on Paul's self-understanding at this critical juncture in his career, the compulsion which drove him on, his goal and tactics, the gospel which he preached and the challenges which he faced both as evangelist and pastor (§29).[9] Equally valuable will it be, before tracing the outlines of the Aegean mission, to consider in general terms the historical settings within which Paul founded his churches, their legal status, structure and character (§30). We can then focus more effectively on the detail of the Aegean mission itself, the particular centres in and from which Paul operated, the churches he established and the letters by which he attempted to counsel and nurture them.

---

probably Galatians, and possibly Philippians, Colossians and Philemon are all to be dated to Paul's Aegean mission. See below, §§31.5-7, 32.5, 32.7, 33.2-3, 34.4-6.

8. Initially with some degree of disparagement: 'the second founder of Christianity' who has 'exercised beyond all doubt the stronger — not the better — influence' than the first (Jesus) (Wrede, *Paul* 180); but subsequently in proper recognition of the debt Christianity owes to Paul — as by Hengel and Schwemer, *Paul* 309. White objects to calling Paul the 'second founder' of Christianity, since the movement was already diverse and dispersed (*Jesus to Christianity* 144). Nevertheless, the title is deserved (if at all), not because Paul was the first to preach the gospel to Gentiles or in Rome or to break out from the matrix of Second Temple Judaism, but because it was his mission which made it impossible for Gentile believers to be retained within the traditional forms of Judaism and because his writings became the most influential reinterpretations of the original traditions and forms of the new movement. See also V. P. Furnish, 'On Putting Paul in His Place', *JBL* 113 (1994) 3-17; R. Morgan, 'Paul's Enduring Legacy', in Dunn, ed., *The Cambridge Companion to St. Paul* 242-55.

9. To avoid any misunderstanding, I should make it clear that this is not a study of Paul's theology (for which see my *Theology of Paul*) but is complementary to it; this section focuses rather on Paul himself, on how he saw himself, on how he pursued his mission, on how he worked, on how he preached and on how he endeavoured to build up the churches he founded.

29.2. Who Did Paul Think He Was?

Somewhat surprisingly, this rather obvious question has rarely been posed quite so bluntly.[10] The question seems to have been largely hidden behind the traditional interest in what Paul taught and the more recent interest in how he acted.[11] But the question, 'How would Paul have thought of himself?', 'How would Paul have introduced himself to a stranger?', remains a valid one, whether posed in the older terminology of 'self-understanding' or 'self-definition', or the more recently fashionable language of 'identity'.[12] Of course, since we are dependent for our answer on what Paul wrote, the question might be more accurately posed as 'Who did Paul *say* he was?'. But I retain the question as asked because Paul himself, as well as his mission, has functioned as a watershed between Judaism and Christianity (more so, in fact, than Jesus). So the question of how Paul thought of himself, if it can be answered adequately, should provide important insights at this crucial juncture in the emergence of Christianity, and indeed in regard to the continuing overlap between Christianity and Judaism. The question as asked, in its English form, has also something of a *double entendre* — both a straightforward question and one which reflects the puzzlement and indignation which Paul evidently provoked for many, both Jews and Gentiles — which sets an appropriate tone as we try to answer it.[13]

In a number of passages in his letters, Paul speaks in explicitly autobiographical terms.[14] Apart from the self-introduction of his letters, where he de-

10. The nearest exception is Niebuhr, *Heidenapostel*. More attention has been given to the famous description of Paul in *The Acts of Paul* — 'a man small in size, bald-headed, bandy-legged, of noble mien, with eyebrows meeting, rather hook-nosed, full of grace' (3.3). As noted by A. J. Malherbe, 'A Physical Description of Paul', *HTR* 79 (1986) 170-75, such a description would not have been seen as unflattering; see further Malina and Neyrey, *Portraits of Paul* 130-45 and 204. Michael Grant cites also Malalas (6th century — a thick grey beard, light bluish eyes, and a fair and florid complexion, a man who often smiled) and Nicephorus Callistus (14th century — beard rather pointed, large nose handsomely curved, body slight and rather bent) (*Saint Paul* 3).

11. Even Barclay, *Jews* (particularly ch. 13) is more concerned with Paul's social identity than with his self-identity, although, of course, there is no clear distinction between the two. But see also his 'Paul among Diaspora Jews: Anomaly or Apostate?', *JSNT* 60 (1995) 89-120.

12. In using the term 'identity' I am conscious both that identity is at least in some degree a social construct and that it should not be regarded as something fixed or single. Precisely because it is in some degree a social construct, a person's identity will inevitably change through time and at any time will be multiple in character (son, Jew, apostle, client, tent-maker, etc.).

13. In this section I draw on my 'Who Did Paul Think He Was? A Study of Jewish Christian Identity', *NTS* 45 (1999) 174-93.

14. See also §21 n. 195 above.

scribes himself most often as 'Paul, an apostle of Jesus Christ',[15] the most relevant are:

- Rom. 11.1 — 'I am an Israelite, of the seed of Abraham, of the tribe of Benjamin'.
- Rom. 11.13 — 'I am apostle to the Gentiles'.
- Rom. 15.16 — 'a minister of Christ Jesus for the Gentiles, serving the gospel of Christ as a priest'.
- 1 Cor. 9.1-2 — 'Am I not an apostle? Have I not seen our Lord? . . . If to others I am not an apostle, at least I am to you'.
- 1 Cor. 9.21-22 — 'To the Jews I became as a Jew, in order that I might win Jews; to those under the law I became as one under the law (though not myself actually under the law) in order that I might win those under the law; to those outside the law I became as one outside the law (though not actually outside the law of God but in-lawed to Christ) in order that I might win those outside the law'.
- 1 Cor. 15.9-10 — 'I am the least of the apostles, not worthy to be called an apostle . . . but by the grace of God I am what I am'.
- 2 Cor. 11.22 — 'Are they Hebrews? So am I. Are they Israelites? So am I. Are they seed of Abraham? So am I. Are they ministers of Christ? . . . I more'.
- Gal. 1.13-14 — 'You have heard of my way of life previously in Judaism, that in excessive measure I persecuted the church of God and tried to destroy it, and that I progressed in Judaism beyond many of my contemporaries among my people, being exceedingly zealous for my ancestral traditions'.
- Gal. 2.19-20 — 'I through the law died to the law. . . . No longer I live, but Christ lives in me'.
- Phil. 3.5-8 — 'circumcised the eighth day, of the people of Israel, of the tribe of Benjamin, a Hebrew of the Hebrews, as to the law a Pharisee, as to zeal a persecutor of the church, as to righteousness which is in the law, blameless. But what was gain to me, these things I have come to regard as loss on account of the Christ. More than that, I regard everything as loss on account of the surpassing value of knowing Christ Jesus my Lord'.

Four striking aspects of Paul's self-identity come to vivid expression in these passages.

---

15. See §29.3 below.

a. 'In Judaism'

It is clear from Gal. 1.13-14 that Paul regarded his 'way of life within Judaism' as something past. However, we need to bear in mind the earlier discussion,[16] to the effect that the 'Judaism' referred to in Gal. 1.13-14 should not be confused with what we today denote by the term 'Judaism' or describe as Second Temple Judaism. The historical term ('Judaism') was coined to describe the Judeans' spirited religio-nationalistic resistance to the attempt of the regional Syrian super-power to enforce an empire-wide homogeneity of religion by suppressing the distinctives of Israel's religion, particularly Torah, circumcision, and laws of clean and unclean. And Gal. 1.13-14 confirms that Paul used the term in this same sense: the 'way of life' he described as 'in Judaism' was his life as a zealous Pharisee, marked by a readiness to persecute, even to destroy those fellow religionists who threatened to compromise the holiness and distinctiveness of this 'Judaism'.[17] The same point emerges from Paul's other look backwards — Phil. 3.5-6. For there too what he had turned his back on and now regarded as so much 'garbage' *(ta skybala)* was particularly the same Pharisaic zeal and righteousness.[18]

So we can certainly say that as a result of his conversion and commission as 'apostle to the Gentiles', Paul no longer thought of himself as belonging to 'Judaism', that is, to the Pharisaic understanding of Israel's heritage, to the zealous faction of what we today call Second Temple Judaism. But can or should we say more? Had Paul, for example, ceased to think of himself as a Jew?

b. Paul the Jew

If Paul no longer thought of himself as 'in Judaism', does it not also follow that he no longer thought of himself as a Jew? For it is difficult to avoid an ethnic sense in the term 'Jew' *(Yehudi, Ioudaios),* the term deriving, as already noted, from the region or territory known as 'Judea' *(Yehudah, Ioudaia).* And Paul remained ethnically Judean in origin, even though initially brought up as a Judean

---

16. See *Jesus Remembered* §§9.1-3; also above, §25.1d-f

17. See again §25.2 above. S. E. Porter, 'Was Paul a Good Jew? Fundamental Issues in a Current Debate', in S. E. Porter and B. W. R. Pearson, eds., *Christian-Jewish Relations through the Centuries* (JSNTS 192; Sheffield: Sheffield Academic, 2000) 148-74, queries identifying the 'Judaism' of Gal. 1.13-14 so closely with Pharisaic Judaism (170-73), but he does not give enough weight to the accompanying phrases, which in effect describe the 'Judaism' being referred to; as a 'zealous' Pharisee, Paul would not have readily agreed that other factions in Israel were (also) 'Judaism'.

18. *Ta skybala* can denote 'excrement' (BDAG 932).

living in the diaspora. It is true that for more than a century *Ioudaios* had been gaining a more religious (not dependent on ethnic) connotation.[19] But recent discussions have concluded that ethnicity remained at the core of Jewish identity.[20] So the question stands: How could Paul have left 'Judaism' behind without leaving behind his religious identity as a Jew?

Something of the ambiguity in which Paul's identity was caught is indicated by two references in his letters. In Rom. 2.17 Paul addresses his interlocutor as one who calls himself a Jew, but he then goes on to indicate his disapproval of the attitudes and conduct which he attributes to the interlocutor (2.17-24). Here he seems to distance himself from the 'Jew'. Yet in Gal. 2.15 Paul continues his appeal to Peter at Antioch by affirming, 'We [two] are Jews by nature and not Gentile sinners'. In this case his continuing identity as a Jew was the basis of his exhortation.

More striking is the fact that a few sentences later in Romans 2 Paul offers a definition of 'Jew' which removes the defining factor from what is outward and visible in the flesh (presumably ethnic characteristics as well as circumcision itself): 'For the Jew [we might translate "the true Jew", or "the Jew properly speaking"] is not the one visibly so, nor is circumcision that which is visibly performed in the flesh, but one who is so in a hidden way, and circumcision is of the heart, in Spirit not in letter.[21] His praise comes not from men but from God' (2.28-29).[22]

---

19. See *Jesus Remembered* §9.2b.

20. Barclay, *Jews* 404; Casey similarly concludes his discussion on 'identity factors', that ethnicity outweighs all the rest (*Jewish Prophet,* especially 14); note also Schiffman's observation that 'Judaism is centred on the Jewish people, a group whose membership is fundamentally determined by heredity', and his argument that even heretics did not lose their 'Jewish status' (*Who Was a Jew?* 38, 49, 61). In 'Who Did Paul Think He Was?' I note that this was precisely why the adoption of Jewish customs by Romans was so frowned upon by the Roman intelligentsia; it was insulting to Roman *dignitas* for another Roman to embrace a foreign identity (180); see, e.g., the texts cited by M. Whittaker, *Jews and Christians: Graeco-Roman Views* (Cambridge: Cambridge University, 1984) 85-91; Feldman, *Jew and Gentile,* particularly 298-300, 344-48. But see also the most fascinating and challenging of recent studies on the subject by the rabbinic scholar D. Boyarin, *A Radical Jew: Paul and the Politics of Identity* (Berkeley: University of California, 1994), who wishes to reclaim Paul as an important Jewish thinker, as one representing 'the interface between *Jew* as a self-identical essence and *Jew* as a construction constantly being remade' (2-3), who maintains that 'Paul's writing poses a significant challenge to Jewish notions of identity' and who in response to Paul wishes to 'deterritorialize Jewishness' and to move towards a 'diasporized (multicultural) Israel' (ch. 10).

21. For detail see my *Romans* 123-24. The seer of Revelation uses similar language — Rev. 2.9 and 3.9.

22. Note how Paul retains the word-play from Gen. 29.35 and 49.8: in Hebrew, 'Jew' = *Yehudi,* and 'praise' = *hodah.* 'In popular etymology it [the patriarchal name Judah *(Yehudah)*] was often explained as the passive of *hodah* "(someone) praised" (Fitzmyer, *Romans* 323). The pun, of course, would probably be lost on Paul's Greek-speaking audiences.

We should not conclude that Paul thereby disowned his Jewish identity. For in fact he was using 'Jew' in a positive way, and he immediately proceeds to affirm 'the advantage' *(to perisson)* of 'the Jew' in 3.1-2; and the contrast between outward appearance and inward reality is one which had been long familiar in the religion of Israel (cf. particularly Jer. 9.25-26) and more widely.[23] At the same time, however, by switching the emphasis away from the outward and visible, Paul in effect was playing down the role of the term 'Jew' as an ethnic identifier: 'Jew' as a term denoting distinctiveness from the (other) nations was no longer relevant; on the contrary, the positive mark of 'the Jew' was nothing observable by others, being determined primarily by relationship with God.[24]

Even more striking is 1 Cor. 9.21-22, cited above. The striking feature is the fact that Paul, even though himself ethnically a Jew, could speak of *becoming* 'as a Jew'. Here, 'to become as a Jew' is obviously to follow the patterns of conduct distinctive of Jews, to 'judaize'.[25] In other words, Paul speaks here as one who did not acknowledge 'Jew' as his own identity, or as an identity inalienable from his person as an ethnic Jew. Instead 'Jew' is being treated almost as a role which he might assume or discard — denoting not so much an actual identity, an identity integral to him as a person, but rather an identity which could be taken on or put off as needs or circumstances demanded.[26] Here again, therefore, it is clear that Paul wanted to disentangle the term 'Jew' from the narrower constraints of ethnicity and to treat it more as denoting a code of conduct or a manner of living.[27]

In short, whereas Paul seems to have been willing to regard his time 'in Judaism' as past, he was unwilling to abandon the term 'Jew' as a self-referential term. As a term marking off 'Jew' ethnically from 'Gentile', or 'Jew' culturally from 'Greek', it still had a functional role;[28] as a term denoting an inner reality

---

23. See especially A. Fridrichsen, 'Der wahre Jude und sein Loeb. Röm. 2.28f.', *Symbolae Arctoae* 1 (1927) 39-49.

24. Note the similar argument regarding circumcision in Phil. 3.3: circumcision is reaffirmed, but redefined in terms of the work of the Spirit in the heart; see my 'Philippians 3.2-14 and the New Perspective on Paul', in *The New Perspective on Paul* ch. 22, (2005) 465-67, (2008) 471-73; also above, §25.1d.

25. See above, §27.4a(iii).

26. C. K. Barrett, *1 Corinthians* (BNTC; London: Black, 1968) 211. See also S. C. Barton, '"All Things to All People": Paul and the Law in the Light of 1 Corinthians 9.19-23', in J. D. G. Dunn, ed., *Paul and the Mosaic Law* (Tübingen: Mohr Siebeck, 1996) 271-85. See also §32 n. 282.

27. Cassius Dio comments on the name 'Jews': 'I do not know how this title came to be given them, but it applies to all the rest of mankind, although of alien race, who affect [*zēlousi* — better, 'emulate'] their customs' (37.17.1 — *GLAJJ* §406 = 2.349, 351).

28. Hence Paul's frequent use of the pairs Jews/Greeks and Jews/Gentiles — Rom. 1.16; 2.9-10; 3.9, 29; 9.24; 1 Cor. 1.22-24; 10.32; 12.13; Gal. 2.15.

and relationship with God in which non-Jews could participate, it still had meaning to be cherished; but as a term giving the distinction between Jew and non-Jew any continuing religious validity, or as signifying a divine partiality towards the 'Jew', its role was at an end.[29]

c. 'I Am an Israelite'

Apart from Gal. 2.15, Paul never called himself a Jew; and even there he uses the term only as a way of claiming common ground with Peter.[30] Paul shows similar ambivalence with regard to other terms (cited above) usually understood to denote national or cultural identity. In Phil 3.5 'Hebrew' is a status which he seems to consign to the rubbish bin (3.7-8). But in 2 Cor. 11.22 Paul affirms his continuing identity as a 'Hebrew' in vigorous rejoinder to those who were operating antagonistically in Corinth; there was something important about himself and his missionary role which could still be expressed by the term, however foolish he thought it to continue investing too much significance in the term (11.21).

Membership of 'the tribe of Benjamin' and descent from Abraham are caught in much the same ambivalence. The former seems also to be something once valued but now discarded as of lasting importance (Phil. 3.5); but in Rom. 11.1 the status is affirmed without disclaimer. And descent from Abraham ('of the seed of Abraham') is again strongly affirmed, albeit polemically in 2 Cor. 11.22, and similarly without qualification in Rom. 11.1. Paul's identity as an 'Israelite' is also asserted in the same polemical context as 'Hebrew' and 'seed of Abraham' (2 Cor. 11.22); and belonging to the race of Israel is part of the heritage discounted in Phil 3.5-7. But again 'I am an Israelite' is affirmed as self-identification *ex anima* and without qualification in Rom. 11.1.[31]

What is striking about the Rom. 11.1 references is that the verse comes after Paul has attempted to redefine both who can be counted as 'Abraham's seed' (ch. 4; also Galatians 3) and what constitutes Israel as Israel (the call of God — Rom. 9.6-13, 24-26).[32] We should recognize that, in so doing, Paul attempts a redefinition of 'Abraham's seed' and of 'Israel' which transcends (or, should we say, absorbs) the ethno-religious distinction indicated by the contrast Jew/Gentile.[33] The significance of Paul's self-identifying confession 'I am an Israelite'

29. Hence Rom. 2.6-11; Gal. 3.28.
30. Only in Acts does Paul declare, 'I am a Jew' (Acts 21.39; 22.3).
31. Note also Rom. 9.4: Paul's kindred according to the flesh 'are [still] Israelites' — 'are', not 'were'; the covenant blessings (9.4-5) now enjoyed by believing Gentiles remain Israel's blessings.
32. See my *Romans* 537; also *Theology of Paul* 510-11.
33. Note that in the climax of his argument in Romans (Romans 9–11), Paul switches

(Rom. 11.1), therefore, becomes clear. That it includes an ethnic identification is not to be disputed; in context that is hardly deniable (especially 11.25-32). But the confession is primarily and precisely an affirmation of identity *as determined by God* and not by distinction from other nations or by conformity to halakhic principles.[34] Indeed, Paul's whole concern was to reassert Israel's identity as primarily determined by God and in relation to God, and thus as transcending ethnic and social distinctions and as absorbing ethnic and social diversity.

d. 'In Christ'

Probably, however, we should allow our appreciation of how Paul thought of himself to be determined primarily by frequency of usage, rather than the few explicit self-references thus far reviewed. That directs us at once to Paul's pervasive use of the phrases 'in Christ' and 'in the Lord' in his letters as denoting self-location, and indeed as Paul's primary reference point for understanding himself as well as his converts.[35] The phrase 'in Christ' at times does service for the recent neologism (not yet used by Paul) 'Christian' and in fact is often translated as 'Christian' in modern translations.[36] Its co-referent in corporate terms is the less frequently used, but obviously important, talk of 'the body of Christ'.[37]

The importance of the self-understanding thereby encapsulated is indicated by Gal. 2.19-20 and Phil. 3.5-8, quoted above. In both cases we see a shift in identity, or in what constitutes self-identity for Paul. He has 'died to the law' (Gal. 2.19), a phrase which epitomizes Paul's conversion, with its concomitant abandonment of what he had previously valued about and for himself (Phil. 3.4-6 — ethnic identity, righteousness as a Pharisee, zealous defence of Israel's cove-

---

from the predominant Jew/Greek, Jew/Gentile usage ('Jew' appears nine times in Romans 1–3) to predominant talk of 'Israel' (in Romans 9–11, 'Israel' appears eleven times, 'Jew' twice); and that in Romans 9–11 the topic is not 'Israel and the church', as so often asserted, but solely 'Israel', that is, his people viewed from God's perspective (see my *Romans* 520; *Theology of Paul* 507-508).

34. As becomes the emphasis in rabbinic Judaism; see C. T. R. Hayward, *Interpretations of the Name Israel in Ancient Judaism and Some Early Christian Writings* (Oxford: Oxford University, 2005) 355.

35. 'In Christ' — eighty-three times in the Pauline corpus (sixty-one, if we exclude Ephesians and the Pastorals); 'in the Lord' — forty-seven times in the Pauline corpus (thirty-nine, if we exclude Ephesians); not to mention the many more 'in him/whom' phrases with the same referent; full details in my *Theology of Paul* §15.2 (with bibliography). See also C. J. Hodge, 'Apostle to the Gentiles: Constructions of Paul's Identity', *BibInt* 13 (2005) 270-88.

36. See, e.g., BDAG 327-28, which gives various instances where the phrases can be treated as periphrases for 'Christian' (328); see further *Theology of Paul* 399 n. 48.

37. *Theology of Paul* 405-406, but noting the variation in usage (n. 76).

nant prerogatives). As a consequence of his encounter with Christ, he counted all that as so much 'garbage' (3.8) in comparison with what now really mattered to him.[38] And what really mattered now was to 'gain Christ', to 'be found in Christ' (3.8-9), to 'know Christ' (3.8, 10), to become like Christ in death as well as resurrection (3.10-11). Alternatively expressed, 'Christ in him' was now the determining and defining character of his living (Gal. 2.20); similarly in Rom. 8.9-11, the indwelling Spirit, 'Christ in you', is what determines Christian status ('belonging to Christ').[39] That was what now determined Paul as a person, his values, his objectives, and his identity. The other identifiers need not and should not be entirely discounted and devalued. But in comparison with being 'in Christ', nothing else really counted for anything very much at all.

One indicator of the shift in Paul's self-understanding is given by the transition from Romans 11 to 12. For in Romans 9–11, as already noted, the concern was exclusively with Israel, including his hopes for ethnic Israel. But in Romans 12 the first social context within which he wanted his readers/hearers to recognize and affirm themselves was the body of Christ (12.3-8).[40] The community called out and constituted by Christ was to be the primary reference by which their identity and mode of living were determined. Paul would hardly have thought otherwise about himself, as his 'in Christ/Lord' language clearly indicates.

So when we ask the question 'Who did Paul think he was?', the simplest answer is the phrase he used evidently of himself in 2 Cor. 12.2 — 'a person in Christ'.[41] He had not ceased to be an ethnic Jew, but he no longer counted that as definitive of his relation to God, and therefore of his identity. At the same time, and bearing in mind the opening remarks on 'identity', we can speak of Paul as having a multiple identity, or of having an identity with different facets. We can agree that the form(s) of his identity took their shape through and their weight from his social relationships, and that his identity changed in terms of shape and weight over time and by virtue of his changing relationships. The key factor,

---

38. See more fully my 'Philippians 3.2-14 and the New Perspective on Paul': 'The sharpness of the contrast is not so much to denigrate what he had previously counted as gain, as to enhance to the highest degree the value he now attributes to Christ, to the knowledge of Christ, and to the prospect of gaining Christ' (*New Perspective on Paul* [2005] 475, [2008] 481).

39. Rom. 8.9 — 'If anyone does not have the Spirit of Christ, that person does not belong to him' — and some of his 'in Christ' references provide the nearest we have to a definition of 'Christian' in Paul's letters. See also A. du Toit, '"In Christ", "in the Spirit" and Related Prepositional Phrases: Their Relevance for a Discussion on Pauline Mysticism', *Focusing on Paul* 129-45.

40. See further my *Romans* 703; *Theology of Paul* 534-35, 548.

41. That Paul intended a self-reference at this point is almost universally agreed among commentators; see also above, §25.5f.

however, is that for Paul himself, his identity was primarily determined by his relationship to Christ, even though that did not entirely de-valorize his other identities (particularly as a circumcised Jew).

29.3. The Apostle

I have left Paul's other chief self-identifier for separate treatment, since it was evidently so important for Paul himself. This is the title 'apostle'. It is clear from the way he introduces himself in most of his letters that this was how Paul wanted to be heard and known:

- Rom. 1.1, 5 — 'Paul, a slave of Jesus Christ, called to be an apostle, set apart for the gospel of God . . . Jesus Christ our Lord, through whom we received grace and apostleship with a view to the obedience of faith among all the nations for the sake of his name';
- 1 Cor. 1.1 — 'Paul, called to be an apostle of Christ Jesus by the will of God';
- 2 Cor. 1.1 — 'Paul, apostle of Christ Jesus by the will of God';
- Gal. 1.1 — 'Paul, apostle, not from human beings nor through a human being, but through Jesus Christ and God the Father';
- Col. 1.1 — 'Paul, apostle of Christ Jesus by the will of God'.[42]

For convenience I repeat the relevant references from §29.2 —

- Rom. 11.13 — 'I am apostle to the Gentiles';
- Rom. 15.16 — 'a minister of Christ Jesus for the Gentiles, serving the gospel of Christ as a priest';
- 1 Cor. 9.1-2 — 'Am I not an apostle? Have I not seen our Lord? . . . If to others I am not an apostle, at least I am to you';
- 1 Cor. 15.8-10 — 'Last of all, as to an abortion, he appeared also to me. For I am the least of the apostles, not worthy to be called an apostle . . . but by the grace of God I am what I am'.

Here we have the answer to the earlier question, 'How would Paul have introduced himself?' 'Apostle of Messiah Jesus/Jesus Christ' was his chosen self-designation, what he would have printed on his 'calling card', and how he in fact did introduce himself in his letters.

---

42. Similarly Eph. 1.1; 1 Tim. 1.1; 2 Tim. 1.1; Tit. 1.1; if these letters are post-Pauline, the openings indicate how established the usage and status had become.

The implication of at least several of these references is that Paul thought it necessary to lay claim to this title ('apostle') and that his claim to it was contested by some. The unusual opening to Galatians, as the first of a sequence of denials/affirmations ('not from human beings nor through a human being, but through Jesus Christ and God the Father'),[43] is especially indicative of an independent apostolic status questioned, at least by those 'causing trouble' in Galatia.[44] Moreover, we have also already observed that Paul did not meet the conditions for recognition/election of an 'apostle' as indicated by Luke (Acts 1.21-22), and that Luke's description of Paul and Barnabas as 'apostles' was probably intended by Luke to be understood as denoting their function as missionaries sent out by the church of Antioch.[45] Paul also knew that (as we might say) lesser 'apostleship';[46] but his consistent insistence that he was an apostle by appointment of God indicates a refusal to be regarded as 'apostle' in any lesser sense than 'those who were apostles before him' (Gal. 1.17).

What, then, did the claim to apostleship and the title 'apostle' signify to Paul?[47]

a. Appointed by the Risen Christ

The basic sense of 'apostle *(apostolos)*' was 'one sent out', so 'delegate, envoy, messenger, authorized emissary'.[48] What gave it the weight which Paul obviously saw in it, and claimed by using it in self-reference, was the fact that the commissioning authority was *Christ,* 'by the will of God'. It was as an emissary of Christ, in accordance with God's will, that he was an apostle, and as such his appointment carried the full weight of that authority behind it. This was what he was insisting on so emphatically in the opening of Galatians.

The authorizing appointment was still more restricted: not simply appointed by Christ (a status and role which could legitimately be claimed for many pioneering evangelists in subsequent centuries), but *appointed by the risen*

---

43. 'Am I now seeking human approval . . . ?' (1.10); 'the gospel that was proclaimed by me is not of human origin; for I did not receive it from a human source, nor was I taught it . . .' (1.11-12); 'I did not confer with any human being, nor did I go up to Jerusalem to those who were already apostles before me . . .' (1.16-17); 'I did not see any other apostle except James. . . . In what I am writing to you, before God, I do not lie!' (1.19-20). See also above, §27 n. 176.

44. See below, §31.7a.

45. See above, §27 n. 108.

46. 2 Cor. 8.23; Phil. 2.25.

47. The bibliography on 'apostle' is extensive; see, e.g., the reviews by H. D. Betz, 'Apostle', *ABD* 1.309-11; J. A. Bühner, *'apostolos', EDNT* 1.142-46; P. W. Barnett, 'Apostle', *DPL* 1.45-51.

48. BDAG 122.

Christ in the course of his resurrection appearances. This is the claim that Paul explicitly makes twice in 1 Corinthians: 'Am I not an apostle? Have I not seen our Lord?' (1 Cor. 9.1); 'last of all, as to an abortion, he appeared also to me' (15.8). In the latter passage Paul makes a twofold assertion:

- the appearance to himself was of the same order and significance as the appearances to Peter, the twelve . . . and 'all the apostles' (15.5-7);[49]
- the appearance to himself was 'last of all', the almost explicit inference being that after Paul, nobody else had been granted an appearance of the risen Christ.[50]

On both points, we should note, Paul was in agreement with Luke: the qualification to be an apostle was a resurrection appearance, because the essential role of an apostle was to bear witness to Jesus' resurrection (Acts 1.22); and the resurrection appearances as such continued only for a limited period (1.1-3).[51]

The claim, therefore, was to a unique status and authority. That was no doubt one of the reasons why Paul's claim to the status was questioned by some, although we have already seen that his claim was in effect acknowledged by the Jerusalem leadership, though possibly with qualifications.[52] But probably the greater question mark was put against Paul's understanding of his apostolic commissioning.

b. Servant of the Gospel

Also worthy of note is the degree to which Paul understood 'apostle' and 'gospel' as in a mutually reinforcing symbiotic relationship:

49. 'All the apostles' seems to have included Barnabas (Gal. 2.9; 1 Cor. 9.5-6) and Andronicus and Junia (Rom. 16.7); see also Reinbold, *Propaganda* 37-39, 40-41, and §22 n. 25 above. Is the plural in 1 Thess. 2.1-12 'so personal to Paul that Silas and Timothy could not be included' in 2.6-7 (an 'epistolary plural'), as A. J. Malherbe, *The Letters to the Thessalonians* (AB 32B; New York: Doubleday, 2000) 144, argues (similarly Reinbold 39-40)? And given Apollos's relatively late appearance on the scene, it is unlikely that he would have been numbered among 'the apostles' referred to in 1 Cor. 15.7.

50. On 'abortion' see my *Theology of Paul* 331 n. 87; the implication of the jibe being that Paul's birth (as a believer) had to be unnaturally hastened in order to ensure his inclusion within the circle of apostles before it finally closed (see §25 n. 142 above). In his review of interpretations Thiselton does not give sufficient attention to the primary sense of *ektrōma* as 'premature birth' (*1 Corinthians* 1208-10). Schrage is better (*1 Korinther* 4.62-63).

51. See above, §22.2b.

52. See again §27 n. 176 above; but we also earlier noted that Paul himself may have been somewhat ambivalent as to whether James (the brother of Jesus) could rightly be called an apostle (§25 n. 205).

- in Rom. 1.1 the two self-introductory phrases, 'called to be an apostle' and 'set apart for the gospel of God', are coterminous;
- as 'a minister of Christ Jesus' his function was to 'serve the gospel of Christ as a priest' (Rom. 15.16);
- as apostle his role was to proclaim the gospel (1 Cor. 15.11);
- Paul's insistence that he was an apostle 'not from human beings nor through a human being but through Jesus Christ and God the Father' (Gal. 1.1) is mirrored in his equally vehement insistence a few sentences later that his gospel was 'not of human origin; for it was not from a human being that I received it, neither was I taught it, but through a revelation of Jesus Christ' (1.11-12).

As has been pointed out by others, Paul's agitation in Galatians 1–2 was not so much in self-defence as in defence of his gospel, because he feared that 'the truth of the gospel' (2.5, 14) was being endangered by the attacks on his evangelistic success as falling short of what God demanded.[53]

The authority which Paul claimed as an *apostle,* therefore, was the authority of the *gospel.*[54] In fact, 'the truth of the gospel' was his first concern; his own apostolic status was secondary to and in service of the gospel. This understanding explains why Paul was willing to acknowledge the prior status and authority of 'those who were apostles before him' (Gal. 1.17) and in effect to acknowledge their right to approve his preaching (2.2). It was more important that the same message should be preached by all the apostles (1 Cor. 15.11), in particular that his preaching of the gospel should be affirmed by the Jerusalem apostles (Gal. 2.6-9), than that his apostleship should be formally acknowledged.[55] Which brings us to the really sensitive issue.

c. To the Gentiles

As already observed, Paul saw his commissioning, apparently from the first, as a commissioning to take the gospel to the Gentiles.[56] Paul never saw himself simply as 'apostle', with some roving commission. He had been specifically commissioned to preach the gospel *among the nations:*[57]

---

53. 'Apostolic authority was conditional upon the gospel and subject to the norm of the gospel' (*Theology of Paul* 572), with bibliography in n. 35; 'apostleship and the gospel were inseparable for Paul' (Stuhlmacher, *Biblische Theologie* 1.249); Hahn, *Theologie* 1.193-95.

54. Schenk emphasizes the character of apostleship as commissioning to proclaim the Easter message ('Selbstverständnisse' 1364-74).

55. See above, n. 52.

56. See above, §25.3c-d.

57. The Greek *ethnē* can be translated equally 'nations' or 'Gentiles', 'the Gentiles' be-

- he had 'received grace and apostleship with a view to the obedience of faith among all the nations for the sake of his name' (Rom. 1.5);
- in his major treatment of 'Israel' he does not hesitate to assert simply, 'I am apostle to the Gentiles' (Rom. 11.13);
- he was 'a minister of Christ Jesus for the Gentiles' (Rom 15.16);
- God chose to reveal his Son in Paul, in order that he might 'preach him among the Gentiles' (Gal. 1.16).

We have already subjected Galatians 1–2 to sufficient examination for the point to be clear that this was where 'the shoe began to pinch' for Paul so far as his role as apostle and servant of the gospel was evaluated by others.[58] The point, however, is too important for our appreciation both of Paul's self-understanding and of how he carried out his commission to be passed over without highlighting it again here. For (1) it was precisely this commission which Paul claimed to have received, to take the good news of Jesus to non-Jews, which proved so controversial in the beginnings of Christianity. So controversial was it indeed, that it caused a schism in the early Jesus movement, a schism which stretched into the next three centuries in the hostile relations between what became the mainstream of Christianity and the so-called Jewish-Christian heretical sects. And (2) it was precisely this commission which caused Paul to formulate 'the truth of the gospel' so clearly and definitively — as an offer of God's acceptance to *all* who believe, without further qualification — and thus to crystallize the heart of the Christian gospel in effect for all time.

It was this understanding of commission, apostle = missionary = evangelist, which gave the Christian concept of apostle its distinctive sense. And not only distinctive, but ground-breaking. For while the concept of 'apostle' = 'messenger, emissary' was self-evident (*apostolos* from *apostellō*, 'send'), and *apostolos* was used in that sense, the sense of 'apostle' as one commissioned to win adherents to one's faith, to convert others, was new. We know of Jewish apologists, concerned to help their fellow Jews to take a proper pride in their religion and to explain its peculiarities to others. We know of wandering philosophers who sought to persuade others of the wisdom of their views. To be sure, the model provided by Jesus, of a summons to radical trust in God in the light of the coming kingdom, had already broken old moulds and was resumed by the first believers in the risen Jesus in their initial preaching in Jerusalem and Judea. But it was this sense of commission to convert others, to win adherents to the new movement from well beyond the boundaries of Second Temple Judaism by sum-

---

ing one way of describing all the nations other than Israel. See also D. J.-S. Chae, *Paul as Apostle to the Gentiles* (Carlisle: Paternoster, 1997); Reinbold, *Propaganda* 164-81.

58. See above, §25.3b-d and §27.3c-d.

moning them to faith in Israel's Christ, which gave the Christian understanding of 'apostle' its distinctive character and established Christianity's character as essentially a missionary religion.[59]

d. Apostle of Israel

Less explicit but, we may judge, equally important for Paul was the conviction that his commission as 'apostle to the Gentiles' was not only in accordance with the will of God but also an extension of Israel's own commission from God. This inference is clearest, once again, in Galatians.

- In Gal. 1.15-16 we have already noted the clear echo of Jer. 1.5 and Isa. 49.1-6 in Paul's description of his conversion/calling.[60] The point, once again, is that Jeremiah had been 'appointed a prophet to the nations' (Jer. 1.5) and that Israel as Yahweh's servant (Isa. 49.3) had been given 'as a light to the nations' (49.6).
- Equally striking is Paul's description of the third strand of the covenant promise made to Abraham — 'In you shall all the nations be blessed' (Gen. 12.3; 18.18)[61] — as 'the gospel preached beforehand' (Gal. 3.8).

Paul could have written in these terms only if he had understood his role as carrying forward God's own agenda for Israel.

The same point follows from what Paul says about his role as 'apostle to the Gentiles' in Romans 9–11. For there he is clear that his role vis-à-vis the nations/Gentiles is part of God's great scheme — the 'mystery' of the divine purpose — to extend mercy to *all,* not least, including Israel (11.13-15, 25-32).[62]

In short, Paul would have strongly resisted the charge that historic Judaism has laid against him, that he was an 'apostate from Israel'. To the contrary, Paul's claim is in effect that he was not only an apostle of Christ Jesus but also an 'apostle *of Israel*'.[63] Sad to say, this self-claim and claim for his apostleship and gos-

---

59. Cf. Schnabel, *Mission* 536-45; Roetzel, *Paul* ch. 2; and see §24 n. 247 above.

60. See above, §25.3d.

61. The Genesis texts can be variously understood (see, e.g., G. J. Wenham, *Genesis* [WBC 1; Waco: Word, 1987] 277-78), but Paul's interpretation is clear. The other strands of the much and variously repeated promise to Abraham (and the patriarchs following him) were the promise of seed and the promise of land (*Theology of Paul* 144).

62. See also A. J. Hultgren, 'The Scriptural Foundations for Paul's Mission to the Gentiles', in S. E. Porter, ed., *Paul and His Theology* (Leiden: Brill, 2006) 21-44.

63. The case was pressed earlier, particularly by Munck, *Paul,* and Jervell, *The Unknown Paul* chs. 3-4 — including the provocative assertion, 'If you interpret Paul solely by

pel have not been adequately appreciated within historic Christianity and ignored within historic Judaism. On this point not least, Paul needs to be listened to afresh, and in his own terms.[64]

e. Eschatological Apostleship

If we are to understand the first generation of Christianity adequately, it is of crucial importance that we take into account the eschatological temper and perspective of the first believers. For they believed that in Jesus Messiah the new age had dawned — not just *a* new age, but *the final* age (*eschaton* = 'last') — in which the ultimate promises of God and hopes for Israel would be realized. As we saw earlier,[65] this focused on two features: Jesus' resurrection as the beginning of the general/final resurrection; and the soon-coming return of Jesus as manifestly Messiah and Lord. This emphasis has hardly appeared again in our tracing the earliest expansion, which took the new movement out of Judea and beyond the eastern seaboard of the Mediterranean — presumably because Luke chose not to highlight this eschatological motivation, which we may assume to have been a factor in that expansion, beyond the echoes in old traditional forms that he took over (Acts 2.17; 3.19-21).

With Paul, however, we can see how this eschatological perspective shaped his understanding of his calling as an apostle — again, not from what Luke tells us of Paul, but from his own letters.

- He recalls how the Thessalonian believers had 'turned to God from idols to serve the living and true God and to await his Son from the heavens' (1 Thess. 1.9-10; as in Acts 3.19-21).
- He seems to have believed that he would still be alive when Jesus returned: 'we who are alive, who are left until the coming *(parousia)* of the Lord . . .'

---

means of his letters you easily lose Paul the Jew. It [the picture of Paul the Jew] has, however, been preserved in the oral tradition that lies behind the Acts of the Apostles' (59); though see above, §29.2b. S. Grindheim, 'Apostate Turned Prophet: Paul's Prophetic Self-Understanding, with Special Reference to Galatians 3.10-12', *NTS* 53 (2007) 545-65, puts the charge into reverse: Paul understood the majority of his fellow Jews, including himself as a Pharisee, as apostates from the God of Israel.

64. See further my 'Paul: Apostate or Apostle of Israel?'; also 'The Jew Paul and His Meaning for Israel', in U. Schnelle and T. Söding, eds., *Paulinische Christologie. Exegetische Beiträge,* H. Hübner FS (Göttingen: Vandenhoeck und Ruprecht, 2000) 32-46; reprinted in T. Linafelt, ed., *A Shadow of Glory: Reading the New Testament after the Holocaust* (New York: Routledge, 2002) 201-15.

65. See above, §23.4a, f.

(1 Thess. 4.15); similarly, 1 Cor. 15.51: 'we will not all die, but we will all be changed'.

- Christ's resurrection was the 'first-fruits of those who have died', that is, the beginning of the (general/final) resurrection (1 Cor. 15.20, 23).
- He encouraged his converts in Corinth to refrain from marriage, because 'the time is short', 'the form of this world is passing away' (1 Cor. 7.29, 31).[66]
- He believed that 'the night is nearly over, and the day [of complete salvation] is near' (Rom. 13.12).

That this perspective shaped Paul's understanding of his apostleship[67] is clearest from three passages in particular:

(1) 1 Cor. 4.9: 'it seems to me that God has put us apostles on display as the grand finale [*eschatous apedeixen*], as those doomed to die [*epithanatious*], because we have been made a spectacle [*theatron*] in the eyes of the world, of angels, and of humankind' (Thiselton). Here he takes up 'the metaphor of a great pageant, in which criminals, prisoners, or professional gladiators process to the gladiatorial ring, with the apostles bringing up the rear as those who must fight to the death'.[68] In other words, he conceives of the whole sweep of history, or of God's programme for the world, as climaxing in the acts of the apostles. The apostles constitute the last act on the stage of cosmic history (watched also by angels). The imagery is somewhat vainglorious, though the imagery is hardly of a 'stage triumph'; in the terms of the metaphor they have been 'condemned to death' *(epithanatios)* in the eyes of the watching cosmos; their public execution would 'bring the curtain down' on the pageant of history.

(2) Rom. 11.13-15: 'I am speaking to you Gentiles. So then, inasmuch as I am apostle to the Gentiles, I magnify my ministry, in the hope that I might provoke my kindred to jealousy, and might save some of them. For if their rejection means reconciliation for the world, what shall their acceptance mean other than

---

66. See below, §32 n. 257.

67. In my earlier treatment of Paul's 'eschatological apostleship' (*Jesus and the Spirit* 111-13), I acknowledged the stimulus I had received from A. Fridrichsen, *The Apostle and His Message* (Uppsala, 1947) — 'this idea that an *apostolate* is to stand in the centre of the eschatologic development between the resurrection and return of the Messiah' (4); O. Cullmann, *Christ and Time* (London: SCM, ³1962) 157-66; and Munck, *Paul* 36-55, though their interpretation was too heavily dependent on a very disputable interpretation of 2 Thess. 2.6-7 (see below, §31 n. 291).

68. Thiselton, *1 Corinthians* 359; see further Schrage, *1 Korinther* 1.340-42. V. H. R. Nguyen, 'The Identification of Paul's Spectacle of Death Metaphor in 1 Corinthians 4.9', *NTS* 53 (2007) 489-501, suggests that the metaphor is drawn more from the Roman spectacle of executing condemned criminals within the arena.

life from the dead?' This is a passage to which we shall return shortly. Here the point to note is Paul's hope and expectation for his apostolic ministry: he pressed forward with his mission to the Gentiles, not because he believed his own people had been cast off by God, and therefore had turned to the Gentiles in despair of his own people; rather, his hope was that his success as apostle to the Gentiles would 'provoke his kindred to jealousy' and bring them to the faith which he preached. In Paul's perspective that 'acceptance' by and of his own people would mean something still more wonderful than 'reconciliation for the world' — in fact, nothing less than 'life from the dead', that is, the final resurrection at the end of the age/history.[69] In other words, Paul hoped that his own mission would trigger the end events, including the coming of the deliverer out of Zion (11.26). That was why it had such overwhelming priority for him.

(3) Col. 1.24: 'Now I rejoice in my sufferings for your sake, and I fill up what is lacking of the afflictions of the Christ in my flesh for the sake of his body, which is the church'. Here Paul, or his co-writer, probably takes up the imagery of Christ's sufferings and death as the eschatological tribulation (commonly referred to as 'the messianic woes') expected as a key antecedent to the age to come.[70] Paul himself had no qualms about the thought of sharing Christ's sufferings,[71] or indeed of himself in some measure fulfilling the role of the Servant of Yahweh.[72] The logic of a suffering still being shared, of course, is of a suffering not yet ended, incomplete. The writer of Colossians, however, is bold enough to regard Paul's apostolic sufferings as actually completing, 'filling up' this *hysterēma* ('lack' or 'deficiency'), with the corollary that the work of redemption/salvation would then be complete.[73] Here again the claim smacks of a vainglorious exaltation of Paul's role.[74] But it is simply

69. 'The eschatological force here is put beyond dispute by the *ek nekrōn,* which elsewhere always denotes resurrection. [And] the rhetorical structure demands that the final phrase should describe something which outstrips the earlier . . . ; here "life from the dead" presented as something more wonderful still than "reconciliation of the world"' (Dunn, *Romans* 658, where I also note that most commentators agree that final resurrection is in view here); see further D. J. Moo, *The Epistle to the Romans* (Grand Rapids: Eerdmans, 1996) 694-96; B. Witherington, *Paul's Letter to the Romans* (Grand Rapids: Eerdmans, 2004) 269.

70. For details see *Jesus Remembered* §11.4c and 395.

71. Particularly Rom. 8.17; 2 Cor. 4.10-12; Phil. 3.10-12; see further my *Theology of Paul* §18.5.

72. See above, §25.3d.

73. See further my *Colossians and Philemon* 114-16; H. Stettler, 'An Interpretation of Colossians 1:24 in the Framework of Paul's Mission Theology', in Ådna and Kvalbein, eds., *The Mission of the Early Church* 185-208; J. L. Sumney, '"I Fill Up What Is Lacking in the Afflictions of Christ": Paul's Vicarious Suffering in Colossians', *CBQ* 68 (2006) 664-80.

74. 'A theologically untenable glorification of the apostle by one of his followers' (H. Hübner, *EDNT* 3.110); others in my *Colossians and Philemon* 116.

the most striking expression of Paul's conviction regarding the importance of his apostolic mission. It was this last apostolic act on the stage of cosmic history which would complete God's purpose in history and trigger 'the consummation of all things'.[75]

It is difficult for us who read such language nearly twenty centuries later — especially when neither the end of history nor the coming of Christ has taken place — to enter with much sympathy into such a conception of Paul's apostolic role. But we need to make the attempt, since it presumably provided much of the motivation and energy which brought about such major results and such lasting effects. Paul's eschatology was integral to his sense of apostolic mission. At the same time, it should always be recalled that the decisive eschatological consideration for Paul was not what was still to happen but what God had already done in and through Christ, particularly in raising him from the dead. That was the eschatological act which determined all else.[76]

f. Church Founder

Despite the final qualification, the last section has left Paul a rather distant and somewhat unnerving figure; the history of those (sects) who looked for an imminent coming of Christ and end of the world hardly inspires confidence in one whose driving force was such an eschatological perspective. It is important, therefore, to recall one other fundamental aspect of Paul's apostolic mission — to found (or plant) churches. This is clearest in 1 Cor. 9.1-2: 'Am I not an apostle? Have I not seen our Lord? . . . If to others I am not an apostle, at least I am to you; for you are the seal of my apostleship in the Lord'. Here the authority of the 'apostle' is very much tied in to the apostle's role in establishing a church: Paul was not apostle to others because he had not converted them, had not founded their churches; but he was to the Corinthians because it was through his evangelism that the church of Corinth had come into existence.[77] In other passages in the Corinthian letters Paul's conviction that he had been commissioned as a church-planting missionary comes to repeated expression:

75. Schnabel's assertion that 'Paul never states that his own missionary work has a central significance for God's plan of salvation for the last days and for the return of Jesus' (*Mission* 945, also 1295-96) has only the controversial 2 Thess. 2.6-7 in view (see n. 67 above).

76. 'Paul's gospel was eschatological not because of what he still hoped would happen, but because of what he believed had already happened' (Dunn *Theology of Paul* 465).

77. N. H. Taylor, 'Apostolic Identity and the Conflicts in Corinth and Galatia', in S. E. Porter, ed., *Paul and His Opponents* (Leiden: Brill, 2005) 99-127, argues that Paul emphasized his founding apostleship to the Galatians and Corinthians in order to regain oversight and authority over these churches.

- 1 Cor. 3.5-15 — 'like a skilled master builder' he laid the foundation;
- 1 Cor. 15.10-11 — he worked harder than the other apostles to bring his audiences to faith;
- 2 Cor. 5.20 — he saw his role as an 'ambassador for Christ'.[78]

This ties in to the agreement to which Paul was party in Jerusalem: that he (and Barnabas) would be responsible for the Gentiles (Gentile believers) (Gal. 2.9). As already noted, Paul did not regard his apostolic commission as something very general; rather, it was specific — to the Gentiles. So it was to that extent limited, limited to the churches for which he was responsible, and Paul seems to have accepted that it was so limited. We will have to return to this subject a little later.[79] Here, however, it is worth noting the symbiotic relation between apostle and church which Paul thus worked with. So when he says that 'God appointed in the church first apostles' (1 Cor. 12.28), he was most likely *not* thinking of the universal church and of apostles with universal authority.[80] Rather he was most likely thinking of 'the church' in the sense that the Corinthian believers came together to be the church in Corinth (11.18; 12.27). The 'apostles' of 12.28 were the apostles who had established them as believers, brought them together to be the body of Christ in Corinth. The apostles appointed to the church in Corinth were, in the first place, Paul himself, and possibly also Apollos.[81] Similarly, Paul describes Andronicus and (his wife?) Junia as 'outstanding among the apostles'. We note that Andronicus and Junia are the only apostles Paul mentions in regard to the Roman Christians, the most likely explanation of which is that Andronicus and Junia were the apostles who founded the church (or one or more of the churches) in Rome.[82]

As a founding apostle, Paul saw it to be his mission to 'lay the foundation' (1 Cor. 3.10); 'that foundation is Jesus Christ' (3.11). In so saying, Paul no doubt

78. See further Schnabel, *Mission* 945-82; S. C. Barton, 'Paul as Missionary and Pastor', in Dunn, ed., *The Cambridge Companion to St. Paul* 34-48 (here 35-39).

79. See further below, §29.4b.

80. 'The apostle exercised authority within a community not as an "apostle of the universal church", but as founder of that community' (Dunn, *Jesus and the Spirit* 274). See also particularly J. Hainz, *Ekklesia. Strukturen paulinischer Gemeinde-Theologie und Gemeinde-Ordnung* (Regensburg: Pustet, 1972) 252-55; and §30.1 below.

81. But see n. 49 above.

82. See below, §33.2b. On Junia as a female name — so Andronicus and Junia possibly the only husband and wife among 'all the apostles' of 1 Cor. 15.7 — see now particularly E. J. Epp, *Junia: The First Woman Apostle* (Minneapolis: Fortress, 2005), with extensive bibliography. For the meaning of the phrase *episēmoi en tois apostolois* as meaning 'outstanding among the apostles', rather than 'well known to the apostles' (as argued by M. H. Burer and D. B. Wallace, 'Was Junia Really an Apostle? A Re-examination of Rom 16.7', *NTS* 47 [2001] 76-91), see Epp 72-78 and Jewett, *Romans* 963.

had in mind the gospel of Christ, which he had been called to proclaim. And this gospel would no doubt have included both the creedal formulae which summed up the beliefs in Christ crucified and risen and the sort of teaching about the life and mission of Jesus which Paul had learned from Peter (Gal. 1.18); as noted already, the many echoes of Jesus tradition which we find in Paul's letters are surely to be regarded as references and allusions to the deposit of Jesus tradition which Paul had passed on when he laid the foundation of a new church.[83]

If then Paul's eschatological motivation seems strange today, we should also recall that it was the same motivation that planted Christianity so enduringly in the Aegean area and beyond, and that it was his apostolic mission in nurturing these churches which established so much of the character of Christianity as it has endured in his letters to these churches. His role as apostle to the Gentiles was thus not simply for the first generation of Christianity but for all generations to follow.

29.4. Paul's Strategy

Given Paul's understanding of his apostolic commission, how did he expect to fulfill it? What was the vision which he pursued?

a. 'From Jerusalem in a Circle' (Rom. 15.19)

In ch. 15, towards the end of his letter to the Romans, Paul takes the opportunity briefly to review his mission thus far:

> [18]. . . what Christ has accomplished through me for the obedience of the Gentiles, by word and deed, by the power of signs and wonders, [19]by the power of God's Spirit; so that from Jerusalem and in a circle round to Illyricum I have completed the gospel of Christ. . . . [23]Now, since I no longer have scope in these regions . . . [28]I will go by way of you to Spain.

Several recent studies have linked this passage to Isa. 66.19-20, and seen in the latter the clue to Paul's strategic vision:[84]

---

83. See *Jesus Remembered* 182 n. 48 and §21.4d above; also Barnett, *Birth* 120-26.

84. R. D. Aus, 'Paul's Travel Plans to Spain and the "Full Number" of the Gentiles of Rom. 11.25', *NovT* 21 (1979) 232-62; Riesner, *Paul's Early Period* 241-53; J. M. Scott, *Paul and the Nations* (WUNT 84; Tübingen: Mohr Siebeck, 1995) 135-62, who make reference back to the unpublished thesis of W. P. Bowers, *Studies in Paul's Understanding of His Mission* (Cambridge PhD, 1976).

[19]From them I will send survivors to the nations,[85] to Tarshish, Put, and Lud, Meshech, Tubal and Javan, and the coastlands far away that have not heard of my fame or seen my glory; and they shall declare my glory among the nations. [20]They shall bring all your kindred from all the nations as an offering to the Lord . . . to my holy mountain in Jerusalem.

There are three noteworthy features of this latter text. (1) It is the first and only time in the Hebrew Bible that a missionary outreach *to* the nations is envisaged. The prophetic oracle in fact is a variation on the promises that the scattered exiles of Israel will be restored to their homeland (66.20)[86] and that there will be an eschatological pilgrimage of the nations to Zion (cf. 66.12).[87] But this form of it is unique: a mission to the nations envisaged as the catalyst for the return of Israel and the pilgrimage of the nations. As the only verse in his Scriptures which entertained that prospect, it is likely that Isa. 66.19 influenced Paul at least to some extent: it alone foreshadowed the mission to which he had committed himself.[88]

(2) This likelihood is strengthened when we appreciate that the principal direction of travel envisaged in the nations listed in Isa. 66.19 is roughly the direction of Paul's mission. In Rom. 15.19 Paul seems to regard his mission thus far as an arc stretching from Jerusalem to Illyricum.[89] Or perhaps we should speak of the first half of an arc,[90] since he clearly envisages a further sweep of the arc, further westwards to include Spain (15.28). The identification of the nations listed in Isa. 66.19 is disputed, but the degree of overlap with Paul's actual itinerary is at least intriguing — at the very least moving from Cilicia, through Asia Minor, through Macedonia/Greece and to the farthest west.[91] Perhaps we

---

85. Those in view are presumably 'survivors' from the judgment on the nations (66.15-16), as in Isa. 45.20 ('survivors of the nations'); see C. Westermann, *Isaiah 40–66* (OTL; London: SCM, 1969) 425; Riesner, *Paul's Early Period* — 'this is the only time, apart from the Servant prophecies, that the Old Testament speaks about proclamation to the Gentiles by human agents' (248).

86. The references are listed in *Jesus Remembered* 393 n. 57.

87. The references are listed in *Jesus Remembered* 394-95 nn. 70, 71, with bibliography. In Isaiah 66 the allusion to 'the wealth of the nations' (v. 12) evokes this theme, since it clearly alludes to the hope that the wealth of the nations will come to restored Israel (Isa. 45.14; 60.5, 11; 61.6).

88. This is Riesner's thesis: 'that Paul read this text as being fulfilled in his own activity' (*Paul's Early Period* 246); 'a prophecy of this sort [Isa. 66.19] must have attracted Paul's attention' (248).

89. See below, §31 n. 116 and §32 n. 482.

90. 'In a circle' can denote not only a complete circle but also a half circle (Riesner, *Paul's Early Period* 242).

91. Reviewed by Riesner, *Paul's Early Period* 250-53. Riesner thinks the most likely identifications are Tarshish = Tarsus, Put = Libya or Cilicia, Lud = Lydia in Asia Minor, Meshech = Cappadocia or Mysia, Tubal = the Caucasus or Bithynia, Javan = Greece or Macedonia, distant is-

should entertain the possibility that this was already the vision which inspired Paul to engage in the earliest mission westwards from Antioch.[92]

(3) Furthermore, it is hardly far-fetched to deduce that when in the same context Paul likens his hoped-for success as his priestly offering of the Gentiles (Rom. 15.16), he was playing on the hope of Isa. 66.20, where it is the diaspora Jews who form the eschatological offering.[93] Paul's Greek could also be understood to speak of an offering made *by* the Gentiles, thus further evoking the varied hopes of the eschatological pilgrimage of Gentiles to Zion to worship there and of the wealth of the nations coming to Jerusalem. It can hardly be accidental that in the same context Paul speaks of the collection which he intended to bring to Jerusalem (as his priority between the two half-arcs of his mission), and does so in terms of the Gentiles sharing their resources with (the poor among the saints in) Jerusalem (Rom. 15.25-27). The collection, in other words, was probably part of Paul's grand strategy to fulfill the mission of Israel to the nations and to fulfill Israel's eschatological hopes in regard to the nations.[94]

James Scott has elaborated the basic thesis here by arguing that a further influence on Paul's missionary strategy was the table of nations in Genesis 10. As already noted, in Gal. 3.8 Paul takes up the language of Gen. 12.3, with the promise of blessing for 'all the nations'. Such talk of 'all the nations' would most naturally evoke the extensive list of nations descended from the three sons of Noah (Shem, Ham and Japheth) according to Gen. 10.1-32. Similarly, when Paul talks of 'the full number of the nations' (Rom. 11.25-26) the thought would probably be of the 70 or 72 nations in the world, in accordance with Deut. 32.8 and Genesis 10.[95] Scott also draws attention to Ezek. 5.5, with its description of Jerusalem as 'in the midst of the nations and the countries in a circle around her', and sees here further influence on Paul's understanding of his mission as 'in a circle' 'from Jerusalem'.[96] The thesis which emerges is that Paul saw his mission as focused on the sphere of Japheth, since the territory traditionally ascribed to Japheth and his sons included Asia Minor and Greece, with Spain as its westernmost portion. 'Interestingly enough, this migration of the sons of Japheth corre-

---

lands = the farthest west. He notes that Tarshish was long viewed with virtual unanimity as Tartessus in western Spain (250), but also that no single writer from antiquity made this equation.

92. Hengel and Schwemer, *Paul* 265; see also 174-76.

93. See also Riesner, *Paul's Early Period* 247.

94. See further Aus, 'Travel Plans' 241-42; Riesner, *Paul's Early Period* 249-50. If part of Paul's motivation for the collection was this eschatological scenario, then it needs to be recalled that he envisaged his mission to Spain as taking place *after* the delivery of the collection to Jerusalem. At the very least, then, we would have to conclude that Paul did not envisage a clear ordering of the final events.

95. Scott, *Paul and the Nations* 135.

96. Scott, *Paul and the Nations* 138-39.

sponds to the intended scope and actual direction of Paul's mission to the nations as described in Romans 15'.[97]

Mention could be made here also of the quotation from Ps. 19.4 in Rom. 10.18 as part of Paul's apologetic for the Christian mission: 'their sound has gone out into all the earth, and their words to the end of the inhabited world'. The use of Ps. 19.4 here is no doubt hyperbolic,[98] but it reflects something of the scope of Paul's vision and strategy, and something of his conviction that both were nearing completion. The language reflects both the 'end of the earth' dimension of Paul's commission[99] and his sense that he had already 'completed *(peplērōkenai)* the gospel of Christ' (Rom. 15.19).[100]

Without subscribing to all details of the theses of Riesner and Scott[101] — given the data, firm conclusions are hardly possible — it is nevertheless likely that Isa. 66.19 provides a shaft of light which illuminates both the rationale of Paul's mission and the compulsion he experienced to reach Spain. If Spain did indeed complete the (half-)circle from Jerusalem, as indicating the limits of Japheth's territory, Paul's compulsion to reach Spain meshes with his hope of winning 'the full number of the Gentiles' to faith (Rom. 11.25) and thus of triggering the climax of God's purpose in history and the resurrection of the dead (11.13-15).

b. 'Where Christ Has Not Been Named' (Rom. 15.20)

The passage from Romans 15 cited at the beginning of §29.4a (15.18-19) continues:

> [19]. . . I have completed the gospel of Christ, [20]thus making it my aim to preach the gospel where Christ has not been named, lest I build on another's foundation.

This appears to be a second principle in Paul's strategy: a commitment to pioneer evangelism, to pursue his mission only in virgin territory. This is what he understood to be his role as 'apostle to the Gentiles'. His success in laying the founda-

97. Scott, *Paul and the Nations* 142. As to when this strategy first occurred to Paul, Scott also argues that Paul already understood his mission in these terms when the division of mission responsibility was agreed in Jerusalem (Gal. 2.7-9); that is, Paul understood his mission territorially — to the nations of Japheth — while Peter's jurisdiction may have included the whole territory of Shem (cf. 1 Pet. 5.13), not just Jerusalem and Judah; which could also explain the conflicts over missionary jurisdiction, since the borders between Shem and Japheth were not clear (149-62).

98. See further my *Romans* 624; Moo, *Romans* 667.

99. See above, §25.3d.

100. The language 'probably reflects his [Paul's] conviction of the pressing imminence of the parousia, leaving all too little time to take the gospel to where it had not so far been heard' (Dunn, *Romans* 864; with further bibliography); Moo, *Romans* 893-94, is doubtful.

101. See, e.g., the critique of Schnabel, *Mission* 1295-99.

tion of the church in Corinth was an example of what he had in mind (1 Cor. 3.10-11). In that passage it is also clear that Paul did not object to others building on the foundation he had laid or watering the seed he had planted — alluding to the follow-up mission of Apollos (3.5-9). The principle was rather intended to distinguish his missionary strategy and to discourage any thought on the part of others of trying to re-lay the foundation of his churches.

The importance of the principle for Paul on this point is clearest in his strong assertions in 2 Cor. 10.13-16:

> [13]We will not boast beyond the proper limits *(eis ta ametra)* but only in accord with the measure of the assignment *(to metron tou kanonos)* which God has apportioned *(emerisen)* to us as our measure *(metrou)*, to reach out even as far as you *(achri kai hymōn)*. [14]For it is not as though in reaching out to you we are overextending ourselves, for it was precisely as far as you *(achri kai hymōn)* that we came with the gospel of Christ. [15]We are not boasting beyond the proper limits *(eis ta ametra)*, in the labours of others; our hope is rather that as your faith grows, our mission will be abundantly enlarged in accordance with our assignment *(kata ton kanona)*, [16]so that we may proclaim the good news in areas beyond you, without boasting in what has been accomplished in someone else's assignment *(en allotriō kanoni)*.

The key word is *kanōn,* which is susceptible to a wide range of interpretation.[102] The most likely alternatives are 'sphere of activity'[103] or 'assignment'.[104] The ambiguity reflects the ambiguity of the agreement reached in Jerusalem with the pillar apostles — 'we to/for the Gentiles, and they to/for the circumcision' (Gal. 2.7-9).[105] As Paul interpreted his calling to be an apostle as 'apostle to the Gentiles', so he interpreted the Jerusalem agreement as recognizing that his assignment or sphere of activity was the non-Jewish nations.[106] 2 Cor. 10.13-16 spells out clearly what that agreement meant for Paul.

---

102. The recent commentary of Harris lists over a dozen ways in which the word has been rendered (*2 Corinthians* 711-12).

103. Or 'province' — LSJ, NRSV, REB, NJB; C. K. Barrett, *2 Corinthians* (BNTC; London: Black, 1973) 265-66.

104. BDAG 507-508; Harris, *2 Corinthians* 712-13. V. P. Furnish, *2 Corinthians* (AB 32A; New York: Doubleday, 1984) 471-72, prefers 'jurisdiction' as embracing 'not only the "right" or "authority" to do something but also the "sphere" within which that authority is to be exercised' (471); but Scott, *Paul and the Nations* 141, 159-62, sees the term as a straight claim to 'territorial jurisdiction' over the Corinthian church (160).

105. See above, §27.3d.

106. 'Ambiguity' is probably the wrong word; Paul plays on the scope of the meaning of the *kanōn* and of the Jerusalem agreement, as embracing the territorial dimension of his assignment, when it became necessary to defend his assignment in territorial terms.

1. The scope of his assignment/assigned sphere determined the scope of any possible boasting, that is, presumably, boasting 'in the Lord' (10.17), in what God was doing through him in accord with his commissioning (10.8, 13).

2. The Corinthians themselves were proof of the extent of his assignment; they indicated and proved the scope of his assigned activity (10.14). The thought here is very similar to that in 1 Cor. 9.1-2: 'If to others I am not an apostle, at least I am to you; for you are the seal of my apostleship in the Lord'.

3. He did not seek to trespass on the assignment or in the assigned sphere of others (10.15-16). The implication, of course, is that he resented any attempt by others to interfere with his assignment or to trespass on his sphere of activity. It was precisely such interference and trespass in Corinth that had occasioned this strong statement of one of his cardinal principles — as the following chapter (2 Corinthians 11) in particular makes very clear.[107] And probably it was the equivalent interference and trespass in the Galatian churches which had crystallized this strong interpretation of the Jerusalem agreement so carefully enunciated in Gal. 2.7-9.

4. He saw such bases as the one he had established at Corinth as launching pads for further missionary outreach, in accordance with his assignment, that is, presumably, for further pioneer missionary work, but with the support of the Corinthians as they continued to grow in their faith (10.15-16).

In short, 2 Cor. 10.13-16 nicely outlines the principles which had guided Paul in the mission he carried out as briefly recalled in Rom. 15.19.

The only qualification to this principle (beyond 1 Cor. 3.5-8, if that is a qualification) is Paul's slight embarrassment in writing to those who were already Christians in Rome: he was keen to minister and to preach the gospel to the Roman believers (Rom. 1.11, 15), even though that would mean building on someone else's foundations (15.20)! Hence the immediate self-correction in 1.11-12: 'I long to see you, that I may share with you some spiritual gift so that you may be strengthened; or rather, so that there may be mutual encouragement among you through each other's faith, both yours and mine'. Paul evidently hesitated to imply that 'the direction of ministry' was one way, as though he was Rome's apostle; rather, ministry would be mutual as between fellow believers.[108]

---

107. It was evidently the 'boasting' of the 'false apostles' in Corinth (11.12-13, 18) which provoked Paul to his own 'boasting' (10.8, 13-17; 11.10, 16-18, 30; 12.1, 5, 6, 9).

108. See further my *Romans* 30-31, 33-34; J. A. Fitzmyer, *Romans* (AB 33; New York: Doubleday, 1993) 248-49; Moo, *Romans* 60. Such embarrassment is much preferable to the suggestion that Paul did not regard the groups in Rome as constituting a properly founded 'church' (as argued by G. Klein, 'Paul's Purpose in Writing the Epistle to the Romans', in K. P.

This too reflects something of the ambiguity of Paul's self-understanding: as 'apostle to the nations', as responsible for the Gentile mission/believers (Gal. 2.7-9), did his responsibility not embrace all Gentile churches, or churches in which Gentile believers were in the majority? It was such ambiguity which resulted in or is reflected by so many of the tensions within the churches of the Gentile mission.

c. Jew First but Also Gentile (Rom. 1.16)

Paul expresses the theological rationale behind his commission in apparently inconsistent terms — the gospel, *his* gospel, as 'the power of God for salvation, to all who believe, to Jew first but also to Greek' (Rom. 1.16). It is important, however, to recognize that this was not simply a matter of practical tactics — reaching out to Gentiles through the Jewish communities — which it was, as we shall see (§29.5b). It was much more a strategic and principled concern: that the gospel was not *de novo, ex nihilo,* but rather the climax of God's saving purpose for Israel and through Israel.

This motif is implicit throughout Paul's letters: the Jesus proclaimed as Lord is Jesus the Christ, the Messiah of Israel's hopes and expectations; the righteousness which the gospel revealed is God fulfilling the obligation he took upon himself in creating the nations and in calling a people to be his own;[109] Paul's mission as apostle to the Gentiles was in implementation of Israel's mission to be a light to the nations;[110] Gentile believers were also the seed of Abraham (Gal. 3; Rom. 4) and were being grafted into the olive tree that was Israel, sustained by its root ([the election of and promises to] the patriarchs).[111] It is true that as a result of Israel's failure to receive the gospel, the *chronological* sequence had changed: 'the full number of the Gentiles' would come in before the salvation of 'all Israel' (Rom. 11.11-15, 25-26). But the *theological* sequence remained unchanged: the blessings now experienced by Gentile believers are those of Israel (9.3-5); 'the gifts and the call of God [to Israel] are irrevocable' (11.29).

This motif in Paul is sometimes questioned or obscured on the basis that his gospel was not defined in terms of a *salvation-history continuity* with the Israel of the past; it was rather defined in terms of an *apocalyptic discontinuity* with the

---

Donfried, ed., *The Romans Debate* [Peabody: Hendrickson, 1991] 29-43; cf. Watson, *Paul, Judaism and the Gentiles* [¹1986] 94-98), since apostles were already associated with the Roman groups (Andronicus and Junia — 16.7) and since he would then be doing precisely what he so fiercely objected to in Galatians and 2 Corinthians 10–13 (see further Dunn, *Romans* liv-lvii). See further below, §33 n. 30.

109. See further *Theology of Paul* §14.2 and below, §33.3a at n. 90.
110. See above, §25.3d(3).
111. The reference is to Rom. 11.16-24; see my *Romans* 659-69 (on 11.16).

past, involving antinomy with what Israel had counted important, and the wholly new start of a new creation.[112] Such an objection reads the contrasts of Paul's rhetoric as statements of theological principle. But metaphors like the ones just mentioned — seed/descendants of Abraham, a growing and maturing olive tree — cannot be read except as elements in an ongoing story, the story of Israel (Romans 9–11), the story of God's unfolding purpose for Israel and his creation.[113] 'Apocalypse', after all, emerged as a genre in Israel's history not only to highlight the complete discontinuity between the present and what is to come but also as the climax of Israel's hopes and expectations for itself and the nations.

The point perhaps becomes clearest in the language of 'mystery', first used in the Pauline corpus in Rom. 11.25. Paul's usage is drawn entirely from Jewish apocalyptic language, where 'mystery' has the sense of divine secrets now revealed by divine agency.[114] The mystery in view here answers precisely to the puzzle of Gentiles coming to faith before (ethnic) Israel: the mystery now revealed is that God had always intended it so; that the 'hardening' come over Israel is only temporary, 'until the full number of the Gentiles has come in'. But that was simply an elucidation of the larger mystery, the mystery of God's purpose 'which has been hidden from the ages and from the generations': that as the climax of his saving purpose for humankind, 'God wished to make known what is the wealth of the glory of this mystery among the nations, which is, Christ in you, the hope of glory' (Col. 1.25-27). Or as Ephesians went on to put it, the mystery of God's purpose had been to bring in the Gentiles as 'fellow heirs, members of the same body, and sharers in the promise in Christ Jesus through the gospel' (Eph. 3.6). It was this mystery which had been revealed to Paul and the saints, and whose implementation had been entrusted to Paul. It was in consciousness of his role in the final part of this cosmic drama that he pursued his calling so urgently (Col. 1.25-29; Eph. 3.1-12). That Colossians and Ephesians at this point simply spell out what was the key 'mystery' for Paul more clearly than Paul's earlier usage[115] is entirely likely,[116] for Paul saw his commission to preach

112. Particularly Martyn, *Galatians;* see further below, §31 n. 381.

113. It is noticeable that the apocalyptic thesis has been based principally on Galatians, since it is much harder to argue it from Romans.

114. First used in Dan. 2.18-19, 27-30 and 4.9 (Theod.), but typical in the classic apocalyptic writings — e.g., *1 En.* 41.1; 46.2; 103.2; 104.10, 12; 106.19; *2 En.* 24.3; *4 Ezra* 10.38; 12.36-38; 14.5; in the DSS, e.g., 1QS 3.23; 4.18; 9.18; 11.3, 5, 19; 1QH 1.21; 2.13; 4.27-28; 7.27; 11.10; 12.13; 1QpHab 7.5, 8, 14; other references in my *Romans* 678. See the still valuable treatment of R. E. Brown, *The Semitic Background of the Term "Mystery" in the New Testament* (FBBS 21; Philadelphia: Fortress, 1968); and cf. J. Coppens, '"Mystery" in the Theology of Saint Paul and Its Parallels at Qumran', in J. Murphy-O'Connor and J. H. Charlesworth, eds., *Paul and the Dead Sea Scrolls* (London: Chapman, 1968) 132-56.

115. As does Rom. 16.25-27, best regarded as an addendum to the letter.

116. Coppens rightly concludes that the use of 'mystery' in the Pauline corpus is not

Christ among the Gentiles as a 'revelation', an 'apocalypse' (Gal. 1.12, 16); and it was in part the mystery revealed in Rom. 11.25 which gave him the reassurance that his mission to the Gentiles was not in discontinuity with God's purpose for Israel but rather was God's way of enacting that purpose (11.11-15).[117] In short, the theology of 'mystery' revealed is not of God's ongoing purpose disrupted and changed but of insight given as to how that purpose is to be fulfilled.

d. A Challenge to the Power of Rome?

Was part of Paul's strategy to build up his churches as a society alternative to the imperial order of Rome? Did he intend his proclamation of Jesus as a challenge to the authority of the emperor? Such a case has been made strongly in recent years.[118] And the logic of the thesis is fairly obvious.[119] (1) It can be argued that in establishing *ekklēsiai* ('churches') in different cities, Paul saw himself as founding a structure to counter the official *ekklēsiai* ('assemblies') of these cit-

---

confined to the role of the Gentiles in God's purpose ('Mystery' 154), but he underestimates the importance of this mystery for Paul's self-understanding, not least as implied in Rom. 11.25.

117. Kim's attempt to refer the unveiling of the 'mystery' of Rom. 11.25-26 to Paul's Damascus conversion experience (*Origin of Paul's Gospel* 95-99, also *Paul and the New Perspective* ch. 7) ignores the implication of the structure of Romans 9–11, that 11.25-26 is presented as the resolution of a long-felt anguish over Israel's failure to respond to the gospel (9.1-3), a failure which was hardly evident at the time of his conversion (see also Moo, *Romans* 714-15).

118. Particularly R. A. Horsley, ed., *Paul and Empire: Religion and Power in Roman Imperial Society* (Harrisburg: Trinity Press International, 1997); also *Paul and Politics: Ekklesia, Israel, Imperium, Interpretation* (Harrisburg: Trinity Press International, 2000); also *Paul and the Roman Imperial Order* (Harrisburg: Trinity Press International, 2004); 'Paul's Assembly in Corinth: An Alternative Society', in D. N. Schowalter and S. J. Friesen, eds., *Urban Religion in Roman Corinth* (HTS 53; Cambridge: Harvard University, 2005) 371-95. See also D. Georgi, *Theocracy in Paul's Praxis and Theology* (Minneapolis: Fortress, 1991); N. Elliott, *Liberating Paul: The Justice of God and the Politics of the Apostle* (Maryknoll: Orbis, 1994); B. Blumenfeld, *The Political Paul: Justice, Democracy and Kingship in a Hellenistic Framework* (JSNTS 210; Sheffield: Sheffield Academic, 2001); N. T. Wright, 'A Fresh Perspective on Paul', *BJRL* 83 (2001) 21-39; also *Paul: Fresh Perspectives* (London: SPCK, 2005) ch. 4; D. G. Horrell, ed., *The Imperial Cult and the New Testament* (= *JSNT* 27.3 [2005]). The situation is well illustrated by Crossan and Reed, *Paul, passim*: 'Imperial divinity was, quite simply, the ideology that held the Roman Empire together' (160). See also n. 330 below.

119. Neatly summarized by Horsley, *Paul and Empire* 1-8, and further 10-24. 'The starting point in recognizing that Paul was preaching an anti-imperial gospel is that much of his key language would have evoked echoes of the imperial cult and ideology'; 'Paul's anti-imperial use of imperial language and symbols' (140, 142); Paul's 'use of *sōtēria* . . . would have been understood as an alternative to that supposedly already effected by Augustus and his successors' (141). Similarly N. T. Wright, 'Paul's Gospel and Caesar's Empire', in Horsley, ed., *Paul and Politics* 160-83 (here 164-70).

ies. (2) Again, for Paul to describe his message as 'gospel' *(euangelion)* could well be seen as deliberately so described in opposition to the 'gospel' of Caesar. The peace brought by Christ (Rom. 5.1) was a more profound 'gospel' than the *pax Romana*. The challenge would be all the more explicit if Paul had derived this key term ('gospel') precisely from such Roman usage.[120] (3) Equally to hail Jesus as 'Lord', exalted to God's right hand and Lord over all earthly powers, could well be seen as a direct challenge to similar aspirations on the part of or assumed for the Roman emperor.[121] This would be all the more unavoidable in those cities where the emperor cult was already well established, such as Pisidian Antioch[122] and Ephesus.[123] Luke's portrayal of the mob's protest against Paul's preaching in Thessalonica fits well with what we might have guessed anyway: the complaint is that Paul and Silas 'are all acting contrary to the decrees of the emperor, saying that there is another king named Jesus' (Acts 17.7).

The point which has come out most strongly in recent study is that the imperial cult was widespread throughout the cities of Greece and Asia Minor — the very cities where Paul was most active.[124] More to the point, it pervaded public life and would have been encountered on a daily basis — in coinage, public in-

---

120. The argument has been long sustained by Strecker; see most recently his *Theology* 337-38; see also G. N. Stanton, 'Jesus and Gospel', *Jesus and Gospel* (Cambridge: Cambridge University, 2004) 9-62.

121. P. Oakes, *Philippians: From People to Letter* (SNTSMS 110; Cambridge: Cambridge University, 2001), fairly asks how the language of the Philippian hymn (Phil. 2.6-11, especially 9-11) would have been heard in the Roman veteran colony of Philippi, with its claim, in effect, that 'Christ has replaced the Emperor as the world's decisive power' (ch. 5). Similarly J. H. Hellerman, *Reconstructing Honor in Roman Philippi: Carmen Christi as Cursus Pudorum* (SNTS 132; Cambridge: Cambridge University, 2005) ch. 6. The ruler cult had 'taken off' with Augustus (Price, *Rituals and Power* 54-62), although of the Julio-Claudians, both Tiberius and Claudius resisted divine honours as absurd, while Gaius Caligula and Nero both demonstrated the absurdity of such a claim; see further D. L. Jones, 'Christianity and the Roman Imperial Cult', *ANRW* 2.23.2 (1980) 1024-32; M. Clauss, *Kaiser und Gott. Herrscherkult im römischen Reich* (Stuttgart: Teubner, 1999) 76-111; also Schnabel, *Mission* 617-21.

122. See above, §27 n. 47.

123. See below, §32.2a.

124. Price, *Rituals and Power,* in particular, has shown how widespread was the imperial cult in Asia Minor; the map on xxv, compared with the map on xxvi of non-imperial temples and theatres, is very striking (see further Price ch. 4; catalogue in 249-74). Note, for example, the presence of the imperial cult in cities mentioned in the NT — Adramyttium, Antioch in Pisidia, Assos, Attalia, Chios, Cnidus, Colossae, Cos, Derba, Ephesus, Hierapolis, Iconium, Laodicea, Miletus, Mitylene, Pergamum, Perge, Philadelphia, Rhodes, Samos, Sardis, Smyrna, Tarsus, Thyatira, Troas (cf. Klauck, *Religious Context* 324). See also S. J. Friesen, *Twice Neokoros: Ephesus, Asia and the Cult of the Flavian Imperial Family* (Leiden: Brill, 1993); B. W. Winter, 'Acts and Roman Religion: The Imperial Cult', *BAFCS* 2.93-103.

scriptions and statues, temples, processions, games and feasts.[125] In other words, it was impossible to ignore or escape the presence of the emperor cult and the challenge which it embodied to anyone who marched by a different drumbeat. The same point emerges when we recall that Roman society was built entirely on a patron-client structure.[126] If free men were to have realistic prospects of bettering their circumstances, they would have to gain the patronage of some more-established person, on whom they depended for subsidy (daily subsistence in the form of food or money) and to whom they would give their support.[127] These patrons in turn were themselves clients of a higher-status patron and would typically 'dance in attendance' on their patron first thing in the morning (the *salutatio*)[128] or accompany their patron on public occasions to form as impressive a retinue as possible.[129] At the top of a rapidly narrowing hierarchy sat the emperor himself, patron of the patrons. The provincial elite held their position as imperial clients and as such were also the principal sponsors of the imperial cult.

125. Most often cited are Price, *Rituals and Power* ch. 5, and P. Zanker, *The Power of Images in the Age of Augustus* (Ann Arbor: University of Michigan, 1988); both are excerpted in Horsley, ed., *Paul and Empire*. See also Klauck, *Religious Context* 288-330. See also §32 n. 78 below.

126. P. Garnsey and R. Saller, *The Roman Empire: Economy, Society and Culture* (Berkeley: University of California, 1987) 148-59, excerpted in Horsley, *Paul and Empire* 96-103; A. Wallace-Hadrill, 'Patronage in Roman Society: From Republic to Empire', in A. Wallace-Hadrill, ed., *Patronage in Ancient Society* (London: Routledge, 1989) 63-87; Chow, *Patronage and Power* 38-82, also excerpted in Horsley, *Paul and Empire* 104-25; brief treatments in *OCD*[3] 348 *(cliens)* and 1126-27 *(patronus);* Horsley, *Paul and Empire* 88-95; P. Lampe, 'Paul, Patrons and Clients', in J. P. Sampley, ed., *Paul in the Greco-Roman World: A Handbook* (Harrisburg: Trinity Press International, 2003) 488-523 (with extensive bibliography). Joubert stresses the importance of distinguishing between patronage and benefaction (*Paul as Benefactor* ch. 2). On the structure of ancient society see Stegemann and Stegemann, *Jesus Movement* 67-95.

127. We should take care, however, not to regard patronage as an all-pervasive phenomenon: 'Patrons did not establish client relationships with "the urban poor". They were great inferiors. They did so with those who possessed the same status as they did, but not their wealth, or with those who were their former slaves but were now their freedmen' (B. W. Winter, *Seek the Welfare of the City* [Grand Rapids: Eerdmans, 1994] 45-47); 'Ordinary citizens did not emerge in the sources as clients of the rich and powerful. In Rome the typical client was someone of moderate means or better' (Meggitt quoting Garnsey, *Famine* 84); 'the only form of patronage that had any impact on the life of the urban plebs was that of patronage by some members of the elite of *collegia . . .*' (*Poverty* 167-70).

128. '*Salutatio,* a formal greeting. . . . Etiquette required a client to attend in formal dress at his patron's house at dawn, to greet him and escort him to work, both for protection and for prestige. . . . His standing to some extent depended on the number and class of those attending him' (*OCD*[3] 1350).

129. B. W. Winter, *After Paul Left Corinth: The Influence of Secular Ethics and Social Change* (Grand Rapids: Eerdmans, 2001) 188-90.

Anyone who refused to work within that structure, as Paul did,[130] could readily be understood as seeking to build an alternative society or counter-structure.

We should not doubt, then, that there was a political dimension to Paul's gospel, and subversive overtones which would have been heard by guests at or visitors to early Christian meals and meetings, not to mention spies and agents of the local authorities, always on the lookout for subversive groups. However, the argument can be greatly oversold.

(1) To argue that Paul drew on the term *ekklēsia* deliberately as a counter to the political citizen assembly ignores two facts. First, political overtones did not attach exclusively to the term; it still retained the basic meaning 'assembly'.[131] Second, the greater influence on Paul was probably the LXX use of the term to translate the 'assembly of Yahweh/Israel *(qahal Yahweh/Israel)*', as indicated by Paul's frequent reference to 'the church(es) of God'.[132] To be sure, Roman authorities were always nervous about 'assemblies',[133] but the use of the word itself did not indicate any more than a gathering.[134]

(2) Similarly, the word *euangelion* (usually in the plural) was in wider use than the good news of Caesar;[135] and the decisive influence on Paul's choice of *euangelion* to denote his message probably came from elsewhere, that is, from the direct influence of Deutero-Isaiah's language on the early Christian tradition. I am thinking particularly of, first, the recollection that Jesus himself had understood his own mission in terms of Isa. 61.1 ('to bring good news [*euangelizasthai*] to the poor')[136] and, second, the direct influence of Isa. 52.7 and 61.1 on Paul himself, as indicated by his quotation of the former in Rom. 10.15, that is, in a passage explaining his understanding of the gospel commission.[137]

---

130. See below, §29.5d.

131. See below, §30.1.

132. Details in §30 n. 13.

133. Garnsey and Saller quote Trajan's observation to Pliny: 'Whatever name we may give for whatever reason to those who come together for a common purpose, political clubs emerge quickly from them' (Pliny, *Ep.* 10.34; *Roman Empire* 158).

134. P. A. Harland, *Associations, Synagogues, and Congregations* (Minneapolis: Fortress, 2003), observes that previous studies have tended to concentrate 'on the ways in which such assemblies were in tension with surrounding society to the neglect of evidence concerning how they continued to live *within* the polis and empire', and notes also the 'lack of evidence for any extensive, imperial-initiated persecution of Christians' in Roman Asia at the end of the first century (12, 13).

135. LSJ 705; *NDIEC* 3.13-14; other examples in Klauck, *Religious Context* 328-29.

136. See *Jesus Remembered* 448-49, 516-17, 662; Hengel and Schwemer, *Paul* 91-92; and further W. Horbury, '"Gospel" in Herodian Judaea', in M. Bockmuehl and D. A. Hagner, eds., *The Written Gospel*, G. N. Stanton FS (Cambridge: Cambridge University, 2005) 7-30.

137. See further *Theology of Paul* 164-69. *Pace* Georgi: 'all attempts to derive the Pauline use of *euangelion* (gospel) from the Septuagint have failed' (*Theocracy* 83).

That is not to deny that Paul and his audiences would have been aware that Paul was offering a very different 'good news' from that of Caesar. But it does suggest that the two would not necessarily have been seen as in direct conflict.

(3) So too, the title 'Lord' was not by any means exclusive to Caesar; it was already a principal way of speaking of the god or goddess of various cults, particularly those from Egypt and the East (notably Isis).[138] Only had it been exclusive to the Caesar cult would the Christian confession 'Jesus is Lord' have necessarily implied a withholding of allegiance to the emperor.[139] In a context of 'lords many' (1 Cor. 8.5) Jesus would have appeared as just another 'lord'. Of course, in speaking to other believers, Paul insisted that 'for us there is one Lord Jesus Christ' (8.6), and could speak of Christ triumphing over the powers and authorities (15.24-27; Col. 2.15). But such talk, if it was voiced outside Christian circles, would likely have been seen as more fanciful than subversive.[140] More relevant here is probably the fact that Paul relinquished the Jesus-tradition talk of the kingdom as a present power capable of challenging the temporal order,[141] and that he seems to have soft-pedalled the emphasis on Jesus as David's son, that is, as a potential claimant to the throne of one of Rome's client kingdoms.[142]

(4) I have already noted Luke's concern to reassure his readers that Christianity's expansion did not threaten Roman authority in any degree[143] — which

138. LSJ 1013 (*kyrios* B); BDAG 577.

139. Such an explicit antithesis becomes apparent only in the early second century, as indicated by Pliny (see above, §21.1e) and particularly in the martyrdom of Polycarp, who refused to swear by the fortune *(tychē)* of Caesar or to revile Christ (*Mart. Pol.* 9–10).

140. The same applies to the title 'Saviour *(sōtēr)*', which certainly became prominent in emperor worship but which was already long familiar in reference to various gods, but also to individual heroes, statesmen and others (W. Foerster, *TDNT* 7.1004-12). Peerbolte notes that Isis was worshipped as the *pansōteira* (*Paul* 60). Martin responds to Wright, 'Paul's Gospel and Caesar's Empire' 173-81 ('Paul's Coded Challenge to Empire: Philippians 3'): 'Wright's recourse to "code" language makes Paul's meaning so obscure and recherché that one wonders how the Philippian congregants could ever have followed it. Wright talks of Paul's subtlety and uses terms like "subversive" and "intrigue"; but these are all scholars' jargon and betray an attempt to treat Paul's writings as unduly sophisticated' (*Philippians* lxx).

141. Most characteristic of Paul is his talk of the kingdom as something still to be inherited (1 Cor. 6.9-10; 15.50; Gal. 5.21; Eph. 5.5; similarly forward looking — 1 Cor. 15.24; 1 Thess. 2.12; 2 Thess. 1.5; 2 Tim. 4.1, 18; cf. Acts 14.22; probably also Col. 4.11; cf. Acts 28.23, 31). The only 'present' references have to do with internal conduct and relationships within the *ekklēsia* (Rom. 14.17; 1 Cor. 4.20); would Col. 1.13 ('He has delivered us from the authority of darkness and has transferred us into the kingdom of the son of his love') have been heard as threatening the empire?

142. Only in the creedal echo of Rom. 1.3-4 does Paul speak of Jesus as descended from David's royal line, and even there in some contrast to his divine sonship (see my *Romans* 12-13).

143. See above, §21 at n. 114.

includes, as we shall see, defusing any politically subversive overtones by depicting Roman authorities ruling that the dissensions in which the new movement
sometimes found itself caught were not really their business.[144] That was no doubt
an apologetic tactic, similar to Josephus's marshalling of imperial edicts favourable to Jewish diaspora communities.[145] But one passage above all suggests that
Paul was equally alert to the dangers in which small gatherings in private homes
might find themselves caught up. This is Rom. 12.9–13.10, addressed to believers
in the capital of the most ruthlessly powerful super-power of his day. Here Paul
draws on traditional Jewish wisdom and Jesus tradition to encourage conduct
which refuses to take offence and which carries out its civic duty faithfully (including the payment of taxes).[146] It is true that the bracketing of the passage with
repeated exhortations to love (12.9; 13.8-10) indicates a motivating compulsion
which would eventually undermine the Roman system. But to live by a different
rationale and impulse is not the same as working for the overthrow of the present
system.[147] The crucial factor in all this must be the lack of any indication, beyond
Acts 17.7-9 (which ends without charges being laid), that Paul's gospel *was* seen
as amounting to a serious political threat during his lifetime.[148]

144. See particularly §31.4c and §34.2e below.

145. See below, §30 n. 90.

146. For details see my *Romans* 738, 759, 768-69; also *Theology of Paul* 674-80; and
below, §33 nn. 250, 251.

147. 'Paul could scarcely have spoken so straightforwardly of the God-given authority
of rulers as he does in Rom 13:1-7 if he had seen the emperor as posing a problem that dominated every other concern' (Klauck, *Religious Context* 329). See also R. Saunders, 'Paul and
the Imperial Cult', in S. E. Porter, ed., *Paul and His Opponents* (Leiden: Brill, 2005) 227-38.

148. Compare the following comments. (1) 'Paul's exhortation to be subordinate to the
authorities (13:1-7) focuses the ethic of nonretaliation on a potentially volatile situation. . . .
There is no "theology of the state" here, beyond the conventional prophetic-apocalyptic affirmation that God disposes the rise and fall of empires and gives the power of the sword into the
hands of the ruler (13:1, 4)' (Elliott, *Liberating Paul* 224). (2) 'The fact that Paul needs to stress
the need for civil obedience . . . implies that, without some such restraining counsel, some
might have heard his teaching to imply that the church was to become a Christian version of the
Jewish "fourth philosophy", owing allegiance to no-one except God and therefore under obligation to rebel violently against human rulers, and to refuse to pay taxes' (Wright, 'Fresh Perspective' 37). (3) L. E. Keck, *Romans* (ANTC; Nashville: Abingdon, 2005), draws attention to
what the passage does *not* say: 'two things are notably absent: a specific reference to the Roman Empire itself, and any mention of Christ, together with the vocabulary of salvation. . . .
The Roman Empire, whether as a whole or in any of its particulars, is not evaluated, neither denounced nor celebrated. . . . Paul gives no hint of the "God or Caesar" issue. . . . One is struck
by its pragmatic, minimalist character' (319-22). R. J. Cassidy, *Paul in Chains: Roman Imprisonment and the Letters of St. Paul* (New York: Crossroad, 2001), argues that Paul's perspective
shifted dramatically between writing Rom. 13.1-7 and the experience of imprisonment in
Rome under Nero, when he wrote Philippians, from the compliant attitude of Rom. 13.1-7 to

All that said, however, it is hard to deny at least something of a more positive answer to the opening question of this section (Was part of Paul's strategy
to build up his churches as a society alternative to the imperial order of Rome?).
A religious movement which saw its identity in terms of the heritage of Israel,
which lived by the good news of Jesus Christ, which owned its primary loyalty
to Jesus as Lord, and which could even see itself as the corporate body of
Christ, characterized by the mutual interdependence and shared obligations of
its members, was indeed in the business of forming an alternative society. This,
we might say, was Paul's equivalent of what Jesus seems to have inculcated: a
communal life lived in the light of the coming kingdom — deeply, but not
openly, subversive.[149]

29.5. Paul's Tactics

If some elements of Paul's strategy are less than wholly clear and have to be deduced from what he says more clearly or from some brief allusions, the position
is only slightly better in regard to the tactics he used to implement his strategic
vision.[150]

a. City Centred

The contrast has often been noted between Jesus' mission around the villages
of Galilee and Paul's around several of the larger conurbations of the eastern
Mediterranean. The contrast is valid. Both Acts and Paul's letters attest that
Paul sought to promulgate his message and establish his churches in large cities — already the imperial foundations in Galatia,[151] and thereafter particularly Thessalonica, Corinth and Ephesus. This would no doubt be for several
reasons.

---

the more critical attitude implied in Phil. 2.15 and 3.20. T. L. Carter, 'The Irony of Romans 13',
NovT 46 (2004) 209-28, argues that Paul writes ironically and that his Roman readers would
have been unlikely to accept what he wrote at face value. Note also the cautionary remarks of
H. Omerzu, 'Paulus als Politiker? Das paulinische Evangelium zwischen Ekklesia und Impe-
rium Romanum', in V. A. Lehnert and U. Rüsen-Weinhold, eds., *Logos — Logik — Lyrik.
Engagierte exegetische Studien zum biblischen Reden Gottes,* K. Haacker FS (Leipzig:
Evangelische Verlagsanstalt, 2007) 267-87.

    149. *Jesus Remembered* §14.9.

    150. For 'strategy' I could have said 'objectives'; in which case, for 'tactics' I could have
said 'strategy'. The distinction I intend is simply between principles and practice.

    151. See above, §27.1c, e.

- In cities Greek would be much more likely to serve as the language of communication; perhaps Paul's experience in Lystra (Acts 14.11-18) had made him realize that he could not function so effectively in a non-Greek-speaking context.
- Cities would have provided much better opportunity for Paul to support himself in gainful employment.[152]
- In such large cities he would find both an established Jewish community and a wider and more varied cross-range of Gentiles, resident aliens *(metoikoi)* who would provide lines of communication to other parts of the non-Jewish world.[153]
- Even small groups of believers could establish themselves in large cities without drawing too much (unwelcome) attention to themselves,[154] whereas such groups might have caused greater provocation in more provincial towns — a lesson learned in Lystra also?
- Large cities always had a hinterland of, or provided the administrative centre for, a larger district or even region; they therefore provided a natural centre from which gospel missionaries could go out to the surrounding towns.

This last point is probably reflected in Paul's frequent references to 'all the churches':[155] particularly 'the churches of Galatia' (1 Cor. 16.1; Gal. 1.2 — only the four cities of Acts 13–14?), 'the churches of Asia' (16.19 — not only Ephesus), 'the churches of Macedonia' (2 Cor. 8.1 — only Philippi and Thessalonica?). The church in Thessalonica seems to have been active in outreach more or less from the first (1 Thess. 1.8); there were 'brothers throughout Macedonia' (4.10).[156] The church in Cenchrea (Rom. 16.1) was presumably founded from Corinth, which it served as Corinth's eastern seaport. 2 Corinthians is addressed to 'the church in Corinth with all the saints in the whole of Achaia' (2 Cor. 1.1; 11.10). And the church in Colossae was planted by Epaphras (Col. 1.7-8), presumably in a mission from the already established church in Ephesus. The references to other churches which acknowledged Paul's leadership/apostleship carry the same implication — Beroea (Acts 20.4), Troas (20.6-12), and possibly Miletus (20.17-38). Perhaps most striking is the evidence of Revelation 2–3 and the letters of Ignatius that several other churches had been successfully planted in Asia Minor, presumably from the bases established by

152. See below, §29.5d.
153. The cosmopolitan composition of the larger Mediterranean cities was often commented on.
154. See above, §29.4d.
155. Rom. 16.16; 1 Cor. 7.17; 14.33; 2 Cor. 8.18; 11.28.
156. See further n. 228 below.

Paul — Smyrna, Pergamum, Thyatira, Sardis, Philadelphia, and Laodicea (Revelation 2–3); and Magnesia, Trallia, and again Philadelphia and Smyrna (Ignatius). The fact that both sequences of letters begin with a letter to Ephesus perhaps indicates that Ephesus was the principal centre from which the missions which planted these other churches had gone forth.

b. To the Synagogue First

We know that there were large Jewish settlements in many of the larger cities of the Roman Empire — notably Alexandria and Syrian Antioch,[157] but also particularly in Asia Minor and Rome itself. According to Philo, Jews were numerous in every city in Asia Minor (*Leg.* 245), and there were Jewish settlers (*apoikoi*) throughout the territory within Paul's compass (*Leg.* 281-82).[158]

In the late third century BCE Antiochus the Great had settled two thousand Jewish families in Lydia and Phrygia to help stabilize the region (Josephus, *Ant.* 12.147-53); in the middle of the second century a sequence of letters sent by the Roman Senate to Asia Minor in support of Jews living there indicates a sizeable Jewish population (*Ant.* 14.185-267; 16.160-78), and the attempt of Governor Flaccus to confiscate the gold collected by Jews in Asia Minor as their part of the Temple tax[159] likewise indicates a sizeable population up country from Ephesus (the Lycus Valley)[160] and beyond.[161] Elsewhere, for example, we know that a Jewish community had been long established in Sardis, and there are numerous references to Jews in Ephesus.[162] The special legal provisions made for such communities, which Josephus takes pains to document, attest both a common sense of identity expressed in the practice of national/religious customs and in the payment of the Temple tax,[163] and a recognition by the Roman au-

---

157. See above, §24 n. 235.

158. On the spread of Jews throughout the Mediterranean, see already J. Juster, *Les Juifs dans l'empire romain. Leur condition juridique, économique et sociale*. Vol. 1 (Paris: Geunther, 1914) 180-209; for sample data see *JAGR* xiv-xv, 1-31; and further §27 n. 181 above and §30 at n. 94.

159. The details come from Cicero's defence of Flaccus (*Pro Flacco* 28.66-69; text in *GLAJJ* §68).

160. Possibly as many as 14,000 adult males; Laodicea was the central point for holding the collection, which presumably also included the Jewish population of Hierapolis and Colossae, the other main cities of the Lycus valley.

161. In Apamea, further up country, Flaccus seized nearly five times as much gold, indicating a much larger Jewish population

162. Further details in Schürer, *History* 3.17-35; P. Trebilco, *Jewish Communities in Asia Minor* (SNTSMS 69; Cambridge: Cambridge University, 1991).

163. 'In the concerns of the Jews of Asia Minor in this period to pay the tax, we see a

thorities that such communities should be recognized and their customs respected.[164]

We should not look back on these Jewish communities through the eyepiece of the Jewish ghettoes of the Middle Ages. They suffered, of course, from the prejudice of Roman intelligentsia against the influence of ethnic groups from the East and their religions.[165] But otherwise they were simply part of the ethnic and cultural mix which was a feature of the great Mediterranean cities, particularly those with seaports. And in several cases, in Asia Minor in particular, we know that the Jewish community was held in high esteem.[166] In Sardis the later synagogue was evidently a large and prestigious building, holding a central location, integrated into a major bath and gymnasium complex.[167] In Miletus a second- or early third-century inscription on a prominent row of seats (the fifth row) in the theatre reads: 'the place of Jews who are also (called) God-worshippers' — prominently reserved seats as ever usually a sign of status.[168] From the same period we find a place reserved for the association of Judean youths at Hypaipa (between Ephesus and Sardis), Jews among the young men's organization at Iasos (southeast of Miletus), and Jews (or perhaps Christians) as members of the local elders' organization at Eumeneia (south of Acmonia).[169] The Noah legend seems to have been adopted in Apamea (it appears on some of their coins), which probably attests Jewish influence or respect for Jewish tradi-

---

strong attachment to the historic land of Israel and to the centrality of the Temple and its worship' (Trebilco, *Jewish Communities* 16).

164. On the Jewish communities elsewhere see below, §§31 nn. 84, 185 and §33 n. 47.

165. 'The Syrian Orontes has long since poured into the Tiber, bringing with it its language and customs' (Juvenal, *Sat.* 3.62-63); Schürer notes that 'for most educated men of the period the Jewish religion was a *barbara superstitio*' (*History* 3.150), referring to Tacitus, *Hist.* 5.2 (*GLAJJ* 2.§281). See also §21 n. 31 above.

166. 'On the borders of the classical world in the early first century, Jewish communities and buildings were fully integrated into local civil and religious life' (Crossan and Reed, *Paul* 214, summing up discussion of synagogue manumissions, 209-14). See, e.g., L. M. White, 'Synagogue and Society in Imperial Ostia: Archaeological and Epigraphic Evidence', in K. P. Donfried and P. Richardson, eds., *Judaism and Christianity in First-Century Rome* (Grand Rapids: Eerdmans, 1998) 30-68 (here 53-67), bibliography in 33 n. 12.

167. The principal archaeological and epigraphic evidence is from a later period (reviewed by Trebilco, *Jewish Communities* ch. 2), but the high Jewish status was presumably the outcome of the deep roots of the Sardis Jews within the city.

168. The titular usage — 'Jews who are also God-fearers' — is curious: had they taken or been accorded the epithet in token of their strict monotheism? Or was the inscription misinscribed and intended to read 'the place of the Jews and those called the God-worshippers'? Or, less likely, was the reference to God-fearers whose devotion to Judaism led them to designate themselves or be designated 'Jews'? See discussion, with further bibliography, in Trebilco, *Jewish Communities* 159-62; photo in Chilton, *Rabbi Paul* 232.

169. Harland, *Associations* 201-202.

tions.[170] The evidence from Acmonia is that the Jewish community there had friends in the highest social circles during our period (50s and 60s); in particular, we hear of one Julia Severa, who was a high priestess of the imperial cult, but who also built the synagogue for the Jews as their patroness.[171] And the important (third-century) Jewish stele from Aphrodisias lists the names of those who had sponsored a building (possibly a soup kitchen), starting with a sequence of Jewish names, followed by a more extensive list of 'God-worshippers', most prominent among them nine city councilors *(bouleutai)* — again testimony to a Jewish community well integrated into a city and well regarded by its leading citizens.[172]

The natural focus for Jewish communities was the synagogue, or prayer-house erected or dedicated for the Jewish communities' use.[173] We know of many such synagogues/prayer-houses[174] but can also assume that where communities were scattered or few in number, the homes of well-to-do Jews would have provided accommodation for the Sabbath gatherings *(synagōgai)*.[175] These synagogues/gatherings would be the locations and means by which such diaspora Jews would maintain, nurture and celebrate their common identity and so provide an obvious point for Jewish visitors to gain entrée to the local Jewish community. Presumably too it was in such gatherings that Jewish travellers who had no previous contacts with local Jews would find the offers of hospitality which spared them the expense and discomfort of the inns or berths on which they had had to depend during their journeys.

Paul himself says nothing about following this practice himself, though we may infer such hospitality by references like Rom. 16.13 (Rufus's mother — 'a mother to me also') and 16.23 ('Gaius, who is host to me and to the whole church'), as well as Paul's commendation of hospitality in 12.13.[176] But the principal evidence from Paul that he did retain his attachment to the synagogue is his reference to the no less than 'five times I have received from the Jews the forty lashes minus one' (2 Cor. 11.24). The reference is undoubtedly to the punishment

---

170. Schürer, *History* 3.28-30; Trebilco, *Jewish Communities* 86-95.

171. Schürer, *History* 3.30-31; Trebilco, *Jewish Communities* 58-60.

172. Schürer, *History* 3.25-26; Trebilco, *Jewish Communities* 152-55; the Aphrodisias inscription is available also in *JAGR* 166-68 and *NDIEC* 9.73-80 (E. A. Judge). On Jewish involvement in Greek and Roman cultural life, see further van der Horst, *Jewish Epitaphs* 99-101; *JAGR* 107-19, 148-51.

173. See, e.g., the data collected in *JAGR* 33-37.

174. The most recent survey is C. Claussen, *Versammlung, Gemeinde, Synagoge. Das hellenistisch-jüdisch Umfeld der frühchristlichen Gemeinden* (Göttingen: Vandenhoeck und Ruprecht, 2002).

175. The synagogue buildings at Priene, Stobi and Dura Europos were originally private houses (Schürer, *History* 3.24, 67; Claussen, *Versammlung* 208).

176. See above, §28 n. 82.

which Jewish communities were permitted to mete out within the jurisdiction of their own synagogues. Although Luke gives no account of such a lashing, Paul was probably alluding to a sequence of punishments he received at the hands of synagogue authorities over a substantial period of his mission. They indicate both synagogue formal disapproval of what Paul was doing — again Luke gives us some flavour of such disapproval[177] — and a determination on the part of Paul to stay within the jurisdiction of the synagogue despite that disapproval being expressed in the punishment of the lash over a period and no less than five times. For Paul so repeatedly to put himself at risk of such a punishment must be counted as substantive testimony that Paul did indeed practise the tactic of initially preaching in the synagogue and that he sustained that practice despite antagonizing many synagogue authorities in doing so.[178]

Luke's account of Paul as a rule beginning his mission in a new city in the synagogue is therefore entirely credible.[179] Such a practice would not have been contrary to his self-understanding as apostle to the Gentiles. Quite the reverse, for it was in the synagogues that he would find those Gentiles who were already most open and amenable to his message.[180] Indeed, the practice is quite what we would expect from an apostle to the Gentiles who also operated on the principle 'to the Jews first, but also to the Gentiles' (§29.4c). His practice of becoming 'as a Jew' to Jews and 'as one under the law' to those under the law was an evangelistic tactic — 'in order that I might win' them (1 Cor. 9.20-21). Of course, the practice demonstrated the same ambiguity as in the division of responsibility agreed in Jerusalem (Gal. 2.7-9), and no doubt contributed to the disagreements on who had the right to instruct Paul's Gentile converts and on what terms; these were tensions which afflicted many of his churches. But it makes best sense of the evidence available to us.

c. God-Fearers and Proselytes

It is a striking fact that many non-Jews were attracted by Judaism, whether by its refined concept of God, its moral standards, its practice of a regular one day in

---

177. Acts 13.45, 50; 14.2; 17.5, 13; 18.6; 19.8-9.

178. A. E. Harvey, 'Forty Strokes save One: Social Aspects of Judaizing and Apostasy', in A. E. Harvey, ed., *Alternative Approaches to New Testament Study* (London: SCM, 1985) 79-96; and further Harris, *2 Corinthians* 801-803.

179. See above, §27 n. 17; and further Hvalvik, 'Paul as a Jewish Believer' 128-33.

180. This was Harnack's view in the opening sentences of his *Mission:* 'The network of the synagogues furnished the Christian propaganda with centres and courses for its development . . .' (1, 431). 'The nearest and surest road to the Gentiles led directly through the synagogue' (Weiss, *Earliest Christianity* 211). See also Theissen, *Social Setting* 102-104.

seven as a day of rest, or its festivals. The fact is striking, because Judaism was, as already noted, a national religion (the religion of the Judeans), and not a cult like the mysteries of Demeter or of Dionysus or of Isis, oriented as they were much more to the movements of the seasons than to any particular *ethnos*.[181] But a fact it is.

Philo and Josephus both speak, albeit in undoubtedly exaggerated terms, of the considerable attractiveness of Jewish customs, including Sabbath and food laws:

- Philo notes that 'throughout the world of Greeks and barbarians, there is practically no state which honours the institutions of any other' but then goes on proudly to boast, 'It is not so with ours. They attract and win the attention of all, of barbarians, of Greeks, of dwellers on the mainland and islands, of nations of the east and the west, of Europe and Asia, of the whole inhabited world from end to end. For, who has not shown his high respect for that sacred seventh day, by giving rest and relaxation from labour to himself and his neighbours, freemen and slaves alike, and beyond these to his beasts? . . . Again, who does not every year show awe and reverence for the fast, as it is called [the Day of Atonement], which is kept more strictly and solemnly than the "holy month" of the Greeks?' (*Mos.* 2.17-23).
- Josephus gives a similar picture: 'Not only have our laws stood the test of our own use, but they have to an ever increasing extent excited the emulation of the world at large. . . . The masses have long since shown a keen desire to adopt our religious observances; and there is not one city, Greek or barbarian, nor a single nation, to which our custom of abstaining from work on the seventh day has not spread, and where the fasts and the lighting of lamps,[182] and many of our prohibitions in the matter of food are not observed' (*Ap.* 2.280, 282; see also 2.123, 209-10).
- We have also already observed the established use of *ioudaïzein*, 'to live like a Jew', to indicate the adoption of Jewish practices by non-Jews.[183]
- The various references to 'proselytes', converts to Judaism, not only in the NT but also in Jewish literature and in some inscriptions,[184] taken with the

---

181. See below, §30 n. 55.

182. 'In particular the Feast of Tabernacles (see the vivid description of the all-night illumination in the Mishnah, *Sukkah* nn. 2-4) and the Feast of Dedication, popularly known as the "Feast of Lights"' (Thackeray, *Josephus* vol. 1 [LCL] 339 n., on *Ap.* 2.118, and referring to *Ant.* 12.325).

183. See §27 n. 255 above.

184. Neatly encapsulated, with bibliography, in BDAG 880. 'In the Roman period, . . . formal conversions to Judaism may perhaps have been less frequent than the looser attachment

preceding data, suggest a substantial spectrum of Gentile attachment to Judaism, from first inquiring interest to full-blown commitment.[185]

- We have also already noted Josephus's report that in Syria many Gentiles had 'judaized' and become 'mixed up' with the Jews during the middle decades of the first century (*War* 2.462-63; 7.45).[186]

- And a string of Roman sources confirms that Judaism exerted considerable attraction for many in Rome itself.[187]

Whether such Gentile adherents or sympathizers were already in the first century regularly or formally referred to as 'God-fearers' or 'God-worshippers' *(theosebeis)* is not really the point.[188] The fact is that there were many such Gentiles, and that Luke's account of Cornelius (Acts 10.2), of Paul addressing himself to Gentiles in the synagogue of Pisidian Antioch as 'those who fear God *(hoi phoboumenoi ton theon)*' (13.16, 26) and winning followers among 'devout *(sebomenoi)* proselytes' and 'devout women' (13.43, 50), and of Paul likewise in Philippi winning Lydia, 'a worshipper of God *(sebomenē ton theon)*' (16.14), in Thessalonica 'a great many devout Greeks' (17.4), and in Corinth Titius Justus,

---

in the form of "God-fearers"' (Schürer, *History* 3.171). Van der Horst notes that only 1 percent of Jewish inscriptions record the identity of a proselyte, though he also observes that many proselytes may not have wished to record that they had been proselytes (*Ancient Jewish Epitaphs* 72). On whether Second Temple Judaism was evangelistic see §24 n. 247 above.

185. See further Feldman, *Jew and Gentile* chs. 6-10.

186. See further §24.8a above.

187. Seneca, *Ep.* 95.47; Persius, *Sat.* 5.176-84; Epictetus 2.9.19-20; Plutarch, *Life of Cicero* 7.6; Juvenal, *Sat.* 14.96-106; Suetonius, *Domitian* 12.2; Cassius Dio 67.14.1-3; texts in *GLAJJ* §§188, 190, 254, 263, 301, 320, 435. See further Hengel and Schwemer, *Paul* 61-80; H. Lichtenberger, 'Jews and Christians in Rome in the Time of Nero', *ANRW* 2.26.3 (1996) 2155-58.

188. *Pace* A. T. Kraabel, 'The Disappearance of the "God-Fearers"', *Numen* 28 (1981) 113-26. But see particularly Schürer, *History* 3.165-68; Hemer, *Book of Acts* 444-47; Trebilco, *Jewish Communities* ch. 7; J. M. Lieu, 'The Race of the God-Fearers', *JTS* 46 (1995) 483-501; I. Levinskaya, *The Book of Acts in Its Diaspora Setting, BAFCS* 5, chs. 4-7, especially the review of the epigraphic evidence in ch. 4; B. Wander, *Gottesfürchtige und Sympathisanten. Studien zum heidnischen Umfeld von Diasporasynagogen* (WUNT 104; Tübingen: Mohr Siebeck, 1998); Ware, *Mission of the Church* 32-47; see also D.-A. Koch, 'The God-Fearers between Fact and Fiction: Two Theosebeis-Inscriptions from Aphrodisias and Their Bearing for the New Testament', *ST* 60 (2006) 62-90. Bruce notes that Kraabel's case for the 'disappearance' of the God-fearers is based on the lack of reference to them in synagogue inscriptions but adds: 'This argument from silence can no more be pressed in relation to God-fearers than it can in relation to freedmen, who are similarly unmentioned in Jewish catacomb inscriptions in Rome' (*Acts* 253; see also n. 184 above). Other bibliography in Fitzmyer, *Acts* 450; Riesner, *Paul's Early Period* 109 n. 5; Ware, *Mission* 33-34 n. 42. See also n. 172 above.

'a worshipper of God' (18.7), is again entirely credible and hardly to be discounted in substance.[189]

One other factor should also be taken into account. In his letters Paul usually addresses substantially Gentile audiences. Most of his letters, however, are peppered with quotations from Scripture, the LXX, and many allusions to scriptural teaching and stories. We should probably infer that Paul was comfortable with the assumption that many if not most of these references would be recognized, that they would resonate in the echo-chamber of a much wider knowledge of Israel's Scriptures. The point then is this: since the LXX was not widely known in the Greco-Roman world, such knowledge could only have been gained if the Gentile readership had already been familiar with and in some cases quite well schooled in these Scriptures, which could only be because they had attended many readings and expositions of these Scriptures in the synagogue on Sabbath days (cf. Acts 15.21).

d. Self-Supporting

Paul is quite explicit in several passages that he thought it important that he should work with his own hands to sustain himself, notably in what is probably his earliest letter — 1 Thessalonians: 'Remember, brothers, our labour and toil, how we worked night and day, so that we might not burden any of you while we proclaimed to you the gospel of God' (2.9-10).[190] And in 1 Corinthians 9 he builds an impressive argument for his right to expect support from those to whom he ministered: the one who plants a vineyard naturally expects to eat its fruit; the ploughman expects to benefit from the crop which results; 'but we have made no use of this right, but we endure anything rather than put an obstacle in the way of the gospel of Christ' (v. 12).[191] Those who serve at the altar share in the meat of

189. J. Lieu, 'The Synagogue and the Separation of the Christians', in B. Olsson and M. Zetterholm, eds., *The Ancient Synagogue from Its Origins until 200 C.E.* (CBNTS 39; Stockholm: Almqvist and Wiksell, 2003) 189-207, questions whether we should accept the Acts testimony, since Luke's 'seductive' picture of the God-fearers in Acts is 'profoundly theological' and not supported by Paul's letters (198). But any recourse to the 'theology and therefore not history' argument is no longer sufficient of itself, and it is hardly clear what would count as evidence either way in Paul's letters (in the following paragraph I adduce about as much as can be said). See also the response by B. Holmberg, 'The Life in the Diaspora Synagogue: An Evaluation', in the same volume 219-323 (here 224-26). Lieu's earlier 'Do God-Fearers Make Good Christians?', in S. E. Porter et al., eds., *Crossing the Boundaries,* M. D. Goulder FS (Leiden: Brill, 1994) 329-45, however, rightly cautions against reading all references to 'god-fearers' within the context of early Christian mission. See also Schnelle, *Paul* 143-45.

190. See particularly Malherbe, *Thessalonians* 148-49, 160-63.

191. That Paul includes Barnabas in his protest — 'Is it only Barnabas and I who have

the sacrificial victims, and, not least, 'the Lord commanded that those who proclaim the gospel should get their living by the gospel' (v. 14). But he immediately goes on to indicate his unqualified refusal to receive any recompense for his work as a preacher; he was determined that his gospel should be 'free of charge' (v. 18). Similarly, he had no hesitation in resolutely defending his policy to the Corinthians in face of criticism from the 'false apostles' (2 Cor. 11.7-21).[192] What caused him to ignore a dominical command so completely? What was the 'obstacle' he feared such dependency might cause to the gospel?

The answer becomes clear as soon as we recall once again the patron-client structure of ancient Roman society.[193] The point, of course, was the mutual obligation implied in a patron-client relationship, the patron providing financial resources, employment, protection, influence, and so on, the client giving the patron his support, providing information and service and acting on the patron's behalf. But it was an unequal relationship, with the patron, by his wealth and position, able to demand complete loyalty from his clients.

The obvious answer to the question why Paul refused to accept financial payment for his preaching, then, is that he wished to avoid entangling himself in such a relationship. The obligation of loyalty to the patron, in return for the financial support it brought him, would have conflicted too much with his primary loyalty to his Lord and the gospel.[194] It is not surprising that Paul expresses his working principle so clearly in 1 Corinthians, since in Corinth the tensions between higher-status members of the congregation — the few powerful and of noble birth (1 Cor. 1.26) — and the majority powerless and of mean birth were, in part at least, tensions of a patron-client society.[195] Paul refused to allow his relations to be caught up in these tensions, just as he refused to accept that baptizing someone made that person his partisan (1.14-17). He did accept financial support from the church in Philippi (Phil. 4.10-19), but these were free gifts, without obligation,

---

no right to refrain from working for a living?' (9.6) — implies that Paul's practice of self-support went back at least as far as his joint mission with Barnabas.

192. Note also Acts 20.34.

193. See above, §29.4d.

194. See D. B. Martin, *The Corinthian Body* (New Haven: Yale University, 1995) 79-86: 'Accepting their money might have led them to regard him as something like their household philosopher — indeed, as their client and themselves as his patrons' (85). Paul's antipathy to such relationships is indicated in his response to the challenge of the 'false apostles' who subsequently appeared in Corinth: 'You put up with it when someone makes slaves of you, or preys upon you, or takes advantage of you, or puts on airs, or gives you a slap in the face' (2 Cor. 11.20).

195. Since only the well-to-do could afford to go to court, those rebuked in 1 Corinthians 6 were presumably higher-status members; regular dining out in a temple (8.10) would also be a possibility only for the nobler-born; and the 'schisms' over the common meal envisaged in 11.17-22 were evidently caused by the well-to-do. See further below, §32.5c.

and he was sure that full return for these gifts would come from God.[196] He must also have depended on sponsorship if he was able to rent out the lecture hall of Tyrannus in Ephesus (Acts 19.9), but Paul presumably saw that as sponsorship of the gospel, rather than as binding him to a client-patron relationship. And presumably he counted such support as he envisaged in expressing hope to be 'sent on his way *(propempō)*' (with food, money, arranging companions, means of travel, etc.)[197] as support for the mission envisaged rather than for himself.

If we accept Paul's self-descriptions of his commitment to support himself by the work of his own hands, that is, presumably, as a tent-maker,[198] two important corollaries follow.[199] One is that his trade must have occupied much of his time — most of the day in fact, otherwise it would have been hard to make ends meet.[200] Consequently, his trade must have largely determined his daily experiences and social status. 'His life was very much that of the workshop — of artisan-friends like Aquila . . . of leather, knives, and awls; of wearying toil; of being bent over a workbench like a slave and of working side by side with slaves . . . of suffering the artisans' lack of status'.[201]

The other corollary is equally fascinating. Given that so much of Paul's time would be spent at his trade in the relative quiet of a leatherworking shop, and knowing Paul's commitment to evangelism,[202] it is probable that he used the time also to forward his missionary work. As Ronald Hock notes: 'It is difficult to imagine Paul *not* bringing up the subject of the gospel during discussions with fellow workers, customers, and others who entered the shop'.[203] This, of course,

---

196. Schnabel sees the key in this case not in friendship or patronage but in *koinōnia* (*Mission* 1448, and further 1446-51). Phoebe also acted at some stage as Paul's 'patron' or 'benefactor' (Rom. 16.2; cf. Acts 18.18), but the circumstances are unknown.

197. BDAG 873; Rom. 15.24; 1 Cor. 16.6, 11; 2 Cor. 1.16.

198. See above, §25 n. 70.

199. Observed most acutely by Hock, *The Social Context of Paul's Ministry.*

200. 'The normal working hours were from sunrise to sunset, but there is evidence that laborers sometimes had to start working before sunrise in order to earn their bread' (Malherbe, *Thessalonians* 148).

201. Hock, *Social Context* 67; though note the cautionary comments of Meggitt, *Poverty* 65, 76-77. Manual labour was typically despised by the social elite as 'vulgar' *(sordidus)* (Cicero, *On Offices* 1.150-51; Plutarch, *Pericles* 1.4–2.2); but see also T. D. Still, 'Did Paul Loathe Manual Labor? Revisiting the Work of Ronald F. Hock on the Apostle's Tentmaking and Social Class', *JBL* 125 (2006) 781-95. Cf. J. H. Neyrey, 'Luke's Social Location of Paul: Cultural Anthropology and the Status of Paul in Acts', in Witherington, ed., *History* 251-79.

202. 'Woe to me if I do not proclaim the gospel' (1 Cor. 9.16) — in the very context in which he defends and explains his determination to be self-supporting!

203. Hock, *Social Context* 41. Archaeology has uncovered numerous small shops in or off ancient Corinth's centre, which provide a fair idea of the sort of conditions Paul would have enjoyed (or endured) when working to support himself in Corinth. Opening as they did straight on to marketplace or thoroughfare, they must have afforded many an opportunity for contact

is speculative, but failure to ask how Paul's evangelism was related to his financial support simply promotes an unrealistic ideal of Paul as apostle.[204]

In sum, Paul was not only a bold strategist but also a tactician with clear principles and priorities and the determination to execute them.

29.6. Paul's Co-workers

Paul sometimes wrote as though the whole responsibility for his mission fell exclusively on his own shoulders. But a survey of Paul's letters, supplemented by information from Acts, reveals an extensive list of colleagues and co-workers *(synergoi)* who deserve mention for their part in Paul's mission.[205]

The most prominent are:

- Barnabas — fellow apostle;[206] the principal colleague of Paul in his early missionary work;[207] the disagreement implied in Gal. 2.13-14 — regarding his cousin Mark, according to Luke (Acts 15.38-39) — did not affect Paul's continuing regard and esteem for him (1 Cor. 9.6; Gal. 2.1, 9, 13; Col. 4.10) or his reputation elsewhere in the Pauline churches (1 Cor. 9.6; Col. 4.10).[208]
- Silas/Silvanus — Paul's principal colleague as he embarked on what became the Aegean mission (Acts 15.40; 16.19, 25, 29; 17.4, 10, 14-15; 18.5;

---

and conversation (Murphy-O'Connor, *St. Paul's Corinth* 167-70; also *Paul* 263-64). In his sarcastic denunciation of early Christian evangelism/instruction, Celsus seems to envisage it being carried on in 'the wooldresser's shop, or the cobbler's, or the washerwoman's shop' (Origen, *c. Cels.* 3.55).

204. F. G. Downing, *Cynics, Paul and the Pauline Churches* (London: Routledge, 1998), argues that Paul deliberately used Cynic-like strategies; but the question is always, How distinctively 'Cynic' were they?

205. The most focused study on this subject is W.-H. Ollrog, *Paulus und seine Mitarbeiter* (WMANT 50; Neukirchen-Vluyn: Neukirchener, 1979). Peerbolte lists fifty-seven individuals connected with Paul mentioned in his letters (*Paul* 228-30), including names towards the end of the list of greetings in Romans 16, where the relationship seems less close, but, surprisingly, omitting Tychicus, Jesus Justus, Persis and Trophimus. Schnabel lists only thirty-eight names (*Mission* 1426-27; further 1428-36, 1439-45).

206. See above, §22 n.25 and §29 n. 49.

207. See further above, §27.1.

208. The reference to Barnabas in 1 Cor. 9.6 is the strongest support for the argument that the Jerusalem council followed the first phase of the Aegean mission (= the Acts 18.22 visit to Jerusalem; see above, §28 at nn. 47, 48), since it could imply that Paul and Barnabas were at that time fellow missionaries. On the other hand, as Conzelmann notes, 'there is no sign of an influence [of Barnabas] on the community' (*1 Corinthians* 154 n. 26); he does not feature in 1 Cor. 1.12-13 or 3.1–4.7.

confirmed by 2 Cor. 1.19); associated with Paul in the writing of 1 and
2 Thessalonians (1 Thess. 1.1; 2 Thess. 1.1); perhaps (with Mark) a channel of Paul's influence to Peter (1 Pet. 5.12).

- Timothy — converted by Paul (Acts 16.1; 1 Cor. 4.17; 1 Tim. 1.2, 18;
  2 Tim. 1.2) and immediately recruited to join Paul and Silas in the Aegean
  mission (Acts 16.3; 17.14-15; 18.5; 2 Cor. 1.19); one of those who accompanied Paul on his last trip to Jerusalem (20.4); one of Paul's *synergoi*
  (Rom. 16.21; 1 Thess. 3.2); Paul's emissary in delicate negotiations with
  the Corinthians (1 Cor. 4.17; 16.10; Acts 19.22) and to other churches
  (Phil. 2.19; 1 Thess. 3.2, 6); most striking is the number of Paul's letters in
  which he associates Timothy with its authorship — 2 Corinthians,
  Philippians, Colossians, 1 and 2 Thessalonians and Philemon.[209] And two
  of the so-called Pastoral Epistles (1 and 2 Timothy) are addressed to him
  personally. Timothy, we may conclude, was Paul's 'right-hand man', his
  senior aide.
- Titus — another of Paul's converts (Tit. 1.4); should probably be ranked
  close behind Timothy in Paul's mission team, despite the surprising absence of his name from Acts;[210] he was closely associated with Paul and
  Barnabas already in the Jerusalem consultation, and was one of its flash-
  points (Gal. 2.1-6); as Paul's 'partner and *synergos*' (2 Cor. 8.23), he was
  the other, and apparently the principal go-between Paul and the Corinthians (2 Cor. 2.13; 7.6, 13-14; 8.6, 16, 23; 12.18); active in 2 Tim. 4.10, and
  the putative recipient of the third of the Pastoral letters (Titus).
- Apollos — a more independent missioner/teacher (Acts 18.24; 19.1); his
  teaching mission in Corinth contributed to partisan tendencies (1 Cor. 1.12;
  3.4) but was warmly affirmed and encouraged by Paul — both were fellow
  servants and *synergoi* whose ministries were complementary and equally
  honoured by God (3.5-9; 4.6; 16.12; also Tit. 3.13).[211]

Special mention should also be made of

- Prisca and Aquila — two of Paul's principal collaborators (Rom. 16.3
  synergoi); they were Paul's hosts and travelling companions (Acts 18.2-3,
  18); they hosted house churches in different centres (Rom. 16.3; 1 Cor.
  16.19; note also 2 Tim. 4.19).[212]

209. 2 Cor. 1.1; Phil. 1.1; Col. 1.1; 1 Thess. 1.1; 2 Thess. 1.1; Phlm. 1.

210. R. G. Fellows pursues the unlikely hypothesis that Timothy and Titus were the
same person — 'Was Titus Timothy?', *JSNT* 81 (2001) 33-58.

211. See also below, §§32.1e, 32.3a, 32.5b.

212. See C. G. Müller, 'Priska und Aquila. Der Weg eines Ehepaares und die
paulinischen Mission', *MTZ* 54 (2003) 195-210.

- Tychicus — 'a beloved brother, a faithful minister, and a fellow servant in the Lord' (Col. 4.7); in the rank of close associates he is numbered only behind Timothy and Titus — emissary of Paul to Colossae (Col. 4.7), and also to Ephesus (Eph. 6.21; 2 Tim. 4.12)[213] and Crete (Tit. 3.12); he was a member of the delegation that accompanied Paul on his last journey to Jerusalem (Acts 20.4). These data suggest that he was a late recruit who came into Paul's inner circle only late in Paul's mission.
- Aristarchus — Col. 4.10, 'fellow prisoner', and Phlm. 24, *synergos;* from Thessalonica (Acts 20.4), but he does not appear to have joined Paul till a later point in his mission;[214] close companion of Paul's according to Acts 19.29; part of the delegation travelling with Paul to Jerusalem (20.4); the only other one mentioned as accompanying 'us' on the voyage to Rome (27.2).

Also of the others specifically named as 'co-workers *(synergoi)*', in addition to Timothy, Titus, Apollos, Prisca, Aquila and Aristarchus:[215]

- Urbanus — Rom. 16.9, *synergos;*
- Epaphroditus — Phil. 2.25, 'my brother and *synergos* and fellow soldier'; 4.18, messenger from Philippi 'and minister to my need';[216]
- Clement 'and my other *synergoi*' — Phil. 4.3;
- Jesus Justus — Col. 4.11, the only other one of his fellow Jewish believers and *synergoi* who had remained with Paul in his imprisonment; possibly to be identified with the Titius Justus of Acts 18.7.[217]
- Mark — his 'failure' (Acts 15.38-39) evidently redeemed later on (Col. 4.10; Phlm. 24, where he is listed as one of Paul's *synergoi;* 2 Tim. 4.11, described as 'useful' to Paul's ministry); possibly a mediator of Paul's influence to Peter (1 Pet. 5.13);
- Luke — Col. 4.14, 'the beloved physician'; Phlm. 24, *synergos;* 2 Tim. 4.11, 'only Luke is with me'; traditionally regarded as the author of Luke-Acts and probably one of the 'we' in the Acts 'we' passages;[218]
- Demas — Col. 4.14, *synergos;* but later regarded as a deserter (2 Tim. 4.10);

213. The subscriptions to the letters to Colossae and Ephesus name Tychicus as the bearer of these letters.

214. Malherbe, *Thessalonians* 67.

215. Schnabel reviews other terms Paul uses to describe his coworkers (*Mission* 1436-37).

216. Also named as the bearer of Philippians in the later subscription.

217. Alternatively, see n. 221 below.

218. See above, §21 nn. 51, 94 and §21.2c-d. Luke and Titus are mentioned as bearers of 2 Corinthians in the subscription to some later manuscripts.

- Philemon — Phlm. 1, 'beloved *synergos*', a man of status (slave-owning, host of the church, guest accommodation), probably converted by Paul (19), and the recipient of the only undisputed personal letter of Paul that has been preserved.

But we should also include such as

- Phoebe — Rom. 16.1, probably bearer of Paul's letter to Rome;[219]
- Epaenetus — Rom. 16.5, first of Paul's converts in Asia, now in Rome;
- Mary — Rom. 16.6, whom Paul knows to be a 'hard worker';[220]
- Andronicus and Junia — Rom. 16.7, kinsfolk, who had been imprisoned with Paul, fellow apostles;
- Ampliatus — Rom. 16.8, 'my beloved in the Lord';
- Stachys — Rom. 16.9, 'my beloved';
- Apelles — Rom. 16.10, 'approved in Christ';
- Tryphaena and Tryphosa — Rom. 16.12, whom Paul knows as 'hard workers';
- Persis — Rom. 16.12, 'the beloved', another 'hard worker';
- Quartus — Rom. 16.23, 'our brother';
- Sosthenes — 1 Cor. 1.1, associated with Paul in the writing of 1 Corinthians;
- Chloe's people — 1 Cor. 1.11, emissaries from the church in Corinth to Paul;
- Crispus — 1 Cor. 1.14, baptized personally by Paul and (formerly?) leader of the synagogue in Corinth (Acts 18.8);
- Gaius — 1 Cor 1.14, also baptized personally by Paul and Paul's host when he wrote Romans (Rom. 16.23);[221]
- (a different) Gaius from Derbe — Acts 19.29; 20.4;
- Stephanas — 1 Corinthians 16, his household baptized personally by Paul, the 'firstfruits of Achaia' and commended by Paul as a worthy leader (vv. 15-17);
- Fortunatus and Achaicus — 1 Cor. 16.17, with Stephanas, emissaries of the church of Corinth to Paul;[222]

219. So explicitly in the subscription to Romans.

220. See S. Schreiber, 'Arbeit mit der Gemeinde (Röm 16.6, 12). Zur versunken Möglichkeit der Gemeindeleitung durch Frauen', *NTS* 46 (2000) 204-26, referring also to Tryphaena, Tryphosa and Persis below.

221. Conceivably Gaius is to be identified with the Titius Justus of Acts 18.7 (otherwise surprisingly not mentioned in 1 Corinthians) — so Gaius Titius Justus (three names according to Roman practice).

222. Stephanas, Fortunatus, Achaicus and Timothy are named as letter-bearers in the subscription at the end of 1 Corinthians in some manuscripts.

- Euodia and Syntyche — Phil. 4.2-3, 'who struggled beside me in the work of the gospel';
- Epaphras — Col. 1.7; 4.12-13, probably evangelist of Colossae and the other cities of the Lycus Valley ('he is one of yourselves, . . . and always strives for you in his prayers . . . he has much labour on your behalf and on behalf of those in Laodicea and those in Hierapolis'), and go-between the Colossian church and Paul; 'fellow prisoner' with Paul (Phlm. 23);
- Onesimus — Col. 4.9; Phlm. 10, 11, the slave who sought out Paul, was converted by him, and became of service to Paul in prison and messenger from Paul to Colossae;
- Apphia — Phlm. 2, 'sister';
- Archippus — Col. 4.17, target of a mysterious exhortation from Paul; Phlm. 2, 'our fellow soldier';
- Onesiphorus — 2 Tim. 1.15, 'he often refreshed me and was not ashamed of my chains' (4.19);
- Trophimus — 2 Tim. 4.20; one of the delegation who accompanied Paul on his last trip to Jerusalem (Acts 20.4), and an occasion for the riot against Paul in Jerusalem (21.29);
- Sopater (from Beroea), Secundus (from Thessalonica), together with Gaius (from Derbe) — the other members of the delegation that accompanied Paul to Jerusalem (Acts 20.4);
- Erastus — Acts 19.22, one of Paul's 'assistants'; 2 Tim. 4.20.

That many of those listed can be identified with some probability as Jews[223] confirms the importance which Paul placed on the 'Jew first but also Gentile' principle undergirding his missionary strategy.

Worthy of separate mention are those who are recalled as acting as Paul's hosts and providing hospitality for him (and probably for a house church):

- Lydia of Philippi (Acts 16.15)
- Jason of Thessalonica (Acts 17.5-7)
- Titius Justus of Corinth (Acts 18.7)[224]
- Aquila and Prisc(ill)a in Corinth and probably elsewhere (Acts 18.2-3)
- Phoebe(?) (Rom. 16.2)

223. R. Hvalvik, 'Named Jewish Believers Connected with the Pauline Mission', in Skarsaune and Hvalvik, eds., *Jewish Believers in Jesus* 154-78, lists a total of twenty-eight, including from the above list Andronicus and Junia, Apollos, Aquila and Prisca, Aristarchus, Barnabas, Crispus, Jesus Justus, John Mark, Silas, So(si)pater, Sosthenes, Stephanas, Timothy, and Tychicus; also Herodion, Jason and Lucius, Mary and Rufus (Rom. 16.6, 11, 13, 21)

224. Or does Luke mean simply that the church met in the house of Titius Justus, since Paul was already lodging with Aquila and Priscilla?

- the mother of Rufus (Rom. 16.13)
- Gaius, also of Corinth (Rom. 16.23)
- (potentially) Philemon (Phlm. 22).

We might well ask, with Roger Gehring, whether part of Paul's strategy was to recruit householders, who could provide meeting space and leadership.[225] The references to Gaius and Stephanas in 1 Cor. 1.14, 16 and to Phoebe and Philemon may well point in that direction.

These are truly remarkable lists: four or five very close associates, Paul's immediate circle and closest aides; four more almost equally as close; fourteen named explicitly as 'co-workers *(synergoi)*'; and about thirty or so others who contributed in a variety of ways to Paul's mission and pastoral care for his churches.[226] If we can speak without too much oversimplification of these as contributing to his mission team, some in regular, close support, others on particular occasions and missions, we find a list of over fifty people, at least ten of them women.[227]

These simple facts immediately make it clear that Paul's mission was in no sense 'a one-man band'. On the contrary, it was always a team mission; he always worked with colleagues and always gave credit, albeit often briefly, to those who worked with him or served as go-betweens for his team and his churches. Indeed, as we have seen, it was an important part of his tactics to base himself in an urban centre, from which ripples of influence could extend to surrounding towns. Such ripples were the colleagues and co-workers[228] — some to extend the mission to further population centres,[229] others to act as emissaries

225. Gehring, *House Church* 185-87.

226. I have not included others who are greeted by Paul in his letters (particularly Rom. 16.13-15), but without indication of any role they played, or someone like Nympha(s), who hosted a church in her (his) home (Col. 4.15) but may only have been known to Paul.

227. A. J. Köstenberger, 'Women in the Pauline Mission', in P. G. Bolt and M. Thompson, eds., *The Gospel to the Nations: Perspectives on Paul's Mission,* P. T. O'Brien FS (Leicester: Inter-Varsity, 2000) 221-47, estimates that 18 percent of Paul's fellow missionaries were women (225).

228. Ollrog notes the close connection between Paul's central mission *(Zentrumsmission)* and the mission of the co-workers *(Paulus* 125-29); see also Reinbold, *Propaganda* 213-24.

229. Whether Paul expected his converts/churches generally to engage in mission has been a subject of recent discussion. In favour of a positive answer, see particularly P. T. O'Brien, *Gospel and Mission in the Writings of Paul* (Grand Rapids: Baker, 1995) chs. 4-5; Ware argues, on the basis particularly of Phil. 1.27-30 and 2.15-16, that Paul's churches needed no exhortation to mission because they were already engaged in this activity (*Mission of the Church* chs. 5-6); Schnabel also discusses the lack of exhortation in Paul's letters to active missionary participation and the evidence for the evangelism of the local communities, including

and to carry correspondence and verbal messages between Paul and his churches. For all that Paul saw himself as 'apostle to the Gentiles', and even primarily responsible for bringing in 'the full number of the Gentiles' (Rom. 11.11-14, 25), it presumably never entered his head that he could do it all as a solo effort. His theology of the body of Christ would have been sufficient to dispatch any such notions.[230] For all his self-assertion, Paul was a team player.

It follows that he must have been a very accomplished leader of men and women who inspired personal loyalty and commitment to his mission, in most of those named, at any rate. Unfortunately, since his letters had to deal so often with controversial issues and individuals who questioned his authority, we hear comparatively little of those who were devoted to him and his cause. But a further glance at people in the above lists like Timothy, Prisc(ill)a and Aquila, Tychicus, Epaphroditus, Philemon and Stephanas gives a quite different side to Paul, his ability to inspire warmth of affection and depth of friendship. Without taking such evidence into consideration, we would be left with a very one-sided picture of Paul; the traditional way of remembering him, as a rather intimidating egotist, needs to be heavily qualified accordingly.

29.7. Paul's Gospel

Can we gain any clear indication of the gospel that Paul preached when he went into a new city and synagogue and was invited to speak to the gathering (as in Acts 13.15)? The chief problem is, of course, that his letters are not evangelistic; they do not constitute examples of such initial preaching; they are letters to often well-established churches, dealing with matters some way down the road from the initial founding of the church. Moreover, we have already noted the difficulty of reading the sermons attributed to Paul in Acts as transcripts of what he actually said on the occasions narrated.[231] Nevertheless, Paul in his letters quite often recalls his readers to their initial experiences of the gospel. Some of these passages, it is true, focus mostly on the character of his preaching and its effect and

---

Phil. 1.5, 1 Cor. 10.31–11.1 and Eph. 4.11 — 'evangelists' (*Mission* 1452-65). Dickson critiques both O'Brien's and Ware's 'overstated affirmation' of congregational mission-commitment and Ollrog's denial (n. 228 above), noting that Paul expected an active mission-commitment on the part of those subsequently described as 'evangelists' (Eph. 4.11) but also that he encouraged more occasional evangelistic opportunities to be grasped (reflected in such passages as 1 Cor. 14.20-25 and 1 Pet. 3.15) and a life-style which promoted the gospel (e.g., 1 Thess. 4.11-12; Phil. 4.5) (*Mission-Commitment* chs. 3-9). See also I. H. Marshall, 'Who Were the Evangelists?', in Ådna and Kvalbein, eds., *The Mission of the Early Church* 251-63.

230. See *The Theology of Paul* §20.

231. See above, §21.3.

not its content.[232] But even so, sufficient information and allusion are there to give us a fair idea of what must have been the main emphases of his initial preaching in several centres at least.[233] And the overlap between the Pauline sermons in Acts and Paul's letters is not so minimal as is sometimes claimed.

Of course, we should not assume that Paul delivered the same message on every occasion or in the same way and terms, and what follows should certainly not be regarded as a sequence which he followed on any or every occasion; but several at least of the following elements would probably have formed the regular thrust of his message.

a. To Turn from Idols to the Living God (1 Thess. 1.9)

The testimony of Acts 14.14-17 and 17.22-31 is that when Paul found opportunity to preach outside the context of the synagogue, the main thrust of his message was to proclaim God as the creator and sustainer of all things who could never be adequately imaged in wood or stone.[234] One might infer, on the other hand, that when he was given opportunity to preach within a synagogue context and took the opportunity to direct his message to the God-fearing adherents and proselytes, he also took for granted that such Gentiles would already have been persuaded of the Jewish understanding of God and focused his message rather on Jesus.[235] The little evidence that we can glean from his letters, however, provides correction to such an assumption. When he reminds the Thessalonian believers that they 'turned to God from idols, to serve a living and true God' (1 Thess. 1.9), that was presumably as a result of his preaching,[236] despite the fact that, accord-

---

232. 1 Cor. 2.1-5; Gal. 3.1-5; 1 Thess. 2.13.

233. The challenge of digging out such allusions is rarely undertaken; a study like O'Brien, *Gospel and Mission,* draws freely from across the board in one or more of Paul's letters. For a more narrowly directed study we have to go back to A. Oepke, *Die Missionspredigt des Apostels Paulus* (Leipzig: Hinrichs, 1920). See also E. P. Sanders, *Paul* (New York: Oxford University, 1991) 22; G. N. Stanton, 'Paul's Gospel', in Dunn, ed., *The Cambridge Companion to St. Paul* 173-84.

234. See above, §27.1d, and below, §31.3b.

235. The famous passage from Juvenal, *Sat.* 14.96-97, envisages (as sufficiently commonplace to be worth satirizing) the non-Jews whose fathers revered the Sabbath and abstained from eating swine's flesh and who 'worship nothing but the clouds and the divinity *(numen)* of the heavens' and who 'in time take to circumcision *(praeputia ponunt)*' (text in *GLAJJ* 2.§301). In Joseph and Asenath, Asenath is converted from worship of 'dead and dumb idols' (8.5; 11.8; 12.5; 13.11) to 'the God of the Hebrews', 'a true God and a living God' (11.10).

236. Harnack described 1 Thess. 1.9-10 as 'the mission-preaching to pagans in a nutshell' *(Mission* 89); critiqued by M. D. Hooker, '1 Thessalonians 1.9-10: A Nutshell — but What Kind of Nut?', in H. Lichtenberger, ed., *Geschichte — Tradition — Reflexion,* M. Hengel

ing to Luke, he preached in the synagogue there, with a message focused on Jesus (Acts 17.1-3). Did he, then, include an Acts 14/17 emphasis as part of some sermons, and was it that which proved effective in the case of most of the Thessalonian Gentile converts?[237] A similar deduction can be drawn from Gal. 4.8-9, which could be counted as a description of the Galatians' conversion, as those who formerly 'did not know God [and] were in slavery to beings that by nature are no gods', but who now 'have come to know God, or rather to be known by God'.[238] The point is the same: whether or not Paul's preaching was directed towards weaning Gentile sympathizers away from idolatry and the worship of 'no gods', that seems to have been the effect in Galatia too. So too in 2 Cor. 5.18-20 he summarizes his commission as 'the message of reconciliation', using the words, 'Be reconciled to God'!

Whether as a sub-theme or as an assumed premise of his preaching, therefore, Paul's gospel did achieve conversion of polytheists to faith in the one God, creator of all things.[239] This, we should not fail to note, was a theme entirely in continuity with Jewish response to Gentile inquirers or would-be proselytes. Paul was in effect requiring of Gentiles responsive to his message that they affirm the Jewish credo (Deut. 6.4 — 'The Lord our God is one Lord') and the first two of the ten commandments (Exod. 20.3-5; Deut 5.7-9). This Jewish understanding of God and belief about God was a fundamental stratum of Paul's gospel which continued to run through his theology at that substratum level, surfacing occasionally in passages like 1 Cor. 8.4-6.[240]

b. Christ Crucified (1 Cor. 1.23; 2.2)

The main emphasis in Paul's evangelistic preaching seems to have been on Jesus Christ. The gospel for Paul was pre-eminently 'the gospel of Christ',[241] 'the gos-

---

FS. Vol. 3: *Frühes Christentum* (Tübingen: Mohr Siebeck, 1996) 435-48: 'the nut in the nutshell is not the gospel preached to pagans, but the epistle addressed to Christian converts' (447).

237. Cf. Heb. 6.1; 9.14. Malherbe rightly notes that Paul does not say that 1.9-10 is what he preached but what the Thessalonians had converted to; also that we should not assume that what is in view was conversion to Jewish monotheism, with Jesus as a second, specifically Christian stage; 'from the start, the presentation of God is Christian, culminating in the saving work of Christ' (*Thessalonians* 132; similarly T. Holtz, *Erste Thessalonicher* [EKK 13; Zürich: Benziger, 1986] 60-61).

238. 'Not knowing God' is equivalent to 'worship of dead idols'; see further, e.g., Martyn, *Galatians* 410.

239. The point was emphasized by Weiss, *Earliest Christianity* 236-48. See also Wilckens, *Theologie* 1/3.54-57.

240. See further my *Theology of Paul* §2, where *inter alia* I note that antipathy to idolatry remained a fixed characteristic of Paul's teaching (and preaching) (32-33).

241. Rom. 15.19; 1 Cor. 9.12; 2 Cor. 2.12; 4.4; 9.13; 10.14; Gal. 1.7; Phil. 1.27; 1 Thess. 3.2.

pel of his [God's] Son' (Rom. 1.9), 'the gospel of the Lord' (2 Thess. 1.8).[242]
Talk of Israel's Messiah, we should also note, would probably provide a natural
opening in preaching to God-fearers, since the theme could hardly have escaped
someone who had heard the Scriptures read and expounded with any regularity,
and the way Paul developed the theme would probably have been less off-putting
than the traditional Jewish messianic hope of a political leader.

Such preaching inevitably would have included at least some basic information about Jesus and about his title 'Christ'. It is hardly credible that intelligent Gentiles would simply accept a message about God's saving purpose
through a cipher, 'Jesus Christ',[243] and would not expect both name and title to
be fleshed out to some substantive degree.[244] The communication of Jesus tradition, to provide the sounding board for such mentions of Jesus' name, is the sub-
text of these references. For example, in 2 Cor. 11.4 Paul refers to preaching of
the 'false apostles' (11.13) as preaching 'another Jesus than the one we proclaimed', implying some unavoidably necessary identification as to this Jesus
was who was being proclaimed. And certainly the Jewishness of Jesus would not
have been hidden. It would have been no news to the Roman believers that Jesus
was of the royal line of David (Rom. 1.3) or that 'Christ became a servant of circumcision' (15.8), or to the Galatians that Jesus was 'born under the law' (Gal.
4.4). The Jewish title 'Messiah/Christ *(christos)*', after all, would have been
meaningless to Gentiles whose affiliation to the synagogue was fleeting or irregular without such explanation.[245] We have echoes of this in some of the uses of
'Christ' where the titular overtone is still evident.[246] For example, in Rom. 15.7
Paul reminds his audiences of how 'the Christ welcomed you'. He recalls promising his Corinthian converts to present them to the Christ as a chaste virgin to

242. But also 'the gospel of God' (Rom. 1.1; 15.16; 2 Cor. 11.7; 1 Thess. 2.2, 8, 9;
1 Tim. 1.11); for Paul it was the same gospel!

243. Such misleading deductions could be drawn from the various creedal statements
which Paul cites (above, §21.4e), until we recall that creedal statements by their nature encapsulate much more extensive stories and teaching and the theological evaluations of these stories
and teaching. 'The use of the name "Jesus" in 1 Thess. 1:10, without an explanatory addendum
such as a title, indicates that Paul talked about Jesus of Nazareth as a person in time and space'
(Schnabel, *Mission* 1388).

244. As Dio Chrysostom observed: 'Whoever really follows anyone surely knows what
the person was like, and by imitating his acts and his words he tries as best he can to make himself like him' (*Or.* 55.4).

245. Hence the common confusion in Greco-Roman sources of *Christos* with the more
familiar name *Chrēstos* (BDAG 1091; and see above, §21.1d).

246. N. A. Dahl, 'The Messiahship of Jesus in Paul', *Jesus the Christ: The Historical
Origins of Christological Doctrine* (Minneapolis: Fortress, 1991) 15-25, notes 'messianic connotations' in 1 Cor. 10.4; 15.22; 2 Cor. 5.10; 11.2-3; Eph. 1.10, 12, 20; 5.14; Phil. 1.15, 17; 3.7
(17 and 24 n. 11); see also my *Theology of Paul* 196-99.

her husband (2 Cor. 11.2). In Philippians he acknowledges that some preach the Christ from envy and selfish ambition but takes comfort in the thought that nevertheless the Christ is being preached (Phil. 1.15, 17). Equally he could recall his preaching as proclamation of the Son of God (2 Cor. 1.19; Gal. 1.16). And in Col. 2.6 the Colossians are reminded that they 'received the tradition of *(parelabete)* Christ Jesus as Lord'.

The most distinctive emphasis of Paul's preaching on Jesus, however, was on Jesus' *crucifixion,* 'the word of the cross' (1 Cor. 1.18), that this degrading execution was not a denial of Jesus' messiahship but actually an expression of the counter-cultural wisdom of God's hidden purpose. In the famous words of 1 Cor. 1.22-25:

> [22]Jews demand signs and Greeks desire wisdom, [23]but we proclaim Christ crucified, a stumbling block to Jews and foolishness to Gentiles, [24]but to those who are the called, both Jews and Greeks, Christ the power of God and the wisdom of God. [25]For God's foolishness is wiser than human wisdom, and God's weakness is stronger than human strength.

Similarly in 1 Cor. 2.2 Paul recalls how 'I decided to know nothing among you except Jesus Christ, and him crucified'. And this was not a new emphasis in Paul's preaching.[247] For in 1 Cor. 15.2 he recalls the message which he had preached to the Corinthians, including the message that 'Christ died for our sins' (15.3), as the gospel proclaimed by all the apostles (15.11). In Gal. 3.1 he reminds the Galatians that 'Jesus Christ was openly portrayed as crucified' before their very eyes. That is, the crucified Christ was so vividly represented to them that it was as though they could see him on the cross with their own eyes.[248] And in the various other evangelistic and confessional formulae echoed by Paul in his letters, it is evident that he was able to take the understanding of Jesus' death as 'for our sins' as a given, part of the foundation (Jesus Christ — 1 Cor. 3.11) laid when the individuals believed, were baptized and became the church in that place.[249]

Paul, in other words, continued the process which must have begun in the earliest days of the new sect, when the first believers searched the Scriptures to make sense of what had happened, and found clear scriptural evidence that

---

247. It is sometimes speculated that after the (comparative) failure of his apologetic preaching in Athens (Acts 17.32-34), Paul decided to change his tack to focus on the scandal *(skandalon)* of the cross.

248. BDAG 867; Betz, *Galatians* 131.

249. See again §21.4e above — including the likelihood of Hellenist innovation (§24.9c)! It is notable that Paul's appeal for unity in Corinth (§32.5b below) was based on his proclamation of Christ crucified (1 Cor. 1.10-25; see also Wilckens, *Theologie* 1/3.70-79).

Jesus was indeed the Messiah of prophetic expectation.[250] Jesus' crucifixion was not his rejection by God, as Saul the persecutor might well have thought (cf. Gal. 3.13), and 'Christ crucified' was not a foolish contradiction to God's purpose (1 Cor. 1.22-25) but actually the expression of God's love for sinners (Rom. 5.8). The traditional understanding of messiahship must therefore be modified, since Jesus was Messiah, and therefore what happened to him showed what messiahship involved, as Scripture could now be seen also to attest (2 Cor. 5.16-21).

c. God Raised Jesus from the Dead (Rom. 10.9)

It is equally clear that a central feature of Paul's proclamation was that God had raised Jesus from the dead. This, we already observed, was the other main emphasis enshrined in the various kerygmatic and confessional formulae which Paul echoes regularly in his letters.[251] What distinguished Paul and his converts was belief 'in him who raised Jesus our Lord from the dead' (Rom. 4.24-25). Conversion was a kind of death which had freed them to 'become another's, the one who was raised from the dead' (7.4). The saving belief expected to be confessed at baptism was 'that God had raised him from the dead' (10.9). Christ was proclaimed as 'raised from the dead'; were it otherwise, their faith would be futile (1 Cor. 15.12, 17). The conversion of the Thessalonians 'to wait for [God's] Son from heaven' presupposed that God had raised him from the dead (1 Thess. 1.9-10) and their belief that 'Jesus died and rose again' (4.15).[252]

Here again we must remind ourselves that from the perspective of nearly two thousand years later it is difficult to appreciate the radical nature of this claim and of its corollaries. For it implied that the events of 'the end of days' were already in train, the culmination of history was in process.[253] This is clearly Paul's presupposition when he elaborates the 'gave himself for our sins' formula in the opening statement of his polemical Galatians: the Lord Jesus Christ 'gave himself for our sins, in order that he might rescue us from the present evil age' (Gal. 1.4).[254] Likewise in his conclusion to the same letter, when he dismisses the controversy as to whether the Gentile believers should be circumcised in order to complete their conversion: 'neither circumcision counts for

---

250. See above, §23.4b.

251. See again §21.4e above.

252. Becker argues that Paul's missionary preaching in Thessalonica had not touched on the theme of resurrection (*Paul* 141, 144-45), but the idea of Jesus' resurrection as the beginning ('firstfruits') of the general resurrection is old (see §23.4a above).

253. On these phrases see *Jesus Remembered* §12.3b; also §23.4a above.

254. See further Martyn, *Galatians* 97-105.

anything, nor uncircumcision, but a new creation' (6.15).[255] Even more explicitly in 2 Cor. 5.17: 'if anyone is in Christ, there is a new creation; the old things have passed away; look, new things have come to be'.[256] Here clearly reflected is the new perspective with which converts saw reality; they saw everything with new eyes; they now saw things from the standpoint of God's apocalyptic purpose, as already coming to effect.[257] It was not just that God had raised Jesus from the dead, but that Jesus' resurrection was the hinge on which God's whole purpose for his people and his creation turned. Jesus' resurrection meant new creation![258]

d. Jesus Is Lord (Rom. 10.9)

Closely bound up with the belief that God had raised Jesus from the dead was the belief that in so doing, God had also exalted Jesus to his right hand as 'Lord'. Paul here was wholly in line with the first Christians in the deductions they drew from Ps. 110.1.[259] But the lordship of Christ was even more central to Paul[260] and must have featured as a prominent part of his preaching. Indeed, Paul could summarize his preaching precisely in these terms: 'we proclaim Jesus Christ as Lord' (2 Cor. 4.5). He could characterize believers everywhere as 'those who call on the name of the Lord Jesus Christ' (1 Cor. 1.2; Rom. 10.12-14). And the (probably baptismal) confession of Rom. 10.9 is precisely the confession with the mouth that 'Jesus is Lord'.[261] It is this confession, with its inference of mastery of and obedience to the one thus confessed, which gives weight to the understanding of baptism which probably already pertained, of the baptisand handing himself or herself over to this new lordship in and through the act of baptism: 'Jesus is Lord' = I hand myself over to Jesus as my Lord! This act and confession was presumably the basis for Paul's frequent exhortations to think and act 'in the Lord',[262] exhortations which presupposed this baptismal confession and com-

255. See again Martyn, *Galatians* 565 n. 64 and 570-74.

256. Discussion of translation and details in Furnish, *2 Corinthians* 314-16; Harris, *2 Corinthians* 432-34.

257. This, we should recall, is similar to both the present and the future tension in Jesus' talk of God's kingly rule (*Jesus Remembered* §12).

258. 'The great and unnerving transmutation of Pharisaic Judaism into Christian Judaism [*sic*] was the proclamation that the general resurrection had already begun when God raised Jesus of Nazareth from the dead' (Crossan and Reed, *Paul* 173).

259. See above, §23.4d.

260. See my *Theology of Paul* §10.4.

261. See above, §21 n. 211.

262. *Theology of Paul* 398 n. 45.

mitment and which were probably urged upon new converts from the time of their baptism (e.g., Rom. 6.17-18).[263]

Did the confession of Jesus as Lord carry with it the implication that Paul worshipped Jesus as God and expected his converts to do so too (cf. John 20.28)? The question is more complex than can be answered with a straightforward Yes or No. Certainly Paul did not hesitate to use texts which spoke of Yahweh in reference to Jesus; we may note particularly the use of the strongly monotheistic Isa. 45.23 in the anticipated universal acknowledgment of the lordship of Christ (Phil. 2.11),[264] and the striking way Paul seems to incorporate Christ within Israel's *Shema* (Deut. 6.4) in 1 Cor. 8.6.[265] What is not clear, however, is the extent to which Paul conceived of the exalted Jesus sharing in God's godhood rather than simply(!) in his (exercise of) lordship.[266] His fairly frequent talk of God as 'the *God* and Father of our *Lord* Jesus Christ'[267] is equally notable, as is his most explicit elaboration of the relation between God and the exalted Christ in 1 Cor. 15.24-28.[268] It is certainly the case that Paul described Christians as 'those who call upon the name of the Lord' (1 Cor. 1.2), invoked Christ (1 Cor. 16.22), besought his aid in prayer (2 Cor. 12.8) and did not hesitate to link God the Father and the Lord Jesus Christ in blessing.[269] But it is also the case that Paul never addresses his prayer-thanks *(eucharisteō, eucharistia)* or his normal petitions *(deomai, deēsis)* to Christ; he never 'glorifies *(doxazō)*' Christ, cultically 'serves *(latreuō, latreia)*' Christ, or 'worships *(proskyneō)*' Christ.[270] More typical is that his thanks and prayers are offered 'through' Christ to God.[271] Equally significant, given that his whole mission was under constant critique from more traditionalist believing Jews, there is never any hint that such Jews found any cause for criticism in Paul's christology of Jesus' lord-

263. See also §29.7i below.

264. See also Rom. 10.13 (citing Joel 2.32).

265. See now G. D. Fee, *Pauline Christology: An Exegetical-Theological Study* (Peabody: Hendrickson, 2007) ch. 15 and §32 n. 272 below.

266. See above, §23 n. 242.

267. Rom. 15.6; 2 Cor. 1.3; 11.31; Col. 1.3; also Eph. 1.3, 17.

268. 'Then comes the end, when he hands over the kingdom to God the Father. . . . For he must reign until he has put all his enemies under his feet. . . . When all things are subjected to him, then the Son himself will also be subjected to the one who put all things in subjection under him, so that God may be all in all' (1 Cor. 15.24-28 NRSV).

269. Rom. 1.7; 1 Cor. 1.3; 2 Cor. 1.2; etc.; also 2 Cor. 13.14 and 2 Thess. 2.16.

270. *Eucharisteō* — Rom. 1.8; 7.25; 14.6; 1 Cor. 1.4; etc.; *eucharistia* — 1 Cor. 14.16; 2 Cor. 4.15; 9.11, 12; etc.; *deomai* — Rom. 1.10; 1 Thess. 3.10; *deēsis* — Rom. 10.1; 2 Cor. 1.11; 9.13-14; etc.; *doxazō* — Rom. 1.21; 3.7; 4.20; 11.36; 15.6, 7, 9; 1 Cor. 6.20; 10.31; etc.; *latreuō* — Rom. 1.9; Phil. 3.3; *latreia* — Rom. 12.1; *proskyneō* — 1 Cor. 14.25. See again §23 n. 292 above.

271. Rom. 1.8; 7.25; Col. 3.17.

ship, that is, criticism because his teaching was thought to infringe the oneness of God and the sole right of God to worship.[272] When Jewish hostility to Paul's attitude to the law, albeit reflected through the Jewish believers, is so clear, it would be indeed odd, if there was a more serious objection to his christology (beyond that implied by 1 Cor. 1.23 and Gal. 3.13), that it was not also reflected in some equivalent to 1 Cor. 1.23.[273]

e. To Wait for His Son from Heaven (1 Thess. 1.10)

Paul's recollection of the Thessalonians' conversion indicates that he had made some mention of Jesus' expected parousia and of the coming tribulation and judgment[274] in his initial preaching in Thessalonica. This would fit with the impression that some of the Thessalonians had deduced from Paul's preaching that 'the day of the Lord' would come any time — with the consequence that the death of some of the Thessalonian converts prior to Christ's coming raised troubling questions for those who expected to be still alive at his coming (4.13-18).[275] It could even be that the confusion on the subject evident at Thessalonica persuaded Paul to give the theme less prominence in his further preaching. For the theme of Jesus' coming is nowhere else so prominent in the letters of Paul as

272. See further *Theology of Paul* 252-60. Jossa finds it 'difficult to maintain this' (*Jews or Christians?* 94). But in the traditions the issue of the claims made regarding Christ as 'blasphemous' is raised only in connection with the designation of Jesus as 'the Son of Man' (Mark 14.64 par. — see *Jesus Remembered* 751-52; by implication Acts 7.55-57), a title never used for Jesus by Paul. The question at the beginning of this paragraph is given more favourable answer by Hurtado (*Lord Jesus Christ;* also 'Paul's Christology', in Dunn, ed., *The Cambridge Companion to St. Paul* 185-98) and by Fee (*Pauline Christology* ch. 11), though they do not give sufficient weight to the reservations (Paul's reserve) just noted; see again §23 n. 292 above. The question whether Paul was a 'Trinitarian' or had 'trinitarian presuppositions' is answered positively by R. C. Fay and A. K. Gabriel, in S. E. Porter, ed., *Paul and His Theology* (Leiden: Brill, 2006) 327-45 and 347-62. Fee prefers to speak of the 'proto-Trinitarian implications' of three 'triadic' passages (1 Cor. 12.4-6; 2 Cor. 13.13; Eph. 4.4-6) (*Pauline Christology* 591-93). And Wilckens describes 1 Cor. 12.4-6 as 'the earliest direct testimony to the Trinitarian reality of God' (*Theologie* 1/3.96).

273. This in response to Capes, 'YHWH Texts and Monotheism in Paul's Christology' 133-34.

274. 'Jesus, who rescues us from the wrath that is coming' (1.10); 'when we were with you, we told you beforehand that we were to suffer affliction/persecution' (3.4); 'the Lord is an avenger in all these things, just as we told you before and kept warning you' (4.6); cf. Acts 17.31. Was an early feature of Paul's preaching that believers must endure the 'birth pangs' of the new age (1 Thess. 5.3) before it could come or they experience it in its fullness (see my *Theology of Paul* §18.5; and further below, §31.6)?

275. See further below, §31.5 at nn. 233 and 234.

in the two Thessalonian letters.[276] On the other hand, we have seen how strongly Paul's apocalyptic expectation continued to feed and sustain his mission.[277] And that was bound to be reflected in greater or less degree in his preaching. So we should not let the relative silence of the subsequent letters lead us to the too simple deduction that he changed his mind and the emphases of his preaching subsequent to Thessalonica.[278]

f. We Have Believed in Christ Jesus (Gal. 2.16)

What Paul looked for in would-be converts is summed up in the one word 'faith': the message which he proclaimed was 'the word of faith'.[279] Christians are 'those who believe',[280] or more explicitly, who 'believe/have faith in Christ',[281] with the corollary that this faith expressed commitment to Jesus as Lord. That such belief in Christ was what Paul characteristically preached for is explicit in Rom. 10.14: 'How are they to call on him [Jesus as Lord — 10.9, 13] in whom they have not believed? And how are they to believe in him of whom they have not heard?'

It is an interesting feature of Paul's preaching, and possibly of considerable significance, that what he called for in his preaching was the response of faith (in Christ), with the corollary of commitment to Jesus as Lord (in baptism). Jesus' own preaching and the preaching described in Acts characteristically called for 'repentance'.[282] But that term and its concomitant 'forgiveness' do not feature in

276. See further *Theology of Paul* §12, particularly 313.

277. See above, §29.7c. The coming 'wrath' is also a feature of Romans (2.5, 8; 3.5; 4.15; 5.9; 9.22; 12.19).

278. See again *The Theology of Paul* §12.

279. Rom. 10.8, 14; 1 Cor. 15.11; also Gal. 1.23. See also §20 n. 30 above.

280. Notably Rom. 1.16; 3.22; 10.4; 13.11; 15.13; 1 Cor. 1.21; 3.5; 15.2; Gal. 3.22; 1 Thess. 2.10, 13; also Eph. 1.13, 19 The aorist tenses (Rom. 13.11; 1 Cor. 3.5; 15.2; Eph. 1.13) refer back to the event of conversion. For the noun *(pistis)* see particularly Rom. 1.5, 8, 17; 3.28, 30; 4.5-20; 5.1-2; 9.30, 32; 10.6, 17; 1 Cor. 2.5; 15.14, 17; Gal. 3.7-26; Phil. 3.9b; 1 Thess. 3.2, 7.

281. Rom. 9.33; 10.11, 14; Gal. 2.16; Phil. 1.29; 'in God' — Rom. 4.5, 24. The only noun phrase fully equivalent to the verbal phrase ('believe in Christ') is *pistis Christou,* which currently is regularly translated as '(the) faith(fullness) of Christ' (see §31 n. 352 below). But since in the key passages in Romans 3–4 and Galatians 2–3 its function is usually to elaborate or specify what the unspecified *pistis* (preceding note) refers to ('faith in what/whom?'), the more obvious understanding is the more traditional 'faith in Christ'. See further *Theology of Paul* §14.8.

282. Matt. 11.21/Luke 10.13; Matt. 12.41/Luke 11.32; Luke 13.3, 5; 15.7, 10; 16.30 (see further *Jesus Remembered* 498-500); Acts 2.38; 3.19, 26; 14.15; 17.30; 26.20.

Paul's reminiscences of his evangelistic preaching.[283] The appropriate inference is that in his preaching Paul did not dwell on his hearers' sins, far less any culpability for Jesus' death that he might have ascribed to them (or to 'the Jews').[284] His message was more an invitation or summons *(kalein)*[285] to accept the message he brought,[286] and for his hearers to commit themselves to the one proclaimed. The emphasis, we may deduce, was not on the need for forgiveness for what had been done in the past but on the challenge to accept the new possibility opened up to them through the death and resurrection of Jesus for a completely new quality of life.

This inference must, of course, be qualified by the 'died for our sins' formula, which Paul presumably inherited from his Hellenist predecessors,[287] and by his understanding of Jesus' death 'as a sin offering' (Rom. 8.3).[288] Also not least by the varied emphasis on the need to be justified (that is, acquitted) by God (as in Rom. 3.28; 4.25–5.1),[289] to be rescued from 'the present evil age' (Gal. 1.4), to be reconciled to God (2 Cor. 5.20-21), and to be saved from the coming judgment on human disowning of God.[290] On the other hand, we should also note how much of these latter emphases are forward-looking, salvation from wrath as the end-product of the process of salvation, and not so much focused on the initial moment of conversion. And in any case, it remains a striking feature of Paul's preaching and of his definitional characterization of Christians as 'believers' that the primary summons in his proclamation was to faith, to believe (in Christ).

283. It appears only in his argument in Rom. 2.4 and in his pastoral counselling in 2 Cor. 7.9-10 and 12.21; 'forgiveness' appears only in Col. 1.14 and Eph 1.7; the verb, only in Rom. 4.7 (a quotation from Ps. 32.1).

284. Contrast the sermons in Acts (see above, §23 n. 288).

285. *Kalein* ('invite, summon') is an important feature of Paul's understanding of the function of the gospel — as the means by which God's *kalein* was effectually heard (Rom. 4.17; 8.30; 9.12, 24; 1 Cor. 1.9; 7.15, 17-24; Gal. 1.6, 15; 5.8, 13; Eph. 4.1, 4; Col. 3.15; 1 Thess. 2.12; 4.7; 5.24; 2 Thess. 2.14 — 'he called you through our gospel'; 1 Tim. 6.12; 2 Tim. 1.9). See further Chester, *Conversion at Corinth* ch. 3.

286. 'Faith comes from hearing *(akoē),* and hearing *(akoē)* through the word of Christ' (Rom. 10.17); see Moo, *Romans* 665-66 n. 27. Note also Gal. 3.2, 5 *(ex akoēs pisteōs):* 'from hearing with faith' (see my *Galatians* 154-55) or 'as a result of the proclamation which elicited faith' (BDAG 36; Martyn, *Galatians* 286-89). The latter phrase is obviously related to *hypakoē pisteōs,* 'the obedience of faith', which Paul's gospel aimed to inculcate (Rom. 1.5); see further my *Romans* 17 and the helpful discussion of Moo, *Romans* 51-53.

287. See above, §24.9c.

288. See my *Romans* 422 and further *Theology of Paul* §9.

289. We need only recall §27.5; though we should also recall Paul's insistence in that dispute that justification was by faith (alone).

290. Rom. 1.18; 2.5, 8; 3.5; 5.9-10; Col. 3.6; 1 Thess. 1.10; 5.9. 1 Thess. 4.6 reminds the Thessalonians of his earlier warnings on the subject.

g. You Will Receive the Holy Spirit

Equally striking is the promise that Paul evidently held out to those who responded in faith. Worthy of more notice than it has traditionally received is the fact that when Paul recalls his audiences to their several conversions, the most common motif in his recollection is their receiving of the Spirit.

- You did not receive a spirit of slavery, falling back into fear; but you received the Spirit of adoption (Rom. 8.15).
- We have received not the spirit of the world but the Spirit which is from God (1 Cor. 2.12).
- In one Spirit you were all baptized into one body . . . and were all drenched with the one Spirit (1 Cor. 12.13).
- God has anointed us, who also has sealed us and given the Spirit as guarantee in our hearts (2 Cor. 1.21-22).
- You show that you are a letter of Christ delivered by us, written not with ink, but with the Spirit of the living God (2 Cor. 3.3).
- Was it by works of the law that you received the Spirit, or by hearing with faith? . . . Having begun with the Spirit are you now being made complete with the flesh? (Gal. 3.2-3)
- In that you are sons, God sent the Spirit of his Son into our hearts crying, 'Abba! Father!' (Gal. 4.6)
- You received the word with joy inspired by the Holy Spirit (1 Thess. 1.6).
- God as the one 'who also gives his Holy Spirit to you' (1 Thess. 4.8).[291]

Also worth noting is that in the closest he comes to providing a definition of a Christian, Paul places the emphasis squarely on the believer's reception of the Spirit: 'If anyone does not have the Spirit of Christ, he does not belong to him'; 'as many as are led by the Spirit of God, they are sons of God' (Rom. 8.9, 14).[292]

---

291. The language reflects Ezek. 36.27 and 37.14 LXX.

292. Recognition of this point was one of the formative insights in my early study of earliest Christianity (*Baptism in the Holy Spirit* 149-50); see further *Theology of Paul* §16. F. W. Horn, *Das Angeld des Geistes. Studien zur paulinischen Pneumatologie* (FRLANT 154; Göttingen: Vandenhoeck und Ruprecht, 1992), plays down the historical reality of the early experiences of the Spirit (61-62, 77-90, 113-14, 201-206); but see the justified protest of V. Rabens, 'The Development of Pauline Pneumatology', *BZ* 43 (1999) 161-79 (here 172); also A. J. M. Wedderburn, 'Pauline Pneumatology and Pauline Theology', in Stanton et al., eds., *The Holy Spirit and Christian Origins* 144-56 (here 145-48); and overall G. D. Fee, *God's Empowering Presence: The Holy Spirit in the Letters of Paul* (Peabody: Hendrickson, 1994); also R. Jewett, 'The Question of the "Apportioned Spirit" in Paul's Letters: Romans as a Case Study', in Stanton et al., eds., *The Holy Spirit and Christian Origins* 193-206. In the same vol-

This emphasis on the gift of the Spirit rather than on forgiveness is the other side of the coin of his emphasis on faith rather than repentance. Again the point is worthy of fuller reflection, that Paul's gospel looked more for a new character of living and of community than for regret over the old way of life, for lives transformed rather than for sins forgiven. Here again the point should not be pushed too hard, for in the exhortations of his letters he does not hesitate to remind the churches that there is an element of 'putting off' as well as of 'putting on' (Rom. 13.12; Col. 3.5-10). Nevertheless, it was the positive forward and upward thrust given by the entrance of the Spirit into his converts' lives on which Paul seems to have laid greatest stress. As the resurrection of Jesus was the other side of his death, so believers' 'walk in newness of life' was the other side of their being baptized into Christ's death (Rom. 6.3-4; 7.6).[293]

h. The Dinner of the Lord

It is clear that among the traditions which Paul passed on to his new churches was the institution of the Lord's Supper (1 Cor. 11.23-26). It was precisely its role in keeping before the community the centrality of Christ (sharing in the body and blood of Christ — 10.16) and of his death (proclaiming the Lord's death till he comes — 11.26) which gave the church's shared meal its distinctive character over against the shared meals of other associations and societies. Presumably it was Paul who established the regular (weekly or monthly) pattern of celebration of the Lord's Supper.[294]

i. How to Live

Given the emphasis of Rom. 6.3-4 and 7.6, we can immediately infer that instruction to inquirers and baptisands would have included ethical guidelines and

---

ume, J. M. G. Barclay, '*Pneumatikos* in the Social Dialect of Pauline Christianity' (157-67), notes that 'the description of the personal experience of a deity as *pneuma* was highly unusual in Greek-speaking antiquity everywhere except in Judaism. . . . Paul employs it [*pneumatikos*] to designate a reality not hitherto attested because it describes a state of affairs believed to be wholly without precedent' (160-65). 'The fear and panic at "enthusiasm" and any *theologia gloriae* which marks out many Protestant theologians is unknown to Paul, for it is not a question of his own glory, but of Christ's' (Luz, 'Paul as Mystic' 141).

293. I continue my protest of *Baptism* that to attribute the Spirit directly to baptism — e.g., Becker, *Paul* 283 ('Baptism in the name of Jesus Christ was the act of conveying the Spirit') — gives an executive power to baptism over the Spirit which no NT writer would have acknowledged.

294. See further §30.6b below.

exhortation.[295] As much is implied by the passages referred to in the final paragraph of §29.7g; or passages like 1 Thess. 4.1-8: 'as you learned from us how you ought to live and to please God . . .';[296] Gal. 5.25: 'If, then, we live in the Spirit — and we do — let us carry out our daily lives under the guidance of the Spirit' (Gal. 5.25);[297] and Rom. 8.13: 'If you live in accordance with the flesh, you will certainly die; but if by the Spirit you put to death the deeds of the body, you will live'.[298] Having been transferred to the lordship of Christ, Paul would expect his converts to live in the 'obedience of faith' (Rom. 1.5)[299] to their new Lord.

Much of that exhortation would be in full continuity with Jewish ethical tradition. We can fairly infer that the character of the paraenesis in Paul's letters would be in continuity with his initial ethical teaching. This would include his insistence on the need to avoid idolatry and sexual license, as we have seen.[300] And, as we will see, Paul's paraenesis regularly echoes the emphases of the Jewish Scriptures and Jewish wisdom.[301] It was precisely Paul's claim that the law is established through faith (Rom. 3.31), that those who walk in accordance with the Spirit fulfill the law (Rom. 8.4), and that the law is fulfilled by loving one's neighbour (Gal. 5.14). Somewhat curiously, not to say contradictory for some, is Paul's equal insistence that (the commandment to circumcise) no longer counts for anything; what matters is keeping the commandments of God (1 Cor. 7.19).[302]

As already noted, a large part of the foundational tradition passed on to churches by the founding apostle, to form a treasury of teaching on which the local

---

295. Weiss, *Earliest Christianity* 253-56. 'It is relatively clear that Paul's initial instruction would have included some guidance on the "vices" which were to be shunned and the "virtues" to be cultivated' (Horrell, *Social Ethos* 78-79).

296. 'This well-rounded statement, expressed in rabbinic terms ("received", "walk", "instruction", "gave"), suggests mature practice in church founding' (Barnett, *Birth* 46). See also D. Lührmann, 'The Beginnings of the Church at Thessalonica', in D. L. Balch et al., eds., *Greeks, Romans and Christians,* A. J. Malherbe FS (Minneapolis: Fortress, 1990) 237-49: 1 Thess. 4.1-12 'shows that "how you ought to live and please God" had been part of Paul's initial preaching in Thessalonica' (249).

297. Martyn's translation (*Galatians* 541).

298. See also Rom. 8.3-4; Gal. 3.3; 5.16; 6.8; and further *Theology of Paul* §23.4.

299. See n. 286 above.

300. See above, §27 n. 207.

301. See below, e.g., §33 n. 256 and §34 n. 390, and note Rom. 2.6-13.

302. For the puzzlement which this last passage causes see, e.g., Hagner, 'Paul as a Jewish Believer' 107-108 and those cited in my *New Perspective on Paul* (2005) 48 n. 199, 50 n. 209, 77 n. 333, (2008) 52 n. 206, 54 n. 217, 85 n. 360. In the light of these passages Hagner's assertion that 'since Christ has come the law is no longer in effect' is too sweeping, despite the qualifications he offers (112).

teachers could draw, would be traditions of Jesus' own teaching and doubtless stories about Jesus himself, that is, an initial deposit of the Jesus tradition.[303] The former (echoes of Jesus' teaching, particularly prominent in the ethical sections of Paul's letters)[304] were presumably in view in Paul's few explicit references to tradition passed on by him (at/as the foundation of the new church).[305] And the latter (stories about Jesus himself) are probably referred to in passages like the following:

- Rom. 6.17 — 'the pattern of teaching to whom/which you were handed over';[306]
- Rom. 15.1-3 — Christ as the model for 'pleasing the neighbour';
- Gal. 6.2 — the parallel thought of bearing one another's burdens and thereby fulfilling 'the law of Christ';
- 1 Cor. 11.1 — Paul himself as a model because he modelled himself on Christ;
- Col. 2.6 — the Colossians should conduct themselves in accord with the tradition of Christ Jesus as Lord which they had received (*parelabete*).

A point worth bearing in mind here is the degree to which the gospel of Paul had a forward look, as well as a backward look to Jesus' death and resurrection. The message of justification which Paul preached looked also to the final justification.[307] The salvation which he proclaimed was the outcome of a process, and salvation would be (finally) accomplished in the day of wrath.[308] He expected a transformed moral life in his converts.[309] We may presume that such emphases were not an afterthought in Paul's teaching but from the first provided a stimulus to a conduct which both was in accordance with the Spirit and looked to the future judgment when Christ returned.[310] On this point too God-fearers

---

303. For convenience I repeat some of what was already said in §§21.4d and f above.

304. E.g., Rom. 12.14; 13.9; 16.19; 1 Cor. 9.14; 13.2; Gal. 5.14; Phil. 4.6; 1 Thess. 5.2, 13, 15.

305. 1 Cor. 11.2; 2 Thess. 2.15; 3.6. Hahn concludes that 'the preaching and theology of the apostle Paul shows on the whole a fundamentally substantial correspondence with Jesus' message' (*Theologie* 1.329).

306. The meaning of the phrase *typon didachēs* ('pattern of teaching') is disputed, but *typos* in the Pauline corpus almost always has a personal reference, and surrender to a person is more likely in mind than surrender to a moral code; see further my *Romans* 343-44.

307. Note the future reference (explicit or implicit) in most of Paul's talk of 'being justified' — Rom. 2.13; 3.20, 24, 26, 28, 30; 4.5; 8.33; Gal. 2.16, 17; 3.8, 11, 24; also 5.5.

308. Particularly Rom. 5.9-10; 11.26; 1 Cor. 3.15; 5.5; 10.33; 1 Thess. 2.16; 2 Thess. 2.10; notable are the present tenses of 1 Cor. 1.18; 15.2; 2 Cor. 2.15. Similarly the noun — particularly Rom. 1.16; 13.11; 2 Cor. 7.10; Phil. 1.19; 1 Thess. 5.8-9; 2 Thess. 2.13.

309. E.g., Rom. 6.4, 19; 7.6; 8.5-9; 1 Cor. 6.9-11; 1 Thess. 4.3-8.

310. Rom. 2.6-13; 14.10-12; 1 Cor. 3.10-17; 2 Cor. 5.10; Gal. 6.8.

would recognize an emphasis ('already' *and* not yet; grace *and* the obedience of faith) with which they were already familiar, and would be the more open to the distinctively Christian emphasis — an obedience of faith made possible by being 'in Christ' and the indwelling Spirit.[311]

To avoid any misunderstanding, I repeat: there are no grounds for concluding that the above features provide some sort of structure or outline of Paul's missionary preaching. But the allusions back to what he preached, how the recipients of his letters were converted, what they believed and experienced, are so numerous and often explicit that they leave little room for doubt that such preaching and such believing and such experiencing formed a common bond among converts in the Pauline/Gentile mission and could be presupposed by Paul even when he was writing to churches he had never visited (Colossae and Rome).

29.8. Paul the Pastor and Letter Writer

We tend to think of Paul as the great missionary evangelist, who brought the gospel to Europe and whose winning of so many Gentiles to the new faith bent the young sapling of Christianity in the direction of its greatest growth. And that is a fair portrayal; as already noted, Paul's stated aim was 'to preach the gospel where Christ has not been named' (Rom. 15.20). But as much if not more of Paul's time and energies were actually spent in *pastoring* the churches of which he had laid the foundations, in nurturing his small congregations through the dangers of infancy and the traumas of youth.[312] This we know from his letters. In his list of labours, life-threatening dangers, toil and hardships in 2 Cor. 11.23-28, the climax of the list is 'the pressure I am under every day, my anxiety for all the churches' (11.28).[313] He was constantly holding up his young churches in his prayers[314] — not just an epistolary convention, but as an expression of deep personal commitment to and concern for them.[315] And, as again already observed,

---

311. See further my *New Perspective on Paul* (2005) 67-88, (2008) 75-97.

312. The topic is still relatively neglected; but see E. Best, *Paul and His Converts* (Edinburgh: Clark, 1988).

313. As regards the 'pressure' Furnish instances questions posed to Paul (e.g., 1 Thess. 4.13–5.11; 1 Cor. 7.8, 11, 12) and the organization of specific projects like the collection (1 Cor. 16.1-4; 2 Corinthians 8–9; Rom. 15.25-28); 'the *anxiety* would refer . . . to Paul's constant worrying, especially with regard to those congregations from which he is separated, that his converts will compromise or even abandon the gospel he has delivered to them' (e.g., Gal. 1.6-9; 3.1-5; 4.14-20) (*2 Corinthians* 537-38). 2 Cor. 2.3-4 is a good example of the 'distress' *(synochē)* Paul experienced regarding the Corinthian church.

314. Rom. 1.9-10; 1 Cor. 1.4; Phil. 1.3-4; Col. 1.3; 1 Thess. 1.2-3; 2.13; 2 Thess. 1.3, 11; 2.13; Phlm. 4; Eph. 1.16.

315. 'We have such a strong yearning for you that we would gladly share with you not

the letters themselves are not evangelistic documents but instruction manuals, dealing principally with issues and problems which often quickly arose in the life of his churches, and dealing with them at both a theological and a practical level. It is Paul the pastor and teacher who meets us in his letters. Without them, if we had only Luke's account of Paul's mission to draw on, we would have a very lop-sided and shallow appreciation of Paul's mission and might well wonder why he left such a gigantic footprint on the character as well as on the history of Christianity.

We will look at each of his letters individually in due course. For the moment, however, it is worth reflecting briefly on some aspects of Paul's letter writing which will help us to appreciate the individual letters when we come to them.[316]

a. The Function and Purpose of the Letter

The basic function of a letter was (and is) to substitute for a face-to-face encounter with another and to carry forward any conversation which writer and recipient could/would have had when they met.[317] In Paul's case, of course, they were necessitated by the distances between Paul and his letter recipients, and by the de-

---

only the gospel of God but also our very selves, because you have become so beloved to us' (1 Thess. 2.8); 'we were made orphans by being separated from you for a short time . . . we longed with great eagerness to see you face to face' (2.17); 'now we live, if you stand firm in the Lord' (3.8); 'begging night and day with the utmost earnestness to see you face to face' (3.10).

316. The latter decades of the twentieth century saw a burst of interest in the practice and character of letter writing in the ancient world; see particularly G. J. Bahr, 'Paul and Letter Writing in the First Century', *CBQ* 28 (1966) 465-77; W. G. Doty, *Letters in Primitive Christianity* (Philadelphia: Fortress, 1973); S. K. Stowers, *Letter Writing in Greco-Roman Antiquity* (Philadelphia: Westminster, 1986); J. L. White, *Light from Ancient Letters* (Philadelphia: Fortress, 1986); Aune, *New Testament* 158-225; A. J. Malherbe, *Ancient Epistolary Theorists* (SBLBS; Atlanta: Scholars, 1988); H. Y. Gamble, *Books and Readers in the Early Church: A History of Early Christian Texts* (New Haven: Yale University, 1995) 36-37; J. Murphy-O'Connor, *Paul the Letter-Writer: His World, His Options, His Skills* (Collegeville: Liturgical, 1995); Longenecker, *Galatians* c-cxix; H.-J. Klauck, *Ancient Letters and the New Testament* (1998; Waco: Baylor University, 2006); M. L. Stirewalt, *Paul: The Letter Writer* (Grand Rapids: Eerdmans, 2003); E. R. Richards, *Paul and First-Century Letter Writing* (Downers Grove: InterVarsity, 2004).

317. The view is of long standing; see, e.g., Doty, *Letters* 27 and n. 13. Often quoted is Seneca's comment to his friend Lucilius, that he preferred that his letters 'should be just what my conversation would be if you and I were sitting in one another's company or taking walks together — spontaneous and easy' (*Ep.* 75.1-2; in Malherbe, *Ancient Epistolary Theorists* 28-29).

lays he frequently found in his travel plans.[318] Even allowing for the rhetoric of such passages, it is clear that Paul would much rather have been present in person to deal with the issues and communications to which his letters responded. The validity of this general observation has to be qualified to some extent at least in regard to his relations with the church in Corinth, where things seem to have gone wrong on one visit (2 Cor. 12.20-21), and where a letter (2.4) and intermediary (Titus — 7.5-16) seem to have been more effective.[319] The contrast between his personal presence and presence by letter was something of which Paul was at times acutely conscious (1 Cor. 5.3-5; 2 Cor. 10.9-11).

An important corollary is that Paul's letters should not be regarded as replacements for the immediacy of direct encounter and of oral/aural communication, as though the letters dispensed with and rendered redundant the teaching and paraenesis previously communicated in the face-to-face encounters. The letters do not constitute a transition from oral to literary. Were that so, we would expect the letters to have included all Paul's evangelistic preaching and a full statement of the tradition(s) he passed on when planting any new church. We would have expected to find letters which were compendia of Paul's message. But they are not. The fact that we can deduce Paul's original oral communication only from allusions like those mentioned in §29.7, including snatches of kerygmatic and confessional formulae and echoes of Jesus tradition, should be sufficient evidence that the letters were a supplement for the foundational earlier preaching and teaching, not a replacement for it.

It is equally important to remember that the great bulk of the recipients of Paul's letters would *not* read them. Probably most were not sufficiently literate to do so anyway. But typically the letter would have been read to the congregation; most recipients would receive the letter by hearing it read to them. In short, reception of the letter would have been an oral/aural event.

b. The Innovations Which Paul Introduced

Paul's epistles were genuine letters. What earlier had been thought of as a special kind of Greek ('biblical Greek'), in reference not least to the language of Paul's letters, we now know to have been the demotic (popular, or 'vulgar') Greek of the time.[320] And we know from the many papyrus letters which have been dis-

---

318. Rom. 1.13; 15.22; 1 Cor. 16.5-9; 2 Cor. 1.8–2.13; 13.1-10; 1 Thess. 2.18.

319. See further M. M. Mitchell, 'New Testament Envoys in the Context of Greco-Roman Diplomatic and Epistolary Conventions: The Example of Timothy and Titus', *JBL* 111 (1992) 641-62.

320. Deissmann, *Light* ch. 2. For the debate on Deissmann's judgment that Paul's letters were not literary compositions but 'real letters' (*Light* 234), see, e.g., Roetzel, *Paul* 72-76.

covered from early in the twentieth century how popular letters were written, particularly the conventions of the initial greeting and the final farewell.[321] To that extent we can recognize clearly how Paul was aware of these conventions, but also how he adapted them and forged his own conventions.[322] Where, for example, the ordinary Greek letter would begin with a greeting, A to B *chairein* ('greeting'), Paul typically transformed the *chairein* into his favourite *charis* ('grace') and supplemented it with the characteristic Jewish greeting, *shalom* = *eirēnē* ('peace') — 'Grace and peace from God our Father and the Lord Jesus Christ'.[323] Likewise, whereas the typical letter of the time ended with a wish for the recipient's good health, having inquired about their health at the beginning, (*errōso, errōsthe,* 'be in good health, farewell'), Paul again typically ended with a formula which recalled his greeting — 'The grace of our Lord Jesus Christ be with you'.[324] And the call 'Greet one another with a holy kiss' seems to be equally distinctive.[325] Such adaptations, or better transformations into expressions of his gospel and theology, were typical of Paul and of the perspective and motivations he sought to inculcate in his converts.

The main innovation, however, was in the body of Paul's letter. To say the least, the amount (and character) of what Paul inserted between the recognizable epistolary opening and conclusion was entirely unusual for a 'letter'.[326] The content of Paul's letters so transformed the letter-type as to pose the question whether Paul's letters are appropriately to be so designated. Are they more appropriately described as discourses or treatises?[327] The issue is hardly worth debating ('a rose by any other name'), since the point is that Paul forged and crafted an obvious means of communication across a distance to his own ends. He did not set himself to write according to some convention or format. The

---

321. Deissmann again deserves the main credit (*Light* ch. 3). The conventions are frequently reviewed; e.g., Doty, *Letters* 21-47; Longenecker, *Galatians* cv-cix; Murphy-O'Connor, *Letter-Writer* ch. 2; Roetzel, *Paul* 81-92; Klauck, *Ancient Letters* 17-25.

322. A. J. Malherbe, *Paul and the Thessalonians* (Philadelphia: Fortress, 1987), justifiably speaks of 'Paul's accomplishment in creating a new, Christian, literary product' (69).

323. Rom. 1.7; 1 Cor. 1.3; 2 Cor. 1.2; Gal. 1.3; Phil. 1.2; Col. 1.2; 1 Thess. 1.1; 2 Thess. 1.2.

324. Rom. 16.20; 1 Cor. 16.23; 2 Cor. 13.13; Gal. 6.18; Phil. 4.23; 1 Thess. 5.28; 2 Thess. 3.18.

325. Rom. 16.16; 1 Cor. 16.20; 2 Cor. 13.12; 1 Thess. 5.26; also 1 Pet. 5.14; Justin, *Apol.* 1.65; see further Thrall, *2 Corinthians* 912-14.

326. 'Paul's letters were inordinately long' (Richards, *Paul* 163); Richards compares the average lengths (number of words) of letters known to us: papyri (87); Cicero (295); Seneca (995); Paul (2,495); 'The church at Rome, when it first received Paul's letter, was probably more stunned by the letter's length than by its content' (164).

327. 'Most theorists assumed that the private letter of friendship was the norm, and felt that the letter should not be a treatise or a dialogue' (Doty, *Letters* 15).

needs of his churches which his letters sought to address determined the structure and content of his letters, as he brought his gospel and theology to bear on these needs.

The same is true of the correlative issue which attracts much attention today — the *rhetoric* of Paul's letters.[328] Should they be classified according to the classic types of ancient rhetoric — judicial (or forensic), deliberative (or advisory) and epideictic (or panegyric)?[329] The answer is probably No! They are, properly speaking, *sui generis*. That is not to deny that Paul knew various rhetorical 'tricks of the trade' and could put them to good use when he wanted.[330] But again it would be misleading to assume that Paul sought to craft his letters in accordance with some rhetorical handbook. Rather, the disagreement among specialists on the discipline should be a reminder of the same point, just made — that is, that Paul's letters are the spontaneous response of Paul's pastoral concern for his churches and were determined by his apprehension of their needs.[331]

However, the fact that we can speak appropriately of the rhetoric of Paul's letters is a further reminder of their oral/aural character. As the rhetorician sought to persuade his listeners by his rhetorical skill and devices, so Paul sought to persuade his audiences of his message and argument. The degree to which he hoped his letters would indeed serve in place of his personal presence and voice is evident in the strength of feeling which they often express.

---

328. The subject is helpfully reviewed by Murphy-O'Connor, *Letter-Writer* 65-113; and F. W. Hughes, 'The Rhetoric of Letters', in K. Donfried and J. Beutler, eds., *The Thessalonians Debate* (Grand Rapids: Eerdmans, 2000) 194-240. The current fascination with rhetorical approaches to Paul's letters is well illustrated by the number of essays devoted to the subject both in *The Thessalonian Debate* and in the parallel volume, Nanos, ed., *Galatians Debate.*

329. See particularly G. A. Kennedy, *New Testament Interpretation through Rhetorical Criticism* (Chapel Hill: University of North Carolina, 1984), and Stowers's review (*Letter Writing,* part 2).

330. Paul's use of the 'diatribe' technique in Romans is well known, and several studies have shown how effectively Paul could use political rhetoric in 1 Corinthians; see particularly Mitchell, *Paul and the Rhetoric of Reconciliation;* L. L. Welborn, *Politics and Rhetoric in the Corinthian Epistles* (Macon: Mercer University, 1997).

331. See, e.g., the critique of Betz's *Galatians* by Longenecker, *Galatians* cxi-cxiii. Roetzel indicates the limitations of approaching Paul's letters in rhetorical terms (*Paul* 76-81). B. W. Winter, 'The Toppling of Favorinus and Paul by the Corinthians', in J. T. Fitzgerald et al., eds., *Early Christianity and Classical Culture,* A. J. Malherbe FS (NovTSupp 110; Leiden: Brill, 2003) 291-306, notes that the *Apologia* of Favorinus (Dio Chrysostom, *Or.* 37) has no 'structure' and 'defies a form critical analysis' (300).

c. Letters as Collaborative Efforts

Several people were usually involved in the composition, production and delivery of each of Paul's letters.

There was, of course, *Paul himself.* How did he go about such writing? Romans, for example, has the appearance of a very carefully structured argument. Did he compose it in one sitting? Surely not; such a lengthy piece would have required several sittings simply to transcribe it.[332] Did he compose/dictate in sections? Did he use previous material?[333] Did he dictate 'off the top of his head',[334] or, more likely, had he sketched the outline of the argument, in part or in whole, before he set about the formal composition, working from notes or even partial drafts?[335] 1 Corinthians, on the other hand, gives the appearance of Paul working through a series of issues, questions and problems referred to him, by letter from Corinth and by report of messengers from Corinth.[336] Galatians, it is true, reads rather like a letter composed in the heat of indignation and anger, and could conceivably have been dashed off in an extended single session. Even here, however, Paul was evidently able to draw on arguments and expositions which must have been the fruit of earlier reflection, and it may well have taken more than one draft to complete.[337] Or again, the famous disruption in the middle of Phil. 3.1 could be readily explained by news coming to Paul during a break in dictation, even overnight.[338]

Then there were *the collaborators,* or *co-authors.* We have already noted that Timothy, Silas and Sosthenes are introduced (severally) as joint authors in no less than seven of Paul's letters (1 and 2 Corinthians, Philippians, Colossians,

332. For an educated guess as to the time that each of Paul's letters would take to write down, see Richards, *Paul* 92, 165; and for the costs involved, 169. For writing materials and procedures see also Klauck, *Ancient Letters* 43-54.

333. For example, the catena of texts in Rom. 3.10-18 was hardly drawn up in the spontaneity of the moment (L. E. Keck, 'The Function of Rom 3:10-18: Observations and Suggestions', in J. Jervell and W. A. Meeks, eds., *God's Christ and His People,* N. A. Dahl FS [Oslo: Universitetsforlaget, 1978] 141-57); and Romans 9–11 looks like a rounded piece which Paul may have used in some previous teaching.

334. Stirewalt suggests several indications of extempore passages (*Paul* 20-23).

335. The *membranae* 'parchments' of 2 Tim. 4.13, regarded as even more important to Paul than his books, probably refer to 'notebooks' which contained material copied from other sources and unpublished material (notes and drafts, work in progress) (Richards, *Paul* 56-57; with reference particularly to T. C. Skeat, 'Especially the Parchments: A Note on 2 Timothy IV.13', *JTS* 30 [1979] 172-77).

336. 1 Cor. 1.11; 5.1; 7.1; 8.1; 12.1; 15.12.

337. Richards, *Paul* 25. See also §32 nn. 413-15 below.

338. Paul's imprisonment (Phil. 1.7, 17), of course, could have meant greater restrictions and possibly lengthier gaps between periods when dictation was possible.

1 and 2 Thessalonians and Philemon).[339] Their role was obviously more than providing companionship while Paul wrote the letters; otherwise they need have been mentioned only in the list of greetings appended to the end of the letters. But in what did their collaboration consist? Did Paul discuss with Timothy and Silas the content of the letters for which they are listed as co-authors? Were they in fact fully co-authors, actually responsible for some of the composition?[340]

A third involvement in the composition of Paul's letters were the *secretaries* or *amanuenses* to whom Paul probably dictated the letters, in accordance with common practice of his day.[341] We know the name of one of these amanuenses — 'Tertius, who wrote the letter' to the Romans (Rom. 16.22). And it is clear from several letters that Paul was in the habit of taking over the pen from the amanuensis at the close of the letter to add a personal note in his own hand:[342] 'See with what large letters I have written to you in my own hand' (Gal. 6.11); 'The greeting, in my own hand, of Paul',[343] adding in 2 Thess. 3.17, 'which is a sign in every letter (of mine); it is the way I write'. The extent of the secretary's involvement in any letter is unclear. Did he simply write to Paul's longhand dictation? A skilled scribe could have used some form of shorthand;[344] but could Paul have afforded the expense of such a skilled scribe? Perhaps Tertius, the only one of Paul's amanuenses actually named, was such a scribe, a fellow Christian (Rom. 16.22), who offered his professional services for Paul's most ambitious literary project. In other cases he would probably have had to depend on less

339. Already noted above (§21 n. 188 and §29 n. 209); also Richards, *Paul* 104, who also notes that 'the practice of named co-senders seems quite rare' (34); similarly Murphy-O'Connor, *Letter-Writer* 18 (further 19-34).

340. Murphy-O'Connor notes that 74 percent of 2 Corinthians 1–9 is written in the first person plural, and only 26 percent in the first person singular, from which he concludes that Timothy must have played a much more significant role in the composition of these chapters (*Paul* 308-309).

341. R. N. Longenecker, 'Ancient Amanuenses and the Pauline Epistles', in R. N. Longenecker and M. C. Tenney, eds., *New Dimensions in New Testament Study* (Grand Rapids: Zondervan, 1974) 281-97 (here 282-88); Richards, *Secretary;* Klauck, *Ancient Letters* 55-60. Murphy-O'Connor (*Letter-Writer* 1-6) and Richards (*Paul* 29) remind us of the materials and skills required of a secretary beyond writing.

342. The practice is widely attested in papyri letters; see Deissmann, *Light* 171-72; Richards, *Secretary* 76-90; J. A. D. Weima, *Neglected Endings: The Significance of the Pauline Letter Closings* (JSNTS 101; Sheffield: JSOT, 1994) 45-50.

343. 1 Cor. 16.21; Col. 4.18; 2 Thess. 3.17.

344. Often cited is Seneca's reference to 'the shorthand symbols by means of which even a rapidly delivered speech is taken down and the hand is able to keep up with the quickness of the tongue' (*Ep.* 90.25). 'The practice was widespread in the empire' (Richards, *Paul* 71; further 67-74; earlier *Secretary* 26-43; Murphy-O'Connor, *Letter-Writer* 8-13); 'we might perhaps think of him taking down a few sentences at a time in this way and then writing them out in longhand while Paul thought out his next few sentences' (Cranfield, *Romans* 4).

skillful (companions acting as) secretaries and to dictate slowly.[345] In addition, we may have to allow the possibility that Paul gave his scribe an outline of what he wanted to say and left it to the secretary to pen it in his own terms and style.[346] This last would not do sufficient justice to the consistency of style and language which is evident through the bulk of Paul's letters. But when we add co-author to secretary, or indeed allow that the co-author might have been the scribe, it could explain some of the unevenness of style (and content) which causes some head-scratching among commentators.[347] And the closeness of such (an) associa-tion(s) in Paul's letter writing gives some weight to the suggestion that Colossians may have been penned by Timothy on Paul's behalf.[348]

Finally, we need to recall again that the letter would have been delivered, probably, by the *messenger (angelos)* reading the letter to the assembled congre-gation.[349] Since the words of the letter would not have been written separately, and probably without (many or any) punctuation marks, the reader of the letter would have had to prepare his or her[350] reading, or, we may say, his or her perfor-mance of the letter with care.[351] How to divide up the words? Where to pause? With what expression should the words be read?[352] As anyone who has heard a dramatic reading of a familiar text knows, such a reading has an interpretative di-mension to it. Should we then envisage Paul schooling his messenger in these readings, to ensure that the words read/heard conveyed the sentiments Paul in-

345. Richards, *Paul* 66-67.

346. Cicero repeatedly asked Atticus to write to their various friends in Cicero's name (*Atticus* 3.15; 11.2, 5, 7); further Murphy-O'Connor, *Letter-Writer* 13-16; Richards, *Paul* 74-79.

347. The puzzle of 2 Cor. 6.14–7.1 springs to mind.

348. See my *Colossians and Philemon,* 38 with other bibliography in n. 47; and below, §34.6.

349. 'I adjure you by the Lord that this letter be read to all the brethren' (1 Thess. 5.27); for possible reasons why the command should have to be given, and with such intensity, see Malherbe, *Thessalonians* 344-45. See also *NDIEC* 7.26-47 on the sending of a private letter, and on the emissaries of Paul's letters (51-56).

350. We may recall that Phoebe was probably the bearer of the letter to Rome (above, §29.6).

351. See further P. J. Achtemeier, '*Omne verbum sonat:* The New Testament and the Oral Environment of Late Western Antiquity', *JBL* 109 (1990) 3-27 (here 15-19); P. J. J. Botha, 'The Verbal Art of the Pauline Letters: Rhetoric, Performance and Presence', in S. E. Porter and T. H. Olbricht, *Rhetoric and the New Testament* (JSNTS 90; Sheffield: Sheffield Academic, 1993) 409-28; W. Dabourne, *Purpose and Cause in Pauline Exegesis* (SNTSMS 104; Cam-bridge: Cambridge University, 1999) ch. 8; W. Shiell, *Reading Acts: The Lector and the Early Christian Audience* (Leiden: Brill, 2004).

352. 'Although it would have to be read aloud as a letter coming from the apostle Paul, the reader would have had to virtually memorize the content for successful delivery' — R. Jewett, *Romans* (Hermeneia; Minneapolis: Fortress, 2007) 40.

tended, perhaps dictating his letter with a view to how he wanted it read?[353] In other words, when we remember that Paul's letters would rarely (if at all) have been read privately, then the reading (aloud, to a gathering) would have been as much a rhetorical event as if Paul himself had been present and spoken personally.

d. Letters as Preserved, Read Often, Copied and Circulated

We should not imagine that each letter sent by Paul was received, read once, and then put away into some strongbox in the house where the congregation met.

- Did Paul make more than one copy of any or all of his letters? That would have been quite in accord with practices of his day.[354]
- Again, the letter may not have been addressed to a single congregation.[355] Did Paul envisage the letter bearer reading the one letter to successive gatherings?[356] Or did he envisage copies being made (after the initial reception) for each of the congregations for their own individual use?
- Again, did Paul always have it in mind that his letter to one congregation should be made available also to others? This was certainly the case with Colossians.[357] Again, copies, rather than a prized original, may have been in view.[358]

353. Cf. R. F. Collins, '"I Command That This Letter Be Read": Writing as a Manner of Speaking', in Donfried and Beutler, eds., *The Thessalonians Debate* 319-39. E. J. Epp, 'New Testament Papyrus Manuscripts and Letter Carrying in Greco-Roman Times', in B. A. Pearson et al., eds., *The Future of Early Christianity*, H. Koester FS (Minneapolis: Fortress, 1991) 35-56, cites a papyrus referring to the letter bearer as one who could expand on the sentiments of the letter: 'The rest please learn from the man who brings you this letter. He is no stranger to us' (46).

354. 'Ancient writers often kept copies of their private letters even when no particular literary merit or topical importance was attached to them; and copies of instructional, administrative letters were all the more likely to be kept. In antiquity, collected editions of letters were nearly always produced by their author or at their author's behest, often from copies belonging to the author. A dossier of Paul's letters would surely have been useful to Paul and his coworkers' (Gamble, *Books and Readers* 101). See further Richards, *Paul* 156-61, who also notes the growing body of opinion that Paul did indeed retain copies of most if not all of his letters (214-15 and n. 25).

355. The letter to the Galatians was addressed 'to all the churches [plural] of Galatia' (Gal. 1.2).

356. Richards argues that the reference to his own handwriting in Gal. 6.11 would have no meaning if the congregations were reading a copy (*Paul* 157 and n. 8).

357. 'When the letter has been read among you, make sure that it is read also in the church of the Laodiceans and that you also read the letter from Laodicea' (Col. 4.16).

358. 'Sharing copies of letters was commonplace' (Richards, *Paul* 158); see further Gamble, *Books and Readers* 96-100.

- Nor can we assume that the letter was given a single reading in any congregation and then simply 'filed away'. On the contrary, we can fairly confidently assume that those with leadership and teaching responsibilities in the different churches would return to the letter again and again, and that the letter would have become part of the stock of teaching and tradition by which the congregation was 'built up'.[359]
- Whatever Paul's own intention on the matter, it would be well to assume that copies were soon made and began to circulate more widely. The more prized Paul's letters were as teaching material, the more they would function like the Jesus tradition and become the common property, first of the local churches, then of the other Pauline foundations in the region.[360] For example, we can guess from the manuscript evidence that Romans was soon circulated more widely in (a) version(s) with chs. 15–16 or ch. 16 omitted.[361] And the evidence of Clement and Ignatius that 1 Corinthians was well known both in Rome and in Asia Minor (and/or Syria) within a generation or two of its composition invites a similar deduction.[362]

In short, the process which resulted, (probably) two generations later, in 2 Peter referring to Paul's letters as 'Scripture' (2 Pet. 3.16) may well have begun very early indeed. That is to say, the influence of Paul's letters and the teaching they contained may well have begun to spread, more or less from the first, in ever-expanding ripples from the churches to which they had been addressed. Of

---

359. As Lindemann observes, if Paul's letters show evidence of reworking and editing, then that implies that these letters were regarded by the communities concerned as an important component of their own tradition (*Paulus im ältesten Christentum* 29).

360. A. Harnack, *Die Briefsammlung des Apostels Paulus* (Leipzig: Hinrichs, 1926), established the consensus view that the collection of Paul's letters was first made in the last quarter of the first century; the exchange of letters in Col. 4.16 was a special case of two sister communities (7). But Richards, *Secretary* 165 n. 169, also *Paul* 218, and D. Trobisch, *Paul's Letter Collection: Tracing the Origins* (Minneapolis: Fortress, 1994), both believe that the Pauline corpus originated with Paul himself. 'The collection of Paul's letters began, as K. Aland has argued on the basis of their textual history, from the time they were first written when neighboring congregations sought copies of Paul's correspondence' (Ellis, *Making* 296-97). See also Gamble, *Books and Readers* 58-63; S. E. Porter, 'When and How Was the Pauline Canon Compiled? An Assessment of Theories', in S. E. Porter, ed., *The Pauline Canon* (Leiden: Brill, 2004) 95-127. See further below, vol. 3.

361. See, e.g., Fitzmyer, *Romans* 49-50.

362. See now A. F. Gregory and P. Foster, in A. Gregory and C. Tuckett, eds., *The Reception of the New Testament in the Apostolic Fathers* (Oxford: Oxford University, 2005) 144-48, 164-67. M. M. Mitchell, 'The Letter of James as a Document of Paulinism?', in R. L. Webb and J. S. Kloppenborg, eds., *Reading James with New Eyes* (LNTS 342; London: Clark, 2007) 75-98, sees in James evidence that the author of James knew a collection of Paul's letters, including at least 1 Corinthians and Galatians.

course we know that some of Paul's letters have been lost;[363] perhaps Paul did not retain a copy in these instances, or they were not so highly prized, or not regarded as of wider interest, or the process envisaged above was disrupted (the letter lost or destroyed) at a very early stage. Such losses, accidental or designed, however, should not detract from the conclusion that those which have been preserved were so because they were prized, read often, copied and circulated.

Overall, the picture which emerges of Paul the apostle is of someone on the cusp of a major transition in religious and cultural history, a man who had a high estimate of himself, or rather of his commission and of the gospel which he believed himself commissioned to preach to Gentiles, a man who pursued the vision given him with relentless and seemingly boundless energy and courage, a man with a visionary strategy and clear-headed tactics, a leader of men and women able to evoke huge loyalty and commitment from many, as well as hostility and vituperation from others, an evangelist with a gospel well thought through and delivered with powerful impact, a pastor whose ministry established Christianity in many places where it took deep root, and whose letters became instruction manuals and theological tracts which shaped future Christianity as no other first-century writer did. Second founder of Christianity indeed!

---

363. At least an earlier letter to the Corinthians (1 Cor. 5.9) and the letter to the Laodiceans (Col. 4.16).

CHAPTER 30

Paul's Churches

During his Aegean mission Paul successfully planted a number of churches. We know a little about these from Acts, but our best insights come from Paul's letters — to the churches in Thessalonica, Corinth, Philippi and Colossae in particular. We will naturally look at these letters in some detail in the subsequent chapters (also his letters to Galatia and Rome, which he probably wrote during this period). But before plunging into the finer detail of the issues and problems he addresses in these letters, it is well to step back and take a more panoramic view of what must have been involved in setting up these churches, what it must have meant for new converts to become 'church', or 'a church (or churches) of God'. Where would such gatherings meet? How would they relate to the local synagogue(s), from which most of the initial membership (including proselytes and God-fearers) would probably have come? How would they have been regarded by others — as a subset of the synagogue, as a religious cult, as an association or club, or just as a group of friends who met regularly? What would their legal status be in the eyes of the local and Roman authorities? What would be their social composition: for example, would they have included elites and slaves, men and women, and on equal terms? How would they have organized themselves?[1] To illuminate such background and contextual information it will be necessary, of course, to draw on Paul's letters to the particular churches mentioned above. But if we can lay, as it were, the infrastructure before examining the particular churches built within that environment, it should be all the more possible to focus attention on the particular issues and situations which occasioned each of the letters when we turn to examine the letters themselves.

---

1. Cf. the questions which stimulated R. L. Wilken, *The Christians as the Romans Saw Them* (New Haven: Yale University, 1984).

30.1. Why 'Church'?

If there is a single term in the NT writings which denotes the existence and character of the embryonic Christian movement in various centres where it became established, that term is *ekklēsia,* 'church'.[2] As already noted (§29.4d), *ekklēsia* in common parlance denoted simply an assembly or gathering of people for some shared purpose. It occurs in this sense in Acts 19.32 and 40, and occasionally in the LXX.[3] It has also been found occasionally in reference to some associations or the business meetings of some clubs.[4] But its predominant usage was to the regularly summoned citizen body in legislative assembly,[5] as again in Acts 19.40.[6] The earliest Christian usage could have been simply to denote the meeting which their coming together constituted — perhaps to avoid the alternative term, *synagōgē,* which was equally capable of signifying a gathering or coming together, but which had already become too much identified as the assembly of Jews, the synagogue.[7] It is not very likely, however, that Paul's use of the term signified, or was understood to signify, a claim that the small groups whom it so categorized should see themselves as the formally constituted citizen body either of the city where they dwelt[8] or of heaven.[9] The fact that Paul can speak both of

2. Statistics in §20 n. 11 above.

3. BDAG 303 cites 1 Kgdms. 19.20; 1 Macc. 3.13; Sir. 26.5.

4. Meeks, *First Urban Christians* 222 n. 24; Harland, *Associations* 106, 182. Examples of *ekklēsia* used for voluntary associations and their meetings are provided by J. S. Kloppenborg, 'Edwin Hatch, Churches and Collegia', in B. H. McLean, ed., *Origins and Method,* J. C. Hurd FS (JSNTS 86; Sheffield: JSOT, 1993) 212-38 (here 215-16 n. 13, 231 n. 65); R. S. Ascough, *Paul's Macedonian Associations* (WUNT 2.161; Tübingen: Mohr Siebeck, 2003) 74.

5. LSJ 509; K. L. Schmidt, *TDNT* 3.513-14.

6. The *ekklēsia* of 19.39 is the *ennomos ekklēsia,* that is, the 'statutory assembly', as distinct from the informal 'gathering *(ekklēsia)*' of 19.32 and 40 (Fitzmyer, *Acts* 660, 662); see further Barrett, *Acts* 2.938.

7. Cf. LSJ 1692 with BDAG 963; see further Schürer, *History* 3.90-91, 95-98.

8. Klauck also notes that *ekklēsia* is used very rarely in the associations and clubs (see n. 4 above) and comments: 'Beneath this unmistakable reserve in terminology there no doubt lies an awareness of the distinction between the private association and the public assembly of citizens' *(Religious Context* 46).

9. Phil. 3.20 — 'our citizenship *(politeuma)* is in heaven'. The term *politeuma* was used frequently for the citizens of a city who were living abroad or in exile — e.g., the *politeuma* of Phrygians devoted to the Great Mother at Pompeii (Harland, *Associations* 35; see further Schürer, *History* 3.88-89; Ascough, *Paul's Macedonian Associations* 77-78, 147-49) — a state of affairs which lent itself to obvious metaphorical application, as in Phil. 3.20. As such the term says nothing as to how Christians should conduct any current civic responsibilities, nor does it constitute a denial that they have such responsibilities (cf. Rom. 13.7!); the thought is of citizenship *in* heaven, not of Christians as a colony *of* heaven. See the excellent note of Bockmuehl, *Philippians* 233-34; also §34 n. 273 below.

ekklēsiai (plural) in a region[10] and of individual *ekklēsiai* (house churches, probably more than one) which met in the same city[11] suggests that the common
sense of 'gathering, meeting' was in mind and was so understood by others who
heard it being used.[12]

The greater influence, I have already suggested, was the LXX use of the
term *ekklēsia* to translate the 'assembly of Yahweh/Israel *(qahal Yahweh/Is-
rael)*', as indicated by Paul's frequent reference to 'the church (or churches) of
God'.[13] We should note that this usage also indicates a background in the
Aramaic-speaking congregations, and that *ekklēsia* emerged as the translation of
qahal,[14] again in preference to *synagōgē*.[15] The point, of course, is that the inspiration for the use of the term *ekklēsia* was almost certainly more theological than
political.[16] Paul's usage was not original to him or to his mission, as his reference
to 'the churches of Judea' (Gal. 1.22) also implies. It embodied not so much a
claim to be a new political entity as a claim to be in direct continuity with the Israel that God called out *(ek-kalein)* to be his people in the world. Here again the
regularity of Paul's use of the plural ('churches') is worth noting: Paul evidently
thought of separate gatherings, in houses or cities, several in a city or region, as
individually 'churches'; the thought of 'the church' as a national or universal entity had not yet come to expression.[17] Wherever a group of believers in Jesus as
Lord came together *(syn-agein),* there was 'the church of God'.

These basic facts immediately raise a number of key questions. Not least,
how did these earliest 'churches' see themselves in relation to the 'synagogues'?
If indeed the first Gentile converts came primarily from the ranks of God-fearers,
that is, from those Gentiles already in a synagogue environment (§29.5c), how
did such converts understand their transition from 'synagogue' adherent to
'church' member? In many ways more important is the further question: How did

10. 1 Cor. 16.1 (Galatia); 16.19 (Asia); 2 Cor. 8.1 (Macedonia); Gal. 1.22 (Judea).

11. Rom. 16.5; 1 Cor. 16.19; Col. 4.15; Phlm. 2. There is wide agreement that the greetings of Rom. 16.14-15 have in view other house churches in addition to the meeting in the
house of Prisca and Aquila (16.5); see §33 n. 55 below.

12. Stegemann and Stegemann, *Jesus Movement* 263; see also above, §29.4d.

13. 'The church of God' — 1 Cor. 1.1; 10.32; 11.22; 15.9; 2 Cor. 1.1; Gal. 1.13. 'The
churches of God' — 1 Cor. 11.16; 1 Thess. 2.14; 2 Thess. 1.4.

14. See also §20 n. 13 above. Note that one of the names claimed by the Qumran community was *qahal el*, 'assembly of God' (1QM 4.10). On the possibility that Jesus spoke of the
qahal Yahweh, see *Jesus Remembered* 513-14.

15. In LXX *qahal* is translated by *ekklēsia* sixty-eight times and by *synagōgē* thirty-six
times; see H.-J. Fabry, *TDOT* 12.546-61 (here 561); details in HR 433 and 1309-10. Note again
Acts 7.38.

16. See also J. Roloff, *ekklēsia, EDNT* 1.412; though note also Stegemann and Stegemann, *Jesus Movement* 262-64.

17. See further *Theology of Paul* 537-40.

outsiders view these new 'churches'? According to Luke's account, a 'church' was typically formed by a sort of breakaway from the synagogue; this is explicitly so in the two centres on which Paul focused his mission — Corinth (Acts 18.7) and Ephesus (19.9). Would such a 'church' have been regarded simply as a rebellious house group, at odds with the synagogue leadership, but still (so far as formal status mattered) within the synagogue community? Would the formation of the 'church' have been seen as a schism within the synagogue, that is, as forming a breakaway or alternative synagogue? Or would 'church' have been seen more or less from the beginning as constituting a different kind of 'gathering' from the congregation of the 'synagogue'?[18] This line of questioning runs on immediately into the still more sensitive issue of the legal status of these new 'churches' — sensitive particularly in view of the Roman authorities' suspicion of new groups.[19]

The issues raised here will require careful treatment below (§§30.3-4), but first it would be wise to seek a little more clarity on what can be said about the physical context of these earliest Christian gatherings in the cities of the Aegean region.

30.2. House Churches — the Archaeological Evidence

It is probably unnecessary to point out that when Paul speaks of the Corinthian believers 'coming together in church' (1 Cor. 11.18), the thought was not of 'church' as place ('in a building'). Rather it was of the individuals themselves coming together to *be* church, *as* church. In view of the later connotations which have become attached to 'church' (= 'building'), it might be less confusing to use terms like 'congregation', 'gathering', 'meeting', 'assembly'. That said, of course, an important question is, Where did the first believers come together in the cities of the Aegean mission? What accommodation did they use for their comings together?

---

18. W. O. McCready, '*Ekklēsia* and Voluntary Associations', in J. S. Kloppenborg and S. G. Wilson, eds., *Voluntary Associations in the Graeco-Roman World* (London: Routledge, 1996) 59-73, suggests the first believers may have 'deliberately selected the term *ekklēsia* because it was different from a contemporary one generally associated with Judaism' (63).

19. See above, §29 n. 133. 'Roman citizens in Corinth may have been puzzled with a "religion" that had such a regular "meeting" *(ekklēsia)* as its essential characteristic. They would certainly have been surprised by the use of the political term *ekklēsia* for a "gathering" which was not that of an association but rather a religious one, yet possessed no statue of their divinity' (Winter, *Corinth* 134).

a. The Archaeological Evidence

Archaeology has uncovered several synagogue buildings which were almost certainly already established in the first century in Italy, Greece and Asia Minor — at Ostia, Rome's port; at Stobi, in Macedonia; on the Aegean island of Delos; at Priene, between Ephesus and Miletus; and probably also Sardis in Asia Minor.[20] Inscriptional evidence, albeit across the first three centuries, enables us to identify thirteen centres in Asia Minor where Jews gathered regularly.[21] So we can certainly assume that on many sites earlier structures functioning as synagogues were built over, and their distinctive synagogue features were forever lost to view. The spread of diaspora Jewish communities was so extensive, and the pattern of 'prayer-houses' already so established in the first century,[22] that we can assume the presence of one or more synagogue structures, or private houses serving as synagogues, wherever there was a significant Jewish community.[23] This would certainly have been the position in the various centres of Jewish settlement during Paul's Aegean mission.[24]

What then of the meeting places of the first believers, when the latter moved out of the immediate synagogue context? Archaeology has uncovered no structure which can be both identified as a church and confidently dated earlier than a century or more beyond Paul. So we have to assume that these meetings took place either in private homes or in larger premises rented for the occasion. Nothing in our sources indicates that the latter was realistic in the great majority of cases.[25] The cost of regular bookings would probably have been beyond the means of the first small groups, and in any case local associations would hardly welcome competing societies to their premises; and temple property would hardly be conducive to a Christian gathering. The only obvious conclusion is that

20. Details in Claussen, *Versammlung* 191-206; plans of the synagogues at Priene, Delos and Ostia in *CHJ* 3.287-90; see also §29 n. 175.

21. Acomonia, Aphrodisias, Ephesus, Hierapolis, Laodicea, Miletus, Pergamum, Philadelphia, Priene, Sardis, Smyrna, Teos and Thyatira (Harland, *Associations* 34 and n. 7).

22. In *Jesus Remembered* 304 n. 226 I note that Philo speaks of 'many [*proseuchas,* prayer-houses] in each section of the city' of Alexandria (*Legat.* 132, 134, 137-38) and refer further to Schürer, *History* 2.425-26 n. 5, 439-40 n. 61 and *NDIEC* 3.121-22 for epigraphical evidence of *proseuchai* in Egypt, Delos and elsewhere. See further *NDIEC* 3.121-22; 4.201-202; 5.148; *JIGRE* 9, 13, 22, 24, 25, 27, 28, 117, 125, 126; Levinskaya, *BAFCS* 5.213-25.

23. See again §29 n. 175 above. 'The evidence indicates that most, if not all, of the earliest synagogues were renovated from existing buildings, usually houses' (White, 'Synagogues' 34; see further his *The Social Origins of Christian Architecture* [2 vols.; Harrisburg: Trinity Press International, 1996, 1997] 1.60-101).

24. See further §29.5b above.

25. Tyrannus's lecture hall in Ephesus (Acts 19.9-10) was an exception; see also below, §32 n. 91.

the first believers met as church in each other's houses, with the wealthiest member and the largest house providing a regular venue for 'the whole church' in different centres.[26] This deduction is strengthened by the various references to house churches (above, n. 11) and by Paul's reference to Gaius as 'host to the whole church', that is, presumably, of Corinth, from which Paul wrote his letter to Rome (Rom. 16.23).[27] The 'whole church' could be a hyperbolic reference to Gaius's hospitality to any Christian passing through Corinth, but it more likely refers to those occasions when all the local believers could meet together (as in 1 Cor. 11.20 and 14.23), as distinct from the several and more frequent(?) smaller gatherings in smaller homes.[28]

What then does archaeology tell us about such homes in the larger cities fringing the Aegean? Some sites are of no help whatever. For example, Thessalonica in Macedonia and Smyrna in Asia Minor, as indeed also Rome, have been so built over that little remains open to view. Fortunately, however, the changing geography and economic fortunes of places like Ostia, Corinth and Ephesus, not to mention Pompeii and Herculaneum, have left substantial remains which are still being worked on and from which we can gain a good grasp of the range of housing stock in such cities during or around our period. Attention has usually been caught by the more substantial properties, occupying most of a small block within a network of streets. But in places the ruins extend above the first-floor level (Ostia in particular) and give us a better idea of what must have been one-room or small apartments in tenement blocks.[29]

Nicholas Purcell sums up the situation well:

> By the imperial period, multi-storey tenement blocks, which were usually known as *insulae,* housed all but a tiny fraction of the population of Rome

---

26. On the private home as a natural and customary location for lectures and teaching in the ancient world, see S. K. Stowers, 'Social Status, Public Speaking and Private Teaching: The Circumstances of Paul's Preaching Activity', *NovT* 26 (1984) 59-82 (particularly 64-73).

27. Keck thinks that Cenchrea was the place of composition (*Romans* 30), but the mention in Rom. 16.1 of 'the church at Cenchrea' is better understood as a reference to another church, in contrast to 'the church' in 16.23 (that is, probably 'the church here', at the place from which the letter was to be sent).

28. See further my *Romans* 910-11. For the early house churches see particularly H. J. Klauck, *Hausgemeinde und Hauskirche im frühen Christentum* (SBS 103; Stuttgart: Katholisches Bibelwerk, 1981); Gehring, *House Church;* on Rom. 16.23 see Klauck 34; Gehring 139, 158-59.

29. The floor plan of the Anaploga villa is from B. Blue, 'Acts and the House Church', *BAFCS* 2.119-222 (here 209), who provides a number of figures and floor plans (193-222), including multi-storey housing (204). See also Murphy O'Connor, *St. Paul's Corinth* 154-58. The photos of Ostia were taken by myself.

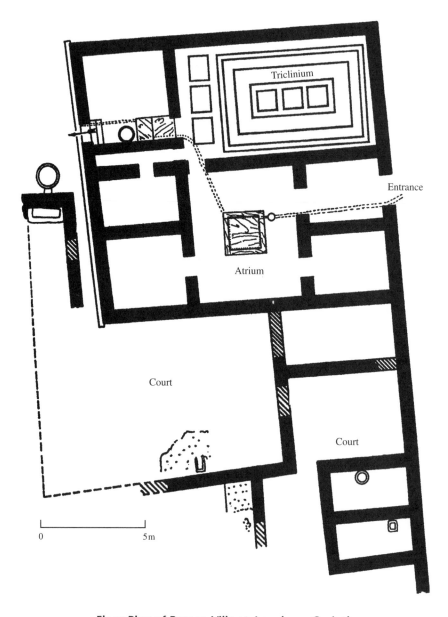

Floor Plan of Roman Villa at Anaploga, Corinth

Roman Tenements in Ostia

and other big cities. Not all this accommodation was of low quality; some was sited in attractive areas, some *cenacula* (apartments) were sufficiently large, those on the lower floors were not inconvenient . . . and many people of quite high status could afford no better.[30]

Juvenal in his *Satires* 3.193-202 gives a vivid picture of the shoddy buildings which during the second half of the first century period must often have been built too hastily and too high by landlords anxious to maximize their rental income:

> We live in a city shored up for the most part with gimcrack stays and props: that's how our landlords arrest the collapse of their property, papering over great cracks in the ramshackle fabric, reassuring the tenants they can sleep secure, when all the time the building is poised like a house of cards. I prefer to live where fires and midnight panics are not quite such common events. By the time the smoke's got up to your third-floor apartment (and you still asleep), your heroic downstairs neighbour is roaring for water and shifting his bits and pieces to safety. If the alarm goes at ground level, the last to fry will be the attic tenant, way up among the nesting pigeons with nothing but the tiles between himself and the weather.[31]

b. The Size of First-Century Churches

What deductions can we make concerning the churches which met within the range of property which literature and archaeology has revealed to us? Given that the majority of any group of converts in any city was likely to be illiterate, lacking in influence and low-born (1 Cor. 1.26), we certainly have to assume that their accommodation would have been at the lower end of the scale. That is to say, if Purcell is correct, most would have lived in multi-storey tenement blocks, perhaps several stories above the ground.[32] Presumably some

---

30. *OCD*[3] 731-32. See also J. E. Packer, 'Housing and Population in Imperial Ostia and Rome', *JRS* 57 (1967) 80-95. 'Whilst the lower floors could be quite spacious and were sometimes rented by members of the elite the higher floors were progressively more subdivided and more densely occupied. The highest floors consisted only of tiny wooden *cellae,* which were rented on a daily basis' (Meggitt, *Poverty* 63-64). See further Rapske, *Paul in Roman Custody* 228-36; Schnabel, *Mission* 593-97; C. Kunst, 'Wohnen in der antiken Grosstadt. Zur sozialen Topographie Roms in der frühen Kaiserzeit', in J. Zangenberg and M. Labahn, eds., *Christians as a Religious Minority in a Multicultural City: Modes of Interaction and Identity Formation in Early Imperial Rome* (London: Clark, 2004) 2-19.

31. As quoted by S. Goodenough, *Citizens of Rome* (London: Hamlyn, 1979) 62.

32. Slaves of course would live in the homes of their masters, freed slaves possibly

gatherings at least took place in such apartments, or at least the larger ones nearer street level. A church in such an *oikos* (usually translated 'house') would consist of only a small group, of, say, up to twelve. Since 'house' inevitably carries connotations of a larger property, such cell groups would probably be better referred to as 'tenement churches'.[33] Again, if Purcell is correct, even the relatively prosperous Aquila and Priscilla could almost certainly have been able to afford no more than a larger ground-floor apartment of a more substantial tenement property, so that the churches which met in their houses (Rom. 16.5; 1 Cor. 16.19) might only have been fifteen or twenty-five strong.

However, it is sufficiently clear that most city groups of early disciples would have included at least some higher-status members.[34] And the probability is that these latter would have invited the local believers to meet as church in their larger property. Gaius has already been mentioned as hosting 'the whole church' in Corinth (Rom. 16.23), making it possible for 'the whole congregation' to come together *(synerchesthai)* 'at the same place *(epi to auto)*' (1 Cor. 11.20; 14.23). And Philemon's house could accommodate both several guests[35] and some slaves.[36] If, then, we should envisage Christians coming together as churches in more substantial houses like the one illustrated above, houses with an atrium and a dining room *(triclinium),* we can certainly assume that larger gatherings were accommodated. How much larger is a matter of some dispute. The best estimates run up to fifty,[37] though quite how such a large group could meet as a single, coherent meeting is less than clear. Were they divided among two or more rooms? When the church met for the common meal, not all, presum-

---

also, and artisans might accommodate themselves in the *tabernae* where their shops were located.

33. R. Jewett has for some years insisted on the more realistic term 'tenement churches' rather than the potentially misleading 'house churches' (with reference to villas uncovered in places like Pompeii and Corinth); see his 'Tenement Churches and Communal Meals in the Early Church', *BR* 38 (1993) 23-43; now also *Romans* 53-55, 64-66. These factors have not yet been taken into account by many commentators; e.g., Schnelle does not consider less than large and fairly luxurious homes (*Paul* 155). But Gehring fairly asks whether the small apartments would be adequate for meetings and suggests that gatherings must have taken place elsewhere, for example, in workshops (*House Church* 147-51). See also D. G. Horrell, 'Domestic Space and Christian Meetings at Corinth: Imagining New Contexts and the Buildings East of the Theatre', *NTS* 50 (2004) 349-69.

34. See below, §30.5.

35. Phlm. 22: 'Prepare a guest room for me', not '*the* guest room'.

36. There is no suggestion that Onesimus, the subject of the letter to Philemon, was the latter's only slave.

37. R. J. Banks, *Paul's Idea of Community* (Exeter: Paternoster, 1980) 40-42; Murphy-O'Connor, *St. Paul's Corinth* 153-58.

ably, could have been accommodated in the triclinium, a fact which probably helps to make sense of the less than satisfactory arrangements for the only church about whose gatherings Paul speaks (Corinth).[38] Certainly numbers able to be accommodated should not be calculated on the bare data of square feet or square metres, since space would presumably be taken up with furnishings and possibly also statuary or ornaments.[39]

The basic point which emerges is that in most cases the earliest house churches must have been fairly small, a dozen or twenty people in all. And even when 'the whole church' in a city or section of a city could meet as church in one place, we may very well be talking of only forty or fifty people, and not necessarily gathered in a single room. The dynamics of church life, of the shared life of believers in most cities, must have been dependent on and to some extent determined by the physical space in which they were able to function as church.

30.3. An Association or a Religious Cult?

I asked earlier how Paul would have understood himself and have introduced himself to others. A similar question can be asked of the first churches. Did the earliest Christians simply invite a neighbour or colleague or visiting fellow countryman to the 'meeting' in their apartment or in the house of a wealthier fellow believer? Probably more important, how would these gatherings have been regarded by others? And potentially most important of all, how would they have been regarded by the local and imperial authorities?[40]

Answers to these questions depend in large part on how much we know about what are variously referred to as 'associations' or 'clubs' *(collegia)*,[41] and religious societies or cults *(thiasoi)* during that period. And since the information from literary sources on the former in particular is modest, it is only in the last

38. See further below, §32.5g.

39. Blue argues that a large house of the period could well accommodate a gathering of a hundred people (*BAFCS* 2.175 and n. 219); but he does not make allowance for the furnishings (couches, tables, etc.), which inevitably would have reduced the space for comfortable meetings. See also D. L. Balch, 'Rich Pompeiian Houses, Shops for Rent, and the Huge Apartment Building in Herculaneum as Typical Spaces for Pauline House Churches', *JSNT* 27 (2004) 27-46; Crossan and Reed, *Paul* 305-15.

40. I prefer to pose the questions thus, rather than in terms of influence, an issue which bedeviled the early history-of-religions attempts to set the development of Christianity within the context of the religions of the day, and which led inevitably to Deissmann's famous question, 'Is it analogy or is it genealogy?' (*Light* 265).

41. 'Association' has become the preferred generic title. See, e.g., Ascough, *Paul's Macedonian Associations* 3 n. 9, who defines 'voluntary associations' as groups 'of men and/or women organized on the basis of freely chosen membership for a common purpose'.

century, with the steadily increasing resources of epigraphical data,[42] that we are in a position even to begin to provide adequate answers.[43]

a. Associations, Cults and Schools

The various groupings can be classified in different ways. Traditionally a three-fold typology has been used based on what seemed to be self-evidently the primary purpose of the association: (1) occupational — particularly trade guilds; (2) cultic — *collegia sodalicia;* (3) burial — *collegia tennuiorum.*[44] Philip Harland, however, distinguishes five common types of association, which provides a more comprehensive and less compartmentalized mapping of the social context within which the earliest Christians in the Aegean cities would have

---

42. That our knowledge depended largely on inscriptions was already apparent in the latter decades of the nineteenth century; see, e.g., Hatch, *Organisation of the Early Christian Churches* 26-28, where he was able to draw on the early collections of inscriptions. Still of immense value is the collection of inscriptional data and its cataloguing by J.-P. Waltzing, *Études historique sur les corporations professionnelles chez les Romains* (4 vols.; Leuven: Peeters, 1895-1900; reprinted Hildesheim: George Olms, 1970). Some sample inscriptions are provided by R. K. Sherk, *The Roman Empire: Augustus to Hadrian* (TDGR 6; Cambridge: Cambridge University, 1988) 233-35. See also S. C. Barton and G. H. R. Horsley, 'A Hellenistic Cult Group and the New Testament Churches', *JAC* 24 (1981) 7-41. The famous Greek inscription recording the minutes of a general meeting of the club known as the Iobacchae in Athens and the regulations adopted by the meeting (in 178 CE) can be found in translation conveniently in Meyer, *The Ancient Mysteries* 96-99. The equally famous inscription from Lanuvium, southeast of Rome, regarding the *cultures Dianae et Antinoi* (136 CE) can be found in translation in Wilken, *Christians* 36-39. Both are discussed at length in E. Ebel, *Die Attraktivität früher christlicher Gemeinden* (WUNT 2.178; Tübingen: Mohr Siebeck, 2004) chs. 1-3; see also Klauck, *Religious Context* 50-53. Ascough provides a useful review of earlier studies in *Paul's Macedonian Associations* 3-10, also his earlier *What Are They Saying about the Formation of Pauline Churches?* (New York: Paulist, 1998) ch. 4. See further N. Tran, *Les membres des associations romaines. Le rang social des* Collegiati *en Italie et en Gaules, sous le haut-empire* (Rome: École Française de Rome, 2006).

43. S. Dill, *Roman Society from Nero to Marcus Aurelius* (London: Macmillan, 1904) ch. 3 'The Colleges and Plebeian Life', demonstrates well how the epigraphical data have opened up to us the world of the great majority of lower-status inhabitants of Roman cities, a point of crucial importance for the study of Christianity's beginnings, since the literature of the period is so dominated by the ancient perception of history as 'the history of kings and queens', or, here we should rather say, the history of consuls and emperors. Of early studies one of the greatest of continuing value is F. Poland, *Geschichte des griechischen Vereinswesens* (Leipzig: Teubner, 1909).

44. Bibliography in Harland, *Associations* 28. Hatch used an eightfold categorization: (1) trade guilds, (2) dramatic guilds, (3) athletic clubs, (4) burial clubs, (5) dining clubs, (6) friendly societies, (7) literary societies, (8) financial societies (*Organisation* 26-27 n. 1).

found themselves.[45] In what follows I group the first four of Harland's categories under the heading of 'associations', maintain a distinction from his fifth (the religious cult), which is sufficiently distinct to warrant a separate category, and add the 'philosophical school', which provides parallels noted by some[46] but too often disregarded.

1. *Associations*

* *Household or familial associations.* Family networks, including slaves and other dependents, could also draw in friends and colleagues.[47] A local house might be adapted and serve for communal use, perhaps with a special room set apart for devotion or performance of sacred ritual.[48] Family language (mother, father, brothers, sisters) occurs in connection with a significant number of associations.[49]

---

45. Harland, *Associations* 29-53. See also R. MacMullen, *Roman Social Relations 50 BC to AD 284* (New Haven: Yale University, 1974) 73-77 (trade associations), 82-86 (neighbourhood and national associations); Chester, *Conversion at Corinth* ch. 8, who justifiably warns against generalisations and blanket assertions in comparing voluntary associations with the Pauline churches (235-36). Harland also justifiably reminds us that 'evidence for social relations in ancient societies is fragmentary in comparison to the data available to a sociologist studying a modern society. . . . What we get, at best, is snapshots of social relations at a particular time and place. It is not always clear how (or whether) we can generalize from these snapshots about the moving picture that is social reality' (15).

46. Particularly E. A. Judge, 'The Early Christians as a Scholastic Community', *JRH* 1 (1960-61) 4-15, 125-37; L. Alexander, 'Paul and the Hellenistic Schools: The Evidence of Galen', in Engberg-Pedersen, ed., *Paul in His Hellenistic Context* 60-84; S. Mason, '*Philosophiai:* Graeco-Roman, Judean and Christian', in Kloppenborg and Wilson, *Voluntary Associations* 31-58; and further S. K. Stowers, 'Does Pauline Christianity Resemble a Hellenistic Philosophy?', in Engberg-Pedersen, ed., *Paul beyond the Judaism/Hellenism Divide* ch. 4; Ascough, *Formation* ch. 2. In his chapter on the formation of the *ekklēsia,* Meeks reviewed four 'models from the environment: the household, the voluntary association, the synagogue and the philosophic or rhetorical school (*Urban Christians* 75-84).

47. Meeks, *Urban Christians* 31, 75-77; A. D. Clarke, *Serve the Community of the Church* (Grand Rapids: Eerdmans, 2000) 64-65; Ascough, *Paul's Macedonian Associations* 30-31.

48. A now-famous example is the so-called villa of the mysteries at Pompeii (diagram in Burkert, *Ancient Mystery Cults* 58; photo in Meyer, *Ancient Mysteries* 61). Others in Klauck, *Religious Context* 63-68; and see n. 23 above.

49. Examples already in Waltzing, *Études* 1.329-30, 446-49, Poland, *Geschichte* 54-55, 72-73, 161, 284, 357, 371-73, and Dill, who cites Mommsen's belief 'that the collegiate life which blossomed so luxuriantly in the early Empire, was modeled on the sacred union of the Roman family' (*Roman Society* 280). See also *NDIEC* 2.91; BDAG 18, 786; Ascough, *Paul's Macedonian Associations* 76-77; Ebel, *Attraktivität* 203-13. Harland criticizes Meeks at this point for arguing that use of such language in the associations was 'rare' (*Associations* 31-33; referring to Meeks, *Urban Christians* 85-88, 225 n. 73; though see also Kloppenborg, 'Edwin

- *Ethnic or regional associations.* Given the network of trade and commerce which linked the countries and cities of the Mediterranean region, not to mention enslaved prisoners of war subsequently freed and the movement of mercenaries, exiled individuals and others, it was natural that fellow countrymen grouped together in foreign cities, even when they had settled there for some time.[50]
- *Neighbourhood associations.* The fact of living or working on a particular street or neighbourhood also provided an occasion for grouping together. Street associations are attested in several cities of Asia, including Ephesus and Smyrna.[51]
- *Occupational associations.* A wide range of such associations is attested in inscriptions — for example, bakers, fishers, farmers, builders, physicians, clothing producers, cleaners, leather cutters, linen workers, dyers, potters, merchants, shippers, and smiths in copper, silver and gold.[52] The range, it should be noted, extended from the manual to what would now be called the professional (purple-dyers, silversmiths and goldsmiths, physicians), but 'the very existence of guilds is a testimony to the identity and pride that characterized workers of many trades'; and in some cases craftsmen or traders attained membership of the city council.[53]

2. *Cult or temple associations.* 'There was an array of such associations in Asia during the Roman era, including those devoted to Apollo, Aphrodite, Artemis, Asclepios, Cybele and Attis, Zeus, and the emperors as gods *(Sebastoi),* as well as messengers of the gods ("angels") or heroes, to name

---

Hatch' 237-38). Chester notes that while familial language is common in Latin inscriptions, it is rare in Greek inscriptions (*Conversion at Corinth* 229-31, citing both Nock and Poland); he goes on, however, to note that 'father' was often used of the one who initiated another into a cult (291 n. 84).

50. Schürer refers, for example, to associations of Tyrians in Delos and Puteoli, and of Sidonians in Athens (*History* 3.108-11). Harland instances associations of Samothracians, Cretans, Sidonians and Pergaians on the island of Rhodes, of Dioscurians in Pergamum, of Alexandrians in Thracia and of Phrygians in Pompeii (*Associations* 34-36)

51. In Apameia, northeast of Colossae, several associations identified themselves by the colonnaded street where they worked — e.g., the artisans of Shoemaker Street and the traders of Bath Street (Harland, *Associations* 37-38). See further A. Bendlin, 'Gemeinschaft, Öffentlichkeit und Identität', in U. Egelhaaf-Gaiser and A. Schäfer, eds., *Religiöse Vereine in der römischen Antike* (STAC 13; Tübingen: Mohr Siebeck, 2002) 9-40 (here 30-32).

52. See the table in Harland, *Associations* 39-40; fuller lists in MacMullen, *Social Relations* 73, and Ascough, *Paul's Macedonian Associations* 17-18; examples in *NDIEC* 3.54-55; 4.17-18; 5.95-114 (a fishing cartel in Ephesus in the mid-50s, with a social 'mix' closely akin to that represented in the Pauline congregations — 110); 7.123-27.

53. Harland, *Associations* 42-44.

just a few'. The mysteries of Isis and Serapis,[54] the Great Mother (Cybele), Demeter and Kore, and Dionysus were well established in Asia. Initiates would participate in a variety of practices, including sacrifice, communal meals, re-enactment of the central myth of the god, sacred processions and hymn-singing. The mysteries devoted to Dionysus (Bacchus) are the best attested in Asia — in cities like Ephesus, Magnesia, Pergamum, Philadelphia and Smyrna.[55]

3. *Philosophical schools.* The most famous were those which inculcated Platonism or Stoicism, the Epicureans, and the Pythagoreans.[56] Joining a philosophical school often involved a 'conversion', acceptance of a new and different way of living.[57] 'They were very much occupied with moral exhortation and teaching; they had authoritative texts that they expounded; they were run by professional teachers who were masters of their traditions; and they were concerned not with devotion to one God, but with understanding the whole class of "divinity" and its relationship to human affairs'.[58]

These three categories can be broadly distinguished in that the associations typically functioned to provide occasions for social gathering, the cults were primarily vehicles for the expression of religious devotion and the desire to defeat death, and the schools were concerned chiefly to promote disciplined thought and reasoned living. At the same time, however, we should not make the mistake of thinking of these different groupings in a rigidly stratified way. The intent of using such a broader classification is to indicate the breadth of Roman society covered by the widespread practice of gathering together in congenial groups for mutual benefit and enjoyment (social, spiritual or intellectual).[59] Nor should we

54. See H. Koester, 'Associations of the Egyptian Cult in Asia Minor', *Paul and His World: Interpreting the New Testament in Its Context* (Minneapolis: Fortress, 2007) chs. 13-14.

55. Harland, *Associations* 45-49. See also Burkert, *Ancient Mystery Cults;* Ascough, *Formation* ch. 3. On the individual mysteries (Eleusis, Dionysus, Attis, Isis and Mithras), see Klauck, *Religious Context* ch. 2; classic literary texts in Meyer, *Ancient Mysteries;* on priestly colleges see J. Rüpke, '*Collegia sacerdotum.* Religiöse Vereine in der Oberschicht', in Egelhaaf-Gaiser and Schäfer, *Religiöse Vereine* 41-67. And note n. 67 below.

56. 'Cynicism was never a formal philosophical school but rather a way of life grounded in an extreme primitivist interpretation of the principle "live according to nature"' (*OCD³* 418).

57. The theme of A. D. Nock's famous *Conversion: The Old and New in Religion from Alexander the Great to Augustine* (London: Oxford University, 1933). Mason also notes that 'the words *epistrophē, conversio,* and *metanoia* routinely characterize the acceptance of philosophy' ('*Philosophiai*' 33).

58. Mason, '*Philosophiai*' 38.

59. 'Thus it appears that in every part of the Roman world, in the decaying little country

make the mistake of assuming that all associations which might be grouped under one of the above heads were homogeneous, though greater homogeneity would be truer of occupational or business associations than the rest.[60] That said, it is still worth drawing attention to several typical features which have bearing on the questions which opened this section.

- Membership of associations was not necessarily exclusive; individuals could participate freely in different associations, or they could express devotion to more than one deity.[61] This was less true of the cults and the schools, though it was a common practice, for example, for elites to undergo initiation into the Eleusinian mysteries, and the influence of the schools cross-fertilized a wide sweep of intellectual thought.
- Nor were the concerns of individual associations limited to the category under which such a taxonomy as above might list them. Burial societies are not included as a separate category, since several associations of different types included provision for burial, in return for monthly payments made by the individual members.[62]

---

town, and in the great trading centres, the same great movement of association is going on apace. It swept into its current every social grade, and every trade, handicraft or profession, the pastil-makers, the green-grocers and unguent sellers of Rome, the muleteers of the Alps, the fullers of Pompeii, the doctors of Beneventum, the boatmen of the Seine, the wine merchants of Lyons' (Dill, *Roman Society* 268).

60. Harland, *Associations* 27-28, 41.

61. S. G. Wilson, 'Voluntary Associations: An Overview', in Kloppenborg and Wilson, *Voluntary Associations* 1-15 (here 9-10). 'From Ostia alone there are over 200 names of *Augustales* who were freedmen also belonging to guilds of woodworkers, barge operators, grain merchants, millers, and of the imperial house' (J. S. Kloppenborg, 'Collegia and *Thiasoi*', in Kloppenborg and Wilson, *Voluntary Associations* 16-30 [here 17]). Bendlin cites two cases where the same individual held the office of *magister* in two and four different *collegia* ('Gemeinschaft' 28-29). Harland notes a law from the late second century which ruled it to be unlawful to belong to more than one guild or association and which indicates that (prior to that law) it had been quite common for someone to belong to more than one association (*Associations* 206). Meeks regarded the exclusivity of Christian groups as an important difference from the voluntary associations (*Urban Christians* 78-79). But in some cases there were regulations which forbad participation in other cults or moving from one fraternity to another (examples in *NDIEC* 1.21-23; Klauck, *Religious Context* 49); and Ascough thinks it reasonable to assume that associations 'at least *de facto* received the primary allegiance of their members' (*Paul's Macedonian Associations* 88).

62. See further Kloppenborg, 'Collegia and *Thiasoi*' 20-23; Bendlin, 'Gemeinschaft' 14; Harland, *Associations* 84-86; Ascough, *Paul's Macedonian Associations* 25-28. There was a custom of a common burial for members of an association, regardless of family ties (*NDIEC* 2.49-50). In a private communication John Kloppenborg commented that 'burial societies are really a fiction of Roman jurists'.

- Associations seem to have existed typically for the non-elite (the urban poor, slaves, freedmen), who would otherwise have lacked regular opportunity for dining out, for titles and honour,[63] and for a good burial. But this class included the great bulk of the population anyway (apart from the elite minority).[64] While there were what we might now call professional associations and working men's clubs,[65] membership of several associations ran across a number of socio-economic levels, with leading citizens or patrons named prominently at the head of lists of members.[66] The schools, naturally, were more intellectually elitist.
- The cults were primarily religious in character and objective, but no association lacked a religious dimension.[67] An occupational association would typically have a patron god or goddess.[68] Associations would typically

---

63. See particularly Tran, *Membres des associations romaines* chs. 1-3; also R. Jewett, 'Paul, Shame and Honor', in Sampley ed., *Paul and the Greco-Roman World* 551-74 (with bibliography).

64. Ascough, *Paul's Macedonian Associations* 51-54.

65. Some associations existed exclusively for slaves and freedmen (Klauck, *Religious Context* 47).

66. Kloppenborg, 'Edwin Hatch' 234-35; B. H. McLean, 'The Agrippinilla Inscription: Religious Associations and Early Church Formation', in B. H. McLean, ed., *Origins and Method*, J. C. Hurd FS (JSNTS 86; Sheffield: JSOT, 1993) 239-70 (here 256-57); *OCD*³ 352. Dill provides several examples: a college of smiths in Tarraconensis, with 15 patrons at the head of the roll, followed by 12 decurions (including two doctors and a soothsayer), 28 'plain plebeians' and several 'mothers' and 'daughters' of the society; a club at Ostia with 9 patrons, 2 holders of quinquennial rank, and 123 plebeians. 'The plebs of many colleges included slaves, and in more than one inscription the men of ingenuous and those of servile birth are carefully distinguished, the slaves being sometimes placed at the bottom of the roll' (*Roman Society* 270-71; on the role of patrons, 273-79). 'From what date the city of Rome's colleges recruited their members from the different professions and from freedmen and slaves in addition, is unknown' (Bendlin, 'Gemeinschaft' 29). See further Harland on 'social networks of benefaction' (*Associations* 97-101, 106-108; and further 140-55); Clarke, *Serve* 65-69.

67. The point was taken early on (Hatch, *Organization* 27-28; Waltzing, *Études* 1.195-255). 'The word [*collegium*] had religious associations even when the object of the club was not primarily worship. Few, if any, *collegia* were completely secular. . . . All ancient societies from the family upwards had a religious basis' (*OCD*³ 352). Consequently the categorization 'cult or temple associations' (2 above) should perhaps be limited to the mystery cults, or 'public religious associations', as in R. S. Ascough, 'Greco-Roman Philosophic, Religious, and Voluntary Associations', in R. N. Longenecker, ed., *Community Formation in the Early Church and in the Church Today* (Peabody: Hendrickson, 2002) 3-19 (here 9).

68. See, e.g., I. Dittmann-Schöne, 'Götterverehrung bei den Berufsvereinen im kaiserzeitlichen Kleinasien', in Egelhaaf-Gaiser and Schäfer, *Religiöse Vereine* 81-96; Ascough, *Paul's Macedonian Associations* 23-24.

hold their meetings in temples.[69] And meetings and shared meals would regularly include ritual acts of devotion, sacrifice or libations to the patron god.[70] The promise held out by the mystery cults of an afterlife must have been particularly attractive to those who feared death.[71]

- Associations did not function as or offer an alternative to the imperial cult.[72] On the contrary, they were thoroughly integrated into it, regularly performing rituals which honoured the *Sebastoi*[73] and participating in the activities of the imperial cult, including sacrifice probably understood (in Asia at this time) as offered to the emperor as to a god.[74]

- Membership of most associations ranged between 15 and 100, typically in the 30s-40s, though some are attested as 200 or more in strength.[75]

- Shared meals were one of the most characteristic features and *raisons d'etre* of associations; indeed, clubs were sometimes described as *eranoi*.[76] Associations would regularly meet (every month or more frequently) to share in a meal,[77] again typically in one of the dining rooms attached to a

---

69. '*Collegia* often held their meetings in temples and their clubhouse *(schola)* might bear the name of a divinity' (*OCD*³ 352).

70. Klauck, *Religious Context* 44-45. 'Honoring gods and goddesses in a variety of ways was a common concern for virtually all types of association and their members' (Harland, *Associations* 73); see the whole section, 'Intertwined Social, Religious, and Funerary Dimensions of Association Life' (61-83). Rüpke attempts a reconstruction of the priestly banquets *(cenae sacerdotales)* ('Collegia sacerdotum' 46-62).

71. See particularly Burkert, *Ancient Mystery Cults* ch. 1; also Chester, *Conversion at Corinth* 273-74.

72. Klauck notes that 'to a small extent the veneration of the emperor also took on the external form of a mystery cult . . . [and] . . . like other mystery cults, sometimes took on the form of an association' (*Religious Context* 315). Notable were the many organizations of *Augustales* (attested in some 2,500 inscriptions); they were composed principally of freedmen, who sometimes organized like a *collegium,* and whose formal responsibilities probably centred on the imperial cult (*OCD*³ 215).

73. *Sebastos,* 'worthy of reverence', Greek rendering of 'Augustus', which became a title for the emperor after Octavian (BDAG 917).

74. Harland, *Associations* chs. 4-5, particularly 121-28, 155-60.

75. Meeks, *Urban Christians* 31; Kloppenborg, 'Collegia and *Thiasoi*' 25-26; Klauck, *Religious Context* 43; Ascough, *Paul's Macedonian Associations* 47. In suggesting to Trajan that an association of firemen might be formed in the province, Pliny indicated that membership would be restricted to 150 (*Ep.* 10.33).

76. *OCD*³ 552; an *eranos* was a 'meal to which each contributed his share' (LSJ 680), a 'potluck' dinner. The practice went back to Homer's time and is still attested in the second century CE; see P. Lampe, 'The Eucharist: Identifying with Christ on the Cross', *Interpretation* 48 (1994) 36-49 (here 38-39 and n. 14).

77. Harland, *Associations* 74-83, with due warning not to be misled by accusations of drunken orgies and incestuous behaviour, which would have only limited validity (74-75), a warning which could equally apply to the allusion in Rom. 13.13; Petronius's vivid account of

temple, which could presumably be rented, and in which the meat consumed would be the residue of animals offered in sacrifice in the temple,[78] though more wealthy associations had their own property, and smaller ones could meet in the bath complexes or in a corner tavern or a private house.[79]

- Technically, associations had to be formally licensed,[80] though unlicensed groups were tolerated as long as they did nothing illegal or offensive.[81] Suspicion and infrequent bans were directed against overtly political or occasionally riotous clubs.[82] For the most part, associations served important

Trimalchio's banquet in *Satyricon* also comes to mind; and see below, n. 229. But note also Burkert's observation that the sacrificial meals were 'realistic, enjoyable festivities with plenty of food, in contrast to the parsimonious everyday life' (*Ancient Mystery Cults* 110).

78. W. W. Willis, *Idol Meat in Corinth* (SBLDS 68; Chico: Scholars, 1985), conveniently provides a sequence of papyri invitations to dine at the table of the lord Sarapis (40-42); see also *NDIEC* 1.5-9. At various temple complexes in the Greco-Roman world, archaeology has regularly uncovered rooms, often opening off a central courtyard, whose function as small dining rooms is attested by the fact that the doorway is off centre, allowing both a couch lengthways on one side of the doorway and another end-on on the other side of the doorway. Three dining rooms were attached to the Asclepion at Corinth, each accommodating eleven persons (see Murphy-O'Connor, *St. Paul's Corinth* 162-67); the dining rooms at the sanctuary of Demeter and Kore would have accommodated only five to nine persons (N. Bookidis, 'Ritual Dining at Corinth', in N. Marinatos and R. Hogg, eds., *Greek Sanctuaries: New Approaches* [London: Routledge, 1993] 45-61 [here 47-49]). For plans of dining facilities attached to other sanctuaries see P. D. Gooch, *Dangerous Food: 1 Corinthians 8–10 in Its Context* (Waterloo: Wilfrid Laurier University, 1993) viii-xvi. See further W. J. Slater, ed., *Dining in a Classical Context* (Ann Arbor: University of Michigan, 1991).

79. See also P. Richardson, 'Building "an Association *(Synodos)* . . . and a Place of Their Own"', in R. N. Longenecker, ed., *Community Formation in the Early Church and in the Church Today* (Peabody: Hendrickson, 2002) 36-56.

80. Augustus enacted the *Lex Iulia* (probably in 7 CE) that every club must be sanctioned by the senate or emperor (*OCD*³ 352). Bendlin deduces from Tacitus, *Ann.* 14.17, that 'the asking for permission in Senate or other local authorities was not the rule' ('Gemeinschaft' 11).

81. Schnelle, *Paul* 154 n. 66, cites M. Öhler, 'Römisches Vereinsrecht und christliche Gemeinden', in M. Labahn and J. Zangenberg, eds., *Zwischen den Reichen* (Tübingen: Francke, 2002) 61: 'At least since the time of Augustus, the formation of clubs and associations had been carefully regulated. A *collegium* could apply to the senate for permission, which was granted when a case could be made that some public good would derive from it and no activities damaging to the state were anticipated. Certain associations that had long existed, including Jewish synagogues, were always licensed on the basis of their tradition. Alongside these there were innumerable unlicensed groups that were tolerated as long as they did nothing illegal or offensive'. See also Ascough, *Paul's Macedonian Associations* 42-46. Kloppenborg, however, observes: 'Roman jurists and some Roman elites *thought* that clubs should be licensed, but there is virtually no evidence to support the contention that the clubs sought such approval' (private communication).

82. See particularly W. Cotter, 'The Collegia and Roman Law: State Restrictions on Voluntary Associations', in Kloppenborg and Wilson, *Voluntary Associations* 74-89. But

aspects of the social, cultural and religious needs of the broad civic community, particularly the middle- and lower-ranking members of society, regularly acting as friendly or welfare societies for their members, including provision of a good burial.[83]

b. Synagogues

Within the social context just sketched out, synagogues had been long accustomed to holding their place.[84] Like associations, synagogues were often named after prominent persons or local neighbourhoods or cities of origin.[85] They more obviously had the appearance of associations, since they had no local shrines or temples (Jerusalem was far away), nor did they observe the normal cultic practices of sacrifice and libation.[86] Indeed, Jewish gatherings had more the appear-

---

Kloppenborg again raises a query: 'Of course, they could be suppressed under some circumstances, but Ilias Arnaoutoglou, "Roman Law and *Collegia* in Asia Minor", in *RIDA* 49 (2002) 27-44, has shown convincingly against Cotter that actions against *thiasoi* in Asia were hardly consistent, constant or organized' (private communication).

83. This last point is Harland's main thesis; see *Associations* particularly 10-14 and chs. 3 and 6. On the various rulings against *collegia,* from the second century BCE to the second century CE, Harland notes the particular context on each occasion (161-69) and concludes that 'most associations would continue to function openly and undisturbed . . . intervention occurred only when associations were caught up in broader disorderly incidents that were not adequately dealt with locally' (166). He also observes that in the severest rulings, collegia of 'ancient foundation' and gatherings 'for religious purposes' were explicitly excused (164, 168); 'when it comes to the province of Asia itself, we have absolutely no evidence of Roman officials dissolving such groups or applying laws regarding associations' (169); 'in general, associations were not anti-Roman or subversive groups' (173). Schürer had already made the point that associations generally enjoyed official toleration in Rome, 'only political clubs being forbidden from the time of Caesar and Augustus' (*History* 3.112). 'For the most part, these groups survived where they did because they reinforced the political *status quo,* rather than being subversive' (Clarke, *Serve* 72, citing the numerous inscriptions from Pompeii which named the political candidates supported by the *collegia*).

84. See, e.g., P. Richardson, 'Early Synagogues as Collegia in the Diaspora and Palestine', in Kloppenborg and Wilson, *Voluntary Associations* 90-109; also 'An Architectural Case for Synagogues as Associations', in Olsson and Zetterholm, eds., *The Ancient Synagogue* 90-117; Clarke, *Serve* ch. 6. Klauck observes that 'the assembly of the members of an association can be called *synagōgē,* "synagogue", in non-Jewish sources too (LSCG 177.93f.; 135.20)' (*Religious Context* 46; referring to F. Sokolowski, *Lois sacrées des cités grecques*); similarly *NDIEC* 4.202.

85. As attested by the evidence from Rome — H. J. Leon, *The Jews of Ancient Rome* (Philadelphia: Jewish Publication Society, 1960) ch. 7; see further below, §33 n. 47.

86. Roman sources, though, do tend to treat Judaism as a cult, a *superstitio* (Mason, *'Philosophiai'* 42).

ance of philosophical schools, as both Philo and Josephus took some pains to point out.[87] The diaspora synagogue 'served as a place for study, discussion of sacred texts, and moral exhortation. Judeans were well known for their disciplined way of life. . . . Joining the group did indeed require "conversion"'.[88]

Of crucial importance was the consistent recognition of and toleration for the rights of Jewish diaspora communities. In particular, Caesar and Augustus had given Jewish synagogues formal recognition, and Caesar expressly exempted Jewish communities from the bans on *collegia*.[89] Josephus makes a point of documenting these decrees and rulings;[90] no wonder, since they secured the toleration of and protection for Jewish laws and customs in the empire. These rights included the right of assembly, the right to administer their own finances (including the exceptional permission for the Temple tax to be collected and transmitted to Jerusalem), jurisdiction over their own members (including the power to administer corporal punishment — 2 Cor. 11.24), freedom from military service (because of the Jewish requirement to observe the Sabbath), and not least in importance, permission not to participate in the imperial cult.[91] In short, the Jewish religion remained throughout our period under the formal protection of the Roman state, although the expression (much used in modern literature) *religio licita* is not actually to be found in the literature of the period.[92]

It is important to underscore the fact that the Jewish *synagōgai* were thus officially regarded as equivalent to, on a par with, the *collegia* and *thiasoi* of

87. Malherbe, *Social Aspects* 54; Mason, *'Philosophiai'* 43-46: in Philo, words built on the root *philosoph-* occur 212 times (e.g., *Mos.* 2.216; *Prob.* 43); Josephus famously represents the Jewish sects (Pharisees, Sadducees, Essenes) as philosophical schools *(philosophiai)* (*War* 2.119; *Ant.* 18.11). Aristobulus (2nd century BCE) seems to have been the first to present Judaism as a philosophical school; see J. J. Collins, *Between Athens and Jerusalem: Jewish Identity in the Hellenistic Diaspora* (New York: Crossroad, 1983) 175-78.

88. Mason, *'Philosophiai'* 42. See also C. Claussen, *Versammlung* ch. 8; also 'Meeting, Community, Synagogue — Different Frameworks of Ancient Jewish Congregations', in Olsson and Zetterholm, eds., *The Ancient Synagogue* 144-67.

89. Philo, *Legat.* 156-58; Josephus, *Ant.* 14.215. 'Pre-70 synagogues were in all respects analogous to collegia, while enjoying greater imperial protection' (Wilson, 'Voluntary Associations' 4). See further Smallwood, *Jews* 133-38.

90. *Ant.* 14.185-267; 16.160-79, including severe warnings to the local authorities in Tralles, Miletus, Pergamum, Halicarnassus, Sardis and Ephesus (14.241-64). Dean Pinter also referred me to *War* 1.200, 282-85; *Ant.* 14.144-48 (14.265-67 on the note on the friendship between Romans and Judeans); 16.48, 53; *Ap.* 2.61. See further Levinskaya, *BAFCS* 5.139-43; Gruen, *Diaspora* ch. 3; bibliography in Fitzmyer, *Acts* 629.

91. Full detail in Schürer, *History* 3.113-23. See further M. Tellbe, *Paul between Synagogue and State: Christians, Jews, and Civic Authorities in 1 Thessalonians, Romans and Philippians* (CBNTS 34; Stockholm: Almqvist and Wiksell, 2001) 26-63.

92. Schürer, *History* 3.117 n. 40; Tellbe, *Paul between Synagogue and State* 54-59.

other national and religious groups — the Jewish ethnic association, the devotees of the cult of Kyrios Yahweh, the practitioners of the philosophy taught by Moses. These *synagōgai* would, of course, have been one of the more homogeneous associations, consisting of Jews as the core members and participants in the synagogue's corporate life. But, as already noted, they were not an exclusive association, for they evidently welcomed non-Jewish adherents and sympathizers (God-fearers) in their gatherings. So too, it is worth repeating, there is sufficient evidence of civic approbation of certain synagogue communities, not least in Asia,[93] so that we can be confident that by and large Jewish synagogue communities were regarded as just another of the wide range of national and religious associations which was such a feature of Roman society.

Equally, we should not imagine that belonging to the synagogue association necessarily precluded diaspora Jews from participation in the practices of other associations. Where Jewish communities were large, we can certainly imagine specifically Jewish trade associations. But we cannot exclude the possibility that in smaller centres a Jew like Aquila participated in the association of tent-makers. Where an association owed devotion to a particular deity, the great majority of Jews would have been inhibited from participation in any gathering where sacrifice or libation was offered. But such scruples may not have excluded them from other social activities. We know that there was a fair range of acculturation and assimilation to local social norms in different Jewish groups.[94] So some participation in neighbourhood associations or trade guilds cannot be excluded. The problems which Paul had to confront in 1 Corinthians 8–10 may not have been confined to liberal Christians.[95]

The issue is further complicated by the possibility that some Jewish synagogue communities had become quite syncretistic. That there were such synagogues in Asia Minor was a common thesis some years ago, a view stimulated by the possibility that Col. 2.18 envisages Jewish worship of angels.[96] But the more strongly emerging consensus is that associations calling themselves *Sabbatistai* or devoting themselves to *Theos Hypsistos* ('God Most High') are better understood as indicative of the power of Jewish beliefs and practices in the formation

---

93. See above, §29.5b.

94. Barclay, *Jews* ch. 11; Harland, *Associations* 195-210, citing evidence, for example, of 'the participation and integration of Jews in civic life but also of Jews' affiliations with or even memberships in the local occupational associations of Hierapolis' (208-209). See also Borgen, '"Yes", "No", "How Far?"'. Cf. L. V. Rutgers's conclusion from his examination of the evidence provided by the catacombs, in *The Jews in Late Ancient Rome* (Leiden: Brill, 1995), that in Rome there was active and self-conscious cultural interaction of Jews with non-Jews; they were *Roman* Jews (263, 268).

95. See below, §32.5e.

96. See my *Colossians and Philemon* 31 and n. 30, 179-84.

of non-Jewish syncretistic cults.[97] In either case, we have evidence of boundaries between Jewish synagogues and other associations which were permeable to powerful beliefs and influential practices. The evidence of Jewish magical practice[98] neither advances nor retards this probability, since magic was a universal para-religious phenomenon at the time, and no doubt good luck charms and amulets were to be found in the household of not a few devout Jews of the period.

This survey of associations and the evidence that Jewish synagogues would usually have blended quite well into the city-scapes (socially and culturally) wherever Jewish communities were to be found, while at the same time able to retain their distinctive customs and practices, provide an invaluable setting for our discussion of how Paul's churches would have been perceived, as well as how they would have seen themselves.

c. Churches

The points of comparison with the churches established by Paul should already be obvious and already suggest answers to the questions which opened this chapter.[99] They were not obviously like a neighbourhood association or trade guild.[100] But since they met in the house of a (probably) prominent citizen, they could be likened to an extension of his (or her) household — a household association.[101] As (in some sense) offshoots of the synagogue, they could have shared

97. Trebilco, *Jewish Communities* ch. 6; Hengel and Schwemer, *Paul* 161-67; Harland, *Associations* 49-50 and nn. 25-26.

98. See particularly P. S. Alexander, 'Incantations and Books of Magic', in Schürer, *History* 3.342-79: 'Magic flourished among the Jews despite strong and persistent condemnation by the religious authority' (342); C. E. Arnold, *Ephesians: Power and Magic* (SNTSMS 63; Cambridge: Cambridge University, 1989); also *The Colossian Syncretism: The Interface between Christianity and Folk Belief at Colossae* (Grand Rapids: Baker, 1996). On magic more generally see Klauck, *Religious Context* 209-31.

99. But it would be unwise to look for a single model; e.g., Ascough suggests that 'the Thessalonians were most analogous to a professional voluntary association while the Philippians were most analogous to a religious association' (*Paul's Macedonian Associations* 14); see also his 'The Thessalonian Christian Community as a Professional Voluntary Association', *JBL* 119 (2000) 311-28. Kloppenborg. 'Edwin Hatch', reviews the earlier debate occasioned by G. Heinrici and Hatch, and the issues arising. See also T. Schmeller, 'Gegenwelten. Zum Vergleich zwischen paulinischen Gemeinden und nichtchristlichen Gruppen', *BZ* 47 (2003) 167-85.

100. Though Meeks observes that 'the *ekklēsia* that gathered with the tentmakers Prisca, Aquila, and Paul in Corinth or Ephesus might well have seemed to the neighbors a club of that sort' (*Urban Christians* 32).

101. Stegemann and Stegemann think 'the institutional character of the *ekklēsia* can best be compared with the popular assemblies; the character of fellowship is best compared with the

the ambiguity of status, as an association or a foreign 'superstition'.[102] With their own distinctive initiation rite and veneration of an exalted hero, they may have seemed an unusual kind of mystery cult.[103] And as groups who were founded by Paul (who resembled an itinerant philosopher) and who, judging by Paul's letters, were nurtured on a diet of doctrinal teaching and moral exhortation, they must have appeared to others more like philosophical schools.[104]

A less expected and more interesting point of contact is Paul's characterization of the new 'churches' as a 'body *(sōma)*', of individual believers as members of Christ or as 'one body in Christ'.[105] Associations or cults could occasionally use the term in self-reference (= 'corporations'), as in Epicurus's characterization of his community as 'a holy body *(hieron sōma)*'.[106] But the main influence or point of comparison is indicated by the way Paul plays on the image: one body, but many members; the unity of the whole depending on the harmony (interaction and cooperation) of all the members. For this was precisely how the image had been used in political philosophy — the city or state as a body, equally dependent on the different ethnic minorities, guilds and political factions working together for the good of the whole.[107] Here again, as with *ekklēsia,* we should hardly infer that Paul thereby set up the individual churches as some sort of competition with or mimicry of the city or state in which these churches had to function.[108] At the same time, the clear assertion that this 'body'

---

ancient household or nuclear family' (*Jesus Movement* 286); 'only the regular meetings, which were connected with common meals, could suggest an analogy with the ancient associations' (281). See also M. Karrer and O. Cremer, 'Vereinsgeschichtliche Impulse im ersten Christentum', in Lehnert and Rüsen-Weinhold, eds., *Logos — Logik — Lyrik* 33-52.

102. Meeks regards the synagogue as 'the nearest and most natural model' for the Christian groups, though he also notes 'how little evidence there is in the Pauline letters of any imitation of the specific organization of the synagogue' (*Urban Christians* 80-81). See also Ascough, *Formation* 21-23.

103. All that Pliny's inquiry found was a *superstitio;* see further Wilken, *Christians as the Romans Saw Them* 15-25, 32-34.

104. 'The Christian faith, as Paul expounds it, belongs with the doctrines of the philosophical schools rather than with the esoteric rituals of the mystery religions' (Judge, 'Early Christians' 135); 'The charges against which Paul defends himself are those that were routinely leveled against the Cynics and other wandering philosophers of his day' (Mason, *'Philosophiai'* 47). Meeks, however, maintains that the Pythagorean and Epicurean schools 'resemble the Pauline communities just to the extent that they take the form of modified households or voluntary associations' (*Urban Christians* 84).

105. Paul's usage is more varied than is usually allowed for (see below, §32 n. 344).

106. Bendlin opens his article with this reference ('Gemeinschaft' 9); cf. BDAG 984.

107. The famous fable of Menenius Agrippa is the best-known example (Livy, *Hist.* 2.32; Epictetus 2.10.4-5); see further H. Lietzmann, *Korinther I/II* (HNT 9; Tübingen: Mohr Siebeck, 1949) 62 (on 12.12); E. Schweizer, *TDNT* 7.1038-39.

108. Though see n. 127 below.

was not a political corporation as such but a body formed by identification with Christ, by being baptized into Christ (1 Cor. 12.13),[109] indicated an identity formed by other than ethnic or social categories — 'neither Jew nor Greek, neither slave nor free, no male and female, but all one in Christ Jesus' (Gal. 3.28).

Even so, the likenesses and differences of the 'churches' to and from the associations, cults and schools of the time would take some time for interested observers and inquirers to recognize and appreciate.

30.4. The Social Composition of Paul's Churches

Until recent decades there was a widespread assumption that the first Christian groups in the Mediterranean cities were predominantly Gentile and of low social status. The caricature of Celsus[110] was usually taken to reinforce 1 Cor. 1.26[111] and to indicate a proletarian movement with only a few leaders of the intellectual calibre of Paul. Over the last generation that picture has decisively changed.[112]

a. Jews and Gentiles

The fact that Paul presented himself as 'apostle to the Gentiles' (Rom. 11.13) and so expressly addresses himself to Gentile converts in several of his letters (as we

109. 1 Cor. 12.13 — 'In one Spirit we were all baptized into one body (cf. Rom. 6.3; Gal. 3.27), whether Jews or Greeks or slaves or free . . .'.

110. Celsus caricatures the Christian message thus: 'Their injunctions are like this. "Let no one educated, no one wise, no one sensible draw near. For these abilities are thought by us to be evils. But as for anyone ignorant, anyone stupid, anyone uneducated, anyone who is a child, let him come boldly". By the fact that they themselves admit that these people are worthy of their God, they show that they want and are able to convince only the foolish, dishonourable and stupid, and only slaves, women, and little children' (Origen, *c. Cels.* 3.44).

111. 'Not many wise, not many powerful, not many well-born' (1 Cor. 1.26).

112. In his too long neglected *Social Pattern of Christian Groups,* E. A. Judge lamented: 'Unfortunately the social stratification of the Christian groups has never been properly investigated, and is perhaps beyond recovery' (51). Judge himself began to remedy the lack in his 'Early Christians' 128-35, and his initial probings were taken further by Theissen, *Social Setting;* A. J. Malherbe, *Social Aspects of Early Christianity* (Baton Rouge: Louisiana State University, 1977); and Meeks, *First Urban Christians* ch. 2, with the conclusion that 'Pauline congregations generally reflected a fair cross-section of urban society' (73); 'the Christian groups were much more inclusive in terms of social stratification and other social categories than were the voluntary associations' (79; Gehring, *House Church* 168-71 defends Meeks's conclusion). On the social diversity of the Corinthian church, see also A. D. Clarke, *Secular and Christian Leadership in Corinth: A Socio-historical and Exegetical Study of 1 Corinthians 1–6* (Leiden: Brill, 1993) chs. 4-7, and Horrell, *Social Ethos* 91-101.

shall see in a moment) has tended to encourage the view that Paul's churches were predominantly or even exclusively Gentile in composition. In the overview of Christianity's earliest history bequeathed to subsequent generations by Baur,[113] Jewish or Jewish-Christian missionaries have typically been regarded as outsiders to Paul's churches. This, it should be noted, was also a by-product of the traditional view that the earliest congregations were uniformly 'orthodox' and that teaching which detracted from 'the truth of the gospel' always came from outside.[114]

The reality was a good deal more confused and hardly uniform. Paul, as we have seen (§29.5b), typically used the local synagogue(s) as the springboard for his mission to Gentile God-fearers. But Luke does indicate that many Jews were also converted,[115] and they would have formed part of the core members round which the earliest churches began to grow. It is true that the Galatian churches seem to have been predominantly or even wholly Gentile in membership. Paul addresses the recipients generally ('you') as those who formerly did not know God and 'were enslaved to beings that by nature are not gods' (Gal. 4.8). And the implication throughout is of later incomers trying to persuade the letter recipients of the need to be circumcised (explicitly in 5.2-3 and 6.12); it is because of Galatians that the Baur thesis has continued to exert as much influence as it has. But even there the recurring first person plural ('we') in the main section of the argument of Galatians (particularly 3.13-14, 23-26; 4.3-6) suggests that Paul had in mind Jewish as well as non-Jewish believers.[116]

Romans is similar to Galatians in that the recipients (chiefly) in view are the Gentile believers in Rome: explicitly in 1.5-6 ('all the nations/Gentiles, among whom you also are called to be Jesus Christ's') and 11.13-32 ('I am speaking to you Gentiles' — 11.13); implicitly in 1.13 and 15.7-12, 15-16. But the 'weak in faith' in view in 14.1–15.6 are most probably believing Jews (and former God-fearers); their scruples regarding food and sacred days are typically Jewish.[117] And a major purpose of Paul's letter is to urge Gentile believers not to assume that they (Gentiles) have replaced the Jews in God's purpose (11.17-24; 12.3, 16) and not to despise or to ride roughshod over the sensitivities of their fellow (Jewish) believers (14.3, 10; 14.13–15.6). The implication is that since Gentile believers were indeed the majority in the Roman congregations, the responsibility was primarily theirs to make the minority Jewish members know that they were fully accepted and respected (14.1; 15.7). We should also note again that brief allusions to the history of Israel, such as we find in 9.6-18 (the patriarchs and the exodus) and 11.2-4 (Elijah),

---

113. See above, §20.3a.

114. See again §20 n. 153 and *Jesus Remembered* §1 at n. 19.

115. Acts 13.43; 14.1; 17.4, 11-12; 18.8; 19.9; 28.24.

116. See my *Galatians* 176-77, 179, 198-200, 213, 216-17; cf. Martyn, *Galatians* 334-36, though he envisages the only Jew included in the 'we' to be Paul himself (323)!

117. See further below, §33.3f(ii).

must mean that Paul could assume a fair knowledge of the LXX on the part of his audiences, a knowledge which he could only assume because he also assumed that the majority of Gentiles in most diaspora churches had been schooled in the Scriptures during their earlier attendance at the synagogue as God-fearers.

In the Corinthian correspondence the situation seems to be much the same. The Gentile predominance in the church(es) of Corinth is nowhere so explicit as in Galatians and Romans. But it is strongly implied by the sequence of problems which Paul tackles in 1 Corinthians, most of which presuppose a not typically Jewish appreciation of rhetoric (1.18–4.20) and the complications which arise from relationships and associations which again are uncharacteristic of Jewish practice (chs. 5–6, 8–10).[118] At the same time, the presence of a group within the Corinthian church which claimed some sort of allegiance to Cephas (1.12) raises the possibility that there were Jewish believers in Corinth who identified themselves in some measure with Cephas, perhaps in the light of the agreement reached between Cephas and Paul, as recorded in Gal. 2.7-9, and who therefore set themselves in some degree over against Paul.[119] But once again the principal evidence is that concerning the dining habits of the Corinthians. The ones who lack 'knowledge' regarding the true nature of idols and whose conscience could not even begin to contemplate eating 'food offered to idols' (8.7-13) were most probably Jews, distinctive as Jews were in the ancient world in their absolute intolerance of idolatry.[120] So once again, we have to envisage mixed congregations, perhaps one or two predominantly Jewish in composition, but, over all, within a predominantly Gentile church.

A glance at the prosopographical data in the two letters which contain most names strengthens in some degree the picture which has emerged. In Paul's greetings in Romans 16, three of those listed are Jews (Andronicus, Junia, and Herodion — vv. 7, 11), though it is likely that Aquila and Prisca, Mary, Rufus and his mother (vv. 3, 6, 13) were also Jews. 'Members of the household of Aristobulus' (16.10) were likely also to have been Jews.[121] That is, one-third or more of those named to whom greetings should be given were probably Jewish. And in Colossians two or three of those with Paul are explicitly identified as Jews ('of the circumcision') — Mark, Jesus Justus, and perhaps also Aristarchus (4.10-11). That is to say, they presumably functioned within the church of the place from which the letter was written. Only three other names are mentioned as sending greetings with the letter (Epaphras, Luke and Demas — 4.12-14).

118. See further below, §32.5.
119. See below, §32 n. 170.
120. See further §32.5e below.
121. 'Aristobulus' was not a Roman name; it appears only twice in *CIL* 6 (17577, 29104) (Lampe, *Paul to Valentinus* 165). See further n. 140 below.

The significance of these findings should not go unnoticed. For one thing they raise again the issue of the ongoing relations between the churches and the synagogues. Were all the Jewish believers wholly detached from the synagogue, or did they see no inconsistency in owning a dual allegiance to 'synagogue' and 'church', perhaps regarding the believers in Messiah Jesus as a (controversial!) renewal group within the Jewish community? Here we also need to bear in mind that in a city where many Jews had settled, the synagogues might themselves have been quite diverse; putting the same point the other way, we should not assume that the several synagogues (gatherings of Jews) in a large city were homogeneous. In which case the first churches might well have been seen as simply part of that diversity and their legal status have been left unquestioned accordingly.[122]

The other corollary to note is that in such mixed congregations there was always likely to be tension as to what 'the truth of the gospel' amounted to, not just for belief about Jesus, but also for the outworking of that belief in practice, in worship, in relations with each other, in ethical standards and on interaction with wider society.[123] In other words, the tensions which came to expression in the Jerusalem consultation and in the subsequent incident in Antioch (§§27.2-4) were

---

122. Tellbe's thesis is 'that the need for socio-political legitimacy in the Graeco-Roman society was a pressing need for the Christian movement not only from the late first century and onward but already in the middle of the first century; and that the interaction between Christians, Jews, and civic authorities played a vital role in forming a specific Christian self-understanding in the early church' (*Paul between Synagogue and State* 4). See particularly 63-74: 'there must have been a crucial concern for them [the early Christians] to identify with Jewish traditions and communities as long as possible, not only in order to claim Jewish rights to form relatively autonomous administrative organizations or to assemble weekly and receive exemption from work on the Sabbath, but also in order to avoid a potential conflict with their civic communities' (73). Contrast Watson's persistent thesis that Paul's goal was to establish a form of Christianity separate and sharply distinctive from the synagogue community (*Paul, Judaism and the Gentiles* [²2007] 51-56, 180-81), which, surprisingly in a sociological study, does not raise the issue of the legal status of the Christian house groups. *Pace* Watson, it would be wiser to use 'sect' to denote a movement still regarded as a sub-group within Second Temple Judaism (cf. Qumran) than a movement which regarded itself as quite separate and alienated from the synagogue communities (e.g., 118); cf. the more careful attempt at definition by White, *From Jesus to Christianity* 129-31.

123. Often referred to is Brown's categorization of the diversity within the varying types of 'Jewish/Gentile Christianity' — at least four diversities: Group 1 — 'Jewish Christian and their Gentile converts, who insisted on *full observance of the Mosaic Law, including circumcision*'; Group 2 — 'Jewish Christian and their Gentile converts, who did *not* insist on circumcision but did require converted Gentiles to keep *some Jewish observances*'; Group 3 — 'Jewish Christian and their Gentile converts, who did *not* insist on circumcision and did *not* require observance of the Jewish ("kosher") food laws'; Group 4 — 'Jewish Christians and their Gentile converts, who did not insist on circumcision or observance of the Jewish food laws and who *saw no abiding significance in Jewish cult and feasts*' (Brown and Meier, *Antioch and Rome* 1-9).

not left behind in homogeneously Gentile churches. On the contrary, we may well envisage that 'the truth of the gospel' and its outworkings were contested truths in some measure in many or most churches. Were it not so, of course, Paul would not have had to write most of his letters as he did!

b. Patrons and Benefactors

Here we have to depend mainly on the evidence of 1 Corinthians. This letter has proved to be a wonderful literary tell, into which during the last generation of scholarship various exploratory shafts have been sunk, revealing aspects and details of a first-century church which earlier generations scarcely began to comprehend.[124] We should not lightly generalize from 1 Corinthians to the rest of the Pauline churches, of course,[125] but in terms of the social composition of Paul's churches 1 Corinthians may have been quite typical.

The major contribution of Gerd Theissen in this area was to highlight the neglected aspect of the famous 1 Cor. 1.26.[126] 'Not many' wise, powerful and of noble birth did not mean 'nobody' of that status. On the contrary, there were a few influential members who came from the upper strata of the very stratified society. The 'wise' would belong to the educated classes; a good education would almost certainly be a privilege limited to the well-to-do. The 'powerful' would be influential people, patrons or clients of the ruling elite. The 'nobly born' would include the wealthy patrician class or local elite, well accustomed to moving among the top echelons of local and regional government.[127] Although a minority in the Corinthian church, their influence would be entirely disproportionate to their numbers. In the social grouping which was the Corinthians' church, they would inevitably be the most influential — the dominant minority.[128]

---

124. Well illustrated by the articles abstracted and reprinted in E. Adams and D. G. Horrell, eds., *Christianity at Corinth: The Quest for the Pauline Church* (Louisville: John Knox, 2004).

125. S. J. Friesen, 'Prospects for a Demography of the Pauline Mission: Corinth among the Churches', in Schowalter and Friesen, eds., *Urban Religion in Roman Corinth* 351-70, justifiably warns against generalizing from what we know of the Corinthian church (353-55).

126. Theissen, *Social Setting* ch. 2; Judge's contribution (n. 112 above) has been largely overlooked.

127. L. L. Welborn, *Politics and Rhetoric in the Corinthian Epistles* (Macon: Mercer University, 1997), notes that the three categories mentioned by Paul 'are the very terms employed by Greek writers from the time of Solon to designate the major class divisions involved in *stasis* [political discord]' (21).

128. Meggitt argues strongly against what he calls the 'new consensus' stemming from Theissen's work. He justly notes that there was no middle class in the ancient world (*Poverty* 7, 41-53) and cautions against using sources from an extremely small clique to draw wider conclusions: 'a context of interpretation needs to be constructed that tries to give voice to the lived reality of the other 99% of the population' (12-13; see also his 'Sources: Use, Abuse, Neglect; The

Here again a study of the names which appear in relation to the Corinthian church gives us some idea of the sort of people Paul would have in mind:

- Crispus (1 Cor. 1.14) had been *archisynagōgos,* 'leader or president of the synagogue', in Corinth, according to Acts 18.8; since upkeep of a synagogue required money, the office was likely to be entrusted to a man of wealth; his role was equivalent to one of the wealthy patrons of an association.[129]
- Erastus (Rom. 16.23) was 'city treasurer', certainly a man of some influence;[130] and if he is indeed the Erastus who laid a pavement 'at his own expense',[131] he would have been a man of substantial private wealth.

Importance of Ancient Popular Culture', in Adams and Horrell, *Christianity at Corinth* ch. 19). But his claim that 1.27-28 refers to 'members of his Corinthian congregation, *without exception*' as the foolish, the weak, low-born and despised dismisses the evidence of 1.26 too lightly (*Poverty* 99). The claim that all the first-century Christians were 'poor', that is, 'living at or near subsistence level, whose prime concern it is to obtain the minimum food, shelter, clothing necessary to sustain life, whose lives are dominated by the struggle for physical survival' (5), certainly discounts the evidence marshalled below and that of 1 Corinthians 8–10 and 11.17-34 in particular (on the latter two passages see particularly G. Theissen, 'Social Conflicts in the Corinthian Community: Further Remarks on J. J. Meggitt, *Paul, Poverty and Survival*', *JSNT* 25.3 [2003] 371-91). Stegemann and Stegemann provide a more realistic analysis by subdividing the traditional two-tier division of elite and nonelite (*honestiores* and *humiliores*): the upper stratum including (1) those belonging to the three orders (*ordines),* senatorial, equestrian, decurional, (2) rich people without *ordo* membership, and (3) retainers of the upper stratum; the lower, the great majority, including (4) the relatively prosperous and relatively poor (*penētes)* and (5) the absolutely poor (*ptōchoi) (Jesus Movement* 288-303). S. J. Friesen, 'Poverty in Pauline Studies: Beyond the So-Called New Consensus', *JSNT* 26 (2004) 323-61, suggests a poverty scale with seven categories ranging from 'below subsistence level' to 'imperial elites', with two-thirds at or below subsistence level, and the better-off in the Pauline churches still only at the level of 'moderate surplus' or 'stable near subsistence' (337-58). See also the reviews of Meggitt by D. B. Martin and G. Theissen, and Meggitt's response, in *JSNT* 84 (2001) 51-94; B. Holmberg, 'The Methods of Historical Reconstruction in the Scholarly "Recovery" of Corinthian Christianity', in Adams and Horrell, *Christianity at Corinth* 255-71 (here 261-71); and n. 157 below.

129. Theissen, *Social Setting* 74-75. Meggitt's objection (*Poverty* 141-43) ignores the widespread convention that payment for the privilege of office-holding was a crucial part of the system, and the synagogue rested on the same base of patronage; see T. Rajak, 'The Jewish Community and Its Boundaries', in J. Lieu et al., eds., *The Jews among the Pagans and Christians in the Roman Empire* (London: Routledge, 1992) 9-28 (here 23-24); Murphy-O'Connor, *Paul* 267.

130. Theissen, *Social Setting* 75-83; Clarke, *Secular and Christian Leadership* 46-56; Winter, *Welfare* ch. 10 — 'city administrator' (192). In suggesting that Erastus might simply be treasurer 'within the church', Meggitt ignores the fuller reference, 'the treasurer of the city' (*Poverty* 136). See also §32 n. 267 below.

131. The inscription is in the museum at Corinth. For more detail see Furnish, *2 Corinthians* 25.

- Stephanas (1 Cor. 1.16; 16.15) had a 'household' quite possibly including slaves[132] — a sure sign of social status and wealth.
- Phoebe (Rom. 16.2) of Cenchrea (the Aegean port of Corinth) was a *prostatis* ('patron, benefactor') of many, including Paul, again a figure of power and influence.[133]
- Gaius (Rom. 16.23) had a house big enough to accommodate 'the whole church'.[134]
- Priscilla and Aquila (1 Cor. 16.19) seem to have run a business, involving travel, itself an expensive business,[135] and to have acted as Paul's host (Acts 18.3; cf. Rom. 16.3-5).
- Sosthenes (1 Cor. 1.1) = the synagogue ruler of Acts 18.17(?).
- 'Chloe's people' (1 Cor. 1.11) were probably slaves or dependent workers.[136]
- Titius Justus also acted as Paul's host according to Acts 18.7.

This list actually comprises a significant proportion of those named who we know belonged to the church of Corinth.[137] We should not assume, of course, that Paul has named all those who identified with the meeting of Jesus messianists in Corinth; we do have to keep in mind Paul's 'not many' in 1 Cor. 1.26. And it is the way of the world that the social elite in any organization tend to attract more public notice than the rest. Nevertheless, the parallel with the associations described in §30.3 is rather striking — the church in Corinth as not untypical of a lower-status association (largely consisting of freedmen, artisans, slaves), with a few high-status patrons. The relevance of all this will become more apparent when we return to a closer examination of 1 Corinthians, since several of the problems which Paul addresses in that letter were evidently caused by some (unnamed) elite members of the church acting in ways incon-

132. Theissen, *Social Setting* 87; Meggitt's caution that slave ownership was not beyond the means of the non-elite (129) is worth pondering, but at least it implies a greater differentiation within the ranks of the 99 percent non-elite than Meggitt allows for.

133. Surprisingly Theissen referred to Phoebe only as a *diakonos* (*Social Setting* 88); but see Meeks, *Urban Christians* 60. Meggitt's argument that *prostatis* does not mean that Phoebe actually was a patron is special pleading (*Poverty* 146-48). See, e.g., B. J. Brooten, 'Iael *prostatēs* in the Jewish Donative Inscription from Aphrodisias', in B. A. Pearson, ed., *The Future of Early Christianity*, H. Koester FS (Minneapolis: Fortress, 1991) 149-62; and further below, n. 169.

134. See above, n. 28; the point is ignored by Meggitt, as also in regard to Philemon, nn. 35-36 above (*Poverty* 134-35).

135. Again a point unjustifiably played down by Meggitt, *Poverty* 133-34.

136. Theissen, *Social Setting* 92-94.

137. Theissen concludes: 'The great majority of the Corinthians known to us by name probably enjoyed high social status' (*Social Setting* 95).

siderate of their fellow members, problems which were all the more serious precisely because they involved the influential patrons and benefactors of the association.[138]

Simply to confirm that the church in Corinth was not necessarily unique in its social composition, we should also recall that in Colossae, slave-owning Philemon could also host a house church (Phlm. 2) and that Nympha(s) likewise was able to host a house church, either in neighbouring Laodicea, or possibly in Colossae also.[139] As owners of (presumably) fairly substantial properties, they too would probably be of higher social status than most other believers in these cities. Similar conclusions can be drawn regarding the members of the likely house churches in Rome, particularly 'those of (the household of) Aristobulus' and 'those of (the household of) Narcissus' (Rom. 16.10, 11). Both were common names, but the manner of reference suggests members of the households of prominent people. The former may indeed refer to retainers of Aristobulus, brother of Herod Agrippa I,[140] and the latter to retainers of the freedman Narcissus who served as one of Claudius's closest aides.[141] Although nothing suggests that Aristobulus and Narcissus were themselves believers, members of a socially powerful household could often be accorded influence for that very reason. And the reference to 'those who labour among you and care for you in the Lord' in 1 Thess. 5.12 suggests individuals like Stephanas in Corinth (1 Cor. 16.15) who

138. E.g., see below, §32.5c.

139. On the unclarity of the location of the house of Nympha(s) see my *Colossians and Philemon* 284.

140. According to Josephus (*War* 2.221), this Aristobulus died as 'a private person (*idiōtēs*)', that is, as distinct from one who held public office or took part in public affairs (LSJ 819). He and Agrippa had lived for a long time in Rome (see above, §26.5b), so it is possible that after Agrippa's return to Judea, Aristobulus had been kept out of the way (under surveillance?) in Rome as surety for his brother's good conduct. Even if he had died (in the late 40s?) some years before Romans was written, his household staff could have retained their identity as *hoi Aristoboulou*, even when merged into another (the imperial?) household (as suggested already by Lightfoot, *Philippians* 174-75); Moo notes that the suggestion is supported by most commentators, since Aristobulus is a rare name in Rome (*Romans* 925 n. 50). The fact that Paul mentions his kinsman Herodion in the very next sentence (Rom. 16.11) may provide added support. Lampe suggests that the household of Aristobulus may be one of the channels through which Christianity infiltrated the capital (*Paul to Valentinus* 165; also 'Paths of Early Christian Mission into Rome: Judaeo-Christians in the Household of Pagan Masters', in S. E. McGinn, ed., *Celebrating Romans: Template for Pauline Theology*, R. Jewett FS [Grand Rapids: Eerdmans, 2004] 143-48).

141. Juvenal, *Sat.* 14.329-31; cf. *CIL* 3.3973; 6.15640 — 'Narcissiani'. After the accession of Nero (54), Narcissus became a victim of Agrippina's vengeance (Tacitus, *Ann.* 13.1), and his household would probably have been absorbed by the emperor's (Lightfoot, *Philippians* 175). Lampe notes that another freedman Narcissus in *CIL* 6.9035 had his own slaves (*Paul to Valentinus* 165).

acted as benefactors and provided leadership *(proistamenous)* in the small Thessalonian congregation, possibly including Jason, in whose house they may still have been meeting (Acts 17.5-7).[142]

c. Slaves and Freedmen

Slavery was a long-established fact of life in the ancient world — as established a fact as 'domestic service' in the Victorian era in Britain and elsewhere. As many as one-third of the inhabitants of most large urban centres would have been slaves.[143] Where warfare had provided the main source of slaves in previous generations (defeated enemies), by this time the children of women in slavery had become the primary source (the status of the father was immaterial).[144] Another possibility was that an individual might sell himself (or be sold) into slavery because of an unpaid debt or to avoid starvation[145] or even to gain a coveted post within an elite household.[146] Twenty-first-century readers need to be reminded that slavery had not yet come to be thought of as essentially immoral or necessarily degrading; it took the slave trade to bring this insight home to Western 'civilization'. It was simply the means of providing labour at the bottom end of the economic spectrum. Consequently, slaves could be well educated, and if their masters were figures of substantial social significance and power, the slaves themselves might be entrusted with considerable responsibility as stewards or in some administrative capacity.[147]

142. *Proistēmi* and *prostatis,* 'patron, benefactor' (Rom. 16.2) come from the same root; whether we translate the verb as denoting leadership or care for (BDAG 870), it probably implies a figure of some status and means. See also below, n. 206.

143. How widespread was ownership of slaves? According to D. C. Verner, *The Household of God: The Social World of the Pastoral Epistles* (SBLDS 71; Chico: Scholars, 1983), it is 'unlikely that more than twenty-five percent of households included slaves, even in the slave centers of the empire' (61); Meggitt, in contrast, maintains that 'slave ownership was not beyond the means of the non-elite' and that 'for many of those just above subsistence level it was not only an economically viable but also a sensible thing to do' [to buy a slave] (*Poverty* 129-31). See also J. A. Harill, 'Paul and Slavery', in Sampley ed., *Paul in the Greco-Roman World* 575-607 (with bibliography).

144. See, e.g., W. W. Buckland, *The Roman Law of Slavery* (Cambridge: Cambridge University, 1908; reprinted 1970) 397-400; W. L. Westermann, *The Slave Systems of Greek and Roman Antiquity* (Philadelphia: American Philosophical Society, 1955) 84-87.

145. Meggitt, *Poverty* 60.

146. Winter, *Welfare* 154-59.

147. See D. B. Martin, *Slavery as Salvation* (New Haven: Yale University, 1990) ch. 1; 'even slaves and ex-slaves became slave-owners, especially those at Rome who belonged to the *familia Caesaris* and prospered from their favoured status . . . slaves can be observed in almost

That said, slavery was completely antithetical to the Greek idealization of freedom, with the slave defined as 'one who does not belong to himself but to someone else' (Aristotle, *Politica* 1.1254a.14) and as one who 'does not have the power to refuse' (Seneca, *De beneficiis* 3.19).[148] Not surprisingly, then, freedom (manumission) was the goal of every slave[149] and was regularly achieved; indeed it would appear that a very substantial proportion of slaves were freed by their masters before their thirtieth birthday.[150] Manumission, however, did not usually bring economic freedom, former slaves being either bound to perform services for their former masters or caught in a client-patron relationship with their former master, with continuing obligation to work on their patron's behalf in return for some remuneration.[151] Even so, some freedmen became very rich and powerful, like Narcissus and Antonius Pallas, both personal secretaries to Claudius, and Numerius Popidius Ampliatus in Pompeii,[152] and in Rome a slave freed by a citizen was normally admitted to citizenship.[153]

It is evident that a good many of the first Christians came from the ranks of slaves. This fact is explicit in the later Pauline letters — in the direct exhortation to both slaves and masters as members of the same church (Colossae) (Col. 3.22–4.1), and in the personal letter to slave-owning Philemon about his now-converted slave Onesimus. The 'household code' of Col. 3.18–4.1 seems to have set a precedent, followed by other letters which in effect span from the close of the first generation into the second and third generations.[154] At all events, such

every area of human activity, the holding public office apart' (K. R. Bradley, *OCD*[3] 1416); 'there were notable distinctions among slaves: the shackled rural slaves, for example, were considerably different from those who managed estates for their masters' (Stegemann and Stegemann, *Jesus Movement* 65, also 86-88).

148. J. A. Glancy, *Slavery in Early Christianity* (Oxford: Oxford University, 2002; Minneapolis: Fortress, 2006), focuses on the common identification of a slave as a 'body', as implying the slave's availability for and vulnerability to sexual exploitation.

149. 'It is the slave's prayer that he be set free immediately' (Epictetus 4.1.33).

150. T. Wiedemann, *Greek and Roman Slavery* (Baltimore: Johns Hopkins University, 1981) 51; S. S. Bartchy, 'Slavery', *ABD* 6.71 ('few persons are known to have reached old age in urban slavery . . . because they had already been released before dying as freedmen/women in their 30s, 40s, 50s or more'); disputed by Bradley in *OCD*[3] 1416 ('most slaves were probably not set free').

151. See, e.g., *NDIEC* 4.103-104. Suetonius reports that Claudius 'reduced to slavery again such [freedmen] as were ungrateful and a cause of complaint to their patrons' (*Claudius* 25.1).

152. The last-named is vividly portrayed by R. Harris, *Pompeii* (London: Hutchinson, 2003).

153. *OCD*[3] 609.

154. Eph. 5.22–6.9 (6.5-9); 1 Pet. 2.18–3.7 (2.18-21); 1 Tim. 2.8-15; 6.1-2 (6.1-2); Tit. 2.1-10 (2.9-10); *Did.* 4.9-11 (4.10-11); *Barn.* 19.5-7 (19.7); *1 Clem.* 21.6-9; Ignatius, *Pol.* 4.1–5.2 (4.3); Polycarp, *Phil.* 4.2-3 (bracketed verses indicate instructions to slaves and/or masters).

passages no doubt reflect a situation which probably pertained from the very early days of the Pauline mission. In Corinth, for example, 'Chloe's people' (1 Cor. 1.11) and Fortunatus and Achaicus (16.17) are quite likely to have been slaves or freedmen.[155]

Particularly interesting, once again, are the number of names in Romans 16 which were common among slaves, freedmen and freedwomen — Andronicus and Junia, Ampliatus, Herodion, Tryphaena and Tryphosa, Persis, Asyncritus, Hermes, Patrobas, Philologus and Julia, and Nereus, as well as the households of Aristobulus and Narcissus.[156] Although the names were common among those of slave origins, we cannot assume that a slave origin was true of those so named in Romans 16. Nevertheless, the fact that more than a half of those greeted in Romans 16 could have been slaves or former slaves, and that a significant proportion must have been slaves or former slaves, strongly suggests that slaves and freedmen/women made up a substantial proportion of the Pauline churches. In this the churches were not unique, since some associations did admit slaves, and many were composed mainly of freedmen. Nevertheless, the likelihood is that such churches consistently drew in a wider range of participants than most clubs and associations.

d. The Poor

The justified stress given to the 'not many' of 1 Cor. 1.26 by Theissen and thereafter should not be allowed to cloak the fact that the great majority of the Pauline congregations, like the great majority of those living in the Roman Empire, were poor. The most recent estimates are that only a tiny proportion (about 3 percent) of an urban population was rich, and that there was no economic middle class. So most of Paul's congregations would have been living near subsistence level.[157] Explicit reference to the poor among the members of Paul's churches is surprisingly lacking, but only until we realize that Paul and his audiences would have taken the harsh realities of their daily lives for granted. However, the exhortation

---

155. Theissen, *Social Setting* 93; Meeks, *Urban Christians* 59; Chester, *Conversion* 242-43; 'Fortunatus' ('blessed, lucky') was especially common among slaves, and 'Achaicus' means 'one who comes from Achaia'.

156. The evidence is carefully scrutinized by Lampe, *Paul to Valentinus* 170-83.

157. Friesen, 'Prospects' 358-70, thus qualifying n. 128 above. On the distinction between the absolutely poor *(ptōchos)* and the relatively poor *(penētes)*, see Stegemann and Stegemann, *Jesus Movement* 88-92. J. Becker, 'Paul and His Churches', in Becker, ed., *Christian Beginnings* 132-210, however, thinks that 'the number of people from the urban, upper middle class [*(sic)*] was proportionally higher than in the general population of a city such as Corinth' (170).

in 1 Thess. 4.11, to 'work with your hands', strongly suggests that the majority of Thessalonian believers were probably manual workers, of low social status.[158]

Somewhat more surprising is the lack of emphasis given to provision for the poor — surprising in the light of the emphasis on the subject in both the Scriptures and the traditions stemming from Jesus himself.[159] But Paul's very willing agreement in Jerusalem to 'remember the poor' (Gal. 2.10) bore fruit in the high priority he obviously gave to the collection for 'the poor among the saints in Jerusalem' (Rom. 15.26).[160] And it is hardly likely that this concern for members of another church (albeit the church in Jerusalem) was unmatched by a similar concern for the poor among his own churches. Noteworthy here is the fact that in giving a typical list of charisms which he expected to be enacted in the body of Christ, Paul makes a point of including 'sharing' and 'doing acts of mercy' (Rom. 12.8), where the thought is most obviously of sharing food or wealth or possessions, and tending the sick, relieving the poor and caring for the aged and disabled, or almsgiving in particular.[161] Widows are also not mentioned as a special concern prior to 1 Tim. 5.3-16,[162] though here too the likelihood is that where believing widows fell on hard times, the Pauline churches recognized a responsibility to help them. In view of the generally low-status membership of Paul's churches, his exhortation that the Corinthians should each week 'put aside and save whatever extra you earn' as a contribution to the collection (1 Cor. 16.2) both echoes the very modest monthly contribution expected in many associations (towards burial costs) and reminds us of the general rule that it is often the poorest who are most generous in such giving.[163]

e. Women

As with associations generally, so particularly in regard to the role of women in public life, we are dependent almost entirely on inscriptional evidence. Women are known to have been involved in associations, that is, mainly in religious asso-

---

158. Meeks, *Urban Christians* 64, drawing on E. Best, *Thessalonians* (BNTC; London: Black, 1972) 176.

159. See *Jesus Remembered* §13.4.

160. See below, §33.4.

161. See further my *Romans* 730-32. No entrance fee or regular (monthly) subscription is envisaged for members of the churches, as was the rule in most associations (Ebel, *Attraktivität* 217), but the system of 'poor relief' may have required some regular giving (and not just from patronal benefactors), as the explicit instruction regarding the collection may imply.

162. The only other reference to widows in the Pauline corpus comes in 1 Cor. 7.8.

163. To be noted, however, is that this is the only financial commitment Paul envisages — not as a weekly or monthly membership subscription, as typically in associations, but for the benefit of others.

ciations,[164] though there is hardly any evidence for their involvement in trade and professional associations.[165] We know of a few associations which existed exclusively for women,[166] but also of women who held office in a number of clubs,[167] particularly in religious associations.[168] Some women also held positions as benefactors and patrons on their own account.[169] Even so, the presence of women in the earliest Christian congregations is a rather striking feature. And not only presence, but active participation and leadership.[170]

I have already noted that no less than nine women were at one time or another members of what we might call Paul's mission team — that is, nearly 20 percent,[171] a notable statistic in a male-dominated society. Not only so, but several of them evidently played significant or leading roles in the Pauline churches:

- Junia (Rom. 16.7), the only woman we know to have been named an apostle;[172]

164. See now C. E. Schultz, *Women's Religious Activity in the Roman Republic* (Chapel Hill: University of North Carolina, 2006) particularly ch. 2.

165. Kloppenborg, 'Collegia and *Thiasoi*' 25.

166. Poland, *Geschichte* 289-91; *NDIEC* 4.15; Ascough, *Paul's Macedonian Associations* 57-58.

167. Poland, *Geschichte* 292-98; McLean, 'The Agrippinilla Inscription' 259-66. Meeks suggests that some of the newer cults initially allowed considerably more freedom for women to hold office alongside men than did the older state cults (*Urban Christians* 25).

168. Ascough, *Paul's Macedonian Associations* 54-59.

169. Women are attested as holding positions such as *archisynagōgos* and *gymnasiarchos* and acting as patrons (*prostatis = patrona*) in the ancient world; see *NDIEC* 4.12-13, 15, 214-19, 242-44; also 6.24-27; R. MacMullen, 'Women in Public in the Roman Empire', *Historia* 29 (1980) 208-18; B. Brooten, *Women Leaders in the Ancient Synagogue* (BJS 36; Chico: Scholars, 1982) particularly ch. 1; van der Horst, *Jewish Epitaphs* 105-109; Brooten, '*Iael prostatēs*' 156-61; Trebilco, *Jewish Communities* ch. 5; C. F. Whelan, 'Amica Pauli: The Role of Phoebe in the Early Church', *JSNT* 49 (1993) 67-85 (here 75-77), drawing particularly on the data from *CIL* documented by Waltzing, *Études;* W. Horbury, 'Women in the Synagogue', *CHJ* 3.358-401 (here 388-401); R. A. Kearsley, 'Women in Public Life in the Roman East: Iunia, Theodora, Claudia Metrodora and Phoebe, Benefactress of Paul', *TynB* 50 (1999) 189-211; B. W. Winter, *Roman Wives, Roman Widows: The Appearance of New Women and the Pauline Communities* (Grand Rapids: Eerdmans, 2003) 173-211; E. A. Hemelrijk, 'City Patronesses in the Roman Empire', *Historia* 53 (2004) 209-45.

170. E. S. Fiorenza, *In Memory of Her* (London: SCM, 1983) 168-84.

171. See above, §29 at n. 227.

172. R. Bauckham, *Gospel Women: Studies of the Named Women in the Gospels* (Grand Rapids: Eerdmans, 2002) ch. 5, makes the fascinating suggestion, inevitably speculative, that Junia was the Latin name chosen by Joanna referred to in Luke 8.3 and 24.10 (her husband, Chusa, chose the name Andronicus); particularly valuable is his rebuttal (172-80) of the argument of M. H. Burer and D. B. Wallace, 'Was Junia Really an Apostle? A Re-examination of Rom 16.7', *NTS* 47 (2001) 76-91. See also above, §29 n. 82, and below, §33.2b.

- Phoebe (Rom. 16.1-2), patron *(prostatis)* of the church in Cenchrea[173] and the first person in the history of Christianity to be formally designated 'deacon';[174]
- Prisca (Rom. 16.3-5) is regularly named before her husband Aquila,[175] probably a fair indicator that she was a leading figure in her own right;
- Mary, Tryphaena, Tryphosa and Persis (Rom. 16.6, 12) are all greeted as 'hard workers', a term which Paul uses elsewhere for those deserving respect and submission (1 Cor. 16.16; 1 Thess. 5.12); notably only these four are so designated in Romans 16;
- Euodia and Syntyche (Phil. 4.2-3) similarly 'struggled beside me in the work of the gospel';
- Lydia (Acts 16.14-15), a businesswomen involved in the expensive provision of purple cloth, mistress of a household and probably an early host of the church in Philippi;
- Nympha (Col. 4.15, or is it Nymphas, a man's name?), who also hosted a house church.
- In addition we should note the regular participation of women in public prophecy in the church in Corinth (1 Cor. 11.2-16), and so quite possibly the functioning of women as regular prophets in 14.29-32, even though Paul had serious misgivings about some women's contributions (14.33-36).[176]
- Nor should we forget Luke's mention of 'women of high standing', 'leading women' who were converted by Paul's preaching in Pisidian Antioch (Acts 13.50), in Thessalonica (17.4), and in Beroea (17.12), and who would probably have gone on to act as benefactors and patrons in the churches established there.

These data, of women taking active participation and leadership roles in Paul's churches, have to be kept in mind when evaluating what Paul has to say about the role of women in his churches.[177]

---

173. See my *Romans* 888-89; and above at n. 133.

174. The seven were elected in Acts 6 to serve *(diakonein)* at tables (6.2) but are not actually described as deacons *(diakonoi)*. The claim that Phoebe was the first formally designated deacon depends on Philippians being dated after Romans (but the 'deacons' of Phil. 1.1 are not named).

175. Prisc(ill)a and Aquila — Acts 18.18, 26; Rom. 16.3; 2 Tim. 4.19. Aquila and Prisc(ill)a — Acts 18.2 (because the couple are mentioned for the first time?); 1 Cor. 16.19 (because of the situation in Corinth implied in 14.33-36?).

176. See below, §32.5f.

177. See again §32.5f below.

f. The Christian Family

A feature of some associations was the use of familial language — father, mother, brother — for patrons and fellow members. The titles 'father of the synagogue' or 'mother of the synagogue' are fairly frequent in the inscriptions.[178] The same is true of Paul's churches. Paul likens himself to a father of his converts and churches on several occasions, responsible both to discipline and to care for them.[179] And 'brother' is a term which occurs well over one hundred times in the undisputed Pauline letters — Paul's usual form of address and appeal to his fellow believers.[180] Presumably the term was intended to embrace the whole congregation (as for the next nineteen centuries!), though Paul does refer specifically to 'sisters' on a number of occasions and calls named fellow believers 'sister'.[181] Paul's usage, then, would not be particularly remarkable, though Meeks suggests that Paul's letters are 'unusually rich in emotional language' and that 'both the number and intensity of the affective phrases in the Pauline letters are extremely unusual'.[182] What would be more distinctive, however, is his assertion that Christ, the central figure to whom the Christian association was devoted, is the eldest of the brothers.[183] Perhaps we should see here one more instance of the influence of the Jesus tradition, in this case the episode in which Jesus was remembered as acknowledging 'whoever does the will of God' as 'my brother and sister and mother' (Mark 3.35).[184]

More striking and most unusual, however, is the fact that families, including children, were evidently regarded as part of the churches. This seems to be implied in 1 Cor. 7.14: the children of a believing parent are not to be regarded as 'unclean' or outside the circle of the community of 'saints'.[185] But it is explicit in

178. Schürer, *History* 3.101; van der Horst, *Jewish Epitaphs* 93-94; *JIWE* 1.5; 2.209, 251, 288, 540, 542, 544, 560, 576, 577, 578, 584; Levinskaya, *BAFCS* 5.191-92; *JAGR* 46-48; P. A. Harland, 'Familial Dimensions of Group Identity II: "Mothers" and "Fathers" in Associations and Synagogues of the Greek World', *JSJ* 38 (2007) 57-79. For the synagogue at Ostia see White, 'Synagogues' 61.

179. 1 Cor. 3.1-2; 4.14-15, 17; 2 Cor. 6.13; 12.14; Gal. 4.19; Phil. 2.22; 1 Thess. 2.7, 11; Phlm. 10. He calls believers 'children of God' several times (Rom. 8.16-17, 21; [9.8]; Phil. 2.15).

180. See above, §20.1(7).

181. Rom. 16.1 (Phoebe); 1 Cor. 7.15; 9.5; Phlm. 2 (Apphia).

182. Meeks, *Urban Christians* 86; though see also n. 49 above; see also Schenk, 'Selbstverständnisse' 1375-82, and note the 'holy kiss' (Rom. 16.16; 1 Cor. 16.20; 2 Cor. 13.12; 1 Thess. 5.26).

183. Rom. 8.29; Col. 1.18; cf. Rom. 8.17; Gal. 4.6-7.

184. See *Jesus Remembered* §14.7.

185. 'Saints, holy ones', of course, is another of Paul's terms for believers; see above, §20.1(8).

the household code of Col. 3.18–4.1, where children are addressed directly, that is, as present in the gathering where the letter would be read out, and as responsible agents despite their youth. In other words, the fictive family of the new Christian association was not understood to replace the normal family structure,[186] but the latter was thought of as embraced within the larger family with God as Father, and Jesus as the firstborn, setting the image for the rest of the family.

A point to be borne in mind is that, in the classic definition of Aristotle, the household was the basic unit of the state.[187] Consequently, we may say that a movement based on houses and households, and using the family as a model, was, inevitably, conforming to the social norms of the day. That tendency became stronger with the adoption of the widespread convention of the household code in Colossians and subsequent Christian letters.[188] The deep (but little apparent on the surface) subversiveness of the Christian house church lay in the subordination of all relationships to the lordship of Christ.

30.5. The Organization of Paul's Churches

It was early on noticed that the Roman associations often mimicked the structure of municipal life in their organization, with heads of societies bearing titles like *magistri, curatores, praefecti* or *praesides,* and officers with titles like tribune or triumvir.[189] The terms *grammateus* ('secretary') and *tamias = quaestor* ('treasurer') appear regularly.[190] *Episkopos* ('overseer, supervisor') and *diakonos* ('assistant') are also attested.[191] In the diaspora synagogues we read regularly of *archisynagōgoi, archontes* ('rulers') and *presbyteroi* ('elders');[192] also occasion-

---

186. Wilson also points out that 'those associations based on a household . . . were an expression of family life, not a substitute for it' ('Voluntary Associations' 14).

187. See particularly Verner, *Household of God* 27-81; here also Meeks, *Urban Christians* 75-77.

188. See my 'The Household Rules in the New Testament', in S. C. Barton, ed., *The Family in Theological Perspective* (Edinburgh: Clark, 1996) 43-63; briefly *Theology of Paul* 666-67.

189. Waltzing, *Études* 1.383-425; Dill, *Roman Society* 267, 269; Bendlin, 'Gemeinschaft' 12-13, also 19-24.

190. Poland notes that the office of 'secretary' can 'be considered to some extent typical of the whole world of associations' and 'is even more widespread than that of treasurer' (*Geschichte* 383, as cited by Klauck, *Religious Context* 46). On 'treasurer' see Poland 375-77, 380-82; Ascough, *Paul's Macedonian Associations* 64 n. 83.

191. *Episkopos* — TDNT 2.612-13; BDAG 379; Poland, *Geschichte* 377, 448; Ascough, *Paul's Macedonian Associations* 80-81. *Diakonos* — Poland 42, 391-92; Ascough 82-83.

192. Schürer, *History* 2.434-38; inscriptional references — *archisynagōgos* (*History* 3.14, 15, 22, 23, 32, 34, 66, 68, 73, 82, 92, 100-101); *archontes* (3.13, 26, 31, 33, 61, 63, 92-95,

ally of a *hypēretēs* or *diakonos* ('assistant'),[193] and a cantor *(psalmo[logos],*
psalmōdos philonomos).[194]

In some degree of contrast, the earliest Pauline churches seem to have
avoided a multiplicity of titles and to have underplayed any concept of formal office. The 'apostle', founder of a church and a continuing authority in that church
— certainly in Paul's view[195] — was the nearest to the chief official in an association and to the 'ruler of the synagogue'.[196] And in the undisputed Pauline letters
we read of Phoebe the *diakonos* in Rom. 16.1, once of *episkopoi*[197] and *diakonoi,*
referred to in the address to the Philippians (Phil. 1.1), though their functions are
quite unclear.[198] But of 'elders' we hear nothing in the early Pauline letters — despite the testimony of Acts that Paul and Barnabas made sure to appoint elders in
the churches of Galatia (Acts 14.23), with the likely implication that this was
Paul's normal practice when he planted a new church.[199]

The hierarchy that Paul does envisage is 'first apostles, second prophets,
third teachers' (1 Cor. 12.28), but in contrast to the shrines and schools the latter
two appear more as functions than offices.[200] In the early Paulines the charism is

---

98-100); *presbyteroi* (3.14, 23, 26, 72, 88, 92, 98, 102). Clarke notes that the office of
gerousiarch, leader of the council of elders, is mentioned in twenty-four inscriptions (*Serve*
133). *Archisynagōgos* was not exclusive to Jewish synagogues (see, e.g., *NDIEC* 1.27; 4.214-
20; Ascough, *Paul's Macedonian Associations* 79-80; and above, n. 84).

193. Schürer, *History* 3.14, 101.

194. Schürer, *History* 3.26, 81; *NDIEC* 1.115-17.

195. 1 Cor. 9.1-2; 12.28; 14.37-38; Gal. 1.6-9; see also above, §29 n. 80.

196. But see n. 102 above.

197. 'Only *episkopos* is likely to have been taken over from the usage of associations'
(Meeks, *Urban Christians* 80).

198. Until the term comes to denote a regular office (1 Tim 3.8-13), the predominant
overtone of *diakonos* in the NT is to denote one who renders a service to others (BDAG 230-
31); cf. J. J. Collins, *Diakonia: Re-interpreting the Ancient Sources* (Oxford: Oxford University, 1990), whose analysis of *diakon-* words in ancient Greek literature and the papyri concludes that the word-group occurred in contexts of three kinds: message, agency and attendance upon a person or in a household. See also J. Reumann, 'Church Office in Paul, Especially
in Philippians', in B. H. McLean, ed., *Origins and Method: Towards a New Understanding of
Judaism and Christianity,* J. C. Hurd FS (JSNTS 86; Sheffield: JSOT, 1993) 82-91; and below,
§34 at n. 262.

199. See above, §27 at n. 97. Kirchenschläger provides a helpful tabulation of ministries
and structures reflected across the NT and Apostolic Fathers ('Entwicklung' 1335-36). But
Kloppenborg rightly warns against assuming a uniform organizational structure in the Pauline
churches ('Edwin Hatch' 232-33).

200. 'Prophet' 'is properly used only of seers and functionaries attached to an established oracular shrine; the unattached seer is called *mantis* or *chremologos.* And it is more often
used of the officials who presided over oracular shrines than of the actual receivers of mantic
inspiration' (*OCD*³ 1259).

the prophecy itself, the actual speaking forth of words given by inspiration, not an innate or God-given ability which may be exercised at will (Rom. 12.6; 1 Cor. 12.8-10). And prophets were prophets because they prophesied regularly; the authority of their prophecies derived from their prophetic inspiration, not from their status as prophets;[201] their prophecies should be tested and evaluated,[202] and others, not so recognized, might well be given to speak an authoritative word of prophecy.[203] Teachers, we may assume, exercised a more learned/acquired skill, in that they were responsible to the community for the stewardship, instruction and interpretation of the community's tradition — reinforcing the likeness of church to synagogue (or to philosophical school). But even so, Paul evidently thought of the charism as the *act* of teaching (Rom. 12.7), a charism which was not confined to the teachers (1 Cor. 14.26; Col. 3.16).[204]

What of individual leaders and leadership groups? Again the role and authority of the apostle was pre-eminent in Paul's eyes. But he does not seem to have thought of the prophets and teachers as exercising leadership outside the spheres of their charisms.[205] Most striking is the fact that in the very troubled situations in Galatia and Corinth, as also in Thessalonica, Paul seems to have been unable to appeal to any leadership to exercise the discipline and authority called for. Where were the elders that Acts tells us Paul appointed in the Galatian churches? Elders are noticeable by their complete absence from the scene in Thessalonica and Corinth,[206] and in Galatians! Instead Paul had to give long-range leadership himself.[207] He had to hope that a 'word of wisdom' (1 Cor. 12.8) would be given to someone in the wholly unsatisfactory circumstances envisaged in 6.1-6 (6.5), or more generally that someone would be enabled to provide guidance in such situations (12.28).[208] Some, he is quick to point out, have exercised such leadership and initiative. Stephanas and his household had appointed themselves *(etaxan heautous)* to some 'ministry *(diakonia)* for the saints' (16.15); that is, presumably, they had seen some service of which the church had need and acted to meet that need without waiting

---

201. See further my *Jesus and the Spirit* 227-33, 280-82. 'Their service is everywhere regarded as a direct gift of the Spirit; and the Church no more chooses prophets than it chooses apostles' (Schweizer, *Church Order* §24c).

202. 1 Cor. 14.29; 1 Thess. 5.19-22.

203. 1 Cor. 11.4-5; 14.1, 5, 24, 31.

204. See further my *Jesus and the Spirit* 236-38, 282-84.

205. Unlike the mother church at Syrian Antioch (Acts 13.1)? See above, §24 at n. 335.

206. Even if we assume that the problems in Corinth were being caused by some of the leaders — the patron, or elite group in the church — it is hardly likely that there was not one to whom Paul could appeal.

207. 2 Thess. 3.6-12; 1 Cor. 5.1-5; 14.37-40.

208. 12.28 — *kybernēseis,* from *kybernētēs,* 'one who is responsible for directing, or piloting a ship'.

to be asked.[209] Paul urges the Corinthian believers to follow their lead, to 'submit' themselves *(hypotassēsthe)* 'to such people and to everyone (who displays the same care and initiative in) working with and toiling for you' (16.16). And similarly Paul urges the Thessalonians to respect and honour *(eidenai)* those who toil among you and who care for you in the Lord and admonish you;[210] esteem them most highly in love because of their work' (1 Thess. 5.12-13). 'Such people' were presumably usually of higher social status, with time and resources to undertake leadership initiatives.[211] But again to be noted is the fact that the authority which Paul wanted his churches to accord to such people was by virtue of their work and service, not because of their social status or because he had appointed them or because they had been elected to some formal office of leadership.[212] And overall the relative lack of titles, official positions and formal rules marks out the Pauline churches from the typical associations of the time.[213]

Equally to be noted is Paul's encouragement to the congregations as a whole to take responsibility as a church for the order and discipline of their meetings. The assembled congregation should deal with the case of 'incest' in 1 Cor. 5.1-5 (5.5-6). The exhortation to respect the hard workers in their midst in Thessalonica is immediately followed by an appeal equally to the congregation as a whole 'to admonish the disorderly, to comfort the discouraged, to help the weak and to be patient with all' (1 Thess. 5.14).[214] And the admonition extends into the final epigrammatic conclusion, where Paul reminds the Thessalonians that it is the responsibility of the congregation as a whole to 'test everything [that is put forward as prophecy], hold fast to what is good [in the prophesying], keep away from every form of evil [again with reference to prophecies]' (5.19-22).[215] In Colossians, similarly, it is the church as a whole

209. Did Paul look to the householders to take leadership (so Gehring, *House Church* 196-210)?

210. 'The three participles . . . name functions rather than offices' (Meeks, *Urban Christians* 134).

211. Theissen, *Social Setting* 87-88; Meeks, *Urban Christians* 134.

212. Conzelmann, *History* 106-107. The point here is *not* that Paul saw no necessity for individual believers to act as leaders; it is rather to underline the character of the leadership that he saw to be necessary in such charismatic communities.

213. Already noted by Weiss, *1 Korintherbrief* xxii-xxv. 'The most striking and obvious difference is the absence of office-bearers in Corinth' (Chester, *Conversion at Corinth* 240).

214. The traditional church view, still in Vatican II's *Lumen Gentium* §12, that the exhortations of 5.14-22 are directed to a leadership group runs clearly counter to what the text actually says, addressed as it is to the generality of 'brothers' in Thessalonica (5.14), that is, the same group who have just been called upon to respect those working among them (5.12). See further Malherbe, *Thessalonians* 316, and for the detail of 5.14, 316-20.

215. See again discussion in Malherbe, *Thessalonians* 332-34.

which has responsibility to 'teach and admonish one another in all wisdom' (Col. 3.16).

Always we must beware of generalizing too lightly from the perspective which Paul provides for us in regard to a mere handful of churches. What we can say, however, is that a consistent picture emerges from his letters to these few churches, and it is one in which formal structures of organization and appointed leadership were markedly lacking. Instead we have to reach for a term like 'charismatic community' if we are to gain an adequate 'feel' for what Paul both sought to accomplish and in the event succeeded in accomplishing[216] — always with the qualification that the outcome seems to have been a very mixed blessing, with, in particular, an alarming degree of instability in the church into which his letters shine most light (Corinth).[217] Hans von Campenhausen's summary description of Paul's 'vision of the structure of the community as one of free fellowship, developing through the living interplay of spiritual gifts and ministries, without the benefit of official authority or responsible "elders"' still seems to be closer to the reality envisaged in Paul's letters than most other formulations.[218]

30.6. Their Meetings

How would outsiders have regarded the actual meetings of Paul's churches? The question is appropriate, since Paul certainly envisaged 'unbelievers *(apistoi)*' and 'outsiders *(idiōtai)*'[219] entering into a gathering of believers (1 Cor. 14.23-24) — presumably invited by a friend, or even attracted off the street by the sounds of the meeting through an open (outer) door. And no doubt the small house churches grew by inviting friends, visiting kinsfolk, fellow synagogue attenders, neighbours and colleagues to come to one of their regular meetings or shared meals.[220] So, what would such visitors think they had come into? Once again we are heavily dependent on what we know of the church in Corinth.

---

216. 'Charismatic community' is the term I have used in *Jesus and the Spirit* (especially 260-65) and *Theology of Paul* 552-62, also 566-71 and 586 n. 108.

217. See further below, §§32.3-7.

218. Von Campenhausen, *Ecclesiastical Authority* 70-71; similarly Wedderburn, *History* 135-38.

219. The *idiōtai,* literally those who relatively lack knowledge and experience of the group, are distinguished from both 'believers' and 'unbelievers' and so probably refer to inquirers or interested visitors, not yet initiated into the group; in religious associations the term is used for non-members who may participate in the sacrifices (BDAG 468).

220. R. J. Banks, *Going to Church in the First Century: An Eyewitness Account* (Beaumont: Christian, 1990), provides an imaginative reconstruction well founded historically.

a. The Regular Worship

Some points of comparison were obvious. Like the synagogue, the church probably met at least weekly.[221] 'On the first day of the week' (1 Cor. 16.2) does not necessarily refer to such a weekly meeting, but it coheres with the reference to such a meeting in Acts 20.7, and it indicates that 'the first day of the week' had a special significance for believers (cf. Rev. 1.10; *Did.* 14.1).[222] It is noteworthy that a regular meeting on a Sunday would have avoided any clash with the synagogue gathering on the Sabbath, which would have allowed Jews, proselytes and God-fearers to maintain their synagogue obligations while also participating in a house church.[223] This avoidance of the Sabbath as the day of meeting would also allow the idea to circulate that the church in any place with a strong Jewish community was a sub-unit of the synagogue.

The typical acts of worship would also be recognizable as such to the outsider, particularly the reading and teaching, the singing and praying (1 Cor. 14.26).[224] The reading would obviously be of Scripture, though not forgetting Paul's letter(s).[225] And the teaching would no doubt include the Jesus tradition and the developing traditions of the regional and other churches;[226] we can confidently assume that stories about Jesus and the (often exciting) exploits of the earliest apostles and missionaries would often be retold, and basic teaching of Jesus

221. Associations typically met once a month, though also on patrons' birthdays and special feast days. At the beginning of Augustus's reign he had limited the associations to meeting once a month, but Jewish synagogues were explicitly exempted in the legislation (Cotter, 'The Collegia and Roman Law' 77-79).

222. Pliny's report of early second-century Christian meetings in Bithynia simply notes that 'it was their habit on a fixed day to assemble . . .' (*Ep.* 10.96.7). But note also Ignatius's encouragement 'to come together more frequently' (*Eph.* 13.1).

223. As we shall see, this possibility of Christians to attend both the synagogue on Saturday and church on Sunday became a continuing bone of contention for Christian leaders through the next three centuries; see vol. 3.

224. *Singing:* note also 1 Cor. 14.15; Col. 3.16-17; Eph. 5.18-20; see further *Jesus and the Spirit* 238-39; *Unity and Diversity* §35 ('Early Christian Hymns'); Meeks, *Urban Christians* 144-45. *Prayers:* note also Rom. 8.15-16, 26-27; 1 Cor. 11.4-5, 13; 14.14-17; see further *Jesus and the Spirit* 239-42; Meeks, *Urban Christians* 147-48. The unformalized and diverse prayers offered by Paul in his letters are presumably typical of prayers in the assembly, and references to prayer give some idea of their content — e.g., Phil. 1.9-10, 19-20; 4.6; Col. 1.9; 1 Thess. 1.2-3; 3.9-10; 2 Thess. 1.11-12.

225. Note again Col. 4.16; and see further above, §29.8d.

226. This practice is implicit in the fairly frequent allusions Paul makes to material from the Jesus tradition (see above, §21.5) and to the practices of 'all the churches' (§29 n. 155), each implying an awareness of both in local churches. See further §30.8 below. 'We may assume that the paraenetic sections of the Pauline letters are fairly close to the sort of exhortations that would have been made orally in the regular meetings' (Meeks, *Urban Christians* 147).

and the first disciples would have been recalled and reinforced. Here too the parallel with synagogue and philosophical school would be most noticeable.[227] Songs and prayers were equally regular features of both associations and *thiasoi,* so it would be primarily the content, not to mention the spiritual impact of the preaching, which would catch and captivate.[228]

Visitors would not necessarily have been surprised by the enthusiasm which was evidently prized and frequently swept over the Corinthian congregation, as indicated by several allusions in 1 Corinthians. The visitors would recognize a familiar type of religious cult.

- 1 Cor. 12.2 — 'You know that when you were pagans, you used to be carried away to idols that were incapable of speech'. An allusion to the Corinthians' own memories of formerly participating in the Dionysiac mysteries is highly probable.[229] In the light of the other references below, Paul's intent was presumably to indicate that inspiration by the Spirit should have a different character.
- 14.12 — 'So then you too, since you are zealous for spirits, seek what builds up the church'. Clearly alluded to is the same appetite for experiences of possession and inspiration, the desire to be taken out of themselves.[230]
- 14.23 — 'If then the whole church comes together in the one place and all speak in tongues, and outsiders or unbelievers enter, will they not say that you are out of your mind *(mainesthe)?*' Although the verb *mainomai* can be used colloquially ('You're mad!'), the context of this chapter suggests a

227. Paul's letters contain several examples of midrashic exposition which would have been familiar in the synagogue (there is no reason to assume that Paul changed his expository style from synagogue to church) — particularly Rom. 4.3-25 (Gen. 15.6), Rom. 10.6-9 (Deut. 30.12-14), 2 Cor. 3.7-18 (Exod. 34.29-35); see further my *Unity and Diversity* ch. 5.

228. Paul often seems to envisage such an effect: Rom. 15.18-19; 1 Cor. 2.4-5; 14.24-25; 2 Cor. 4.5-6; *plērophoria* — 'with full conviction' (Rom. 15.29 v.l.; Col. 2.2; 4.12; 1 Thess. 1.5).

229. 'Dionysiac festivals were ubiquitous throughout the Greek world. . . . Festivals of Dionysus were often characterized by ritual licence and revelry, including reversal of social roles, cross-dressing by boys and men, drunken comasts in the streets, as well as widespread boisterousness and obscenity' (*OCD*³ 481). For recent discussion of 12.2 see Thiselton, *1 Corinthians* 912-16. It was in Corinth that Pausanias, a century later, heard the story of Pentheus, torn limb from limb by the female revellers in celebrating the mystery of Dionysus (*Description of Greece* 2.6).

230. The thought seems to be of an irresponsible yielding of oneself to such experiences without concern for what spirit was inspiring or with what effect (cf. Thiselton, *1 Corinthians* 1107); a modern parallel would be similar irresponsibility in experimentation with drugs, where the 'high' was what mattered above all else.

close parallel to the thought of John 10.20 ('He has a demon and is out of his mind [*mainetai*]'), again with possible Dionysiac/Bacchic overtones.[231]

Whatever the precise facts of the matter, Paul was clearly concerned lest the gatherings of believers in Corinth should give the impression that they were just another rowdy and ecstatic religious cult in quest of 'out of this world' experiences to make more endurable the harshness of daily life. Presumably he was all too conscious of the bad publicity which meetings of some clubs generated; the warning against 'reveling and drunkenness, debauchery and licentiousness' (Rom. 13.13) no doubt had in mind the notoriety enjoyed by some associations.[232] As Paul sought to avoid the slightest smell of subversiveness in Rom. 12.9–13.10, so in 1 Corinthians he was evidently anxious to leave as little room for confusing the church of Corinth with a riotous assembly — the concern being to avoid not so much punitive action by the authorities as an unsavoury reputation among the citizenry.

b. The Shared Meal

If 1 Corinthians is any guide, the young churches, like most associations, met regularly to share a common meal: Paul envisages the Corinthian believers coming together 'to share in (eat) the dinner of the Lord' (1 Cor. 11.20). Indeed, if we take 11.18 and 20 as more or less synonymous, the Corinthians came together in/ as church for that purpose; their sharing in the Lord's meal was what constituted them as 'church'.[233] This again would be no surprise to any outsider, since eating together seems to have been one of the main purposes of most associations and religious cults. The meal at Corinth would be regarded as an *eranos*.[234] As we shall see below (§32.5g), the problems at Corinth may have been caused precisely because the shared meal there was too much like the typical Greco-Roman dinner party, with participants graded in accordance with social status. Furthermore, a striking feature of Paul's treatment of the subject, too little noticed, is that in 10.21 he does not hesitate to draw a parallel with the meals which took

231. Cf. BDAG 610.

232. Similarly Varro, *R. R.* 3.2.16 (in MacMullen, *Social Relations* 77-78); Philo, *Legat.* 312; *Flacc.* 4, 136; on which see T. Seland, 'Philo and the Clubs and Associations of Alexandria', in Kloppenborg and Wilson, *Voluntary Associations* 110-27; also Ascough, *Paul's Macedonian Associations* 85-87. These 'outsider' criticisms, of course, should not be taken as objective characterizations of such gatherings; see above, n. 77.

233. As Paul had already said: 'Because the bread is one, we though many are one body, for we all partake of the one bread' (10.17).

234. See above, n. 76.

place in temples or at the table of Sarapis.[235] It was precisely the closeness of the parallel which made it necessary for Paul to insist that the Corinthian believers could not, must not sit both at the table of such idols and at the table of the Lord.

Several further features of these shared meals call for comment. For one thing it is not clear whether the church fellowship meals took place as frequently as once a week, or whether Paul was thinking of occasions when the whole congregation came together 'in the same place' (11.20) — perhaps such gatherings of the whole church were less frequent, with smaller meetings in apartments and smaller house churches in between. Presumably, since believers gathered in someone's home, the host at the meal was the householder. Again we need to ask whether each of the gatherings was a 'coming together to eat the Lord's dinner/feast *(deipnon)*' (11.20). Paul's language could imply that only some of the gatherings were for a shared meal; there were other comings together for other purposes (cf. 14.26).[236] Or it could imply that every coming together 'to the same place' was for the purpose of eating together.

We should not fail to note that 'the Lord's Supper' was a complete meal, which would begin, we may suppose, in Jewish fashion, with the blessing, breaking and sharing of the bread. Paul's own description is explicit that the sharing of the cup took place 'after the meal', at the close of the meal (11.25).[237] The point is obscured by the fact that the term 'supper' in 'the Lord's Supper' is an old-fashioned term and now more misleading than helpfully descriptive.[238] The term Paul uses in 11.20 is *deipnon,* which refers to the main meal of the day, eaten in the evening; 'the Lord's dinner' would be a more accurate translation, however crassly it may ring in the modern ear. No doubt, a large part of the attraction of the churches, as with the associations generally, was the companionship (fellowship) and conviviality of these meals (not to mention a share in better food than many might be able to provide for themselves). The complete meal character of 'the dinner of the Lord' also carries an important theological corollary: to the extent that we can speak of the Lord's Supper in Corinth as a sacramental meal —

---

235. See n. 78 above.

236. So, e.g., Becker, *Paul* 252.

237. See particularly O. Hofius, 'The Lord's Supper and the Lord's Supper Tradition: Reflections on 1 Corinthians 11.23b-25', in B. F. Meyer, ed., *One Loaf, One Cup: Ecumenical Studies of 1 Cor. 11 and Other Eucharistic Texts* (Macon: Mercer University, 1993) 75-115 (here 80-96); and further my *Theology of Paul* §22. As I point out there, this implication of a single meal framed by the broken bread and the cup 'after dinner' weakens the suggestion that what Paul envisaged in 1 Corinthians 11 was a two-phase meal: a 'first table' of several courses, followed by a break; and a 'symposium' (drinking party) as a 'second table' (610-11), as argued, e.g., by Lampe, 'Eucharist' 37-40.

238. In some cultures 'supper' refers only to a drink and a light snack before bed. The now much more commonly used term, 'eucharist', is even more remote from a complete meal.

as we can (10.16) — a key consideration is that the sacramental character embraced the whole meal, beginning with the shared bread and ending with the shared cup. Integral to the religious character of the meal was its shared character;[239] for Paul the whole meal was to be shared in conscious memory of Jesus' last supper and, as in the earliest Jerusalem gatherings, probably in conscious continuation of Jesus' own table-fellowship.[240]

A final feature worthy of note is one which would certainly have struck the casual or interested visitor. That was the absence of any libation to the gods or patron deity in particular. As already noted, other associations would typically have celebrated their meal in a temple. In religious associations priests of the cult deity would have played a prominent role,[241] and we know that diaspora Jews from priestly families still retained the title 'priest'.[242] But the earliest Christians refused any link with a temple — apparently not even acknowledging any dependency on the Temple in Jerusalem. To eat the meat of animals sacrificed in the local temples was abhorrent to them. They poured no libations to any god(s). They named no individuals as priest nor paid respect to them as such.[243] Their ritual of broken bread and shared wine must have appeared very tame in comparison, not to say dishonouring to the ancient gods. Did they even deserve the name of a religious cult? Their reverence for Jesus and worship of the one God (whom Jews also confessed) certainly constituted them a cult in the taxonomy of the day. But it must have appeared to many a strange kind of cult — and perhaps all the more attractive for that very reason![244]

c. One or More Meetings?

An enduring problem emerging from 1 Corinthians, the only text we can draw on extensively for the first-generation Pauline churches, is how we should envisage

---

239. The theme of sharing is the main emphasis in 10.16-30: *koinōnia*, 'participation/sharing in' — 10.16 (twice); *koinōnos*, 'partner, one who take part in with someone else' — 10.18, 20; *metechō*, 'share/partake in' — 10.17, 21, 30; see more fully *Theology of Paul* 615-20.

240. See *Jesus Remembered* §14.8 and above, §23.2d.

241. E.g., in the regulations of the Iobacchi: 'The priest shall perform the customary services at the meeting and the anniversary in proper style, and shall set before the meeting the drink-offering for the return of Bacchos and pronounce the sermon' (111-16; Meyer, *Ancient Mysteries* 98).

242. Schürer, *History* 3.22, 23, 34, 61, 95, 99.

243. Lohse, *Paulus* 145; see further my *Theology of Paul* §20.3 — 'Community without Cult' (543-48).

244. Cf. Judge, 'The Social Identity of the First Christians' 212; also 'Did the Churches Compete with Cult Groups?', in J. T. Fitzgerald et al., eds., *Early Christianity and Classical Culture*, A. J. Malherbe FS (NovTSupp 110; Leiden: Brill, 2003) 501-24; Barton and Horsley 'Hellenistic Cult Group' 39-40; Meeks, *Urban Christians* 140.

the relation of chs. 10–11 to chs. 12–14. Were all gatherings a combination of the two functions: to worship in the setting of a shared meal? The likelihood is that the two meetings were distinct, perhaps taking place on different days of the week.[245] Whereas ch. 14 seems to envisage a meeting for worship, with participants arriving more or less together (14.26), ch. 11 envisages individuals arriving at different times (11.33), with resulting problems. This accords also with Pliny's early second-century report that the Bithynian Christians met twice on their special day: before daylight for worship, and again later to share in their meal together (*Ep.* 10.96.7). At the same time, we should not assume that all or the only comings together of the first Christians were formal meetings; visits to friends, outings together during precious free time, shared meals however simple would provide countless opportunities for the sharing of faith and exploration of its implications.

All this leaves unresolved the question whether unbelievers and outsiders were admitted to the Lord's dinner. The implication of 14.23-24, that such could be present when believers came together as church, may apply only to gatherings for worship. At the same time, we should not assume that the shared meals had a specially sacred character which disbarred unbelievers and outsiders from sharing in them.[246] Was every shared meal 'the Lord's dinner'? Was the bread broken and the wine drunk at every meal 'in remembrance' of Jesus (11.24-25)? We have already noted the same ambiguity with regard to Luke's references to the 'breaking of bread'.[247] And it would be unduly hasty to assume that the hospitality which a Christian couple like Aquila and Priscilla extended to fellow believers and others would have had a markedly different character (in their eyes) from the meals shared when the whole church gathered in one place.[248] Whether or not the Lord's table was seen as an evangelistic opportunity in these early years, we can be fairly confident that Christian hospitality did result in many guests and visitors coming to faith in the Lord of their hosts.

Finally we need to ask whether the first Christian groups asked for and received permission for their meetings.[249] There is no hint whatsoever of such asking, not even in the politically sensitive exhortations to believers in the empire's capital city (Romans). The probability is either that they assumed, or hoped, that their meetings were too small to attract suspicion,[250] or that in effect they were

---

245. Klauck, *Hausgemeinde* 37; Gehring, *House Church* 171-73; see the brief discussion in Gnilka, *Die frühen Christen* 302-303.

246. Rom. 14.6 clearly implies that thanks were offered to God at all meals.

247. See again §23.2d above.

248. The reverse situation (believers dining as guests of an unbeliever) is clearly envisaged in 1 Cor. 10.27-30, with believers able to give thanks for what they received (10.30).

249. See above, nn. 80, 81.

250. 'Did Christians pass "informal" scrutiny by city officials because their Jewish hero and their appeal to Jewish tradition cloaked them as a Jewish society?' (Cotter, 'Collegia' 88).

continuing to shelter under the authorizations given to the synagogue by Caesar and his successors.[251] This again is the implication of Luke's account of Roman authorities' reactions to the Jesus sect in the early days: the disagreements which resulted in believers meeting separately from the synagogue as such were 'disputes about words and names and about your [the Jews'] own law'; they should resolve such disputes among themselves and not trouble the authorities (Acts 18.15).[252] This certainly seems to be the most likely situation pertaining during Paul's Aegean mission.[253] The continuing link, even if ruptured, with the wider Jewish community (at least as perceived from 'outside') presumably reassured both God-fearers and subsequently other Gentile inquirers that they were not entering a political club which would result in their names appearing on some list of potential troublemakers.

30.7. Boundaries

Sociology has taught us that group identity and group boundaries are mutually complementary.[254] The group is constituted as a group by the boundaries that distinguish it as a group and from other groups. Boundaries are part of group definition and are indispensable to the identity of the group; the clearer the boundaries, the clearer the identity; the more confused or ambiguous the boundaries, the more confused or ambiguous the identity. Social anthropologists have also pointed out that the human body is an image of society; as the body is a bounded system, so society can be defined as a body by its boundaries.[255] So, for Paul to define the churches he founded as the body of Christ in different centres, or as 'one body in Christ', implies such a bounded system, a clear sense of identification with and difference from, of 'others' and 'outsiders'.[256]

251. This understanding — that they were members of a Jewish synagogue/association — presumably is what made it possible for believers to escape the obligation of the imperial cult (Winter, *Welfare* 136-43).

252. Malherbe's generalization seems fair: 'In the first century Christians were criticized for social rather than political reasons' (*Social Aspects* 21); see further above, §29.4d, and below, §31.4c.

253. The 'Jewish tax' (the Temple tax) did not become an issue for the authorities (who should pay and so accept identification as Judeans/Jews) until after the Temple's destruction; see vol. 3.

254. A lesson I learned years ago from H. Mol, *Identity and the Sacred* (Oxford: Blackwell, 1976): 'It is precisely the boundary . . . which provides the sense of identity' (57-58).

255. Particularly influential has been the work of Mary Douglas, *Natural Symbols: Explorations in Cosmology* (London: Barrie and Jenkins, 1973).

256. See also Meeks, *Urban Christians* 94-96.

It has been apparent from earlier discussion that the emergence of the Jesus sect within Second Temple Judaism involved a questioning of previous boundaries, and a breaking down or pushing back of old boundaries.[257] The same issue arises once again with Paul's mission, particularly so in this chapter as we have looked at the churches he founded and how they would have appeared to others. Given not least the Jewish character of the chief missionaries and of the gospel they preached, how clearly defined and distinctive were the groups that converts would be joining? What boundaries defined the groups' identity over or through which converts would have to pass in becoming members of one of these groups?

There are various boundaries of course, and we should not assume that they were all of the same kind or functioned in the same way. We may distinguish, for example,

- *rigid* boundaries, whose once-for-all crossing was a *sine qua non* of membership;
- *variable* boundaries, where different members of the group attributed differing values to the beliefs or traditions or rituals expected of members;
- *permeable* (or soft or fluid) boundaries, through which individuals could pass back and forth;
- *non-exclusive* boundaries, which permitted membership of more than one group; and
- *shifting* boundaries, as a group tightened or slackened its requirements of membership.[258]

a. Baptism

The most obvious boundary marker for the religious association focused on Jesus as Lord was baptism in the name of this Jesus. Paul evidently did not put tremendous store on the performance of baptism (1 Cor. 1.14-17), but he had no doubt as to the power of its symbolism (baptized into Christ's death) and could assume that everyone he wrote to, and not just in Rome, had been baptized (Rom. 6.4). If anything is to be reckoned a *sine qua non* of membership of the Pauline churches, presumably baptism 'in the name of Jesus Christ' is the obvious contender. It is just such a ritual act, probably in most cases performed in a group or

257. See *Jesus Remembered* §14.8 and above, at the end of §24.7a; also my 'Boundary Markers in Early Christianity', in J. Rüpke, ed., *Gruppenreligionen im römischen Reich* (STAC 43; Tübingen: Mohr Siebeck, 2007) 49-68.
258. Meeks prefers to speak of 'gates in the boundaries' (*Urban Christians* 105-107). Here, of course, the parallel with the body ceases to apply.

even public context,[259] which would normally be required to mark a convert's passing over of the boundary marking off the new sect.

Every religious association at the time of Paul probably practised some form of initiation ritual. I have already noted the early suggestion of the history-of-religions school that Christian baptism or the significance Paul attributed to it was derived from the contemporary mystery cults, and there I pointed out the differences too lightly glossed over by the early history-of-religions scholars.[260] Particularly relevant in this case are the probability both that the purification rituals of the mystery cults were part of the preparation for the initiation and not part of the initiation itself, and that the initiation rituals themselves were far more elaborate, involving 'things recited', 'things shown' and 'things performed'.[261] Nevertheless, the fact that entry into membership of a church required such a ritual act of initiation would not have been strange to outsiders. Its significance in terms of the baptisand becoming servant of the exalted Lord named in the ceremony would not be strange either.[262] Nor indeed the idea of thereby somehow passing from death to life.[263] And if indeed 'manifestations of the Spirit'[264] (including inspired utterance and extraordinary doings),[265] regularly accompanied Christian initiation,[266] then this too may not have appeared out of the ordinary to any who witnessed such events. The chief differences would probably have been seen as the exclusivity and accompanying moral transformation which was im-

259. We do not know the circumstances in which baptism was performed in the earliest days of Christianity. The Acts accounts suggest a public event, or at least not a secret event (2.41; 8.12-13, 38; 10.47-48; 16.15; 18.8; 19.5), though the baptism of Paul himself may have been rather private (9.18) and the baptism of the jailer in Philippi is envisaged as taking place during the night (16.33 — 'without delay'). See further Meeks, *Urban Christians* 150-52.

260. See above, §20.3b.

261. OCD² 716; see further Burkert, *Ancient Mystery Cults* ch. 4; Klauck, *Religious Context* 86-89; Meeks, *Urban Christians* 152-53.

262. See above, §23.2a; if indeed baptism 'in the name of' echoed the banking imagery of transferring ownership to the one named (as we today write a cheque 'to the name of') (details and bibliography in BDAG 713), then this too would have resonated in the commercial world in which Paul could move with some ease.

263. Cf. Lucius's own report: 'the very rite of dedication itself was performed in the manner of a voluntary death and of a life obtained by grace' (Apuleius, *Metamorphoses* 11.21); translation by J. G. Griffiths, *Apuleius of Madauros: The Isis-Book (Metamorphoses, Book XI)* (Leiden: Brill, 1975) 52.

264. I use the phrase of Paul, *phanerōsis tou pneumatos* (1 Cor. 12.7), which Paul evidently saw as synonymous with 'diversity of charisms', 'diversity of acts of service', 'diversity of activities' (12.4-6).

265. Gal. 3.2-5; 1 Cor. 1.5-7; 12.13 as the means of entrance upon the life and activity of the charismatic body of Christ. The picture given in Acts (2.1-4; 8.17-18; 10.44-46; 19.6) is not far removed from what Paul evidently had in mind. See further my *Jesus and the Spirit* ch. 8.

266. Further discussion in *Theology of Paul* §§16.3-4 and 17.2.

plied in the Christian rite. Whereas it was possible for the individual to be initiated into more than one mystery cult, baptism implied an initiation into Christ
which made it impossible to regard membership of the church as simply one
among a number of similar or competing loyalties; I think of the rebukes of
1 Cor. 1.11-13 and 10.14-23. And whereas initiation into another cult might have
little or no social and moral consequences,[267] baptism implied both acceptance
of a definitively different group identity (the body of Christ — 12.13) and a radical moral transformation (6.9-11).

The equivalent for proselytes entering Judaism was, of course, circumcision. As we have already seen, that was regarded as a, if not the, defining characteristic of a 'Jew'.[268] It has become equally clear earlier on that Paul no longer
regarded circumcision as a requirement for Gentile believers in Jesus, a position
he held to consistently throughout his mission.[269] To that extent he must have regarded baptism in the name of Christ as substituting for circumcision — a case of
abandoning completely one boundary marker and replacing it with another. It is
sometimes argued that Paul abandoned two of the traditional ritual requirements
laid on the proselyte (circumcision and Temple sacrifice) but retained the third
(proselyte baptism).[270] But firm evidence for proselyte baptism in the period
prior to the destruction of the Temple is lacking. It is more likely that proselyte
baptism was introduced in the post-70 period, perhaps in place of a Temple sacrifice which could no longer be offered. Certainly where ritual baths were available and ritual purifications were regularly practised, we can assume that the
proselyte would undergo regular purification. But there is no indication that the
first immersion in a *miqwe* was accorded the significance of an initiation, a
crossing-the-boundary ceremony.[271] And such considerations must have been a
good deal less relevant to diaspora Jews who lived far from the Temple and could
hope to worship there at best occasionally. The desire for some kind of purifica-

267. Chester, *Conversion at Corinth* 270-71.

268. Paul uses 'circumcision' to designate Jews as a whole; see above, §27.2a and
n. 117.

269. See above, §§27.3d and 27.5; and note Gal. 5.2-6; 6.15; 1 Cor. 7.19; Rom. 2.28-29;
Phil. 3.3.

270. But as Collins notes: 'The requirements of baptism and sacrifice are not attested
before the end of the first century' ('A Symbol of Otherness' 171). That baptism was the equivalent of circumcision was a central part of Calvin's justification for paedobaptism (*Institutes*
4.16.3-5).

271. See further Beasley-Murray, *Baptism* 18-31; L. H. Schiffman, 'At the Crossroads:
Tannaitic Perspectives on the Jewish-Christian Schism', in E. P. Sanders, ed., *Jewish and Chris-
tian Self-Definition*. Vol. 2 (Philadelphia: Fortress, 1981) 115-56 (here 127-31); R. L. Webb,
John the Baptizer and Prophet (JSNTS 62; Sheffield: Sheffield Academic, 1991) 122-28;
S. J. D. Cohen, 'The Rabbinic Conversion Ceremony', in *Beginnings of Jewishness* 198-238
(here 222-25).

tion ritual would have been well understood by practising Jews, but Paul's effective replacement of circumcision with baptism for Gentile converts must have been a major factor in the breaches with the synagogue which Paul's establishment of new churches regularly caused.

b. Other Boundaries

Paul seems in effect to have insisted on several other boundaries. *Faith in Christ* was presumably a *sine qua non* also, the complement of the baptism which expressed the faith (as implicit in Rom. 10.9-10).[272] Hence the characteristic appellation of members of the new churches as 'believers',[273] distinctive, even if only as an 'in-house' self-designation, in the lack of any sense that the designation needed to be elaborated as 'believers in a particular heavenly being'.[274] At the same time it was evidently appreciated that the faith called for constituted some sort of clarification or qualification or modification (what is the best word?) of the Jewish requirement that proselytes join the confession of God as one (Deut. 6.4). Such a corollary would hardly escape believing Jews or converted God-fearers, since the adaptation of the *Shema* in 1 Cor. 8.6 is fairly obvious to anyone familiar with Deut. 6.4.[275] Here is a case of a shifting boundary as the full significance of who Jesus was and of how he relates/d to God became a matter of steadily deepening reflection. Presumably Paul did not see this identification of the church(es) with Christ (the body of Christ) as supplanting set-apartness to God as the key marker and boundary (as baptism in effect supplanted circumcision) but understood such faith in Christ as a filling out of traditional Jewish faith in God as one.[276]

The *ethnic identity* of the elect people of God was another boundary which Paul's commission to take the good news of Jesus to the Gentiles put into question. The issue evidently troubled Paul, though it was only in his major letter to Rome that he was able to address it in detail (Romans 9–11), as we shall see (§33.3e). Was this a case of boundaries abolished, or pushed back, or redefined? And whereas Paul could evidently sit light to a third identity marker of Judaism, the Temple in Jerusalem,[277] his attitude to the Mosaic law, the fourth 'pillar of

272. See above, §29.7f.
273. See above, §20.1(5).
274. But see Lane Fox's comment in §20 n. 30 above.
275. For brief review and discussion see Thiselton, *1 Corinthians* 636-38.
276. Which no doubt was why Paul saw no problem in adapting the *Shema* in 1 Cor. 8.6, or in quoting scriptural texts referring to Yahweh in reference to Christ; see earlier discussion in §§23.4d, h and §29.7d and my *Theology of Paul* 244-60.
277. Particularly 1 Cor. 3.16-17; 6.19; 2 Cor. 3.7-11; 6.16; Gal. 4.25. For recent discus-

Judaism',[278] is a good deal more ambiguous than is normally appreciated, again as we shall see (§33.3d).

In particular, we should note again that Paul's hostility to *idolatry* and to *illicit sexual relations (porneia)* remained as firm and as unyielding as that of any traditional Jewish community.[279] He was as urgent about the need for holiness[280] and the separation thereby involved from more typically Gentile morality as any of his diaspora Jewish predecessors.[281] In contrast, again if 1 Corinthians is any guide, other members of his churches evidently felt more relaxed about participation in festive meals on temple premises (1 Corinthians 8) or about consorting with prostitutes (5.9–6.20). Here boundaries were variable within individual churches, as observed (or not observed) diversely by the church's members.

Given what has already been said about the importance of *shared meals,* in the local community as well as in the church, it should occasion no surprise that the greatest tensions emerged at this point. So far as the Jewish laws governing the meal table were concerned, Paul's own teaching displays some variation. He had made a major issue of it in Antioch (Gal. 2.11-17),[282] but in the different circumstances he evidently knew of in Rome he could be more relaxed in his encouragement of those with different views on the issue to be tolerant and accepting of one another (Rom. 14.1–15.6). However, more relevant to our present discussion is the evidence of tensions within the Corinthian church, or between some members of it and Paul, over the issue of involvement with the wider community. Members of the social elite would inevitably feel pressure to attend civic festivals and functions which involved sacrifice to one or more of the gods and to participate in festive meals in one or other of the city's prominent temples. Here the problem was that of overlapping groups and overlapping boundaries. Believers who were also members of a social elite or clients of politically prominent

---

sion see A. L. A. Hogeterp, *Paul and God's Temple: A Historical Interpretation of Cultic Imagery in the Corinthian Correspondence* (Leuven: Peeters, 2006) part 3.

278. See my *Partings* ch. 2 ('The Four Pillars of Second Temple Judaism').

279. Idolatry — Rom. 1.23; 1 Cor. 8.4; 10.14, 20-21; 1 Thess. 1.9. Paul was as fiercely critical of the sexual license practised in Hellenism as the writer of the Wisdom of Solomon (Rom. 1.21-27). The Corinthian Christians are told to 'flee from *porneia*' (1 Cor. 6.18) and to drive out the licentious person from their midst (5.13). *Porneia* is the most prominent of 'the works of the flesh' and in his vice-lists (Gal. 5.19; also Eph. 5.3; Col. 3.5; 1 Thess. 4.3).

280. As well as the epithet 'saints *(hagioi)*' (see above, §20.1[8]), the language of sanctification/set-apartness occurs regularly in Paul's letters: *hagiazein* — Rom. 15.16; 1 Cor. 1.2; 6.11; 7.14; 1 Thess. 5.23; *hagiasmos* — Rom. 6.19, 22; 1 Cor. 1.30; 1 Thess. 4.3-4, 7; 2 Thess. 2.13. To the extent that baptism implied cleansing, the implication was of cleansing from previous impurity (cf., e.g., 1 Cor. 6.9-11).

281. 'The emphasis in Paul's paraenesis, however, is not upon the maintenance of boundaries, but upon internal cohesion' (Meeks, *Urban Christians* 100; see further 100-101).

282. See above, §§27.4-5.

figures would inevitably have found themselves pulled different ways. Was the solution to cut ties with one or other, to retreat behind an exclusive boundary?[283] Should the friend of eminent and influential citizens turn his or her back on them and eschew the opportunities which continuing social intercourse might provide for witness and preaching? As we shall see, Paul's attempt to square this circle is among the most interesting of the advice he gives (§32.5e).

The issue of boundaries was not solved during Paul's Aegean mission. Nor indeed, we may say, has it ever been finally resolved. For that very reason, however, the situations which initially posed these questions and the initial attempts by Paul and others to address them in a theologically and socially responsible way are all the more instructive for subsequent generations.

30.8. The Christian Network

One feature which would probably have marked out the emerging Pauline churches from the religious and other associations of the time was the self-awareness of belonging to a movement which was spreading over the Mediterranean world and the network of communication for which Paul was largely responsible. Neighbourhood and business (commerce and craft) associations were typically very local.[284] Religious cults, worshippers of Isis for example, would no doubt have been aware of many shrines and temples to Isis, but indications that they thought it necessary to maintain communication with other temple foundations are thin on the ground.[285] Schools, however, had a worldwide presence.[286] And synagogues presumably maintained a lively consciousness that the freedom to practise their religion was a consequence of their being natives of a

---

283. Paul contrasts temple meals and church meals as mutually exclusive (1 Cor. 10.20-21), but while that precluded a believer from attending the former, did it preclude an unbeliever from attending the latter? But, as already noted, Meeks stresses the exclusivity of the Christian groups in contrast to the typical voluntary associations (*Urban Christians* 78; supported by McCready, *'Ekklēsia'* 62).

284. 'While there is little to suggest extra-local links between professional associations, there are some important exceptions' (Kloppenborg, 'Collegia and *Thiasoi'* 27 n. 19); but see also Harland, *Associations* 36.

285. 'Once established, local cults remained largely autonomous and could take quite divergent forms from one locality to another' (Wilson, 'Voluntary Associations' 3). Chester, in dialogue with R. S. Ascough, 'Translocal Relationships among Voluntary Associations and Early Christianity', *JECS* 5 (1997) 223-41, notes that some types of associations did have translocal links, notably Dionysiac artists and athletes, but otherwise such links were not typical of associations (*Conversation at Corinth* 257-59). See also Ascough's attempt to demonstrate translocal links for many associations (*Paul's Macedonian Associations* 91-100).

286. Mason, *'Philosophiai'* 39.

Temple state (Judea),[287] a dependency which they expressed in payment of the Temple tax.

How much Paul communicated his vision and grand strategy to the Aegean churches, we do not know. But several features in his letters suggest that he inculcated a sense of belonging to and responsibility in relation to a large network of churches, with the Jerusalem congregations as the mother church.

- Paul's greeting to the saints in Corinth reminds them that they number themselves with 'all those who in every place call on the name of the Lord Jesus Christ' (1 Cor. 1.2). And his deliberate references to 'all the churches' no doubt had this perspective in mind too.[288]
- Paul's epistolary commendations of the churches to which he wrote should not be regarded as merely formal. He commends the Romans that their faith is spoken of 'in all the world' (Rom. 1.8). Similarly the Thessalonians, that they had become an example to all the believers in Macedonia and Achaia; in every place their faith had become known, and in these regions the story of Paul's evangelistic success in Thessalonica was well known (1 Thess. 1.7-9); they loved all the brothers throughout Macedonia (4.10). Similarly the Colossians, for what he had heard of their faith and love (Col. 1.4). Paul's pride in his tactic of self-support was well known not only in Corinth but 'in the region of Achaia' (2 Cor. 11.10).[289]
- The fact that Paul was able to greet so many individuals in Rome whom he obviously knew implies that he had met them at various times during his earlier mission, that is, met them elsewhere than in Rome. This also means that they had traveled to Rome or were frequent visitors there.[290]
- Paul's own travels around the network of his churches should not be regarded as exceptional. Apollos was not the only travelling professional teacher to visit (some of) Paul's churches; 1 Cor. 9.5 implies that 'the other apostles and the brothers of the Lord and Cephas' likewise traveled widely; and the incomers to the churches of Galatia, Corinth (2 Corinthians 10–13) and Philippi (Phil. 3.2) may well have traveled some distance.

287. The decrees cited by Josephus (above, n. 90) regularly refer to Hyrcanus, high priest of the Jews (*Ant.* 14.185-267; 16.160-79).

288. See above, §29 n. 155.

289. Jervell also points out that those who speak of a tradition like Acts 18.12-17 as 'local tradition' overlook the fact that such a ruling would have been important not only for the local community itself but also for other communities; 'mission reports would be passed not only to the commissioning community, but be part of the mission proclamation in establishing new communities. In this way the local tradition would have spread around' (*Apg.* 463).

290. See above, §28 n. 65.

- Likewise the messengers who passed between Paul and his churches — Chloe's people, Stephanas, Fortunatus and Achaicus, Titus (Corinth),[291] Timothy (Thessalonica), Epaphroditus (Philippi),[292] Tychicus, Onesimus and Epaphras (Colossae) — indicate a vigorous and extensive communication system between Paul and his churches, and probably among his churches as well.[293] Similarly, the 'letters of recommendation' referred to in 2 Cor. 3.1 presuppose some system soon established where such letters were given to believers to provide introductions to churches visited in the course of their travels.

- Paul speaks on several occasions of 'hearing' reports which evidently circulated round various churches,[294] implying a regular transmission of news between Paul and his churches and between churches.

- Although Paul at this stage evidently did not think of a world 'church' and spoke of individual congregations as the body of Christ in the city of residence (1 Cor. 12.27),[295] the sense of different congregations being united with Christ corporately must have served as a bond of major significance among these congregations.

- The collection which Paul spent many months gathering for the poor among the Jerusalem church was a remarkable feat of organization which involved many churches — 'the assemblies [plural] of Galatia' (1 Cor. 16.1, 'the assemblies of Macedonia' (2 Cor. 8.1) and Achaia (Rom. 15.26; 2 Cor. 9.2) — and which must have required extensive travel around and among these churches.[296] Probably, however, it was only a more intensive use of the Christian network than normal.

291. Theissen notes that of the seventeen persons or circles of people named in connection with Corinth, nine engaged in travel (*Social Setting* 92).

292. Note the frequency of communication implied in Phil. 2.19-30: (1) news of Paul's imprisonment had reached Philippi; (2) Epaphroditus had been sent with the Philippians' gift; (3) news of his illness when with Paul had reached Philippi; (4) probably (though not necessarily) news of the Philippians' concern for Epaphroditus had come back to Epaphroditus; (5) Paul was now about to send Epaphroditus back; (6) he hoped then to send also Timothy; and not least, (7) Paul hoped to come himself. News of the tensions implicit in Phil. 4.2-3 must also have been communicated to Paul.

293. Malherbe speaks of 'the formation of a network by which information about churches was communicated' (*Social Aspects* 65); McCready refers to a paper by T. A. Robinson, who noted that 'early churches fostered trans-local links in a way that stood in substantial contrast to voluntary associations' (*Ekklēsia* 63).

294. 1 Cor. 5.1; 11.18; Gal. 1.23; Phil. 1.27, 30; 2.26; 4.9; Col. 1.4, 9; 2 Thess. 3.11; Phlm. 5.

295. See my *Theology of Paul* 540-41, 550-52.

296. Rom. 15.25-28; 1 Cor. 16.1-2; 2 Corinthians 8–9; cf. Acts 20.4. Note Paul's ability to use one group of churches to stir another group to emulation (2 Cor. 8.1-7; 9.2-4).

We should not be misled, then, into thinking that, because he used the term *ekklēsia* for individual churches, Paul saw them each as independent and autonomous. It is true that the concept of the church as the universal body of Christ does not emerge in the Pauline corpus till the later letters, and it may indeed be an elaboration rather than an articulation of his own thought.[297] But he certainly did not think of them as independent and autonomous from each other. They each represented Christ, were Christ's body in their place of residence (1 Cor. 12.27); they had a common identity. Not only so, but Paul's churches had been founded by him; whoever else might have claim to be their apostle, *he* certainly was their apostle. He was their father in Christ. And he fully expected them to share a family likeness. The gospel which he had preached to them was what all the apostles preached in founding churches (1 Cor. 15.11). His repeated appeal in his Corinthian letters to what was true for 'all the churches' implied a shared identity. And that identity included the sense of shared indebtedness to the mother church of Jerusalem, equivalent to the identity expressed in the diaspora Jewish synagogues in their payment of the annual Temple tax. Paul did not make much use of the idea of the new groups of believers as 'the people of God',[298] but his conviction that they as the called of God (Rom. 9.24) had been grafted into the one olive tree of Israel (11.17-24) implied a belief in the corporate identity of the believers, Jews with Gentiles, on which the later Pauline letters could build.

30.9. Conclusion

What then was the attraction of the first Christian churches in a world where an amazing range of associations, religious cults and philosophical schools, not to mention synagogues, offered companionship and enjoyment, security in the face of death, and instruction in the good life? No single answer could possibly cover the range of factors or the range of individual cases. But in the light of the above some educated guesses can be hazarded, the most obvious being:

- The transforming and deeply emotional impact of Paul's message, as attested regularly in his letters. 'Conversion' in the full-rounded sense of the word was evidently a profound and life-altering experience for many, an experience of renewal and transformation, of being cleansed, enlightened and set free.[299] Experiences of acceptance love, joy, peace to which Paul

297. See my '"The Body of Christ" in Paul', in M. J. Wilkins and T. Paige, eds., *Worship, Theology and Ministry*, R. P. Martin FS (JSNTS 87; Sheffield: JSOT, 1992) 146-62; also below, §34 at n. 377 and §37.1d.

298. Rom. 9.25, 26; 11.1-2; 15.10; 2 Cor. 6.16.

299. Rom. 8.2; 12.2; 1 Cor. 6.9-11; 2 Cor 3.12-18; 4.6; Gal. 5.1.

regularly refers must have been sufficiently common for such references to resonate with the recipients of his letters.[300] The Christians themselves, of course, attributed all this to the Spirit of God.

- Harnack justifiably drew attention to the more striking experiences of the Spirit and of power, such as are indicated in passages like Gal. 3.5 and 1 Corinthians 12 and 14, the overcoming of demons through exorcism, the promise of healing for sickness, as well as the care shown and provision made in the early churches for the sick, the poor and slaves.[301]
- We should certainly not underestimate the powerful attraction of a hope for immortal life, guaranteed by the resurrection of Christ, so vividly highlighted in 1 Corinthians 15.
- A sense of being bound up with and belonging to one who had already conquered death, of sharing in his relationship of sonship to God, both in experience and in lived practice (Rom. 8.14-17; 'in Christ').
- The attraction that had always been exerted by the synagogue on those with serious religious concerns, now enhanced by the fascinating focus on a crucified and resurrected Jew (including immersion in his teaching),[302] and without the inhibiting demand for circumcision and complete judaizing.
- The wholeness of the Christian 'package', which in the event may be said to have combined the strengths of each of the other models in an exceptional way: life beyond the grave, self-transcending spiritual experiences, the enjoyment of shared meals, the character, comfort and satisfaction of religious devotion, and the mental stimulation of instruction in sacred texts and life-tested traditions.[303]

---

300. Rom. 5.1, 5; 8.6; 14.17; 15.13; 2 Cor. 5.14; Gal. 5.6, 22; Phil. 2.1-2; 4.7; Col. 1.8; 3.15; 1 Thess. 1.3; 3.6, 12; 2 Thess. 1.3.

301. Harnack, *Mission* book 2 chs. 2-5. Harnack's evidence stretches across three centuries, but passages like Rom. 12.6-8, 15.19, 1 Cor. 12.8-10, 28, Gal. 3.5 and 6.2 are evidence enough for the first generation. The impact of miracles, particularly exorcisms, is likewise stressed by MacMullen, *Paganism* 95-96 ('*That* was what produced converts. Nothing else is attested'), and Peter Brown, *The World of Late Antiquity from Marcus Aurelius to Muhammad* (London: Thames and Hudson, 1971) 55 (cited by Ashton, *Religion* 166-70).

302. Nock denied that imitation of Jesus was a factor in the attraction of Christianity (*Conversion* 210), but he ignores the continuing effect of the Jesus tradition and then written Gospels, which, to be fair, is more implicit than explicit.

303. Cf. Nock: 'The success of Christianity is the success of an institution which united the sacramentalism and the philosophy of the time. It satisfied the inquiring turn of mind, the desire for escape from Fate, the desire for security in the hereafter; like Stoicism, it gave a way of life and made man at home in the universe, but unlike Stoicism it did this for the ignorant as well as for the lettered. It satisfied also social needs and it secured men against loneliness' (*Conversion* 210-11).

- We should not over-emphasize, but we should certainly not exclude, the likelihood that what attracted some of the poorer members was the attractiveness of attending gatherings where they could enjoy a good meal or at least one markedly better than their normal daily fare — the 'rice-Christians' of the first century.
- Nor should we ignore socio-economic factors; in particular, Meeks highlighted the possibility that many of the most active and prominent members of Paul's circle may have suffered from 'high status inconsistency', so that 'the intimacy of the Christian groups [might have] become a welcome refuge' from the anxiety and loneliness they had previously experienced.[304]
- In more general terms we should certainly include the openness of membership to a range of social status, different races and sexes, and even whole families,[305] inculcating a sense of 'family', of truly belonging despite such differences, of mattering to God and his Christ and to fellow believers.

All this is presumably embraced in Paul's boast in the gospel as 'the power of God for salvation to all who believe, Jew first but also Gentile' (Rom. 1.16).

304. Meeks, *Urban Christians* ch. 2 (here 73) and 191.

305. 'A first key to the success of the Christian communities is certainly to be found in their openness to non-Christians of both sexes. . . . Openness is a fundamental mark of the Christian communities and at the same time the great difference over against pagan associations: with the Christians of both sexes there is no restriction of membership in accordance with criteria of gender and social origin' (Ebel, *Attraktivität* 215-16).

CHAPTER 31

The Aegean Mission: Phase One

31.1. The Aegean Mission

The next phase of Luke's record of Christian beginnings (Acts 16–20) is usually referred to as 'the second and third missionary journeys of Paul'. This is based on a misperception and is a misnomer.[1] What we actually have is the account of a sustained mission around the coasts of the Aegean Sea.[2] Luke presents it as a coherent and integrated unit. It has a clear beginning: the mission was entered upon with several marks of divine prompting (16.6-9). And it has a clear end: that period of mission, as indeed Paul's whole period of unrestrained missionary work, is climaxed and concluded with a speech which has the appearance of Paul's last will and testimony (20.18-35). In between, the initial circuit of the northern and western side of the Aegean (chs. 16–17) is followed by a lengthy stay in Corinth, Paul's effective headquarters for eighteen months and more (ch. 18). Subsequently, Ephesus, on the other side of the Aegean, evidently served similarly as Paul's headquarters for a further two to three years (ch. 19). A trip back to Antioch between these two halves is passed over in the briefest of terms (18.22-23) and was evidently not regarded by Luke as particularly significant.

This account accords well in substance with what we know of and can deduce about Paul's missionary work from his own letters. We have already noted the likelihood that the incident at Antioch occasioned a breach not only with Barnabas but also with the church of Antioch and, *a fortiori,* with the leadership of the church in Jerusalem (§27.6). In which case it is probable that Paul more or less cut his links with Antioch: he could no longer serve as a missionary (apostle)

---

1. Cf. Knox, *Chapters* 25-26.
2. Already noted by Weiss, *Earliest Christianity* 277; White also prefers to speak of 'the Aegean mission' (*Jesus to Christianity* ch. 8).

of a church which had not backed him in the Antioch incident over the terms on which Jews and Gentiles should be able to associate within the mixed (Jew/Gentile) churches established by Paul (Gal. 2.11-21). The movement into the Aegean region, therefore, was much more like the establishment of a separate or even independent mission than the extension of the mission from Antioch into a second missionary journey. Paul's fierce resentment at encroachments on his mission subsequently is clearly expressed in subsequent letters,[3] and the terms of independence on which he worked are clearly indicated in 2 Cor. 10.13-16.[4]

Moreover, it is worth repeating, the Aegean mission was the heart of Paul's missionary work for Paul himself. Apart from Galatians and Romans (and Titus), all the letters written by Paul or in his name were to churches founded in this period (or individuals connected with these churches): Philippi, Thessalonica, Corinth, Ephesus, and also Colossae, only a hundred miles or so from the Aegean coast. More important in the long term, most of the letters sent by Paul himself (including, I believe, Galatians) were written during this period from his Aegean bases.[5] Noteworthy is the fact that Paul himself also seems to recall the move into Macedonia as a new beginning: he commends the Philippians for their participation with him 'in the beginning of the gospel' (Phil. 4.15).[6] And he certainly regarded the closure of this period as the end of what was to be the main phase of his work as an apostle (Rom. 15.18-21); hence the heightened significance of his letter to the Romans, as an expression of his mature theology summing up his understanding of the gospel as he closed the main chapter of his life's work as an apostle.[7] So the Aegean mission was indeed the principal period of Paul's missionary work and the one which has made the most lasting impact on Christian development and thought.

We can be fairly confident, then, that Luke has drawn the main thread of his narrative from good information. Particularly noticeable is the appearance of the first and second of the 'we' sections of Acts, in effect bracketing the Aegean mission itself (16.10-17; 20.5-15).[8] These suggest first-hand involvement in the

3. Particularly Gal. 1.6-9, 2 Cor. 12.11-13 and Phil. 3.2.

4. See above, §29.4b.

5. See below, §§31.5-7, 32.5, 7 and 33.3. I opt with some hesitation for the view that Philippians, Philemon and Colossians were written from Rome (see below, §§34.4-6), though scholarly opinion is completely divided on the subject, with many thinking it more likely that at least Philemon (and Colossians) was written from Ephesus (see the end of §34.3).

6. Referring, most obviously, to his arrival in Philippi; see, e.g., O'Brien, *Philippians* 531-32; Bockmuehl, *Philippians* 263.

7. For this reason I use Romans as the template for my attempt to describe Paul's theology (*The Theology of Paul,* and see below, §33.3a).

8. On the suggestion that Paul engaged in a Macedonian mission already in the 40s, see above, §28.1c.

beginning and end of the Aegean mission proper, or at least the ability of the author of Acts to draw on first-hand testimony.[9] And the fact that Luke can name a key figure in each of the three first church plantings (Philippi, Thessalonica, Corinth) who provided hospitality and who thus may well have become hosts of the resulting house congregation[10] indicates likely first-hand sources of information about these plantings.

At the same time, it should not escape notice that Luke's account is exceedingly episodic in character, focusing on specific incidents,[11] with often brief linking narratives. The episodes in Philippi and Ephesus in particular well exemplify how highly accomplished Luke was as a raconteur. Inevitably, as with all such selective history-writing (all good history-writing is selective), many readers are left wondering about the gaps and the silences of the narrative: how much more must have happened during Paul's lengthy stays in Corinth and Ephesus than Luke's parsimonious account allows us to see?[12] And why, oh why, does Luke not give any indication of the activity which was to give Paul his lasting influence — his letters?

As usual, of course, Luke takes the opportunity to advance his own concerns.

- The reader is regularly reminded that the mission was ever at divine initiative and with divine approval.[13]
- The success in attracting to faith both Jews[14] and God-fearing Gentiles is fairly regular,[15] as also the hostility of the local Jewish community.[16]
- The theme of the gospel's superiority over other spiritual forces is effectively developed.[17]
- The encounter with Greek philosophy in Athens enables Luke to further the theme that the gospel's encounter with paganism includes the proclamation of God (17.22-31).

9. See further above, §21.2.

10. Lydia (Acts 16.15), Jason (Acts 17.5-7) and Titius Justus (Acts 18.7).

11. The imprisonment consequent on an exorcism (16.16-40), the encounter with Athenian intellectuals (17.16-34), the ruling of Gallio (18.12-17), the defeat of magic and subsequent uproar in Ephesus (19.11-20, 23-41), and the farewell discourse at Miletus (20.17-35).

12. He gives no hint of the extended problems Paul faced in his relations with the Corinthian church (see below, §§32.3-7), and the question of an unrecorded crisis in Ephesus has long fascinated students of Acts and of Paul (see below, §32.2e).

13. Acts 16.6-10, 14; 18.9-10; 19.11-12.

14. Acts 16.1; 17.4, 11-12; 18.4, 8, 19-20, 24-28.

15. Acts 16.14; 17.4, 12, 34; 18.4, 7.

16. Acts 17.5, 13; 18.6, 12-17; 19.9; 20.3, 19.

17. Acts 16.16-18; 19.11-20.

- And the apologetic theme is steadily maintained, that the new movement and its missionaries pose no threat to the civic authorities and should be treated with respect.[18]

So far as we can tell, however, such an agenda was well rooted in the information available to Luke and would have been entirely consistent with Paul's own assessment of the character and success of his mission.

31.2. The Beginnings of the Aegean Mission

a. In Search of a Mission Field

Acts 15.40–16.8 reports briefly the journey of Paul, together with his new co-missioner Silas, westward from Antioch and Cilicia, through the Cilician Gate, revisiting the churches founded in Galatia during the earlier mission from Antioch. As usual, Luke focuses on the main character, Paul, and his account gives the impression of a man whose sense of missionary vocation was as strong as ever but who was completely uncertain as to where he should exercise that mission.

- 'The truth of the gospel' which Paul had so vigorously asserted and defended in Jerusalem and Antioch (Gal. 2.5, 14) presumably continued to fire the same burning passion to preach that gospel among non-Jews without reference to circumcision or other 'works of the law' (2.16).
- He had recruited Silas, apparently a leading Jerusalemite (Acts 15.22, 40),[19] presumably with a view (in part at least) to retaining as much goodwill and support from that quarter as possible.[20] As Paul's letters confirm, Silas was to be Paul's principal colleague during the first phase of the Aegean mission (§29.6).
- In Lystra he added Timothy to his team (16.1). Timothy had presumably been converted during Paul's earlier visit(s),[21] though Acts 14 itself says nothing of this.[22] According to Luke, Paul made a point of having Timothy

---

18. Acts 16.35-39; 18.12-17; 19.23-41.

19. See above, §27 nn. 234, 235.

20. Silas may be one of the very few who stood firm with Paul in the incident in Antioch (see above, §27.6).

21. 1 Cor. 4.17 ('my beloved and faithful child'), 1 Tim. 1.2 ('my loyal child in the faith'), 1.18 ('my child'), 2 Tim. 1.2 ('my beloved child'). See also §29.6.

22. Timothy's mother ('Eunice' by name, according to 2 Tim. 1.5) had married a Greek (Acts 16.2). Such intermarriage was strongly discouraged within most Jewish commu-

circumcised (16.3), since he was known to be the offspring of a mixed marriage — a Jewish mother and a Greek father.[23] If so, this would have been another eirenic act by Paul, demonstrating both his own view that circumcision was of no intrinsic importance (either way)[24] but also his recognition that it was a distinctive mark of Jewishness.[25] The action, we may fairly note, was consistent with his own stated mission policy (1 Cor. 9.20) and also confirms that 'Jew first, but also Gentile' was an active principle of Paul's mission strategy (§29.4c).[26]

---

nities (recalling not least Nehemiah 9–10) but still took place often enough. The fact that Timothy had not been circumcised may also indicate that his mother had ceased to practise as a Jew. On the other hand, 2 Tim 3.15 speaks of Timothy as having been taught the Scriptures of his people from his childhood, so it may be that it was Timothy's Greek father who refused to allow him to be circumcised. Regarded as an uncircumcised Jew, Timothy presumably did not attend the synagogue, but conceivably his parents were wealthy enough for his mother to have some Torah scrolls of her own. At any rate, Timothy's mother was sufficiently open to this Jewish gospel to have become a believer herself (was her husband now dead?). See further vol. 3.

23. The principle of matrilineal descent was not yet (formally) in operation in the first century (S. J. D. Cohen, 'The Matrilineal Principle', *Beginnings of Jewishness* ch. 9), but Lüdemann responds that it 'was probably already part of a *halachah*' (*Early Christianity* 175, referring to Schiffman, 'Tannaitic Perspectives' 121). Despite the misgivings of many, Luke's account of Timothy having a Jewish mother and of that weighing with Paul, in view of the number of Jews in places where he intended to exercise his mission with Timothy's assistance (16.3), is quite plausible. Cohen disagrees: Timothy was not a Jew (*Beginnings* 363-77, with review of opinions on all sides of the issue); but was the issue quite so clear-cut for Paul (or Luke) when the identity of Paul's mission (Jewish? something other?) was precisely what was at stake and stood in question? Barrett's discussion (*Acts* 2.761-62), which shows how confused the issue has become, does not take sufficient account of the confusion of categories involved in proclaiming a Jewish Messiah to Gentiles, often in the presence of Jews.

24. Gal. 5.6; 6.15; 1 Cor. 7.19.

25. The report that Paul himself circumcised Timothy is often regarded as quite inconsistent with Paul's opposition to circumcision elsewhere (Acts 15.2; Gal. 2.3-5; 5.2-4; probably already in the view reported in Gal. 5.11!). See, e.g., the reviews in Haenchen, *Acts* 480-82, and (more sympathetically) Fitzmyer, *Acts* 575-76; bibliography in Jervell, *Apg.* 414 n. 36; Becker regards the report as a blatant contradiction which 'deserves no credence' (*Paul* 127); Lüdemann, however, changed his mind and comes down strongly in favour of historicity (*Early Christianity* 174-77); Chilton thinks Timothy is the author of the 'we' travel diary and therefore would have remembered the event (*Rabbi Paul* 146-49), even though 16.3 is not a 'we' passage. Luke explains the matter clearly enough: if the son of a Jewish mother was regarded as a Jew, by many or most Jews, then Timothy was a Jew (this is clearly what Luke understood to be the case). Since he was a Jew, Timothy's lack of circumcision would have been an affront to most Jews. Paul had no problem with the circumcision of Jews (1 Cor. 7.18a); it was the insistence that *Gentile* believers *had* to be circumcised to which he objected (§27.3). See also Hvalvik, 'Paul as a Jewish Believer' 135-39.

26. Cf. Wilson, *Luke and the Law* 64-65. Jervell pushes the point: '. . . all missionaries

Paul's Aegean Mission

- Paul (and Silas) had evidently decided to revisit the churches established during his evangelism as a missionary of the church of Antioch (Acts 13–14), a decision which is consistent with Paul's well-attested pastoral concern for his churches (§29.8). But it may also indicate a concern on Paul's part to ensure that these churches did not follow the path chosen by Peter and the Antiochenes (Gal. 2.11-14). If so, however, this is another point at which Luke seems rather to tell his story from the standpoint of Jerusalem: for, according to Luke, Paul and Silas delivered the 'apostolic decree' to these churches (Acts 16.4).[27] In contrast, as we shall see, Paul's

---

in Acts are Jews. This is not a matter of tactics or accommodation for Luke, but of the character of the gospel as promise to Israel' (*Apg.* 414). He also justifiably warns against overlooking the fact that Paul was 'a complicated and many-layered man with great inner tensions'; 'his theology is not unequivocal/clear-cut *(eindeutig),* which is true also for his view of the law' (414-15).

27. This is the last mention of the 'apostolic decree' during the Aegean mission at least,

letter to the Galatians is better understood as Paul's vigorous attempt to resist such pressure and to retain these churches within his own sphere of influence.[28]

The most natural route for an extended mission westwards was through Apamea and Colossae to Ephesus on the Aegean coast (16.6): Ephesus was the principal city of Roman Asia,[29] and Paul's city-centred mission tactic (§29.5a) had probably already been shaped by his time in Syrian Antioch and in his missionary outreach from Antioch (chs. 13–14). Luke, however, narrates that having been forbidden by the Spirit to go into Asia (16.6), the mission team attempted to head northwards into Bithynia, a region with several well-established and significant coastal cities and Jewish settlements (cf. 1 Pet. 1.1).[30] But, says Luke, they were once again prevented by the Spirit (16.7). A more northerly route through Phrygia and Galatia (16.6) would indeed lead to Bithynia. So this is often taken to be the journey in which churches were established in (northern) Galatia, to which the letter to the Galatians was written (cf. also 18.23).[31] But the reasons for declining to identify the cities of Acts 13–14 with 'Galatia' have long since been exploded.[32] Not only so, but the

------

which strengthens the likelihood that the decree emerged as or has become the settled practice of the churches within Antioch's sphere of influence. See above, §27.3e.

28. See above, §29.4b, and below, §31.7.

29. See below, §32.2a.

30. Schürer, *History* 3.35-36.

31. E.g., Fitzmyer, *Acts* 578; Murphy-O'Connor, *Paul* 159-62, 185-93; White, *Jesus to Christianity* 198-99. Breytenbach observes that German scholarship tends to assume the North Galatian interpretation as *communis opinio* (*Paulus und Barnabas* 103), illustrated by Gnilka, *Paulus* 62, and Lohse, *Paulus* 98-99; but contrast Weiss, *Earliest Christianity* 279, Stuhlmacher, *Biblische Theologie* 1.225-27, and Hengel and Schwemer, *Paul* 475 n. 1359. Uniquely Crossan and Reed hypothesize that Paul pressed north to Pessinus etc. on Paul's *first* journey through the region and arbitrarily dispense with Acts 14.21-28 (*Paul* 231).

32. 'There is virtually nothing to be said for the north Galatian theory. There is no evidence in Acts or in any non-testamentary source that Paul ever evangelized the region of Ancyra and Pessinus, in person, by letter, or by any other means' (Mitchell, *Anatolia* 2.3). Breytenbach also points out that there is no evidence of Jews in Ancyra and Pessinus and no evidence of Christianity in central Anatolia before Constantine (*Paulus und Barnabas* 140-48). Martyn regards Gal. 1.21 (Paul's pre-Jerusalem conference missionary work was in 'the territories of Syria and Cilicia') as a sufficient rebuttal of S. Mitchell (*Galatians* 184-85 n. 240, following the usual 'North Galatia' argument — e.g., Kümmel, *Introduction* 298). But it is entirely possible that Paul chose not to remind his Galatian audiences that it was while he was still a missionary of Antioch that he had established the Galatian churches (see also above, §25 n. 223). It is disappointing to observe how, in maintenance of a particular hypothesis, a proper preference for the testimony of Paul over that of Acts transposes into outright rejection of the testimony of Acts; cf. T. Witulski, *Die Adressaten des Galaterbriefes* (FRLANT 193;

most natural understanding of Luke's description in Acts 16.6 ('they went through the region of Phrygia and Galatia') actually excludes a more northerly route.[33] Besides which, according to Luke, the option of heading into Bithynia became an option only after the natural choice of heading directly into Asia had been frustrated.[34]

Göttingen: Vandenhoeck und Ruprecht, 2000), who concludes that the secondary character of Acts means that the question of Galatians' addressees should be investigated without reference to Acts (222). Where do such scholars think Luke derived the account and chronology of Acts 13–14 from — entirely his imagination?

33. 'It is hardly conceivable that the *Galatikē chōra* mentioned here [Acts 16.6] is the region of north Galatia, which lay some 200 kilometers as the crow flies north-east of any natural route between Lystra and the region of Mysia. On the contrary, the phrase is naturally understood as denoting the country of Phrygia Paroreius, on either side of Sultan Dag, an area that was ethnically Phrygian, but which lay partly in the province of Galatia and partly in Asia' (Mitchell, *Anatolia* 2.3 n. 8; cf. Strabo, *Geog.* 12.8.14, 577). Riesner notes that 'immediately north of Iconium a semi-desert begins'; 'it is difficult to imagine a mission in the steppe region of eastern Phrygia' (*Paul's Early Period* 282; further 281-91). Taylor likewise notes the absence of Roman roads and the difficulty of the terrain envisaged by the North Galatia hypothesis ('Roman Empire' 2438-40). On Acts 18.22-23 and 19.1, Mitchell adds: 'Again there is no reason to look beyond the natural geographical interpretation of this journey, from Syria through the Cilician Gates on to the plateau, across Lycaonia to the communities of Derbe, Lystra, Iconium, and Pisidian Antioch, and thence through the rest of Phrygia Paroreius to Apamea, and down the Maeander valley to the west coast. The region around Derbe, Lystra, Iconium, and Antioch was all part of the province of Galatia in the mid–first century AD, and the expression *Galatikē chōra,* both here and in the earlier passage [16.6], naturally refers to it.' Mitchell summarizes Appendix I, 'Provincial Boundaries in Asia Minor, 25 BC–AD 235', thus: 'in the mid-first century it was as natural to refer to the churches of Antioch, Iconium, Lystra, and Derbe as churches of Galatia, as it was to call that of Corinth a church of Achaea' (*Anatolia* 2.4). On the extent and boundaries of the province of Galatia see also R. K. Sherk, 'Roman Galatia: The Governors from 25 BC to AD 114', *ANRW* 2.7.2 (1980) 954-1052 (here 958-59 and map at 960). Scott argues that Paul's missionary strategy was determined by the table of nations in Genesis 10 (see above, §29.4a), in which Gomer would include both North, ethnic Galatians and South, non-ethnic Galatians (*Paul and the Nations* ch. 4).

34. The reference here would be to Phrygia, since it was that part of the region (loosely described by Luke as 'the Phrygian and Galatian region') which still lay open to them once they had traversed Galatia to(wards) the borders of Asia. In 18.23 Luke describes the equivalent journey as 'travelling one place after another *(kathexēs)* through the region of Galatia and Phrygia', perhaps because on the latter occasion he continued more directly west; see again n. 33 above and Hemer, *Book of Acts* 120. See also Breytenbach, *Paulus und Barnabas* 113-19; French, *BAFCS* 2.53-54, 56-57. On any thesis, the route of the journey from 'opposite Mysia' to Troas (16.7-8) is far from clear; see, e.g., Barrett, *Acts* 2.770-71; Talbert, *Barrington Atlas* maps 62, 56 and 52; C. Breytenbach, 'Probable Reasons for Paul's Unfruitful Missionary Attempts in Asia Minor (A Note on Acts 16:6-7)', in C. Breytenbach and J. Schröter, eds., *Die Apostelgeschichte und die hellenistische Geschichtsschreibung,* E. Plümacher FS (AGAJU 57; Leiden: Brill, 2004) 157-69.

Luke gives no indication that this was a preaching mission (which he was quite capable of doing with brief summary statements). The impression is rather of a prevailing uncertainty among the mission team, looking for new centres of operation in the aftermath of the breach with Antioch. Those passed by included such important centres of Jewish settlement as Apamea, Sardis, Smyrna and Pergamum as well as Ephesus.

That Luke attributes the mission team's lack of clear goals to the Spirit should not be regarded as merely a Lukan device. Had it been such, we would have expected the guidance given to be positive, as elsewhere in Acts,[35] rather than the negatives of 16.6-7.[36] And Luke would probably have presented it as guidance given to Paul himself, rather than the vague 'they/them'. Moreover, Paul himself certainly attests a reliance on the Spirit for guidance.[37] Quite likely, then, we should envisage not some specific prophetic word (as implied in 13.3) or vision (as in 16.9) but simply an inner conviction shared by the team; such too could be heard as the voice of the Spirit (cf. 8.29; 10.19). A striking implication is often ignored: that this whole journey of several hundred miles was undertaken without any clear sense of positive direction.

According to 16.9-10, however, the uncertainty was ended in the coastal port of Troas[38] with a vision; as in earlier episodes (chs. 9 and 10), the vision is given considerable weight in determining fresh and unexpected courses of action.[39] At the same time we should note that some process of evaluation of the vision is implied in 16.10, a process in which the team as a whole was involved (*symbibazontes*).[40] It is an attractive speculation (but only that, despite its long

---

35. Cf. Acts 8.29; 10.19; 11.12; 13.2, 4; 15.28; 19.21; 21.4.

36. Chilton fancifully suggests that the interdict was voiced by Silas, who wanted to preserve the whole region for the Petrine mission (*Rabbi Paul* 149), though, as Becker notes, 1 Pet. 5.12 may suggest that Silas 'went over to the Petrine mission' (*Paul* 183) at a later date.

37. E.g., 'walking in accordance with the Spirit' (Rom. 8.4, 14; Gal. 5.16, 18, 25); see further *Jesus and the Spirit* 222-25; R. Banks, 'The Role of Charismatic and Noncharismatic Factors in Determining Paul's Movements in Acts', in Stanton et al., eds., *The Holy Spirit and Christian Origins* 117-30.

38. On Troas see, e.g., Taylor, 'Roman Empire' 2441-42.

39. Again a modernist scepticism in regard to visions (cf. Haenchen's review of the psychological reasons adduced to 'explain' the vision — *Acts* 489) should not blind us to the fact of such visions in the past and of the importance often attached to them; interpretation of dreams had been practised as an art in Greek circles from the fifth century BCE onwards (*OCD*[3] 497); Joseph and Daniel are the most familiar Jewish practitioners. Notable is the fact that the vision is neither of Christ nor of an angel (cf. 18.9-10; 23.11; 27.23-24); would we today have described it more as a dream ('in the night')? Either way the psychology might be relevant: through the subconscious God was perceived as speaking a message which the unconscious mind may have been blocking.

40. *Symbibazō*, 'to draw a conclusion in the face of evidence; conclude, infer' (BDAG

pedigree) that Luke himself was 'the man from Macedonia', as signalled by the first 'we' at 16.10.[41] At all events the 'us' of the vision is matched by the 'us' of those who concluded that they were being called to take a major step forward in mission by crossing into Europe.[42]

b. The Founding of the Church in Philippi

The city of Philippi was an obvious target for Paul as he edged further west in search of a mission centre.

* Luke describes it as 'a leading city of (that) part *(meridos)* of Macedonia' (16.12).[43]
* It was also a Roman colony.[44] As a Roman colony it enjoyed autonomy, ex-

---

956-57). Note again the plural: Paul had the vision; the team drew the conclusion. We know from Paul's letters how insistent he was that prophetic revelation should be 'tested/evaluated' by others (1 Cor. 14.29; 1 Thess. 5.19-22). Was a mission strategy shaped by Isa. 66.19 a factor (see above, §29.4a)? Riesner notes that after Bithynia (Tubal), the next goal mentioned in Isa. 66.19 is Greece or Macedonia (*Paul's Early Period* 293).

41. Ramsay, *St. Paul* 201-203.

42. See the map (p. 665) above. We should not overstate the significance of the step at this point: Europe was not thought of as a quite different continent (Barrett, *Acts* 2.766, 772); the importance often attributed to the crossing from Asia Minor is an anachronistic expression of European self-importance. A. N. Wilson, *Paul: The Mind of the Apostle* (London: Sinclair-Stevenson, 1997), waxes lyrical about the long-term effect on 'European civilization' (137).

43. The text is somewhat confused, but see Metzger, *Textual Commentary* 444-46; Barrett, *Acts* 2.778-80; Fitzmyer, *Acts* 584; P. Pilhofer, *Philippi*. Vol. 1: *Die erste christliche Gemeinde Europas* (WUNT 87; Tübingen: Mohr Siebeck, 1995) 159-65. Sherwin-White gives Luke 'full marks for [this] description of the city . . . [it] suggests the eye-witness. . . . The numbered districts of Macedonia were unique, and hence the correct term, which even in its garbled form has the ring of an official designation, was not understood outside the province' (*Roman Society* 93-94); similarly Pilhofer 164. *Meris,* 'part', often appears in inscriptions and papyri in the sense 'district' (BDAG 632; Hemer, *Book of Acts* 113-14 n. 31). Pilhofer provides several maps of Philippi and its environs (17, 50, 62, 75).

44. Mark Antony had founded a colony there for Roman veterans of the battles of 42 BCE, which had resulted in the victory of Antony and Octavian over the assassins of Caesar. After Octavian's decisive triumph over Antony at Actium (31 BCE) Octavian had settled still more veterans there, as well as the partisans of Antony expelled from Italy (Fitzmyer, *Acts* 584). See further L. Bormann, *Philippi. Stadt und Christengemeinde zur Zeit des Paulus* (NovTSupp 78; Leiden: Brill, 1995) part 1; Pilhofer, *Philippi* ch. 1, with inscriptional and archaeological data reviewed on 1-34 (though note the brief critique of both Bormann and Pilhofer in Bockmuehl, *Philippians* 7-8); Oakes, *Philippians* ch. 1 (photos 6-9); more briefly H. L. Hendrix, 'Philippi', *ABD* 5.313-17; Taylor, 'Roman Empire' 2444-46; Murphy-O'Connor, *Paul* 211-13.

emption from tribute and taxation, and was administered by Roman law, as in effect part of Italy itself.[45]

* It lay on the Egnatian Way (Via Egnatia), the principal east-west land route from the Adriatic port of Dyrrachium to Byzantium. Did Paul see himself taking a first step on the road to Rome itself?

The only evidence of a Jewish community in Philippi at that time is what Luke tells us in Acts 16.[46] The impression given by Luke's narrative is that Paul and his companions spent their first few days in the city searching for a house synagogue, but without success. In the absence of Jewish hospitality, where did they stay? Luke makes no suggestion that they went to the marketplace and began preaching there, as an itinerant philosopher might have done. Instead, they waited for the Sabbath and went ('outside the city gate') to where they 'supposed' (presumably from information gleaned in the preceding days) there might be a *proseuchē* — that is, a Jewish assembly, not necessarily a building, for Sabbath prayer and Torah instruction.[47]

Paul's tactics were as before. Whatever the size of the prayer gathering, Paul evidently had opportunity to speak with the women gathered there.[48] His witness won a prominent merchant, Lydia by name, who is described as 'one who worshipped God', that is, a God-fearer. Possibly she had already been attracted to Judaism in her home town of Thyatira in Asia, where subsequently a Sambatheion, probably a 'Sabbath House', is attested.[49] In other words, Paul's tactics (§29.5), already well tested in Galatia (according to Acts 13.26, 43-44; 14.1), proved their effectiveness once more in Philippi. But also to be noted is the implication of 16.16, that even after becoming settled in Lydia's house (16.15), Paul and his mission team continued to attend the place of prayer *(proseuchē).* They did not immediately hive off into a small prayer group on their own in Lydia's house. They continued to regard themselves as part of the Jewish assem-

---

45. E.g., Barrett, *Acts* 2.780; fuller details on Roman colonies in Lake and Cadbury, *Beginnings* 4.190, and *OCD*[3] 364. Hellermann overemphasizes the Roman character of Philippi (*Reconstructing Honor* chs. 3-4).

46. See further Pilhofer, *Philippi* 231-34. Paul's letter to the Philippians also suggests a predominantly or exclusively Gentile congregation (see below, §34.4). Bockmuehl also notes 'the complete absence of quotations from the Old Testament' (*Philippians* 9).

47. On the location of 'the (place of) prayer', see Taylor, 'Roman Empire' 2446-48; Pilhofer, *Philippi* 165-73, followed by Bockmuehl, *Philippians* 14-15. On the widespread Jewish presence in the Aegean region, see above, §30.2a.

48. The implication is probably that only or predominantly women were present, so a formally constituted synagogue/'prayer-house' is presumably not in view (so, e.g., Bruce, *Acts* 358; Tellbe, *Paul between Synagogue and State* 220-23; others in Jervell, *Apg.* 421 n. 79); Jervell himself is less sure (421-22); Schnabel has no doubt that it was a synagogue (*Mission* 1153).

49. Schürer, *History* 3.19.

bly and the *proseuchē* as the place where they would find those most prepared for and open to their message.

Lydia was a woman with a substantial business in luxury goods (only the wealthy could afford clothes which had been treated with the expensive purple dyes).[50] She also had a house big enough to provide hospitality for the band of four, and household servants. That presumably meant she was an unmarried daughter or widow.[51] Luke makes a point of attributing her attentive openness *(prosechein)* to the Lord (16.14); this notable success would have been an important vindication of their coming to such a less promising location as Philippi. Her baptism (16.15) correlates with her heart being opened to pay attention to Paul's words; in baptism her attentiveness became commitment.[52] Her offer of hospitality (16.15) may well mean that she became host of the embryonic Christian fellowship.[53] Her subsequent non-appearance in Paul's letter to the Philippians could have many reasons, of which only one is her absence on business.[54]

The story which follows (16.16-40) is one of the most vivid in Luke's second volume. It begins with a slave girl who 'had a spirit of divination *(pythōn)*' and whose fortune-telling ability brought her owners substantial income (16.16). Luke tells how she used to follow Paul and his companions, crying out, 'These men are servants of the Most High God, who proclaim to you a way of salvation' (16.17). This went on for many days until Paul 'very much annoyed' summarily exorcised the spirit from her (16.18).

The implication of the language used by Luke (16.16-17) is that the girl spoke as in a trance: she was inspired, like the priestess at Delphi, by Apollo, who was symbolized by a snake (the python); like the Delphi priestess (called the Pythia), she 'gave oracles *(manteuomenē)*' (in a trance or in ecstasy).[55] Her utter-

---

50. So, e.g., Luke 16.19; Josephus, *War* 6.390; Taylor ('Roman Empire' 2448-49) and Meggitt (*Poverty* 69) are more cautious. The imperial monopoly on purple goes back at least to Nero, which could suggest that Lydia was of freed status, a member of 'Caesar's household' (*NDIEC* 2.25-32 [here 28]; but see also *NDIEC* 3.54). Pilhofer cites inscriptions attesting purple-dyers from Thyatira in both Thessalonica and perhaps Philippi itself (*Philippi* 175-82), though see Ascough, *Paul's Macedonian Associations* 22 n. 33, and Bockmuehl notes that Lydia is described as a *porphyropōlis* ('dealer in purple') rather than a *porphyrobaphos* ('dyer in purple') (*Philippians* 5).

51. The name could indicate slave origin ('the Lydian' — e.g., Weiss, *Earliest Christianity* 281), but Hemer notes that the name was also found among women of social standing (*Book of Acts* 231). For women as house owners see *NDIEC* 4.93.

52. 'Household' here need not include children, since the term was as commonly used to include household slaves and retainers (see, e.g., P. Weigandt, *EDNT* 2.502).

53. See further Pilhofer, *Philippi* 234-40.

54. Zahn suggested that her name was actually Euodia or Syntyche (Phil. 4.2), called 'the Lydian' to distinguish her from other merchants in purple (Lake and Cadbury, *Beginnings* 199).

55. Though W. Foerster notes that 'from the beginning of the Roman imperial period

ance is quite conceivable in the circumstances, since it required only a superficial knowledge of Jewish apologetics or of early Christian preaching. 'The Most High God' was an obvious title for Jews to use in speaking of God,[56] even though it would probably cause confusion given the many high gods in Greco-Roman polytheism.[57] And 'the (or a) way of salvation' echoes language evidently quite common in the early mission.[58] One can well imagine, for example, a dim-witted slave girl, who had picked up phrases used of and by the missionaries, following them round and calling them out in the way Luke records; such a case would be attributed to possession in the common understanding of the time.[59]

That Paul responded, after many days of this, with annoyance (the same word is used in 4.2), has an authentic ring (16.18). Luke does not dress up the episode as Paul acting out of compassion or out of a desire to confront evil head on. Paul's exorcism followed the normal pattern:[60] invoking the power and authority of the name of one whose own power as an exorcist was already well known, and perhaps already legendary ('the name of Jesus Christ').[61] The success here would be indicated by the fact that the girl fell silent and ceased to function as an oracle giver. A less satisfying note is that the girl immediately drops from the story, with nothing said as to whether Paul and the others tried to help her in any way;[62] notably, she does not become a convert.[63]

---

pythōn was also used for a ventriloquist' (*TDNT* 6.918), the demon speaking through her; see further Barrett, *Acts* 2.785; T. Klutz, *The Exorcism Stories in Luke-Acts* (SNTSMS 129; Cambridge: Cambridge University, 2004) 214-17, 243-44.

56. It appears over one hundred times in the LXX for Yahweh. See further Bruce, *Acts* 360; Trebilco, *Jewish Communities* ch. 6. Barrett concludes that the term was used 'sporadically' in Hellenistic Judaism (*Acts* 2.786).

57. 'A deliberate *double entendre* commonly encountered in Jewish writings from Asia Minor and elsewhere: Jews and Christians knew the true *theos hypsistos* to be the God of Israel' (Bockmuehl, *Philippians* 8; citing Hemer, *Book of Acts* 231, and P. Trebilco, 'Paul and Silas — "Servants of the Most High God" [Acts 16.16-18]', *JSNT* 36 [1989] 51-73; see also Pilhofer, *Philippi* 182-88; Klauck, *Magic and Paganism* 68-69; Schnabel, *Mission* 606-15).

58. On the use of *hodos* ('way') to characterize the new Jewish sect, see above, §20.1(14). 'Salvation' is a particularly Lukan theme (cf. I. H. Marshall, *Luke: Historian and Theologian* [Exeter: Paternoster, 1970], whose thesis is that 'the idea of salvation supplies the key to the theology of Luke' [92]), but familiar (in verb or noun) in all strands of earliest Christianity.

59. 'Possession was believed to attend the "young and the somewhat simple" of either sex. . . . Private practitioners were quick to exploit the possibilities, and spells for obtaining a prophecy made ample use of a child's transparency to God' (Lane Fox, *Pagans and Christians* 208).

60. Cf. Matt. 12.27; Luke 9.49; and further *Jesus Remembered* 675-77.

61. See further *Jesus Remembered* 673-77.

62. Cf. F. S. Spencer, 'Out of Mind, Out of Voice: Slave-Girls and Prophetic Daughters in Luke-Acts', *BibInt* 7 (1999) 133-55 (here 146-50); Klauck, *Magic and Paganism* 72-73. Klutz suggests some reasons for Luke's silence, none of them very satisfactory (*Exorcism Stories* 260-62).

63. A contrast with Lydia, of which L. M. White, 'Visualizing the "Real" World of Acts

The tale now unfolds with rapid strokes (16.19-24), the story-teller well into his stride, though no longer as a personal participant (the 'we' disappears after 16.17). The owners of the slave girl (probably a small syndicate) saw that their hope of gain had 'gone out' with the spirit.[64] More concerned for profit than for their slave, they made a citizen's arrest and hauled Paul and Silas before the magistrates. As Roman citizens in a Roman colony, they would carry weight with the duumvirs responsible for administering the law; with slavery such an important economic factor in ancient society, responsibility for loss of slave value was a serious matter. Their charge, however, was not of robbery. Instead, Luke tells us, they adopted a tactic repeated countless times in the history of communities the world over: the appeal to prejudice against small ethnic minorities commonly known for their peculiar customs. 'These men are disturbing our city; they are Jews and are advocating customs that are not lawful for us as Romans to adopt or observe' (16.20-21).[65] Such prejudice among Roman intellectuals against the Jews for their customs of circumcision and dietary regulations is well attested for the period. In view of the tensions between Paul and 'the Jews' elsewhere in Luke's narrative, it is important to appreciate the fact that in Philippi it was precisely as a Jew that Paul suffered.[66]

That popular resentment among the local mob could be counted on against 'strange superstitions' from the east would be consistent with all this,[67] as also the readiness of magistrates to concede to such pressure on the assumption that those charged were guilty of some serious crime and worthy of punishment. The punishment is not merely salutary but severe: they are stripped, beaten publicly (by the 'rodbearers' of 16.35) and put into the innermost cell with their feet in stocks.[68] Why did Paul not claim his Roman citizenship (as in 22.25)? Possibly

---

16: Towards Construction of a Social Index', in White and Yarbrough, eds., *The Social World of the First Christians* 234-61 (here 256-59), probably makes too much.

64. The verb is the same as in verse 18: their hope of profit 'went out' with the spirit — a nice Lukan pun.

65. 'The formulation of the charge against Paul at Philippi . . . is positively archaic. But though it is unusual, it is not entirely unparalleled in Julio-Claudian usage. It is perhaps characteristic that it is in an isolated Roman community in the Greek half of the Roman empire that the basic principle of Roman "otherness" should be affirmed, whereas in Italy the usual custom prevailed of treating alien cults on their merits' (Sherwin-White, *Roman Society* 82; see further 80-83). Fitzmyer, *Acts* 587, quotes Cicero on the Roman penal code: 'No one shall have gods for himself, either new or foreign gods, unless they are officially recognized' (*De legibus* 2.8.19).

66. See also Klutz, *Exorcism Stories* 247-51.

67. The severe persecution of the Jewish community of Alexandria in 38, under Caligula, would have been well known round the eastern Mediterranean (see Schürer, *History* 1.389-91).

68. 'Such summary punishment was the usual procedure in dealing with minor breaches

because a charge of depriving slave owners of the value of their property or of teaching foreign superstitions (in a Roman colony) would have involved a protracted trial with an uncertain outcome;[69] and a beating with *fustes* was comparatively light in contrast to the severe scourging with the *flagellum* envisaged in 22.25.[70]

The climactic scene is vivid (16.25-34): Paul and Silas not at all downcast; their prayer and singing hymns to God (at midnight!) holding the other prisoners' attention (rather than inciting abuse); the earthquake leaving all doors opened and all fetters unfastened; the dramatic reversal of fortune for the jailer, who comes trembling to Paul and Silas, asks 'What must I do to be saved?' (16.30) and becomes a believer (16.31-33). Of course, it all sounds too good to be true. But presumably this is how the story quickly circulated within the church at Philippi, if not also further afield. And Paul would certainly see 'salvation' as secured through 'belief in the Lord Jesus', however much such belief would have to be spelled out in any particular case.[71] The baptisms of the jailer and his entire household (16.33) apparently took place in the middle of the night, so presumably they were not baptized by immersion in the local river! — more likely at a well in the courtyard.

Equally, if not still more enjoyable for the retellers of this story in the Philippian church would be the sequel (16.35-39). The two magistrates either have qualms about their too peremptory judgment and try to shuffle the affair under the carpet, or they are satisfied that a sufficient warning and example had been given; the departure of the main culprits from the city should effectively 'close the book'. The appropriate officers[72] are dispatched to send them on their way without further fuss. Paul, however, himself a Roman citizen (a fact not previously disclosed), and therefore exempt from such arbitrary punishment, is able to humble the authorities: they had exceeded their authority (a charge against Roman citizens had to be investigated properly), and were themselves liable to serious retribution (cf. 22.29).[73] The public apology thus secured was presumably, in Paul's

---

of the peace' (Taylor, 'Roman Empire' 2454); *coercitio* was 'the right, held by every magistrate with imperium, of compelling reluctant citizens to obey his orders and decrees, by inflicting punishment' (*OCD*³ 355).

69. Weiss, *Earliest Christianity* 283; Haenchen, *Acts* 504; see further Rapske, *Paul in Roman Custody* 129-34.

70. Taylor, 'Roman Empire' 2457-58.

71. See *Theology of Paul* 371-85. Luke also describes the faith of the jailer's household as 'belief in God' (16.34), confirming both Luke's and Paul's emphasis that non-God-fearing Gentiles had first to be converted to (belief in) God (see above, §27.1e, and below, §31.3b).

72. *Rabdouchoi* — literally those who carried the bundles of rods and axes symbolizing their master's authority to inflict corporal or capital punishment, the lictors, equivalent to policemen (see further Lake and Cadbury, *Beginnings* 4.200).

73. The relevant Roman laws are indicated by Lake and Cadbury, referring to Cicero, *In*

mind, not simply a matter of rubbing his persecutors' face in the dirt or of retrieving his own honour (cf. 1 Thess. 2.2) but of establishing the status of the fragile new community, free from the spite of any other important citizens they happened to offend.[74] The fact that Paul and Silas nevertheless leave the city more or less at once (16.39-40) implies that there was some face-saving on both sides.

This is the first church of the Pauline mission that we can clearly identify from Paul's letters whose founding is recorded. As we might expect, the vividly told tale serves Luke's various purposes well: a further triumph over magic; a miraculous example of divine providence (though not attributed to divine intervention as such), with acquisition of further converts as a direct result; and the respect of Roman authorities wrested from them unwillingly but nevertheless formally accorded by them.[75] But the space Luke gives to the episode is as much explained by the fact that it was a great story in itself. Although parallels of such miraculous deliverance from jail can be readily produced from the literature of the time,[76] it is hard to doubt that this story, with all its detail, was the story the Philippian church told about its own foundation,[77] though how soon it took place after Paul's arrival in Philippi we cannot say; Luke gives no time indicator.[78] Paul

---

Verrem 5.66 (*Beginnings* 4.201); Sherwin-White, *Roman Society* 58-59; Fitzmyer, *Acts* 589; *OCD*³ 355, 1267-68 (*provocatio);* also Taylor, 'Roman Empire' 2455-57; Barrett, *Acts* 2.801; 'The *Duoviri* left themselves open to severe punishment for they could be deprived of office and disqualified from any further government service for having violated the rights of Roman citizens in a Roman colony' (Tajra, *Trial* 29, referring to Dio Cassius 60.24.4; quoted also by Barrett 2.805). On the issue of Paul's Roman citizenship, see above, §25.1c.

74. Whether the tactic was successful may depend on the interpretation of Phil. 1.27-30 (see further §34.4 below).

75. See also Klutz, *Exorcism* 239-40.

76. L. T. Johnson, *The Acts of the Apostles* (Collegeville: Liturgical, 1992), cites Ovid, *Metamorphoses* 9.782-83; 15.669-78; Lucian of Samosata, *Lover of Lies* 22 (300). The parallel with Euripides' account of the deliverance of the Bacchanals and of Dionysus in *Bacchae* 443-50, 586-602, was first made by Celsus (Origen, *c. Cels.* 2.34); see further Lake and Cadbury, *Beginnings* 4.196-97; Haenchen, *Acts* 501; Weaver, *Plots of Epiphany* 264-71. See also §23 n. 177 above.

77. Cf. Jervell, *Apg.* 430-31; less sanguine is Omerzu, *Prozess* 124-66 (summary 164). Barrett justifiably observes: 'There is nothing incredible in an earthquake [in the eastern Mediterranean], but the reader does not expect one to be violent enough to release all the prisoners in the town gaol, yet gentle enough to do them no harm, and sufficiently localized to be, it seems, unnoticed by the town officials' (*Acts* 2.776, 794; though see also 794-95). Luke, however, does not question the story he was told. If he was much too credulous in simply passing on such a story, there is also something pathetic about the fact that the story 'gave offence'(!) to nineteenth-century scholars (reviewed by Haenchen, *Acts* 500-501). See also Ashton, *Religion* 171-78.

78. Murphy-O'Connor reckons that Paul must have wintered in Philippi (48-49) (*Paul* 214-15).

himself recalls various miracles (including Luke's favourite 'signs and wonders') as part of his missionary success,[79] though never explicitly an exorcism as such. A not insignificant detail is the fact that Luke has rightly recorded the popular designation *(stratēgoi)* for the two chief officials in the Roman colony (16.20, 22, 35-36, 38).[80] We should also observe that Paul himself recalled being beaten with rods (2 Cor. 11.25) and being 'shamefully treated *(hybristhentes)* in Philippi' (1 Thess. 2.2).[81] Here in particular, the much fuller account of what happened in Philippi, even when the first person ('we') narrative comes to an end (16.18), suggests that Luke had much richer sources of information here than in any of the preceding episodes.[82]

c. The Founding of the Church in Thessalonica

Whatever the circumstances of Paul's departure from Philippi, the obvious next destination was Thessalonica, the capital of the province and nearly one hundred miles further west along the Egnatian Way.[83] Given the importance of Thessalonica, both for east-west and north-south communication,[84] we can envisage it as having a significant Jewish population, if mainly traders and merchants, even

79. Rom. 15.18-19; 2 Cor. 12.12; Gal. 3.5.

80. The official title was praetors or duumvirs *(duoviri)*, but *stratēgoi* was a popular designation for them in inscriptions (BDAG 947-48); see also Lake and Cadbury, *Beginnings* 4.194-95; Bruce, *Acts* 362; Pilhofer, *Philippi* 193-99; D. B. Saddington, 'Military and Administrative Personnel in the New Testament', *ANRW* 2.26.3 (1996) 2408-35 (here 2429-30); Taylor, 'Roman Empire' 2452-53.

81. 'The verb *hybrizō* is perfectly apt to describe the punishment of a Roman citizen without even the semblance of a trial' (Murphy-O'Connor, *Paul* 214).

82. Did Luke remain in Philippi when the others moved on (16.40)? The fact that the 'we' narrative resumes at the same point (Philippi) on Paul's final journey back to Jerusalem (20.5-6) is strongly suggestive of such a hypothesis. Pilhofer concludes from his study of Acts 16 that Luke was especially knowledgeable about Macedonia and particularly Philippi, a fact which strengthens the possibility that Luke himself came from Philippi (*Philippi* 204-205, 248-49).

83. For a map of the route see Pilhofer, *Philippi* 202. Paul's team passes through Amphipolis and Apollonia (17.1) without pausing to preach; for Haenchen the mention of a synagogue in Thessalonica 'seems to suggest that there was no such synagogue in Amphipolis and in Apollonia' (*Acts* 506). Hemer suggests that these were the stopping places on the journey from Philippi to Thessalonica, dividing the journey into three stages of about 30, 27 and 35 miles (*Book of Acts* 115); but to cover such distances in three days by foot would have required some of Caesar's famous forced marches; Lake and Cadbury conclude, as a natural though not necessary inference, that Paul must have used horses (*Beginnings* 4.202).

84. On the history and archaeology see Riesner, *Paul's Early Period* 337-41 (outline map 418); on the socio-religious context see below, n. 245.

though supporting epigraphical data are slim,[85] and the modern city has prevented much excavation of the site. But the move would be consistent with Paul's missionary strategy and tactics: both the focus on a major city and the use of Sabbath and synagogue to expound his gospel (17.2-3).[86] According to Luke, the pattern which had emerged in the mission from Antioch (13.44–14.20) was repeated: initial interest and positive response among Jews and Gentile sympathizers,[87] followed by Jewish opposition, resulting in civic unrest and departure to another city (17.1-16). The pattern is one which Luke no doubt shaped or extended, but he assuredly did not invent it. For Paul himself vividly recalled the character and effectiveness of his preaching among Gentiles in Thessalonica (1 Thess. 1.5–2.13), and also the 'distress' experienced by the new converts (1.6) at the hand of their own countrymen (2.14), as probably including incitement from Jewish sources (2.15-16).[88]

A feature of Paul's evangelistic tactic is brought to the fore in this sequence — the appeal to and exposition of Scripture as providing proof of the claims made regarding Jesus (17.2-3, 11).[89] Although the tactic had in effect been acted

85. Schürer, *History* 3.65-67; no epigraphical evidence of a synagogue has been uncovered, but we know of a Samaritan community there at a later date (66-67); see also Riesner, *Paul's Early Period* 344-48; Levinskaya, *BAFCS* 5.154-57; Tellbe, *Paul between Synagogue and State* 86-90; Ascough, *Paul's Macedonian Associations* 192-202. See further C. von Brocke, *Thessaloniki — Stadt des Kassander und Gemeinde des Paulus* (WUNT 125; Tübingen: Mohr Siebeck, 2001) ch. 1.

86. It is taken for granted that a substantial number of God-fearing Greeks, including a fair number of women of high social status, were participating in the synagogue devotions. Once again we should note that the Jewish community in a major city was not a small, despised group but of sufficient social status to attract significant numbers of Gentile adherents.

87. 'Many of the God-fearing Greeks and not a few of the leading women' (17.4); 'not a few Greek women and men of high standing' (17.12). For a useful discussion of why Paul's message proved so attractive to the Thessalonians, see C. A. Wanamaker, *1 and 2 Thessalonians* (NIGTC; Grand Rapids: Eerdmans, 1990) 10-16. The language of the letter, addressed to Gentiles, 'in large part would be fully comprehensible only to someone . . . who knew [Jewish] Greek' (Holtz, *Erste Thessalonicher* 10).

88. Wanamaker, *1 and 2 Thessalonians* 8. Paul recalls warning the Thessalonian converts that they should expect to suffer distress or persecution (1 Thess. 3.3-4), but whether such a warning preceded the actual suffering they experienced (1.6) or was a warning before Paul and the others hurriedly left (Acts 17.10) is not clear. See also 2 Cor. 6.4-5; 11.23-27. Riesner notes that of the twenty-five pieces of information in Luke's account of the founding of the Thessalonian church, eighteen or nineteen are either directly or indirectly confirmed by 1 Thessalonians — 'on the whole . . . quite admirable findings for an ancient historian' (*Paul's Early Period* 367). Von Brocke estimates the historical value of 17.1-10 very highly (*Thessaloniki* 188-271). On 1 Thess. 2.14-16 see below, n. 269.

89. The central claim should probably best be translated as, 'This is the Messiah, Jesus whom I am proclaiming to you' (NRSV) (similarly 18.5, 28). In contrast, the Thessalonian let-

out in the speech in Pisidian Antioch (particularly 13.32-37), Luke said nothing of it during the rest of the mission from Antioch. But here it constitutes the whole of the message delivered by Paul in the synagogues of Thessalonica and Beroea. Noticeable also is the fact that in describing Paul's approach, Luke uses for the first time, though regularly thereafter, a different verb: *dialegomai*, which expresses the idea of a conversation, discussion or argument, involving the exchange of opinions.[90] Did Luke thereby intend to suggest a change of tactic — from preaching to dialogue? We may deduce that the various shifts in focus of emphasis reflect at least in part Luke's editorial decisions, to prevent the reports of successive preachings from becoming too repetitive. But the emphasis on scriptural proof of the claims made for Jesus is one which both Luke and Paul shared,[91] and discussion/argument over key Scriptures is certainly implied in Paul's treatment of passages like Gen. 15.6 and Lev. 18.5,[92] so there is no call to play the one emphasis off against the other here.

According to Luke the Thessalonian synagogue-focused mission lasted only for three Sabbaths, but a lengthier period focused on Jason's house is probably implicit (17.5-6), and 1 Thess. 2.9 and Phil. 4.16 certainly suggest a longer period[93] — perhaps another example of Luke's concertina-ing of history? On the other hand, as already noted, the report that Paul's preaching attracted mainly Gentiles, and that it provoked Jewish resentment at and opposition to preaching to Gentiles, is confirmed by 1 Thess. 1.6 and 2.14-16.[94] A further indication that Luke has been able to draw on good tradition is the mention of Jason (17.5-9), without introduction or further identification, as one whose name was sufficiently well known. It is not said whether he was a Jew or Gentile (the Greek name in itself is not decisive on the point),[95] but he was evidently a man of some

ters are devoid of quotations from the OT, though 1 Thessalonians contains several allusions (2.4, 16; 4.5, 6, 8; 5.8, 22). Even so, however, the letters hardly exclude the likelihood that Paul would have begun his mission in the synagogue (Malherbe, *Thessalonians* 58).

90. BDAG 232. Contrast the verbs used earlier of Paul's mission: 'proclaimed *(katangellein)* the word of God' (13.5); 'spoke the word of the Lord' (13.44-46); 'speaking boldly *(parrēsiazesthai)* for the Lord' (14.3); 'proclaimed the good news *(euangelizesthai)*' (14.21; 16.10); 'spoke *(lalēsai)* the word' (14.25; 16.6).

91. Luke 24.27, 44-47; e.g., 1 Cor. 15.1-4.

92. Rom. 4.3-22; Gal. 3.6-14; Rom. 10.5; Gal. 3.12.

93. Kümmel, *Introduction* 256; several months (Haenchen, *Acts* 510-11); 'only a couple of months' (Brown, *Introduction* 464); at least two or three months (Malherbe, *Thessalonians* 59-61); 'about three months' (Schnelle, *Paul* 146).

94. The description of their 'jealousy' *(zēlōsantes)* again may include an allusion to Jewish 'zeal' *(zēlos)* to maintain Jewish ethnic and religious distinctives in the face of assimilating or syncretistic pressures of a major Greek city; on this 'zeal' see above, §25.2c.

95. Though if this Jason is the same as the Jason of Rom. 16.21, the latter is described as a 'kinsman' of Paul; Luke probably thought he was a Gentile (Malherbe, *Thessalonians* 63).

substance, with a house large enough to provide such hospitality[96] and where the 'brothers' could meet.[97] He may have provided the work of which Paul speaks in 1 Thess. 2.9, though characteristically Luke only alludes to such day-to-day details in passing later on.[98] Here also it is noteworthy that Luke was well aware of the proper title for the authorities in Thessalonica ('politarchs').[99]

The accusations against Paul and Silas (in absentia) and Jason reflect the degree to which religion and politics of state were closely related in those days. They also express the sort of exaggerated populist rhetoric so readily drawn upon in all ages on such occasions of public confrontation.[100] To 'turn the world (or empire) upside down' was to threaten the foundations of established order and custom; new ideas can always provide an excuse for populist conservative reaction, though if Paul's teaching in Thessalonica included a strong eschatological emphasis,[101] one can see how the accusation might arise. So too any proclamation of a new focus for religious commitment linked to talk of God's kingdom[102] could be readily presented in populist rhetoric as a seditious threat to Caesar's rule (cf. Luke 23.2), however far-fetched the accusation might seem to a more objective onlooker.[103]

---

96. The implication of the tale is that Paul and Silas were not present in Jason's house at the time of the disturbance. Luke the story-teller evidently felt no need to complete every pedantic detail (cf. 14.20, 22, and the silence in 16.19 regarding Timothy and the one implied by the 'we').

97. But Jervell thinks that 'there is no talk of founding a congregation, because the converts should continue to belong to the synagogue' (*Apg.* 435). Acts 20.4 reports that two of the church delegates who accompanied Paul on his last journey to Jerusalem were from Thessalonica, Aristarchus (Col. 4.10) and Secundus.

98. Acts 18.3; 20.34; cf. Haenchen, *Acts* 511-12: 'We can only take the true measure of the extraordinary accomplishment of this missionary when, to all the other difficulties which he had to combat, and which Luke mentions in part, we add the constant need for money' (512). See further §29.5d above.

99. See above, §21 n. 100. Barrett summarizes the discussion well (*Acts* 2.814).

100. Equally typical of such charge and counter-charge, of course, is Luke's characterization of the opposition roused by 'the Jews' as a 'rabble, layabouts' (*agoraioi*, 'the crowd in the marketplace'; the parallel with Plutarch, *Aemilius Paulus* 38.3, is sometimes cited — Malherbe, *Thessalonians* 64); 'they raised a mob' *(ochlopoiēsantes)* and 'started a riot *(ethoryboun)* in the city' (17.5). Omerzu thinks that the reference to a *crimen maiestatis* is a redactional link to Luke 23.2-5 but that the *ochlopoieō* may reflect the historical reproaches levelled against Jason (*Prozess* 219-20).

101. Cf. 1 Thess. 5.1-11; 2 Thess. 2.1. 'The eschatological content of the preaching (cf. 2 Th 2:5-7, with its veiled allusion to the removal of the imperial power) might well have been construed as contravening one or more of Caesar's decrees' (Bruce, *Acts* 371-72). According to 1 Thessalonians, Paul also warned of coming affliction/persecution (3.3-4) and of the unexpectedness of the coming of 'the day of the Lord' (5.2; 'you know').

102. Cf. Acts 14.22; 19.8; 20.25; 1 Thess. 2.12; 2 Thess. 1.5.

103. Hemer, *Book of Acts* 167, indicates the 'decrees of Caesar' which might be in view,

The people at large, as well as the authorities, were bound to be disturbed by such accusations (17.8-9). The authorities take security (bail money)[104] from Jason and the others, presumably to guarantee the departure of Paul and Silas, and then let them go.[105] The response suggests that they recognized the realities of the situation and knew how to defuse a potentially dangerous situation involving an uncontrolled mob. Use of the mob was a well-known demagogic tactic within the history of Greek democracy, so they would not be short of precedents. But it is interesting, and somewhat curious, that Luke does not take the opportunity to underline the lack of threat posed by Paul and the vindication of the rights of the new association (as he does in 16.35-39 and 18.12-17). Perhaps he was more constrained by the reports he actually received than he is usually given credit for.

d. Evacuation to Beroea

Luke narrates that Paul and Silas slipped away by night,[106] though it would take more than one day's journey to reach Beroea (about forty-five or fifty miles to the southwest).[107] Why there? Beroea lay on the road to central and southern Greece but was several miles south of the main road, the Egnatian Way. So the suggestion that it was during this phase that Paul went as far as Illyricum (Rom. 15.19), that is, continued westward on the Via Egnatia, is that much less likely.[108]

citing E. A. Judge, 'The Decrees of Caesar at Thessalonica', *RTR* 30 (1971) 1-7; see also K. P. Donfried, 'The Cults of Thessalonica and the Thessalonian Correspondence', *NTS* 31 (1985) 336-56, reprinted in *Paul, Thessalonica and Early Christianity* (London: Clark, 2002) 21-48 (here 32-35); Tajra, *Trial* 36-42. Omerzu is not persuaded by Judge (*Prozess* 200-202). J. K. Hardin, 'Decrees and Drachmas at Thessalonica: An Illegal Assembly in Jason's House (Acts 17.1-10a)', *NTS* 52 (2006) 29-49, suggests rather that both the charges and the seizure of payment relate to the imperial restrictions on voluntary associations: the charges are of political orientation, and the politarchs exacted payment for the formation of an unauthorized group (though see above, §30 nn. 81-83).

104. *Lambanein to hikanon* = the Roman legal term *satis accipere*, 'take bail' (BDAG 472).

105. Sherwin-White, *Roman Society* 95-97. The success in deflecting the charge of treason may imply that Jason had some standing in the city or friends in high places (Malherbe, *Thessalonians* 63).

106. 'Most writers . . . think that the passive in [1 Thess.] 2:17 ("we were made orphans") signifies that Paul's absence was imposed on him' (Malherbe, *Thessalonians* 61); see also von Brocke, *Thessaloniki* 268-71.

107. J. D. Wineland, *ABD* 1.678 (fifty miles); Barrett, *Acts* 2.817 (forty-five miles).

108. Conceivably, news of Claudius's edict expelling Jews from Rome (49) reached Paul about this time and quickly squashed any thought of proceeding directly to Rome (Riesner, *Paul's Early Period* 359-60).

Cicero described Beroea as *oppidum devium,* 'a town lying off the high road, out of the way' (*In Pisonem* 36.89), which made it a good place for flight.[109] However, it was not an insignificant urban centre,[110] and there is some (later) evidence of a (significant) Jewish presence there.[111] So to that extent it furthered Paul's strategic and tactical goals. But the main reason may simply have been that Beroea lay outside Thessalonica's jurisdiction; the departure of Paul and Silas thus far from Thessalonica may have been all that was required to meet the bail conditions laid on Jason and the others (Acts 17.9).[112]

Here the pattern of Luke's narrative repeats with interesting variations (17.10-13). On arrival Paul and Silas head at once for the synagogue. Here however the response from the local Jews is presented as much more positive: they were more 'noble', 'fair-minded' (REB), received the word eagerly, and 'scrutinized or critically examined *(anakrinontes)*' the Scriptures daily to see if the texts supported the interpretation put upon them by Paul and Silas. The implication is that the synagogue in Beroea functioned as a house of study where the scrolls were kept and where members of the Jewish community could attend daily (not just on the Sabbath) for Scripture study. According to Luke the success was greater among the local Jews ('many', as opposed to the 'few' in Thessalonica), with a similar number of Gentile women of high status ('not a few' on both occasions) and Gentile men, also of high social standing.[113] The resulting church presumably consisted of Jews and Gentiles. The reference to Sopater of Beroea in 20.4[114] indicates that the church became established, even though it is mentioned nowhere else.

In a re-run of the mission from Antioch (14.19), trouble is caused by Jews from the main city of mission (Thessalonica) stirring up hostility to Paul, who is quickly removed from the scene (17.13). The report that Paul alone was sent off (17.14)[115] presumably indicates that he was the main exponent of the new message and so drew the fire of the opposition on to himself. That his companions

109. Barrett, *Acts* 2.817.

110. Lucian described it as 'large and populous *(megalē kai polyanthrōpos)*' (*Lucius* 34).

111. Schürer, *History* 3.67, 68.

112. Thessalonica was 'a free city which lay outside the Roman jurisdiction. . . . Paul exploits the fact that there was no inter-city jurisdiction or authority except that of the Roman governor. . . . There is no evidence that the police forces of different cities ever acted in concert' (Sherwin-White, *Roman Society* 96-98).

113. Women had a significant position within Macedonian society, and grave inscriptions suggest that women constituted 50 percent of the proselytes and 80 percent of the God-fearers (Riesner, *Paul's Early Period* 351).

114. Is Sopater of 20.4 to be identified with Sosipater of Rom. 16.21?

115. 'The brothers' send Paul away — presumably indicating that an embryonic church was already beginning to form.

escorted him to Athens (probably by sea) before returning to Beroea (17.15) suggests either that they feared for his safety or that they wished to introduce him
personally to friends or relations in Athens. Again, a key consideration would be
that Athens was under a different jurisdiction; the hope would presumably be
that in removing the chief occasion for unrest wholly from the region, those who
remained might escape any further persecution — a vain hope in light of 1 Thess.
1.5-6 and 2.14.[116] A communication from Paul (17.15) which his companions
were to take back to Thessalonica (that Silas and Timothy should join him as
soon as possible) foreshadows the extensive letter writing and network of communication Paul was soon to establish for his churches.

31.3. Confrontation in Athens

The move to Athens is not presented by Luke as part of Paul's mission strategy.
The implication is rather that Paul might well have settled in Thessalonica and
made that city his mission centre, had his time there not been curtailed by events.
The moves to Beroea and Athens were forced upon him, and the impression
given by Luke's account is that Paul did not see the latter as a promising base for
his work. The presence of Jews in Athens is well attested,[117] and Luke indicates
that there was the usual body of non-Jewish sympathizers (God-fearers) in attendance at the synagogue (Acts 17.17). But once again, as in Thessalonica, Paul's
speaking in the synagogue is presented in terms of dialogue *(dielegeto)* rather
than proclamation *(euangelizesthai),* and in Athens is passed over without further comment (17.17). Unusually in Acts, for the rest of Paul's time in Athens the
Jewish community and the attendant God-fearers do not feature. Instead, Luke
evidently saw the opportunity to present another confrontation for the gospel:
this time not with magic (as in Cyprus) or simplistic paganism (as in Lystra) or
fortune-telling as a business (as in Philippi) but with sophisticated Greek philosophy. The main interaction takes place, unusually in Paul's mission, though more
understandable in Athens, in the marketplace, and again in dialogue: *dielegeto*
(17.17);[118] *syneballon* (17.18).[119]

116. Riesner again notes that a strategy drawn from Isa. 66.19 LXX would have not only
Macedonia but all of Greece in view (*Paul's Early Period* 295).

117. Schürer, *History* 3.65; Levinskaya, *BAFCS* 5.158-62.

118. Haenchen notes that Plutarch, *Cic.* 24.5, uses *dialegomai* for the teaching methods
of a peripatetic philosopher (*Acts* 517 n. 6).

119. *Symballō,* 'to engage in mutual pondering of a matter, converse, confer' (BDAG
956). Schnabel sees Acts 17.22-31 as an example of Paul's dialogical method of explaining the
gospel (*Mission* 1392-1404).

a. 'What Has Athens to Do with Jerusalem?'

Luke's description of the Athenians and the foreigners who had taken residence there, as interested in nothing other than 'talking or hearing about the latest novelty' (REB), is rather dismissive (Acts 17.21).[120] But it catches quite well both the continuing attraction for Roman philhellenists of Athens as the city which more than any other evoked and preserved the greatness of Greek culture,[121] and the sense of decadence and somewhat faded glory which had probably characterized Athens for many decades.[122] The fact remains, however, that Athens was the historic and famed centre of Greek culture and retained its reputation for learning as a famous university town — 'learned Athens', as Ovid described it (*Ep.* 2.38).

Its reputation for philosophical innovation began with Socrates, who had been sentenced to death in 399 BCE, and the Academy founded by Plato in about 385 BCE continued to attract philosophers and would-be philosophers for some nine centuries. Its other local philosopher of note was Epicurus, who established his school (the Garden) in about 306/307 and taught there till his death in 270. The Epicureanism which Paul would have confronted in Athens (Acts 17.18) was a practical philosophy whose objective was to secure a happy life and to maximize the experience of pleasure.[123] Among other things, it taught that the soul could not survive the death of the body (giving freedom from fear of death) and that the gods do not interfere with the natural world (giving freedom from fear of the supernatural).[124] Subjects for dialogue between Paul and local Epicureans, and the likelihood that Paul's arguments would find little resonance with Epicureans, are at once clear.

---

120. It draws upon (and panders to) well-known characterizations of Athens, which suggest to some that the portrayal is drawn from literature (or familiar gossip) rather than from personal acquaintance (see Barrett, *Acts* 2.833).

121. 'From the 50s BC on philhellenism prompted Roman nobles, then emperors, to become benefactors of the city' (*OCD*³ 205; see further 'Philhellenism' 1159-60).

122. See further Taylor, 'Roman Empire' 2463-64, 2467; Barrett, *Acts* 2.833-34; Haenchen, *Acts* 517 n. 2, cites Horace's reference to 'empty Athens' (*Ep.* 2.2.81); 'essentially a mediocre university town dedicated to the conservation of its intellectual heritage' (Murphy-O'Connor, *Paul* 108).

123. 'We say that pleasure is the beginning and end of the blessed life' (Epicurus, *Ep. Men.* 128); see further A. A. Long and D. N. Sedley, *The Hellenistic Philosophers* (2 vols.; Cambridge: Cambridge University, 1987) 1.112-25 and 2.114-29.

124. 'Gods exist, atomic compounds like everything else, but take no thought for the cosmos or any other, living an ideal life of eternal, undisturbed happiness — the Epicurean ideal. . . . The soul is composed of atoms, all extremely small but distinguished by shape into four kinds. . . . At death the component atoms are dispersed' (*OCD*³ 533). See further Long and Sedley, *Hellenistic Philosophers* 1.65-72, 139-49 and 2.64-75, 143-54. Extensive bibliography in *OCD*³ 534.

The more influential Stoicism which Paul encountered (17.18) had been founded in Athens by Zeno, who in the first decades of the third century BCE taught so regularly in the Stoa Poecile ('Painted Colonnade') on the northwest section of the marketplace *(agora)*[125] in Athens that his philosophy took its name from the location (Stoicism).[126] Reformulated by Chrysippus, in the latter half of the third century,[127] Stoicism taught that the aim of the philosopher should be to live in harmony with nature, guided by the cosmic reason which Stoics identified with God and which manifests itself both in providence and in human reason.[128] To live in harmony with this reason is the only good; everything else is a matter of indifference.[129] A sophisticated philosophy like Stoicism obviously had many other aspects, not to mention points of dispute among its adherents, but at least in the broad outline just indicated, it would obviously have provided more points of contact with Jewish monotheism than did Epicureanism, points on which Paul could hope to build in any dialogue.

It would have taken a more astringent historian than Luke to pass up the opportunity to depict an encounter between Paul and such philosophies which could so appropriately be identified with Athens. In developing the theme as he does, Luke in effect poses Tertullian's later question, 'What has Athens to do with Jerusalem? What has the Academy to do with the Church?'.[130] What has the proclamation of the Jewish Messiah Jesus to do with the Greek intellectual tradition so deeply rooted in Athens? The answer provided by Luke's account is fascinating. He does not indicate points of specific contact or dispute Paul might have had with these philosophies, but, as we shall see, the speech attributed to Paul does seek to build on some crucial common or overlapping ground with the Stoics in particular. At the same time, however, the Christian challenge and confrontation is set out at two points: traditional Jewish revulsion at Gentile idolatry, and the specifically Christian claims for Jesus, particularly Jesus' resurrection.

125. The site was excavated in 1981 and is clearly visible today.

126. The fact that Luke reports Paul as encountering representatives of only these two schools of philosophy, Epicureans and Stoics, at least indicates Luke's awareness of how closely associated with Athens the two schools were.

127. *OCD³* 329, 1446.

128. Cicero describes Chrysippus's views: 'He says that divine power resides in reason and in the mind and intellect of universal nature. He says that god is the world itself, and the universal pervasiveness of its mind' (*De natura deorum* 1.39; Long and Sedley, *Hellenistic Philosophers* 1.323 and 2.321-22).

129. 'Zeno represented the end as: "living in agreement". This is living in accordance with one concordant reason, since those who live in conflict are unhappy. His successors expressed this in a more expanded form, "living in agreement with nature". . . . Chrysippus wanted to make this clearer and expressed it thus: "living in accordance with experience of what happens by nature"' (Stobaeus 2.75.11–2.76.8; Long and Sedley, *Hellenistic Philosophers* 1.394 and 2.389-90).

130. Tertullian, *De Praescriptione Haereticorum* 7.

The reaction of Paul (17.16) to the many statues and representations of the gods in Athens (a feature noted by other ancient historians)[131] was characteristically Jewish; the verb is strong — *parōxyneto,* 'outraged' (REB), 'deeply distressed' (NRSV). Nothing aroused Jewish contempt for the other religions of the Mediterranean and Mesopotamian world so much as idolatry. On their side, polytheists found such Jewish abhorrence puzzling and atheistic, even though the austere worship of the supreme God as invisible did attract some. On the whole, however, this was one of the points of mutual incomprehension between Jew and Gentile which helped protect Jewish distinctiveness.

The initial impression gained by the adherents of these older (as they would see them) philosophies was, however, dismissive and disparaging — particularly, no doubt, on the part of the Epicureans. The term used of Paul, *spermologos* ('babbler, chatterer') (17.18), evokes the image of one who made his living by picking up scraps, a scavenger and peddler of second-hand opinions.[132] The charge of proclaiming 'foreign deities *(daimonia)'* echoes that brought against Socrates.[133] This was no doubt deliberate on Luke's part, since the trial and death of Socrates 450 years earlier was one of the most famous episodes in Athens' history. The implication of Luke's description is that Paul was both misunderstood and a teacher of integrity, like Socrates himself.

In Luke's perspective, then, and despite the presence of a Jewish synagogue, the Athenians seem to have had little conception of a coherent and ancient theistic system like Judaism. In particular, they could make little sense of Paul's preaching about Jesus. According to Luke, they thought Paul was proclaiming two new 'foreign deities' (17.18), that is, presumably, Jesus and Resurrection *(Anastasis)*.[134] From this we may deduce that Paul focused his teaching on the central features of the Christian message (§29.7c) and that without a context (knowledge of Jewish history and religion), the argument proved meaningless to those who heard to him.

The climax of the narrative is Paul being brought before the Areopagus

---

131. References in Fitzmyer, *Acts* 604; Taylor, 'Roman Empire' 2465-66. H. M. Martin's 'Athens', *ABD* 1.516-17, provides a helpful overview of the antiquities still visible in Athens, many of which Paul would have seen for himself (see also Lake and Cadbury, *Beginnings* 4.209-10; D. W. J. Gill, 'Achaia', *BAFCS* 2.444-46).

132. BDAG 937; Taylor, 'Roman Empire' 2467-68.

133. Particularly in Xenophon, *Memorabilia* 1.1.1, and Plato, *Apology* 24B; see further Lake and Cadbury, *Beginnings* 4.212.

134. This was how Chrysostom understood it, as have many since (Haenchen, *Acts* 518 n. 1). But Barrett thinks it unlikely that Paul would have used the noun much (the creedal forms he echoes in his letters use verbs — 'God raised him') and suggests that the Athenian comment (referring to plural deities) is primarily intended to recall the story of Socrates (*Acts* 2.831). Jervell thinks the suggestion hardly valid in view of 17.32 (*Apg.* 444).

(17.19), that is, the ancient court which took its name from traditionally meeting at or on a construction at[135] the *Areios pagos,* the 'hill of Ares',[136] northwest of the Acropolis. Its powers at this time are obscure, but the Areopagus may well still have been Athens' chief court, with power to try crimes of any kind and with some supervisory responsibility regarding public morality, foreign cults and the like.[137] Luke does not make it clear whether Paul was formally arrested.[138] But in the event Paul is not charged with any crime or misdemeanor, and the scene simply peters out (17.32-34) without any formal closure. The implication is that the court had power to demand a hearing of any new teaching; the echo of Socrates' trial remains strong.

None of this is to dispute that Luke was able to draw on good tradition here. We know from 1 Thess. 3.1 that Paul spent some time in Athens.[139] The depiction of Athens is certainly recognizable from what we know of it at this period, from both literary and archaeological sources.[140] We also know from Paul's letters both that his antipathy to idolatry was as vehement as that of any other Jew,[141] and that the resurrection of Jesus was at the centre of his gospel (§29.7c). Moreover, had the story been entirely Luke's contrivance, we might have expected his account to end with a greater success than he reports in 17.34 (cf. 19.11-20). In contrast, the two named individuals who did become believers (Dionysius the Areopagite and a woman named Damaris) may have been among his informants or explicitly featured in the reports he received.[142]

---

135. It is difficult to imagine a council meeting on the hill in its present condition, though a terrace could have been built on and out from it, providing a sufficient surface for a gathering of leading citizens. Taylor argues that it would have met at the Royal Stoa, in the northwest corner of the Agora ('Roman Empire' 2470-71).

136. 'Ares' = the Greek god of war = Roman 'Mars', hence 'Mars Hill'.

137. Taylor, 'Roman Empire' 2469-70; Barrett, *Acts* 2.831-32, referring particularly to T. D. Barnes, 'An Apostle on Trial', *JTS* 20 (1969) 407-19. Josephus reports that the Athenians were known to punish impiety with severity: 'the penalty decreed for any who introduced a foreign god was death' (*Ap.* 2.262-68). 'Under the Roman Principate it ranked with the *boulē* and the assembly *(ekklēsia)* as one of the major corporations of Athens' (*OCD*³ 152).

138. The verb *epilabomenoi* is ambiguous and could simply denote Paul's being taken along somewhat unwillingly (cf. BDAG 374).

139. But how to square Paul's own recollection that Paul sent Timothy from Athens back to Thessalonica (1 Thess. 3.1-2) with Acts 17.14-15 and 18.1 is not clear (see further below, nn. 196, 226).

140. See also Hemer, *Book of Acts* 116-17.

141. See above, §29.7a.

142. Cf. Hemer, *Book of Acts* 208-209.

b. Paul's Speech to the Areopagus (Acts 17.22-31)

The speech which follows is one of the briefest of the more substantial speeches in Acts and would take less than two minutes to declaim. A typically cultured rhetorical opening, 'Athenians, I see how extremely religious *(deisidaimonesterous)* you are in every way' (17.22),[143] provides an immediate point of contact: by giving place for an altar 'to an unknown god' (17.23), the Athenians have demonstrated their readiness to ensure that no manifestation of the deity is overlooked.[144] This provides an opening for the assertion that Paul proclaims no new god but one they themselves had already acknowledged, albeit inadequately (17.23). At the same time, however, the objective is to proclaim this unknown god as the only God.

The speech immediately (17.24) makes the link with the Jewish axiom that there is one God ('the God') who has created all things ('the world and everything in it'). He is the sole sovereign ('Lord of heaven and earth'). The claim is wholly consistent and continuous with fundamental Jewish self-understanding and apologetic, as enshrined also in the Jewish Scriptures.[145]

It follows, with the same traditional logic, that this God does not dwell in shrines 'made with human hands' (17.24).[146] Nor is he dependent on anything made or provided by human beings (17.25). The relation is completely the reverse: humanity is wholly dependent on God for everything, from life and breath itself to everything else.[147] The implication is that humankind understands itself only when it understands its fundamental dependence on God, with the corollary that such an understanding calls for an appropriate worship. The line of argument would have been meaningful both to Epicureans (God needs nothing from human hands) and to Stoics (God as the source of all life).[148]

---

143. *Deisidaimonesterous* denotes here, of course, not our modern sense of 'superstitious' (KJV) but 'devout, religious': 'I perceive that you are very devout people'; see the full discussion in Barrett, *Acts* 2.835-36.

144. As many commentaries note, there are several attestations to 'altars of unknown gods' in Athens (Pausanias 1.1.4; Philostratus, *Apollonius* 6.3; Diogenes Laertius 1.110). See particularly Lake in *Beginnings* 5.240-46; P. W. van der Horst, 'The Altar of the "Unknown God" in Athens (Acts 17:23) and the Cults of "Unknown Gods" in the Graeco-Roman World', *Hellenism-Judaism-Christianity: Essays on Their Interaction* (Kampen: Kok Pharos, 1994) 165-202; Taylor, 'Roman Empire' 2472-75.

145. Gen. 1.1; Exod. 20.11; Ps. 145.6; Isa. 42.5; Wis. 9.1, 9; 2 Macc. 7.23; similarly Matt. 11.25 and Acts 4.24. That God was creator of all things was a familiar belief in Greek circles (cf. Plato, *Timaeus;* Epictetus 4.7.6).

146. Using again *cheiropoiētos,* as in 7.48; see above, §24 n. 125.

147. Isa. 42.5; 57.15-16; Wis. 9.1-3; 2 Macc. 14.35.

148. Texts in Barrett, *Acts* 2.841; Fitzmyer, *Acts* 608; Jervell, *Apg.* 447 n. 235. See further D. L. Balch, 'The Areopagus Speech: An Appeal to the Stoic Historian Posidonius against

The chief thrust of the argument, however, continues to draw on fundamental tenets of Jewish monotheism (17.26-27). Humankind is made from one common stock,[149] an idea less familiar to Greek thought.[150] God fixed the seasons and the boundaries of the nations.[151] His objective was that they should seek God,[152] recognizing that only in relation to and dependence on this beneficent and overseeing God would they be able to recognize their status and function as individuals and peoples.[153] The verbs used here ('if perhaps they might grope for [psēlaphēseian] him and find him') capture well the sense of uncertain reaching out in the dark of those moved and motivated by such considerations of natural theology — God at work in and manifest in an obscure way in the world.[154]

The clinching consideration is that this Creator God has not created a hunger for God within humankind only to leave it unsatisfied (17.27-28). This same sovereign Lord is not far from each of his human creatures. Again the thought is drawn immediately from the Scriptures.[155] But precisely at this point, one or two sayings from Greek poets can be cited as amounting to the same thing. The first, if it is a quotation, has an unknown source — 'in him we live and move and are'.[156] But the second is drawn from the Stoic poet Aratus, *Phaenomena* 5 — 'We too are his family'.[157] At this point the Jewish-Christian understanding of

---

Later Stoics and the Epicureans', in D. L. Balch et al., eds., *Greeks, Romans and Christians,* A. J. Malherbe FS (Minneapolis: Fortress, 1990) 52-79; Klauck, *Magic and Paganism* 81-95; G. W. Hansen, 'The Preaching and Defence of Paul', in I. H. Marshall and D. Peterson, eds., *Witness to the Gospel: The Theology of Acts* (Grand Rapids: Eerdmans, 1998) 295-324 (here 309-12).

149. Gen. 1.27-28; 10.32.

150. Dibelius, *Studies* 35-37: 'This is Old Testament and Christian preaching' (35); Fitzmyer, *Acts* 609.

151. Gen. 1.14; Deut. 32.8; Ps. 74.17; Wis. 7.18; 1QM 10.12-16; see further Dibelius, *Studies* 29-34; Haenchen, *Acts* 523-24 nn. 5-6; Wilson, *Gentiles* 201-205.

152. Deut. 4.29; Pss. 14.2; 53.2; Isa. 55.6; 65.1; cf. Wis. 13.6. Haenchen sets the revelation of creation and the revelation of Torah too much in contrast (*Acts* 524 n. 1); but see only Psalm 19 (he should have learned better from Haydn)! The thought that finding God is impossible, though he is not far from us, was present in popular philosophy too (Jervell, *Apg.* 449, citing Seneca, *Ep.* 41.1 and Dio Chrysostom, *Or.* 12.28).

153. The same point is made in 14.17; cf. Philo, *Spec. Leg.* 1.36. Paul presses it hard in Rom. 1.19-25.

154. See further Fitzmyer, *Acts* 609-10.

155. Ps. 145.18; Jer. 23.23.

156. Lake regarded it as a quotation from Epimenides (*Beginnings* 5.246-51; see also Bruce, *Acts* 384-85). If not a quotation, the language echoes Stoic (and pre-Stoic) beliefs (see further Dibelius, *Studies* 47-54; Barrett, *Acts* 846-49); however, Fitzmyer, *Acts* 610, rebuts Haenchen's contention that it was 'a received Stoic formulation' (*Acts* 524 n. 3).

157. Cited already by Aristobulus, frag. 4 (Eusebius, *Praep. evang.* 13.12.6; Charlesworth, *OTP* 2.841).

the relationship between God and humankind draws close to some traditional Greek religious sentiments and provides a bridge across which apologists could attempt to venture in the hope of drawing their audiences over to their own side.

But the apologetic effort is not expended in simply looking for points of contact and possible cross-over (17.29). The challenge to what any Jew would regard as an inferior and inadequate conception of God must be made. The point of common perception ('we are God's offspring') therefore provides the basis for the thoroughly Jewish corollary that God should not be represented by images of gold, silver or stone or any work of human imagination.[158] Such a critique of popular non-Jewish religion would not be new to sophisticated philosophers.[159]

In 17.30 what has been an apology for the Jewish understanding of God becomes an evangelistic thrust. Such misunderstanding should not be seen as a form of ignorance (cf. 14.16) and should now be repented of. In the face of the clearer understanding of God and of God's relation to humankind just outlined, idolaters should repent of their idolatry.

The conclusion follows in a rush (17.31). Repentance is necessary, since the same God who began all things will bring all things to a conclusion with a day of judgment. The concept of a day of judgment is again thoroughly Jewish[160] and was carried over into Christian theology as a basic datum.[161] The further description ('he will judge the world in righteousness') is drawn directly from the Psalms.[162] Once again, then, the language is thoroughly Jewish in its conception — 'righteousness' understood as God fulfilling the obligation he accepted when he created human society.[163] It would have had meaning for such an audience: 'righteousness' as referring particularly to the prescribed duties towards the gods. But one wonders what impact such a brief allusion to the theme of final judgment could have had in such a context as is envisaged. At this point the cameo character of Luke's presentation, simply alluding in a phrase to a whole theme requiring a much fuller exposition, diminishes the credibility of the picture here painted.

Still more audacious and straining on credulity would have been the abrupt allusion to the 'man appointed (that is, to serve as judge)' in the final judgment. The thought would not have been new to a Jewish audience.[164] But what a Greek

---

158. See, e.g., Deut. 4.28; Isa. 40.18-19; 44.9-20; Wis. 13.10-19; Ep. Jer.; *Sib. Or.* 3.8-45.

159. Barrett, *Acts* 2.850, cites Seneca, *Ep.* 31.11; Lucretius 1.63-80; Plutarch, *De Superstitione* 6 (167DEF).

160. E.g., Isa. 2.12; 34.8; Dan. 7.9-11; Joel 2.1-2; Amos 5.18; Zeph. 1.14–2.3; 3.8; Mal. 4.1; see further F. Büchsel, *TDNT* 3.933-35.

161. E.g., Rom. 2.5, 16; 1 Thess. 5.2; 2 Thess. 1.10.

162. Pss. 9.8; 96.13; 98.9.

163. Cf., e.g., Pss. 31.1; 35.24; 45.8; Isa. 26.2; 45.21. See below at §33 n. 90.

164. As already noted, the legendary heroes Abel and Enoch were already speculated as having such a role (§21 n. 173).

audience would have made of it is much less clear. The final straw would have been talk of resurrection from the dead. The idea of a man ascended to heaven would be familiar in both Jewish and Greek thought.[165] But resurrection from the dead was a peculiarly Jewish conception, implying, as it presumably would, a resurrection of the body. Luke cannot have been unaware of the offensive character of such an abrupt and bald declaration.[166] It is almost as though he wanted to set in the sharpest possible contrast the fundamental claim of Christianity and the mocking rejection of the Athenian sophisticates which follows (17.32).

This is the extent to which the Christian story is drawn upon. But the terms used to do so are worth noting.

- Jesus is not identified, and so the story of his continuity with Israel's history and prophecy is not a factor — in marked contrast to the speeches to Jews (Acts 2 and 13 in particular).
- At the same time, the point is clearly implied that the message about Jesus and his resurrection can only be rightly understood within the context of Jewish belief in the one God and Creator of all.
- Jesus is named only as a 'man whom he [God] has appointed', so that the basic monotheistic thrust of the overall speech is not compromised and the misunderstanding implicit in the philosophers' impression in 17.18 (that Paul was a proclaimer of foreign divinities) is corrected.
- In focusing the Christian challenge on the idea of final judgment and resurrection, no mention is made of the cross.

In short, the christology is subordinated to the theology; the developing christological distinctives of Christian faith are subordinated to the prior task of winning appropriate belief in God. At the same time, the focus on resurrection in both 17.18 and 31 confirms that in a Greek context as well as a Jewish the claim that God had raised Jesus from the dead stood at the centre of the Christian gospel. Whether or not Luke presented this as some model for Christian apologetic to sophisticated Gentile audiences is less clear, but his account of the relatively modest success of the attempt (17.32-34) was probably realistic.

It need hardly be stated that such a brief exposition and abrupt reference to the resurrection of an unidentified man would hardly have done justice to the occasion. But is the central thrust credible as a speech of Paul? NT scholars have

165. See, e.g., A. F. Segal, 'Heavenly Ascent in Hellenistic Judaism, Early Christianity and Their Environment', *ANRW* 2.23.2 (1980) 1333-94; Dunn, *Christology in the Making* 17-19.

166. See particularly N. T. Wright, *The Resurrection of the Son of God* (London: SPCK, 2003) 32-84.

differed on this, particularly those who do not like the idea of natural theology and who want to insist that the gospel is nothing more or less than the proclamation of Jesus — Christ crucified for our sins and raised from the dead.[167] But Paul's chief theological statement, his letter to the Christians in Rome, contains a clear natural theology in its opening statement (Rom. 1.19-32).[168] Paul also preserves a memory of the mockery of Greek sophisticates at the gospel: the proclamation of Christ crucified, 'to Gentiles, folly' (1 Cor. 1.23), as also the memory of his limited success in winning such people for the gospel: 'not many wise in worldly terms' (1 Cor. 1.26). And the thought of Jesus as final judge is certainly part of Paul's theology.[169] So here too Luke was drawing on a clear perception and possibly even some memory of how Paul attempted to engage Greek wisdom with an essentially Jewish message regarding God, elaborated with the distinctively Christian belief in the resurrection of Jesus. Even here Luke shows himself a good practitioner of Thucydides' dictum (§21.3).[170]

The conclusion is briefly told (17.32-34). The message with its call to repentance for idolatrous conceptions of God might have struck a chord with some; Jewish apologetic would no doubt already be familiar to any who were 'groping after God' (17.27). But such a hopelessly brief allusion to the distinctive Christian claims regarding judgment and resurrection would have been bound to meet with incomprehension and dismissal, and a lengthier exposition would have demanded too great a leap in basic assumptions and conceptuality for most. Those more comfortable with their own philosophies or inattentive to what Paul would have said would indeed have been dismissive (particularly the Epicureans). Assuming a more sustained presentation by Paul, others might well have wished to hear more.

167. As, classically, Dibelius: 'It has been shown that the theology of the Areopagus speech is absolutely foreign to Paul's own theology, that it is, in fact, foreign to the entire New Testament' (*Studies* 71, referring back to 58-64); the attempt, in effect, to exclude Acts from the NT is curious! 'In terms of content the speech contradicts Pauline theology so strongly that even in its basic traits we cannot credit it to the apostle to the Gentiles' (Becker, *Paul* 128). 'If the speech had not been in Acts, we would not have concluded that Paul was its author' (Jervell, *Apg.* 456). Schnelle assumes that Paul would have preached as he theologizes in Romans (*Paul* 146). Contrast the more measured judgment of Fitzmyer, *Acts* 602. Fitzmyer's bibliography on the Areopagus speech stretches to more than four pages (613-17).

168. Cf. his earliest letter, written not long after Paul's time in Athens — 1 Thess. 1.9-10 (see §29.7a above). We should, of course, not regard Rom. 1.19-32 as the only way Paul might have attempted to engage with broader religious sensibilities (cf. Lüdemann, *Early Christianity* 193-94). See also Porter, *Paul of Acts* chs. 6 and 7 (conclusions on 150 and 170).

169. Rom. 1.16; 2 Cor. 5.10; cf. 1 Cor. 6.2.

170. See, e.g., F. F. Bruce, 'The Speeches in Acts — Thirty Years After', in R. J. Banks, ed., *Reconciliation and Hope,* L. L. Morris FS (Exeter: Paternoster, 1974) 53-68 (here 64-65); and further B. Gärtner, *The Areopagus Speech and Natural Revelation* (Uppsala: Almqvist and Wiksell, 1955).

The actual recruits who took the step of believing were few — 'some men'. Among them Luke's sources recalled Dionysius, a member of the Areopagus council, a man of high social status, and a woman named Damaris. Of neither do we hear any more in the NT.[171] But it is not even clear whether a viable church was established. Paul is recalled as having left almost straight away (18.1), an unusual step for him where a new church was there to be nurtured. Athens does not feature in Acts after 18.1, nor does the only other NT reference (1 Thess. 3.1) tell us anything. And elsewhere Stephanas of Corinth is given the honour of being called 'the first convert in Achaia' (1 Cor. 16.15).[172] All told, the experiment in meeting Greek philosophy in Athens head-on does not appear to have been a great success and probably left its most lasting influence in Paul's formulations in Romans 1 and 1 Corinthians 1 (not to mention Acts 17).[173]

31.4. The Founding of the Church in Corinth

A move to Corinth, the next obvious target location (in 50 or 51),[174] allows Luke to develop his portrayal of Paul's mission with significant details. (1) He provides, for the first time, details of how Paul sustained himself financially (18.2-3). (2) The regular pattern, of initial preaching to Jews followed by opposition, is met by a second denunciation of Jewish intransigence and announcement that the gospel will thenceforth be taken to the Gentiles (18.4-6). (3) A clearer picture than ever before is provided of the transition from a synagogue-centred ministry to a house church (18.7-8). (4) Corinth is clearly signalled as a centre in which Paul's mission became established over a lengthy period (18.9-11). (5) The Roman authorities give a judgment favourable to the legal status of the church by

171. According to Eusebius, Dionysius became the first bishop of Corinth (*HE* 3.4.10; 4.23.3).

172. 'We may make the well-founded historical assumption that Paul did not have much missionary success in Athens, for an Athenian community has no recognizable role in his plans for his mission, journeys and collection. Moreover it is only around 170 CE that we hear of a Christian community in Athens' (Lüdemann, *Early Christianity* 194, citing Eusebius, *HE* 4.23.2-3).

173. But see C. Gempf, 'Before Paul Arrived in Corinth: The Mission Strategies in 1 Corinthians 2:2 and Acts 17', in P. J. Williams et al., eds., *The New Testament in Its First-Century Setting*, B. W. Winter FS (Grand Rapids: Eerdmans, 2004) 126-42, who critiques Ramsay's suggestion that Paul left Athens disillusioned and consequently changed his tactics in Corinth (*St. Paul* 252). Jervell draws the conclusion that for Luke the Gentile mission is not a matter of the Areopagus speech or directed to Gentiles apart from Jews but has to do with God-fearers in the synagogues (*Apg.* 455).

174. Murphy-O'Connor, *St. Paul's Corinth* 139-50; on the journey from Athens to Corinth, a minimum of two days, see Murphy-O'Connor *Paul* 256-59.

ruling that it still belongs within the protected sphere of the Jews' national religion (18.12-17).

a. Corinth

Corinth,[175] two days' journey from Athens, met all Paul's criteria for a strategic centre for his mission. Although almost completely destroyed by a Roman army in 146 BCE, it had been re-founded as a Roman colony by Julius Caesar in 44 BCE. Its location, on the isthmus linking Achaia to the Peloponnese, made it a natural centre for trade and commerce both north and south, and east and west; it was Caesar who first projected the construction of a canal between the Aegean and the Gulf of Corinth to facilitate movement of trade (Suetonius, *Julius* 44), a project which Caligula and particularly Nero attempted to put into effect (Suetonius, *Gaius* 21; *Nero* 19).[176] The first colonists for the most part were freed slaves (Strabo 8.6.23), that is, not Romans as such but probably many of those enslaved in Rome's then-recent conquest of the East (Syrians, Jews, Egyptians). However, freedmen often became very successful businessmen,[177] and with such natural advantages as Corinth possessed its commercial success was assured.

> Once the colony was securely based, it attracted entrepreneurs from Greece and the major trading countries of the E. Mediterranean. Such infusions of new capital in a prime commercial situation inevitably generated more wealth, and within 50 years of its foundation many citizens of Corinth were men of very considerable means. The clearest evidence of this is an inscription commemorating L. Castricius Regulus, who assumed the presidency of the first restored Isthmian Games sometime between 7 BC and AD 3. He refurbished the facilities, which had not been used for a century, and offered a banquet to all the inhabitants of the colony. . . . Commercial development demanded banking facilities, and by the mid-1st century AD Corinth was an important financial center (Plutarch, *Mor.* 831A).[178]

175. The most useful of recent summary of the evidence regarding Roman Corinth is provided by Furnish, *2 Corinthians* 4-22; see also Thiselton, *1 Corinthians* 6-12.

176. The texts are conveniently cited by Murphy-O'Connor, *St. Paul's Corinth* 110.

177. In the decades prior to Paul's arrival in Corinth, one of the most successful businessmen and most prominent in the city's hierarchy of public offices was the freedman Gnaeus Babbius Philenus (Furnish, *2 Corinthians* 10, 12; Thiselton, *1 Corinthians* 8-9).

178. Murphy-O'Connor, 'Corinth', *ABD* 1.1136; see also his *Paul* 258. Corinthian bronze was particularly prized (see Murphy-O'Connor, *St. Paul's Corinth* index 'Bronze'). See also R. M. Grant, *Paul in the Roman World: The Conflict at Corinth* (Louisville: Westminster John Knox, 2001) ch. 2.

By the time of Paul's sojourn in Corinth it had a population of about 80,000[179] and had become once again a senatorial province (since 44), which meant that Rome's chief representative was a proconsul. As already noted, our knowledge of the proconsul for 51-52 (or 52-53), Lucius Iunius Gallio,[180] enables us to date Paul's time in Corinth with remarkable precision (Acts 18.12-17). Corinth's municipal government mirrored that of republican Rome, with senior magistrates *(duoviri)* assisted by two *aediles,* responsible for commercial and financial litigation.[181] In an honour-shame culture, the greatest honour Corinth could bestow on an individual was presidency of the Isthmian Games, celebrated every two years; Paul could have attended the Games of 51.[182]

Corinth has been well excavated and gives a good impression of what Paul must have seen during his time there.[183] The central area, with colonnades to north and south, was dominated on the west by the large temple devoted to the imperial cult, but other temples and altars also featured prominently.[184] The *bēma* ('tribunal'), from which official pronouncements would be delivered, referred to in 18.12, has a prominent central position, though flanked by shops on either side. The road to Lechaeum, Corinth's northwestern outlet to the Gulf of Corinth, was obviously a prominent thoroughfare, again flanked with shops and prominent structures. I have already suggested that a shop like one of them, perhaps even opening on to a principal thoroughfare, might have been Paul's workspace during his working day as a tent-maker.[185]

We can be confident that a good many Jews had settled in Corinth, even

179. Winter, *Corinth* 294.

180. See above, §28.1b.

181. Erastus (Rom. 16.23; above, §30.4b) may have been or become one of these. On the civic leadership in Corinth and the related status and power, see Clarke, *Secular and Christian Leadership* chs. 2-3; and on the thoroughly Roman character of Corinth see Winter, *Corinth* 7-22.

182. These games are probably alluded to in 1 Cor. 9.24-27.

183. Schowalter and Friesen, eds., *Urban Religion in Roman Corinth,* contains several essays summarizing and drawing on the relevant archeological data.

184. Furnish lists particularly temples to Apollo and Athena, to Tyche and Aphrodite, an impressive Asclepium (about half a mile north of the forum), and the cult of Demeter and Kore, and probably also the cults of Isis and Sarapis (*2 Corinthians* 15-20). Of the Asclepium, Murphy-O'Connor remarks, 'It may well have been the closest the city got to a country-club with facilities for dining and swimming' (*St. Paul's Corinth* 165; further 162-67). On the mystery cults in first-century Corinth see Chester, *Conversion* 303-16. See further N. Bookidis, 'Religion in Corinth: 146 BCE to 100 CE', in Schowalter and Friesen, eds., *Urban Religion in Roman Corinth* 141-64 (particularly 151-63); and on the much-exaggerated and much-misunderstood issue of sacred prostitution in Corinth, see J. R. Lanci, 'The Stones Don't Speak and the Texts Tell Lies: Sacred Sex at Corinth', in the same volume (205-20).

185. See above, §29.5d and n. 203.

though the epigraphical evidence is of uncertain date, and the oft-referred-to syn-agogue inscription — [*syna*]*gōgē Hebr*[*aiōn*] — may be as late as the fourth or fifth century CE.[186] But in a vigorous cosmopolitan centre such as Corinth, the principal competitors for the young church would likely have been the already well-established religious and civic cults, and the greatest social pressure would most likely come from the overlapping networks (associations, professional col-leagues, business associates) to which converts still belonged.

b. Paul Finds His Mission Centre

Acts 18.1-17, together with the two letters to the Corinthians, gives us the fullest and most detailed record of the establishment of a church and its early history available to us. For Luke it was important that this successful foundation was the result of a happy combination of providential events and divine assurance pro-vided directly. In particular, the foundation period was bracketed by two events involving the Roman authorities. The first was the beginning of one of the most fruitful partnerships in all Paul's career as a missionary, when the expulsion of Jews from Rome provided the occasion for Paul to meet up with Aquila and Priscilla (18.2-3).[187] The second was the favourable ruling of the proconsul Gallio in Corinth itself, which ensured that the manipulation of public sentiment against the missionaries (as in Thessalonica) could not happen in Corinth (18.12-16). More important, probably for Paul himself, was a vision of the Lord (Jesus) which gave Paul the initial confidence he needed to settle himself in Corinth for a lengthy ministry (18.9-11). That God could thus be seen to be behind and direct-ing Paul's mission was of first importance for both Paul and Luke.

For the historian it is also important that so much of the detail can be cor-roborated and located within the wider history of the period. The expulsion of Jews from Rome can be dated to 49, and Gallio's period of office can be dated likewise with some precision to 51-52 (or 52-53).[188] The mention of the names Priscilla and Aquila, Titius Justus and Crispus, and also Sosthenes, with detail of

---

186. Schürer, *History* 3.65-66; Murphy-O'Connor, 'Corinth' 1138; Levinskaya, *BAFCS* 5.162-64.

187. On Prisc(ill)a and Aquila see above, §29.6. That husband and wife both practised the trade or profession of tent-making is possible; see *NDIEC* 2.17, 27; 4.235. Becker envis-ages Paul's initial period in Corinth as a time of want and thus doubts that 'Paul came across Priscilla and Aquila so quickly after his arrival in Corinth' (*Paul* 149).

188. See §28.1b above. Sherwin-White notes the unlikelihood that Luke could have gained knowledge of the name 'Gallio' and his office from public records (*Roman Society* 104-107); reminiscences of one or more of those involved or on the sidelines are much the more ob-vious source.

status and location, as usual give some assurance that Luke had good sources to draw on.[189] And although the pattern of synagogue preaching and rejection is characteristic of Luke, even here there are indications that resistance from local Jews accompanied the foundation of the church in Corinth (1 Cor. 1.22-23) and that there was a Jewish dimension to the tensions within the Corinthian church itself.[190]

The meeting with Aquila and Priscilla must have been the first confirmation to Paul that Corinth might provide a settled base for him (18.1-3). If indeed the couple had been expelled from Rome because of disturbances occasioned by claims made within the Jewish community there regarding Jesus as the Christ (§21.1d), we can assume that Aquila and Priscilla were already Christian before they met Paul[191] and that they had already demonstrated their leadership qualities in the intra-Jewish debates in Rome. This is borne out here by the fact that Luke includes no record of their being converted by Paul. Their arrival in Corinth was 'recent' (18.2); possibly the abruptness of their expulsion meant that they had had to give all their attention to business affairs and had not been able to continue 'agitating' on behalf of Christ; or perhaps, having been warned off by events in Rome, they kept their heads down after their arrival in Corinth. Even so, their mutual commitment (as well as their mutual trade) probably ensured that they and Paul 'hit it off' together.[192] As earlier noted, Aquila and Priscilla probably ran a substantial business (in tent-making or, more generally, leather-working) and were well-to-do, their apartments large enough to host the local churches in Corinth and subsequently in Rome.[193] They could therefore take Paul on and provide him with a living wage. Luke says nothing more at this point, but we have already seen what strong views Paul himself held on the importance he attached to being self-supporting (§29.5d). The fact that Corinth was such a successful business centre, with a very buoyant market for tents and the like, may also have been a factor in Paul's deciding to settle there.[194]

189. See further Jervell, *Apg.* 463-64. R. G. Fellows, 'Renaming in Paul's Churches: The Case of Crispus-Sosthenes Revisited', *TynB* 56 (2005) 111-30, argues for the likelihood that Crispus and Sosthenes was the same person.

190. Cf. 1 Cor. 1.12; 8–10; 2 Corinthians 11; see further below, §32.5.

191. See, e.g., Murphy-O'Connor, *Paul* 263; otherwise Jossa, *Jews or Christians?* 129.

192. Paul's references below to the couple indicate a particularly warm bond between them (§29.6).

193. 1 Cor. 16.19; Rom. 16.5.

194. See also Thiselton, *1 Corinthians* 17-19, 23, who quotes D. Engels, *Roman Corinth* (Chicago: University of Chicago, 1990), on the likely demand for such products: 'tents for sheltering visitors to the Spring games, awnings for the retailers in the forum, and perhaps sails for merchant ships'. It is not coincidental that we hear of Paul's trade only in connection with Corinth (Acts 18.3).

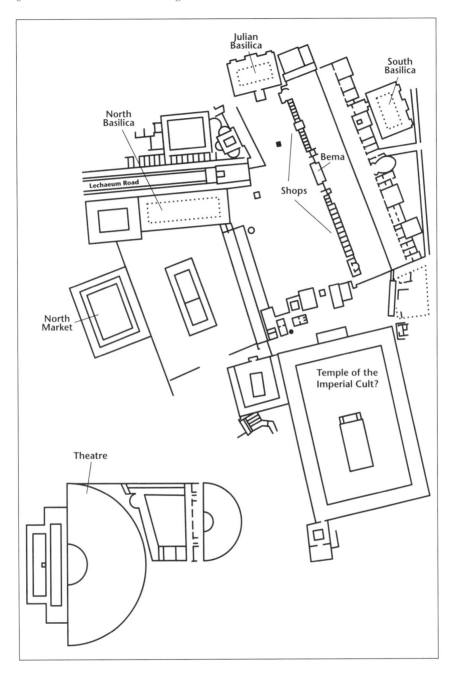

Corinth

Whatever evangelism Paul could undertake while working, his main evangelistic effort was once again in the synagogue, on the Sabbath (18.4). Despite the tiredness which such physical labour must have caused,[195] he did not take the day off but continued to use the synagogue as the obvious place in which to argue his case (§29.5b): 'he kept on arguing his case *(dielegeto)* and trying to persuade *(epeithen)* both Jews and Greeks' (18.4). Here again Luke takes it for granted that there were Greek proselytes and/or God-fearers who attended the Corinthian synagogue on the Sabbath. However, when Silas and Timothy arrived from Macedonia (18.5),[196] Paul may have been able to devote himself (more fully) to preaching. Probably they brought funds from the Macedonian churches.[197] But possibly also the larger team allowed a better balance between work and ministry. The involvement of Silas and Timothy in the early days of the Corinthian church is attested also by Paul.[198]

Paul's own recollection of the impact of his preaching and evangelistic efforts can be said to complement Luke's brief account, though the few details only coincide at one or two points.

- His preaching focused on 'Christ crucified' (1 Cor. 1.23; 2.1)[199] and was evidently addressed to 'Jews and Greeks' (1.22), as Luke had claimed (Acts 18.4); 'testifying that the Messiah was Jesus' is Luke's version of Paul's 'proclaiming Christ crucified'.

- The imminent coming of Jesus and final judgment were evidently as much a part of Paul's message in Corinth (1 Cor. 1.7-8) as it had been in Thessalonica (1 Thess. 1.10; 5.2). Of this Luke says nothing.

- Paul's preaching was characterized more by spiritual than rhetorical impact (1 Cor. 2.1-5), rather as in Thessalonica (1 Thess. 1.5); and the conversions in Corinth were attended by an abundance of spiritual gifts (1 Cor. 1.5, 7), rather as in Galatia (Gal. 3.5). Here too, but rather more strangely, Luke is silent.

195. Cf. 1 Cor. 4.11-12; 2 Cor. 11.27.

196. 1 Thess. 3.1-2 seems to imply that Timothy and Silas were with Paul in Athens (see, e.g., Lake and Cadbury, *Beginnings* 4.224; Kümmel, *Introduction* 257)? Does this mean that Luke knew a tradition which differed from the recollections of Paul (Jervell, *Apg.* 439) or that he has over-compressed his narrative (cf. Bruce, *Acts* 374-75; Barrett, *Acts* 865)? Malherbe notes a variety of possible solutions (*Thessalonians* 70-71), and see n. 226 below.

197. Cf. 2 Cor. 11.8-9; Phil. 4.15; so, e.g., Haenchen, *Acts* 539; Lüdemann, *Early Christianity,* 203.

198. 1 Cor. 4.17; 16.10-11; 2 Cor. 1.19; 1 Thess. 1.1 — written from Corinth.

199. That this preaching (1 Cor. 1.1-2) preceded the writing of 1 Thessalonians undermines Becker's argument that 'in the light of the Corinthian problems the apostle transforms his election theology [of 1 Thessalonians] into a special theology of the cross peculiar to him' (*Paul* 206).

• The resulting church predominantly consisted of lower-status people (slaves and freedmen and women), though also of a few well-educated, well-born and socially/politically influential individuals (1 Cor. 1.26),[200] such as Crispus (Acts 18.8; 1 Cor. 1.14).

Once again, according to Luke, the opposition of the bulk of the Jewish community to the proclamation that 'the Messiah was Jesus'[201] led to a frustrated denunciation: they were rejecting a message to which Gentiles were responding positively and with joy; the obvious corollary was that the Christian message should be taken more directly to the Gentiles (18.6).[202] Whether this was simply an outburst of frustrated concern on Paul's part (cf. 13.51) or a Lukan motif (or both), it is obviously not intended as final.[203] And as before, despite the opposition of the bulk of the Jewish community, some among the listeners were convicted and believed. Titius Justus, possibly referred to again in Col. 4.11, is named first (Acts 18.7). For, although he was a God-fearer (his name suggests that he was a Roman citizen),[204] his house is mentioned, presumably because it provided the base for the new congregation to meet. The dynamics are those of a schism in the synagogue community, but the implication that the new church met next door to the parent body gives the report a peculiar piquancy.

More important was the conviction of Crispus (18.8), the *archisynagōgos* or president of the synagogue, regarding Messiah Jesus as Lord.[205] To win such a prominent Jew was a confirmation that other Jews as well as Paul saw the new teaching as wholly consistent with and a fuller/further expression of their ancestral religion. This is the fourth household to be recorded as committing themselves to the new sect,[206] and again it is not clear whether a family is in view or simply the household slaves and retainers. Paul remembered the occasion well, having personally baptized Crispus (1 Cor. 1.14).

---

200. See, e.g., Clarke, *Secular and Christian Leadership* 41-45.

201. The same approach as in Thessalonica (17.2-3) and Beroea (17.11) is implied.

202. The account uses language similar to that in 13.45, but the denunciation is stronger than in 13.46, and fiercer even than the final denunciation in 28.25-28. The other two denunciations provide a scriptural rationalisation (13.47; 28.26-27). But here an allusion to Ezek. 33.3-5 is judged sufficient (cf. Acts 20.26-27).

203. Paul continues his strategy of going first to the synagogue (18.19; 19.8) and in engaging first with his fellow Jews where possible (28.17, 23). 'The repudiation is directed locally; it refers only to the synagogue in Corinth' (Jervell, *Apg.* 459-60). See further §29.5b. For a more negative judgment on the Lukan motif, see Haenchen, *Acts* 539-40; Sanders, *The Jews in Luke-Acts* ch. 3 and 275-77 (on 18.1-17); but also Jervell's response (459 n. 306).

204. See above, §29 at nn. 217 and 221.

205. 'Trusted the Lord' is sufficient indication that a life-determining decision was made.

206. Cf. Acts 10.48; 16.15, 33.

The note that many other Corinthians who heard (Paul or about Crispus) 'believed and were baptized' (18.8) presumably refers primarily to the rest of the synagogue community (Jews and God-fearers) who joined the breakaway group, but it could include those attracted to the gatherings in the house of Titius Justus. Luke evidently did not share either Paul's knowledge or his opinion that the household of Stephanas were his first converts in Achaia (1 Cor. 16.15). He also missed the opportunity to report the conversion of another local notable, Gaius.[207]

Not least of significance for Paul must have been the vision of the Lord (Christ) which came to him in the night (a dream?) (18.9-10).[208] On this occasion it is the assurance that the Lord would be with him to protect him and to add many to his newly founded church ('my people are many in this city') which is presented as decisive in causing Paul to settle for a long period in Corinth (18.11).[209] And indeed it probably was this token of heavenly approval which caused Paul to make Corinth the first headquarters of what was by now clearly a mission independent both of Antioch and of the local synagogue. Paul does recall a considerable degree of trepidation in his early preaching in Corinth (1 Cor. 2.3), but also an abundance of visionary experiences over the years (2 Cor. 12.7). He also thought of the believing Gentiles as one with God's people.[210] So Luke's portrayal is entirely consistent with Paul's own recollections and subsequent reflections.

That there was much more to the story of the Corinthian church's beginnings is clear from the letter which 'takes the lid off' a first-century church as no other document for the first few centuries does — 1 Corinthians. Luke must have known at least some of the much fuller story, but it was clearly his deliberate style to focus on particular events, which he no doubt regarded as key events in the larger story, even if his resulting history is somewhat spasmodic in character. I have already drawn heavily on the fuller data provided by 1 Corinthians in §30 above (particularly §§30.4-7). But it is worth noting that the social composition of the church, as reflected in 1 Corinthians, must have been a factor from the very early days of its existence. The factional spirit which Paul contests so vigorously in that letter was evidently rooted in some degree in the fact that the Corinthian believers had been

207. 1 Cor. 1.14; Rom. 16.23.

208. Luke often credits visions as playing a decisive role in shaping a policy and determining a course of action (cf. 9.10; 10.3; 11.5; 16.9-10), but there is nothing implausible in that, given the fervency of the new movement. The 'extraordinary character of the revelations' which Paul experienced (2 Cor. 12.7) would not, of course, have made him think lightly of such a vision.

209. The language used ('a great people') echoes Acts 15.14 and may well indicate a scriptural template for the report (Josh. 1.9; Isa. 41.10; 43.5; Jer. 1.8, 19; also Matt. 28.20). Jews and God-fearing Gentiles would be primarily in mind, at least initially (cf. Jervell, *Apg.* 460-61 and n. 312).

210. Rom. 9.25-26; 15.10; 2 Cor. 6.16.

baptized by different individuals (1 Cor. 1.11-16). So there were tensions from the first. And although Apollos presumably arrived on the scene after Paul's departure (cf. Acts 18.27-28), the tensions between the 'not many' intellectual, politically active, higher-status members and the majority rest (1.26), as reflected in the later chapters of the letter, cannot have been long in emerging. Of all this Luke says nothing; as elsewhere, he chooses not to recount such unpleasantness, though no doubt the seeds were already sprouting which produced the unpleasant growths tackled in Paul's subsequent correspondence (§§32.4-7).

c. The Ruling of Gallio

The only other episode Luke chose to relate (or knew of) during (towards the end of?) the eighteen months of Paul's sojourn in Corinth (autumn 51?)[211] was of particular importance for Luke's history, but also, no doubt, for Paul's mission (18.12-17). This was the ruling of the proconsul Gallio on, in effect, the status of the church/assembly newly established by Paul, although it is not clear at what stage during Paul's time in Corinth or during Gallio's time as proconsul the events now described took place. The pattern of Jewish opposition takes a significant turn here. It is 'the Jews' once again who take the lead — that is, obviously, the bulk of the Jewish community following the defection(?) of some of their leading members, or the leaders who succeeded Crispus. But on this occasion, instead of trying to manipulate either the city's elite, as in Antioch and Iconium (13.50; 14.5), or the mob, as in Lystra, Thessalonica and Beroea (14.19; 17.5, 13), they take their case directly to the highest court in the region. The charge is also significantly different — not of fomenting civil and political unrest, as in Thessalonica (17.6-7; cf. 16.20-21), but of 'persuading people to worship God contrary to the law' (18.13). The last phrase is ambiguous, probably deliberately so. On the one hand, it would be intended to trigger Roman suspicion of new sects and various rulings in the past which had been handed down to prevent such sects from making inroads into the traditional and civic cults (with consequent disturbance of civic functions and good order).[212] On the other, it would express the synagogue's real complaint: that Jews and God-fearers affiliated to the synagogue were being encouraged to worship without regard to the (Jewish) law (that is, its distinctively Jewish features).[213]

211. Barrett, *Acts* 2.871. See above, §28.1b.
212. Cf. Lake and Cadbury, *Beginnings* 4.227; Sherwin-White, *Roman Society* 101-102; Winter, *BAFCS* 2.98-103.
213. Weiss noted that the imperial edicts which secured Jewish rights permitted them to live in accordance with their law, so that departure from the law could be counted a breach of the edict (*Earliest Christianity* 304).

The peremptory ruling which followed (there was no need even for Paul to respond), addressed to all the participants as 'Jews' (18.14-15), was of supreme importance for the young Christian church. 'If it was a crime or wicked fraud, (which) you Jews (bring before me), I would have been justified in accepting your complaint. But if it is questions regarding words and labels and the law which you observe, you must see to it yourselves; I have no intention of acting as judge in these matters'.[214]

In the first place, the ruling refuted the suggestion that the believers in Messiah Jesus were in breach of any Roman law, whether in their worship or in their evangelism. In the second place, it affirmed that the disputes between the young church and the synagogue were internal to the Jewish community,[215] issues to be determined within their own jurisdiction.[216] The consequences of such a ruling and precedent from such a prominent Roman authority would have been immense.[217] (1) On the legal and political front, the young churches would be freed at a stroke from the threat of criminal actions against them. They could shelter under the legal protection afforded to synagogues — a vitally important immunity in an empire constantly fearful of combinations and associations which might foster unrest against the state.[218] (2) On the social and theological side it was equally important that the new groups of disciples should be recognized as part of diaspora Judaism. Nascent Christianity was not yet seen as something distinct from its parent religion; the young churches were still recognized

214. As Sherwin-White notes: 'The narrative in fact agrees very well with the workings of *cognitio extra ordinem*. It is within the competence of the judge to decide whether to accept a novel charge or not. In the middle of the second century there were proconsuls of Asia who were ready to refuse to accept even the generally recognized charges against Christians, and to dismiss them out of hand' (*Roman Society* 99-100, 102; see further 99-104). Similarly Taylor, 'Roman Empire' 2486-87. Cf. Omerzu, *Prozess* 263-64, 269.

215. The reference to 'words and labels *(peri logou kai onomatōn)*' (18.15) may refer to the arguments as to whether Jesus was indeed 'Messiah', but also to whether the new *ekklēsia* could indeed be regarded as part of the Jewish community (just another *synagōgē*).

216. Such Jewish jurisdiction is implicit in Paul's submission to synagogue discipline/punishment in 2 Cor. 11.24.

217. Since Corinth modelled itself on Rome (Winter, *Corinth* 19), the influence of a ruling established there would have carried all the more weight; 'this brother [Gallio] of Seneca the philosopher was himself a leading jurist, and therefore his ruling was of importance' (279); see also his 'Rehabilitating Gallio and His Judgement in Acts 18:14-15', *TynB* 57 (2006) 291-308. L. V. Rutgers, 'Roman Policy toward the Jews: Expulsions from the City of Rome during the First Century C.E.', in Donfried and Richardson, eds., *First-Century Rome* 93-116, notes that Rome had no settled policy on such matters, and legal precedents were important (94-96).

218. The precedent had been established a century earlier by the local magistrates in Sardis confirming that the resident Jews had the right to decide their own 'affairs and controversies with one another' (Josephus, *Ant.* 14.235); see further above, §30 n. 90.

to be both continuous and of a piece with the network of Jewish synagogues scattered round most of the Mediterranean world.

With this ruling the case was brusquely dismissed (18.16 — 'he drove them away from the rostrum'). Why 'all' should then seize and beat Sosthenes, the ruler of the synagogue (18.17), is hardly self-evident. If 'all' denotes the Jewish plaintiffs, we presumably have to envisage that they had cause for complaint against Sosthenes: had he also joined the disciples of Messiah Jesus (cf. 1 Cor. 1.1), a second (successive?) president of the synagogue? Or was he more accommodating to the new sect ('the Jews' were not so united after all)? Alternatively, if the 'all' refers to the market layabouts, is this a case where the Jewish community was not so highly regarded within the city,[219] so that the adverse ruling gave opportunity to express antagonism against an ethnic minority group?[220] Either way, Gallio left the Jewish community to its own affairs and to stew in their own juice; 'none of this was a cause of concern for Gallio' (18.17). The ruling, with its beneficial effects for the young church, was left unchanged. The promise to Paul in particular of protection while in Corinth (18.10) had not failed.

How long Paul stayed on in Corinth after Gallio's ruling we do not know. Perhaps he decided to take a break quite soon thereafter (18.18),[221] since he would have been assured by the ruling as to the young church's security and may well have concluded that it could be safely left on its own for some time as a result. Whatever the chronological details, the other important feature of his stay in Corinth was that the settled period gave him opportunity to start and develop correspondence with the churches he had earlier founded. As already noted, Luke tells us nothing of this, but arguably the correspondence begun during Paul's time in Corinth was his greatest legacy left to subsequent Christians. During the eighteen or more months when Corinth served as Paul's mission centre, he certainly wrote one letter (to Thessalonica) and probably (but the point is disputed) two others, 2 Thessalonians and Galatians.

31.5. Paul's First Letter to the Thessalonians

1 Thessalonians is one of three Pauline letters that we can date with reasonable precision within a two-year span.[222] It was obviously written in the roughly two

---

219. Cf. 19.34; but contrast 13.50; 14.2, 19; 17.5, 13. Cf. Barrett's discussion (*Acts* 2.875).

220. See particularly M. V. Hubbard, 'Urban Uprisings in the Roman World: The Social Setting of the Mobbing of Sosthenes', *NTS* 51 (2005) 416-28.

221. Luke uses the expression *hēmeras hikanas* elsewhere (Acts 9.23, 43; 27.7) to denote a lengthy period of time ('many days') — but days rather than weeks (27.7!).

222. The others are 1 Corinthians and Romans (see below, §32.5 and §33.3).

years during which Paul was based in Corinth; that is, probably between 50 and 52, and most likely quite soon after Paul had reached Corinth.[223]

a. Why Did Paul Write 1 Thessalonians?

Paul had evidently been worried about the small group of believers he had left behind in Thessalonica — not surprisingly, in view of the circumstances which resulted in his own hasty departure from there. His anxiety is clearly signalled in 1 Thess. 3.1, 5:[224] when he[225] could no longer bear *(stegontes)* it (not knowing how they were), he had sent back Timothy[226] 'to establish and encourage' them, lest they be 'agitated or disturbed *(sainesthai)* by these afflictions *(thlipsesin)'* (3.2-3),[227] of which he had forewarned them (3.3-4). He was really concerned that the pressures they experienced had caused them to abandon the faith and the Lord to whom they had pledged themselves in baptism (3.5). But Timothy had then returned with very encouraging news — good news, gospel news *(euangelizamenou)* indeed: their faith was strong; they were 'standing firm in the

---

223. Acts 18.4 ('he used to argue every Sabbath in the synagogue') implies both that Paul had to work every other day of the week to sustain himself (see above, §29.5d) and so could only use the Sabbaths for direct evangelism, and that this must have been the state of affairs for some weeks prior to the coming of Silas and Timothy. Holtz notes the lack of greetings in the letter (*Erste Thessalonicher* 11), which suggests an early stage in the life of both churches, before links had been established.

224. Malherbe speaks of Paul's 'utter desolation' (*Thessalonians* 189).

225. The plural 'we' could simply be an 'authorial plural' (Malherbe 70, 86-89).

226. Donfried argues that the 'in Athens' refers to the city in which Paul decided to be left alone, rather than to the place where the decision was made — 'Was Timothy in Athens? Some Exegetical Reflections on 1 Thess. 3.1-3', *Paul, Thessalonica* 209-19.

227. *Thlipsis* ('trouble that causes distress' — BDAG 457) occurs three times in 1 Thessalonians (1.6; 3.3, 7), and again in 2 Thessalonians (1.4, 6); the verb *(thlibō)* is used in 1 Thess. 3.4 and 2 Thess. 1.6, 7. Most assume that the reference is to the suffering which the Thessalonians experienced at the hands of others: NRSV translates 'persecutions'; J. M. G. Barclay, 'Conflict in Thessalonica', *CBQ* 55 (1993) 512-30, prefers 'social harassment' (514). Malherbe thinks that 3.7 indicates 'internal distress' rather than external pressures (*Thessalonians* 77, 193), but Paul's own experience of 'persecution' could be referred to in 3.7, and it does not follow that the one reference (3.7) carries all the others with it. The tie-in with the events recalled in Acts 17.5-9 and their sequel is still the most persuasive. See Holtz, *Erste Korintherbrief* 49, who refers appropriately to 2 Cor. 4.8-12 and 11.23-33; Wanamaker, *1 and 2 Thessalonians* 81, responding directly to Malherbe; and especially T. D. Still, *Conflict at Thessalonica: A Pauline Church and Its Neighbours* (JSNTS 183; Sheffield: Sheffield Academic, 1999): '. . . external (i.e. observable, verifiable), non-Christian opposition which took the forms of verbal harassment, social ostracism, political sanctions and perhaps even some sort of physical abuse, which on the rarest occasions may have resulted in martyrdom' (217).

Lord' (3.6-8). Given uncertainty as to when Timothy was sent back to Thessalonica, how long he was there, and when he came on to Corinth, and assuming that Paul wrote very soon after Timothy's arrival, that must point to a date for writing the letter still quite early in Paul's sojourn in Corinth — probably in 50.[228]

The resultant letter[229] was certainly intended to maintain the line of communication reopened by Timothy's coming[230] and *to encourage the Thessalonian believers in the face of continued suffering and distress*.[231] The conjunction and frequency of words denoting or referring to distress and suffering, whether imposed from without or experienced within, makes it hard to conclude otherwise.[232] This is evidently the dominant pastoral theme, with the problem caused by the death of some of Paul's converts (4.13-18) as a particular case in point.[233] The fact that some had died ('fallen asleep') (4.13) need not imply a

228. Kümmel, *Introduction* 257, and further 258-60: 'several months . . . between Paul's separation from the Thessalonians and the writing of the letter to them' (260); 'four months after Paul's departure from Thessalonica' (Malherbe, *Thessalonians* 72). There is a strong consensus in favour of 50 (or 51) as the date of composition; bibliography in R. Jewett, *The Thessalonian Correspondence: Pauline Rhetoric and Millenarian Piety* (Philadelphia: Fortress, 1986) 53 nn. 18, 19; Schnelle, *History* 44 n. 82. Jewett agrees (spring 50), although he regards that as *preceding* the Jerusalem conference (Gal. 2.1-10); but see §28.1 above.

229. The older fascination with the possibility that 1 Thessalonians is a combination of two (or more) letters is well answered by Kümmel, *Introduction* 260-62, and Schnelle, *History* 47-48; see further Jewett, *Thessalonian Correspondence* 33-46. It is remarkable that Murphy-O'Connor should feel able to speak of features of what appears to be a single letter as 'psychologically impossible', 'totally out of character' and 'out of the question' (*Paul* 105-108); one would have hoped that exegetes had long since learned that such sweeping judgments are impossible to justify in regard to historical individuals of whom too little is known to sustain such judgments. Wanamaker surprisingly opts for the minority view that 2 Thessalonians preceded 1 Thessalonians (*1 and 2 Thessalonians* 37-45), though the considerations adduced never rise beyond the level of one among other plausible, some more compelling, readings of the data; see already Kümmel 263-64.

230. For the possibility that Paul was responding to a letter from Thessalonica brought by Timothy, see Malherbe, *Thessalonians* 75-77; the *peri de* ('now concerning') formula of 4.9, (13) and 5.1 could imply questions raised by the Thessalonians, either by letter or by word through Timothy.

231. See also Tellbe, *Paul between Synagogue and State* 94-104.

232. *Hypomonē* ('patience, endurance') — 1.3; *thlipsis/thlibō* (see n. 227 above) — 1.6; 3.3, 4, 7; *paschō* ('suffer') — 2.2, 14; *hybrizō* ('treat in an insolent and spiteful manner') — 2.2; *agōn* ('a struggle against opposition') — 2.2; *diōkō* ('persecute') — 2.15; *anankē* ('distress, calamity, pressure') — 3.7; some have died (4.13-17).

233. See discussion in M. Konradt, *Gericht und Gemeinde. Eine Studie zur Bedeutung und Funktion von Gerichtsaussagen im Rahmen der paulinischen Ekklesiologie und Ethik im 1 Thess und 1 Kor* (BZNW 117; Berlin: de Gruyter, 2003), 128-34. That Paul turns to the problem only after he had already launched into some more general paraenesis (4.1-12) suggests

lengthy period of time between Paul's departure from Thessalonica and his receiving news via Timothy. The echo of the killing of the Lord Jesus and the
prophets (2.14-15) suggests that the opposition which confronted the recent converts may have been a factor in their early death, even though there is no indication that any had suffered martyrdom as such.[234] But without knowing the age
range of the first converts, and bearing in mind that illness and disease regularly
carried away younger men and women still in their prime, there is little problem
in envisaging circumstances in which two or three had died in the interval before
Timothy returned to Paul.

The other dominant feature of the letter is the *eschatological emphasis* it
reveals both in Paul's earlier preaching and as a factor in their 'distress' and in
Paul's continued teaching and exhortation. He reminds them that in responding
to his message, they had turned to God 'and to wait for his Son from heaven'
(1.10). The Lord's 'coming' (parousia) is a repeated theme in the letter[235] and
presumably also featured in his church-founding teaching, since it was the death
of some before that parousia which caused the worries addressed in 4.13-18.[236]
An unusually high proportion of Paul's use of the title 'Lord *(kyrios)'* occurs in
the Thessalonian letters,[237] suggesting that his early proclamation of Jesus as
Lord was oriented to a marked degree toward Jesus' coming (again) as Lord, or
perhaps more accurately, towards Christ's present exaltation and soon return.[238]
His teaching seems to have included talk of imminent suffering (3.3-4), of God's
'wrath' (1.10) and (final) 'punishment' (4.6). And his continuing concern for
their final salvation,[239] and for presenting them holy, complete and blameless be-

---

that it was not the primary occasion or reason for the letter. This consideration tells against the
thesis of C. R. Nicholl, *From Hope to Despair in Thessalonica: Situating 1 and 2 Thessalonians* (SNTSMS 126; Cambridge: Cambridge University, 2004), that 1 Thessalonians is primarily intended to address a crisis of confidence, even despair, caused by the death of some (the
day of the Lord would be a day of wrath), with the rest of the letter read in light of this thesis.
But he is justified in questioning whether what the letter had in view was an 'eschatological enthusiasm' which was not essentially forward-looking.

234. But see those referred to by Malherbe, *Thessalonians* 62; and Still in n. 227 above.
Tellbe suggests that the Thessalonian Jews accused Paul of being a false prophet (*Paul between
Synagogue and State* 107-15).

235. *Parousia* — 2.19; 3.13; 4.15; 5.23; 2 Thess. 2.1, 8, 9; half of all the Pauline uses of
the term come in Thessalonians; only one of the seven in the other Paulines refers to Christ's
parousia (1 Cor. 15.23), whereas six of the seven in Thessalonians refer to Christ's parousia
(only 2 Thess. 2.9 does not).

236. See also §29.7e above.

237. About 16 percent of all the occurences in Paul, when the Thessalonian letters themselves make up less than 8 percent of the Pauline corpus.

238. Cf. Hahn, *Titles* 89-103.

239. *Sōzō* — 1 Thess. 2.16; 2 Thess. 2.10; *sōtēria* — 1 Thess. 5.8-9; 2 Thess. 2.13. 'Sal-

fore the Lord Jesus at his parousia (2.19; 3.13; 5.24), is obvious. In particular, they need not worry about those who have died before Christ's coming, for the latter would in no way be disadvantaged. On the contrary, at the 'last trump' 'the dead in Christ' will rise first and will join those still alive to meet the Lord 'in the air', to welcome him and escort him on his triumphant return to earth (4.13-18).[240] Their primary concern should rather be to ready themselves for the coming of 'the day of the Lord' (like a thief in the night),[241] which otherwise might catch them unprepared, and to live lives accordingly (5.1-9), exhortations which presumably featured in Paul's earlier preaching too (4.2; 5.1).

b. What Does the Letter Reveal about the Thessalonian Believers and Their Context?

One of the more fascinating aspects of the letter is the difficulty it poses to later readers in using it to envisage anything much about the lives of the recipients or their circumstances, apart from their initial experience in conversion (1.5-6; 2.13) and the 'persecution' they evidently continued to experience (no doubt as reported by Timothy) (3.6-7). We glean something of Paul's preaching and teaching, as already indicated, as also of his own tactics (2.9) and deep concerns for the young church (3.1-5). There are possible allusions to criticisms made of Paul's methods and message in 2.3-7[242] and some self-defence

---

vation' for Paul, it should not be forgotten, is the future goal towards which Paul looked and directed his converts (see my *Theology of Paul* 471).

240. The image indicated by the combination of terms *parousia* (4.15) and *apantēsis* ('meet') (4.17) is of a visit by a high-ranking official or ruler to a city with his entourage, when he would be met on his approach by a deputation of leading citizens and escorted into the city (E. Peterson, *TDNT* 1.380-81; A. Oepke, *TDNT* 5.859-60; Crossan and Reed, *Paul* 167-71; see further my *Theology of Paul* 299-300). Wanamaker (*1 and 2 Thessalonians* 175-76) and Malherbe (*Thessalonians* 277) recognize the technical usage but do not see how it fits here; but we should not assume that Paul had a completely consistent conception of how the parousia and attendant events would be related (see my *Theology of Paul* 314-15, 492-93). As Holtz notes (*Erste Thessalonicher* 203), the key factor is that the meeting is envisaged as taking place on the Lord's *descent* from heaven (4.16 — *katabēsetai ap' ouranou*), that is, to earth.

241. This is a classic example of a motif of Jesus' teaching which had been absorbed into earliest Christian paraenesis without it being thought necessary, each time it was used, to recall that Jesus first coined the image (see further *Jesus Remembered* §8.1e).

242. 'Our appeal is not from deceit, nor from impure motives, nor with deceit. . . . Neither did we ever use flattering language, as you know, nor any pretext for greed, as God is our witness. Nor did we seek glory from human beings, either from you or from others. Although we might have made harsh demands on you as apostles of Christ' (2.3, 5-7). 'Was he being compared to the stereotype of the crude and avaricious wandering Cynic philosopher peddling his message?' (Brown, *Introduction* 461); see further Holtz, *Erste Thessalonicher* 93-95. Malherbe, however, sees standard language used to describe the ideal philosopher and thinks

in 2.9-10.[243] However, apart from 1.9 ('turned to God from idols'), we gain little sense of the religious competition in Thessalonica, even though we know
from other sources that the imperial cult was strong[244] and that the cults of
Serapis and Dionysus were prominent and well integrated with the civic
cult.[245] It is certainly possible to read 4.4[246] against the background of the
strong sexual element in the mystery cult of Cabirus, the most distinctive of the
Thessalonian cults;[247] it is arguable that the dismissive reference to those who

---

that hypotheses of Paul responding to opposition in Thessalonica 'shatter on the cordiality and
warmth of the letter' (*Thessalonians* 79-80, 141-44). According to Malherbe (66), the use of
topoi common to Greek philosophical discourses (notably 2.7-8) suggests that the
Thessalonian believers had listened with understanding to popular philosophers; see further his
'"Gentle as a Nurse": The Cynic Background to 1 Thessalonians 2', *NovT* 12 (1970) 203-17,
and 'Exhortations in 1 Thessalonians', *NovT* 25 (1983) 238-56, both reprinted in *Paul and the
Popular Philosophers* (Minneapolis: Fortress, 1989) 35-48, 49-66. See further J. G. Cook, 'Pagan Philosophers and 1 Thessalonians', *NTS* 52 (2006) 514-32.

243. 'You are witnesses, and God, how holy, just and blameless we were to you believers' (2.10).

244. See J. R. Harrison, 'Paul and the Imperial Gospel at Thessaloniki', *JSNT* 25 (2002)
71-96. The presence of the imperial cult was presumably a factor in the accusations referred to
in Acts 17.7 (see above, §31.1c).

245. C. Edson, 'Cults of Thessalonica', *HTR* 41 (1948) 153-204; K. P. Donfried, 'Cults
of Thessalonica', *NTS* 31 (1985) 336-56, reprinted in *Paul, Thessalonica* 21-48; Jewett,
Thessalonian Correspondence 123-32; H. Koester, 'Archaeology and Paul in Thessalonike',
Paul and His World 38-54. The socio-religious situation in Thessalonica is well summarized by
Wanamaker, *1 and 2 Thessalonians* 3-6.

246. It is God's will 'that each of you know how *heautou skeuos ktasthai*'. The phrase *to
heautou skeuos ktasthai* has caused much puzzlement. *Skeuos* can mean 'instrument' and have the
sense 'penis' (BDAG 928), which fits well with the strong phallic symbolism in the cults of Dionysus and Cabirus (Donfried, *Paul, Thessalonica* 30-31). Hence the regular translation 'control
your own body', with strong sexual overtones (so, e.g., Wanamaker, *1 and 2 Thessalonians* 152-
53; J. E. Smith, 'Another Look at 4Q416 2 ii.21, a Critical Parallel to First Thessalonians 4:4',
CBQ 63 [2001] 499-504). But '(gain) control' is an unusual sense for *ktasthai*, which more naturally means 'gain possession, acquire'. The other ancient interpretation, 'acquire a wife', has parallels in the phrase 'to take a wife' and still conveys some implication of threat from sexual license
but also depends on an unusual sense for *skeuos* (favoured by Holtz, *Erste Thessalonicher* 157-58;
B. Witherington, *Women in the Earliest Churches* [SNTSMS 59; Cambridge: Cambridge University, 1988] 67-68; Malherbe, *Thessalonians* 226-28; M. Konradt, '*Eidenai hekaston hymōn to
heautou skeuos ktasthai . . .* Zu Paulus' sexualethischer Weisung in 1 Thess 4,4f.', *ZNW* 92 [2001]
128-35). J. M. Bassler, '*Skeuos*: A Modest Proposal for Illuminating Paul's Use of Metaphor in
1 Thessalonians 4:4', in White and Yarbrough, eds., *The Social World of the First Christians* 53-
66, builds hypothesis upon hypothesis by proposing that *skeuos* refers to virgin partners (cf.
1 Thess. 4.4 with 1 Cor. 7.37) — *skeuos = parthenos;* but the interpretation of *parthenos* in 1 Corinthians 7 as denoting spiritual marriage is less than likely (see §32 n. 256).

247. Donfried, *Paul, Thessalonica* 25-31; Jewett, *Thessalonian Correspondence* 127-
32, 165-78, reads in a lot in his elaborate suggestion for the success of Paul's proclamation: that

say 'Peace and security' (5.3) is an allusion to imperial sloganeering;[248] and the warnings against drunkenness (5.6-8) could certainly have cult or association banquets in mind.[249] But otherwise the paraenesis in chs. 4–5 is fairly standard, albeit with a strong eschatological motivation (5.1-9; cf. Rom. 13.11-14). We could even deduce some hesitation within the Thessalonian assembly about spiritual enthusiasm and prophecy: 'Do not quench the Spirit; do not despise prophecy' (5.19-20).[250] But even if the case is pressed for 'mirror-reading' from the letter the situation addressed, the results are meagre.[251]

Of the social composition of the church, their status in Thessalonica and involvement in the life of the city, we learn nothing, beyond some possible hints. If the church met in Jason's house (Acts 17.5), then we can think at most of a group of about forty or forty-five. 1 Thess. 1.9 (they had 'turned to God from idols') is sometimes pressed to the conclusion that the Thessalonian church was exclusively Gentile in composition;[252] a Jewish minority, however, is by no means excluded, as in fact suggested by Acts 17.4 ('some' Jews, 'a great many' Greeks, and 'not a few' leading women).[253] More problematic is the contrast be-

---

the integration of the Cabirus cult into the civic cult had left a vacuum for the craftsmen and labourers of Thessalonica who had previously seen Cabirus as their redeemer figure and principal benefactor, a vacuum which Paul's message of the new saviour figure, Jesus, filled (particularly 165-66). See Koester's scathing comments: 'From Paul's Eschatology to the Apocalyptic Scheme of 2 Thessalonians', *Paul and His World* 55-69 (here 57-58).

248. H. L. Hendrix, 'Archaeology and Eschatology at Thessalonica', in B. A. Pearson, ed., *The Future of Christianity,* H. Koester FS (Minneapolis: Fortress, 1991) 107-18, with bibliography 112 nn. 13, 14; von Brocke, *Thessaloniki* 167-85; Tellbe, *Paul between Synagogue and State* 125-26 (further 126-30).

249. See above, §30 n. 232.

250. Jewett deduces from 1 Thess. 5.12-13 that the status and action of the Thessalonian leaders was being criticized by an ecstatically inclined congregation (*Thessalonian Correspondence* 102-104), but in that case the exhortations to the congregation in 5.19-20 would have been rather foolhardy, even with the accompanying command that they (the same congregation) should 'test everything' (5.21).

251. While Jewett's warning is valid (*Thessalonian Correspondence* 118) that we should not assume that all the congregation's troubles came from outside (as suggested by Acts 17), the mirror reflection is *en ainigmati* (1 Cor. 13.12), too enigmatic, too puzzling (REB) for firm conclusions to be drawn. Donfried summarizes the argument of his 'The Epistolary and Rhetorical Context of 1 Thessalonians 2:1-12' in K. P. Donfried and J. Beutler, eds., *The Thessalonians Debate: Methodological Discord or Methodological Synthesis?* (Grand Rapids: Eerdmans, 2000) 31-60, as follows: 'One should neither define 1 Thess. 2.1-12 as an apology nor read this text in mirror fashion as if Paul were countering specific charges that had been leveled against him' (*Paul, Thessalonica* xxxi); further discussion of 2.1-12 in Part 1 of the *Thessalonians Debate* volume.

252. The fact that Paul does not quote from the OT in 1 Thessalonians (though see n. 89 above) could suggest an audience for the letter unfamiliar with Scripture.

253. Barnett regards 1 Thessalonians as 'Jewish Christianity adapted for non-Jewish readers. Its messianic and apocalyptic categories of thought are thoroughly Jewish' (*Birth* 43).

tween, on the one hand, the inferences which may be drawn from 2 Cor. 8.2 that the churches of Macedonia were very poor, and from 1 Thess. 4.11 ('work with your hands') that the Thessalonian believers were manual labourers, and, on the other, the implication of Acts 17.4 that Paul recruited not a few influential people during his brief mission. But again, once allowance is made for Luke's hyperbole,[254] a picture not so very different from that of 1 Corinthians emerges: a church composed predominantly of lower-status freedmen and artisans, with a smaller number of higher-status individuals more accustomed to and capable of giving leadership (1 Thess. 5.12-13).[255]

More striking, however, is the contrast with 1 Corinthians, in that 1 Thessalonians gives the impression of a small, rather introverted group, active in spreading their message (1.8), but otherwise too caught up in their own beliefs of an imminent dawning of 'the day of the Lord' and of their own salvation to be much concerned with questions of involvement with the life of the city in which they lived. Two verses give a flavour of the mood of the letter (Paul's own perspective at the time of writing) and of the perspective he encouraged the Thessalonians to adopt.

- 4.11-12 — 'We urge you . . . to make it your ambition to live a quiet life (hēsychazein),[256] to mind your own affairs, and to work with your own hands, just as we instructed you, so that you may behave properly towards outsiders (tous exō) and be dependent on no one'.
- 5.4-7 — '. . . you are all sons of light[257] and sons of day. We are not of the night or of darkness. . . . Those who sleep, sleep at night, and those who get drunk are drunk at night. But we are of the day. . . .'

254. Besides which, Luke's account focuses only on the initial reactions and says nothing of others who may have been converted during the mission (probably) based in Jason's house.

255. 'The fragments of available evidence point to a somewhat narrower range of social levels in the Thessalonian church than in other Pauline congregations; it appears to have consisted mainly of what Wayne Meeks describes as the "typical" Christian in the Pauline churches, "a free artisan or small trader"' (Jewett, *Thessalonian Correspondence* 120-22); similarly Riesner, *Paul's Early Period* 350, 376-78; see also Ascough, *Paul's Macedonian Associations* 169-76.

256. 'Of conduct that does not disturb the peace. Christian leaders endeavoured to keep their members free of anything that might be construed as disturbance of public order' (BDAG 440). *Hēsychazein* 'had long described withdrawal from active participation in political and social affairs' (Malherbe, *Thessalonians* 247). 'Paul is here proscribing the boisterous political rabble-rousing behaviour by clients on behalf of their patrons in *politeia*' (Winter, *Welfare* 48-53).

257. The antithesis between 'sons of light' and 'sons of darkness' is particularly typical of the Qumran community (e.g., 1QS 1.9; 2.16-17; 3.24-26; 1QM 1.1, 9-16).

The implication of 4.11-12 is of a group operating with an 'insider/outsider' attitude,[258] who should keep their heads down, avoid entanglements with wider society, and provide as far as possible for their own needs.[259] The implication of 5.4-7 is of a group whose self-awareness was constituted by apocalyptic antitheses between day and night, light and darkness, being awake and being asleep, being sober and being drunk.[260] As those who belong to the day, to the light, they should have as little as possible to do with those who belong to the night, to darkness.[261]

Linking all these emphases and clues together, the impression I receive is of a group whose eschatological message and persecution from fellow residents had turned them to a large extent in upon themselves — what we today might classify as a characteristically sectarian (or cultic) mentality. The letter counsels that they should let their lives be wholly determined by the prospective and imminent return of Christ; they should live as those for whom the day has already dawned, their quality of moral living distinguishing them from those still of the night; they should keep themselves to themselves, and do what has to be done to support themselves, but otherwise maintain their focus on being ready to welcome Christ in his parousia.[262] The Thessalonian congregation, in other words,

258. J. S. Kloppenborg, '*Philadelphia, theodidaktos* and the Dioscuri: Rhetorical Engagements in 1 Thessalonians 4.9-12', *NTS* 39 (1993) 265-89, notes that Paul's use of *philadelphia* ('fraternal love') is highly unusual, since elsewhere it 'is almost unanimously used of actual kin relations', whereas Paul applies the term to extra-familial relationships (272-74); but a new sense of family (Paul makes intensive use of *adelphos,* 'brother', throughout the two Thessalonian letters) probably carried the implication of an equivalent restriction of fraternal love to the (new, fictive) family-circle.

259. Malherbe sees a detachment in attitude (as with Seneca) rather than in action from society (*Thessalonians* 246-52), but his discussion (continued in 252-60, also 56 and 62) does not take enough account of the fact that the attitude inculcated was not that of the Stoic but that of apocalyptic eschatology, as reflected in NT categorization elsewhere of others as 'those outside' (Mark 4.11 — 'the mystery of the kingdom'; 1 Cor. 5.12-13 — judgment) and by the immediate sequel (1 Thess. 4.13–5.11).

260. On the imagery see Plevnik, *Paul and the Parousia* 105-106, 108-10; Dunn, *Romans* 786-88 (on the parallel Rom. 13.11-12).

261. Brown speaks of 'the strange exclusivity of this Christian group whose converts abandoned the public religion' (*Introduction* 460). Here again Malherbe, *Thessalonians* 294-96, 305-306, does not give enough weight to the implications of antitheses so expressive of an eschatological and apocalyptic (rather than a philosophical) mind-set.

262. The *ataktoi* ('disorderly, obstinate, insubordinate') who are to be admonished in 5.14 are probably best understood as those who refused to buckle down to this sort of self-discipline while they waited — the same people probably subsequently in view in 2 Thess. 3.6-12 (cf. Jewett, *Thessalonian Correspondence* 104-105; Holtz, *Erste Thessalonicher* 251-52; Wanamaker, *1 and 2 Thessalonians* 196-97). Ascough draws parallels with disturbances within voluntary associations (*Paul's Macedonian Associations* 181-84). See also below, n. 285.

was being encouraged to be a sort of Christian equivalent to the Qumran community,[263] and forerunner of the many apocalyptic sects which have spattered the
history of Christianity.[264]

This is a sobering conclusion to reach — especially for those who regard
the earliest churches as models to be emulated by their modern successors, and
especially for those who want to treat Paul's letters as timeless, to be dutifully
heeded as applicable to every and any situation in the present. Of course, there
are many elements and features of the letter which do emphasize Christian
distinctives relevant to all times and circumstances: most obviously the repeated
stress on 'faith, love and hope';[265] 'Lord' hardly ceases to be Paul's favourite title for Christ; Paul's distinctive 'in Christ' is already in play;[266] and the
kerygmatic formulae echoed in 4.14 and 5.10[267] assuredly confirm that these
emphases were already regular features of Paul's preaching. Yet, it is also true
that 1 Thessalonians lacks the emphases which so distinguish the Pauline
Hauptbriefe (Romans, 1-2 Corinthians and Galatians) and which much more
clearly define Pauline theology. Particularly noticeable are the absence of any
clear allusion to, let alone statement of, Paul's most distinctive formulation of
the gospel as 'justification by faith',[268] and the denunciation of 'the Jews' in

263. Donfried finds several 'possible contacts between Paul and the Essene community
in Jerusalem' (*Paul, Thessalonica* xxxiv-xxxv, 7-13, 221-31), but the links may simply reflect
shared background rather than 'contact'.

264. This is in line with the earlier view represented by Lightfoot, von Dobschütz and
others; see Jewett's brief review (*Thessalonian Correspondence* 138-40). Jewett's rebuttal
(140) fails to appreciate the extent to which Paul himself shared that view. And if a strong realized element ('millenarian radicalism') was already prominent in the Thessalonian church prior
to the writing of 1 Thessalonians, as he argues ('They refused to prepare for a future *parousia*
of Christ because in principle they were experiencing and embodying it already in their ecstatic
activities' — 176), then Paul would surely have responded emphatically on that point. It is
hardly necessary to explain the dismay caused by the death of some before the parousia in
terms of 'divinization' drawn from the Cabirus cult (176-77), or that the church's leaders required support because they had been criticized for not manifesting the divinity of the redeemer
figure in their own persons (170). This is reading-in on a grand scale. A stronger realized element is indicated only later, in 2 Thess. 2.2, but otherwise the emphasis on 'impending crisis'
(Jewett 161) and 'imminent salvation' (Wanamaker, *1 and 2 Thessalonians* 10) seems apposite,
though Wanamaker himself largely follows Jewett.

265. *Pistis* ('faith') — 1.3, 8; 3.2, 5-7, 10; 5.8; *agapē* ('love') — 1.3; 3.6, 12; 5.8, 13;
elpis ('hope') — 1.3; 2.19; 4.13; 5.8; as a triad — 1.3 and 5.8.

266. 'In Christ' — 2.14; 4.16; 5.18; 'in the Lord' — 3.8; 4.1; 5.12.

267. See above, §21.4e.

268. This formulation becomes a basis for tracing a development in Paul's theology (see
the brief review and bibliography in Schnelle, *History* 53-55; also *Paul* 188-91). But how could
Paul have taken the stand that he did in Jerusalem and Antioch without adopting a clear view on
the non-applicability of 'works of the law' to Gentiles or a teaching which had to apply to

2.14-16.[269] Of course, there may be good reasons for this, some of which we will explore below (§31.7). There is no need to doubt or deny that Paul's gospel in Thessalonica called for a response of faith.[270] And the offence of 2.14-16 can be softened by noting the particular circumstances which provoked Paul to speak with a momentary petulance and anger to which he never fell prey again in his subsequent correspondence. But when 1 Thessalonians is set alongside Paul's other letters, it is hard to avoid the deduction that in his preaching in Thessalonica and in this his first extant letter, he let an apocalyptic and eschatological perspective dominate his teaching and his counsel to an extent which he subsequently came either to regret or to modify significantly.[271]

---

mixed congregations? Lohse justifiably warns against overdependence on word statistics (*Paulus* 211-14).

269. The sharpness of the denunciation causes many to infer that the passage is a later interpolation, but Paul was evidently sensitive about 'persecution' of Gentile believers by traditionalist Jews (Gal. 4.29); see also my *Partings* (²2006) 193 and n. 32; *Theology of Paul* 507 n. 40; and further C. J. Schlueter, *Filling Up the Measure: Polemical Hyperbole in 1 Thessalonians 2.14-16* (JSNTS 98; Sheffield: Sheffield Academic, 1994); Still, *Conflict at Thessalonica* 24-45; Davies, 'Paul' 717-19; Malherbe, *Thessalonians* 167-79; Schnelle, *Paul* 179-81; Konradt, *Gericht und Gemeinde* 73-93. As Schwemer notes, the 'wrath' envisaged could refer to the recent disasters experienced in Israel — Antipas's defeat by Aretas, Caligula's attempt to have his statue erected in the Jerusalem temple, Agrippa's horrific death, increasing political unrest, and the famines of the 40s ('Verfolger' 173-75); similarly M. Bockmuehl, '1 Thessalonians 2:14-16 and the Church in Jerusalem', *TynB* 52 (2001) 1-31. Weiss suspected that the lines 'were written shortly after the breach with the synagogue at Corinth' (*Earliest Christianity* 295). Hengel quotes R. L. Rubinstein, *My Brother Paul* (New York: Harper and Row, 1972) 115, as speaking of a 'family dispute' and as claiming that Paul's 'harshness [in 1 Thess. 2.14-16] was not unlike that of the members of the Community of the Scrolls' ('Early Christianity' 7-8). J. S. Lamp, 'Is Paul Anti-Jewish? *Testament of Levi* 6 in the Interpretation of 1 Thessalonians 2:13-16', *CBQ* 65 (2003) 408-27, draws particular attention to the close parallel between 2.16c and *T. Levi* 6.11. Grindheim sees 2.14-16 as 'a characteristically Pauline contribution to the intra-Jewish discussion regarding the sins of Israel. Paul's verdict is not fundamentally different from the views found in apocalyptic literature. He understands the history of Israel to be a history of apostasy' ('Apostate Turned Prophet' 546-50, here 549).

270. Kim's 'Justification by Grace and through Faith in 1 Thessalonians', *Paul and the New Perspective* 85-100, is an over-reaction, though understandable in the light of developmental theses as in §27 n. 298 above. See also Riesner, *Paul's Early Period* 394-403; 'the formulae of faith appearing frequently in this writing presuppose that the Thessalonians were already familiar with information the apostle only needed to recall by means of keywords' (415).

271. But see also above, §29.7e.

31.6. Paul's Second Letter to the Thessalonians

Opinion is divided roughly 50/50 as to whether Paul himself wrote 2 Thessalonians or someone later, in his name.[272] Given the diversity of Paul's undisputed letters, the arguments claimed to be decisive for the latter position are quite surprising, since they seem to depend on a rather wooden use of word- and style-statistics and an unwillingness either to allow sufficiently for different situations calling forth different responses or to accept that Paul could have so written (the same is true of 1 Thess. 2.14-16).[273] The cooler reality is that there are no decisive stylistic reasons against attributing the letter to Paul, bearing in mind the changed circumstances presupposed in 2 Thessalonians[274] (not to mention any influence from a secretary or amanuensis — Timothy?);[275] and that while it is hardly difficult to envisage several possible scenarios to explain why the letter was written,[276] those who advocate a later (pseudonymous) authorship are much

272. In recent years the arguments for non-Pauline authorship put forward by W. Trilling, *Untersuchungen zum zweiten Thessalonischerbrief* (Leipzig: St. Benno, 1972), also *Der zweite Brief an die Thessalonischer* (EKK 14; Zürich: Benziger,1980) 22-26, have been widely persuasive, particularly in German scholarship (bibliography in Schnelle, *History* 317; otherwise Wilckens, *Theologie* 1/3.66).

273. Schnelle, e.g., certainly exaggerates when he speaks of 'a fundamental difference' between the eschatological instructions in 1 and 2 Thessalonians, and of 2 Thess. 2.1-12 envisaging 'a completely different course of events' which 'deviates so strongly' from that in 1 Thessalonians (*History* 316, 318). On such criteria many writers would find some of their works being classed as 'inauthentic'! Murphy-O'Connor comments scathingly: 'They invoke differences of style and vocabulary, but in a highly selective way which prejudges the conclusion' (*Paul* 110).

274. See particularly Jewett, *Thessalonian Correspondence* 3-18 (particularly 10-12); Wanamaker, *1 and 2 Thessalonians* 17-28 (particularly 21-28); Malherbe, *Thessalonians* 364-74 (particularly 365-68). 'What modern Pauline scholarship in fact has discovered is that Paul's style and vocabulary are brilliantly situational; the variations are comprehensible when one takes the unique circumstances of each letter into account' (Jewett 12). 'There is either no, or at most insufficient, attention given to how the changes in the situation in Thessalonica may have caused Paul to consciously adopt a different style at points to achieve his present goal, not the one he had when he wrote 1 Thessalonians. All Paul's letters, after all, have their peculiarities (von Dobschütz 1909: 43)' (Malherbe 367).

275. Cf. Donfried, *Paul, Thessalonica* 55-56; see above, §29.8c.

276. 'II Thess is most comprehensible . . . if Paul himself wrote II Thess a few weeks after he had written I Thess, when the first letter was still in his mind' (Kümmel, *Introduction* 268). Koester's counter-argument that 'such a situation [as is implied in 2.1-2] is hardly possible just a few weeks after the writing of the first letter' (*Introduction* 2.242) betrays a lack of familiarity with apocalyptic or enthusiastic sects. Donfried has no difficulty in envisaging one of Paul's co-workers sending the letter 'not long after' 1 Thessalonians ('2 Thessalonians and the Church of Thessalonica', *Paul, Thessalonica* 49-67 [here 56]).

more hard-pressed to envisage the situation which might have called for the letter to be written at a later date.[277]

More or less all agree that the key to the situation envisaged is 2.1-3:

> [1]With reference to the coming *(parousia)* of our Lord Jesus Christ and our assembling with him, we beg you [2]not to be quickly shaken out of your composure, nor to be alarmed either by spirit or by word or by letter, as though from us, to the effect that the day of the Lord has come *(enestēken)*. [3]Do not let anyone deceive you in an any way; for [it will not come] unless the apostasy happens first and the man of lawlessness, the son of perdition, is revealed.

It is important to observe that the issue addressed takes up one of the main themes of 1 Thessalonians — 'the coming *(parousia)* of the Lord Jesus Christ'.[278] After the usual epistolary opening (1.1-2), the regular thanksgiving (1.3-4) and prayer (1.11-12) are elaborated to recall and reinforce the other main themes of 1 Thessalonians:

- the persecutions *(diōgmos)* and afflictions *(thlipsis)* which they were still enduring, possibly at a more severe level (1.4);
- the suffering which will precede and make them worthy of the kingdom of God (1.5);
- the triumphant revelation of the Lord Jesus from heaven with his mighty angels (1.7) to repay those who afflict them with affliction (1.6), to relieve those afflicted (1.7), and to inflict punishment *(ekdikēsis)* on those who do not know God and those who have not obeyed the gospel of the Lord Jesus (1.8-9), a glorious coming on that day (1.10).[279]

---

277. 'No forgery hypothesis so far has been able to offer a credible explanation for the origin of the letter and its relation to 1 Thessalonians' (Wanamaker, *1 and 2 Thessalonians* 28), with reference to I. H. Marshall, *1 and 2 Thessalonians* (NCBC; London: Marshall, Morgan and Scott, 1983) 40-45; it is 'difficult to imagine a setting where a letter specifically addressed to the Thessalonians by Paul would be relevant and convincing to a non-Thessalonian church some thirty or more years after the Apostle's death' (Donfried, *Paul, Thessalonica* 66).

278. See n. 235 above.

279. *Thlipsis* — see above, n. 227; suffering — 1 Thess. 2.14; 2 Thess. 1.5; worthy of the kingdom of God — 1 Thess. 2.12; 2 Thess. 1.5; angelic participation in the parousia — 1 Thess. 4.16; 2 Thess. 1.7; the vengeance/punishment *(ekdikēsis)* of the Lord — 1 Thess. 4.6; 2 Thess. 1.8; the saints to share in his glory — 1 Thess. 2.12; 2 Thess. 1.10; believers assembling with the Lord at his parousia (1 Thess. 4.14-17; 2 Thess. 2.1); the day of the Lord — 1 Thess. 5.2, 4; 2 Thess. 1.10; 2.2. The fierceness of the expectation of judgment in 2 Thess. 1.6-9 is anticipated in the talk of divine 'wrath' (1 Thess. 1.10; 2.16; 5.9). Note also 'the word of the Lord' in 1 Thess. 4.15 — probably a word of prophecy (see my *Theology of Paul* 303 n. 45; Malherbe, *Thessalonians* 267-70) — and the reference to 'spirit' and 'word' in 2 Thess.

The problem, however, seems to be that the last motif, 'the day of the Lord', had become a matter of contention and confusion among the Thessalonian believers, and to that subject Paul turns immediately after the opening preliminaries.[280] Evidently there had been reports, involving a word of prophecy or some teaching given or some letter claimed to be from Paul or some combination of two or three, to the effect that the day of the Lord had already come (2.2).[281] How 'the day of the Lord' was related to 'the coming of the Lord Jesus Christ' (2.1) is not clear. The obvious implication of Paul's earlier teaching was that the two were synonymous (1 Thess. 5.2-5), both still future-imminent, the parousia emphasizing the glorious return of Jesus, the 'day of the Lord' picking up the threatening overtones which had been a classic feature of its usage in the prophets.[282] But something had caused many of the Thessalonian believers to conclude that the climactic end events were already in train — perhaps as a deduction from the belief that in Jesus' resurrection 'the resurrection of the dead' had already begun;[283] perhaps stimulated by Paul writing in 1 Thess. 2.16 that God's wrath 'has come upon them [the Jews who opposed the gospel] *eis telos*'.[284] The result seemingly had been that some of the Thessalonian believers had concluded that the parousia and final judgment were almost upon them. In consequence they were behaving irresponsibly *(ataktōs)* (3.6, 11) by failing to work and meddling in others' affairs (3.11)[285] — presumably eating others' bread and proving a bur-

---

2.2. The earlier influential study by W. Wrede, *Die Echtheit des zweiten Thessalonischerbrief untersucht* (Leipzig: Heinrichs, 1903), had made much of such parallels: they could hardly be explained as accidental or by Paul 'slavishly following' his earlier letter. Similarly Schnelle: 'Only the hypothesis of the literary dependence of 2 Thessalonians on 1 Thessalonians can adequately explain these agreements' (*History* 321-22). But 'slavishly following' is an unacceptable exaggeration, and the parallels of language, thought and sequence are readily explicable in letters to the same church, written by the same person, within a few months of each other, and to the same situation as it had developed within that time frame.

280. *Pace* Malherbe, who thinks that to treat response to the error indicated in 2.2 as Paul's main concern is 'an unjustified assumption that minimizes the importance Paul attached to behavior in chaps. 1 and 3' (*Thessalonians* 351-52); compare, however, the delay in 1 Thessalonians before Paul addresses the concerns indicated in 1 Thess. 4.13-18.

281. Paul does not say how he knew this but later mentions that he had 'heard' about the goings-on in Thessalonica (3.11); the Christian grapevine was already well developed (see §30.8 above).

282. Isa. 2.12-17; 22.5; Ezek. 7.5-12; 13.6-9; 30.3; Joel 1.15; 2.11, 31; Amos 5.18-20; Obad. 15; Zeph. 1.14-15; Mal. 4.5.

283. See above, §23.4a. The tension, after all, is not so dissimilar from that in Jesus' teaching that the kingdom of God has come, and is yet to come; see *Jesus Remembered* §§12.4-6.

284. *Eis telos* can be variously rendered: 'in the end, finally', 'to the end, until the end', 'forever, through all eternity' (BDAG 998).

285. English translations of 3.11 cannot reproduce the word-play in the Greek — *mēden*

den to the rest (3.8)[286] — a state of affairs already threatening in the earlier letter (1 Thess. 5.14) but given an added seriousness and urgency by the irresponsible belief about the day of the Lord having already come.

At all events Paul was so alarmed by the news of this new 'spin' to his earlier teaching that he wrote immediately on hearing about it. That is to say, the letter was most likely written from Corinth within the same year as 1 Thessalonians — 50 or 51.[287] To be noted is the fact that the crisis caused by this new teaching was generated purely from within — no doubt under the pressure of continued opposition and harassment from local authority figures and from within the synagogue,[288] but primarily, it would appear, out of internal tensions regarding and reflection on the parousia of Jesus. This, it should also be noted, is consistent with the portrayal of the Thessalonian church drawn from 1 Thessalonians (§31.5) — of a group wholly focused on the hope of the parousia, the principal emphasis of their (successful) witness and proclamation, doing what they had to do to maintain body and soul, but otherwise with their backs largely turned to the world around them.

Paul's response was to outline what he believed was still to take place before that great and terrible day — the coming of 'the man of lawlessness, the son of perdition' (2.3) — introducing one of the most enigmatic passages in the NT (2.3-12):

> [3]That day will not come unless the apostasy happens first and the man of lawlessness, the son of perdition, is revealed. [4]He opposes and exalts himself over every so-called god or object of worship, so that he takes his seat in the temple of God, proclaiming himself to be God. . . . [6]And you know what is now restraining him, so that he may be revealed in his own time. [7]For the mystery of lawlessness is already at work; only he who restrains him will do so until he is out of the way. [8]And then the lawless one will be revealed, whom the Lord Jesus will do away with by the breath of his mouth and destroy at the appearance of his coming, [9]whose coming is by the activity of the Satan, in every miracle and sign and wonder that is false, [10]and with every

---

ergazomenous alla periergazomenous, 'not doing any work but meddling/being busybodies' (BDAG 800). The inference is probably that the individuals referred to were so caught up with their convictions that they spent time disrupting the work of other believers by their continual attempts to propagate their views.

286. Winter suggests that Paul was trying to wean the Thessalonian believers from the system of patronage as a permanent means of support (*Welfare* 53-60); but see the criticisms of Kloppenborg, *'Philadelphia'* 276-77 n. 46, and Jewett, *Romans* 67-69.

287. So the great majority of those who accept Pauline authorship of 2 Thessalonians.

288. In 1.8 Gentiles are probably in view in the reference to 'those who do not know God' (Ps. 79.6; Jer. 10.25; Jdt. 9.7; 2 Macc. 1.27; Gal. 4.8), and Jews in the reference to 'those who do not obey the gospel of our Lord Jesus' (Rom. 10.16, 21; 11.31; 15.31).

deceit of injustice for those who are perishing, because they did not receive the love of the truth so as to be saved. [11]Therefore God sends them an effective delusion so that they believe the lie, [12]in order that all may be condemned who did not believe the truth but took pleasure in injustice.

The imagery used here is probably drawn from language used of apocalyptic-like opponents of Israel in the past — the prince of Tyre, who said, 'I am a god; I sit in the seat of the gods' (Ezek. 28.2), and Antiochus Epiphanes, who profaned the Temple and exalted himself, considering himself greater than any god (Dan. 11.31, 36)[289] — the trepidation presumably increased by memory of Caligula's recent repetition of 'the abomination of desolation'.[290] But what 'that which restrains' *(to katechon)* refers to and who 'he who restrains' *(ho katechōn)* may be (2.6, 7) has baffled commentators for generations.[291] Particularly relevant is Paul Metzger's demonstration that the idea of various retarding factors which delayed the end was not unusual in apocalyptic circles.[292] His own favoured solution is the dominant view of the Fathers, going back to Tertullian,[293] that what was in view is Rome, the *imperium Romanum,* which could equally be represented by the person of the emperor.[294] In a situation where a small group was suffering ha-

289. Dan. 11.36 — *hypsōthēsetai epi panta theon;* 2 Thess. 2.4 — *hyperairomenos epi panta legomenon theon.*

290. See above, §26.5a.

291. Suggestions include God or the Holy Spirit, a divine or heavenly power, the gospel or Paul's own mission; review in BDAG 532; Wanamaker, *1 and 2 Thessalonians* 250-52; P. Metzger, *Katechon: II Thess 2,1-12 im Horizont apokalyptischen Denkens* (BZNW 135; Berlin: de Gruyter, 2005) 15-47. The possibility that Paul saw his own mission as a restraining factor — he still had to preach Christ to 'the full number' of Gentiles (Rom. 11.13, 25) — would fit with Paul's sense of eschatological apostleship (§29.3e above), as O. Cullmann clearly perceived, 'Le caractere eschatologique du devoir missionnaire et de la conscience apostolique de S. Paul. Étude sur le *katechon (-ōn)* de II Thess. 2.6-7', *RHPR* 16 (1936) 210-45. Satan is depicted as a blocking factor in 1 Thess. 2.18 (cf. Rom. 1.13; 15.22).

292. Metzger, *Katechon* 133-276, summarized (276) as (1) the full number predestined (Revelation, *4 Ezra, 2 Baruch*), (2) the appointed time (2 Peter, *4 Ezra, 2 Baruch,* Qumran), (3) God or his forbearance (*4 Ezra, 2 Baruch,* Qumran), (4) the search for the worthy (Revelation), (5) the awaited repentance (*4 Ezra, b. Sanh.* 97b), (6) the one who restrains (Ps.-Philo, *LAB*), (7) Rome (Revelation, *4 Ezra*). Ps.-Philo, *LAB* 51.5, *quousque reveletur qui tenet,* 'until he is revealed who restrains', appears initially promising but is equally enigmatic; see H. Jacobson, *A Commentary on Pseudo-Philo's 'Liber Antiquitatum Biblicarum'* (Leiden: Brill, 1996) 2.1104.

293. Metzger, *Katechon* 15-20.

294. Metzger refers particularly to *4 Ezra* 5.3, 6; also 11.45-46; Rev. 17.10, 15-18; 19.2 (*Katechon* 166-74, 210-11, 276, 293-95). On *4 Ezra* 5.3, 6 see M. E. Stone, *Fourth Ezra* (Hermeneia; Minneapolis: Fortress, 1990) 110-11. On the Revelation passages see Aune, *Revelation,* vol. 3 *ad loc.;* on 'the eschatological antagonist' (antichrist) see 2.751-55; with striking parallels in *2 Bar.* 40.1-3, *Sib. Or.* 5.33-34 and *Asc. Isa.* 4.2, 6.

rassment or persecution from local bodies, a cryptic reference to the power of Rome as a restraining force would be not altogether surprising, the attitude not dissimilar to the recognition of Rome's role in the divinely ordered scheme of things which Paul articulates in Rom. 13.1-7.[295] In other words, the relevant orderliness of civil/imperial government was actually preventing the outbreak of unrestrained hostility to and persecution of the young church, a view not far from Luke's portrayal of Paul's own experience in Philippi and Corinth.[296]

Whatever the solution to the enigma, the main fact is that Paul saw that several important events had still to transpire before the parousia of the Lord Jesus. Apparently he had already told the Thessalonians this when he was with them (2.5) — a further indication that his teaching in Thessalonica had been both intensive and extensive in relation to the imminent return of Jesus. Similarly he repeated his teaching, first given when he was with them and in his former letter (2.15; 3.6), on how they should conduct themselves in the light of the imminent parousia (3.6, 10): following the example he had set (3.7-9; 1 Thess. 2.9-10), they should work quietly *(hēsychias)* and earn their own bread (3.11-12; 1 Thess. 4.11). His final instructions, to deal firmly with those who ignored his teaching on the subject, give a fascinating glimpse into the earliest form of Christian community discipline that we know of: the church should not associate or mingle with them, in the hope of shaming them (3.14); they should not regard them as enemies but admonish them as brothers (3.15). Unfortunately, we have no knowledge of the success or otherwise of this pastoral counsel. But again there is a clear sense of the febrile and fractious character of such an apocalyptically oriented sect — a salutary reminder that this too was part of earliest Christianity.

In all this, it is worth repeating, Paul's teaching was consistent with Jesus' own teaching on the coming of the kingdom: imminent, but with an interval prior to its full coming.[297] Given the depressing history of Christian millenarian and apocalyptic enthusiasm, it is not unimportant to appreciate that, while fully convinced of the eschatological character of his commission (§29.3e), Paul did not allow himself to become caught up in such enthusiasm. In effect, he observed the answer which (according to Luke) Jesus gave to a similar question about the coming of the kingdom (Acts 1.6): 'It is not for you to know the times and seasons which the Father has set in his own authority, but . . . you will be my witnesses . . . to the end of the earth' (1.7-8). With similar effect, turning from his attempt to correct the Thessalonians (2 Thess. 2.3-12), Paul includes in his reassurance of them (2.13–3.5) a request for their prayers for his mission: 'pray

---

295. Cf. also the ambiguity of Paul's conception of who rules 'this age' — 'the rulers of this age' (1 Cor. 2.6, 8); 'the god of this age' (2 Cor. 4.4). See also the end of n. 291 above.

296. See above, §§31.1b, 4c.

297. See again *Jesus Remembered* 435.

for us that the word of the Lord may make speedy progress and be glorified, as it does with you' (3.1).

31.7. Paul's Letter to the Galatians

Galatians is one of the more flexibly dated of Paul's letters. Those who think that it preceded the Jerusalem conference (Acts 15) date it to about 48.[298] Those who think it was written during Paul's time in Ephesus date it to 53 or 54.[299] Those who think the closeness of the argument to that of Romans implies a date closer to that of the latter, favour a date of 55/56.[300] I have already indicated reasons why I do not think the first alternative makes best sense of the historical data.[301] And the similarity in the line of thought between Galatians and Romans hardly requires a closeness in their dates of composition,[302] unless we have to assume a volatility in Paul's theologizing which goes well beyond the evidence of his writings themselves.[303]

a. The Circumstances Which Occasioned the Letter

In my view, the strongest likelihood is that Paul wrote Galatians while he was still in Corinth, within a year of the two Thessalonian letters, that is, some time in 52.[304] I envisage the sequence of events somewhat as follows. Following Paul's failure to win the argument in Antioch (Gal. 2.11-17) and his departure as (in effect) an independent missionary,[305] the church in Antioch endeavoured to ensure

298. For whom Galatians 2 = Acts 11 (using the accustomed shorthand); see §27 n. 139 above.

299. E.g., Fitzmyer, *Acts* 636; Murphy-O'Connor, *Paul* 184.

300. E.g., Becker suggests it was written on the way from Troas to Macedonia (2 Cor. 7.5; Gal. 4.13) (*Paul* 262). Schnelle recognizes only two possibilities: Galatians was written during Paul's stay in Ephesus, or the much more favoured alternative (bibliography in n. 255): Galatians written after 1 and 2 Corinthians and just before Romans (*History* 94-95, 106); similarly Wilckens, *Theologie* 1/3 ch. 19.

301. See above, §27.3a.

302. 'One should consider only with the greatest caution the argument that the thematic proximity of the letters to the Galatians and to the Romans also allows us to conclude their temporally proximate composition' (Riesner, *Paul's Early Period* 290; directed especially at U. Borse, *Der Standort des Galaterbriefes* [BBB 41; Cologne: Hanstein, 1972]). Murphy-O'Connor considers 'the hypothesis of the proximity of Galatians to 2 Corinthians and Romans . . . to be without foundation' (*Paul* 181).

303. On those who think that Acts 15 = Acts 18.22, see above, §28 at n. 47.

304. Here I follow Weiss, *Earliest Christianity* 296-97.

305. See above, §27.6.

that the guidelines (for Jew/Gentile fellowship) thus established at Antioch were being followed in the churches established in missions from Antioch. That would mean primarily the churches of Syria and Cilicia. It was probably during this process (we need assume only about six months or so) that the 'rules of fellowship' which we know as 'the apostolic decree' took firm shape.[306] However, since the churches of Galatia had also been established by mission from Antioch, by Paul and Barnabas — or Barnabas and Paul, as probably the Antioch church preferred to remember the mission team — the question must inevitably have risen whether the same rules should not be expected to apply there too. Possibly then or independently, some more traditionalist Jewish believers saw that Paul's failure in Antioch gave them the opportunity to attempt to reverse his earlier victory in Jerusalem (2.1-10); the faction represented by those whom Paul in his letter to the Galatians dubs the 'false brothers' (2.4) springs to mind.[307] Even if a satisfac-

---

306. See above, §27.3e Note again that the letter of Acts 15.23-29 was addressed to 'the Gentile brothers in Antioch, Syria and Cilicia'. The closer to the Jerusalem conference the actual emergence of these rules as formally agreed, the more understandable is it that Luke may have been given to understand or gained the impression (from Jerusalem sources) that they had been the product of the conference itself.

307. This may be hinted at in Gal. 2.4-5: the false brothers 'sneaked in to spy on our freedom . . . to whom . . . we did not yield submission, in order that the truth of the gospel might remain for *you*'; in Paul's mind the challenge which he faced in Jerusalem merged into the threat posed in Galatia. Is this an indication that the faction referred to there had gained more influence in the Jerusalem church? Similarly Martyn, *Galatians* 217-19. The basic thesis that Paul's 'opponents' were 'Jewish Christian missionaries', first suggested by the Anti-Marcionite Prologue to Galatians, and a lynchpin of Baur's reconstruction (see above, §20.3a), continues to persuade the majority of commentators (Kümmel, *Introduction* 298-301; Schnelle, *History* 102, bibliography n. 282; Schnabel, *Mission* 1024-26). The recent alternative, an oddly ordered thesis of M. D. Nanos, *The Irony of Galatians: Paul's Letter in First-Century Context* (Minneapolis: Fortress, 2002) — influenced by N. Walter, 'Paulus und die Gegner des Christusevangeliums in Galatien', in W. Kraus and F. Wilk, eds., *Praeparatio evangelica. Studien zur Umwelt, Exegese und Hermeneutik des Neuen Testaments* (WUNT 98; Tübingen: Mohr Siebeck, 1997) 273-80 — that Paul writes to 'righteous Gentiles within Jewish synagogue communities' (75-83) and against (non-Christian) Jewish 'opponents', Jewish representatives of local Galatian synagogues (an intra- or inter-Jewish rather than an intra- or inter-Christian dispute), justifiably recognizes the degree of ambiguity of identity involved in clear demarcation of 'Jew' from 'Christian' at this time (the thesis is already clear in Nanos 6-7, 12-13; see also his 'Intruding "Spies" and "Pseudo-Brethren": The Jewish Intra-Group Politics of Paul's Jerusalem Meeting [Gal 2:1-10]', in S. E. Porter, ed., *Paul and His Opponents* [Leiden: Brill, 2005] 59-97). But the thesis runs aground on the obvious implications: (1) that 'gospel' was already more or less a technical term for 'the good news about Christ' (Gal. 1.6-9; 2.5, 7, 14; cf. 2 Cor. 11.4; Nanos offers the improbable translation of 1.6, 'a different message of good', but leaves elaboration of this till the last chapter); (2) that in Paul's defence in Galatians 1–2 the authority and authorization of the Jerusalem apostles was crucial to both sides of the confrontation in which Paul found himself; and (3) that 'the false brothers' (2.4) claimed 'falsely' to be fellow

tory *modus vivendi* for mixed Jew/Gentile churches was becoming established in Syria and Cilicia, the more thoroughgoing Gentile churches of Galatia may have seemed to call its wider viability into question. Jewish prerogative had to be reasserted, otherwise (in their judgment) the continuity of election and covenant, that is, of God's whole saving purpose, would be put in serious jeopardy.[308]

Whatever the actual course of events, a strong faction had come among or emerged within the churches in Galatia, claiming that in order to be recognized as believers in Messiah Jesus and to participate in Israel's heritage, the Gentile believers had to go the whole way and become proselytes by being circumcised.[309] Wherever they came from, those whom Paul refers to as 'those who are upsetting you' (5.12),[310] they obviously claimed to have the backing of the Jerusalem leadership.[311] Only so is it possible to make sense of Paul's vigorous but careful statement of his relationship with the Jerusalem leadership, particularly in 1.10–2.10;[312] he must have been responding to claims made by the incomers and to what they had said about Paul.[313] By the time Paul wrote Galatians, the faction had been propagating their view with considerable effect; many of the

---

believers (rather than 'falsely' to be fellow Jews! — 150-51). W. Schmithals refines his Gnostic hypothesis to the extent of postulating 'a Jewish Christian enthusiasm of Gnostic provenance' ('Judaisten in Galatien?', *Paulus* 39-77). J. L. Sumney, who has given more attention to the subject of Paul's opponents than anyone else, provides a recent overview — 'Studying Paul's Opponents: Advances and Challenges', in Porter, ed., *Paul and His Opponents* 7-58 (here 17-24).

308. M. Winger, 'Act One: Paul Arrives in Galatia', *NTS* 48 (2002) 548-67, deduces that on his earlier visit(s) Paul had not preached to the Galatians about the law; if 'Act One', though, includes a visit following the Antioch incident, the suggestion would be much less likely.

309. That the key demand was for the Galatian Gentile believers to be circumcised is clearly indicated in Gal. 5.2-12, though already implicit in 2.3-5; there is no dispute on this point.

310. Martyn prefers to refer to them as 'the Teachers' (to avoid Paul's pejorative language) but agrees that they were 'Christian-Jewish evangelists' coming from outside the Galatian churches who referred to their message as 'the gospel' and regarded the law as 'the good news for Gentiles' (*Galatians* 14, 18, 117-26; here 120-22, also 132-35).

311. *Pace* J. L. Sumney, *'Servants of Satan', 'False Brothers' and Other Opponents of Paul* (JSNTS 188; Sheffield: Sheffield Academic, 1999): 'there is no evidence that they are authorized or claim to be authorized by any segment of the Jerusalem church' (307-308); but he completely ignores the key data.

312. Martyn notes also and particularly the offensiveness of the reference to Jerusalem in Gal. 4.25 (*Galatians,* particularly 460-66).

313. See above, §27.3c. Initially at least, it need not have been a hostile (or overtly hostile) account of Paul: that he was actually subordinate in authority to the Jerusalem leadership and had his authorization in mission from them; that Paul had taken them only through the first stage of initiation and actually practised circumcision himself (5.11), alluding (probably) to Paul's own circumcision of Timothy among them (for different interpretations of 5.11 see my *Galatians* 278-80 and above, n. 25).

Galatians were being convinced and accepting circumcision (6.12-13).[314] A particularly persuasive argument seems to have been that if the Galatian Gentiles were to have any hope of sharing in the blessings promised through Abraham, they had to follow Abraham's example and to be circumcised as he had been.[315] All this apparently was happening while Paul was on the last part of his journey to Corinth and during the early months of his sojourn there.[316]

Again, whatever the finer details, we can assume that a Paul partisan in Galatia took opportunity to seek out Paul in Corinth or to send a message through to him, apprising him of what was happening.[317] Paul evidently reacted with astonishment and anger (1.6). The first or most successful of his early church-foundings as missionary to the Gentiles were being lost to the gospel. The failure in Antioch must have been bad enough for someone as strong-willed and as sure of his vocation as Paul. But now to learn that the agreement won with so much effort in Jerusalem was in danger of being reversed must have been intolerable for him. If the dominantly Gentile churches of Galatia lost sight of what was central to the gospel, then it would be hard, perhaps even impossible, to maintain that gospel in the other churches he had gone on to establish. No doubt he called for pen and ink, papyrus and scribe at the earliest opportunity and began to dictate.

The strength of this hypothesis is that all the relevant data fit neatly within it.

- It fits with the sequence indicated in Acts 13–14, 15–18; although first place should certainly be given to Paul's own first-hand account of events, so far as they can be deduced from his letters, it would be irresponsible in terms of historical method to ignore Acts, especially when the basic information provided by Luke can be shown to fit with a very viable hypothesis.

---

314. The present tenses of the verb 'circumcise' in 5.3 and 6.13 suggest an ongoing process: some had already accepted circumcision, and others were seriously contemplating it; the incomers were 'trying to compel [them] to be circumcised (6.12); see my *Galatians ad loc.* C. E. Arnold, '"I am astonished that you are so quickly turning away" (Gal. 1.6): Paul and Anatolian Folk Belief', *NTS* 51 (2005) 429-49, suggests that 'the deep-seated concern of the Galatians to maintain their favour with the gods through scrupulous observance of cultic requirements and the performance of good works would have inclined them to accept the message of Paul's opponents' (449) — a suggestion which would help make sense of the sequence of thought in Gal. 4.8-10.

315. See below, n. 350.

316. Martyn dates the letter earlier, while Paul was still in Philippi or Thessalonica (*Galatians* 19), but does not allow for the full implementation of the policy which probably resulted from Antioch's refusal to back Paul against Peter.

317. Ramsay suggested it was Timothy (*St. Paul* 189-92), though in that case it would presumably have carried some weight if Paul had associated Timothy with the writing of Galatians, as he had done with the two letters to Thessalonica.

- Paul refers to his preaching the good news to the Galatians *to proteron* (Gal. 4.13). The natural sense of the last phrase is 'earlier, formerly', and though it can be used in the sense 'once', the more obvious meaning is 'the first time'.[318] This fits with the hypothesis of repeated visits: Acts 13–14 recounts the first visit; Acts 16, the second visit.
- The references to Barnabas in 2.1, 9, 13 imply that the Galatians knew whom Paul was referring to; but Barnabas was Paul's colleague only during his mission from Antioch (Acts 13–14) and not in his subsequent missionary work.[319]
- The anger and surprise expressed by Paul that his Galatian converts should be 'so quickly *(tacheōs)* turning away' from God (1.6) has the smack of rhetorical exaggeration, so that the timescale envisaged is indeterminable;[320] but again it fits well with a shorter rather than a longer timescale between Paul's mission and that of the Antioch/Jerusalem missionaries.
- There is a striking difference between the Thessalonian letters and Galatians: in the former Paul made hardly anything of his apostolic status (only 1 Thess. 2.7), but in the latter he insisted on it with surprising vehemence (Gal. 1.1); and thereafter he almost always made a point of introducing himself as 'apostle of Christ Jesus'.[321] The obvious inference to be drawn is that something happened between the writing to Thessalonica and the letter to Galatia which made Paul think it imperative that he assert his apostolic status forcibly and unequivocally. That 'something' is most likely the report he received from Galatia about the incursions of the missionaries from Antioch/Jerusalem and about their calling in question the independence of his gospel and its authority.

318. BDAG 888-89; '4:13 on the basis of the more usual meaning presupposes rather two visits of Paul to Galatia' (Kümmel, *Introduction* 302, 303), but all that can be claimed is consistency with, rather than proof of, the hypothesis (see further my *Galatians* 233-34).

319. Martyn suggests that the Galatians' knowledge of Barnabas came from the Teachers (*Galatians* 17 n. 15), but it is unclear why the Teachers should even mention Barnabas to the Galatians if Barnabas had not been one of their founding apostles. Conversely, the failure to mention Barnabas in Gal. 4.13-15, which Martyn finds 'scarcely credible' if Barnabas had in fact accompanied Paul on his first visit to the Galatians (*Galatians* 185), can readily be understood if Paul chose not to mention that their conversion was due in part to one who had sided with 'the men from James' in Antioch (2.13); whereas mention of Barnabas as party to the preceding agreement in Jerusalem (2.7-9) could only strengthen Paul's case.

320. *Tacheōs* could refer alternatively (or also) to the speed with which the Galatians had succumbed to the message of the incoming missionaries (*Galatians* 40).

321. Rom. 1.1; 1 Cor. 1.1; 2 Cor. 1.1; Col. 1.1 (though not the friendly letters of Philippians and Philemon); also Eph. 1.1; 1 Tim. 1.1; 2 Tim. 1.1; Tit. 1.1. See also below, n. 327.

- Equally the hypothesis makes best sense of other changes in emphasis between the Thessalonian letters and Galatians, referred to above.[322] It would have been precisely in response to the challenge which the news from Galatia posed to him, that Paul found it necessary to restate his understanding of the gospel and to recall and resharpen the sharper edge which the confrontation with Peter had prompted him to give to his formulation of that gospel.[323]

- Conversely, a comparison between the Thessalonian letters and Galatians suggests that in the light of the confusion among the Thessalonian believers, Paul drew back from his earlier emphasis on the imminent parousia of the Lord. He did not abandon his future apocalyptic eschatology, but he switched the focus of his apocalyptic theology from future to past, from what Christ would do when he came (again) to what God has done in the (first) coming of Christ.[324]

I therefore remain in little doubt that the most obvious candidates for the epithet 'Galatians' are the churches founded by Paul during his mission from Antioch with Barnabas as his colleague, the mission which Luke describes in his own terms in Acts 13–14.[325]

The letter itself can be most simply described as *a restatement of Paul's gospel.* Despite the urgency of its writing, Paul planned its structure with some care.[326]

322. See the final paragraph of §31.5.

323. Against Strecker and those who have followed him (Schnelle, *History* 107); see above, §27 n. 298.

324. Contrast 1 Thess. 1.10; 4.13–5.11 and 2 Thess. 1.5–2.12 with Gal. 1.4; 4.4; 5.14-15. Martyn pays special attention to the 'apocalyptic theology in Galatians' (*Galatians* 97-105)

325. A strong tradition in critical scholarship takes Gal. 3.1 literally: the 'foolish Galatians' could only be the descendants of the Celts who invaded central Anatolia in the third century BCE and settled the region north of Antioch, Iconium etc., and after whom the larger Roman province (including Antioch, Iconium, etc.) was named (see, e.g., Kümmel, *Introduction* 298; Becker, *Paul* 272; Gnilka, *Paulus* 73; Schnelle, *History* 97; Martyn, *Galatians* 15-17). It apparently has not occurred to these scholars that Paul could have been speaking with heavy irony: 'you residents of province Galatia who are acting like the ignorant and uncouth Celts from whom the province is named!' They also ignored Weiss's observation that on the North Galatia hypothesis, Paul would have preached in a town like Ancyra, whose population was no longer made up of 'Galatians' in the national sense but of Greeks, Romans, Syrians and Jews, 'people whom the name "Galatian" would have suited just as well or as ill as it did the inhabitants of Lystra' (*Earliest Christianity* 298).

326. The following exposition will necessarily be brief, but I will refer frequently to my *Galatians* for fuller detail; see also my *The Theology of Paul's Letter to the Galatians* (Cambridge: Cambridge University, 1993).

b. Paul's Defence against Misrepresentations and Allegations of the Incoming Missionaries: Three Strands (Galatians 1–2)

(i) *Apologia pro vita sua*. Galatians begins explosively, in disregard for courteous epistolary form, with a blunt assertion of Paul's apostolic authority: 'Paul, apostle — not from human beings nor through a human being, but through Jesus Christ and God the Father who raised him from the dead' (1.1).[327] Similarly, dispensing with the conventional thanksgiving and prayer for the recipients, Paul immediately rebukes them for their 'desertion'[328] from the gospel which he had preached to them and which they had received from him (1.6-9).[329] That Paul felt personally slighted by what the Galatians had done, as presumably had been reported to him, is evident from 1.10. His language suggests that the incomers had spoken of Paul rather dismissively as attempting improperly to 'persuade *(peithō)*' the Galatians (and thus to impress God).[330] Likewise the implied charge (1.10) that he had been a mere 'man-pleaser' *(ēreskon)* (presumably in accepting Gentile believers without the embarrassing inconvenience of circumcision) was a well-known jibe in the ancient world,[331] and would have been particularly wounding for a man of such strong conviction and vocation as Paul.

Paul's response was to insist with renewed vehemence that the gospel he

327. Contrast the greeting of 1 Thessalonians, with no reference to his being an apostle and a willingness to speak of his role as apostle as one shared with Silvanus and Timothy (1 Thess. 2.7), suggesting that Paul did not find it necessary to assert his authority as apostle prior to the Galatians confrontation, which then established his more characteristic self-introduction thereafter (1 Cor. 1.1; 2 Cor. 1.1; Rom. 1.1; Col. 1.1); does the absence from Phil. 1.1 reflect that the congregation had been established before Paul became so sensitive on the subject? J. Frey, 'Paulus und die Apostel. Zur Entwicklung des paulinischen Apostelbegriffs und zum Verhältnis des Heidenapostels zu seinen "Kollegen"', in Becker and Pilhofer, eds., *Biographie und Persönlichkeit des Paulus* 192-227 (including extensive bibliography), suggests that 1 Thessalonians reflects a broader concept of 'apostle' (199-201; on Acts 14.4, 14 — 196-98; the full suggested development is set out in clear tabular form on 211).

328. *Metatithesthai*, 'turn away', can have the sense of 'desert, defect'; Diogenes Laertes 7.166 refers to Dionysius the Turncoat *(ho metathemenos)*, who left the Stoics and adopted Epicureanism (BDAG 642); 2 Maccabees uses the same language to describe the apostasy of the Hellenistic Jews from their ancestral religion (2 Macc. 4.46; 7.24; 11.24). See further Dunn, *Galatians* 39-40; Martyn, *Galatians* 108.

329. On Paul's rebuke ('I am astonished that . . .') as ironic, see particularly Nanos, *Irony* 39-51, drawing on N. A. Dahl, 'Paul's Letter to the Galatians: Epistolary Genre, Content and Structure', in Nanos, ed., *Galatians Debate* 117-42 (here 117-30).

330. 'Since Plato philosophers and others have regarded the "art of persuasion" as something rather negative and unfitting. Rhetoric became identified with deception, slander, and even sorcery' (Betz, *Galatians* 54-55).

331. W. Foerster, *TDNT* 1.456; Betz, *Galatians* 55 nn. 111, 112. The equivalent noun *(areskeia)* regularly had a negative sense, 'obsequiousness'.

had preached to the Galatians was *not* his own but had been given him directly 'through a revelation of Jesus Christ' (1.11-12). And he proceeded to remind them that it was this revelation (1.13-16)[332] which had transformed him from a persecutor to a proclaimer of the faith he had once tried to destroy (1.23), that it was this revelation which had commissioned him to preach the gospel to them ('among the Gentiles')[333] and which provided the only authorization he had ever received or required so to preach.

(ii) Interwoven with this defence and vindication of Paul's apostolic credentials was a testy but carefully formulated description of his relationship with the Jerusalem leadership (1.1–2.10). Here, in contrast to 1 Thessalonians, mirror-reading produces a sufficiently clear image of *the four charges to which Paul evidently found it necessary to respond* both bluntly and with not so subtle innuendo.[334]

1. *The authority for Paul's mission (apostleship) and gospel was derived from or came through the Jerusalem apostles.*

Paul could not hold back his rebuttal even beyond the first line of the letter (1.1, already quoted above). Lest there be any doubt, he repeats the assertion with repeated emphasis: 'the gospel preached by me is not of human origin; for it was not from a human being that I received it, neither was I taught it . . .' (1.11-12).

2. *Paul learned the gospel on his visit to Jerusalem following his conversion, and it was thus from or through the Jerusalem apostles that he gained authorization for his mission.*

Paul is equally emphatic in rebuttal: on receiving the revelation, 'I did not immediately consult with flesh and blood, nor did I go up to Jerusalem to those who were apostles before me' (1.16-17). It was only three years later that he went up to Jerusalem; during his fifteen-day visit he stayed with Cephas, but the other apostles he did not see, only James the Lord's brother (1.18-19). The added oath — 'What I write to you, please note, before God, I am not lying' (1.20) — indi-

---

332. There is an obvious link in Paul's thought between 1.12 ('I received it through a *revelation* [*apokalypsis*] of Jesus Christ') and 1.16 (God was pleased 'to *reveal* [*apokalypsai*] his Son in me, in order that I might preach him among the Gentiles').

333. See further above, §§25.3c-d.

334. Cf. the much-referred-to article of Barclay, 'Mirror-Reading a Polemical Letter'. Though I agree with much of his hypothesis at this point, Martyn is more confident than the evidence allows of his ability to reconstruct a very full version of the Teachers' message (*Galatians* 120-26, 302-6 ['The Teachers' Sermon']; cf. Sanders, *Paul* 54-55). The exercise is valuable but becomes somewhat pernicious when it serves him as justification for discounting some of what Paul says and implies as the view of the Teachers! See further nn. 378, 391 and 398 below.

cates clearly how seriously Paul regarded the charges leveled against him and how important he saw it to set the record straight.[335] During the subsequent fourteen years (2.1) he had remained out of touch with Jerusalem, 'unknown by sight to the churches of Judea' (including Jerusalem) and known only by favourable reputation (1.21-24).

3. *Paul had acknowledged his dependency on and subordination to the Jerusalem leadership by going to Jerusalem to lay his gospel before them and thus to gain their approval. The corollary presumably was that the gospel which now came to the Galatians with the authorization of Jerusalem supplemented and overrode the gospel preached by Paul.*

Paul here had to respond with greater subtlety.[336] He had gone up to Jerusalem, not because he had been summoned by the Jerusalem apostles, but 'in accordance with a revelation' (2.2); his authorization again came directly from heaven. It was true that he had 'laid before them the gospel which [he] preached among the Gentiles' and that, in doing so, he had had a real concern 'lest somehow [he] was running or had run in vain' (2.2). In other words, he acknowledged that without the affirmation of his gospel by the Jerusalem apostles, his mission might have been 'in vain *(eis kenon)*', that is, without effective purpose or success.[337] But he goes on to make three things clear:

- The attempt by the traditionalist faction in Jerusalem ('the false brothers') to 'compel' the circumcision of the Gentile believer Titus, who had come up with Paul and Barnabas, did not gain the Jerusalem apostles' support (2.4-6).
- In refutation of those who claimed that Gentile believers must be circumcised, Paul was able to report the formal recognition and seal of approval given to his mission by the Jerusalem apostles; they had acknowledged that his commission to the uncircumcised was equivalent to Peter's apostolate to the circumcised (2.6-9).[338]
- At the same time, his wording would indicate to any informed reader that the acknowledgment which he had given to the Jerusalem apostles at that

335. For fuller exposition, particularly of what the passage tells us about Paul's early development as a Christian, see above, §25.5a and n. 187.

336. For what follows see further §27.3c above.

337. The implication is that the gospel for Paul was so much the outworking and climax of God's purpose for and through Israel that failure of the Jerusalem apostles to affirm it would render it a dead letter (Dunn, *Galatians* 94-95; cf. Martyn, *Galatians* 192-93).

338. But it is an open question whether the form of words used in the agreement (2.8) constituted a recognition of Paul's 'apostleship', as distinct from the God-given success of his mission; see above, §27 n. 176.

time (2.2 — 'those held in repute'), an esteem in which others still held them (2.6 — 'those reputed to be something'; 2.9 — 'those reputed to be pillars'), he could no longer accord to them (2.6 — 'what they once were makes on difference to me, God shows no partiality'), presumably in the light of the Antioch incident and the news of the incursion in Galatia.

4. *Paul had not been supported in the stand he took against Cephas (and James) in Antioch. By implication, the authority which stemmed from Jeru-salem, and which had been thus acknowledged by the church of Antioch, should be followed by the churches founded in mission from Antioch.*

Here Paul was in more of a trap, for if indeed the Antiochenes had accepted the counsel/demands of 'those from James', following the lead given by Cephas, Barnabas and the rest of the Jewish believers (as is most probably the case),[339] then Paul could not deny it, and consequently his whole case was in danger of collapsing. The only alternative was to recall the episode in his own terms (2.11-14) and to restate and elaborate the argument he had used (ineffectively) against Peter in Antioch (2.14-21).

(iii) *Apologia pro evangelio suo.* As clear as it is that Paul felt the need to defend himself and to spell out in some detail his relationships with Jerusalem, his real concern and objective was to *defend, explain and reaffirm the gospel* in response to which the Galatians had come to faith. The self-defence of chs. 1–2 was not motivated by personal pique or self-importance, but because the gospel for non-Jews was so bound up with his commission to the Gentiles. Paul's anxiety reaches fever-pitch and his language becomes most aggressive when he finds it necessary to re-assert the gospel that he had preached: 'Even if we or an angel from heaven preach to you a gospel contrary to what we preached to you, let him be accursed! (1.8, repeated for emphasis in 1.9); to 'the false brothers', 'not even for an hour did we yield submission, in order that the truth of the gospel might remain with you' (2.5); the Jerusalem apostles 'saw that I had been entrusted with the gospel for the uncircumcision . . . and gave to me and Barnabas the right hand of fellowship' (2.7-9); in Antioch Cephas 'stood condemned', and 'the rest of the Jews joined him in playing the hypocrite'; 'they were not walking straight towards the truth of the gospel' (2.11-14).

It was presumably as the climax to these assertions of the crucial importance of his gospel that Paul restated what for him was its essence (2.16-21) before going on to present a more developed argument to expound the gospel as he understood it (chs. 3–4). As we have already seen (§27.5), one of the primary features of the gospel for Paul was that its reception depended only on faith, that

---

339. See above, §27.6. Had Paul told this story to the Galatians, or did they hear it first from the incoming traditionalist Christian Jews?

it could come to effective implementation only through the channel of trust, that is, through acceptance of the message about Jesus the Christ and the responding faith in, commitment to this Jesus (as Lord).[340] Any further requirement which compromised the sole demand for 'faith in Christ' actually negated the gospel's central assertion that God accepts only those who trust him, that God can draw back into a right relationship with himself only those who rely on him with the helplessness of mortal humankind (2.16). The realization that codes and rules (the law), which served to define others (Gentiles) as 'sinners' (2.17)[341] and which constituted walls of separation (2.18)[342] that were actually nullifying the grace of God (2.21), had been for Paul himself[343] like passing from death to life, a dying to the law as the basis for acceptability to God and a living for God through Christ (2.19-20). It is this thematic statement, so deeply rooted in his own experience, that Paul goes on to develop and argue for in more detail.

c. A Fuller Exposition of Paul's Gospel (Gal. 3.1–5.12)

The reports communicated to him had evidently given Paul a clear enough idea of what the incoming missionaries had said to his Galatian converts and what had worked so persuasively upon them to convince them that they ought to be circumcised. Having vented his first outburst of outrage and set the record straight as to his own curriculum vitae, Paul turns in more measured terms to respond to these arguments.

(i) *The importance of their own experience of God's Spirit* (3.1-5). As he had rooted his initial appeal firmly in his own experience, as to the source of his

---

340. But the lordship of Jesus is not particularly brought out, far less emphasized, in Galatians; apart from the opening greeting (1.3) and closing farewell (6.18), *kyrios* is used of Jesus only in 1.19, 5.10 and 6.14 — should we see here another sign that in the light of the overblown expectations of the Thessalonians (see above, at n. 237), Paul modified his language and emphases to some extent?

341. On 2.17 see above, §27 n. 260.

342. The imagery is of the law as constituting a wall of separation between righteous and sinner, between Jew and Gentile, as in *Ep. Aris.* 139-42 and Eph. 2.14 (*mesotoichon*, 'dividing wall'); cf. Isa. 5.2, 5. If Paul were to insist that Gentiles observe the laws governing table-fellowship, he would be building the very things he had demolished — 'the observances of the law through which the boundaries between Israel and the goyim were established' (U. Wilckens, 'Zur Entwicklung des paulinischen Gesetzesverständnis', *NTS* 28 [1982] 154-90 [here 170]); cf. Martyn, *Galatians* 256.

343. That Paul speaks here (2.18-21) with the intensity of a personal experience of awakening and total reorientation should not be downplayed, however much he may have wanted his experience to be read as typical of the coming to faith as a passing from death to life; also, the destruction of the law as a 'dividing wall' was integral to this experience (n. 342).

commission and understanding of the gospel (1.15-16; 2.18-20), so in restating the gospel, Paul turns at once to the Galatians' equivalent experience. Paul could be confident that his Galatian audiences would know what he was talking about, because they could remember how the crucified Christ had been portrayed so vividly *(proegraphē)* before their eyes (3.1).[344] Still more important, Paul knew from the success of his evangelism that they would remember that they had experienced God's full acceptance in being given to share in his Holy Spirit,[345] and they had done so simply by 'hearing with faith' and not by observing any requirement of the Torah (3.2-5).[346] It was this success, after all, which had proved so persuasive for the 'pillar apostles' in Jerusalem (2.7-9).[347]

This repeated emphasis on experience has important theological corollaries. Paul's understanding of the gospel was *rooted in experience,* his own and that of others. Here are clear instances of the creative and transforming power of a lively spiritual experience. It did not conform to or allow itself readily to be pigeon-holed into the language and categories of their already existing traditions. Rather, as the molten lava of a volcanic eruption breaks open old surfaces and carves out new channels, so the power of molten experience forced language and life-patterns into new forms and expressions. Paul's gospel was not primarily and not only a sequence of theological affirmations to be deduced from Israel's history or Scriptures, or even from his knowledge of Jesus; rather, primarily for him, the gospel was rooted in an experience of the living God revealing himself through Jesus the Christ and his will to humankind in a personal and transforming way.

(ii) *Understanding Scripture aright* (3.6-18). At the same time, Paul's conviction regarding the gospel did not rest in experience alone. Having appealed to

---

344. BDAG 867; Betz, *Galatians* 131.

345. 'This reception of the "Spirit" is the primary datum of the Christian churches in Galatia' (H. D. Betz, 'Spirit, Freedom, and Law: Paul's Message to the Galatian Churches', *SEÅ* 39 [1974] 145-60 [here 146]); see also D. J. Lull, *The Spirit in Galatia: Paul's Interpretation of* Pneuma *as Divine Power* (Chico: Scholars, 1980) ch. 3; C. H. Cosgrove, *The Cross and the Spirit: A Study in the Argument and Theology of Galatians* (Macon: Mercer University, 1988). What this experience of the Spirit included is indicated in 3.5 and 4.6; see further §27 at n. 125 above.

346. The phrase *akoē pisteōs* is ambiguous. Most prefer to take *akoē* in the sense 'that which is heard', 'message' (BDAG 36) — so, 'by believing what you heard' (NRSV, NIV, NJB), 'by believing the gospel message' (REB), or 'as the result of a message which elicited (only) faith' (BDAG); see further Martyn, *Galatians* 286-89. But in the nearest parallel Paul stresses the importance of 'hearing' (Rom. 10.14-18), and he would have been well aware of the Hebrew understanding of obedient or heedful hearing (Rom. 1.5; 15.18; 2 Cor. 10.5; *hypakoē,* 'obedience', and *akoē* coming from the same root, *akouō,* 'to hear'; hence also Gal. 4.21); see further S. K. Williams, 'The Hearing of Faith: *AKOĒ PISTEŌS* in Galatians iii', *NTS* 35 (1989) 82-93: '"the hearing of faith", that "hearing" which Christians call *faith*' (90).

347. See further §§27.2b and 27.3d-e above.

their experience, Paul goes on immediately to develop his case by expounding a key passage and motif of his people's Scriptures. Although the argument was probably developed in response to Scripture-based expositions by the other missionaries in Galatia, it would be no less true that a Scripture base for his own understanding of the gospel was of major importance for Paul. Had he been unable to mount such an argument, a credible argument, at least to his own Pharisee-trained eyes, one might well wonder what he would have done or what he would have made of the 'revelation' he had received. The question is a non-starter, however, since it was precisely the symbiotic relation between his experience (and knowledge) of Jesus the Christ and his well-founded grasp of Jewish Scripture which proved so compelling for Paul.[348]

As already suggested, the incoming missionaries (from Antioch, or direct from Jerusalem?) had probably seized upon the fact that the Galatians had been converted to what was still in essence a Jewish sect, the messianic sect of the Nazarene. Apart from anything else, it was the God of Israel that Paul proclaimed to non-Jews. Jesus could not have been proclaimed as 'Christ' in a Gentile context without some explanation of that name, or filling out of why that name/title should be used — Jesus, Israel's Messiah. Was such a vivid 'placarding' of 'Jesus Christ as crucified' (3.1) not accompanied or supplemented by some explanation of why he was crucified? To understand their experience as experience of 'the Spirit' would presumably require some instruction on the subject from Israel's Scriptures. With such a basis on which to build, the incoming missionaries could readily go on to the obvious corollary: if you have come thus far in accepting the heritage of Israel, you should obviously go the whole way and unite yourselves with the heirs of Abraham by being circumcised as Abraham was circumcised.[349] Only so, they would insist, could the Galatians legitimately claim to share in the blessings promised to Abraham's descendants.[350]

---

348. Here is one of the points on which Paul agreed with the incoming missionaries: that the gospel was in continuity with and a filling out (fulfilling) of the Scriptures.

349. The classic statement of the view that it was the other missionaries who introduced talk of Abraham's seed — that the blessings promised to Abraham were to his descendants (Israel, the Jews) — is that of C. K. Barrett, 'The Allegory of Abraham, Sarah, and Hagar in the Argument of Galatians' (1976), *Essays on Paul* (London: SPCK, 1982) 154-70 (particularly 159-65); also *Freedom and Obligation* (London: SPCK, 1985) 22-24; now greatly elaborated by Martyn, *Galatians* (see n. 334 above), who is followed by Murphy-O'Connor, *Paul* 196-98.

350. Eleazar's rebuke to the uncircumcised proselyte Izates, on finding the latter reading the law of Moses, gives the flavour of their argument: 'In your ignorance, O king, you are guilty of the greatest offence against the law and thereby against God. For you ought not merely to read the law but also, and even more, to do what is commanded in it. How long will you continue to be uncircumcised? If you have not yet read the law concerning this matter, read it now, so that you may know what an impiety it is that you commit' (Josephus, *Ant.*

It is important to realize that Paul agreed with the central point in the argument thus put to the Galatians: that their new status before God could/should be defined as 'sons/seed of Abraham', 'heirs' of the 'promise(s)' made to Abraham;[351] at the heart of this new status was their participation in 'the blessing of Abraham' (3.14). For Paul, however, that new status was granted to those who *believed;* it was a status which could be defined as *hoi ek pisteōs,* 'those whose identity is from faith, who believe as Abraham believed'.[352]

Paul's exposition focuses on three texts from Genesis which made clear to him the mode of this relationship, the scope of the blessing, and the means by which non-Jews could be incorporated in the promised seed.

1. Gen. 15.6 — 'Abraham believed God, and it was reckoned to him for righteousness' (3.6). Abraham's believing was the key to the right relationship with God. So, his faith is what characterizes the relationship into which God led him and promised to his seed. So 'those *ek pisteōs'* are 'sons of Abraham', who believed as he believed (3.7).[353]

20.44-45). The normal sequence is indicated by Trypho, who urges Justin, 'first be circumcised, then (as is commanded in the law) keep the Sabbath and the feasts and God's new moons, and, in short, do all the things that are written in the law, and then perhaps you will find mercy from God' (*Dial.* 8.4).

351. 'Sons/seed of Abraham' — 3.7, 29; 4.22, 30. Inheriting the blessing promised to Abraham — 3.8-9, 14, 16-18, 22, 29; 4.7, 23, 28, 30.

352. *Ek pisteōs* is a key term in the exposition of ch. 3: 3.7, 8, 9, 11, 12, 22, 24 (also 5.5); it is clearly parallel to *dia pisteōs* (3.14), and obviously an elaboration of the *ek pisteōs* of 2.16. Note again that the *pistis* in 3.7 denotes trust as Abraham trusted (3.6), not as Christ trusted (or was Christ justified by faith?). The attempt of R. B. Hays, *The Faith of Jesus Christ: The Narrative Substructure of Galatians 3:1–4:11* (Grand Rapids: Eerdmans, ²2002) 170-73, 176-77, to argue that with the *hoi ek pisteōs* of 3.7 no parallel is being drawn between Abraham's believing and the Galatians' faith, I find frankly incredible (cf. Romans 4); that Scripture preaches the gospel that God 'is to justify the nations *ek pisteōs*' (3.8, referring to Gen. 12.3 and 18.18) obviously matches God reckoning Abraham righteous in that he believed (3.7, referring to Gen. 15.6). Martyn does maintain that *pistis* in 3.7 includes a reference to 'the faith of Christ enacted in his death' (*Galatians* 299), but there is nothing to show that the 'faith' in view is different from Abraham's believing (it is noticeable that Martyn does not attempt to press this fuller meaning on *pistis* in 3.8 — 300); B. W. Longenecker, *The Triumph of Abraham's God: The Transformation of Identity in Galatians* (Edinburgh: Clark, 1998), equally avoids the crucial nexus of 3.6-8 (95-115); see further §27 n. 289 above, and the fuller statement of my argument — '*EK PISTEŌS:* A Key to the Meaning of *PISTIS CHRISTOU'*, in J. R. Wagner, ed., *The Word Leaps the Gap,* R. B. Hays FS (Grand Rapids: Eerdmans, 2008) 351-66.

353. Paul subsequently expounded this passage in detail in Romans 4; I have already indicated how important it was in traditional Jewish self-understanding (§27.4b above); see further my *Galatians* 159-61.

2. Gen. 12.3/18.8 — 'In you shall all the nations be blessed' (3.8). This, the third strand of the promise to Abraham,[354] Paul describes as 'gospel'. He does so because the promise anticipates that God purposed to justify the nations/Gentiles and to do so in the same way, *ek pisteōs* (3.8-9).

At this point Paul inserts a parenthesis which has caused considerable confusion (3.10-14). It consists in a brief elaboration of the theme of divine blessing by the counterpoint of divine curse.[355] The basic point seems to be that the law/Torah should not be seen as the means by which the promise of blessing to the nations is implemented. Curse has proved to be the more natural language and inevitable terms of the law (3.10); the law is a matter of doing, not of believing, and it is through believing that each is justified (3.11-12); the curse of the law was exhausted in Christ on the cross (3.13), so that the blessing of Abraham could come in Christ Jesus to those, Jew and Gentile, who receive the promised Spirit through faith (3.14). Whatever the precise details of Paul's exposition,[356] the primary thrust of his argument is in elaboration of 'the blessing of Abraham' promised to 'all the nations': that God justifies Gentiles (Galatians and others) in the same way that he justified Abraham; and all *ek pisteōs* are thus most justly to be described as 'sons of Abraham'.

3. Gen. 13.15/17 LXX; 15.18; 17.8; 24.7 — '. . . and to your seed' (3.16). The promise was to Abraham 'and his seed *(sperma)*'. Here Paul engages in some rather neat word-play, based on the fact that the word used, *sperma*,

---

354. There were three strands to the promise to Abraham: seed (Gen. 13.16; 15.5; 17.2-4, 19; 18.18; 22.17; 26.4), land (12.7; 13.14-17; 15.18-21; 17.8; 26.3), and blessing to the nations (12.3; 18.18; 22.18; 26.4). The promise of seed was obviously the crucial element in Paul's dispute with the other missionaries. The promise of land was also important (it still is in Middle East politics!) and had already been elaborated in the way Paul was to do in Rom. 4.13 (cf. Sir. 44.21; 2 *Bar.* 14.13; 51.3; see further my *Romans* 213). But the third strand was relatively neglected in Jewish thought; see J. R. Wisdom, *Blessing for the Nations and the Curse of the Law: Paul's Citation of Genesis and Deuteronomy in Gal. 2.8-10* (WUNT 2.133; Tübingen: Mohr Siebeck, 2001) 36-42.

355. See further Wisdom, *Blessing for the Nations.* The theme was perhaps part of the other missionaries' appeal (C. K. Barrett, *Paul: An Introduction to His Thought* [London: Chapman, 1994] 31; Martyn, *Galatians* 325).

356. For fuller exposition see my *Galatians* 168-80; also *Theology of Paul* 361-62, 374, 153, 225-27; also *The New Perspective on Paul* (2005) 38-41, (2008) 41-44 (with bibliography). On the puzzle of 3.10 note Grindheim's argument: 'If Paul's implicit indictment of the sins of the covenant people is dependent on Jeremiah, it implies that Paul finds the same fundamental error with them as did Jeremiah: lack of trust in the Lord and lack of loyalty to him. After the coming of Christ, the sin of disloyalty manifested itself as failure to believe in Jesus' ('Apostate Turned Prophet' 564).

is singular, and therefore can be referred immediately to Christ, Abraham's principal descendant (in terms of God's fulfilling the promise made to Abraham). Paul's point was not to deny that *sperma* is a collective noun and can be fairly translated 'descendants' (he was, of course, fully aware of that fact, as 3.29 indicates). His point was rather to indicate how the full sweep of Abraham's blessing was to be achieved: if the promise to Abraham's seed included blessing to 'all the nations', then 'all the nations' blessed were *de facto* Abraham's seed; and this was accomplished by the fact that all believers (Gentile as well as Jew) were incorporated in Christ, the pre-eminent seed.[357] And since the promise (to Abraham) had already proved itself thus effective through faith — Galatian Gentiles had actually entered into that blessing — the law was thereby rendered irrelevant to the fulfilment of the promise and its gospel (3.17-18).

An interesting question is whether Paul would have developed this argument had it not been for the Christian Jewish mission insisting that the Galatian Gentiles needed to be circumcised if they were to be truly Abraham's seed and so heirs of the blessings promised to Abraham and his seed. The degree of artificiality in Paul's argument (as it seems to modern readers) was presumably forced upon Paul by the need to counter the other preaching which was so undermining the gospel as Paul understood it. Crucial to Paul's gospel were its three strands: justification by faith (like Abraham); experiencing the gift of God's Spirit (the blessing promised to Abraham); finding their new identity 'in Christ' (Abraham's seed). That he could tease out the Genesis texts so central to Israel's identity in just these terms was of indescribable importance to Paul.

(iii) *Why then the law?* (3.19–4.11). Having explained that the law was irrelevant to the promise/gospel, Paul evidently felt it necessary to restate what he saw to be the purpose of the law. This presumably was because the other missionaries had insisted, rather as Eleazar had to Izates,[358] that it was the greatest impiety to claim a share in Israel's bounty without observing the law given by God to Israel.

The terms of Paul's response are again much debated. A strong tradition of

---

357. As a collective singular, 'seed' was inherently ambiguous and invited some rhetorical play on the identity of the 'seed'. Although rabbinic literature does not identify Abraham's 'seed' as the Messiah (Str-B 3.553), the obvious link between the seed of David ('seed' taken as singular in 2 Sam. 7.12-14!) and the seed of Abraham (suggested by Ps. 89.3-4) naturally invited a messianic interpretation for more Jewish teachers than Paul (M. Wilcox, 'The Promise of "Seed" in the New Testament and the Targumim', *JSNT* 5 [1979] 2-30; F. F. Bruce, *Commentary on Galatians* [NIGTC; Grand Rapids: Eerdmans, 1982] 173). See further my *Galatians* 183-85.

358. See n. 350 above.

scholarship sees in Paul's language (3.19-24) evidence of a deep antipathy to and rejection of the law as such: it simply increased sin (3.19); it was not of divine origin (3.19); it could not make alive (3.21); it was an imprisoning power like the power of sin (3.22-24).[359] However, such an interpretation, I believe, misses Paul's point. How could he, a Jew, deny the clear testimony of his Scriptures that the law was given by God through Moses to instruct and direct the people of Israel? In my view, Paul's concern was rather to demonstrate how the law, as an integral part of God's dealings with his people Israel, was *complementary* to, rather than in direct antithesis to, God's purpose as revealed in the promise(s) to Abraham.

I read these same verses differently:

- 3.19 — the law 'was added *(prosetethē)*', that is, by God (a divine passive), not to nullify or qualify the original promise (3.15), but for a different purpose;
- 3.19 — the law was given 'for the sake of *(charin)* transgressions', that is, in order to provide some sort of remedy for transgressions, that is, by providing the sacrificial system by which atonement could be made for transgressions;[360]
- 3.19 — the law was 'ordered through angels *(diatageis di' angelōn)*', that is, by God (who else?) through angelic attendants,[361] and 'by the hand of (the pre-eminent) mediator (Moses)',[362] whereas the promise was made immediately by God and directly to Abraham;

359. See, e.g., those cited in my 'Was Paul against the Law?', in *The New Perspective on Paul* (2005) 261-63, (2008) 267-69, and nn. 10, 12-16. A negative connotation in this passage, as indicating that God was wholly absent from the giving of the law [so that it sneaked in against his will?!], is crucial to Martyn's whole interpretation of Galatians, as his repeated reference to the passage (that is, to his understanding of the passage) makes clear (*Galatians* particularly 28, 36, 356-58, 364-70).

360. *Charis,* 'for the sake of, on account of' has, if anything, a positive ring to it (LSJ, *charis* VI.1); without knowing Rom. 5.20 (not yet written!), the audience was hardly likely to hear the phrase in the sense 'in order to provoke or produce' transgressions (as by Betz, *Galatians* 165-67; Barrett, *Paul* 81; Martyn, *Galatians* 354-55).

361. Martyn's rendering of *dia* as 'by' angels is tendentious (*Galatians* 356-57). More likely the allusion is to the angels popularly thought to have attended on God at Sinai (Deut. 33.2 LXX; *Jub.* 1.29–2.1; Philo, *Som.* 1.143; Josephus, *Ant.* 15.136; *Apoc. Mos.* preface). See further T. Callan, 'Pauline Midrash: The Exegetical Background of Gal. 3.19b', *JBL* 99 (1980) 549-67. The thought was familiar to other NT writers (Acts 7.38, 53; Heb. 2.2); the language is similar in Acts 7.53 *(eis diatagas angelōn)* and Heb. 2.2 *(di' angelōn),* and it would never have occurred to these writers that such language could constitute a denial of the divine origin (through angelic intermediacy) of the law.

362. 'By the hand of' is a Semitic idiom = 'through' (*TDNT* 9.430-31) and probably echoes the phrasing of Lev. 26.46. Betz notes that 'by the hand of Moses' became almost a formula in the LXX (*Galatians* 170). See further Longenecker, *Galatians* 140-43.

- 3.21 — the purpose of the law was never to 'make alive', only the promise given by God himself could do that;[363] by implication the role of the law was rather to order life,[364] not to make alive, so that the two (promise and law) are not (to be set) against each other;[365]
- 3.23-25 — the law had a temporary role in 'protecting' Israel during the epoch when 'everything was under the power of sin', restricted *(ephrouroumetha)*[366] and disciplined like a youth with his *paidagōgos,*[367] till the time of maturity had come, until the coming of Christ, the fulfilment of the promise, and the fuller realization that justification (of Gentile as well as Jew) is *ek pisteōs*.

Only so, I believe, by this more subtle argument, could Paul have hoped to counter the otherwise highly plausible and persuasive arguments of the incoming missionaries. For Paul to have rejected the law out of hand would have played into the hands of his Galatian opponents. His rejoinder would have been so easy to dismiss, since it is so obvious to anyone who respects the Scriptures of Israel that the law is of divine origin and divine purpose. Unless Paul could show that he took that divine origin seriously and could see a divine purpose in the law, his response to the other missionaries would have been laughed out of court.[368]

A lengthy conclusion follows (3.26–4.11). Paul reiterates his central point: it is 'through this faith' that all (who believe) are 'sons of God in Christ Jesus' (3.26). But the reiteration carries the exposition one step further: those *ek*

363. 'The verb "make alive" in its usage, mostly biblical, almost always describes a work exclusive to God (2 Kgs. 5.7; Neh. 9.6; Job 36.6; Ps. 71.20; *Jos. Asen.* 8.3, 9; 12.1; 20.7; *Ep. Aris.* 16; John 5.21; Rom. 4.17; 1 Cor. 15.22) or to his Spirit, a particularly NT emphasis (John 6.63; Rom. 8.11; 1 Cor. 15.45; 2 Cor. 3.6; 1 Pet. 3.18' (Dunn, *Galatians* 192-93).

364. The implication comes from the verb used in 3.19 — the law 'ordered *(diatageis)* through angels'; *diatassō* has the sense 'to give (detailed) instructions as to what must be done' (BDAG 237-38).

365. See further my *Galatians* 192-93. The possible confusion is rooted in Lev. 18.5 ('in doing them [God's commandments] a person shall live by them' — referred to in 3.12), which initially referred to the way life should be lived within the covenant people, as both the parallel Deut. 30.19-20 and the earliest commentary on Lev. 18.5, Ezek. 20.5-26, clearly imply; see further my *The New Perspective on Paul* (2005) 65-67, (2008) 73-75.

366. The principal sense of *phroureō* is 'guard, watch over' (as in its other three NT uses — 2 Cor. 11.32; Phil. 4.7; 1 Pet. 1.5); so a protective custody (see further my *Galatians* 197-98).

367. *Paidagōgos* denoted the slave (usually) who conducted a boy to and from school (BDAG 748). The role, sometimes abused, was essentially a positive one — to protect and guard his charge and to provide instruction and discipline as necessary; see particularly D. J. Lull, '"The Law Was Our Pedagogue": A Study in Galatians 3:19-25', *JBL* 105 (1986) 481-98; N. H. Young, '*Paidagōgos:* The Social Setting of a Pauline Metaphor', *NovT* 29 (1987) 150-76.

368. See further my *Theology of Paul* §6.

pisteōs/dia pisteōs are not only sons of Abraham but 'sons of God'. This is a neat way to tie up the double motif of Israel as God's son[369] and Christ as God's Son: to believe as Abraham believed is to be a son of Abraham, to belong to Israel's sonship; to be in Christ is to be seed of Abraham, son of God. Crucial is the being in Christ; it is that which both relativizes all distinctions of race, class and gender and provides the only and ultimate grounding for relationships between those 'in Christ'.[370] Greeks who have believed into Christ need have no sense of inferiority or disadvantaged status in reference to native-born Jews (3.27-29).

Once again Paul hastens to make it clear that he does not dismiss Israel's claim to its special relationship with God (4.1-7).[371] It is simply that Israel and the Jewish missionaries in Galatia are 'behind the times'. Israel is still 'heir' of the promises but is like a child or adolescent who has not yet attained his majority, become of age; as such, Israel (and the missionaries) are 'no different from a slave', like all belonging to 'the present evil age' (1.4), 'enslaved under the elemental forces *(stoicheia)* of the world' (4.1-3).[372] But the purposed time of fulfilment has come, with the coming of Christ, God's Son, who has opened the way from the enslavement of the juvenile under the law to the status of mature sons. This status the Galatians share with other believers in Christ, through receiving the divine gift of the Spirit of the Son, crying 'Abba! Father!' — no longer a slave but a son (4.4-7).[373]

Back in the old age, the enslavement of the Galatians was to 'beings that by nature are no gods' (4.8).[374] But now if they turn their backs on the fulfilled

---

369. For Israel as God's son, see particularly Exod. 4.22; Jer. 31.9; Hos. 11.1; also, e.g., Deut. 14.1; Isa. 43.6; Hos. 1.10 (further my *Christology* 15).

370. Gal. 3.28 (or 26-28) is almost universally regarded as a baptismal formula. See also Fiorenza, *In Memory of Her* ch. 6.

371. The significance of this passage is missed by Martyn and those who follow him (Longenecker, *Triumph* 46), since it clearly presupposes a historical process and transition (whether it is called 'salvation history' or not is neither here nor there), during which Israel passes through the phases of childhood and adolescence but *is nevertheless an heir*. It is easy to become confused, since Paul groups unbelieving Jews and Gentiles in the same boat, both in an enslaved status, the law functioning in effect as one of the 'elemental forces'. See further my *Galatians ad loc.,* and below, nn. 373 and 402.

372. For the *stoicheia* see my *Colossians and Philemon* 149-50 and bibliography there; add now M. C. de Boer, 'The Meaning of the Phrase *ta stoicheia tou kosmou* in Galatians', *NTS* 53 (2007) 204-24.

373. That there is a conscious echo of Exodus motifs and themes, particularly in the contrast between slavery and sonship, is well argued by S. Keesmaat, *Paul and His Story: (Re)interpreting the Exodus Tradition* (JSNTS 181; Sheffield: Sheffield Academic, 1999) ch. 5.

374. Witulski sees here and in the *stoicheia* references to the imperial cult (*Adressaten* 128-52) and hypothesizes that Gal. 4.8-20 was originally a separate letter written to South Galatia and only combined with the rest of Galatians by a post-Pauline redactor; but see n. 372.

promise of the Spirit and allow themselves to be persuaded to observe Sabbaths and feast days, as *de rigueur*,[375] they would simply be putting themselves back into that old age, the age of confinement and slavery (4.9-10). The very thought and prospect exasperated Paul and brought him to near despair (4.11).

(iv) *A personal plea, and tour de force* (4.12–5.1). Paul's main exposition is complete, but he could not refrain from personalizing the issue. He reminds his audiences of the bonds of affection which had bound them to one another from his first coming (4.12-15). They should recognize equally that the motives of the other missionaries were more mixed: the latter began by denying what was obvious to Paul and should be obvious to Paul's converts; they 'wish to shut you out *(ekkleisai)*' (4.17), to deny that the Galatian believers were already inheritors of the promise, in order to provoke a zeal *(zēloute)* like that of the most zealous of converts to traditional Judaism[376] — very different from Paul's maternal concern to bring them into full conformity to Christ (4.19).[377]

The depth of Paul's concern and fears is evident in his readiness to present a reading on the theme of sons of Abraham 'against the grain' of the Genesis texts (4.21-29) — probably, as already indicated, in response to the incoming missionaries' claims that the line of Abraham's inheritance ran to and through his son Isaac.[378] The basic point of Paul's rejoinder is his observation (or agreement) that sonship of Abraham was of two kinds: the one defined by slavery, the other by promise. The types of these two sons are the son of Hagar the slave girl

375. Paul alludes to a further aspect of *ioudaïzein* ('live as a Jew') on which the other missionaries evidently insisted on the part of the Galatians but of which we would otherwise have been unaware — the importance of observing Sabbath and the feasts which marked the Jewish calendar, an important aspect of 'Torah piety'; for details see my *Galatians* 227-29; also 'Echoes of Intra-Jewish Polemic in Paul's Letter to the Galatians', *JBL* 112 (1993) 459-77, reprinted in *The New Perspective* ch. 9, here (2005) 232-35, (2008) 238-41; Martyn, *Galatians* 414-18; references in Schnelle, *History* 102-103). Less likely is Witulski's suggestion of a reference to the festal calendar of the imperial cult (*Adressaten* 158-68), since in the context of Galatians a reference to Jewish festivals is much more probable (the absence of specific reference to 'Sabbaths' is hardly decisive against such a reference).

376. See further again my *Galatians* 238-39 and 'Echoes' 235-38.

377. Here the process of salvation (see my *Theology of Paul* §18) is vividly expressed in a striking variation on the image of the labour involved in giving birth to a child — a personalisation of the labour pains which bring forth the age to come (cf. Mark 13.8; Rom. 8.22-23; Col. 1.24). See also B. R. Gaventa, 'The Maternity of Paul: An Exegetical Study of Galatians 4.19', in R. T. Fortna and B. R. Gaventa, eds., *Studies in Paul and John*, J. L. Martyn FS (Nashville: Abingdon, 1990) 189-201; cf. Martyn, *Galatians* 42-31; Roetzel, *Paul* 50-52.

378. See above, n. 349. On the use of the Isaac/Ishmael contrast particularly in rabbinic Judaism, see Longenecker, *Galatians* 200-206. It is less clear that the other missionaries would have identified the Galatian believers with Ishmael (Barrett, 'Allegory' 161-62; Martyn, *Galatians* 434) — not least since Ishmael was already circumcised before Isaac was born (Gen. 17.23).

(Ishmael), and Isaac, the son promised to Abraham (the son of Sarah). Hagar speaks of Sinai[379] and so also of those, 'the present Jerusalem',[380] who identify with the Sinaitic covenant, the Torah (4.24-25).[381] In contrast to the slavery typified by Hagar, Sarah speaks of freedom, 'the Jerusalem above', the children of promise, born in accordance with the Spirit (4.26-29).[382]

To be presented with such a reading,[383] not so controversial in terms of the hermeneutics of the time,[384] would not have been so galling to the other missionaries, as the coda with which Paul concludes. He picks up the tradition that Ishmael teased or made fun of the younger Isaac (Gen. 21.9 LXX) and sees in it a typological foreshadowing of Jewish hostility to the gospel for the Gentiles (4.29). And such is his anxiety and irritation at what had been happening in Galatia that he quotes the angry words of Sarah (4.30): 'Throw out the slave girl and her son; for the son of the slave girl will never inherit with the son of the free' (Gen. 21.10). It is an invitation directed, of course, to the Galatian churches, to reject and eject the traditionalist missionaries from their midst. And though Paul's use of the verse could be heard as anticipating and even validating subsequent Christian anti-Semitism,[385] it is important to appreciate that his motivation

---

379. The point of connection ('Hagar-Sinai') as understood by Paul has eluded elucidation (*Galatians* 251-52).

380. For Martyn, this reference to Jerusalem would have proved the most offensive to the 'Teachers' (*Galatians* 28, 462-66).

381. Martyn's article 'Apocalyptic Antinomies in Paul's Letter to the Galatians', *NTS* 31 (1985) 410-24, remains basic in his more developed *Galatians* (particularly 36-41, 449-50, 456-57; see my *Galatians* 244, 252). It is quite important, however, to grasp that Paul does not work here with an antithesis between 'covenant' and 'law' (*pace* Martyn, *Galatians* 347 — Paul 'declares with polemical emphasis a divorce between the covenant and the *nomos*'; cf. 454-56). On the contrary, he thinks of 'two covenants', one of them 'from Mount Sinai' (4.24); the term 'covenant' itself is neutral. The same term *(diathēkē)* is used in 3.15, 17 but in the sense 'last will and testament' (BDAG 228); the contrast in 3.15-29 is between 'promise' (seven times) and 'law' (eight times), not between 'covenant' and 'law'. See further my 'Did Paul Have a Covenant Theology?', *The New Perspective on Paul* ch. 20, here (2005) 426-29, (2008) 432-35.

382. Paul does not hesitate to link the fulfilment of the promise to the reception of the Spirit, as he has already done in 3.14, thus reinforcing his claim that the reality of the Galatians' experience of the Spirit confirms that they are indeed already heirs of the promise (4.6-7).

383. The reworking of the same promise/Torah contrast in Rom. 4.13-16 is notably less provocative.

384. Paul was quite aware that he was drawing a deeper meaning from the Genesis stories than was apparent on the surface: 'such things are to be interpreted allegorically' (4.24). Alexandrian Judaism at least was well versed in the practice of allegorical interpretation, and Jerusalem as a heavenly ideal was familiar in Jewish apocalyptic thought (for details see my *Galatians* 247-48, 253-54).

385. Betz justifiably points to the contrast between the commanded 'throw out' here and the criticized 'shut out' in 4.17 (*Galatians* 250-51); but see also my *Galatians* 258-59.

was eschatological rather than racial. That is to say, he wanted all, Jew and Gentile, to enter into 'the fullness of the time' (4.4) begun with the coming of Christ; for Jew to remain in the relative slavery of being 'under the law' (in contrast to the liberty of the Spirit) was bad enough, but for believing Gentile to abandon that liberty in favour of that slavery was more than Paul could stomach (4.31–5.1).[386]

(v) *To accept circumcision was to abandon Christ* (5.2-12). The corollary was obvious; the gloves were now off! What the other missionaries were actually offering the Galatian believers was a choice between circumcision and Christ, between the law and grace; to choose the former was to cut themselves off from Christ, to fall away from grace (5.2-5); or as he had put it earlier, to choose the flesh and forget the Spirit (3.3).[387] The key was still faith: 'faith operating effectively through love' was really what they should be concerned for; the law measured by circumcision was a needless distraction (5.6).[388] He could only hope that they would hear what he was saying and ignore the blandishments and innuendos of the other missionaries. Better for the troublemakers to have themselves castrated than to have the Galatians circumcised (5.7-12)![389]

d. Living Responsibly — by the Spirit (Gal. 5.13–6.10)

The fact that Paul includes in the midst of his exhortation a reminder that the Galatians should support their (own) teachers (6.6) presumably implies that before leaving or passing on from these new Galatian churches, Paul had made arrangements to ensure appropriate teaching on such matters.[390] They would have

---

386. That Paul experienced his conversion as 'liberation' should never be ignored (5.1), that is, liberation from his heavily regulated life as a Pharisee, which he came to see, with hindsight, as a form of slavery; see further *Theology of Paul* 388-89, 434-35.

387. Sumney argues that there is insufficient evidence that the opponents in Galatia attached great theological significance to circumcision ('Studying Paul's Opponents' 24), which rings oddly with the implication that circumcision was regarded as the essential mark of covenant membership.

388. See further my 'Neither Circumcision nor Uncircumcision, but . . .', in *The New Perspective on Paul* ch. 13; also Martyn, *Galatians* 472-74.

389. The crudity of Paul's final expostulation (5.12) should not be downplayed, however much it may be excused in terms both of the times and of the strength of Paul's feelings (see my *Galatians* 282-84). That an allusion should be seen to the self-castration practised by devotees of Attis and the Mother Goddess (the *galli*) in central Anatolia certainly cannot be ruled out (for details see particularly S. Elliott, *Cutting Too Close for Comfort: Paul's Letter to the Galatians in Its Anatolian Cultic Context* [JSNTS 248; London: Clark, 2003]) and would have made the remark even more shocking to Paul's interlocutors.

390. Cf. Acts 14.23, and see above, §27.1f.

been responsible for reinforcing the traditions with which Paul himself had endowed the churches (§29.7i). How much these teachers had been able to withstand or counter the incomers' appeal to customs and traditions well rooted in the law, it is impossible to say; Paul expresses no sense of disappointment with regard to these teachers, only with regard to his converts generally.

We can readily envisage the other missionaries making their case for law-observance in that the law showed so clearly how those who called upon the name of the Lord should live, how they should conduct themselves. Despite their own teachers (6.6), this may well have been a major concern for Gentile converts, having committed themselves to a new Lord, and still inquiring what that new commitment should mean for their daily lives and relationships.[391] To such inquiry the incoming missionaries no doubt gave a straightforward and attractive answer: to the descendants and heirs of Abraham, God gave the law precisely in order to show them how to live as his people. Probably they also pointed out the corollary of living without the law as such to direct and regulate their way of life: the alternative to living Jewishly (*ioudaïzein* — 2.14) was to live as Gentile sinners (*ex ethnōn hamartōloi* — 2.15) lived; without the law, license would prevail.

Whether the other missionaries so argued, Paul was certainly alive to the persuasiveness of the argument for the law. His response is essentially that living by the Spirit is a third option[392] which has the strength and attractiveness of both the other alternatives but which avoids the weakness of both and is alive to the dangers of both.

- The freedom of the Spirit is a freedom not for self-indulgence but to serve one another (5.13).[393]
- The law is summed up in the commandment to 'love your neighbour as yourself',[394] and the motivating power of love ensures that those who live

391. Betz, *Galatians* 273; J. Barclay, *Obeying the Truth: A Study of Paul's Ethics in Galatians* (Edinburgh: Clark, 1988) 60-74.

392. Note the repetition and variation:
- 5.16 — Walk *(peripatein)* by the Spirit
- 5.18 — led *(agesthai)* by the Spirit
- 5.22 — the fruit *(karpos)* of the Spirit
- 5.25 — live *(zēn)* by the Spirit, follow *(stoichein)* the Spirit
- 6.8 — sow *(speirein)* to the Spirit

See further *Galatians* 295-96; *Theology of Paul* 642-49.

393. It is unnecessary to assume that in 5.13 Paul turned to address a 'second front' (Galatian enthusiasts), as originally suggested by W. Lütgert, *Gesetz und Geist. Eine Untersuchung zur Vorgeschichte des Galaterbriefes* (Gütersloh: Bertelsmann, 1919); the dangers were obvious (Kümmel, *Introduction* 301; Dunn, *Galatians* 285-86); see above, §30 at n. 232.

394. Another echo of Jesus' teaching: the focus on Lev. 19.18 is peculiarly Christian and

by that priority fulfil[395] what the law was intended to safeguard and promote (5.14-15).

- What the Spirit wants is the opposite of what the flesh wants (5.16-17):[396] the latter seeks only the satisfaction of its own appetites and desires,[397] which is what incapacitates it for a share in God's kingdom (5.19-21); but the Spirit bears fruit in the character of those who follow the Spirit, preeminently love (5.22-26).

- A Spirit-directed life[398] is quite different from one 'under the law' (5.18); hence the earlier exasperated questions of 3.2-3. The law is certainly not against such a love-motivated life (5.23), nor (by implication) can the law as such produce such character; so the Galatian converts in effect gain nothing (and lose everything) if they put themselves (back) under the law.

---

most likely was an innovation by Jesus himself; see *Jesus Remembered* 584-86, also *Galatians* 291-92.

395. The perfect tense (*peplērōtai*, 'is fulfilled') 'is probably to be translated "the whole law has found its full expression in a single word" or "is summed up under one entry"' (BDAG 828). Jewish tradition did not baulk at the thought of summing up the law in a single formulation; the tradition of Hillel summing up 'the whole law' in the negative form of the golden rule (*b. Shabb.* 31a) is well known. Paul obviously understood 'fulfilling the whole law *(ho pas nomos)*' (5.14) as different from 'being obliged to do the whole law *(holon ton nomon)*' (5.3); it is the difference between a requirement to live as a Jew (5.3) and a motivation to love the other (5.14), the difference spelled out in these verses (see further my *Galatians* 289-91). Martyn attempts to resolve the tension between 5.3 and 5.14 by speaking of the 'two voices' of the law: the law of Sinai that curses, and what he calls 'the original, pre-Sinaitic Law, consisting of God's single, promising word', even 'the Abrahamic Law' (*Galatians* 502-14). But this seems to cut across the clear distinction in Galatians 3 between the promise and the law (contrast his 347 cited in n. 381 above), and to identify Lev. 19.18 (Gal. 5.14) with the promise rather than the law of Sinai simply confuses the issue. It makes better sense to see Paul as distinguishing different functions of the law, some of them now passé, others still in effect; see my *Theology of Paul* §§6, 14, 23.

396. For the notion of existential conflict between Spirit and flesh see *Galatians* 297-300; *Theology of Paul* 477-82. Integral to Paul's argument is the insight that a relationship with God too much understood in terms of flesh ('circumcision in the flesh'; 3.3; 4.23, 29; 6.12-13) is as dangerous a reliance on 'flesh' as 'satisfying the desires of the flesh' (5.16); hence the definition of 'those who belong to Christ' as those who 'have crucified the flesh' (5.24). On the scope of Paul's understanding of 'flesh' see *Theology of Paul* 62-73.

397. 'The works of the flesh' (a typical 'vice-list') contrasted with 'the fruit of the Spirit (a Christian 'virtue-list'); for further details see *Galatians* 302-13; *Theology of Paul* 662-65.

398. 'Walk' = 'conduct oneself' is a typically Jewish metaphor (e.g., Exod. 18.20; Deut. 26.17; Josh. 22.5; Pss. 81.13; 86.11; Prov. 14.2; Isa. 57.2; 1QS 3.18-4.26; further F. J. Helfmeyer, *TDOT* 3.396-99) and untypical of Greek thought (H. Seesemann, *TDNT* 5.941). It may have been used by the incoming missionaries, since the OT speaks typically of 'walking in [God's] laws/statutes' (e.g., Exod. 16.4; 1 Kgs. 6.12; Jer. 44.23; Ezek. 5.6-7). The fact that the embryonic Christian movement was known as 'the way' (§20.1[14]) implies that from the beginning it was seen as a 'way' to be 'walked'.

- If law is still desired, the Galatians should think rather in terms of 'the law of Christ' (6.2); that is, they should form their living on the template provided by Christ, in the same spirit of gentleness, love of neighbour and absence of self-concern which Christ so exemplified (6.1-5).[399]
- What is finally at stake is the same: God's judgment on the lives they will have led. Here again, however, the way forward is not in terms of doing the law but in terms of 'sowing to the Spirit' in order to 'reap (the harvest of) eternal life', though the latter still requires sustained commitment and persistence (6.7-10).[400]

e. Conclusion (Gal. 6.11-18)

At this point Paul evidently took the pen in his own hand and rounded off this passionate letter with his own personally penned appeal. In it he shows how sharply antithetical to each other are his gospel (the gospel) and the message ('gospel'?) of the incoming traditionalists. The latter focuses on the issue of circumcision, but their motives (their real motives, he implies) are mixed. They want the Galatians circumcised because that will prove to their fellow Jews that they are still true to their ancestral traditions and thus assuage any hostility within Judaism to the message of the crucified Messiah (6.12).[401] They want the Galatian Gentiles to be circumcised 'in the flesh' in order that they may continue to boast in the privileges and prerogatives God has bestowed on ethnic Israel as in effect exclusive to Israel (6.13). The message of the cross, however, has transformed and rendered null all such discriminatory values. In this new world, this new creation,[402] neither circumcision nor uncircumcision counts for anything

---

399. By 'the law of Christ' Paul probably had in mind the way in which Jesus lived in relation to the law, as exemplified in the Jesus tradition which they knew, and as summed up in the love command (5.14); see further *Galatians* 321-24; *Theology of Paul* 649-58; Martyn, *Galatians* 554-58; Longenecker, *Triumph* 83-89; Wilckens, *Theologie* 1/3.159 n. 69, 164.

400. The importance of such exhortations in Paul's paraenesis is often missed; see further *The New Perspective on Paul* (2005) 74-80, (2008) 82-89.

401. Nanos interprets 6.12 (they try to compel the Galatian believers to be circumcised 'only that they may not be persecuted for the cross of our Lord') in terms of a Jewish community suffering 'status disapproval and loss of legal rights and privileges' (*Irony* 223) because they had failed to compel those who claimed the prerogatives of Jewish status to become fully part of the acknowledged Jewish community; but that would hardly be described as 'persecution for the cross of Christ'!

402. The 'antinomy' between 'new creation' and (implied) old creation (6.15) is central to Martyn's understanding of Paul's apocalyptic theology. But he sets his apocalyptic schema in too sharp antithesis to the whole idea of redemptive history — that is, of a purpose of God unfolding in and through history. His emphasis properly characterizes the 'revelation' which Christ constituted for Paul but does not do sufficient justice to the extent to which Paul sees God's saving purpose as a

(6.14-15).[403] This is what 'the Israel of God' needs to learn — that it is constituted by 'this rule' and should order its life by 'this rule' (6.16).[404]

f. The Aftermath

What was the result of Paul's letter to the Galatians? Did they hear his rebuke and
appeal and 'throw out' (4.30) the other missionaries? Or did Paul's stand in regard to the Galatian churches gain as little success as his stand in Syrian Antioch
(2.11-17)? The evidence is lacking for a clear answer. Some see the clue in Paul's
subsequent instructions regarding the collection Paul went on to make for the
church in Jerusalem.[405] According to 1 Cor. 16.1-2 Paul had given instructions to
the churches of Galatia in regard to the collection, implying a further letter in
which, perhaps, he took up the most controversial points of Galatians which the
other missionaries had disputed.[406] But in his subsequent letters regarding the
collection, only the churches of Macedonia and Achaia are mentioned as contributing to the collection (2 Cor. 9.2-4; Rom. 15.26); the churches of Galatia are noticeable by their absence. A plausible deduction from this is that the other missionaries were able to exploit Paul's over-reaction and potentially offensive
statements in Galatians and continued to win support from the Galatian Gentile
believers. In consequence of which they did not respond positively to Paul's second letter and did not participate in the collection.[407] In other words, the mission
from Antioch or Jerusalem succeeded in drawing the Galatian churches within
their sphere of influence and out of the circle of Paul's churches, the churches of
the Gentile mission. The letter to the Galatians, however, was preserved, either

---

historical process: Abraham as progenitor of seed; the giving of the law as having a role prior to
Christ; Christ coming in 'the fullness of time'; the growing up of heirs from minority (= slavery) to
majority (the gift of the Spirit). In Jewish (and Paul's!) perspective, apocalypse is the climax of
God's saving purpose for his people Israel, not a whole new start. Responses to Martyn's overem-
phasis on apocalyptic discontinuity are a reminder that the two emphases are not incompatible; see
my *Theology of Galatians* 36-52; Longenecker, *Triumph* ch. 1; Hays, *Faith of Jesus Christ* xxxv-xl.

403. See again n. 388 above.

404. Just who Paul thinks to be encompassed by/within 'the Israel of God' here (6.16) is
unclear and much disputed; cf., e.g., my *Galatians* 344-46 and Martyn, *Galatians* 574-77; see
also G. K. Beale, 'Peace and Mercy upon the Israel of God: The Old Testament Background of
Galatians 6,16b', *Biblica* 80 (1999) 204-33. Becker speaks for the majority when he concludes
that Paul has taken the 'salvific term' 'Israel of God' from Judaism and reclaimed it for the
church (*Paul* 464-65).

405. Particularly Martyn, *Galatians* 29-34. Contrast Schnelle, who deduces from Gal.
2.10 and silence otherwise on the subject that the collection was already complete (*History* 95).

406. Martyn refers to 4.25-27, 3.19-20, and 6.16 (*Galatians* 28-29).

407. Cf. Lüdemann, *Paul* 86-87.

by Paul himself retaining a copy or by its being circulated more widely before the Galatian churches turned their back firmly on Paul.

The alternative is that Paul's letter succeeded in its objective: most in the Galatian churches continued to espouse and live by the gospel proclaimed by Paul and rejected the overtures from Antioch/Jerusalem. Paul's instructions to the Galatians regarding the collection need not have involved a letter; instructions as in 1 Cor. 16.2-4 hardly required a letter and could have been delivered by verbal message. The absence of the Galatian churches from the subsequent references to the collection need not imply that the Galatian churches failed to contribute to the collection: the churches of Asia are not mentioned either, and it is hardly likely that they failed or refused to contribute; and, according to Acts 20.4, the list of delegates accompanying Paul on his last trip to Jerusalem included Gaius from Derbe, and Timothy (representing Lystra?), as well as Tychicus and Trophimus from Asia.[408] It is even possible that Paul mentioned only the churches of Macedonia and Achaia, since they were most proximate to Corinth (and Rome) and their example would serve as a greater spur to the Corinthians (2 Cor. 9.2-4). Or that, as things turned out, Paul saw the collection as primarily the fruit of his Aegean mission.

Whatever the facts of the case, the key fact is that Paul's letter to the Galatians was preserved, whether by the churches of Galatia themselves or because it was circulated early on or because Paul himself kept a copy. And thus it became an integral part of the Pauline heritage and corpus and in due course part of Christian Scripture, to serve as an enduring statement of the truth of the gospel as Paul perceived it.

In terms of the letter's wider impact, we may justifiably speculate that, whatever the outcome in Galatia itself, the more conservative traditionalist faction within the spectrum which was emerging Christianity would not have reacted favourably to the insulting language used by Paul.[409] Knowledge of and reaction to the letter may well have prompted the further excursions into 'Paul's territory', of which he complains in 2 Cor. 10.12-18 and Phil. 3.2, and presumably contributed to the hostility which met Paul in his final visit to Jerusalem (Acts 21.20-36). It may well be also that Paul himself, with hindsight, realized that in his letter to the Galatians he had spoken unwisely, perhaps even unfairly, so that his later more measured letter on the subject (Romans) benefited from and expressed more carefully his understanding of the gospel. We will have to bear in mind such possibilities in the chapters that follow.

---

408. As so often, when data from Acts do not fit with a thesis drawn more or less exclusively from Paul's letters, those data are simply discounted (as by Martyn, *Galatians* 227 n. 81, who also dismisses Georgi's suggestion that Paul's silence about Galatia may indicate that the Galatians' representatives had not yet arrived in Corinth).

409. Brown, *Introduction* 473-74, referring particularly to Gal. 2.14; 4.24-25; 5.12; 6.12-13.

CHAPTER 32

The Aegean Mission: Phase Two

32.1. Intermission

a. A Scrappy Account

The information provided by Luke for the second phase of Paul's Aegean mission is much less satisfactory for the historian (18.18–19.41).

- It begins with Paul undertaking what appears to be a Nazirite vow at the beginning of a lengthy trip back to Palestine (18.18-21), a trip which Luke treats in such a cursory fashion that Paul's destination is unclear and its purpose left wholly unexplained (18.22).
- The absence of indication of any companions for the trip is also rather odd, given Luke's normal practice in describing such journeys.[1]
- Paul's return to the Aegean theatre, described with equal brevity (18.23), is interrupted by twin episodes regarding Apollos (18.24-28) and twelve 'disciples' in Ephesus (19.1-7), which suggests that there was already a church established in Ephesus prior to Paul's major mission there, and which therefore raises questions about Paul's strategy (§29.4b).[2]
- Paul's own mission in Ephesus is described with similar brevity (19.8-12), Luke preferring to give greater attention to two episodes, from one of which Paul seems to have been strangely absent, and the other 'in the

---

1. Acts 13.4, 13, 51; 14.21, 24-27; 15.40; 16.6-12; 17.1; 18.8; 20.3-6; 21.1-17; 27.1-2; the only other exception is 20.1-3.

2. 'In reality there already existed in Ephesus, when Paul actually came to the city — 18.26 is proof — a Jewish-Christian community which however still lived in the fellowship of the synagogue with the other Jews' (Haenchen, *Acts* 547); similarly Lüdemann, *Early Christianity* 209.

wings' as it were (19.13-20, 23-41), with Paul himself only featuring some-what awkwardly between the two episodes in a note about his travel plans (19.21-22).

- Although Luke makes some point of indicating Paul's concern for the churches he has founded,[3] he makes no effort here to describe what we know from Paul's Corinthian correspondence to have been extensive com-munication and correspondence between Paul and the church in Corinth during his time in Ephesus. Luke's references to Paul's intention to go on to Macedonia and Achaia and to his sending Timothy and Erastus to Mace-donia while Paul remained in Asia (19.21-22) are so vestigial as to raise se-rious questions either as to how much Luke knew or as to whether he wanted to cover up something.
- Completely unmentioned is the possibility that Paul might have spent some time in prison during his sojourn in Ephesus, a possibility which has pro-vided the basis for various hypotheses to the effect that Paul also wrote 'the prison epistles' — Philippians, Philemon (and Colossians?) — during that imprisonment.[4]

As usual, the indications of Luke pursuing his own agenda are clear.

That Paul undertook a vow is part of what has been called Luke's 're-judaisation' of Paul,[5] that is, his attempt to show Paul more as a practising Jew than Paul's own letters imply — especially if he had not long since written his letter to the Galatians.

- The return to the church (in Jerusalem) and to Antioch (18.21-22) masks the strained relations which Paul's letters indicate or imply with these two centres, whose authority Paul had previously acknowledged but now ques-tioned (Gal. 2.6).[6]
- The integration of both Apollos and the twelve disciples into the Pauline mission (Acts 18.24–19.7) ensures that the line of gospel history runs with-out serious divergence or confusion from Jerusalem through the Hellenist mission (8.14-17; 11.22-24) and on in Paul's mission.
- The twin episodes also underline how central, the *sine qua non,* for Luke was the gift of the Spirit in the process/event of becoming a disciple/Chris-tian (19.2-6).

---

3. Acts 14.21-23; 15.41–16.5; 20.2, 17-38.
4. See below, §32.2e.
5. Much referred to is P. Vielhauer, 'On the "Paulinism" of Acts', in Keck and Martyn, eds., *Studies in Luke-Acts* 33-50 (here 37-43).
6. See above, §27.3c.

- The parallel between Peter and Paul is extended with an equivalent mention of the amazing miracles for which each was responsible (5.15; 19.11-12).
- The triumph over evil spirits, charlatan exorcists and magic in Ephesus (19.12-20) provides a most striking climax to an important strand in Luke's narrative (8.13, 18-24; 13.6-12); 'the word of God grew mightily and prevailed' (19.20).
- The outcome of the near riot in Ephesus is another brick in the wall of Luke's attempt to depict the new movement as in itself no threat to Rome's law and order.

At the same time, the very scrappiness of Luke's account probably indicates that he had been able to make use of reports and traditions which did not neatly fit together. The fact that Luke devotes substantial space to two episodes in which Paul, though named, is not actually at the centre of the story (making four such episodes in two chapters — 18.12-17, 24-28; 19.13-19, 23-41) is a strange procedure for one for whom Paul was the principal figure and great hero. But Luke tells them as he does, presumably because the stories came to him in this form. As in most cases, the words are the words of the story-teller (Luke), but the stories he most probably drew from earlier sources and eyewitnesses. So, while we can properly regret that he did not make more effort to fill in the blanks more fully, we can also take some reassurance from the fact that he did not weave a much more coherent and rounded narrative. How much more we can say as to the historical value of the individual reports and narrative links is a subject for fuller discussion.

b. Initial Contact with Ephesus (Acts 18.19-21)

That Paul should have planned a mission to and in Ephesus would fully accord with his overall strategy (§29.4a) — Ephesus being the capital of the Roman province of Asia and ideally sited for expansion both inland and through the Aegean.[7] Quite possibly he saw the sense of an initial, passing visit to reconnoitre 'the lie of the land'; with his mission being now so well established in Corinth, it was time to consider setting up base in another major centre. Paul's stated intention to return, 'God willing' (18.21), is a typical Pauline promise with qualification.[8]

The circumstances of such an initial visit in Luke's account are determined by Paul's determination to travel on to Palestine (18.19-20), to which we must return (§32.1d). And Luke does provide an answer to the conundrum posed above

---

7. See further below, §32.2a.
8. Rom. 1.10; 15.32; 1 Cor. 4.19; 16.7; but also in wider use (BDAG 448).

— as to whether there was a church in Ephesus prior to Paul's mission. The clear implication of the initial contact is that there was no church already there: Paul went, as usual, to the synagogue (18.19). The favourable response there mirrored an initially positive reaction in other centres;[9] no split within or from the synagogue is in view. The key factor is that when Paul left Ephesus, he left Priscilla and Aquila behind, and they continued in effect as representatives of Paul's mission, with the implication that their continued witness would have been within the synagogue in Ephesus. And if and when they succeeded in winning interest in Jesus Messiah, or even in establishing a gathering (house church) of Jesus messianists within or attached to the Ephesus synagogue, the resultant meeting (church) could hardly be described as a non-Pauline foundation.[10] The fact that Paul on his return to Ephesus once again began in the synagogue (19.8) suggests, as Luke presumably intended, that we can speak only of the foundation of the Ephesian church in the period which followed.

There is no reason to see a contrivance of Luke's here. Priscilla and Aquila were obviously a couple with means who probably had business links or even branches of their business in Ephesus, as well as in Corinth and Rome.[11] That would explain both why they accompanied Paul on this first visit to Ephesus, and presumably stayed on there when Paul himself continued his journey to Palestine, and why they would not have seen themselves as missionaries or evangelists (they were preoccupied with the affairs of business). The sequel of Priscilla and Aquila not preaching themselves but taking Apollos aside (in the synagogue) to bring him up to date with the beliefs of the Jesus movement (18.26) provides a coherent and consistent picture. Given a free hand, Luke might well have been tempted to attribute Apollos's being brought fully within the fold to the instruction of Paul himself. As we shall note further below, the fact that Luke does not bend his narrative to show that Apollos was confirmed by one or other of leading figures, like Peter and John (8.14-17) or Barnabas (11.22-24), is a firm indication of Luke's faithfulness to the traditions he received on the subject.[12]

9. Acts 13.42-43; 14.1; 17.4, 11-12.

10. 'Prisca, and Aquila . . . were the real founders of the church at Ephesus' (Murphy-O'Connor, *Paul* 171-72); similarly Becker, *Paul* 151-52. Note the reference to 'the brothers' in 18.27. The implication is that Apollos's preaching within the synagogue attracted those already convinced by Paul's initial preaching and/or Priscilla's and Aquila's continued witness. If Priscilla and Aquila opened their house to such believers, Apollos would probably have taken part in the house-group discussions and worship and won their support for his visit to Corinth. At all events, 'the brothers' were sufficiently conscious of their identity as Jesus-believers to communicate with the more-established church in Corinth, where a breach with the synagogue had already occurred. See also Schnabel, *Mission* 1217-19.

11. See further §31.4b above.

12. See also P. Trebilco, *The Early Christians in Ephesus from Paul to Ignatius* (WUNT 166; Tübingen: Mohr Siebeck, 2004) 125-27.

c. Did Paul Undertake a Vow?

Luke tells us that, before leaving Achaia, Paul[13] undertook a vow at Corinth's Aegean seaport, Cenchrea (18.18).[14] The vow which Luke envisages was probably analogous to the Nazirite vow described in Num. 6.1-21, in which case the vow was not to cut his hair during a specified period. So presumably what is described in conjunction with it here ('he had his hair cut') would be Paul's final haircut before the vow took effect.[15] Since such a vow could only be completed at the central sanctuary (offering up the previously unshorn hair — Num. 6.18), the implication of Acts 21.23-24 is probably that the vow was maintained until Paul's final visit to Jerusalem.

For those who see Paul's attitude to the law, and particularly its rituals, as (almost wholly) negative, the account indicates the creative hand of Luke.[16] But Paul's attitude to the law was not so negative as is often portrayed.[17] And, as with the earlier episode of Timothy's circumcision (16.3),[18] such an action would have been wholly consistent with Paul's stated pastoral tactics, as expressed in 1 Cor. 9.20.[19] Moreover, Luke does not emphasize the Jewish character of the vow here, and in 21.23-26 he does not relate Paul's recommended action as fulfilment of the vow made earlier; it is more likely that he passes on reports whose substance and significance he himself did not fully appreciate.[20] Consequently, it would be unwise to dismiss the action reported here as merely a Lukan fabrication. And if we take the report seriously, as a traditionally Jewish vow made by Paul in preparation for a visit to the homeland, perhaps in recognition that the un-

---

13. Luke's syntax could refer to Aquila as taking the vow, but Paul as the central figure of the narrative is probably intended. Haenchen briefly reviews secondary literature on the subject (*Acts* 545).

14. Another of Luke's vague time references, 'many days' (18.18; see §31 n. 221), added to the period prior to the Gallio ruling, leaves room for various sub-missions in the region; the church at Cenchrea was to have the redoubtable Phoebe as its patron (Rom. 16.1-2).

15. Lake and Cadbury, *Beginnings* 4.230; Haenchen, however, thinks that the reference must be to the completion of a vow (*Acts* 543 n. 2, 546); Jervell wonders whether Luke understood the regulations relating to the vow (*Apg.* 466). *NDIEC* 4.114-15 refers to Juvenal's account of sailors shaving their heads, presumably in fulfilment of vows taken during a dangerous sea journey (*Sat.* 12.81), a parallel which Taylor finds suggestive ('Roman Empire' 2488). See also below, §34 at n. 18.

16. Haenchen, *Acts* 543; H. Conzelmann, *Die Apostelgeschichte* (HNT 7; Tübingen: Mohr Siebeck, 1963) 107; Lüdemann, *Early Christianity* 205.

17. See my *Theology of Paul* §§6, 14 and 23; *New Perspective on Paul* (2005) 63-80, (2008) 71-89.

18. See above, §31.2a.

19. See above, §29.5b.

20. See also Barrett's discussion (*Acts* 2.877-78).

dertaking was somewhat hazardous, the appropriate inference to draw is that the vow was an expression of Paul's willingness to go some way towards meeting the concerns of his fellow Jewish believers in regard to his own respect for and observance of the law and the ancestral customs. Which suggests, in turn, that Paul intended his visit to Syria to be one of reconciliation. A Nazirite vow would demonstrate Paul's willingness to follow the Torah in matters of personal spiritual discipline, it would demonstrate his 'good faith' to the Torah conservatives in Antioch (and Jerusalem), and hopefully it would heal any continuing rift with them.[21] The report that he undertook such a vow is not confirmed by Paul in his letters, but that hardly counts as a counter-argument, since there was no obvious occasion for him to refer to it.

d. Why the Visit to Palestine?

It was possible to sail direct to Caesarea, or at least without calling at the northern Syrian ports. So even if the (implied) intention was to go only to Antioch, availability of passage or adverse winds may have left Paul no option other than to go to Caesarea.[22] And once there, a trip to Jerusalem would have been hard to avoid.

Despite his awareness of Paul's unpopularity in Jerusalem,[23] Luke passes over the visit in almost embarrassed silence — 'having gone up and greeted the church [Jerusalem itself is not mentioned], he went down to Antioch'. Nothing is said about a meeting with James or the elders (as in 21.18), or of Paul reporting his further successes (as in 15.12 and 21.19); Luke's previous reports to that effect had been brief enough, so why he excluded any similar description is certainly a puzzle and inevitably raises questions as to the reason for and success of the visit.

Mention of the visit to Antioch is almost as brief: beyond the fact that Paul 'spent some time *(chronon tina)* there', nothing more is said. Luke was presumably content thus to reaffirm the impression that the threads linking Paul's mis-

---

21. The Western text adds to Paul's speech, 'I must at all costs keep the approaching festival in Jerusalem', but does not specify which feast.

22. Lake and Cadbury, *Beginnings* 4.231; Haenchen, *Acts* 547-48. 'Syria' (18.18; as in 20.3) could simply refer to the eastern Mediterranean seaboard (Palestine being treated as a subprovince of Syria at that time) and therefore would be inclusive of a visit to either Jerusalem or Antioch or both. But in Acts it would more naturally be taken to refer to Syria proper (15.23, 41; 21.3), and with the visit to Jerusalem passed over without the city itself being named (18.22), the implication is that Paul wished primarily to visit Antioch, the church which first formally commissioned him (13.3).

23. Acts 9.29; 21.21, 27-36.

sion to the mother churches of Syria remained unbroken. Nothing more need be said. And since Luke had passed over in total silence the earlier confrontation in Antioch and the likely breach with Antioch (§27.6), there was evidently nothing else of substance that he could report.

These minimalist reports, however, have naturally intrigued historians, who tend either to dispute whether the visits took place or to build them up into something more significant. Was Luke as confused over this reported fourth visit of Paul to Jerusalem as he seems to have been over the reported second visit (11.30)?[24] Would Paul have undertaken the lengthy and potentially hazardous journey to and from to Syria/Palestine for a visit which seems to have been so inconsequential? Would Paul have returned to Antioch or Jerusalem so soon after the breach in Antioch occasioned by the representatives of James (Gal. 2.11-14), particularly if he had so recently been required to resist the encroachments of missionaries from Antioch or Jerusalem in Galatia (§31.7)? Alternatively, perhaps Luke has confused or has conflated the accounts of different visits to Jerusalem and the conference in Jerusalem only took place on this third or fourth visit (Gal. 2.1-10 = Acts 18.22a), followed by the incident in Antioch (Gal. 2.11-14 = Acts 18.22b).[25]

Each of the scenarios envisaged can be filled out and fitted into what we know from Paul's letters. But there is really no good reason here to depart from Luke's own account, and too little reason to attribute it to his own creativity. If the test of *cui bono?* applies, Luke has made such a hash of drawing anything from a visit which advances his several concerns that it was hardly worth his inclusion of the visit.[26] And there seems to be no good reason for Luke to have transferred the account of Acts 15 from Acts 18.22 to its present location, if indeed Acts 18.22 was the occasion for the major conference and agreement in Jerusalem. More to the point, given what we already know of Luke's practice of drawing a veil over unpleasant and fractious relations between Paul and the leadership in Jerusalem and Antioch,[27] the brevity of Luke's account in 18.22 suggests that here we have another case where Luke had reports of such a visit but was embarrassed at the fuller details he knew but chose not to record.[28]

So why would Paul have undertaken such a visit, especially after he had given vent to the fierce polemic of Galatians? A partial answer could be, of course, that after several years absence from his homeland and home congrega-

24. See above, §25.5g.

25. See above, §28 nn. 47 and 48. Haenchen traces the first instance of the view back to Jakob Cappellus (*Acts* 544 n. 6).

26. The fact that the journey is 'wholly without point' 'shows that Luke once again has to do with tradition'; 'no special Lukan interest is visible in it' (Jervell, *Apg.* 467-68).

27. See above, §21.2d.

28. Weiss, *Earliest Christianity* 307.

tion he felt the need for a furlough, for some break from the intensity of his evangelistic and pastoral responsibilities (cf. 2 Cor. 11.28). In a day of modern ease of travel (by train and plane) we naturally stand in some awe at the time and effort which such a return visit would have involved. But seasoned travellers like Paul readily undertook lengthy journeys, officials and envoys from Rome to Asia Minor and beyond, merchants and emissaries criss-crossing the Mediterranean, every year or more frequently, and the homeward journey, by ship, may have been relatively inviting for the time it gave Paul for reflection and prayer and the possibility to visit new churches in the intermediate ports of call.

Another possibility is that Paul paid a brief, private visit to Jerusalem in order to discharge the vow he had taken in Cenchrea (Acts 18.18),[29] though in that case it is again surprising that Luke made nothing of it, since such a visit would presumably have advanced the portrayal of Paul's relations with Jerusalem that Luke wanted to promote.

More likely, however, the concerns which resulted in Paul going to Jerusalem in Gal. 2.1-2 were still a major factor for Paul. If it had been important for Paul at that earlier time to ensure that the Jerusalem leadership recognized and affirmed his gospel and its success (Gal. 2.2),[30] then it would still be as important to ensure that recognition and affirmation now. It would be particularly important to have the agreement of Gal. 2.6-9 reconfirmed, especially in the wake of the Antioch incident and the repercussions in Galatia.[31] If indeed the crisis in Galatia had been the sequel to Paul's defeat in Antioch (§31.7a), it became all the more important that the earlier agreement with the pillar apostles should be restated and affirmed afresh. We do not know the result of Paul's letter to the Galatian churches; quite likely he himself did not yet know the outcome. Or was his decision to go to Jerusalem to reassert his agreed commission occasioned by some report (from the person who delivered and read the letter to the Galatian churches?) as to the response it had provoked? In any case, crucial for Paul himself would be renewed ratification of 'the gospel for the uncircumcision' (Gal. 2.7) by the Jerusalem leadership. Unless his gospel was reaffirmed and the demand for Gentile believers to be circumcised (and undertake other works of the law) was countermanded by the Jerusalem leadership, there was bound to be continued interference in Paul's mission from law-insistent Jewish believers. And Paul would have wanted to avoid such interference if at all possible. A visit to the Jerusalem leadership was the one action which might secure the restatement of the Gal. 2.6-9 agreement. Similarly, if the incomers to Galatia had been sent from or claimed the authority of Antioch as the mother church of the Galatian

29. Hvalvik, 'Paul as a Jewish Believer' 139-41.
30. See above, §27.3c.
31. Cf. Barrett, *Acts* 2.880-81.

plantings, a visit to Antioch to have the Jerusalem agreement at least reaffirmed there too would have been unavoidable.

If this provides the likely rationale for Paul's visit to Jerusalem and Antioch, then Luke's silence about the details of the visit and its outcome once again is pregnant with implication of a visit which did not succeed in its purpose.[32] Any attempt by Paul for a renewed recognition of and support for his mission probably did not win the assent he had hoped for. Relations remained strained. And the breach with the Antioch congregation was probably not healed.[33] The indications of subsequent encroachments upon Paul's mission (2 Corinthians 10–13; Philippians 3) should probably be seen as confirmation of Paul's lack of success in Jerusalem and Antioch.

Perhaps we should also infer that this lack of success made Paul realize he had to make a still greater effort to rebuild bridges between the Gentile and Jewish missions, by raising a collection for the mother church in Jerusalem from as many of his own church foundations as he could recruit to the cause.[34] This would certainly explain why the collection for Jerusalem became precisely such a major priority for Paul in the second phase of his Aegean mission, as the letters certainly written during that period attest;[35] perhaps, indeed, it was his visit to the church (in Jerusalem, 18.22) which had brought home to Paul how many of the believers there were poor and in need of support from alms. By thus making good the one 'condition' to which he had willingly given assent in the earlier Jerusalem agreement (Gal. 2.10),[36] Paul demonstrated his own good faith and commitment to that agreement, made conjointly with the Jerusalem leadership, and

32. The fact that Paul apparently travelled alone, without the support of any one or more of his growing band of co-workers (§29.6), may also indicate that he undertook the trip to Jerusalem without the support and perhaps against the strong advice of such co-workers. The outcome was what they had feared!

33. Contrast Taylor, who argues that this visit to Antioch effected a degree of reconciliation with the leaders of the Antioch (and Jerusalem) churches, indicated by the diminution of animosity towards these churches and of Paul's earlier defensiveness regarding his apostolic status (*Paul* ch. 7).

34. For Taylor the reconciliation included Paul's 'rejoining the collection project', and the anonymous brother of 2 Cor. 8.18 was probably a prominent member of the Antioch church seconded by them to assist Paul in the collection (*Paul* 200-203).

35. 1 Cor. 16.1-4; 2 Corinthians 8–9; Rom. 15.25-28.

36. Those who prefer to date Galatians to the second phase of Paul's Aegean mission see Gal. 2.10 as a further reference to the collection, just as those who identify Gal. 2.1-10 with Acts 11.30 see Gal. 2.10 as an allusion to the famine aid, which Acts 11.30 says was the purpose of that visit. However, it is not at all clear whether the final clause of Gal. 2.10 ('the very thing which I have eagerly done') need refer to any particular fund-raising exercise; it may simply assert that Paul always had been concerned 'to remember the poor' and continued to be so. See above, §27.3d at n. 186, and below, §33.4.

presumably hoped that by so doing he would encourage (or shame) them into re-affirming its key clauses as well.

Paul's decision to return to the main focus of his mission (in the Aegean) by land would be understandable as it allowed further visits to the churches of the earlier mission from Antioch.[37] Without knowing either how the letter to the Galatians had been received or how the trip to Jerusalem and Antioch turned out, we naturally remain much in the dark over the trip. But we can infer with some confidence that Paul would have wanted either to consolidate whatever success he had gained with the letter and/or the visit or to bolster his supporters if one or both had failed in their purpose. The other main objective would probably have been to recruit the Galatians to the new plan to gather a collection from among his churches for the poor in Jerusalem; 1 Cor. 16.1 indicates that it was the churches of Galatia to whom Paul had first given instructions on how to go about gathering contributions to the collection. This suggests, whatever the outcome of the letter (Galatians) and the visit, that Paul had been able to retain the Galatian churches within his sphere of influence for at least the next stage of his work.

e. Enter Apollos (Acts 18.24-28)

The interlude in Paul's Aegean mission allows Luke to insert the story of how Apollos was drawn into the Pauline circle by Priscilla and Aquila. With Barnabas, Apollos is one of the most intriguing figures in earliest Christian history; the several brief references to him only serve to stir curiosity still further.[38] Not least in the fascination he exerts is the fact that, as 'a native of Alexandria' (18.24), Apollos is the one man (of whom we know among the earliest believers) who provides a clear link between earliest Christianity and Alexandria — Alexandria being the second greatest city in the Roman Empire, a major centre of learning and of Jewish settlement and the source of most of the diaspora Jewish literature which we still possess (including the Greek translation of the Scriptures, the LXX, several of the writings preserved in the Apocrypha and the extensive expository writings of the Jewish philosopher Philo, Paul's older contemporary). The description of Apollos which follows gives some credibility to the suggestion that the beginnings of Christianity in Alexandria were not entirely 'orthodox' (to use the later term).[39]

---

37. Acts 13.14–14.23; 15.41–16.5; on the travel itinerary envisaged in 18.23, see above, §31.2 at n. 32. For the reasons already given (§31.1), this should not be described as the beginning of 'the third missionary journey'.

38. Acts 18.24; 19.1; 1 Cor. 1.12; 3.4-6, 22; 4.6; 16.12; Tit. 3.13.

39. See further vol. 3; also n. 41 below.

This Alexandrian background makes all the more intriguing the description that Apollos was 'a learned or eloquent man *(anēr logios)*,[40] well versed in or powerful in (his exposition of) the Scriptures' (18.24). There is an open invitation here to imagine one who expounded the Scriptures in the manner of the Wisdom of Solomon or of a Philo or other Hellenistic Jewish apologists.[41] Since these writings provide examples of how diaspora Judaism confronted wider Hellenistic religion and philosophy, both exemplary for and alternative to Christian apologetic, we can well understand how it is that Apollos appears in the NT as a somewhat ambivalent figure, and how some could attribute the authorship of Hebrews to him.[42]

The impression that Apollos was a figure somewhat on the edge of mainline developments[43] is confirmed by the description here (18.25-26). He had been 'instructed (catechized) in the way of the Lord';[44] he was 'aglow with the Spirit'; 'he spoke and taught accurately the traditions about Jesus' (cf. 28.31). But he had been baptized only with 'the baptism of John'; his instruction in 'the way of the Lord' indicates further influence from Baptist traditions;[45] and his knowledge of the way was not wholly accurate. The implication is that his knowledge of Jesus came from reports of Jesus' ministry prior to his death and resurrection (the 'Galilean gospel'), perhaps even from the period of overlap with the ministry of John the Baptist (John 3.26):[46] he had responded to the challenge made by Jesus himself, responding in the way the first disciples had done — by undergoing the baptism which the Baptist had instituted. Whatever the uncertainty, Luke's description confirms that for him John's baptism marked the beginning, but only the beginning, of the gospel.[47]

---

40. On *logios* see Lake and Cadbury, *Beginnings* 4.233; BDAG 598.

41. 'It is difficult to imagine that an Alexandrian Jew with precisely these qualifications . . . could have escaped the influence of Philo' (Murphy-O'Connor, *Paul* 275).

42. Bibliography in Kümmel, *Introduction* 402; Schnelle, *History* 367.

43. Cf., e.g., those referred to by Jervell, *Apg.* 470 n. 376.

44. No indication is given of where and by whom this happened; but D adds that it happened in Apollos's homeland, Alexandria. As Barrett notes, this 'is by no means impossible. There was a very large Jewish community in Alexandria, and in the constant coming and going between that city and Jerusalem there must have been some Jews who had accepted and were concerned to spread the new faith' (*Acts* 2.888).

45. Cf. Mark 1.3 pars. Is the prominence given to 'the way' in Ephesus (18.25-26; 19.9, 23) perhaps an indication of a wider influence from Baptist traditions? But 'the way' was an early description for the new movement; see §20.1(14) above.

46. See *Jesus Remembered* 350-55. But knowing only the baptism of John (18.25) does not necessarily mean that he was a disciple of the Baptist as such; 'the baptism of John' could serve as a generic description of a baptism of repentance, in distinction from baptism in the name of Jesus.

47. Cf. 1.22; 10.37; 13.24-25.

There must have been many such as Apollos — men and women who had heard and responded to early or incomplete or distorted accounts of Jesus and the gospel as it had begun to be proclaimed in Jerusalem, by the Hellenists and in the mission of Paul. In the early years of a movement like Christianity, defining characteristics and boundaries are always less distinct than hindsight cares to admit. It was precisely one of the major functions and achievements of both Paul and Luke to fill out the Christian identity, its characteristics and boundaries. The key question would be whether such individuals should be regarded as already full disciples, or how should their deficiency be rectified? In this and the next episode Luke gives his answer. In the case of Apollos it was important that his teaching of Jesus tradition was accurate, that he had received the baptism associated with John the Baptist, and that he spoke boldly in the synagogue.[48] But the decisive consideration was probably that he was 'aglow with the Spirit'.[49] In consequence, all that he needed was some further instruction. Unlike the 'disciples' in the following episode, he apparently did not need to be baptized in the name of Jesus: John's baptism complemented by the gift of the Spirit was sufficient — as in the case of the first disciples themselves (1.5).[50] In contrast, it was precisely because they had no inkling of the Spirit that the twelve dealt with next by Paul had to go through the whole initiation procedure (19.2-6). In both cases it was the presence or absence of the Spirit which was decisive; the assessment of Priscilla and Aquila on the issue was as Paul's. For Luke once more it is the coming of the Spirit which is the central and most crucial factor in conversion-initiation and in Christian identity.[51]

48. Cf. 9.27-28; 13.46; 14.3; 19.8.

49. Does *zeōn tō pneumati* mean 'with burning zeal', as BDAG 426 and the major English translations (Shauf, *Theology as History* 138 n. 62), or 'aglow with the Spirit', as Chrysostom and many commentators (Shauf 138 n. 63). That a reference to the Holy Spirit is intended seems likely in view of Paul's use of the same phrase in Rom. 12.11; since Luke uses other language to describe the action of the Spirit in and on individuals, he probably owes the phrase to the tradition/report he heard about the episode (see my *Baptism* 88; also 70; Haenchen, *Acts* 550 n. 8; Lüdemann, *Early Christianity* 209; Bruce, *Acts* 402; Barrett, *Acts* 2.888). Speaking boldly (*parrēsiazesthai*) is something Luke associates with Paul (Acts 9.27-28; 13.46; 14.3; 19.8; 20.26) and probably also reflects Paul's sentiments (cf. 1 Thess. 2.2; *parrēsia* — 2 Cor. 3.12; 7.4; Phil. 1.20; Col. 2.15; Phlm. 8); for the Pauline assumption that the Spirit inspires such boldness in speech, see Rom. 15.18-19; 1 Cor. 2.4; 2 Cor. 3.12 (in context); 4.13; 1 Thess. 1.5.

50. Lüdemann misses the point when he infers from the two stories being set in parallel that Apollos received the Holy Spirit only by being instructed (*Early Christianity* 211); similarly Jervell in deducing that 'if someone has only John's baptism, then he does not know the Spirit' (*Apg.* 470, 475).

51. As in Acts 2.38; 8.15-17; 9.17; 10.44-47; 11.15-17; 19.2-6; see again my *Baptism* 90-102.

The episode plays a further role, for Apollos became a prominent figure within the Aegean mission, as Luke knew well (18.26-28). We know also from 1 Corinthians that Apollos became a focus for some dissatisfaction and disaffection regarding Paul,[52] a kind of George Whitefield to Paul's John Wesley, as we might say. In other words, in his case there was a real danger of an off-centre or out-of-focus kind of Christianity developing round Apollos, particularly as he had rhetorical skills which Paul evidently lacked.[53] It was therefore important for Luke to be able to tell the story of how Apollos, for all his fervency in Spirit and accurate knowledge about Jesus, still had to be and in the event was instructed more accurately in 'the way of God' (18.25-26). Any challenge or even threat he may have been thought to pose to the Pauline mission[54] is defused by the report of his fervency in Spirit and fuller instruction by those prominent members of the Pauline team, Priscilla and Aquila. The point being made is that the Christianity established in the Aegean region was the Christianity of Paul and his team.[55] That Paul did regard Apollos as a fellow worker subsequently is confirmed by 1 Cor. 16.12, with Priscilla and Aquila also close at hand (1 Cor. 16.19).

The account here was probably derived ultimately from Priscilla and Aquila, or even from Apollos himself.[56] Luke's willingness to leave the anomaly of Apollos's status as unclear as he has suggests that Luke has told the story as he heard it, even though it jars somewhat with his own presentation of the exclusive Jerusalem-centred origins for the new movement. And even if Apollos came somewhat 'out of the blue', there is no reason to doubt Luke's account of a letter of recommendation being written by the Ephesian 'brothers' to Corinth (18.27); such letters of commendation evidently became a common practice as believers travelled from place to place[57] and a major means of cementing the scattered churches into a single identity. Nor is there any reason to doubt Apollos's connection with the Corinthian church,[58] since it is so strongly confirmed by Paul in 1 Corinthians 1–4, where his ministry in succession to Paul and the power and effectiveness of his speaking are also clearly implied. The way he helped the be-

52. 1 Cor. 1.12; 3.4-7; 4.6. See further below, n. 203.

53. Cf. Acts 18.24, 28; 1 Corinthians 1–4; 2 Cor. 10.10.

54. Cf. 1 Cor. 1.12; 3.4-7; 4.6-7. M. Wolter, 'Apollos und die ephesinischen Johannesjünger (Act 18:24–19:7)', *ZNW* 78 (1987) 49-73, argues that Luke's portrayal reflects the rivalry between Paul and Apollos in Corinth and makes it clear that the authority to convey the Spirit belonged exclusively to Paul.

55. Jervell, *Apg.* 472.

56. Contrast Becker: 'Acts 18:24-28 as a whole is hardly historically reliable' (*Paul* 153).

57. Rom. 16.1; Col. 4.7-17; cf. 2 Cor. 3.1. See also §30.8 above.

58. On the elaboration in D, to the effect that the original suggestion for Apollos to go to Corinth came from 'certain Corinthians staying in Ephesus', see Metzger, *Textual Commentary* 467-68; Barrett, *Acts* 2.890-91.

lievers there, Luke tells us, was by vigorously refuting the Jews in Corinth on the central issue that the Messiah was Jesus (as in 17.3 and 18.5). Here we may note again that, although the Corinthian church had already established itself separately from the synagogue, substantial discussion about Jesus and the messianic prophecies between them is still envisaged, though it took place 'in the open, publicly'. Gallio had been right: this was still a Jewish sect and an intra-Jewish argument.

f. Disciples without the Spirit! (Acts 19.1-7)

> [1]While Apollos was in Corinth, Paul passed through the interior regions and came to Ephesus, where he found some disciples. [2]He said to them, 'Did you receive the Holy Spirit when you became believers?' They replied, 'No, we have not even heard that there is a Holy Spirit'. [3]Then he said, 'Into what then were you baptized?' They answered, 'Into John's baptism'. [4]Paul said, 'John baptized with the baptism of repentance, telling the people to believe in the one who was coming after him, that is, Jesus'. [5]On hearing this, they were baptized in the name of the Lord Jesus. [6]When Paul had laid hands on them, the Holy Spirit came upon them, and they spoke in tongues and prophesied. [7]Altogether there were about twelve of them.

Although Luke makes no effort to link the two episodes (those of Apollos and the twelve 'disciples'), it is difficult to avoid the conclusion that the two stories came to him together, and with some implication that they were indeed linked. Both are set in Ephesus; both feature an imperfectly instructed advocate of 'the way of the Lord' or 'disciples' requiring to be better taught; and for both the 'baptism of John' had evidently been the committal point of their believing. The major difference between the two stories seems to lie in the fact that Apollos already had the Spirit, and so did not need to be baptized in Jesus' name (18.25-26); whereas the others, not having the Spirit, were treated as new converts (19.2-6).[59] The probable inference is that the twelve had been won to belief by Apollos as a result of his charismatic preaching, but prior to Apollos's further instruction by Priscilla and Aquila — though their declared lack of knowledge about the Spirit (19.2) is still a surprise on most scenarios. Perhaps we should best infer that they were neither Jews nor God-fearers but rather somewhat peripheral Gentiles who therefore lacked what all Jews and almost all God-fearers (and hearers of the Baptist) would have been able to take for granted in reference to the Spirit of God.[60]

---

59. See again my *Baptism* 83-87; also Bruce, *Acts* 406-407; Schnabel, *Mission* 1216-17.

60. See further Shauf, *Theology as History* 105-10, 144-61. For bibliography on the puzzle of the Ephesian 'disciples' see also, e.g., Bruce, *Acts* 406, and my *Baptism* 84. Jervell

Once again the vagueness of Luke's account and the conundrum which it poses — how could 'disciples' (19.1) 'have not even heard that there is a Holy Spirit' (19.2)? — suggests a report which Luke passes on rather than contrives for his own ends. To be sure, the episode serves one of Luke's principal concerns: to document the gift of the Spirit as the key factor in determining Christian identity (19.2-6).[61] But that was probably the reason why he included it rather than evidence that he created such an anomalous episode; and the portrayal of Paul's concern in Acts 19.2 is entirely of a piece with Paul's own priorities indicated in Gal. 3.2.[62] Moreover, visible manifestations of the Spirit's coming upon new converts (Acts 19.6) is by no means only a Lukan motif (8.18; 10.46). Paul evidently had witnessed such manifestations in his converts,[63] though neither Luke nor Paul implies that such manifestations are inevitable or uniform or necessarily of a particular kind. All in all, however, it is difficult to avoid the conclusion that whoever first told this story either heard it from Paul himself or knew Paul very well.

It is worth noting two other assumptions within the story of the twelve 'disciples'.[64] First, that the status of disciple/believer presupposes baptism. The sequence of Paul's questions is telling: 'Did you receive the Holy Spirit when you believed?' If not, 'Into what then were you baptized?' (19.2-3). Second, that baptism in the name of Jesus would normally be part of a response to the call to believe in Jesus climaxing in the gift of the Spirit (2.38; 19.5-6).[65] As regards the further laying on of hands (19.6), the implication seems to be that laying on of

---

(*Apg.* 477-78) rightly objects to the anachronism of Haenchen's comment that 'Paul wins over the sects' (*Acts* 557). Trebilco thinks it quite possible that there were followers of John the Baptist in Ephesus around 52 CE (*Early Christians* 130-32), though how that relates to the twelve's having been won to discipleship by Apollos is unclear.

61. Luke highlights it by having Paul ask the crucial question: 'Did you receive the Holy Spirit when you believed?' (19.2). The question of baptism is secondary to that (19.3). Discipleship without the Spirit is self-evidently a contradiction in terms. See above, n. 51.

62. Acts 19.2 — 'Did you receive the Holy Spirit when you believed?' Gal. 3.2 — 'Did you receive the Spirit by works of the law or by hearing with faith?' For Paul too it is reception of the Spirit which constitutes a person as a member of Christ (Rom. 8.9; 1 Cor. 12.13; Gal. 3.2-3); see further my *Theology of Paul* §16.

63. Cf. Rom. 15.18-19; 1 Cor. 1.4-5; Gal. 3.5; 4.6.

64. Luke actually says, 'The men in all were *about (hōsei)* twelve in number' (19.7). It is hardly likely, then, that he saw them as some kind of equivalent to 'the twelve'; otherwise he would have avoided using the *hōsei*.

65. The various accounts provided by Luke, including Acts 8.14-17 and 10.44-48, can hardly be taken to indicate Luke's belief that baptism bestowed the Spirit; it is simply an inaccurate rendering of Luke's account (as of Luke 3.21-22) for Fitzmyer to say that 'the episode emphasizes Christian baptism as a baptism in the Spirit' (*Acts* 642), or for Jervell to say, 'The difference between John's baptism and Jesus' baptism lies in the bestowal of the Spirit' (*Apg.* 475); see again my *Baptism* 90-102.

hands is a beneficial aid, particularly when the normal, simpler procedure (repentance/belief and baptism) has not 'worked' for some reason (as in 8.17); but Luke makes no effort to depict laying on of hands as a norm to be followed in every case, and Paul says nothing at all on the subject.

32.2. The Founding of the Church in Ephesus

According to Luke, in returning to the Aegean mission in late 52 or early 53, Paul had followed the route which had been denied him on his previous trek through the Anatolian highlands (Acts 16.6), descending to Ephesus (19.1) either via the Lycus[66] and Meander Valleys or through the next more northerly valley of the Cayster, near whose mouth Ephesus lay.[67] Whether or not it had been Paul's intention to make Ephesus his base on his earlier journey through Galatia and Phrygia (16.6), Ephesus, situated on the other side of the Aegean from Corinth, was the obvious focus for a second phase of the Aegean mission. The initial visit indicated in 18.19-21 could only have confirmed its potential and whetted Paul's appetite to open a new base for his mission there.

a. Ephesus

After a somewhat turbulent history in the affairs of Rome, Augustus had chosen Ephesus to be the capital of the province of Asia.[68] Located near the mouth of the Cayster River, it was strategically positioned for both land and sea routes, a major travel hub, particularly important in lying at the westward end of the ancient Persian and still-much-used trade routes from the Euphrates. Strabo regarded Ephesus as the largest commercial centre in Asia Minor west of the Taurus (*Geog.* 14.1.24).[69] Moreover, unlike the location of its greatest potential rival, Pergamum, that of Ephesus also afforded excellent opportunities for expansion

---

66. The route would probably have included Colossae, though only in transit (cf. Col. 2.1).

67. Hemer thinks that the phrase *ta anōterika merē* ('the upper regions, the interior') more likely refers to 'the traverse of the hill-road reaching Ephesus by the Cayster valley' (*Book of Acts* 120).

68. In what follows I draw particularly on Trebilco, *Early Christians* ch. 1; and R. E. Oster, 'Ephesus', *ABD* 2.542-49; see also P. Scherrer, 'The City of Ephesos from the Roman Period to Late Antiquity', in Koester, ed., *Ephesos* 1-25 (here 5-8); Murphy-O'Connor, *Paul* 166-71; Schnabel, *Mission* 1206-14. Fuller bibliography in Shauf, *Theology as History* 127-28 n. 9.

69. Oster, 'Ephesus' 543.

as the centre of the imperial presence in the region. Unsurprisingly, then, during the reign of Augustus Ephesus benefited from the general prosperity engendered by the *pax Romana* and experienced tremendous growth, receiving the highly prized title 'the first and greatest metropolis of Asia', which it used in inscriptions of the period.[70] Aqueducts were constructed, streets (re)paved, market-places enlarged, monuments and statues erected, temples dedicated and many fine buildings constructed, all expressive of the Romanization of the city. During the Roman period the population of the city is generally estimated at between 200,000 and 250,000,[71] making Ephesus the third-largest city, after Rome and Alexandria.

Ephesus was also unsurpassed as a religious centre. It was the home of many cults,[72] but the cult which dominated all was the worship of Artemis. 'It was the cult of the Ephesian Artemis which, more than anything else, made Ephesus a centre of religious life during our period'[73] — 'Artemis of the Ephesians' (Acts 19.28, 34). And its influence extended deeply into the civic, economic and cultural life of the city, as, of course, Acts 19.23-41 clearly implies. The temple of Artemis, the Artemesium, stood outside the city wall and was widely regarded as one of the seven wonders of the world, 'the ornament of the whole province' (*IvEph* 18b.1-3), its magnificence a testimony not only to the dedication of Ephesus to Artemis but also of the privilege and prosperity which accrued to the principal custodians of the cult of the goddess.[74] Luke shows how well attuned he was to the pride which Ephesus invested in the temple of Artemis

70. Trebilco refers, e.g., to *IvEph* 647, 1541, 1543, and refers also to Oster, 'Ephesus' 543.

71. L. M. White, 'Urban Development and Social Change in Imperial Ephesos', in Koester, ed., *Ephesos* 27-79, estimates a population of 180,000 to 200,000 (41-49).

72. Oster provides a tabular summary of the cults documented for Ephesus ('Ephesus' 548). See also *NDIEC* 6.196-202 and the essays by S. Friesen and J. Walters in Koester, ed., *Ephesos* 229-50 and 281-309 respectively.

73. Trebilco, *Ephesus* 19; see further 19-30; note his brief discussion of the much-disputed issue of whether Artemis was venerated as a goddess of fertility (22-23); also his earlier 'Asia', *BAFCS* 2.291-362 (here 316-50). Fitzmyer cites another of the *Inschriften von Ephesos*: 'Since the goddess Artemis, leader of our city, is honored not only in her own homeland, which she has made the most illustrious of all cities through her own divine nature, but also among Greeks and barbarians . . .' (*Acts* 658-59). See also the earlier note by L. R. Taylor, 'Artemis of Ephesus', in Lake and Cadbury, *Beginnings* 5.251-56; and further *NDIEC* 4.74-81.

74. Trebilco (*Ephesus* 20) cites the epigramist Antipater of Sidon: 'I have set eyes on the wall of Babylon on which is a road for chariots, and the statue of Zeus by the Alphaeus, and the hanging gardens, and the colossus of the Sun, and the huge labour of the high pyramids, and the vast tomb of Mausolus; but when I saw the house of Artemis that mounted to the clouds, those other marvels lost their brilliancy, and I said, "Lo, apart from Olympus, the Sun never looked on aught so grand"' (*The Greek Anthology* 9.58).

when he has the town clerk of Ephesus quiet the riotous crowd with the opening words: 'Citizens of Ephesus, who is there that does not know that the city of Ephesus is the temple keeper *(neōkoros)* of the great Artemis?' (Acts 19.35).[75] We know of two major annual festivals in honour of Artemis — the Artemesia in March-April, and the larger celebration of Artemis's birthday in May-June — which would have featured competitions, processions and banquets, both attracting many visitors from elsewhere in the Greek-speaking world.[76] The wealth accruing to the temple would have been staggering in its amount, and as elsewhere, given that no one would dare to violate such a temple sanctuary, the Artemesium would have provided a secure bank deposit for many wealthy citizens, as Dio Chrysostom confirms *(Or.* 31.54).[77]

Almost as important, and politically still more important, was the presence of the imperial cult in Ephesus. Already in 29 BCE Augustus had granted it the right to dedicate sacred precincts to Dea Roma and Divus Iulius (Cassius Dio 51.20.6-7). Although Ephesus was only the third city in Asia to be given permission to establish a provincial imperial cult as such (dedicated to the reigning emperor), after Pergamum and Smyrna, and only during the subsequent reign of Domitian (89/90 CE), there were many facets of the imperial cult which Ephesus enjoyed, including reverence for other members of the imperial family and the numerous festivals, processions and games associated with the cult. It would be impossible for any resident of Ephesus to be unaware of or unaffected by the imperial cult.[78] Moreover, it is important to appreciate that the imperial cult would

---

75. *Neōkoros* became a title particularly for those cities in Asia which were granted the honour of building an official temple of the imperial cult, but it was used characteristically, as here, for Ephesus as the keeper of the temple of Artemis (Hemer, *Book of Acts* 122 n. 60; Fitzmyer, *Acts* 661; BDAG 670; see also Sherwin-White, *Roman Society* 89 n. 4). According to this speech Ephesus is keeper of 'that which fell from the sky *(diopetēs)'* (19.35). That meteorites became sacred objects is also understandable (Lake and Cadbury, *Beginnings* 4.250; Bruce, *Acts* 420; Trebilco, 'Asia' 351-53; BDAG 250-51), though the term by this time might have been extended to denote the heavenly origin of the image of the multi-breasted Artemis. Either way the allusion could serve as an implied riposte to the Pauline/Jewish dismissal of idols as 'made with hands' (19.26) (Lake and Cadbury 4.250).

76. C. Thomas has complied a fascinating epigraphic catalogue of foreigners in imperial Ephesos ('At Home in the City of Artemis', in Koester, ed., *Ephesos* 66-79).

77. See further Trebilco, *Ephesus* 25-26.

78. See above, §29 nn. 124, 125. 'Imperial cults permeated community life. . . . Imperial cults were an aspect of urban life encountered often and in diverse forms'; 'Imperial worship touched all or most aspects of life in the cities of Asia. . . . No other symbolic system had such a range of effective meaning'; 'The vitality of the festivals, the distribution of imperial cults throughout urban areas, and the importance of imperial temples all imply widespread participation' (Trebilco, *Ephesus* 34-35, 37, citing S. J. Friesen, *Imperial Cults and the Apocalypse of John: Reading Revelation in the Ruins* [New York: Oxford University, 2001] 75, 126, 128).

in no way have been regarded as a competitor to the cult of Artemis, or vice-versa. We know that from the middle of the first century 'the Kouretes, who were responsible for the mysteries of Artemis and whose members were part of the governing order of the city, consistently called themselves not only "*eusebeis*", but also "*philosebastoi*"',[79] that is, loyal to (or also responsible for) the cult of the deified emperors.[80]

As in many other cities in Asia, Ephesus contained a large Jewish population.[81] There is indication of Jewish settlement already in the third century BCE, and Josephus makes a point of itemizing the privileges and rights which had been agreed and regularly reaffirmed for Jews in Ephesus during the century prior to Paul's visit, including exemption from military service, right of assembly, and permission to maintain their own rites and customs and to collect the Temple tax.[82] The fact that Josephus takes such pains to record these official guarantees of Jewish rights indicates both that these rights were sometimes challenged by the Ephesian authorities and that there were continuing tensions caused by the special privileges granted to the Jews, but also that the Jewish community had sufficiently prominent, wealthy and well-connected members to ensure the maintenance of their rights when they were challenged. In this connection, it should be noted that some Jews in Ephesus possessed Roman citizenship, several of whom would no doubt have played significant roles within the city, in its civic and commercial life. Although no synagogue has yet been found in Ephesus, the existence of one or more synagogues/meeting places is implied in the permission 'to come together for sacred and holy rites in accordance with their laws' (Josephus, *Ant.* 14.227). An inscription from the Roman period also mentions *archisynagōgoi* and presbyters.[83] So there is no reason to doubt the testimony of Luke that there was at least one synagogue in Ephesus (Acts 18.19, 26; 19.8).

In terms of modern archaeology, Ephesus is the highlight of most modern visits to Pauline sites or the churches of the Apocalypse of John (Revelation).

---

79. Trebilco, *Ephesus* 36, citing G. M. Rogers, 'The Mysteries of Artemis at Ephesos', in H. Friesinger, ed., *100 Jahre Österreichische Forschungen in Ephesos. Akten des Symposions Wien 1995* (Vienna: Österreichischen Akademie der Wissenschaften, 1999) 241-50 (here 247-50).

80. *Sebastos* = the Latin *Augustus,* which became an imperial title. See also Price, *Rituals and Power* 62-65; Price also notes that 'the Sebastoi seem to have served as an important way of avoiding the bluntness of direct sacrifice to the emperor himself' (216).

81. Schürer, *History* 3.22-23; though *NDIEC* 4.231-32 notes the surprisingly little epigraphical evidence for Jewish presence in Ephesus.

82. Josephus, *Ant.* 14.223-30, 234, 237-40, 262-64, 304-305, 313-14; 16.58-65, 167-68, 172-73. See also Philo, *Legat.* 315. See further Schürer, *History* 3.129-30; Levinskaya, *BAFCS* 5.143-48.

83. Schürer, *History* 23. See further Trebilco, *Ephesus* 43-49.

Many of the temples and structures postdate Paul's time in Ephesus, but it is still possible to gain a fair sense of the city which he experienced.[84] Two of the major thoroughfares linking the upper and lower parts of the city have been well preserved, and more recent excavations of residences on either side of Curetes Street, which leads to the upper agora much developed under Augustus, have added greatly to knowledge of housing in the early centuries. Particularly striking is the proximity of the lower, the commercial agora to the theatre, so that the sequence of events described in Acts 19.29 (the crowd rushing from the nearest open space into the theatre) is easily imagined.[85]

b. Paul's Second Mission Centre

Luke's account of Paul's entry upon what was to be the second crucial phase of his Aegean mission leaves much to be desired. The initial visit to Ephesus (18.19-21) was understandably brief. But the fact that Paul by his absence in the East missed Apollos presumably increased the subsequent sense in Corinth that Apollos was an independent figure, in the eyes of some, worthy of more respect than Paul.[86] And the account of Paul's encounter with the twelve 'disciples' (§32.1f), although located in Ephesus, is strangely unrelated to Paul's subsequent mission there: were the twelve integrated into the church which soon became independent of the synagogue in Ephesus (19.9)? why did Luke leave the episode so detached?

Typical of Luke, however, is the brevity of his description of what was probably the most crucial and successful period of mission in Paul's whole career (Acts 19.8-10). He was evidently content to sketch it in briefest outline — focusing on the schism within the synagogue and the emergence of an independent church more engaged with the wider community. With the instinct of a good story-teller he knew that the account of earliest Ephesian Christianity would be better served by the vivid episodes to follow.

Worth noting, however, is that while the pattern of preaching within[87] and

---

84. Oster provides a useful summary of the major excavations and restorations ('Ephesus' 544-48).

85. The theatre could seat 24,000. Deissmann cites an inscription (*Light* 112-13) which seems to presuppose that meetings of the Ephesian citizen assembly *(ekklēsia)* were held in the theatre; see also Bruce, *Acts* 418-19.

86. See below, §32.3a.

87. That the subject of Paul's preaching is 'the kingdom of God' is one of Luke's ways of maintaining continuity between the foundation teaching of the mother community (Acts 1.5), the mission of the Hellenists (8.12), and Paul's mission from beginning to end (14.22; 19.8; 20.25; 28.23, 31).

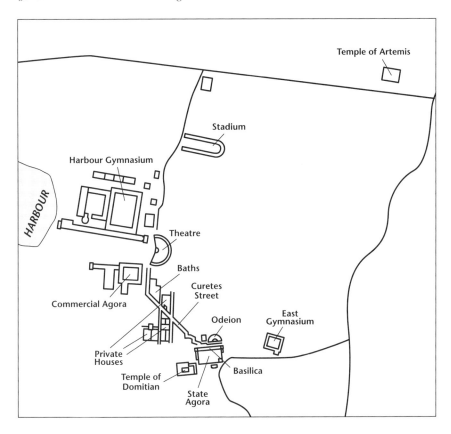

Ephesus

opposition from the synagogue is repeated, Luke's account has some significant modifications. The potentially sympathetic response already foreshadowed in 18.20 is confirmed; for as much as three months Paul is able to preach the word boldly. And, rather strikingly, no mention is made of God-fearing Gentiles. Differently from earlier synagogue proclamations,[88] Luke here suggests an openness to the message which characterized the bulk of the congregation. It was only after three months that opposition arose, and only among 'some' (not 'the Jews'); indeed the 'some' are clearly a minority in the face of the community as a whole.[89] Certainly if Luke had wanted to portray a breakdown between the Pau-

---

88. Acts 13.50; 14.2; 17.5, 13.

89. Note how in Luke's narrative the Jewish opposition in the diaspora synagogues seems to become less severe, first in Corinth (18.4) — as Barrett observes, after leaving the

line gospel and 'the Jews' as complete and irrevocable,[90] he completely missed the opportunity to press home the point in relation to one of the major Mediterranean centres of the Jewish diaspora.

Nevertheless a split did occur. Quite why this needed to happen is unclear, but presumably the confrontation of two factions within the synagogue — 'the disciples' (19.9) and the group (presumably of traditionalists) which stirred up opposition to Paul — evidently made for an intolerable atmosphere in the Sabbath gatherings. The departure of one of the factions (most obviously the newer group), to form a new synagogue, was a sensible solution. The picture has a familiar ring to anyone acquainted with factionalism within a church or congregation. Here we should note that Luke describes a separation and not an expulsion — simply that Paul 'left them, taking the disciples with him' (19.9) — and that he records no recriminations on either side. Evidently it would be inaccurate to speak of a confrontation between synagogue (as such) and church in Ephesus.

Luke further narrates that Paul thereafter, indeed for a further two years, 'argued daily in the lecture hall of Tyrannus' (19.9).[91] The implication is that Paul quickly found a platform for his proclamation, though presumably 'the disciples' also met in homes for worship and fellowship. The inference should not be ignored that Paul must have gained wealthy backers by this time (some of the Asiarchs of 19.31?), since he was able to hire a lecture hall. The subsequent report in 20.34 that Paul continued to work to support himself need not run counter to this. No doubt conscious of the potential anomaly, the Western text adds that he debated daily 'from the fifth hour till the tenth' (11.00 a.m. till 4.00 p.m.), that is, during the normal Mediterranean siesta[92] — a plausible guess, allowing Paul the earlier morning and later afternoon for his tent-making. The implication, then, is that the departure from the synagogue was also a move to a mission more immediately directed to the wider citizenship of Ephesus and indeed to the more leisured and intellectual strata of the society. The wide-reaching effect (19.10 — 'all the residents of Asia heard the word of the Lord')

---

synagogue in Corinth, a further eighteen months elapsed before the Jews took serious action against him (18.11-12; *Acts* 2.902) — and then in Ephesus, so that the final openness of the Jews in Rome (28.17-24, 30-31) comes as less of a surprise. Luke also does not give any hint of a coordinated opposition stemming from Thessalonica, Corinth or Galatia during this period.

90. As argued, e.g., by Sanders, *The Jews in Luke-Acts*.

91. The detail of the location (the hall of Tyrannus) and the time notes (three months, two years) give some confidence as to Luke's sources, even regarding the brief record in 19.8-10 (Haenchen, *Acts* 560). Tyrannus is otherwise unknown, but the name *Tyrannos* has been found in first-century Ephesian inscriptions (Hemer, *Book of Acts* 120; Fitzmyer, *Acts* 648; Trebilco, *Early Christians* 144 n. 173).

92. Lake and Cadbury, *Beginnings* 4.239.

is obviously exaggerated. But it indicates how important a centre Ephesus was: many travelling to the capital from all over the province would no doubt take the opportunity to hear lectures like those of Paul. Luke makes a point of indicating that the message continued to be heard by (and appeal to) Jews as well as Greeks (similarly 19.17).

The significance of the next two years of mission in Ephesus (19.10) can hardly be exaggerated.[93] For Paul to have lectured for two years in the same setting indicates an extensive range of subjects, texts and traditions covered during that period. We have to envisage a large syllabus covering exposition of many Scriptures, instruction in Jesus tradition, and elaboration of the characteristic Pauline themes that we know of from his letters. This is not to say that Ephesus should be seen as marking a major development in Pauline theology. What we can envisage, however, is a systematic presentation of his gospel and its outworking, already developed perhaps in more piece-meal fashion in less sustained preaching and teaching. This picture in turn involves the recognition that his letters should not be seen as simply off-the-cuff compositions in response to particular questions; rather he was able to draw on many expositions and arguments already well honed by such presentations and by discussions and arguments which they presumably sparked off.[94] Particularly noteworthy is Paul's own testimony, at the time of writing 1 Corinthians, so well into or even through the two-year period, that he had decided to stay on in Ephesus till Pentecost, 'for a wide door for effective work has opened to me, and there are many adversaries' (1 Cor. 16.8-9). How the latter note correlates with our other hints regarding the opposition which confronted Paul[95] is a matter of speculation.

Moreover, Ephesus was ideally suited as a centre for an expansive mission. Since Ephesus was the capital of the province, there was frequent travel to and from it. We can well imagine mission teams being sent out from it, southwards to Magnesia and Miletus, north to Smyrna and Pergamum, and up the river valleys to the cities of the Lycus Valley (Laodicea, Hierapolis and Colossae), to Sardis, Philadelphia and to Thyatira.[96] This is not merely a matter

93. Acts 20.31 indicates that Paul spent longer in Ephesus, three years, than anywhere else.

94. 'We may assume that Paul's letters, for example Romans and certain passages of the two letters to the Corinthians, contain brief summaries of lectures and to some extent the much reduced quintessence of what Paul taught in public over a period of two or three years in the "school of Tyrannus" in Ephesus' (Hengel, *Acts* 11). Similarly Lohse, *Paulus* 183-84. Hultgren speculates that Rom. 3.23-26a was the conclusion to a homily delivered by Paul on the Day of Atonement in a synagogue in Ephesus (*Paul's Gospel and Mission* 62-64).

95. See §§32.2d and e below.

96. Similarly Murphy-O'Connor, *Paul* 174-75. On the beginnings of Christianity in

of imagination, since we can see from Col. 1.5-8 and 4.12-13 that this is how the Lycus Valley mission came about; Paul's reference to 'the churches of Asia' (1 Cor. 16.19) indicates a well-developed church-planting programme;[97] and letters were being written to churches in most of the other cities mentioned above over the next two generations (Revelation 2–3 and Ignatius). Even if the actual origins of the church at Ephesus are uncertain, then, it was probably Paul's choice of it as centre of the eastern Aegean mission which largely accounts for the prominence it came to enjoy within early Christian history. As we shall see, it was from there that Paul wrote some of his various Corinthian epistles (and visited Corinth at least once — 2 Cor. 2.1). As already noted, many think that it was from prison in Ephesus (cf. 2 Cor. 11.23) that Paul wrote Philippians, Colossians and Philemon.[98] The letter to the Ephesians speaks for itself.[99] And as we shall see in volume 3, 1 and 2 Timothy are also associated with Ephesus, and there is an ancient tradition also linking the apostle John in his later years to Ephesus. Ephesus, then, marked a crucial and important stage in Paul's mission and in the early development of Christianity. It is disappointing, then, that Luke does not give more detail of such matters, although the following two episodes do mark out the significance of the Ephesus phase in Luke's own way.[100] In any case, he would have no difficulty in gathering the material he has used.[101]

c. Paul's Extraordinary Miracles and a Further Triumph over Syncretism and Magic

Characteristic of Luke is his report that handkerchiefs (sweat-rags) and scarves (aprons) which had had physical contact with Paul were effective in healings and exorcisms (Acts 19.11-12).[102] These 'not just ordinary' miracles are equivalent

---

these Asian cities see further Schnabel, *Mission* 820-38, 1231-48. Cf. Becker: 'the Christianity in Pergamum and Thyatira is Pauline. Revelation campaigns against it from the Jewish-Christian position' (*Paul* 158).

97. Note also Paul's own report that 'a wide door for effective work' had been opened for him in (or from) Ephesus (1 Cor. 16.8-9).

98. The question again is whether the crisis alluded to in 1 Cor. 15.32 and 2 Cor. 1.8-9 can be correlated with the events recorded here. See below, §32.2e.

99. See further below, §37.1.

100. Trebilco laments how little we learn from both Paul's letters and from Acts about the Ephesian church itself (*Early Christians* 101-103, 152, 171).

101. Barrett (*Acts* 2.902) dismisses Haenchen's sceptical questions in reference to 19.8-10 (*Acts* 560) as 'pointless' and 'ill-thought-out'; they 'do nothing to destroy the historical worth of vv. 8-10'.

102. As Shauf rightly emphasizes, 19.11 is consistent with Luke's narrative elsewhere,

to the similar range of healings and exorcisms attributed to Peter's shadow in 5.15. Luke has played up such reports, of course, just as we today might want to play them down;[103] Paul's own view of his miracles was more ambivalent.[104] But if indeed the episode engendered an atmosphere of awe and enthusiasm (19.17),[105] it would not be at all surprising that such cures did take place. The belief that spiritual power can be conveyed through physical means is at the root of Christian teaching on the sacraments, and of healing ministry more generally, as well as of the long tradition of relics within Christianity. Similar beliefs among the believers in Ephesus would no doubt ensure that the stories Luke retells here were circulating within the Ephesian church long before Luke wrote them down.[106]

The following episode of the would-be Jewish exorcists who attempt unsuccessfully to exorcise 'by the Jesus whom Paul proclaims' (19.13)[107] reminds us that Jews had quite a reputation as exorcists in the ancient world.[108] And of course we also know of other successful exorcists of the period.[109] But the 'seven sons of a Jewish high priest named Sceva' (19.14) sound something like a circus act, and that is probably how they should be regarded.[110] Their title would certainly be contrived: whatever corruption there might have been in the high priestly families in Jerusalem, one can scarcely conceive of an outcome like this. On the other hand it is very possible to envisage a varied bunch of 'con artists', or even of renegade Jews who tried to sell themselves as what we might call 'strolling exorcists'.[111] We also know of such characters from other literature of the

that '*God* did extraordinary miracles *through* Paul' (*Theology as History* 171-72). It is also worth noting that Luke does not attribute all illness to evil spirits.

103. Shauf reviews the embarrassment which modern commentators have experienced in assessing the report (*Theology as History* 111-13).

104. Rom. 15.19; but also 2 Cor. 12.11-12. Haenchen ignores the former text and overplays the latter (*Acts* 563, following Käsemann).

105. As in 5.11-16; the prominence of 'the name of the Lord' in both contexts (chs. 3–4; 19.17) is not accidental; see further above, §23.2g.

106. 'The stories about Paul's successful healings . . . and of the marked lack of success of the sons of Sceva were no doubt told with delight — and probably with some exaggeration — by Ephesian Christians, and listened to by Luke with equal pleasure' (Barrett, *Acts* 2.903).

107. The final note, that the demoniac drove them 'out of that house' (19.16), may suggest that they had been called in by a householder to deal with a member of the household thought to be possessed by a demon.

108. Schürer, *History* 3.342-43, 352-58.

109. Mark 9.38/Luke 9.49; Matt. 12.27/Luke 11.19; Acts 8.7; 16.18; Josephus, *Ant.* 8.45-49; Justin, *Dial.* 85.3; Lucian, *Philops.* 16.

110. Barrett refers to Juvenal, *Sat.* 6.544, where the fortune-telling Jewess is described as *magna sacerdos* (*Acts* 2.909); see his full discussion and other references to secondary literature.

111. In which case, of course, the fact that no one knows of such a Jewish high priest

time.[112] The parallels with the accounts of Simon and Bar-Jesus in Acts 8 and 13 are noteworthy. In each case Luke recounts a confrontation of the new Jewish sect with forms of corrupt or syncretistic Judaism,[113] not just unbelieving Judaism,[114] and the resultant victory of the disciples of Messiah Jesus. The implicit message is clear: true continuity with earlier Judaism and the true fulfilment of Jewish heritage is to be found in 'the word of the Lord', not in such syncretistic compromises with wider religious beliefs and practices in the Hellenistic world.[115]

The story tells us much about the practice of exorcism in the ancient world (19.14-16). The technique of the would-be exorcists would presumably be the standard one, as indeed we can see from other accounts. The key to successful exorcism was to be able to call to upon a spiritual power stronger than that which was oppressing the sufferer.[116] The formula used here was the regular one: 'I adjure (horkizō) you by the name of . . .'.[117] The fact that the name of Jesus was used here is a reminder that Jesus was known to have been a highly successful exorcist in his time: to be able to call on Jesus was to call on that power which had proved itself in earlier exorcisms; in later magical papyri the name of Jesus is one of those evoked in exorcistic formulae.[118]

(see, e.g., Fitzmyer, *Acts* 649-50) is neither here nor there. 'This is a "stage name" of the seven' (Klauck, *Magic and Paganism* 100); Klauck also refers to Juvenal's caricature of a Jewish beggar-woman who traffics in interpretations of dreams as 'a handmaid of the laws of Jerusalem, high priestess of the tree and reliable messenger of the highest heaven' (*Sat.* 6.542-47). Jervell surprisingly concludes that Luke does not intend to depict the would-be exorcists as charlatans (*Apg.* 481-82).

112. Particularly Lucian's *Alexander the False Prophet.*

113. Samaria was part of Israel's traditional territory; bar-Jesus was a Jewish magician; and the would-be exorcists are presented as sons of a Jewish high priest.

114. As Jervell, *Apg.* 483.

115. Note also the contrast between 16.16-18 and 19.13-16: a successful exorcism by Paul in Philippi demonstrates the power of the name of Jesus Christ in the right hands over black magic, whereas the lack of success in an attempted exorcism in Ephesus demonstrates the perils of illegitimate use of Jesus' name.

116. Cf. Acts 3.6, 16; 4.10, 12; see further G. H. Twelftree, *Jesus the Exorcist* (WUNT 2.54; Tübingen: Mohr Siebeck, 1993) 38-43.

117. See, e.g., Janowitz, *Magic* 41-42; S. E. Porter, 'Magic in the Book of Acts', in M. Labahn and B. J. L. Peerbolte, *A Kind of Magic: Understanding Magic in the New Testament and Its Religious Environment* (LNTS 306; London: Clark, 2007) 107-21 (here 119-20). Cf. its use, in reverse, in Mark 5.7, and the equivalent used by Paul in 16.18. For a full discussion of the sense of *horkizō* as not itself carrying magical connotations, see Shauf, *Theology as History* 202-10.

118. For details see *Jesus Remembered* 670-77. Bruce notes that the use of Jesus' name as a healing formula was censured by leading rabbis (*Acts* 410). Shauf argues vigorously that Luke did not intend to portray the episode of 19.13-17 as the triumph of Christian miracle over

The rather amusing sequel (the demoniac overpowering the would-be exorcists and driving them out of the house naked and wounded) serves as a serious cautionary tale. Paul was successful as an exorcist (it is implied) because he was a disciple of Jesus and could therefore call upon the name of Jesus legitimately and with effect (16.18). 'The seven sons of Sceva', in contrast, were trying simply to manipulate formulae, depending on technique (and their impressive title). The lesson would be clear: spiritual power can be self-destructive in the wrong hands or where attempts are made to use it illegitimately. Only the one who follows in close discipleship upon Jesus and is led by his Spirit can act thus in his name.[119]

According to Luke many were awe-struck by news of this episode, and many of those who became believers renounced their former magical practices, publicly burning their books with magical formulae and incantations (19.17-19).[120] Interestingly, he not only indicates that many of the believers had practised magic previously (19.18) but seems to imply that it was only some time after their commitment of faith that they confessed their practices.[121] This would not be surprising, given the melting-pot character of much religion of the time, and that magic had not such a negative connotation then as it has now.[122] Ironically the same action (burning of books) could be the sign (then as now) both of the clearest break with an old way of life (when done of one's own volition) and of attempts at thought control (when done by others).[123] The cost, fifty thousand pieces of silver, would amount to a substantial fortune.[124] In all this there is nothing that stretches historical credibility.[125]

---

magic (*Theology as History* 177-226), in dispute with Garrett, *Demise of the Devil* ch. 5. In this section I distinguish syncretism (19.13-17) from magic (19.18-20).

119. A similar lesson is implied in 8.20-24; cf. also 13.8-11 and again 16.16-18. At the same time we should recall that Luke did retain the tradition of Luke 9.49-50: it is Christ, not his disciples, who determines just who can act in his name.

120. 'They would no doubt resemble the papyri edited and published by K. Preisendanz in *Papyri Graecae Magicae* (1928, 1931) [see Betz, *Greek Magical Papyri*]. . . . Ephesus was noted for such products and the term *Ephesia grammata* was current' (Barrett, *Acts* 2.913, referring to Plutarch, *Symp.* 7.5.4, and Clement of Alexandria, *Strom.* 5.8.45.2), as already Lake and Cadbury, *Beginnings* 4.240. See further Fitzmyer, *Acts* 651; Trebilco, *Early Christians* 150-51.

121. Probably before the congregation, as subsequently laid down in *Did.* 4.14; cf. *2 Clem.* 8.3; *Barn.* 19.12.

122. See above, §24 n. 187. The equivalent today could include over-reliance on prescribed drugs and sleeping pills.

123. For ancient examples see Lake and Cadbury, *Beginnings* 4.243.

124. 'A worker's wage for 137 years with no days off' (BDAG 128); cf. Josephus, *Ant.* 17.189.

125. Luke simply reports the story he heard; the story did not require him to signify

d. Confrontation with State Religion (Acts 19.23-41)

After inserting a brief note on Paul's plans, Luke devotes the rest of his account of the foundation of the Ephesian church to a confrontation pregnant with significance for the future of Christianity within the Roman Empire.[126] For as already indicated, the cult of Artemis (Diana) in Ephesus was one of the greatest cults in the Mediterranean world, and Artemis herself was one of, if not the most popular of, the Hellenistic deities. So, for the new belief in Jesus to be seen so quickly as a threat to the Ephesian cult would say much about infant Christianity's divine warrant.

The story as told by Luke is highly plausible:[127] the clustering of artefact makers and traders round the so-famous shrine, making a living from the pilgrim traffic and curious visitors (19.24);[128] the new wave of religious enthusiasm causing the pilgrim traffic to diminish, so threatening the livelihood of these artisans (19.26-27);[129] the ease with which a demagogic speaker like Demetrius the silversmith could play on fears and local indignation to whip up a riot (19.25-29);[130] the

whether he doubted the authenticity of such a high priest, Sceva (*pace* Haenchen, *Acts* 565). It is astonishing that Lüdemann should think that a form-critical analysis in itself gives sufficient proof of unhistoricity (*Early Christianity* 214).

126. Luke gives only the vaguest of time references — 'about that time' (Acts 19.23). But if Paul departed immediately after the episode (20.1), it must have happened late in his time there — that is, in 55.

127. Barrett (*Acts* 2.917) is again justifiably dismissive of Haenchen's objections (*Acts* 576-77) to the historicity of the episode as 'superficial and unconvincing'. The history master who loftily determines what could or should have happened in such an episode knows too little of history. Lüdemann similarly confuses criticism of Luke's story-telling technique with a judgment against the historicity of the episode as a whole (*Early Christianity* 220). Disappointingly, Murphy-O'Connor simply follows Haenchen in regarding the episode as 'a vehicle created by Luke' (*Paul* 300). German scholarship continues to see very little if anything of historical value in Acts 19, as illustrated by M. Fieger, *Im Schatten der Artemis. Glaube und Ungehorsam in Ephesus* (Bern: Lang, 1998), and M. Günther, *Die Frühgeschichte des Christentum in Ephesus* (Frankfurt: Lang, 1998). But see those cited by Schnabel, *Mission* 1223; and further Trebilco, *Early Christians* 104-107, 157-70.

128. 'Silversmiths' (*argyrokopoi*) in Ephesus are well attested in inscriptions of the city (see Hemer, *Book of Acts* 235). 'Silver shrines' (in miniature), as distinct from terracotta souvenirs, have not been discovered, nor are they referred to in ancient sources, but silver statuettes of Artemis have and are (Lake and Cadbury, *Beginnings* 4.245-46).

129. Sixty years later the younger Pliny records the devastation of the old cults by the success of Christianity in Bithynia (*Ep.* 10.96). Worth noting is the fact that it was the economic impact of Paul's mission which provoked the opposition in Ephesus, as in Philippi (Acts 16.19).

130. Rather cleverly Luke has Demetrius not only attest to the success of the new religion (19.26) but also express the primary Jewish and Christian protest against the other reli-

likelihood that Paul's preaching had again attracted the support of influential local figures (19.31 — some of the Asiarchs);[131] the rush from the agora into the theatre;[132] and the near riot defused by the town clerk by his appeal both to the sacred traditions regarding Artemis (19.35-36) and to Rome's heavy disapproval of such an irregular assembly (19.38-40).[133] As well as his reporting of such local details,[134] Luke's knowledge of the names of those involved attests a well-informed source for the story: Demetrius, Gaius and Aristarchus (19.29 — members of Paul's team),[135] and Alexander 'put forward' to speak by the Jews (19.33).[136]

Two features of the episode were of particular importance for Luke. One is the fact that 'the Jews' were caught up in the riot and were regarded as on the same side as those threatening Artemis.[137] It was 'the Jews' who put Alexander forward

---

gions of the time — the fundamental conviction that gods made with hands are not gods at all (cf. 7.41; 17.24, 29); see also above, §§27.1e and §31.3b.

131. The Asiarchs were holders of high office in the league of Greek cities in the Roman province; three or four may have held office at any one time, but former office holders probably retained the title. Since the function of the league was to promote the imperial cult, Paul's friendship with some of the Asiarchs sounds odd. But the title probably was largely honorific, and the office almost certainly was awarded only to men of wealth and high social status. See above, §21 n. 101.

132. Lake and Cadbury cite a good parallel in an inscription from Cnidus (*Beginnings* 4.248). See also above at n. 85.

133. The 'town clerk' was probably the secretary or chief executive officer of the civic assembly, responsible for drafting and publishing its decrees. That he should be fearful for the city's standing of the consequences of an irregular assembly getting out of hand (they could easily serve as a cloak for seditious activities), and was one of very few men who could have commanded sufficient respect from the crowd, is wholly to be expected. See further Sherwin-White, *Roman Society* 83-88, with illuminating parallel from Dio Chrysostom, *Or.* 46.14; 48.1-3; 38.38 (84). 'It seems that some of the wealth of Artemis got into the city treasury and that the town clerk might not have welcomed an inquiry' (Barrett, *Acts* 2.935).

134. W. Weren, 'The Riot of the Ephesian Silversmiths (Acts 19,23-40): Luke's Advice to His Readers', in R. Bieringer et al., eds., *Luke and His Readers,* A. Denaux FS (BETL 182; Leuven: Leuven University, 2005) 441-56: 'The text is permeated with words and ideas that present a faithful picture of daily life in Ephesus during the second half of the first century CE, and its flourishing Artemis cult' (453). P. Lampe, 'Acts 19 im Spiegel der ephesischen Inschriften', *BZ* 36 (1992) 59-76, had already observed that most of the notes of local colour appear in the Demetrius episode (70), though including the redactional speech of the town clerk (76). For earlier comments to the same effect see §21 n. 102 above.

135. Here described as *synekdēmoi,* 'travelling companions'; see further above, §29.6.

136. See also Jervell, *Apg.* 494-96. Barrett considers the possibility that Alexander became (or was already) a Christian and was the source for some of Luke's information (*Acts* 934).

137. 'The narrative in Acts sits comfortably with the suggestion that this threat to religious (and economic) stability was perceived to have come from the Jews . . . it is probably too early for the Christians to have been identified as a separate group by those outside Judaism who had no close contact with Christians' (*NDIEC* 4.10).

'to make a defence before the people' (19.33). Some of the crowd wanted him to speak,[138] but it was his being recognized as a Jew which triggered the manic response of the crowd in the two-hour-long chant 'Great is Artemis of the Ephesians!' (19.34). The implication, therefore, is that Alexander was a representative Jew, in good standing outside the Jewish community, and regarded as able to speak (presumably) on its behalf; but also that the crowd saw their grievance as directed against a Jewish teaching.[139] And indeed, since Demetrius's speech had characterized Paul's message as directed against idolatry (19.26), it is difficult to see 'the Jews' distancing themselves from it. In other words, in a subtle way (too subtle for many commentators!), Luke has included the message of Paul within the defence attempted by Alexander. 'The Jews' of Ephesus are still not shown as hostile to Paul. In this way, not overtly but clearly enough, Luke is able to bring out once again that 'the way' preached by Paul was fully continuous and consistent with and not yet to be readily distinguished from the religion of 'the Jews' properly understood now (as he would say) in the light of Jesus.[140]

Even more important, men holding leading positions within the province (Asiarchs) are shown as among Paul's friends (19.31), and the town clerk quiets the riotous assembly by pointing out the lack of legal grounds for any complaint against the disciples of Jesus (19.35-41).[141] Once again, as in 18.12-17, the new Jewish sect is shown to be still part of Jewish national religion and to constitute no threat to civic cult or Roman authority.[142] The judgment that Gaius and Aristarchus (and Alexander?) were neither sacrilegious nor blasphemers of Artemis was as important to note 'for the record' as Gallio's earlier judgment that the dispute in Corinth was an internal Jewish affair. The one meant that the way of Jesus still ran within the confines of the Jewish ethnic religion recognized by Roman authority; the other, that 'the way', like its parent Judaism, could not as such be considered a threat to traditional Greek religion. In short, in Ephesus, as in Corinth, the two main centres of the Pauline mission, Christianity was deemed to

138. *Synebibasen*, 'instructed, advised' — but the precise meaning of the verb is unclear; Fitzmyer translates, 'made suggestions to' (*Acts* 660).

139. Cf. Shauf, *Theology as History* 251-53.

140. See also Jervell, *Apg.* 492.

141. 'Neither temple robbers nor blasphemers of the goddess' (19.37): the former was a charge sometimes brought against Jews (Rom. 2.22!); the latter could be seen as the corollary to Judaism's exclusive monotheism (see Lake and Cadbury, *Beginnings* 4.251).

142. See further R. F. Stoops, 'Riot and Assembly: The Social Context of Acts 19:23-41', *JBL* 108 (1989) 73-91: the town clerk's speech 'identifies opposition to the Way, rather than the Way itself, as the source of trouble and threat to the established order' (88). Shauf critiques the suggestion that 19.23-40 is part of a political apologetic by Luke (*Theology as History* 258-62), but it is the apologetic effect of the various rulings and outcomes in Acts 16–18 with which Luke was no doubt concerned, rather than to present the authorities themselves in a positive way.

be of a piece with and able to shelter quite legitimately under the same legal banner as Judaism. And in both cases we can infer from subsequent letters and references to the churches in both centres that Paul's foundation endured and the churches expanded.[143]

e. The Crisis in Asia

One of the most intriguing puzzles for the historian in regard to this phase of Paul's Aegean mission is how to correlate Luke's account with Paul's own reference back to a crisis he seems to have experienced during this period. In 2 Corinthians 1 Paul speaks of

> [8]. . . the affliction we experienced in Asia; for we were so utterly, unbearably crushed that we despaired of life itself. [9]Indeed, we felt that we had received the sentence of death *(to apokrima tou thanatou),* so that we would rely not on ourselves but on God who raises the dead. [10]He who rescued us from so deadly a peril will continue to restore us; on him we have set our hope that he will rescue us again.

What was this crisis, this 'deadly peril' which brought Paul to despair and to the sense that death was inevitable? The commentary by Murray Harris has provided one of the most thorough and recent of discussions.[144] He first notes what can be said with some confidence:

- it occurred 'in (the province of) Asia'; since other references show that Paul was not unwilling to specify Ephesus when what he was thinking of took place there (notably 1 Cor. 15.32), the larger reference here implies an event which took place elsewhere in Asia;[145]
- since it is hardly likely that such a severe crisis would have left little or no mark on 1 Corinthians, the crisis itself must have occurred between the writing of 1 and 2 Corinthians;[146]

---

143. On Ephesus, see particularly Trebilco, *Early Christians* parts 2-4; and further in vol. 3.

144. Harris, *2 Corinthians* 164-82.

145. Similarly Trebilco, *Ephesus* 80-81. But it is less likely that it happened on the trip from Ephesus to Troas, since Paul's reference to his arrival in Troas is much more positive than if he had just survived a life-threatening crisis (2 Cor. 2.12).

146. 'The intensity of feeling with which Paul refers to the incident suggests that it happened fairly recently, and the use of the disclosure formula *(For we do not want you to be ignorant)* suggests that the Corinthians are learning of it for the first time' (Furnish, *2 Corinthians* 122).

- the crisis had a devastating effect on Paul, as 2 Cor. 1.8-9 clearly attests; even if he writes, as usual, with rhetorical effect, the sense of one brought to his knees and despair of this life is inescapable; Harris justifiably notes the exceptional language used by Paul.[147]

Of the various possibilities which have been proposed to identify 'the affliction experienced in Asia', the following are most worthy of note:[148]

- Paul literally 'fought with beasts' in Ephesus (1 Cor. 15.32).[149] This is rendered unlikely by several factors: Paul used the phrase *kata anthrōpon,* which probably signifies that he did not intend to be taken literally;[150] the absence of any (other) record of such an event, an event which Luke for one would hardly have passed over in silence;[151] as a Roman citizen Paul would have been exempt from such an ordeal; and the stadium at Ephesus was probably not used for beast-fighting in the first two centuries.[152]
- The riot described in Acts 19.23-41. The problem here is that, as it stands, Luke's account leaves no room for such a major attack on Paul himself; Luke reports that Paul was strongly discouraged from becoming involved

147. 'The effect of the double *hyper* in 1:8 is dramatic: *kath' hyperbolēn* hyper *dynamin,* "beyond measure, beyond my capacity [to cope with]". This self-confession is unparalleled, especially when seen against the background of Paul's confident assertion that "nothing is beyond my power in the strength of him who makes me strong!" (Phil. 4:13, TCNT). In the light of . . . (4.8), "despairing, but not utterly desperate" (Furnish, *2 Corinthians* 252), Paul's frank admission . . . (1:8), "we utterly despaired even of remaining alive", is singular' (Harris, *2 Corinthians* 165-66).

148. For fuller discussion and detail see Furnish, *2 Corinthians* 122-24; Thrall, *2 Corinthians* 115-17; Trebilco, *Ephesus* 75-81, 83-87; Harris, *2 Corinthians* 166-72.

149. This identification of 1 Cor 15.32 with 2 Cor. 1.8-11 goes back to Tertullian.

150. 'The phrase "humanly speaking" is equivalent to "figuratively speaking" and shows that his fighting with beasts is not to be taken literally' (Bruce, *Paul* 295). A. J. Malherbe, 'The Beasts at Ephesus', *JBL* 87 (1968) 71-80, has shown that the term *thēriomacheō* ('fight with wild animals') appears frequently in Cynic-Stoic diatribe to describe the wise man's struggle against his own passions and against his opponents, and Ignatius uses the same word to describe his experience as a prisoner — 'from Syria to Rome I am fighting with wild animals, bound to ten leopards, that is, a detachment of soldiers' (*Rom.* 5.1; BDAG 455; Trebilco, *Ephesus* 58 n. 29).

151. The late second-century *Acts of Paul and Thecla* does contain an account of Paul being condemned to fight with beasts, but at the crucial point Paul has a conversation with one of the lions (whom he had previously baptized), and in the ensuing slaughter both the lion and Paul are spared (Elliott, *Apocryphal New Testament* 378-79).

152. Harris, *2 Corinthians* 167, cites G. E. Bean, *Aegean Turkey: An Archaeological Guide* (London: Benn, 1966) 170-71.

in the disturbance (19.30-31) and apparently followed the advice (20.1). Of course, Luke's account may be far from complete, and though it does strengthen the implication of fierce opposition to Paul and his message, a specific link between the Demetrius riot and 2 Cor. 1.8-11 has to be left entirely to the imagination.

• Sufferings alluded to in 2 Cor. 1.5 (his sharing 'the sufferings of Christ') and 12.7 ('the thorn in the flesh'). But the former is part of a regular motif in Paul and probably refers to the more diverse trials and tribulations which Paul had to endure during his ministry;[153] and the latter seems to have been a more sustained ailment, whose removal he sought three times, petitions which were rejected (12.8-10)![154] Neither matches the short and unusually sharp crisis envisaged in 1.8-11.[155]

• Paul spent some of his time in Ephesus in prison.[156] Such a spell in prison could be alluded to in 2 Cor. 6.5 ('imprisonments') and 11.23 ('far more imprisonments'), also in Paul's three references to 'fellow prisoner';[157] since several imprisonments seem to be in view in 11.23, and we know of only the brief night in prison in Philippi (Acts 16.24-34) prior to the writing of 2 Corinthians, an imprisonment in Ephesus is quite possible;[158] and where else could Epaphras, who evangelized the Lycus Valley cities, presumably from Ephesus, have shared prison with Paul? As already noted, this theory is the basis for the view that Paul wrote one or more of his letters while imprisoned in Ephesus.[159]

---

153. Rom. 8.17-18; 2 Cor. 4.11-12, 16-17; Col. 1.24; similarly with the 'catalogues of suffering' so prominent in 2 Corinthians — 4.8-11; 6.4-10; 11.23-27; 12.10; 2 Cor. 1.10 itself envisages future crises; see further my *Theology of Paul* 482-87; S. Hafemann, 'The Role of Suffering in the Mission of Paul', in Ådna and Kvalbein, eds., *The Mission of the Early Church* 165-84.

154. Harris, however, favours an association between 2 Cor. 1.8-11 and 12.7 (*2 Corinthians* 171-72). But see Thrall, *2 Corinthians* 118.

155. Furnish notes that the near-fatal illness of Epaphroditus (Phil. 2.27) is described as such (*2 Corinthians* 123). See further Thrall, *2 Corinthians* 115-16.

156. Famously argued by G. S. Duncan, *St. Paul's Ephesian Ministry* (London: Hodder and Stoughton, 1929); see also 'Important Hypotheses Reconsidered VI: Were Paul's Imprisonment Epistles Written from Ephesus?', *ExpT* 67 (1955-56) 163-66; 'Paul's Ministry in Asia — the Last Phase', *NTS* 3 (1956-57) 211-18.

157. Rom. 16.7 (Andronicus and Junia), Col. 4.10 (Aristarchus, presumably the same as in Acts 19.29), Phlm. 23 (Epaphras). Several regard the 'fellow prisoner' as figurative (prisoners of Christ?), but in that case why just these four should be so described is hardly clear (Dunn, *Colossians and Philemon* 275-76). According to Rom. 16.4 Prisca and Aquila 'risked their necks for my sake'.

158. *1 Clem.* 5.6 says that Paul was imprisoned ('bore chains') seven times.

159. See further below, §34.3e. However, Thrall notes that 'the proposed evidence in

Here as elsewhere in Luke's narrative we are left in the dark. It is entirely possible, of course, that, as with the Hellenists in Acts 6.1-6 and 8.1-4 and the Antioch incident in 15.36-41, Luke has chosen to draw a veil over a very unpleasant incident (this or some other), which in this case proved almost fatal to Paul. And a period in jail in Ephesus or elsewhere in Asia must be envisaged if Paul's references to several imprisonments and to 'fellow prisoners' are to be accommodated. But of the circumstances of the crisis or the imprisonment as such, we know too little — nothing whatsoever, apart from these allusions — so that hypotheses depending on any of the above possibilities are never going to be strong enough to bear much if any weight.[160] It is likely, however, that the crisis affected Paul severely, and that 2 Corinthians bears the marks left by it on Paul's own mission and theology, as we shall see.[161]

32.3. Between Ephesus and Corinth

However, intriguing as it is to attempt to fill the gaps in Luke's narrative by speculating about Paul's time in Ephesus, even more intriguing events were happening on the other side of the Aegean, in Corinth. About some of these we have good information from the Corinthian letters, information which, together with supporting information from other historical sources, provides more reliable ground for fleshing out the ongoing situation there. Above all, of course, Paul's response to the events in Corinth has gifted future generations with what we now call 1 and 2 Corinthians, so that what happened in Corinth proved to be of much fuller and more lasting significance than the events in Ephesus.

Philippians for an imprisonment which could be identified with the *thlipsis* of 2 Cor. 1.8 is not very convincing' (*2 Corinthians* 117). And since the collection was such a major concern of Paul during this period, the absence of any reference or allusion to the collection in the 'prison epistles' must count strongly against dating them to the Ephesus sojourn.

160. For one imaginative reconstruction, related to the murder in 54 of M. Junius Silanus, proconsul of Asia, and involving a possible friendship between Paul and Silanus, see Bruce, *Paul* 295-98, with critique by Harris, *2 Corinthians* 167.

161. Note again Dodd, 'The Mind of Paul' 83-128; also Furnish, *2 Corinthians* 124-25; Harris, *2 Corinthians* 174-82.

a. After Paul Left Corinth

Bruce Winter gave the title *After Paul Left Corinth* to his investigation of the question 'Why had Paul not dealt with some, if not all, of the problems he addressed in 1 Corinthians while he was in Corinth?'[162] His suggested answer is that 'the problems which arose subsequent to Paul's departure did so partly because the Christians were "cosmopolitans", i.e., citizens of this world and, in particular citizens or residents of Roman Corinth'.[163] In particular, Winter argues that in the period following Paul's departure from Corinth (about 52), several important developments took place in or related to Corinth which had a considerable impact on the Corinthian Christians. He highlights three or four:[164]

- A provincial or federal imperial cult was created in about 54, which from then on was celebrated annually in Corinth;[165] Winter suggests that Paul's reference to the 'so-called gods on earth' (1 Cor. 8.5) might have this development in particular in mind.[166]
- The Isthmian Games may have been moved to the nearby site of Isthmia at this time. It was the custom of the president of the Games to give civic dinners to those who held citizenship in Corinth, and Winter argues that 'the "right" *(exousia)* of some to eat in the idol temple [8.9] may well have been connected with these games'.[167]
- There is evidence that three severe grain shortages occurred in Corinth during the early days of the Corinthian church, and Winter hypothesizes that 'the present distress' (7.26) might have been caused by famine.[168]
- Winter also notes that the city authorities controlled the marketplaces and wonders whether the special provision to allow Jews to provide their own specially slaughtered meat might have been withdrawn, perhaps in the wake of the unrest occasioned by the unsuccessful civil action brought against Paul (Acts 18.12-17). Given the report of Gallio's attitude to the episode and its sequel (18.17), this is less likely; but if there is anything to the specu-

---

162. Winter, *Corinth* 1.

163. Winter, *Corinth* 27.

164. Winter, *Corinth* 5-7.

165. Winter, *Corinth* 5, referring to A. J. S. Spawforth, 'Corinth, Argos and the Imperial Cult: *Pseudo-Julian, Letters 198*', *Hesperia* 63.2 (1994) 211-32.

166. Further B. W. Winter, 'The Achaean Federal Imperial Cult II: The Corinthian Church', *TynB* 46.1 (1995) 169-78; also *Corinth* 281-82 — 'so-called gods', 'i.e., popularly but erroneously called gods' (282).

167. See Winter, *Welfare* ch. 9, especially 168-74; also *Corinth* ch. 12.

168. Winter, *Corinth* 7, noting that the term 'distress' *(anankē)* is linked with the word for 'famine' in literary sources — e.g., Thucydides 3.82.2; 85.2. See further Winter 216-24.

lation, it could help explain the quandary which believers might find themselves in when invited to dine at another's house (1 Cor. 10.25-30).[169]

In addition, there are the developments which took place within the church in Corinth itself and which we find referred to or hinted at in Paul's letters themselves.

- The coming of Apollos to Corinth while Paul was still further east (Acts 18.27–19.1) clearly made a great impact on many of the Corinthian believers, as Paul readily acknowledges (1 Cor 3.5-9). The success of Apollos's ministry (Acts 18.27-28) must have made him seem to not a few a more effective evangelist and teacher than Paul himself — a fact not hidden by Paul's insistence that Apollos (only) watered the seed planted by Paul, and that it was God who gave the (substantial?) growth. At all events, Apollos became a focus of some factionalism in Corinth, and if he had been successful in winning many new converts and adherents, they in particular would presumably have claimed, 'I belong to Apollos' (1 Cor. 1.12; 3.4).
- Did Cephas/Peter visit Corinth during the two years or so after Paul left Corinth? This has been a subject of reflection and dispute for many years, and no clear or firm answer is possible.[170] But the possibility cannot be excluded, and the fact that his name functioned in some measure like Apollos's as a rallying cry for some of those disaffected from Paul (1 Cor. 1.12) has to be explained somehow.

169. Fuller exposition in Winter, *Corinth* ch. 13; see also below, n. 292.
170. That Cephas did visit Corinth has been strongly argued by Weiss, *1 Korinther;* T. W. Manson, 'The Corinthian Correspondence', *Studies in the Gospels and Epistles* (Manchester: Manchester University, 1962) 190-209; and C. K. Barrett, 'Cephas and Corinth', *Essays on Paul* (London: SPCK, 1982) 28-39 (others in Cullmann, *Peter* 55 n. 64). 1 Cor. 9.5 is hardly clear-cut evidence. But a plausible allusion has been detected in 3.10 ('someone else is building on' the foundation laid by Paul), since the sequence 3.5-9 (referring to Apollos), 3.10-15 (referring to Cephas? — cf. Wilckens, *Theologie* 1/3.17) is matched by the Paul-Apollos-Cephas sequence in 3.22. Barrett also draws particular attention to 15.11 ('Whether it was I or they, so we proclaim and so you have come to believe'), where the 'they/we' can naturally be taken to include the first- and last-named witnesses of Christ's resurrection just referred to (15.5, 8). Barrett also sees further allusions in 2 Cor. 2.17; 3.1; 5.12; 10.7, 12-18; and 11.4-5, 13. See also his 'Sectarian Diversity at Corinth', in T. J. Burke and J. K. Elliott, eds., *Paul and the Corinthians,* M. Thrall FS (NovTSupp 109; Leiden: Brill, 2003) 287-302. Hengel, *Petrus* 106-29, sees repeated indications of continuing tension between Peter and Paul: 1 Cor. 3.10-15 is an 'indirect polemic' against the foundational role of Peter (25-27; see above, §23.3b); 15.9-10 ('I worked harder than them all') is probably directed against Peter (110); 2 Cor. 10.4-5 may indicate that Peter laid more stress on Jesus' life and teaching (116-17); and Peter may lie behind 2 Corinthians 10–13 (117-20) and be in mind in the reference to the 'super-apostles' (125). See further below, §35.1d.

- Did the repercussions of Paul's continuing dispute/disagreement with Jerusalem and Antioch[171] reach as far as Corinth? Not initially, it would seem (unless Cephas came advocating the practice which he had followed in Antioch), but probably subsequently, as 2 Corinthians 10–13 probably implies. The incoming missionaries were perhaps traditionalist Jewish believers emboldened by any failure of Paul to achieve rapprochement in his trip to Jerusalem and Antioch referred to in Acts 18.23.[172]

So much of this is speculative that it is hard to build strong hypotheses on it. However, such speculation, rooted as it is, and as far as it can be, in the scattered and fragmentary data of the period and the various hints in our texts, is a worthwhile reminder that the situations envisaged and addressed in Paul's letters were by no means static. Rather, they were in constant flux, as new members joined the church, as the networks (plural) to which the members belonged changed or rubbed against each other causing friction, as personal relationships and loyalties (patron-client) were put in question by the new loyalty (to Jesus as Lord, and to Paul his apostle), as individuals learned more of their faith and reflected on what it demanded of them, and so on.[173] So, once again, it is not difficult to envisage changing circumstances which Paul saw as requiring his personal intervention and explicit instruction. It is more important that we today gain a sense of a church coming to be, 'warts and all', than that we can be fully confident as to the precise character and detail of the circumstances.

b. Maintaining Communication with Corinth

In between the two episodes of Acts 19 in which Paul is off-stage, Luke makes a point of including a note on Paul's resolve to go through Macedonia and Achaia, and then on to Jerusalem, and thereafter Rome, but adds that he sent Timothy and Erastus to Macedonia while he himself stayed on in Asia (Acts 19.21-22). With such a cursory note Luke encapsulates months and years of high ambition coupled with chronic indecision. The note certainly has an authentic ring to it. Paul was well known for his seeming vacillation on his travel plans,[174] as, presumably, circumstances, opportunities and demands upon him changed almost by the day. His concern for his churches, and particularly to visit Corinth, is well at-

171. See above, §32.1d.

172. See further below, §32.7b.

173. The point about overlapping networks is well developed by C. K. Robertson, *Conflict in Corinth: Redefining the System* (New York: Lang, 2001).

174. Rom. 1.10-13; 2 Cor. 1.15-18; here cf. particularly 1 Cor. 16.5-9; see also Acts 20.3-4.

tested, as also his sending of Timothy as his emissary.[175] Paul himself signals his determination to reach Rome following a visit to Jerusalem.[176] And 19.22 confirms the vital role in maintaining communication played by Paul's co-workers.[177] Even with points of unclarity remaining (why no mention of Titus?), the details of these two verses, therefore, are probably more easily correlated with the information which emerges from Paul's letters than any others in Acts.[178]

But here above all the reader of Acts, familiar with Paul's correspondence, cannot help wondering why Luke fails to mention the intensive communication between Paul and the church in Corinth during this period —

- news, quite possibly brought by Apollos from Corinth,[179] which caused Paul to write;
- a first letter, the 'previous letter' (1 Cor. 5.9), probably from Ephesus;
- reports, a letter and messengers from Corinth to Paul in Ephesus, perhaps over a (short) period of time (1 Cor. 1.11; 16.17);
- a possible visit by Timothy to investigate the initial reports (1 Cor. 4.17?);[180]
- Paul urged (presumably in Ephesus) Apollos to visit Corinth 'with the other brothers', possibly at the request of the Corinthians,[181] though Apollos showed the same ambivalence as Paul (1 Cor. 16.12);
- 1 Corinthians, sent from Ephesus (1 Cor. 16.8, 19-20), probably carried by Timothy (1 Cor. 4.17; 16.10-11);[182]

175. 1 Cor. 4.14-21; 16.1-11; 2 Cor. 1.16; 2.12-13; Phil. 2.19-23.

176. Rom. 1.13; 15.24-25; 2 Cor. 1.16; 10.16.

177. See above, §29.6 and §30.8. The Erastus here (19.22) was probably different from the man of the same name mentioned in Rom. 16.23, 'the city treasurer' of Corinth, but he is mentioned again in 2 Tim. 4.20. 2 Cor. 8.16-24 also attests that Paul sent some of his team (Titus and others) ahead to organize or coordinate the collection.

178. The fact that Paul's planning was made 'in the Spirit' is the first of the notes to this effect in chs. 19–21, which emphasize how much Paul's controversial trip to Jerusalem was undertaken with sensitivity to the mind of the Spirit (19.21; 20.22-23; 21.4, 11). The 'must' also indicates a sense of divine compulsion behind Paul's movements which no doubt Paul and Luke shared (note the repetition of the theme in 23.11 and 27.24).

179. Murphy-O'Connor, *Paul* 184, 276.

180. Murphy-O'Connor, *Paul* 279.

181. See below, n. 193.

182. Trebilco thinks it less likely that 1 Cor. 4.17 and 16.10 refer to Timothy as the deliverer of 1 Corinthians to the Corinthians, since otherwise Timothy would have been mentioned as a co-author of the letter (as in six of Paul's other letters) (*Ephesus* 57-58); but if he was going personally to Corinth, he would not have sent his greetings in the letter; on 1 Cor. 16.10 see n. 392 below.

- Titus visited Corinth, probably from Ephesus, and probably to help organize the collection (2 Cor. 8.6a; 12.18);
- a painful visit by Paul to Corinth (2 Cor. 2.1);[183]
- the 'letter of tears' from Paul, probably in Ephesus (2 Cor. 2.4, 9; 7.8, 12), and probably carried by Titus — that is, a second visit of Titus;
- Paul appears to have arranged to meet Titus in Troas on Titus's return from Corinth[184] but could not find him there and went on to Macedonia (2 Cor. 2.12-13), where he met Titus and received with joy the news that the Corinthians had been reconciled to Paul (7.6-16);
- 2 Corinthians (possibly more than one letter), written after Paul had left Ephesus and met Titus with his good news (the 'letter of tears' had been effective), and probably delivered by Titus on a third visit to check the progress of the collection (2 Cor. 8.6b, 16-24);
- plans for a third visit to Corinth by Paul (2 Cor. 12.14, 21; 13.1-2), which eventuated in his last visit to Corinth, during which he wrote his letter to Rome (§33.2).

The communication between Paul and Corinth was intensive because of the successive crises in Paul's relationship with the church there.[185] And though the intensity of this communication is only a heightened example of Paul's more general practice of maintaining communication with his churches, the Corinthian correspondence is particularly rich and rewarding, not least because so many letters were involved and because it 'takes the lid off' a first-century church as no other Christian literature of the first two or three centuries does. The Corinthian correspondence, therefore, will repay some careful study.

183. Did the visit proposed in 1 Cor. 16.5-7 (= Acts 19.21?) become the 'painful visit'? And does 1 Cor. 16.5-7 imply that such a visit followed soon after the dispatch of the letter, or is the vacillation of Acts 19.21-22 a better guide to Paul's movements?

184. The most direct route between Corinth and Ephesus was by sea, about a week's journey; but Paul had evidently seen an opportunity for mission work further north in Asia (2 Cor. 1.12) and for visiting the churches of Macedonia, and so arranged to meet Titus *en route*.

185. M. M. Mitchell, 'Paul's Letters to Corinth: The Interpretive Intertwining of Literary and Historical Reconstruction', in Schowalter and Friesen, eds., *Urban Religion in Roman Corinth* 307-38, rightly stresses the importance of recognizing 'that Paul's letters were themselves primary *agents* in the unfolding of the historical scenario (not just witnesses to it)' (322, elaborated in 322-35).

32.4. The First of Paul's Letters to the Corinthians

1 Cor. 5.9: 'I wrote to you in the letter not to become mixed up with sexually immoral people'. This is all that Paul says about his first letter (usually referred to as letter A of Paul's Corinthian correspondence). Some judge it unlikely that a letter of Paul would have been lost (especially when so much Corinthian correspondence was evidently prized) and so infer that it has been retained within the extant Corinthian correspondence.[186] But none of the passages nominated for the content of letter A actually deals with the problem referred to in 1 Cor. 5.9-13. So the most likely solution is that letter A has indeed been lost, as most agree. This, of course, is a sobering conclusion to reach, since it could imply that the Corinthians were not sufficiently impressed by the letter to think it worth retaining and copying for wider use. It is probably simpler, however, to deduce that this first letter was fairly brief, perhaps hastily written, and was superseded by the more extensive and more carefully expressed 1 Corinthians.

The most thorough attempt to illuminate the early exchange with the Corinthians is still that of John Hurd, who devoted a whole monograph to investigating what gave rise to 1 Corinthians. His thesis is that Paul had written at some length in letter A, and that his letter prompted several assertions and questions which the Corinthians sent to Paul and to which Paul replied in 1 Corinthians.[187] Our present 1 Corinthians, then, would be an elaboration and clarification of what he had said in letter A. Had that been the case, however, it is likely that Paul would have referred back to his previous letter on several of the occasions in which he was restating his earlier teaching. And the fuller we suppose letter A to have been, the more puzzling its disappearance. In fact, as Hurd accepts, nothing in 1 Corinthians encourages the thesis that Paul's earlier teaching had caused controversy or had been largely misunderstood or that Paul himself abandoned some earlier emphases or radically transformed his message.[188] The weakness of Hurd's argument is that it is too introverted, assuming that the content of 1 Corinthians can be explained in effect wholly and solely in terms of the interaction be-

186. E.g., 2 Cor. 6.14–7.1; 1 Cor. 6.12-20; 9.24–10.22; 11.2-34; 15.1-58; 16.13-24. For advocates of such hypotheses see Kümmel, *Introduction* 276-77; Schnelle, *History* 62-64.

187. J. C. Hurd, *The Origin of 1 Corinthians* (London: SPCK, 1965) ch. 5 — 'The Corinthians' Letter to Paul'; ch. 6 — 'The Contents of Paul's Previous Letter'; set out in tabular form, 290-93. Horrell finds Hurd's reconstruction of the list of subjects in the Corinthians' letter to Paul 'highly plausible' (*Social Ethos* 90).

188. 'Nowhere in 1 Corinthians did Paul indicate that he had changed his mind, or that he had been mistaken or shortsighted' (Hurd, *Origin* 220). The observation weakens Hurd's further thesis that Paul's first preaching in Corinth had been more enthusiastic and less cautious than the teaching of 1 Corinthians, and that many of the attitudes of the Corinthians (reproved or revised in 1 Corinthians 7–15) were a reflection of that first preaching (*Origin* ch. 8, and again 290-93).

tween Paul and the Corinthians. But we have already noted (§32.3a) the likelihood that much of the stimulus for 1 Corinthians came from the changing situation in Corinth and in the Corinthian church itself.

Why did Paul write with the warning of 1 Cor. 5.9? The word he uses, 'become mixed up with *(synanamignysthai)*', was presumably the one he used in the previous letter. It implies a regular association with, time spent together, close friendship.[189] The likely inference to be drawn is that one or two of the more prominent members of the church had continued, as before, to make use of prostitutes for sexual pleasure or to accept the favours of the female companions on hand at banquets, in accordance with the mores and social practices of the time.[190] News of this had come to Paul, perhaps with a note that no one was rebuking the person in view (he presumably belonged to the social elite), or that some of the other male members of the church were continuing to attend upon or to go about with this man. Paul wrote at once to urge that no one should consort with such a man. The letter may have been brief and allowed the misunderstanding which Paul seeks to correct in 1 Cor. 5.9-13. So there Paul both clarifies what he had intended (he was speaking only of sexually immoral believers), broadens the exhortation to include other practices which believers should avoid (being greedy, involved in idolatry, verbally abusive, drunkards, extortionate), and urges a more rigorous policy in the case in point (expulsion of 'the evil man' from their midst) (5.10-11, 13). The implication, it should be noted, is that the strong advice of the previous letter had not been taken or had been ineffective. Either way, the person referred to must have continued within the assembly at Corinth during the period covered by Paul's first two letters. The sexual license of some of the higher-status members of the church in Corinth continued to be a major concern for Paul (1 Corinthians 5–6) — a further reminder of the reality of one of Paul's two most important foundations (the churches in Corinth and Ephesus).

32.5. The Second of Paul's Letters to the Corinthians
(1 Corinthians)

We do not know how the first letter was received in Corinth, beyond the inference from 1 Cor. 5.10 that it had been misunderstood or (wilfully?) misinter-

---

189. See also Thiselton, *1 Corinthians* 409.

190. See particularly Winter, *Corinth* 81-93. The quotation from Cicero (90) is particularly apposite: 'If there is anyone who thinks that youth should be forbidden affairs even with courtesans, he is doubtless eminently austere, but his view is contrary not only to the licence of this age, but also to the custom and concessions of our ancestors. For when was this not a common practice? When was it blamed? When was it forbidden? When, in fact, was it that what is allowed was not allowed *(quod licet, non liceret)*' *(Pro Caelio* 20.48).

preted. At any rate, its principal instruction had not been acted on (1 Cor. 5.11, 13). The news of this by itself might have taken only a week or two to reach Paul. But it came as part of a much more extensive sequence of communications. These must have taken some time to reach Paul, and Paul's composition of a reply must have taken some time also.[191] A more precise date than 53-54 for the letter cannot be achieved.

a. The Sources of Information

Paul's sources of information for 1 Corinthians were evidently threefold:

- There was a letter from the church in Corinth — presumably from the bulk of the members and representative of their concerns; the topics of the letter are probably signalled by the phrase *peri de* ('now concerning'), which begins a sequence of sections of 1 Corinthians,[192] in which Paul, presumably, addresses questions and issues raised by the Corinthians' letter.[193]
- The letter was probably brought by Stephanas, Fortunatus and Achaicus (1 Cor. 16.17), who may have provided the additional information about the scandals addressed in 1 Corinthians 5–6 and the issues/disorders dealt with in 11.2-16 and 17-34;[194] Paul's awareness that 'some' of the Corinthians were saying 'There is no resurrection of the dead' (15.12) is likely to

191. No one disputes the Pauline authorship of 1 Corinthians; *1 Clement* contains several indisputable allusions to the letter — see D. A. Hagner, *The Use of the Old and New Testaments in Clement of Rome* (NovTSupp 34; Leiden: Brill, 1973) 196-209; Gregory and Tuckett, *Reception* 144-48, and further 164-67 (Ignatius), 205-207 (Polycarp). Despite some comments to the contrary, 1 Corinthians is one of the most carefully constructed of all Paul's letters; the features of the letter which have sometimes been taken to indicate that several letters have been amalgamated are easily understood in terms of Paul turning his attention from one issue to another (see Schnelle, *History* 62-66; Thiselton, *1 Corinthians* 36-41).

192. *Peri de* ('now concerning') — 7.1, 25; 8.1, 4; 12.1; 16.1, 12; see BDAG 798.

193. *Peri de* at the beginning of a subject is usually taken as indicating a subject raised in the letter from Corinth (bibliography, e.g., in Trebilco, *Ephesus* 68 n. 75), despite M. M. Mitchell, 'Concerning *peri de* in 1 Corinthians', *NovT* 31 (1989) 229-56. The letter therefore probably raised at least the following subjects:

    7.1-24 — sexual relations between husband and wife;

    7.25-40 — the unmarried;

    8.1–11.1 — the problem of food offered to idols;

    12.1–14.40 — the role of spiritual gifts in worship;

    16.1-4 — arrangements for the collection;

    16.12 — a possible visit of Apollos.

194. These three were probably the unnamed sources referred to in 5.1 ('it is reported') and 11.18 ('I keep hearing').

go back to his three informants as well;[195] Paul's commendation of the Stephanas delegation (16.15-18) would signal his approval of their initiative in apprising him of these further problems in the Corinthian assembly.

- 'Chloe's people' (1.11), presumably slaves or business agents who happened to be in Ephesus on Chloe's business, are explicitly cited as the source for the information about the Corinthians' (incipient) factionalism (1.12); Paul names this source presumably because it was not part of the official delegation from Corinth.

An interesting feature is the sequence in which Paul dealt with the information he had received. He does not deal with the matters raised in the formal letter first; instead he deals with the issues which had come to him by word of mouth.[196] This may reflect Paul's preference for oral rather than written reports; he could question the reporter at first hand and clarify any points of uncertainty or possible confusion. But it also probably indicates the likelihood that the Corinthians' letter had not raised the subjects orally reported to Paul, with the implication that the church as an assembly was unwilling to confront the issues which some members' conduct was posing to them. In contrast, the fact that Paul tackles these issues before turning to the questions raised by the letter indicates just how seriously Paul regarded both the situations orally reported to him and the church's blindness in regard to how dangerous they were.[197]

b. An Appeal to Avoid Factionalism (1 Corinthians 1–4)

After the opening pleasantries, in which he recalls the enthusiastic beginnings of the church in Corinth (1.4-9), Paul turns at once to an appeal for unity:

> I appeal to you, brothers, through the name of our Lord Jesus Christ, that you all speak as one and that there be no divisions *(schismata)* among you, but that you be made complete *(katērtismenoi)* in the same mind and the same conviction. (1.10)

As Margaret Mitchell in particular has argued, this verse probably indicates the theme of the whole letter[198] and suggests that it was the factionalism underlying

---

195. The way Paul introduces these topics (11.2, 17; 15.1-2) suggests that what he had heard had brought home to him how much his original teaching was being ignored or forgotten.

196. The first *peri de,* in 7.1 — 'Now concerning the matters about which you wrote' — clearly denotes the transition to the subjects raised by the letter.

197. In what follows I draw upon my brief treatment in *1 Corinthians* (NTG; Sheffield: Sheffield Academic, 1995).

198. Mitchell, *Paul and the Rhetoric of Reconciliation.*

or expressed in the subsequent issues addressed in the letter which was Paul's principal or primary concern in writing the letter. 1 Cor. 11.18 certainly indicates that there actually were 'schisms' in the church (or so the report to Paul affirmed), and other references[199] imply that the bitter fruit of division was a major factor in the other issues.

The question whether the four slogans of 1.12[200] indicate two or four parties actually already at loggerheads in Corinth has fascinated researchers ever since Baur's now-famous essay on the subject.[201] That there were tensions in the Corinthian church is certain, but whether they can be successfully linked to the slogans is not at all clear.

- We can be sure that there were several Pauline loyalists — Crispus, Gaius and Stephanas for a start (1.14, 16). And Paul's defensiveness in 4.3 and 9.3 assuredly indicates his awareness that others had been criticizing him.[202]
- Again, it is evident that Apollos's time in Corinth had won him not a few admirers, not least because of his rhetorical proficiency. The repetition of the Apollos slogan in 3.4, Paul's account of their respective roles (3.5-9), and the further reference to Apollos in 4.6 ('I have applied all this to Apollos and myself for your benefit') no doubt indicate that the comparison between Paul and Apollos made by some Corinthians (to the detriment of Paul) was a major factor in the first subject of Paul's exposition (1.18–4.21).[203]

199. 'Quarrels' (1.11), 'jealousy and quarreling' (3.3), 'puffed up (*physiousthe* — 'have an exaggerated self-conception') on behalf of one against another' (4.6), 'these arrogant people' (4.19), 'boasting' (5.6), 'grievances' and legal proceedings between members (6.1), 'factions' (11.19), 'disorder' (14.33). Mitchell notes the overtones of such other verses as 6.19 ('You do not belong to yourselves'), 7.22 ('God has called you in peace') and 10.32 ('I please all in all things'); 1 Corinthians 12 'employs the most common *topos* in ancient literature for unity' (*Paul* 120, 123, 147-49, 161).

200. 'I am of Paul', 'I am of Apollos', 'I am of Cephas', 'I am of Christ'. The genitive formulation could be translated 'I belong to', or 'I belong to the party of'.

201. See above, §20 n. 129. For a brief review of the debate see Kümmel, *Introduction* 272-75; and on the history-of-religions standpoint see Schnelle, *History* 66-70.

202. 1 Cor. 4.3 — 'With me it is a very small thing that I should be judged by you or by any human court'; 9.3 — 'This is my defence to those who would examine me'. In both cases the legal imagery and terminology are prominent.

203. 1 Cor. 4.6 makes it clear that a right evaluation of the relative roles of Apollos and himself is the main concern of 3.4 to 4.6 at least. P. F. Beatrice, 'Apollos of Alexandria and the Origins of the Jewish-Christian Baptist Encratism', *ANRW* 2.26.2 (1995) 1232-75, argues that Apollos was one of Paul's chief opponents (1251-60): 'One gets the clear impression that Paul was trying to demolish Apollos' theological construction from its foundation, based on baptism and wisdom.' (1245); '*Ho adikēsas* [2 Cor. 7.12] is no other than Apollos himself' (1247); the 'thorn in the flesh' (2 Cor. 12.7) was Apollos of Alexandria (1248)! Cf. Watson, *Paul, Judaism and the Gentiles* [[1]1986] 82-84, [[2]2007] 152-56; D. P. Ker, 'Paul and Apollos — Colleagues or

- As for the Cephas slogan: whether or not Peter had visited Corinth subsequent to Paul's visit,[204] it remains likely that wherever we can detect a Jewish dimension to one of the issues addressed by Paul, we may well infer that those who followed a more characteristically Jewish line cited Cephas, the apostle to the circumcised, as their pattern and precedent.
- What the Christ slogan signifies is the least obvious[205] — perhaps no more than a rejoinder on the part of those who disapproved of such partisan-sounding slogans and who responded by claiming their loyalty was to Christ alone.[206]

At all events, it is interesting that such a small church as Corinth evidently was[207] could produce such tensions.

Two observations help clarify the situation envisaged in 1.12. One is that the divisions in Corinth should not be exaggerated. Paul's rejoinder to the slogans in 1.13 ('Has Christ been divided? Was Paul crucified for you? Or were you baptized in the name of Paul?') indicates that he was in fact most critical of the Paul slogan. It is the *party-spirit* that he criticizes, not different *parties*. This observation is strengthened when we note that Paul treats Apollos as an ally, speaks of him positively, doing so without any sense of tension between them (3.5-9; 16.12). Also, it is no less striking that on the issues where a Jewish perspective is most evident, in chs. 5–6 (sexual license), 8, 10 (idolatry) and 11 (patriarchalism), Paul's basic counsel is traditionally Jewish in character. All this suggests that what we see behind 1 Corinthians are more in the nature of tensions and disagreements rather than outright splits and well-defined parties.[208] And Nils Dahl may hit more closely to the mark when he argues that the internal troubles in the church of Corinth were caused by opposition to Paul and Paul's teaching on various issues important to the community.[209] The note of self-defence and exasperation at various points in 1 Corinthians[210] surely indicates that such opposition to Paul and reaction to his teaching was a factor in the Corinthian crisis.

Rivals?', *JSNT* 77 (2000) 75-97. Contrast Bruce: 'every mention he [Paul] makes of him [Apollos] is marked by friendliness and confidence' (*Paul* 257). See also n. 54 above.

204. See above, n. 170.

205. See again §20 n. 129 above.

206. Paul seems to agree: 'Let no one boast in human (leaders)' (3.21).

207. See above, §30.2b.

208. In objecting to Baur's thesis, Munck, 'The Church without Factions', *Paul and the Salvation of Mankind* 135-67, preferred to speak of 'cliques' and 'bickerings'.

209. N. A. Dahl, 'Paul and the Church at Corinth according to 1 Corinthians 1–4', in W. R. Farmer et al., eds., *Christian History and Interpretation,* J. Knox FS (Cambridge: Cambridge University, 1967) 313-35, reprinted in Adams and Horrell, *Christianity at Corinth* ch. 5.

210. 1 Cor. 1.17; 3.1-3; 4.3-4, 18-21; 8.1-3; 9.1-6; 10.33; 11.16; 14.37-38; 16.10-11.

The other observation is that we should not assume the tensions in the Corinthian church to have been theological (doctrinal) in character. On the contrary, as we shall see, they were primarily social and ethical. Paul certainly draws upon theological principles to deal with them, particularly his christology;[211] but while beliefs about baptism seem to have been a factor in the Corinthian factionalism, the issue was more by whom or in whose name one had been baptized (1.13-17) rather than the theology of baptism;[212] the only doctrinal issue dealt with as such is the question of the resurrection of the body, which Paul leaves to the end (ch. 15). Somewhat surprisingly, despite the turn from 'doctrine' to 'religion' at the beginning of the twentieth century, the assumption still prevailed through the early history-of-religion attempts to illuminate 1 Corinthians that theological tenets were at the heart of the challenges confronting Paul. Here the quest for pre-Christian Gnosticism (see above, §20.3c) found fruitful ground, by reading Paul's talk of 'wisdom' and 'spiritual' against the later Gnostic systems, or by presupposing a proto-Gnostic background to Paul's language.[213] Alternatively, given the probable influence of Apollos on some of the Corinthians, a more likely sounding board is provided by the kind of Hellenistic Jewish interaction with the philosophies of the day such as we find in Philo,[214] though broader Stoic influence can also be posited,[215] as indeed a not necessarily ideologically motivated spiritual elitism or enthusiasm.[216] But the use of catchwords like

211. Christ crucified (1.18-31); 'bought with a price' (6.19); 'for whom Christ died' (8.11); one Lord, exclusive (10.21); body of Christ (12.12-27); first fruits of the resurrection (15.20).

212. Cf. Chester, *Conversion* 290-94; see also below, nn. 286 and 379 on ch. 10.1-13 and on 15.29 respectively.

213. Notably U. Wilckens, *Weisheit und Torheit* (Tübingen: Mohr Siebeck, 1959); Schmithals, *Gnosticism in Corinth*. But see the measured evaluation of R. M. Wilson, 'How Gnostic Were the Corinthians?', *NTS* 19 (1972-73) 65-74; also 'Gnosis and Corinth', in M. D. Hooker and S. G. Wilson, eds., *Paul and Paulinism,* C. K. Barrett FS (London: SPCK, 1982) 102-19; Chester, *Conversion* 277-80, 284-90; and further my *1 Corinthians* 34-41.

214. B. A. Pearson, *The Pneumatikos-Psychikos Terminology in 1 Corinthians* (SBLDS 12; Atlanta: Scholars, 1973); R. A. Horsley, 'Pneumatikos vs. Psychikos: Distinctions of Spiritual Status among the Corinthians', *HTR* 69 (1976) 269-88; also 'Gnosis in Corinth: 1 Corinthians 8.1-6', *NTS* 27 (1981) 32-52, reprinted in Adams and Horrell, *Christianity at Corinth* ch. 8; J. A. Davis, *Wisdom and Spirit: An Investigation of 1 Corinthians 1.18–3.20 against the Background of Jewish Sapiential Traditions in the Greco-Roman Period* (Lanham: University Press of America, 1984); G. E. Sterling, '"Wisdom among the Perfect": Creation Traditions in Alexandrian Judaism and Corinthian Christianity', *NovT* 37 (1995) 355-84.

215. As by T. Paige, 'Stoicism, *eleutheria* and Community at Corinth', in Wilkins and Paige, eds., *Worship, Theology and Ministry in the Early Church,* 180-93, reprinted in Adams and Horrell, *Christianity at Corinth* ch. 16.

216. Originally by W. Lütgert, *Freiheitspredigt und Schwarmgeister in Korinth* (Göttingen: Bertelsmann, 1908), though in combination with an early form of the Gnostic hy-

'knowledge' and 'spiritual' are too widespread in ancient religion and philosophy to allow us to deduce a particular set of beliefs or ideology from their use in 1 Corinthians, any more than we can make equivalent deductions from the slogans in 1.12.[217] And in recent study it has become clearer that the primary backgrounds to chs. 1–4 are rhetoric and the issues of status and influence in which rhetoric often played a decisive part.

The point should have been clear enough from the way Paul introduced the subject and played on it.[218] But it was L. L. Welborn who first made the point that the terms used by Paul in the opening chapters echo those used of political factionalism in the city-states — *schisma* ('schism'), *eris* ('strife'), *meris* ('party'), 'puffed up' (4.6), echoing 'the caricature of the political windbag'. 'The real problem addressed in 1 Corinthians 1–4 is one of partisanship . . . it is a power struggle, not a theological controversy, which motivates the writing of 1 Corinthians 1–4 . . . Paul's goal in 1 Corinthians 1–4 is not the refutation of heresy, but . . . the prevention of *stasis* (strife, discord)'.[219] It is the nexus between wisdom and

---

pothesis — *pneumatikoi* in the sense of 'enthusiasts *(Schwärmer)*'. Fee makes an explicit link to eschatology — 'spiritualized eschatology' (*1 Corinthians* 12); but on the eschatology hypothesis note the discerning observations of J. M. G. Barclay, 'Thessalonica and Corinth: Social Contrasts in Pauline Christianity', *JSNT* 47 (1992) 49-74; and see further below, n. 227. More recent attempts to categorize have tended to eschew elaborate descriptions: J. Murphy-O'Connor, *The Theology of the Second Letter to the Corinthians* (Cambridge: Cambridge University, 1991), speaks simply of 'the Spirit-people' (14); and A. Lindemann, *Der erste Korintherbrief* (HNT; Tübingen: Mohr Siebeck, 2000), attributes (some of) the Corinthians' position simply to 'spiritual enthusiasm' (14).

217. H. Koester, 'The Silence of the Apostle', in Schowalter and Friesen, *Urban Religion in Roman Corinth* 339-49, argues that the Corinthians were drawing on Jesus tradition transmitted by Peter or Apollos, regarded as a secret wisdom and connected to an act of mystery initiation: 'Paul does not allow such sayings to carry the authority of Jesus, and thus he denies the Corinthians the right to rely on such sayings. . . . His message of Christ crucified does not permit Jesus to stand as an authority for sayings that have the power to save. . . . The entire polemic of 1 Corinthians must be seen as an argument against understanding the new message about Jesus as a mystery religion' (345-46). But the thesis reads far too much into or behind the text, and the connections drawn between different passages of 1 Corinthians are contrived.

218. 1 Cor. 1.17 — 'Christ sent me to proclaim the gospel, not with eloquent wisdom.' (Thiselton translates the last phrase, *ouk en sophia logou*, as 'not with clever rhetoric' — *1 Corinthians* 109, 145-46); 1.20 — 'Where is the wise? Where is the scribe? Where is the debater of this age?'; 2.1 — 'When I came to you, brothers, I did not come with high-sounding rhetoric or a display of cleverness' (Thiselton); 2.4-5 — 'My speech and my proclamation were not with persuasive words of wisdom, but in demonstration *(apodeixis)* of the Spirit's power' (*apodeixis* being a technical term in rhetoric to denote a compelling conclusion drawn out from accepted premises — Weiss, *1 Korinther* 50); 2.13 — 'These things we speak not in words taught by human wisdom.' See also B. W. Winter, *Philo and Paul among the Sophists* (Grand Rapids: Eerdmans, ²2002) 148-50, 155-64.

219. L. L. Welborn, 'On the Discord in Corinth: 1 Corinthians 1–4 and Ancient Poli-

eloquence[220] and between rhetoric and social status[221] which provides the chief keys to these four chapters — as Mitchell was able to demonstrate when she built on Welborn's findings her overarching thesis that 1 Corinthians was not against particular parties or siding with a particular party but was directed against the factionalism which characterized social relationships in Corinth and elsewhere.[222]

In face of this emphasis on rhetorical ability as proof of wisdom, Paul made no pretence to any great rhetorical ability — although his disavowal in 2.3-5 uses rhetorical tricks. His tactic was different.

- First, he sets his face against the values which gave such weight and status significance to such matters — the cross, the foolishness of God's redemptive purpose being wrought through a crucified man, is the measure of a divine Wisdom which has turned the values of society upside down (1.18-25); their own assembly, with its small minority of wise, powerful and well-born, was itself proof that God's values are focused in Christ (1.26-31); the terms he used to describe his entry into Corinth were 'consciously anti-sophistic'.[223]

---

tics', *JBL* 106 (1987) 85-111, reprinted in *Politics and Rhetoric in the Corinthian Epistles* ch. 1 (here 3-6). Cf. Clarke, *Secular and Christian Leadership* 93 ('personality-centred politics'); Grant, *Paul in the Roman World* 27-30.

220. D. Litfin, *St. Paul's Theology of Proclamation: 1 Corinthians 1-4 and Greco-Roman Rhetoric* (SNTSMS 79; Cambridge: Cambridge University, 1994), cites Eduard Norden, the doyen of study in this area, that 'we will simply fail to grasp the import of 1 Cor. 1.17-2.5 unless we remember that Paul wrote these words at a time when it was not possible to be considered wise without being eloquent' (244). Note also Winter's argument that there was a high-profile sophistic movement (the so-called Second Sophistic) already active in mid-first-century Corinth, and that Paul's opponents, in 2 Corinthians 10-13 as well as 1 Corinthians 1-4, were well trained in Greek rhetoric and can indeed be classified as adherents to the sophistic tradition *(Philo and Paul)*.

221. See further S. Pogoloff, *Logos and Sophia: The Rhetorical Situation of 1 Corinthians* (SBLDS 134; Atlanta: Scholars, 1992).

222. See also Martin, *Corinthian Body* 55-68: 'since Paul infiltrates his rhetoric with so many status terms, much, if not all, of the conflict among the Corinthians must have centred on issues of status' (61). Chester also sees most of the problems in the church of Corinth as caused by competition among the leading figures for honour and status (*Conversion at Corinth* 240-44, 246-52). In all this it is not helpful to allow Paul's response to be characterized in Baurian terms of 'opposition' to Paul; the tensions and problems addressed evidently arose not so much from 'opponents' as from differing views on how to live in a non-Christian world and to relate to the social world of Corinth; see A. Lindemann, 'Die paulinische Ekklesiologie angesichts der Lebenswirklichkeit der christlichen Gemeinde in Korinth', in R. Bieringer, ed., *The Corinthian Correspondence* (BETL 125; Leuven: Leuven University, 1996) 63-86; also *Erste Korintherbrief* 11-14.

223. Winter, *Corinth* 42-43.

- Second, he appeals to their own experience of the convicting power of his own poor-rhetorical preaching (2.4-5); it is this same Spirit which enables (should enable) them to appreciate God's wisdom and what really matters (2.6-16).[224] Here the appeal is like that in Galatians (Gal. 3.3; 5.25), that they remain true to that power which had entered and begun to transform their lives when they first responded to the gospel.

- Third, again as with the Galatians (Gal. 5.13-26; 6.7-9), Paul reminds the Corinthians that it is how they go on from their beginning which matters (1 Cor. 3.10-15);[225] he warns them that it is possible to 'ruin/corrupt/destroy *(phtheirein)*' the work that God has begun in them, the temple *(naos)* of God that they have become by virtue of the indwelling Spirit (3.16-17).[226]

- Finally, he renews the contrast already developed in 1.18-31 by setting over against each other their ideal of wealth, royal honour and power (4.8),[227] and its attendant arrogance (4.18-19), with the reality of apostolic disrepute and vagrancy (4.9-13),[228] and at the same time the genuine paternal care which Paul exhibited in his dealings with them (4.14-17) — a different kind of kingdom and power (4.20-21).

224. Murphy-O'Connor thinks that Paul made a mistake here 'by turning the spirit-people into figures of fun'; 'his whole purpose is to mystify them and thereby reduce them to confused silence amid the laughter of all the others who hear the letter read aloud' (*Paul* 282-84).

225. On 1 Cor. 3.13-15 see particularly Konradt, *Gericht und Gemeinde* 258-78.

226. Hogeterp notes that 'the term *naos* may more specifically designate the inner sanctum of the Temple, as distinct from the invariably general term for the Temple complex, *to hieron*' (*Paul and God's Temple* 322-23), and the association of the Temple with God's Spirit in Wis. 9.1-18, Pseudo-Philo 8.108-14 and 1QS 8–9 (327-31). See also F. W. Horn, 'Paulus und der Herodianische Tempel', *NTS* 53 (2007) 184-203.

227. 1 Cor. 4.8 has provided the main support for the view that the Corinthians had an 'overrealized eschatology' and were behaving as though the age to come was already consummated (Thiselton, *1 Corinthians* 358; see his earlier, much-referred-to 'Realized Eschatology at Corinth', *NTS* 24 [1978] 510-26, abstracted in Adams and Horrell, *Christianity at Corinth* ch. 7). But Barclay notes that the language may say more of Paul's perspective than of the Corinthians: 'Their Spirit-filled lives are not an early experience of the future; they simply consider themselves to have reached the heights of human potential' ('Thessalonica and Corinth' 64). Similarly Martin: 'The problem with this interpretation is that there is no evidence that the Corinthians claim these benefits as a result of first learning about such eschatological benefits through Christian preaching and then transferring them to present experience' (*Corinthian Body* 105). The 'realized eschatology' hypothesis to explain the attitudes of the Corinthian believers shares some of the same defects as the pan-Gnostic hypothesis (above n. 213).

228. Note the deliberate repetition in 4.10 of the same words and themes used in 1.26-27: 'we are fools *(mōroi)* . . . ; we are weak *(astheneis)* . . . ; we are without honour'. In the final sentence (4.13) the double use in self-description of *perikatharma* and *peripsēma,* both denoting 'dirt scraped off', is also noteworthy.

Worth noting at this point is the way in which Paul completes the radical re-evaluation which he sees the gospel as making of the social markers of 1.26: the foolish but deep wisdom of the cross in contrast to the wisdom of this age (1.17–2.16); the birth to Paul through the gospel (4.15) as providing the more important model for conduct (4.16-17) than being well-born in this age; the power of the kingdom of God as of a quite different order from the power of the powerful (4.18-21).

c. The Clash of Value Systems (1 Corinthians 5–6)

As already noted (§30.4b), it was Gerd Theissen who first drew effective attention to the social stratification in the Corinthian church as indicated in 1.26: for example, that all the people named in connection with the church of Corinth seem to have been of high social status, and that the only ones named by Paul as baptized by himself personally were also of high social status. One of the weaknesses of Theissen's valuable analysis, however, was his assumption that high status entailed high social integration; whereas the very transition (conversion) into a marginal religious movement must have involved a high degree of status inconsistency or status dissonance.[229] The consequential stresses are nowhere more clearly evident than in the issues confronted in 1 Corinthians 5–11.

In this section I deal with the first two problems: sexual license and the readiness of some members to resort to litigation to resolve disagreements with other members of the church. These, I have already suggested (§32.5a), seem not to have been mentioned in the Corinthians' letter to Paul — a fact which is revealing as to the stresses they caused, one of the principal stresses, it would appear, being the unwillingness of most of the Corinthian church members to face up to the reality of these situations.

Chs. 5–6 always did pose something of a conundrum to commentators: how could the Corinthians have been so silent, even 'arrogant/conceited' *(pephysiōmenoi),* over a case of sexual license *(porneia)*[230] 'which is not (found/tolerated)[231] among the Gentiles' (5.1-2)? And how could they be unmoved at members taking one another to court (6.1, 6)? John Chow provided the most plausible answer.[232] The reason for the silence of the Christian community is

---

229. As pointed out by Meeks, *Urban Christians* 69-70. But note Horrell's counter-critique *(Social Ethos* 100-101).

230. On *porneia* see my *Theology of Paul* 92-93, 121-23 and (on the present passage) 690-92.

231. See Thiselton, *1 Corinthians* 385-86: 'Even the virtually unshockable Catullus expresses utter abhorrence at such a sexual relationship' (386, referring to Catullus, *Poems* 74 and 88-90).

232. Chow, *Patronage and Power* 130-41; similarly Clarke, *Secular and Christian Leadership in Corinth* 73-88; Meggitt is dubious *(Poverty* 149-53).

probably that those involved were rich patrons, one or more of the powerful and nobly born mentioned in 1.26. It was the individual's social prestige, and the degree to which less-well-to-do members of the congregation were dependent on his patronage, which kept the bulk of the Corinthian church silent.[233] To offend such a one could have entailed serious social consequences for livelihood and social acceptability. The very viability of the church itself may have been at stake if its existence depended on the protection and benefaction of such a powerful figure within the legal and social establishment of Corinth. Certainly when Paul talks of arrogance in 5.2, we may well envisage a congregation whose quiet acquiescence to such behaviour Paul saw as reflecting the 'arrogance' of the powerful figure able to act with such disregard for established mores. At the same time it should be noted that Paul's rebuke is directed more to the church than to the individual himself, and that he expected the church to deal with the situation themselves rather than simply to obey his peremptory commands.

Less speculative, but equally informative, is the patronal hypothesis to resolve the issue of how the Corinthians could be so unmoved by the fact of one member taking another to court.[234] For particularly in a Roman colony, the right to prosecute was not granted to all; resort to the courts was a prerogative of those of high social rank and power.[235] 1 Cor. 6.2 and 4 provide two further clues: what was in view was a 'trivial case' (6.2), that is, presumably a civil rather than a criminal case;[236] and the

233. Winter infers that the father was not deceased, so that the form of incestuous liaison (son with father's wife) was one for which Roman law provided no leniency, and observes that if the case was taken to court, it 'might have involved public humiliation for the father as an incompetent *paterfamilias* who would suffer that which Romans most feared — shame which resulted in a complete loss of *dignitas*' (*Corinth* 49, 51). Subsequently he argues that 'Paul was seeking to wrest the community from the grasp of the patrons, who sought to exercise their control over other Christians' (193).

234. Some associations forbad members to take fellow members to court (Ascough, *Paul's Macedonian Associations* 60-61; Chester, *Conversion* 252-54).

235. 'If the defendant was a parent, a patron, a magistrate, or a person of high rank, then charges could not be brought by children, freedmen, private citizens and men of low rank respectively. Generally, lawsuits were conducted between social equals who were the powerful *(hoi dynatoi)* of the city, or by a plaintiff of superior social status and power against an inferior. . . . Social status and legal privilege were clearly connected in the Roman Empire. . . . (In Corinth) the nature of society was such that those who belonged to its upper echelons were given over to seeking primacy in *politeia* by using vexatious litigation as an acceptable means of doing so' (Winter, *Welfare* 107-108, 113, 121). Winter cites in particular P. Garnsey, *Social Status and Legal Privilege in the Roman Empire* (Oxford: Clarendon, 1970). See further Winter, *Corinth* ch. 4; also Chow, *Patronage* 123-30; Martin, *Corinthian Body* 76-79. Meggitt points to examples of litigation in which both parties came from the ranks of the non-elite (*Poverty* 122-25), but it remains unlikely that 'the urban poor' would have sufficient time and resources to go to court; Meggitt's 'non-elite' are too undifferentiated.

236. Winter, *Welfare* 107.

description of what was at issue as 'everyday matters *(biōtika)*' (6.4) suggests that the case in view was a dispute over inheritance (a prominent subject of litigation under Roman law), the plaintiff claiming to have been defrauded *(adikeisthei)* of his rights of property or inheritance (6.7-8).[237] Since the legal system of the time markedly favoured those of higher status against those of lower rank,[238] all the circumstances of the case in Corinth would be satisfied if we envisage a wealthy patron taking a socially inferior fellow believer to court over some disputed inheritance.

In both cases we see the clash of value systems. In both cases Paul saw a failure to recognize that conversion to the new loyalty to Christ meant a complete break with the old mores and patterns of social relationship[239] and with all self-indulgent behaviour (6.9-10):[240] resort to prostitutes and courtesans was no longer a 'right' to be claimed (6.12), whether in casual sex or at banquets, even for those high on the scale of social prestige and wealth (6.12-20);[241] taking a brother to court, however customary in 'high society', was equally unacceptable (6.1-8).[242] In the case of the intolerable incest, strong disciplinary action was necessary, and Paul sets himself as it were over the assembled church met under the power of their new and only patron, the Lord Jesus, charging them to purge the malice and evil from their midst (5.3-8, 13), rendering Deut. 17.17 as a command.[243] Was this the same problem as the one he addressed in his first letter (5.9)? At all events, both 5.9-13 and 6.9-20 are clear enough evidence that the

237. Chow, *Patronage* 125-27.

238. See also Clarke, *Leadership* 62-68.

239. 'Paul's sharp criticism of their practice is implicit in the very first word of (6.1): *tolma* . . . "How can you dare . . . ?"' (Horrell, *Social Ethos* 137).

240. On the references to 'the effeminate and practising homosexuals' (6.9), see my *Theology of Paul* 122 n. 103.

241. See again Winter, *Corinth* 81-93, and n. 190 above. See further my *Theology of Paul* 690 n. 80; and note the much-quoted statement of Apollodorus (mid-fourth century BCE): 'We have courtesans for pleasure, concubines for the day-to-day care of the body, and wives to bear legitimate children and to maintain faithful guardianship of household affairs' (Pseudo-Demosthenes, *Orations* 59.122).

242. 'The civil courts by convention provided another appropriate arena to conduct a power struggle within the church as it would in any association'; 'some Christians appear to have had no qualms adopting the ethos of *politeia* at this point, for this was how citizens had long used the civil courts to pursue enmity relationships' (Winter, *Corinth* 66, 75). As noted above (n. 234), some voluntary associations prohibited litigation between members over disputes which arose in meetings, but Paul forbad all recourse to litigation (255-56). Was Paul as politically motivated, seeing the Christian *ekklēsia* as an 'alternative' society, as R. A. Horsley suggests in '1 Corinthians: A Case Study of Paul's Assembly as an Alternative Society', in Horsley, ed., *Paul and Empire* 242-52, reprinted in Adams and Horrell, *Christianity at Corinth* ch. 18 (here 232)?

243. On what was in view in 1 Cor. 5.5, see my *Theology of Paul* 691 n. 85; Thiselton, *1 Corinthians* 395-400.

old value systems continued to hold sway for several of the Corinthian believers. Here again conversion had (should have) involved a decisive shift in loyalty and the beginning of moral and personal transformation which made such retrogression to the earlier socially acceptable practices no longer even conceivable for believers. What society deemed acceptable may nevertheless have the power to corrupt, like leaven whose influence steadily spreads through the whole (5.6-8).[244] An insistence on the right to indulge in sensual pleasures (6.12) was no longer acceptable for those whose bodies were members of Christ and shrines of the Holy Spirit (6.13-20). The body is 'the sphere in which commitment to Christ becomes real'.[245]

d. The Clash between Old and New Settings (1 Corinthians 7)

In 7.1 Paul turns for the first time to the letter addressed to him by the church in Corinth.[246] In his answer to the Corinthians' questions about marriage and divorce, it quickly becomes evident that here too were issues caused by the fact that the young Christians were caught in the tensions of societal expectations and overlapping networks as they rubbed against and provoked friction for those who had begun to call upon the name of the Lord Jesus Christ (1.2).[247] What did the new loyalty to Christ mean for marriage, for the unmarried, for those married to unbelievers? In other words, how did the new loyalty to Christ affect the most ba-

244. For the image of leaven as a corrupting influence which spreads through the whole till the whole is corrupted, cf. Mark 8.15 pars., and more widely H. Windisch, *TDNT* 2.904-905.

245. Murphy-O'Connor, *Paul* 285.

246. There is a widespread consensus that 7.1b — 'It is good for a man not to touch/ have physical intimacy with a woman' — is a quotation from the letter rather than a statement of Paul's own view. See, e.g., those cited by Schrage, *1 Korinther* 53 n. 11, who observes that the likelihood of this being the case had already been recognized by Tertullian and Origen; see further Thiselton, *1 Corinthians* 498-500; G. D. Fee, '1 Corinthians 7:1-7 Revisited', in T. J. Burke and J. K. Elliott, eds., *Paul and the Corinthians*, M. Thrall FS (NovTSupp 109; Leiden: Brill, 2003) 197-213. The conclusion, of course, tells strongly against the popular view that Paul was extremely ascetic and hostile to the very thought of sexual intercourse, as does what Paul actually says in the following verses! Though see also D. Zeller, 'Der Vorrang der Ehelosigkeit in 1 Kor 7', *ZNW* 96 (2005) 61-77. In *The Theology of Paul* I point out that Paul was evidently not intending to present a full treatise on marriage, but only to answer the questions put to him (694).

247. See again Robertson, *Conflict in Corinth*. G. Beattie, *Women and Marriage in Paul and His Early Interpreters* (LNTS 296; London: Clark International, 2005), notes that the context of Paul's teaching on marriage is dominated by concern to avoid *porneia* (19-36); *porneia* — 5.1 (twice); 6.13, 18; 7.2; *porneuō* — 6.18; 10.18 (twice); *pornē* — 6.15, 16; *pornos* — 5.9, 10, 11; 6.9.

sic unit of society, the marital household?[248] The social standing of those who raised the questions addressed in 7.1-9 is unclear, though we should note that in 7.12-16 it is primarily the believing wife of an unbelieving husband who seems to be in view, and in the counsel of 7.21-24 it is only slaves (not masters) who are addressed.

(i) In the first case, Paul's advice is markedly progressive: marriage should be seen as a genuine partnership in which sexual relations are assumed to be the norm (7.3-4), and even a dedication to prayer should not override these mutual rights and obligations (7.5).[249] It is evident that he saw marriage as the only appropriate context for sexual activity (7.2-4),[250] and, recognizing that sexual desire was natural and important,[251] his conclusion was that marriage was the right thing for many/(most?), even though not his own preferred option (7.8-9, 36-38). On the question of divorce he was able to cite the clear teaching of Jesus (7.10-11) but recognized that such teaching had to be qualified or adapted to the circumstances in which some believers now found themselves — married to an unbelieving partner who could insist on a divorce (7.1-16).[252] Here particularly the new social grouping (the church) found itself cutting across and grating against the conventions and expectations of the old social grouping (the household).

Very illuminating is Paul's view of how and whether their response to God's call necessarily demanded a change in their physical and social situation. His answer was: not necessarily. Whether they were circumcised or uncircumcised was no longer of importance; whatever the circumstances in which

248. It is noticeable that Paul's treatment follows the sequence of the 'household rules', which were common in the ancient world and which became a feature of subsequent NT letters (Col. 3.18–4.1; Eph. 5.22–6.9; etc.) — husbands and wives (7.1-16), children (7.14) and slaves (7.21-24); also that the moderating ideals were those more widely cherished for their social value — *enkrateia,* 'self-control' (7.5, 9), and *euschēmōn,* 'good order' (7.35). See, e.g., D. Balch, 'Household Codes', *ABD* 3.318-20; also '1 Cor. 7.32-35 and 'Stoic Debates about Marriage, Anxiety and Distraction', *JBL* 102 (1983) 429-39; and further below, §34 n. 394.

249. Despite inferences which may be drawn to the contrary, Paul does not regard either the state of marriage or the state of celibacy as a charism (7.7); the charism in this case is rather the enabling to exert self-control or to divert sexual energy into acts of prayerful activity, at least for a time (see also Thiselton, *1 Corinthians* 513-14).

250. 'What runs counter to much first-century practice is the fact that the Christian husband does not have authority over his own body, but his wife does. He therefore cannot indulge his sexual passions outside marriage, however much this may have been accepted in first-century society' (Winter, *Corinth* 228). 'These verses amount to nothing less than a sexual revolution' (Barrett, *Paul* 139).

251. Martin's argument that Paul 'rejected desire or passion as a proper motivation for sexual intercourse' is a very tendentious reading of 1 Cor. 7.9 (*Corinthian Body* 209-17); Paul does not use *epithymia,* 'desire', in ch. 7.

252. By this period in Roman law divorce could be initiated by either husband or wife (*OCD*³ 929).

they were called, they could live out that call within these circumstances (7.17-20).[253] Slaves should indeed take any opportunity to become free,[254] but since their relationship to Christ relativized all other relationships, they could still serve him even as a slave of another (7.21-24).[255]

(ii) In dealing with the second main question posed by the Corinthians, regarding those betrothed or engaged,[256] Paul reveals his own predilections more clearly: he would prefer them not to marry. However, with pastoral sensitivity he makes it clear that this is only his own view, even though he speaks as one approved by God (7.25). His concern once again was for his audience to recognize that they may need to choose between the socially desirable and the priority of their devotion to the Lord. A husband or wife will quite properly want to please his or her partner and has to be concerned about 'the affairs of the world' (7.32-35), and Paul was anxious to avoid more occasions for clashes between such conventional responsibilities and the responsibility of the believer to Christ. The clash was all the more severe in view of the shortness of the time (7.26, 29),[257] the nearness of the parousia,[258] perhaps signalled in Paul's view by the sequence of famines which may have afflicted the region around that time.[259] For Paul that had become a major factor in his own decision not to marry. But here again, Paul shows himself equally sensitive to the fact that others may judge their personal circumstances differently, and he repeatedly encourages those who decide they

253. It is important here to recognize that Paul did not regard status (e.g., slavery) as a 'calling'; the 'call' in these verses is the call of conversion, as commentators now agree.

254. See particularly S. S. Bartchy, *MALLON CHRĒSAI: First-Century Slavery and the Interpretation of 1 Corinthians 7:21* (SBLDS 11; Missoula: Scholars, 1973); Horrell, *Social Ethos* 161-67.

255. See further my *Theology of Paul* 698-701, with bibliography.

256. Paul uses both *parthenos* ('virgin') (7.25, 28, 34, 36-38) and *agamos* ('unmarried') (7.8, 11, 32, 34). So *parthenos* probably here refers not to one 'unmarried' (REB) and to more than just 'one not yet married' (Thiselton); 7.36, 38 imply something equivalent to an engagement ('his *parthenos*'), as most modern ETs recognize — e.g., 'his fiancée' (NRSV, NJB), 'the girl to whom he is betrothed' (REB); also Witherington, *Women in the Earliest Churches* 37-38.

257. It is difficult to avoid the conclusion that Paul thought the end of the present age to be imminent (see also above, §29.3e; see further *Theology of Paul* 393-94), though Thiselton warns that Paul's language may be taken too literally (*1 Corinthians* 580-83), and Schnelle cites Epictetus (3.22.69), that 'in view of how things are at present, and the situation at the front, the Cynic must be unhindered from placing himself entirely in the service of God, must be able to travel freely among people without being hindered by bourgeois obligations, unbound by personal connections' (*Paul* 58 and n. 3).

258. The *hōs mē* ('as though not') of 7.29-31 became a *locus classicus* of patristic and Reformation exegesis in expositions of the appropriate mode of Christian existence in the world; see further my *1 Corinthians* 57, and *Theology of Paul* 697 n. 114.

259. See above, n. 168.

should marry to do so and to feel confident that they were doing the right thing (7.28a, 35b, 36, 38).[260]

(iii) A final word to widows, women who were often still quite young when widowed,[261] takes the same line: remarriage is not the wisest course, in his own view; but they are wholly free to remarry if they think it right and proper to do so, though 'only in the Lord' (7.39-40).

In all this there is a sense of the uncomfortableness of individual believers having too many ties and responsibilities which may divert them from their primary responsibility to Christ the Lord. But it is an uncomfortableness which Paul recognized had to be lived with during the present age. He certainly gave no counsel to 'come out' from the world or to adopt an ascetic life-style as the only way of living in the present age.[262] Though he himself did not share the pressures and responsibilities of married life, he was entirely understanding of these pressures and responsibilities and encouraging of those married or contemplating marriage to live out these responsibilities. In so doing he gives both a realistic depiction of how to cope with the clash between old setting and new loyalty and a model of sensitive pastoral counselling for later generations.[263]

e. The Clash of Rights (1 Corinthians 8–10)

The next issue raised by the Corinthians concerned *eidōlothyta*, 'meat offered to an idol' (8.1), and Paul's response seems to go off at a tangent in the midst of his discussion of the subject (chs. 8, 10) to defend his own actions in declining a position of financial dependency on others (ch. 9). What is often missed, however, is the fact that the three chapters are tied together by the common theme of *rights:* when and when not, why and why not to exercise or claim them.[264]

260. On the ambivalent *hyperakmos* (7.36), which lexicographers have taken as either 'past one's prime, beyond marriageable age' or 'at one's sexual peak' or even 'with strong passions' (BDAG 1032; NRSV), see Winter: 'The verbal form neither suggested that the person had reached menopause if a woman nor impotence through age if a man. It was used to refer either to a woman who had reached puberty and therefore could engage in sexual intercourse and safely conceive, or to the sexual drives or passions of either sex' (*Corinth* 249 and the important n. 46); see also Martin, *Corinthian Body* 219-26; Thiselton, *1 Corinthians* 593-98.

261. Twelve was the marriageable age for women, and young girls were often married to much older men; the older husbands frequently died when their wives were still young (*OCD*[3] 928, 1621). See also §24 at n. 47 above.

262. See also A. S. May, *'The Body for the Lord': Sex and Identity in 1 Corinthians 5–7* (JSNTS 278; London: Clark International, 2004) chs. 7-9.

263. See further my *Theology of Paul* 695, 698.

264. 'This dialogue between the Corinthians and Paul on the Christian concept of freedom is in general the most profound discussion of this theme that early Christianity has to offer' (Becker, *Paul* 212).

The point is often missed, even though the theme is signalled by the repeated use of *exousia,* itself best translated as 'right' (8.9; 9.4-6, 12, 18). Obscuring the point, however, most modern translations render *exousia* in 8.9 by 'freedom' (NIV, NJB) or 'liberty' (NRSV, REB).[265] Again, as in 6.12, the issue is focused in the claim *exesti,* 'it is right, permitted, proper', of 10.23. Here too, however, much earlier discussion was misled by use of the same term in passages like Mark 2.26 and 10.2 and by the inference drawn that what Paul had in mind was a further aspect of his discussion of the law (or law) — 'it is legal', 'all things are lawful' (NRSV) — and that his treatment was a further example of his refusal to rely on the law as a guide to Christian conduct.[266] But what is rather in view is probably social custom and the rights of some (Roman citizens in particular) to participate in civic banquets and other such celebrations.[267] Since these banquets were typically celebrated in one of Corinth's larger temples, or in honour of the imperial family or one or other of the gods worshipped in Corinth, the meat dishes provided inevitably came from the unused carcasses of the animals sacrificed in the temple or as part of the relevant cult. On special festival days the whole population might hope to be able to participate, even if only at the fringe, of such feasts. This at once posed a severe question and threat to all members of the Corinthian church who were Jews or who had been strongly influenced by Jewish beliefs and praxis. For idolatry was totally unacceptable to Jewish sensibility. The second commandment was fundamental; the thought of God being in any degree adequately imaged in wood and stone was intolerable to them.[268]

The question came down to whether the other members, particularly those of higher social status who could anticipate being regularly invited and expected

265. The 'liberty' *(eleutheria)* actually claimed (9.1, 19; 10.29) is liberty to exercise (or forgo) the *exousia.*

266. Often cited is the summation of C. K. Barrett, 'Things Sacrificed to Idols', *Essays on Paul* (London: SPCK, 1982) 40-59: 'Paul is nowhere more unJewish than in this *mēden anakrinontes* ["not raising questions" — 1 Cor. 10.25, 27]', 'an attitude of extraordinary liberalism' (49, 50).

267. Theissen was again first to highlight the likelihood that the issue arose because those of high social status and integrated into the public life of the city would find it difficult to avoid participating in such public functions and festivities (*Social Setting* 130), with particular reference to Erastus, the 'city treasurer' (Rom. 16.23). It is Winter, however, who brought home most effectively that the issue was one of 'rights' — the 'civic privilege which entitled Corinthians to dine on "civic" occasions in a temple' (*Welfare* ch. 9, 'Civic Rights'). 'Candidates for election promised to perform important benefactions for their fellow [Roman] citizens upon election, such as fund . . . banquets'; 'The president of the [Isthmian] games was expected to entertain the citizens at a feast' (168, 172, 174; also *Corinth* 93-96, 280-81). 'It would seem that there was a long-established convention in the ancient world for people of status or power to articulate their actions on the basis that "all things are permitted"' (*Corinth* 81).

268. See above, §29.7a.

to join in such banquets, should feel free to exercise their right to do so.[269] It is because the issue is about such rights that Paul interjects into the discussion a careful statement regarding his own rights as an apostle (ch. 9), as an example of whether and how such rights should be exercised. It should be noted at once that he does not deny these rights, either his as an apostle or theirs as citizens of Corinth; his concern was rather how believers should deal with the clash between their rights and their responsibilities to fellow believers. The fact that Paul concludes by extending his discussion of rights even to private guest-dining (10.23-30), thus to the whole range of friendship and association beyond the circle of the congregation, shows how alive he was to the problem of overlapping networks and how concerned he was to indicate a way in which these overlaps could be sustained without damaging the church.

The issue, then, was not so much one of 'knowledge' *(gnōsis),* even though that term features prominently in ch. 8 (8.1, 7, 10, 11).[270] The 'knowledge' that an idol was nothing in the world and that God is one was a knowledge which Paul shared (8.4), but it was appealed to by feast-participators not so much as an article of faith but rather as a means of justifying the exercise of their prior right — a rationalizing of a preferred mode of conduct rather than a desire to determine conduct in accordance with faith.

Paul's response was clear. He affirms his (the Christian) belief in God as one but draws different inferences from it. Some Corinthians concluded that as idols were 'nothing', eating *eidōlothyta* was a matter of no consequence. Paul read the credo differently (8.5-6): it signified that the gods of the Corinthian temples were of no consequence, including the 'so-called gods and lords' of the imperial cult(!);[271] and even if their influence was all too real in Corinthian society,

269. As Theissen observed, Paul addresses himself almost exclusively to those who claimed the right to participate in temple celebrations and feasts (*Social Setting* 137). Here again we should not ignore likely tensions of social dissonance and status inconsistency (Meeks, *Urban Christians* 70); the knowledge (and assertion) that 'an idol is nothing' would hardly commend even an important social figure to the promoters and officials of the cult in question. Cf. and contrast Barclay, 'Thessalonica and Corinth'. Becker highlights the tensions and dilemmas well: 'Was it not a danger for the polis when Christians scorned the official gods, who guaranteed the well-being of the city? If someone no longer wanted to swear to a business contract by recognized gods, was that person still a reliable contractual partner? If a Christian woman and wife of a pagan man no longer wanted to pay homage to the household gods with the whole family, could she still be trusted with household affairs? If a family no longer responded to invitations to go to the temple, could one in the long run maintain social relations with that family?' (*Paul* 248).

270. The mention of *gnōsis* of course was seen as proof of the Gnostic hypothesis by its proponents; see above, n. 213.

271. See above, n. 166. The balance of 8.5a and b catches well the ambivalence Paul probably felt about acknowledging what was the reality confronting him daily in cities like

the Jewish/Christian credo affirmed that the only God worthy of unreserved worship was God the Father, the source of all things, and the only Lord worthy of total obedience was the Lord Jesus, the agent of God's creative power.[272] The corollary implicit in 8.7-13 is that obedience to this Lord should put at least a large question mark against conduct which involved any degree of recognition or acknowledgment of the claims of other (so-called) gods and lords.

The more explicit response is that believers should allow their conduct to be at least influenced, if not determined, by how it actually affects other believers (8.7-13). On the central matter of rights, Paul counsels, these should always be trumped by love (8.1) — love of God (8.3) and love of neighbour, that is, a due sense of responsibility for one's fellow believer.[273] The fact was that some in the Corinthian assembly saw eating *eidōlothyta* as a betrayal of their faith, as a deadly toxic and corrosive influence (8.7).[274] It was equally the case that such

---

Corinth and Ephesus, that is, the reality of the imperial cult in particular and how it determined so much of political manoeuvring and the social round.

272. Remarkable here is the way Paul expands (if that is the best word) the *Shema* ('The Lord our God, the Lord is one') to include Christ: 'for us there is one God, the Father, . . . and one Lord, Jesus Christ'. That Paul here speaks of Christ in terms of the language of divine agency used in the wisdom tradition particularly of divine Wisdom (Prov. 3.19; 8.22-31; Wis. 8.4-6; Philo, *Det.* 54; *Heres* 199) is generally recognized; see further my *Christology* ch. 6; also *Theology of Paul* 272-75 (with bibliography); R. Cox, *By the Same Word: Creation and Salvation in Hellenistic Judaism and Early Christianity* (BZNW 145; Berlin: de Gruyter, 2007) 141-61; and above, §29.7d. Fee vigorously disputes this consensus (*Pauline Christology* 595-619), but (1) he almost entirely ignores the parallel passages (John 1.1-18; Heb. 1.1-3), where the echoes of wisdom language are more explicit and which indicate that this line of reflection was well established in earliest Christianity; (2) he makes a highly questionable differentiation between personified Wisdom and wisdom as a divine attribute; and (3) he questions whether Paul even knew the Wisdom of Solomon, despite listing (Pauline!) 'allusions' to this work familiar to Pauline scholars for over a century. There is a woodenness of exegesis here which would question whether any use of the phrase 'to be or not to be' could be regarded as an allusion to Hamlet's words. More sound is the conclusion of W. L. Knox, *St. Paul and the Church of the Gentiles* (Cambridge: Cambridge University, 1939, 1961): 'The divine Wisdom, the pattern and agent of creation and the divine Mind permeating the cosmos, was identified with Jesus not as a matter of midrashic exposition which could be used and thrown aside, but as an eternal truth in the realm of metaphysics; . . . whether he [Paul] realised it or not, he had committed the Church to the theology of Nicaea' (178).

273. Theissen sums up the burden of Paul's expectations of the higher-status members of the congregation as 'love-patriarchalism' (*Social Setting* 107-10), which fits well here, but elsewhere Paul's rebuke of these members is too strong to be summed up under that heading; see further Horrell, *Social Ethos* ch. 4.

274. Paul describes them consistently as 'weak' (8.7, 9-12; 9.22). The term is expressive of a 'strong' perspective, which sees such scruples as a weakness in faith (cf. Rom. 14.1-2; 15.1). But the important point is that recognition of the reality of such scruples should condition the behaviour of the 'strong'.

believers, seeing those with more robust knowledge on the subject eating *eidōlothyta* in one of the Corinthian temples (8.10), might be encouraged to do the same and thus to act in contradiction to their conscience,[275] thereby even destroying their faith and their relationship with Christ (8.11) and certainly causing them extreme anguish of spirit (8.12).[276] So to act, so to damage the faith and peace of mind of one for whom Christ had died, was to act in disregard of Christ himself. After all, if rights were what was at issue, the *exousia* to participate in such meals/banquets (8.9), they should be willing to forgo these rights for the sake of their fellow believers. 'If food causes my brother to stumble, I will never eat meat lest I cause my brother to stumble' (8.13).

As an example of how Christian behaviour should be expressed as freedom to *refuse* rights and not just freedom to *claim* them, Paul puts forward his own case: of his apostolic right and his refusal to claim it (ch. 9).[277] This was the right in particular to look to his converts and those he taught for financial support, to be provided with food and drink — in principle, provision for a wife as well (9.4-6).[278] The case is built on obvious precedents of those who could properly expect to benefit from the labour (9.7), from a scriptural ruling[279] to the same effect (9.8-12), from the precedent of priestly service (9.13),[280] and is capped by reference to an explicit command of the Lord, 'that those who proclaim the gospel should get their living by the gospel' (9.14). But Paul makes clear how important it was for him (and Barnabas — 9.6) to decline that right (9.12) and to support themselves by the work of their own hands (9.18). Paul's rationale was presumably that he could thereby avoid being obligated to any wealthy individual or being caught in a patron-client relationship.[281] But here the point being made is that

---

275. 'Conscience *(syneidēsis)*' is a critical factor in all this for Paul (1 Cor. 8.7, 10, 12; 10.25, 27-29); on the concept and experience of 'conscience' and related bibliography, see *Theology of Paul* 54-55 n. 16.

276. To be noted is that Paul envisages the damage being done by those of tender conscience *acting* against or in defiance of their conscience, not simply by their *witnessing* others acting in ways they disapproved of.

277. The self-defence of ch. 9 was not so much of a tangent, since he had been criticized at just this point for not claiming his apostolic right (9.3). Lüdemann sees a further case of an anti-Pauline attack on Paul's apostleship (*Opposition* 65-72).

278. The context makes it clear that the issue was not simply the right to be married or to be accompanied by a wife but the right to receive financial support for both, not simply for himself alone.

279. 1 Cor. 9.9 cites Deut. 25.4, but if 9.10 quotes a text, its source is unknown.

280. The priest eating meat left over from the sacrifices (Num. 18.8, 31; Deut. 18.1-3) would be an appropriate precedent in the circumstances.

281. See above, §30.5d. P. Marshall, *Enmity in Corinth: Social Conventions in Paul's Relations with the Corinthians* (WUNT 2.23; Tübingen: Mohr Siebeck, 1987), analyzes the situation envisaged in ch. 9 in terms of the conventions governing friendship: acceptance of gifts

preaching the gospel was such an all-important priority for him that *anything* — any social entanglement like a patron-client relationship — which might hinder or conflict with that responsibility should thereby be avoided (9.16-18).

It was this principle which gave Paul the freedom to shape his policy and tactics to the different social contexts and groupings within which and to which he ministered, the freedom to be 'all things to all' (9.22).[282] It was the freedom to live like a Jew, when appropriate (9.20), and the freedom equally to live like a non-Jew,[283] when appropriate (9.21), or the freedom (in the case of *eidōlothyta*) to observe others' scruples (9.22).[284] A final consideration is that the exercise of such freedom, in refusing to claim legitimate rights, is also a valuable exercise in self-control (9.25), and indeed necessary if self-indulgence was not to prevent the successful completion of the process of personal salvation (9.26-27).

In ch. 10 Paul returns to the question raised by the Corinthians about *eidōlothyta*. Those who want to exercise their right as believers to take part in civic and religious banquets, despite the immorality which was regularly a feature of such occasions, should bear in mind the example of the Israelites, their spiritual ancestors, in the wilderness (10.1). They too had experienced the equivalent of being baptized into Christ (10.2); they too enjoyed the equivalent of the bread and cup of the Lord's table (10.3-4). Nevertheless they died in the wilderness (without reaching the goal of the promised land) (10.5). Why? Because they lusted for what was evil: they practised idolatry; they ate and drank as part of their festival in honour of the golden calf (Exod. 32.6); they indulged in sexual immorality;[285] and as a result 23,000 of them perished in a single day (10.6-8). The warning for those who indulged themselves by participation in the feasts and festivals of Corinth could hardly be clearer (10.9-13).[286]

---

establishes friendship; refusal of gifts creates enmity (summary on 396-98). He suggests that Paul's refusal of aid from the Corinthians, when he had accepted gifts from Philippi, 'insulted and dishonoured them, treated them as inferiors and showed that he did not love them' (246). Similarly Murphy-O'Connor, *Paul* 305-307.

282. Here again it is important that 9.19-23 not be regarded as a self-standing statement of missionary policy; its function and scope are determined by its role in illustrating and forwarding Paul's argument about rights and freedom not to claim them. Paul had rights and obligations in reference to the law, which he does not deny (9.21), but here the freedom for the higher priority and obligation to preach the gospel to as many as possible (9.19, 22b-23) was foremost in his mind.

283. See above, §29.2b.

284. Paul does not give a balancing clause ('to the strong I became strong') (as in 9.20-21), since it was precisely the freedom/right to partake in idol-feasts, in disregard for the scruples of others, to which Paul objects in 8.7-13.

285. For the evidently intentional overtones of 'rose up to play' (10.7, quoting Exod. 32.6), see Thiselton, *1 Corinthians* 734-35.

286. Again we should note that the focus of Paul's criticism is not some defective view

Paul did not hesitate to press the issue to a straight either-or, such was his inherited and still-powerful antipathy to idolatry (10.14). It was not possible to appreciate the full significance of the Christians' shared meal — as a sharing in the very blood and body of Christ himself (10.16-17) — without drawing the unavoidable conclusion that partaking of the table of the Lord was wholly incompatible with feasting at a table dedicated to an idol (10.21).[287] It was not that an idol was anything of itself (10.19), but Scripture alerts us to the malign forces behind such idols (10.20),[288] and it is not possible to give ground to such forces without provoking the Lord to the 'jealousy *(zēlos)*' which destroyed the Israelites (10.22). Here the strong discouragement of 8.7-13 against participation in temple meals for the sake of the 'weaker brother' becomes outright rejection of any compromise policy; in the case of idolatry, there could be no 'both-and'.[289]

Having given such forthright and rigorous instruction, Paul qualifies it by indicating that he had in mind only the formal feasts and festivals of the various city cults and not day-to-day social intercourse between believers and unbelievers; the combination is similar to 5.9-13.[290] Here the issue of 'right' *(exesti)* was more complex (10.23); the key was once again not to allow the outcome to be determined by one's own advantage but to consider the effect (beneficial or otherwise) on the other (10.24). Paul envisages the situation where a believer is invited to a meal.[291] For Paul there was no question of refusing the invitation simply because the host was not a member of the church. If meat was served, as would be quite likely, there was a fair to strong chance that it had come from the meat market as supplied from the temples; but not necessarily so, since other sources of supply were available.[292]

---

of baptism and the Lord's Supper but the behaviour of the Corinthians as wholly inappropriate to those who had experienced such spiritual realities; see also above at n. 212 (on 1.17) and below, n. 379 (on 15.29); Chester, *Conversion* 342.

287. For invitations 'to dine at the banquet of the Lord Sarapis', see above, §30 n. 78.

288. Deut. 32.17; 1 Cor. 10.20-21 is the only occasion on which Paul speaks of demons (also 1 Tim. 4.1).

289. As Gooch clearly shows, it would have been impossible to treat meals in temples as purely secular and to dissociate them from the religious rites for which the temple primarily existed *(Dangerous Food)*.

290. It is important to note that 10.23–11.1 is not simply a 'loose thread' (Fee, *1 Corinthians* 476) or 'conciliatory afterthought and summary of his argument' (Horsley, '1 Corinthians' 233) but gives a ruling which enabled Paul's Corinthian converts to maintain social relationships despite the prohibition on attending banquets in temple property. See further *Theology of Paul* 702-704.

291. *Pace* Horrell, *Social Ethos* 146, the situation envisaged must be that of an invitation to a meal in someone's home; the meat served in a temple would of course have come from the temple sacrifices, which Paul had set his face against; see again *Theology of Paul* 702-704.

292. J. J. Meggitt, 'Meat Consumption and Social Conflict in Corinth', *JTS* 45 (1994) 137-41, points out that poor-quality meat would have been more widely available from 'cookshops

Paul's counsel was that the believer should accept such a dish without question; after all, it was ultimately God's provision (Ps. 24.1) (10.25-27). Only if someone else asserted that the meat had come from a temple should the believer decline the dish. Again, not for his own sake so much as for the effect his eating *eidōlothyta* would have on the other (10.28-29). Here again, Paul is uncomfortable with what he says: there was no answer which would be gladly accepted by all, and Paul was unwilling for his own conscience to be subservient to another's (10.29-30). But at least the principles are clear, even if their application is not always clear-cut:

- Idolatry should be avoided with firm resolution.[293]
- The commitment made to Jesus as Lord (in baptism) was to be an exclusive loyalty which, unlike most other religious devotions, did not permit multiple loyalties (attending meals in honour of other gods); sharing in the table of the Lord constituted both an identity marker and a boundary marker.[294]
- Since an idol is nothing and 'the earth is the Lord's' (10.26), one could eat *eidōlothyta unwittingly* without damage to faith and relationships with other believers;[295] one believer's conscience is not prescriptive for another's conscience.
- It was the *conscious* partaking of *eidōlothyta* as such which Paul deemed unacceptable, knowing that it might hinder an inquirer or cause a brother to stumble.
- More determinative than 'my right' should be 'what builds up (the community)' (8.1, 10; 10.23);[296] love of the brother should have first place in such considerations (8.1; 10.24).[297]

(*popinae* and *ganeae*)', wineshops (*tabernae* or *cauponae*) and elsewhere (also *Poverty* 109-12). D.-A. Koch, '"Alles, was *en makellō* verkauft wird, esst . . .". Die *macella* von Pompeji, Gerasa und Korinth und ihre Bedeutung für die Auslegung von 1 Kor 10,25', *ZNW* 90 (1999) 194-291, concludes that meat for sale in the typical *macellum* may or may not have had its origin in cultic slaughtering. I have already noted Winter's suggestion (above at n. 169) that a further factor may be that in Corinth official provision had previously been made in the market complex for the Jewish community to secure kosher meat and other foods and that, as a move against the Jews, the provision of 'suitable food' was officially withdrawn from the Corinthian meat market, thus depriving Christians of meat not offered to idols (*Corinth* 293-95, 297-301). See also D. W. Gill, 'The Meat-Market at Corinth (1 Corinthians 10:25)', *TynB* 43 (1992) 389-93.

293. Here again it is important to note that Paul did not abandon Israel's traditional hostility to idolatry (see my *Theology of Paul* 702-704).

294. Meeks, *Urban Christians* 159-60.

295. Worthy of note is that Paul's advice in 10.25, and in an issue which was very much bound up with the identity of some believers, is in effect 'Don't ask, don't tell'!

296. See further below, nn. 360, 361.

297. For criticism of Theissen's famous summing up Paul's counsel in terms of 'love patriarchalism', see Horrell, *Social Ethos* particularly ch. 4; Jewett, *Romans* 65-69.

- In determining what to do in controversial issues, a critical factor for Paul was whether he could give thanks for what he did (10.30), whether he was doing it 'for the glory of God' (10.30).
- Similarly, whether he was doing it mindful of its effect on others (including the impression made on others) and for their benefit, or simply to satisfy himself or to gain honour from others (10.32-33), was critical for Paul.

Here again Paul sets an example, as he did not hesitate to claim (11.1), of how Christians should handle controversial subjects and of the priorities they should observe in their mutual relationships.

f. The Tension between Household and Church (1 Cor. 11.2-16)

From 11.2 Paul turns away from the problems of shifting boundaries and clashing cultures to tensions within the church of Corinth itself as evidenced in their gatherings. This was by no means a case of Paul or the Corinthians turning their back on the wider society and becoming wrapped up in their own problems, for the problems were in part caused by values and priorities which had governed former conduct and life-style being assumed on the part of some as still appropriate for the communal life of the new association. And throughout 1 Corinthians, Paul shows himself more than a little aware of the adverse or negative impression which conduct within the Christians' meetings might make on their neighbours, with consequences for the standing of the church and its evangelistic outreach.

In making this transition, it is noticeable that in ch. 11 Paul does not refer to the Corinthians' letter — not till 12.1. The appropriate inference is probably that the information to which he responds had come to him by word of mouth, again probably from Stephanas and his companions. As in chs. 1–10, in other words, Paul seems to prefer to deal first with the oral reports he had received about the conduct of the Corinthian worship and their shared meals (ch. 11) before turning to the issue raised formally by the Corinthians themselves (chs. 12–14). The inference may also again be justified that the bulk of the Corinthian believers were more accepting of the conduct referred to in ch. 11 than Paul was, and that by putting his treatment of this conduct prior to the concerns the Corinthians had raised (chs. 12–14), Paul was in effect rebuking them for their unconcern.

The tension exposed in 11.2-16 (and probably 14.33b-36) is one occasioned by the fact that the believers met in homes, *the tension caused by the same space serving as both home and meeting place of church.*[298] The problem arose because

---

298. The clue was provided by my colleague S. C. Barton, 'Paul's Sense of Place: An Anthropological Approach to Community Formation in Corinth', *NTS* 32 (1986) 225-46; see my *1 Corinthians* 75.

the ingrained patriarchalism of ancient society came to such definitive expression precisely in the household. Within the household, regarded as the basic unit of society, the primary fact was *patria potestas,* the absolute power of the *paterfamilias* over the other members of the household.[299] Well-to-do single women and widows could have a considerable degree of independence in practice, but even so they were still legally under the guardianship of their family's senior male member. Wives, however, had no choice but to be subordinate and submissive.[300] So when wives or women of the household began to take active and prominent part in worship, and not in some cult centre or elsewhere away from the home, but in the area so clearly marked out by male dominance, tensions were almost bound to emerge.

This seems to have been the case in Corinth: women prophesying and praying (aloud) in the assembled congregation, acting in ways that would have been deemed inappropriate in the home. The issue was provoked because the women were praying and prophesying with their heads uncovered. This is sometimes taken to indicate the problem to be that women were worshipping in uninhibited ecstasy, with hair loose and dishevelled, too much like the devotees of Dionysus.[301] And given what Paul tells us of Corinthian worship in chs. 12–14,[302] that may indeed have been a contributory factor, though if that was the main thrust of Paul's concern, we might have expected him to deal with it entirely in ch. 14, devoted as that chapter is to such problems in the Corinthian worship gatherings.

Paul's response, however, indicates that it was two (other) aspects which most troubled him. One was the implications of the women's conduct for male hierarchy. Very revealing is the fact that Paul introduces the subject not by indicating the problem or issue being addressed (as in 5.1, 6.1 and 8.1). Instead he begins by reasserting the proper relationship of man and woman, or, perhaps more accurately, of husband and wife:[303] the *anēr* is head *(kephalē)*[304] of the *gynē* (11.3); the *anēr* is the image and glory of God, while the *gynē* is the glory of the *anēr* (11.7). In all this, Paul evidently draws on the (second) creation narrative in Genesis 2:

299. See *OCD³* 1122-23. There were variations in Greek and Jewish law, but the basic fact held true throughout the Mediterranean world that the household was essentially a patriarchal institution. Meggitt justifiably warns against exaggerating the reality of *patria potestas* in practice (*Poverty* 27-28).

300. The exhortation to wives to 'be subject *(hypotassesthe)* to your husbands' (Col. 3.18; Eph. 5.24) simply conformed to current mores; for details see my *Colossians and Philemon* 247.

301. See particularly Fiorenza, *In Memory of Her* 227; and further my *1 Corinthians* 72-74. But see also C. H. Cosgrove, 'A Woman's Unbound Hair in the Greco-Roman World', *JBL* 124 (2005) 675-92 (here 678-86).

302. Particularly 1 Cor. 12.2; 14.12, 23.

303. The issue is easily confused, since *anēr* can mean both 'man' and 'husband', and *gynē* can mean both 'woman' and 'wife'.

304. On the ambiguity of *kephalē,* 'head' or 'source', see Thiselton's full discussion (*1 Corinthians* 812-23).

woman comes from man (2.22); woman was created on account of man (2.18). Since the man and woman of Genesis 2 provide the ideal of marital union (2.24), the thought is particularly of husband and wife. Paul, in other words, uses a theology of created order to support the social convention of *patria potestas* as still determinative for the way women/wives function in the house church. The qualifications he makes in 11.11-12 point towards a more balanced relationship 'in the Lord' but do not question the fundamental principles drawn out in 11.3 and 7.

It is likely that Paul's brief reversion to the subject in 14.33b-36 works from the same premise.[305] For there what is probably in view was a situation where women prophets were taking part in the evaluation of prophetic utterances which Paul called for in 14.29. Paul refers to the motivation somewhat patronizingly as their 'wanting to learn', but the revealing detail is that they should 'ask their own husbands at home' (14.35). In other words, church should not be confused with home: for a wife to question her husband in public, as one prophet might scrutinize the prophecy of another, was improper.[306] A wife should be 'subject' (*hypotassesthai* — that word again) to her husband (14.34); and as in 11.3-7, the Torah is appealed to in support (14.34).[307] In short, even though Paul recognized that 'in the Lord' (11.11) there is no difference in status between man and woman (Gal. 3.28), he refrained from calling in question the basic structure of household authority.

That Paul was highly mindful of the impression which his churches might make on the wider public is indicated by his second consideration in 11.2-16. He maintains that a man did not cover his head when praying or prophesying (11.4),[308] the theological rationale being that as the image and glory of God, he should not hide that (11.7). In contrast, a woman should cover herself,[309] for as the glory of *man,* it was inappropriate that she worship *God* unveiled.[310] But such

305. 1 Cor. 14.34-35/36 is frequently regarded as an interpolation (e.g., Horrell, *Social Ethos* 184-95; Murphy-O'Connor, *Paul* 290; Lohse, *Paulus* 136); see my *Theology of Paul* 589 and further bibliography in Thiselton, *1 Corinthians* 1150.

306. See particularly Fiorenza, *In Memory of Her* 230-33; Witherington, *Women in the Earliest Churches* 90-104; Thiselton, *1 Corinthians* 1158-60, with further bibliography; though see also Beattie, *Women and Marriage* 56-58.

307. A particular passage is not specified, but presumably the reference is to Gen. 3.16 as then currently interpreted in Jewish circles.

308. R. E. Oster, 'Use, Misuse and Neglect of Archaeological Evidence in Some Modern Works on 1 Corinthians', *ZNW* 83 (1992) 52-73, finds unambiguous archaeological evidence that in Roman worship men usually did cover their heads (67-69), so the grounds of Paul's assertion are unclear.

309. That a veil or other head covering is in view, rather than hair as itself a covering, is clear from the language used; see P. T. Massey, 'The Meaning of *katakalyptō* and *kata kephalēs echōn* in 1 Corinthians 11.2-16', *NTS* 53 (2007) 502-23.

310. As M. D. Hooker argued, 'Authority on Her Head: An Examination of 1 Corinthi-

theological argument was evidently not the major consideration. This is indicated rather by the language of 'shame' and 'honour' which in 11.2-16 and
14.33b-36 has particular prominence,[311] and by Paul's recourse to talk of 'what
is proper' and in accordance with 'nature' (11.13, 14).[312] The appeal is to some
convention of the day, that it was as 'shameful' for a man to pray or prophesy
with his head covered, as for a woman to pray or prophecy with her head uncovered — as shameful, indeed, as for a woman to have her hair cropped close or
shaved off (11.4-6).[313] It was shameful too for a wife to speak out in the house
church in which presumably her husband was a leading figure (14.35). In a society dominated by honour/shame considerations,[314] Paul was in effect appealing
to that widespread sensibility of what was right and acceptable. The appeal of
11.13-15 was to what everyone knew to be 'proper', what everyone 'naturally'
('of course') saw as a matter of 'disgrace'.

Such counsel is evidence of just how little Paul saw the new social reality of
church as challenging these established conventions of home and society. Of
course, his primary concern was probably the impression his churches were liable
to make on a society almost wholly subservient to such conventions and values. In
other matters (chs. 1–7) he was outspoken in his challenge, but here he himself evidently shared too much of the mind-set to call it into radical question.[315] His

---

ans 11.10', *From Adam to Christ: Essays on Paul* (Cambridge: Cambridge University, 1990)
113-20, the veil constitutes her 'authority' *(exousia)* [or 'right'] to pray in her own right to God,
even though she is the glory of *man;* see further *Theology of Paul* 589-90; cf. Beattie, *Women
and Marriage* 47-51. Winter suggests that the puzzling reference to 'the *angeloi*' in 11.10
should not be referred to the 'angels' (with allusion to Gen. 6.1-4) but to 'messengers', that is,
information-gatherers who reported back to those who sent them (the civic authorities) what
was being said in these strange 'meetings' *(Corinth* 136-38). See also discussion in
Witherington, *Women in the Earliest Churches* 78-90; C. S. Keener, *Paul, Women and Wives:
Marriage and Women's Ministry in the Letters of Paul* (Peabody: Hendrickson, 1992) ch. 1.

311. *Aischros,* 'shameful' (only 11.6 and 14.35 in the undisputed Paulines); *kataischynō,*
'dishonour, put to shame' (11.4, 5; used seven times elsewhere by Paul); *atimia,* 'dishonour,
disgrace' (11.14); *prepon,* 'fitting, seemly, proper' (11.13).

312. To live in harmony with the natural order was a particularly Stoic ideal, but the appeal is probably broader — to how things are constituted, 'how things are' (Thiselton, *1 Corinthians* 844-46).

313. The sexual connotations should not be missed: 'for a married woman in *Roman* society to appear in public without a hood sent out signals of sexual availability or at very least a
lack of concern for respectability' (Thiselton, *1 Corinthians* 5, citing A. Rouselle, 'Body Politics in Ancient Rome', in G. Duby and M. Perot, eds., *A History of Women in the West I: From
Ancient Goddesses to Christian Saints* [Cambridge: Harvard University, 1992] 296-337, and
Martin, *Corinthian Body* 229-49, who notes that part of the classical Greek wedding was the
unveiling of the bride [233-34]).

314. Malina, *New Testament World* ch. 2.

315. It is sometimes suggested that it was for similar reasons that Paul dropped the 'no

qualifications are limited to 'in the Lord' (11.11), though his abrupt refusal to engage in any further discussion of the matter (11.16) probably betrays a degree of disquiet on the counsel he was giving.[316] This is not the Paul who provided a model of theological instruction, robust ethical prioritisation and pastoral sensitivity in the earlier chapters.

g. The Tensions between Rich and Poor (1 Cor. 11.17-34)

By the way he introduces the two issues treated in ch. 11, Paul implies that they came to him in the same way (presumably also by oral report from Stephanas and the other messengers from Corinth).[317] Whereas in the former case he begins with commendation that the Corinthians have maintained the traditions he taught them ('I praise you' — 11.2), in the latter he begins with a sharp rebuke: 'I do not praise you'. Evidently the proper ordering of prayer and prophecy in worship was not so contentious a subject; perhaps only one or two were being petulant or provocative (the *tis,* 'someone', of 11.16?). But the conduct of the common meal was something else (11.17-22). Here what was at stake was not so much divergent doctrine or theological influence from other cults, as had been suggested by the early history-of-religions researchers, but the social stratification of the Corinthian church and the assumption on the part of some (the socially secure and well-to-do) that the association of Jesus Christ should be enjoyed much as other associations were.[318]

From what Paul had been told, the Corinthians' gathering to eat together had become an occasion of schism and factionalism (11.18 — *schismata;* 11.19 — *haireseis*):[319] they were treating 'the dinner of the Lord' as though it was the sort of dinner party typical of other associations. To the extent that the host provided any of the food or drink, we may envisage the host's social equals reclining

---

longer male and female' when he repeated the thought of Gal. 3.28 in 1 Cor. 12.13 (e.g., Horrell, *Social Ethos* 86).

316. 'The final comment reads rather like a rather embarrassed or indeed bad-tempered attempt to forestall further discussion on the subject' (*Theology of Paul* 588), as, significantly, perhaps also 14.35-36.

317. Winter, *Corinth* 159-63, argues that 11.18 should be translated 'I believe a certain report' rather than 'I believe it for the most part' (BDAG 633).

318. Here again it was Theissen who first observed that the problems were those of social integration (*Social Setting* ch. 4). Winter suggests that Corinth was in the midst of a grain shortage when Paul wrote; 'some Christians seem to have made no move at the dinner to share with the "have-nots" during this grain shortage' (*Corinth* 157).

319. *Hairesis* was the term used by Josephus for the different 'sects' within Second Temple Judaism and in Acts for the 'sect' of the Nazarenes; see above, §20.1(15). Paul uses it only once elsewhere (Gal. 5.20), as a danger implicitly confronting the Galatian believers.

in the triclinium while the rest sat on benches in the atrium, as also different quality of food and drink being served to the guests of different social status.[320] Alternatively, or also, to the extent that the Lord's dinner was an *eranos* meal, with participants bringing their own contributions, there was even more scope for the factionalism which Paul deplored. For each was going ahead as though the meal was his own, and some were getting drunk while others went hungry (11.21)![321] It would appear from 11.33 that some arrived early (or promptly) and began eating straight away[322] — presumably the more leisured well-to-do, whose contribution would be substantial. But others arrived later, presumably slaves and freedmen with obligations to patrons, whose contribution was much less (in both quality and quantity), the result being that they had to 'feast' on the left-overs and their own meagre contributions.

At all events, it seems impossible to escape the inference that social inequality, a degree of party-spirit, and lack of concern, perhaps even disdain, on the part of the better-off for the poorer members of the church was at the root of the problems addressed by Paul. Paul's response was incisive:

- He could not praise *(epaineō)* such conduct; to those who set much store by public compliment and commendation,[323] this was a cutting rebuke.[324]
- The Lord's dinner was not an occasion simply to satisfy hunger; they should attend to that need in their own homes (11.22, 34).
- When they came together to eat, they should wait for one another *(ekdechesthe)* (11.33)[325] so that they might share together, as one, in the dinner of the Lord.

320. See the passages from Pliny, *Ep.* 2.6; Juvenal, *Sat.* 5.80-91; Martial, *Epigrams* 3.60 and 4.85, cited by Murphy-O'Connor, *St. Paul's Corinth* 159-60, abstracted in Adams and Horrell, *Christianity at Corinth* 134-35. See also Lampe, 'Eucharist' (above, §30 n. 237); Thiselton, *1 Corinthians* 860-62.

321. See above, §30 at n. 232.

322. Winter argues that *prolambanō* in 11.21, usually translated in terms of doing something before the usual time (BDAG 872), is better translated 'devours'; 'it was during the meal that each one "took" or "devoured" his or her own dinner' (*Corinth* 144-51).

323. See LSJ 603; H. Preisker, *TDNT* 2.586-87; P. Arzt-Grabner et al., *1 Korinther* (PKNT 2; Göttingen: Vandenhoeck und Ruprecht, 2006) 169-70.

324. It is hardly accidental that Paul's modest use of *epaineō* is focused in 1 Corinthians 11 (vv. 2, 17, 22 [twice]), otherwise only Rom. 15.11. Chester argues that the problems at the common meal were caused by important figures competing for honour (*Conversion* 246-52).

325. Winter again argues for an unusual meaning for *ekdechomai;* rather than 'to remain in a place or state and await an event or the arrival of someone, so "expect, wait"' (BDAG 300), Winter argues for 'to receive one another' in the sense of sharing food and drink (*Corinth* 151-52). But the thrust of the exhortation remains the same.

- By so acting, they 'were humiliating *(kataischynete)* those who have nothing *(tous mē echontas,* the have-nots)'[326] — in church the poor should be honoured as much as the rich and not so put to shame (11.22).
- They 'were despising, treating with contempt the church of God' (11.22); the failure to recognize that the gathered assembly as a whole was the body of Christ, as well as the blessed bread (10.16), meant that the inconsiderate were eating and drinking judgment on themselves (11.29).[327]

Two points are worthy of further emphasis. For one thing, we should note that Paul did not hesitate to condemn outright such factionalism and disregard of rich for poor within the congregation. Their coming together in such a way could result in condemnation rather than blessing (11.34): 'for this reason many among you are weak and ill, and some have died' (11.30); the sanctity of sharing the body and blood of Christ (10.16) should not — nay, dare not — be treated lightly.[328] Paul's hope, however, was that such a severe judgment, when accepted by those responsible for the problems, would be a learning experience ('disciplined by the Lord') which would result in their salvation (11.32).[329]

The other is the central position Paul obviously attributed to the sharing of the body and blood of Christ (10.16) as the key elements in the shared meal, spanning the whole meal, giving the meal its sacramental character. It was the bonding effect of that shared meal which Paul sought to maintain, the bonding to Christ and with other participants. That was the real identifying factor and boundary marker — not so much the meal itself, or even the bread and wine as such, but the experience of their sharing in the meal, in the bread and the wine, in shared devotion to the one Lord and in mutual concern one for the other.[330]

---

326. At this point Meggitt's argument that the Corinthian Christians were all 'poor' becomes very forced: 'those not having are . . . those not having the bread and the wine of the eucharist' (*Poverty* 118-22). But the reference to members having homes of their own where their needs could be satisfied (11.22) and the implication that the dinner of the Lord had become a time of excess (11.21) surely imply a higher-status lower-status tension.

327. For a fuller exposition of Paul's own theology of the Lord's Supper, see my *Theology of Paul* 613-23.

328. See further my *Theology of Paul* 612-13. Worth pondering is Chester's parting shot: '"Magical sacramentalism" has provided modern Christian scholars with an effective talisman to shield them from the uncomfortable fact that Paul held views concerning the sacraments, and indeed the demonic, which they would find distasteful and primitive' (*Conversion* 342).

329. Konradt rightly emphasizes the beneficial effect intended by the judgment: a matter not of condemnation but of discipline in order to escape condemnation (*Gericht und Gemeinde* 448, discussion 439-51); cf. the *Pss. Sol.* references in §33 n. 105 below.

330. See above, §30 n. 239.

h. The Tensions of Diverse Charisms (1 Corinthians 12–14)

Having dealt with issues reported to him, Paul returns to the questions raised by the Corinthians — what they evidently referred to as *pneumatika* ('spiritual things'),[331] but Paul preferred to speak of as *charismata* (what has been freely and graciously given, so 'gifts').[332] The distinction is probably indicative, for the former evidently encouraged a focus on the experience of the gift, on the experience of inspiration, as an end in itself, whereas the latter rather focuses on the outcome of the inspiration, on the gracious effect of the gift on others.[333] Whether or not that distinction can be pushed all the way, it certainly sums up the major thrust both of Paul's critique of the Corinthians' worship and of his evaluation of the gifts experienced in the Corinthian assembly.

The key problem is signalled at once: Paul reminds his audience that 'when you were Gentiles you used to be carried away to idols that were incapable of speech' (12.2).[334] Despite the questionings of some,[335] the likelihood is that Paul here recalls their (or at least some prominent Corinthians') experiences of ecstatic rapture in their former religious practice. While the wording itself ('carried away to dumb idols') is open to different interpretations, Paul's subsequent characterization of the Corinthians as 'zealots for spirits' (14.12), that is, in context, presumably eager for experiences of inspiration,[336] and his warning of the danger of so surrendering to the experience of speaking in tongues as to give any outsider the impression that they were out of their mind and had lost control of themselves (*mainesthe* — 14.23), almost certainly carries with it the implication that 12.2 refers disapprovingly to such experiences in the Corinthians' past.

In particular, the incipient factionalism of the Corinthian church was again evident in the esteem being placed by those so gifted in certain eye-catching

---

331. Since Paul uses the genitive form in 12.1 *(pneumatikōn)*, the reference could conceivably be to 'spiritual persons', as in 2.13; but his explicit use of the neuter in 14.1, where *pneumatika* seems to resume the discussion begun in 12.1, should probably be regarded as decisive.

332. 1 Cor. 12.4, 9, 28, 30, 31 — a particularly Pauline term (sixteen times in the Pauline corpus) and only once elsewhere in the NT (1 Pet. 4.10).

333. See my early treatment of the subject in *Jesus and the Spirit* 205-209; and on *charisma* as the effect or expression of grace *(charis)*, as grace coming to concrete manifestation, see also *Theology of Paul* 553-54.

334. The reference expresses the typically Jewish disdain for idols as mute (G. D. Fee, *The First Epistle to the Corinthians* [NICNT; Grand Rapids: Eerdmans, 1987] 578, cites, e.g., Hab. 2.18-19; Ps. 115.5; 3 Macc. 4.16) in contrast to the living God, and for Gentiles as typically idolatrous; most prefer to translate *ethnē* in 12.2 as 'pagans' rather than 'Gentiles/nations', since Paul is obviously referring to a state or status which characterized their past.

335. See the convenient and careful discussion of Thiselton, *1 Corinthians* 911-16.

336. See *Jesus and the Spirit* 233-34.

charisms, particularly speaking in tongues; the fact that Paul devotes more or less the whole of chapter 14 to countering what he regarded as a considerable over-evaluation of the experience of speaking in tongues in terms of community bene-fit puts the point beyond dispute. At the same time, he implies there was a kind of competitive prophesying, with one prophet out-speaking his prophetic utterance and another pressing for the meeting's attention (14.29-33a), as well as the likely embarrassment of wives of prophets publicly questioning their husband's proph-ecy (14.33b-36).[337] So the problem was not simply limited to speaking in tongues.

Those who argue that the same social factors and tensions were probably in play here are most probably on the right track.[338] For in the religious culture of the day we can well imagine that experiences of exaltation, being taken out of oneself, and manifestly so by the inspired speech produced, were highly prized and regarded as a matter of prestige; one who enjoyed such experiences of inspi-ration was manifestly more 'spiritual' than others.[339] Something like this is obvi-ously implied in Paul's teaching in 12.14-26: some thought their gifts and contri-butions to the common worship as more important, more honourable than others;[340] some even may well have been acting as though their gifts constituted all that the community needed.[341] As in the disorder over the common meal (11.17-34), the inevitable consequence was that some (low-status) members were being discounted, their contribution to worship being regarded as lacking, coming short of the higher gifts (*hysteroumenō* — 12.24).[342] The fact that Paul poses the point in terms of 'weakness' (*asthenēs* — 12.22), 'shamefulness' (*aschēmōn* — 12.23), 'dishonour' *(atimos)* and 'honour' (*timē* — 12.23-24) again puts the point beyond dispute. By implication, categorizing other believers in such terms, terms used by those who sought high social regard and success, was a major factor in the factionalism and divisions in the Corinthian church (12.25 — *schisma*). The ideal Paul paints at the end of his exposition of the body of Christ (12.25-26) — the members of the body having concern for one another, sharing together both in an individual's suffering and in an individual's renown and prestige *(doxa)* — suggests that the reality in the church of Corinth was quite other.

337. See above, §32.5f.
338. See above, §20.3d.
339. See particularly Martin, *Corinthian Body* 88-92.
340. 1 Cor. 12.21 — 'The eye cannot say to the hand, "I have no need of you", or the head to the feet, "I have no need of you"'.
341. 1 Cor. 12.17 — 'If the whole body was an eye, where would the hearing be? If the whole body were hearing, where would the sense of smell be?'
342. A well-supported variant (p[46] D F G etc.) reads the active, *hysterounti,* which can be taken in the sense 'inferior' (BDAG 1044).

(i) Paul's response was much more measured than in the sharp rebukes of chs. 5, 6 and 11. With the rhetoric of repeated emphasis he drives his points home:

- The gifts are diverse, but the source of each and all is 'the same' — 'the *same* Spirit', 'the *same* Lord', 'the *same* God' (12.4, 5, 6, 8, 9 11); no scope here for pride in superior endowment.
- Every member of the assembly is gifted by God: 'to *each* is given the manifestation of the Spirit'; 'the Spirit distributes individually to *each*'; 'God set the members, *each* one of them, in the body as he wished' (12.7, 11, 18); to despise any member or any gift was to despise God and his Spirit.
- Most noticeable of all is the insistent emphasis on unity, on oneness: '*one* Spirit' (12.9, 11); many members but *one* body (12.12 [twice], 14, 20); 'in *one* Spirit we were all baptized into *one* body . . . and all were given to drink of *one* Spirit' (12.13); the Corinthian factionalism was denying and disabling that oneness.

Particularly striking is the way Paul adapts (12.14-26) the familiar political image of the state or city as a body, its strength and prosperity depending on the various ethnic and trade groups cooperating for the greater good of the whole.[343] Here again this would not necessarily be seen as subversive; 'the body of Christ',[344] if the language reached the ears of the authorities, would most likely be seen simply as an adaptation of the logic of mutual interdependence in state or city to the ridiculously small sect meeting within its borders. Nevertheless, the theology of a unity which depended on the grace of God to establish it, on the gracious gifting of the Spirit for its flourishing and on the greater honour due to the inferior members (12.24) was a profound transformation of the older political model.[345] The body of Christ was not a threat to the body politic, but it was a differently bounded system[346] — embracing on equal terms Jews and Greeks,

343. See *Theology of Paul* 550 nn. 102, 103, and Mitchell, *Paul* 157-61, with reference particularly to Livy, *Historia* 2.32; Epictetus 2.10.4-5. M. V. Lee, *Paul, the Stoics, and the Body of Christ* (SNTSMS 137; Cambridge: Cambridge University, 2006), argues that Paul's usage was influenced by the Stoic understanding of the universe as a body, an understanding which informed Stoic social ethics.

344. Too little noted is the fact that the image of 'the body of Christ' was not yet fixed and formalized in Paul's teaching: 'the bread which we break is . . . participation in the body of Christ' (1 Cor. 10.16); 'just as the body is one and has many members . . . so also is the Christ' (12.12); 'you are Christ's body and individually members' (12.27); 'we are all one body in Christ' (Rom. 12.5).

345. Martin, *Corinthian Body* 92-96.

346. The insight of Mary Douglas, *Natural Symbols: Explorations in Cosmology* (London: Barrie and Jenkins, 1973), into the correlation between the social body (culture, system)

slaves and free (12.13). To be part of that system, to find meaning, life and vocation in and through that system, to be thus bound up with others in a functioning unity enabled by God, in which members truly respected and cared for one another, that did become something radically different from a social system which was geared to maintaining status and to generating power, praise and honour for its most prominent citizens.

There are two other notable features of Paul's concept of the Christian assembly in Corinth as the body of Christ in Corinth.[347] One is that the body of Christ, the worshipping congregation in Corinth, was for Paul a *charismatic community* — the 'functions' of the various organs being understood as charisms[348] rather than different ethnic, social or business interests. The community's effective functioning therefore depended primarily on the Spirit and the 'manifestations of the Spirit', rather than on human ability or social status. The other is that Paul saw the *mutual interdependence of the body* working out through what we might call a system of checks and balances: most notably, a message in a tongue[349] needing to be complemented by interpretation;[350] prophecy requiring discernment of spirits;[351] but also healings and miracles depending on faith (12.9-10).[352] The more eye-catching gifts of 12.8-10 are balanced by the hierarchy of authority and value to the community (apostles, prophets, teachers)

---

and the physical body has been seminal here; so particularly for Meeks, *Urban Christians* 97-98, and J. Neyrey, 'Perceiving the Human Body: Body Language in 1 Corinthians', *Paul in Other Words: A Cultural Reading of His Letters* (Louisville: Westminster, 1990) 102-46.

347. 1 Cor. 12.27 — 'You (Corinthians) are the body of Christ (in Corinth) and individually *(ek merous)* members of it'.

348. This is the language Paul uses in the parallel passage in Romans: 'not all the members have the same function *(praxin)*'; they have different charisms (Rom. 12.4, 6).

349. The several descriptions in ch. 14 of speaking in tongues imply that, for Paul, (1) it was a tongue = a language (part of the normal range of meaning of *glōssa*), by means of which the individual communicated with God (14.2) — very likely what he referred to as the 'language of angels' in 13.1, as known elsewhere in the Judaism of the period (*T. Job* 48-50; *Apoc. Abr.* 17; *Asc. Isa.* 7.13–9.33; *Apoc. Zeph.* 8.3-4); (2) it was experienced as a benefit for the speaker (14.4) — Paul thanks God that he speaks in tongues more than they (14.18); and (3) it bypassed the mind and was independent of the speaker's thought processes (14.14-15) and so was technically 'ecstatic' (standing outside of oneself), though one may think of 'cool' ecstasy as well as of 'hot' ecstasy.

350. The term *hermēneia* and its cognates in biblical Greek embrace the sense of "translation" as well as "interpretation" (LSJ 690; BDAG 393), which fits well with the understanding of 'tongues' as languages (see n. 349 above).

351. The point is implicit in the list of 12.10 but explicit in 14.29 and 1 Thess. 5.19-22 (cf. 1 Cor. 2.13-15). See *Jesus and the Spirit* 233-36, and further *Theology of Paul* 557 n. 136.

352. 'Faith' here understood as a charism given to some and not others; see further *Jesus and the Spirit* 211-12, and my *Romans* 721-22 (on Rom. 12.3), 727-28 (on 12.6), 797-98 (on 14.1), and 828-29 (on 14.23).

and the inclusion of the more organizing gifts of 'helpful deeds *(antilēmpseis)* and provision of guidance *(kybernēseis)*' in 12.28.[353] At its best Paul envisaged the charismatic body of Christ as equally gifted to organize itself and to exercise its own self-discipline — which was no doubt why he was so upset by what he had had to deal with in chs. 5–6 and 11.

(ii) To Paul's discussion of *pneumatika/charismata* we owe one of his most and justly famous pieces of writing — the so-called hymn to love (1 Corinthians 13). This is what replaces the priority of seeking praise and honour, what he calls the 'far better *(hyperbolēn)* way' (12.31). Without love, 'the greatest *(meizona)*[354] gifts' (12.31) are worth nothing.[355] The examples were evidently chosen to help the Corinthians achieve the proper evaluation of what they counted as the greatest gifts: speaking in tongues (in the first place), prophecy, understanding of 'the mysteries and all knowledge *(gnōsin)*', having 'all faith', even the surrender of all possessions and 'handing over their body' (13.1-3).[356] In each case what seems to be in view was the Corinthians' high regard for experiences of inspiration, in which they could hope to learn what was hidden from ordinary mortals, through which they could experience total surrender, and of which they could expect to boast *(kauchēsōmai)*.[357] It is fairly obvious that the description of love in 13.4-7 likewise has the objectionable priorities of some of the Corinthian believers in view: love as patient and kind, love as not 'zealous' (as in 14.12), not heaping praise on oneself *(perpereuetai)*, not having an exaggerated self-conception *(physioutai)*, not behaving with ill-mannered impropriety *(aschēmonei)*,[358] not preoccupied with one's own concerns, not becoming irritated (presumably at the attention paid to other, lesser-gifted members), and so on. Worthy of particular note is the final assertion that all their knowledge (Paul's

353. *Jesus and the Spirit* 252-53; Thiselton translates 'various kinds of administrative support and ability to formulate strategies' (*1 Corinthians* 1018-22).

354. *Meizōn* is comparative ('greater') but frequently serves for the superlative ('greatest'); Thiselton, *1 Corinthians* 1025-26.

355. It should occasion no surprise that Paul reverts to love as the key to communal integration and harmony — as in Gal. 5.13–6.2 and Rom. 12.9–13.10, and in all cases in reflection of the same prominence which Jesus gave to love of neighbour (see above, §31 n. 399, and below, §33 at n. 260).

356. Note the correlation with the charisms listed in 12.8-10: speaking in tongues (always last in Paul's listing), prophecy, faith, utterance of knowledge.

357. Note 14.2: speaking in tongues as 'speaking mysteries in the Spirit'. The parallel with the experience of being raptured to the third heaven described in 2 Cor. 12.2-4 (on which see above, §25.5f) should also be noted: possibly an 'out of the body' experience in which were heard 'inexpressible words which no one is permitted to speak', and which understandably gave ground for boasting (Paul uses *kauchaomai* five times in 12.1-9). On the reading *kauchēsōmai* in 1 Cor. 13.3, rather than *kauthēsomai* ('that I should be burned'), see Metzger, *Textual Commentary* 563-64; Thiselton, *1 Corinthians* 1042-44.

358. Thiselton's translation (*1 Corinthians* 1049).

included), all their experience of inspiration (Paul's included) was incomplete (13.9); that even though he spoke as a mature adult in reference to their childish behaviour (13.11; cf. 14.20), even so they all (Paul included) still only saw indistinctly (through a mirror), enigmatically *(en ainigmati)*[359] — a rebuke indeed to any who thought they either knew it all or could have it all here and now.

(iii) Having spelled out the character of the assembled congregation as charismatic community (ch. 12), and of love as the *sine qua non* (ch. 13), Paul then turns to practical instruction. Here the focus is on prophecy as the most desirable gift because it is the most beneficial to the assembly. The opening sentence provides the appropriate headline: 14:1 — 'Pursue love (the top priority), and strive for *(zēloute) pneumatika* (a concession to their way of thinking about the charisms), but rather that you might prophesy (the greatest of the gifts — 12.31)'. The key criterion is *oikodomē,* 'edification, community benefit'; here it receives even more emphasis than in Paul's dealing with the selfish attitudes expressed by some Corinthians in regard to *eidōlothyta* (chs. 8, 10).[360] As Winter notes, 'The concept of "building up" *(oikodomei)* is not found in pagan religious language. "Edification" was a unique term which Paul coined for the Christian faith which reflects the responsibility individuals should assume for the welfare of others as a matter of "religious" obligation'.[361]

Here again the implication is clear that Paul judged the behaviour of too many of the Corinthian believers to have more the character decried in 13.4-5 than that of *oikodomē.* On that criterion the superior value of prophecy is clear:

- the tongues-speaker speaks only to God; nobody else understands what is being said; only the tongues-speaker is 'built up' thereby (14.2, 4);
  ○ whereas prophecy speaks to other people, for their *oikodomē* and encouragement and comfort; those who prophesy build up the church (14.3-5, 31);
- tongues-speaking is like notes played on an untuned stringed instrument or like a trumpet played badly; the sounds are unintelligible, incapable of conveying any meaning, like a foreign language (14.7-12);

359. Mirrors at that time were made of polished bronze, so that a degree of distortion of the image was inevitable; 'through/by means of a mirror' may imply that Paul was not thinking of seeing his own image, but of seeing items only by their reflection; *ainigma* has the sense of 'that which requires special acumen to understand because it is expressed in puzzling fashion, "riddle"', though it can also denote 'indirect mode of communication, "indirectly"' (BDAG 27, 397; discussion in Thiselton, *1 Corinthians* 1068-69).

360. *Oikodomeō* — 1 Cor. 8.1, 10; 10.23; 14.4, 17 (used only three times elsewhere in Paul); *oikodomē* — 14.3, 5, 12, 19 (seven other times in the undisputed Paulines, five of them elsewhere in the Corinthian correspondence).

361. Winter, *Welfare* 175.

- whereas speech which conveys meaning benefits the hearer — providing revelation, knowledge, prophecy, teaching (14.6, 26, 30);
- tongues-speaking does not even benefit the mind of the tongues-speaker; and anyone who overhears the tongues-speaking cannot say 'Amen', even when the tongues-speaker is giving thanks (14.14, 16-17);[362]
  - whereas prophecy engages the mind;[363] so speaking or singing in tongues, though valuable, should always be complemented by speech intelligible and beneficial to the understanding of the hearers (14.13-19);[364]
- the Corinthians' lack of concern that the mind was not engaged in tongues-speech was a sign of their spiritual immaturity (14.20); they were failing to appreciate that tongues were a sign of judgment[365] and would appear like a form of madness to an outsider or unbeliever who wandered into the meeting (14.22-23);
  - whereas prophecy, though intended for the benefit of believers (14.22), was much more likely to bring home to such an unbeliever or outsider the truth about himself and to win from him the confession that God was truly in their midst (14.24-25).

The corollaries which Paul draws from this exposition for the Corinthians' regular worship (14.26) are straightforward. The priority was that 'all things should be done for *oikodomē*' (14.26). In practical terms, this meant that:

- only two or three should speak in a tongue, each in turn, and with the interpretation (if an interpreter was present to interpret) after each (14.27);
- no one should speak in tongues in the assembly unless there was someone who would/could interpret the tongue; otherwise the tongues-speaker should be silent (14.28);
- likewise, only two or three prophets should speak, while the rest evaluated what was said (14.29);[366]

362. This is the only time in the NT in which 'Amen' is used in the liturgical context of actual worship.

363. Contrast Philo's conception of prophecy as ecstatic, the mind evicted by the arrival of the Spirit (particularly *Heres* 259-66).

364. In *Jesus and the Spirit* I wondered whether in practical terms Paul's primary concern was not to prevent a sequence of speaking in tongues; any speaking in a tongue must always be followed by speaking in the vernacular (248).

365. See further *Jesus and the Spirit* 230-32.

366. 1 Cor. 14.29 probably refers responsibility for evaluation to the other prophets here, though in 1 Thess. 5.21 the responsibility is that of the congregation as a whole (see *Jesus and the Spirit* 281).

- if another prophet received a revelation to convey, the first prophet should give way; prophetic contributions should be in sequence; the prophet had sufficient control to refrain from speaking (even though still feeling inspired to speak) (14.30-32);[367]
- wives (of prophets) should not question (take part in the evaluation of) the prophecy when it was their husbands who prophesied; that would be shameful; rather in public they should show their respect for their husbands and ask their questions at home (14.34-35).[368]

Paul somewhat spoils the effect of his highly reasoned exposition by insisting rather peremptorily that his instruction had to be acknowledged as 'a command of the Lord'; here is one place where he certainly exercised his apostolic muscle (14.37-38).[369] But the closing summary resumes the voice of sweet reasonableness in the conciliatory exhortation: 'So then, brothers, eagerly desire *(zēloute)* to prophesy and do not forbid *(kōlyete)* to speak in tongues; but let everything be done in the right way *(euschēmonōs)* and in order/orderly sequence *(kata taxin)*' (14.39-40). Unfortunately, in the subsequent history of Christianity the final exhortation (14.40) has been taken out of context and too often set up as the governing instruction for all worship. I suspect that Paul would often have preferred the relative disorder of the Corinthians' worship to the regimented orderliness of much subsequent worship.[370] But certainly the word was highly appropriate for the overheated worship when the whole church came together in first-century Corinth.

i. Disagreement on the Significance of Jesus' Resurrection and the Resurrection of the Body (1 Corinthians 15)

Paul has left the one clearly 'doctrinal' issue to the last. The reason may be simply that he thought the social factionalism was much the more pressing danger to the unity and health of the Corinthian assembly. Or perhaps he did not see the opinions or confusions of a few (15.12) as so very serious. Either way, his attitude would mark a fascinating and important difference with the very high value placed on doctrinal uniformity in subsequent centuries. What is certainly the

---

367. Most commentators take 14.32 ('the spirits of prophets are [to be] subject to prophets') to refer to each prophet's ability to control his or her own inspiration (as implied also in 14.30).

368. See above, §32.5f.

369. See further *Jesus and the Spirit* 275-80.

370. The observation was frequently made in the early days of the twentieth-century charismatic movement; see, e.g., those referred to in my *Baptism* 4 n. 12.

case is that Paul engages with the issues as a matter of vigorous discussion and exhortation rather than, as in the preceding issues, as a matter for discipline and forthright rebuke.[371] Even in the opening assertion of the foundational importance of the resurrection, belief in which seems to have been common ground between Paul and the Corinthians in view (15.11-12), the thrust is more to remind them of that importance than to instruct them in it afresh (15.1-19).[372]

The subject called for treatment since 'some' of the Corinthian believers were saying, 'There is no resurrection of the dead' (15.12). That cannot mean that these individuals denied that Jesus had been raised; the 'some of you' (15.12) is evidently included in the 'you' who 'believed' the proclamation that 'Christ has been raised from the dead' (15.11-12). What Paul had in mind must rather have been the denial that those who died would be raised in the age to come. The issue was not whether 'Christ has been raised *from* the dead' but whether such a thing as resurrection *of the dead* is conceivable.[373] That it is 'the dead' who are in view is repeated no less than thirteen times in 15.12-52. So clearly what was in dispute was what happened after death and to the dead.[374]

Clearly implied here is the typically Greek thought that physical matter was antithetical to the spirit, that while the soul could be saved, liberated from its physical bondage, the material body itself would corrupt to death and nothingness.[375] In Greek thought the dead did not live again in bodily existence; the

371. The strongest element of rebuke comes at 15.32-34, where, rather noticeably, the 'sin' referred to is to the social habits which the wrong understanding of the resurrection encourages (too casual eating and drinking, bad company), and where in accusing such of 'lack of knowledge *(agnōsia)*', intended to cause them 'shame *(entropē)*', Paul seeks to exert social pressure more than to threaten divine judgment (as in 11.29, 34).

372. On the importance of this creedal confession (1 Cor. 15.3-5/6/7) and the centrality of the resurrection of Christ in the first Christian and Paul's preaching, see above, §21.4e, §23.4a and §29.7c.

373. See particularly M. de Boer, *The Defeat of Death: Apocalyptic Eschatology in 1 Corinthians 15 and Romans 5* (Sheffield: JSOT, 1988).

374. This focus tells decisively against the thesis that the problem addressed by Paul was the belief that resurrection could/should already be experienced in this life — a popular interpretation during the height of the 'Gnostic fever' (bibliography in Thiselton, *1 Corinthians* 1173 n. 32; add C. M. Tuckett, 'The Corinthians Who Say "There Is No Resurrection of the Dead" [1 Cor 15,12]', in Bieringer, ed., *Corinthian Correspondence* 247-75) — influenced of course by 2 Tim. 2.18.

375. The negative, dualistic Greek attitude is summed up in the classical pun *sōma sēma*, 'the body a tomb (of the soul)', and in the much-quoted saying of Empedocles about the 'alien garb of the flesh' (quoted by E. Schweizer, *sōma*, *TDNT* 7.1026-27). The influence of Homer, where *sōma* always means 'dead body, corpse' (LSJ 1749), was no doubt still strong, with the usage continued into the LXX and the non-Pauline NT (see W. Baumgärtel, *TDNT* 7.1045). The fact that Paul never uses *sōma* with that connotation is in itself significant here.

physical body did not rise again.[376] This inference is confirmed by the second phase of the discussion, beginning with the response (of the 'some') to what Paul has said so far: 'How are the dead raised? With what kind of body do they come?' (15.35). The questions in effect attempted rhetorically to pose Paul with a (to their way of thinking) *reductio ad absurdum*. For the typically Greek worldview it was simply inconceivable, absurd, to think of the physical body being raised again to life after death had intervened. Alternatively expressed, the problem for the Corinthian deniers was not the idea of a postmortem existence.[377] The problem was how such postmortem existence could be conceived when envisaged in terms of and as the result of *resurrection*. The belief in postmortem existence made too little sense for them when it was predicated as consequent on resurrection of the dead, for 'resurrection' implied resurrection of the *body*.

Paul responds in turn to the two assertions/questions by careful argument (15.12, 35).

- If there is no resurrection of the dead, then Christ was not raised, which would falsify the whole Christian message (15.13-17) and destroy Christian hope for life beyond this life: 'If in this life only we have been hoping in Christ, we are of all people most to be pitied' (15.18-19).
- Christ's resurrection shows that there *is* resurrection of the dead, resurrection life 'in Christ', as there is death at the end of this life 'in Adam' (15.20-22); the resurrection of Christ is the basis of Christian faith in the exaltation of Christ. As the beginning of the harvest of resurrected people (15.23), it entails the full harvest as integral to the final triumph of God (15.24-28).[378]
- So Christian hope is not limited to this life; otherwise why should people 'be baptized on behalf of, or for the sake of, the dead'?[379] Otherwise a life

376. See particularly Wright, *Resurrection of the Son of God* 32-84.

377. The other principal traditional interpretation of 15.12 (Thiselton, *1 Corinthians* 1172-73).

378. On 15.24-28 see also above, §23.4h, and §29 at n. 268.

379. See Thiselton's careful review of the interpretations offered for Paul's puzzling talk of baptism 'on behalf/for the sake of the dead' (*1 Corinthians* 1242-49); Thiselton translates 'have themselves baptized for the sake of the dead' and understands it as referring to 'the decision of a person or persons to ask for, and to receive baptism as a result of the desire to be united with their believing relatives who have died' (1248), following M. Raeder, 'Vikariasttaufe in 1 Cor 15:29?', *ZNW* 46 (1955) 258-61. M. F. Hull, *Baptism on Account of the Dead (1 Cor 15:29): An Act of Faith in the Resurrection* (Atlanta: SBL, 2005), reviews more than forty interpretations and argues that Paul is holding up one group within the Corinthian community as a laudable example for the entire community, namely those who have undergone the rite of baptism on account of their belief that the dead (believers) are destined for life — though since baptism in response to the gospel of 15.3ff. would anyway have that implication,

The Aegean Mission: Phase Two

of sufferings and martyrdom would be pointless,[380] and living for present pleasure would be the more obvious option (15.29-34).

More to the main point at issue:

- Hope beyond death is not a matter of either resurrection of this body or of no body; this body dies like a grain of wheat in the ground and 'comes to life *(zōopoieitai)*' in a *different* body, for there are different bodies, heavenly as well as earthly (15.36-41).
- The decisive contrast is between two kinds of body, a *sōma psychikon* and a *sōma pneumatikon* (15.44). To bring out the contrast Paul employs a kaleidoscope of variations.[381] The former is characterized by its subjection to decay and death; it is *choïkos,* 'made of dust *(chous)*';[382] it is 'flesh and blood';[383] it is mortal; it dies; Adam is the archetype. The latter is the opposite: it is not subject to decay and death; it is spiritual; it is appropriate to heaven; the archetype is the risen Christ.[384]

---

it is unclear why Paul should so refer to it in 15.29. The suggestion of J. E. Patrick, 'Living Rewards for Dead Apostles: "Baptised for the Dead" in 1 Corinthians 15.29', *NTS* 52 (2006) 71-85, that what was in view was a practice of baptizing in order to honour now-dead apostles, makes little sense either, since the only apostles in view in Corinth, including in relation to the Corinthians' baptisms (1.12-13), were all still very much alive.

380. Paul envisages his tribulations in Ephesus using the image of being mauled to death in the arena by wild animals; see above, at n. 149.

381. 42, 50	*phthora/aphtharsia*	'corruption'/'incorruption'
43	*atimia/doxa*	'dishonour'/'glory'
43	*astheneia/dynamis*	'weakness'/'power'
44-46	*sōma psychikon/sōma pneumatikon*	'natural body'/'spiritual body'
47-49	*choïkos/epouranios*	'earthly'/'heavenly'
50	*sarx kai haima/ —*	'flesh and blood'/ —
52	*hoi nekroi/aphthartoi*	'the dead'/'incorruptible'
53-54	*phtharton/aphtharsia*	'corruptible'/'incorruption'
54	*thnēton/athanasia*	'mortal'/'immortality'.

382. Paul no doubt was thinking of the Genesis passages: 2.7 — 'the Lord God formed the man, dust *('aphar)* from the ground' (15.45 picks up the second half of the verse); 3.19 — 'dust *('aphar)* you are, and to dust *('aphar)* you shall return'.

383. It should be noted that the sequence of contrasts runs through 15.50, so that 'flesh and blood' clearly belongs with the first of the paired terms in n. 381; it is obviously synonymous with 'natural body' and 'earthly (body)'; the resurrection body is not 'flesh and blood'; the influential view of J. Jeremias, '"Flesh and Blood Cannot Inherit the Kingdom of God" (1 Cor. 15:50)', *NTS* 2 (1955-56) 151-59 (here 152), that in 15.50 Paul turns his attention to living persons (referred to as 'flesh and blood'), leaves the point unaffected. See further my '"How Are the Dead Raised? With What Body Do They Come?" Reflections on 1 Corinthians 15', *SWJT* 45 (2002-3) 4-18.

384. Paul's insistence that it was not the spiritual which was first but the natural (15.46)

The measure of Paul's theological acumen and sophistication is seen here more clearly than almost anywhere else in his letters, for in this carefully constructed argument he was evidently attempting to characterize the resurrection of the dead by developing what was a unique double contrast.

One is between *psychē* ('soul') and *pneuma* ('spirit'). The Hebrew Scripture on which Paul was drawing (Gen. 2.7) did not make a clean distinction between 'soul' and 'spirit'. So when it depicted human existence as the divine breath *(ruach = pneuma)* infusing the *adam* formed from the dust of the earth, the result was that 'the *adam* became a living soul *(nephesh = psychē)*' (2.7), 'flesh' in which was 'the breath *(ruach)* of life' (6.17; 7.15). But for Paul that did not mean that resurrection life should be conceived as the soul or spirit separating, far less escaping, from the earthly body of flesh (and blood). Earthly existence had its own wholeness — *sōma psychikon* — not a physical body with a 'soul' in it but a 'soulish body', the human/earthly mode of existence raised above the level of mere dust by its soulish dimension. Resurrection existence, however, was distinct and different — *sōma pneumatikon* — a different kind of wholeness of existence, made possible by the action of the Spirit and patterned on Christ's resurrection.

The other contrast was the distinction between *sarx* ('flesh') and *sōma* ('body'), a distinction which was peculiarly Paul's. Hebrew had no separate word for 'body'; the typical sense of the Hebrew *basar* is of the 'flesh' of the material body. And Greek made relatively little distinction between *sarx* and *sōma*, both denoting the body in its physical materiality. But Paul seems to have deliberately pulled the two senses apart, in *sōma* retaining the Hebraic sense of the whole person, while using *sarx* with a negative connotation more reminiscent of Greek's dualistic tendency.[385] So 'body' is not to be confused with 'flesh' or simply identified as 'flesh'. 'Body' had more the character of mode of existence, embodied existence, enabling communication with other bodies.[386]

---

suggests that the Corinthians may have been arguing somewhat as Philo, that the two creation narratives (Genesis 1 and 2) referred to 'two types of men, the one a heavenly *(ouranios)* man, the other an earthly *(gēinos)*' *(Leg.* 1.31), with the latter first and an archetype of the second (cf. Barrett, *Paul* 112; and particularly Sterling, '"Wisdom among the Perfect"' 357-67; S. Hultgren, 'The Origin of Paul's Doctrine of the Two Adams in 1 Corinthians 15.45-49', *JSNT* 25 [2003] 343-70, disagrees); possibly we should see here the influence of Apollos (Murphy-O'Connor, *Paul* 281; and see above, at n. 214). Paul argues in contrast that the order is Adam, then Christ, that is, the resurrected Christ; the 'heavenly *(epouranios)*' in 15.49 is clearly the *resurrected* Christ *(Theology of Paul* 289).

385. The two spectrums of his usage overlap (Rom. 8:13; 1 Cor. 6:16). But more characteristic of Paul is the use of a more negative phrase to qualify the otherwise neutral 'body' — for example, 'body of sin' (Rom. 6:6), 'mortal body' (Rom. 8:11), whereas 'flesh' is more regularly negative without any qualifying phrase or adjective (most strikingly Rom. 8:3-12).

386. For fuller exposition see *Theology of Paul* 55-61.

In all this I have avoided the term 'physical' as too misleading in 'fleshing' out Paul's contrasts.[387] It should be clear from the above that 'physical body' is not an adequate translation of *sōma psychikon*. Yet, it should also be clear that the *sōma psychikon* is characterized by the decay and corruption ('dust to dust') of the mortal body. Equally it should be clear that it is difficult to conceive of a 'body' as 'physical' which is not characterized by subjection to decay, corruption and death; Paul's antithesis between 'flesh' and 's/Spirit' does not abstract 'flesh' from its physical character.[388] Difficult as it is to grasp Paul's conceptualization of the *sōma pneumatikon*, it is clearly not characterized by what happens to flesh and blood; in Paul's thought, the transformation of resurrection takes the person into a quite different bodily realm, characterized by incorruption, glory, the over-coming of death and heavenly power.[389]

The eirenic character of Paul's debate with 'some' of the Corinthians should be noted. He did not refute them with an antithetical denial. He did not say, 'Of course the dead physical bodies are raised to physical/fleshly life in the final resurrection'. He recognized for his own part that the negatives of 'flesh and blood' existence incapacitated the flesh from being the resurrection's mode of existence. But at the same time, he did not lapse into an 'immortality of the soul' acceptance of their over-negative antipathy to bodily existence. He retained the Hebrew appreciation of the wholeness of human existence, of the human being existing simultaneously in both a physical environment and a spiritual environment, and his conception of the resurrection as resurrection of the body, resurrection to bodily existence, was his attempt to find a middle way between Greek and Hebrew conceptualities which would provide common ground for both. Unfortunately the subtlety of Paul's conception of 'the resurrection of the dead' and of 'the resurrection of the body' escaped those who followed him (as probably also the Corinthians!).[390] But the blurring of the clear distinctions which he drew has not benefited subsequent theology, and the re-confusion of 'body' with 'flesh', with consequent transfer of the negatives Paul uses of flesh to physical function, and to the sexual func-

---

387. Cf. and contrast M. J. Harris, *Raised Immortal: Resurrection and Immortality in the New Testament* (Grand Rapids: Eerdmans, 1985) 121-33; Wright, *Resurrection of the Son of God* 343-60.

388. See again *Theology of Paul* 62-73.

389. Martin's repeated reminder is important: in the ancient world Paul's distinction would not have been understood as a distinction between matter and non-matter, 'spirit' being conceptualized as a kind of 'stuff', a rarified substance, high on the spectrum or hierarchy of essences (*Corinthian Body* 6-15, 21-25, 108-17, 123-29).

390. Luke did not help by characterizing Jesus' resurrection body as 'flesh and bones' (Luke 24.39), and Ignatius established the subsequent consensus by talking of Jesus' resurrection as resurrection of the flesh (*Smyrn.* 3.1).

tioning of the physical body in particular, has been disastrous for the main-stream of Western Christian tradition.

j. Some Concluding Concerns (1 Corinthians 16)

Two other matters raised by the Corinthians' letter are dealt with briefly. Reference to the collection (16.1) clearly implies that the subject had already been talked about (Paul did not need to explain what it was). Whether that was during the time he spent in Corinth (§31.4) or, as I suspect, in earlier communications from Ephesus is not at all clear — perhaps in Timothy's (earlier?) visit (4.17), or even in the earlier letter (§32.4). The note reminds us that the communication between Paul and Corinth was much more extensive than we have firm evidence for (§32.3b). At any rate, all that Paul judged now to be required was the basic instruction on how the money was to be raised for the collection (16.2). How this passage contributes to our fuller knowledge of the collection will be discussed more fully below (§33.4).

As typically in his letters, Paul goes on to talk about his hopes and plans to visit Corinth with his equally typical ambivalence (16.5-9).[391] His protestations on the point must have worn thin for many of his letter recipients. But we can well envisage Paul as genuinely torn between the opportunities and demands of the changing circumstances of his mission and his churches. His uncertainty as to Timothy's arrival in Corinth (16.10-11)[392] similarly reminds us that conditions of travel were so subject to unexpected constraints that no firm timetable could be guaranteed.

The other subject raised by the Corinthian letter was Apollos's return to Corinth, evidently requested by the Corinthians — a clear indication of the favourable impression Apollos had made on the believers in Corinth and of his influence on the church there. Interestingly, Paul strongly favoured that return visit; he 'strongly urged' Apollos to go (16.12). Apollos himself, however, was much more resistant to returning (he was 'not at all willing to come now') — perhaps because he too disapproved of the factionalism among the Corinthians and the use of his name therein ('I am of Apollos'). He would come when a favourable opportunity arose (16.12).

A final exhortation re-enforcing the importance of their acting 'in love' (16.13-14) gives way to a strong commendation of Stephanas, Fortunatus and Achaicus (16.15-18),[393] and some greetings from 'the churches of Asia' and the

---

391. Rom. 15.22-32; 2 Cor. 13.1-10; 1 Thess. 2.17–3.11; Phlm. 22.

392. 1 Cor. 16.10 is better translated 'whenever Timothy comes', rather than 'if Timothy comes' (Thiselton, *1 Corinthians* 1330).

393. Winter wonders whether the service that the household of Stephanas had provided was financial assistance in the midst of famine (*Corinth* 195-99).

local believers (though Apollos is not mentioned) (16.19-20). Typically Paul appends a greeting in his own hand (16.21) and a closing prayer for grace and reassurance of his love for them (16.23-24). But the intervening anathema against 'anyone who does not love the Lord' (16.22) reveals something of his continuing frustration over the intractableness shown by (too many of) the Corinthians, just as his repetition of the liturgical 'slogan' *maranatha,* 'Our Lord, come!' (16.22), indicates a longing for such frustrations to be brought to an end.

32.6. The Third of Paul's Letters to the Corinthians

The most intriguing of Paul's correspondence with the church in Corinth is the letter he refers to in 2 Cor. 2.1-4, 9 and 7.8-12:[394]

> I wrote as I did, so that when I came I might not suffer pain *(lypēn)* from those who should have made me rejoice. . . . For I wrote out of deep distress and anguish of heart and with many tears, not to cause you pain *(lypēthēte)* but to let you know the abundant love I have for you. (2.3-4)
>
> I wrote for this reason, to know your proven character and whether you are obedient in all things. (2.9)
>
> If I offended *(elypēsa)* you by what I wrote, I do not regret it; if I were to regret it, for I see that that letter offended you *(elypēsen),* even if only briefly, I now rejoice, not because you were made sad *(elypēthēte),* but because you became sorry *(elypēthēte)* enough to repent. . . . So then, although I wrote to you, it was not on account of the wrongdoer, nor on account of the one who was wronged, but in order that your devotion on our behalf might be made clear to you before God. (7.8-9, 12)

The occasion for this letter is hopelessly unclear. Possibly Timothy, on his return to Ephesus, brought news which caused Paul to react in despair and/or anger; perhaps (some of) the Corinthians had indeed treated Timothy with disdain, as Paul had feared (1 Cor. 16.11 — 'let no one despise [*exouthenēsē* him').[395] Or Titus may have returned from his first visit (to move forward the organization of

---

394. Paul plays on the theme of *lypē,* 'sorrow, grief', intensively in these two passages: in 2.1-7 and 7.8-11 *lypē* is used five times, and *lypeō* eleven times; so it is important to appreciate that *lypeō* has a range of nuance: 'to cause severe mental or emotional distress, "vex, irritate, offend, insult"', through 'to experience sadness or distress, "become sad, sorrowful, distressed"' (BDAG 604), rather than to translate each occurrence by using the same terms.

395. *Exoutheneō* — 'to show by one's attitude or manner of treatment that an entity has no merit or worth, *disdain;* to have no use for something as beneath one's consideration, *reject disdainfully;* to regard another as of no significance and therefore worthy of maltreatment, *treat with contempt*' (BDAG 352).

the collection — 2 Cor. 8.6a; 12.18) with the distressing news. Or again, if we should fit in the 'painful visit' (referred to in 2 Cor. 2.1) to this sequence, we could further envisage that Timothy's or Titus's return prompted Paul to make that visit, which in turn left Paul dismayed or even distraught[396] and caused him to leave after a brief visit and to write 'the letter of tears'; this would fit well with the sequence 2.1-4.[397] In any case, the chief value of such speculation is to remind us how frequent was the communication between Paul and Corinth.

And what was the trouble which caused Paul such anguish? We are similarly in the dark on this too.

- Possibly it was further news about the scandal Paul had dealt with in 1 Cor. 5.1-5, that the congregation was still not grasping the nettle, perhaps adamantly refusing to do so (for the reasons considered in connection with that passage — §32.5c).[398]
- Perhaps it was further news regarding the one or more referred to in the earlier (first) letter to Corinth (1 Cor. 5.9); his/their outrageous behaviour was continuing, and the danger alluded to in 5.6-8 had become acute (2 Cor. 12.21). The whole community *must* recognize and confront the danger to themselves before it poisoned the whole church. Something stronger than the strong instructions of 5.11-13 was required.
- Alternatively, the crisis was one of personal relationship, Paul being accused (maliciously) by a prominent member of the church of deceit and of exploiting the Corinthians (2 Cor. 12.14-17; 13.1). A likely explanation for this distrust would be the collection (that Paul was using the money collected for his own ends, perhaps even to 'line his own pocket').[399] Some-

396. Something of that response may be conveyed by the allusions in 2 Cor. 12.21 and 13.2.

397. That 'the painful visit' took place after 1 Corinthians and before 'the severe letter' is a common consensus; see, e.g., Thrall, *2 Corinthians* 53-56; Harris, *2 Corinthians* 57-58.

398. But Kümmel justifiably dismisses the thought 'that Paul, who wrote 1 Cor 6:12ff; 1 Thess 4:3ff; Rom 13:12, should have subsequently taken so lightly [2 Cor 2:6ff] a grave case of sexual misbehavior' (*Introduction* 283); see also Thrall, *2 Corinthians* 61-65.

399. In considering 'the prevailing view' that the offence was 'an outrageous insult', Thrall notes Zahn's observation that nowhere in the LXX or the NT does *adikeō* (7.2, 12) have the sense of 'insult' or 'slander'; rather it means 'to inflict injury of an illegal kind upon a person or thing' (*2 Corinthians* 67; cf. BDAG 20, and Matt. 20.13, where 'I am doing you no wrong' [*ouk adikō se*] has the sense 'I am not cheating you'). Thrall concludes that some kind of illegal injury was in view and suggests that 'after Paul arrived in Corinth on his second visit, one of the church members handed over to him for temporary safekeeping the money he had saved to contribute to the collection. This money was then stolen, in circumstances which suggested that some other member of the congregation was responsible. But this man denied the charge. It was Paul's word against his, and the church was uncertain whom to believe. Because the apostle's

thing like this would fit well with the further reference to Titus in this connection (12.17-18) and would explain the depth of personal anguish experienced by Paul at such questioning of his own integrity.[400]

Whatever the case, the episode confirms that the church in Corinth was very far from being a 'pure' church, with clearly defined and observed moral boundaries. The anguish which the episode caused to Paul, and the irritation or even insult which his letter caused to the Corinthians, however temporarily, is an indication of just how delicate and febrile were both the community's *esprit* and Paul's relations with them. That said, the letter seems to have served its purpose (Paul more effective in writing than when present in person?): the anguish-causer had been 'punished *(epitimia)*' by the majority (2.6); and the Corinthians' sorrow over the whole episode and their display of devotion to Paul had been balm indeed to his wounded spirit and (presumably) secured their reconciliation (7.6-13).

What the letter expressed beyond Paul's personal anguish is also unclear. Presumably it contained a forthright denunciation of whatever it was that caused Paul such distress. And presumably it called for forthright action, or for the action which the congregation as a whole had been unwilling to take. As with the first letter (1 Cor. 5.9) there is no indication that it contained more, and it might have been something very brief, dealing only with the case in point. Whatever its content, it was probably carried by Titus, sent back (perhaps) when he had not long returned from there.

Has the letter been retained? It is very unlikely that 'the letter of tears' is to be equated with 1 Corinthians itself; 1 Corinthians hardly fits Paul's description of it.[401] Possibly, however, it has been retained by incorporation within 2 Corinthians, as chs. 10–13.[402] And if 2 Corinthians reached its present form by amal-

---

view of the matter was not immediately accepted, he began to suspect that other members of the congregation . . . might have had something to do with the theft. Since he was unable to persuade them to take action against the man he suspected, he returned to Ephesus. He then wrote a letter which caused a revulsion of feeling amongst the Corinthians and moved them to further investigation, which resulted in the offender's confession and punishment' (67-68). Mitchell suggests that the anger and suspicion directed against Paul were caused by Paul taking upon himself the authority to organize the collection (2 Corinthians 8), an authority he had previously accorded to the Corinthians themselves (1 Cor. 16.3) ('Paul's Letters to Corinth' 328-35); the language, however, implies a more serious charge. See further below on 12.16 (n. 491).

400. On 'the painful visit' see further Harris, *2 Corinthians* 54-59; Murphy-O'Connor attributes the problem to a judaizing intruder challenging Paul's authority (*Paul* 293-95), but there is no indication in the information regarding 'the painful visit' that the 'false apostles' of 2 Cor. 11.13 were already involved.

401. See Thrall, *2 Corinthians* 57-61, and Harris, *2 Corinthians* 5-7, for brief consideration of what the latter calls 'this time-honoured view'.

402. See below, n. 407.

gamating a number of letters, then that must be judged quite probable. However, since I question that particular hypothesis (see §32.7a), I am left no alternative to the hypothesis that the letter was not retained, either by the Corinthians or by Paul, and so was not available for copying, distributing more widely and (ultimately) adding to the collection of Paul's letters. Given that its most prominent feature was the distress, offence and sadness which it expressed and caused, it may be judged very likely that none of the principal parties to its composition, delivery and receipt thought it worth retaining and happily saw to its destruction when good relations were restored.[403]

32.7. The Fourth of Paul's Letters to the Corinthians (2 Corinthians)

a. The Puzzle of 2 Corinthians

2 Corinthians is potentially the most rewarding of Paul's letters, but also the most problematic and frustrating of all his writings.[404] Given what we know about Paul's relations and communication with Corinth, we might have expected to be able to slot 2 Corinthians into the sequence of these links with relative ease. But that is far from being the case.

For one thing, any links with 1 Corinthians are surprisingly elusive. There is clear reference back to the third letter; indeed, just as we only know of the first letter from the reference in 1 Cor. 5.9, so we only know of the third letter from the references in 2 Corinthians (§32.6). But of reference back to the presumably much more substantial 1 Corinthians, there is nothing to speak of. When he had dealt with so many subjects in 1 Corinthians, and so extensively and with such care, we might have expected some allusion to what he had previously said or to how the Corinthians had reacted to it. It is almost as though the two (sets of) letters had been written to different churches. As we shall see in a moment, there are obvious reasons why Paul's own changed circumstances and the new threat which Paul saw to be confronting the Corinthians could have so dominated 2 Corinthians as to blank out such references back. But their absence is nevertheless surprising.

The other major problem is whether 2 Corinthians is the letter as Paul wrote it. As it stands, the letter falls into three clear and disjointed parts — chs.

---

403. See further Harris, *2 Corinthians* 3-8.

404. '. . . the most personal, moving, profound, and difficult letter in the whole corpus, a letter that reveals him [Paul] as a man, an apostle, and a theological thinker at great depth' (Barrett, *Paul* 15).

1–7, chs. 8–9 and chs. 10–13. The three sections lack clear connection between them, and the tone of each section is quite different from that of the others. The unity of chs. 1–7 is also questionable, with Paul's personal apologia of 1.8–2.13 and 7.5-16 seemingly interrupted by the extensive apologia for his ministry (2.14–7.4), and the latter itself seemingly interrupted or interpolated awkwardly by 6.14–7.1. And chs. 8–9 deal with the organization of the collection twice. Not surprisingly, then, a strong tradition of scholarship has inferred that 2 Corinthians itself is an amalgamation of different letters — typically four or five letters in all (chs. 1–7 perhaps incorporating material from an earlier letter, ch. 8, ch. 9 and chs. 10–13).[405] The strongest cases can be made for chs. 8–9 as independent letters,[406] and for chs. 10–13 either as 'the letter of tears'[407] written prior to 2 Corinthians (1–9) or as a fifth letter, written subsequent to 2 Corinthians.[408]

For myself, such hypotheses have the advantage of making some sense of the puzzling factors indicated above. My only problem is with envisaging the situation and the motivation which caused some anonymous collector or editor to chop off the introductions and conclusions to each letter and simply to stick the torsos together in such an awkward way as to raise the questions which the various amalgamation hypotheses are designed to resolve. Why not retain them as complete letters? Nothing was obviously to be gained by giving the impression that Paul wrote only two letters to the Corinthians rather than, say, five or more. If the editor felt so free to 'top and tail' the letters in question, what prevented

---

405. The most influential reconstruction along these lines has been that of G. Bornkamm, 'Die Vorgeschichte des sogenannten Zweiten Korintherbriefes', *Geschichte und Glaube. Gesammelte Aufsätze,* vol. 4 (Munich: Kaiser, 1971) 162-94. Scriba envisages nine Corinthian letters in all, plus the later addition of 2 Cor. 6.14–7.1 ('Von Korinth nach Rom' 168-69). Mitchell proposes a version of the five-letter hypothesis ('Paul's Letters to Corinth' 317-21).

406. See particularly H. D. Betz, *2 Corinthians 8 and 9* (Hermeneia; Philadelphia: Fortress, 1985).

407. E.g., Becker, *Paul* 216-21, and particularly Horrell, *Social Ethos* 296-312. But Schnelle justifiably responds: 'If chapters 10–13 are part of the "tearful letter", then it is very remarkable that Paul does not mention the incident that had caused such pain and was supposed to have occasioned the letter in the first place. The opponents whom he battles in 10–13 have no connection to the individual member of the congregation in 2.3ff' (*History* 81-82); similarly Murphy-O'Connor, *Paul* 255.

408. See particularly Thrall, *2 Corinthians* 5-20, who also argues that ch. 8 was part of a single letter (chs. 1–8), with ch. 9 a separate, subsequent letter (36-43; bibliography 47-49). T. Schmeller, 'Die Cicerobriefe und die Frage nach der Einheitlichkeit des 2. Korintherbriefs', *ZNW* 95 (2004) 181-208, suggests that the compilations in the Ciceronian letter corpora make a chronologically arranged fusion of Pauline letters in 2 Corinthians more plausible. The whole debate has been thoroughly reviewed by Harris, *2 Corinthians* 8-51; Harris himself favours the 'traditional hypothesis', 2 Corinthians as a unity (11-33), and notes that the hypothesis has stronger support in contemporary scholarship than is often recognized (42-43).

him from exercising the same freedom to edit the material into a more coherent unit?[409] Or if he was careful to excise greetings, thanksgivings and farewell, would we not have expected him to take care to ensure better links between the sections?[410] Furthermore, unless the editing was done very early indeed, then we might have expected copies of one or more of these independent letters to have been made and circulated more widely,[411] which would almost certainly have left some mark in the textual tradition. But of that there is none.

I do not believe that the puzzle of 2 Corinthians is finally resolvable. The unavoidable fact is that all the data of the letter in its present form are capable of supporting a variety of hypotheses. What is frustrating in this, as in other debates on the beginnings of Christianity, is the unwillingness of some to make allowances for changes of circumstance or information or mood which might provide a perfectly adequate explanation of the various infelicities and disjunctures which grate on the ear of the twentieth- or twenty-first-century reader of such documents. The inadequacy of our historical imagination is often a greater problem than the puzzling data of a letter like 2 Corinthians.

For what it is worth, my own suspicion is that the puzzle of 2 Corinthians was of Paul's own making. It is likely that he was in transit when he wrote the letter. In his anxiety to learn how 'the letter of tears' and Titus's (second) visit had been received, Paul had gone to Troas to meet Titus on his way back from Corinth; but not finding Titus there, he had gone on into Macedonia (2 Cor. 2.12-13), where he met Titus to hear the good news which Titus brought, that the Corinthians had repented, as Paul had hoped, and were eager to be reconciled (7.5-16). Paul's most obvious next step, we might think, would have been to hasten on through Macedonia to Corinth in person. But evidently not.

A plausible scenario is as follows. Paul had already entered Macedonia before he met Titus. Knowing that a messenger could travel a good deal faster than he could, Paul consequently decided to write to the Corinthians immediately to express his delight with the outcome and that that particular breach had been healed. Whether he made this decision at once, or after continuing his journey through Macedonia, cannot be determined. At each of the Macedonian churches he would certainly have been called upon to spend some time preaching and teaching. At one or more points, perhaps initially from Titus himself, he received

409. White, e.g., characterizes chs. 8–9 as one or two 'fragmentary letters' (*Jesus to Christianity* 205; the various partition hypotheses are helpfully laid out — 204-207), but letters shorn of opening and closing are hardly 'fragmentary'. Contrast J. D. H. Amador, 'Revisiting 2 Corinthians: Rhetoric and the Case for Unity', *NTS* 46 (2000) 92-111.

410. For a possible scenario see Thrall, *2 Corinthians* 45-47.

411. See above, §29.8d. But see also Harris, *2 Corinthians* 41-42; the lack of clear attestation of reference to 2 Corinthians in the first half of the second century (see, e.g., Thrall, *2 Corinthians* 2-3; Harris, *2 Corinthians* 2-3) hardly helps the case either way.

The Aegean Mission: Phase Two

news of a group of incoming missionaries who were causing fresh problems in Corinth, partly feeding on old grievances and partly stimulating new ones. Here again Paul had to decide whether to go to Corinth personally or to write, but the thought of another painful visit was too much (2 Cor. 1.23). In any case, time and setting did not permit the careful composition of a letter, as it had with 1 Corinthians and would with Romans. So we may quite plausibly envisage Paul beginning to dictate his letter without a clear structure in mind. In the first part he took the opportunity to indicate the crisis he had experienced in Asia and to explain his vacillation over whether to come personally or not. Under the pressure of composition, this personal apologia went off at something of a tangent into a broader apologia for his ministry,[412] in which he took a few swipes at the incoming missionaries, before expressing his relief at the good news brought by Titus more fully. Since he was also anxious for Titus to continue to promote the collection, it may have been most convenient, in the circumstances, simply to supplement an already half-drafted exhortation regarding the collection (ch. 8) with another (ch. 9). And finally, before Titus left with the letter, and perhaps on hearing further reports about the unfolding situation in Corinth,[413] perhaps even after travelling with Titus to the next city and church,[414] Paul felt compelled to add a final outburst in response to the new challenge posed by the incoming missionaries (chs. 10–13).[415] Then without more delay, and without taking time to polish the letter and to dictate a fairer copy, he sent it off straight away.

Of course, this reconstruction is as speculative as the others. In this debate

---

412. Harris observes that apologetic features are characteristic of all three major sections of 2 Corinthians (*2 Corinthians* 46-47). Paul uses the term *apologeomai* ('defend oneself') in 12.19. On 2 Cor. 6.14–7.1 see Harris's review of the discussion (14-25); he notes that whereas earlier influential studies viewed the paragraph as a non-Pauline interpolation, the most recent studies have defended its Pauline authorship and its integrity in the context (15); he wonders in conclusion whether 'Paul had composed it at an earlier time, under Essene influence, and now incorporated it . . . as a digressive appeal to the Corinthians to sever their ties with paganism' (25).

413. Lietzmann famously regarded the possibility that 'a sleepless night of constant wakefulness' intervened as sufficient explanation for the disjuncture between chs. 1–9 and chs. 10–13 (*Korinther* 139); 'Paul dictated the letter with interruptions, so the possibility of unevenness is antecedently present' (Kümmel, *Introduction* 292).

414. Harris points out that each of Paul's letters (apart from Philemon) would have taken time to compose — 'perhaps days or even weeks or months'! — and hypothesizes not merely 'dictation pauses' but several stages of composition (*2 Corinthians* 31, 43-44, 50-53).

415. In Schnelle's view, all that is necessary is to presuppose that news of a changed situation in Corinth reached Paul between chs. 1–9 and 10–13 (*History* 86-87); he suggests that Titus brought that news, but also that chs. 1–9 were first dictated after Titus had left for Corinth (86), but does not explain how the reference to the return of Titus in 2 Cor. 7.6-16 fits into his reconstruction. Murphy-O'Connor's dismissal of such an explanation as 'psychologically impossible' (*Paul* 254) unfortunately evidences the same 'fundamental flaw' of the historian's superior knowledge which he himself criticizes a page earlier.

speculation is all we have, in which case it is probably wiser to work with the 2 Corinthians we have, rather than to make historical hypotheses depend on literary hypotheses regarding the unity (or otherwise) of 2 Corinthians. And since it is quite possible to envisage a scenario in which our 2 Corinthians is more or less as it left Paul's hands (as, for example, above),[416] I will indeed work with 2 Corinthians as it stands, though without making much depend on the letter being composed as a unity, far less at a single 'sitting'. In any event, (the bulk of) 2 Corinthians was probably written in the autumn of 55.

b. What Was the Challenge Posed by the Incoming Missionaries?

We do well to recall what a fast-changing situation has to be envisaged in Corinth. The church had been first established at the beginning of the 50s.

- Within about two years of Paul's first departure from Corinth, a particular crisis regarding one or two prominent members of the church called forth a strong rebuke from Paul (§32.4).
- Shortly afterwards problems had mounted in the church of Corinth, posed by various developments, primarily political and social, and mostly social in character, though with theological ramifications, which called forth the carefully written 1 Corinthians. The letter confirms that Paul faced a good deal of personal criticism from within the church, again more social than ideological in character.
- Not long after there was still further bad news of personal disaffection and accusation which Paul found very wounding and to which he responded in 'the letter of tears' (§32.6).
- At some stage a group of incoming missionaries added their own criticism of Paul's mission, provoking the counter-attack particularly of 2 Corinthians 10–13, though, as 2 Corinthians now stands, strangely mixed with Paul's relief at the Corinthians' positive response to 'the letter of tears' and with concern now (in the wake of that positive response) to promote the collection more vigorously.

With such a disparate community as the church of Corinth and such a febrile atmosphere as pervaded that church, the introduction of a further catalyst into that

---

416. 'If II Cor is understood as an actual letter out of a unique complicated historical situation, it is comprehensible as a historical substance' (Kümmel, *Introduction* 292). Also worthy of note is Kümmel's earlier observation that 'in antiquity there are no parallels' 'for someone other than the original author piecing together several of his letters, leaving out some parts and reworking other parts' (262).

volatile mix was bound to be explosive. But who were the incoming missionaries, and what was the challenge they brought?[417]

Paul's references to them can hardly be regarded as dispassionately descriptive, but the references do nevertheless give us a fairly clear idea of what they stood for, and so of the confusion their coming caused the Corinthian believers. There are two key sets of information. First, *they were Christian missionaries or preachers* — 'servants of Christ' (11.23), 'apostles of Christ' (11.13); they 'proclaimed Jesus', their message included promise of reception of the Spirit, they came with the 'gospel' (11.4). Paul was highly critical of them: they were 'servants of Satan' (11.14-15), 'false apostles' (11.13); they preached 'another Jesus', promised 'a different Spirit', came with 'a different gospel' (11.4).[418] But clearly in so saying he was both echoing and endeavouring to counter the claims that they themselves had made, claims that had been accepted by most of the Corinthian believers.

Second, they were *Jews*[419] who made a boast of being 'Hebrews',[420] 'Israelites' and 'seed of Abraham' (11.22). Not only so, but the parallels with Paul's two other most outspoken challenges to other Jewish preachers are also striking: 'a different gospel' (Gal. 1.6), an emphasis on being 'seed of Abraham' (Galatians 3), boasting of traditional Jewish/Israelite identity (Phil. 3.5).[421] Notable is the fact that they presented themselves to the Corinthians as 'ministers of righteousness' (2 Cor. 11.15), a reference back to the antithesis of ch. 3, and an echo (though no more than that) of the principal bone of contention between Paul and his Jewish Christian adversaries (e.g., Gal. 2.21; Phil. 3.9).

In the light of this information, it is hardly possible to conclude other than that the incomers were Jewish missionaries who saw themselves in at least some degree as part of the counter-mission, or, perhaps less polemically, as the follow-up mission which sought to correct or complete Paul's mission. The absence of

417. They have been the subject of many studies and hypotheses; see, e.g., the recent reviews in Furnish, *2 Corinthians* 48-54; Thrall, *2 Corinthians* 926-45; Harris, *2 Corinthians* 67-87.

418. It is not necessary to envisage the other missionaries as promulgating a much different christology — e.g., Jesus as a 'divine man *(theios anēr)* (D. Georgi, *The Opponents of Paul in Second Corinthians* [Philadelphia: Fortress, 1986] 271-77; cf. Thrall, *2 Corinthians* 667-70) — otherwise Paul could hardly have failed to respond to it. Paul's rhetoric (cf. Gal. 1.6-9) was designed primarily to signal that their message was not the same as his own; but the difference might only be a different emphasis on the cross and on the necessity to share in Christ's suffering (cf. Gal. 2.19, 3.1 and 6.14 with 2 Cor. 4.7–5.21) and a different evaluation of the importance of apostles having served as one of Jesus' disciples during Jesus' own mission (cf. Gal. 2.6 with 2 Cor. 5.16).

419. Becker describes them curiously as 'former Jews' (*Paul* 222).

420. See above, §25 at n. 37; cf. Rom. 2.17, 23; 3.27; 4.2; Gal. 6.13-14.

421. See above, §31.7b, and below on Phil. 3.2 (§34.4a).

any mention of or allusion to circumcision, as one of the demands made by the incomers, is not sufficient to disturb this conclusion. All that need be envisaged is a group who tailored their message or tactics to the situation they found in Corinth. That would include the faction who identified in at least some measure with Cephas/Peter (1 Cor. 1.12).[422] Since Peter was (known to be) (the) apostle to Jews/the circumcision, this faction would have provided obvious contact points for the incomers. At the same time, Peter had accepted a gospel of uncircumcision for Gentile converts (Gal. 2.6-9), and the Cephas faction, having lived in community with uncircumcised Gentile believers in Corinth, might well have been hard to persuade that their fellow (Gentile) believers now must be circumcised. In the transition process of God-fearer to proselyte, circumcision was usually at the end of the process. The fact that Paul nowhere mentions the law *(nomos)* in 2 Corinthians (but note ch. 3) is perhaps a reflection of a greater subtlety of approach than in Galatia.

The adaptation of the incomers to the Corinthian situation is also implied by what appears to be their drawing on some of the earlier criticisms levelled against Paul: that his skills in speaking and rhetoric were poorly developed (2 Cor. 10.10; 11.6); that Paul fell short of the normal standards of friendship in refusing to accept financial support from the Corinthians (11.7-11; 12.13-18); earlier factional bitterness had been renewed, old wounds re-opened and old accusations revived (12.19–13.2). Their evident emphasis on 'signs and wonders and miracles', and probably also 'visions and revelations',[423] as evidence of their apostleship (12.1, 11-12), also plugged in well to the equally evident appeal of the manifestly supernatural against which Paul had cautioned (some of) the Corinthians in 1 Corinthians 12–14. Given the degree of disaffection in regard to Paul,[424] it should occasion no surprise that an incoming group who saw their task as making good (or better) what Paul had already done (but inadequately) should latch on to that disaffection and try to turn it to their own account.[425]

The most intriguing aspect of the information and clues we have regarding the incoming missionaries is their relation to Jerusalem. The discussion here has

---

422. See above, at n. 204.

423. Worth noting is the parallel with the Jewish opposition in view in Col. 2.18, where *nomos* is equally absent from the vocabulary, even though the Jewish character of the challenge being confronted is clear (see below, §34.6c).

424. Rehearsed at the beginning of this section.

425. Such playing off the Corinthian factionalism against Paul is all that need be inferred (cf. Murphy-O'Connor, *Paul* 302-304 and n. 44); the assumption of some rapprochement between the incoming 'Judaizers' and earlier 'proto-Gnostics', as Harris still argues (*2 Corinthians* 77-87; cf. Kümmel, *Introduction* 285-86), is neither plausible nor required by the data (see above, n. 213). Becker's characterization of them seems to reflect a Lutheran Reformation which saw the threat of the second front in terms of *Schwärmerei* (*Paul* 223).

focused on the references to the 'super *(hyperlian)* apostles' (11.5; 12.11). Is the reference to the 'false apostles' to the incomers themselves?[426] Or to the apostles of Jerusalem, the 'pillar apostles' (Gal. 2.9)?[427] And if the latter, is the description Paul's own, or that of the incomers? Since Paul seems to compare himself with 'the super-apostles' ('in no way inferior' — 11.5; 12.11), whereas he ranks himself ahead of the incomers ('far greater', 'far more', 'to a much greater degree', 'many times' — 11.23), the phrase probably does have in view the Jerusalem leadership.[428] This likelihood is strengthened by what seems to be Paul's strong interpretation of the Jerusalem agreement on division of labour (Gal. 2.7-9) in 2 Cor. 10.13-16: for Paul, the agreement was agreement that the twin missions, to the circumcision and to the uncircumcision, should not interfere in each other's territory.[429] But in his view, this was precisely what the Jewish incoming missionaries were doing, and Paul would probably assume from this that it was with the approval, tacit or otherwise, of Jerusalem.

Although the relation between chs. 10–13 and the preceding chapters is mired in controversy, we should also note various references in the earlier chapters which can be taken as allusions to the incoming missionaries, written perhaps when the seriousness of their challenge had not yet become apparent. In particular, the incomers seem to have relied on 'letters of recommendation' (3.1) on which to base their authority and in order to make their influence effective with the Corinthians. These would certainly be letters from other churches. And if they were to have the desired effect, they would have to be letters from the more established and/or highly regarded of the new churches or from leading figures known and esteemed by all. The church of Jerusalem or the 'super-apostles' based there would be obvious candidates. Likewise, the fact that Paul immediately goes into a comparison and contrast between his own ministry and that of Moses (3.4-18) strongly suggests that the incoming missionaries presented their

426. Conzelmann, *History* 111; Thrall's conclusion (*2 Corinthians* 671-76).

427. Argued for by E. Käsemann in an influential article in *ZNW* 41 (1942) 33-71, reprinted as *Die Legitimität des Apostels. Eine Untersuchung zu II Korinther 10–13* (Darmstadt: Wissenschaftliche Buchgesellschaft, 1956), and supported by Barrett, *2 Corinthians* 30-32.

428. 'It is surely inconceivable that he [Paul] should say "I reckon I am just as good as the servants of the Devil". . . . False brothers and false apostles he can have no dealings with; of super-apostles and pillars he speaks with nothing worse than irony' (Barrett, *Paul* 35). Harris also suggests that the phrase refers to the original apostles, the Twelve, and that it is not a derogatory description of the Twelve coined by Paul, but either the description used by Paul's opponents or, more probably, the apostle's own 'ironic description of the exalted view of the Twelve held by the "false apostles"' (*2 Corinthians* 75-76). In contrast, Sumney, having identified the 'super-apostles' with the 'intruders' (*'Servants of Satan'* 112-15), concludes that 'there is no justification for associating it [this anti-Pauline mission] with the Jerusalem church' (307).

429. See above, §29.4b.

mission in line with that of Moses — the kind of apologetic appeal to Moses which we find in other Hellenistic Jewish writings.[430] That more traditionalist Christian Jews should appeal to Moses as consistent with their preaching the good news of Jesus (11.4) would be hardly surprising.

The most obvious solution to the question regarding the identity of the incoming missionaries, therefore, is that they saw themselves as part of continuing outreach from the more traditionalist Jewish mission, supported by the Jerusalem leadership, explicitly or tacitly. They thought Paul's preaching was deficient and defective and that his converts needed to be still more thoroughly converted. In order to secure their success, they came with commendations from highly respected churches 'in the homeland' and made great play of their manifest charisms. They played on the Corinthians' ideas of friendship and honour. And in order to discredit Paul, they also allied with some of the most disaffected of the Corinthian believers and encouraged the complaints and charges which had previously been levelled against Paul by one or more of the Corinthians. 2 Corinthians was, *inter alia,* Paul's response to these threats to one of his most treasured and potentially most important church foundations, and as the dimensions of the threat became clearer to him, so, it would appear, his response became much more outspoken and confrontational.

c. A Very Personal Statement (2 Cor. 1.1–2.13; 7.5-16)

After the initial greeting (1.1-2), Paul more or less dispenses with the normal thanksgiving and plunges at once into a reflection on suffering and the comfort provided by God, as a sharing in the sufferings of Christ and the comfort provided by Christ (1.3-7). This theme was evidently in the forefront of his mind as his frequent return to the theme in the following chapters indicates.[431] But what prompted the initial reflection was evidently the crisis he himself had endured in Asia, which had brought him near to death (1.8-11).[432]

---

430. Cf. §24 n. 132 above, and particularly Georgi, *Opponents* ch. 3. The debate occasioned by Georgi is briefly reviewed by Thrall, *2 Corinthians* 238-39, 246-48.

431. 2 Cor. 4.7–5.5; 6.4-10; 11.23–12.10; 13.4.

432. A. E. Harvey, *Renewal through Suffering: A Study of 2 Corinthians* (Edinburgh: Clark, 1996): 'For the first time in his extant letters, and possibly for the first time in the entire philosophical and religious literature of the West, we find the experience of involuntary and innocent suffering invested with positive value and meaning *in itself*'; 'the moment at which Paul experienced this reality and grasped its significance for the Christian life can be plausibly identified with his near-death experience recorded in 2 Corinthians 1.8' (31, 121). On the nature of this crisis, see above, §32.2e. The fact that Paul does not elaborate on it here may indicate a lack of planning for the letter, or, of course, he might have assumed that the Corinthians already knew about it.

But then his main concern vis-à-vis the Corinthians begins to emerge. With implied reference to earlier criticisms[433] and (probably) these criticisms as reinforced by the newcomers,[434] Paul insists on his personal integrity and appeals to the mutual esteem in which they held each other (1.12-14). A particular bone of contention was evidently Paul's vacillation over his plans to visit Corinth again; we may assume that Titus had reported both Paul's seeming equivocations to the Corinthians and the Corinthians' dissatisfaction back to Paul. Paul replies with a nice rhetorical play on 'yes' and 'no': just as the gospel does not say 'yes' and 'no' at the same time, neither does Paul in his dealings with them (1.17-20). God's faithfulness (*pistos de ho theos* — 1.18), displayed in the 'yes' of Christ (1.19) and the anointing with the Spirit (1.21-22), calls forth the appropriate human response ('Amen' — 1.20), a corresponding faithfulness as the expression and measure of their mutual relationship.[435]

Protests apart, the real reason for Paul's continued absence was that he did not want to repeat his painful visit (1.23–2.1). That had resulted in mutual pain and anguish, expressed in and caused by 'the letter of tears' he had written following that visit (2.2-4).[436] However the 'punishment' meted out to the offending party had been sufficient (2.6); it was time now to reach out in love and to forgive him (2.8-10), lest the opportunity for reconciliation be lost (2.11). This said, Paul reverts back to his travel itinerary, recollecting the restless mood which had prevented him from settling in Troas, despite the opportunities for mission there, until he knew the outcome of that letter (2.12-13). At which point, perhaps without clear idea of what still needed to be said in the rest of the letter, Paul probably allowed himself to go off at a tangent into a broader apologia for his ministry (§32.7d), only to pick up where he had left off in a further (initially intended as concluding?) recollection of the relief brought to him by Titus's arrival with the good news of the Corinthians' response (7.5-16). They had initially been offended by the letter but had then been moved to deep regret and repentance regarding their part in the breach with Paul (presumably, their giving credit to the

---

433. The reference to 'fleshly wisdom' (2.12) harks back to the confrontation in 1 Corinthians 1–4.

434. 'Fleshly weapons' (2 Cor. 10.4); *eilikrineia*, 'sincerity, purity of motive' (1.12; 2.17).

435. The underlying theological argument is lost in the Greek and easily missed without an awareness of the resonances of the language in Hebrew thought: *pistos* ('faithful') and *amēn* both reflect the Hebrew root *'mn*, whose basic idea was the 'constancy' (of things) and 'reliability' (of persons); the human 'Amen' echoes God's faithfulness (*'emunah*) (see particularly A. Jepsen, *TDOT* 1.319-23). Closely linked in Israel's thought is God's faithfulness in causing to stand (*qwm*), that is, in fulfilling his word and establishing or maintaining his covenant with Israel (see J. Gamberoni, *TDOT* 12.598-600), which Paul presumably echoes in his confidence that 'it is God who establishes (*bebaiōn*) us with you in Christ'.

436. On the 'severe letter' see above, §32.6.

false accusation against Paul). Their contrition and desire to make amends made up for all the previous pain (7.11-13) and confirmed the confidence in them which he had expressed to Titus (7.14). Titus himself had been caught up in the emotion of it all: he well recalled how his own mind had been set at rest by their response (7.13, 15), and it was no doubt the vividness of his report to Paul which had caused Paul to rejoice so strongly and to reaffirm his confidence in them.

This much, we can be confident, was Paul's primary/initial response to the Corinthians; he would have been keen to dash off a further letter to express his relief and joy at Titus's news. But whether it was simply that he found himself with sufficient time to dictate a longer letter or other news brought by Titus caused him substantial misgiving, for some reason he allowed his personal apologia to expand into a lengthy excursus in the course of dictating, before reverting to his initial mood and delight at Titus's main news.

d. An Apologia for His Ministry (1) (2 Cor. 2.14–4.6)

Something prompted Paul to embark on an exposition of his ministry:

- by contrasting his ministry with that of Moses (2.14–4.6);
- by reflecting on the paradox of divine power in and through human frailty (4.7–5.10);
- by emphasizing that his ministry had been given him by God (5.11-21);
- by further reflection on the paradox of a ministry proclaiming salvation available now having to be carried out through and despite tremendous difficulty and opposition (6.1-10).
- A return to the earlier theme (6.11-13) was interrupted with the awkward inclusion of what possibly had been a pre-formed exhortation (6.14–7.1), before he completed the transition back to the earlier theme (7.2-4).

However awkward the section within 2 Corinthians, or puzzling its origin within the sequence of Paul's communications with Corinth, the chapters contain some of the profoundest of Paul's theologizing about the cross of Christ and about its impact on human suffering, that of apostolic ministry in particular.

The digression begins with a diverse collection of metaphors, unusual even for Paul, who delighted to play with a whole range of metaphors in his attempts to make his message as vividly real to his audiences as possible.[437] Here the metaphors are the Roman triumph (2.14),[438] the sweet smell *(euōdia)* of sac-

---

437. See, e.g., *Theology of Paul* §13.4.

438. Latin *triumphus* = Greek *thriambos;* here the verb is *thriambeuō* (on the debate regarding its precise meaning, see BDAG 459).

rifice (particularly the burnt offering) (2.15-16),[439] and the opposite of the peddler with his tricks to entice purchase (2.17). Paul likens his mission to that of a
defeated and enslaved enemy led in triumph through Rome by God victorious in
his Christ (2.14).[440] The metaphor is dark, since the defeated captives were either enslaved or executed,[441] but Paul did not hesitate to think of himself as a
slave of Christ,[442] and the thought of dying and death as his lot as an apostle
(and indeed as a necessary part of the salvation process) had been sparked off by
the crisis in Asia (1.8-9) and becomes a leit-motif of this lengthy digression.[443]
Paul was equally ready to use the metaphor of sacrifice in a variety of ways[444]
and does not hesitate here to liken his ministry to the animal or offering burnt in
sacrifice to release a sweet smell — again a reflection of the necessity of his dying in order for his ministry to have effect, whether of life or death. The thought
that his ministry has such contrasting effects and the implication of personal
integrity (the defeated but uncompromising enemy, the pure sacrifice) lead into
the contrast between the sincerity of his ministry (now vindicated by the
church's response to 'the letter of tears') and the insincerity of the huckster trying to peddle his dubious wares[445] (alluding not too subtly to the new challenge
confronting his church in Corinth).

With the transition in thought thus signalled, Paul launches into a more
open polemic against the incoming missionaries who have begun to challenge
Paul's message with dubious means. They had come with letters of recommendation,[446] whereas Paul needed no such letters; the effect of his ministry on the Corinthians themselves was proof enough that he had been authorized by God and

---

439. *Osmē euōdias,* 'pleasing odour', occurs forty-six times in LXX, usually in reference to the burnt offering (Gen. 8.21; Exod. 29.18; etc.); see further Harris, *2 Corinthians*
248-49.

440. The 'in the Christ' seems to refer to the 'us' who are led triumph by God.

441. See particularly S. J. Hafemann, *Suffering and the Spirit: An Exegetical Study of
2 Cor. 2:14–3:3* (WUNT 2.19; Tübingen: Mohr Siebeck, 1986) 18-39; P. B. Duff, 'Metaphor,
Motif, and Meaning: The Rhetorical Strategy behind the Image "Led in Triumph" in 2 Corinthians 2:14', *CBQ* 53 (1991) 79-92; cf. Thrall, *2 Corinthians* 191-95; Harris, *2 Corinthians*
243-46.

442. Rom. 1.1; 1 Cor. 7.22; Gal. 1.10; Phil. 1.1 (Col. 4.12).

443. See above, n. 432.

444. Rom. 12.1; 15.16; 1 Cor. 5.7; Phil. 2.17; 4.18.

445. *Kapēleuō* — 'trade in, peddle, huckster'; 'Because of the tricks of small tradesmen
. . . the word almost comes to mean *adulterate*' (BDAG 508; and further Thrall, *2 Corinthians*
212-15; Harris, *2 Corinthians* 253-54).

446. 'The Greek letter of introduction, the *systatikē epistolē,* was a distinct epistolary
type, and its use was common in antiquity' (Thrall, *2 Corinthians* 218). Whoever provided the
letters (Jerusalem?), they were presumably highly respected proponents of a Moses ministry
and the law-keeping which it implied.

was an instrument of God's purpose (3.1-3). Here, once again, it should be noted that Paul immediately appeals to the mark of the Spirit in their lives as the inescapable proof that his message was from Christ.[447]

The character of the challenge, of which he had learned from Titus, is clearly indicated in these verses (3.3-18). For the key term in the passage (3.1–4.6) is 'ministry' *(diakonia),*[448] and the key question is 'sufficiency/competency' *(hikanotēs)* for ministry.[449] Paul proceeds to develop a sharp contrast between two forms of ministry — that represented by Moses and that represented by the Pauline mission. Why should Paul have taken this tack? Most obviously because the incoming missionaries were making much of Moses as their precedent and norm,[450] and primarily, presumably, with reference to Moses' exceptional closeness to God as the one who was given the law written on tablets of stone; as those who stood directly in the succession from Moses, the incomers could claim his authority and expect the appropriate respect from the Corinthians.[451]

Paul's response works with a sequence of strong antitheses:

- not ink   but the Spirit (3.3)
- not tablets of stone   but tablets of fleshly hearts (3.3)
- old covenant   new covenant (3.6, 14)
- not of letter   but of Spirit (3.6-7)
- ministry of death   ministry of life (3.6-7)
- ministry of condemnation   ministry of justification (3.9)
- fading glory   surpassing glory (3.7-11)

The contrast between the ministry the incomers represented and that of Paul is not simply between the remote authority of letters of recommendation written from afar and the immediacy of lives transformed by the Spirit, but the same contrast is at the heart of the difference between Paul's ministry and theirs. Here again it is the life-giving impact of the Spirit in the hearts of the Corinthians which marks the difference from a faith to be learned from written instruction.

In talking of 'tablets of *stone*' (3.3), Paul was clearly alluding to the Exodus accounts using the same phrase.[452] This invited the contrast with the new

447. As consistently in his earlier correspondence — 1 Thess. 1.5-6; Gal. 3.2-5; 1 Cor. 1.5-7 — and already here (2 Cor. 1.21-22).

448. *Diakonia* — 3.7, 8, 9 (twice); 4.1; *diakonos* — 3.6; *diakoneō* — 3.3.

449. *Hikanos* — 2.16; 3.5; *hikanotēs* — 3.5; *hikanoō* — 3.6.

450. Note the double contrast Paul makes with the incomers and with Moses: 'not as so many' (2.17), 'not as some' (3.1); 'not just as Moses' (3.13).

451. See above, at n. 430.

452. Exod. 24.12; 31.18 and particularly 34.1, 4; see also 32.15-16; 34.28-29.

covenant of Jer. 31.31-34,[453] and with the equivalent promise in Ezekiel that Israel's 'heart of *stone*' would be replaced by a 'heart of flesh',[454] where it is God's Spirit which achieves the obedience God looks for (11.19; 36.27). The implication is almost explicit: Paul's Spirit ministry was the fulfilment of Jeremiah's and Ezekiel's prophecies and therefore achieved the existential realization of what the written law could only set out at the surface level. The law of itself, as 'letter' (*gramma*),[455] could not achieve such an end; what it did was to spell out the condemnation which falls on the law-breaker. The law of itself could not 'make alive';[456] only the Spirit could do that — as evidenced, once again, in and through Paul's ministry.

Very boldly, in the following paragraph Paul essays to establish his contrast and claim by offering a radically different interpretation of the key passage in which the high esteem of the other missionaries for Moses was rooted — Exod. 34.29-35.[457] In bringing the law down from Mount Sinai, Moses' face had shone with the reflected glory of God, so much so that he had to put a veil over his face when speaking to the people (for they were afraid); but when he went into the presence of the Lord (in the tent of meeting he subsequently had constructed), he removed the veil. Paul rather arbitrarily assumes that the shining of Moses' face faded after a time (he did not cover his face with a veil permanently)[458] and sees in that a symbol of the passing/past glory of the covenant he brought (the Sinai law).[459] With even more nimble footwork he depicts the veil between Moses and the people as a veil still standing between the people and the law (the old covenant). This allows Paul to read Exod. 34.34 (LXX) as a type of

---

453. It is hard to doubt that an allusion to Jer. 31.31-34 was intended; see, e.g., *Theology of Paul* 147 and the bibliography in n. 103 there; also Wilckens, *Theologie* 1/3.115 n. 96.

454. Paul's unusual phrase 'fleshly hearts' (3.3) must have been prompted by its use in Ezek. 11.19 and 36.26-27; see also Harris, *2 Corinthians* 264-65.

455. *Gramma* here is not to be identified simply with *nomos* ('law'); as in Rom. 2.28-29, *gramma* focuses rather on the law as written, visible, external; see further *Theology of Paul* 149; *New Perspective on Paul* (2005) 433-34, (2008) 439-40; Thrall, *2 Corinthians* 235; Davies, 'Paul' 721-23; cf. BDAG 205-206; otherwise S. Grindheim, 'The Law Kills but the Gospel Gives Life: The Letter-Spirit Dualism in 2 Corinthians 3.5-18', *JSNT* 84 (2001) 97-115.

456. The point Paul had already made in Gal. 3.21; see above, §31 at n. 363.

457. On 2 Cor. 3.12-18 as a 'midrash' on Exod. 34.29-35, see, e.g., those cited in *Theology of Paul* 148 nn. 105, 106; Harris, *2 Corinthians* 277; 'This section is clearly based on the story in Exod. 34.29-35' (Thrall, *2 Corinthians* 238).

458. On whether 'fading' is an adequate translation of *katargoumenēn* in 3.7 and on Paul's obviously deliberate play on the term (3.7, 11, 13, 14), see *Theology of Paul* 148 and *New Perspective on Paul* (2005) 431, (2008) 437 n. 31; Harris, *2 Corinthians* 284-85, 290-91, 297-300, 304.

459. Paul makes great play with the image of the veil: *kalymma* — 3.13-16; *kekalymmenon* ('veiled') — 4.3.

what happens when one goes into the Lord = turns to the Spirit:[460] the veil is taken away (2 Cor. 3.16).[461] This is what the Corinthians had done as a result of Paul's ministry; they were like Moses, enjoying the immediate presence of God, reflecting God's glory in ever greater degree (3.18 — the effect of the same Spirit),[462] not like the Moses whose veiled law *(gramma)* and its continuing role they (and the incomers) were failing to understand.

It was having this ministry that kept Paul going; he had nothing to be ashamed of and had no need to resort to the dubious tactics of others (4.1-2). The veil hiding the light of 'the gospel of the glory of the Christ' he attributes to 'the god of this age' (4.3-4). But Paul sees his commission as precisely the proclamation of this Christ in order that 'the light of the knowledge of the glory of God in the face of Christ' might shine to dispel the darkness from the hearts of many others as it had already for Paul and his converts (4.5-6).[463]

e. An Apologia for His Ministry (2) (2 Cor. 4.7–7.4)

Characteristic of the unplanned composition of the letter, Paul's thought seems to ricochet from the thought of the glory expressed in his gospel (the manifestation of the transforming glory of God in the face of Jesus Christ — 4.6) to the contrasting paradox of the inadequacy of those who proclaim that gospel. The following meditation on suffering as an integral part of Christian experience, and of the minister of the gospel in particular,[464] is as profound a train of theological reflection as we find anywhere in early Christian literature.

The primary thought is that human weakness ('earthenware jars'), destructive opposition,[465] and the repeated intimations of mortality (Paul's daily experi-

460. In keeping with his emphasis on the Spirit in this passage, as the life-giving activity of God already so powerfully experienced by his converts, Paul hermeneutically identifies 'the Lord' of Exod. 34.34 with the Spirit (3.17) as the power which liberates from the blinkered attitudes exemplified by the ministry of the incoming missionaries. See again *Theology of Paul* 422 and n. 51, and especially Harris, *2 Corinthians* 311-12.

461. Exod. 34.34 (LXX) — 'whenever Moses went in *(eiseporeueto)* before the Lord, he would remove *(periereito)* the veil'; 2 Cor. 3.16 — 'whenever he turned *(epistrepsē)* to the Lord, the veil was taken away *(periaireitai)*'. See further *Theology of Paul* 326 n. 40, 421-22; an allusion is generally recognized (Thrall, *2 Corinthians* 268-69; Harris, *2 Corinthians* 306-309).

462. Harris, *2 Corinthians* 317-18; for discussion of the imagery see Thrall, *2 Corinthians* 290-95.

463. That Paul here evokes his own conversion experience as typical of Christian conversion is likely; see above, §25 n. 134; Harris, *2 Corinthians* 336-37 (bibliography in n. 112).

464. The thought is primarily of the Christian minister (apostolic suffering), but not exclusively so; the 'we' includes believers as a whole (*Jesus and the Spirit* 327).

465. On the imagery used in 4.8-9, see, e.g., Harris, *2 Corinthians* 341-45.

ence) are not to be allowed to command primary attention or to distract from the more important fact of life itself (4.7-12). There is a dynamic synergism between death and life which provides a wholly different perspective on such negatives. As Jesus[466] had shown, the dying *(nekrōsis)* of human mortality is not the whole story and not the final word. But neither is it to be ignored or excluded from the story, as though it was something strange or antithetical to the purpose of God for the ministry of his word. *The dying and rising of Jesus show how the synergism works:* the very reality of human dying makes it clear that the life displayed in and proclaimed through the minister is not his own, but the life of Jesus.[467] In fact, it is the acceptance of the suffering and dying as a *sharing in the suffering and dying of Jesus*[468] (and not something to be fretted over or resisted) which makes the proclamation of life so effective (4.10-13).[469] This is the faith which gives the proclamation its power: the confidence that as God raised Jesus from the dead,[470] so the affliction suffered and the wasting away of mortality are trumped by the inward renewing of the Spirit with its sure promise of final transformation into the resurrection body (4.13–5.4).[471] And once again, it is the Spirit already received and experienced which serves as the first instalment of this process and guarantee of its completion (5.5).[472]

It is this which gives the confidence to continue ministry in the present — a

---

466. Note how Paul refers simply to 'Jesus' (not 'Jesus Christ' or 'the Lord Jesus') throughout this section — 4.10-14 (six times); it was the mortal Jesus that Paul had in mind.

467. As in Rom. 6.4-8, the thought is that the 'newness of life' experienced by the believer is in some sense an 'already' sharing in the resurrection life of Christ, but that until the dying with Christ has completed its course, the complete sharing with Christ in resurrection is part of the 'not yet' of the resurrection body.

468. This is a major motif in Paul's soteriology; see *Theology of Paul* §18, where I attempt to fill out what has been a much too neglected aspect of Paul's theology and gospel. M. J. Gorman has developed the theme in *Cruciformity: Paul's Narrative Spirituality of the Cross* (Grand Rapids: Eerdmans, 2001).

469. Murphy-O'Connor regards the 'extraordinary statement' of 4.10-11 as 'the summit of 2 Corinthians, and the most profound insight ever articulated as to the meaning of suffering and the nature of authentic ministry' *(Paul* 314).

470. In 4.14 Paul echoes one of the new movement's fundamental credos; see above, §21.4e.

471. The chapter division obscures the fact that 5.1-5 is the climax of a larger unit of exposition — 4.16–5.5; on the continuity of thought across the chapter division see Furnish, *2 Corinthians* 288; and further *Theology of Paul* 488-90. The sequence of thought is very similar to that of Rom. 8.18-24. On the imagery of 5.1-4 see particularly Thrall, *2 Corinthians* 357-70, and Harris, *2 Corinthians* 369-91, although the 'nakedness' envisaged in 5.3 is simply the other side of the belief of some Corinthians that 'there is no resurrection of the dead' (1 Cor. 15.12), and is not distinctively 'proto-gnostic' (Harris) (cf. Thrall 374-80).

472. Note again how in 5.5 Paul picks up the thought already expressed in 1.22 and 3.3, 16-18.

matter of faith, and not sight (5.6-7). It has its 'down' side — being 'away from the Lord' (5.6-9). And it requires determined dedication; it is not a downhill ride all the way from the mountain peak of conversion; the crucified Christ will also be the judge on the final day (5.10).[473] This proper reverence *(phobos)* for him who is Lord[474] and awareness that God knows us better than we do ourselves is what ensures that ministry is not a matter of commending oneself — another swipe at those (the other missionaries) who, in Paul's view, relied too much on making a pleasing or eye-catching impression (5.11-12). If he appeared distracted, it was for God; but to the Corinthians he spoke with common sense (5.13).[475] The key factor was the gospel with its message of the love of God manifested in the death of Christ, for that death spelled the death of every and any life lived merely to impress others or merely to enjoy oneself.[476] The death of Christ for all made possible a living for others, as Christ had lived and died (5.14-15). This is the way Christ should be apprehended; a merely human point of view (which Paul himself had once shared) could make no sense of how Christ had lived and died. The transformation of values and perspectives which becoming 'in Christ' involved brought a totally new view of reality — 'new creation' (5.16-17). This was what it meant to be a minister of the gospel, of the new covenant: having been reconciled to God through Christ, to proclaim the reconciliation with God which Christ's death had made possible. As it was 'in Christ' that God acted decisively to deal with human sin and failure, so it is 'in Christ' that the right standing with God is effected and right living for God becomes a realistic possibility (5.18-21).[477]

Once again, Paul in his dictation seems to have become carried away with the wonder and excitement of his gospel: that the transforming grace of God can be ex-

---

473. It is important to recognize that Paul's theology included expectation of a judgment (by Christ!) for believers, an impartial judgment, as in Rom. 2.6-11; see *New Perspective on Paul* (2005) 72-80, (2008) 80-89.

474. Thrall, *2 Corinthians* 401-402

475. 'If we were out of our senses, it was for God; if we are in our right mind, it is for you' (5.13 — BDAG 350), which is perhaps an allusion to Paul's own experience of ecstasy (see §25.5f above), but possibly a reflection of the character of Paul's message and the quality of his commitment as perceived by the incomers; options in Harris, *2 Corinthians* 417-18.

476. '. . . one died for all, so all died' (5.14) — probably an aspect of Paul's Adam theology; see *Theology of Paul* 208-12; also A. J. M. Wedderburn, '2 Corinthians 5:14 — a Key to Paul's Soteriology?', in T. J. Burke and J. K. Elliott, eds., *Paul and the Corinthians,* M. Thrall FS (NovTSupp 109; Leiden: Brill, 2003) 267-83.

477. On the metaphor of reconciliation see *Theology of Paul* 228-30, and on the imagery of 5.20-21 see 217 and 221-22; there is a full discussion in A. Bash, *Ambassadors for Christ: An Exploration of Ambassadorial Language in the New Testament* (WUNT 2.92; Tübingen: Mohr Siebeck, 1997), here 87-116; also Harris, *2 Corinthians* 449-56. Wilckens emphasizes that God is the reconciler rather than the reconciled (*Theologie* 1/3.123).

perienced *now,* that salvation can begin to become a reality *now* (6.1-2).[478] And
once again the thought ricochets back to the contrast between the enticingly easy
way offered by the other missionaries (6.3) and the reality which (true) ministers of
God experienced — 'afflictions, calamities, distress, beatings, imprisonments, ri-
ots, hard labour, sleepless nights, hunger' (6.4-5), which prompts in turn the characterization of how he responds to such depressing challenges — 'in purity, understanding, patience, kindness, the Holy Spirit, sincere love, declaring the truth, the
power of God' (6.6-7) — and the concluding acceptance of the inevitable dialectic
of ministry, which involves 'honour and dishonour, ill-repute and good repute, de-
ceivers and truthful, unknown and well known, dying and, look, we live, disciplined and not killed, grieving but always rejoicing, poor and making many rich,
having nothing and possessing everything'. Paul cherished no allusions as to how
he was regarded; the facts that he was rejected, slandered and ignored, that he knew
real suffering, sorrow and poverty meant very little to him. The dialectical facts that
in it all and despite it all he remained true to his calling and by his ministry he enriched so many — that was what mattered to him above all else (6.8-10).

Quite what happened at this point in the letter or in Paul's dictation will
never become clear. 6.11-13 read rather like the last gasp of a sustained personal
apologia which had the character of an intense emotional catharsis. In opening
himself so fully and frankly to the Corinthians, he had left himself vulnerable to
unfavourable interpretation and misconstrual. All he could do now was to appeal
to them to respond as openly and as generously as he had attempted to do. It
would make psychological sense if Paul, quite drained by the effort, broke off his
dictation. Here again we could readily imagine him moving on another stage of
his journey through Macedonia before returning to his dictation. Perhaps before
picking up where he left off, he included a short pre-formed exhortation on the
continuing relevance of Israel's obligation to holiness, to a set-apartness to God
which required a set-apartness from anything which destroyed that holiness and
rendered impure (6.14–7.1).[479] The passage does ring oddly with Paul's teaching
on holiness and purity elsewhere, but it did put the challenge before the more casual of the Corinthian believers in stark either-or terms, and so it can count as one
of the most extreme expressions of concerns he expressed elsewhere in the Corinthian correspondence.[480] Or again, having dictated the further section of his

478. The double 'now' in his reading of Isa. 49.8 is particularly effective.

479. On the lengthy debate as to whether 2 Cor. 6.14–7.1 is an interpolation or whatever,
see, e.g., Harris, *2 Corinthians* 14-25 (n. 412 above), with bibliography. T. Schmeller, 'Der
ursprüngliche Kontext von 2 Kor 6.14–7.1. Zur Frage der Einheitlichkeit des 2. Korintherbriefs', *NTS* 52 (2006) 219-38, suggests that the passage originally came between chs. 1–9
and chs. 10–13, providing the connection between the two parts, though why the passage was
then subsequently moved to its present position is hardly obvious.

480. The command in 1 Cor. 5.6-8 to 'clean out the old leaven' in connection with the

immediate response to the good news brought by Titus (7.2-16), he could even be envisaged him leaving it to his secretary/scribe to make a fair copy of the whole before dispatching it. In any case, the circumstances of the letter's composition are so hidden from us that any number of scenarios could be envisaged to explain the character of the letter at this point.

f. Concerning the Collection (2 Corinthians 8–9)

As with 6.11–7.4, we have similar difficulties in explaining how chs. 8–9 became part of the letter.[481] But here again it would be unjustified and unwise to exclude possibilities such as that ch. 8 formed a first draft of what Paul wanted to say on this subject after hearing the encouraging news brought by Titus. At a later point in the journey through Macedonia Paul could have set himself to write afresh (ch. 9), and in the event decided simply to use both drafts. As indicated earlier, such hypotheses at least have the advantage of not having to conclude that a later editor chopped off introductions and conclusions of independent letters; Paul as himself editor of a letter somewhat thrown together (because of the circumstances of composition) is a more credible thesis.

Since the collection is a subject requiring a full treatment, I will leave further consideration of chs. 8–9 till §33.4 below.

g. Confrontation (2 Corinthians 10–13)

Whether Paul had simply paused for a break or had received fresh information in the interim (a more likely scenario),[482] the appeal of chs. 10–13 ends up as the final section of his letter. He begins with a mildness of tone mingled with sarcasm (10.1-2), which quickly escalates into a full-blown polemical apologia, more sustained in intensity than anything he had written before (even to the Galatians).[483]

Passover lamb reflects the same concern to purge the community of all that might render it impure, and the antithesis between 'the table of demons' and 'the table of the Lord' in 1 Cor. 10.20-21 is quite as sharp.

481. See above, at n. 406; Harris provides a brief survey of views (*2 Corinthians* 26-29).

482. Murphy-O'Connor hypothesizes that Paul took the opportunity after writing 2 Corinthians 1–9 and before going on to Corinth (2 Cor. 9.4) to evangelize further west, to Illyricum (Rom. 15.20) (*Paul* 316-19); similarly Schnabel, *Mission* 1250-51; but *mechri tou Illyrikou*, 'as far as Illyricum' (Rom. 15.19), need not be taken to imply a mission *in* Illyricum; anywhere relatively close to the border between Macedonia and Illyricum could be roughly described by the phrase = '(more or less) as far as (the border of) Illyricum'; similarly Wedderburn, *History* 125; see also Hengel and Schwemer, *Paul* 261.

483. Paul was aware of its possible effect on the Corinthians — 10.9.

What evidently irritated Paul to the point of anger was the way the incomers had presented themselves as far more worthy of respect than Paul and the extent to which the Corinthians had been taken in (as Paul saw it) by them. The key word is 'boasting', and much of the fascination of the passage is the degree to which Paul was so 'needled' by their claims that he found it necessary to indulge in boasting on his own account.[484]

- The incomers disparaged Paul's authority and disparaged his persona: he was 'subservient *(tapeinos)*' when with them but 'bold *(tharrō)*' when absent from them (10.1);[485] '"his letters", they say, "are weighty and powerful, but his personal presence *(parousia)* is weak,[486] and his speech is contemptible *(exouthenēmenos)*"' (10.10).[487]
- They commended themselves by categorizing, measuring and comparing themselves with one another in a self-conscious self-promoting manner (10.12) and had no sense of going beyond their remit when they interfered in Paul's mission (10.13-16).
- Their preaching of Jesus and the gospel put the emphasis in the wrong places (11.4).[488]
- They presented themselves as apostles (11.13), 'ministers of righteousness' (11.15), and claimed the right to be (entirely) supported by the church in Corinth, 'taking advantage *(lambanei)*'[489] of the Corinthians' generosity (11.20) and disparaging Paul's tactic of supporting himself as both unfriendly, demeaning, a sign of his weakness (11.7-9, 11-12, 18, 21, 29),[490] and simply 'wrong' (12.13).

484. *Kauchaomai,* 'to boast, be proud of' — 10.8, 13, 15, 16, 17 (twice); 11.12, 16, 18 (twice), 30 (twice); 12.1, 5 (twice), 6, 9; *kauchēsis,* 'boasting' — 11.10, 17.

485. It is likely that Paul is using here the language of accusations levelled against him (note how Paul reverts to the same theme in 11.7 and 12.21); for *tapeinos* as denoting someone acting in a servile manner, see BDAG 989; and further Thrall, *2 Corinthians* 602-603; Harris, *2 Corinthians* 669-71.

486. 'For more than two centuries "rhetorical delivery" had encompassed both speech and "bodily presence"; this included appearance and a stage presence' (Winter, *Corinth* 35).

487. The language of contempt *(exoutheneō)* was part of the discourse of the Corinthian letters (1 Cor. 1.28; 6.4; 16.11).

488. See above, n. 418.

489. For this unusual use of *lambanō* see BDAG 584. The exegetical key is 12.16 (Harris, *2 Corinthians* 785); see below, n. 491.

490. In saying that he 'robbed/plundered *(esylēsa)* other churches' (11.8), Paul may be alluding to the charge of malpractice levelled against him (see above, n. 399); the echo of such an indiscriminate charge ('other churches', plural) would help resolve any tension with Phil. 4.15 (only Philippi provided such support, presumably through 'the brothers from Macedonia' — 2 Cor. 11.9).

- They made a lot of their Jewish pedigree (11.22) and boasted of their exploits as ministers of Christ (11.23-29).
- They boasted of the visions and revelations which they had been granted (12.1-7) and of the miracles they had wrought (12.11-12).
- They even accused Paul of deceit[491] and fraud[492] in the matter of giving and receiving, probably taking up the previous insinuations that Paul's endeavours through Titus for the collection were in his own self-interest (12.16-18; 13.1).[493]

Paul's rejoinder was robust.

- Their criteria were wrong; they were operating in accordance with the normal criteria of human society; in accusing him of walking 'according to the flesh' *(kata sarka),* they showed little appreciation of what the warfare between *sarx* and *pneuma,* 'flesh and Spirit', was all about (10.2-4);[494] their arrogance *(hypsōma)* was against the knowledge of God (10.5); Paul was quite prepared to take them on (10.6).[495]
- He demanded the respect that one Christian owed to another (10.7).[496]
- Paul would certainly speak as boldly as he wrote when he next saw them (10.11); he may be untrained *(idiōtēs)* in rhetoric,[497] but not in knowledge of the gospel and of what they needed to hear (11.6).
- Paul's authority was the authority of his commission, of which the Corinthians were proof (10.13-16);[498] not self-commendation counts, but the commendation of the Lord (10.17-18).
- It remained a matter of personal pride, however foolish, that he had not been a financial burden on the Corinthian believers (cf. 1 Cor. 9.15), and he would continue so to act in his relations with them — an expression of

491. 2 Cor. 12.16 — 'but crafty fellow *(panourgos)* that I am, I entrapped you by trickery *(dolō hymas elabon)'* — presumably taking up language used by his opponents (e.g., BDAG 754; Thrall, *2 Corinthians* 849-51; Harris, *2 Corinthians* 889).

492. Note the double insistence that neither Paul nor Titus had 'taken advantage' of them *(epleonektēsa,* 'exploit, outwit, defraud, cheat') in 12.17-18 (BDAG 824).

493. On the nature of the trickery and exploitation imputed, see again Thrall 855-57 and above, n. 399.

494. Paul alludes to one of his favourite themes, which would already have been familiar to the Corinthians: *sarx* — 1 Cor. 1.26; 3.3; 15.50; 2 Cor. 1.17; 5.16; and the intense focus on the Spirit in the Corinthian correspondence; see further *Theology of Paul* 65-66, 477-82.

495. See further Thrall, *2 Corinthians* 614-18.

496. The point is developed in Rom. 14.1-12.

497. See, e.g., Thrall, *2 Corinthians* 676-78; Winter, *Philo and Paul* 223-28.

498. On 10.13-16 see above, §29.4b.

his love for them, not at all a making light of their friendship (2 Cor. 11.7-21).[499]

- Paul's anger at the overblown and deceitful claims made by the incoming missionaries, and their mischievous criticisms and accusations levelled against him, spills over in outright condemnation of them as 'false apostles, dishonest workmen, disguising themselves as apostles of Christ', but in reality 'servants of Satan', the master of such deceptive disguise (11.12-15)[500] — the gloves are off!

- In mounting frustration and irritation Paul succumbs to the challenge to measure himself against the 'false apostles', to play them at their own game, or, as he would rather see it, to play the fool (11.1, 16-17),[501] but in his own terms. What follows is the antithesis of an 'achievements-list'[502] or a *cursus honorum:*[503] a catalogue of what the world would regard as catastrophes, of repeated physical punishment,[504] suffering and danger, of sustained pressure *in extremis,* climaxing in what he counted as his greatest burden (his 'worrying for all the churches') and the bathos of his escape from Damascus (let down in a basket through a window in the wall!) (11.23-33).[505] His boast, if he must boast, is of his weakness (11.30; 12.5)! And even when he slips the restraints still more to boast of his own visions and revelations,[506] it is with the immediate qualification of the 'thorn in the

---

499. Again implicit is an allusion to the other missionaries' criticism that Paul was not acting towards the Corinthians in the spirit of friendship, that is, in giving and receiving (Marshall, *Enmity* 225-33).

500. In *Life of Adam and Eve* 9.1 Satan 'transformed himself into the brightness of angels' to deceive Eve again; that Paul may have known the tradition is suggested by his recollection of the serpent's (earlier) deception of Eve a few verses earlier (2 Cor. 11.3).

501. Note the frequency of *aphrōn* ('foolish') and *aphrosynē* ('foolishness') in these chapters: *aphrōn* — 11.16, 19; 12.6, 11; *aphrosynē* — 11.1, 17, 21.

502. See, e.g., Thrall, *2 Corinthians* 755-58.

503. C. Forbes, 'Comparison, Self-Praise and Irony: Paul's Boasting and Conventions of Hellenistic Rhetoric', *NTS* 32 (1986) 1-30: an 'ironic parody of self-praise and comparisons of his opponents' (16); see also U. Heckel, *Kraft in Schwachheit. Untersuchungen zu 2 Kor 10–13* (WUNT 2.56; Tübingen: Mohr Siebeck, 1993) 149-59; Winter, *Philo and Paul* 234-36. M. Ebner, *Leidenslisten und Apostelbrief. Untersuchungen zu Form, Motivik und Funktion der Peristasenkataloge bei Paulus* (Würzburg: Echter, 1991), sees parallels with the labours of Hercules (161-72).

504. 'Paul's body must have also been covered with deep scars from these chastisements, because scourging left behind numerous and deep wounds' (Becker, *Paul* 173-74).

505. The *faux*-solemnity of the oath of 11.31 ('God knows that I am not lying') heightens the ludicrousness of boasting about the contents of such a list and about such a climax to the list (11.32-33), probably in conscious contrast to the honour of being first soldier to scale the wall of a besieged town (Murphy-O'Connor, *Paul* 320).

506. On the heavenly journey in view (12.2-4), see above, §25.5f. The argument of P. R.

flesh'[507] and the realization that much more important was the grace which sustained him and the experience of God's power coming to its full effect in and through his weakness (12.1-10).[508] After that 'the signs of his being an apostle' are affirmed dismissively as still missing the point (12.11-12).

- A final affirmation of his policy of not being a burden to them and a strong rebuttal of any false dealing in the matter of the collection (12.14-18; 13.1) is mingled with forebodings over his coming visit: that he will find them continuing to be riven with factionalism[509] and tolerating loose living (12.20-21); that he will have to exercise strong discipline (13.2-4),[510] not as a matter of proving himself, but that they may do what is good *(to kalon)* and demonstrate their well-ordered maturity *(katartisis)*[511] (13.5-9); and that he will be able to exercise the ministry given him — to build up and not to tear down (13.10).[512]

A final urging to put things in order *(katartizō)* and an appeal to live in harmony[513] and peace (13.11) is a fitting close to such a sequence of troubled

---

Gooder, *Only the Third Heaven? 2 Corinthians 12.1-10 and Heavenly Ascent* (LNTS 313; London: Clark, 2006), that 2 Cor. 12.1-10 recalls a *failed* ascent to heaven, takes too little account of 12.2-4 as Paul's prime example of 'revelations of extraordinary quality', which could be expected to cause him to be 'elated' (12.7).

507. The 'thorn in the flesh' cannot be identified with any confidence, most likely some painfully irritating and recurring malady; full discussion in Thrall, *2 Corinthians* 809-18, who, if pressed for a decision, opts for migraine.

508. Note how Paul harks back to the theme which dominated the earlier chapters — his discovery that life comes through sharing in Christ's suffering and death (1.5; 4.7-12; 5.14-15, 21; 6.4-10), here, the power of Christ coming to its fullest expression in and through all-too-human weakness (12.7-10), knitting the letter together as a thematic whole. Cf. 1 Cor. 1.18-31, where divine Wisdom is seen most clearly in the all-too-human suffering of Jesus. See further Heckel, *Kraft in Schwachheit* 206-14, and §5.

509. *Eris* ('strife, discord, contention') — 1 Cor. 1.11; 3.3; 2 Cor. 12.20; *zēlos* ('jealousy, envy') — 1 Cor. 3.3; 2 Cor. 12.20. The rest of the list should not be regarded as drawn from some standard vice-list: *thymos* ('outburst of anger'), *eritheia* ('dispute, outbreak of selfishness'), *katalalia* ('slander, defamation'), *psithyrismos* ('secret gossip, tale-bearing'), *physiōsis* ('conceit'), *akatastasia* ('disorder, unruliness'), all unusual in Paul's other vice-lists (the closest parallel is Gal. 5.19-21), indicate clearly the nature of Paul's foreboding in regard to the Corinthian church as such.

510. Note the final recurrence to the 'power in weakness' theme, that is, Christ's power in the human weakness of his servants (13.3-4).

511. On *katartisis* see Harris, *2 Corinthians* 927-28.

512. Note the reference back to the theme of *oikodomē*, 'building up' (10.8; 12.19; 13.10). Paul may have been comparing and contrasting his commission with that of Jeremiah (Jer. 1.10), especially as Jeremiah's commission 'to the nations' (1.5) seems also to have influenced Paul's sense of commission (see above, §25.3d[3]). Note the solemn way Paul reaffirms this vocation: 'We are speaking before God in Christ' (12.19).

513. 2 Cor. 13.11 — *to auto phroneite,* 'think the same thing'.

and troublesome correspondence. Somewhat ironically, but in the last analysis highly appropriate, is the fact that the parting benediction was to become the principal liturgical benediction of future generations of the Christian church: 'The grace of our Lord Jesus Christ, and the love of God, and the fellowship of (*koinōnia,* 'sharing in') the Holy Spirit be with you all' (13.13).

h. The Aftermath

In Paul's other correspondence we have no firm evidence of how successful or otherwise the letter proved to be. Uniquely in the Corinthian correspondence we are enabled to follow through the misunderstandings over the first letter and the highs and lows which were consequent upon 'the letter of tears'. And while we cannot be very clear on how 1 Corinthians was received, we are in a position to deduce that 2 Corinthians, despite all the angst which it expressed, was well received. The key fact is that when Paul did arrive back in Corinth, he stayed there for no less than three months (Acts 20.3). This will have been the time, as is generally agreed, during which he composed his letter to Rome[514] — a massive undertaking which would have required calmness and ability to concentrate without continuous distraction.

The seemingly inescapable inference is that 2 Corinthians (in whatever form it reached Corinth) proved successful. The forebodings which had clouded the final paragraphs of 2 Corinthians (12.19–13.10) either failed to materialize or were soon dispelled by what proved to be the warmth of his reception. The outpouring of regret and affection which had resulted from 'the letter of tears' (7.6-13) probably ensured that Paul's further vigorous protest and sarcasm (chs. 10–13) evoked a fresh round of contrition at the too favourable response given to the incoming missionaries. The charges of malpractice were presumably withdrawn, the Corinthians accepted the good faith of Paul's policy of supporting himself,[515] and those whose life-style had caused such distress either reformed their conduct or withdrew from the assembly. Whether the 'false apostles' were in effect expelled or simply went on their way, the need for a sustained apologia for his own ministry disappeared. The resulting time spent in Corinth must have been one of the calmest and most rewarding of all Paul's ministry. That is not to say that the church of Corinth, having been an archetype of what could go wrong in a church, thereafter became a model approaching the ideal which 'the New Testament church' has often been held up to be. But that is a further story for a further volume *(1 Clement).*

514. See below, §33.2.
515. But perhaps he was the house-guest of Gaius during this time (Rom. 16.23).

The Close of a Chapter

33.1. A Final Circuit

As usual, Luke's account of the close of the Ephesus-centred phase of Paul's Aegean mission leaves many questions unanswered. The implication is that Paul left Ephesus because of the disturbances there (Acts 19.23-41) — the first such enforced departure for about four years on Luke's timescale. At the same time, the obvious deduction is that the trip to Macedonia (20.1-2) is the one referred to by Paul himself in 2 Corinthians (2 Cor. 2.12-13; 7.5-7), though Luke gives no hint whatsoever of the tensions between Paul and the church in Corinth or of Paul's personal inner turmoil reflected in these latter passages. As in other accounts covering days and weeks of travel, Luke describes the trip solely as one of successful pastoral ministry,[1] and as though Paul was travelling alone.

In his usual cursory fashion, when he does not want (for whatever reason) to elaborate his story, Luke simply mentions that Paul 'came to Greece, where he spent *(poiēsas)* three months' (Acts 20.2-3).[2] This hints at the sequel to the story left unresolved with 2 Corinthians: that Paul had followed up his letter(s) to Corinth by going on from Macedonia to Corinth in person. Luke's silence on the multiple tensions between Paul and the church of Corinth, however, has the regrettable corollary that he has no place to describe what we must assume (given that Paul stayed there as long as he did) was a welcome reunion, happy resolution of all (or almost all) suspicions, and healing of the much-bruised relationship.

Most baffling of all is Luke's silence on what must have been Paul's two principal priorities for his time in Corinth: the composition of his letter to the Christians in Rome, and the final preparations to gather in and organize the trans-

---

1. Cf. Acts 14.21-22; 16.4-5; 18.23.
2. For this use of *poiein* see Barrett, *Acts* 2.946.

port of the collection to Jerusalem. As noted at the end of §32, the former would have taken many days, and the sojourn in Corinth must have been such as to enable him to give the concentration which such a carefully composed letter would require. And the latter would have demanded a good deal of communication with the contributing churches,[3] organizing travel and hospitality for the gathering delegates and the onward travel to Jerusalem, and ensuring the security of the collection itself, with all the multitudinous but inescapable, time-consuming details involved. But Luke gives us no hint of any of this. More than any other of his editorial decisions, Luke's silence here must count as a dereliction of his responsibility as a historian. For, as we shall, both matters were of first importance for Paul, indeed the climax of his career, so that the gap Luke leaves here detracts more than any other from the value of his history of Christianity's beginnings.

The one hint that Luke has retained here in regard to the collection is in the list of the persons who accompanied Paul on his journey back to Jerusalem (20.4) — Sopater of Beroea, Aristarchus and Secundus of Thessalonica, Gaius of Derbe, Tychicus and Trophimus of Asia, as well as Timothy.[4] In Luke's account the reasons for the company are not given; as in 20.1-2, Luke often does not bother to mention companions. It is only Paul's letters that enable us to deduce that those named were almost certainly the representatives of the churches appointed by them to accompany the collection to Jerusalem (1 Cor. 16.3; 2 Cor. 8.23),[5] partly for safety reasons (the sum of money was no doubt large), but also to express in personal terms the sense of fellowship and spiritual debt owed by the diaspora churches to the mother church in Jerusalem (Rom. 15.27). What is noticeable is that they came from the principal theatres of Paul's mission: southern Galatia, Macedonia and Asia, though the absence of any one named from Achaia or Corinth itself remains a puzzle.[6] It is this representativeness of the group, that they could represent the full sweep of the Pauline mission to the Gentiles, which gives

3. The organization had been in hand for well over a year (1 Cor. 16.2-3; 2 Cor. 9.2).

4. Luke never mentions Paul's other close lieutenant in dealing with Corinth (Titus) — why, we don't know. Timothy is mentioned after Gaius (presumably since he also came from Galatia), but his native town/region is not mentioned (Lystra, 16.1), again presumably since he was a member of Paul's team more than a delegate of Lystra/Galatia.

5. As most agree; see Jervell, *Apg.* 498 and those mentioned in his n. 558.

6. Possibly the abruptness of the departure (20.3) came before the local arrangements were made or the delegates of the churches appointed, though that is unlikely, given that Achaia had been ready for a year (2 Cor. 9.2) and given Paul's commendation of Achaia's giving in Rom. 15.26. Or could it even be that Paul himself, now wholly reconciled to and one with the church in Corinth, was regarded by the Corinthians as himself sufficiently representative of their concerns — a fitting sequel to the months of suspicion as to Paul's motives and dealings reflected in 2 Corinthians (see above, §§32.6-7)? The absence of Philippi from the list might be covered by Acts 20.6; was Luke himself ('we') Philippi's delegate? Lüdemann's scepticism at this point is unwarranted (*Early Christianity* 225).

the clue: that this was Paul's (last) great effort to heal the breach with Jerusalem and the mission to Jews. All the more disappointing, then, that we have to piece together the significance of this enterprise from what Paul's letters tell us and are left by Luke in the dark as to its outcome. The disappointment is all the greater since the 'we' narrative picks up again at 20.5, most probably signalling that the narrator himself had joined the party, possibly even as one of the delegates.[7]

If we stick with Luke's account before examining Romans and the collection with the care they deserve, the next detail of interest is the fact that 'the Jews' re-emerge at the end of the three months as a united opposition[8] — the inference being that those who hatched the plot represented the bulk of the Jewish community in Corinth in their continuing opposition to the way of Jesus. Alternatively, since Corinth is not actually mentioned, and the plot is mentioned in close connection with Paul's travel plans, 'the Jews' may represent those Jews with whom Paul had been planning to travel directly to Jerusalem on a pilgrim ship.[9] For the plan itself we have the corroborating testimony of Rom. 15.25. The last-minute change of plan (20.3 — for Paul himself to return through Macedonia, rather than sail directly for Syria) was typical of the chopping and changing in his plans for which Paul had often to apologize.[10]

According to 20.5 Paul's companions (the delegates) were sent ahead to Troas — possibly in order to confuse any hostile intent, or to allow Paul one last visit to the churches of Macedonia. Did he already sense that this might be his last chance to see these churches which were so dear to his heart? But as so often, Luke covers the many miles in a few words. Of interest is his note that Paul remained at Philippi for Passover (20.6) — celebrated as a traditional feast, though now, presumably, with additional Christian significance.[11] The surprisingly long time taken for the journey from Philippi to Troas (five days; contrast 16.11)[12]

7. 'It is noteworthy that the "we-sections" begin again in Philippi, where they ceased in xvi.16. The obvious conclusion is that whatever may be the relation between the we-sections and the final form of Acts they represent the experience of someone who was in Philippi during the period of Paul's preaching in Thessalonica, Athens, Corinth, and Ephesus, and went with him from Philippi to Jerusalem, and ultimately to Rome' (Lake and Cadbury, *Beginnings* 4.253).

8. Note that it is in Corinth or Greece (not at all in Ephesus) that opposition from 'the Jews' recurs (cf. 18.12, 28 with 18.19 and 19.10, 17, 33-34; though note also 21.27-29).

9. Ramsay, *St. Paul* 287. That such pilgrims could be hostile to Paul is indicated in 21.27. See also below, n. 369.

10. Rom. 1.10-13; 1 Cor. 16.5-9; 2 Cor. 1.15-18; 1 Thess. 2.18. Lüdemann regards Rom. 15.25 as indicating an unchangeable resolve to travel directly to Jerusalem and so deduces that the itinerary of Acts 20.1-3 refers to the earlier trip to Jerusalem (18.22) (*Early Christianity* 224-25) — a strange mixture of rigidity and creative imagination in exegesis.

11. Luke 22.1, 7-20; cf. 1 Cor. 5.7-8.

12. But *achri,* usually marking a continuous extent of time up to a point, could be rendered 'within' five days (BDAG 160).

could be explained by adverse winds. Luke shows no embarrassment at presupposing the existence of a church at Troas whose founding he has not narrated (but cf. 2 Cor. 2.12).

Acts 20.7 gives us the first clear indication that Christians had begun to meet on Sunday.[13] The implication is that Paul delayed so long in Troas (despite his desire to reach Jerusalem in time for Pentecost — 20.16) because he wanted to share in the Sunday gathering.[14] The purpose of the gathering was 'to break bread' (20.7). Elsewhere in Acts this phrase denotes a shared meal,[15] but the enacted memory of the last supper may well have been part of it,[16] the whole meal being regarded as 'the dinner of the Lord', about which Paul had written quite recently to the Corinthians.[17]

The tragi-comic episode which follows is vividly recalled — the narrator was present in person (20.7b-12):[18] Paul going on talking hour after hour (again hints of foreboding and final farewells); the lights; the young man, Eutychus, sitting in the inset of a high window, dozing off and falling down; the immediate shock at his stillness (the narrative assumes he was dead); Paul ever the one to take the lead. The account of the healing action may reflect the influence of the similar exploits of Elijah and Elisha,[19] but that influence could as well have been on Paul himself (as he pondered what to do) as on Luke. It will not be accidental to Luke's scheme of things that a miracle of raising from the dead is thus attributed to Paul, as it had been to Peter in 9.40-41.

The details of Luke's account of the next stage of the journey (20.13-16)

---

13. Cf. 1 Cor. 16.2; Rev. 1.10; *Did.* 14.1; Ignatius, *Magn.* 9.1; *Barn.* 15.9; Pliny, *Ep.* 10.96.7.

14. The chronology of these verses — leaving Philippi after Passover, five days' travel, Sunday meeting — has encouraged the chronologists to calculate that the journey must have been undertaken in 57 CE (Jewett, *Dating Paul's Life* 47-50; Hemer, *Book of Acts* 169, 216), which is very plausible, though see Barrett's demurral (*Acts* 952); Fitzmyer prefers the spring of 58 (*Acts* 666).

15. As in 2.42 and most obviously in 27.35-36 (see below, §34 n. 179).

16. The Sunday in question was close to Passover (20.6).

17. 1 Cor. 11.20-26; cf. subsequently *Did.* 14.1; see above, §30.6b. The second breaking of bread in the middle of the night (Acts 20.11) must assuredly denote the opportunity to assuage hunger. In fact, it would have been (and is) typical of Jewish hospitality on such an occasion that a lengthy period of fellowship took place round the meal table and was interspersed with opportunities to partake of fresh supplies of food and drink (to think in terms of a modern sermon and eucharist would be anachronistic). See also Barrett, *Acts* 950-51, 955; contrast Haenchen, 'only a Eucharist without the proper character of a meal' (*Acts* 586), and Fitzmyer, who thinks the celebration of the eucharist was continued after some hours of Paul's discourse (*Acts* 669) — receiving the host for a second time in the same eucharist?!

18. There is no need to postulate a different 'we', as Dibelius and others have suggested (Jervell, *Apg.* 504).

19. 1 Kings 17.21 and 2 Kings 4.34-35; details in Barrett, *Acts* 954-55.

are among the most realistic of all Luke's historical recollections:[20] the special arrangement made by Paul to cross the Troas peninsula by foot while the others sailed round from Troas to Assos (20.13);[21] the island-by-island progress down the coast, each a day's sailing apart — Mitylene, Chios, Samos — and on to Miletus (20.14-15); the possibility for Ephesian believers to trek down to Miletus for a meeting with Paul (20.17-18); and the day-by-day account of the itinerary to Cos, Rhodes, to Patara (on the south of the Asia Minor land mass), and by-passing Cyprus to Tyre (21.1-3). The Aegean mission had come to its end.

We can imagine something of Paul's anguish in having to bypass Ephesus, the second main centre of his Aegean mission. The earlier part of the trip had probably taken the character of a sequence of farewell visits,[22] so that not to in-clude a visit to Ephesus itself must have been a trying, possibly heart-rending de-cision for Paul. Why then did he bypass Ephesus? Possibly because the earlier cri-sis at Ephesus had been more serious than Luke has let on; Paul could not be sure of his safety there.[23] But the reason Luke gives (in effect, to save time)[24] would have been sufficient explanation, even if Luke does not elucidate it. For there could have been no more appropriate time than the feast of Pentecost to offer the firstfruits of the Gentile mission in Jerusalem (the collection) and to acknowledge to Jerusalem the debt which Gentile experience of the Spirit owed (Rom. 15.16, 27). However, given the importance of Ephesus for Paul's Aegean mission, it was entirely fitting that Luke should include a speech to the Ephesian 'elders', a speech which catches well the sense of a chapter coming to its end, the end of the Aegean mission, the imminent end of Paul's mission as a whole, and the forebod-

20. Is it so difficult to imagine Luke many years later recalling this farewell journey of Paul, as Thornton suggests (*Zeuge* 276; followed by Jervell, *Apg.* 499-500, but also 506)?

21. 'The open water from Troas to Assos in the stormy north-east wind, prevalent about five days out of seven, can be most unpleasant in a small boat. Those who are only acquainted with modern steamers have no notion of the misery which can be caused by the Mediterranean' (Lake and Cadbury, *Beginnings* 4.257-58). Perhaps the difficult sail to Troas (20.6) had made the land journey to Assos more attractive for Paul.

22. This is not simply a deduction from the character of the speech provided in Acts 20.18-35; Paul himself was concerned at how his trip to Jerusalem would turn out (Rom. 15.31); even if it proved a success, Paul's intention was to go to Rome and on to Spain, rather than to return to the Aegean (Rom. 15.19, 23, 28).

23. See above, §32.2e.

24. Ephesus was not the most direct route (Lake and Cadbury, *Beginnings* 258). But Miletus was some thirty miles to the south of Ephesus, so it would be questionable how much time Paul saved by bypassing Ephesus; perhaps the captain gave him no choice in the matter. 'Samos would have been a more convenient meeting place' (Conzelmann, *Apg.* 116). Barrett wonders whether, in view of the considerable sum of money he was carrying, Paul might have felt safer in Miletus than in the great city of Ephesus (*Acts* 960). See also Rapske, 'Travel' 16-17, and discussion by Trebilco, *Early Christians* 173-74.

ing of his own death. This is how Luke chose to bring down the curtain on the Aegean mission. Paul chose to do it by writing his letter to the Christians in Rome.

33.2. The Reasons for Romans

Important as the collection was for Paul, much the most precious fruit to grow to maturity in the three months he spent in Corinth was his letter to the Christians in Rome. This was written while he was guest at the home of Gaius, whose house also served as the meeting place when 'the whole church (in Corinth)' came together (Rom. 16.23).[25] It was Gaius too, perhaps, or Phoebe, another of Paul's benefactors (Rom. 16.1-2), who was able to provide or finance the use of a skilled secretary or amanuensis, Tertius (Rom. 16.22), something particularly desirable in such a major composition, and itself signalling the care with which Paul set about composing the letter.[26] We need not imagine Paul spending day after day for the whole period on the letter. But neither is there any hint that he continued to work to maintain himself. More likely what detained him for so long in Corinth was the business of organizing the collection and the gathering to Corinth of the various delegates. But no doubt there would be long gaps when little more could be done and he could devote himself to the drafting and final composition of the letter.

a. Why the Letter to Rome?

There has been a surprisingly brisk debate about the reasons why Paul wrote Romans[27] — the briskness being partly the result of one or other favoured answer being pushed to the exclusion of others. In fact, it is easy to discern more than one motive in Paul's writing:

- to commend Phoebe to the Roman believers (Rom. 16.1-2); this motive need not unduly exaggerate the significance of these verses, for Phoebe probably acted as the bearer of the letter, and perhaps also as Paul's personal representative in reading and expanding on the letter to the various groupings in Rome, a role in which Paul could have coached her (see again §28.8c);[28]

25. See further above, §30.2a.
26. See further above, §29.8c.
27. See, e.g., A. J. M. Wedderburn, *The Reasons for Romans* (Edinburgh: Clark, 1988); K. P. Donfried, *The Romans Debate* (Peabody: Hendrickson, ²1991) part 1; K. Haacker, *Der Brief des Paulus an die Römer* (THNT 6; Leipzig: Evangelische Verlagsanstalt, 1999) 11-14; Schnelle, *History* 110-12, 127; Jewett, *Romans* 80-88.
28. Paul calls on the Roman congregations to 'assist her in whatever matter she may

- to prepare the congregations in Rome for his planned visit; this had been a trip long contemplated,[29] as was natural — how could the apostle to the Gentiles not preach in the capital city of the empire?[30]
- to canvas support from the Roman congregations for his intended mission to Spain (15.24, 28);[31] both verses imply that his own visit to Rome would be *en passant,* and Paul is explicit in his hope that they would send him on his way with financial and other support *(propemphthēnai);*[32]
- to gain the Roman Christians' support for his imminent visit to Jerusalem; its outcome was uncertain, in Paul's perspective (15.31), so support from the centre of the empire would be welcome;[33]
- to advise on problems among the Roman congregations,[34] which he pre-

---

have need of you' (Rom. 16.2). Jewett argues that Phoebe's role as patron of his projected Spanish mission (n. 31 below) was crucial and that the matter *(pragma)* of 16.2 is 'her missionary patronage' *(Romans* 89-91), but his translation gives the *pragma* ('matter, affair') a definiteness lacking in the Greek — 'whatever she needs in the matter', rather than 'whatever matter she may need help with'. He thinks it unlikely that the impoverished congregations could help her in her business (89) — but they could nevertheless 'participate in a credible manner' in the Spanish mission (88)!

29. Rom. 1.10-15; 15.23-24, 29, 32; Acts 19.21.

30. But it is not necessary to argue that, since he refused to 'build on someone else's foundation' (Rom. 15.20), Paul must have regarded Rome as lacking an apostolic foundation and have seen his task as establishing the church in Rome (cf. Klein and Watson in §29 n. 108 above): the lavish congratulations of 1.8 and 15.14 would be deceitful on that view; the degree of embarrassment experienced by Paul precisely on this point (see §29.4b) is clearly evident in 1.11-15; and anyway, Paul knows that there were apostles already associated with Rome — Andronicus and Junia (16.7). The reason why Paul did not use the term 'church' when speaking of the Roman believers as a whole (only in 16.5 — the house church of Prisca and Aquila) is less likely because he thought the church had not yet been founded and more likely because the congregations were still under the aegis of the synagogues, with only the household gathering of Prisca and Aquila as clearly distinct from any synagogue; cf. M. Nanos, *The Mystery of Romans: The Jewish Context of Paul's Letter* (Minneapolis: Fortress, 1996).

31. See now particularly Jewett, *Romans* 80-89. Jewett is the first to pay close attention to what would be involved in undertaking a mission in Spain, given, not least, the lack of Jewish settlement there and that Greek was not widely known (74-79), though the upshot is to raise questions about the viability of such a mission and about the realism of such an ambition. That the ambition was again inspired by Isa. 66.19 is nonetheless still possible (Riesner, *Paul's Early Period* 305).

32. *Propempō —* 'to assist someone on making a journey, *send on one's way* with food, money, by arranging for companions, means of travel, etc.' (BDAG 873).

33. Particularly argued by J. Jervell, 'The Letter to Jerusalem', in Donfried, *Romans Debate* 53-64.

34. Particularly P. S. Minear, *The Obedience of Faith: The Purpose of Paul in the Epistle to the Romans* (London: SCM, 1971); other bibliography is in my *Romans* lvii; also J. P. Sampley, 'The Weak and the Strong: Paul's Careful and Crafty Rhetorical Strategy in Romans

sumably learned through communications from one or other of those known personally to him and greeted in ch. 16; problems are hinted at in 12.14–13.7 and explicitly in 14.1–15.7, where Paul's experience of dealing with not too dissimilar situations in Corinth could stand him in good stead;
• to provide what Günther Bornkamm called Paul's 'last will and testament'; that is, Paul took the opportunity to draw together the insights and lessons he had learned in his missionary work to provide a synthesis of his theology.[35]

To say again, it is not necessary to play off these various 'reasons' against each other; Paul could certainly have had several in mind. What needs to be explained above all, however, is why the letter takes the form it does, why it goes into such detail, and why it is so dominated by the challenge of Jewish and Gentile believers recognizing and respecting each other as equal recipients of the gospel. Almost all of the above reasons, taken individually, fail to explain why such a lengthy exposition of his gospel was deemed necessary. For example, there is no hint that 'works of the law' or 'seed of Abraham' were issues in Rome; Paul's concern here is a reflection much more of the issues he had debated earlier, in Antioch and Galatia and no doubt elsewhere. Was it necessary to have such an extensive put-down of Jewish presumption (as we will see), if the real target was Gentile presumption and intolerance (as indicated in 11.17-24 and 14.1)?[36] Did Paul need to set out his gospel so fully simply in order to

---

14:1–15:13', in White and Yarbrough, eds., *The Social World of the First Christians* 40-52; W. L. Lane, 'Social Perspectives on Roman Christianity during the Formative Years from Nero to Nerva', in Donfried and Richardson, *First-Century Rome* 196-244 (here 199-202). See now particularly P. F. Esler, *Conflict and Identity in Romans: The Social Setting of Paul's Letter* (Minneapolis: Fortress, 2003): 'Paul seeks to reconcile Judeans and Greeks by reminding them of the new common ingroup identity that they share. . . . Paul had a particular purpose in writing to the Judean and non-Judean Christ-followers in Rome, in that he was attempting to exercise leadership over them' (133); the attempt illustrated by 7.1-6 (224-27).

35. G. Bornkamm, 'The Letter to the Romans as Paul's Last Will and Testament', in Donfried, *Romans Debate* 16-28: 'This great document, which summarizes and develops the most important themes and thoughts of the Pauline message and theology and which elevates his theology above the moment of definite situations and conflicts into the sphere of the eternally and universally valid, this letter to the Romans is the last will and testament of the Apostle Paul' (27-28). Similarly N. Dahl, 'The Missionary Theology in the Epistle to the Romans', *Studies in Paul* 70-94; Becker, *Paul* 262; E. Lohse, *Der Brief an die Römer* (KEK; Göttingen: Vandenhoeck und Ruprecht, 2003), describes the character of Romans as 'a sum(mation) of the gospel', pointing to the many passages which take up and develop thoughts and motifs which Paul had already used in his earlier letters (46; similarly *Paulus* 212-14).

36. In an extensive discussion of Romans (in excess of three hundred pages) Esler devotes only four of them to Rom. 2.1–3.20, a passage full of indicators of Paul's concern and how he sought to work it out, and less than one page to the climaxes of 11.25-32 and 15.7-13 (*Conflict and Identity* 150-54, 305-306, 354).

commend Phoebe, or to prepare the Roman congregations for his visit, or to deal with the pastoral problems in Rome?[37] After all, his reference to and quotation of various credal or kerygmatic summaries, and without further elaboration,[38] shows how much he could take for granted that they shared a faith in common. A much briefer letter of introduction or exhortation would have met these aims.

That Paul felt it necessary to spell out the gospel which he intended to preach in Spain would provide a better explanation, were it not for the fact that the Jewish/Gentile dimension of the letter would seem singularly inappropriate for a situation where there were, apparently, few if any Jews.[39] Again, while the extensive apology for his gospel would make a great deal of sense in view of Paul's imminent trip to Jerusalem, where he could expect to be quizzed and challenged in regard to it yet once more, it is less easy to see the logic of addressing this apology to the Roman believers and how he could hope for them to make any difference to what was to happen in Jerusalem. And for all its extent and theological contents, Romans can hardly count as a systematic statement of Paul's theology in the round, since it makes no attempt to expound and explain important features, for example, of Paul's christology and ecclesiology as we know them from his other letters. Nevertheless, the scope and length of the letter does seem to demand a reason somewhat as substantial as these.

What does become clear from the letter itself is that Paul saw himself at the end of what had been the most energetic, trying and fruitful periods of his mission.

- He had 'completed (the preaching of) the gospel of Christ *(peplērōkenai to euangelion tou Christou)* from Jerusalem and in a sweep round to Illyricum' (Rom. 15.19).[40] Clearly implied is
  - Paul's grand mission strategy;[41]
  - his conviction that a major segment had been completed;
  - and presumably his sense that he should move on to the next stage, presumably under the continuing impression that time was short.[42]

---

37. 'It is not the problems of a local church but the universal gospel and Paul's own mission which in this letter provide the point of departure for theological discussion' (Dahl, 'Missionary Theology' 78).

38. Rom. 1.3-4; 3.24/25-26; 4.24-25; 5.6, 8; 7.4; 8.11, 32, 34; 10.9; 14.15; see *Theology of Paul* 174-77.

39. Jewett, *Romans* 74-75.

40. See my *Romans* 864; Moo, *Romans* 895-96; Haacker, *Römer* 308.

41. See above, §29.4a.

42. See above, §29.3e; the *peplērōkenai* (15.19) echoes the *plērōma* ('full number') of 11.25.

- He no longer had scope/opportunity *(topos)* in these (Aegean) regions (15.23). The perspective is revealing:
  - given that he saw his task as planting the gospel securely in the major cities of the region, leaving it to the local believers to spread the gospel to surrounding cities and towns, his task in the Aegean was indeed complete;
  - even so, his dealings with Corinth were a reminder that his 'care for all the churches' was an ongoing burden, so that, again, the eschatological imperative must have been a major driving force.

In these circumstances, and given the relative calm of his few weeks in Corinth, Paul probably concluded that it was time to reflect on his mission to date, on its character, on the tensions and dissensions it had provoked, on what had proved to be most important in the gospel he had been preaching, on what needed to be carefully thought through and set down. No doubt the exercise was partly at least with a view to the apologia he might have to make in Jerusalem, and partly at least to persuade the Roman believers of the scope and implications of his gospel. But Paul's primary objective, I suspect (with Dahl and Lohse), was to think through his gospel in the light of the controversies which it had occasioned and to use the calm of Corinth to set out both his gospel itself and its ramifications in writing with a fullness of exposition which the previous trials and tribulations had made impossible and which would have been impossible to sustain in a single oral presentation.

As we shall see, what emerges clearly from Romans is that it was the tensions and issues that had been there from the beginning, in the confrontations in Jerusalem, in Antioch, in Galatia and (differently) in Corinth, which continued to preoccupy Paul's attention and to demand the sustained treatment which was now possible. These were the tensions and issues in a gospel which proclaimed a Jewish Messiah to a non-Jewish world: whether Gentile and Jew were in equal need of the gospel; how the God of Israel's justifying grace could extend to Gentiles; how the gospel, as compared with the Torah, deals with the reality of sin, the weakness of the flesh, and the power of death; in view of the gospel for all who believe, where Israel stands in the purpose of God; and how all this should work out in Rome itself. The fact that this letter is explicitly addressed to Gentiles,[43] and yet is so dominated by Jewish issues or, better, with the issue of the Jewishness of the gospel (how do Jew and Gentile stand in relation to each other, and how should they view each other before God? what is the role of the Torah for believers? who or what is 'Israel'?), has caused so much puzzlement among its interpreters.[44] And yet in effect it is precisely what occasions this puzzlement which

---

43. Rom. 1.6, 13; 11.13-32; 15.7-12, 15-16.
44. Esler insists on using the term 'Judean' (rather than 'Jew') for *Ioudaios* (*Conflict*

explains why the letter was written. For Paul's mission caused an equivalent puzzlement among many of his fellow Christian Jews (and probably many Gentile believers too); and, indeed, it is probably fair to conclude that it caused Paul some puzzlement as well, as he sought to respond to the call which he believed with all his heart had come to him on the Damascus road. Like a great thinker who has had to await retirement before he can find the time to set down his mature reflection, fruit of many individual controversies and essays, so Paul, arguably the greatest of Christian theologians, found just enough time in Corinth to set down this synthesis of his understanding of the most controversial aspect of his life's work: that the good news of Jesus Messiah is for all who believe.

b. The Congregations in Rome

How well did Paul know Rome and the circumstances of those to whom he addresses his letter? He would know well, of course, that it was the capital of the Roman Empire, whose *imperium* and influence he had sampled in centres like Philippi, Thessalonica and Ephesus. The history of Corinth and the fact that Corinth modelled itself so closely on Rome would have left him in no doubt as to how Roman power was exercised. Those he personally knew in Rome (Rom. 16.3-15) he must have met during their journeyings elsewhere,[45] and from such who were or had been previously resident in Rome he must have learned much about Rome.[46]

Almost certainly he would have known that there were many Jews living in Rome.[47] For example, he may have known some of the descendants of the Jews

---

and Identity 62-74) but does not take sufficient account of the fact that a more religious identity for *Ioudaios* had become increasingly common from the first century BCE as a result of an increasing number of proselytes, who by virtue of their acceptance of circumcision and 'judaizing' could be regarded as *Ioudaioi* (*Jesus Remembered* 262-63; J. C. Walters, *Ethnic Issues in Paul's Letter to the Romans* [Valley Forge: Trinity Press International, 1993] 58-59). Equally significant is Paul's redefinition of *Ioudaios* in non-ethnic terms (Rom. 2.28-29, a passage which Esler surprisingly passes over with minimal comment, and 1 Cor. 9.20, *Ioudaios* as an identity which Paul could assume or not). And we should recall the observation of Cassius Dio that the title *Ioudaioi* is given not only to those who come from *Ioudaia* (Judea), 'but it applies also to all the rest of mankind, although of alien race, who affect *(zēlousi)* their customs' (37.17.1 — *GLAJJ* 2.349, 351; see also W. Gutbrod, *TDNT* 3.370).

45. Jewett suggests that Paul may have met during their exile from Rome, not only Aquila and Prisca, but also Epainetus, Mary, Andronicus and Junia, Ampliatus, Urbanus, Stachys, Apelles, Herodion, Tryphaena, Tryphosa, Persis, Rufus and his mother (*Romans* 60-61).

46. In what follows I draw on my *Romans* xlv-liv.

47. Perhaps as many as 40,000 or 50,000 in the middle of the first century — Leon, *Jews of Ancient Rome* 135-36; A. D. Clarke, 'Rome and Italy', *BAFCS* 2.455-81 (here 464-68); 'at least

enslaved and taken to Rome in 62 BCE by Pompey after the latter's capture of Jerusalem (Philo, *Leg.* 155).[48] The expulsion of many Jews from Rome by Claudius was still a recent memory and had made possible Paul's abiding friendship with Prisca and Aquila (Acts 18.1-3).[49] And several of those whom he knew personally and to whom he sent his greetings were Jews — Andronicus, Junia and Herodion explicitly (*syngenēs*, 'compatriot, kin' — 16.7, 11), but also probably Prisca and Aquila, Mary, Rufus and his mother (16.3, 6, 13).[50] Add in Paul's experience of Jewish communities in the major Roman cities of his mission, their rights, the respect and sometimes suspicion in which they were held, and we can safely infer that Paul would have had a fair idea of the circumstances and overall low status of the large Jewish community in Rome.[51]

30,000' (Barclay, *Jews in the Mediterranean Diaspora* 295); 20,000 is the estimate of R. Penna, *Paul the Apostle*. Vol. 1: *Jew and Greek Alike* (Collegeville: Liturgical, 1996) 19-47 (here 30 and n. 53), and of R. Brändle and E. Stegemann, 'The Formation of the First "Christian Congregations" in Rome in the Context of the Jewish Congregations', in Donfried and Richardson, *First-Century Rome* 117-27 (here 120). See also the classic study of G. La Piana, 'Foreign Groups in Rome during the First Centuries of the Empire', *HTR* 20 (1927) 183-403 (here 341-93); Smallwood, *Jews* 201-10; Gruen, *Diaspora* ch. 1; M. H. Williams, 'The Shaping of the Identity of the Jewish Community in Rome in Antiquity', in Zangenberg and Labahn, eds., *Christians as a Religious Minority in a Multicultural City* 33-46. The names of no less than eleven synagogues have been identified — Leon ch. 7; Levinskaya, *BAFCS* 5.182-85; *JIWE* 2 index (539-40); summarized by Jewett, *Romans* 57 (with bibliography). P. Richardson, 'Augustan-Era Synagogues in Rome', in Donfried and Richardson, *First-Century Rome* 17-29, takes up from Leon and notes that four or five of the synagogues can be dated to the first century: those of the Hebrews, the Augustesians, the Agrippesians, the Volumnesians, and probably the Herodians (19-28). Synagogues could not be named after such powerful individuals (Augustus himself; Marcus Agrippa, Augustus's right-hand man; Herod the Great; Volumnius, probably a tribune of Syria) without their knowledge and permission, which implies a degree of status accorded to and integration achieved by these synagogues. Leon's argument that the Rome synagogues lacked a central controlling organisation, each synagogue organizing and directing its own affairs separately, is generally accepted (168-70; see, e.g., Levinskaya 185-92; Penna, *Paul* 1.27-34).

48. See §24.2a above for the possibility that the Libertini in Jerusalem mentioned in Acts 6.9 were descendants of such Jews who had been taken captive from Judea into slavery in Rome and subsequently freed (Philo, *Legat.* 155). Most of the names in the list of greetings in 16.3-15 were common among slaves, freedmen and freedwomen — including the Jews Junia and (probably) Rufus; see above, §30 at n. 156.

49. See above, §31.4b.

50. Lampe, *Paul to Valentinus* 74-75. Numbers of Christians in Rome at this time are often assumed to be quite small (Spence suggests approximately 250-500 [*Parting* 286-87]), but less than ten years later they could be described as 'a great multitude' (*1 Clem.* 6.1) and 'vast numbers (*multitudo ingens*)' (Tacitus, *Ann.* 15.44.2-4), when accused of starting the fire of Rome in 64; from which Jewett reckons that the number must have grown to several thousand by then (*Romans* 61-62).

51. 'It was precisely the low grade of many Jewish occupations and Jewish poverty that

Paul's knowledge would presumably extend to the beginnings of the Christian movement in Rome.[52] His gratitude to God that their faith was being proclaimed throughout the world (1.8) need not be dismissed as mere formal pleasantry but reminds us of the network of communication which quickly developed among the churches of the diaspora.[53] His friendship with Prisca and Aquila would have informed him of the circumstances — the unrest in the Roman synagogues occasioned by (the preaching of) Chrestus/Christ — which had occasioned their departure from Rome.[54] In addition, Paul evidently knew leaders of several of Rome's house churches (16.3-15).[55] Above all, he knew personally Andronicus and Junia, his kinsfolk, with whom he had spent some time in prison (16.7). More to the point, he describes them as 'outstanding among the apostles, who were in Christ before me' (16.7).[56] In Paul's parlance one of the chief marks of an apostle was that he or she was (commissioned to be) a church-founder; it will be recalled that Paul made much of this in writing to the Corinthians — even if some did not regard Paul as an apostle, at least he was apostle to the Corinthians, because he had brought them to faith (1 Cor. 9.1-2).[57] To be noted is the fact that in the NT the only ones to be linked directly to Rome as 'apostles' are Andronicus and Junia. In Paul's perspective (apostles as church founders), that presumably means that he regarded them as among the first to bring the gospel to Rome, the founders of one or more of the Roman congregations.[58] That he refers

evoked the contempt of Roman authors' (S. Applebaum, 'The Social and Economic Status of the Jews in the Diaspora', in S. Safrai and M. Stern, eds., *The Jewish People in the First Century,* vol. 2 [Assen: Van Gorcum, 1976] 701-27 [here 721]). See also Penna, *Paul* 1.38-40, who laments how little we know of the Jewish community in Rome (45-46).

52. Lampe provides an impressive demonstration of the likelihood that the earliest Christians (and so also the earliest churches) were concentrated in Trastevere (Transtiberinus) and Porta Campena, both where the poorest of Rome's residents lived, and perhaps already also on the Aventine and in Mars Field (Campus Martinus), both more mixed, socially (*Paul to Valentinus* chs. 3-4); summarized in 'Early Christians in the City of Rome: Topographical and Social Historical Aspects of the First Three Centuries', in Zangenberg and Labahn, eds., *Christians as a Religious Minority in a Multicultural City* 20-32. See more briefly Lichtenberger, 'Jews and Christians in Rome' 2158-60. See also A. du Toit, '"God's Beloved in Rome" (Rom 1:7): The Genesis and Socio-Economic Situation of the First-Generation Christian Community in Rome', *Focusing on Paul* 179-202; and above, §30.2a.

53. See §30.8 above.

54. See above, §28 nn. 40, 41, 44.

55. Five different groupings/congregations can be discerned in Romans 16; see, e.g., my *Romans* lii; Jewett, *Romans* 61. Lampe thinks that seven or eight different house or apartment groups can be postulated (*Paul to Valentinus* 359-60); similarly Schnabel, *Mission* 812-13.

56. See my *Romans* 894-95; Fitzmyer, *Romans* 739; and above, §29 n. 82 above.

57. See further §29.3f above.

58. See more fully my *Romans* 894-95, and above, §29 at n. 82; cf. Fitzmyer, *Romans* 33; Bauckham, 'Jesus and the Jerusalem Community' 71-72. However, there is no tradition to

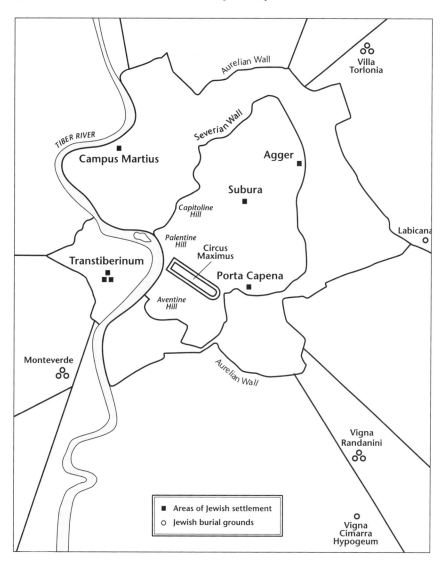

Rome, Showing the Location of Jewish Communities

to them as apostles 'in Christ before me' also presumably signals that he recognized their precedence before himself in the ranks of apostles.[59] Whatever their precise status, therefore, we can be sure that Paul's knowledge of the beginnings of Christianity in Rome was quite extensive.

Paul would have known, then, that the gospel of Messiah Jesus had first come to Rome within the context of the Jewish synagogues, one or several.[60] Whether or not this gospel was open to Gentiles from the first, or reflected the opening to Gentiles made by Hellenist believers, or indeed was influenced at some remove by the earliest reports of the Pauline mission, we cannot say.[61] But evidently Gentiles were drawn in quite quickly — presumably God-fearers who

---

that effect. Despite Andronicus and Junia being named 'apostles' in Rome, Brändle and Stegemann assert that no missionary activity in Rome is known to us ('Formation' 127). Other influence of Jewish merchants (or slaves) cannot of course be excluded or of visitors returning to Rome from a pilgrim feast in Jerusalem (cf. Acts 2.10; see, e.g., Schnelle, *History* 112; Lampe, *Paul to Valentinus* 165; Schnabel, *Mission* 804-805; R. Hvalvik, 'Jewish Believers and Jewish Influence in the Roman Church until the Early Second Century', in Skarsaune and Hvalvik, eds., *Jewish Believers in Jesus* 179-216 [here 187-89]); Becker suggests that 'unknown Christians, who were won by the mission of Stephen, were the first to promote Christ in Rome' (*Paul* 336); with a view to Acts 28.13-24, Lampe draws attention to the Puteoli-Rome trade axis, the harbour of Puteoli rather than of Ostia being the main gateway of Rome to the East (9-10). Lampe, 'Paths of Early Christian Mission into Rome: Judaeo-Christians in the Households of Pagan Masters', in S. McGinn, ed., *Celebrating Romans: Template for Pauline Theology,* R. Jewett FS (Grand Rapids: Eerdmans, 2004) 143-48, also suggests that 'it was through the Jewish members of the households mentioned in Rom. 16.10 in particular 'that Jewish-Christianity found one of its ways into the city of Rome' (148). On the later tradition attributing the foundation of the Roman church to Peter, see Fitzmyer 29-30: 'There is no reason to think that Peter spent any major portion of time in Rome before Paul wrote his letter, or that he was the founder of the Roman church or the missionary who first brought Christianity to Rome' (30).

59. The commendation of Andronicus and Junia as 'outstanding among the apostles' and 'in Christ before me' is neatly complemented by Paul's own self-assessment as 'the least of the apostles' (1 Cor. 15.9), though more effective in preaching the gospel (15.10-11).

60. Often cited is the note of Ambrosiaster (fourth century) that the Romans 'embraced faith in Christ, though according to Jewish rite, without seeing any sign of miracles and without any of the apostles' (*PL* 17.46; see, e.g., Fitzmyer, *Romans* 30-31; Moo, *Romans* 4). Brown argues that 'the dominant Christianity at Rome had been shaped by the Jerusalem Christianity associated with James and Peter, and hence was a Christianity appreciative of Judaism and loyal to its customs' (Brown and Meier, *Antioch and Rome* 110). See further Brown's response to criticism of his views — 'Further Reflections on the Origins of the Church of Rome', in Fortna and Gaventa, eds., *Studies in Paul and John* 98-115.

61. There is nothing to support the further alternative that the earliest Roman 'Christianity' was a quite different form of belief in/about Jesus (e.g., a 'Q Christianity'). On the contrary, it is noticeable that Paul takes it for granted that the believers in Rome had been converted by the same gospel that he preached.

had participated in varying degrees in the life of one or other of the Rome synagogues. Quite possibly it was the fact that the message of Christus (Chrestus) was attracting so many Gentiles which provoked the unrest reported by Suetonius, and possibly those who were targetted for expulsion were primarily those Jewish individuals (like Aquila and Prisca) who had been most active in such evangelism.[62]

We can even make a confident guess that Paul would have been well informed as to the current circumstances of the Christians in Rome; after all, he knew personally members of the five (or more) apartment churches in Rome (Rom. 16.3-16).[63] From the presence of Christian Jews in Rome, greeted by Paul (16.3-15), we can deduce that with Claudius's death (54) the likelihood is that Claudius's edict lapsed and Jews like Aquila and Priscilla, Andronicus and Junia returned to Rome to claim property, revive business interests, and so forth.[64] It was this return which probably explains the friction which Paul addresses in Rom. 14.1–15.6: that in the absence of Christian Jewish leadership, the direction of several/most of the apartment churches passed to non-Jews; and that the Gentile leadership had to be encouraged to welcome (back) the returning Jewish believers — for reasons which will become clearer below; 'Welcome the one who is weak in faith . . .'; 'Welcome one another' (14.1; 15.7).[65] Apart from anything else, the need to counter such a Gentile 'takeover' of the infant Christian movement in Rome would explain Paul's insistence that Gentile believers should not adopt a supercilious attitude towards the Jews who were their fellow believers.[66] It should be noted, however, that Paul

62. See again §28 nn. 40, 41, 44. J. C. Walters, 'Romans, Jews, and Christians: The Impact of the Romans on Jewish-Christian Relations in First-Century Rome', in Donfried and Richardson, *First-Century Rome* 175-95, suggests that it was 'aggressive proselytizing' which attracted the scrutiny of Roman administrators (181-82). Lane suggests that the decree was directed against the members of only one or two specific synagogues ('Roman Christianity' 204).

63. See above, n. 55.

64. The extent and effectiveness of the decree anyway are uncertain. Tacitus notes that the decree to expel astrologers from Italy (in 52) was 'stringent but ineffectual' (*Ann.* 12.52).

65. This was the case argued particularly by W. Wiefel, 'The Jewish Community in Ancient Rome and the Origins of Roman Christianity', *Judaica* 26 (1970) 65-88, reprinted in Donfried, *Romans Debate* 85-101, which has proved persuasive for many; see, e.g., Walters, *Ethnic Issues* ch. 3; Fitzmyer, *Romans* 33, 77-78; Moo, *Romans* 13, 19; Brändle and Stegemann, 'Formation' 126-27; Jewett, *Romans* 61. See also A. Pitta, 'The Strong, the Weak and the Mosaic Law in the Christian Communities of Rome (Rom. 14.1–15.13)', in Zangenberg and Labahn, eds., *Christians as a Religious Minority in a Multicultural City* 90-102; Hvalvik, 'Jewish Believers' 192-96. Whether we should speak of 'opponents' of Paul in Rome is another question; see S. E. Porter, 'Did Paul Have Opponents in Rome and What Were They Opposing?', in S. E. Porter, ed., *Paul and His Opponents* (Leiden: Brill, 2005) 149-68.

66. Rom. 11.17-24; 12.3; 14.3, 10; 15.1. It is presumably Paul's sense that he was addressing (primarily) a predominantly Gentile audience which explains the data in n. 43 above. A. A. Das, *Solving the Romans Debate* (Minneapolis: Fortress, 2007), follows S. K. Stowers, *A Rereading of Romans* (New Haven: Yale University, 1994), in arguing that Romans is addressed to a Gentile au-

assumed that Jewish believers (returnees) were seeking to be part of these (Gentile) churches, rather than attempting to form their own (Jewish exiles only) churches. How well integrated the several apartment congregations were with each other it is hardly possible to say, though Paul seems to have been confident that his letter would reach 'all who are in Rome, called to be saints' (1.7). Nor can we be sure of the relationships between the house churches and the synagogues at this time.[67] Despite the common deduction made by many that the house churches from 49 on were quite separate from the Jewish community,[68] the degree of their independence is unclear, partly because most of the Gentile believers had probably been God-fearing adherents of one of the Rome synagogues,[69] and partly because the legal status of the house churches would be still dependent on their being assumed to be an offshoot of the Jewish community.[70]

---

dience. But 14.1–15.7 makes most sense if more traditionalist Jewish believers are in view (see below at n. 270), and the greetings of ch. 16, which include several identifiably Jewish (see above, at n. 50), obviously envisage those to be greeted as members of the congregations addressed (rather than as 'third parties', as Das argues). The most obvious conclusion is the broad consensus that the congregations were mixed, with non-Jewish believers in the majority; see also Watson, *Paul, Judaism and the Gentiles* (²2007) 175-91. Lampe estimates the Jewish component of the Roman Christians in Romans 16 as 15 percent ('The Roman Christians of Romans 16', in Donfried, ed., *Romans Debate* 216-30 [here 225]), a figure Spence thinks is too low (*Parting* 277).

67. The evidence of Acts 28 is too enigmatic and may be too much coloured by Luke's programme for firm deductions to be made; see further below, §34.3c.

68. E.g., Schnelle: the expulsions of 49 'accomplished the final separation between the Christian community and the synagogue' (*History* 112); Lichtenberger, 'Jews and Christians in Rome' 2168, 2173; Hvalvik, 'Jewish Believers' 198-99. Spence concludes a lengthy study entitled '"Christianity" and the Synagogue of Rome' by noting, 'It is certain that by the time Paul wrote to the Christians in Rome, there existed a social community distinct from the synagogue and consisting of ethnic-Jews and ethnic-Gentiles brought together by faith in Jesus Christ'; his thesis is that 'the expulsion [in 49 under Claudius] resulted in either the establishment of a Christian community in Rome distinct from the Jewish community or hastened its development' (*Parting of the Ways* 117). But his discussion is flawed by repeated reference to the 'church' as a clearly defined entity (e.g., 31-32, 60-61) — he dismisses the significance of the absence of *ekklēsia* from Rom. 1.7 too lightly (281-83); and the appeal to Acts 28 (10, 114) is undermined by Luke's failure to mention any believers in Rome itself (see again §34.3c below).

69. For several centuries subsequently Christian leaders found it necessary to exhort their congregations not to attend Jewish synagogues and not to observe Jewish feasts and customs (see my *Partings* [²2006] xix-xx, 344-46), so it is entirely likely that God-fearing Gentiles saw their faith in Messiah Jesus as an extension of their earlier adherence to a synagogue community.

70. See above, §30 n. 122, and §31.4c. But I cannot follow the thesis of Mark Nanos that the Roman believers were still wholly 'under the authority of the synagogue' (*The Mystery of Romans* 30-31, 72-75); see, e.g., my critique in *Theology of Paul* 675 n. 9 and 684 n. 59. In contrast, Watson still maintains (though with less emphasis) his thesis that Paul tried to persuade his Roman readers 'to make a final break with the Jewish community. He wishes to turn a failed reform-movement into a sect' (*Paul, Judaism and the Gentiles* [¹1986] 106; [²2007] 188, 260,

In addition it is hardly stretching probability to assume that communication between Rome and Corinth, between which centres there would have been continual coming and going, brought Paul regular news of the political and social conditions of the believers in Rome. Such must be the source of Paul's awareness of the vulnerability of the Roman congregations implied in the counsels of 12.14-21 (petty persecution and insult) and 13.1-7 (the importance of respecting the power civic authorities). Rom. 13.7 ('Render to everyone their dues, tribute to whom tribute is due, tax to whom tax is due')[71] may well provide an illuminating shaft of light into the situation in Rome in the mid-50s. For we know from Tacitus (*Ann.* 13) that in the year 58 there was persistent public complaint regarding indirect taxes *(vectigalia),* so it is quite likely that at the time of writing (two years earlier?) indirect taxation was already a sensitive issue for Jewish and Christian traders, tempted as they must have been to question whether the tax-collectors *(publicani)* were demanding too much over the set rate of tax.[72] At any rate, it is very likely that the otherwise unexpected advice to the Roman believers to 'pay their taxes' was prompted by Paul's knowledge of the situation confronting the Christian groupings in Rome.

None of this puts in question the main contention of §33.2a, for the great weight of the exposition of the body of the letter (1.16–11.36) is hardly likely to find sufficient reason or explanation in Paul's knowledge of the particularities of the Roman Christians' circumstances in Rome. But it does reinforce the point that the exposition was not a merely theoretical or abstract exercise on Paul's part but was born of his experience of mission in many Roman cities and had very direct relevance to the situation of the churches in Rome.

33.3. Paul's Letter to Rome

Whereas 2 Corinthians raises continuing (and unanswerable) questions about its unity as a single letter, what used to be described as the 'integrity' of Romans is

---

343), an intention which is nowhere explicit in Romans and which runs counter to the theological logic of passages like 4.11-12; 9.3-4; 11.17-24; 15.7-12, 25-27; the confusing evidence of Acts 28.17-24 (see §§34.3c-d below) should not be ignored completely.

71. The distinction between *phoros* ('tribute') and *telos* ('tax') corresponds to the difference between *tributum* (direct taxes from which Roman citizens would have been exempt in Italy and colony-cities) and the more substantial *vectigalia* (initially revenue from rents on state property, but in Paul's time extended to cover indirect taxes as well, mainly customs duties); for details see *OCD*[3] 1583, 1228.

72. See particularly J. Friedrich, W. Pöhlmann and P. Stuhlmacher, 'Zur historischen Situation und Intention von Römer 13,1-7', *ZTK* 73 (1976) 131-66; followed, e.g., by my *Romans* liii-liv; Fitzmyer, *Romans* 35-36, 78-79; Lohse, *Römer* 358.

of minor consideration. A view popular two generations ago (that ch. 16 was actually addressed to Ephesus) has been largely abandoned.[73] And questions about the ending of the letter (particularly the status of 16.25-27)[74] do not affect the body of the letter. Nor indeed are currently popular discussions regarding the appropriate rhetorical classification for the letter — epideictic, deliberative, protreptic, or what?[75] — proving very helpful in clarifying the impact which the main thrust of the letter must have had on the first audiences in Rome.[76]

a. The Main Thrust of the Letter

There should be little doubt as to the principal theme of Romans. It is given in the opening section of the letter. By that I refer not only to 1.16-17, which is almost universally agreed to be the thematic statement for the letter as a whole. I refer also to 1.1-5. Here again it is usually recognized that Paul provides a (more) widely known credal statement (1.3-4) in order to serve as his calling-card and reassurance of good faith.[77] What needs to be emphasized, more than is often the case, however, is that these opening verses serve also as a statement of Paul's gospel, indicating what is central to it.[78] The importance of the passage for the letter as a whole is indicated by the way Paul disrupts the customary epistolary opening (self-introduction, naming recipients) by inserting this statement of 'the gospel of God'. Paul's tactic is the same as the one he employed in writing to the Galatians, whose unexpected opening and vehemence must have rivetted the attention of the Galatian congregations when they heard it read to them.[79] Similarly here, and in what was a much more carefully planned and worded letter, the opening part of chapter 1 must have been intended to signal to the Roman audiences what lay at the heart of the gospel for Paul.

73. See, e.g., Schnelle, *History* 118-19, 127; Murphy-O'Connor, *Paul* 324-28; and particularly H. Gamble, *The Textual History of the Letter to the Romans* (Grand Rapids: Eerdmans, 1977), and Lampe, *Paul to Valentinus* 153-64.

74. See, e.g., Metzger, *Textual Commentary* 533-36.

75. See, e.g., Donfried, *Romans Debate* — essays by Wuellner, Stirewalt and Aune in particular; and Jewett, *Romans* 41-46.

76. It should be clear that in what follows I draw on my *Romans* and *Theology of Paul* (itself set out as an exposition of Paul's theology at the time he wrote Romans), even where I do not cite them specifically.

77. For the debate on whether Paul adapted or modified an earlier formula, see my *Romans* 5-6, 11-16; also *Theology of Paul* 242-43; Jewett, *Romans* 103-109.

78. Moo, *Romans* 25; N. T. Wright, 'The Letter to the Romans', *New Interpreter's Bible* (Nashville: Abingdon, 2002) 10.415-16, 419. Barnett sees the credo of Rom. 1.1-4 as both summarizing 'the teaching of the apostles' and serving as a template for Paul's synagogue teaching (*Birth* 92). In contrast, Esler largely ignores the christology of key passages like 1.3-4, 3.22-26 and 8.3, 32-34 (*Conflict and Identity* 136-37, 155-68, 244, 265-66).

79. See above, §31.7b.

> ¹. . . the gospel of God ²which was promised beforehand through his
>   prophets in the holy Scriptures. ³It concerns his Son
>   who was descended from the seed of David in terms of the flesh,
>   ⁴and who was appointed Son of God in power in terms of the spirit of
>   holiness as from the resurrection of the dead,
> Jesus Christ our Lord, ⁵through whom we received grace and apostleship
>   with a view to the obedience of faith among all the nations for the
>   sake of his name.

In this neatly compressed summary statement Paul gives clear expression to what was evidently of first importance in his understanding of the gospel which he shared with the recipients of the letter:[80]

- The fact of central importance is that the gospel is about Jesus, God's son: both his life and mission as son of David, and his resurrection from the dead as Lord. With epigrammatic conciseness Paul highlights both the fact that Jesus is the royal Messiah ('seed of David') of Israel's hopes and expectations,[81] and the fact that this same Jesus is now exalted Lord, in whom the resurrection of the dead has already begun.[82]
- The first emphasis is underlined by the introduction's explicit assertion that this gospel, of this Jesus, is the fulfilment of the prophetic promises of Israel's Scriptures (1.2).
- The second emphasis is elaborated by drawing from the whole statement of faith Paul's own commission as apostle to the nations/Gentiles; it is this gospel which he has been commissioned to preach,[83] this gospel by means of which he is to bring Gentiles to 'the obedience of faith' (1.5) — among whom, of course, are (most of) the Roman believers themselves (1.6).

What thus becomes immediately clear from this finely contrived formulation is Paul's double intent in this letter: to make clear both *the integrally Jewish charac-*

---

80. Paul could evidently assume that 'gospel' would be a familiar term to the Roman believers, and with the connotations which were distinctive of Christian usage; the development of this distinctively Christian usage seems to have been largely due to Paul himself (*Theology of Paul* 164-69), but he could evidently assume that the usage would be familiar in congregations he had never visited personally.

81. The political overtones of the confession (Jesus as Israel's royal Messiah) are evident, but expressed as Paul has done, it is unlikely that they would have been recognized by any spies in the Roman congregations.

82. See above, §23.4a.

83. Paul's apostolic commissioning is emphasized, but evidently it did not need to be defended as in Galatians. Here again it is a striking fact that Paul could assume so much on the part of his Roman audiences.

ter of the gospel, and that precisely this gospel is the good news he has been commissioned to bring *before the nations;*[84] and to underline that it is in Jesus, God's son, that the double character of the gospel and of his own commission comes together, Jesus Christ our Lord as the fulcrum point on which everything turns. As he reminds them a few sentences later in solemn affirmation: it is *God* he serves in the gospel of his *Son* (1.9).

> [16]I am not ashamed of the gospel, since it is the power of God for salvation to all who believe, Jew first but also Gentile. [17]For the righteousness of God is being revealed in it from faith to faith — as it is written, 'He who is righteous by faith shall live'.

Here too, with wonderful economy of language, Paul succeeds in setting out the key emphases which he wanted to bring out in his letter.

- Central to Paul's concern, as apostle and writer of Romans, was his conviction that the gospel is *to all who believe, Jew first but also Gentile.* This is not a simple statement of (naïve) universalism ('to all who believe'); the 'all' Paul had in mind, here as elsewhere in Romans,[85] was the 'all' that transcends and breaks down the barrier between Jew and Greek,[86] between Jews and Gentiles.[87]
- The means by which the gospel achieves its goal of salvation is *faith,* that is, self-evidently in view of the preceding statement of 'the gospel' (1.3-4),

---

84. It is precisely this double aspect (*Jewish* gospel to the *nations*) which explains Paul's constant side-glances to the (ethnic) Jewish element among the Rome apartment congregations (see above, §33.2a).

85. 'In all the nations' (1.5); 'to all who believe' (1.16); 'to all who believe' (3.22); 'father of all who believe' (4.11); 'to all the seed' (4.16); 'to all' (5.18); 'gave his Son for us all' (8.32); 'to all who believe' (10.4); 'all who believe' (10.11); 'he is Lord of all, rich towards all who call upon him' (10.12); 'everyone who calls upon the name of the Lord' (10.12); 'God has confined all in disobedience in order that he might have mercy on all' (11.32); 'all the nations, all the peoples' (15.11); echoed in the 'all's of 1.18, 29; 2.1, 9, 10; 3.9, 12, 19, 20, 23; 5.12.

86. 'Jew and Greek' — Rom. 1.16; 2.9-10; 3.9; 10.12. The importance of Paul's juxtaposition of Jew and Greek should not be missed, and the phrase should not be regarded as simply a variation of 'Jew and Gentile'. The latter was a Jewish perspective (no non-Jew would call himself a 'Gentile'; 'Gentiles', it should not be forgotten, translates *ethnē,* 'nations'). But 'Greek' was a self-identification of pride ('Greek and barbarian' was a perspective on the world equivalent to 'Jews and Gentiles', as Paul well knew — 1.14). So Paul's 'Jew and Greek' embraces the two dominant ethnic and cultural perspectives which his mission confronted in the cities of Asia Minor, Macedonia and Greece. See also C. D. Stanley, '"Neither Jew nor Greek": Ethnic Conflict in Graeco-Roman Society', *JSNT* 64 (1996) 101-24.

87. 'Jews and Gentiles' — Rom. 3.29; 9.24.

faith in the Jesus of 1.3-4.[88] It is because the gospel is so directed (to 'the obedience of *faith*' — 1.5) that it can have its immediate impact on both Jew and Gentile: to Jew first, since this Jesus is Messiah, son of David; but also and equally to Gentile, since (by implication) its saving effect on Gentiles is not dependent on their ceasing to be Gentiles (that is, by becoming 'Jews', proselytes to Judaism).

• More fully explained, the gospel 'works' by revealing, bringing to direct expression, *the righteousness of God.* No one with knowledge of Israel's Scriptures, as we may assume also for Gentile God-fearers, could fail to recognize a major motif of Israel's theology and understanding of how God conducts his dealings with his creation and his chosen people (Israel).[89] For the phrase expresses God's enactment of the obligation he had accepted in so creating and so choosing: to sustain and save both.[90] For Jews the phrase had an inescapably covenant connotation: it denoted God's *saving* righteousness[91] and merged naturally into thought of God's 'faithfulness'.[92] Since it was revealed

88. Precisely what this 'faith' involves will be one of Paul's principal concerns to elucidate in the letter — particularly Romans 4 and 9.30–10.13.

89. The fact that Paul introduces the term without explanation can only mean that he was assuming that his Roman audiences would be familiar with the term, and with the connotation he was drawing from it. The point does not depend on earlier usage of the phrase 'the righteousness of God' as such; see, e.g., Hultgren, *Paul's Gospel and Mission* 18-26. The theological focus and framework of the christology ('the gospel of God', 'the righteousness of God') should not be missed (Wilckens, *Theologie* 1/3.172).

90. For 'righteousness' as a relational term, denoting that which meets the obligations laid upon the individual by the relationship of which he or she is part, see my *Theology of Paul* 341-44 and the bibliography there. I also note that the relational character of God's righteousness undercuts the traditional debates of post-Reformation theology as to whether 'the righteousness of God' is a subjective or objective genitive, 'an activity of God' or 'a gift bestowed by God' — a case of unnecessary and unjustified either-or exegesis (344). M. A. Seifrid, 'Righteousness Language in the Hebrew Scriptures and Early Judaism', in Carson et al., *Justification and Variegated Nomism* 1.415-42, warns against putting too much stress on the relational aspect of 'righteousness'; but see my *New Perspective on Paul* (2005) 58-60, (2008) 63-65.

91. In the Hebrew Bible *tsedhaqah* ('righteousness') is often better translated 'deliverance' or 'vindication' (e.g., Pss. 51.14; 65.5; 71.15; Isa. 46.13; 51.5-8; 62.1-2; Mic. 6.5; 7.9).

92. Here Seifrid has some justification for his criticism of N. T. Wright, who repeatedly defines divine righteousness as 'the covenant faithfulness of God' ('Romans and the Theology of Paul', in D. M. Hay and E. E. Johnson, eds., *Pauline Theology.* Vol. 3: *Romans* [Minneapolis: Fortress, 1995] 30-67). The fact remains, however, that for Paul 'righteousness' and 'faithfulness' would have been overlapping terms, both expressing aspects of the Hebrew *'emeth,* whose basic sense is 'that on which others can rely' (A. Jepsen, *'aman, TDOT* 1.313); see also Lohse, *Paulus* 199-204. But there is scope for confusion here, since the other key term, *pistis,* covers the spectrum 'faith/faithfulness', and the issue of where *pistis* lies on that spectrum in Paul's usage lies close to the heart of Paul's argument in Romans (see below, §33.3c, and further my 'Faith, Faithfulness', *NIDB* 2.407-23).

by the gospel, 'the power of God for *salvation*', Paul had surely done enough to ensure that the recipients of his letter would understand this 'righteousness' as *saving* righteousness.[93]

- But again, as of crucial importance, Paul insists that the medium through which this righteousness comes to saving effect is *faith*. He underscores the point: 'from faith to faith'.[94] And he reinforces it with a scriptural warrant or proof, drawn from Hab. 2.4: 'He who is righteous by faith shall live'. But he quotes it in such a way that the 'by faith' can have maximum reference — both to the way in which a person becomes 'righteous' and to the way in which the 'righteous' should live.[95] In so doing, in effect Paul gives more flesh to the earlier and otherwise puzzling 'obedience of faith' (1.5): that faith (in God and now in his Christ) is the only basis for a saving relationship with God and so also the only means by which that relationship can be sustained — obedience as the expression and fruit of faith, not obedience to Torah as something different.

Here again it becomes clear that Paul's whole *raison d'etre* as an apostle was to bridge the divide which had characterized God's purpose from the first choice of Abraham, of Isaac and not Ishmael, of Jacob and not Esau, of Israel out of Egypt, to show that in the fullness of God's purpose God's saving righteousness now reaches out to embrace *all,* Gentile as well as Jew. He believed from his heart that he had been commissioned to implement that eschatological purpose. His mission had been devoted to that task.[96] Now it was time, in the maturity of all his experience of that mission, from the perspective of mission accomplished in the Aegean, to set out his understanding of the gospel of God's saving righteousness. Clear too are the twin aspects of this gospel, and their symbiotic rela-

---

93. It was Luther's realization that this is what Paul had in mind — 'God's righteousness' as saving righteousness ('the righteousness by which through grace and sheer mercy God justifies us through faith'), and not God's righteousness as his 'justice' ('that justice whereby God is just and deals justly in punishing the unjust') — which gave birth to the Reformation and to the key Reformation doctrine of 'justification by faith' (*Luther's Works,* ed. J. Pelikan [St. Louis: Concordia, 1960] 34.336-37, as cited by R. Bainton, *Here I Stand* [London: Hodder and Stoughton, 1951] 65; full quotation in my *New Perspective on Paul* [2005] 187, [2008] 193). See also E. Lohse, 'Martin Luther und die Römerbrief des Apostels Paulus — Biblische Entdeckungen', *KD* 52 (2006) 106-25.

94. On the different ways that the double affirmation of faith's importance can be taken, see my *Romans* 43-44; and further Jewett, *Romans* 143-44.

95. Hab. 2.4 Heb. — 'the righteous (man) by his faith(fulness) shall live';

    Hab. 2.4 LXX — 'the righteous out of my faith(fulness) shall live';

    Paul — 'the righteous out of faith shall live'.

For details see my *Romans* 44-46; Jewett, *Romans* 144-46.

96. See further above, §29.3.

tionship: (1) that the gospel is thoroughly Jewish in character, is indeed Israel's good news about God, but also that precisely as such it is also good news for non-Jews; and (2) that the response which the gospel seeks to provoke and by which its power comes to saving effect is *faith,* faith which not only receives righteousness from God but which also lives out that righteousness from day to day.

This double definition of Paul's gospel — both the gospel which comes to focus in Jesus Messiah, God's son and 'our Lord', and the gospel as bringing the saving power of God to effect — is what Paul goes on to work out in detail through the rest of his letter to Rome.

b. The Human Plight, Jew as well as Gentile (Rom. 1.18–3.20)

The obvious point needs to be made that in what follows Paul was not so much preaching the gospel as explaining its rationale, the need for its good-news message. In so doing, he set a pattern for future systematic statements of Christian theology.

(i) *1.18-32.* As good news for all, Paul starts by setting out his understanding of the human condition without that good news, apart from faith. The picture drawn is bleak: of human impiety and unrighteousness *(adikia),*[97] stemming from human suppression of the truth of God (1.18-20); alternatively expressed, it is the picture of humans' unwillingness to accept their status as creatures of the Creator, their refusal to accept their dependency on God (to glorify him and give him thanks), and their assumption that they are wise enough to live the life which expresses their fullest potential (1.21-22).

Paul seems to be starting his story at the same point as his Scriptures, with God in creation and the human failure to live on the terms that God had set for his creation (Genesis 2–3).[98] So clearly he had in view humankind *(anthrōpoi —* 1.18) as a whole. But he proceeds to lay out the indictment in the terms (familiar to him) of Jewish polemic against and disdain for the other nations. He focuses on the two sins which provoked the sharpest condemnation in Israel's sacred writings:

---

97. *Adikia* ('unrighteousness') is obviously set over against the lead theme of God's *dikaiosynē* ('righteousness') (1.17).

98. Whether there is an allusion specifically to Adam is disputed (see, e.g., my *Romans* 60-61; Haacker, *Römer* 51), but at least a broad allusion to the creation and 'fall' narratives of Genesis is beyond dispute. J. R. Levison, 'Adam and Eve in Romans 1.18-25 and the Greek *Life of Adam and Eve*', *NTS* 50 (2004) 519-34, sees strong correspondences between the two writings, particularly in that 'the glory of God has been exchanged for the reign of divine anger and death, and natural human dominion has been exchanged for unnatural subservience to the creation' (534).

- idolatry: 'they changed the glory of the incorruptible God for the mere likeness of corruptible man, birds, beasts and reptiles'; 'they worshipped and served the creature rather than the Creator' (1.23, 25);[99]
- the sexual licence which Israel so often associated with idolatry: the 'uncleanness of dishonouring their bodies among themselves'; 'disgraceful passions' of female and male homosexual practice (1.24, 26-27).[100]

In both cases Paul would have been well aware that these sins had besmirched Israel's own history.[101] Finally, he itemizes

- sins which document the kind of dysfunctional society created by minds disqualified *(adokimos)* for appropriate human existence by their own disqualification *(edokimasan)* of God — 'jealousy, murder, rivalry, deceit, spite, etc.' (1.28-31).

This listing is similar to vice-lists drawn up by various religious and moral philosophers.[102] But the predominant thrust of the indictment is very much in terms of Jewish condemnation of what Jews saw to be characteristic failings of Gentile societies. Likewise the understanding of the self-destructive consequences of persistently self-indulgent behaviour as God's wrath *(orgē)*, as deliberately determined by God,[103] and not simply the outworking of fate or arbitrary decisions of the gods, is characteristically Jewish.

(ii) *2.1-29*. It should not be surprising then that Paul, in rhetorical mode, spies, as it were, one or more members of his audiences heartily applauding this sweeping condemnation of human impiety and unrighteousness (2.1). Almost certainly the interlocutor envisaged by Paul was a Jew; the distinctively Jewish character of the first two items on the threefold indictment should put that identification beyond doubt.[104] But the point becomes still clearer when we notice that

99. The echoes of Isa. 44.9-20 and particularly Wisdom of Solomon 11–15 are notable in these verses; see, e.g., my *Romans* 56-62; Fitzmyer, *Romans* 283-84; Lohse, *Römer* 89-90.

100. For references see my *Romans* 65-66; Fitzmyer, *Romans* 289; Haacker, *Römer* 53 n. 64.

101. The most explicit echoes in 1.23 are of Ps. 106.20 and Jer. 2.11 (see, e.g., Jewett, *Romans* 160-61).

102. See *Theology of Paul* 123-24, 662-65 (with bibliography).

103. Particularly striking is the threefold *paredōken*, 'God gave them over' — 1.24, 26, 28; see also Moo, *Romans* 99-102.

104. With the majority, I see 2.1 as addressed to a Jewish interlocutor; see, e.g., Konradt, *Gericht und Gemeinde* 501-502 (bibliography in n. 120); Wilckens, *Theologie* 1/3.175; Becker characterizes the whole of 1.8–3.20 as 'a dialogue with Jewish Christians' (*Paul* 358). The attempt to argue in contrast that it is a Gentile interlocutor whom Paul has in view (particularly by Stowers, *A Rereading of Romans* 100-104, and R. M. Thorsteinson, *Paul's Interlocutor in*

in his exchange with this interlocutor Paul echoes what were also typical Jewish assumptions about Israel's own favoured relationship with God. It was not that Jews denied their failings; it was rather that many Jews rationalized their disobedience as not meriting the same punitive judgment as God dispenses to Gentile sins (2.3).[105] Paul's response to the interlocutor, secure in the favour of God despite his sin, was blunt. Such an attitude treated lightly God's goodness and forbearance and did not appreciate that as deep a repentance was required from a Jew for his sins as from a Gentile for the same sins (2.4-5). Such an attitude failed to recognize the even-handedness and impartiality of God, which Israel's own Scriptures regarded as the most fundamental given about God's acting as judge (2.6, 11).[106] In final judgment 'glory and honour' would be accorded to *all* who brought good to effect, Jew first but also Gentile (2.7, 10); but wrath and distress would be the lot of *all* who out of selfish ambition brought evil to effect, Jew first but also Gentile (2.8, 9). Once again, the primary thought is of 'all' as transcending the distinction between Jew and Gentile, the default-setting of a Jewish perspective on humanity as whole:[107] Jews as 'first', but first in condem-

---

Romans 2 [CBNTS 40; Stockholm: Almqvist and Wiksell, 2003]) does not sufficiently take into account that the indictment of 1.18-32, while universal in scope, uses characteristic Jewish polemic against the idolatry and promiscuity of other nations. Esler (*Conflict and Identity* 151), while recognizing the Jewish character of the critique in 1.18-32, is scathingly dismissive of the view that 2.1 has a Jewish target, since Paul could hardly accuse Jews generally of idolatry (doing the same things). Jews, however, readily recalled idolatrous episodes of their own history (of which the episode of the golden calf was only the first), and *eidōlolatria* could be used more generally (as in Col. 3.5); he ignores the echo of Wis. 15.1-4 in 2.1-6 (n. 105 below), and he leaves unexplained why Paul turns to talk of 'having the law' (2.14) before he turns from the non-Jew to the 'Jew' in 2.17. Similarly, in suggesting that Paul already had in mind the tensions of Rom. 14.1–15.6, Jewett misses the point that in ch. 14 it is the 'weak' (Jewish) traditionalist who 'judges' the other (14.3), the same term as in 2.1 (*Romans* 197-98, 839-40). Cf. O. Wischmeyer, 'Römer 2.1-24 als Teil der Gerichtsrede des Paulus gegen die Menschenheit', *NTS* 52 (2006) 356-76.

105. The attitude critiqued in 2.1-6 is the attitude which we find once again in the Wisdom of Solomon (15.1-4 — 'even if we sin, we are yours') and in the *Psalms of Solomon:* the psalmist is confident that 'those who act lawlessly [one of his favourite phrases] will not escape the condemnation of the Lord' (the same phrase as in Rom. 2.3), whereas God will spare the devout and grant them mercy; he destroys the sinner but (only) disciplines the righteous (*Pss. Sol.* 3; 9.6-7; 13.5-12; 16.11-15); see my *Theology of Paul* 115-17; also P. J. Tomson, '"Die Täter des Gesetzes werden gerechtfertigt werden" (Röm 2,13). Zu einer adäquaten Perspektive für den Römerbrief', in M. Bachmann, ed., *Lutherische und Neue Paulusperspektive* (WUNT 182; Tübingen: Mohr Siebeck, 2005) 183-221, especially 191-99.

106. Rom. 2.6: God renders to each according to his works (Ps. 62.12 and Prov. 24.12, regularly repeated in Jewish writings); 2.11: there is no partiality with God (Deut. 10.17; 2 Chron. 19.7; Sir. 35.12-13; etc.). For more detail see my *Romans* 85, 88-89; on the latter, see particularly J. Bassler, *Divine Impartiality: Paul and a Theological Axiom* (SBLDS 59; Chico: Scholars, 1982).

107. Note again that the whole world/humankind could be summed up as 'Jews and

nation as first in commendation; and Gentiles as standing on equal terms before the impartial judge.

Paul's tactics begin to become clearer at this point. He wanted it to be appreciated that his fellow Jews too fall under the indictment which he has drawn up against humankind as a whole. That indictment had been drawn up in fact on the basis of Israel's own law; he had ended the indictment by referring to 'the decree *(dikaiōma)* of God' (1.32), as something known to all. The terms of judgment (2.6, 11) he draws directly from Israel's Scripture. But now he refers, for the first time, explicitly to the Torah as the measure of judgment (2.12). And he does so in a way that makes it clear that simply *having* that law (Israel's prized and privileged possession) was no advantage to Jews. His mind was evidently still on the distinction between Jew and Gentile marked by the law, the distinction between being 'within the law *(en nomō)*' and 'lawless *(anomōs)*' (2.12), between 'having the law' and 'not having the law' (2.14). Paul insists, as many of Israel's teachers had before him,[108] that 'it is not the hearers of the law who are righteous before God, but the doers of the law who will be counted righteous *(dikaiōthēsontai)*' (2.13). But he insists equally, spelling out the implications of divine impartiality, that Gentiles do not need to 'have' the law or be 'within' the law to know what God requires of them,[109] and that it is how they have acted on the basis of that knowledge which will be judged by God, through Jesus Christ (2.14-16). That he insists is also his gospel (2.16). In short, the fact that Israel has been given the law does not of itself secure a favourable judgment for Israel.

Having as it were little by little unveiled the identity of his interlocutor, Paul at last brings him out fully into the open: 'you are called "Jew *(Ioudaios)*"' (2.17). At the same time, he states clearly what it is that gives the 'Jew' his distinctive identity: it is the fact the he 'relies on the law and boasts in God' (2.17). Paul here clearly refers to Israel's sense of having been chosen by God to be his own people[110] and having been given, not least as a mark of God's favour, the Torah, the terms of the covenant relationship into which God had graciously en-

---

Gentiles *(ethnē)'* = 'Jews and the nations *(ethnē)*', just as the whole world/humankind could be summed up as 'Greeks and barbarians'.

108. E.g., Deut. 4.1, 5-6, 13-14; 30.11-14; 1 Macc. 2.67; 13.48; Philo, *Cong.* 70; *Praem.* 79; Josephus, *Ant.* 20.44; *m. 'Abot* 1.17; 5.14.

109. For the exegetical debates on these verses, see, e.g., Fitzmyer, *Romans* 309-11; Moo, *Romans* 148-53; Haacker, *Römer* 64-65; Jewett, *Romans* 212-15.

110. Definitive here was Deut. 32.8-9: 'When the Most High gave each nation its heritage, when he divided all mankind, he laid down the boundaries for peoples according to the number of the sons of God; but the Lord's share was his own people, Jacob was his allotted portion' (REB, following the reading of 4QDeutʲ and LXX). Other references are in *Theology of Paul* 35 n. 32 and 43 n. 84. See further E. W. Nicholson, *God and His People: Covenant and Theology in the Old Testament* (Oxford: Clarendon, 1986); Sanders, *Paul,* index 'Election'. For a particularly fine expression of Israel's confidence in election, see 1 Chron. 16.14-22 = Ps. 105.7-15.

tered with Israel.[111] It is this sense of being a privileged people, or rather the presumption which followed from that, which Paul seeks to puncture. The interlocutor's sense of being specially favoured is clear: 'you are instructed from the law, sure that you are a guide to the blind, a light for those in darkness, an instructor of the foolish, a teacher of the young, having the embodiment of knowledge and of truth in the law' (2.18-20). Paul sums up the attitude particularly with the term *boasting*: the 'Jew' boasts in God and in the law (2.17, 23). And the context makes it clear that the boasting is not in terms of self-achievement, as maintained by important strands of interpretation stemming from the Reformation, but boasting of *privilege,* boasting in regard to, even over against, the much less favoured 'lawless' nations/Gentiles.[112]

Paul pricks the bubble of presumption in strong rhetorical style by pointing out that Jews also break the commandments (2.21-24)[113] and that circumcision is only of benefit for those who actually practise the law (2.25). Here again he goes straight to the key issue — circumcision, not as a demand being made of Gentile believers by Jewish believers (as in Galatia), but as the Jew's badge of his identity as belonging to the nation chosen by God, as that which attests his belonging within the circle of God's favour, just as the absence of circumcision attests the Gentile's standing outside that circle. Once again, as in 2.6-11, Paul insists that it is the fulfilling the law rather than bearing the mark of the law which matters (2.26). The uncircumcised who do the law are more commended by God than the circumcised who break the law (2.27). As Israel's teachers had long insisted, what mattered with God is circumcision of the heart and not the outwardly visible mark in the flesh (2.28-29).[114]

(iii) *3.1-20.* As if it was not already sufficiently clear, Paul acknowledges that his drawing the 'Jew' so firmly into his indictment of human sin must sound odd to Jewish ears and to anyone well versed in the Scriptures. He has his interlocutor ask in puzzlement: 'What then is the advantage of the Jew, or what is the value of circumcision?' (3.1). Paul was obviously well aware that in so completely discountenancing the 'Jew', he put a massive question mark against the

---

111. For this sense of privilege, as exemplified by Bar. 3.36–4.4, see my *Romans* lxviii-lxxi.

112. The point is now more generally recognized; see, e.g., Sanders, *Paul, the Law and the Jewish People* 33; Moo, *Romans* 160; Haacker, *Römer* 68; Wright, 'Romans' 446; Jewett, *Romans* 223. *Pss. Sol.* 17.1 and *2 Bar.* 48.22-24 ('We shall always be blessed; at least, we did not mingle with the nations. For we are all a people of the Name') catch the mood well (Lohse, *Römer* 109-10). Further bibliography appears in my *New Perspective on Paul* 9-10.

113. He is able to quote Isa. 52.5 in support of his indictment (Rom. 2.24); see further my *Romans* 113-16.

114. Deut. 10.16; Jer. 4.4; 9.25-26; Ezek. 44.9; 1QpHab 11.13; 1QS 5.5; 1QH 10[= 2].18; Philo, *Spec. Leg.* 1.305.

whole of Israel's tradition, the choice of Israel, the Scriptures themselves. As we shall see, Paul's indictment was aimed only at Israel's *presumption* and not at Israel's election as such (chs. 9–11), but he was not yet in a position in the flow of his exposition to deal with the dilemma which the indictment of his fellow 'Jew' was already posing. The very fact, however, that he interjects the questions of 3.1 is a reminder that in this letter, addressed primarily to the Gentile believers in Rome, the status of Israel and the relationship of Jew and Gentile before God were at the heart of what he wanted to say in the letter.

At this stage all that Paul can do is to insist that despite what he had been saying,

- Israel had been favoured by God (3.2),
- Israel's unfaithfulness *(apistia)* had not changed God's covenant faithfulness *(pistis, dikaiosynē)* towards Israel (3.3-5),
- God's righteousness *(dikaiosynē)* includes his exercise of judgment on sin (3.5-6); the truth *(alētheia)* of God remains firm.[115]

In the least-well-organized part of this careful composition, Paul allows himself to acknowledge the line which his thought could follow: that if God remains faithful to the unfaithful, then he is exercising saving righteousness to the unrighteous, and human sin is in effect promoting such divine goodness (3.5-8). But until he has developed his exposition more fully, he can only dismiss the thought with indignation.

The upshot of the indictment is that Jews and Greeks appear together on the charge sheet as 'all under sin' (3.9). In proof Paul draws together a catena of passages, which in original setting again were more characteristic of Israel's dismissal of its enemies, but which Paul subverts, in the light of his indictment, to apply to all, Jew as well as Gentile (3.10-18).[116] In the final summing up Paul again indicates explicitly that his concern has been to draw Jews within the universal indictment on human sin: the passages just cited are addressed to 'those within the law, in order that every mouth might be stopped [Jews' as well as Gentiles'] and all the world become liable to God's judgment. For by works of the law shall no flesh be justified *(dikaiōthēsetai)* before him, for through the law

---

115. In 3.3-7 the play on the Hebrew root *'aman,* giving both the sense of 'truth' *('emeth)* and 'faithfulness' *('emunah),* and so overlapping with *dikaiosynē* in its sense of 'covenant faithfulness', should not be missed; see also above, n. 92.

116. See my *Romans* 149-51: 'it can hardly be accidental that . . . all the Psalm quotations work with an antithesis between those self-consciously favoured by God and the rest variously described as the fool, the unrighteous, the lawless, the wicked, the sinner' (151). The catena, here subverted, reflects attitudes similar to the intra-Jewish denunciations that we find in the *Psalms of Solomon* (Albi, *Scripture* 174-77).

comes the knowledge of sin' (3.19-20). In the history of interpretation, the last verse has been too quickly read out of context. Certainly it is a statement of the universal incapacity of human beings to stand before God in their own strength.[117] The same point had been clearly indicated in 1.18-32: that when humankind disowns God and relies on its own wisdom, the results are disastrous for human society. But Paul's concern in all this has been to ensure that his fellow Jews did not presume that they were exempt from this judgment. And 'works of the law' is a distinctively Jewish expression to indicate the obedience Israel reckoned as required of them to maintain their covenant status and set-apartness to God and from others.[118] As a phrase summarizing what had been said earlier, 'works of the law' certainly cannot refer to Israel's *dis*obedience (2.21-24); its most obvious summary reference is to Israel's attitude referred to in 2.17-20 and embodied in the rite of circumcision — 'works of the law' as the obedience to the law which distinguished Jews from Gentile 'sinners'.[119] No, says Paul, that is not the function of the law: the law does not simply define sin and warn against sin; the law brings sin to conscious awareness, the very awareness of the seriousness of their own sins which so many of his fellow Jews seemed to be lacking (2.1-5). *All* are under sin, Jew as well as non-Jew (3.9).

c. The Gospel's Solution to the Human Plight (3.21–5.11)

(i) *3.21-31*. Having spelled out the severity of the human plight, embracing Jew as well as Gentile, Paul returns to his main subject as signalled in 1.16-17 — the righteousness of God, attested by the law and the prophets but now revealed apart from the law (3.21). Paul thus at once re-emphasizes the balance that he maintains throughout the letter between recognizing the revelation which God had entrusted to Israel in the law and through the prophets ('the oracles of God' — 3.2) and recognizing that the righteousness of God so attested is not simply, no longer

---

117. Ps 143.2 — 'no living person will be justified before you'; cf. particularly Job 9.2; Ps. 14.1; *1 En.* 81.5; 1QH 17[= 9].14-16. The same passage is alluded to in the parallel Gal. 2.16 (§27 at n. 287).

118. In Paul's vocabulary, 'works of the law' (Gal. 2.16) = 'living as a Jew' (Gal. 2.14). Fitzmyer, *Romans* 338, and Lohse, *Römer* 126-27, fail to note that in 4QMMT the sect's understanding of 'works of the law' is what led the sectarians to 'separate' from the rest of the people; see further §27.4a-b above; also *Theology of Paul* 354-59; also *New Perspective on Paul* (2005) 14-15, 22-26, (2008) 15-16, 23-28. The expression 'has its place exclusively in the confrontation with the Judaizers' (Haacker, *Römer* 83-84). Jewett ignores the distinctively Jewish significance of 'works of the law' (*Romans* 266-67).

119. See again *New Perspective on Paul* (2005) 41-43, (2008) 44-47. This is one of my more controversial theses.

simply, for those who know the law and live within the law (Jews), but for all. This is the righteousness of God now revealed most definitively in Jesus Christ, the concerned action of God for salvation 'through faith in Jesus Christ to *all* who believe' (3.22), since *all* stand in need of that saving action (3.23). Here Paul brings together the two main thrusts of the letter (§33.3a) in what is evidently the heart of his understanding of the gospel: God's righteousness comes to saving effect in Jesus Christ (3.24)[120] and through faith in him (3.22).[121]

The mystery of how God so achieves this act of redemption is Jesus' death on the cross (3.25-26). Here Paul evidently felt no need to emphasize the shocking character of Jesus' crucifixion, as he had in earlier letters.[122] Instead he draws on what was probably a way of speaking about Jesus' death which he knew (through his contacts) to be already familiar to the Roman believers,[123] and which in consequence he had no need to elaborate — to our loss! The imagery he draws on is one familiar to any religion in the ancient world, the imagery of sacrifice. But not any sacrifice: the allusion is explicitly to the cult of Jerusalem and to the specific sacrifices of the Day of Atonement.[124] This presumably is part of what Paul meant when he talked about the righteousness of God 'attested by the law and the prophets' (3.21): God had given a way of dealing with the sin which disrupted the covenant relation with his people, namely, the sin offering and the scapegoat.[125] God has provided Jesus as that means of atonement *(hilastērion)*.

120. In his discussion of 'righteousness' Esler's rather selective style of exegesis seems to ignore the fact that the key motif here is 'the righteousness of God' *(Conflict and Identity* 159-68).

121. Faith in Christ is central to Paul's exposition, which makes unlikely the currently popular view that, in the phrase *pistis Christou* (3.22; also 3.26; Gal. 2.16, 20; 3.22; Phil. 3.9), Paul refers to the 'faithfulness of Christ' (details and bibliography in *Theology of Paul* 379-85 and *New Perspective on Paul* [2005] 39-40 n. 164, [2008] 43 n. 169). That Paul's gospel centres on God's action in and through Christ is obvious (1.3-4; 4.24-25; 5.6-21; etc.), but Paul's concern particularly in Romans was also that the gospel functions by evoking faith in this Christ (particularly 10.14-17) and works its saving effect by evoking this faith (1.16-17; 3.27–4.22; etc.). Esler dismisses the 'subjective genitive' view with his usual robustness *(Conflict and Identity* 157-59); see also Jewett, *Romans* 276-78, and above, §27 n. 289.

122. Gal. 3.1; 6.14; 1 Cor. 1.18-25.

123. It is widely agreed that Paul draws on a familiar formula; see, e.g., my *Romans* 163-64; Jewett, *Romans* 270-71.

124. The allusion is inescapable, since the key term here, *hilastērion,* can refer only to the cover of the ark of the covenant on which blood was sprinkled on the Day of Atonement (references in my *Romans* 170-71). The sin offering as 'means of atonement' at the 'place of atonement' is obviously in view; see also Moo, *Romans* 231-37; Lohse, *Römer* 134-35.

125. These were probably understood as two aspects of the same act of atonement; the same formula is used for both sin offering and scapegoat (11QTemple 26.10, 27.2 — 'and they shall be forgiven'; *m. Sheb.* 1.7 — 'makes atonement for the Israelites'); see further my *Romans* 171-72; *Theology of Paul* 218-19. This view is controversial (see, e.g., Jewett, *Romans*

How the sacrificial logic worked is nowhere made explicit; my own suggestion is that the sacrificer identified himself with the sin offering (by laying his hand[s] on the animal), thus transferring his sin to the animal, so that the death of the animal meant the destruction of that deadly virus (sin); but the logic is much disputed.[126] All that Paul affirms here is that Christ's death as sacrifice has demonstrated God's righteousness (again the key term):[127] in passing over *(paresin)* former sins;[128] in dealing (as righteous judge) with the sin which had so disrupted human relationship with God (1.18-3.20); and in making effective God's justifying/treating as righteous the one who believes in/identifies with this Jesus.[129] Here again it should be noted that the theology implies an affirmation of Israel's sacrificial cult; it was because God had given this means of atonement that Jesus could be this means of atonement. Whether he or the Jerusalem believers who made the same credal formulation thought that Jesus' death had thereby rendered the sacrificial cult now redundant remains unclear.[130]

In a striking and much misunderstood manner, Paul at once returns to the theme of 'boasting': 'Where then is boasting?' (3.27). It was a theme of which, we recall, he had made so much in heavily ironic fashion in writing to Corinth, his current place of residence (2 Corinthians 10–12). And it will not be coincidental that the boasting he criticized there was that of the Jewish missionaries who made so much of their Jewish pedigree (11.22). But here what Paul presumably had in mind was the hardly unrelated boasting which earlier in this letter he had attributed to his typically Jewish interlocutor (Rom. 2.17, 23) — that is, a boasting in the privileged status before the God of Israel over the (other) nations. Paul confirms this a few sentences later when he in effect challenges any idea

---

285-87), but Paul certainly thought of Jesus' death in terms of both — Rom. 8.3 *(peri hamartias* = as sin offering) and 2 Cor. 5.21 (where the transfer of sin to another is clearly in view, as most explicit in the scapegoat ritual); see again *Theology of Paul* 212-18.

126. *Theology of Paul* 218-23, with bibliography.

127. Note how Paul plays on the theme: '. . . to demonstrate his righteousness *(dikaiosynēs)* . . . that he might be just *(dikaion)* and justifier *(dikaiounta)* . . .' — echoing the similar play in 3.3-7 (see above, n. 115).

128. *Paresis,* which occurs only here in the Greek Bible, denotes 'passing over', not in the sense of 'overlooking, disregarding', but as 'letting go unpunished, with penalty remitted' (BAGD *'paresis'*); see also Jewett, *Romans* 289-90.

129. For Paul this trust in = identification with Jesus was the beginning of the 'in Christ' process, whereby the death of Jesus works through the life of the believer as indicated in 2 Cor. 4.7-18 and as taken up again in Rom. 8.17-23 (see again my *Theology of Paul* §18). He alludes to the schema here only briefly, perhaps assuming that the Roman believers would already be sufficiently familiar with it (through his colleagues already teaching in the apartment churches in Rome), but knowing that he would return to it, as to other themes so far only alluded to (3.1-8), in subsequent chapters.

130. See above, §§23.5 and 24.9c.

that God (Israel's God) is God of Jews only (3.29); *that* was what such Jewish boasting in effect claimed. It is precisely this aspect of his preceding indictment to which Paul so immediately returns, as the first and most important corollary of his understanding of his gospel of the righteous-reckoning God, which confirms once again that it was precisely this aspect of their shared gospel which he was so anxious to explain and defend in this carefully written letter.[131]

He insists that such boasting is excluded. How so? Not by 'the law *(nomos)* of works', the law as enacted in works, but through 'the law *(nomos)* of faith', the law enacted from faith (3.27).[132] Their common gospel was that a person is justified by faith apart from works of the law (3.28); God's acceptance was not channelled through or fundamentally dependent on their doing what the law laid down. This was what Paul had insisted on in effect from the start of his missionary work, and explicitly at the confrontation with Peter at Antioch, and vehemently in his letter to the Galatians (Gal. 2.16). The fundamental principle is the same as in Rom. 3.20: the creature does not, cannot stand before God on the basis of what he does, but only on the basis of humble trust and gratitude (1.21). But again it is the particular aspect of that fundamental truth — that Jewish missionaries should not try to impose legal observances ('works of the law') on Gentile believers as a *sine qua non* of faith — which Paul had most in mind. It was the law defined by distinctively Jewish works, like circumcision and the laws of clean and unclean, which gave the impression that God was an exclusively Jewish God, and not God of Gentiles also (3.29). Such a position was ridiculous for a Jew to maintain, since Israel's most basic creed is that 'God is one' (Deut. 6.4), which means that he is God of *all* the nations. This carried the further corollary that God deals with all alike (the 'all' here explicit as 'Jews and Gentiles', 'circumcision and uncircumcision') — 'from faith', 'through faith' (3.30). And lest anyone infer from this that faith therefore renders the law invalid, Paul concludes by affirming that the law can only be effectively fulfilled through faith (hence 'the law of faith' in 3.27); *what God demands from his human creatures first and foremost is their trust in him.*

131. It is surprising how earlier neo-orthodox exegesis referred at once to 'pride in accomplishments', 'boasting in one's self (Sich-Rühmen)' (as still in Moo, *Romans* 247; Lohse, *Römer* 137), despite the obvious reference back to 2.17, 23 (but see *New Perspective on Paul* 9-10 and n. 38). In pressing for a wider reference, Jewett, *Romans* 295-96, plays down the connected train of thought: boasting (3.27) → justification from works (of the law) (3.28) → God of Jews only (3.29).

132. That Paul had in mind the Torah is much disputed, but note again the train of thought: 'law of faith' (3.27) → 'faith establishes the law' (3.31); see further *Theology of Paul* 634-42. Haacker, e.g., observes that the question 'What kind of law?' implies a plurality of laws (*Römer* 93), but the question is more like 'What kind of law is the "law of faith"?'. Paul's answer is indicated in passages like Gal. 5.6, 14 and Rom. 14.23; cf. Moo, *Romans* 254-55.

(ii) *4.1-25*. At this point (4.1) Paul turns to Abraham as the appropriate test case for his gospel. That would have been entirely understandable for the Roman believers, for anyone familiar with Jewish heritage would be well aware that Abraham, the father of the nation, was regarded both as the archetype of the proselyte (one who turned away from idolatry to the one true God)[133] and as the archetype of the devout Jew.[134] He could therefore serve as the test-case for the legitimacy or otherwise of boasting before God on the basis of law-observance (4.2). The key text was Gen. 15.6: 'Abraham believed God, and it was reckoned to him for righteousness' (4.3). Paul would know well the strong Jewish tradition which understood that text in relation to the larger Abraham story, and in particular, by reference to one of the profoundest acts of obedience that Abraham (or anyone) could enact — the readiness to offer the life of his son Isaac in sacrifice (Genesis 22). In this tradition Abraham's *faith* was understood as his *faithfulness;* such unquestioning obedience could be and was counted a ground of boasting.[135]

Paul's response is much more carefully and plausibly argued than his earlier treatment of Gen. 15.6 and of Abraham's 'seed' in Galatians 3–4; perhaps his earlier attempt had not been as successful in persuading fellow Jewish believers as he had hoped.[136] Here instead he starts from the basic contrast between a human contract (involving payment for work done) and the divine-human covenant whereby God accepts humans who trust him despite their characteristic 'ungodliness' (4.4-5), alluding back to 1.18. This is how the 'reckoned' of Gen. 15.6 should be understood: the reckoning of a favour, not of a debt (4.4);[137] the ap-

---

133. *Jub.* 12.1-21; Josephus, *Ant.* 1.155; *Apoc. Abr.* 1-8; see further my *Romans* lxix-lxx and 204-205; N. Calvert-Koyzis, *Paul, Monotheism and the People of God: The Significance of Abraham Traditions for Early Judaism and Christianity* (JSNTS 273; London: Clark International, 2004) 123-36.

134. Note already Gen. 26.5: the promise is repeated to Isaac 'because Abraham obeyed my voice and kept my charge, my commandments, my statutes and my laws'. For full treatment see G. W. Hansen, *Abraham in Galatians: Epistolary and Rhetorical Contexts* (JSNTS 29; Sheffield: Sheffield Academic, 1989) 175-99; B. Ego, 'Abraham als Urbild der Toratreue Israels. Traditionsgeschichtliche Überlegungen zu einem Aspekt des biblischen Abrahambildes', in F. Avemarie and H. Lichtenberger, eds., *Bund und Tora. Zur theologischen Begriffsgeschichte in alttestamentlicher, frühjüdischer und urchristlicher Tradition* (WUNT 92; Tübingen: Mohr Siebeck, 1996) 25-40.

135. 'Was not Abraham found faithful when tested, and it was reckoned to him as righteousness?' (1 Macc. 2.52); cf. James 2.21 ('Was not our ancestor Abraham justified by works when he offered his son Isaac on the altar?'). See further references in my *Romans* 200-202.

136. Rom. 4.3-22 is one of the finest examples of exposition of a biblical text available to us from the Second Temple period: the text stated (4.3); its terms explained — 'reckoned' (4.4-8), 'believed' (4.9-21), each by means of auxiliary texts drawn in (Ps. 32.1-2; Gen. 17.5); and the conclusion drawn (4.22).

137. Cf. M. Cranford, 'Abraham in Romans 4: The Father of All Who Believe', *NTS* 41 (1995) 71-88, particularly 76-83.

peal, in effect, is to Israel's recognition that God's election of Israel was an act of pure grace.[138] This sense of 'reckoning' is also demonstrated in reference to the relation to God of another of Israel's heroes (4.6-8): for David, despite his grievous sin, was forgiven, his sin *not* 'reckoned' (Ps. 32.1-2).[139]

A key issue for Paul is that Gen. 15.6 comes well before Genesis 22 (the offering of Isaac), as indeed before Genesis 17 (the circumcision of Abraham), in the story of Abraham. Abraham exemplifies one who is 'reckoned righteous' through faith ('Abraham believed God') and apart from the law, so Abraham's faith should not be simply conflated with his subsequent faithfulness. It is this fact which makes Abraham the father of 'all who believe', not just of the circumcised but also of the uncircumcised, and of the circumcised not because of their circumcision but because of their believing as Abraham believed before he was circumcised (4.9-12).[140] The promise to Abraham, therefore, did not come to Abraham on the basis of what he went on to do but on the basis of his faith. So to make the fulfilment of that promise, to make entry into the heritage of Abraham, dependent on doing what the law laid down was actually to render faith invalid and to nullify the promise (4.13-14).[141] The law had a different purpose: to serve as a measure of God's judgment (4.15).[142] That is why the promise is enacted *ek pisteōs* ('from faith'): in order that it may come to *all* Abraham's descendants, not just to Jews alone, but to all who share Abraham's faith (4.16), rather than just those who are 'heirs *ek nomou*

138. Deut. 4.32-40; 6.10-12, 20-23; 7.6-8; 8.17-18; etc. See also O. Hofius, '"Rechtfertigung des Gottlosen" als Thema biblischer Theologie', *Paulusstudien* (WUNT 51; Tübingen: Mohr Siebeck, 1989, ²1994) 121-47, who demonstrates that *iustificatio impii* as a theme in Paul's theology is deeply rooted in the Old Testament. 'The Old Testament knows and attests the justification of the ungodly very well. It is an act of God which he brings himself to do out of free love and mercy toward his guilt-laden chosen people Israel' (Stuhlmacher, *Biblische Theologie* 1.331).

139. See further my *Romans* 205-207 and *New Perspective on Paul* (2005) 45-46, (2008) 49-50; J.-N. Aletti, 'Romains 4 et Genèse 17. Quelle énigme et quelle solution?', *Biblica* 84 (2003) 305-25.

140. The same point had formed the beginning of Paul's equivalent treatment in Gal. 3.6ff.

141. It is here that the argument of Romans 4 comes closest to the earlier argument of Galatians 3 — as indicated by the key term 'promise *(epangelia)*': Rom. 4.13, 14, 16, 20; Gal. 3.14, 16-18, 21-22, 29. The promise that Abraham 'should be heir of the world' (Rom. 4.13) would presumably have raised not a few eyebrows in Rome itself (Haacker, *Römer* 106; Jewett, *Romans* 325-26), though Paul was actually reflecting an idea which was widespread in several strands of Jewish thought at the time (see my *Romans* 213).

142. One of the things Paul does in Romans which he did not develop in Galatians is to spell out the role of the law in its continuing force: it was never intended to 'make alive' (Gal. 3.21), and its role in protecting Israel was temporary (3.22-25) (see above, §31 n. 363 and the following notes); but only in Romans does Paul indicate the law's continuing role in defining and judging sin (Rom. 3.20; 4.15; 5.13; 7.7; see further *Theology of Paul* 133-37).

(from law)' (4.14). That is how the promise to Abraham that he would be 'father of many nations' (Gen. 17.5 LXX) comes to its fulfilment (4.17).[143]

And what is this 'faith'? What is the believing of Abraham which was reckoned as righteousness? Paul's answer (4.17-21) is one of the profoundest expositions of 'faith' in any language. It was trust in God as the one 'who gives life to the dead and calls things which have no existence into existence' (4.17): in one so-powerful sentence Paul both underlines that the effectual power involved is entirely God's (human participation is the participation of the dead and the non-existent!) and foreshadows the central expression of that power in the raising of Jesus from the dead (4.24-25). In Abraham's case the equivalent was giving life to Sarah's womb, when both Abraham and Sarah were long past child-bearing (4.19); for only as an act of divine *fiat* could the promise of descendants be fulfilled. So that faith in this case could be nothing more than sheer trust — the dead and non-existent dependent wholly on the life-giving act of God. And despite the hopelessness of his situation, Abraham 'believed' (4.18); he did not doubt God's promise but was 'fully convinced that what he had promised he was able also to do' (4.20-21), giving the glory to God which humankind typically failed to do (1.21). It was *precisely this faith,* not his subsequent faithfulness, which 'was reckoned to him for righteousness' (3.22; Gen. 15.6).

All that remained was to remind the Roman audiences that the story of Abraham's believing and being reckoned righteous was archetypal for all who believe. For as Abraham believed in the life-giving God in respect of the promise of a son, so the gospel calls for faith in the same life-giving God 'who raised Jesus our Lord from the dead' (4.23-24). The final clauses elaborate the already traditional formula[144] by summarizing the double effect of Jesus' death-resurrection: the wiping out of transgressions and the drawing back into a positive relation with God (4.25).

(iii) *5.1-11.* Paul concludes this second main section of his exposition by drawing out the implications of his gospel: 'Therefore, having been justified from faith, we [Jew and Gentile] have peace in relation to God through our Lord Jesus Christ' (5.1). Typically, however, he does not linger there, at the wonder of being accepted by God solely 'through faith'. Naturally he rejoices in the privilege granted only to priests and (in human society) to ambassadors, of being accorded access into the innermost sanctum, into the very presence of the king himself (5.1-2).[145] And, notably, in this concluding paragraph, he returns to the theme of 'boasting' — the point at which his critique of Jewish presumption had

---

143. This, the main thrust of Romans 4, as in Galatians 3, is often missed; see *New Perspective on Paul* (2005) 43-45, (2008) 47-49.

144. *Theology of Paul* 175; Jewett, *Romans* 341-42.

145. See my *Romans* 247-48; Fitzmyer, *Romans* 396; Jewett, *Romans* 349-50.

been at its sharpest (2.17, 23; 3.27). Boasting is appropriate, not in privileged status over others, but rather in God's grace, at the prospect of the restoration of and to the glory God had intended for his human creation (5.2, alluding back to 3.23, and forward to 8.17-21).[146] But Paul quickly qualifies even that thought, rather as he had done more than once in his fourth letter to the Corinthians,[147] by turning to the reality of human suffering as experienced all too vividly by believers. As in the fool's boasting in 2 Corinthians 11–12, it is the realistic appreciation of the fact of that suffering of which he is the more proud — particularly because of the positive benefits of such suffering in character building and in carrying forward the salvation process (5.3-4). And again, as so often in his earlier letters,[148] it is the experience of the Spirit, in this case of the love of God 'poured out in our hearts' (the vividness of the image reflects the vividness of the experience), which gives him a secure basis for such hope and reflection (5.5).

The wonder of this gospel draws from Paul yet one more paean of praise to this so gracious God: the God who does it all for human salvation purely out of his love — love, that is, for the weak, for the ungodly, for sinners, for those who had set their faces against him (5.6-10). Likewise the process of salvation brought into effect by the gospel (1.16) is summed up as the movement from cross to resurrection, from death to life, from justification and reconciliation to salvation (5.9-10). Significantly, Paul returns yet again, as already noted, to the theme of 'boasting'. Boasting is appropriate, but only in that process of salvation with all its suffering, and in reconciliation with God (5.3-5, 11).[149] And thus Paul rounds off the story begun with God's creation and the failure of the human creature to acknowledge the Creator, now completed with the sure hope of sharing (again) in God's glory and the fullness of salvation.

d. The Story of Salvation Retold in Its Cosmic Dimensions (5.12–8.39)

Paul at this point seems at first to be simply carrying on an unbroken flow of argument: 'Therefore, . . .' (5.12). But in fact, he is about to recapitulate the whole argument of the preceding chapters.[150]

---

146. Jewish tradition interpreted the 'fall' in terms of Adam having been deprived of the 'glory' of God (see, e.g., my *Romans* 167-68).

147. See above, §32.7.

148. E.g., Gal. 3.3-5, 14; 4.6; 5.25; 1 Cor. 2.10-16; 12.13; 2 Cor. 1.22; 5.5.

149. Cf. S. J. Gathercole, *Where Is Boasting? Early Jewish Soteriology and Paul's Response in Romans 1–5* (Grand Rapids: Eerdmans, 2002) 260-62.

150. The structure of Romans at this point is much debated, particularly whether ch. 5 ends the first section of the exposition (1.18–5.21) or begins the second (5.1–8.39); e.g.,

(i) As 1.18 began with humankind's initial and continuing failure to acknowledge God, so 5.12 re-begins with the entry of sin and death into and their continuing hold over human experience. And as 5.1-11 looked forward to the coming glory, the sure hope and promise of final salvation, so 8.31-39 will end with a similarly confident hope of final vindication at the last judgment and assurance of the never-failing love of God in Christ for the trials and tribulations up to that day.[151] But it is not a simple re-telling of the same story. The first telling (1.18–5.11) focused on the Jew/Gentile dimension of the gospel, on, as we might say, the horizontal and social dimension of a good news which is to *all* who believe. The second telling (5.12–8.39) changes focus, and the lead players on the stage change also — no longer Jew and Gentile, but cosmic powers which bear ineluctably on human experience, particularly sin and death, or, more in the character of the second telling, the personified powers of Sin and Death.[152] Whether or not it is wholly accurate, or helpful, to characterize them as cosmic powers, the fact from which Paul obviously moves out is that these terms encapsulate human experience of constraints far beyond human choice and social convention.

- *Death* most obviously is a power to which all humankind must bow the knee in submission, sooner or later.
- But *Sin* too for Paul was a power experienced willy-nilly as, we might say, the compulsion to seek self-advantage, to measure and evaluate all things by their perceived benefit or otherwise to ourselves — the power which typically transforms legitimate 'desire' into self-indulgent and self-corrupting 'lust'.[153]

These are the actors which dominate the next three chapters.[154]

Has the story changed — no longer the issue of how Gentiles can be reckoned acceptable to/accepted by God? And if so, do these chapters function as a

---

Haacker opts for the first alternative (as I did in *Romans*), while Lohse and Jewett opt for the second. A division at 5.11/12, as suggested here, is uncommon, but see Witherington, *Romans* 132. As will become apparent, I see Romans 1–11 as Paul telling the story of the gospel in three different ways: 1.18–5.11 — good news for Jew and Gentile; 5.12–8.39 — good news about the law; 9.1–11.36 — good news about Israel; for a more concise presentation see my 'Paul's Letter to Rome: Reason and Rationale', in V. A. Lehnert and U. Rüsen-Weinhold, eds., *Logos — Logik — Lyrik. Engagierte exegetische Studien zum biblischen Reden Gottes,* K. Haacker FS (Leipzig: Evangelische Verlagsanstalt, 2007) 185-200 (here 194-200).

151. As 5.9-10 picked up the talk of 'salvation' in 1.16, so 8.31-34 picks up the talk in 1.17 of God's 'righteousing'.

152. On these powers see *Theology of Paul* §5.

153. In Paul's usage *epithymia* moves between the meanings; see BDAG 372.

154. In Romans 5–8, *hamartia*, 'sin' (singular), appears 41 times — chs. 5 (6), 6 (16), 7 (14) and 8 (5); *thanatos*, 'death', 21 times — chs. 5 (6), 6 (7), 7 (5) and 8 (3).

kind of parenthesis between the chapters on either side dominated by the Jew/ Gentile and Israel issues? To some extent the answer is Yes, but not entirely. For other elements are one by one introduced into the retelling and help ensure that the earlier focus is not lost.

- *Flesh* too is soon introduced as a prominent player on the stage[155] — denoting the weakness of the human condition, the natural corruption of mortality, but also the moral corruption of the person who focuses primarily or solely on satisfaction of the human appetites and becomes dominated by them, and linking back to the earlier critique in 2.28 and 3.20.[156]
- Countering this increasing emphasis on 'flesh', at about the same time, we are re-introduced to *Spirit,* that is, the Holy Spirit[157] — the power which answers to the power of Sin, both meeting the power of Sin now and ensuring the final triumph over both powers of Sin and Death, and the power which Israel had always hoped for, both within, the circumcision of the heart (2.29),[158] and in final resurrection (1.4).
- Most striking of all, *Law* makes an early entrance on stage (5.13) and becomes a key player (5.20), characterizing a power whose time is past (6.14-15; 7.1-6),[159] a power subverted by the stronger power of Sin (Rom. 7.7–8.2) and the weakness of the flesh (8.3), and yet still a measure of what God requires of his human creation, whose fulfilment the more powerful Spirit enables (8.4). That Paul speaks explicitly to 'those who know the law' (7.1) recalls 3.19 and functions as a reminder that the law/Torah is what binds the two stories together.[160]

(ii) *5.12-21.* So the retelling of the story begins, this time with humankind particularized in the figure of Adam,[161] the one through whom Sin and Death

155. *Sarx,* 'flesh' — 7.5, (14), 18, 25; 8.3-9, 12-13.

156. See *Theology of Paul* 62-70.

157. *Pneuma,* 'Spirit' — 7.6, and the great Spirit-chapter 8 (twenty times) — 8.2, 4-6, 9-11, 13-16, 23, 26-27.

158. The hope of future circumcision of the heart (Deut. 30.6; *Jub.* 1.23) is obviously equivalent to the hope of the law written in the heart (Jer. 31.31-34) and of the promised Spirit (Ezek. 11.19; 36.27)

159. Note the echo of the argument of Gal. 3.19-29; see above, §31.7c(iii). As, e.g., Moo notes, 'the word "law", usually referring to the Mosaic law, occurs more times in Romans (seventy-four) than in all the other letters of Paul combined (forty-seven); Paul devotes an entire chapter to it (7), and it recurs in relationship to almost every topic Paul treats (cf., e.g., 2:12-16; 4:13-15; 5:13-14, 20; 6:14, 15; 8:2-4; 9:31–10:5; 13:8-10)' (*Romans* 27).

160. The reference is, once again, to the Torah; see my *Romans* 359-60.

161. The Hebrew *adam,* of course, means 'man', that is, 'humankind, human being'; see *Theology of Paul* 82-84.

gained their terrible hold over the tribe of Adam (5.12-14). The relation between the two Paul acknowledges is unclear: death reigned even before sin was reckoned (5.13-14), but death is also to be reckoned as the outcome of sin (5.12);[162] the bottom line is the same as in 1.18-32.[163] It is the law (5.14 — Paul clearly thinks of the law of Moses) which defines sin and makes one conscious of sinning (5.13); this has been Paul's repeated theme (3.20; 4.15); it is the only function of the law as such which so far he has set over against the law understood in terms of 'works'.[164] But quickly the picture darkens: for in defining to be sin what humankind may have been thoughtlessly unaware of as sin, the law actually increases transgressions, thus both multiplying sins and tightening Sin's stranglehold on human character until its outworking in death (5.20). So it was not the law which provided an answer to the power of Sin and Death; it provided a measure of sin, and a means whereby atonement for sins could be made (3.22, 25), but not an effective counter to the power of Sin. In fact, integral to this telling of the gospel is *the tragedy of the Law:* the fact that it was subverted in its purpose and became a negative rather than a positive force in human/Israel's experience, subverted by Sin's power and the flesh's weakness. Such an exposition obviously forms a continuation of the critique of Paul's fellow Jews' assumption that the law, doing (the works of) the law, was the way of and to salvation.

Although the telling has gone only from Eden to Sinai in this opening statement (5.12-14), Paul delays no longer in introducing what the gospel proclaims as the answer to the power of sin and death — Christ as fulfilling an equivalently more than individual or historical (mythological) role, Christ as a second Adam, or as he had described him in the Corinthian correspondence, Christ 'the last Adam' (1 Cor. 15.45). This is an astonishing theological step for Paul to have taken in regard to a man who had been active in the land of Israel less than thirty years earlier. It was no longer simply a matter of believing that Jesus himself had been exalted to heaven to sit at God's right hand and assume dominion over 'all things': that was what God had always intended for his human creation from the beginning (according to Ps. 8.4-6).[165] The really astonishing

162. The meaning of the final clause of 5.12 (*'eph' hō* all sinned') is unclear: *epi* has a wide range of usage (BDAG 363-67). But it seems to envisage a connection between the sin and death of Adam and the sin and death of everyone — Adam as inaugurating a humanity susceptible to the power of Sin and (therefore) subject to the power of Death. See discussions and reviews of Fitzmyer, *Romans* 408-10, 413-17; Moo, *Romans* 321-29; Jewett, *Romans* 375-76.

163. Paul leaves open the question whether death was always part of the divine plan in creating humanity or whether it was the consequence of sin; see further my *Theology of Paul* 94-97, 124-26.

164. Though the implications of 'the law of faith' (3.27) and of the law being established through faith (3.31) are still to be worked out.

165. The conviction that Ps. 110.1 had been fulfilled in Jesus ('Sit at my right hand until

feature was that what Jesus had done could be said to have the same sort of influence and effect on humankind in general ('all') as had the (historical/mythical?)
figure of Adam. He could be spoken of as somehow summing up all humankind
in himself, as Adam alone had previously stood for all humankind. But Adam
stood for death, Christ for life (as again in 1 Cor. 15.21-22). It is the wonder of
this parallel and contrast which fills Paul's vision for the rest of Romans 5: the
grace which far surpassed the trespass, the justification which far outweighed the
condemnation, the life which far surmounted the death, the righteousness which
overwhelmed the sinfulness (5.15-19). One purple passage (5.6-11) is followed
by another, its rhetorical power too easily diminished by fussing over the fine detail of words and syntax.

Having introduced these players on stage — Sin, Death and (the) Law —
Paul proceeds to deal with them in turn, to show how the gospel speaks to the
challenge of each; 'flesh' is brought on in ch. 7 as the plot becomes more complex, and 'Spirit' becomes the story's real hero in ch. 8. In each case, each of
what are now the three chapters (6, 7 and 8), Paul proceeds in the same way. First
he expresses the clarity of the gospel's *indicative:* what Christ has done and what
has already happened to believers through their commitment and baptism. But
then he turns to the gospel's *imperative,* where the continuing power of Sin and
Death and the continuing weakness of the flesh have to be factored into a more
realistic assertion of believers' responsibilities and capabilities.

(iii) *6.1-23.* Sin is the first to be tackled. Paul's talk of sin's increase being
more than matched by the abundant overflow of grace (5.20-21) provides the occasion for Paul to recall the jibe which he had angrily denounced at an earlier
point:[166] 'Are we to persist in sin in order that grace might increase?' (6.1). His indignant response is that such an attitude completely fails to appreciate the epochal
transition that Christ has effected and that being baptized into Christ effected for
the baptisand (6.2-4).[167] Jesus' death means that he is beyond Sin's power, and
Jesus' resurrection means that he is beyond Death's power (6.7-10). So those who

---

I make your enemies a footstool for your feet') quickly merged in earliest christology with
God's purpose in creation, to 'put everything in subjection under adam's/man's feet' (Ps. 8.6);
see particularly 1 Cor. 15.25-27 and, further, *Theology of Paul* 200-201, 248-49.

166. Rom. 3.8 — 'Let us do evil that good might come of it'.

167. Rom. 6.1-11 is not an exposition of baptism (as typically Wilckens, *Theologie*
1/3.197; 'the baptized are brought into justification by baptism [cf. Rom 6:6-14]' —
Stuhlmacher, *Biblische Theologie* 1.353); rather baptism is the first of the powerful images
by which Paul attempts to draw out the transformation which has already been theirs and
the ongoing transformation of which the Christian life consists. See further *Theology of
Paul* 443-44, 447-48, 451-52; Jewett, *Romans* 400. See also S. Sabou, *Between Horror and
Hope: Paul's Metaphorical Language of Death in Romans 6:1-11* (Bletchley: Paternoster,
2005).

have united their lives with his have been united with Jesus in his death — Paul's further and more refined reflection on the theme which had dominated so much of 2 Corinthians.[168] This does not mean that the process which was completed in Christ himself has already been worked through and completed in those united with him; the full equivalent to his resurrection lies still ahead (6.5):[169] 'if we have died with Christ, we believe that we shall also live with him' (6.8). They have been crucified with him in order that the body of sin (= the flesh) might be done away with (6.6); but this process will not be completed till their own resurrection. At the same time, the transforming power of Christ's resurrection (= the Spirit) is already at work,[170] and therefore the enabling no longer to serve Sin (6.4, 6).

This emphasis on what has already happened (the indicative) becomes the basis for Paul's exhortation (the imperative). The Roman Christians have to start from the fact of their being 'in Christ'; their responsibility is to let his deadness to sin and aliveness to God come to expression in their lives individually and corporately (6.11). That means a resolute No to Sin; in particular, an honest recognition that human desire *(epithymia)* can easily be corrupted and perverted by that power (6.12). What is required is a constant handing oneself in all one's parts *(melē)*, dimensions, relationships (all that makes up the person) to God (6.13).[171] And not to think that a simple submission to the Law is going to be sufficient means to achieve that goal (6.14-15). Here again the two retellings overlap: as far as the traditional Jewish believer was concerned, the law was the obvious way to submit before the covenant God: 'under the Law' was the answer to or protection from being 'under Sin'. But Paul had already indicated that the law is ineffective before the power of Sin (5.20), and he would shortly explain his own painful recognition that the Law in itself was not in experience a channel of grace (7.7–8.3). He would also climax this retelling by highlighting the power of the Spirit as the great Enabler (ch. 8). But here his concern was evidently to spell out the importance of the imperative in stark terms. Even for believers, in Christ, there was a responsibility to consciously and carefully withhold themselves from submission to that self-centred, self-promoting instinct (Sin), and with equal deliberation and care to hand themselves over to the power of righteousness (6.16-18).[172]

---

168. See above, §32.7.

169. Rom. 6.5 — 'If we have been knit together with the very likeness of Jesus' death, we shall certainly also be knit together with the very likeness of his resurrection'. That the future tense in 6.5b is a temporal rather than a logical future is the majority view; see *Theology of Paul* 470; Haacker, *Römer* 128; Lohse, *Römer* 191; Jewett, *Romans* 401-402.

170. Paul had already developed the theme in 2 Cor. 3.3–5.5 and will return to it in Rom. 8.2-8, 12-14, 17-25.

171. *Melē* is difficult to translate felicitously — usually 'members', but as denoting all that constitutes the person; see my *Romans* 337; Moo, *Romans* 384.

172. In 6.16-20 Paul uses *dikaiosynē*, 'righteousness', with its double force: both as re-

They had to obey: not the impulses of self-indulgence which ever tightened the grip of Sin and could end only in death, but as those 'under grace', slaves of God (happy paradox), with all the ready obedience of the slave of a great and good master, in all the matters which he indicated to be right (6.19-23). In short, the indicative did not render the imperative unnecessary; rather the indicative made the imperative possible to obey.

(iv) *7.1-25.* Paul now turns to the Law.[173] With different and somewhat convoluted imagery he makes the same opening point: that the death of Christ has freed those bound by the law in order to be united with Christ (7.1-4). Once again reference to the Law brings the second telling into overlap with the first: for it is archetypically the Jew who is bound by the law; and it is this bond(age) which would withhold the freedom of union with Christ from others.[174] But quickly Paul develops the imagery into a headline statement which he will expand in the two chapters to follow. First, the most complete statement of the factors involved in the human (including Jewish) condition, with the further complication of 'flesh' introduced for the first time:

- 'When we were in the *flesh* the passions of *sins* which operate through the *law* were effective in what we were and did so as to bear fruit for *death*' (7.5).

Then his summary statement of what the gospel has made possible:

- 'But now we have been released from the law, having died to that by which we were confined *(kateichometha),*[175] so that we might serve in newness of Spirit and not in oldness of letter' (7.6).

---

calling its primary usage in the letter — God's saving action on behalf of those to whom he has committed himself (1.17; 3.21-22, 25-26) — and the right living which is an expression of that saving righteousness in and through the lives of those in a positive relation with God. As such it serves as the positive alternative to sin, that is, both the power of Sin and the actual sinning which Sin engenders.

173. Note the parallel between 7.1 ('I speak [*lalō*] to those who know the law') and 3.19 ('whatever the law says it says [*lalei*] to those within the law'). It is widely recognized here that the Jewish law is in view (e.g., Fitzmyer, *Romans* 455-57; Esler, *Conflict and Identity* 224-25; Lohse, *Römer* 206; Jewett, *Romans* 430). P. J. Tomson, 'What Did Paul Mean by "Those Who Know the Law"? (Rom 7.1)', *NTS* 49 (2003) 573-81, argues that Paul assumes the Romans' knowledge of Jesus' strict teaching on the marriage law.

174. This is the point which Paul saw was at stake in the confrontation with Peter in Antioch (Gal. 2.11-16); see above, §27.5.

175. *Kateichometha* (echoing 1.18) is used here in the same sense as *synkleiomenoi* ('confined') in Gal. 3.23; the train of thought is similar.

Here the last antithesis ('newness of Spirit, not oldness of letter') recalls both the exposition of 2 Corinthians 3[176] and the earlier affirmation of what the 'Jew *(yehudah)*' should be all about if he is to win praise *(hodah)* from God (Rom. 2.28-29).

Paul evidently took a deliberate decision in composing the letter to make what must have been heard by many Jewish and Jewish-sympathizing believers as an extreme statement regarding the law (7.5-6). The tactic was the same as in Gal. 3.15-18 — to pose the antithesis between promise and law, between grace/ Spirit and law in such a way as to command the strict attention of the congregations listening to the letter being read. The rhetorical ploy in each case is the same: the strong statement invites the rejoinder, 'Why then the law?' (Gal. 3.19); and here in response to the even stronger assertion of Rom. 7.5-6, 'What then shall we say? That the law is sin?' (7.7). And thus Paul begins his most striking defence of the Law.[177] For with the introduction of the flesh to the exposition (7.5), he can unfold the plot in its full complexity.

Paul resumes his earlier evocation of the Adam story and 'the fall' (5.12-21). He speaks with existential intensity in the voice of Adam[178] — Adam who would not have known the archetypal sin of covetousness had it not been for the law telling him not to covet (7.7). But Sin grasping the opportunity provided by the commandment 'You shall not covet' stirred up covetousness in him (7.8).[179]

---

176. See above, §32.7d.

177. That a 'defence of the law' is an appropriate description of the passage should be obvious from the sequences 7.7-12, 13-14, 16-17, 22-23, though it is too little recognized (see *Theology of Paul* 156-58); here once again Esler's and Jewett's desire to show the letter's bearing on the situation in Rome (*Conflict and Identity* 239; *Romans* 440) prevents them from seeing Paul's deeper concern to understand the role of the law in relation to the gospel.

178. The reference of the 'I' of 7.7-25 is much disputed; see the full treatments of J. Lambrecht, *The Wretched "I" and Its Liberation: Paul in Romans 7 and 8* (Leuven: Peeters, 1992); B. Dodd, *Paul's Paradigmatic "I": Personal Example as Literary Strategy* (JSNTS 177; Sheffield: Sheffield Academic, 1999) ch. 7; H. Lichtenberger, *Das Ich Adams und das Ich der Menschheit. Studien zum Menschenbild in Römer 7* (WUNT 164; Tübingen: Mohr Siebeck, 2004). 'The Adamic ideal-biography is at the same time the autobiography of the man Paul'; 'at this point the generic or ideal and the individual, autobiographical I coincide' (O. Wischmeyer, 'Paulus als Ich-Erzähler. Ein Beitrag zu seiner Person, seiner Biographie and seiner Theologie', in E.-M. Becker and P. Pilhofer, eds., *Biographie und Persönlichkeit des Paulus* [WUNT 187; Tübingen: Mohr Siebeck, 2005] 88-105 [here 101-102]). Appeal to Rom. 5.13 as indicating that the law was not in existence in Adam's time (as by Esler, *Conflict and Identity* 234-36; Jewett, *Romans* 442 and n. 22) ignores the fact that whereas in Rom. 5.12-21 Adam is the beginning of the cosmic story, in 7.7-12 Adam is the archetype of human experience of the power of Sin (as in *2 Bar.* 54.19). That the command to Adam (not to eat of the tree of the knowledge of good and evil) already embodied or at least expressed the law of God was probably taken for granted in Jewish thought (see, e.g., my *Romans* 379-80; Lichtenberger ch. 15).

179. That wrong desire, lust, or covetousness was the root of all sin was an already es-

The Creator God had warned him that 'in the day you eat of it [the fruit of the tree of the knowledge of good and evil], you shall die' (Gen. 2.17). But Sin (the serpent) had deceived him (through his consort) (3.13), that is, by reassuring her that if she ate, 'You will not die' (3.4), and so he had died (Rom. 7.9-11).[180] So it was not the Law's fault: the law remains holy. Here Paul qualifies the earlier outright antithesis between Spirit and 'letter *(gramma)*' which had been at the heart of his apologia for his ministry in 2 Cor. 3.3-6. He evokes the same antithesis in Rom. 7.5-6, only to clarify it. The law itself is not *gramma; gramma* is more to be identified with the law manipulated by Sin.

How this travesty has come about Paul goes on to explain. The law's function of defining sin and bringing sin to consciousness is what the sin-provoking power of Sin manipulates (7.13). And it does so by fastening upon the weakness of the flesh: it is the legitimate appetite of the flesh which Sin turns in upon itself into greed and self-aggrandizement; it is desire *(epithymia)* which Sin turns in upon itself into its negative counterpart lust, covetousness *(epithymia)* (7.14).[181] So the typical person ('I') finds himself or herself caught in a double bind.

- On the one hand, the *self* is divided: with the mind knowing what is good and wanting to do it, but as flesh, ensnared by Sin, doing what is evil (7.15-20).
- And on the other, the *law* is divided: it is 'the law of *God*', holy, just and good (7.12), which the mind recognizes and affirms; but at the same time, it is the dupe of sin, 'the law of *sin*', manipulated by sin and increasing the self's enslavement (7.21-23).[182]

Paul ends with a cry of despair at the picture of (him)self that he has painted: 'Wretched man am I! Who will deliver me from the body of this death?' (7.24). But it is a cry demanded by the rhetoric of the dilemma he has posed. In reality, he knows that the cry has already been answered through Christ; so he rounds off his defence of the law by affirming the double division in self and law which is

---

tablished theologoumenon in Jewish thought, as James 1.15 confirms; see again my *Romans* 380; Lichtenberger, *Das Ich* ch. 16.

180. The no doubt deliberate echo of Gen. 3.13 ('the serpent deceived me and I ate') in Rom. 7.11 ('sin seizing its opportunity through the commandment deceived me and through it killed me') is generally recognized.

181. See above, n. 153.

182. The parallel between 7.18-20 (the divided 'I') and 7.21-23 (the divided law) has been too little noticed by Romans commentators (*Theology of Paul* 472-77). 'The law of sin (and death)' (7.23, 25; 8.2) can be safely regarded as Paul's summary reference to the process described in 7.7-11, 13.

the consequence of being in the flesh, and which, presumably, will continue as long as the flesh endures (7.25).[183]

(v) *8.1-39.* For all the complexity of the plot which Paul has now elaborated in this second telling of the story of the gospel, there is still one major player whose entrance has been signalled, but who has yet to come fully on stage — the Holy Spirit. This is the nearest that Paul comes to the ancient device of *deus ex machina;* when the plot has become impossibly complex, and the melodrama of human existence has reached its most pathetic nadir, the solution is unveiled in a few words. If humankind is divided within between the competing impulses and desires of the self, and if the law is divided as both 'the law of God' and 'the law of sin', then the double act of Christ and the Spirit provides the answer. Why was the law so unable to provide the answer? — Paul again looks rhetorically (or asks his reader actually to look) at Jewish believers sitting on one side of the congregation. Because in face of the weakness of human flesh (as just described), it had become a tool of sin and death (8.2-3). But God's Son had met the problem of the flesh, by coming 'in the very likeness of sinful flesh',[184] and by his death he had effected what the sin offering did — that is, had condemned and done away with 'sin in the flesh' (8.3).[185] Consequently, those who are united with Christ ('in Christ') can experience liberation from the flesh's negative impulses (passions) by which Sin and Death had previously entrapped them (8.1-2). And the Spirit in turn had similarly trumped the power of Sin and Death, liberating the law from their manipulation, with the consequence that those who live in accordance with the Spirit, and not in accordance with the flesh can now fulfil what the law really demands (8.4-6).[186] For it is impossible for those who

183. The arguments that 7.25b is a gloss (popular in the German commentary tradition, e.g., Lichtenberger, *Das Ich* 154-60, and Jewett, *Romans* 456-58; but see Haacker, *Römer* 149, and Lohse, *Römer* 224-25) or that the 'chain-link interlock' means in effect that 7.25a and 7.25b are not spoken by the same person (Longenecker, *Rhetoric at the Boundaries* 88-93; found persuasive by Klauck, *Ancient Letters* 225-26) do not give enough attention to the fact that in 8.10, 12-13 and 17-25 Paul faces up to the same condition as in 7.25b; 7.25a is as much an expression of hope (8.24-25), of the 'not yet', as it is of faith realized, the 'already'. See further *Theology of Paul* 472-82. Similarly Stuhlmacher ignores 8.10, 12-13 when he continues to insist that 'Rom. 7:7-25 and 8:1-17 are to be contrasted with one another' (*Biblische Theologie* 1.282).

184. For the exegetical issues and theological implications of this phrase see my *Romans* 421-22; Moo, *Romans* 479-80; Lohse, *Römer* 231; Jewett, *Romans* 483-84.

185. For a reference to the sin offering in the phrase 'concerning sin', see, e.g., Moo, *Romans* 480, and those referred to by him in n. 49, and by Haacker, *Römer* 152 n. 15.

186. Those who doubt that Paul could put the law and Spirit together in positive relationship simply miss the rhetoric of the exposition; precisely that paradoxical combination prevented Paul from abandoning his heritage completely and from preaching a Christianity of mystic experience and charismatic enthusiasm. See *Theology of Paul* §23 (here 642-49), also

live on the level of the flesh — seeing the satisfaction of their basic appetites and instincts as their *raison d'etre* — to please God; they will always be in captivity to the law of sin and death, unable to submit to the law of God (8.7-8).

Paul was entirely confident, writing as he was, seeking to win his audiences' welcome to Rome, that he knew what the true state of affairs was in Rome. Yet once more he pins his faith in them on the fact that they have received the Spirit;[187] indeed, more clearly than anywhere else he states bluntly that the *sine qua non* of belonging to Christ is possession of the Spirit of Christ (8.9). This is what it means to be 'in Christ' or to have Christ 'in me' — 'Christ in you' being obviously synonymous with 'having the Spirit' (8.9-10).[188] Not that this is the end of the story; as he had qualified the indicatives of 6.1-10 and 7.1-6 with the imperatives of 6.11-23 and the dividedness of 7.14-25, so now Paul reminds his audiences that though the process of salvation has begun and begun decisively, it is still to be completed.[189] Though the Spirit is already making alive and producing righteousness, the body is still dead; death has still to work out its final claim to power in the dying of the flesh (8.10). Only when the Spirit's life-giving work climaxes in life given to the mortal body — that is, the resurrection — will the process of salvation be complete (8.11).

And as in ch. 6 the reassurance that the outworking of Christ's resurrection in their lives will be completed led to a series of exhortations, so Paul drives home the point here immediately by urging in strong terms that the Roman believers should not live for the flesh. That was still evidently an all too real possibility — even for those 'in Christ' (8.1). And if they did so, it would not be possible for the Spirit to complete the work of defeating the power of Sin and Death; 'you will die!' Only if they put to death those aspects of their selfish,

---

Stuhlmacher, *Biblische Theologie* 1.266; J. L. Martyn, '*Nomos* plus Genitive Noun in Paul: The History of God's Law', in J. T. Fitzgerald et al., eds., *Early Christianity and Classical Culture*, A. J. Malherbe FS (NovTSupp 110; Leiden: Brill, 2003) 575-87; Lohse, *Römer* 230; Wilckens, *Theologie* 1/3.208-10; 'under the power of sin and flesh, the law was distorted and became an instrument concerning honor for oneself and one's group. But in Christ the law regains its proper spiritual function, which leads to genuine life (7:10-14; 8:4)' (Jewett, *Romans* 481). C. Grappe, 'Qui me délivera de ce corps de mort? L'Esprit de vie! *Romains* 7,24 et 8,2 comme elements de typologie adamique', *Biblica* 83 (2002) 472-92, suggests a twofold allusion to Adam in the contrast of 'this body of death' (7.24) with 'the Spirit of life'. For bibliography on the debate on how 'the law of the Spirit' should be understood, see, e.g., Schnelle, *History* 128.

187. See again §29.7g above.

188. See again §29 at n. 39 above.

189. As earlier in 5.1-10 and in Gal. 3.3; 6.8; 2 Cor. 4.16–5.10. Fee denies that Paul envisaged any continuing internal struggle with sin in his theologizing (*God's Empowering Presence* 537-39, 547, 556, 559), but it is difficult to make sense of an exhortation such as 6.12-13, a statement such as 8.10 and a warning such as 8.12-13 other than in terms of moral choices to be repeatedly made (the powers of sin and death to be constantly resisted).

self-assertive living would the life of the Spirit flourish and grow fruitful (8.12-13).[190] That is what it meant in existential reality to be a son of God — to be led by the Spirit (8.14).[191] It is not a fearful checking of the rule-book to see whether one had been guilty of some minor infringement ('a spirit of slavery, falling back into fear')[192] — that was how it had been with Luther before he discovered that God's righteousness was his saving, not his punitive, righteousness — but 'the Spirit of adoption', a joyful, often intense sense of being God's child, echoing the distinctive prayer of Jesus, crying 'Abba! Father!', and knowing that, wonder of wonders, being united with Christ, we share Jesus' own sonship (8.15-16).[193]

Ever since the near-death experience of the crisis in Asia (2 Cor. 1.8-9),[194] Paul could not rejoice in the experience of God's Spirit/grace without at once remembering that God's saving righteousness works itself out in the midst of, and indeed through the trials and tribulations of, the Christian and especially the apostolic life. So here, the thought of sharing in God's inheritance together with Christ ('heirs together with Christ') is at once tempered by the cautionary note: 'provided that we suffer with him in order that we might also be glorified with him' (8.17). And with this thought Paul opens up once again the whole cosmic dimension of the story whose second telling began with Adam (5.12). For the suffering which tempers and refines and matures (5.3-5), in preparation for the restoration of and to the glory of man/Adam as the image and glory of God (8.18), is a suffering shared with creation as a whole. The degree to which the created order is dysfunctional and out-of-joint is a reflection of the human shortfall from the glory of God (3.23); as the creation participated in the results of human disobedience,[195] so creation shares the 'futility' (8.20 — *mataiotēs*) of humankind consequent upon turning its back on God (1.21 — *mataioomai*).[196] But

---

190. Here particularly we see the danger of taking the indicative of 6.1-4, 7.1-6 and 8.1-11 in isolation from what follows in each case.

191. Paul picks up the same theme elaborated in other terms in Gal. 5.16-26; see above, §31.7d.

192. Bultmann's shrewd observation that 'the hidden side of "boasting" . . . is the fear which the man who is concerned for himself has, a fear which arises . . . from zeal in the works of the Law' (*Theology* 1.243) well highlights the fear which actually motivates so much fundamentalism. Here again the contrast between a spirit of slavery and a spirit of sonship is probably a deliberate echo of Exodus language (Keesmaat, *Paul and His Story* ch. 2).

193. That the language, practice and experience echo that of Jesus is highly probable; see *Jesus Remembered* 711-18.

194. See above, §32.2e and n. 432.

195. There is a strong allusion here to Gen. 3.17-19. See also H. A. Hahne, *The Corruption and Redemption of Creation: Nature in Romans 8.19-22 and Jewish Apocalyptic Literature* (LNTS 336; London: Clark, 2006).

196. These are the only passages where Paul uses these terms; cf. 1 Cor. 3.20; 15.17

the gospel is a message of hope — at the cosmic level as well as the personal level. For though the liberation of creation from corruption awaits 'the revelation of the sons of God' (8.19-21), they share a common suffering-with-promise — the suffering of labour pains prior to the birth of the child (8.22). It is this sense of out-of-jointness, of already knowing the life-giving power of the Spirit but having to express it still through 'the body of death' (7.24; 8.10), with all the attendant frustrations and failings which Paul knew all too well, which is actually a sign of the Spirit working towards the final stage of salvation, the second stage of adoption,[197] that is, 'the redemption of the body' (8.23). Here again, as in 2 Cor. 4.7–5.5, Paul boldly transforms the 'problem of suffering' into a promise of full deliverance.

With this thought Paul is well into the final chapter of his second telling of the gospel story at the cosmic level. The thought of continued suffering and 'groaning' is further lightened by a threefold assurance:

- that the picture just sketched is the nature of Christian hope: not invested in the present state of affairs, 'what is seen', but confidence in God and in God fulfilling his purpose as engendering the patience of hope (8.25);
- that 'the Spirit also helps us in our weakness', doing for us what we cannot do for ourselves in maintaining communion with God, in and through the very honesty of our inability to find the right words to pray and the right things to ask for (8.26-27);
- and the assurance that God works out his eternal purpose, to restore his created order to his image so clearly embodied in his Son, and to do so precisely in and through all that happens (8.28-30).

The assured climax of it all is the final appearing before God on the day of judgment, when what will count first and foremost and finally will be God's love for his human creation as expressed in the death of his Son.[198] The image of effective sacrifice merges into that of the effective intercessor at God's right hand,

---

(mataios). This passage provides a quite different strand for Christian ecological concern than those which emphasize human domination over or stewardship for the non-human.

197. It will be no mere coincidence that Paul uses the metaphor of 'adoption (huiothesia)' twice within the same paragraph: 'the Spirit of adoption', which begins the process of claiming back the individual (8.15), and final adoption, that is, 'the redemption of the body' (8.23), where the conceptuality elaborated in 1 Cor. 15.42-57 is clearly in play, as also in Rom. 8.11.

198. It is probable that Rom. 8.32 echoes Gen. 22.16 and the earliest reflection on the sacrifice of Isaac (the Aqedah), which may have been already current in Jewish thought (Theology of Paul 224-25; Lohse, Römer 255 and n. 5), though the point can be easily overstated, as several warn (Fitzmyer, Romans 531-32; Moo, Romans 540 n. 18; Jewett, Romans 537-38).

pleading our case and ensuring our final acquittal (8.31-34). The cluster of imagery here becomes confusing: 'Christ in you' (8.10) has given way to the Son who is the elder brother of a large family (8.29), and now reverts to the law-court imagery of judgment and acquittal (justification). Quite how Paul meshed the imagery of union with Christ, in death and resurrection, with the family imagery of shared sonship, with the sacrificial imagery of the son (Isaac) offered by the father (Abraham), with the sin offering (8.3), with the first and final verdict of acquittal is not clear. Indeed, the multiplicity of images and the fact that they do not all easily integrate with one another or complement each other has caused endless debate within subsequent Christian scholarship as one commentator emphasizes one image to the virtual exclusion of the rest, and another subordinates the rest to a different image, and so on in an endless round of theological debate. It is important, then, simply to note that Paul himself did not attempt to integrate these images and was content to lay them side by side, presumably in an attempt to indicate the many-faceted promise of the gospel and in the hope that different images would resonate more powerfully with different audiences as his letter was listened to, studied and pondered.[199]

The final thought is another purple passage where Paul expresses his full assurance that all the suffering endured by believers — he could readily illustrate from his own experience — would never be sufficient to overwhelm the love of God (8.35-37). As the first telling had climaxed in the sure confidence of the individual suffering believer in final salvation (5.1-11), so the second telling maintains its cosmic perspective: nothing in all creation, neither Death (the last enemy — 1 Cor. 15.26), nor Life(!), nor anything that may threaten human individuality and experience has the capacity to separate 'from the love of God in Christ Jesus our Lord' (8.38-39).

e. What Then of Israel (Romans 9–11)?

At this point we may well envisage Paul stopping in his dictation and sending Tertius home to return next day. The mental application, not to mention the theological concentration involved in the second telling of the gospel story (5.12–8.39) and the spiritual exaltation expressed in the final paragraphs, must have left Paul drained. What we may imagine was important at that moment was time for a break, time to allow reflection on the development of what was becoming a treatise, time to consider whether the threads and thrust of his exposition were still clear. So it is significant that when dictation resumed, Paul turned abruptly to the

---

199. See further *Theology of Paul* 328-33; also *New Perspective on Paul* (2005) 85-86, 88, (2008) 94-95, 97.

question of Israel — not, it should be noted, to the question of how Israel related to 'the church', as though 'the church' was already formulated in Paul's mind as equivalent to 'Israel', let alone as superseding Israel.[200] As already noted, the term 'church' (singular) appears only once in the letter in reference to Rome itself, and only in reference to one of the apartment congregations in Rome (16.5). And earlier it was observed that *ekklēsia* would most likely have been originally understood in its sense of 'assembly', without any marked distinction in connotation from its near synonym 'synagogue' (§§30.1, 3-4). More to the point here, the subject matter of chs. 9–11 is exclusively 'Israel'; even when Gentile believers are brought fully into view, they are done so under the imagery of branches grafted into the olive tree which is Israel (11.17-24). Having told the story of the gospel in terms of Jew and Gentile, and retold it in cosmic terms, Paul in effect turns to yet a third telling, the gospel as the story of Israel.

Why this exclusive focus on Israel? The most obvious answer is that Paul was preaching a gospel which was/is Jewish through and through. It centred on the Messiah of Israel, son of David (1.3). It drew its principal category of God's saving righteousness entirely from Israel's understanding of God having committed himself to be their God and they to be his people (1.16-17). Paul's exposition had set out to puncture the presumption of the 'Jew' (2.1-29), provoking the earlier question, 'What then is the advantage of being a Jew?' (3.1). He had emphasized repeatedly that God's saving righteousness was for *all* who believed, Jew first but also Gentile. He had argued to his own satisfaction that believing Abraham rather than faithful Abraham was the pattern to be emulated (ch. 4). He had set out a different portrayal of the law as the key to understanding both its continuing function (as the measure of sin) and its failure to provide an answer to the power of sin — different, that is, from the assumption that having the law and living a committed (and distinctively Jewish) life as required by the law ('works of the law') was what God demanded above all else (5.12–8.4). And not least, in the final section of the preceding exposition he had freely drawn on categories which Scripture used of Israel — 'saints', 'those who love God', 'the called', 'firstborn' (8.27-30)[201] — and used them of his gospel to all who believe. Paul clearly expected his audiences to understand that the blessings to which they were heir were the blessings of Israel.

(i) *9.1-29.* Such a claim naturally raised again the question of 3.1: What then of Israel itself? That this was indeed Paul's line of thought is indicated by the

---

200. It needs to be constantly repeated that the subject of chs. 9–11 is not 'the church and Israel', as so often assumed. The theme is simply 'Israel' (*Theology of Paul* 507, and more fully, 504-509).

201. For documentation of these as self-referential terms in Jewish literature, see my *Romans* 19-20, 481, 485.

way he opens the next section — precisely by reaffirming the blessings of Israel as the blessings *still* of Israel (9.4-5).[202] The very items which he had already claimed for his gospel and for believing Gentiles — particularly 'adoption', 'glory', 'the promises',[203] and the Messiah[204] — are (still) the privileges of *Israel.* It is precisely because these are Israel's blessings that the problem to be addressed in chs. 9–11 arises. If they are Israel's blessings, why has Israel failed to enter into them as they come through the gospel — the Spirit of adoption, the promised new covenant, the Messiah Jesus?[205] And if they are being claimed (instead) by believing Gentiles, are they no longer Israel's? Paul's immediate response, as already noted — but it is important to take the point on board — is that the blessings are still Israel's. Here we should note its plight restated in terms of the third story: not now human sinfulness (including Jews); not now human slavery to the dominion of Sin and Death; but now Israel's (for Paul) inexplicable failure to recognize Israel's Messiah and to respond positively to the gospel of this Christ.

So the question is posed afresh, and still more sharply.[206] If this is the case — that these are still Israel's blessings, and the word of God has not failed (9.6) — then what does it mean to be 'Israel'? The question introduces a convoluted argument; whether Paul had used it before or crafted it for this letter does not change the fact that it would have required careful thought and composition in his dictation.[207] It is convoluted precisely because Paul wanted to hold together

202. The present tense of 9.4 ('who are Israelites') obviously carries over into the following catalogue: 'whose are the adoption, the glory and the covenants, the law, the service and the promises; whose are the fathers and from whom is the Christ' (9.4-5).

203. Adoption — Rom. 8.15; glory — 5.2; 8.18, 21; promises — 4.13-20; for the other items on the list see again my *Romans* 527-28.

204. Rom. 9.5 is the clearest example of where *Christos* in Paul retains its titular sense — 'the Messiah' (*Theology of Paul* 198). On the issue of whether Paul speaks of Christ as God here, see my *Theology of Paul* 255-57; Lohse, *Römer* 269-70; H.-C. Kammler, 'Die Prädikation Jesu Christi als "Gott" und die paulinische Christologie. Erwägungen zur Exegese von Röm 9,5b', *ZNW* 94 (2003) 164-80; Jewett, *Romans* 567-69.

205. That Israel's refusal of the gospel caused Paul's anguish is implicit in the opening verses (9.1-2), particularly in the echo of Moses' willingness to be destroyed (9.3 — *anathema*) if only Israel's sin (the golden calf) would be forgiven (Exod. 32.32). That Israel's refusal was in mind would probably have been obvious to the Roman audiences (not least in view of the indictment of ch. 2 climaxing in talk of Israel's faithlessness in 3.3), but in chs. 9–11 Paul chooses to unfold this fact more slowly (10.21), just as he had slowly unveiled his interlocutor in ch. 2 as the self-styled 'Jew'.

206. Each telling of the gospel story raises its immediate question: 'What advantage has the Jew?' (3.1); 'Is the law sin?' (7.7); and now, 'Has the word of God failed?', and, in effect, 'Who/What is Israel?' (9.6). That it is precisely these three questions which are raised confirms the strongly Jewish focus sustained throughout the letter.

207. There is a roundedness to chs. 9–11 which suggests that Paul may have formulated and used its line of argument at some earlier stage. But if so, it does not follow that chs. 9–11

what must have seemed to others two incompatible assertions: that the blessings of the *gospel* (to all) are the blessings of Israel; and yet they remain *Israel's* blessings. It is convoluted because Paul begins by redefining 'Israel', not least so that *Gentiles* can be included within that definition (9.24); but also he could not let go the promises to Israel in its *ethnic identity,* and his argument ends up by so reaffirming (11.26); the word of God has *not* failed.

At first the exposition of who or what is 'Israel' seems straightforward. Paul points out that the promise came down from Abraham not through physical descent alone (Isaac and not Ishmael), and not by virtue of any good or bad they could have done (Jacob and not Esau, still in the womb).[208] So 'Israel' is not to be defined in terms of ethnic identity or law-keeping (9.6-12). Rather 'Israel' is defined in terms of God's call, as the 'called' of God:[209] not embracing all Abraham's offspring, but 'in Isaac shall your seed be called *(klēthēsetai)'* (9.7); the purpose of God stands in terms of election, 'not from works but from him who calls *(kalountos)'* (9.12).[210]

Paul does not hide the seeming arbitrariness of this choice made by God; it is a consequence of the corollary affirmation that human beings can do nothing to achieve their salvation and are wholly dependent on the promise and grace of God.[211] So he at once faces up to the harshness of what he has affirmed: that there is a dark side of those not called — the Esaus and the Pharaohs of this world (9.13, 17), the shadow counterpart to Jacob and Moses' Israel. His theological rationale has three elements:

- nothing should detract from the sovereignty of the Creator God, who has the power of the potter to determine what he makes and for what purpose

---

form an awkward insertion into the letter. On the contrary, it suggests rather both that Paul had reflected for some time on the issues here discussed and that he gave this exposition final form precisely as the third account of his gospel and in many ways as the climax of Romans. See further, e.g., Fitzmyer, *Romans* 540-41; Moo, *Romans* 547-54; Wright, 'Romans' 620-26.

208. The references are to Gen. 21.12 and 18.10, 14, the first of a sequence of quotations from the Jewish Scriptures which are such a feature of these chapters.

209. Here the play on *klētoi* ('called' — 8.28) with *kaleō* ('call' — 8.30; 9.7, 12, 24-25) and possibly also with *ekklēsia* ('church') should not be missed. Davies speaks fittingly of 'an over-arching monotheism of grace which can embrace the differences that now separate Jews and Christians and hold them together' ('Paul' 727).

210. In 9.11-12 'doing good or evil' is not simply equivalent to 'works (of the law)'; Paul could never have thought of 'doing evil' as a demand of the law. God's sovereign election/call is 'dependent *neither* on any human activity of good or evil, *nor* on the demonstration of covenant faithfulness' (*New Perspective on Paul* [2005] 46, [2008] 50).

211. 'The idea of "election" — i.e. of having been chosen out and pre-ordained by God unto salvation — is an immediate and pure expression of the actual religious experience of grace' (R. Otto, *The Idea of the Holy* [London: Oxford University, 1923] 91).

(9.19-21);[212] presumably Paul and his audiences would think of individuals who seemed destined (not least in character) for different levels and functions of society, and of peoples seemingly destined for a tragic role in human history; nothing is to be gained by closing one's eyes to or denying what can only be experienced as either blind or malicious fate or as God's seeming arbitrariness in the unfolding of human history and heritage;

• the most fundamental character of the sovereign God's dealings with humankind is *mercy* — '"I will have mercy on whom I have mercy . . ."' [Exod. 33.19]; so it is not a matter of who wills or who runs but of God who shows mercy' (Rom. 9.15-16); this is the central element of Paul's faith in God to which he clings to the last (11.30-32);

• this play between divine (arbitrary-seeming) sovereignty and assurance of God's mercy will provide the twist in the plot of the story of Israel by which Paul will resolve the paradox of the two sides of God's purpose: that Israel itself is now experiencing the dark side of God's purpose, 'vessels of wrath made ready for destruction' (9.22-23), so that 'the vessels of mercy' may be seen to be determined by God's call, 'not only from Jews but also from Gentiles' (9.24);[213] or alternatively expressed, that Israel itself, like the 'I' and the law in 7.14-20, is divided, the tension between flesh and Spirit of ch. 8 mirrored in the tension between ethnic Israel and the Israel of God's call.[214]

This last point is reinforced by a sequence of quotations from Hosea and Isaiah: the Hosea references emphasizing that Israel's very nature is as a people 'called' — the 'non-people' called 'my people', the 'not-loved loved', a 'not-my-people called sons of the living God' (9.25-26); the Isaiah references reminding that Israel's hope in the past had focused in a remnant (9.27-29).[215]

(ii) *9.30–10.21*. Where does that leave the question of Israel? The troubling fact, from Paul's perspective, was that Israel, despite pursuing the law (as the measure) of righteousness, had not reached it, had not attained that righteousness. Why? Because they had assumed it was simply or pre-eminently a matter of doing what the law laid down ('as if it was a matter of works'); the attitude

212. The quotation from Isa. 29.16 in 9.20 is clear, as is the allusion in 9.21 to the image of the creator God as a potter moulding his clay, popular in Jewish thought (e.g., Ps. 2.9; Isa. 41.25; 45.9; Jer. 18.1-6; Sir. 33.13; 1QS 11.22).

213. Although the story in terms of 'Jew and Gentile' (chs. 1–5) has been replaced by the story of Israel ('Jew/Gentile [Greek]' — chs. 1–5 [five times] and chs. 9–11 [once]; 'Israel' — chs. 1–8 [none] and chs. 9–11 [eleven times]), the reversion here to the terms of the first telling is a reminder that it is the same story being thus told in different ways.

214. I develop this way of reading chs. 9–11 in *Theology of Paul* §19.

215. Rom. 9.25-26 — Hos. 2.1, 23; 9.27-29; Isa. 1.9; 10.22-23.

critiqued under the motif of 'boasting' in both 2.17-24 and 3.27-31 (and earlier in Gal. 2.14-16) will at least in part be in view (9.31-32).[216] Whereas Gentiles, despite not pursuing righteousness as measured by the law, have attained the goal that Israel had sought. Why? Because they had realized that the key was faith, faith as distinct from works and independently of works (9.30, 32). The crucial difference was brought out into the open by their respective attitudes to God's Messiah Jesus: to a law-obedience-as-what-mattered attitude, Jesus had proved 'a stumbling and a rock of offence' (again as God had intended), but to believers Jesus was the true basis for confidence — Isa. 28.16 providing a neat expression of the two-handedness of God's purpose (9.33).[217]

If the talk of Israel 'pursuing a law of righteousness', and doing so ineffectively 'as if it was from works' (9.31-32), is somewhat obscure, Paul repeats the analysis of Israel's plight in alternative terms. He commends his fellow Jews for their 'zeal for God' (10.2), just as he had for their pursuit of the law of righteousness (9.31). But as one who had himself been 'zealous' for God, he knew well that he had been operating from a false understanding of the righteousness of God.[218] As he had been, so Israel also generally had been too much concerned to establish its own righteousness, as something which was peculiarly Israel's *(tēn idian dikaiosynēn)* and not available to those outside its bounds.[219] In consequence, when that saving righteousness had been extended to Gentiles, Paul's fellow Jews had in effect disowned it. They had failed to recognize that the coming of the Messiah had brought 'an end *(telos)*[220] to the law as the means to righteousness' (10.4), a righteousness conceived by them as open only to (ethnic) Israel and those who joined themselves to (ethnic) Israel. Whereas 'the righteousness of God' (again the key theme of the letter) is 'for all who believe' (again the central claim of the gospel) (10.4).

216. See above, §27.4-5, and §§33.3b(ii) and c(i).

217. Isa. 28.16 in 9.33: 'Behold, I place in Sion a stone of stumbling and a rock of offence; and he who believes in me shall not be put to shame'.

218. See above, §25.2c; cf. V. M. Smiles, 'The Concept of "Zeal" in Second-Temple Judaism and Paul's Critique of It in Romans 10:2', *CBQ* 64 (2002) 282-99.

219. This is the probable connotation of *idios,* though the point is disputed; see my *New Perspective on Paul* 10-11 and n. 40, where I also observe that the link between 'zeal' and 'establishing (Greek *stēsai,* Hebrew *hēqim*) their own *(idian)* righteousness' has been largely missed (my *Romans* 588, with reference particularly to Sir. 44.20; 45.23; 1 Macc. 2.27); see also Jewett, *Romans* 617-18.

220. *Telos* can mean also 'goal'; both 'end' and 'goal' can fit here, as the fairly even split among commentators illustrates, but the echo of the argument of Gal. 3.19-29 (particularly 22-25) strongly suggests that it was the end of an era which Paul had principally in mind (*Theology of Paul* 368-69; cf. the discussions of R. Badenas, *Christ the End of the Law: Romans 10:4 in Pauline Perspective* [JSNTS 10; Sheffield: JSOT, 1985]; Fitzmyer, *Romans* 584-85; Moo, *Romans* 636-42; Haacker, *Römer* 206-209; Lohse, *Römer* 291-93; Jewett, *Romans* 619-20), but Esler overemphasizes the point in his reading of 10.4-13 (*Conflict and Identity* 285-87).

To press home the point Paul essays a bold distinction between two classic texts referring to the function and keeping of the law. One is Lev. 18.5, which he had cited briefly in Gal. 3.12: 'The one who does these things will live by them'. For Paul this summed up the role of the law for Israel, as dictating the way in which the people should live and as promising (length of) life to those who ordered their lives accordingly (10.5).[221] The other is Deut. 30.12-14. That it was originally intended to encourage the keeping of the law is clear: the commandment is not too hard and not too far away, neither in heaven nor far across the sea, so that you have to seek it out in order to know what it is; 'No, the word is very near to you; it is in your mouth and in your heart *so that you can do it*' (30.14). But we know that the thought of knowledge of God's will not having to be searched for in heaven or across the sea provoked reflection on the passage in terms of divine Wisdom (Bar. 3.29-30) and in terms of 'the good' (Philo, *Post.* 84-85).[222] The imagery, in other words, invited the insight that the law was actually the expression of something still greater and more universal — divine Wisdom,[223] 'the good' which was the goal of religious philosophy.[224] It is this line of reflection on which Paul draws. For him this more transcendent reality of which Deuteronomy speaks is nothing other than the word of faith. It comes to focus not in the Torah but in Christ and in the gospel, 'the word of faith' which Paul and the other Christian missionaries preached (10.6-8).[225]

The line of exposition is not so contrived as it first appears — and as it

221. This was the original sense of Lev. 18.5, as its earliest elaboration in Ezek. 20.5-26 indicates, and as the parallel exhortations elsewhere in Jewish literature confirm (e.g., Deut. 4.1; 5.32-33; 30.15-20; Neh. 9.29; Prov. 3.1-2; Bar. 4.1; *Ep. Aris.* 127; Philo, *Cong.* 86-87; *4 Ezra* 7.21). The promise element was already being interpreted as a promise of life beyond death/eternal life (CD 3.20; Mark 10.17), but it is not clear that Paul was reading it in that extended way here. See my *New Perspective on Paul* (2005) 65-67, (2008) 73-76; cf. Moo, *Romans* 647-50; 'the word *zēsetai* has for the apostle not an eschatological meaning, but it characterizes the essence of law-righteousness' (Lohse, *Römer* 294).

222. Bar. 3.29-30 — 'Who has gone up into heaven and got it and brought it down from the clouds? Who has gone across to the other side of the sea and found it, and will gain it with choice gold?' (towards the end of a hymn to divine Wisdom, subsequently identified with 'the book of the commandments of God' — 4.1). Philo, *Post.* 84-85 — 'What he describes as "close by" and "near" is the good. For it is not necessary, he [Moses] says, "to fly up into heaven" or to go "to the other side of the sea" in searching for what is good. For it is "near" and "close by" for each. . . . "For", he says, "it is in your mouth and in your heart and in your hands"' (Philo using the LXX version). See more fully my *Romans* 602-605.

223. Baruch's claim, like that of ben Sira (Sir. 24.23), was precisely that the otherwise inaccessible wisdom of God, that which partook of God's very character as manifest in creation, was in fact actually accessible in and as the Torah (Bar. 3.37–4.1)

224. W. Grundmann, *agathos, TDNT* 1.11-12.

225. Cf. J. P. Heil, 'Christ, the Termination of the Law (Romans 9:30–10:8)', *CBQ* 63 (2001) 484-98.

may have appeared to Paul's Roman audiences when they first heard it. On fuller consideration, after more careful instruction in and study of Paul's teaching in the letter, Paul could probably expect them to recognize two earlier clues to a fuller understanding of his exposition of Deut. 30.12-14. One was what he had just said about Christ as the *telos* of the law (10.4); Christ had in effect replaced the law in God's scheme of salvation.[226] The other was the much earlier description of the law as 'the law of faith' (3.27), along with Paul's insistence that faith actually establishes the law (3.31). This was presumably why Paul could ignore the final clause of Deut. 30.14 ('so that you can do it') in good conscience. For in his view, the law could only be 'done' through faith; what God required in terms of the law could only be met by those who lived 'from faith', from that basic trust in and dependence on God, or, alternatively expressed, who 'walked in accordance with the Spirit' (8.4). So Deut. 30.12-14 could be justifiably read as calling for the faith which is the *only* way to do or fulfil what God expects of his human creatures. And as before, that faith is now focused by the gospel in Christ. Consequently, Deuteronomy's talk of 'in your mouth' can be referred to the baptismal confession called for by the gospel, that 'Jesus is Lord'; and 'in your heart' can be referred to the belief called for by the gospel that 'God raised him from the dead' (10.9-10). This ties back into the Isa. 28.16 passage already quoted (9.33): 'Everyone [the 'all' again, and on this occasion inserted into the quotation][227] who believes in him shall not be put to shame' (10.11). And to ram the point home yet once more, Paul insists on the 'all', Jew as well as Greek; the Lord whom they confess is 'Lord of *all,* rich to *all* who call upon him, for "*everyone* who calls upon the name of the Lord shall be saved" [Joel 2.32]' (10.12-13).[228]

The thought of the gospel as the more/most/final effective revelation of divine Wisdom prompts Paul to a fuller statement of the current tragedy of Israel. For the means by which faith is inculcated is by hearing the gospel preached (10.17); and for the gospel to be preached requires preachers commissioned by God and his Christ, as Isaiah's talk of those who 'proclaim good news' (Isa. 52.7) foreshadowed (10.14-15).[229] And such there have been — Paul was one among

226. In recent literature cf. particularly Donaldson, *Paul and the Gentiles.*

227. First noted by E. E. Ellis, *Paul's Use of the Old Testament* (Grand Rapids: Eerdmans, 1957) 140; see further Jewett, *Romans* 631-32.

228. The clear reference to Christ of a prophecy which envisages the survivors of Jerusalem calling upon God (Joel 2.32) is very striking (see also above, §23.4d). There is an analogous train of thought behind the use of Deut. 30.12-14: that the Torah is in an important sense the embodiment of divine Wisdom, now even more completely embodied in Christ and in 'the word of faith'. On the significance of identifying Christ in terms of Wisdom, see my *Christology* 168-96 and *Theology of Paul* 266-81.

229. The quotation of Isa. 52.7 suggests that the Isaianic vision of the preacher of good

many. The trouble was that Israel had not believed the message, as again Isaiah had foreshadowed in the same passage (Isa. 53.1) (10.16). The gospel had indeed gone to Israel, as indeed to the ends of the earth. But Israel had not responded. Deut. 32.21 provided the next clue: that in the mystery of the divine purpose for Israel he was seeking to provoke Israel to jealousy by a non-nation (10.19).[230] In consequence, whereas, again in the words of Isaiah (65.1), God had been found (through the gospel) by Gentiles who had not sought him, Israel had proved to be recalcitrant; as expressed once more by the same passage (65.2), God had 'stretched out his hands' in vain 'to a disobedient and obstinate people' (10.20-21). The conundrum of the dark side of God's purpose and of the divided Israel had not yet been resolved.

(iii) *11.1-36.* This now-clear indictment of Israel's disobedience, like that of the earlier indictment of his fellow Jews' faithlessness (3.3), prompts for Paul once again the question both of God's faithfulness and of his continuing purpose for his people (ethnic) Israel: 'Has God repudiated his people?' (11.1). It is the same issue being posed as in 9.6; has the argument not progressed? Yes indeed, for the threads which will contribute to the answer have been individually drawn out and can now be woven into the final pattern — the inference that the dark side of God's saving purpose paradoxically may embrace Israel itself (9.22-24), the tradition that only a remnant of Israel will remain faithful (9.27-29), and the hint provided by Deuteronomy that God will provoke Israel to jealousy by those who hitherto were not his people (10.19). So Paul can confidently reject the possibility that God has rejected his people by drawing the threads together.

- There are those Israelites who have responded to the gospel — himself for a start (11.1), and those foreshadowed by God's answer to Elijah of the many more than Elijah who had not bowed the knee to Baal (11.2-4 — 1 Kgs. 19.18).[231] 'So too in the present time, there is a remnant in accordance with the election of grace', demonstrating again — and here too the third telling intersects with the first — that being 'Israel' (or being a 'Jew')

---

news lay behind Paul's use of the term 'gospel', as also behind Jesus' preaching (*Theology of Paul* 167-69; *Jesus Remembered* 656), though Paul may also have been conscious of the political overtones of the term 'gospel' (see above, §29.4d; Jewett, *Romans* 639-40).

230. On the crucial role of Deut. 32.21 in helping resolve Paul's puzzle, see R. H. Bell, *Provoked to Jealousy: The Origin and Purpose of the Jealousy Motif in Romans 9–11* (WUNT 2.63; Tübingen: Mohr Siebeck, 1994); Jewett, *Romans* 644-47; also Esler, *Conflict and Identity* 288-93; otherwise M. Baker, 'Paul and the Salvation of Israel: Paul's Ministry, the Motif of Jealousy, and Israel's Yes', *CBQ* 67 (2005) 469-84.

231. Perhaps with the unspoken inference that Jewish non-believers are equivalent to the worshippers of Baal? Cf. A. Lindemann, 'Paulus und Elia. Zur Argumentation in Röm 11,1-12', in Lehnert and Rüsen-Weinhold, eds., *Logos — Logik — Lyrik* 201-18.

is not a matter of works like circumcision (2.25-29) but wholly of grace (11.5-6).

• Israel, Paul now confirms the suggestion of 9.22-23, is experiencing the dark side of God's call. 'The elect' are not simply identical with ethnic Israel. That only a remnant has responded to God's grace implies that the rest (of ethnic Israel) have been 'hardened'. Paul does not hesitate to reaffirm the harshness of the earlier analysis of the role of Pharaoh within God's purpose (9.17-18)[232] and of the divine potter's deliberately making vessels 'for dishonourable use', 'vessels of wrath' (9.21-22), and to apply that analysis directly to 'the rest' of Israel (11.7), confirming it from Israel's own Scriptures (11.8-10).[233]

• But the way to see this, as a phase in God's dealings with Israel and in the outworking of his saving purpose, is in terms of the success of the Gentile mission. As the bright side of Pharaoh's hardening was Israel's deliverance from slavery, so the bright side of Israel's failure has been 'salvation for Gentiles'. The thread of divine purpose is seen in the sequence — Israel's trespass → Gentiles' salvation → provoking Israel to jealousy → the full and complete triumph of God's saving purpose for Israel ('how much more' — 11.11-12).

This last, Paul makes it clear, was the inspiration behind his own mission: as apostle to the Gentiles, not giving up on his own people, but seeing the success of his mission as a crucial factor in winning his own people to faith, to the experience of salvation, and in hope that that further success would herald the final resurrection, 'life from the dead' (11.13-15).[234]

The for Paul happy prospect of Israel's coming reintegration into God's saving purpose leads him at once to reflect back on the beginning of the process: how God's saving purpose began to come to lasting effect with the promises to the patriarchs. It was that set-apartness (holiness) to this saving purpose which ensures that what has grown from that root shares in the same holiness (11.16). And what has grown from the root is Israel, imaged as a cultivated olive tree (11.17-24).[235] Into this tree the Gentile believers (imaged as shoots from a wild

---

232. It is not necessary to resolve the issue of whether Pharaoh was hardened or hardened himself (see my *Romans* 554-55); here it is plain that the hardening is the action of God — 'the rest were hardened' (*epōrōthēsan*, divine passive).

233. Rom. 11.8 — Deut. 29.4; Rom. 11.9-11 — Ps. 69.22-23. As in 3.10-18, what was a curse directed against Israel's enemies is turned against Israel itself (my *Romans* 649-50).

234. On the eschatology here and its implications for Paul's own self-understanding as apostle, see above, §29.3e(2).

235. In Jewish writings Israel had occasionally been likened to an olive tree (Jer. 11.16; Hos. 14.6); the olive was the most widely cultivated fruit tree in the Mediterranean area.

olive) have been grafted. Some of the original branches have been broken off, that is true. But that is no occasion for pride on the part of the newly grafted-in branches; they are sustained only by the richness of the original root (11.17-18), and they may equally be broken off in turn, if they fail in faith (11.19-21). As in 2.6-11 the even-handed impartiality of God can be taken as a basic given (11.22). Gentile believers therefore must not make the same mistake as the original Jewish branches — the mistake of 'boasting *(katakauchaomai)'*[236] in their privilege (of being part of the olive tree) over those not part of it (11.18). If they have been 'unnaturally' grafted in,[237] how much more easily will the natural branches be grafted back into their own olive tree if and when they believe (11.23-24).[238] This is the first and firm striking of a chord (warning against Gentile presumption, as he had earlier warned against Jewish presumption) which Paul will play repeatedly in the final section of the letter;[239] so we can justifiably infer that in so dictating this warning he already had in mind the situation in the Roman congregations to be addressed in ch. 14.

And so the third telling of the story reaches its own climax. The answer to the puzzles and questions posed in 9.6 and 11.1 can be revealed as the unveiling of the 'mystery' of God's saving purpose.[240] 'Hardening in part has come over Israel, until the full number of the Gentiles has come in; and so all Israel will be saved' (11.25-26). Here he holds together the double sense of 'Israel', or, alternatively expressed, both sides of the divided Israel. He does not let go the sense of ethnic Israel: the unbelieving majority of ethnic Jews is the partial hardening of Israel (or hardening of part of Israel).[241] The 'all Israel' must at least include 'all (the ethnic) Israel' that has been hardened.[242] At the same time, Israel defined as and by the call of God is not lost sight of: the 'all Israel' will include the wild

236. *Katakauchaomai,* 'boast at the expense of another, *boast against, exult over'* (BDAG 517), a more virulent form of a term so central to the earlier critique of Jews — *kauchaomai* (2.17, 23), *kauchēma/kauchēsis* (3.27; 4.2).

237. See P. F. Esler, 'Ancient Oleiculture and Ethnic Differentiation: The Meaning of the Olive-Tree Image in Romans 11', *JSNT* 26 (2003) 103-24.

238. The imagery, of course, is forced: branches cut off wither and die; they cannot be grafted back. But Paul, of course, rests his hope at this point in the miracle-working God.

239. Rom. 12.3; 14.3, 10; 15.1.

240. *Mystērion,* 'mystery', understood by Paul as the final (eschatological) purpose of God hidden from the generations but now revealed in Christ and through the apostles, becomes a major motif in subsequent Pauline literature — particularly Col. 1.26-27; 2.2; 4.3 and Eph. 1.9; 3.3-4, 9; 5.32; 6.19. See above, §29 n. 114; Jewett, *Romans* 687-89.

241. On the ambiguity of the phrase *apo merous* ('partial' or 'in part'), see Moo, *Romans* 717 n. 28; Jewett, *Romans* 699-700.

242. On the debate as to the scope of the reference of *'all* Israel', see particularly Moo, *Romans* 720-23, including his distinction between 'all Israel' and 'every Israelite' (722 n. 55), of which Jewett needs to take note (*Romans* 702).

branches grafted in as well as the natural branches re-grafted (11.23-24), will include the Gentile 'non-people' now called 'my people' (9.24-25). So Paul has no hesitation in reaffirming Isaiah's hope (Isa. 59.20-21) for Israel of a reconstituted covenant with Israel (11.26-27), no hesitation in reaffirming God's election and call of Israel (11.28-29).[243] Israel's time on the dark side of God's purpose, as enemies of and disobedient to God's purpose expressed in and through the gospel, will end in God's mercy (11.28, 30). Israel's experience, in fact, is the paradigm for God's saving purpose for *all:* to absorb human disobedience and limit its effect 'in order that he might have mercy on *all*' (11.31-32).[244]

How far did Paul think through the ramifications of this extraordinary climax to his wrestling with a problem which caused him such personal anguish we cannot say. It is, after all a 'mystery' which he was unveiling; that is, he was attempting to express the inexpressible — the way God was working out his purpose for Israel and for humankind. And he was all too conscious that he was attempting in effect to draw from the unplumbable depths of the divine purpose. He signals this clearly in the closing doxology — in praise of God alone, be it noted — by summing up what Jewish prophet and wisdom had long perceived as the mystery of God's mind and purposes[245] in the unusual terms 'unfathomable *(anexeraunētos)*' and 'incomprehensible *(anexichniastos)*', terms which Paul evidently dredged up to express just this sense that he was skirting the unknowable

243. Very striking is the fact that Jesus does not feature explicitly in this last chapter; even the prospect of 'the deliverer' to come 'out of Zion' is neither distinctively nor specifically Christian. It is as though Paul is doing here what he did in 10.6-13: as he there pressed through the particularity of the Torah to the still richer wisdom of God, so here he presses behind the gospel to the immeasurable mystery of the purposes of the merciful God. See also *Theology of Paul* 527-28; Davies, 'Paul' 726-28.

244. Whether Paul's theology here can be simply classified as 'universalistic' is not as clear as it may seem; the 'all', as from the beginning of the letter, is directed particularly to the Jew/Gentile divide, which his own mission set out to overcome — all, Jew as well as Gentile. That Paul thought in terms of a *Sonderweg* for Israel — that is, of Israel being 'saved' by virtue of its election, through the law rather than the gospel — is unlikely, though argued for by Gager, *Reinventing Paul* 59-61 (drawing particularly on F. Mussner, L. Gaston and S. Stowers). But Paul clearly thought of God's call, the same call, as embracing both Gentiles and Jews (9.11-12, 24), and of the gospel calling for faith in Christ as universal in its outreach (10.6-18; 11.28-32); why otherwise would he have been so troubled by Israel's rejection of the gospel (9.1-3)? See further R. Hvalvik, 'A "Sonderweg" for Israel: A Critical Examination of a Current Interpretation of Romans 11.25-27', *JSNT* 38 (1990) 87-107; T. L. Donaldson, 'Jewish Christianity, Israel's Stumbling and the *Sonderweg* Reading of Paul', *JSNT* 29 (2006) 27-54; B. W. Longenecker, 'On Israel's God and God's Israel: Assessing Supersessionism in Paul', *JTS* 58 (2007) 26-44. Other bibliography in Lohse, *Römer* 321-22, and Jewett, *Romans* 702.

245. Rom. 11.34 is quoted directly from Isa. 40.13, and 11.35 is a variant version of Job 41.3 LXX, closer in fact to the not very clear Hebrew.

and inexpressible (11.33-35). The bottom line for Paul was that as Creator God, the all, everything, was not only 'from' and 'through' God but also 'for/to' him (11.36).

f. How This Good News Should Come to Expression in the Roman Congregations (Rom. 12.1–15.13)

Having told the story of 'God's saving righteousness', from beginning to end, from creation to consummation, and done so no less than three times, Paul could draw breath and take a lengthy pause before turning to the still-pressing issue of how this gospel should impact the lives of those to whom he was writing. In other letters he had been forced by the urgency of the messages coming to him — from Thessalonica, Galatia and Corinth — to address the various issues and crises confronting both them and him with some immediacy. In this case, in contrast, in the relative leisure and calm of Corinth, at the close of his successful missioning in the Aegean area, he had been able to work through in considerable detail the content and character of the gospel which had been his principal message as 'apostle to the Gentiles' — and not simply for his own self-satisfaction, or even necessarily for an immediate purpose. It was rather that the challenges which had surfaced again and again in his mission and in his attempts to maintain positive relations with the home churches in Judea and Antioch had repeatedly been occasioned by the difficulties of reconciling the gospel of a *Jewish* Messiah with a vocation to preach this Messiah among the *Gentiles.* The composition of Romans gave him the opportunity to work these issues through as thoroughly as we have now seen. But having done this, there were still specific issues of which he knew in Rome, and which needed to be addressed, some a direct expression of the tensions he had laid bare particularly in his third telling of the gospel's story. To these he now turned.

(i) *12.1-8.* The initial exhortation is a finely formed appeal *(parakalō)* drawing on the imagery of Israel's cult and neatly implying the superiority of the gospel to the law (12.1-2). The sacrifices which they were now called to offer were their own bodies, with the inference that their social (bodily) relations with others should be as much a matter of careful devotion as ever they maintained in bringing their sacrifices to the altar.[246] When they refuse to be conformed to this age and when they allow the Spirit to transform them by the renewal of their minds (an exhortation to the same effect as those in 8.12-14), the prospect is that

---

246. *Theology of Paul* 543-45, with particular reference to E. Käsemann, 'Worship in Everyday Life: A Note on Romans 12', *New Testament Questions of Today* (London: SCM, 1969) 188-95.

they will be granted a better insight into the will of God than the insight Jews gained from the Torah.[247]

The fact that Paul had redefined Israel to make room for believing Gentiles should not give his mainly Gentile audiences occasion to preen themselves as though they were peculiarly special in God's sight (12.3). It was true that their identity as believers was not given by ethnic Israel, neither the land nor the 'works of the law' typical of the 'Jew'. But they were nevertheless members of a body of people; many and diverse as they were, they were 'one body in Christ, and individually members of one another' (12.4-5). This reworking of the well-known metaphor of civic unity (the city or state as a body)[248] must have struck the Roman audiences with particular force. Their unifying bond was not their dwelling in the imperial capital or the genius of Rome or loyalty to the person of the emperor but their union with Christ. Given that vital difference, and that the 'functions' of the body were not ethnic or trade or neighbourhood associations but the charisms given to each (12.6), the exhortation was the same as in other uses of the body imagery elsewhere: that the different members should exercise their different functions for the good of the whole (12.6-8). Paul does not press the last point, as he had to do in writing to the church in Corinth (1 Cor. 12.7 — did Paul find that the message had been heard and acted on when he arrived there?); presumably no reports of charismatic competition and confusion in the Roman congregations had been reported to him. So he could simply present the community-as-body imagery redefined in terms of Christ and charism, and leave the imagery to work its familiar application on the Roman assemblies.

(ii) *12.9–13.14*. As important as it was that they should learn how to regard each other and how to conduct themselves towards each other, it was still more important that they learn how to conduct themselves in relation to others, especially since they were little groups living in the midst of the capital of the fearsome empire that was Rome. As the headline, and forming a bracket with 13.8-10, stands the call to love: 'Let love be without pretence' (12.9).[249] After an initial elaboration of that imperative, reminding of the need to show respect to one another, to be 'aglow with the Spirit', to be 'steadfast in affliction, and maintain the practice of hospitality' (12.10-13), there follows a mélange of traditional

247. Even if the contrast between 2.18 and 12.2 was not picked up on first hearing, Paul would no doubt have expected it to be noticed when the letter was studied more carefully: the (false) confidence of the 'Jew' that 'you know the will of God *(to thelēma tou theou)* and approve the things that matter *(dokimazeis ta diapheronta),* being instructed from the law' (2.18), is obviously answered by the Roman believers' enabling 'to discern what is the will of God *(eis to dokimazein ti to thelēma tou theou)*' through the renewing of their minds (12.2).

248. See above, §30.3c

249. Cf. particularly Esler, *Conflict and Identity* 322-30.

Jewish wisdom regarding human relationships,[250] including various nuggets of Jesus' wisdom.[251] Diaspora Jews had long learned the need to conduct themselves circumspectly when living in foreign lands and in unsympathetic circumstances: to sympathize with others in their joys and sorrows (12.15); to live in harmony, neither cherishing proud thoughts nor over-estimating one's own wisdom (12.16); to live peaceably with all, so far as possible (12.18); to leave vengeance to God (12.19); and willingly to offer an enemy food or drink (12.20).[252] And Jesus' teaching on how to respond to persecution, to curses, to actions directed against them of evil intent should be at the front of their minds — not independently of the accumulated wisdom, be it noted, but as part of it. The implication is obvious: that Paul knew, or strongly suspected, that the little Christian groups meeting in tenement apartments were very vulnerable in a city where government spies and informers were always on the lookout for potentially subversive groups,[253] where pin-prick acts of persecution and discrimination (ethnic, social, religious) would be a common experience and where there was the constant danger of over-reaction bringing still closer attention to the existence and character of the little gatherings. In such circumstances Paul's advice is not that the Roman believers should agitate or secretly organize or preach/teach against the state; that would be an impossible counsel of madness. It was rather that they should show themselves good neighbours and citizens so that the body of Christ in Rome could grow with as little constraint as possible and its common life prove fruitful in the way Jesus had taught.[254]

That an understanding of 12.9-21 along these lines is moving in the direction intended by Paul is confirmed by the fact that he then turns explicitly to the Roman Christians' relation with the state and its officials — from the petty persecution of fellow residents to the overwhelming power of the state itself (13.1-7).[255] Here too it is the conjoint wisdom of Israel and of Jesus on which Paul

---

250. 12.15 — Sir. 7.34;   12.19 — Lev. 19.18 and Deut. 32.35;
    12.16 — Prov. 3.7 and Isa. 5.21;   12.20 — Prov. 25.21-22;
    12.17 — Prov. 3.4;   12.21 — *T. Ben.* 4.3.
    12.18 — Ps. 34.14 [LXX 33.15];
251. 12.14 — Luke 6.27-28/Matt. 5.44   12.18 — Mark 9.50.
    12.17 — Luke 6.29/Matt. 5.39

252. The imagery of 'heaping coals of fire on someone's head' remains obscure; see my *Romans* 750-51; Fitzmyer, *Romans* 657-58; Moo, *Romans* 788-89; Jewett, *Romans* 777-78.

253. Livy's account of the suppression of the Bacchanalia in 186 (*Hist.* 39.8-19) gives a good indication of the suspicion with which the authorities regarded foreign cults and of the way in which they could gather information (see Benko, 'Pagan Criticism' 1066-67).

254. See *Jesus Remembered* §14, especially 607-11.

255. 'The parenesis of Rom. 12:1–15:13, including 13:1-7, should not be understood as a general ethic formulated by Paul, but as part of a situational ethic addressed to circumstances of a given time and place' (Tellbe, *Paul between Synagogue and State* 171, further 177-82).

draws: that the city and imperial authorities should be respected as the divinely appointed means of providing good government, law and order (13.1-4),[256] so that submission to their authority was a matter not simply of fearing their punitive power but of conscience (recognizing the justice of wrong being punished) (13.5); and that, as Jesus had instructed, the due demands of the authorities for tax purposes should be fully complied with (13.6-7).[257] Here again there is absolutely no sense that Paul was encouraging a proactive counter-culture which was likely to bring the wrath of the authorities down upon the heads of the little gatherings of Christians. Rather we need to speak of a form of political quietism — the living as a good citizen which would ensure that the Christian assemblies could focus on their primary responsibility as Christians, to build up the body of Christ and to live and spread the message of God's Son.

This obligation to pay all that was due from the individual believers allows the transition to the more positive counterpart, that the Roman believers should be noted above all for their love of one another and of the neighbour (13.8-10). This climax to the sequence of exhortations beginning in 12.9 once again draws together the wisdom of Israel as highlighted and brought to focus in Jesus' own teaching. There should be little doubt that Jesus was remembered as picking out Lev. 19.18 ('You shall love your neighbour as yourself'), giving it an unprecedented prominence and holding it forward as the quintessence of the law regarding human relationships (Mark 12.31 pars.).[258] It is this awareness of Jesus tradition, which Paul could assume was shared among the Roman congregations, that Paul now presents as the summation *(anakephalaioutai)*[259] and fulfilment *(plērōma)*[260] of the law as a whole; the same assertion as he had made in Gal. 5.14 — 'the whole law is fulfilled *(peplērōtai)* in one word, "You shall love your neighbour as yourself"'.[261] Assumed also is the line of thought from 'the law of

---

256. Prov. 8.15-16; Jer. 7.26; Dan. 4.17, 25, 32; 5.21; Wis. 6.3-4; see further my *Romans* 761-62, and more fully W. Schrage, *Die Christen und der Staat nach dem Neuen Testament* (Gütersloh: Gütersloher, 1971) 14-28. Although the imperial cult could not but loom large over Paul's mission (Horsley, *Paul and Empire* 20-24), and particularly in Rome, its heart, the subordination of the authorities to the gods was still conventional; see further N. Elliott, 'Romans 13:1-7 in the Context of Imperial Propaganda', in Horsley, *Paul and Empire* 184-204; Jewett, *Romans* 789-92; and above at §29 nn. 147, 148.

257. Rom. 13.7 — Mark 12.17 pars.; see *Jesus Remembered* 623-24, 635-36, 650-51.

258. See *Jesus Remembered* 584-86.

259. For the meaning of this rare word, see BDAG 65 and H. Schlier, *TDNT* 3.681-82.

260. *Plērōma* is usually taken here in the sense of 'fulfilling' (BDAG 830), doing all that the law demands; see my *Romans* 780-81; Jewett assumes reference particularly to the love feasts of the early communities (*Romans* 814-15). Esler is typical of those who think Paul had finished with the law, but here, e.g., he completely fails to relate his discussion to 3.27, 31 and 8.2-4, which hardly feature in his treatment (*Conflict and Identity* 333-35).

261. See above, §31 n. 395.

faith' (Rom. 3.27) to the 'love command' — expressed explicitly in Gal. 5.6 (what counts is 'faith operating effectively through love'): that the law is not fulfilled by demanding obedience to any particular commandments ('works of the law'), but by living towards God and the neighbour out of love.

At this point Paul could have turned immediately to his other major concern regarding the congregations in Rome (14.1–15.6), since the dominant chord of love will be struck again there to resolve the discords of disputes there (14.15). But first Paul evidently thought it necessary to remind his audiences of the eschatological urgency of their situation[262] — the only time in Romans that he plays this card in his paraenesis, in striking contrast to the Thessalonian correspondence and (but less so) to the Corinthian correspondence (especially 1 Cor. 7.26, 29).[263] The shortness of the time still available for his mission and for the work of saving righteousness to achieve its goal was ever in the background of Paul's mind, even when he made no explicit reference to it.[264] So here, the concern comes to expression in the reminder that the final goal of 'salvation' was nearer than when they first believed (13.11). He draws on the imagery of approaching dawn to urge that they should already be living as those who belong to the (coming) day and not to the night (13.12-13). The double allusion should not be missed, on the one hand to Jesus' own teaching that his disciples should live in the light of the coming kingdom,[265] and on the other to the conduct often thought to be typified by the late-night revelries of various associations,[266] reminiscent, indeed, of conduct previously tolerated in the church of Corinth itself (1 Cor. 11.21)! The key is their commitment to and union with Christ (now under the imagery of putting on a fresh suit of clothes, and the mien appropriate to the dress)[267] — a reminder of the crucial exhortation of 8.12-13 and of how its implementation should be effected (Rom. 13.14).

(iii) *14.1–15.6.* But now Paul can give his full attention to the one subject of which he had been informed and which caused him concern regarding the relations within and between the different apartment gatherings of believers in Rome — the 'differences of opinion *(dialogismoi)*' between the advocates of differing patterns of conduct (14.1).[268] The situation seems to be as already indi-

---

262. See further my *Romans* 786-88; Jewett, *Romans* 820-21.

263. See above, §32 at n. 257.

264. See again §29.3e.

265. See again *Jesus Remembered* 607-11.

266. See above, §30 nn. 77, 232. Petronius's vivid account of Trimalchio's banquet in *Satyricon* 15.26.6–15.78.8, written quite probably within about ten years of Paul's letter to Rome, gives a fair idea of what Paul must have had in mind.

267. Most see baptismal terminology here, though Paul is hardly calling for a repeated baptism (my *Romans* 790-91).

268. The phrase used by Paul, *diakriseis dialogismōn,* is difficult to translate effectively

cated:[269] that following the expulsion from Rome (in 49) of the Christian Jews who had established these early tenement congregations, their membership and leadership had become predominantly Gentile in character. In consequence, the typical gathering for a shared meal ('the dinner of the Lord') had ceased to be restricted by or to observe the shared-meal traditions of their more traditional Jewish members. But in the two years since the death of Claudius (54) and the consequent lapse of his edict of expulsion, Jews, including those who believed in Messiah Jesus, had begun to return to Rome — Jews like Prisca and Aquila. Many of the Christian Jews who had sought to resume participation in the various house churches must have found the fact that the shared meals now made no concession to Jewish scruples disconcerting, to say the least. They found that even when a welcome (back) was extended to them, it was in effect with a view to persuading them to accept the new *modus vivendi* and its theological rationale — that they too should feel free to partake of unclean foods in good conscience (14.1).

Whether this suggested reconstruction of the situation envisaged by Paul is on the right lines or not, the designation of one side of the dispute as 'weak in faith', who 'eat only vegetables' (14.1-2), most obviously refers to Jewish believers[270] and those (former 'God-fearers') who shared Jewish sensibilities on these matters.[271] The inference is confirmed by the subsequent talk of 'clean *(katharos)*' and 'unclean *(koinos)*', since both inevitably evoke the Jewish tradition of clean and unclean, and the latter *(koinos)* in particular is distinctively Jewish.[272] On the other side of the disagreement were those who 'had faith to eat ev-

---

— something like 'the means or processes by which (differing) opinions are evaluated and the differences resolved'; see further my *Romans* 798-99. Jewett observes that parallels and the context suggest that it was the opinion of the 'weak' which was being scrutinized by the dominant group (*Romans* 836).

269. See above at n. 65.

270. See, e.g., Moo, *Romans* 828-31; Schnelle, *History* 122-23; Lohse, *Römer* 372-74; the fullest recent discussion is by M. Reasoner, *The Strong and the Weak: Romans 14.1–15.13 in Context* (SNTSMS 103; Cambridge: Cambridge University, 1999). While avoidance of all meat was not required by Jewish law and tradition, the fear that meat was tainted by idolatry was ever present in diaspora Jewish communities, and it is quite likely that any special provision for a Jewish meat market had been withdrawn at the time of Claudius's edict and not yet re-established (cf. above, §32 nn. 169, 292). Josephus reports that on a visit to Rome in about 64, Jewish priests 'had not forgotten the pious practices of religion, and supported themselves on figs and nuts' (*Life* 14). And James, brother of Jesus, was remembered as abstaining from animal flesh (Eusebius, *HE* 2.23.5). See further my *Romans* 799-802.

271. The attraction of various Romans to Jewish practices is a regular theme in the Roman literature of the period (e.g., Plutarch, *Cic.* 7.6; Seneca, *Ep.* 108.22; Suetonius, *Domitian* 12.2; Cassius Dio 67.14.1-3; and further my *Jesus, Paul and the Law* 145-46).

272. See above, §26 n. 60; and my *Romans* 818-19, 825-26.

erything' (14.2) — most obviously Gentiles (and liberal Jews like Paul himself) who now believed that the laws of clean and unclean were no longer relevant to the life of faith. Similarly with the other bone of contention, given less attention in Paul's treatment — the question whether Christians should observe the Sabbath and other Jewish festivals (14.5-6).[273] Here were two of the cases where, in Paul's view, faith in Christ had become the most important factor in ordering relationships among believers; and as such, faith re-valued and de-prioritized those laws which inhibited such relationships as those between Jews and Gentiles, even when both were believers. This, we can say, was an example of 'the law of faith' (3.27) coming to effect through and as love of neighbour, in this case the Christian neighbour. The 'weak in faith' evidently felt the need to bolster or support their faith by maintaining these traditional restrictions; the attitude and conduct were what Paul had encountered long ago in Antioch (Gal. 2.11-14).[274] Those less inhibited regarded the attitude and corresponding conduct as 'weak'.

The perspective, of course, is that of those less inhibited (referred to as 'the strong' in 15.1), a perspective which Paul shared (14.14); in contrast, those so designated might well have regarded themselves as 'the strong', that is, strong in traditions that still mattered. But despite his own perspective on such issues, Paul's concern here was nevertheless that *both* attitudes and modes of conduct should be properly respected and made room for in their common life. Paul, it should be noted, had not changed his view from that expressed in Gal. 2.11-18. There, in Antioch and in Galatia, the problem had been that Jewish believers were insisting that Gentile believers should 'live like Jews *(ioudaïzein)*' (Gal. 2.14). Here the shoe was on the other foot, with Gentile believers trying to browbeat their Jewish fellow believers to disregard and abandon their traditional praxis. In each case 'the truth of the gospel' was at stake: one in the insistence that faith alone was not sufficient; the other in failure fully to love the Christian brother or sister.[275]

It is important to grasp that the disagreement in Rome was by no means trivial — simply a question of diet, or even of vegetarians vs. meat-eaters, or sim-

---

273. The Sabbath and other Jewish festivals proved attractive to many non-Jews (Philo, *Mos.* 2.21; Josephus, *Ap.* 2.282; Col. 2.16; Juvenal, *Sat.* 14.96, 105-106; see also Leon, *Jews* 12-14; my *Romans* 805-806) and continued to exert this fascination for several centuries (E. Lohse, *TDNT* 7.32-34; my *Partings* [²2006] xix-xx, 344-46).

274. See above, §27.4. Despite Nanos, *Mystery* 103-39, it should be self-evident that those 'weak in faith' can hardly be unbelieving Jews; cf. R. A. J. Gagnon, 'Why the "Weak" at Rome Cannot Be Non-Christian Jews', *CBQ* 62 (2000) 64-82.

275. The issue in Rome was not the same as that which had been a major problem in Corinth: then it had been about 'idol-food', here it is about the laws of clean and unclean (foods); then it was a matter of social intermixing with non-believers, here it is an internal issue between believers. That the key to resolving both problems was the same — love (1 Cor. 8.1; Rom. 14.15) — should not blind us to the differences between the situations envisaged.

ply a matter of avoiding certain work-tasks on the Sabbath. On the contrary, as we have seen, the laws of clean and unclean in particular stood at the heart of Jewish identity: they defined and enacted Israel's sense of holiness (set-apartness) to God (Lev. 20.22-26); the importance of maintaining the laws of clean and unclean in forging the identity of 'Judaism' had been sealed with the blood of martyrs (1 Macc. 1.62-63).[276] Their continuing rootedness in Jewish-Christian identity is vividly illustrated in Peter's recorded insistence that he had 'never eaten anything common *(koinos)* or unclean *(akathartos)*' (Acts 10.14) and in his withdrawal from Jew-Gentile table-fellowship in Antioch (Gal. 2.11-14). So it is no wonder that there were still many believing Jews who regarded the maintenance of these laws as integral to their identity as believing Jews. Much the same could be said of their continuing assumption that the Sabbath law had still to be observed: it had similarly been seen as a hallmark of belonging to the covenant people,[277] and the Jesus tradition shows that Jesus' disputes with Pharisees on the need to observe the Sabbath laws continued to reverberate in the communities who retold that tradition.[278] So there were issues of personal integrity, definitions of what this new sect (Christianity) stood for, at stake here.[279] How they handled such questions would determine the character of the movement hereafter.[280]

Paul's counsel can be summed up succinctly:

(1) Each group stood on dangerous ground in its attitude to the others: those who regarded themselves as more liberated from such restrictions would tend to '*despise (exouthenein)*' the more scrupulous, whereas the more tradition-alist believers would tend to 'condemn *(krinein)*' those who disregarded such traditions (14.3). There is a sharp psychological insight here, since more or less any grouping that shares a common ideology will have a spectrum of opinion in their understanding and implementation of that ideology, and the temptation will always be what Paul saw it to be: for those embracing a tighter understanding to regard others who disagreed as apostates from 'the true faith',[281] and for those in-

276. See above, §26.3b; also §27.4 again.

277. The Sabbath was also fundamental to Jewish identity (e.g., Exod. 31.16-17; Isa. 56.6; Ezek. 20.16; 1 Macc. 1.43; Josephus, *Ant.* 11.346).

278. *Jesus Remembered* 566-69.

279. 'What is at stake in 14:1–15:13 is thus ultimately the complex issue of the continuity and discontinuity between Judaism and Christian belief' (Tellbe, *Paul between Synagogue and State* 167).

280. Reasoner shows how well 14.1–15.6 has been prepared for earlier in the letter (summed up in *Strong and Weak* 225), though the question is whether the letter builds up to chs. 14–15 (as the point of the letter) or whether chs. 14–15 are the most immediately pressing test case for the theology laid out earlier.

281. Jewett notes that 'Paul himself had experienced such contempt on the part of the

terpreting the common ideology more loosely to despise the more scrupulous for their narrow-mindedness and rigidity.[282] The modern attitudes of and to the various fundamentalisms of twenty-first-century religions provide all the illustration that might be needed.

(2) Both sides should recognize and acknowledge that *both* attitudes may be acceptable to God: 'Who are you to condemn the slave of someone else? It is before his own master that he stands or falls. And he shall stand, for the master is able to make him stand' (14.4). Speaking particularly to the traditionalist, Paul insists that there is not a simple right and wrong in these matters; *both* may be right — that is, in the eyes of the Lord Jesus Christ. It was not necessary that one be wrong in order for the other to be right — a salutary lesson for any fundamentalist tendency. 'The truth of the gospel' is richer and more diverse than any single grasp of it.

(3) Each individual should make up his or her own mind before God (14.5b). That should be the primary consideration in such controversial matters: 'For no one lives *for himself* and no one dies *for himself.* For if we live, we live *for the Lord;* and if we die, we die *for the Lord*' (14.7-8). Here is a blunt reminder that for all the assertions of religious identity and personal integrity, there was a good deal of self-concern, self-assertion and self-serving in the expression of both attitudes.

(4) The test which Paul offers to discern the appropriateness both of one's own conduct and that of the other is whether one can and does 'give thanks to God' *for* what he or she does and *in* what he or she does (14.6). The same point as before is driven home: that relationships with God embrace a *range* of beliefs and life-styles among those who own Jesus as Lord (14.9). It may be hard for some to acknowledge that what is not acceptable to *us* may nevertheless be acceptable to *God,* but this is precisely what Paul insists upon.

(5) In consequence, no one should attempt to impose his or her own conscience on others, since 'each of us will have to give account of himself to God' (14.10-12).[283] Paul does not speak of 'conscience *(syneidēsis)*' here as he had in

---

Corinthians, because of his inelegant style of speaking (2 Cor 10:10)' and that 'the experience of such social contempt by persons of minority status is visible in Jonathan's prayer in 2 Macc. 1:27 for the Jewish exiles scattered among the Gentiles' (*Romans* 839).

282. W. S. Campbell, 'The Rule of Faith in Romans 12:1–15:13', in D. M. Hay and E. E. Johnson, eds., *Pauline Theology.* Vol. 3: *Romans* (Minneapolis: Fortress, 1995) 259-86, catches well the balance of Paul's two-handed rebuke: 'Gentiles must not regard observance of the Jewish law as incompatible with Christian faith, and Jews must not regard it as essential to Christian faith' (283)

283. The echo of Rom. 2.6-16 would of course be recognized in fuller study of the letter, as Paul no doubt intended; that Paul could hold these passages together with 8.31-34 should be given more attention in studies of Paul's theology than is frequently the case (see *New Perspective on Paul* [2005] 72-80, [2008] 80-89).

1 Corinthians 8-10,[284] but the counsel already given in 14.5b and 14.6 has the same implication; and Paul's subsequent teaching that conduct must be the expression of faith, otherwise it is sin (14.22-23), makes the same point. Conduct which springs from faith and expresses gratitude to God is acceptable to God; in consequence, it should also be acceptable to fellow believers, even when it is different from how their faith finds expression.

Having primarily directed his remarks to the 'weak in faith' in 14.4-12, Paul turns his attention to those less inhibited by traditionalist (Jewish) scruples. They have a special obligation, the obligation of love (14.15), echoing the advice given to the 'know-alls' in 1 Corinthians 8 and summed up in Rom. 14.13: 'not to put an occasion for offence or downfall in the brother's way'.

(6) If the 'weak' should not 'condemn' the 'strong', neither should the 'strong' 'despise' the 'weak'. Rather, those less bound by tradition should *respect* the traditionalists' scruples: 'to the one who reckons something profane, to that person it *is* profane' (14.14b). This, we should recall, is Paul speaking, Paul who personally was 'convinced in the Lord Jesus that nothing is profane in itself' (14.14a).[285] He acts out the counsel he is giving by defending the traditionalists in retaining the very scruples which he himself rejected.

(7) The less scrupulous should recognize that by encouraging their fellow believers to act against their conscience/faith, they may actually destroy that person (14.15), that is, destroy their faith by encouraging them to 'eat with offence' (14.20).[286] This is what Paul seems to have in mind when he talks about the brother being 'deeply upset on account of food' (14.15) — that is, not merely experiencing a feeling of indignation or revulsion at the conduct of the other, but being drawn into conduct which is contrary to their faith and so deeply unsettling.

(8) The kingdom priorities are 'not a matter of eating and drinking, but of righteousness, peace and joy in the Holy Spirit' (14.17). To be noted here are both the echo of Jesus' own kingdom life-style, expressed not least in the openness of his table-fellowship,[287] and Paul's typical reference back to the experience of the Spirit as the fundamental fact of Christian life and community.[288]

---

284. 1 Cor. 8.7, 10, 12; 10.25, 27-29.

285. An echo of Jesus' teaching on true purity, as recalled/interpreted in Mark 7.15-19, is generally recognized (*Jesus Remembered* 573-77), as also the exhortation not to judge one another in 14.13 (Mark 9.42 pars.) and the allusion in 14.17 to the kingdom of God in relation to food and drink (*Theology of Paul* 191-92); bibliography in each case in Jewett, *Romans* 858, 859-60, 863.

286. The phrase probably means 'eats with an offended, bad conscience' (cf. 1 Cor. 8.7, 10-11): 'the weak' stumbles by actually *following the example* of the 'strong', rather than simply by *seeing* the 'strong' eat (my *Romans* 826).

287. See *Jesus Remembered* 599-607.

288. See again §29.7g above.

(9) Not to be ignored is the impression made on those outside by Christian attitudes and conduct with regard to other Christians: selfish lack of concern for the others would attract contempt (14.16); acting out of genuine concern for the others would be approved by people in general (14.18). The less prominence given to this note in the equivalent counsel of 1 Corinthians 8 and 10 (10.32-33) is a reminder that the situations envisaged by Paul in each case were different.[289]

(10) But the same priority as in 1 Corinthians applies here too: 'the building up *(oikodomē)* of one another' (14.19; 15.2).[290] That is what it means to act *kata agapēn,* 'in terms of love' (14.15): not thinking first and foremost of one's own prerogatives, far less advantage, but thinking of how to benefit the other and of how the whole community can most flourish.

(11) So the bottom line for the 'strong' is that they should be ready voluntarily to restrict their own liberty for the sake of the other: 'It is a fine thing not to eat meat or drink wine or anything by which your brother stumbles' (14.21). Paul presses home this point at the beginning of ch. 15: 'We the strong ought to support the weaknesses of those without strength, and not to please ourselves; let each of us please his neighbour' (15.1-2). The authority for this strong exhortation is two-fold: the teaching of Jesus on the priority of 'loving the neighbour',[291] but also the character of Jesus' own mission itself, 'for Christ did not please himself' (15.3).[292] Paul's concluding hope, appropriately, is that the Roman audiences will 'live in harmony' among themselves and 'with one mind *(homothymadon)* and one voice' 'glorify the God and Father of our Lord Jesus Christ' (15.5-6).

g. In Conclusion (Rom. 15.7-13)

Finally, lest the overall main thrust of the letter as a whole has been lost to sight in the finer detail of mutual relationships within the Roman apartment churches,

289. 'By formulating his argument in an oblique fashion, Paul is able to treat a delicate Jew-Gentile problem without exacerbating the tensions in Rome' (Walters, *Ethnic Issues* 87).

290. See above, §32 at nn. 360, 361.

291. This is the only passage in which Paul speaks of 'the neighbour *(plēsion)*' apart from the two references to Lev. 19.18: 'you shall love your neighbour as yourself' (Rom. 13.9-10 and Gal. 5.14); so it is most probable that he had in mind Jesus' teaching which prioritized Lev. 19.18 (see above, at n. 260).

292. The Scripture which Paul cites — 'The reproaches of those who reproach you have fallen on me' (Ps. 69.9) — is somewhat unexpected, but Paul presumably refers it to Jesus' suffering and death as essentially 'for others' (so most). That Paul did light on this verse strengthens the likelihood that Psalm 69 featured in very early reflection on and telling of Jesus' crucifixion (*Jesus Remembered* 777), and note also the quotation of Ps. 69.26 in Acts 1.20. According to Jewett, 'this is the only instance in the Pauline letters where a biblical precedent is cited for Jesus' passion' (*Romans* 879), though we should not forget 3.25 and 8.3.

Paul neatly draws out the final sequence of exhortations to reinforce that principal message. They are to 'welcome one another' (Jew and Gentile, traditionalist
and non-traditionalist), just as Christ 'welcomed' them (15.7). For this is precisely in accord with the very purpose of Christ's whole life and mission. He 'became servant of the circumcised' (15.8). Why? 'For the sake of the *truth* of God'
— that is, the reliability and integrity of God and constancy of his purpose.[293]
That purpose is and, Paul would say, always has been twofold (15.8-9): both to
confirm the promises of the fathers (Paul does not back away one step from the
affirmations of 9.4 and 11.29), and so that 'the Gentiles should give praise to
God for his mercy' ('mercy', the very term to which Paul had pinned his hope
from first to last in chs. 9–11).[294] Here is confirmation, if confirmation were
needed, that Paul's gospel, his apostleship and mission, had in view, always had
as its primary motivation, the realization of precisely that vision: the promises to
Israel fulfilled, and Gentiles praising God for mercy. Here as the climax of this
letter, the letter in which he laid out most carefully and most completely his understanding of the gospel and of how God's saving righteousness was coming
into its full effect, Paul sums up his hope and prayer: that Jews and Gentiles
would rejoice together and together praise God (15.9-11);[295] that Isaiah's vision
of the Messiah's rule embracing the nations (Gentiles) and of the Gentiles finding their hope in him (Isa. 11.10) would now, finally, be realized (15.12). It was
that hope which Paul especially wished should be experienced in overflowing
measure by the Roman congregations (15.13).

h. A Look Back, a Look Forward, and
Farewell Greetings (Rom. 15.14–16.27)

With such a conclusion to such a treatise, all that was necessary now was to reit-
erate his confidence in the Romans (15.14) and to apologize graciously for writing at such length. He had wanted to set out clearly ('rather boldly') his under-

---

293. The evocation once again, and in this climactic passage, of the thought of God's
truth (*ʾemeth, alētheia*) should again not be missed; see nn. 92, 115 above; Haacker, *Römer* 296;
Wright, 'Romans' 747. Jewett again loses sight of the larger picture (Romans as a definitive
statement of Paul's gospel), which enhances rather than 'undercuts' its direct relevance to the
social context (*Romans* 891).

294. *Eleeō* — 9.15, 18; 11.30-32; *eleos* — 9.23; 11.31; 15.9.

295. Rom. 15.9 — Ps. 18.49 = 2 Sam. 22.50; 15.10 — Deut. 32.43; 15.11 — Ps. 117.1;
15.12 — Isa. 11.10. See further B. Schaller, 'Christus, "der Diener der Beschneidung . . ., auf
ihn werden die Völker hoffen". Zu Schriftzitate in Röm 15,7-13', in D. Sänger and M. Konradt,
eds., *Das Gesetz im frühen Judentum und im Neuen Testament,* C. Burchard FS (Göttingen:
Vandenhoeck und Ruprecht, 2006) 261-85.

standing of his commission: 'the grace given him from God [as in 1.5], to be a minister of Christ Jesus for the Gentiles', to bring the Gentiles to God as a kind of priestly sacrifice, 'sanctified by the Holy Spirit' (15.15-16). He was even prepared (no doubt with a twinkle in his eye) to 'boast *(kauchēsis)* in Christ Jesus' in this work for God (15.17),[296] for its substance was what Christ had accomplished through him in bringing the Gentiles to the obedience of faith (15.18, again in echo of 1.6). It was the manifest success of this mission ('signs and wonders, the power of God's Spirit') and the completion of the Aegean mission (15.19) which provided an opportunity for his long-intended visit to Rome itself (15.22-23). His hope was that this visit would be a staging-post on his mission to regions beyond (Spain), after he had delivered the collection made among his churches for the poor among the saints in Jerusalem (15.24-29), which he hoped would be well received (but feared might not) (15.30-31), as a joyful prologue to his coming to them (15.32-33).

All that remained to do was to commend Phoebe, his ambassador (16.1-2), to send greetings to those he knew well or as acquaintances or as names he had become familiar with (16.3-16), to append a final exhortation (16.17-20) and greetings from some in Corinth (16.21-23), and to sign off.

i. The Aftermath

How long it took Paul to complete this composition and to ensure its dispatch in a fair copy we do not know. Perhaps he made a copy at least of the body of the letter for his own retention and future use. At any rate, we can well imagine that it was well through his three months' stay in Corinth before he was ready to send Phoebe on her way with it.

How was the letter received in Rome? We have no way of knowing, apart from the fact that Clement (of Rome), writing about forty years later, was evidently familiar with it and seems to draw on it at several points.[297] And the implication of the letter's retention, even in different text-forms, is that the letter was treasured, much studied and much copied, probably also for wider distribution. Here again, however, sad to say, Acts lets us down; indeed, the disjunction between what we learn of the Roman congregations from Paul's letter to Rome and

---

296. Recall the importance of 'boasting' in Paul's first exposition of his gospel (2.17, 23; 3.27; 4.2; 5.2-3, 11).

297. Gregory and Tuckett, *Reception* 148-51, referring particularly to *1 Clem.* 32.2 (Rom. 9.5), 32.4–33.1 (Rom. 5.21–6.2a), and 35.5-6 (Rom. 1.29-32). Penna deduces from 1 Peter that Paul's letter to the Romans 'did in certain ways resonate positively with the Romans, but that the community on the whole and especially its leaders remained partially faithful to its [1 Peter's] own moderately Judaizing tradition' (*Paul* 1.54-56).

Acts' portrayal of the Roman Jewish community in Acts 28 is one of the most disappointing and frustrating of all the Lukan lacunae. For, as we shall see (§34.3c), Luke gives only brief indication of awareness that there were already churches/congregations of believers in Messiah Jesus in Rome itself when he recounts Paul's final arrival there (Acts 28.14-15). Going out from the letter itself, we would have expected to hear of excited Christians greeting Paul in Rome itself, eager either to hear from him or to engage him in discussion and debate (not least over what he had written to them). But of such Luke tells us nothing; it evidently neither fitted his style nor was the focus of his concern. But the irritating result is that we lose the opportunity of evaluating how the letter was received in Rome and how its counsel was acted upon — all the more frustrating when the assemblies there, within the next few years, were to suffer their most severe outburst of persecution (§35.2). What we would have given to know whether Paul's teaching was a crucial factor in sustaining them for the time of trial soon to come upon them!

On one point, however, we should pause — in regard to the widespread assumption that church and synagogue in Rome had become quite separate by this time. The implication of Acts 28 is at least that there was still a positive dialogue being pursued. And the fact that 1 Peter seems to have been written from Rome (1 Pet. 5.13) and may have been written exclusively for a Christian Jewish readership,[298] points in a different direction. Paul's letter to Rome itself, given its character, may have provided grist for such open and even positive dialogue, though the possibility that the death of Paul (and Peter) was in part contrived by ultraconservative Jewish Christians in Rome, pursuing there the same agenda as they had in Galatia and Philippi, has also to be considered.[299] At all events, whatever its immediate reception, the letter was preserved and no doubt proved to be an invaluable instruction and discussion manual for the congregations then and thereafter, and more widely, as it became more widely dispersed. The abiding outcome, need it be added, was that it came to be seen and continues to be perhaps most important single expression of gospel and theology ever penned.

33.4. The Collection

Paul's other main preoccupation during his three-month stay in Corinth was no doubt the final arrangements for the collection. This was the collection being

---

298. See below, §37.3.

299. Brown infers that Clement's talk of jealousy and envy 'refers to betrayal by their fellow Christians' (Brown and Meier, *Antioch and Rome* 124-27), thinking of 'ultraconservative Jewish Christians' of Group 1 in Brown's categorization (see §30 n. 123 above). See also Lampe, *Paul to Valentinus* 82-84.

made around the churches of the Pauline mission for the poor among the believers in Jerusalem (Rom. 15.26). It was clearly a matter of considerable importance for Paul: the very fact that he devotes so much attention to it, and across three letters, puts it among his primary concerns.[300] So it obviously dominated much of his thought and planning during the Ephesus-based Aegean mission. Moreover, as already indicated, the correlation of the reference to 'church delegates' in speaking of the collection (1 Cor. 16.3; 2 Cor. 8.23), and the list of church representatives who were to accompany Paul on the journey to Jerusalem (Acts 20.4), can only mean that the three months in Corinth were largely devoted to coordinating the organization of the gathering of these delegates, of their hospitality and sea passage to Israel, and of the security of the collection itself. However, the origins of the collection are somewhat disputed, as also, to some extent, its theological rationale.

a. The Origins of the Collection

The issue here is how to correlate Gal. 2.10 with the enterprise of the collection itself. In Gal. 2.7-9, we may recall, Paul reports the hard-won agreement made with the Jerusalem leadership, to the effect (i) that Gentile believers need not be circumcised and (ii) that there should be two missions of equal status and equally to be recognized as preaching the good news of Messiah Jesus — a mission to (fellow) Jews (by Cephas/Peter) and a mission to non-Jews (by Paul and Barnabas).[301] In 2.10, however, Paul adds that the only stipulation made by the Jerusalem apostles was 'that we should remember the poor — the very thing', Paul notes, 'which I have eagerly done'.

One of the important questions raised by 2.10 is whether this stipulation was some sort of qualification to the agreement of 2.7-9. The question can be posed more precisely: did any or all of the Jerusalem leadership regard this codicil to the agreement as some sort of concession which safeguarded the more traditional Jewish view of covenant obligation — the giving of alms being regarded as a crucially important expression of covenant-obligated 'righteousness'?[302] If the answer is in the affirmative, that would give the subsequent collection a considerable significance. For in making the collection, Paul would then be acting in a way that recognized or even agreed with the Jerusalem leadership's concern to maintain at least some element of 'covenantal nomism': that non-Jews' acceptance of the gospel must (also) be evidenced by alms-giving. Equally possible,

---

300. 1 Cor. 16.1-4; 2 Corinthians 8–9; Rom. 15.25-32.
301. See above, §27.3d.
302. See again the final part of §27.3d.

however, indeed more likely in Paul's case, Paul himself understood the stipulation of 2.10 as simply an important part of Jewish heritage which he himself continued to regard as important for his mission also — though without any overtones that such an active concern was a 'work of the law', without which faith in Christ could not be counted as righteousness.[303]

The other important issue in relating Gal. 2.10 to the collection is whether 2.10 in effect marked the beginning of the collection. In other words, did Paul have in mind from the Jerusalem agreement onwards, and did he actually begin to plan the collection from the beginning of his work as an independent missionary? Or did the Antioch incident produce some hiatus in the original intention?[304] Alternatively, does the mention of the stipulation (Gal. 2.10) in the letter to the Galatians indicate that the collection was already a preoccupation of Paul's?[305] This last question, of course, is bound up with the dating of Galatians. And those who date Galatians closer to Romans and within the latter phase of the Aegean mission can correlate 2.10 closely with the concerns expressed in the letters written during that period (1 and 2 Corinthians and Romans). Indeed, 2.10 becomes for some the key indicator that Galatians should be so dated.[306]

I see things somewhat differently. As already indicated, the most plausible dating for Galatians, in my view, is during the first phase of the Aegean mission, when Paul was based at Corinth.[307] Were it the case that Paul was already actively sponsoring the collection, he would surely have made more of it in the letter itself, explicitly calling on the Galatians for their support (as he does in the Corinthian letters).[308] Nothing in Galatians correlates with 1 Cor. 16.1 — 'the directions I gave to the churches of Galatia'.[309] Nor is there any hint in the Thessalonian correspondence that Paul was already active in raising funds for the collection. At the time of the Jerusalem agreement, and at the time of writing to

303. This is no doubt one of the implications Paul intended his audiences to draw from the fact that he followed 2.10 with his account of the Antioch incident (2.11-14) and of its significance (2.15-18); see above, §27.4-5.

304. Thrall, *2 Corinthians* 504-506, in some agreement with D. Georgi, *Remembering the Poor: The History of Paul's Collection for Jerusalem* (1965; ET Nashville: Abingdon, 1992) ch. 2. Thrall's discussion (503-20) is the best informed of the more recent treatments.

305. Knox, *Chapters* 37-40; Lüdemann, *Paul* 80, 107-108; Lohse, *Paulus* 89.

306. See above, §28 at n. 49. 'As soon as Paul left Jerusalem and began his second missionary journey throughout the northern Mediterranean, he started a campaign for funds to relieve the poverty of the Jerusalem community' (S. McKnight, 'Collection for the Saints', *DPL* 143-47 [here 143]).

307. See above, §31.7a.

308. Becker implausibly suggests that the Galatians had completed their collection and independently taken it to Jerusalem, prior to the entry of the 'Judaizers' (*Paul* 24-25).

309. See further A. J. M. Wedderburn, 'Paul's Collection: Chronology and History', *NTS* 48 (2002) 95-110 (here 96-101).

the Galatians, it is most likely that in Gal. 2.10 Paul was simply affirming his long-standing and sustained eagerness as a Jesus-believer to maintain the traditional Jewish concerns for the 'poor',[310] a concern he continued to enact during his days as a church founder without reference to and prior to the idea of the collection as such.[311]

The collection, I suggest, was rather the crystallization of this concern, following the failure of Paul's attempted rapprochement alluded to in Acts 18.22-23,[312] and was seen by Paul as a way of healing the breach with Jerusalem (and Antioch) which had been tragically deepened by the Antioch incident. The implication of 1 Cor. 16.1, then, is that on his third trip through Galatia (Acts 18.23) Paul had given the churches of Galatia directions regarding the collection. And it was these directions that he repeated in 1 Cor. 16.1-3, once he had settled in Ephesus.[313] In 1 Cor. 16.1 Paul refers to the collection as something already known about. So we can well envisage Paul speaking of his new idea for reconciliation with the mother church to all the assemblies he had to deal with, personally or by messenger or by written communication. This, together with the evidence of 2 Corinthians 8–9, confirms that the collection was a major preoccupation of Paul during this second phase of the Aegean mission and probably implies that it was only with the second phase that it became such a preoccupation.

b. The Uniqueness of the Collection

The thesis of Deborah Watson documents the marked difference between provision for the poor in Greco-Roman and in Jewish society.[314] In the former, giving between individuals was restricted largely to other citizens (the patron-client

310. '"Remember the poor" refers back to the historic, habitual Jewish concern for the poor which continues in the Christian church, and not to the collection. The admonition to "remember the poor" is an indication that the Jerusalem leaders, too, are aware that the prevailing tendency in the Graeco-Roman world is to forget the poor, not to remember them. Because aid to the poor is central to the godly life, and perhaps because circumcision has been waived for Gentile Christians, the Jerusalem leaders are emphasizing the non-negotiable nature of this practice' (D. Watson, *Paul's Collection in Light of Motivations and Mechanisms for Aid to the Poor in the First Century World* [Durham PhD, 2006] ch. 7).

311. It is not necessary to deduce from what Paul regarded as a breach of faith in Antioch (Gal. 2.11-14) that Paul's eagerness to 'remember the poor' slackened, as Georgi suggested (*Remembering* 45-46). But I agree with Georgi that organization of the collection began only after Galatians (49-50).

312. See above, §32.1d.

313. Similarly Riesner, *Paul's Early Period* 297.

314. *Paul's Collection* chs. 2-4.

structure).[315] Likewise, public benefaction was similarly oriented towards the citizenry and always looked for an appropriate return in terms of honour.[316] The needs of the very poor were not in view. The monthly corn dole, in at least several large cities as well as Rome, was again restricted to citizens and would often have been inadequate for the full number of poor citizens; non-citizens were again not catered to. And subsidized grain during famine would again be beyond most of low status.

Traditional Jewish provision was markedly different and explicitly included the poor and the resident alien.[317] Prophetic condemnation of injustice done to the poor is a distinctive feature of Jewish communal ethic.[318] Watson concludes appropriately: 'care for and giving to the poor constituted a major component of daily Jewish life'.[319]

In both cases, however, the international character of the collection as envisaged by Paul makes it stand out. Charitable provision in the Greco-Roman world, such as it was, depended on steps taken by local rulers for their own people. And Jewish provision was likewise characteristically local in character. The Temple tax, which did indeed require the transportation of substantial sums from many different nations to Jerusalem, was for Temple overheads and community sacrifices.[320] Josephus does record a case of a more international character. This was when Queen Helena of Adiabene, visiting Jerusalem in 46 or 47, discovered a city hard pressed with famine and took immediate steps to secure provisions in Alexandria and Cyprus for distribution among the needy. Her son, Izates, when he learned of the famine, likewise 'sent a great sum of money to leaders of the Jerusalemites' and relieved the extreme pressure of famine for many (*Ant.* 20.51-53). But Paul's vision of a collection from churches in at least three different regions round the Aegean and for the relief of poverty in a quite distant country looks to be quite exceptional. As an extension of the Jewish tradition of care for all needy residents of the land, it says a great deal as to the extent to which Paul saw the scattered Christian congregations as part of a single community, in direct continuity with the people of God, Israel, and consequently with responsibilities of love (practical concern) for the well-being of one another.

315. See above, §29 n. 126.

316. 'Love of honour *(philotimia)*' was the appropriate term (LSJ 1941).

317. E.g., Exod. 23.10-11; Lev. 19.9-10; 23.22; Deut. 14.28-29; 24.19-22.

318. Notably Isa. 58.6-7, 9-10; Amos 2.6-8; 5.11-12; 8.4-6; on the crucial character of almsgiving in Jewish spirituality see above, §27 nn. 187, 188.

319. Conclusion to Watson, *Paul's Collection* ch. 3, 'Motivations and Mechanisms for Aid to the Poor: Jewish'.

320. Sanders, *Judaism* 156.

c. The Practicalities of the Collection

It is worth noting the several indications that Paul gave much thought and time to the business of organizing the collection, to ensuring its security and to recruiting the delegates who in Jerusalem would represent the churches who had contributed to the collection. Even so, it may be recalled, Paul's activity on this front may have aroused suspicion that he was lining his own pockets.[321]

(i) *1 Cor. 16.1-4* — the directions given to the church of Corinth, as they had been given to the churches of Galatia (16.1):

- On the first day of the week, each should put aside some money (some appropriate portion of his income), saving it up so that when Paul arrived, the collection would (be) already (to) be gathered in (16.2). It is not entirely clear here whether Paul expected individuals to gather their contributions at home, or the church to keep some central fund. Either would have its hazards: individuals near the top of some tenement would have little security; but a growing central sum, even if held by Gaius or Erastus, would also attract unfavourable attention. But the implication is probably that the money saved each week should be paid in to a central fund only when Paul arrived.[322]
- Paul would then either give letters of introduction to the delegates chosen by the Corinthian church to accompany the gift to Jerusalem, or Paul would also go in person (16.3-4).

The passage indicates an early stage in the planning:

- the subject had already been talked about; 16.1 implies that Paul was not introducing a new topic unfamiliar to the Corinthians;
- the instruction to build up the collection over a number of (many?) weeks (16.2) implies that a fairly lengthy period was expected to elapse before it was ready;
- Paul seems to envisage the possibility that the collection would be taken by the emissaries appointed by the church of Corinth; no other churches or emissaries are mentioned, though we can safely assume that Paul would already have been thinking of a collection contributed to by many/most of the churches he had founded. More to the point, Paul was still unclear

---

321. See above, §32.6, particularly n. 399, on the possible implications of 2 Cor. 7.2, 12; 8.20-21; 12.18; 13.1.

322. Georgi, *Remembering* 54. The contrast with the associations restricted to a monthly subscription (§30 n. 62) should not be exaggerated here. See also Fee, *1 Corinthians* 813-14; Schrage, *1 Korinther* 4.428-29.

whether he himself should take or go with the collection to Jerusalem. Perhaps the failure of the trip to Jerusalem in Acts 18.22-23 was still too raw; perhaps he was thinking of a sequence of gifts taken by representatives of different groups of churches, and not yet of a single large collection.

(ii) *2 Corinthians 8–9* — The movement to-and-fro of Titus between Paul and Corinth on the business of the collection has already been noted.[323] Here we note the others involved:

- the mysterious brother 'famous among the churches' and formally appointed *(cheirotonētheis)*[324] by the churches to be Paul's companion in this service (8.18-19);
- the (equally unnamed) brother sent by Paul to accompany Titus (8.22);[325]
- the brothers (plural), the delegates *(apostoloi)* of the churches (8.23)[326] — presumably the two unnamed brothers just referred to;
- the brothers sent by Paul, specifically to ensure that the collection has been gathered in (9.3-5) — presumably the same brothers as in 8.18-22.[327]

The impression is clear here of a quickened tempo. Paul writing from Macedonia is able to confirm that the collection from the Macedonian churches has already been (almost) completed. Indeed, Achaia (Corinth not included) was fully prepared, and had been for a year (9.2)[328] — the business had been long in hand. So Paul is anxious that the reconciled Corinthians demonstrate (9.13) the strength of their commitment to (him and to) the project by ensuring that the gathering in of the contributions is already well advanced by the time he (and the delegates from Macedonia) arrive in Corinth.

323. See above, §32.3b.

324. '*Cheirotonein* is a technical term and describes the process of electing envoys by the raising of hands in the assembly' (Betz, *2 Corinthians 8 and 9* 74 and n. 287).

325. For the identity of the two 'brothers' and possible reasons why Paul did not name them, see Betz, *2 Corinthians 8 and 9* 72-74; Thrall, *2 Corinthians* 557-62.

326. This usage ('apostles' = delegates, envoys) may reflect the Corinthians' terminology, since 'apostle' is a term Paul guarded jealously, though he takes it up very positively here — '*apostoloi* of the churches, the glory of Christ'. J. C. Hurd, 'Reflections concerning Paul's "Opponents" in Galatia', in Porter, ed., *Paul and His Opponents* 129-48, argues implausibly that the two 'brothers' were appointed and sent from Jerusalem to look after the collection in Paul's presumed absence and were the ones who caused the heartache and anger by their preaching in Galatia (145).

327. This confusing repetition of talk of Titus's companions ('brothers') leads to the suggestion that 2 Corinthians 8 and 9 were originally separate drafts of the same communication (see above, §32.7a).

328. See further Betz, *2 Corinthians 8 and 9* 92-93.

(iii) *Rom. 15.25-28, 31* — Somewhat surprisingly, for the first time the re-cipients for whom the collection is being made are specified. Earlier references spoke only of 'the collection for the saints' (1 Cor. 16.1), though it was clearly implied that it was the saints in Jerusalem that Paul had in mind (16.3). 2 Cor. 8.4 and 9.12 similarly refer simply to 'the service for the saints', but it is clearly im-plied that the giving is intended to relieve poverty (8.9, 13-15), 'the needs *(hysterēmata)* of the saints' (9.12). But now Paul is quite specific: the collection is for 'the poor among the saints in Jerusalem' (Rom. 15.26).[329] What is unclear is whether this was a sudden emergency (one of the periodic famines which would affect the poorer members of any community in particular). Or did Paul view the situation in the church of Jerusalem as endemic — the conversion of many poorer Jews within Judea to faith in Messiah Jesus putting a strain on the common fund in Jerusalem, if it was still operating in the way Luke described (Acts 2.44-45; 4.32-37)?[330] Either way, Paul's knowledge of the situation in Je-rusalem suggests that he kept himself informed of developments there. And ei-ther way, the passage suggests that when Paul wrote Romans the collection was more or less complete, and he was about to set off to Jerusalem to deliver it per-sonally (15.28). More disturbing is the implication of his request to the Romans to pray 'that my service for Jerusalem might be acceptable *(euprosdektos)* to the saints' (15.31).[331] Paul evidently had some foreboding, as well he might, that the collection would *not* prove 'acceptable' to the saints in Jerusalem!

(iv) *Acts 20.4* — As already noted (§33.1), the names mentioned here are most obviously to be correlated with representatives appointed by the churches to accompany the collection (2 Cor. 8.23). It is possible that other delegates joined him on Paul's final trip round the northern shore of the Aegean, from Philippi and Troas, or Miletus in particular.[332] Since a large delegation would be

---

329. An earlier view that the Jerusalem believers described themselves as 'the Poor' is now generally discounted; see, e.g., my *Romans* 875-76; Fitzmyer, *Romans* 722.

330. See above, §23.1d.

331. Paul uses *euprosdektos* twice in this context (15.16, 31). Hogeterp notes that the ac-ceptability of offerings of Gentiles was controversial within late Second Temple Judaism (*Paul and God's Temple* 287-88). See further Jewett, *Romans* 936-37.

332. As suggested, e.g., by K. F. Nickle, *The Collection: A Study in Paul's Strategy* (London: SCM, 1966) 69, though delegates from Tyre, Ptolemais and Caesarea are much less likely, since they could hardly be counted as representative of Paul's mission. Wedderburn points out that it would have made little sense for delegates from Asia to travel west to Corinth, only to travel east again to Jerusalem ('Paul's Collection' 105-107). Much as Paul may have de-sired Roman participation (Nickle 69-70; cf. Rom. 12.13 with 2 Cor. 8.4), the timing virtually rules it out: the letter to Rome could not have been sent in time enough for a collection to have been made or a delegate to be appointed and to reach Corinth in time to join the party; Paul would have been much more explicit on the subject; and anyway, Rome was not one of his churches.

expensive in terms of subsistence and travel costs, there must have been a good reason for their number.[333]

We have no means of knowing how large the collection was in its sum total. Although it was made up of contributions from believers, the great majority of whom were very poor themselves (1 Cor. 1.26; 2 Cor. 8.2), the few more wealthy members of the contributing churches may have made significant donations. It must have been a substantial sum, otherwise the cost of travel and subsistence for such a large delegation would have eaten up a large portion of what would otherwise have been added to the collection itself. At any rate it was liable to be bulky or heavy (presumably it was exchanged into the more portable gold), and the band of delegates would be necessary to ensure its safe delivery. That the major portion of the journey was made by sea is understandable in the circumstances.[334]

d. The Language of the Collection

The language Paul uses and presses home in 2 Corinthians 8–9, much of it distinctive to these chapters, shows how deeply he felt on this score.[335] Moreover, it provides the clearest evidence of the practical outworking of Paul's theology, and indeed, surprisingly to many, of how similar that outworking was to the Jewish logic of human acts of righteousness as what should be expected from the people of God.[336]

(i) *charis* — 8.1, 4, 6, 7, 9, 16, 19; 9.8, 14, 15 (also 1 Cor. 16.3); *eucharistia* — 9.11, 12. *Charis,* of course, is one of the key words of Paul's gospel, with the basic meaning of 'grace'.[337] In its usage in these chapters, however, it embraces a mini-theology in itself: 'the grace of God' as something 'given' among/to the churches of Macedonia (8.1; 9.8, 14);[338] the collection as itself *charis,* a 'generous undertaking, gift' (8.4, 6-7, 19; also 1 Cor. 16.3); the 'generous act' of Christ as the motivation for the collection (8.9); *charis* in the sense of 'thanks' (8.16; 9.15), *eucharistia,* 'thanksgiving' (9.11, 12), as the appropriate response to such generosity.

---

333. Thrall, *2 Corinthians* 512-13.

334. See further Murphy-O'Connor, *Paul* 345-46.

335. The term used in 1 Cor. 16.1, *logeia,* means simply 'collection' (Georgi, *Remembering* 53; see further Thiselton, *1 Corinthians* 1318; Arzt-Grabner et al., *1 Korinther* 507).

336. Cf. the listing by Harris, *2 Corinthians* 554-55.

337. See *Theology of Paul* 319-23.

338. Georgi notes the singular use of *charis,* 'even though proper Greek usage would have suggested — indeed required — the plural. But for Paul there is only one divine grace, no matter how varied it may appear in its visible results' (*Remembering* 97). See also Beckheuer, *Paulus und Jerusalem* 126-33.

(ii) *eulogia* — 9.5, 6. A similar point is made by calling the collection *eulogia,* which usually denotes the act of speaking in favourable terms — 'good speaking', so 'praise' or 'blessing'. Here it seems to be pressed to the sense of 'good action', so 'generous gift'.[339] Actions must follow what would otherwise be empty words.

(iii) *perisseuō/perisseuma* — 8.2, 7, 14; 9.8, 12. The chapters 'abound' with the imagery of overflowing abundance *(perisseuō/perisseuma)* as denoting the character, hyperbolically, of course, of the generosity called for and expressed in the collection (8.7, 14)[340] — extraordinary because of the 'extreme poverty' of the givers (8.2) — but again mirroring Jesus' generosity (8.9) and the appropriate response of those who have themselves received so much (9.8, 12).[341] Other terms all indicate the warmth of the response which Paul thereby encouraged in the Corinthians and in their participation in the collection: 'love', *agapē* (8.7, 8, 24), a key word in Paul's theology and paraenesis;[342] 'eagerness', *spoudē* (8.7, 8, 16, 17, 22), as in Rom. 12.8; 'readiness', *prothymia* (8.11, 12, 19; 9.2; only here in Paul);[343] and 'zeal', *zēlos* (9.2). The concentration of these terms in 2 Corinthians 8–9 is again noteworthy.

(iv) *haplotēs* — 8.2; 9.11, 13. The force of *haplotēs* here is disputed, whether the basic meaning of 'simplicity, sincerity' can stand here — so 'sincere concern, simple goodness, which gives itself without reserve, "without strings attached", "without hidden agendas"' (as also in Rom. 12.8).[344] Alternatively, Paul here presses a fresh layer of significance on the term, as he does with *charis, eulogia, koinōnia* and *hypostasis* — so 'generosity, liberality' (NRSV). But in any case, the repeated use of the term (seldom elsewhere), as with several of the words listed here, gives a clear signal of the attitude which Paul sought to inculcate.

(v) *authairetos* — 8.3, 17. The unusual *authairetos,* only here in the NT, implies Paul's desire that the Corinthians' participation in the collection, like that of Titus, should be 'self-chosen, of his own accord'[345] — the 'natural' outwork-

---

339. BDAG 409; see also Beckheuer, *Paulus und Jerusalem* 153-74.

340. A similar point is made by calling the collection *hadrotēs,* 'abundance, this lavish gift' (8.20), and by characterizing it as 'filling up, supplying' *(prosanaplēroō)* others' needs (9.12).

341. To be noted also is the way Paul uses *autarkeia* in 9.8, a favourite virtue of Cynics and Stoics ('self-sufficiency', without requiring aid from others) (cf. BDAG 152). Paul uses the term to denote a 'sufficiency' made possible precisely by the sharing of scarce resources.

342. See, e.g., my *Theology of Paul* 656-61.

343. Georgi refers particularly to 1 Chronicles 29, where the verb *prothymeisthai* is used seven times (*Remembering* 108-109). Betz notes that *prothymia* is not a specifically Christian term (*2 Corinthians 8 and 9* 65).

344. BDAG 104; Thrall, *2 Corinthians* 523-24, 591.

345. It can have the sense of 'undertaking the duty at one's own expense' (LSJ 275).

ing of their faith and experience of grace, and not simply a response to Paul's appeal.[346]

(vi) *diakonia/diakoneō* — 8.4, 19, 20; 9.1, 12, 13 (also Rom. 15.25, 31). *Diakonia* is the regular term for 'service, ministry'; again Paul takes it for granted that such acts of service (as the collection) on behalf of others are the fruit of Christian concern for one another (as in Rom. 12.7, 1 Cor. 12.7 and 16.15). That Paul can speak of this service/ministry being 'tested, approved' (*dokimē* — 9.13),[347] that is, by their readiness to take part in the collection, is also to be noted; words alone affirming concern for fellow believers in need are never enough.[348]

(vii) *leitourgia* — 9.12. This is one of the most fascinating of the terms used by Paul, since it also denotes 'service'. But in classical Greek usage it was the standard term for 'public service' in Athens and elsewhere, 'the usual designation for a service performed by an individual for the state or public cult'.[349] What is interesting is that this public service was expected of rich men at their own expense; it helped channel their competitiveness in a public-spirited direction. By implication, Paul compares the obligation of those so enriched by the grace of God to make the equivalent public benefaction for the sake of their poorer fellow believers.

(viii) *koinōnia* — 8.4; 9.13. *Koinōnia* in the sense of 'sharing, participation in' is an important term for Paul.[350] Here he pushes the term into active mode as 'active participation in this ministry to the saints', the collection (8.4): *koinōnia* as sharing the poverty of fellow believers (by helping alleviate it) is again the outworking of the participation in Christ (1 Cor. 10.16) and in his Spirit (Phil. 2.1) that is to be expected; 'fellowship' cannot only be passive, it must also be active.[351]

---

346. Another unusual usage is *hypostasis* (9.4), but the sense of 'plan, project, undertaking' has gained strong support in recent years (BDAG 1040-41; Furnish, *2 Corinthians* 427-28; Thrall, *2 Corinthians* 568-70; each acknowledging debt to H. Koester, *TDNT* 8.572-89).

347. Similarly in 8.8 — 'I am testing *(dokimazōn)* the genuineness of your love' — overtones here of the suspicions which had blighted the earlier relations between Paul and the Corinthian church. And note also 8.2 — the 'severe test' of affliction.

348. *Endeixis,* 'demonstration, proof' (8.24), makes a similar point: the collection will demonstrate the reality of their love.

349. BDAG 591; *OCD*[3] 875.

350. See *Theology of Paul* 561-62, 616-17, 709; *koinōnia* is predominantly a Pauline term within the NT — thirteen of its nineteen occurrences in the NT appear in the undisputed Paulines (Rom. 15.26; 1 Cor. 1.9; 10.16 [twice]; 2 Cor. 6.14; 8.4; 9.13; 13.13; Gal. 2.9; Phil. 1.5; 2.1; 3.10; Phlm. 6).

351. J. Hainz, 'KOINŌNIA bei Paulus', in L. Bormann et al., eds., *Religious Propaganda and Missionary Competition in the New Testament World,* D. Georgi FS (NovTSupp 74; Leiden: Brill, 1994) 375-91 (here 378-80). A complementary point is made by *isotēs* (8.13, 14),

(ix) *kalos* — 8.21; *agathon ergon* — 9.8; *dikaiosynē* — 9.9, 10; *hypotagē* — 9.13. These remaining terms are also fascinating, for they are a reminder that Paul did not hesitate to call his converts to do 'what is good' *(kala)*, to encourage them to appreciate that God wanted them to 'abound in every good work *(ergon agathon)*'. Such 'submission *(hypotagē)* to the confession of the gospel' was appropriate, whereas the 'submission' called for in the Jerusalem meeting was not (Gal. 2.5).[352] Most striking of all is the repeated use of what was a key term in Paul's definition of the gospel, but used here more in terms that the Jerusalem and Antiochene traditionalists would appreciate: *dikaiosynē,* the term so central to Paul's exposition of his gospel in Romans, in the sense of (God's) 'righteousness',[353] but here in the sense of a 'righteous act' which meets the demands of the law in regard to social responsibility for others.[354] The usage emerges immediately from the little catena of texts from (Jewish) Scripture which Paul echoes or quotes in the first half of this final paragraph:

- 9.6 — 'whoever sows sparingly will also reap sparingly, and whoever sows generously will also reap generously' — cf. Prov. 11.24;
- 9.7a — 'each one should give as he has decided in his heart, not reluctantly or under compulsion' — cf. Deut. 15.10;
- 9.7b — 'God loves a cheerful giver' = Prov. 22.8a LXX;
- 9.9 — 'he has scattered abroad, he has given to the poor; his righteousness endures for ever' = Ps. 112.9 LXX (speaking of 'the righteous');
- 9.10a — 'he who supplies seed for the sower and bread for food' = Isa. 55.10;
- 9.10b — 'the harvest of your righteousness' — cf. Hos. 10.12 LXX.

Paul was clearly rooting his appeal for the Corinthians to participate in the collection in the Jewish understanding of 'righteousness' as the responsibility which follows from Israel's covenant standing, responsibility to share the cove-

---

with its encouragement for 'equality, fairness' in distribution between believers, as those prospering help out others in need; see further Georgi, *Remembering* 84-89; Betz, *2 Corinthians 8 and 9* 67-68; Thrall, *2 Corinthians* 539-40; Joubert, *Paul as Benefactor* 140-44.

352. Cf. Betz, who over-interprets the phrase as a reference to a document (*2 Corinthians 8 and 9* 122-25). But as Georgi notes, 'The *hypotagē tēs homologias* in this verse is to become *hypakoē tēs pisteōs,* later, in the Epistle to the Romans (Rom. 1:5)' (Georgi, *Remembering* 105); we might add by way of comparison, Rom. 6.17 — 'you have been handed over to the pattern of teaching'.

353. See above, §33.3a.

354. The awkwardness felt by commentators at the thought of Paul using this key term in such a way is well illustrated by Georgi, *Remembering* 99-101; Furnish, *2 Corinthians* 448-49; Thrall, *2 Corinthians* 580-83.

nant blessings (prosperity of crop and fruit) with those less fortunate in the community. The fact that this entirely Jewish concern (an aspect of 'covenantal nomism') was supplementary to what for Paul was presumably the primary motivation (the grace of God in Christ evoking the gracious act) should not be ignored.[355] Nor should it be allowed to diminish the fact that Paul did draw upon this very Jewish social ethic and presumably saw it as wholly of a piece with his theology of 'righteousness' already developed in Galatians and soon to be expounded fully in Romans.

e. The Theology of the Collection

What did Paul intend by the collection? The terminology just reviewed has already provided a large part of the answer.

At one level, and perhaps the most enduringly pastoral level, the collection was simply an act of Christian compassion — a highly practical expression of concern for fellow believers in need,[356] an enactment of Paul's vision of the body of Christ,[357] albeit, and uniquely, at an international level.

It was for Paul the inevitable outworking of the experience of grace, of God's boundless generosity in providing for humankind's welfare, and particularly of his acceptance of the ungodly sinner (Jew as well as Gentile) and gift of the Spirit to the weak and incapable. The *charis* of 'generous giving' was of a piece with the *charis* of 'thanks' as the proof of and response to the *charis* of God.[358]

At the same time, these seemingly simple and straightforward principles had become entangled in the controversies which Paul's gospel and mission had occasioned among the earliest Christian congregations. The collection was clearly Paul's attempt to heal the breach with the mother congregations in regard to the wider Mediterranean mission, to restore the fractured *koinōnia* of Jews and Gentiles.[359] So it was caught up in the ambiguities of the status of uncircumcised

---

355. Betz plays down the likelihood that Paul's thought here was shaped by LXX references, rather than by more widespread proverbial usage (*2 Corinthians 9 and 9* 103-15), but the quotations (from memory) and allusions are for the most part too concentrated and too clear to leave the matter in much doubt. Indicative of the discomfort observed in n. 354 is his comment: 'It is remarkable that Paul could speak of human righteousness in a way not unlike that found in Jewish authors' (115) — why 'remarkable'?

356. As in Rom. 12.13; 1 Cor. 16.15; Gal. 6.2, 10; Phil. 2.25; 4.16.

357. 1 Cor. 12.26; Rom. 12.8.

358. See further §33.4d above.

359. The point is usually put under the heading of 'the unity of the church', an expression of that unity (e.g., Nickle, *Collection* 111-29; earlier bibliography in 111 n. 112; Schrage, *1 Korinther* 4.426), but the attempt to heal a fractured unity is a more appropriate characterization.

Gentile believers — ambiguous for many/most of the Jewish believers in Messiah Jesus.

Should the collection, then, be seen as a direct implementation of the codicil added to the Jerusalem agreement in Gal. 2.10? No doubt it was so viewed by some. Paul himself must have been aware of this possible interpretation of the action and may well have been willing for it to be so interpreted, in the hope that it might facilitate rapprochement with Jerusalem. Indeed, his exposition of the obligation laid upon believers, Corinthian Gentiles specifically, in terms of 'good works', 'submission' and 'righteousness',[360] suggests that Paul was quite ready to encourage such an interpretation.[361] Quite possibly Paul's own (thoroughly Jewish) conviction, that acceptance (by God) within the community of believers should be manifested in the fruit of transformed character and in lives typified by service and care of the other, was anyway sufficiently similar to the traditionalists' insistence on 'works of the law'[362] for Paul to judge that he could promote the collection in the terms he did, without yielding any ground on his fundamental of justification through faith alone.[363]

Still more pressing, should the collection be seen as a fulfilment of the prophetic hope for Gentiles to come in bearing gifts to the Lord, a vision particularly prominent in Isaiah?[364] Paul himself certainly plays on that idea in his talk of his priestly commission to make 'the offering of the Gentiles acceptable' (Rom. 15.16). The passage echoes the Isaianic vision (Isa. 66.20), a verse which, as we saw earlier (§29.4a), may well have contributed significantly to Paul's whole mission strategy.[365] So, once again we have to ask, in using such language, was

---

360. Note again that 'righteousness' could have the sense of 'almsgiving' (§27 n. 189), also Berger's observation that almsgiving could be presented as a substitute for Temple sacrifice and circumcision ('Almosen für Israel'). Luke seems to interpret the collection in such terms, if we are to follow Acts 24.17 (Jervell, *Apg.* 571) — another case where Luke's narrative reflects more of the Jerusalem version of Paul's mission. In Gal. 2.10 it is unclear whether 'the poor' were (to be) understood as a specific reference to the Jerusalem congregations as such, or whether the Jerusalem poor would have simply been the most obvious example of a more general concern (see again §27 n. 186 above).

361. The fact that 2 Corinthians 8 and 9 could have begun as drafts of different letters (§32.7a) might well suggest that Paul was uncertain of the wisest way of making his appeal for the collection.

362. See again my *New Perspective on Paul* 67-80.

363. He had attempted to maintain the same 'both-and' in Galatians; see 2.6-9, 11-18, etc., but also 2.10b; 5.6b, 13; 6.2.

364. Isa. 18.7; 45.14; 60.5-7, 9, 11, 13; 61.5-6.

365. See above, §29 n. 84, and especially Riesner, *Paul's Early Period* 249-50. See also D. J. Downs, '"The Offering of the Gentiles" in Romans 15.16', *JSNT* 29 (2006) 173-86, who argues that the phrase 'the offering of the Gentiles' should be read as a subjective genitive.

Paul showing his willingness for the collection to be so understood?[366] Indeed, the whole enterprise could have been part of Paul's hope and strategy for Israel to be 'provoked to jealousy' by Gentile response to the gospel (Rom. 10.19; 11.13-14).[367] If so, it was a dangerous tactic. For Isaiah's vision could easily be interpreted in terms of glorifying the nation of Israel; the gifts brought by the Gentiles were to enrich the restored people of Israel. The vision was most naturally fulfilled by the Gentiles becoming proselytes.[368] Paul, of course, would have resisted that corollary. The collection could even be presented as a Christian equivalent to the Temple tax, signifying the centrality of Jerusalem for the diaspora believers, and even the Jerusalem church's right to an equivalent to the Temple tax from the diaspora churches.[369] Again, Paul would no doubt have demurred. For him the collection was simply a recognition of mutual interdependence even among believers in countries far apart (Rom. 15.26), and a particular acknowledgment by Gentile believers of the spiritual blessings they had received through their participation in the heritage of Israel (15.27).

Presumably this ambiguity which hung around the collection like a cloak was a major factor in what appears to have been the failure of the collection, as Paul had feared might be the case (Rom. 15.31).[370] But that belongs to the final act of Paul's story (§34). Here it is more appropriate to conclude with Paul's hope that the collection would help heal old wounds and draw Jew and Gentile, Jew and

---

366. Possibly the puzzling reference in Rom. 15.28 to Paul 'sealing the fruit to them' (presumably the Jerusalem church) was a way of giving the business a more formal, almost commercial character, as well as indicating that Paul wanted to put his own personal stamp on the enterprise ('my service' — 15.31), his presence (he would hope) guaranteeing the safe delivery of the collection; see also Fitzmyer, *Romans* 723; Jewett, *Romans* 931-32.

367. McKnight, 'Collection' 146. Rom. 11.13-14 certainly indicates that such thoughts were in Paul's mind at the time. But the point should not be pressed, for Paul still had in mind to go to Spain, a totally new area of mission; the end could be not yet (Thrall, *2 Corinthians* 513)! Nickle notes that the passage cited in 2 Cor. 9.10 (Isa. 55.10) includes the assurance that God's word will accomplish its purpose (*Collection* 137); cf. Rom. 9.6!

368. The texts are assembled in *Jesus Remembered* 394-95 nn. 70 and 71.

369. The point was pressed in a famous article by K. Holl, 'Der Kirchenbegriff des Paulus in seinem Verhältnis zu dem der Urgemeinde', *Gesammelte Aufsätze zur Kirchengeschichte* (Tübingen: Mohr, 1928) 2.44-67. On the Temple tax and the parallels and differences between the Temple tax and Paul's collection, see Nickle, *Collection* 74-93. McKnight suggests that the collection might have been administered along with the Temple tax, Paul accompanying both funds to hand them over to the Temple and the Jerusalem community ('Collection' 144); but though the suggestion of Paul sheltering under the protection afforded to the transmission of the Temple tax is attractive, it is hardly likely that diaspora synagogues would regard Paul as an appropriate representative to convey the Temple tax itself. Thrall notes that in Philo the bearers of the Temple tax to Jerusalem were called *hieropompoi*, not *apostoloi* as in 2 Cor. 8.23 (*2 Corinthians* 554, with reference to Philo, *Legat.* 216; *Spec. Leg.* 1.77-78).

370. See further below, §34.1e.

Greek, into genuinely mutual acceptance and communal worship and service —
the vision he held out in that climactic paragraph of his letter to Rome (15.7-13).

33.5. The Testament of Paul (Acts 20.17-38)

The composition of the letter to the Christians in Rome and the dispatch of the
delegation to convey the collection to Jerusalem provided a highly fitting climax
to Paul's Aegean mission. The Aegean mission had been the principal focus of
his mission work and was to bear its most enduring fruit. But Luke, who mentions neither Paul's epistolary correspondence nor the collection, chose to mark
the end of the Aegean mission, and effectively the end of Paul's career as a pioneering peripatetic missionary, in a different way. He has Paul deliver a farewell
speech to the elders of the other of his two principal bases for the Aegean mission — Ephesus — what turns out, in effect, to be Paul's last will and testimony,
Paul's only recorded speech to fellow believers.[371]

a. From Where Did Luke Derive the Speech?

Within Jewish circles the genre of testament was already well established.[372]
Characteristic of the genre was the presentation of some revered figure from the
past, prior to his death, giving farewell instruction to his immediate circle, drawing appropriate lessons from his own life, and warning of evil times ahead. Such
testaments attributed to some or all of the twelve patriarchs were already in circulation and probably also one attributed to Job.[373] Luke does not make use of
the genre as such, but the motivation seems to be similar.[374] Paul, who is about to
be separated for good from all of his churches, takes the opportunity to review
the character of his main missionary work, to forewarn of future dangers and to
draw appropriate lessons for his churches.[375]

---

371. 'The setting in Miletus is most likely historical then; Paul probably did give a speech
in Miletus, and this was known to Luke from tradition' (Trebilco, *Early Christians* 174-75).

372. It was modelled principally on Genesis 49, but note also Joshua 23; and cf. 1 Samuel 12 and 1 Macc. 2.49-70.

373. For the *Testaments of the Twelve Patriarchs* and the *Testament of Job,* see *OTP* vol.
1. The Testaments have 'a loose format: The ideal figure faces death and causes his relatives and
intimate friends to circle around his bed. He occasionally informs them of his fatal flaw and ex-
horts them to avoid certain temptations; he typically instructs them regarding the way of righteousness and utters blessings and curses. Often he illustrates his words . . . with descriptions of
the future as it has been revealed to him in a dream or vision' (773). See also Fitzmyer, *Acts* 674.

374. Note particularly Acts 20.24-25.

375. 'The speech is formally directed to the community leaders from Ephesus, but

The emphases are the ones which Luke assumed that Paul would have wanted to give. But the fact that he depicts Paul's audience as 'the elders' from Ephesus (20.17), who are also addressed as 'overseers' in 20.28, despite the fact that Paul nowhere refers to 'elders' in any of his letters from this whole period, suggests that Luke wrote more than half consciously with an eye to the churches of his own day.[376] Most intriguing of all, verses 29-30 express a mood of foreboding which we more naturally associate with documents written towards the end of the century, and their language, as also verses 24 and 28, have given some credibility to the quite popular suggestion that Luke was also the actual author of the Pastoral Epistles.[377]

Luke certainly takes the opportunity to underscore several of his principal themes which run through Acts:

- 'the counsel of God' (20.27) as the ultimate determiner of the most decisive events;[378]
- the Spirit of God as the inspiring and ordering power behind the church and its mission (20.22-23, 28);[379] the mission which began with such clear signs of the Spirit's direction (13.2, 4; 16.6-7) ends on a similar note of conviction;
- Paul as one who received his ministry from the Lord Jesus[380] to serve as the great model of the committed missionary and teacher;[381]
- the repeated theme of witness-bearing (20.21, 23, 24);[382]

---

serves the whole Christian church. Paul himself is the sole example for the church, and as such he gives orders for the time after his death. He appears here as the sole founder of the communities. He is, in other words . . . presented as something like a "chief apostle" (Oberapostel)' (Jervell, *Apg.* 509, also 515).

376. See Trebilco, *Early Christians* 187-86, and above, §27 at n. 97; though note also Phil. 1.1 (on which see below, §34.4c).

377. See particularly S. G. Wilson, *Luke and the Pastoral Epistles* (London: SPCK, 1979). E.g., the perspective of 20.28 is closer to that of the later epistles than to anything in the undisputed Pauline letters: 'take heed to yourselves' (1 Tim. 4.16), 'overseers' (1 Tim. 3.1-7; Tit. 1.7), Spirit-appointed leaders (cf. 1 Tim. 4.14; 2 Tim. 1.6), also elders (20.17; 1 Tim. 5.17; Tit. 1.5); and note the thought of shepherding the flock in 1 Pet. 5.2-3. Barrett summarizes Wilson's list of parallels (*Acts* 965). See further Trebilco, *Early Christians* 189-95.

378. A particularly Lukan motif within the NT (Luke 7.30; Acts 2.23; 4.27-28; 5.38-39; 13.36; 20.27).

379. See also Acts 4.8, 31; 5.32; 6.5; 7.55; 8.29, 39; 10.19-20, 47; 13.2, 4, 9; 15.28; 16.6-7.

380. Acts 20.24; cf. 9.15-16; 18.9-10; 22.17-21; 26.16-18.

381. Acts 20.19-21, 24-27, 31, 34-35. S. Walton, *Leadership and Lifestyle: The Portrait of Paul in the Miletus Speech and 1 Thessalonians* (SNTSMS 108; Cambridge: Cambridge University, 2000) ch. 4, argues that 'Luke presents Paul as both the model of the discipleship lived and taught by Jesus, and the model of leadership in the tradition of Jesus' (134).

382. Acts 1.8, 22; 2.32; 3.15; 5.32; 10.41; 13.31; 22.15; 26.16.

- Paul's preaching in Acts, summarized in 20.21, as repentance towards God and faith towards Jesus as 'our Lord';[383] in Paul's letters themselves, note the equivalent balance of 1 Thess. 1.9-10, though 'repentance' is hardly a characteristically Pauline term;[384]
- the gospel as about the grace of God and the kingdom of God,[385] and calling for repentance towards God as well as for faith in the Lord Jesus Christ (20.21, 24-25, 32);[386]
- the tension between a message directed to both Jews and Greeks (cf. 19.10, 17)[387] but also threatened by 'the plots of the Jews' (20.19, 21);[388]
- and, not least, the subtle reinforcement of the message that Christianity (consisting of Jews and Greeks) fully shares Israel's identity (20.28 and 32).[389]

However, Luke has not simply created the speech from his own theological priorities; there are several indications that his own theological emphases may have been as much shaped by the reports and traditions available to him.[390]

- Thus we note Paul's sense of being under criticism from within his churches (20.18, 26-27, 33), a surprising feature for the reader of Acts, but familiar from Paul's letters themselves.[391]

383. E.g., Acts 13.38; 16.31; 17.30; 19.4; 26.18. It was important for Luke that God as much as Jesus was the content of the proclamation to the Greeks (particularly 14.15-17 and 17.22-31).

384. *Metanoia* ('repentance') appears in the Pauline corpus only in Rom. 2.4 and 2 Cor. 7.9-10; the verb *metanoeō* ('repent') only in 2 Cor. 12.21.

385. See also Acts 1.3; 8.12; 14.22; 19.8; 28.23.

386. Repentance — 2.38; 3.19; 5.31; 8.22; 11.18; 17.30; 20.21; 26.20; faith — 4.4; 9.42; 10.43; 11.17, 21; 13.12, 48; 14.1, 9, 23, 27; 15.7, 9; 16.31, 34; 18.8, 27; 19.2, 4; 20.21; 26.18.

387. Acts 9.15; 13.44-48; 17.4, 11-12, 17; 18.4-7; 19.8-10, 17. But in characterizing Paul's mission, as earlier (14.1; 18.4; 19.10, 17), as directed to both 'Jews and Greeks', Luke has retained an authentically Pauline understanding of his mission (Rom. 1.16; 10.12; 1 Cor. 1.24; 10.23; 12.13; Gal. 3.28; Col. 3.11).

388. See also Acts 12.3, 11; 13.50; 14.3, 4, 19; 17.5; 18.6, 12; 19.9; 20.3; 22.30.

389. Israel as God's inheritance (e.g., Num. 18.20; Deut. 32.9; Jer. 10.16; 51.19; Sir. 44.23) and the people of Israel as 'the holy ones/saints' (e.g., Deut. 33.3; Pss. 16.3; 34.9; Dan. 7.18; 8.24; Tob. 8.15; Wis. 18.9). That these terms are addressed to Gentile believers is Luke's way of indicating that both the vision of James (15.15-17) and the commission of Paul (26.18) were fulfilled in Paul's mission.

390. Cadbury lists fourteen 'Pauline expressions' in the speech (*Beginnings* 5.412-13); other bibliography is found in Trebilco, *Early Christians* 177 n. 89, and see further 178-86.

391. That Paul felt himself to be under criticism for various aspects of his ministry is well attested in his letters — over his travel plans (2 Cor. 1.15-18), on his preaching (1 Cor. 1.17–2.4; 2 Cor. 10.10; 11.6), on his refusal to accept financial help (1 Corinthians 9; 2 Cor.

- So too the emphasis on Paul's suffering (20.19, 23) is something on which Acts has not particularly dwelt, whereas Paul speaks of his 'chains' and 'afflictions' on several occasions in his letters.[392]

- 'Serving the Lord' (20.19) is Paul's language,[393] not Luke's, as also the terms 'humility'[394] and 'what is in your best interests (ta sympheronta)' (20.20).[395] Paul also recalls his tears (2 Cor. 2.4), as well as danger from his own people and hindrances put in his way by 'the Jews'.[396]

- The mention of 'house to house' ministry (20.20) reminds us that Paul's chief work was often carried through in house churches, whereas Luke concentrated more on the initial ministry in the synagogues. Both 'in public and from house to house' implies that his teaching was always consistent: he did not say one thing in private and another in public; there was no esoteric teaching for a privileged inner circle.

- The reference to the church as 'obtained through the blood of his own' (20.28)[397] is a theological reflection on the cross unique in Acts,[398] but once again it should be noted that reference to the blood of Christ (on the

---

11.7-11), and so on. Already in his earliest letter he felt it necessary to appeal to his converts' knowledge of his conduct (1 Thess. 1.5).

392. Cf. particularly Phil. 1.17, and note the strong motif in 2 Corinthians (§32.7).

393. Rom. 1.1; 12.11; 14.18; 16.18; Gal. 1.10; Phil. 1.1.

394. E.g., Rom. 12.16; 2 Cor. 10.1; Phil. 2.3.

395. 1 Cor. 6.12; 7.35 v.l.; 10.23, 33 v.l.; 12.7; 2 Cor. 8.10; 12.1 v.l. (BDAG 960).

396. 2 Cor. 11.26; 1 Thess. 2.14-16.

397. Acts 20.28 is one of the most difficult verses in Acts, not to mention the whole New Testament. The chief difficulty arises in the final clause — '. . . the church of God, which he obtained through the blood of his own'; or should we better translate 'through his own blood' (cf. NIV)? The text caused such puzzlement (God's own blood?) that some of the scribes responsible for making copies of Luke's book evidently attempted to improve or clarify it — particularly by reading 'the church of the Lord, which he obtained through his own blood' (cf. Heb. 9.12). REB prefers this as the correct reading, but a good rule in textual criticism is that the more difficult text is most likely to be original. NRSV and NJB, in contrast, read 'the blood of his own Son', assuming a reference in the phrase like that explicitly given in Rom. 8.32. On the textual issues see Metzger, *Textual Commentary* 480-82; B. D. Ehrman, *The Orthodox Corruption of Scripture* (New York: Oxford University, 1993) 87-88; and further Sellner, *Das Heil Gottes* 467-80.

398. Rather than assume a simplistic or, alternatively, a highly sophisticated statement of God's action in Christ (cf. 2 Cor. 5.19), we should probably see here a not very clearly expressed reference to the death of Jesus. Even so, the christology is beyond anything else we have read in Acts (Jesus as 'God's own'). Not only so, but nowhere else in Acts does Luke attribute a saving significance to the cross, whether as an act of martyrdom or as a sacrifice. Conceivably Luke himself was not entirely clear on the significance of the cross: all the other references to it in Acts express a suffering-vindication motif (see above, §23.4g). But possibly it is simply a jumbled reference to the more familiar and clearly formulated teaching of Paul.

cross) is a regular feature in Paul's letters,[399] though never as a reference to God's blood.

- Paul's emotional commitment to his churches (20.19, 31), his admonishing his converts, and his concern for 'the weak' (20.35) are reflected much more clearly in Paul's letters than elsewhere in Acts hitherto.[400]
- The language of 20.32 is particularly Pauline in character: 'I commend you . . . to God and to the message of his grace *(charis),* which is able to build you up *(oikodomēsai)* and to give you the inheritance *(klēronomia)* among all who are set apart' (to some extent also that of v. 33).[401]
- Prior to 20.34 Luke has said virtually nothing about Paul maintaining himself by his own labour, a point of principle for Paul himself.[402]
- And the implication that Paul modelled his conduct on the teaching of Jesus is again lacking in Acts but is a feature of Paul's letters.[403]

Although several of these features read more as Luke's formulation of Pauline emphases, the suggestion that Luke was justified in portraying this as Paul's last will and testimony is a view which can be maintained with some confidence.[404] Indeed, it is difficult to avoid the conclusion that, whether through tra-

---

399. Rom. 3.25; 5.9; 1 Cor. 10.16; 11.25, 27; Col. 1.20.

400. E.g., 1 Cor. 16.17-19; 2 Cor. 2.4; 6.11-13; 7.2-16; Gal. 4.19; 1 Thess. 2.17-20; 3.10. *Noutheteō* ('admonish') is an exclusively Pauline word in the NT, apart from here.

401. 'Grace' (nearly two-thirds of the NT occurrences of *charis* appear in the Pauline corpus); God's ability/power (Rom. 16.25; 2 Cor. 9.8); 'upbuilding' (1 Cor. 8.1, 10; 10.23; 14.1, 17; 1 Thess. 5.11; though also Acts 9.31); 'inheritance' (Rom. 4.13-14; 8.17; 1 Cor. 6.9-10; Gal. 3.18) among the sanctified (Rom. 15.16; 1 Cor. 1.2; though also Acts 26.18); for the full phrase ('inheritance among the sanctified') cf. particularly Eph. 1.18 and Col. 1.12. Coveting, acquisitive desire (20.33) is a theme which appears nowhere else in Acts but is a common Pauline concern (e.g., Rom. 7.7-8; 1 Cor. 10.6; Gal. 5.16, 24).

402. A point of principle and pride for Paul (1 Cor. 4.12; 9.15-18; 2 Cor. 11.7-11; 1 Thess. 2.9; 2 Thess. 3.8; see further §29.5d). The verse here adds the information that his labour provided for the needs also of those with him. But concern that the more able should assist the weaker was certainly another Pauline concern (Rom. 15.1-2; Gal. 6.2)

403. Rom. 6.17; 13.14; 15.1-5; 1 Cor. 11.1; Phil. 2.5; Col. 2.6; see further *Theology of Paul* 189-95. Paul was quite ready to put himself forward as an example of Christian conduct (1 Cor. 4.16; 11.1; Gal. 4.12; 1 Thess. 2.9-12; 4.11; 2 Thess. 3.6-10).

404. Haenchen quotes Dodd (disapprovingly): '. . . so many echoes of the language of the Pauline epistles, that we must suppose . . . that he [Luke] worked upon actual reminiscences of Paul's speech upon this or some similar occasion' (*Acts* 591 n. 8); Barrett's quotation from Bauernfeind, 'the spirit of this speech is the spirit of Paul, but not the letter (Buchstabe) of the Pauline letters known to us' (*Acts* 964), may be nearer the mark. 'One must reckon with authentic reminiscences, even if, obviously, the speech as such has been conceived by Luke. . . . The speech is determined both by Lukanisms as also by Paulinisms' (Jervell, *Apg.* 516). Walton concludes from a close comparison of the Miletus speech with 1 Thessalonians 'that the

dition or through personal awareness of Paul's thought, Luke's attempt to represent Paul's mind at this point has been very successful.

b. The Speech Itself

There are two dominant motifs in the speech, as typical of the testament genre: an apologia for the past life and an exhortation/warning for the future.

The apologia comes first:

- Paul has 'served the Lord with all humility and tears, enduring the trials that came to me through the plots of the Jews' (20.19);
- he has been faithful in proclaiming his message of 'repentance toward God and faith toward our Lord Jesus' (20.20-21);
- he goes now to Jerusalem, fully prepared for the imprisonment and persecution awaiting him, and determined to 'finish my course and the ministry that I received from the Lord Jesus, to testify to the good news of God's grace' (20.22-24).[405]

The link to the warning of troublesome times ahead is made by Paul's disclaiming personal responsibility for what is to happen (20.26-27). Then comes the exhortation and warning:

- the Ephesian elders/overseers[406] have responsibility 'to shepherd the church of God (or the Lord)' (20.28);[407]
- there will be danger from without — after Paul's departure 'savage wolves will come in among you, not sparing the flock' (20.29);
- and danger from within — 'some even from your own group will come distorting the truth in order to entice the disciples to follow them' (20.30).

thought of the two texts, and often its verbal expression, runs remarkably parallel' and that 'Luke knows Pauline tradition independently of the epistles' (*Leadership* 185, 212).

405. The sense of the weightiness of the commission is somewhat as in 2 Cor. 5.18-20, but the language is the same as that in 2 Tim. 4.7 ('I have completed my course').

406. On *episkopos* ('overseer') here see particularly Fitzmyer, *Acts* 678-79.

407. In terms of the constantly underlying question of Christian identity, there are several important features in this verse. (1) 'The flock' is a well-established OT image of God's people (Ps. 78.52, 71; Isa. 40.11; Jer. 23.2; Ezek. 34; Mic. 5.4). (2) This evocation of 'Israel imagery' for the churches founded by Paul is enhanced by use of the term 'acquire', used of God's choice of Israel in the Greek translations of Isa. 43.21 and Mal. 3.17. (3) 'The church of God' is the regular OT usage ('assembly' of God), indicating that each gathering of believers, followers of the Way, Gentile as well as Jew, was of a piece with and in direct continuity with the congregation of Israel (see above, §20.1[14]).

- 'Keep awake' (20.31) continues the same mood of eschatological foreboding.[408]

The premonition that false teaching will arise in the future, from influences both without and within, again has the ring of later letters in the New Testament;[409] the mood is that of the end of an epoch, *fin de siècle*.[410]

A reminder that Paul had been so warning them for three years and commendation of the audience 'to God and the message of his grace' (20.31-32) could have made a suitable closure to the speech; but instead, somewhat surprisingly, it marks a final transition back to the apologia:

- 'I coveted no one's silver or gold or clothing' (20.33);[411]
- 'I worked with my own hands to support myself and my companions' (20.34);
- he thus left them an example of how to support the weak, in the spirit of Jesus' own teaching: 'It is more blessed to give than to receive' (20.35).[412]

The dark cloud of foreboding is almost tangible in the influence it has on the scene. Although the speech refers only to Paul's uncertainty as to what will happen in Jerusalem (20.22) and mentions only predictions from the Spirit that 'imprisonments and persecutions' await him (20.23),[413] it is already clearly im-

408. Cf. Mark 13.35, 37; 1 Thess. 5.6; 1 Pet. 5.8; Rev. 3.2-3; 16.15.

409. 1 Tim. 4.1-3; 2 Tim. 4.3-4; 2 Pet. 2.1-3; 3.3-4; similarly *Did.* 16.3 and other second-century Christian writings; cf. also the warnings in Matt. 7.15, 10.16 and John 10.12, and the situation envisaged in 1 John 2.19.

410. Acts 20.29 became the basis of the subsequent view that heresy was always from outside the church, subsequent and secondary to orthodoxy — a view largely unquestioned until Bauer in 1934 (*Jesus Remembered* 5).

411. The denial here echoes Paul's sense of responsibility towards his churches in money matters (cf. 1 Cor. 9.12, 15; 2 Cor. 7.2; 11.7-11), though the tone is again that of a final statement of accounts (the model perhaps provided by 1 Sam. 12.3-5).

412. The explicit quotation of a saying of Jesus is unusual in Paul (only in 1 Cor. 7.10, 9.14 and 11.23-26). But he seems to echo and allude to other teaching of Jesus at various points in his ethical exhortation (see *Jesus Remembered* 182 n. 48). The saying, then, is further evidence for a common store of Jesus tradition circulating orally in the early churches, not all of which was eventually included in the written Gospels (the nearest parallel would be Luke 6.35-36, 38). For other sayings preserved outside the canonical Gospels which may well go back to Jesus himself, see Luke 6.5 D and *GTh* 82 (*Jesus Remembered* 172). See further Haenchen, *Acts* 594-95 n. 5; Fitzmyer, *Acts* 682.

413. Luke does not pause to resolve the tension between Paul's decision to go to Jerusalem 'bound in the Spirit' (Acts 20.22) and a Spirit-inspired prophecy that he should *not* go (21.4) (see further my *Unity and Diversity* §44.3). We know, of course, that Paul had his own forebodings (Rom. 15.31).

plied that these will mark the end of Paul's mission.[414] Paul goes on to insist that his life has no value and that his only desire is to 'finish the course'[415] and the ministry he had received from the Lord Jesus (20.24). And the emotionally wrenching scene at the end of the speech as the elders take final farewell of Paul ('grieving that they would not see him again') underlines the finality of the departure; the weeping reinforces the impression that a final testament has been delivered (cf. Gen. 50.1-4). Nor is the emotional tension ever relieved throughout the rest of the journey to Jerusalem: the farewell to the believers in Tyre echoes that at Miletus (21.5-6);[416] during his stay in Caesarea in the house of Philip, one of the seven (6.5),[417] the prediction of the prophet Agabus is explicit — Paul will be imprisoned and handed over to the Roman authorities (21.11);[418] and Paul himself reiterates his readiness to die (21.13). Luke could hardly have made it any more plain that this sequence did indeed mark not only the end of Paul's Aegean mission but also the end of his whole ministry as a church-founding missionary, with the end of his course already anticipated.

414. It is widely accepted that the speech assumes Paul's death; see particularly G. Ballhorn, 'Die Miletrede — ein Literaturbericht', in Horn, ed., *Ende* 37-47 (here 45-47).

415. Typical athletic imagery; cf. 1 Cor. 9.24-27; Phil. 3.13-14; and especially 2 Tim. 4.7.

416. The church in Tyre was presumably founded by the Hellenist mission (Acts 11.19).

417. On Philip see above, §24.7; 'the seven' already have an established status in the early tradition, like 'the twelve'. 'The four unmarried daughters who used to prophesy' (21.9) sounds like a vivid recollection rather than contrived (they don't contribute any prophecy!). Haenchen maintains that the account was grounded in oral tradition, even though discounting the force of the 'we' (*Acts* 604-605). Further discussion in Barrett, *Acts* 994. Von Dobbeler wonders whether Philip's house was actually a house-community, perhaps more like the spiritual centre of a prophetic-charismatic form of Christianity including women prophets (*Philippus* 221-22).

418. In the light of 21.8-12, the time spent by Luke ('we') with Philip and the encounter with Agabus could have provided Luke with invaluable information about the earlier phases of the Jesus movement; Lüdemann, e.g., thinks that the material is traditional and historically reliable (*Early Christianity* 233-35); and see Barrett, *Acts* 986-87.

PART NINE

THE END OF THE BEGINNING

CHAPTER 34

The Passion of Paul

Nothing shows us Luke's priorities in writing the Acts of the Apostles more clearly than the final section of that book. For the last eight chapters (chs. 21–28) are devoted to the final acts in Paul's career. In this, Acts is obviously structured in parallel to Luke's Gospel, with the narrative there likewise building up to the climax of Jesus' mission, usually described as 'the passion narrative' (Luke 19.29–23.56).[1] Since the Acts narrative likewise focuses on the final trials and sufferings of Paul (arrest, near scourging, hearing before the Jewish council, threats of assassination, formal trial before the Roman governor, two years' imprisonment, hearing before the Jewish king, near-death experiences at sea and on land), it is appropriate to give the chapters a similar title — 'the passion of Paul'.[2]

---

1. Cf. H. Omerzu, 'Das Schweigen des Lukas', in Horn, ed., *Ende* 127-56 (here 154-55). The extent of the gospel 'passion narrative' depends on whether it includes the events prior to Palm Sunday and the resurrection narratives.

2. The parallels between the two passion narratives are quite extensive:

	Luke	*Acts*
Determined to go to Jerusalem	9.51, 53; 13.33; 18.31	19.21; 20.3, 16
Jerusalem as where destiny must be unfolded	13.33	20.22-23
passion predictions on the road to Jerusalem	9.44; 18.31-33	21.11; cf. 28.17
abandoned by his supporters	disciples	Jerusalem church
hearing before Jewish council	22.66-71	22.30–23.10
trial before Roman governor	23.1-5, 13-25	24.1-23
hearing before Jewish king	23.6-11	26.1-32
repeated pronouncements of innocence	23.4, 14, 22	23.9; 25.25; 26.32; 28.21
vindication	ch. 24	28.1-10
open ending	24.44-53	28.30-31

In fact, Luke devotes a full quarter of his total narrative to the account of Paul's passion. This is a substantially greater proportion than he gave to the passion narrative in the Gospel (though by pushing so much of the Jesus tradition into the final journey to Jerusalem, starting in Luke 9.51, Luke does lessen the contrast). He also pays much more attention to the passion of Paul than he does to the trial and martyrdom of Stephen, the first Christian martyr (Acts 6–7). And the contrast with the briefest of references to the execution of James, brother of John (12.2), is quite astonishing. Clearly Paul was Luke's great hero, the hero of the earliest expansion of the Jesus sect. All other activity, even in the church of Jerusalem, let alone the mission of Peter and other missionaries, is eclipsed, and Paul stands alone, centre-stage, even his companions being allowed to play only shadowy roles (including Luke himself — the 'we' of the beginning [21.1-18] and latter stages of this final section of Acts [27.1-28.16]).

Not least of importance is the fact that Paul completes the course that Luke obviously intended for Acts, by bringing the gospel, apparently for the first time, to Rome. The programme outlined in 1.8 is completed: the expanding circles of mission from Jerusalem (chs. 1–5) to Samaria and Judea (chs. 6–12), from Antioch into the peninsula formed by Asia Minor (chs. 13–15), and from there into the Aegean (chs. 16–20), reach their natural climax in the journey to Rome (chs. 21–28). And it is completed precisely in the completion of the commission given to Paul himself (alone) to carry Christ's name before 'the Gentiles and kings and the sons of Israel' (9.15-16):[3] in the repeated sequence of trials and hearings, before the sons of Israel (22.1-22; 23.1-10), before the Gentile governors (24.1–25.12), and, as the climax, before the Jewish king (25.13–26.32). There is no point in regretting the exclusiveness of this final focus and the information which Luke passed over or deliberately excluded in order to achieve this 'spotlight' effect on Paul. We should rather appreciate what he has left to us and draw on it to best effect to round off the story of Paul's final contribution to the making of Christianity.

The fact that Luke has made so little of Paul's earlier sufferings, largely ignoring the events catalogued by Paul himself in 2 Cor. 11.23-27, gives Acts too the character of 'a passion narrative with a lengthy introduction'.

3. Which is one of the reasons why the commission is repeated in 22.15, 17-21 and 26.16-18.

34.1. Arrest in Jerusalem

a. The Attempted Rapprochement (Acts 21.17-26)

As in Luke 19, so in Acts 21, there is no clear break marking the beginning of the passion narrative proper. The warning bells ring repeatedly on Paul's final journey to Jerusalem: the foreboding of the farewell speech (20.24-25), the heart-wrenching leave-takings at Miletus (20.37-38) and Tyre (21.5-6), the warnings of coming disaster by prophecy (21.4) and prophet (21.11), and the consequent anguish of both Paul and his friends (21.12-14).[4] So the reader is quite prepared for the frosty reception of Paul by 'James and all the elders' in Jerusalem itself.[5] To be sure, they praise God for the news Paul brings of the success of his mission among the Gentiles (21.19-20). But their immediate verbal response, according to Luke, is to tell Paul:

> [20]You see, brother, how many tens of thousands *(myriades)* there are of those who have believed among the Jews, and they are all zealots *(zēlōtai)* for the law. [21]They have been informed about you that you teach defection *(apostasian)* from Moses, telling all the Jews who live among the Gentiles that they should not circumcise their children or walk in accordance with the customs.

In Luke's narrative these comments come as something of a surprise. The last time James appeared in Acts he had been presented as a conciliatory figure seeking to support the Gentile mission (15.13-29). Luke has omitted the indications of increasing strain with the Jerusalem leadership which we learn from Paul himself.[6] But, much as Luke might have wanted to present an eirenic rapport between Paul and the Jerusalem church, that option was no longer possible. In the light of Paul's letters, the report given by James is particularly illuminating:

- The success of the Jewish mission has brought in 'myriads' of 'zealots' — a term which evokes all the passionate commitment to Israel's set-apartness to God and from the (other) nations, and fiery readiness to prevent potential compromise and adulteration of that ideal of Israel's holiness, by violent means if necessary; Paul as Saul had been such a 'zealot', as both Luke (22.3) and Paul attest (Gal. 1.13-14; Phil. 3.6).[7]

---

4. See the end of §33.5. As Lake and Cadbury note, Luke makes no attempt to indicate whether Paul arrived in time for Pentecost — despite Acts 20.16 (*Beginnings* 4.270).

5. Becker contrasts the hospitality Paul had enjoyed with Peter on his earlier visit to Jerusalem with the absence of any thought of hospitality provided by James (*Paul* 454).

6. Particularly Gal. 2.11-21; 2 Corinthians 11.

7. The 'zeal' here in view was understood as a reflection of divine zeal/jealousy (see §25 nn. 102-104) and alludes to the 'zeal' of such as Phinehas (Num. 25.6-13; Sir. 45.23-24) or

- They had been informed or instructed (by those whose zeal made them virulent opponents of Paul's mission) that Paul was an apostate[8] who told diaspora Jews to abandon circumcision and the customs by which Jews characteristically ordered their lives.

The portrayal rings true.[9] Quite apart from Luke's apparently being present (21.18), the portrayal matches too closely the picture given by Paul's letters to be readily dismissed;[10] and it is all the more persuasive because Luke has so studiously ignored the tensions between Jerusalem and Paul which Paul's letters attest. Moreover, the false reports about Paul's mission are just what we might have expected when such 'zeal' fed upon news and rumours of Paul's mission, and they accord well with the dismissal of Paul in subsequent Jewish-Christian writings.[11]

The passage is extremely important, then, in that it provides invaluable information about the beginnings of Christianity in Jerusalem:

- it tells us about the strength of the Jerusalem church — 'myriads who have believed';[12]
- it tells us about the character of the Jerusalem church — 'they are all zealots for the law';
- and it confirms that the Jerusalem church was a seething cauldron of suspi-

---

Mattathias (1 Macc. 2.19-27). On Saul the 'zealot' see further §25.2c above. Within a few years 'Zealot' was the name taken by the instigators of the revolt against Rome (Josephus, *War* 4.160-61), and though Luke uses it here of religious (and not military) zeal, its use nevertheless reflects the mounting nationalistic and political tension of these days; see also *Jesus Remembered* 272-73.

8. The term *apostasia* ('apostasy, defection') is often used in a political sense, 'rebellion' (e.g., Josephus, *Life* 43; *Ap.* 1.135-36; *Ant.* 13.219), but also of religious apostasy, especially in the LXX (Josh. 22.22; 2 Chron. 29.19; 33.19; Jer. 2.19; 1 Macc. 2.15) (H. Schlier, *TDNT* 1.513-14).

9. The account 'is perfectly trustworthy' (Bornkamm, *Paul* 99); 21.21 'gives reliable historical information about the possible consequences of Pauline preaching and praxis among Jews and about the reservations of the Jerusalem community over Paul' (Lüdemann, *Early Christianity* 236).

10. The rumour could have arisen from a prejudiced account of Paul's letter to the Galatian churches.

11. See vol. 3.

12. The report echoes the hyperbolic numbers of 2.41, 4.4, 5.14 and 6.7 (see above, §21 n. 78). But we need not doubt that the sect of the Nazarene had attracted and won substantial numbers of Jews, a point on which Jervell lays particular emphasis; his Festschrift (ed. D. Hellholm et al.) was entitled *Mighty Minorities? Minorities in Early Christianity* (Oslo: Scandinavian University Press, 1995), to mark what the editors regarded as Jervell's main challenge to NT scholarship in his 'Mighty Minorities?', *ST* 34 (1980) 13-38, reprinted in *The Unknown Paul: Essays on Luke-Acts and Early Christian History* (Minneapolis: Augsburg, 1984) 26-52.

cion regarding Paul, and probably of outright hostility ('zealots') to the opening of the gospel to the Gentiles.[13]

To this subject we will have to return in §36.1 below.

James himself, however, is presented consistently with his previous portrayal, as one willing or eager to seek compromise, a viable *modus vivendi* for both parties, which might hold both extremes together. As in 15.19-20, where the compromise offered was the terms of the 'apostolic decree',[14] here the compromise proffered by James and the elders is also carefully calibrated (21.22-24).[15] They do not themselves disown these rumours (21.22), or Luke has refrained from passing such information on. Instead they suggest that Paul should disprove the rumours by his own action, by showing that he himself still lived in observance of the law (21.23-24).[16] Obviously this was not the time to engage in theological debate on the role of the law for believers; passions needed to be cooled first. We may presume that it was such considerations which secured Paul's agreement; after all, he did not regard himself as an apostate or as one who had abandoned the law.[17] Here Paul shows himself as eirenic as James had in the earlier Jerusalem council (Gal. 2.9).

---

13. On the justification of the charge Haenchen provides an array of views (*Acts* 609 n. 2).

14. See above, §27.3e. The decree itself is recalled in 21.25. Some read the verse as though James was informing Paul of something new to him (e.g., Weiss, *Earliest Christianity* 5; Hahn, *Mission* 84-85; Hengel, *Acts* 117; Achtemeier, *Quest for Unity* 14-15, 32; Fitzmyer, *Acts* 694). But Luke could hardly have intended such a meaning (he had already shown Paul delivering the letter itself to his early foundations — 16.4). Nor does the text require us to read it that way (cf. Barrett, *Acts* 2.1014-15). Rather the repetition increases the sense that a formal statement was being made.

15. Brandon talked of Paul being 'trapped by James into compromising himself with his Gentile followers' (*The Fall of Jerusalem* xvi, 150-51). And Barrett speaks too hastily of 'the sham of James's proposal' (*Acts* 2.1000); but see the fuller discussion (1000-1001). In contrast, Pratscher warns against interpreting Luke's silence too negatively (*Herrenbruder* 95-100).

16. Porter deduces that the Jerusalem leadership shared the suspicions they voiced and that they took the opportunity to 'put Paul in his proper place as subordinate to the Jerusalem leaders' (*Paul of Acts* 175, 179-80, 185).

17. Similarly Porter, *Paul of Acts* 181-85. On Paul's own attitude to the law and customs see above, §33.3d(iv) and (v); also *Theology of Paul* §§6, 14, 23; also 'Paul, Apostate or Apostle?'; cf. Jervell, *Apg.* 529. Barrett is again unduly harsh: 'The question is whether Paul was prepared to use a special occasion such as the one described in order to suggest something that was not true, namely that he too was regularly observant of the Law as understood within Judaism. Readiness to do this is not covered by 1 Corinthians 9.' But his subsequent comment is more perceptive: 'Paul was in fact a Jewish Christian of a kind that could hardly continue to exist after the first generation — a fact that was not clearly seen by Luke' (*Acts* 2.1012-13).

The advice was that Paul should join with four men, presumably believing Jews, who were about to discharge a vow they had made, should go through the rite of purification with them, and should pay for the shaving of their heads (21.23-24). The vow in question was a Nazirite vow (Num. 6.1-21). The period of the vow having been completed, those involved could now shave their heads.[18] If Paul's vow at Cenchrea had anything of the same character (18.18) Paul would have been able to discharge it at the same time. But Luke says nothing of this. Alternatively the hope may have been that Paul would be willing to shoulder all the expenses of the Nazirites.[19] Certainly the process described follows the rules for the discharge of a Nazirite vow (21.26).[20] Even if Paul himself had not undertaken such a vow, or if the vow of 18.18 did not last so long,[21] the fact that he had returned from outside the holy land meant that he had to purify himself for seven days.[22] Where did Paul get the money necessary to pay for the men's expenses? Possibly from the unmentioned collection![23]

b. The Compromise Fails

When the process was almost complete (21.27),[24] disaster struck. Paul had been seen with Trophimus, who accompanied Paul from Corinth (20.4) and who, we deduce, must have been one of the commissioners appointed to take the collection to Jerusalem[25] — but Luke says nothing of this. Trophimus, a Gentile believer, had been seen in Paul's company in the city itself (21.29), but in the fe-

---

18. A purification is not part of the vow in Numbers 6 as such, but it was impossible to avoid being rendered impure in day-to-day life (as Num. 6.9 recognized), and the need for purification in order to participate in the cult was a standard feature of Israel's religion (see, e.g., Josephus, *War* 5.227, referring to the purity regulations of Leviticus 11–15 and Numbers 19).

19. Agrippa I seems to have done this a few years earlier (41), according to Josephus, *Ant.* 19.294.

20. Num. 6.13-15; 6.21 seems to envisage the payment of a further offering.

21. See above, §32.1c.

22. Haenchen, *Acts* 610 n. 3, 612; and further 611-12; Bruce, *Acts* 447; Hvalvik, 'Paul as a Jewish Believer' 141-43. The Nazirite vow was binding for thirty days (*m. Nazir* 6.3).

23. Hengel and Schwemer, *Paul* 255; Berger, *Theologiegeschichte* 162. Barrett envisages James announcing, 'perhaps to Paul's dismay, "We shall use part of this gift to pay the expenses of our four poor Nazirite brothers, and will do so in your name"' (*Acts* 2.1001).

24. The sequence is unclear: Paul's purification was already complete (21.26), so the incomplete purification of 21.27 presumably refers to that of the four men. As Lake and Cadbury suggest (*Beginnings* 4.274), it is possible that the different vows were completed over a sequence of days, so that Paul, as 'manager' of the group, would have entered the Temple more than once to announce, or 'notify' (Barrett, *Acts* 2.1016), the completion of the several vows.

25. See §33.4c above.

vered atmosphere of suspicion indicated in 21.21, it would have been hardly surprising that rumours quickly circulated (maliciously, no doubt, on the part of some) that Paul had taken Trophimus into the Temple, thus defiling the Temple with Gentile impurity.[26] The rumour could have been that Paul had broken the ultimate taboo, of taking Trophimus beyond the court of the Gentiles, through the barrier warning Gentiles of death if they passed beyond it, and into the court of Israel.[27] But even a rumour of Trophimus parading in the court of the Gentiles could have been a sufficient spark to ignite the fires of fear and anger which immediately erupted. That no thought was given to the possibility that Trophimus was a potential or even an actual proselyte, heralding the incoming of the Gentiles to Zion at the end of the age,[28] would again be consistent with a zealotic suspicion and commitment to defend Israel's holiness at any cost. Of course, the Jews from Asia (who make the accusation) are not identified as disciples, but the implication is that their attitude was little different from that of the 'zealots' among the Jerusalem disciples.

The marketplace gossip that Paul was 'teaching everyone everywhere against our people, our law and this place' (21.28) would certainly have created a highly charged atmosphere where almost any act of sacrilege could be attributed to Paul. The accusation itself strongly echoes that levelled against Stephen in 6.13 ('he speaks against this holy place and the law'); Paul sparked off opposition and hostility like that which brought about Stephen's martyrdom. The allusion will be deliberate on Luke's part. The additional factor here ('against the people') well echoes the zealot's determination to protect the boundaries separating Jew from Gentile at all costs.

The account of the riot is neatly drawn and quite plausible (21.30-36).[29] The crowd gathers, stirred more by passion and prejudice than by clear information. The object of its hostility is seized and dragged away from the sacred spot,

26. The default position of Jewish rulings on the subject was that Gentiles should be assumed to be defiled by unpurified corpse impurity and by idolatry *(m. 'Abod. Zar.);* see also Sanders, *Judaism* 72-76.

27. Notices fixed prominently on this fence — two of them have been discovered (see further Lake and Cadbury, *Beginnings* 4.274-75; Fitzmyer, *Acts* 698; Barrett, *Acts* 2.1020) — warned Gentiles that the penalty for breaching this barrier was death. This was virtually the only power of capital punishment which Judea retained. The fence, therefore, was a visible sign and symbol of Israel's obligation to keep itself apart from the nations (cf. Eph. 2.14) — the obligation which zealots were sworn to defend.

28. *Jesus Remembered* 394-95 (nn. 70, 71) But 'the (pilgrim) Jews from Asia' who started the riot (21.27) might have known Trophimus the Ephesian from earlier contact.

29. 'The many concrete details, often without clear meaning for the story's content, speak also more for a written source than for individual, oral reports. Luke has not only a source at his disposal, but possesses also private information, namely as a co-worker of Paul' (Jervell, *Apg.* 537).

out through the gates;[30] the Temple authorities take steps to ensure their property is protected.[31] The fortress Antonia abutted the northwest side of the Temple platform, with two stairs giving access directly on to it, so that in times of unrest a detachment of the local garrison could rapidly be deployed,[32] here led by the commander of the garrison troops himself. The cause of the trouble (Paul) was the obvious person to arrest — if only to calm the situation and to allow fuller inquiry. The information offered on the spot is inevitably confused (21.34); we can guess what one account was (21.28), but what was the other?! The cohort beats an orderly retreat, protecting their presumably injured prisoner from the mob's further violence and taking him back up the stairs.[33] The crowd is incensed at the loss of its prey. Luke knows how to tell a good story.

A moment of humour relieves the intensity of the drama. The tribune is surprised that Paul knows Greek (21.37). He had assumed, or had been informed, that the riot centred on an Egyptian 'who recently stirred up a revolt and led four thousand men of the sicarii out into the wilderness' (21.38). The Egyptian in question we know about also from Josephus.[34] A few years earlier an 'Egyptian false prophet' had led a crowd (Josephus says about 30,000) by a circuitous route from the desert to the Mount of Olives with the promise that they would be able to seize the city. They had been quickly dispersed (with many deaths) by vigorous action from the procurator Felix, but the Egyptian himself had escaped. Luke's information indicated a much smaller crowd (4,000) and characterized them as 'sicarii' ('dagger men'). This was the name given to those in the early days of the Jewish revolt (begun in 66) who used daggers *(sica, sikarion)* to assassinate their political opponents. Josephus indicates that the sicarii ('a new species of bandits') emerged during Felix's procuratorship, that is, during the 50s *(War* 2.254),[35] so the tribune's confusion on the matter is not implausible, and otherwise, the report shows good knowledge of the period.

Paul's reply gives information nowhere else available to us (21.39). He was not only a native of Tarsus (which we might have deduced from 9.30 and 11.25), but he had also been a citizen of that notable metropolis.[36] More to the point of Luke's account, Paul identifies himself as a Jew. He responds to the confusion regarding his identity (21.37) by taking his stand simply as a Jew. This self-

30. We should presumably assume that the gates in view were those to the inner courts, the Temple proper.

31. Cf. the account in *m. Sanh.* 9.6, cited in §25 at n. 113 above.

32. Josephus, *War* 5.243-44; Schürer, *History* 1.366.

33. But it is not necessary to conclude that Paul was badly injured (Barrett, *Acts* 2.1018, 1032-33; in response to Haenchen, *Acts* 618 and Weiser, *Apg.* 607).

34. Josephus, *War* 2.261-63; also *Ant.* 20.169-72.

35. See further Barrett, *Acts* 2.1025-26.

36. See above, §25.1b.

designation further undermines the impression which some have taken from Luke's references to the hostility of 'the Jews' elsewhere,[37] that Christian identity had become wholly divorced from Jewish identity. Here the leading proponent of Gentile Christianity identifies himself straightforwardly as (still) a Jew: Jewish and Christian identity still overlap and here merge in the person of Paul himself. Here too Luke's account reflects Paul's own self-understanding: he thought of himself more naturally as an 'Israelite' (Rom. 11.1; 2 Cor. 11.22), and though he was more circumspect in his use of 'Jew' in self-reference (1 Cor. 9.20), when he sought to build or maintain bridges with his more conservative fellow–believing Jews, he used it quite naturally of himself (Gal. 2.15).[38]

The closing scene is somewhat contrived: Paul, securely guarded on the steps rising above the Temple platform, is able to calm the howling mob, as the tribune and his cohort had failed to do (21.40). But Luke the story-teller relishes the drama of the scene he describes — Paul motioning with his hands, a great and expectant hush quieting the crowd, and Paul beginning to speak in his native Aramaic tongue.[39]

c. Paul's First Defence

For the second time Luke recounts Paul's conversion — this time from Paul's own lips (as also the third, in Acts 26),[40] his personal *apologia* (22.1). As before, the constant focal point of the speech remains the encounter between Jesus and Paul;[41] and the climax is the commissioning of Saul/Paul to take the gospel to the Gentiles.[42] But here there are two principal shifts in emphasis. The first is the emphasis on Paul's Jewish identity, training and zeal, as one who even after his conversion went naturally to the Temple to pray (22.3, 17), and on Ananias as 'a devout observer of the law' (22.12). The other is the way the speech passes over the element of commissioning early in the encounter[43] and leaves the commissioning till the subsequent vision of Paul in the Temple (22.17-21). Clearly Luke's intention was to make the commission to go to the Gentiles literally the climax of the

---

37. E.g., Acts 13.50; 17.5; 20.3, 19.

38. See above, §§25.1d, 29.2.

39. Paul was, of course, fluent in his native language (2 Cor. 11.22; Phil. 3.5). Bruce suggests the parallel of someone regarded as a traitor (by, e.g., Irish nationalists) being able to address a hostile crowd in the vernacular (*Acts* 454).

40. See the synoptic parallels in *Jesus Remembered* 212, and above, §25.3.

41. Acts 22.7-10; cf. 9.4-6 and 26.14-16.

42. Acts 22.15, 21; cf. 9.15-16 and 26.16-18, 23.

43. On the Damascus road encounter itself (26.16-18) or in the meeting with Ananias (9.15-16; contrast 22.15).

speech. And the dramatic reasoning behind this telling is equally obvious: it was the confirmation that this 'apostate' was so blatantly threatening Israel's set-apartness from the other nations, and thus undermining Israel's holiness as God's chosen people, which was bound to infuriate a nationalistic crowd.[44]

The handiwork of Luke is, as ever, very obvious.

- Luke sets the speech itself (22.1-21) in a framework, with 21.37-40 as preface and 22.22-29 as sequel, the former in which Paul identifies himself as a Jew (21.39), and the latter in which he identifies himself as a Roman citizen (22.25-28). Thus Paul in himself reflects the character of a Christianity which spans from Jerusalem to Rome.
- The speech begins with a reassertion by Paul that 'I am a Jew' (22.3) and climaxes in a vision of Jesus (22.17-18)[45] giving Paul the commission to go 'far away to the Gentiles' (22.21). This is precisely the tension which characterized the first beginnings of Christianity, in Acts as well as Paul's letters.
- Although a Jew of the diaspora (it was diaspora Jews who had started the trouble — 21.27), Paul had been brought up in Jerusalem itself, taught by one of the greatest rabbis of the time (Gamaliel) and educated 'strictly *(kata akribeian)* according to our ancestral law', a 'zealot *(zēlōtēs)*' for God (22.3). Paul spoke their language 'from inside'.
- Equally striking is the strong emphasis on Ananias's Jewish identity — 'a devout man according to the law and well spoken of by all the Jews living in Damascus' (22.12); on the Jewish character of Paul's commission to bear witness[46] for the Righteous One 'to every person' (22.14-15), with its echoes of Moses', Isaiah's, Jeremiah's and the Servant's commission;[47]

44. It is worth noting that it was this threat which infuriated the crowd, not the implied identification of Jesus as 'Lord' (22.19) in the role of 'the Lord' in Isa. 6.8 (see n. 47 below).

45. As in 10.10 and 11.5, Luke has no hesitation in describing it as a vision seen 'in ecstasy'; it is Luke's way of denying that the vision was contrived (Paul was not controlling things).

46. Acts 22.15 and 22.16 (as also Stephen — 22.20) are the only occasions on which Luke uses the term 'witness' of other than the apostles, with which it was otherwise tightly linked (1.8, 22; 2.32; 3.15; 5.32; 10.39, 41; also 13.31), and the closest he comes to conceding Paul's own fierce insistence that he was an apostle every bit as much as the earlier witnesses of the risen one (1 Cor. 9.1-2; 15.8-11; Gal. 1.1, 15-16).

47. First, Paul was appointed not simply to do but to know God's will (22.10, 14-15) — the aspiration of every pious Jew (Pss. 40.8; 143.10; 2 Macc. 1.3; Rom. 2.18).

Second, the one he saw was 'the righteous one' (22.14) — echoing the language particularly of Wis. 2.12-20 and 5.1-5.

Third, the one who appointed Paul was 'the God of our fathers' (21.14), as in 7.32 probably an allusion to the commissioning vision of Moses in Exod. 3.15.

Fourth, as with Isaiah, the vision takes place in the Temple (Isa. 6.1); as with Isaiah,

and not least on Paul's own continuing identification with the Temple (22.17), where he receives his commission to the nations (22.21).[48]

None of this will have been accidental. Luke was making a clear point by means of this section: Paul, and the movement he represents, shared a double character and a double loyalty. He (and it) were both Jewish, standing well within the traditions of his people, but also with rights and obligations within and to the wider world.[49] It was this twofold identity which caused all the problems now unfolding: fellow Jews who would not recognize the wider obligation as articulated by Paul; Roman authorities uncertain as to the continuing Jewish identity of Paul and what he represented. This is a theme Luke plays upon constantly in this and the following chapters, as Paul becomes a kind of shuttlecock batted back and forth between the two spheres; the physical to-ing and fro-ing of the main character in steadily clarifying the (contested) definition of Christianity's identity is the subplot being played out in these chapters.

Did Paul deliver this speech in these circumstances? The dramatic context sketched out by Luke is not at all so far-fetched as many assume. In a day when public oratory was the principal means of disseminating information and canvassing public support for policy, the tradition of crowds giving a hearing to speeches would be well established. As usual, Luke would feel no obligation either to provide a transcript of what Paul actually said or to refrain from recording any speech. In accordance with the conventions of historical writing of the day, it was enough for Luke and his readers that he could represent what Paul could or would have said on the occasion in question. The variation in the three accounts of Paul's conversion, reproduced by one and the same author, is itself a sufficient reminder both of the liberty Luke as an author evidently felt in retelling

---

Paul's first reaction is to confess his unfitness (Isa. 6.5; Acts 22.19-20); and like Isaiah, Paul is 'sent' and 'goes' (22.21) at the behest of 'the Lord' (Isa. 6.8). Most striking is the link provided to Luke's theme of Jewish rejection, already highlighted in 13.46-47 and 18.6, and foreshadowing the final word of 28.25-28, where the same passage is cited (Isa. 6.9-10). As with Isaiah, Paul is given the depressing information that his own people will not accept his testimony (22.18), but nevertheless, like Isaiah, he must continue to speak his message to his people (to Jew as well as Gentile; cf. 3.25, 13.47 and 26.18), as Paul in fact did, according to 28.17-24 and 30-31.

Finally, the mission was 'to the Gentiles' (22.21), echoing Jer. 1.5 and Isa. 49.6, though less clearly than in Paul's own words in Gal. 1.15-16.

48. The Lukan Paul is 'eager to admit that he still continued to pray in the Temple after his conversion'. 'The commission to bear witness "to the Gentiles" is thus conferred on Paul in the very heart of Judaism's religious cult, in the precincts of the Jerusalem Temple' (Fitzmyer, *Acts* 707, 708-709; see also Jervell, *Apg.* 545, 547).

49. Haenchen picks up only one side of the double point: for Luke 'there is no fundamental gulf between Judaism and Christianity, the continuity between the two is unbroken, and Christianity can claim to be tolerated like Judaism' (*Acts* 631).

the same story and of the fact that this was quite acceptable historiographical technique for the time.[50]

At the same time it should already be clear how closely Luke was able to stick to Paul's own agenda:

- the recollection of Paul's past as a Pharisee strict (see n. 144 below) and full of 'zeal' *(zēlos)* for God (Gal. 1.13-14; Phil. 3.5-6);
- the centrality of the encounter with Jesus on the approach to Damascus (1 Cor. 15.8); 'the brightness/glory *(doxa)* of the light' (22.11) ties in to Paul's own recollection of the event (2 Cor. 4.4-6);[51]
- Paul's insistence that he was every much a 'witness' (Luke's term) of the resurrected Jesus as the first apostles (1 Cor. 9.1-2; n. 46 above);
- his commission as very much in the character of the earlier commissionings of the prophets of Israel (Gal. 1.15-16; n. 47 above);
- above all, his commission to take the gospel of Jesus Messiah to the nations (Gal. 1.16; Rom. 1.5; 11.13).

As before, Luke's freedom in retelling the story in his own terms[52] can be regarded as quite acceptable in terms of historical narrative when the central theme of the retelling echoes so resonantly with Paul's own concerns in the matter. It is even possible that, following his three years in Arabia and Damascus (Gal. 1.17-18), Paul needed a further commissioning boost before embarking on his evangelistic work in Syria and Cilicia (Gal. 1.21-23) — one of the abundant revelations to which Paul confesses in 2 Cor. 12.6.[53]

d. The Sequel (Acts 22.22-29)

In the face of renewed uproar, the tribune has Paul taken into the barracks (the fortress Antonia at the top of the steps, overlooking the Temple area) for interrogation. In this sequel Luke continues to play off the mutual incomprehension of both Jew and Gentile as to who Paul was and what he was about. The crowd has heard Paul identify himself wholeheartedly with his ancestral religion but cannot accept his commission to go to the Gentiles. The centurion on the other hand has learned from his first mistake: Paul is a Jew (and not 'the Egyptian'). But now he

---

50. See above, §21.3; and here Barrett, *Acts* 2.1032-33.

51. See above, §25.3b.

52. Note, e.g., the link with the martyrdom of Stephen (7.58; 22.20).

53. Lüdemann's conclusion that 'Paul's vision in the temple is certainly unhistorical' is more 'certain' than any historian can be on such an issue (*Early Christianity* 240).

makes a second: he assumes that as a Jew Paul is no different from most other Jews and so can be subjected to the arbitrary punishments allowed under Roman law. And when informed that Paul is in fact a Roman citizen, he can hardly believe it (22.25-28). Luke dwells on the confusion at some length, since it is representative of his whole endeavour: to show that Paul is a typical and properly representative Christian; that is, a Jew through and through, but also a Roman citizen. As he spans two worlds, so the faith he represents can command a hearing in both worlds.

The procedure set in motion by the centurion was a common one — to interrogate a prisoner by means of physical torture (22.24-25).[54] And torture it would have been, since the Roman scourge was usually a flail with knotted cords, or possibly in a severe flagellation with pieces of metal or bone inserted into the leather straps.[55] Quite possibly it was the prospect of such a severe beating which caused Paul on this occasion to identify himself as a Roman citizen.[56] The point was that the law explicitly safeguarded Roman citizens from such arbitrary punishment (16.37).[57] The reaction of the tribune and those who had illegally tied Paul (22.29) is a fair reflection of the seriousness of what they had done as a breach of Roman law.

The interplay between centurion, tribune and Paul is a fine piece of storytelling: the tension builds as Paul is stretched out and tied securely at a whipping post or on a bench in preparation for the fearful scourging; the bombshell dropped by Paul and the incredulity and fear of the centurion and the tribune are vividly evoked; and finally the turning of the tables is highly effective — in contrast to the tribune's citizenship by purchase, Paul had been born a citizen (22.28).[58] But it serves Luke's point still more by underlining the depth of Paul's second identity, this time as a Roman citizen — something necessary, since the

---

54. 'To interrogate with scourging', i.e., the form of torture usual for non-Romans and slaves (Haenchen, _Acts_ 633). See also Rapske, _Paul in Roman Custody_ 139-40.

55. Illustrations in Rapske, _Paul in Roman Custody_ 447.

56. Unlike Acts 16.23, where the beating may have been relatively much less severe; see above, §31 at n. 70.

57. Interrogation of a Roman citizen by torture was forbidden by the Lex Porcia and the Lex Julia (details in Haenchen, _Acts_ 634 n. 4; see also Sherwin-White, _Roman Society_ 71-74; and §31 nn. 68, 73 above).

58. We know that Roman citizenship was sold during the reign of Claudius (Cassius Dio 60.17.5-7). 'The "great sum" which Lysias paid . . . was the bribe given to the intermediaries in the imperial secretariat or the provincial administration who put his name on the list of candidates for enfranchisement' (Sherwin-White, _Roman Society_ 154-55). On Paul's Roman citizenship, see above, §25.1c. Omerzu agrees that Paul's appeal to his Roman citizenship in the context of an interrogation by torture was part of the tradition on which Luke drew (_Prozess_ 379-80, 382).

emphasis on Paul's Jewish identity had been so thoroughly reinforced in the preceding paragraphs.

e. What Had Happened to the Collection?

In all this not a word is said by Luke about the collection, which had been Paul's primary motivation in coming to Jerusalem. Luke does allow the spotlight on Paul to include Trophimus briefly within its half-shadow (21.29), Trophimus, as we have seen, probably being one of the representatives of the churches in Asia charged with bringing the collection safely to Jerusalem. And later Luke has Paul mentioning that his purpose was to bring 'alms and offerings' to his nation (24.17).[59] It is typical of Luke to highlight these two actions, which were at the very heart of Jewish piety: as already noted, in the Judaism of the period 'almsgiving' was more or less synonymous with 'righteousness';[60] and in the context 'offerings' can hardly mean anything other than the means to offer sacrifices in the Temple. Luke, in other words, plays upon the ambiguity of the collection which we noted in §33.4e above. As so often, he presents Paul in the terms which more traditionalist Jewish believers who nevertheless sympathized with Paul's mission might have preferred. That is, he emphasizes Paul's continuing Jewishness — in this case his willingness to go along with a more traditionalist interpretation of such a substantial gift coming from Gentiles, such as James probably looked for in pressing the codicil of the concord achieved in Jerusalem (Gal 2.6-10), to 'remember the poor'.[61]

If so, the point is that Luke passes over the principal purpose which had been in Paul's mind: that the collection should serve as an outstretched hand to Jerusalem from the churches of the Pauline mission, an expression of gratitude, a living out of *koinōnia,* and a healing of the breach which had opened up between the Pauline churches and the mother church of Jerusalem.[62] More poignantly to

59. In view of Paul's description of the collection as a 'service' *(diakonia)* (see §33.4d above), an allusion to it in 21.19 in Paul's talk of his *diakonia* (albeit 'among the Gentiles') cannot be excluded. D. J. Downs, 'Paul's Collection and the Book of Acts Revisited', *NTS* 52 (2006) 50-70, argues that there is no direct reference or even allusion in Acts to the collection.

60. See §27 n. 189 above.

61. See again §§27.3d and 33.4e above. Taylor takes up the suggestion of Dibelius and others that the delivery of the collection is narrated in Acts 11.27-30, which Luke chose to include with the other Antioch material, leaving its outcome unclear (*Paul* 52 [bibliography in n. 5], 216-17). D.-A. Koch, 'Kollektenbericht, "Wir"-Bericht und Itinerar. Neue(?) Überlegungen zu einem alten Problem', *NTS* 45 (1999) 367-90, suggests that Luke's source may have included a statement of accounts of the collection delegation (378-81).

62. The contrast in terminology for the collection is striking — cf. particularly §33.4d above.

the point, by referring to the collection only in terms which the Jerusalem leadership could recognize and resonate with, Luke makes his silence regarding the outcome of Paul's collection all the more puzzling. If the collection permitted such a traditionalist interpretation, why did Luke not follow through the obvious inference by narrating how the collection was welcomed and accepted joyfully and with much gratitude?

Instead, there is nothing — complete silence — all the more painful from Paul's perspective, since he had invested so much time and effort in achieving the collection. So what did happen to it? What were the other delegates, like Trophimus or Aristarchus (27.2), doing all this while and during the unfolding drama of Paul's trials and imprisonment? Once again, silence, unrelieved and ominous. All we are left with are speculations: was Paul expected to use some of the collection in taking up the suggestion of James in 21.24? Later on, when we read that Governor Felix was hoping for a bribe from Paul (24.26), are we likewise to infer that Felix knew of this substantial sum of money (still in the hands of Paul's companions?) and hoped that Paul might use it to make the bribe? Or did Paul draw on the collection for his own support during the long months of imprisonment?[63]

Or should we infer, rather, that the acceptance of the collection was dependent in James's view on Paul proving his *bona fides* as a devout Jew (21.23-26), after which James would have been able to receive the collection understood in terms of the earlier agreement (Gal. 2.10)?[64] In which case, presumably, the failure of the compromise and the resultant riot would have made it virtually impossible for James to accept the collection; such acceptance would be too easily interpreted as James accepting the collection on *Paul's* terms, which would leave the Jerusalem leadership exposed to the outright hostility of the more extreme 'zealots'.[65] Or was the collection actually accepted out of public gaze, and the delegates (Gentiles all) encouraged to go home quietly?[66]

The whole issue remains obscure. And the obscurity is heightened by Luke's more or less exclusive focus on Paul. The delegates themselves would at

---

63. Ramsay finds such suggestions incredible and deduces that Paul must have been able to draw on resources from hereditary property (*St. Paul* 310-12).

64. This possibility I had suggested earlier (*Unity and Diversity* [²1990] 257, [³2006] 277-78); similarly Bauckham, 'James and the Jerusalem Church' 479; see further Murphy-O'Connor, *Paul* 348-51; Joubert, *Paul as Benefactor* ch. 6. Schnabel treats the issue far too casually (*Mission* 1001-2).

65. Cf. Haenchen, *Acts* 613-14; Jervell, *Apg.* 529-30.

66. Georgi suggests that it 'was received as if "on the side", accompanied by whispers; quite a blow to the delegation', hence Luke's silence on the subject (*Remembering* 126); cf. Wehnert, *Reinheit* 271. F. W. Horn, 'Die letzte Jerusalemreise des Paulus', in Horn, ed., *Ende* 15-35, justifiably warns against posing the straight alternative of either acceptance or rejection as possibly too simple (34).

best have had to remain in hiding, since their active presence in Jerusalem could only exacerbate the suspicions regarding Paul. Perhaps they withdrew from Jerusalem itself and were able to send in supplies by a neutral intermediary (using the collection money?) to one who now needed such financial support as much as any of the 'poor'. Or possibly they left the money with some banker, or through such a one, deposited in the Temple, in the hope that once the crisis was over, it could be properly delivered and its resources drawn on for the intended 'poor among the saints in Jerusalem'.

Given, however, Luke's total silence regarding any support given to Paul by the Jerusalem leadership in the following chapters, and equally total silence about the outcome of the collection, it is hard to shake off the suspicion that the collection was *not* welcomed and possibly not even received by the Jerusalem church — as Paul had feared might be the case (Rom. 15.31) — so deep was the antipathy which had grown up in Jerusalem and in the Jerusalem church itself towards Paul in the meantime, of which 21.20-21, 27-28 is probably a fair reflection.[67] In which case, this was another example of internal dissension within the new churches over which Luke has chosen to draw a veil.[68] Worse still, it would mean that the strategy in which Paul had invested so much of himself, in a supreme effort to hold the churches of the Pauline mission together with the churches of Palestine, had failed![69] The politics of church and state in Jerusalem had made such a rapprochement impossible to achieve. For all that he had achieved in the Aegean mission (and subsequently in the influence wrought by his letters), this climactic attempt to maintain the oneness of gospel and church, from Jerusalem to Illyricum, Rome and beyond, proved to be in vain. Perhaps in more peaceful times Paul could have succeeded, but in the circumstances of the late 50s the breach could not be healed. Since Luke could not end his story of Paul and the Jerusalem church on a high note, he evidently decided to draw a veil of silence over the whole, focusing the spotlight so intently on Paul as to prevent his readers from seeing anything more of the Jerusalem church.

34.2. Trials and Tribulations

The narrative from Acts 22.30 through 26.32 is somewhat frustrating for the historian, the sequence of events being recorded, in contrast to all the previous se-

---

67. Lüdemann, *Opposition* 59-62; Becker, *Paul* 455-57. The older interpretation that the collection was welcomed is still maintained by Nickle, *Collection* 70-72.

68. As in Acts 6.1-6, 8.1-4 and 15.36-41.

69. We must return to the question of the impact on the Pauline churches of such a rejection in vol. 3.

quences, in laborious and long-winded detail.[70] But of course Luke was not writing for the historian. He was telling the story of Christianity's beginnings as a good story-teller would. The laboured detail and several repetitions have the effect of almost mesmerizing the listener and of slowly winding up the dramatic tension until its amazing climax in 26.28-29, when King Agrippa speaks (in effect) with the voice of the intended listener to Luke's story. Agrippa has, as it were, to shake himself free of the mesmerizing effect of Paul's testimony/Luke's story, so powerful has become the appeal of the faith Paul proclaims. And Paul's reply, 'I pray to God, that whether in a short or a long time, not only you but also all who hear me today would become such as I am' (26.29), no doubt has in view not only those within the narrative but also those caught up in listening to its being read to them.

a. The Hearing before the Jewish Council (Acts 22.30–23.11)

For the third time in successive chapters Luke sets out a contrast between Jewish hostility and Roman protection. The two preceding examples were part of the same episode, where Paul was attacked by and defended himself against the Jerusalem mob. But at Roman insistence (22.30) the next stage was naturally to have Paul confront his peers in a hearing before a council of Jewish leaders, presided over by the high priest. Here will be clarified, the tribune hopes (22.30; 23.28), the issue of whether Paul was acting on behalf of or against his people. Luke also effectively indicates the power of Rome vis-à-vis the Jewish authorities.[71] The tribune, identified as Claudius Lysias in 23.26, has the authority (no doubt in the name of the procurator) to summon the leading Jews in a sanhedrin/council,[72] not to try Paul as though he fell within their jurisdiction, but for them to elucidate Paul's status and the facts behind the riot in the Temple court. The issue is still, What is the real identity of Paul and of the movement he represents?

    The hearing makes no progress whatsoever. Paul starts by attesting his clear

---

70. E.g., Barrett notes with regard to 23.12-35 that 'Luke's main story would have been adequately served if he had written: The tribune, hearing of a plot against Paul's life, sent him by night and under guard to Caesarea' (*Acts* 2.1071).

71. As usual the simple reference to 'the Jews' allows the inference that Luke was setting the Jewish nation as a whole over against Christianity. But that hardly makes sense of his repeated emphasis in these two chapters on Paul's own Jewish identity. And on Roman lips, an indiscriminate reference to 'the Jews' would hardly be surprising.

72. As usual (see *Jesus Remembered* 271 n. 75), 'the sanhedrin' would be more accurately described as a council of leading Jews convened to consider a particular issue put before them of potential national importance.

conscience before God (23.1).[73] And the high priest[74] immediately orders those close to Paul to strike him on the mouth (23.2). Why he should take offence at Paul's opening sentence is not clear. Possibly the use of Greek (language and/or conceptions) was offensive in the circumstances, or even Paul's mention of God, or that he spoke without awaiting an invitation/direction to do so. Paul's claim to have a clear conscience in itself would hardly merit such a response. But hostility towards one whom the high priest no doubt already regarded as a renegade Pharisee could help explain what would have been an unjustified and peremptory act.

Paul responds in angry and equally peremptory fashion (23.3).[75] To call down God's judgment on the high priest and to call him a 'white-washed wall'[76] was a devastating denunciation of such a powerful figure.[77] Paul's apology when rebuked (23.4) is at best ambiguous and probably sarcastic: 'I did not realize that he was high priest' (23.5).[78] The Scripture cited by Paul — 'You shall not speak evil of a leader of your people' (Exod. 22.28) — certainly has something of a sarcastic ring, since whoever was president of the council would be 'a ruler of the people'. The irony is deepened since the high priest was acting illegally in calling for the punishment of one who had not yet been tried or found guilty,[79] whereas it is Paul who cites the law in accusing the high priest of breaching it: Paul is more law-abiding than the high priest!

73. Did Luke envisage Paul addressing the council in Aramaic (Luke does not say so) or Greek (with an eye to the tribune and his soldiers nearby — 22.30 and 23.10)? The question has some point here, since Paul starts by attesting his 'good conscience', a conception (conscience) lacking in Hebrew, and only recently acceptable as good Greek (see, e.g., Bruce, *Acts* 463-64). Does this betray Luke's later perspective? The introduction is certainly Pauline (cf. Rom. 9.1; 2 Cor. 1.12; 2 Tim. 1.3), but less appropriate here (in front of the Jewish assembly) than in 24.16.

74. Ananias, son of Nedebaeus, was high priest from about 47 to 58; this fits with the chronology of Paul's final visit to Jerusalem probably in 57 (§28.1). He had been sent to Rome by the governor of Syria in 52 under suspicion of involvement in disturbances between Jews and Samaritans, but pleas on behalf of the Jews by Agrippa II had been effective in securing his acquittal (Josephus, *War* 2.232-46; *Ant.* 20.118-36). The affair will have done him no harm in the eyes of his own people, and he was then probably at the height of his power, remembered subsequently for his wealth and influence, both of which he retained even after he was replaced as high priest. See further Hemer, *Book of Acts* 170-71.

75. The contrast with Jesus' demeanour in Luke 23 is striking.

76. Paul's response seems to be a mixture of allusion to Deut. 28.22 (God's punitive 'strike' against Israel's disobedience) and Ezek. 13.10-15 (whitewash obscuring the weaknesses of a wall ready to collapse; cf. Matt. 23.27); the Qumran sectarians made the same sort of allusion to Ezek. 13.10 in their criticism of the Jewish leadership — 'those who build the wall and cover it with whitewash' (CD 8.12).

77. Ananias may already have used his wealth to support his political manoeuvering; he was murdered at the outbreak of the Jewish revolt a few years later (66) (Josephus, *War* 2.441-42).

78. On the range of possible interpretations of this utterance, see Barrett, *Acts* 2.1061-62.

79. Cf. Lev. 19.15; John 7.51.

Thereafter Paul, apparently assuming that he has little chance of a fair hearing, plays the factional card. The council is composed of both Sadducees and Pharisees, who disagreed on whether there would be a resurrection of the dead. Paul seizes this wedge between Pharisees and the high priestly party, already evident in the early days of the beginning of the way (5.33-39), and drives it deeper. He speaks as a Pharisee[80] and is able to claim that the whole issue of the validity of the new movement boils down to the question of 'the hope of the resurrection of the dead' (23.6).[81] Here is one somewhat drastic way to defend and maintain a continuing Jewish identity, that is, by siding with one faction within Second Temple Judaism over against another.[82] The tactic succeeds to the extent that Paul wins support from his (erstwhile) fellow Pharisees, but at the cost of the whole council degenerating into violent argument (23.7-9). The tribune, fearing that Paul might be torn apart by the factions, intervenes for the third time and rescues Paul once more (23.10). A further vision strengthens Paul's hand in the course he has taken: he would bear witness in Rome (23.11).[83]

In regard to the hearing itself, Luke evidently wanted those who received his account to infer that Paul had concluded that the hearing gave no prospect of reconciliation between the two ends of the spectrum there facing each other — the official guardians of Israel's cult and Torah, and Paul representing the Nazarene sect's outreach into the ranks of Gentile proselytes and God-fearers. The breach was deep, the hostility sharp. The question left hanging, however, is whether rapprochement was still possible between those whose position was nearer to the middle of the spectrum — the Pharisees, who also believe in the resurrection of the dead, and some of whose members were also believers (15.5), and the thousands of believers still zealots for the law (21.20), whose absence

80. By 'son of Pharisee' Paul may refer to his being a disciple of Gamaliel (22.3; cf. 1 Cor. 4.17; 1 Tim. 1.2; 2 Tim. 1.2); see above, §25 n. 60.

81. The Pharisees had embraced the still fairly recent view (only a couple of centuries old) that beyond death the faithful (or all human beings) could expect resurrection (see *Jesus Remembered* 396 n. 83, 821-23). The Sadducees, on the other hand, were conservative in their beliefs and practices (as so often with the ruling class in a society); if it was not in the Torah, then it should not or need not be embraced (Josephus, *Ant.* 18.16). Excluded on this criteria was not only belief in the resurrection but also interest in the burgeoning hierarchy of angels and spirits which was also a feature of the intertestamental period (Bruce, *Acts* 466); hence the consideration of Acts 23.8-9 (on which see Fitzmyer, *Acts* 719; Barrett, *Acts* 2.1065-66; F. Parker, 'The Terms "Angel" and "Spirit" in Acts 23,8', *Biblica* 84 [2003] 344-65).

82. The concerns over the justification for this line of defence (noted by Barrett, *Acts* 2.1064) make too little allowance both for the exigencies of the situation portrayed or for the dramatic license which Luke permitted himself (see also Haenchen, *Acts* 638).

83. The motif occurs also in 18.9-10 and 27.23-24; the assurance that Paul would reach Rome agrees with Paul's own hopes on the subject (Rom. 1.10-13; 15.24, 28-29, 32), which probably were sustained by such visions.

from the whole affair has an ominous ring. The question, in other words, remains hanging whether the breach is between Judaism and what was to become 'Christianity', or more accurately between different factions within the religion of the Jews, or even between Jewish-Christianity and Paul![84]

As ever, we cannot be sure that such a confrontation did take place in just these terms. Luke could well have had good firsthand reports to draw on here, and the events described, though surprising, are hardly implausible.[85] Paul's identification of himself as a Pharisee accords with Phil 3.5, and he shared Luke's conviction that the resurrection of Jesus was absolutely central to Christian faith.[86] Perhaps more to the point, whatever the finer details, Luke's portrayal has certainly hit the nerve of Jewish factionalism of the period,[87] and of earliest Christianity's role within that factionalism.

b. The Plot against Paul and Its Sequel (Acts 23.12-35)

Luke does not allow the dramatic tension to slacken one whit. Now 'the Jews', or at least a die-hard group of Jews (more than forty in number), plot to assassinate Paul (23.12-13),[88] and involve the same alliance of hostile authorities ('high

84. In Luke's own day the point would be the basis of any possible rapprochement between Christians and Pharisees (by then the only surviving and dominant party within a Judaism recovering from the failure of the 66-70/73 revolt). This assertion of common ground of shared hope becomes a repeated feature of the final chapters of Acts (24.15; 26.6-8; 28.20).

85. Baur's comment — 'we can scarcely imagine that a single expression undesignedly let fall by the Apostle regarding the resurrection could have kindled so fierce a fire' (*Paul* 216) — shows how little even he knew of the intensity which religious factionalism could occasion. Weiss is similarly sceptical (*Earliest Christianity* 374 n. 108); and Becker — that the Pharisees would form a common front with Paul against the Sadducees is 'already a glaring distortion of historical truth' (*Paul* 453). In contrast, Barrett, *Acts* 2.1053-55, is justifiably critical of Haenchen's nit-picking scepticism (*Acts* 639-43). Similarly Fitzmyer, *Acts* 715-17, with reference to Weiser, *Apg.* 615. See also Lüdemann, *Early Christianity* 245-56. Omerzu concludes that the account is not traditional and goes back entirely to Luke (*Prozess* 395-96).

86. E.g., Rom. 10.9; 1 Cor. 15.14, 17.

87. Haenchen, e.g., shows no appreciation of the factionalism inherent in the 'zeal' referred to in Acts 21.21 and 22.3; and on Paul's assertion that he is a Pharisee (23.6), he rashly pronounces, 'No proof should really be necessary that here it is not the historical Paul who speaks' (*Acts* 641, 643). Hvalvik fairly responds: 'It is hardly inconceivable that the historical Paul could have said, "With regard to the resurrection, I am a Pharisee"' ('Paul as a Jewish Believer' 150).

88. Whether those in view could have been called 'sicarii', those who assassinated political opponents with knives (see above, at n. 35), is not clear; Luke does not use the term here. But as already noted, according to Josephus the sicarii began to operate during the governorship of Felix (*War* 2.254). We can readily imagine, therefore, a group of Jews dedicated to the cause of

priests and elders') that opposed Peter and John initially (4.5, 8, 23) in complicity (23.14). The plot was simple: to ask the tribune for a further hearing, on the way to which Paul would have been assassinated (23.15).[89] In this way the contrast between Jewish hostility to Paul and Roman protection for Paul can be still more sharply drawn. More to the larger point, within Luke's overarching scheme this is the climax of Jewish hostility to Paul; from this point onwards Jewish hostility and its effectiveness steadily diminish.

Within Luke's larger scheme, it is also striking that the only one who rallies to Paul's support from within his own community is one who belongs to his own immediate family circle (his nephew).[90] The young man hears of the plot, gains entrance to the barracks where Paul was being held, and tells Paul (23.16). How the nephew learned of the plot Luke does not say; the story-teller prefers to leave such details to the audience's imagination. The fact that the nephew had free access (as a relative) to Paul in custody[91] renders all the more eloquent Luke's silence regarding any other visitors who supported him. Paul in turn sends him to inform the tribune of the plot (23.17-21).[92] Significantly, it is to the Romans that he turns: there is no help to be looked for within Judaism or even the Jerusalem church. Paul's isolation is complete; he depends wholly on Roman protection. The tribune responds immediately by having Paul taken under heavy escort (about half the Jerusalem garrison!)[93] to the governor (Felix) in

---

Israel maintaining its national identity in clear distinction from Roman interference and the corruption of Greek influences. Such a group could both regard Paul as a traitor (21.21, 28) and be willing to take the most extreme measures to remove him. We may refer to Josephus's report that Felix bribed the high priest Jonathan's most trusted friend 'to bring in the brigands to attack Jonathan and kill him' (*Ant.* 20.163; *War* 2.256 attributes the murder to sicarii). The episode here, therefore, does not lack in historical plausibility, however dramatic Luke's retelling of it.

89. Luke no doubt would intend his readers to indulge in some dark humour at the thought of the plotters having condemned themselves to death by the failure of their plot; the Greek says literally 'put themselves under an anathema', that is, committed themselves to destruction (Deut. 13.15; 20.17; Josh. 6.21; etc.) if they did not succeed in their enterprise. Hence, presumably, the repeated reference to the vow not to eat till Paul was dead (23.12, 14, 21), just in case the reader or listener missed the point.

90. This is the first we hear of Paul having relatives in Jerusalem. But why not? With whom had he stayed when he first came to Jerusalem as a student? Luke's technique is only to introduce such characters as and when the story-line requires it.

91. 'Paul was as much in protective custody at this point as he was a remand prisoner' (Rapske, *Paul in Roman Custody* 149).

92. The full report of the plot in 23.16-21 has the same purpose and effect as the repetition of 10.1–11.18 — to add weight to the episode, here by highlighting the sharp contrast between 'the Jews' on the one side and Paul in his almost complete isolation within his own people on the other.

93. Details in Barrett, *Acts* 2.1078; on the size of the Roman garrison in Jerusalem see *NDIEC* 6.159-61; on the plausibility of such a heavy escort, see Rapske, *Paul in Roman Cus-*

his headquarters in Caesarea, with a letter further rehearsing the situation and his finding that Paul was guilty of no serious charge;[94] it was all a matter of internal Jewish disagreement (23.22-30). The overnight transfer to the 'praetorium' in Caesarea[95] is successful, and the governor prepares for a formal hearing (23.31-35).

In all this it is surprising, we might think, that there is no mention of the brothers or the disciples or the believers rallying round Paul or involved in representations on his behalf. The tensions within the Jewish community are evidently reflected in the tensions within the sect of the Nazarene (cf. 6.1–8.2).[96] Why would Luke omit such a notice when it would have strengthened the sense of a Jesus movement united in brotherly concern? The upshot, once again, is to highlight the protective role of the Roman tribune. And Luke takes the opportunity to underline the Gallio ruling (18.14-15): that the complaints made by Jewish authorities against Paul (and his mission) were purely internal matters, an entirely Jewish affair, and of no interest to the Roman overlords. Here again, of course, we have no way of corroborating Luke's account. All we can say is that the detail and the circumstances are entirely plausible for the time.[97] And as someone who was in Caesarea for some of the time (27.1, 'we'), Luke may have had contacts

---

tody 153-55. Since Antipatris is too far (some forty miles) for a single day's march, the reference to traveling 'during the night' (23.31) could imply an extended day's march which reached its destination only late at night. The main body of the escort with Paul could then return (23.32), since the area of greatest danger had been left behind.

94. As with the speeches, Luke would feel free to compose a letter with terms and sentiments which he thought to be appropriate and which reflected the generally favourable attitude towards Paul on the part of the Roman authorities during this whole period. The letter is written in proper, formal style, giving the name of the sender, the intended recipient with his title as a superior official ('most excellent/Excellency'), and the appropriate greeting. That an inferior Roman official might well refer a potentially explosive issue to his superior, to avoid responsibility if things went wrong, is wholly understandable; the younger Pliny is known to us because as the emperor's administrator or legate in Bithynia from 110 AD, he kept writing to Emperor Trajan for advice on such tricky questions. It is also hardly surprising that the commander of the Jerusalem garrison, Claudius Lysias, comes over as one ready to bend the truth and to present himself in the most favourable light (rescuing Paul because he was a Roman citizen); the representation would hardly be unfair to the tribune. On Lysias's action see further Sherwin-White, *Roman Society* 54-55.

95. The 'praetorium' was the official residence of a provincial governor. Here it refers to the palace which Herod the Great had built for himself, and which now evidently served also as the procurator's military headquarters and garrison. See further Rapske, *Paul in Roman Custody* 155-58.

96. 'It is reasonable to guess that during his two years of trial and imprisonment in Palestine they [the Jerusalem leaders] preferred to sever relations with him to prevent the sect as a whole becoming involved in the issue' (Judge, 'Early Christians' 14).

97. Here, as elsewhere, Barrett's (*Acts* 2.1070-71) and Jervell's (*Apg.* 565) comments are eminently sensible; see also Omerzu, *Prozess* 398-420.

within the Roman garrison there who could keep him informed of events as they had unfolded.

c. On Trial before Governor Felix (Acts 24.1-27)

The trial before Governor Felix,[98] which Luke now recounts, is the first and only trial proper, as is confirmed by the regularly recurring legal terminology.[99] That the case against Paul was given a formal hearing would have had to be assumed even if Luke had said nothing of it, so we can be confident that he draws here on good tradition and possibly eyewitness reports or reminiscences.[100] At the same time, Luke was also evidently aware of the rhetorical style and flourishes which characterized such set pieces and introduces both the brief prosecution speech (24.2-4)[101] and the speech for the defence (24.10-11) accordingly.[102] The account indicates how much the control of affairs had slipped from Jewish hands. High Priest Ananias now comes down to Caesarea as a petitioner rather than as

---

98. Unusually, Felix had been a slave who had been freed by Emperor Claudius; but he seems to have been a favourite of the emperor, and Claudius was known for giving too much power to freedmen. He was procurator of Palestine from 52/53-59/60, a period of growing unrest (the Jewish revolt broke out in 66), for which his maladministration was blamed (see further Schürer, *History* 1.460-66). His servile origins will not have helped when opinion turned against him at court; Tacitus summed him up in one of the better one-liners of the period: 'he exercised the power of a king with the spirit of a slave' (*Hist.* 5.9). See further D. W. J. Gill, 'Acts and Roman Policy in Judaea', *BAFCS* 4.15-26 (here 21-25).

99. Acts 24.1, 2, 8, 10, 13, 14, 19, 20, 22.

100. The names — Ananias and Tertullus (otherwise unknown to us) — are usually taken as demonstrating Luke's reliance on tradition, and the representation of Felix is certainly in character (cf., e.g., Lüdemann, *Early Christianity* 249-50; Jervell, *Apg.* 573-74). Sherwin-White quotes Mommsen's judgment that the narrative was 'an exemplary account of the provincial penal procedure *extra ordinem*' (similarly Tajra, *Trial* 115, with reference to both Paul's appearances before the governors Felix and Festus) and concludes for himself, 'The account of the trial before Festus and Felix is sufficiently accurate in all its details' (*Roman Society* 48, 68; see further 48-53). See further Omerzu, *Prozess* 422-56.

101. Particularly the flattering introduction and address, 'Your Excellency' (24.2), the note of respectful gratitude for favours received (24.3), the promise to be brief and the request for a hearing 'with your (customary) graciousness' (24.4).

102. The speeches are so conventional, they summarily rehearse previous episodes, and they serve to advance Luke's own agenda (Christianity as a legitimate Jewish sect; see particularly 24.14-15), that the hand of Lukan construction can hardly be denied (did the prosecution speech indeed last for only eleven lines?); see, e.g., Jervell, *Apg.* 573 and those cited by him (n. 241). The one feature which suggests that Luke may have been drawing on some recollection of the events is the allusion to Paul's purpose in coming to Jerusalem, namely, to deliver the collection (24.17).

president of the court, with only 'some elders' in attendance. And the case now rests in the hands of a professional spokesman ('rhetor') — Tertullus. The Latin name need not imply that he was not himself a Jew, but Luke makes no attempt to bring out the point either way.[103]

The first two points of accusation use the image of pestilence and riot: 'this man is a source of disease, a plague carrier'; 'he foments discord/strife/rebellion' (24.5). Two more frightening prospects could not be put before the governor of a province.[104] The intention would be to throw as much mud as possible at 'the sect of the Nazarenes'. The accusation is directed against Paul as such, but no attempt is made to exculpate the other Nazarenes from the implication that the dangers were posed by Paul in his role as ringleader of the sect.[105] A specific charge of desecrating the Temple (24.6) summarizes the initial accusation (21.28); it is not so important for the story-telling that the charge needed to be spelled out more fully.[106]

In Luke's presentation, Paul shows himself equally familiar with the conventions of formal rhetoric and well able to perform accordingly: 'I cheerfully make my defence, knowing that for many years you have been a judge over this nation' (24.10). Such an expression of confidence in Felix's judgment need not have been entirely misplaced: Felix's marriage to Drusilla (24.24) would have given him an unusual degree of knowledge of Jewish affairs;[107] and in other cases he seems to have been amenable to sensible argument.[108] Paul's response (24.11) both underlines his traditional piety (he had come up to Jerusalem to

103. See further Barrett, *Acts* 2.1093-94.

104. 'The charge was precisely the one to bring against a Jew during the Principate of Claudius or the early years of Nero' (Sherwin-White, *Roman Society* 51).

105. The reader is expected to recall such episodes as 15.2, 17.5-8, 18.12-17, 19.23-41 and 21.27-36.

106. The Western text includes reference to the part played by Claudius Lysias (24.6c-8a), but the verses are generally regarded as a later elaboration (Metzger, *Textual Commentary* 490).

107. Drusilla was the youngest daughter of Herod Agrippa I. According to Josephus, she was born in 37/38 and married Azizus, king of Syrian Emesa, in 53. She had previously been betrothed to Epiphanes, son of Antiochus, king of Commagene, but he 'had rejected the marriage since he was not willing to convert to the Jewish religion'. And the marriage to Azizus went ahead only after he had consented to be circumcised (*Ant.* 20.139). She is said to have been very beautiful, and Felix was able to persuade her to leave Azizus and to marry him instead (*Ant.* 20.141-44). The reports are thus conflicting: how much did the insistence on conversion and circumcision reflect Drusilla's own views (she was still less than twenty years old when she married Felix)? And was her abuse of traditional Jewish marriage law an aberration or characteristic (there was presumably no question of Felix being circumcised)? The fact that Luke bothers to mention her here suggests that he saw her presence as some kind of confirmation that the Jewish character of Paul's message was recognized by Felix.

108. Josephus, *Ant.* 20.178.

worship) and shows the unreality of the charge of trouble-making: he had been in Jerusalem for only twelve days — hardly time to foment a rebellion![109] The reply accords both with Paul's own stated policy of conduct within Jewish contexts (1 Cor. 9.20) and with the low-key policy advocated by James and followed by Paul in 21.23-26.[110]

Paul goes on to 'confess' (24.14) that the accused 'sect' worships 'the ancestral God' in accordance with the Scriptures, and that they share the same hope of resurrection, of both just and unjust (24.15).[111] Paul meets the exaggerations of the prosecution (24.5-6) with his own exaggeration: Ananias, as a Sadducee, did *not* believe in the resurrection; and only those among the elders who were Pharisees would have done so (23.8). But the exaggeration serves primarily, and not unfairly, to underline the chief point (for both Paul and Luke): that the Jesus sect was as consistently traditional in worship and as thoroughgoingly scriptural in belief as any other section of the Jewish people. Particularly notable is the theocentric focus of the confession: 'I worship our ancestral God . . . having hope in God' (24.14-15).

Paul's traditional piety is further stressed: he endeavoured always to have a clear conscience not only towards God but also towards people generally (including his fellow Jews) (24.16); he had come to bring alms to his people and to offer sacrifices (24.17); when the trouble began in the Temple, he had been completing the rites of purification (24.18). The only possible ground of accusation against him was his affirmation of belief in the resurrection of the dead (24.19-21).[112] Luke (and Paul) continue to insist on the substantial overlap and direct continuity between Christianity and the ancestral faith of Israel.[113] He was no renegade or apostate careless of Israel's founding principles and continuing priorities.

In response Felix adjourns the case and rules that Paul should be kept in liberal custody until the tribune Lysias came down from Jerusalem.[114] Luke says that Felix had 'a more accurate knowledge of the things concerning the Way'.

---

109. On the reckoning of the twelve days see Bruce, *Acts* 478, and Barrett, *Acts* 2.1102-3.

110. Acts 24.12 is interesting, since it indicates that there were several synagogues, or gathering places (for different interest groups or nationalities), within the city (cf. 6.9).

111. Cf. Dan. 12.2; John 5.28-29; Rev. 20.12-15.

112. There was no one to speak to the charge arising from the riot in the Temple (24.19); Sherwin-White notes that 'Roman law was very strong against accusers who abandoned their charges' (*Roman Society* 52).

113. Haenchen, *Acts* 658-59.

114. The ruling was that his friends (*hoi idioi*, his own people) should not be prevented from attending to him (see further Rapske, *Paul in Roman Custody* 171-72; Barrett, *Acts* 2.1113); this was the chance for Luke to report the local Christians' solidarity with and provision for Paul, but he only alludes to it.

The claim is somewhat surprising, though Luke's reference to 'the Way' rather than 'the sect of the Nazarenes' (24.5) could suggest that Felix had indeed some knowledge of the Jesus movement. An effective procurator would have agents and spies everywhere. But having a Jewish wife, Drusilla (24.24), would have given him an insight into national politics unusual among his predecessors. In which case, he did not really need a fuller report from Lysias, and the reason for the adjournment was simply an excuse (Luke certainly does not follow up the point in his account).

One of the most intriguing episodes in Luke's narrative is his account of Felix's private interviews with Paul during the days following (24.24-25). The descriptions of the subject of their conversations are interesting. 'Faith in Christ Jesus' would be the agenda as perceived by both Paul and Luke;[115] Paul sought to convert the procurator. 'Righteousness, self-control and coming judgment', on the other hand, evoke something of the character of a philosophical debate. 'Righteousness', to be sure, is a thoroughly and almost distinctively Jewish term, in its usage as denoting fulfilment of the obligations placed on the individual by membership of a people or a covenant;[116] but in Greek thought it would be comprehensible in the more abstract sense of 'justice'. The case is quite the opposite with the second item, 'self-control', for that occurs frequently in Greek thought and seldom in LXX and NT.[117] In the former it is a key term as an ideal of philosophical ethics — self-control in regard to all human desires (including food, drink and sex). On the other hand, 'coming judgment' (not final judgment) would be familiar within both circles of thought.[118] Either way, Luke portrays Paul as 'getting through' to Felix. Felix's response — to delay and put off the vital existential choice, between fleeting political power (he was deposed within two years) and a settled faith with its resulting self-discipline — makes him the unenviable paradigm of the temporizer.[119]

This pattern of events (frequent private conversations) continued for two years, Luke indicating his confident suspicion that Felix was hoping for a bribe

---

115. See, e.g., 11.24; 15.9; 20.21; Rom. 1.17; 3.22; Gal. 2.16.

116. See above, §33 n. 90.

117. E.g., Sir. 18.30; 1 Cor. 7.9; Gal. 5.23. Stowers argues that Romans is greatly concerned with the problem of self-mastery (*Rereading of Romans* ch. 2), though the references to 5.3-4, 7.18 and 12.3 (45, 73, 82) hardly make a convincing case.

118. In the OT cf., e.g., Isa. 13.6-16; Joel 2.1-2; Zeph. 1.14–2.3.

119. The portrayal of Felix as giving private hearings to Paul is a nice story-line, and not implausible. But the parallel with the encounter between Herod Antipas and John the Baptist is striking (both rulers stole other men's wives; and cf. particularly Mark 6.20), and Luke's omission of the Mark 6 tradition in his own Gospel may be a further example of his readiness to delay the impact of certain episodes till his second volume (see above, §21.2d). See also Mason, *Josephus* 176-77.

(24.26). Such an attitude on the part of Felix would have been quite in character.[120] As already noted, according to Josephus, Felix bribed the most trusted friend of Jonathan the high priest to arrange for Jonathan's murder by the *sicarii*.[121] And in any event it would be unusual for highly placed Roman officials not to accept gifts and favours which would help ensure their future prosperity.[122] Is there an implication that Felix knew of the money, the alms of 24.17, that is the collection(!), which Paul had brought up to Jerusalem with him, and that it was still technically in Paul's control (it had *not* been delivered to the Jerusalem church)? The picture of Felix summoning Paul frequently for private consultation evokes the impression of a man as much drawn by the character of Paul and his message as he was repelled by the consequences which would inevitably follow from acceptance of that message.

Luke tells us that Felix remained in office for a further two years,[123] during which time he kept Paul in prison as a favour to 'the Jews' (24.27). We know that Felix was recalled in 59 or 60.[124] Josephus reports that the leaders of the Jewish community in Caesarea pursued him to Rome with accusations of maladministration, but that Nero spared him at the entreaty of Felix's brother, the influential freedman Pallas, who had been a favourite of Claudius (*Ant.* 20.182). The fact that the complaint was brought only by the local Jewish leadership could conceivably mean that Felix's attempt to curry favour with 'the Jews' (the representative leadership in Jerusalem; cf. 25.9) by leaving Paul in custody had some success. But with such few facts to hand, such correlation between Acts and Josephus is hazardous, especially as the portrayal here conforms to Luke's consistent attempt to portray the representative Jews of a place as uniformly hostile to Paul.

d. The Tension Mounts (Acts 25)

In many ways ch. 25 is the strangest chapter in Acts. The business of Paul in Roman custody has already been drawn out for more than three chapters. And nothing would have been easier for Luke than to concertina the events narrated in this chapter into a brief sentence or two. Even if the appeal to Caesar is the dramatic high point of the chapter (25.11-12), Luke, short of space on his roll or anxious

120. Haenchen thinks the two portrayals of Felix (24.24-25 and 26) are incompatible (*Acts* 662)!

121. See above, n. 88.

122. Josephus tells us that the only ones left in prison by Festus's successor, Albinus, were those unable to pay an appropriate bribe (*War* 2.273).

123. See above, §28 n. 15.

124. See above, §28.1b.

to move the narrative on, could readily have included it at the end of the speech in ch. 26.

Why then this slow build-up to the confrontation with Agrippa in ch. 26? The obvious answer is that Luke is a supremely accomplished story-teller. The function of the chapter is to build up the suspense. The trial before Felix had been adjourned. The two years following could be passed over in a sentence or two. Nothing had been resolved. But now, under the new procurator, Festus,[125] the tension can be ratcheted up afresh with a compelling rhythm. Like a musical crescendo which mounts up and then falls back, only to build again and mount still higher to a powerful climax, so the passion narrative of Paul builds to its climax. It begins with Festus taking the unusual step of leaving his headquarters to go up to Jerusalem (25.1). That he should make one of his first priorities a visit to Jerusalem is a reminder of the increasing tensions of the period (increasing brigandage, or guerilla actions)[126] and of the importance of commanding Jerusalem as Israel's capital and heart. The chief priests and other leading Jews request that Paul be transferred back to Jerusalem (25.2-3). That he was high on the agenda of the chief priests[127] and other leading Jews is equally understandable: the threat which Paul's mission to the Gentiles was seen to represent and embody, a threat to Jewish national identity and integrity, would have made his case stand out, whatever the other grievances of the time. Festus is shown as first standing firm before Jewish demands (25.4-5) but then as willing to accommodate them (25.9), opening up the possibility of dirty work at the crossroads (25.3).[128]

In the hearing which follows at Caesarea (25.6-7) Luke does not linger over details, indicating neither specific charges ('many weighty complaints') nor refutation. His concern was evidently to set the scene with broad brushstrokes and to evoke the atmosphere of continuing charge and denial. The important points for the reader to note would be the threatening attitude of the Jews,[129] the absence of proof in support of the charges (25.7), and Paul's blanket denial of any offence — whether against the law or the Temple or Caesar (25.8). The last

125. According to Josephus, Festus was a much stronger and fairer procurator than either his predecessor (Felix) or his successor (Albinus): he took firm action against bands of dissidents and handled with sensitivity a tricky situation regarding a wall constructed in the Temple area (*Ant.* 20.185-95). The way he is portrayed in the following narrative conforms with this broad picture.

126. See above, at n. 35.

127. The high priest at that time was one Ishmael (Schürer, *History* 2.231), but the narrative no longer depends on such details (cf. 23.1-5).

128. What were Luke's sources for postulating a further plot against Paul? Presumably these were not the same men as vowed to starve themselves in 23.13; two years had elapsed! Did Luke simply assume an equivalent strategy? In the increasingly tense and fervid atmosphere of the late 50s and early 60s (the Jewish revolt began in 66), such a supposition would not necessarily be far-fetched.

129. Acts 25.7 — they 'stood around him'; similarly 25.18.

(against Caesar) is a surprising new element in the charges, but it could reflect the similar tactics used against Jesus (particularly Luke 23.2), or an understandable attempt to bring home to the authorities the fundamentally subversive character of Paul's work as seen by the plaintiffs.[130]

'I appeal to Caesar' is one of the dramatic highlights of Luke's account (25.10-11)[131] and provides a watershed, since it transposes the story of Paul on trial from a relatively minor, internal dispute within Judea and Judaism to the world stage of a prospective trial before the ruler of the Roman Empire, the master of the civilized world as they then knew it (25.12). At this point, the mounting climax moves from minor to major key. The transition is marked by the disappearance of 'the Jews'; they take no part in the second half of the narrative, to be replaced as representative of Jewish interests (26.2-3) by the much more pliable Agrippa (25.13–26.32). Of course — and this is the point — the appeal to Caesar has resolved nothing, simply ensured that Paul will not be handed back to Jewish jurisdiction (presumably Paul's own chief concern). But with the introduction of King Herod Agrippa II to the scene, the build-up to Paul's last great self-testimony (ch. 26) begins afresh, with the sort of marking-time dialogue which imparts no new information but simply stretches out the suspense still more (25.13-27). This is Luke the story-teller and dramatist *par excellence* at work.

Agrippa II was son of Agrippa I.[132] He had been only sixteen when his father died (44 CE). Emperor Claudius had decided he was too young to inherit and appointed a Roman governor instead (Josephus, *Ant.* 19.360-63). In the intervening years, however, he had been given more and more of the northeastern territories of Herod the Great's former kingdom.[133] His interest in and knowledge of

---

130. Cf. Acts 16.21; 17.7; 24.5.

131. Nothing is said of it at this point, but Paul exercises the right of the Roman citizen — to be tried by the emperor (in this case Emperor Nero, whose first five years, 54-59, were remembered as a period of good rule). Festus would know of Paul's citizenship as a matter of court record (23.27) and would have no reason to deny the citizen's right (see Sherwin-White, *Roman Society* 63-67; Schürer, *History* 1.369; Rapske, *Paul in Roman Custody* 186-88; Bruce, *Acts* 488-89; further bibliography in Fitzmyer, *Acts* 746), even if he was under no binding obligation to do so (Lentz, *Paul* 144-53). Luke could evidently assume that as one of Roman citizenship's most ancient and most basic rights, it would be well known to his readers (Hemer, *Book of Acts* 130-31 n. 92).

132. On Agrippa I see above, §26.5b. Bernice (or Berenice), who accompanies Agrippa II (25.13; 26.30), was Agrippa II's sister. She had been twice widowed, and a third marriage had failed. She took an active political part in proceedings in her own right (Josephus, *War* 2.310-14, 333-34; *Life* 343, 355) and seems to have settled into the role of acting as consort or hostess to the unmarried Agrippa, inevitably giving rise to otherwise unfounded rumours of incest (*Ant.* 20.145). She subsequently became mistress of Titus, conqueror of Jerusalem (details in Schürer, *History* 1.479). See further Bruce, *Acts* 491; Hemer, *Book of Acts* 173-74 n. 27.

133. Josephus, *War* 2.247, 252; 3.56-57; *Ant.* 20.138, 159.

Jewish law and tradition was probably common knowledge:[134] sufficient at least to justify Festus's seeking out his advice (25.14, 22, 26) and Paul's subsequent compliment (26.3). It was thus a very astute move on Festus's part to consult Agrippa: to have such an acknowledged authority on Jewish affairs to advise and approve his judgment on Paul would provide excuse enough for Festus either for giving way to the pressures of the Jewish council or for resisting them.[135]

And so, like a well-staged play, with the grand processional entry ('with great pageantry') of Agrippa and his consort, followed by the military staff, the chief notables and finally Paul himself (25.23),[136] and then the prologue spoken by Festus, rehearsing well-known details (25.24-27), Luke at last brings us to the great climax of Paul's final defence and proclamation (ch. 26). It should be noted that the scene is not portrayed as a formal trial: no formal indictment is brought against Paul — on the contrary, he is declared innocent (25.25), for the second or third time (23.29; 25.18) — and there is no speech for the prosecution (as before Felix). The format rather is that of a hearing (but in a magnificent setting), designed to give Paul's final complete self-testimony maximum effect. The final sentences in particular (25.26-27) give Paul the perfect opening: the slate that is to provide the charge before Caesar is blank; let Paul write on it what he will.

On the question of historicity, we again need entertain no doubt as to the main outlines of the tale.[137]

- The portrayals of Procurator Festus (25.1) and of King Agrippa (25.13) are in character with what we know of them from elsewhere.
- The variation in time notes — 'three days', 'not more than eight or ten days', 'many days' (25.1, 6, 14) — suggests more than arbitrary choice.
- Even the pageantry of the final scene would fit well with the ancient love of display and as a setting for what comes close to a 'show trial'.

134. Agrippa's reputation is disputed, but he seems to have functioned in Rome as a spokesman for Jewish causes; he is remembered as having engaged in legal discussion with the famous Rabbi Eliezer ben Hyrcanus; and it may have been at Agrippa's insistence that the non-Jewish husbands of his sisters were first circumcised (Schürer, *History* 1.471-76).

135. 'The complication and prolongation of the trial of Paul arose from the fact that the charge was political — hence the procurators were reluctant to dismiss it out of hand — and yet the evidence was theological, hence the procurators were quite unable to understand it' (Sherwin-White, *Roman Society* 51).

136. Any film director worth his salt would recognize the potential of the scene.

137. Barrett (*Acts* 2.1121-23) responds effectively to the arguments of Haenchen (*Acts* 668-70) — 'an exaggerated analysis of difficulties' (Fitzmyer, *Acts* 742) — and Weiser (*Apg.* 637-39) against the substantial historicity of Luke's record. Haenchen in particular seems to assume that Luke's dramatic license in 25.23-27 undermines the historical value of the episode entirely (*Acts* 678-79). See also Omerzu, *Prozess* 466-95 (discussion limited to 25.1-12).

• The appeal to Caesar provides the only obvious historical explanation for Paul's being transferred to Rome in Roman custody.[138]

But the detailed exchanges probably owe most to Luke's historical imagination and dramatic flair: he does not bother to specify the charges brought against Paul (25.7); Paul's response is equally vague (25.8, 10-11; apart from the reference to the Temple in 25.8); and presumably Luke had no record to draw on of any private conversation between Festus and Agrippa (25.14-22). On the other hand, given a degree of virulent hostility to Paul on the part of at least some of the Jewish leadership in Jerusalem, the narrative has an overall plausibility which would fully satisfy Luke's canons of historiography. And somewhat surprisingly, Luke does little to advance his central claim that the movement which Paul led was Jewish through and through;[139] he must have thought the point sufficiently secure. Here it is the demands of the unfolding drama which override all else.

e. The Hearing before Governor Festus and King Agrippa (Acts 26)

Luke's whole Pauline passion narrative has been building towards this scene, which forms the climax of the book of Acts in the same way that the crucifixion provides the climax of the Gospels.[140] Now, at last, Paul has opportunity to make a final and determinative defence (Luke will make no attempt to indicate that he was given a subsequent opportunity before Emperor Nero). This is no mere repetition of Paul's self-defence in ch. 22 for the sake of emphasis, but the Lukan Paul's definitive answer to his Jewish critics — addressed explicitly to the king of the Jews.[141] Moreover, it should also be noted that this speech, together with the account of Paul's conversion itself (ch. 9), brackets the main body of Paul's missionary work. Hence its character: it hardly addresses the accusations laid against him but reviews the course and rationale of his whole life. Only so can the turns in his

---

138. The fact that Paul's citizenship provides the only explanation for his being taken to Rome is the strongest proof that his Roman citizenship was not a Lukan fiction (see above, §25.1c).

139. Contrast even 25.19 with 23.6 and 24.14-15.

140. Note particularly: the near conversion of Agrippa (26.28) parallels that of the thief on the cross (only in Luke 23.40-43); and the affirmation of Paul's innocence by both Festus and Agrippa (26.31-32) parallels the similar assessments of both Pilate and Herod regarding the case against Jesus (the latter again only in Luke 23.14-15).

141. This is one important difference from the Gospel passion narrative: the Roman governor, Festus, in effect hands over the proceedings to Agrippa; this is to be entirely an intra-Jewish affair. Hence Paul's address is to 'King Agrippa' (26.2, 19).

life which have occasioned the accusations be properly appreciated. This is Paul's 'apology', Luke's version of Paul's own *apologia pro vita sua*.[142]

At first (26.3-4) it seems as though Paul is simply recalling his pre-conversion life-style.[143] But the difference is that the claim here envisages no break, no before and after (conversion): Paul is speaking of 'my way of life from my youth, from the beginning'; he expects the testimony of his contemporaries to his strict Pharisaism to stand him in good stead in the present;[144] and he speaks to Agrippa both of 'our religion *(thrēskeia)*' (26.5), as of a religion still common to both, of 'our twelve tribes' (26.7), as of a national and religious identity shared, and of the first believers as still members of the synagogue (26.11). The key move, as in 23.6, is to focus the point at issue in the accusation against Paul on *Israel's* hope for the resurrection of the dead, the distinctively Pharisaic conviction (26.6-8). Left implicit is the claim that the hope and promise given to their fathers and central to all Israel's daily worship and aspiration has been fulfilled — by the resurrection of Jesus. Of course, Agrippa might have replied to Paul's challenge,[145] that even if he did believe 'that God raises the dead', his hope was to share in the *final* resurrection, not in the possibility of a single individual being resurrected prior to the new age. But in the present context the question makes its point: this (Christian) belief in the resurrection of Jesus is a Jewish belief and a Jewish hope realized.

The account then follows the now-familiar sequence of Paul's conversion story, retold in more detail and with story-teller variations (to maintain interest),[146] but constructed round the same core of the verbal encounter between the

142. Bruce, *Acts* 496. The noun *(apologia)* was used in 22.1; here it is the verb (26.1-2, twice; 26.24). Paul's own *apologia* came in Galatians 1–2 (see above, §31.7b).

143. Cf. Gal. 1.13-14; Phil. 3.5; Acts 22.3-5. Paul says 'All the Jews know . . .' in the way we today would say 'Everyone knows . . .' (26.4).

144. Cf. 21.24 — '. . . you live in observance of the law'; 23.6 — 'I am a Pharisee'. The assertion allows some adaptability, since 26.4 may limit this form of life-style to his time 'among my people and in Jerusalem' (cf. 1 Cor. 9.20). Note again that the description of the Pharisees as 'the strictest sect of our religion' employs one of the terms used regularly by Josephus to describe the 'sect of the Pharisees' — *akribēs* ('strict, exact, scrupulous'), *akribeia* ('exactness, precision'); as also 22.3 (*Jesus Remembered* 269 n. 67). Paul and Luke both reflect a more widespread admiration for the Pharisees at the care they took over their religious observances.

145. 'Why is it judged unbelievable for you [plural] that [if in fact] God raises the dead?' (26.8); see Haenchen, *Acts* 684.

146. It betrays a literary mind-set to envisage Luke garnering the different traditions from different milieus and using them more or less unaltered (Jervell, *Apg.* 599). New in the performance variations is the information that Paul's early persecution was authorized by the chief priests (plural) (26.10, but cf. 22.5). That there was a judicial process which resulted in some being condemned to death seems to strain the facts somewhat (cf. 22.4), though Paul's own recollection of his career as persecutor uses very violent language (Gal. 1.13 — 'tried to

The Passion of Paul

risen Jesus and Saul the persecutor (26.14-16).[147] The major divergence is that Paul's commissioning to the Gentiles takes place at the point of encounter itself.[148] The terms are crucial for the Lukan Paul's *apologia:*

- He had been appointed directly by the Christ from heaven to be an 'assistant and witness' (26.12). Even here Luke refrains from using the term 'apostle', but nonetheless the commission sets Paul fully at one with those originally commissioned by the risen Christ (1.8, 22; 10.41) and reflects Paul's own testimony to having seen and been commissioned by Christ.[149]
- He had been sent to the nations/Gentiles (26.17). The commission itself (26.18, and again 26.23) is spelled out in phrases which deliberately echo

---

destroy'), which was reflected also in his reputation among the early churches (9.21; Gal. 1.22; cf. Gal. 4.29 and 1 Thess. 2.14-15). Also new is the claim that Saul the persecutor 'punished them often in all the synagogues and tried to force them to blaspheme' (26.11). Quite what is in view here is unclear. 'Blasphemy' properly speaking was insult to the divine majesty. Luke can hardly mean that Saul tried to force Jewish believers to blaspheme God as such. But he could mean that Saul sought from them a confession which he would then have regarded as blaspheming God, that is, as making claims for Jesus which detracted from the honour due to God alone (cf. Luke 5.21; Mark 14.62-64; see *Jesus Remembered* 751-52). Or, less likely, that he tried to force them to deny Jesus as their Lord, and thus to blaspheme against his God-given status and glory, that is, blasphemy in Paul's (but not Saul's) ears (as in Pliny, *Ep.* 10.96.5 — *maledicerent Christo*). The reference to persecution 'even to foreign cities' is equally hyperbolic (no city other than Damascus is ever mentioned), but the phrase has an insider's perspective (literally, 'even to cities outside', that is, outside the land of Israel). Also new is the information that the heavenly voice addressed Paul/Saul in Hebrew/Aramaic (26.14), despite the fact that it is a Greek proverb which follows (or to be more precise, it is known only in Greek).

147. Cf. 9.4-6; 22.7-8, 10; and see again *Jesus Remembered* 210-12. Here, however, a proverbial tag, well known in classical literature (details in L. Schmid, *TDNT* 3.664-65; Barrett, *Acts* 1158; further bibliography in Fitzmyer, *Acts* 759), has been added to the risen Jesus' first words: 'it is hard for you to kick against the goads'. The metaphor is obviously that of the ox being prodded to pull steadily or to make a straight furrow; it probably expressed 'futile and detrimental resistance to a stronger power, whether it be that of a god, of destiny, or of man' (Schmid 664). The popular view persists that pricks of conscience were in mind, Saul struggling to free himself from the memory of his part in Stephen's death (7.58; 8.1) or from enslavement to covetous desire (cf. Rom. 7.7-12). The problem with both explanations is that none of Paul's own explicit recollections of his pre-Christian experience bears testimony to such pangs of conscience (cf. Gal. 1.13-14; Phil. 3.5-6), nor does the substantial persecution envisaged here (26.10-11) give any hint of such. The wonder of the Damascus road encounter for Paul was that Christ confronted him in his full fury as a persecutor (1 Cor. 15.9-10), not as one eaten up with doubt or guilt over what he was doing.

148. Contrast 9.15-16; 22.15, 21.

149. Cf. Gal. 1.12 and 15-16; 1 Cor. 9.1-2; 15.8-10. The indication of further visions of Christ refers directly to Acts 18.9-10; 22.17-21; 23.11; cf. 27.23-24. But Paul himself also refers to many visions which he received (2 Cor. 12.1-10).

the commission of the Servant of Yahweh: 'to open their eyes' (Isa. 42.7) and 'to turn them from darkness to light' (Isa. 42.6-7, 16). Paul is evidently depicted here as fulfilling the role of the Servant, the role of Israel (49.3).[150] Here again is clearly reflected Paul's own conviction that with the death and resurrection of Jesus, the time and possibility had arrived for the fulfilment of Israel's responsibility to be a light to the Gentiles.[151]

- The final phrase of 26.18 ('a share among those made holy by faith in me') recalls Paul's final testament (20.32) and carries the same overtones of a characteristic Pauline thought: that Gentile Christian identity is to be moulded into the distinctive Jewish heritage.[152]

- The claim that Paul's initial mission was in Damascus, Jerusalem and Judea (26.19-20) before going to the Gentiles of course reflects Luke's own version of the story of Paul's mission (Acts 9, 13).[153] But it also reflects Paul's own assertion that he had fully proclaimed the good news from Jerusalem (Rom. 15.19), and it reinforces Paul's own missionary theology of 'Jew first, but also Gentile' and the hopes he had expressed in Rom. 11.11-15.[154] It was evidently important for Luke (as for Paul) that the even-handedness of Paul's outreach was maintained.

- Above all, Paul insists that his message is nothing other than what the prophets and Moses had predicted: 'that the Messiah would suffer, and that as first of the resurrection of the dead, he was to proclaim light both to the people and to the nations' (26.23). As with the earliest Christian self-understanding and preaching,[155] the core message about the Nazarene stands in direct continuity with the authoritative Scriptures of Israel. But what stands out more clearly now than before is that the openness of the gospel to the Gentiles is equally part of that identity and of that continuity, as being part of Israel's own commission to serve as 'a light to the nations' (Isa. 49.6, already cited in 13.47).

The concluding paragraph (26.24-32) effectively maintains the dramatic quality of the scene while highlighting still further Luke's chosen emphases. The speech is cut short, outlining the final spoken words still more clearly as the

---

150. See above, §25.3d.

151. Gal. 1.15-16; 3.8, 13-14, 23-29; 4.1-7; see further Jervell, *Apg.* 594.

152. Romans chs. 4, 9–11; the themes of the whole verse are closely parallel to those in Col. 1.12-14.

153. The presentation of Paul as a preacher of repentance (26.20) accords more with Luke's emphasis (cf., e.g., Luke 3.8-14) than Paul's, who hardly uses the terminology in his letters (see above, §33 n. 384).

154. See above, §33 n. 86 and n. 234.

155. Luke 24.45-47; Acts 2.23-24.

speech's climax (26.23). The reaction of Festus (26.24 — 'Paul, you are mad') seems uncalled for,[156] except that it again brings out the exceptional character of the Christian claim — Christ risen from the dead, a light to both Jew and Gentile (26.22-23). The appeal to Agrippa to bear testimony on Paul's behalf is a dramatic masterstroke (Paul addresses the king boldly, man to man): 'King Agrippa, do you believe the prophets? I know that you believe!' (26.27). As one well informed of Jewish affairs and doubtless familiar with the Scriptures, Agrippa could hardly fail to acknowledge that what Paul was saying was 'the sober truth' (26.25). And the reaction of Agrippa (26.28 — 'You are trying to persuade me to become a Christian')[157] likewise indicates not so much the power of Paul's presentation as what should be the inherent appeal of this so Jewish message to this so Jewish king. Paul's reply has a noble dignity and brings the scene to a fitting end on a note of pathos: Paul truly believed that nothing would bring greater benefit to his audience than their acceptance of his message, to share his faith and vision — though not his chains (26.29).

Like the calm coda following the emotion-draining climaxes of the second movement of Bruckner's Seventh Symphony or Tchaikovsky's 'Romeo and Juliet' Overture, the final paragraph of this most dramatic of all Luke's scenes winds down quietly and gently to a close (26.30-32). Surprisingly, nothing more is said in public by the principals; but dramatically that allows Paul to have the last word, and the effect of his words to continue ringing in the ears of audience and reader. The concluding episode is in complete contrast — no formal gather-

---

156. Presumably Festus was reacting to the talk of resurrection (cf. 17.32), though possibly also the thought of having the same national religion for all the diverse nations would have made little sense to the representative of an empire whose policy was to respect the distinctive national features of its subject peoples. For Haenchen, Luke intends 'to show that the Roman official and the Roman state which he represents are not capable of dealing with these theological questions — as the Jew Agrippa was' (*Acts* 688).

157. The character of Agrippa's reply is not altogether clear. KJV's 'Almost thou persuadest me to be a Christian' has become more or less proverbial, with its tantalizing suggestion that Paul in his final days in Judea almost succeeded in converting the one remaining (and last) Jewish king. Some contemporary translations maintain something of this tradition: 'A little more, and your arguments would make a Christian of me' (JB/NJB; similarly REB); cf. Jervell, 'It is in no way intended ironically, but expresses a certain agreement, though without drawing the consequences' (*Apg.* 597). But most assume a note of irony or of questioning intended in the words: 'In a short time you think to make me a Christian!' (RSV, a too free rendering of the Greek); 'Do you think that in such a short time you can persuade me to be a Christian?' (NIV; similarly GNB and NRSV). Either way, the dramatic impact is powerful. None of these translations, however, quite reflects the ambiguity of the final clause, which could be better rendered, 'to act (as) a Christian', possibly even 'to play the Christian' (Lake and Cadbury, *Beginnings* 4.323; Bruce, *Acts* 506; Barrett, *Acts* 1169-71; Fitzmyer, *Acts* 754 disagrees), and which thus probably contains a stronger note of sarcasm. This is only the second time the term 'Christian' occurs, and significantly it appears in a formal Roman setting (11.26; see above, §24.8d).

ing or consultation but simply the sound of the departing dignitaries talking among themselves. The point is that they are in total agreement: there are no grounds for Paul's imprisonment or death. And even if Agrippa has not been persuaded of what Paul affirmed, he is clear that Paul is totally innocent (26.31-32), Luke thus ending the scene as he began it (25.25). Nonetheless, Paul must go to Rome: the privilege accorded the Roman citizen, even though the charges against him have been judged vacuous by the most competent authorities, still provides the occasion and means for the divine plan to be fulfilled. He must go to Caesar, and that meant, as any reader would know, to Rome! The final and most crucial step to 'the end of the earth' (1.8) is about to be taken.

As to the historical detail (in sum):

- Once again we need have no doubt that Paul was heard by Festus and that he was sent to Rome for his case to be settled. As already noted, Luke's account accords well with what we know of Festus and Agrippa from Josephus, though we may have to allow a fair degree of dramatic licence for the final scene (26.24-29).
- The speech itself is constructed round the same two features as before — the encounter with Jesus[158] and the sending of Paul to the Gentiles.[159] These were also the constants of Paul's own recollection of the event.[160]
- The references to 'Jesus the Nazarene' (26.9)[161] and to 'the saints' (26.10) also have a primitive ring.

Otherwise, 26.2-23 is simply one variant of what must have been an often-told tale, elaborated in part and, of course, adapted to the circumstances (26.6-8, 21), but whether by Luke or by Paul himself would hardly make much difference. As observed before, if Luke could record without qualm three such variant accounts of the same event (Paul's conversion), he would hardly expect his readers to have qualms about the veracity of his portrayal of Paul on the ground of these variations.

34.3. And So to Rome

Following the slow-paced chapters of much talk and little movement, Acts 27 comes as a welcome contrast. It is all action and little talk. Dramatically it serves to slacken completely the suspense built up over the past two chapters, and after

---

158. Acts 9.4-6; 22.7-10; 26.14-16.
159. Acts 9.15-16; 22.15, 21; 26.16-18, 23.
160. 1 Cor. 9.1-2; Gal. 1.15-16.
161. Cf. Acts 2.22; 6.14; see above, §20.1(16).

a calm interlude (27.1-12) it allows a quite different tension to build again, this time round the prospect of natural danger and disaster. Compositionally, the chapter's function is like that of the Saturday following Good Friday and leading into the resolution of Easter Sunday in the Gospel.[162]

a. Shipwreck (Acts 27)

The story unfolds easily and naturally. Paul and his companions — 'we' and Aristarchus, one of the original delegation (20.4) — are transferred to the custody of a detachment under the command of a centurion named Julius of the Augustan Cohort (27.1-2).[163] The ship was based in the Aegean and served the coastal cities; the inference is that Julius expected to pick up a more substantial vessel for the more demanding trip to Rome at one of the larger cities in Asia Minor. The prevailing wind of the region throughout summer is westerly or northwesterly, so a course to the east and north of Cyprus was able to use the island for shelter for much of the journey, before crossing to the south coast of Asia Minor, where it could pick up a strong westerly current (27.4).[164] At Myra Julius's hope was fulfilled: a larger vessel was there, bound for Italy (27.5-6). It had probably run northwards from Alexandria to Asia Minor, where it could work its way westwards along the coast. The ship was presumably a grain carrier (27.37);[165] Rome continued to depend on the grain of Egypt to feed its impoverished masses, and the maintenance and security of the grain traffic was a major objective of state policy. The orders of Julius the centurion might well have envisaged the likelihood of being able to combine his escort duty with that of supervising a grain shipment; hence, perhaps, his choice of a sea route in preference to the overland route.

It is clear from the ensuing account that the events took place late in the

---

162. Murphy-O'Connor, *Paul* 351-54, follows M.-E. Boismard and L. Lamouille, *Les Actes des deux apôtres* (3 vols.; EB; Paris: Gabalda, 1990) 2.225-26, 260, in arguing that Acts 27.1–28.16 has been formed by the integration and elaboration of two sources.

163. We have inscriptional evidence of auxiliary cohorts being granted the honorific title 'Augusta' (see Broughton, *Beginnings* 5.443; Hemer, *Book of Acts* 132-33 n. 96; Bruce, *Acts* 511-12). This detachment had been given escort duty, whether as a regular or as exceptional duty. Since the other prisoners are incidental to the story, Luke says no more about them (until 27.42); how serious their crimes were we do not know, but as the sequel indicates, Paul as a Roman citizen would have higher status and be accorded freer access to the centurion and the captain. We are to assume that the terms of Paul's custody continued to allow such favours (cf. 24.23), as also freedom to visit 'his friends' (the church) at Sidon (cf. 11.19; 15.3) and to enjoy some hospitality superior to the harshness of shipboard travel (27.3; cf. 28.14).

164. Lake and Cadbury, *Beginnings* 4.326.

165. For details see Bruce, *Acts* 513; Barrett, *Acts* 2.1185.

Paul's Journey to Rome

sailing season (27.9, 12). Both captain and centurion were evidently anxious to reach Rome before the season closed down: presumably the financial rewards for a late-season cargo of grain made the risk worthwhile, and escort duty through the winter in foreign parts or the prospect of the lengthy overland route in early winter were evidently less appealing. In the event, however, the winds were against them (presumably the northwester), prevented them crossing the southern Aegean and forced them southwards, to the shelter of Crete's southern flank (27.7-8).[166] By tradition, and no doubt on the basis of earlier costly experience, no journeys were attempted in the open sea after November 11.[167] The two preceding months were regarded as dangerous. This fits with the timing indicated by Luke: 'the fast' (27.9) is the Day of Atonement, Yom Kippur, which usually falls in late September or early October.[168] Since 'even the fast was already passed', they were well into the danger period (27.9-12).

The loss of 'much time' (27.9) battling against the contrary winds would

166. J. Smith, *The Voyage and Shipwreck of St. Paul* (London: Longmans, Green, [3]1866) 75-76; Hemer, *Book of Acts* 134-35 n. 102.

167. See above, §28 at n. 72.

168. In 59 CE it fell on October 5 (see further Bruce, *Acts* 515; Barrett, *Acts* 2.1188). We should not overlook the clear implication that Paul and his companions continued to observe this distinctively Jewish holy day (cf. 20.6, 16).

readily suggest to such a seasoned traveller as Paul, who had already been ship-wrecked three times (2 Cor. 11.25), that there was too little realistic hope of any further progress, let alone of reaching Italy without loss of life (27.10). It would be in character that he should choose to make his views known to those responsible for the voyage (even if he was unfamiliar with this particular route); the scene is not implausible.[169] The centurion was evidently in charge: he had commandeered the vessel, or as a grain carrier it would have been on imperial service. But he evidently consulted not only the captain and owner (27.11) but also other experienced crewmen and travellers (27.12) before making up his mind or reaching a consensual decision. In the event, there was majority agreement that their wisest course was to winter in a Cretan port; the only disagreement with Paul was that the majority thought it worth taking the chance to reach a harbour (Phoenix) which would be more secure from the winter storms.[170]

The gentle southwester soon gives way to 'a violent [literally 'typhonic'] wind, called the Northeaster *(eurakylōn)*' (27.13-15).[171] Once round Cape Matala, about six miles to the west of Fair Havens, they would be unable to prevent themselves from being driven away from the shore. In the crisis, the crew takes the familiar emergency actions in such a plight (27.16-20): securing the dinghy, running stout ropes (literally 'helps') under the hull to help prevent the timbers starting apart or splitting; the use of a sea anchor[172] to prevent the drifting ship from turning broadside to the wind; and subsequently, and more unwillingly, lightening the ship by throwing overboard (some of) the cargo,[173] and then all but essential gear (cf. 27.29, 38). The danger was that they would be driven on to the Syrtes, the much-feared sandbanks off the coast of Libya, where they would be pounded to destruction and almost certain death.

In an interlude, Paul is shown to give way to the so very human temptation to say, 'I told you so' (27.21). More positively, even in the extreme discomfort and distress of a ship pounded unceasingly, he had received one more vision or audition

169. *Pace* Haenchen, *Acts* 709.

170. Phoenix faced 'southwest and northwest' (not 'northeast and southeast', as RSV). Probably modern Phineka is meant; see Lake and Cadbury, *Beginnings* 4.329-30; Haenchen, *Acts* 700-701 n. 7; Hemer, *Book of Acts* 139; Barrett, *Acts* 2.1192-93.

171. 'There is a noted tendency of a south wind in these climes to back suddenly to a violent north-easter, the well-known *gregale*. . . . *Euraquilo* is an unusual, but logically formed, nautical term which a traveler is likely to have heard from sailors speaking a Latin or mixed jargon, and precisely apposite to the circumstances of Paul's voyage' (Hemer, *Book of Acts* 141-42); on *eurakylōn* see further Barrett, *Acts* 2.1194; M. Reiser, 'Von Caesarea nach Malta. Literarischer Charakter und historische Glaubwürdigkeit von Act 27', in Horn, ed., *Ende* 49-73 (here 63-67).

172. The Greek says simply 'letting down the gear'. The technical language in this passage, as also in 27.40, is unclear. See also Rapske, 'Travel' 33-34.

173. Rapske ('Travel' 31-35) and Wallace and Williams (*Three Worlds* 22) point out the difficulty of jettisoning a cargo of grain.

(27.23-24), his last in Acts, but the first and only time of an angel.[174] The angel's message is strikingly God-centred: it is God to whom Paul belongs and who stands at the focus of Paul's worship (27.23); it is God who is affirmed to be in sovereign control of events and of those caught up in them (27.24); and it is faith in this God which Paul affirms (27.25). Thirteen or fourteen days would be about the time taken to drift (across the Adria) from Crete to Malta (27.27-29).[175] The soundings (27.28), using a lead weight, accord with an approach to Malta from the east.

An attempt to escape by (some of) the crew is foiled by Paul (27.30-32). Such action by (some of) the sailors is understandable in the circumstances (they were nearing land), but their abandoning ship would have left it without skilled crew. That it was Paul who realized what was happening and alerted the centurion, who would likely be his closest companion apart from Luke and Aristarchus, makes for a better story but is not implausible. But did Paul and Luke misunderstand what could have been a legitimate and praiseworthy attempt by the crew to anchor the bow? And did Paul mean the soldiers to cut the dinghy adrift, thus decreasing the chances of any kind of orderly disembarkation, should the weather improve?[176]

That the closeness of land (27.28-29) would have roused Paul's spirits is also in character. As one who had remained buoyant and resilient in the face of repeated setbacks in the past, and one who had demonstrated his natural leadership many times before, he takes the lead in giving encouragement. This was the nature and effect of his faith, as his letters repeatedly confirm.[177] In this case in particular, he had been given an assurance as to the safety of his companions, and he was not embarrassed to speak it forth as his own personal conviction (27.33-34). Therefore he urges them to take food 'for your preservation' (*sōtēria*, 'salvation');[178] that Luke refers to a sharing of what supplies of bread remained is almost certain (27.35-36).[179] The more significant feature for Luke is that Paul

---

174. Why an angel here? Presumably because a Gentile crew would have no idea who 'the Lord' was; but then Paul could have provided an explanation sufficient for the occasion in a sentence or two. If this is Luke's contrivance, it shows him to be an author sensitive to the severe constraints of the situation. Alternatively he recalls a Paul who displayed that sensitivity on the occasion itself. A pagan audience would find no difficulty in giving meaning to 'a messenger of the God whose I am and whom I worship' (27.23).

175. Smith, *Voyage* 124-26. The Adria (27.27) was the sea bounded by Italy, Malta, Crete and Greece. On the unlikely possibility that the island was not Malta but Mljet in the Adriatic, or the peninsula of Kefallinia near Epirus, see Rapske, 'Travel' 36-43.

176. See Lake and Cadbury, *Beginnings* 335-36. 'Paul by this course of action would have doomed the ship to run aground' (Haenchen, *Acts* 706).

177. E.g., 2 Cor. 1.3-11; 4.7-18; 12.7-10; Phil. 1.15-26; 4.10-13.

178. The translations paraphrase — e.g., 'it will help you survive' (NRSV), 'your lives depend on it' (REB).

179. Despite the sequence, 'took bread, gave thanks (*eucharistēsen*) to God, and broke

'gave thanks to God before them all'. It is as a witness for God, the one God of Israel, that Paul stands out in his endurance, his perceptiveness and his leadership.

With the long-drawn-out crisis evidently about to be resolved, there was no
point in trying to save any of the remaining cargo (27.38).[180] The lighter the ship,
the more likely that the waves would carry it through any shoals or over any
rocks as they made the decisive attempt to bring it to safety or to beach it. In the
event the only hope was to try to beach the ship (27.39-41).[181] The desperate attempt met disaster at 'a place of two seas' (literally), that is, presumably, a sand-
bar or patch of shallows which divided deeper water on two sides or where two
currents clashed;[182] there they ran aground, and with the bow stuck fast, the stern
began to be battered and broken by the power of the surf.

The soldiers plan to kill the prisoners (27.42), a natural reaction of the escort; they would be held responsible, should the prisoners have escaped in the
confusion.[183] It is noteworthy that Luke does not attribute the centurion's
counter-order to the urging of Paul (27.43); Luke makes no attempt to give Paul a
leading role in the final denouement.[184] The centurion, presumably already impressed by Paul, might well consider that it would be in his own interest if he was
able, after all and despite everything, to bring this probably innocent Roman citizen safely to Rome. But Luke no doubt would like us to deduce that the centurion

---

it', a eucharist can hardly be in view (*pace* Klauck, *Magic and Paganism* 112). The actions are
simply those of a normal Jewish meal, with the thanksgiving, breaking of bread and its distribution (not mentioned here) as the first act of the meal, by means of which all present can share in
the blessing of the bread (cf. Luke 9.16; 24.30) (Haenchen, *Acts* 707 n. 3; cf. Barrett, *Acts*
1208-10). In the circumstances what was needed was not a symbolic piece of bread but sufficient bread to give them strength for the final stage of the long-running crisis (27.34), and not a
private celebration between Paul, Luke and Aristarchus but a break-fast for everyone which
gave 'nourishment *(trophē)*' to all (27.38). This conclusion is bound to reflect back on the earlier references to 'breaking bread' (2.46; 20.7, 11). In each case there is nothing in the text
which points to the conclusion that Luke intended to describe any more than a shared meal (see
also 20.7a and 11-12).

180. The exactness of the numbers of those on board is striking — 276 (27.37). Was
there a roll call at this point, as would be appropriate with first light (27.33), given the likelihood of serious injuries or loss of crew overboard in the hazardous conditions of the last thirteen days? At any rate the number is best explained as a reminiscence; it seems to have no symbolic significance. An ocean-going ship would have been quite capable of carrying twice as
many (Hemer, *Book of Acts* 149-50). Josephus records the foundering *(baptisthēnai)* of his ship
in the sea of Adria, with a company of some 600 (*Life* 15).

181. The seamanship involved is elucidated by Smith, *Voyage* 134, 138-39; Hemer,
Book of Acts 150-51.

182. Probably 'a bank of soft clay in the middle of the entrance to St. Paul's Bay'
(Haenchen, *Acts* 708); see further Smith, *Voyage* 139-41.

183. Cf. Acts 12.19; 16.27.

184. Contrast 27.9-10, 21-26, 30-32, 33-36.

was still more impressed by Paul's earlier reassurance (27.24); his detachment need have no fear of losing their charges — all would be saved. And so it proves: the swimmers make their own way, and the rest, using planks or 'some pieces (or persons?) from the ship', head for the shore. In a tone of appropriate thankfulness and triumph, Luke concludes one of his most dramatic episodes — 'And thus came everyone safely to land' (27.44).

It is hard to doubt that Luke saw in this episode a paradigm of Paul's mission: a laboured but definite progress; an unbelieving and reactionary crew (playing the same role as 'the Jews' elsewhere); a supportive Roman officer; above all God's manifest reassurance and deliverance from the most perilous of situations; and an outcome which can be described as 'salvation'. The parallel particularly with the preceding events would provide redoubled confirmation for the reader that as God delivered Paul from the perils of the deep, so his promise of deliverance from hostile Jews and Gentiles (26.17) could be firmly relied on. Come what may, God would fulfil his purpose by having Paul preach the good news in the very heart of the empire.

The shipwreck had been a favourite feature of ancient story-telling, at least since Homer's *Odyssey*. And many assume that Luke has simply followed ancient convention, drawing on such stories known to him for the impressive range of nautical details which are a feature of his account.[185] On the other hand, stormy passages and shipwrecks were common in Mediterranean travel; in 2 Cor. 11.25-26, written a few years prior to this episode, Paul recalls that he had already been shipwrecked three times, had been adrift at sea for a night and a day, and was no stranger to dangers at sea. Luke himself, presumably, had experienced his own share of such hazards, whether with Paul or on other occasions. It would be a surprise, then, if his narrative was drawn solely from literary precedents; almost certainly he had his own memories, for example of the details he records in verses 16-19.[186]

---

185. E.g., there are echoes of Homer in verses 29 and 41; see further Bruce, *Acts* 508-509, and particularly D. R. MacDonald, 'The Shipwrecks of Odysseus and Paul', *NTS* 45 (1999) 88-107. Fitzmyer notes the accounts which are often invoked for comparison, particularly Lucian's *Navigium*. But he adds, 'At most, such accounts reveal the literary form that Luke makes use of in this chapter; to none of them is the Lucan account actually indebted' (*Acts* 768). C. H. Talbert and J. H. Hayes, 'A Theology of Sea Storms in Luke-Acts', in Moessner, ed., *Jesus and the Heritage of Israel* 267-83, provide a useful catalogue of comparative material (268-71).

186. Smith's *Voyage* is still highly regarded (Bruce, *Acts* 510 and Barrett, *Acts* 2.1178). Barrett adds, 'It might almost be said that the writer's knowledge of the sea and of sailors is too good for us; he uses what are plainly technical terms, some of which are otherwise unknown so that we can only guess at their meaning' (1178). Similarly R. Chantal, *Paul de Tarse en Méditerranée. Recherches autour de la navigation dans l'antiquité (Ac 27–28,16)* (Paris: Cerf, 2006), concludes: the account 'through its fullness, its precision and the technical details of nautical documentation ... constitutes within antique literature an incontestable and irreplaceable source for the history of navigation in the first century as well as for our knowledge of Paul of Tarsus' (192).

If the details of the storm and of the desperate measures taken, vivid as they are, do not settle the question of the chapter's historical value, there are others which do suggest that through the story-teller's artistry there are clear historical reminiscences to be detected. We may mention, in sequence:

- the names of the centurion and his cohort and of Paul's companions (27.1-2);
- the details of the itinerary, including lesser-known place-names like Cnidus, Salmone and Cauda, and the approach to Malta (27.7, 16, 39-41);
- the name of the 'typhonic wind', 'Eurakylon (Northeaster)' (27.14);
- and the numbers involved (27.37).

Notable also is the restraint of the story-teller. We read of no overtly supernatural intervention beyond the reassurance provided by an angel in a dream or vision (27.23-24): Luke, who elsewhere delights to draw parallels between Paul and Jesus, ignores the opportunity suggested by Luke 8.22-25. No miracle is attributed to Paul beyond the prediction of 27.26; otherwise his advice is simply good sense born of experience (27.10, 31). He is indomitable, but not divine (contrast 28.6). And though he is 'the focal point of the action',[187] that is consistent with the Paul we know from his letters as well as from Acts;[188] and even then, as already noted, Luke makes no attempt to give Paul a leading role in the climactic scene (27.42-44).[189]

Above all there is the appearance of the story-teller in first-person terms ('we'), beginning at 27.1. Some suggest that this too is simply a feature taken over from the genre of sea journeys;[190] but much the most obvious conclusion to draw from the 'we' form is that the writer intended his readers to understand that he himself had been present, an eyewitness of and participant in the events described.[191] In fact, therefore, the simplest and most obvious conclusion to draw is

187. 'Paul always stands in the limelight. He is never at a loss for advice' (Haenchen, *Acts* 709, 711). Haenchen regards these as 'errors of the Lucan portrait of Paul' (711).

188. Barrett justifiably protests against Haenchen's over-reaction (*Acts* 2.1178-79). Haenchen makes far too much of Paul's prisoner status — 'a highly suspect prisoner *(crimen laesae majestatis)*' (*Acts* 700 n. 5); but, according to Luke, Paul had already been declared innocent by the responsible authority (26.31-32).

189. In the event it is *not* Paul the prisoner who 'saves them all' (Haenchen, *Acts* 709).

190. See §21 n. 50 above.

191. Lake and Cadbury's judgment — 'Much the most natural view is that it really represents the actual experiences of Paul and his friends, but it is possible that the narrative has been coloured in a few details by traditional accounts of shipwrecks' (*Beginnings* 4.324) — is still one of the fairest. Contrast the consistent scepticism which is a feature of the dominant German commentary tradition; e.g., Lüdemann concludes that verses 6-44 (without redaction additions) 'are the result of Luke's readings and probably have no point of reference in history' (*Early Christianity* 259-60). Otherwise Thornton, *Zeuge* 313-41, who concludes: 'I regard it as

that the chapter, as indeed the rest of the book, was written by one who had been a companion of Paul throughout this particular journey, and, indeed, all the way to Rome (the final 'we' is at 28.16). Where so much remains unclear, the simplest and most obvious solution is probably the best.

b. The Verdict Is Delivered on Paul (Acts 28.1-10)

The episode on Malta *(Melitē)* is a cameo and summary of the long-drawn-out crisis confronting Paul. The scene, though similar to other accounts of shipwreck, could be drawn from memory: the locals speaking in an unknown dia-lect;[192] their uncommon kindness, nonetheless; the fire, the rain and the cold. As is usual in Luke's story-telling, however, the focus tightens on to the chief participants (Paul and the locals); the rest of the ship's complement fade into the background. But the verisimilitude of the scene is sustained: Paul, not commanding but quick to help (cf. 20.34); a torpid viper caught up with the bundle of sticks and stirred by the heat of the fire; the superstitious but understandable reaction of the locals.

As with 'the Jews' earlier, the viper threatening Paul's life leads onlookers to the conclusion that he is a criminal; although he has escaped the perils of the sea, he has not escaped the due reward of his crimes; the goddess Justice has had the last word (28.3-4).[193] But Paul's survival (he shakes the viper off, unharmed)[194] causes them to change their mind: not a murderer but a god; justice *has* had the last word (28.5-6). Luke evidently wanted this to be the final verdict on the accusations brought against Paul. This is indicated not only by the fact that Luke allows the verdict of the Maltese to stand unchecked: 'justice' has indeed spoken, and clearly in Paul's favour.[195] It is indicated also by the fact, al-

---

quite conceivable that the actual source for Acts 27f. was Luke's memory' (341); J. M. Gilchrist, 'The Historicity of Paul's Shipwreck', *JSNT* 61 (1996) 29-51 — 'an eyewitness record, but written-up after a considerable lapse of time' (29); Jervell, who is impressed by the many nautical details and the eyewitness character of the story *(Apg.* 611-14); and Reiser provides a scathing critique of those who see Acts 27 as purely literary fiction ('Von Caesarea nach Malta').

192. Luke calls them *barbaroi,* that is, not able to converse in Greek, the international language of the day; see further Barrett, *Acts* 2.1220-21.

193. 'Justice' is quite often personified as a goddess in Greek literature, named by Hesiod as the daughter of Zeus and Themis (G. Schrenk, *TDNT* 2.181).

194. There are no poisonous snakes on Malta now, but was it always so? *Echidna* denoted a snake thought to be poisonous. See Hemer, *Book of Acts* 153. This was one of the details used in the construction of the longer end added to Mark's Gospel (Mark 16.9-20), probably in the second century (Mark 16.18), and which more recently has been given special significance by snake-handling sects.

195. In the overall construction of Acts this final judgment of the people ('he is a god')

ready noted, that the trial before Caesar stands suspended through the concluding phase of Luke's narrative: the final verdict *has* been given; nothing more need be said, and nothing that happens beyond the horizon of Luke's account can alter the verdict already given. But it is indicated also by the fact that the Jews in Rome have no accusations or complaints to bring against Paul (28.21): those ('the Jews') who have been the principal movers and instigators against Paul (28.19) now have nothing to say against the man himself. The verdict from on high has in effect quashed their accusations also; there is no charge or counter-charge between Paul and his people to be resolved (28.19, 21). Paul can proceed as no longer an accused criminal and apostate. A fresh start can be made in preaching and teaching the gospel to his own people (28.22-31).

The sequel (28.7-10) functions as a corollary to the verdict just given: Paul is received as a celebrated figure;[196] nothing is said of Paul as prisoner or in custody, or of the other survivors of the wreck — these details are now irrelevant; miracles of healing (28.8-9) confirm Paul's standing as a medium of healing power (divinely authorized and attested);[197] the locals continue to be truer representatives of heaven's judgment on Paul as they heap his party ('us') with honours at the end of their stay. Nor, somewhat surprisingly, is anything said about Paul preaching to the people. Rather, the whole episode has a celebratory character — celebration in effect at the vindication of Paul. Nor, surprisingly, is any-

---

is remarkable (28.6). A repeated feature of earlier scenes was Luke's determination to show how false ideas of God were rejected and to demonstrate the folly of confusing God with human beings or idols — Simon (8.10, 20-24), Peter (10.25-26), Herod (12.20-23), Paul and Silas (14.11-18), the Athenian shrines and idols (17.22-31). But here, quite exceptionally, Luke allows Paul to be reckoned a god, with Paul making no attempt to qualify or correct the opinion. We cannot conclude from this that Luke wanted Paul to be thought of in these terms, abandoning his earlier consistent strategy and emphasis. Rather he lets the judgment stand, precisely as the reversal of the earlier verdict of Paul's guilt (28.4): Paul's god-likeness here is rather the measure of his innocence and of his stature as the spokesman for the one true God. See also M. Labahn, 'Paulus — ein *homo honestus et iustus*. Das lukanische Paulusportrait von Acts 27–28 im Lichte ausgewählter antiker Parallelen', in Horn, ed., *Ende* 75-106.

196. The hospitality accords with the traditions of hospitality of the time, though we should also note that it was limited to three days. Luke did not think it important to indicate the accommodation provided for the party for the next three months (28.11).

197. The description of the illness of Publius's father is remarkably detailed (28.8) — not just a 'fever' (cf. Luke 4.38-39) but also 'dysentery' (a term which occurs nowhere else in biblical Greek). Such detail would normally indicate use of tradition, and here probably Luke's own personal recollection; similarly with the otherwise unknown name Publius (Poplios). The illness is not attributed to demonic interference, and Luke's description of the healing effected by Paul mirrors normal technique of prayer and laying on of hands (cf. 6.6; 8.15, 17; 13.3), without reference to the name of Jesus (contrast 3.6, 16; 4.10, 30; 16.18). Paul himself had earlier recalled performing various miracles (Rom. 15.19; 2 Cor. 12.12), so Luke's record of Paul's success as a healer is probably based on his own clear recollections of the time.

thing said of the Maltese coming to faith. The period is represented solely as a celebration from beginning to end of Paul's vindication and authorization from on high.

c. 'And So We Came to Rome' (Acts 28.11-22)

In February (probably of the year 60), more favourable winds began to blow, and sea travel became safe enough again.[198] They found passage in a ship also from Alexandria (cf. 27.6), and probably also a grain carrier which had cut its timing at the end of the previous season just too fine.[199] The detail of the route (Syracuse, Rhegium, Puteoli) must surely be drawn from personal reminiscence, the timetable dependent on the variable winds. Puteoli, near modern Naples, was the main port in southern Italy, and passengers were usually disembarked there (five days vigorous walk from Rome) while the grain continued to Ostia, which had recently replaced Puteoli as Rome's own port.[200] The fact that Paul was still in custody and was one of a band of prisoners guarded by a detachment of soldiers remains out of view for Luke; the wishes of the Christian group (Paul, Luke and Aristarchus) are granted without demur. One could imagine the centurion giving Paul permission to inquire whether there were fellow believers in Puteoli,[201] and even to accept their hospitality for a few days;[202] but the implication that the centurion was willing to tolerate further delay in bringing his other prisoners to Rome seems more dubious. Conceivably, however, he left Paul with a token guard and proceeded directly to Rome with the rest of his party. At all events, it is significant that a church was already established in Puteoli.[203]

Christians from Rome itself give formal welcome to Paul and his party at Appii Forum (about forty-three miles south of Rome) and at the Three Taverns (about thirty-three miles south of Rome), both on the Appian Way (28.15) — ap-

198. Hemer, *Book of Acts* 154.

199. See further Rapske, 'Travel' 22-29. The ship's figurehead was the *Dioskyroi,* the heavenly twins Castor and Pollux, twin sons of Zeus. These legendary twin sons of Zeus and Leda were regarded as the patron deities of navigation; the ship had taken their name as its own, for obvious reasons (Lake and Cadbury, *Beginnings* 4.343-44). Luke may even see significance in the name under whose patronage Paul's ship sailed — perhaps suggesting that the Christian (28.14-15) and Jewish brothers (28.17, 21) whom Paul was soon to encounter were likewise twin siblings of the one God, brothers of Paul and so of one another.

200. Hemer, *Book of Acts* 154-55 and n. 155.

201. Cf. Acts 18.2; 19.1; 21.4.

202. Rapske notes the likelihood that Ignatius was also able to partake of hospitality while being taken as a prisoner to Rome ('Travel' 20, and further 17-21).

203. We learn from Josephus of a Jewish community in Puteoli (*Ant.* 17.328).

parently two different parties.[204] Who these 'brothers' were Luke does not say. As with the most significant breakthrough in 11.20, so with the foundation of the church in what Luke would regard as the capital of the world, Luke passes it over with the briefest of references. This is one of the most aggravating features of Luke's narrative. For we know from Paul's letter to Rome that there was already a significant number of Christians in Rome. But Luke was evidently determined to focus Paul's sojourn in Rome entirely on his interaction with the Jewish community there. It is not the portrayal of a supportive Christian community on which Luke chooses to focus his final description of Paul, valuable as that would have been.[205] Rather, as soon becomes apparent, his concern was evidently to sketch out the final encounters between Paul and the representatives of his own people settled in Rome. It is possible that the believers who met Paul outside Rome are included in the 'we' who 'came to Rome' (28.16). but again Luke leaves this point wholly unclear. What was important for Luke was the arrival of Paul's party in Rome; even the Roman believers, having met Paul's party, are left on one side.

At the end of the journey Luke recalls (the last of the 'we' references) that Paul was after all a prisoner and briefly describes the conditions of his continuing custody (28.16).[206] The terms of his custody remained as liberal as they had been from the beginning (24.23).[207] The thought of Paul chained to his guard (28.20) has evoked many an imaginative scenario of Paul still preaching and seeking to convert his succession of captors; but they may well have some basis in historical fact.[208]

We know that there was a strong Jewish community in Rome at this

204. Is there any suggestion that the element of factionalism, or at least different apartment churches in Rome which did not entirely see eye to eye (Rom. 14.1–15.6; see above, §33.3f[iii]), is reflected at this point? *1 Clem.* 5.5 notes that Paul had to endure 'jealousy and strife', possibly a reference to his reception in Rome (cf. Barrett, *Acts* 2.1235-36).

205. Cf. and contrast, e.g., Acts 4.32-35; 9.31; 14.21-23. Acts 28.15 rules out the possibility that Luke wanted to attribute the coming of Christianity to Rome as the work of Paul (as Haenchen, *Acts* 730). Nor can we safely infer from Luke's account that the believers in Rome were now quite separate from the synagogues. The narrowness of Luke's focus leaves such issues unresolvable from his account.

206. On who Luke refers to as the 'soldier guarding him' (28.16), see Hemer, *Book of Acts* 199-200; Rapske, *Paul in Roman Custody* 174-77; Saddington, 'Military and Administrative Personnel in the New Testament' 2418; Barrett, *Acts* 2.1233.

207. The harsh conditions and treatment often endured in prisons as such is well documented by C. S. Wansink, *Chained in Christ: The Experience and Rhetoric of Paul's Imprisonments* (JSNTS 130; Sheffield: Sheffield Academic, 1996) ch. 1.

208. Cf. Phil. 1.12-18 and see further below, §34.4d. Josephus narrates of Agrippa's imprisonment in Rome (prior to the death of Tiberius) that the centurion guarding him and chained to him 'should be of humane character', and 'that he should be permitted to bathe every day and receive visits from his freedmen and friends' (*Ant.* 18.203).

time,[209] and an encounter between Paul and some representative Jews from one or several of the Roman synagogues is not unlikely.[210] In the manner of the typical Lucan summary dialogue (cf. 25.14-21), Paul rehearses the basic facts of his case — from his own perspective (28.17-20). The salient points are:

- his complete innocence of both the charges and the suspicions entertained against him — he has done nothing against either the people or the ancestral customs (28.17);[211]
- Jewish hostility countered by Roman conviction of his innocence (28.18; a repeated motif in chs. 21–26);
- Paul's denial of any antipathy towards his own nation (28.19).[212]
- On the contrary, the issue for Paul remains completely 'in-house' — what is at issue is 'the hope of Israel' (28.20).[213]

In other words, from Luke's perspective (as from Paul's), the coming together in Rome was not of representatives of different and hostile peoples or religions but of fellow members ('brothers') of the same people and religion.

For their part the Roman Jews accept Paul's assurances (28.21-22). Surprisingly, in the light of the hostility of the Jews regularly recorded by Luke in his account of many of Paul's missions, none of the accusations regularly brought against Paul elsewhere (in Asia Minor, Macedonia and Greece) had reached their ears. Even the implacable animosity of the Jews of Jerusalem (sustained over two years) had not been reported to them.[214] What are we to make of this?[215] At the least we have to say that Luke did not wish to depict the opposition of 'the Jews' to Paul himself as so total and complete as his earlier narrative seemed to indicate. 'The Jews' of Jerusalem were not so representative of 'the Jews' elsewhere; so far as the whole body of the Jews in Rome was concerned, Paul's claim that the primary issue focused on 'the hope of Israel' (28.20) was one they could examine without prejudice. On the other hand, they knew that 'this sect' which Paul represented was 'everywhere spoken against';[216] but Luke was evidently concerned to

209. See above, §33.2b.

210. The verb used, 'call together' (28.17), need not indicate Paul's presumption of an authority he did not possess ('summon, convene'), since it can have the lighter sense of 'invite to a gathering' (cf. 10.24).

211. Cf. Acts 21.21, 28; 24.12-13; 25.8.

212. Cf. Acts 22.3; 23.6; 24.14; 26.4-5.

213. Cf. Acts 23.6; 24.15; 26.6-7.

214. Even though there was regular contact between the Roman Jews and Judea (cf. Acts 2.10).

215. Haenchen regards it as 'unbelievable', 'impossible' (*Acts* 727).

216. Could this be a reflection of the hostility to the message of Jesus Messiah which

show that the Roman Jews saw this to be distinct from any charges against Paul himself. They were anxious therefore to hear what Paul's views on the subject were. Despite its bad reputation, they still saw the movement Paul represented as a Jewish 'sect' and were open to Paul's account of it.

d. The Final Scene (Acts 28.23-31)

Luke might have continued the previous scene without a break, but evidently he wanted to depict the major encounter as a separate scene. The scene just completed had in fact simply cleared the ground of the now-irrelevant accusations against Paul and had established the Roman Jews' openness to Paul's message. The final scene could then focus exclusively on this lasting image of Paul as Christian missionary and apologist.

And what is this image that Luke was so concerned to depict? Paul as preaching the gospel to Gentiles? Paul as building up the church? Paul as bearing witness before Caesar? No. His concern evidently was to portray Paul making a final statement about the relation of his gospel to Israel and to the Gentiles.[217] To the end of his defining description of earliest Christianity, this remains his primary concern: that Christianity can only understand itself in relation to the people of the law and the prophets as well as by means of their message, and that the salvation which this Christianity proclaimed is also for the other nations as well.

The response is as on the earlier occasions: some were being persuaded or convinced; others were disbelieving (28.24).[218] Luke uses the imperfect tense to indicate that this was not a once-for-all outcome;[219] rather a process of ongoing debate and dialogue had been begun whose tendency and likely outcome followed the same twofold pattern but which presumably continued through the next two years (28.30-31). The implication is that that this twofold response continued to characterize the response of the Jews into the time beyond Luke's narrative.

---

had occasioned the expulsion of many (believing) Jews from Rome eleven years earlier (see above, §21.1d)? But what does it say about the continuing attitude within the Roman synagogues to the apartment churches of Rome?

217. The twin emphases of Paul's testimony were the kingdom of God and Jesus (28.23). The fact that this twofold emphasis recurs in the very last verse (28.31) indicates that the choice of themes was neither accidental nor frivolous. As with the repeated emphasis in 1.3 and 6, Luke evidently wanted the continuity with Jesus' own proclamation of the kingdom in the Gospel to be clear beyond doubt. Equally fundamental to Paul's gospel was the claim that Jesus fulfilled the hopes of Israel as embodied in the law and the prophets (13.27; 24.14-15; 26.22-23; cf. particularly Luke 4.16-21; 24.25-27, 44-46; Acts 2.30-31; 3.18-26; 8.30-35; 10.43).

218. Acts 13.43-45; 14.1-2; 17.4-5, 10-13; 18.4-6, 19-20; 19.8-9; 23.6-9.

219. Contrast the aorist tenses of Acts 17.4 and 19.26.

To be noted is the fact that Paul's final word (28.25-28) does not follow a uniform rejection of his message by the Jews of Rome; in this final scene there is no more talk of 'the Jews' acting as a single body in animosity or hostility towards Paul.[220] Quite the contrary: Luke notes that the visitors leave, still disagreeing, even after Paul has made his denunciation. This confirms that Luke did not intend the quotation from Isa. 6.9-10[221] to be seen as Paul washing his hands of 'the Jews'; it simply indicates once more the mixed response that Paul's message would continue to receive from his own people.[222] A significant factor is that the text was part of Isaiah's commission. Notable also here is the fact that the quotation begins with the words of Isaiah's commission — 'Go to this people' (28.26), which by implication functions also as Paul's commission. In its function within canonical Isaiah the text certainly was not intended to put Isaiah off from fulfilling his commission in prophesying to his people; another sixty chapters of just such prophecy follow on this commission! And in the context so skilfully set out by Luke, the probability is that he intended the quotation here too to be understood in this light: that is, that Paul, who had drawn so much of his own commission from Isaiah,[223] would have understood Isaiah as indicating the course (and frustrations) of Paul's mission to his own and Isaiah's people, not as calling on him to end it in dismissive denunciation.

Acts 28.28[224] therefore should not be understood as Paul's final turn away from and rejection of his people in favour of the Gentiles — any more than the earlier denunciations of 13.46 and 18.6.[225] The idea of 'the salvation of God' be-

---

220. Contrast Acts 13.50; 14.4; 17.5; 18.12; 22.30; 23.12.

221. Isa. 6.9-10 was a passage much reflected on in early Christian writing, since it helped provide an answer to one of the most puzzling questions of all for the first Christians: why the Jews should have rejected their own Messiah in such large-scale numbers (Matt. 13.14-15/Mark 4.12/Luke 8.10; John 12.39-40; Rom. 11.7-8). The text serves this purpose here too (cf. the 'hardening' motif in 7.51, 19.9 and 28.27 with that in Rom. 11.25).

222. See J. Jervell, *Luke and the People of God: A New Look at Luke-Acts* (Minneapolis: Augsburg, 1972) particularly 49 and n. 21, and 63; also *Apg.* 629; cf. Barrett, *Acts* 2.1246. The crucial nature of this final passage for the issue of Luke's attitude to the Jews is indicated by J. B. Tyson, ed., *Luke-Acts and the Jewish People* (London: SCM, 1988); see particularly the essay by Tyson, 'The Problem of Jewish Reception in Acts' 124-37 (especially 124-27); also R. L. Brawley, *Luke-Acts and the Jews* (SBLMS 33; Atlanta: Scholars, 1987) 75-77. L. E. Keck, 'The Jewish Paul among the Gentiles: Two Portrayals', in J. T. Fitzgerald et al., eds., *Early Christianity and Classical Culture,* A. J. Malherbe FS (NovTSupp 110; Leiden: Brill, 2003) 461-81, concludes by asking: 'Is Luke-Acts itself evidence of a struggle to keep the wild olive grafted into the root?' (481).

223. See Acts 13.47, 22.17-21 and 26.18, 23.

224. 'Let it therefore be known to you that this salvation of God has been sent to the Gentiles; they will listen' (28.28).

225. *Pace* E. Haenchen, 'The Book of Acts as Source Material for the History of Early

ing known 'to the nations' is an allusion to Ps. 67.2,[226] a passage which expresses the thought of God's faithfulness to Israel as part of his universal saving concern for all nations. The same point had been implicit in the multiple allusions to Isaiah in Luke 2.30-32:[227] the salvation of God for all peoples, Gentiles as well as Jews. In his description of John the Baptist (Luke 3.4-6) Luke had extended the quotation of Isa. 40.3-5 to climax in the phrase 'all flesh shall see the salvation of God', to make the same point: Israel is most true to its heritage when it recognizes God's saving concern for the other nations as well. Just the same point was made by Luke in the opening scene of Jesus' ministry in Jesus' exposition of the prophecy from Isa. 61.1-2: the commission of Jesus was for Gentile as well as Jew (Luke 4.18-27). And, by no means least, it was the same point that Luke recalls James, brother of Jesus, as making in his crucial ruling in the Jerusalem council by his quotation from Amos: the restoration of Israel is with a view to the rest of humanity seeking the Lord (15.16-18).[228]

The implication here, then, is that the 'turn to the Gentiles' is simply part of God's larger scheme of salvation and does not imply a rejection of Israel. That is to say, the Lukan Paul is no different from the Paul of Romans 9–11: the mixed and largely negative response of the Jews to the gospel of Messiah Jesus and the positive response of the Gentiles is simply a phase in the larger purposes of God to include all, Jew and Gentile, within his saving concern. In other words, what Luke records is not so much a final scene as a definitively typical scene — the ongoing debate between believers in Messiah Jesus and traditional Jews as definitive for Christianity; the debate continues, some Jews being persuaded, others disbelieving.[229] So it was and so, Luke implies, it will continue to be, for this is the inevitable consequence of Christianity's own identity, given its foundational beliefs in the kingdom of Israel's God and in Jesus as Messiah and Lord.

Christianity', in L. E. Keck and J. L. Martyn, eds., *Studies in Luke-Acts* (Philadelphia: Fortress/ London: SPCK, 1966) 258-78: 'Luke has written the Jews off' (278); heavily reinforced by Sanders, *The Jews in Luke-Acts,* particularly 80-83, 297-99; and insisted on by D. Schwartz, 'The End of the Line: Paul in the Canonical Book of Acts', in W. S. Babcock, ed., *Paul and the Legacies of Paul* (Dallas: Southern Methodist University, 1990) 3-24 (here 10 and 313-14 n. 38). But see my 'The Question of Antisemitism in the New Testament', in J. D. G. Dunn, ed., *Jews and Christians: The Parting of the Ways AD 70 to 135* (WUNT 66: Tübingen: Mohr Siebeck, 1992/Grand Rapids: Eerdmans, 1999) 177-212 (here 187-95); also *Partings* §8.4; similarly Hvalvik, 'Jewish Believers' 197, with other bibliography in n. 95; and Sellner, *Das Heil Gottes* 383-402, 494.

226. Cf. Ps. 98.3 and Isa. 40.5.

227. Isa. 42.6; 46.13; 49.6; 52.10.

228. See further above, §27.3e.

229. Omerzu observes that too little attention is paid to the disparity between the detailed reports of chs. 21–26 and the brevity of the Rome narrative in 28.16-31 and concludes that only 28.16, 23 and 30-31 contain traditional material ('Schweigen' 128, 155-56).

The fade-out scene is entirely positive. The implication is that Paul remained in custody (28.16, 20), but at his own expense (in a rented apartment?), sustained by the financial gifts of his supporters.[230] Nothing is said of the progress of the case against Paul or of an appearance before Caesar (even though implied in 27.24).[231] And nothing continues to be said of the Roman believers, or even of Paul's own co-workers, or, once again, of any letters Paul might have written; the focus remains tight upon Paul himself.

The significant points that Luke evidently wanted to remain with his readers were twofold.

- The chief features of Paul's message — 'proclaiming the kingdom of God and teaching what related to the Lord Jesus Christ' — match the initial emphasis of Acts (1.3) and continue to imply complete continuity with the preaching of Jesus.
- Paul 'continued to welcome all who came to him', preaching this message 'with all boldness and without hindrance *(akōlytōs)*'.[232] In context that can mean nothing other than a sustained proclamation to all, Jew as well as Gentile. Despite the depressing but realistic prognosis provided by Isaiah (28.26-27), the obligation to preach to *all* the good news of God's kingdom and of Jesus as Messiah and Lord remained unbroken, and the final picture is of Paul continuing to fulfil this commission into the undisclosed future.[233]

And thus Luke gives his final answer to the question which motivated the telling of his tale from the first. What is this movement which we now call Christianity? It is the extension of Israel, of Isaiah's commission to Israel, of Israel's

---

230. On the conditions of the liberal custody, see Rapske, *Paul in Roman Custody* 177-82, 236-39, 322-33, 381-85.

231. Is this because the outcome of the trial before Nero was unsuccessful in the event, and Paul suffered martyrdom (as tradition relates; see below, §34.7)? Quite probably, Luke, having already alluded to the trial before Nero (27.24) and earlier to Paul's death (20.25), did not want to end his narrative on this note. Hence the earlier emphasis that the vindication has already been given, and not by the emperor, but by divine warrant (28.1-7). Even this sobering issue is set to one side so that the narrative can reach the conclusion to which it has been driving.

232. The latter is a legal term, 'without let or hindrance'; see Barrett, *Acts* 2.1253. See further D. L. Mealand, 'The Close of Acts and Its Hellenistic Vocabulary', *NTS* 36 (1990) 583-97 (here 589-95), the term referring, perhaps, to the 'unrestricted' use Paul had of his rented accommodation.

233. Cf. D. Marguerat, 'The Enigma of the Silent Closing of Acts (28:16-31)', in Moessner, ed., *Jesus and the Heritage of Israel* 284-304; slightly fuller in *First Christian Historian* ch. 10; and on the open-endedness of Acts see further L. Alexander, 'Reading Luke-Acts from Back to Front', in Verheyden, ed., *Unity of Luke-Acts* 419-46, reprinted in Alexander, *Acts in Its Ancient Literary Context* 207-29.

commission to be a light to the Gentiles. It is a movement which Paul embodies. It is a movement which can only understand itself in relation to Israel, to the hope of Israel, as fulfilling that hope and contributing to its further fulfilment. It is a movement which can be true to itself only in ongoing dialogue with Jews, both those who respect it and are open to its claims, but also those who dispute it and reject its claims. Only thus will it be true to its own character and commission as called by God to proclaim the salvation of God to all.

e. The Prison Epistles

The historian of Christianity's beginnings, however, must step out of Luke's spotlight, to avoid being blinded by it, and must attempt to discern what was happening in the surrounding shadows. In two areas it is necessary to say something and possible to do so.

One is on a subject close to Paul's own heart, 'his anxiety for all the churches'. For if Paul's imprisonment was as liberal as Luke says (28.16, 30-31), then he would certainly have been able to receive visitors and messengers from the various churches of his mission. And equally, he would have been able to maintain some of the pattern of correspondence which he had developed during the Aegean mission. It is to this period of imprisonment that we should probably date the 'prison' epistles: Philippians, Philemon and the disputed Colossians.[234] Attractive as it is to refer the latter two in particular to an earlier Ephesian imprisonment,[235] the weight of consideration points more likely to a Roman origin for the letters — in particular:[236]

- An Ephesian imprisonment is at best a deduction from Paul's reference to a crisis experienced in Asia (2 Cor. 1.8), which sounds as though it was much shorter and sharper than the liberal conditions envisaged for Rome.[237]

---

234. Presumably the letter to the Laodiceans was written at the same time and was probably carried by the same messengers as were responsible for the letters to Philemon and Colossians (Col. 4.15). The implication of 4.15 is that the house church hosted by Nympha(s) was in Laodicea.

235. The view of a majority of non-English-language commentators, including Murphy-O'Connor, *Paul* 175-79, 183; see also above, §28 n. 52. The most important factor in favour is the proximity of Colossae to Ephesus (only about 120 miles away).

236. See particularly P. T. O'Brien, *Commentary on Philippians* (NIGTC; Grand Rapids: Eerdmans, 1991) 19-26; Schnelle, *History* 131-33; also *Paul* 367-69; Bockmuehl, *Philippians* 25-32; Wilckens, *Theologie* 1/3.40-42.

237. A minority view is that Caesarea was the place from which the prison epistles were

- The failure to speak of the collection in letters from Ephesus would be inexplicable in view of the collection's importance in other letters of the Ephesus-centred mission (1 and 2 Corinthians, Romans).[238]
- The references to 'the praetorium' ('throughout the whole praetorium') and to 'the saints of the household of Caesar'[239] in Phil. 1.13 and 4.22 are most obviously to be read as references to the imperial guard in Rome, from whose ranks the prison guard would presumably have been drawn, and to the imperial slaves in Nero's palace.[240]

Although no certainty can be achieved on the question, therefore, I will follow the working hypothesis that the three letters in view were indeed written during Paul's Roman imprisonment and examine them next (§§34.4-6).

The actual sequence of the letters is an unsolvable problem. None of them can have been written very early in Paul's imprisonment. The to-and-fro movements to and from Philippi — news of Paul's imprisonment, the gift brought by Epaphroditus, news of Epaphroditus's illness and the distress it caused in Philippi — must have covered many weeks.[241] Similarly the timescale presupposed in Philemon and Colossians — news of Paul's imprisonment reaching Colossae, the presumably less easily managed trip of the slave Onesimus to the imprisoned Paul, his conversion by Paul and period of service on behalf of Paul — all imply a similarly lengthy period. However, it does not really matter which order the letters are dealt with; I choose to leave Colossians to the last, simply because that fits better with the circumstances which I envisage to lie behind the composition of the letter by someone other than Paul, but with Paul's approval (§34.6).

The other crucial task, of course, is to inquire what actually happened to Paul himself, how his imprisonment ended, and, inevitably, how his life ended,

---

sent (e.g., Kümmel, *Introduction* 324-32, 346-49; see §28 n. 52 again). But regular communication between Caesarea and Philippi in particular is much more difficult to envisage than between Rome and Philippi, and death was a much less probable outcome of the imprisonment in Caesarea than of that in Rome.

238. Cf. Wedderburn, 'Paul's Collection' 102. Brown thinks that Paul would have mentioned the Philippians' contribution to the collection had he been looking back from prison in Rome (*Introduction* 496); but the letter focuses almost exclusively on the close personal relationship between Paul and the church in Philippi (see §34.4b below).

239. That is, officials, servants and slaves in the emperor's administration and service.

240. Bockmuehl notes the unlikelihood that Ephesus would have had a 'praetorium', since Asia was a senatorial rather than an imperial province. He notes also that the vast majority of the imperial civil service were based in the West; of 660 individuals identified in inscriptions as *Caesaris* ('belonging to Caesar'), about 70 percent lived in Rome, and 96 percent were either in Rome, Italy or North Africa (*Philippians* 28, 30-31).

241. See, e.g., Martin-Hawthorne, *Philippians* xlviii-xlix; and below, §§34.4a(i) and (iv).

how his passion was completed. Besides which, any more that can be deduced about the apartment churches in Rome in the period building up to the persecution under Nero will be a bonus (§34.7).

34.4. Paul's Letter to the Philippians

a. Introductory Matters

(i) *Date.* As just indicated, it is most likely that Philippians was written/dictated by Paul (and Timothy) during Paul's period of liberal custody in Rome, that is, about 61 or 62. Could we be more confident that Paul spent some time in jail in Ephesus, the letter could be referred to that earlier period, in which case the letter would have to be dated to about 55. Since Paul's thought was already well developed by then, the six- or seven-year time difference need not be regarded as particularly significant. Rome was more distant from Philippi than Ephesus, but Philippi stood on the main east-west highway, the Via Egnatia, along which there was regular and heavy traffic from the capital of the empire to the east.[242] Given regular communication through casual and specific visits, the sequence of news passing back and forth between Paul and Philippi need have lasted no more than a year.

(ii) *Unity.* Next to 2 Corinthians, Philippians has proved to be the most popular candidate for the thesis that some NT letters in their present canonical form were actually produced by combining the whole or parts of different letters.[243] In this case the thesis is that Philippians has been formed by the combination of two or three different letters.[244] The basic rationale is straightforward: in particular, the transition from 3.1 to 3.2 (or 3.1a to 3.1b) is very abrupt; a calm sequence of exhortation is suddenly interrupted by the warning, 'Beware of the dogs . . . !' (3.2). Since this could be readily explained as the seam between dif-

242. The journey by land from Philippi to Rome would have taken about four weeks (Schnelle, *History* 133; also *Paul* 369). See further above, §31.2b.

243. Becker notes that Polycarp, in his letter to the Philippians, refers both to Paul writing letters (plural) to the Philippians and to 'his epistle' (*Phil.* 3.2; 11.3) (*Paul* 313); the plural could possibly refer to the canonical Philippians and a lost letter.

244. Bibliography, e.g., in Brown, *Introduction* 497-98; Bormann provides a useful tabulation of the diverse theories partitioning Philippians into three parts (*Philippi* 110, 115). Murphy-O'Connor (*Paul* 216-30) typifies the confidence of those who argue against a single letter: phrases like 'it is inconceivable', 'unacceptable assumption', 'we must assume' suggest an attempt to narrow historical options unduly in order to strengthen the case for the favoured hypothesis; and attempts to penetrate into Paul's consciousness ('Paul quickly realized', 'Paul's self-absorption', he 'was sending contradictory messages') are more imaginative than historical.

ferent letters, it becomes more plausible to explain other tensions in the letter as similar, if less obvious, seams. I have some problems with this thesis.

- If, *ex hypothesi,* we assume that later editors felt free to truncate or amend Paul's letters in order to unite them in a single letter, why did they not make the transition smoother? In other words, the hypothesis does not solve the problem of the abrupt transition.
- If, conversely, they respected what the revered Paul wrote so much that they would not have modified or amended Paul's text, how can we then infer that they felt free to chop off the letter framework and possibly other sections of one or more letters in order to combine them into a single letter form?
- The lack of good precedents and parallels for such a practice in the literary world of the day leaves it as a hypothesis almost entirely dependent on its internal plausibility.

On the contrary, there is no difficulty in envisaging a number of scenarios which could have resulted in the letter leaving Paul in its present form. The most obvious one is the likelihood that Paul's custody, liberal as it was, did not permit extended periods of dictation. Consequently, composition may have had to be spread over a number of days, including one or two intervals (court officials, for example, demanding an interview), in the course of which reports of a serious development at Philippi sparked off an angry passage, perhaps to be inserted at its present awkward point, since time did not permit a revision or a fair copy.[245]

(iii) *Opponents.* Assuming that such an insertion (3.2–4.1) was occasioned by news of the arrival in Philippi of a group whom Paul regarded as a threat to the church he had established, can we identify the group? The most obvious conclusion to be drawn from 3.2-6 is that they were a group who stressed their Jewish pedigree and who presumably argued that the commitment and status of the uncircumcised Gentile believers in Philippi was both defective[246] and indicative of their immaturity (cf. 3.15). Paul does not speak of them as incomers, but if the

---

245. For other arguments in favour of the letter's integrity see Kümmel, *Introduction* 332-35; O'Brien, *Philippians* 10-18; J. T. Fitzgerald, 'Philippians, Epistle to the', *ABD* 5.320-22; Schnelle, *History* 135-38; and further Bockmuehl, *Philippians* 20-25; Martin-Hawthorne, *Philippians* xxx-xxxiv.

246. The characterization of those warned against as 'the mutilation *(katatomē)*' reflects the equivalent characterization of Jews as 'the circumcision *(peritomē)*' and the similar 'play' on the cutting involved in circumcision as in Gal. 5.12. The invective in both cases is fierce: 'Beware of the dogs'; since Homer 'dog' had been a slightly dismissive insult throughout the Mediterranean world (LSJ 1015).

Jewish community in Philippi was as small as Acts 16.13 seems to imply, it is more likely that they were recent arrivals in Philippi.

Were they Christians/believers in Messiah Jesus? Probably yes. They would not have constituted such a threat to the Pauline believers otherwise. Paul's playing off his knowledge of Christ against the value of Jewish privilege (3.7-11) should probably be seen as pointing in the same direction. Similarly, to call them 'enemies of the cross of Christ' (3.18) would have had more bite if those being targetted thought of themselves as belonging to the crucified Messiah. The parallel of 3.5 with 2 Cor. 11.22 (those who made much of their identity as Hebrews, that is, who clung to a traditional or conservatively Jewish identity) suggests that the parallel extends to 2 Cor. 11.4 and even Gal. 1.6-9 (they preached what Paul regarded as a different gospel and another Jesus).

Were the incomers emissaries from Jerusalem? The description of the traditional Jewish believers in Jerusalem (Acts 21.20-21) has an eerie echo of the position from which Paul distances himself in Phil. 3.5-7. So one could readily and plausibly envisage those Jerusalem believers who were so antagonistic to Paul taking upon themselves or commissioning others to visit some of Paul's churches to carry the fight against Paul's 'apostasy' into the assemblies founded in the Pauline mission. However, that there was a specific link to Jerusalem, let alone to a particular individual like James, is less likely; in that case we would have expected passages in Philippians parallel to the disclaimers in Gal. 1.17-24 (Paul's gospel is independent of Jerusalem) and 4.25 (the present Jerusalem as a situation of slavery) and to the dismissive comments regarding the 'super-apostles' of 2 Cor. 11.5 and 12.11. The evidence demands no more than a continued campaign, deriving ultimately from Jerusalem, or as part of the aftermath of the confrontation in Antioch, and pursued (perhaps) spasmodically and by different groups, without central coordination but of similar motivation and character — and all reflecting the tensions within the new movement which Paul had attempted to address at length in his letter to Rome.

Were such opponents a single group, or were there different groups and challenges? The key evidence here is the reference in Phil. 3.18-19 to what sound like libertarians ('their god is their belly and their glory is their shame'), a group, in other words, possibly quite different from the traditionalists implied in 3.4-6.[247] In fact, however, such language seems to have become established around

247. When the heyday of the Gnostic hypothesis was beginning to fade, an influential thesis was that of H. Koester, 'The Purpose of the Polemic of a Pauline Fragment', *NTS* 8 (1961-62) 317-32, who envisaged Jewish Gnostic perfectionists who maintained a 'radicalized spiritualistic eschatology . . . typical of early Christian Gnosticism' (331). Schnelle thinks of 'Hellenistic Jewish Christian missionaries that combined Judaizing and enthusiastic elements' (*History* 140-41). Fitzgerald provides a concise review of the debate ('Philippians'

this period in Jewish polemic against what was perceived as apostasy.[248] Its use in such conventional polemic means that it cannot be used to identify particular viewpoints. The fact that *T. Mos.* 7 can employ such language in what was probably an attack on Pharisees[249] may be sufficient indication that the language belongs to the category of disinformation propaganda or to the imaginative caricature of a polemic of suspicion such as both Christianity and Judaism were to suffer from in subsequent centuries. So Paul may well have had in view the same group as in 3.2-6 and simply drew, rather cavalierly, on these terms to label what he regarded as the group's irresponsibility.[250]

(iv) *Occasion.* In the light of this we can conclude that the occasion for the letter seems to have been fivefold:

- The Philippians had sent him financial support through Epaphroditus; this is a thank you letter (4.18).
- During his time with Paul, Epaphroditus had fallen seriously ill, and news of his illness had reached back to Philippi; Epaphroditus himself was also homesick and concerned about the distress his illness would cause among his friends in Philippi; Paul was therefore sending him back, presumably as the bearer of the letter (2.25-30).
- Christian Jewish missionaries had reached Philippi and were demeaning the status of the Philippian believers because they lacked the marks which attest the people of God's covenant (3.2-6); Paul responds with the same strength of feeling that characterized Galatians and 2 Corinthians 10–13.
- Paul still hoped to be released and to be able to visit Philippi again (1.26; 2.24); his hopes and intentions for such visits are a frequent feature of his letters.[251]
- Paul also took the opportunity of the letter to offer some pastoral counsel on strained relationships, which presumably had been reported to him (4.2-4).

---

323). W. Cotter, 'Our *Politeuma* Is in Heaven: The Meaning of Philippians 3.17-21', in B. H. McLean, ed., *Origins and Method,* J. C. Hurd FS (JSNTS 86; Sheffield: JSOT, 1993) 92-104, sets the passage in the context of the criticisms often levelled at the voluntary associations (98-101; see above, §30 n. 232).

248. Philo, *Virt.* 182; 3 Macc. 7.11; *T. Mos.* 7.4.

249. Note particularly *T. Mos.* 7.9.

250. Cf. O'Brien, *Philippians* 26-35.

251. Rom. 15.23-24; 1 Cor. 16.5-6; 2 Cor. 13.1; Gal. 4.20; 1 Thess. 2.17-18; Phlm. 22. Such a desire, of course, conflicts with Paul's long-term plan to use Rome as a base or springboard for a mission to Spain (Rom. 15.23-24, 28). But four or five years had passed since he formulated that hope, and his time in Rome may well have revealed to him the impracticality of his earlier ambition. Besides which, Paul was notorious for changing his travel plans (cf. Rom. 1.13; 2 Cor. 1.12–2.13; 12.14-21; 1 Thess. 2.17-18)!

b. A Letter of Friendship

Most commentators on the Pauline letters regard, quite rightly, the letter to Philippi[252] as the warmest and most joyful of all Paul's extant letters.[253] There is nothing of the assertiveness which expands the greetings in Galatians and Romans. The following thanksgiving (1.3-11) is more extended than that of 1 Corinthians, curtailed as the latter is by Paul's immediate appeal for unity (1 Cor. 1.10), less fraught than that of 2 Corinthians and warmer than that of either of the Thessalonian letters. It offers the usual thanksgivings, prayers and reassurances. But notable is the immediate recollection of the way the Philippians had shared *(koinōnia)* in the gospel from the beginning (1.5). Unusually, he cites their mutual affection: 1.7 can be rendered both 'because I hold you in my heart' and 'because you hold me in your hearts' — perhaps deliberately to embrace both meanings. He stresses again their 'mutual sharing *(synkoinōnous)* in God's grace', both in his bonds/imprisonment and in the defence *(apologia)* and confirmation *(bebaiōsis)* of the gospel (1.7).[254] His affirmation of longing for them and his prayer for them has a particular intimacy: he longs for them 'with the affection *(splanchna)* of Christ Jesus' (1.8), a phrase which occurs only here; and the exuberant prayer that their love might 'overflow *(perisseuein)*' likewise uses language unusual in his letter openings (1.9). And the prayer for discernment *(aisthēsis)* and enabling 'to approve what is really important *(dokimazein ta diapheronta)*' indicates a strong confidence in their spiritual maturity.[255]

The immediate sequel to this opening is not to teach or exhort the Philippian believers but to reassure them of his own well-being and of the positive outcomes of his imprisonment (1.12-18). Paul remains confident of his future deliverance *(sōtēria)* 'through your prayers and the supply of the Spirit of Jesus Christ' (1.19) and only wants that 'deliverance' to include the sparing of his life, 'for you', 'for your progress and joy in faith', in order that he might be able to come to them again to give them fresh grounds for boasting in Christ Jesus

252. I do not intend the heading 'A Letter of Friendship' to denote a technical form, though it is popularly so used; see, e.g., G. D. Fee, *Philippians* (NICNT; Grand Rapids: Eerdmans, 1995) 2-7, 12-14 ('a Christian "Hortatory Letter of Friendship"'). Here as with Paul's other letters, there is a danger of labelling the letter and then critiquing Paul for failure to observe some of the conventions of the form. Bockmuehl's remarks on the subject are judicious (*Philippians* 33-40).

253. There is a richer concentration of *chara* ('joy') and *chairō* ('rejoice') in Philippians than in the rest of Paul's letters: *chara* (5) — 1.4, 25; 2.2, 29; 4.1; *chairō* (8) — 1.18 (twice); 2.17, 18, 28; 3.1; 4.4, 10; cf. Romans (3, 4), 1 Corinthians (0, 4), 2 Corinthians (5, 8), Galatians (1, 0), 1 Thessalonians (4, 2), 2 Thessalonians (0, 0). Note also the frequency of the *koinōnia* ('sharing') word-group: 1.5; 2.1; 3.10; 4.14.

254. See Wansink, *Chained in Christ* 138-45.

255. In Rom. 12.1-2 this enabling evidences the renewal of the mind.

(1.24-26). He remains equally confident that the Philippians will continue to share his passion for the gospel and the sufferings which such outreach entails (1.27-30).[256]

The appeals and exhortations which follow are again evidence of a particular warmth and intimacy. Paul appeals to their experience of 'encouragement in Christ', of the 'consolation of love' and of 'sharing *(koinōnia)* in the Spirit' (2.1), and trusts that they will 'complete my joy' by being of one mind, motivated by the same love, thinking as one (2.2), doing nothing out of selfish ambition or self-conceit, but 'in humility regarding others as better than themselves' (2.3), and looking not to their own interests but to those of others (2.4). The concern is not so much (or not at all) that Paul had heard anything which gave him pause: the Philippian church was not at all like its near Macedonian neighbour in Thessalonica, disturbed by eschatological anxieties, or like the church in Corinth, with its dangerous tendencies to factionalism. The concern here is that a maturing congregation will continue to mature. So there was no need for Paul to instruct or rebuke on particular issues of belief or conduct; rather, he could use the opportunity to set the sights of the Philippian believers on the ultimate model and goal of Christ (2.5-11) and to encourage them in the ongoing process of 'working out their salvation' (2.12), confident of the divine enabling to do so (2.13, as in 1.6). A community life with which onlookers cannot find fault will make their witness all that more effective and demonstrate the effectiveness of the gospel which he had preached to them (2.14-16).[257] So even if Paul's life was not spared, his death would be a joyous sacrifice and thank-offering of their faith, a matter for their mutual rejoicing (2.17-18).

The warmth of the relationship between Paul and the church in Philippi is reflected also in the family and filial warmth between Paul and his chief co-worker, Timothy (2.20-23). And the tenderness of the relations between Epaphroditus and his fellow believers in Philippi, as also Paul's resonance with them, has already been noted (3.26-30).[258]

The insertion of the warning passage (3.2-21) and the brief exhortation to Syntyche and Euodia to be of the same mind (4.2-3) are bracketed with repeated calls to 'rejoice' (3.1; 4.4) and reassurance of Paul's joy over them — 'my beloved and longed-for brothers, my joy and my crown' (4.1). And the closing paragraphs return to the same theme (4.10). There is a marked tranquility in the gentle exhortation and assurance of 4.5-9 (surprising, given Paul's circum-

256. Ware argues that 1.27-30 implies the Philippians' own active missionary work (*Mission* ch. 5).

257. See below, n. 270.

258. See further R. Metzner, 'In aller Freundschaft. Ein frühchristlicher Fall freundschaftlicher Gemeinschaft (Phil 2.25-30)', *NTS* 48 (2002) 111-31.

stances). And particularly poignant are Paul's reflections on the Philippians' fellowship with him and support for him from the beginning, and his evident pleasure and satisfaction that it was the church of Philippi which had continued to support him financially in his present situation (in prison) — 'a fragrant offering, a sacrifice acceptable and pleasing to God' (4.15-18).[259] Even the very personal letter of Paul to Philemon does not contain such warmth of feeling and expression. If Paul had a favourite church, it would have been the church in Philippi.

c. What Do We Learn about the Philippian Church?

The letter to Philippi is remarkable as one side of a personal conversation between close friends. As mutual confidants their conversation focuses on the matters which form the bond linking them together. It is not surprising, therefore, that we gain little information about the Philippian believers and the situation of their church; such whispered intimacies say much about the two parties' mutual affection, and any allusions to their circumstances are frustratingly allusive.

Thus we learn that there were two groups of office-bearers, or probably more accurately, two leadership roles which had already emerged in Philippi — 'overseers *(episkopoi)* and deacons *(diakonoi)*' (1.1). It will hardly be coincidental that these become the titles for regular offices or roles in the churches of the next generation.[260] Whether the structures of church organization which we see in 1 Timothy 3 and Titus 1 were already emerging in Philippi, it is not possible to determine now. Certainly some leadership and administrative functions must be attributed to the *episkopoi* and *diakonoi* of Philippi.[261] But how well defined or

---

259. Bormann sees the letter of thanks (4.10-20) 'as the key to understanding the relation between Paul and the Philippian community' (*Philippi* ch. 6.3; and further chs. 7-8). Pilhofer notes that 'the business *(logos)* of giving and receiving' (4.15) was the first and most important *raison d'etre* for some associations' existence (*Philippi* 147-52). See also BDAG 601; and further G. W. Peterman, *Paul's Gift from Philippi: Conventions of Gift Exchange and Christian Giving* (SNTSMS 92; Cambridge: Cambridge University, 1997) 53-68, who argues that 'in each point of his response the apostle corrects a possible Greco-Roman understanding of the significance of the gift with a Jewish understanding of it' (158-59); Ascough, *Paul's Macedonian Associations* 139-44, 149-57.

260. I assume here that the Pastoral Epistles (1 and 2 Timothy and Titus), where these offices/roles are clearly well established, reflect the period between about 80 and 100; see vol. 3 and, in the meantime, my *Unity and Diversity* §30.1. Schnelle sees the presence of overseers and deacons already in Philippi as a further indication that Philippians was written later (from Rome) rather than earlier (from Ephesus), that is, only about six years after the church was founded (*History* 132).

261. 'That Paul should refer to two definite groups in the prescript of his letter suggests

(alternatively) amorphous or embryonic these functions were some twelve years after the church began, and to what extent the use of these titles indicates a drawing on religious or secular precedents, we cannot tell.[262] It is significant, for example, that when Polycarp wrote to Philippi about fifty years later, there was no one there claiming or who could claim the title *episkopos*.[263] So, some sort of structure we can certainly see, but its outlines remain obscure.

The only individual Philippian believers whose names we learn, apart from Epaphroditus, are Euodia and Syntyche and Clement (4.2-3). The two women seem to have had some sort of falling out, but Paul makes so little of it that it cannot have been very serious.[264] More important, Paul's mention of them, and the fact that he regards their falling out as sufficiently serious for him to name them publicly in a letter to be read to the assembled believers, probably implies that they were among the leaders of the church.[265] The fact that they are commended by Paul because they 'struggled along with me in the gospel' suggests that they formed part of Paul's mission team during his Macedonian mission, which confirms their prominence within the local assembly. Clement is the only one named of a number of 'co-workers'.[266] What is not clear is whether they functioned in

---

that they have special, self-evident authority' (O'Brien, *Philippians* 48). Martin-Hawthorne are sympathetic to the early interpretation (Chrysostom) of the phrase in the sense, 'bishops who are also deacons', 'overseers who serve' (*Philippians* 11-12).

262. J. Reumann, 'Contributions of the Philippian Community to Paul and to Earliest Christianity' *NTS* 39 (1993) 438-57, concludes that *episkopoi* and *diakonoi* were titles adopted by the Philippians themselves for leaders in the house churches (449-50); the suggestion is taken up by Bormann, *Philippi* 210-11. Pilhofer similarly suggests that the title *episkopoi* reflects a specifically Philippian phenomenon, a local usage within associations, although evidence for such usage is sparse (*Philippi* 140-47); see further Ascough, *Paul's Macedonian Associations* 80-81, 131-32. Bockmuehl is less impressed (*Philippians* 53-55). The most common inference made is that the *episkopoi* and *diakonoi* had been responsible for collecting and transmitting the financial gifts made by the Philippian church to Paul (e.g., Murphy-O'Connor, *Paul* 217; Wedderburn, *History* 134). See further Reumann, 'Church Office in Paul' 82-91.

263. If there had been, Polycarp would probably have referred to him or counselled submission to him, as Ignatius does regularly (*Eph.* 1.3; 3.2; 4.1; 6.1; *Magn.* 6.1; 7.1; *Trall.* 2.1; 3.1; *Phld.* 8.1; *Smyrn.* 8.1-2; 9.1).

264. However, N. A. Dahl, 'Euodia and Syntyche and Paul's Letter to the Philippians', in White and Yarbrough, eds., *The Social World of the First Christians* 3-15, thinks the disagreement between these two 'outstanding and influential members of the church in Philippi' was the chief problem faced by Paul. But Tellbe's description of 'a community in disharmony' is overstated; he thinks it was related to the opposition the community faced (*Paul between Synagogue and State* 228-30). O'Brien voices similar cautions (*Philippians* 478-80).

265. Ascough, *Paul's Macedonian Associations* 134-35, and further 136-38.

266. Is the one addressed in 4.3 Paul's unnamed 'true yoke-fellow *(syzyge)*' or someone called Syzygos? No one can tell for sure, but as a name it is nowhere else attested (cf. O'Brien,

this role only while Paul was actively present among them, or whether they continued to promote the mission Paul had begun.

The fact that none of those named have recognizably Jewish names suggests that the Philippian congregation was predominantly Gentile.[267] This would accord with the depiction in Acts of a minimal Jewish constituency in Philippi (Acts 16.13). Although we can conclude from Phil. 3.2-6 that incoming Jewish missionaries or emissaries were ruffling some feathers (particularly Paul's!), there is nothing in the letter itself to suggest that the pattern of Galatia and Corinth was being repeated, that is, that the Pauline converts in Philippi had welcomed the incomers and were being enticed by them to abandon the central message of Paul's gospel. Their undivided loyalty to Paul was one of the factors which gave them a special place in Paul's heart.

The generosity of the Philippian believers is certainly indicated (particularly 4.15-18), and the dedication of their messenger Epaphroditus was presumably a reflection of the Philippian church's own commitment to support Paul (2.30). Other allusions to their requests to God and their needs (4.6, 19) are fairly formal (though no doubt entirely sincere) and tell us nothing about the Philippian believers' circumstances and particular needs. So we cannot say anything about the composition of the church, or about the members' social status and relative standing in Philippi itself,[268] though the implication of 2 Cor. 8.3 is that they were not particularly well off.[269] Likewise the talk of being 'in the midst of a crooked and perverse generation, in which you shine like stars in the world, holding fast the word of life' (2.15-16) has too much of a formal character to give us any clear idea as to whether the church in Philippi was very active in evangelism,[270] or was coming under any particular pressure from neighbours or offi-

---

Philippians 480-81). Could this be a reference to Luke (Bockmuehl, *Philippians* 241)? Other possibilities in Martin-Hawthorne, *Philippians* 242.

267. As Kümmel notes, 3.3 assumes that the readers are not circumcised Jews (*Introduction* 322). Oakes deduces the likelihood that, given the high percentage of Roman citizens in Philippi (he estimates 40 percent), it is likely that the church in Philippi had a similar unusually high percentage of Roman members (he estimates 36 percent); 'no other city in which Paul founded a church is likely to have had this many Romans' (*Philippians* 76).

268. Pilhofer notes that there are no Thracian names among the sixty-four Philippian Christians known to us from the first six centuries, which suggests a church focused in the city itself, the Roman colony (*Philippi* 240-43).

269. The Macedonians had contributed to the collection 'beyond their means' (2 Cor. 8.3); see further Ascough, *Paul's Macedonian Associations* 118-22.

270. Ware argues that the *epechein* of 2.16 means 'holding forth [not 'holding fast'] the word of life' (*Mission* 256-70); Dickson disagrees strongly (*Mission-Commitment* 107-14); O'Brien thinks the rendering 'hold fast' is preferable (*Philippians* 297). An interesting contrast with 1 Thess. 1.7-8 and Rom. 1.8 is the fact that the thanksgiving in Phil. 1.3-11 makes no mention of the Philippians' activity in spreading their faith.

cials. One would expect the earlier allusion to the Philippians' 'opponents' to be more detailed if there was an active opposition and repression (1.28),[271] and the suffering of the Philippian believers referred to in 1.29-30 could be as much a reflection of their sharing in Paul's current suffering, perhaps by sacrificial giving and support through Epaphroditus.[272]

One intriguing allusion is to 'our citizenship in heaven' (3.20), which, once again, is too allusive to provide useful information, but which could imply a rather small close-knit group, living lives divorced from the cares and responsibilities of citizens and able to concentrate on their higher citizenship and on their mutual relationships and support for Paul.[273] One consequent disappointment is that nothing in the letter coheres with or confirms the Acts account of the church's foundation (Acts 16.12-40): no reference to Lydia or to one who might have been recognizable as the jailer of Acts 16; only a hint of tensions with prominent citizens (1.28?), but no echoes of a miraculous release from prison, and no allusion to still-cowed authorities. Of course, there could be many reasons for this (Lydia might have been long departed from Philippi; apart from 4.15, there was no occasion in the letter itself to refer back to such founding events). But it does strengthen the impression of a community living to a large extent in their own world, without very much active involvement in or interaction with the wider world.[274]

271. The 'severe test of affliction' (2 Cor. 8.2) probably refers primarily to the Thessalonians (cf. 1 Thess. 1.6; 2.14; 3.3; 2 Thess. 1.4). Did the authorities' mistake in overreaching their authority in dealing with Paul and Silas initially (Acts 16.19-40) provide something of a shield for the church there? But see also Bormann, *Philippi* 217-24. Such opposition as there was, referred to in 1.27-30, is better understood as local, rather than tied into what is in view in 3.2ff. (see particularly Oakes, *Philippians* 84-89).

272. Oakes also argues that the suffering envisaged in 1.28 was economic (*Philippians* 89-96)

273. In discussing the term *politeuma* as applied to Jewish communities, Schürer observes that it can refer to 'quite a small civilian community . . . which is organized like a city commune and enjoys a measure of independent existence alongside the city commune; in this sense the term always refers to a group of different nationality from the local community as a whole' (*History* 3.88). Pilhofer notes that the *politeuma* of the Roman citizens of the colony was through their belonging to the *tribus Voltinia* (*Philippi* 118-34), which suggests that Paul was setting his 'citizenship of heaven' as a deliberate and more important alternative — alternative also to his own belonging to 'the tribe of Benjamin' (3.5). See also Bockmuehl, *Philippians* 233-35; Martin-Hawthorne, *Philippians* 231-32; and §30 n. 9 above. This is the only clear allusion to the current political context of the letter; but see also n. 274.

274. Was Paul's urging that they should 'conduct their lives *(politeuesthe)* worthily of the gospel of the Christ' (1.27) a further echo of a Philippian slogan, that Philippians should live 'worthily of their city' (Pilhofer, *Philippi* 136-37)? *Politeuesthe* could be rendered 'discharge your obligations as citizens' (BDAG 846); 'the word *politeuesthai* here carries the dual sense of exercising the rights and public duties of free and full citizenship' (Bockmuehl, *Philippians* 97-98).

d. What Do We Learn about Paul's Circumstances and the Roman Congregations?

Very valuable here is the indication that Paul was able to use his time of imprisonment to continue his work of evangelism (1.12-13). That it was well known throughout the whole praetorian guard that his 'imprisonment was in Christ' must mean that the soldiers guarding him, or officer interrogating him, had been sufficiently impressed by Paul's testimony to speak about it fully and freely among the rest of the praetorian guard. Possibly Paul succeeded in converting one or several of the guards (as their spell of duty rotated). The thought is enticing and has given rise to many novellistic speculations about such Christians. Certainly the parting greeting from 'the saints in Caesar's household' (4.22) must mean that the Christian gospel had already begun to spread and take root even in the households of the rich and powerful, and it is natural to see the influence of Paul himself in all this, as his further comments confirm.

More important, Paul tells us that the effect of such ministry on his guards had encouraged most of his 'brothers in the Lord' to give testimony to their own faith with boldness and without fear (1.14). This is consistent with the picture reflected in Paul's letter to Rome, where the impression given by Rom. 12.9–13.7 is of a community of small apartment churches who needed to keep their heads down to avoid drawing hostile suspicions on to them.[275] Should we then deduce that Paul's presence among them had indeed encouraged them to lift their heads and to engage in more overt evangelism. It would be hugely ironic if this was indeed the case and if, as a result, the attention of the authorities was being drawn to this new Jewish sect, with the most unfortunate of outcomes two or three years later in the Neronian persecution of the Roman Christians.[276]

Paul adds that the preaching was two-edged. Some of the Roman believers were preaching 'out of envy and rivalry', though others out of goodwill (1.15). The former Paul accuses of acting out of 'false motives' and 'selfish ambition *(eritheia)*, not sincerely, but thinking to increase the distress of my imprisonment' (1.17-18). This is also consistent with the impression given by Rom. 14.1–15.7 of a degree of factionalism among the Roman congregations, some perhaps favourable to the more traditionally Jewish understanding of the new faith, others (the majority) more favourable to the Pauline view that characteristic Jewish praxis (observing the laws of clean and unclean, and the Sabbath) should not be required of non-Jewish believers. What is illuminating and possibly disturbing here is the further inference that some within the Roman congregations were positively antagonistic to Paul. Were we able with any confidence to link the infor-

275. See above, §33.3f(ii).
276. See also below, §35 n. 36.

mation of Rom. 14.1–15.7 with the information of Phil. 1.15-18, the most obvious corollary would be that the more traditionalist Jewish believers and their Gentile supporters became quite hostile to the law-free version of the gospel preached by Paul and his supporters.[277]

This snippet of information once again underlines how narrow was the focus of Luke's account of Paul's arrival in Rome and of his two years in custody there, even if, as already noted, the allusion to two different welcoming groups (Acts 28.15) may have included some awareness not only of Christian groups already well established in Rome but also of tensions between them.

The other gleanings derivable from Philippians in regard to Paul's own circumstances are even more intriguing. For in expressing himself as fully and freely as he does to the Philippians, he shows just how uncertain he was at the time of writing as to the outcome of his trial. At first he seems confident of his deliverance *(sōtēria)* (1.19), but does he mean by that, his freedom, his acquittal and release? At once, however, he goes on to reflect on his possible death (1.20-23): he was ready to die, even desired death ('to depart and be with Christ') (1.23); he was ready to be, as it were, the libation poured over the sacrifice of their faith (2.17); but he still felt (hoped?) in his heart of hearts that he would be freed and be able to visit them again (1.24-26; 2.24).

In the meantime, his imprisonment was sufficiently light for Paul to maintain communication with (some/many of) the Roman believers (1.14), for him to instruct Timothy and write this letter with him as co-author (1.1; 2.19-23), for Epaphroditus to deliver the gifts of the Philippians and to minister to Paul's needs in some way (2.25, 30) and for Paul to talk of sending Epaphroditus back to Philippi (2.28). Paul's own contentment in a threatening and oppressive situation — the several references to his 'chains' (1.7, 13, 14. 17) are hardly metaphorical — is particularly marked in the closing paragraphs (4.11-13): his ability to thrive whether well-fed or hungry (4.12); his confidence in the enabling of God to confront and survive the sharpest distresses (4.13); his delight in the gifts brought by Epaphroditus (4.18); the assurance that 'God will fully supply every need of yours according to his riches in glory in Christ Jesus' (4.19), no doubt rooted in his own experience of such supply. All of which is consistent with the final scene of Acts, of Paul held in light custody, content with his lot, able to preach the gospel (and to write letters to his churches), but with a trial of uncertain outcome ahead of him.

---

277. For fuller discussion see O'Brien, *Philippians* 100-105; Martin-Hawthorne, *Philippians* 45-48.

e. Christ as the Pattern

The most striking feature of the letter to Philippi is the consistent way in which Paul presents Christ as a pattern, a pattern both to which the Philippian believers are to be conformed and in accordance with which they should mould their attitudes and conduct.[278] This is significant, since the letter is so relaxed, and since, for the most part, Paul was not framing his christology with a polemical edge. Unlike earlier letters, where references to what was believed about Jesus were often determined by misunderstandings and confusion,[279] here Paul was evidently able to choose his own terms and imagery.

The most powerful expression is what is usually regarded as a hymn in praise of Christ cited by Paul in 2.6-11:[280]

> [5]Think this among yourselves which you think in Christ Jesus
> (or, which was in Christ Jesus),[281]
> [6]who being in the form of God
> did not count equality with God something to be grasped *(harpagmos),*
> [7]but emptied himself,
> taking the form of a slave,
> becoming in the likeness of human beings.
> And being found in form as man,
> [8]he humbled himself
> becoming obedient to death,
> death on a cross.
> [9]Wherefore God exalted him to the heights
> and bestowed on him the name which is over every name,

278. Oakes argues that 'the theme of suffering provides the most notable structural feature of the letter: an extended three-fold parallel between Paul, Christ and the Philippians' (*Philippians* 77). See also Wilckens, *Theologie* 1/3.246, 249.

279. In particular, regarding the parousia (1 and 2 Thessalonians), regarding the revelation of Christ in the gospel (Galatians and 2 Corinthians 10–13), regarding the nature of God's wisdom expressed in Christ and the implications of Jesus' resurrection (1 Corinthians).

280. Still valuable is R. P. Martin's review of the discussion on this point, *A Hymn of Christ: Philippians 2:5-11 in Recent Interpretation and in the Setting of Early Christian Worship* (SNTSMS 4; Cambridge: Cambridge University, 1967, ²1983; 3rd ed., Downers Grove: InterVarsity Press, 1997); his bibliography runs to twenty-five pages, and in Martin-Hawthorne, *Philippians,* to nearly seven tightly packed pages (92-98; see also lxiv-lxxviii). There is no way of telling when the hymn was composed prior to the writing of the letter, and when Paul learned it, or indeed whether Paul himself composed it.

281. See discussion of the alternative renderings in Bockmuehl, *Philippians* 122-24; Oakes, *Philippians* 188-93; Martin-Hawthorne, *Philippians* 106-109; since 'Christ Jesus' is the subject of the hymn that follows, the issue is not of fundamental importance.

¹⁰that at the name of Jesus every knee should bow . . .
¹¹and every tongue confess that Jesus Christ is Lord,
to the glory of God the Father.

It is fashionable today to draw attention to the political and social implications of the hymn.[282] I share what is a minority opinion, that the hymn is formulated so as to evoke the contrasting parallel of Adam.[283] The parallel is not precise, but the action of the hymn mirrors the purpose which God had in creating Adam/man/humankind and the way that purpose was frustrated by Adam's disobedience in paradise, as the story is told in Genesis 1–3. And it resolves the tragedy of Adam's disobedience by portraying a Jesus who out-Adams Adam by achieving a destiny far beyond what even Adam could have hoped for.

- 2.6a — like Adam, he was in the form *(morphē)* of God (cf. Gen. 1.27);[284]
- 2.6b — like Adam, he was tempted to grasp equality with God (Gen. 3.5);[285]

282. See above, §29 n. 121. For Hellerman, *Reconstructing Honor* ch. 6, the hymn describes Jesus' *cursus pudorum* (career of shame) set in deliberate contrast to the Roman lust for a *cursus honorum* (career of honour).

283. I refer to my *Christology* ch. 4, particularly 114-21; also *Theology of Paul* 281-88 (with bibliography). I agree with Barrett — 'it is hard to doubt that *to be on an equality with God* was intended to evoke the story of Adam. It recalls much too clearly the temptation to which Adam fell' (*Paul* 108); and Wilckens — 'the articular phrase *to einai isa theō* in v. 6c is clearly a linguistic signal of the allusion to the history of Paradise' (*Theologie* 1/3.247 n. 14, also 205). The line of interpretation seems to have been more conducive to systematicians than to NT exegetes; cf. particularly K.-J. Kuschel, *Born before All Time? The Dispute over Christ's Origin* (London: SCM, 1992) 243-66; and J. Macquarrie, *Jesus Christ in Modern Thought* (London: SCM, 1990) 55-59; other NT scholars are listed in my *Theology of Paul* 286 n. 95. T. H. Tobin, 'The World of Thought in the Philippians Hymn (Philippians 2:6-11)', in J. Fotopoulos, ed., *The New Testament and Early Christian Literature in Greco-Roman Context,* D. E. Aune FS (NovTSupp 122; Leiden: Brill, 2006) 91-104, suggests that speculation regarding the 'heavenly man' of Gen. 1.27, as evidenced by Philo (*Opif.* 134-35; *Leg.* 1.31-32), was known to Paul.

284. Whether *morphē* is synonymous or not with the *eikōn* of Gen. 1.27 is not entirely to the point, since an allusion by definition is not a one-to-one correlation (*morphē theou* is obviously used in antithesis to *morphē doulou* in 2.7). But note the dismissive comments of Fee, *Philippians* 209-10, and *Pauline Christology* 390-93. 'The problem is that the undeniable counter-analogy between Philippians 2 and Genesis 3 *in general* is not easily pinned down in *particulars*' (Bockmuehl, *Philippians* 133).

285. The debate on *harpagmos* is never ending; does it mean 'snatching', or something to be snatched or grasped retentively? For recent discussion see Bockmuehl, *Philippians* 129-31. Bockmuehl follows (in particular) N. T. Wright, '*Harpagmos* and the Meaning of Philippians 2.5-11', *The Climax of the Covenant* (Edinburgh: Clark, 1991) 62-90, in taking *harpagmos* as something already possessed to be exploited to one's own advantage (130). However,

- 2.7 — unlike Adam (Gen. 3.6-7), however, he refused the temptation but nevertheless accepted the lot of humankind which was the consequence of Adam's sin, that is, enslavement to corruption (Gen. 3.19) and sin,[286]
- 2.8 — and submitted voluntarily to the death which had been the consequence of Adam's sin (Gen. 2.19);[287]
- 2.9-11 — consequently, he was super-exalted *(hyperypsōsen)* not only to the lordship over all things, which had been God's original purpose for Adam/humankind (Ps. 8.5b-6),[288] but above and beyond that, to share fully in the lordship which hitherto had been the sole prerogative of God (the allusion to Isa. 45.23 is unmistakable).[289]

The key point is that this hymn in praise of Christ is put forward as an encouragement to the Philippian believers to put others first (2.3-4); Christ's attitude and mission is the model for their own conduct in regard to each other. It seems, in other words, that Paul continued to develop the line of thought he had first clearly articulated in 1 Cor. 15.21-22 and 44-54, and still further in Rom. 5.12-21 and 7.7-11, drawing out the parallel and contrast between Adam and Christ still more fully:

Adam	*Christ*
death	life
natural	spiritual

Martin justifiably asks why *harpagmos* (from *harpazein,* 'to seize, snatch') would be used, and how one who was equal with God could use this status to his own advantage (what higher 'advantage' could there be than equality with God?) (*Hymn* lxix-lxx). S. Vollenweider, 'Der "Raub" der Gottgleichheit. Ein religionsgeschichtlicher Vorschlag zu Phil 2.6(-11)', *NTS* 45 (1999) 413-33, finds the key to 2.6b in the biblical, Jewish and Hellenistic traditions about the usurpation of equality with God by kings and rulers (cf. Isa. 14.12-15 and the hubris of god-like kings such as Alexander, who 'robbed' their position). I translate 'grasp' to reflect the ambiguity in the term and continue to find the Adam allusion as the most likely key to explain how Christ could both be 'in the form of God' and yet be tempted to grasp something other or further (so also BDAG 133).

286. Cf. Ps. 8.5a; Wis. 2.23; Rom. 5.12-14, 21a; 8.3; Gal. 4.4; Heb. 2.7a, 9a.

287. Cf. Wis. 2.24; Rom. 5.12-21; 7.7-11; 1 Cor. 15.21-22.

288. Cf. 1 Cor. 15.27, 45; Heb. 2.7b-8, 9b.

289. It should always be remembered that in Paul's use of the Adam parallel, *Christ supersedes and outperforms Adam:* note the 'how much more' of Rom. 5.15-17 and the contrast between 'living soul' and 'life-giving Spirit' in 1 Cor. 15.45 in particular. So here, the 'super-exalt' and 'the name above every name' (Phil. 2.9) play the same role. In the dispute over the extent of Paul's Adam christology, then, the way forward, exegetically, is not to dispute or deny the Adam typology but to understand better how and why Paul uses the Adam motif.

man of dust	man of heaven
perishable/mortal	imperishable/immortal
trespass	free gift
condemnation	justification
disobedience	obedience[290]

The two men provide two types of humanity; it is the type modelled by Christ which should provide the pattern for Christian attitudes and relationships.[291]

This template in fact functions throughout Philippians, more clearly than in any of Paul's other letters, 2 Corinthians apart, as the key to Paul's soteriology:

- he longs for them with the compassion of Christ Jesus (1.8);
- his imprisonment is 'in Christ' (1.13);[292]
- 'the spirit of Christ' is a/the means to Paul's salvation (1.19);
- for Paul 'living is Christ' (1.21);
- Paul wants to be 'with Christ' (1.23);
- he wants the Philippians to live their lives 'in a manner worthy of the gospel of Christ' (1.27);
- his and their suffering is on Christ's behalf (1.29);
- they are to think as Christ thought (2.5);[293]
- his hopes and planning are 'in the Lord' and seek to reflect Christ's concerns (2.19-24);
- knowing Christ, gaining Christ and being found in him are his whole ambition (3.8-10);
- his goal is to share Christ's sufferings and to be conformed to his death (3.10);

---

290. The disobedience/obedience antithesis (as most explicitly in Rom. 5.19) confirms that Paul saw the parallel/antithesis between Adam and Christ as extending over Jesus' life and death and not just beginning with his resurrection (*pace* Fee, *Pauline Christology* 522-23); Hebrews developed the same line of thought (Heb. 2.6-9 and 5.8-9).

291. The great majority think that the hymn attributes the decision of 2.6-7 to Christ prior to his birth (pre-existence) as the most obvious understanding of 2.7 (see, e.g., Martin, *Hymn* xix-xxiii; Fee, *Philippians* 202-203 and n. 41; Bockmuehl, *Philippians* 131-32; the essays by L. D. Hurst and G. F. Hawthorne in R. P. Martin and B. J. Dodd, eds., *Where Christology Began: Essays on Philippians 2* [Louisville: Westminster John Knox, 1998] 84-110; Hahn, *Theologie* 1.207-208), though I continue to find persuasive the fact that the predominant Adam/Christ contrast in Paul is between Adam's life-death and Christ's death-(resurrection) life (see further *Theology of Paul* 286-88).

292. The 'in Christ'/'in the Lord'/'in him' phrases occur regularly in all of Paul's letters (apart from 2 Thessalonians) but are particularly prominent here: 1.1, 13, 14, 26; 2.1, 5, 19, 24, 29; 3.1, 3, 9, 14; 4.1, 2, 4, 7, 10, 13, 19, 21.

293. See above, §21 n. 207.

- Christ has made him his own, and he strives for 'the prize of the upward call of God in Christ Jesus' (3.12-14);[294]
- he looks for their 'body of humiliation' to 'be conformed to the body of his glory' (3.21);
- he 'can do all things through the one who strengthens him' (4.13);
- and he is confident that God's 'riches in glory in Christ Jesus' 'will fully satisfy their every need' (4.19).

Indeed, it is this emphasis which gives the contrasting parallel with Adam such resonance: as Adam had provided the pattern for human behaviour apart from Christ, so Christ provides the pattern and the enabling for human behaviour 'in Christ', in conformity to Christ, and with Christ.

f. The Christ-Pattern Contrasted with the Torah-Pattern

The other most striking feature of Philippians is the apparent insertion of a fierce warning and self-apologia (3.2-21) in the midst of this otherwise very warm and friendly letter. I have already drawn heavily on the passage to illuminate Paul's understanding of his past and of what his conversion meant to him,[295] just as I have indicated the likelihood that the outburst of 3.2ff. was occasioned by news of incomers seeking to extend the victory at Antioch, some twelve years earlier, to the churches of the Pauline mission (§34.4a). Here, however, it is appropriate to focus attention on the way Paul formulates his understanding of how the process of salvation works, since this is probably the last and clearest expression of his theologizing on the subject. That the pattern of Christ was still influencing Paul's thinking is indicated by the parallel between 2.6-11 and 3.7-11.[296]

That Paul sets in contrast his old understanding of righteousness *(dikaiosynē)* over against his new understanding 'in Christ' is obvious (3.4-11). What is insufficiently appreciated, however, is the terms in which he does so.

(i) It is certainly the case that the negative side of the contrast includes both his pride in ethnic and religious identity and his claims as a zealous and 'blameless *(amemptos)*' Pharisee. What is often missed, however, is that Paul also expects the Philippians to be 'without blemish *(amemptos)*' (2.15), and hopes that 'in the day of Christ' they will be 'pure and blameless *(eilikrineis kai aproskopoi)*'

---

294. As elsewhere, Paul holds himself out as an exemplar too (3.17; 4.9), but only because he himself was endeavouring to conform his life and mission to the template of Christ (1 Cor. 4.16-17; 11.1).

295. See above, §25 *passim.*

296. See, e.g., Marguerat, 'Paul et la Loi' 271-72; I would press beyond to see the two aspects of 3.4-6 in parallel to the two aspects of 2.6.

having produced a harvest of righteousness *(karpon dikaiosynēs)* that comes through Jesus Christ' (1.10-11).

The point is that Paul could have expressed his hopes and goals in such terms before he was converted. His conversion did not change his desire to be blameless or hope for outcomes from his life and conduct which could be described as 'righteous' in character.[297] This is markedly different from the tradition of interpretation which infers that a 'blameless' life and 'righteous' conduct cannot be expected of justified sinners. Paul evidently understood soteriology not simply in terms of a changed status, but also in terms of a person being transformed and producing 'righteous fruit'.

(ii) Equally striking is the way Paul integrates his diverse models and vocabulary of salvation.

- It is those who worship by God's Spirit who are 'the circumcision' (3.3).
- He integrates the forensic imagery of 'righteousness' with the language of being 'in Christ' (3.9) and with an easy familiarity which has defeated generations of commentators.
- His confidence in knowing Christ is tempered by his awareness that full conformity to Christ's death and hope of attaining the resurrection from the dead is 'not yet' and is not finally assured ('if somehow') (3.10-11).[298]
- Similarly, his confidence that Christ has already made him his own is balanced by his clear sense that he has a race still to complete, and that completion will require the maximum effort from him if he is to win the prize at its end (3.12-14).

This maturest of Paul's theologizing about the factors and processes by which salvation comes about and is completed has rarely been appreciated in its full scope.[299]

297. In 3.12 — 'Not that I have already reached the goal *(teteleiōmai)'* — there may also be a backward glance to his old attitude, since the claim to be 'perfect *(teleios)'* featured in Second Temple Judaism in the praise of heroes of the past, such as Noah (Sir. 44.17), and in assurance among the Qumran covenanters that they were 'perfect' in their understanding and observance of Torah (1QS 1.8; 2.2; 3.9-11; 8.18; 9.8-9, 19); see further Gathercole, *Where Is Boasting?* 182-90. But we should also note that according to Col. 1.28, Paul himself hoped to present his converts *teleios* ('complete', 'mature', 'perfect') in Christ, and that here he immediately addresses himself to 'as many as are *teleioi'* (Phil. 3.15)!

298. The 'if somehow' indicating 'a degree of contingency', which, however, as Bockmuehl observes, is 'often underrated by commentators' (*Philippians* 217). In contrast, Martin-Hawthorne hear only a note of humility on Paul's part (*Philippians* 200; cf. O'Brien, *Philippians* 412-13), though without observing the consistent note of 'eschatological reserve' in so many of Paul's exhortations (see *Theology of Paul* 497-98).

299. See further my *New Perspective on Paul* ch. 22, with bibliography.

As the latest of his reflections on his gospel, this passage also confirms that the issues reflected in it permeated Paul's thinking and were formative factors of first importance in his theology. It was not that the challenge in view in 3.2 and 18-19 seems to have been particularly serious in Philippi itself; nothing that Paul says implies that the Philippian believers were being tempted to follow the lead given by these 'opponents'. But whatever it was that sparked Paul off in 3.2 was certainly sufficient to recall to his mind the issues which had shaped the formulation of his gospel and which had provided a counterpoint to most of his mission. Still central to his gospel and his theology were the issues whether Jewish identity and praxis were a determinative factor in standing before God and how knowing Christ and being in Christ should work out in character and life.

34.5. Paul's Letter to Philemon

The second letter which can be referred to Paul's imprisonment in Rome is his personal letter to Philemon on the subject of the latter's slave Onesimus.[300]

a. Philemon

We can tell a good deal about the recipient:

- He was well-to-do: he had a house large enough to host the church in the city where he lived (2) and to provide a guest room (22); he was a slave-owner, probably of several slaves (otherwise Onesimus's absence would have been particularly awkward for Philemon, a fact to which Paul would presumably have referred).[301]
- He probably lived in Colossae.[302]
- He seems to have been a successful businessman who presumably met Paul on his travels (Paul had not yet visited Colossae — Col. 2.1) and who had been converted through Paul's ministry (19).[303]

---

300. In what follows I draw on my *Colossians and Philemon*. J. A. Fitzmyer, *Philemon* (AB 34C; New York: Doubleday, 2000), as usual contains a massive bibliography (43-78).

301. M. Barth and H. Blanke, *The Letter to Philemon* (Grand Rapids: Eerdmans, 2000), observe that if Onesimus was a house-born slave, 'the possibility cannot be excluded that Philemon was his physical father' (138); see further on Philemon (137-41).

302. See below, n. 332. This implies that the Onesimus of Phlm. 10 was also the Onesimus of Col. 4.9, well known to the Colossians ('one of yourselves').

303. Murphy-O'Connor suggests that he had been converted by Epaphras (the founder of the church in Colossae) 'as Paul's agent' (*Paul* 236).

- He was close to Paul (Paul addresses him as 'beloved') and must have worked with him for some time as one of his 'co-workers' (1).
- He was probably leader of the church which met in his home (2), perhaps functioning as its patron.[304]

b. The Occasion

The letter's primary object was evidently to intercede on Onesimus's behalf. It is clear that Onesimus had wronged his master in some way (18). But beyond that the picture is obscure.

The traditional view is that Onesimus had robbed Philemon and run away; he subsequently met Paul, through some mutual contact, or while both were in prison. The problems with this view are twofold. One would have expected the converted Onesimus to express some repentance for his theft and flight[305] and Paul to have reassured Philemon on this score in the letter; but Paul says nothing on the subject. The other is that it is difficult to envisage the circumstances in which Paul could have met Onesimus in prison. If Paul was under 'house arrest', an imprisoned runaway would hardly have been housed with him. And if Paul's imprisonment was more severe, how could Paul, himself a prisoner, 'send' a runaway back to Philemon (12; Col. 4.8-9)?

Recently an alternative view has gained increasing support.[306] It was evidently quite common for a slave who in some way had put himself in the wrong with his master to seek out a friendly third party to ask the latter to intercede on his behalf with his offended master. This makes better sense of the language of the letter, not least the 'if' clause of v. 18 ('If he has wronged you in any way or owes you anything'), which probably refers to an issue where Philemon thought he had a legitimate grievance against Onesimus, but where Onesimus felt he was

304. 'The hearts of the saints have been refreshed through you' (7) probably implies a wider mission but would presumably be intended by Paul to include the saints in Colossae.

305. A slave's flight would constitute an act of robbery in itself, since the slave was the property of the owner (Justinian, *Digest* 47.2.61).

306. The suggestion is not new, but P. Lampe's brief article 'Keine "Sklavenflucht" des Onesimus', *ZNW* 76 (1985) 135-37, brought the alternative to the fore and has proved influential since then; see, e.g., B. M. Rapske, 'The Prisoner Paul in the Eyes of Onesimus', *NTS* 37 (1991) 187-203 (here 195-203); S. Bartchy, *ABD* 5.307-308; Fitzmyer 17-18, 20-23. Fitzmyer cites the most relevant passage from Justinian's *Digest* 21.1.17.4, and the much-referred-to letter of Pliny to Sabinianus (*Ep.* 9.21); another translation of the Pliny letter in my *Colossians and Philemon* 304-305 n. 13. Wansink remains doubtful (*Chained in Christ* 186-88), preferring to argue that Philemon had sent Onesimus to deliver support and to serve Paul in prison (188-98); Barth and Blanke also remain unimpressed (*Philemon* 141, 227-28); S. R. Llewelyn notes a number of difficulties with Lampe's interpretation (*NDIEC* 8.41-44).

being blamed unfairly. The situation, then, would be that Onesimus sought out Paul as a potential intercessor on his behalf. The time Philemon had already spent with Paul and the debt Philemon presumably felt he owed to Paul (19) would have been sufficient to convince Onesimus that Paul's was the support he most needed to gain. However Onesimus contrived the meeting with Paul, he had been converted by Paul during the latter's time in prison ('my child Onesimus, whose father I became while in chains' — 10) and had become dear to Paul, attending to his various needs in prison (11, 13).[307]

c. Place of Writing

All this, of course, bears on the question of where Paul wrote the letter. Here the case for a letter sent from Ephesus is at its strongest, since it is much easier to envisage a slave from Colossae seeking out Paul in Ephesus, only about 120 miles distant, whereas a slave finding passage to Rome (or Caesarea), or covering such a journey by foot, is much harder to envisage. Paul's request for a guest room to be prepared for him also makes better sense if the request came from Ephesus, Paul looking for release from the crisis in Ephesus to the relative calm of Colossae.[308]

However, the whole question of whether we have sufficient historical data to support the hypothesis of an Ephesian imprisonment remains a critical, perhaps a decisive, factor in the discussion. It is more difficult to envisage how Paul could have converted Onesimus and how Onesimus could have assisted Paul during the intense crisis envisaged in 2 Cor. 1.8-10 than supporters of the Ephesian hypothesis allow. Whereas the imprisonment envisaged in Acts 28.16, 30 would allow just the sort of access to Paul which the letter to Philemon presupposes.

The other factor is the close relation between Paul's letter to the Colossians and his letter to Philemon. The close correlation between Col. 4.9-14 and Phlm. 23–24, with their overlapping cast of characters (Onesimus, Epaphras, Mark, Aristarchus, Demas, Luke), strongly suggests that the two letters were written in close conjunction. Moreover, the concluding exhortations of Colossians confirm that Paul still looked for opportunities to preach his gospel, even in prison (Col. 4.3-4). The fact that this had to be put as a request for their prayers (contrast the more buoyant optimism of Phil. 1.12-18) perhaps suggests that the conditions of Paul's imprisonment had worsened. So, if Colossians was the last letter written with Paul's own approval,[309] that is, written from Rome, some time before his

---

307. In Col. 4.9 Onesimus is called 'the faithful and beloved brother'.
308. Fitzmyer comes down hesitantly in favour of Ephesus (*Philemon* 9-11).
309. See below, §34.6.

death, then Philemon too should presumably be referred to Paul's time under house arrest in Rome during the latter part of the two years of Acts 28.30.

It remains true that for Onesimus to seek out Paul in Rome would have been a massive and bold undertaking, though hardly beyond imagination ('all roads lead to Rome'). Though at the same time, that such journeys should have been envisaged by Onesimus and Paul may simply remind us that the mutual relationships between all three of the main characters were of an extraordinary quality.

d. The Letter Itself

What then was Paul hoping for in writing the letter? As a fugitive slave Onesimus could quite properly be punished by beatings, chains, branding, or worse.[310] But a potential crisis of that sort does not seem to be in view in the letter; how could Paul compensate Philemon (18-19) if such a penalty was in order? If, on the other hand, the nature and seriousness of Onesimus's wrongdoing were themselves an issue, and if Onesimus's enlisting of Paul's good offices was itself not an unacceptable action, then the language used in 15-17 is quite as might be expected.

> [15]Perhaps it was for this reason that he was separated from you for a time, in order that you might have him back for ever, [16]no longer as a slave, but more than a slave, as a beloved brother, especially to me, but how much more to you, both in the flesh and in the Lord. [17]If therefore you count me as a partner, welcome him as you would me.

Paul's main concern, then, was for a positive reconciliation between Philemon and Onesimus.[311] Similarly, Paul's readiness to let Philemon understand the breach in the way he chose ('If he has wronged you in any way or owes you anything, charge it to my account' — 18) displays the touch of an experienced mediator, recognizing as he did that in a master-slave dispute the master held all the cards.

At the same time we should note how persuasive ('manipulative' would be an unsympathetic description) Paul could be in encouraging Philemon to act in the Christian way that Paul deemed to be appropriate.[312] It begins with the

---

310. See, e.g., Rapske, 'Prisoner Paul' 189-90; Bartchy, *ABD* 5.307-308; other bibliography in my *Colossians and Philemon* 306 n. 14; now also Barth and Blanke, *Philemon* 26-31.

311. M. Wolter, *Der Brief an die Kolosser; Der Brief an Philemon* (ÖTKNT 12; Gütersloh: Mohn, 1993) 233-34.

312. For similar rhetorical persuasiveness cf. Pliny's letter to Sabinianus (*Ep.* 9.21).

fact that the letter to Philemon is also addressed to the church in Philemon's house (2). That is to say, what might have been regarded as a purely personal matter between Paul and Philemon was to be shared not only with Apphia and Archippus (2),[313] but also with the church which met in Philemon's house. The inference is that the letter would have been read openly at a meeting of the house church, which can be assumed to be the usual practice when a letter was received from Paul. This should not be regarded as an underhanded way of pressuring Philemon,[314] even though the social mixture in the meeting could have proved embarrassing for Philemon in the circumstances.[315] Rather we should infer that Paul saw this to be the appropriate way in which even important personal decisions should be made, as a shared responsibility, even as they shared the same faith (6). And presumably, Paul must have felt he knew Philemon well enough to know that Philemon would share that understanding of how the body of Christ (in Colossae) should work — otherwise his tactic was likely to backfire!

The pressure builds from v. 8: 'Though I am bold enough in Christ to command you to do your duty, I would rather appeal to you on account of love' (8-9) — again a not too subtle way of indicating restraint on his part in the hope of encouraging similar restraint on Philemon's. The appeal to love is reinforced by sentimental reference to Paul's old age, to his special affection for Onesimus ('my son', 'my own heart'),[316] to the transformation in Onesimus (from *achrēston,* 'useless', to *euchrēston,* 'useful') and to the value to Paul of Onesimus's present service during his imprisonment (9-13). But particularly striking is the fine mixture of pressure and pleading in Paul's fuller requests in 14-16 and 19-21:

> [14]I resolved to do nothing without your consent, so that your goodness might not be by compulsion but of your own free will. . . . [19]I, Paul, have written with my own hand: I will repay; not to mention that you owe me in addition your very self. [20]Yes, brother, let me have some benefit from you in the Lord; refresh my heart in Christ. [21]Confident of your obedience I have written to you, knowing that you will do even more than I say.

---

313. Apphia is usually regarded as Philemon's wife, and Archippus is often taken to be their son, though Paul identifies him only as 'our fellow-soldier'.

314. Cf. N. R. Peterson, *Rediscovering Paul: Philemon and the Sociology of Paul's Narrative World* (Philadelphia: Fortress, 1985) 99-100.

315. The meeting would presumably have included members who were also slaves (cf. Col. 3.22-25) and also children (3.20).

316. Paul uses the term *splanchna,* 'heart', three times in Philemon (7, 12, 20; he uses the term only five times elsewhere in his letters). 'The frequent use of the word in this short letter shows how personally Paul was involved in the matter' (H. Koester, *TDNT* 7.555).

These entreaties would allow Philemon to respond with dignity and generosity in a way that would both maintain and display his honour.[317] Vv. 15-16 could be taken to suggest that Paul expected Philemon to take Onesimus back as his slave and looked primarily for a transformed relationship ('no longer as a slave, but more than a slave, as a beloved brother . . .'). But the final verses leave the door open (no doubt deliberately) for Philemon to take the hint that Paul was hoping for something more in terms either of Onesimus's manumission[318] or of his return (probably as a freedman) to Paul (21).[319]

e. Paul's Attitude to Slavery

Since the letter is the only one which is addressed directly to the subject of slavery, it is worth pausing to summarize what it tells us about Paul's attitude to slavery. We need to remind ourselves of the harsh facts about slavery in the first century.

- In the ancient world slavery was accepted as an integral part of society and as essential to its economic functioning.
- While *treatment* of slaves was recognized as a moral issue, the *fact* of slavery itself was not; it was primarily the revulsion against the slave trade in the modern period in Europe and North America which has made slavery so repulsive morally.
- In the absence of modern democracy it would have been impossible to conceive of an effective political protest against the institution; slave revolts had been put down with ruthless cruelty.[320]
- The most effective amelioration of the slave's lot had to depend on the master's kindly treatment of the slave and on his continuing positive patronage after the slave's manumission.

In this context the most important counsel in the letter is v. 16, already quoted: 'no longer as a slave, but more than a slave, as a beloved brother, . . . both in the flesh and in the Lord'. Such teaching put into practice from the heart would transform and enrich any social relationship, whatever its continuing outward

317. Cf. particularly J. M. G. Barclay, 'Paul, Philemon and the Dilemma of Christian Slave-Ownership', *NTS* 37 (1991) 161-86 (here 170-75).

318. A very substantial proportion of slaves were freed before their thirtieth birthday (see §30 n. 150 above).

319. See my *Colossians and Philemon* 344-45; Fitzmyer, *Philemon* 35-36, each with bibliography.

320. See also Barth and Blanke, *Philemon* 31-33.

form, and, if sustained over time, was bound to undermine and diminish any radical inequality between the partners.[321]

34.6. The Letter to the Colossians

There is probably only one other letter which calls for attention as written during Paul's imprisonment — the letter to Colossae, though a strong body of opinion regards Colossians, along with 2 Thessalonians,[322] as deutero-Pauline, written some time after Paul's death and in his name.[323] If it was written during Paul's imprisonment, then the earthquake which devastated the Lycus Valley cities in 60/61[324] could well be regarded as a *terminus ad quem* before which the letter must have been written. The earthquake can hardly have left Colossae undamaged, and perhaps in ruins. And though we do not know whether the Colossian church survived beyond the earthquake, the absence of any allusion to the earthquake in the letter points more to a date before 60/61. Given the likelihood that Paul's imprisonment ran from 60 to 62, that would allow up to about half of that period for the letter to be written before news of the earthquake and its effects reached Paul.

a. The Church of Colossae

Colossae lay on or close to one of the main east-west routes through Anatolia. The valley of the river Meander runs east from near Ephesus and about one hundred miles upstream is joined by the river Lycus, whose valley in turn provided the most accessible route to the central plateau and thus a major artery of east-west communication during the Greek and Roman periods.[325] The fertile Lycus

---

321. See further Bartchy, *MALLON CHRĒSAI;* R. Gayer, *Die Stellung des Sklaven in den paulinischen Gemeinden und bei Paulus* (Bern: Lang, 1976) 175-82, 296-309; Barclay, 'Dilemma' 175-86. Fitzmyer provides a useful summary of slavery in antiquity and on flight from slavery (*Philemon* 25-29); fuller in Barth and Blanke, *Philemon* 9-31; on manumission (Barth and Blanke 41-53).

322. See above, §31.6.

323. See, e.g., A. Standhartinger, *Studien zur Entstehungsgeschichte und Intention des Kolosserbriefs* (NovTSupp 94; Leiden: Brill, 1999); also 'Colossians and the Pauline School', *NTS* 50 (2004) 572-93; and the review by R. M. Wilson, *Colossians and Philemon* (ICC; London: Clark International, 2005) 9-19; and further below, §34.6b.

324. Tacitus, *Ann.* 14.27.1 (cited below, n. 397). According to J. B. Lightfoot, *Colossians and Philemon* (London: Macmillan, 1875, ³1879), the Armenian version of Eusebius's *Chronicle* dates the earthquake subsequent to the burning of Rome in 64 (38-40).

325. W. M. Ramsay, *Cities and Bishoprics of Phrygia* (2 vols.; Oxford: Oxford University, 1895, 1897) 5.

Valley also encouraged settlement and supported three prominent cities — Laodicea and Hierapolis, with Colossae a further ten miles upstream. Four or five centuries before the time of the NT Colossae had been populous, large and wealthy,[326] its wealth due both to its position on the main road from Ephesus and Sardis to the Euphrates and to its wool industry. But by the early years of the Roman Empire its significance had been much reduced, in contrast to Laodicea (an administrative and financial centre) and Hierapolis (famous for its hot mineral springs).[327] Just how important or otherwise Colossae was deemed to be is a matter of some debate: Strabo (12.8.13) describes it as a *polisma* ('small town'), though he uses the same term for Athens; but Pliny refers to it as one of Phrygia's 'most famous towns'.[328]

There were probably substantial Jewish communities in the Lycus Valley cities. In the late third century BCE Antiochus the Great had settled two thousand Jewish families in Lydia and Phrygia to help stabilize the region (Josephus, *Ant.* 12.147-53). As already noted, Philo says that Jews were numerous in every city of Asia Minor (*Legat.* 245). And the attempt by Flaccus to seize the Temple tax in Laodicea,[329] presumably gathered from the nearby cities, suggests a large number of male Jews in the region.[330] Colossae itself could have had as many as two or three thousand Jewish residents, including families.

The church of Colossae was founded probably in the second half of the 50s CE. It was not established by Paul himself, although he may have passed nearby on his journey through Phrygia to Ephesus in about 52 (Acts 18.23; 19.1).[331] Its foundation seems rather to have been the result of evangelism by Epaphras (Col. 1.6-7), who was a native of Colossae (4.12) and who may have been responsible for the evangelism of the Lycus Valley cities (4.13). Presumably Epaphras was converted by Paul during Paul's sojourn in Ephesus (Acts 19.8-10), as also Philemon, another resident of Colossae (Phlm. 19).[332] If so, the founding of the church in Colossae may provide the only clear example of Paul's likely tactic of establishing an evangelistic centre in a major city (here Ephesus) from which in-

326. Herodotus, *Hist.* 7.30; Xenophon, *Anabasis* 1.2.6.

327. See also Murphy-O'Connor, *Paul* 231-34.

328. Pliny, *Nat. Hist.* 5.145. See further, e.g., E. M. Yamauchi, *New Testament Cities in Western Asia Minor* (Grand Rapids: Baker, 1980) 155-61; C. E. Arnold, 'Colossae', *ABD* 1.1089-90.

329. Cicero, *Pro Flacco* 28.68; text in *GLAJJ* §68 (196-98).

330. 'A little more than twenty pounds of gold' seized at Laodicea could indicate as many as 14,000 male Jews. See Trebilco, *Jewish Communities* 13-14; further details in my *Colossians and Philemon* 21 and n. 4.

331. Col. 2.1 indicates that Paul was not known personally to a fair number of the Colossian believers.

332. That Philemon also lived in Colossae is almost universally inferred from the parallels between Col 4:9-14 and Phlm. 23-24.

dividual or teams of evangelists would go out to cities within striking distance from Ephesus (cf. Acts 19.26).[333]

It is not possible to say how large the church of Colossae was at this time. The reference to the church which gathered in the house of well-to-do Philemon (Phlm. 2) implies that there were other house churches. And the house churches of Laodicea in particular may have functioned as part of the same Christian community (Col. 2.1; 4.15-16). The 'household rules' (3.18–4.1) also imply a household 'model' for the Colossian church(es), in which both slaves and children were full members of the congregation (both are directly addressed in 3.20, 22-25). The social status and social mix of the Colossian believers is also clearly implied in the 'household rules' (slave-owners and slaves), but more than that is a matter of speculation.

What we can say, however, is that the Colossian church was probably composed of Jews as well as Gentiles, though mainly of the latter. This is a deduction, inevitably somewhat speculative, from several considerations.

- We may suppose that Epaphras followed Paul's own tactic in going first to the synagogue to preach his message of Messiah Jesus.[334] Colossae having such a substantial Jewish population, there were probably several assembly places for Sabbath prayers and Torah instruction. And presumably, in Colossae as elsewhere, there were Gentiles who were sufficiently impressed by or attracted to the beliefs and praxis of the local Jews as to attend some of the synagogues, even on a regular basis. Epaphras would probably have made his initial converts from within their number.[335]
- The implication of several passages in Colossians is that the recipients were predominantly Gentiles who through the gospel had now been given to share in privileges hitherto known only to Israel:
  - 1.12 — God 'has qualified you to share the inheritance of the saints in the light';[336]
  - 1.27 — the 'mystery' of God's purpose ('which is Christ in you, the hope of glory') now being 'made known among the nations';[337]
  - 2.13 — 'you who were dead in the transgressions and uncircumcision of your flesh' now 'made alive with him'.[338]

---

333. See further above, §29.5a.

334. See above, §29.5b.

335. See again above, §29.5a and n. 228.

336. The combination of 'inheritance', 'light' and 'saints' is unquestionably Jewish in character, with the most notable parallels from the DSS — e.g., 1QS 11.7-8; 1QH 11.10-12, and the frequent contrast between the Qumranites as 'the sons of light' and others as 'the sons of darkness' (1QS 1.9-10; 3.24-25; 4.7-13; 1QM *passim*). See further my *Colossians and Philemon* 75-78.

337. On 'mystery' see above, §29 n. 114 and §33 n. 240.

338. A distinctively Jewish perspective; see below, at n. 362.

- Also implied is some concern that 'Greek and Jew, circumcision and uncircumcision' should mutually recognize the others' full acceptance before God 'in Christ' (3.11). And the reference in 4.11 to 'the only ones from (the) circumcision among my co-workers' similarly implies a concern on the part of the writer to assure the recipients that Paul's own mission team reflected a similar make-up of circumcision and uncircumcision.

The character of the letter indicated here, and of the gospel which the letter assumes, are also directly relevant to clarifying the situation which the letter presupposes and was evidently intended to meet.

b. Who Wrote Colossians?

The answer to this question cannot be found simply by reference to the opening word of the letter: 'Paul . . . to the saints in Colossae' (Col. 1.1-2). For the facts both that pseudepigraphy seems to have been common and accepted in the ancient world[339] and that there was no obvious sense of authorial copyright in such ancient writings introduce considerations to the discussion which we today are no longer in a position fully to evaluate.

A crucial factor here is the fact that the style of Colossians seems to be so different from that of undisputed Pauline letters that it cannot have been written by the same person.[340] That in itself need not be a decisive factor, since, as we have already noted, Paul may well have used an amanuensis, and it is not at all inconceivable that, in some circumstances, Paul may even have left it to his amanuensis to pen the actual letter itself in his own language and style.[341]

Here the key may be to remember that Timothy is named as co-author with Paul (Col. 1.1), as he is in five other of Paul's letters.[342] A variation in style between Colossians and these others would seem to be most obviously explained

---

339. See again vol. 3 on the subject of pseudepigraphy; in the meantime I may refer to my 'Pseudepigraphy', *DLNT* 977-84; Standhartinger, *Studien* ch. 2; and §37 n. 209 below.

340. Very influential here have been the findings of W. Bujard, *Stilanalytische Untersuchungen zum Kolosserbrief als Beitrag zur Methodik von Sprachvergleichen* (SUNT 11; Göttingen: Vandenhoeck und Ruprecht, 1975). E. Schweizer, *The Letter to the Colossians* (London: SPCK, 1982), thinks they are decisive: 'The letter can neither have been written nor dictated by Paul' (18-19); further bibliography in my *Colossians and Philemon* 35 n. 42.

341. See above, §29.8c and n. 346 (the reference to Cicero, *Atticus* 3.15; 11.2, 5, 7). Wilson, however, wishes to dispose of the 'amanuensis theory' once and for all as 'a desperate expedient' (*Colossians* 31).

342. 1 and 2 Thessalonians, 2 Corinthians, and the two other 'prison epistles', Philippians and Philemon.

The Passion of Paul

by the fact that the *two* styles are the different styles of the *two* authors. That is to say, Paul may well (presumably did) take primary responsibility for the other five letters for which he claimed that Timothy was jointly responsible; but in this case, he left it to Timothy to craft the letter in his own terms, but as a letter sent by them *both*. After all, if we take the ascriptions of authorship in the letter openings seriously, we should properly describe most of Paul's letters as 'the letters of Paul and . . .'. When Paul made such a point of attributing the letters to joint authorship, we are probably unfair in failing to give more of the credit for the letters to his fellow author. At the very least, if we take these ascriptions seriously (and there is no reason why not), we have to envisage Paul discussing the content and the form of the letter with Timothy, dictating it to him (and considering any changes Timothy may have suggested), and reading any draft as well as the final form to Timothy to ensure that Timothy was entirely happy to have the letter attributed to him as co-author. In which case it is just as easy to see some reversal in the roles in the case of Colossians. Not that Paul wrote to Timothy's dictation. Rather that he left it to Timothy to write the letter *as a letter from them both*. If, for example, Philippians, as a letter composed by Paul, could be attributed also to *Timothy*, why should a letter composed by Timothy not be attributed also to *Paul* — Paul content to add the final personal note (4.18) in his own hand?[343]

The attraction of this solution is that it could explain the features which have hitherto pushed commentators to conclude that Colossians is post- or deutero-Pauline. I refer not simply to the differences in style but also the distinctiveness of the Colossians christology and the emergence of new features like the 'realized eschatology' of 2.11-12 and 3.1 and the 'household rules' of 3.18–4.1.[344] At the same time, a date within the lifetime of Paul avoids the problems that attach to a post-Pauline dating: particularly the lack of any reference to the earthquake which almost destroyed Colossae in 60 or 61 and the difficulty of envisaging the function in a letter composed some years later of the references to several persons (4.7-17) who were involved with Paul in the early 60s (Phlm. 23-24) but who presumably moved on after Paul's death.[345]

The parallel between Colossians and Philemon, the latter being regarded

---

343. I develop here the suggestion of Schweizer, *Colossians* 23-24; see further my *Colossians and Philemon* 35-39 and n. 47; cf. Chilton, *Rabbi Paul* 248-50. F. C. Burkitt, *Christian Beginnings* (London: University of London, 1924), made a similar suggestion with regard to Silvanus in reference to 1 and 2 Thessalonians (132).

344. The marked overlap between Colossians and Ephesians is a problem more for the latter, since the consensus is that Colossians provided something of a model for Ephesians, though it may be that the same person who drafted Colossians to express Paul's views felt that much freer to use Colossians as a sort of template for the more ambitious Ephesians. See further below, §37.1a.

345. See further my *Colossians and Philemon* 35-39.

almost universally as written by Paul, greatly strengthens the case for Colossians as a letter written while Paul was still alive, though in prison (4.3, 10, 18) and perhaps unable to do more than add his signature (4.18). For the closeness of the parallel between Col. 4.10-14 and Phlm. 23-24 is best explained by the closeness of timing of the two letters, while the differences — particularly the absence of Jesus Justus (Col. 4.11), the lack of reference to Philemon in Colossians and the lack of reference to Tychicus (4.7-9) in Philemon — can be explained partly by the different purposes of the two letters and partly by some gap, though not long, between the sending of the two letters.[346] One possible scenario is that before Onesimus could leave with the personal letter to Philemon, Paul was somehow prevented from composing another letter, or the terms of his imprisonment became more severe. In such circumstances he may only have been able to commission and approve the letter penned by Timothy and to add his personal greeting, and request that his chains be remembered (4.18), before the letter could be dispatched with Tychicus in company with Onesimus to Colossae (4.9).

c. The Danger Threatening the Church at Colossae

Why should Paul write (or authorize) a letter to a fairly minor church which he had never visited? The implication of 1.7-8 is that news had come from Epaphras which occasioned some anxiety. If Onesimus (4.9) was the slave of Philemon (Phlm. 10-16), then he too could have brought news from Colossae. The references to Tychicus and Mark (Col. 4.7-10), not to mention Phlm. 22, also suggest a concern to maintain communication with the Colossian believers. And the warnings which evidently form the central section of the letter (2.8-23) certainly signal an anxiety concerning the self-understanding and self-confidence of the Colossian Christians. What was the problem or danger envisaged?

Most attempts to answer this question have spoken freely of 'the Colossian heresy' or of the Colossian 'errorists' or have used similar phrases. Such language betrays the perspective of an established faith (an 'orthodoxy') newly challenged by radicals or revisionists. But such a perspective only emerged in second-century Christianity and is wholly anachronistic here. The 'philosophy' of 2.8 and the 'regulations' of 2.20 might well have been long established, beside which the gospel of Paul and the small house-meetings of believers in Messiah Jesus would have seemed brash and callow.

---

346. The different reference to Archippus (presumably a member of the household of Philemon and Apphia, possibly their son) — warm greeting (Phlm. 2), admonition (Col. 4.17) — suggests that some concern regarding Archippus's ministry *(diakonia)* had arisen between the two letters, but not that he had left the community, as Murphy-O'Connor suggests *(Paul* 236-37).

Nor does the letter itself suggest that the Colossian church was facing a great crisis, confronted by a group of teachers, internally or externally, endeavouring to subvert the gospel on which the church had been founded. It should not be assumed that the crisis which occasioned Paul's letter to the Galatians or 2 Corinthians 10–13 provides a pattern for all the problems confronted in the Pauline letters.[347] The contrast between the fierce denunciations of Galatians and 2 Corinthians 10–13 and the relatively relaxed tone of Colossians as a whole, including the exhortations of Col. 2.8-23, indicate a quite different occasion for the letter.[348]

Indeed, the implication of 2.8-23 is that the practitioners of (an) older established 'philosophy' and religious system had contrasted the 'captivating' power of their own beliefs and praxis with the beliefs and praxis of the Pauline converts (2.8), had 'passed (negative) judgment' on the latters' rituals and festivals (2.16), and had acted as though they themselves were umpires with the authority (of ancient tradition) to 'disqualify' the Christian belief and praxis (2.18) as ineffectual and unfit for purpose. The challenge confronting the letter writer, then, was probably not so much to counter a 'false teaching' as to encourage the Colossian believers to hold up their heads in the face of a denigrating dismissal by a long-established religious system and to maintain confidence in their beliefs regarding Christ and what he had done.

What then was the older system beside which the Colossian believers found it difficult to hold up their heads? Two main answers have been offered.

The dominant view in the latter half of the twentieth century was that the threat posed was that of *gnosticizing syncretism*.[349]

• The term 'philosophy' ('love of wisdom') (2.8) had long been used of a systematic treatment of a theme, practical as well as speculative, and so for various schools of 'philosophy'.[350] The term thus invites identification of the other teaching as a typically Hellenistic mix of religious philosophy.

347. The assumption reflects the continuing influence of Baur's reconstruction of Christianity's early history, as a running battle between a Petrine faction and a Pauline faction (see §20.3 above).

348. See particularly M. D. Hooker, 'Were There False Teachers in Colossae?', *From Adam to Christ* (Cambridge: Cambridge University, 1990) 121-36.

349. The classic and very influential presentation is that of E. Lohse, *Colossians and Philemon* (Hermeneia; Philadelphia: Fortress, 1971). As an expert on Gnosticism, Wilson provides a particularly valuable review of the discussion on 'the Colossian heresy' (*Colossians and Philemon* 35-58); his conclusion is that 'the Colossian "heresy" belongs somewhere at an early stage in the development . . . on a trajectory which leads from Qumran and Jewish apocalyptic on the one hand to the developed Gnostic systems of the second century on the other', but allowing for 'other possible influences, from mysticism or magic or from Wisdom circles, or from quite non-Jewish sources' (57-58).

350. O. Michel, *TDNT* 9.172-79.

- The emphasis in the letter on 'wisdom' (1.9, 28; 2.3, 23; 3.16; 4.5), 'insight' (1.9; 2.2), and 'knowledge' (1.6, 9-10; 2.2-3; 3.10) suggests a typically Gnostic (or gnosticizing) regard for spiritual self-awareness.
- The references to 'the elements of the universe' and the cosmic powers of 2.10 and 15 likewise suggest a belief that only by establishing a right relationship with the cosmic powers could one hope to 'gain entry' to the 'pleroma *(plērōma)*' (2.9) and participate in the divine 'fullness' (2.10) — language typical of the later Gnostic systems.
- The language of 2.18 is particularly critical:[351] it seems to indicate a practice of worshipping angels; and talk of 'things seen on entering' is highly reminiscent of the 'things recited', 'things shown' and 'things performed'[352] in the initiations into the mystery religions.[353]

The thesis fits well with a persistent view that religious syncretism was widespread in Asia Minor. There is attestation of worship of angels in western Asia Minor;[354] of at least one cult of God Most High and 'his holy angels'; of associations calling themselves 'Sabbatistai'; and the practice of magic was widespread.[355] That there were Jewish elements involved in this syncretistic mix is not to be doubted; magic was a universal para-religious phenomenon at the time, and no doubt good-luck charms and amulets were to be found in the household of not a few devout Jews of the period. Insofar as this broader picture is relevant to the Colossian 'philosophy', it remains unclear whether it should be regarded as a Jewish syncretistic group or as a non-Jewish group which had absorbed some Jewish elements.

On the considerations marshalled by Lohse the issue is equally unclear.

- Judaism had long been described as a 'philosophy' by its influential apologists (Aristobulus, Philo, and soon Josephus).[356]

---

351. 'Let no one disqualify you, taking pleasure in humility and the worship of the angels, which things he had seen on entering . . .'.

352. *OCD*[2] 716.

353. Influential here was the earlier exposition of M. Dibelius, 'The Isis Initiation in Apuleius and Related Initiatory Rites', in F. O. Francis and W. A. Meeks, *Conflict at Colossae* (Missoula: Scholars, 1973) 61-121.

354. BDAG 459.

355. C. E. Arnold, *The Colossian Syncretism: The Interface between Christianity and Folk Belief at Colossae* (WUNT 2.77; Tübingen: Mohr Siebeck, 1995).

356. E.g., 4 Maccabees is set out as a philosophical discourse in defence of 'our [Jewish] philosophy' (5.22-24); Philo had no difficulty in presenting biblical teaching and Jewish piety as a kind of philosophy; and Josephus did not hesitate to commend the different sects of Judaism as *philosophiai* (see Michel, *TDNT* 9.181-82).

- Talk of 'wisdom' and 'knowledge' is hardly specific to or distinctive of Gnostic systems; it was widespread in Second Temple Judaism as well.[357]
- Although 'pleroma' does become a technical term in the later Gnostic systems, the thought of divine fullness was already familiar in Hellenistic Judaism, as again Philo attests.[358]
- And the prepositional phrase 'worship of angels' can readily be understood as worship offered *by* angels, rather than worship offered *to* angels, which would fit with one of the great traditions of Jewish visionary apocalypses.[359]

An alternative source for what evidently worried the letter writers was one or more of *the synagogues in Colossae*. If the church in Colossae emerged from the synagogue, as in Corinth and Ephesus (Acts 18.6-7; 19.9), then, as in other centres of the Pauline mission, their relationship to the synagogues could well have been uncertain and a matter of some controversy. In this situation the venerable 'philosophy' which was disparaging the new house churches is most likely to have been the venerable 'philosophy' of Second Temple Judaism, an ethnic religion well established and well respected in the vicinity. The problem would have been from the synagogue's side that here were former God-fearers now finding their religious quest satisfied apart from the synagogue, and satisfied in terms which the synagogues were bound to see as in some degree competitive with their own. Members of the synagogue community who had relished the respect and support of such God-fearers would naturally feel both aggrieved and indignant at such johnny-come-latelies trying to upstage them.

Such *a priori* reasoning chimes in well with the data of the letter itself, where a certain preoccupation with aspects of Jewish identity is clearly evident.

- Col. 1.12 has already been mentioned — God 'has qualified you to share the inheritance of the saints in the light'.[360]
- The talk of 'alienation' in 1.21 smacks of a Jewish perspective, as more explicitly in Eph. 2.12 ('aliens from the commonwealth of Israel, and strangers to the covenants of promise').[361]

357. Examples in my *Colossians and Philemon* 70-71, 131-32.

358. The idea of God or his Spirit as filling the world was a common topos in Greek thought (e.g., Seneca, *De beneficiis* 4.8.2; Aristides, *Orationes* 45.21), as also in Jewish writing (Jer. 23.24; Ps. 139.7; Philo, *Leg.* 3.4; *Gig.* 47; *Conf.* 136; *Mos.* 2.238). The language need not be drawn from or presuppose a feature of the Colossian 'philosophy' as such.

359. Isa. 6.2-3; Dan. 7.10; *1 En.* 14.18-23; 36.4; 39–40.

360. As noted in n. 336 above, the terms are characteristically Jewish terminology.

361. This language of alienation (*apallotrioō*) occurs in the NT only here and in Eph. 2.12 and 4.18.

- Another Jewish perspective is the repeated reference to circumcision (Col. 2.11 — as a positive metaphor; 4.11) and the circumcision/uncircumcision contrast (2.13; 3.11); who but a Jew would use 'uncircumcision' as a pejorative term?[362]
- Likewise the emphasis evidently being placed by those who 'passed judgment' on the church in regard to food and drink,[363] and festivals, new moon and Sabbaths[364] — all characteristically and some distinctively Jewish concerns.
- Similarly, 2.21 ('Do not touch, do not taste, do not handle') most probably echoes typically Jewish fears lest physical contact render impure (as in Lev. 5.3), fears particularly evident in the Judaism of the period.[365]
- Nor should the echo of the distinctively Jewish antipathy to idolatry and *porneia* ('sexual license') in Col. 3.5 go unnoticed.

Similar concerns can be cited within a wider religious framework, but none of the concerns indicated above is strange to, and several are distinctive of, Second Temple Judaism ('saints', circumcision, Sabbath, antipathy to idolatry). Calendar piety, food laws, circumcision and rejection of idolatry were not just random elements of some syncretistic cult but the norms and markers which gave Jews their identity.[366] So the most obvious proponents of the Colossian 'philosophy' are one or more of the Jewish synagogues. They probably prided themselves on the venerable age and sophistication of their religion ('philosophy'). They no doubt resented the claims being made by the Colossian church that its members, Gentile as well as Jew, were fully participant in Israel's distinctive heritage. And they presumably judged these claims to be disqualified because the Christians were not maintaining the practices which hitherto had been regarded as distinctive markers of the heritage of Abraham, Moses, David and Elijah. The echo in 2.22 ('human commandments and teachings') of the Jesus tradition's criticism of Jewish/Pharisaic tradition (Mark 7.7/Matt. 15.9) is unlikely to be accidental; it suggests a critical interaction which consciously drew on that tradition.

---

362. As again in Eph. 2.11, on which see §37 n. 34 below.

363. Cf. Dan. 1.3-16; 10.3; Add. Esth. 14.17; *Jos. Asen.* 8.5.

364. E.g., 1 Chron. 23.31; Neh. 10.33; Ezek. 45.17; Hos. 2.11; 1 Macc. 10.34.

365. As particularly in 1QS 6–7 and *T. Mos.* 7.9-10 — 'Do not touch me lest you pollute me . . .'.

366. W. Schenk, 'Der Kolosserbrief in der neueren Forschung (1945-1985)', *ANRW* 2.25.4 (1987) 3327-64 (here 3351-53); Sanders, *Schismatics* 190 (further 190-93).

d. 'The Worship of Angels'

This hypothesis makes good sense of the single most puzzling and contested phrase in Colossians — 'the worship of angels' (2.18).

Various second-century sources describe (or accuse) Jews of worshipping angels.[367] But more characteristic of Judaism is warning against such worship.[368] So if this is what Col. 2.18 had in view, and the Jews of (some of) the Colossian synagogues were the target, then it must have indeed been a rather syncretistic Judaism. But since the thesis of such a syncretistic Judaism is not well attested elsewhere for this period, even by hostile witnesses like the second-century sources just alluded to, consideration has to be given to the alternative way of rendering the prepositional phrase, even if the more obvious way of taking it is as 'worship offered to angels'.

That a subjective genitive rendering is entirely plausible ('worship rendered by angels') has long been maintained by Fred Francis and those who have followed him.[369] In the light of the considerations just marshalled, a subjective genitive reading becomes all the more likely, since (as already mentioned) such worship features prominently in several Jewish apocalypses. More to the point, there is clear evidence in various Jewish sources of the period of an aspiration to join in or with such worship.[370] The cumulative evidence invites us, therefore, to envisage one or more Jewish synagogues in Colossae who understood their Sabbath worship as joining with the worship of the angels in heaven. The self-discipline and mortification (2.18, 23) which they practised as part of their purity, dietary and festal traditions were presumably regarded by them as requisite for such spiritual (mystical) experiences.[371] And consequently they looked down on what must have seemed to be the relative poverty of the worship of the Jews and non-Jews who had formed a new assembly (church) in the city.

367. *Kerygma Petri; Apology of Aristides* 14.4; Celsus in Origen, *c. Cels.* 1.25 and 5.6.

368. *Apoc. Zeph.* 6.15; *Apoc. Abr.* 17.2; Philo, *Fug.* 212; *Som.* 1.232, 238; also Rev. 19.10 and 22.9.

369. F. O. Francis, 'Humility and Angel Worship in Colossae', in Francis and Meeks, *Conflict at Colossae* 163-95. See particularly T. J. Sappington, *Revelation and Redemption at Colossae* (JSNTS 53; Sheffield: JSOT, 1991); C. Stettler, 'The Opponents at Colossae', in S. E. Porter, ed., *Paul and His Opponents* (Leiden: Brill, 2005) 169-200; other bibliography in my *Colossians and Philemon* 29 n. 27; I. K. Smith, *Heavenly Perspective: A Study of the Apostle Paul's Response to a Jewish Mystical Movement at Colossae* (LNTS 326; London: Clark International, 2006); cf. H. W. Attridge, 'On Becoming an Angel: Rival Baptismal Theologies at Colossae', in L. Bormann et al., eds., *Religious Propaganda and Missionary Competition in the New Testament World,* D. Georgi FS (NovTSupp 74; Leiden: Brill, 1994) 481-98.

370. Most strikingly in *T. Job* 48-50, *Apoc. Abr.* 17 and *Apoc. Zeph.* 8.3-4; and no less strikingly in the Qumran scrolls, notably the *Songs of the Sabbath Sacrifice* (4Q400-405).

371. For data see my *Colossians and Philemon* 178-79, and on the difficult verse 23, see 194-98.

e. The Message of the Letter

Whatever the danger threatening the Colossian church was, the concern of the letter was evidently to counter that threat and to provide sound counsel for the Colossian believers' faith and conduct, not least in the light of that threat. It is significant, then, that Paul and Timothy conclude the opening pleasantries (1.1-11 — greeting, thanksgiving and prayer) with a specific claim as to what the Colossian believers have received in accepting the gospel (1.12-14): that is, both a share in Israel's 'inheritance' and a new status with God's Son (rescued from the authority of darkness and transferred into the kingdom of God's Son; redemption and forgiveness). In face of denigratory criticism from the synagogue(s), the claim to share in Israel's inheritance is at once reasserted without qualification, and the distinctive benefits of the gospel message are set out with bold strokes.

Contrary to many commentators, however, it is not the claims made for Christ in the gospel which appear to lie at the heart of the issue between the letter writers and the Colossian 'philosophy'. The great 'hymn' (as it is usually described) in praise of Christ (1.15-20), which is immediately attached to this opening statement, is not set out in polemical fashion but is given as grounds for the recipients' own faith and hope (1.4-5, 11-14). And the defence in 2.8-23 focuses not on Christ but on the traditions being cited (2.8), on food, drink, festivals (2.16) and purity (2.20-23). Certainly, who Christ is and what Christ has done provide the secure basis for the letter's denial of the importance of these traditions and practices.[372] But the issue is not, as often suggested, that Christ's role was being challenged by the 'philosophy'.[373] The claims made about Christ are simply there to boost the Colossians' self-esteem to withstand the denigrating criticisms of their own lack of ancient tradition, of ritual, festival and rule. The point, of course, is that what Christ had done for them and was doing in them (1.27; 3.3-4) rendered such praxis nugatory and irrelevant. But that claim as such, evidently, was not the point of conflict with the 'cultured despisers' in the Colossian synagogue(s).

At the same time, the Colossian christology marks a significant consolidation and step forward in Pauline christology. Distinctive of the letter are the following features:

- talk of 'the kingdom of [God's] beloved Son' (1.13);[374]

---

372. Col. 2.6-7, 9-15, 17, 19, 20; 3.1-4.

373. Commentators have been too easily distracted by the reference to 'the worship of angels' in 2.18.

374. The unusual formula 'Son of his love' seems to be a Semitic form (BDF §165),

- the cosmic sweep of the 'hymn' — 'all things created through him and for him' (1.16);[375]
- the cosmic body is identified with 'the church' (1.18),[376] although later (2.19) the church is depicted as the trunk of the body, Christ being the head;[377]
- he has reconciled 'all things' (1.20);[378]
- Christ himself as 'God's mystery, in whom all the treasures of wisdom and knowledge are hidden' (2.2-3), 'the mystery of Christ' (4.3);[379]
- the nearest the Pauline corpus comes to a statement of incarnation — 'in him the whole fullness of deity dwells bodily' (2.9);[380]
- the unique expression of the Christus Victor theme — Christ leading 'the rulers and authorities' in triumph in the chariot of his cross (2.15);[381]
- believers not only died with Christ but already raised with him (2.20; 3.1).[382]

---

equivalent to 'beloved son' (cf. Eph. 1.6 — 'the beloved'). For Israel's king as God's son, see particularly 2 Sam. 7.14; Pss. 2.7; 89.26-27; 4Q174 (4QFlor.) 1.10-19; 4Q246 2.1. The nearest to this language in the earlier Paul is 1 Cor. 15.24-28.

375. A fuller expression of 1 Cor. 8.6 (see above, §32 n. 272; and §29.7d). That language used of the wisdom of God in Jewish wisdom tradition is similarly used here of Christ is generally recognized (1.15-17, 18b); documentation in *Colossians and Philemon* 87-94, 97-99, and bibliography on 1.15-20 in 83 n. 5 (see again §32 n. 272 above). Murphy-O'Connor is confident in his ability to detect Pauline revisions of an original hymn and of Paul's motivations for the revisions (*Paul* 242-46).

376. If the hymn used the ancient Greek thought likening the cosmos to a body (the classic text is Plato's *Timaeus* 31B-32C), and if 'the church' has been added by way of explanation, the step being taken was extraordinary, 'the church' being presented as the focus or beginning of Christ's effective rule over the cosmos. The thought at least anticipates the even more extraordinary Eph. 1.22-23.

377. Schenk, 'Selbstverständnisse' 1411-15; see further my '"The Body of Christ" in Paul'.

378. The verb is the uniquely compounded *apokatallassō*, which appears in literary Greek only here, in 1.22 and Eph. 2.16. The phrase 'all things' takes further the earlier thought of Rom. 5.10; 1 Cor. 7.11; 2 Cor. 5.18-20 but is anticipated in some measure in Jewish hope (Isa. 11.6-9; 65.17, 25; *Jub.* 1.29; 23.26-29; *1 En.* 91.16-17; Philo, *Spec. Leg.* 2.192).

379. Elaborating the earlier 1.26-27, itself taking up the language of earlier letters (Rom. 11.25; 1 Cor. 2.1, 7; 4.1); the terminology is also taken up strongly in Ephesians (see again §29 n. 114 above; and my *Colossians and Philemon* 119-21). Col. 2.3 also ties the mystery to the wisdom language of 1.15-17 (also 1.9 and 28).

380. An elaboration of 1.19 — 'in him all the fullness of God was pleased to dwell'. See above, n. 358, and further my *Colossians and Philemon* 99-102, 151-52.

381. Elaborating the imagery of 2 Cor. 2.14 (see above, §32 n. 438; and further *Colossians and Philemon* 167-70).

382. In the earlier use of the imagery, participation with Christ in his resurrection was still seen as future (Rom. 6.5, 8; 8.11; even Phil. 3.10-11, 21).

In Colossians we see the transition to the great Wisdom/Logos christologies of the second and third centuries already well under way.

In order to boost the Colossian believers' confidence in their status as genuine participants in the good news of Jesus Messiah stemming from Israel, Paul and Timothy reemphasize the claim which so identified and distinguished Paul's conception of his calling and mission: that he had been specially commissioned to reveal the long-hidden mystery of God's purpose, 'to make known what is the wealth of the glory of this mystery among the nations, which is Christ in you, the hope of glory' (1.25-27).[383] Implicit in this is a rebuttal of the Colossian synagogues and traditionalist Jews, that far from being in any position to disparage the Gentile believers of Colossae, the latter were in possession of the key to the mystery of God's purpose, a mystery to which the non-believing Jews were still blind.[384] In a word, the key is Christ, 'in whom all the treasures of wisdom and knowledge are hidden' (2.3). This includes, not least, the traditions they had received *(parelabete)*[385] about this Christ which should provide the continuing basis for their conduct *(peripateite)* (2.6-7). Here, we might note in passing, Paul evidently saw complete consistency between the Jesus tradition he knew to have been passed on to the Colossians and the bold christological assertions being made in the letter; it was the same Jesus Christ who provided a pattern for their daily living as well as the key to unlock the divine mystery and who was the central theme of their devotion.[386]

As already noted, the response to the disparaging critique directed at the Colossian church from one or more of the Colossian synagogues is focused in 2.8-23. Any role which the Colossian philosophy attributed to 'the elemental forces *(ta stoicheia)* of the world' and 'the (heavenly) rulers and authorities' has been trumped by the gospel of Christ.[387] 'In him dwells *all* the fullness of the de-

383. On 1.24 see above, §29.3e.

384. A characteristic feature of the 'mystery' motif in Jewish writings is the claim (of the individual or group) that the resolution of the mystery has been revealed to them (and by implication, not to others); see again §29 n. 114 above.

385. As is generally recognized, *paralambanō* is more or less a technical term for receiving tradition, and the verb is most often used by Paul in this sense (1 Cor. 11.23; 15.1, 3; Gal. 1.9, 12; Phil. 4.19; 1 Thess. 2.13; 4.1; 2 Thess. 3.6).

386. Col. 2.6-7 is one of the most important, usually missed, confirmations that a substantial body of traditions about Christ Jesus as Lord must have been passed on when churches were first founded (it could be assumed that this had been the case in Colossae). That this tradition was to determine their conduct *(peripatein)* presumably means that it included the sort of Jesus tradition which formed the core of the Synoptic Gospels.

387. The debate on the meaning and reference of *stoicheia* is considerable, but it probably encapsulates the all-too-common belief (even today) that human beings have to live their lives under the influence or sway of primal and cosmic forces, however precisely conceptualized; for an effective summary of the case see R. P. Martin, *Colossians and Philemon* (NCBC;

ity in bodily form'; he 'is the head of all rule and authority' (2.9-10); he has wholly disarmed and defeated such powers (2.15). This also means that any hold which such forces and powers might have had on their lives has been broken: their lack of circumcision has been fully met in the death of Christ, itself a kind of circumcision (2.11); their new life was a sharing in Christ's resurrection life (2.12-13); and their transgressions and any indictments which the law might bring against them had been wiped out and cancelled (2.13-14). The correlation here with Gal. 4.1-10 should not be missed: it was what Paul regarded as the over-exaltation of the law and the way it was being understood to disqualify uncircumcised Gentiles from full participation in its benefits (not least for direct-ing conduct) to which he was objecting so strongly, even if the Colossian syna-gogues were not pressuring the Gentile believers to accept that logic themselves.

The point at which pressure was evidently being exerted was in regard to the rules and rituals which the Colossian synagogues regarded as indispensable — the traditional Jewish rules regarding food and drink and festivals (2.16, 20-23), and the more distinctive claim to join with the 'worship of angels' (2.18).[388] In the view of the Colossian synagogues, failure to observe these rules and to en-joy such worship 'condemned *(krinein)*' and 'disqualified *(katabrabeuein)*' the Colossian believers (2.16, 18).[389] The response is again robust. This was just the same mistake that Paul had confronted in Galatia: such an insistence on certain laws as indispensable was tantamount to regarding the law as itself one of the 'el-emental forces' (2.20; Gal. 4.9-10). Moreover, it failed to recognize that the be-lievers were already experiencing in Christ the reality only foreshadowed in such rules and worship (2.17-19), and it bred arrogance and self-deception (2.18, 23).

The basis for Christian conduct was rather to recognize what had already happened in their lives: they had been raised with Christ and should therefore set their minds on what is above and not on what is on the earth (3.1-2); their old lives were dead, and their real life was 'hidden with Christ in God' (3.3). That was where their hope should be fixed (3.4). This basic starting point should de-termine their conduct from then on: both that which they should avoid (3.5-11) and that which they should cultivate (3.12-17). The paraenesis uses imagery ('put off', 'put on') and forms (vice-lists, virtue-lists) which were common in the

---

London: Marshall, Morgan and Scott, 1973) 10-14; and further my *Colossians and Philemon* 148-51. The 'rulers and authorities' take up the more varied terminology and conceptuality of 1.16 (on which see my *Colossians and Philemon* 92-93) but are a variant expression of the same range of belief about the cosmos and the cosmic powers which influenced or determined human destiny.

388. See above, nn. 363, 364 and §34.6d.

389. *Brabeuō* has the primary meaning 'award a prize (a *brabeion*)' in a contest; hence *katabrabeuō* (only here in biblical Greek and not much attested elsewhere) means 'decide against' as an umpire, and so 'rob of a prize' (BDAG 515).

ethical systems of the ancient world.[390] Noticeable, however, is the characteristic Jewish antipathy to *porneia* ('sexual immorality') and idolatry (3.5), as well as the characteristic Jewish emphasis on praxis. More distinctively Christian is the holding forth of Christ as the image of God to which they were being conformed (3.10) and the assertion that in Christ national, religious and social discrimination is now at an end (3.11). The commendation of humility would jar with most of their fellow residents, as with Greek thought generally (3.12),[391] and the emphasis on forgiving as the Lord forgave and on the central motivation of love (3.13-14) can be safely regarded as echoes of distinctive elements in the Jesus tradition.[392]

All this would map out a different character of living from the one promoted by the Colossian synagogues. Paul and Timothy no doubt hoped that by providing such a range of guidelines and exhortations, in place of the rituals and rules advocated by the disparaging Jewish neighbours, they would have enabled the Colossian believers to maintain their own priorities and live out their own convictions with confidence. Presumably it is no mere coincidence that the paraenesis climaxes in a commendation of their worship — meditating on the word of Christ, teaching and admonition, singing with thankfulness — and by inculcating an attitude of gratitude to God (3.16-17).[393] This would be the answer to any claim on the part of the synagogue congregations that their worship reached heights which the believers could never experience. Quite the contrary, says Paul!

The final block of paraenesis (3.18–4.1) comes as something of a surprise, for the author(s) seem to take up a familiar theme of ancient moralizing — the importance of household management *(oikonomia)*. Moreover, they take it up in the terms familiar from other such *Haustafeln:* particularly both assumed and confirmed is the centrality and dominance of the *paterfamilias,* as husband, father and master, and the expectation that the wife should 'be subject' to her husband.[394] But notable is the assumption that children and slaves would be fully part of the Christian gathering; as already noted, they are addressed directly (3.20, 22). And the whole is suffused with a Christian spirit by the constant reference to their common Lord:

390. *Theology of Paul* 123-24, 662-65.

391. W. Grundmann, *TDNT* 8.1-4, 11-12.

392. *Jesus Remembered* 182 n. 48, 590.

393. For detail see *Colossians and Philemon* 235-41.

394. Details again in *Colossians and Philemon* 242-47; see also my 'The Household Rules in the New Testament', in S. C. Barton, ed., *The Family in Theological Perspective* (Edinburgh: Clark, 1996) 43-63. I gladly acknowledge my indebtedness in particular to D. Balch, *Let Wives Be Submissive: The Domestic Code in 1 Peter* (Missoula: Scholars, 1981). See also Witherington, *Women in the Earliest Churches* 47-54.

- 3.18 — 'wives, be subject to your husbands, as is fitting in the Lord';
- 3.20 — 'children, obey your parents . . . for this is pleasing in the Lord';
- 3.22 — 'slaves, obey in everything . . . fearing the Lord'
- 3.23 — 'whatever you do, put yourself wholly into it, as to the Lord';
- 3.24 — 'the master you are slave to is Christ';
- 4.1 — 'masters, grant your slaves what is just and fair, knowing that you also have a master in heaven'.[395]

In this reaffirmation and adaptation of the common understanding of the importance of household order, the intention was presumably twofold. In part, such exhortation recognized the pivotal place which the household held in the good ordering of society. Paul and Timothy could give such instruction knowing that it would reassure any visitors to (or informers within) the Colossian congregation that the Christians were good citizens, as civically responsible as any of their neighbours.[396] This would also be an effective rejoinder to any suggestion on the part of the Colossian synagogue community that the Colossian believers, lacking the discipline and ritual of the law, must be less responsible in their family and civic duties. In part too, however, and as with the relationship Paul sought to encourage between Philemon and Onesimus, it set the relationships which constituted the household within the more fundamental relationship of the several parties (individually and together as a household) with the one Lord in whom they believed and to whom they had committed themselves. This was the way in which, at the end of his mission, Paul still saw the Christian message as impacting the social and political conditions of his time, as a yeast which steadily permeates and transforms the whole, not necessarily in its visible workings and forms, but in its inward character and motivating spirit.

f. The Aftermath

As with almost all of Paul's letters we have no information as to how the letter to the Colossians was received or of its impact. Here again a critical factor was probably the earthquake which ravaged the Lycus Valley in 60-61. According to Tacitus, Laodicea was badly damaged, and although he does not refer to damage suffered by Colossae, it is scarcely likely that Colossae escaped serious damage;[397] the un-

---

395. See also J. M. G. Barclay, 'Ordinary but Different: Colossians and Hidden Moral Identity', *ABR* 49 (2001) 34-52.

396. The intention, in other words, was much the same as in the exhortations given to the believers in Rome (Rom. 12.9–13.7; cf. also 4.5-6), an encouragement to responsible citizenship (see above, §33.3f[ii]).

397. 'In the Asian province one of its famous cities, Laodicea, was destroyed by an

reliable Orosius (early fifth century) states that all three Lycus Valley cities 'fell by earthquakes' (*Hist. adv. paganos* 7.7.12).[398] But even if the Colossian group of believers survived the earthquake of 60/61, we do not know whether Colossae was extensively rebuilt.[399] It is possible that most members of the Colossian church who survived resettled elsewhere, possibly in Laodicea, which, again as Tacitus tells us, was able speedily to re-establish itself.

Perhaps more striking is the fact that neither of the subsequent two Christian leaders who wrote letters to churches in Asia Minor[400] included Colossae in their correspondence. Does that suggest that the Colossian church as such did not survive? Here it may be significant that while we have firm information about the importance in the history of Christianity of the other two cities of the Lycus Valley (Hierapolis and Laodicea),[401] we hear nothing more of Colossae.

This also raises the question of what happened to the letter to Colossae itself. Was it saved from the destruction wrought by the earthquake, unlike, perhaps, the letter to the Laodiceans (Col. 4.16)?[402] Or did Timothy retain a copy, perhaps for use in further attempts to retain and promote the heritage of Paul? In all this we can do no more than speculate.

34.7. When Did Paul Die?

Luke ends his account of Christianity's beginnings with the fading sunset of Paul in custody for two years (about 60-62) in Rome. Although Luke knew all too well that Paul had been taken to Rome in order to stand trial before the emperor, he made no attempt to round off his story with an account of that trial. It is very unlikely that Luke did not know the outcome of any trial at the end of the two-year period: the option of arguing that Acts was written before the trial, and possibly to influence the trial,[403] is ruled out by the normal dating of Luke's Gospel,

---

earthquake in this year, and rebuilt from its own resources without any subvention from Rome' (Tacitus, *Ann.* 14.27.1).

398. The odd fact that the mound marking the site of Colossae has never been excavated means that we have no archaeological evidence to draw on.

399. There is some inscriptional and numismatic evidence for Colossae's continuance as a Roman city, but evidently it never recovered its former glory.

400. The seer of Revelation (Revelation 2–3) and Ignatius.

401. An early tradition places the graves of Philip and his four daughters at Hierapolis (Eusebius, *HE* 3.31.4; 5.24.2). Laodicea was one of the churches to which the seer of Revelation wrote (Rev. 3.14-25), and the Council of Laodicea met in about 363. Its site has not been properly excavated either.

402. Conceivably it was the exchange of the two letters (Col. 4.16) which resulted in the one being lost and the other preserved.

403. See above, §21 n. 52.

which all recognize to have used Mark's Gospel, itself usually dated to the late 60s or early 70s. Moreover, Luke has already shown clearly what the appropriate verdict should be, as voiced before Paul was shipped to Rome by both Agrippa II and the Roman governor Festus (Acts 26.31-32). This verdict had been confirmed for his readers by the episode in Malta following the shipwreck: Paul's escape from the viper's venom proved to the onlookers that he was not a criminal but a god (28.4-6)! And Luke himself had prepared his readers and their audiences for Paul's death in the speech which Paul had earlier delivered in Miletus (20.25, 29). Not only so, but we should recall that Luke's tendency was to gloss over several of the most negative incidents in the history of Christianity's expansion.[404]

So the most obvious conclusion to draw is that Luke indeed knew all too well that the trial of Paul at the end of the two-year period had gone badly for Paul and that he had been summarily executed, immediately or a little later.[405] This, however, was not the note on which Luke wanted to end his history. Rather it was the fact that in depicting Paul freely preaching the gospel in Rome, Luke had reached the climax and end of his stated programme — to describe the way the witness to Christ spread from Jerusalem, through Judea and Samaria, and to 'the end of the earth' in Rome (1.8).[406] The open-ended portrayal of ongoing proclamation of Christ and God's kingdom (28.30-31), with the implication that this was the ongoing task of those who continued to bear witness to Christ, was much preferable. Apart from anything else, it invited the readers and audiences of second-generation Christianity to continue the same story in bearing the same witness in their own situations.[407]

So much for Luke's Acts. Is there any other information or traditions on which to draw? Three offer some pointers.

(1) The Pastoral Epistles are most probably to be read as letters written in

---

404. Particularly the incident at Antioch and the opposition which Paul faced in Galatia, Corinth (2 Corinthians 10–13) and Philippi (Phil. 3.2-21). As Haenchen observes, Luke nowhere prepared his readers for a happy outcome (*Acts* 731).

405. Omerzu, 'Schweigen' 156. P. R. McKechnie, 'Judean Embassies and Cases before Roman Emperors, AD 44-66', *JTS* 56 (2005) 339-61, observes that over a period of about two decades, rulings seem to have been consistently given in favour of the Jerusalem priesthood, even against some Roman procurators, which suggests that when Nero heard the case against Paul, he would have ruled against him. The earlier suggestion (by Ramsay, Lake and Cadbury) that the case never came to trial and lapsed was based on a mistaken dating of an edict (Bruce, *Paul* 376-77).

406. See above, §22 n. 53. See also Lichtenberger, 'Jews and Christians in Rome' 2152-53; W. F. Brosend, 'The Means of Absent Ends', in Witherington, ed., *History* 348-62.

407. See further B. S. Rosner, 'The Progress of the Word', in I. H. Marshall and D. Peterson, eds., *Witness to the Gospel: The Theology of Acts* (Grand Rapids: Eerdmans, 1998) 215-33 (here 229-33); and above, n. 233.

the spirit of Paul some twenty or thirty years later.[408] But even so, they may incorporate earlier material from Paul or well-grounded traditions about Paul. In reference to Paul himself and his fate, the most interesting is 2 Timothy, particularly 2 Tim. 4.9-18. The letter speaks of Paul's 'first defence', which he had had to face alone, and of his 'rescue from the lion's mouth' (4.16-17). This could suggest that there had been a first trial, which Paul had survived, though now he was facing a second, which could and probably would end in his death (4.6-7).[409] Particularly poignant are the sense of having been almost abandoned ('only Luke is with me' — 4.11) and the requests for the cloak to be brought which he had left behind in Troas, 'also the books and above all the parchments *(membranas)*' (4.13).[410] The most plausible inference to draw from this is that after his first trial, Paul's imprisonment was made more severe, being held, perhaps, in a cold, dank dungeon, where a cloak would be no longer a luxury but a necessity in winter (4.21), and where opportunity to leave his own archive in good order was now urgent.

By itself, 2 Timothy would only extend the story-line of Acts by including a first trial, without implying Paul's release.[411] But when the other two Pastorals are included, it may be inferred that Paul was released after his first (or second) trial and was able to travel back into the Aegean region.[412] Indeed, the travel plans in 1 Timothy (3.14-15) and Titus (3.12) are reminiscent of Paul's earlier hopes and intentions, and if they are to be correlated with the sober pessimism of 2 Tim. 4.6-7, we have to envisage a much more extensive further period of mission of Paul in the Aegean area and Greece (Nicopolis), followed by a further imprisonment (reason unattested) prior to his final trial and, presumably, death. For my own part, I doubt whether this is the best way to read these data. I suspect some of it is a reworking of Paul's previous itineraries, and that the only data which bear directly on the question of Paul's end is the 2 Tim. 4.6-18 passage. It may even be that we should see in 4.9-18 a note from Paul which he was able to have smuggled out of his final, more severe imprisonment.[413] That would at least fill out the picture

---

408. See below, vol. 3.

409. 'I am already being poured out as a libation, and the time of my departure has come. I have fought the good fight, I have finished the race . . .' (4.6-7); contrast Phil. 3.12-14.

410. See above, §29 n. 335.

411. That 2 Timothy and the information it offers should be considered independently from the other two Pastorals is strongly argued by M. Prior, *Paul the Letter-Writer and the Second Letter to Timothy* (JSNTS 23; Sheffield: JSOT, 1989), followed by Murphy-O'Connor, *Paul* 357-59.

412. 1 Tim. 1.3; 2 Tim. 1.18; 4.20; Tit. 1.5; 3.12.

413. This suggestion first occurred to me when I read the note, of similar character, which William Tyndale managed to have smuggled out of his imprisonment; the note was framed and hung on the wall of Tyndale House, Cambridge.

which Acts leaves with us: that after being held in custody for two years, Paul was put on trial. Despite being abandoned by his friends(!), the trial ended in a reprieve, but a temporary reprieve, since he was still held in prison, but under more severe conditions. The second trial resulted in his execution.

How does such speculation correlate with what we know of the situation in Rome during this period? The most important factor is that, after the first five years of his reign, which were hailed as a golden age by contemporary poets, Emperor Nero's character and rule began to degenerate, that is, in 59, following his arranging to have his mother murdered (Tacitus, *Ann.* 15.67).[414] The following five years culminated in the fire of Rome, blamed on the Christians. I will return to this subject in §35. The point is that during that five years, 59-64, Nero became less and less rational and predictable. Josephus tells us of some Jewish priests who had been sent by the procurator Felix as prisoners to Rome 'to render account to Caesar' 'on a slight and trifling charge', who were still being held in custody there in 64, that is, after at least four or five years (*Life* 13-14). It is entirely possible, then, that Nero chose arbitrarily to regard the accusations against Paul more seriously than had Festus. And if, during his imprisonment, Paul's message had indeed succeeded in penetrating the praetorium and Nero's civil service (Phil. 1.13), it is likely that news of this would have incited Nero's advisers against the representative of this further example of Levantine 'superstition' penetrating (and corrupting) Roman society. The scenario suggested by 2 Tim. 4.6-18 is entirely consistent with all this and again points to an execution of Paul in 62, or possibly as part of the anti-Christian pogrom in 64.

(2) The second possibly relevant tradition is that contained in *1 Clem.* 5.6-7 — speaking of Paul:

> [6]Seven times he bore chains; he was sent into exile and stoned; he served as a herald in both the East and the West; and he received the noble reputation for his faith. [7]He taught righteousness to the whole world and came to the limit (*terma*) of the West, bearing witness before the rulers. And so he was set free from this world and transported up to the holy place, having become the greatest example of endurance.

The seven imprisonments may indicate information extending beyond the Acts 28 imprisonment.[415] But the key issue here is the sense of the phrase 'the limits of the West'. The most natural interpretation is that Spain is intended.[416] Certainly some

---

414. For further detail see, e.g., *OCD*[3] 1037-38.

415. Haacker, *Römer* 311; though if the 'far more imprisonments' of 2 Cor. 11.23 referred to as many as three or four, then the imprisonments of Jerusalem, Caesarea and Rome would make up the seven; we know so little regarding several items on the 2 Corinthians 11 list.

416. H. Lona, *Der erste Clemensbrief* (KAV; Göttingen: Vandenhoeck und Ruprecht, 1998) 165; earlier bibliography in BDAG 935-36. Strabo describes Spain as 'the most westerly

commentators wonder whether Clement simply took this from Rom. 15.24 and 28, on the assumption that Paul actually reached his goal.[417] Otherwise his account could reflect Paul's own recollection (15.19) of his mission, as in both the east ('from Jerusalem') and the west ('in a sweep round to Illyricum'). However, it must be remembered that Clement was writing from Rome, and it is hard to envisage him meaning anything other than a point west of Rome by the phrase he used.[418] In any case, the sequence 'having come to the limit of the West and having borne witness before the rulers, he thus departed from this world' suggests that the appearance before 'the rulers' led directly to his death.

(3) The third testimonies can be grouped together as coming from more than a century later than the event of Paul's death. The first is the famous Muratorian fragment, which simply notes that Luke left out from Acts both the passion of Peter 'and also the departure of Paul from the city on his journey to Spain'. Here, more than in the case of *1 Clement,* the mention of departing from Rome *en route* for Spain is so strongly reminiscent of Paul's own intentions in Rom. 15.24 and 28 as to suggest that it is derived from that letter.[419] The other is the account of Paul's martyrdom in the *Acts of Paul* 11, which contains a novelistic elaboration of what was presumably an earlier tradition that Paul was executed by Nero during Nero's persecution of Christians after the great fire of Rome; the form of execution is specified as beheading (11.5).[420] Interestingly, the *Acts* show no interest in or knowledge of a mission to Spain, even though that tradition would have provided more grist for the novelist's mill.[421]

Eusebius infers from 2 Timothy that Luke wrote Acts during Paul's two-year imprisonment in Rome and that Paul had been released after a successful

---

point, not only of Europe, but of the whole inhabited world' (3.1.4). Ellis notes that Philostratus (*Apol.* 5.4) speaks of Gades (Cadiz) as the *terma* of Europe (*Making* 281). Murphy-O'Connor suggests that the hostility Paul experienced from the Roman church (2 Tim. 4.16) may be explained by the failure of his mission to Spain (*Paul* 361-63).

417. E.g., Lüdemann, *Early Christianity* 266; and again BDAG 935-36.

418. H. Löhr, 'Zum Paulus-Notiz in 1 Clem 5,5-7', in Horn, ed., *Ende* 197-213 (here 207-209), though he notes that *terma* could mark 'the West' as the goal or turning point in a chariot or foot race (LSJ 1777). Sanders had already observed that 'if it ["*terma* of the West"] means "goal of the West", in the sense of "Paul's fixed destination", then Rome will do very well' (*Paul* 16).

419. Omerzu, 'Schweigen' 129. B. Wander, 'Warum wollte Paulus nach Spanien?', in Horn, ed., *Ende* 175-95, concludes that the final judgment on the question whether Paul actually did embark on a Spanish mission has to be *non liquet* (194). The absence of reliable traces, even legends, of missionary activity by Paul in Spain itself is telling.

420. Texts in *NTA* 2.260-63; Elliott, *Apocryphal New Testament* 385-88.

421. *The Acts of Peter* begins with such a novelistic narrative of Paul's departure from Rome for Spain (1-3) (*NTA* 2.287-89; Elliott, *Apocryphal New Testament* 399-401). Schnabel presses the case for the view that Paul was released from his (first) Roman imprisonment and engaged in a mission in Spain (*Mission* 1273-83).

first defence before coming to Rome for a second time and suffering martyrdom there (*HE* 2.22.1-8). Whether the *Acts of Paul* provides the basis for Eusebius's further report that 'Paul was beheaded in Rome itself' (*HE* 2.25.5) during Nero's persecution is not clear. But Eusebius also attests that the title of 'Peter and Paul' 'is still given to the cemeteries there', and he attributes the tradition to a Christian writer 'Caius, who lived when Zephyrinus was bishop of Rome' (198-217) and who identifies the Vatican and the Ostian Way as the two sites specially revered in connection with the two apostles (2.25.6-7).[422] He also cites Dionysius, bishop of Corinth, claiming that Peter and Paul both 'taught in Italy in the same place and were martyred at the same time' (2.25.8), and later Origen for the tradition that Paul 'was martyred in Rome under Nero' (3.1.3).

In all this, the impulse towards hagiography and to claiming apostolic foundation of specific churches[423] had long been obscuring what little historical data there were available even then, so that little more can be usefully gleaned from such evidence. On any hypothesis problems remain:

- the silence of Acts, if Paul was released from prison and went on to more missionary work;
- the difficulty of integrating the testimony of 2 Timothy with that of the other two Pastorals;
- the difficulty of integrating 1 Timothy and Titus (further Aegean mission, but nothing about Paul going to Spain) with *1 Clem.* 5.6-7 (Paul reached 'the limits of the West', but nothing about other mission).[424]

At best we probably have to settle for the conclusion that Paul was executed under Nero, and probably at the command of Nero, some time between 62 and 64.[425] The lack of a competing tradition for the death of Paul can be regarded as sufficient confirmation for at least this historical conclusion.

---

422. The full statement is provided below in §35.3. Recent archaeological investigations in Rome under both St. Peter and St. Paul without the Walls suggest that the two churches were indeed built on the sites of their burials and/or executions; see also Bruce, *Paul* 450-54. But more elaborate claims should be at best tentative: as Barrett notes, 'there is theological appropriateness if something less than historical conviction in the rough inscription on the fourth-century sepulchral slab in S. Paolo fuori le Mura: PAULO APOSTOLO MART.'; and see §35 n. 53 below.

423. Dionysius claimed that his own church, Corinth, had been founded by both Peter and Paul (Eusebius, *HE* 2.25.8).

424. Murphy-O'Connor suggests a single summer of mission to Spain (a failure), followed by a further year in Illyricum and thence back into Macedonia and to Ephesus (*Paul* 363-64).

425. This also is the conclusion of Becker, *Paul* 476, and Schnelle, *Paul* 384-86. Murphy-O'Connor allows for some further five or so years of missionary work following his release, before Paul returned to Rome to support the Christians there during continuing persecution from Nero, to perish during Nero's final year, in late 67 or early 68 (*Paul* 368-71).

CHAPTER 35

The Voiceless Peter

In comparison with the mission of Paul, what we know of Peter's mission is lamentably little. If only Peter had had someone like Luke to record his doings and adventures, what a tale might have come down to us! The thought should make us all the more grateful to and for Luke. For if we knew about Paul only what his letters tell us, how impoverished would our knowledge of his mission be. What guesses and speculations we would have had to make in order to fill out the historical background of each of Paul's letters. Unfortunately, however, we are in a much worse case with Peter. For whereas we have at least several letters which we can attribute to Paul's composition or dictation with full confidence, with Peter we can have no such confidence; even the letter known as 1 Peter is usually regarded as a later composition or compilation.[1] And without a Luke tracking Peter's footsteps, all we have are hints we may discern and inferences we may draw. There are a number of these, but all in all we find ourselves in a darkened room, with only a few pinprick shafts of light illuminating tiny patches of a large area and wondering how the patches can be linked into a coherent overall picture.

35.1. The Later Mission of Peter

The account of Peter's leadership in the earliest days of the new sect in Jerusalem and the story of his early mission were as full (or as bare) as most of Luke's account of Paul's mission (§26). That sequence ended with Peter going off-stage, somewhat mysteriously, 'to another place' (Acts 12.17).[2] Thereafter, however, he

1. See further below, §37.3a.
2. See above, §26 at n. 130.

remains off-stage in Luke's drama, appearing only briefly, though decisively, in Luke's account of the Jerusalem council (15.7-11). Beyond that, nothing. The allusions and hints elsewhere do little to compensate.

a. Peter at the Jerusalem Council and at Antioch

It is worth recapping what we learned about these two episodes (§27), from Peter's perspective. At the consultation in Jerusalem the issue, as both Luke and Paul agree, was whether it was necessary for Gentile believers to be circumcised before they could be regarded as full members of the sect of the Nazarene. The meeting agreed, in the end, that circumcision was not necessary. What proved to be the determinative consideration was the recognition, on all sides, that the grace of God had been given to and through Paul for effective evangelism among Gentiles quite apart from circumcision (Paul — Gal. 2.7-9), or, alternatively, that the Spirit of God had been given to believing Gentiles without their being circumcised (Peter — Acts 15.7-9). Paul recalls the encounter from his perspective; he does not record any testimony provided by Peter. Luke tells the story probably more from Jerusalem's perspective, giving the credit primarily to Peter; the testimony of Paul (and Barnabas) is only confirmatory for Peter's decisive role (15.12).

The most straightforward way to regard the two accounts is as has been suggested: they are two versions of the same event.[3] That Paul emphasizes his own part in the decision is wholly understandable, especially in the light of the need he evidently perceived to underline the authority of his gospel in the face of the crisis confronting him in Galatia. That in so doing he plays down the role of Peter, if that is what he has done, simply tells us something of the strains Paul felt in his relationship with the 'pillar' apostles.[4] From a Jerusalem perspective, as represented by Luke, however, it was equally important that the precedent provided by Peter should be given the credit it deserved.[5] That meant giving prominence to an episode in the early mission of Peter which provided such a precedent — the conversion of the Roman centurion Cornelius (Acts 10.1–11.18). In evaluating the two different versions of the Jerusalem decision, we should avoid setting them out as mutually exclusive alternatives. If Luke in his narrative has given the Cornelius episode a prominence and significance which was only recognized later, that should not be allowed to diminish the importance of the prece-

---

3. See above, §§27.3a-b.
4. See above, §27.3c.
5. Cf. P. Perkins, *Peter: Apostle for the Whole Church* (1994; Minneapolis: Fortress, 2000) 119.

dent. And Paul's account should not be regarded as dispassionate and wholly even-handed, as though Paul alone provided reliable historical information — a mistake too often made in evaluating the comparative treatments of Paul and Luke on any historical event.

The crucial factor is that the case made for a Gentile mission which did not require circumcision of Gentile believers was agreed to, whether the case was made by Peter or by Paul. More to the point, Peter played a significant part in that agreement. Even if it was only to give his hand in recognition and fellowship to Paul, as one of the accepted leaders of the new sect (Gal. 2.9), that was no small matter. And since, on either version, it involved a recognition that the grace/Spirit of God was breaking through beyond the traditional understanding of Gentile conversion, that says something too about Peter's priorities and his willingness to recognize and respond to the radical departure from older norms which the breakthrough entailed. Moreover, it requires only a small amendment to or elaboration of Paul's account for a fuller role in the affair to be accorded to Peter. Since he was the acknowledged first among the original disciples of Jesus, Peter's readiness to recognize that God willed a circumcision-free Gentile mission was bound to be a factor of first importance.

Here, in short, at the Jerusalem council we should probably see Peter functioning as a vital middle-man between the more conservative believers who insisted that circumcision was an indispensable mark of God's people and the more radical Paul.

The subsequent incident at Antioch is harder to evaluate, precisely because we only have the one account — that of Paul (§27.4); Luke is silent. This also means that we have no voice which speaks for Peter in this case. In Paul's recollection, we are left with the impression of a Peter who is fearful and hypocritical, inconsistent and unprincipled (Gal. 2.11-14). But here, quite as clearly as with the previous episode in Jerusalem, we can be confident that Paul is giving a very one-sided view of the confrontation.[6] I have already indicated the sort of case which can and probably should be made for Peter (§27.4d). What emerges was probably a conflict between principle and pragmatism, a disagreement, not so much on the principles involved, as on how the principles apply to the situation in view. The principle was clear, and agreed![7] The question was whether other principles were also to be considered, and whether the practicalities called for some softening of the principle in the case in point. It is not difficult to envisage here the sort of considerations which must have weighed with Peter — particu-

---

6. 'The picture of Peter is deliberately unflattering because Paul wishes to demonstrate the probity of his own character by contrast' (Perkins, *Peter* 117-18).

7. Note again Gal. 2.15-16: 'We are Jews by nature . . . knowing that no human being is justified by works of the law, but only through faith in Jesus Christ'.

larly the holiness of God's people Israel as marked by their separateness from the (other) nations. As the one especially commissioned to take the gospel to his own people, he must have felt the pressure to demonstrate his *bona fides* as a devout Jew, in order, not least, to ensure that his fellow Jews would give him a hearing as one of themselves. Such tugs-of-war between principle and pragmatism will always be a feature of corporate decision-making. It is all too easy for those who insist on the principle to accuse the other of compromise, although the art of securing agreement between differing emphases, political, social, or religious, will inevitably involve some 'compromise'. Just as the pragmatist will ever be tempted to accuse those who insist on the principle *tout simple* of naïvete or fundamentalism.

Here again, then, we should probably find Peter somewhere in the middle, between on the one hand, the 'certain individuals from James' (Gal. 2.12), insisting that Jewish believers should 'live as Jews', and on the other, Paul drawing out the principle of justification by faith alone in rigorist terms. That the compromise enacted by Peter was not seen as denying the grace of God to Gentiles is presumably indicated by the unanimous support given to it by the other Jewish believers, including Barnabas, Paul's own chief ally and colleague in Gentile mission. And the probability that the Antioch church as a whole sided with Peter against Paul[8] strongly suggests that the many Gentile believers in Antioch also agreed that Peter's action and the resulting compromise were wholly appropriate in the situation in Antioch and its daughter churches — Gentile believers conforming to Jewish laws of clean and unclean sufficiently to allow the practice of eating together to resume.[9]

The Peter who emerges from these episodes was neither voiceless nor unprincipled. He was rather the necessary foil to Paul's all-out mission to Gentile God-fearers and proselytes. He was the bridge between the conservative James and the radical Paul. He did not succeed in maintaining the link in this case. But the Paul who subsequently encouraged similar-looking compromises in Corinth and Rome, and who made such a priority of the collection from his churches for the poor of Jerusalem's church, certainly recognized and affirmed the principles and pragmatics on which Peter's action at Antioch had presumably been based. Having fought for and successfully maintained his own principle, Paul himself became more Petrine-like in policy and practice. The influence of Peter on Paul, even allowing for the Antioch incident, should not be underplayed.

---

8. See above, §27.6.

9. I suggest above that 'the apostolic decree' (Acts 15.29) indicates the way the compromise was worked out in these churches sooner or later under the Jerusalem church's guidance (§27.3e).

b. Peter the Missionary

Paul's own recollection is that Peter had been entrusted with a commission very like his own. The recognition of the Jerusalem leadership that Paul 'had been entrusted with the gospel for the uncircumcision' was a corollary to the prior, already-acknowledged recognition that Peter 'had been entrusted with the gospel for the circumcision', with 'the apostleship of the circumcision' (Gal. 2.7-8). Paul's mission to Gentiles was the counterpart of Peter's mission to his fellow Jews. Paul never resiles from that agreement or disowns it. Implicit, then, in all Paul's mission is the recognition that Peter was engaged in the same mission among their own people.[10]

This mission is clearly alluded to in 1 Cor. 9.5, where Paul refers to what was obviously common knowledge: that Cephas, like other apostles and the brothers of the Lord, was accompanied by his believing wife when he travelled. Since the issue in view is the support which visiting apostles, preachers and teachers should be able to expect from the congregations to which they ministered, the implication is that Cephas/Peter did undertake a good many such journeys and visits.[11] Whether we should think of visits like those referred to in Acts 9.32 — that is, pastoral and teaching visits — or evangelistic visits to synagogues, in Palestine or further afield, we cannot say.

Notable is the sequence in 1 Cor. 15.3-11, where Peter is in effect included in no less than three or four of the resurrection appearances listed — to himself alone (15.5), to the twelve (15.5), to the more than five hundred (15.6), and presumably to 'all the apostles' (15.7). Equally notable is the fact that Paul affirms that they all share and preach the same gospel; 'whether it was I or they, so we preach and so you have believed' (15.11). The contrast (if that is an appropriate word) with Gal. 2.7 ('the gospel for the circumcision/the gospel for the uncircumcision') should not be missed. In Paul's view he and the rest preached one and the same gospel; he and Peter did not differ in the gospel they preached.

That Peter was committed to mission work, whether breaking new ground or helping consolidate churches that had already been established, probably explains why he disappears from the Jerusalem scene entirely after the Jerusalem council. His absence when Paul makes his final and fateful journey to Jerusalem

10. Becker wonders, 'Was the Antiochene quarrel for Peter perhaps only an interlude?' (*Paul* 101-102).

11. 1 Cor. 9.5 carries the intriguing implication that Peter was accompanied by his wife on (at least some of) his trips. That he was married is, of course, indicated in early Jesus tradition (Mark 1.29-31 pars.), but the implication carries the further corollary that Peter's missionary work was by no means so strenuous and hazardous as Paul's, perhaps suggesting that his mission was more focused on teaching than on evangelism. For details see Thiselton, *1 Corinthians* 679-82 and those referred to by him.

is particularly noticeable, as is the fact that he is never mentioned at any point during Luke's account of the passion of Paul. The obvious inference is that James had become the effective and recognized leader of the Jerusalem church, though not only because of Peter's absence elsewhere.

c. Where Did Peter Exercise His Commission?

The two references from 1 Corinthians give no indication of where Peter carried out his commission. Luke's Acts limits Peter's explicit mission to the coastal region of Palestine.[12] 'The churches of/in Judea' (Gal. 1.22; 1 Thess. 2.14) should perhaps be attributed to Peter's mission.[13]

Here it becomes appropriate to raise again the issue of whether Peter visited and preached in Corinth itself. Even if the evidence is insufficient to demonstrate that he did so,[14] important indicators as to Peter's significance stand out. The name of Cephas/Peter was well known to the Corinthian believers. They had been told from the outset that he had been the first to witness the risen Christ (1 Cor. 15.5). Paul could refer to the missionary or pastoral travels and visits of Cephas as something they were familiar with (9.5). Some people in Corinth held him in particularly high esteem and used his name as a kind of slogan or banner (1.12). In the last case we may presume that something of the differences (of emphasis) known to exist between Paul and Peter allowed some of Paul's Corinthian converts to take some sort of stand alongside Peter on issues in which they found a degree of fault with Paul.[15] Even in this quintessentially Pauline foundation, the name of Cephas/Peter resonated loudly — and, it should not be ignored, did so not least because Paul made clear to the Corinthians how important Cephas had been for the beginnings of Christianity and still was. This still does not provide sufficient evidence for us to conclude that Peter had visited Corinth in person. But it does make the implication so much stronger that Peter did not confine his mission to the eastern seaboard of the Mediterranean but most likely, in enacting his apostolic commission, made evangelistic visits to centres with significant diaspora Jewish communities and pastoral visits to churches with a substantial Jewish presence, and so became known among the churches of the Pauline mission.[16]

---

12. As does the pseudo-Clementine literature (*Hom.* 7–8) (Elliott, *Apocryphal New Testament* 436-38).

13. Barnett, *Birth* 32.

14. See above, §§32.3a (particularly n. 170), 32.5b, 32.7b. See, e.g., Perkins, *Peter* 10-11.

15. In §32 I suggested that those upholding more traditionalist Jewish tendencies were the most likely to rally round the name of Cephas (see again §32 n. 170).

16. 'Peter's stature within the early Christian community cannot be denied by any-

Should Peter be seen behind the incursions into the Pauline mission churches — Galatia, Corinth (2 Corinthians 10–13) and Philippi? Nothing in the language Paul uses invites such an inference. In Galatians Paul freely acknowledged his own indebtedness to Peter (Gal. 1.18) and the warmth of the agreement with the pillar apostles (including Peter) at Jerusalem (2.9). The distancing parenthesis — 'what they once were makes no difference to me; God shows no partiality' (2.6) — is a relatively mild assertion that Cephas's previous status was of little continuing importance for Paul. It is quite different from the outrage Paul expresses regarding the 'other gospel which is not another' brought by the incomers to Galatia (1.6-7). In Paul's perspective 'the gospel for the circumcision' preached by Peter was the same gospel as his own (2.7, 15-16); the only difference was that it was differently targeted. That was why Paul was so indignant over Peter's conduct in Antioch: his action was undermining 'the truth of the [agreed] gospel' (2.14). If Paul did not spare Peter from his tongue-lashing in Antioch (2.11-14), it is unlikely that he would have failed to identify Peter as the source of the 'other gospel which is not another', had Peter indeed been behind it. Since there were others more traditionalist than Peter strongly represented within the new movement, there are a good many other more plausible candidates for the instigation to convert more fully Paul's converts.

The same applies to Corinth and Philippi. The 'super-apostles' of 2 Cor. 11.5 and 12.11 were characterized more by quality of rhetoric and miracle-working, not by the precedence and pre-eminence which marked out Peter.[17] And it is hard to see Paul thinking of Peter when he warned against 'the dogs' in Phil. 3.2. Identifications and associations which had a greater appeal when the beginnings of Christianity were seen in terms of Baur's antithesis between Paul and Peter lose more or less all appeal when it is remembered that there was a strong traditionalist wing of the new movement and that Peter himself is so regularly remembered as somewhere in the middle trying to hold the two ends of the spectrum together.

On the subject of Peter's mission the most intriguing reference is to be found in the letter associated with his name — 1 Pet. 1.1: 'Peter, apostle of Jesus Christ, to the chosen sojourners of the diaspora in Pontus, Galatia, Cappadocia, Asia and Bithynia'. Does this signify that Peter fulfilled his commission in these territories?[18] The region is a coherent one, roughly the bulk of Asia Minor north

---

one. Even gentile converts in Galatia and Corinth who have had no contact with Peter or the Petrine mission recognize that he is one of the leading disciples of the Lord' (Perkins, *Peter* 118; see also 120).

17. But see also above, §32 nn. 427, 428.

18. Interestingly, Eusebius seems to be aware that a positive answer to the question is only a deduction from 1 Pet. 1.1: 'Peter seems *(eoiken)* to have preached to the Jews of the dispersion in Pontus and Galatia and Bithynia, Cappadocia and Asia' (*HE* 3.1.1-2). Mitchell is

of the Taurus Mountains, stretching along the Black Sea coast from the Aegean to the borders of Armenia.[19] It overlaps the regions of Paul's mission — certainly Asia, unless the inference is that the northern half of Asia is intended, and possibly Galatia, unless the territory of Galatia contiguous with Bithynia and Pontus is in view (North Galatia). But otherwise it covers the bulk of Asia Minor for which we have no other early record of mission. Moreover, we know that there were Jewish communities in many of the cities in these regions.[20] And we also know from Pliny's letter to Trajan that Christianity was deeply rooted and widely influential in Bithynia half a century later (*Ep.* 10.96). So it is entirely likely that there was vigorous Christian evangelism carried out in these territories during the middle decades of the first century, and by no means impossible that Peter himself was involved in such mission, or at least in helping to establish the churches founded by others.[21]

Little more can be said. The evidence of 1 Pet. 1.1 simply names 'the sojourners/strangers of the diaspora' in these regions as the intended recipients of the letter. But it does clearly imply that they were predominantly Jews: the term 'elect' is, as with Paul, taken over from Jewish self-designation; but 'diaspora' was already established as a technical term for the 'dispersion' of Israelites among the nations.[22] And the fact that it is Peter who is named as the author of a letter so directed presumably indicates that the Christians of these regions had particular cause to be linked with Peter. But beyond that the faint light from the passage fails altogether.

---

more sanguine: 'In so far as the gospel was taken here in the early years of the Church, the evangelist was surely Peter, who addressed the Jews of Pontus, Galatia, Cappadocia, Asia, and Bithynia in his first epistle' (*Anatolia* 2.3).

19. For more detail see, e.g., P. J. Achtemeier, *1 Peter* (Hermeneia; Minneapolis: Fortress, 1996) 83-85; Achtemeier wonders whether the Pauline missionary areas in Asia Minor such as Pamphylia, Pisidia, Lycaonia, Cilicia and Phrygia have been deliberately excluded (83, 85).

20. 1 Macc. 15.15-24 records a letter sent by the Roman consul in support of Jews to various places, including to Ariarathes of Cappadocia (15.22). Philo speaks of 'colonies *(apoikias)*' (of Jews) sent out 'into most parts of Asia as far as Bithynia and the remotest corner of Pontus' (*Legat.* 281). Aquila, husband of Priscilla and one of Paul's co-workers, came from Pontus (Acts 18.2). Jews from Cappadocia, Pontus and Asia are included in the list of those who witnessed the first Christian Pentecost (Acts 2.9). From Bithynia there are several inscriptions attesting the presence of Jewish synagogues. See further Schürer, *History* 3.3-4, 34-36; and on Asia see above, §29 n. 162; also J. H. Elliott, *1 Peter* (AB 37B; New York: Doubleday, 2000) 316-17.

21. 1 Pet. 1.12 seems to envisage others than the letter writer as the church founders; that Peter's role was more that of a shepherd (cf. 1 Pet. 5.1-3) in regard to churches already founded may be suggested, as in Acts 9.32.

22. Details in Elliott, *1 Peter* 313-14. See further §37.3c(i) below.

d. Peter the Rock and the Pastor

We should not fail to include the inferences which may be drawn from the Gospels, particularly Matthew and John.

In Matthew Peter is held in particular esteem. Not only does Matthew repeat the traditions which present Peter as the leading figure among Jesus' disciples, but he includes material distinctive to his Gospel which reinforces the impressions from the Jesus tradition.[23] The play on Peter's name in Matt. 16.17-19 is especially noteworthy, and not simply because that passage became (in due course) the foundation for the church of Rome's claim to supremacy among the apostolic sees of the early church: 'You are Peter *(Petros),* and on this rock *(petra)* I will build my church'.[24] The significance of this passage for subsequent Christianity we can return to later (volume 3). Here what should be noted is that the tradition of Peter being named also Cephas *(kepha', 'rock')* is well attested by Paul,[25] so that in the traditions on which Matthew drew — that is, already in the first generation — the passage must reflect an appreciation of Peter high enough for such a passage to be formulated. It is true that in his distinctive material Matthew presents Peter as a or the representative disciple:

- 14.28-29 — he represents 'little faith' discipleship (14.31);
- 15.15 — he speaks for the rest in asking for explanation of a parable;
- 16.19 — the power to bind and loose is later granted to the disciples as a whole (18.18 — in more or less exactly the same words);
- 18.21 — it is Peter who asks and is instructed about forgiveness;
- 18.24-27 — he pays the temple tax for Jesus and himself.

But 16.17-19 ensures that Matthew intended Peter to be seen as *primus inter pares* in confession and in representative significance. And whatever we make of Matthew's theology or ecclesiology, the weightiness he attributes to Peter must be rooted in memory of Peter either functioning in such a weighty manner or in his being revered already during his life as at least one of the foundational figures on whom the church(es) of the second and subsequent generations was being built.[26]

23. See *Jesus Remembered* 507-11 and 540 nn. 250, 251.

24. The text is inscribed around the inside of the dome of St. Peter's in Rome. On the traditional debate between Catholic and Protestant as to whether Matthew wanted *Petros* and *petra* to be understood as synonyms (Peter is the rock of the church) or as distinct (*petra* is the confession made by *Petros*), see Cullmann, *Peter* 212-42; Luz, *Matthäus* 471-83.

25. 1 Cor. 1.12; 3.22; 9.5; 15.5; Gal. 1.18; 2.9, 11; also John 1.42. See also Perkins, *Peter* 40-41.

26. Cf. Barnett, *Jesus* 244.

John's Gospel reflects a similar weight of tradition regarding Peter, particularly in the Johannine equivalent to the confession of Jesus at Caesarea Philippi (John 6.68-69) and in the episode of Jesus washing the disciples' feet (13.5-10); in the resurrection narrative Peter is the first to enter the empty tomb (20.6-7). But most striking is the prominent role of Peter in what appears to be an addendum to the Gospel, consisting of John 21. Here most noteworthy is the special post-Easter commission given exclusively to Peter and given three times: 'Tend my lambs' (21.15); 'shepherd my sheep' (21.16); 'tend my sheep' (21.17). Presumably it is not by chance that 1 Peter represents Peter as counseling his readers to 'shepherd the flock of God', appealing to the example of 'the chief shepherd' (Christ) (1 Pet. 5.2-4). The obvious inference to be drawn is that Peter was thought of as himself a great shepherd, well able to instruct his fellow elders (5.1) in the art of shepherding and no doubt serving as himself an example of what a shepherd should be. And again, the fact that the shepherd motif appears in two traditions linked specifically to Peter strongly suggests that the tradition was well rooted in early memories of how Peter carried out his commission from his Lord.[27]

Added to the other traditions and allusions already reviewed, the few pinpricks of light into the darkened room are nevertheless sufficient to enable us to gain an impression of a man held in high esteem across a wide range of the earliest churches for his mission among his fellow Jews, revered as an example of discipleship (including its failings) and as providing a solid platform for faith in Christ, and deeply respected as a pastor of the Christian flock.

e. Peter in Rome

The only city of importance associated with the name of Peter which has not so far been mentioned is Rome. There are several churches which claim Peter as their apostolic founder. The most obvious one is Jerusalem, where he was evidently the leading figure in the first years of the new sect destined to become Christianity. Antioch can claim him to an extent too,[28] for although he did not establish the church there, the lead he gave, which led to the confrontation with Paul in Galatians 2, was probably followed by the church as a whole. So he set the pattern for the church of Antioch and its daughter churches in Syria and Cilicia. The claim of Corinth is the least substantial, being probably based on inferences drawn from 1 Corinthians.[29]

27. Perkins, *Peter* 37-38.

28. Eusebius names Peter as the first bishop of Antioch (*HE* 3.36.2), though earlier he names Euodius as Antioch's first bishop (3.22).

29. See above, §34 n. 423. As Perkins observes: 'Clearly, every major see sought to begin its ecclesiastical history with apostolic founders' (*Peter* 43).

So far as Rome itself is concerned, it is clear enough that Peter did not first establish the church(es) there.[30] Nor, for that matter, did Paul. There were already small apartment-groups of believers meeting in Rome before Paul arrived there. And his earlier letter to Rome shows no awareness of Peter's having been there or expectation of his arrival. Nor does Luke give any hint to the contrary, even though an association of Peter with Rome would have rounded off the plot of Acts (from Jerusalem to Rome) more effectively than he did with Paul alone. The obvious conclusion is that if Peter came to Rome, he did not arrive there during the two years of Paul's imprisonment (Acts 28.30-31).[31] At all events, his influence in Rome, as apostle to the circumcision, suggests that several at least of the Roman apartment churches maintained their Jewish-Christian character and that the advice of Rom. 14.1–15.6 continued to provide effective guidelines for their common life, guidelines of which Peter could well have approved.

However, the reason why Peter (and Paul) can be described as the founding apostles of the church of Rome is not that they were the first Christians there or first established the church there but that they died there. This point brings us to the next great calamity to befall the infant movement of Jesus messianists.

35.2. Persecution under Nero

As we have already seen (§§33.2-3), the outlines of the early years of Christianity in Rome are at best sketchy:

- apartment congregations established through the early ministry of Andronicus and Junia and others (Rom. 16.7), which won Gentile converts in significant numbers;
- disturbances within the Roman synagogues over the messiahship claimed for Jesus by such Jewish believers, resulting in expulsion of those identified as the most significant leaders and troublemakers;
- tensions between predominantly Gentile congregations and Jewish believers returning after the lapse of Claudius's decree of expulsion (14.1; 15.8);

30. The story of Peter coming to Rome during the reign of Claudius to drive home his earlier defeat of Simon Magus is told in great detail in the apocryphal *Acts of Peter* (see Elliott, *Apocryphal New Testament* 390-426; Schneemelcher-Wilson, *NTA* 2.271-321) and briefly reported in grandiose terms but without detail by Eusebius (*HE* 2.14). This all can be safely regarded as novelistically fanciful elaboration of Luke's account of their encounter in Acts 8. See further Perkins, *Peter* 140-47, 152-56.

31. See the history of the debate as to whether Peter resided in Rome in Cullmann, *Peter* 72-81.

- tensions between those wanting to continue maintaining characteristically Jewish traditions of clean and unclean and those claiming freedom from such scruples (14.1–15.7);
- consciousness of the vulnerability of the small groups to harassment and worse from authorities ever on the lookout for trouble-making factions (12.9–13.7);
- increasing rivalry in regard to Paul during the latter's imprisonment in Rome and in the way the gospel continued to be preached (Phil. 1.15-18);
- the spreading influence of Paul's continuing witness, even despite his chains (Acts 28.16; Phil. 1.12-13);
- increased boldness in the proclamation of the gospel to others (Phil. 1.14).

All this suggests the likelihood that the new movement would come more and more to public attention. However much Paul had counseled the Roman believers to 'keep their heads down' (Rom. 12.9–13.7), it is likely that Paul's presence in Rome and the increasing boldness of his and their witness to their new faith would make them more and more visible to vigilant authorities and informers.

This is probably the background to the most infamous of the episodes which darkened the earliest history of Christianity. In 64, during the tenth year of Nero's principate, a fire swept through Rome, the jerry-built high-rise apartments providing ready fuel to the flames.[32] I have already cited Tacitus's account of the sequel: how rumours that Nero was responsible for setting or spreading the fire — conceivably to clear the ground for his grandiose Domus Aurea (house of gold).[33] To scotch such rumours Nero looked for scapegoats and found them in those being described as 'Christians'. Since this name always and only appears initially in some sort of confrontation with Roman authorities,[34] the most plausible explanation is that this group was identified as such by those responsible for securing Rome from all internal threats. The briefer note from Suetonius[35] suggests that Suetonius relied on sources similar to that of Tacitus. The outline just sketched above is consistent with this suggestion: the increased evangelistic activity on the part of the Roman believers was sufficient to draw attention to this new and repugnant 'superstition'.[36]

---

32. See Juvenal, *Sat.* 3.193-202, cited above, §30.2a.

33. But modern historians are virtually unanimous in dismissing the view that Nero himself started the fire; see, e.g., R. Holland, *Nero: The Man behind the Myth* (Phoenix Mill: Sutton Publishing, 2000) 160-64.

34. See above, §24 n. 274.

35. 'Punishment was inflicted on the Christians *(Christiani),* a class *(genus)* of men given to a new and evil-doing/nefarious/criminal *(maleficus)* superstition' *(Nero* 16.2).

36. Tacitus's description *(Ann.* 15.44.2 — §21.1c) need not imply that the 'Christians' were already widely recognized as a body distinct from the Roman synagogues, as most infer

Tacitus's horrific account is worth repeating for the vivid picture it paints:

First, then, those who confessed *(fatebantur)* were arrested; next, on their disclosures vast numbers *(multitudo ingens)* were convicted, not so much on the count of arson as for hatred of the human race *(odio humani generis)*. And derision accompanied their end: they were covered with wild beasts' skins and torn to death by dogs; or they were fastened on crosses and, when daylight failed, were burned to serve as lamps by night. Nero had offered his gardens for the spectacle, and gave an exhibition in his Circus, mixing with the crowd in the habit of a charioteer, or mounted on his car. Hence, in spite of a guilt, which had earned the most exemplary punishment, there arose a sentiment of pity, due to the impression that they were being sacrificed not for the welfare of the state but to the ferocity of a single man. (*Ann.* 15.44.4-5)[37]

The picture hardly needs elaborating; but some notes should be made.

- Presumably we have to envisage that torture was applied in many cases, causing some at least to 'confess'.
- The numbers envisaged ('vast numbers') indicate that the movement had been expanding rapidly — perhaps a further testimony to the effectiveness of Paul's witness in jail and to that of the increased evangelism which he evidently stimulated.[38]

(see above, §33 n. 68) and as Spence in particular argues (*Parting* 119-37, 170; though see also 235-37); the identification could have been as a result of Nero's agents looking for a scapegoat and becoming aware of 'Christians' as a distinct group. Holland wonders whether some Christians might have seen the fire in apocalyptic terms and thus provoked the hostility of their fellow residents (*Nero* 177-79). Tellbe argues that Paul's advice in Rom. 14.1–15.6 expedited the 'parting of the ways' between the Christians and synagogue and thus paved the way for Nero's being able to distinguish Christians from Jews in 64 (*Paul between Synagogue and State* 193). G. Theissen, 'Paulus — der Unglückstifter. Paulus und die Verfolgung der Gemeinden in Jerusalem und Rom', in E.-M. Becker and P. Pilhofer, eds., *Biographie und Persönlichkeit des Paulus* (WUNT 187; Tübingen: Mohr Siebeck, 2005) 228-44, conjectures that Nero's attention was drawn to the Christians by Paul's appeal (242-43). See also Jossa, *Jews or Christians?* 129-35 and nn. 27 and 33, who draws attention to the *Chronicle* of Sulpicius Severus, who reports that Titus determined to destroy the Jerusalem Temple 'in order that the religion of the Jews and Christians should be more completely exterminated' (2.30.7), and to Tertullian's observation that the 'school' of Christianity insinuated its claims 'under cover of a very famous religion [Judaism] and one certainly permitted by law' (*Apol.* 21.1).

37. Tacitus, *Ann.* 15.44.2-5; see more fully above, §21.1c, with accompanying notes.

38. Though Origen observes that only 'a few, whose number could easily be enumerated, have died occasionally for the sake of the Christian religion' (*c. Cels.* 3.8), which suggests that the 'vast numbers' may well be an exaggeration.

- As already noted, Tacitus's attribution to them of 'hatred of the human race' echoes his similar savage criticism of Judaism[39] and suggests the assumption on the part of the authorities that the 'Christians' still shared the traditional Jewish impulse to separateness from other nations; it is not yet clear that the 'Christians' were anything other than a sub-set of the much more venerable Judaism.[40]
- That crosses were chosen as the implement of their torture indicates a knowledge of the focal point of their message — Christ crucified and raised from the dead.
- Crucifixion also almost certainly implies that those so cruelly executed were not Roman citizens, perhaps suggesting a high proportion of non-Jews.[41]
- Although the church must have been decimated by the persecution, the pity which Nero's cruelty evoked in the mind of many of Rome's residents must have watered the ground well, into which the blood of the martyrs fell as seed to take root and grow to flower in the days ahead.

And what of Peter?

35.3. The Martyrdom of Peter

The only tradition which calls for consideration is that Peter was one of the Christians who perished in the persecution initiated by Nero following the great fire of Rome in 64. The tradition presupposes that Peter came to Rome, presumably some time in the early 60s.[42] The inference is more precarious than at first appears, since neither Ignatius (writing to Rome in the second decade of the second century) nor Justin Martyr (himself martyred in Rome in ca. 165) makes any reference to Peter's having been present in Rome or having died there. Such a reference might have been expected from Ignatius in particular, since to be able to name Peter as bishop in Rome[43] or as preceding Ignatius in the way of martyrdom in Rome would have been grist for his mill. The only reference to Peter and Paul by Ignatius is to their apostolic authority, in contrast to his own status as a condemned man *(katakritos)* (Ignatius, *Rom.* 4.3).[44] At best we may infer that the

---

39. See above, §21 n. 23.

40. See further §21.1c above. Smallwood discusses whether there was any Jewish involvement in the denunciation of the 'Christians' (*Jews* 218-19).

41. Lampe, *Paul to Valentinus* 82-84.

42. But see again §26 n. 130 above.

43. In 1 Peter, Peter describes himself only as a 'fellow elder' (1 Pet. 5.13).

44. 'I am not enjoining you as Peter and Paul did. They were apostles, I am condemned;

naming of Peter and Paul conjointly in a letter to Rome was an allusion to their status as revered figures particularly in Rome, with Peter named (understandably) before Paul. But more than that is speculative.[45]

The earliest and weightiest indication that Peter was in Rome is the greeting sent by 1 Peter from 'the church in Babylon' as the place from which the letter was sent (1 Pet. 5.13). That the reference provides sufficient proof of Peter's presence and active ministry in Rome is dependent on two deductions drawn from the text. One is that 'Babylon' is code for Rome; this is widely accepted, since there are no traditions linking Peter with Mesopotamia, and by this time Babylon had long ceased to be a city of any significance; and its function as a code for the imperial decadence of the capital of the current super-power is also attested in Revelation.[46]

The other deduction is that 1 Peter provides information regarding Peter himself, or at least of the way Peter was recalled in the following generation. Here the naming of Silvanus and Mark as close companions of Peter (5.12-13) is particularly relevant.[47] Silvanus/Silas had also been a close companion of Paul, particularly during the first phase of Paul's Aegean mission.[48] So it is quite possible to conceive of Silvanus acting as a go-between for the two apostles, or of Silvanus linking up with Peter, perhaps in the latter part of Paul's mission (he disappears from view after Corinth),[49] or in Rome after Paul's death. Mark, we recall, had been part of the earliest mission team of Barnabas and Paul (according to Acts 15.38) and, despite a breach with Paul (15.39), had subsequently become one of his close companions during Paul's (final?) imprisonment (probably) in Rome (Phlm. 24; Col. 4.10).[50] So again, it is entirely plausible to knit the notes together and infer that after Paul's death Mark had joined Peter when the latter came to Rome and began to minister there.

The supporting evidence from the early period is slight,[51] and the more ex-

---

they were free, until now I have been a slave. But if I suffer, I will become a freed person who belongs to Jesus Christ, and I will rise up, free, in him. In the meantime I am learning to desire nothing while in chains' (Ignatius, *Rom.* 4.3). See further R. J. Bauckham, 'The Martyrdom of Peter in Early Christian Literature', *ANRW* 2.26.1 (1992) 539-95 (here 563-66).

45. 'Ignatius may not be referring to the martyrdom of Peter and Paul but to their respective Epistles. Ignatius employs the topos of his own unworthiness to give orders in his other epistles, *To the Trallians* (3.3) and *To the Ephesians* (3.1)' (Perkins, *Peter* 139).

46. Rev. 14.8; 16.19; 17.5; 18.2, 10, 21. See further Achtemeier, *1 Peter* 353-54; Aune, *Revelation* 2.829-31; Elliott, *1 Peter* 882-87.

47. On the significance of Peter as *martys,* 'witness' (5.1), see Bauckham, 'Martyrdom' 540-41.

48. See above, §§29.6 and 31.2.

49. Acts 18.5; 2 Cor. 1.19; 1 Thess. 1.1; 2 Thess. 1.1.

50. See also Irenaeus, *Adv. haer.* 3.1.1; Eusebius, *HE* 2.15.2.

51. Bauckham argues that *Asc. Isa.* 4.2-3 and *Apoc. Pet.* 14.4 refer to Peter's execution,

plicit testimony is later and of increasingly dubious value as the hagiographical incense begins more and more to obscure the historian's view. Clement, notably, seems to be more concerned to laud Paul; his mention of Peter in the same context is tantalizingly obscure: 'We should set before our eyes the good apostles. There is Peter, who because of unjust jealousy bore up under hardships not just once or twice, but many times; and having borne his witness *(martyrēsas)* he went to the place of glory that he deserved' (*1 Clem.* 5.3-4). Again, all that can be safely deduced from this reference is that Clement, writing from Rome, may well have had in mind, and intended his audience to recall, the traditions of Peter's suffering and death in Rome itself.[52]

The best of the later data is provided by Eusebius, in the passage already cited in reference to Paul. His description of the persecution of Nero focuses on these two:

> It is related that in his [Nero's] time Paul was beheaded in Rome itself, and that Peter was likewise crucified, and the title of 'Peter and Paul', which is still given to cemeteries there, confirms the story, no less than does a writer of the church named Caius, who lived when Zephyrinus was bishop of Rome. Caius in a written discussion with Proclus, the leader of the Montanists, speaks as follows of the places where the sacred relics of the apostles in question are deposited: 'But I can point out the trophies of the Apostles, for if you will go to the Vatican or to the Ostian Way you will find the trophies of those who founded this church'. And that they both were martyred at the same time Dionysius, bishop of Corinth, affirms in this passage of his correspondence with the Romans: 'By so great an admonition you bound together the foundations of the Romans and Corinthians by Peter and Paul, for both of them taught together in our Corinth and were our founders, and together also taught in Italy in the same place and were martyred at the same time'. (*HE* 2.25.8)

The legends gathering around the names of the two great apostles are evident here: particularly, as already noted, the attribution of the founding of the churches of both Corinth and Rome to both Peter and Paul, and the claim that Peter and Paul taught together in both cities. But the testimony is traced back to the late second century (Caius and Dionysius), not much more than a century beyond the likely date for their deaths.[53] And the traditions of the places where the two

---

probably in Rome and under Nero ('Martyrdom' 566-77), though the allusions can bear little weight.

52. *Martyreō* probably already bore the sense of 'bear witness (unto death), bear witness (by martyrdom)' (BDAG 618); cf. already 1 Tim. 6.13. See also Bauckham, 'Martyrdom' 553-63.

53. Irenaeus, writing in the same period, knows the same tradition: Peter and Paul

apostles had been buried and were still revered (the Vatican and the Via Ostia) can be given higher credence.[54] Whether their martyrdoms 'at the same time' is part of the legendary tendency to draw the two together, it is not possible to say. But the distinct methods of their execution — Paul by the sword, Peter by crucifixion — have the ring of faithful witness transmitted through the following generations.[55] Eusebius subsequently adds the further detail that 'at the end he [Peter] came to Rome and was crucified head downwards, for so he had demanded to suffer', a tradition which he attributes to Origen in the third volume of the latter's commentary on Genesis (*HE* 3.1.1-3).[56]

Here again, as with Paul (§34.7), the lack of any competing tradition can probably be counted as sufficient endorsement of the central fact: that Peter was executed in Rome, probably during the Neronian persecution, in 64. If any care was taken to make Peter's execution special, rather than as one of the many variations of Nero's lustful cruelty, that may suggest that Peter's status as a or the leading member of the Christians was recognized by the authorities, and that it was decided that his death should be mockingly fitting to the message which he had proclaimed of the crucified Christ. He was probably buried in the necropolis on Vatican Hill, beside the site of his execution.[57]

---

preached in Rome and laid the foundations of the church (*Adv. haer.* 3.1.2). Cullmann's discussion is a model of scholarly reserve (*Peter* 116-31). Contrast M. D. Goulder, 'Did Peter Ever Go to Rome?', *SJT* 57 (2004) 377-96, who thinks the likelihood of Peter having visited Rome is remote, and that Peter probably died in Jerusalem about the year 55 (see further n. 54 below).

54. The circus and gardens of Nero, where Tacitus says the execution of Christians took place, were on the site now occupied by the Vatican (*Ann.* 15.44.5). 'The claim that the bones of Peter were found [under the main altar of St. Peter's basilica] is dubious' (Brown and Meier, *Antioch and Rome* 97 n. 201); see Cullmann's extensive discussion (*Peter* 131-56), and now particularly J. Zangenberg, 'Gebeine des Apostelfürsten? Zu den angeblich frühchristlichen Gräbern unter der Peterskirche in Rom', in Zangenberg and Labahn, eds., *Christians as a Religious Minority in a Multicultural City* 108-38. A broken ossuary discovered in 1953 on the site of the Franciscan monastery Dominus Flevit had a rough Hebrew inscription 'Simeon bar Jonah', which opens the possibility that Peter had actually been buried in Jerusalem; details are in P. B. Bagatti and J. T. Milik, *Gli scavi del 'Dominus Flevit'*. Part 1: *La necropolis del periodo romano* (Jerusalem: Tipografia dei PP. Francescani, 1958), and J. Finegan, *The Archaeology of the New Testament* (Princeton: Princeton University, 1969) 245-46. However, if the inscription refers to Cephas/Peter, it is odd that there is no tradition to that effect. And were it true, Peter being such an important figure in earliest Christianity, one would have thought that reverence for Peter would have ensured that his place of burial was properly commemorated.

55. Bauckham argues forcibly that John 21.18-19 — the risen Jesus' words to Peter: 'When you grow old, you will stretch out your hands . . .' — is an allusion to Peter's crucifixion ('Martyrdom' 545-50; see also earlier Cullmann, *Peter* 88-89).

56. For a little more detail and earlier bibliography see *ODCC* 1261.

57. See further Perkins, *Peter* 38; Elliott, *1 Peter* 886 n. 809; and n. 54 above.

35.4. The Lasting Significance of Peter

Peter does not feature much (if at all) as author of writings which make up the New Testament. It is such writings, the only ones assuredly from the first generation of Christianity, which have ensured that the influence of Paul remains vital for any form of Christianity which puts the New Testament at its heart. Nor is there much evidence of Peter actually evangelizing and founding churches in the way that Paul did, or of his sustaining a mission which decisively shaped the emerging churches of the Aegean region in particular. Peter's significance, however, matches and at several points surpasses that of Paul, and it is for these points that his memory is so revered throughout Christianity.[58]

- He was one of Jesus' earliest disciples and was evidently regarded as the leader of the disciple group, one of Jesus' inner circle, along with the brothers James and John.
- The creedal statement of 1 Cor. 15.3-7 confirms that he was known in all the churches founded on the faith assertions of that statement, as the most highly privileged and most authoritative first witness to the resurrected Jesus.[59]
- The Acts traditions of the earliest period of the mother church of Jerusalem are clear that Peter was the leading figure among the core 'twelve' (Acts 1–5).
- His significance as much the pre-eminent foundation member of 'the church of God' is indicated by his early nickname 'Cephas' and role as a 'pillar' apostle.[60]
- Paul evidently saw him as the key figure linking back to the mission of Jesus: his first post-conversion visit to Jerusalem was with the specific purpose of 'getting to know' Peter (Gal. 1.18), which can only mean that Paul regarded Peter as the principal conduit through which he would gain access to the Jesus tradition.
- His role as the most respected and authoritative transmitter and performer of the Jesus tradition throughout the earliest years is probably confirmed by the subsequent tradition that Mark's Gospel is in effect a record of such preaching and teaching (Papias).[61]

---

58. See also the summing up of Dschulnigg, *Petrus* 205-207.

59. On the grounds that the appearance to Peter was what proved decisive in establishing that most central element of Christian faith, it is Peter (rather than Paul) who has often been regarded as 'the second founder of the Christian church' — as in A. C. McGiffert, *A History of Christianity in the Apostolic Age* (Edinburgh: Clark, 1897) 48.

60. See above, §23.3b.

61. The point is pressed by M. Hengel, *Studies in the Gospel of Mark* (London: SCM, 1985) ch. 1; also *Petrus* 58-78; Bauckham, *Jesus and the Eyewitnesses* chs. 7 and 9. 'Behind

- Peter's success as apostle/missionary to his fellow Jews was fully and freely acknowledged by Paul (Gal. 2.7-9), and the agreement in Jerusalem designated Peter as having the pre-eminent responsibility for the mission to Jews, equivalent to the responsibility accorded to Paul for the mission to non-Jews.
- In the agreement of Gal. 2.7-9 'the Petrine apostolate is accepted as the norm',[62] Paul's mission being understood as complementary.
- His missionary work was also well known and highly respected well beyond the shores of Palestine, though the only territory in which he is actually recalled as ministering in our primary sources is the eastern seaboard of the Mediterranean (Acts 9.32-43).
- Peter fully accepted, and was probably converted to recognition, that God was welcoming non-Jews on equal terms with Jews, without requiring them to become proselytes (Acts 10.1–11.18; Gal. 2.7-9).
- This openness to the unexpected grace/Spirit of God, together with his commission to bear testimony of Jesus Messiah to his fellow Jews, probably meant that in the crisis in Jerusalem and the confrontation in Antioch he was able to see both sides, to recognize the important elements of each and to chart a course between them which had the prospect (if not at once the effect) of success in holding the two sides together.[63]
- His association with the role of shepherd probably attests a ministry of support particularly of congregations of believing Jews, which took him increasingly and probably more or less permanently away from Jerusalem.[64]
- A brief ministry in Rome itself and his consequent death, most likely during the Neronian persecution in 64, gave him the iconic status of witness-bearer pre-eminent and ensured that the church(es) of Rome would look back to him, as well as to Paul, as providing the sure foundation on which their church(es) were built.[65]

---

such a "revolutionary work" *an authority must stand*' (Hengel, 'Eye-witness Memory' 92). The written Gospels will, of course, be a principal focus of attention in vol. 3.

62. Becker, *Paul* 91.

63. It is this intermediary role which explains how Peter could become 'the focal point for the unity of the whole Church' (Dunn, *Unity and Diversity* §76.6); cf. Hengel, *Petrus* 84; M. Bockmuehl, 'Peter between Jesus and Paul: The "Third Quest" and the "New Perspective" on the First Disciple', in T. D. Still, ed., *Jesus and Paul Reconnected: Fresh Pathways into an Old Debate* (Grand Rapids: Eerdmans, 2007) 67-102.

64. 'The journeys of the apostle Simon Peter evidently served as a rule to visit already existing communities, not ones established by Peter himself' (Reinbold, *Propaganda* 79).

65. The order of the two names (Peter and Paul) in *1 Clem.* 5.2-7, Ignatius, *Rom.* 4.3, and Irenaeus, *Adv. haer.* 3.3.2, 'betrays the established rank of the two men in Roman evaluation' (Brown and Meier, *Antioch and Rome* 123).

CHAPTER 36

Catastrophe in Judea

If Peter had no one to speak for him in regard to the final twenty years of his life and mission, the case is even worse for the other principal figure of first-generation Christianity — James, the brother of Jesus. The only passage in Acts in which he takes centre stage is Luke's account of the Jerusalem council (Acts 15.13-21). Otherwise, James is a figure largely lost in the mist of Christianity's beginnings, only emerging two or three times into the full light. Otherwise he comes across as an almost sinister figure in the wings, the few references to him, both by Paul and by Luke, heavy with troublesome overtones.

36.1. The Church in Jerusalem

The picture given by Luke is of an expansion of the new movement (embryonic Christianity), particularly under Paul, which proceeded without serious checks, even during Paul's imprisonment. The first major setback, the persecution of the Christians in Rome under Nero, Luke leaves over the horizon. The history of the mother church, in contrast, had been much more mixed. Already within the first fourteen years it had suffered serious setbacks: first, in the early 30s in the execution of Stephen and consequent persecution (effectively of the Hellenists); and second, in the early 40s in the execution of one of Jesus' inner circle, James brother of John.[1] Thereafter, such limited supply of information as we have largely dries up, and we are left once again with pinpricks of light to illumine a dark room, confronted by the challenge to somehow gain a picture of the whole room by joining up the little pools of light illuminated for us.[2]

1. See above, §§24.6 and 26.5c.
2. The James ossuary discovered in 2002, with the inscription 'Jacob [= James], son of

1077

a. The Leadership of James

The item of information in which we can have most confidence is that James, the brother of Jesus, was the leading figure in the Jerusalem church from the early 40s to the early 60s.[3] As indicated earlier (§23.3), 'the twelve' as such seem to have faded from the scene quite quickly. And Peter, having been most prominent in the early years in Jerusalem itself, seems to have become more mission-oriented, and no longer to have regarded Jerusalem as his main base of operation. With the other James (brother of John) eliminated, and John apparently not a front-line figure, the way was left for James (brother of Jesus) to become in effect the sole leader in Jerusalem. This is certainly the impression given by the sequence of references to James, from Peter's effective departure from Jerusalem (Acts 12.17) onwards:

- 1 Cor. 15.7 — apart from Cephas/Peter, James is the only one personally named in the list of witnesses to the resurrected Jesus (Paul adds his own name to the list);[4] that just these three are named suggests both that they were generally understood to have been singled out by the risen Christ and that their witness to the resurrected Jesus was recognized as particularly important.[5]
- Gal. 1.19 — the fact that on his first post-conversion visit to Jerusalem Paul specifically mentions James, and only James, apart from his host Peter suggests that James was already the most prominent figure in the Jerusalem assembly after Peter.
- Acts 12.17 — that the departing Peter sends his message explicitly 'to James and the brothers' (not to the rest of the twelve/apostles) suggests that

---

Joseph, brother of Yeshu'a [= Jesus]', is almost certainly a fake, and anyway would add nothing to our knowledge of James; see further C. A. Evans, *Jesus and the Ossuaries* (Waco: Baylor University, 2003) 112-22; J. Magness, 'Ossuaries and the Burials of Jesus and James', *JBL* 124 (2005) 121-54.

3. For a review of the traditional debate as to whether James was a half brother of Jesus, e.g., J. Painter, 'Who Was James? Footprints as a Means of Identification', in B. Chilton and J. Neusner, eds., *The Brother of Jesus* (Louisville: Westminster John Knox, 2001) 10-65 (here 10-24).

4. That James may well have become more sympathetic to Jesus' mission, after initial suspicion or hostility (Mark 3.20-21; John 7.5), is quite likely, in view of Acts 1.14; 1 Cor. 15.7 may well have been an appearance to a believer (like all the others, apart from the appearance to Paul); see above, §22 n. 78, and *Jesus Remembered* 862-64.

5. See further M. Hengel, 'Jakobus der Herrenbruder — der erste "Papst"?', *Paulus und Jakobus. Kleine Schriften III* (WUNT 141; Tübingen: Mohr Siebeck, 2002) 549-82 (here 560-61, 578). On the possibility that the two appearances, to Cephas and to James (1 Cor. 15.5, 7), may come from 'rival' lists, see particularly Pratscher, *Herrenbruder* 35-46.

James was already the most prominent figure in relation to 'the brothers' and probably implies that he was the obvious partner or successor to Peter as the principal leader in Jerusalem.[6]

- The fact that Paul names James first among the 'pillar apostles' at the Jerusalem consultation (Gal. 2.9) matches Luke's account of the same event, where James appears in effect as chairman of the meeting (Acts 15.13-21).
- On Paul's final visit to Jerusalem, it was to James that he reported (21.18), not even to 'James and all the elders'; Luke notes that 'all the elders were present', but the clear implication is that James presided over the gathering.
- All this accords well with the fact that James, rather than Peter, is subsequently remembered (anachronistically) as the first 'bishop of Jerusalem'.[7]

The evidence is all consistent and no obvious alternative offers itself. Nor, so far as we can see, was there any degree of shared leadership — as Peter/Cephas could be said to have shared leadership with John, or with the rest of the twelve, or even with the seven chosen in Acts 6. It is true that a system of 'elders' appears quite soon (already in Acts 11.30), probably the community of believers adapting to the traditional organizational structure of Jewish communities and synagogues (§23.3e). It is also true that 'elders' supplement 'apostles' as representing the whole Christian community in Luke's account of the Jerusalem council.[8] But in that account James is the one who speaks with greatest authority and as one whose judgment (or decision) is what determines the outcome (15.19-20),[9] even though the subsequent letter is sent in the name of 'the apostles and elders' (15.23). So although in the final scene (21.18-25) the response and advice to Paul is given chorus-like by James and 'all the elders', the implication is probably that it was James who, as in ch. 15, spoke for them all. Now, of course, there is no indication of James exercising formal authority over the church in Jerusalem — nothing equivalent to the exhortations and rebukes in Paul's letters to his churches.[10] In

6. See above, §23.3d.

7. Eusebius cites Clement of Alexandria's *Hypotyposes* (*HE* 2.1.3); also *HE* 2.23.1; 3.7.8; 7.19.1; ps.-Clem., *Recog.* 1.43; the two introductory epistles to the pseudo-Clementines (see below, §36.1d); more detail in Painter, *Just James* 190. In *Recog.* 1.72 it is James who sends Peter to Caesarea to confront Simon Magus (presumably running the accounts of Acts 8 and 10 together).

8. Acts 15.2, 4, 6, 22, 23; 16.4. Bauckham suggests that the elders absorbed some of the twelve/apostles who had remained in Jerusalem ('James and the Jerusalem Church' 437-38), though Luke clearly wanted to ascribe the decision made in Acts 15 to the apostles as such, as well as the elders.

9. See above, §27 n. 324.

10. The letter of James can be regarded as an epitome of James's teaching, but it is far more general than the specifics which are such a feature of Paul's letters; see below, §37.2.

each case James is depicted as speaking on behalf of the community. Nevertheless, for nearly two decades following the death of Herod Agrippa, James could fairly be said to have functioned as the apostle of the Jerusalem church, or even as prefiguring the monarchical bishop of the later centuries.[11]

b. The Role of James at the Jerusalem Council

It is worth reverting to the two episodes in Jerusalem and Antioch yet again, since, uniquely, they involve all three of the principal actors in first-generation Christianity — James, Peter and Paul. They therefore are of incomparable value in providing clues as to the way these three interacted and as to their mutual relationships. The story of these episodes has already been rehearsed fully from Paul's perspective (§§27.3-4) and recalled briefly from Peter's perspective (§35.1a). But it is important also to clarify a little more fully James's part in both episodes.

A possible reading of the Jerusalem council is that no less than four or five parties/factions were involved: the 'false brothers' at one end (Gal. 2.4-5; Acts 15.5); Paul at the other (Gal. 2.6-9); with James, Peter and Barnabas somewhere in between.[12] But in both Paul's and Luke's accounts Paul and Barnabas make a common front,[13] so that although Paul focuses attention on the recognition given to his own commission (Gal. 2.6-9), on the subject of mission to the uncircumcised, Paul and Barnabas at this point stood together. And likewise, although Paul focuses on the counterpart mission of Peter, and Luke on James's ruling on the matter, the clear implication of the Gal. 2.7-9 agreement is that Peter and James likewise stood together (with John).

Here the point needing to be re-emphasized is the fact of James's being fully party to that agreement. James who, as we shall see, comes to be regarded, with some justification, as the arch-conservative within the earliest Christian movement, seems fully to have recognized and agreed with the gospel for the uncircumcised. That is, he acknowledged and accepted that in extending his grace/Spirit to uncircumcised Gentiles who believed in Messiah Jesus, God was truly at work, and in a precedent-creating way. Whatever happened thereafter, that was a momentous decision which James took, acknowledged leader of the Jerusalem church, the mother church, as he already was. Even if Paul describes

---

11. Hengel, 'Jakobus' 561-63.

12. Painter envisages six factions (*Just James* 73-78); he covers much the same ground as in *Just James* in 'James and Peter: Models of Leadership and Mission', in Chilton and Evans, eds., *The Missions of James, Peter, and Paul* 143-209 (here 180-87).

13. Note the plurals of Gal. 2.5 and 9; Acts 15.12, 22.

the episode in a way most favourable to himself and the Gentile mission, the key fact is that James gave his right hand in formal agreement with that mission. Whatever happened thereafter should not be allowed to cloud or to detract from that crucial agreement. For it was that agreement which made it possible for the expanding movement to hold together, even to the degree that it did. It was that agreement which prevented the mission pioneered by Paul from splintering away to become one of the many movements which flare and flourish for a few generations and then fade away.[14] And it was the participation of James in the agreement which ensured that it would have such an outcome. James, in other words, became in this agreement one of the architects and foundations of a Christianity which embraced Jew and Gentile without discrimination.

Equally important, Luke's presentation of James undercuts any evaluation of James as a stereotypically backward-looking reactionary; the James of Acts 15[15] is not to be characterized (from a Pauline perspective) as an unwilling supporter of the Gal. 2.7-9 agreement. On the contrary, James in Acts 15.13-21 simply presents a different way of understanding what he fully acknowledged God to be doing in looking so 'favourably on the Gentiles' (15.14). As already stressed, James was not opposed to the Gentile mission of Paul. Rather, he saw the Gentile mission in terms which integrated it into his understanding of God's purpose for the restoration of Israel: the intention of the rebuilding of David's tent was that 'the rest of humanity might seek the Lord, even all the Gentiles upon whom my name has been named' (15.16-17). And as already indicated, this vision of the unfolding purpose of God was not so very different from that of Paul, particularly as expressed in Romans 9–11 and 15.9-12.[16] James is represented/remembered, in fact, as holding forth a variant of the prophetic hope for the eschatological pilgrimage of the nations to Zion, that is, of the *liberal* Jewish hope that Gentiles would share fully in the blessings which flowed from the anticipated ingathering of the dispersed tribes of Israel.[17]

The difference between James and Paul, then, was not one of theological principle; nor would Paul have disputed the citation of Amos 9.11-12 as now be-

14. E.g., Marcionite communities, or the Catholic Apostolic Church (for brief details, see, e.g., *ODCC* 1033-34, 306, respectively), or the strange case of Shabbetai Tsevi (*Enc. Rel.* 13.192-94).

15. I have already suggested that Luke's portrayal of James is not his own but represents how Luke's Jerusalem sources remembered James and told their side of the Jerusalem agreement (§27.3e).

16. See above, §27 at nn. 212-16. S. McKnight, 'A Parting within the Way: Jesus and James on Israel and Purity', in B. Chilton and C. A. Evans, eds., *James the Just and Christian Origins* (Leiden: Brill, 1999), sees James as carrying forward Jesus' own agenda for the restoration of Israel (102-11).

17. See the data in *Jesus Remembered* 394-95 nn. 70-71.

ing eschatologically realized in the success of the mission to Gentiles. The difference was more of halakhic principle, of the appropriate outworking of the theology and of the text. James agreed readily enough that Gentile believers must not be required to be circumcised and to keep the law of Moses (15.6, 19). But he differed from Paul in regard to how the law still bore upon Gentile believers. Paul could still insist on avoiding *porneia* and idolatry, while sitting loose to the various food and other laws which regulated table-fellowship between Jew and non-Jew. James assumed rather that Gentiles brought within restored Israel should maintain the minimum standards of the non-Jews (aliens) who chose to live in the midst of Israel (15.20).[18] The difference was between a conception of Israel still focused in the land and conscious of the continuing boundaries of God's people Israel, and a conception of Israel breaking through such boundaries and determined only by the call of God and by faith in his Christ.

Bauckham's thesis highlights a further factor which probably pushed James and Paul apart. For it can be fairly deduced that the Jerusalem church, and James in particular, saw it as his/their responsibility to exercise oversight over the developing Christian mission, including, in particular, the Gentile mission.[19] This inference is sustained by several factors:

- the centrality of Jerusalem for any Jewish view of the world, implying its right to issue rulings which determined halakhic practice in diaspora communities;
- the different conception of Gentile converts as aliens resident in the midst of the people, requiring their observance of the terms of 'the apostolic decree';
- the probability that the pressures on the Pauline churches to 'judaize' probably stemmed (ultimately) from Jerusalem;
- the address of the letter of James 'to the twelve tribes of the diaspora' (James 1.1);
- the high regard in which James is held both in Jewish-Christian literature[20] and in the gnostically inclined *Gospel of Thomas* (logion 12) suggests an influence which reached well beyond Jerusalem.

18. I follow here the thesis of Bauckham, whose several essays on James through the 1990s have been particularly insightful and persuasive; see above, §27 n. 222; and on the terms of the apostolic decree see §27 nn. 199-203. McKnight ('Parting' 108-11) and Ådna ('James' Position at the Summit Meeting') also follow Bauckham here.

19. Bauckham, 'James the Just and the Jerusalem Church' 450-51; 'James in the period of his supremacy in Jerusalem was no merely local leader, but the personal embodiment of the Jerusalem church's constitutional and eschatological centrality in relation to the whole developing Christian movement, Jewish and Gentile' (450).

20. See below, §36.1d.

Paul, as we have seen, did not want his mission to become independent of Jerusalem and in effect gave his life to maintain the link and continuity with Jerusalem. But the claim of James and Jerusalem to exercise hegemony over the whole expanding mission of the Jesus sect must have been a major stumbling block for Paul.

In short, the picture of James which emerges is a good deal more nuanced than is usually the case when James is understood simply as a foil to Paul — a natural temptation, since Paul holds such a strong place within Christian Scripture. James was much more a partner than an opponent in the great enterprise which was emerging Christianity — a critical partner, indeed, but sharing much more of the vision of Paul and, presumably, a similar loyalty to the one who had been his brother than the references to him in Acts and Paul at first suggest.

c. The Role of James in the Antioch Incident

As with Peter, it is the subsequent incident at Antioch which throws some of these conclusions into question, or at least calls in question the lasting value of the Jerusalem agreement. For if Peter's behaviour at Antioch seems hard to comprehend, following the Jerusalem agreement as it did, not to mention Peter's time with Jesus, then the role of James appears to be equally problematic. For, as we recall, Peter's 'separation' from table-fellowship with the believing Gentiles must have been motivated by the arrival of the group 'from James'; Paul's account is almost explicit on this point (Gal. 2.12).[21] Nor does it put any strain on Paul's words to deduce that the group from James made it clear to Peter that they were speaking on behalf of James and with the authority of James. That at once speaks volumes for the authority accorded to James, even by Peter himself: that a word from James should cause Jesus' own leading disciple to withdraw from an openness of fellowship with which he himself was quite easy[22] is quite amazing.

The fact that in this incident Peter proved himself a turncoat (as Paul saw it), to be followed by all the other Jewish believers, including Paul's own colleague Barnabas, should serve as a caution to us in evaluating the role of James. For the blame for the incident can be too easily heaped on James, as though his was the primary breach of faith and as though it was simply his own strong per-

21. See above, §27.4 at n. 275. L. T. Johnson, *Brother of Jesus, Friend of God: Studies in the Letter of James* (Grand Rapids: Eerdmans, 2004), plays down the role of James in the Antioch incident (7-9).

22. Whether because of his time with Jesus, who had practised an amazingly open table-fellowship (*Jesus Remembered* §14.8), or as a result of his encounter with Cornelius (Acts 10.1–11.18; see above, §26.3).

sonality that browbeat the others and compelled them to follow his treacherous lead. But given the character of Peter and Barnabas, it is not so likely that they acted as they did simply because James was represented to them as demanding that they should so act. Rather we should infer that the considerations adduced by the group from James must have been very weighty for Peter and Barnabas. And if weighty for them, then, we can justifiably infer, they must have been equally or more weighty for James. In other words, the implication is that there were considerations or new factors to be taken into account which caused James (and Peter and Barnabas) to draw different corollaries from the Jerusalem agreement from those drawn by Paul.

We have already considered the factors which probably weighed with Peter and Barnabas. Presumably they weighed all the more heavily with James (§27.4d):

- the holiness of the people of Israel;
- the responsibility of the believing Jews as the vanguard of Israel's restoration to bring their fellow Israelites along with them;[23]
- the rising tide of Jewish nationalism and unrest under Roman rule, which would make it all the more desirable to demonstrate conformity with Israel's traditions;
- in such circumstances Gentiles truly wanting to participate in the heritage of Israel could surely be expected to conform more fully to Jewish scruples (to 'judaize') than had been the practice in the community of Jesus believers in Antioch.

Markus Bockmuehl has drawn attention to a further factor which may have weighed particularly with James,[24] namely the possibility that some (in this case including James) regarded Antioch as part of the land of Israel.[25] From such a perspective, the mission to the circumcised, seeking the restoration of Israel, could be reckoned to include Antioch. As Jesus may have carried his own mission 'to the lost sheep of the house of Israel' (Matt. 10.5-6) to the borders of Tyre

---

23. As Pratscher points out, the group 'from James' are not to be identified with the 'false brothers' of Gal. 2.4: the requirements they presumably insisted on applied not to the Gentiles but only to the Jewish believers; from James's perspective they did not constitute a breach of the Jerusalem agreement but its implementation (*Herrenbruder* 80-85).

24. Bockmuehl, 'Antioch and James the Just' 155-98; also *Jewish Law* 61-70.

25. Bockmuehl, 'Antioch and James the Just' 169-79; see also M. Hengel, '*Ioudaioi* in the Geographical List of Acts 2:9-11 and Syria as "Greater Judea"', *BBR* 10 (2000) 161-80. The boundaries of the promised land are variously reckoned — including as extensively as from the Euphrates to the Nile (Gen. 15.18), or, in this case, to include the land all the way to the Taurus Mountains (including Syria) (Ezek. 47.15-17; 48.1).

and Sidon (Mark 7.31),[26] so it is quite conceivable that James, in implementation of the same mission,[27] sought to ensure that its outreach to Antioch should be in accord with the same hope for Israel's restoration.[28] After all, if the eschatological focus on Jerusalem was still strong — Jerusalem as the focal point for the climactic events of Israel's restoration and/or Jesus' return — it would be most natural for those centred there to attempt to conform the outlying regions of Israel to what was happening in Jerusalem.[29] In this case the factor which weighed also with Peter would not simply be James's authority but the theological and eschatological significance still clustered round Jerusalem. The 'fear' of which Paul accused Peter (Gal. 2.12) could then be understood not simply as fear of individuals (believing or unbelieving Jews) so much as fear that he was after all compromising the Jewish destiny, Israel's restoration. In other words, the exhortation from James was not so much aimed at thwarting the Gentile mission but rather as ensuring the integrity of the mission to the circumcised. The ambiguity of the dual responsibilities agreed at Jerusalem (2.9) gave James the right so to insist, and it was an argument that Peter and Barnabas could not deny.

Even if we are only partially correct in attributing these several considerations to those responsible for the 'schism' in the Antioch church, the key point is that James was much less 'out on a limb' on this matter than is often represented. On the contrary, if a case can be made for Peter and Barnabas, as having acted with a high degree of pragmatic responsibility, then an even stronger case can be made for James, located as he was at the centre of an increasingly sensitive Christian Jewish identity crisis. In short, James can and should be regarded as having acted much more responsibly and with much more integrity than Paul's brief account is usually taken to imply.

d. James the Traditionalist

However we may interpret the role of James in the Jerusalem council and the incident at Antioch, the impression is hard to escape that the church of Jerusalem,

---

26. *Jesus Remembered* 322-23, 515.

27. Matt. 10.5-6 was presumably retained in the memory of at least some in Jerusalem as a statement of their own agenda.

28. 'The new mission should not be conducted in such a way as to compromise Jesus' mission to Israel' (Bockmuehl, 'Antioch and James the Just' 179-89; here 187).

29. This thesis dovetails well with Bauckham's argument that the apostolic decree draws on the prohibition of Leviticus 17–18 in reference to Gentiles living 'in the midst of' the house of Israel ('James and the Jerusalem Church' 459-61); but if the decree as such only emerged later (as most agree, but see above, §27 nn. 229, 231), it cannot be regarded as a factor in the Antioch incident itself.

as headed and represented by James, became the centre of the traditionalist and conservative wing of the Messiah Jesus movement as it expanded through the missions of Paul and Peter.

In the light of the intensity of Paul's denial of influence from Jerusalem (Gal. 1.17-22), it is almost impossible to avoid the conclusion that the 'trouble-makers' in Galatia referred to Jerusalem as the fountainhead of all authority, including for their own mission.[30] Whether this was with Jerusalem's and James's explicit authorization, the fact remains that Jerusalem provided the incomers with their inspiration to proselytize Paul's converts. And if the Galatian churches had been founded by missionaries from Antioch (Paul and Barnabas), then it could be inferred that the theological considerations which had proved determinative at Antioch were being simply extended to a predominantly Gentile situation, where the integrity of a mission conceived primarily in terms of Israel's restoration was understood to require God-fearers to become full proselytes.[31]

The same considerations weigh with the interventions in both Corinth (2 Corinthians 10–13) and Philippi (Phil. 3.2-21).[32] For in both Paul evidently confronted Jewish missionaries of the gospel of Messiah Jesus who insisted on their traditional identity as Hebrews and descendants of Abraham (2 Cor. 11.22; Phil. 3.5). The parallels between Gal. 1.13-14 and Phil. 3.5-6, and between Gal. 1.6-9 and 2 Cor. 11.4, are probably sufficient to confirm that the threat which Paul perceived was of the same character and claimed the same authorization and legitimacy. Again the implication is of a source for a narrower, more law-conformist understanding of Christianity, and the most obvious identification of that source is Jerusalem, whether specifically James or not.[33]

Most striking is Luke's portrayal of the Jerusalem church in the encounter with James and the elders in Acts 21 — 'myriads who have believed' and 'all zealots for the law' (21.20).[34] Such a report must mean, even allowing for Luke's (or his report's) exaggeration, that the believers were by then (57) a major element in the population of Jerusalem. Given that the political situation in Judea at that time was becoming steadily more serious,[35] the description of the Christians as 'zealots

---

30. See above, §31.7a.

31. We recall again that the letter bearing the apostolic decree (Acts 15.23-29) is addressed to 'the Gentile brothers in Antioch, Syria and Cilicia' (15.23) and that Paul, in talking about mission work which may well have included Galatia, simply referred to his activity in Syria and Cilicia (Gal. 1.21). See above, §27 n. 319.

32. See more fully above, §§32.7b and 34.4a(iii).

33. Ps.-Clem., *Recog.* 4.35, warns that no teacher is to be believed unless he brings from Jerusalem the testimonial of James the Lord's brother — a significant echo of 2 Cor. 3.1. The involvement of James himself is questioned by Pratscher, *Herrenbruder* 89-93.

34. See again above, §34.1a.

35. Josephus, *War* 2.223-38; *Ant.* 20.97-124; fuller analysis in Smallwood, *Jews* 272-84.

for the law' can only mean that they were heavily influenced by the rising nation-alism (marked by more fervent devotion to the national religion), with a propor-tion, no doubt, active among the ranks of those becoming increasingly restless un-der Roman rule and increasingly inclined to resist it.[36] That Luke represents these Christian 'zealots' as deeply suspicious of Paul's mission in its impact on diaspora Jews confirms, if confirmation were needed, that Jerusalem must have been a pri-mary source of the Christian Jewish opposition which Paul's mission repeatedly experienced. But does it also imply that the James of Acts 21.18ff. had changed in views and in the degree of openness which the James of Acts 15.13-21 had ex-pressed? The question is too bound up with the problem of distinguishing Luke's portrayal from that of his sources, and the difficulty of fully evaluating both the state of the political situation in Jerusalem in 57 and how it might have impacted the Christian community. But even with such indeterminacies, it is important to note again that the course of action urged by James and the elders (15.22-25) was a potentially viable compromise, quite in tune with the policy envisaged in the ap-ostolic decree[37] and not uncongenial to Paul's own stated principles (1 Cor. 9.20). James, in other words, who has already been depicted as praising God over the success of Paul's mission (21.20), is further presented as seeking an honourable compromise, consistent with both his principles and that of Paul. This James is a much more conciliatory figure than he is usually thought to be.[38] It is true, of course, that he features no more in Acts, at no point being presented as coming to Paul's aid in trial or in prison. But we do not know how much such silence is the consequence of Luke's editorial choice;[39] and it should perhaps be recalled that Luke also reports that the Roman synagogue communities had heard no adverse reports about Paul from Judea (28.21).

Not least of importance is the fact that James is regarded highly within the continuing Jewish-Christian traditions of the second century preserved in the pseudo-Clementine literature.[40] There James appears as the head of the Jerusa-

---

36. Josephus does not use the term 'Zealot' until the beginning of the Jewish revolt proper (*War* 4.160-61), that is, not till 66, about nine years later than the encounter between Paul and James. But I have already noted that the sicarii were already active during the procuratorship of Felix, that is, during the 50s (*War* 2.254) (see above, §34 at n. 35). So 'Zealot' may well already have become indicative of political activism and not simply of religious zeal.

37. Luke makes the point by including here a further reference to the apostolic decree (Acts 21.25).

38. Cf. Ward's conclusion: 'We find no evidence that James was a "rigorous legalist" nor "a representative of the strict Jewish-Christian tendency" nor even a "Christian Pharisee"' ('Jesus of Jerusalem' 786).

39. I have already noted that Luke is equally silent about support given to Paul during his imprisonment in Rome by the Roman congregations; in some contrast to Phil. 1.12-17, which I take to be referring to Rome (see above, §34.4a, particularly n. 240).

40. See particularly Pratscher, *Herrenbruder* 121-50 (summary 149-50). I have already

lem church from the first, 'ordained bishop in it by the Lord' (*Recog.* 1.43). Peter and the other apostles are depicted as subordinate to James and as having to give account of their work to him.[41] And the pseudo-Clementines are introduced by letters in which Peter addresses James as 'the lord and bishop of the holy church', and Clement addresses 'James, the lord and the bishop of bishops, who rules Jerusalem, the holy church of the Hebrews, and the churches everywhere excellently founded by the providence of God'.[42] Since the various Jewish-Christian groupings are consistently regarded by 'catholic' Christian writers as conservative in regard to the law and the Jewish way of life,[43] it puts no pressure on the data to infer that James was regarded as a hero and exponent of these emphases which remained fundamental to many Jews who came to faith in Messiah Jesus. The fact also that such Jewish-Christian sects regarded Paul as an outright opponent[44] indicates that such conciliatory attitudes which James himself may have counselled had long been swept away by a complete schism between the heirs of James and the heirs of Paul.[45]

Of particular interest is the way James is described by Hegesippus, who, Eusebius tells us, 'belongs to the generation after the Apostles' (*HE* 2.23.3):

> He was called 'the Just' by all men from the Lord's time to ours, since many are called James, but he was holy from his mother's womb. He drank no wine or strong drink, nor did he eat flesh; no razor went upon his head; he did not anoint himself with oil, and he did not go to the baths. He alone was allowed

---

noted that only the *Gospel of the Hebrews* 7 contains an account of the appearance to James (1 Cor. 15.7); see *Jesus Remembered* 863 n. 171; Painter, *Just James* 184-86.

41. E.g., *Recog.* 1.17, 72; 4.35; *Hom.* 1.20; 11.35.

42. *ANF* 8.215, 218.

43. 'They practise circumcision, persevere in the customs which are according to the law and practise a Jewish way of life, even adoring Jerusalem as if it were the house of God' (Irenaeus, *Adv. haer.* 1.26.2). Other patristic references are in my *Unity and Diversity* (³2006) 258 n. 10.

44. In *Epistula Petri* 2.3 Peter refers to one who is obviously Paul as 'the man who is my enemy'; see further again in *Unity and Diversity* (³2006) 260, and below, n. 69.

45. The fact that James is held in high regard also in Gnostic literature (*GTh* 12 — 'James the righteous, for whose sake heaven and earth came into being'; *First* and *Second Apocalypses of James* in Schneemelcher, *NTA* 1.313-41) suggests an interesting history of these Gnostic texts and groups, which will be followed up in vol. 3; for the moment for more detail see Pratscher, *Herrenbruder* ch. 3; R. P. Martin, *James* (WBC 48; Waco: Word, 1988) xli-lxi; Hengel, 'Jakobus' 551-59; Painter, *Just James* 159-81. Bauckham justifiably concludes: 'Some historical reality must lie behind this legendary greatness' ('James and the Jerusalem Church' 427; also 451). Pratscher notes that none of the different Gnostic groups displays an anti-Pauline attitude, indicating that the genuine Jewish Christian tradition (as in the pseudo-Clementines) did not play a decisive role in shaping the Gnostic presuppositions (*Herrenbruder* 177).

to enter the sanctuary, for he did not wear wool but linen, and he used to enter alone into the temple and be found kneeling and praying for forgiveness for the people, so that his knees grew hard like a camel's because of his constant worship of God, kneeling and asking forgiveness for the people. So from his excessive righteousness he was called the Just and Oblias, that is in Greek, 'Rampart of the people' and righteousness, as the prophets declare concerning him. . . . [On inquiry being made of James] what was the 'gate of Jesus', he said that he was the Saviour. Owing to this some believed that Jesus was the Christ. . . . as many as believed did so because of James. (*HE* 2.23.4-9)[46]

Particularly striking are the three titles given to James — 'the Just', 'Oblias' (Greek for 'Rampart of the people') and 'Righteousness'. Bauckham has argued persuasively that the term 'Oblias' should be seen in the context of the earliest church's understanding of itself as the eschatological temple, rather as the Qumran community did.[47] As Oblias, the 'rampart', he protected the city through his prayers;[48] 'James as the rampart compares only with Peter as the rock'.[49] As Bauckham also notes, talk of 'the gate of Jesus' accords with this imagery, and, presumably with Ps. 118.20 in mind, depicts Jesus as the gate into the eschatological temple.[50]

The picture which emerges has a striking consistency, especially if we allow for changing circumstances (the rising tide of Jewish nationalism and fanaticism) and for the degree of hero-worship in the later Jewish-Christian writings. James must have been a considerable figure who commanded a high degree of respect and whose word carried a considerable weight of authority during his life. Whether he retained the degree of openness to the Gentile mission, as indicated in both accounts of the Jerusalem council, it is no longer possible to say.[51]

46. Epiphanius repeats and elaborates this tradition (*Pan.* 78.14.1-6); Painter, *Just James* 211-13. See also Pratscher, *Herrenbruder* 103-21.

47. Bauckham, 'James and the Jerusalem Church' 441-50, referring *inter alia* to 1 Pet. 2.5; Eph. 2.20; 1 Cor. 3.11; Gal. 2.9; Rev. 3.12; 21.14.

48. R. Bauckham, 'For What Offence Was James Put to Death?', in Chilton and Evans, eds., *James the Just* 199-232 (here 206-10); also 'Jesus and the Jerusalem Community' 69. Epiphanius also knows the name for James, 'Oblias, which means "wall"' (*Pan.* 78.7.7).

49. Bauckham, 'James and the Jerusalem Church' 449.

50. Bauckham, 'What Offence?' 208-10, and further 210-18; see also Hengel, 'Jakobus' 563-66 ('Der "Offenbarungsmittler"'). On the other features of Hegesippus's account see Painter, *Just James* 125-27.

51. The pseudo-Clementines include the belief that a mission to the Gentiles was required: 'Since it was necessary for the nations to be called in the place of those who remained unbelievers so that the number that was shown to Abraham might be fulfilled, the saving proclamation of the kingdom of God was sent out into the whole world' (*Recog.* 1.42.1 Latin ver-

But that agreement was crucial to the development of Christianity and made it possible both to retain a strongly Jewish tradition within emerging Christianity (the letter of James!) and for a document like Matthew (not to mention Paul!) to maintain its positively integrative vision (Jew and Gentile) as a thoroughgoing Christian perspective.[52] Whether the later James drew back from an earlier more conciliatory position, and what he or the church in Jerusalem would have looked like had it not been for the catastrophe of the 60s, we will never know. But these unanswerable questions should not be allowed to detract from the predominantly positive image left to us particularly by Luke in Acts 15.

36.2. The Death of James

Of the three principal actors on the stage of first-generation Christianity, only with James do we have really firm evidence regarding his death and the circumstances of his death. This is primarily because the event is referred to by Josephus, though other possibly early traditions complement and may well fill out Josephus's information.

a. Josephus

Josephus briefly notes the execution of James in his account of the events which marked the transition from the unexpected death of Festus to the arrival of Albinus, his successor as governor of the province of Judea in 62. According to Josephus (*Ant.* 20.200-203), the high priest, Ananus, 'who followed the sect of the Sadducees, who are cruel in their judgments beyond all the Jews' (20.199), seized the opportunity afforded by the hiatus between Festus's death and Albinus's arrival to act against James and certain others.

> He convened the judges of the Sanhedrin and brought before them a man named James, the brother of Jesus who was called the Christ [or the so-called Christ], and certain others. He accused them of having transgressed the law and delivered them up to be stoned. Those of the inhabitants of the city who were considered the most fair-minded and who were strict in observance of the law were offended at this. (20.200-201)

---

sion; see also 1.50.2); my comments here draw on F. Stanley Jones, *An Ancient Jewish Christian Source on the History of Christianity: Pseudo-Clementine* Recognitions *1.27-71* (Atlanta: Scholars, 1995) 72.

52. B. Witherington, *The Brother of Jesus* (San Francisco: HarperSanFrancisco, 2003) describes him as 'James the Jewish-Gentile Mediator' (109).

The outcome is that those so offended (who 'bore it with difficulty') appealed to King Agrippa II, and some of them went out to meet Albinus on the way to complain, the ground of offence being that Ananus had no authority to convene such a Sanhedrin without Albinus's consent (20.202). Albinus responded angrily, and Agrippa deposed Ananus from the high priesthood, which he had held for only three months (20.203).

As noted in *Jesus Remembered,* this is the reference to Jesus in Josephus in which we can invest greatest confidence.[53] It should not escape notice that the reference to Jesus is a consequence of the primary reference to James — even in this incidental way, the death of James was more significant in Josephus's history than that of Jesus — though it should also be noted that James is identified precisely by the fact that he was brother of this Jesus, called 'the Christ'. It follows that the reason why James was singled out by Ananus is because of his status in relation to the Christ — that is, most probably, because of his leadership of the sect of 'Christians' in Jerusalem. Whether the 'certain others' were also members of the same sect is not indicated.[54]

The accusation against them is that they had transgressed the law. The echo of the charges against Stephen (Acts 6.11, 13-14) is interesting, since the two passages are independent of each other. Moreover, those who protest against Ananus's high-handed action are themselves described as 'strict *(akribeis)* in reference to the laws', a description which Josephus uses as characteristic of the Pharisees.[55] In the light of these two observations, a twofold inference may very well be justified. The first is that the action of Ananus was rooted in and expressive of a deeply felt factional dispute, in which the ground of complaint was actually a disagreement on the law, on how it should be interpreted and observed (a halakhic dispute); the history of inter-factional dispute within Judaism and in relation to the new Jesus sect provides sufficient precedent for such a violent way being chosen to resolve the dispute. The second is that the 'strict' may have been a good deal more sympathetic with James than with the priestly faction; this would accord with the evidence from Acts that many Pharisees joined the sect (Acts 15.5), that even the Christian Paul succeeded in winning some support from the Jerusalem Pharisees (23.6-10), and that the Jerusalem believers (headed by James) were themselves consistently zealous for the law (21.20).[56]

---

53. *Jesus Remembered* 141.

54. Hengel assumes that they are other unnamed Jewish Christians ('Jakobus' 551).

55. *Jesus Remembered* 269 n. 67.

56. Pratscher, *Herrenbruder* 255-60. C. A. Evans, 'Jesus and James: Martyrs of the Temple', in Chilton and Evans, eds., *James the Just* 233-49, wonders whether 'Paul's visit and the controversy that ensued may very well have contributed to the high priestly opposition towards James' (236).

That the action against James was occasioned by factional rivalry, the new high priest seizing the opportunity of the interregnum between procurators to make a pre-emptive strike against a hated rival,[57] is more plausible than that the underlying reason was a political dispute between those who held divergent attitudes to Roman rule. It is true, of course, that by 62 the storm clouds of the revolt which broke out four years later were already gathering. So, one could conceive of James as one of the few moderating voices caught between the extreme factions who, as so often in such conflicts, is regarded as treacherous by one or other (or both) sides and whose elimination simply deepens the polarisation between the extremists.[58] This would certainly accord with the internecine policies which were already evident in the assassinations by the sicarii and which became such a horrific feature of the subsequent siege of Jerusalem (69-70).[59] But Josephus, whose later descriptions of the factions does not spare them, gives no hint that such factors were in play in the execution of James.

That James was executed by stoning is also significant, since it sounds like a properly judicial execution, and less of the lynching that Stephen's execution seems to have deteriorated into. Of the offences for which stoning was the due penalty, the most obvious alternatives are blasphemy (Lev. 24.13-16, 23) and enticing the people to worship other gods (Deut. 13.6-10).[60] We have already seen that the charge of blasphemy may well have been in play in the trial of Jesus (Mark 14.61-64),[61] a charge which is echoed in Luke's account as the immediate cause of Stephen's execution (Acts 7.56-59). So it is very likely that James could have been accused of something similar, especially in light of the claims being made regarding Jesus, based particularly on Ps. 110.1, and evidently from very early on within Jerusalem itself.[62] The other alternative, of deceiving the people and enticing them to go astray after another god, falls in line with another version of the judgment against Jesus, that he was 'a magician and a deceiver of the people' (Justin, *Dial.* 69.7),[63] and could indicate a growing opposition within the Je-

57. See particularly J. S. McLaren, 'Ananus, James and Earliest Christianity: Josephus' Account of the Death of James', *JTS* 52 (2001) 1-25; cf. Barnett, *Jesus* 322.

58. On the political turmoil as it might have affected the situation, see, e.g., Martin, *James* lxiv-lxix. Curiously it is Ananus himself who later during the Jewish revolt fills the role of a moderate voice which is silenced by extremists, thus ending the hope of a negotiated peace (Josephus, *War* 4.151).

59. See below, §36.4.

60. See particularly Bauckham, 'What Offence?' 218-32, particularly 223-29.

61. *Jesus Remembered* 751-52.

62. See above, §23 at n. 91 and 23.4d. As Bauckham notes, it is possible that Sadducees and Pharisees differed over the definition of 'blasphemy', the Sadducees defining it more broadly, the Pharisees more narrowly ('What Offence?' 223-25), which would be consistent with Josephus's note that the 'strict' disapproved of Ananus's action.

63. See G. N. Stanton, 'Jesus of Nazareth: A Magician and a False Prophet Who De-

rusalem hierarchy to the claims being made for Jesus within the Messiah-Jesus sect.[64] Such opposition came to full flower in the situation reflected in John's Gospel two or three decades later,[65] so it is possible that Ananus was an early exponent of opposition to the Messiah-Jesus sect on these grounds. In either case, factional dis-information and tendentious misrepresentation could well have played a part; the opposition of the 'strict' suggests that there was something of the 'kangaroo court' or 'show trial' in the proceedings against James. But even if we cannot be sure about the grounds for James's execution, Josephus still gives us a clear glimpse of the sort of factionalism, both against the Messiah-Jesus sect and between the other sects of late Second Temple Judaism, which must have been a feature of the early 60s, as the Judean factions began to tear themselves apart.

b. Hegesippus

Very noticeable is the fact that Eusebius gives a far more extensive account of the martyrdom of James than he does of either Paul or Peter.[66] He is able to cite the same key passage from Josephus (*Ant.* 20.197-203), though he prefaces it with another briefer quotation from Josephus — a passage not in the traditional text of Josephus: 'And these things happened to the Jews [the destruction of Jerusalem] to avenge James the Just, who was the brother of Jesus the so-called Christ, for the Jews killed him in spite of his great righteousness' (*HE* 2.23.20).

But Eusebius's main and extensive account of the death of James is drawn from Hegesippus, whose narrative continues from the point reached above (§36.1d). Hegesippus describes how the scribes and Pharisees appealed to James at Passover to deny the error concerning Jesus, and to do so standing on the pinnacle of the temple in order to be clearly seen. They put the question to him, 'O just one, to whom we all owe obedience, since the people are straying *(planatai)* after Jesus who was crucified, tell us what is the gate of Jesus?'. James replies in

---

ceived God's People?', in J. B. Green and M. Turner, eds., *Jesus of Nazareth: Lord and Christ* (Grand Rapids: Eerdmans, 1994) 164-80; and further *Jesus Remembered* 689-94.

64. Bauckham favours this second alternative ('What Offence?' 225-29). Evans suggests that 'Jesus and James may very well have advanced the same agenda over against the Temple establishment, and both suffered the same fate at the hands of essentially the same people' ('Jesus and James' 249), though the suggestion does not accord well with the Hegesippus quotation in §36.1.

65. See my 'Let John Be John — a Gospel for Its Time', *Das Evangelium und die Evangelien* (ed. P. Stuhlmacher; Tübingen: Mohr, 1983) 309-39 = *The Gospel and the Gospels* (Grand Rapids: Eerdmans, 1991) 293-322; and further in vol. 3.

66. See above, §§34.7 and 35.3.

a loud voice, 'Why do you ask me concerning the Son of Man? He is sitting in heaven on the right hand of the great power, and he will come on the clouds of heaven' (*HE* 2.23.13).

Many are convinced by James's testimony, making it clear to the scribes and Pharisees that they have made a mistake.

> So they went up and threw down the Just, and they said to one another, 'Let us stone James the Just', and they began to stone him since the fall had not killed him, but he turned and knelt saying, 'I beseech thee, O Lord, God and Father, forgive them, for they know not what they do'. . . . And a certain man among them, one of the laundrymen, took the club with which he used to beat out the clothes, and hit the Just on the head, and so he suffered martyrdom. And they buried him on the spot by the temple, and his gravestone still remains by the temple. He became a true witness both to Jews and to Greeks that Jesus is the Christ, and at once Vespasian began to besiege them. (*HE* 2.23.14-18)[67]

The claim that Hegesippus 'belongs to the generation after the Apostles' (*HE* 2.23.3) makes his account potentially of considerable value, though the mistaken date,[68] the attribution of the action against James to 'the scribes and Pharisees',[69] and the degree to which the testimony and final words of James seem to have been crafted on the template of the Gospel tradition of Jesus' trial and death[70] naturally

67. Eusebius earlier quotes Clement of Alexandria's *Hypotyposes* regarding James the Just, 'who was thrown down from the pinnacle of the temple and beaten to death with a fuller's club' (*HE* 2.1.5). And in *Demonstratio evangelica* 3.5 Eusebius also records that it was James's testimony to Jesus as the Son of God which resulted in James being 'thrown with stones' by the high priests and teachers of the Jewish people.

68. The death of James can be reliably dated to 62 (the interregnum between Festus and Albinus), whereas the revolt against Rome did not begin until 66 and Vespasian did not begin to plan the siege of Jerusalem till 68, though it was only in early 70 (April) that Titus was able to begin the siege itself (Schürer, *History* 1.499-503).

69. In ps.-Clem., *Recog.* 1.70.7 it is Paul who threw James from the top of the stairs!

70. *Eusebius*

Why do you ask me concerning the
    Son of Man?
He is sitting in heaven on the right hand
    of the great power,
and he will come on the clouds
    of heaven.

Mark 14.62

You will see the
    Son of Man
sitting on the right hand
    of the power,
and coming with the clouds
    of heaven.

Eusebius

I beseech thee, O Lord, God and
Father, forgive them,
for they know not what they do.

Luke 23.34

Father, forgive them,
for they know not what they do.

call for considerable caution as to the weight which can be placed on the account. The key point, however, is the confirmation from Hegesippus that James was stoned, also that the cause of the action taken against James was his preaching of Jesus. The further detail provided by Hegesippus cannot have been gleaned from Josephus.

The account of Hegesippus is similar to what we find in the Gnostic *Second Apocalypse of James:* the decision to stone James, casting him down from the pinnacle of the temple, and on finding him still alive stoning him, while he prayed (at much greater length):

> But [when] they [looked upon him], they observed [that he was still alive(?). Then] they arose(?) [and went down], seized him and [abused] him, dragging him to the ground. They stretched him out, rolled a stone on his abdomen, and trampled him with their feet, saying, '(O you) who have gone astray!' Again they raised him up, since he was (still) alive, made him dig a hole, and made him stand in it. When they had covered him up to his abdomen, they stoned him in this manner. (61-62)[71]

The extra detail (rolling the stone on James, etc.) could be imaginative elaboration. But also to be noted is that the speech earlier attributed to James ends with a prophecy that the temple will be torn down 'to the ruin and derision of those who are in ignorance' (60). This latter echoes the warning of the temple's destruction in the Jesus tradition (Mark 14.58)[72] and implies that the action against James was motivated by the high priestly faction — that is, it is more in accord with Josephus's record of a move against James by the high priest. So it is possible that the tradition here was drawn from an earlier source, however much now elaborated, and even that Hegesippus and the *Second Apocalypse* were both drawing on an earlier tradition describing a more elaborate stoning.[73] It is important here to recall that the sentence of stoning included both casting down the condemned person from a high place and the actual stoning thereafter.[74]

At all events, we can be confident that the tradition of James being sentenced to judicial execution by stoning is well rooted in history, that the move against James was at high priestly instigation, and that the reason was the intersectarian rivalry provoked (probably) by the success of the early preaching and claims about Jesus.

---

71. Following the translation of W.-P. Funk, 'The Second Apocalypse of James', in Schneemelcher, *NTA* 1.339. Pratscher sets out the pseudo-Clementine, Hegesippus and *2 Apoc. Jas.* traditions synoptically (*Herrenbruder* 239-40).

72. See *Jesus Remembered* 631-34 and above, §24.4c. On the parallels with the Jesus tradition and Stephen's martyrdom, see Pratscher, *Herrenbruder* 252-54.

73. Bauckham, 'What Offence?' 201-206.

74. Bauckham, 'What Offence?' 203, 205.

36.3. What Happened to the Jerusalem Church?

There is no indication in our traditions that the action against James was part of or precipitated a more general persecution of the Jerusalem believers. The facts that Ananus's action was opposed by the 'strict' (Pharisees) and that Ananus himself was deposed for his precipitate action would tell against such a hypothesis anyway. So we may presume that the Jerusalem church continued more or less as before James's death. The tradition that Symeon, another brother of Jesus, succeeded James[75] is basically plausible, the line of succession passing horizontally (to brothers) rather than vertically (to a son), as in the caliphate tradition,[76] though we can hardly assume that there was a formal transition of authority in such a confused setting.

The Jewish revolt against Rome broke out four years later. Should we assume that followers of Jesus would have been opposed to such violent action? The subsequent history of Christianity would hardly suggest that it must have been so. And the fact that Luke has James describing the Jerusalem believers as 'zealots of the law' (Acts 21.20) just nine years before the outbreak of the war, a war initiated by 'Zealots' (a title of which Luke could hardly have been ignorant), suggests that there would probably have been some (many?) Christians who, initially at least, supported the revolt.[77]

However, the only tradition relating to the outbreak of the war is what is known as 'the flight to Pella' tradition, to the effect that early in the war the main body of Christians in Jerusalem fled from Jerusalem across the Jordan to the Perean city of Pella, one of the cities of the Decapolis.[78] The tradition comes down to us from two sources: Eusebius, *HE* 3.5.3, and Epiphanius, who refers to it three times in different writings.[79]

---

75. Eusebius, *HE* 3.11.1; 4.22.4. Eusebius calls him 'the son of Clopas . . . another cousin of the Lord'; see also Painter, *Just James* 144-47; and further Bauckham, *Jude and the Relatives of Jesus* 79-94. Typically, Lüdemann argues that this mention of Symeon being appointed to succeed James stands in conflict with the Pella tradition, since the latter, in his view, excludes a return to Jerusalem ('Successors' 209).

76. Already evident in the succession to the high priesthood (see Jeremias, *Jerusalem* 377-78). See above, §23 n. 199.

77. The case was argued particularly by Brandon, *The Fall of Jerusalem* ch. 9, particularly 179-80. Jossa dismisses the suggestion: 'what is certain is that they did not take part in the war' (*Jews or Christians?* 136).

78. D. G. Reid, 'Pella, Flight to', *DLNT* 900-902, indicates the location of Pella with a nice conciseness: 'Pella was located at the base of the foothills in the northern Jordan valley, about two miles east of the Jordan river and eighteen miles south of the Sea of Galilee' (900). For the history of Pella and archaeological data see R. H. Smith, 'Pella', *ABD* 5.219-21.

79. There may also be an echo of the tradition in the pseudo-Clementines: 'Those who believe in him will be led, through the wisdom of God, to a fortified place of the land, as if to

The people of the church of Jerusalem were commanded by an oracle given by revelation before the war to those in the city who were worthy of it to depart and dwell in one of the cities of Perea which they called Pella. To it those who believed on Christ migrated from Jerusalem. (Eusebius, *HE* 3.5.3)

This heresy of the Nazoreans exists in Beroea in the neighbourhood of Coele Syria and the Decapolis in the region of Pella. . . . For from there it took its beginning after the exodus from Jerusalem when all the disciples went to live in Pella because Christ had told them to leave Jerusalem and to go away since it would undergo a siege. Because of this advice they lived in Perea after having moved to that place, as I said. There the Nazorean heresy had its beginning. (Epiphanius, *Pan.* 29.7.7-8; similarly 30.2.7 — 'Ebion's preaching originated here')

When the city was about to be taken by the Romans, it was revealed in advance to all the disciples by an angel of God that they should remove from the city, as it was going to be completely destroyed. They sojourned as emigrants in Pella . . . in Transjordania. . . . (But after the destruction of Jerusalem, then they had returned . . . they wrought great signs.) (Epiphanius, *Treatise on Weights and Measures* 15)[80]

It is possible that Epiphanius was dependent for this tradition on Eusebius,[81] but there are sufficient differences to suggest that they were independent[82] and that they attest variant versions of a historical tradition.[83]

---

life, and preserved because of the battle that will afterwards come to destroy those who have not been persuaded because of their doubt' (*Recog.* 1.37.2 [Jones]; similarly 1.39.3). See further C. Koester, 'The Origin and Significance of the Flight to Pella Tradition', *CBQ* 51 (1989) 90-106; further bibliography in Bauckham, 'Jesus and the Jerusalem Community' 79 n. 58.

80. I draw here on G. Lüdemann, 'The Successors of Earliest Christianity: An Analysis of the Pella Tradition', *Opposition to Paul in Jewish Christianity* 200-213 (here 203).

81. Lüdemann, 'Successors' 203-204 and 309-10 n. 16; J. Verheyden, 'The Flight of the Christians to Pella', *ETL* 66 (1990) 368-84.

82. Koester, 'Origin' 94-95; followed by Reid, 'Pella' 901; and particularly J. Wehnert, 'Die Auswanderung der Jerusalemer Christen nach Pella. Historisches Faktum oder theologische Konstruktion?' *ZKG* 102 (1991) 231-55 (responding to Verheyden); see also Painter, *Just James* 121-22.

83. It is unlikely that Pella was a target of Vespasian's campaign down the Jordan Valley in 68, since it was a Hellenistic city and pro-Roman, and Josephus's account of that campaign does not mention Pella (*War* 4.413-39); Gadara, the capital of Perea, was also spared (4.413-18). See further S. S. Sowers, 'The Circumstances and Recollection of the Pella Flight', *TZ* 26 (1970) 315-20 (here 307-10). Lüdemann thinks that Eusebius's comment in *Demonstratio evangelica* 6.18.14 ('the apostles and disciples of our Saviour, and all the Jews that believed on him, being far from the land of Judea, and scattered among the other nations, were enabled at that time to escape the ruin of the inhabitants of Jerusalem') 'seems to leave no room for the Pella tradition' ('Successors' 310 n. 17); but taken as literally as Lüdemann suggests, the report

One of the most fascinating aspects of this tradition is the possibility that it reflects in some degree the section of the 'little apocalypse' (Mark 13), or at least its Lukan version — Luke 21.20-21, 24:

> When you see Jerusalem surrounded by armies, then know that its desolation has drawn near. Then those who are in Judea must flee to the mountains, and those in the midst of it [Jerusalem] must leave it, and those in the countryside must not enter it . . . and Jerusalem will be trampled on by the Gentiles, until the times of the Gentiles are fulfilled.

This looks like an elaboration of the tradition preserved in Mark, which speaks only of 'the abomination of desolation set up where it ought not to be' (Mark 13.14). Since the Markan tradition itself may be an elaboration of the Jesus tradition in the light of Caligula's attempt to have an image of himself erected in the Jerusalem temple,[84] a logical deduction would be that the further elaboration in the Lukan version reflects the subsequent and far more severe crisis which confronted Jerusalem with the besieging armies of Vespasian and subsequently Titus.[85] At the very least it is possible that Eusebius's tradition knew of a prophetic utterance/oracle, itself stimulated by the 'little apocalypse' tradition, which was uttered within the Jerusalem church at worship, as it became evident that the initial successes of the revolt could not be sustained against the full might of Rome and that the capture and destruction of Jerusalem were inevitable.

The fact that Pella is remembered by Epiphanius as the seat of the Jewish-Christian sects is also relevant. For, as we have seen, some of their distinctive characteristics are precisely those which come to expression in Acts 21.20-21 as

---

would leave Judea wholly bereft of Christians in the mid-60s, which can hardly have been Eusebius's intention. Such pressing of the data to yield a more constricted meaning than is warranted is typical of Lüdemann's style. Carleton Paget responds to Lüdemann: 'The principal problem with the arguments of those who would deny much historical worth to the Eusebian tradition of a flight to Pella is that they cannot explain in a convincing way the quite specific reference to a flight to Pella. Why Pella of all places?' ('Jewish Christianity' 747-48). See also Painter, *Just James* 144-47.

84. See above, §21 n. 293 and §26.5a at n. 96. Brandon argues that Matthew's setting of the 'abomination' 'in the holy place' (that is, the actual entry of the Roman conquerors into the sanctuary) would have implied a delay of any flight until it was far too late (*The Fall of Jerusalem* 173-74); but this ignores the likelihood that Matthew was content simply to reproduce a passage which had been shaped by the earlier crisis.

85. The famous observation of C. H. Dodd that the Lukan version is drawn more from the language of the OT (and so could predate the actual siege of Jerusalem) than from the siege itself ('The Fall of Jerusalem and the "Abomination of Desolation"' [1947], *More New Testament Studies* [Manchester: Manchester University, 1968] 69-83) is weakened by the likelihood that Luke's account is a further elaboration of the already elaborated Mark 13. See also *Jesus Remembered* 417-18.

features of the Jerusalem church: high regard for James, devotion to the law, and suspicion/denigration of Paul.[86] The Pella tradition, therefore, might well provide the link between the Jerusalem church and the Jewish-Christian sects of subsequent centuries: *Ebionaioi* is a transliteration of the Hebrew/Aramaic for 'poor', perhaps reflecting the fact that some of the Jerusalem believers may have embraced their poverty out of conviction, thinking of themselves as 'the Poor';[87] and the 'Nazoreans' obviously reflects, retains and maintains the tradition of the first Christians being known as the 'Nazarenes'.[88] That is to say, there may well be a direct line of continuity between the more conservative traditionalists under James and the subsequent teachings of Ebionites and Nazoreans.[89]

The further tradition that those who had fled to Pella returned to Judea after the destruction of Jerusalem (at n. 80 above) would also fit with this scenario: that the more conservative of those who had fled to Pella remained there, while the rest returned to re-establish churches in Judea. But this takes us into the discussion of volume 3. All that need be noted here is that the church of Jerusalem ceased to exist as such for at least some years during and after the Jewish war against Rome. Some, more fiercely nationalistic than the others, probably fought in the war and probably perished during the horrific siege of Jerusalem. The bulk fled before flight was impossible, either early in the conflict,[90] or before Titus closed the lines of escape which initially existed during the siege.[91] Of these, the

86. See again my *Unity and Diversity* §54.2; also D. F. Wright, 'Ebionites', and D. A. Hagner, 'Jewish Christianity', *DLNT* 313-17, 583-87.

87. This is not to say that Paul referred to the Jerusalem Christians as a whole as 'the poor'; that is not the obvious meaning of Rom. 15.26 ('the poor among the saints in Jerusalem'). But the tradition of 'the Poor' as a title is established within the traditions of Second Temple Judaism (Pss. 69.32; 72.2; *Pss. Sol.* 5.2, 11; 10.6; 15.1; 18.2; 1QpHab 12.3, 6, 10; 1QM 11.9, 13; 4Q171 2.10), so conceivably it could have been embraced by some in Jerusalem. See further E. Bammel, *TDNT* 6.888-902; but see also L. E. Keck, 'The Poor among the Saints in the New Testament', *ZNW* 56 (1965) 100-129; and '"The Poor among the Saints" in Jewish Christianity and Qumran', *ZNW* 57 (1966) 54-78; see also R. J. Bauckham, 'The Origin of the Ebionites', in P. J. Tomson and D. Lambers-Petry, eds., *The Image of the Judaeo-Christians in Ancient Jewish and Christian Literature* (WUNT 158; Tübingen: Mohr Siebeck, 2003) 162-81.

88. See above, §20.1(16).

89. Koester points out the unlikelihood that any claim was made that some of the original apostles were among those who fled to Pella (Epiphanius would have been quick to deny it). Epiphanius calls the refugees who fled to Pella 'disciples' and 'disciples of the apostles' (96; Reid, 'Pella' 901). See further B. Van Elderen, 'Early Christianity in Transjordan', *TynB* 45 (1994) 97-117.

90. Both Eusebius (*HE* 3.5.3) and Epiphanius (*Pan.* 29.7.8) make this claim. As Reid notes, Josephus says that many Jews fled from Jerusalem immediately after the initial Jewish victory over the Twelfth Legion in November 66 (*War* 2.556), and local Christians may have joined that exodus ('Pella' 902).

91. Despite M. Hengel, *Studies in the Gospel of Mark* (London: SCM, 1985) 16-17, the

more conservative, perhaps despairing of God's favour for Israel, probably settled permanently in Transjordan, their descendants evolving into the Jewish-Christian sects of the patristic period. But others returned to Judea and to the ruined Jerusalem to pick up the pieces and to resume a Christian presence in the land of Israel, Palestine.

36.4. The Fall of Jerusalem

Like the fall of Constantinople in 1453, the fall of Jerusalem in 70 marks one of the great turning points in the history of the Mediterranean world. Its effects and aftermath will be one of the main subjects of volume 3. Here, however, it marks a natural closure point for volume 2: the fall of Jerusalem providing the other 'book-end' for the story of a Christianity which 'began from Jerusalem'.

The Jewish War as such is not really part of the story of emerging Christianity, even if, as noted above, some or many of the Jerusalem believers may have been active participants in the war, fighting for Israel and in this role seeing themselves as servants of Israel's God. The point is, however, that the failure of the Jewish revolt marked the end of Second Temple Judaism. The destruction of the Temple knocked over, until the present day, what had been one of the four pillars of Judaism. The different sects which had made for such diversity and factionalism within Second Temple Judaism disappeared, if not overnight, very quickly thereafter, though the heirs of the Pharisees became slowly and increasingly the voice of continuing Judaism. The Judaism which survived the catastrophe of 70 CE soon became something different, in diversity certainly, but in character also, as focused more on Torah than Temple.

And this is important for the story of Christianity, for Second Temple Judaism was the matrix and womb of embryonic Christianity. The sect of the Nazarene was a constituent part of the diversity of late Second Temple Judaism. This meant that with the fall of Jerusalem, marking the effective end of Second Temple Judaism, the sect of the Nazarene was orphaned and had to learn to understand itself in relation to the new reality which emerged after 70 CE. Again, to describe and understand that process is part of the task of volume 3. Here however it is important to appreciate something of the sequence of events which brought both Judaism (and emergent Christianity) to that transition point.

Josephus has provided the definitive account of the Jewish War, written only a few years after its conclusion (probably the latter half of the 70s), by one who had been an active participant in most of the events narrated. The war, which

---

besieged inhabitants of Jerusalem were given several opportunities to escape if they so chose (see particularly Josephus, *War* 5.420-23)

had threatened for a long time, might never have erupted had it not been for increasing insensitivity by the Roman procurators, particularly the last (Florus), fanning the flames of growing insurgency by the sicarii and other dissidents.[92] War became inevitable when the fortress of Masada was occupied as an action of open rebellion and the daily sacrifice for the emperor in the Jerusalem temple was suspended at the instigation of Eleazar, son of Ananias the high priest (*War* 2.408-10).[93] There was an immediate division within Jerusalem between (1) the peace party, primarily the chief priests, the Pharisaic notables, and those related to the Herodian house, and (2) the insurgents. The former initially held the Upper City but were forced to abandon it by the fury of the mob, who proceeded to set fire to the palaces of Ananias, the high priest, and of King Agrippa and Berenice. They also set fire to 'the public archives, eager to destroy the money-lenders' bonds and to prevent recovery of debts, in order to win over a host of the poor against the rich, sure of impunity' (2.427). Next to fall was the fortress Antonia, with its garrison put to the sword (2.430). And the next day High Priest Ananias, who had been in hiding, was caught and killed by the rebels (2.441). These events were accompanied by much savage butchery between factions, both in Jerusalem itself and in other cities in Judea and Syria and as far afield as Alexandria between Jews and Gentiles (2.442-48, 457-98).

The initial Roman response, in the autumn of 66, under Cestius Gallus, governor of Syria, ended with their forces being ambushed and routed in a gorge near Beth-Horon (2.499-555). At this point, Josephus reports, 'many distinguished Jews abandoned the city as swimmers desert a sinking ship' (2.556). Well aware that the Romans would return in force, the Jews committed to the revolt appointed two commanders to defend the capital, Joseph ben Gorion and High Priest Ananus, and others for the provinces. As Schürer notes: 'It is characteristic that, in contrast to the later period of the war, the men in whose hands power lay at this stage belonged entirely to the upper classes. It was the chief priests and eminent Pharisees who led the country's defence organization.'[94]

Josephus himself was one of those commissioned by the Jerusalem hierarchy, in his case to command the forces in Galilee. He narrates at length (2.569-646) his limited success and the civil strife among the fragmenting factions (particularly the opposition of John of Gischala), which made his task so difficult.

92. More detail in Smallwood, *Jews* 284-92. M. Goodman, *Rome and Jerusalem: The Clash of Civilizations* (London: Penguin, 2007), provides an excellent summary treatment of the Jewish revolt and a shrewd analysis of its background.

93. 'The suspension of the sacrifice for the emperor was tantamount to an open declaration of revolt against the Romans' (Schürer, *History* 1.486). See also Josephus, *War* 2.197, 341; the move was not unopposed (2.412-17). On sacrifice by Gentiles in the Temple of Jerusalem see further Schwartz, *Studies in the Jewish Background of Christianity* 102-16.

94. Schürer, *History* 1.489. For fuller detail see Smallwood, *Jews* 298-302.

Meanwhile Nero appointed the experienced Vespasian to quell the rebellion, and he, setting out from his base in Antioch, quickly subdued Galilee, mostly without a fight (Sepphoris had quickly declared itself for the Romans). A major stand was made at the strong fortress of Jotapata, to which Josephus had retreated in April or May 67 (*War* 3.141).[95] There he led a heroic resistance (3.150-288 — Josephus is his own effective publicist). And when it fell, in June/July 67 (3.316-39), he was able to persuade the survivors to commit suicide but survived himself to be presented before his conqueror, Vespasian (3.383-98). This provided opportunity for another meeting with the Roman general in which he predicted that Vespasian would become emperor (3.399-402). The prophecy, together with Roman admiration for a doughty foe, resulted in Josephus being treated leniently and in effect joining the staff of Vespasian (3.408). Other resistance in Galilee was soon crushed, and by the end of 67 the revolt in northern Palestine was over (4.120).

The reduction of the south was proceeding (including Perea and the Jordan Valley), and Jerusalem itself was about to be tackled when news of Nero's death reached Vespasian (June 68), who suspended military operations until the situation in Rome became clear. He had resumed operations in 69 when the competition to become Nero's successor erupted into war between the claimants to the throne. The initial success of the Western legions' choice (Vitellius) stirred the Eastern legions to promote the cause of Vespasian. On July 1, 69, Vespasian was proclaimed emperor in Egypt, quickly recognized as emperor throughout the East, and with the murder of Vitellius in December 69, he was left as undisputed ruler of the Roman world. With wider demands commanding his attention, Vespasian entrusted the completion of the Jewish War, the capture of Jerusalem above all else, to his son Titus (*War* 4.658).

In the meantime (68-69) Jerusalem had been suffering what was in reality a bloody civil war between different factions (4.121-365). The most fanatical of the nationalists were the Zealots, headed by John of Gischala, who dispatched other leaders of the rebellion as traitors with savage fury, including Ananus, who as high priest had been responsible for securing the execution of James, who led the opposition to the Zealots, and whom Josephus describes as 'a man of profound sanity, who might possibly have saved the city, had he escaped the conspirators' hands' (4.151, 193-207, 305-25). During this period many fled from Jerusalem, and conceivably this was when the Jerusalem believers could have fled.[96]

---

95. On Jotapata see Josephus, *War* 3.158-60; Schürer, *History* 1.493 n. 37; R. D. Sullivan, 'Iotape (place)', *ABD* 3.444-45.

96. Schürer, *History* 1.498. Josephus notes that the Zealot guards were willing to let such deserters go if they paid the price, 'the result being that the wealthy purchased their escape and the poor alone were slaughtered' (*War* 4.379).

As Titus gathered his strength for the final siege, the situation in Jerusalem became even worse when Simon bar-Giora, who had ravaged the south during the hiatus of Roman control, was invited into Jerusalem to oppose John. The result was that Jerusalem found itself under the control of two tyrants, rather than just one, Simon managing to blockade the Zealots within the Temple (4.566-84). And the internecine warfare took a further turn for the worse when the Zealots split and Eleazar, one of the original Zealots, managed to take possession of the inner Temple, leaving John holding the outer court and Simon the city (5.1-20).[97] The ensuing destruction included the burning of almost all the reserves of corn, which might have sufficed the city for many years of siege (5.25).

Once the siege was established the miseries of famine quickly fastened on the city, still crowded with refugees (5.424-38; 6.193-222); 'no other city ever endured such miseries, nor since the world began has there been a generation more prolific in crime' (5.442).[98] Though initially Titus encouraged deserters and sent them into the country, wherever they chose to go (5.20-422), latterly, as the siege works grew steadily more constrictive, Titus had escapees scourged and crucified in view of the defendants on the city walls, 'five hundred or sometimes more being captured daily . . . and so great was their number, that space could not be found for the crosses nor crosses for the bodies' (5.450-51). In August 70 the defences had been so reduced and the Romans were pressing so closely to the Temple that the daily sacrifice, which had been offered continually throughout, finally ceased (6.94). Despite fanatical resistance the Temple compound steadily came into Roman control, by fire and sword, and in the final attack (August 30, 70) the Temple itself was set on fire and destroyed (6.250-53), despite general reverence for the sanctuary and Titus's explicit command that it should be spared (6.240-42, 260-66).[99] Also destroyed by fire were the Temple's treasury chambers, 'in which lay vast sums of money, vast piles of raiment and other valuables', since they were 'the general repository of Jewish wealth, to which the rich had consigned the contents of their dismantled houses' (6.282). Titus then gave his troops permission to burn and sack the city, and first the Lower City and then the Upper City was subjugated, until by late September all Jerusalem was in flames (6.353-408).

And thus fell Jerusalem. And thus ended Second Temple Judaism. And thus was marked the end of the beginning of Christianity. The Jewish War contin-

---

97. Josephus likens the new development to 'a faction bred within a faction, which like some raving beast for lack of other food at length preyed upon its own flesh' (5.4) and describes the continued fighting as 'converting the sanctuary into a charnel-house of civil war' (5.19).

98. Schürer provides a succinct version of Josephus's more wordy account (*History* 1.501-508).

99. Was the burning of the Temple deliberate? See discussion by Smallwood, *Jews* 325-26.

ued until the lengthy subjugation of the last redoubt (Masada) was achieved in 73. But it is the destruction of the Temple in 70 which marked the end of the era.

What makes Josephus's account so depressing is not simply the horrific description of the hardships and starvation endured by the besieged. More depressing even than that is his record of the factionalism which sparked off the revolt and the internecine warfare between the factions in Jerusalem itself, which quickly extinguished even the remotest possibility of withstanding the Roman siege engines. In these final months the folly and self-destructiveness of factionalist politics and policies within situations of severe challenge and crisis were demonstrated as never before and never since. The distant observer can only wonder whether or to what extent the other faction of Second Temple Judaism, the sect of the Nazarene, was involved in the calamity. Alternatively, was there something about the sect — one thinks at once of the tradition of the life and teaching of Jesus the Nazarene — which cooled the hotter heads and held back even traditionalist believers in Jesus Messiah either from taking up arms or from involvement in what the dispassionate observer must have known was a futile attempt to resist the power of Roman arms? The extent to which, if at all, Christians were involved in the fall of Jerusalem we will never know. The extent to which Christianity was affected by the fall of Jerusalem belongs to the next stage in tracing Christianity in the making.

CHAPTER 37

The Legacy of the First-Generation Leadership

The 60s were a period of unmitigated disaster for earliest Christianity. Within the space of a mere two years (62-64), it would appear that the three most prominent figures among the leadership of the Jesus sect, Paul, James and Peter, were cut down and killed. In 64 the fury of Nero decimated the rapidly growing Roman assemblies. And in the madness of the Jewish revolt (66-70), the mother church in Jerusalem was either caught up in the maelstrom or had to abandon what the Jewish believers there also regarded as the centre of the world and the hinge on which the future would turn. Other than the execution of Jesus himself, the body of his disciples had never received such a sequence of blows within such a short space of time. And never since has Christianity experienced such a devastating decade, to be bereft of all its principal leaders and to lose its place in the centres both of salvation history and of the history of Western empire in such a short span of years.

The story was not finished, of course, although, as we shall see, our knowledge of Christianity's history goes into a dark tunnel for much of the following decades, illuminated only by a few individual and somewhat scattered figures, documents and epigrapha. The combination of the ending of Acts and the absence of a coherent sequence of letters like those of Paul is like a turning off of the few floodlights which picked out various highpoints and deepened various shadows in the earliest decades. This turning off the lights is another aspect of the disaster of the 60s. Presumably Luke found it more appropriate to end his account before the disasters struck, and presumably in the hope that the steady progress of the first generation would inspire his own and the next generation to rally and to continue the work of spreading the word in the darker days that followed the 60s.

How newly emerging leaders and those unaffected by the disasters of the 60s (the double catastrophe was limited to Rome and to Palestine) consolidated the traditions of Jesus and girded themselves afresh for the future will be the subject of volume 3. But before drawing the history of the first generation of Christian faith and life to a close, it is important to appreciate that the special heritage of the first three great leaders of Christianity was not lost or allowed to disappear. Each of the three has a document attributed to him, documents which are best understood as attempts to represent the teaching of each and to preserve what each stood for, not simply as an act of pietas, but because their message was of continuing importance, even though they themselves had been taken from the churches which reverenced their memory. The three documents are Ephesians (Paul), the letter of James and the first letter of Peter. Ephesians was fittingly described by F. F. Bruce as 'the quintessence of Paulinism',[1] and *mutatis mutandis,* equivalent titles could probably serve just as well for the other two.[2]

37.1. Paul — the Letter to the Ephesians

The letter to the Ephesians is one of the most attractive documents in the NT. Its mood of elevated composure, sustained prayer, and uninhibited confidence in God (particularly chs. 1 and 3), as well as its vision of the church united, growing to maturity and loved, though still facing a fearsome adversary (chs. 2, 4, 5, 6), must have inspired the first audiences to which it was read, as it still does today.

a. Why Most Scholars Have Concluded That Ephesians Was Not Written by Paul

Several features of Ephesians are quite distinctive within the Pauline corpus.

- Unlike the other letters of the Pauline corpus, this one is not directed to a particular church or situation or person.[3] The absence of both specified addressees in the original text and of Paul's customary list of greetings are

---

1. Bruce, *Paul* ch. 36. 'Ephesians has the aim of propagating a definite picture of Paul. . . . The author of Ephesians appears to presuppose a positive picture of Paul in the Church and he believes he can continue that without more ado' (Lindemann, *Paulus im ältesten Christentum* 42). A quite popular view, as in Knox, *Church of Gentiles* 184, is that Ephesians was intended as an introduction to the first collection of Paul's letters.

2. 'Both writings [1 and 2 Peter] have the character of testaments of the apostle [Peter] before his martyrdom' (Hengel, *Petrus* 18-19).

3. The words 'in Ephesus' (1.1), which most modern translations still include, are not present in the earliest and best manuscripts; and second-century references to the letter do not know it as sent to Ephesus; see E. Best, *Ephesians* (ICC; Edinburgh: Clark, 1987), 98-101.

matched by the absence of reference to particular situations or problems known or reported to the author. If Ephesians was intended as a circular letter,[4] it would be unlike any other letter that Paul wrote.[5]

- The style of the letter is also distinctive: chs. 1–3 in particular are pleonastic, marked by repetitions and redundancies.[6] Anyone familiar with the other Pauline letters will recognize that Ephesians is exceptional at this point.

- Even more striking is the exceptionally close relationship between Ephesians and Colossians.[7] Such identical phraseology can be explained only if both letters were written at the same time or, more likely (given the differences already noted), by one letter deliberately drawing on the other. Most examinations of the data have concluded that the character of the interdependence is best explained as Ephesians using Colossians, in part at least, as a model.[8]

- The perspective seems to be second generation: 'the apostles' are looked back to as the foundation period (2.20) and distinguished as 'holy' (3.5).[9] The self-reference in 3.1-13 at first looks to be strong evidence of Pauline

---

4. The nearest parallels, significantly, are James and 1 Peter, though in these cases particular recipients are still specified.

5. More typically, if Col. 4.16 is any guide, Paul expected letters addressed to particular congregations to be circulated to other churches; see above, §29.8d.

6. Note, e.g., the long sentences which constitute 1.3-14 and 4.11-16 (single sentences in Greek) and the repetition and piling up of adjectives, phrases and clauses such as we find in 1.17-19, 2.13-18 and 3.14-19.

7. Cf. particularly:

Eph.	Col.	Eph.	Col.	Eph.	Col.
1.15-17	1.3-4, 9-10	4.16	2.19	5.22, 25	3.18-19
2.5	2.13	4.31-32	3.8, 12	6.5-9	3.22–4.1
2.16	1.20-22	5.5-6	3.5-6	6.21-22	4.7
4.2	3.12	5.19-20	3.16		

See further G. H. van Kooten, *The Pauline Debate on the Cosmos: Graeco-Roman Cosmology and Jewish Eschatology in Paul and in the Pseudo-Pauline Letters to the Colossians and the Ephesians* (Leiden: Brill, 2001): review of previous analyses (191-258) and van Kooten's synopsis (259-309). Van Kooten argues that the author of Ephesians was also familiar with 1 and 2 Corinthians, probably 1 Thessalonians, and possibly Romans (251-54).

8. See, e.g., Kümmel, *Introduction* 357-63; Schnelle, *History* 300-303, 307-308; the minority view (that Paul himself was the author) includes M. Barth, *Ephesians* (AB; 2 vols.; New York: Doubleday, 1974), and F. F. Bruce, *The Epistles to the Colossians, to Philemon and to the Ephesians* (NICNT; Grand Rapids: Eerdmans, 1984). Detailed discussion in Best, *Ephesians* 6-40, and A. T. Lincoln, *Ephesians* (WBC 42; Dallas: Word, 1990) xlvii-lxxiii.

9. For the earlier Paul all believers had been 'sanctified, set apart as holy' (1 Cor. 1.2; 6.11; 7.14) and could be addressed as 'saints, holy ones' (Rom. 1.7; 8.27; 12.13; 15.25; 1 Cor. 6.1-2; etc.).

authorship, but the measure of boasting goes well beyond what Paul had previously claimed for his own role.[10] And even with 3.1 and 4.1, the addition of the definite article turns the humble self-designation of Phlm. 1 and 9 ('a prisoner of Christ Jesus') into something more like an honorific title ('the prisoner of the Lord').

• The theological perspective seems to have moved beyond that of the earlier Paulines, and even that of Colossians. The cosmic christology of Col. 1.17-19 has grown into the cosmic ecclesiology of Eph. 1.22-23. The 'church', characteristically the local congregation (in house, city or region) in the earlier Paulines has become consistently the universal church.[11] The law, so prominent a theme in Romans and Galatians, is mentioned only briefly in 2.15, even though the message of good news for Gentiles is the same. And the eschatology is more consistently 'realized': 'salvation' as already accomplished (2.5, 8; 6.17);[12] the recipients are already raised and seated with Christ 'in the heavenly places' (2.6);[13] the church is envisaged as reaching into future generations (3.21); and there is no reference to Christ's coming again (contrast 4.15).

All in all, the evidence is most consistent with the hypothesis that the letter was written by a disciple of Paul some time after Paul's death.[14] The reason, we may guess, was to celebrate Paul's faith and apostolic achievements, using Colossians as a kind of template, and to ensure that his message was not lost to view but adapted to the changing circumstances of the post-60s. Alternatively expressed, we may say that Ephesians was an attempt to formulate Paul's legacy ('Paulinism'!) for the second-generation Christians and to give this synthesis of his heritage a fitting liturgical setting for use in church gatherings, to provide matter for meditation and worship as well as for instruction.[15] The close link

10. Contrast, e.g., Rom. 11.13, 25; 16.25-26; 1 Cor. 7.40; 14.37-38; 2 Cor. 10.13-18; 12.1-13.

11. Eph. 1.22; 3.10, 21; 5.23-25, 27, 29, 32.

12. For the earlier Paul 'salvation' was future (Rom. 5.9-10; 13.11; 1 Cor. 3.15), the end result of a process of 'being saved' (1 Cor. 1.8; 2 Cor. 2.15). Rom. 8.24-25 is not an exception; see my *Romans* 475-76.

13. On 'the heavenly places *(ta epourania),* see Best, *Ephesians* 115-19 (bibliography n. 23).

14. The issue of pseudepigraphy (an author claiming falsely to be someone else) is one I will deal with fully in vol. 3. In the meantime I may refer to my 'Pseudepigraphy', *DLNT* 977-84.

15. In the heyday of 'pan-liturgism' in NT studies (seeing baptismal and liturgical formulations scattered throughout the NT), it is noteworthy that both Ephesians and 1 Peter could be regarded as examples of extended liturgical forms; see particularly J. C. Kirby, *Ephesians: Baptism and Pentecost* (London: SPCK, 1968); and further my *Unity and Diversity* §36.1.

with Colossians, the mention of Tychicus in particular (6.21-22) and the fact that the letter became closely associated with Ephesus all suggest a letter written in the province of Asia, perhaps as early as the 70s.[16]

b. A Prayerful Reflection on the Wonder of the Gospel of Paul (Ephesians 1–3)

After the opening, using the regular Pauline formulae of self-description ('apostle') and greeting ('grace and peace'), the first three chapters unfold as a great prayer and meditation (1.3–3.21). They begin with as profound a meditation on the blessing and purpose of God as we will find anywhere in the Bible. The blessing reaches from the beginning of time (1.4) to climax in the fullness of time, with everything summed up 'in Christ' (1.10), and with the Spirit as the guarantee of the final redemption (1.14), all in accordance with God's good pleasure and will (1.5, 9, 11).[17] The key to the whole is given by the tenfold repetition of one of Paul's distinctive phrases: 'in Christ'. But equally significant is the God-centredness of the whole passage, marked particularly by the repeated emphasis that all has happened and happens 'to the praise of his glory' (1.6, 12, 14).

Also noteworthy is the characteristically Jewish language and thought: 'Blessed be God' (1.3) runs in the train of Jewish prayer;[18] God's unconditional choice of those to be holy (1.4),[19] to be adopted as his children (1.5),[20] to share in God's inheritance and be his possession (1.11, 14), as before with Israel;[21] the 'mystery' of God's purpose much reflected on in Daniel and at Qumran.[22] The blending of this with the 'in Christ' motif does indeed take us to the heart of Paul's understanding of his gospel.

The prayer (1.15-23) follows the pattern of Paul's letters[23] but quickly moves beyond the more typical Pauline prayer for wisdom and fuller understanding (1.17-18) to an almost ecstatic reflection on the working of God's mighty

---

16. The hypothesis that Ephesians signals the existence of a Pauline school at Ephesus and the beginning of a collection of Paul's letters is discussed by Trebilco, *Early Christians* 90-94.

17. Typically Pauline is the talk of 'redemption through his blood' and 'the riches of his grace' (1.7), but untypically Pauline in the same verse is the talk of 'forgiveness of trespasses' (1.7).

18. Cf., e.g., Pss. 41.13; 72.18-19; the *Shemoneh 'Esreh* (Eighteen Benedictions) (see Schürer, *History* 2.455-63).

19. E.g., Exod. 19.6; Lev. 19.2; Num. 15.40; Deut. 7.6-8; 14.2; Ps. 16.3; Dan. 7.18, 21-22.

20. Cf. Rom. 9.4. 'The beloved' was a favourite name for Israel (e.g., Deut. 33.12; Isa. 5.1).

21. 'Inheritance' — see, e.g., Gen. 12.2-3; Deut. 32.9; Jer. 10.16; God's possession — cf. Exod. 19.5; Deut. 14.2.

22. See above, §29 n. 114 and §33 n. 240.

23. Cf. particularly Rom. 1.8-15; 1 Cor. 1.4-9; Col. 1.3-8.

power (1.19). This power can only be fully appreciated when its outworking has been recognized in God's raising Christ from the dead and seating him at his right hand, far above every other name that may be named (1.20-21). Most mysterious (most wonderful, most glorious for the author) is that Christ's lordship, in accordance with Ps. 110.1, is 'for the church, which is his body, the fullness of him who fills all in all' (1.22-23). Quite what the exotic vision envisages is hardly clear, but the implication is that the church, Christ's body, is the place and medium in and through which God is bringing his purpose for creation as a whole to its completion, the church as in effect the prototype and test-bed for reconciliation between peoples and between humankind and the creation of which it is part. The writer, inspired by Paul's own faith in God and in his Christ, by Paul's own hopes and vision, sketches a vision of his own to encourage those who were to hear the letter read to them and to give them fresh hope and renewed commitment.

One of the most valuable things the writer does is to pull apart what had been the two central entwined themes of Paul's gospel: (1) the symbiotic relationship between divine grace and human faith (2.1-10), and (2) the breaking down of the boundary which had hitherto kept God's people (Israel) separate as God's people from the other nations (2.11-22).

(1) The picture the author paints of the human condition, apart from God's mercy, is as bleak and desolate as anything Paul wrote earlier:[24] 'dead through trespasses and sins' (2.1, 5); daily conduct determined by the standards of contemporary society and the spirit of the age (2.2); and living motivated by the satisfaction of merely human appetites, 'following the desires of flesh and senses' (2.3). The gospel is of divine initiative in the face of such human lostness and enslavement, signalled by the three great words — God's mercy, love and grace (2.4-5); particularly effective is the repeated emphasis of one of Paul's key gospel words ('grace') in 2.5, 7 and 8, matching the threefold repetition of 'in Christ Jesus' (2.6, 7, 10). The divine remedy to the human plight is equally striking: those dead, now made alive together with Christ (2.5); those in captivity to 'the ruler of the power of the air' (2.2), now raised with Christ and seated with him in the heavenly places (2.6); human weakness and self-indulgence transformed into the doing of good works (2.10).

Here of particular note is the way the writer has pulled apart one of Paul's key phrases, 'the works *of the law*', that which was obligatory upon Jews as members of Israel, the covenant people.[25] The primary question for Paul had

---

24. Cf. particularly Rom. 1.18-32; 2 Cor. 4.3-4.

25. See above, §27.4a(v). Although Paul speaks of 'works' without adding 'of the law' in Rom. 4.2, 6; 9.12, 32; 11.6, the implication is that he is using shorthand for the fuller phrase, as I. H. Marshall, 'Salvation, Grace and Works in the Later Writings in the Pauline Corpus', *NTS* 42 (1996) 339-58, recognizes (345).

been whether these works were obligatory (also) for Gentile believers. Paul's response had been clear: only faith was necessary; to require works of the law in addition to faith was to subvert the gospel of justification by faith alone.[26] Here the thought seems to have broadened out to refer to human effort in general as inadequate to the demands of salvation; salvation can be accomplished only by grace alone through faith alone.[27] This was hardly a misunderstanding of Paul. On the contrary, it was embedded in Paul's earlier formulations — that no individual or people can achieve acceptance by God by his/her/its own efforts.[28] This was the theological reasoning which underpinned Paul's more specific assertion that 'works of the law' should not be required as essential for justification. But, like so much else in Paul (and in Ephesians), it was a theological insight well grasped and understood *within* Jewish tradition, and a fundamental credo within its primary textbook of covenantal nomism — Deuteronomy, 'the book of the law'.[29] That is presumably why Paul could appeal to it (he did not need to argue for it) in making the more specific claim that works of the law were a threat to that fundamental principle. The writer to the Ephesians, in other words, anticipated the understanding of Paul which was to become the key theologoumenon of the Reformation,[30] though without falling into the false corollaries that Judaism is a religion solely of 'works' or that 'good works' have no place in the process of salvation: 'We are what he has made us, created in Christ Jesus for good works, which God has prepared beforehand to be our way of life' (2.10).[31]

(2) The other strand of Paul's gospel, now disentangled from the first, as Paul never quite had done, is the fact that this same gospel is for Gentiles as much as for Jews. This, we recall, was the central motivation of Paul, appointed as he believed himself to have been, as apostle to the Gentiles.[32] By separating out this strand of Paul's apostleship and gospel, Ephesians highlights its distinc-

---

26. Rom. 3.28; 9.30-32; Gal. 2.15-16; see §27.5 above.

27. The writer does the same with the critique of 'boasting' (2.9), which reverts to the more fundamental critique of boasting in 1 Cor. 1.29, 31 without becoming confused with the more distinctively Jewish boasting in the privilege of election (as in Rom. 2.17-23; 3.27-29; see above, §33 at nn. 112 and 131).

28. Rom. 4.4-5; 9.11, 16; 11.6; see again §27.5 above.

29. As again Marshall recognizes ('Salvation, Grace and Works' 350-52, 357); see my *Paul and the New Perspective* (2005) 45, (2008) 49, and above, §33 n. 138.

30. A. T. Lincoln (with A. J. M. Wedderburn), *The Theology of the Later Pauline Letters* (Cambridge: Cambridge University, 1993) 135-36. 'Long before Augustine and Luther, the author of Ephesians already interpreted the Pauline phrases "works of the law" and "works" in terms of general human accomplishment' (Das, *Paul, the Law and the Covenant* 272).

31. See further my *Paul and the New Perspective* (2005) 51-54, (2008) 55-58 (ch. 1 §3.4).

32. See above, §29.3c.

tive character and gives it the prominence it was due in this restatement of 'the quintessence of Paulinism'.

A critical factor for interpretation here is to recognize that the issue is set up as from a Jewish perspective on Gentile disqualification from the grace already spoken of (2.5, 7, 8). The assumption expressed — not dismissed, but presupposed as the starting point for the affirmation of the gospel's message — is that God's saving purpose for humankind had hitherto been worked out through Israel, and that Gentiles had hitherto been strangers to that grace.[33] Characteristic of Jewish self-understanding was the conviction that circumcision was a positive identity marker 'in the flesh', which set Jews apart definitively from other nations as God's elect nation (cf. Phil. 3.4-5). It is a Jewish perspective which divides the world into 'the uncircumcision' and the 'circumcision' — the whole range of differences focused in this one feature (as in Gal. 2.7-9).[34] Eph. 2.12 lists the blessings from which Gentiles had previously been disqualified, in ascending order of importance: 'without Christ, alienated from the people (or citizenship — *politeia*) of Israel, strangers to the covenants of promise, having no hope and without God in the world'. It was this state of whole nations, not only the deadness and enslavement of the individual, that Paul's gospel had addressed.

The gospel is the same — 'in Christ' (2.13). 'In Christ' these disqualifications are rendered null; 'in Christ' those hitherto 'far off' have now been brought 'near' (2.13, 17); Christ is and has proclaimed peace between the alienated nations (2.14, 17).[35] The key to understanding the passage is the recognition that the writer sees the two hostilities/alienations as interrelated. He assumes the Jewish view that Gentiles, by definition cut off from the grace provided through Israel's God-given covenant(s), are distant from God[36] and in need of reconciliation with God.[37] But that enmity had become entangled and confused with enmity between Jew and Gentile. Both were expressed in 'the dividing wall'

33. On this passage see particularly T. L. Yee, *Jews, Gentiles and Ethnic Reconciliation: Paul's Jewish Identity and Ephesians* (SNTSMS 130; Cambridge: Cambridge University, 2005) chs. 2-3.

34. Only Jews regarded the lack of circumcision as something negative; in contrast, the Greeks typically regarded circumcision as a form of mutilation. The added note that circumcision was 'made . . . by human hands' (2.11) is an indication that the writer saw this evaluation of 'circumcision . . . in the flesh', as a boundary separating Gentiles from God's grace, to be mistaken.

35. Eph. 2.13-18 is a nicely structured passage (a chiasmus), where the repeated references to 'far off/near' and 'peace' (2.13-14, 17; echoing Isa. 57.19) bracket the central imagery of hostility reconciled 'in him' (2.14-16); see R. Schnackenburg, *Ephesians* (Edinburgh: Clark, 1991) 106.

36. Cf. Isa. 49.1; 66.18-19; Acts 2.39.

37. Cf. Rom. 5.10; Col. 1.21.

(2.14), symbolizing Gentile exclusion from the presence of God.[38] But the main barrier was formed by the law, with particular reference to the rules (especially purity and food rules) which reinforced the separation of Jew from Gentile (2.15).[39] At the heart of Paul's gospel (himself a Jew) was the claim that God in Christ had resolved both alienations and that *the one could not be reconciled in isolation from the other.* This the writer grasps, in insisting that the two being made one was integral to peace with God (2.14-15); reconciliation of either was possible only as reconciliation of each with the other (2.16). The final imagery of 2.18 is of the reconciled people now able to pass through the barrier which had previously divided them, together to celebrate their reconciliation in joint worship made possible by their common participation in the one Spirit. The outcome is not a new national or international entity but individuals of all nations now sharing in privileges previously thought to be limited to Israel as a nation — 'fellow citizens with the saints and members of the household of God' (2.19) — the old divisive temple of Jerusalem replaced by a community built on apostles and prophets, Christ as the keystone[40] that locks all together, growing conjointly into 'a holy temple in the Lord' and dwelling place for God.[41] This is the gospel's potential that would bring the vision of 1.22-23 to actuality.

Not content with this restatement of the gospel climaxing in the vision of the two alienated peoples bonded together in one holy temple in Christ, the writer goes on to insist that it was the promulgation of this gospel and the pursuit of this vision which had been what Paul was all about. It is as though the author feared that in a post-70 situation, with churches more and more predominantly Gentile in composition, this central aspect of Paul's mission might be forgotten and downplayed — as indeed subsequently became the case. So he deliberately continues on the theme

38. The 'dividing wall' is probably an allusion to the barrier which marked off 'the court of the Gentiles' from 'the court of Israel' in the Jerusalem temple, and which Gentiles could not breach except on pain of death; see above, §34 n. 27.

39. Cf. Acts 10.9-16, 28, 34-35; Gal. 2.11-16; Col. 2.16, 21; see above, §§26.3, 27.4 and 34 at n. 363. In his earlier formulations Paul spoke summarily of these as 'works of the law'; here, with the potentially confusing term 'works' stripped out, it is 'the law with its commandments and ordinances'.

40. The image is either of the keystone or capstone, since the apostles and prophets fill the role of foundation (Lincoln, *Ephesians* 155-56), or of the first stone laid in the foundation, providing the alignment for all the other parts of the foundation (Schnackenburg, *Ephesians* 124). The metaphor was drawn from Isa. 28.16 (understood as foundation) and in early Christian apologetic was often combined with Ps. 118.22 (Matt. 21.42; Rom. 9.33; 10.11; 1 Pet. 2.4, 6-8).

41. The imagery of a people as the mode of God's presence and action in the world is drawn from Scripture (cf. Exod. 19.5-6; Lev. 26.11-12; Ezek. 37.27), and the usage here reflects the early conviction that the community of believers in Messiah Jesus were the eschatological temple (see above, §23 at n. 202 and §36 at n. 47).

of 2.11-22 by stressing that it was 'on behalf of you Gentiles' that Paul had been imprisoned (3.1) and that it was precisely Paul's commission to preach this gospel (3.2). He picks up the language Paul had used in his own great attempt to wrestle with the 'mystery' of God's purpose for Israel (Rom. 11.25), taking its elaboration further than did Colossians (Col. 1.26-27).[42] *This* was the great mystery of God's saving purpose, long hidden but now made known to Paul by revelation, revealed to apostles and prophets by the Spirit (3.3-5): 'that the Gentiles have become fellow heirs, members of the same body, and sharers in the promise in Christ Jesus through the gospel' (3.6). *This* was the gospel to which Paul had been commissioned and for which he had been engraced and empowered (3.7).[43]

In a passage becoming ever more florid and encomiastic in character, the theme of Paul's commission and the wonder of his message is elaborated:

> To me, the least of all the saints, was given this grace to preach to the Gentiles the good news of the boundless riches of Christ, and to enlighten everyone about God's mysterious plan . . . so that through the church the richly varied wisdom of God might be made known to the rulers and authorities in the heavenly places. This was in accordance with the eternal purpose that he has brought to effect in Christ Jesus our Lord, in whom we have boldness in access to God with confidence through faith in him. (3.8-12)

This already rich meditation on the significance of Paul's commission is rounded off with one of the most beautiful and uplifting prayers in the whole of Jewish or Christian Scripture:

> That he (the Father)[44] may grant you, in accordance with the riches of his glory, to be strengthened with power through his Spirit in your inner being, that the Christ may dwell through faith in your hearts,[45] being rooted and grounded in love, that you may be empowered to comprehend with all the saints what is the breadth and length and height and depth,[46] and to know the

---

42. See again §29 n. 114 above; also C. C. Caragounis, *The Ephesian Mysterion* (Lund: Gleerup, 1977).

43. Cf. Rom. 1.5; 15.15-16; 1 Cor. 9.17; 15.10; Gal. 2.7-9; Col. 1.29. See also Wilckens, *Theologie* 1/3.283.

44. 'The Father from whom every family in heaven and on earth takes its name', or, as we might say, receives its identity (3.15); as with Paul, the writer had no difficulty in affirming both God's special relation with Israel and his universal Fatherhood.

45. This is a prayer for fellow Christians: the writer had no hesitation in using language which some would regard as appropriate only as a prayer for conversion; powerful images of spiritual relationship respond more to the reality of experience than to the logic of theological propriety.

46. The four dimensions of God's love (Lincoln, *Ephesians* 207-13; Schnackenburg, *Ephesians* 150-51).

love of Christ that surpasses knowledge, so that you might be filled with all
the fullness of God *(plērōma tou theou)*. (3.16-19)

What Colossians had dared to attribute to the human Christ — 'in him the
whole fullness of deity *(plērōma tēs theotētos)* dwells bodily' — Ephesians holds
forth as a prayerful possibility for believers. What Ephesians itself had held out
as a vision of the church, the body of Christ, 'the fullness of him who fills all in
all' (1.22-23), is now held out as an aspiration for believers individually and col-
lectively. The goal for the church is nothing less than to embody the presence and
the love of God in the way that Christ did! No mystic could aspire to more. In the
spirit of deep devotion thus expressed, the prayerful meditation is completed
with a fitting doxology (3.20-21).

c. An Exhortation in Pauline Character (Ephesians 4–6)

Paul's regular practice in his letters had been to attach a sequence of appropriate
exhortations to the main body of his letter. Here, although chs. 1–3 have been
more prayer than exposition, the same practice is followed. Characteristically
Pauline is the appeal that the audiences to which the letter was read should lead
their lives in a manner expressive of the grace which had called them to faith
(4.1), with a very un-macho (then as now) humbleness and meekness in self-
esteem, patience and forbearance in love and an eager determination to maintain
the unity of the Spirit and the peace which benefits all (4.2-3).[47]

The confession which follows (4.4-6) is a more carefully structured and liturgical formula than anything in the earlier Paul: in particular, the triadic structure ('one Spirit, one Lord, one God'); and the four 'all's of the climax reminding
those making the confession that the ultimate foundation of Christian unity is
God, both in his oneness and in his allness as Creator.

Equally Pauline is the imagery of the church as the body of Christ (Rom.
12.4-8; 1 Cor. 12.4-31). Notable are the continuation of the insight that the body
is constituted and functions by grace *(charis)* and gift *(dōrea)* (4.7-8),[48] the recognition of the mutual interdependence which makes it possible for the body to
function effectively as one (4.12),[49] and the emphasis on a body which is still

47. Cf. Rom. 12.3; 1 Cor. 4.6; Gal. 6.1; Phil. 2.3; Col. 3.12.

48. Eph. 4.8 cites Ps. 68.18, a passage which lauds Yahweh's triumph over Israel's enemies, now read as a description of Christ's exaltation (cf. 1 Cor. 15.24-26; Col. 2.15). In contrast to Psalm 68, Ephesians speaks of Christ giving, rather than receiving, gifts; but there is a
Targum of Psalm 68 which refers it to Moses and reads it similarly (Moses giving the law), so
the Ephesians' reading need not have sounded strange (discussion in Lindars, *New Testament
Apologetic* 52-53; Lincoln, *Ephesians* 243-44; Best, *Ephesians* 379-82).

49. The punctuation of 4.12 is disputed: either 'to equip the saints for the work of minis-

growing towards maturity, the mark of which is Christ (4.13). But equally characteristic of Ephesians, the imagery is developed: the church is no longer simply
the church in Corinth (as in 1 Cor. 12.27) but the universal church of Ephesians;
the gifts are the established ministries of apostle, prophet, evangelist, pastor and
teacher (Eph. 4.11)[50] and do not include the 'occasional' ministerings of prophecy, helping, and the like, which is a feature of the earlier lists (Rom. 12.8; 1 Cor.
12.28); the maturity looked for includes an ability to resist false teaching and deceit (Eph. 4.14), a typically second-generation concern;[51] and the head of the
body is no longer simply a *part* of the body (as in 1 Cor. 12.21), but Christ is
head over the body (Eph. 4.15).[52] The change of emphasis allows the author to
maintain the image of the church as the body of Christ, while both asserting its
dependence on Christ for its proper functioning and affirming the central bond of
love (4.16).[53]

There follows a section of more general, more or less all-purpose exhortation, which stretches from 4.17 to 5.20. Unlike earlier Pauline letters, this one
seems to have no particular situation in view. The first part (4.17-24) parallels
2.1-10 in structure: a reminder of the audiences' Gentile past (4.17-19), of their
conversion (4.20-21), and of God's purpose for them (4.22-24). As in 2.11-12,
the warning presupposes a Jewish perspective: that Gentile conduct was characterized by the futility *(mataiotēs)* of their vaunted reason and surrender to sexual
excess, impurity and greed (4.17-19).[54] 'You did not so learn the Christ' (4.20)!
Not only is Christ the head of the body (a visionary conception of the church),
but also in his own life and mission, Jesus has provided the model for conduct expected of those 'in him' (4.21).[55] To live in accordance with this teaching is to
put away the old life and through renewal of mind (self-perception) to put on a

---

try' (ministry is what the saints do) or 'to equip the saints, for the work of ministry' (the ministry is that of the apostles, prophets etc.). The former is more in line with the earlier Pauline vision of a body in which all members have 'ministry' (1 Cor. 12.5); the latter is more in line with
a more institutionalized concept of church in which ministry is focused more tightly on appointed officers. See discussion in Lincoln, *Ephesians* 253-55; S. H. T. Page, 'Whose Ministry?
A Re-appraisal of Ephesians 4:12', *NovT* 47 (2005) 26-46.

50. The first, second and fifth featured strongly in the earlier Pauline passages, but not
evangelist and pastor.

51. Acts 20.28-31; a consistent concern in the Pastorals.

52. See also my '"The Body of Christ" in Paul', and the note with bibliography in Best,
Ephesians 189-96.

53. Discussion in Lincoln, *Ephesians* 261-64; Best, *Ephesians* 409-13.

54. Cf. Rom. 1.21-31.

55. Here, as with Col. 2.6-7, the most obvious implication is that the writer is referring
to a store of traditions about Jesus' teaching and life which he could assume would have been
part of regular catechetical teaching and would be familiar among all churches; see further below, n. 59.

new life being created in accordance with God and his will (4.22-24) — the writer neatly combining the contrast between a mode of living determined by deceitful desire and the aspiration for one which is patterned in accordance with God's intention in creating humankind in the first place.[56]

The familiar imagery of change of clothes to denote new life (4.22, 24)[57] is developed in the following paragraphs by vivid reminders of what has (should have) been 'put off' (4.25): falsehood (4.25), anger cherished beyond nightfall (4.26), misappropriation of what belongs to others (4.28), speech which rots relationships (4.29), as well as bitterness, indignation, shouting, slander and all malice (4.31); sexual license, impurity of any kind, greed (5.3); and obscenity, foolish talk and coarse jesting *(eutrapelia)* (5.4).[58] In contrast, the new life is (to be) marked by truth-speaking and a sensitivity to mutual interdependence (4.25), by honest work with a view to being able to help others out with any surplus gained (4.28), by speech which is a means of grace to others (4.29), and by kindness, tender-heartedness and readiness to forgive as those forgiven by God in Christ (4.32)[59] — imitators of God,[60] and loving others as Christ loved us (5.1-2) — a life marked by thankfulness (5.4). They are in large part based on age-old wisdom, familiar among both Greek and Jewish moralists, but of no less value for that; Christian paraenesis agreed with and willingly drew on the best expressions of moral responsibility, particularly Jewish wisdom,[61] though rooted in the forgiveness and love of Christ (4.32; 5.2) and enabled by the Spirit (4.30).

In 5.6-14 the imagery changes from putting off and putting on to another

---

56. Cf. Rom. 8.29; 13.14; 2 Cor 3.18; Col. 3.10.

57. 'Put off *(apothesthai)*' — cf. Rom. 13.12; Col. 3.8; Jas. 1.21; 1 Pet. 2.1; 'put on *(endysasthai)'* — Rom. 13.12, 14; Gal. 3.27; Col. 3.10, 12; 1 Thess. 5.8. Selwyn was one of the first to draw attention to this prominent feature of Christian paraenesis (*First Peter* 393-400); see also E. Schweizer, 'Traditional Ethical Patterns in the Pauline and Post-Pauline Letters and Their Development (Lists of Vices and House-Tables)', in E. Best and R. M. Wilson, eds., *Text and Interpretation* (Cambridge: Cambridge University, 1979) 195-209; further bibliography in *Theology of Paul* 662-65.

58. *Eutrapelia,* only here in biblical Greek, is defined by Aristotle as the middle term between the extremes of buffoonery and boorishness (*Ethica Nichomachea* 2.7.13; BDAG 414).

59. Note the echo of Jesus' teaching — Matt. 6.14 (*Jesus Remembered* §14.6); as in Col. 3.13. Other echoes of Jesus' teaching: 4.26 — Matt. 5.22; 4.29 — Matt. 15.11; 5.1 — Matt. 5.45; 5.5 — inheriting the kingdom of God (*Jesus Remembered* 386), in the form taken up by Paul (1 Cor. 6.9-10; Gal. 5.21); 5.28-30 — elaboration of the love command (Mark 12.31 pars.; *Jesus Remembered* §14.5a).

60. See R. A. Wild, '"Be Imitators of God": Discipleship in the Letter to the Ephesians', in F. Segovia, ed., *Discipleship in the New Testament* (Philadelphia: Fortress, 1985) 127-43.

61. In particular, 4.24 picks up the language of Wis. 9.3; 4.25 uses the words of Zech. 8.16; the exhortation of 4.26-27 elaborates Ps. 4.4; 4.30 echoes Isa. 63.10; and 5.2 echoes Exod. 29.18. For such blending of traditional Jewish wisdom and Jesus' teaching see also Rom. 12.14-21 (§33 nn. 250, 251) and James (§37.2c below).

familiar contrast between light and darkness, between a life in the light, open to and reflecting light's searching rays, and a life full of hidden shamefulness.[62] The elaboration of the contrast here is a blend of the conventional and the more distinctively Christian. All would agree that goodness, righteousness and truth are desirable virtues (5.9), that a religious person will want to learn 'what is pleasing' to God (5.10), and that part of the effectiveness of the imagery of light lies in the power of light to expose what would otherwise be hidden from sight (5.11-13). The distinctive Christian claim is that the light (the real, the most effective light) is 'in the Lord' (5.8). Equally characteristic of Paul's teaching is the claim that discernment of what please the Lord (5.10) is given by renewal of the mind and through the Spirit.[63] Eph. 5.14 — 'Sleeper, awake! Arise from the dead, and the Christ will shine upon you' — may be a snatch of an early Christian hymn.[64] The paragraph is rounded off with more general aphoristic exhortation and a contrast between drunkenness and the exuberance which is typically a mark of the Spirit's infilling (5.18).[65] The fullness of the Spirit is manifested not in debauchery but in inspirational and heartfelt praise,[66] a life lived out of a spirit of thankfulness to God the Father through the Lord Jesus Christ (5.19-20).

A striking feature of what appears to be Ephesians' development of material from Colossians is the elaboration (5.21–6.9) of what seems to have been the first Christian attempt to adapt the regular pattern of household economy for Christian usage (Col. 3.18–4.1).[67] We may envisage the same motivation here: to demonstrate the good citizenship of small house churches, which might otherwise be deemed subversive of traditional social values,[68] and to bear witness to

62. In the OT cf., e.g., Pss. 36.9; 82.5; Prov. 4.14-19; Eccl. 2.13; as noted earlier, a prominent contrast in the DSS is between 'the sons of light' (the Qumran covenanters) and 'the sons of darkness' (the rest). In the NT see, e.g., Matt. 6.22-23; Acts 26.18; 2 Cor. 4.6; Col. 1.12-13; 1 Pet. 2.9; 1 John 1.6.

63. Rom. 12.2; 1 Cor. 2.14-15; Phil. 1.9-10; 1 Thess. 5.19-22. The power of light to expose the unsavoury and shameful recalls such passages as John 3.20 and 1 Cor. 14.24-25 and echoes the warning notes of Mark 4.21-22 and Rom. 13.11-14.

64. Discussion in Lincoln, *Ephesians* 331-32, and Best, *Ephesians* 497-500.

65. The recall of the story of Pentecost (Acts 2.1-4, 12-16) may be intentional. Worth noting is that for the writer, being filled with the Spirit is not regarded as a once-for-all event; the exhortation is to be (constantly or repeatedly) filled with the Spirit; see further Fee, *God's Empowering Presence* 658-753.

66. A living hymnody has been a mark of spiritual vitality throughout the history of Christianity, and Christian renewal movements have always been marked by a fresh creative round of new song.

67. See above, §34 at n. 394. The Colossian household rules probably provided the precedent also for 1 Pet. 2.18–3.7; cf., e.g., Tit. 2.1-10; *Did.* 4.9-11; *1 Clem.* 21.6-9.

68. In the history of Christianity, and of religions generally, new sects/cults are generally held in suspicion on this point.

the quality and character of the Christian household.[69] Here again the core teaching is fairly conventional (good ethics are not an exclusively Christian prerogative). But here too the conventional is transformed by the Christian sense that all relationships have to be lived 'in the Lord' and with the unselfish and sacrificial love of Christ as the pattern and inspiration.

The Christian adaptation begins at once: that wives should be subject to their husbands was the social and moral currency of the day (5.22);[70] and the headship of the husband is reaffirmed (5.23-24) as Paul had done before (1 Cor. 11.3). But the exhortation is softened by prefacing it with a call to be subject to one another (5.21), and by the reminder that Christ's headship over the church is the model (5.23-24); the paradigm for the husband is Christ as lover and saviour, not as lord and master (5.25).[71] This emphasis on the husband's responsibility to love his wife with the self-sacrificial love of Christ is repeated several times in 5.25-33:

- Christ gave himself to make the church ready to be united with him — taking up the imagery of the bath of purification which the bride would take prior to and in preparation for the wedding ceremony (5.25-27);[72]
- Jesus' emphasis on loving your neighbour 'as yourself' (Lev. 19.18) is taken up with the reminder of just how well one looks after oneself (5.28-30);
- the great mystery of marriage, of two becoming one flesh (Gen. 2.24 is quoted), mirrors the relation of Christ and the church, which works because love and respect provide the mutual bond (5.31-33).[73]

The second pairing within the household code (as in Col. 3.20-21) is children and parents (6.1-4). As with the submissiveness of wives, so the obligation of obedience to parents (6.1) was a widely recognized virtue in the ancient world, though again qualified by 'in the Lord'.[74] As in Col. 3.20, a notable variation from other such codes is that children are addressed as responsible members of

---

69. See again Schweizer, 'Traditional Ethical Patterns'.

70. Twenty-first-century readers who find this offensive should perhaps recall that U.K. marital law, which treated wives as the property of their husbands, was changed only in the nineteenth century.

71. See also Keener, *Paul, Women and Wives* chs. 4-6.

72. The imagery of the bridal bath is usually referred to baptism (see particularly R. Schnackenburg, *Baptism in the Thought of St. Paul* [Oxford: Blackwell, 1964] ch. 1), though the imagery is corporate (the church lives in the time between betrothal and the wedding ceremony at the parousia — cf. 2 Cor. 11.2; Rev. 19.7-8; 21.2, 9-10), and the cleansing is evidently a spiritual cleansing which comes 'by the word' (cf. 1 Cor. 6.11; Tit. 3.5-6; Heb. 10.22).

73. It is the husband who is called to love, for the love in view is not marital or family love so much as the sacrificial and non-self-serving love of the more powerful for the less advantaged.

74. The phrase, however, is missing in some important manuscripts.

the congregation, but here with the scriptural injunction of Exod. 20.12 drawn in to reinforce it (6.2-3). As with Paul, the author thought it entirely appropriate to apply a promise relating to Israel's prosperity in the promised land to Gentile believers elsewhere in the Mediterranean world.[75] The parallel injunction to fathers is conventional (6.4), recognizing parental responsibility for training and disciplining *(paideia)* their offspring, but again tempered with the reminder that the training and instruction should be 'of the Lord'.

The other pairing, slaves and masters, is modelled closely on Col. 3.22-25, where again it is noticeable that slaves were being regarded as full members of the congregation to whom the letter would be read. Again the Christianizing of the rule is prominent: obey your earthly masters as you obey Christ (6.5), 'as slaves of Christ, doing the will of God from the heart' (6.6), 'as to the Lord' (6.7), 'knowing that whatever good we do, we will receive the same again from the Lord' (6.8). And masters should remember that both slave and master have the same Master in heaven, bearing in mind the divine impartiality (6.9).[76]

The closing sequence (6.10-20) is one of the most vivid portrayals of the Christian life as a spiritual struggle. It evidently draws on well-established Jewish motifs, particularly that of Yahweh as a divine warrior and of the armour which Yahweh dons to effect judgment on human sin and social injustice.[77] The adaptation of familiar imagery is a textbook example of how living tradition works, not merely repeating or recycling old material, but allowing it to stimulate fresh formulations which absorb and create it anew for changing circumstances and audiences.

- The opposing forces are no less than the cosmic powers, the intangible influences, which bear upon humankind, whether conceptualized as 'the devil' (6.11)[78] or as multiform in existential impact (6.12).[79]
- They can only be withstood 'in the strength of the Lord's power' (6.10, 13), a spiritual power which alone is adequate to defeat such destructive forces: the belt of truth, the breastplate of righteousness (6.14),[80] shoes as readiness

75. A reflection, perhaps, of the Jacobean 'solution' to the problem of Gentile membership of a Jewish church (Acts 15.15-21); see above, §§27.3e and 36.1b.

76. Divine impartiality is an important element in Paul's exposition in Rom. 2.11 (see above, §33 n. 106); elsewhere in the NT, see Acts 10.34; Col. 3.25; Jas. 2.1.

77. Isa. 59.12-18; Wis. 5.17-20.

78. Cf. Eph. 2.2; 4.27; Jas. 4.7; 1 Pet. 5.8-9.

79. Cf. Rom. 8.38-39; 1 Cor. 15.24-26; Col. 1.16; 2.15; 1 Pet. 3.22. To what extent such language was already seen as metaphorical for social pressures or the *Zeitgeist* is debated; see particularly W. Wink, *Naming the Powers* (Philadelphia: Fortress, 1984), and further *Theology of Paul* §5; Best, *Ephesians* 174-80.

80. The latter draws directly on Isa. 59.17 and Wis. 5.18.

for the gospel of peace (6.15),[81] the shield of faith (6.16),[82] the helmet of salvation[83] and the sword of the Spirit, which is the word of God (6.17).[84]

• The final exhortation departs from the imagery of warfare, but it could be said that it stresses the need for communication with the Commander (prayer 'in the Spirit') and for a cooperative effort in the ongoing struggle (6.18-20). It is striking how the language reverts to the theme of Paul's mission — 'to make known with boldness the mystery of the gospel' (6.19), in a formulation probably modelled on Paul's personal request in Col. 4.2-4 but adapted to the restatement of Paul's commission in Eph. 3.1-13.

The conclusion (6.20-21) is almost verbatim Col. 4.7-8, and the final benediction is an elaboration of Paul's usual prayer for grace and peace (6.23-24).

d. A Church Epistle

On returning to Ephesians and reading it afresh, what struck me most was the vision of the church which the letter reverts to again and again. Not a particular church, like all Paul's earlier letters, but 'church' as an almost ideal figure, church as all churches should be and cannot be except as the one, whole church.

• God's family through Jesus Christ (1.5) and heirs (1.14, 18);
• Christ's lordship as 'for the church, which is his body, the fullness of him who fills all in all' (1.22-23);
• the two estranged peoples become one new humanity, reconciled to God in one body (2.15-16);
• 'fellow citizens with the saints and members of the household of God' (2.19);
• 'a holy temple in the Lord', 'a dwelling place for God' (2.21-22);
• 'fellow heirs, members of the same body, joint participants in the promise' (3.6);
• through the church the wisdom of God is to be made known to the rulers and authorities in the heavenlies (3.10);
• 'to God be glory in the church and in Christ Jesus' (3.21);

---

81. There is probably an echo of Isa. 52.7, a passage also echoed in Acts 10.36 and cited in Rom. 10.15.

82. In Wis. 5.19 the shield is 'holiness'; the adaptation is appropriate, since faith was such a defining characteristic of Christian discipleship.

83. In Wis. 5.18 the helmet is 'impartial justice', but in 1 Thess. 5.8 Paul had already spoken of 'the hope of salvation' as a helmet.

84. The imagery again reflects older usage (Isa. 49.2; Hos. 6.5; cf. Heb. 4.12).

- one body, with gifted leadership and ministry for the building up of the body, a body sustained by the nourishment which flows from the head (4.4, 12-13, 15-16);
- children of light (5.8);
- Christ the head of the body, the church (5.23-24);
- and, most lavish, the church as the betrothed of Christ, prepared for the wedding ceremony, loved with sacrificial love by her husband (5.25-27, 29-30, 32).

This sustained focus — strongly affirming Paul's role in the cosmic drama being viewed, always reverberating with the steady drumbeat of 'in Christ', fully aware of the church's reliance on the Spirit, and constantly looking beyond to the final purpose and glory of God — makes Ephesians such a fitting tribute to Paul and fully deserving of the accolade of providing 'the quintessence of Paulinism'.

37.2. James — the Letter of James

The letter attributed to James is one of the most exciting of the earliest Christian writings. For more than any other, the undisputed letters of Paul apart, James puts us in touch with first-generation Christianity. Moreover, whereas the letters of Paul give us invaluable information about the earliest churches of the Gentile mission, the letter of James gives us an unparalleled insight into the embryonic Christianity of Palestine and probably of Jerusalem itself. And whereas Paul's several letters, correlated with information from Acts, enable us to make triangulations which help fix more firmly the knowledge we have about the predominantly Gentile churches and about Paul's own gospel and theology, James is almost the only window we have into the Jerusalem church and its influence in the 50s and 60s of the first century.

Unfortunately James has suffered from the unavoidable comparison with Paul. This is principally because Paul is the only uncontested voice within the NT from the first generation and in effect dominates the canonical space beyond the Gospels.[85] The result is that James suffers by way of comparison, particularly because for generations of Protestant commentators (who gave the lead in the development of a properly critical study of the NT), Paul has been the one who most clearly defined what Christianity is and what the gospel is. Compared

---

85. R. Bauckham, who climaxes his work on James in *James: Wisdom of James, Disciple of Jesus the Sage* (London: Routledge, 1999), observes that this is more a Western problem, since Eastern Orthodoxy arranges the NT canon in a different order — Gospels, Acts, James and the other Catholic Epistles, Pauline letters, Revelation (115).

with the weighty theology of Paul's correspondence, the letter of James seems lightweight, if not misguided.[86] Worse still, for nearly two centuries of scholarship influenced by Baur, influenced at least to the extent of being fascinated by the question 'Who were Paul's opponents?', the most obvious available answer was James himself,[87] with the letter of James regarded as providing at least some supportive evidence.[88] I have already indicated in §36.1 that there is much more to be said on behalf of James than is usually claimed, and one of the key questions here is what the letter of James may contribute to that reassessment. More to the point, it is of crucial importance for a well-proportioned view of Christianity's beginnings that the letter of James be pulled out of Paul's shadow and read for itself and for what it tells us of those beginnings quite apart from Paul.[89]

a. Who Is James?

The letter begins, 'James, a slave of God and of the Lord Jesus Christ' (1.1). Clearly implied is that this James is well known and needs no further or more elaborate introduction. Of the other Jameses mentioned in the beginning of Christianity,[90] only James the brother of John, one of the original three confidants of Jesus and of the initial triumvirate of the Jerusalem church, could meet that description, except that his early execution (ca. 42) almost certainly rules him out.[91] The only other obvious answer to the question is James the brother of

---

86. The most famous expressions are the much-quoted comments of Luther: it 'contains nothing evangelical'; 'it teaches nothing about him [Jesus]'; James and Paul cannot be harmonized; 'it is no apostolic letter (but) a right epistle of straw'; see F. Mussner, *Der Jakobusbrief* (HTKNT; Freiburg: Herder, ³1975) 42-47.

87. E.g., see §32 nn. 427, 428 above.

88. For those who regard the letter as directed polemically against Paul or his hyper-Pauline disciples, see Schnelle, *History* 397. Bultmann's treatment of James in his *New Testament Theology*, as typical of viewing James through Pauline spectacles, is nicely documented by Johnson, *Brother of Jesus* 238-40. M. Hengel continues in the tradition in his 'Der Jakobusbrief als antipaulinische Polemik', *Paulus und Jakobus* 511-48, regarding the letter 'as a masterpiece of early Christian polemic', 'an artistic, subtle polemic' (525), not limited to 2.14-26, though the further suggestion that Paul's missionary work is in view in 3.1-12 and 4.13-16 (529-39) lacks plausibility.

89. L. T. Johnson, *The Letter of James* (AB 37A; New York: Doubleday, 1995), speaks with justification of the need to break 'the Pauline fixation' which has distorted the evaluation of James (111-14).

90. Son of Zebedee (brother of John); son of Alphaeus (one of the twelve); son of Mary (James the small/younger); father of Judas; see BDAG 464.

91. See above, §§23.3c and 26.5c.

Jesus. That there could be any doubt on the matter is testimony to how little appreciated are both the dominance which this James achieved over the mother
church and his influence not simply in Jerusalem but further afield.[92]

The usual considerations thought to weigh against James as the author[93]
are not as compelling as regularly asserted:

- The Greek is too good[94] and the rhetorical quality of the letter too accomplished for it to have been composed by the brother of a Galilean artisan.

Since the breakdown of the earlier dichotomy between Hellenistic Judaism and
Palestinian (that is, *not* Hellenized) Judaism, this argument has been almost
wholly discredited.[95] James was the leader of the church in Jerusalem for most
of thirty years and could hardly have functioned in leadership there without at
least a speaking/hearing capacity in Greek. Since we can fairly infer that his
ministry must have included preaching to or some occasions for teaching the
regular and substantial flow of diaspora pilgrims, particularly for the pilgrim
feasts, the obvious language of communication would have been Greek. And
even if his own spoken Greek was not as polished as that of the letter, it is
hardly implausible to envisage any attempt to put James's teaching into written
form being polished by a fellow disciple more fluent in written Greek than
James himself.[96]

- James the brother of Jesus would surely have introduced himself as such.[97]

This is actually an argument which tells as much if not more strongly against
pseudonymity. A pseudonymous author would surely have emphasized precisely
this claim, that he wrote in the name of Jesus' own brother, whereas the self-

92. See above, §36.1d.

93. This is still the majority view; see, e.g., the review of nineteenth- and twentieth-century
scholarship on the issue in Johnson, *James* 150-51, 154-56; Schnelle, *History* 384-88 n. 11.

94. J. B. Mayor, *The Epistle of St. James* (London: Macmillan, ²1897), after intensive
study of James's Greek style, famously concluded: 'On the whole I should be inclined to rate
the Greek of this Epistle as approaching more nearly to the standard of classical purity than that
of any other book of the N.T. with the exception perhaps of Hebrews' (ccxvi).

95. As Schnelle acknowledges (*History* 385); see above, §24 nn. 21, 31; further bibliography in Martin, *James* lxx.

96. Bauckham, *James* 24, mentions that Josephus, even though he could write Greek
quite competently, nevertheless employed assistants to polish his Greek (*Ap.* 1.50). And see
further Hengel, 'Jakobusbrief' 520-21. Neither Bauckham nor Hengel (523) nor Johnson
(*James* 7-10, 116-18) thinks that the quality of Greek and rhetoric need be counted against the
view that the letter was written by a Christian leader of the first generation from Jerusalem.

97. Schnelle, *History* 386.

introduction, limited to use of the honorific title 'slave of God',[98] attests a person who was most secure in and confident of his authority and who knew that it would be recognized without more fanfare.[99]

- Had the famous James of Jerusalem stood behind the letter, there would not have been such a strong degree of hesitation over accepting the letter as authoritative (canonical) for the Christianity of the Mediterranean region.[100]

It is equally possible that the letter of James initially was only known to and used by more traditionalist Christian Jewish congregations, that it was thought by others to express an outmoded understanding of Christianity by the predominantly Gentile churches, and that the name of James was too much tarnished by the high regard in which he was held in communities becoming regarded as heretical by 'mainstream' Christianity.[101] As John's Gospel and even Paul were regarded with suspicion in the second century as being too much favoured by Gnostics and Marcion, so the letter of James was probably regarded as having too narrow an appeal and as too close to the other end of the spectrum to be embraced wholeheartedly. But just as the inherent merit and authority of both Paul's and John's writings ensured their more universal acceptance by the second century, so the character of the letter of James, and perhaps also the regard for the brother of Jesus and one of the first leaders of the mother church, was sufficient to ensure its wider influence and acceptance.[102]

- The social context, particularly the polemic against the rich, reflects the situation towards the end of the first century.[103]

Again it can equally be the case that James of Jerusalem reflected the antagonism felt by many of the poorer elements within Judea against the rapaciousness of some of the wealthy landowners and merchants. We know that such tensions were a factor in the final explosion in Jerusalem, and no doubt these tensions

---

98. Martin, *Slavery as Salvation.*

99. Contrast Paul, who had to emphasize his title 'apostle' precisely because it was contested (see above, §§29.3; 31.7 at n. 321).

100. Details in Kümmel, *Introduction* 405. Johnson makes a case for *1 Clement* and the Shepherd of Hermas knowing and using James, though recognizing that the influence is strongest in Alexandria and Jerusalem (*Brother of Jesus* 52-60, 69-70; and further 45-100); see also Gregory and Tuckett, eds., *Reception* 297-98, 305, 312-14, 320-21. On James and the *Didache* see Gregory and Tuckett, eds., *Trajectories* 193-95, 204-207, 210-11.

101. See §36.1d above.

102. We will consider these issues more fully in vol. 3.

103. Emphasized particularly by Schnelle, *History* 388-90.

were building up well before then.[104] It would hardly be surprising that the young Christian community, among whom poverty was widely known to be endemic,[105] should have shared in these tensions, and that James should have articulated them in some of his exhortations and preaching.

- The character of the letter smacks more of diaspora than of Palestinian Judaism.[106]

The letter of James indeed shares some of the characteristics of Wisdom literature, such as could certainly be found in a centre of diaspora Judaism such as Alexandria.[107] But any suggestion that apocalyptic interest and enthusiasm dominated the Judaism of Palestine, to the exclusion of Wisdom, works with far too sweeping generalisations and with categories treated as though they were mutually exclusive.[108] Ben Sira is a classic expression of wisdom tradition, so well rooted in Second Temple Judaism that it almost came to be counted as part of the canon of Jewish Scripture;[109] and, as we shall see, ben Sira was one of the main influences on James. Not only so, but both Qumran and Jesus of Nazareth provide classic examples of a scope of teaching which included both apocalyptic and wisdom material.[110]

- The attitude to the law is not what we would have expected from someone as committed to the Temple and ritual law as James of Jerusalem seems to have been.

104. Signalled not least by the destruction of the public archives in the early days of the revolt ('eager to destroy the money-lenders' bonds and to prevent the recovery of debts') — Josephus, *War* 2.427. See further Goodman, *The Ruling Class of Judea*.

105. I refer to the no doubt well-informed concern which caused Paul to make the collection such a high priority in the latter years of his Aegean mission (see above, §33.4), as well as the implications of Acts 11.29 and Gal. 2.10.

106. Davids, *James* 10, cites H. A. A. Kennedy, 'The Hellenistic Atmosphere of the Epistle of James', *Expositor* ser. 8, 2 (1911) 37-52: 'It seems difficult for any unprejudiced enquirer to evade the conclusion that the Jewish writer of this Epistle moved with more than ordinary freedom in the region of Hellenistic culture' (51).

107. Exemplified by Pseudo-Phocylides (see below, n. 129).

108. See particularly T. C. Penner, *The Epistle of James and Eschatology* (JSNTS 121; Sheffield: Sheffield Academic, 1996), who concludes: 'the content of James is essentially a type of eschatological wisdom for the community awaiting the impending reversal and exaltation of the righteous' (259).

109. See, e.g., P. W. Skehan and A. A. Di Lella, *The Wisdom of Ben Sira* (AB 39; New York: Doubleday, 1987) 20.

110. Qumran: e.g., 1QM (apocalyptic); 4Q184, 185 (wisdom). Jesus: kingdom of God (apocalyptic); Sermon on Plain/Mount (wisdom); on Jesus see *Jesus Remembered* §§12.4 and 15.8a-b. See also Johnson, *Brother of Jesus* 18-19.

The weakness here is twofold. First, the argument again operates from the perspective of Pauline controversy. It is being assumed that James must be the foil or even antithesis to Paul's insistence that faith does not require to be supplemented by such works of the law as circumcision and concerns for ritual purity; James, the assumption is, would not write on the law without affirming what Paul denied.[111] But perhaps James was no more enamoured of the laws of ritual purity than Jesus was (cf. Matt. 15.16-20); perhaps like Jesus, he wanted to press more deeply into the law (cf. Matt. 5.21-48). That his teaching was heavily influenced by that of Jesus will become apparent below, so that a more subtle engagement with the law should rather be inferred.

Second, we have here another example of the one document per community (here per person) hypothesis which has bedevilled so much of recent discussion of the Q material/document embodied in the Synoptic tradition.[112] That is to say, it is being assumed that a letter of James would have provided a complete range of his views, would have provided a comprehensive theology of James. But that simply does not follow. Even Paul's most carefully laid out exposition of his gospel and theology (Romans) is not a comprehensive statement of what he believed. And in such a brief letter as James what should be looked for are characteristic rather than comprehensive expressions of his understanding of and devotion to the law. To approach the letter of James with an already clear-cut view of what James of Jerusalem would have believed regarding the law, usually inferred from Gal. 2.12, Acts 21.20-21 and Hegesippus, and to conclude that the letter of James is incompatible with that inferred view, is simply poor scholarship. The letter should rather be counted as at least possible evidence for the views of James of Jerusalem, at least as providing inferences as potentially valid as those drawn from other passages. And if the letter suggests that James might not have been such a conservative traditionalist as he is so often thought to have been, then these considerations need to be given due weight in any attempt to reconstruct earliest Christianity and to evaluate its constituent parts.

In short, the arguments usually marshalled against attributing the letter of James to James of Jerusalem, the brother of Jesus, are not strong enough to overturn the most obvious implication of the heading of the letter: that the teaching which follows was the teaching of earliest Christianity's most famous James. The most obvious is still the most probable.[113]

---

111. James does respond to a Pauline argument about faith and works, as we shall see (§37.2d[v]); but as we shall also see, it does not follow that James must have affirmed all that Paul denied.

112. See again *Jesus Remembered* 149-52.

113. Cf. Johnson, *Brother of Jesus:* 'The evidence provided by the letter fits comfortably within that provided by our other earliest and best sources (Paul, Acts, Josephus), whereas it fits only awkwardly if at all within the framework of the later and legendary sources that are used for most reconstructions' (3).

To this should be added the inference from the rest of the opening: 'James . . . to the twelve tribes which are in the diaspora' (1.1). The 'diaspora', we recall, is shorthand for the natives of the land of Israel (not just Judea) who had been scattered abroad, initially largely eastwards (Nineveh and Babylon), and latterly westwards (in particular, Alexandria, Cyrenaica, Asia Minor, Rome); 'the twelve tribes' would not be a fanciful attempt to recall and re-create the accounts of early settlement in the land of Israel but expresses a consciousness of large bodies of Israelites/Judeans/Jews in the eastern as well as western diaspora.[114] The significance of taking this reference seriously, and not simply as a spiritualized reference to Christians seen as a new Israel, is threefold.

- It ties in with Jesus' own vision of a restored Israel, one of the points at which the letter of James can be seen to be in direct continuity with Jesus' own mission.
- It correlates with the picture of James sketched out in §36, in connection both with the Acts account of the Jerusalem council and with James's role in the incident at Antioch (§§36.1b-c).
- It reinforces the centrality of Jerusalem, since such a letter, addressed to the full sweep of Israelites and Jews scattered abroad, could only have been composed from a Jerusalem-as-the-centre-of-Israel/Judaism perspective and thus must express the views of one who was regarded as having authority in regard to Israel's exiles.[115]

All this points strongly to James of Jerusalem as the one whose views are set out in writing under his name.

What it does not necessarily imply, however, is that the letter was composed by James himself.[116] It is just as likely that the teaching contained in the letter was teaching which James was known to have given and which had been remembered, and perhaps early on partially transcribed for wider circulation. It

---

114. It should be recalled that many more Judeans/Jews lived outside the Holy Land than in it (see above, §27 n. 181). D. C. Allison, 'The Fiction of James and Its *Sitz im Leben*', *RB* 108 (2001) 529-70, revives the view that the letter was written to non-Christian Jews as well as Christians.

115. Similarly Bauckham, *James* 13-21, who refers to the 'practice of letters from the authorities in Jerusalem to Jews in the Diaspora, giving directions on cultic and other legal matters . . . evidenced as early as the late fifth century BCE by a letter to the Jewish colony at Elephantine in Egypt' (19), and *inter alia* by the letter from James to the churches of Syria and Cilicia in Acts 15.23-29 (20). Similarly K.-W. Niebuhr, 'Der Jakobusbrief im Licht frühjüdischer Diasporabriefe', *NTS* 44 (1998) 420-43. Both Bauckham and Niebuhr are critiqued by Mitchell, 'James, a Document of Paulinism?' 84 n. 33. See also J. S. Kloppenborg, 'Diaspora Discourse: The Construction of *Ethos* in James', *NTS* 53 (2007) 242-70; and n. 214 below.

116. Here I distance myself somewhat from Bauckham, *James* 23-25.

could well be that either after the death of James or even after the destruction of Jerusalem, the bolder step was taken of putting that material together in its present form for a circulation more widespread than James himself had ever achieved, but reflective of the widespread influence he had exerted in his lifetime.[117] The hope would have been, presumably, to reaffirm the centrality of Jerusalem for the surviving Jesus movement in Palestine and its supporters in the diaspora. And what better medium would there have been but a letter from James of Jerusalem containing the best or most characteristic of his teaching. This is the hypothesis which I favour and which leads me to approach the letter as containing the legacy of this James.

b. Is This a Letter?

The answer can be given immediately — No! It has a letter opening, 'James . . . to the twelve tribes . . . greeting' (1.1), but it has no closing formulations which would normally end a letter; its sequence of teaching simply stops. So at best the 'letter' of James has only a partial epistolary framework.

When we turn to the body of the letter[118] and look for the sort of progression of thought which might be expected in a letter, we are similarly disappointed. On almost any definition of 'letter', James does not constitute a coherent letter. This should at once make us cautious about applying a literary analysis which assumes that a real letter is being examined.[119] The letter, I believe, is best read as a compendium of James's teaching, a transcription of characteristic emphases and regularly repeated sayings and themes, without too much attempt being made to adapt it more fittingly to a letter format. The nearest parallel within the Jesus community would be the Q material, and we should probably see the letter of James coming together in a similar way to the transcription of Jesus tradition in Q, and in a similar lumpy conjunction of what had

---

117. Martin (*James* lxxii) notes two passages of possible relevance here: 'James wrote a single epistle and some claim that it was published by another under his name' (Jerome, *De vir. ill.* 2); 'This is the discourse that James [the] Just spoke in Jerusalem, [which] Mareim, one [of] the priests wrote' (*2 Apoc. Jas.* 44.13-17). Burkitt suggested that 'in the "Epistle of James" we have a free Greek rendering of an original Aramaic discourse made by James . . . to some Jewish-Christian community, very likely that of Jerusalem itself. It was rescued from oblivion by the Greek-speaking Gentile-Christian Church of Aelia, when they were beginning to adopt St. James as their ecclesiastical ancestor' (*Christian Beginnings* 70).

118. I shall continue to speak of the letter of James, rather than the 'letter' of James, to avoid needless pedantry.

119. Of recent literature Bauckham (*James* 62) refers particularly to H. Frankemölle, 'Das semantische Netz des Jakobusbriefes. Zur Einheit eines umstrittenen Briefes', *BZ* 34 (1990) 161-97; L. Thurén, 'Risky Rhetoric in James?', *NovT* 37 (1995) 262-84.

originated as disparate material. In other words, as the Synoptic tradition is Jesus tradition, so the letter of James can properly and illuminatingly be classified as James tradition.

The structure of the letter is a matter of continuing debate, particularly as to whether there is any real continuity and coherence of theme and content,[120] or whether the more subtle links by catchword indicate more care in composition than at first appears. There is greatest agreement on the internal coherence of the three sections 2.1-13, 2.14-26 and 3.1-12, but the following sections are also quite substantial and coherent in themselves (3.13-18; 4.1-10; 4.11/13-17; 5.1-6; 5.7-11; 5.12/13-18). And the same can be said for at least some of the briefer sections in ch. 1. One plausible analysis is provided by Bauckham, whose work on James has been so fruitful and who in his treatment of the letter notes the frequent observation that 1.2-27 introduces virtually every topic that is expounded at greater length in chs. 2–5:[121]

	Ch. 1	Chs. 2–5	
1.	1.2-4	2.1-13	Partiality and the law of love
2.	1.5-8	2.14-26	Faith and works
3.	1.9-11	3.1-12	The tongue
4.	1.12	3.13-18	True and false wisdom
5.	1.13-15	4.1-10	A call to the double-minded to repent
6.	1.16-17	4.11-12	Against judging one another
7.	1.18	4.13-17	Denunciation of merchants
8.	1.19-20	5.1-6	Denunciation of landowners
9.	1.21	5.7-11	Holding out till the parousia
10.	1.22-25	5.12	Speaking the whole truth
11.	1.26	5.13-18	Prayer
12.	1.27-28	5.19-20	Reclaiming those who err

The point is not that each of the twelve sections suggested for ch. 1 matches the corresponding section in chs. 2–5.[122] It is rather that there are thematic and verbal links between the content of ch. 1 and the content of chs. 2–5

---

120. M. Dibelius, *Der Brief des Jakobus* (KEK; Göttingen: Vandenhoeck und Ruprecht, [11]1964) = M. Dibelius and H. Greeven, *James* (Hermeneia; Philadelphia: Fortress, 1975), is the classic exposition; he was of the view that a compiler without theological expertise had gathered an anthology of paraenetic sayings out of traditional material (*Jakobus* 19).

121. Bauckham, *James* 71-72; in the above table the titles refer only to the sections in chs. 2-5. Other analyses of structure and outline are provided and reviewed by Martin, *James* xcviii-civ.

122. Bauckham, of course, recognizes a degree of arbitrariness in his division, and that the chapters could be subdivided differently.

which appear to be deliberate, and that the material of ch. 1 seems to be more closely related to the sections of chs. 2–5 than these sections are to each other:[123]

1.12	those who love him	2.5
1.25	the law of freedom	2.12
1.26	tongue, bridle	3.2, 5-9
1.6	wisdom, wise	3.13, 15, 17
1.8	double-minded	4.8
1.9-10	bring low/exalt	4.10
1.22, 23, 25	doer	4.11
1.10-11	transience of wicked	4.14
1.3-4, 12	endurance, endure	5.11
1.16	err, error	5.19-20

Bauckham also notes the sequence of catchwords which evidently serve to link the material in ch. 1,[124] as well as the regular pattern marking the sections of chs. 2–5, often beginning with a personal address ('brothers') or (a) question(s)[125] and ending with an aphorism which rounds off or sums up the section.[126] The evidence is such, then, that, however the structure is analyzed and the details assessed, there are sufficient indications of a careful rather than arbitrary composition.

There can be little dispute that the letter of James belongs to the genre of Wisdom literature, beginning classically with the book of Proverbs.[127] In Proverbs we find a similar combination of lengthier exhortations, often introduced by an address to 'my child' (chs. 1–9),[128] and lists of aphorisms apparently randomly sequenced (chs. 10–31). As already noted, the Wisdom of Jesus ben Sira provides another close parallel, not to mention the aphoristic wisdom of Jesus of

---

123. After reviewing and documenting the different literary forms in James, particularly aphorisms, similitudes and parables (*James* 29-60), and the literary structure of the letter (61-73), Bauckham concludes: 'So it seems that [ch. 1] is a collection of aphorisms, carefully compiled in order to introduce all the main themes of [chs. 2-5]' (72).

124. Particularly 'lack' (1.4-5), 'temptation/tempt' (1.12-13), 'anger' (1.19-20) and 'religious/religion' (1.26-27).

125. 'Brothers' (2.1, 26; 3.1; 4.11; 5.7, 12, 19), a question (2.2-4; 3.13), questions (2.14-16; 4.1; 5.13-14) and 'anyone among you' (3.13; 5.13, 14); see further Bauckham, *James* 64-65.

126. Jas. 2.13, 26; 3.12b, 18; 4.10, 17; 5.12, 20; see further Bauckham, *James* 65-66, 68-69; 'it is therefore clear that the twelve sections are carefully crafted as self-contained entities' (66).

127. For a helpful review see Johnson, *James* 29-46.

128. Prov. 1.8, 10, 15; 2.1; 3.1, 11, 21; 4.10, 20; 5.1, 7; 6.1, 3, 20; 7.1; subsequently 19.27; 23.15, 19, 26; 24.13, 21; 27.11.

Nazareth collected in the Q material. On a broader canvas we could mention also the Sentences of Pseudo-Phocylides,[129] the *Sayings of the Fathers (Pirqe 'Abot)* and the *Sayings of Rabbi Nathan ('Abot R. Nathan),*[130] or even the meditations of Marcus Aurelius.[131] In fact, the tradition is more or less universal, stretching from Confucius in the East to Native American sages in the West (a European-centred perspective, I admit). Evidently every generation has produced individuals who in their own search for wisdom for living have collected and treasured the sayings and thoughts of great figures of the present and near past who spoke with perception and humour that brought illumination and relief to the weary searcher; we need only think of such as Pascal's *Pensées* or Benjamin Franklin's *Poor Richard's Almanack,* or indeed the tradition of recording notable passages in a 'commonplace book'.[132]

It is much the most obvious understanding of how the letter of James came about to deduce that James was a noted teacher whose teaching and wisdom were similarly valued, and that the content of the letter is representative of the wisdom which his teaching conveyed. The parallels also underline the probability that it was others who valued James's teaching more perhaps than he did himself, and that it was someone else who gathered up what was regarded as his choicest repertoire and formulated it for wider dispersal in the form which has come down to us as the letter of James.

c. The Oral James Tradition

The letter of James is even more fascinating when we consider that it is probably the transcription of teaching James gave orally, which was known only in oral mode during his life and initially after his death. In which case, the letter gives us an unparalleled insight into the way the oral tradition of the earliest Christian community/ies functioned.[133] The fascination is not least in that the

129. P. W. van der Horst, *OTP* 2.565-82; also *The Sentences of Pseudo-Phocylides* (Leiden: Brill, 1978); also 'Pseudo-Phocylides and the New Testament', *ZNW* 69 (1978) 187-202, where he lists the following parallels: Jas. 3.1ff., 3.6, 5.4 and 5.12 with Ps.-Phoc. 20, 27, 19 and 16 (202).

130. For introduction see M. B. Lerner in S. Safrai, ed., *The Literature of the Sages* (CRINT 2.3; Assen: Van Gorcum, 1987) 263-81 and 369-79 respectively.

131. C. R. Haines, *Marcus Aurelius* (LCL; Harvard: Heinemann, 1916, revised 1930).

132. I inherited such a loose-leaf notebook from a Canadian uncle.

133. In framing their reviews of James's relationship with contemporary moralists and Jewish wisdom tradition under the headings 'Literary Connections' and 'Literary Relationships', Dibelius (*Jakobus* 43-53) and Johnson (*James* 16-48) typify the *literary* mind-set of twentieth-century students of earliest Christianity.

letter of James gives us an even clearer insight into that process than does the Synoptic tradition and therefore may also help illuminate the way in which the Jesus tradition functioned in oral mode. This is because, more clearly than in the case of Jesus, we can discern the major sources on which James seems to have drawn and the way in which James worked with this pre-existing tradition to produce his own teaching. The potential for illuminating the more hidden years of the oral period of earliest Christian tradition is therefore considerable. In all this it is well to remember that wisdom teaching above all other forms of verbal communication is designed for oral communication; throughout human history, we could well say, the role of the aphorism has been precisely to encapsulate wise insight and counsel in oral form crafted to lodge itself in the memory of the auditor.[134]

That the teaching of the letter of James is deeply rooted in the Jewish wisdom tradition is easily demonstrated by listing the passages where there are echoes of, and occasionally direct quotations from, particularly Proverbs and ben Sira.[135]

James	*Proverbs*	*ben Sira*	*Wisdom*
1.2	—	2.1	3.4-5
1.3	27.21	—	—
1.5	2.3-6	—	—
1.13	—	15.11-20	—
1.19	15.1	5.11	—
1.21	—	3.17	—
2.6	14.21	—	—
2.23	—	—	7.27
3.2	—	14.1	—
3.6	16.27	5.13	—
3.10	—	5.13; 28.12	—
3.13	—	3.17	—
4.6 (quotation)	3.34	—	—
4.11	—	—	1.11
4.14	27.1	—	—
5.3	—	29.10	—
5.6	—	—	2.10, 12
5.20 (quotation)	10.12	—	—

---

134. Kenneth Bailey describes 'a community that can create (over the centuries) and sustain in current usage up to 6,000 wisdom sayings' (quoted in *Jesus Remembered* 206).

135. For convenience I draw on the list of citations and allusions provided by Aland[26]. For a broader survey, see Martin, *James* lxxxvii-xciii.

It is interesting that the echoes and allusions illustrate how wisdom teachers (and tradition) functioned. There are some direct quotations (not only from Proverbs).[136] But in most cases it is questionable whether we should speak of a deliberate echo or allusion, as though the element of teaching would only make sense when the auditor consulted Proverbs or ben Sira for himself or herself. Rather we should speak of common themes, the shared wisdom of the ancients. This was true of Proverbs, in that its indebtedness to earlier wisdom teachings is not hidden.[137] And ben Sira in turn is clearly heavily influenced by Proverbs, even though he makes no direct quotation from Proverbs. Rather he evidently found in Proverbs stimulus to convey the same or similar teaching, but in his own words.[138] So with James: he has evidently absorbed the teaching of Proverbs and ben Sira (and others), but he has re-minted it in his own style.

What needs to be more appreciated is the fact that James does so in a similar way with the other wisdom teaching which most obviously influenced him and shaped his own teaching — the wisdom of Jesus of Nazareth. That James does allude to and echo the wisdom of Jesus is well known and not disputed. We may cite the most widely accepted references previously listed,[139] though various commentators have claimed to find many more:[140]

---

136. Jas. 2.8 — Lev. 19.18; 2.11 — Exod. 20.13-14; 2.23 — Gen. 15.6; 4.6 — Prov. 3.34; 5.4 — Isa. 5.9; 5.5 — Jer. 12.3; 5.20 — Prov. 10.12.

137. The strikingly close parallels between Prov. 22.17–23.19 and the Egyptian *Wisdom of Amenemope* (*ANET* 421-24) has been often noted; see further W. McKane, *Proverbs* (London: SCM, 1970) 51-208.

138. 'The role of a sage is to express *as his own wisdom in his own formulation* the wisdom he has gained from his intensive study of the tradition' (Bauckham, *James* 79). Bauckham also quotes appositely ben Sira's self-description of the wisdom teacher: 'When an intelligent person hears a wise saying, he praises it and adds to it' (Sir. 21.15a) (76); and he illustrates the point effectively, 'When Ben Sira echoes the words of the well-known Deuteronomic commandment to love God (Sir. 7:29-30), he surely expected his readers to recognize the allusion and to understand him as interpreting the commandment by adding . . . the duty of respecting God's priests' (79-80; see further 75-81, 83-91). The argument is repeated in R. Bauckham, 'James and Jesus', in Chilton and Neusner, eds., *The Brother of Jesus* 100-137 (here 114-15).

139. *Jesus Remembered* 182 n. 49.

140. E.g., P. Davids, *James* (NIGTC; Grand Rapids: Eerdmans, 1982), lists thirty-six, with nine more general parallels in thought (47-48); P. J. Hartin, *James and the Q Sayings of Jesus* (JSNTS 47; Sheffield: Sheffield Academic, 1991), lists twenty-six close associations or allusions (141-42; with further bibliography); see also Bauckham, 'James and Jesus' 116-17, with particular reference to the privately published and little-known D. B. Deppe, *The Sayings of Jesus in the Epistle of James* (1989). W. H. Wachob and L. T. Johnson, 'The Sayings of Jesus in the Letter of James', in B. Chilton and C. A. Evans, eds., *Authenticating the Words of Jesus* (Leiden: Brill, 1999) 431-50 (reprinted in *Brother of Jesus* 136-54), follow Deppe in working from the above seven plus 4.2 — Matt. 7.7/Luke 11.9. J. S. Kloppenborg, 'The Emulation of the Jesus Tradition in the Letter of James', in R. L. Webb and J. S. Kloppenborg, eds., *Reading*

James	Jesus tradition	*Gospel of Thomas*
1.5	Matt. 7.7/Luke 11.9	92, 94
2.5	Matt. 5.3/Luke 6.20b	54
4.9	Matt. 5.4/Luke 6.21b	—
4.10	Matt. 23.12/Luke 14.11	—
5.1	Luke 6.24-25	—
5.2-3a	Matt. 6.20/Luke 12.33b	76.2
5.12	Matt. 5.34-37	—

What has not been given sufficient attention, however, is the way James works with the Jesus tradition. He does not cite it as a quotation, as though there was a firm text to be cited and repeated as such. It is questionable whether he even alludes to particular sayings, as one might allude to an already established text, or as though his teaching and its force could only be appreciated by reference to that text. This observation highlights yet once more the danger of approaching the question of dependence as from a literary perspective, as though the only knowledge the letter of James could evidence of Jesus tradition was from knowledge of a written text, like the Sermon on the Mount (or Plain). To treat James as valuable at this point only as confirmation that there was already a Q document in writing is simply to confess failure to appreciate what oral tradition was and how its dispersal and transmission functioned.[141]

In the letter of James we see teaching of Jesus which has been absorbed and become the lifeblood of a teacher's teaching and a community's paraenesis. It is not the teaching of Jesus respectfully preserved and paraded for repeated consideration. It is the teaching of *James,* but a teaching which has been impacted, shaped and moulded by different wisdom traditions and particularly by the memory of what and how Jesus taught.[142] This, we can see from the letter of

---

James with New Eyes (LNTS 342; London: Clark, 2007) 121-50, refines Hartin's discussion and lists ten parallels with Q material, plus Jas. 5.12/Matt. 5.33-37 (tabulated 148-50). Note also the eighteen parallels or links between Matthew and James (fourteen of them from the Sermon on the Mount) listed by Martin, *James* lxxv-lxxvi. Barnett sets out some twenty instances synoptically (*Birth* 126-33).

141. Cf. Schnelle: 'Both James and the Sermon on the Mount are embedded in a common stream of tradition that is indebted to a kind of Jewish Christianity with a strong sapiential element' (*History* 393). But Kloppenborg thinks it 'makes best sense if James is aware not merely of "Q tradition" but of the document itself, to be sure in a somewhat elaborated, pre-Matthean form' ('Emulation' 124), maintaining his thesis of several editions of a Q document (but see again *Jesus Remembered* 147-60).

142. Bauckham documents several examples of how sayings of Jesus have been creatively re-expressed by James (*James* 84-85, 88-91; and 'James and Jesus' 117-22). Kloppenborg develops Bauckham's thesis by appeal to the rhetoricians' practice of *aemulatio* — 'the restating of predecessors' ideas in one's own words' ('Emulation' 133).

James, was how the Jesus tradition was appropriated and continued to mould the lives of the first Christians through the teaching of James. It is not, of course, as though James (or his letter) replaced the Jesus tradition; that was all the while being maintained, circulated, performed, interpreted in the ways still evident in the Synoptic tradition (and still more freely in the Johannine tradition, and beyond in the streams of tradition running into the *Gospel of Thomas*). We see, rather, the way the Synoptic material was reflected on and how it provided the paraenetic framework and became part of the moral equipment for a generation taught by James of Jerusalem. And what we would have experienced, no doubt, were we able to situate ourselves in one of the Jerusalem assemblies being taught by James, is the way use of words, turns of phrase, and play of idiom and illustration sent reverberations through the community's own store of wisdom and Jesus tradition to trigger recollections of other teaching and stimulate still deeper reflection on the theme being taught.[143]

It is necessary to insist on the point that the letter was not the first time that this teaching had been given. Nor did the transcription of it change its essential character, even when the author took care to structure it as he did. Rather we should see in the units and sections of the letter genuine recollections of teaching given by James and evidence of the influence he exercised and impact he made, evidence precisely in the fact that this is the teaching of James as it was remembered and in the event transcribed. Nor need we regard the transcription as providing some kind of pure form of James's teaching, or as a freezing either of the tradition or of the traditioning process.[144] It corresponds more closely to the essentially oral character of James's teaching during his leadership in Jerusalem that the letter should be regarded as illustrative of his teaching, as to both manner and content, and as also providing an illustration and precedent for the continuing creative re-expression of the Jesus tradition and Christian paraenesis.

143. This is what J. M. Foley, *Immanent Art: From Structure to Meaning in Traditional Oral Epic* (Bloomington: Indiana University, 1991) chs. 1-2, calls the 'metonymic reference' of a performance, whereby an audience can fill out allusions made by the performer by reference to the community's already well-stocked knowledge of the tradition being played on (see my 'Altering the Default Setting' 151-52 = *New Perspective on Jesus* 95). Kloppenborg's description of *aemulatio* is very similar: 'The practice of *aemulatio* presupposes, on the one hand, that the audience will normally be able to identify the intertext that the author is paraphrasing, and thus will see how the author aligns himself or herself with the *ethos* of the original speaker. On the other, it assumes that the audience will appreciate the artistry of paraphrase and application of the old maxim to a new rhetorical situation' ('Emulation' 141).

144. The ongoing process can be seen particularly in *Didache* (J. S. Kloppenborg, '*Didache* 1.1–6.1, James, Matthew, and the Torah', in Gregory and Tuckett, eds., *Trajectories* 193-221), and to some extent in the Shepherd of Hermas (J. Verheyden, 'The Shepherd of Hermas', in Gregory and Tuckett, eds., *Reception* 293-329).

d. The Enduring Emphases of James's Teaching

In its character as oral tradition, particularly as aphoristic tradition, the material in the letter of James can be ordered and grouped diversely. The same feature is sufficiently evident in the different ways the Synoptic Gospels have ordered and grouped Jesus' teaching. And in the case of James, even allowing for the linkwords and thematic links in the letter as it is, we remain in the spirit of the tradition and honour the memory of James the teacher if we do not merely or slavishly follow the particular sequencing of the remembered teaching of James which the letter has provided but highlight the emphases evident in the letter however its content is ordered. We can be confident that, whoever transcribed these teachings, this represents, not exhaustively but characteristically, the wisdom teaching current in the church of Jerusalem during the first generation of Christianity under the leadership of James, brother of Jesus. Five themes in particular catch the eye.[145]

(i) *Maturity/perfection.* The term *teleios* appears more often in the letter of James than in any other NT writing (1.4 [twice], 17, 25; 3.2). *Teleios* has the sense of 'that which has reached or achieved its goal or end, or which meets the highest standard':

- so of God's gift ('perfect') (1.17) and of the law ('perfect') (1.25);
- of the complete effect *(teleios)* of patience/endurance ('let endurance have its full effect' — 1.4), bringing the patient person to maturity *(teleios)* and completeness *(holoklēros);*[146]
- of faith brought to completion *(eteleiōthē)* by works (2.22);
- of one who makes no mistake in speaking, a 'perfect' *(teleios)* man (3.2).

The emphasis helps confirm that the teaching of James was not evangelistic, directed to non-believers, but was directed primarily towards bringing believers to the maturity God intended for them. Of such perfection God's giving and God's law were understood to be the pattern and means for that goal to be achieved.[147]

Here the lengthier exhortation on the responsibilities of the teacher and the danger of an undisciplined tongue (3.1-12) can be included.[148] For the teacher is

145. Cf., e.g., Davids, *James* 34-57; Martin, *James* lxxix-lxxxvi; Johnson, *Brother of Jesus* 245-59.

146. *Holoklēros,* 'complete and meeting all expectations, "with integrity, whole, complete, undamaged, intact, blameless"' (BDAG 703).

147. On this point James is not far from the Dead Sea community in its goals, or indeed the other very Jewish document in the NT — Hebrews (see vol. 3).

148. The danger of the human tongue was a common theme in Judaism; see C. A. Evans, 'Comparing Judaisms: Qumranic, Rabbinic, and Jacobean Judaisms Compared', in Chilton and

ideally the 'perfect man' (3.2) precisely because he has full control of his speech, of his tongue. The power of the tongue, of spoken words, to lead or direct a person down a particular course is stressed; it is like the bridle on a horse (as already 1.26), like the rudder of a great ship (3.3-4). And the danger of an undisciplined tongue is vividly illustrated by the small fire which can set ablaze a whole forest (3.5b-6) and the untamed wild beast (3.7). The same tongue can both bless and curse (3.9-10), a feature as much contradictory to the intended role of the human tongue as a spring which produces both fresh and brackish water, or a fig tree which produces olives (3.11-12). Here is evident the concerns of one who was himself a teacher and who was highly sensitive to both the importance and the necessity of his role, as to its potential and its dangers, so much so that he discouraged would-be teachers from taking on the role unless they were prepared to bear that responsibility (3.1). One senses the voice of James in all this, an element of autobiography, and an indication of how important teaching to maturity was in the earliest Jerusalem church.

(ii) *Wisdom.* As we have already seen, the whole letter can be classified as wisdom teaching. But it is no surprise, and characteristic of the genre, that 'wisdom' *(sophia)* is itself held out as something to be sought. Typical of James's re-expressing older tradition is the combination in 1.5-8 of the similarly early exhortation in Prov. 2.3-6 to search out wisdom from God and the urging of Jesus to ask from God in confidence (Matt. 7.7). The theme is resumed in 3.13-18, where James follows in the tradition of Jewish wisdom in describing the wisdom from above in a sequence of attractive similes (Sir. 24.13-21) or a tumbling kaleidoscope of descriptive adjectives (Wis. 7.22-26). It is significant that for James the adjectives are all drawn from moral discourse: 'pure, peaceable, gentle/courteous, willing to yield/compliant, full of mercy and good fruits, non-judgmental/impartial, genuine/sincere' (3.17). The parallels with Paul's description of love (1 Cor. 13.4-6) and of the fruit of the Spirit (Gal. 5.22-23) are obvious. For James, we may say, the wisdom from God is another way of referring to the work of the Spirit and to the outworking of love (cf. 2.8-13).

The bulk of ch. 4 and 5.7-11 is another example of typical wisdom emphases interlaced with a more apocalyptic and more distinctively Christian perspective. In a sequence of related exhortations it develops an increasingly sharp contrast between a life lived according to everyday norms (the wisdom from below, as he might have said) and a life oriented by the wisdom from above (implied)

Neusner, eds., *Brother of Jesus* 161-83 (here 166-68). And conciseness *(brachylogia)* was prized in the Hellenistic world; see L. T. Johnson, 'Taciturnity and True Religion: James 1:26-27', in D. L. Balch et al., eds., *Greeks, Romans and Christians,* A. J. Malherbe FS (Minneapolis: Fortress, 1990) 329-39: 3.1-12 'is a marvel of brevity, compressing a variety of conventional motifs with unconventional conciseness' (336).

and particularly by the prospect of the Lord's coming. The one arises from conflicting cravings for life's pleasures (4.1), from desires/lusts which provoke conflict (4.2),[149] from an asking which seeks only one's own satisfaction (4.3). It is a form of friendship with the world that is hostile to God (4.4), pays no heed to the spirit which God has implanted in each (4.5), and repeats the basic sin of prideful disregard of God (4.6). The other asks from God (for his wisdom) in humility and is open to the grace from God (4.2, 6, 10).

The theme of life's transience is similarly a wisdom theme, played on also by Jesus,[150] here giving Christian sensibility its cautionary attitude in forward planning, 'If the Lord wills', 'Deo volente' (4.15). Here, it should be noted, the boasting that is critiqued (4.16) is not the boasting in works of the law or in ethnic identity, as in Paul, but the boasting of false confidence in the course of the world continuing unabated and in the values of everyday society continuing to determine the world order (4.13). Similarly, the particularly Christian hope for the coming of the Lord (Jesus) becomes a primary factor in strengthening the patience and endurance (5.7-8, 10-11) encouraged in 1.3-4. The loosely attached repetition of Jesus' exhortation to avoid oaths and to assert intentions by a simple Yes or No (5.12) arises out of the same concern for a life uncluttered by conflicting goals and motivated simply by God's wisdom and the Lord's coming.

Here again we may see how the earliest Jerusalem community under James's guidance may have attempted to shield itself not only from the commonly recognized dangers of desire-becoming-lust but also from what it perceived as a religion not informed by the wisdom from above and a manner of living motivated by the priorities of this-worldly enterprise. Possibly in the warnings against murder, fighting and warfare we may even see a reflection of the deteriorating social and political circumstances of the late 50s in Jerusalem and around.

(iii) *Prayer.* James takes it for granted that in the quest for wisdom, prayer has an integral place: 'If any of you lacks wisdom, ask God, who gives to all generously and ungrudgingly, and it will be given you' (1.5). The fuller counsel draws on Jesus' teaching on the subject of effective prayer (Mark 11.23-24 par.), reinforced by James's warning against 'double-mindedness' (1.6, 8). The theme is taken up again in the sequence of 3.14–4.3, in the contrast between, on the one hand, wisdom from above, with its fruit of gentle considerateness and harvest of peaceful relations (3.17), and, on the other, the selfish, self-seeking greed which

---

149. That 'desire *(epithymia)*' when indulged (lust) gives birth to sin, and sin, in due course, gives birth to death was already emphasized in the familiar theme of 1.14-15. That wrong desire, lust, or covetousness was the root of all sin was an already established theologoumenon in Jewish thought (Philo, *Opif.* 152; *Decal.* 142, 150, 153, 173; *Spec. Leg.* 4.84-85; *Apoc. Mos.* 19.3; *Apoc. Abr.* 24.10; Str-B 3.234-37).

150. Matt. 6.25-33; Luke 12.16-21; cf. Ps-Phoc. 116-21.

asks wrongly, only with a view to one's own pleasures (3.14-16; 4.1-3). The final exhortation on the theme elaborates the wisdom of mutual concern particularly for the needy (5.13-18):

> ¹³Are any among you suffering? They should pray. . . . ¹⁴Are any among you sick? They should call for the elders of the church¹⁵¹ and have them pray over them, anointing them with oil in the name of the Lord. ¹⁵The prayer of faith will save the sick, and the Lord will raise them up; and anyone who has committed sins will be forgiven. ¹⁶Therefore confess your sins to one another, and pray for one another, so that you may be healed.¹⁵² The prayer of the righteous is powerful and effective . . . ¹⁷⁻¹⁸[instancing Elijah's successful prayer that it might not rain and then that it should rain].

The inclusio formed by 1.5-8 and 5.13-18 underscores the importance which James attached to prayer. And if the latter passage reflects in any degree the experience and practices of the Judean churches during the 50s and 60s — as we may assume to be the case, otherwise the words would be empty posturing and would have been less likely to be preserved — they are a further important testimony to the character and spirituality of these churches.

(iv) *Warnings to the rich.* A particular emphasis in the same sweep of teaching is the repeated warning against the transience of riches, and the folly of investing self-esteem and identity in such temporary impressiveness (like the flower that withers with the rising sun) (1.9-11). The elaborated exhortation not to pander to the rich when they attend the assembly (2.1-4) is of a piece with Jesus' warnings against Pharisees who expected the best seats in the village assemblies (Mark 12.38-39).¹⁵³ But it assumes a more sharply critical note reminiscent of the famous denunciations of prophets like Amos, when it not only recalls that God has 'chosen the poor in the world to be rich in faith and to be heirs of the kingdom' but goes on to denounce the rich for oppressing the poor and dragging them into court (2.6).¹⁵⁴ In the further accusation that the rich 'blaspheme the good *(kalon)* name

---

151. That the elders of the church are to be called, rather than someone with gifts of healing, may imply a degree of institutionalizing of the charismata, equivalent (in the Jerusalem tradition) to Eph. 4.11-12 (see above, n. 49) and subsequently the Pastorals (see vol. 3).

152. The confidence expressed in the power of prayer here should not be discounted, not least in that it reflects the same confidence as expressed by Jesus (Mark 11.23-24 par.) continuing in the Jerusalem church. The relation between faith and healing is presumably the same as that indicated by Paul in 1 Cor. 12.9 (see my *Jesus and the Spirit* 210-12), though only as exercised by the elders (n. 151). The procedure of prayer (and confession) and anointing with oil in the name of the Lord seems to be already well established (cf. Acts 3–5).

153. See *Jesus Remembered* 306-307.

154. See further P. H. Davids, 'The Test of Wealth', in Chilton and Evans, eds., *The Missions of James, Peter, and Paul* 355-84.

which is invoked over you' (2.7), we may also see an echo of persecution, using legal means, of those who named the name of Jesus the Christ.

The most striking expression of antipathy towards the rich, however, comes in 5.1-6. Here we find the closest parallel to the denunciations of the rich for their exploitation of the poor familiar from such as Amos and Isaiah.[155]

> [1]Come now, you rich people, weep and wail, for the miseries that are coming to you. [2]Your riches have rotted, and your clothes are moth-eaten. [3]Your gold and silver have rusted, and their rust will be evidence against you, and it will eat your flesh like fire. . . . [4]Listen! The wages of the labourers who mowed your fields, which you have kept back by fraud, cry out, and the cries of the harvesters have reached the ears of the Lord of hosts. [5]You have lived on the earth in luxury and in pleasure; you have fattened your hearts in a day of slaughter. [6]You have condemned and murdered the righteous one, who does not resist you.

Such denunciations, of course, could fit many situations in which Christianity found itself during its beginning period. But one of these is the period prior to the revolt of 66, when arguably the rapaciousness of many landlords was a factor in driving smallholders and tenant farmers into brigandage. The facts that it is attributed to James but also that it nowhere indicates that the catastrophe of 70 were a fitting judgment on such evils[156] and rounds off its denunciation simply with what looks like a reminiscence of the execution of Jesus (5.6) suggest that this was a denunciation first formulated within the pre-66 situation of Judea, and (why not?) by James himself.

The insight into the conditions of the earliest Christian assemblies in Jerusalem and Judea is stark. It is certainly consistent with the repeated indications of the poverty prevailing in the Jerusalem church. And notably it takes up a theme of God's favour for the poor and readiness to avenge the injustices suffered by the poor, which so marked the teaching both of the prophets of old and of Jesus himself.

(v) *The law and works.* In many ways the most intriguing feature of James's exhortations is his emphasis on the law, 'the perfect law of liberty' (1.25; 2.12). His emphasis on the importance of not simply hearing but also of *doing* the word/the law (1.22-25; 4.11) is characteristic of Jewish teaching,[157] of Jesus (Matt. 7.24-27) and equally of Paul (Rom. 2.13). His concern for the welfare of orphans and wid-

---

155. See above, §33 n. 318; cf. Ps.-Phoc. 22-47.

156. 'In a day of slaughter' (5.5) is lifted from Jer. 12.3, in a similar denunciation of exploitation.

157. Cf., e.g., Deut. 4.1, 5-6, 13-14; 30.11-14; Ezek. 33.30-31; 1 Macc. 2.67; 13.48; Philo, *Cong.* 70; *Praem.* 79; Josephus, *Ant.* 20.44; *m. 'Abot* 1.17; 5.14; see further Evans, 'Comparing Judaisms' 169-72.

ows in their distress as the mark of religion that is 'pure and undefiled' (1.27) is equally characteristic of Judaism,[158] and of the religion practised by Paul.[159] Equally James's readiness to sum up the law in terms of Lev. 19.18 ('You shall love your neighbour as yourself') (Jas. 2.8; 4.12)[160] is undoubtedly to be traced to the direct influence of Jesus' teaching to the same effect, and Paul was no different (Rom. 13.8-10).[161] Nor can we put any distance between James and Paul in regard to James's commendation of impartiality (2.9; cf. Rom. 2.11), or in regard to his affirmation that 'mercy triumphs over judgment' (2.13; cf. Rom. 11.30-32).[162]

The issue which has captivated generations of scholars, however, comes in the next passage — James's famous rebuke that 'faith without works is dead' (2.14-26). Interpretation of this passage provides the classic example of a 'Paul-fixation' in Protestant scholarship which has skewed its perception of this letter, of the teacher behind it, and indeed of Paul himself.[163] In so saying, I do not doubt that the passage evidences a reaction to Paul's teaching, but just what that reaction was and what it amounted to have been too quickly subsumed under and locked into a gospel/law antithesis, whose antithetical sharpness is of little or no help in understanding any of the proponents or the issues in this interaction.

That there is some degree of reaction against Paul's teaching on justification by faith is hard to dispute. In my view the key and decisive consideration is the close parallel between Paul's most considered statement of his gospel at this point (Rom. 3.27–4.22) and Jas. 2.18-24:

	Romans	James
Issue posed in terms of faith and works	3.27-28	2.18
Significance of claiming 'God is one'	3.29-30	2.19
Appeal to Abraham as test case	4.1-2	2.20-22
Citation of proof text — Gen. 15.1	4.3	2.20-22
Interpretation of Gen. 15.6	4.4-21	2.23
Conclusion	4.22	2.24

158. Particularly Deut. 10.18; 14.29; 16.11, 14; 24.17-21; 26.12-13; 27.19.

159. This is documented particularly by the importance Paul placed on the collection (above, §33.4), including as an expression of 'righteousness' (§33.4d). As Johnson rightly notes, Paul predominantly uses the term 'work *(ergon)*' in precisely the same sense as James; 'Paul and James were both moral teachers within the symbolic world of Torah' (*James* 58-64).

160. Reference to judging 'the neighbour *(plēsion)*' is presumably the antithesis to loving the neighbour; 2.8 and 4.12 are the only times James uses the term *plēsion* (see also §33 n. 291 above).

161. *Jesus Remembered* 584-86, and above, §33 at n. 258. Johnson finds further allusion to Leviticus 19 in James (*Brother of Jesus* 123-25).

162. See further Johnson, *Brother of Jesus* 12-14.

163. Bauckham makes the same complaint (*James* 113-20).

Equally noticeable is James's espousing the interpretation of Gen. 15.6 by reference to Abraham's offering of Isaac (the Aqedah — Genesis 22), which was indeed the standard for his day in Jewish circles[164] but which Paul implicitly challenges by his exposition of Abraham's believing in Gen. 15.6 in terms solely of trust.[165] In the face of this parallel and contrast, it is hard to doubt that one reflects knowledge of the other.[166] And since James is the more polemical,[167] the most obvious inference is that the James version is responding to the Paul version.[168] This, of course, does not mean that the letter of James, or the historical James, knew and referred to Paul's letter to the Romans as such, though that is not impossible. Rom. 3.27–4.22, we may assume, was not the first time that Paul had essayed precisely that argument and exposition — here again we must avoid the literary mind-set which so easily slips into thinking of a written document as a once-only expression of a particular view. The impression given by the letter to Rome is rather of a final setting down of arguments and expositions which had been used and reworked by Paul on many previous occasions. All that need be assumed, therefore, is that word of Paul's teaching on this point had been conveyed to Jerusalem, no doubt as part of the rumours and exaggerations which, according to James in Acts 21.21, had reached the conservative traditionalists in Jerusalem and prejudiced them against Paul. Whatever the precise details, the most obvious explanation for such mirror-imaging is that James was remembered as responding in some sense and in some degree to what he had heard of Paul's teaching on Abraham's faith.[169]

What is interesting, in any case, is the way in which James responds. For, rather like Ephesians, he separates the issue of 'works' from 'works of the law', a

---

164. See above, §33 at nn. 134 and 135.

165. Christian appreciation of Abraham's conduct in Genesis 22 should not allow itself to be locked into a gospel/law or faith/works antithesis (either the first-century or the sixteenth-century antithesis); the positive potency of Genesis 22 for Christian (and other) reflection is well demonstrated by R. W. L. Moberly, *The Bible, Theology, and Faith: A Study of Abraham and Jesus* (Cambridge: Cambridge University, 2000).

166. Johnson's claim that 'James *never* connects *erga* to the term "law" *(nomos)*' *(James* 30, 60) is effectively met by M. A. Jackson-McCabe, *Logos and Law in the Letter of James* (NovTSupp 100; Leiden: Brill, 2001) 243-53, by reference particularly to Jas. 1.25: whoever pays continual attention to the 'perfect law of liberty' is/becomes 'a doer of work *(poiētēs ergou)*'; all *erga* are *erga logou,* that is, of the word *(logos)* which finds written expression in the Torah (244-45).

167. Particularly striking is the dismissal that belief in God as one has any relevance to the issue: 'Even the demons believe — and shudder!' (2.19).

168. *Pace* Bauckham, *James* 127-31. Barnett thinks that 'clearly James is responding to Paul's teaching in Galatians' *(Jesus* 319), though the parallels with Romans are much fuller.

169. Here again I have to demur from Bauckham, *James* 127-31, whose treatment of James otherwise I find very persuasive.

phrase which he never uses. It is clear enough from the sequence 2.8-26 that what he says about 'works' (2.14ff.) is wholly consistent with his emphasis on the need to fully carry out *(teleite)* (the demands of) the law (2.8). But what he is emphasizing is the importance of faith coming to expression in obedience to God (2.21-23) and in active concern for the welfare of others (2.15-16, 25).[170] Concerns for ritual purity or the purity of table-fellowship are not in view. It is almost as though James deflects the sort of criticism of Paul represented in Acts 21.21, not by refuting Paul, but rather by emphasizing what Paul also emphasized — the importance of faith coming to expression in love-motivated, love-expressing action (Gal. 5.6), the importance of those baptized into Christ continuing to live lives commanded by and expressive of righteousness (Romans 6). In other words, Jas. 2.14-26 is best read as James standing between Paul and Paul's Christian-Jewish critics to mediate between them by using the same Gen. 15.6 passage to make points that Paul would have wanted to make on his own account and in his own terms. This, we might appropriately say, is the voice of the James of Acts 15, or even of Acts 21, looking for common ground, trying to bring in a further dimension in which James and Paul were in agreement.[171]

In so doing, incidentally, James confirms that it was the Gentile issue (how freely the gospel could be offered to Gentile believers) which was the major bone of contention between Paul and other Jewish missionaries.[172] It was precisely by bypassing the issues which so traumatized the Gentile mission — whether Gentile believers must be circumcised and whether devout Jews could eat with Gentile believers except on strict terms — that the letter of James in effect defuses the antagonism between Paul and his Christian Jewish critics. By taking up what could have been a sharp criticism of Paul's gospel (cf. Rom. 3.8) and turning it into an exhortation that Paul could only have agreed with (that living faith will come to expression in doing good),[173] James could have hoped to undercut the misguided interpretations of Paul's teaching and to highlight a paraenetic emphasis which was also part of Paul's teaching.

170. On Rahab's action as a 'sign' and expression of her faith see Bauckham, *James* 124-25.

171. Cf. Mitchell's thesis: 'The author of the Letter of James knows some collection of Paul's letters, and writes *from within Paulinism* (rather than in opposition to Paul), creating a compromise document which has as one of its purposes reconciling "Paul with Paul" [1 Corinthians with Galatians] and "Paul with the pillars"' ('James, a Document of Paulinism?' 79). See also Stuhlmacher, *Biblische Theologie* 2.59-69; Wilckens, *Theologie* 1/3.362-65.

172. Cf. Bauckham, *James* 128, 134.

173. It requires frequent repetition that Paul regarded 'works' (as distinct from 'works of the law') as something good and desirable — Rom. 2.6-7; 13.3; 15.18; 1 Cor. 3.13-14; 9.1; 15.58; 16.10; 2 Cor. 9.8; 10.11; Gal. 6.4; Phil. 1.22; 2.30; Col. 1.10; 3.17; 1 Thess. 1.3; 5.13; 2 Thess. 1.11; 2.17.

Not least of importance is the fact that the letter of James stands so firmly in the course of the Jesus tradition. The readiness to sum up the law in the love command, one of the law's commands (Lev. 19.18 — 'Love your neighbour as yourself'), and the consistent focus on the moral and ethical issues of human relationship are entirely consistent with the spirit of the Jesus tradition and things that James no doubt learned from Jesus and the Jesus tradition. Indeed the teaching of James is just what several students of the Q tradition assume to have been the character of the teaching in continuing Galilean communities of Jesus' followers, only it is linked to James of Jerusalem and gives us some clear indications of how the Jerusalem church must have lived with and out of the Jesus tradition. Here too James well complements Paul, by giving insight into how the first Christian congregations must have continued to be taught by and in the spirit of the Jesus tradition for daily living and relationships, even while the Easter faith was being worked out in doctrinal terms by such as Paul.[174] The living Jesus tradition, long and continuously reflected on, must have been the lifeblood of Paul's 'in Christ' as much as his own teaching.

e. Is the Letter of James Christian?

This question of whether the letter of James is Christian recurs every so often in NT scholarship. One can understand why, when looking from the perspective of developed Christianity, for from that perspective the letter is so characteristically Jewish and so undistinctively Christian. Jesus is mentioned (explicitly) only twice: 'James, a servant . . . of the Lord Jesus Christ' (1.1); 'Surely you do not retain your faith in our glorious Lord Jesus Christ while showing partiality' (2.1). 'The coming of the Lord' as judge (5.7-9) almost certainly refers to Jesus. And the talk of healing 'in the name of the Lord' (5.14-15) recalls the atmosphere of Acts 3–4 (§§23.2a, g). But there is no explicit reference to Jesus' life, death and resurrection, apart from the ambiguous 5.6 ('You have condemned and murdered the righteous one, who does not resist you'). And the examples of patient suffering are the prophets and Job (5.10-11),[175] in contrast, for example, to 1 Pet. 2.18-23. Presumably this undistinctively Christian character of the letter was one of the major reasons why it took so long for the letter to be accepted as part of the Christian canon. But in view of the possibility that elements of the Jerusalem church fleeing from Jerusalem to Transjordan became one of the main roots of

---

174. James could be seen as pressing for more weight to be given to the Jesus tradition than Paul may have been seen to have done (cf. Pratscher, *Herrenbruder* 215-16).

175. See P. Gray, 'Points and Lines: Thematic Parallelism in the Letter of James and the *Testament of Job*', *NTS* 50 (2004) 406-24.

Ebionism (§36.3), we should not fail to note that this christology of James is already beyond the adoptionism characteristic of Ebionism,[176] and the letter's talk of Jesus as Lord is wholly of a piece with Paul's. Here again it is important to appreciate that the letter may be representative of only James's paraenesis as distinct from his theology.

A negative answer to the question can, of course, also be countered by noting the importance of the 1.1 and 2.1 references and the indications that the Jesus tradition is an integral part of the warp and woof of the wisdom being taught (§37.2c). But the more important riposte is that the question is misdirected. Rather than asking what is inevitably a rather anachronistic question, the more illuminating question to be asked is, What does this letter tell us about embryonic Christianity? The answer to this latter question ensures that the letter of James is able to make its full contribution to our understanding of Christianity in the making.

- It reveals to us a community which was in direct continuity with the wisdom traditions of Second Temple Judaism and drew on the same resources.
- It reveals to us a community which saw itself in direct continuity with Jesus of Nazareth and drew deeply on the tradition of his teaching for its own pattern of living.
- It reveals to us a community which did not set the conviction of Jesus' glorification and lordship in any sort of antithesis with the tradition of his teaching but saw the two as entirely coherent and consistent with each other.
- It reveals how the Jesus tradition, material such as was grouped into the Sermon on the Plain/Mount, must have functioned in the instruction and paraenesis of so many fledgling Christian communities, not only in Palestine but further afield.
- It suggests how the disparate Gentile and Jewish congregations of the first century could find common ground and mutual respect the one for the other precisely in the Jesus tradition, in the way it was being formulated and continuously re-expressed and in the insights and emphases being drawn from it for daily conduct and mutual relationships. After all, in the end of the day, it was precisely this character of the letter of James which secured its recognition as Christian Scripture across the churches of the third and fourth centuries.

176. The Ebionites 'want him to be only a prophet and man and Son of God and Christ and mere man . . . who attained by a virtuous life the right to be called Son of God' (Epiphanius, *Pan.* 30.18.6); see further my *Unity and Diversity* 260-62.

The letter of James, then, is an invaluable testimony to a past age, to a time when in effect Christian and Jewish believers in Messiah Jesus were more or less synonymous. It also is an invaluable reminder of how Jewish was the Jesus tradition and that this continuity of wisdom tradition from Second Temple Judaism through Jesus is integral to the character of the Christianity that emerged from the catastrophes of Rome 64 and Jerusalem 70. This is the legacy of James.

37.3. Peter — the Letter of Peter (1 Peter)

In the case of Paul we know so much about his theology and concerns that there is little difficulty in recognizing Ephesians as a legitimate attempt to sum up what was deemed to be of lasting value in his theology. Even in the case of James, the inferences which may readily be drawn from Paul's few allusions to him, and from Acts, are sufficiently consistent with the letter of James to give us confidence that the letter can appropriately be regarded as a compendium or (re)collection of James's own teaching. But with Peter the position is different. So voiceless is Peter in the material so far examined that we do not really know what a Petrine theology or letter would look like. Unlike Paul and James, 1 Peter has virtually nothing to be compared with, nothing which would enable us to make with confidence the sort of case made for Ephesians and the letter of James. The references and allusions to Peter in the Pauline correspondence, especially when compared with the Gospels and Acts, provide at best a very ambiguous picture, indicating an individual who had considerable leadership qualities and who played a major role in preaching to his fellow Jews but whose distinctive views are not clearly evident and who played a questionable role in one of the major issues which confronted the sect of the Nazarene. Here the disappointment in regard to the speeches attributed to Peter in Acts is considerable. For though there is plenty of evidence that Luke was drawing on primitive material in Acts 2, 3 and 10 (§21.3), any attempt to correlate these primitive elements with 1 Peter has limited success.[177] Indeed, the more 'authenticity' is attributed to the Petrine speeches in Acts, the weaker (not stronger) the case for Petrine authorship of 1 Peter!

So, how Petrine is 1 Peter?

---

177. Though see J. H. Elliott, *1 Peter* (AB 37B; New York: Doubleday, 2000) 25-27, with further bibliography in n. 9. For what might be claimed as the teaching specifically of Peter in the Acts sermons, see §26.6 above.

a. Who Wrote 1 Peter?

The arguments regarding the authorship of 1 Peter are similar to those regarding the letter of James. Here too we have an explicit self-introduction: 'Peter, apostle of Jesus Christ to the elect sojourners of the diaspora of Pontus, Galatia, Cappadocia, Asia and Bithynia' (1 Pet. 1.1). And unlike for the letter of James, there is no question as to who this 'Peter' is; no one would have doubted or questioned that this is the Peter known, no doubt, to all believers as the leading disciple of Jesus, and probably also as the first leader of the church in Jerusalem, and primarily responsible for the mission to fellow Jews. But as with the letter of James, the consensus of modern scholarship is that this letter cannot have been written by Peter himself and is probably pseudonymous, coming from the pen of a second-generation Chris-tian.[178] The recent magisterial commentary by Paul Achtemeier can serve as indicating the main arguments which have proved too weighty for most to ignore or discount.[179]

- As with the letter of James, the quality of the Greek of 1 Peter puts a question mark against the likelihood that this letter was written by a Galilean fisherman.[180] Although warning against exaggerating the quality of 1 Peter's Greek, Achtemeier judges 1 Peter as belonging 'stylistically with the best prose of the NT'. The author had evidently 'enjoyed some level of formal education', so that it is 'rather difficult to imagine someone like the Peter described in the Gospels as having possessed such knowledge and skills'.[181]

These considerations are as weighty as they are in the case of James. And if they are regarded as less than persuasive in James's case,[182] then it would seem to fol-

178. Schnelle, *History* 400-401; for those who regard Peter himself as the author see Elliott, *1 Peter* 118 n. 35 (considerations marshalled in favour of Peter as author are summarized on 119-20).

179. Achtemeier, *1 Peter* (Hermeneia; Minneapolis: Fortress, 1996). Achtemeier devotes the largest part of his introduction to the question of authorship (1-43), with much data regarding 1 Peter's relation to other aspects of earliest Christian tradition and context directed to the answer to that question. In contrast, Elliott leaves the question of authorship till late in his introduction (*1 Peter* 118-30). Elliott's most weighty points (120-23) are similar to those of Achtemeier.

180. Kümmel, *Introduction* 423.

181. Achtemeier, *1 Peter* 2, 4, 6. 'While one may surely presume some facility in Greek even among Palestinian fishermen in the first century who lacked formal education, the kind of Greek found in this epistle was probably beyond such a person, and hence the language was in all likelihood not given its present form by Simon Peter' (4-5). 'Its relatively polished Greek contains few vulgar elements and reveals an author of some education' (Elliott, *1 Peter* 64; with documentation [64-68], and further 120).

182. See above, §37.2a. If the tradition of Acts 4.13 is given weight — that Peter and

low that someone who evidently travelled much more widely through the eastern Mediterranean, no doubt having to become proficient in Greek in order to communicate effectively, would have been at least as capable of writing 1 Peter as James was of writing the letter of James. The frequently canvassed possibility that Silvanus acted as Peter's secretary or amanuensis should also be given due weight (5.12), given not least the allowance that we have found it necessary to make in the case of Paul for a substantial role of the fellow sender and/or amanuensis in some of his letters.[183] It is certainly true that Silvanus is not introduced as a fellow writer (as he was by Paul in his Thessalonian correspondence), but according to 5.12 the author does say, 'Through *(dia)* Silvanus . . . I have written to you briefly'. Since we know too little as to how variously a writer might have described his dependence on a scribe, we can hardly dismiss the possibility that this is how the writer chose to indicate his debt to Silvanus for helping him craft the letter.[184] Similarly, the fact that 1 Peter shows 'overwhelming dependence on the Greek version of the OT' could be explained, as so often in OT quotations in the NT, either by a writer using LXX for such correspondence or by a secretary who translated any quotations or allusions drawing on the Hebrew or Aramaic text into the Greek versions more familiar to the letter's recipients. In all this, it is necessary to liberate the discussion from being controlled unwittingly by the modern parallel of a 'secretary' expected by the 'boss' to transcribe exactly what was dictated and nothing more.

John were *agrammatoi* ('unlearned, illiterate') and *idiōtai* ('untrained') — it both applies to James too and refers to their capacity as perceived thirty years earlier. That Mark acted as Peter's *hermēneutēs* (Eusebius, *HE* 3.39.15) is not as decisive as some claim (e.g., Schnelle, *History* 400), since *hermēneutēs* can denote 'interpreter' or 'expounder' (perhaps as a catechist), as well as 'translator' (*PGL* 549).

183. See above, §29.8c. For bibliography of those who favour a secretary hypothesis see Elliott, *1 Peter* 123 n. 37. Achtemeier comments that 'the more room one gives to Silvanus's own literary creativity in solving the problem of the language of the letter, the less one is able to ascribe it in any meaningful way to Peter' (*1 Peter* 8-9). But does the comment do justice to the fact that many of Paul's letters claim joint authorship?

184. 'The ideas were Peter's, but Silvanus composed the letter' (Barnett, *Jesus* 305-306). Achtemeier (*1 Peter* 7-9, 349-50) makes too much of 'the fact that in the one example we have [in the NT] where a scribe is acknowledged (Rom 16:22), the language is quite different'; but he also observes that Eusebius mentions a letter written 'through *(dia)* Clement' which was actually written by Clement (*HE* 4.23.11). It is true that we know nothing of Silvanus's linguistic ability (350), but that neither helps nor hinders the task of interpreting what 5.12 means by the phrase 'through Silvanus'. The phrase is usually taken to refer to the bearer of the letter, not its scribe (Schnelle, *History* 401 n. 70; Elliott, *1 Peter* 124); examples from Ignatius and the documentary papyri are given by E. R. Richards, 'Silvanus Was Not Peter's Secretary: Theological Bias in Interpreting *dia Silouanou . . . egrapsa* in 1 Peter 5:12', *JETS* 43 (2000) 417-32.

• The lack of personal reminiscences of the life of Jesus is 'something one would surely [not] expect in a letter from one who had accompanied him from Galilean ministry to resurrection'.[185]

Here yet once again it would appear that an argument is being driven by the pervasive 'one-document fallacy':[186] that when only one literary document is available to us, it either must have been the only document that the person produced or community treasured, or it must contain the whole of what that person or community believed and practised. The absence of reference to Jesus' pre-passion mission is such a standard feature of almost all the NT letters that not too much should be made of the same feature in 1 Peter.

• 'The strongly Pauline flavour of the letter, in both its language and its contents,[187] and the evident use of other early Christian traditions seem unexpected from one who would surely have had his own understanding and expression of the Christian faith'.[188]

The issue of influence from Paul or whether 1 Peter is too Pauline in character to be the work of Paul's 'opposite number' in the mission field, is another instance of a discussion being undermined by our ignorance as to what a document from Peter wholly independent of Paul would look like.[189] The occasional glimpses we have of Peter in Paul's letters are sufficient to reveal a Peter who was the pri-

---

185. Achtemeier, *1 Peter* 9-10. The self-reference to a 'witness of the sufferings of Christ' (5.1) refers to 2.22-25, verses which are 'patently drawn from Isaiah 53' (1 Pet. 2.24-25 — Isa. 53.4-6, 12); other suggested reflections 'are evanescent at best' (9-10). Kümmel, *Introduction* 424, is typical of modern critics who find it 'scarcely conceivable' that Peter could write such a letter without referring to the example of Jesus — despite 2.21-24!

186. *Jesus Remembered* 150-51.

187. See Berger, *Theologiegeschichte* 383-94; Achtemeier notes, e.g., 'typically Pauline words and phrases' like *en Christō* (3.16; 5.10, 14), *apokalypsis* (1.7, 13; 4.13), *diakoneō* (1.12; 4.10) and *charismata* (4.10)', but he notes also the absence of many key Pauline concepts and wonders 'how much of the "Pauline" flavour of 1 Peter is the result of a common use of early liturgical or confessional material' (*1 Peter* 15-19).

188. Achtemeier, *1 Peter* 1-2.

189. Achtemeier draws an oddly phrased conclusion: 'The very absence of identifiably Petrine elements in the letter argues strongly for some internal association with the apostle Peter; otherwise, it is difficult to imagine why the letter would have been ascribed to him' (*1 Peter* 43). I agree, but I remain puzzled how Achtemeier might document 'identifiable Petrine elements' apart from 1 Peter itself. A similar response is due to D. G. Horrell, 'The Product of a Petrine Circle? A Reassessment of the Origin and Character of 1 Peter', *JSNT* 86 (2002) 29-60, who argues that there is no substantial evidence to link the letter to a specifically Petrine group.

mary source for much of Paul's own knowledge of the Jesus tradition (Gal. 1.18), who agreed warmly with Paul's taking the gospel to the Gentiles and without circumcision (2.6-9), and who was a respected missionary figure in the Pauline church in Corinth.[190] The only point at which he took a different stand from that of Paul was in Antioch, and that after he had acted out his own willingness to 'live like a Gentile' (Gal. 2.14).[191] The gospel they agreed was for Gentile as well as Jew, not a different gospel, but the same gospel — and for the same church. It would be hardly surprising, then, if Peter and Paul saw eye to eye on a good many features, such as we find in 1 Peter. Indeed, precisely because we know so little of Peter's own theology (apart from 1 Peter), we can hardly avoid the counter-question: whether on the points of agreement there was as much or even more influence from Peter on Paul than vice-versa, whether some of Paul's teaching is as much 'Petrine' as 1 Peter is 'Pauline'! The fact that 1 Peter shares as much with Paul as it does, therefore, should not be so surprising or so objectionable as it often appears to be.[192] Rather it should be counted as further evidence indicating a figure who was probably more eirenic and conciliatory than either Paul or James and whose lasting reputation as someone able to 'oversee' *(episkopos)* others and to act as a shepherd (1 Pet. 5.1-4) is preserved in his subsequent title as the first pope of Rome.[193]

190. See above, §§35.1b-c.

191. It is all too easy, in looking at the issue from a Pauline perspective, to give the Antioch incident an undue weight in assessing Peter's subsequent and wider influence (see, e.g., Kümmel, *Introduction* 423; Wedderburn, *History* 77-78).

192. Common features 'reflect, not ideas unique to Paul that were then borrowed by the Petrine author, but features typical of the early Christian proclamation and teaching in general, upon which both authors drew. . . . Many of the themes common to Paul and 1 Peter, moreover, were interpreted differently by each author. . . . The Petrine author constructed, on the basis of the same tradition known to Paul, a distinctive pastoral message and spoke with a distinctive voice. . . . It is high time for 1 Peter to be liberated from its "Pauline captivity" and read as a distinctive voice of the early Church' (Elliott, *1 Peter* 38-40; bibliography in n. 17). Elliott's judgment is given thoroughgoing support by J. Herzer, *Petrus oder Paulus? Studien über das Verhältnis des Ersten Petrusbriefes zur paulinischen Tradition* (WUNT 103; Tübingen: Mohr Siebeck, 1998). See also Brown and Meier, *Antioch and Rome* 134-39. Stuhlmacher describes the message of 1 Peter as 'a kind of golden mean between Paulinism and the Jewish Christian tradition of faith' (*Biblische Theologie* 2.84).

193. M. Konradt has tried to correlate the relationship between 1 Peter, Paul and James to common tradition rooted in Antioch that was developed differently after the incident — M. Konradt, 'Der Jakobusbrief als Brief des Jakobus. Erwägungen zum historischen Kontext des Jakobusbriefes im Lichte der traditionsgeschichtlichen Beziehungen zum 1 Petr und zum Hintergrund der Autorfiktion', in P. von Gemünden, M. Konradt and G. Theißen, eds., *Der Jakobusbrief. Beiträge zur Rehabilitierung der "strohernen Epistel"* (Beiträge zum Verstehen der Bibel 3; Münster: Lit, 2003) 16-53; and 'Der Jakobusbrief im frühchristlichen Kontext: Überlegungen zum traditionsgeschichtlichen Verhältnis des Jakobusbriefes zur Jesusüber-

• The 'situation in Asia Minor reflects a time later than one could assume Peter had lived'.[194]

This is a very difficult argument on which to gain a proper handle. I have already noted that the addressees of the letter ('the elect sojourners of the diaspora of Pontus, Galatia, Cappadocia, Asia and Bithynia' — 1.1) suggest that the Christians of these regions had particular cause to be linked with Peter. More than that we cannot say. Since we know nothing of the beginnings of Christianity in Pontus, Cappadocia and Bithynia, we can hardly exclude the possibility that 1 Pet. 1.1 provides evidence for beginnings during Peter's life and mission.[195] Achtemeier's own careful consideration of the historical situation envisaged in 1 Peter is that it probably reflects unofficial harassment rather than official policy and 'persecution' that was local rather than regional, from which he concludes that the references to persecution in 1 Peter are 'of no value in seeking to determine whether Simon Peter could still have been alive when they occurred'.[196]

A somewhat different point is the complete lack of tension in the letter between Christians and Jews,[197] such as the evidence of Paul's letters would lead us to expect in a letter of Paul's great counterpart in the twin missions to Jews and to Gentiles. But, as with the equivalent argument in regard to the letter of James, there may be a danger here of Pauline spectacles distorting our twenty-first-century view of the first-century Christian mission. The evidence of intra-Christian tension during that period comes predominantly from Paul and focuses on Paul's own understanding and execution of his apostolic commission. It is

---

lieferung, zur paulinischen Tradition und zum 1 Petr', in J. Schlosser, ed., *The Catholic Epistles and the Tradition* (BETL 176; Leuven: Peeters, 2004) 169-210 (I owe these references to Lutz Doering).

194. Achtemeier, *1 Peter* 2.

195. *Pace* L. Goppelt, *Der erste Petrusbrief* (KEK; Göttingen: Vandenhoeck und Ruprecht, 1978) 64; Schnelle, *History* 401.

196. Achtemeier, *1 Peter* 23-36, citing the conclusion on 35-36. Similarly Elliott, *1 Peter* 97-103, concludes: 'The manner in which Christian suffering is mentioned, described, and addressed in this letter points not to organized Roman persecution as its cause but to local social tensions deriving from the social, cultural, and religious differences demarcating believers from their neighbors. . . . The letter presupposes a situation in which the addressees were not being treated as "enemies of the state" but were made victims of social discrimination because of their similarity to Israel in their distinctiveness and nonconformity, and because of their adherence to an exotic Israelite sect stigmatized as "Christian"' (103). Achtemeier dates the letter to between 80 and 100, 'most likely in the earliest years of that range' (*1 Peter* 50), and Elliott to between 73 and 92 (*1 Peter* 138).

197. Achtemeier, *1 Peter* 39; Schnelle takes it to be significant that 'the problematic associated with the incident in Antioch (Gal. 2.11-14) is entirely missing from the letter' (*History* 400).

quite possible that in regions and churches where Gentile numbers were not significant and Paul's influence was not strong, the congregations were untroubled
by 'the Gentile question', with Gentile believers content to judaize or for their
fellowship to be determined along the lines of 'the apostolic decree'.

All in all, then, the issue of authorship is a good deal more intangible, and
the possibility that Peter was himself the author of 1 Peter a good deal more open
than has often been thought to be the case. It is at this point that the question
'Why Peter?' becomes more relevant, especially when posed in the light of what
has already become apparent about the living tradition and the traditioning processes of the period.

b. Why Peter?

1 Peter has several striking features of relevance here, all in terms of the traditions being drawn on.

1. One is the strong *influence of the language and thought of the Jewish
Scriptures.* As Achtemeier notes, '1 Peter abounds in OT language. . . . Virtually
all of the imagery of 1 Peter is drawn from its writings. . . . The traditions contained in the sacred writings of Israel informed the thought of the author of this
epistle'.[198]

1.15	Lev. 11.44-45; 19.2	2.21	Isa. 53.9
1.24	Isa. 40.6-7	2.24	Isa. 53.4-6, 12
1.25	Isa. 40.8-9	3.8	Ps. 34.13-17
2.3	Ps. 33.9 LXX	3.14-15	Isa. 8.12-13
2.6	Isa. 28.16	4.8	Prov. 10.12
2.7	Ps. 117.22 LXX	4.14	Isa. 11.2
2.8	Isa. 8.14	4.18	Prov. 11.31 LXX
2.9	Isa. 43.21	5.5	Prov. 3.34 LXX
2.10	Hos. 1.6, 9; 2.25	5.8	Ps. 22.14
2.12	Isa. 10.3		

Here is evidence not necessarily for the thought of a particular individual and for
how much he himself had been influenced by the LXX, but more for the influence of the Scriptures on the language of instruction and paraenesis used in the
earliest churches.

---

198. Achtemeier, *1 Peter* 12; documentation also in nn. 110-16. Again I draw on the text
and marginal notes of Aland[26], citing only clear quotations and omitting the many more allusions. A full list of OT citations and allusions is provided by Elliott, *1 Peter* 13-16. 'Arguably
the most Jewish-sounding letter of the New Testament' (Barnett, *Jesus* 308).

2. Somewhat as with the letter of James, there is clear evidence of *influence from the Jesus tradition*, particularly from Jesus' remembered teaching about responding to unjust abuse and persecution.[199]

1 Peter	*Jesus tradition*
1.6; 4.13	Matt. 5.12
1.10-12	Matt. 13.17
1.17	Luke 11.2
2.12b	Matt. 5.16b
2.19-20	Luke 6.32-33/Matt. 5.46-47
3.9, 16	Luke 6.28/Matt. 5.44
3.14	Matt. 5.10
4.5	Matt. 12.36
4.7	Luke 21.36
4.14	Luke 6.22/Matt. 5.11
5.6	Luke 14.11
5.7	Matt. 6.25-34

Once again, it is not a question of allusion or of literary dependence whether 1 Peter can provide support for a particular form of a saying of Jesus. It is more a matter of what such obvious similarity of thought and expression tells us about the way teaching of Jesus was remembered and absorbed and used in the paraenesis of emerging Christianity. Consequently, it is also not so much a question of whether the evidence of 1 Peter is sufficient to indicate a personal relationship between the author of 1 Peter and Jesus.[200] It is more a matter of how an early believer instructed in the Jesus tradition, or even a prominent disciple of Jesus himself, drew together teaching whose substance and imagery can be traced back to Jesus and into Jesus' own exhortation and instruction.

3. The other notable feature is 1 Peter's *use of early Christian tradition, liturgical, catechetical or paraenetic,* which we may deduce was widely familiar in the earliest Christian churches. Again, for convenience, I cite Achtemeier's documentation:[201]

199. Already referred to in *Jesus Remembered* 182 n. 49, to which I have added some examples indicated by Achtemeier, *1 Peter* 10-12, and Elliott, *1 Peter* 24. G. Maier, 'Jesustradition im 1. Petrusbrief', in D. Wenham, ed., *Gospel Perspectives*. Vol. 5: *The Jesus Tradition outside the Gospels* (Sheffield: JSOT, 1984) 85-128, offers a more extensive list (tabulated 127-28) which does not include all those listed here.

200. As Achtemeier suggests (*1 Peter* 11).

201. Achtemeier, *1 Peter* 21-23, with bibliography in nn. 205-208; Schnelle, *History* 409-11. 1 Peter became a fruitful quarry for the excavation of hymnic and catechetical material in the first half of the twentieth century; see again my *Unity and Diversity* §§35.3f-g and 36.1;

hymnic or confessional forms	e.g., 1.18-21; 2.21-25; 3.18-22
catechetical topoi	e.g., 1.18-21; 3.18-22
hortatory traditions	e.g., 2.21-25
persecution traditions	e.g., 1.6; 4.1.

In this case also the temptation is to look for firm forms, established formulae, fixed tradition. But more likely we have evidence of teaching, both content and form, being transmitted and circulated among the earliest congregations by founding apostles and visiting teachers, taking a variety of shapes recognizable across a wide range of churches, so that a document like 1 Peter could evoke a wide range of associations and other traditions already familiar in individual churches.[202] Only so could a letter like 1 Peter commend itself and gain a respectful hearing across such a diversity of churches as are presumably indicated in the list of addressees (1.1).

The question, then, is how such a document should be able to claim the authorship of Peter, and to do so successfully, without, so far as we are aware, any doubts being expressed regarding it.[203] Presumably it was not simply its immersion in Scripture, its knowledgeable handling of the Jesus tradition, its obvious familiarity with early church traditions which persuaded people — unless, of course, these were known to be characteristic of Peter's teaching and preaching style! Certainly it cannot be considered an adequate explanation to assume that a body of teaching (or even already a letter) was discovered and attributed to Peter, simply because he was known as such a major figure in the early history of Christianity and because claiming his authorship would give the resulting letter an authority it could not otherwise have. Nor is it adequate, in my view, to infer that some unknown disciple simply contrived the letter from his own resources and passed it off as Peter's, for the same reason.[204] Such logic is self-contradictory, in that it envisages a situation where Peter was very highly

---

other bibliography in Kümmel, *Introduction* 419-20 nn. 7-13, who thinks it possible that several hymns have been worked into 1 Peter (421); and in Elliott, *1 Peter* 8-10, 28-30, who proceeds to catalogue a more extensive list of creedal and hymnic forms, and baptismal, liturgical and hortatory traditions (30-37).

202. Elliott's list (n. 198 above) consists mainly of motifs, phrases and fragments.

203. It was probably already known to Clement and Polycarp; see the detailed discussion of probable and possible allusions in Elliott, *1 Peter* 138-49; 'with the single exception of 1 John, 1 Peter is the only one of the Catholic Epistles whose authority was never questioned; "it is second only to the Gospels and the Pauline Epistles in the extent of the influence which it exercised on the language and thoughts of writers widely separated from each other in place and in circumstances"' (148-49, quoting F. H. Chase in *HDB* 3.781).

204. A common failing in critical scholarship, from which Achtemeier is not exempt, is to postulate an unknown Christian of sufficient theological stature to compose 1 Peter, while disputing that Peter himself could have been such a figure.

respected but where nothing of what he taught or his manner of teaching was known or recalled. In *Jesus Remembered* I protested against the assumption which has set so many questers of the historical Jesus off on the wrong foot: that Jesus made so little impact during his mission that nothing can be discerned of that impact from this side of the first Easter.[205] Here I have to make the same protest with regard to Peter. Should we indeed complement the impact-less Jesus with an impact-less Peter (and leave Paul as the undisputed impact-maker in the field of first-generation Christianity)? Such would indeed be a dereliction of historical responsibility, and, much as it might appeal to some residual Protestant suspicion that Peter has been oversold in Roman Catholic tradition, its manifest unfairness cries out. It is much more plausible to assume that Peter was a figure who made a considerable impact on his generation, above all in and through the mission for which he had prime responsibility, among his fellow Jews. And to assume, furthermore, and in consequence, that much of his most characteristic and influential teaching was recalled within the oral traditions of the churches where he ministered most often and most effectively. That 1 Peter was quite probably sent from Rome (5.13)[206] most naturally suggests that in the two years (or whatever) during which Peter was in Rome prior to his execution, he made such an impact there that in some sense 1 Peter is the manifestation and expression of that impact.

The problem of giving due weight both to the self-introduction (1.1) and to the critical issues which have dominated the evaluation of 1 Peter during the last two centuries is usually resolved in terms of pseudonymity.[207] And in principle I have no problem with that conclusion.[208] But the most plausible form of the pseudonymous thesis is that a subsequently formulated teaching or written document, which belongs firmly within the authoritative stream of teaching/writing that began with the figure named, for that reason can be attributed to that figure and recognized as his without falsehood or impropriety.[209] And while such a the-

---

205. See also *New Perspective on Jesus* ch. 1.

206. Kümmel, *History* 422-23; Lichtenberger, 'Jews and Christians in Rome' 2165; and particularly Elliott, *1 Peter* 131-34. Schnelle, however, thinks Asia Minor is more likely, noting *inter alia* that 'Babylon' as a code word for the totalitarian claim of the Roman state is not documented until after 70 CE — referring to Rev. 14.8; 16.19; 17.5; 18.2, 20, 21 (*History* 402-403). Often cited here is C.-H. Hunzinger, 'Babylon als Deckname für Rom und die Datierung des 1. Petrusbriefes', in H. G. Reventlow, ed., *Gottes Wort und Gottes Land,* H.-W. Hertzberg FS (Göttingen: Vandenhoeck und Ruprecht, 1965) 67-77.

207. Bibliography in Elliott, *1 Peter* 125 n. 38.

208. See again my 'Pseudepigraphy', *DLNT* 977-84.

209. See particularly D. G. Meade, *Pseudonymity and Canon* (WUNT 39; Tübingen: Mohr Siebeck, 1986). Achtemeier draws on N. Brox, *Falsche Verfasserangaben. Zur Erklärung der frühchristlichen Pseudepigrapha* (SBS 79; Stuttgart: Katholisches Bibelwerk, 1975) 72-74: 'More widely attested . . . was the notion that students who in their writings enun-

sis can work well with an Isaiah or a Paul, where the fountainhead of authority had left a literary deposit which continued to inspire further writing in his name, the problem once again with Peter is that we have nothing to compare 1 Peter with. Granted that Peter was a highly influential figure who made a lasting impact on earliest Christianity, we have no literary evidence of that impact — apart, that is, from 1 Peter itself. *Which is precisely the point!* If 1 Peter has a distinctive character, even where that includes influence from Paul, then why the unwillingness to attribute that character to Peter?[210] That need not mean that Peter wrote the letter himself, but the attribution of the letter to Peter has to have a better explanation than that some individual or church thought it a good idea to attribute their own composition to Peter.[211] The most obvious explanation is that 1 Peter does represent the teaching of Peter, was from the beginning recognized as such and quickly came to be accepted as such. Which could mean that Peter himself composed the letter 'through Silvanus', or, equally, that a close colleague or disciple (Silvanus, Mark? — 5.13) put together teaching he knew from Peter into a letter which was (and still is) a fitting tribute to the quality, character and content of what Peter was remembered as teaching and preaching. The latter would also help explain why a 'Finally' appears just over half-way through the letter, the letter being made up by putting together the material from some characteristic exhortatory material of Peter delivered at different times.

c. The Legacy of Peter

The legacy of Peter down through the history of Christianity is nowhere more starkly expressed than in the words of Jesus to Peter in Matthew's Gospel, words inscribed round the base of the dome in St. Peter's in Rome: 'Tu es Petrus, et super hanc petram aedificabo ecclesiam meam' ('You are Peter and on this rock I will build my church' — Matt. 16.18). But that is a legacy which began to be as-

---

ciated a master's teachings were obliged to attribute that writing not to themselves, but to the one who originated such doctrine' (40), citing *inter alia* students of the Pythagorean school who routinely attributed their writings to its founder, and Tertullian who enunciated the principle that what disciples publish should be regarded as their master's work (*Adv. Marc.* 4.5).

210. To observe that 'ascription of the letter to Peter would have been intended to identify its message as reflective of and consistent with the actual witness and pastoral concerns of the Apostle Peter' (Elliott, *1 Peter* 125; and further 127-30) almost amounts to the same thing! 1 Peter is attestation to 'the actual witness and pastoral concerns of the Apostle Peter'!

211. Contrast Kümmel: 'It cannot be determined why this Gentile Christian seized precisely upon the authority of Peter unless the place of writing provided the occasion for him to do so' (*Introduction* 424). See also N. Brox and F.-R. Prostmeier, summarized by Elliott, *1 Peter* 126-27.

serted only subsequently, and with more and more vigour in later centuries. Viewed from the first century, and by the immediate heirs of Peter, following his execution in Rome in 64, the best claimant to embody and express the legacy of Peter is the first letter attributed to him. It has several striking sequences and themes.

(i) *The letter is probably written primarily for Jewish believers.* This is suggested by two repeated motifs in particular:

- It is addressed to an Israel scattered from the land, 'resident in foreign lands' (*parepidēmoi* — 1.1), sojourners/exiles and 'aliens' (*paroikia* — 1.17; *paroikoi* — 2.11).[212] The imagery was a familiar one in the Mediterranean world, where exile for political or other reasons was common, but here it no doubt draws on the strong sense of diaspora Jews that they were suffering the curse of Deut. 28.63-68.[213]
- The recipients are described in distinctively Jewish terms: they are 'elect' (*eklektoi* — 1.1; 2.4, 9); the grace they have received is in fulfilment of what the prophets prophesied (1.10); theirs is the responsibility that God laid upon Israel (1.15-16), 'You shall be holy, for I am holy' (Lev. 11.44-45; 19.2); likewise the language of Exod. 19.6 is taken up in 2.9 — 'You are a chosen race, a royal priesthood, a holy nation'; and the other intense use of Israel's Scriptures in self-reference has already been documented.[214]

212. On the political, legal and social status of the *paroikoi,* see particularly Elliott, *1 Peter* 94, and the full treatment in his earlier *A Home for the Homeless: A Sociological Exegesis of 1 Peter, Its Situation and Strategy* (1981; Minneapolis: Fortress, ²1990) 59-118; '*Paroikoi,* "by-dwellers", were distinguished legally from complete strangers *(xenoi)* and belonged to an institutionalized class ranked socially below the citizen population and above freed-persons, slaves, and complete strangers' (*1 Peter* 94). In some dispute with Elliott, R. Feldmeier, *Die Christen als Fremde. Die Metapher der Fremde in der antiken Welt, im Urchristentum und im 1. Petrusbrief* (WUNT 64; Tübingen: Mohr Siebeck, 1992), argues strongly that the language is a metaphor for Christian self-understanding, strangers in a world estranged from God.

213. A theme given particular attention by N. T. Wright; see *Jesus Remembered* 393 nn. 57, 58.

214. In a private communication Doering strongly disagrees: 'What is distinctive about 1 Pet is that it without qualms and argument transfers Israel epithets to Gentiles. Again, the image of Peter may be relevant: primarily associated with the mission to the circumcised (as compared with Paul), Peter has nevertheless become associated with the mission to the Gentiles as well (Acts 10–11; as compared with James)'. In his 'First Peter as Early Christian Diaspora Letter', in K.-W. Niebuhr and R. Wall, eds., *Catholic Epistles and Apostolic Traditions* (Waco: Baylor University, forthcoming), however, Doering demonstrates that 1 Peter fits well with the tradition of letters written to the Jewish diaspora and is closely modeled on the analogy of Jewish diaspora experience.

These are perspectives which we find also in Paul: Paul liked to use the language of Israel's special relationship with God for his own (Gentile) converts;[215] and the imagery of 'living stones' being built into a spiritual house, and the recipients as 'a holy priesthood offering spiritual sacrifices' (2.5), is very Pauline in character.[216]

Where a difference becomes apparent is in 1 Peter's talk of 'Gentiles'. At no point does the letter seem to envisage Gentiles as believers: Gentiles rather form the population within which the believers live as aliens (2.12).[217] And whereas Paul often recalls the recipients of his letters to their own Gentile past (as in Gal. 4.8), here the letter recalls that the recipients used to do 'what the Gentiles desire to do' (1 Pet. 4.3) — 'Gentiles' again as 'others'. It is true, and very striking, that the letter refers to the recipients' past in remarkably strong terms: indulging 'desires in their former ignorance' (1.14);[218] 'the futile way of life inherited from your ancestors' (1.18); 'called out of darkness' (2.9); 'going astray like sheep' (2.25).[219] But this is all consistent with the in-house character of prophetic exhortation and rebuke, or expressive of a conviction that the realization of eschatological hope highlights the ignorance, futility and darkness of the old age.[220] A notable contrast is the different use made of Hos. 2.25 ('I will have pity on "Not-pitied", and I will say to "Not-my-people", "You are my people"'). In Rom. 9.24-25 Paul uses this verse to signal that God's call of *Gentiles* as well as Jews is in accord with his pattern of election; but in 1 Pet. 2.9-10 the verse is simply a further statement of God's saving purpose for his elect people.[221]

It is not that 1 Peter contests the possibility of Gentile believers participating in Israel's heritage. The impression is more of one who has had to deal pri-

215. E.g., 'saints' (Rom. 1.7; 15.25-26; 1 Cor. 1.2; etc.); 'elect' (Rom. 8.33; Col. 3.12); for further details see my *Romans* 19-20 (on 1.7) and 502-503 (on 8.33).

216. Particularly Rom. 15.16 (for detail see again *Romans* 859-61). Should the closer parallel of 2.5 with Eph. 4.12 be attributed to influence from Peter on the Pauline legacy?

217. '"Gentiles" as designation for outsiders opposed to insiders (2:12) and their God (2:12; 4:2-4), in continuity with Israelite usage' (Elliott, *1 Peter* 96). M. Sordi, *The Christians and the Roman Empire* (ET 1988; London: Routledge, 1994), notes that 2.12 (Christians maligned as evildoers) recalls Tacitus's libel that Jews feel only hate and enmity (hostile odium) against all others (*Hist.* 5.5.1), but also that it echoes charges brought against the Stoics (32-34).

218. But not 'ignorance of God', as Elliott suggests (*1 Peter* 96).

219. The general view is that these references indicate a Gentile audience (Kümmel, *Introduction* 418-19; Schnelle, *History* 403-404). Elliott, however, notes a sequence of indicators of Israelite origin, maintaining that 'readers of a predominantly Israelite origin were presumed among the Fathers', before concluding that 'the author reckoned with a mixed audience — some of Israelite roots and some of pagan origin' (*1 Peter* 95-97).

220. 1 Pet. 2.25, of course, is a quotation from Isa. 53.6.

221. Doering again disagrees, referring particularly to 2.10 and 4.3-4, which in his view clearly refer to the 'pagan' past of the addressees.

marily with believers among the Jews of the diaspora, living in hostile Gentile territory. This could well be the legacy of a Peter who never saw himself only in relation to Paul, either as some sort of opponent or rival, or as dependent on him for his best ideas. This sounds more like a Peter who took his commission to his fellow Jews with utmost seriousness, whose theological and pastoral teaching was determined by that focus. This is a Peter who shared many traditions and emphases with Paul but framed them in his own terms. More important, this is a Peter who had never given up hope that the gospel was for his own people and whose impact on diaspora Jewish believers was probably of immense significance in holding Christianity within its Jewish framework or at least ensuring that its Jewish character would not be lost.

(ii) A repeated emphasis in 1 Peter is *the centrality of Christ in the fulfilment of Israel's prophecy and in achieving salvation.* I sequence the points systematically:

- Like Paul, 1 Peter blesses 'the God and Father of our Lord Jesus Christ' (1.3) — a characteristically but not distinctively Pauline formulation.
- Christ's saving ministry had been 'predestined before the foundation of the world' and 'made manifest at the end of the times' (1.20-21) — a distinctive variation of the more widespread Christian belief that Christ was the eschatological enactment of God's purpose for humankind from the beginning.[222]
- The prophets, inspired by the Spirit (now revealed to be the Spirit) of Christ predicted his sufferings and glory (1.10-11) — again a distinctive variation of a common early Christian theme.
- The understanding of being 'ransomed . . . by the precious blood of Christ, as of a lamb without defect or blemish' (1.18-19) draws on the same sacrificial imagery as Paul, and the use of Isa. 8.14 and 28.16 in reference to Jesus as the precious stone laid in Zion, a cause of stumbling (1 Pet. 2.6, 8), is a reminder that both were able to draw on a much more widespread use of at least one 'stone' testimony regarding Jesus.[223]
- The application of Isaiah 53 to Jesus' vicarious suffering and death (2.22-24) is the most explicit in the NT, a passage at best alluded to in Acts 3–4 but explicitly referred to in 8.32-35, and presupposed by Paul.[224]
- The theme of Christ once suffering for sins, 'the righteous for the unrighteous', is resumed in 3.18 and underlies the thought through to 4.1; the passage may be an already extensive elaboration of an early Christian hymn

222. See Goppelt, *Erste Petrusbrief* 125-26; Dunn, *Christology* 236-37.
223. See above, §23 at n. 96.
224. See again §23 at n. 94, and §33 n. 144.

('put to death in the flesh, and made alive in/by the Spirit') climaxing in the confessional formula in 3.22 ('he is at the right hand of God, having gone to heaven, with angels and authorities and powers made subject to him').[225]

- Unique to 1 Peter in the NT is the first statement of what became called in subsequent centuries the 'harrowing of hell' — here the basic idea that Christ, 'put to death in the flesh, but made alive in the Spirit', 'went and proclaimed to the spirits in prison' (the disobedient in the days of Noah) (3.18-20), alluded to again in 4.6 ('the gospel was proclaimed also to the dead').[226]
- Equally typical of early Christian confessional language, but equally distinctive, is the talk of God 'who gave us new birth to a living hope through the resurrection of Jesus Christ from the dead' (1.3).
- Like Paul (Rom. 1.5), 1 Peter makes it clear from the outset that the Christian is called to 'obedience (to Christ)' (1.2, 14, 22).
- The characteristic Pauline *en Christō* ('in Christ') motif is not lacking (3.16; 5.10, 14).
- The theme of suffering for the sake of Christ who suffered for them emerges repeatedly in the last two chapters as a linking theme (4.1, 12-16; 4.19–5.1; 5.9-10), including the familiar Pauline theme of sharing Christ's sufferings (4.13).
- The expectation of Christ's return as setting in train final judgment is clear in several passages (1.7; 4.5; 5.4), with further allusions in 4.13 and 17, 5.6 and 10. The lively hope of an imminent 'end of all things' (4.7) is as clear as in the Synoptic tradition and in Paul, still retained even a full generation after Jesus' own mission.

Setting out 1 Peter's christology in this systematized (and rather contrived) way has the advantage of bringing out how fully developed was that christology, as rounded as Paul's, but with its own distinctive elements and formulations. Notable is the fact that Jesus is not remembered simply as a teacher. His significance embraces the whole sweep of history, from before the foundation of the world to the end of all things. His suffering and death are not simply an event in the past which can inspire those who suffer in the present, but, as for Paul, the reality of the suffering and resurrected Christ is a present force sustaining and giving them hope for the future. Here the frustrations at being unable to hear the voiceless Peter at last begin to be resolved, as we begin to sense an individual

---

225. See the recent review by Elliott, *1 Peter* 693-97, and further 697-705.

226. On the *descensus Christi ad infernos,* see again Elliott, *1 Peter* 706-10, with extensive bibliography 709 n. 420.

with a powerful message focused on Christ which must have made a lasting impact on so many of his fellow believing Jews to whom he ministered.

(iii) The letter teaches *why and how Christians must expect to suffer*. If there is any single theme which dominates 1 Peter, it is the theme of suffering, both the sufferings of Christ (1.11; 2.21-24; 3.18; 4.1) and the suffering which believers must anticipate as their lot in this age:[227]

- The initial talk of rejoicing in suffering various trials, in recognition that suffering is a means of testing and proving the genuineness of their faith (1.6-7), strikes two characteristic Pauline notes (e.g., Rom. 5.3-5; 2 Cor. 12.9-10), the latter deeply rooted in Jewish wisdom tradition.
- A particular concern seems to have been with the harsh conditions and unjust beatings which Christian slaves had to endure (2.18-20). This is the first development of the suffering theme in the letter, so it is striking that the thought turns first to the suffering of slaves. Equally noticeable is the fact that in 1 Peter's adaptation of the 'household rules', initially (so far as we can tell) drawn into Christian paraenesis in Col. 3.18–4.1, it is the exhortation to slaves which is put first, rather than the rules for wives and husbands (as in Col. 3.18-19 and Eph. 5.22-25). Moreover, it is the main emphasis in the exhortation, whereas the exhortation in Col. 3.22-25 has no thought of the slave's unjust suffering. The memory of Jesus' own unjust suffering, as giving comfort and an example to follow, is distinctive to 1 Peter.
- As with Rom. 12.14 and 17, 1 Pet. 3.9 draws on Jesus' teaching on how to respond to curses and abuse (cf. Luke 6.27-29) — a further testimony to the way in which the recollection of what Jesus himself had warned about and taught must have comforted and instructed first-generation converts.
- The theme returned to in 3.13-17 seems to be broader: unjust suffering in general (3.13-14, 17), occasions when their faith and hope were being questioned and challenged (4.15-16) and situations where they were being maligned and abused as being 'Christian' (4.16).[228] Jesus is again cited as the pre-eminent case of one whose suffering was for a positive purpose and with a good outcome.
- Yet another extended exhortation rounds off the theme — 4.12-19. Christians should expect a fiery trial (4.12); they can rejoice that they share in

227. 'The suffering of Christ as consolation and pattern for the suffering Christians' (Wilckens, *Theologie* 1/3.370-74). As has often been pointed out, twelve of the forty-two uses of *paschō* ('suffer') in the NT occur in 1 Peter. Other documentation in Schnelle, *History* 404.

228. 1 Pet. 4.16 is the only other passage in the NT (apart from Acts 11.26 and 26.28) where the title 'Christian (*christianos*)' appears; see above, §20 n. 5. Horrell argues that 4.16 indicates a stage where what was a hostile label, a form of stigma, is coming to be borne with pride by insiders ('The Label *Christianos*', particularly 376-81).

Christ's sufferings and, accordingly also, that they will participate in his glorious return (4.13); being reviled for the name of Christ is a blessing, since it means that the Spirit of God rests upon them (4.14); to suffer as a 'Christian' is not a cause for shame but a cause to glorify God for that name (4.16).[229] Consequently 'those who suffer in accordance with God's will (should) entrust themselves to a faithful Creator, while continuing to do good' (4.19).

- The final element in the motif is a reminder that in the world fellow believers (*adelphotēs* — 'family group, fellowship') are suffering similarly, an assurance of God's support and strengthening, and an affirmation of the hope that the suffering will be temporary, to be succeeded by the summons 'to God's eternal glory in Christ' (5.9-10).

All this provides some invaluable insights into the congregations for which this teaching had been crafted: that slaves were a prominent proportion of these congregations — presumably many of the Jewish slaves in the Western diaspora finding a new hope in the gospel of Messiah Jesus; and that the low social status of the Christians generally left them vulnerable to suspicion and provocation on the part of fellow residents and suspicious authorities in their towns and cities. While many of the features of the teaching are fully shared with Paul, and presumably quite common elsewhere in earliest Christianity, the comfort to be found in the way Jesus suffered (and not just in the fact that his suffering was vicarious) is a distinctive chord which 1 Peter adds to the theme.[230]

(iv) 1 Peter teaches about *living in a hostile world*. Underlying the whole letter is the thought of the congregations of Jewish messianists being confronted by and having to live within a society whose values and authorities are antagonistic to their own.

- The note is struck immediately in the characterization of the letter's recipients as living in exile (1.1), sojourners and 'aliens' (1.17; 2.11), the exile providing an image of this life as a temporary residence in a hostile context

229. A. Puig i Tàrrech, 'The Mission according to the New Testament: Choice or Need?', in A. A. Anatoly et al., eds., *Einheit der Kirche im Neuen Testament. Dritte europäische orthodox-westliche Exegetenkonferenz in Sankt Petersburg, 24-31 August 2005*. (WUNT 218; Tübingen: Mohr Siebeck, 2008): 'The judicial pressure against Christians would seem to be confirmed in 4.15-16 (see also 2.14). Likewise, in 3.15 terminology does not exclude a judicial context: the formula *aiteō logon* ('ask the reason') fits with a judicial interrogation and *apologia* ('answer') indicates the right to reply of somebody being interrogated in court' (n. 27).

230. Suffering is not such a prominent theme in James, but see P. H. Davids, 'Why Do We Suffer? Suffering in James and Paul', in Chilton and Evans, eds., *The Missions of James, Peter, and Paul* 435-66.

(1.17-18; 2.11-12), exiled from where one's true inheritance and citizenship lie (1.4; cf. Phil. 3.20; Heb. 11.13-16).[231]

- Equally striking, in terms of comparison with Paul, is the similar attitude to the state, which follows from being *paroikoi* in a strange land. As Paul strongly advised the Roman believers not to react to persecution but to honour the civic authorities and to be good citizens (Rom. 12.9–13.7), so 1 Peter advises the sojourning believers to be good neighbours and to honour the authorities, including the emperor (2.11-17; 4.14).

- The letter summons believers to keep the ten commandments and the laws faithfully (avoiding murder, adultery, robbery or crime — 4.3, 15), while also showing complete respect for those who are not Christians (2.17).[232] That such ethical commitment of the believers, alongside worship, was/became characteristic for Asian Christianity is suggested by Pliny's report to Trajan (*Ep.* 10.96): the Christians solemnly swear 'not to commit any crime, but to avoid theft, robbery, adultery, not to break a trust or deny a deposit when they are called for it' (cf. 4.15).[233]

- The fact that the exhortation to slaves focuses almost entirely on their vulnerability to harsh and unjust treatment (2.18-20) and that the subsequent passages assume the likelihood of hostility and abuse (3.9, 14-17; 4.16) is a salutary reminder of how exposed the earliest believers in Messiah Jesus were to antagonisms from those unsympathetic to their faith.

- An interesting feature is the assumption in the household rules that believing wives may well have unbelieving husbands (3.1-6) but that the wives of Christian husbands will also be Christian (3.7).[234] Both indicate that the pattern of Christianity attracting more women than men was an early feature. More to the point here, though, is the implied patriarchal character of the social context in which the first Christians had to operate: when the head of the family converted, his household naturally followed him, but when the wife was converted, she was often unaccompanied by her husband and had to dress and to conduct herself most circumspectly to avoid seeming to challenge his authority.

---

231. The metaphorical usage is familiar also in the LXX — Lev. 25.23; 1 Chron. 29.15; Pss. 38.13; 118.19 (Achtemeier, *1 Peter* 126 n. 38).

232. I owe this point to Puig i Tàrrech, who also notes: 'This is the most likely sense of the difficult word *allotriepiskopos* (4.15): the believers must not interfere in the affairs of the other social groups or associations (the famous *haeteriae*) and respect everybody'. On the difficulty of determining the sense of *allotriepiskopos* see BDAG 47: 'one who meddles in things that do not concern the person, a busybody', or 'concealer of stolen goods', or even 'spy, informer, revolutionist'.

233. Full text above, §21.1e.

234. See also Achtemeier, *1 Peter* 217.

- Presumably the exhortations not to be conformed to older patterns of conduct (1.14; 4.2-3), to conduct themselves among the Gentiles in a praiseworthy manner (*kalos* — 2.12), to avoid deceit and seek peace (3.10-11) and to be doers of good (3.11, 13, 16-17) were also a way of marking off the Christian way of life from that of others around them.
- A regular feature of 1 Peter is the reminder of the hope that believers cherished (1.3, 13, 21; 3.5, 15) and of the divine judgment to be expected (1.17; 2.12; 4.5-6), a judgment from which believers themselves would not be exempt (4.17-18), both emphases providing a perspective which could help them withstand the deceitful attractions of the present society, with its various slings and arrows.

In short, 1 Peter provides a sustained and well-thought-through theology and rationale for a Christianity which in the early centuries found itself too different in its beliefs, values and praxis from contemporary society and social mores to be wholly comfortable in that environment. The Christianity which in the West subsequently became a state religion, an established structure within the political establishment, found it much harder to come to terms with 1 Peter and to live responsibly from it.

(v) A final theme is *the church as envisaged in 1 Peter.* The letter also provides a couple of brief glimpses into the corporate life of the Christian congregations for which the letter was constructed.

- The mention of 'elders' (5.1, 5) is reminiscent of the Jerusalem church (§23.3e), as of Jas. 5.14, again suggesting an organization which drew on the synagogue model and perhaps indicating structures which regarded themselves as synagogues.
- The image of a shepherd tending his flock (5.2-4) was one perhaps particularly associated with Peter himself (cf. John 21.15-17) and may suggest Peter's influence in the way the congregations he ministered to thought of themselves and of those who ministered among them.
- The very Pauline understanding of congregations functioning charismatically (4.10-11), each with a charism *(charisma),*[235] whether of word or of service, and dependent on words and grace to be given to exercise the charism (cf. Rom. 12.3-8; 1 Corinthians 12), suggests churches that continued to live by the Spirit (cf. Gal. 5.25–6.2) and to recognize leaders who emerged through their ministry and pastoral care (cf. 1 Cor. 16.15-18; 1 Thess. 5.12-13).
- As elsewhere in earliest Christianity, baptism plays an important role in marking the beginning of the process of salvation, though the definition is

235. Outside of the Pauline corpus, *charisma* occurs in the NT only in 1 Pet. 4.10.

interesting — 'not as the washing away of bodily pollution, but as a pledge to God of, or appeal to God for *(eperōtēma eis theon),* a good conscience' (3.21).[236]

- The author has a concept of the church as universal — 'your brotherhood throughout the world' (5.9). 'Throughout the text, the author refers to the community in a broad sense, without making a clear distinction between a local congregation and the universal church. The only territorial references are at the beginning (1.1: the five Roman provinces) and at the end (5.9: 'the whole world').[237]

In all this we should not forget that this Peter may represent a voice of Jewish belief in Christ and its outworkings in daily life which is otherwise almost entirely lost to us from the first century. I refer to the voice of diaspora Jews who came to believe in Jesus Messiah, doing so principally through the mission of Peter, apostle to the circumcision. With Paul we hear and gain insight into the character of earliest Gentile Christianity and to the mixed congregations where Gentile believers predominated. With the letter of James, and to some extent through Acts (Luke so often telling his story from a Jerusalem perspective), we hear the voice of moderate Jewish believers in Jerusalem, intense in their own terms. But with 1 Peter it is probably the Messiah Jesus congregations principally made up of Jewish believers in the Western diaspora which we can listen into, encountering the sort of preaching and teaching which established and sustained them. If so, 1 Peter does a service of incalculable value, since otherwise the establishment of what was becoming Christianity in these regions and circles remains almost wholly unknown to us.

37.4. The End of the Beginning

To what point(s), then, have we reached in our attempt to trace the first generation of Christianity in the making?

a. The Story Thus Far

Within forty years a movement which had come to life in the days following the death of Jesus the Nazarene had grown through a troubled childhood into

---

236. See my *Baptism in the Holy Spirit* 217-18.

237. Puig i Tàrrech, 'Mission' n. 28, who also notes that the term used here is *kosmos* and not *oikoumenē:* 'The perspective is as universal as possible, even beyond the borders of the Empire. Similarly, Diognetus 6.2: "There are Christians in all the cities of the world"'.

vigorous adolescence. From beginnings almost entirely in Jerusalem and Judea it had spread widely, initially or perhaps even primarily, it would appear, in and through the Jewish diaspora. The firm records available to us give indication of considerable expansion in Syria, in the south and west of the Asia Minor peninsula, in Macedonia, Greece and in commercial centres of Italy. They also indicate a movement which began as a Jewish sect but in its considerable appeal to non-Jews was already beginning to become something else. However, given that the expansion appears typically to have begun in diaspora synagogues and communities, and among Gentiles previously attracted to Jewish beliefs and customs, it is likely that the sect of Jesus Messiah also gained footholds in other diaspora communities, in Alexandria and Cyrenaica in the West in particular, and in the Eastern diaspora in Mesopotamia and eastern Syria. Such traditions as there are on this subject will be looked at more carefully in volume 3.

In all this, of course, we are talking about only small cell groups — tenement and apartment congregations and house churches, many groups possibly only of a dozen or so members. Often, it would appear, there would have been only one congregation as such ('the whole church') even in a city as large as Corinth, whereas in such centres there were probably several synagogues. The tenement and apartment groups and congregations would be largely hidden from general view, in back streets and in poorer parts of the town or city, in contrast to the temples and cults often in public and prominent settings. So the size and number of first-century Christian churches should not be exaggerated, nor the wide scatter of the little cell groups be taken too quickly to indicate a large-scale movement. Only in Jerusalem (Acts 21.20) and in Rome (Tacitus, *Ann.* 15.44.2-5) do we have indications of substantial early expansion. A modern calculation based on modern experience of new religious movements suggests that the number of Christians by this period may only have been about 3,000 in total,[238] though that hardly takes account of the 'many thousands' of Acts 21.20 or the 'vast numbers' of Tacitus (*Ann.* 15.44.2). In contrast, Bo Reicke estimates 40,000 believers and adherents by the year 67, including perhaps 25,000 in Palestine, Transjordan and Syria, at least 5,000 in Asia Minor, and possibly 2,000 in Greece and Italy.[239] But whatever the facts, now unrecoverable, the seed had been sown widely; the salt (or yeast) was beginning to have its effect.

We have no way of telling just how seriously the calamities of the 60s affected the new movement. Again their impact on the post-70 literature, both Jew-

238. R. Stark, *The Rise of Christianity* (San Francisco: HarperSanFrancisco, 1996, 1997) 5-7.

239. Reicke, *New Testament Era* 302-303. As Schnabel notes, Elliott thinks the figure for Asia Minor is conservative (*1 Peter* 89); Schnabel wonders whether there could have been as many as 150,000 in Asia Minor by the year 100 (*Mission* 848).

ish and Christian, will be a matter for discussion in volume 3. But the devastating effects, as they must have been in Jerusalem and Rome, were unlikely to have been so serious elsewhere. We do not know how much the Jewish believers in Syrian Antioch, Alexandria, Libya and Cyrene were caught up in the serious disturbances which were part of the wider reaction to the Jewish revolt (Josephus, *War* 7.41-62, 409-50). But it is likely that elsewhere, in Asia Minor and in the Aegean region at any rate, the effects of the Jewish revolt were not so serious for the young Christian groups. If the letters of the seer of Revelation, of Ignatius and of the younger Pliny are any guide, the growth of the young churches continued without much, if any, serious abatement.

This is where the three letters examined in §37 may well have played their part and themselves constitute testimony to a movement which gathered up the legacy of the first-generation leaders and found in that legacy a clear confirmation of their shared and distinctive beliefs, continuing inspiration for the ongoing task of spreading the gospel of Jesus Christ and the necessary encouragement to live lives patterned in accordance with its promises and traditions. These letters, then, are not so much the last wills and testaments of a movement fatally wounded by the catastrophes of the 60s but the charters for the heirs of these leaders, on the basis of which the next phase of Christianity in the making would be brought about.

So where have we reached in our attempt to trace Christianity in the making? In particular, how do our findings so far answer the questions raised at the beginning of this volume? These, it may be recalled, focused primarily on the double issue of continuity between Jesus and the embryonic Christianity which emerged after his death (§20.2, 'From Jesus to Paul') and of how a Jewish sect became a Gentile religion (§20.3). And always lurking behind the scenes has been the issue of whether earliest Christianity, properly so called, was a single movement or in fact diverse movements, whether the historical reality of 'Christianity in the making' in the period 30-70 is best described as 'Christianity' (or 'embryonic Christianity') or as 'Christianities', a scattering of movements whose integrated coherence cannot simply be assumed. It is appropriate to round off this volume with some summary reflections on these three crucial issues.

b. What Degree of Continuity Did the First Christians Maintain with the Mission and Message of Jesus?

The issue of continuity, it will be recalled, arises for two main reasons: first, because so little interest in the pre-Easter mission and teaching of Jesus seems to be reflected in the earliest Christian writings; and second, because the claims made in regard to Jesus seem to have transformed his own message (focusing on the kingdom of God) into something else (focusing on the Lord Jesus Christ). Drawing together our various findings, what answers begin to emerge?

- It is an undoubted fact that the conviction that God had raised Jesus from the dead and had exalted Jesus to his right hand transformed Jesus' first disciples and their beliefs about Jesus. It is also natural that they should have focused their earliest preaching and teaching on filling out the consequences of that basic belief.
- The elaboration of these fundamental convictions gave rise to some astonishing assertions, which attributed to Jesus a share in functions previously ascribed in Jewish thinking only to God and in worship previously reserved only for God.[240] These certainly seem to transcend anything that Jesus was remembered as saying about himself. However,
  - the assertion that Jesus was Messiah was an integral part of the Jesus tradition from the first;
  - in the light of the tradition in Mark 14.62-64 it is at least arguable that such early Christian beliefs about Jesus are in direct continuity with Jesus' own hope and expectation;
  - and the degree to which the christological passages in the Synoptic Gospels bear evidence of subsequent reflection on what Jesus had said also attests the degree to which the first Christians' christological reflections were fed by the Jesus tradition itself.
- There are indications of some development in the earliest reflections on the significance of Jesus' death — from an interpretation consistent with a continuing participation in the Temple cult, to an interpretation of Jesus' death as the definitive sin offering and Day of Atonement scapegoat, which, by implication, made the Temple sacrificial cult redundant for believers in Messiah Jesus. However, as we saw in *Jesus Remembered,* it is hard to avoid the conclusion that Jesus had foreseen his own death as an integral part of the mission he had been sent to fulfill.
- The other most striking feature of the earliest days was the vitality of the spiritual experience of the first believers, attributed to the outpouring of God's Spirit upon them. This upwelling (or downpouring) of spiritual exuberance was not simply a feature of the earliest Jerusalem community but also proved to be decisive in the opening of the gospel to non-Jews. What also was striking, however, was the close link which was established, apparently from the first, between such experience and the foundational convictions about Jesus.[241] It was the closeness of this link which prevented

240. Particularly Acts 2.33; 1 Cor. 8.6; Phil. 2.10-11.
241. E.g., Acts 1.5 and 11.16; 2.33 (again); Rom. 8.9, 15-16; Gal. 3.1-5; 4.4-7; Heb. 2.3-4.

the spiritual enthusiasm from spinning off into a different kind of religious movement.

- The care with which Acts represents the first preachers as continuing the theme of the kingdom of God in their preaching suggests that the chief theme of Jesus' own preaching remained influential in at least some parts of the new movement.
- Perhaps above all, we have noted again and again that there are indications and evidence that the tradition of Jesus' own teaching and the character of his own mission constituted a continuing force, particularly in the paraenesis of the wide range of congregations reflected in the letters of the NT. Again and again they give pointers to a mass of traditional material which they could assume and, more important, assume that their readers/ auditors were familiar with.[242] During this whole period, when we have as yet no clear evidence of the Jesus tradition having been written down (at least, written down extensively), it can safely be assumed that the oral Jesus tradition was widely circulating and widely known in many individual, diverse forms and combinations.

In short, the degree of disjunction between the mission of Jesus and the post-Easter gospel should not be exaggerated. The fact that the Jesus tradition could be presented (in the subsequent Gospel format) as *gospel,* that is, as expression of the preaching and teaching of the early churches, should not be discounted and set aside, as is so often the case.

Most intriguing, however, is the continuity/discontinuity between the expectation of Jesus himself and that of the post-Easter believers. To be sure, as already noted, it could be argued that Jesus' expectation was at least in part fulfilled by what Christians believe happened to Jesus (his resurrection and exaltation).[243] But the whole issue of the first Christians' imminent expectation of the return (parousia) of Jesus from heaven remains unclear, both as to its origin (did Jesus himself expect to return?) and as to the effect of its disappointment ('the delay of the parousia'). In fact, there is little indication in the literature of the first generation that 'the delay of the parousia' was regarded as a problem: a degree of imminent expectation seems to have been a sustained feature of Paul's own Christ-devotion to the end (e.g., Phil. 4.5), and James is remembered "as warning that 'the Judge is standing at the doors!' (Jas. 5.9). But to what extent did the disasters of the 60s change things? The deaths of the three first-generation leaders and the disaster of the destruction of Jerusalem and the temple

242. For Paul see again *Jesus Remembered* 182 n. 48; in §37 note again Eph. 4.20-21 (nn. 55, 59 above); and §§37.2c and 37.3b.

243. See *Jesus Remembered* 750-52, 818-24, 867-70, 874-76.

in 70 CE must surely have influenced Christian eschatological thinking in at least some measure — particularly if Jesus' own prediction of the temple's destruction and the coming of the Son of Man were already seen in Christian circles as heralding the end time.[244] Inevitably, then, we draw this volume to a close by noting that the impact of the transition to the second generation of leadership and of the disaster of 70 on earliest Christian reflection regarding Jesus himself will be one of the subjects requiring close attention in volume 3.

c. From Judaism to Christianity

That it was indeed Christianity, properly so called, which emerged in the earliest 30s of the Common Era need not be doubted. Whatever the degree of continuity between Jesus and Paul, there is no question of the direct continuity between the sect of the Nazarenes and the 'Christianity' identified by Ignatius. But was that 'Christianity' as distinct from 'Judaism', as Ignatius seems to imply? That a 'parting of the ways', or, as I prefer, 'several partings of the ways', between Judaism and Christianity took place increasingly in the period following 70 CE is again hardly to be disputed. But what was the situation in the period between 30 and 70, the period covered by this volume? How far had the ways parted, if at all, by the time the three great leaders of first-generation Christianity had been executed? Here too the picture has become clearer as a result of the investigations of this volume.

- The early descriptions of the Messiah Jesus followers as 'the sect of the Nazarenes' assuredly sets the new movement firmly within the spectrum of the 'sects' which made up a substantial proportion of Second Temple Judaism. The first Christians were all Jews. Christianity began as a sect, a messianic sect, within Second Temple Judaism.
- It is certainly hard to deny the thoroughgoing Jewish character of the earliest and first-generation community of Messiah Jesus in Jerusalem. This is clearly attested in Acts, in the continued attachment to the Temple, and in the continuing devoted practice of the law, and it is confirmed by the various hints in the letters of Paul that the main opposition to his own mission stemmed from Jerusalem.
- The clearest breach between 'Judaism' and one of the leaders of the new sect (Paul) is in Gal. 1.13-14, the only use of the term 'Judaism' in the NT. But, set in context, the text serves more clearly to remind us both of the di-

---

244. Mark 13.3-27; Wright does not hesitate to correlate the 'coming of the son of man' precisely with the destruction of Jerusalem and the Temple (*Jesus and the Victory of God* 362).

versity within Second Temple Judaism and that the 'Judaism' which Paul left behind in his conversion was the particular form of Second Temple Judaism in which he had been trained and out of which had grown his zeal as a persecutor of the new sect. The 'Judaism' of Gal. 1.13-14 is only part of what today is identified as Second Temple Judaism; alternatively expressed, it is only one of what some prefer to speak of as first-century Judaisms.

• The burgeoning claims for Christ already referred to do not seem to have caused particular tension with fellow Jews. Even though the idea of a crucified Messiah seems to have been offensive to many Jews, the Jewish believers in this crucified Messiah seem to have been able to thrive in Jerusalem itself. And the issue left only a small mark in the Pauline correspondence. That Jesus was Messiah seems to have been so uncontroversial that Messiah = Christ quickly began to lose its titular significance (controversial in reference to Jesus?) and become a proper name for Jesus. And there is no evidence in the Pauline letters that even the more exalted claims regarding Christ were a bone of contention between Paul and his more traditionalist Jewish brothers; his own monotheistic faith is repeatedly affirmed. The issue will reappear with some force in volume 3, but the most obvious inference that can be drawn in regard to the first generation is that the claims being made for Jesus may have seemed to most Jews little different in character from the speculations elsewhere in Second Temple apocalyptic and mystical reflection regarding famous heroes exalted to heaven and angelic intermediaries.

• The main bone of contention for the first generation was undoubtedly the Mosaic law: to what extent should Gentile believers be expected to observe the Torah. It should be noted at once that there is no real evidence that any Christian missionary was antinomian, encouraging a total disregard for the law. Paul himself affirmed (most of) the ten commandments; his antipathy to *porneia* and to idolatry was Jewish through and through. But against the law as a 'dividing wall' (Eph. 2.14) separating Jew from Gentile, Paul reacted strongly. The problem was that it was just such 'works of the law' as circumcision and the laws of clean and unclean which gave the body of Jews their distinctive life-style and character. Consequently, to abandon such laws, or even to sit loose to them, was a step which relatively few of Paul's fellow Jews could countenance. Consequently, too, the churches which grew up under Paul's tutelage may simply have been too un-Jewish for most Jews to regard as part of the Jewish community,[245] although the

---

245. As W. A. Meeks, 'Breaking Away: Three New Testament Pictures of Christianity's Separation from the Jewish Communities', in J. Neusner and E. S. Frerichs, eds., *'To See Our-*

point has always to be made with the qualification that we know too little about the diversity of diaspora Judaism to be fully confident in asserting what would and would not have been unacceptable within the range of diaspora synagogues.

• At the same time, insofar as the legal standing of the Christian house groups was an issue with any civic authorities, it is likely that they continued to find shelter *de facto* under the special provisions usually in force for Jewish synagogues, with the issue whether the 'Christians' were in actual fact a separate entity from the Jewish community in any city only beginning to be posed towards the end of our period.

The outcome is that as we take leave of first-generation Christianity, we should probably recognize that a tearing apart between embryonic Christianity and Second Temple diaspora Judaism was beginning to happen. In theology and ethics the continuity was firm and clear. Legally, most small churches in effect probably continued to shelter under the legal status of the synagogues. But sociologically, there were more and more churches which were probably predominantly Gentile in composition and beginning to develop a life-style which was distinct from Judaism. As we shall see, the picture continues to be far from clear, since for several centuries Christians had to be discouraged from attending the synagogue on the Sabbath and from observing Jewish practices and feasts.[246]

Here again, however, we should recognize that the disaster of 70 would have posed an issue which could not be escaped by the following generations. For consistent within the early Christian leadership was a strong affirmation of the movement's Jewishness. Christian hope could still be expressed in terms of 'the restoration of Israel' (Acts 1.6). The incoming of Gentiles could still be seen either as expanding the definition of 'Israel' (Romans 9–11) or as an integral corollary to the return of the diaspora exiles and the rebuilding of the ruins of David's dwelling (Acts 15.16-18). But the destruction of the Jerusalem temple must have called in question any continuing hope expressed in terms of Israel's restoration. How would the two strands (restoration of Israel, incoming of Gentiles) survive that disaster? How would Jewish and Gentile believers now regard each other? If Paul's vision of the mixed church, Jew and Gentile worshipping in harmony, was unlikely of realization *sociologically*, was his vision of an 'Israel'

---

selves as Others See Us': Christians, Jews, 'Others' in Late Antiquity (Chico: Scholars, 1985) 93-115, famously asserted: '*Theologically* it is correct to say that the Scriptures and the traditions of Judaism are a central and ineffaceable part of the Pauline Christians' identity. *Socially,* however, the Pauline groups were never a sect of Judaism. They organized their lives independently from the Jewish associations of the cities where they were founded, and apparently, so far as the evidence reveals, they had little or no interaction with the Jews' (106).

246. For the present see my *Partings,* especially ²2006 xi-xxx.

consisting of those called by God, Jew first but also Gentile, sustainable *theolog-ically?* Transformation of a concept like 'Israel' can go only so far before becoming a different concept. What would happen on this front in the wake of 70?

d. The Character of Christianity at the End of the First Generation

Finally, we should not fail to note again that the Christianity which was to emerge from the disasters of the 60s was a very mixed bag. From early on the Hellenists had marked a spectrum which quite quickly began to move well beyond the eschatological messianic sect focused in Jerusalem. The Pauline mission to the Gentiles was the catalyst for a further stretching of the spectrum. And the likelihood, as we saw, is that Paul's attempt to heal the resulting breach between the churches of the Gentile mission and Jerusalem failed. But the spectrum and the tension involved are not to be reduced in effect to Peter vs. Paul, as Baur tended to argue, or to Paul vs. James, as the heirs of Luther have preferred. The spectrum was (or the spectra were) a good deal more complex than that, with

- the very conservative Jewish believers (the 'false brothers', 'false apostles') marking one end,
- one or more of the (predominantly Gentile) factions who challenged Paul in places like Corinth at the other end,
- and James, Peter and Paul somewhat spread from right to left in between.

The somewhat uncomfortable fact is that first-generation Christianity was never the pure ideal church which subsequent generations imagined as 'the apostolic age' or for whose return radical reformers longed. As already indicated, it is likely that the conservative Jewish end fed into what came to be designated as the Jewish Christian (heretical) sects. And it is equally tempting to match that development by linking the other end of the spectrum to the Gnosticism which was to emerge with increasing strength in the second century. Whether this was so or the extent to which this was so will be an important part of the agenda for volume 3. A particular issue will be whether the effective loss of the Jerusalem end of the spectrum was a foreshortening of the spectrum which changed the character of the whole.

A further issue for the internal self-understanding and identity of the new movement is what effect the transition from the characteristically charismatic form of the first generation to the second and subsequent generations would have. For the Spirit-inspired and Spirit-justified character of the early developments of embryonic Christianity was inseparable from these developments —

specifically the Jerusalem Pentecost and the subsequent Gentile Pentecosts. The tension between charisma and office, already familiar from Israel's history in the frequent tensions between prophet and priest/cult, soon re-emerged in the new movement in the tensions between 'Hebrew' and 'Hellenist' and between halakhic rulings sent down from Jerusalem and a Pauline counsel to be ruled by the Spirit. How would these tensions play out in the generations following 70? In the 'routinization' or 'institutionalization' of charisma, as Weber suggested? Or in a further extension of the spectrum or a further tearing of the fragile unity of Christianity? Always to be borne in mind are the questions whether what emerged as 'Christianity' in the second century answers fully to the sweep and diversity of the impact made by Jesus, by his resurrection and by the experience of the (his) Spirit; and whether in its diverse developments the 'Christianity' of the second century was becoming (or had already become) something different in character from the Christianity of the first generation.

These are the central issues which emerge for me at the end of volume 2 and which should be borne in mind as we turn to volume 3. In the meantime, however, it should simply be reiterated that the three principal leaders of the first generation can properly be said together to represent the enduring character and range of first-generation Christianity — a Christianity integrally Jewish/OTish in character, with a gospel of salvation for Gentile as well as Jew, embracing both Jew and Gentile on the common ground of faith in Messiah/Christ Jesus, inspired by the mission and teaching, the death and resurrection of Jesus, devoted to the one God through this Christ, and motivated and enabled by the same Spirit.

Abbreviations

	Other Early Christian Literature. ET and ed. W. F. Arndt and F. W. Gingrich. 2nd edition revised by F. W. Gingrich and F. W. Danker (Chicago: University of Chicago, 1979)
BBB	Bonner biblische Beiträge
BBR	*Bulletin for Biblical Research*
BCE	Before the Christian Era, or Before the Common Era
BDAG	W. Bauer, *A Greek-English Lexicon of the New Testament and Other Early Christian Literature.* 3rd edition of BAGD, revised by F. W. Danker (Chicago: University of Chicago, 2000)
BDF	F. Blass, A. Debrunner and R. W. Funk, *A Greek Grammar of the New Testament* (Chicago: University of Chicago/Cambridge: University of Cambridge, 1961)
Beginnings	*The Beginnings of Christianity.* Part 1: *The Acts of the Apostles.* Ed. F. J. Foakes Jackson and K. Lake (London: Macmillan). Vol. 1: *Prolegomena* I (1920). Vol. 2: *Prolegomena* II (1922). Vol. 3: *The Text of Acts,* by J. J. Ropes (1926). Vol. 4: *English Translation and Commentary,* by K. Lake and H. J. Cadbury (1933). Vol. 5: *Additional Notes,* by K. Lake and H. J. Cadbury (1933)
BETL	Bibliotheca ephemeridum theologicarum lovaniensium
BibInt	*Biblical Interpretation*
BJRL	*Bulletin of the John Rylands University Library of Manchester*
BJS	Brown Judaic Studies
BNTC	Black's New Testament Commentaries
BR	*Biblical Research*
BU	Biblische Untersuchungen
BZ	*Biblische Zeitschrift*
BZNW	Beihefte zur Zeitschrift für die neutestamentliche Wissenschaft
ca.	*circa,* about, approximately
CBNTS	Coniectanea biblica: New Testament Series
CBQ	*Catholic Biblical Quarterly*
CBQMS	*CBQ* Monograph Series
CE	Christian Era, or Common Era
cf.	compare
ch(s).	chapter(s)
CHJ	*The Cambridge History of Judaism* (Cambridge: Cambridge University). Vol. 2: *The Hellenistic Age.* Ed. W. D. Davies and L. Finkelstein (1989). Vol. 3: *The Early Roman Period.* Ed. W. Horbury et al. (1999)
CIJ	*Corpus inscriptionum judaicarum*

CIL	*Corpus inscriptionum latinarum*
CRINT	Compendia Rerum Iudaicarum ad Novum Testamentum
DLNT	*Dictionary of the Later New Testament and Its Developments.* Ed. R. P. Martin and P. H. Davids (Downers Grove: InterVarsity, 1997)
DNTB	*Dictionary of New Testament Background.* Ed. C. A. Evans and S. E. Porter (Downers Grove: InterVarsity, 2000)
DPL	*Dictionary of Paul and His Letters.* Ed. G. F. Hawthorne and R. P. Martin (Downers Grove: InterVarsity, 1993)
DSS	Dead Sea Scrolls
EB	Études bibliques
ed(s).	edited by, editor(s)
EDNT	*Exegetical Dictionary of the New Testament.* Ed. H. Balz and G. Schneider (ET; Grand Rapids: Eerdmans, 1990-93)
e.g.	*exempli gratia,* for example
EKK	Evangelisch-katholischer Kommentar zum Neuen Testament
Elliott, *Apocry-phal New Testament*	J. K. Elliott, ed., *The Apocryphal New Testament* (Oxford: Clarendon, 1993)
Enc. Rel.	*The Encyclopedia of Religion.* Ed. M. Eliade. 16 vols. (New York: Macmillan, 1987)
Ep(p).	*epistola(e),* letter(s)
ET	English translation
et al.	*et alii,* and others
ETL	*Ephemerides theologicae lovanienses*
ExpT	*Expository Times*
FBBS	Facet Books, Biblical Series
FRLANT	Forschungen zur Religion und Literatur des Alten und Neuen Testaments
FS	Festschrift, volume written in honour of
GLAJJ	*Greek and Latin Authors on Jews and Judaism.* Ed. M. Stern. 3 vols. (Jerusalem: Israel Academy of Sciences and Humanities, 1976-84)
GNB	Good News Bible
HDB	J. Hastings, ed., *A Dictionary of the Bible.* 5 vols. (Edinburgh: Clark, 1898-1904)
HNT	Handbuch zum Neuen Testament
HR	E. Hatch and H. A. Redpath, *Concordance to the Septuagint and Other Greek Versions of the Old Testament.* 2 vols. (Oxford: Clarendon Press, 1897-1906)
HTKNT	Herders theologischer Kommentar zum Neuen Testament

HTR	*Harvard Theological Review*
HTS	Harvard Theological Studies
ICC	International Critical Commentary
IDB	*Interpreter's Dictionary of the Bible*
IEJ	*Israel Exploration Journal*
IG	*Inscriptiones graecae*
inscr.	inscription
IvEph	*Die Inschriften von Ephesos.* Ed. H. Wankel. 8 vols. in 11 (Bonn: Habelt, 1979-84)
JAC	*Jahrbuch für Antike und Christentum*
JAGR	*The Jews among the Greeks and Romans: A Diasporan Sourcebook.* Ed. M. H. Williams (London: Duckworth, 1998)
JB	Jerusalem Bible
JBL	*Journal of Biblical Literature*
JCSD	*Jewish and Christian Self-Definition* (London: SCM). Vol. 1: *The Shaping of Christianity in the Second and Third Centuries.* Ed. E. P. Sanders (1980). Vol. 2: *Aspects of Judaism in the Graeco-Roman Period.* Ed. E. P. Sanders et al. (1981). Vol. 3: *Self-Definition in the Graeco-Roman World.* Ed. B. E. Meyer and E. P. Sanders (1982)
JECS	*Journal of Early Christian Studies*
JETS	*Journal of the Evangelical Theological Society*
JIGRE	*Jewish Inscriptions of Graeco-Roman Egypt.* Ed. W. Horbury and D. Noy (Cambridge: Cambridge University, 1992)
JIWE	*Jewish Inscriptions of Western Europe.* Ed. D. Noy (Cambridge: Cambridge University). Vol. 1: *Italy, Spain and Gaul* (1993). Vol. 2: *The City of Rome* (1995)
JJS	*Journal of Jewish Studies*
JPT	*Journal of Pentecostal Theology*
JQR	*Jewish Quarterly Review*
JR	*Journal of Religion*
JRH	*Journal of Religious History*
JRS	*Journal of Roman Studies*
JSHJ	*Journal for the Study of the Historical Jesus*
JSJ	*Journal for the Study of Judaism*
JSNT	*Journal for the Study of the New Testament*
JSNTS	*JSNT* Supplement Series
JSS	*Journal of Semitic Studies*
JTS	*Journal of Theological Studies*
KAV	Kommentar zu den Apostolischen Vätern
KD	*Kerygma und Dogma*

KEK	Kritisch-exegetischer Kommentar über das Neue Testament. H. A. W. Meyer.
KJV	King James Version, or Authorized Version
LAB	*Les antiquités bibliques.* 2 vols. (Paris: Cerf, 1976)
LBT	Library of Biblical Theology
LCL	Loeb Classical Library
LD	Lectio divina
LNTS	Library of New Testament Studies (incorporating JSNTS)
LS	C. T. Lewis, with C. Short, ed., *A Latin Dictionary* (Oxford: Clarendon, 1879)
LSJ	H. G. Liddell and R. Scott, revised by H. S. Jones, *A Greek-English Lexicon* (Oxford: Clarendon, ⁹1940); with supplement (1968)
LXX	Septuagint
MM	J. H. Moulton and G. Milligan, *The Vocabulary of the Greek Testament* (London: Hodder, 1930)
ms(s)	manuscript(s)
MTZ	*Münchener theologische Zeitschrift*
NCBC	New Century Bible Commentary
NDIEC	*New Documents Illustrating Early Christianity* (Sydney: Macquarie University/Grand Rapids: Eerdmans). Vols. 1-5, ed. G. H. R. Horsley (1981, 1982, 1983, 1987, 1989). Vols. 6-9, ed. S. R. Llewelyn (1992, 1994, 1998, 2002)
NEB	New English Bible (NT 1961; OT and Apocrypha 1970)
NICNT	New International Commentary on the New Testament
NIDB	*The New Interpreter's Dictionary of the Bible.* Ed. K. D. Sakenfeld. 4 vols. (Nashville: Abingdon, 2006-9)
NIDNTT	*New International Dictionary of New Testament Theology.* Ed. C. Brown. 4 vols. (Grand Rapids: Eerdmans, 1975-85)
NIGTC	New International Greek Testament Commentary
NIV	New International Version (1978)
NJB	New Jerusalem Bible (1985)
NovT	*Novum Testamentum*
NovTSupp	Supplement to *NovT*
NRSV	New Revised Standard Version (1989)
NT	New Testament
NTA	*New Testament Apocrypha*
NTG	New Testament Guides
NTS	*New Testament Studies*
NTTS	New Testament Tools and Studies

OCD[2]	*The Oxford Classical Dictionary.* 2nd edition. Ed. N. G. L. Hammond and H. H. Scullard (Oxford: Clarendon, 1970)
OCD[3]	*The Oxford Classical Dictionary.* 3rd edition. Ed. S. Hornblower and A. Spawforth (Oxford: Clarendon, 2003)
ODCC	*The Oxford Dictionary of the Christian Church.* Ed. F. L. Cross and E. A. Livingstone. 2nd edition (Oxford: Oxford University, 1983; 3rd edition, 1997)
OT	Old Testament
ÖTKNT	Ökumenischer Taschenbuch-Kommentar zum Neuen Testament
OTP	*The Old Testament Pseudepigrapha.* Ed. J. H. Charlesworth. 2 vols. (London: Darton, 1983-85)
pace	with due respect to, but differing from
par(s).	parallel(s)
passim	here and there, throughout
PGL	*Patristic Greek Lexicon.* Ed. G. W. H. Lampe (Oxford: Clarendon, 1968)
PKNT	Papyrologische Kommentare zum Neuen Testament
PL	*Patrologia latina.* Ed. J. Migne
QD	Quaestiones disputatae
RAC	*Reallexikon für Antike und Christentum.* Ed. T. Kluser et al. (Stuttgart, 1950-)
RB	*Revue biblique*
REB	Revised English Bible (1989)
RGG	*Religion in Geschichte und Gegenwart.* 3rd edition. Ed. K. Galling. 7 vols. (Tübingen: Mohr Siebeck, 1957-65)
RHPR	*Revue d'histoire et de philosophie religieuses*
RIDA	*Revue internationale des droits de l'antiquité*
RSV	Revised Standard Version (NT 1946, OT 1952, Apocrypha 1957)
RTR	*Reformed Theological Review*
SBL	Society of Biblical Literature
SBLDS	SBL Dissertation Series
SBLMS	SBL Monograph Series
SBLSBS	SBL Sources for Biblical Study
SBS	Stuttgarter Bibelstudien
Schneemelcher, *NTA*	W. Schneemelcher and R. M. Wilson, *New Testament Apocrypha* (Cambridge: Clarke). Vol. 1: *Gospels and Related Writings* (revised edition, 1991). Vol. 2: *Writings Related to the Apostles; Apocalypses and Related Subjects* (revised edition, 1992)

Schürer, *History*	E. Schürer, *The History of the Jewish People in the Age of Jesus Christ,* revised and ed. G. Vermes and F. Millar. 4 vols. (Edinburgh: Clark, 1973-87)
SEÅ	*Svensk exegetisk årsbok*
SJT	*Scottish Journal of Theology*
SNTSBull.	*Society for New Testament Studies Bulletin*
SNTSMS	Society for New Testament Studies Monograph Series
ST	*Studia theologica*
STAC	Studien und Texten zu Antike und Christentum
Str-B	H. Strack and P. Billerbeck, *Kommentar zum Neuen Testament.* 4 vols. (Munich: Beck, 1926-28)
SUNT	Studien zur Umwelt des Neuen Testaments
SWJT	*Southwestern Journal of Theology*
TCNT	Twentieth-Century New Testament
TDGR	Translation Documents of Greece and Rome
TDNT	*Theological Dictionary of the New Testament.* Ed. G. Kittel and G. Friedrich (ET; Grand Rapids: Eerdmans, 1964-76)
TDOT	*Theological Dictionary of the Old Testament.* Ed. G. J. Botterweck and H. Ringgren (ET; Grand Rapids: Eerdmans, 1974-)
THNT	Theologischer Handkommentar zum Neuen Testament
TLZ	*Theologische Literaturzeitung*
TRE	*Theologische Realenzyklopädie*
TSAJ	Texte und Studien zum Antiken Judentum
TynB	*Tyndale Bulletin*
TZ	*Theologische Zeitschrift*
UBS	The United Bible Societies, *The Greek New Testament,* 4th edition. Ed. B. Aland et al. (Stuttgart: Deutsche Bibelgesellschaft, 1993)
UTB	Uni-Taschenbücher
v., vv.	verse, verses
v.l.	*vario lectio,* variant reading
vol(s).	volume(s)
WBC	Word Biblical Commentary
WMANT	Wissenschaftliche Monographien zum Alten und Neuen Testament
WUNT	Wissenschaftliche Untersuchungen zum Neuen Testament
ZKG	*Zeitschrift für Kirchengeschichte*
ZNW	*Zeitschrift für die neutestamentliche Wissenschaft*
ZTK	*Zeitschrift für Theologie und Kirche*

Bibliography

Commentaries

Acts

Barrett, C. K. *The Acts of the Apostles.* 2 vols. ICC. Edinburgh: Clark, 1994-98.

Boismard, M.-E., and L. Lamouille. *Les Actes des deux apôtres.* 3 vols. EB. Paris: Gabalda, 1990.

Bruce, F. F. *The Acts of the Apostles.* NICNT. Grand Rapids: Eerdmans, 1990, 3rd ed.

————. *The Book of the Acts.* Grand Rapids: Eerdmans, 1988, 2nd ed.

Conzelmann, H. *Die Apostelgeschichte.* HNT 7. Tübingen: Mohr Siebeck, 1963.

Dunn, J. D. G. *The Acts of the Apostles.* Peterborough: Epworth, 1996.

Fitzmyer, J. A. *The Acts of the Apostles.* AB 31. New York: Doubleday, 1998.

Haenchen, E. *The Acts of the Apostles.* ET Oxford: Blackwell, 1971.

Harnack, A. *Die Apostelgeschichte.* Leipzig: Hinrich, 1908.

Jervell, J. *Die Apostelgeschichte.* KEK. Göttingen: Vandenhoeck und Ruprecht, 1998.

Johnson, L. T. *The Acts of the Apostles.* Collegeville: Liturgical, 1992.

Pesch, R. *Die Apostelgeschichte.* 2 vols. EKK 5. Zürich: Benziger, 1986.

Preuschen, E. *Die Apostelgeschichte.* HNT 4/1. Tübingen: Mohr Siebeck, 1912.

Schille, G. *Die Apostelgeschichte des Lukas.* THNT 5. Berlin: Evangelische, 1983.

Schneider, G. *Die Apostelgeschichte.* 2 vols. HTKNT 5. Freiburg: Herder, 1980-82.

Weiser, A. *Die Apostelgeschichte.* 2 vols. ÖTKNT 5/l. Gütersloh: Gütersloher, 1981-85.

Witherington, B. *The Acts of the Apostles: A Socio-Rhetorical Commentary.* Grand Rapids: Eerdmans, 1998.

Romans

Dunn, J. D. G. *Romans.* WBC 38. Dallas: Word, 1988.

Fitzmyer, J. A. *Romans.* AB 33. New York: Doubleday, 1993.

Haacker, K. *Der Brief des Paulus an die Römer*. THNT 6. Leipzig: Evangelische Verlagsanstalt, 1999.

Jewett, R. *Romans*. Hermeneia. Minneapolis: Fortress, 2007.

Keck, L. E. *Romans*. ANTC. Nashville: Abingdon, 2005.

Lohse, E. *Der Brief an die Römer*. KEK. Göttingen: Vandenhoeck und Ruprecht, 2003.

Moo, D. J. *The Epistle to the Romans*. NICNT. Grand Rapids: Eerdmans, 1996.

Witherington, B. *Paul's Letter to the Romans*. Grand Rapids: Eerdmans, 2004.

Wright, N. T. 'The Letter to the Romans'. In *New Interpreter's Bible*. Vol. 10. Nashville: Abingdon, 2002.

1 Corinthians

Arzt-Grabner, P., et al. *1 Korinther*. PKNT 2. Göttingen: Vandenhoeck und Ruprecht, 2006.

Barrett, C. K. *1 Corinthians*. BNTC. London: Black, 1968.

Conzelmann, H. *1 Corinthians*. Hermeneia. Philadelphia: Fortress, 1976.

Fee, G. D. *The First Epistle to the Corinthians*. NICNT. Grand Rapids: Eerdmans, 1987.

Lietzmann, H. *Korinther I/II*. HNT 9. Tübingen: Mohr Siebeck, 1949.

Lindemann, A. *Der erste Korintherbrief*. HNT 9/1. Tübingen: Mohr Siebeck, 2000.

Schrage, W. *1 Korinther*. EKK 7/4. Düsseldorf: Benziger, 2001.

Thiselton, A. C. *1 Corinthians*. NIGTC. Grand Rapids: Eerdmans, 2000.

Weiss, J. *1 Korinther*. KEK. Göttingen: Vandenhoeck und Ruprecht, 1910.

Wolff, C. *Der erste Brief des Paulus an die Korinther*. Vol. 2. THNT 7/2. Berlin: Evangelische, 1982.

2 Corinthians

Barrett, C. K. *2 Corinthians*. BNTC. London: Black, 1973.

Betz, H. D. *2 Corinthians 8 and 9*. Hermeneia. Philadelphia: Fortress, 1985.

Furnish, V. P. *2 Corinthians*. AB 32A. New York: Doubleday, 1984.

Harris, M. J. *2 Corinthians*. NIGTC. Grand Rapids: Eerdmans, 2005.

Thrall, M. *2 Corinthians*. 2 vols. ICC. Edinburgh: Clark, 1994-2000.

Galatians

Betz, H. D. *Galatians*. Hermeneia. Philadelphia: Fortress, 1979.

Bruce, F. F. *Commentary on Galatians*. NIGTC. Grand Rapids: Eerdmans, 1982.

Burton, E. de W. *Galatians*. ICC. Edinburgh: Clark, 1921.

Dunn, J. D. G. *Galatians*. BNTC. London: Black, 1993.

Esler, P. F. *Galatians*. London: Routledge, 1998.

Lightfoot, J. B. *Saint Paul's Epistle to the Galatians*. London: Macmillan, 1865.

Longenecker, R. N. *Galatians.* WBC 41. Dallas: Word, 1990.

Martyn, J. L. *Galatians.* AB 33A. New York: Doubleday, 1997.

Mussner, F. *Der Galaterbrief.* HTNT 9. Freiburg: Herder, [3]1977.

Ramsay, W. M. *A Historical Commentary on St. Paul's Epistle to the Galatians.* London: Hodder and Stoughton, 1900.

Vouga, F. *An die Galater.* HNT 10. Tübingen: Mohr Siebeck, 1998.

Ephesians

Barth, M. *Ephesians.* 2 vols. AB 34, 34A. New York: Doubleday, 1974.

Best, E. *Ephesians.* ICC. Edinburgh: Clark, 1987.

Bruce, F. F. *The Epistles to the Colossians, to Philemon and to the Ephesians.* NICNT. Grand Rapids: Eerdmans, 1984.

Lincoln, A. T. *Ephesians.* WBC 42. Dallas: Word, 1990.

Muddiman, J. *The Epistle to the Ephesians.* BNTC. London: Continuum, 2001.

Schnackenburg, R. *Ephesians.* Edinburgh: Clark, 1991.

Philippians

Bockmuehl, M. *The Epistle to the Philippians.* BNTC. London: Black, 1997.

Fee, G. D. *Philippians.* NICNT. Grand Rapids: Eerdmans, 1995.

Gnilka, J. *Der Philipperbrief.* HTNT 10/3. Freiburg: Herder, 1976, 2nd ed.

Hawthorne, G. F., and R. P. Martin. *Philippians.* WBC 43. Nashville: Nelson, 2004, 2nd ed.

Lightfoot, J. B. *Philippians.* London: Macmillan, 1878, 4th ed.

O'Brien, P. T. *Philippians.* NIGTC. Grand Rapids: Eerdmans, 1991.

Colossians and Philemon

Barth, M., and H. Blanke. *The Letter to Philemon.* Grand Rapids: Eerdmans, 2000.

Dunn, J. D. G. *The Epistles to the Colossians and to Philemon.* NIGTC. Grand Rapids: Eerdmans, 1996.

Fitzmyer, J. A. *The Letter to Philemon.* AB 34C. New York: Doubleday, 2000.

Hübner, H. *An Philemon; An die Kolosser; An die Epheser.* HNT 12. Tübingen: Mohr Siebeck, 1997.

Lightfoot, J. B. *Colossians and Philemon.* London: Macmillan, 1875, 1879, 3rd ed.

Lohse, E. *Colossians and Philemon.* Hermeneia. Philadelphia: Fortress, 1971.

Martin, R. P. *Colossians and Philemon.* NCBC. London: Marshall, Morgan and Scott, 1973.

Schweizer, E. *The Letter to the Colossians.* London: SPCK, 1982.

Wilson, R. M. *Colossians and Philemon.* ICC. London: Clark International, 2005.

Wolter, M. *Der Brief an die Kolosser; Der Brief an Philemon.* ÖTKNT 12. Gütersloh: Mohn, 1993.

1 and 2 Thessalonians

Best, E. *The First and Second Epistles to the Thessalonians.* BNTC. London: Black, 1972.
Holtz, T. *Die erste Brief an die Thessalonicher.* EKK 13. Zürich: Benziger, 1986.
Malherbe, A. J. *The Letters to the Thessalonians.* AB 32B. New York: Doubleday, 2000.
Marshall, I. H. *1 and 2 Thessalonians.* NCBC. London: Marshall, Morgan and Scott, 1983.
Trilling, W. *Der zweite Brief an die Thessalonischer.* EKK 14. Zürich: Benziger, 1980.
Wanamaker, C. A. *1 and 2 Thessalonians.* NIGTC. Grand Rapids: Eerdmans, 1990.

James

Davids, P. *James.* NIGTC. Grand Rapids: Eerdmans, 1982.
Dibelius, M., and H. Greeven. *James.* Hermeneia. Philadelphia: Fortress, 1975.
Johnson, L. T. *The Letter of James.* AB 37A. New York: Doubleday, 1995.
Martin, R. P. *James.* WBC 48. Waco: Word, 1988.
Mayor, J. B. *The Epistle of St. James.* London: Macmillan, 1897, 2nd ed.
Mussner, F. *Der Jakobusbrief.* HTKNT 13/1. Freiburg: Herder, 1975, 3rd ed.

1 Peter

Achtemeier, P. J. *1 Peter.* Hermeneia. Minneapolis: Fortress, 1996.
Brox, N. *Der erste Petrusbrief.* EKK 21. Zürich: Benziger, 1979.
Elliott, J. H. *1 Peter.* AB 37B. New York: Doubleday, 2000.
Goppelt, L. *A Commentary on I Peter.* 1978. Grand Rapids: Eerdmans, 1993.
Selwyn, E. G. *The First Epistle of St. Peter.* London: Macmillan, 1947.

Other Works

Achtemeier, P. J. 'Omne verbum sonat: The New Testament and the Oral Environment of Late Western Antiquity'. *JBL* 109 (1990) 3-27.
————. *The Quest for Unity in the New Testament Church.* Philadelphia: Fortress, 1987.
Adams, E., and D. G. Horrell, eds. *Christianity at Corinth: The Quest for the Pauline Church.* Louisville: Westminster John Knox, 2004.
Ådna, J. 'James' Position at the Summit Meeting of the Apostles and the Elders in Jerusalem (Acts 15)'. In *The Mission of the Early Church to Jews and Gentiles,* edited by J. Ådna and H. Kvalbein, 125-61. Tübingen: Mohr Siebeck, 2000.

Ådna, J., and H. Kvalbein, eds. *The Mission of the Early Church to Jews and Gentiles.* WUNT 127. Tübingen: Mohr Siebeck, 2000.

Akenson, D. H. *Saint Paul: A Skeleton Key to the Historical Jesus.* New York: Oxford University, 2000.

Aland, K. *Synopsis Quattuor Evangeliorum.* Stuttgart: Württembergische Bibelanstalt, 1964.

Albi, M. C. *'And Scripture Cannot Be Broken': The Form and Function of the Early Christian Testimonia Collections.* NovTSup 96. Leiden: Brill, 1999.

Aletti, J.-N. 'Romains 4 et Genèse 17. Quelle énigme et quelle solution?' *Biblica* 84 (2003) 305-25.

Alexander, L. C. *Acts in Its Ancient Literary Context: A Classicist Looks at the Acts of the Apostles.* LNTS 298. London: Clark, 2005.

——. 'Paul and the Hellenistic Schools: The Evidence of Galen'. In *Paul in His Hellenistic Context,* edited by T. Engberg-Pedersen, 60-84. Minneapolis: Fortress, 1995.

——. 'The Pauline Itinerary and the Archive of Theophanes'. In *The New Testament and Early Christian Literature in Greco-Roman Context,* D. E. Aune FS, edited by J. Fotopoulos, 151-65. Leiden: Brill, 2006.

——. 'The Preface to Acts and the Historians'. In *History, Literature and Society in the Book of Acts,* edited by B. Witherington, 73-103. Cambridge: Cambridge University, 1996.

——. *The Preface to Luke's Gospel: Literary Convention and Social Convention in Luke 1.1-4 and Acts 1.1.* SNTSMS 78. Cambridge: Cambridge University, 1993.

——. 'Reading Luke-Acts from Back to Front'. In *The Unity of Luke-Acts,* edited by J. Verheyden, 419-46. Leuven: Leuven University, 1999.

Alexander, P. S. 'Incantations and Books of Magic'. In Schürer, *History* 3.342-79.

Allison, D. C. 'The Fiction of James and Its Sitz im Leben'. *RB* 108 (2001) 529-70.

——. *The Jesus Tradition in Q.* Harrisburg: Trinity, 1997.

Amador, J. D. H. 'Revisiting 2 Corinthians: Rhetoric and the Case for Unity'. *NTS* 46 (2000) 92-111.

Anderson, R. D. *Ancient Rhetorical Theory and Paul.* Kampen: Kok Pharos, 1996.

Applebaum, S. 'The Social and Economic Status of the Jews in the Diaspora'. In *The Jewish People in the First Century,* edited by S. Safrai and M. Stern, 2.701-27. Assen: Van Gorcum, 1976.

Arnold, C. E. *The Colossian Syncretism: The Interface between Christianity and Folk Belief at Colossae.* WUNT 2.77. Tübingen: Mohr Siebeck, 1995.

——. *Ephesians: Power and Magic.* SNTSMS 63. Cambridge: Cambridge University, 1989.

——. '"I Am Astonished That You Are So Quickly Turning Away" (Gal. 1.6): Paul and Anatolian Folk Belief'. *NTS* 51 (2005) 429-49.

Ascough, R. S. 'Greco-Roman Philosophic, Religious, and Voluntary Associations'. In *Community Formation in the Early Church and in the Church Today,* edited by R. N. Longenecker, 3-19. Peabody: Hendrickson, 2002.

——. *Paul's Macedonian Associations.* WUNT 2.161. Tübingen: Mohr Siebeck, 2003.

——. 'The Thessalonian Christian Community as a Professional Voluntary Association'. *JBL* 119 (2000) 311-28.

————. 'Translocal Relationships among Voluntary Associations and Early Christianity'. *JECS* 5 (1997) 223-41.

————. *What Are They Saying about the Formation of Pauline Churches?* New York: Paulist, 1998.

Ashton, J. *The Religion of Paul the Apostle.* New Haven: Yale University, 2000.

Attridge, H. W. 'On Becoming an Angel: Rival Baptismal Theologies at Colossae'. In *Religious Propaganda and Missionary Competition in the New Testament World,* D. Georgi FS, edited by L. Bormann et al., 481-98. Leiden: Brill, 1994.

Aune, D. E. 'Magic in Early Christianity'. *ANRW* 2.23.2 (1980) 1507-57.

————. *The New Testament in Its Literary Environment.* Philadelphia: Westminster, 1987.

————. 'Recent Readings of Paul Relating to Justification by Faith'. In *Rereading Paul Together: Protestant and Catholic Perspectives on Justification,* edited by D. E. Aune, 188-245. Grand Rapids: Baker, 2006.

Aus, R. D. 'Paul's Travel Plans to Spain and the "Full Number" of the Gentiles of Rom. 11.25'. *NovT* 21 (1979) 232-62.

Avemarie, F. *Die Tauferzählungen der Apostelgeschichte.* WUNT 139. Tübingen: Mohr Siebeck, 2002.

Avemarie, F., and H. Lichtenberger, eds. *Auferstehung — Resurrection.* WUNT 135. Tübingen: Mohr Siebeck, 2001.

Badenas, R. *Christ the End of the Law: Romans 10:4 in Pauline Perspective.* JSNTS 10. Sheffield: JSOT, 1985.

Bahr, G. J. 'Paul and Letter Writing in the First Century'. *CBQ* 28 (1966) 465-77.

Baker, M. 'Paul and the Salvation of Israel: Paul's Ministry, the Motif of Jealousy, and Israel's Yes'. *CBQ* 67 (2005) 469-84.

Balch, D. L. '*akribōs . . . grapsai.* (Luke 1:3)'. In *Jesus and the Heritage of Israel,* edited by D. Moessner, 229-50. Harrisburg: Trinity, 1999.

————. 'The Areopagus Speech: An Appeal to the Stoic Historian Posidonius against Later Stoics and the Epicureans'. In *Greeks, Romans and Christians,* A. J. Malherbe FS, edited by D. L. Balch et al., 52-79. Minneapolis: Fortress, 1990.

————. *Let Wives Be Submissive: The Domestic Code in 1 Peter.* Missoula: Scholars, 1981.

————. 'Rich Pompeiian Houses, Shops for Rent, and the Huge Apartment Buildings in Herculaneum as Typical Spaces for Pauline House Churches'. *JSNT* 27 (2004) 27-46.

————. 'Stoic Debates about Marriage, Anxiety and Distraction'. *JBL* 102 (1983) 429-39.

Ballhorn, G. 'Die Miletrede — ein Literaturbericht'. In *Das Ende des Paulus,* edited by F. W. Horn, 37-47. Berlin: de Gruyter, 2001.

Bammel, E. 'Galater 1.23'. *ZNW* 59 (1968) 108-12.

Banks, R. J. *Paul's Idea of Community.* Exeter: Paternoster, 1980.

————. 'The Role of Charismatic and Noncharismatic Factors in Determining Paul's Movements in Acts'. In *The Holy Spirit and Christian Origins,* J. D. G. Dunn FS, edited by G. N. Stanton et al., 117-30. Grand Rapids: Eerdmans, 2004.

Barclay, J. M. G. 'Conflict in Thessalonica'. *CBQ* 55 (1993) 512-30.

————. 'Deviance and Apostasy'. In *Modelling Early Christianity,* edited by P. F. Esler, 114-27. London: Routledge, 1995.

————. *Jews in the Mediterranean Diaspora from Alexander to Trajan (323 BCE–117 CE).* Edinburgh: Clark, 1996.

————. 'Mirror Reading a Polemical Letter: Galatians as a Test Case'. *JSNT* 31 (1987) 73-93.

————. *Obeying the Truth: A Study of Paul's Ethics in Galatians.* Edinburgh: Clark, 1988.

————. 'Ordinary but Different: Colossians and Hidden Moral Identity'. *ABR* 49 (2001) 34-52.

————. 'Paul among Diaspora Jews: Anomaly or Apostate?' *JSNT* 60 (1995) 89-120.

————. 'Paul, Philemon and the Dilemma of Christian Slave-Ownership'. *NTS* 37 (1991) 161-86.

————. 'Pneumatikos in the Social Dialect of Pauline Christianity'. In *The Holy Spirit and Christian Origins,* J. D. G. Dunn FS, edited by G. N. Stanton et al., 157-67. Grand Rapids: Eerdmans, 2004.

————. 'Thessalonica and Corinth: Social Contrasts in Pauline Christianity'. *JSNT* 47 (1992) 49-74.

Barnes, T. D. 'An Apostle on Trial'. *JTS* 20 (1969) 407-19.

Barnett, P. *The Birth of Christianity: The First Twenty Years.* Grand Rapids: Eerdmans, 2005.

————. *Jesus and the Rise of Early Christianity: A History of New Testament Times.* Downers Grove: InterVarsity, 1999.

Barrett, C. K. 'The Allegory of Abraham, Sarah, and Hagar in the Argument of Galatians' (1976). In *Essays on Paul,* 154-70. London: SPCK, 1982.

————. 'Cephas and Corinth'. In *Essays on Paul,* 28-39. London: SPCK, 1982.

————. 'Christocentricity at Antioch'. In *On Paul,* 37-54. London: Clark, 2003.

————. 'The End of Acts'. In *Geschichte — Tradition — Reflexion,* M. Hengel FS. Vol. 3: *Frühes Christentum,* edited by H. Lichtenberger, 545-55. Tübingen: Mohr Siebeck, 1996.

————. *Essays on Paul.* London: SPCK, 1982.

————. *Freedom and Obligation: A Study of the Epistle to the Galatians.* London: SPCK, 1985.

————. 'The Historicity of Acts'. *JTS* 50 (1999) 515-34.

————. *Jesus and the Word and Other Essays.* Edinburgh: Clark, 1995.

————. *Luke the Historian in Recent Study.* London: Epworth, 1961.

————. *On Paul: Essays on His Life, Work and Influence in the Early Church.* London: Clark, 2003.

————. 'Paul and Jerusalem'. In *On Paul,* 1-26. London: Clark, 2003.

————. *Paul: An Introduction to His Thought.* London: Chapman, 1994.

————. 'Paul: Councils and Controversies'. In M. Hengel and C. K. Barrett, *Conflicts and Challenges in Early Christianity,* 42-74. Harrisburg: Trinity, 1999.

————. 'Pauline Controversies in the Post-Pauline Period'. *NTS* 20 (1974) 229-45.

————. 'Paul: Missionary and Theologian'. In *On Paul,* 55-72. London: Clark, 2003.

————. 'Quomodo historia conscribenda sit'. *NTS* 28 (1982) 303-20.

———. 'Sectarian Diversity at Corinth'. In *Paul and the Corinthians,* M. Thrall FS, edited by T. J. Burke and J. K. Elliott, 287-302. Leiden: Brill, 2003.

———. 'Things Sacrificed to Idols'. In *Essays on Paul,* 40-59. London: SPCK, 1982.

———. 'The Third Gospel as a Preface to Acts? Some Reflections'. In *The Four Gospels,* F. Neirynck FS, edited by F. Van Segbroeck, 2.1451-66. Leuven: Leuven University, 1992.

Bartchy, S. S. 'Community of Goods in Acts: Idealization or Social Reality?' In *The Future of Early Christianity,* H. Koester FS, edited by B. A. Pearson et al., 309-18. Minneapolis: Fortress, 1991.

———. 'Divine Power, Community Formation, and Leadership in the Acts of the Apostles'. In *Community Formation in the Early Church and in the Church Today,* edited by R. N. Longenecker, 89-104. Peabody: Hendrickson, 2002.

———. *MALLON CHRĒSAI: First-Century Slavery and the Interpretation of 1 Corinthians 7.21.* SBLDS 11. Missoula: Scholars, 1973.

Barth, M., et al. *Paulus — Apostat oder Apostel?* Regensburg: Pustet, 1977.

Barton, S. C. '"All Things to All People": Paul and the Law in the Light of 1 Corinthians 9.19-23'. In *Paul and the Mosaic Law,* edited by J. D. G. Dunn, 271-85. Tübingen: Mohr Siebeck, 1996.

———. 'Paul's Sense of Place: An Anthropological Approach to Community Formation in Corinth'. *NTS* 32 (1986) 225-46.

Barton, S. C., and G. H. R. Horsley. 'A Hellenistic Cult Group and the New Testament Churches'. *JAC* 24 (1981) 7-41.

Bash, A. *Ambassadors for Christ: An Exploration of Ambassadorial Language in the New Testament.* WUNT 2.92. Tübingen: Mohr Siebeck, 1997.

Bassler, J. M. *Divine Impartiality: Paul and a Theological Axiom.* SBLDS 59. Chico: Scholars, 1982.

———. '*Skeuos:* A Modest Proposal for Illuminating Paul's Use of Metaphor in 1 Thessalonians 4:4'. In *The Social World of the First Christians,* W. A. Meeks FS, edited by L. M. White and O. L. Yarbrough, 53-66. Minneapolis: Fortress, 1995.

Bauckham, R. J. 'The Eyewitnesses and the Gospel Tradition'. *JSHJ* 1 (2003) 28-60.

———. 'For What Offence Was James Put to Death?' In *James the Just,* edited by B. Chilton and C. A. Evans, 199-232. Leiden: Brill, 1999.

———. *God Crucified: Monotheism and Christology in the New Testament.* Carlisle: Paternoster, 1998.

———. *Gospel Women: Studies of the Named Women in the Gospels.* Grand Rapids: Eerdmans, 2002.

———. 'James and Jesus'. In *The Brother of Jesus,* edited by B. Chilton and J. Neusner, 100-137. Louisville: Westminster John Knox, 2001.

———. 'James and the Gentiles (Acts 15.13-21)'. In *History, Literature and Society in the Book of Acts,* edited by B. Witherington, 154-84. Cambridge: Cambridge University, 1996.

———. 'James and the Jerusalem Church'. *BAFCS* 4.415-80.

———. 'James, Peter, and the Gentiles'. In *The Missions of James, Peter, and Paul,* edited by B. Chilton and C. Evans, 91-142. Leiden: Brill, 2005.

———. *James: Wisdom of James, Disciple of Jesus the Sage.* London: Routledge, 1999.

————. *Jesus and the Eyewitnesses: The Gospels as Eyewitness Testimony.* Grand Rapids: Eerdmans, 2006.

————. 'Jesus and the Jerusalem Community'. In *Jewish Believers in Jesus: The Early Centuries,* edited by O. Skarsaune and R. Hvalvik, 55-95. Peabody: Hendrickson, 2007.

————. *Jude and the Relatives of Jesus in the Early Church.* Edinburgh: Clark, 1990.

————. 'Kerygmatic Summaries in the Speeches of Acts'. In *History, Literature and Society in the Book of Acts,* edited by B. Witherington, 154-84. Cambridge: Cambridge University, 1996.

————. 'The Martyrdom of Peter in Early Christian Literature'. *ANRW* 2.26.1 (1992) 539-95.

————. 'The Parting of the Ways: What Happened and Why'. *ST* 47 (1993) 135-51.

————, ed. *The Book of Acts in Its Palestinian Setting* (= *BAFCS* 4). Grand Rapids: Eerdmans, 1995.

Bauer, W. *Orthodoxy and Heresy in Earliest Christianity.* 1934, 1964. ET Philadelphia: Fortress, 1971.

Baur, F. C. 'Die Christuspartei in der Korinthischen Gemeinde, der Gegensatz des petrinischen und paulinischen Christentums in der ältesten Kirche, der Apostel Petrus in Rom'. *Tübinger Zeitschrift für Theologie* 4 (1831) 61-206.

————. *The Church History of the First Three Centuries.* 1853. ET 2 vols. London: Williams and Norgate, 1878, 1879.

————. *Paul: The Apostle of Jesus Christ.* 1845. ET 2 vols. London: Williams and Norgate, 1873, 1875.

Beale, G. K. 'Peace and Mercy upon the Israel of God: The Old Testament Background of Galatians 6,16b'. *Biblica* 80 (1999) 204-33.

Beasley-Murray, G. R. *Baptism in the New Testament.* London: Macmillan, 1963.

Beatrice, P. F. 'Apollos of Alexandria and the Origins of the Jewish-Christian Baptist Encratism'. *ANRW* 2.26.2 (1995) 1232-75.

Beattie, G. *Women and Marriage in Paul and His Early Interpreters.* LNTS 296. London: Clark International, 2005.

Becker, E.-M. 'Autobiographisches bei Paulus'. In *Biographie und Persönlichkeit des Paulus,* edited by E.-M. Becker and P. Pilhofer, 67-87. Tübingen: Mohr Siebeck, 2005.

Becker, E.-M., and P. Pilhofer, eds. *Biographie und Persönlichkeit des Paulus.* WUNT 187. Tübingen: Mohr Siebeck, 2005.

Becker, J. 'Paul and His Churches'. In *Christian Beginnings,* edited by J. Becker, 132-210. Louisville: Westminster John Knox, 1993.

————. *Paul: Apostle to the Gentiles.* Louisville: John Knox, 1993.

————, ed. *Christian Beginnings: Word and Community from Jesus to Post-apostolic Times.* 1987. Louisville: Westminster John Knox, 1993.

Beckheuer, B. *Paulus und Jerusalem. Kollekte und Mission im theologischen Denken des Heidenapostels.* Frankfurt: Lang, 1997.

Bell, R. H. *Provoked to Jealousy: The Origin and Purpose of the Jealousy Motif in Romans 9–11.* WUNT 2.63. Tübingen: Mohr Siebeck, 1994.

Bellinger, W. H., and W. R. Farmer, eds. *Jesus and the Suffering Servant: Isaiah 53 and Christian Origins.* Harrisburg: Trinity, 1998.

Ben-Chorin, S. *Paulus. Der Völkerapostel in jüdischer Sicht.* Munich: DTV, 1970.

Bendlin, A. 'Gemeinschaft, Öffentlichkeit und Identität'. In *Religiöse Vereine in der römischen Antike,* edited by U. Egelhaaf-Gaiser and A. Schäfer, 9-40. Tübingen: Mohr Siebeck, 2002.

Ben-Dov, M. *Historical Atlas of Jerusalem.* 2000; New York: Continuum, 2002.

Benko, S. 'The Edict of Claudius of A.D. 49'. *TZ* 25 (1969) 406-18.

———. 'Pagan Criticism of Christianity During the First Two Centuries'. *ANRW* 2.23.2 (1980) 1055-1118.

Berger, K. 'Almosen für Israel. Zum historischen Kontext der paulinischen Kollekte'. *NTS* 23 (1976-77) 180-204.

———. *Theologiegeschichte des Urchristentums. Theologie des Neuen Testaments.* Tübingen: Francke, 1994.

———. 'Volksversammlung und Gemeinde Gottes. Zu den Anfängen der christlichen Verwendung von "Ekklesia"'. *ZTK* 73 (1976) 167-207.

Bernheim, P.-A. *James, Brother of Jesus.* London: SCM, 1997.

Bertone, J. A. *The Law of the Spirit: Experience of the Spirit and Displacement of the Law in Romans 8:1-16.* New York: Lang, 2005.

Best, E. *Paul and His Converts.* Edinburgh: Clark, 1988.

Betz, H. D. 'Paul's Ideas about the Origins of Christianity'. In *Paulinische Studien,* 272-88. Tübingen: Mohr Siebeck.

———. 'Spirit, Freedom, and Law. Paul's Message to the Galatian Churches'. *SEÅ* 39 (1974) 145-60.

Beyschlag, K. *Simon Magus und die christliche Gnosis.* WUNT 16. Tübingen: Mohr Siebeck, 1974.

Bickerman, E. J. *The Jews in the Greek Age.* Cambridge: Harvard University, 1988.

———. 'The Name of Christians'. *HTR* 42 (1949) 109-24.

Bieringer, R., ed. *The Corinthian Correspondence.* BETL 125. Leuven: Leuven University, 1996.

Blue, B. 'Acts and the House Church'. *BAFCS* 2.119-222.

Blumenfeld, B. *The Political Paul: Justice, Democracy and Kingship in a Hellenistic Framework.* JSNTS 210. Sheffield: Sheffield Academic, 2001.

Bockmuehl, M. 'Antioch and James the Just'. In *James the Just,* edited by B. Chilton and C. A. Evans, 155-98. Leiden: Brill, 1999.

———. *Jewish Law in Gentile Churches.* Edinburgh: Clark, 2000.

———. '1 Thessalonians 2:14-16 and the Church in Jerusalem'. *TynB* 52 (2001) 1-31.

Bockmuehl, M., and D. A. Hagner, eds. *The Written Gospel,* G. N. Stanton FS. Cambridge: Cambridge University, 2005.

Bond, H. K. *Caiaphas: Friend of Rome and Judge of Jesus?* Louisville: Westminster John Knox, 2004.

———. *Pontius Pilate in History and Interpretation.* SNTSMS 100. Cambridge: Cambridge University, 1998.

Bookidis, N. 'Religion in Corinth: 146 BCE to 100 CE'. In *Urban Religion in Roman Cor-*

inth, edited by D. N. Schowalter and J. Friesen, 141-64. Cambridge: Harvard University, 2005.

———. 'Ritual Dining at Corinth'. In *Greek Sanctuaries: New Approaches,* edited by N. Marinatos and R. Hogg, 45-61. London: Routledge, 1993.

Borgen, P. 'Catalogues of Vices, the Apostolic Decree, and the Jerusalem Meeting'. In *Early Christianity,* 233-51.

———. *Early Christianity and Hellenistic Judaism.* Edinburgh: Clark, 1996.

———. 'Militant and Peaceful Proselytism and Christian Mission'. In *Early Christianity,* 45-69.

———. '"Yes", "No", "How Far?"': The Participation of Jews and Christians in Pagan Cults'. In *Paul in His Hellenistic Context,* edited by T. Engberg-Pedersen, 30-59. Minneapolis: Fortress, 1995.

Bormann, L. 'Autobiographische Fiktionalität bei Paulus'. In *Biographie und Persönlichkeit des Paulus,* edited by E.-M. Becker and P. Pilhofer, 106-24. Tübingen: Mohr Siebeck, 2005.

———. *Philippi. Stadt und Christengemeinde zur Zeit des Paulus.* NovTSupp 78. Leiden: Brill, 1995.

Bornkamm, G. 'The Letter to the Romans as Paul's Last Will and Testament'. In *Romans Debate,* edited by K. P. Donfried, 16-28. Peabody: Hendrickson, 1991.

———. *Paul.* London: Hodder and Stoughton, 1969.

———. 'Die Vorgeschichte des sogenannten Zweiten Korintherbriefes'. In *Gesammelte Aufsätze.* Vol. 4: *Geschichte und Glaube,* 162-94. Munich: Kaiser, 1971.

Borse, U. *Der Standort des Galaterbriefes.* BBB 41. Cologne/Bern, 1972.

Botermann, H. *Das Judenedikt des Kaisers Claudius. Römischer Staat und Christiani im 1. Jahrhundert.* Stuttgart: Steiner, 1996.

Botha, P. J. J. 'The Verbal Art of the Pauline Letters: Rhetoric, Performance and Presence'. In *Rhetoric and the New Testament,* edited by S. E. Porter and T. H. Olbricht, 409-28. Sheffield: Sheffield Academic, 1993.

Böttrich, C. '"Ihr seid der Tempel Gottes". Tempelmetaphorik und Gemeinde bei Paulus'. In *Gemeinde ohne Tempel / Community without Temple,* edited by B. Ego et al., 411-26. Tübingen: Mohr Siebeck, 1999.

Bousset, W. *Kyrios Christos.* 1913, 1921. ET Nashville: Abingdon, 1970.

Bowker, J. '"Merkabah" Visions and the Visions of Paul'. *JSS* 16 (1971) 157-73.

———. 'Speeches in Acts: A Study in Proem and Yelammadenu Form'. *NTS* 14 (1967-68) 96-111.

Bowman, J. *Samaritan Documents Relating to Their History, Religion and Life.* Pittsburgh: Pickwick, 1976.

Boyarin, D. *A Radical Jew: Paul and the Politics of Identity.* Berkeley: University of California, 1994.

Bradshaw, P. F. *Daily Prayer in the Early Church.* London: SPCK, 1981.

———. *The Search for the Origins of Christian Worship: Sources and Methods for the Study of Early Liturgy.* Oxford: Oxford University, 1992.

Brändle, R., and E. Stegemann. 'The Formation of the First "Christian Congregations" in Rome in the Context of the Jewish Congregations'. In *Judaism and Christianity in*

First-Century Rome, edited by K. P. Donfried and P. Richardson, 117-27. Grand Rapids: Eerdmans, 1998.

Brandon, S. G. F. *The Fall of Jerusalem and the Christian Church.* London: SPCK, 1951.

Brawley, R. L. *Luke-Acts and the Jews.* SBLMS 33. Atlanta: Scholars, 1987.

Brehm, H. A. 'The Meaning of *Hellēnistēs* in Acts in Light of a Diachronic Analysis of *helēnizein'.* In *Discourse Analysis and Other Topics in Biblical Greek,* edited by S. E. Porter and D. A. Carson, 180-99. Sheffield: Sheffield Academic, 1995.

―――. 'Vindicating the Rejected One: Stephen's Speech as a Critique of the Jewish Leaders'. In *Early Christian Interpretation of the Scriptures of Israel,* edited by C. A. Evans and J. A. Sanders, 266-99. Sheffield: Sheffield Academic, 1997.

Breytenbach, C. *Paulus und Barnabas in der Provinz Galatien.* AGAJU 38. Leiden: Brill, 1996.

―――. 'Probable Reasons for Paul's Unfruitful Missionary Attempts in Asia Minor (a Note on Acts 16:6-7)'. In *Die Apostelgeschichte und die hellenistische Geschichtsschreibung,* E. Plümacher FS, edited by C. Breytenbach and J. Schröter, 157-69. Leiden: Brill, 2004.

Brooten, B. J. 'Iael prostatēs in the Jewish Donative Inscription from Aphrodisias'. In *The Future of Early Christianity,* H. Koester FS, edited by B. A. Pearson et al., 149-62. Minneapolis: Fortress, 1991.

―――. *Women Leaders in the Ancient Synagogue.* BJS 36. Chico: Scholars, 1982.

Brosend, W. F. 'The Means of Absent Ends'. In *History, Literature and Society in the Book of Acts,* edited by B. Witherington, 348-62. Cambridge: Cambridge University, 1996.

Brown, R. E. 'Further Reflections on the Origins of the Church of Rome'. In *Studies in Paul and John,* J. L. Martyn FS, edited by R. T. Fortna and B. R. Gaventa, 98-115. Nashville: Abingdon, 1990.

―――. *An Introduction to the New Testament.* New York: Doubleday, 1997.

―――. *The Semitic Background of the Term "Mystery" in the New Testament.* FBBS 21. Philadelphia: Fortress, 1968.

Brown, R. E., K. P. Donfried, et al., eds. *Peter in the New Testament.* London: Chapman, 1974.

Brown, R. E., and J. P. Meier. *Antioch and Rome: New Testament Cradles of Catholic Christianity.* London: Chapman, 1983.

Brox, N. *Falsche Verfasserangaben. Zur Erklärung der frühchristlichen Pseudepigrapha.* SBS 79. Stuttgart: Katholisches Bibelwerk, 1975.

Bruce, F. F. *New Testament History.* London: Marshall, Morgan and Scott, 1969.

―――. *Paul: Apostle of the Free Spirit.* Exeter: Paternoster, 1977.

―――. 'The Speeches in Acts — Thirty Years After'. In *Reconciliation and Hope,* L. L. Morris FS, edited by R. J. Banks, 53-68. Exeter: Paternoster, 1974.

Buck, C., and G. Taylor. *Saint Paul: A Study in the Development of His Thought.* New York: Scribner, 1969.

Buckland, W. W. *The Roman Law of Slavery.* Cambridge: Cambridge University, 1908; reprinted, 1970.

Bujard, W. *Stilanalystische Untersuchungen zum Kolosserbrief als Beitrag zur Methodik von Sprachvergleichen.* SUNT 11. Göttingen: Vandenhoeck und Ruprecht, 1975.

Bultmann, R. 'Paul' (1930). In *Existence and Faith,* 130-72. London: Collins, 1964.

————. *The Theology of the New Testament.* 2 vols. ET London: SCM, 1952, 1955.

Bunine, A. 'La date de la première visite de Paul à Jérusalem'. *RB* 113 (2006) 436-56, 601-22.

Burer, M. H., and D. B. Wallace. 'Was Junia Really an Apostle? A Re-examination of Rom 16.7'. *NTS* 47 (2001) 76-91.

Burfeind, C. 'Paulus muss nach Rom. Zur politischen Dimension der Apostelgeschichte'. *NTS* 46 (2000) 75-91.

Burkert, W. *Ancient Mystery Cults.* Cambridge: Harvard University, 1987.

Burkitt, F. C. *Christian Beginnings.* London: University of London, 1924.

Byrskog, S. *Story as History — History as Story.* WUNT 123. Tübingen: Mohr Siebeck, 2000.

Cadbury, H. J. 'Commentary on the Preface of Luke'. *Beginnings* 2.489-510.

————. 'The Greek and Jewish Traditions of Writing History'. *Beginnings* 2.7-29.

————. *The Making of Luke-Acts.* New York: Macmillan, 1927.

————. 'The Speeches in Acts'. *Beginnings* 5.402-27.

————. 'The Tradition'. *Beginnings* 2.209-64.

Callan, T. 'Pauline Midrash: The Exegetical Background of Gal. 3.19b'. *JBL* 99 (1980) 549-67.

Calvert-Koyzis, N. *Paul, Monotheism and the People of God: The Significance of Abraham Traditions for Early Judaism and Christianity.* JSNTS 273. London: Clark International, 2004.

Cameron, R., and M. P. Miller. *Redescribing Christian Origins.* Atlanta: SBL, 2004.

Campbell, D. A. 'An Anchor for Pauline Chronology: Paul's Flight from "the Ethnarch of King Aretas" (2 Corinthians 11:32-33)'. *JBL* 121 (2002) 279-302.

————. 'Paul in Pamphylia (Acts 13.13-14a; 14.24b-26): A Critical Note'. *NTS* 46 (2000) 595-602.

Campbell, R. A. *The Elders: Seniority within Earliest Christianity.* Edinburgh: Clark, 1994.

Campbell, W. S. '"All God's Beloved in Rome!" Jewish Roots and Christian Identity'. In *Celebrating Romans: Template for Pauline Theology,* R. Jewett FS, edited by S. E. McGinn, 67-82. Grand Rapids: Eerdmans, 2004.

————. *Paul and the Creation of Christian Identity.* LNTS 322. London: Clark, 2006.

————. 'Romans III as a Key to the Structure and Thought of the Letter'. *NovT* 23 (1981) 22-40.

————. 'The Rule of Faith in Romans 12:1–15:13'. In *Pauline Theology.* Vol. 3: *Romans,* edited by D. M. Hay and E. E. Johnson, 259-86. Minneapolis: Fortress, 1995.

Cancik, H. 'The History of Culture, Religion, and Institutions in Ancient Historiography: Philological Observations concerning Luke's History'. *JBL* 116 (1997) 673-95.

Capes, D. B. *Old Testament Yahweh Texts in Paul's Christology.* WUNT 2.47. Tübingen: Mohr Siebeck, 1992.

————. 'YHWH Texts and Monotheism in Paul's Christology'. In *Early Jewish and Christian Monotheism,* edited by L. T. Stuckenbruck and W. E. S. North, 120-37. London: Clark International, 2004.

Cappelletti, S. *The Jewish Community of Rome from the Second Century* BCE *to the Third Century* CE. Leiden: Brill, 2006.

Capper, B. 'Community of Goods in the Early Jerusalem Church'. *ANRW* 2.26.2 (1995) 1730-74.

———. 'The Palestinian Cultural Context of Earliest Christian Community of Goods'. *BAFCS* 4.323-56.

Caragounis, C. C. *The Ephesian Mysterion: Meaning and Content.* Lund: Gleerup, 1977.

Carleton Paget, J. 'Jewish Christianity'. *CHJ* 3.731-75.

———. 'Jewish Proselytism at the Time of Christian Origins: Chimera or Reality?' *JSNT* 62 (1996) 65-103.

Carrington, P. *The Primitive Christian Catechism.* Cambridge: Cambridge University, 1940.

Carson, D. A., P. T. O'Brien, and M. A. Seifrid, eds. *Justification and Variegated Nomism: A Fresh Appraisal of Paul and Second Temple Judaism.* Vol. 1: *The Complexities of Second Temple Judaism.* WUNT 2.140. Tübingen: Mohr Siebeck, 2001.

———, eds. *Justification and Variegated Nomism: A Fresh Appraisal of Paul and Second Temple Judaism.* Vol. 2: *The Paradoxes of Paul.* WUNT 2.181. Tübingen: Mohr Siebeck, 2004.

Carter, T. L. 'The Irony of Romans 13'. *NovT* 46 (2004) 209-28.

Case, S. J. *The Evolution of Early Christianity.* Chicago: University of Chicago, 1914.

Casey, P. M. *From Jewish Prophet to Gentile God: The Origin and Development of New Testament Christology.* Cambridge: Clarke, 1991.

Cassidy, R. J. *Paul in Chains: Roman Imprisonment and the Letters of St. Paul.* New York: Crossroad, 2001.

———. *Society and Politics in the Acts of the Apostles.* Maryknoll: Orbis, 1988.

Casson, L. *Travel in the Ancient World.* London: Allen and Unwin, 1974.

Catchpole, D. R. 'Paul, James and the Apostolic Decree'. *NTS* 23 (1976-77) 428-44.

Chae, D. J.-S. *Paul as Apostle to the Gentiles: His Apostolic Self-Awareness and Its Influence on the Soteriological Argument in Romans.* Carlisle: Paternoster, 1997.

Chantal, R. *Paul de Tarse en Méditerranée. Recherches autour de la navigation dans l'antiquité (Ac 27–28,16).* LD 206. Paris: Cerf, 2006.

Chester, A. *Messiah and Exaltation: Jewish Messianic and Visionary Traditions and New Testament Christology.* WUNT 207. Tübingen: Mohr Siebeck, 2007.

Chester, S. J. *Conversion at Corinth: Perspectives on Conversion in Paul's Theology and the Corinthian Church.* London: Clark, 2003.

Chibici-Revneanu, N. 'Ein himmlischer Stehplatz. Die Haltung Jesu in der Stephanusvision (Apg 7.55-56) und ihre Bedeutung'. *NTS* 53 (2007) 459-88.

Chilton, B., and C. A. Evans, eds. *James the Just and Christian Origins.* Leiden: Brill, 1999.

———, eds. *The Missions of James, Peter, and Paul: Tensions in Early Christianity.* NovTSupp 115. Leiden: Brill, 2005.

Chow, J. K. *Patronage and Power: A Study of Social Networks in Corinth.* JSNTS 75. Sheffield: JSOT, 1992.

Clark, A. C. 'The Role of the Apostles'. In *Witness to the Gospel: The Theology of Acts,* edited by I. H. Marshall and D. Peterson, 169-90. Grand Rapids: Eerdmans, 1998.

Clarke, A. D. 'Rome and Italy'. *BAFCS* 2.455-81.

———. *Secular and Christian Leadership in Corinth: A Socio-Historical and Exegetical Study of 1 Corinthians 1–6*. Leiden: Brill, 1993.

———. *Serve the Community of the Church*. Grand Rapids: Eerdmans, 2000.

Clauss, M. *Kaiser und Gott. Herrscherkult im römischen Reich*. Stuttgart: Teubner, 1999.

Claussen, C. 'Meeting, Community, Synagogue — Different Frameworks of Ancient Jewish Congregations'. In *The Ancient Synagogue from Its Origins until 200 C.E.*, edited by B. Olsson and M. Zetterholm, 144-67. Stockholm: Almqvist and Wiksell, 2003.

———. *Versammlung, Gemeinde, Synagoge. Das hellenistisch-jüdisch Umfeld der frühchristlichen Gemeinden*. Göttingen: Vandenhoeck und Ruprecht, 2002.

Cohen, S. J. D. 'Adolph Harnack's "The Mission and Expansion of Judaism": Christianity Succeeds Where Judaism Fails'. In *The Future of Early Christianity,* H. Koester FS, edited by B. A. Pearson et al., 163-69. Minneapolis: Fortress, 1991.

———. *The Beginnings of Jewishness: Boundaries, Varieties, Uncertainties*. Berkeley: University of California, 1999.

———. 'Crossing the Boundary and Becoming a Jew' (1989). In *Beginnings of Jewishness,* 140-74.

Collins, J. J. *Between Athens and Jerusalem: Jewish Identity in the Hellenistic Diaspora*. New York: Crossroad, 1983.

———. 'Cult and Culture: The Limits of Hellenization in Judaea'. In *Hellenism in the Land of Israel,* edited by J. J. Collins and G. E. Sterling, 38-61. Notre Dame: University of Notre Dame, 2001.

———. *Diakonia: Re-interpreting the Ancient Sources*. Oxford: Oxford University, 1990.

———. 'A Symbol of Otherness: Circumcision and Salvation in the First Century'. In *'To See Ourselves as Others See Us': Christians, Jews, 'Others' in Late Antiquity,* edited by J. Neusner and E. S. Frerichs, 163-86. Chico: Scholars, 1985.

Collins, R. F. '"I Command That This Letter Be Read": Writing as a Manner of Speaking'. In *The Thessalonian Debate,* edited by K. P. Donfried and J. Beutler, 319-39. Grand Rapids: Eerdmans, 2000.

Colpe, C. 'The Oldest Jewish-Christian Community'. In *Christian Beginnings,* edited by J. Becker, 75-102. Louisville: Westminster John Knox, 1993.

———. *Die religionsgeschichtliche Schule. Darstellung und Kritik ihres Bildes vom gnostischen Erlösermythus*. Göttingen: Vandenhoeck und Ruprecht. 1961.

Conzelmann, H. *History of Primitive Christianity*. Nashville: Abingdon, 1973.

———. *The Theology of St. Luke*. 1953, 1957. ET London: Faber and Faber, 1961.

Cook, J. G. 'Pagan Philosophers and 1 Thessalonians'. *NTS* 52 (2006) 514-32.

Coppens, J. '"Mystery" in the Theology of Saint Paul and Its Parallels at Qumran'. In *Paul and the Dead Sea Scrolls,* edited by J. Murphy-O'Connor and J. H. Charlesworth, 132-56. London: Chapman, 1968.

Cosgrove, C. H. *The Cross and the Spirit: A Study in the Argument and Theology of Galatians*. Macon: Mercer University, 1988.

———. 'Did Paul Value Ethnicity?' *CBQ* 68 (2006) 268-90.

———. 'A Woman's Unbound Hair in the Greco-Roman World'. *JBL* 124 (2005) 675-92.

Cotter, W. 'The Collegia and Roman Law: State Restrictions on Voluntary Associations'.

In *Voluntary Associations in the Graeco-Roman World,* edited by J. S. Kloppenborg and S. G. Wilson, 74-89. London: Routledge, 1996.

———. 'Our *Politeuma* Is in Heaven: The Meaning of Philippians 3.17-21'. In *Origins and Method: Towards a New Understanding of Judaism and Christianity,* J. C. Hurd FS, edited by B. H. McLean, 92-104. Sheffield: JSOT, 1993.

Cox, R. *By the Same Word: Creation and Salvation in Hellenistic Judaism and Early Christianity.* BZNW 145. Berlin: de Gruyter, 2007.

Cranford, M. 'Abraham in Romans 4: The Father of All Who Believe'. *NTS* 41 (1995) 71-88.

Crossan, J. D., and J. L. Reed. *In Search of Paul: How Jesus' Apostle Opposed Rome's Empire with God's Kingdom.* San Francisco: HarperSanFrancisco, 2004.

Crossley, J. G. *Why Christianity Happened: A Sociohistorical Account of Christian Origins (26-50 CE).* Louisville: Westminster John Knox, 2006.

Cullmann, O. 'Le caractère eschatologique du devoir missionnaire et de la conscience apostolique de S. Paul. Etude sur le *katechon (-on)* de II Thess. 2.6-7'. *RHPR* 16 (1936) 210-45.

———. *Christ and Time.* London: SCM, 1962.

———. *The Earliest Christian Confessions.* London: Lutterworth, 1949.

———. *Peter: Disciple, Apostle, Martyr.* London: SCM, 1962.

———. 'Samaria and the Origins of the Christian Mission'. In *The Early Church,* 183-92. London: SCM, 1956.

Cummins, S. A. *Paul and the Crucified Christ in Antioch: Maccabean Martyrdom and Galatians 1 and 2.* SNTSMS 114. Cambridge: Cambridge University, 2001.

Dabourne, W. *Purpose and Cause in Pauline Exegesis.* SNTSMS 104. Cambridge: Cambridge University, 1999.

Dahl, N. A. 'The Crucified Messiah'. In *Jesus the Christ: The Historical Origins of Christological Doctrine,* 27-47. Minneapolis: Fortress, 1991.

———. 'The Doctrine of Justification: Its Social Function and Implications' (1964). In *Studies in Paul,* 95-120.

———. 'Euodia and Syntyche and Paul's Letter to the Philippians'. In *The Social World of the First Christians,* W. A. Meeks FS, edited by L. M. White and O. L. Yarbrough, 3-15. Minneapolis: Fortress, 1995.

———. 'The Messiahship of Jesus in Paul'. In *Jesus the Christ: The Historical Origins of Christological Doctrine,* ed. D. H. Juel, 15-25. Minneapolis, Fortress. 1991.

———. 'The Missionary Theology in the Epistle to the Romans'. In *Studies in Paul,* 70-94.

———. 'Paul and the Church at Corinth according to 1 Corinthians 1–4'. In *Christian History and Interpretation,* J. Knox FS, edited by W. R. Farmer, et al., 313-35. Cambridge: Cambridge University, 1967.

———. 'Paul's Letter to the Galatians: Epistolary Genre, Content and Structure'. In *The Galatians Debate,* edited by M. Nanos, 117-42. Peabody: Hendrickson, 2002.

———. *Studies in Paul: Theology for the Early Christian Mission.* Minneapolis: Augsburg, 1977.

Das, A. A. 'Another Look at *ean mē* in Galatians 2:16'. *JBL* 119 (2000) 529-39.

———. *Paul and the Jews.* Peabody: Hendrickson, 2003.

————. *Solving the Romans Debate.* Minneapolis: Fortress, 2007.

Davids, P. H. 'James and Peter: The Literary Evidence'. In *The Missions of James, Peter, and Paul,* edited by B. Chilton and C. Evans, 29-52. Leiden: Brill, 2005.

————. 'The Test of Wealth'. In *The Missions of James, Peter, and Paul,* edited by B. Chilton and C. Evans, 355-84. Leiden: Brill, 2005.

————. 'Why Do We Suffer? Suffering in James and Paul'. In *The Missions of James, Peter, and Paul,* edited by B. Chilton and C. Evans, 435-66. Leiden: Brill, 2005.

Davies, J. G. *He Ascended into Heaven.* Bampton Lectures 1958. London: Lutterworth, 1958.

Davies, W. D. *Paul and Rabbinic Judaism.* London: SPCK, 1948, 1981, 4th ed.

————. 'Paul and the People of Israel'. *NTS* 24 (1977-78) 4-39.

————. 'Paul: From the Jewish Point of View'. *CHJ* 3.678-730.

Davis, J. A. *Wisdom and Spirit: An Investigation of 1 Corinthians 1.18–3.20 against the Background of Jewish Sapiential Traditions in the Greco-Roman Period.* Lanham: University Press of America, 1984.

de Boer, M. *The Defeat of Death: Apocalyptic Eschatology in 1 Corinthians 15 and Romans 5.* Sheffield: JSOT, 1988.

Deichgräber, R. *Gotteshymnus und Christushymnus in der frühen Christenheit.* Göttingen: Vandenhoeck und Ruprecht, 1967.

Deissmann, A. *Light from the Ancient East.* London: Hodder and Stoughton, 1927.

————. *Paul: A Study in Social and Religious History.* New York: Harper Torchbook, 1927.

de Jonge, M. *Christology in Context: The Earliest Christian Response to Jesus.* Philadelphia: Westminster, 1988.

Delling, G. *Worship in the New Testament.* 1952. London: Darton, Longman and Todd, 1962.

Deutschmann, A. *Synagoge und Gemeindebildung. Christliche Gemeinde und Israel am Beispiel von Apg 13,42-52.* BU 30. Regensburg: Pustet, 2001.

Dexinger, F. 'Limits of Tolerance in Judaism: The Samaritan Example'. *JCSD* 2.88-114.

Dibelius, M. *Paul.* Edited and completed by W. G. Kümmel. London: Longmans, 1953.

————. *Studies in the Acts of the Apostles.* London: SCM, 1956.

Dickson, J. P. *Mission-Commitment in Ancient Judaism and in the Pauline Communities.* WUNT 2.159. Tübingen: Mohr Siebeck, 2003.

Dietzfelbinger, C. *Die Berufung des Paulus als Ursprung seiner Theologie.* WMANT 58. Neukirchen-Vluyn: Neukirchener, 1985.

Dill, S. *Roman Society from Nero to Marcus Aurelius.* London: Macmillan, 1904.

Dittmann-Schöne, I. 'Götterverehrung bei den Berufsvereinen im kaiserzeitlichen Kleinasien'. In *Religiöse Vereine in der römischen Antike,* edited by U. Egelhaaf-Gaiser and A. Schäfer, 81-96. Tübingen: Mohr Siebeck, 2002.

Dodd, B. *Paul's Paradigmatic "I": Personal Example as Literary Strategy.* JSNTS 177. Sheffield: Sheffield Academic, 1999.

Dodd, C. H. *The Apostolic Preaching and Its Developments.* London: Hodder and Stoughton, 1936, 1944.

————. *The Bible and the Greeks.* London: Hodder and Stoughton, 1935.

———. 'The Framework of the Gospel Narrative'. In *New Testament Studies,* 1-11. Manchester: Manchester University, 1953.

———. 'The Mind of Paul'. In *New Testament Studies,* 67-128. Manchester: Manchester University, 1953.

Donaldson, T. L. 'Jewish Christianity and the Sonderweg Reading of Paul'. *JSNT* forthcoming.

———. *Paul and the Gentiles: Remapping the Apostle's Convictional World.* Minneapolis: Fortress, 1997.

———. 'Zealot and Convert: The Origin of Paul's Christ-Torah Antithesis'. *CBQ* 51 (1989) 655-82.

Donfried, K. P. 'The Cults of Thessalonica and the Thessalonian Correspondence'. *NTS* 31 (1985) 336-56.

———. 'The Epistolary and Rhetorical Context of 1 Thessalonians 2:1-12'. In *The Thessalonians Debate,* edited by K. P. Donfried and J. Beutler, 31-60. Grand Rapids: Eerdmans, 2000.

———. *Paul, Thessalonica and Early Christianity.* London: Clark. 2002.

———. '2 Thessalonians and the Church of Thessalonica'. In *Paul, Thessalonica,* 49-67.

———. 'Was Timothy in Athens? Some Exegetical Reflections on 1 Thess. 3.1-3'. In *Paul, Thessalonica,* 209-19.

———, ed. *The Romans Debate.* Peabody: Hendrickson, 1991.

Donfried, K. P., and J. Beutler, eds. *The Thessalonians Debate: Methodological Discord or Methodological Synthesis?* Grand Rapids: Eerdmans, 2000.

Donfried, K. P., and P. Richardson, eds. *Judaism and Christianity in First-Century Rome.* Grand Rapids: Eerdmans, 1998.

Donne, B. *Christ Ascended: A Study in the Significance of the Ascension of Jesus Christ in the New Testament.* Exeter: Paternoster, 1983.

Doty, W. G. *Letters in Primitive Christianity.* Philadelphia: Fortress, 1973.

Downing, F. G. *The Church and Jesus: A Study in History, Philosophy and History.* London: SCM, 1968.

———. *Cynics, Paul and the Pauline Churches.* London: Routledge, 1998.

Downs, D. J. 'Paul's Collection and the Book of Acts Revisited'. *NTS* 52 (2006) 50-70.

Dschulnigg, P. *Petrus im Neuen Testament.* Stuttgart: Katholisches Bibelwerk, 1996.

Duff, P. B. 'Metaphor, Motif, and Meaning: The Rhetorical Strategy behind the Image "Led in Triumph" in 2 Corinthians 2:14'. *CBQ* 53 (1991) 79-92.

Duncan, G. S. 'Important Hypotheses Reconsidered VI: Were Paul's Imprisonment Epistles Written from Ephesus?' *ExpT* 67 (1955-56) 163-66.

———. 'Paul's Ministry in Asia — the Last Phase'. *NTS* 3 (1956-57) 211-18.

———. *St. Paul's Ephesian Ministry.* London: Hodder and Stoughton, 1929.

Dunn, J. D. G. 'Altering the Default Setting: Re-envisaging the Early Transmission of the Jesus Tradition'. *NTS* 49 (2003) 139-75.

———. 'The Ascension of Jesus: A Test Case for Hermeneutics'. In *Auferstehung — Resurrection,* edited by F. Avemarie and H. Lichtenberger, 301-22. Tübingen: Mohr Siebeck, 2001.

———. *Baptism in the Holy Spirit.* London: SCM, 1970.

———. '"The Body of Christ" in Paul'. In *Worship, Theology and Ministry in the Early*

1200

Church, R. P. Martin FS, edited by M. J. Wilkins and T. Paige, 146-62. Sheffield: JSOT, 1992.

———. 'The Book of Acts as Salvation History'. In *Heil und Geschichte. Die Geschichtsbezogenheit des Heils und das Problem der Heilsgeschichte in der biblischen Tradition und in der theologischen Deutung,* edited by J. Frey, H. Lichtenberger and S. Krauter. Tübingen: Mohr Siebeck, 2009.

———. 'Boundary Markers in Early Christianity'. In *Gruppenreligionen im römischen Reich,* edited by J. Rüpke, 49-68. Tübingen: Mohr Siebeck, 2007.

———. *Christology in the Making: A New Testament Inquiry into the Origins of the Doctrine of the Incarnation.* London: SCM/Grand Rapids: Eerdmans, 1980, 1989 (1996), 2nd ed.

———. *1 Corinthians.* Sheffield: Sheffield Academic, 1995.

———. 'Did Paul Have a Covenant Theology?' In *The New Perspective on Paul,* ch. 20.

———. 'Echoes of Intra-Jewish Polemic in Paul's Letter to the Galatians'. *JBL* 112 (1993) 459-77.

———. '4QMMT and Galatians'. *NTS* 43 (1997) 147-53.

———. 'The Household Rules in the New Testament'. In *The Family in Theological Perspective,* edited by S. C. Barton, 43-63. Edinburgh: Clark, 1996.

———. '"How Are the Dead Raised? With What Body Do They Come?" Reflections on 1 Corinthians 15'. *Southwestern Journal of Theology* 45 (2002-3) 4-18.

———. 'How New Was Paul's Gospel? The Problem of Continuity and Discontinuity'. In *Gospel in Paul,* R. N. Longenecker FS, edited by L. A. Jervis and P. Richardson, 367-88. Sheffield: Sheffield Academic, 1994.

———. 'Jesus and Ritual Purity: A Study of the Tradition History of Mark 7.15'. In *Jesus, Paul and the Law,* 89-107.

———. *Jesus and the Spirit: A Study of the Religious and Charismatic Experience of Jesus and the First Christians.* London: SCM, 1975.

———. *Jesus, Paul and the Law: Studies in Mark and Galatians.* London: SPCK, 1990.

———. *Jesus Remembered.* Grand Rapids: Eerdmans, 2003.

———. 'The Jew Paul and His Meaning for Israel'. In *Paulinische Christologie. Exegetische Beiträge,* H. Hübner FS, edited by U. Schnelle and T. Söding, 32-46. Göttingen: Vandenhoeck und Ruprecht, 2000.

———. 'KYRIOS in Acts'. In *Jesus Christus als die Mitte der Schrift,* O. Hofius FS, edited by C. Landmesser et al., 363-78. Berlin: de Gruyter, 1997.

———. 'Lightfoot in Retrospect'. In *The Lightfoot Centenary Lectures. To Commemorate the Life and Work of Bishop J. B. Lightfoot (1828-89)* (= *Durham University Journal* 94 [1992]), 71-94.

———. '"A Light to the Gentiles": The Significance of the Damascus Road Christophany for Paul'. In *The Glory of Christ in the New Testament: Studies in Christology,* G. B. Caird FS, edited by L. D. Hurst and N. T. Wright, 251-66. Oxford: Clarendon, 1987.

———. 'Mark 2.1–3.6: A Bridge between Jesus and Paul on the Question of the Law'. *NTS* 30 (1984) 395-415.

———. 'Matthew's Awareness of Markan Redaction'. In *The Four Gospels,* F. Neirynck FS, edited by F. Van Segbroeck, 1349-59. Leuven: Leuven University, 1992.

———. '"Neither Circumcision Nor Uncircumcision, but . . ."'. In *The New Perspective on Paul,* ch. 13.

———. *The New Perspective on Paul.* WUNT 185. Tübingen: Mohr Siebeck, 2005; revised, Grand Rapids: Eerdmans, 2007.

———. 'Once More — Gal. 1.18: *historēsai Kēphan*'. *ZNW* 76 (1985) 138-39.

———. 'On History, Memory and Eyewitnesses: In Response to Bengt Holmberg and Samuel Byrskog'. *JSNT* 26 (2004) 473-87.

———. *The Partings of the Way between Christianity and Judaism and Their Significance for the Character of Christianity.* London: SCM. 1991, 2006, 2nd ed.

———. 'Paul: Apostate or Apostle of Israel?' *ZNW* 89 (1998) 256-71.

———. 'Paul's Conversion — a Light to Twentieth-Century Disputes'. In *Evangelium — Schriftauslegung — Kirche,* P. Stuhlmacher FS, edited by J. Ådna et al., 77-93. Göttingen: Vandenhoeck und Ruprecht, 1997.

———. 'Paul's Letter to Rome: Reason and Rationale'. In *Logos — Logik — Lyrik. Engagierte exegetische Studien zum biblischen Reden Gottes,* K. Haacker FS, edited by V. A. Lehnert and U. Rüsen-Weinhold, 185-200. Leipzig: Evangelische Verlagsanstalt, 2007.

———. 'Q1 as Oral Tradition'. In *The Written Gospel,* G. N. Stanton FS, edited by M. Bockmuehl and D. A. Hagner, 45-69. Cambridge: Cambridge University, 2005.

———. 'The Question of Antisemitism in the New Testament'. In *Jews and Christians: The Parting of the Ways AD 70 to 135,* edited by J. D. G. Dunn, 177-212. Tübingen: Mohr Siebeck, 1992.

———. 'The Relationship between Paul and Jerusalem according to Galatians 1 and 2'. *NTS* 28 (1982) 461-78.

———. 'Social Memory and the Oral Jesus Tradition'. In *Memory in the Bible and Antiquity,* edited by L. T. Stuckenbruck et al., 179-94. Tübingen: Mohr Siebeck, 2007.

———. *The Theology of Paul's Letter to the Galatians.* Cambridge: Cambridge University, 1993.

———. *The Theology of Paul the Apostle.* Grand Rapids: Eerdmans, 1998.

———. 'Towards the Spirit of Christ: The Emergence of the Distinctive Features of Christian Pneumatology'. In *The Work of the Spirit: Pneumatology and Pentecostalism,* edited by M. Welker, 3-26. Grand Rapids: Eerdmans, 2006.

———. *Unity and Diversity in the New Testament: An Inquiry into the Character of Earliest Christianity.* London: SCM, 1977, 1990, 2006, 3rd ed.

———. 'Who Did Paul Think He Was? A Study of Jewish Christian Identity'. *NTS* 45 (1999) 174-93.

———, ed. *The Cambridge Companion to St. Paul.* Cambridge: Cambridge University, 2003.

———, ed. *Paul and the Mosaic Law.* WUNT 89. Tübingen: Mohr Siebeck, 1996.

Dupont, J. 'Ascension du Christ et don de l'Esprit d'après Actes 2:33'. In *Christ and Spirit in the New Testament,* C. F. D. Moule FS, edited by B. Lindars and S. S. Smalley, 219-28. Cambridge: Cambridge University, 1973.

———. 'The First Christian Pentecost'. In *The Salvation of the Gentiles: Studies in the Acts of the Apostles,* 35-59. 1967. ET New York: Paulist, 1979.

———. 'La nouvelle Pentecôte (Ac 2,1-11). Fête de la Pentecôte'. In *Nouvelles études sur les Actes des Apôtres,* 193-98. Paris: Cerf, 1984.

———. *The Sources of Acts: The Present Position.* London: Darton, Longman and Todd, 1964.

du Toit, A. 'Encountering Grace: Towards Understanding the Essence of Paul's Conversion Experience'. In *Focusing on Paul,* 57-75.

———. *Focusing on Paul: Persuasion and Theological Design in Romans and Galatians.* BZNW 151. Berlin: de Gruyter, 2007.

———. '"God's Beloved in Rome" (Rom 1:7). The Genesis and Socio-Economic Situation of the First Generation Christian Community in Rome'. In *Focusing on Paul,* 179-202.

———. '"In Christ", "in the Spirit" and Related Prepositional Phrases: Their Relevance for a Discussion on Pauline Mysticism'. In *Focusing on Paul,* 129-45.

———. 'A Tale of Two Cities: "Tarsus or Jerusalem" Revisited'. *NTS* 46 (2000) 375-402.

Ebel, E. *Die Attraktivität früher christlicher Gemeinden.* WUNT 2.178. Tübingen: Mohr Siebeck, 2004.

Ebner, M. *Leidenslisten und Apostelbrief. Untersuchungen zu Form, Motivik und Funktion der Peristasenkataloge bei Paulus.* Würzburg: Echter, 1991.

Edson, C. 'Cults of Thessalonica'. *HTR* 41 (1948) 153-204.

Egelhaaf-Gaiser, U., and A. Schäfer, eds. *Religiöse Vereine in der römischen Antike.* STAC 13. Tübingen: Mohr Siebeck, 2002.

Ego, B. 'Abraham als Urbild der Toratreue Israels. Traditionsgeschichtliche Überlegungen zu einem Aspekt des biblischen Abrahambildes'. In *Bund und Tora. Zur theologischen Begriffsgeschichte in alttestamentlicher, frühjüdischer und urchristlicher Tradition,* edited by F. Avemarie and H. Lichtenberger, 25-40. Tübingen: Mohr Siebeck, 1996.

Elliott, J. H. *A Home for the Homeless: A Sociological Exegesis of 1 Peter, Its Situation and Strategy.* 1981. Minneapolis: Fortress, 1990.

———. 'The Jewish Messianic Movement'. In *Modelling Early Christianity,* edited by P. F. Esler, 75-95. London: Routledge, 1995.

Elliott, N. *Liberating Paul: The Justice of God and the Politics of the Apostle.* Maryknoll: Orbis, 1994.

———. 'Romans 13:1-7 in the Context of Imperial Propaganda'. In *Paul and Empire,* edited by G. H. R. Horsley, 184-204. Harrisburg: Trinity, 1997.

Elliott, S. *Cutting Too Close for Comfort: Paul's Letter to the Galatians in Its Anatolian Cultic Context.* JSNTS 248. London: Clark, 2003.

Elliott-Binns, L. E. *Galilean Christianity.* London: SCM, 1956.

Ellis, E. E. '"The End of the Earth" (Acts 1:8)'. *BBR* 1 (1991) 123-32.

———. *The Making of the New Testament Documents.* Leiden: Brill, 1999.

———. *Paul's Use of the Old Testament.* Grand Rapids: Eerdmans, 1957.

Engberg-Pedersen, T., ed. *Paul beyond the Judaism/Hellenism Divide.* Louisville: Westminster John Knox, 2001.

———, ed. *Paul in His Hellenistic Context.* Minneapolis: Fortress, 1995.

Epp, E. J. *Junia: The First Woman Apostle.* Minneapolis: Fortress, 2005.

———. 'New Testament Papyrus Manuscripts and Letter Carrying in Greco-Roman

Times'. In *The Future of Early Christianity,* H. Koester FS, edited by B. A. Pearson et al., 35-56. Minneapolis: Fortress, 1991.

Esler, P. F. 'Ancient Oleiculture and Ethnic Differentiation: The Meaning of the Olive-Tree Image in Romans 11'. *JSNT* 26 (2003) 103-24.

―――. *Community and Gospel in Luke-Acts: The Social and Political Motivations of Lucan Theology.* SNTSMS 57. Cambridge: Cambridge University, 1987.

―――. *Conflict and Identity in Romans: The Social Setting of Paul's Letter.* Minneapolis: Fortress, 2003.

―――. 'Making and Breaking an Agreement Mediterranean Style: A New Reading of Galatians 2:1-14'. *BibInt* 3 (1995) 285-314.

―――, ed. *Modelling Early Christianity: Social-Scientific Studies of the New Testament in Its Context.* London: Routledge, 1995.

Evans, C. A. 'Comparing Judaisms: Qumranic, Rabbinic, and Jacobean Judaisms Compared'. In *The Brother of Jesus,* edited by B. Chilton and J. Neusner, 161-83. Louisville: Westminster John Knox, 2001.

―――. 'Jesus and James: Martyrs of the Temple'. In *James the Just,* edited by B. Chilton and C. A. Evans, 233-49. Leiden: Brill, 1999.

―――. *Jesus and the Ossuaries.* Waco: Baylor University, 2003.

―――. 'Paul and "Works of Law" Language in Late Antiquity'. In *Paul and His Opponents,* edited by S. E. Porter, 201-26. Leiden: Brill, 2005.

Evans, C. F. 'The Kerygma'. *JTS* 7 (1956) 25-41.

Fairchild, M. R. 'Paul's Pre-Christian Zealot Associations: A Re-examination of Gal. 1.14 and Acts 22.3'. *NTS* 45 (1999) 514-32.

Falk, D. K. 'Jewish Prayer Literature and the Jerusalem Church in Acts'. *BAFCS* 4.267-301.

Farmer, W. R. 'James the Lord's Brother, according to Paul'. In *James the Just,* edited by B. Chilton and C. A. Evans, 133-53. Leiden: Brill, 1999.

Fee, G. D. '1 Corinthians 7:1-7 Revisited'. In *Paul and the Corinthians,* M. Thrall FS, edited by T. J. Burke and J. K. Elliott, 197-213. Leiden: Brill, 2003.

―――. *God's Empowering Presence: The Holy Spirit in the Letters of Paul.* Peabody: Hendrickson, 1994.

―――. *Pauline Christology: An Exegetical-Theological Study.* Peabody: Hendrickson, 2007.

―――. 'Paul's Conversion as Key to His Understanding of the Spirit'. In *The Road from Damascus,* edited by R. N. Longenecker, 166-83. Grand Rapids: Eerdmans, 1997.

Feldman, L. H. *Jew and Gentile in the Ancient World: Attitudes and Interactions from Alexander to Justinian.* Princeton: Princeton University, 1993.

―――. 'Reflections on Rutgers's "Attitudes to Judaism in the Greco-Roman Period"'. *JQR* 86 (1996) 153-70.

Feldman, L. H., and M. Reinhold, eds. *Jewish Life and Thought among the Greeks and Romans: Primary Readings.* Minneapolis: Fortress, 1996.

Feldmeier, R. *Die Christen als Fremde. Die Metapher der Fremde in der antiken Welt, im Urchristentum und im 1. Petrusbrief.* WUNT 64. Tübingen: Mohr Siebeck, 1992.

Fellows, R. G. 'Renaming in Paul's Churches: The Case of Crispus-Sosthenes Revisited'. *TynB* 56 (2005) 111-30.

Ferguson, E. *Backgrounds of Early Christianity.* Grand Rapids: Eerdmans, 1993, 2nd ed.

Fieger, M. *Im Schatten der Artemis. Glaube und Ungehorsam in Ephesus.* Bern: Lang, 1998.

Fiensy, D. A. 'The Composition of the Jerusalem Church'. *BAFCS* 4.213-36.

Filson, F. V. *A New Testament History.* London: SCM, 1965.

Fiorenza, E. S. *In Memory of Her: A Feminist Theological Reconstruction of Christian Origins.* London: SCM, 1983.

Fitzmyer, J. A. 'The Authorship of Luke-Acts Reconsidered'. In *Luke the Theologian: Aspects of His Teaching,* 1-26. London: Chapman, 1989.

———. 'The Designations of Christians in Acts and Their Significance'. In Commission Biblique Pontificale, *Unité et diversité dans l'église,* 223-36. Rome: Libreria Editrice Vaticana, 1989.

Foley, J. M. *Immanent Art: From Structure to Meaning in Traditional Oral Epic.* Bloomington: Indiana University, 1991.

Forbes, C. 'Comparison, Self-Praise and Irony: Paul's Boasting and Conventions of Hellenistic Rhetoric'. *NTS* 32 (1986) 1-30.

Fornara, C. W. *The Nature of History in Ancient Greece and Rome.* Berkeley: University of California, 1983.

Fossum, J. E. *The Name of God and the Angel of the Lord: Samaritan and Jewish Concepts of Intermediation and the Origin of Gnosticism.* WUNT 36. Tübingen: Mohr Siebeck, 1985.

Francis, F. O., and W. A. Meeks. *Conflict at Colossae.* Missoula: Scholars, 1973.

Frankemölle, H. *Frühjudentum und Urchristentum. Vorgeschichte-Verlauf-Auswirkungen (4. Jahrhundert v. Chr. bis 4. Jahrhundert n. Chr.).* Stuttgart: Kohlhammer, 2006.

———. 'Das semantische Netz des Jakobusbriefes. Zur Einheit eines umstrittenen Briefes'. *BZ* 34 (1990) 161-97.

Fredriksen, P. *From Jesus to Christ: The Origins of the New Testament Images of Jesus.* New Haven: Yale University, 1988.

———. 'Judaism, the Circumcision of Gentiles, and Apocalyptic Hope: Another Look at Galatians 1 and 2'. *JTS* 42 (1991) 532-64.

French, D. H. 'Acts and the Roman Roads of Asia Minor'. *BAFCS* 2.49-58.

———. 'The Roman Road-System of Asia Minor'. *ANRW* 2.7.2 (1980) 698-729.

Frenschkowski, M. 'Galiläa oder Jerusalem? Die topographischen und politischen Hintergründe der Logienquelle'. In *The Sayings Source Q and the Historical Jesus,* edited by A. Lindemann, 535-59. Leuven: Leuven University, 2001.

Frey, J. 'Paulus und die Apostel. Zur Entwicklung des paulinischen Apostelbegriffs und zum Verhältnis des Heidenapostels zu seinen "Kollegen"'. In *Biographie und Persönlichkeit des Paulus,* edited by E.-M. Becker and P. Pilhofer, 192-227. Tübingen: Mohr Siebeck, 2005.

Fridrichsen, A. *The Apostle and His Message.* Uppsala, 1947.

———. 'Der wahre Jude und sein Loeb. Röm. 2.28f.'. *Symbolae Arctoae* 1 (1927) 39-49.

Friedrich, J., W. Pöhlmann, et al. 'Zur historischen Situation und Intention von Römer 13,1-7'. *ZTK* 73 (1976) 131-66.

Friesen, S. J. *Twice Neokoros: Ephesus, Asia and the Cult of the Flavian Imperial Family.* Leiden: Brill, 1993.

Fuller, M. E. *The Restoration of Israel: Israel's Re-gathering and the Fate of the Nations in Early Jewish Literature and Luke-Acts.* BZNW 138. Berlin: de Gruyter, 2006.

Fuller, R. H. *The Foundations of New Testament Christology.* London: Lutterworth, 1965.

Funk, R. W., and R. W. Hoover. *The Five Gospels: The Search for the Authentic Words of Jesus.* New York: Macmillan/Polebridge, 1993.

Furnish, V. P. *The Theology of the First Letter to the Corinthians.* Cambridge: Cambridge University, 1999.

Fusco, V. 'La discussione sul protocattolicesimo nel Nuovo Testamento. Un capitolo di storia dell'esegesi'. *ANRW* 2.26.2 (1995) 1645-91.

Gager, J. G. *Reinventing Paul.* New York: Oxford University, 2000.

———. 'Some Notes on Paul's Conversion'. *NTS* 27 (1981) 697-704.

Gagnon, R. A. J. 'Why the "Weak" at Rome Cannot Be Non-Christian Jews'. *CBQ* 62 (2000) 64-82.

Gamble, H. Y. *Books and Readers in the Early Church: A History of Early Christian Texts.* New Haven: Yale University, 1995.

———. *The Textual History of the Letter to the Romans.* Grand Rapids: Eerdmans, 1977.

Garnsey, P. *Social Status and Legal Privilege in the Roman Empire.* Oxford: Clarendon, 1970.

Garnsey, P., and R. Saller. *The Roman Empire: Economy, Society and Culture.* Berkeley: University of California, 1987.

Garrett, S. R. *The Demise of the Devil: Magic and the Demonic in Luke's Writings.* Minneapolis: Fortress, 1989.

Garrison, R. *Redemptive Almsgiving in Early Christianity.* JSNTS 77. Sheffield: JSOT, 1993.

Gärtner, B. *The Areopagus Speech and Natural Revelation.* Uppsala: Almqvist and Wiksell, 1955.

Gasque, W. W. *A History of the Criticism of the Acts of the Apostles.* Tübingen: Mohr Siebeck, 1975.

Gathercole, S. J. 'The Petrine and Pauline Sola Fide in Galatians 2'. In *Lutherische und Neue Paulusperspektive,* edited by M. Bachmann, 309-27. Tübingen: Mohr Siebeck, 2005.

———. *Where Is Boasting? Early Jewish Soteriology and Paul's Response in Romans 1– 5.* Grand Rapids: Eerdmans, 2002.

Gaventa, B. R. *From Darkness to Light: Aspects of Conversion in the New Testament.* Philadelphia: Fortress, 1986.

———. 'The Maternity of Paul: An Exegetical Study of Galatians 4.19'. In *Studies in Paul and John,* J. L. Martyn FS, edited by R. T. Fortna and B. R. Gaventa, 189-201. Nashville: Abingdon, 1990.

Gayer, R. *Die Stellung des Sklaven in den paulinischen Gemeinden und bei Paulus.* Bern: Lang, 1976.

Gehring, R. W. *House Church and Mission.* Peabody: Hendrickson, 2004.

Gempf, C. 'Before Paul Arrived in Corinth: The Mission Strategies in 1 Corinthians 2:2 and Acts 17'. In *The New Testament in Its First-Century Setting,* B. W. Winter FS, edited by P. J. Williams et al., 126-42. Grand Rapids: Eerdmans, 2004.

———. 'Public Speaking and Published Accounts'. *BAFCS* 1.259-303.

Georgi, D. *The Opponents of Paul in Second Corinthians*. Philadelphia: Fortress, 1986.
———. *Remembering the Poor: The History of Paul's Collection for Jerusalem*. 1965. ET Nashville: Abingdon, 1992.
———. *Theocracy in Paul's Praxis and Theology*. Minneapolis: Fortress, 1991.
Gerhardsson, B. 'The Secret of the Transmission of the Unwritten Jesus Tradition'. *NTS* 51 (2005) 1-18.
Gilbert, G. 'The List of Nations in Acts 2: Roman Propaganda and the Lukan Response'. *JBL* 121 (2002) 497-529.
Gilchrist, J. M. 'The Historicity of Paul's Shipwreck'. *JSNT* 61 (1996) 29-51.
Gill, D. W. J. 'Achaia'. *BAFCS* 2.433-53.
———. 'Acts and Roman Policy in Judaea'. *BAFCS* 4.15-26.
———. 'Acts and Roman Religion: Religion in a Local Setting'. *BAFCS* 2.80-92.
———. 'Acts and the Urban Elites'. *BAFCS* 2.105-18.
———. 'The Meat-Market at Corinth (1 Corinthians 10:25)'. *TynB* 43 (1992) 389-93.
Glancy, J. A. *Slavery in Early Christianity*. Oxford: Oxford University, 2002.
Gnilka, J. *Die frühen Christen. Ursprünge und Anfang der Kirche*. Freiburg: Herder, 1999.
———. *Paulus von Tarsus. Zeuge und Apostel*. Freiburg: Herder, 1996.
Goguel, M. *The Birth of Christianity*. London: George Allen and Unwin, 1953.
Gooch, P. D. *Dangerous Food: 1 Corinthians 8–10 in Its Context*. Waterloo: Wilfrid Laurier University, 1993.
Goodenough, S. *Citizens of Rome*. London: Hamlyn, 1979.
Gooder, P. R. *Only the Third Heaven? 2 Corinthians 12.1-10 and Heavenly Ascent*. LNTS 313. London: Clark, 2006.
Goodman, M. *Judaism in the Roman World: Collected Essays*. Leiden: Brill, 2007.
———. *Mission and Conversion: Proselytizing in the Religious History of the Roman Empire*. Oxford: Clarendon, 1994.
———. 'The Persecution of Paul by Diaspora Jews'. In *Judaism in the Roman World*, 145-52.
———. *Rome and Jerusalem: The Clash of Civilizations*. London: Penguin, 2007.
———. *The Ruling Class of Judaea: The Origins of the Jewish Revolt against Rome AD 66-70*. Cambridge: Cambridge University, 1987.
Goppelt, L. *Apostolic and Post-apostolic Times*. London: Black, 1970.
Gorman, M. J. *Cruciformity: Paul's Narrative Spirituality of the Cross*. Grand Rapids: Eerdmans, 2001.
Goulder, M. D. 'Did Peter Ever Go to Rome?' *SJT* 57 (2004) 377-96.
———. 'The Jewish-Christian Mission, 30-130'. *ANRW* 2.26.3 (1996) 1979-2037.
———. *Paul and the Competing Mission in Corinth*. Peabody: Hendrickson, 2001.
———. *A Tale of Two Missions*. London: SCM, 1994.
———. *Type and History in Acts*. London: SPCK, 1964.
Grant, M. *Saint Paul: The Man*. Glasgow: Collins Fount, 1978.
Grant, R. M. *Paul in the Roman World: The Conflict at Corinth*. Louisville: Westminster John Knox, 2001.
Grappe, C. 'Qui me délivrera de ce corps de mort? L'Esprit de vie! Romains 7,24 et 8,2 comme éléments de typologie adamique'. *Biblica* 83 (2002) 472-92.

Gray, P. 'Points and Lines: Thematic Parallelism in the Letter of James and the Testament of Job'. *NTS* 50 (2004) 406-24.

Green, J. B. *The Death of Jesus.* WUNT 2.33. Tübingen: Mohr Siebeck, 1988.

―――. 'Internal Repetition in Luke-Acts: Contemporary Narratology and Lucan Historiography'. In *History, Literature and Society in the Book of Acts,* edited by B. Witherington, 283-99. Cambridge: Cambridge University, 1996.

Green, M. *Evangelism in the Early Church.* Grand Rapids: Eerdmans, 1970, 2003.

Gregory, A. *The Reception of Luke and Acts in the Period before Irenaeus.* WUNT 2.169. Tübingen: Mohr Siebeck, 2003.

Gregory, A., and C. Tuckett, eds. *The Reception of the New Testament in the Apostolic Fathers.* Oxford: Oxford University, 2005.

―――, eds. *Trajectories through the New Testament and the Apostolic Fathers.* Oxford: Oxford University, 2005.

Grindheim, S. 'Apostate Turned Prophet: Paul's Prophetic Self-Understanding, with Special Reference to Galatians 3.10-12'. *NTS* 53 (2007) 545-65.

―――. 'The Law Kills but the Gospel Gives Life: The Letter-Spirit Dualism in 2 Corinthians 3.5-18'. *JSNT* 84 (2001) 97-115.

Gruen, E. S. *Diaspora: Jews amidst Greeks and Romans.* Cambridge: Harvard University, 2002.

Gunkel, H. *Die Wirkungen des Heiligen Geistes nach der populären Anschauung der apostolischen Zeit und der Lehre des Apostels.* Göttingen: Vandenhoeck und Ruprecht, 1888.

―――. *Zum religionsgeschichtlichen Verständnis des Neuen Testaments.* Göttingen: Vandenhoeck und Rupecht, 1903.

Günther, M. *Die Frühgeschichte des Christentum in Ephesus.* Frankfurt: Lang, 1998.

Haacker, K. 'Paul's Life'. In *The Cambridge Companion to St. Paul,* edited by J. D. G. Dunn, 19-33. Cambridge: Cambridge University, 2003.

―――. 'Die Stellung des Stephanus in der Geschichte des Urchristentums'. *ANRW* 2.26.2 (1995) 1515-53.

―――. *The Theology of Paul's Letter to the Romans.* Cambridge: Cambridge University, 2003.

―――. *Der Werdegang eines Apostels.* SBS 171. Stuttgart: KBW, 1997.

Haenchen, E. 'The Book of Acts as Source Material for the History of Early Christianity'. In *Studies in Luke Acts,* edited by L. E. Keck and J. L. Martyn, 258-78. Nashville: Abingdon, 1966.

Hafemann, S. 'The Role of Suffering in the Mission of Paul'. In *The Mission of the Early Church,* edited by J. Ådna and H. Kvalbein, 165-84. Tübingen: Mohr Siebeck, 2000.

―――. *Suffering and the Spirit: An Exegetical Study of 2 Cor. 2:14–3:3.* WUNT 2.19. Tübingen: Mohr Siebeck, 1986.

Hagner, D. A. 'Paul as a Jewish Believer — according to His Letters'. In *Jewish Believers in Jesus: The Early Centuries,* edited by O. Skarsaune and R. Hvalvik, 96-120. Peabody: Hendrickson, 2007.

Hahn, F. *Christologische Hoheitstitel.* Göttingen: Vandenhoeck und Ruprecht, 1963, 1995, 5th ed. ET *The Titles of Jesus in Christology.* London: Lutterworth, 1969.

————. *Mission in the New Testament.* London: SCM, 1965.

Hainz, J. *Ekklesia. Strukturen paulinischer Gemeinde-Theologie und Gemeinde-Ordnung.* Regensburg: Pustet, 1972.

————. 'KOINONIA bei Paulus'. In *Religious Propaganda and Missionary Competition in the New Testament World,* D. Georgi FS, edited by L. Bormann et al., 375-91. Leiden: Brill, 1994.

Hansen, G. W. *Abraham in Galatians: Epistolary and Rhetorical Contexts.* JSNTS 29. Sheffield: Sheffield Academic, 1989.

————. 'The Preaching and Defence of Paul'. In *Witness to the Gospel: The Theology of Acts,* edited by I. H. Marshall and D. Peterson, 295-324. Grand Rapids: Eerdmans, 1998.

Hardin, J. K. 'Decrees and Drachmas at Thessalonica: An Illegal Assembly in Jason's House (Acts 17.1-10a)'. *NTS* 52 (2006) 29-49.

Harill, J. A. 'Paul and Slavery'. In *Paul in the Greco-Roman World,* edited by J. P. Sampley, 575-607. Harrisburg: Trinity, 2003.

Harland, P. A. *Associations, Synagogues, and Congregations.* Minneapolis: Fortress, 2003.

————. 'Familial Dimensions of Group Identity II: "Mothers" and "Fathers" in Associations and Synagogues of the Greek World'. *JSJ* 38 (2007) 57-79.

Harnack, A. *Die Briefsammlung des Apostels Paulus.* Leipzig: Hinrichs, 1926.

————. *The Constitution and Law of the Church in the First Two Centuries.* London: Williams and Norgate, 1910.

————. *The Date of the Acts and of the Synoptic Gospels.* London: Williams and Norgate, 1911.

————. *History of Dogma.* Vol. 1, 1886. ET 1894. New York: Dover, 1961.

————. *Luke the Physician: The Author of the Third Gospel and the Acts of the Apostles.* London: Williams and Norgate, 1907.

————. *The Mission and Expansion of Christianity in the First Three Centuries.* London: Williams and Norgate/New York: Harper Torchbook, 1908, 1962.

————. *What Is Christianity?* 1900. ET London: Williams and Norgate, 1901, 1904, 3rd ed.

Harris, M. J. *Raised Immortal: Resurrection and Immortality in the New Testament.* Grand Rapids: Eerdmans, 1985.

Harrison, J. R. 'Paul and the Imperial Gospel at Thessaloniki'. *JSNT* 25 (2002) 71-96.

Hartin, P. J. *James and the Q Sayings of Jesus.* JSNTS 47. Sheffield: Sheffield Academic, 1991.

Hartman, L. *'Into the Name of the Lord Jesus': Baptism in the Early Church.* Edinburgh: Clark, 1997.

Harvey, A. E. 'Forty Strokes save One: Social Aspects of Judaizing and Apostasy'. In *Alternative Approaches to New Testament Study,* edited by A. E. Harvey, 79-96. London: SCM, 1985.

————. *Renewal through Suffering: A Study of 2 Corinthians.* Edinburgh: Clark, 1996.

Hatch, E. *The Organization of the Early Christian Churches.* London: Longmans, 1888.

Hay, D. M. *Glory at the Right Hand: Psalm 110 in Early Christianity.* SBLMS 18. Nashville: Abingdon, 1973.

—————. 'Paul's Understanding of Faith as Participation'. In *Paul and His Theology,* edited by S. E. Porter, 45-76. Leiden: Brill, 2006.

Hays, R. B. *The Faith of Jesus Christ: The Narrative Substructure of Galatians 3:1–4:11.* Grand Rapids: Eerdmans, 2002, 2nd ed.

Hayward, C. T. R. *Interpretations of the Name Israel in Ancient Judaism and Some Early Christian Writings.* Oxford: Oxford University, 2005.

Head, P. 'Acts and the Problem of Its Texts'. *BAFCS* 1.415-44.

Heckel, U. *Kraft in Schwachheit. Untersuchungen zu 2. Kor 10–13.* WUNT 2.56. Tübingen: Mohr Siebeck, 1993.

Heil, J. P. 'Christ, the Termination of the Law (Romans 9:30–10:8)'. *CBQ* 63 (2001) 484-98.

Heinrici, G. *Das Urchristentum.* Göttingen: Vandenhoeck und Ruprecht, 1902.

Heitmüller, W. *'Im Namen Jesu'. Eine sprach- und religionsgeschichtliche Untersuchung zum Neuen Testament, speziell zur altchristlichen Taufe.* Göttingen: Vandenhoeck und Ruprecht, 1903.

—————. *Taufe und Abendmahl bei Paulus. Darstellung und religionsgeschichtliche Beleuchtung.* Göttingen: Vandenhoeck und Ruprecht, 1903.

—————. 'Zum Problem Paulus und Jesus'. *ZNW* 13 (1913) 320-37.

Hellerman, J. H. *Reconstructing Honor in Roman Philippi: Carmen Christi as Cursus Pudorum.* SNTS 132. Cambridge: Cambridge University, 2005.

Hemelrijk, E. A. 'City Patronesses in the Roman Empire'. *Historia* 53 (2004) 209-45.

Hemer, C. J. *The Book of Acts in the Setting of Hellenistic History.* WUNT 49. Tübingen: Mohr Siebeck, 1989.

—————. 'The Name of Paul'. *TynB* 36 (1985) 179-83.

Hendrix, H. L. 'Archaeology and Eschatology at Thessalonica', In *The Future of Christianity,* H. Koester FS, edited by B. A. Pearson, 107-18. Minneapolis: Fortress, 1991.

Hengel, M. *Acts and the History of Earliest Christianity.* London: SCM, 1979.

—————. *The Atonement: A Study of the Origins of the Doctrine in the New Testament.* London: SCM, 1981.

—————. *Between Jesus and Paul: Studies in the Earliest History of Christianity.* London: SCM, 1983.

—————. *Crucifixion.* London: SCM, 1977.

—————. 'Early Christianity as a Jewish-Messianic, Universalistic Movement'. In M. Hengel and C. K. Barrett, *Conflicts and Challenges in Early Christianity,* 1-41. Harrisburg: Trinity, 1999.

—————. 'Erwägungen zum Sprachgebrauch von Christos bei Paulus und in der "vorpaulinischen" Überlieferung'. In *Paul and Paulinism,* C. K. Barrett FS, edited by M. D. Hooker and S. G. Wilson, 135-59. London: SPCK, 1982.

—————. 'Eye-Witness Memory and the Writing of the Gospels'. In *The Written Gospel,* G. N. Stanton FS, edited by M. Bockmuehl and D. A. Hagner, 70-96. Cambridge: Cambridge University, 2005.

—————. 'The Geography of Palestine in Acts'. *BAFCS* 4.27-78.

—————. *The 'Hellenization' of Judaea in the First Century after Christ.* London: SCM, 1989.

———. '*Ioudaioi* in the Geographical List of Acts 2:9-11 and Syria as "Greater Judea"'. *BBR* 10 (2000) 161-80.

———. 'Der Jakobusbrief als antipaulinische Polemik'. *Paulus und Jakobus* 511-48.

———. 'Jakobus der Herrenbruder — der erste Papst?' *Paulus und Jakobus* 549-82.

———. 'Judaism and Hellenism Revisited'. In *Hellenism in the Land of Israel,* edited by J. J. Collins and G. E. Sterling, 6-37. Notre Dame: University of Notre Dame, 2001.

———. *Judentum und Hellenismus.* WUNT 10. Tübingen: Mohr Siebeck, 1988, 3rd ed. ET *Judaism and Hellenism.* London: SCM, 1974.

———. 'Der Lukasprolog und seine Augenzeugen. Die Apostel, Petrus und die Frauen'. In *Memory in the Bible and Antiquity,* edited by L. T. Stuckenbruck et al., 195-242. Tübingen: Mohr Siebeck, 2007.

———. 'Paul in Arabia'. *BBR* 12 (2002) 47-66.

———. 'Paulus und die Frage einer vorchristlichen Gnosis'. In *Paulus und Jakobus,* 473-510.

———. *Paulus und Jakobus.* Vol. 3 of *Kleine Schriften.* WUNT 141. Tübingen: Mohr Siebeck, 2002.

———. *The Pre-Christian Paul.* London: SCM, 1991.

———. *Property and Riches in the Early Church: Aspects of a Social History of Early Christianity.* London: SCM, 1974.

———. '"Sit at My Right Hand!" The Enthronement of Christ at the Right Hand of God and Psalm 110.1'. In *Studies in Early Christology,* 119-225. Edinburgh: Clark, 1995.

———. *The Son of God.* ET London: SCM, 1976.

———. *Der unterschätzte Petrus. Zwei Studien.* Tübingen: Mohr Siebeck, 2006.

———. *The Zealots.* 1961, 1976, 2nd ed. ET Edinburgh: Clark, 1989.

Hengel, M., and A. M. Schwemer. *Paulus zwischen Damaskus und Antiochien.* Tübingen: Mohr Siebeck, 1998. ET (of previously untranslated MS) *Paul between Damascus and Antioch.* London: SCM, 1997.

Herzer, J. *Petrus oder Paulus? Studien über das Verhältnis des Ersten Petrusbriefes zur paulinischen Tradition.* WUNT 103. Tübingen: Mohr Siebeck, 1998.

Hill, C. C. *Hellenists and Hebrews: Reappraising Division within the Earliest Church.* Minneapolis: Fortress, 1992.

Hock, R. F. *The Social Context of Paul's Ministry: Tentmaking and Apostleship.* Philadelphia: Fortress, 1980.

———. 'A Support for His Old Age: Paul's Plea on Behalf of Onesimus'. In *The Social World of the First Christians,* W. A. Meeks FS, edited by L. M. White and O. L. Yarbrough, 67-81. Minneapolis: Fortress, 1995.

Hodge, C. J. 'Apostle to the Gentiles: Constructions of Paul's Identity'. *BibInt* 13 (2005) 270-88.

Hofius, O. 'The Fourth Servant Song in the New Testament Letters'. In *The Suffering Servant: Isaiah 53 in Jewish and Christian Sources,* edited by B. Janowski and P. Stuhlmacher, 163-88. Grand Rapids: Eerdmans, 2004.

———. 'Gal. 1.18: *historēsai Kēphan*'. *ZNW* 75 (1984) 73-85.

———. 'The Lord's Supper and the Lord's Supper Tradition: Reflections on 1 Corinthians 11.23b-25'. In *One Loaf, One Cup: Ecumenical Studies of 1 Cor. 11 and Other Eucharistic Texts,* edited by B. F. Meyer, 75-115. Macon: Mercer University, 1993.

―――. '"Rechtfertigung des Gottlosen" als Thema biblischer Theologie'. In *Paulusstudien,* 121-47. WUNT 51. Tübingen: Mohr Siebeck, 1994.

Hogeterp, A. L. A. *Paul and God's Temple: A Historical Interpretation of Cultic Imagery in the Corinthian Correspondence.* Leuven: Peeters, 2006.

Holl, K. 'Der Kirchenbegriff des Paulus in seinem Verhältnis zu dem der Urgemeinde'. In *Gesammelte Aufsätze zur Kirchengeschichte,* 2.44-67. Tübingen: Mohr, 1928.

Holland, R. *Nero: The Man behind the Myth.* Phoenix Mill: Sutton Publishing, 2000.

Holmberg, B. 'The Life in the Diaspora Synagogue: An Evaluation'. In *The Ancient Synagogue from Its Origins until 200 C.E.,* edited by B. Olsson and M. Zetterholm, 219-323. Stockholm: Almqvist and Wiksell, 2003.

―――. 'The Methods of Historical Reconstruction in the Scholarly "Recovery" of Corinthian Christianity'. In *Christianity at Corinth,* edited by E. Adams and D. G. Horrell, 255-71. Louisville: Westminster John Knox, 2004.

―――. *Paul and Power: The Structure of Authority in the Primitive Church as Reflected in the Pauline Epistles.* Lund: Gleerup, 1977.

Holtz, T. 'Der antiochenische Zwischenfall (Gal. 2.11-14)'. *NTS* 32 (1986) 344-61.

―――. 'Zum Selbstverständnis des Apostels Paulus'. *TLZ* 91 (1966) 331-40.

Hooker, M. D. 'Authority on Her Head: An Examination of 1 Corinthians 11.10'. In *From Adam to Christ,* 113-20.

―――. *From Adam to Christ: Essays on Paul.* Cambridge: Cambridge University, 1990.

―――. '1 Thessalonians 1.9-10: A Nutshell — but What Kind of Nut?' In *Geschichte — Tradition — Reflexion,* M. Hengel FS. Vol. 3: *Frühes Christentum,* edited by H. Lichtenberger, 435-48. Tübingen: Mohr Siebeck, 1996.

―――. 'Were There False Teachers in Colossae?' In *From Adam to Christ,* 121-36.

Horbury, W. '"Gospel" in Herodian Judaea'. In *The Written Gospel,* G. N. Stanton FS, edited by M. Bockmuehl and D. A. Hagner, 7-30. Cambridge: Cambridge University, 2005.

―――. 'Jewish and Christian Monotheism in the Herodian Age'. In *Early Jewish and Christian Monotheism,* edited by L. T. Stuckenbruck and W. E. S. North, 16-44. London: Clark International, 2004.

―――. 'Women in the Synagogue'. *CHJ* 3.358-401.

Horn, F. W. *Das Angeld des Geistes. Studien zur paulinischen Pneumatologie.* FRLANT 154. Göttingen: Vandenhoeck und Ruprecht, 1992.

―――. 'Die letzte Jerusalemreise des Paulus'. In *Das Ende des Paulus,* 15-35.

―――. 'Paulus und der Herodianische Tempel'. *NTS* 53 (2007) 184-203.

―――. 'Der Verzicht auf die Beschneidung im frühen Christentum'. *NTS* 42 (1996) 479-505.

―――, ed. *Das Ende des Paulus.* BZNW 106. Berlin: de Gruyter, 2001.

Horrell, D. G. 'Domestic Space and Christian Meetings at Corinth: Imagining New Contexts and the Buildings East of the Theatre'. *NTS* 50 (2004) 349-69.

―――. 'The Label *Christianos:* 1 Peter 4:16 and the Formation of Christian Identity'. *JBL* 126 (2007) 383-91.

———. 'The Product of a Petrine Circle? A Reassessment of the Origin and Character of 1 Peter'. *JSNT* 86 (2002) 29-60.

———. *The Social Ethos of the Corinthian Correspondence: Interests and Ideology from 1 Corinthians to 1 Clement.* Edinburgh: Clark, 1996.

Horsley, G. H. R. 'The Politarchs'. *BAFCS* 2.419-31.

Horsley, R. A. '1 Corinthians: A Case Study of Paul's Assembly as an Alternative Society'. In *Paul and Empire,* 242-52.

———. 'Gnosis in Corinth: 1 Corinthians 8.1-6'. *NTS* 27 (1981) 32-52.

———. 'Pneumatikos vs. Psychikos: Distinctions of Spiritual Status among the Corinthians'. *HTR* 69 (1976) 269-88.

———, ed. *Christian Origins.* Minneapolis: Fortress, 2005.

———, ed. *Paul and Empire: Religion and Power in Roman Imperial Society.* Harrisburg: Trinity, 1997.

———, ed. *Paul and Politics: Ekklesia, Israel, Imperium, Interpretation.* Harrisburg: Trinity, 2000.

———, ed. *Paul and the Roman Imperial Order.* Harrisburg: Trinity, 2004.

Hubbard, M. V. 'Urban Uprisings in the Roman World: The Social Setting of the Mobbing of Sosthenes'. *NTS* 51 (2005) 416-28.

Hughes, F. W. 'The Rhetoric of Letters'. In *The Thessalonians Debate,* edited by K. P. Donfried and J. Beutler, 194-240. Grand Rapids: Eerdmans, 2000.

Hultgren, A. J. *Paul's Gospel and Mission: The Outlook from His Letter to the Romans.* Philadelphia: Fortress, 1985.

———. *The Rise of Normative Christianity.* Minneapolis: Fortress, 1994.

———. 'The Scriptural Foundations for Paul's Mission to the Gentiles'. In *Paul and His Theology,* edited by S. E. Porter, 21-44. Leiden: Brill, 2006.

Hultgren, S. 'The Origin of Paul's Doctrine of the Two Adams in 1 Corinthians 15.45-49'. *JSNT* 25 (2003) 343-70.

Hunter, A. M. *Paul and His Predecessors.* London: SCM, 1940, 1961, 2nd ed.

Hurd, J. C. *The Origin of 1 Corinthians.* London: SPCK, 1965.

———. 'Reflections concerning Paul's "Opponents" in Galatia'. In *Paul and His Opponents,* edited by S. E. Porter, 129-48. Leiden: Brill, 2005.

Hurtado, L. W. *How on Earth Did Jesus Become a God? Historical Questions about Earliest Devotion to Jesus.* Grand Rapids: Eerdmans, 2005.

———. *Lord Jesus Christ: Devotion to Jesus in Earliest Christianity.* Grand Rapids: Eerdmans, 2003.

———. *One God, One Lord: Early Christian Devotion and Ancient Jewish Monotheism.* Philadelphia: Fortress, 1988.

———. 'Paul's Christology'. In *The Cambridge Companion to St. Paul,* edited by J. D. G. Dunn, 185-98. Cambridge: Cambridge University, 2003.

———. 'Pre-70 C.E. Jewish Opposition to Christ-Devotion'. *JTS* 50 (1999) 35-58.

Hvalvik, R. 'Jewish Believers and Jewish Influence in the Roman Church until the Early Second Century'. In *Jewish Believers in Jesus: The Early Centuries,* edited by O. Skarsaune and R. Hvalvik, 179-216. Peabody: Hendrickson, 2007.

———. 'Named Jewish Believers Connected with the Pauline Mission'. In *Jewish Be-*

lievers in Jesus: The Early Centuries, edited by O. Skarsaune and R. Hvalvik, 154-78. Peabody: Hendrickson, 2007.

———. 'Paul as a Jewish Believer — according to the Book of Acts'. In *Jewish Believers in Jesus: The Early Centuries,* edited by O. Skarsaune and R. Hvalvik, 121-53. Peabody: Hendrickson, 2007.

———. 'A "Sonderweg" for Israel: A Critical Examination of a Current Interpretation of Romans 11.25-27'. *JSNT* 38 (1990) 87-107.

Hyldahl, N. *Die paulinische Chronologie.* Leiden: Brill, 1986.

Isser, S. 'The Samaritans and Their Sects'. *CHJ* 3.569-95.

Jackson-McCabe, M. A. *Logos and Law in the Letter of James.* NovTSupp 100. Leiden: Brill, 2001.

Jacobs, A. S. 'A Jew's Jew: Paul and the Early Christian Problem of Jewish Origins'. *JR* 86 (2006) 258-86.

Janowitz, N. *Magic in the Roman World.* London: Routledge, 2001.

Janowski, B., and P. Stuhlmacher, eds. *The Suffering Servant: Isaiah 53 in Jewish and Christian Sources.* Grand Rapids: Eerdmans, 2004.

Jaubert, A. *La notion d'alliance dans le judaïsme aux abords de l'ère chrétienne.* Paris: Éditions du Seuil. 1963.

Jeffers, J. S. *Conflict at Rome: Social Order and Hierarchy in Early Christianity.* Minneapolis: Fortress, 1991.

———. *The Greco-Roman World of the New Testament: Exploring the Background of Early Christianity.* Downers Grove: InterVarsity, 1999.

Jeremias, J. '"Flesh and Blood Cannot Inherit the Kingdom of God" (1 Cor. 15:50)'. *NTS* 2 (1955-56) 151-59.

———. *Jerusalem at the Time of Jesus: An Investigation into the Economic and Social Conditions during the New Testament Period.* London: SCM, 1969.

Jervell, J. 'The Future of the Past: Luke's Vision of Salvation History and Its Bearing on His Writing of History'. In *History, Literature and Society in the Book of Acts,* edited by B. Witherington, 104-26. Cambridge: Cambridge University, 1996.

———. 'The Letter to Jerusalem'. In *Romans Debate,* edited by K. P. Donfried, 53-64. Peabody: Hendrickson, 1991.

———. *Luke and the People of God: A New Look at Luke-Acts.* Minneapolis: Augsburg, 1972.

———. 'The Mighty Minority' (1980). In *The Unknown Paul,* 26-51.

———. *The Theology of the Acts of the Apostles.* Cambridge: Cambridge University, 1996.

———. *The Unknown Paul: Essays on Luke-Acts and Early Christian History.* Minneapolis: Augsburg, 1984.

Jervis, L. A., and P. Richardson, eds. *Gospel in Paul: Studies on Corinthians, Galatians and Romans,* R. N. Longenecker FS. JSNTS 108. Sheffield: Sheffield Academic, 1994.

Jewett, R. 'The Agitators and the Galatian Congregation'. *NTS* 17 (1970-71) 198-212.

———. *Dating Paul's Life.* London: SCM, 1979.

———. 'The Question of the "Apportioned Spirit" in Paul's Letters: Romans as a Case

Study'. In *The Holy Spirit and Christian Origins,* J. D. G. Dunn FS, edited by G. N. Stanton et al., 193-206. Grand Rapids: Eerdmans, 2004.

———. 'Tenement Churches and Communal Meals in the Early Church'. *BR* 38 (1993) 23-43.

———. *The Thessalonian Correspondence: Pauline Rhetoric and Millenarian Piety.* Philadelphia: Fortress, 1986.

Johnson, L. T. *Brother of Jesus, Friend of God: Studies in the Letter of James.* Grand Rapids: Eerdmans, 2004.

———. *Religious Experience in Earliest Christianity: A Missing Dimension in New Testament Studies.* Minneapolis: Fortress, 1998.

———. 'Taciturnity and True Religion: James 1:26-27'. In *Greeks, Romans and Christians,* A. J. Malherbe FS, edited by D. L. Balch et al., 329-39. Minneapolis: Fortress, 1990.

Jones, A. H. M. *Cities of the Eastern Roman Provinces.* Oxford: Oxford University, 1971.

Jones, F. S. *An Ancient Jewish Christian Source on the History of Christianity: Pseudo-Clementine Recognitions 1.27-71.* Atlanta: Scholars, 1995.

Jones, J. L. 'Christianity and the Roman Imperial Cult'. *ANRW* 2.23.2 (1980) 1024-32.

Jossa, G. *Jews or Christians? The Followers of Jesus in Search of Their Own Identity.* WUNT 202. Tübingen: Mohr Siebeck, 2006.

Joubert, S. *Paul as Benefactor: Reciprocity, Strategy and Theological Reflection in Paul's Collection.* Tübingen: Mohr Siebeck, 2000.

Judge, E. A. 'The Decrees of Caesar at Thessalonica'. *RTR* 30 (1971) 1-7.

———. 'Did the Churches Compete with Cult Groups?' In *Early Christianity and Classical Culture,* A. J. Malherbe FS, edited by J. T. Fitzgerald et al., 501-24. Leiden: Brill, 2003.

———. 'The Early Christians as a Scholastic Community'. *JRH* 1 (1960-61) 4-15, 125-37.

———. 'Judaism and the Rise of Christianity: A Roman Perspective'. *TynB* 45 (1994) 355-68.

———. 'The Social Identity of the First Christians: A Question of Method in Religious History'. *JRH* 11 (1980) 201-17.

———. *The Social Patterns of Christian Groups in the First Century.* London: Tyndale, 1960.

Juel, D. *Messianic Exegesis: Christological Interpretation of the Old Testament in Early Christianity.* Philadelphia: Fortress, 1988.

Jüngel, E. *Paulus und Jesus. Eine Untersuchung zur Präzisierung der Frage nach dem Ursprung der Christologie.* Tübingen: Mohr Siebeck, 1967.

Juster, J. *Les Juifs dans l'empire romain. Leur condition juridique, économique et sociale.* Vol. 1. Paris: Geunther, 1914.

Käsemann, E. 'The Beginnings of Christian Theology' (1960). In *New Testament Questions of Today,* 82-107.

———. 'The Disciples of John the Baptist in Ephesus' (1952). In *Essays on New Testament Themes,* 136-48. London: SCM, 1964.

———. *Die Legitimität des Apostels. Eine Untersuchung zu II Korinther 10–13.* Darmstadt: Wissenschaftliche Buchgesellschaft, 1956.

———. *New Testament Questions of Today.* London: SCM, 1969.

———. 'New Testament Questions of Today' (1957). In *New Testament Questions of To-day,* 1-22. London: SCM, 1969.

———. 'On the Subject of Primitive Christian Apocalyptic' (1962). In *New Testament Questions of Today,* 108-37.

———. *Perspectives on Paul.* 1969. ET London: SCM, 1971.

———. 'Worship in Everyday Life: A Note on Romans 12'. In *New Testament Questions of Today,* 188-95.

Kaye, B. N. 'Lightfoot and Baur on Early Christianity'. *NovT* 26 (1984) 193-224.

Kearsley, R. A. 'The Asiarchs'. *BAFCS* 2.363-76.

———. 'Women in Public Life in the Roman East: Iunia, Theodora, Claudia Metrodora and Phoebe, Benefactress of Paul'. *TynB* 50 (1999) 189-211.

Keck, L. E. 'The Function of Rom 3:10-18: Observations and Suggestions'. In *God's Christ and His People,* N. A. Dahl FS, edited by J. Jervell and W. A. Meeks, 141-57. Oslo: Universitetsforlaget, 1978.

———. 'The Jewish Paul among the Gentiles: Two Portrayals'. In *Early Christianity and Classical Culture,* A. J. Malherbe FS, edited by J. T. Fitzgerald et al., 461-81. Leiden: Brill, 2003.

———. 'The Poor among the Saints in Jewish Christianity and Qumran'. *ZNW* 57 (1966) 54-78.

———. 'The Poor among the Saints in the New Testament'. *ZNW* 56 (1965) 100-129.

Keck, L. E., and J. L. Martyn, eds. *Studies in Luke Acts.* Nashville: Abingdon, 1966.

Keener, C. S. *Paul, Women and Wives: Marriage and Women's Ministry in the Letters of Paul.* Peabody: Hendrickson, 1992.

Keesmaat, S. C. *Paul and His Story: (Re)Interpreting the Exodus Tradition.* JSNTS 181. Sheffield: Sheffield Academic, 1999.

Kennedy, G. A. *New Testament Interpretation through Rhetorical Criticism.* Chapel Hill: University of North Carolina, 1984.

Kennedy, H. A. A. *St. Paul and the Mystery Religions.* London: Hodder and Stoughton, 1914.

Ker, D. P. 'Paul and Apollos — Colleagues or Rivals?' *JSNT* 77 (2000) 75-97.

Kertelge, K., ed. *Mission im Neuen Testament.* QD 93. Freiburg: Herder, 1982.

———, ed. *Paulus in den neutestamentlichen Spätschriften.* QD 89. Freiburg: Herder, 1981.

Kim, K.-J. *Stewardship and Almsgiving in Luke's Theology.* JSNTS 155. Sheffield: Sheffield Academic, 1998.

Kim, S. 'The Jesus Tradition in 1 Thess 4.13–5.11'. *NTS* 48 (2002) 225-42.

———. *The Origin of Paul's Gospel.* WUNT 2.4. Tübingen: Mohr Siebeck, 1981; Grand Rapids: Eerdmans, 1984, 2nd ed.

———. *Paul and the New Perspective: Second Thoughts on the Origin of Paul's Gospel.* WUNT 140. Tübingen: Mohr Siebeck, 2002.

Kippenberg, H. G. *Garizim und Synagoge. Traditionsgeschichtliche Untersuchungen zur samaritanischen Religion der aramäische Periode.* Berlin: de Gruyter, 1971.

Kirby, J. C. *Ephesians: Baptism and Pentecost.* London: SPCK, 1968.

Kirchenschläger, W. 'Die Entwicklung von Kirche und Kirchenstruktur zur neutesta-mentlichen Zeit'. *ANRW* 2.26.2 (1995) 1277-1356.

Klauck, H.-J. *Ancient Letters and the New Testament.* 1998. ET Waco: Baylor University, 2006.

———. *Hausgemeinde und Hauskirche im frühen Christentum.* SBS 103. Stuttgart: Katholisches Bibelwerk, 1981.

———. *Magic and Paganism in Early Christianity: The World of the Acts of the Apostles.* London: Clark, 2000.

———. *The Religious Context of Early Christianity: A Guide to Graeco-Roman Religions.* 1995. ET Edinburgh: Clark, 2000.

Klausner, J. *From Jesus to Paul.* London: Allen and Unwin, 1943.

Kloppenborg, J. S. 'Collegia and Thiasoi'. In *Voluntary Associations in the Graeco-Roman World,* edited by J. S. Kloppenborg and S. G. Wilson, 16-30. London: Routledge, 1996.

———. 'Diaspora Discourse: The Construction of Ethos in James'. *NTS* 53 (2007) 242-70.

———. 'Didache 1.1–6.1, James, Matthew, and the Torah'. In *Trajectories through the New Testament and the Apostolic Fathers,* edited by A. Gregory and C. M. Tuckett, 193-221. Oxford: Oxford University, 2005.

———. 'Edwin Hatch, Churches and Collegia'. In *Origins and Method: Towards a New Understanding of Judaism and Christianity,* J. C. Hurd FS, edited by B. H. McLean, 212-38. Sheffield: JSOT, 1993.

———. 'The Emulation of the Jesus Tradition in the Letter of James'. In *Reading James with New Eyes: Methodological Reassessments of the Letter of James,* edited by R. L. Webb and J. S. Kloppenborg, 121-50. London: Clark, 2007.

———. *Excavating Q: The History and Setting of the Sayings Gospel.* Minneapolis: Fortress, 2000.

———. *'Philadelphia, theodidaktos* and the Dioscuri: Rhetorical Engagements in 1 Thessalonians 4.9-12'. *NTS* 39 (1993) 265-89.

———. 'The Theodotus Synagogue Inscription and the Problem of First-Century Synagogue Buildings'. In *Jesus and Archaeology,* edited by J. H. Charlesworth, 236-82. Grand Rapids: Eerdmans, 2006.

Kloppenborg, J. S., and S. G. Wilson, eds. *Voluntary Associations in the Graeco-Roman World.* London: Routledge, 1996.

Klutz, T. *The Exorcism Stories in Luke-Acts.* SNTSMS 129. Cambridge: Cambridge University, 2004.

Knox, J. *Chapters in a Life of Paul.* London: SCM, 1950, 1989, 2nd ed.

Knox, W. L. *St. Paul and the Church of Jerusalem.* Cambridge: Cambridge University, 1925.

———. *St. Paul and the Church of the Gentiles.* Cambridge: Cambridge University, 1939, 1961.

Koch, D.-A. 'Alles, was *en makello* verkauft wird, esst . . .'. Die *macella* von Pompeji, Gerasa und Korinth und ihre Bedeutung für die Auslegung von 1 Kor 10,25'. *ZNW* 90 (1999) 194-291.

————. 'The God-Fearers between Fact and Fiction. Two Theosebeis-Inscriptions from Aphrodisias and Their Bearing for the New Testament'. *ST* 60 (2006) 62-90.

————. 'Kollektenbericht, "Wir"-Bericht und Itinerar. Neue(?) Überlegungen zu einem alten Problem'. *NTS* 45 (1999) 367-90.

Koester, C. 'The Origin and Significance of the Flight to Pella Tradition'. *CBQ* 51 (1989) 90-106.

Koester, H. 'Epilogue: Current Issues in New Testament Scholarship'. In *The Future of Early Christianity,* H. Koester FS, edited by B. A. Pearson et al., 46-76. Minneapolis: Fortress, 1991.

————. 'From Paul's Eschatology to the Apocalyptic Scheme of 2 Thessalonians'. In *Paul and His World,* 55-69.

————. '*Gnōmai Diaphoroi:* The Origin and Nature of Diversification in the History of Early Christianity'. *HTR* 58 (1965) 279-318.

————. *Introduction to the New Testament.* Vol. 1: *History, Culture and Religion of the Hellenistic Age;* vol. 2: *History and Literature of Early Christianity.* ET Philadelphia: Fortress, 1982.

————. 'One Jesus and Four Primitive Gospels'. *HTR* 161 (1968) 203-47.

————. *Paul and His World: Interpreting the New Testament in Its Context.* Minneapolis: Fortress, 2007.

————. 'The Purpose of the Polemic of a Pauline Fragment'. *NTS* 8 (1961-62) 317-32.

————. 'The Silence of the Apostle'. In *Urban Religion in Roman Corinth,* edited by D. N. Schowalter and J. Friesen, 339-49. Cambridge: Harvard University, 2005.

————, ed. *Ephesos: Metropolis of Asia.* HTS 41. Cambridge: Harvard Divinity School, 1995, 2004.

Konradt, M. *Gericht und Gemeinde. Eine Studie zur Bedeutung und Funktion von Gerichtsaussagen im Rahmen der paulinischen Ekklesiologie und Ethik im 1 Thess und 1 Kor.* BZNW 117. Berlin: de Gruyter, 2003.

Köstenberger, A. J. 'Women in the Pauline Mission'. In *The Gospel to the Nations: Perspectives on Paul's Mission,* P. T. O'Brien FS, edited by P. G. Bolt and M. Thompson, 221-47. Leicester: Inter-Varsity, 2000.

Kraabel, A. T. 'The Disappearance of the "God-Fearers"'. *Numen* 28 (1981) 113-26.

Kraeling, C. H. 'The Jewish Community of Antioch'. *JBL* 51 (1932) 130-60.

Kraft, H. *Die Entstehung des Christentums.* Darmstadt: Wissenschaftliche Buchgesellschaft, 1981.

Kramer, W. *Christ, Lord, Son of God.* London: SCM, 1966.

Kraus, W. *Zwischen Jerusalem und Antiochia. Die "Hellenisten", Paulus und die Aufnahme der Heiden in das endzeitliche Gottesvolk.* SBS 179. Stuttgart: Katholisches Bibelwerk, 1999.

Kremer, J. *Pfingstbericht und Pfingstgeschehen. Eine exegetische Untersuchung zu Apg 2,1-13.* SBS 63/64. Stuttgart: KBW, 1973.

————, ed. *Les Actes des Apôtres. Tradition, redaction, théologie.* BETL 48. Gembloux: Duculot, 1979.

Kretschmar, G. 'Himmelfahrt und Pfingsten'. *ZKG* 66 (1954-55) 209-53.

Kruse, C. G. 'The Price Paid for a Ministry among the Gentiles: Paul's Persecution at the

Hands of the Jews'. In *Worship, Theology and Ministry in the Early Church,* R. P. Martin FS, edited by M. J. Wilkins and T. Paige, 260-72. Sheffield: JSOT, 1992.

Kuhn, H. W. *Ältere Sammlungen im Markusevangelium.* Göttingen: Vandenhoeck und Ruprecht, 1971.

Kümmel, W. G. *Introduction to the New Testament.* Nashville: Abingdon, 1975.

———. *The New Testament: The History of the Investigation of Its Problems.* ET Nashville: Abingdon, 1972.

Kunst, C. 'Wohnen in der antiken Großstadt. Zur sozialen Topographie Roms in der frühen Kaiserzeit'. In *Christians as a Religious Minority in a Multicultural City,* edited by J. Zangenberg and M. Labahn, 2-19. London: Clark, 2004.

Labahn, M. 'Paulus — ein homo honestus et iustus. Das lukanische Paulusportrait von Acts 27–28 im Lichte ausgewählter antiker Parallelen'. In *Das Ende des Paulus,* edited by F. W. Horn, 75-106. Berlin: de Gruyter, 2001.

Lake, K. 'The Apostolic Council of Jerusalem'. *Beginnings* 5.195-212.

———. 'The Communism of Acts 2 and 4–6 and the Appointment of the Seven'. *Beginnings* 5.140-51.

———. 'The Day of Pentecost'. *Beginnings* 5.111-21.

Lambrecht, J. *The Wretched "I" and Its Liberation: Paul in Romans 7 and 8.* Leuven: Peeters, 1992.

Lamp, J. S. 'Is Paul Anti-Jewish? Testament of Levi 6 in the Interpretation of 1 Thessalonians 2:13-16'. *CBQ* 65 (2003) 408-27.

Lampe, P. 'Acts 19 im Spiegel der ephesischen Inschriften'. *BZ* 36 (1992) 59-76.

———. 'Early Christians in the City of Rome: Topographical and Social-Historical Aspects of the First Three Centuries'. In *Christians as a Religious Minority in a Multicultural City,* edited by J. Zangenberg and M. Labahn, 20-32. London: Clark, 2004.

———. 'The Eucharist: Identifying with Christ on the Cross'. *Interpretation* 48 (1994) 36-49.

———. *From Paul to Valentinus: Christians at Rome in the First Two Centuries.* Minneapolis: Fortress, 2003.

———. 'Keine "Sklavenflucht" des Onesimus'. *ZNW* 76 (1985) 135-37.

———. 'Paths of Early Christian Mission into Rome: Judaeo-Christians in the Household of Pagan Masters'. In *Celebrating Romans: Template for Pauline Theology,* R. Jewett FS, edited by S. E. McGinn, 143-48. Grand Rapids: Eerdmans, 2004.

———. 'Paul, Patrons and Clients'. In *Paul in the Greco-Roman World,* edited by J. P. Sampley, 488-523. Harrisburg: Trinity, 2003.

———. 'Paulus — Zeltmacher'. *BZ* 31 (1987) 256-61.

———. 'The Roman Christians of Romans 16'. In *Romans Debate,* edited by K. P. Donfried, 216-30. Peabody: Hendrickson, 1991.

Lanci, J. R. 'The Stones Don't Speak and the Texts Tell Lies: Sacred Sex at Corinth'. In *Urban Religion in Roman Corinth,* edited by D. N. Schowalter and J. Friesen, 205-20. Cambridge: Harvard University, 2005.

Lane, W. L. 'Social Perspectives on Roman Christianity during the Formative Years from Nero to Nerva'. In *Judaism and Christianity in First-Century Rome,* edited by K. P. Donfried and P. Richardson, 196-244. Grand Rapids: Eerdmans, 1998.

Lane Fox, R. *The Classical World: An Epic History of Greece and Rome.* London: Penguin, 2005.

———. *Pagans and Christians in the Mediterranean World from the Second Century AD to the Conversion of Constantine.* 1986. London: Penguin, 1988.

Lang, F. 'Paulus und seine Gegner in Korinth und in Galatien'. In *Geschichte — Tradition — Reflexion,* M. Hengel FS. Vol. 3: *Frühes Christentum,* edited by H. Lichtenberger, 417-34. Tübingen: Mohr Siebeck, 1996.

La Piana, G. 'Foreign Groups in Rome during the First Centuries of the Empire'. *HTR* 20 (1927) 183-403.

Larsson, E. 'Die Hellenisten und die Urgemeinde'. *NTS* 33 (1987) 205-25.

———. 'Temple-Criticism and the Jewish Heritage: Some Reflexions on Acts 6–7'. *NTS* 39 (1993) 379-95.

Legasse, S. 'Paul's Pre-Christian Career according to Acts'. *BAFCS* 4.365-90.

Lehnert, V. A., and U. Rüsen-Weinhold, eds. *Logos — Logik — Lyrik. Engagierte exegetische Studien zum biblischen Reden Gottes,* K. Haacker FS. Leipzig: Evangelische Verlagsanstalt, 2007.

Lentz, J. C. *Luke's Portrait of Paul.* SNTSMS 77. Cambridge: Cambridge University, 1993.

Leon, H. J. *The Jews of Ancient Rome.* Philadelphia: Jewish Publication Society, 1960.

Levinskaya, I. *The Book of Acts in Its Diaspora Setting* (= *BAFCS* 5). Grand Rapids, Eerdmans 1996.

———. 'The Italian Cohort in Acts 10:1'. In *The New Testament in Its First-Century Setting,* B. W. Winter FS, edited by P. J. Williams et al., 106-25. Grand Rapids: Eerdmans, 2004.

Levison, J. R. 'Adam and Eve in Romans 1.18-25 and the Greek *Life of Adam and Eve'. NTS* 50 (2004) 519-34.

Lichtenberger, H. *Das Ich Adams und das Ich der Menschheit. Studien zum Menschenbild in Römer 7.* WUNT 164. Tübingen: Mohr Siebeck, 2004.

———. 'Jews and Christians in Rome in the Time of Nero: Josephus and Paul in Rome'. *ANRW* 2.26.3 (1996) 2142-76.

———, ed. *Geschichte — Tradition — Reflexion,* M. Hengel FS. Vol. 3: *Frühes Christentum.* Tübingen: Mohr Siebeck, 1996.

Liechtenham, R. *Die urchristliche Mission. Voraussetzungen, Motive und Methoden.* Zürich: Zwingli, 1946.

Lietzmann, H. *Mass and Lord's Supper.* 1926. ET Leiden: Brill, 1954.

Lieu, J. M. 'Do God-Fearers Make Good Christians?' In *Crossing the Boundaries,* M. D. Goulder FS, edited by S. E. Porter et al., 329-45. Leiden: Brill, 1994.

———. 'The Race of the God-Fearers'. *JTS* 46 (1995) 483-501.

———. 'The Synagogue and the Separation of the Christians'. In *The Ancient Synagogue from Its Origins until 200 C.E.,* edited by B. Olsson and M. Zetterholm, 189-207. Stockholm: Almqvist and Wiksell, 2003.

Lightfoot, J. B. *Essays on the Work Entitled "Supernatural Religion".* London: Macmillan, 1889.

———. 'St. Paul and the Three'. In *Saint Paul's Epistle to the Galatians,* 292-374. London: Macmillan, 1865.

Lincoln, A. T., and A. J. M. Wedderburn. *The Theology of the Later Pauline Letters.* Cambridge: Cambridge University, 1993.

Lindars, B. *New Testament Apologetic: The Doctrinal Significance of the Old Testament Quotations.* London: SCM, 1961.

Lindemann, A. 'Die paulinische Ekklesiologie angesichts der Lebenswirklichkeit der christlichen Gemeinde in Korinth'. In *The Corinthian Correspondence,* edited by R. Bieringer, 63-86. Leuven: Leuven University, 1996.

―――. *Paulus im ältesten Christentum. Das Bild des Apostels und die Rezeption der paulinischen Theologie in der frühchristlichen Literatur bis Marcion.* Tübingen: Mohr Siebeck, 1979.

―――. 'Paulus und Elia. Zur Argumentation in Röm 11,1-12'. In *Logos — Logik — Lyrik. Engagierte exegetische Studien zum biblischen Reden Gottes,* K. Haacker FS, edited by V. A. Lehnert and U. Rüsen-Weinhold, 201-18. Leipzig: Evangelische Verlagsanstalt, 2007.

―――, ed., *The Sayings Source Q and the Historical Jesus.* BETL 158. Leuven: Leuven University 2001.

Linton, O. 'The Third Aspect: A Neglected Point of View'. *ST* 3 (1949) 79-95.

Litfin, D. *St. Paul's Theology of Proclamation: 1 Corinthians 1–4 and Greco-Roman Rhetoric.* SNTSMS 79. Cambridge: Cambridge University, 1994.

Lohfink, G. *Die Himmelfahrt Jesu. Untersuchungen zu den Himmelfahrts- und Erhöhungstexten bei Lukas.* Munich: Kösel, 1971.

―――. *Die Sammlung Israels. Eine Untersuchung zur lukanischen Ekklesiologie.* Munich: Kösel, 1971.

Lohmeyer, E. *Galiläa und Jerusalem.* Göttingen: Vandenhoeck und Ruprecht, 1936.

Löhr, H. 'Zum Paulus-Notiz in 1 Clem 5,5-7'. In *Das Ende des Paulus,* edited by F. W. Horn, 197-213. Berlin: de Gruyter, 2001.

Lohse, E. 'Das Evangelium für Juden und Griechen. Erwägungen zur Theologie des Römerbriefes'. In *Rechenschaft vom Evangelium. Exegetische Studien zum Römerbrief,* 1-19. Berlin: de Gruyter, 2007.

―――. *Paulus. Eine Biographie.* Munich: Beck, 1996.

Long, A. A., and D. N. Sedley. *The Hellenistic Philosophers.* 2 vols. Cambridge: Cambridge University, 1987.

Longenecker, B. W. 'On Israel's God and God's Israel: Assessing Supersessionism in Paul'. *JTS* 58 (2007) 26-44.

―――. *Rhetoric at the Boundaries.* Waco: Baylor University, 2005.

―――. *The Triumph of Abraham's God: The Transformation of Identity in Galatians.* Edinburgh: Clark, 1998.

Longenecker, R. N. 'Ancient Amanuenses and the Pauline Epistles'. In *New Dimensions in New Testament Study,* edited by R. N. Longenecker and M. C. Tenney, 281-97. Grand Rapids: Zondervan, 1974.

―――. *New Wine into Fresh Wineskins: Contextualizing the Early Christian Confessions.* Peabody: Hendrickson, 1999.

―――, ed. *Community Formation in the Early Church and in the Church Today.* Peabody: Hendrickson, 2002.

1221

————, ed. *Contours of Christology in the New Testament.* Grand Rapids: Eerdmans, 2005.

————, ed. *The Road from Damascus: The Impact of Paul's Conversion on His Life, Thought, and Ministry.* Grand Rapids: Eerdmans, 1997.

Löning, K. 'The Circle of Stephen and Its Mission'. In *Christian Beginnings,* edited by J. Becker, 103-31. Louisville: Westminster John Knox, 1993.

————. 'Paulinismus in der Apg'. In *Paulus in den neutestamentlichen Spätschriften,* edited by K. Kertelge, 202-34. Freiburg: Herder, 1981.

Lüdemann, G. 'The Acts of the Apostles and the Beginnings of Simonian Gnosis'. *NTS* 33 (1987) 420-26.

————. *Early Christianity according to the Traditions in Acts: A Commentary.* London: SCM, 1989.

————. *Opposition to Paul in Jewish Christianity.* Minneapolis: Fortress, 1989.

————. *Paul, Apostle to the Gentiles: Studies in Chronology.* 1980. ET Philadelphia: Fortress, 1984.

————. *Primitive Christianity: A Survey of Recent Studies and Some New Proposals.* 2002. ET London: Clark, 2003.

————. 'The Successors of Earliest Christianity: An Analysis of the Pella Tradition'. In *Opposition to Paul in Jewish Christianity,* 200-213.

————. *Untersuchungen zur simonianischen Gnosis.* Göttingen: Vandenhoeck und Ruprecht, 1975.

Lührmann, D. 'The Beginnings of the Church at Thessalonica'. In *Greeks, Romans and Christians,* A. J. Malherbe FS, edited by D. L. Balch et al., 237-49. Minneapolis: Fortress, 1990.

Lull, D. J. '"The Law Was Our Pedagogue": A Study in Galatians 3:19-25'. *JBL* 105 (1986) 481-98.

————. *The Spirit in Galatia: Paul's Interpretation of Pneuma as Divine Power.* Chico: Scholars, 1980.

Lütgert, W. *Freiheitspredigt und Schwarmgeister in Korinth.* Göttingen: Bertelsmann, 1908.

————. *Gesetz und Geist. Eine Untersuchung zur Vorgeschichte des Galaterbriefes.* Gütersloh: Bertelsmann, 1919.

Luz, U. 'Paul as Mystic'. In *The Holy Spirit and Christian Origins,* J. D. G. Dunn FS, edited by G. N. Stanton et al., 131-43. Grand Rapids: Eerdmans, 2004.

Maccoby, H. *The Mythmaker: Paul and the Invention of Christianity.* London: Weidenfeld and Nicolson, 1986.

————. *Paul and Hellenism.* London: SCM, 1991.

MacDonald, D. R. 'The Shipwrecks of Odysseus and Paul'. *NTS* 45 (1999) 88-107.

Macdonald, J. *The Theology of the Samaritans.* London: SCM, 1964.

MacDonald, M. Y. *The Pauline Churches: A Socio-Historical Study of Institutionalization in the Pauline and Deutero-Pauline Writings.* SNTSMS 60. Cambridge: Cambridge University, 1988.

Mack, B. *The Christian Myth.* New York: Continuum, 2001.

MacMullen, R. *Paganism in the Roman Empire.* New Haven: Yale University, 1981.

————. *Roman Social Relations 50 BC to AD 284.* New Haven: Yale University, 1974.

————. 'Women in Public in the Roman Empire'. *Historia* 29 (1980) 208-18.

Maddox, R. *The Purpose of Luke-Acts.* Edinburgh: Clark, 1982.

Magness, J. 'Ossuaries and the Burials of Jesus and James'. *JBL* 124 (2005) 121-54.

Maier, G. 'Jesustradition im 1. Petrusbrief'. In *Gospel Perspectives.* Vol. 5: *The Jesus Tradition outside the Gospels,* edited by D. Wenham, 85-128. Sheffield: JSOT, 1984.

Maile, J. F. 'The Ascension in Luke-Acts'. *TynB* 37 (1986) 29-59.

Malherbe, A. J. *Ancient Epistolary Theorists.* SBLSBS 19. Atlanta: Scholars, 1988.

————. 'The Beasts at Ephesus'. *JBL* 87 (1968) 71-80.

————. 'Exhortations in 1 Thessalonians'. *NovT* 25 (1983) 238-56.

————. '"Gentle as a Nurse": The Cynic Background to 1 Thessalonians 2'. *NovT* 12 (1970) 203-17.

————. *Paul and the Popular Philosophers.* Minneapolis: Fortress, 1989.

————. *Paul and the Thessalonians.* Philadelphia: Fortress, 1987.

————. 'A Physical Description of Paul'. *HTR* 79 (1986) 170-75.

————. *Social Aspects of Early Christianity.* Baton Rouge: Louisiana State University, 1977.

Malina, B. J. *The New Testament World: Insights from Cultural Anthropology.* London: SCM, 1983.

Malina, B. J., and J. H. Neyrey. *Portraits of Paul: An Archaeology of Ancient Personality.* Louisville: Westminster John Knox, 1996.

Manson, T. W. 'The Corinthian Correspondence'. In *Studies in the Gospels and Epistles,* edited by M. Black, 190-209. Manchester: Manchester University, 1962.

Marguerat, D. 'The Enigma of the Silent Closing of Acts (28:16-31)'. In *Jesus and the Heritage of Israel,* edited by D. Moessner, 284-304. Harrisburg: Trinity, 1999.

————. *The First Christian Historian: Writing the 'Acts of the Apostles'.* SNTSMS 121. Cambridge: Cambridge University, 2002.

————. 'Paul et la loi. Le retournement (Philippiens 3,2–4,1)'. In *Paul, une théologie en construction,* edited by A. Dettweiler et al., 251-75. Geneva: Labor et Fides, 2004.

Marshall, I. H. 'Acts and the "Former Treatise"'. *BAFCS* 1.163-82.

————. *Last Supper and Lord's Supper.* Exeter: Paternoster, 1980.

————. *Luke: Historian and Theologian.* Exeter: Paternoster, 1970.

————. 'Salvation, Grace and Works in the Later Writings in the Pauline Corpus'. *NTS* 42 (1996) 339-58.

————. 'Who Were the Evangelists?' In *The Mission of the Early Church,* edited by J. Ådna and H. Kvalbein, 251-63. Tübingen: Mohr Siebeck, 2000.

Marshall, I. H., and D. Peterson, eds. *Witness to the Gospel: The Theology of Acts.* Grand Rapids: Eerdmans, 1998.

Marshall, P. *Enmity in Corinth: Social Conventions in Paul's Relations with the Corinthians.* WUNT 2.23. Tübingen: Mohr Siebeck, 1987.

Martin, D. B. *The Corinthian Body.* New Haven: Yale University, 1995.

————. *Slavery as Salvation.* New Haven: Yale University, 1990.

Martin, R. P. *A Hymn of Christ: Philippians 2:5-11 in Recent Interpretation and in the Setting of Early Christian Worship.* Downers Grove: InterVarsity, 1997, 3rd ed.

Martyn, J. L. 'Apocalyptic Antinomies in Paul's Letter to the Galatians'. *NTS* 31 (1985) 410-24.

————. 'Nomos plus Genitive Noun in Paul: The History of God's Law'. In *Early Christianity and Classical Culture*, A. J. Malherbe FS, edited by J. T. Fitzgerald et al., 575-87. Leiden: Brill, 2003.

Mason, S. 'Chief Priests, Sadducees, Pharisees and Sanhedrin in Acts'. *BAFCS* 4.115-77.

————. '*Philosophiai*: Graeco-Roman, Judean and Christian'. In *Voluntary Associations in the Graeco-Roman World*, edited by J. S. Kloppenborg and S. G. Wilson, 31-58. London: Routledge, 1996.

Matthews, C. R. *Philip: Apostle and Evangelist.* NovTSupp 105. Leiden: Brill, 2002.

Mattingly, H. B. 'The Origin of the Name Christiani'. *JTS* 9 (1958) 26-37.

Mazar, B. *The Mountain of the Lord: Excavating in Jerusalem.* New York: Doubleday, 1975.

McCoy, W. C. 'In the Shadow of Thucydides'. In *History, Literature and Society in the Book of Acts*, edited by B. Witherington, 3-23. Cambridge: Cambridge University, 1996.

McCready, W. O. 'Ekklesia and Voluntary Associations'. In *Voluntary Associations in the Graeco-Roman World*, edited by J. S. Kloppenborg and S. G. Wilson, 59-73. London: Routledge, 1996.

McGiffert, A. C. *A History of Christianity in the Apostolic Age.* Edinburgh: Clark, 1897.

McKechnie, P. R. 'Judean Embassies and Cases before Roman Emperors, AD 44-66'. *JTS* 56 (2005) 339-61.

McKnight, S. 'Covenant and Spirit: The Origins of the New Covenant Hermeneutic'. In *The Holy Spirit and Christian Origins*, J. D. G. Dunn FS, edited by G. N. Stanton et al., 41-54. Grand Rapids: Eerdmans, 2004.

————. *A Light among the Gentiles: Jewish Missionary Activity in the Second Temple Period.* Minneapolis: Fortress, 1991.

————. 'A Parting within the Way: Jesus and James on Israel and Purity'. In *James the Just*, edited by B. Chilton and C. A. Evans, 102-11. Leiden: Brill, 1999.

McLaren, J. S. 'Ananus, James and Earliest Christianity: Josephus' Account of the Death of James'. *JTS* 52 (2001) 1-25.

————. *Power and Politics in Palestine: The Jews and the Governing of Their Land 100 BC-AD 70.* JSNTS 63. Sheffield: Sheffield Academic, 1991.

McLean, B. H. 'The Agrippinilla Inscription: Religious Associations and Early Church Formation'. In *Origins and Method*, 239-70.

————, ed. *Origins and Method: Towards a New Understanding of Judaism and Christianity*, J. C. Hurd FS. JSNTS 86. Sheffield: JSOT, 1993.

Mealand, D. L. 'The Close of Acts and Its Hellenistic Vocabulary'. *NTS* 36 (1990) 583-97.

Meeks, W. A. 'Breaking Away: Three New Testament Pictures of Christianity's Separation from the Jewish Communities'. In *'To See Ourselves as Others See Us': Christians, Jews, 'Others' in Late Antiquity*, edited by J. Neusner and E. S. Frerichs, 93-115. Chico: Scholars, 1985.

————. *The First Urban Christians: The Social World of the Apostle Paul.* New Haven: Yale University, 1983.

Meeks, W. A., and R. L. Wilken, eds. *Jews and Christians in Antioch in the First Four Centuries of the Common Era.* Missoula: Scholars, 1978.

Meggitt, J. J. 'Meat Consumption and Social Conflict in Corinth'. *JTS* 45 (1994) 137-41.

———. *Paul, Poverty and Survival.* Edinburgh: Clark, 1998.

———. 'Sources: Use, Abuse, Neglect. The Importance of Ancient Popular Culture'. In *Christianity at Corinth,* edited by E. Adams and D. G. Horrell, ch. 19. Louisville: Westminster John Knox, 2004.

Meissner, S. *Die Heimholung des Ketzers. Studien zur jüdischen Auseinandersetzung mit Paulus.* WUNT 2.87. Tübingen: Mohr Siebeck, 1996.

Menoud, P. H. 'The Meaning of the Verb *porthein:* Gal. 1.13, 23; Acts 9.21'. In *Jesus Christ and the Faith,* 47-60. Pittsburgh: Pickwick, 1978.

Merkel, H. 'Der Epheserbrief in der neueren Diskussion'. *ANRW* 2.25.4 (1987) 3176-212.

Merklein, H. 'Die Ekklesia Gottes. Der Kirchenbegriff bei Paulus und in Jerusalem'. In *Studien zu Jesus und Paulus,* 296-318.

———. '"Nicht aus Werken des Gesetzes . . .". Eine Auslegung von Gal 2,15-21'. In *Studien zu Jesus und Paulus,* 2.303-15. Tübingen: Mohr Siebeck, 1998.

———. *Studien zu Jesus und Paulus.* WUNT 43. Tübingen: Mohr Siebeck, 1987.

———. 'Zur Entstehung der urchristlichen Aussage vom präexistenten Sohn Gottes'. In *Studien zu Jesus und Paulus,* 247-76.

Metzger, B. M. 'Ancient Astrological Geography and Acts 2:9-11'. In *Apostolic History and the Gospel,* F. F. Bruce FS, edited by W. W. Gasque and R. P. Martin, 123-33. Exeter: Paternoster, 1970.

———. 'Considerations of Methodology in the Study of the Mystery Religions and Early Christianity'. *HTR* 48 (1955) 1-20.

———. *A Textual Commentary on the Greek New Testament.* London: United Bible Societies, 1971, 1975.

Metzger, P. *Katechon. II Thess 2,1-12 im Horizont apokalyptischen Denkens.* BZNW 135. Berlin: de Gruyter, 2005.

Metzner, R. 'In aller Freundschaft. Ein frühchristlicher Fall freundschaftlicher Gemeinschaft (Phil 2.25-30)'. *NTS* 48 (2002) 111-31.

Meyer, E. *Ursprung und Anfänge des Urchristentums.* 3 vols. Stuttgart: J. G. Cotta, 1921-23.

Meyer, M. W., ed. *The Ancient Mysteries: A Sourcebook; Sacred Texts of the Mystery Religions of the Ancient Mediterranean World.* San Francisco: Harper, 1987.

Minear, P. S. *The Obedience of Faith: The Purpose of Paul in the Epistle to the Romans.* London: SCM, 1971.

Mitchell, M. M. 'Concerning *peri de* in 1 Corinthians'. *NovT* 31 (1989) 229-56.

———. 'The Letter of James as a Document of Paulinism?' In *Reading James with New Eyes: Methodological Reassessments of the Letter of James,* edited by R. L. Webb and J. S. Kloppenborg, 75-98. London: Clark, 2007.

———. 'New Testament Envoys in the Context of Greco-Roman Diplomatic and Epistolary Conventions: The Example of Timothy and Titus'. *JBL* 111 (1992) 641-62.

———. *Paul and the Rhetoric of Reconciliation: An Exegetical Investigation of the Language and Composition of 1 Corinthians.* Louisville: Westminster John Knox, 1993.

———. 'Paul's Letters to Corinth: The Interpretive Intertwining of Literary and Historical Reconstruction'. In *Urban Religion in Roman Corinth,* edited by D. N. Schowalter and J. Friesen, 307-38. Cambridge: Harvard University, 2005.

Mitchell, M. W. 'Reexamining the "Aborted Apostle": An Exploration of Paul's Self-Description in 1 Corinthians 15.8'. *JSNT* 25 (2003) 469-85.

Mitchell, S. *Anatolia: Land, Men, and Gods in Asia Minor.* 2 vols. Oxford: Clarendon, 1993.

Mitford, T. B. 'Roman Cyprus'. *ANRW* 2.7.2 (1980) 1285-1384.

Moessner, D. P. 'The Appeal and Power of Poetics (Luke 1:1-4)'. In *Jesus and the Heritage of Israel,* 84-123.

———. 'The Meaning of *kathexēs* in the Lukan Prologue as a Key to the Distinctive Contribution of Luke's Narrative among the "Many"'. In *The Four Gospels, F. Neirynck FS,* edited by F. Van Segbroeck, 2.1513-28. Leuven: Leuven University, 1992.

———. 'The "Script" of the Scriptures in Acts: Suffering as God's "Plan" *(boulē)* for the World for the "Release of Sins"'. In *History, Literature and Society in the Book of Acts,* edited by B. Witherington, 218-50. Cambridge: Cambridge University, 1996.

———, ed. *Jesus and the Heritage of Israel.* Harrisburg: Trinity, 1999.

Moffatt, J. *An Introduction to the Literature of the New Testament.* Edinburgh: Clark, 1918.

Moore, G. F. 'Christian Writers on Judaism'. *HTR* 14 (1922) 197-254.

Morgan, R. 'Paul's Enduring Legacy'. In *The Cambridge Companion to St. Paul,* edited by J. D. G. Dunn, 242-55. Cambridge: Cambridge University, 2003.

Moule, C. F. D. *The Birth of the New Testament.* London: Black, 1962, 1981, 3rd ed.

———. 'The Christology of Acts'. In *Studies in Luke Acts,* edited by L. E. Keck and J. L. Martyn, 59-85. Nashville: Abingdon, 1966.

———. 'Once More, Who Were the Hellenists?' *ExpT* 70 (1958-59) 100-102.

———. *The Origin of Christology.* Cambridge: Cambridge University, 1977.

———. *The Phenomenon of the New Testament.* London: SCM, 1967.

———. 'The Post-resurrection Appearances in the Light of Festival Pilgrimages'. *NTS* 4 (1957-58) 58-61.

Mount, C. *Pauline Christianity: Luke-Acts and the Legacy of Paul.* NovTSupp 104. Leiden: Brill, 2002.

Müller, C. G. 'Priska und Aquila. Der Weg eines Ehepaares und die paulinischen Mission'. *MTZ* 54 (2003) 195-210.

Müller, P.-G. 'Der "Paulinismus" in der Apg'. In *Paulus in den neutestamentlichen Spätschriften,* edited by K. Kertelge, 157-201. Freiburg: Herder, 1981.

Munck, J. *Paul and the Salvation of Mankind.* London: SCM, 1959.

Murphy-O'Connor, J. 'The Cenacle — Topographical Setting for Acts 2:44-45'. *BAFCS* 4.303-21.

———. 'Gal 2:15-16a: Whose Common Ground?' *RB* 108 (2001) 376-85.

———. *The Holy Land.* Oxford: Oxford University, 1998.

———. *Paul: A Critical Life.* Oxford: Clarendon, 1996.

———. *Paul the Letter-Writer: His World, His Options, His Skills.* Collegeville: Liturgical, 1995.

————. *The Theology of the Second Letter to the Corinthians.* Cambridge: Cambridge University, 1991.

Mussner, F. '"In den letzten Tagen" (Apg. 2,17a)'. *BZ* 5 (1961) 263-65.

Nanos, M. D. 'Intruding "Spies" and "Pseudo-Brethren": The Jewish Intra-group Politics of Paul's Jerusalem Meeting [Gal 2:1-10]'. In *Paul and His Opponents,* edited by S. E. Porter, 59-97. Leiden: Brill, 2005.

————. *The Irony of Galatians: Paul's Letter in First-Century Context.* Minneapolis: Fortress, 2002.

————. *The Mystery of Romans: The Jewish Context of Paul's Letter.* Minneapolis: Fortress, 1996.

————. 'What Was at Stake in Peter's "Eating with Gentiles" at Antioch?' In *The Galatians Debate,* ch. 15.

————, ed. *The Galatians Debate.* Peabody: Hendrickson, 2002.

Neudorfer, H.-W. 'The Speech of Stephen'. In *Witness to the Gospel: The Theology of Acts,* edited by I. H. Marshall and D. Peterson, 275-94. Grand Rapids: Eerdmans, 1998.

————. *Der Stephanuskreis in der Forschungsgeschichte seit F. C. Baur.* Giessen: Brunnen, 1983.

Neufeld, V. H. *The Earliest Christian Confessions.* NTTS 5. Grand Rapids: Eerdmans, 1963.

Neyrey, J. H. 'Luke's Social Location of Paul: Cultural Anthropology and the Status of Paul in Acts'. In *History, Literature and Society in the Book of Acts,* edited by B. Witherington, 251-79. Cambridge: Cambridge University, 1996.

————. *Paul in Other Words: A Cultural Reading of His Letters.* Louisville: Westminster John Knox, 1990.

————. 'Perceiving the Human Body: Body Language in 1 Corinthians'. In *Paul in Other Words,* 102-46.

Nguyen, V. H. R. 'The Identification of Paul's Spectacle of Death Metaphor in 1 Corinthians 4.9'. *NTS* 53 (2007) 489-501.

Nicholl, C. R. *From Hope to Despair in Thessalonica: Situating 1 and 2 Thessalonians.* SNTSMS 126. Cambridge: Cambridge University, 2004.

Nicklas, T., and M. Tilly, eds. *The Book of Acts as Church History: Text, Textual Traditions and Ancient Interpretations.* BZNW 120. Berlin: de Gruyter, 2003.

Nickle, K. F. *The Collection: A Study in Paul's Strategy.* London: SCM, 1966.

Niebuhr, K.-W. *Heidenapostel aus Israel.* WUNT 62. Tübingen: Mohr Siebeck, 1992.

————. 'Der Jakobusbrief im Licht frühjüdischer Diasporabriefe'. *NTS* 44 (1998) 420-43.

————. '"Judentum" und "Christentum" bei Paulus und Ignatius von Antiochien'. *ZNW* 85 (1994) 218-33.

————. 'Die paulinische Rechtfertigungslehre in der gegenwärtigen exegetischen Diskussion'. In *Worum geht es in der Rechtfertigungslehre?* edited by T. Söding, 105-30. Freiburg: Herder, 1999.

————. 'Tora ohne Tempel. Paulus und der Jakobusbrief im Zusammenhang frühjüdischer Torarezeption für die Diaspora'. In *Gemeinde ohne Tempel / Community without Temple,* edited by B. Ego et al., 427-60. Tübingen: Mohr Siebeck, 1999.

Nobbs, A. 'Cyprus'. *BAFCS* 2.279-89.

Nock, A. D. *Conversion: The Old and New in Religion from Alexander the Great to Augustine.* London: Oxford University, 1933.

―――. 'Early Gentile Christianity and Its Hellenistic Background' (1928) and 'Hellenistic Mysteries and Christian Sacraments' (1952). In *Essays on Religion and the Ancient World,* 2 vols., edited by J. Z. Stewart, 1.49-133 and 2.791-820. Oxford: Clarendon, 1972.

―――. 'Paul and the Magus'. *Beginnings* 5.164-88.

―――. *St. Paul.* Oxford: Oxford University, 1938, 1946.

Nolland, J. 'Uncircumcised Proselytes?' *JSJ* 12 (1981) 173-94.

Norris, F. W. 'Antioch on the Orontes as a Religious Center I: Paganism before Constantine'. *ANRW* 2.18.4 (1990) 2322-79.

North, J. L. 'Jesus and Worship, God and Sacrifice'. In *Early Jewish and Christian Monotheism,* edited by L. T. Stuckenbruck and W. E. S. North, 186-202. London: Clark International, 2004.

Novak, D. *The Image of the Non-Jew in Judaism: An Historical and Constructive Study of the Noahide Laws.* Lewiston: Mellen, 1983.

Oakes, P. *Philippians: From People to Letter.* SNTSMS 110. Cambridge: Cambridge University, 2001.

O'Brien, P. T. *Gospel and Mission in the Writings of Paul.* Grand Rapids: Baker, 1995.

Oepke, A. *Die Missionspredigt des Apostels Paulus.* Leipzig: Hinrichs, 1920.

Ogg, G. *The Chronology of the Life of Paul.* London: Epworth, 1968.

Öhler, M. *Barnabas. Die historische Person und ihre Rezeption in der Apostelgeschichte.* WUNT 156. Tübingen: Mohr Siebeck, 2003.

―――. 'Die Jerusalemer Urgemeinde im Spiegel des antiken Vereinswesens'. *NTS* 51 (2005) 393-415.

Ollrog, W.-H. *Paulus und seine Mitarbeiter.* WMANT 50. Neukirchen-Vluyn: Neukirchener, 1979.

Olsson, B., and M. Zetterholm, eds. *The Ancient Synagogue from Its Origins until 200 C.E.* CBNTS 39. Stockholm: Almqvist and Wiksell, 2003.

Omerzu, H. 'Paulus als Politiker? Das paulinische Evangelium zwischen Ekklesia und Imperium Romanum'. In *Logos — Logik — Lyrik. Engagierte exegetische Studien zum biblischen Reden Gottes,* K. Haacker FS, edited by V. A. Lehnert and U. Rüsen-Weinhold, 267-87. Leipzig: Evangelische Verlagsanstalt, 2007.

―――. *Der Prozess des Paulus. Eine exegetische und rechtshistorische Untersuchung der Apostelgeschichte.* BZNW 115. Berlin: de Gruyter, 2002.

―――. 'Das Schweigen des Lukas'. In *Das Ende des Paulus,* edited by F. W. Horn, 127-56. Berlin: de Gruyter, 2001.

Oster, R. E. 'Use, Misuse and Neglect of Archaeological Evidence in Some Modern Works on 1 Corinthians'. *ZNW* 83 (1992) 52-73.

Overman, J. A. '*Kata Nomon Pharisaios:* A Short History of Paul's Pharisaism'. In *Pauline Conversations in Context,* C. J. Roetzel FS, edited by J. C. Anderson et al., 180-93. London: Sheffield Academic, 2002.

Packer, J. E. 'Housing and Population in Imperial Ostia and Rome'. *JRS* 57 (1967) 80-95.

Page, S. H. T. 'Whose Ministry? A Re-appraisal of Ephesians 4:1'. *NovT* 47 (2005) 26-46.

Paige, T. 'Stoicism, *eleutheria* and Community at Corinth'. In *Worship, Theology and Ministry in the Early Church,* R. P. Martin FS, edited by M. J. Wilkins and T. Paige, 180-93. Sheffield: JSOT, 1992.

Painter, J. 'James and Peter: Models of Leadership and Mission'. In *The Missions of James, Peter, and Paul,* edited by B. Chilton and C. Evans, 143-209. Leiden: Brill, 2005.

————. *Just James: The Brother of Jesus in History and Tradition.* Columbia: University of South Carolina, 1997.

————. 'Who Was James? Footprints as a Means of Identification'. In *The Brother of Jesus,* edited by B. Chilton and J. Neusner, 10-65. Louisville: Westminster John Knox, 2001.

Palmer, D. W. 'Acts and the Ancient Historical Monograph'. *BAFCS* 1.1-29.

Parker, F. 'The Terms "Angel" and "Spirit" in Acts 23,8'. *Biblica* 84 (2003) 344-65.

Parsons, M. C. *The Departure of Jesus in Luke-Acts: The Ascension Narratives in Context.* JSNTS 21. Sheffield: JSOT, 1987.

————. 'The Text of Acts 1:2 Reconsidered'. *CBQ* 50 (1988) 58-71.

Patrick, J. E. 'Living Rewards for Dead Apostles: "Baptised for the Dead" in 1 Corinthians 15.29'. *NTS* 52 (2006) 71-85.

Pearson, B. A. *The Pneumatikos-Psychikos Terminology in 1 Corinthians.* SBLDS 12. Atlanta: Scholars, 1973.

————. 'A Q Community in Galilee?' *NTS* 50 (2004) 476-94.

Pearson, B. A., et al., eds. *The Future of Early Christianity,* H. Koester FS. Minneapolis: Fortress, 1991.

Peerbolte, L. J. L. *Paul the Missionary.* Leuven: Peeters, 2003.

Penna, R. *Paul the Apostle: A Theological and Exegetical Study.* Vol. 1: *Jew and Greek Alike.* Collegeville: Liturgical, 1996.

Penner, T. C. *The Epistle of James and Eschatology.* JSNTS 121. Sheffield: Sheffield Academic, 1996.

————. *In Praise of Christian Origins: Stephen and the Hellenists in Lukan Apologetic Historiography.* New York: Clark International, 2004.

Perkins, P. *Gnosticism and the New Testament.* Minneapolis: Fortress, 1993.

————. *Peter: Apostle for the Whole Church.* 1994. Minneapolis: Fortress, 2000.

Pervo, R. I. *Profit with Delight: The Literary Genre of the Acts of the Apostles.* Philadelphia: Fortress, 1987.

Pesch, R. 'Voraussetzungen und Anfänge der urchristlichen Mission'. In *Mission im Neuen Testament,* edited by K. Kertelge, 11-70. Freiburg: Herder, 1982.

Pesch, R., et al. '"Hellenisten" und "Hebräer"'. *BZ* 23 (1979) 87-92.

Peterman, G. W. *Paul's Gift from Philippi: Conventions of Gift Exchange and Christian Giving.* SNTSMS 92. Cambridge: Cambridge University, 1997.

Peterson, N. R. *Rediscovering Paul: Philemon and the Sociology of Paul's Narrative World.* Philadelphia: Fortress, 1985.

Pfleiderer, O. *Primitive Christianity.* ET London: Williams and Norgate, 1906.

Philip, F. *The Origins of Pauline Pneumatology.* WUNT 2.194. Tübingen: Mohr Siebeck, 2005.

Pilhofer, P. *Philippi*. Vol. 1: *Die erste christliche Gemeinde Europas*. WUNT 87. Tübingen: Mohr Siebeck, 1995.

Piper, R. A. *Wisdom in the Q-tradition: The Aphoristic Teaching of Jesus*. SNTSMS 61. Cambridge: Cambridge University, 1989.

―――, ed. *The Gospel behind the Gospels: Current Studies on Q*. NovTSupp 75. Leiden: Brill, 1995.

Pitta, A. 'The Strong, the Weak and the Mosaic Law in the Christian Communities of Rome (Rom. 14.1–15.13)'. In *Christians as a Religious Minority in a Multicultural City,* edited by J. Zangenberg and M. Labahn, 90-102. London: Clark, 2004.

Plevnik, J. *Paul and the Parousia: An Exegetical and Theological Investigation*. Peabody: Hendrickson, 1996.

Plümacher, E. 'Die Apostelgeschichte als historische Monographie'. In *Les Actes des Apôtres. Traditions, rédaction, théologie,* edited by J. Kremer, 457-66. Leuven: Leuven University, 1979.

―――. 'The Mission Speeches in Acts and Dionysius of Halicarnassus'. In *Jesus and the Heritage of Israel,* edited by D. Moessner, 251-66. Harrisburg: Trinity, 1999.

Pogoloff, S. *Logos and Sophia: The Rhetorical Situation of 1 Corinthians*. SBLDS 134. Atlanta: Scholars, 1992.

Pokorny, P. *The Genesis of Christology: Foundations for a Theology of the New Testament*. Edinburgh: Clark, 1987.

Poland, F. *Geschichte des griechischen Vereinswesens*. Leipzig: Teubner, 1909.

Popkes, W. 'Leadership: James, Paul, and Their Contemporary Background'. In *The Missions of James, Peter, and Paul,* edited by B. Chilton and C. Evans, 323-54. Leiden: Brill, 2005.

Porter, S. E. 'Did Paul Have Opponents in Rome and What Were They Opposing?' In *Paul and His Opponents,* 149-68.

―――. 'Magic in the Book of Acts'. In *A Kind of Magic: Understanding Magic in the New Testament and Its Religious Environment,* edited by M. Labahn and L. J. L. Peerbolte, 107-21. London: Clark, 2007.

―――. *The Paul of Acts*. WUNT 115. Tübingen: Mohr Siebeck, 1999.

―――. 'Was Paul a Good Jew? Fundamental Issues in a Current Debate'. In *Christian-Jewish Relations through the Centuries,* edited by S. E. Porter and B. W. R. Pearson, 148-74. Sheffield: Sheffield Academic, 2000.

―――. 'The "We" Passages'. *BAFCS* 2.545-74.

―――. 'When and How Was the Pauline Canon Compiled? An Assessment of Theories'. In *The Pauline Canon,* edited by S. E. Porter, 95-127. Leiden: Brill, 2004.

―――, ed. *Paul and His Opponents*. Leiden: Brill, 2005.

―――, ed. *Paul and His Theology*. Leiden: Brill, 2006.

Pratscher, W. *Der Herrenbruder Jakobus und die Jakobustradition*. FRLANT 139. Göttingen: Vandenhoeck und Ruprecht, 1987.

Price, S. R. F. *Rituals and Power: The Roman Imperial Cult in Asia Minor*. Cambridge: Cambridge University, 1984.

Purvis, J. D. 'The Samaritans'. *CHJ* 2.591-613.

―――. 'The Samaritans and Judaism'. In *Early Judaism and Its Modern Interpreters,* edited by R. A. Kraft and G. W. E. Nickelsburg, 81-98. Atlanta: Scholars, 1986.

Rabens, V. 'The Development of Pauline Pneumatology'. *BZ* 43 (1999) 161-79.

Raeder, M. 'Vikariasttaufe in 1 Cor 15:29?' *ZNW* 46 (1955) 258-61.

Räisänen, H. 'Galatians 2.16 and Paul's Break with Judaism'. In *Jesus, Paul and Torah,* 112-26.

———. 'Die "Hellenisten" der Urgemeinde'. *ANRW* 2.26.2 (1995) 1468-1514.

———. '"The Hellenists": A Bridge between Jesus and Paul?' In *Jesus, Paul and Torah,* 149-202.

———. *Jesus, Paul and Torah: Collected Essays.* JSNTS 43. Sheffield: JSOT, 1992.

———. *Paul and the Law.* WUNT 29. Tübingen: Mohr Siebeck, 1983.

———. 'Paul's Call Experience and His Later View of the Law'. In *Jesus, Paul and Torah,* 15-47.

Rajak, T. 'The Jewish Community and Its Boundaries'. In *The Jews among the Pagans and Christians in the Roman Empire,* edited by J. M. Lieu et al., 9-28. London: Routledge, 1992.

Ramsay, W. M. *The Bearing of Recent Discovery on the Trustworthiness of the New Testament.* London: Hodder and Stoughton, 1915.

———. *The Cities and Bishoprics of Phrygia.* 2 vols. Oxford: Oxford University, 1895, 1897.

———. *The Cities of St. Paul: Their Influence on His Life and Thought.* London: Hodder and Stoughton, 1907.

———. *St. Paul the Traveller and the Roman Citizen.* London: Hodder and Stoughton, 1896.

Ramsey, A. M. 'What Was the Ascension?' *SNTSBull.* 2 (1951) 43-50.

Rapske, B. M. 'Acts, Travel and Shipwreck'. *BAFCS* 2.1-47.

———. *The Book of Acts and Paul in Roman Custody* (= *BAFCS* 3). Grand Rapids: Eerdmans, 1994.

———. 'The Prisoner Paul in the Eyes of Onesimus'. *NTS* 37 (1991) 187-203.

Rau, E. *Von Jesus zu Paulus. Entwicklung und Rezeption der antiochenischen Theologie im Urchristentum.* Stuttgart: Kohlhammer, 1994.

Read-Heimerdinger, J. *The Bezan Text of Acts.* JSNTS 236. London: Sheffield Academic, 2002.

Reasoner, M. *The Strong and the Weak: Romans 14.1–15.13 in Context.* SNTSMS 103. Cambridge: Cambridge University, 1999.

Reicke, B. *The New Testament Era.* London: Black, 1969.

Reinbold, W. *Propaganda und Mission im ältesten Christentum. Eine Untersuchung zu den Modalitäten der Ausbreitung der frühen Kirche.* Göttingen: Vandenhoeck und Ruprecht, 2000.

Reinhardt, W. 'The Population Size of Jerusalem and the Numerical Growth of the Jerusalem Church'. *BAFCS* 4.237-65.

Reiser, M. 'Von Caesarea nach Malta. Literarischer Charakter und historische Glaubwürdigkeit von Act 27'. In *Das Ende des Paulus,* edited by F. W. Horn, 49-73. Berlin: de Gruyter, 2001.

Reitzenstein, R. *Hellenistic Mystery Religions: Their Basic Ideas and Significance.* 1910. ET Pittsburgh: Pickwick, 1978.

Rengstorf, K. H. 'The Election of Matthias: Acts 1.15ff.'. In *Current Issues in New Testa-*

ment Interpretation, O. A. Piper FS, edited by W. Klassen and G. F. Snyder, 178-92. New York: Harper and Row, 1962.

Reumann, J. 'Church Office in Paul, Especially in Philippians'. In *Origins and Method: Towards a New Understanding of Judaism and Christianity,* J. C. Hurd FS, edited by B. H. McLean, 82-91. Sheffield: JSOT, 1993.

———. 'Contributions of the Philippian Community to Paul and to Earliest Christianity'. *NTS* 39 (1993) 438-57.

———. 'Justification in Pauline Thought: A Lutheran View'. In *Rereading Paul Together: Protestant and Catholic Perspectives on Justification,* edited by D. E. Aune, 108-30. Grand Rapids: Baker, 2006.

Richards, E. *Acts 6:1–8:4: The Author's Method of Composition.* SBLDS 41. Missoula: Scholars, 1978.

Richards, E. R. *Paul and First-Century Letter Writing.* Downers Grove: InterVarsity, 2004.

———. *The Secretary in the Letters of Paul.* WUNT 2.42. Tübingen: Mohr Siebeck, 1991.

Richardson, P. 'An Architectural Case for Synagogues as Associations'. In *The Ancient Synagogue from Its Origins until 200 C.E.,* edited by B. Olsson and M. Zetterholm, 90-117. Stockholm: Almqvist and Wiksell, 2003.

———. 'Augustan-Era Synagogues in Rome'. In *Judaism and Christianity in First-Century Rome,* edited by K. P. Donfried and P. Richardson, 17-29. Grand Rapids: Eerdmans, 1998.

———. 'Building an Association *(Synodos)* . . . and a Place of Their Own'. In *Community Formation in the Early Church and in the Church Today,* edited by R. N. Longenecker, 36-56. Peabody: Hendrickson, 2002.

———. 'Early Synagogues as Collegia in the Diaspora and Palestine'. In *Voluntary Associations in the Graeco-Roman World,* edited by J. S. Kloppenborg and S. G. Wilson, 90-109. London: Routledge, 1996.

———. *Israel in the Apostolic Church.* SNTSMS 10. Cambridge: Cambridge University, 1969.

Riesner, R. 'Das Jerusalemer Essenerviertel und die Urgemeinde. Josephus, Bellum Judaicum V 145; 11QMiqdasch 46, 13-16; Apostelgeschichte 1-6 und die Archäologie'. *ANRW* 2.26.2 (1995) 1775-1922.

———. *Paul's Early Period: Chronology, Mission Strategy, Theology.* Grand Rapids: Eerdmans, 1998.

———. 'Synagogues in Jerusalem'. *BAFCS* 4.179-211.

Ritmeyer, L., and K. Ritmeyer. *Jerusalem in the Year 30 A.D.* Jerusalem: Carta, 2004.

Ritschl, A. *Die Entstehung der altkatholischen Kirche.* Bonn: Marcus, 1850, 1857, 2nd ed.

Robbins, V. K. 'The We-Passages and Ancient Sea Voyages'. In *Perspectives on Luke-Acts,* edited by C. H. Talbert, 215-42. Edinburgh: Clark, 1978.

Robertson, C. K. *Conflict in Corinth: Redefining the System.* New York: Lang, 2001.

Robinson, J. A. T. 'The Most Primitive Christology of All?' In *Twelve New Testament Studies,* 139-53. London: SCM, 1962.

———. *Redating the New Testament.* London: SCM, 1976.

Robinson, J. M., P. Hoffmann, et al. *The Critical Edition of Q*. The International Q Project. Leuven: Peeters, 2000.

Robinson, J. M., and H. Koester. *Trajectories through Early Christianity*. Philadelphia: Fortress, 1971.

Roetzel, C. *Paul: The Man and the Myth*. Edinburgh: Clark, 1999.

Roloff, J. *Die Kirche im Neuen Testament*. Göttingen: Vandenhoeck und Ruprecht. 1993.

Rosner, B. S. 'The Progress of the Word'. In *Witness to the Gospel: The Theology of Acts,* edited by I. H. Marshall and D. Peterson, 215-33. Grand Rapids: Eerdmans, 1998.

Rothschild, C. K. *Luke-Acts and the Rhetoric of History*. WUNT 2.175. Tübingen: Mohr Siebeck, 2004.

Rowland, C. *Christian Origins*. London: SPCK, 1985.

———. *The Open Heaven: A Study of Apocalyptic in Judaism and Early Christianity*. London: SPCK, 1982.

Rüpke, J. 'Collegia sacerdotum. Religiöse Vereine in der Oberschicht'. In *Religiöse Vereine in der römischen Antike,* edited by U. Egelhaaf-Gaiser and A. Schäfer, 41-67. Tübingen: Mohr Siebeck, 2002.

Rutgers, L. V. 'Attitudes to Judaism in the Greco-Roman Period: Reflections on Feldman's Jew and Gentile in the Ancient World'. *JQR* 85 (1995) 361-95.

———. *The Jews in Late Ancient Rome*. Leiden: Brill, 1995.

———. 'Roman Policy toward the Jews: Expulsions from the City of Rome during the First Century C.E.'. In *Judaism and Christianity in First-Century Rome,* edited by K. P. Donfried and P. Richardson, 93-116. Grand Rapids: Eerdmans, 1998.

Saddington, D. B. 'Military and Administrative Personnel in the New Testament'. *ANRW* 2.26.3 (1996) 2408-35.

Safrai, S., ed. *The Literature of the Sages*. CRINT 2.3. Assen: Van Gorcum, 1987.

Sampley, J. P. '"Before God, I Do Not Lie" (Gal. 1.20): Paul's Self-Defence in the Light of Roman Legal Praxis'. *NTS* 23 (1977) 477-82.

———. 'The Weak and the Strong: Paul's Careful and Crafty Rhetorical Strategy in Romans 14:1–15:13'. In *The Social World of the First Christians,* W. A. Meeks FS, edited by L. M. White and O. L. Yarbrough, 40-52. Minneapolis: Fortress, 1995.

———, ed. *Paul in the Greco-Roman World: A Handbook*. Harrisburg: Trinity, 2003.

Sanders, E. P. 'Jewish Association with Gentiles and Galatians 2.11-14'. In *Studies in Paul and John,* J. L. Martyn FS, edited by R. T. Fortna and B. R. Gaventa, 170-88. Nashville: Abingdon, 1990.

———. *Judaism: Practice and Belief, 63 BCE–66 CE*. London: SCM, 1992.

———. *Paul*. New York: Oxford University, 1991.

———. *Paul and Palestinian Judaism*. London: SCM, 1977.

———. *Paul, the Law and the Jewish People*. Philadelphia: Fortress, 1983.

Sanders, J. T. 'The First Decades of Jewish-Christian Relations: The Evidence of the New Testament (Gospels and Acts)'. *ANRW* 2.26.3 (1996) 1937-78.

———. *The Jews in Luke-Acts*. Philadelphia: Fortress, 1987.

———. *The New Testament Christological Hymns: Their Historical Religious Background*. SNTSMS 15. Cambridge: Cambridge University, 1971.

———. *Schismatics, Sectarians, Dissidents, Deviants: The First One Hundred Years of Jewish-Christian Relations*. London: SCM, 1993.

Sandmel, S. *The Genius of Paul: A Study in History.* Philadelphia: Fortress, 1958.

Sandnes, K. O. *Paul — One of the Prophets?* WUNT 2.43. Tübingen: Mohr Siebeck, 1991.

Sappington, T. J. *Revelation and Redemption at Colossae.* JSNTS 53. Sheffield: JSOT, 1991.

Satterthwaite, P. E. 'Acts against the Background of Classical Rhetoric'. *BAFCS* 1.337-79.

Saunders, R. 'Paul and the Imperial Cult'. In *Paul and His Opponents,* edited by S. E. Porter, 227-38. Leiden: Brill, 2005.

Schäfer, P. *Judeophobia: Attitudes toward the Jews in the Ancient World.* Cambridge: Harvard University, 1997.

―――. 'New Testament and Hekhalot Literature: The Journey into Heaven in Paul and Merkavah Mysticism'. *JSS* 35 (1985) 19-35.

Schäfer, R. *Paulus bis zum Apostelkonzil.* WUNT 2.179. Tübingen: Mohr Siebeck, 2004.

Schaller, B. 'Christus, "der Diener der Beschneidung . . . , auf ihn werden die Völker hoffen". Zu Schriftzitate in Röm 15,7-13'. In *Das Gesetz im frühen Judentum und im Neuen Testament,* C. Burchard FS, edited by D. Sänger and M. Konradt, 261-85. Göttingen: Vandenhoeck und Ruprecht, 2006.

Scharlemann, M. H. *Stephen: A Singular Saint.* AnBib 34. Rome: Pontifical Biblical Institute, 1968.

Schenk, W. 'Die ältesten Selbstverständnis christlicher Gruppen im ersten Jahrhundert'. *ANRW* 2.26.2 (1995) 1355-1467.

―――. 'Der Kolosserbrief in der neueren Forschung (1945-1985)'. *ANRW* 2.25.4 (1987) 3327-64.

Schenke, H.-M. 'Four Problems in the Life of Paul Reconsidered'. In *The Future of Early Christianity,* H. Koester FS, edited by B. A. Pearson et al., 318-28. Minneapolis: Fortress, 1991.

Schenke, L. *Die Urgemeinde. Geschichtliche und theologische Entwicklung.* Stuttgart: Kohlhammer, 1990.

Scherrer, P. 'The City of Ephesos from the Roman Period to Late Antiquity'. In *Ephesos: Metropolis of Asia,* edited by H. Koester, 1-25. Cambridge: Harvard Divinity School, 1995, 2004.

Schiffman, L. H. 'At the Crossroads: Tannaitic Perspectives on the Jewish-Christian Schism'. *JCSD* 2.115-56.

―――. *Who Was a Jew?* Hoboken: Ktav, 1985.

Schille, G. *Anfänge der Kirche. Erwägungen zur apostolischen Frühgeschichte.* Munich: Kaiser, 1966.

Schlueter, C. J. *Filling Up the Measure: Polemical Hyperbole in 1 Thessalonians 2.14-16.* JSNTS 98. Sheffield: Sheffield Academic, 1994.

Schmeller, T. 'Die Cicerobriefe und die Frage nach der Einheitlichkeit des 2. Korintherbriefs'. *ZNW* 95 (2004) 181-208.

―――. 'Gegenwelten. Zum Vergleich zwischen paulinischen Gemeinden und nichtchristlichen Gruppen'. *BZ* 47 (2003) 167-85.

―――. 'Der ursprüngliche Kontext von 2 Kor 6.14–7.1. Zur Frage der Einheitlichkeit des 2. Korintherbriefs'. *NTS* 52 (2006) 219-38.

Schmidt, D. D. 'Rhetorical Influences and Genre: Luke's Preface and the Rhetoric of Hellenistic Historiography'. In *Jesus and the Heritage of Israel,* edited by D. Moessner, 27-60. Harrisburg: Trinity, 1999.

Schmithals, W. *Gnosticism in Corinth.* 1965. ET Nashville: Abingdon, 1971.

———. 'Judaisten in Galatien?' In *Paulus,* 39-77.

———. *Paul and James.* 1963. London: SCM, 1965.

———. 'Paulus als Heidenmissionar und das Problem seiner theologischen Entwicklung'. In *Jesu Rede von Gott und ihre Nachgeschichte im frühen Christentum,* W. Marxsen FS, edited by D.-A. Koch, 235-51. Gütersloh: Mohn, 1989.

———. *Paulus, die Evangelien und das Urchristentum.* Leiden: Brill, 2004.

———. 'Probleme des "Apostelkonzils" (Gal 2,1-10)'. In *Paulus,* 5-38.

———. *Theologiegeschichte des Urchristentums. Eine problemgeschichtliche Darstellung.* Stuttgart: Kohlhammer, 1994.

Schnabel, E. J. *Early Christian Mission.* Vol. 1: *Jesus and the Twelve;* vol. 2: *Paul and the Early Church.* Downers Grove: InterVarsity, 2004.

Schnackenburg, R. *Baptism in the Thought of St. Paul.* Oxford: Blackwell, 1964.

Schneckenburger, M. *Über den Zweck der Apostelgeschichte.* Bern: Fischer, 1841.

Schneemelcher, W. *Das Urchristentum.* Stuttgart: Kohlhammer, 1981.

Schneider, G. 'Gott und Christus als Kyrios nach der Apostelgeschichte'. In *Begegnung mit dem Wort,* H. Zimmermann FS, edited by J. Zmijewski and E. Nellessen, 161-73. Bonn: Hanstein, 1980.

———. 'Stephanus, die Hellenisten und Samaria'. In *Les Actes des Apôtres. Traditions, rédaction, théologie,* edited by J. Kremer, 215-40. Gembloux: Duculot, 1979.

Schnelle, U. *The History and Theology of the New Testament Writings.* 1994. London: SCM, 1998.

———. *Paul: His Life and Theology.* 2003. Grand Rapids: Baker, 2005.

Schowalter, D. N., and J. Friesen, eds. *Urban Religion in Roman Corinth.* HTS 53. Cambridge: Harvard University, 2005.

Schrage, W. *Die Christen und der Staat nach dem Neuen Testament.* Gütersloh: Gütersloher, 1971.

Schreiber, S. 'Arbeit mit der Gemeinde (Röm 16.6, 12). Zur versunken Möglichkeit der Gemeindeleitung durch Frauen'. *NTS* 46 (2000) 204-26.

Schröter, J. 'Heil für die Heiden und Israel. Zum Zusammenhang von Christologie und Volk Gottes bei Lukas'. In *Die Apostelgeschichte und die hellenistische Geschichtsschreibung,* E. Plümacher FS, edited by C. Breytenbach and J. Schröter, 285-308. Leiden: Brill, 2004.

———. 'Jerusalem und Galiläa. Überlegungen zur Verhältnisbestimmung von Pluralität und Kohärenz für die Konstruktion einer Geschichte des frühen Christentums'. *NovT* 42 (2000) 127-59.

———. 'Lukas als Historiograph. Das lukanische Doppelwerk und die Entdeckung der christlichen Heilsgeschichte'. In *Die antike Historiographie und die Anfänge der christlichen Geschichtsschreibung,* edited by E.-M. Becker, 237-62. Berlin: de Gruyter, 2005.

Schultz, C. E. *Women's Religious Activity in the Roman Republic.* Chapel Hill: University of North Carolina, 2006.

Schwartz, D. R. *Agrippa I: The Last King of Judaea.* Tübingen: Mohr Siebeck, 1990.

———. 'The End of the Line: Paul in the Canonical Book of Acts'. In *Paul and the Legacies of Paul,* edited by W. S. Babcock, 3-24. Dallas: Southern Methodist University, 1990.

———. *Studies in the Jewish Background of Christianity.* Tübingen: Mohr Siebeck, 1992.

Schweizer, E. *Church Order in the New Testament.* ET London: SCM, 1961.

———. 'Concerning the Speeches in Acts'. In *Studies in Luke Acts,* edited by L. E. Keck and J. L. Martyn, 208-16. Nashville: Abingdon, 1966.

———. *Erniedrigung und Erhöhung bei Jesus und seinen Nachfolgern.* Zürich: Zwingli, 1962.

———. *The Lord's Supper according to the New Testament.* Philadelphia: Fortress, 1967.

———. 'Traditional Ethical Patterns in the Pauline and Post-Pauline Letters and Their Development (Lists of Vices and House-Tables)'. In *Text and Interpretation,* M. Black FS, edited by E. Best and R. M. Wilson, 195-209. Cambridge: Cambridge University, 1979.

Schwemer, A. M. 'Erinnerung und Legende. Die Berufung des Paulus und ihre Darstellung in der Apostelgeschichte'. In *Memory in the Bible and Antiquity,* edited by L. T. Stuckenbruck et al., 277-98. Tübingen: Mohr Siebeck, 2007.

———. 'Paulus in Antiochien'. *BZ* 42 (1998) 161-80.

———. 'Verfolger und Verfolgte bei Paulus. Die Auswirkungen der Verfolgung durch Agrippa I. auf die paulinische Mission'. In *Biographie und Persönlichkeit des Paulus,* edited by E.-M. Becker and P. Pilhofer, 169-91. Tübingen: Mohr Siebeck, 2005.

Scott, J. M. *Paul and the Nations.* WUNT 84. Tübingen: Mohr Siebeck, 1995.

Scriba, A. 'Von Korinth nach Rom. Die Chronologie der letzten Jahre des Paulus'. In *Das Ende des Paulus,* edited by F. W. Horn, 157-73. Berlin: de Gruyter, 2001.

Seccombe, D. 'Was There Organized Charity in Jerusalem before the Christians?' *JTS* 29 (1978) 140-43.

Seeberg, A. *Der Katechismus der Urchristenheit.* 1903. Republished Munich: Kaiser, 1966.

Segal, A. F. 'Heavenly Ascent in Hellenistic Judaism, Early Christianity and Their Environment'. *ANRW* 2.23.2 (1980) 1333-94.

———. *Paul the Convert: The Apostolate and Apostasy of Saul the Pharisee.* New Haven: Yale University, 1990.

———. *Rebecca's Children: Judaism and Christianity in the Roman World.* Cambridge: Harvard University, 1986.

Seifrid, M. A. *Justification by Faith: The Origin and Development of a Central Pauline Theme.* NovTSupp 68. Leiden: Brill, 1992.

———. 'Righteousness Language in the Hebrew Scriptures and Early Judaism'. In *Justification and Variegated Nomism,* vol. 1, edited by D. A. Carson et al., 415-42. Tübingen: Mohr Siebeck, 2001.

Seland, T. 'Once More — the Hellenists, Hebrews and Stephen: Conflict and Conflict-Management in Acts 6–7'. In *Recruitment, Conquest, and Conflict: Strategies in*

Judaism, Early Christianity, and the Greco-Roman World, edited by P. Borgen et al., 169-207. Atlanta: Scholars, 1998.

———. 'Philo and the Clubs and Associations of Alexandria'. In *Voluntary Associations in the Graeco-Roman World,* edited by J. S. Kloppenborg and S. G. Wilson, 110-27. London: Routledge, 1996.

———. 'Saul of Tarsus and Early Zealotism: Reading Gal 1,13-14 in Light of Philo's Writings'. *Biblica* 83 (2002) 449-71.

Sellner, H. J. *Das Heil Gottes. Studien zur Soteriologie des lukanischen Doppelwerks.* BZNW 152. Berlin: de Gruyter, 2007.

Shauf, S. *Theology as History, History as Theology: Paul in Ephesus in Acts 19.* BZNW 133. Berlin: de Gruyter, 2005.

Sherk, R. K. *The Roman Empire: Augustus to Hadrian.* TDGR 6. Cambridge: Cambridge University, 1988.

———. 'Roman Galatia: The Governors from 25 BC to AD 114'. *ANRW* 2.7.2 (1980) 954-1052.

Sherwin-White, A. N. *Roman Society and Roman Law in the New Testament.* Oxford: Clarendon, 1963.

Shiell, W. *Reading Acts: The Lector and the Early Christian Audience.* Leiden: Brill, 2004.

Simon, M. *St. Stephen and the Hellenists in the Primitive Church.* London: Longmans Green, 1958.

Skarsaune, O. *In the Shadow of the Temple: Jewish Influences on Early Christianity.* Downers Grove: InterVarsity, 2002.

Skarsaune, O., and R. Hvalvik, eds. *Jewish Believers in Jesus: The Early Centuries.* Peabody: Hendrickson, 2007.

Skeat, T. C. 'Especially the Parchments: A Note on 2 Timothy IV.13'. *JTS* 30 (1979) 172-77.

Slater, W. J., ed. *Dining in a Classical Context.* Ann Arbor: University of Michigan, 1991.

Slee, M. *The Church in Antioch in the First Century C.E..* JSNTS 244. London: Clark International, 2003.

Slingerland, D. 'Acts 18:1-17 and Luedemann's Pauline Chronology'. *JBL* 109 (1990) 686-90.

———. 'Acts 18:1-18, the Gallio Inscription, and Absolute Pauline Chronology'. *JBL* 110 (1991) 439-49.

Smallwood, E. M. *The Jews under Roman Rule from Pompey to Diocletian.* Leiden: Brill, 1981.

Smiles, V. M. 'The Concept of "Zeal" in Second-Temple Judaism and Paul's Critique of It in Romans 10:2'. *CBQ* 64 (2002) 282-99.

Smith, D. E. *From Symposium to Eucharist: The Banquet in the Early Christian World.* Minneapolis: Fortress, 2003.

Smith, I. K. *Heavenly Perspective. A Study of the Apostle Paul's Response to a Jewish Mystical Movement at Colossae.* LNTS 326. London: Clark International, 2006.

Smith, J. *The Voyage and Shipwreck of St. Paul.* London: Longmans Green, 1866.

Smith, J. Z. *Drudgery Divine: On the Comparison of Early Christianities and the Religions of Late Antiquity.* Chicago: University of Chicago, 1990.

Soards, M. L. *The Speeches in Acts: Their Content, Context and Concerns.* Louisville: Westminster John Knox, 1994.

Sohm, R. *Kirchenrecht.* 1892. Munich: Duncker und Humblot, 1923.

Sordi, M. *The Christians and the Roman Empire.* ET 1988. London: Routledge, 1994.

Sowers, S. S. 'The Circumstances and Recollection of the Pella Flight'. *TZ* 26 (1970) 315-20.

Spence, S. *The Parting of the Ways: The Roman Church as a Case Study.* Leuven: Peeters, 2004.

Spencer, F. S. 'Neglected Widows in Acts 6:1-7'. *CBQ* 56 (1994) 715-33.

————. 'Out of Mind, Out of Voice: Slave-Girls and Prophetic Daughters in Luke-Acts'. *BibInt* 7 (1999) 133-55.

————. *The Portrait of Philip in Acts: A Study of Roles and Relations.* JSNTS 67. Sheffield: JSOT, 1992.

Spicq, C. 'Les dénominations du Chrétien'. In *Vie chrétienne et pérégrination selon le Nouveau Testament,* 13-57. Paris: Cerf, 1972.

Squires, J. T. *The Plan of God in Luke-Acts.* SNTSMS 76. Cambridge: Cambridge University, 1993.

Standhartinger, A. 'Colossians and the Pauline School'. *NTS* 50 (2004): 572-93.

————. *Studien zur Entstehungsgeschichte und Intention des Kolosserbriefs.* NovTSupp 94. Leiden: Brill, 1999.

Stanley, C. D. '"Neither Jew nor Greek": Ethnic Conflict in Graeco-Roman Society'. *JSNT* 64 (1996) 101-24.

Stanton, G. N. 'Jesus and Gospel'. In *Jesus and Gospel,* 9-62. Cambridge: Cambridge University, 2004.

————. *Jesus of Nazareth in New Testament Preaching.* SNTSMS 27. Cambridge: Cambridge University, 1974.

————. 'Paul's Gospel'. In *The Cambridge Companion to St. Paul,* edited by J. D. G. Dunn, 173-84. Cambridge: Cambridge University, 2003.

————. 'Stephen in Lucan Perspective'. In *Studia Biblica 1978,* 3 vols., edited by E. A. Livingstone, 3.35-60. Sheffield: JSOT, 1980.

Stanton, G. N., B. W. Longenecker, et al., eds. *The Holy Spirit and Christian Origins,* J. D. G. Dunn FS. Grand Rapids: Eerdmans, 2004.

Stegemann, E. W., and Stegemann, W. *The Jesus Movement: A Social History of Its First Century.* Minneapolis: Fortress, 1999.

Stegemann, W. 'War der Apostel Paulus ein römischer Bürger?' *ZNW* 78 (1987) 200-229.

Stendahl, K. *Paul among Jews and Gentiles.* Philadelphia: Fortress, 1977.

Sterling, G. E. *Historiography and Self-Definition: Josephus, Luke-Acts and Apologetic Historiography.* NovTSupp 64. Leiden: Brill, 1992.

————. '"Opening the Scriptures": The Legitimation of the Jewish Diaspora and the Early Christian Mission'. In *Jesus and the Heritage of Israel,* edited by D. Moessner, 199-225. Harrisburg: Trinity, 1999.

————. '"Wisdom among the Perfect": Creation Traditions in Alexandrian Judaism and Corinthian Christianity'. *NovT* 37 (1995) 355-84.

Stettler, C. 'The Opponents at Colossae'. In *Paul and His Opponents,* edited by S. E. Porter, 169-200. Leiden: Brill, 2005.

Stettler, H. 'An Interpretation of Colossians 1:24 in the Framework of Paul's Mission Theology'. In *The Mission of the Early Church,* edited by J. Ådna and H. Kvalbein,
185-208. Tübingen: Mohr Siebeck, 2000.

Still, T. D. *Conflict at Thessalonica: A Pauline Church and Its Neighbours.* JSNTS 183.
Sheffield: Sheffield Academic, 1999.

—————. 'Did Paul Loathe Manual Labor? Revisiting the Work of Ronald F. Hock on the
Apostle's Tentmaking and Social Class'. *JBL* 125 (2006) 781-95.

Stirewalt, M. L. *Paul: The Letter Writer.* Grand Rapids: Eerdmans, 2003.

Stoops, R. F. 'Riot and Assembly: The Social Context of Acts 19:23-41'. *JBL* 108 (1989)
73-91.

Stowasser, M. 'Am 5,25-27; 9,11f. in der Qumranüberlieferung und in der Apostelgeschichte. Text- und traditionsgeschichtliche Überlegungen zu 4Q174 (Florilegium) III 12/CD VII 16/Apg 7,42b-43; 15,16-18'. *ZNW* 92 (2001) 47-63.

Stowers, S. K. 'Does Pauline Christianity Resemble a Hellenistic Philosophy?' In *Paul beyond the Judaism/Hellenism Divide,* edited by T. Engberg-Pedersen, ch. 4. Louisville: Westminster John Knox, 2001.

—————. *Letter Writing in Greco-Roman Antiquity.* Philadelphia: Westminster, 1986.

—————. *A Rereading of Romans.* New Haven: Yale University, 1994.

—————. 'Social Status, Public Speaking and Private Teaching: The Circumstances of
Paul's Preaching Activity'. *NovT* 26 (1984) 59-82.

Strange, W. A. 'The Jesus-Tradition in Acts'. *NTS* 46 (2000) 59-74.

Strecker, G. *Theology of the New Testament.* Berlin: de Gruyter, 2000.

Streeter, B. H. *The Primitive Church.* London: Macmillan, 1930.

Strelan, R. *Strange Acts: Studies in the Cultural World of the Acts of the Apostles.* BZNW
126. Berlin: de Gruyter, 2004.

Stuckenbruck, L. T. '"Angels" and "God": Exploring the Limits of Early Jewish Monotheism'. In *Early Jewish and Christian Monotheism,* edited by L. T. Stuckenbruck
and W. E. S. North, 45-70. London: Clark International, 2004.

Stuckenbruck, L. T., and W. E. S. North, eds. *Early Jewish and Christian Monotheism.*
JSNTS 263. London: Clark International, 2004.

Stuckenbruck, L. T., et al., eds. *Memory in the Bible and Antiquity.* WUNT 212.
Tübingen: Mohr Siebeck, 2007.

Stuhlmacher, P. *Biblische Theologie des Neuen Testaments.* 2 vols. Göttingen:
Vandenhoeck und Ruprecht, 1992, 1999.

—————. '"The End of the Law": On the Origin and Beginnings of Pauline Theology'. In
Reconciliation, Law, and Righteousness: Essays in Biblical Theology, 134-54.
1981. ET Philadelphia: Fortress, 1986.

—————. 'Isaiah 53 in the Gospels and Acts'. In *The Suffering Servant: Isaiah 53 in Jewish
and Christian Sources,* edited by B. Janowski and P. Stuhlmacher, 147-62. Grand
Rapids: Eerdmans, 2004.

—————. 'Matt 28:16-20 and the Course of Mission in the Apostolic and Postapostolic
Age'. In *The Mission of the Early Church,* edited by J. Ådna and H. Kvalbein, 17-
43. Tübingen: Mohr Siebeck, 2000.

Suhl, A. 'Paulinische Chronologie im Streit der Meinungen'. *ANRW* 2.26.1 (1995) 939-
1188.

————. *Paulus und seine Briefe.* Gütersloh: Gütersloher, 1975.

Sumney, J. L. '"I Fill Up What Is Lacking in the Afflictions of Christ": Paul's Vicarious Suffering in Colossians'. *CBQ* 68 (2006) 664-80.

————. *'Servants of Satan', 'False Brothers' and Other Opponents of Paul.* JSNTS 188. Sheffield: Sheffield Academic, 1999.

————. 'Studying Paul's Opponents: Advances and Challenges'. In *Paul and His Opponents,* edited by S. E. Porter, 7-58. Leiden: Brill, 2005.

Tabor, J. D. *Things Unutterable: Paul's Ascent to Paradise in Its Greco-Roman, Judaic, and Early Christian Contexts.* Lanham: University Press of America, 1986.

Tajra, H. W. *The Trial of St. Paul.* WUNT 2.35. Tübingen: Mohr Siebeck, 1989.

Talbert, C. H. *Theological Themes and the Genre of Luke-Acts.* SBLDS 20. Missoula: Scholars, 1974.

Talbert, C. H., and J. H. Hayes. 'A Theology of Sea Storms in Luke-Acts'. In *Jesus and the Heritage of Israel,* edited by D. Moessner, 267-83. Harrisburg: Trinity, 1999.

Talbert, R. J. A., ed. *Barrington Atlas of the Greek and Roman World.* Princeton: Princeton University, 2000.

Tannehill, R. *The Narrative Unity of Luke-Acts: A Literary Interpretation.* 2 vols.. Philadelphia: Fortress, 1986, 1990.

Tatum, G. *New Chapters in the Life of Paul: The Relative Chronology of His Career.* CBQMS 41. Washington, D.C.: Catholic Biblical Association of America, 2006.

Taylor, J. 'The Jerusalem Decrees (Acts 15.20, 29 and 21.25) and the Incident at Antioch (Gal 2.11-14)'. *NTS* 47 (2001) 372-80.

————. 'The Roman Empire in the Acts of the Apostles'. *ANRW* 2.26.3 (1996) 2436-2500.

————. 'St. Paul and the Roman Empire: Acts of the Apostles 13–14'. *ANRW* 2.26.2 (1995) 1189-1231.

————. 'Why Did Paul Persecute the Church?' In *Tolerance and Intolerance in Early Judaism and Christianity,* edited by G. N. Stanton and G. Stroumsa, 99-120. Cambridge: Cambridge University, 1998.

————. 'Why Were the Disciples First Called "Christians" at Antioch?' *RB* 101 (1994) 75-94.

Taylor, L. R. 'Artemis of Ephesus'. *Beginnings* 5.251-56.

Taylor, N. H. 'Apostolic Identity and the Conflicts in Corinth and Galatia'. In *Paul and His Opponents,* edited by S. E. Porter, 99-127. Leiden: Brill, 2005.

————. *Paul, Antioch and Jerusalem.* JSNTS 66. Sheffield: Sheffield Academic, 1992.

————. 'Popular Opposition to Caligula in Jewish Palestine'. *JSJ* 32 (2001) 54-70.

————. 'Stephen, the Temple, and Early Christian Eschatology'. *RB* 110 (2003) 62-85.

Taylor, V. *The Formation of the Gospel Tradition.* London: Macmillan, 1935.

Tcherikover, V. *Hellenistic Civilization and the Jews.* Philadelphia: Jewish Publication Society of America, 1959.

Tellbe, M. *Paul between Synagogue and State: Christians, Jews, and Civic Authorities in 1 Thessalonians, Romans and Philippians.* CBNTS 34. Stockholm: Almqvist and Wiksell, 2001.

Theissen, G. *The Gospels in Context: Social and Political History in the Synoptic Tradition.* ET Minneapolis: Fortress, 1991.

————. 'Hellenisten und Hebräer (Apg 6,1-6). Gab eine Spaltung der Urgemeinde?' In *Geschichte — Tradition — Reflexion,* M. Hengel FS. Vol. 3: *Frühes Christentum,* edited by H. Lichtenberger, 323-43. Tübingen: Mohr Siebeck, 1996.

————. 'Paulus — der Unglückstifter. Paulus und die Verfolgung der Gemeinden in Jerusalem und Rom'. In *Biographie und Persönlichkeit des Paulus,* edited by E.-M. Becker and P. Pilhofer, 228-44. Tübingen: Mohr Siebeck, 2005.

————. *Psychological Aspects of Pauline Theology.* Edinburgh: Clark, 1987.

————. 'Social Conflicts in the Corinthian Community: Further Remarks on J. J. Meggitt, *Paul, Poverty and Survival*'. *JSNT* 25 (2003) 371-91.

————. *Social Reality and the Early Christians.* Minneapolis: Augsburg Fortress, 1992.

————. *The Social Setting of Pauline Christianity.* Philadelphia: Fortress, 1982.

Theobald, M. 'Der Kanon von der Rechtfertigung (Gal 2,16; Röm 3,28)'. In *Studien zum Römerbrief,* 164-225. Tübingen: Mohr Siebeck, 2001.

Thiede, C. P. *Simon Peter.* Exeter: Paternoster, 1986.

Thielman, F. *Paul and the Law: A Contextual Approach.* Downers Grove: InterVarsity, 1994.

Thiselton, A. C. 'Realized Eschatology at Corinth'. *NTS* 24 (1978) 510-26.

Thomas, C. 'At Home in the City of Artemis: Religion in Ephesos in the Literary Imagination of the Roman Period'. In *Ephesos: Metropolis of Asia,* edited by H. Koester, 66-79. Cambridge: Harvard Divinity School, 1995, 2004.

Thornton, C.-J. *Der Zeuge des Zeugen. Lukas als Historiker der Paulusreisen.* WUNT 56. Tübingen: Mohr Siebeck, 1991.

Thorsteinson, R. M. *Paul's Interlocutor in Romans 2.* CBNTS 40. Stockholm: Almqvist and Wiksell, 2003.

Thurén, L. 'Risky Rhetoric in James?' *NovT* 37 (1995) 262-84.

Tobin, T. H. 'The World of Thought in the Philippians Hymn (Philippians 2:6-11)'. In *The New Testament and Early Christian Literature in Greco-Roman Context,* D. E. Aune FS, edited by J. Fotopoulos, 91-104. Leiden: Brill, 2006.

Tomson, P. J. 'Gamaliel's Counsel and the Apologetic Strategy of Luke-Acts'. In *The Unity of Luke-Acts,* edited by J. Verheyden, 585-604. Leuven: Leuven University, 1999.

————. *Paul and the Jewish Law: Halakha in the Letters of the Apostle to the Gentiles.* Assen: Van Gorcum, 1990.

————. '"Die Täter des Gesetzes werden gerechtfertigt warden" (Röm 2,13). Zu einer adäquaten Perspektive für den Römerbrief'. In *Lutherische und Neue Paulusperspektive,* edited by M. Bachmann, 183-221. Tübingen: Mohr Siebeck, 2005.

Tran, N. *Les membres des associations romaines. Le rang social des collegiati en Italie at en Gaules, sous le haut-empire.* École française de Rome, 2006.

Trebilco, P. 'Asia'. *BAFCS* 2.291-362.

————. *The Early Christians in Ephesus from Paul to Ignatius.* WUNT 166. Tübingen: Mohr Siebeck, 2004.

————. *Jewish Communities in Asia Minor.* SNTSMS 69. Cambridge: Cambridge University, 1991.

————. 'Paul and Silas — "Servants of the Most High God" (Acts 16.16-18)'. *JSNT* 36 (1989) 51-73.

Trilling, W. *Untersuchungen zum zweiten Thessalonicherbrief.* Leipzig: St. Benno, 1972.

Trobisch, D. *Paul's Letter Collection: Tracing the Origins.* Minneapolis: Fortress, 1994.

Troeltsch, E. *The Social Teaching of the Christian Churches.* 1912. ET London: George Allen and Unwin, 1931.

Tuckett, C. M. 'The Corinthians Who Say "There Is No Resurrection of the Dead" [1 Cor 15,12]'. In *The Corinthian Correspondence,* edited by R. Bieringer, 247-75. Leuven: Leuven University, 1996.

Turner, M. *Power from on High: The Spirit in Israel's Restoration and Witness in Luke-Acts.* Sheffield: Sheffield Academic, 1996.

———. 'The Spirit and Salvation in Luke-Acts'. In *The Holy Spirit and Christian Origins,* J. D. G. Dunn FS, edited by G. N. Stanton et al., 106-13. Grand Rapids: Eerdmans, 2004.

———. 'The Spirit of Christ and "Divine" Christology'. In *Jesus of Nazareth: Lord and Christ; Essays on the Historical Jesus and New Testament Christology,* I. H. Marshall FS, edited by J. B. Green and M. Turner, 413-36. Grand Rapids: Eerdmans, 1994.

Tyson, J. B., ed. *Luke-Acts and the Jewish People.* London: SCM, 1988.

van Bruggen, J. *Paul: Pioneer for Israel's Messiah.* Phillipsburg: P & R, 2005.

van der Horst, P. W. 'The Altar of the "Unknown God" in Athens (Acts 17:23) and the Cults of "Unknown Gods" in the Graeco-Roman World'. In *Hellenism–Judaism–Christianity: Essays on Their Interaction,* 165-202. Kampen: Kok Pharos, 1994.

———. *Ancient Jewish Epitaphs: An Introductory Survey of a Millennium of Jewish Funerary Epigraphy (300 BCE–700 CE).* Kampen: Kok Pharos, 1991.

———. 'The Jews of Ancient Cyprus'. In *Jews and Christians in the Graeco-Roman Context,* 28-36. Tübingen: Mohr Siebeck, 2006.

———. 'Peter's Shadow: The Religio-Historical Background of Acts 5.15'. *NTS* 23 (1976-77) 204-12.

———. *The Sentences of Pseudo-Phocylides.* Leiden: Brill, 1978.

Van Elderen, B. 'Some Archaeological Observations on Paul's First Missionary Journey'. In *Apostolic History and the Gospel,* F. F. Bruce FS, edited by W. W. Gasque and R. P. Martin, 151-61. Exeter: Paternoster, 1970.

Vanhoye, A. 'Personnalité de Paul et exégèse paulinienne'. In *L'Apôtre Paul: Personnalité, style et conception du ministere,* edited by A. Vanhoye, 3-15. Leuven: Leuven University, 1986.

van Kooten, G. H. *The Pauline Debate on the Cosmos: Graeco-Roman Cosmology and Jewish Eschatology in Paul and in the Pseudo-Pauline Letters to the Colossians and the Ephesians.* Leiden: Brill, 2001.

van Unnik, W. C. 'Luke's Second Book and the Rules of Hellenistic Historiography'. In *Les Actes des Apôtres. Traditions, rédaction, théologie,* edited by J. Kremer, 37-60. Leuven: Leuven University, 1979.

———. *Tarsus or Jerusalem: The City of Paul's Youth.* London: Epworth, 1962.

Vegge, T. *Paulus und das antike Schulwesen. Schule und Bildung des Paulus.* BZNW 134. Berlin: de Gruyter, 2006.

Verheyden, J. 'The Flight of the Christians to Pella'. *ETL* 66 (1990) 368-84.

———. 'The Unity of Luke-Acts'. In *The New Testament and Early Christian Literature* in *Greco-Roman Context,* D. E. Aune FS, edited by J. Fotopoulos, 3-56. Leiden: Brill, 2006.

―――, ed. *The Unity of Luke-Acts.* BETL 142. Leuven: Leuven University, 1999.

Verner, D. C. *The Household of God: The Social World of the Pastoral Epistles.* SBLDS 71. Chico: Scholars, 1983.

Verseput, D. J. 'Paul's Gentile Mission and the Jewish Christian Community: A Study of the Narrative in Galatians 1 and 2'. *NTS* 39 (1993) 36-58.

Vielhauer, P. 'On the "Paulinism" of Acts'. In *Studies in Luke Acts,* edited by L. E. Keck and J. L. Martyn, 33-50. Nashville: Abingdon, 1966.

Vollenweider, S. 'Der "Raub" der Gottgleichheit. Ein religionsgeschichtlicher Vorschlag zu Phil 2.6(-11)'. *NTS* 45 (1999) 413-33.

von Brocke, C. *Thessaloniki — Stadt des Kassander und Gemeinde des Paulus.* WUNT 125. Tübingen: Mohr Siebeck, 2001.

von Campenhausen, H. *Ecclesiastical Authority and Spiritual Power in the Church of the First Three Centuries.* 1953. ET London: Black, 1969.

von Dobbeler, A. *Der Evangelist Philippus in der Geschichte des Urchristentums.* Tübingen: Francke, 2000.

von Dobschütz, E. *Christian Life in the Primitive Church.* London: Williams and Norgate, 1904.

―――. *Ostern und Pfingsten.* Leipzig, 1903.

von Weizsäcker, C. *The Apostolic Age of the Christian Church.* 2 vols. London: Williams and Norgate, 1907.

Vouga, F. *Geschichte des frühen Christentums.* Tübingen: Mohr Siebeck, 1994.

Wachob, W. H., and L. T. Johnson. 'The Sayings of Jesus in the Letter of James'. In *Authenticating the Words of Jesus,* edited by B. Chilton and C. A. Evans, 431-50. Leiden: Brill, 1999.

Wagner, G. *Pauline Baptism and the Pagan Mysteries.* ET Edinburgh: Oliver and Boyd, 1967.

Wahlen, C. 'Peter's Vision and Conflicting Definitions of Purity'. *NTS* 51 (2005) 505-18.

Walasky, P. W. *'And So We Came to Rome': The Political Perspective of St. Luke.* SNTSMS 49. Cambridge: Cambridge University, 1983.

Wallace, R., and W. Williams. *The Three Worlds of Paul of Tarsus.* London: Routledge, 1998.

Wallace-Hadrill, A., ed. *Patronage in Ancient Society.* London: Routledge, 1989.

Walter, N. 'Apostelgeschichte 6.1 und die Anfänge der Urgemeinde in Jerusalem'. *NTS* 29 (1983) 370-93.

―――. 'Paulus und die Gegner des Christusevangeliums in Galatien'. In *Praeparatio evangelica. Studien zur Umwelt, Exegese und Hermeneutik des Neuen Testaments,* edited by W. Kraus and F. Wilk, 273-80. Tübingen: Mohr Siebeck, 1997.

Walters, J. C. *Ethnic Issues in Paul's Letter to the Romans.* Valley Forge: Trinity, 1993.

―――. 'Romans, Jews, and Christians: The Impact of the Romans on Jewish-Christian Relations in First-Century Rome'. In *Judaism and Christianity in First-Century Rome,* edited by K. P. Donfried and P. Richardson, 175-95. Grand Rapids: Eerdmans, 1998.

Walton, S. '*Homothymadon* in Acts: Co-location, Common Action or "Of One Heart and

Mind"?' In *The New Testament in Its First-Century Setting,* B. W. Winter FS, edited by P. J. Williams et al., 89-105. Grand Rapids: Eerdmans, 2004.

———. *Leadership and Lifestyle: The Portrait of Paul in the Miletus Speech and 1 Thessalonians.* SNTSMS 108. Cambridge: Cambridge University, 2000.

Waltzing, J.-P. *Études historique sur les corporations professionnelles chez les Romains.* 4 vols. Leuven: Peeters, 1895-1900.

Wander, B. *Gottesfürchtige und Sympathisanten. Studien zum heidnischen Umfeld von Diasporasynagogen.* WUNT 104. Tübingen: Mohr Siebeck, 1998.

———. 'Die sogenannten "Gegner" im Galaterbrief'. In *Logos — Logik — Lyrik. Engagierte exegetische Studien zum biblischen Reden Gottes,* K. Haacker FS, edited by V. A. Lehnert and U. Rüsen-Weinhold, 53-70. Leipzig: Evangelische Verlagsanstalt, 2007.

———. *Trennungsprozesse zwischen Frühen Christentum und Judentum im 1. Jh. n. Chr.* Tübingen: Francke, 1994.

———. 'Warum wollte Paulus nach Spanien?' In *Das Ende des Paulus,* edited by F. W. Horn, 175-95. Berlin: de Gruyter, 2001.

Wansink, C. S. *Chained in Christ: The Experience and Rhetoric of Paul's Imprisonments.* JSNTS 130. Sheffield: Sheffield Academic, 1996.

Ward, R. B. 'James of Jerusalem in the First Two Centuries'. *ANRW* 2.26.1 (1992) 779-812.

Ware, J. P. *The Mission of the Church in Paul's Letter to the Philippians in the Context of Ancient Judaism.* NovTSupp 120. Leiden: Brill, 2005.

Watson, D. *Paul's Collection in Light of Motivations and Mechanisms for Aid to the Poor in the First-Century World.* Durham PhD, 2006.

Watson, F. *Paul, Judaism and the Gentiles.* SNTSMS 56. Cambridge: Cambridge University, 1986, 2007, 2nd ed.

Weatherly, J. A. *Jewish Responsibility for the Death of Jesus in Luke-Acts.* JSNTS 106. Sheffield: Sheffield Academic, 1994.

Weaver, J. B. *Plots of Epiphany: Prison-Escape in Acts of the Apostles.* BZNW 131. Berlin: de Gruyter, 2004.

Wedderburn, A. J. M. 'The "Apostolic Decree": Tradition and Redaction'. *NovT* 35 (1993) 362-89.

———. *Baptism and Resurrection: Studies in Pauline Theology against Its Graeco-Roman Background.* WUNT 44. Tübingen: Mohr Siebeck, 1987.

———. '2 Corinthians 5:14 — a Key to Paul's Soteriology?' In *Paul and the Corinthians,* M. Thrall FS, edited by T. J. Burke and J. K. Elliott, 267-83. Leiden: Brill, 2003.

———. *A History of the First Christians.* London: Clark, 2004.

———. 'Pauline Pneumatology and Pauline Theology'. In *The Holy Spirit and Christian Origins,* J. D. G. Dunn FS, edited by G. N. Stanton et al., 144-56. Grand Rapids: Eerdmans, 2004.

———. 'Paul's Collection: Chronology and History'. *NTS* 48 (2002) 95-110.

———. *The Reasons for Romans.* Edinburgh: Clark, 1988.

———. 'Traditions and Redaction in Acts 2.1-13'. *JSNT* 55 (1994) 27-54.

———. 'The "We"-Passages in Acts: On the Horns of a Dilemma'. *ZNW* 93 (2002) 78-98.

————. 'Zur Frage der Gattung der Apostelgeschichte'. In *Geschichte — Tradition — Reflexion*, M. Hengel FS. Vol. 3: *Frühes Christentum*, edited by H. Lichtenberger, 302-22. Tübingen: Mohr Siebeck, 1996.

Wehnert, J. 'Die Auswanderung der Jerusalemer Christen nach Pella. Historisches Faktum oder theologische Konstruktion?' *ZKG* 102 (1991) 231-55.

————. *Die Reinheit des "christlichen Gottesvolkes" aus Juden und Heiden*. FRLANT 173. Göttingen: Vandenhoeck und Ruprecht, 1997.

————. *Die Wir-Passagen der Apostelgeschichte*. Göttingen: Vandenhoeck und Ruprecht, 1989.

Weima, J. A. D. *Neglected Endings: The Significance of the Pauline Letter Closings*. JSNTS 101. Sheffield: JSOT, 1994.

Weinel, H. *St. Paul: The Man and His Work*. London: Williams and Norgate, 1906.

Weinrich, O. 'Gebet und Wunder. Zwei Abhandlungen zur Religions- und Literaturgeschichte'. In *Religionsgeschichtliche Studien*, 147-79. Darmstadt: Wissenschaftliche Buchgesellschaft, 1968.

Weiss, J. *Earliest Christianity: A History of the Period AD 30-150*. 2 vols. ET 1937. New York: Harper Torchbook, 1959.

Welborn, L. L. 'On the Discord in Corinth: 1 Corinthians 1–4 and Ancient Politics'. *JBL* 106 (1987) 85-111.

————. *Politics and Rhetoric in the Corinthian Epistles*. Macon: Mercer University, 1997.

Wells, G. A. *The Jesus Myth*. Chicago: Open Court, 1999.

Wendel, U. *Gemeinde in Kraft. Das Gemeindeverständnis in den Summarien der Apostelgeschichte*. Neukirchen-Vluyn: Neukirchener, 1998.

Wendland, P. *Die hellenistisch-römische Kultur in ihren Beziehungen zu Judentum und Christentum*. Tübingen: Mohr Siebeck, 1907.

Wengst, K. *Christologische Formeln und Lieder des Urchristentums*. Gütersloh: Gütersloher, 1972.

Wenham, D. 'Acts and the Pauline Corpus II: The Evidence of Parallels'. *BAFCS* 1.215-58.

Weren, W. 'The Riot of the Ephesian Silversmiths (Acts 19,23-40): Luke's Advice to His Readers'. In *Luke and His Readers*, A. Denaux FS, edited by R. Bieringer et al., 441-56. Leuven: Leuven University, 2005.

Werner, M. *The Formation of Christian Dogma*. 1941. ET London: Black, 1957.

Westerholm, S. *Perspectives Old and New on Paul: The "Lutheran" Paul and His Critics*. Grand Rapids: Eerdmans, 2004.

Westermann, W. L. *The Slave Systems of Greek and Roman Antiquity*. Philadelphia: American Philosophical Society, 1955.

Whelan, C. F. '*Amica Pauli:* The Role of Phoebe in the Early Church'. *JSNT* 49 (1993) 67-85.

White, J. L. *Light from Ancient Letters*. Philadelphia: Fortress, 1986.

White, L. M. *The Social Origins of Christian Architecture*. 2 vols. HTS 42. Harrisburg: Trinity, 1996, 1997.

————. 'Synagogue and Society in Imperial Ostia: Archaeological and Epigraphic Evidence'. In *Judaism and Christianity in First-Century Rome,* edited by K. P. Donfried and P. Richardson, 30-68. Grand Rapids: Eerdmans, 1998.

———. 'Urban Development and Social Change in Imperial Ephesos'. In *Ephesos: Metropolis of Asia,* edited by H. Koester, 27-79. Cambridge: Harvard Divinity School, 1995, 2004.

———. 'Visualizing the "Real" World of Acts 16: Towards Construction of a Social Index'. In *The Social World of the First Christians,* W. A. Meeks FS, edited by L. M. White and O. L. Yarbrough, 234-61. Minneapolis: Fortress, 1995.

White, L. M., and O. L. Yarbrough, eds. *The Social World of the First Christians,* W. A. Meeks FS. Minneapolis: Fortress, 1995.

Whittaker, M. *Jews and Christians: Graeco-Roman Views.* Cambridge: Cambridge University, 1984.

Wiedemann, T. *Greek and Roman Slavery.* Baltimore: Johns Hopkins University, 1981.

Wiefel, W. 'The Jewish Community in Ancient Rome and the Origins of Roman Christianity'. *Judaica* 26 (1970) 65-88.

Wilckens, U. *Die Missionsreden der Apostelgeschichte.* WMANT 5. Neukirchen-Vluyn: Neukirchener, 1963.

———. *Theologie des Neuen Testaments.* Vol. 1: *Geschichte der urchristlichen Theologie.* 4 vols. Neukirchen-Vluyn: Neukirchener, 2003.

———. *Weisheit und Torheit.* Tübingen: Mohr Siebeck, 1959.

———. 'Zur Entwicklung des paulinischen Gesetzesverständnis'. *NTS* 28 (1982) 154-90.

Wilcox, M. 'The Promise of "Seed" in the New Testament and the Targumim'. *JSNT* 5 (1979) 2-30.

Wild, R. A. '"Be Imitators of God": Discipleship in the Letter to the Ephesians'. In *Discipleship in the New Testament,* edited by F. Segovia, 127-43. Philadelphia: Fortress, 1985.

Wilken, R. L. *The Christians as the Romans Saw Them.* New Haven: Yale University, 1984.

———. *The Myth of Christian Beginnings.* London: SCM, 1979.

Williams, M. H. 'The Shaping of the Identity of the Jewish Community in Rome in Antiquity'. In *Christians as a Religious Minority in a Multicultural City,* edited by J. Zangenberg and M. Labahn, 33-46. London: Clark, 2004.

Williams, S. K. 'The Hearing of Faith: *akoē pisteōs* in Galatians iii'. *NTS* 35 (1989) 82-93.

Willis, W. W. *Idol Meat in Corinth.* SBLDS 68. Chico: Scholars, 1985.

Wilson, A. N. *Paul: The Mind of the Apostle.* London: Sinclair-Stevenson, 1997.

Wilson, M. 'Cilicia: The First Christian Churches in Anatolia'. *TynB* 54 (2003) 15-30.

Wilson, R. M. 'Gnosis and Corinth'. In *Paul and Paulinism,* C. K. Barrett FS, edited by M. D. Hooker and S. G. Wilson, 102-19. London: SPCK, 1982.

———. 'How Gnostic Were the Corinthians?' *NTS* 19 (1972-73) 65-74.

———. 'Simon and Gnostic Origins'. In *Les Actes des Apôtres. Traditions, rédaction, théologie,* edited by J. Kremer, 485-91. Leuven: Leuven University, 1979.

Wilson, S. G. *The Gentiles and the Gentile Mission in Luke-Acts.* SNTSMS 23. Cambridge: Cambridge University, 1973.

———. *Luke and the Law.* SNTSMS 50. Cambridge: Cambridge University, 1983.

————. 'Voluntary Associations: An Overview'. In *Voluntary Associations in the Graeco-Roman World,* edited by J. S. Kloppenborg and S. G. Wilson, 1-15. London: Routledge, 1996.

Winger, M. 'Act One: Paul Arrives in Galatia'. *NTS* 48 (2002) 548-67.

Wink, W. *Naming the Powers.* Philadelphia: Fortress, 1984.

Winter, B. W. 'The Achaean Federal Imperial Cult II: The Corinthian Church'. *TynB* 46 (1995) 169-78.

————. 'Acts and Food Shortages'. *BAFCS* 2.59-78.

————. 'Acts and Roman Religion: The Imperial Cult'. *BAFCS* 2.93-103.

————. *After Paul Left Corinth: The Influence of Secular Ethics and Social Change.* Grand Rapids: Eerdmans, 2001.

————. 'Official Proceedings and the Forensic Speeches in Acts 24–26'. *BAFCS* 1.305-36.

————. *Philo and Paul among the Sophists.* Grand Rapids: Eerdmans, 2002.

————. 'Rehabilitating Gallio and His Judgement in Acts 18:14-15'. *TynB* 57 (2006) 291-308.

————. *Roman Wives, Roman Widows: The Appearance of New Women and the Pauline Communities.* Grand Rapids: Eerdmans, 2003.

————. *Seek the Welfare of the City: Christians as Benefactors and Citizens.* Grand Rapids: Eerdmans, 1994.

————. 'The Toppling of Favorinus and Paul by the Corinthians'. In *Early Christianity and Classical Culture,* A. J. Malherbe FS, edited by J. T. Fitzgerald et al., 291-306. Leiden: Brill, 2003.

Wischmeyer, O. 'Paulus als Ich-Erzähler. Ein Beitrag zu seiner Person, seiner Biographie und seiner Theologie'. In *Biographie und Persönlichkeit des Paulus,* edited by E.-M. Becker and P. Pilhofer, 88-105. Tübingen: Mohr Siebeck, 2005.

————. 'Römer 2.1-24 als Teil der Gerichtsrede des Paulus gegen die Menschenheit'. *NTS* 52 (2006) 356-76.

————, ed. *Paulus. Leben — Umwelt — Werk — Briefe.* Tübingen: Francke, 2006.

Wisdom, J. R. *Blessing for the Nations and the Curse of the Law: Paul's Citation of Genesis and Deuteronomy in Gal. 3.8-10.* WUNT 2.133. Tübingen: Mohr Siebeck, 2001.

Witherington, B. *The Brother of Jesus.* San Francisco: HarperSanFrancisco, 2003.

————. *The Paul Quest: The Renewed Search for the Jew of Tarsus.* Downers Grove: InterVarsity, 1998.

————. *Women in the Earliest Churches.* SNTSMS 59. Cambridge: Cambridge University, 1988.

————, ed. *History, Literature and Society in the Book of Acts.* Cambridge: Cambridge University, 1996.

Witulski, T. *Die Adressaten des Galaterbriefes. Untersuchungen zur Gemeinde von Antiochia ad Pisidiam.* Göttingen: Vandenhoeck und Ruprecht, 2000.

Wolter, M. 'Apollos und die ephesinischen Johannesjünger (Act 18:24–19:7)'. *ZNW* 78 (1987) 49-73.

Wrede, W. *Die Echtheit des zweiten Thessalonicherbrief untersucht.* Leipzig: Heinrichs, 1903.

—————. *Paul.* London: Philip Green, 1907.

—————. 'The Task and Methods of "New Testament Theology"'. In *The Nature of New Testament Theology,* edited by R. Morgan, 68-116. London: SCM, 1973.

Wright, N. T. *The Climax of the Covenant: Christ and the Law in Pauline Theology.* Edinburgh: Clark, 1991.

—————. 'A Fresh Perspective on Paul'. *BJRL* 83 (2001) 21-39.

—————. *Paul: Fresh Perspectives.* London: SPCK, 2005.

—————. 'Paul's Gospel and Caesar's Empire'. In *Paul and Politics: Ekklesia, Israel, Imperium, Interpretation,* edited by R. A. Horsley, 160-83. Harrisburg: Trinity, 2000.

—————. *The Resurrection of the Son of God.* London: SPCK, 2003.

—————. 'Romans and the Theology of Paul'. In *Pauline Theology.* Vol. 3: *Romans,* edited by D. M. Hay and E. E. Johnson, 30-67. Minneapolis: Fortress, 1995.

Yamauchi, E. M. *New Testament Cities in Western Asia Minor.* Grand Rapids: Baker, 1980.

Yee, T. L. *Jews, Gentiles and Ethnic Reconciliation: Paul's Jewish Identity and Ephesians.* SNTSMS 130. Cambridge: Cambridge University, 2005.

Young, N. H. '*Paidagōgos:* The Social Setting of a Pauline Metaphor'. *NovT* 29 (1987) 150-76.

Zangenberg, J. 'Gebeine des Apostelfürsten? Zu den angeblich frühchristlichen Gräbern unter der Peterskirche in Rom'. In *Christians as a Religious Minority in a Multicultural City,* edited by J. Zangenberg and M. Labahn, 108-38. London: Clark, 2004.

Zangenberg, J., and M. Labahn, eds. *Christians as a Religious Minority in a Multicultural City: Modes of Interaction and Identity Formation in Early Imperial Rome.* London: Clark, 2004.

Zanker, P. *The Power of Images in the Age of Augustus.* Ann Arbor: University of Michigan, 1988.

Zeller, D. 'Theologie der Mission bei Paulus'. In *Mission im Neuen Testament,* edited by K. Kertelge, 164-89. Freiburg: Herder, 1982.

—————. 'Der Vorrang der Ehelosigkeit in 1 Kor 7'. *ZNW* 96 (2005) 61-77.

—————. *Die weisheitlichen Mahnsprüche bei den Synoptikern.* Würzburg: Echter, 1977.

Zetterholm, M. *The Formation of Christianity in Antioch: A Social-Scientific Approach to the Separation between Judaism and Christianity.* London: Routledge, 2003.

Zmijewski, J. 'Die Aufnahme der ersten Heiden in die Kirche nach Apg 10,1–11,18'. *ANRW* 2.26.2 (1995) 1554-1601.

Zwiep, A. W. *The Ascension of the Messiah in Lukan Christology.* NovTSupp 87. Leiden: Brill, 1997.

—————. '*Assumptus est in caelum:* Rapture and Heavenly Exaltation in Early Judaism and Luke-Acts'. In *Auferstehung — Resurrection,* edited by F. Avemarie and H. Lichtenberger, 323-49. Tübingen: Mohr Siebeck, 2001.

—————. *Judas and the Choice of Matthias.* WUNT 2.187. Tübingen: Mohr Siebeck, 2004.

—————. 'The Text of the Ascension Narratives (Luke 24.50-3; Acts 1.1-2, 9-11)'. *NTS* 42 (1996) 219-44.

Index of Scriptures and Other Ancient Writings

References in the Old and New Testaments printed in **bold** indicate
that some exegesis or exposition is offered on these pages.

Index of Authors

Subject Index